Janson's
History of Art

Janson's History of Art

THE WESTERN TRADITION

Eighth Edition

PENELOPE J. E. DAVIES

WALTER B. DENNY

FRIMA FOX HOFRICHTER

JOSEPH JACOBS

ANN M. ROBERTS

DAVID L. SIMON

Prentice Hall
Upper Saddle River   London   Singapore
Toronto   Tokyo   Sydney   Hong Kong   Mexico City

Editorial Director: Leah Jewell
Editor in Chief: Sarah Touborg
Senior Sponsoring Editor: Helen Ronan
Editorial Project Manager: David Nitti
Editorial Assistant: Carla Worner
Media Director: Brian Hyland
Media Editor: Alison Lorber
Director of Marketing: Brandy Dawson
Senior Marketing Manager: Laura Lee Manley
Marketing Assistant: Ashley Fallon
Senior Managing Editor: Ann Marie McCarthy
Assistant Managing Editor: Melissa Feimer
Senior Operations Specialist: Brian Mackey
Production Liaisons: Barbara Cappuccio and Marlene Gassler
AV Project Manager: Gail Cocker
Cartography: Peter Bull Art Studio
Senior Art Director: Pat Smythe
Site Supervisor, Pearson Imaging Center: Joe Conti
Pearson Imaging Center: Corin Skidds, Robert Uibelhoer, and Ron Walko
Cover Printer: Lehigh-Phoenix Color
Printer/Binder: Courier/Kendallville

This book was designed by
Laurence King Publishing Ltd, London.
www.laurenceking.com

Senior Editor: Susie May
Copy Editor: Robert Shore
Proofreader: Lisa Cutmore
Picture Researcher: Amanda Russell
Page and Cover Designers: Nick Newton and Randell Harris
Production Controller: Simon Walsh

Cover image: Titian, *Man with a Blue Sleeve*. ca. 1520. Oil on canvas,
32 x 26"(81.2 × 66.3 cm). The National Gallery, London.

Library of Congress Cataloging-in-Publication Data
Janson, H. W. (Horst Woldemar)
Janson's history of art : the western tradition / Penelope J.E. Davies ... [et. al]. -- 8th ed.
p. cm.
Includes bibliographical references and index.
ISBN 978-0-205-68517-2 (hardback)
1. Art--History. I. Davies, Penelope J. E., II. Janson, H. W. (Horst Woldemar), History of art.
III. Title. IV. Title: History of art.
N5300.J29 2009b
709--dc22
2009022617

10 9 8 7 6 5 4 3 2 1

Prentice Hall
is an imprint of

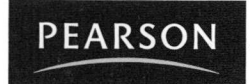

www.pearsonhighered.com

ISBN 10: 0-205-68517-X
ISBN 13: 978-0-205-68517-2
Exam Copy ISBN 10: 0-205-69518-3
ISBN 13: 978-0-205-69518-8

Contents

Preface

WELCOME TO THE EIGHTH EDITION OF JANSON'S CLASSIC TEXTBOOK, officially renamed *Janson's History of Art* in its seventh edition to reflect its relationship to the book that introduced generations of students to art history. For many of us who teach introductory courses in the history of art, the name Janson is synonymous with the subject matter we present.

When Pearson/Prentice Hall first published the *History of Art* in 1962, John F. Kennedy occupied the White House, and Andy Warhol was an emerging artist. Janson offered his readers a strong focus on Western art, an important consideration of technique and style, and a clear point of view. The *History of Art*, said Janson, was not just a stringing together of historically significant objects, but the writing of a story about their interconnections—a history of styles and of stylistic change. Janson's text focused on the visual and technical characteristics of the objects he discussed, often in extraordinarily eloquent language. Janson's *History of Art* helped to establish the canon of art history for many generations of scholars.

Although revised to remain current with new discoveries and scholarship, this new edition continues to follow Janson's lead in important ways: It is limited to the Western tradition, with a chapter on Islamic art and its relationship to Western art. It keeps the focus of the discussion on the object, its manufacture, and its visual character. It considers the contribution of the artist as an important part of the analysis. This edition maintains an organization along the lines established by Janson, with separate chapters on the Northern European Renaissance, the Italian Renaissance, the High Renaissance, and Baroque art, with stylistic divisions for key periods of the modern era. Also embedded in this edition is the narrative of how art has changed over time in the cultures that Europe has claimed as its patrimony.

WHAT'S NEW IN JANSON'S HISTORY OF ART?

"The history of art is too vast a field for anyone to encompass all of it with equal competence."

H. W. JANSON, from the Preface to the first edition of *History of Art*

Janson's History of Art in its eighth edition is once again the product of careful revision by a team of scholars with different specialties, bringing a readily recognized knowledge and depth to the discussions of works of art. We incorporate new interpretations such as the reidentification of the "Porticus Aemilia" as Rome's Navalia, or ship-shed (p. 186); new documentary evidence, such as that pertaining to Uccello's *Battle of San Romano* (p. 538); and new interpretive approaches, such as the importance of nationalism in the development of Romanticism (Chapter 24).

Organization and Contextual Emphasis

Most chapters integrate the media into chronological discussions instead of discussing them in isolation from one another, which reflected the more formalistic approach used in earlier editions. Even though we draw connections among works of art, as Janson did, we emphasize the patronage and function of works of art and the historical circumstances in which they were created. We explore how works of art have been used to shore up political or social power.

Interpreting Cultures

Western art history encompasses a great many distinct chronological and cultural periods, which we wish to treat as distinct entities. So we present Etruscan art as evidence for Etruscan culture, not as a precursor of Roman or a follower of Greek art. Recognizing the limits of our knowledge about certain periods of history, we examine how art historians draw conclusions from works of art. The boxes called *The Art Historian's Lens* allow students to see how the discipline works. They give students a better understanding of the methods art historians use to develop art-historical arguments. *Primary Sources*, a distinguishing feature of Janson for many editions, have been incorporated throughout the chapters to support the analysis provided and to further inform students about the cultures discussed, and additional documents can be found in the online resource, MyArtsLab. (See p. xix for more detail.)

Women in the History of Art

Women continue to be given greater visibility as artists, as patrons, and as an audience for works of art. Inspired by contemporary approaches to art history, we also address the representation of women as expressions of specific cultural notions of femininity or as symbols.

Objects, Media, and Techniques

Many new objects have been incorporated into this edition to reflect the continuous changes in the discipline. The mediums we discuss are broad in scope and include not only modern art forms such as installations and earth art, but also the so-called minor arts of earlier periods—such as tapestries, metalwork, and porcelain. Discussions in the *Materials and Techniques* boxes illuminate this dimension of art history.

The Images

Along with the new objects that have been introduced, every reproduction in the book has been reexamined for excellence in quality, and when not meeting our standards has been replaced. Whenever possible we obtain our photography directly from the holding institutions to ensure that we have the most accurate and authoritative illustrations. Every image that could be obtained in color has been acquired. To further assist both students and teachers, we have sought permission for electronic educational use so that instructors who adopt *Janson's History of Art* will have access to an extraordinary archive of high-quality (over 300 dpi) digital images for classroom use. (See p. xix for more detail on the Prentice Hall Digital Art Library.)

New Maps and Timelines

A new map program has been created to both orient students to the locations mentioned in each chapter and to better tell the story of the chapter narrative. Readers now can see the extent of the Eastern and Western Roman Empires, as well as the range of the Justinian's rule (p. 236). They can trace the migration routes of tribes during early medieval times (p. 314) and the Dutch trade routes of the seventeenth century (p. 702). This enriching new feature provides an avenue for greater understanding of the impact of politics, society, and geography on the art of each period. End of chapter timelines recap in summary fashion the art and events of the chapter, as well as showing key contemporaneous works from previous chapters (for example, pp. 345 and 759).

Chapter by Chapter Revisions

The following list includes the major highlights of this new edition:

CHAPTER 1: PREHISTORIC ART

Expands upon the methods scholars (both art historians and anthropologists) use to understand artwork, including, for instance, feminist interpretations. Includes new monuments such as Skara Brae and Mezhirich. A new box explains dating techniques.

CHAPTER 2: ANCIENT NEAR EASTERN ART

This chapter is expanded to include a discussion of Jerusalem.

CHAPTER 3: EGYPTIAN ART

Now includes a tomb painting from the pre-Dynastic age, and a discussion of jewelry. A new box names the major Egyptian gods.

CHAPTER 4: AEGEAN ART

Improved images and a reconstruction of Mycenae enhance the discussion of Aegean art.

CHAPTER 5: GREEK ART

This chapter is tightened to allow space for longer discussion of Greek sanctuaries, and the inclusion of Hellenistic works outside of the Greek mainland, such as the Pharos at Alexandria. The issue of homosexuality in fifth-century Athens is addressed, as well as women's roles in life and art. A new box deals with the issue of repatriation of works of art such as the Elgin marbles.

CHAPTER 6: ETRUSCAN ART

The range of artworks is increased to include, for instance, terra-cotta revetments and terra-cotta portraits.

CHAPTER 7: ROMAN ART

This chapter includes new interpretations such as the reidentification of the "Porticus Aemilia" as Rome's Navalia or ship-shed. It also has been tightened to allow space for more Republican works (such as the terra cotta pediment from Via di San Gregorio and the Praeneste mosaic) and a wider discussion of life in Pompeii. There is some rearrangement of art works to improve the chronological flow.

CHAPTER 8: EARLY CHRISTIAN AND BYZANTINE ART

A new section on early Jewish art is added, including three images of early synagogue wall paintings and mosaics (Dura Europos and Hammath Tiberias). Coverage of Late Byzantine art is increased, as is discussion of liturgical and social history.

CHAPTER 9: ISLAMIC ART

The relationship of Islamic art to early Jewish and Christian medieval art is accentuated.

CHAPTER 10: EARLY MEDIEVAL ART

Includes an expanded discussion and reorganization of Viking art, which is now placed later in the chapter.

CHAPTER 11: ROMANESQUE ART

Coverage of secular architecture is broadened to include the bridge at Puente la Reina on the pilgrimage route to Santiago de Compostela and a new section on the crusades and castle architecture.

CHAPTER 12: GOTHIC ART

This chapter is tightened to allow space for added focus on secular objects and buildings with the inclusion of a Guillaume de Machaut manuscript illumination and Westminster Hall from the royal palace in London. There is also expanded discussion of courtly art and royal iconography in later Gothic monuments.

CHAPTER 13: ART IN THIRTEENTH- AND FOURTEENTH-CENTURY ITALY

Organization now places less emphasis on religious architecture. Siena's Palazzo Pubblico is added. There is a more focused discussion of Tuscany, and a briefer treatment of Northern Italy and Venice. Images of key works of art, including Nicola and Giovanni Pisano and the Arena chapel are improved. Two maps in the chapter outline Italian trade routes and the spread of the plague in the 1340s.

CHAPTER 14: ARTISTIC INNOVATIONS IN FIFTEENTH-CENTURY NORTHERN EUROPE

Discussion of the *Très Riches Heures du Duc de Berry* is enlarged, and reproductions contrasting aristocratic "labors" and the images of peasants are added. Treatment of works by Van Eyck, Van der Weyden and Bosch is revised and sharpened. A new map of centers of production and trade routes in Northern Europe illustrates the variety of media produced in the region.

CHAPTER 15: THE EARLY RENAISSANCE IN FIFTEENTH-CENTURY ITALY

Reorganized for better flow and student comprehension, this chapter now begins with the Baptistery competition illustrating reliefs by both Ghiberti and Brunelleschi. It then looks at architectural projects by Brunelleschi and Alberti in Florence as a group, considering their patronage and function as well as their form. New art illustrates Brunelleschi's innovations at the Duomo, while his work at San Lorenzo is expanded to include the Old Sacristy. Section on domestic life has been revised, but it still offers a contextualized discussion of works such as Donatello's *David*, Uccello's *Battle of San Romano* and Botticelli's *Birth of Venus*. This section now includes the Strozzi cassone at the Metropolitan Museum of Art in New York and Verrocchio's *Lady with a Bunch of Flowers*. The discussion of Renaissance style throughout Italy is revised for greater clarity.

CHAPTER 16: THE HIGH RENAISSANCE IN ITALY, 1495–1520

A discussion of the portrait of Ginevra de' Benci is now included, permitting a revised discussion of the *Mona Lisa*. The section on the Stanza della Segnatura is revamped to focus on *The School of Athens*. Treatment of Giorgione and Titian is reorganized and revised to reflect current discussions of attribution and collaboration. A new Titian portrait, *Man with a Blue Sleeve*, is included.

CHAPTER 17: THE LATE RENAISSANCE AND MANNERISM IN SIXTEENTH-CENTURY ITALY

Florence in the sixteenth century is reorganized and refreshed with new images, including a view of the architectural context for Pontormo's *Pietà*. Michelangelo's New Sacristy is treated in terms of architecture as well as sculpture. Ducal Palaces of the Uffizi and the Pitti and of the Boboli Gardens receives a new focus. Cellini's Saltceller of Francis I is discussed in its Florentine context. Treatment of Il Gesù is revamped. New images enliven the Northern Italian art section and Sofonisba Anguissola's *Self Portrait* is compared to Parmigianino's. There is a revised consideration of Palladio, and a new Titian, *The Rape of Europa*, exemplifies the artist's work for elite patrons.

CHAPTER 18: RENAISSANCE AND REFORMATION IN SIXTEENTH-CENTURY NORTHERN EUROPE

Discussion of France, as well as Spain, is revised and images are improved. Includes new images and discussions of Cranach and Baldung: Cranach's *Judgment of Paris* in New York replaces another version of this theme, while Baldung is represented by his woodcut of *The Bewitched Groom* of 1544. The discussion of Holbein is enlivened by consideration of his *Jean de Dinteville and Georges de Selve* ("The Ambassadors"), allowing examination of him as an allegorist as well as a portraitist. Gossaert is now represented by the *Neptune and Amphitrite* of 1516, while a new Patinir, the triptych of *The Penitence of Saint Jerome*, represents the landscape specialty of that region.

CHAPTER 19: THE BAROQUE IN ITALY AND SPAIN

Chapter content benefits from insights gained through recent exhibitions and from the inclusion of new architectural image components. New illustrations better expand understanding of the Roman Baroque and the role of the Virgin in Spanish art, including a view of the Piazza Navonna that shows Bernini's *Four Rivers Fountain* and as well as Borromini's church of S. Agnese, a cut-away of Borromini's complex star-hexagon shaped church,

S. Ivo, and one of Murillo's many depictions of the *Immaculate Conception* (St. Petersburg).

CHAPTER 20: THE BAROQUE IN THE NETHERLANDS

The importance of trade, trade routes and interest in the exotic is explored in this chapter. Gender issues—and the relationship between men and women—and local, folk traditions (religious and secular) play a role here in the exploration of the visual culture and social history. New images include: Peter Paul Rubens' *The Raising of the Cross*—the entire open altarpiece; Peter Paul Rubens' *Four Studies of the Head of a Negro*; Jacob Jordaens' *The King Drinks*; Judith Leyster's *The Proposition*; Rembrandt van Rijn's *Bathsheba with King David's Letter*, and Vermeer's *Officer and Laughing Girl*.

CHAPTER 21: THE BAROQUE IN FRANCE AND ENGLAND

New scholarship from the *Poussin and Nature: Arcadian Visions* exhibition in 2008 informs a more developed discussion of this artist's work. A fuller discussion of the role of the 1668 Fire of London and the re-building of St. Paul's Cathedral, in addition to a three-dimensional reconstruction of St. Paul's and a modern reconstruction of Sir Christopher Wren's plan of the city of London drawn just days after the fire, expands the coverage of this architect.

CHAPTER 22: THE ROCOCO

Expresses in greater depth the concept of the Rococo, the role of Madame da Pompadour and the expansion of the Rococo style in Germany. New images include Francois Boucher's *Portrait of Madame de Pompadour* (Munich); Jean-Simeon Chardin's *The Brioche (the Dessert)* and Egid Quirin Asam's interior and altar of the Benedictine Church at Rohr. Sections of this chapter are reorganized to accommodate the removal of Marie-Louise Élisabeth Vigée-Lebrun, Sir Thomas Gainsborough and Sir Joshua Reynolds to Chapter 23.

CHAPTER 23: ART IN THE AGE OF THE ENLIGHTENMENT, 1750–1789

Slightly restructured, the chapter keeps Neoclassicism and early Romanticism separated, thus making them more clearly defined. Joshua Reynolds, Thomas Gainsborough, and Vigée-Lebrun are placed here and into the context of Neoclassicism and Romanticism. Antonio Canova also is moved to this chapter to emphasize his importance in the development of Neoclassicism. Image changes include Joseph Wright's more clearly Romantic *The Old Man and Death*; Ledoux's Custom House with the entrance to the Saltworks at Arc-et-Senans; as well as the addition of Canova's tomb of Archduchess Maria Christina.

CHAPTER 24: ART IN THE AGE OF ROMANTICISM, 1789–1848

This chapter is tightened and has several new images. William Blake is now represented by *Elohim Creating Adam* and Corot by *Souvenir de Montrefontaine (Oise)*. Frederick Church's *Twilight in the Wilderness* is added. The discussion of architecture is changed by placing the Empire style at the very end, thus keeping the Neoclassical revival together.

CHAPTER 25: THE AGE OF POSITIVISM: REALISM, IMPRESSIONISM, AND THE PRE-RAPHAELITES, 1848–1885

Includes a number of image changes to better focus discussions. These include: Monet's *Gare St. Lazare*; Rossetti's *Proserpine*; Nadar's portrait *Édouard Manet*; and Le Gray's *Brig on the Water*.

CHAPTER 26: PROGRESS AND ITS DISCONTENTS: POST-IMPRESSIONISM, SYMBOLISM, AND ART NOUVEAU, 1880–1905

Now incorporates discussions of vernacular, or amateur, photography, represented by Henri Lartigue's *Avenue du Bois de Bologne*; *Woman with Furs*, and the advent of film, represented by Thomas Edison's *New Brooklyn to New York via Brooklyn Bridge*.

CHAPTER 27: TOWARD ABSTRACTION: THE MODERNIST REVOLUTION, 1904–1914

Discussion of the formal and stylistic developments between 1904 and 1914 that culminated in abstractionism is tightened and the number of images reduced.

CHAPTER 28: ART BETWEEN THE WARS

More compact discussion structured around the impact of World War I and the need to create utopias and uncover higher realities, especially as seen in Surrealism.

CHAPTER 29: POSTWAR TO POSTMODERN, 1945–1980

Polke is placed here from Chapter 30, thus putting him within the context of an artist influenced by Pop Art. David Hammons is moved to Chapter 30. Betye Saar's *Shield of Quality* adds a woman to the discussion of African-American artists.

CHAPTER 30: THE POSTMODERN ERA: ART SINCE 1980

Architecture is reduced, and fine art is expanded. Neo-Expressionism benefits from the addition of Julian Schnabel's *The Exile*. The multi-culturalism of the period receives greater emphasis, especially feminism. Barbara Kruger is placed in a more feminist context with inclusion of a new image, *Untitled (We Won't Play Nature to Your Culture)*. The discussion of African-American identity is broadened by the placement of David Hammons here, and by the addition of Kara Walker's *Insurrection (Our Tools Were Rudimentary, Yet We Pressed On)*. Fred Wilson's *Mining the Museum* is also included. The discussion of González-Torres now stresses his involvement with the AIDS crisis. The importance of large-scale photography for the period is reinforced by the addition of Andreas Gursky's *Shanghai*. The truly global nature of contemporary art is strengthened by the addition of El Antsui's *Dzesi II*.

Acknowledgments

We are grateful to the following academic reviewers for their numerous insights and suggestions on improving Janson:

Amy Adams, College of Staten Island

Susan Benforado Baker, University of Texas Arlington

Jennifer Ball, Brooklyn College

Dixon Bennett, San Jacinto College – South

Diane Boze, Northeastern State University

Betty Ann Brown, California State University – Northridge

Barbara Bushey, Hillsdale College

Mary Hogan Camp, Whatcom Community College

Susan P. Casteras, University of Washington

Cat Crotchett, Western Michigan University

Tim Cruise, Central Texas College

Julia K. Dabbs, University of Minnesota – Morris

Adrienne DeAngelis, University of Miami

Sarah Diebel, University of Wisconsin-Stout

Douglas N. Dow, Kansas State University

Kim Dramer, Fordham University

Brian Fencl, West Liberty State College

Monica Fullerton, Kenyon College

Laura D. Gelfand, The University of Akron

Alyson A. Gill, Arkansas State University

Maria de Jesus Gonzalez, University of Central Florida

Bobette Guillory, Carl Albert State College

Bertha Steinhardt Gutman, Delaware County Community College

Marianne Hogue, University of North Carolina – Wilmington

Stephanie Jacobson, St. John's University

Ruth Keitz, University of Texas – Brownsville

Joanne Kuebler, Manhattan College

Adele H. Lewis, Arizona State University

Lisa Livingston, Modesto Junior College

Diane Chin Lui, American River College

B. Susan Maxwell, University of Wisconsin-Oshkosh

Paul Miklowski, Cuyahoga Community College

Charles R. Morscheck Jr., Drexel University

Elaine O'Brien, California State University – Sacramento

Matthew Palczynski, Temple University

Jason Rosenfeld, Marymount Manhattan College

Phyllis Saretta, The Metropolitan Museum of Art

Onoyom Ukpong, Southern University and A & M College

Kristen Van Ausdall, Kenyon College

Marjorie S. Venit, University of Maryland

Linda Woodward, Montgomery College

Ted M. Wygant, Dayton Beach Community College

The contributors would like to thank John Beldon Scott, Whitney Lynn, and Nicole Veilleux for their advice and assistance in developing this edition. We also would like to thank the editors and staff at Pearson Education including Sarah Touborg, Helen Ronan, Barbara Cappuccio, Marlene Gassler, Cory Skidds, Brian Mackey, David Nitti, and Carla Worner who supported us in our work. At Laurence King Publishing, Susie May, Kara Hattersley-Smith, Julia Ruxton, Amanda Russell, and Simon Walsh oversaw the production of this new edition.

Faculty and Student Resources for Teaching and Learning with *Janson's History of Art*

PEARSON/PRENTICE HALL. We are pleased to present an outstanding array of high quality resources for teaching and learning with *Janson's History of Art*. Please contact your local Prentice Hall representative (use our rep locator at www.pearsonhighered.com) for more details on how to obtain these items, or send us an email at art.service@pearson.com.

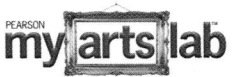 www.myartslab.com Save time, improve results. MyArtsLab is a robust online learning environment providing you and your students with the following resources:

Complete and dynamic e-book
Illustrated and printable flashcards
Unique "Closer Look" tours of over 125 key works of art
Pre-and post-tests for every chapter of the book
Customized study plan that helps students focus in on key areas
Primary Sources with critical thinking questions
Writing Tutorials for the most common writing assignments

Available at no additional charge when packaged with the text. Learn more about the power of MyArtsLab and register today at www.myartslab.com

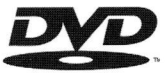 THE PRENTICE HALL DIGITAL ART LIBRARY. Instructors who adopt *Janson's History of Art* are eligible to receive this unparalleled resource containing every image in *Janson's History of Art* in the highest resolution (over 300 dpi) and pixilation possible for optimal projection and easy download. Developed and endorsed by a panel of visual curators and instructors across the country, this resource features images in jpeg and in PowerPoint, an instant download function for easy import into any presentation software, along with a zoom and a save-detail feature.

COURSESMART eTEXTBOOKS ONLINE is an exciting new choice for students looking to save money. As an alternative to purchasing the print textbook, students can subscribe to the same content online and save up to 50% off the suggested list price of the print text. With a CourseSmart eTextbook, students can search the text, make notes online, print out reading assignments that incorporate lecture notes, and bookmark important passages for later review. For more information, or to subscribe to the CourseSmart eTextbook, visit www.coursesmart.com.

CLASSROOM RESPONSE SYSTEM (CRS) IN CLASS QUESTIONS (ISBN: 0-205-76375-8). Get instant, classwide responses to beautifully illustrated chapter-specific questions during a lecture to gauge students' comprehension—and keep them engaged. Contact your local Pearson representative for details.

MYTEST (ISBN: 0-205-76391-X) is a commercial-quality computerized test management program available for both Microsoft Windows and Macintosh environments.

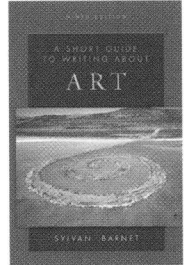 A SHORT GUIDE TO WRITING ABOUT ART, 10/e (ISBN: 0-205-70825-0) by Sylvan Barnet. This best-selling text has guided tens of thousands of art students through the writing process. Students are shown how to analyze pictures (drawings, paintings, photographs), sculptures and architecture, and are prepared with the tools they need to present their ideas through effective writing. Available at a discount when purchased with the text.

INSTRUCTOR'S RESOURCE MANUAL WITH TEST BANK (ISBN: 0-205-76374-X, download only) is an invaluable professional resource and reference for new and experienced faculty, containing sample syllabi, hundreds of sample test questions, and guidance on incorporating media technology into your course.

Introduction

WHY IN 1962 DID ANDY WARHOL MAKE A PAINTING ENTITLED *Gold Marilyn Monroe* (fig. **I.1**)? This almost 7-foot-high canvas was produced shortly after the death of the Hollywood screen star and sex symbol. It was not commissioned and obviously Monroe never "sat" for it, an activity that we generally associate with portraiture. Instead, Warhol

worked from a press photograph, a still from the 1953 movie *Niagara*, which he cropped to his liking and then transferred onto canvas using **silkscreen**. This process involves mechanically transferring the photograph onto a mesh screen, or in this case several screens, one for each color, and pressing printing ink through them onto canvas. Warhol then surrounded Marilyn's head with a field of broadly brushed gold paint.

Warhol's painting is not a conventional portrait of Monroe but rather a pastiche of the public image of the film star as propagated by the mass media. Warhol imitates the sloppy, gritty look and feel of color newspaper reproductions of the period, when the colors were often misregistered, aligning imperfectly with the image, and the colors themselves were "off," meaning not quite right. The Marilyn we are looking at is the impersonal celebrity of the media, the commodity being pushed by the film industry. She is supposedly glamorous, with her lush red lipstick and bright blond hair, but instead she appears pathetically tacky because of the grimy black ink and the garish color of her blond hair as it becomes bright yellow and her flesh tone turns pink. Her personality is impenetrable, reduced to a sad, lifeless public smile. Prompted by Monroe's suicide, *Gold Marilyn Monroe* presents the real Marilyn—a depressed, often miserable person, who, in

this textureless, detailless, unnaturalistic image, is becoming a blur fading into memory. Warhol has brilliantly expressed the indifference of the mass media, whose objective is to promote celebrities by saturating a thirsty public with their likenesses but which tells us nothing meaningful about them and shows no concern for them. Monroe's image is used simply to sell a product, much as the alluring and often jazzy packaging of Brillo soap pads or Campbell's soup cans is designed to make a product alluring without telling us anything about the product itself. The packaging is just camouflage. As a sentimental touch, Warhol floats Marilyn's head in a sea of gold paint, embedding her in an eternal realm previously reserved for use in icons of Christ and the Virgin Mary, which immerse these religious figures in a spiritual aura of golden, heavenly light (see fig. 13.22). But Warhol's revered Marilyn is sadly dwarfed by her celestial gold surrounding, adding to the tragic sense of this powerful portrait, which trenchantly comments on the enormous gulf existing between public image and private reality.

If we turn the clock back some 200 years and look at a portrait by the Boston painter John Singleton Copley, we again see an image of a woman (fig. **I.2**). But, made as it was in a different time and context, the story surrounding the painting is entirely different. The sitter is Freelove Olney Scott, and she is presented as a refined-looking woman, born, we would guess, into an aristocratic family, used to servants and power. As a matter of fact, we have come to accept Copley's portraits of colonial Bostonians, such as Mrs. Joseph Scott, as accurate depictions of their subjects

I.1 Andy Warhol, *Gold Marilyn Monroe*. 1962. Synthetic polymer paint, silk-screened, and oil on canvas, 6'11¼" × 4'9" (2.11 × 1.44 m). Museum of Modern Art, New York. Gift of Philip Johnson 316.1963

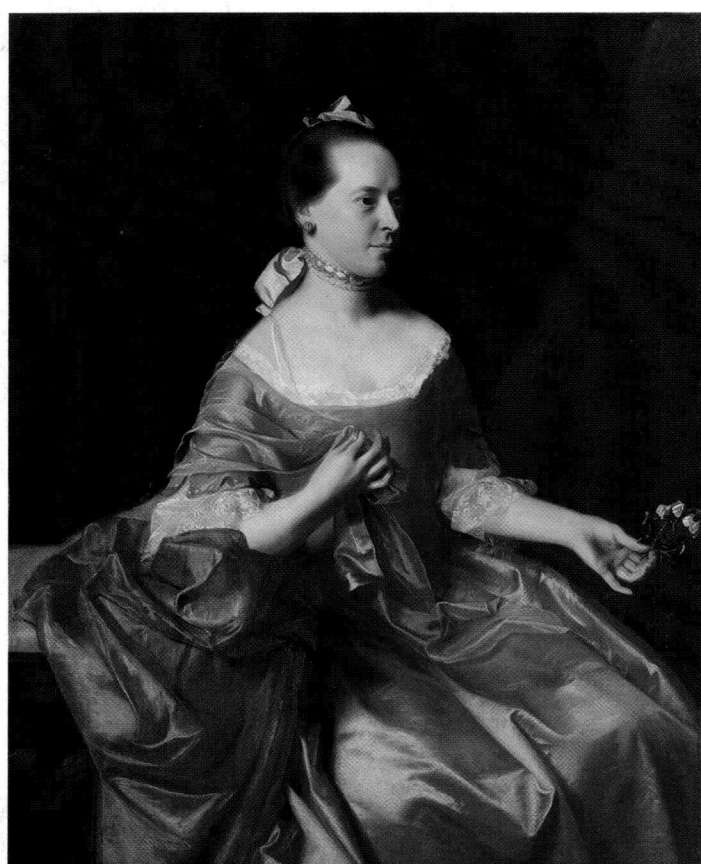

I.2   John Singleton Copley, *Mrs. Joseph Scott*. Oil on canvas, 69½ × 39½" (176.5 × 100 cm). The Newark Museum, Newark, New Jersey. 48.508

and lifestyles. But many, like Mrs. Scott, were not what they appear to be. So, who was Mrs. Scott? Let's take a closer look at the context in which the painting was made.

Copley is recognized as the first great American painter. Working in Boston from about 1754 to 1774, he became the most sought-after portraitist of the period. Copley easily outstripped the meager competition, most of whom actually earned their living painting signs and coaches. After all, no successful British artist had any reason to come to America. The economically struggling colonies were not a strong market for art. Only occasionally was a portrait commissioned, and typically, artists were treated like craftsmen rather than intellectuals. Like most colonial portraitists, Copley was largely self-taught, learning his trade by looking at black-and-white prints of paintings by the European masters.

As we can see in *Mrs. Joseph Scott*, Copley was a master of painting textures, which is all the more astonishing when we remember that he had no one to teach him the tricks of the painter's trade. His pictorial illusions are so convincing, we think we are looking at real silk, ribbons, lace, pearls, skin, hair, and marble, quite the opposite of Warhol's artificial Marilyn. Copley's contemporaries also marveled at his sleight of hand. No other colonial painter attained such a level of realism.

But is Copley just a "face painter," as portraitists were derogatorily called at the time, offering mere resemblances of his sitters and their expensive accoutrements? Is this painting just a means to replicate the likeness of an individual in an era before the advent of photography? The answer to both questions is a resounding "no." Copley's job was not just to make a faithful image of Mrs. Scott, but to portray her as a woman of impeccable character, limitless wealth, and aristocratic status. The flowers she holds are a symbol of fertility, faithfulness, and feminine grace, indicating that she is a good mother and wife, and a charming woman. Her expensive dress was imported from London, as was her necklace. Copley undoubtedly copied her pose from one of the prints he had of portraits of British or French royalty.

Not only is Mrs. Scott's pose borrowed, but most likely her clothing is as well, for her necklace appears on three other women in Copley portraits. In other words, it was a studio prop, as the dress may have been too. In fact, except for Mrs. Scott's face, the entire painting is a fiction designed to aggrandize the wife of a newly wealthy Boston merchant who had made his fortune selling provisions to the occupying British army. The Scotts were *nouveau-riche* commoners, not titled aristocrats. By the middle of the eighteenth century, rich Bostonians wanted to distinguish themselves from the multitude, and so, after a century of trying to escape their British roots, from which many had fled to secure religious freedom, they now sought to imitate the British aristocracy, even to the point of taking tea in the afternoon and owning English Spaniels, a breed that in England only aristocrats were permitted to own.

Joseph Scott commissioned this painting of his wife, as well as a portrait of himself, not just to record their features, but to show off the family's wealth. The pictures were extremely expensive and therefore status symbols, much as a Rolls-Royce or a Tiffany diamond ring are today. The portraits were displayed in the public spaces of their house so that they could be readily seen by visitors. Most likely they hung on either side of the mantel in the living room, or in the entrance hall. They were not intended as intimate affectionate resemblances destined for the bedroom. If patrons wanted cherished images of their loved ones, they would commission miniature portraits, which captured the likeness of the sitter in amazing detail and were often so small they could be encased in a locket that a woman would wear on a chain around her neck, or a gentleman would place in the inner breastpocket of his coat, close to the heart.

Warhol and Copley worked in very different times, a fact that has tremendous effect on the look and meaning of their portraits. Their paintings were made to serve very different purposes, and consequently they tell very different stories. And because art always serves a purpose, it is impossible for an artist to make a work that does not represent a point of view and tell a story, sometimes many stories. As we will see, great artists tell great and powerful stories. We shall find that an important key to unraveling these stories is understanding the context in which the work was made.

THE POWER OF ART AND THE IMPACT OF CONTEXT

In a sense, art is a form of propaganda, for it represents an individual's or group's point of view, and this view is often presented as truth or fact. For centuries, art was used by church and state to propagate their importance, superiority, and greatness. *The Alba Madonna* (fig. **I.3**), for example, was designed to proclaim the idealized, perfect state of existence attainable through Catholicism in sixteenth-century Italy, while the Arch of Titus (fig. **I.4**) was erected to reinforce in the public's mind the military prowess of the first-century Roman emperor. Even landscape

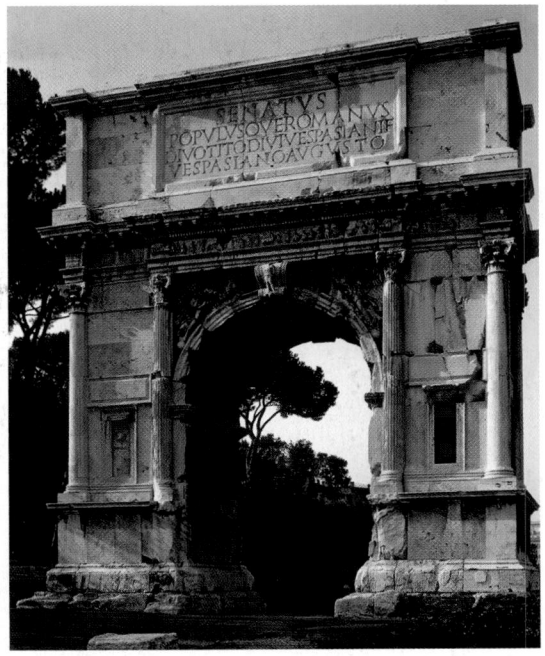

I.4   Arch of Titus, Forum Romanum, Rome. ca. 81 CE (restored)

paintings and still lifes of fruit, dead game, and flowers made in the seventeenth century are loaded with moral messages, and are far from simple attempts to capture the splendor and many moods of nature or show off the painter's finesse at creating a convincing illusionistic image.

Epitomizing the power of art is its ability to evoke entire historical periods. The words "ancient Egypt" will conjure up in most people's minds images of the pyramids, the Sphinx, and flat stiff figures lined up sideways across the face of stone (fig. **I.5**). Or look at the power of Grant Wood's famous 1930 painting

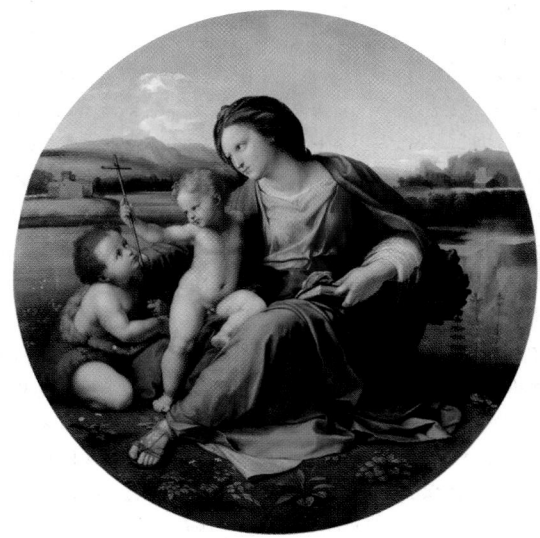

I.3   Raphael, *The Alba Madonna*. ca. 1510. Oil on panel transferred to canvas, diameter 37¼" (94 cm). Image courtesy of the Board of Trustees, National Gallery of Art, Washington, D.C., Andrew W. Mellon Collection, 1937.1.24. (24)

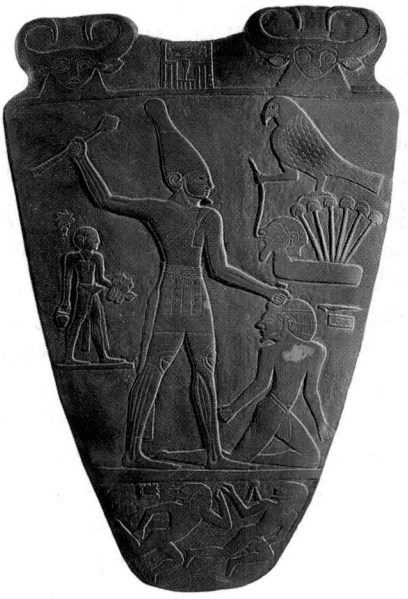

I.5   Palette of King Narmer, from Hierakonpolis. ca. 3150–3125 BCE. Slate, height 25" (63.5 cm). Egyptian Museum, Cairo

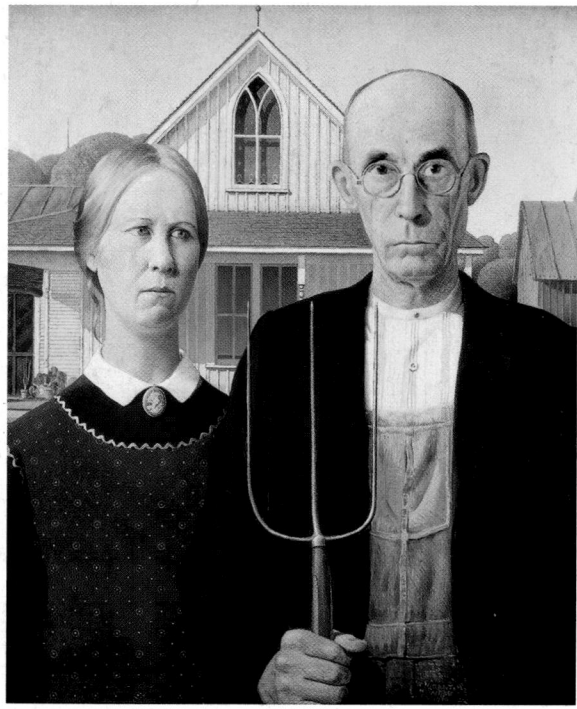

I.6 Grant Wood, *American Gothic*. 1930. Oil on beaverboard, 30¹¹/₁₆" × 25¹¹/₁₆" (78 × 65.3 cm). Unframed. Friends of American Art Collection. 1930.934. The Art Institute of Chicago

Many art historians, critics, and other viewers found the picture remarkably beautiful—glittering and shimmering with a delicate, ephemeral otherworldy aura. Many, especially Catholics, however, were repulsed by Ofili's homage to the Virgin and were infuriated. Instead of viewing the work through Ofili's eyes, they placed the painting within the context of their own experience and beliefs. Consequently, they interpreted the dung and graphic imagery—and perhaps even the black Virgin, although this was never mentioned—as sacrilegious. Within days of the opening of the exhibition, the painting had to be placed behind a large Plexiglas barrier. One artist hurled horse manure at the façade of the Brooklyn Museum, claiming, "I was expressing myself creatively," a defense often offered for Ofili. Another museum visitor sneaked behind the Plexiglas barrier and smeared the Virgin with white paint in order to cover her up. The biggest attack came from New York's mayor, Rudolph Giuliani, a Catholic, who was so outraged that he tried, unsuccessfully, to stop city funding for the museum. The public outrage at Ofili's work is just part of a long tradition that probably goes back to the beginning of image making. Art has consistently provoked anger, just as it has inspired pride, admiration, love, and respect, and the reason is simple: Art is never an empty container but rather a vessel loaded with meaning, subject to multiple interpretations, and always representing someone's point of view.

American Gothic (fig. **I.6**), which has led us to believe that humorless, austere, hardworking farmers dominated the American hinterlands at the time. The painting has virtually become an emblem of rural America for the period.

American Gothic has also become a source of much sarcastic humor for later generations, which have adapted the famous pitchfork-bearing farmer and his sour-faced daughter for all kinds of agendas unrelated to the artist's original message. Works of art are often later appropriated to serve purposes quite different from those initially intended, with context heavily influencing the meaning of a work. The reaction of some New Yorkers to *The Holy Virgin Mary* (fig. **I.7**) by Chris Ofili reflects the power of art to provoke and spark debate, even outrage. The work appeared in an exhibition titled *Sensation: Young British Artists from the Saatchi Collection*, presented at the Brooklyn Museum in late 1999. Ofili, who is a Briton of African descent, made an enormous picture of a black Virgin Mary using tiny dots of paint, glitter, map pins, and collaged images of genitalia from popular magazines. Instead of hanging on the wall, this enormous painting rested on two large wads of elephant dung, which had been a signature feature of the artist's large canvases since 1991. Elephant dung is held sacred in some African cultures, and for Ofili, a devout Catholic who periodically attends Mass, the picture was a modernization of the traditional presentation of the elemental sacredness of the Virgin, with the so-called pornographic images intended to suggest both procreation and hovering naked angels. While intentionally provocative, the picture was not conceived as an attack on the Catholic religion.

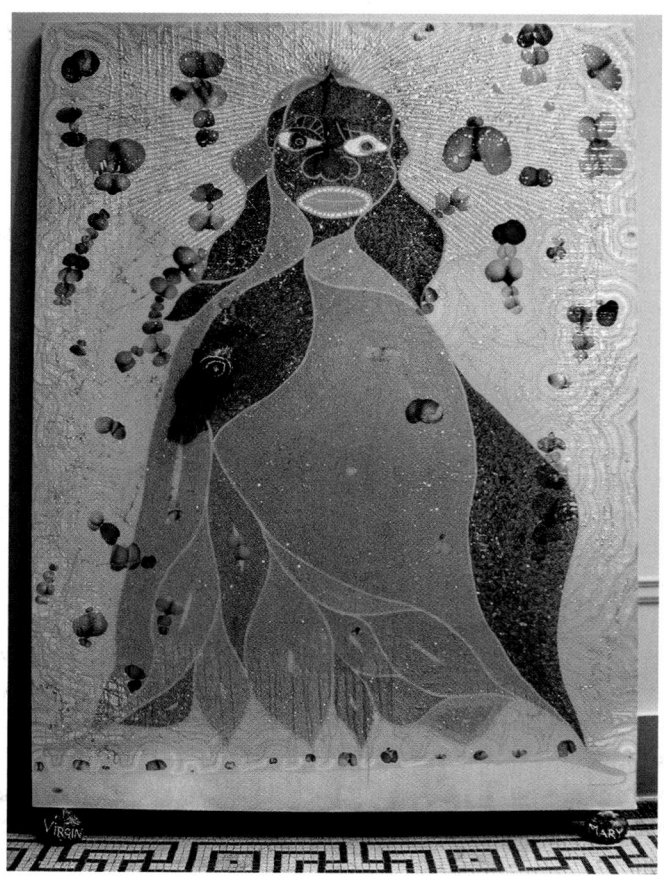

I.7 Chris Ofili, *The Holy Virgin Mary*. 1996. Paper, collage, oil paint, glitter, polyester resin, map pins, and elephant dung on linen, 7'11" × 5'11⅝" (2.44 × 1.83 m). Victoria Miro Gallery, London

Because the context for looking at art constantly changes, our interpretations and insights into art and entire periods evolve as well. For example, when the first edition of this book was published in 1962, women artists were not included, which was typical for textbooks at the time. America, like most of the world, was male-dominated and history was male-centric. Historically, women were expected to be wives and mothers, and to stay in the home and not have careers. They were not supposed to become artists, and the few known exceptions were not taken seriously by historians, who were mostly male. The feminist movement, beginning in the mid-1960s, overturned this restrictive perception of women. As a result, in the last 40 years, art historians—many of them female—have "rediscovered" countless women artists who had attained a degree of success in their day. Many of them were outstanding artists, held in high esteem during their lifetimes, despite the enormous struggle to overcome powerful social and even family resistance against women becoming professional artists.

One of these "lost" women artists is the seventeenth-century Dutch painter Judith Leyster, a follower, if not a student, of the famed Frans Hals. Over the subsequent centuries, Leyster's paintings were either attributed to other artists, including Hals and Gerrit van Honthorst, or they were labeled "artist unknown." At the end of the nineteenth century, however, Leyster was rediscovered in her own right through an analysis of her signature, documents, and style, and her paintings were gradually restored to her name. It was only with the feminist movement that she was elevated from a minor figure to one of the more accomplished painters of her generation, one important enough to be included in basic histories of art. The feminist movement provided a new context for evaluating art, one that had an interest in rather than a denial of women's achievements and a study of issues relating to gender and how they appear in the arts.

A work like Leyster's *Self-Portrait* (fig. **I.8**) is especially fascinating from this point of view. Its size and date (ca. 1633) suggest that this may have been the painting the artist submitted as her presentation piece for admission into the local painters' guild, the Guild of St. Luke of Haarlem. Women were not generally encouraged to join the guild, which was a male preserve that reinforced the professional status of men. Nor did women artists generally take on students. Leyster bucked both traditions, however, as she carved out a career for herself in a man's world. In her self-portrait, she presents herself as an artist armed with many brushes, suggesting her deft control of the medium—an idea that the presentation picture itself was meant to demonstrate. On the easel is a segment of a genre scene of which several variations are known. We must remember that at this time artists rarely showed themselves working at their easels, toiling with their hands: They wanted to separate themselves from mere artisans and laborers, presenting themselves as intellectuals belonging to a higher class. As a woman defying male expectations, however, Leyster needed to declare clearly that she was indeed an artist. But she cleverly elevates her status by not dressing as an artist would when painting. Instead, she appears as her patrons do in their portraits, well-dressed and well-off. Her mouth is open, in what is called a

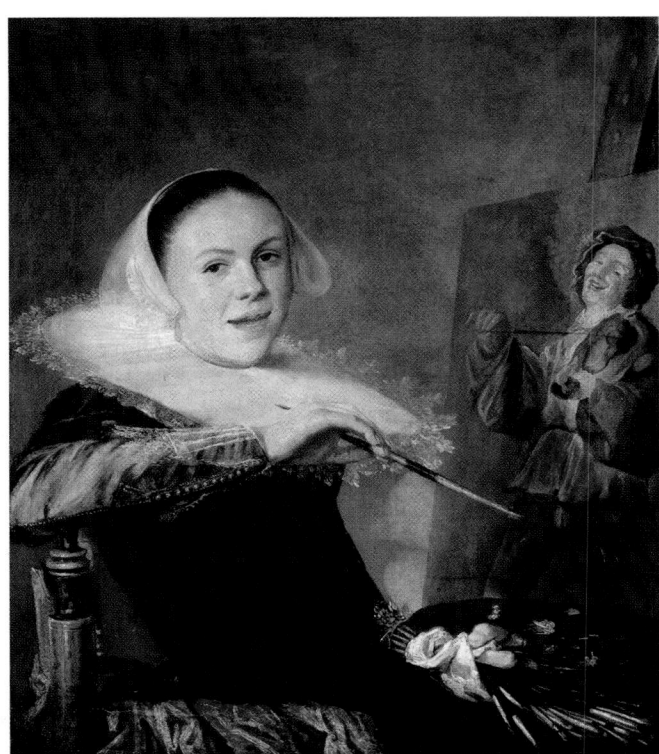

I.8   Judith Leyster, *Self-Portrait*. ca. 1633. Oil on canvas, 29⅜ × 25⅝" (72.3 × 65.3 cm). National Gallery of Art, Washington, D.C. Gift of Mr. and Mrs. Robert Woods Bliss

"speaking likeness" portrait, giving her a casual but self-assured animated quality, as she appears to converse on equal terms with a visitor, or with us. Leyster, along with Artemisia Gentileschi and Marie-Louise-Élisabeth Vigée-Lebrun, who also appear in this book, was included in a major 1976 exhibition titled *Women Artists 1550–1950*, which was shown in Los Angeles and Brooklyn, and played a major role in establishing the importance of women artists.

WHAT IS ART?

Ask most people "What is art?," and they will respond with the words "an oil painting" or "a marble or bronze sculpture." Their principal criterion is that the object be beautiful—whatever that may be—although generally they will probably define this as the degree to which a painting or sculpture is real looking or adheres to their notion of naturalism. Technical finesse or craft is viewed as the highest attribute of art making, capable of inspiring awe and reverence. Epitomizing these values is Greek and Roman sculpture, such as the fourth-century BCE sculpture the *Apoxyomenos (Scraper)* (fig. **I.9**), which for centuries was considered the high point of fine art. To debunk the myth that art is only about technique and begin to get at what it is really about, we return to Warhol's *Gold Marilyn Monroe*. The painting is rich with stories, one of which is how it poses questions about the meaning of art, how it functions, and how it takes on value, both financial and aesthetic. Warhol even begs the question of the significance of technical finesse in art making, an issue raised by the fact that he wants to give us the impression that he may not have even touched this painting himself. We have already seen how he appropriated someone else's photograph of Monroe, not even taking his own. Warhol then instructed his assistants to make the screens for the printing process. They may also have prepared the canvas, screened the image with the colors Warhol selected, and even painted the gold to Warhol's specifications.

By using assistants to make his work, Warhol is telling us that art is not necessarily about the artist's technical finesse, but about communicating an idea using visual language. The measuring stick for quality in art is the quality of the statement being made, or its philosophy, as well as the quality of the technical means for making this statement, even if not executed by the artist. Looking at *Gold Marilyn Monroe* in the flesh at New York's Museum of Modern Art is a powerful, even unforgettable experience. Standing in front of this large canvas, we cannot help but feel the

empty glory of America's most famous symbol of female sexuality and stardom. Because the artist's vision, and not his touch, is the relevant issue for the production of this particular work, it is of no consequence that Warhol makes it seem as though he never laid a hand on the canvas except to sign the back. We shall see shortly, however, that the artist's touch is indeed often critical to the success of a work of art, which is especially true for art made before 1900.

Warhol openly declared that his art was not about his technical ability when he named his midtown Manhattan studio "The Factory." By doing so, he told us that art was a commodity, and that he was manufacturing a product, even a mass-produced one. The factory churned out over a thousand paintings and prints of Marilyn based on the same publicity still. All Warhol appeared to do for the most part was sign them, his signature reinforcing the importance people placed on the idea of the artist's signature itself being an essential part of the work. Ironically, most Old Master paintings, dating from the fourteenth through the eighteenth centuries, are not signed; and despite giving the public the impression that he had little involvement in his work, Warhol was a workaholic and very hands-on in the production of his art.

Moreover, artists have been using assistants to help make their pictures for centuries. Peter Paul Rubens, an Antwerp painter working in the first half of the seventeenth century and one of the most famous artists of his day, had an enormous workshop that cranked out many of his paintings, especially the larger works. His assistants often specialized in particular elements such as flowers, animals, or clothing, for example, and many went on to become successful artists in their own right. Rubens would design the painting, and then assistants, trained in his style, would execute individual parts. Rubens would then come in at the end and pull the painting together as needed. The price the client was willing to pay often determined how much Rubens himself participated in the actual painting of the picture: Many of his works were indeed made entirely by him, and therefore commanded the highest prices. Rubens's brilliant flashy brushwork was in many respects critical to the making of the picture. Not only was his handling of paint considered superior to that of his assistants, the very identity of his paintings—their very life, so to speak—was linked to his unique genius in applying paint to canvas, almost as much as it was to the dynamism of his dramatic compositions. His brushwork complemented his subject matter. The two went hand in hand.

Warhol was not the first artist to make art that intentionally raised the issue of what art is and how it functions. This distinction belongs to the humorous and brilliant Parisian Marcel Duchamp, one of the most influential artists of the twentieth century. In 1919, Duchamp took a postcard reproduction of Leonardo da Vinci's *Mona Lisa*, which hangs in the Louvre Museum in Paris, and drew a moustache on the sitter's face (fig. **I.10**). Below he wrote the letters, "L.H.O.O.Q.," which when pronounced in French is *elle a chaud au cul*, or "She's got the hots." Duchamp was poking fun at the public's fascination with the mysterious smile on the Mona Lisa, which had intrigued

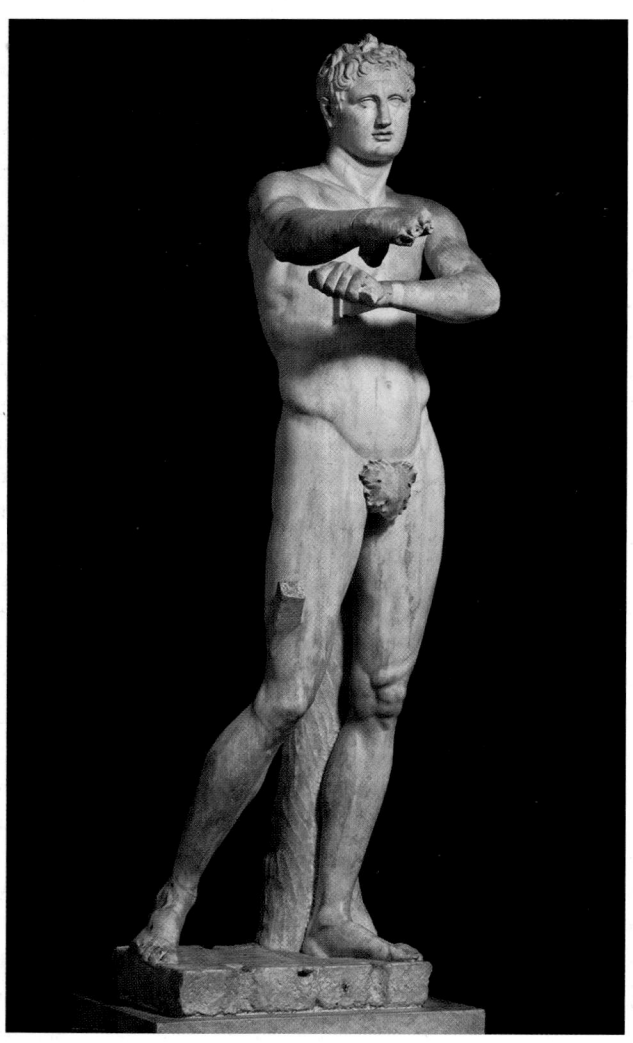

I.9 *Apoxyomenos (Scraper)*. Roman marble copy, probably after a bronze original of ca. 330 BCE by Lysippos. Height 6'9" (2.1 m). Musei Vaticani, Rome

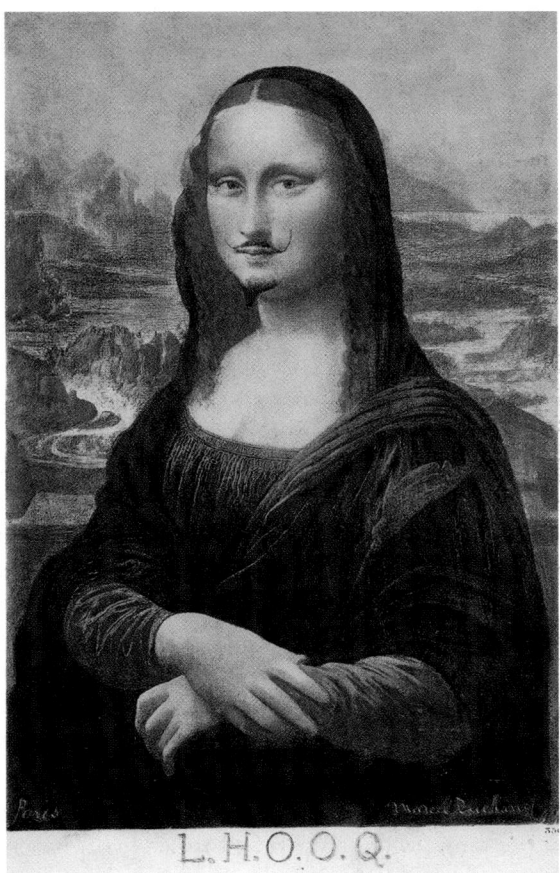

I.10 Marcel Duchamp, *Mona Lisa (L.H.O.O.Q.)*. 1919. Rectified readymade; pencil on a postcard reproduction, 7 × 4⅞" (17.8 × 12 cm). Private collection

and while intellectually engaging us in a most serious manner, it can also provide us with a smile, if not a good belly laugh. Many historians today consider *Mona Lisa (L.H.O.O.Q)* as important as Leonardo's *Mona Lisa*, and put the two artists on the same plane of importance.

ART AND AESTHETICS: THE ISSUE OF BEAUTY

Mona Lisa (L.H.O.O.Q.) also raised the issue of aesthetics, which is the study of theories surrounding art, including the definition of beauty and the meaning and purpose of art. Duchamp selected the *Mona Lisa* for appropriation for many reasons, one of them no doubt being that many people considered it the greatest and therefore the most beautiful painting ever made. Certainly, it was one of the most famous paintings in the world, if not the most famous. In 1919, most of those who held such a view had probably never seen it and only knew if from reproductions, probably no better than the one Duchamp used in *Mona Lisa (L.H.O.O.Q.)*. And yet, they would describe the original painting as beautiful, but not Duchamp's comical version.

Duchamp called altered found objects such as *Mona Lisa (L.H.O.O.Q.)* "readymades" (for other examples, see *Bicycle Wheel*, fig. 27.29, and *Fountain*, fig. 28.2), and he was adamant that these works had no aesthetic value whatsoever. They were not to be considered beautiful; they were aesthetically neutral. What interested Duchamp were the ideas that these objects embodied once they were declared art.

Despite his claim, Duchamp's readymades can be perceived as beautiful, in ways, of course that are quite different from Leonardo's *Mona Lisa*, but beautiful all the same. *Mona Lisa (L.H.O.O.Q.)* has an aura about it, an aura of wit and ideas that are specific to Duchamp. As a result, this slightly altered cheap color postcard is a compelling work of art. The qualities that attract us to it, which we can describe as its beauty, could not be further from those of Leonardo's *Mona Lisa*, which have more to do with composition, color, and paint handling. Ultimately, beauty, in many respects, can be equated with quality, which to a large degree hinges on the power of the statement, not some pre-conceived notion of visual beauty.

Beauty is not just a pretty colorful picture or a perfectly formed, harmonious nude marble figure such as the *Apoxymenos*. Beauty resides as well in content and how successfully this content is made visual. This book is intended to suggest the many complex ways that quality, and thus beauty, manifests itself in art. Some of the greatest paintings are grotesque, depicting horrific scenes that many people do not find acceptable, but they are nonetheless beautiful—scenes such as beheadings, crucifixions (fig. **I.11**), death and despair, emotional distress, and the brutal massacre of innocent women and children. Like Duchamp's *Mona Lisa (L.H.O.O.Q.)*, these works possess an aura that makes them riveting, despite the repulsiveness of their subject matter. They have quality, and to those who recognize and feel this quality, this

viewers for centuries and eluded suitable explanation. Duchamp irreverently provided one: She is sexually aroused. With the childish gesture of affixing a moustache to the image, Duchamp also attacked bourgeois reverence for Old Master painting, as well as the age-old ideal of oil painting representing the pinnacle of art.

Art, Duchamp is saying, can be made by merely drawing on a mass-produced reproduction. Artists can use any imaginable medium in any way in order to express themselves: not just oil on canvas or cast bronze or chiseled marble He is announcing that art is about ideas that are made visually, and not necessarily about craft. In this deceptively whimsical work, which is actually rich in ideas, Duchamp is telling us that art is anything someone wants to call art—which is not the same as saying it is good art. Furthermore, he is proclaiming that art can be small, since *Mona Lisa (L.H.O.O.Q.)* is a fraction of the size of its source, the *Mona Lisa*. By appropriating Leonardo's famous picture and interpreting it very differently from traditional readings (see pages 564–66), Duchamp suggests that the meaning of art is not fixed forever by the artist, that it can change and be reassigned by viewers, writers, collectors, and museum curators, who may use it for their own purposes. Lastly, and this is certainly one of Duchamp's many wonderful contributions to art, he is telling us that art can be fun, that it can defy conventional notions of beauty,

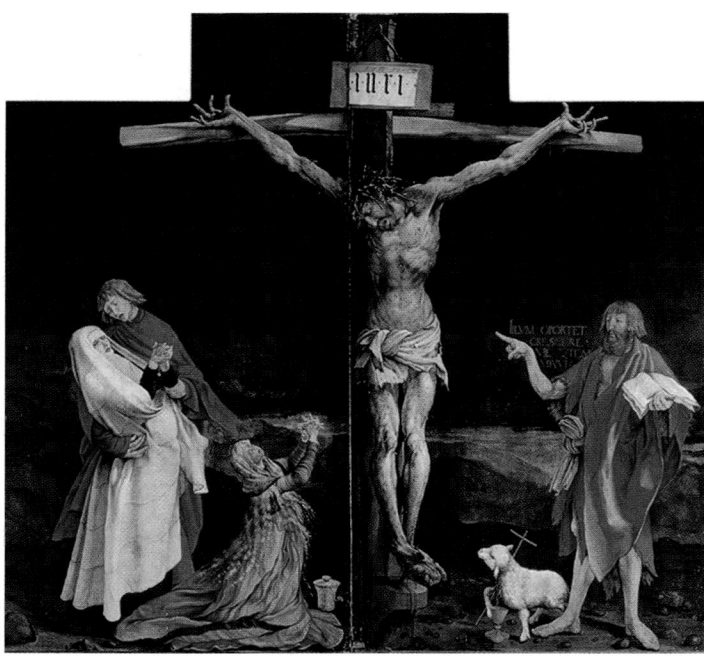

I.11 Matthias Grünewald, *The Crucifixion* (center panel). ca. 1509/10–15. Oil on panel, 9'9½" × 10'9" (2.97 × 3.28 m). Musée d'Unterlinden, Colmar, France

makes them beautiful. Others will continue to be repulsed and offended by them, or at best fail to find them interesting.

ILLUSIONISM AND MEANING IN ART

The Roman historian Pliny tells the story about the competition between the Greek painters Zeuxis and Parrhasius to see who could make the most realistic work. Zeuxis painted grapes so real that birds tried to eat them. But it was Parrhasius who won the competition when he made a painting of a curtain covering a painting. So realistic was the work that Zeuxis asked him to pull back the curtain covering his painting only to discover that he was already looking at the painting.

Pliny's story is interesting, because despite a recurring emphasis on illusionism in art, the ability to create illusionistic effects and "fool the eye" is generally not what determines quality in art, and if it were, thousands of relatively unknown artists today would be considered geniuses. As we just discussed, quality in art comes from ideas *and* execution. Just being clever and fooling the eye is not enough.

A look at the sculpture of twentieth-century artist Duane Hanson shows us how illusionism can be put in the service of meaning to create a powerful work of art. Hanson's 1995 sculpture *Man on a Mower* (fig. **I.12**) is a work that is too often appreciated only for its illusionistic qualities, while the real content goes unnoticed. Yet, it is the content, not the illusionism itself, that makes this sculpture so powerful. Hanson began making his sculptures in the late 1960s, casting his figures in polyester resin, and then meticulously painting them. He then dressed them in

real clothing, used real accessories (including wigs and artificial eyeballs), and placed them with real bits of furniture. Most viewers are startled to discover his sculptures are not real people, and many have tried to interact with his characters, which include museum guards, tourists, shoppers, house painters, and sunbathers.

But Hanson's art is about more than just a visual sleight of hand. He is also a realist and a moralist, and his art is filled with tragic social commentary. By "realist," we mean that his sculpture is not limited to attractive, beautiful, and ennobling people, objects, and situations, but instead focuses on the base, crude, and unseemly. In *Man on a Mower*, which, with the exception of the lawnmower and aluminum can, is painted cast bronze, we see an overweight man clutching a diet soda. He dwarfs the riding mower he sits on. His T-shirt, baseball hat, pants, and sneakers are soiled. He is ordinary, and the entire sculpture is remarkably prosaic.

Man on a Mower is a tragic work. We see disillusionment in the man's eyes as he blankly stares off into space. The diet soda he holds suggests that he is trying to lose weight but is losing the battle. Cutting grass is another metaphor for a losing battle, since the grass is going to grow back. This work also represents the banality of human existence. What is life about? The monotony of cutting grass. In this last work, made when he knew he was dying of cancer, Hanson captured what he perceived to be the emptiness of human existence and contemporary life in the modern world. The illusionism of the sculpture makes this aura of alienation and lack of spirituality all the more palpable. This man is us, and this is our life, too. He embodies no poetry, nobility, or heroism. Our twentieth-century *Man on a Mower* has no fine causes or beliefs to run to as he confronts the down-to-earth reality of life and death.

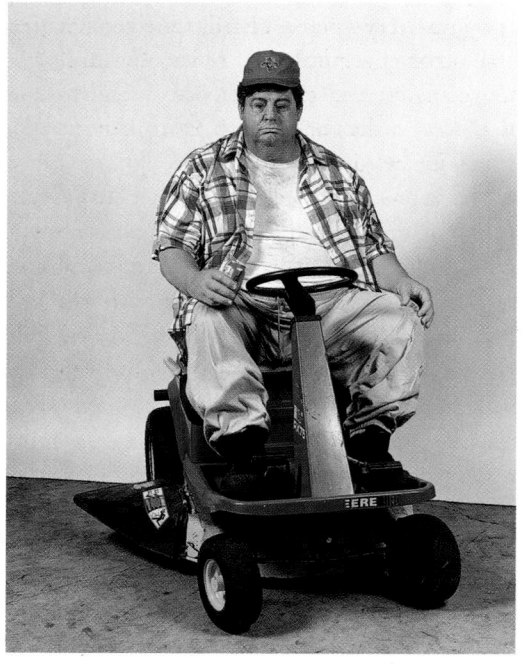

I.12 Duane Hanson, *Man on a Mower*. 1995. Bronze, polychromed in oil, with mower. Life-size. Courtesy Van de Weghe Fine Art, New York

CAN A MECHANICAL PROCESS BE ART? PHOTOGRAPHY

The first edition of this book did not include photography, reflecting on attitude dating back to the introduction of photography in 1839 that the medium, because it was largely a mechanical process, was not an art form, or certainly not one that had the same merit as painting and sculpture. Within the last 25 years, however, photography has been vindicated. Along with video and film, it has been elevated to the status of one of the most important artistic mediums, perhaps even outstripping painting. Pictures from the nineteenth and twentieth centuries that had interested only a handful of photography insiders suddenly became intensely sought-after, with many museums rushing to establish photography departments and amass significant collections. In other words, it took well over 125 years for people to understand photography and develop an eye for the special qualities and beauties of the medium, which are so radically different from those of the traditional twin peaks of the visual arts, painting and sculpture.

We need only look at a 1972 photograph titled *Albuquerque* (fig. **I.13**) by Lee Friedlander to see how photography operates as an artistic medium. In his black-and-white print, called a gelatin silver print since the pre-exposed paper surface consists of silver in a gelatin solution, Friedlander portrays a modern America which, he suggests, has been rendered vacuous and lifeless by modernity and twentieth-century technology. How does he make such a statement? The picture obviously has a haunting emptiness, for it contains no people and is instead filled with strange vacant spaces of walkway and street that appear between the numerous objects, such as a fire hydrant, street signs, and traffic light, that pop up everywhere. A hard, eerie geometry prevails, as seen in the strong verticals of poles, buildings, and wall. Cylinders, rectangles, and circles can be found throughout the composition, even in the background apartment building and the brick driveway in the foreground.

Despite the stillness and sense of absence, the picture is busy and restless. The vertical elements create a vibrant staccato rhythm, which is reinforced by the asymmetrical composition lacking a focus or center, and by the powerful intersecting diagonals of the street and foreground wall. Friedlander crafted his composition so carefully he gets the shadow of the hydrant to parallel the street. Disturbing features appear everywhere. There is a lopsided telephone pole, suggesting collapse. And there is the pole for a street sign, the top of which has been cropped, that visually cuts a dog in two while casting a mysterious shadow on a nearby wall. The fire hydrant appears to be mounted incorrectly, sticking too far out of the ground. The car on the right has been brutally cropped and appears to have a light pole sprouting from its hood. The entire picture is dominated by technology and synthetic, industrial, or mass-produced objects. Nature has been cemented over, reduced to a few straggly trees in the middle ground and distance and the thriving weeds surrounding the

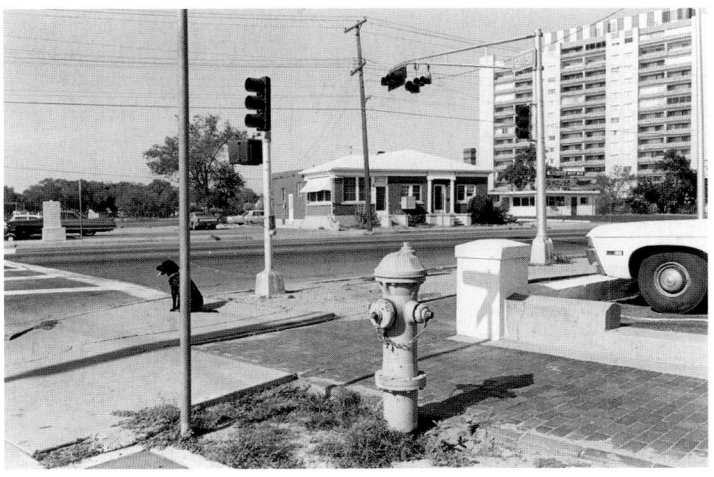

I.13 Lee Friedlander, *Albuquerque.* 1972. Gelatin silver print, 11 × 14" (27.9 × 35.6 cm)

hydrant. In this brilliant print, Friedlander powerfully suggests that technology, mass-produced products, and a fast fragmented lifestyle are spawning alienation and a disconnection with nature. Friedlander also suggests that modernization is also making America homogeneous—if it were not for the title, we would have no idea that this photograph was taken in Albuquerque, New Mexico.

Friedlander did not just find this composition. He very carefully made it. He not only wanted a certainly quality of light for his picture, but probably even waited for the sun to cast shadows that aligned perfectly with the street. When framing the composition, he meticulously incorporated a fragment of the utility cover in the lower left foreground, while axing a portion of the car on the right. Nor did the geometry of the picture just happen. He made it happen. Instead of a soft focus that would create an atmospheric blurry picture, he used a deep focus that produces a sharp crisp image filled with detail, allowing, for example, the individual rectangular bricks in the pavement to be clearly seen. The strong white tones of the vertical rectangles of the apartment building, the foreground wall, and the utility box blocking the car on the left edge of the picture were most likely carefully worked up in the darkroom, as was the rectangular columned doorway on the house. Friedlander has exposed the ugliness of modern America in this hard, cold, dry image, and because of the power of its message has made an extraordinarily beautiful work of art, the kind of image that has elevated photography into the pantheon of art.

HOW ARCHITECTURE TELLS STORIES

An art form that is basically abstract and functional might be seen as a poor candidate for telling stories, conveying messages, and disseminating propaganda. And yet it can. We see Gianlorenzo Bernini doing it in 1657 when he was asked by Pope Alexander XVII to design a large open space, or piazza, in front of St. Peter's

Cathedral in Rome. Bernini's solution was to create a plaza that was defined by a colonnade, or row of columns, resembling arms that appear to embrace visitors maternally, welcoming them into the bosom of the church (fig. **I.14**). He thus anthropomorphized the building by emphasizing the identification of the church with the Virgin Mary. At the same time, the French architect Claude Perrault was commissioned to design the façade of Louis XIV's palace, the Louvre in Paris (fig. **I.15**). To proclaim the king's grandeur, he made the ground floor, where the day-to-day business of the court was carried out, a squat podium. In contrast, the second floor, where the royal quarters were located and Louis would have held court, was much higher and grander and served as the main floor, clearly supported by the worker-bee floor. Perrault articulated this elevated second story with a design that recalled Roman temples, thus associating Louis XIV with imperial Rome and worldly power. The severe geometry and symmetry of the building reflect the regimented order and tight control of Louis XIV's reign.

At first glance, it seems hard to project any story onto Frank Lloyd Wright's Solomon R. Guggenheim Museum (fig. **I.16**), a museum that, when it was built between 1956 and 1959, was largely dedicated to abstract art. Located on upper Fifth Avenue in New York and overlooking Central Park, the building resembled for many a flying saucer; it was certainly radically different from the surrounding residential apartment buildings, and for that matter, almost anything built anywhere up to that time. But if we had to guess, we would probably first divine that the building might be a museum, for the exterior resembles a work of art—a giant nonobjective sculpture. Made of reinforced concrete, the building even seems as though it were made from an enormous mold that formed its continuous upward spiral, which from any one side appears to consist of enormous, weighty, massive horizontal bands. There is no mistaking this structure for an apartment complex or office building.

Wright conceived the Guggenheim in 1945–46, when he received the commission, and his personal goal was to create an organic structure that deviated from the conventional static rectangular box filled with conventional rectangular rooms. The building is designed around a spiral ramp (fig. **I.17**), which is meant to evoke a spiral shell, and this ramp is what defines the design of the exterior. Wright also thought of the interior as a ceramic vase, for it is closed at the bottom, widens as it rises, and is "open" at the top since it is capped by a spectacular light-filled, cone-shaped glass roof. Essentially, the museum is a single ramp-lined space, although there are a handful of galleries off the ramp and separate spaces for offices, auditorium, and bookstore, for example. Wright expected visitors to take an elevator to the top of the ramp, and then slowly amble down its 3 percent gradient, gently pulled along by gravity. Because the ramp was relatively narrow, viewers could not stand too far back from the art, which seemed to float on the curved walls, enhancing the fluid effect of Wright's curved, organic design. As a result, visitors were forced into a more intimate relationship with the art. At the same time, however, they could look back across the open space of the room

to see where they had gone, comparing the work in front of them to a segment of the exhibition presented on a sweeping distant arc, Or they could look ahead as well, to get a preview of where they were going.

Not only do visitors see the art, they also see other visitors, sometimes just as distant specks, winding their way down the ramp. The building has a sense of continuity and mobility that Wright viewed as an organic experience, analogous to traveling along the continuous winding paths of the adjacent Central Park, which was designed in the nineteenth century to capture and preserve nature in the encroaching urban environment. Wright's enormous "room" reflects nature not only in its spiral shell design, but also in the organic concave and convex forms that can be seen from the top of ramp and that reflect the subtle eternal movement of nature. Wright even placed a lozenge-shaped pool on the ground floor, directly opposite the light entering from the skylight above, the two architectural touches reinforcing a sense of nature. Art historians have also likened the sense of constant

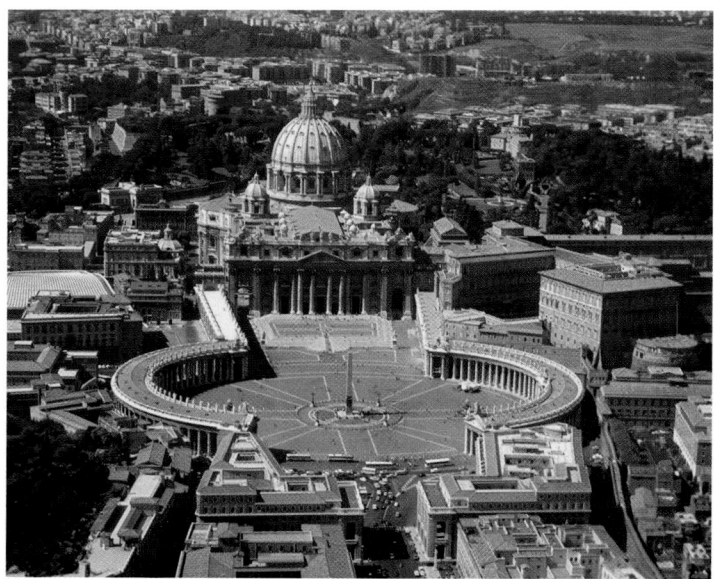

I.14 St. Peter's, Rome. Nave and façade by Carlo Maderno, 1607–15; colonnade by Gianlorenzo Bernini, designed 1657

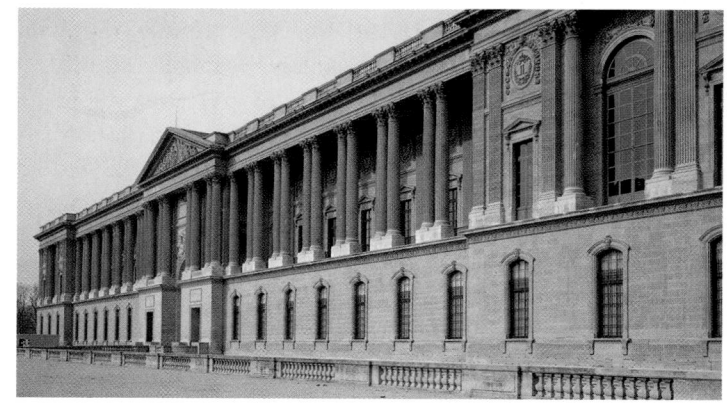

I.15 Claude Perrault. East front of the Louvre, Paris. 1667–70

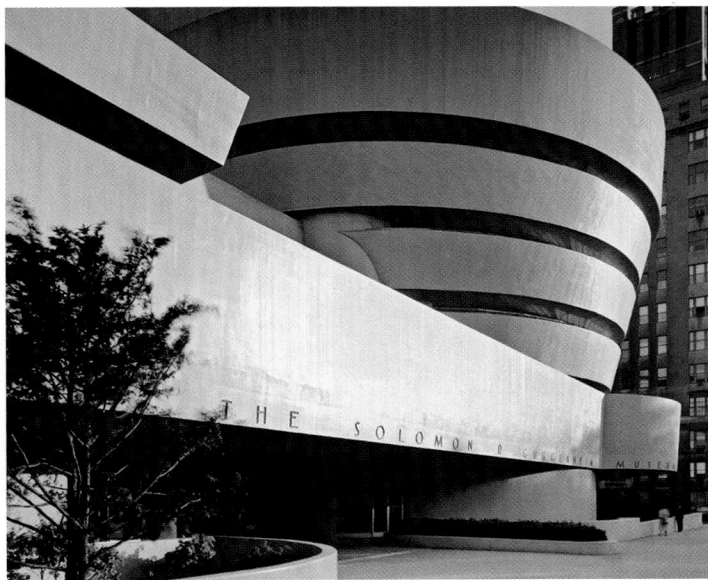

1.16 Frank Lloyd Wright. The Solomon R. Guggenheim Museum, New York. 1956–59

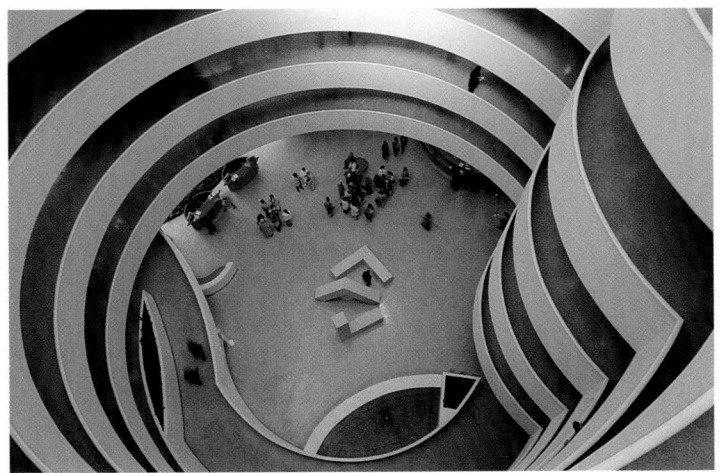

1.17 Frank Lloyd Wright. Interior of the Solomon R. Guggenheim Museum, New York. 1956–59

movement in Wright's seemingly endless ramp—which most people now ascend rather than descend because exhibitions begin at the foot of the ramp—to the American frontier, the ramp embodying "the expansive, directionless response of the frontiersman to limitless space," as expressed by James Fenimore Cooper's Natty Bumppo, Herman Melville's whaling chase, Mark Twain's Mississippi, and Walt Whitman's Open Road. Far-fetched as this may sound, we must remember that Wright was born in the Midwest in the nineteenth century, when it was still rural, and beginning with his earliest mature buildings, his designs, such as the Robie House (see fig. 26.39), were meant to capture the vast spread of the plains and were carefully integrated into the land.

If Wright's austere, abstract sculptural design for both the exterior and interior undermines his attempt to evoke nature, the building still retains a sense of open space and continuous

movement. Unlike any other museum, the Guggenheim has a sense of communal spirit, for here everyone is united in one large room and traveling the same path.

EXPERIENCING ART

You will be astonished when you see first-hand much of the art in this book. No matter how accurate the reproductions here, or in any other text, they are no more than stand-ins for the actual objects. We hope you will visit some of the museums where the originals are displayed. But keep in mind that looking at art, absorbing its full impact, takes time and repeated visits. In many respects, looking at art is no different than reading a book or watching a film—it requires extensive, detailed looking, a careful reading of the image or object, perhaps even a questioning of why every motif, mark, or color is used. Ideally, the museum will help you understand the art. Often, there are introductory text panels that tell you why the art has been presented as it is and what it is about, and ideally there will be labels for individual works that provide further information. Major temporary exhibitions generally have a catalog, which adds further information and sometimes another layer of interpretation. But text panels, labels, and catalogues generally reflect one person's reading of the art: Keep in mind there are usually many other ways to approach or think about it.

Art museums are relatively new. Before the nineteenth century art was not made to be viewed in museums, so when you are looking at work in a museum, you are often viewing it out of the original context in which it was meant to be seen. Much work can still be seen in its original context—churches, cathedrals, chateaux, public piazzas, and archaeological sites. Ultimately, however, art can be found everywhere—in commercial galleries, corporate lobbies and offices, places of worship, and private homes. It is displayed in public spaces, from subway stations and bus stops to public plazas and civic buildings such as libraries, performing arts centers, and city halls. University and college buildings are often filled with art, and the buildings themselves are art. The chair you are sitting in and the house or building you are reading this book in are also works of art—maybe not great art, but art all the same, as Duchamp explained. Even the clothing you are wearing is in a sense art, and for you it is a way to make a personal statement. Everywhere you find art, it is telling you something, and supporting a point of view.

Art is not a luxury, as many people would have us believe, but an integral part of daily life. It has a major impact on us, even when we are not aware of it, for we feel better about ourselves when we are in environments that are visually enriching and exciting. Most important, art stimulates us to think. Even when it provokes and outrages us, it broadens our experience by making us question our values, attitudes, and worldview. This book is an introduction to this fascinating field that is so intertwined with our lives. After reading it, you will find that the world will no longer look the same.

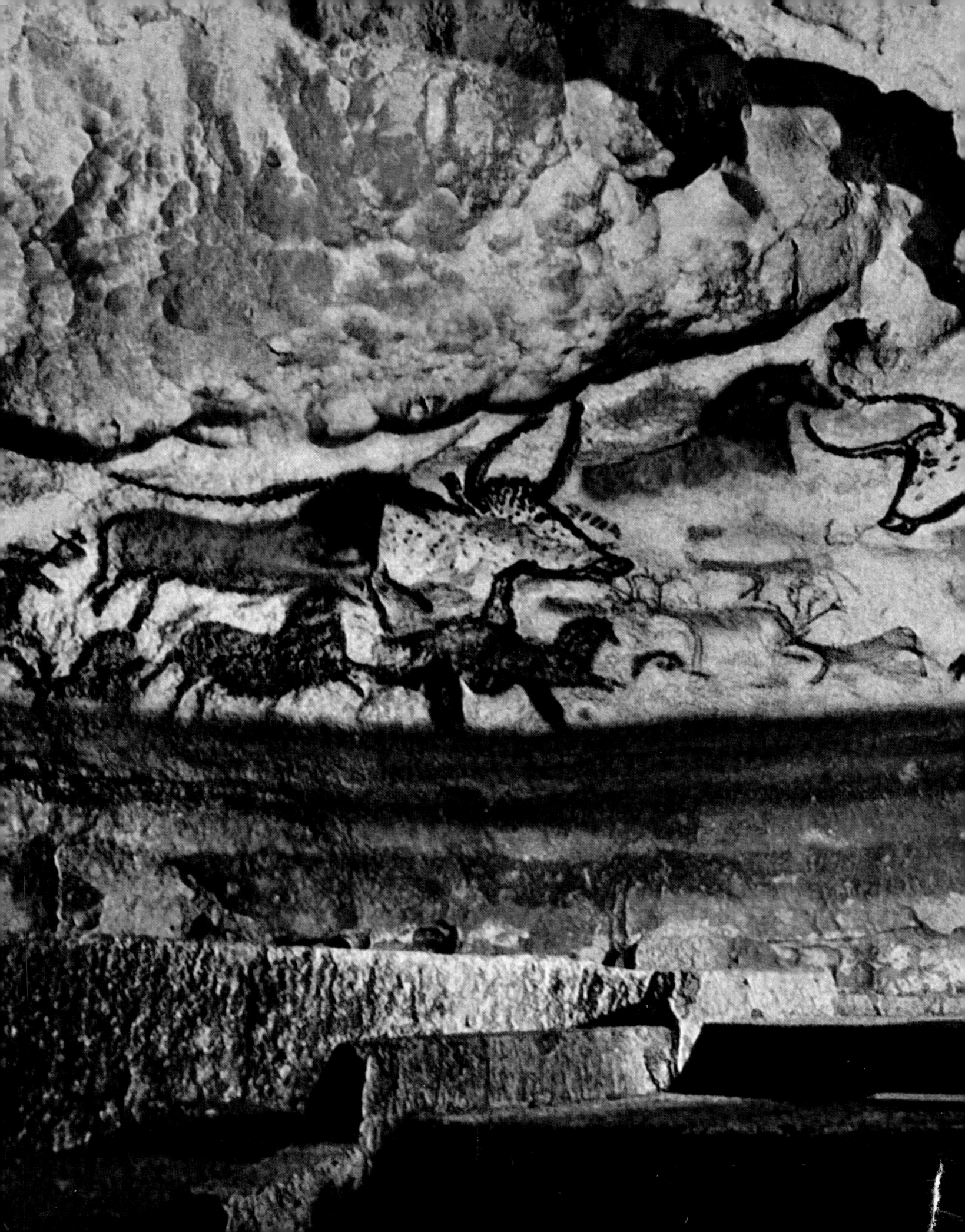

CHAPTER 1

Prehistoric Art

W HEN MODERN HUMANS FIRST ENCOUNTERED PREHISTORIC cave paintings in the 1870s, they literally could not believe their eyes. Although the evidence indicated that the site at Altamira in Spain dated to around 13,000 BCE, the paintings had been executed with such skill and sensitivity that historians initially considered them forgeries

(see fig 1.1). Since then, some 200 similar sites have been discovered all over the world. As recently as 1994, the discovery of a cave in southeastern France (see fig. 1.2) brought hundreds more paintings to light and pushed back the date of prehistoric painting even further, to approximately 30,000 BCE. Carved objects have been discovered that are equally old.

These earliest forms of art raise more questions than they answer: Why did prehistoric humans spend their time and energy making art? What functions did these visual representations serve? What do the images mean? Art historians often use contemporaneous written texts to supplement their understandings of art; prehistoric art, however, dates to a time before writing, for which works of art are among our only evidence. Art historians therefore deploy scientific and anthropological methods in their attempts to interpret them. Archaeologists report new finds with regularity, so the study of prehistoric art continues to develop and refine its interpretations and conclusions.

Fully modern humans have lived on the earth for over 100,000 years. At first they crafted tools out of stone and fragments of bone. About 40,000 years ago, they also began to make detailed representations of forms found in nature. What inspired this change? Some scholars suppose that image making and symbolic

language are the result of the new structure of the brain associated with *homo sapiens sapiens*. Art emerges at about the time that fully modern humans moved out of Africa and into Europe, Asia, and Australia, encountering—and eventually displacing—the earlier Neanderthals (*homo neanderthalensis*) of western Eurasia. On each of these continents, there is evidence of representational artwork or of body decoration contemporary with *homo sapiens sapiens*. Tens of thousands of works survive from this time before history, the bulk of which have been discovered in Europe. Many are breathtakingly accomplished.

The skill with which the earliest datable objects are executed may have been the product of a lengthy and lost period of experimentation in the techniques of carving and painting, so the practice of art making may be much older than the surviving objects. All the same, some scholars argue that a neurological mutation related to the structure of the brain opened up the capacity for abstract thought, and that symbolic language and representational art were a sudden development in human evolution. Whatever led to the ability to create art, whether a gradual evolutionary process, or a sudden mutation, it had an enormous impact on the emergence of human culture, including the making of naturalistic images. Such works force us to reevaluate many of our assumptions about art and the creative process, and raise fundamental questions, not least of which is why human beings make art at all.

Detail of figure 1.8, *Hall of the Bulls,* Lascaux Cave, Dordogne, France

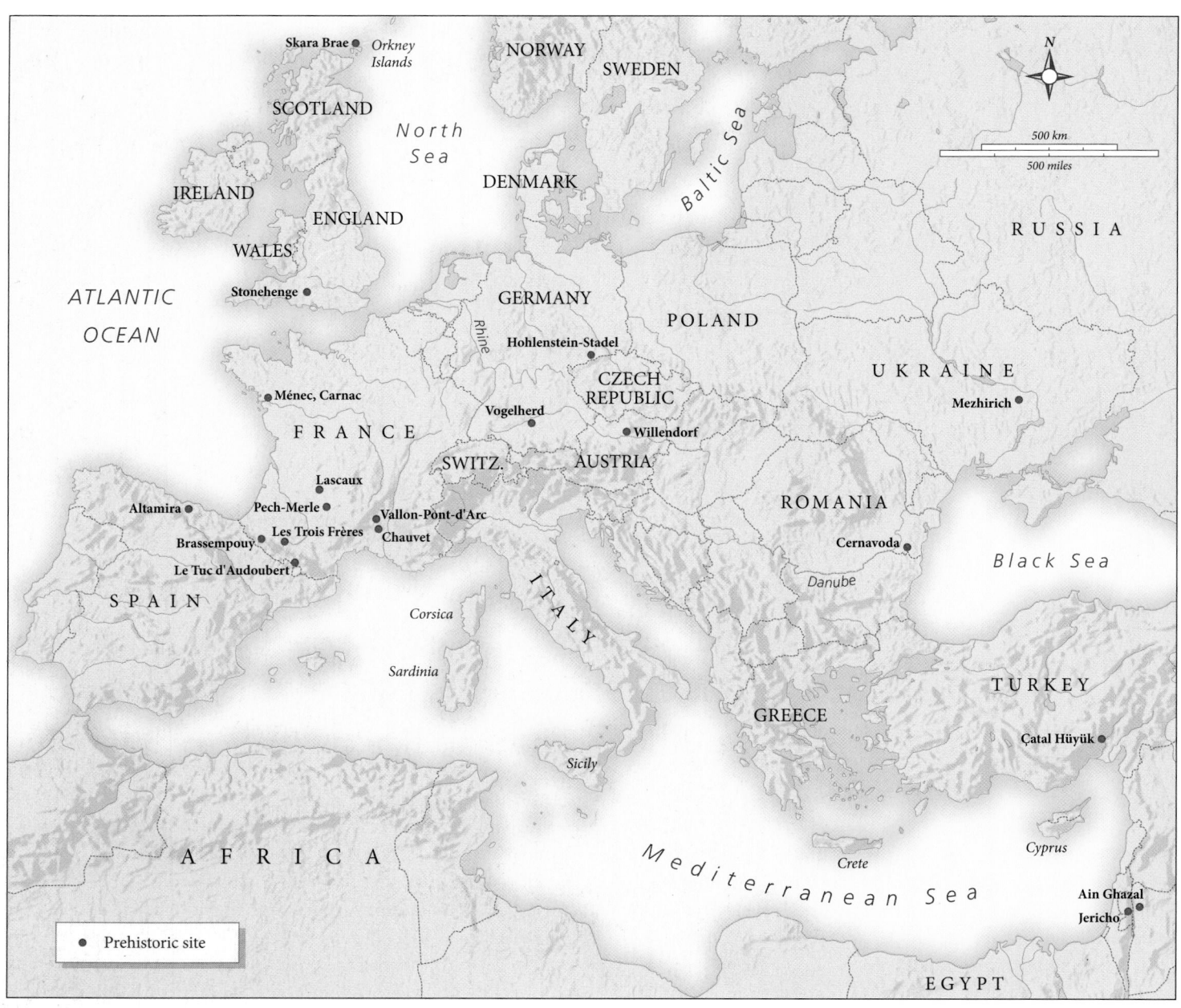

Map 1.1   Prehistoric Europe and the Near East

PALEOLITHIC ART

Upper Paleolithic painting, drawing, and sculpture appeared over a wide swath of Eurasia, Africa, and Australia at roughly the same time, between 10,000 and 40,000 years ago (map **1.1** and *Informing Art*, page 9). This time span falls in the Pleistocene era, more commonly known as the Ice Age, when glaciers (the extended polar ice caps) covered much of the northern hemisphere. The Lower and Middle Paleolithic periods extend back as far as 2 million years ago, when earlier species of the *homo genera* lived. These cultures crafted stone tools, which they sometimes decorated with abstract patterns. The end of the most recent Ice Age corresponded with the movement of fully modern humans out of Africa and into Europe, newly habitable as the warming climate caused the glaciers to recede.

Prehistoric paintings first came to light in 1878 in a cave named Altamira, in the village of Santillana del Mar in northern Spain. As Count Don Marcelino Sanz de Sautuola scoured the ground for flints and animal bones, his 12-year-old daughter, Maria, spied bison, painted in bold black outline and filled with bright earth colors (fig. **1.1**), on the ceiling of the cave. There, and in other more recently discovered caves, painted and engraved images predominantly depict animals. The greatest variety known is in the vast cave complex of Chauvet, near Vallon-Pont-d'Arc in southeastern France, named after one of the spelunkers who discovered it in 1994. Here, the 427 animal representations found to date depict 17 species, including lions, bears, and aurochs (prehistoric oxen), in black or red outlines (fig. **1.2**), and are sometimes polychromatic (containing several colors). Abstract shapes may accompany the animals, or appear alone, such as those depicted

1.1 *Wounded Bison*, Altamira, Spain.
ca. 15,000–10,000 BCE

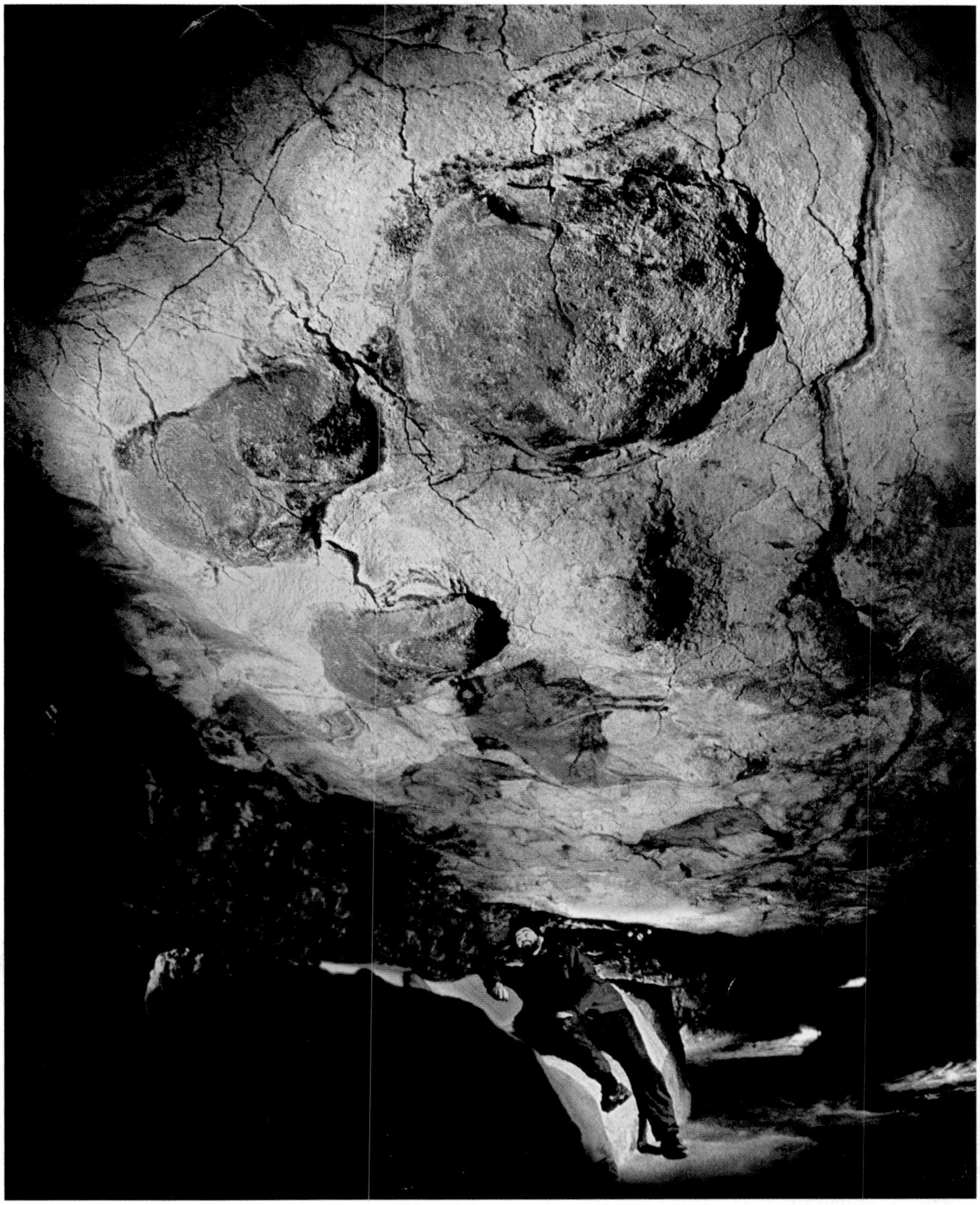

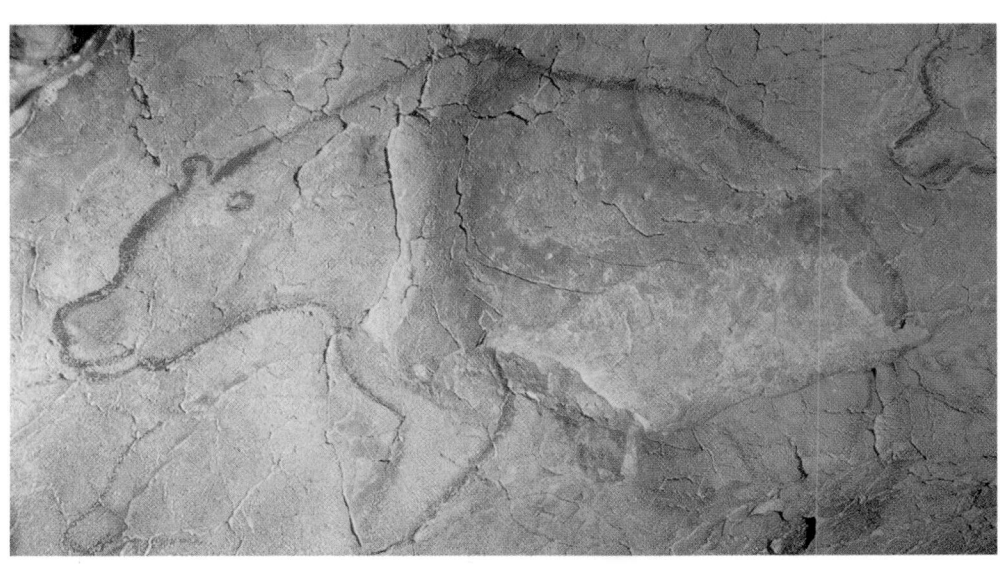

1.2 *Bear*, Recess of the Bears,
Chauvet Cave, Vallon-Pont-d'Arc,
Ardèche Gorge, France.
ca. 30,000–28,000 BCE

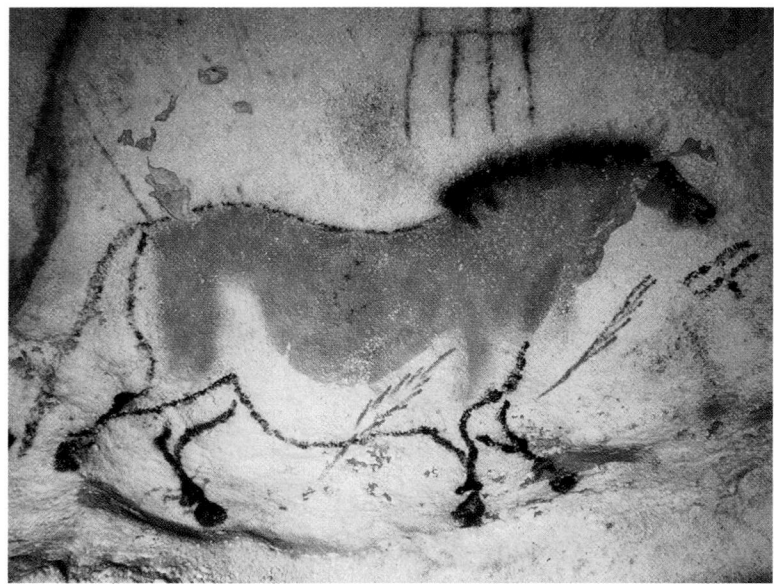

1.3 *Chinese Horse*, Lascaux Cave, Dordogne, France. ca. 15,000–13,000 BCE

silhouette (see *Materials and Techniques*, page 5). In rare instances, images depict human or partly human forms. At Chauvet, for instance, archaeologists identified the lower half of a woman painted on a projection of rock. At Les Trois Frères, a site in the French Pyrenees, a human body depicted with its interior muscles and anatomy supports an animal head with antlers. At Lascaux, a male stick figure with a birdlike head lies between a woolly rhinoceros and a disemboweled bison, with a bird-headed stick or staff nearby (fig. **1.4**).

On first assessing the Altamira paintings toward the end of the nineteenth century, experts declared them too advanced to be authentic and dismissed them as a hoax. Indeed, though cave art may represent the dawn of art as we know it, it is often highly sophisticated. Like their counterparts at Chauvet and elsewhere, the bison of Altamira were painted from memory, yet their forms demonstrate the painters' acute powers of observation and skill in translating memory into image. Standing at rest, or bellowing or rolling on the ground, the bison behave in these paintings as they do in the wild. The painters' careful execution enhances the appearance of nature: Subtle shading (modeling) expresses the volume of a bison's belly or a lioness's head, and the forward contour of an animal's far leg is often rendered with a lighter hue to suggest distance.

Initially, scholars assigned relative dates to cave paintings by using stylistic analysis, dating them according to their degree of **naturalism**, that is, how closely the image resembled the subject

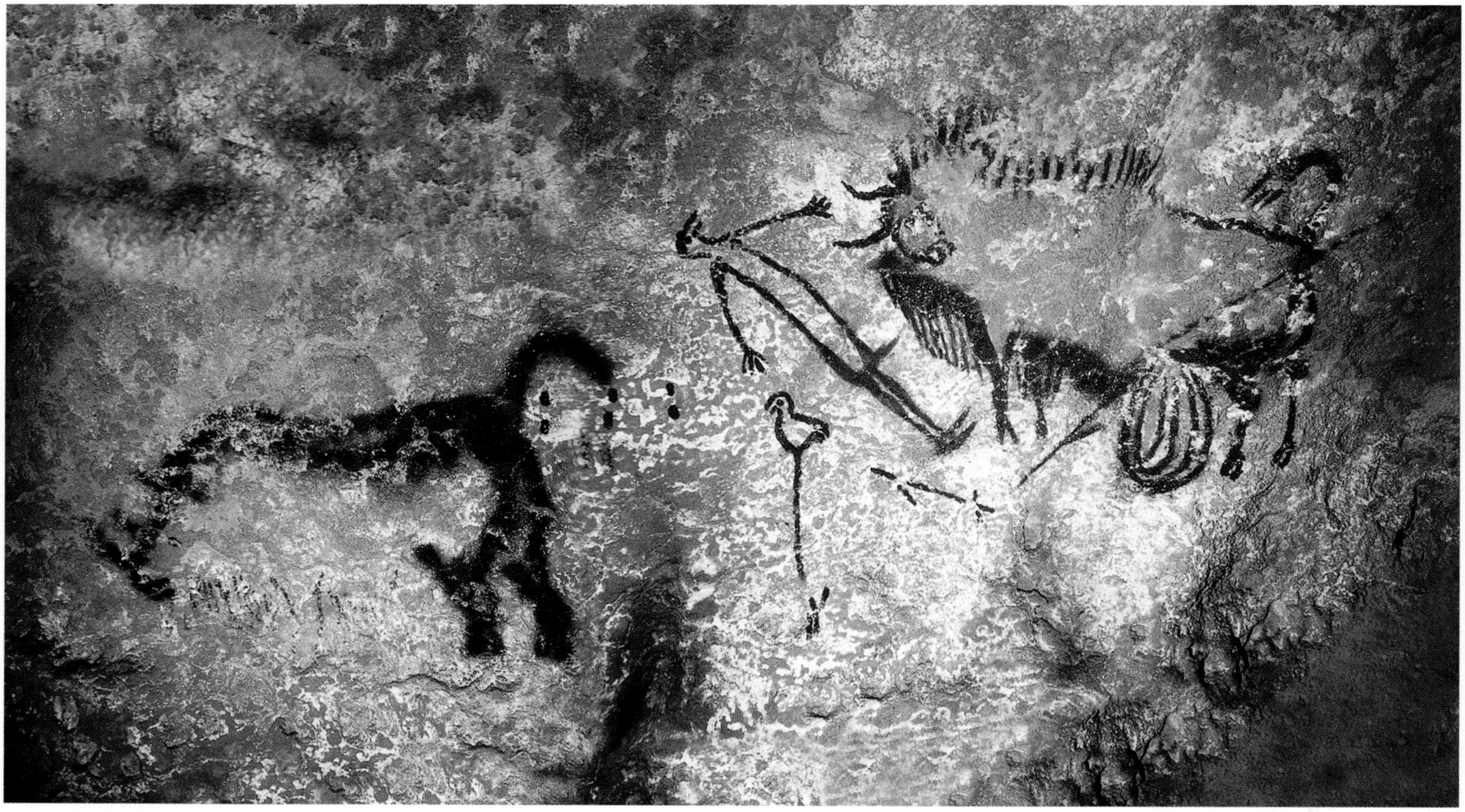

next to the *Chinese Horse* at Lascaux in the Dordogne region of France (fig. **1.3**). Scholars have interpreted these as weapons, traps, and even insects. Human hands occasionally feature on the cave walls, stamped in paint or, more usually, in negative

1.4 *Rhinoceros, Wounded Man, and Bison*, Lascaux Cave, Dordogne, France. ca. 15,000–13,000 BCE

Cave Painting

Paleolithic cave artists used a wide variety of techniques to achieve the images that have survived. Often working far from cave entrances, they illuminated the darkness using lamps carved out of stone and filled with fat or marrow. Archaeologists have found several of these lamps at Lascaux and elsewhere. Sometimes, when the area of rock to be painted was high above ground level, they may have built scaffolds of wood, which they stabilized against the wall by driving the poles into the limestone surface.

They prepared the surface by scraping the limestone with stone tools, bringing out its chalky whiteness as a background. They then engraved some images onto the wall, with a finger if the limestone was soft enough, or with a sharp flint. Sometimes they combined this technique with the application of color. They created black using vegetal charcoal and perhaps charred bones. Ocher, a natural iron ore, provided a range of vivid reds, browns, and yellows. For drawing—outlines of animals, for instance—they deployed charcoal and ocher in chunks, like a crayon; to generate paint, they ground the minerals into powder on a large flat stone. By heating them to extremely high temperatures, they could also vary the shades of red and yellow. They could then blow these mineral powders through tubes of animal bone or reed against a hand held up with fingers splayed to the rock surface to make hand silhouettes.

To fill in animal or human outlines with paint, they mixed the powders with blenders, which consisted of cave water, saliva, egg white, vegetal or animal fat, or blood; they then applied the colors to the limestone surface, using pads of moss or fur, and brushes made of fur, feather, or chewed stick. Some scholars understand, by experimentation, that pigment was often chewed up in the mouth and then blown or spat directly onto the walls to form images. In some cases, like the *Spotted Horse* of Pech-Merle or at Chauvet, artists applied paint in dots, leading to what some scholars describe as a "pointilliste" effect. They achieved this by covering the palm with ocher before

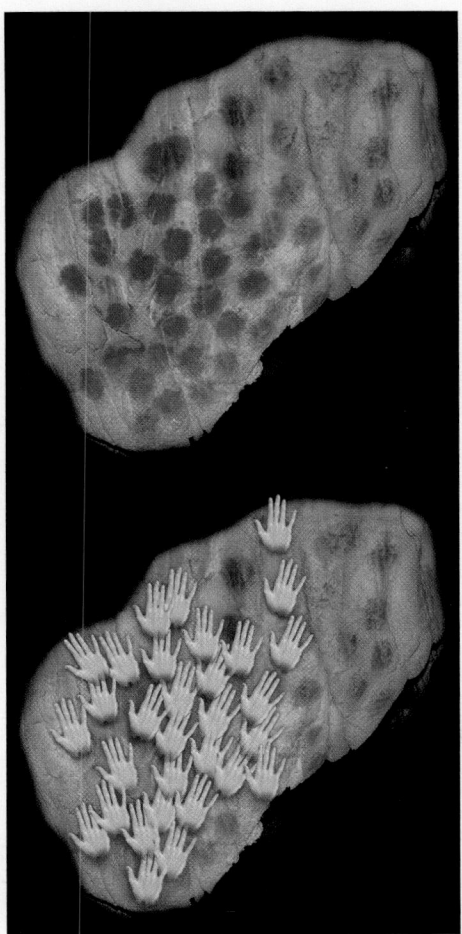

Hand dots in the Brunel Chamber at Chauvet. Large dots were made by covering the palm with paint and applying it to the wall. In places, fingers are just visible.

pressing it against the limestone. Analysis of these marks has yielded rich results: Not only can archaeologists identify individual artists by their handprint, but they have even been able to determine that women and adolescents were at work as well as men.

---

in nature. As art historians at that time considered naturalism the most advanced form of representation, the more naturalistic the image, the more evolved and, therefore, the more recent it was considered to be. Radiocarbon dating has since exposed the flaws in this approach, however (see *Informing Art*, page 17). Judged to be more recent in the overall sequence on account of their remarkable naturalism, some of the paintings at Chauvet in fact proved to be among the earliest on record, dating to about 32,000 years ago. It is thus a mistake to assume that naturalism was a Paleolithic artist's—or any artist's—inevitable or only goal. A consistent use of conventions in depicting individual species (bulls at Lascaux shown in profile but with frontal horns, for instance) defies nature; these are not **optical images**, showing an animal as one would actually see it, but **composite** ones, offering many of the details that go toward making up the animal portrayed, though not necessarily in anatomically accurate positions. As the "stick man" at Lascaux may illustrate, artists may have judged their success by standards quite removed from naturalism.

Interpreting Prehistoric Painting

As majestic as these paintings can be, they are also profoundly enigmatic: What purpose did they serve? The simplest view, that they were merely decorative—"art for art's sake"—is highly unlikely. Most of the existing paintings and engravings are readily accessible, while many more that once embellished caves that open directly to the outside have probably perished. But some, at Lascaux and elsewhere, lie deep inside extended cave systems, remote from habitation areas and difficult to reach (fig. **1.5**). In these cases, the power of the image may have resided in its making, rather than in its viewing: the act of painting or incising the image may have served some ritual or religious purpose.

After the images' initial discovery, scholars turned to approaches developed by ethnographers (anthropologists who study cultural behavior) to interpret cave paintings and engravings. Most often, they have attributed the inspiration for these works to magico-religious motives. Thus, early humans may have perceived an image as equivalent to the animal it represented; to

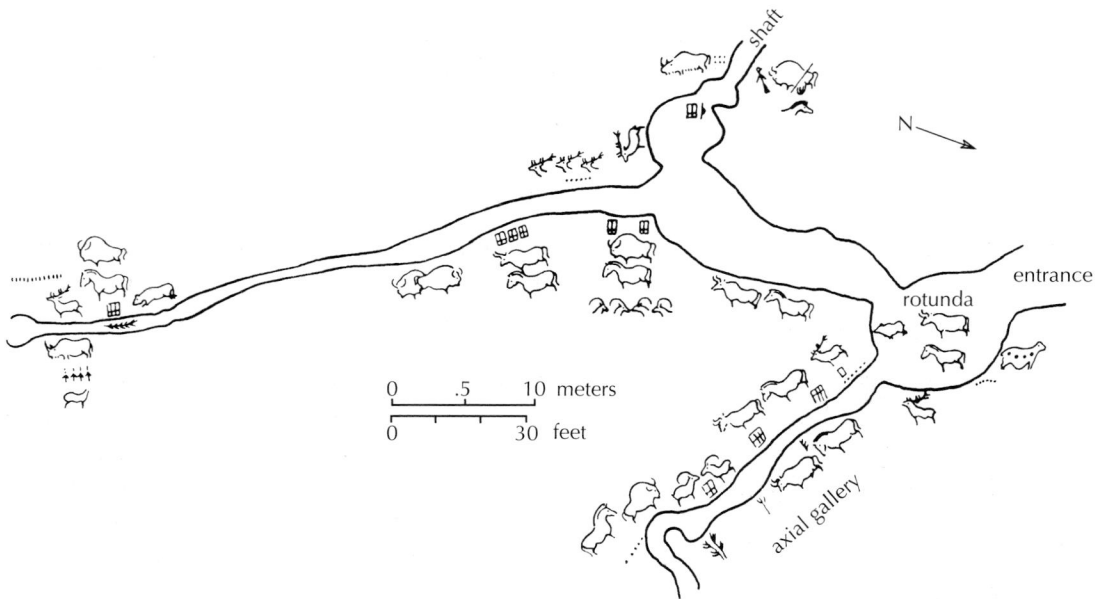

1.5 Schematic plan of Lascaux Cave system (based on a diagram by the Service de l'Architecture, Paris)

create or possess the image was to exert power over its subject, which might improve the success of a hunt. Gouge marks on cave walls indicate that in some cases spears were cast at the images (fig. **1.6**). Similarly, artists may have hoped to stimulate fertility in the wild—ensuring a continuous food supply—by depicting pregnant animals. A magico-religious interpretation might explain the choice to make animals appear lifelike, and to control them by fixing them within outlines; conversely, human fear of falling victim to the same magic may account for the decidedly unnaturalistic, abstract quality of the "stick figure" at Lascaux.

More recent theories concerning shamanism—a belief in a parallel spirit world accessed through alternative states of con-sciousness—build upon the earlier ethnographic interpretations, arguing that an animal's "spirit" was evident where a bulge in the wall or ceiling suggested its shape, as with the *Spotted Horses* (see fig. 1.6) at Pech-Merle in southwestern France. The artist's or shaman's power brought that spirit to the surface. Some scholars have cast the paintings in a central role in early religion, as images for worship. Others focus on a painting's physical context—this means examining relationships between figures to determine, in the absence of an artificial frame, a ground-line or a landscape, whether multiple animal images indicate individual specimens or a herd, and whether these images represent a mythical past for early communities. Do Lascaux's *Rhinoceros, Wounded Man, and Bison* (see fig. 1.4) constitute separate images or the earliest known narrative—the gory tale of a hunt, perhaps, or a shaman's encounter with his spirit creature? Multiple animal engravings, one on top of another, as at Les Trois Frères (fig. **1.7**), may have recorded animal migrations throughout the passing seasons.

Assessing physical context also means recognizing that a cave 15 feet deep is a very different kind of space from another over a mile deep, and was possibly used for different purposes. Paintings in the spacious Hall of the Bulls at Lascaux and the stick man at the same site, located at the bottom of a 16-foot well shaft, may have functioned differently. It means factoring in the experiential aspects of caves: In order to reach these images, a prehistoric viewer had to contend with a precarious path, eerie flickering lights, echoing sounds, and the musty smells that permeate sub-terranean spaces, all of which added texture to the viewing process (fig. **1.8**). Most important, recent interpretations acknowledge that one explanation may not suffice for all times and places. For instance, even if sympathetic magic makes sense of the *Chinese Horse* from Lascaux with its distended belly (see fig. 1.3), it hardly explains the art at Chauvet, where fully 72 percent of the animals represented were not hunted, judging by organic remains found in the cave.

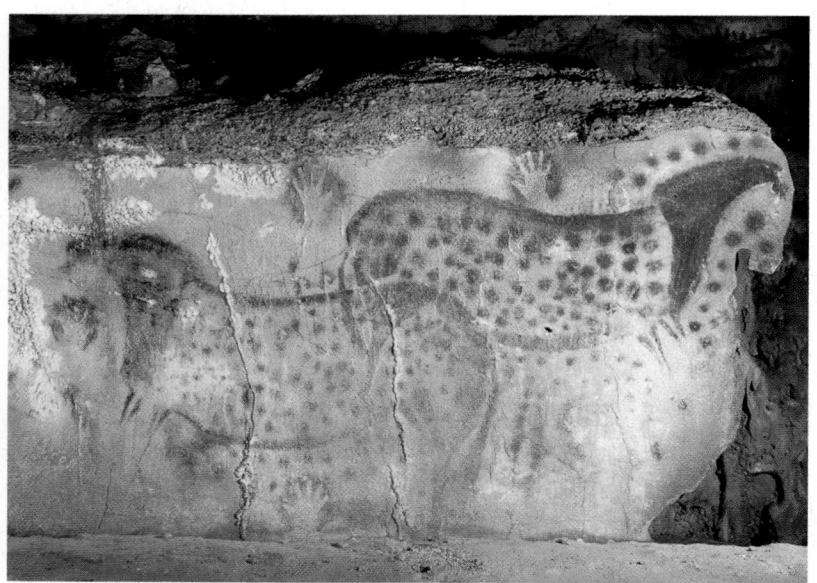

1.6 *Spotted Horses and Human Hands*, Pech-Merle Cave, Dordogne, France. Horses ca. 16,000 BCE; hands ca. 15,000 BCE. Limestone, approximate length 11'2" (3.4 m)

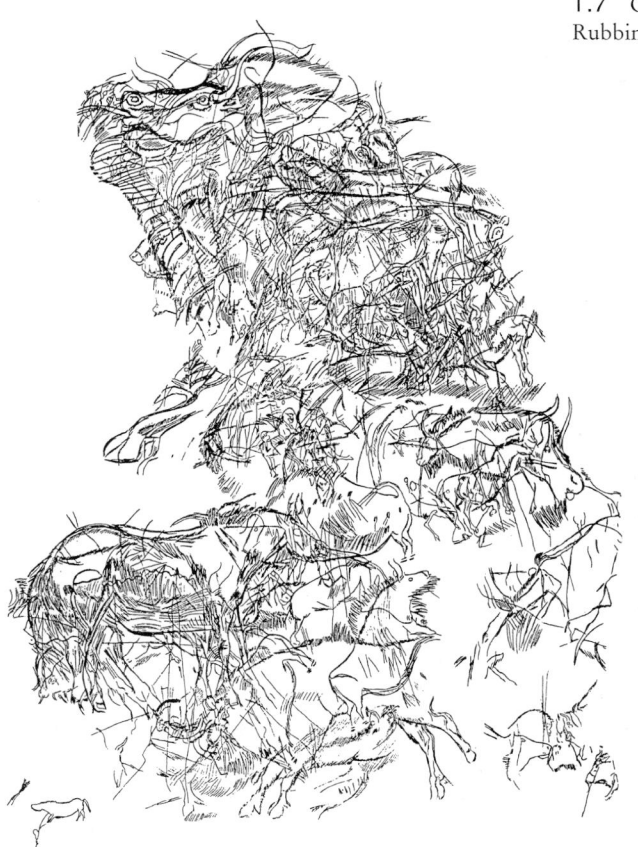

Paleolithic Carving

Prehistoric artists also carved and modeled sculptures in a variety of materials. At just under a foot high, a carved figure from Hohlenstein-Stadel in Germany (fig. **1.9**) represents a standing creature, half human and half feline, crafted out of mammoth ivory. Although it is now in a poor state of preservation, the creation of this figure, with rudimentary stone tools, was clearly an arduous business. It involved splitting the dried mammoth tusk, scraping it into shape, and using a sharp flint blade to incise such features as the striations on the arm and the muzzle. Strenuous polishing followed, using powdered hematite (an iron ore) as an abrasive. Exactly what the figure represents is unclear. Like the hybrid figures painted on cave walls (see fig. 1.4), it may represent a human dressed as an animal, possibly for hunting purposes. Some prehistorians have named these composite creatures shamans or "sorcerers," who could contact the spirit world through ritualistic behavior.

As in cave paintings, animals were frequent subjects for sculpture. A miniature horse from a cave in Vogelherd along the Danube River in Germany, and a pair of interlocked ibexes, date

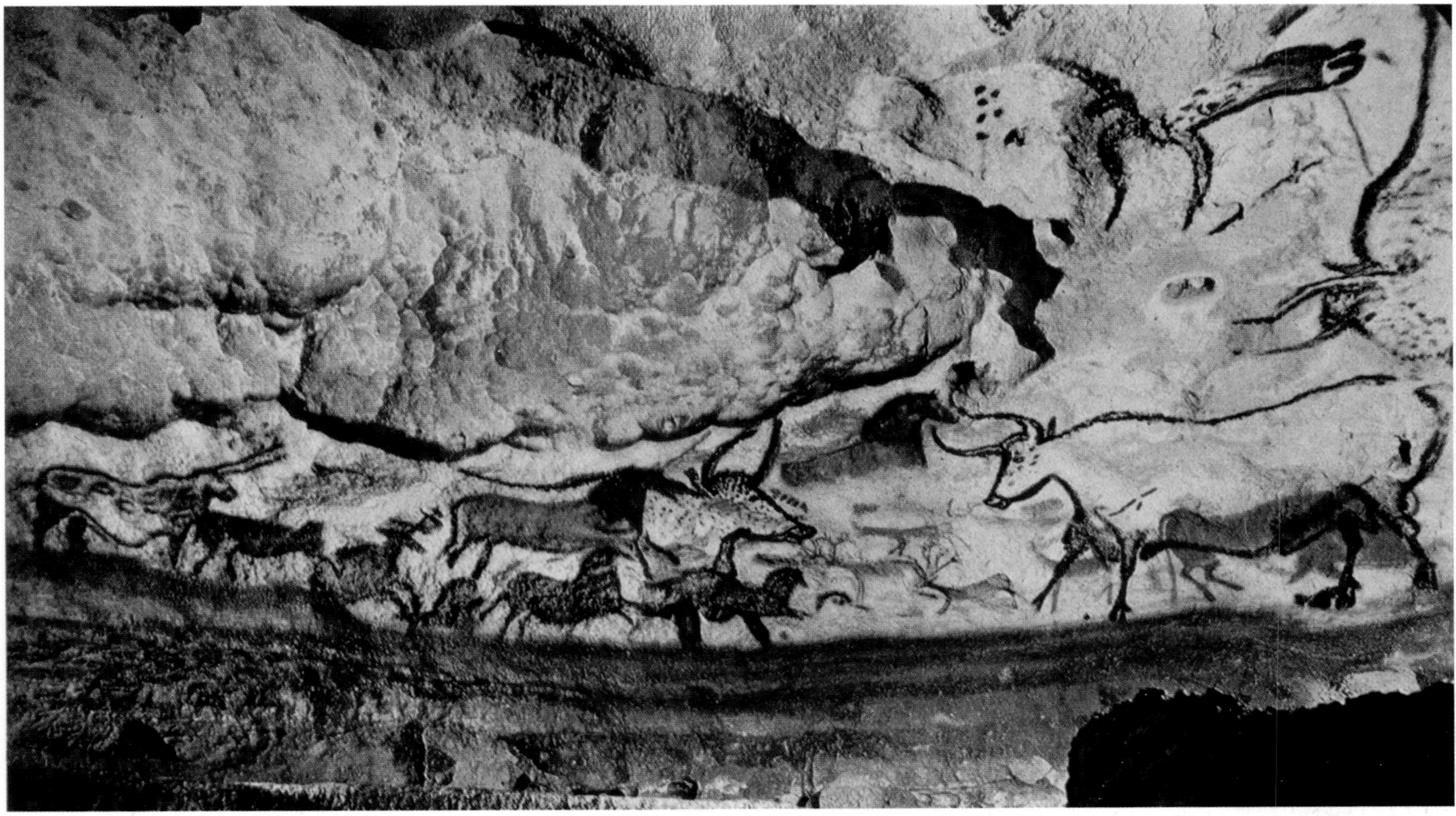

1.8 *Hall of the Bulls,* Lascaux Cave, Dordogne, France. ca. 15,000–13,000 BCE. Largest bull approximate length 11'6" (3.5 m)

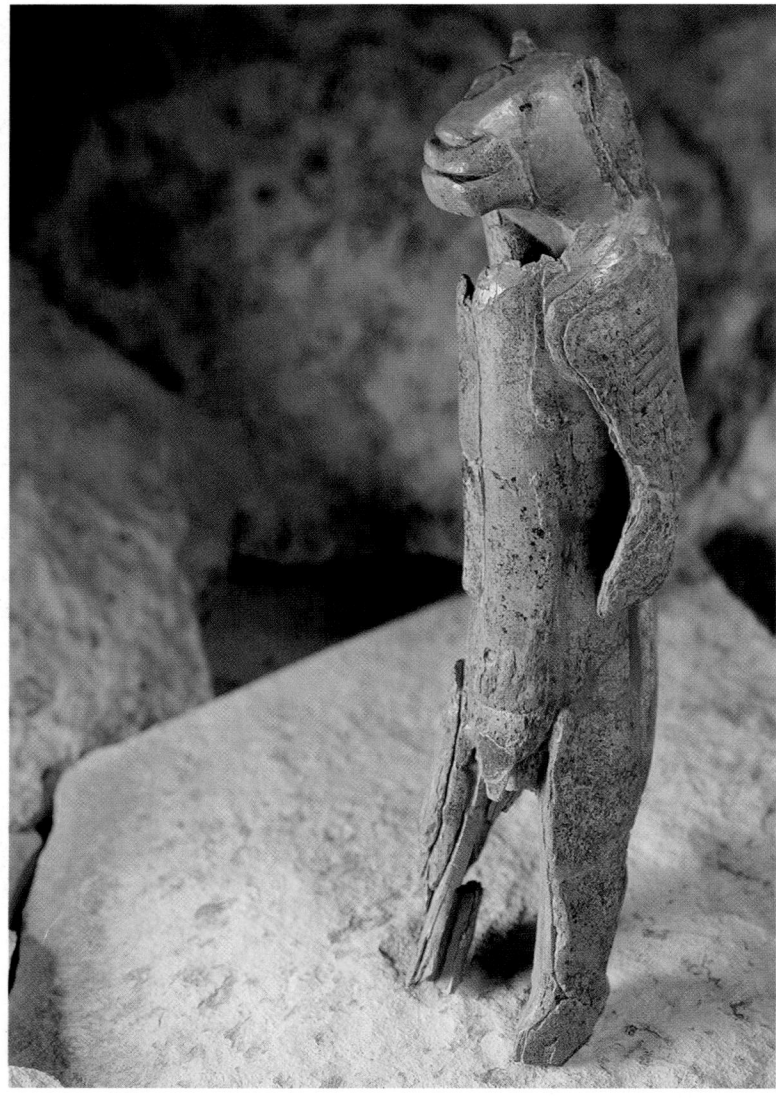

1.9 Hybrid figure with a human body and feline head, from Hohlenstein-Stadel (Baden-Württemberg), Germany. ca. 30,000 BCE. Mammoth ivory, height 11½" (29.6 cm). Ulma Museum, Ulm, Germany

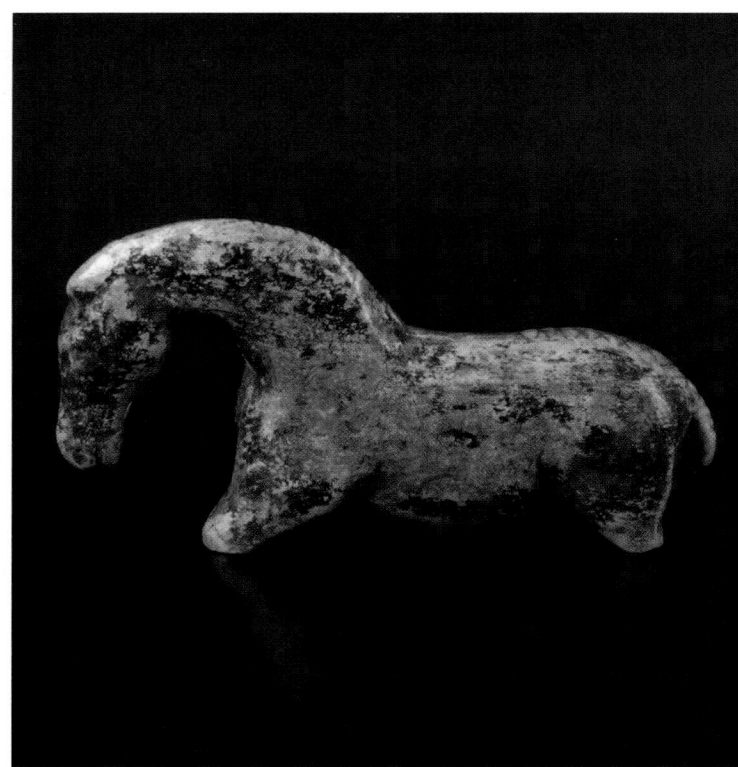

1.10 *Horse,* from Vogelherd Cave, Germany. ca. 28,000 BCE. Mammoth ivory, height 2" (5 cm). Institut für Urgeschichte, Universität Tübingen

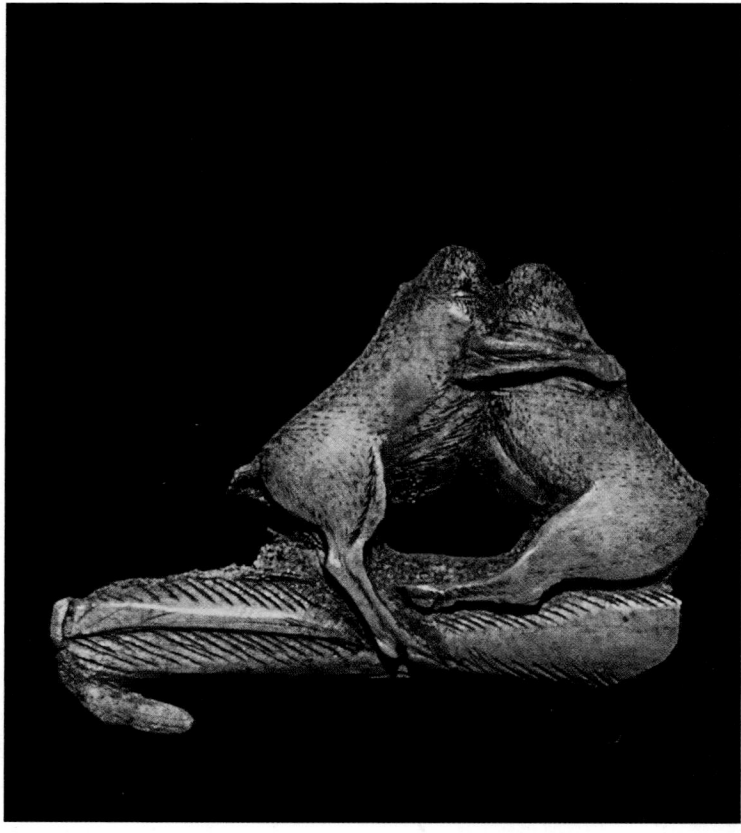

1.11 *Spear Thrower with Interlocking Ibexes,* Grotte d'Enlène, Ariège, France. ca. 16,000 BCE. Reindeer antler, 3½ × 2¾" (9 × 7 cm). Musée de l'Homme, Paris

to the beginning and end of the Upper Paleolithic era (figs. **1.10** and **1.11**). The horse is one of many portable carvings in woolly mammoth ivory created around 28,000 BCE. A small hole between its front legs suggests that it was a pendant. The ibexes, carved from reindeer antler around 13,000 BCE, functioned as a spear-thrower. Once attached to a spear by the hook at the end of its shaft, it allowed a hunter to propel the weapon more effectively. The sculptor had an eye for strong outlines and finished the surface with painstaking care, marking the ibexes' coats with nicks from a stone tool and working up a high polish.

Just as cave artists sometimes transformed bulges in rock walls into painted animals, so, deep within a cave at Le Tuc d'Audoubert in the French Pyrenees, around 13,000 BCE, a sculptor used clay to build up a natural outcropping of rock into two bison (fig. **1.12**); a calf originally stood by the front legs of the right-hand figure. Each sculpture is about 2 feet long; their forms

Telling Time: Labels and Periods

While geologists have developed methods for dividing time based on the age of the Earth, historians have used the activity of tool-making as the defining feature when measuring human time. For the era before the written word (prehistory), patterns apparent in stone tools serve as the basis for distinguishing different cultures. The Stone Age stretches from about 2 million years ago to about 2000 BCE.

Prehistorians divide this broad span of time into the Paleolithic or Old Stone Age (from the Greek *palaio-*, meaning "ancient," and *lithos*, meaning "stone"), the Mesolithic or Middle (*meso-*) Stone Age, and the Neolithic or New (*neo-*) Stone Age. The Paleolithic era reaches from 2 million years ago to about 10,000 BCE and the Mesolithic from about 10,000 to 8000 BCE. The Neolithic era spans from about 8000 to about 2000 BCE. At some time during the third millennium BCE, humans in some parts of the world replaced stone tools with tools made of metal, ushering in the Bronze Age in Europe and Asia.

Specific human cultures reached these phases at different times: The beginning of the Neolithic era appears to start earlier in western Asia than in Europe, for example. Yet the broad span of the Paleolithic era requires further refinement, and excavations of Paleolithic sites provide another framework for dividing time. The oldest material is at the bottom of an excavation, so scholars call the oldest Paleolithic era the Lower Paleolithic (ending about 100,000 years ago). The middle layers of Paleolithic excavations—thus the Middle Paleolithic era—date from 100,000 to about 40,000 years ago. The most recent layers in such excavations are called the Upper Paleolithic, and date from about 40,000 to around 8000 BCE.

Archaeologists have used many sites and different types of tools and tool-making technologies to identify specific culture groups within the Upper Paleolithic period. For example, they name the Aurignacian culture for Aurignac, a site in western France. The objects from this culture date from about 34,000 to 23,000 BCE. The Gravettian culture is named for La Gravette, a site in southwestern France, and dates from about 28,000 to 22,000 BCE. The most recent of these cultures is the Magdalenian, named for a site in southwestern France called La Magdaleine, with dates ranging from around 18,000 to 10,000 BCE. Many of these terms were coined in the nineteenth century, when the study of prehistoric culture first took root.

The Paleolithic Age

Lower Paleolithic	**2,000,000–100,000 BCE**
Middle Paleolithic	**100,000–40,000 BCE**
Upper Paleolithic	**40,000–10,000 BCE**
Aurignacian	34,000–23,000 BCE
Gravettian	28,000–22,000 BCE
Solutrean	22,000–18,000 BCE
Magdalenian	18,000–10,000 BCE
Mesolithic	**10,000–8000 BCE**
Neolithic	**8000–2000 BCE**

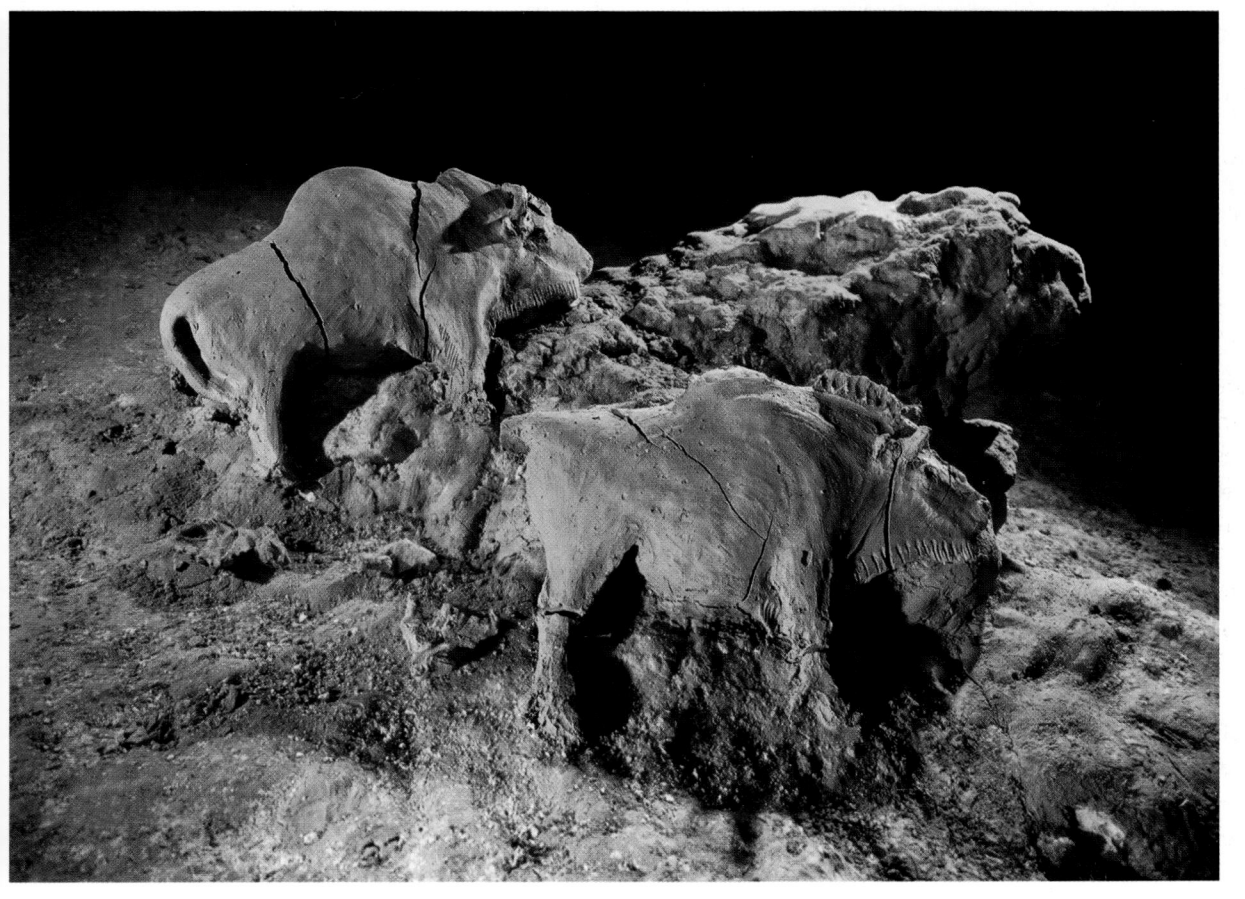

1.12 *Two Bison*, Le Tuc d'Audoubert Cave, Ariège, France. ca. 13,000 BCE. Clay, length 23⅝" (60 cm)

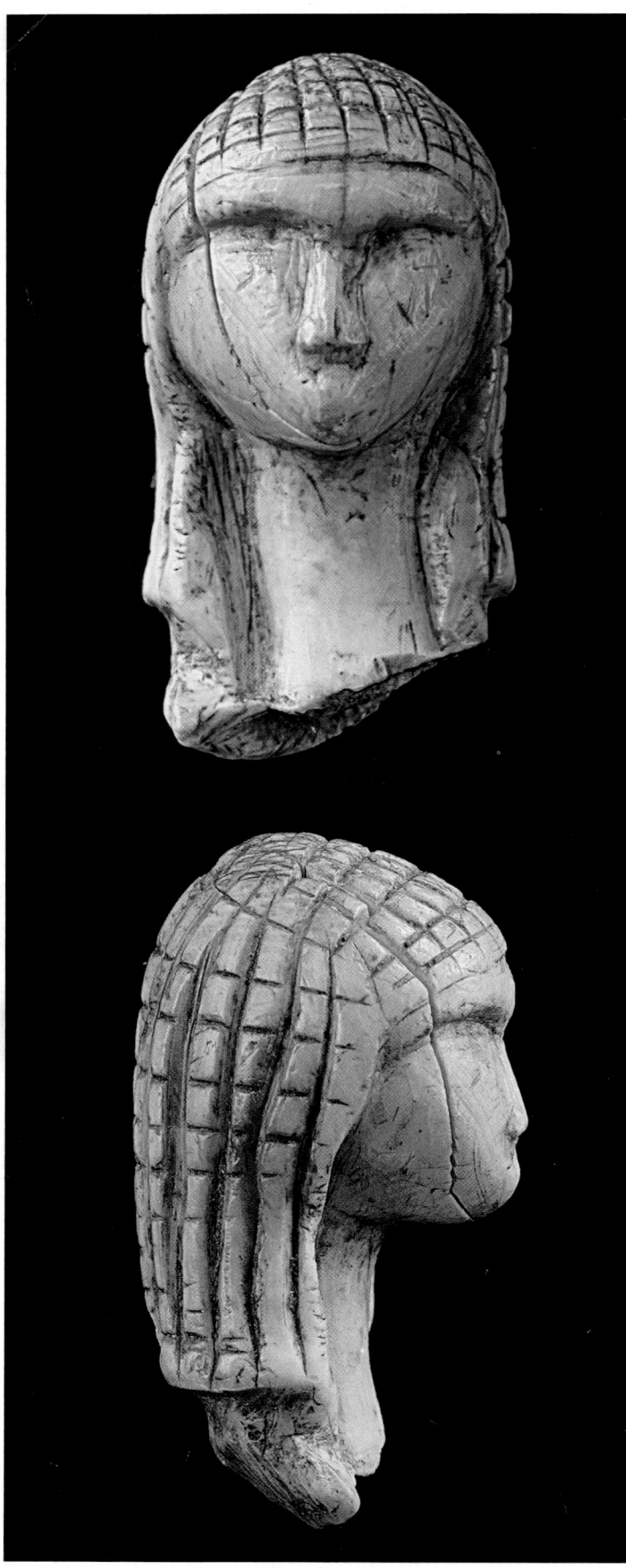

1.13 *Woman from Brassempouy*, Grotte du Pape, Brassempouy, France. ca. 22,000 BCE. Ivory, height 1½" (3.6 cm). Musée des Antiquités Nationales, Saint-Germain-en-Laye

swell and taper to approximate the mass of a real bison. Despite the three-dimensional character of the representations (notice the fullness of the haunch and shoulder and the shaggy manes), the sculptures share conventions with cave paintings: The artist rendered them in fairly strict profile, so that they are viewable from one side only, but once again the function of the object is unclear to us. Among the human footprints found near this group are those of a two-year-old child. Along with the baby's handprint in a cave at Bedeilhac in France, and the women's handprints at Chauvet, these caution us against simply reconstructing Paleolithic works of art as the ritual centerpieces of a male-dominated hunting society.

Women were frequent subjects in prehistoric sculpture, especially in the Gravettian period (see *Informing Art*, page 9). In fact, so far do female images outnumber male images at that time that they may be evidence of a matrilineal social structure. In the late nineteenth century, a group of 12 ivory figurines were found together in the Grotte du Pape at Brassempouy in southern France. Among them was the *Woman from Brassempouy* (fig. **1.13**) of about 22,000 BCE. The sculpture is almost complete, depicting a head and long elegant neck. At a mere 1½ inches long, it rests comfortably in the hand, where it may have been most commonly viewed. Also hand-sized is the limestone carving of the nude *Woman of Willendorf* of Austria, from about 28,000 to 25,000 BCE (fig. **1.14**). Discovered in 1908, her figure still bears traces of ocher rubbed onto the carved surface. Both figurines are highly abstract. Instead of rendering the female form with the naturalism found in the representations of animals, the artist reduced it to basic shapes. In the case of the *Woman from Brassempouy*, the artist rendered the hair schematically with deep vertical gouges and shallow horizontal cross-lines. There is no mouth and only the suggestion of a nose; hollowed-out, overhanging eye sockets and holes cut on either side of the bridge of the nose evoke eyes. The quiet power and energy of the figure reside in the dramatic way its meticulously polished surface responds to shifting light, suggesting movement and life.

The abstract quality of the *Woman of Willendorf* appears to stress a potent fertility. This kind of abstraction appears in many other figurines as well; indeed, some incomplete figurines depict only female genitalia. Facial features are not a priority: schematically rendered hair covers the entire head. Emphasis rests on the figure's reproductive qualities: Diminutive arms sit on pendulous breasts, whose rounded forms are echoed in the extended belly and copious buttocks. Genitalia are shown between large thighs.

The terminology applied to figures like the *Woman from Brassempouy* and the *Woman of Willendorf* in the past has complicated our interpretations of them. At the time of the first discovery of such female figurines in the mid-nineteenth century, scholars named them "Venus" figures: Venus is the Roman goddess of love (Aphrodite in the Greek world), whom ancient sculptors portrayed as a nude female; nineteenth-century archaeologists believed the prehistoric figures to be similar to the Roman goddess, in function if not in form. Today, we tend to avoid such anachronisms in terminology. We do not know whether the

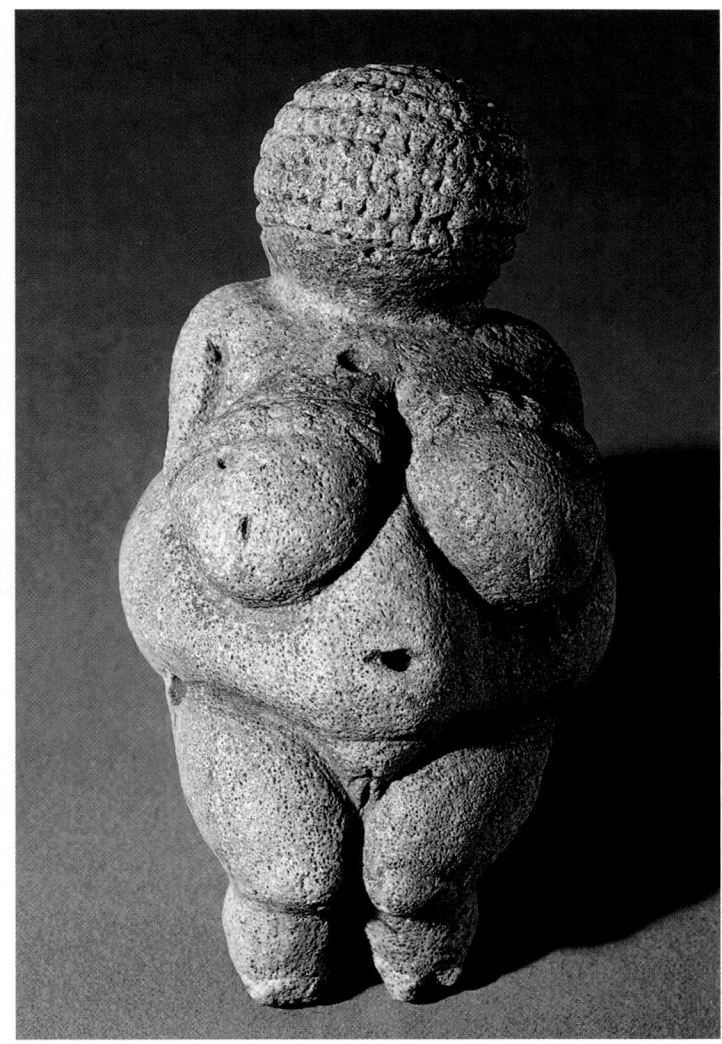

1.14 *Woman of Willendorf*. ca. 28,000–25,000 BCE. Limestone, height 4⅜" (11.1 cm). Naturhistorisches Museum, Vienna

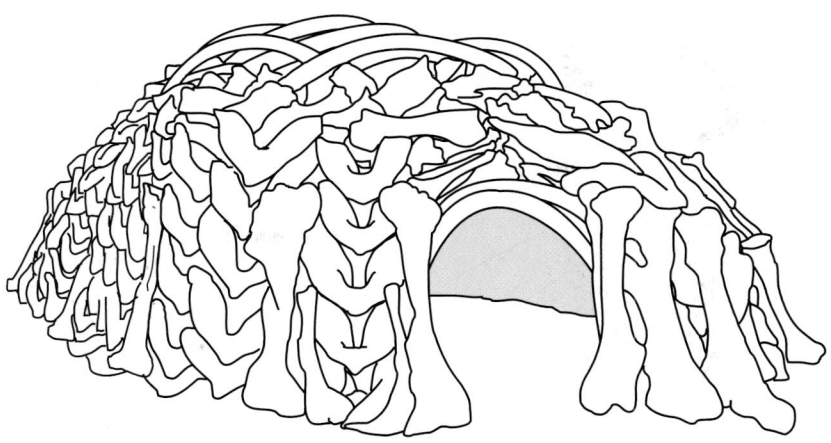

1.15 House at Mezhirich, Ukraine. 16,000–10,000 BCE. Mammoth bone

Woman of Willendorf represents a specific woman, or a generic or ideal woman. Indeed, she may not represent the idea of woman at all, but rather the notion of reproduction or, as some have argued, the fertile natural world itself. The emphasis on the reproductive features has suggested to many that she may have been a fertility object; the intention may have been to ensure a successful birth outcome rather than an increase in the number of pregnancies. According to one feminist view, the apparently distorted forms of figures like this specifically reflect a woman's view of her own body as she looked down at it. If so, some of the figures may have served as obstetric aids, documenting different stages of pregnancy to educate women toward healthy births. Moreover, this may indicate that at least some of the artists were women.

Paleolithic Houses

In the Paleolithic period, people generally built small huts and used caves for shelter and ritual purposes. In rare cases, traces of dwellings survive. At Mezhirich, in the Ukraine, a local farmer discovered a series of oval dwellings with central hearths, dating to between 16,000 and 10,000 BCE (fig. **1.15**). The distinctive feature of these huts was that they were constructed out of mammoth bones: interlocked pelvis bones, jawbones and shoulder blades provided a framework, and tusks were set across the top. The inhabitants probably covered the frame with animal hides. Archaeological evidence shows that inside these huts they prepared foods, manufactured tools, and processed skins. Since these are cold-weather occupations, archaeologists conclude that the structures were seasonal residences for mobile groups, who returned to them for months at a time over the course of several years.

NEOLITHIC ART

Around 10,000 BCE, the climate began to warm, and the ice that had covered almost a third of the globe started to recede, leaving Europe with more or less the geography it has today. New vegetation and changing animal populations caused human habits to mutate, especially in relation to their environment. In the Neolithic period, or New Stone Age, they began to build more substantial structures, choosing fixed settlement places on the basis of favorable qualities such as a water supply, rather than moving seasonally. Instead of hunting and gathering what nature supplied, they domesticated animals and plants. This gradual change occurred at different moments across the world; in some places, hunting and gathering are still the way of life today.

Settled Societies and Neolithic Art

The earliest evidence of these adjustments to environmental shifts appears in the fertile regions of the eastern Mediterranean and Mesopotamia, between the Euphrates and Tigris rivers. A small settlement developed in the ninth millennium BCE by the Jordan River at the site of Jericho, of biblical fame, in the present West Bank territory. Over time its inhabitants built houses of

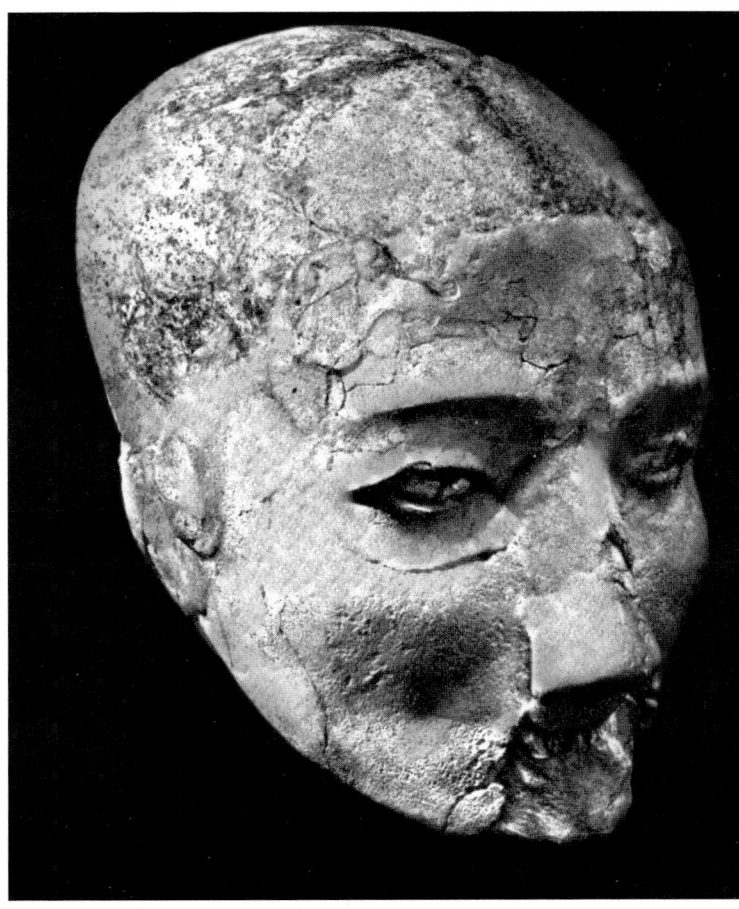

sun-baked mud brick on stone foundations. They plastered the floors and crafted roofs of branches and earth. Skeletal remains indicate that they buried the bodies of their dead beneath the floors; they displayed the skulls separately above ground, reconstructing them with tinted plaster to resemble flesh, and crafting eyes of seashell fragments (fig. 1.16). The subtlety of their modeling, and the close observation of the interplay between flesh and bone, make these works remarkably lifelike, each as individual as the skulls they encased. Perhaps these funerary practices reflect a concept of an afterlife; at the very least, they suggest a respect for the dead or even ancestor worship. Around 7500 BCE, the people of Jericho, now numbering over 2,000, dug a wide ditch and raised a solid stone wall around their town, which by this time had expanded to cover some 10 acres. Built with only the simplest stone tools, the wall was 5 feet thick and over 13 feet high. Into it they set a massive circular tower, perhaps one of several, 28 feet tall and 33 feet in diameter at the base, with a staircase inside providing access to the summit (fig. 1.17). The wall may have functioned as a fortification system against neighboring settlements, or as a barrier against rising floodwaters. With its construction, monumental architecture was born.

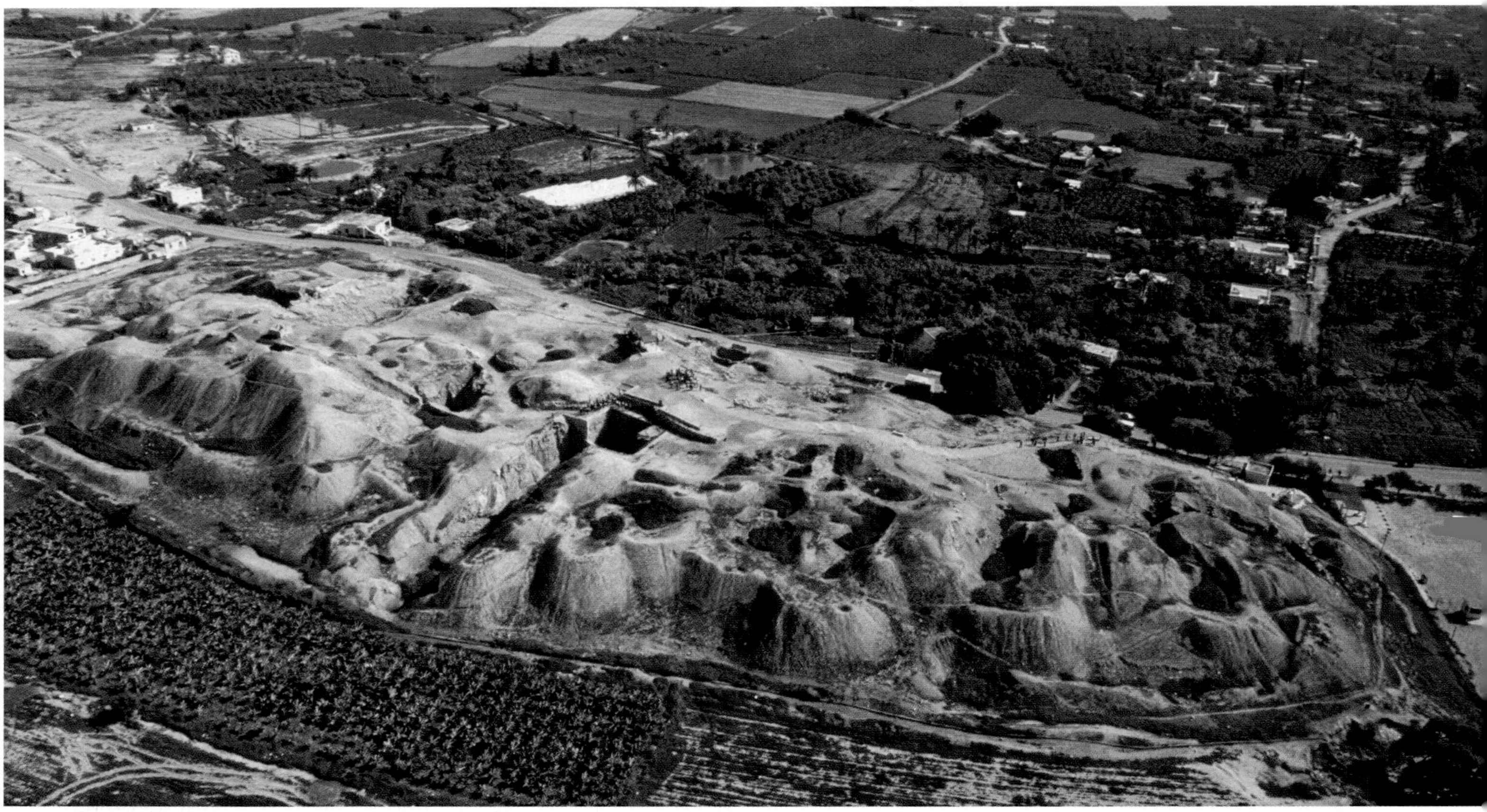

1.17 Jericho, Jordan (aerial view)

At Ain Ghazal, near Amman in Jordan, over 30 fragmentary plaster figures, dating to the mid-seventh millennium BCE, represent a starkly different sculptural tradition from the Jericho heads (fig. 1.18). Some are only bust-size, but the tallest statues, when restored, are 3 feet in height, and constitute the first known large-scale sculptures. Conservators have studied the construction technique of these figures, and conclude that large size was the motivating force behind their design, directly resulting in their flat, shallow appearance. These investigations have shown that artists applied plaster to bundles of fresh reeds, bound with cordage, which they kept horizontal during the assembly process. They added the legs separately, then applied paint and added cowrie shells for eyes, darkened with bitumen (a black, tarlike substance) for pupils. Once the plaster was dry, they stood the fragile figures upright and probably added wigs and clothing. Like the Jericho heads, the figures may have represented ancestors. Alternatively, as some of the bodies are two-headed, they may have had a mythical function.

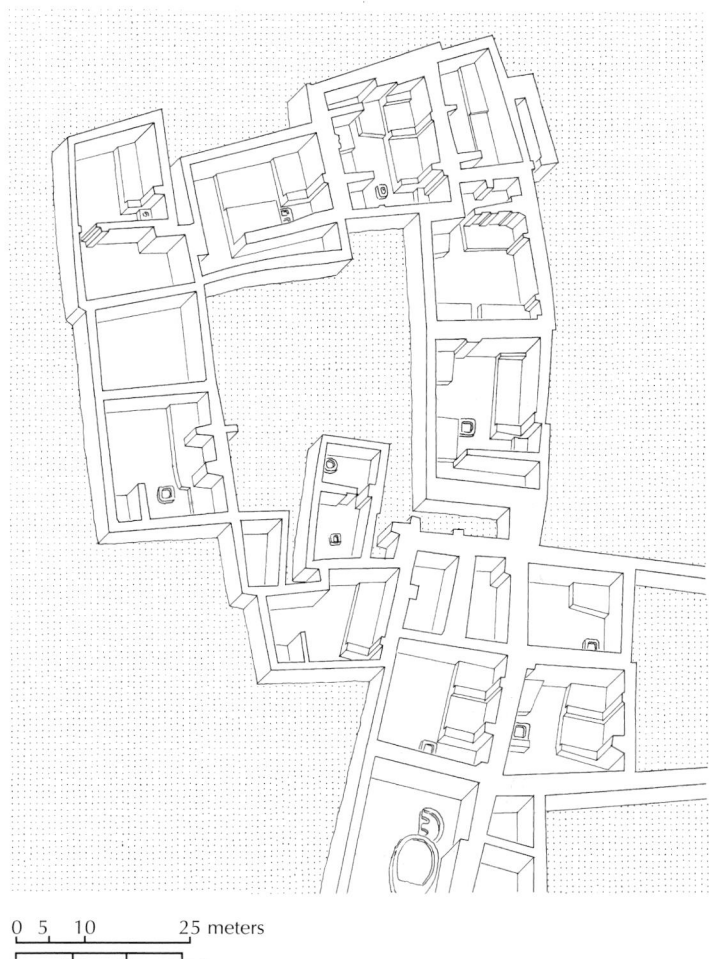

0 5 10   25 meters

0   25   50   75 feet

1.19   Reconstruction of Çatal Hüyük, Turkey

ÇATAL HÜYÜK In Anatolia (modern Turkey), excavations since 1961 have revealed a Neolithic town at Çatal Hüyük, dating from about 7500 BCE, a thousand years later than Jericho (see map 1.1). Flourishing through trade in ores—principally obsidian, a highly valued glasslike volcanic stone, used to make strong, sharp blades—the town developed rapidly through at least 12 successive building phases between 6500 and 5700 BCE. Its most distinctive feature is that it lacked streets, and the mud-brick and timber houses had no doors at ground level: Each house stood side by side with the next, accessed by ladder through a hole in the roof that doubled as a smoke vent (fig. 1.19). The advantages of this design were structural—each house buttressing the next—and defensive, since any attacker would have to scale the outer walls before facing resistance on the rooftops. The design also made economic use of available building stone and provided thick-walled insulation. The rooms inside accommodated activities ranging from working and cooking to sleeping, on platforms lining the walls. As at Jericho, burials were beneath the floor.

In most of the rooms at Çatal Hüyük, plaster covered the walls; often it was painted. Many of the paintings depict animal hunts, with small human figures running around disproportionately large bulls or stags. The images have a static quality, quite

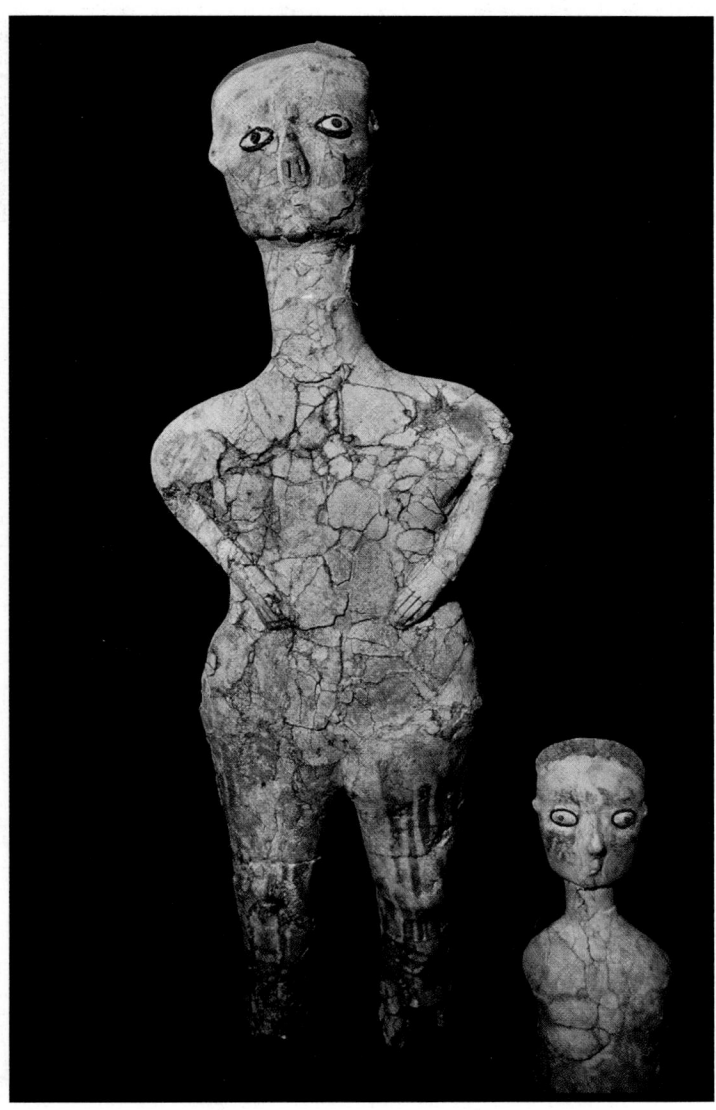

1.18   Human figures, from Ain Ghazal, Jordan. ca. 6750–6250 BCE. Height of larger figure 33" (84 cm). Department of Antiquities, Amman

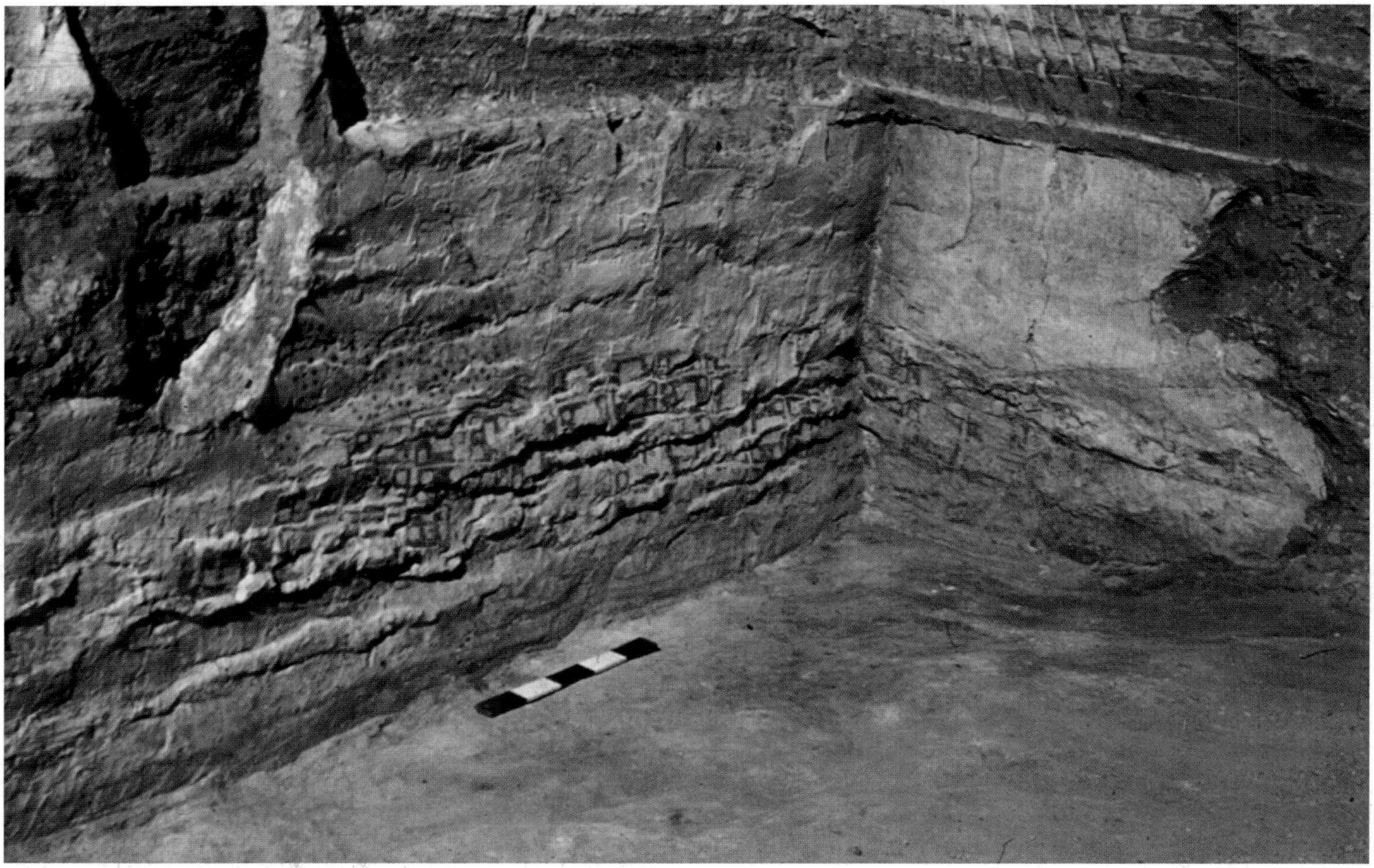

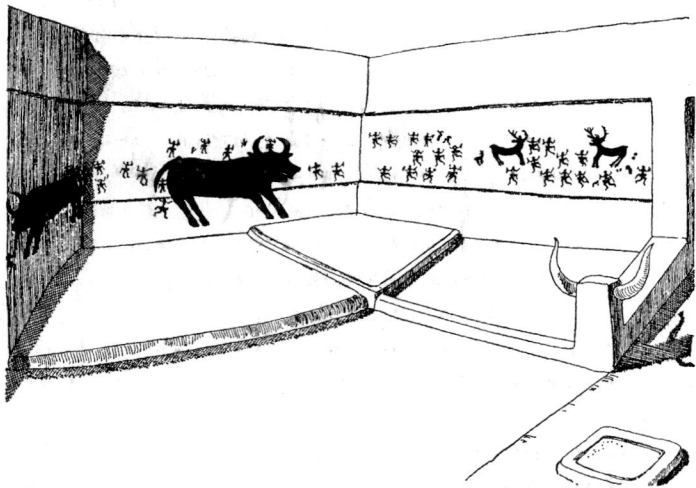

1.20 *View of Town and Volcano*, Shrine VII.14, Çatal Hüyük. ca. 6000 BCE. Wall painting

unlike the earlier cave paintings that seem to embody motion. One unusual painting in an early room appears to depict rows of irregular blocklike houses, and probably represents Çatal Hüyük itself (fig. **1.20**). Above the town, a bright red feature spotted with black and topped with black lines and dots may represent Hasan Dag, a twin-peaked volcano in view of the town. If archaeologists have properly identified this site, the image is the first known landscape painting. It may indicate a sense of community in this early settlement, with inhabitants specifically identifying themselves with place. Some archaeologists speculate that the more ornate rooms at Çatal Hüyük functioned as shrines; in some of them, bulls' horns and plaster breasts may have signified fertility (fig. **1.21**).

OVEN-FIRED POTTERY A number of new technologies that developed during the Neolithic period collectively suggest the beginnings of specialization. As the community could count on a regular food supply, some of its members were able to devote time to acquiring special skills. These included pottery, weaving, and the smelting of copper and lead. Oven-fired pottery is extremely durable, and often survives in the form of discarded shards. Though absent from early Jericho, a great variety of clay vessels painted with abstract forms survive in regions stretching from Mesopotamia, where pottery may have originated in the sixth millennium BCE, to Egypt and Anatolia, where it was discovered at Çatal Hüyük (see map 1.1) and other settlements. Archaeologists have found pottery from this period in the Balkans, and by about 3500 BCE the technology of pottery making appeared in western Europe.

1.21 *Animal Hunt.* Restoration of Main Room, Shrine A.III.1, Çatal Hüyük. ca. 6000 BCE (after Mellaart)

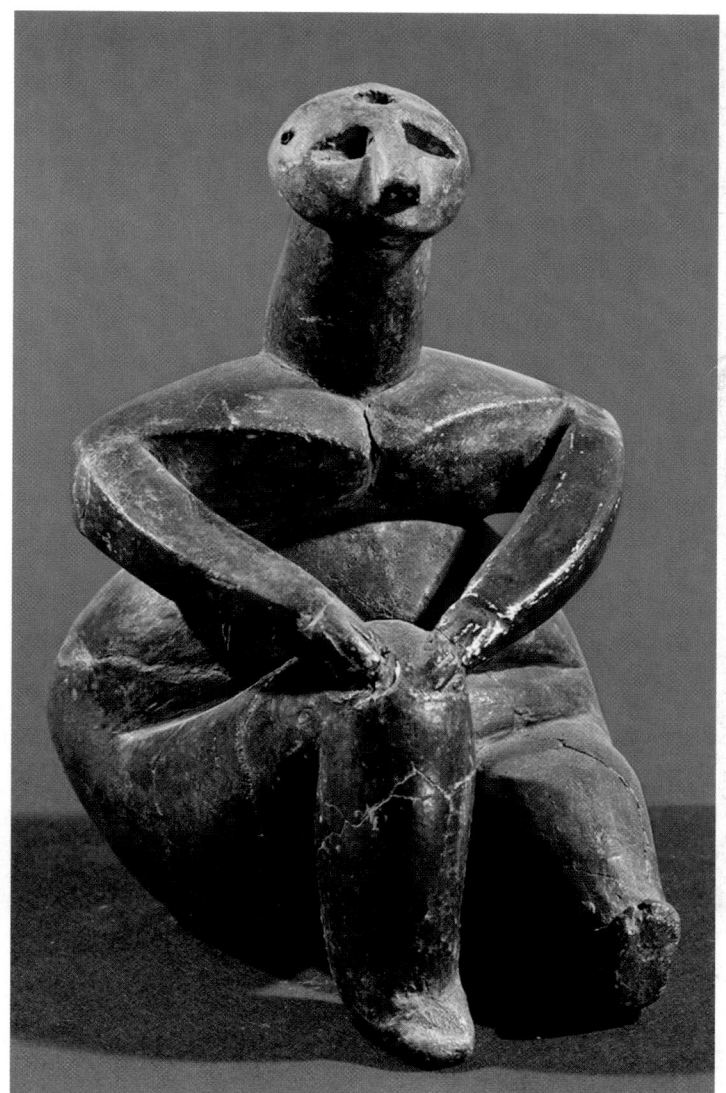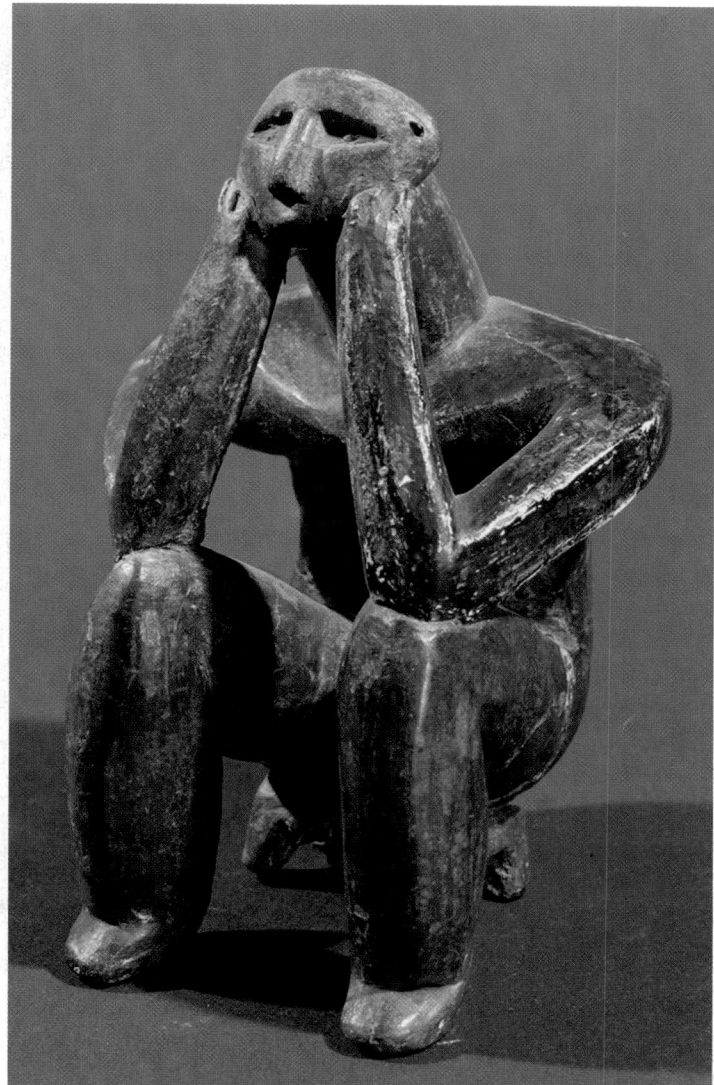

1.22 Female and male figures, from Cernavoda, Romania. ca. 3500 BCE. Ceramic, height 4½" (11.5 cm). National Museum of Antiquities, Bucharest

In Europe, artists also used clay to fashion figurines, such as a woman and man from Cernavoda in Romania, of about 3500 BCE (fig. 1.22). Like the *Woman of Willendorf* and the Ain Ghazal figurines, they are highly abstract, yet their forms are more linear than rounded: The woman's face is a flattened oval poised on a long, thick neck, and sharp edges articulate her corporeality—across her breasts, for instance, and at the fold of her pelvis. Elbowless arms meet where her hands rest on her raised knee, delineating a triangle and enclosing space within the sculptural form. This emphasizes the figurine's three-dimensionality, encouraging a viewer to look at it from several angles, moving around it or shifting it in the hand. The abstraction highlights the pose; yet, tempting as it may be to interpret this, perhaps as coquettishness, we should be cautious about reading meaning into it, since gestures can have dramatically different meanings from one culture to another. Found in a tomb, the couple may represent the deceased, or mourners; perhaps they were gifts that had a separate purpose before burial.

Architecture in Europe: Tombs and Rituals

Neolithic people of western and northern Europe framed their dwellings mostly in wood, with walls of wattle (branches woven into a frame) and daub (mud or earth dried around the wattle) and roofs of thatch, which rarely survive. At Skara Brae, on the island of Orkney just off the northern tip of Scotland, is a group of ten houses built of stone, dating to between 3100 and 2600 BCE. The builders sunk them into mounds for protection against the harsh weather, and connected them by covered passages. A typical house had a square room, with walls of flat unmortared stones (fig. 1.23). Driftwood and whalebone supported a roof of turf thatch. At the center of the room was a hearth for cooking, and the inhabitants built furniture—such as beds and shelving—out of large flat stones.

It was a concern for ceremonial burial and ritual, rather than for protection, that inspired Neolithic people of western and northern Europe to create monumental architecture. They defined spaces for tombs and rituals with huge blocks of stone

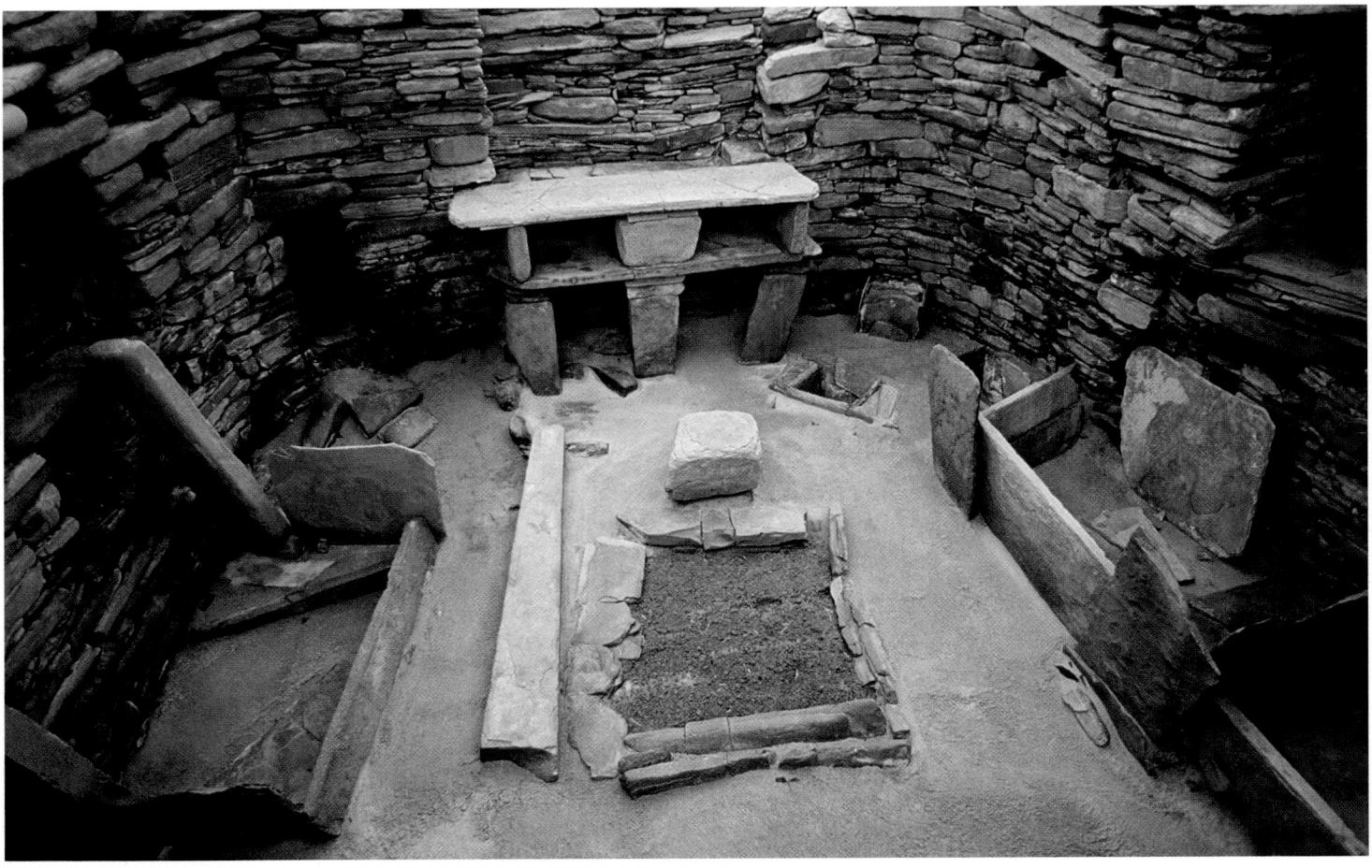

1.23 House at Skara Brae, Orkney, Scotland. ca. 3100–2600 BCE

known as **megaliths**. Often they mounted the blocks in a **trilithic** (three-stone) **post-and-lintel** arrangement (with two upright stones supporting a third horizontal capstone) (see fig. 1.25) to construct tombs for the dead with one or more chambers. Termed **dolmen** tombs, they were both impressive and durable. At some sites, upright megaliths known as **menhirs** marked out horizontal space in distinct ways, and perhaps served as ritual centers. Between 4250 and 3750 BCE at Ménec, in the Carnac region on the south coast of Brittany (see map 1.1), over 3,000 megaliths set upright at regular intervals in long, straight rows stretch out over 2 miles (3 km). Typically, the smaller stones of about 3 feet in height stand at the eastern end, and, gradually, the height of the stones increases, reaching over 13 feet at the western end (fig. 1.24). Scholars argue that the lines, with their east–west orientation, gauged the sun's position in the sky at different times of the year, functioning as a calendar for an agrarian people whose sustenance depended on the sun's cycle. Quarrying, shaping, transporting, and erecting these blocks was an extraordinary feat. Quite apart from remarkable engineering expertise, it required a highly efficient organization of manpower. The resulting monument, with its simple repeated forms identical in shape yet diverse in size, static yet cast into motion by the sun's slow and constant passage, has a calm grandeur and majesty that imposes quiet order on the open landscape.

Often, megaliths appear in circles, known as cromlechs. This is the prevalent arrangement in Britain, where the best-known megalithic structure is Stonehenge, on the Salisbury Plain (figs. **1.25** and **1.26**). What now appears as a unified design is in fact the result of at least four construction phases, beginning with a huge ditch defining a circle some 330 feet in diameter in the white chalk ground, and an embankment of over 6 feet running around the inside. A wide stone-lined avenue led from the circle to a pointed gray sandstone (sarsen) megalith, known today as the Heel Stone. By about 2100 BCE, Stonehenge had grown into a horseshoe-shaped arrangement of five sarsen trilithls, encircled by a ring of upright blocks capped with a lintel; between the rings was a circle of smaller bluestone blocks. Recent excavations exposed remains of a similar monument built of wood 2 miles (3 km) away, as well as remnants of a village. Archaeologists believe the structures are related.

Exactly what Stonehenge—and its nearby counterpart—signified to those who constructed them is a tantalizing mystery. Many prehistorians believe that Stonehenge, like Ménec, marked the passing of time. Given its monumentality, most also concur that it had a ritual function, perhaps associated with burial; its careful circular arrangement supports this conjecture, as circles are central to rituals in many societies. Indeed, these two qualities led medieval observers to believe that King Arthur's magician, Merlin, created Stonehenge, and it continues to draw crowds on

Dating Techniques

One of the chief concerns of archaeologists and art historians, regardless of the period in which they conduct research, is to be able to place works of art in a historical context. This means that dating an object is of paramount importance. Scholars assign two types of date: relative dates and absolutes dates. A relative date indicates that one object is older or more recent than another. To determine these dates, archaeologists tend to use stratigraphy: An object found at a lower layer or *stratum* of an excavation is normally older than an object found above it. The relative chronology of one site can be transferred to another site if objects of a similar kind appear at both. Pottery is a useful indicator of relative date for most ancient cultures because it is so durable that it exists in great profusion, often in an uninterrupted sequence.

Absolute dating assigns a calendar date to an object. In historical cultures (those with written documents), written records might preserve a date. For instance, building inscriptions indicate that the Athenians constructed the Parthenon between 447 and 432 BCE. Researchers have developed numerous other methods for establish-

ing absolute dates. These include radiometric dating, which works well for dating organic materials up to approximately 40,000 years old. Living organisms contain radioactive isotopes (such as carbon-14) that decay at a known rate after its death. By measuring the level of isotopes in organic material, archaeologists can gauge when it lived. Though effective, this method requires destroying part of the object, and can only establish when an organism died, not when an artist turned it into an artifact.

Some other techniques measure radiation levels. For instance, thermoluminescence is an effective dating technique for objects containing crystalline materials that have been exposed to high temperatures—such as pottery, which has been fired. Heat releases electrons trapped in the object's crystalline lattice, resulting in a "zeroing" radiation moment. Thereafter, electrons accumulate again. By measuring the luminescence (light, which is proportional to the number of electrons released) of the object during a second heating, archaeologists can determine the length of time since the zeroing event.

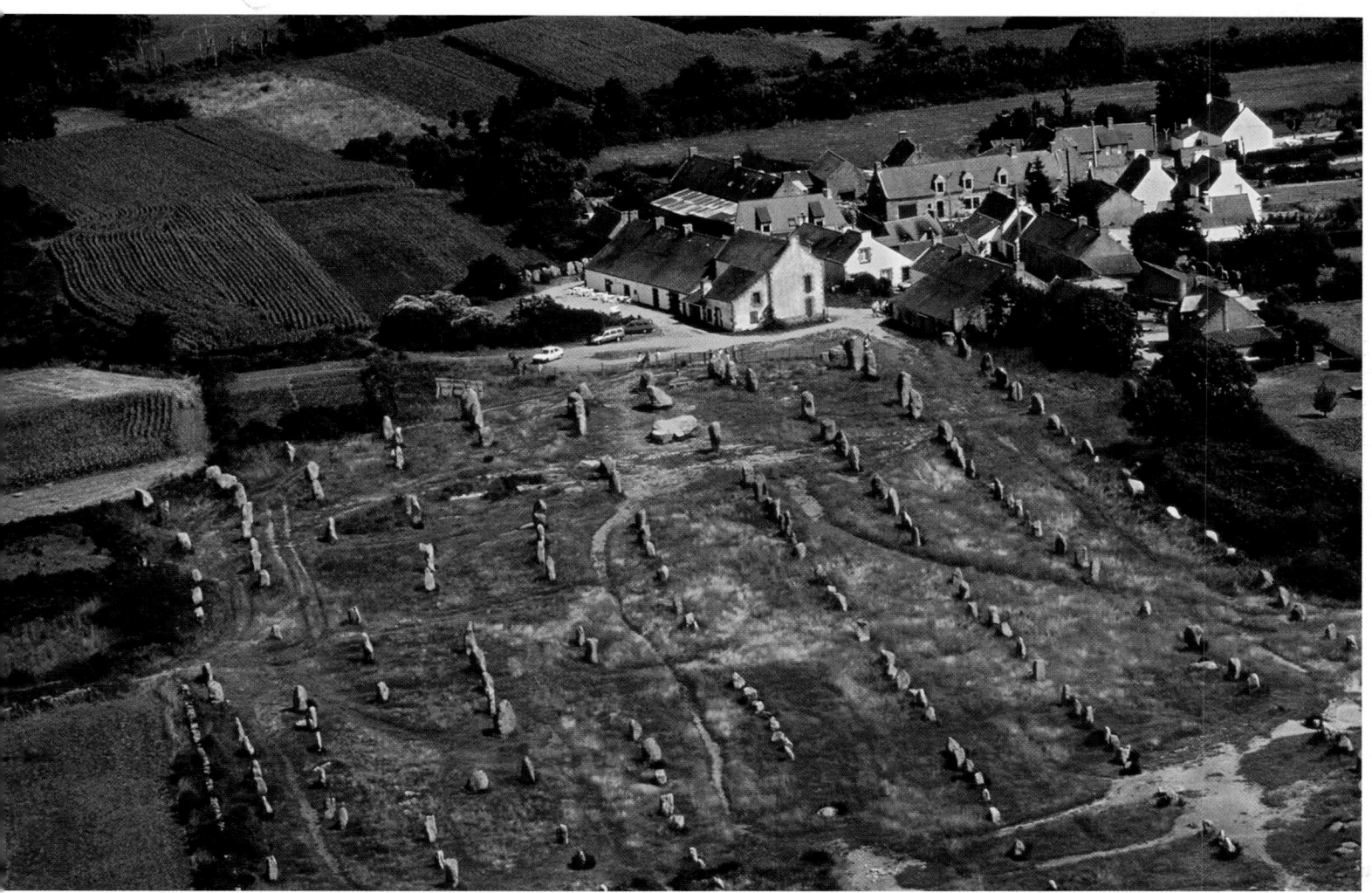

1.24   Menhir alignments at Ménec, Carnac, France. ca. 4250–3750 BCE

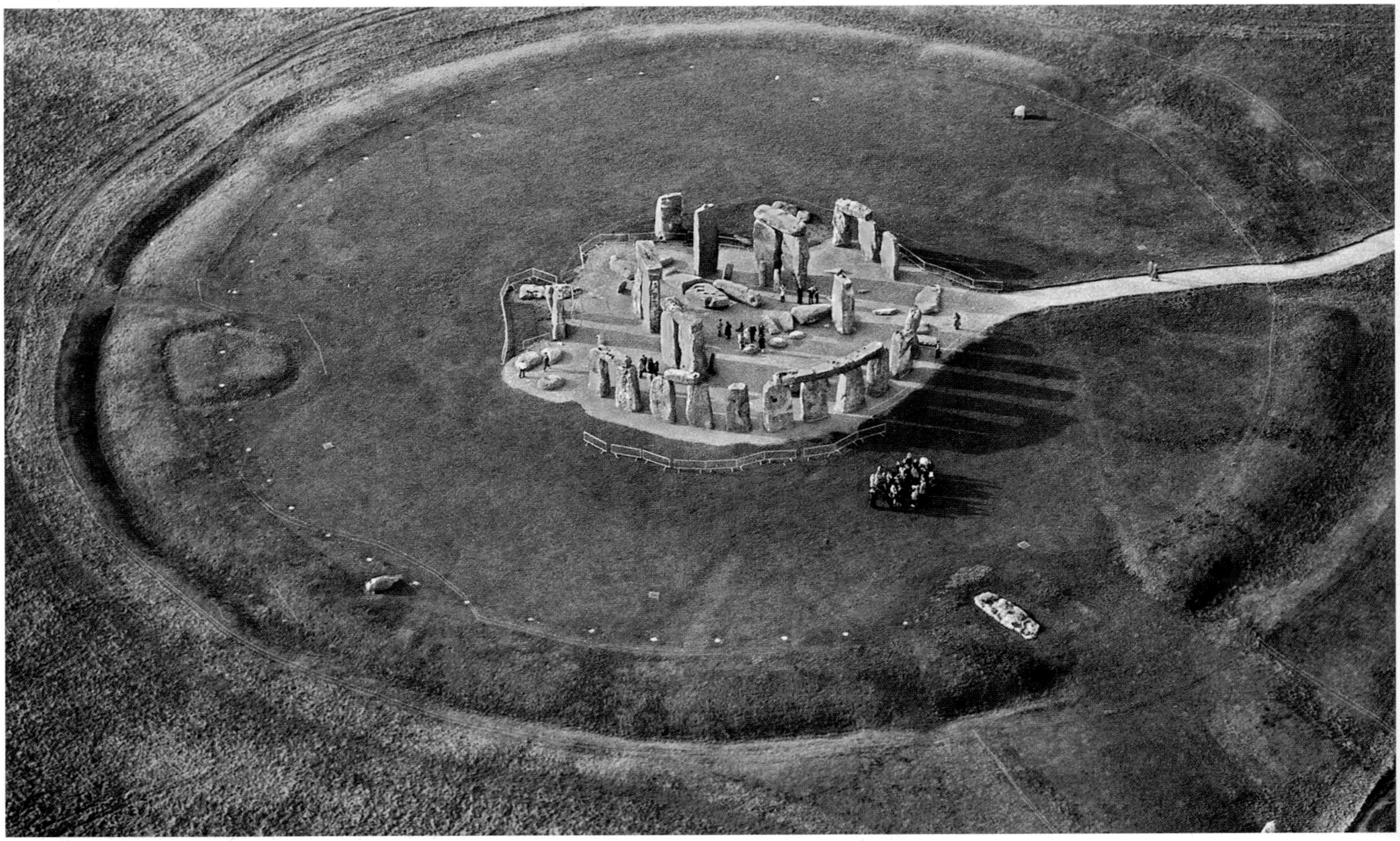

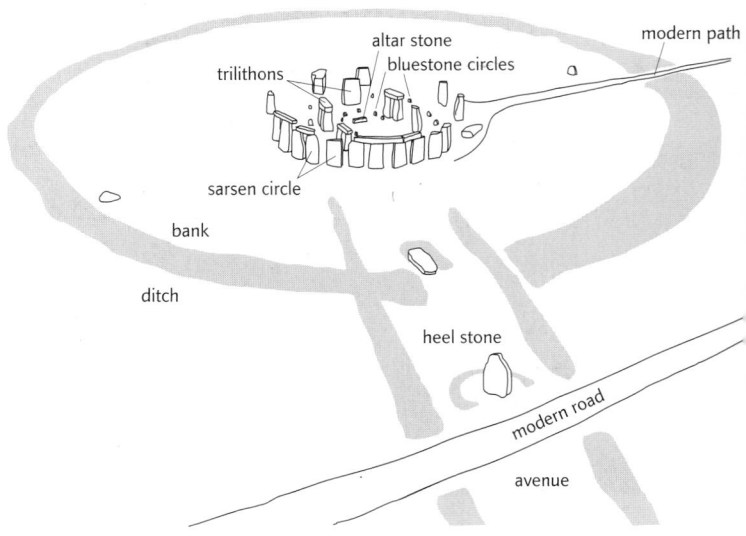

1.25 Stonehenge (aerial view), Salisbury Plain, Wiltshire, England. ca. 2100 BCE. Diameter of circle 97' (29.6 m)

summer solstices. What is certain is that, like Ménec, Stonehenge represents tremendous organization of labor and engineering skill. The largest trilith, at the center of the horseshoe, soars 24 feet, supporting a lintel 15 feet long and 3 feet thick. The sarsen blocks weigh up to 50 tons apiece, and traveled 23 miles (37 km) from the Marlborough Downs; the bluestones originated 200 miles (320 km) away, in the Welsh Preseli mountains. The blocks reveal evidence of meticulous stone working. Holes hollowed out of the capstones fit snugly over projections on the uprights (forming a mortise-and-tenon joint), to make a stable structure. Moreover, upright megaliths taper upward, with a central bulge, visually implying the weight they bear, and capturing an energy that gives life to the stones. The lintels are worked in two directions, their faces inclining outward by about 6 inches to appear vertical from the ground, while at the same time they curve around on the horizontal plane to make a smooth circle. Art historians usually associate this kind of refinement with the Parthenon of Classical Athens (see fig. 5.40).

Prehistoric art raises many questions. While we know humans began to express themselves visually during the prehistoric age, there are no written records to explain their intentions. Even so, by the end of the era, people had established techniques of painting, sculpting, and pottery making, and begun to construct

monumental works of architecture. They developed a strong sense of the power of images and spaces: They recognized how to produce naturalistic and abstract figures, and how to alter space in sophisticated ways.

1.26 Diagram of original arrangement of stones at Stonehenge

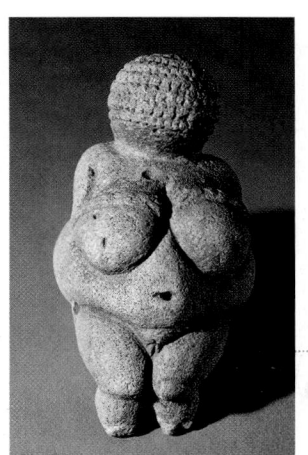

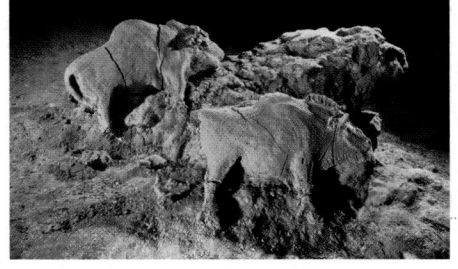

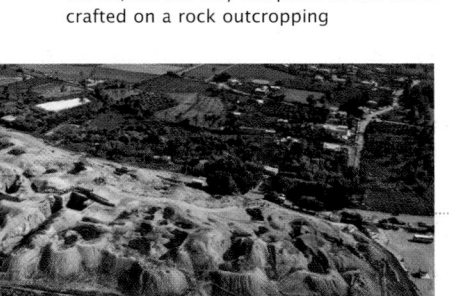

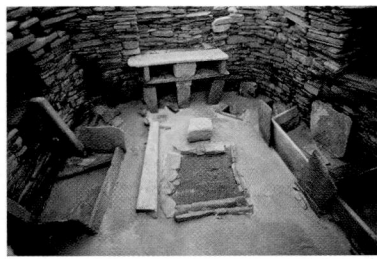

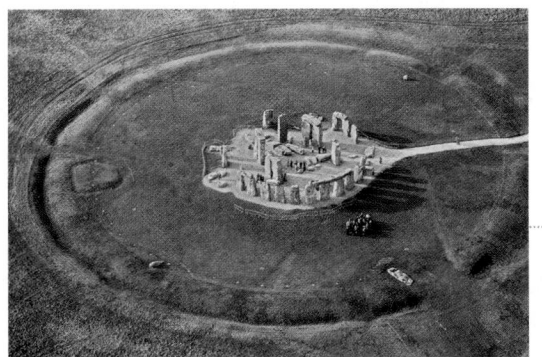

ca. 28,000–25,000 BCE
Woman of Willendorf

16,000–10,000 BCE Mammoth bone houses at Mezhirich

ca. 13,000 BCE Clay sculpture of two bison crafted on a rock outcropping

ca. 7500 BCE Jericho's fortification system; beginning of monumental architecture

ca. 3100–2600 BCE
Stone houses at
Skara Brae

ca. 2100 BCE Final phase of construction at Stonehenge

40,000 BCE

30,000 BCE

20,000 BCE

10,000 BCE

5000 BCE

4000 BCE

3000 BCE

2000 BCE

◄ ca. 38,000 BCE Humans produce the earliest objects classed as "art"

◄ ca. 32,000 BCE Oldest-known cave paintings, at Chauvet

◄ ca. 10,000 BCE Earth's climate gradually begins to warm

◄ Sixth millennium BCE Pottery may have originated in Mesopotamia

◄ ca. 3500 BCE Pottery manufacturing appears in Western Europe

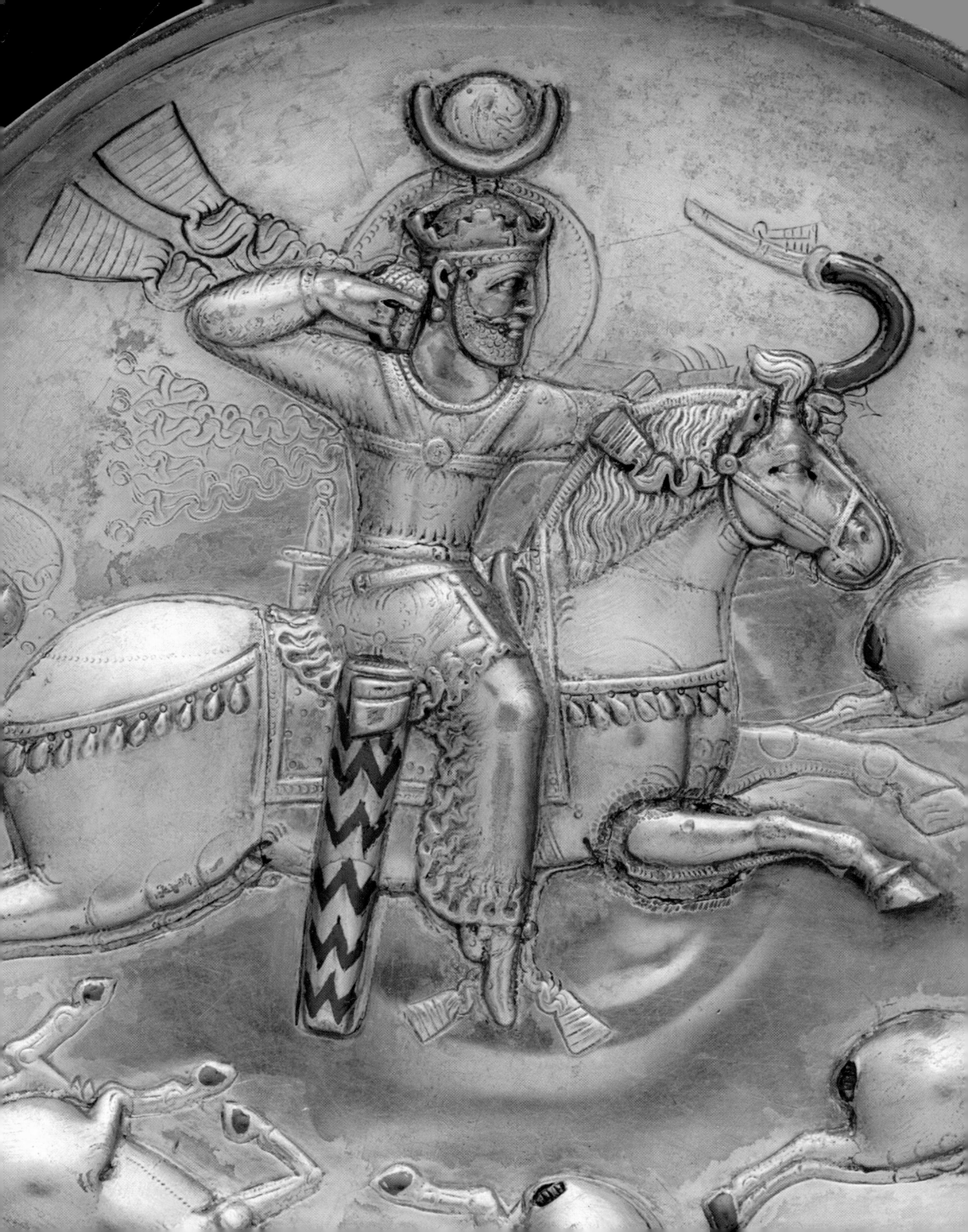

CHAPTER 2

Ancient Near Eastern Art

GROWING AND STORING CROPS AND RAISING ANIMALS FOR FOOD, the signature accomplishments of Neolithic peoples, would gradually change the course of civilization. Not long before they ceased to follow wild animal herds and gather food to survive, people began to form permanent settlements. By the end of the Neolithic era, these settlements grew

beyond the bounds of the village into urban centers. In the fourth millennium bce, large-scale urban communities of as many as 40,000 people began to emerge in Mesopotamia, the land between the Tigris and Euphrates rivers. The development of cities had tremendous ramifications for the development of human life and for works of art.

Although today the region of Mesopotamia is largely an arid plain, written, archaeological, and artistic evidence indicates that at the dawn of civilization lush vegetation covered it. By mastering irrigation techniques, populations there exploited the rivers and their tributaries to enrich the fertile soil even further. New technologies and inventions, including the wheel and the plow, and the casting of tools in copper and bronze, increased food production and facilitated trade. As communities flourished, they grew into city-states with distinct patterns of social organization to address the problems of urban life. Specialization of labor and trade, mechanisms for the resolution of disputes, and construction of defensible walls all required a central authority and government.

It was probably the efficient administration that developed in response to these needs that generated what may have been the earliest writing system, beginning around 3400–3200 bce, consisting of pictograms pressed into clay with a stylus to create inventories. By around 2900 bce, the Mesopotamians had refined the pictograms into a series of wedge-shaped signs known as **cuneiform** (from *cuneus*, Latin for "wedge"). They used this system for administrative accounts and the Sumerian *Epic of Gilgamesh* in the late third millennium bce. Cuneiform writing continued through much of the ancient era in the Near East and formed a cultural link between diverse groups who established power in the region. With the invention of writing, we enter the realm of history.

The geography of Mesopotamia had other profound effects on developing civilizations. Unlike the narrow, fertile strip of the Nile Valley in Egypt, protected by deserts on either side, where urban communities now also began to thrive, Mesopotamia is a wide, shallow trough, crisscrossed by the two rivers and their tributaries and with few natural defenses. People wanting to exploit its fertile soil constantly traversed the region, entering easily from any direction. Indeed, the history of the ancient Near East is a multicultural one; city-states were constantly at war with one another and only sometimes united under a single ruler. Still, Mesopotamian visual culture retains a surprisingly constant character. Two dominant themes emerge: Art enabled and reflected political power; and Mesopotamians used visual narrative, exploring strategies for telling stories through art.

Detail of figure 2.33, *Peroz I (457–483) or Kavad I hunting rams.*

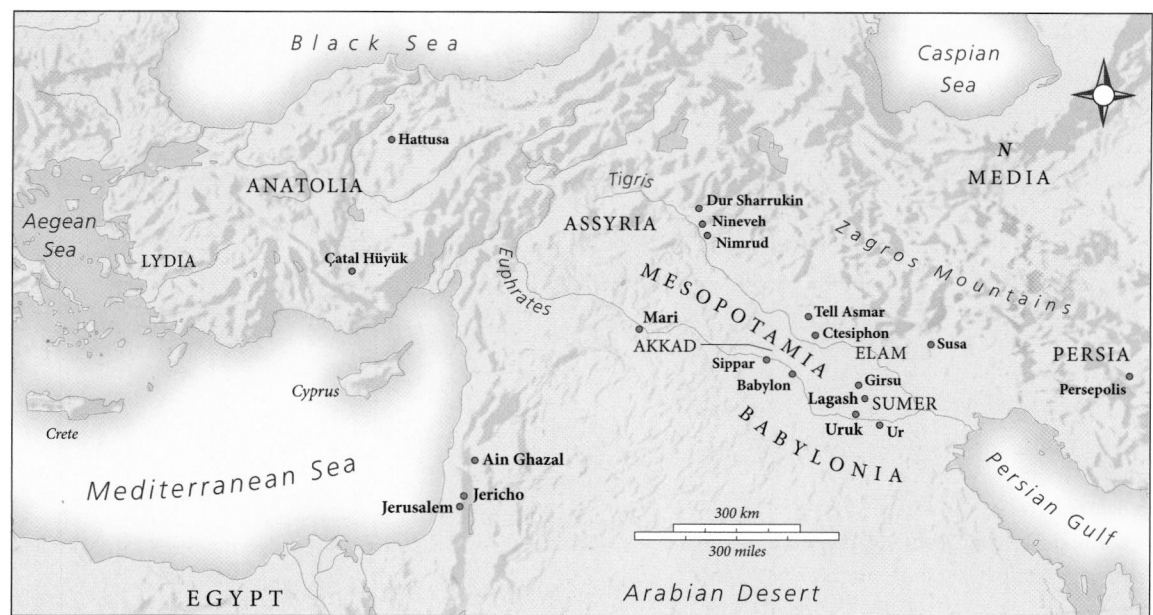

Map 2.1   The Ancient Near East

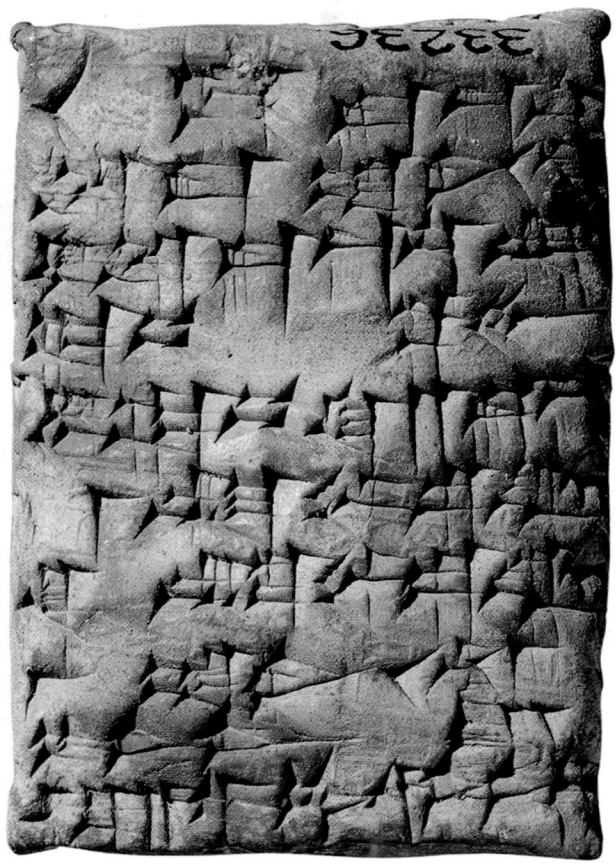

2.1   Babylonian deed of sale. ca. 1750 BCE. This deed graphically shows the impressions made by the stylus in the soft clay. Department of Western Asiatic Antiques, No. 33236. The British Museum, London

SUMERIAN ART

The first major civilization in Mesopotamia was in the southern region of Sumer, near the junction of the Tigris and Euphrates rivers, where several city-states flourished from before 4000 BCE (map **2.1**) until about 2340 BCE. Who the Sumerians were is not clear; often scholars can establish linkages between peoples through common linguistic traditions, but Sumerian is not related to any other known tongue. Archaeological excavations since the middle of the nineteenth century have unearthed many clay tablets with cuneiform writing including inventories and lists of kings, as well as poetry (fig. **2.1**). Many of the earliest excavations concentrated on Sumerian cities mentioned in the Bible, such as Ur (the birthplace of Abraham) and Uruk (the biblical Erech). Along with architecture and writing, works of art in the form of sculpture, **relief**, and pottery inform us about Sumerian society.

For Sumerians, life itself depended on appeasing the gods, who controlled natural forces and phenomena such as weather and water, the fertility of the land, and the movement of heavenly bodies. Each city had a patron deity, to whom residents owed both devotion and sustenance. The god's earthly steward was the city's ruler, who directed an extensive administrative staff based in the temple. As the produce of the city's land belonged to the god, the temple staff took charge of supplying farmers with seed, work animals, and tools. They built irrigation systems, and stored and distributed the harvest. Centralized food production meant that much of the population could specialize in other trades. In turn, they donated a portion of the fruits of their labor to the temple. This system is known as theocratic socialism.

Mud Brick

Mud brick was made primarily from local clay. Raw clay absorbs water, and then cracks after drying. As a binding agent and to provide elasticity and prevent cracking, Sumerian builders would add vegetable matter, such as straw, to the clay. By forcing the mud mixture into wooden frames, the brick makers obtained uniformly rectangular bricks. They then knocked the molded bricks out of the frames and placed them in the sun to bake. To erect walls, they joined the bricks together with wet clay. One disadvantage of mud brick is that it is not durable. The Sumerians would therefore seal important exterior walls with bitumen, a tarlike substance, or they would use glazed bricks. Sometimes they covered interior walls with plaster.

Mud brick is not a material that readily excites the imagination today (in the way that, for instance, marble does), and because it is so highly perishable, it has rarely survived from ancient times to indicate how Sumerian temples might once have looked. However, more recent examples of mud-brick architecture like the kasbahs (citadels) south of Morocco's Atlas mountains, at Aït Ben Haddou and elsewhere, reveal the extraordinary potential of the material. There, the easy pliability of mud brick allows for a dramatic decorative effect that is at once man-made and in total harmony with the natural colors of the earth. Notice, too, the geometric designs echoed in the woodwork of doorways and windows. First constructed in the sixteenth century CE, these buildings undergo constant maintenance (recently funded by UNESCO) to undo the weather's frequent damage. Naturally, Sumerian temples may have looked quite different, but the kasbahs serve as a useful reminder that mud-brick construction can produce magnificent results.

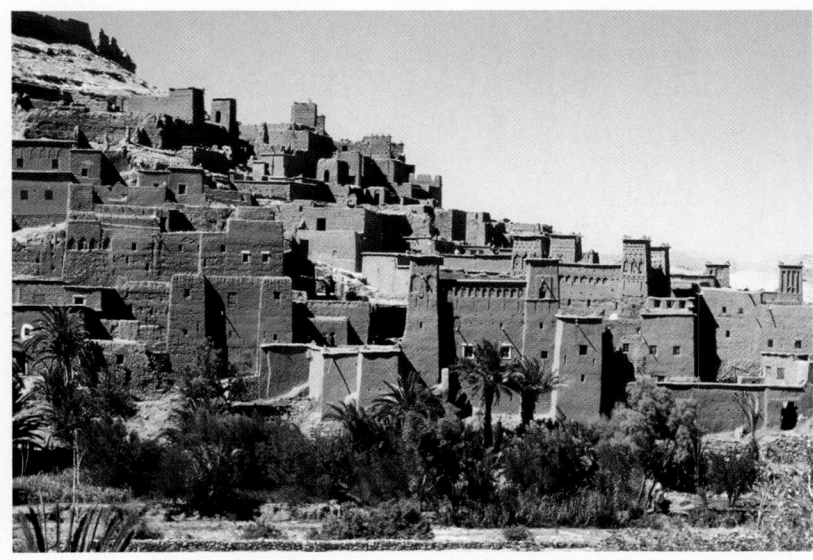

Mud-brick kasbahs at Aït Ben Haddou, Morocco

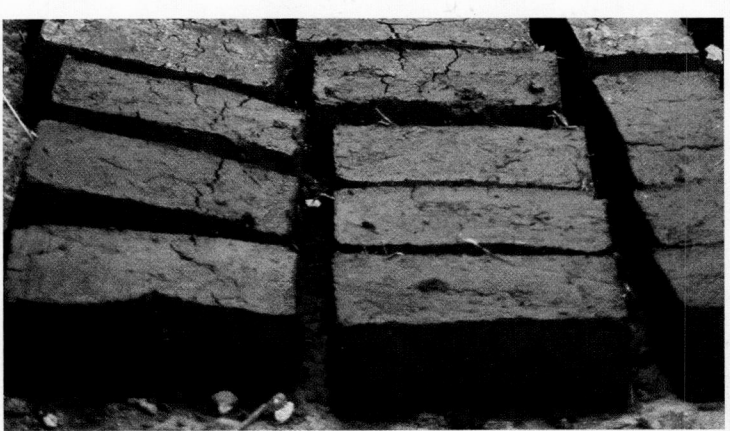

Mud bricks at Aït Ben Haddou, Morocco

Temple Architecture: Linking Heaven and Earth

The temple was the city's architectural focus. Good stone being scarce, Sumerians built predominantly with mud brick covered with plaster. (See *Materials and Techniques*, above).

Scholars distinguish two different types of Sumerian temple. "Low" temples sat at ground level. Usually their four corners were oriented to the cardinal points of the compass. The temple was tripartite: Rooms serving as offices, priests' quarters, and storage areas lined a rectangular main room, or **cella**, on its two long sides. The essential characteristics of "high" temples were similar, except that a platform raised the building above ground level; these platforms were gradually transformed into squat, stepped pyramids known as **ziggurats**. The names of some ziggurats—such as Etemenanki at Babylon ("House temple, bond between heaven and earth")—suggest that they may have been links or portals to the heavens, where priest and god could commune.

At approximately 40 to 50 feet high (at Warka and Ur), ziggurats functioned analogously as mountains, which held a sacred status for Sumerians. A source of water flowing to the valleys, mountains were also a place of refuge during floods, and symbolized the Earth's generative power. Indeed, Sumerians knew their mother goddess as the Lady of the Mountain. Significantly, raised platforms made temples more visible. Mesopotamian texts indicate that the act of seeing was paramount: In seeing an object and finding it pleasing, a god might act favorably toward those who made it. The desired response of a human audience, in turn, was wonder. Finally, there was probably a political dimension to the high platform: It emphasized and maintained the priests' status by visually expressing their separation from the rest of the community.

Around 3500 BCE, the city of Uruk (present-day Warka and the biblical Erech) emerged as a center of Sumerian culture, flourishing from trade in its agricultural surplus. One of its temples, the White Temple, named for its whitewashed brick surfaces, probably honored the sky-god Anu, chief of the Sumerian gods (fig. **2.2**). It sits on a 40-foot mound constructed by filling in the ruins of older temples with brickwork, which suggests that the site itself was sacred (fig. **2.3**). Recessed brickwork articulated its sloped sides. A system of stairs and ramps led counterclockwise around the mound, culminating at an entrance in the temple's long north side. This indirect approach is characteristic of Mesopotamian temple architecture (in contrast to the direct axial approach favored in Egypt), and the winding ascent mirrored a visitor's metaphorical ascent into a divine realm. From three sides, members of the community could also witness the ceremonial ascent of priests and leaders who had exclusive access to the temple. Enough survives of the superstructure to indicate that thick buttressed walls surrounded a central, rectangular hall (cella) housing a stepped **altar**. Along the long sides of the cella were smaller rooms, creating an overall tripartite layout typical of the earliest temples.

Uruk was the home of the legendary king Gilgamesh, hero of an epic poem that describes his adventures. Gilgamesh purportedly carved his tale on a stone marker—which suggests the importance of narrative in Sumerian culture. The epic credits Gilgamesh with building the city walls of Uruk and the Eanna, a temple of Inanna (goddess of love and war) or Ishtar. The poem describes the temple's gleaming walls, built with "kiln-fired brick." In the Eanna precinct, archaeologists found several temples whose walls were decorated with colored stone or painted clay cones set into plaster to form mosaic patterns. (See *Primary Source*, page 25.)

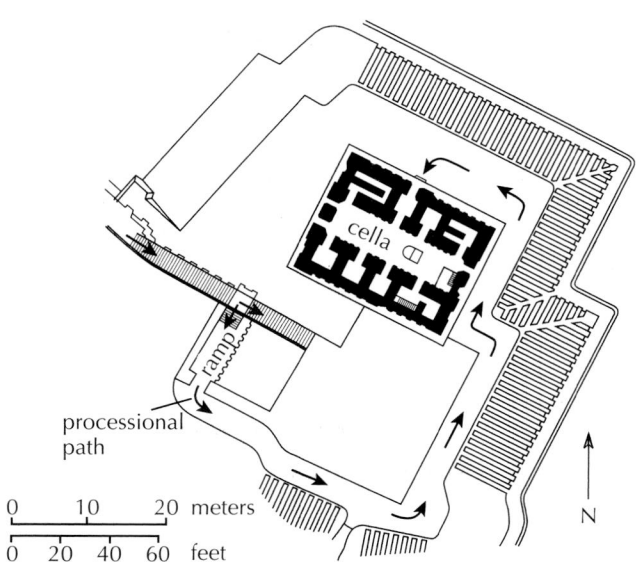

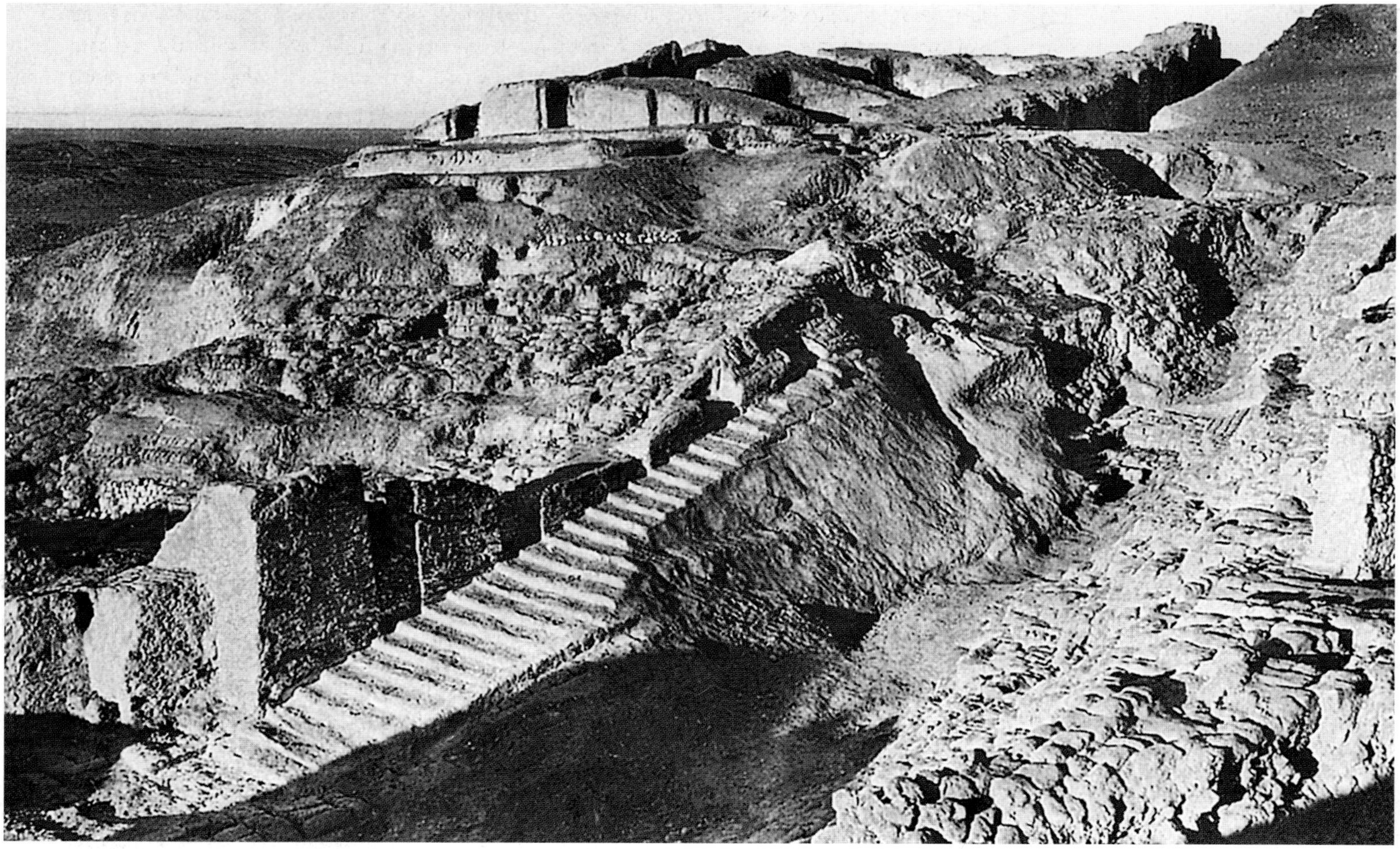

cella

ramp

processional
path

0   10   20 meters
0 20 40 60 feet

N

2.2   Plan of the White Temple on its ziggurat (after H. Frankfort)

2.3   Remains of the White Temple on its ziggurat. ca. 3500–3000 BCE. Uruk (Warka), Iraq

The Gilgamesh Epic

One of the earliest written epics, the Gilgamesh epic survives on cuneiform tablets. Although the earliest texts to survive come from Akkadian tablets written after 2150 BCE, the text itself dates to the Sumerian era, about 2800 BCE. The surviving parts of the epic recount the tale of Gilgamesh, the king of Uruk, who first battles, then befriends the wild man Enkidu. When his friend dies, Gilgamesh goes in search of a way to defeat death, but eventually returns to Uruk, accepting his own mortality. This excerpt from the beginning of the poem describes (with gaps from the sources) Gilgamesh's accomplishments as king.

Anu granted him the totality of knowledge of all.
He saw the Secret, discovered the Hidden,
he brought information of (the time) before the Flood.
He went on a distant journey, pushing himself to exhaustion,
but then was brought to peace.
He carved on a stone stela all of his toils,
and built the wall of Uruk-Haven,
the wall of the sacred Eanna Temple, the holy sanctuary.

Look at its wall which gleams like copper(?),
inspect its inner wall, the likes of which no one can equal!
Take hold of the threshold stone—it dates from ancient times!
Go close to the Eanna Temple, the residence of Ishtar,
such as no later king or man ever equaled!
Go up on the wall of Uruk and walk around,
examine its foundation, inspect its brickwork thoroughly.
Is not (even the core of) the brick structure made of kiln-fired brick,
and did not the Seven Sages themselves lay out its plans?
One square mile is devoted to city, one to palm gardens, one to lowlands, the open area(?) of the Ishtar Temple,
three leagues and the open area(?) of Uruk it (the wall) encloses.
Find the copper tablet box,
open the … of its lock of bronze,
undo the fastening of its secret opening.
Take out and read the lapis lazuli tablet
how Gilgamesh went through every hardship.

Source: The Epic of Gilgamesh, tr. Maureen Gallery Kovacs (Stanford, CA: Stanford Univ. Press, 1989)

Sculpture and Inlay

The cella of Uruk's White Temple would once have contained a cult statue, which is now lost. Yet a female head dating to about 3100 BCE, found in the Eanna sanctuary of Inanna at Uruk, may indicate what a cult statue looked like (fig. **2.4**). The sculptor carved the face of white limestone, and added details in precious materials: a wig, perhaps of gold or copper, secured by the ridge running down the center of the head, and eyes and eyebrows of colored materials. Despite the absence of these features, the sculpture has not lost its power to impress: The abstraction of its large eyes and dramatic brow contrasts forcefully with the delicate modeling of the cheeks. Flat on the back, the head was once attached to a body, presumably made of wood, and the full figure must have stood near life-size.

TELL ASMAR A group of sculptures excavated in the 1930s at a temple at Tell Asmar illustrates a type of limestone, alabaster, and gypsum figures that artists began to make about 500 years after the carving of the Uruk head (fig. **2.5**). Ranging in height from several inches to 2½ feet, these figures probably originally stood in the temple's cella. They were purposely buried near the altar along with other objects, perhaps when the temple was rebuilt or redecorated. All but one of the figures in this group stand in a static pose, with hands clasped between chest and waist level. The style is decidedly abstract: On most of the standing male figures, horizontal or zigzag ridges define long hair and a full beard; the arms hang from wide shoulders; hands are clasped around a cup; narrow chests widen to broad waists; and the legs are cylindrical. The male figures wear fringed skirts hanging from a belt in a stiff cone shape, while the women have full-length drapery. Most scholars identify the two larger figures as cult statues of Abu, god of vegetation, and his consort. The others figures probably represent priests, since the fringed skirt is the dress of the priesthood. Some statues of this kind from elsewhere are inscribed with the name of the god and of the worshiper who dedicated the statue.

The poses and the costumes represent conventions of Sumerian art that later Mesopotamians adopted. Most distinctive are the faces, dominated by wide, almost round eyes. Dark inlays

2.4 *Female Head*, from Uruk (Warka), Iraq. ca. 3200–3000 BCE. Limestone, height 8" (20.3 cm). Iraq Museum, Baghdad

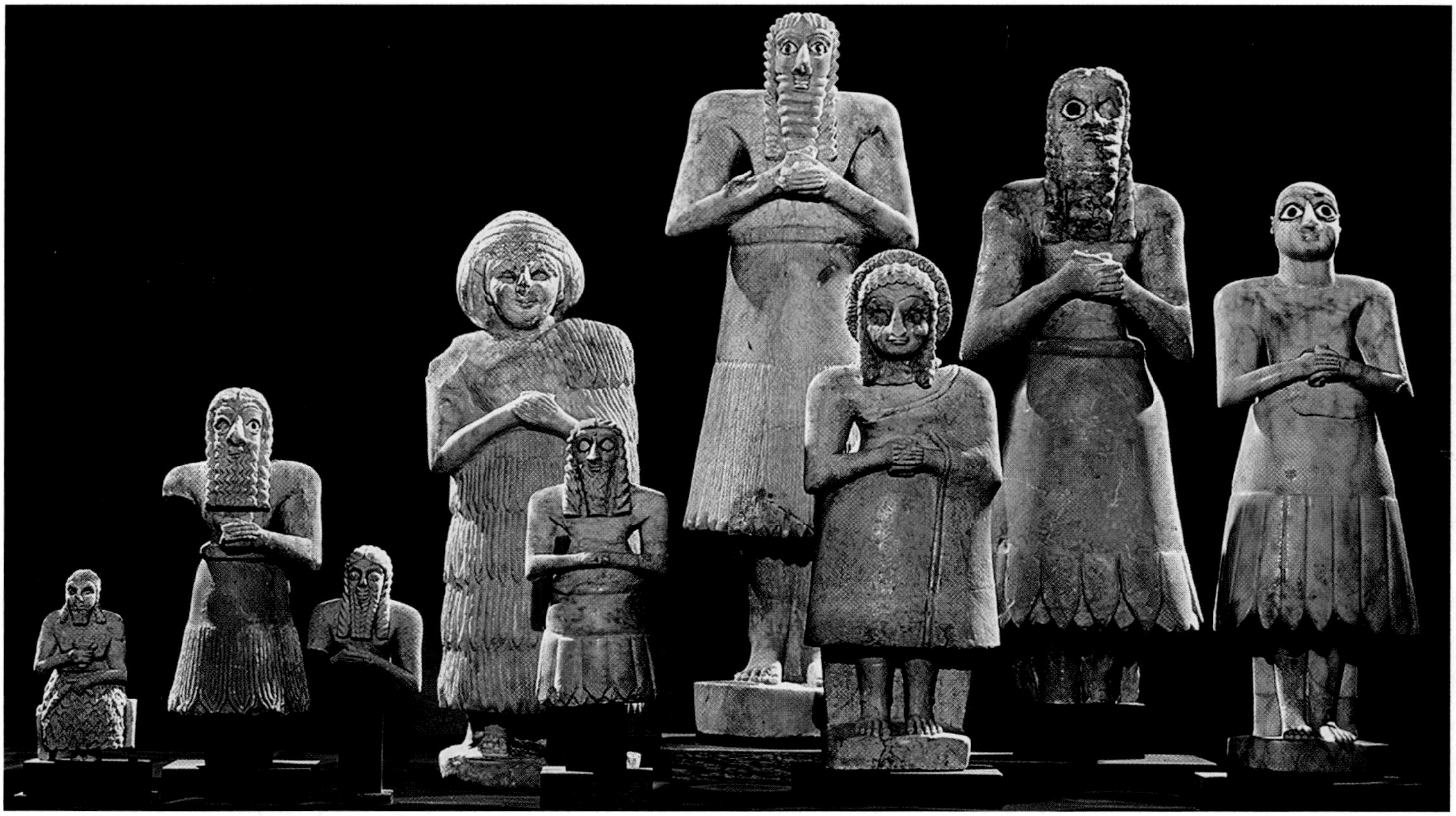

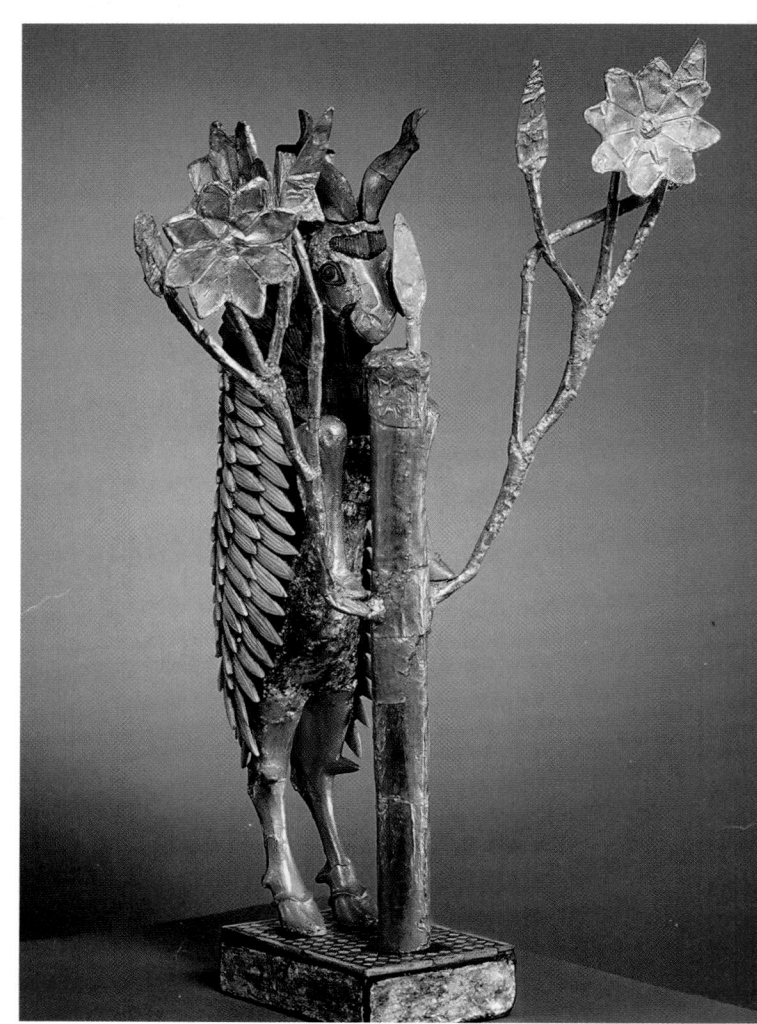

2.5 Statues from the Abu Temple, Tell Asmar, Iraq. ca. 2700–2500 BCE. Limestone, alabaster, and gypsum, height of tallest figure approx. 30" (76.3 cm). Iraq Museum, Baghdad, and The Oriental Institute Museum of the University of Chicago

of lapis lazuli and shells set in bitumen accentuate the eyes, as do powerful eyebrows that meet over the bridge of the nose. As noted above, seeing was a major channel of communication with gods, and the sculptures may have been responding to the god's awe-inspiring nature with eyes wide open in admiration. Enlarged eyes were also a conventional means of warding off evil in Mesopotamia, known today as an **apotropaic device**. Several of these statues were in the Iraq Museum, and were looted during recent unrest in Baghdad (see *The Art Historian's Lens*, page 29).

THE ROYAL CEMETERY AT UR The Sumerian city of Ur in southern Mesopotamia first attracted archaeologists because of its biblical associations. Its extensive cemetery was well preserved under the walls of King Nebuchadnezzar II's later city, and Leonard Woolley discovered a wide variety of Sumerian objects in excavations there during the 1920s. The cemetery contained some 1,840 burials dating between 2600 and 2000 BCE. Some were humble, but others were substantial subterranean structures and contained magnificent offerings, earning them the designation

2.6 *Goat in Thicket (Ram and Tree)*, one of the pair from the Great Death Pit in the Royal Cemetery of Ur, Muqaiyir, Iraq. ca. 2600 BCE. Wood, gold, lapis lazuli, height 20" (50.8 cm). University Museum, University of Pennsylvania, Philadelphia

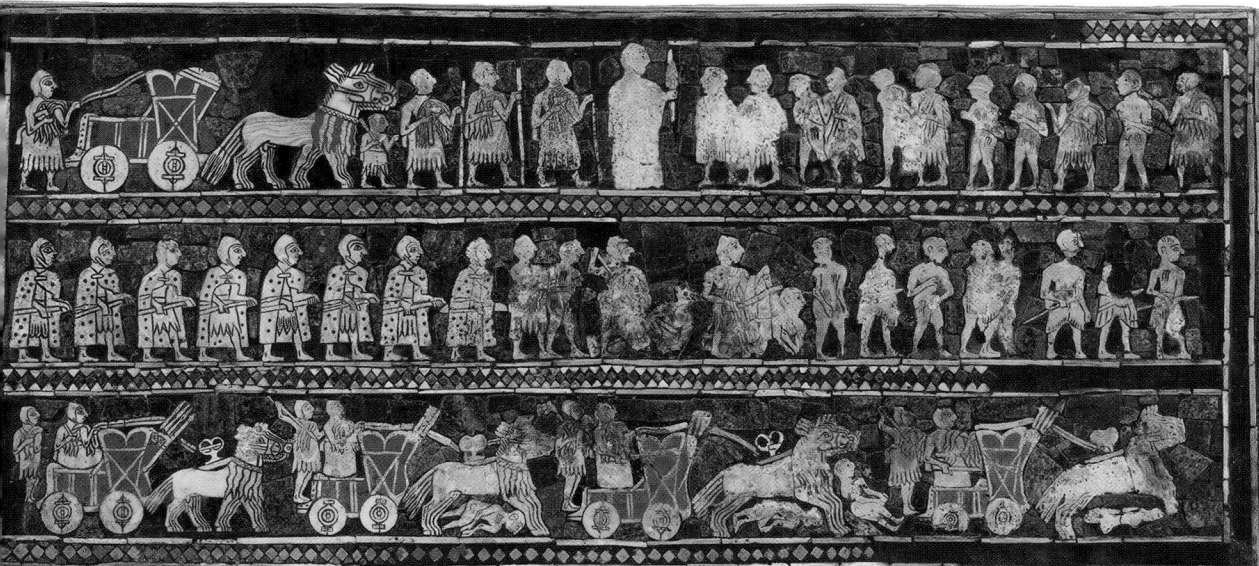

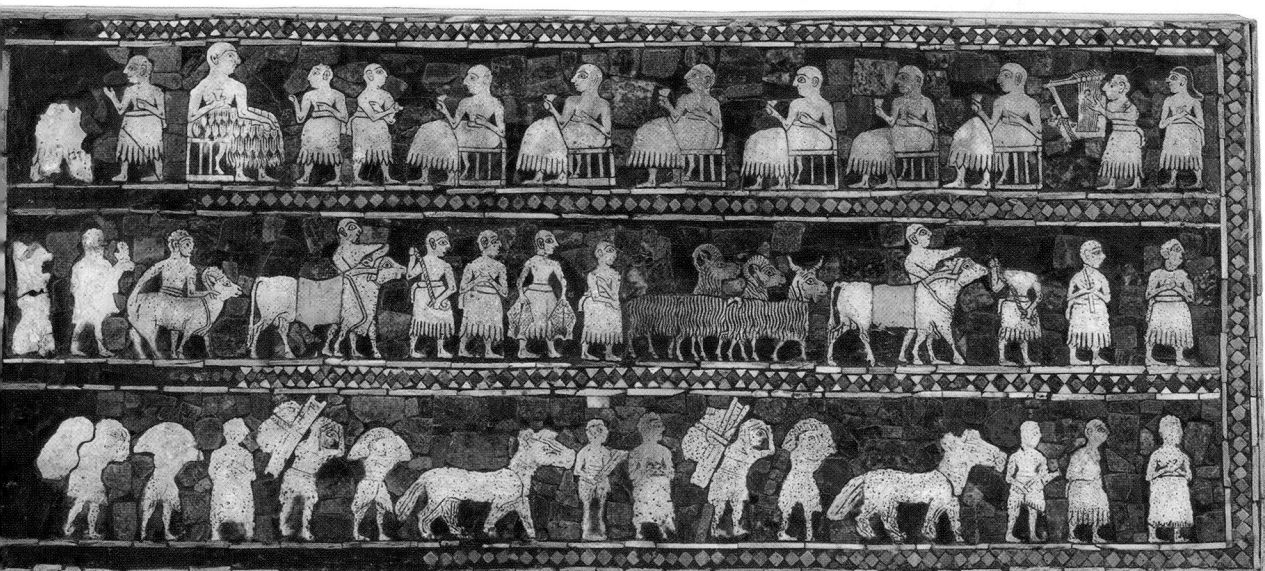

2.7 *Royal Standard of Ur*, front and back sides. ca. 2600 BCE. Wood inlaid with shell, limestone, and lapis lazuli, height 8" (20.3 cm). The British Museum, London

of "royal graves," even though it remains uncertain whether the deceased were royalty, priests, or members of another elite. So-called Death Pits accompanied the wealthiest burials. Foremost among them was the Great Death Pit, in which 74 soldiers, attendants, and musicians were interred, apparently drugged before lying down in the grave as human sacrifices. Even in death, the elite maintained the visible trappings of power and required the services of their retainers. These finds suggest that Sumerians may have believed in an afterlife.

Among the many kinds of grave goods Woolley found in the Royal Cemetery were weapons, jewelry, and vessels. Many of the objects display the great skill of Sumerian artists in representing nature. A pair of wild goats rearing up on their hind legs against a flowering tree probably functioned as stands for offerings to a deity. Gold leaf is the dominant material, used for the goat's head, legs, and genitals, as well as for the tree and a cylindrical support strut rising from the goat's back in the one shown here (fig. **2.6**). Lapis lazuli on the horns and neck fleece complements the shell

fragments decorating the body fleece and the ears of copper. The base is an intricately crafted pattern of red limestone, shell, and lapis lazuli. Images on cylinder seals show that a bowl or saucer would have been balanced on the horns and the support cylinder. The combination of the goat (sacred to the god Tammuz) and the carefully arranged flowers (rosettes sacred to Inanna) suggests that the sculpture reflects Sumerian concerns about fertility, both of plants and animals.

Visual Narratives

Two objects from the Royal Cemetery at Ur offer glimpses of the development of visual narrative in Mesopotamia. The *Royal Standard of Ur*, of about 2600 BCE, consists of four panels of red limestone, shell, and lapis lazuli inlay set in bitumen, originally attached to a wooden framework (fig. **2.7**). The damaged side panels depicted animal scenes, while the two larger sections show a military victory and a celebration or ritual feast, each unfolding in

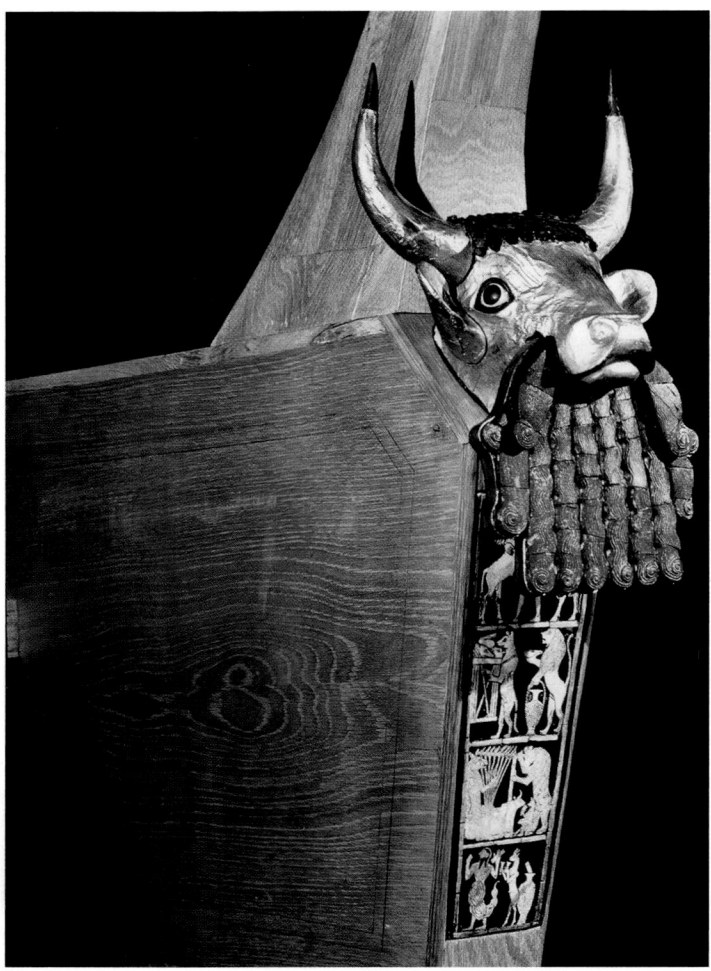

2.8 *Bull Lyre*, from the tomb of Queen Pu-abi, Ur (Muqaiyir), Iraq. ca. 2600 BCE. Wood with gold, lapis lazuli, bitumen, and shell, reassembled in modern wood support. University Museum, University of Pennsylvania, Philadelphia

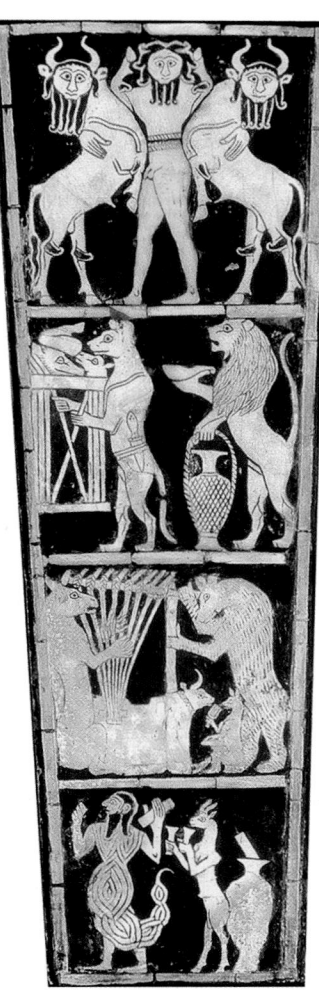

2.9 Inlay panel from the soundbox of lyre, from Ur (Muqaiyir), Iraq. ca. 2600 BCE. Shell and bitumen, 12¼ × 4½" (31.1 × 11.3 cm). University Museum, University of Pennsylvania, Philadelphia

three superposed **registers**, or horizontal bands. Reading from the bottom, the "war" panel shows charioteers advancing from the left, pulled by onagers (wild asses), and riding over enemy bodies. In the middle register, infantry soldiers do battle and escort prisoners of war, stripped of armor and clothing. At the top, soldiers present the prisoners to a central figure, whose importance the artist signals through his position and through his larger size, a device known as **hieratic scale**; his head even breaks through the register's frame to emphasize his importance. In the "banquet" panel, figures burdened with booty accompany onagers and animals for a feast. Their dress identifies them as travelers from northern Sumer and probably Kish, the region later known as Akkad. In the top register, the banquet is already underway. Seated figures raise their cups to the sound of music from a nearby harpist and singer; a larger figure toward the left of the scene is presumably a leader or king, perhaps the same figure as on the "war" side. Together, the panels represent the dual aspects of kingship: the king as warrior, and the king as priest and mediator with the gods. Despite the action in the scenes, the images have a static quality, which the figures' isolation emphasizes (a staccato treatment): Their descriptive forms (half frontal, half

profile) rarely overlap. This, and the contrasting colored materials, give the narrative an easy legibility, even from a distance.

On excavating the *Royal Standard of Ur*, Woolley envisioned it held aloft on a pole as a military standard, and named it accordingly. In fact, it is unclear how the Sumerians used the object. It may have been the sounding-box for a stringed instrument, an object that was commonly deposited in burials. In one of the cemetery's most lavish graves, the grave of "Queen" Pu-abi, Woolley discovered a lyre decorated with a bull's head of gold gilt and lapis lazuli, dating to ca. 2600 BCE (fig. **2.8**), comparable to the lyre on the *Standard*. On its sounding-box, a panel of shell inlaid in bitumen depicts a male figure in a heraldic composition, embracing two human-faced bulls and facing a viewer with a frontal glare (fig. **2.9**). In the lower registers, animals perform human tasks such as carrying foodstuffs and playing music. These scenes may have evoked a myth or fable that contemporary viewers knew either in written or in oral form, and that was perhaps associated with a funerary context. In some cultures, fantastic hybrid creatures, such as the bulls or the man with a braided, snakelike body in the bottom scene, served an apotropaic function.

Losses Through Looting

The archaeologist's greatest nemesis is the looter, who pillages ancient sites to supply the world's second largest illicit business: the illegal trade in antiquities. The problem is worldwide, but recent publicity has focused on Iraq, where thousands of archaeological sites still await proper excavation. Looters are often local people, living in impoverished conditions but supported and organized by more powerful agents; just as frequently, looters work in organized teams, arriving on site with jackhammers and bulldozers, wielding weapons to overcome whatever meager security there might be. Often employing the most sophisticated tools, such as remote-sensing and satellite photography, they move quickly and unscrupulously through a site, careless of what they destroy in their search for treasure. Loot changes hands quickly as it crosses national borders, fetching vast sums on the market. Little or none of this fortune returns to local hands.

Even more is at stake in these transactions than the loss of a nation's heritage. Only a fraction of the value of an archaeological find resides in the object itself. Much more significant is what its findspot—the place where it was found—can tell archaeologists, who use the information to construct a history of the past. An object's location within a city or building reveals how it was used. A figurine, for instance, could be a fertility object, doll, or cult image, depending on its physical context. The exact level, or stratum, at which archaeologists find an object discloses when it was in use. On some sites, stratigraphy (reading levels/strata) yields very precise dates. If an object comes to light far from its place of manufacture, its findspot can even document interactions between cultures.

A 1970 UNESCO Convention requires member states to prohibit the importation of stolen antiquities from other member states, and offers help in protecting cultural property that is in jeopardy of pillage. To date, 115 countries are party to the convention.

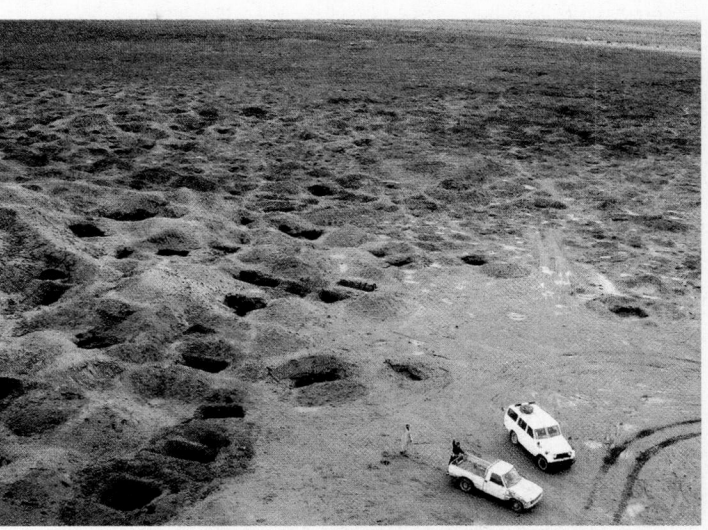

Looters at the archaeological site of Isin, southern Iraq, January 2004

Cylinder Seals

The Mesopotamians also produced vast numbers of cylinder seals, which the administration used to seal jars and secure storerooms. The seals were cylindrical objects usually made of stone, with a hole running through the center from end to end. A sculptor carved a design into the curved surface of the seal, so that when the owner impressed it in soft clay, a raised, reverse image would unfold, repeated as the cylinder rolled along. Great quantities of seals and sealings (seal impressions) have survived. Many are of modest quality, reflecting their primarily administrative purpose, but the finest examples display a wealth of detail and a high level of sculptural expertise. With subjects ranging from divine and royal scenes to monumental architecture, animals, and daily activities, the seals provide critical information about Mesopotamian existence and values. The sealing illustrated here appears to show the feeding of the temple herd, which provided a significant portion of the temple's wealth (fig. 2.10). The human figure's distinctive costume and hat may identify him as a priest-king; some have seen the large vessels as a reference to sacred offerings, and excavators found one such vase, measuring nearly 3 feet in height, in the Eanna precinct at Uruk, dating to ca. 3200 BCE.

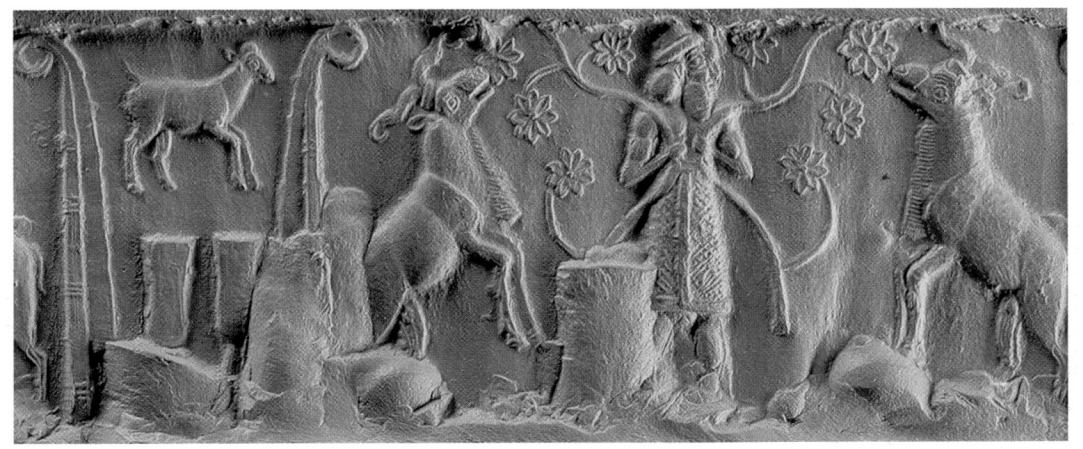

2.10 *Priest-King Feeding Sacred Sheep*, from vicinity of Uruk (Warka), Iraq. ca. 3300 BCE. Cylinder sealing, height 2⅛" (5.4 cm), diameter 1¾" (4.5 cm). Staatliche Museen zu Berlin, Preussischer Kulturbesitz, Vorderasiatisches Museum

ART OF AKKAD

Around 2350 BCE, Sumerian city-states began to fight over access to water and fertile land. Gradually, their social organization was transformed as local "stewards of the god" positioned themselves as ruling kings. The more ambitious tried to enlarge their domains through conquest. Semitic-speaking people (those who used languages in the same family as Hebrew and Arabic) from the northern region gradually assumed positions of power in the south. Although they adopted many features of Sumerian civilization, they were less bound to the tradition of the city-state. Sargon (meaning "true king") conquered Sumer, as well as northern Syria and Elam (to the northeast of Sumer) in about 2334 BCE (see map 2.1), basing himself in the city of Akkad (a site unknown today, but probably to the northwest of Sumer, near present-day Baghdad). Akkadian then became the language of authority in Mesopotamia. Sargon's ambitions were both imperial and dynastic. He combined Sumerian and Akkadian deities in a new pantheon, hoping to break down the traditional link between city-states and their local gods, and thereby to unite the region in loyalty to his absolute rule. Under his grandson, Naram-Sin, who ruled from 2254 to 2218 BCE, the Akkadian Empire stretched from Sumer in the south to Elam in the east, and then to Syria in the west and Nineveh in the north.

Sculpture: Power and Narrative

Akkadian rulers increasingly exploited the visual arts to establish and reflect their power. A magnificent copper portrait head found in a rubbish heap at Nineveh, dated to between 2250 and 2200 BCE and sometimes identified as Naram-Sin himself (fig. **2.11**), derives its extraordinary power from a number of factors: The intended view of the portrait was from the front, and this **frontality** makes it appear unchanging and eternal. The abstract treatment of beard and hair (which is arranged like a Sumerian king's) contrasts with the smooth flesh to give the head a memorable simplicity and strong symmetry, which denote control and order. The intricate, precise patterning of hair and beard testifies to the metalworker's expertise in hollow casting (see *Materials and Techniques*, page 128). Furthermore, at a time before many people understood the science of metallurgy, the use of cast metal for a portrait demonstrated the patron's control of a technology that most associated primarily with weaponry. In its original form, the portrait probably had eyes inlaid with precious and semiprecious materials, as other surviving figures do. The damage to the portrait was probably incurred during the Medes' invasion of Nineveh in 612 BCE. The enemy gouged out its eyes and hacked off its ears, nose, and lower beard, as if attacking the person represented. Many cultures, even today, practice such acts of ritualized vandalism as symbolic acts of violence or protest.

The themes of power and narrative combine in a 6½-foot **stele** (upright marker stone) erected in the Akkadian city of Sippar during the rule of Naram-Sin (fig. **2.12**). The stele commemorates Naram-Sin's victory over the Lullubi, people of the Zagros mountains in eastern Mesopotamia, in relief. This time the story does not unfold in registers; instead, ranks of soldiers, in composite view, climb the wavy contours of a wooded mountain. Their ordered march contrasts with the enemy's chaotic rout: As the victorious soldiers trample the fallen foe underfoot, the defeated beg for mercy or lie contorted in death. Above them, the king's large scale and central position make his identity clear. He stands isolated against the background, next to a mountain peak that suggests his proximity to the divine. His horned crown, formerly an exclusive accoutrement of the gods, marks him as the first Mesopotamian king to deify himself (an act that his people did not unanimously welcome). The bold musculature of his limbs and his powerful stance cast him as a heroic figure. Solar deities shine auspiciously overhead, as if witnessing his victory.

The stele of Naram-Sin still communicated its message of power over a thousand years later. In 1157 BCE, the Elamites of southwestern Iran invaded Mesopotamia and seized it as war

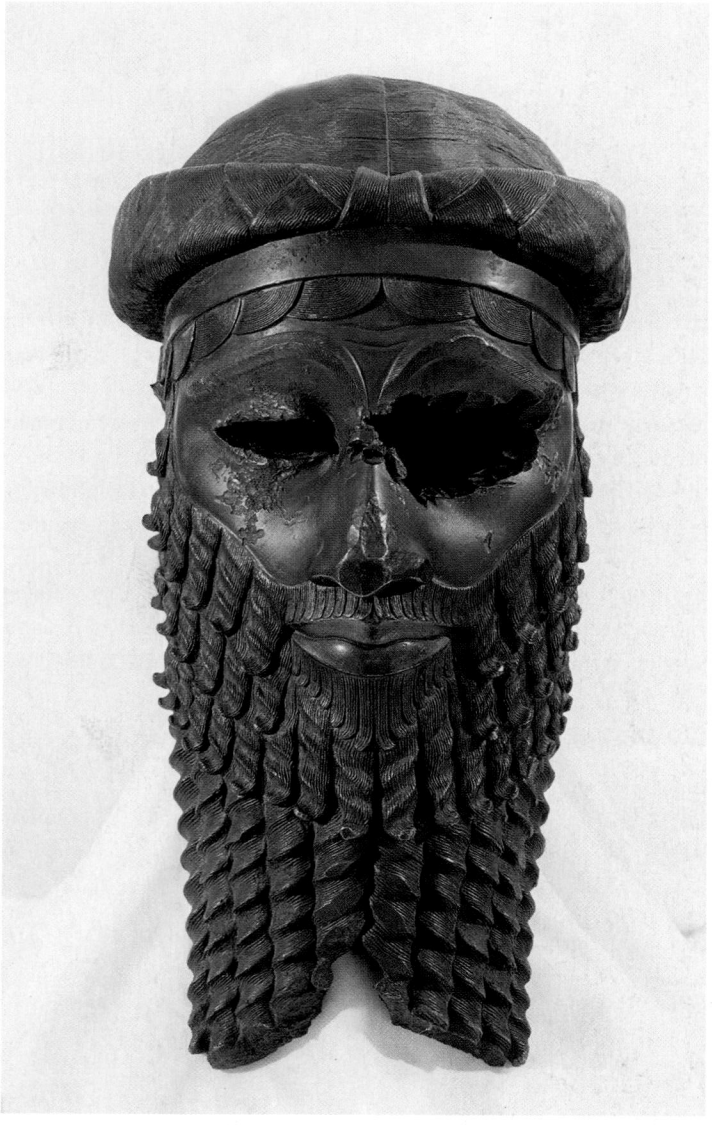

2.11 *Head of an Akkadian Ruler*, from Nineveh (Kuyunjik), Iraq. ca. 2250–2200 BCE. Copper, height 12" (30.7 cm). Iraq Museum, Baghdad

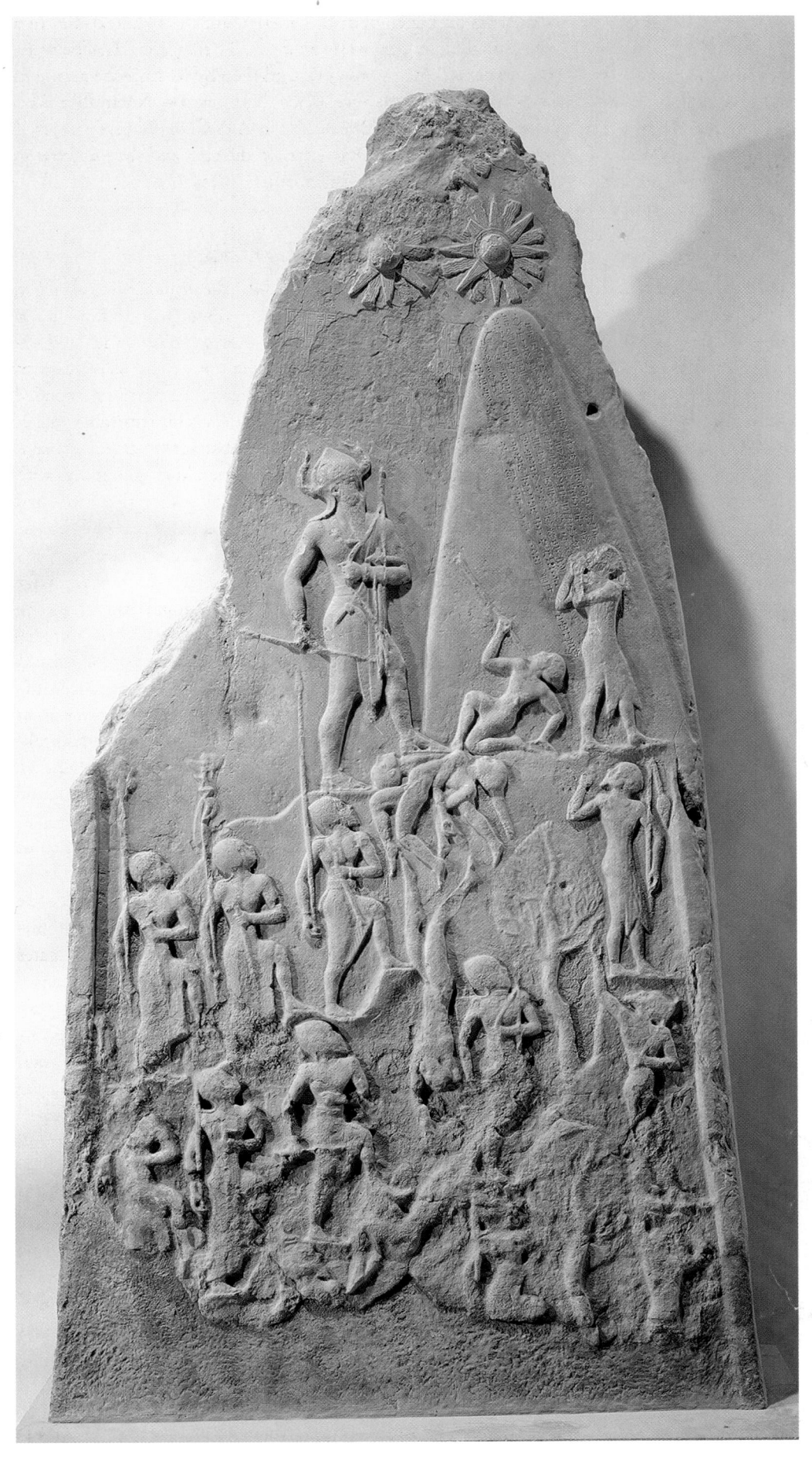

2.12 Stele of Naram-Sin.
r. 2254–2218 BCE. Height 6'6" (2 m).
Musée du Louvre, Paris

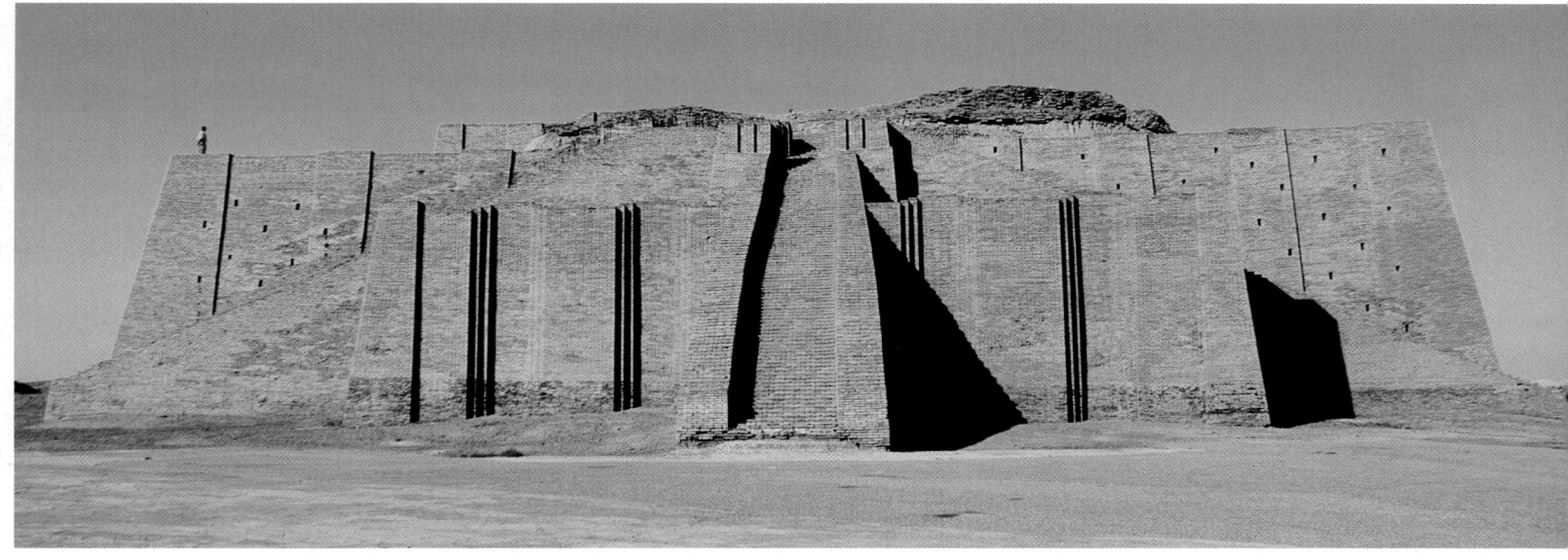

2.13 Great Ziggurat of King Urnammu, Ur, Muqaiyir, Iraq. ca. 2100 BCE

booty. An inscription on the stele records that they then installed it in the city of Susa (see map 2.1). By capturing the defeated city's victory monument, they symbolically stole Naram-Sin's former glory and doubly defeated their foe.

NEO-SUMERIAN REVIVAL

The rule of the Akkadian kings came to an end when a mountain people, the Guti, gained control of the Mesopotamian Plain in about 2230 BCE. The cities of Sumer rose up in retaliation and drove them out in 2112 BCE, under the leadership of King Urnammu of Ur (the present-day city of Muqaiyir, Iraq, and the birthplace of the biblical Abraham), who united a realm that was to last 100 years. As part of his renewal project, he returned to building on a magnificent scale.

Architecture: *The Ziggurat of Ur*

Part of Urnammu's legacy is the Great Ziggurat at Ur of about 2100 BCE, dedicated to the moon god, Nanna (Sin in Akkadian) (fig. **2.13**). Its 190-by-130-foot base soared to a height of 50 feet in three stepped stages. The base consisted of solid mud brick faced with baked bricks set in bitumen, a tarry material used here as mortar. Although not structurally functional, thick **buttresses** (vertical supporting elements) articulate the walls, giving an impression of strength. Moreover, a multitude of upward lines adds a dynamic energy to the monument's appearance. Three staircases, now reconstructed, converged high up at the fortified gateway. Each consisting of 100 steps, one stood perpendicular to the temple, the other two parallel to the base wall. From the gateway, a fourth staircase, which does not survive, once rose to the temple proper. The stairways may have provided an imposing setting for ceremonial processions.

Sculpture: *Figures of Gudea*

Contemporary with Urnammu's rule in Ur, Gudea became ruler of neighboring Lagash (in present-day Iraq), a small Sumerian city-state that had retained independence after the collapse of Akkad. Reserving the title of king for Lagash's city-god, Ningirsu, Gudea promoted the god's cult through an ambitious reconstruction of his temple. According to inscriptions, Ningirsu appeared to Gudea in a dream after the Tigris River had failed to rise and instructed him to build the temple.

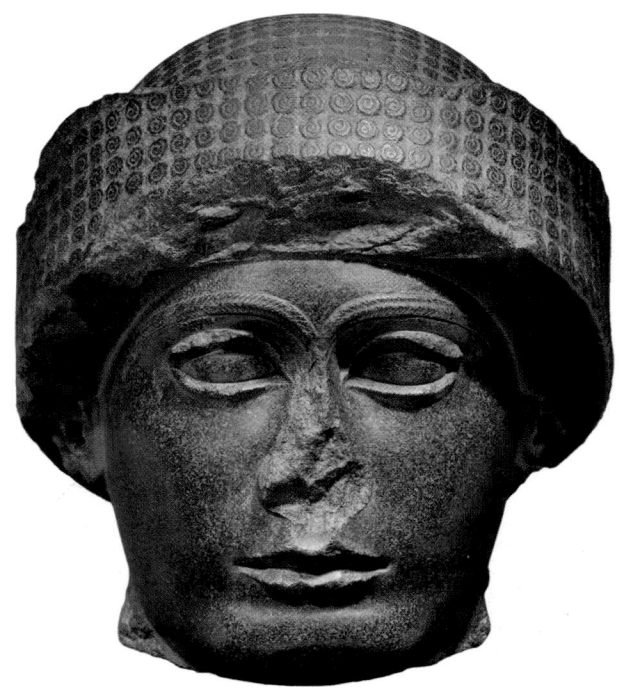

2.14 Head of Gudea, from Lagash (Telloh), Iraq. ca. 2100 BCE. Diorite, height 9⅛" (23.2 cm). Museum of Fine Arts, Boston. Francis Bartlett Donation of 1912. 26.289

Texts on Gudea Figures from Lagash and Surrounding Areas, ca. 2100

Gudea, the ruler of Lagash, commissioned numerous temples and many figures of himself to be placed in the temples. Many of these figures (compare figs. 2.14 and 2.15) are inscribed with cuneiform texts that provide insight into the function of each image.

In this excerpt, the god Ningirsu speaks to Gudea, encouraging him to rebuild his temple:

When, O faithful shepherd Gudea,
Thou shalt have started work for me on Eninnu, my royal abode,

I will call up in heaven a humid wind.
It shall bring thee abundance from on high
And the country shall spread its hands upon riches in thy
    time.
Prosperity shall accompany the laying of the foundations of my
    house.
All the great fields will bear for thee;
Dykes and canals will swell for thee;
Where the water is not wont to rise
To high ground it will rise for thee.
Oil will be poured abundantly in Sumer in thy time,
Good weight of wool will be given in thy time.

Source: H. Frankfort, *The Art and Architecture of the Ancient Orient*, 4th ed. (New Haven: Yale University Press, 1970, p. 98).

Of the building itself, nothing now remains. Yet some 20 examples of distinctive statues representing Gudea survive. He had dedicated (or given as an offering) the images at the temple and in other shrines of Lagash and vicinity (figs. **2.14** and **2.15**), and they served as a mark of his piety, at the same time as they also extended the Akkadian tradition of exalting the ruler's person. Carved of diorite, a dark stone that was as rare and expensive as it was hard to work, they testify to Gudea's great wealth. Whether standing or seated in pose, the statues are remarkably consistent in appearance: Often wearing a thick woolen cap, Gudea has a long garment draped over one shoulder, and clasps his hands across his front in a pose similar to statues from Tell Asmar of 500 years earlier. Like those figures, Gudea's eyes are wide open, in awe. The highly polished surface and precise modeling allow light to play upon the features, showcasing the sculptors' skills. Rounded forms emphasize the figures' compactness, giving them an impressive monumentality.

In the life-size seated example shown in figure 2.15, Gudea holds the ground plan of Ningirsu's temple on his lap. Inscriptions carved on the statue reveal that the king had to follow the god's instructions meticulously to ensure the temple's sanctity. The inscriptions also provide Gudea's motivation for building the temple, and his personal commitment to the project: By obeying the god, he would bring fortune to his city. (See *Primary Source*, above.) Following Ningirsu's instruction, Gudea purified the city and swept away the soil on the temple's site to expose bedrock. He then laid out the temple according to the design that Ningirsu had revealed to him, and helped manufacture and carry mud bricks.

BABYLONIAN ART

The late third and early second millennia BCE were a time of turmoil and warfare in Mesopotamia. The region was then unified for over 300 years under a Babylonian dynasty. During the reign of its most famous ruler, Hammurabi (r. 1792–1750 BCE), the city of Babylon assumed the dominant role formerly played by Akkad and Ur. Combining military prowess with respect for Sumerian tradition, Hammurabi cast himself as "the favorite shepherd" of the sun-god Shamash, stating his mission "to cause justice to prevail in the land and to destroy the wicked and evil, so that the strong might not oppress the weak nor the weak the strong." Babylon retained its role as cultural center of Sumer for more than 1,000 years after its political power had waned.

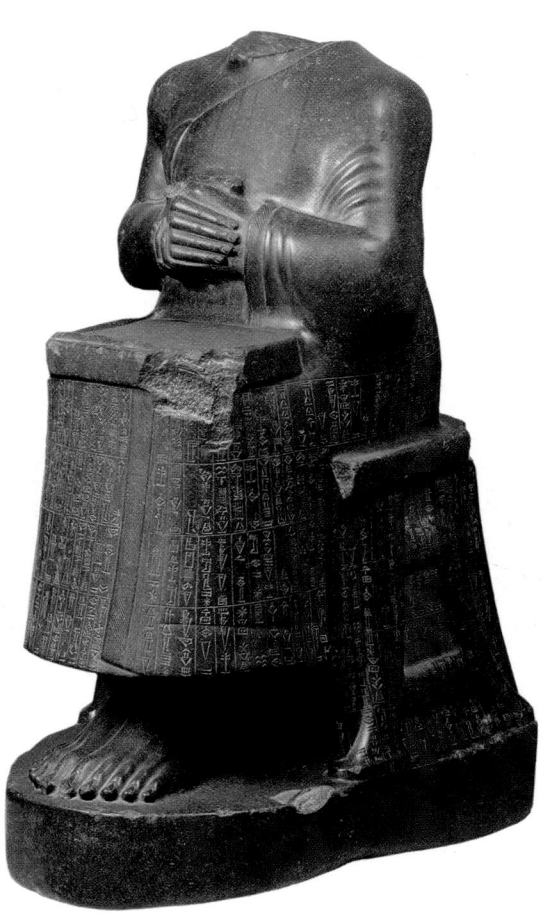

2.15 Seated statue of Gudea holding temple plan, from Girsu (Telloh), Iraq. ca. 2100 BCE. Diorite, height approx. 29" (73.7 cm). Musée du Louvre, Paris

The Code of Hammurabi

Posterity remembers Hammurabi best for his law code. It survives as one of the earliest written bodies of law, engraved on a black basalt stele reaching to over 7 feet in height (fig. **2.16**). The text consists of 3,500 lines of Akkadian cuneiform, and begins with an account of the temples Hammurabi restored. The largest portion concerns commercial and property law, rulings on domestic issues, and questions of physical assault, detailing penalties for noncompliers (including the renowned Hebrew Bible principle of "an eye for an eye"). (See *Primary Source*, page 35.) The text concludes with a paean to Hammurabi as peacemaker.

At the top of the stele, Hammurabi appears in relief, standing with his arm raised in greeting before the enthroned sun-god Shamash. The god's shoulders emanate sun rays, and he extends his hand, holding the rope ring and the measuring rod of kingship; this single gesture unifies both the scene's composition and the implied purpose of the two protagonists. The image is a variant on the "introduction scene" found on cylinder seals, where a goddess leads a human individual with his hand raised in salute before a seated godlike figure, who bestows his blessing. Hammurabi appears without the benefit—or need—of a divine intercessor, implying an especially close relationship with the sun-god. Still, the smaller scale of Hammurabi compared to the seated god expresses his status as "shepherd" rather than god himself. The symmetrical composition and smooth surfaces result in a legible image of divinely ordained power that is fully in line with Mesopotamian traditions. Like the stele of Naram-Sin, Hammurabi's stele later became war booty, when the Elamites carried it off to Susa.

ASSYRIAN ART

Babylon fell around 1595 BCE to the Hittites, who had established themselves in Anatolia (present-day Turkey). When they departed, they left a weakened Babylonian state vulnerable to other invaders: the Kassites from the northwest and the Elamites from the east. Although a second Babylonian dynasty rose to great heights under Nebuchadnezzar I of Isin (r. 1125–1104 BCE), the Assyrians more or less controlled southern Mesopotamia by the end of the millennium. Their home was the city-state of Assur, sited on the upper course of the Tigris and named for the god Ashur.

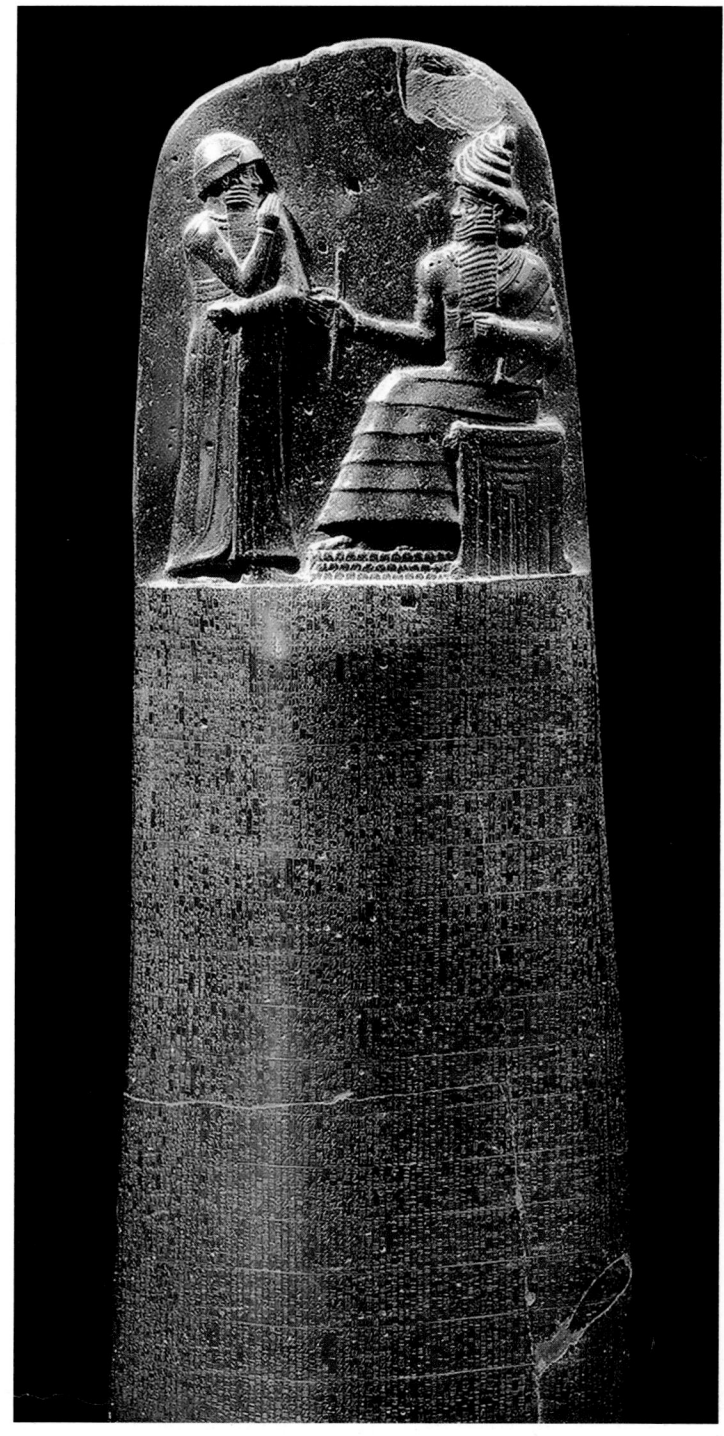

2.16 Upper part of stele inscribed with the Law Code of Hammurabi. ca. 1760 BCE. Diorite, height of stele approx. 7' (2.1 m); height of relief 28" (71 cm). Musée du Louvre, Paris

Art of Empire: Expressing Royal Power

Under a series of able rulers, beginning with Ashur-uballit (r. 1363–1328? BCE), the Assyrian realm expanded. At its height, in the seventh century BCE, the empire stretched from the Sinai peninsula to Armenia; the Assyrians even invaded Egypt successfully in about 670 BCE (see map 2.1). They drew heavily on the artistic achievements of the Sumerians and Babylonians, but adapted them to their own purpose. The Assyrians' was clearly an art of empire: propagandistic and public, designed to proclaim and sustain the supremacy of Assyrian civilization, particularly through representations of military power. The Assyrians continued to build temples and ziggurats based on Sumerian models, but their architectural focus shifted to constructing royal palaces. These grew to unprecedented size and magnificence, blatantly expressing royal presence and domination.

The Code of Hammurabi

Inscribed on the stele of Hammurabi in figure 2.16, the Code of Laws compiled by King Hammurabi offers a glimpse of the lives and values of Babylonians in the second millennium BCE.

Prologue

When Anu the Sublime, King of the Anunaki, and Bel, the lord of Heaven and earth, who decreed the fate of the land, assigned to Marduk, the over-ruling son of Ea, God of righteousness, dominion over earthly man, and made him great among the Igigi, they called Babylon by his illustrious name, made it great on earth, and founded an everlasting kingdom in it, whose foundations are laid so solidly as those of heaven and earth; then Anu and Bel called by name me, Hammurabi, the exalted prince, who feared God, to bring about the rule of righteousness in the land, to destroy the wicked and the evil-doers; so that the strong should not harm the weak; so that I should rule over the black-headed people like Shamash, and enlighten the land, to further the well-being of mankind. …

The Code of Laws [excerpts]

If any one bring an accusation against a man, and the accused go to the river and leap into the river, if he sink in the river his accuser shall take possession of his house. But if the river prove that the accused is not guilty, and he escape unhurt, then he who had brought the accusation shall be put to death, while he who leaped into the river shall take possession of the house that had belonged to his accuser. …

If any one bring an accusation of any crime before the elders, and does not prove what he has charged, he shall, if it be a capital offense charged, be put to death. …

If any one steal the property of a temple or of the court, he shall be put to death, and also the one who receives the stolen thing from him shall be put to death. …

If any one steal cattle or sheep, or an ass, or a pig or a goat, if it belong to a god or to the court, the thief shall pay thirtyfold; if they belonged to a freed man of the king he shall pay tenfold; if the thief has nothing with which to pay he shall be put to death …

If any one break a hole into a house (break in to steal), he shall be put to death before that hole and be buried …

If any one be too lazy to keep his dam in proper condition, and does not so keep it; if then the dam break and all the fields be flooded, then shall he in whose dam the break occurred be sold for money, and the money shall replace the corn which he has caused to be ruined. …

If any one be on a journey and entrust silver, gold, precious stones, or any movable property to another, and wish to recover it from him; if the latter do not bring all of the property to the appointed place, but appropriate it to his own use, then shall this man, who did not bring the property to hand it over, be convicted, and he shall pay fivefold for all that had been entrusted to him. …

If a man wish to separate from a woman who has borne him children, or from his wife who has borne him children: then he shall give that wife her dowry, and a part of the usufruct of field, garden, and property, so that she can rear her children. When she has brought up her children, a portion of all that is given to the children, equal as that of one son, shall be given to her. She may then marry the man of her heart. …

If a son strike his father, his hands shall be hewn off.

If a man put out the eye of another man, his eye shall be put out.

If he break another man's bone, his bone shall be broken.

If a builder build a house for some one, and does not construct it properly, and the house which he built fall in and kill its owner, then that builder shall be put to death.

If it kill the son of the owner, the son of that builder shall be put to death.

If it kill a slave of the owner, then he shall pay slave for slave to the owner of the house. …

Source: *World Civilizations Online Classroom* "The Code of Hammurabi" tr. L. W. King (1910). Edited by Richard Hooker www.wsu.edu:8080/2dee. © 1996.

Note: The Epilogue of *The Code of Hammurabi* appears at www.myartslab.com.

The proclamation of Assyrian royal power began well outside the palace, as is clear in the plan for the city of Dur Sharrukin (present-day Khorsabad, Iraq), where Sargon II (r. 721–705 BCE) had his royal residence (fig. **2.17**). Though much of the city remains unexcavated, archaeologists estimate that it covered an area of nearly a square mile, enclosed within an imposing mud-brick fortification wall. To reach the palace, a visitor had to cross the city, traversing open plazas and climbing broad ramps. On the northwest side, a walled and turreted citadel closed the ziggurat and the palace off from the rest of the town and emphasized their dominant presence. Enclosing temple and palace, the citadel revealed the privileged relationship between the king and the gods. Both structures stood atop a mound 50 feet high, which

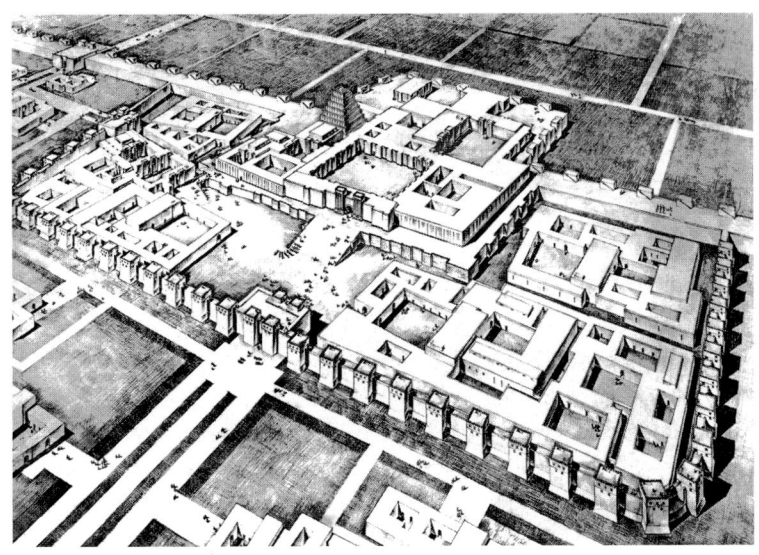

2.17 Reconstruction drawing of the citadel of Sargon II, Dur Sharrukin (Khorsabad), Iraq. ca. 721–705 BCE (after Charles Altman)

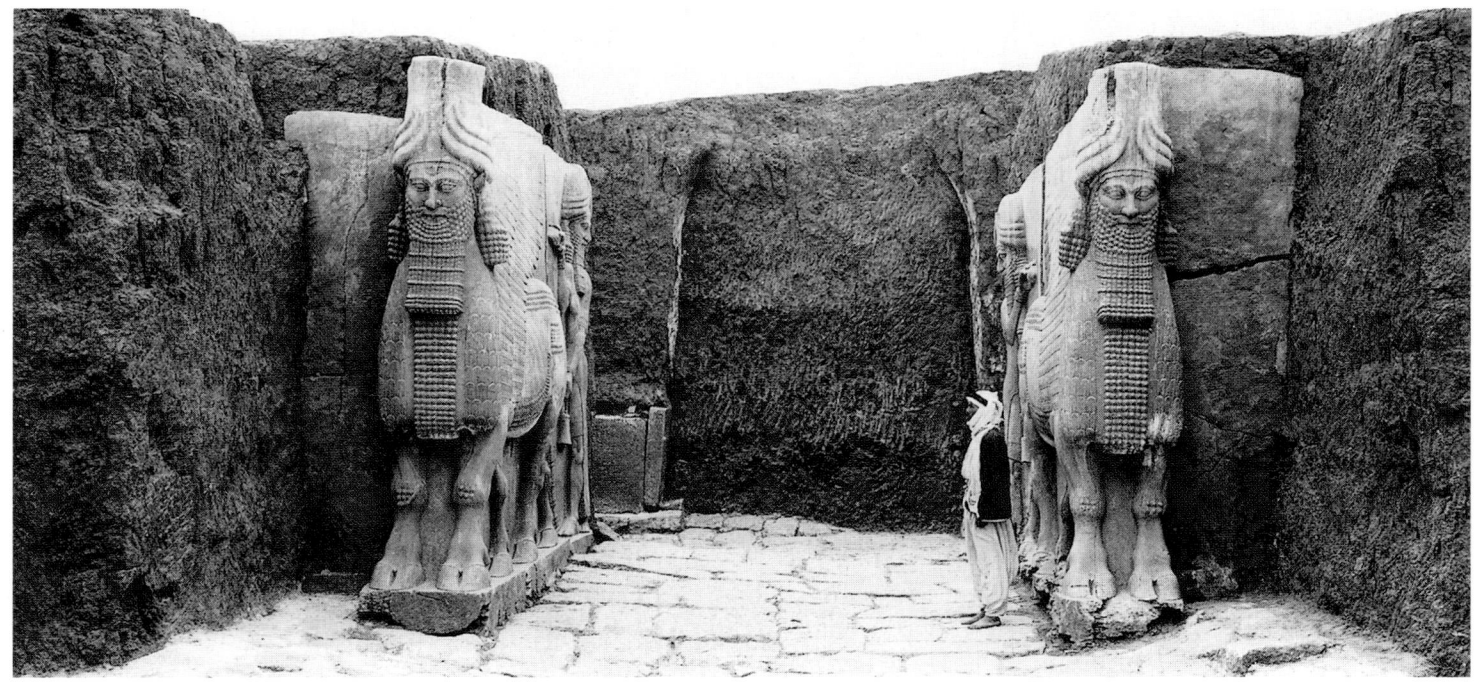

2.18 Gate of the citadel of Sargon II, Dur Sharrukin (Khorsabad), Iraq (photo taken during excavation). 742–706 BCE

raised them above the flood plain and expressed the king's elevated status above the rest of society. The ziggurat had at least four stages, each about 18 feet high and of a different color, and a spiral ramp wound around it to the top.

The palace complex comprised about 30 courtyards and 200 rooms, and monumental imagery complemented this impressive scale. At the gateways stood huge, awe-inspiring guardian figures known as **lamassu**, in the shape of winged, human-headed bulls (fig. **2.18**). The illustration here shows the lamassu of Khorsabad during excavation in the 1840s; masons subsequently sawed up one of the pair for transportation to the Louvre in Paris. The massive creatures are almost in the round (fully three-dimensional

and separate from the background). Carved out of the limestone of the palace wall, they are one with the building. Yet the addition of a fifth leg, visible from the side, reveals that the sculptor conceived of them as deep relief sculptures on two sides of the stone block, so that the figures are legible both frontally and in profile. From the front, the lamassu appear stationary, yet the additional leg sets them in motion when seen from the side. With their tall, horned headdresses and deep-set eyes, and the powerful muscularity of their legs and bodies, all set off by delicate patterning of the beard and feathers, they towered over any approaching visitor, embodying the king's fearful authority. The Assyrians may have believed the hybrid creatures had the power to ward off evil

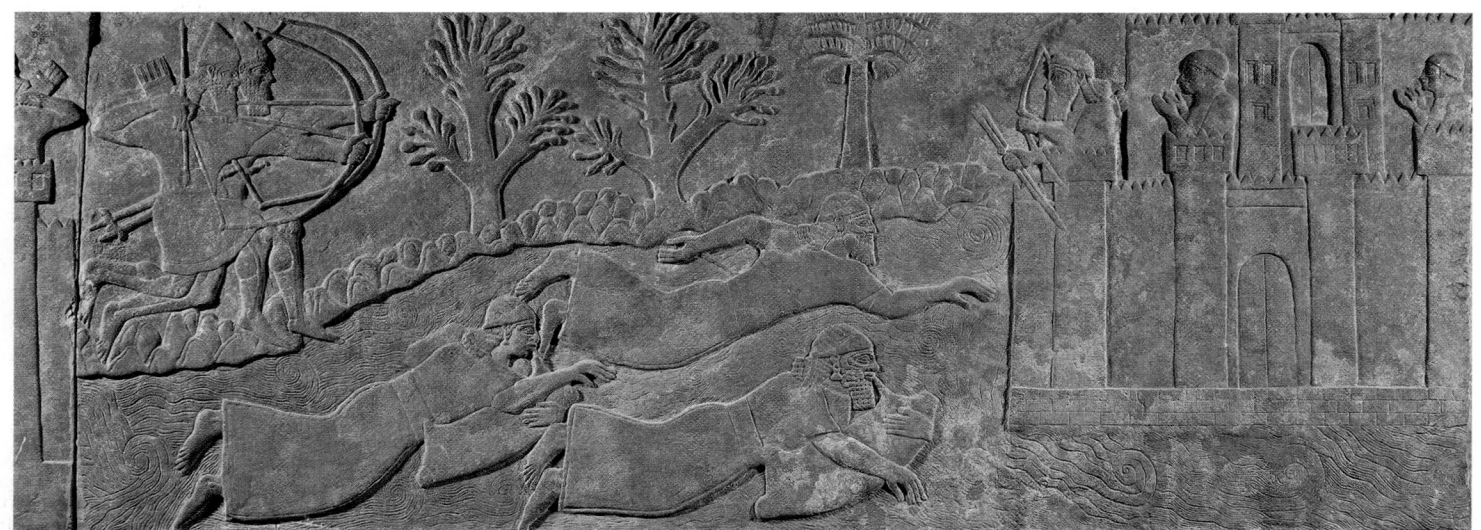

2.19 *Fugitives Crossing River*, from the Northwest Palace of Ashurnasirpal II, Nimrud (Calah), Iraq. ca. 883–859 BCE. Alabaster, height approx. 39" (98 cm). The British Museum, London

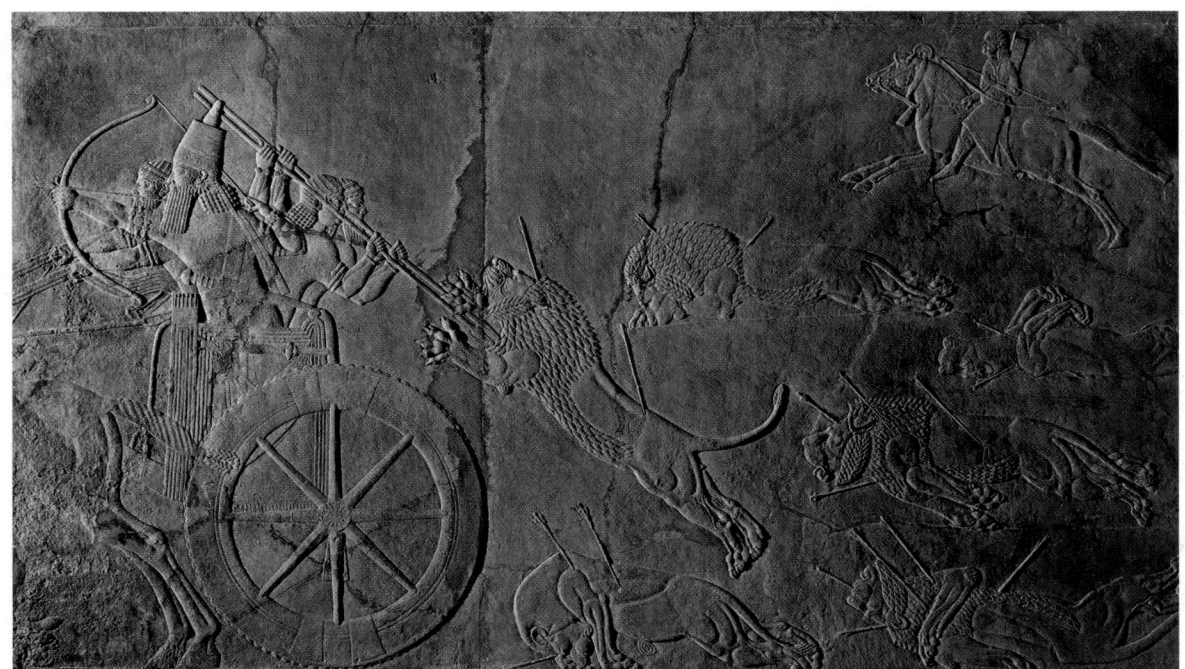

2.20 Lion Hunt relief, from the North Palace of Ashurbanipal, Nineveh. ca. 645 BCE. The British Museum, London

spirits. Contemporary texts indicate that sculptors also cast lamassu in bronze, but because these images were later melted down, none now survives.

Once inside a royal palace, a visitor would confront another distinctive feature of Assyrian architecture: upright gypsum slabs called **orthostats**, with which builders lined the lower walls. Structurally, the slabs protected the mud brick from moisture and wear, but they served a communicative purpose as well. On their surfaces, narrative images in low relief, painted in places for emphasis, glorified the king with detailed depictions of lion hunts and military conquests (with inscriptions giving supplementary information). In these reliefs, the Assyrian forces march indefatigably onward, meeting the enemy at the empire's frontiers, destroying his strongholds, and carrying away booty and prisoners of war. Actions take place in a continuous band, propelling a viewer from scene to scene, and repetition of key images creates the impression of an inevitable Assyrian triumph. This detail (fig. **2.19**), from the Northwest Palace of Ashurnasirpal II (r. 883–859 BCE) at Nimrud (ancient Kalah, biblical Calah, Iraq), shows the enemy fleeing an advance party by swimming across a river on inflatable animal skins. From their fortified city, an archer—possibly the king—and two women look on with hands raised. The artist intersperses landscape elements with humans, yet shows no concern to capture relative scale, or to depict all elements from a single viewpoint. This suggests that the primary purpose of the scenes was to recount specific enemy conquests in descriptive detail; depicting them in a naturalistic way was not critical.

As in Egypt (discussed in Chapter 3), royal lion hunts were staged events that took place in palace grounds. Royal attendants released animals from cages into a square formed by troops with shields. Earlier Mesopotamian rulers hunted lions to protect their subjects, but by the time of the Assyrians, the activity had become more symbolic, ritually showcasing the king's strength and serving as a metaphor for military prowess. On a section of Assyrian relief from the North Palace of Ashurbanipal (r. 668–627 BCE) at Nineveh, dating to roughly 645 BCE (fig. **2.20**), the king races forward in his chariot with bow drawn, leaving wounded and dead lions in his wake. A wounded lion leaps at the chariot as attendants plunge spears into its chest. Its body is hurled flat out in a clean diagonal line, its claws spread and mouth open in what appears to be pain combined with desperate ferocity. To ennoble the victims of the hunt, the sculptor contrasted the limp, contorted bodies of the slain animals with the taut leaping lion and the powerful energy of the king's party. Yet we should not conclude that the artist necessarily hoped to evoke sympathy for the creatures, or to comment on the cruelty of a staged hunt; it is more likely that by ennobling the lions the sculptor intended to glorify their vanquisher, the king, even more intensely.

LATE BABYLONIAN ART

Perpetually under threat, the Assyrian Empire came to an end in 612 BCE, when Nineveh fell to the Medes (an Indo-European-speaking people from western Iran) and the resurgent Babylonians. Under the Chaldean dynasty, the ancient city of Babylon had a final brief flowering between 612 and 539 BCE, before the Persians conquered it. The best known of these Late Babylonian rulers was Nebuchadnezzar II (r. 604–ca. 562 BCE), builder of the biblical Tower of Babel, which soared 270 feet high and came to symbolize overweening pride. He was also responsible for the famous Hanging Gardens of Babylon, numbered among the seven wonders of the ancient world compiled by Greek historians by the second century BCE.

The Royal Palace

The royal palace at Babylon was on almost the same scale as Assyrian palaces, with numerous reception suites framing five huge courtyards. Instead of facing their buildings with carved stone, the Late Babylonians adopted baked and **glazed brick**, which they molded into individual shapes. Glazing brick involved putting a film of glass over the brick's surface. Late Babylonians used it both for surface ornament and for reliefs on a grand scale. Its vivid coloristic effect appears on the courtyard façade of the Throne Room and the Processional Way leading to the Ishtar Gate and the gate itself, now reassembled in Berlin (fig. **2.21**). A framework of brightly colored ornamental bands contains a procession of bulls, dragons, and other animals, set off in molded brick against a deep blue background. The animals portrayed were sacred: White and yellow snake-necked dragons to Marduk, the chief Babylonian god; yellow bulls with blue hair to Adad, god of storms; and white and yellow lions to Ishtar herself, goddess of love and war. Unlike the massive muscularity of the

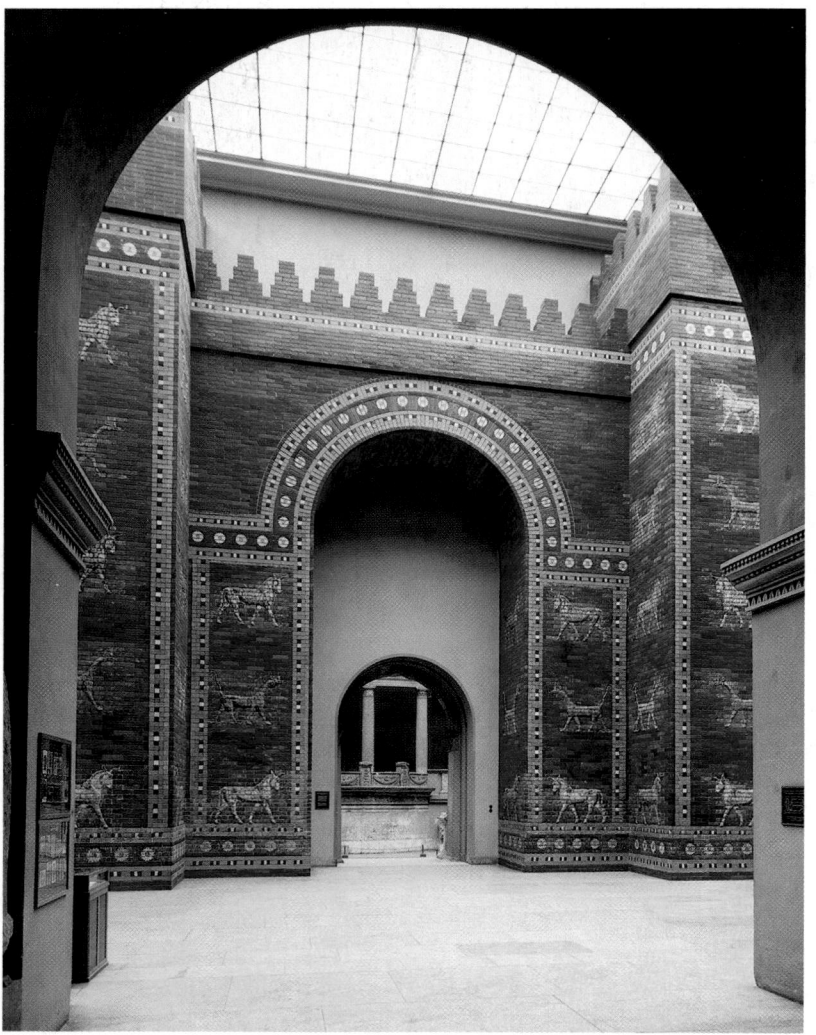

2.21   Ishtar Gate (restored), from Babylon, Iraq. ca. 575 BCE. Glazed brick originally 40' high (12.2 m). Staatliche Museen zu Berlin, Preussischer Kulturbesitz, Vorderasiatisches Museum

lamassu, their forms are light and agile-looking, arrested in a processional stride that slowly accompanies ceremonial processions leading to the archway of the gate.

REGIONAL NEAR EASTERN ART

Alongside the successive cultures of Mesopotamia, a variety of other cultures developed in areas beyond the Tigris and Euphrates. Some of them invaded or conquered contemporaneous city-states in Mesopotamia, as did the Hittites in the north and the Iranians in the east. Others, such as the seagoing Phoenicians on the Mediterranean coast to the west, traded with the people of Mesopotamia and in so doing spread Mesopotamian visual forms to Africa and Europe.

The Hittites

The Hittites were responsible for Babylon's overthrow in 1595 BCE. An Indo-European-speaking people, they had probably entered Anatolia from southern Russia in the late third millennium BCE and settled on its rocky plateau as one of several cultures that developed independently of Mesopotamia. As they came into contact with Mesopotamian traditions, the Hittites adopted cuneiform writing for their language, and preserved details of their history on clay tablets. Emerging as a power around 1800 BCE, they rapidly expanded their territory 150 years later under Hattusilis I. Their empire extended over most of present-day Turkey and Syria, which brought them into conflict with the imperial ambitions of Egypt. The Hittite Empire reached its apogee between 1400 and 1200 BCE. Its capital was Hattusa, near the present-day Turkish village of Bogazköy. Fortification walls protected the city, constructed of huge, irregularly shaped stones that were widely available in the region. At the city gates, massive limestone lions and other guardian figures protruded from the blocks that formed the **jambs** (fig. **2.22**). The Lion Gate is 7 feet high, and though badly weathered, the figures still impress visitors with their ferocity and stark frontality. These powerful guardians probably inspired the later Assyrian lamassu (see fig. 2.18).

The Phoenicians

The Phoenicians, too, contributed a distinctive body of work to Near Eastern art. Living on the eastern coast of the Mediterranean in the first millennium BCE in what is now Lebanon, they developed formidable seafaring skills, which led them to found settlements farther west in the Mediterranean (most notably on the North African coast and in Spain). They became a linchpin in the rapidly growing trade in objects—and ideas—between East and West. The Phoenicians were especially adept in working metal and ivory, and in making colored glass. They readily incorporated motifs from Egypt and the eastern Mediterranean coast, as seen in the open-work ivory plaque illustrated here (fig. **2.23**), on which is poised an Egyptian winged sphinx. The plaque dates to the

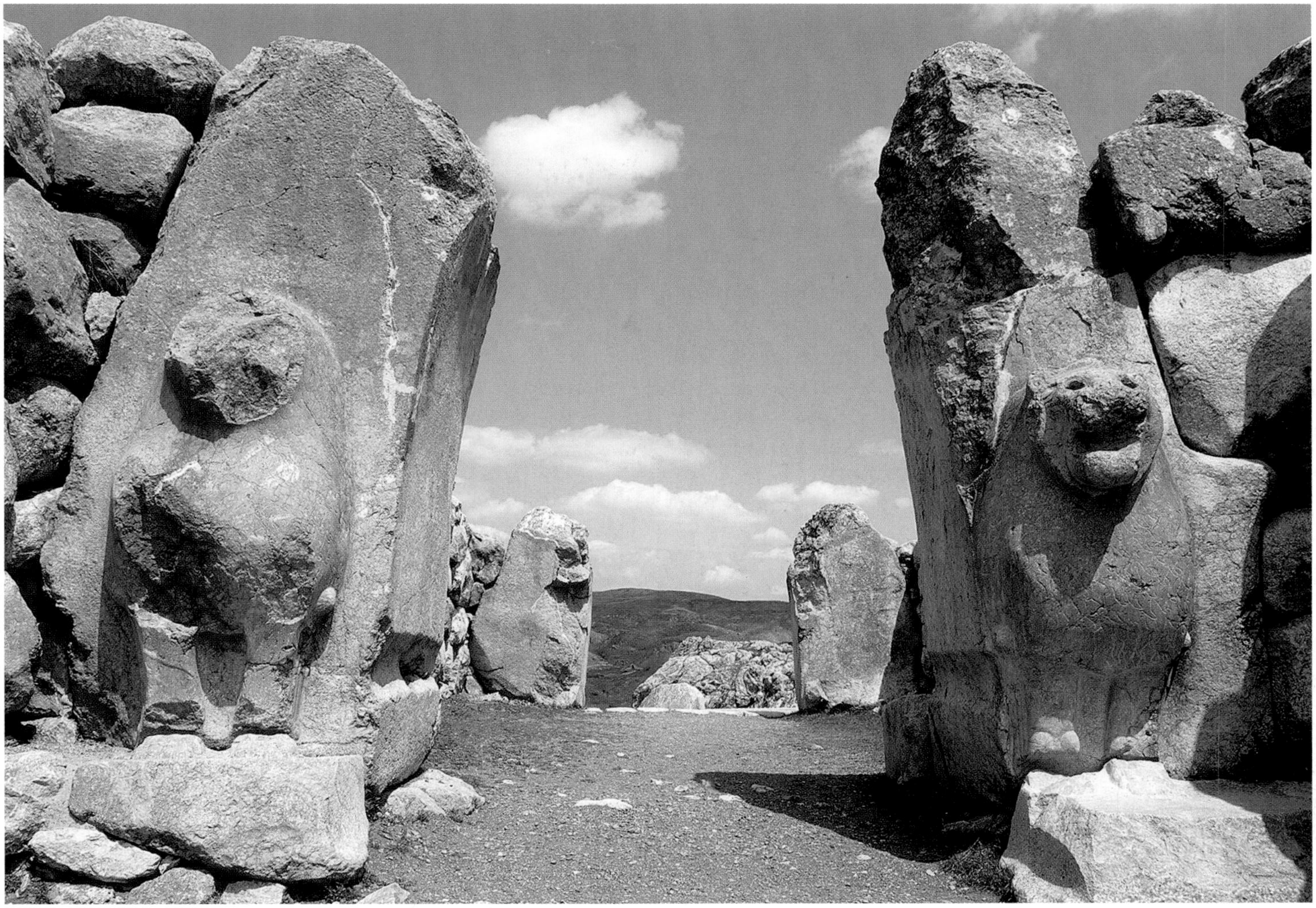

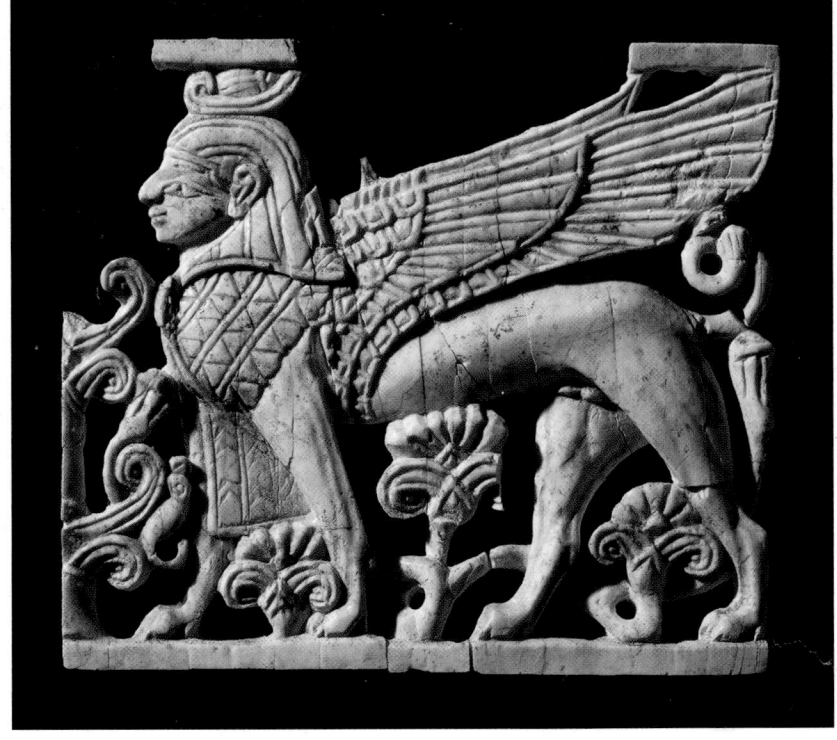

2.22　The Lion Gate, Bogazköy, Anatolia (Turkey). ca. 1400 BCE

2.23　Phoenician ivory plaque depicting a winged sphinx, found at Fort Shalmaneser, Nimrud (ancient Kalhu), northern Iraq. ca. 8th century BCE. The British Museum, London

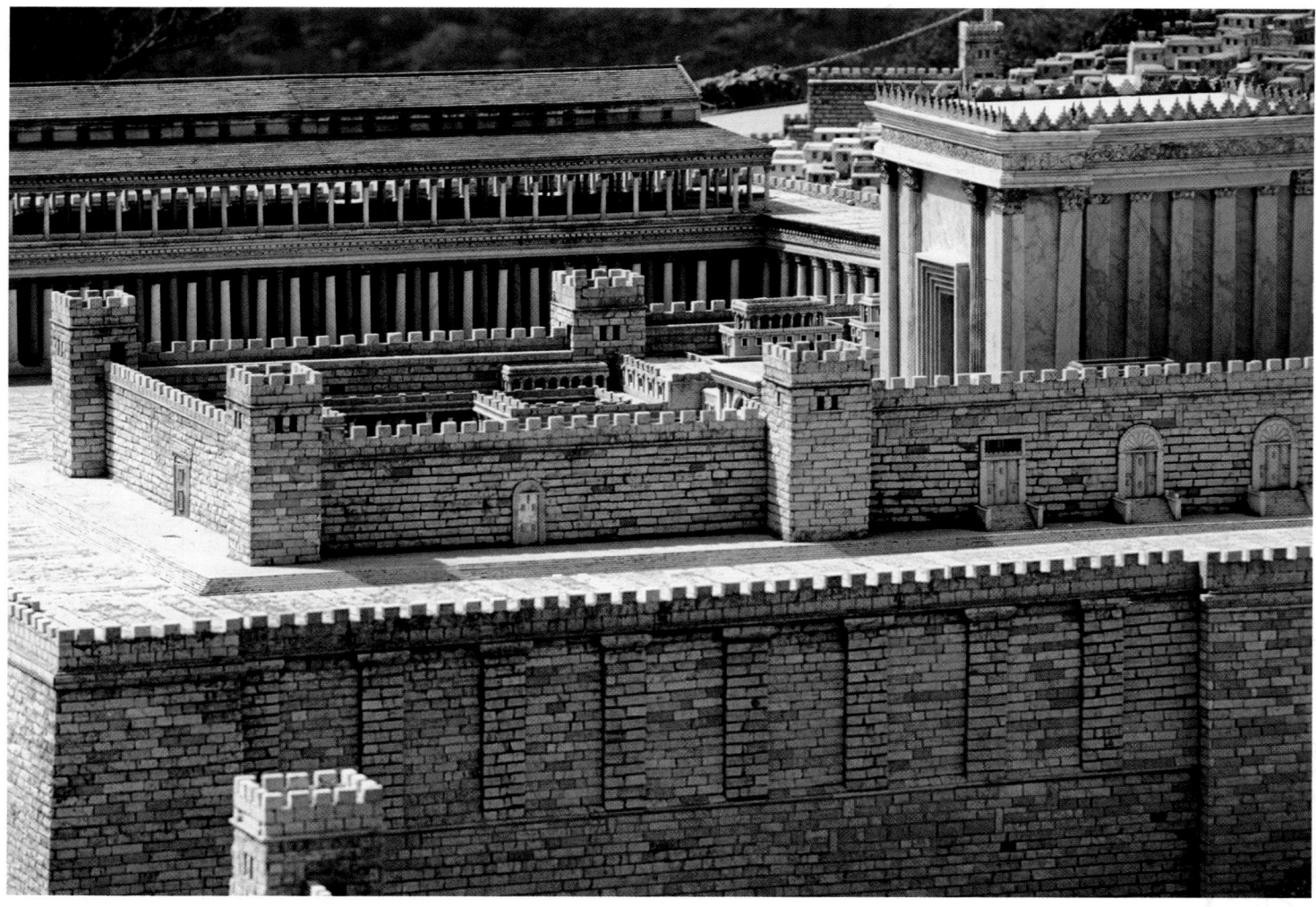

2.24 Temple of Solomon (reconstruction), Jerusalem. ca. 457–450 BCE

eighth century BCE, and came to light in Fort Shalmaneser at Nimrud, the Assyrian capital where the conquering Assyrian kings had probably taken it as booty. Though the details are Egyptian—its wig and apron, the stylized plants—the carver has reduced its double crown to fit neatly within the panel, suggesting that what mattered was a general quality of "Egyptianness" rather than an accurate portrayal of Egyptian motifs. The rounded forms and profile presentation translate the Egyptian motif into a visual form more familiar to Mesopotamian eyes.

The Hebrews

According to later tradition, the Akkadians expelled the Hebrews from Mesopotamia in about 2000 BCE. The latter settled in Canaan, on the eastern Mediterranean, before moving to Egypt in around 1600 BCE. There, they were bound into slavery. Moses led their flight from Egypt into the Sinai desert, where they established the principles of their religion. Unlike other Near Eastern peoples, the Hebrews were monotheistic. Their worship centered on Yahweh, who provided Moses with the Ten Commandments, a set of ethical and moral rules. After 40 years, they returned to Canaan, which they named Israel. King David, who ruled until

961 BCE, seized the city of Jerusalem from the Canaanites, and began to construct buildings there worthy of a political and religious capital for Israel, including a royal palace. His son, Solomon, completed a vast temple for worship, now known as the First Temple (fig. 2.24). The temple stood within a sacred precinct on Mount Moriah (the present-day Temple Mount), where, according to the scriptures, the patriarch Abraham had prepared to sacrifice his son, Isaac. Archaeological evidence for the massive building is controversial, and literary descriptions are incomplete. According to the Hebrew Bible, Solomon covered the entire temple and the altar inside with gold. For the inner sanctuary, which held the Ark of the Covenant (a chest containing the Commandments), sculptors created two monumental cherubim (angels depicted as winged children) out of gilded olive wood. They also covered the walls with carvings of cherubim, palm trees, and flowers. Brass pillars stood at the front of the temple, with pomegranate-shaped **capitals**. King Hiram of Tyre (Phoenicia) is credited with providing resources for the construction of the temple, such as materials and artisans, which is further evidence of the close connections between Near Eastern cultures.

Babylonian forces under King Nebuchadnezzar II destroyed the temple in 587/86 BCE, forcing the Israelites into exile. Upon their return in 538, they built the temple anew, and under Herod the Great, king of Judea from 37 BCE to 4 CE, the Second Temple was raised up and substantially enlarged. Roman soldiers razed this rebuilding in the reign of the emperor Vespasian, in the first century CE. The only vestige of the vast complex Herod commissioned is the western wall, known today as the Wailing Wall.

IRANIAN ART

Located to the east of Mesopotamia, Iran was a flourishing agricultural center in Neolithic times, starting in about 7000 BCE. During that period, Iran became a gateway for migrating tribes from the Asiatic steppes to the north as well as from India to the east. While it is distinctive, the art of ancient Iran still reflects its intersections with the cultures of Mesopotamia.

Early Iranian Art

The early nomadic tribes left no permanent structures or records, but the items they buried with their dead reveal that they ranged over a vast area—from Siberia to central Europe, from Iran to Scandinavia. They fashioned objects of wood, bone, or metal, and these diverse works share a common decorative vocabulary, including animal motifs used in abstract and ornamental ways. They belong to a distinct kind of portable art known as **nomad's gear**, including weapons, bridles, buckles, **fibulae** (large clasps or brooches), and other articles of adornment, as well as various kinds of vessels.

The handleless beaker in figure **2.25**, dating to about 4000 BCE, originates from a pottery-producing center at Susa on the Shaur River. On the surface of its thin shell of pale yellow clay, a brown **glaze** defines an ibex (mountain goat), whose forms the painter has reduced to a few dramatic sweeping curves. The circles of its horns reflect in two dimensions the cup's three-dimensional roundness. Racing hounds above the ibex stretch out to become horizontal streaks, and vertical lines below the vessel's rim are the elongated necks of a multitude of birds. This early example of Iranian art demonstrates the skill of the potter in both the construction of the cup and its sensitive painted design. It prefigures a later love of animal forms in the nomadic arts of Iran and Central Asia.

The Persian Empire: Cosmopolitan Heirs to the Mesopotamian Tradition

During the mid-sixth century BCE, the small kingdom of Parsa to the east of lower Mesopotamia came to dominate the entire Near East. Under Cyrus the Great (r. 559–530/29 BCE), ruler of the Achaemenid dynasty, the people of Parsa—the Persians—overthrew the king of the Medes, then conquered major parts of Asia Minor in ca. 547 or 546 BCE, and Babylon in 538 BCE. Cyrus assumed the title "king of Babylon," along with the broader ambitions of Mesopotamian rulers. The empire he founded continued to expand under his successors. Egypt fell in 525 BCE, while Greece only narrowly escaped Persian domination in the early fifth century BCE. At its height, under Darius I (r. 521–486 BCE) and his son Xerxes (r. 485–465 BCE), the territorial reach of the Persian Empire far outstripped the Egyptian and Assyrian empires combined. It endured for two centuries, during which it developed an efficient administration and monumental art forms.

Persian religious beliefs related to the prophecies of Zoroaster (Zarathustra) and took as their basis the dualism of good and evil, embodied in Ahuramazda (Light) and Ahriman (Darkness). The cult of Ahuramazda focused its rituals on fire altars in the open air; consequently, Persian kings did not construct monumental

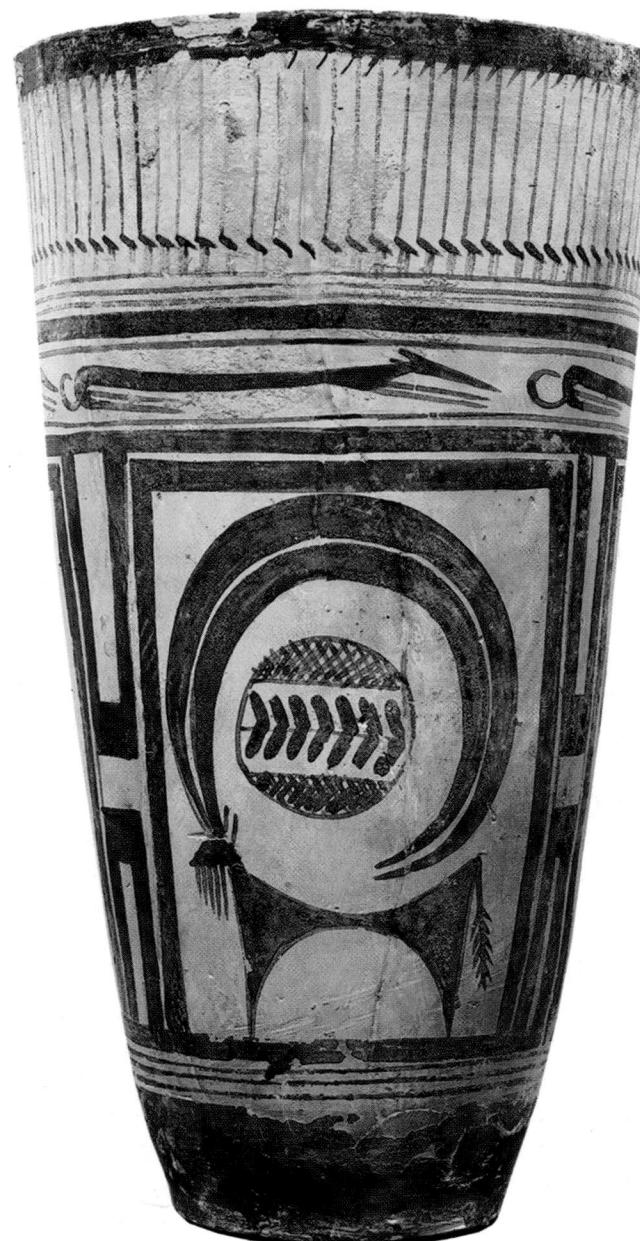

2.25 Painted beaker, from Susa. ca. 4000 BCE. Height 11¼" (28.3 cm). Musée du Louvre, Paris

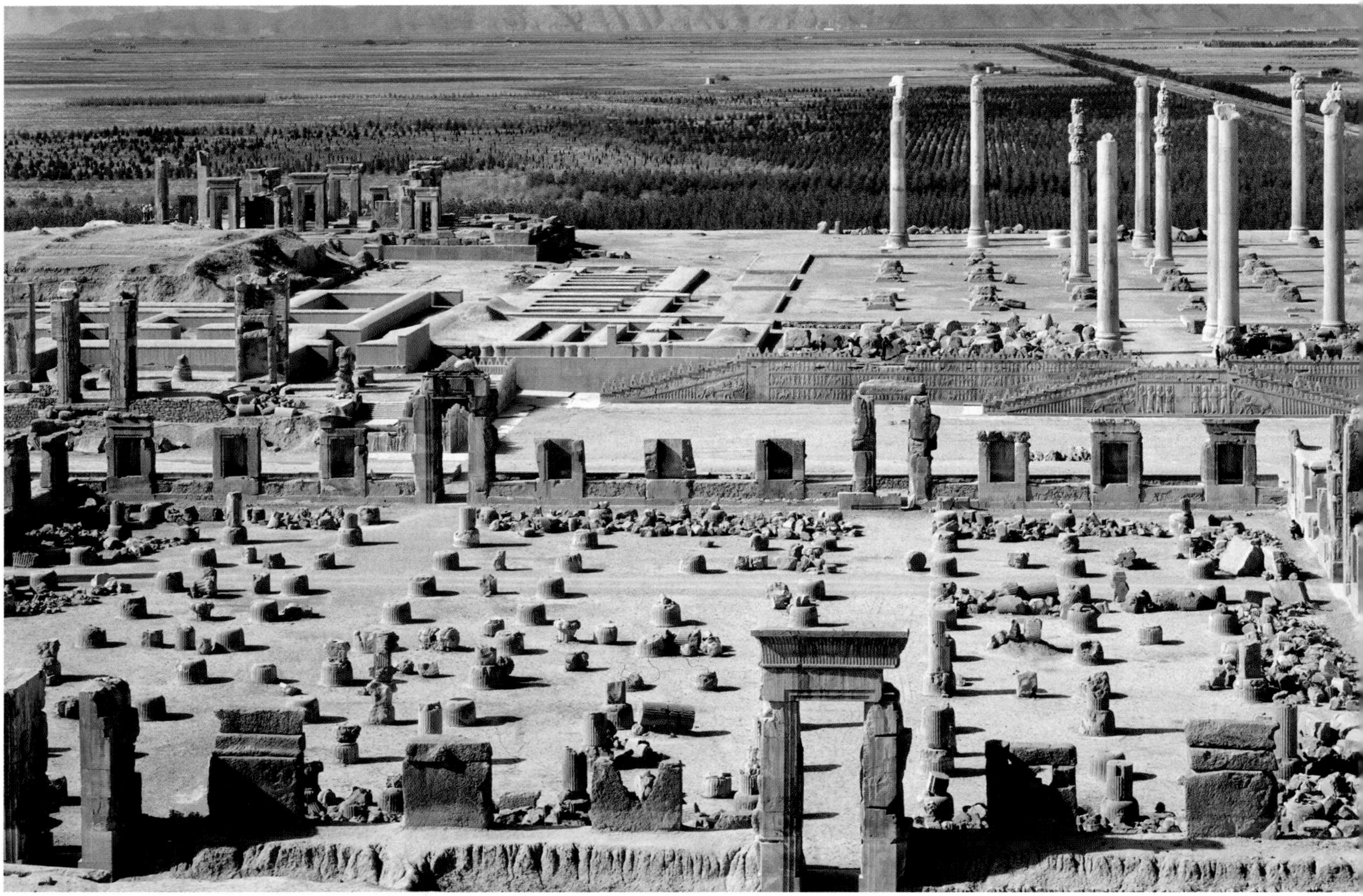

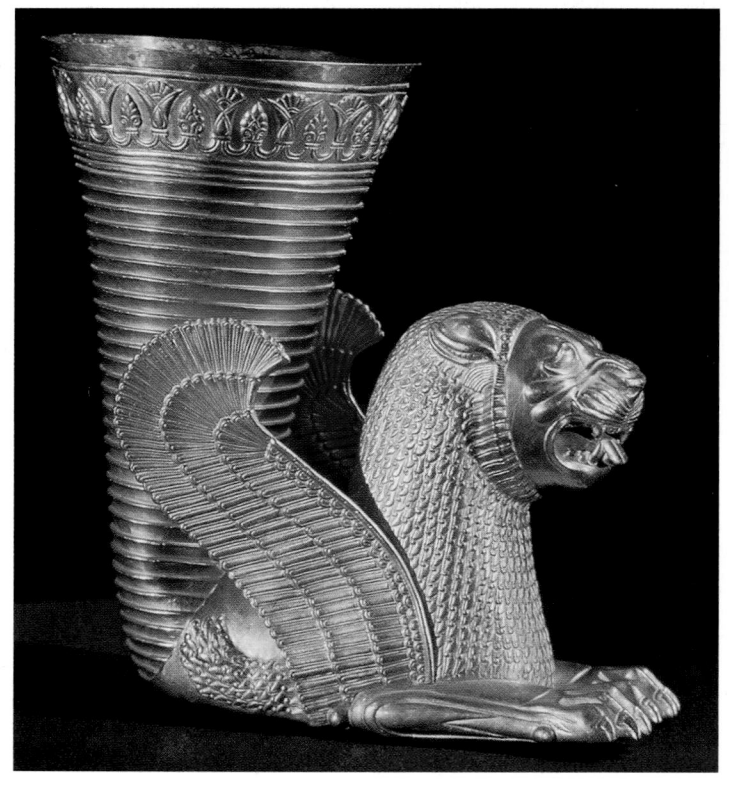

2.26 Palace of Darius and Xerxes, Persepolis. 518–460 BCE

religious architecture. Instead they concentrated their attention and resources on royal palaces, which were at once vast and impressive.

PERSEPOLIS Darius I began construction on the most ambitious of the palaces, on a plateau in the Zagros highlands at Parsa or Persepolis, in 518 BCE. Subsequent rulers enlarged it (fig. **2.26**). Fortified and raised on a platform, it consisted of a great number of rooms, halls, and courts laid out in a grid plan. The palace is a synthesis of materials and design traditions from all parts of the far-flung empire; brought together, they result in a clear statement of internationalism. Darius boasts in his inscriptions that the palace timber came from Lebanon (cedar), Gandhara and Carmania (yaka wood), and its bricks from Babylon. Items for palace use (such as the golden **rhyton**, or ritual cup, in fig. **2.27**), were of Sardian and Bactrian gold, Egyptian silver, and ebony, and Sagdianan lapis lazuli and carnelian. To work these materials, the Achaemenids brought in craftsmen from all over the empire, who

2.27 Achaemenid rhyton. 5th–3rd centuries BCE. Gold.
Archaeological Museum, Tehran, Iran

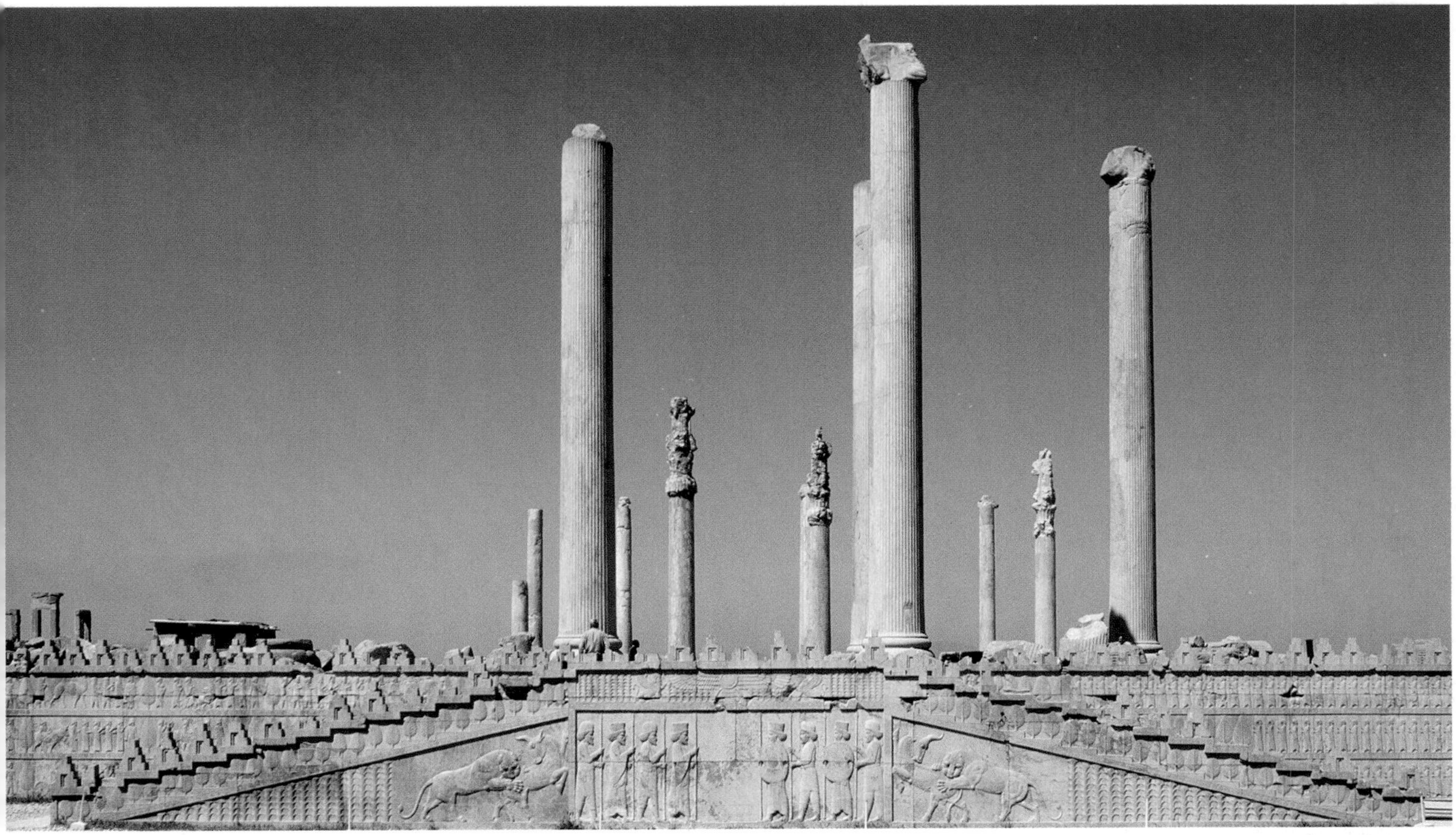

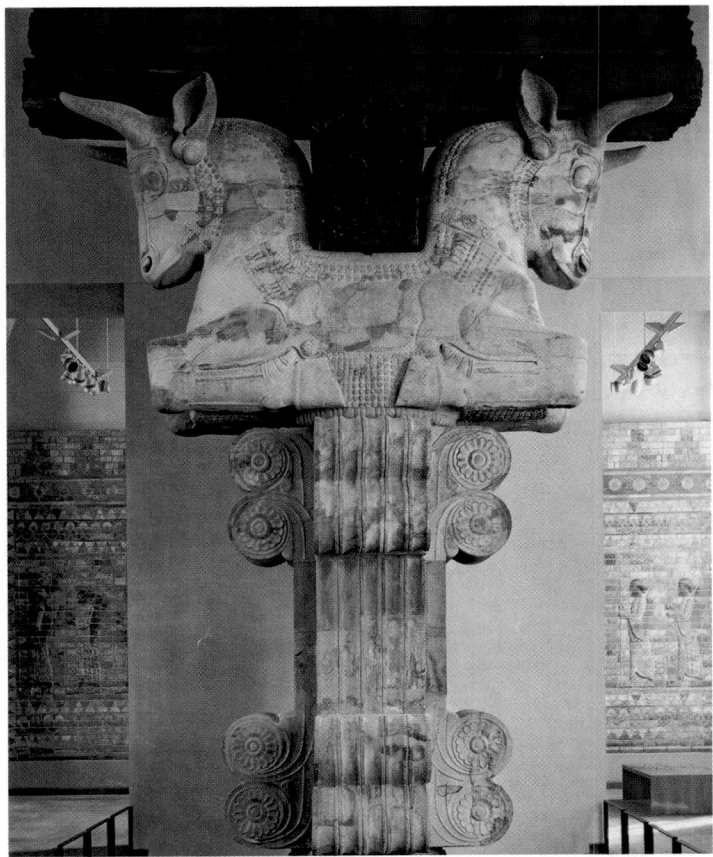

2.28 Audience Hall of Darius and Xerxes, Persepolis, Iran. ca. 500 BCE

then took this international style away with them on returning to their respective homes. The gold-worker responsible for the rhyton shaped it as a senmurv, a mythical creature with the body of a lion sprouting griffin's wings and a peacock's tail. It belongs firmly to the tradition of Mesopotamian hybrid creatures.

Visitors to the palace were constantly reminded of the theme of empire, beginning at the entrance. There, at the massive "Gate of All the Lands," stood colossal winged, human-headed bulls, like the Assyrian lamassu (see fig. 2.18). Inside the palace, architects employed columns on a magnificent scale. Entering the 217-foot-square Audience Hall, or *apadana*, of Darius and Xerxes, a visitor would stand amid 36 columns, which soared 40 feet up to support a wooden ceiling. A few still stand today (fig. **2.28**). The concept of massing columns in this way may come from Egypt; certainly Egyptian elements are present in the vegetal (plantlike) detail of their bases and capitals. The form of the shaft, however, echoes the slender, fluted column shafts of Ionian Greece (see fig. 5.8). Crowning the column capitals are "cradles" for ceiling beams composed of the front parts of two bulls or similar creatures (fig. **2.29**). The animals recall Assyrian sculptures, yet their truncated, back-to-back arrangement evokes animal motifs of Iranian art, as seen in the form of the rhyton.

2.29 Bull capital, from Persepolis. ca. 500 BCE. Musée du Louvre, Paris

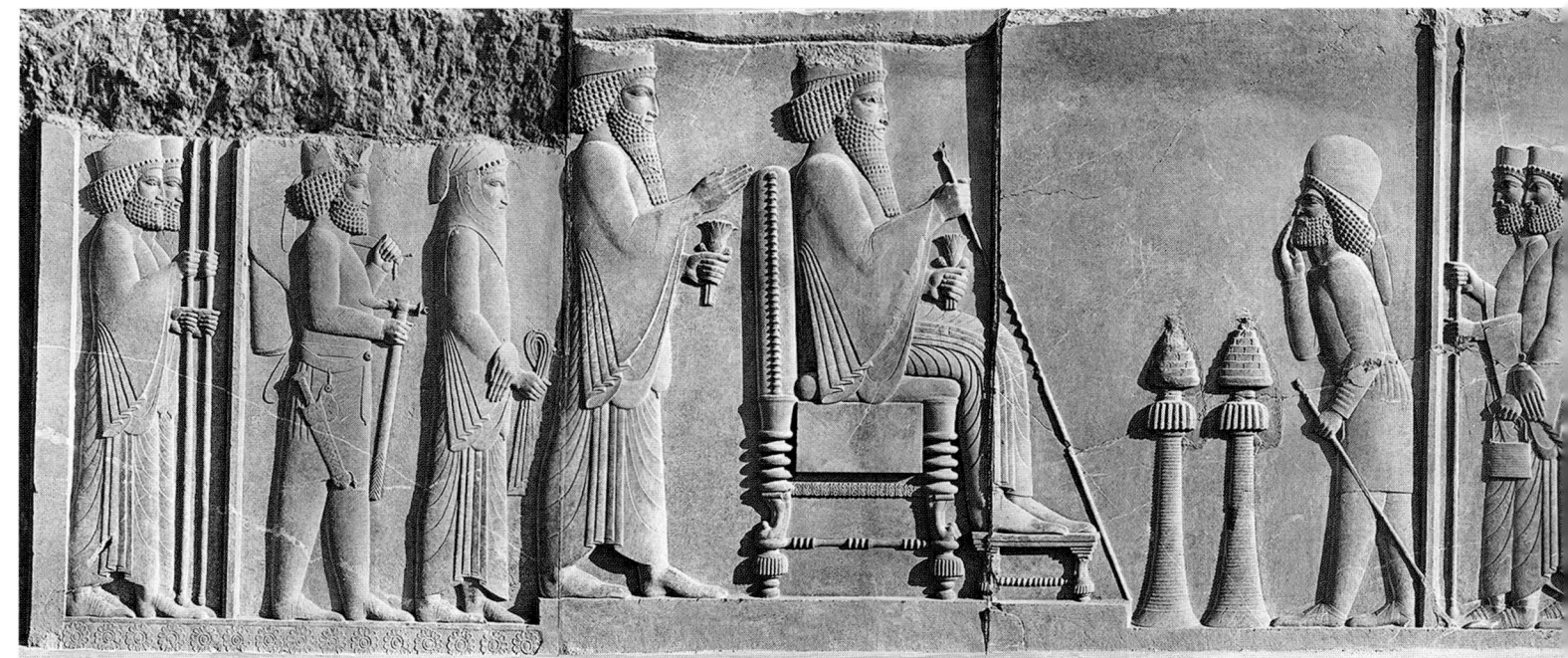

2.30 *Darius and Xerxes Giving Audience*. ca. 490 BCE. Limestone, height 8'4" (2.5 m). Archaeological Museum, Tehran, Iran

In marked contrast to the military narratives of the Assyrians, reliefs embellishing the platform of the Audience Hall and its double stairway proclaim a theme of harmony and integration across the multicultural empire (fig. **2.30**). Long rows of marching figures, sometimes superposed in registers, represent the empire's 23 subject nations, as well as royal guards and Persian dignitaries. Each of the nations' representatives wears indigenous dress and brings a regional gift—precious vessels, textiles—as tribute to the Persian king. Colored stone and metals applied to the relief added richness to a wealth of carved detail. The relief is remarkably shallow, yet by reserving the figures' roundness for the edge of their bodies (so that they cast a shadow), and by cutting the background away to a level field, the sculptors created an impression of greater depth. Where earlier Mesopotamian reliefs depict figures in mixed profile and frontal views, most of these figures are in full profile, even though some figures turn their heads back to

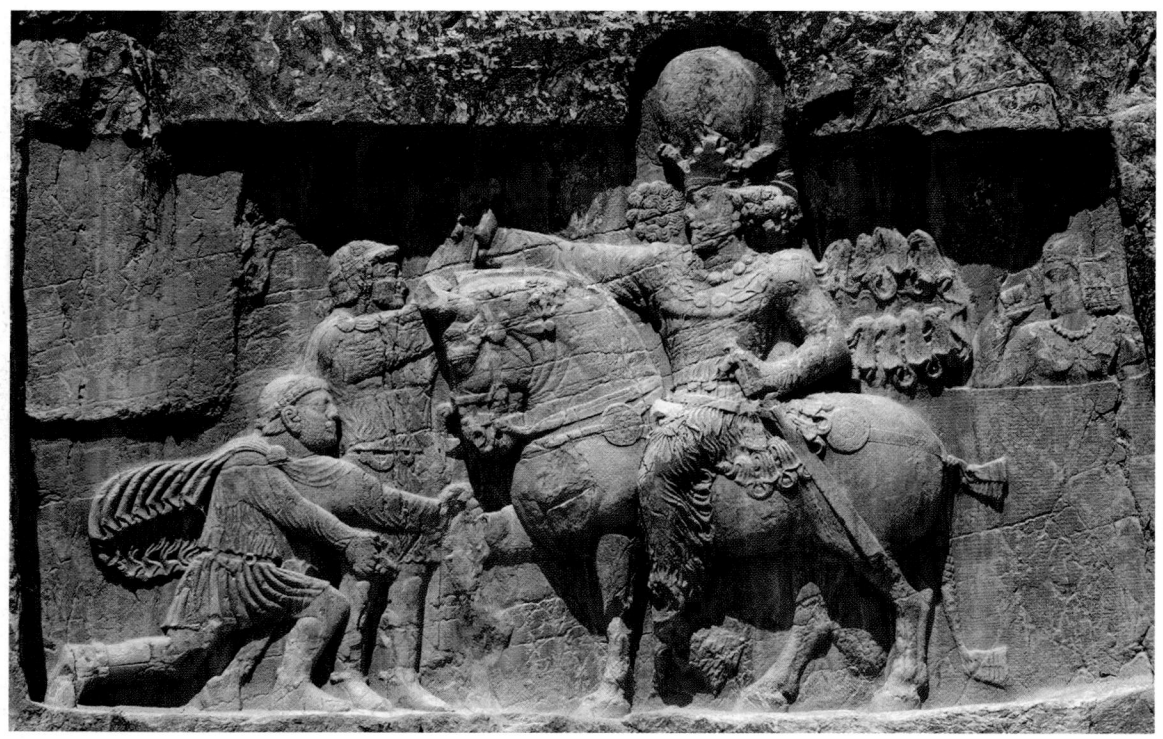

2.31 *Shapur I Triumphing over the Roman Emperors Philip the Arab and Valerian*, Naksh-i-Rustam (near Persepolis), Iran. 260–272 CE

address those who follow. Through repetition of the walking human form, the artists generated a powerful dynamic quality that guides a visitor's path through the enormous space. The repetition also lends the reliefs an eternal quality, as if preserving the action in perpetual time. If, as some believe, the relief represents the recurring celebration of the New Year Festival, this timeless quality would be especially apt.

The Achaemenid synthesis of traditions at Persepolis demonstrates the longevity and flexibility of the Near Eastern language of rulership. The palace provides a dramatic and powerful setting for imperial court ritual on a grand scale.

Mesopotamia Between Persian and Islamic Dominion

Rebuffed in its attempts to conquer Greece, the Persian Empire eventually came under Greek and then Roman domination, but like many parts of the Greek and Roman empires, it retained numerous aspects of its own culture. The process began in 331 BCE with Alexander the Great's (356–323 BCE) victory over the Persians, when his troops burnt the palace at Persepolis in an act of symbolic defiance. After his death eight years later, his generals divided his realm among themselves, and Seleukas (r. 305–281 BCE) inherited much of the Near East. The Parthians, who were Iranian nomads, gained control over the region in 238 BCE. Despite fairly constant conflict, they fended off Roman advances until a brief Roman success under Trajan in the early second century CE, after which Parthian power declined. The last Parthian king was overthrown by one of his governors, Ardashir or Artaxerxes, in 224 CE. This Ardashir (d. 240 CE) founded the Sasanian dynasty, named for a mythical ancestor, Sasan, who claimed to be a direct descendent of the Achaemenids, and this dynasty controlled the area until the Arab conquest in the mid-seventh century CE.

Ardashir's son, Shapur I (r. 240–272 CE), proved to be Darius' equal in ambition, and he linked himself directly to the Persian king. He expanded the empire greatly, and even succeeded in defeating three Roman emperors in the middle of the third century CE. Two of these victories Shapur commemorated in numerous reliefs, including an immense panel carved into rock at Naksh-i-Rustam, near Persepolis, where Darius I and his successors had previously located their rock-cut tombs (fig. **2.31**). The victor, on horseback, raises his hand in a gesture of mercy to the defeated "barbarian," who kneels before him in submission. This was a stock Roman scene, recognizable to Roman viewers, and this quotation gives the relief an ironic dimension, for the victorious Shapur here expropriates his enemy's own **iconography** of triumph. Elements of style are typical of late or provincial Roman sculpture, such as the linear folds of the emperor's billowing cloak. However, Shapur's elaborate headdress and clothing, his heavily caparisoned horse, and his composite pose are all distinctly Near Eastern.

Roman and Near Eastern elements are combined again in Shapur I's palace (242–272 CE) at Ctesiphon, near Baghdad, with its magnificent brick, barrel-vaulted audience hall, or **iwan** (fig. **2.32**). It was a Roman practice to exploit the **arch** to span huge spaces (see fig. 7.61), and the architect used it here to enclose a space 90 feet high, typical of the Near Eastern tradition of large-scale royal building. The registers of arched blank windows or **blind arcades** may derive from Roman façades, such as those in the stage buildings of theaters or ornamental fountains (see fig. 7.7). Yet the shallowness of the arcades creates a distinctly

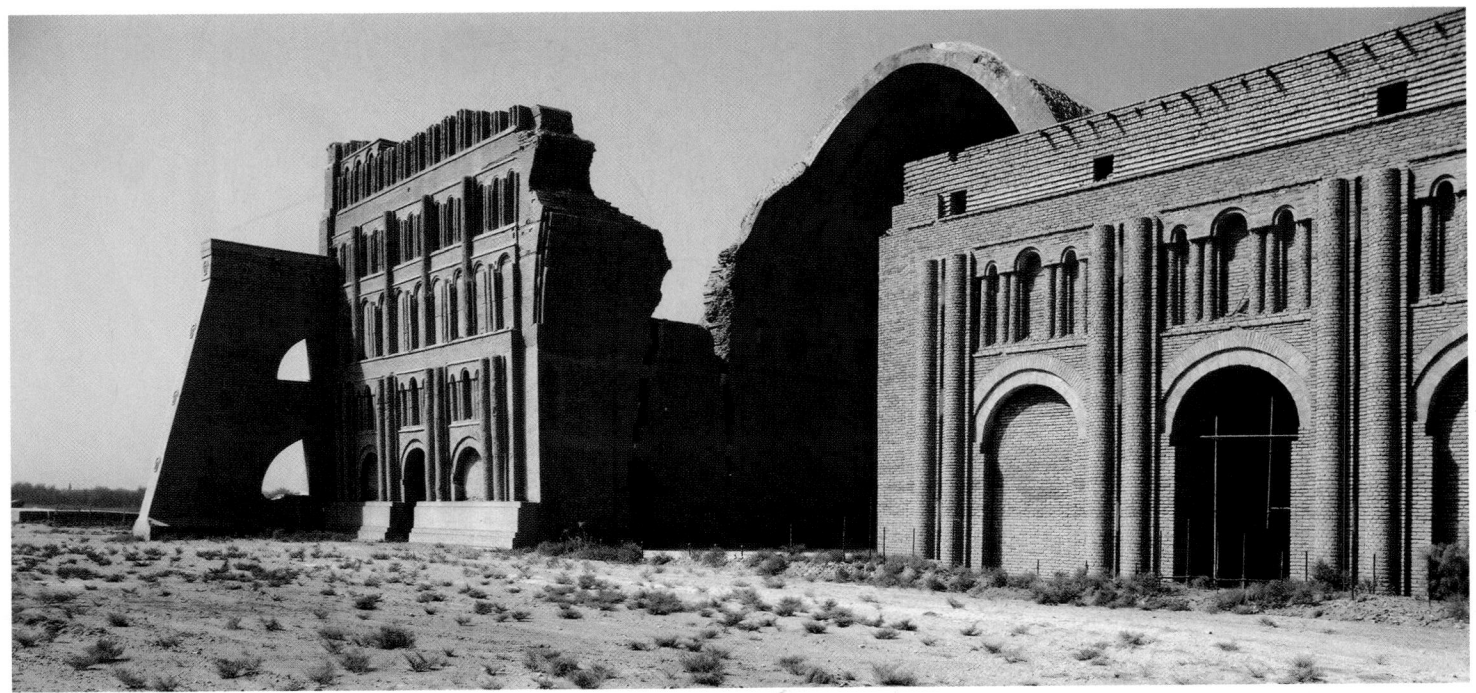

2.32 Palace of Shapur I, Ctesiphon, Iraq. 242–272 CE

eastern surface pattern, in turn subordinated to an awe-inspiring entryway.

Metalwork continued to flourish in the Sasanian period, using a wide variety of techniques. Hunting scenes were a popular subject, as seen in figure 2.33, a late fifth-century CE silver bowl that probably represents King Peroz I hunting gazelles. A metalworker turned the bowl on a lathe, and hammered out the king and his prey from behind (a technique known as **repoussé**), before applying gilt and inlaying details such as the horns of the animals and the pattern on the quiver, with **niello**, a compound of sulphur. The hunting subject continues a tradition known to Assyrians, as well as to Egyptians and Romans. Sasanians exported many of their wares to Constantinople (see map 8.1) and to the Christian West, where they had a strong impact on the art of the Middle Ages. Artists would manufacture similar vessels again after the Sasanian realm fell to the Arabs in the mid-seventh century CE, and these served as a source of design motifs for Islamic art as well (see Chapter 9).

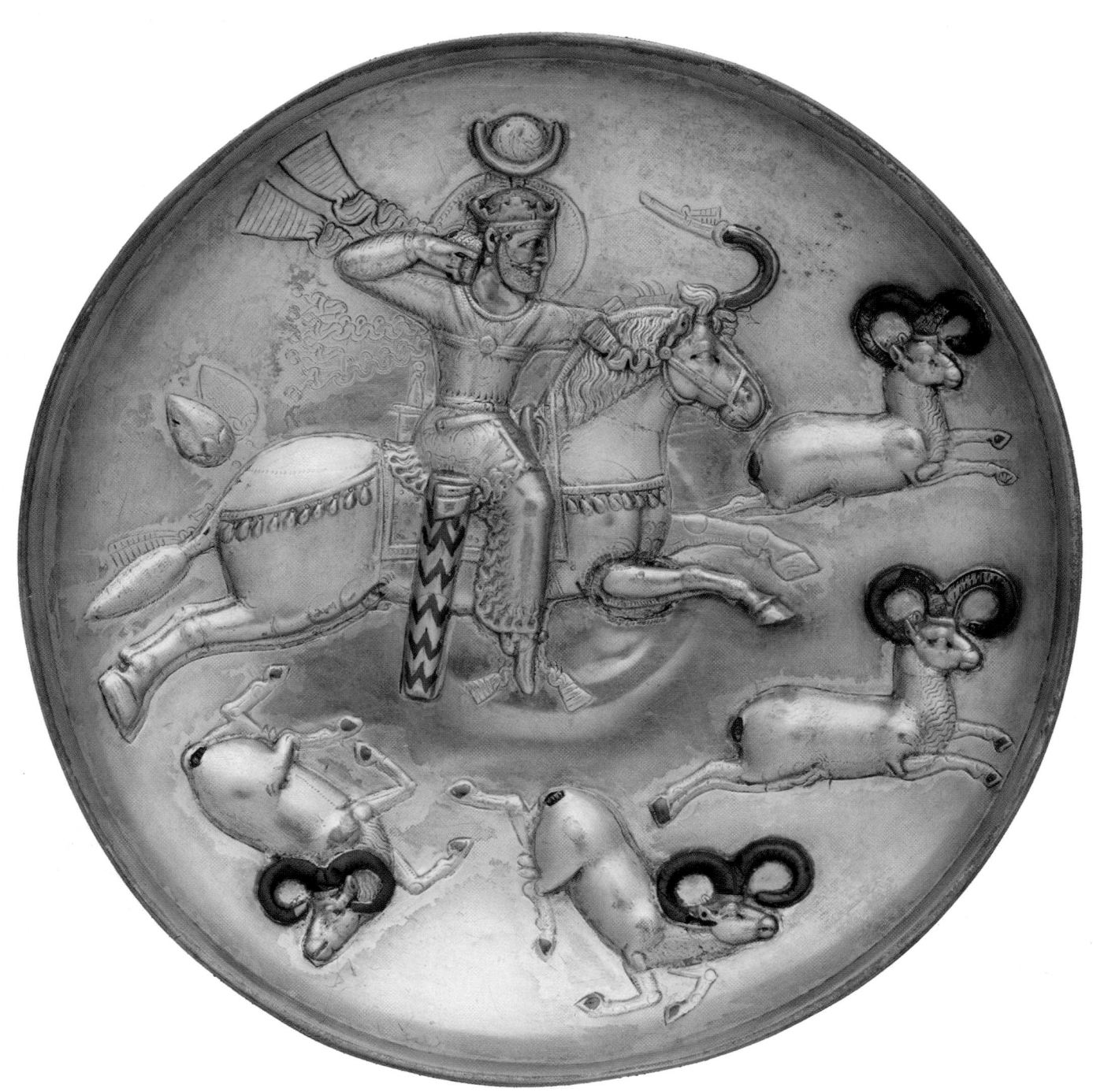

2.33 *Peroz I (457–483) or Kavad I hunting rams.* 5th–6th century CE. Silver, mercury gilding, niello inlay, diameter 8⅝" (21.9 cm), height 1⅞" (4.6 cm). Metropolitan Museum of Art, New York, Fletcher Fund, 1934 (34.33)

ca. 4000 BCE
Handleless beaker
from Susa

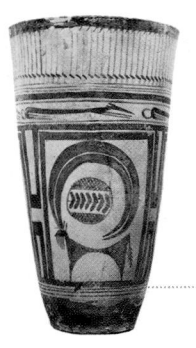

Ancient
Near Eastern Art

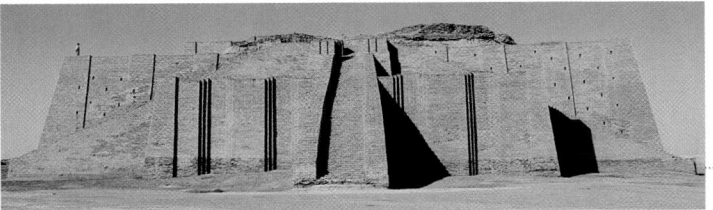

ca. 2600 BCE The *Royal Standard of Ur*

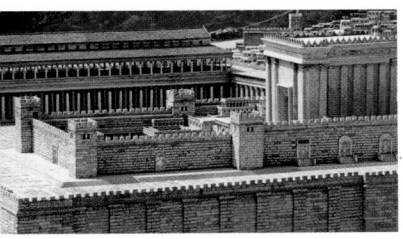

ca. 2100 BCE King Urnammu commissions the Great Ziggurat at Ur

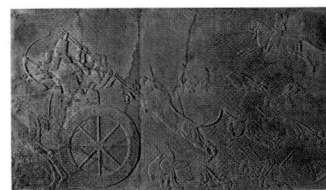

ca. 957 BCE Solomon's Temple is completed
in Jerusalem

ca. 668–627 BCE Assyrians construct
the North Palace of Ashurbanipal

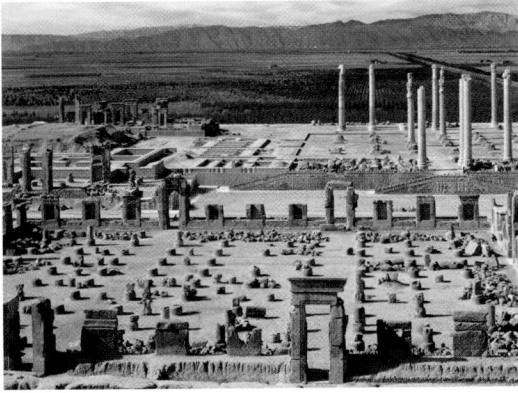

ca. 518 BCE Construction of the Persian palace
at Persepolis begins

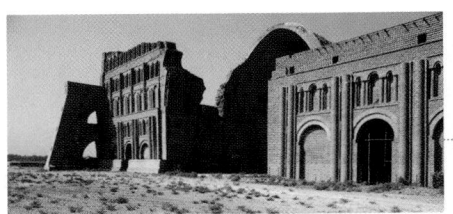

242–272 CE Shapur I's palace at Ctesiphon built

4000
BCE

3500
BCE

3000
BCE

2500
BCE

2000
BCE

1500
BCE

1000
BCE

500
BCE

0

500
CE

◄ ca. 3500 BCE Sumerian city of Uruk emerges
ca. 3500 BCE Pottery manufacturing appears in
western Europe

ca. 3100–2600 BCE Neolithic stone houses at
Skara Brae

◄ ca. 2900 BCE Mesopotamians begin using
cuneiform writing

◄ ca. 2350 BCE Conflict begins among Sumerian city-
states over access to water and fertile land

◄ after 2150 BCE Earliest surviving Akkadian tablets
of the *Epic of Gilgamesh*
ca. 2100 BCE Final phase of construction at
Stonehenge

◄ ca. 1792–1750 BCE Hammurabi rules Babylon

◄ ca. 1595 BCE The Hittites conquer Babylon

◄ 1400–1200 BCE Apogee of the Hittite Empire

◄ 612 BCE Nineveh falls to the Medes and resurgent
Babylonians; end of the Assyrian Empire
ca. 604–562 BCE Reign of the Late Babylonian ruler
Nebuchadnezzar II
ca. 559–530/29 BCE Rule of Cyrus the Great, who
leads Persians to overthrow the Medes

◄ 331 BCE Alexander the Great defeats the Persians

◄ 224 CE Ardashir founds the Sasanian dynasty

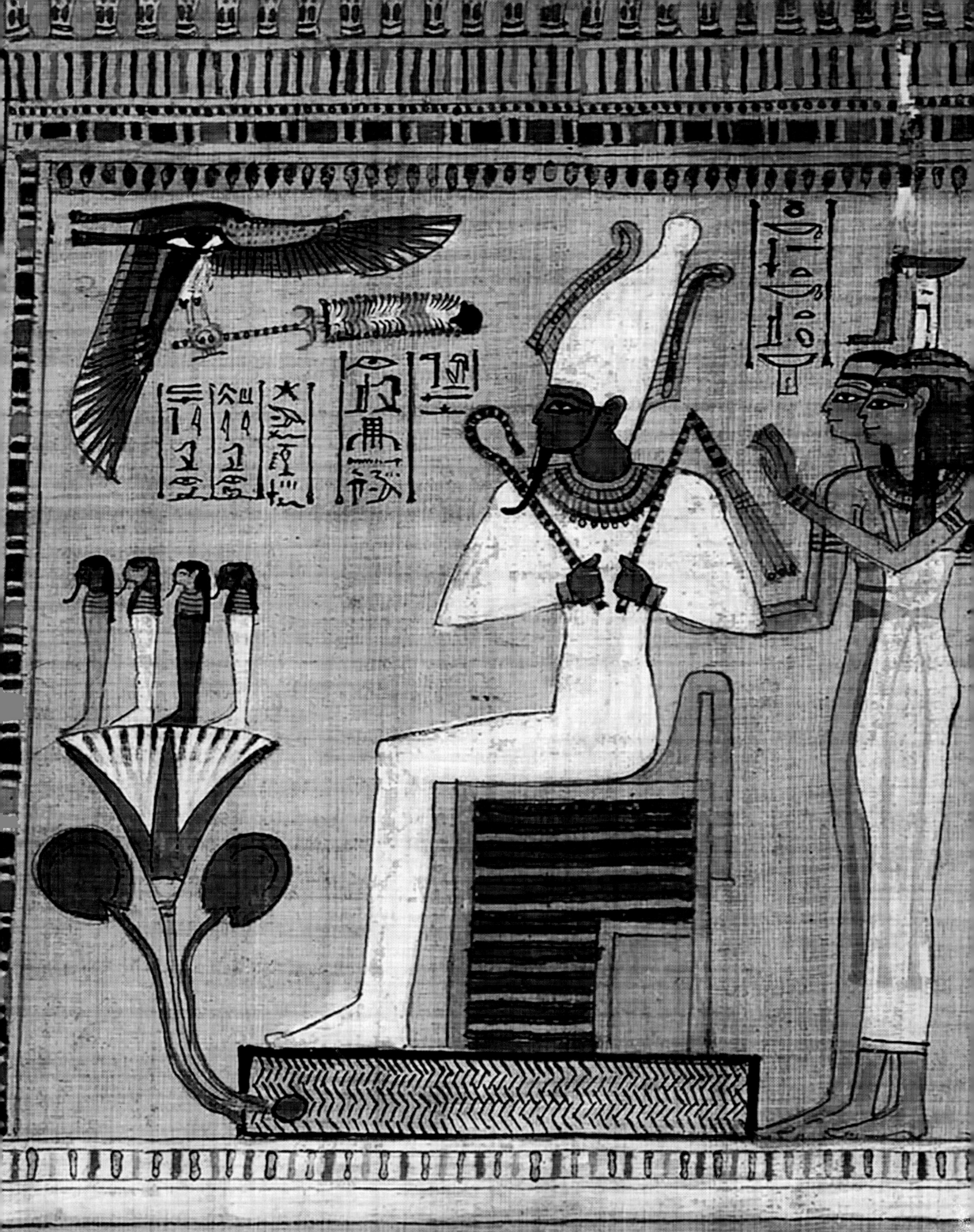

Egyptian A

EGYPT HAS LONG FASCINATED THE WEST. THE ANCIENT GREEKS AND the Romans knew and admired Egypt, and Renaissance collectors and scholars took up their esteem. Napoleon's incursions into Egypt in the late eighteenth century brought artifacts and knowledge back to France and stimulated interest throughout Europe. European-sponsored excavations have been

going on in Egypt since the nineteenth century, sometimes, as in the case of the discovery in 1922 of the tomb of King Tutankhamun, with spectacular results.

One reason that ancient Egypt enthralls us is the exceptional technique and monumental character of its works of art. Most surviving objects come from tombs, which Egyptians built to assure an afterlife for the deceased. They intended the paintings, sculptures, and other objects they placed in the tombs to accompany the deceased into eternity. Thus, Egyptian art is an art of permanence. In fact, the fourth-century BCE Greek philosopher Plato claimed that Egyptian art had not changed in 10,000 years. The reality is more complex, but it is fair to say that most Egyptian artists did not strive for innovation or originality, but adhered instead to traditional formulations that expressed specific ideas. Continuity of form and subject is a characteristic of ancient Egyptian art.

Egyptian artists executed works of art mainly for the elite patrons of a society that was extremely hierarchical. Contemporary with the Egyptian development of writing around 3000 BCE there emerged a political and religious system that placed a god-king (called a pharaoh from the New Kingdom on) in charge of the physical and spiritual well-being of the land and its people. Many of the best-known works of Egyptian art exalted

these powerful rulers, and express the multifaceted ways that Egyptians envisioned their king: as a human manifestation of the gods, as a god in his own right, as a beneficent ruler, and as an emblem of life itself. Royal projects for the afterlife dominated the landscape and provided the model for elite burials. These two categories of art—royal commissions and funerary objects—constitute a large proportion of surviving Egyptian art. Religion accounts for the predominance of both types of art.

Egyptian geography also played a formative role in the development of art. The land was established on the course of the Nile River in North Africa, exploiting the natural protection of the surrounding desert, or "red land." The river floods annually, inundating the land on either side. As it recedes, the water leaves a dark strip of soil fertilized by silt. The Egyptians called this rich soil the "black land." They irrigated and farmed it, and regularly produced surplus food. This allowed them to diversify and develop a complex culture. Egypt's agrarian society depended on the annual flooding of the Nile to survive. The king had to assure continuity of life through intercession with the gods, who often represented natural forces. (See *Informing Art*, page 52.) The chief deity was the sun, whom they worshiped as Ra-Horakhty. In matters concerning the afterlife, the deities Osiris, Isis, and Horus played key roles. Osiris was the mythical founder of Egypt, and Isis was his consort. Osiris's brother Seth (god of chaos) murdered him, and having dismembered him, scattered his remains far and wide. Isis eventually recovered them, and reassembled them

Detail of figure 3.41, *The Weighing of the Heart and Judgment by Osiris*

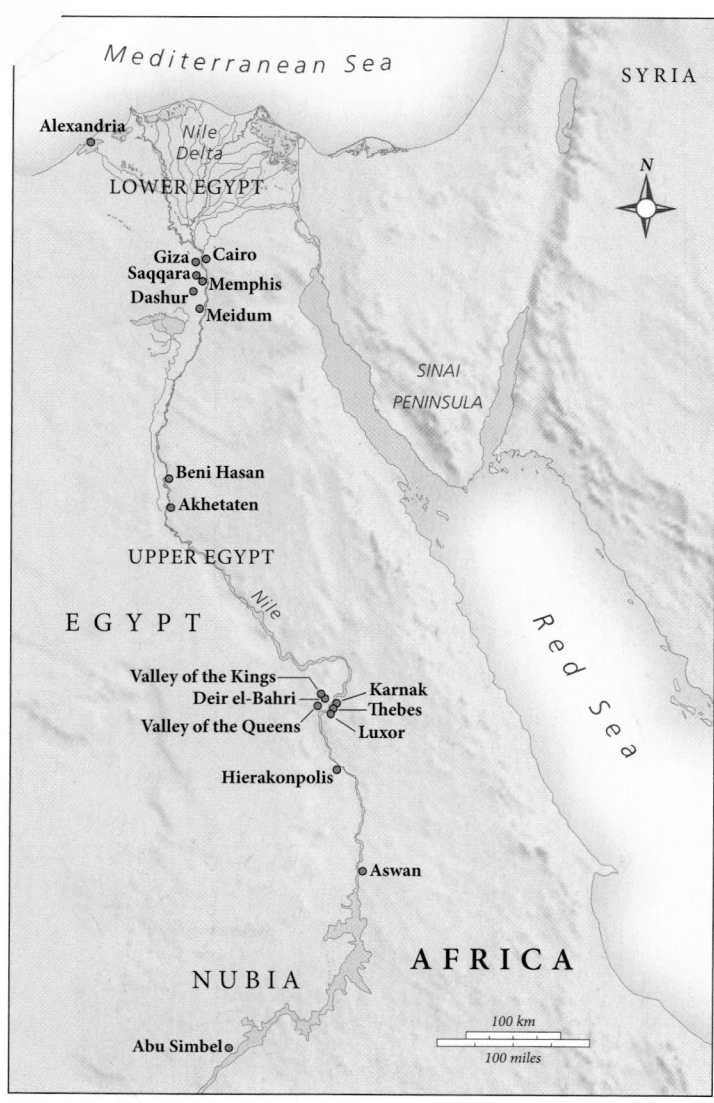

Map 3.1 Ancient Egypt

between present-day Aswan and the point where the river fans out into the Delta, near present-day Cairo. Lower Egypt, in the north, consists mainly of the vast Delta, from ancient Memphis to the Mediterranean. In Upper Egypt, independent cities shared a rich culture that archaeologists know as Naqada II/III (from the location where they first discovered it). One of those cities was Hierakonpolis, where a number of well-constructed tombs contained valuable furnishings. In one, known as Tomb 100 and probably built for a ruler, paintings embellished the walls (fig. **3.1**). Human figures with rectangular torsos, stick limbs, and simple round heads ride in boats, and engage in battle with one another. Unlike later Egyptian tomb paintings, the design is not arranged in registers (rows). A group of animals at the top sit on a ground-line, but the painter dispersed most of the figures freely against the background. In the lower left corner, a figure raises a stick against three smaller figures, who may be prisoners. This scheme will reappear in later Egyptian art (see fig. 3.2).

With time, the culture of Upper Egypt spread northward, ultimately dominating the centers of Lower Egypt. Tradition maintained that the first king of the first dynasty founded the city of Memphis, at the mouth of the Nile Delta, uniting Upper and Lower Egypt (map **3.1**). The traditional division of Egypt into two distinct regions arises from the Egyptian worldview, which saw the world as a set of dualities in opposition: Upper and Lower Egypt; the red land of the desert and the black land of cultivation; the god of the earth (Geb) balanced by the sky (Nut); Osiris (god of civilization) opposed to Seth (god of chaos). The king had to balance the forces of chaos and order, and bring *ma'at* (harmony or order) to the world. Recognizing this worldview has led some scholars to question the traditional explanation that Upper and Lower Egypt were independent regions unified by King Narmer. Instead, they argue that this division was an imaginative reconstruction of the past.

to create the first mummy (an embalmed and wrapped body). From it she conceived her son, Horus, who avenged his father's death by besting Seth in a series of contests. Gods took many forms: Ra might appear as a falcon-headed man; Osiris as a mummy. Egyptians called the king himself the son of Ra and saw him as the human embodiment of Horus. As an equal to the gods, he controlled the land, the future, and the afterlife. A large priesthood, an administrative bureaucracy, and a strong military assisted him.

PREDYNASTIC AND EARLY DYNASTIC ART

The origins of Egyptian culture stretch back into the Neolithic period. By at least 5000 BCE, humans were growing crops and domesticating animals in the Nile Valley. Settlements there gradually transformed into urban centers.

According to tradition, Egypt initially consisted of two regions. Upper Egypt, in the south, includes the Nile Valley

The Palette of King Narmer

The *Palette of King Narmer* (fig. **3.2**), dated to around 3000 BCE, visually expressed the concept of the king as unifier. A **palette** is a stone tablet with a central depression for grinding the protective paint that Egyptians applied around their eyes to protect them from ailments and the sun's glare. Its size—more than 2 feet high—suggests that it was not for ordinary use, but was probably reserved for a ceremony to ornament a cult statue. This ritual function may explain its findspot (where it was found) in the temple of Hierakonpolis, where it had been buried along with other offerings to the god Horus.

Shallow relief carvings in registers decorate both sides of the *Palette*. At the top of each side, in the center, **hieroglyphs** spell out Narmer's name, within an abstract rendering of the king's palace. The Egyptians developed hieroglyphs as a writing system at about the same time as the Mesopotamians were inventing cuneiform, and used them in both religious and administrative contexts. They called them "god's words"; the Greeks later saw them as sacred carvings, and their name for them, derived from

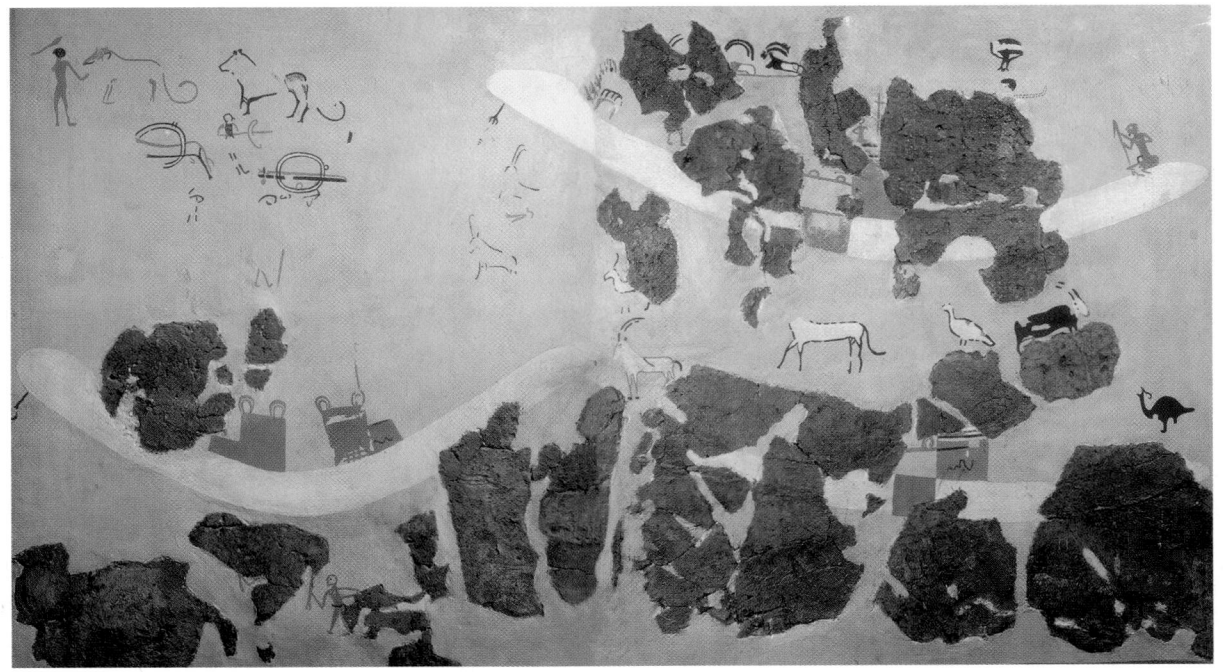

3.1 *People, boats, and animals.* First example of an Egyptian decorated tomb chamber showing people, boats and animals in the late predynastic Tomb 100 at Hierakonpolis. ca. 3000 BCE. Height 43.3″ (110 cm). Egyptian Museum, Cairo

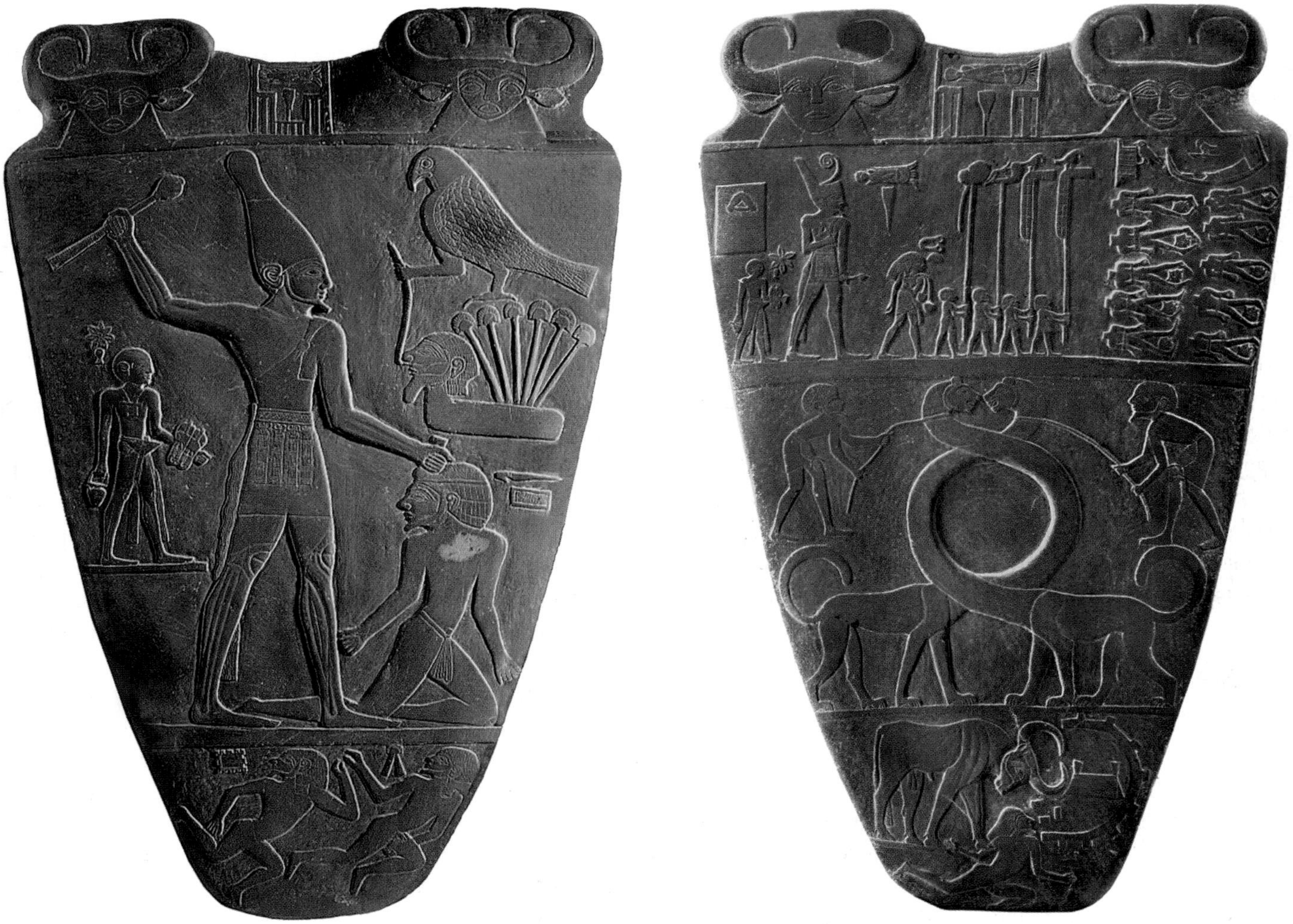

3.2 *Palette of King Narmer* (both sides), from Hierakonpolis. ca. 3150–3125 BCE. Slate, height 25″ (63.5 cm). Egyptian Museum, Cairo

Egyptian Gods and Goddesses

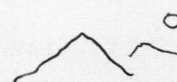

Religion permeated every aspect of Egyptian life. According to Egyptian belief, the gods not only created the world, but remained involved in its existence. From artistic and textual evidence, we know the names of over 1,500 deities, some of whom are named below. The Egyptians conceived of their gods in myriad human, animal, and hybrid forms, and assigned numerous functions to them, which evolved over the course of time.

AMUN: One of Egypt's most important gods, associated with the sun, creation, and fertility. When combined with Ra as Amun-Ra in the Middle and New Kingdoms, he became the supreme Egyptian god. Usually represented as a man with a double plumed crown, a ram, or a human with a ram's head.

ANUBIS: God of the dead and embalming. Usually depicted as a jackal or another canine, or as a man with a jackal's head.

ATEN: A manifestation of the sun-god, supreme and only god under Akhenaten. Represented by the disk of the sun, emanating rays ending in hands.

HAPY: God of the inundation of the Nile, associated with life-giving and creation. Usually represented as a man with a swollen belly.

HATHOR: One of Egypt's most important goddesses. Mother or wife of Horus, wife or daughter and "Eye" of Ra, mother or wife of the king. Goddess of the sky, of women, female sexuality, and motherhood, of foreign lands, of the afterlife, and of joy, music, and happiness, and cow-goddess. Shown as a woman in a long wig or in a vulture cap with cow horns and a sun-disk, or as a cow.

HORUS: God of the sky, of the sun, and of kingship, with whom the living king was associated. Son of Isis and Osiris. Represented as a falcon or hawk, or as a man with a falcon's head.

ISIS: Egypt's most important goddess. Sister and wife of Osiris, mother and protector of Horus, and mother of the king. Cosmic goddess, goddess of magic, and protector of the dead. Usually represented as a woman crowned with the hieroglyphic throne sign, or with horns and a sun-disk.

MA'AT: Personification of truth, justice, and order. Represented as a woman with a tall feather headdress, or as a feather.

NEPHTHYS: Sister of Isis, funerary goddess. Represented as a woman.

NUT: Personification of the heavens, associated with thunder, rain, and stars, and with resurrection. Mother of Isis, Osiris, Nephthys, and Seth. Usually shown as a woman, often with limbs or body extended across the sky.

OSIRIS: One of Egypt's chief deities. Ruler of the underworld, god of death, resurrection, and fertility, and associated with the king. Murdered and dismembered by his brother, Seth, he was reassembled by his consort Isis and sister Nephthys, and brought back to life. Represented as a white or black mummy, often wearing the white crown of Upper Egypt.

RA: The most important Egyptian deity. Creator, king and father of the king. Combined with Ra-Horakhty as the morning sun. Often shown as a sun-disk surrounded by a cobra, or as a man with a hawk's head and headdress with a sun-disk.

SETH: Brother of Osiris and Isis, who murdered Osiris; brother and husband of Nephthys. Desert deity, associated chiefly with chaos, violence, and destruction. Represented as an animal with a curved head, or as a man with a curved animal head.

THOTH: Moon-god, associated with writing and knowledge. Represented as an ibis, a baboon, or an ibis-headed man with a writing palette.

---

the Greek words *hieros* (sacred) and *gluphein* (to carve), has endured. Flanking the hieroglyphs, heads of cows represent the sky goddess, locating the king in the sky. On one side of the *Palette* (shown on the left), King Narmer holds a fallen enemy by the hair, as he raises his mace—an emblem of kingship—with the other hand. The king appears in the composite view that will be the hallmark of Egyptian two-dimensional art: with a frontal view of eye, shoulders, and arms, but a profile of head and legs. He wears the white crown of Upper Egypt and from the belt of his kilt hangs the tail of a bull, a symbol of power that Egyptian kings would wear as part of their ceremonial dress for 3,000 years. The large scale of his figure compared with others immediately establishes his authority. For his part, the enemy, like those in the bottom register, is stripped of clothing as an act of humiliation. Behind the king, and standing on his own ground-line, an attendant carries the king's sandals. Hieroglyphs identify both the sandal-carrier and the enemy. To the right of Narmer appears a falcon resting on a papyrus stand, which grows from a human-headed strip of land; the falcon holds a rope tethered to the face.

On the other side of the *Palette* (on the right in fig. 3.2), Narmer appears in the highest register, now wearing the red crown of Lower Egypt. Flanked by the sandal-carrier and a long-haired figure, he follows four standard-bearers to inspect the decapitated bodies of prisoners, arranged with their heads between their legs. In the larger central register are two animals, each roped in by a male figure. They twist their long necks to frame a circle in the composition. The symmetrical, balanced motif may represent *ma'at*. Similar beasts occur on contemporary Mesopotamian cylinder seals, and may have influenced this design. In the lowest register, a bull representing the king attacks a city and tramples down the enemy.

The *Palette* communicates its message by combining several different types of signs on one object. Some of these signs—the king, attendants, and prisoners—are literal representations. Others are symbolic, such as the depiction of the king as a bull, denoting his strength. **Pictographs**, small symbols based on abstract representations of concepts, encode further information: In the falcon and papyrus group, the falcon represents Horus, whom the Egyptians believed the king incarnated, while the human-headed papyrus stand represents Lower Egypt, where papyrus grew abundantly. A possible interpretation is that this pictograph expresses Narmer's control of that region. Finally, the artist included identifying texts in the form of hieroglyphs. Together, the different signs on the *Palette of King Narmer* drive home important messages about the nature of Egyptian kingship: The king embodied the unified Upper and Lower Egypt, and though human, he occupied a divine office, as shown by the placement of his name in the sky, the realm of Horus.

As Horus's manifestation on earth, the king provided a physical body for the royal life force (*ka*) that passed from monarch to succeeding monarch. Positioned at the pinnacle of a highly stratified human hierarchy (indicated by his scale), the king was between mortals and gods, a kind of lesser god. His role was to enforce order over its opposing force, chaos, which he does on the *Palette* by overcoming foreign foes and establishing visible authority over them.

THE OLD KINGDOM: A GOLDEN AGE

The *Palette of King Narmer* offers an image of kingship that transcends earthly power, representing the king as a divinity as well as a ruler. The kings of the Old Kingdom (Dynasty Three to Dynasty Six, ca. 2649–2150 BCE) found more monumental ways to express this notion. Other dynasties would emulate their works of art for the following two millennia. (See *Informing Art*, page 54.)

Old Kingdom Funerary Complexes

During the Old Kingdom, Egyptians fashioned buildings to house the day-to-day activities of the living mainly out of perishable materials, with the result that little now survives. The bulk of archaeological evidence comes instead from tombs. The great majority of the population probably buried their dead in shallow desert graves, but the elite had the resources to build elaborate funerary monuments with luxury provisions for the afterlife. The survival of these tombs is no accident; they were purposely constructed to endure.

These structures had several important functions. As in many cultures, tombs gave the deceased a permanent marker on the landscape. They expressed the status of the dead and perpetuated their memory. Generally a rectangular mud-brick or stone edifice marked an early elite or royal burial (fig. **3.3**), known today as a **mastaba**, from the Arabic word for "bench." Plaster covered its exterior sloping walls, which were painted to evoke a niched palace façade. Often this superstructure was solid mud brick or filled with rubble, but sometimes it housed a funerary chapel or storerooms for equipment needed in funerary rituals. These monuments also served a critical function in ensuring the preservation of a deceased individual's life force, or *ka*. Egyptians considered the *ka* to live on in the grave, and in order to do so, it required a

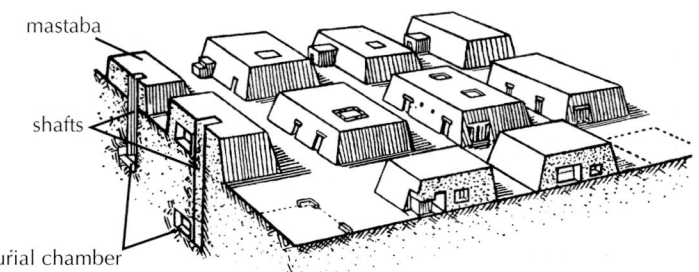

3.3   Group of mastabas, 4th Dynasty (after A. Badawy)

place to reside for eternity. This need led embalmers to go to great lengths to preserve the body through mummification (a process that they only perfected in the Eleventh and Twelfth Dynasties). The mummified body was usually placed within a **sarcophagus** (a stone coffin) and buried in a chamber at some depth below the mastaba, surrounded by subsidiary chambers for funerary apparatus. Egyptians believed that a statue could serve as a surrogate home for the *ka* in the event that the embalmers' efforts failed and the body decayed, so they set a sculpture within the burial chamber. They also equipped their tombs with objects of daily life for the *ka*'s enjoyment.

THE FUNERARY COMPLEX OF KING DJOSER   Out of this tradition emerges the first known major funerary complex, that of the Third Dynasty King Djoser (Netjerikhet), at Saqqara (figs. **3.4**, **3.5**, and **3.6**), who ruled between 2630 and 2611 BCE. On the west side of the Nile, Saqqara was the **necropolis** (cemetery or city of the dead) of the capital city of Memphis in Lower Egypt. Encircling the entire complex is a rectangular stone wall stretching over a mile in length and 33 feet high. The dominant feature of the complex is a stepped pyramid, oriented to the

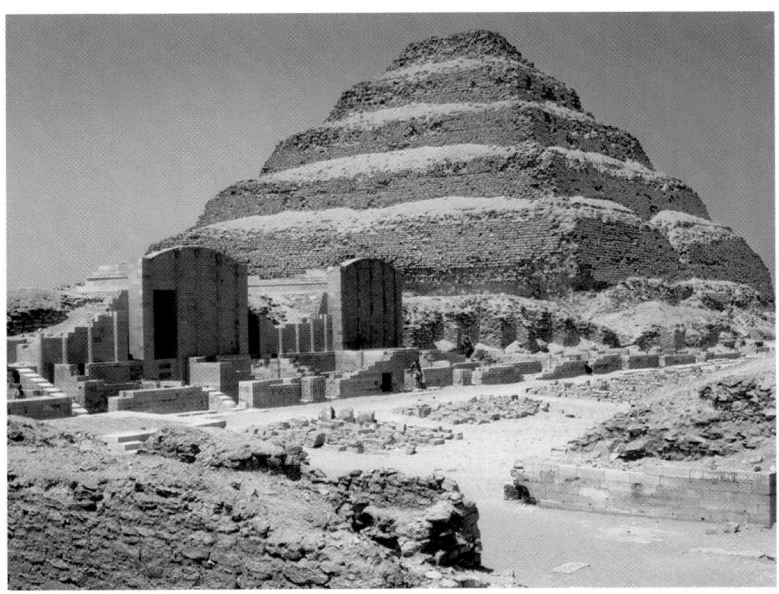

3.4   Imhotep. Step pyramid and funerary complex of King Djoser, Saqqara. 3rd Dynasty. ca. 2681–2662 BCE

Major Periods in Ancient Egypt

In Egyptian society, a king's life was the measure of time. To organize the millennia of Egyptian culture, scholars use a chronology devised in the third century BCE by the priest-historian Manetho, who wrote a history of Egypt in Greek for Ptolemy I, based on Egyptian sources. He divided the list of Egyptian kings into 31 dynasties, beginning with the First Dynasty shortly after 3000 BCE. Modern scholars have organized the dynasties into kingdoms, beginning with the Old Kingdom, which covers from ca. 2649 BCE to 2150 BCE. The period before this, between prehistory and the First Dynasty, is known as the Predynastic period. Further subdivisions include the Middle Kingdom (ca. 2040–1640 BCE) and the New Kingdom (ca. 1550–1070 BCE).

Scholars still debate the actual dates for these broad periods and even for the reigns of kings, as Manetho's list offered only a relative chronology (that is, the order in which kings succeeded one another) rather than absolute dates.

Major Periods in Ancient Egypt

ca. 5450–2960 BCE—Predynastic

ca. 2960–2649 BCE—Early Dynastic (Dynasties 1, 2)

ca. 2649–2150 BCE—Old Kingdom (Dynasties 3–6)

ca. 2040–1640 BCE—Middle Kingdom (Dynasties 11–13)

ca. 1550–1070 BCE—New Kingdom (Dynasties 18–20)

---

cardinal points of the compass (figs. 3.4 and 3.5). It began as a 26-foot-high mastaba, which the enclosure wall would originally have concealed. Over the course of years it rose to its towering 204-foot height as builders added progressively diminishing layers of masonry to its form. These layers resulted in the emergence of a kind of a staircase, perhaps the means by which the king could ascend to the gods after death. The treads of the "steps" incline downwards and the uprights outwards, giving the structure an impressively stable appearance. A chamber cut into the rock about 90 feet beneath the pyramid and lined with Aswan granite contained the burial, and additional chambers held funerary provisions. North of the pyramid was a labyrinthine funerary temple, where the living performed offering rituals for the dead king.

The buildings in the burial complex reproduce the palace architecture inhabited by the king while alive. The niched enclosure wall evokes a palace façade. In the palace, large courts accommodated rituals of kingship; similarly, a large court to the south of the pyramid may have housed rituals for receiving tribute or asserting royal dominion. Shrines of Upper and Lower Egypt flanked a smaller oblong court to the east, which may have been the site of the *sed*-festival, a ceremony that celebrated the king's 30-year jubilee and rejuvenated his power. Unlike palace structures, however, many of the buildings in the funerary complex are nonfunctional: Of 14 gateways indicated in the enclosure wall, only one (on the southeast corner) allows entrance, while the rest are false doors. Likewise, chapels dedicated to local gods were simply façades with false doors, behind which was a fill of rubble, sand, or gravel. Furthermore, while architects chose perishable materials for palaces—primarily mud brick—they constructed the funerary complex entirely in limestone: It was built to last. All the

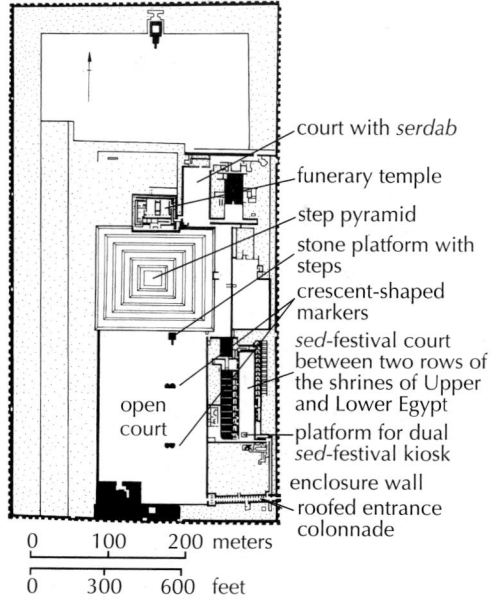

court with *serdab*

funerary temple

step pyramid

stone platform with steps

crescent-shaped markers

sed-festival court between two rows of the shrines of Upper and Lower Egypt

open court

platform for dual *sed*-festival kiosk

enclosure wall

roofed entrance colonnade

0   100   200 meters

0   300   600 feet

3.5   Plan of the funerary district of King Djoser, Saqqara (Claire Thorne, after Lloyd and Müller)

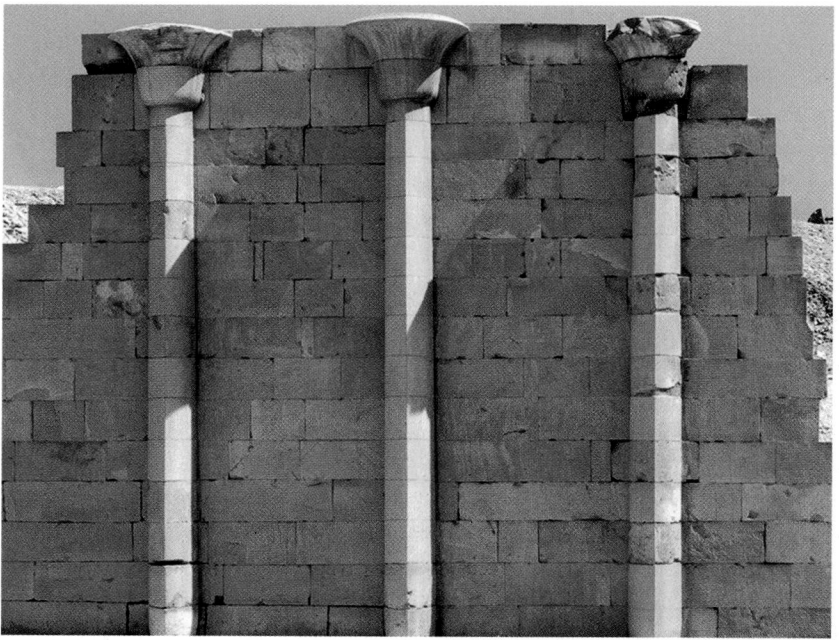

3.6   Papyrus-shaped half-columns, North Palace, funerary complex of King Djoser, Saqqara

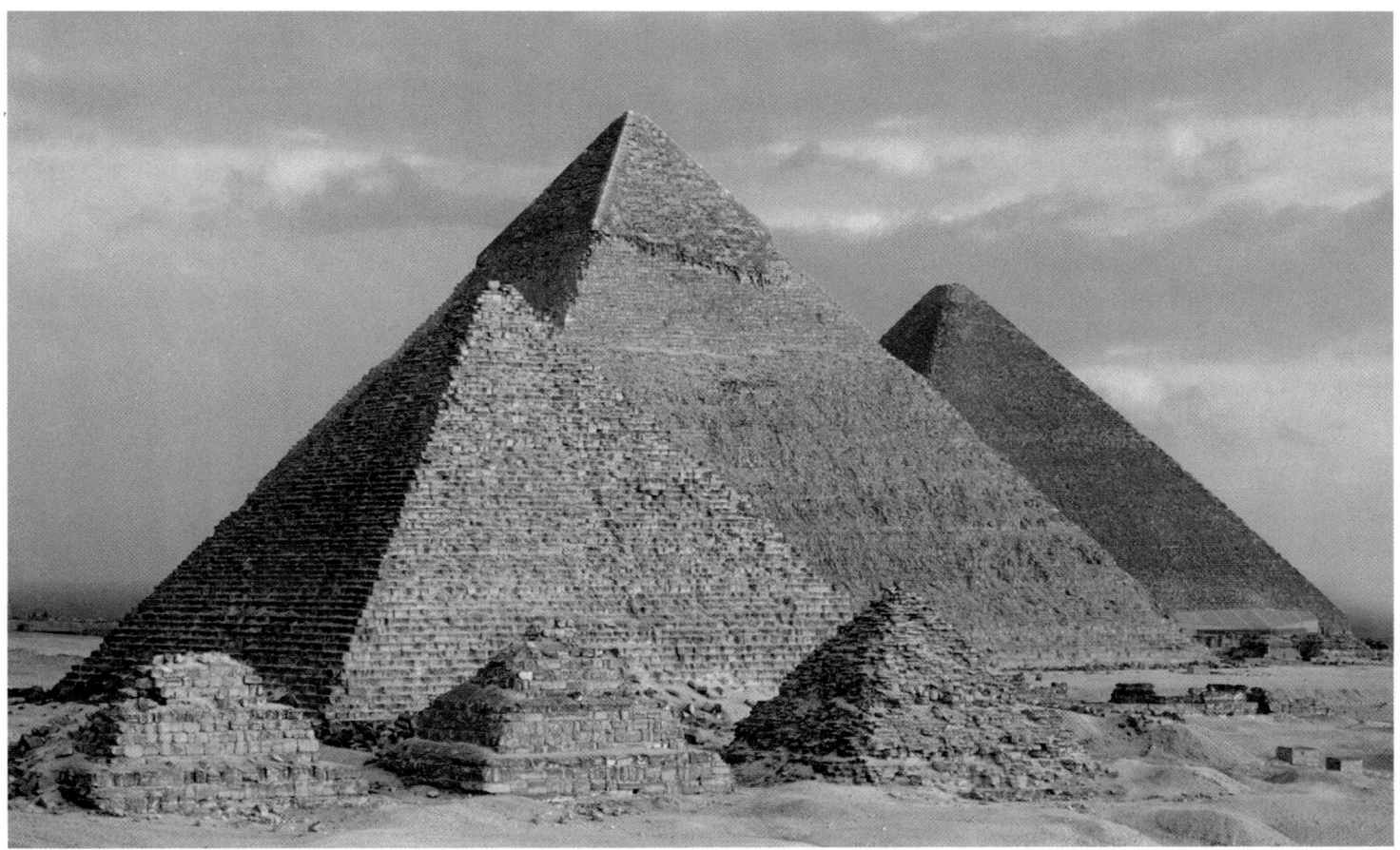

3.7 The pyramids of Menkaure, ca. 2533–2515 BCE, Khafra, ca. 2570–2544 BCE, and Khufu, ca. 2601–2528 BCE, Giza

same, masons treated the durable limestone to mimick the perishable fabrics of the palace: They dressed the limestone blocks of the enclosure wall to resemble the niched façades of mud-brick architecture. Additionally, the now reconstructed façade of a shrine echoes the form of an Upper Egyptian tent building, with tall poles supporting a mat roof that billows in the wind. Engaged columns imitate the papyrus stems or bundled reeds that Egyptian builders used to support mud-brick walls, with capitals shaped to resemble blossoms (fig. 3.6). Paint over the stone lintels disguised them as wood, and inside the tomb chamber, blue and green tiles covered false doors to imitate rolled-up reed matting.

Many elements of the complex served as permanent settings for the dead king to perpetually enact rituals of kingship—rituals that maintained order among the living. The installation of a life-sized seated statue of the king in a **serdab** (an enclosed room without an entrance) to the east of the funerary temple assured his presence in the complex. Two holes in the serdab's front wall enabled his *ka*, residing in the statue, to observe rituals in his honor and draw sustenance from offerings of food and incense. The entire complex was oriented north–south, and the king's statue looked out toward the circumpolar stars in the northern sky. With these provisions, his *ka* would remain eternally alive and vigilant.

Inscriptions on statue fragments found within the complex preserve the name of the mastermind behind its construction, a high official at Djoser's court and high priest of Ra named Imhotep. Egyptians in Imhotep's own time and beyond credited him with advancing Egyptian culture through his wisdom and knowledge of astronomy, architecture, and medicine; they regarded him so highly that they deified him. This complex, the first large-scale building constructed entirely in stone, preserves at least one of his legacies. Scholars often identify him as the first named architect in history.

The Pyramids at Giza: Reflecting a New Royal Role

Other kings followed Djoser's lead, but during the Fourth Dynasty, ca. 2575–2465 BCE, funerary architecture changed dramatically. To the modern eye, the most obvious change is the shift from a step pyramid to a smooth-sided one. A pyramid at Meidum attributed to Sneferu, the founder of the Fourth Dynasty, underlines the deliberateness of the transformation. It was originally built as a step pyramid, but its steps were later filled in to produce smooth sides.

The best-known pyramids are the three Great Pyramids at Giza (fig. **3.7**), commemorating Sneferu's son, Khufu (the first and largest pyramid), Khafra (r. 2520–2494) (a somewhat smaller one), and Menkaure (r. 2490–2472) (the smallest pyramid). (See *Materials and Techniques*, page 56.) Throughout the ages since

Building the Pyramids

In spite of much research, many aspects of pyramid design remain a mystery to Egyptologists. Elevations of other types of building—palaces and pylons, for instance—are preserved on the walls of New Kingdom tombs and temples, and a few plans survive. Pyramid architects may have worked from similar guidelines. Orienting the pyramids to the cardinal points of the compass appears to have been critical, and the architects probably achieved this by observing the stars. The greatest deviation is a meager 3 degrees east of north, in the pyramid of Djoser.

During the Old and Middle Kingdoms, builders constructed a pyramid's core out of local limestone. Quarries are still visible around the Great Pyramids and the Great Sphinx (fig. a and see fig. 3.9). For the casing (the outer surface), they must have brought Tura limestone and Aswan granite from quarries some distance away, as these are not local materials. Using copper tools, levers, and rope, workers cut channels in the rock and pried out blocks averaging 1½ to 5' in length but sometimes much larger. Somehow they hauled these blocks overland, on hard-packed causeways built for that purpose. Some scholars believe teams of men or oxen pulled them on sleds, basing this view primarily upon a tomb painting showing 172 men dragging a huge statue of the Twelfth Dynasty king Djehutihopte on a sled. When documentary filmmakers tried to replicate the process using blocks of stone, it proved extraordinarily slow and cumbersome. Yet estimates of 2.3 million stone blocks in the pyramid of Khufu, constructed within 23 years, suggest that quarries must have moved stone at tremendous rates: approximately 1,500 men had to produce at least 300 blocks a day. In Hatshepsut's mortuary temple, late nineteenth century archaeologist William Flinders Petrie discovered models of wooden cradles in the shape of a quarter-circle. If four cradles were fitted to the four sides of a block of stone, these frames would have allowed a small team of men to roll a block relatively quickly.

Archaeological remains of pyramids indicate that methods of construction evolved over time. In early pyramids, builders used a buttressing technique, with inclined layers around a central core, diminishing in height from inside out (fig. b). They then set a smooth outer casing of cut stones at an angle to the ground. When this technique proved unstable at the beginning of the Fourth Dynasty, architects turned to courses of stone, built up layer by layer. They designed outer casing blocks as right-angled trapezoids and set them level to the ground as the pyramid rose (fig. c). Scholars believe that workers constructed ramps to raise blocks into place as the monument grew, but still debate the ramps' design; since builders dismantled them after use, they have left little trace in the archaeological record. The simplest solution would be a linear ramp leading up to one face of the pyramid, made out of debris left over from building. As the pyramid grew, however, the slope would have become so steep that workers would have needed steps to haul the blocks up. At this point, they could only have maneuvered the blocks with levers. A spiraling ramp, which worked its way around the pyramid at a shallower incline, would have concealed the base corners of the pyramid, making calculations difficult for surveyors, and it would have been hard to construct at the highest levels. Another alternative is a ramp zigzagging up one side of the monument. One scholar proposes that workers used sand and rubble ramps for roughly the lowest sixth of the Great Pyramid, followed by stone ramps at the higher levels, resting on the untrimmed outer steps. As they removed the ramps, the builders would have smoothed out the outer casing blocks to form a slope.

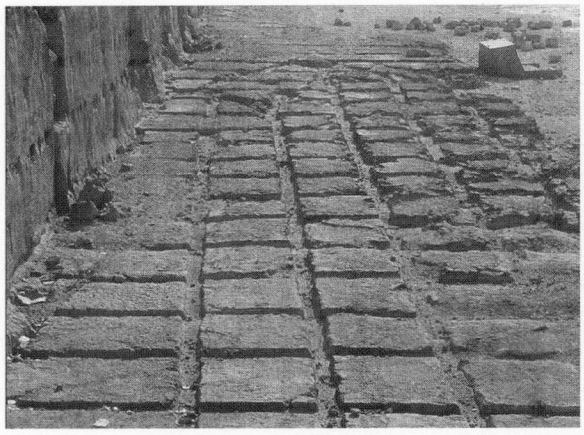

(a) Limestone quarry to the north of the Pyramid of Khafra

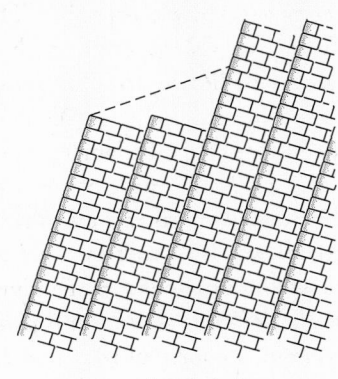

Buttressing Technique
Third Dynasty

(b) Buttressing technique

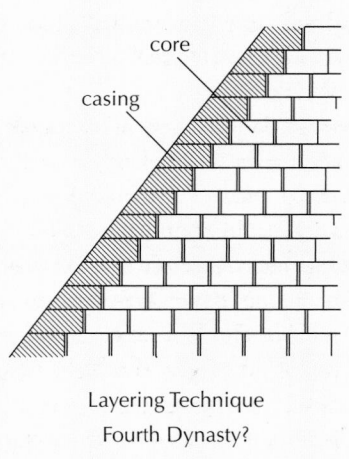

core

casing

Layering Technique
Fourth Dynasty?

(c) Layering technique

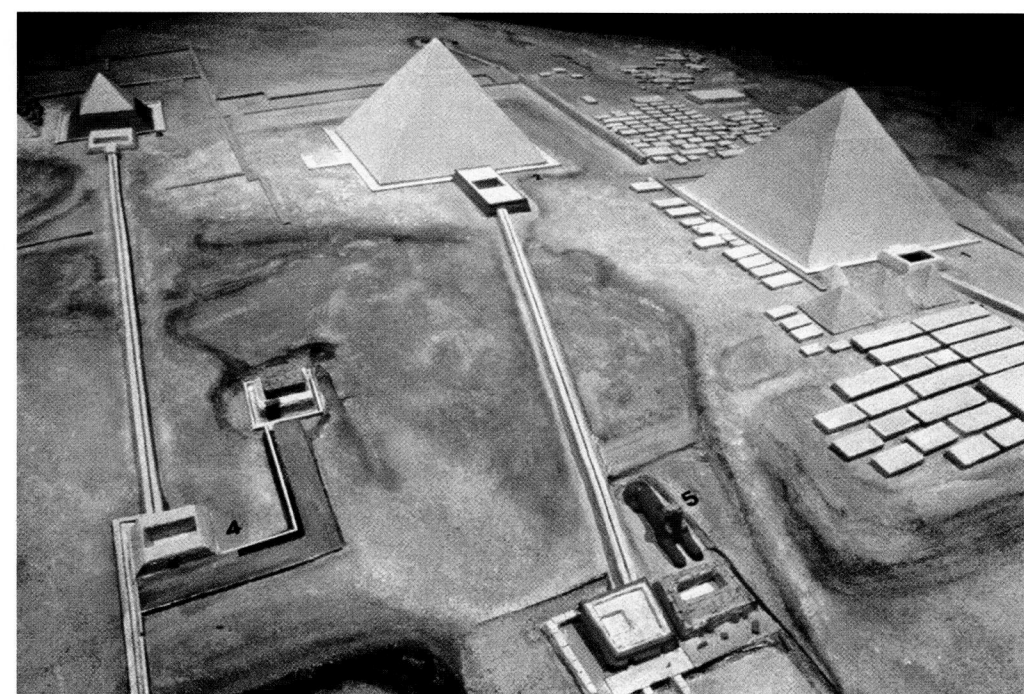

3.8 Model of the Great Pyramids, Giza: Menkaure (left), Khafra (middle), Khufu (right)

their construction, the pyramids have continued to fascinate and impress (see *The Art Historian's Lens*, page 75.) Their lasting grandeur derives both from their sheer monumentality (Khafra's covers 13 acres at the base, and still rises to a height of about 450 feet) and from their extraordinary simplicity. On a square plan, their four surfaces, shaped as equilateral triangles, taper up from the desert sand toward the sky. At any time of day, one side will hold the sun's full glare, while another is cast into shadow. Before Islamic builders plundered their stone, each pyramid was dressed with white limestone, preserved now only on the pinnacle of the pyramid of Khafra; at the tip of each, moreover, was a thin layer of gold. On Khafra's pyramid, a course of red granite set off the limestone's whiteness at ground level. The entrance to each pyramid was on its north face, and somewhere within the solid stone mass, rather than below ground, the architect concealed a burial chamber in the hopes of foiling tomb robbers (see fig. 3.3). Encircling each pyramid was an enclosure wall, and clustered all around were smaller pyramids and mastabas for members of the royal family and high officials.

Like Djoser's complex at Saqqara and most subsequent royal burials, Fourth Dynasty burials took place on the Nile's west bank, the side of the setting sun, across from living habitations on the east bank (fig. **3.8**). Yet in contrast to Djoser's complex, where the compact arrangement was laid out on a north–south axis, the architects at Giza set out the monuments on an extended east–west axis. At the start of the funeral ceremony, attendants transported the body westward across the Nile. Once beyond the land under cultivation, the procession reached the valley temple, connected to the Nile by a canal. In the valley temple of Khafra is a central T-shaped hallway, where floors of white calcite set off walls and pillars of costly red Aswan granite. Light cascaded in through slits in the upper walls and the red granite roof.

Beyond the valley temple, a raised and covered causeway led westward into the desert for about a third of a mile (0.2 km) to the funerary temple, adjoined to the pyramid's east face. Here an embalmer preserved the dead king's body, and the living perpetuated the cult for his *ka*. Again, a rich variety of hard stone made for a vivid coloristic effect; relief sculptures probably added to the funerary temple's decoration, but most have perished over time. Next to the valley temple of Khafra stands the Great Sphinx, carved from an outcropping of rock left after quarrying stone (fig. **3.9**). (Like pyramid, sphinx is originally a Greek term.) Uncomfortable with human representation in art, later Islamic residents of Giza damaged the massive sculpture, obscuring details of its face, and the top of the head is also missing. Still, scholars believe that the sculptors combined a portrait of Khafra (or possibly Khufu) with the crouching body (and thus strength) of a lion. Its vast scale also proclaims the king's power.

The change in funerary architecture suggests a shift in the way Egyptians perceived their ruler. The smooth-sided pyramid was the shape of the *ben-ben*, a sacred stone relic in Heliopolis, center of the sun cult. These monumental tombs may therefore have emphasized the solar aspect of the king's person; indeed, the change in building practice coincides more or less with the king's adoption of the title "son of Ra." The change in orientation for the complexes also meant that the king's funerary temple did not face the northern stars, as before, but the rising sun in the east, which signified eternity through its daily rising and setting. In contrast to the funerary complex for Djoser (see figs. 3.4 and 3.5), the Giza complex contains no buildings for reenacting rituals of kingship. This suggests that the perpetual performance of these rituals was no longer the dead king's task. Now, his role was to rise to the sun-god on the sun's rays, perhaps symbolized by the pyramid's sloping sides, and to accompany him on his

Excerpt from the Pyramid Text of Unis (r. 2341–2311 BCE)

King Unis of the Fifth Dynasty built a pyramid at Saqqara on the walls of which were inscribed a series of incantations and prayers for the afterlife of the pharaoh. So-called Pyramid Texts such as these were placed in tombs throughout Egyptian history for both royal and nonroyal burials. Some of their formulas were adapted for different versions of the Book of the Dead. Though the earliest text to survive dates from about 2320 BCE, the prayers may have been composed much earlier.

The Resurrection of King Unis

A pale sky darken, stars hide away,
Nations of heavenly bowmen are shaken,
Bones of the earth gods tremble—
All cease motion, are still, for they have looked upon Unis,
  the King,

Whose soul rises in glory, transfigured, a god,
Alive among his fathers of old time, nourished by ancient mothers.

The King, this is he! Lord of the twisty ways of wisdom
(whose very mother knew not his name),
His magnificence lights the black sky,
His power flames in the Land of the Risen—
Like Atum his father, who bore him;
And once having born him, strong was the Son more than
  the Father!

The *Kas* of the King hover about him;
Feminine spirits steady his feet;
Familiar gods hang over him;
Uraei (cobras) rear from his brow;
And his guiding Serpent precedes:
"Watch over the Soul! Be helpful, O Fiery One!"
All the mighty companions are guarding the King!

Source: *Ancient Egyptian Literature: An Anthology*, tr. John I. Foster (Austin, TX: University of Texas Press, 2001)

endless cycle of regeneration. Texts in the form of chants or prayers inscribed on the interior walls of some later Old Kingdom pyramids express this conception of the role of the king vividly.

The *Primary Source* text reproduced above, from the pyramid of Unis in Saqqara, dates to about 2320 BCE and describes the king's resurrection and ascension.

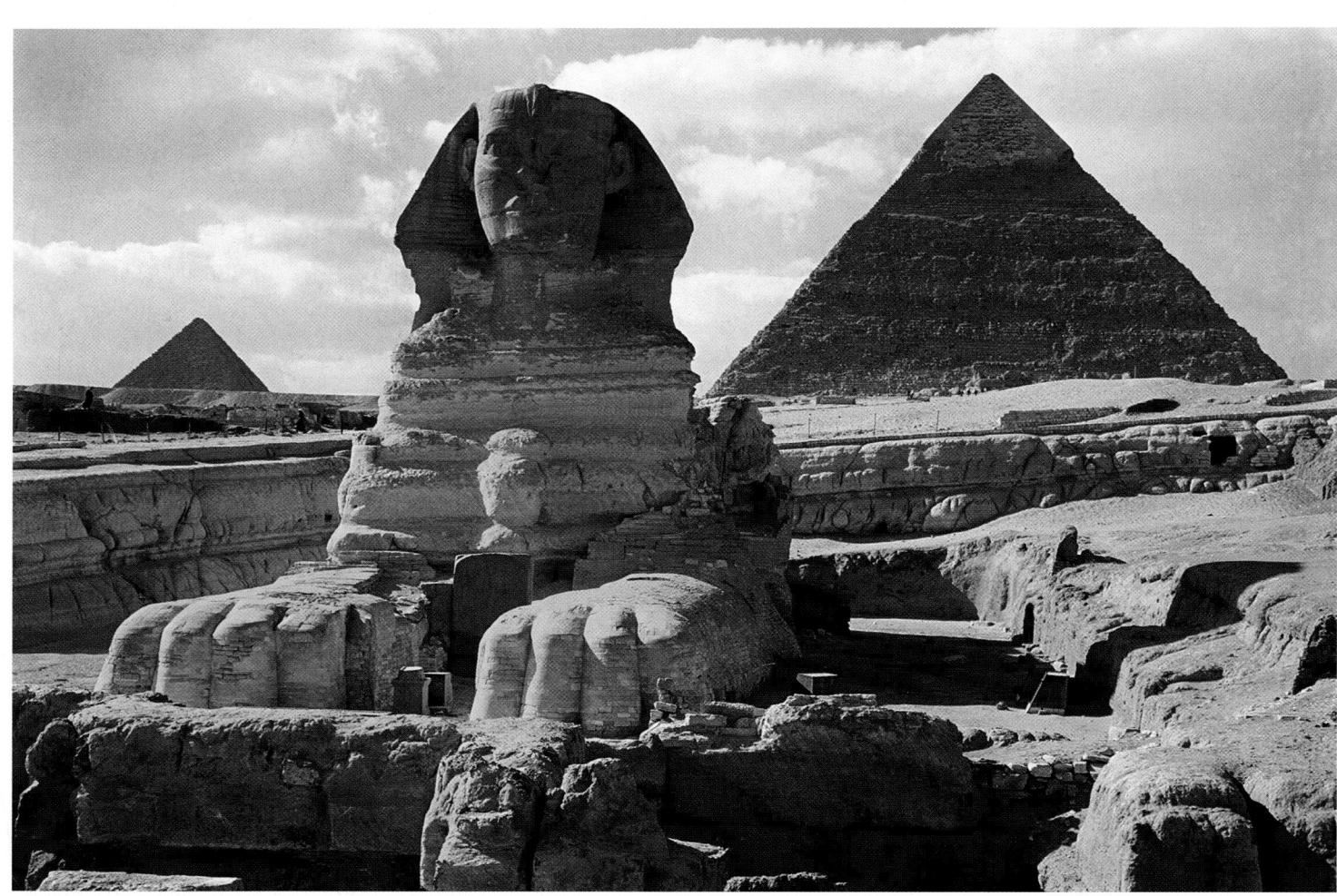

3.9   The Great Sphinx, Giza. ca. 2570–2544 BCE. Sandstone, height 65' (19.8 m)

Representing the Human Figure

In the hall in the valley temple of Khafra, a series of indentations in the paving show that 23 seated statues of the king once lined its walls. Archaeologists discovered one of these almost intact and six in poorer condition, interred in the temple floor. The best-preserved statue represents the seated king in a rigidly upright and frontal pose (fig. **3.10**). This pose allowed him to watch—and thus take part in—rituals enacted in his honor; frontality gave him presence. Behind him, the falcon Horus spreads his wings protectively around his head. Like the *Palette of King Narmer*, this sculpture neatly expresses qualities of kingship. Horus declares the king his earthly manifestation and protégé, and the king's muscular form indicates his power. The smooth agelessness of the latter's face bespeaks his eternal nature, while the sculpture's compact form gives it a solidity that suggests permanence. The intertwined plants —papyrus and perhaps sedge—carved between the legs of his chair

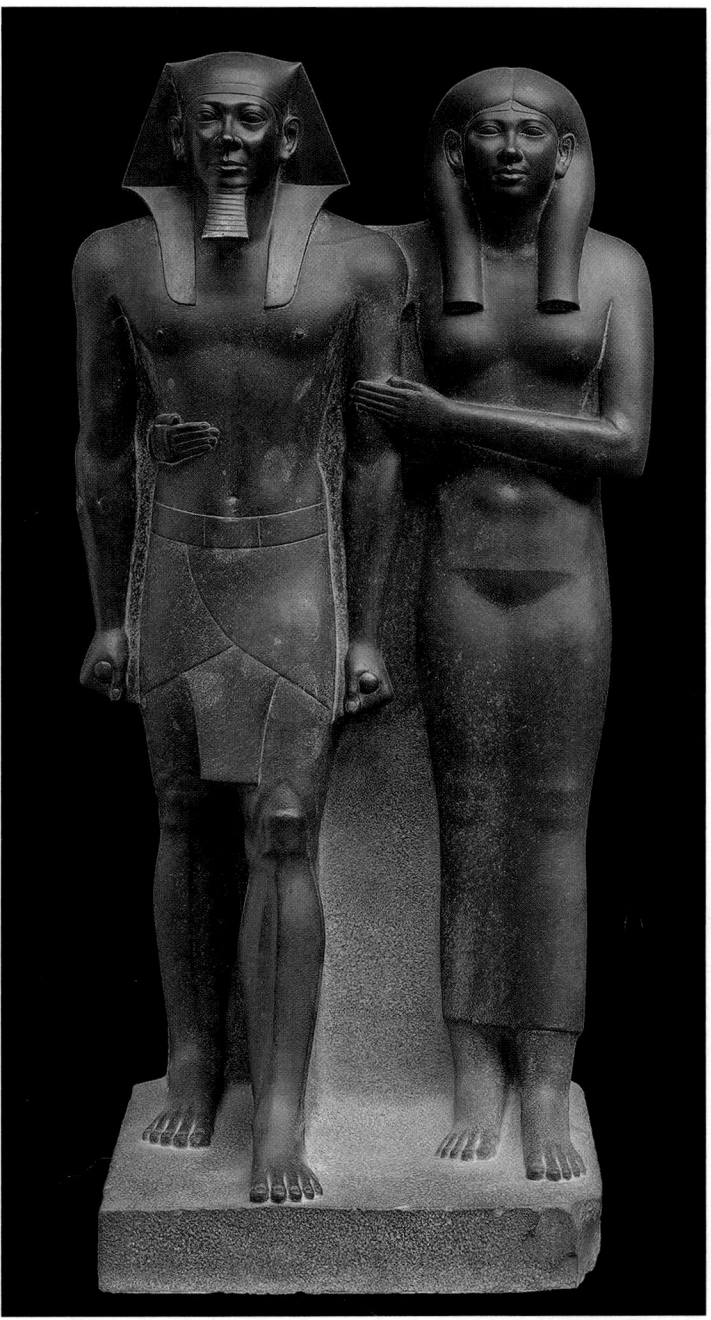

3.11 Menkaure and His Wife, Queen Khamerernebty II, from Giza. ca. 2515 BCE. Slate, height 54½" (138.4 cm). Museum of Fine Arts, Boston. Harvard University—Boston Museum of Fine Arts Expedition

are indigenous to both Lower and Upper Egypt, indicating the territorial reach of royal authority and the unity of the land. Even the stone used for his image expresses the king's control of distant lands: Diorite came from the deserts of Nubia. A hard stone, it lends itself to fine detail and a high polish, and the strong Egyptian light pouring in through the temple's louvered ceiling and reflected off the white calcite pavement must have made the figure glisten.

A slightly later, three-quarter-life-size group in schist represents King Menkaure and his chief wife Khamerernebty II (fig. **3.11**). It shares important features with the statue of Khafra. Carved in one piece with an upright back slab, it exhibits a similar

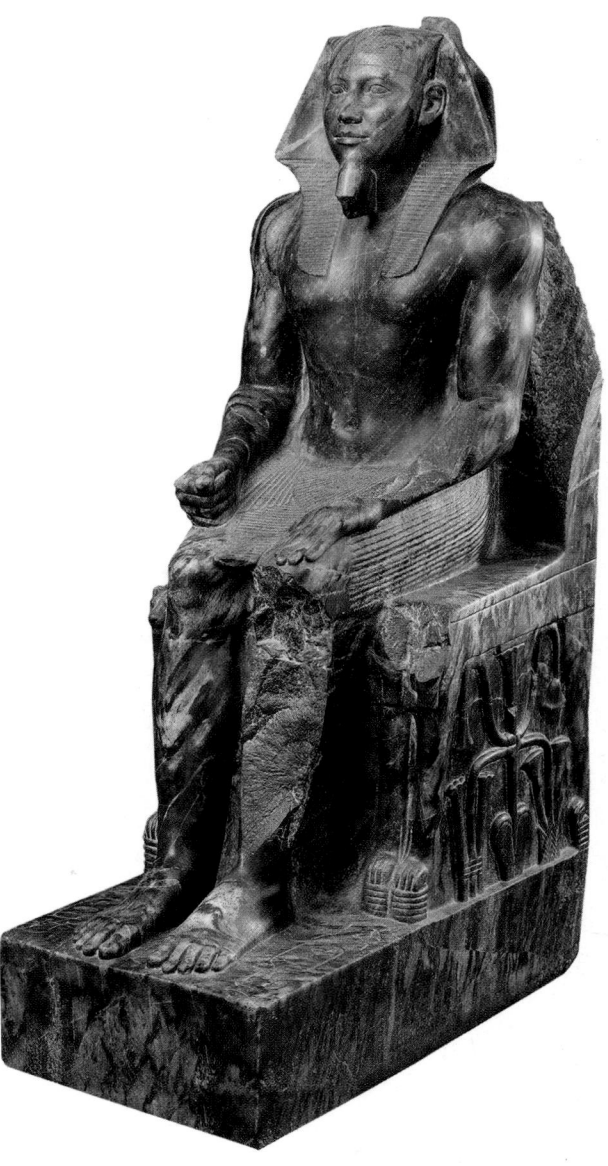

3.10 *Khafra*, from Giza. ca. 2500 BCE. Diorite, height 66" (167.7 cm). Egyptian Museum, Cairo

rigid frontality. One reason for this may have been the sculpture's intended location and function. This group, too, may have come from the king's valley temple.

The artist depicted Menkaure and his queen with several characteristics in common. Of almost identical height, both are frozen in a motionless stride with the left foot forward. Though the king is more muscular than Khamerernebty, and though she is draped in a thin dress hemmed at her ankles while he is half nude, smooth surfaces and a high polish characterize both bodies. Menkaure's headdress even echoes the form of Khamerernebty's hair. These common qualities establish an appearance of unity, and the queen's embrace further unifies the pair.

In some cases, traces of paint show that sculptors added details to their work in color, though whether they always painted statues carved in high-quality hard stone is hard to assess. A pair of Fourth Dynasty sculptures from a mastaba tomb at Meidum are carved from limestone, which is softer than diorite and does not yield such fine surface detail (fig. **3.12**). Here, the artist painted

skin tones, hair, garments, and jewelry, using the standard convention of a darker tone for a male, a lighter tone for a female. Rock-crystal pupils so animate the eyes that, in later years, fearful robbers gouged the eyes out of similar figures before looting the tombs they occupied. Inscriptions identify this pair as Rahotep and his wife Nofret, and describe their social status: He is a government official and she is a "dependent of the king." Like the royal portraits, these figures are represented with ritualized gestures and in full frontality.

This rigid frontality is the norm for royal and elite sculptures in the round. In relief and painting, there is also a remarkable consistency in stance among royal and elite subjects. The standard pose, as illustrated on the *Palette of King Narmer* (see fig. 3.2) and on a wooden stele found in the mastaba of a court official of Djoser, Hesy-ra, at Saqqara (fig. **3.13**), is altogether nonnaturalistic. In the case of the latter, frontal shoulders and arms and a frontal kilt combine with a profile head (with a frontal eye) and legs; the figure has two left feet, with high arches and a single toe.

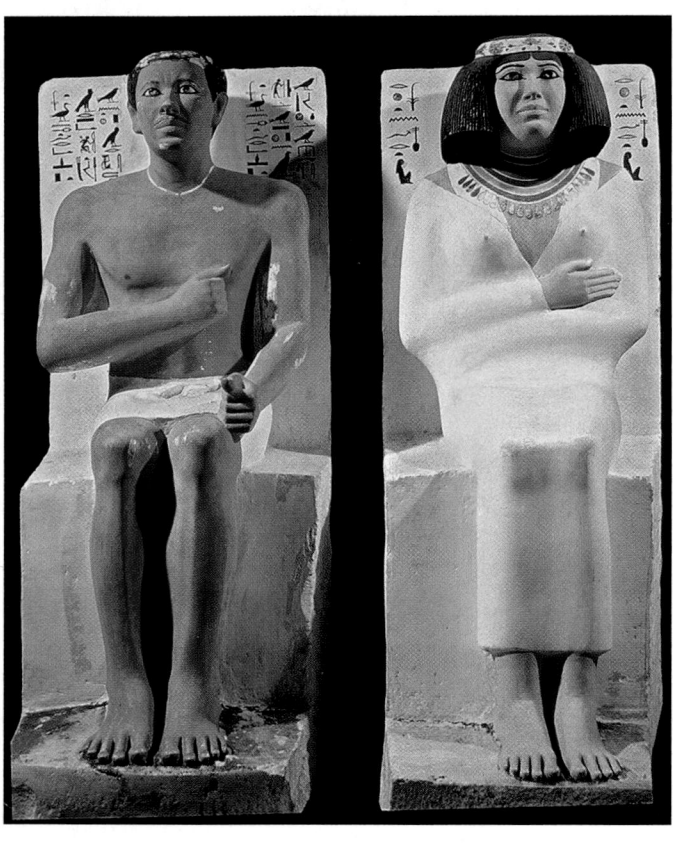

3.12   Prince Rahotep and His Wife, Nofret. ca. 2580 BCE. Painted limestone, height 47¼" (120 cm). Egyptian Museum, Cairo

3.13   *Relief Panel of Hesy-ra*, from Saqqara. ca. 2660 BCE. Wood, height 45" (114.3 cm). Egyptian Museum, Cairo

3.14   Grid showing proportional guidelines for relief panel of Hesy-ra.

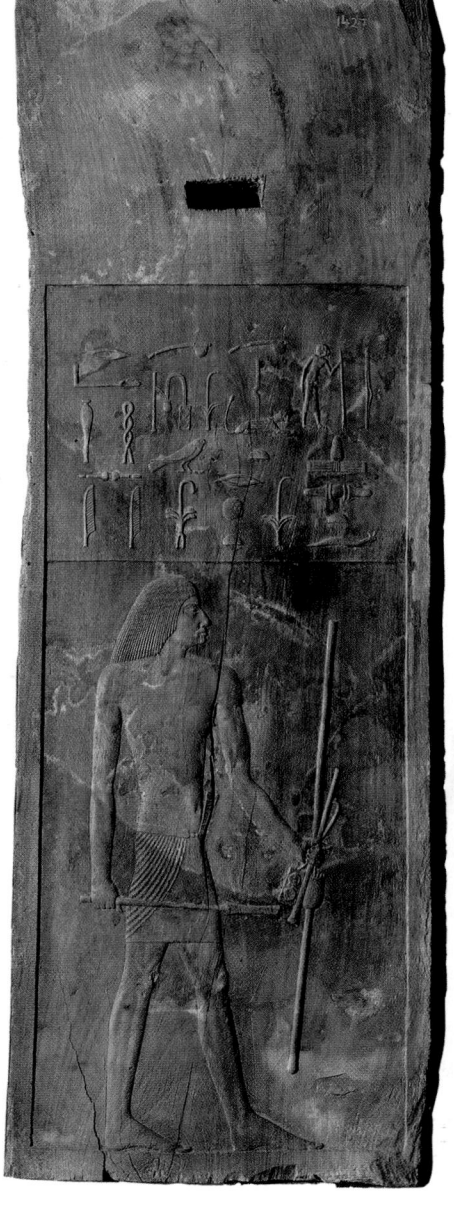

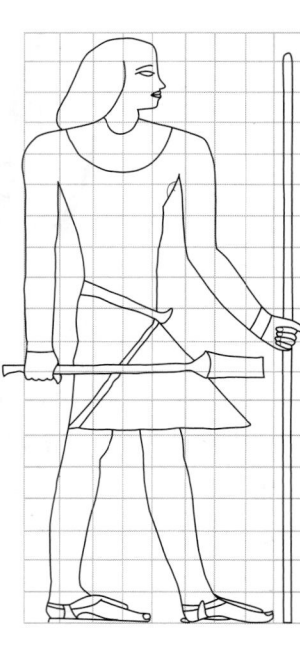

The representation is conceptual or intellectual rather than visual: The artist depicts what the mind knows, not what the eye sees. This artificial stance contributes to the legibility of the image, but it also makes the figure static.

THE CANON Body proportions are also consistent enough in royal and elite sculpture in the round and in relief and painting to suggest that artists relied on guidelines for designing the human image. In fact, traces of such guidelines are still visible on reliefs and paintings. This **canon** (set of rules) began in the Fifth Dynasty with a grid superimposed over the human image: One vertical line ran through the body at the point of the ear, and as many as seven horizontal lines divided the body according to a standard module. Over time, the guidelines changed, but the principle of the canon remained: Although body-part measurements might vary from person to person, the relationship between parts remained constant. With that relationship established, an artist could make a human portrait at any scale, taking the proportions of body parts from copybooks. Unlike later systems of perspective, where a figure's size suggests its distance from a viewer, in the Egyptian canon size signaled social status.

For elite male officials, there were two kinds of ideal image, each representing a different life stage. One is a youthful, physically fit image, like that of Hesy-ra (see fig. 3.13). In the other, a paunch, rolls of fat, or slack muscles, and signs of age on the face indicate maturity. A painted limestone figure of a scribe, perhaps

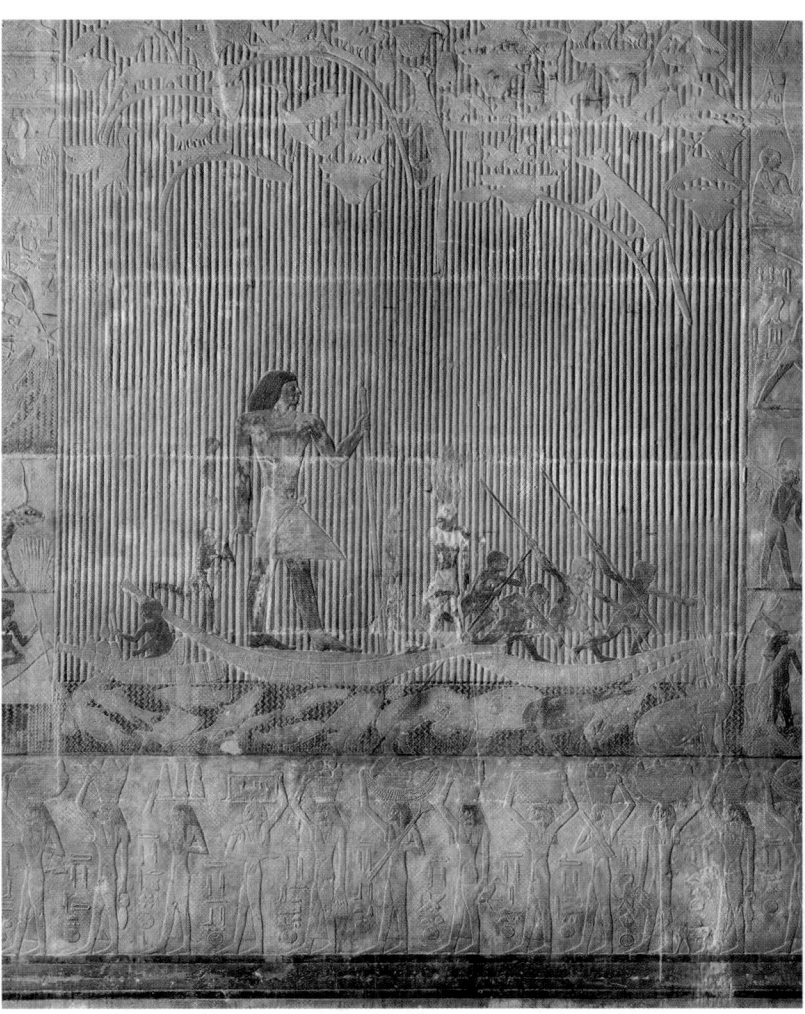

3.16 *Ti Watching a Hippopotamus Hunt*, Tomb of Ti, Saqqara. ca. 2510–2460 BCE. Painted limestone relief, height approx. 45" (114.3 cm)

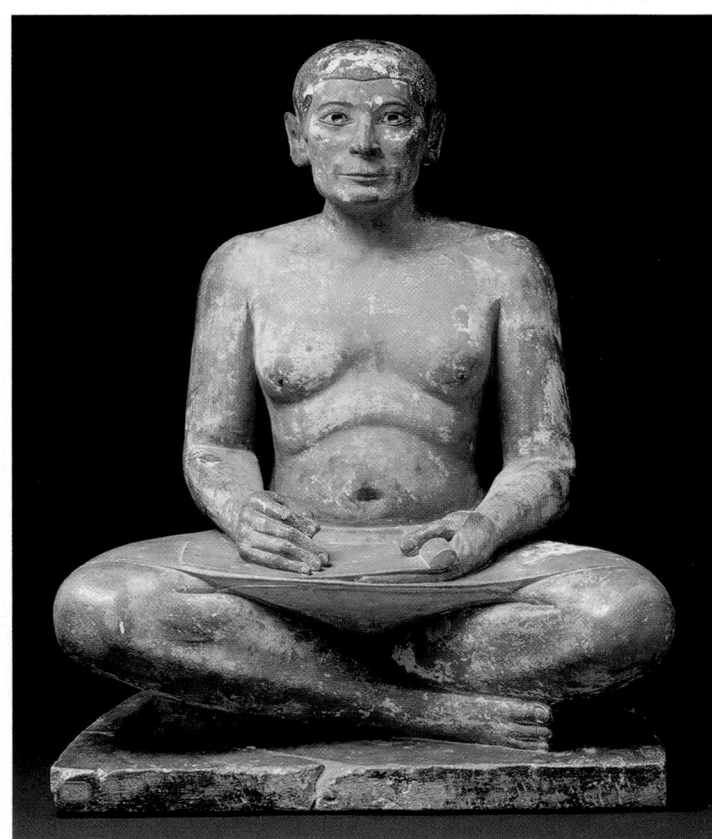

3.15 *Seated Scribe*, from Saqqara. ca. 2400 BCE. Limestone, height 21" (53.3 cm). Musée du Louvre, Paris

named Kay, from his mastaba at Saqqara, is an example of the second type (fig. **3.15**). He is depicted rigidly upright and frontal but, unlike Hesy-ra, his body shows signs of slackening, in the sallow cheeks, sagging jaw, and loose stomach. Since Egyptian society was mostly illiterate, a scribe had high status; indeed, the artist depicted the figure seated on the floor in the act of writing, the very skill in which his status resided. The image reinforces his social status: It shows an official who has succeeded in his career, eats well, and relies on subordinates to do physical work on his behalf.

These conventions of pose, proportion, and appearance applied only to the highest echelons of society—royalty and courtiers. By contrast, the lower the status of the subject, the more relaxed and naturalistic their pose. Once the conventions were established, ignoring them could even result in a change of meaning for a figure, especially a change of status, from king or official to servant or captive. Fine low-relief paintings in the tomb chapel of Ti, a high official during the Fifth Dynasty, at Saqqara encapsulate the correlation between rank and degree of naturalism neatly (fig. **3.16**). In one section, Ti stands on a boat in a thicket of papyrus, observing a hippopotamus hunt. He stands rigidly in the traditional composite view, legs and head in profile, torso and eye frontal, while hunters, shown on a smaller scale, attack their prey from a second boat in a variety of active poses that more closely resemble nature. Zigzagging blue lines beneath the boats denote the river, where hippopotami and fish—on the lowest rung of the natural world—swim about in naturalistic poses. Similarly, nesting birds and predatory foxes freely inhabit the papyrus blossoms overhead.

PAINTINGS AND RELIEFS Like statues in tombs, paintings and reliefs played a role in the Egyptian belief system. Images such as *Ti Watching a Hippopotamus Hunt* (see fig. 3.16) allowed the deceased to continue activities he or she had enjoyed while alive. They also functioned on metaphorical levels. The conquest of nature, for instance, served as a metaphor for triumph over death. Death was the realm of Osiris, as god of the underworld, and so were the life-giving waters of the Nile, because of his regeneration after Seth had murdered him. Osiris was the god of fertility and resurrection, to whom Egyptians could liken the deceased. And, because Isis hid Horus in a papyrus thicket to protect him from Seth, they saw a papyrus stand as a place of rebirth, much like the tomb itself. Traditionally, too, a boat was the vehicle that carried the *ka* through its eternal journey in the afterlife. By contrast, Egyptians viewed the crop-destroying hippopotamus as an animal of evil and chaos, and so as the embodiment of the destructive Seth, lord of the deserts. Thus, meanings specific to its funerary context may have encoded the entire painting. Other Old Kingdom tomb paintings depict family members buried alongside the principal tomb owner, or as company for the *ka* in the afterlife. Some scenes depict rituals of the cult of the dead (that is, rituals in honor of the dead), or portray offerings and agricultural activities designed to provide the *ka* with an eternal food supply. In these scenes, the deceased typically looks on, but does not participate.

THE MIDDLE KINGDOM: REASSERTING TRADITION THROUGH THE ARTS

The central government of the Old Kingdom disintegrated with the death of the Sixth Dynasty king Pepy II in around 2152 BCE. This led to the turbulent First Intermediate Period, which lasted over a century and when local or regional overlords fostered antagonisms between Upper and Lower Egypt. The two regions reunited in the Eleventh Dynasty, as King Nebhepetra Mentuhotep or Mentuhotep II (ca. 2061–2010 BCE) gradually reasserted regal authority over all of Egypt. The late Eleventh, Twelfth and Thirteenth Dynasties make up the Middle Kingdom (ca. 2040–1640 BCE), when much of the art deliberately echoed Old Kingdom forms, especially in the funerary realm. The art asserted continuity with the golden days of the past. Sculptures of some members of the royal family, however, also show breaks with tradition.

Royal Portraiture: Changing Expressions and Proportions

A fragmentary quartzite sculpture of Senwosret III (r. 1878–1841 BCE) indicates a rupture with convention in the representation of royalty (fig. **3.17**). Rather than sculpting a smooth-skinned, idealized face, untouched by time—as had been done for over 1,000 years—the artist depicted a man scarred by signs of age. His brow creases, his eyelids droop, and lines score the flesh beneath his eyes. Scholars have described the image as "introspective," and reading it against the background of Senwosret III's troubled campaign of military expansion in Nubia to the south, they see the portrait's physical imperfections as reflections of the king's stress. Facial expressions or signs of age, however, can signify different things to different societies, and it is equally likely that the tight-lipped expression reflects a new face of regal authority, projecting firm resolve. Sculptors of this time tended to combine the aged face with a body that was still youthful and powerful.

As facial expressions became more naturalistic in royal images of this time, so the canon of proportions changed too. This is clear if we compare the Old Kingdom sculpture of Queen Khamererebty (see fig. 3.11) with a sculpture of Lady Sennuwy (fig. **3.18**), the wife of a provincial governor, found at Kerma in Upper Nubia. Depictions of women during the Middle Kingdom

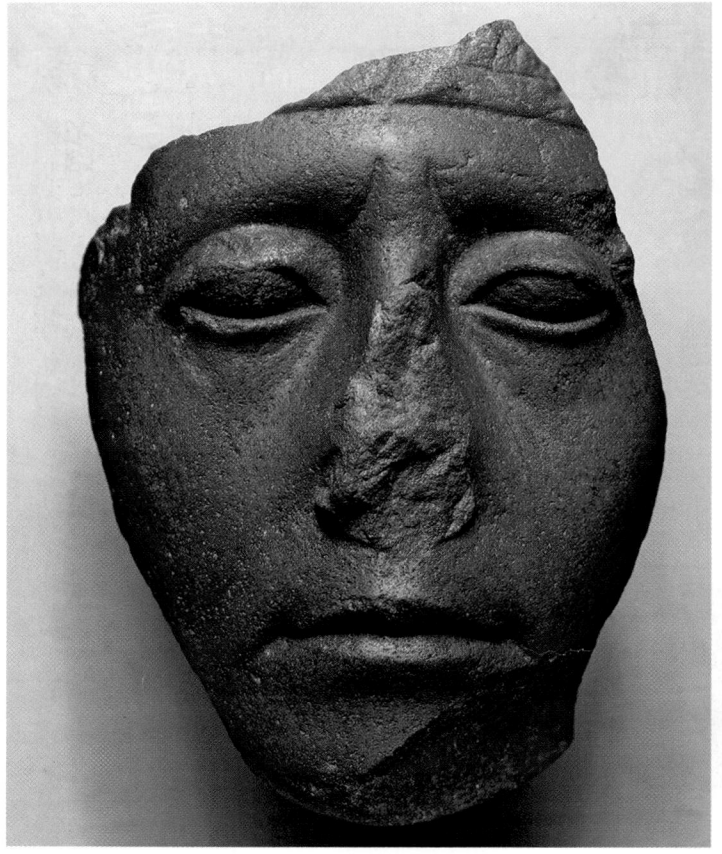

3.17 *Senwosret III*. ca. 1850 BCE. Quartzite, height 6½" (16.5 cm). Metropolitan Museum of Art, New York. Purchase, Edward S. Harkness Gift, 1926 (26.7.1394)

have increasingly narrower shoulders and waists, and slimmer limbs. Males have proportionally smaller heads, and lack the tight musculature of their Old Kingdom counterparts. Though subtle, these changes distinguish representations of the human body from period to period.

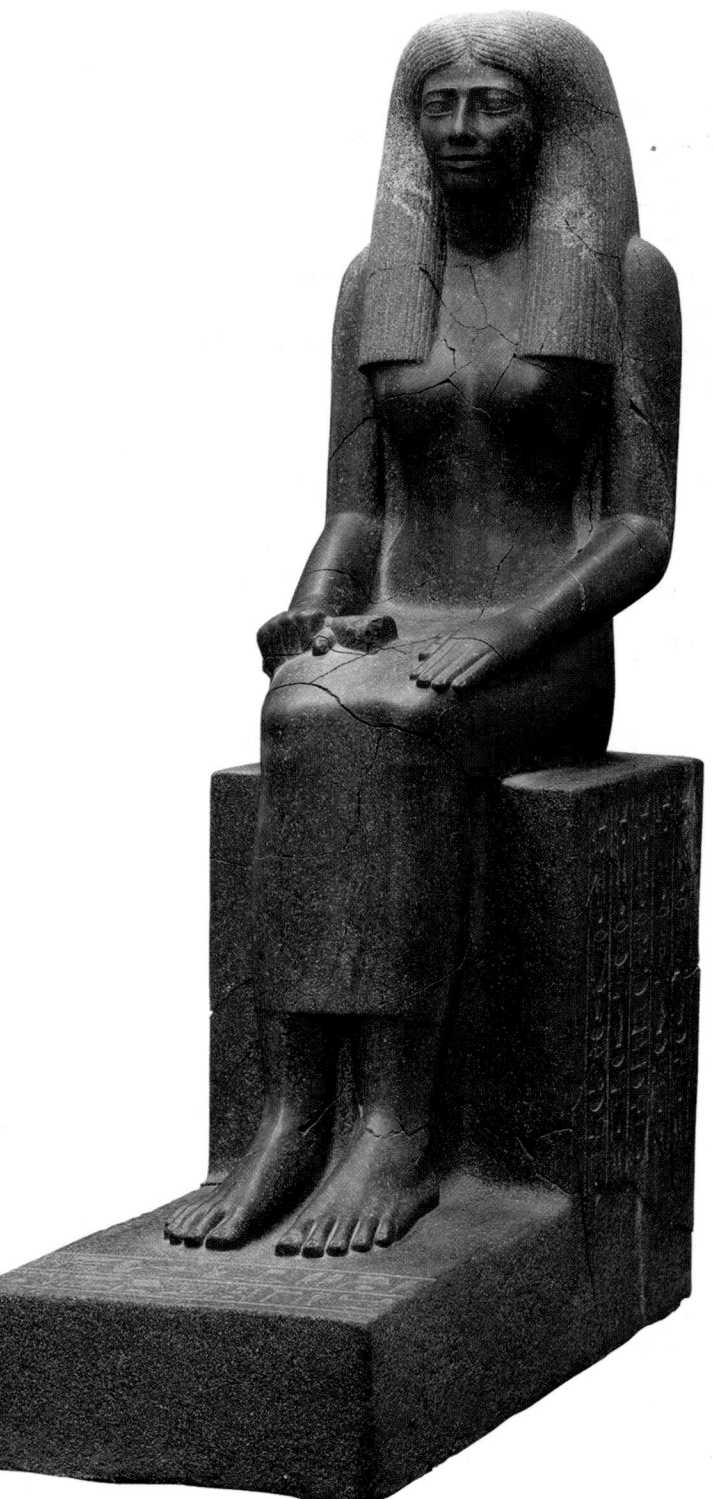

3.18 *Lady Sennuwy*. ca. 1920 BCE. Granite, height 67¾" (172 cm), depth 45⅞" (116.5 cm). Museum of Fine Arts, Boston. Harvard University—Boston Museum of Fine Arts Expedition. 14.720

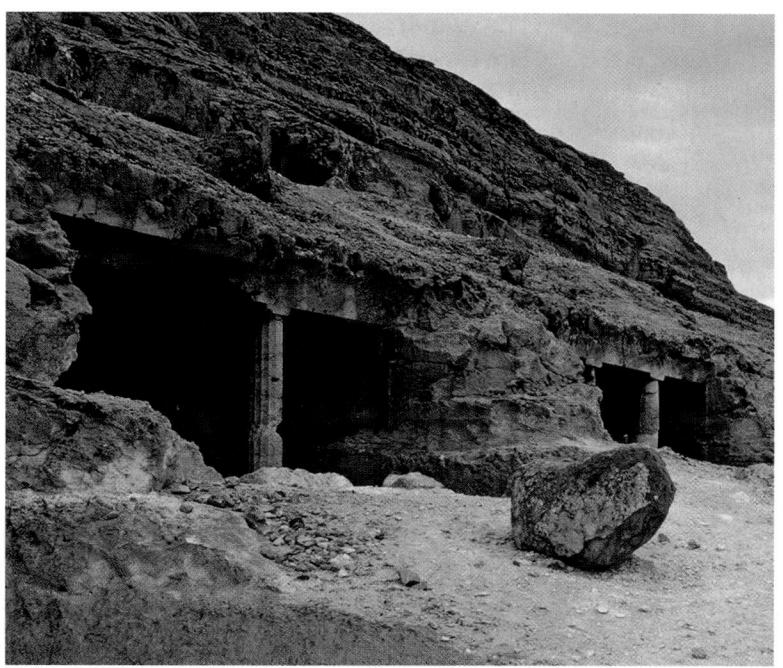

3.19 Rock-cut tombs, Beni Hasan, B-H 3-5, 11th and 12th Dynasties. ca. 1950–1900 BCE

Funerary Architecture

Burial patterns among court officials and other members of the elite stayed relatively constant during the Middle Kingdom, with most choosing interment in sunken tombs and mastabas. Already known in the Old Kingdom, rock-cut tombs were especially popular at this time. Fine examples still exist at Beni Hasan, the burial place of a powerful ruling family of Middle Egypt in the Eleventh and Twelfth Dynasties (fig. **3.19**). The tombs were hollowed out of a terrace of rock on the east bank of the Nile and offered stunning views across the river. Inside, a vestibule led to a columned hall and burial chamber, where a niche framed a statue of the deceased (fig. **3.20**). As in Old Kingdom tombs, paintings and painted relief decorated the walls. The section illustrated in figure **3.21**, from the restored tomb of Khnum-hotep, shows workers restraining and feeding oryxes (a type of antelope trapped in the desert and raised in captivity as a pet).

As in the Old Kingdom, tomb owners believed the paintings provided nourishment, company, and pastimes for the dead. The living placed a wide variety of objects in tombs along with the dead, including objects made of **faience**, a glass paste fired to a shiny opaque finish. The figurine shown in figure **3.22** came from a tomb in Thebes, and represents a schematized woman. Her legs stop at the knees, possibly to restrict her mobility, or because legs were not essential to her function. The artist delineated her breasts and pubic area, and painted a cowrie-shell girdle to emphasize her belly and hips. Her function may have been as a fertility object, to enhance family continuity among the living and regeneration of the dead into a new life in the beyond. Egyptians associated the blue-green color of the faience with fertility, regeneration, and the goddess Hathor.

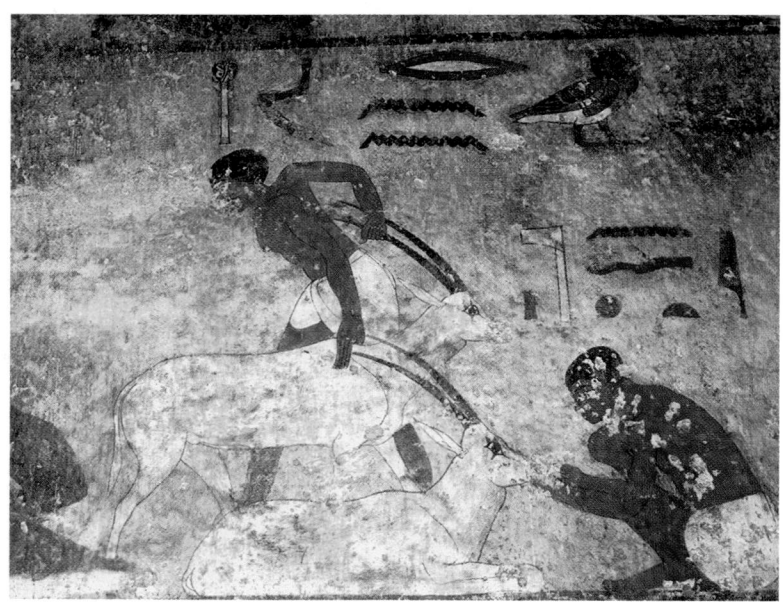

3.21 *Feeding the Oryxes*. Tomb of Khnum-hotep, Beni Hasan. ca. 1928–1895 BCE. Wall painting (detail)

Often, the living buried jewelry with the deceased. Egyptians used jewelry widely, for daily personal adornment, for formal occasions such as court audiences, to bedeck cult statues, and to protect mummies. Many of the surviving pieces show extraordinary technological skill on the part of the jewelers. In the pyramid complex at Dahshur, the tomb of Mereret, a royal woman at the court of Senwosret III, contained two valuable pectorals, or large pendants. One is designed as a shrine with lotus-capital columns, within which two sphinxes trample enemies underfoot. With one raised forepaw, they support a cartouche of the king's name (fig. **3.23**). A vulture spreads its wings overhead. In wearing the pectoral, Mereret broadcast Senwosret's power to overcome foes and assert order. At the same time, the pectoral expressed royal wealth: The jeweler fashioned it in **cloisonné** (a metalworking technique often used for enamel), using a gold framework for valuable stones brought from afar: carnelian from the eastern desert, turquoise from Sinai, and lapis lazuli from present-day Afghanistan. As a mummy ornament, the pectoral may have offered protection against malevolent forces.

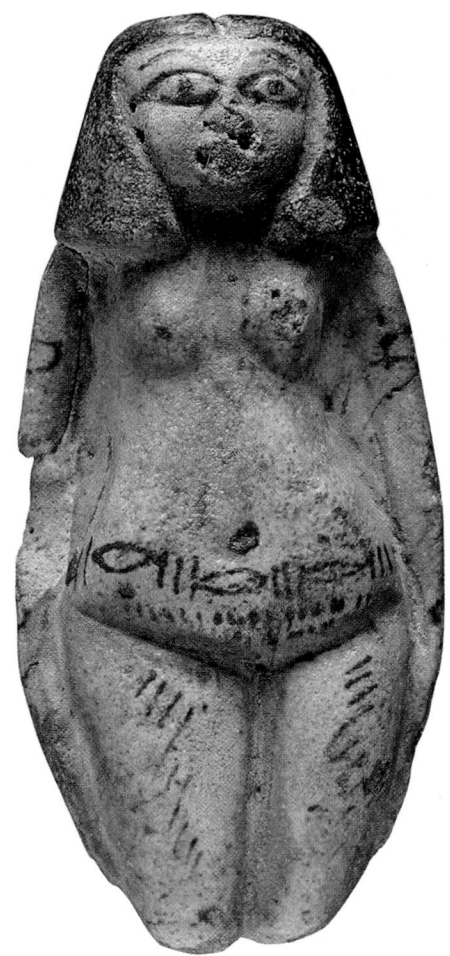

3.22 *Female Figurine*, from Thebes. 12th–13th Dynasties. Faience, height 3⅓" (8.5 cm). The British Museum, London. Courtesy of the Trustees

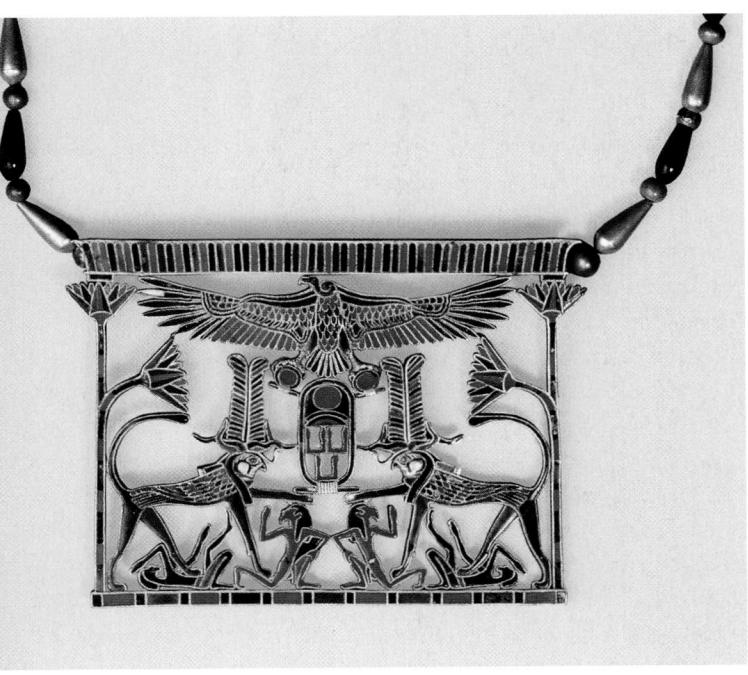

3.23 Pectoral of Mereret, from tomb in pyramid complex of Senwosret III at Dahshur. 12th Dynasty. Gold, carnelian, lapis lazuli, and turquoise, height 2⅖" (6.1 cm). Egyptian Museum, Cairo

The stability of the Middle Kingdom was not to last. As central authority weakened after about 1785 BCE, local governors usurped power. During the Twelfth Dynasty, immigrants from Palestine known as the Hyksos (a Greek rendering of the Egyptian for "rulers of foreign lands") moved into the Nile Delta, gaining control of the area and forcing the king southward to Thebes. The era of their control is known as the Second Intermediate Period.

THE NEW KINGDOM: RESTORED GLORY

The first king of the Eighteenth Dynasty, Ahmose (r. 1550–1525 BCE), finally expelled the Hyksos from Egypt. The 500 years after their expulsion—covering the Eighteenth, Nineteenth, and Twentieth Dynasties—are designated the New Kingdom. They constitute a time of renewed territorial expansion and tremendous prosperity for Egypt, and a time when the arts flourished. Tremendous architectural projects were accomplished along the full length of the Nile, centering on the region of Thebes (present-day Luxor). Of these projects, many of the secular buildings, including palaces and forts, were made of mud brick and have perished. Stone tombs and temples, however, retain a measure of their former glory.

Royal Burials in the Valley of the Kings

Changes in burial practices expose a major difference between the Old Kingdom and the New. Having witnessed the loss of order that allowed plundering of royal burials, Eighteenth Dynasty kings abandoned the practice of marking their tombs with pyramids. Instead, they excavated tombs out of the rock face in the Valley of the Kings west of Thebes, and their entrances were concealed after burial. Excavations have revealed that in these tombs a corridor led deep into the rock to a burial chamber flanked by storage rooms. Decorating the burial chamber were paintings of the king with Osiris, Anubis, and Hathor, funerary deities who assured his passage from this world to the next. Rituals of the funerary cult took place away from the tomb, over a rocky outcropping to the east, at a temple on the edge of the land under cultivation.

HATSHEPSUT'S TEMPLE The best-preserved example of a New Kingdom funerary temple is that of the female king Hatshepsut (ca. 1478–1458 BCE) (fig. 3.24). Hatshepsut was the chief wife—and half-sister—of Thutmose II. On his death in 1479 BCE, power passed to Thutmose III, his young son by a minor wife. Designated regent for the young king, Hatshepsut ruled with him as female king until her death in 1458 BCE. She justified her unusual rule by claiming that her father, Thutmose I, had intended her to be his successor.

Nestled in the cliffside at Deir el-Bahri, Hatshepsut's temple sat beside the spectacular Eleventh Dynasty temple of

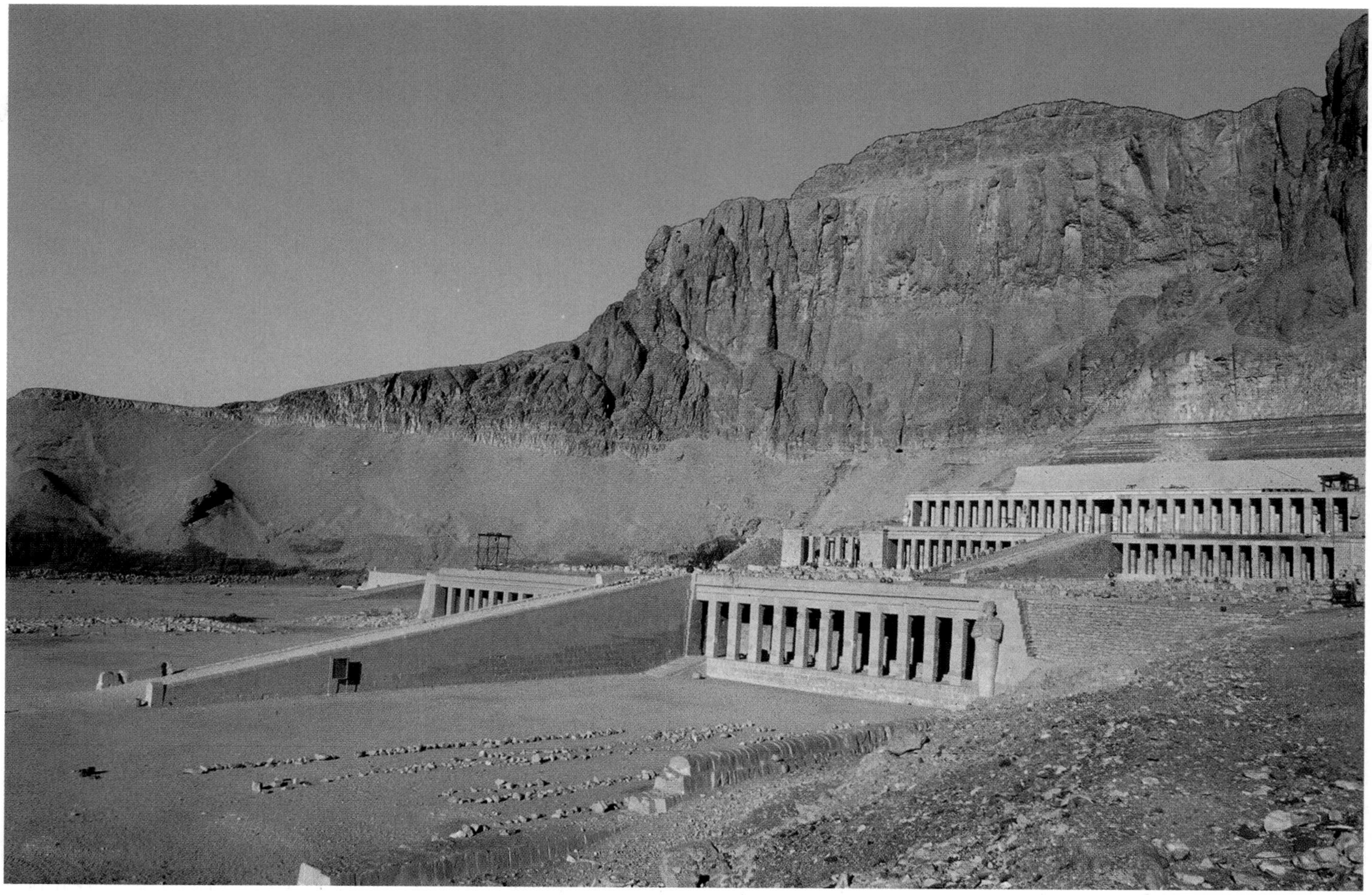

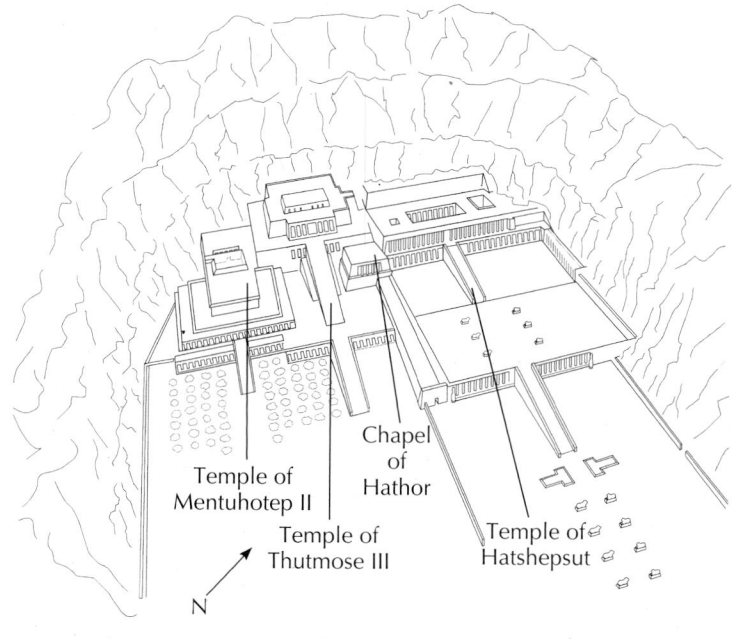

3.24 Temple of Hatshepsut, Deir el-Bahri. ca. 1478–1458 BCE

Mentuhotep II (fig. **3.25**), who had reunited Egypt over 500 years earlier during the Middle Kingdom. Senenmut, the architect who designed Hatshepsut's temple, may have modeled some of its features after this earlier temple, with its crowning pyramid or mastaba and terraces extending into the cliff face. Hatshepsut's temple is a striking response to its physical setting. Its ascending white limestone courts, linked by wide ramps on a central axis, echo the desert's strong horizontal ground-line and the clifftop above. Meanwhile, the bright light and shadows of the colonnades create a multitude of vertical lines that harmonize with the fissures of the cliff. With its clean contours, the royal structure imposes order on the less regularized forms of nature, just as the king's role was to impose order on chaos. At the time of its construction, a causeway led from a valley temple by the Nile to the funerary temple. Trees lined the entrance way, and paired sphinxes faced each other. Cut into the rock at the farthest reach of the temple was the principal sanctuary, dedicated to Amun-Ra, god of the evening sun. Smaller chapels honored Anubis, god of embalming, and Hathor, goddess of the west. An altar dedicated to Ra-Horakhty stood on the upper terrace.

Throughout the complex, painted relief sculptures brought the walls to life, describing battles, a royal expedition to the land of Punt in search of myrrh trees for the terraces, and scenes of

3.25 Reconstruction of Temples, Deir el-Bahri, with temples of Mentuhotep II, Thutmose III, and Hatshepsut (after a drawing by Andrea Mazzei, Archivio White Star, Vercelli, Italy)

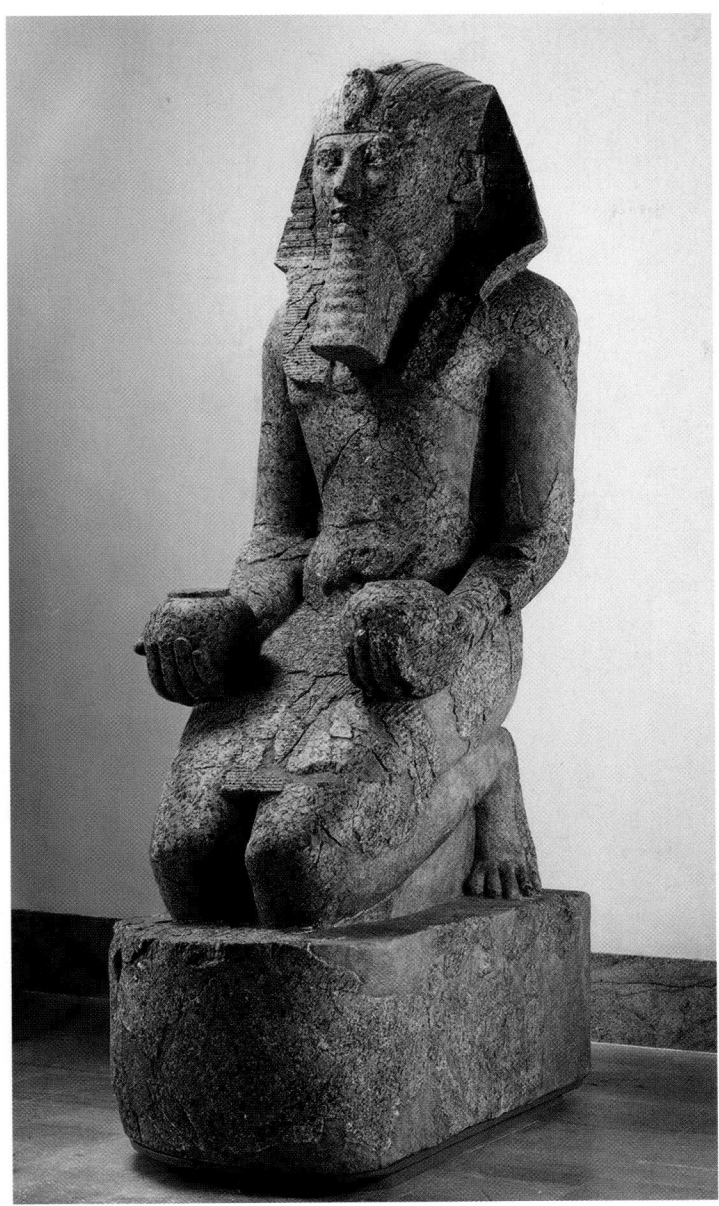

3.26 *Kneeling Figure of King Hatshepsut*, from Deir el-Bahri.
ca. 1473–1458 BCE. Red granite, height approx. 8'6" (2.59 m).
Metropolitan Museum of Art, New York. Rogers Fund, 1929 (29.3.1)

Deir el-Bahri. At some point after Hatshepsut's death, the uraeus cobras were meticulously removed from the granite sphinxes and seated statues at her mortuary complex. Perhaps the intention was to repudiate her royal descent. By the forty-second year of Thutmose III's reign, a more systematic elimination of her images and removal of her name from inscriptions was underway. Workmen smashed her statues and buried the fragments in two pits in front of the temple complex. Still, Hatshepshut's temple remains a monument to her memory. Archaeologists have recently identified an obese mummified body in an unmarked tomb in the Valley of the Kings as her mortal remains.

Temples to the Gods

Besides building their own funerary temples, Eighteenth Dynasty kings expended considerable resources on temples to the gods, such as the Theban divine triad: Amun, his consort Mut, and their son Khons. At Karnak and nearby Luxor, successive kings built two vast temple complexes to honor this triad, and on special festivals divine boats conveyed the gods' images along waterways between the temples.

THE TEMPLE OF AMUN-RA At the Temple of Amun-Ra (a manifestation of the god Amun) at Karnak, a vast wall encircled the temple buildings (fig. **3.27**). Entering the complex, a visitor walked through massive **pylons**, or gateways built as monuments to individual kings (and sometimes dismantled as building proceeded over the years). As a ceremonial procession moved within the buildings, these pylons marked its progress deeper and deeper into sacred space. Within the complex, a vast **hypostyle** hall (room with many columns) was the farthest point of access for all but priests and royalty (fig. **3.28**). Here, a forest of columns would awe the mind, their sheer mass rendering the human form almost insignificant. The architect placed the columns close to one another to support a ceiling of stone lintels which had to be shorter than wooden lintels to prevent them from breaking under their own weight. Nevertheless, the columns are far heavier than they needed to be, with the effect that a viewer senses the overwhelming presence of stone all around—heavy, solid, and permanent. Beyond the hall, a sacred lake allowed the king and priests to purify themselves before entering the temple proper. They proceeded through smaller halls, sun-drenched courts, and processional ways decorated with **obelisks**, tall stone markers topped by pyramid-shaped points, and chapels where they would pause to enact ceremonies. Every day the priests would cleanse and robe the images of the gods, and offer sacred meals to nourish them. The king and the priests conducted these rituals away from the public eye, with the result that they gained power for being shrouded in mystery.

Essential to the temple's ritual functioning was its metaphorical value: It symbolized the world at its inception. The columns of the hypostyle hall represented marsh plants in stylized form: Their capitals emulated the shape of papyrus flowers and buds—so that the building evoked the watery swamp of chaos out of

Thutmose I legitimizing his daughter's rule. Sculptures of the king and deities abounded. One of eight colossal red-granite statues from the third court (fig. **3.26**) depicts Hatshepsut kneeling as she makes an offering of two spherical jars. An inscription on the base records that the king is presenting *ma'at* (order) to Amun. Since kingship was a male office, she wears the regalia of a male king: a kilt, a false beard, and the **nemes headdress**, the striped cloth worn by kings. Although she is visibly female in some images, in this and many others she is depicted without breasts.

Sometime after Hatshepsut's demise, Thutmose III (r. 1479–1425) constructed his own temple between his mother's and Mentuhotep's, with the purpose of eclipsing Hatshepsut's. He designated his own temple as the destination of the divine boat carrying the statue of Amun in the Festival of the Wadi, held at

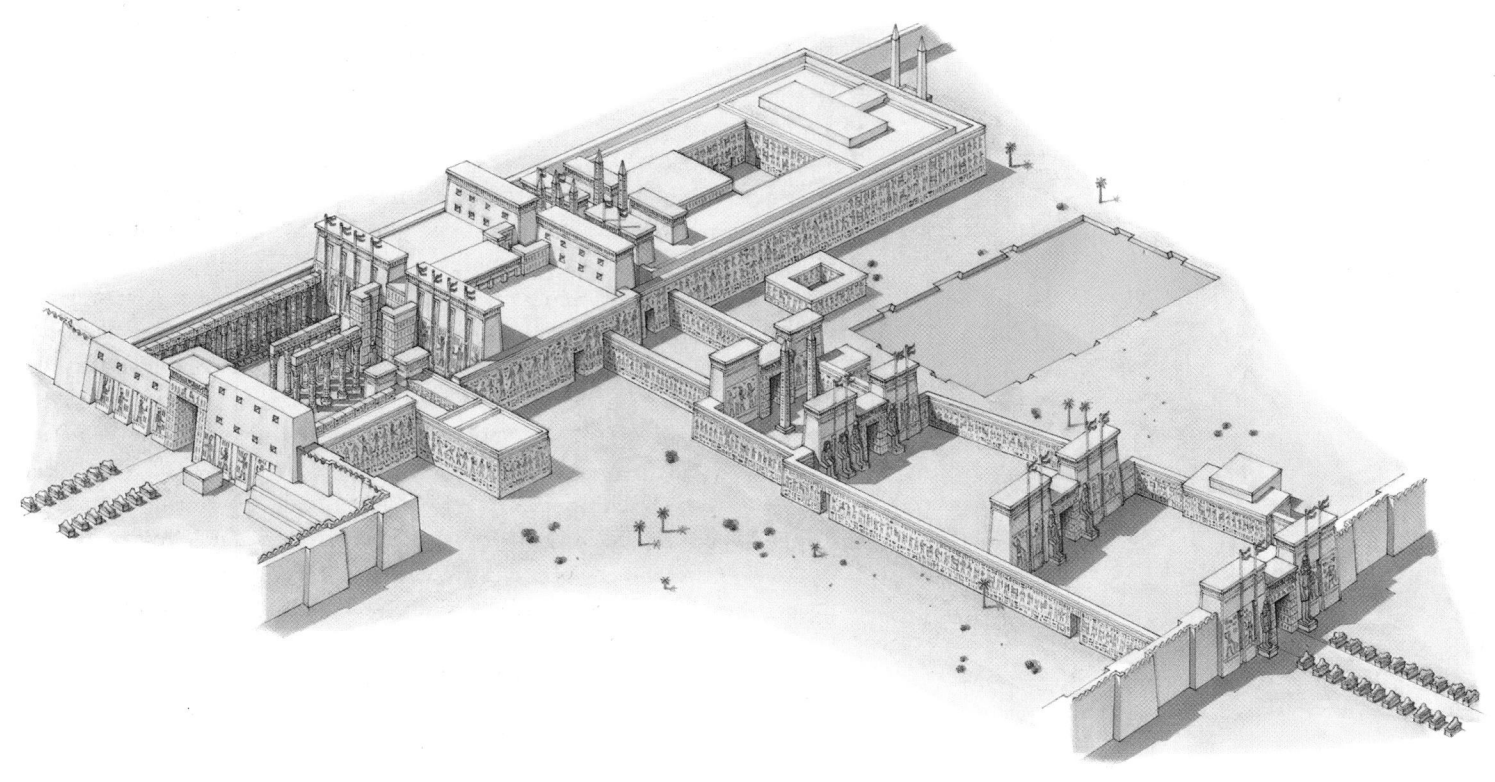

3.27 Reconstruction drawing of Temple of Amun-Ra, Karnak, Thebes

which the mound of creation emerged. The temple was thus the king's exhortation in stone to the gods to maintain cosmic order.

Throughout the complex, a distinctively Egyptian form of decoration covered the pylons and hall and enclosure walls: **sunken relief**. In this technique, the sculptor cut sharp outlines into the stone's face, and modeled the figures within the outlines, below the level of the background, rather than carving away the surface around figures to allow them to emerge from the stone. Light shining onto the stone's surface then cast shadows into the outlines, animating the figures without compromising the solid planar appearance of the wall. This type of relief was especially popular for decorating hard stone, since it required less carving away.

The subject of the reliefs at Karnak was the king's relationship with the gods. In one section, from the north exterior wall of the hypostyle hall, an upper register shows Seti I sacking the Hittite city of Kadesh on the Orontes River, and, in a lower register, his Libyan campaign (fig. **3.29**). Following convention, the king and his horse-drawn chariot are frozen against a background filled with hieroglyphs and soldiers, whose smaller scale glorifies the king's presence. The figures of the king and his horse are also cut more deeply than surrounding figures, resulting in a bolder outline. The king's might and the ruthless efficiency of his forces seem to assure victory, although neither battle was, in fact, decisive. Through his conquest of foreign forces, the king established order, *ma'at*.

3.28 Hypostyle hall of Temple of Amun-Ra, Karnak, Thebes. ca. 1290–1224 BCE

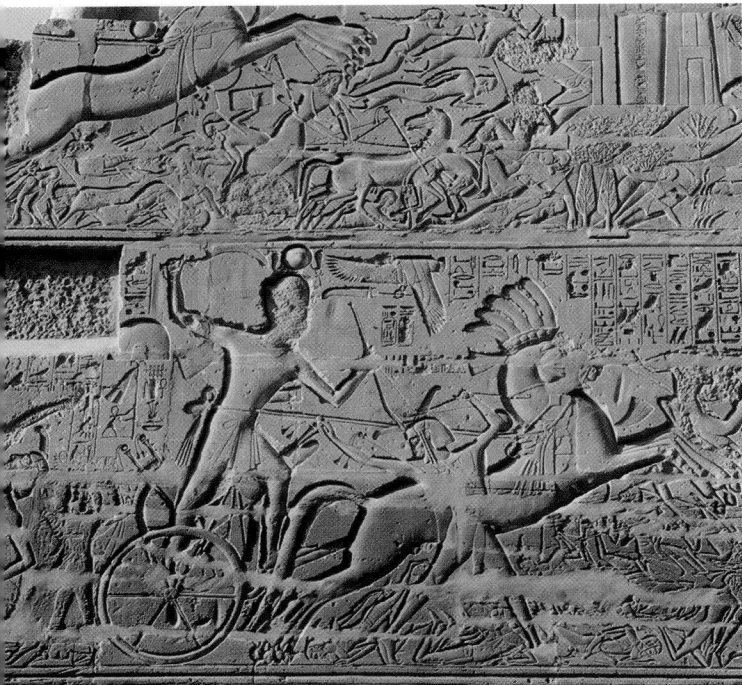

ABU SIMBEL Seti I's son, Ramesses II, ruled for 67 years during the Nineteenth Dynasty (ca. 1290–1224 BCE). He commissioned more architectural projects than any other Egyptian king, including a monumental temple dedicated to himself and Amun, Ra-Horakhty, and Ptah, carved into the sandstone at Abu Simbel on the west bank of the Nile (fig. **3.30**). Location alone made an eloquent statement: With the temple, the king marked his claim to the land of Kush in Lower Nubia, which was the origin of precious resources of gold, ivory, and animal pelts. A massive rock façade substitutes for a pylon, where four huge seated statues of the king almost 70 feet high flank the doorway, dwarfing any approaching visitor. Between the statues' legs, small figures represent members of the royal family. A niche above the entrance holds an image of Amun, who is shown as a falcon-headed figure crowned by a sun disk. Flanking this deeply carved sculpture are sunk-relief depictions of Ramesses holding out a statue of the

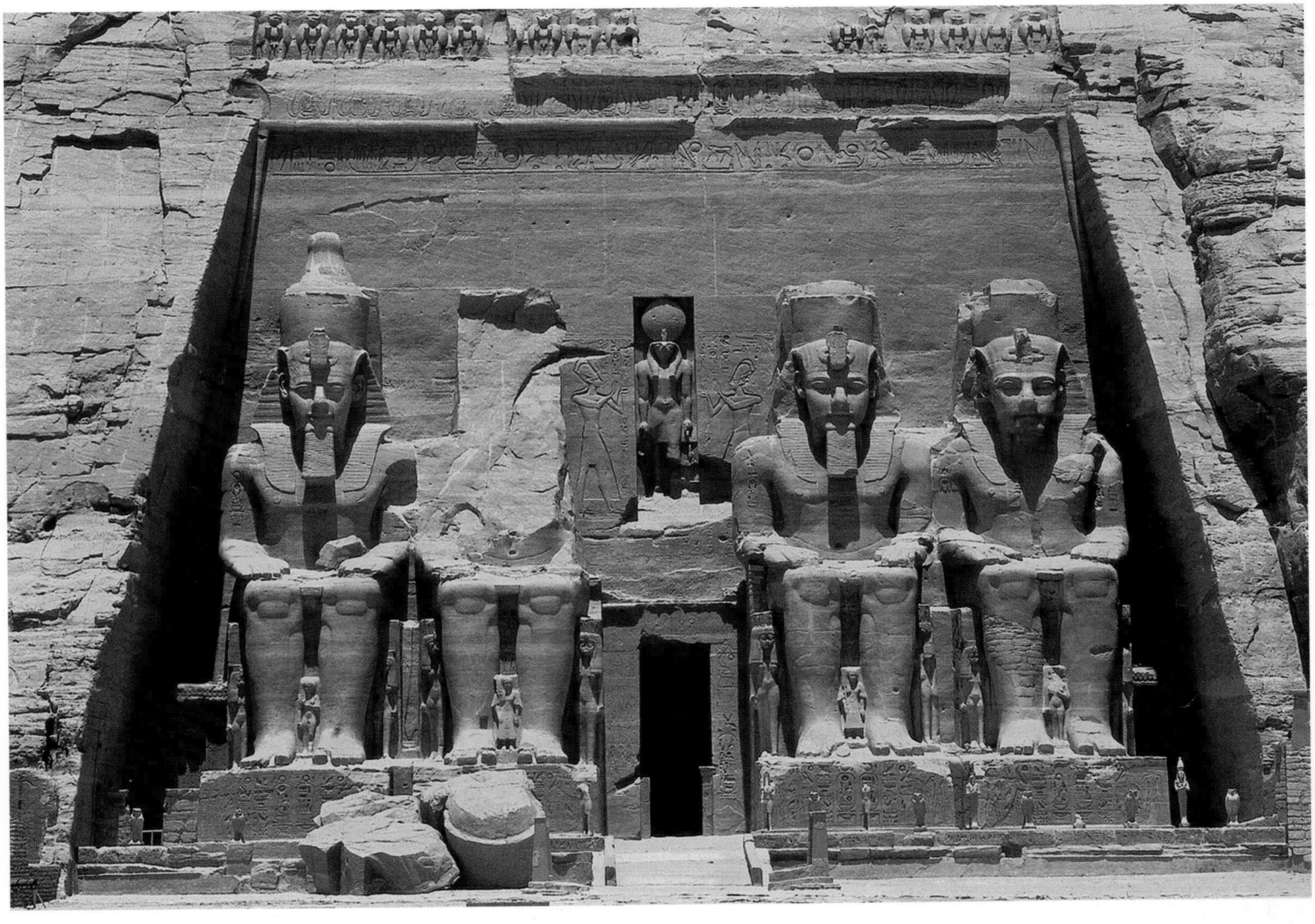

3.30 Temple of Ramesses II, Abu Simbel. 19th Dynasty. ca. 1279–1213 BCE

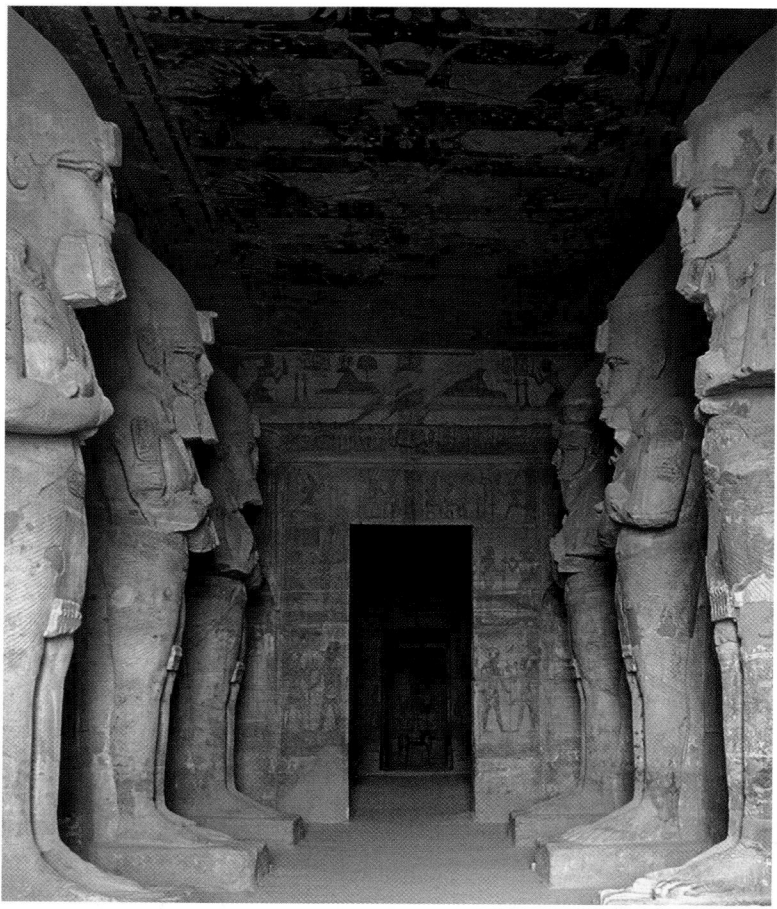

3.31   Interior of Temple of Ramesses II, Abu Simbel. 19th Dynasty. ca. 1279–1213 BCE

goddess of order, Ma'at, to the god. The image thus demonstrates the king's role as keeper of terrestrial order at the gods' request. On the interior of the temple are more colossal figures of Ramesses, shaped from the same rock as the columns behind them. Their size (32 feet high) and frontality presented an awe-inspiring sight to priests who conducted rituals inside (fig. 3.31).

Ramesses commissioned a second, complementary temple about 500 feet away from his own, in honor of his wife, Nefertari, and Hathor. Here, too, sculptors cut figures into the rock as a façade for the temple, which, though colossal in scale, was significantly smaller than Ramesses' temple. The topographical relationship between the two temples may be significant. Their central axes, when extended forward, intersected in the Nile's life-giving waters, so their locations may express the generative force embodied in the royal couple. This relationship has hardly been visible since the 1960s, when engineers moved the temple of Ramesses upward nearly 700 feet to raise it above flood levels resulting from the construction of the Aswan Dam.

Block Statues

In the New Kingdom, a type of sculpture known since the late Old Kingdom experienced fresh popularity. This was the block statue, where the artist reduced the body, shown seated on the

ground with knees drawn up to the chest and wrapped in a cloak, to a cubic abstraction. Above the block is a portrait head, and feet protrude at the bottom; sometimes arms are folded across the knees. Like the more conventional full-body sculptures, these images functioned as seats for the *ka* in tombs. When they first appear in the Sixth Dynasty, the figures are found in model funerary boats, transporting the dead to the cult center of Osiris at Abydos. They may, therefore, represent the deceased as a being sanctified by this journey in the afterlife. The example illustrated in figure **3.32** may come from the temple at Karnak. It presents two portraits. Above is the head of Senenmut, a high official at the court of Hatshepsut and Thutmose III and master of works for the temple at Deir el-Bahri. Below Senenmut's head is a very small head, portraying Nefrua, daughter of Hatshepsut and Thutmose II. Featuring the sidelock of hair that identifies her as a child, her head emerges from the block in front of Senenmut's face, as if held in an embrace, perhaps reflecting his protective role as her tutor. Omitting anatomical features in favor of the block form left an ample surface for a hieroglyphic text of prayers or dedications.

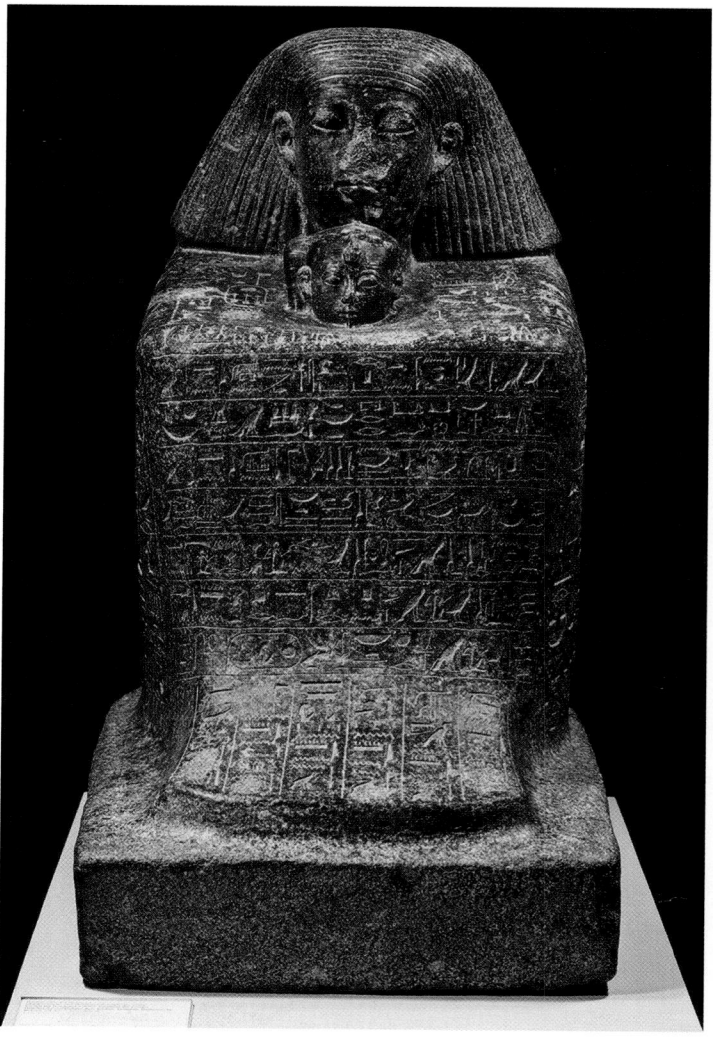

3.32   *Senenmut with Nefrua*, from Thebes. ca. 1470–1460 BCE. Granite, height approx. 3'½" (107 cm). Ägyptisches Museum, Berlin

Images in New Kingdom Tombs

New Kingdom artists continued to paint tomb chapels with scenes similar to those in Old and Middle Kingdom tombs. In the New Kingdom, however, additional images showed the deceased worshiping deities whose interventions could ease their transition to the next world—most typically, Osiris and Anubis. In the tomb chapel that featured in the annual festival of the Wadi at Thebes, when the living crossed to the west bank of the Nile and feasted with the dead, artists also painted banquet scenes. Music, dance, and wine were sacred to Hathor, who could lead the dead through the dangerous liminal phase between death and the after-life. A fragment of painting from the Tomb of Nebamun at Thebes (ca. 1350 BCE) shows that painters still employed hierarchical conventions established in the Old Kingdom 1,000 years previously (fig. **3.33**). While elite diners sit in rigid composite view (half profile, half frontal) in an upper register, musicians and dancers below move freely in pursuit of their crafts. A flute player and a clapper have fully frontal faces, and they even turn the soles of their feet to face a viewer—an extreme relaxation of elite behavior. The nude dancers twist and turn, and the loosened, separated strands of the entertainers' long hair further animate their painted images. The freedom of movement inherent in these figures has suggested to some that works from contemporary Crete may have been available for these painters to study. Art historians have gone so far as actually to attribute paintings elsewhere to artists from this Aegean island culture.

New Kingdom artists and patrons also followed Middle and Old Kingdom precedents in designing sculpted tomb images. Some reliefs executed for an unfinished tomb in Thebes belonging to Ramose, vizier for Amenhotep III (ca. 1375 BCE), depict Ramose's brother, Mai, and his wife, Urel (fig. **3.34**). The relief is shallow, but the carving distinguishes different textures with great mastery. The composite postures and the gestures of the wife embracing her husband reflect conventions going back at least to the Old Kingdom; all the same, the canon of proportions differs from earlier representations, and some of the naturalism seen in other New Kingdom works informs the profiles of this couple. The united front that husband and wife present through eternity may be compared to a New Kingdom love song that extols the joy of spending "unhurried days" in the presence of one's beloved. (See www.myartslab.com.)

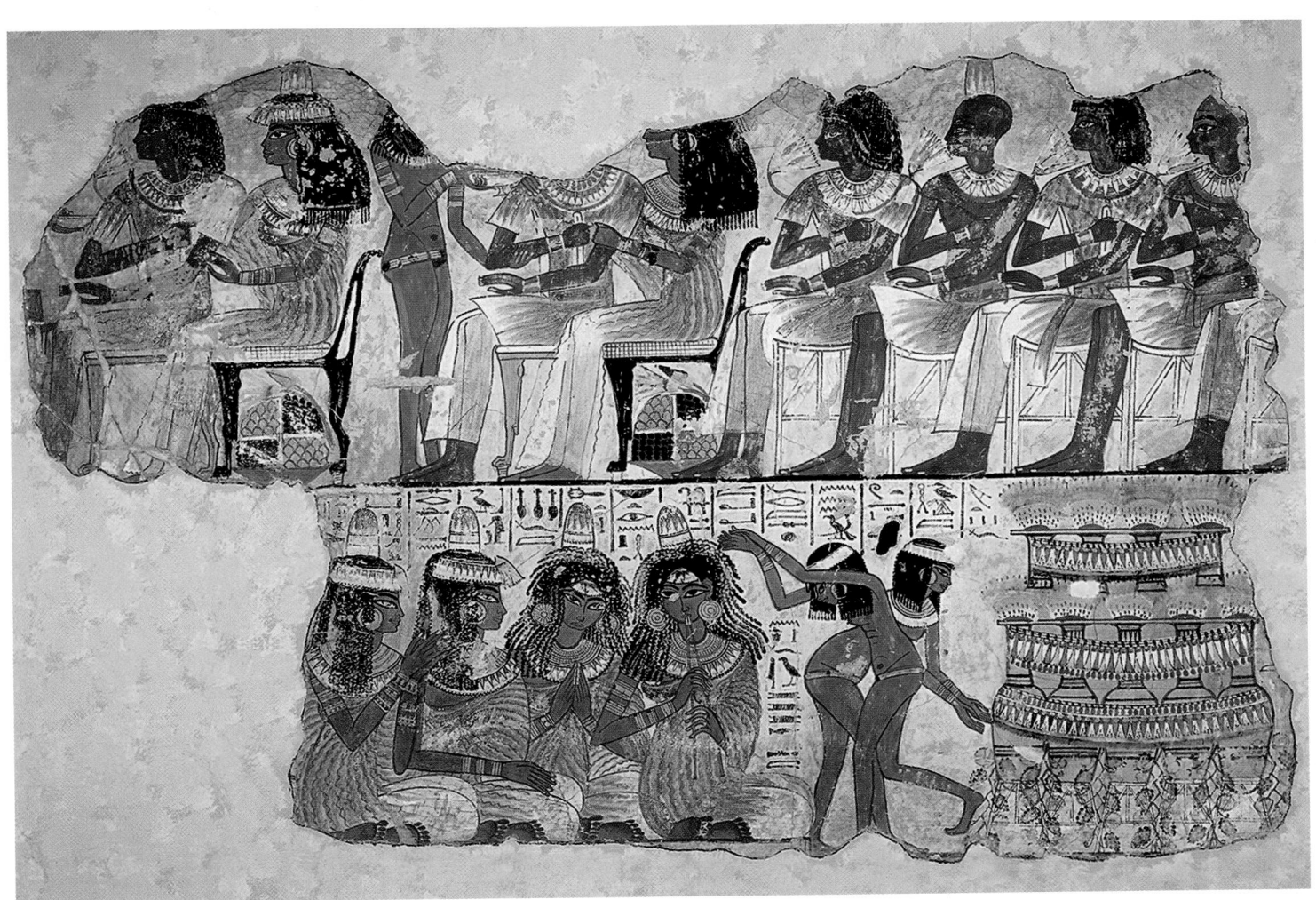

3.33 *Musicians and Dancers*, from the Tomb of Nebamun, Thebes. ca. 1350 BCE. Wall painting, painted plaster, height 24" (61 cm). The British Museum, London

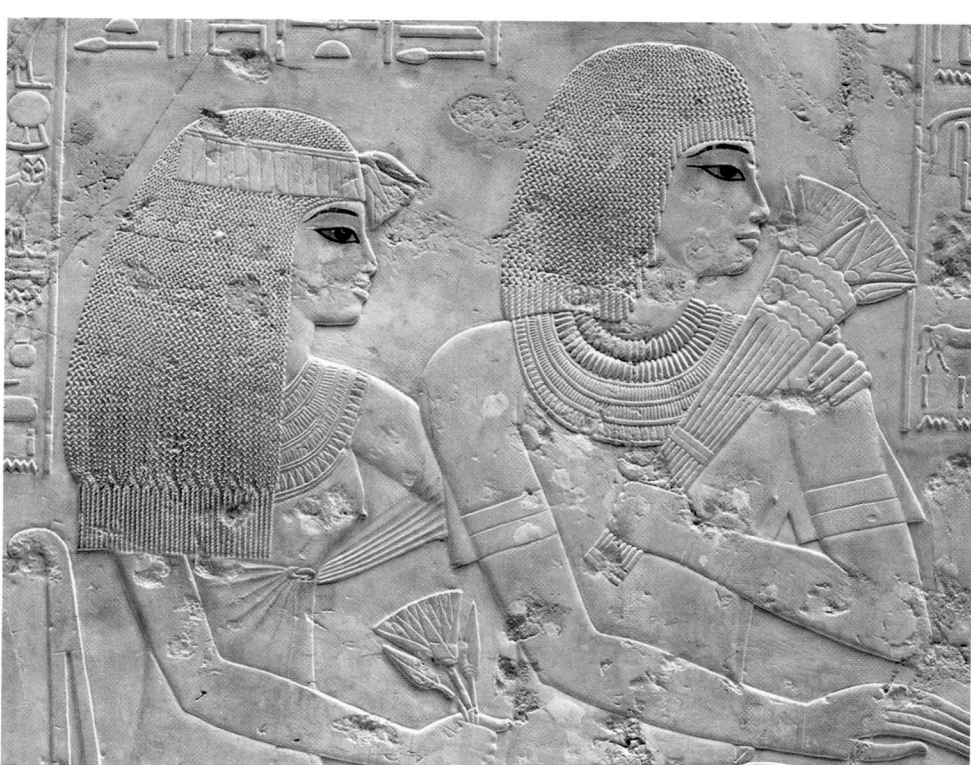

3.34 *Mai and His Wife, Urel,*
Tomb of Ramose, Thebes. ca. 1375 BCE.
Limestone relief detail

AKHENATEN AND THE AMARNA STYLE

Amenhotep III, whom Ramose served as vizier, raised the level of devotion to the sun-god during his reign (1391–1353 BCE). In temple complexes at Karnak and elsewhere, the king established wide open-air courtyards where Egyptians could worship the sun in its manifestation as a disk (or Aten) in the sky. Aten worship increased dramatically under his son, Amenhotep IV, who stressed the sun's life-giving force and began to visualize the god not in the traditional guise of a falcon-headed figure, but as a disk that radiated beams terminating in hands. Enraged by the young king's monotheistic vision of Aten, a powerful conservative priesthood thwarted his attempts to introduce this new cult to traditional religious centers such as Thebes. In response, Amenhotep IV established a new city devoted entirely to Aten on the Nile's east bank in central Egypt. He named his new city Akhetaten (now known as Amarna), meaning "horizon of Aten," and changed his own name to Akhenaten, "beneficial to Aten." Akhenaten's belief in Aten as the source of life found expression in the "Hymn to Aten" which is sometimes attributed to the king. This text (see www.myartslab.com) expresses joy in the daily rising of the sun by describing the world coming back to life at its appearance. Akhenaten's new cult and fledgling city lasted only as long as its founder; after his death, his opponents razed the city to the ground. Still, archaeological remains suggest that Akhenaten built temples in the contemporary style, using massive pylons and obelisks, as at Karnak, but with an emphasis on open-air courts directly exposed to the sun's glare.

The Amarna Style

Sculptures of Akhenaten and his family break dramatically with long-established conventions for depicting royal subjects. In numerous depictions, the figure of Akhenaten exhibits radically different proportions from those of previous kings. A colossal figure of Akhenaten installed at the temple of Amun-Ra in Karnak between 1353 and 1335 represents the king with narrow shoulders lacking in musculature, and with a marked pot belly, wide hips, and generous thighs (fig. **3.35**). His large lips, distinctive nose and chin, and narrow eyes make his face readily recognizable. The Amarna style, which was not reserved for the king's image but influenced representations of court officials and others as well, specifically emphasized naturalism in the body. Still, these unusual portraits of Akhenaten have puzzled scholars. Some dismiss them as caricatures, yet such expensive and prominent images must have had the king's approval. There have also been attempts to diagnose a medical condition from these representations, by reading the king's features as symptoms of Frolich's Syndrome, a hormonal deficiency that produces androgynous (both male and female) characteristics. Possibly he simply intended his "feminized" appearance to capture the androgynous fertile character of Aten as life-giver.

Group representations of Akhenaten with his family—his consort Nefertiti and three oldest daughters—are equally remarkable for the apparent intimacy among the figures. This is clear on a sunk-relief scene on an altar stele, of the kind that Egyptians would erect in small shrines in their homes and gardens (fig. **3.36**). Beneath the disk of the sun, its life-giving beams radiate downward with hands at their terminals. Attenuated reed columns

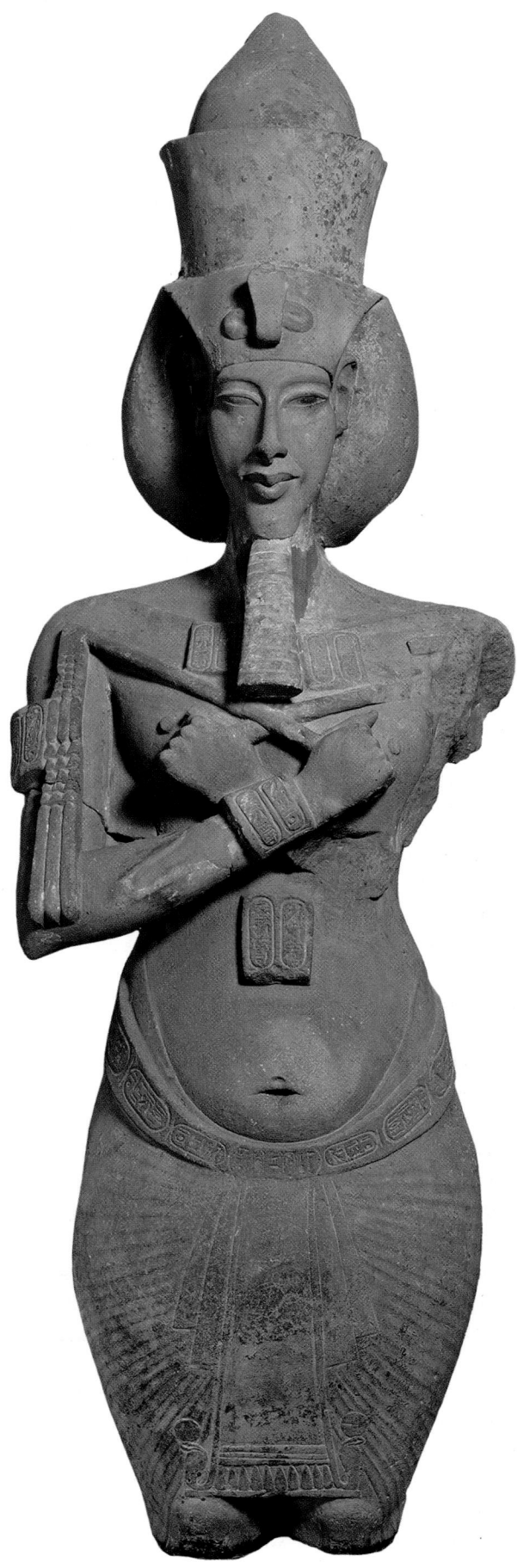

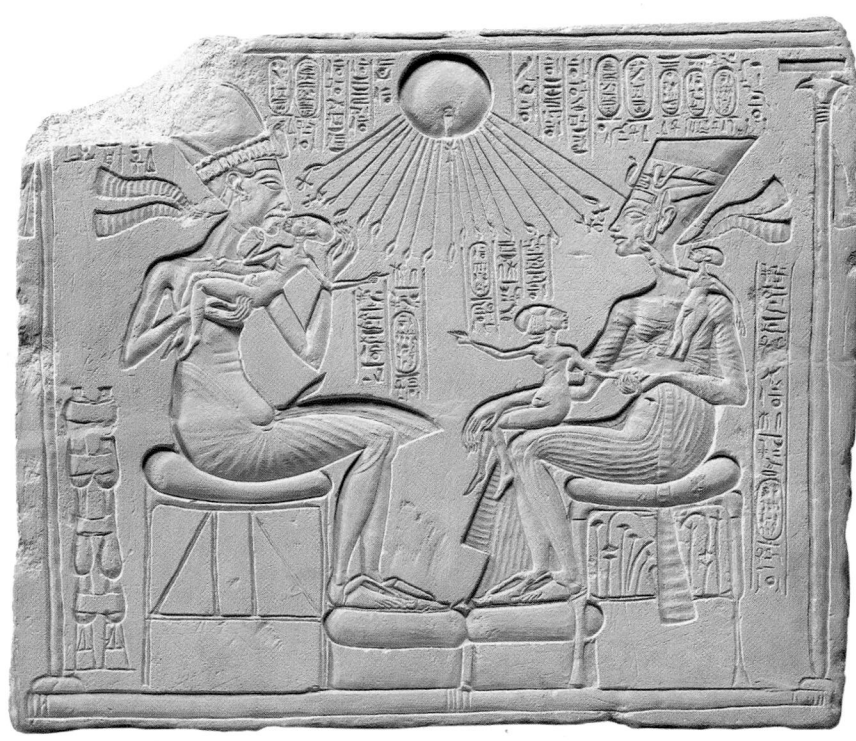

3.36 *Akhenaten and His Family*. ca. 1355 BCE.
Limestone, 12¾ × 15¼" (31.1 × 38.7 cm). Staatliche Museen zu Berlin, Preussischer Kulturbesitz, Ägyptisches Museum

suggest that the scene takes place within a garden pavilion, which is stocked with wine jars. The king and his consort sit facing each other on stools. They hold three lively daughters, who clamber on their laps and in their arms, uniting the composition with animated gestures that reach across the relief in marked contrast to the static quality of scenes of other times. The deliberate emphasis on the daughters' childishness marks a change: In the past, artists had represented children with a hieroglyphic pictograph of an adult in miniature, sucking a finger. The emphasis on children epitomizes the regeneration that the royal couple represent, and especially the king as manifestation of Aten.

QUEEN TIY The surprising transience implicit in the children's youthfulness and animated gestures on the altar also characterizes a one-third-life-size portrait of Akhenaten's mother Queen Tiy, chief wife of Amenhotep III (fig. **3.37**). Using the dark wood of the yew tree, with precious metals and semiprecious stones for details, the artist achieved a delicate balance between idealized features and signs of age. Smooth planes form the cheeks and abstract contours mark the eyebrows, which arch over striking eyes inlaid with ebony and alabaster. Yet the downturned mouth and the modeled lines running from the sides of the nose to the mouth offer careful hints of the queen's advancing years.

The sculpture went through two stages of design: Initially, the queen wore gold jewelry and a silver headdress ornamented with golden cobras, which identified her with the funerary goddesses Isis and Nephthys. A wig embellished with glass beads and topped with a plumed crown (the attachment for which is still

3.35 *Akhenaten*, from Karnak, Thebes. 1353–1335 BCE. Sandstone, height approx. 13' (3.96 m). Egyptian Museum, Cairo

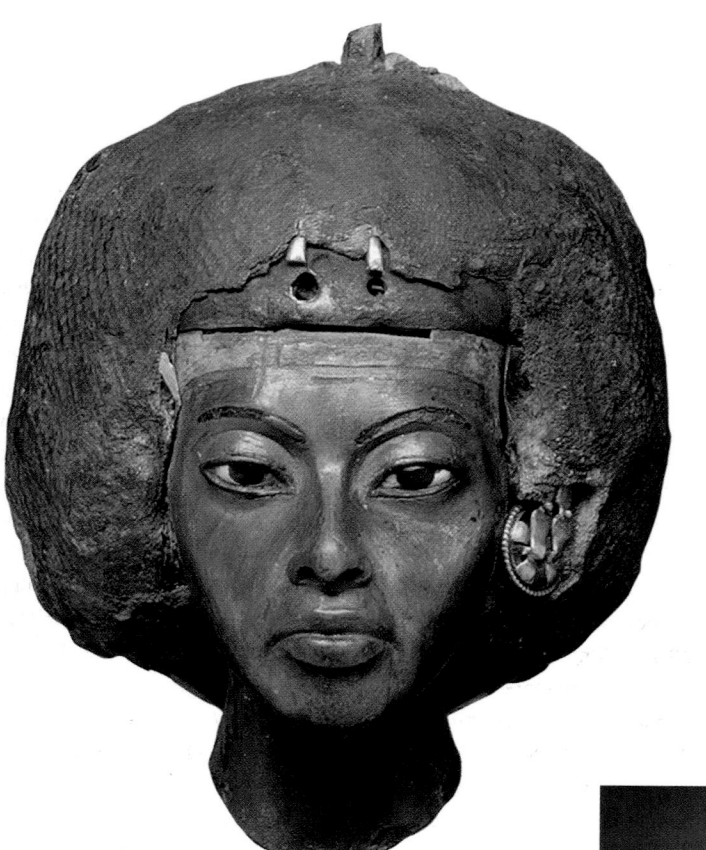

3.37 *Queen Tiy*, from Kom Medinet el-Ghurab.
ca. 1352 BCE. Yew, ebony, glass, silver, gold, lapis lazuli,
cloth, clay, and wax, height 3¾" (9.4 cm).
Staatliche Museen zu Berlin, Preussischer Kulturbesitz,
Ägyptisches Museum

extant) later concealed this headdress. Although excavators discovered the sculpture with funerary paraphernalia for her husband, Amenhotep III, these changes indicate that it was adapted to suit the beliefs of Akhenaten's new monotheistic religion.

PORTRAITS OF NEFERTITI As with Akhenaten's images, early depictions of Nefertiti emphasize her reproductive capacity by contrasting a slender waist with large thighs and buttocks. Sculptures from the second half of Akhenaten's reign, however, are less extreme. At Amarna, archaeologists discovered the studio of the king's chief sculptor, Tuthmosis, whom court records call "the king's favorite and master of the works." This yielded sculptures at every stage of production: heads and limbs of quartzite and jasper, and torsos of royal statues to which they could be affixed. Plaster casts were found, modeled from clay or wax studies taken from life. The most famous of these sculptures is a bust of Nefertiti, plastered over a limestone core and painted—a master portrait, perhaps, from which artists could copy other images (fig. **3.38**). The sculpture's left eye lacks the inlay of the right, showing that

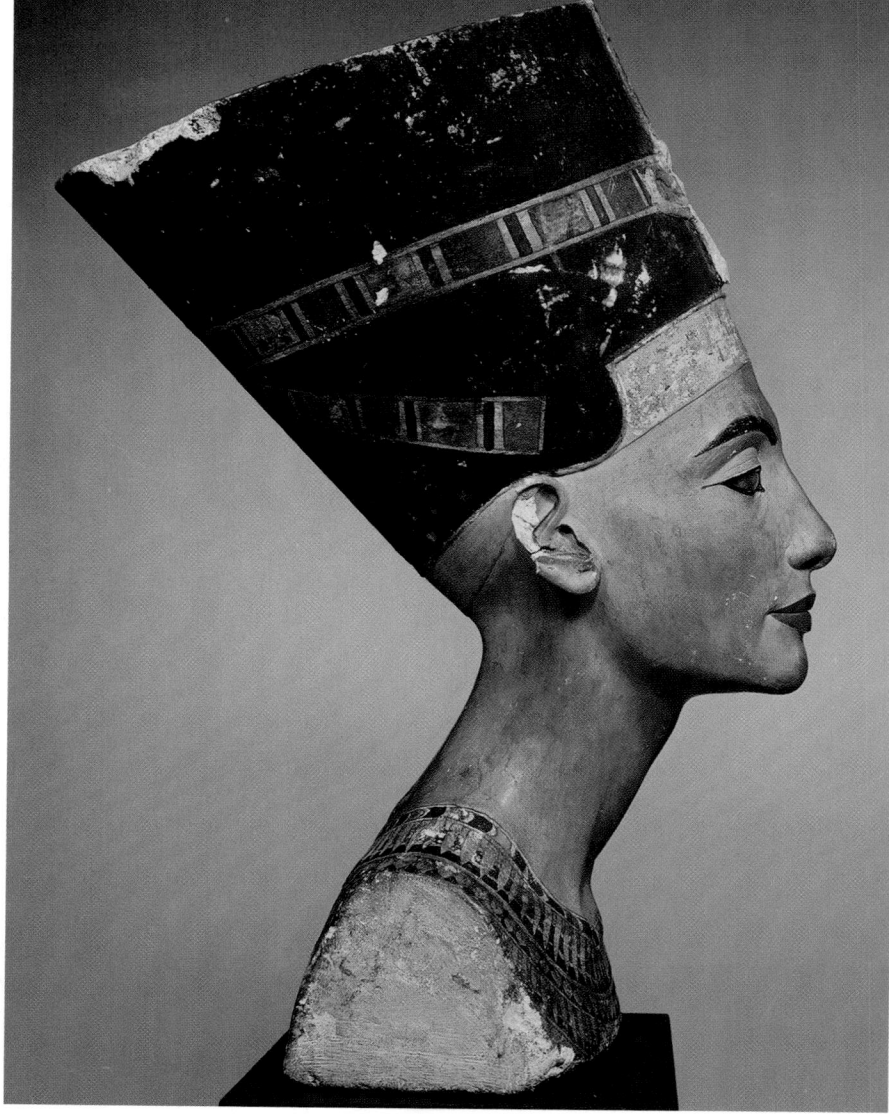

3.38 *Queen Nefertiti*. ca. 1348–1336/35 BCE.
Limestone, height 19" (48.3 cm).
Staatliche Museen zu Berlin,
Preussischer Kulturbesitz, Ägyptisches Museum

Interpreting Ancient Travel Writers

A great many Greeks went to Egypt; some, as might be expected, for business, some to serve in the army, but also some just to see the country itself.

—Herodotus

One of the primary sources available to art historians is the writing of ancient travelers. Despite the dangers of travel in antiquity, from shipwrecks to thievery, Egypt became a prime destination for curiosity-seekers, beginning around 1500 BCE, and peaking during the first and second centuries CE. Locals did what they could to entice travelers. In Roman times, men from Busiris, near Giza, would climb the pyramids' slippery slopes as a tourist attraction. Some early travelers painted or scratched their names on works of art, among them Hadrian's wife, Sabina. Others made a crucial—if complex—contribution to our knowledge of ancient monuments by writing about their journeys. Born in the early fifth century BCE in Halicarnassos (present-day Bodrum, Turkey), Herodotus spent the best part of his adulthood traveling throughout the Mediterranean and the Near East. His account of his Egyptian travels still survives. In the late first century BCE, the Greek geographer Strabo also wrote a valuable description of his experiences in Egypt and elsewhere.

These authors saw the "great wonders" at first hand, at a time when much more survived of them than is the case today. Often, their accounts supply vital information for reconstructions, or other details, such as the names of artists, architects, or patrons; but it is a mistake to accept the writers' words uncritically. These ancient travelers had different priorities from the modern art historian, and this fact would certainly have affected the accuracy of their accounts. Herodotus, for instance, was much more interested in religion than in works of art or architecture. This results in him giving considerably less detailed or precise information about artistic monuments than we might desire. It is also all too easy to forget that even ancient travelers visited Egypt at least a millennium after the pyramids and other monuments had been built. Furthermore, they relied on traditions handed down by guides and other locals, who, research shows, were often misinformed. Herodotus insists that the blocks of Khufu's pyramid were all at least 30 feet long, when 3 feet would have been more accurate. He also attributes the work to slaves, thus denigrating Khufu as a tyrant. Local priests may have broadcast this view in the fifth century BCE to please their Persian rulers. A long tradition among scholars of giving greater credence to classical texts than other types of evidence has led, in many instances, to an undue acceptance of ancient authors' words as "truth," even when archaeological evidence paints a different picture.

the bust remained unfinished, but an extraordinary elegance still derives from the sculptor's command of geometry, which is at once precise—the face is completely symmetrical—and subtle. The sculptor abandoned this piece and another similar head in the workshop when he moved from Amarna to Memphis after Akhenaten's death in 1335 BCE and the subsequent razing of his city.

Tutankhamun and the Aftermath of Amarna

Shortly after Akhenaten's death, a young king ascended the throne. Married to Akhenaten's daughter, even perhaps himself one of Akhenaten's sons, Tutankhaten was only nine or ten when he became king. Possibly under the influence of the priests of Amun, he restored the royal residence to Memphis and resurrected the orthodox religion of Egypt that Akhenaten had rejected. He changed his name to Tutankhamun to reflect the monarchy's renewed alliance with Amun, before dying unexpectedly at the age of 19. His sudden death has inspired numerous murder and conspiracy theories, but recent scientific studies of his mummy point to natural causes.

Tutankhamun's greatest fame results not from his life, but from his death and the discovery of his tomb in 1922 by the British archaeologist Howard Carter. Although robbers had entered the tomb twice, much of it remained untouched when Carter found it (fig. **3.39**). With a stairway, corridor, and four chambers, the tomb is uncharacteristically small for a royal burial, leading scholars to suppose that a nonroyal tomb might have

been hastily coopted for the king at the time of his unanticipated death. All the same, offerings buried with him lacked nothing in volume or quality. Indeed, the immense value of the objects makes it easy to understand why grave robbers have been active in Egypt ever since the Old Kingdom. The tomb contained

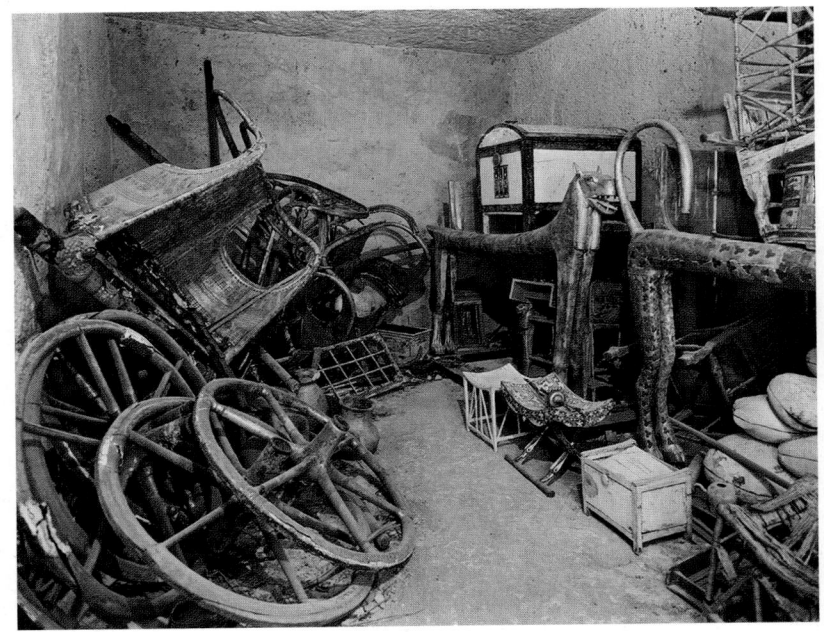

3.39   Tomb of Tutankhamun. 18th Dynasty

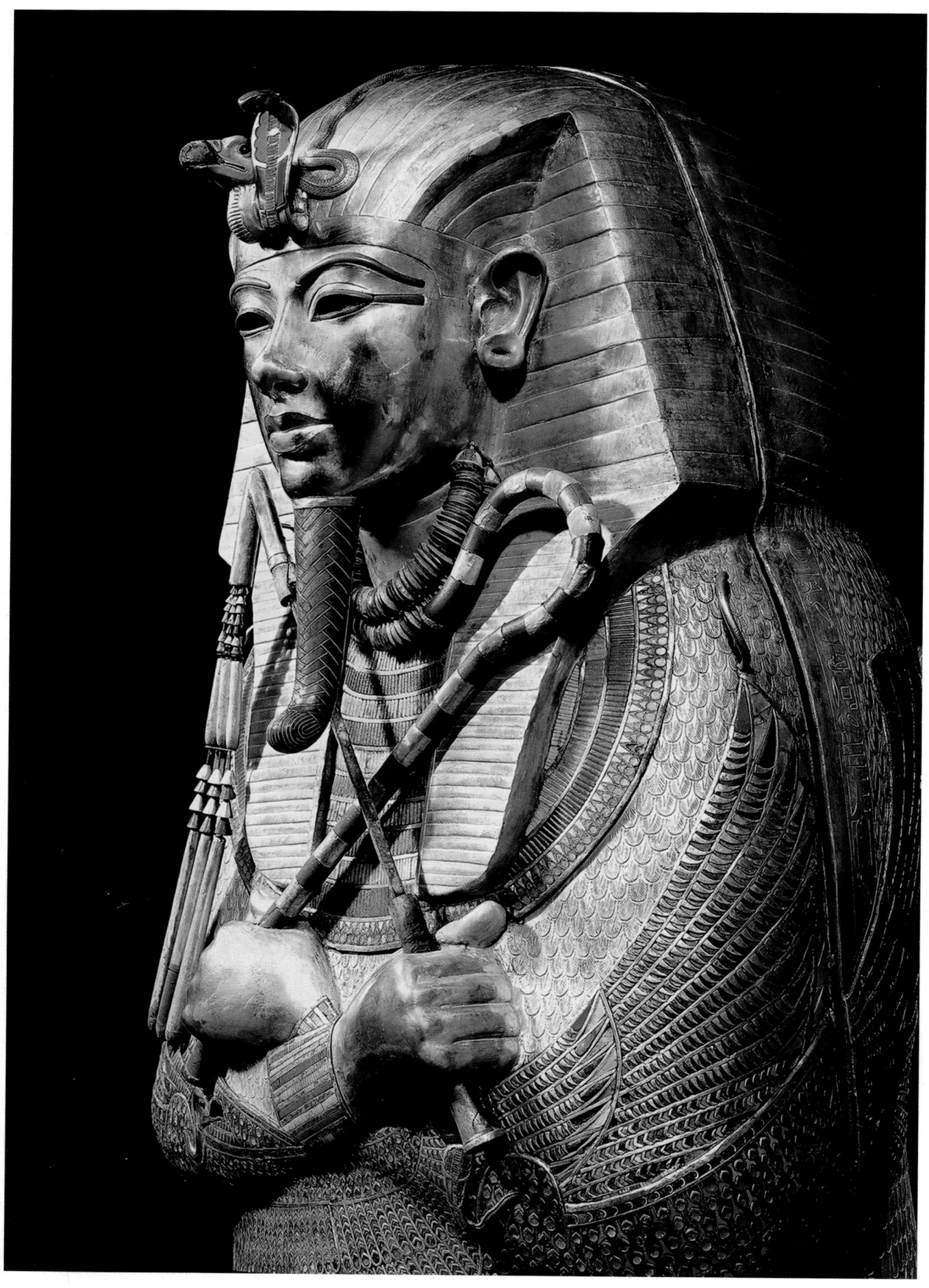

The Book of the Dead

This text is an incantation from Plate III of the Papyrus of Ani in the British Museum, from the latter half of the Eighteenth Dynasty. It accompanies the weighing of the soul illustrated in the closely related The Book of the Dead of Hunefer (see fig. 3.40).

Saith Thoth the righteous judge of the cycle of the gods great who are in the presence of Osiris: Hear ye decision this. In very truth is weighed the heart of Osiris, is his soul standing as a witness for him; his sentence is right upon the scales great. Not hath been found wickedness [in] him any; not hath he wasted food offering in the temples; not hath he done harm in deed; not hath he let go with his mouth evil things while he was upon earth.

Saith the cycle of the gods great to Thoth [dwelling] in Hermopolis [the god's cult-center along the Nile in Upper Egypt]: Decreed is it that which cometh forth from thy mouth. Truth [and] righteous [is] Osiris, the scribe Ani triumphant. Not hath he sinned, not hath he done evil in respect of us. Let not be allowed to prevail Amemet [Ammut, the devourer of souls] over him. Let there be given to him cakes, and a coming forth in the presence of Osiris, and a field abiding in Sekhet-hetepu [Field of Peace] like the followers of Horus.

---

funerary equipment, such as coffins, statues, and masks, as well as items used during the king's lifetime, such as furniture, clothing, and chariots. Many of the objects feature images of Tutankhamun battling and overcoming foreign enemies, as part of his kingly duty to maintain order amid chaos. Three coffins preserved the king's mummified corpse, the innermost of which is gold and weighs over 250 pounds. Most impressive is the exquisite workmanship of its cover, with its rich play of colored inlays against polished gold surfaces (fig. **3.40**). The number and splendor of the objects in the burial of a minor king like Tutankhamun make the loss of the burial finery of powerful and long-lived kings all the more lamentable.

Tutankhamun's short-lived successor, the aged Ay, continued the process of restoring the old religion. He married Tutankhamun's widow, perhaps to preserve, rather than usurp, succession to the throne. Head of the army under Tutankhamun and last king of the Eighteenth Dynasty, Horemheb completed the restoration process: He set out to erase all traces of the Amarna revolution, repairing shattered images of the traditional gods and rebuilding their temples; but the effects of Akhenaten's rule lived on in Egyptian art for some time to come.

PAPYRUS SCROLLS: *THE BOOK OF THE DEAD*

Inscriptions on walls and furnishings accompanied royal burials like Tutankhamun's. Yet in the Middle Kingdom, the desire to include the prayers and incantations that accompanied kings to the afterlife spread to other classes of patrons. By the New Kingdom, these patrons commissioned scribes to make illustrated funerary texts such as *The Book of the Dead* which first appeared in the Eighteenth Dynasty. This is a collection of over 200 incantations or spells that ultimately derived from the Coffin Texts of the Middle Kingdom, which scribes copied onto scrolls made of papyrus reeds. The popularity of *The Book of the Dead* in the New Kingdom signals a change in Egyptian beliefs about the afterlife: Any member of the elite could enjoy an afterlife, as long as the deceased had lived in accordance with *ma'at* and could pass tests imposed by the gods of the underworld. In order to ensure that the deceased had the knowledge required to do this and progress to the hereafter, relatives generally placed a version of *The Book of the Dead* inside the coffin or wrapped within the mummy bandaging itself. Among the scenes illustrating the book are the funeral procession, the weighing of the heart, and the provision of nourishment for the dead.

One of the finest surviving examples is *The Book of the Dead of Hunefer*, dating from about 1285 BCE. The scene representing the weighing of the heart and Osiris' judgment of the dead in Chapter 125 (see *Primary Source*, above) conforms to a well-defined type that many workshops shared (fig. **3.41**). Derived from traditional tomb painting, its imagery has been adapted to the format of the scroll to be a continuous narrative, repeating protagonists in one scene after another without a dividing framework. At the left, Anubis, the jackal-faced guardian of the underworld, leads Hunefer into the Hall of the Two Truths. Anubis then weighs Hunefer's heart, contained in a miniature vase, against the ostrich feather of Ma'at, who symbolized divine order and governed ethical behavior. Ma'at's head appears on the top of the scales. Thoth, the ibis-headed scribe, records the outcome. Looking on with keen interest is Ammut. Made up of the parts of various ferocious beasts—the head of a crocodile, the body and forelegs of a lion, and the hindquarters of a hippopotamus—she was the devourer of those whose unjust life left them unworthy of an afterlife.

The deceased had to swear to each of the deities seen overhead that he or she had lived according to *ma'at*. When he had been declared "true of voice," Horus presented him to his father, Osiris, shown with emblems of kingship, wrapped in a white mummy-like shroud, and seated in a pavilion floating above a lake of natron, a salt used for preserving the body. With him are Isis and her sister Nephthys, mother of Anubis and protector of the dead. In front of the throne, the four sons of Horus stand on a white lotus blossom, symbol of rebirth. Also considered the gods of the cardinal points, they protected the internal organs that were removed as part of the embalming process and placed in containers known

3.40 Cover of the coffin of Tutankhamun. 18th Dynasty. Gold, height 72" (182.9 cm). Egyptian Museum, Cairo

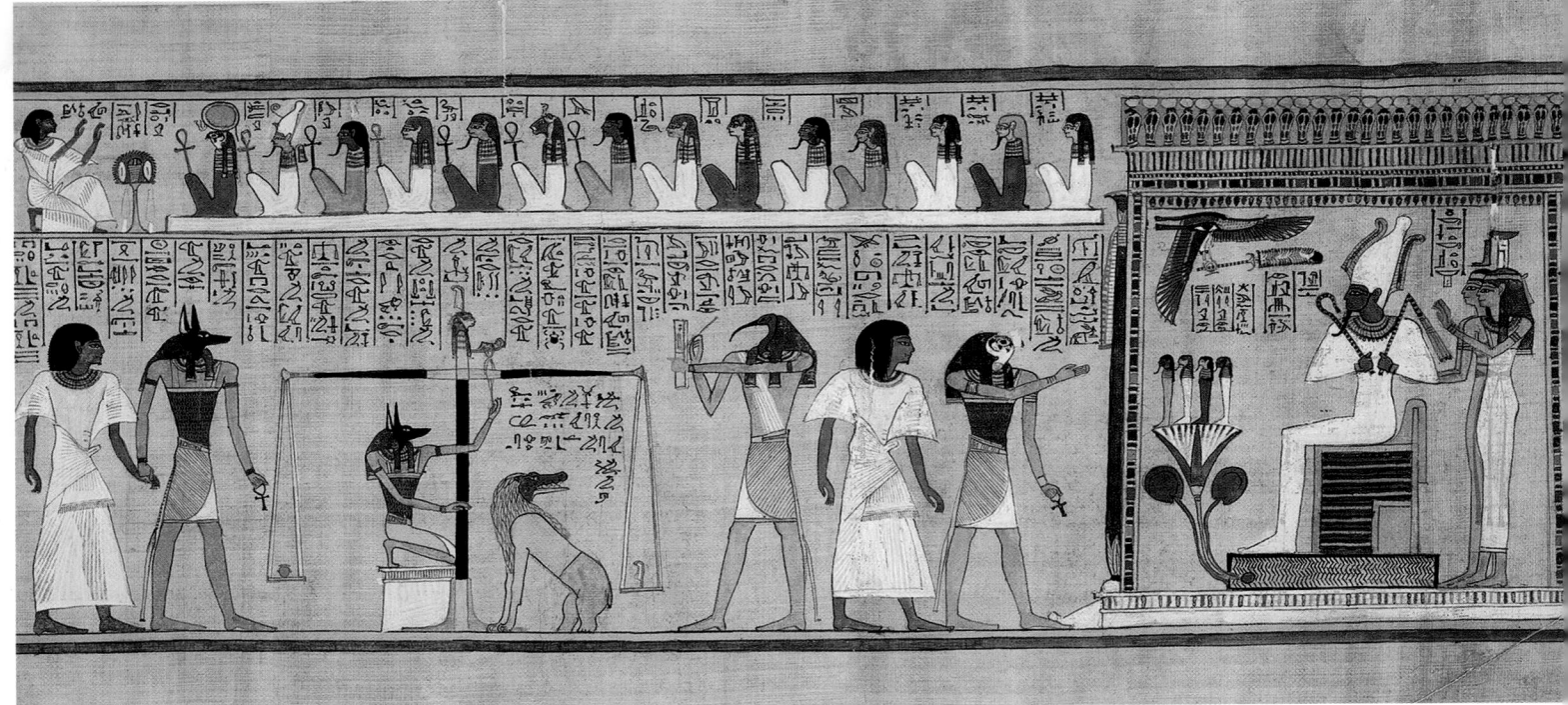

3.41 *The Weighing of the Heart and Judgment by Osiris*, from *The Book of the Dead of Hunefer*. 1285 BCE. Painted papyrus, height 15⅝" (39.5 cm). The British Museum, London

as canopic jars. Above, Horus, identified by the eye he lost in his struggle with Seth, called the udjat eye, bears an ostrich feather, representing the favorable judgment of Ma'at. In the afterlife, as on earth, the desire for order was paramount.

LATE EGYPT

Tutankhamun's revival of the cult of Amun and the ancient sources of *The Book of the Dead* demonstrate that New Kingdom Egyptians deeply venerated the traditions of the past. Even as Ramesses II extended the borders of his realm to the south and the east, the cult centers at Luxor and Karnak absorbed great wealth and developed great influence. About 1076 BCE, barely 70 years after the end of the reign of Ramesses III, priests began to exert more and more power, until during the Twenty-first Dynasty the cult of Amun dominated Egypt. Thereafter, successive groups of foreigners controlled the area, including Nubians, Persians, and Macedonians, and the era known as the New Kingdom comes to an end.

The final phase of ancient Egypt belongs to the history of Greece and Rome. Alexander the Great conquered Egypt and founded the city of Alexandria before his death in 323 BCE. His general, Ptolemy (d. 284 BCE), became king of the region, and established a dynasty that lasted nearly 300 years, until the death of Ptolemy XIV or Caesarion, Cleopatra's son by the Roman dictator Julius Caesar. In 30 BCE, the Roman general Octavian, soon to be the emperor Augustus, claimed Egypt as a Roman province. Despite its lack of autonomy, Egypt flourished economically

under the Greeks and Romans. In the Ptolemaic period, Alexandria became one of the most vibrant centers of culture and learning in the Hellenistic world, and its port ensured a lively trade that reached as far as China and India. In Roman times, the Nile's life-giving waters made Egypt the chief source of grain in the empire, earning it the title of Rome's granary. But in addition to this commercial function, Egypt provided Rome and its successors with inspiring models of kingly power and imagery that lasted through the ages.

For some 3,000 years, from the era of the pyramids down to the time of the Ptolemies, Egyptian kings built magnificent structures that expressed their wealth and their control over the land and its resources. All aspects of royal patronage demonstrated the intimate link between the king and the gods. Building in stone and on a grand scale, Egyptian kings sought to impress a viewer with the necessity and inevitability of their rule. The formulas for representing the power of the king are as old as Egypt itself.

Egyptian kings and other elite patrons built structures for both the living and the dead. The objects and images placed in their tombs for the afterlife offer a modern viewer a glimpse of the material goods that they enjoyed in their lifetimes. The tombs provided a safe haven for the body and the soul (*ka*) of the deceased. They were built to endure, and they were equipped with numerous representations of the dead. These representations were also designed to last by virtue of being made of the most permanent of materials. Permanence was also sought through the consistent use of conventions for representing the patron. The longevity of Egyptian art forms testifies to the longevity of Egyptian social structures, political organization, and beliefs.

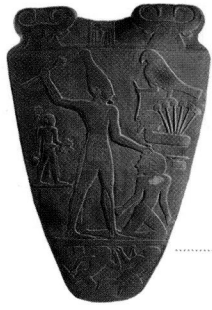

ca. 3150–3125 BCE
The *Palette of King Narmer*

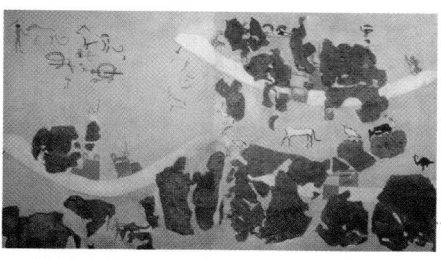

ca. 3500–3200 BCE Predynastic painting at Hierakonpolis

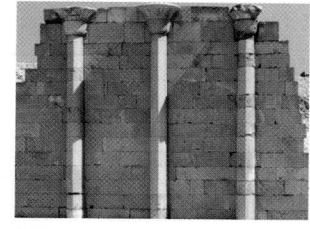

2630–2611 BCE Rule of King Djoser, and construction of his mortuary complex at Saqqara

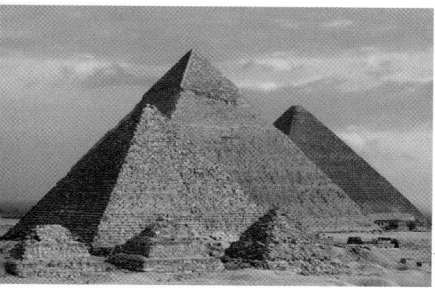

a. 2575–2465 BCE The Fourth Dynasty, and construction of the three Great Pyramids at Giza

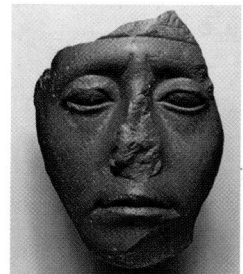

ca. 1870s–1840s BCE Naturalistic sculpture of King Senwosret III

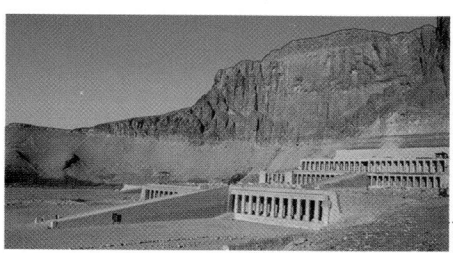

ca. 1458 BCE King Hatshepsut dies; her mortuary temple was designed by Senenmut

ca. 1348–1336/35 BCE Plaster and limestone portrait bust of Akhenaten's wife, Nefertiti

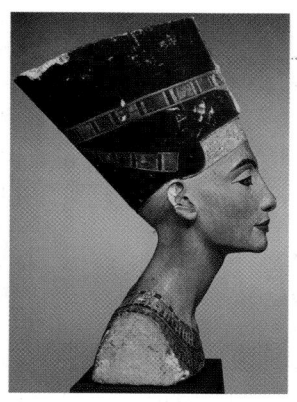

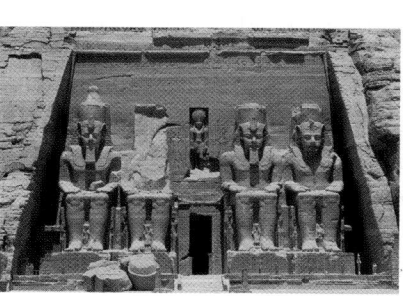

ca. 1290–1224 BCE Rule of King Ramesses II, who commissioned a monumental temple at Abu Simbel

Egyptian Art

5000 BCE

◄ ca. 5000 BCE Human settlements along the Nile Valley

4500 BCE

ca. 4250–3750 BCE Neolithic menhirs at Ménec

4000 BCE

3500 BCE

ca. 3500 BCE Pottery manufacturing appears in western Europe

3000 BCE

◄ ca. 2900 BCE Mesopotamians begin using cuneiform writing

2500 BCE

ca. 2100 BCE Final phase of construction at Stonehenge

2000 BCE

◄ ca. 2040 BCE Beginning of the Middle Kingdom

◄ 1792–1750 BCE Hammurabi rules Babylon after 1785 BCE The Hyksos gain control of the Nile Delta

◄ ca. 1595 BCE The Hittites conquer Babylon ca. 1550–1525 BCE Rule of King Ahmose; expulsion of the Hyksos from Egypt

1500 BCE

◄ ca. 1400–1200 BCE Apogee of the Hittite Empire

◄ ca. 1353–1335 BCE Rule of King Akhenaten; new religious center at Amarna

1000 BCE

ca. 957 BCE Solomon's Temple is completed in Jerusalem

500 BCE

◄ 323 BCE Alexander the Great dies, leading to Ptolemy's kingdom of Egypt

0

◄ 30 BCE Roman general Octavian proclaims Egypt a Roman province

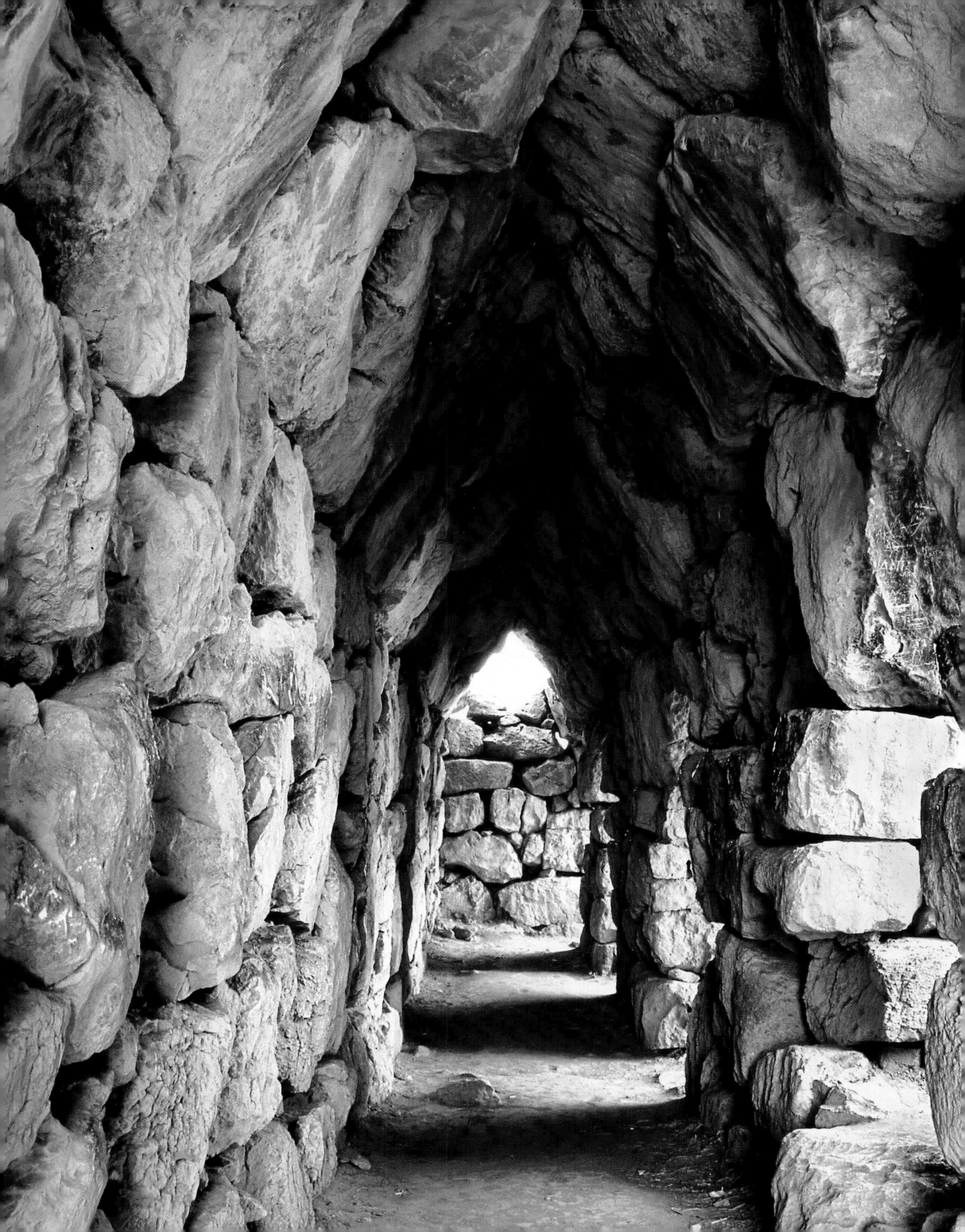

CHAPTER 4

Aegean Art

T HE MEDITERRANEAN WAS ONE OF THE PRIMARY HIGHWAYS THAT connected the cultures of antiquity. With North Africa on the south, Asia on the east, and Europe on the west and north, this body of water brought disparate cultures into contact for both trade and conflict. The Greeks named one branch of the Mediterranean, between Greece and Turkey, the

Aegean Sea, and on islands and peninsulas there several closely related but distinct cultures developed in the third and second millennia BCE. The Cycladic culture emerged on the islands forming an irregular circle between the Greek mainland and the island of Crete. The British archaeologist Sir Arthur Evans named the culture on the island of Crete Minoan, because the later Greeks associated Crete with the legendary King Minos, son of the Greek god Zeus, and a mortal princess, Europa. The culture on the mainland is called Helladic, from the Greek *Hellas*. Together, these separate cultures formed a civilization we know today as Aegean, after the sea that both separates and unites them.

Until the second half of the nineteenth century, Aegean civilization was known principally from *The Iliad* and *The Odyssey*, epic tales of gods, kings, and heroes attributed to the eighth-century BCE Greek poet (or group of poets) known as Homer. His story of the siege of Troy and its aftermath still excites the modern imagination. Prompted by these stories, and curious to determine whether they had a factual basis, German archaeologist Heinrich Schliemann excavated sites in Asia Minor and Greece during the 1870s. Following his lead, Arthur Evans began excavations in Crete in 1900. Since then, a great deal of archaeological evidence has come to light, some consistent with, but much contradicting, Homer's tales. Although writing has been found in

Minoan and Mycenaean contexts, it is not bountiful and scholars are still working on its decipherment. (Note the absence of *Primary Source* boxes in this chapter.) Consequently, we understand less about Aegean civilization than we do about the cultures of Egypt or the ancient Near East.

There is evidence of human habitation throughout the Aegean as early as the Paleolithic period, though settlements spread and grew mainly in the Neolithic and Early Bronze ages. Scholars divide the Aegean Bronze Age into three phases: Early, Middle, and Late, each of which is further subdivided into three phases, I, II, and III. Archaeologists often prefer these relative dates to absolute dates, because the chronology of the Aegean Bronze Age is so open to debate. The Early phase (ca. 3000–2000 BCE) corresponds roughly to the Predynastic and Old Kingdom period of Egypt, and Sumerian and Akkadian culture in Mesopotamia. The Middle phase (ca. 2000–1600 BCE) is contemporaneous with the Middle Kingdom in Egypt and the rise of Babylon in Mesopotamia. And the Late phase (ca. 1600–1100 BCE) is contemporaneous with the Second Intermediate Period and the New Kingdom in Egypt, the Hittite overthrow of Babylon, and the rise of the Assyrians in Mesopotamia. A mass destruction of Aegean sites, from a cause still unknown to us, led to significant depopulation in about 1200 BCE, and, despite a slight resurgence, by 1100 BCE the Aegean Bronze Age had come to an end.

The different cultures of the Aegean produced distinct art forms. Stylized marble representations of the human figure and

Detail of figure 4.20, Corbeled casemate at Tiryns, Greece

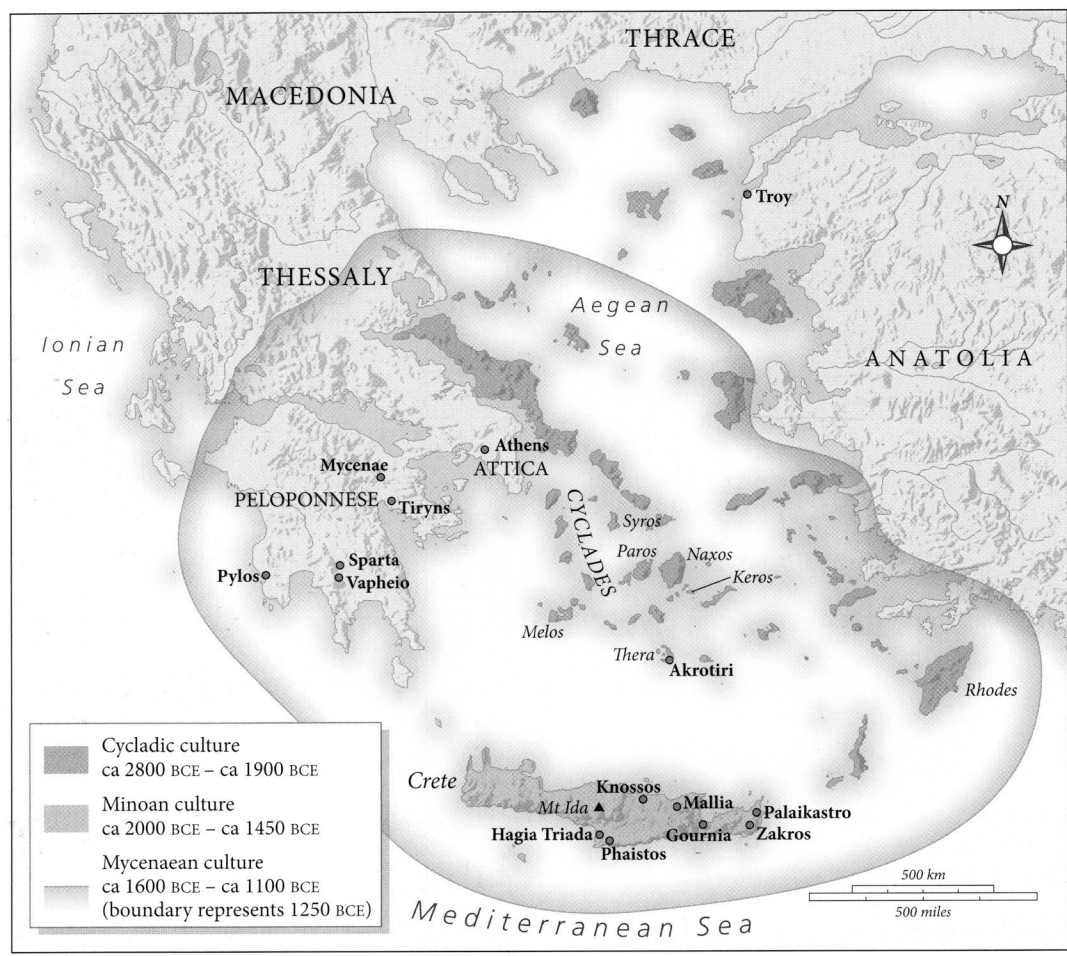

Map 4.1 The Bronze Age Aegean

EARLY CYCLADIC ART

Information about the culture of the Cyclades comes entirely from the archaeological record, which indicates that wealth accumulated there early in the Bronze Age as trade developed, especially in obsidian, a dark volcanic stone. Funerary practice reflects this prosperity. At the beginning of the Early Bronze Age, around 2800 BCE, the islanders started to bury their dead in stone-lined pits sealed with stone slabs, known today as cist graves. Although they lacked large-scale markers, some of these graves contained offerings, such as weapons, jewelry, and pottery. Potters crafted their wares by hand in the Early Cycladic period, and in addition to drinking and eating vessels, they produced flat round objects with handles, decorated with incised or stamped spirals and circles, and sometimes with abstract renderings of ships (fig. **4.1**).

Archaeologists nickname them "frying pans" because of their shape, but they may in fact have been **palettes** for mixing cosmetics, or, once polished, served as an early kind of mirror.

Some Cycladic burials included striking figures, usually female, carved from the local white marble. The Early Cycladic II example illustrated here represents the prevalent type (fig. **4.2**). The figure is nude, with arms folded across the waist, and toes extended. The flat body has a straight back, and a long, thick neck supports a shield-shaped face at a slight angle. The artist used abrasives, probably emery from the island of Naxos, to distinguish details on the figure, such as a ridgelike nose, small pointed breasts, a triangular pubic area, and eight toes. Traces of pigments on a few figures indicate that the artist painted on other details, including eyes, hair, jewelry, and body markings similar to tattoos.

Female figures of this type are always standing (or reclining). They come in many sizes (the largest reaching 5 feet long and the smallest only a few inches), but their form is consistent enough to indicate a governing canon of proportions, as with Egyptian sculptures (see Chapter 3). All the same, a number of figures clearly stand outside this canon. For instance, some appear to be pregnant. There are also some male figures. These are usually seated and play a musical instrument, such as a flute or a harp, like the player illustrated in figure **4.3**.

frescoes are paramount in the Cyclades. Large palaces with elaborate adornments on their walls dominate on Crete. Citadels and grave goods remain from the Greek mainland. In the absence of extensive writing, these works of art provide valuable insights into Aegean practices and ideals. The fact that the tales of Homer and Greek myths look back to these cultures testifies to their importance in the development of later Greek culture.

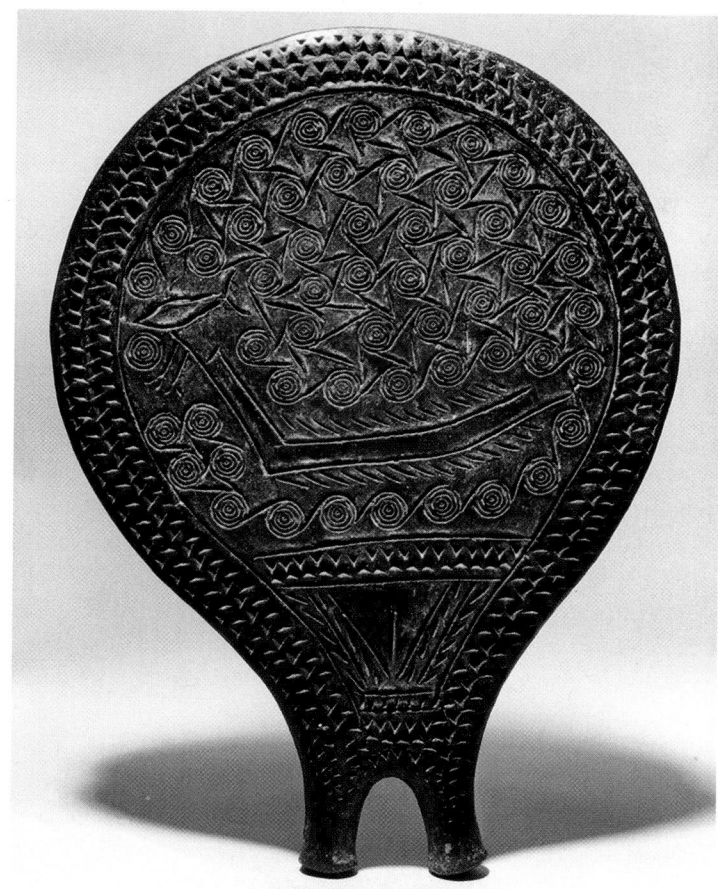

4.1 "Frying pan," from Chalandriani, Syros. Early Cycladic II. ca. 2500–2200 BCE. Terra cotta, diameter 11" (28 cm), depth 2⅜" (6 cm). National Archaeological Museum, Athens

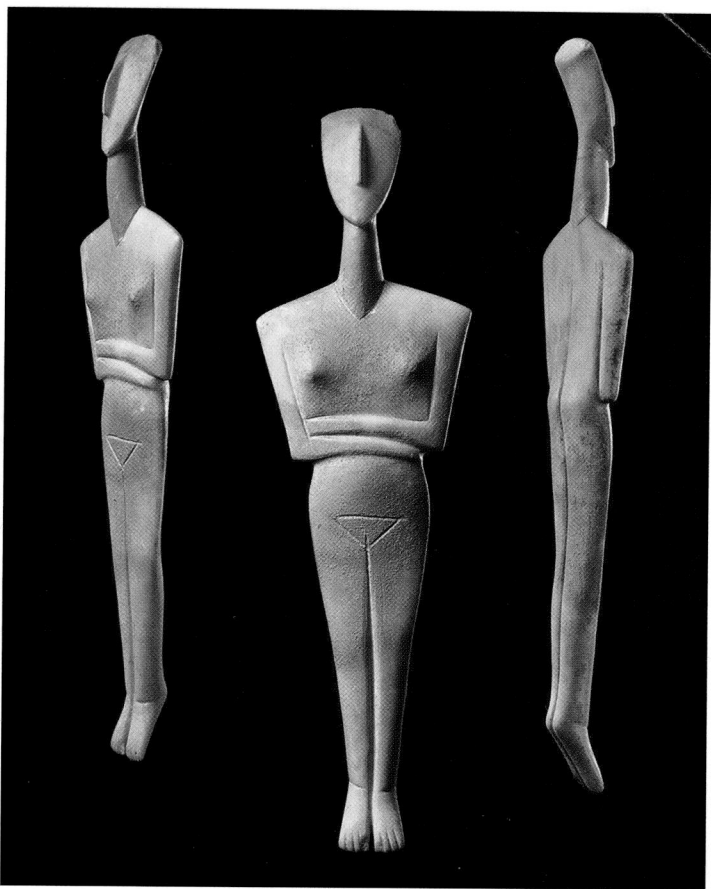

4.2 Figure, from the Cyclades. ca. 2500 BCE. Marble. Height 15¾" (40 cm). Nicholas P. Goulandris Foundation. Museum of Cycladic Arts, Athens. N.P. Goulandris Collection, No. 206

For many years, archaeologists called these figures Cycladic "idols," and pictured them playing a central role in a religion focusing on a mother goddess. More recently scholars have offered two other plausible explanations for their functions. Perhaps sculptors crafted them purely for funerary purposes, to represent servants or surrogates for human sacrifices, or even for the body of the deceased. Alternatively, they may have served a different function before burial, possibly within household shrines. Although most have come to light in a reclining position, they may once have been propped upright. Some examples show signs of repair with wire, which is a strong indication that people used—and valued—them before depositing them in graves.

Most likely, no single explanation applies to all of them. The greatest obstacle to determining their function is our general ignorance about their **provenance**, that is, where and how they were found and their subsequent history. The simplicity and clear geometry of the figures appeals to a twentieth- and twenty-first-century aesthetic that favors understated and clean geometric forms. Those qualities and the luscious white marble used to form the figures have led to their widespread appearance on the art market, often without any record of archaeological context. In

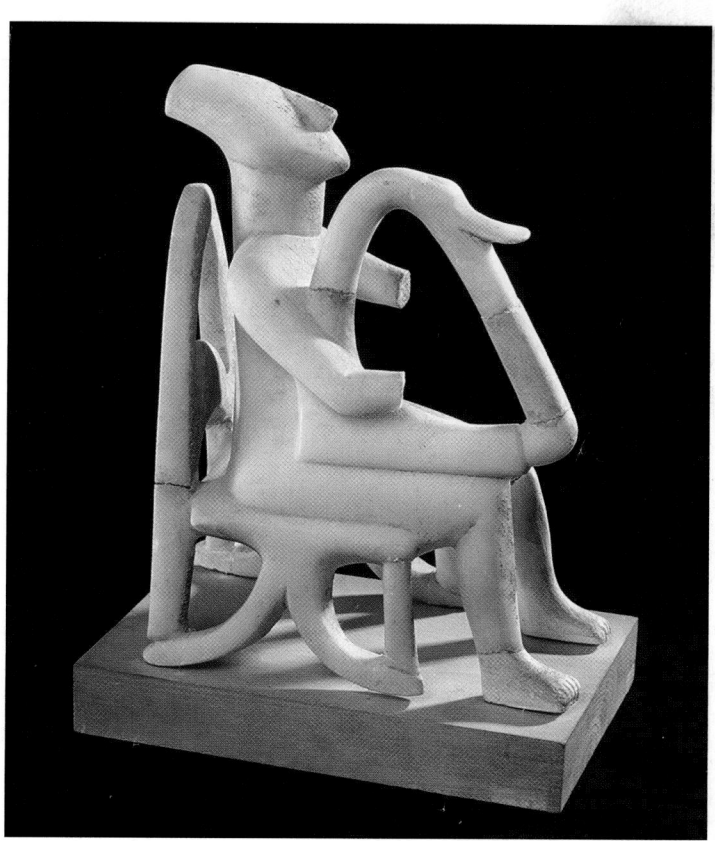

4.3 *Harpist*, from Amorgos, Cyclades. Latter part of the 3rd millennium BCE. Marble. Height 8½" (21.5 cm). Museum of Cycladic Art, Athens

order to better interpret these figures, archaeologists need to know their exact findspots, whether in a burial context or in living quarters.

The carved figures of women and musicians that survive from these Aegean islands seem to look back to Paleolithic and Neolithic figures, such as the *Woman of Willendorf* (see fig. 1.14). Yet the characteristic pattern of these figures—the canon that they followed—is distinct to these islands (and to Crete, where some examples have surfaced). The tradition of making figural imagery in the marble native to these islands would become a dominant feature of later Greek art.

MINOAN ART

Archaeologists have found a wider range of objects and structures on the island of Crete than on the Cyclades. This large island, south of the Cyclades, and about 400 miles (640 km) northwest of Egypt, stretches over 124 miles (200 km) from east to west, divided by mountain ranges, and with few extensive areas of flat, arable land (map **4.1**). This geography, along with continuous migration throughout the Bronze Age, encouraged diversity and independence among the population: Minoan communities tended to be small and scattered. All the same, as a result of inhabiting an island that is centrally placed in the Mediterranean, Minoans became skilled seafarers and developed a powerful fleet of ships.

The major flowering of Minoan art occurred about 2000 BCE, when Crete's urban civilizations constructed great "palaces" at Knossos, Phaistos, and Mallia. At this time, the first Aegean script, known as Linear A, appeared. This is known as the First Palace period, comprising Middle Minoan I and II. Little evidence of this sudden spurt of large-scale building remains, as all three early centers suffered heavy damage, probably from an earthquake, in about 1700 BCE. A short time later, the Minoans built new and even larger structures on the same sites. This phase constitutes the Second Palace period, which includes Middle Minoan III and Late Minoan IA and IB. An earthquake demolished these centers, too, in about 1450 BCE. After that, the Minoans abandoned the palaces at Phaistos and Mallia, but the Mycenaeans, who gained control of the island almost immediately, occupied Knossos.

The "Palace" at Knossos

The buildings of the Second Palace period are our chief source of information for Minoan architecture. The largest is the structure at Knossos, which its excavator, Arthur Evans, dubbed the Palace of Minos (figs. **4.4** and **4.5**). In fact, the city of Knossos may have been the most powerful Cretan center of the Middle and Late Bronze Age, with its most impressive structures dating from between 1700 and 1400 BCE. These included courts, halls, shrines, workshops, storerooms (housing vast clay jars for oil and other provisions), and perhaps residential quarters, linked by corridors,

staircases, and porticoes. Frequent **light wells** (open spaces reaching down through several floors) illuminated and ventilated interior spaces (as seen in fig. **4.6**). Other amenities in the buildings included a system of clay pipes for drainage. Conspicuously lacking are exterior fortifications to protect the complex. Given their strength at sea, the Minoans may have had little fear of invasion.

As well-preserved as it appears, the present complex is a little deceptive: Evans reconceived and reconstructed much of it in concrete when he worked there between 1900 and 1932 (see *The Art Historian's Lens*, page 87). The original builders at Knossos framed the walls with timbers and constructed them out of rubble masonry or mud brick. Some they built of **ashlar masonry** (cut and dressed stone), which gave them a more ornamental appearance. Columns, often made of wood with a stone base, supported the porticoes. Their form was unusual: A smooth shaft tapered downward from a generous cushionlike capital. Often the shaft was oval in cross section rather than round. Wall paintings suggest that capitals were painted black and the shaft red or white. The origin of this type of column remains a mystery.

At first glance, the plan of the complex (see fig. 4.4) may appear confusing and haphazard. This probably explains why later Greek legend referred to it as the labyrinth, home of the Minotaur, a half-human, half-bull creature who devoured the youths the Athenians offered him in tribute, and whom the hero Theseus killed after penetrating the maze. Coupled with the natural defenses of the island's geography, this mazelike arrangement of rooms, and a general lack of emphasis on entrances, may have been part of a moderate internal defensive strategy. The small size of the rooms and the careful control of the sun's penetration into living spaces through light wells may also have been deliberate decisions to keep the buildings cool in hot weather.

Moreover, the design does have an underlying logic. At its core is a large central court, onto which important rooms opened. The court divides the plan on an approximately north–south axis. On the west, a corridor running north–south separates long, narrow storerooms from rooms of less uniform shapes close to the court; the latter rooms may have performed a ceremonial role. An east–west corridor divides the east wing into (perhaps) a workshop area on the north side, and grander halls on the south. The complex appears to grow outward from the court, and using flat (rather than pitched) roofs would have greatly facilitated the building of additional structures. Compared to Assyrian and Persian palaces, such as the citadel of Sargon II at Dur Sharrukin (fig. 2.17) or the palace of Darius and Xerxes at Persepolis (fig. 2.26), the overall effect at Knossos is modest; individual units are relatively small and the ceilings low. Still, the rich decoration of some of the interior walls made for a set of elegant spaces. We should also remember that much of what remains belongs to subterranean or ground-floor levels, and archaeologists have long believed that grander rooms existed on a lost upper level.

Exactly how the grand structures of Crete functioned, and who lived in them, is still a subject of debate. As noted above, Arthur Evans described the complex at Knossos as a "palace" when he first excavated it (assigning royal names to various

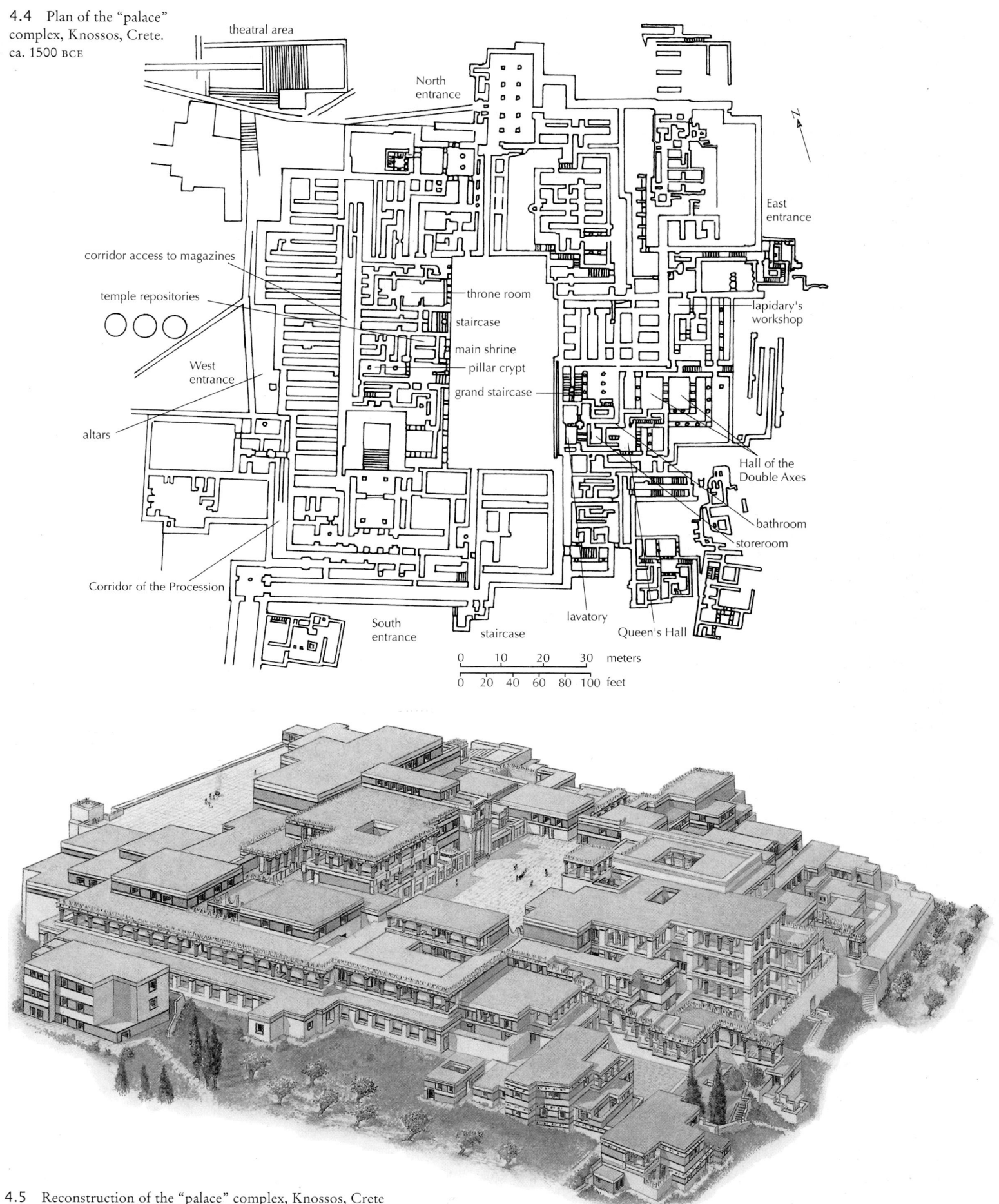

4.4 Plan of the "palace" complex, Knossos, Crete. ca. 1500 BCE

theatral area

North entrance

East entrance

corridor access to magazines

temple repositories

throne room

lapidary's workshop

staircase

West entrance

main shrine

pillar crypt

grand staircase

altars

Hall of the Double Axes

bathroom

storeroom

Corridor of the Procession

South entrance

staircase

lavatory

Queen's Hall

| 0 | 10 | 20 | 30 | meters |
| 0 | 20 40 | 60 | 80 100 | feet |

4.5 Reconstruction of the "palace" complex, Knossos, Crete

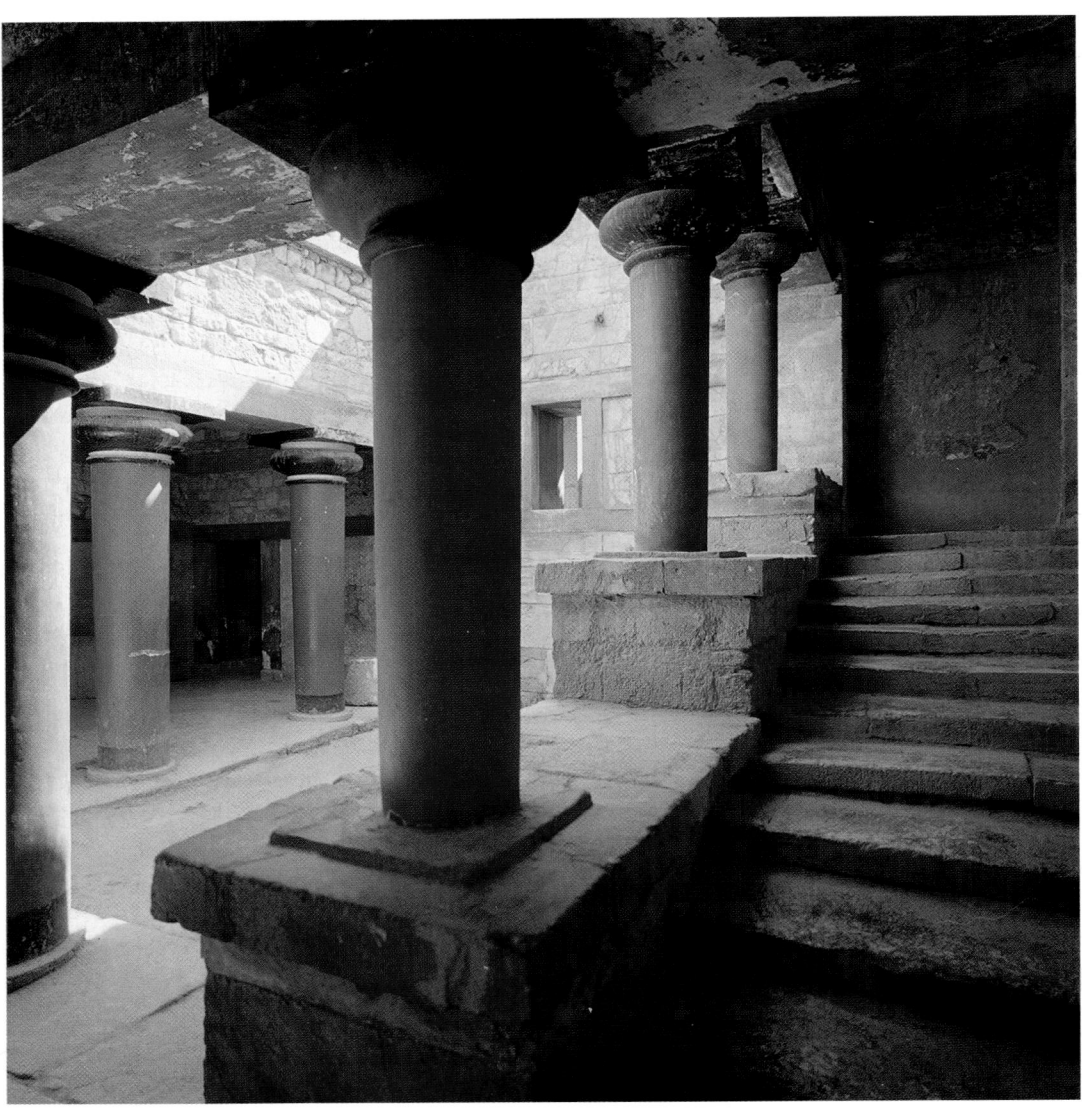

4.6 Staircase, east wing, "palace" complex, Knossos, Crete

rooms), and the term stuck, regardless of its accuracy. Evans conceived of the complex as a palace or an elite residence for several reasons. He was reacting partly to recent discoveries on the Mycenaean mainland, described below, and partly to the presence of a grand room with a throne. But the social and political realities of Evans's own homeland may have been even more influential in his thinking: He would have been familiar with the large palaces that the extended royal family occupied in late Victorian England. In fact, excavation of the complex at Knossos suggests that a variety of activities went on there. Extensive storage areas support a hypothesis that the palace was a center of manufacturing, administration, and commerce. Additionally, some spaces that seem ceremonial, such as the great court with its triangular raised causeway, and small shrine-like rooms with apparently religious paraphernalia, suggest that political and sacred activities occurred there too. There is no reason to believe that the Minoans segregated these activities as neatly as we often do today. Moreover, there is no evidence to suggest that the functions of the various complexes, at Knossos and elsewhere, were identical, or that they remained constant over time.

Wall Paintings: Representing Rituals and Nature

Grand rooms within the complexes at Knossos and elsewhere were decorated with paintings. Archaeologists found most of them in extremely fragmentary condition, so that what we see today is the result of extensive restoration, which may not always be entirely reliable. Vibrant mineral colors characterize the frescoes, applied to wet or dry plaster in broad washes without shading, in a technique known as **buon fresco**; wide bands of geometric patterns serve as elaborate frames. The prevalent subjects of paintings at Knossos go a long way toward supporting a hypothesis of ritual activity there. For instance, a miniature Second Palace period painting, dating to around 1500 BCE, depicts a crowd of spectators attending an event—a ritual or a game perhaps (fig. **4.7**). Art historians know it as the *Grandstand Fresco*. A tripartite building features at the center, which scholars identify as a shrine because of the stylized bulls' horns on its roof and in front of its façade. On either side sit two groups of animated women, bare-breasted and dressed in flounced skirts. Above and

Two Excavators, Legend, and Archaeology

In the mid-nineteenth century, most scholars believed that Homer's epic tales of the Trojan War and its aftermath, *The Iliad* and *The Odyssey*, were merely the stuff of legend. But just a few decades later, that view had radically changed. Two extraordinary men were key figures in bringing about that change. One of them was Heinrich Schliemann (1822–1890). The German-born son of a minister, Schliemann became wealthy through a succession of business ventures and retired at the age of 41. From a young age, he had been fascinated by Homer's world of gods and heroes, vowing to learn ancient Greek (one of about 15 languages he would eventually master). He became convinced that a historical framework supported Homer's poetry, and during his extensive travels, he learned that a handful of archaeologists believed the Turkish site of Hissarlik to be the site of Homer's Troy. After gaining permission from the Turkish government to excavate there, he began working officially in 1871. Among the spectacular finds he described in print was "Priam's Treasure," a hoard of vessels, jewelry, and weapons made of precious metals, which he named after Homer's king of Troy. Then, turning his attention to Mycenae, Schliemann discovered the shaft graves of Circle A, some of which contained magnificent objects, such as the gold mask in figure 4.27.

Schliemann was also intrigued by the site of Knossos on Crete, but he was unable to purchase the land. The opportunity fell instead to Arthur Evans (1851–1941), the son of a renowned British naturalist, and himself Keeper of the Ashmolean Museum in Oxford. By 1900, he had begun excavating the so-called Palace of Minos at Knossos with extraordinary results. In 1911, in recognition of his contribution to the field of archaeology, Evans received a knighthood.

Until recently, scholars judged these two early archaeologists very differently. They deemed Schliemann's excavation technique destructive and considered Schliemann himself little more than a treasure hunter. Some scholars questioned whether he actually discovered "Priam's Treasure" as a hoard, or whether he assembled sporadic finds to make more of a news splash. Tales of his excavations have been embellished into myth in their own right. By some accounts, Schliemann had his Greek wife, Sofia, model ancient jewelry. Of late, scholars have recognized the unfairness of assessing Schliemann by modern scientific standards, and they have acknowledged his critical role in igniting scholarly and popular interest in the pre-Hellenic world.

Evans's reputation has fared better than Schliemann's, largely because of his close attention to stratigraphy, that is, using layers of deposit in excavations to gauge relative time. Geologists had developed this technique in the seventeenth and eighteenth centuries and archaeologists still use it today in a refined form. Evans employed it to assess the relative positions of walls and other features, and it led him to establish a relative chronology for the entire site. His designations of Early, Middle, and Late Minoan periods defined an essential historical framework for the Aegean world as a whole in the Bronze Age. Evans's work at Knossos included a considerable amount of reconstruction. His interventions help to make the site comprehensible to laypeople, but can also mislead an unknowing viewer. In fact, it was Evans, not the Minoans, who built much of what a visitor now sees at Knossos. One significant consequence of Evans's restorations at Knossos is that they have kindled debate among conservators about how much to restore and how to differentiate visually between ancient ruin and modern reconstruction.

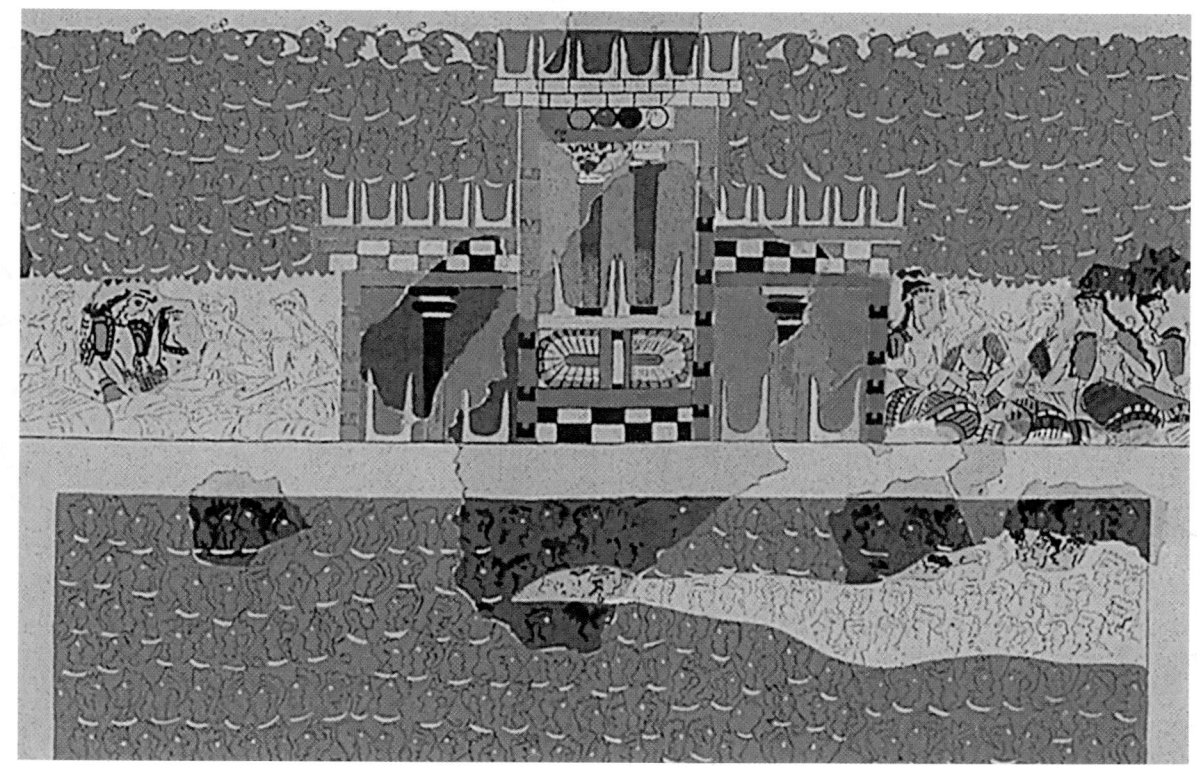

4.7 *Grandstand Fresco*, from Knossos, Crete. ca. 1500 BCE. Archaeological Museum, Iráklion, Crete

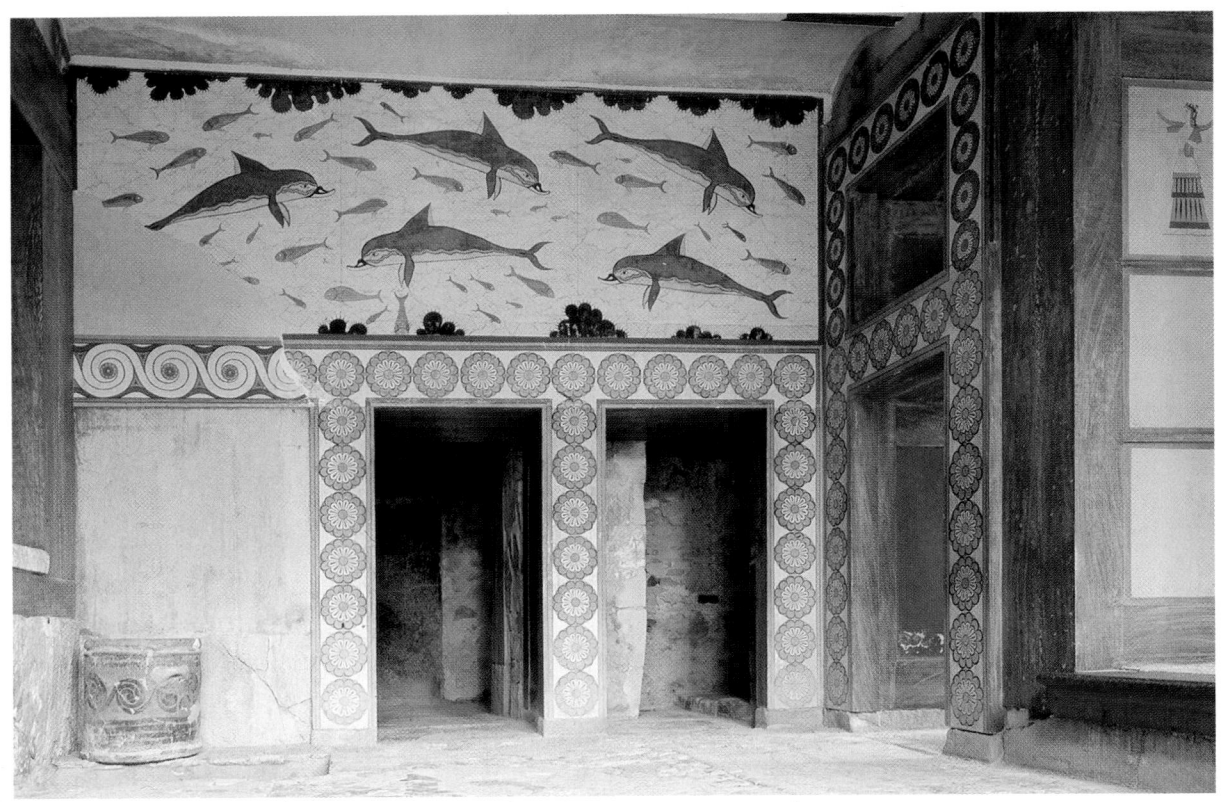

4.8 The "Queen's Megaron," from Knossos, Crete. ca. 1700–1300 BCE. Archaeological Museum, Iráklion, Crete

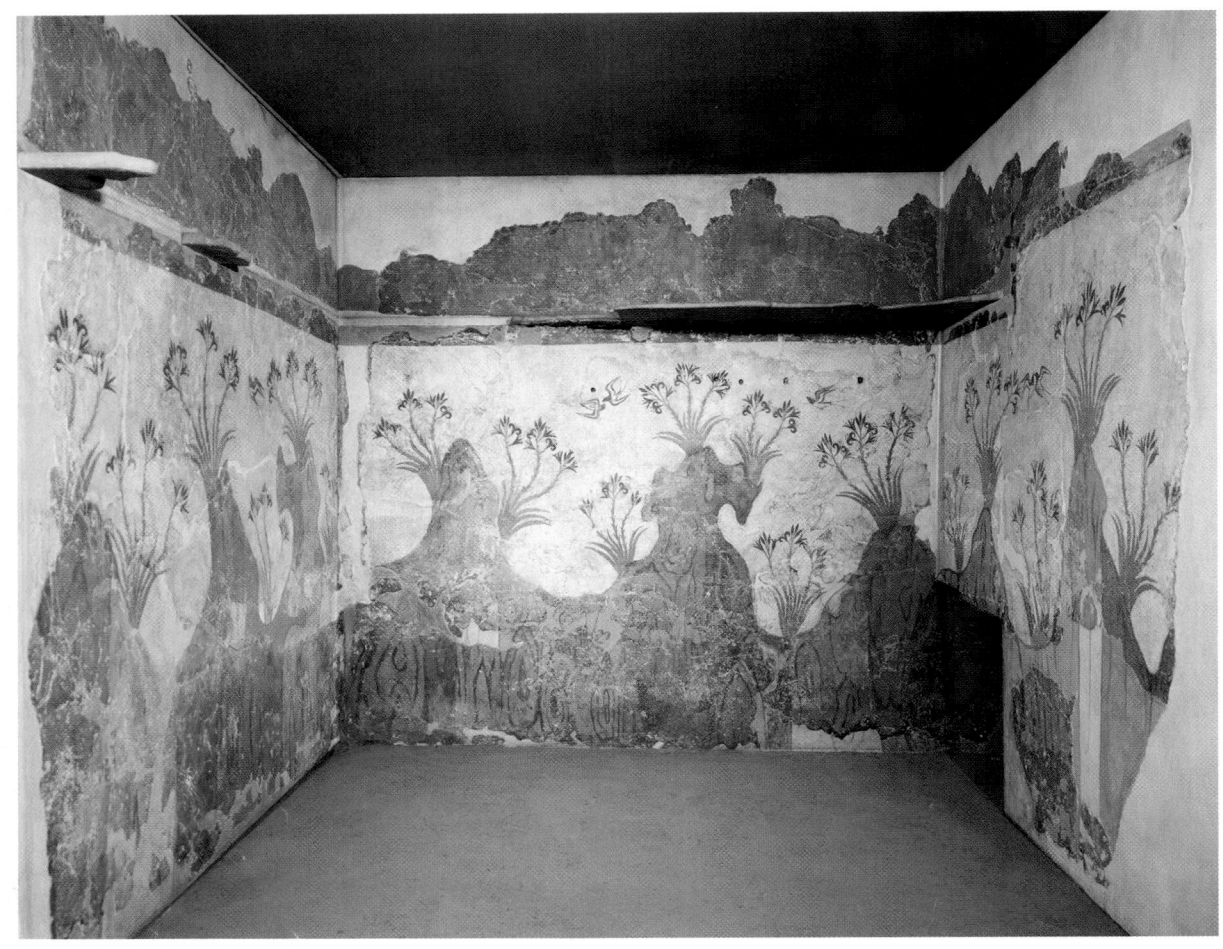

4.9 *Spring Fresco*, from Akrotiri, Thera. ca. 1600–1500 BCE. National Archaeological Museum, Athens

below, the painter used countless disembodied heads as a short-hand technique to denote the crowd, rendered with simple, impressionistic black strokes, on a swath of brown for males and white for females. The crowd figures are smaller in scale than the central women, suggesting that they are of lesser importance. The fresco may represent an event that took place in the palace's central court, as archaeologists have unearthed remains of a tripartite room on the west side of the court.

In many other Minoan paintings, nature is the primary subject. A painting found in fragments in a light well has been restored to a wall in the room Evans called the "Queen's Megaron" in Knossos' east wing (fig. 4.8), though some have contended that it actually belongs on the floor. Blue and yellow dolphins swim against a blue-streaked cream background, cavorting with small fish. Within the upper and lower frames, multilobed green forms represent plants and rocks. Sinuous outlines suggest the creatures' forms, while the curving, organic elements throughout the composition animate the painting. Such lively representations of nature occur frequently in Minoan art in a variety of mediums, and the many images of sea creatures probably reflect the Minoans' keen awareness of and respect for the sea. The casual quality of Minoan images contrasts forcefully with the rigidity and timelessness of many Egyptian representations, even though there is good evidence for contact between Minoan artists and Egypt.

PAINTED LANDSCAPES IN A SEASIDE TOWN In the mid-second millennium BCE, a volcano erupted on the Cycladic island of Thera (present-day Santorini), about 60 miles (96 km) north of Crete. The eruption covered the town of Akrotiri in a deep layer of volcanic ash and pumice. Beginning in 1967, excavations directed by Spyridon Marinatos and then Christos Doumas uncovered houses dating from the Middle Minoan III phase (approximately 1670–1620 BCE) preserved up to a height of two stories. On their walls was an extraordinary series of paintings.

Landscapes dominate. In a small ground-floor room, a rocky landscape known as the *Spring Fresco* occupies almost the entire wall surface (fig. 4.9). The craggy terrain undulates dramatically, its dark outline filled with rich washes of red, blue, and ocher—colors that were probably present in the island's volcanic soils—with swirling black lines to add texture within. Sprouting from its surface, lilies flower in vivid red trios, while swallows dart between them, painted in a few graceful black lines.

In other rooms at Akrotiri, painters inserted humans into the landscape. Often they are life-size, but sometimes smaller, as in a painting on the upper section of at least three walls in a large second-floor room (fig. 4.10). The scene reflects the town's role as a harbor: A fleet of ships ferries passengers between islands, set within a sea full of leaping dolphins. The ships vary, some being under sail and some rowed by oarsmen, but the painter's brush describes them all carefully. The same is true of the islands, each of which features a port city with detailed stone architecture. Crowds of people watch the spectacle from streets, rooftops, and windows. The painting may represent an actual event—a memorable expedition to a foreign land, perhaps, or an annual festival.

Minoan Pottery

Like the wall paintings, Minoan painted pottery was inspired by the natural world of the Aegean. Minoan potters painted their vessels sensitively with lively organic forms that enhance the curving shapes of the vases. By the Middle and Late Minoan periods, they manufactured pottery on the wheel, allowing for a variety of rounded forms and many sizes. Minoans used large and rough vessels for storage, while inhabitants of the "palaces" used the finest wares, which were often very thin-walled. Minoans also exported these "eggshell" ceramics in great quantities to markets all around the Mediterranean, creating one of the first major international industries.

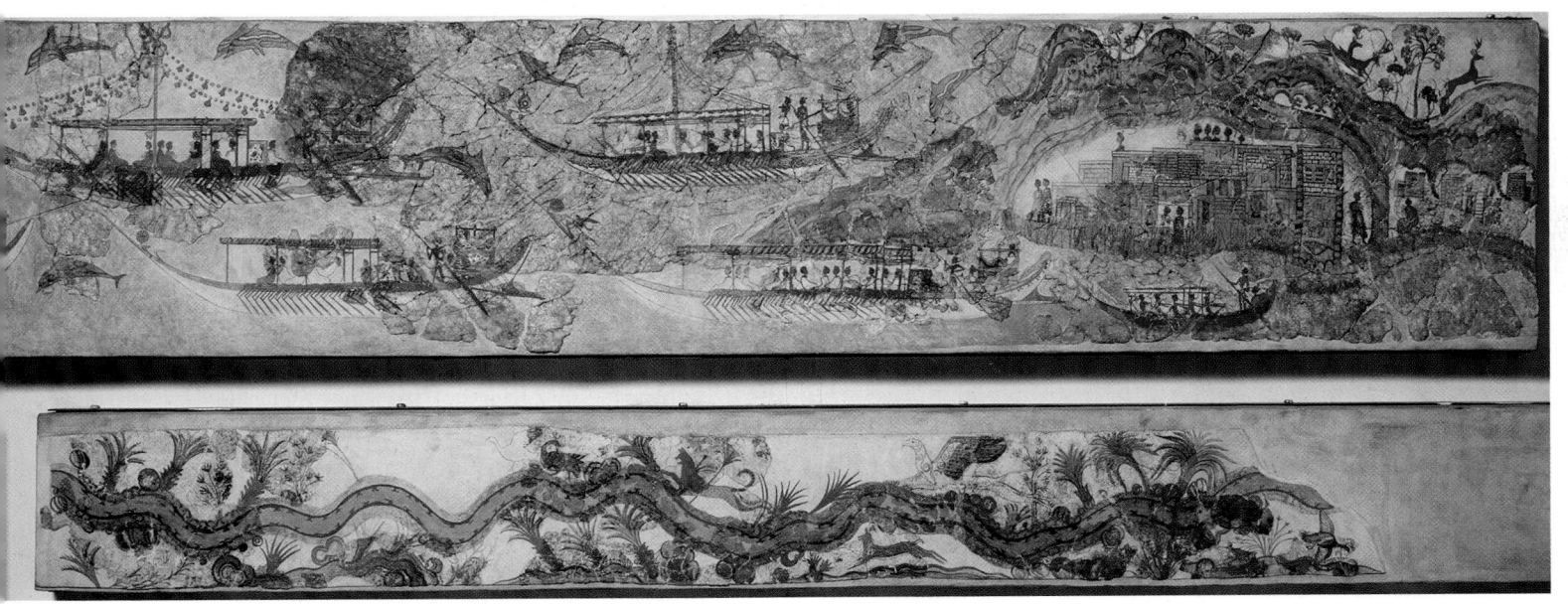

4.10 *Flotilla Fresco*, from Akrotiri, Thera. ca. 1600–1500 BCE. National Archaeological Museum, Athens

KAMARES WARE The shape of a vase from Phaistos in southern Crete, dating to the Middle Minoan II period (about 1800 BCE), illustrates the organic approach of many Minoan potters to their wares (fig. **4.11**). Its neck curves upward into a beak shape, which the vase painter has emphasized by giving it an eye. Bold curvilinear forms in white, red, orange, and yellow stand out against a black background to form abstracted sea horses, which endow the vessel with life and movement. This style, known today as Kamares ware, first appears at the beginning of the Middle Minoan phase and took its name from the cave on Mount Ida where it originally came to light.

MARINE MOTIFS Marine motifs gained prevalence in the pottery of the slightly more recent Late Minoan IB phase. A stirrup jar, with two round handles flanking its narrow spout, makes a vivid example of this "marine style." A wide-eyed black octopus swirls its tentacles around the body, contrasting with the light eggshell-colored clay (fig. **4.12**). Clumps of algae float between the tentacles. As with Minoan wall paintings, an extraordinarily dynamic and naturalistic quality energizes the painting. Moreover, the painting's forms express the shape of the vessel they decorate: The sea creature's rounded contours emphasize the jar's swollen belly, while the curves of its tentacles echo the curved

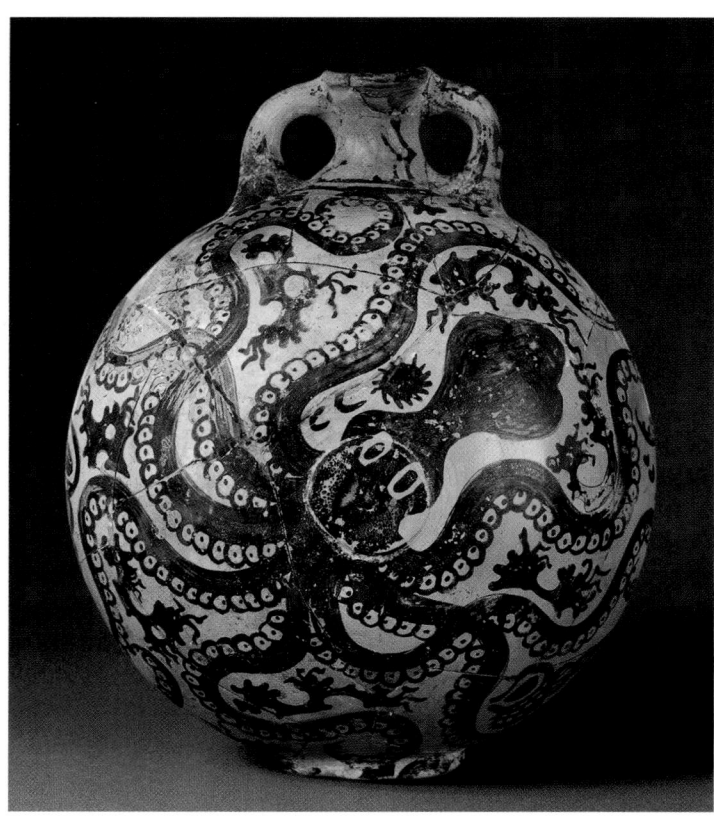

4.12 *Octopus Vase*, from Palaikastro, Crete. ca. 1500 BCE. Height 11" (28 cm). Archaeological Museum, Iráklion, Crete

handles. Exactly beneath the spout, the end of a tentacle curls to define a circle of the same size as the jar's opening.

Carved Minoan Stone Vessels

From an early date, Minoan artists also crafted vessels of soft stone, either from black steatite (soapstone), which was locally available, or from stones imported from other Aegean islands. They carved it with tools of a harder stone, hollowing out the interior with a bow-driven drill before finishing surfaces with an abrasive, probably emery. Traces of gold on some pieces reveal that the stone was often gilded. Fragments of such works were discovered at Hagia Triada on the southern side of Crete, including a black steatite vessel known as the *Harvester Vase*, with a large hole at the top and a smaller hole at the base (fig. **4.13**). This type of vessel was used for pouring liquid offerings or drinking. Later Greeks called it a rhyton (plural rhyta), and archaeologists suppose that, like many stone vessels, it had a ceremonial use.

Only the upper part of the rhyton survives. Twenty-seven slim, muscular men, mostly nude to the waist and clad in flat caps and pants, seem to move around the vessel in a lively rhythm and with raucous energy. Their dynamic movement is a counterpart to the animated imagery on Minoan pots and wall paintings. Hoisting long-handled tools over their shoulders, four bare-headed singers bellow with all their might. Their leader's chest is so distended that his ribs press through his skin. A single long-haired

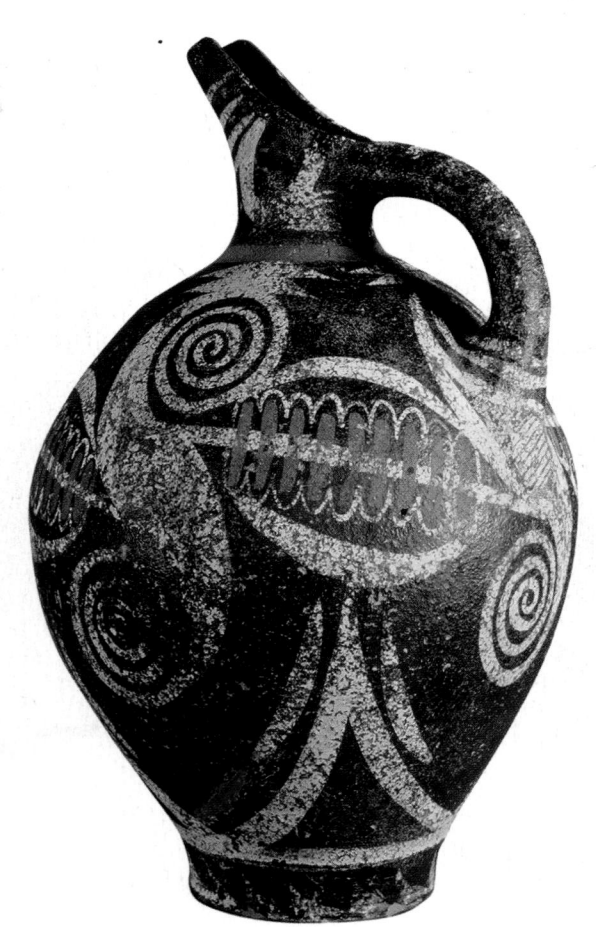

4.11 Beaked jug (Kamares ware), from Phaistos. ca. 1800 BCE. Height 10⅝" (27 cm). Archaeological Museum, Iráklion, Crete

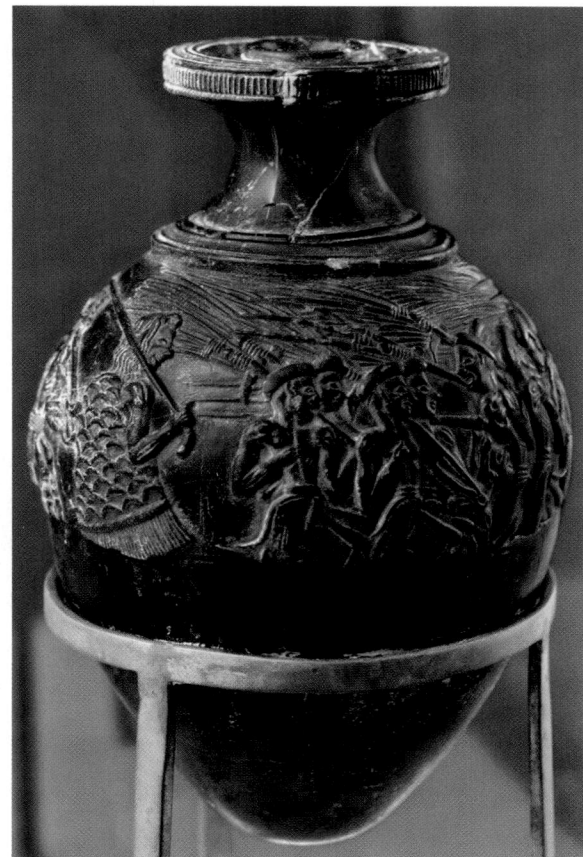

4.13 *Harvester Vase*, from Hagia Triada. ca. 1500–1450 BCE. Steatite (soapstone), width 4½" (11.3 cm). Archaeological Museum, Iráklion, Crete

Excavators have discovered similar vessels elsewhere in Crete, for instance at the palace at Zakros, on the east coast of Crete, and contemporaneous Egyptian tomb paintings depict Cretans carrying bull-headed rhyta, suggesting that the civilizations with which Minoans traded identified them with these distinctive vessels. The prevalence of the bull motif, coupled with evidence of altars decorated with horns, suggest that bulls played a part in Minoan religious ritual. Rhyta are often found smashed to pieces. Although later vandalism or earthquakes might account for the damage, their smashed state suggests that ceremonial vessels were ritually destroyed after use.

Religious life on Minoan Crete centered on shrines and on natural places deemed sacred, such as caves, mountain peaks, or groves. No temples or large cult statues have been discovered. Archaeologists did find two small-scale faience statuettes from

male in a scaly cloak, holding a staff, seems to head the procession. The leader of the singers holds a sistrum, a rattle that originated in Egypt. This detail and the composite depiction of the men's bodies provide evidence of contact between Crete and Egypt.

Interpretations of the scene depend partly on identifying the tools carried by the crowd and the objects suspended from their belts. If they are hoes and bags of seed corn, then the subject may be a sowing festival; if, instead, they are winnowing forks and whetstones, it is more likely a harvest festival. Alternatively, some see the scene as a warriors' triumph, while still others see a representation of forced labor. In the absence of further evidence, either archaeological or written, debate about the meaning of the image will certainly continue.

Another magnificent rhyton in the shape of a bull's head comes from Knossos, and dates to the Second Palace period (about 1500–1450 BCE) (fig. **4.14**). Like the *Harvester Vase*, it is carved from steatite, with white shell inlaid around the muzzle. For the eyes, the artist inserted a piece of rock crystal, painted on the underside with a red pupil, black iris, and white cornea, so that it has a startlingly lifelike appearance. The horns, now restored, were once of gilded wood. Light incisions in the steatite, dusted with white powder, evoke a shaggy texture and variegated color in the animal's fur. The vessel was filled through a hole in the neck, and a second hole below the mouth served as a spout.

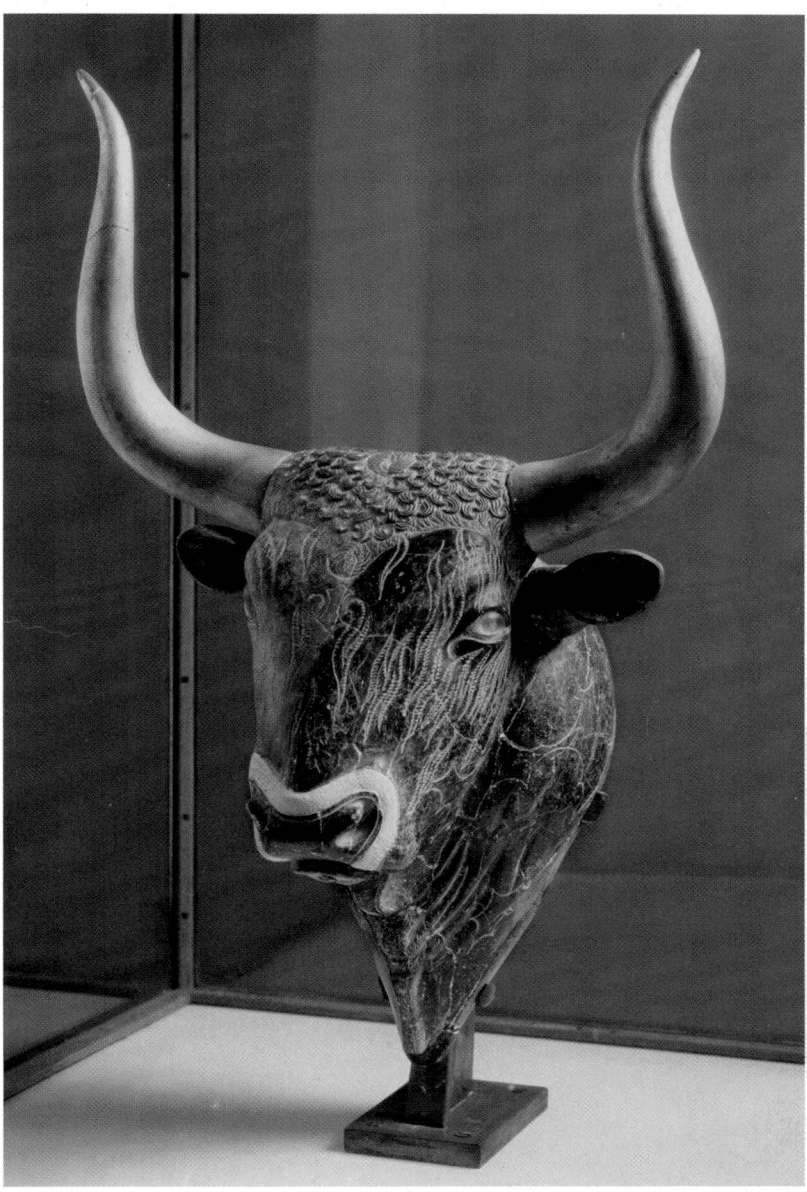

4.14 Rhyton in the shape of a bull's head, from Knossos, Crete. ca. 1500–1450 BCE. Serpentine, steatite, crystal, and shell inlay (horns restored), height 8⅛" (20.6 cm). Archaeological Museum, Iráklion, Crete

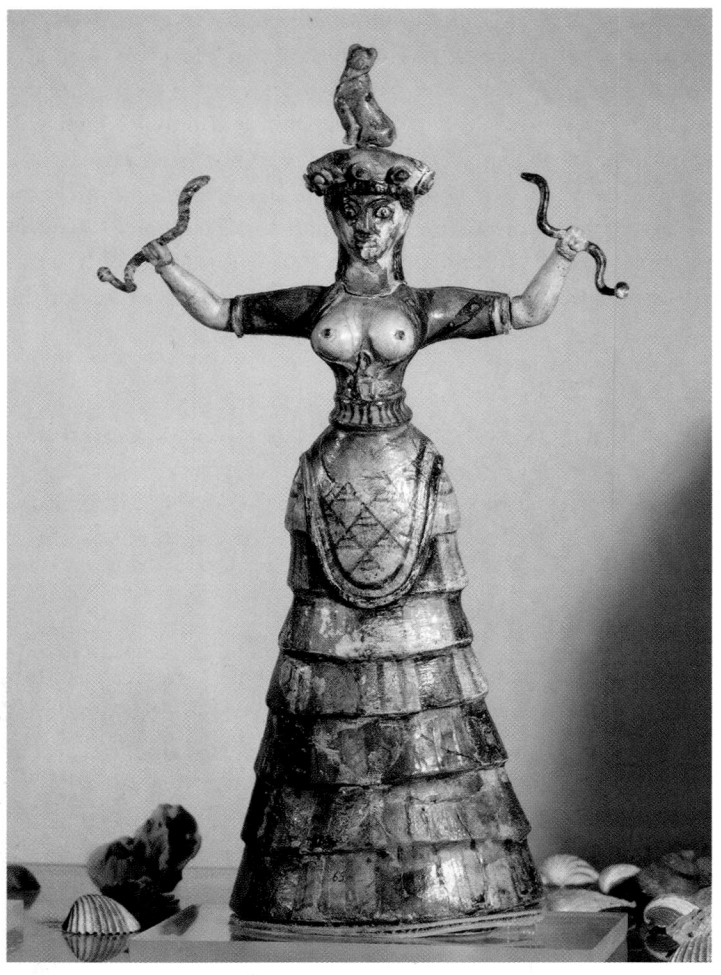

4.15 *Snake Goddess*, from the palace complex, Knossos, Crete. ca. 1650 BCE. Faience, height 11⅝" (29.5 cm). Archaeological Museum, Iráklion, Crete

the Middle Minoan III phase (about 1650 BCE) at Knossos. One shows a female figure raising a snake in each hand and wearing a headdress topped by a feline creature (fig. **4.15**). She is clad in a flounced skirt similar to those worn by women in the *Grandstand Fresco* (see fig. 4.7), and bares her breasts. Her tiny waist is another consistent feature of Minoan representations of humans, like the men on the *Harvester Vase* (see fig. 4.13). These statuettes came to light along with remnants of furniture in pits sunk in the floor of a room on the west side of the central court. Because some ancient religions associated snakes with earth deities and male fertility, and because of this statuette's bared breasts, some scholars have associated them with a mother goddess or ritual attendants, and identified the room as a shrine.

Late Minoan Art

It is unclear what brought Minoan civilization to an end. In the past, scholars argued that the eruption of the volcano on the island of Thera may have hastened its decline. Recent discoveries and dating of the volcanic ash from the eruption, however, indicate that the civilization on Crete survived this natural disaster, though perhaps in a weakened state. About 1450 BCE (Late Minoan II), invaders from the Greek mainland, whom archaeologists call Mycenaeans, took over the complexes on Crete. They established themselves in the center at Knossos until around 1375 BCE, when Knossos was destroyed and the Mycenaeans abandoned most of the island's sites. During the period of Mycenaean control, however, artists at Knossos worked in Minoan styles.

The fragmentary *Toreador Fresco* dates from the Mycenaean occupation of Knossos (Late Minoan II–IIIA), and appears to

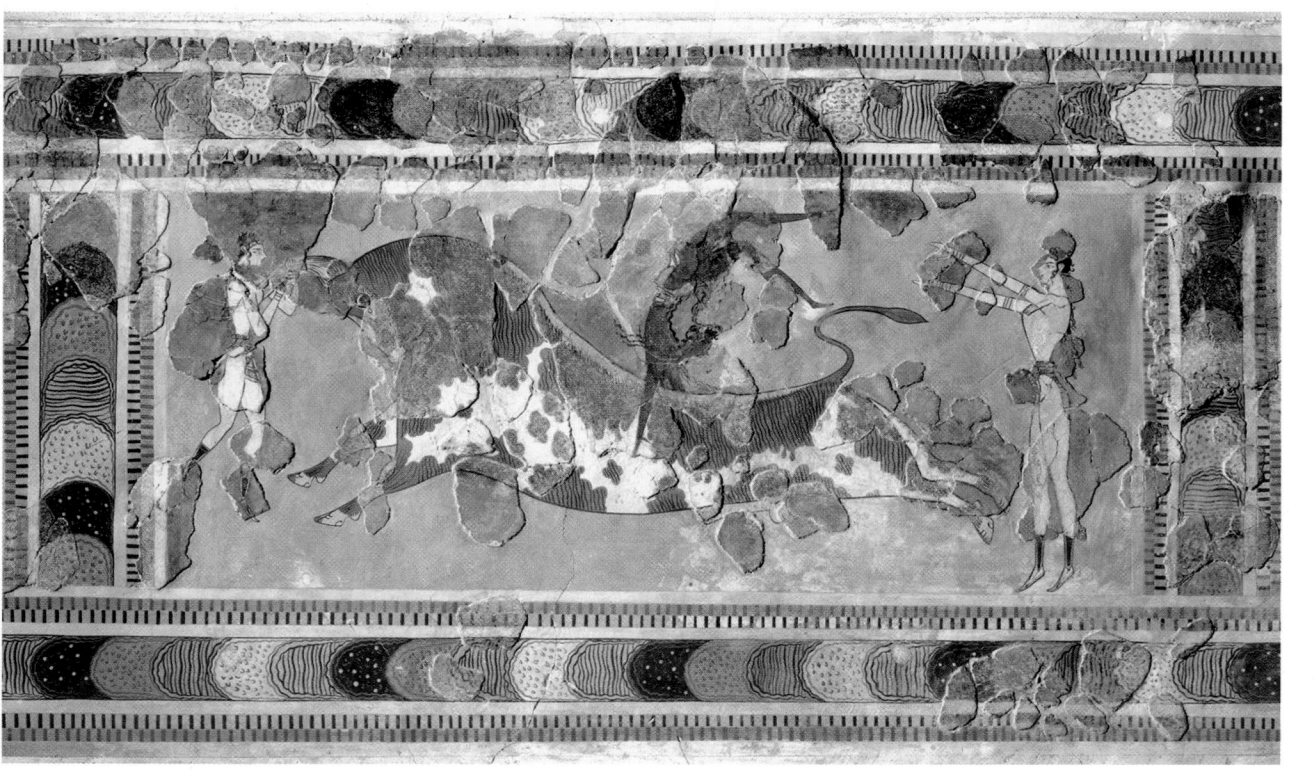

4.16 *Toreador Fresco*, from the palace complex, Knossos, Crete. ca. 1550–1450 BCE (restored). Fresco. Height including upper border approx. 24½" (62.3 cm). Archaeological Museum, Iráklion, Crete

have been one of a series that decorated an upper room in the northeast part of the palace (fig. **4.16**). Against a deep-blue background, a white-skinned figure clad in a kilt clasps the horns of a huge curvaceous bull, painted at a full gallop. Behind the bull, a similar white-skinned figure stands on tiptoe with arms outstretched, while above the bull's back, a dark-skinned figure performs a backward somersault. The figures have long limbs and small waists, and they are painted in profile. The strong washes of color, and animated though somewhat stylized poses, demonstrate the continuity of Minoan practice into the Late period.

Scholars continue to debate the meaning of this scene. Although most agree that such bull-leaping performances had a ritual function, the purpose of the activity and the identity of the participants remain unclear. Following the widespread Mediterranean convention for distinguishing gender by skin tone, Arthur Evans identified the light-skinned figures as female and the darker one as male. In this case, the presence of women in such a prominent role in Minoan imagery may serve as evidence of their importance in ritual activities. Others have seen the three figures as sequential representations of the same person, taking part in a coming-of-age initiation ceremony in which boys cast off their earlier "feminine" guise and emerge as fully masculine.

MYCENAEAN ART

By the time the Mycenaeans conquered Crete in about 1450 BCE, they had been building cities of their own on the Greek mainland since the start of the Late Helladic period, ca. 1600 BCE. They probably made early contact with Minoan Crete, which exerted important influences on their own culture. From the dating of Mycenaean sites and the objects discovered in them, archaeologists place the height of the culture between about 1500 and 1200 BCE (Late Helladic III). The most imposing remains are the citadels at sites that Homer named: Mycenae, Pylos, and Tiryns. The culture takes its name from the first of these, the legendary home of King Agamemnon, who led the Greek forces in Homer's account of the Trojan War.

Architecture: Citadels

At the beginning of the Second Palace period on Crete, growing settlements throughout the Greek mainland, including at Mycenae itself (figs. **4.17** and **4.18**), centered around large structures known as citadels (when fortified) or palaces. In some of them, most particularly Pylos on the southern coast of the

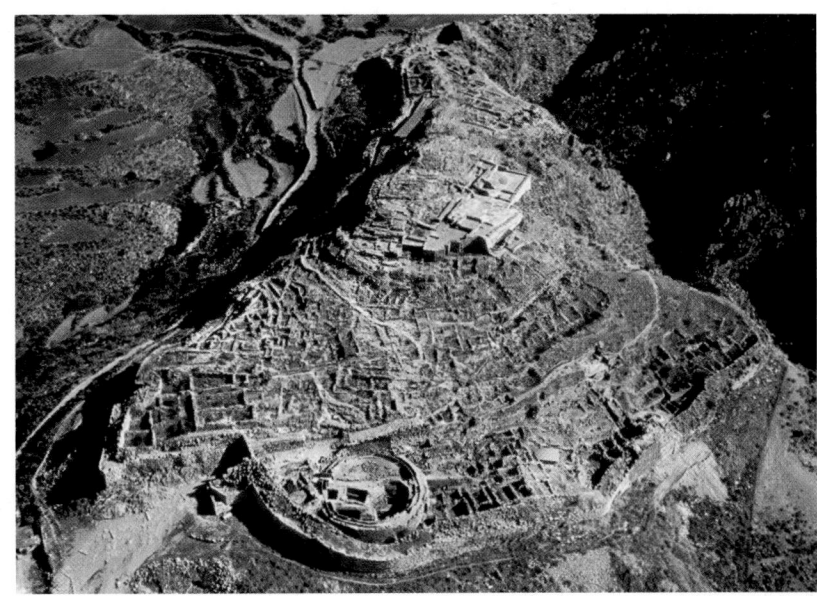

4.17 Aerial view of Mycenae, Greece. ca. 1600–1200 BCE

4.18 Reconstruction of Mycenae, Greece

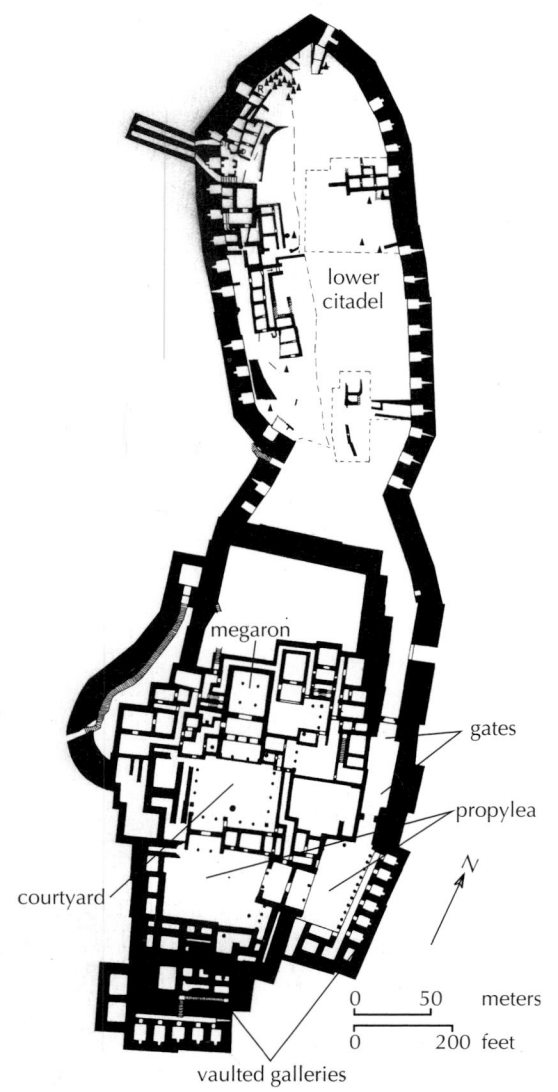

lower
citadel

megaron

gates

propylea

courtyard

N

0   50   meters

0   200 feet

vaulted galleries

4.19   Plan of palace and citadel at Tiryns, Greece. ca. 1400–1200 BCE

provide water during a siege, have led scholars to regard the Mycenaeans as quite different from the Minoans, with a culture focused primarily on warfare. The contrast is often stated in terms that imply an essential character difference between nature-loving Minoans and warmongering Mycenaeans. Homer's characterizations of the kings of this era and, in fact, his entire narrative of the Trojan War, only reinforce modern ideas about the Mycenaeans as warlike. The poet describes the city of Tiryns, set on a rocky outcropping in the plain of Argos in the northeastern Peloponnesus, as "Tiryns of the Great Walls." We should note, however, that Mycenaean fortifications date to after the destruction of Minoan centers, so the Mycenaeans may have been responding to a new set of political and social circumstances.

The inhabitants at Tiryns fortified their citadel in several stages around 1365 BCE (fig. **4.19**). Like the slightly later walls at Mycenae, those at Tiryns consist of massive blocks of limestone, weighing as much as 5 tons. For most of the wall, the blocks were irregularly shaped (or polygonal), wedged together with smaller stones and fragments of pottery. At entrances or other highly visible places, the stones might be saw-cut and dressed, or smoothed with a hammer. In its final form, the outer wall at Tiryns was a full 20 feet thick, and a second inner wall was just as impressive. Centuries later, the massiveness of these walls so awed the Greeks that they declared them the work of the Cyclopes, a mythical race of one-eyed giants. Even today, archaeologists term such walls "Cyclopean."

Builders designed the fortifications at Tiryns carefully to manipulate any visitor's approach to the residents' military advantage, just as the slightly earlier Hittite fortifications did (see fig. **2.22**). A narrow fortified ramp circled the walls, so that an aggressor approaching in a clockwise direction would have his nonshield-bearing side vulnerable to attack by defenders on the walls. If an aggressor reached the entrance, two sets of fortified **propylons** (gateways) presented further obstacles: Inhabitants could trap the aggressor between the propylons and attack from above. Within the walls, rooms and passages known as **casemates** provided storage for weapons (fig. **4.20**). They also offered safety for townspeople or soldiers during an assault. The gallery passage was built using a **corbel** technique: Each course of masonry projects slightly beyond the course below it, until the walls meet in an irregular arch to cover the span (fig. **4.21**). When a corbel roofs an entire space, as it does here, it is called a **corbel vault**.

A corbel arch served effectively to create the Lioness Gate at Mycenae of about 1250 BCE. When the inhabitants enlarged the city walls to improve its defenses, they built this gate as a principal entrance into the citadel (fig. **4.22**). Two massive stone posts support a huge lintel to form the opening. Above the lintel, a corbel arch directs the weight of the heavy wall to the strong posts below it. The corbel thus relieves the weight resting on the vast stone lintel, which itself weighs 25 tons; this form of construction is known as a **relieving triangle**. To seal the resulting gap, the builders inserted a triangular gray limestone slab above the lintel, carved with a huge pair of animals, probably lionesses. They stand in a **heraldic pose** (as mirror images of each other), with their

Peloponnesian region (see map 4.1), archaeologists found clay tablets inscribed with a second early writing system, which they dubbed Linear B because of its linear character and because it derived, in part, from earlier Minoan Linear A. Architect and classical scholar Michael Ventris decoded the system in 1952. The tablets proved to have been inventories and archival documents, and the language of Linear B was an early form of Greek. The inhabitants of these Late Bronze Age sites, therefore, were the precursors of the Greeks of more recent times.

The Linear B tablets refer to a *wanax* ("lord" or "king"), suggesting something of a Mycenaean social order, so it is reasonable to suppose that Mycenaean citadels and palaces may have incorporated royal residences. The inhabitants of many of these sites gradually enclosed them with imposing exterior walls. They exploited the sites' topography for defense purposes, and often expanded and improved their walls in several building phases. They constructed these fortifications of large stone blocks laid on top of each other, creating walls that were at times 20 feet thick. These walls, and tunnels leading from them to wells that would

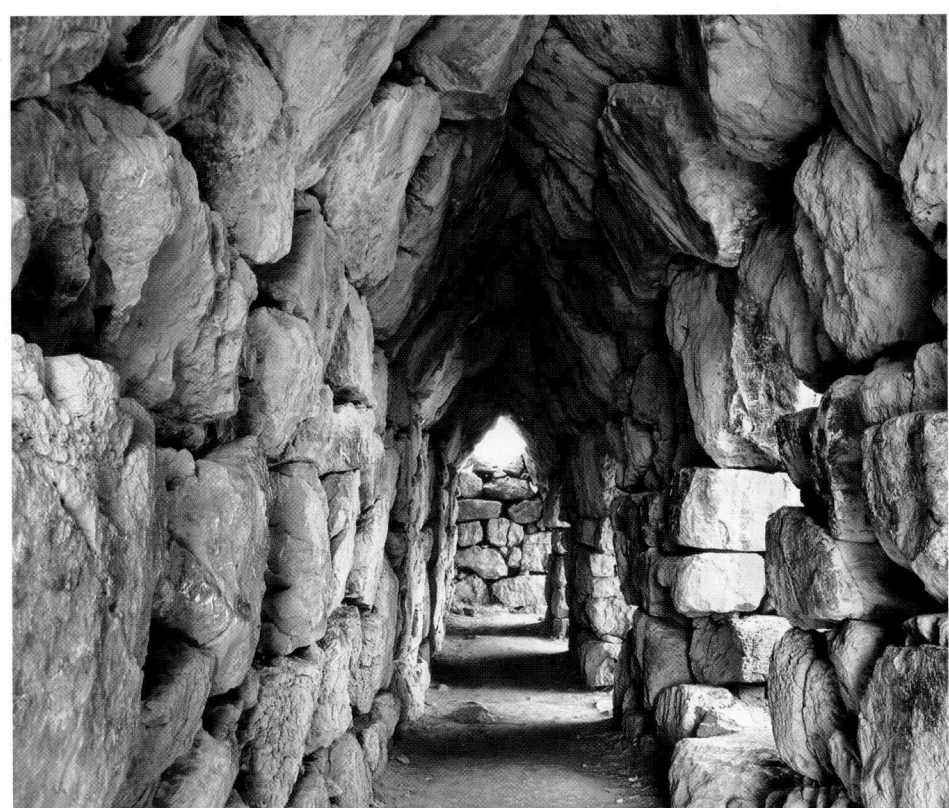

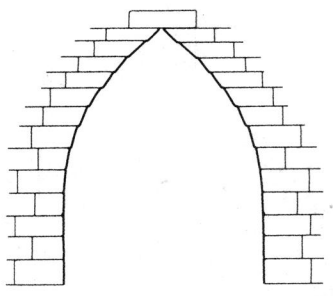

4.21 Drawing: corbel arch

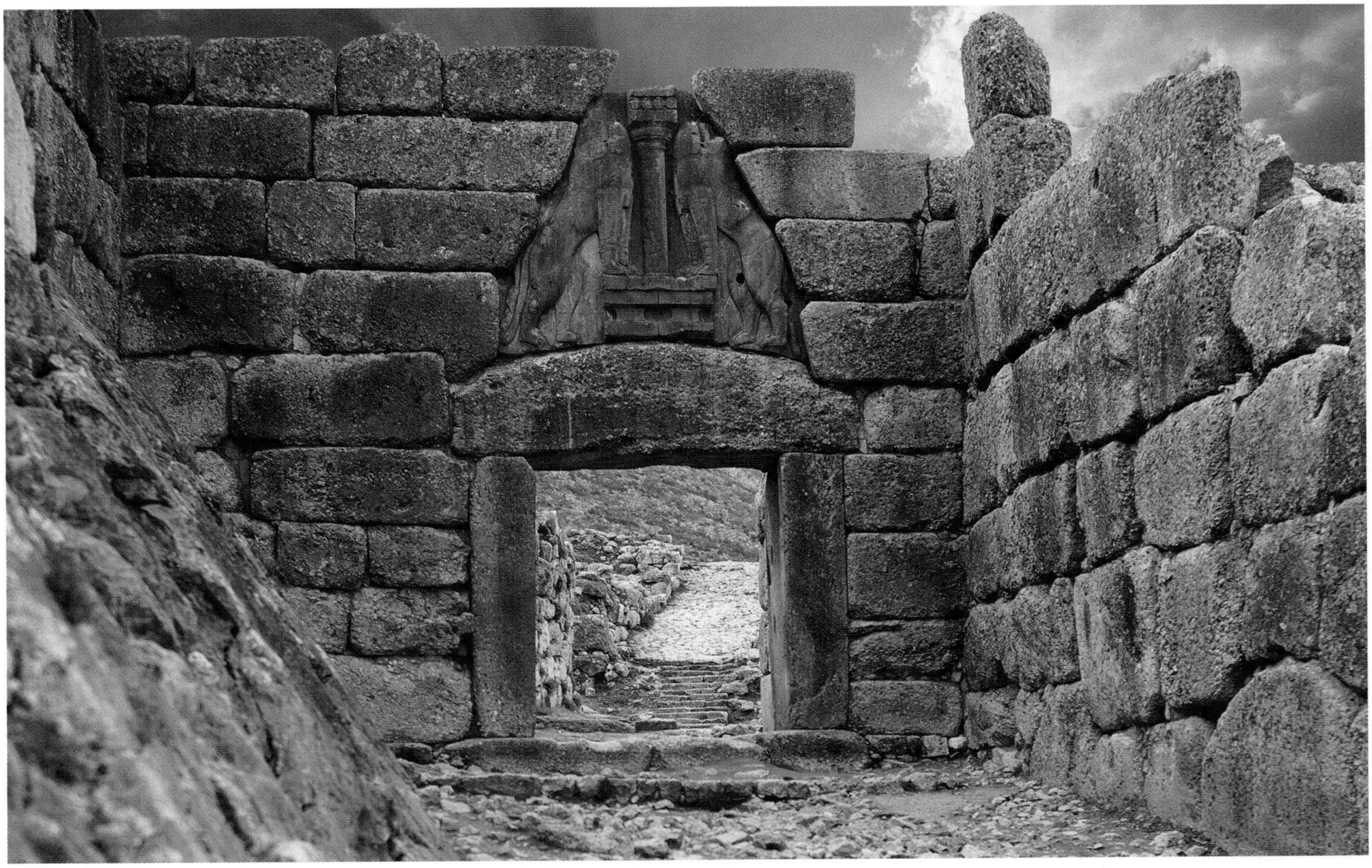

4.22 The Lioness Gate, Mycenae, Greece. ca. 1250 BCE

front paws on a pair of altars of a Minoan type, and flanking a tapering Minoan-style column, which may have supported another element of some kind. Dowel holes in their necks suggest that their heads were added separately, in wood or a different stone. At almost 10 feet high, this relief is the first large-scale sculpture known on the Greek mainland. The lionesses function as guardians, and their tense, muscular bodies and symmetrical design suggest an influence from the Near East. Mycenaeans ventured all over the Mediterranean, including Egypt and Anatolia, and Hittite records suggest contact with a people who may have been Mycenaean. Similar structures such as the Hittite Lion Gate at Bogazköy in Anatolia (fig. 2.22) may have suggested the concept of animal guardians at the gate of a palace.

The fortifications of Mycenaean citadels protected a variety of buildings (see figs. 4.17 and 4.18). These interior structures were built of rubble in a timber framework, as in Minoan palaces, sometimes faced with limestone. The dominant building was a **megaron**, a large rectangular audience hall. At Tiryns (see fig. 4.19) the megaron lay adjacent to an open courtyard. Two columns defined a deep porch that led into a vestibule and then into the hall. The hall contained a throne and a large central hearth of stuccoed clay, surrounded by four columns supporting the roof beams. Above the hearth, the ceiling may have been left open to the sky or covered by a raised roof, allowing smoke to escape and light to enter.

The design of a megaron is essentially an enlarged version of simple houses of earlier generations; its ancestry goes back at least to Troy in 3000 BCE. A particularly well-preserved example survives at the southern Peloponnesian palace of Pylos of about 1300 BCE. There, the hearth is set into a plastered floor decorated to resemble flagstones of varied ornamental stone (fig. **4.23**). A rich decorative scheme of wall paintings and ornamental carvings enhanced the megaron's appearance. The throne stands against the northeast wall, and painted griffins flank it on either side, similar

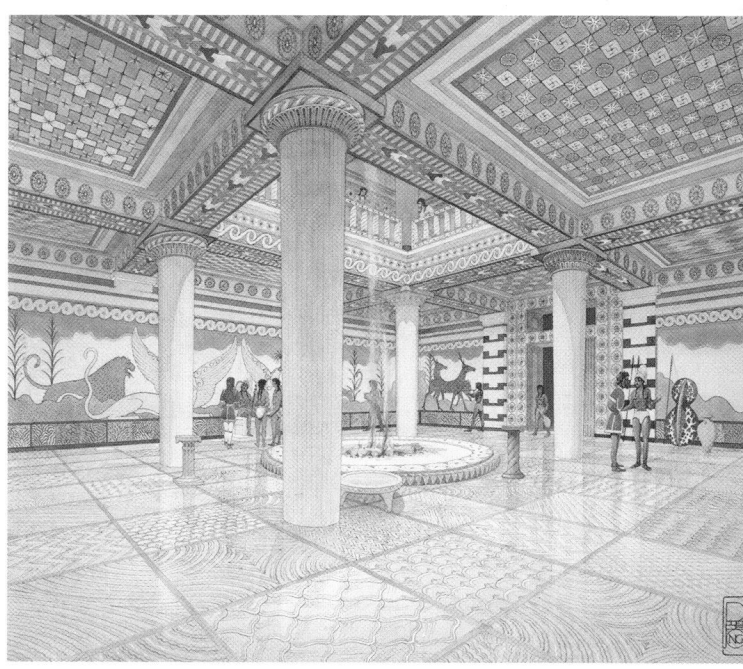

4.23   Reconstruction of megaron at Pylos. ca. 1300–1200 BCE

to those decorating the throne room at Knossos, elaborated under Mycenaean rule. Other elements of the decoration, such as the shape of the columns and the ornament around the doorways, reveal further Minoan influence at Pylos.

Mycenaean Tombs and Their Contents

At the end of the Middle Helladic period at Mycenae, ca. 1600 BCE, the ruling elite began to bury their dead in deep rectangular shafts, marking them at ground level with stones shaped like stelai. The burials were distributed in two groups (known as

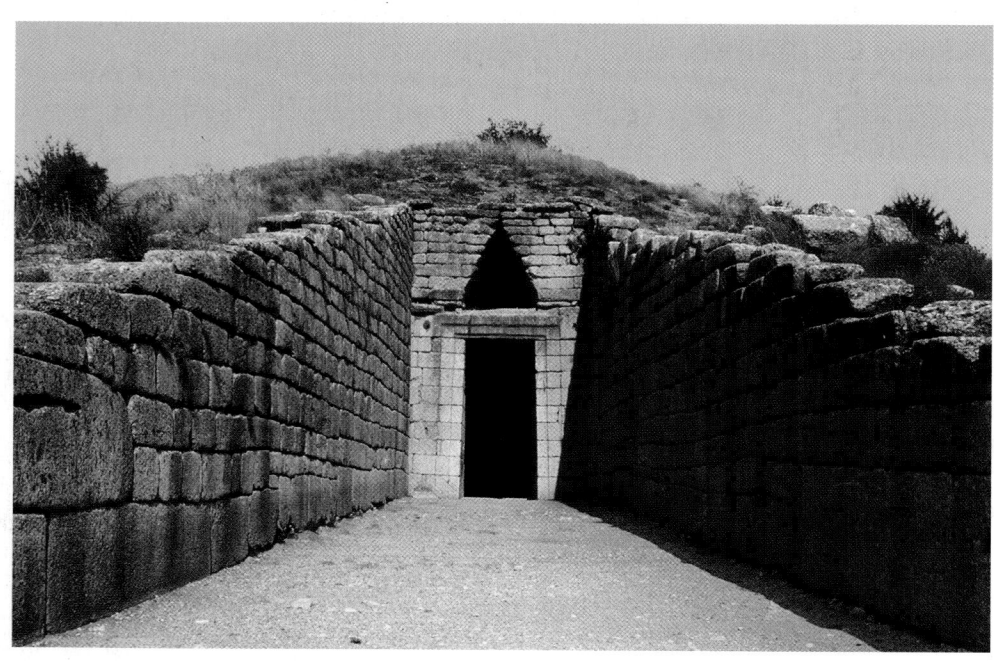

4.24   "Treasury of Atreus," Mycenae, Greece. ca. 1300–1250 BCE

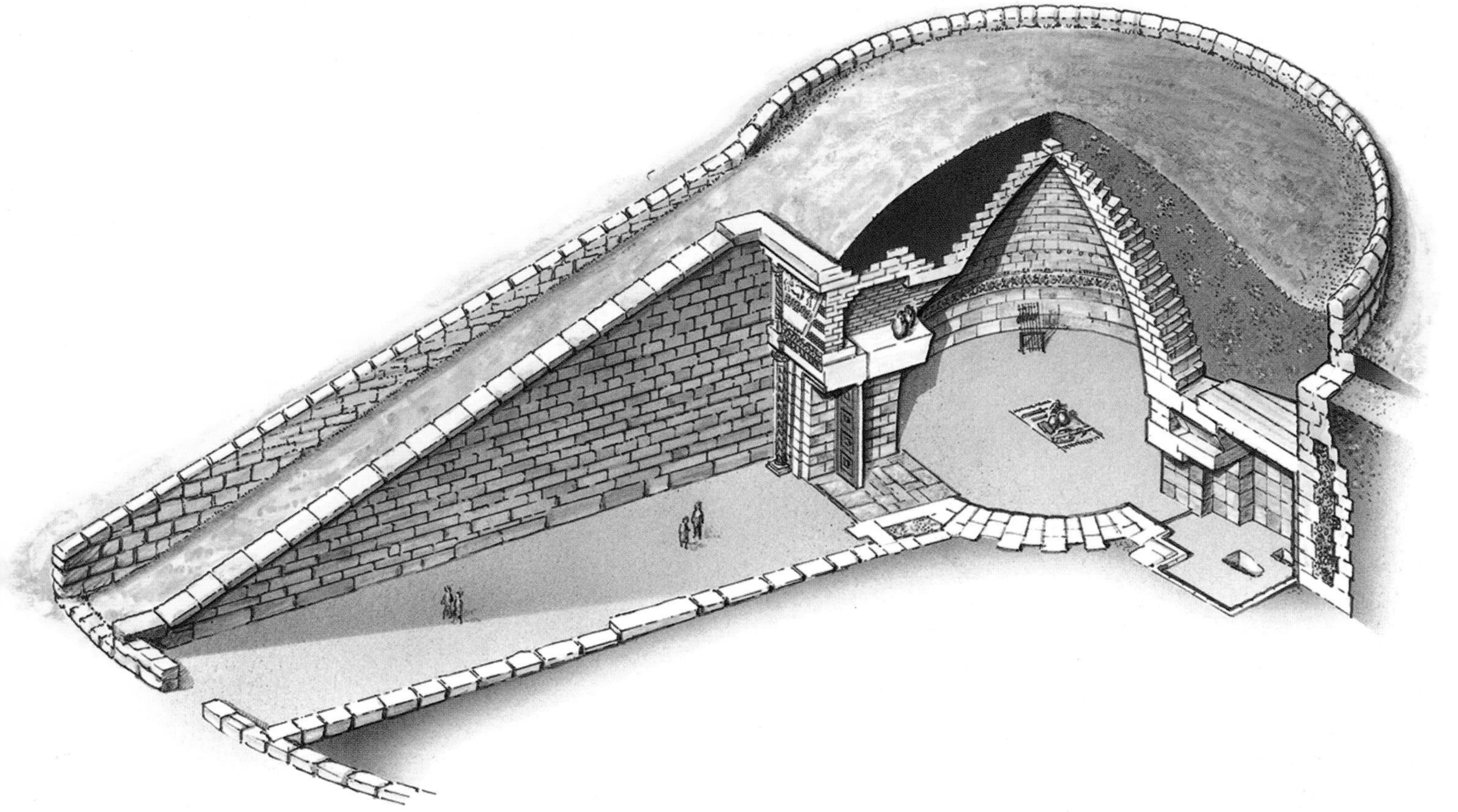

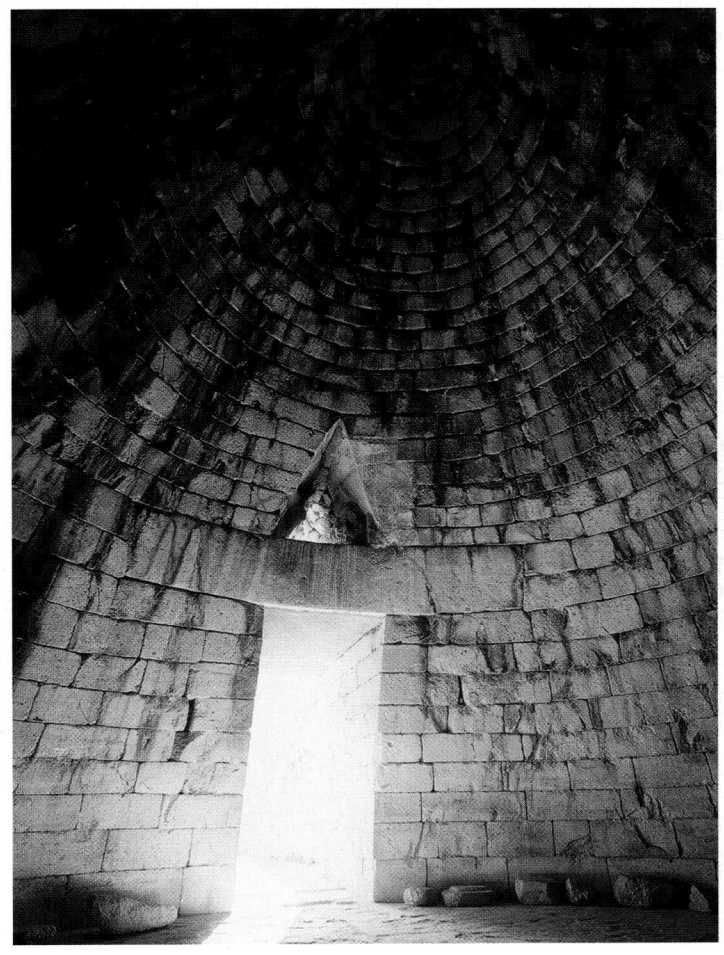

4.25 Reconstruction of "Treasury of Atreus," Mycenae, Greece

Grave Circles A and B), which later generations eventually set off and monumentalized with a low circular wall. As time passed, the elite built more dramatic tombs, in a round form known as a **tholos**. Over 100 tholoi are known on the mainland, nine of them near Mycenae.

One of the best-preserved and largest of these tombs is at Mycenae. Dubbed the "Treasury of Atreus" after the head of the clan that Homer placed at Mycenae, it dates to about 1250 BCE (Late Helladic III B). A great pathway, or **dromos**, lined with carefully cut and fitted ashlar masonry, led to a spectacular entrance (figs. **4.24** and **4.25**). The door slopes inward, in a style associated with Egyptian construction. Flanking the opening were columns of Egyptian green marble, carved with spirals and zigzags. Above the doorway, small columns framed decorative marble bands that concealed a relieving triangle.

The tomb itself consisted of a large circular chamber dug into sloping ground and then built up from ground level with a corbel vault: Courses of ashlar blocks protruded inward beyond one another up to a capstone (fig. **4.26**). When built in rings rather than parallel walls (as at Tiryns, see fig. **4.20**), the corbel vault

4.26 Interior of "Treasury of Atreus," Mycenae, Greece

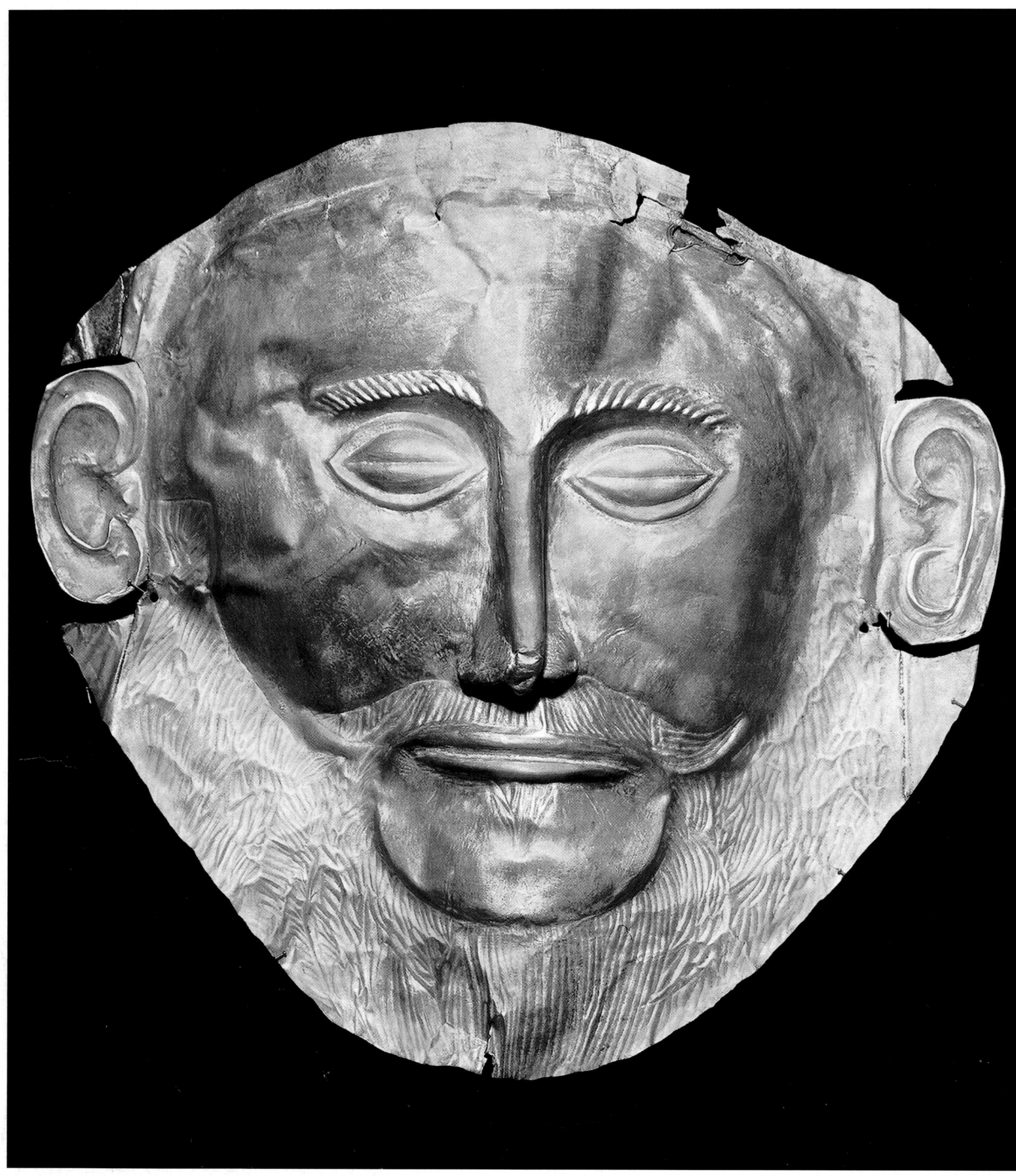

4.27 *Mask of Agamemnon*, from shaft grave, Grave Circle A, Mycenae, Greece. ca. 1600–1500 BCE. Gold, height 12" (35 cm). National Archaeological Museum, Athens

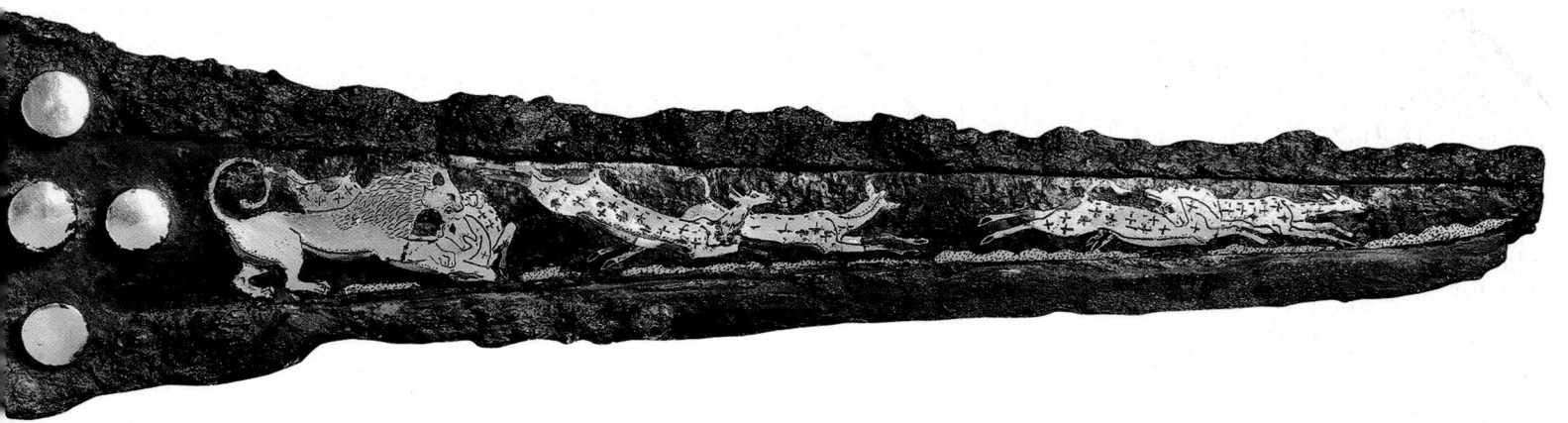

4.28 Inlaid dagger blade, from shaft grave IV, Grave Circle A, Mycenae, Greece. ca. 1600–1550 BCE. Length 9⅜" (23.8 cm). National Archaeological Museum, Athens

results in a beehive profile for the roof. Gilded rosettes may once have decorated the ashlar blocks of the vault to resemble a starry sky. The vault rose 43 feet over a space 48 feet in diameter. Architects would not dare such a large unsupported span again until the Pantheon of Roman times (see Chapter 7). To one side of the main room, a small rectangular chamber contained subsidiary burials. Earth covered the entire structure, helping to stabilize the layers of stone and creating a small hill, which was encircled with stones.

METALWORK Like the Great Pyramids of Egypt, these monumental *tholos* tombs exalted the dead by drawing attention to themselves. As a result, they also attracted robbers throughout the ages, and the grave goods that once filled them have long been dispersed. Many of the earlier shaft graves also contained lavish burial goods, ranging from luxurious clothing and furniture to fine weaponry. On excavating Grave Circle A, Heinrich Schliemann discovered five extraordinary death masks of hammered gold, covering the faces of dead males. Although far from naturalistic, each mask displays a distinct treatment of physiognomy: Some faces are bearded while others are clean-shaven. This suggests that the goldsmiths individualized the masks somewhat to correspond to the deceased's appearance. On finding one of them in 1876 (fig. **4.27**), Schliemann telegraphed a Greek newspaper, "I have gazed on the face of Agamemnon." Since modern archaeology places the mask between 1600 and 1500 BCE, and the Trojan War—if it happened—would date to about 1300–1200 BCE, this could not in fact be a mask of Agamemnon, despite its title. But it may represent a Mycenaean king of some stature, given the expense of the materials and the other objects found near it. Among the weapons in the graves were finely made ornamental bronze dagger blades, some of them inlaid with spirals or figural scenes in gold, silver, and niello (a sulfur alloy that bonds with silver when heated to produce a shiny black metallic finish). The example in figure **4.28** depicts a lion preying on gazelles; the dagger's owner claims the lion's predatory strength.

THE *VAPHIO CUPS* While the burial method used in the shaft graves is distinctively Mycenaean, the treasures found within them raise an interesting question about the interactions between Minoans and Mycenaeans. Many objects show Minoan influence, while others appear so Minoan that they must have come from Crete or been created by Cretan craftsmen. Two gold cups from a Mycenaean tomb at Vaphio near Sparta, in the southern Peloponnesus, are particularly intriguing (fig. **4.29**). Probably crafted between 1500 and 1450 BCE, they are made of two skins of gold: The outer layer was embossed with scenes of bull-catching—a theme with Minoan roots—while the inner lining is smooth. A cylindrical handle was riveted to one side. On one cup, bull-trappers try to capture the animal with nets, while on the other, a cow is set out to pasture to entice a bull into captivity. The subject matter of the cups suggests that they refer to one another, yet they are not, strictly speaking, a pair. One cup has an upper border framing the scene, but the other does not, and stylistic analyses suggest that different artists crafted them. Where the cups or the artists originated is a matter for debate. For some, the "finer" cup (with the pasture scene) must be Minoan on account of its peaceful quality, and the other a more violent Mycenaean complement made by a Mycenaean—or a Minoan—artist. What the cups underline is how little we understand about the interplay between, and the movements of, Minoan and Mycenaean artists, and, indeed, how arbitrary and subjective our attempts to distinguish between them may be.

Sculpture

Mycenaean religious architecture apparently consisted of modest structures set apart from the palaces. At these small shrines, Mycenaeans worshiped a wide variety of gods. Names recorded on Linear B tablets indicate that some of them, such as Poseidon, are the predecessors of the later Olympian gods of Greece. The Greek Poseidon was the god of the sea, and was probably of some importance to the seafaring Mycenaeans.

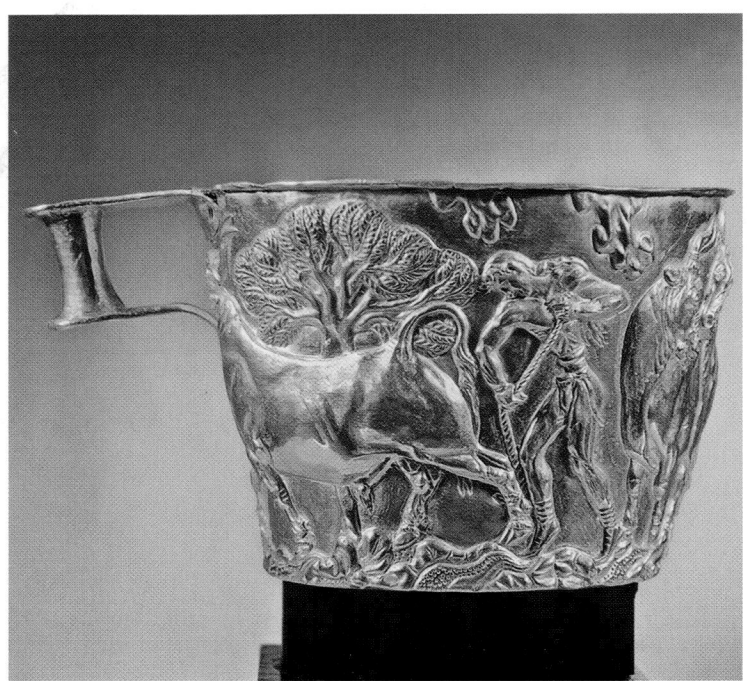
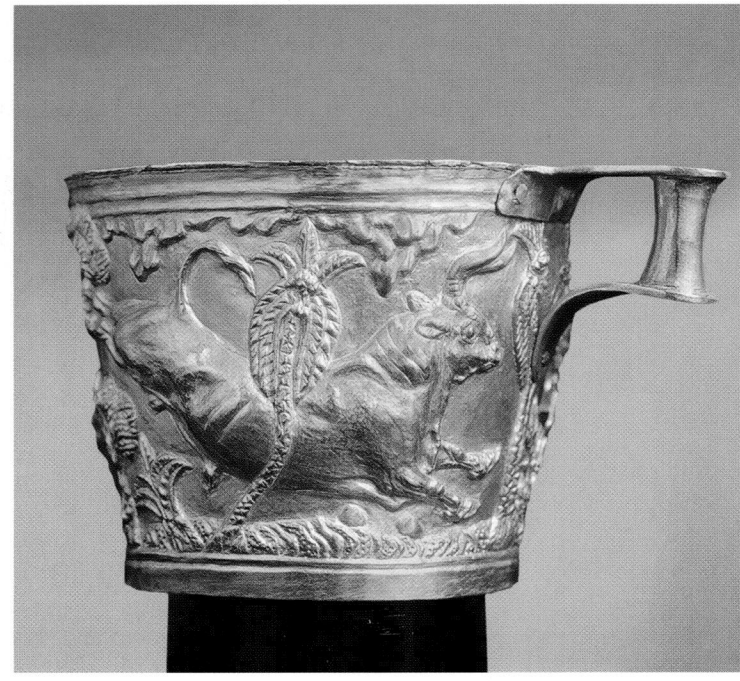

4.29 *Vaphio Cups.* ca. 1500–1450 BCE. Gold, height 3½" (3.9 cm). National Archaeological Museum, Athens

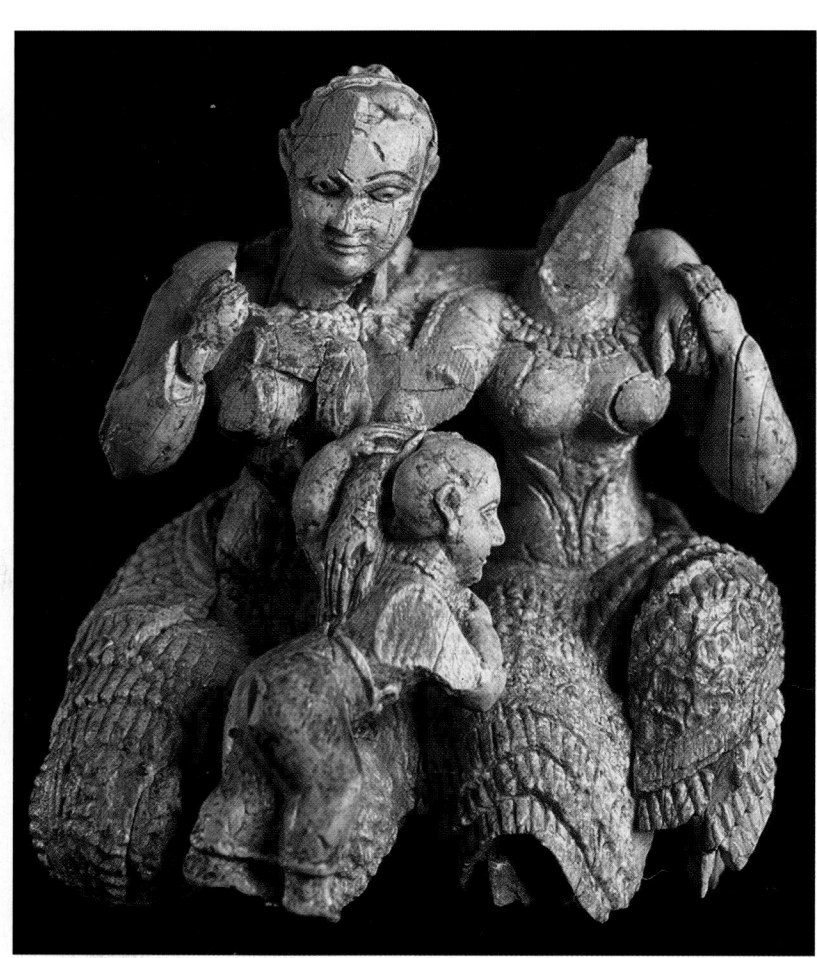

4.30 *Three Deities*, from Mycenae, Greece. 14th–13th century BCE. Ivory, height 3" (7.5 cm). National Archaeological Museum, Athens. Ministry of Culture Archaeological Receipts Fund. 7711

Free-standing sculptures are rare, but one small, finely carved ivory group depicting two kneeling women with a young child came to light in a shrine next to the palace at Mycenae in 1939 (fig. **4.30**). The women wear flounced skirts similar to the one worn by the Minoan *Snake Goddess* (see fig. 4.15), suggesting that the work came from Crete or was carved by an artist from Crete working on the Greek mainland for Mycenaean patrons. Yet the material is ivory, and probably originated in Syria or Egypt, documenting Mycenaean trade links. The figures' intertwined limbs and the child's unsettled pose describe a transient moment. For some scholars, the close physical interaction among the figures suggests that this small object is a rendering of a family group, including grandmother, mother, and child. Others argue that it represents three separate divinities, one of whom takes the form of a child.

Along with the "Treasury of Atreus," with its echoes of Egypt, and the Lioness Gate, which is a blend of Minoan and Near Eastern influences, this sculpture and others that survive from Bronze Age Greece reveal a culture with contacts throughout the Mediterranean. Whether those contacts came as a result of war or trade, the culture of Mycenaean Greece was receptive to the ideas and forms of other regions. Despite its warlike and dynamic character, Mycenaean civilization collapsed around 1200 or 1100 BCE, probably in the chaos caused by the arrival of new peoples on the Greek mainland. Whether or not the inhabitants of these powerful citadels actually took part in a legendary ten-year-long siege of Troy in Asia Minor, their descendants believed they did. For the Greeks, the Mycenaean Age was an age of heroes.

Aegean Art

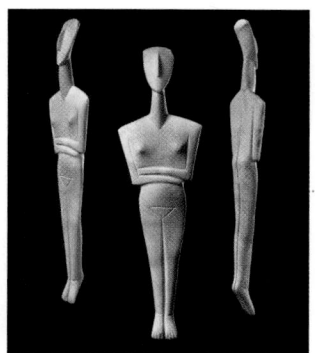

ca. 2500 BCE White marble Cycladic figurines

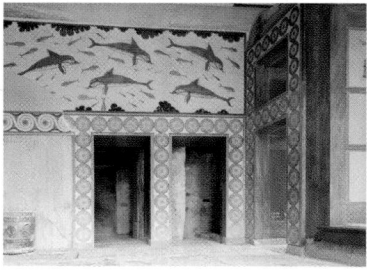

ca. 1700–1300 BCE Minoans construct the Second "Palace" at Knossos

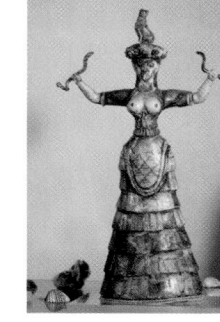

ca. 1650 BCE *Snake Goddess* from Knossos

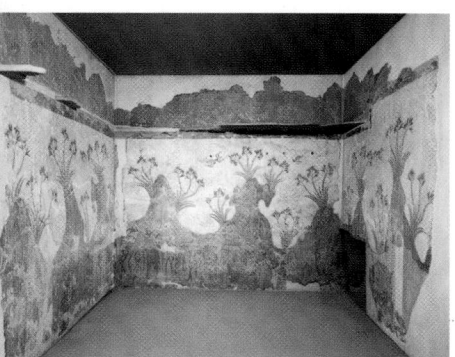

ca. 1600–1500 BCE *Spring Fresco* at Akrotiri, Thera

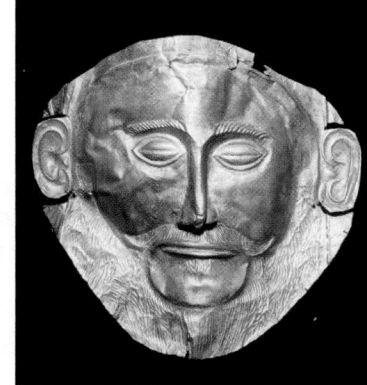

ca. 1600–1500 BCE Mycenaean death masks of hammered gold

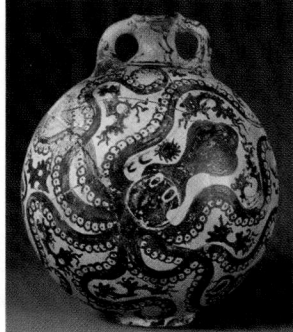

ca. 1500 BCE *Octopus Vase*, an example of Minoan "marine style" pottery

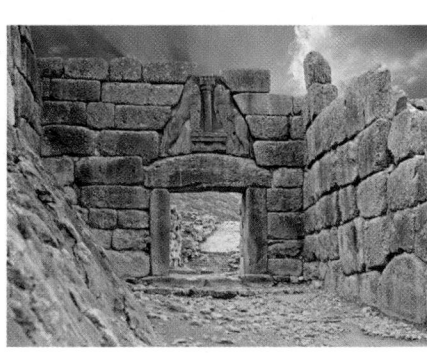

ca. 1250 BCE Construction of the Lioness Gate at Mycenae

3000 BCE

2750 BCE

2500 BCE

2250 BCE

2000 BCE

1750 BCE

1500 BCE

1250 BCE

1000 BCE

◄ ca. 2800 BCE Cycladic Islanders start to bury their dead in stone-lined pits

ca. 2575–2465 BCE Egypt's 4th Dynasty; construction of the three Great Pyramids at Giza

ca. 2100 BCE King Urnammu commissions the Great Ziggurat at Ur
ca. 2100 BCE Final phase of construction at Stonehenge

◄ ca. 2000 BCE Minoans build the first "palaces" on Crete, and develop Linear A

◄ ca. 1792–1750 BCE Hammurabi rules Babylon

◄ ca. 1500 BCE Volcano erupts on Thera
ca. 1500–1200 BCE Height of Mycenaean culture

◄ ca. 1450 BCE Earthquake demolishes Knossos and other Minoan centers; Mycenaeans invade Crete

ca. 1290–1224 BCE King Ramesses II rules Egypt, and commissions a monumental temple at Abu Simbel

◄ ca. 1200 BCE Depopulation of Aegean sites

◄ 8th century BCE *The Iliad* and *The Odyssey*, attributed to Homer

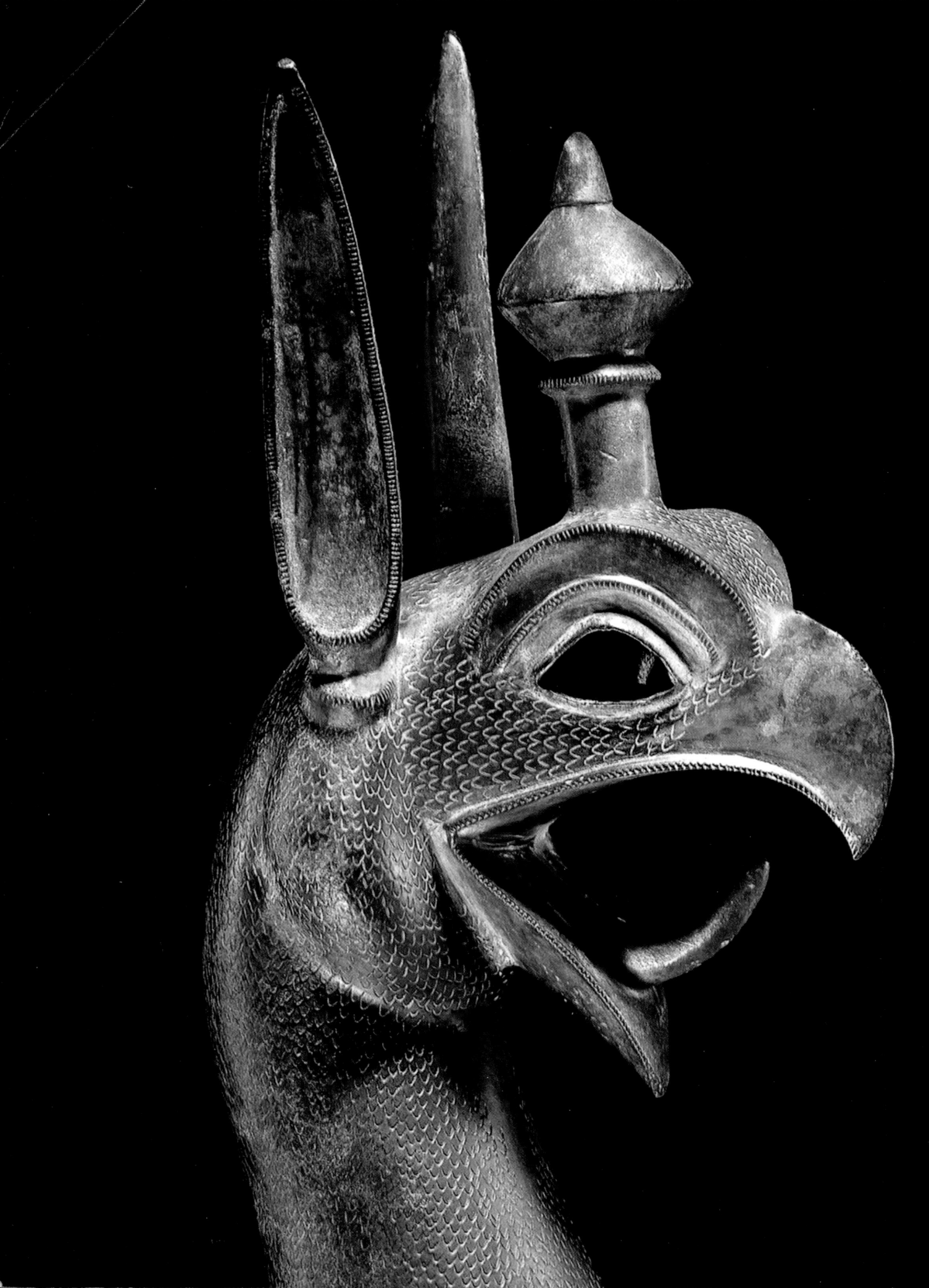

CHAPTER 5

Greek Art

GREEK ARCHITECTURE, SCULPTURE, AND PAINTING ARE immediately recognizable as ancestors of Western civilization. A Greek temple recalls countless government buildings, banks, and college campuses, and a Greek statue evokes countless statues of our own day. This is neither coincidental nor inevitable: Western civilization has carefully

constructed itself in the image of the Greek and Roman worlds. Through the centuries, these worlds have represented a height of cultural achievement for Western civilization, which looked to them for artistic ideals as well as for philosophical models such as democracy.

The great flowering of ancient Greek art was just one manifestation of a wide-ranging exploration of humanistic and religious issues. Artists, writers, and philosophers struggled with common questions, preserved in a huge body of works. Their inquiries cut to the very core of human existence, and form the backbone of much of Western philosophy. For the most part, they accepted a pantheon of gods, whom they worshiped in human form. (See *Informing Art*, page 105.) Yet they debated the nature of those gods, and the relationship between divinities and humankind. Did fate control human actions, or was there free will? What was the nature of virtue? Greek thinkers conceived of many aspects of life in dualistic terms. Order (*cosmos* in Greek) was opposed to disorder (*chaos*), and both poles permeated existence. Civilization— which was, by definition, Greek—stood in opposition to an uncivilized world beyond Greek borders; non-Greeks were "barbarians," named for the nonsensical sound of their languages to Greek ears ("bar-bar-bar-bar"). Reason, too, had its opposite: the

irrational, mirrored in light and darkness, in man and woman. In their art as in their literature, the ancient Greeks addressed the tension between these polar opposites.

Trying to understand the visual culture of the worlds on which Western civilization so deliberately modeled itself presents a special challenge for the art historian: It is tempting to believe that something familiar on the surface holds the same significance for us today as it did for Greeks or Romans. Yet scholars have discovered time and time again that this is a dangerous fallacy.

A further complication in studying Greek art is that there are three separate, and sometimes conflicting, sources of information on the subject. First, there are the works themselves—reliable, but only a fraction of what once existed. Secondly, there are Roman copies of Greek originals, especially sculptures. These works tell us something about important pieces that would otherwise be lost to us, but pose their own problems. Without the original, we cannot determine how faithful a copy is, and sometimes multiple copies present several different versions of a single original. This is explained by the fact that a Roman copyist's notion of a copy was quite different from ours: It was not necessarily a strict imitation, but allowed for interpreting or adapting the work according to the copyist's taste or skill or the patron's wishes. Moreover, the quality of some Greek sculpture owed much to surface finish, which, in a copy, is entirely up to the copyist. If the original was bronze and the copy marble, not only would the finish differ dramatically, but the copyist might alter the very composition to

Detail of figure 5.6, Griffin-head protome from a bronze tripod-cauldron, from Kameiros, Rhodes

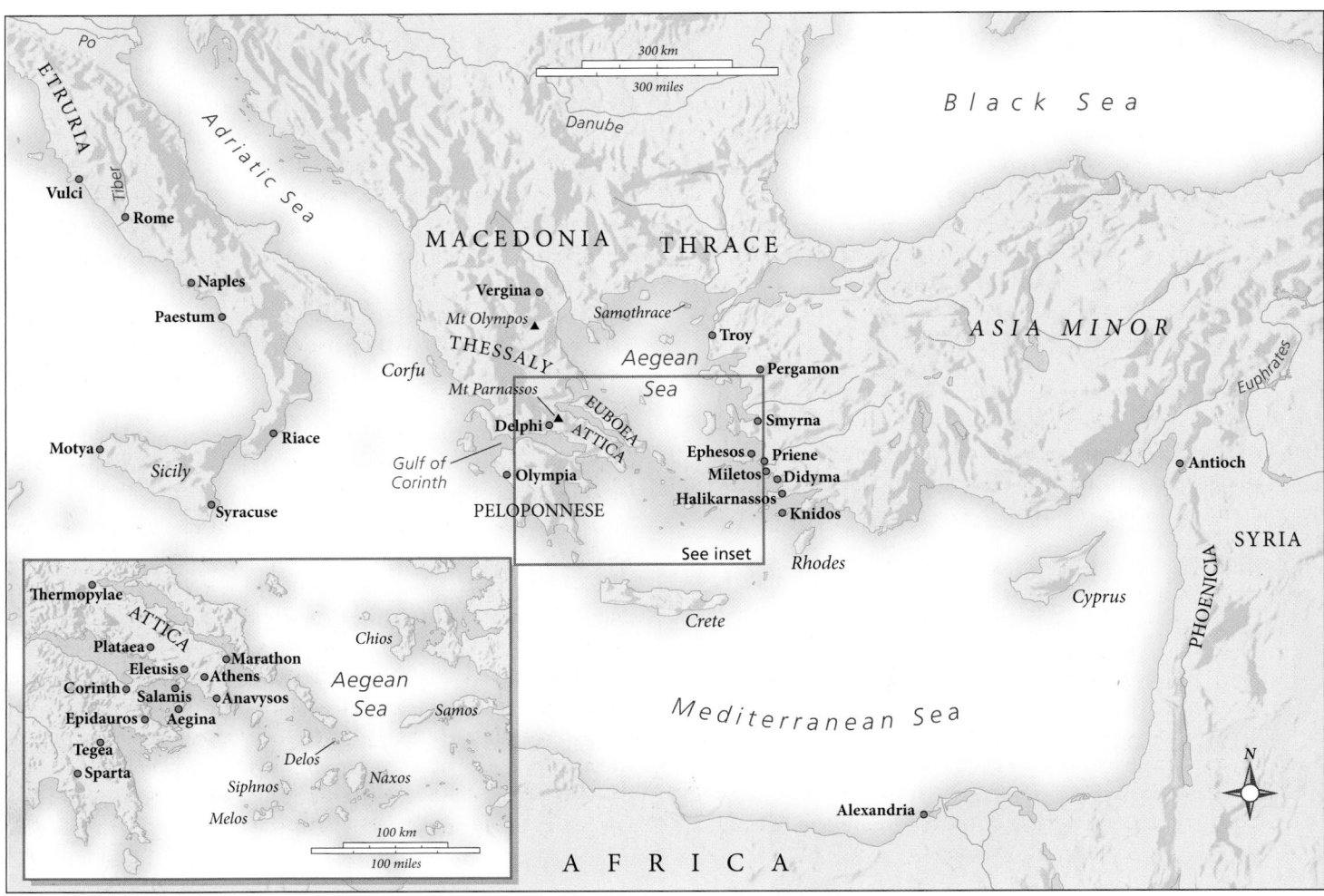

Map 5.1   Greece in the Archaic and Classical periods

accommodate the different strengths of stone and bronze. In rare cases, works that appear to be copies because of their general style or subject matter are of such high quality that we cannot be sure that they really are copies. Lastly, Roman copies tend to come to light in Roman contexts, which allows archaeologists to glean information about Roman collectors but not about the contexts in which Greeks displayed the originals.

The third source of information about Greek works is literature. The Greeks were the first Western people to write at length about their artists. Roman writers incorporated Greek accounts into their own; many of these survive, although often in fragmentary condition. These written sources offer a glimpse of what the Greeks considered their significant achievements in architecture, sculpture, and painting. They name celebrated artists and monuments, but often deal with lost works and fail to mention surviving Greek works that we number among the greatest masterpieces of their time. Weaving these strands of information into a coherent picture of Greek art has been the difficult task of archaeologists and art historians for several centuries.

THE EMERGENCE OF GREEK ART: THE GEOMETRIC STYLE

The first Greek-speaking groups came to Greece about 2000 BCE, bringing a culture that soon encompassed most of mainland Greece, the Aegean Islands, and Crete. By the first millennium BCE, they had colonized the west coast of Asia Minor and Cyprus. In this period we distinguish three main subgroups: the Dorians, centered in the Peloponnese; the Ionians, inhabiting Attica, Euboea, the Cyclades, and the central coast of Asia Minor; and the Aeolians, who ended up in the northeast Aegean (map 5.1). Despite cultural differences, Greeks of different regions had a strong sense of kinship, based on language and common beliefs. From the mid-eighth through the mid-sixth centuries BCE, Greeks spread across the Mediterranean and as far as the Black Sea in a wave of colonization. At this time, they founded settlements in Sicily and southern Italy, collectively known as Magna Graecia, and in North Africa.

After the collapse of Mycenaean civilization described in the last chapter, art became largely nonfigural for several centuries. In the ninth century BCE, the oldest surviving style of Greek art

Greek Gods and Goddesses

All early civilizations and preliterate cultures had creation myths to explain the origin of the universe and humanity's place in it. Over time, these myths evolved into complex cycles that represent a comprehensive attempt to understand the world. Greek gods and goddesses, though immortal, behaved in human ways. They quarreled, and had offspring with one another's spouses and often with mortals as well. Their own children sometimes threatened and even overthrew them. The principal Greek gods and goddesses, with their Roman counterparts in parentheses, are given below.

ZEUS (Jupiter): son of Kronos and Rhea; god of sky and weather, and chief Olympian deity. After killing Kronos, Zeus married his sister HERA (Juno) and divided the universe by lot with his brothers: POSEIDON (Neptune) was allotted the sea, and HADES (Pluto) received the underworld, which he ruled with his queen, PERSEPHONE (Proserpina).

Zeus and Hera had several children:
   ARES (Mars), the god of war
   HEBE, the goddess of youth
   HEPHAISTOS (Vulcan), the lame god of metalwork and the forge

Zeus also had numerous children through his love affairs with other goddesses and with mortal women, including:
   ATHENA (Minerva), goddess of crafts, war, intelligence, and wisdom. A protector of heroes, she became the patron goddess of Athens, an honor she won in a contest with Poseidon. Her gift to the city was an olive tree, which she caused to sprout on the Akropolis.
   APHRODITE (Venus), the goddess of love, beauty, and female fertility. She married Hephaistos, but had many other liaisons. Her children were HARMONIA, EROS, and ANTEROS (with Ares); HERMAPHRODITOS (with Hermes); PRIAPOS (with Dionysos); and AENEAS (with the Trojan prince Anchises).
   APOLLO (Apollo), god of the stringed lyre and bow, who therefore both presided over the civilized pursuits of music and poetry, and shot down transgressors; a paragon of male beauty, he was also the god of prophecy and medicine.
   ARTEMIS (Diana), twin sister of APOLLO, virgin goddess of the hunt and the protector of young girls. She was also sometimes considered a moon-goddess with SELENE.
   DIONYSOS (Bacchus), the god of altered states, particularly that induced by wine. Opposite in temperament to Apollo, Dionysos was raised on Mount Nysa, where he invented winemaking; he married the princess Ariadne after the hero Theseus abandoned her on Naxos. His followers, the goatish satyrs and their female companions, the nymphs and humans who were known as maenads (bacchantes), were given to orgiastic excess. Yet there was another, more temperate side to Dionysos' character. As the god of fertility, he was also a god of vegetation, as well as of peace, hospitality, and the theater.
   HERMES (Mercury), the messenger of the gods, conductor of souls to Hades, and the god of travelers and commerce.

---

developed, known today as the Geometric Style because of the predominance of linear designs. Artists created works of painted pottery and small-scale clay and bronze sculpture in this style. The forms are closely related: the types of figures found in sculpture often adorned the pottery.

Geometric Style Pottery

As quickly as pottery became an art form, Greek potters began to develop an extensive, but fairly standardized, repertoire of vessel shapes (fig. 5.1), and adapted each type to its function. Making and decorating vases were complex processes, usually performed

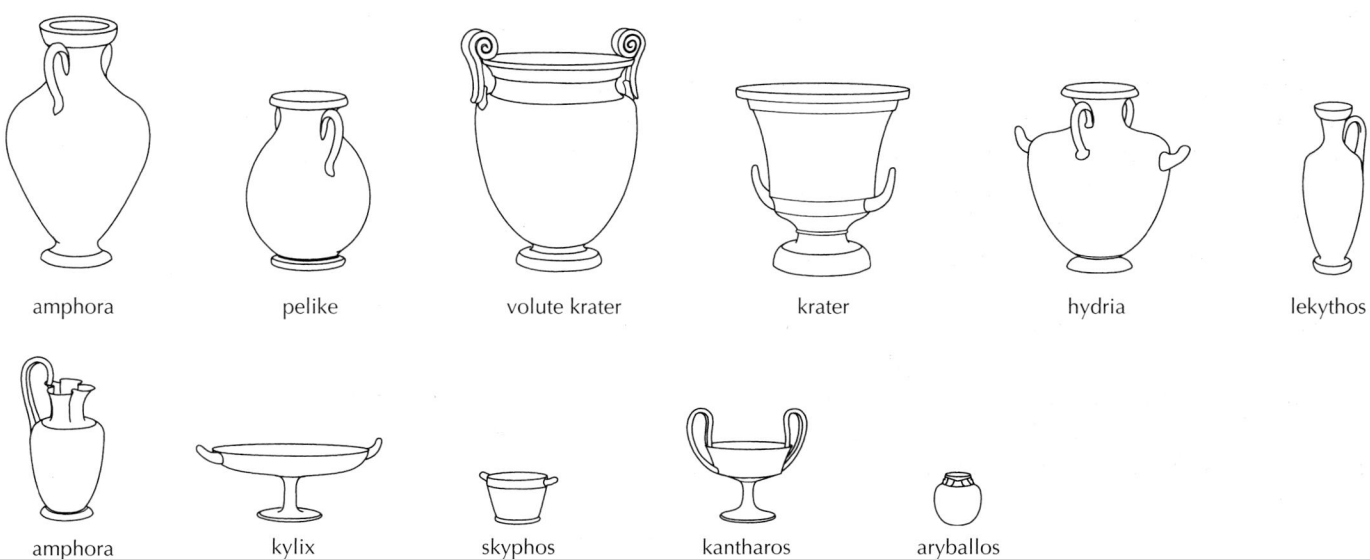

amphora   pelike   volute krater   krater   hydria   lekythos

amphora   kylix   skyphos   kantharos   aryballos

5.1   Some common Greek vessel forms

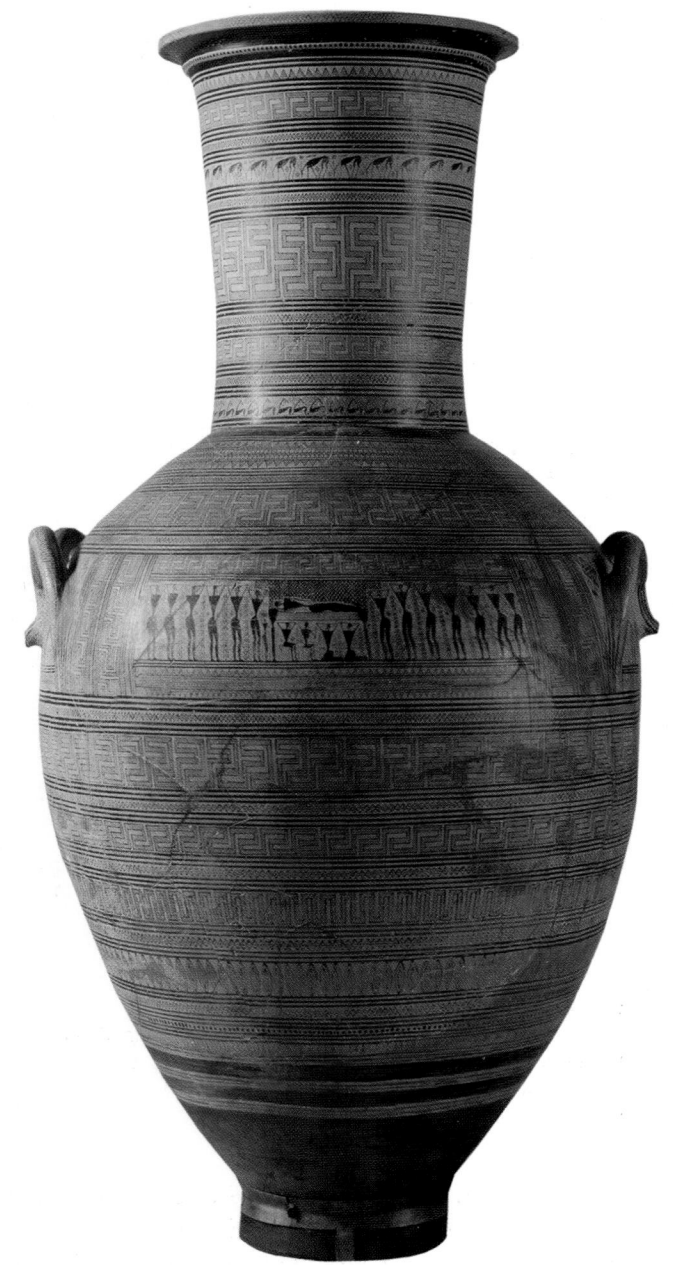

the lasting epic poems *The Iliad* and *The Odyssey*, tales of the Trojan War and the return home of one of its heroes, Odysseus, to Ithaka.

The vase shown here, from a cemetery near the later Dipylon gate in northwestern Athens, dates to around 750 BCE (fig. **5.2**; see fig. 5.37). Known as the Dipylon Vase, it was one of a group of large vessels Athenians used as funerary markers over burials. Holes in its base allowed mourners to pour liquid offerings (libations) during funerary rituals; the libations filtered down to the dead buried below. In earlier centuries, Athenians had placed the ashes of their dead inside vases, choosing the vase's shape according to the sex of the deceased: They placed a woman's remains in a belly-handled amphora, a type of vase they used more commonly for storing wine or oil; a man's ashes were stored in a neck-amphora (a wine jar with a long neck). Since the early first millennium, Athenians had also used **kraters** as burial markers, large bowl-like vessels in which they normally mixed wine with water (see fig. 5.1). The shape of the vase illustrated here shows that the person buried beneath was a woman; its monumentality indicates that she was a woman of considerable means.

The amphora is a masterpiece of the potter's craft. At over 5 feet tall, it was too large to be thrown in one piece. Instead, the potter built it up in sections, joined with a clay slip (clay mixed with water or another liquid). A careful proportional scheme governed the vessel's form: Its width measures half of its height and the neck measures half the height of the body. The potter placed the handles so as to emphasize the widest point of the body. Most of the decoration is given over to geometric patterns dominated by a **meander** pattern, also known as a maze or Greek key pattern (fig. **5.3**), a band of rectangular scrolls, punctuated with bands of lustrous black paint at the neck, shoulder, and base. The geometric design reflects the proportional system of the vase's shape. Single meander patterns run in bands toward the top and bottom

5.2 Dipylon Vase. Late Geometric belly-handled amphora, from the Dipylon Cemetery, Athens. ca. 750 BCE. Height 5'1" (1.55 m). National Archaeological Museum, Athens

by different artisans. Each pottery shape presented its own challenges to the painter, and some became specialists at decorating certain types of vases. Large pots often attracted the most ambitious craftsmen because they provided a generous field on which to work. At first painters decorated their wares with abstract designs, such as triangles, "checkerboards," and concentric circles. Toward 800 BCE, human and animal figures began to appear within the geometric framework, and in elaborate examples these figures interact in narrative scenes. This development occurred at about the time the alphabet was introduced (under strong Near Eastern influence), and contemporaneous, too, with the compositions of the poet (or group of poets) known as Homer, who wrote

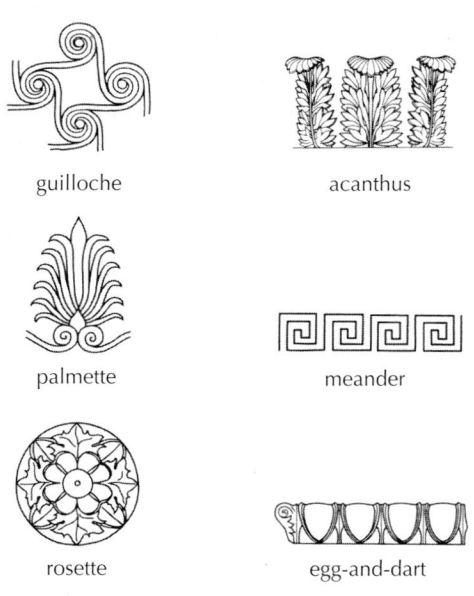

guilloche

acanthus

palmette

meander

rosette

egg-and-dart

5.3 Common Greek ornamental motifs

of the neck; the triple meander encircling the neck at the center emphasizes its length. The double and single meanders on the amphora's body appear stocky by contrast, complementing the body's rounder form. On the neck, deer graze, one after the other, in an identical pattern circling the vase. At the base of the neck, they recline, with their heads turned back over their bodies, like an animate version of the meander pattern itself, which moves forward while turning back upon itself. These animal **friezes** prefigure the widespread use of the motif in the seventh century BCE.

In the center of the amphora, framed between its handles, is a narrative scene. The deceased lies on a bier, beneath a checkered shroud. Standing figures flank her with their arms raised above their heads in a gesture of lamentation; four additional figures kneel or sit beneath the bier. Rather than striving for naturalism, the painter used solid black geometric forms to construct human bodies. A triangle represents the torso, and the raised arms extend the triangle beyond the shoulders. The scene represents the *prothesis*, part of the Athenian funerary ritual, when the dead person lay in state and public mourning took place. For the living, a lavish funeral was an occasion to display wealth and status, and crowds of mourners were so desirable that families would hire professionals for the event. Thus the depiction of a funeral on the vase is not simply journalistic reportage but a visual record of the deceased person's high standing in society.

Archaeologists have found Geometric pottery in Italy and the Near East as well as in Greece. This wide distribution reflects the important role of not only the Greeks but also the Phoenicians, North Syrians, and other Near Eastern peoples as agents of diffusion around the Mediterranean. What is more, from the second half of the eighth century onward, inscriptions on these vases show that the Greeks had already adapted the Phoenician alphabet to their own use.

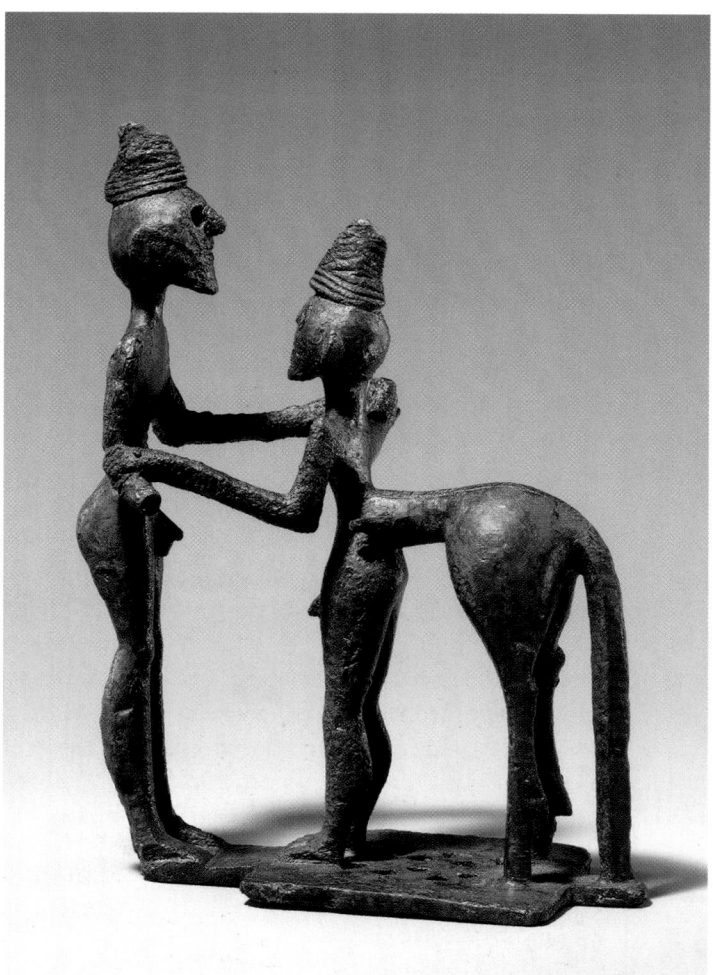

5.4 *Man and Centaur*, perhaps from Olympia. ca. 750 BCE. Bronze, height 4⅜" (11.1 cm). Metropolitan Museum of Art, New York. Gift of J. Pierpont Morgan, 1917. 17.190.2072

Geometric Style Sculpture

A small, bronze sculptural group representing a man and a centaur dates to about the same time as the funerary amphora, and there are similarities in the way the artist depicted living forms in both works of art (fig. **5.4**). Thin arms and flat, triangular chests contrast with rounded buttocks and legs. The heads are spherical shapes, with beards and noses added. The metalworker cast the sculptural group in one piece, uniting the figures with a common base and through their entwined pose. Indeed, the figures obviously interact, revealing the artist's interest in narrative, a theme that persists throughout the history of Greek art. The figures' helmets suggest that their encounter is martial, and the larger scale of the man may indicate that he will prevail in the struggle. It is hard to say whether the artist was referring to a story known to the audience. Many scholars believe the male figure represents the hero Herakles, son of Zeus and a mortal woman, who fought centaurs many times in the course of his mythical travails. The group probably came to light in the great Panhellenic (all-Greek) sanctuary at Olympia, home of the Olympic games. This sanctuary, like the Panhellenic sanctuary at Delphi, home of the

Panhellenic games (see fig. 5.19), was not specific to one city-state: People from cities all over the Greek world routinely visited it for festivals and to make dedications to the gods, which accounts for its gradual monumentalization. There was a distinct rise in dedications there and at Delphi in the eighth century BCE, especially of small metal objects. Judging by the figurative quality of the sculptural group, by the costliness of the material, and the complexity of the technique, it was probably a sumptuous votive offering.

THE ORIENTALIZING STYLE: HORIZONS EXPAND

Between about 725 and 650 BCE, a new style of art emerged in Greece that reflects strong influences from the Near East and Egypt. Scholars call this the Orientalizing period, when Greek art and culture rapidly absorbed Eastern motifs and ideas, including hybrid creatures such as griffins and sphinxes. This movement led to a vital period of experimentation, as artists strove to master new forms.

Miniature Vessels

The Orientalizing style replaced the Geometric in many Greek city-states, including Athens. One of the foremost centers of its production, though, was Corinth, at the northeastern gateway to the Peloponnese. During this period, Corinth came to dominate colonizing ventures to the west, as well as the trade in pottery exports. Its workshops had a long history of pottery production, and at this time vase painters learned to refine a black gloss slip, which they used to create silhouette or outline images. By incising the slip, they could add fine detail and vivacity to their work. They particularly specialized in crafting miniature vessels like the vase shown here, which is a Proto-Corinthian **aryballos** or perfume jar, dating to about 680 BCE (fig. **5.5**). Despite its small size, intricate decoration covers the vase's surface. Around the shoulder stalks a frieze of animals, reminiscent of Near Eastern motifs and of the frieze on the Dipylon Vase (see figs. 2.21 and 5.2). Bands of real and imaginary animals are a hallmark of Corinthian and other Orientalizing wares: They cover later vases from top to bottom. A **guilloche pattern** ornaments the handle, and meander patterns enliven the edge of the mouth and the handle (see fig. 5.3). The principal figural frieze offers another early example of pictorial narrative, but the daily-life scenes that are characteristic of Geometric pottery yield here to the fantastic world of myth.

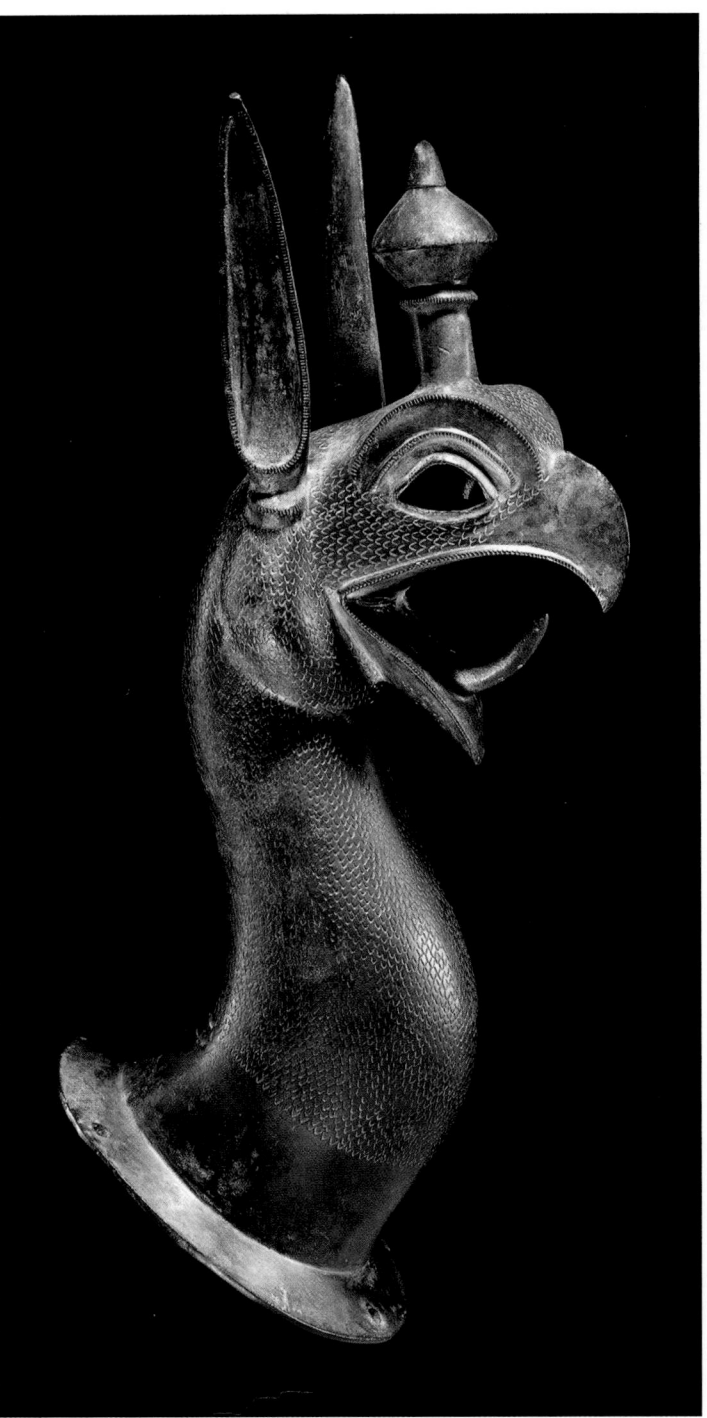

5.6   Griffin-head protome from a bronze tripod cauldron, from Kameiros, Rhodes. ca. 650 BCE. Cast bronze. The British Museum, London

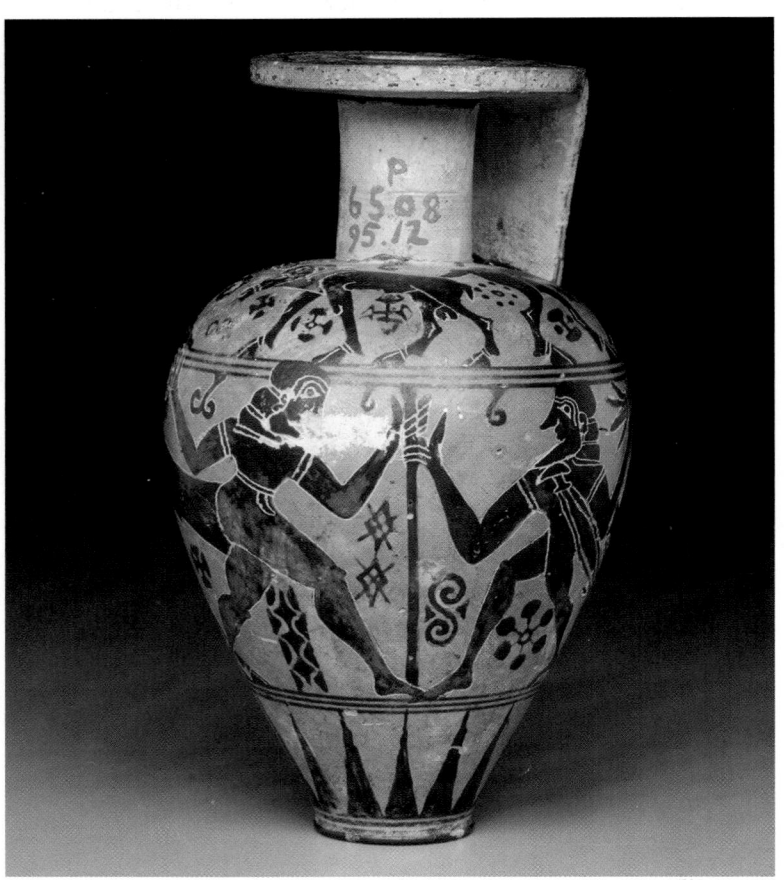

5.5   The Ajax Painter. Aryballos (perfume jar). Middle Proto-Corinthian I A, 690–675 BCE. Ceramic, height 2⅞" (7.3 cm), diameter 1¾" (4.4 cm). Museum of Fine Arts, Boston. Catharine Page Perkins Fund. 95.12

On one side, a stocky nude male wielding a sword runs toward a vase on a stand. On the side shown here, a bearded male struggles to wrest a scepter or staff from a centaur. According to one theory, the frieze represents a moment in Herakles' conflict with a band of centaurs on Mount Pholoë. In Greek mythology, centaurs were notoriously susceptible to alcohol, and the mixing bowl for wine represented on the other side may indicate the reason for their rowdiness. Others interpret the "Herakles" figure as Zeus, brandishing his thunderbolt or lightning. No matter how one reads this scene, it was clearly meant to evoke a myth. Greeks buried vessels like this aryballos in tombs as offerings for the dead, and dedicated them in sanctuaries throughout the Greek world.

BRONZE TRIPODS Among the costliest dedications in Greek sanctuaries during the Geometric and Orientalizing periods were bronze tripod cauldrons, large vessels mounted on three legs. Some of them reached truly monumental proportions, and the dedication was not only an act of piety, but also a way to display status through wealth. From the early seventh century BCE, bronze-workers producing these vessels in the Orientalizing style attached **protomes** around the edge of the bowl—images of sirens (winged female creatures) and griffins, which were fantasy creatures known in the Near East. The cast protome shown here, from the island of Rhodes, is a magnificently ominous creature, standing watch over the dedication (fig. **5.6**). The boldly upright ears and the vertical knob on top of the head contrast starkly with the strong curves of the neck, head, eyes, and mouth, while its menacing tongue is silhouetted in countercurve against the beak. The straight lines appear to animate the curves, so that the dangerous hybrid seems about to spring.

ARCHAIC ART: ART OF THE CITY-STATE

During the course of the seventh and sixth centuries BCE, the Greeks refined their notion of a **polis**, or city-state. Once merely a citadel, a place of refuge in times of trouble, the city came to represent a community and an identity. They governed these city-states in various ways, including monarchy (from *monarches*, "sole ruler"), aristocracy (from *aristoi* and *kratia*, "rule of the best"), tyranny (from *tyrannos*, "king"), and oligarchy (from *oligoi*, "the few," a small ruling elite). The citizens of Athens ruled their city-state by democracy (from *demos*, "the people"). The path to democracy was a slow one, starting with the reforms of Solon, a statesman of the late sixth century. Even after Perikles' radical democratic reforms of 462 BCE, women played no direct role in civic life, and slavery was an accepted practice, as it was throughout the Greek world. With the changing ideal of the city-state came transformations in its physical appearance. Scholars know the artistic style of this time as Archaic (from *archaios*, Greek for "old"). Architects began to design monumental buildings in canonical styles, while artists started to explore human movement and emotion.

The Rise of Monumental Temple Architecture

Early Greeks worshiped their gods in open-air sanctuaries. The indispensable installation for cult (religious practice) rituals was an altar, where priests performed sacrifices standing before the worshiping community of the Greek polis. Increasingly, though, Greeks built temples to accompany these altars. Usually the entrance of the temple faced east, toward the rising sun, and the altar stood to the east of the temple. The chief function of a temple was not so much to house rituals, most of which occurred outside the building, but to provide safe shelter for the cult image of the god to whom the temple was dedicated, and to store valuable dedications. At some point in the seventh century BCE, they began to design temples in stone rather than wood. Corinthian architects were probably the first to make the change, designing in a style known as Doric, named for the region where it originated. From there, the concept spread across the isthmus of Corinth to the mainland and up to Delphi and the island of Corfu, then rapidly throughout the Hellenic world. A second style, the Ionic, soon developed on the Aegean Islands and the coast of Asia Minor. The style known as Corinthian did not develop until the late fifth century BCE (see page 142).

Greeks recognized the importance of this architectural revolution even as it happened: Architects wrote treatises on their buildings—the first we know of—and the fame they achieved through their work has lasted to this day. Writing in the first century BCE, the Roman architect Vitruvius described the Greek styles of architecture, and his work has been central to our understanding of Greek building. However, our readings of his text have been mediated through early modern commentators and illustrators, who wrote of Doric and Ionic "orders" rather than "types," which is a better translation of Vitruvius' "*genera*." The distinction is important: "Order" suggests an immutable quality, a rigid building code, when in fact there is a subtle but rich variation in surviving Greek architecture.

The essential, functioning elements of Doric and Ionic temples are very similar, though they vary according to the building's size or regional preferences (fig. **5.7**). The nucleus of the building—its very reason for existing—is its main chamber, its cella or **naos**. This chamber housed the god's image. Often, interior columns lined the cella walls and helped to support the roof, as well as visually framing the cult statue. Approaching the cella is a porch or **pronaos**, and in some cases architects added a second porch behind the cella, making the design symmetrical and providing

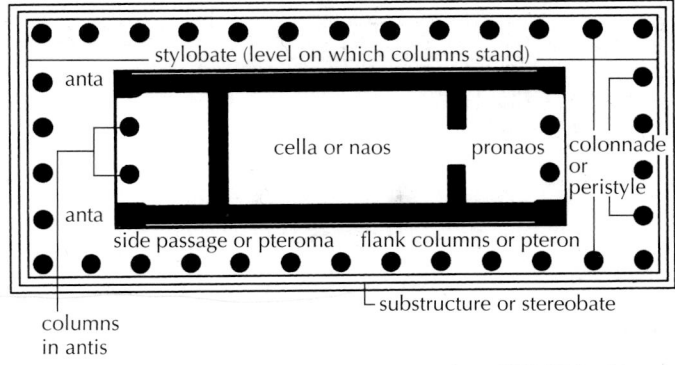

5.7 Ground plan of a typical Greek peripteral temple (after Grinnell)

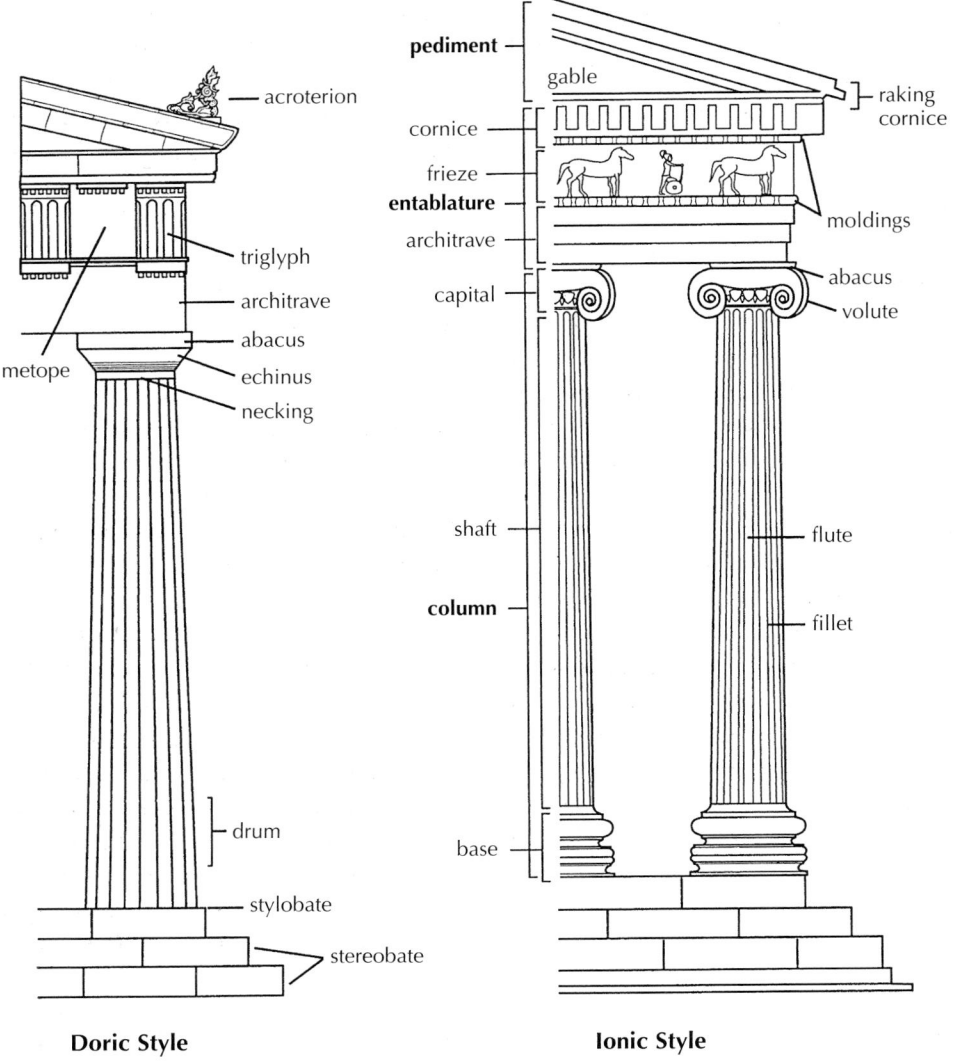

Doric Style   **Ionic Style**

5.8 Doric and Ionic styles in elevation

space for apparatus used in rituals and religious dedications. In large temples, a colonnade or **peristyle** surrounds the cella and porches; Vitruvius called this type a **peripteral temple**. The peristyle commonly consists of 6 to 8 columns at front and back, and usually 12 to 17 along the sides, counting the corner columns twice; the largest temples of Ionian Greece had a double colonnade. The peristyle added more than grandeur: It offered worshipers shelter from the elements. Being neither entirely exterior nor entirely interior space, it also functioned as a transitional zone, between the profane world outside and the sanctity of the cella. Some temples stood in sacred groves, and the strong vertical form of the columns integrated the building with the environment of trees. Echoed again by columns inside the cella, the peristyle also unified the exterior and interior of the building.

Differences between the Doric and Ionic styles are apparent in a head-on view, or elevation. Many terms that Greeks used to describe the parts of their buildings, shown in figure **5.8**, are still in common usage. The building proper rests on an elevated level (the **stylobate**), normally approached by three steps, known as the **stereobate**. A **Doric column** consists of a shaft, usually

marked by shallow vertical grooves, known as **flutes**, and a capital, made up of a flaring, cushionlike **echinus** and a square tablet called the **abacus**. The **entablature** includes all the horizontal elements that rest on the columns: the **architrave** (a row of stone blocks directly supported by the columns); the **frieze**, made up of alternating triple-grooved **triglyphs** and smooth or sculpted **metopes**; and a projecting horizontal cornice, or **geison**. The architrave in turn supports the triangular **pediment** and the roof elements.

An **Ionic column** differs from a Doric column in having an ornate base, perhaps designed initially to protect the bottom from rain. Its shaft is more slender, less tapered, and the capital has a double scroll or **volute** below the abacus. Masons left a sharp angle where the flutes met, instead of flattening it as on Doric columns. The Ionic column lacks the muscular quality of its mainland cousin. Instead, it evokes a growing plant, like a formalized palm tree, a characteristic it shares with its Egyptian predecessors, though it may not have come directly from Egypt. Above the architrave, the frieze is continuous, not broken up visually into triglyphs and metopes.

Greek builders created temples, whether Doric or Ionic, out of stone blocks fitted together without mortar. This required them to shape the blocks precisely to achieve smooth joints. Where necessary, metal dowels or clamps fastened the blocks together. With rare exceptions, they constructed columns out of sections called **drums**, and stonemasons fluted the entire shaft once it was in position. They used wooden beams for the ceiling, and terra-cotta tiles over wooden rafters for the roof. Fire was a constant threat.

Why and how either style came to emerge in Greece, and why they came together into succinct systems so quickly, are questions that still puzzle scholars. Remains of the oldest surviving temples show that the main features of the Doric style were already established soon after 600 BCE. It is possible that the temple's central unit, the cella and porch, derived from the plan of the Mycenaean megaron (see fig. 4.23), either through continuous tradition or by way of revival. If this is true, this relationship may reflect the revered place of Mycenaean culture in later Greek mythology. Still, a Doric column shaft tapers upward, not downward like the Minoan-Mycenaean column. This recalls fluted half-columns in the funerary precinct of Djoser at Saqqara of over 2,000 years earlier (see fig. 3.6). In fact, the very notion that temples should be built of stone and have large numbers of columns was an Egyptian one, even if Egyptian architects designed temples for greater internal traffic. Scholars believe that the rise of monumental stone architecture and sculpture must have been based on careful, on-the-spot study of Egyptian works and the techniques used to produce them. The opportunity for just such a study was available to Greek merchants living in trading camps in the western Nile Delta, by permission of the Egyptian king Psammetichus I (r. 664–610 BCE).

Some scholars see Doric architecture as a petrification (or turning to stone) of existing wooden forms, so that stone form follows wooden function. Accordingly, triglyphs once masked the ends of wooden beams, and the droplike shapes below, called **guttae**, mimic the wooden pegs that held them in place. Metopes evolved from boards that filled gaps between triglyphs to guard against moisture. Some derivations are more convincing than others, however. The vertical subdivisions of triglyphs hardly seem to reflect the forms of three half-round logs, as some have suggested, and column flutings need not have developed out of tool marks on a tree trunk, since Egyptian builders also fluted their columns and yet rarely used timber for supporting members. The question of how well function explains stylistic features faces the architectural historian repeatedly.

DORIC TEMPLES AT PAESTUM Whatever the reason for the emergence of the Doric and Ionic styles, architects continued to refine them throughout Greek times. The early evolution of Doric temples is evident in two unusually well-preserved examples located in the southern Italian polis of Paestum (ancient Poseidonia), where a Greek colony flourished during the Archaic period. The residents dedicated both temples to the goddess Hera, wife of Zeus; however, they built the Temple of Hera II almost a century after the Temple of Hera I (fig. **5.9**). The differences in their proportions are striking. The Temple of Hera I (on the left

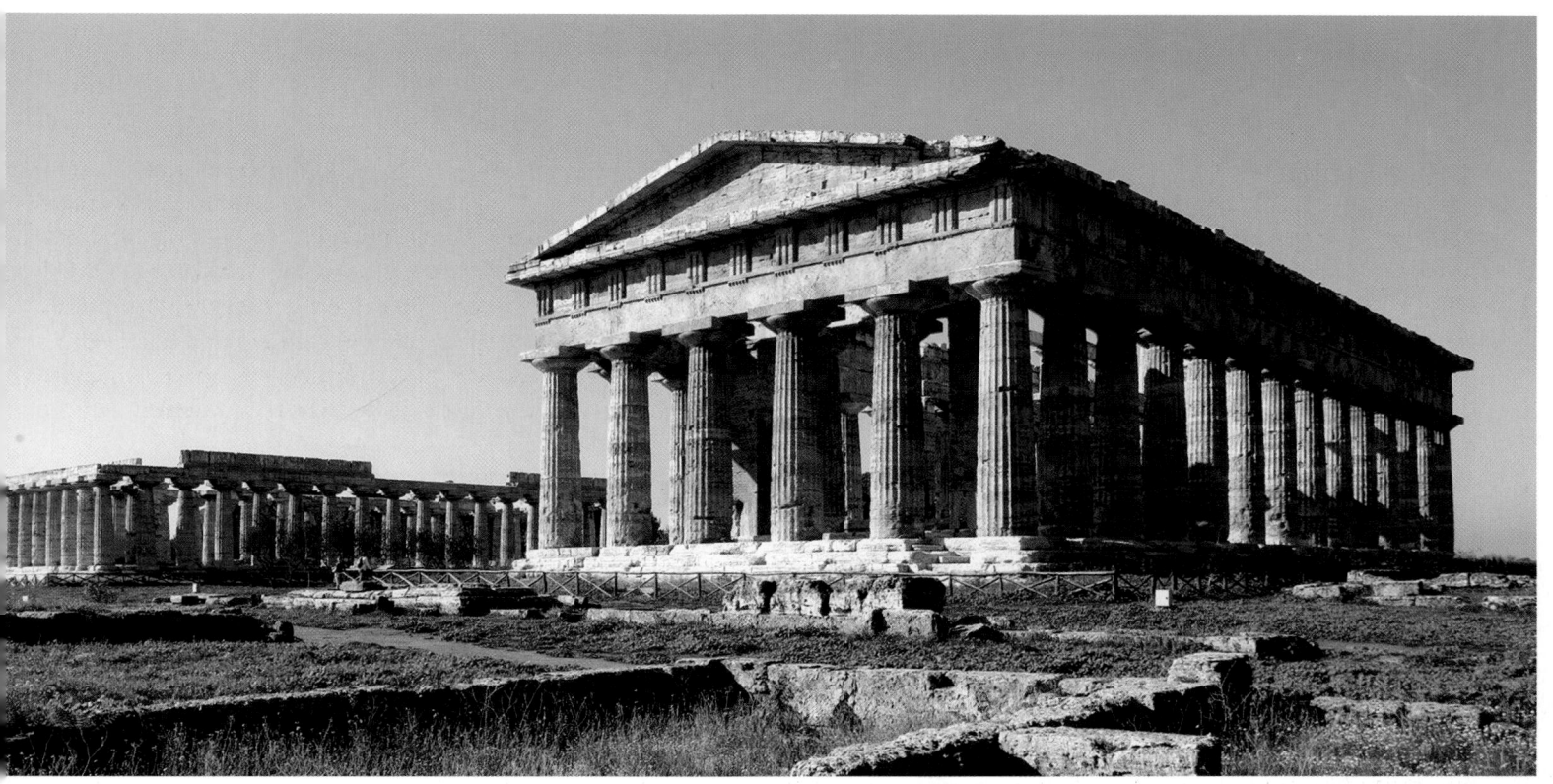

5.9 The Temple of Hera I ("Basilica"), ca. 550 BCE, and the Temple of Hera II ("Temple of Poseidon"), Paestum. ca. 460 BCE

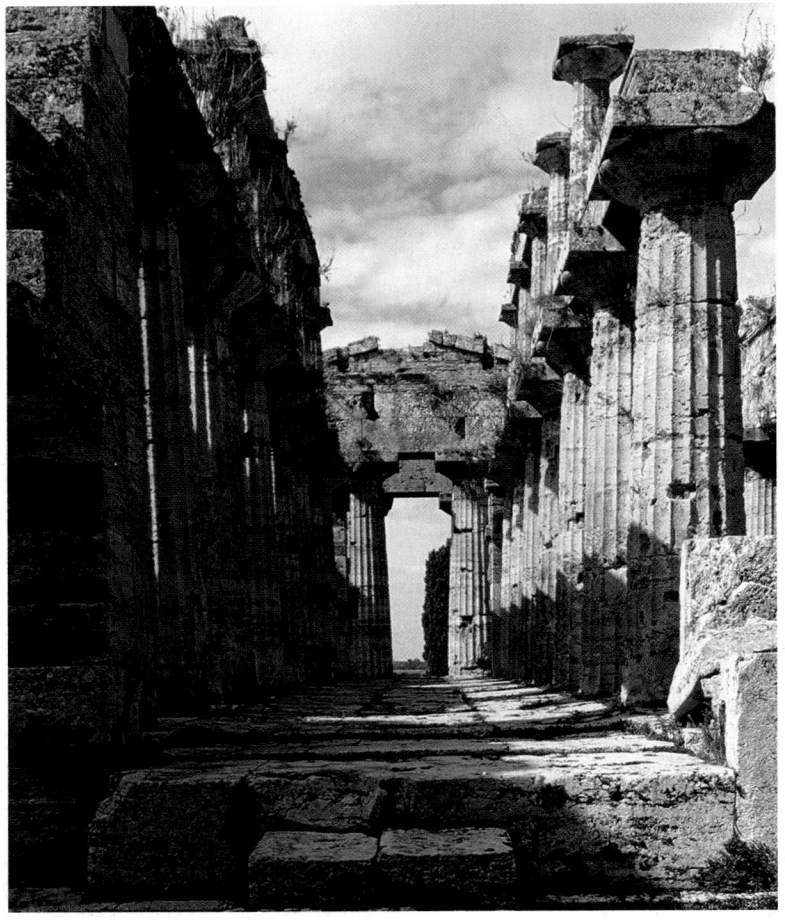

5.10   Interior of Temple of Hera II. ca. 500 BCE

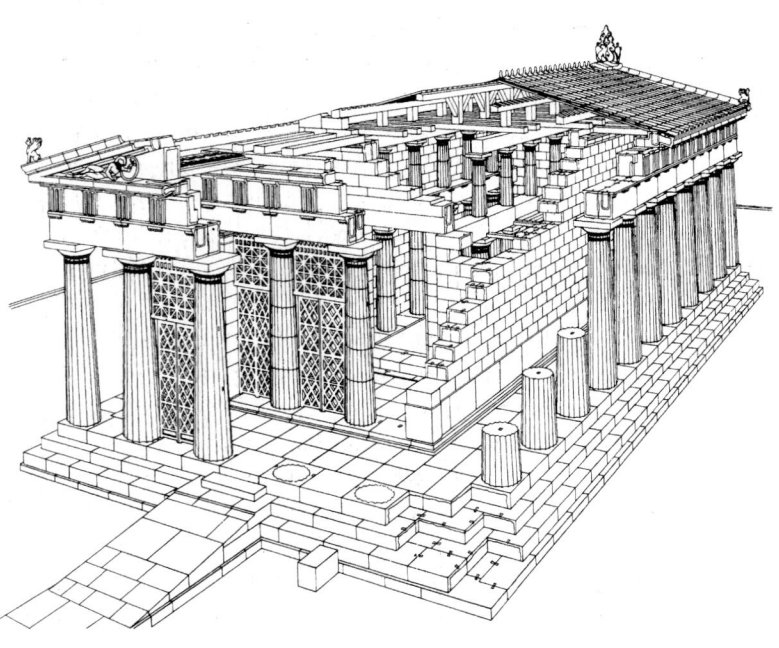

5.11   Sectional view (restored) of Temple of Aphaia, Aegina.
ca. 500–480 BCE

of fig. 5.9) appears low and sprawling—and not just because so
much of the entablature is missing—whereas the Temple of Hera
II looks tall and compact. One reason is that the Temple of Hera I
is **enneastyle** (with nine columns across the front and rear), while
the later temple is only **hexastyle** (six columns). Yet the difference
in appearance is also the result of changes to the outline of the
columns. On neither temple are the column shafts straight from
bottom to top. About a third of the way up, they bulge outward
slightly, receding again at about two-thirds of their height. This
swelling effect, known as **entasis**, is much stronger on the earlier
Temple of Hera I. It gives the impression that the columns bulge
with the strain of supporting the superstructure and that the slender tops, although aided by the widely flaring capitals, can barely
withstand the crushing weight. The device, seen also in the mono-
liths at Stonehenge, adds an extraordinary vitality to the building—a sense of compressed energy awaiting release.

Being so well preserved, the Temple of Hera II shows how the
architect supported the ceiling in a large Doric temple (fig. **5.10**).
Inside the cella, the two rows of columns each support a smaller
set of columns scaled in such a way that the tapering seems
continuous despite the intervening architrave. Such a two-story
interior is first found at the Temple of Aphaia at Aegina around
the beginning of the fifth century BCE. A reconstruction drawing
of that temple (fig. **5.11**) illustrates the structural system in detail.

EARLY IONIC TEMPLES   The Ionic style first appeared about
a half-century after the Doric. With its vegetal decoration, it
seems to have been strongly inspired by Near Eastern forms.
The closest known parallel to the Ionic capital is the **Aeolic** capital, found in the region of Old Smyrna, in eastern Greece, and in
the northeast Aegean, itself apparently derived from North
Syrian and Phoenician designs. Leading cities of Ionian Greece
commissioned the earliest Ionic temples in open rivalry with one
another. Little survives of these vast, ornate buildings. One of
them, the Temple of Artemis at Ephesos, gained tremendous

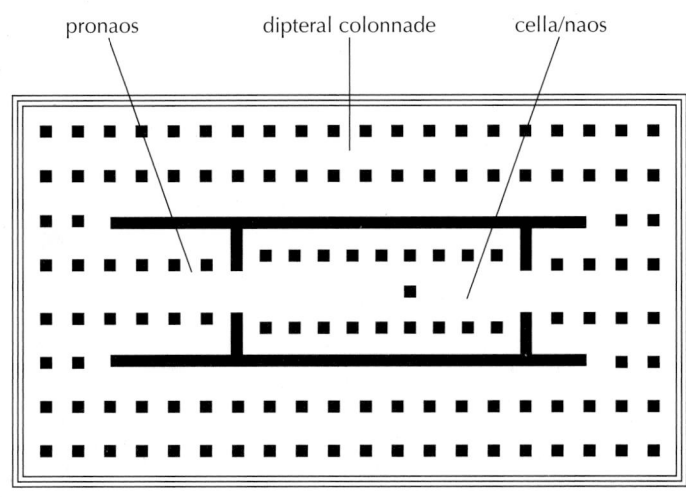

5.12   Restored plan of Temple of Artemis at Ephesos,
Turkey. ca. 560 BCE

fame in antiquity, and earned a place among the seven wonders of the ancient world. The Ephesians hired Theodoros of Samos to work on its foundations in about 560 BCE, shortly after he and another architect, Rhoikos, had designed a vast temple to Hera on the island of Samos. The temple's subsequent architects, Chersiphron of Knossos and his son Metagenes, wrote a treatise on it. The temple was **dipteral** (with two rows of columns surrounding it) (fig. **5.12**), and this feature emphasized the forestlike quality of the building, as did its vegetal capitals. In this much, it resembled the temple on Samos. Yet in other respects the Temple of Artemis clearly outshone Hera's: It was larger, and it was the first monumental building constructed mostly of marble. These Ionic colossi had blatant symbolic value: They represented their respective city's bid for regional leadership.

STONE SCULPTURE

According to literary sources, in the eighth century BCE Greeks erected simple wooden sculptures of their gods for worship in sanctuaries; but since wood deteriorates, none of them now survives. In about 650 BCE, sculptors, like architects, made the transition to working in stone, and so began one of the great traditions of Greek art.

KORE AND KOUROS Early Greek statues clearly show affinities with the techniques and proportional systems used by Egyptian sculptors, whose work Greek artists could observe first hand in the Nile Delta. Two are illustrated here: one a small female figure of about 630 BCE, probably from Crete (fig. **5.13**); the other a life-size nude male youth of about 600 BCE (fig. **5.14**), known as the *New York Kouros* because it is displayed in the Metropolitan Museum of Art. Like their Egyptian forerunners (see figs. 3.10 and 3.11), the statues are rigidly frontal, and conceived as four distinct sides, reflecting the form of the block from which the sculptor carved them. Like Menkaure, the Greek male youth is slim and broad-shouldered; he stands with his left leg forward, and his arms by his sides, terminating in clenched fists. His shoulders, hips, and knees are all level. Both figures have stylized, wiglike hair like their Egyptian counterparts, and like some Near Eastern sculptures (see fig. 2.11). All the same, there are significant differences. First, the Greek sculptures are truly freestanding, without the back slab that supports Egyptian stone figures. In fact, they are the earliest large stone images of the human figure that can stand on their own. Moreover, Greek sculptures incorporated empty space (between the legs, for instance, or between arms and torso), whereas Egyptian figures remained embedded in stone, with the spaces between forms partly filled. Early Greek sculptures are also more stylized than their Egyptian forebears. This is most evident in the large staring eyes, emphasized by bold arching eyebrows, and in the linear treatment of the anatomy: The sculptor appears almost to have etched the male youth's pectoral muscles and rib-cage onto the surface of the stone, whereas the Egyptian sculptor modeled Menkaure's musculature. Unlike Menkaure, the male youth is nude. Earlier cultures, like the Egyptians, forced nudity on slaves, whereas ancient Greeks considered public nudity acceptable for males, but not for females. Accordingly, like most early Greek female sculptures, this one is draped, in a close-fitting garment that reveals her breasts but conceals her hips and legs.

Dozens of Archaic sculptures of this kind survive throughout the Greek world. Some have come to light in sanctuaries and cemeteries, but most were found in reused contexts, which complicates any attempt to understand their function. Scholars describe them by the Greek terms for maiden (**kore**, plural korai) and youth (**kouros**, plural kouroi), terms that gloss over the

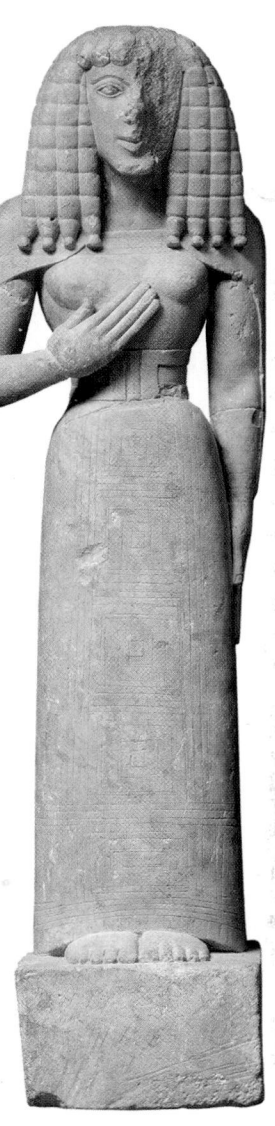

5.13 *Kore (Maiden).* ca. 630 BCE. Limestone, height 24½" (62.3 cm). Musée du Louvre, Paris. Fletcher Fund, 1932. (32.11.1)

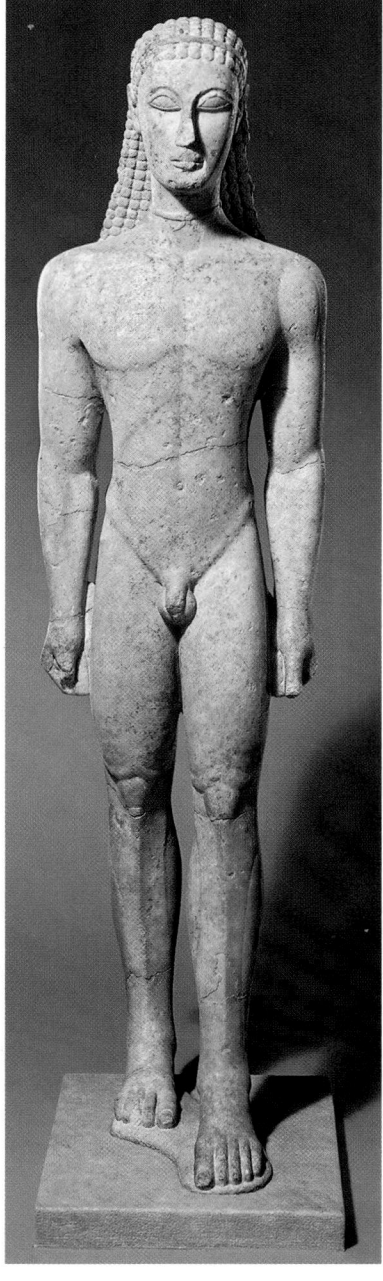

5.14 *New York Kouros (Youth).* ca. 600–590 BCE. Marble, height 6'1½" (1.88 m). Metropolitan Museum of Art, New York

difficulty of identifying their function. Some bear inscriptions, such as the names of artists ("'So-and-so' made me") or dedications to various deities, chiefly Apollo. The latter, then, were votive offerings. But in most cases we do not know whether the sculptures represent the donor, a deity, or a person deemed divinely favored, such as a victor in the athletic games that were so central to ancient Greek life. Those placed on graves probably represent the person buried beneath.

Sculptors made no clear effort to give the statues portrait features, so the images can represent an individual only in a general way. It might make sense to think of them as ideals of physical perfection and vitality shared by mortals and immortals alike, given meaning by their physical context. What is clear is that only the wealthy could afford them, since many were well over life-size and carved from high-quality marble. Indeed, the very stylistic cohesion of the sculptures may reveal their social function: By

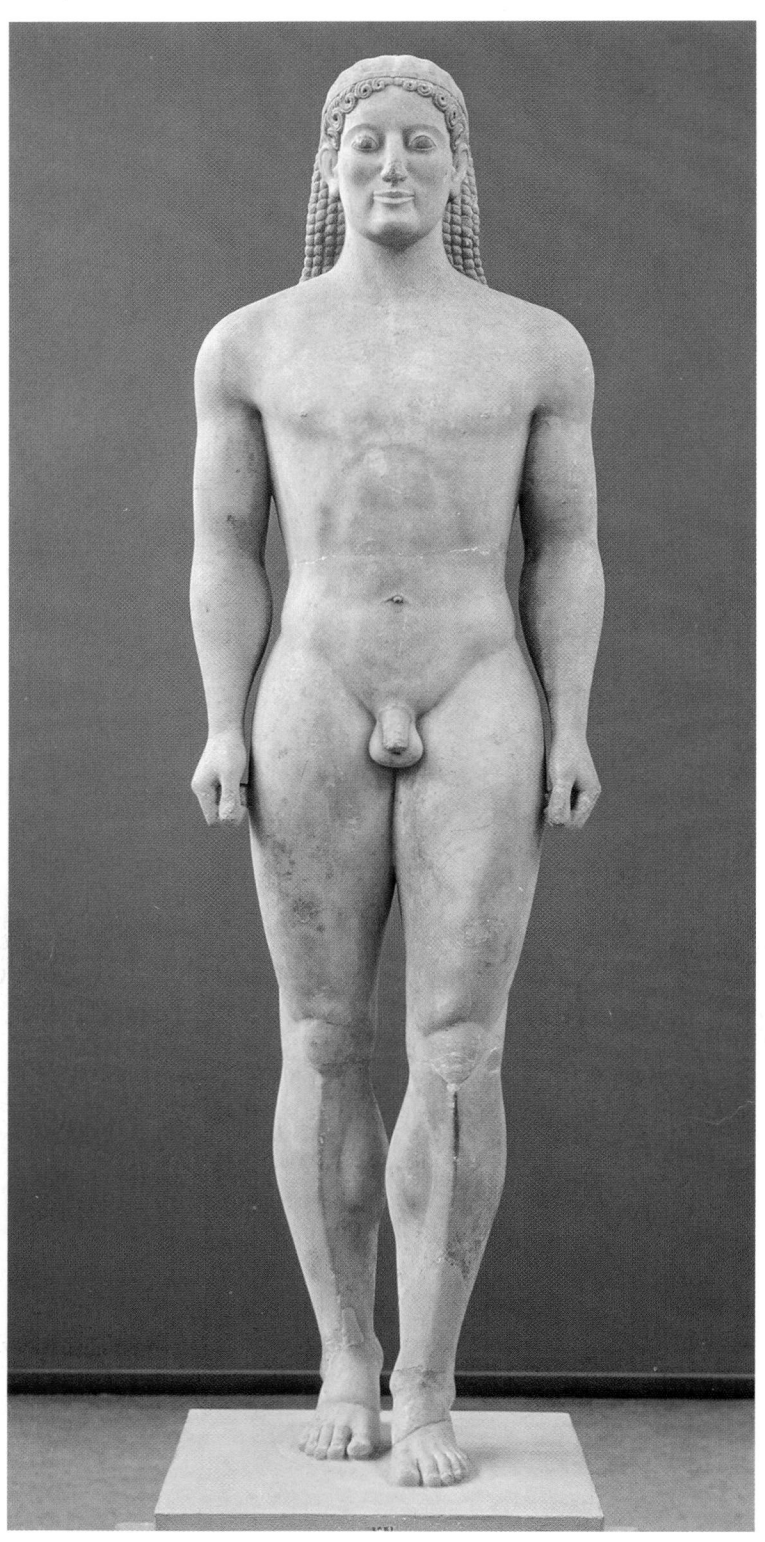

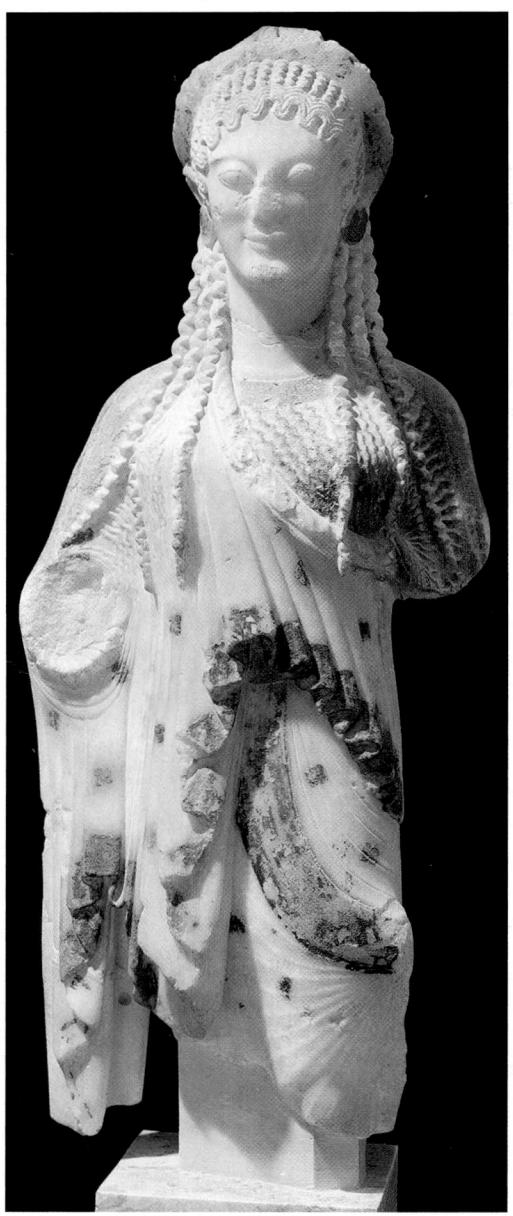

5.16 *Kore*, from Chios (?). ca. 520 BCE. Marble, height 21⅞" (55.3 cm). Akropolis Museum, Athens

5.15 *Kroisos (Kouros from Anavysos)*. ca. 540–525 BCE. Marble, height 6'4" (1.9 m). National Museum, Athens erecting a sculpture of this kind, a wealthy patron declared his or her status and claimed membership in ruling elite circles.

DATING AND NATURALISM The Archaic period stretches from the mid-seventh century to about 480 BCE. Within this time frame, there are few secure dates for free-standing sculptures. Scholars have therefore established a dating system based upon the level of naturalism in a given sculpture. According to this system, the more stylized the figure, the earlier it must be. Comparing figures 5.14 and **5.15** illustrates how this model works. An inscription on the base of the latter identifies it as the funerary statue of Kroisos, who died a hero's death in battle. Like all such figures, it was painted, and traces of color are still discernible in the hair and the pupils of the eyes. Instead of the sharp planes and linear treatment of the *New York Kouros* (see fig. 5.14), the sculptor of the kouros from Anavysos modeled its anatomy with swelling curves; a viewer can imagine flesh and sinew and bones in the carved stone. A greater plasticity gives the impression that the body could actually function. The proportions of the facial features are more naturalistic as well. The face has a less masklike quality than the *New York Kouros*, though the lips are drawn up in an artificial smile, known as the **Archaic smile**, that is not reflected in the eyes. Based on these differences, scholars judge the *Kroisos* more "advanced" than the *New York Kouros*, and date it some 75 years later. Given the later trajectory of Greek sculpture, there is every reason to believe that this way of dating Archaic sculpture is more or less accurate (accounting for regional differences and the like). All the same, it is worth emphasizing that it is based on an assumption—that sculptors, or their patrons, were striving toward naturalism—rather than on factual data.

There is more variation in types of kore than in types of kouros. This is partly because a kore is a clothed figure and therefore presents the problem of how to relate body and drapery. It is also likely to reflect changing habits or local styles of dress. The kore in figure **5.16**, from about 520 BCE, was a dedication on the Akropolis of Athens, though she probably came from Chios, an island of Ionian Greece. She has none of the severity of the earlier kore from Crete. She wears the light Ionian **chiton** (a rectangle of fabric draped and fastened at the shoulder by pins) under the heavier diagonally shaped himation, which replaced the earlier peplos (plain woolen garment) in fashion. The layers of the garment still loop around the body in soft curves, but the play of richly differentiated folds, pleats, and textures has almost become an end in itself. Color played an important role in such works, and is unusually well preserved in this example.

Architectural Sculpture: The Building Comes Alive

Soon after the Greeks began to dedicate stone temples, they also started to use architectural sculpture to articulate their buildings and bring them to life. Indeed, early Greek architects such as Theodoros of Samos were often sculptors as well. Traces of

pigment show that these sculptures were normally vividly painted. (See *Materials and Techniques*, page 223.)

The Egyptians had been covering walls and columns with reliefs since the Old Kingdom. Their carvings were so shallow (see fig. 3.28) that they did not break the continuity of the surface and had no volume of their own. Thus, like the reliefs on Assyrian, Babylonian, and Persian buildings, they related to their architectural setting in the same way as wall paintings (see figs. 2.19 and 2.20). Another kind of architectural sculpture in the Near East, however, seems to have begun with the Hittites: the lamassu protruding from stone blocks that framed the gateways of fortresses or palaces (see fig. 2.22). Directly or indirectly, this tradition may have inspired the carving over the Lioness Gate at Mycenae (see fig. 4.22).

THE TEMPLE OF ARTEMIS, CORFU The façade of the early Archaic Temple of Artemis on the island of Corfu, built soon after 600 BCE, suggests that the Lioness Gate relief, which was still visible in the sixth century, is a conceptual ancestor of later Greek architectural sculpture (figs. **5.17** and **5.18**). Sculpture on the temple is confined to the pediment, a triangle between the ceiling and the roof that serves as a screen to protect the wooden rafters behind it from moisture. Technically, the pedimental sculptures are in high relief, like the guardian lionesses at Mycenae. However, the sculptor undercut the figures so strongly that they are nearly detached from the background, and appear to be almost independent of their architectural setting. Indeed, the head of the central figure actually overlaps the frame; she seems to emerge out of the pediment toward a viewer. This choice on the sculptor's part heightens the impact of the figure and strengthens her function.

Although the Greeks of Corfu dedicated their temple to Artemis, the figure represents the snake-haired Medusa, one of

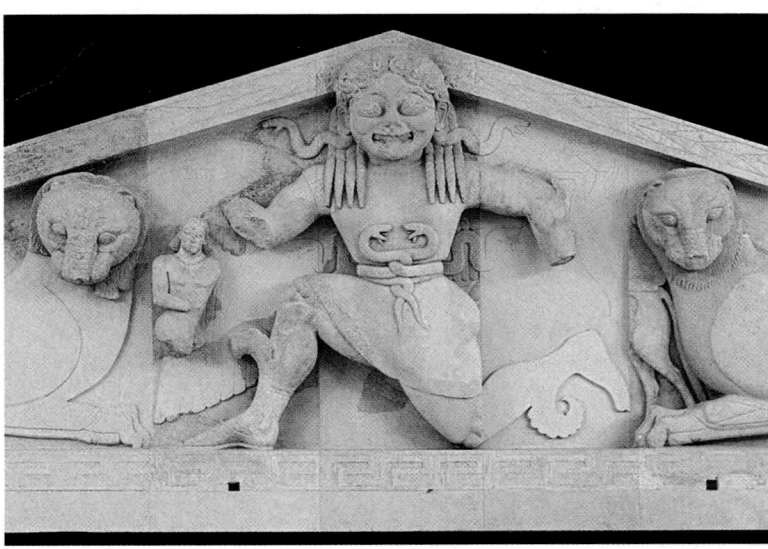

5.17 Central portion of west pediment of Temple of Artemis, Corfu, Greece. ca. 600–580 BCE. Limestone, height 9'2" (2.8 m). Archaeological Museum, Corfu

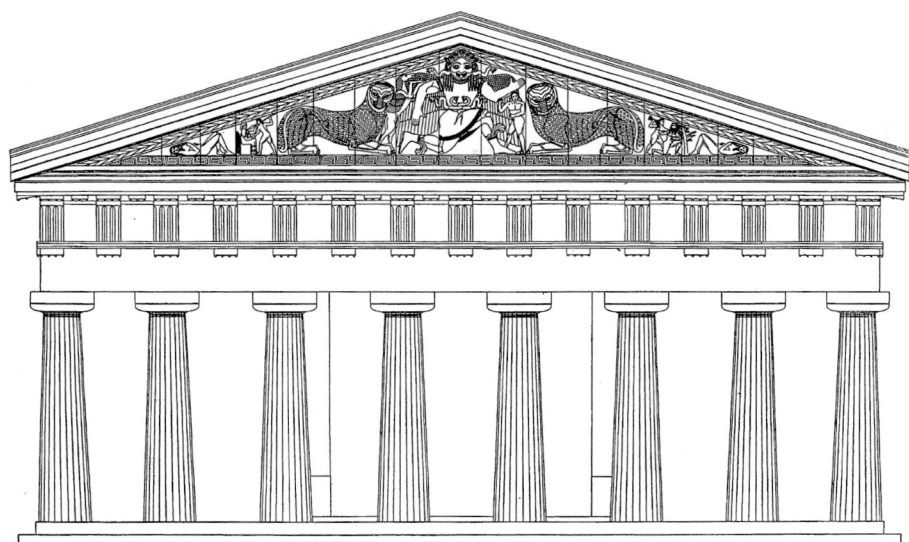

5.18 Reconstruction drawing of west front of Temple of Artemis, Corfu (after Rodenwaldt)

the Gorgon sisters of Greek mythology. Medusa's appearance was so monstrous, the story went, that anyone who beheld her would turn to stone. With the aid of the gods, the hero Perseus managed to behead her using her reflection in his shield to guide his sword. Traditionally, art historians have interpreted the figure of Medusa as a protective device, used to ward evil spirits away from the temple. However, scholars now argue that she served as a visual commentary on the power of the divinity: As a mistress of animals, she exemplifies the goddess' power and dominance over Nature. To emphasize this, two large feline creatures flank Medusa, in a heraldic arrangement known from the Lioness Gate and from earlier Near Eastern examples.

To strengthen the sculptures' message, the designer included narrative elements in the pediment as well. In the spaces between and behind the main group, the sculptor inserted subsidiary figures. On either side of Medusa are her children, the winged horse Pegasus, and Chrysaor, who will be born from drops of the blood she sheds when Perseus decapitates her. Pegasus was a symbol of Corinth. Since Corfu was Corinth's colony, the winged horse reminded residents of Corinth's control. Logically speaking, Pegasus and Chrysaor cannot yet exist, since Medusa's head is still on her shoulders; and yet their presence in the heraldic arrangement alludes to the future, when Perseus will have claimed the Gorgon's power as his own—just as the sculptor has here, in the service of Artemis. To bring the story to life, the sculptor fused two separate moments from a single story, in what is known as a **synoptic narrative.** Two additional groups filled the pediment's corners. They may depict Zeus and Poseidon battling the giants (a gigantomachy), a mortal race who tried to overthrow the gods. If so, they strike a cautionary note for a viewer, warning mortals not to aim higher than their natural place in the order of things, since the gods destroyed the giants for their overreaching ambitions.

With their reclining pose, the felines fit the shape of the pediment comfortably. Yet in order to fit Pegasus and Chrysaor between Medusa and the felines, and the groups into the corners,

the sculptor carved them at a significantly smaller scale than the dominant figures. Later solutions to the pediment's awkward shape suggest that this one, which lacks unity of scale, was not wholly satisfactory.

Aside from filling the pediment with sculpture, Greeks often affixed free-standing figures, known as **acroteria**, above the corners and center of the pediment, to soften the severity of its outline (see fig. 5.20). In Ionic buildings, female statues or **caryatids** might substitute for columns to support the roof of a porch (see figs. 5.20 and 5.51). Sculptors also decorated the frieze. In Doric temples, they would often embellish the metopes with figural scenes. In Ionic temples, they treated the frieze with a continuous band of painted or sculpted decoration. For the frieze as for the pediment, the designer frequently selected mythological subjects with a topical relevance.

THE SIPHNIAN TREASURY, DELPHI These Ionic features came together in a building constructed at Delphi shortly before 525 BCE by the people of the Ionian island of Siphnos. Delphi was the site of an important Panhellenic sanctuary to Apollo, to which people traveled from all over Greece to consult its oracle (fig. 5.19). The sanctuary gradually came to incorporate a theater and a stadium as well as several temples. Individuals and cities made dedications there, such as statues and spoils of war, and many cities built treasuries on the course of the principal thoroughfare, the Processional Way, to store their votive offerings. Treasuries resembled miniature temples, and typically had an ornate quality. Although the Treasury of the Siphnians no longer stands, archaeologists can reconstruct its appearance from surviving blocks (figs. **5.20** and **5.21**). Two caryatids supported the architrave of the porch. Above the architrave was a magnificent sculptural frieze (see fig. 5.21), part of which depicts the mythical battle of the gods against the giants, possibly also seen at Corfu. At the far left, the two lions pull the chariot of Themis, and tear apart an anguished giant. In front of them, Apollo and Artemis advance

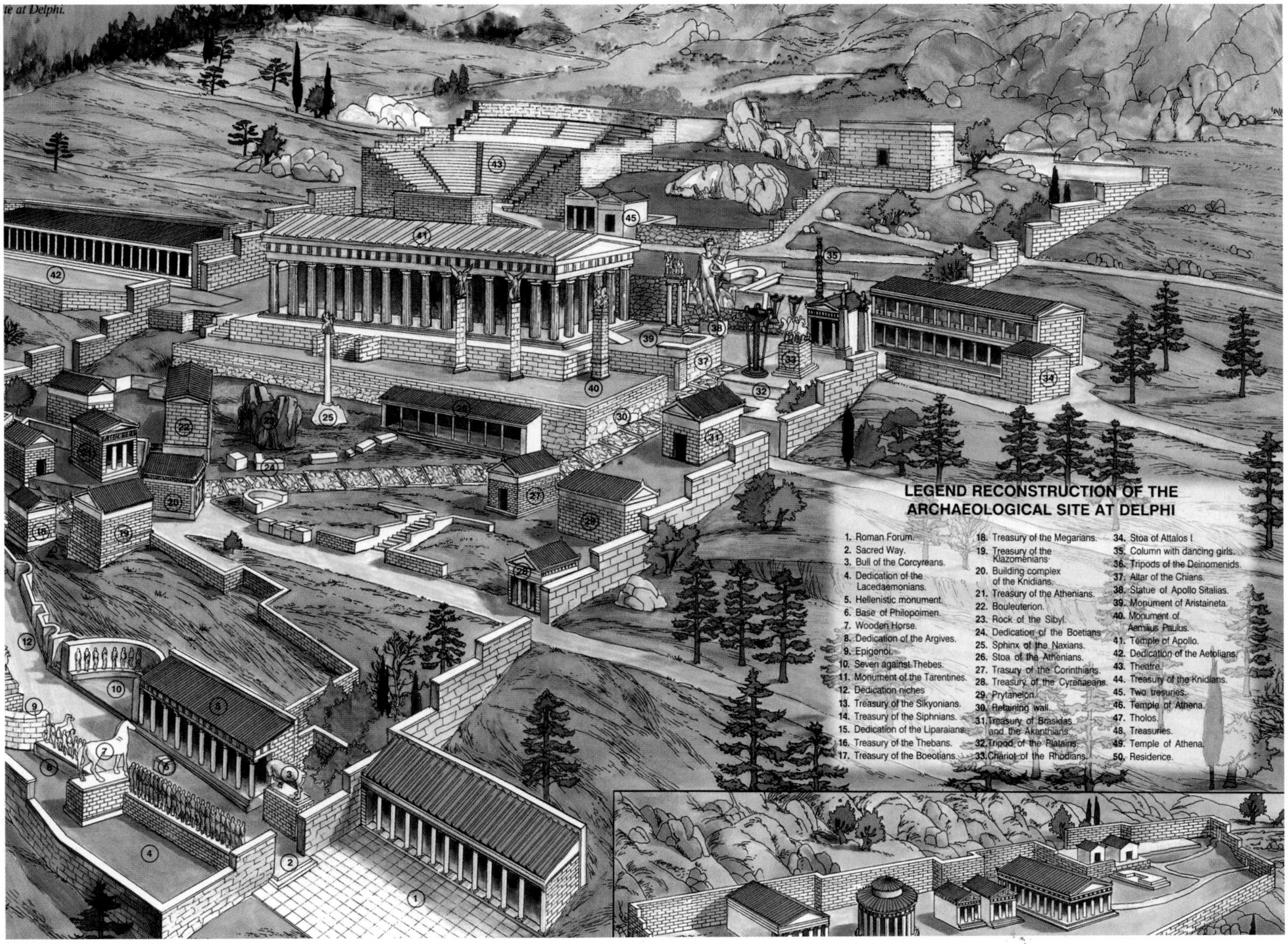

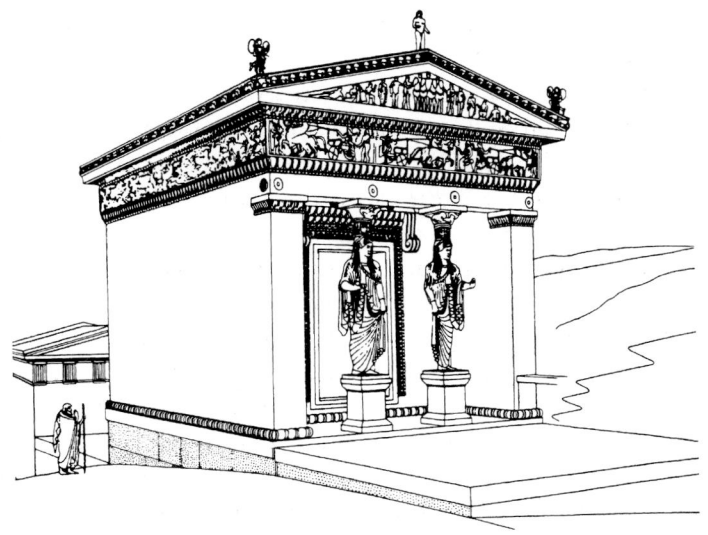

5.19 Plan of Sanctuary of Apollo in ancient times, Delphi

LEGEND RECONSTRUCTION OF THE ARCHAEOLOGICAL SITE AT DELPHI

1. Roman Forum.
2. Sacred Way.
3. Bull of the Corcyreans.
4. Dedication of the Lacedaemonians.
5. Hellenistic monument.
6. Base of Philopoimen.
7. Wooden Horse.
8. Dedication of the Argives.
9. Epigenoi.
10. Seven against Thebes.
11. Monument of the Tarentines.
12. Dedication niches
13. Treasury of the Sikyonians.
14. Treasury of the Siphnians.
15. Dedication of the Liparaians.
16. Treasury of the Thebans.
17. Treasury of the Boeotians.
18. Treasury of the Megarians.
19. Treasury of the Klazomenians.
20. Building complex of the Knidians.
21. Treasury of the Athenians.
22. Bouleuterion.
23. Rock of the Sibyl.
24. Dedication of the Boetians.
25. Sphinx of the Naxians.
26. Stoa of the Athenians.
27. Treasury of the Corinthians.
28. Treasury of the Cyrenaeans.
29. Prytaneion.
30. Retaining wall.
31. Treasury of Brasidas and the Akanthians.
32. Tripod of the Plataians.
33. Chariot of the Rhodians.
34. Stoa of Attalos I.
35. Column with dancing girls.
36. Tripods of the Deinomenids.
37. Altar of the Chians.
38. Statue of Apollo Sitalias.
39. Monument of Aristaineta.
40. Monument of Aemilius Paulus.
41. Temple of Apollo.
42. Dedication of the Aetolians.
43. Theatre.
44. Treasury of the Knidians.
45. Two treasuries.
46. Temple of Athena.
47. Tholos.
48. Treasuries.
49. Temple of Athena.
50. Residence.

together, shooting arrows, originally added in metal, into a phalanx of giants. Stripped of his armor, a dead giant lies at their feet. Though the subject is mythical, its depiction provides historians with a wealth of detail on contemporary weaponry and military tactics.

Astonishingly, the relief is only a few inches deep from front to back. Within that shallow space, the sculptors (scholars discern more than one hand) created several planes. They carved the arms and legs of those nearest a viewer in the round. In the second and third layers, the forms become shallower, yet even those farthest from a viewer do not merge into the background. The resulting relationships between figures give a dramatic sense of the turmoil of battle and an intensity of action not seen before in narrative reliefs. As at Corfu, the protagonists fill the sculptural field from top to bottom, and this compositional choice enhances the frieze's power. It is a dominant characteristic of Archaic and Classical Greek art, and in time sculptors sought ways to fill the triangular field of the pediment, too, while retaining a unity of scale. Taking

5.20 Reconstruction drawing of Treasury of the Siphnians, Sanctuary of Apollo, Delphi. ca. 525 BCE

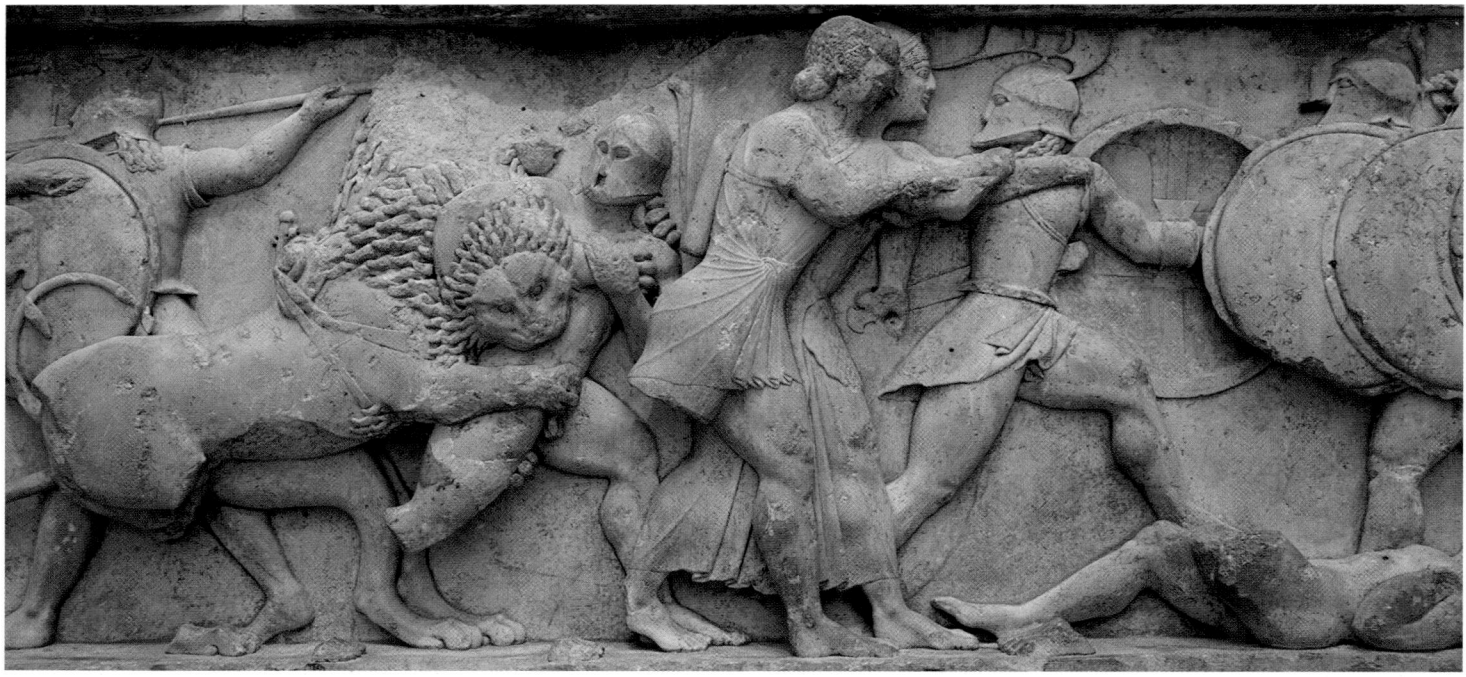

5.21 *Battle of the Gods and Giants*, from the north frieze of the Treasury of the Siphnians, Delphi. ca. 530 BCE. Marble, height 26" (66 cm). Archaeological Museum, Delphi

their cue, perhaps, from friezes such as that found on the Siphnian Treasury, they introduced a variety of poses for figures, and made great strides in depicting the human body in naturalistic motion. The pediments of the Temple of Aphaia at Aegina illustrate this well (see fig. 5.11).

PEDIMENTS OF THE TEMPLE OF APHAIA AT AEGINA

In ca. 480 BCE, the Aeginetans replaced the sculptures in the east pediment of their Temple of Aphaia. Scholars hypothesize that the Persian invasion of Greece may have caused damage to the earlier sculptures. The new pediment (fig. **5.22**) depicts the first sack of Troy, by Herakles and Telamon, king of Salamis. The west pediment, which was not replaced at the time and dates from about 500–490 BCE, shows the second siege of Troy (recounted in *The Iliad*) by the Greek king Agamemnon, who was related to Herakles. The pairing of subjects commemorates the important role the heroes of Aegina played in both legendary battles—and, by extension, at Salamis, where their navy helped to overcome the Persians in 480. The use of **allegory** to elevate historical events to a universal plane is a frequent strategy in Greek art.

The figures of both pediments are fully in the round, independent of the stone background. For centuries, those of the east pediment lay in pieces on the ground, and scholars now debate their exact arrangement. All the same, they can determine the relative position of each figure within the pediment with reasonable accuracy, since the designer introduced a range of action poses for the figures, so their height, *but not their scale*, varies to suit the gently sloping sides of the pedimental field. In the center stands the goddess Athena, presiding over the battle between Greeks and Trojans that rages on either side of her. Kneeling

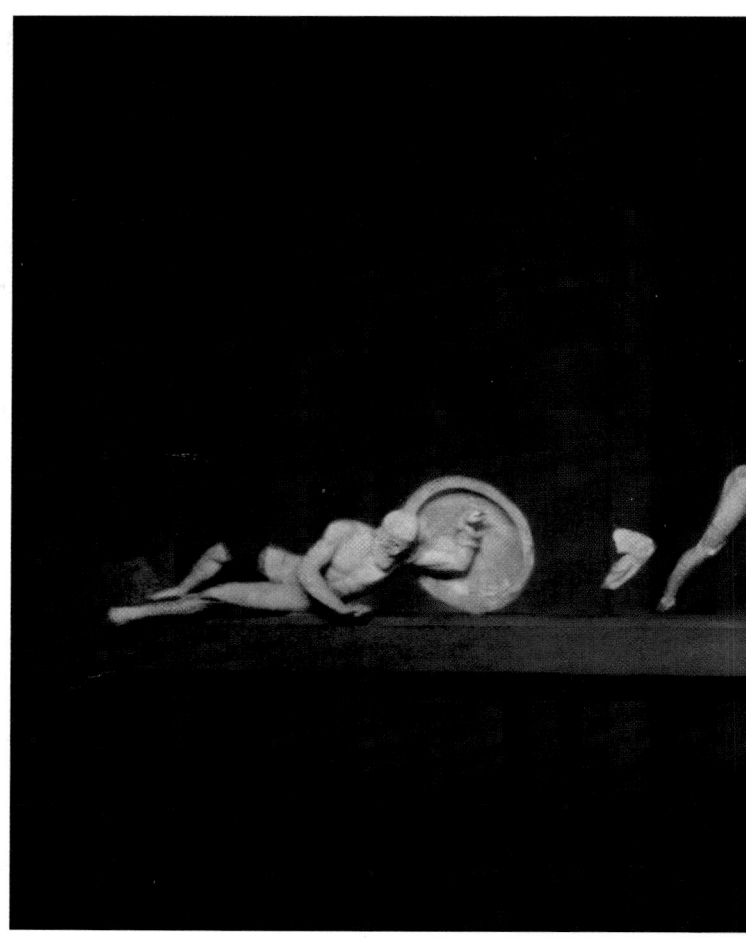

5.22 Reconstruction of the east pediment of the Temple of Aphaia, Aegina. Greek, ca. 500–480 BCE. Glyptothek, Staatliche Antikensammlungen, Munich, Germany

archers shoot across the pediment to unite its action. The symmetrical arrangement of poses on the two halves of the pediment creates a balanced design, so that while each figure has a clear autonomy, it also exists within a governing ornamental pattern.

A comparison of a fallen warrior from the west pediment (fig. **5.23**) with its counterpart from the later east pediment (fig. **5.24**) exposes the extraordinary advances sculptors made toward naturalism during the decades that separate them. As they sink to the ground in death, both figures present a clever solution to filling the difficult corner space. Yet while the earlier figure props himself up on one arm, only a precariously balanced shield supports the later warrior, whose full weight seems to pull him irresistibly to the ground. Both sculptors contorted their subjects' bodies in the agonies of death: The earlier sculptor crosses the warrior's legs in an awkward pose, while the later sculptor twists the body from the waist, so that the left shoulder moves into a new plane. Although the later warrior's anatomy still does not fully respond to his pose (note, for instance, how little the pectorals stretch to accommodate the strenuous motion of the right arm, and the misplaced navel), his body is more modeled and organic than the earlier warrior's. He also breaks from the head-on stare of his predecessor, turning his gaze to the ground that confronts him.

The effect suggests introspection: The inscrutable smiling mask of the earlier warrior yields to the suffering and emotion of a warrior in his final moments of life. Depictions of suffering, and how humans respond to it, are among the most dramatic developments of late Archaic art.

Vase Painting: Art of the Symposium

A similar experimentation with figural poses and emotion occurred in Archaic vase painting, which replaced the Orientalizing style as workshops in Athens and other centers began to produce extremely fine wares, painted with scenes from mythology, legend, and everyday life. The difference between Orientalizing and Archaic vase painting is largely one of technique. On the aryballos from Corinth (see fig. 5.5), the figures appear partly as solid silhouettes, partly in outline, or as a combination of the two. Toward the end of the seventh century BCE, influenced by Corinthian products, Attic vase painters began to work in the **black-figured** technique: They painted the entire design in black silhouette against the reddish clay, and then incised internal details into the design with a needle. Next, they painted white and purple over the black to make chosen areas

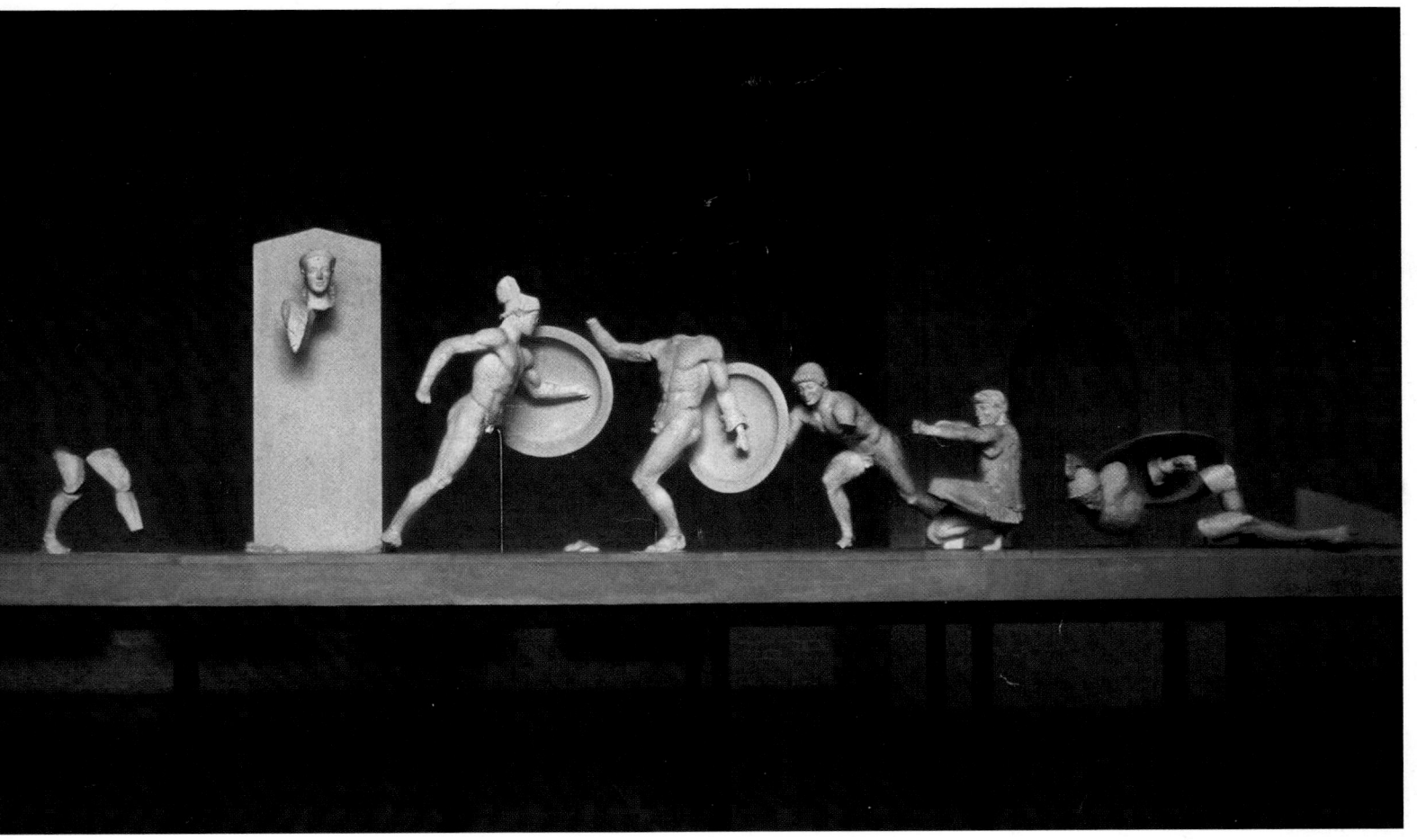

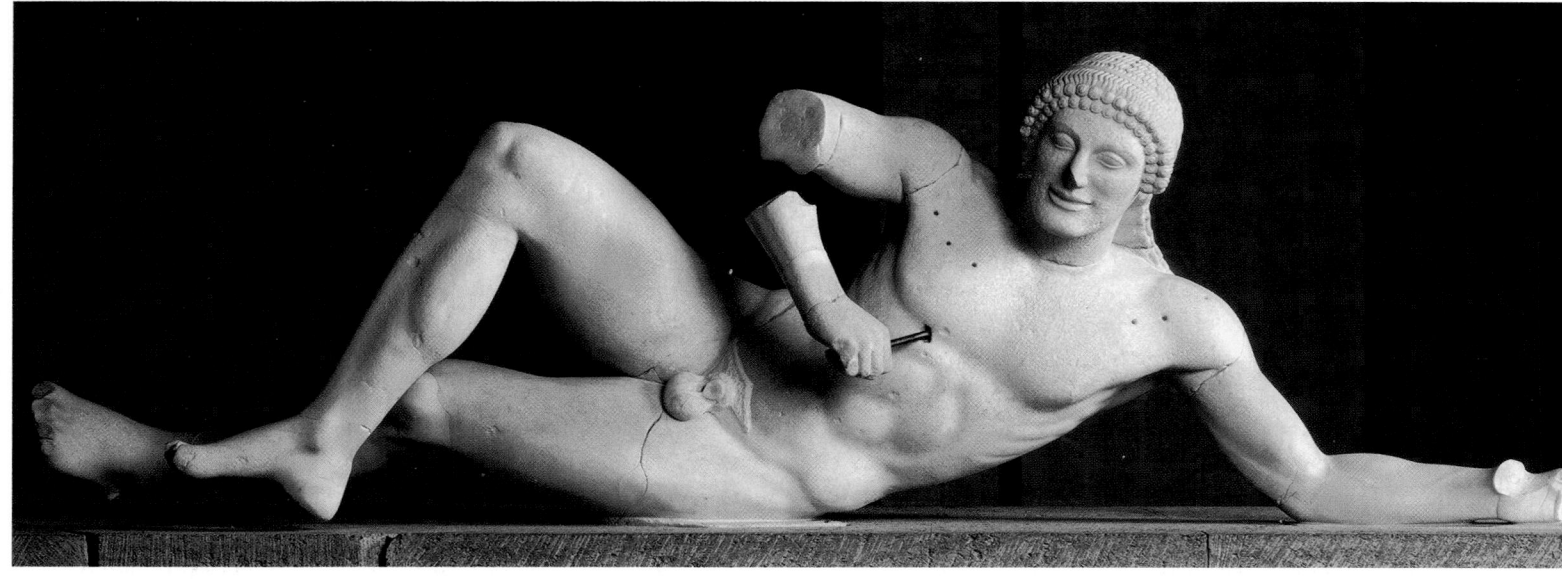

5.23 *Dying Warrior*, from west pediment of the Temple of Aphaia. ca. 500–490 BCE. Marble, length 5'2½" (1.59 m). Staatliche Antikensammlungen und Glyptothek, Munich

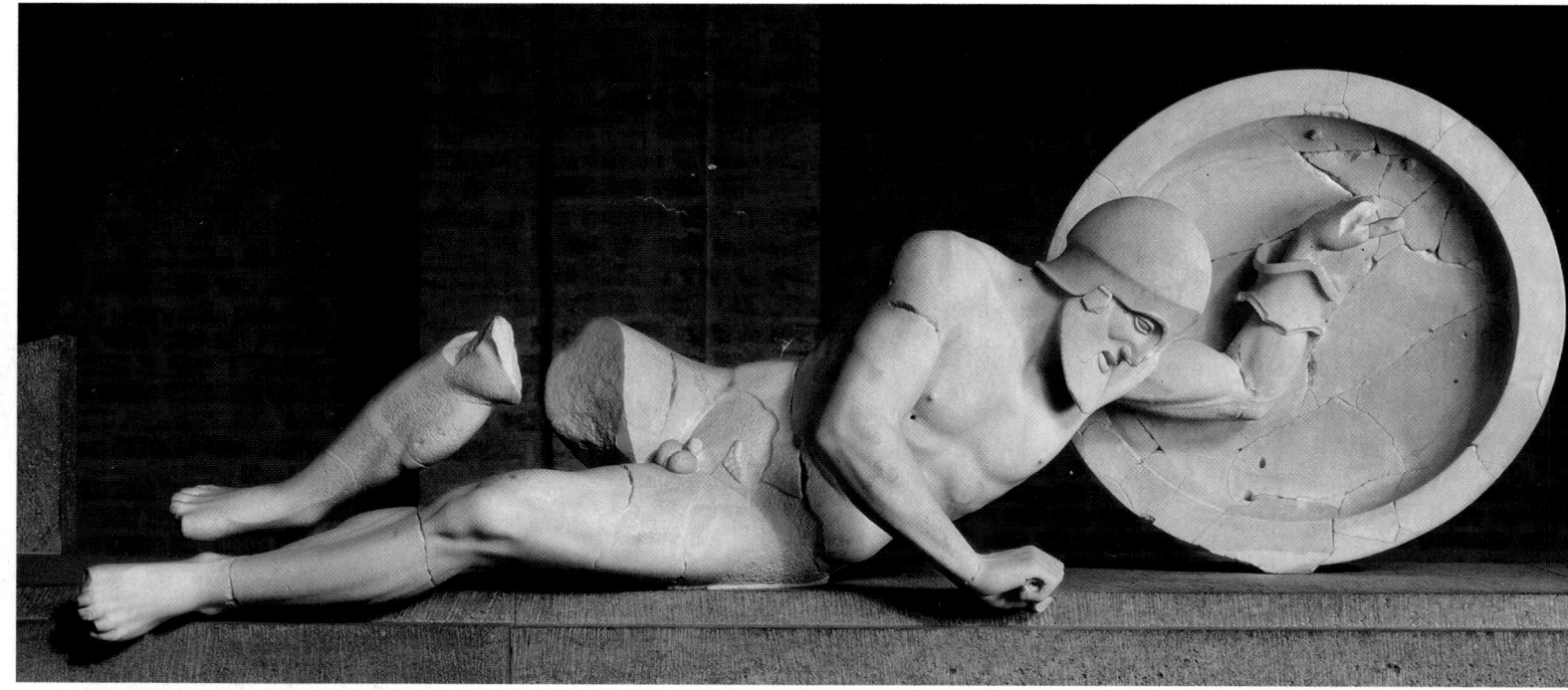

5.24 *Dying Warrior*, from east pediment of the Temple of Aphaia. ca. 480 BCE. Marble, length 6' (1.83 m). Staatliche Antikensammlungen und Glyptothek, Munich

stand out. The technique lent itself to a two-dimensional and highly decorative effect. This development marks the beginning of an aggressive export industry, the main consumers of which were the Etruscans. Vast numbers of black-figured vases were found in Etruscan tombs. Thus, although in terms of conception these vases (and later red-figured vessels) represent a major chapter in Greek (and specifically Athenian) art, with regard to their actual use, painted vases are a major component of Etruscan culture, both visual and funerary.

Greeks used the vases illustrated in these pages to hold wine. For everyday use, they generally poured wine from plainer, unadorned vases. They reserved decorated vases for special occasions, like the **symposium** (*symposion*), an exclusive drinking party that was a central feature of Greek life. Symposia were exclusively for men and courtesans; wives and other respectable citizen women did not attend. Participants reclined on couches around the edges of a room, and a master of ceremonies filled their cups from a large painted mixing bowl (a krater) at the center. Music, poetry, storytelling, and word games accompanied the festivities. Often the event ended in lovemaking, which is frequently depicted on drinking cups. Sometimes this was homosexual in orientation, since it was not unusual in the fifth century BCE for a mature Greek man to have a younger male lover, for whom he acted as a social and political mentor. There was also a serious side to symposia, as described by Plato and Xenophon, which centered on debates about politics, ethics, and morality. The great issues that Greeks pondered in their philosophy, literature, and theater—the nature of virtue, the value of an individual man's life, or mortal relations with the gods, to name a few—were mirrored in, and prompted by, the images with which they surrounded themselves.

After the middle of the sixth century BCE, many of the finest vessels bear the signatures of the artists who made them, indicating the pride that potters and painters alike took in their work. In many cases, vase painters had such distinctive styles that scholars can recognize their work even without a signature, and use modern names to identify them. Dozens of vases (in one instance, over 200) might survive by the same hand, allowing scholars to trace a single painter's development over many years.

A fine example of the black-figured technique is an Athenian amphora signed by Exekias as both potter and painter, dating to the third quarter of the sixth century BCE (fig. 5.25). The painting shows the Homeric heroes Achilles and Ajax playing dice. The episode does not exist in surviving literary sources, and its appearance here hints at a wide field of lost traditions that may have inspired Exekias. The two figures lean on their spears; their shields are stacked behind them against the inside of a campaign tent. The black silhouettes create a rhythmical composition, symmetrical around the table in the center. Within the black paint, Exekias incised a wealth of detail, focusing especially upon the warriors' cloaks; their intricately woven texture contrasts with the lustrous blackness of their weapons.

The extraordinary power of this scene derives from the tension within it. The warriors have stolen a moment of relaxation during a fierce war; even so, poised on the edge of their stools, one heel raised as if to spring into action, their poses are edgy. An inscription on the right reads "three," as if Ajax is calling out his throw. Achilles, who in his helmet slightly dominates the scene, answers with "four," making him the winner. Yet many Greek viewers would have understood the irony of the scene, for when they return to battle, Achilles will die, and Ajax will be left to bear his friend's lifeless body back to the Greek camp, before falling on his own sword in despair. Indeed, Exekias himself would paint representations of the heroes' tragic deaths. This amphora is the first known representation of the gaming scene, which subsequently became popular, suggesting that vase paintings did not exist in artistic isolation; painters responded to one another's work in a close and often clever dialogue.

Athenian vase painters seem to have intended most of the scenes on their vessels for a male audience. There are cases, however, when vases reflect female life and appear to be intended for a female audience. A black-figured **hydria** (water jar) by the

Priam Painter is one such vase (fig. **5.26**). The belly of the water jug shows a scene in a columned fountain house, where three women collect water into hydriai from animal-headed spigots, and a fourth supports a hydria on her head. Their poses, with knees and arms raised, allow the painter to experiment with figural movement. The animated gesture of a fifth woman reflects the fact that, for Athenian women, the daily outing to the public fountain house was the only opportunity to leave the confines of the home; the fountain house represented a rare chance to socialize outside the immediate family.

Despite its decorative potential, the silhouettelike black-figured technique limited artists to incision for detail, leading them to develop the reverse procedure of leaving the figures red and filling in the background. This **red-figured** technique gradually replaced the older method between 520 and 500 BCE. The effects of the change would become increasingly evident in the decades to come, but they are already discernible on an amphora of about

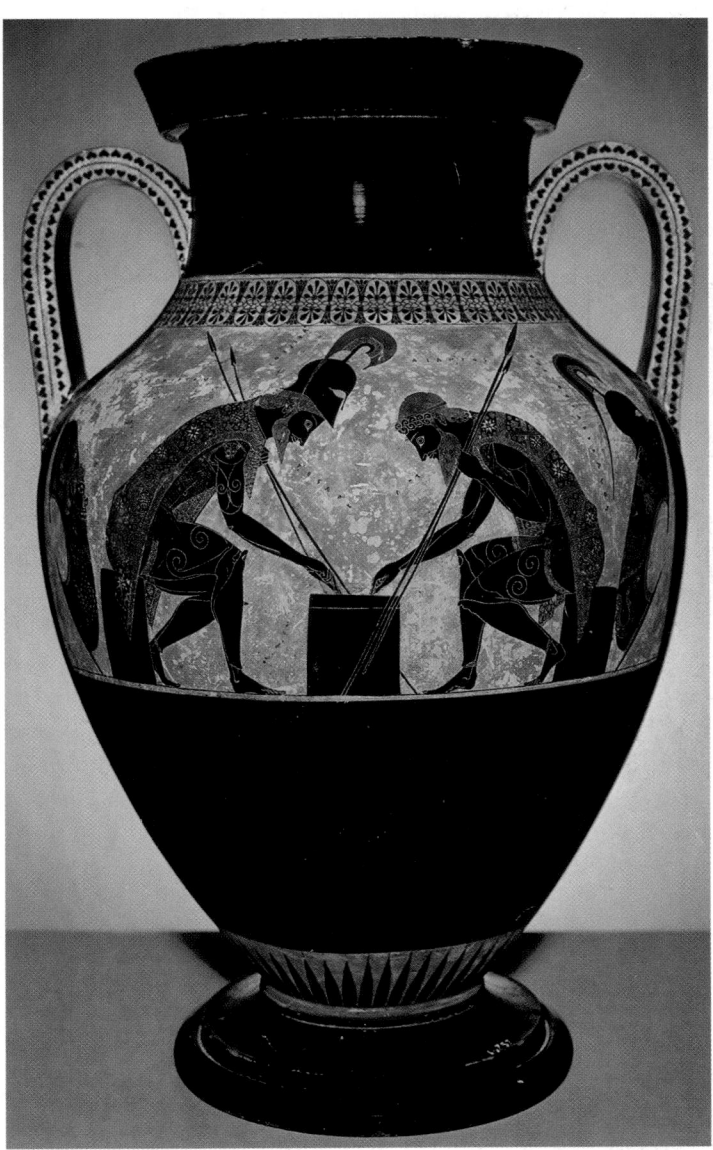

5.25 Exekias. *Achilles and Ajax Playing Dice*. Black-figured amphora. ca. 540–530 BCE. Height 2' (61 cm). Vatican Museums

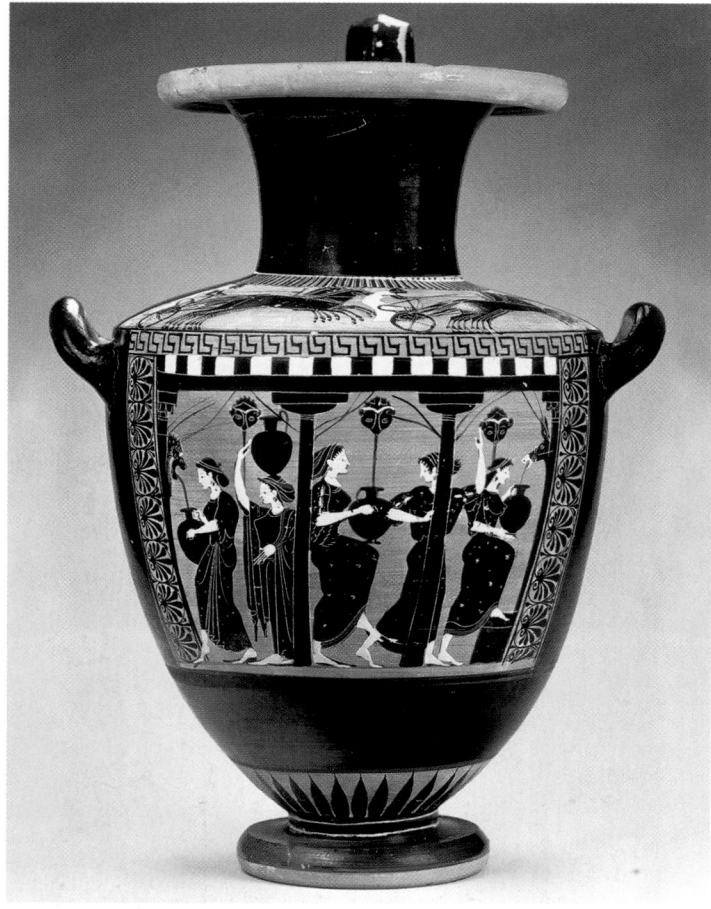

5.26 Priam Painter. *Women at a fountain house*. 520–510 BCE. Black-figured hydria. Ceramic. Height 20⅞" (53 cm). Museum of Fine Arts, Boston, William Francis Warden Fund, 1961. 61.195

510–500 BCE, signed by Euthymides (fig. **5.27**). No longer is the scene so dependent on profiles. The painter's new freedom with the brush translates into a freedom of movement in the dancing revelers he represents. They cavort in a range of poses, twisting their bodies and showing off Euthymides' confidence in rendering human anatomy. The shoulder blades of the central figure, for instance, one higher than the other, reflect the motion of his raised arm. The turning poses allow Euthymides to tackle **foreshortening**, as he portrays the different planes of the body (the turning shoulders, for instance) on a single surface. This was an age of intensive and self-conscious experimentation; indeed, so pleased was Euthymides with his painting that he inscribed a taunting challenge to a fellow painter: "As never Euphronios."

On a slightly later **kylix** (wine cup) by Douris, dating to 490–480 BCE, Eos, the goddess of dawn, tenderly lifts the limp body of her dead son, Memnon, whom Achilles killed after their mothers sought the intervention of Zeus (fig. **5.28**). Douris traces the contours of limbs beneath the drapery, and balances vigorous outlines with more delicate secondary strokes, such as those indicating the anatomical details of Memnon's body. The dead weight of Memnon's body contrasts with the lift of Eos' wings, an ironic commentary, perhaps, on how Zeus decided between the two warriors by weighing their souls on a scale that tipped against

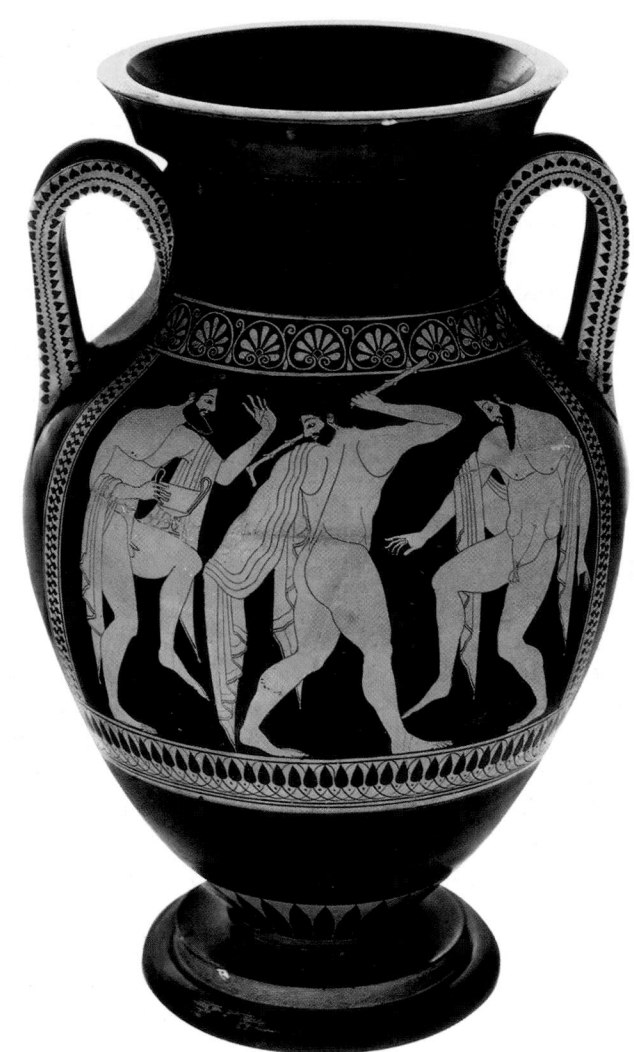

5.27 Euthymides. *Dancing Revelers*. Red-figured amphora. ca. 510–500 BCE. Height 2' (60 cm). Museum Antiker Kleinkunst, Munich

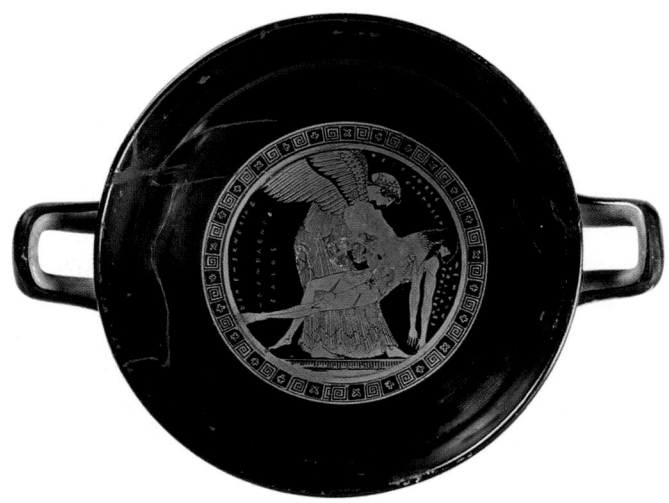

5.28 Douris. *Eos and Memnon*. Interior of an Attic red-figured kylix. ca. 490–480 BCE. Ceramic. Diameter 10½" (26.7 cm). Musée du Louvre, Paris

Memnon. After killing him, Achilles stripped off Memnon's armor as an act of humiliation, and where the figures overlap in the image, the gentle folds of Eos' flowing chiton set off Memnon's nudity. His vulnerability in turn underlines his mother's desperate grief at being unable to help her son.

At the core of the image is raw emotion. Douris tenderly exposes the suffering caused by intransigent fate, and the callousness of the gods who intervene in mortal lives. In this mythological scene, Athenians may have seen a reflection of themselves during the horrors of the Persian Wars of 490–479 BCE. Indeed, an inscription brings the vase into the realm of everyday life, with the signatures of both painter and potter, as well as a dedication typical of Greek vases: "Hermogenes is beautiful."

THE CLASSICAL AGE

The beginning of the fifth century BCE brought crisis. A number of Ionian cities rebelled against their Persian overlords, and after Athens came to their support, the Persians invaded the Greek mainland, under the leadership of Darius I. At the Battle of Marathon in 490 BCE, a contingent of about 10,000 Athenians, with a battalion from nearby Plataea, repulsed a force of about 90,000 Persians. Ten years later, an even larger force of Persians returned under Darius' son, Xerxes I. Defeating a Spartan force at Thermopylae, they took control of Athens, burning and pillaging temples and statues. The Greeks fought them again at Salamis and Plataea in 480–479 BCE, and finally defeated them. These battles were defining moments for the Greeks, who first faced destruction in their cities, and then emerged triumphant and confident after the horrors of invasion. At least in Athens, Persian destruction of public monuments and space is visible in the archaeological record, and, for archaeologists and art historians, signals the end of the Archaic period. The period stretching from the end of the Persian Wars to the death of Alexander the Great in the late fourth century BCE is known as the Classical Age. During this time, architects and sculptors alike sought visual harmony in proportional systems, and artists achieved a heightened naturalism in depicting the human form.

The struggle against the Persians tested the recently established Athenian democracy. Athens emerged from the war as the leader of the Delian League, a defensive alliance against the Persians, which quickly evolved into a political and economic empire that facilitated many architectural and artistic projects. The Classical era was when the playwrights whose names are still so familiar—Aristophanes, Aeschylus, Sophocles, and Euripides—were penning comedies and tragedies for performance at religious festivals, and thinkers like Socrates and Plato, and then Aristotle, engaged in their philosophical quests. Perhaps the most influential political leader of the day was Perikles, who came to the forefront of Athenian public life in the mid-fifth century BCE, and played a critical role in the city's history until his death in 429 BCE. An avid patron of the arts, he focused much of his attention on beautifying the city's highest point or Akropolis.

Classical Sculpture

The Persian sack of 480 BCE left the Athenian Akropolis in ruins. Among many statues that were once dedications there and were later excavated from the debris, one kouros stands apart (fig. **5.29**). Archaeologists sometimes attribute it to the Athenian sculptor Kritios, and know it as the *Kritios Boy*. On account of its

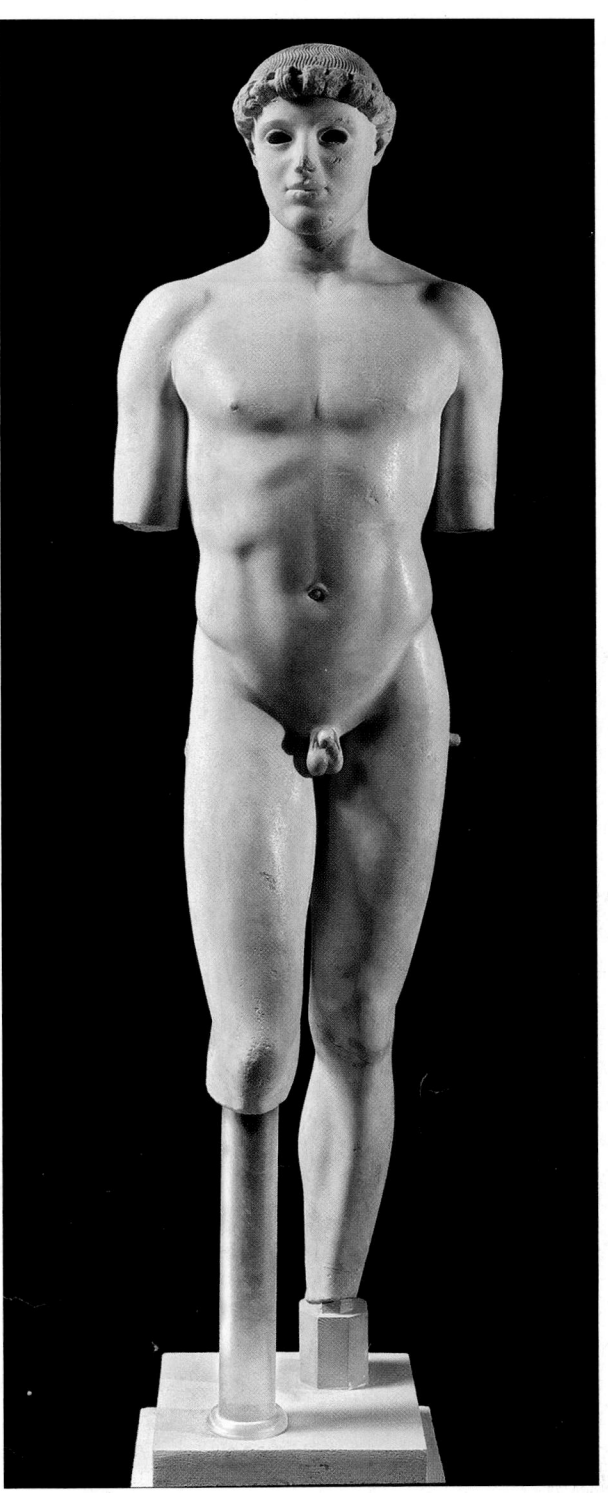

5.29 *Kritios Boy*. ca. 480 BCE. Marble, height 46" (116.7 cm). Akropolis Museum, Athens

and rigid. The *Kritios Boy* has one leg forward like earlier kouroi, yet an important change has occurred. The sculptor has shifted the youth's weight, creating a calculated asymmetry in the two sides of his body. The knee of the forward leg is lower than the other, the right hip is thrust down and in, and the left hip up and out. The axis of the body is not a straight vertical line, but a reversed S-curve. Taken together, these small departures from symmetry indicate that the youth's weight rests mainly on the left leg, while the right leg acts as a prop to help balance the body.

The *Kritios Boy* not only stands; he stands at ease. The artist masterfully observed the balanced asymmetry of this relaxed natural stance, which is known to ancient art historians as a **chiastic pose** (from "χ," the Greek letter *chi*), and to Renaissance art historians as **contrapposto** (Italian for "counterpoise"). The leg that carries the main weight is called the engaged leg, the other, the free leg. This simple observation led to radical results, for with it came a recognition that if one part of the body is engaged in a task, other parts respond. Bending the free knee results in a slight swiveling of the pelvis, a compensating curvature of the spine, and an adjusting tilt of the shoulders. This unified approach to the body led artists to represent movement with a new naturalism. Indeed, even though the *Kritios Boy* is at rest, his muscles suggest motion, and the sculpture has life; he seems capable of action. At the same time, the artist recognized that strict adherence to nature would not always yield the desired result. So, as in the later Parthenon (see pages 131–37), refinements are at work. The sculptor exaggerated the line of muscles over the pelvis to create a greater unity between thighs and torso, and a more fluid transition from front to back. This emphasized the sculpture's three-dimensionality, and encouraged a viewer to move around it.

The innovative movement in the musculature gives a viewer the sense, for the first time, that muscles lie beneath the surface of the marble skin, and that a skeleton articulates the whole as a real organism. A new treatment of the flesh and the marble's surface adds to this impression: The flesh has a soft sensuousness that is quite alien to earlier kouroi, and the sculptor has worked the surface of the marble to a gentle polish. Gone, also, is the Archaic smile. The face has a soft fleshiness to it, especially marked around the chin, which is characteristic of sculpture in the early Classical period. The head is turned slightly away from the front, removing the direct gaze of earlier kouroi and casting the figure into his own world of thought.

A sculpture discovered in the Graeco-Punic settlement of Motya in western Sicily exhibits a similar sensuousness (see map 5.1 and fig. **5.30**). Like the *Kritios Boy*, it represents a youth standing in a sinuous chiastic pose, his head turned from a frontal axis. The sculptor has used the fine fabric of a charioteer's tunic to "mask" the full curves of the body, revealing the flesh while simultaneously concealing it. Athletic contests were a prominent component of male life in Greece and its colonies. Greeks viewed physical prowess as a virtue, and victors in games won a measure of fame. Sculptures like this one, set up in public places, commemorated their success.

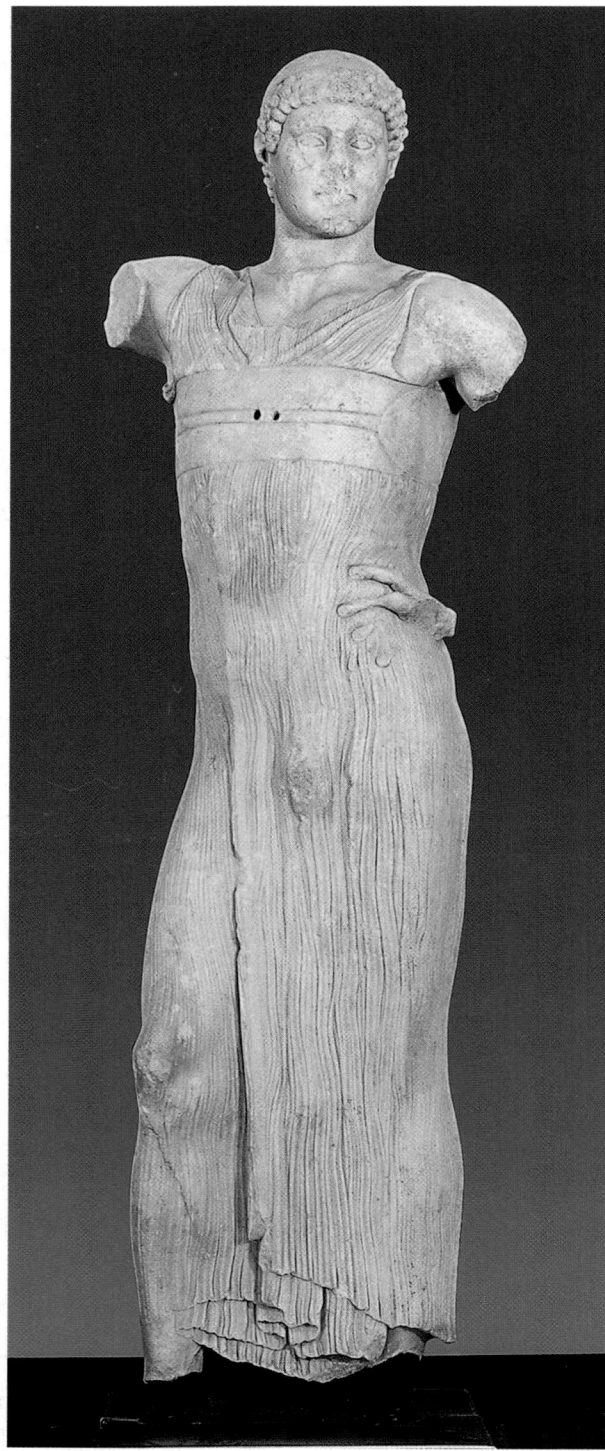

5.30 *Charioteer from Motya*, Sicily. ca. 450–440 BCE. Marble, height 6'3" (1.9 m). Museo Giuseppe Whitaker, Motya

findspot, they date it to shortly before the Persian attack. It differs significantly from earlier, Archaic kouroi (see figs. 5.14 and 5.15), not least because it is the first surviving statue that stands in the full sense of the word. Although the earlier figures are in an upright position—instead of reclining, sitting, kneeling, or running—their stance is really an arrested walk, with the body's weight resting evenly on both legs. This pose is nonnaturalistic

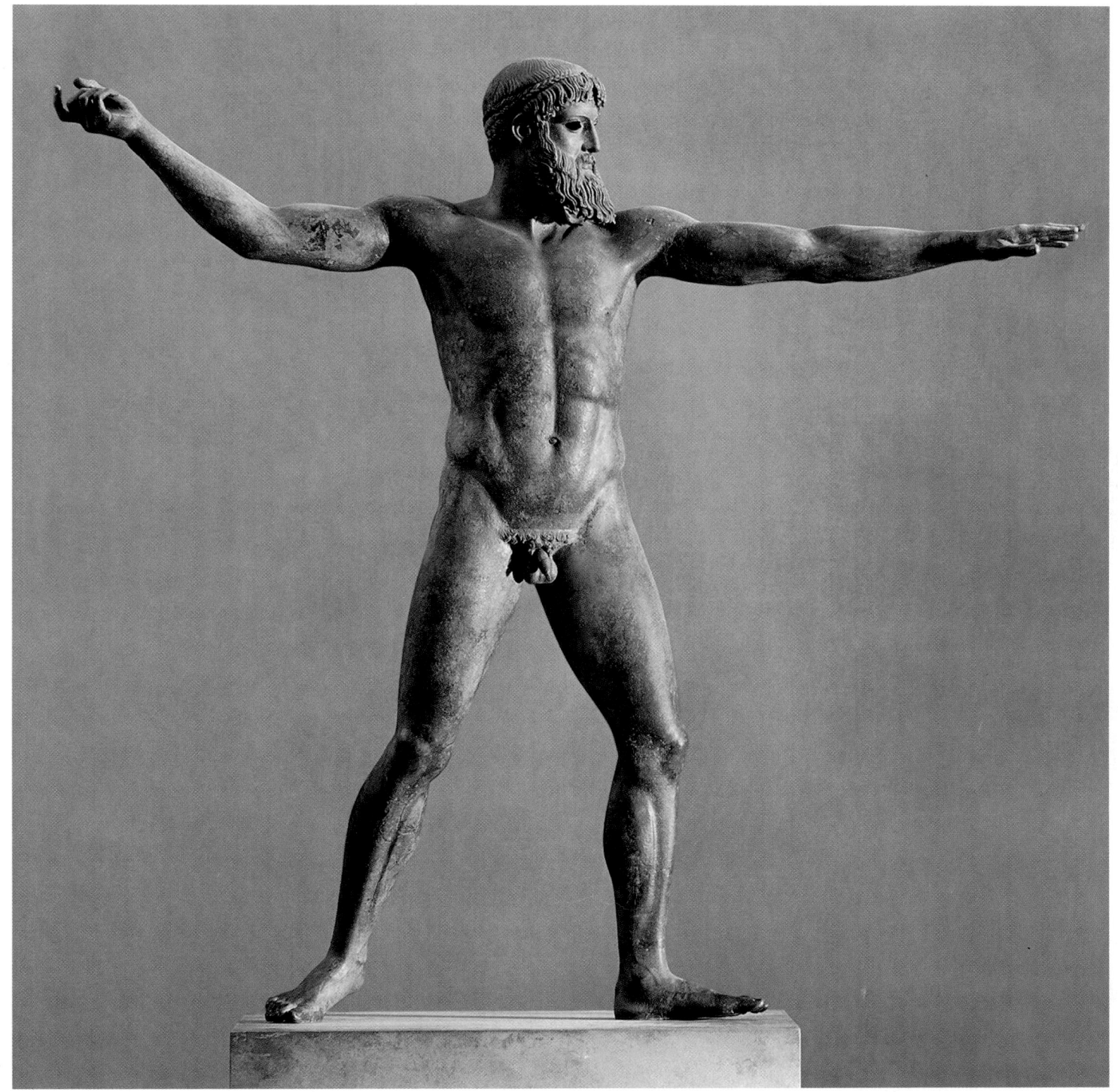

5.31 *Zeus.* ca. 460–450 BCE. Bronze, height 6'10" (1.9 m). National Archaeological Museum, Athens.
Ministry of Culture Archaeological Receipts Fund. 15161

The *Kritios Boy* marks a critical point in Greek art. One of the changes it engendered was a wholehearted exploration of the representation of movement, another hallmark of early Classical sculpture. A magnificent nude bronze dating to about 460–450 BCE recovered from the sea near the Greek coast (fig. **5.31**) was probably in the cargo of a Roman vessel that sank on its voyage to Italy. At almost 7 feet tall, it depicts a spread-eagled male figure in the act of throwing—probably Zeus casting a thunderbolt, or Poseidon throwing his trident. In a single figure, the sculptor captures and contrasts vigorous action and firm stability. The result is a work of outright grandeur, expressing the god's awe-inspiring power. The piece shows off not only the artist's understanding of bodies in motion, but also an expert knowledge of the strengths of bronze, which allowed the god's arms to stretch out without support. (See *Materials and Techniques*, page 128.) Some ten years later, in about 450 BCE, a sculptor named Myron created a

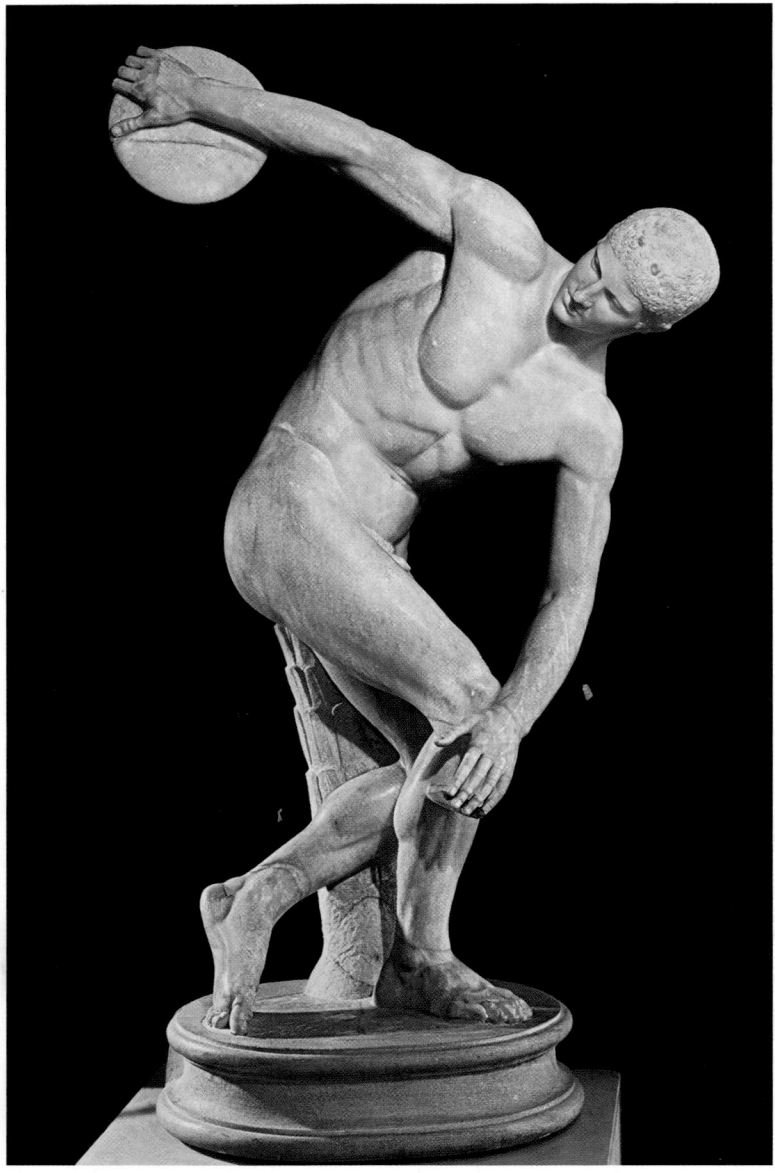

5.32 *Diskobolos* (*Discus Thrower*). Roman copy after a bronze original of ca. 450 BCE by Myron. Marble, life-size. Museo delle Terme, Rome

bronze statue of another athlete, a discus thrower, the *Diskobolos*, which earned great renown in its own time. Like most Greek sculptures in bronze, it is known to us only from Roman copies (fig. **5.32**). (See www.myartslab.com.) If the bronze Zeus suggested impending motion by portraying the moment before it occurred, Myron condensed a sequence of movements into a single pose, achieved through a violent twist of the torso that brings the arms into the same plane as the legs. The pose conveys the essence of the action by presenting the coiled figure in perfect balance.

THE *DORYPHOROS*: IDEALS OF PROPORTION AND HARMONY Within half a century of the innovations witnessed in the *Kritios Boy*, sculptors were avidly exploring the body's articulation. One of those sculptors was Polykleitos of Argos, whose most famous work, the *Doryphoros* (*Spear Bearer*) (fig.

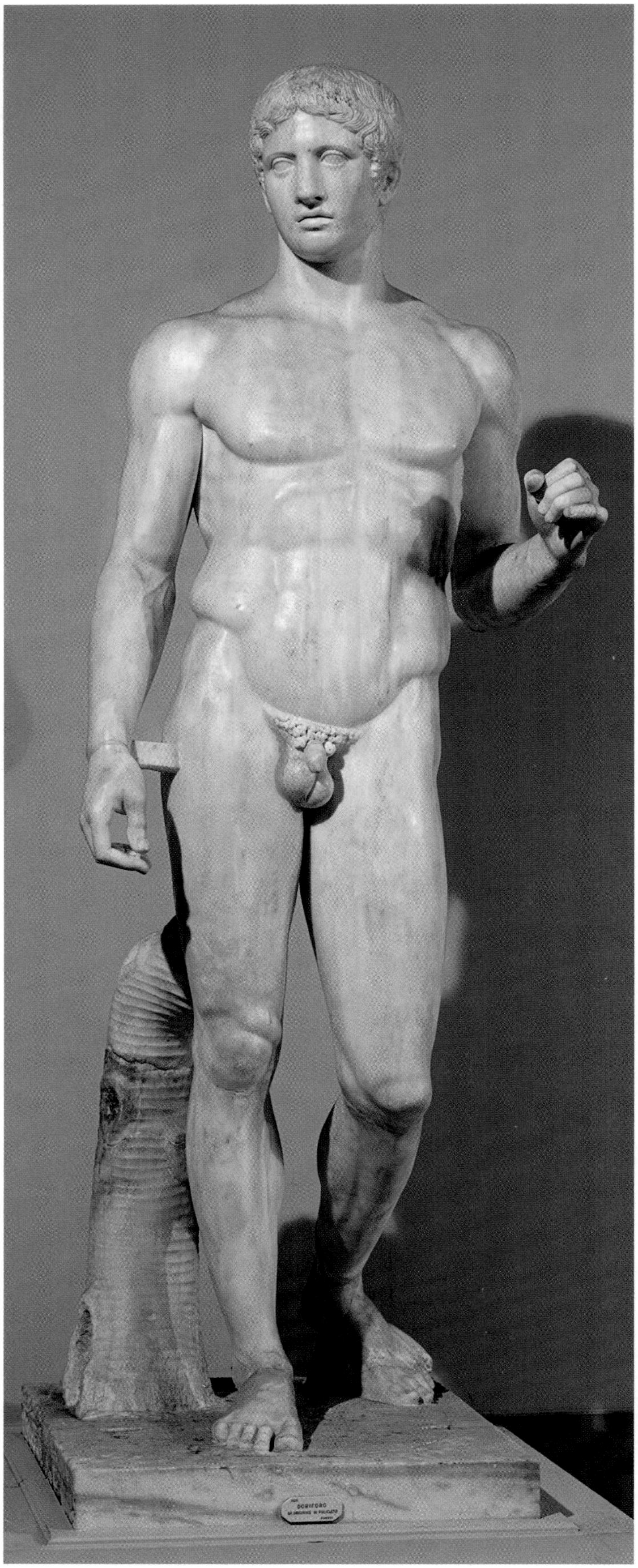

5.33 *Doryphoros* (*Spear Bearer*). Roman copy after an original of ca. 450–440 BCE by Polykleitos. Marble, height 6'6" (2 m). Museo Archaeologico Nazionale, Naples

5.33), is known to us through numerous Roman copies. In this sculpture, the chiastic pose is much more emphatic than in the *Kritios Boy*, the turn of the head more pronounced. Polykleitos seems to delight in the possibilities the pose offers, examining how the anatomy on the two sides of the body responds to it. The "working" left arm balances the engaged right leg in the forward position, and the relaxed right arm balances the free left leg. Yet, in this sculpture, Polykleitos did more than study anatomy. He explored principles of commensurability, *symmetria*, where part related to part, and all the parts to the whole: He proposed an ideal system of proportions, not just for individual elements of the body but for their relation to one another and to the body as a whole. He also addressed *rhythmos* (composition and movement). According to one ancient writer, Greeks knew this work as his *kanon* (canon, meaning "rule" or "measure"). (See www.myartslab.com.) Egyptian artists had earlier aimed to establish guidelines for depiction based on proportion. Yet for Polykleitos, the search for an ideal system of proportions was more than an artist's aid: It was rooted in a philosophical quest for illumination, and in a belief that harmony (*harmonia*)—in the universe, as in music and in all things—could be expressed in mathematical terms. Only slightly later than this sculpture, Plato would root his doctrine of ideal forms in numbers, and acknowledge that beauty was commonly based on proportion. Philosophers even referred to works of art to illustrate their theories. Moreover, beauty was more than an idle conceit for Classical Athenians; it also had a moral dimension. Pose and expression reflected character and feeling, which revealed the inner person and, with it, *arete* (excellence or virtue). Thus contemplation of harmonious proportions could be equated with the contemplation of virtue. (See *Primary Source*, page 133.)

Much of the *Doryphoros'* original appearance may have been lost in the copy-making process: Bronze and marble differ greatly in both texture and presence. Surviving Greek bronzes are extremely rare, and when a pair of over-life-size figures was found in the sea near Riace, Italy, in 1972, they created a sensation (fig. **5.34**). Their state of preservation is outstanding, and shows off to advantage the extraordinarily fine workmanship. Greek sculptors used a refined version of the lost-wax technique familiar to Near Eastern artists. The process differs radically from cutting away stone, since the technique is additive (the artist builds the clay model in the first phase of the process). Further, where marble absorbs light, a bronze surface reflects it, and this led sculptors to explore a variety of surface textures—for hair and skin, for instance. They could add different materials for details: These statues have ivory and glass-paste eyes, bronze eyelashes, and copper lips and nipples. Statue A (or *Riace Warrior A*), shown here, has silver teeth. Who these figures represented is still unknown: a pair of heroes, perhaps, or warriors. They may have formed part of a single monument. Though they strike similar poses, the men have differing body types, which has led some scholars to date them apart and attribute them to two separate sculptors. They could equally be the work of a single artist exploring the representation of character and age.

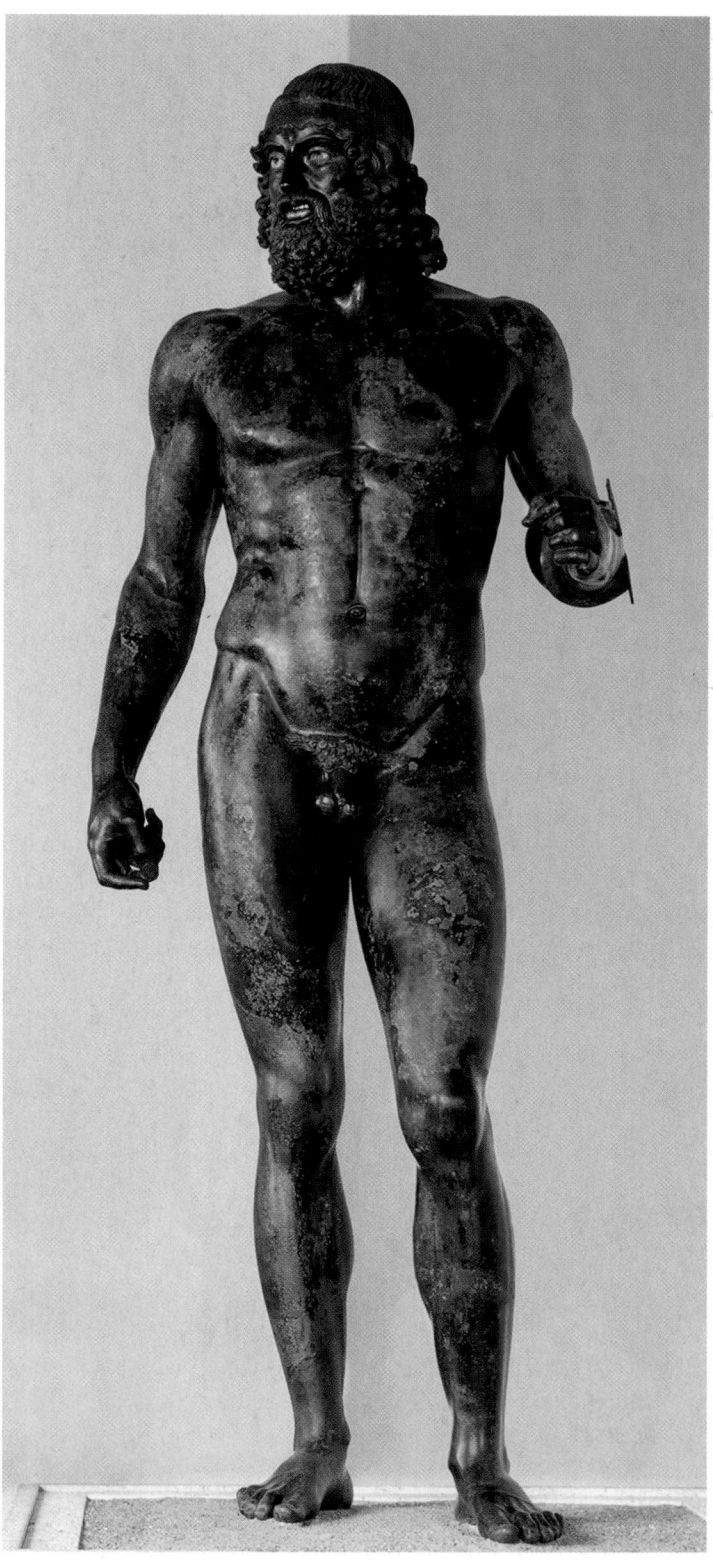

5.34 *Riace Warrior A*, found in the sea off Riace, Italy. ca. 450 BCE. Bronze, height 6'8" (2.03 m). Museo Archaeologico, Reggio Calabria, Italy

THE SCULPTURES OF THE TEMPLE OF ZEUS, OLYMPIA
The Riace bronzes may once have stood in a sanctuary, where Greeks customarily celebrated great men. There, they were in the presence of the gods, whose temples featured additional sculpture

The Indirect Lost-Wax Process

Zeus (see fig. 5.31) is one of the earliest surviving Greek statues that was made by the indirect lost-wax process. This technique enables sculptors to create spatially freer forms than they can in stone. They make projecting limbs separately and solder them onto the torso, and no longer need to support them using unsightly struts. Compare, for example, the freely outstretched arms of the *Zeus* with the strut extending from hip to drapery on the *Aphrodite of Knidos* (see fig. 5.56).

The Egyptians, Minoans, and early Greeks had often made statuettes of solid bronze using the *direct* lost-wax process. The technique was simple. The sculptor modeled his figure in wax; covered it with clay to form a mold; heated out the wax; melted copper and tin in the ratio of nine parts to one in a crucible; and poured this alloy into the space left by the "lost wax" in the clay mold. Yet, because figures made in this way were solid, the method had severe limitations. A solid-cast life-size statue would have been prohibitively expensive, incredibly heavy, and prone to developing bubbles and cracks as the alloy cooled. So from the eighth through the sixth centuries BCE, the Greeks developed the *indirect* lost-wax method, which allowed them to cast statues hollow and at any scale.

First, the sculptor shaped a core of clay into the basic form of the intended metal statue, before covering this core with a layer of wax to the thickness of the final metal casting, and carving the details of the statue carefully in the wax. The figure was then sectioned into its component parts—head, torso, limbs, and so on. For each part, the artist applied a heavy outer layer of clay over the wax and secured it to the inner core with metal pegs. The package was then heated to melt the wax, which ran out. Molten metal—usually bronze, but sometimes silver or gold—was then poured into the space left by this "lost wax." When the molten metal cooled, the outer and inner molds were broken away, leaving a metal casting—the statue's head, torso, or arm—and these individual sections were then soldered together to create the statue. The sculptor completed the work by polishing the surface, chiseling details such as strands of hair and skin folds, and inlaying features such as eyes, teeth, lips, nipples, and dress patterns in ivory, stone, glass, copper, or precious metal.

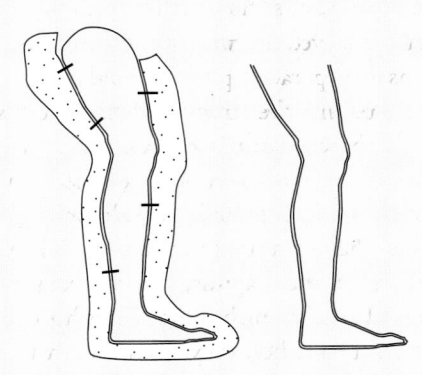

The indirect lost-wax process

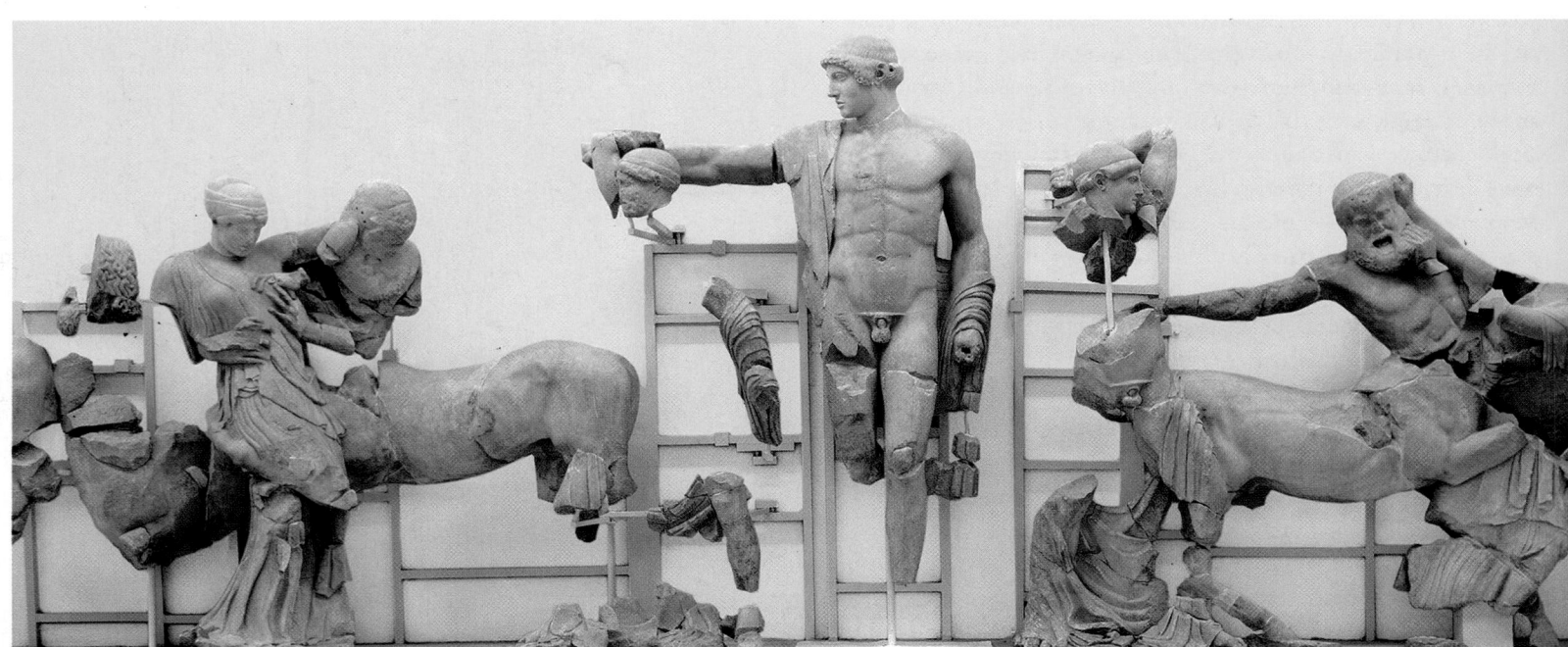

5.35 Photographic reconstruction (partial) of *Battle of the Lapiths and Centaurs*, from west pediment of Temple of Zeus at Olympia. ca. 460 BCE. Marble, slightly over-life-size. Archaeological Museum, Olympia as ornamentation. The chief temple in the sanctuary at Olympia honored Zeus. Spoils from a victory of Elis over its neighbor Pisa in 470 BCE provided funds for the temple's construction, to a design by the architect Libon from Elis. Its fragmentary pediments, perhaps the work of Ageladas from nearby Argos in about 460 BCE, are highpoints of the early Classical style, and are reassembled in the Archaeological Museum at Olympia. In the east pediment, mythology provides an analogy for the recent victory, as at Aegina. The subject is the triumph of Pelops over Oinomaos, king of Pisa, in a chariot race, for which the prize was the hand of the king's daughter, Hippodameia. Pelops (for whom the Peloponnesos is named) was an important figure for Greeks, for they credited him with founding the athletic games at Olympia. Yet he prevailed in the race by trickery, with the result that he and his descendants, including Agamemnon, king of Mycenae, lived under a curse. Thus, the myth was topical in a second way: Pelops' example served as a warning against foul play to Olympic contestants as they paraded past the temple.

The west pediment represents the struggle of the Lapiths, a tribe from Thessaly, with the centaurs (a centauromachy) (fig. 5.35). Centaurs were the offspring of Ixion, king of the Lapiths, and Hera, whom he tried to seduce while in Olympos (with the result that Ixion was chained forever to a fiery wheel in Tartarus). As half-brothers of the Lapiths, the centaurs were guests at the wedding of the Lapith king Peirithoös and Deidameia. Unable to tolerate alcohol, they got into a drunken brawl with the Lapiths, who subdued them with the aid of Peirithoös' friend Theseus.

At the center of the composition stands the commanding figure of Apollo. His outstretched right arm, the strong turn of his head, and his powerful gaze show his engagement in the drama, as he wills the Lapiths to victory. At the same time, his calm, static pose removes him from the action unfolding around him; he does not help physically. To the left of Apollo, the centaur king, Eurytion, has seized Hippodameia. Both figures are massive and simple in form, with soft contours and undulating surfaces. The artist entangled them in a compact interlocking group, which is quite different from the individual conflicts of the Aegina figures. Moreover, the artist expressed their struggle in more than action and gesture: The centaur's face mirrors his anguish, and his pain and desperate effort contrast vividly with the calm on the young bride's face. In setting the centaurs' evident suffering against the emotionlessness of the Lapiths, the pediment draws a moral distinction between the bestial centaurs and the civilized humans, who share in Apollo's remote nobility. Apollo, god of music and poetry but also of light and reason, epitomizes rational behavior in the face of adversity. By partaking in divine reason, humans triumph over animal nature. This conflict between the rational and the irrational, order and chaos, lay at the heart of Greek art, both in its subject matter and in its very forms. It exposes the Greeks' sense of themselves, representing civilization in the face of barbarianism—always neatly encapsulated in the Persians.

Like the west pediment, the east pediment may have had a local relevance, encouraging fair play among Olympic competitors.

The metopes were certainly topical: They depict the labors of Herakles, Pelops' great-grandson, who according to legend laid out the stadium at Olympia. Narrative scenes had been a feature of metopes since the early sixth century BCE, but at Olympia the designer exploited the pictorial and dramatic possibilities fully for the first time. The metope illustrated here, which was inserted prominently over the entrance on the temple's east side, shows Atlas returning to Herakles with the apples of the Hesperides (fig. 5.36). Atlas was one of the Titans, the race of gods before the Olympians, and it was his charge to support the Earth on his shoulders. Herakles agreed to hold the world for him, and thus persuaded Atlas to go to the gardens of the Hesperides to fetch the apples in fulfillment of his final labor. On returning, Atlas refused to accept his burden back, until Herakles cheated him into doing so. In the metope, Herakles supports a cushion (which held the globe) on his shoulders, with the seemingly effortless assistance of a young Athena. He eyes the apples as he tries to conceive of a way to trick Atlas into giving them up. This is not the grim combat so characteristic of Archaic Greek art (see figs. 5.23 and 5.24); the burly Herakles has assumed the thoughtful air that is central to the Classical spirit. The figures have all the characteristics of early Classical sculpture: fleshy faces (often described as "doughy"), an economy of pose and expression, and simple, solemn drapery.

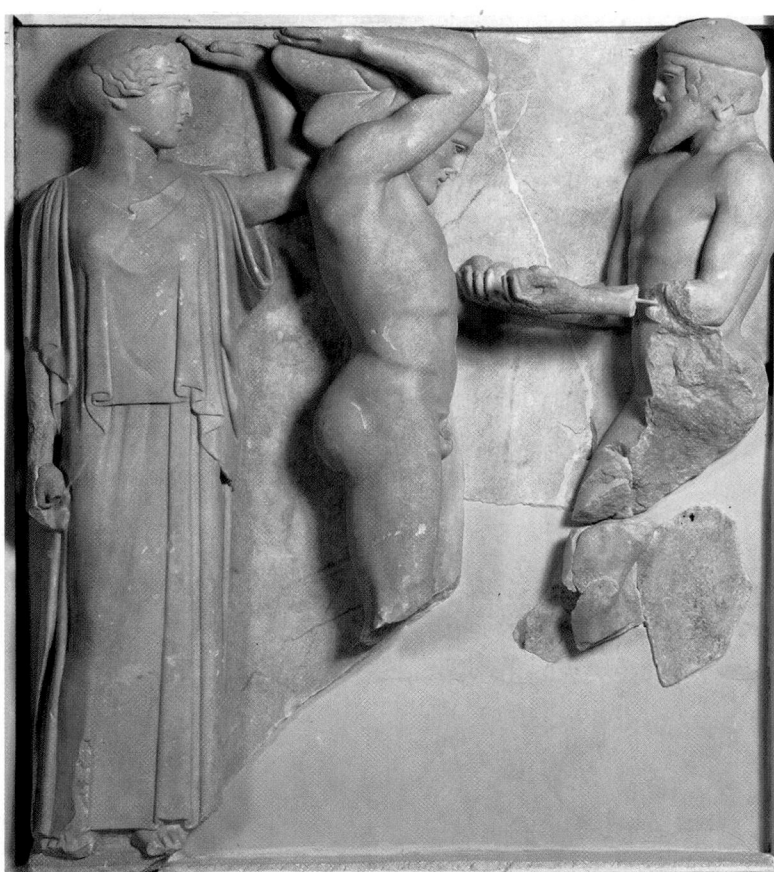

5.36 *Atlas Bringing Herakles the Apples of the Hesperides.* ca. 460 BCE. Marble, height 63" (160 cm). Archaeological Museum, Olympia

5.37 Plan of the agora at Athens

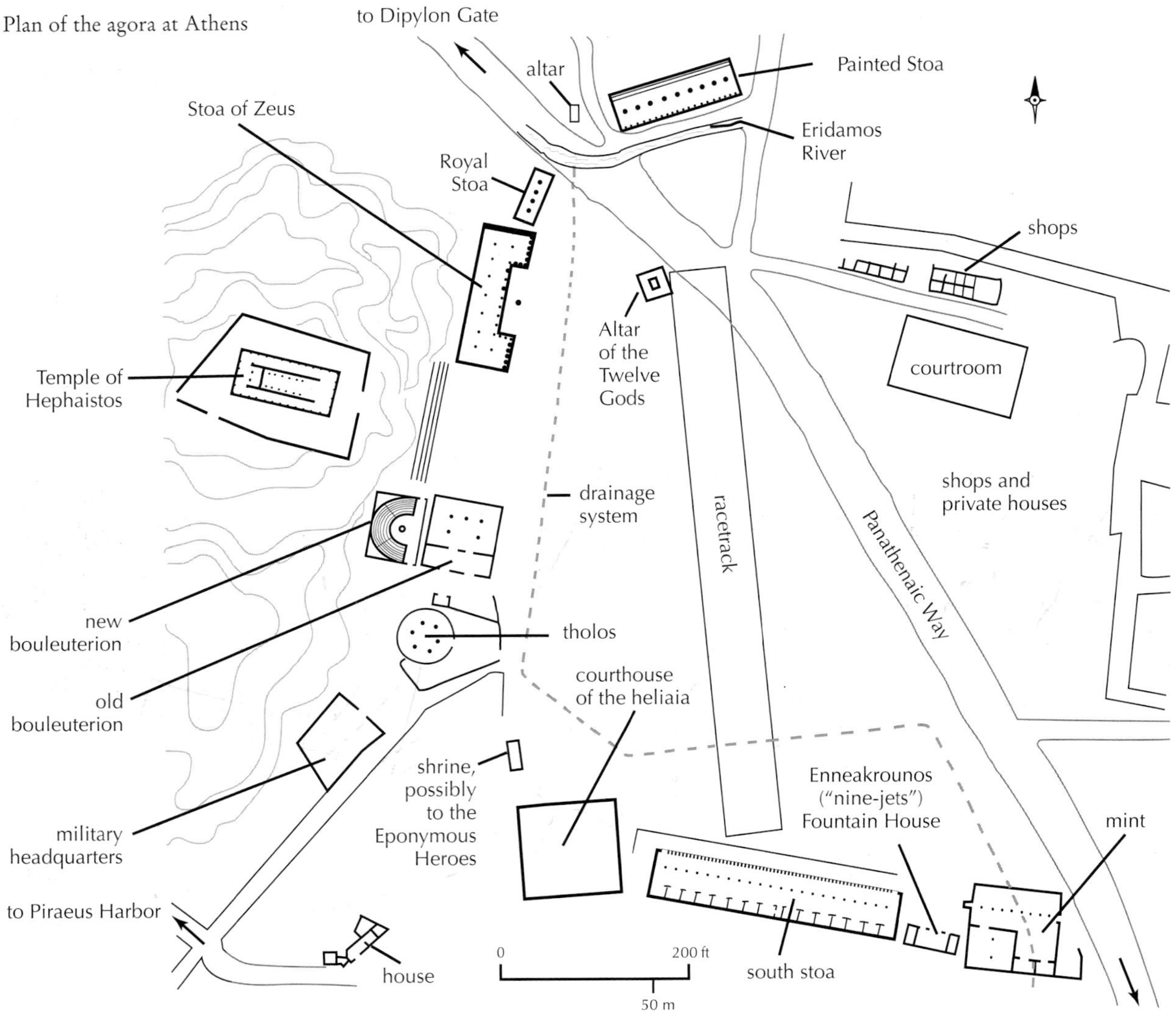

to Dipylon Gate

altar

Painted Stoa

Stoa of Zeus

Royal Stoa

Eridamos River

shops

Altar of the Twelve Gods

courtroom

Temple of Hephaistos

drainage system

racetrack

Panathenaic Way

shops and private houses

new bouleuterion

old bouleuterion

tholos

courthouse of the heliaia

military headquarters

shrine, possibly to the Eponymous Heroes

Enneakrounos ("nine-jets") Fountain House

mint

to Piraeus Harbor

house

0   200 ft

50 m

south stoa

to Acropolis

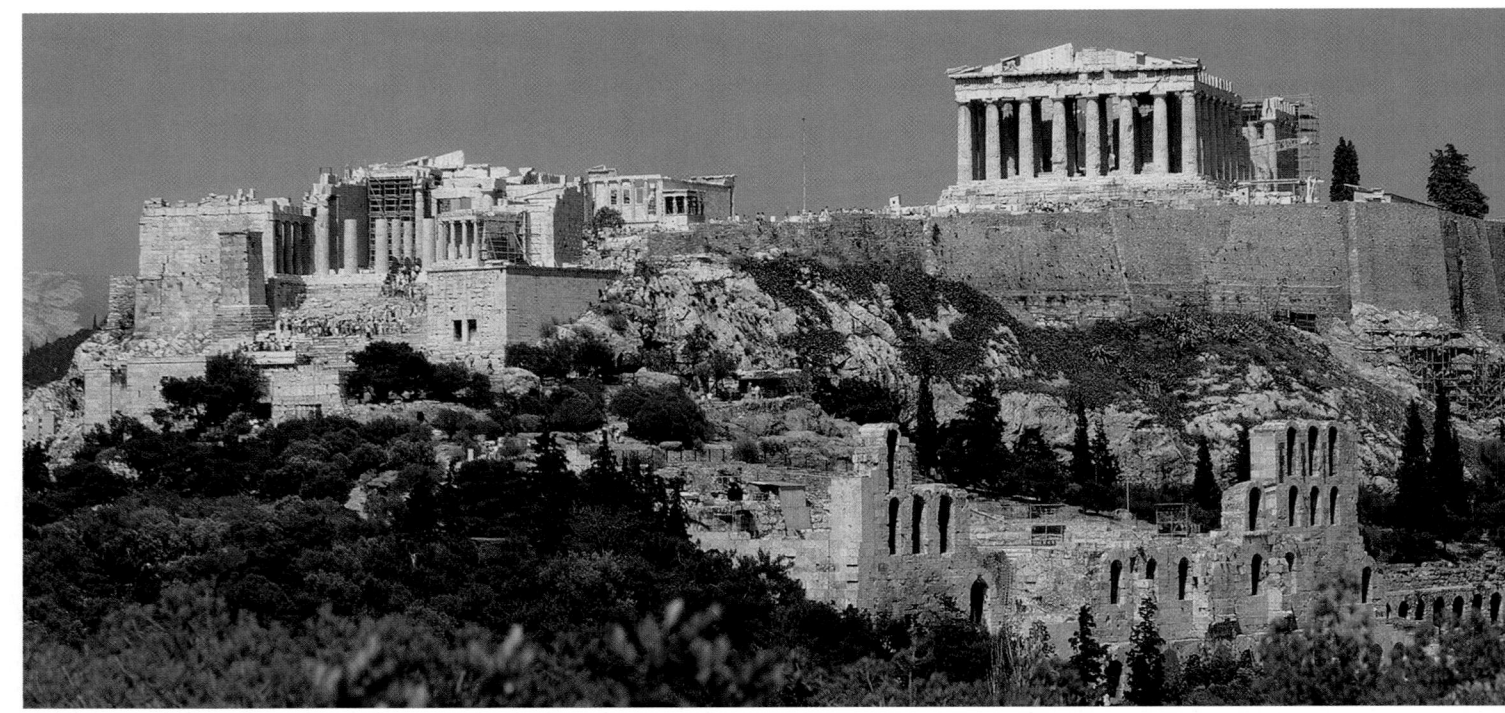

5.38 Akropolis (view from west), Athens. Propylaia, 437–432 BCE; with Temple of Athena Nike, 427–424 BCE

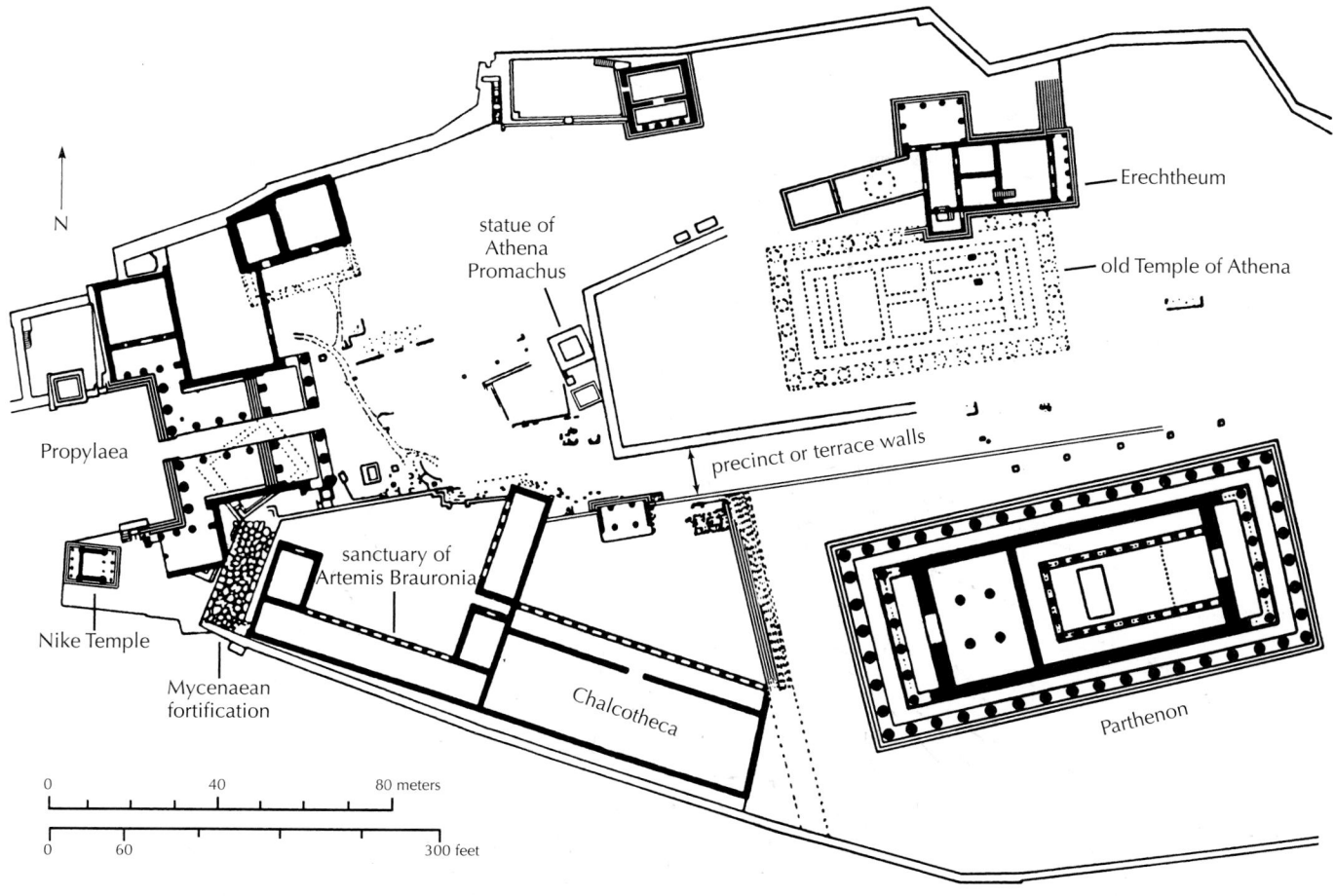

Architecture and Sculpture on the Athenian Akropolis

As in many Greek cities, the principal centers of Athenian public life were the agora and the Akropolis. The agora (fig. **5.37**) was primarily a marketplace, but as time passed Athenians dedicated temples and civic buildings such as stoas (colonnaded porticoes) there, and the space took on a monumental character. The Akropolis had been a fortified site since Mycenaean times, around 1250 BCE (figs. **5.38** and **5.39**). During the Archaic period, it was home to at least one sizeable temple dedicated to the city's patron goddess, Athena, as well as several smaller temples or treasuries, and votive statues. For over 30 years after the Persian sack of 480 BCE, the Athenians left the sacred monuments on the Akropolis in ruins, as a solemn reminder of the enemy's ruthlessness. This changed in the mid-fifth century BCE, with the emergence of Perikles into political life. Perikles' ambitions for Athens included transforming the city—with its population of about 150,000—into the envy of the Mediterranean world. His projects, which the democratic assembly approved, began on the Akropolis. Individually and collectively, the structures there expressed the ideals of the Athenian city-state, and have come to exemplify Classical Greek art at its height. (See www.myartslab.com.)

THE PARTHENON The dominant temple on the Akropolis is the Parthenon (fig. **5.40**). Perikles conceived it to play a focal role in the cult of Athena, though there is no evidence that Athenians used it directly for cult practices; there is no altar to the east, and the chief center of cult practice remained on the site of the Erechtheion, north of the Parthenon (see fig. **5.51**). Built of gleaming white marble from nearby Mount Pentelikon, the Parthenon occupies a prominent site on the southern flank of the Akropolis. From there it dominates the city and the surrounding countryside, a brilliant landmark against the backdrop of mountains to the north, east, and west. Contemporary building records, and a biography of Perikles written by the Greek historian Plutarch, indicate that two architects named Iktinos and Kallikrates oversaw its construction between 447 and 432 BCE. To meet the expense of building the largest and most lavish temple of its time on the Greek mainland, Perikles resorted in part to funds collected from the Delian League, its allies against the Persians. Perhaps the Persian danger no longer seemed real; still, the use of these funds weakened Athens' position in relation to its allies. Centuries later, Plutarch still remembered accusations against Perikles for adorning the city "like a harlot with precious stones, statues, and temples costing a thousand talents."

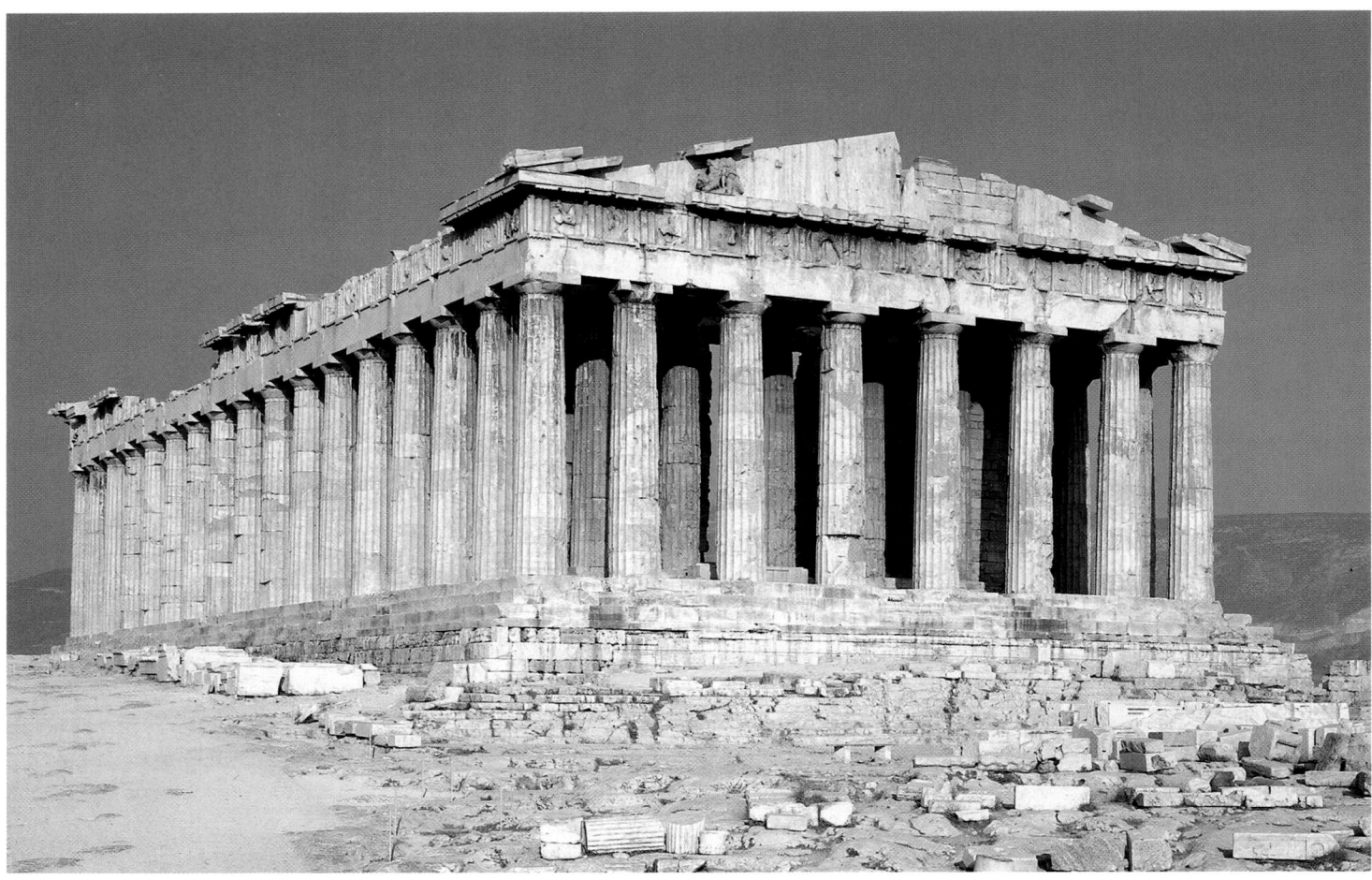

5.40   Iktinos and Kallikrates. The Parthenon (view from the west). Akropolis, Athens. 447–432 BCE

When read against the architectural vocabulary of Classical Greece, the Parthenon emerges as an extraordinarily sophisticated building. Its parts integrate fully with one another, so that its spaces do not seem to be separate, but to melt into one another. Likewise, architecture and sculpture are so intertwined that discussion of the two cannot be disentangled. The temple stood near the culminating point of a grand procession that wound its way through the agora and onto the Akropolis during the Panathenaic festival in Athena's honor; as magnificent as it was to observe from a distance, it was also a building to experience from within. Imitating the grandiose temples of Archaic Ionia, the Parthenon featured an **octastyle** (eight-column) arrangement of its narrow ends. This was unusually wide, offering a generous embrace and enough space for an arrangement of a U-shaped colonnade in the cella and an enormous statue of Athena by the famed sculptor Pheidias. She stood with one hand supporting a personification of Victory, and a shield resting against her side. Pheidias fashioned the figure out of ivory and gold (a combination known as **chryselephantine**), supported on a wooden armature (fig. **5.41**). It was extraordinarily valuable, and the building's forms drew visitors in to view it. Like all peripteral temples, the encircling colonnade gave the impression that a visitor could approach the temple from all sides. In fact, a prostyle porch of six columns (where the columns stand in front of the side walls, rather than between

them) mediated entry to the cella at the east end, and to an **opisthonaos** (rear room), on the west, containing four tall, slender Ionic columns. The porches are unusually shallow. This allowed light into the cella, which otherwise came in through two large windows on either side of the cella's main entrance. In its combination of a well-lit interior and the rational articulation of the interior space with a colonnade, the Parthenon initiated a new interest in the embellishment of interior space.

Compared with the Temple of Hera II at Paestum (see fig. 5.9, right), the Parthenon appears far less massive, despite its greater size. One of the reasons for this is a lightening and an adjusting of proportions since the Archaic period. The columns are more slender, their tapering and entasis less pronounced, and the capitals are smaller and less flaring. Practical necessity partly determined the diameter of the columns: For convenience and economy, the architects reused many drums from the earlier Parthenon, still unfinished at the time of the Persian sack. Yet how these columns would relate to the rest of the building was a matter for new design. Their spacing, for instance, is wider than in earlier buildings. The entablature is lower in relation to their height and to the temple's width, and the **cornice** (protruding horizontal element) projects less. The load the columns carry seems to have decreased, and as a result the supports appear able to fulfill their task with a new ease.

Aristotle (384–322) BCE

The Politics, from Book VIII

The Politics is a counterpart to Plato's Republic, *a treatment of the constitution of the state. Books VII and VIII discuss the education prescribed for good citizens. Drawing is included as a liberal art—that is, a skill not only useful but also conducive to higher activities. Yet painting and sculpture are said to have only limited power to move the soul.*

There is a sort of education in which parents should train their sons, not as being useful or necessary, but because it is liberal or noble. ... Further, it is clear that children should be instructed in some useful things—for example, in reading and writing—not only for their usefulness, but also because many other sorts of knowledge are acquired through them. With a like view they may be taught drawing, not to prevent their making mistakes in their own purchases, or in order that they may not be imposed upon in the buying or selling of articles [works of art], but perhaps rather because it makes them judges of the beauty of the human form. To be always seeking after the useful does not become free and exalted souls. ...

The habit of feeling pleasure or pain at mere representations is not far removed from the same feeling about realities; for example, if any one delights in the sight of a statue for its beauty only, it necessarily follows that the sight of the original will be pleasant to him. The objects of no other sense, such as taste or touch, have any resemblance to moral qualities; in visible objects there is only a little, for there are figures which are of a moral character, but only to a slight extent, and all do not participate in the feeling about them. Again, figures and colors are not imitations, but signs, of character, indications which the body gives of states of feeling. The connexion of them with morals is slight, but in so far as there is any, young men should be taught to look ... at [the works] of Polygnotus, or any other painter or sculptor who expresses character.

Source: Aristotle, *The Politics*, ed. Stephen Everson (NY: Cambridge University Press, 1988)

Like Polykleitos, Iktinos and Kallikrates grappled with issues of commensurability. The governing principle behind their design was a ratio of 9:4 or $2x + 1:x$. Thus, for instance, the 8 (x) columns across the façades answer seventeen ($2x + 1$) columns along the sides. Additionally, the ratio of the spacing between two columns (the **intercolumniation**) to the diameter at the lowest point of the column was 9:4. It was not just a matter of design convenience, but an attempt to produce harmony through numerical relationships. Libon of Elis first used this proportional scheme in the Temple of Zeus at Olympia. Iktinos and Kallikrates employed it pervasively in the Parthenon, though never dogmatically. In fact, despite the relative precision the formula dictated, they built intentional departures from the design's strict geometric regularity into the Parthenon (as architects did in other temples). For instance, the columns are not vertical, but lean in toward the cella (the corner columns in two directions), and the space between the corner column and its neighbors is smaller than the standard intercolumniation of the colonnade as a whole. Moreover, the stepped platform on which the temple rests is not fully horizontal, but bows upward, so that the center of the long sides is about 4 inches higher than the corners. This curvature reflects up through the temple's entablature, and every column capital is slightly distorted to fit the bowed architrave. That these irregularities were intentional is beyond doubt, as masons tailormade individual blocks to accommodate them. Why they were desirable is less clear.

When architects first introduced irregularities into temple architecture, some 100 years earlier, they may have intended to solve drainage problems. Yet in the Parthenon, they are so exaggerated that scholars consider them to be corrections of optical illusions. For instance, when viewed from a distance, straight horizontals appear to sag, but if the horizontals curve upward, they look straight. When seen close up, a long straight line seems to curve like the horizon; by exaggerating the curve, the architects could make the temple appear even larger than it was. These two apparently contradictory theories could work in tandem, since different optical distortions would prevail depending on a viewer's vantage point. What is certain is that these refinements

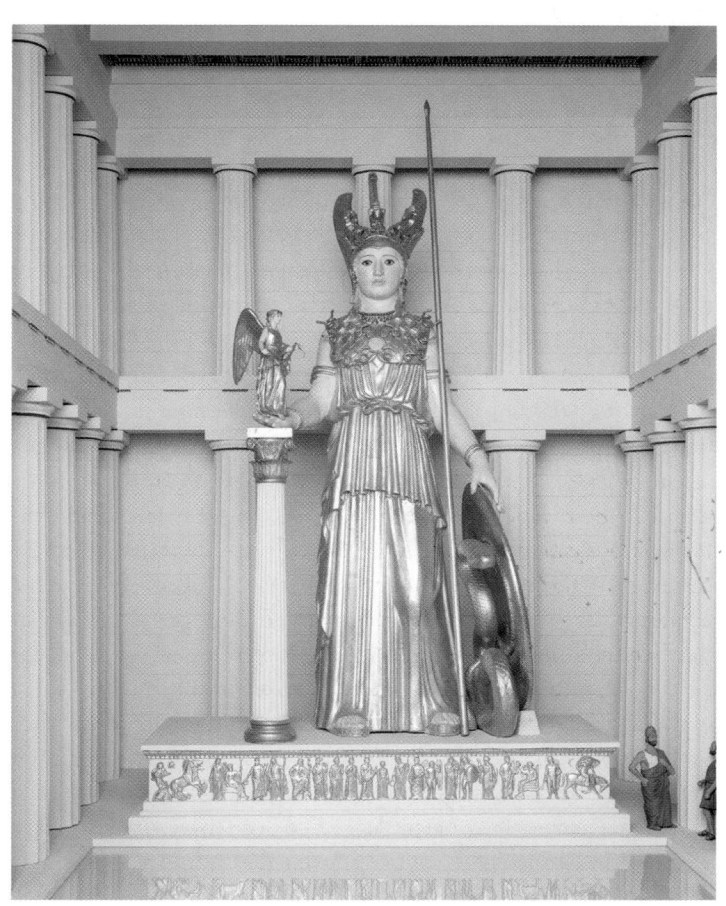

5.41 Model of *Athena Parthenos* by Pheidias. ca. 438 BCE. Royal Ontario Museum, Toronto

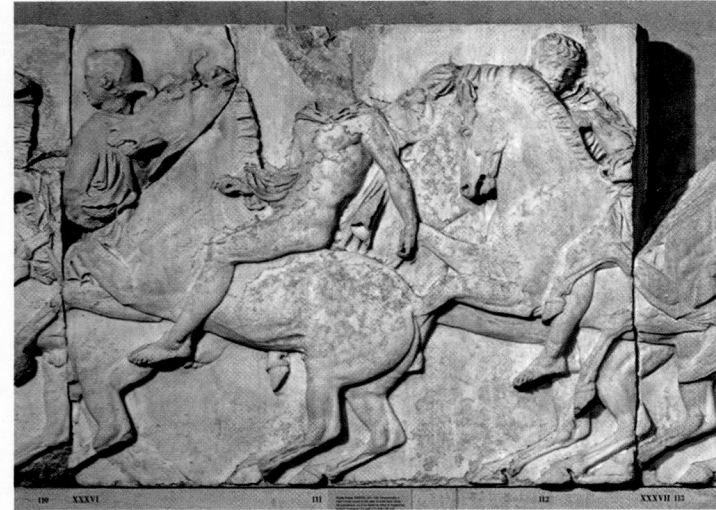
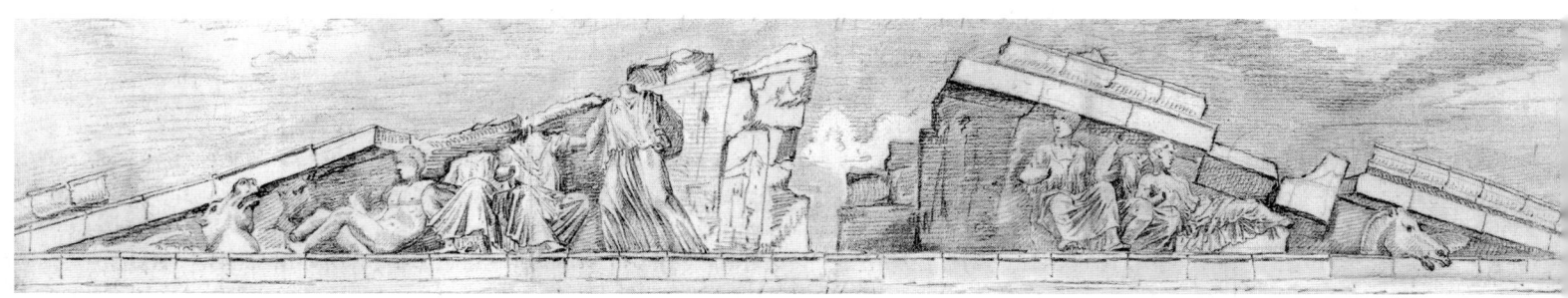

Repatriation of Cultural Heritage

In 2008, a new Acropolis Museum in Athens opened for preliminary viewing. Swiss-French architect Bernard Tschumi designed the museum to hold finds from the Akropolis; but it also incorporates a hall to house the Elgin Marbles from the Parthenon, a move designed to put pressure on the British Museum in London to send them home. Ever since 1978, when UNESCO established a department entitled the Intergovernmental Committee for Promoting the Return of Cultural Property to its Countries of Origin or its Restitution in Case of Illicit Appropriation, the Elgin Marbles have stood at the center of a heated debate on the repatriation of antiquities: Should museums around the world be required to return objects of cultural value to their countries of origin? And should museums purchase works of art that have been illegally trafficked? Recently, the Italian government made headlines by publicly requesting the return of objects illegally looted from Italy and purchased (generally in good faith) by museums in the United States. And to celebrate the successful outcome of negotiations with museums such as the Metropolitan Museum of Art in New York, the Boston Museum of Fine Arts, and the Getty, it mounted a free exhibition of works of art that had "come home," in the Italian president's Quirinal Palace.

The issues might seem straightforward, but repatriation and museum acquisition of illegally trafficked objects are actually complex questions. It is understandable that a country should want to retain its cultural heritage. Moreover, for archaeologists, objects removed by looting lose much of their value (see *The Art Historian's Lens*, page 29). Yet the grand-scale return of works of art to their home countries would cut the heart out of many established museums with valuable educational functions. Should all objects be returned, or just the more outstanding works of art—in which case, who should make such a qualitative judgment? If repatriation were to apply only to recent acquisitions, how long must an object's pedigree be to make it legal? If looting is inevitable, is it better that a museum purchase illegal objects and display them publicly, or that they should disappear into private collections? Is it better for a work of art to decay in its home country if conditions there prevent adequate preservation, or to be maintained elsewhere? And what if an individual or museum purchased antiquities legally from an invading force (such as the Ottoman authorities, who controlled Greece in Lord Elgin's day)? Such issues are not easily resolved.

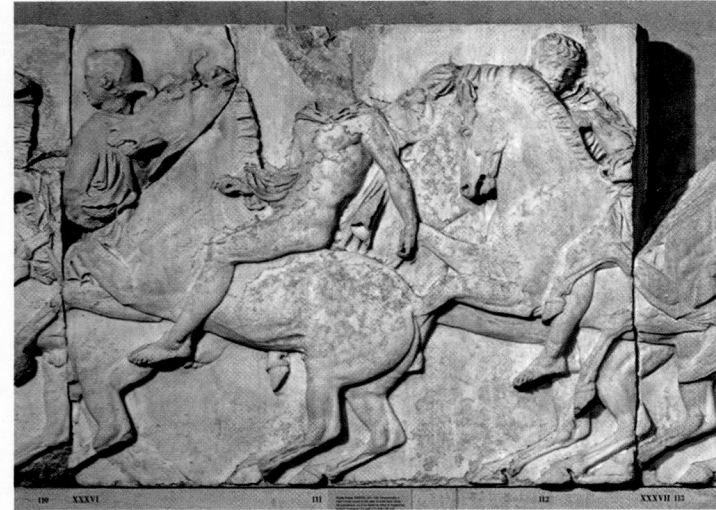

North frieze of the Parthenon

give the temple a dynamic quality that it might otherwise lack. Rather than sitting quietly on its platform, the building derives energy from its swelling forms as if it were about to burst out of its own skin; through the refinements, the temple comes alive.

THE PARTHENON SCULPTURES The largest group of surviving Classical sculptures comes from the Parthenon, which had a more extensive decorative program than any previous temple. The sculptures have a vivid and often unfortunate history.

Christians converted the temple into a church, probably in the sixth century CE, and much of the decoration on the east side was destroyed or vandalized. In 1687, Venetian cannon fire ignited ammunition that the Turkish forces were storing in the temple. The west pediment figures survived the explosion, but not the war's aftermath. They shattered when a crane dropped them while removing them so that the Venetian commander could take them to Venice. Over 100 years later, Lord Elgin, British ambassador to Constantinople, purchased what he could of the temple's

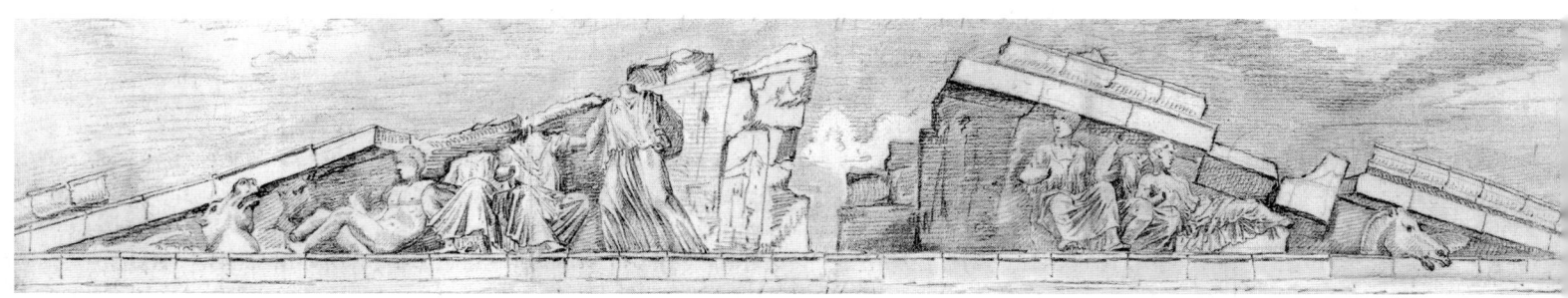

5.42 Jacques Carrey. Drawings of east pediment of the Parthenon. 1674 CE. Bibliothèque Nationale, Paris

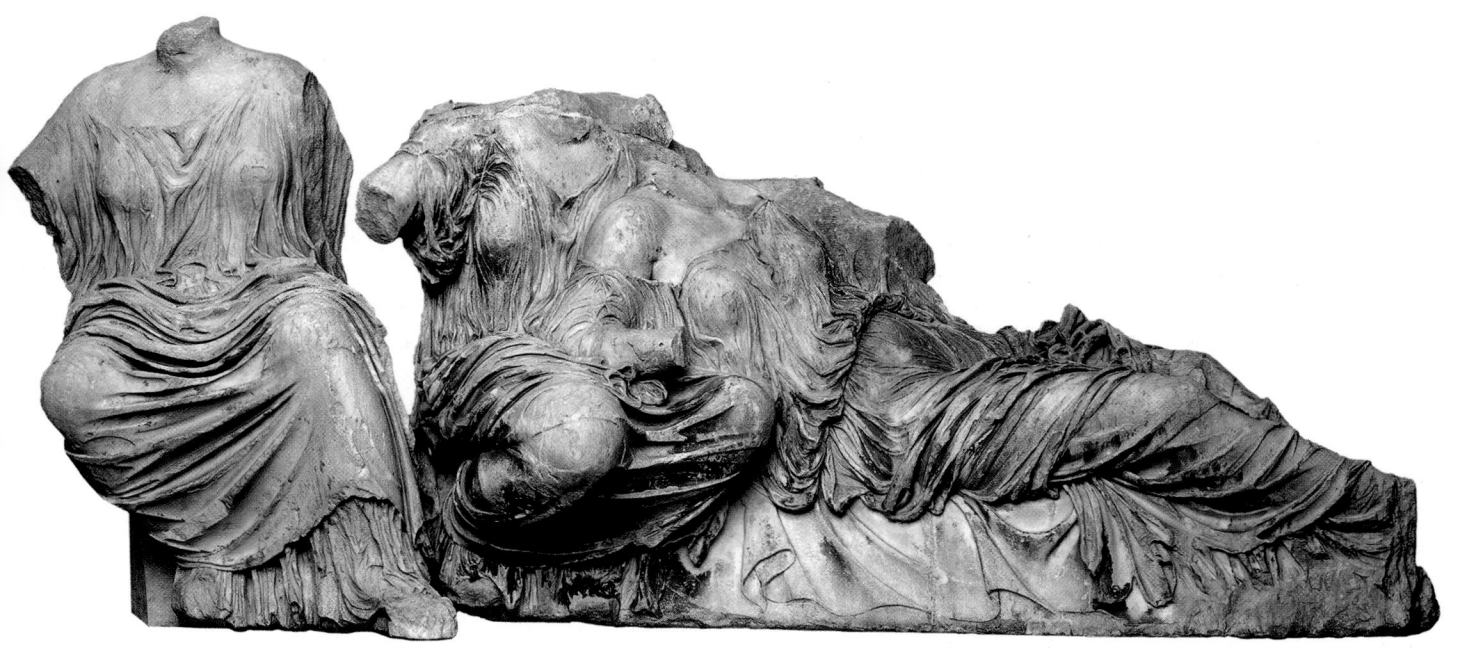

5.43　Three goddesses, from east pediment of the Parthenon. ca. 438–432 BCE. Marble, over-life-size. The British Museum, London

decoration from the Turks and shipped it to England. In 1816, needing money, he sold it to the British Museum. Today, the Elgin Marbles, as they are known, stand at the center of a heated debate on the repatriation of national treasures. (See *The Art Historian's Lens*, page 134.)

Thirteen years before the explosion in the Parthenon, an artist named Jacques Carrey was traveling in Athens as part of the retinue of the French ambassador to the Ottoman court. He executed a series of drawings of surviving Parthenon sculptures, which, along with literary sources, have become invaluable resources for understanding the decorative program as a whole (fig. **5.42**). Like the sculptures on the Temple of Zeus at Olympia, the Parthenon sculptures had topical relevance. The west pediment portrayed the struggle between Athena and Poseidon to be Athens' patron deity. The east pediment represented the birth of Athena from the head of Zeus, in the presence of other gods. All but the central figures survive, and Carrey's drawing allows for a confident reconstruction of their arrangement. Bursting from the left corner is the upper body of Helios, the sun-god, whose rearing horses draw him into view. Balancing him in the right corner, Selene, the moon-goddess, or Nyx, the night, sinks away with her horses. These celestial gods define the day's passing, and place the scene in an eternal cosmic realm. To the right of Helios, a nude male figure in a semireclining position is probably Dionysos. On the other side of the pediment, a closely knit group of three female deities was long identified as Hestia, Dione, and Aphrodite. A recent analysis of the group sees them instead as Leto, Artemis, and Aphrodite (fig. **5.43**).

As a group, the pediment figures are strikingly impressive. Like the building in which they are embedded, their forms are strong and solid, yet their implied power contrasts with their languid poses and gains strength from the contrast. The female group is a masterpiece of swirling drapery, which disguises the sheer bulk of the marble. The garments cling to the bodies beneath as if wet, both concealing and revealing flesh. Yet the drapery does not follow the lines of the body, as it does on the *Charioteer of Motya* (see fig. 5.30), so much as struggle with them, twisting around the legs in massive folds. The effect is extraordinary: Although a viewer can only see the deities from a frontal vantage point, as if the figures were two-dimensional, the curves of the deeply cut folds echo their forms in **section** (i.e., along a plane made by an imaginary vertical slice from front to back), and thereby broadcast their three-dimensionality. The effect goes against nature; yet the sculptor, possibly Pheidias himself, could better express nature through the *appearance* of truth than through truth itself. This optical device is a sculptural equivalent of the deliberate distortions in the temple's architecture.

Running the whole way around the building (rather than just at the ends, as at Olympia) was a full program of metopes, numbering 92 in all, depicting scenes of violent action. On the west side, sculptors described the battle of the Greeks against the Amazons (an Amazonomachy), a mythical race ruled by their warrior women. Metopes on the north side portrayed the Sack of Troy (the *Ilioupersis*), the conclusion of the Trojan War, when Greek forces fought the Trojans over Paris' abduction of Helen, wife of Menelaus, brother of King Agamemnon. On the east side, the gods fought the giants. The metopes of the south side mostly depict the Battle of the Lapiths and the Centaurs, already seen at Olympia. The four cycles come together to form a thematic whole: All depict the tension between the civilized and uncivilized worlds, between order and chaos; and all are therefore allegories for the Athenian victory over the Persians. Historical events are cloaked again in the guise of myth; myth elevates life so that the triumph of order over chaos has a preordained inevitability. Little survives of the metope cycles except for those on the south side, which are relatively well preserved. Their quality

Plutarch (ca. 46–after 119 CE)

Parallel Lives of Greeks and Romans, from the lives of Perikles and Fabius Maximus

A Greek author of the Roman period, Plutarch wrote Parallel Lives *to show that ancient Greece matched or exceeded Rome in its great leaders. Comparing Perikles (d. 429 BCE) with Fabius Maximus (d. 203 BCE), he concludes that Perikles' buildings surpass all the architecture of the Romans. Plutarch is the only ancient source to say that Pheidias was the overseer of Perikles' works.*

But that which brought most delightful adornment to Athens, and the greatest amazement to the rest of mankind; that which alone now testifies for Hellas that her ancient power and splendour, of which so much is told, was no idle fiction—I mean his construction of sacred edifices. ... For this reason are the works of Perikles all the more to be wondered at; they were created in a short time for all time.

Each one of them, in its beauty, was even then and at once antique; but in the freshness of its vigour it is, even to the present day, recent and newly wrought. Such is the bloom of perpetual newness, as it were, upon these works of his, which makes them ever to look untouched by time, as though the unfaltering breath of an ageless spirit had been infused into them.

His general manager and general overseer was Pheidias, although the several works had great architects and artists besides. Of the Parthenon, for instance, with its cella of a hundred feet in length, Kallicrates and Iktinus were the architects. ...

By the side of the great public works, the temples, and the stately edifices, with which Perikles adorned Athens, all Rome's attempts at splendour down to the times of the Caesars, taken together, are not worthy to be considered, nay, the one had a towering preeminence above the other, both in grandeur of design, and grandeur of execution, which precludes comparison.

Source: *Plutarch's Lives*, vol. 3, tr. Bernadotte Perrin (Cambridge: Harvard University Press, 1916)

---

varies dramatically: Not all of them are as successful as the ballet-like choreography of figure **5.44**, which reminds us that a vast crew of workers must have been engaged in completing the Parthenon in such a short period: They executed two pediments and the frieze in under ten years (ca. 440–432 BCE).

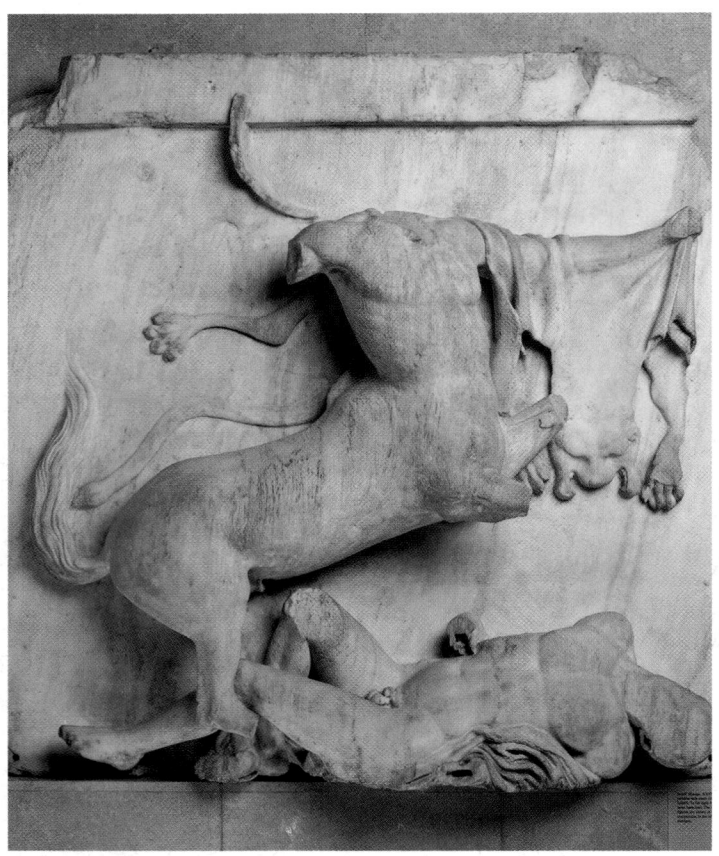

5.44 *Lapith and Centaur*, metope from south side of the Parthenon. ca. 440 BCE. Marble, height 56" (142.2 cm). The British Museum, London

The Parthenon is often viewed as the perfect embodiment of the Classical Doric style. Although this may be the impression from the outside, it is far from accurate. At architrave level within the peristyle, a continuous sculpted frieze runs around all sides of the building, in a variation of the Ionic style (see fig. 5.8). In a continuous sculpted band, some 525 feet long (fig. **5.45**), the frieze depicts a procession, moving from west to east, propelling the viewer around the temple, drawn close to the building to read the images. Horsemen jostle with musicians, water-carriers, and sacrificial beasts. Figures overlap to create the illusion of a crowd, even though the relief is only inches deep. Frenzied animals underline the calm demeanor of the human figures (see *The Art Historian's Lens*, page 134), who have the ideal proportions of the *Doryphoros*.

According to the traditional view, the procession depicted in the frieze is the Panathenaic procession, part of a festival held annually to honor Athena in the presence of the other Olympian gods, and on a grander scale every four years. The figures and their groupings are typical of the participants in these processions, and the frieze represents an idealized event, rather than a specific moment. If this view is correct, the frieze is remarkable in that for the first time it exalts mortal Greeks by depicting them in a space usually reserved for divine and mythological scenes. The most problematic aspect of the relief is the detail in figure **5.46**, from the center of the east end of the temple, where there are five unidentified figures, three of them young. Two of the young figures carry stools on their heads, while the third, in a group with one of the adults, handles a piece of cloth. According to the traditional view, the cloth is a new robe for Athena, woven by Athenian girls and women and depicting Athena's triumph against the giants in the gigantomachy. An alternative and controversial theory, however, places the entire frieze in the realm of myth, interpreting this scene as the three daughters of Erechtheus, a legendary king of Athens. According to Athenian myth, the oracle at Delphi

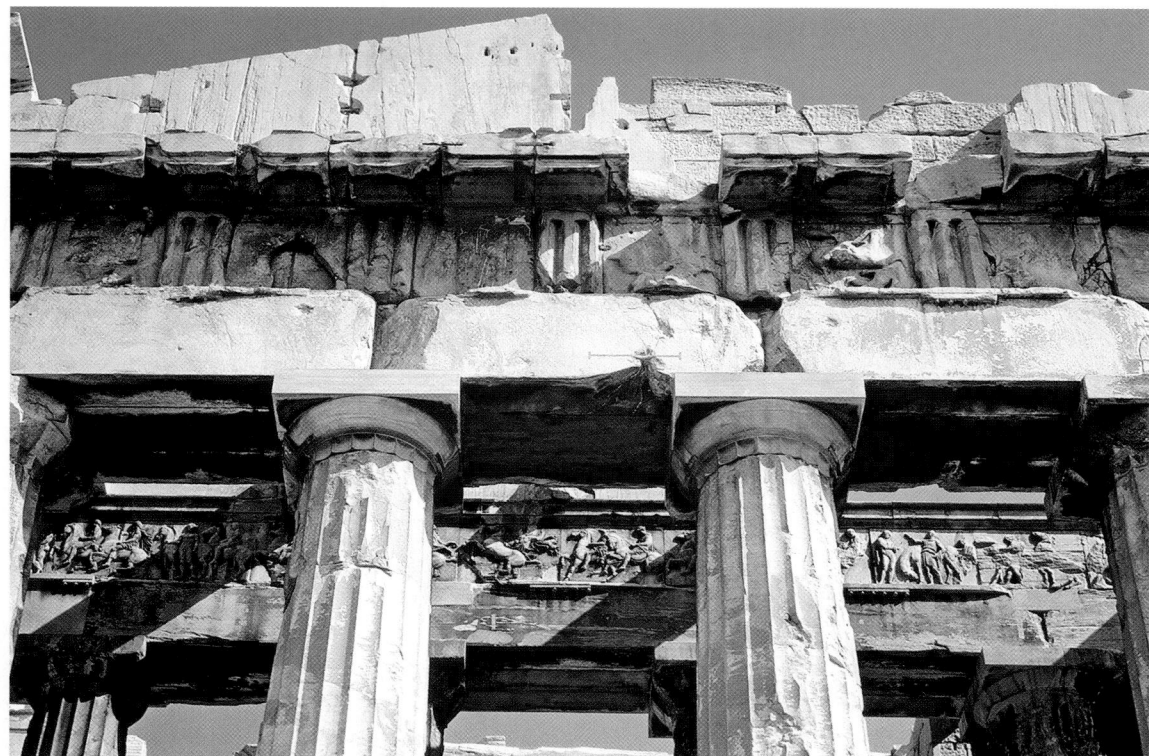

demanded the death of one of Erechtheus' daughters if Athens was to be saved from its enemies. Here, one of the daughters calmly receives the garment in which she will be sacrificed. The myth had obvious resonance for Athens after its victory over the Persians, and the playwright Euripides made it the subject of a tragedy.

Whatever the meaning of the frieze, its iconography integrated Athenians and divine space, time, and ritual practice in a unity that reflected the Athenians' sense of superiority and self-confidence. The problem of the frieze is exacerbated by the discovery, during the building's recent preservation and reconstruction, that the pronaos featured another frieze in its upper well. Nothing survives of this frieze, but if it was thematically connected with the frieze around the cella, we lack a crucial piece of evidence for a secure identification and interpretation of the iconography.

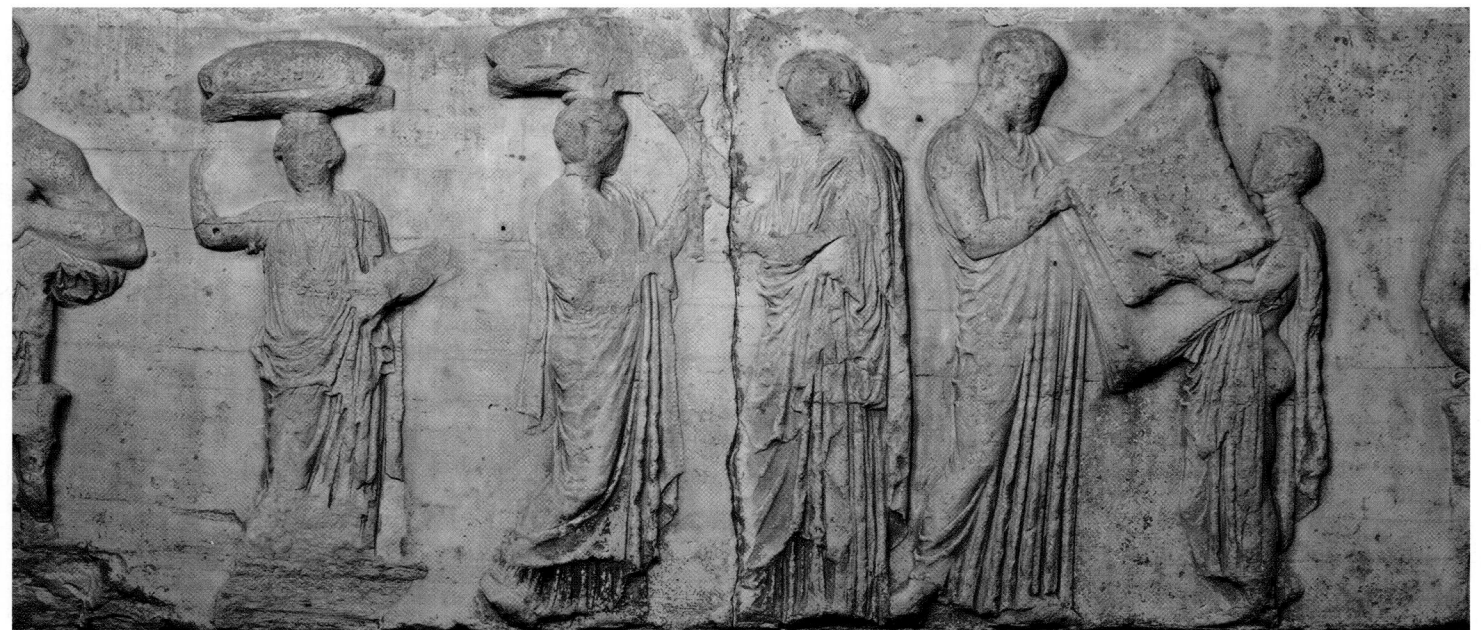

5.46 East frieze of the Parthenon. ca. 440 BCE. Marble, height 43" (109.3 cm). The British Museum, London

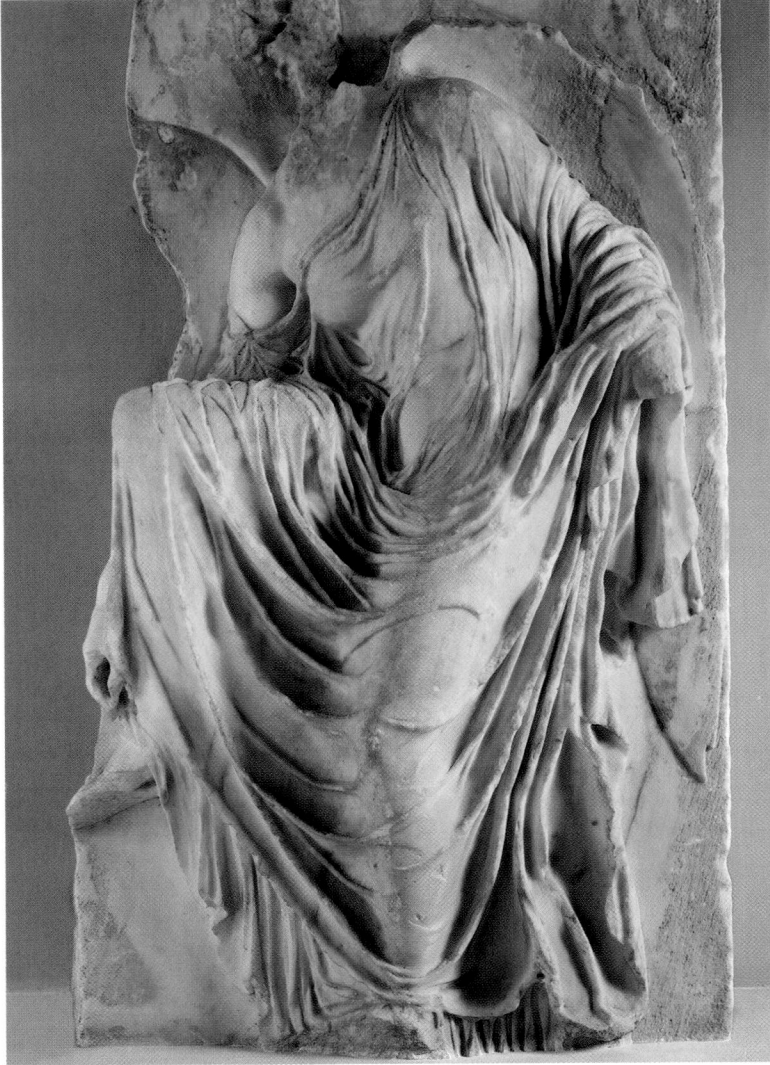

5.47 *Nike*, from balustrade of Temple of Athena Nike. ca. 410–407 BCE. Marble, height 42" (106.7 cm). Akropolis Museum, Athens

THE PHEIDIAN STYLE According to Plutarch, the sculptor Pheidias was chief overseer of all the artistic projects that Perikles sponsored. (See *Primary Source*, page 136.) Ancient literary sources attribute few works directly to his hand: His huge sculpture of Athena Parthenos, and a second chryselephantine colossus of a seated Zeus in the Temple of Zeus at Olympia, aroused extreme admiration, not only due to their religious roles, but also because of their vast size and the sheer value of the materials employed. An equally large bronze sculpture of Athena that stood on the Akropolis facing the Propylaia was also by the master sculptor. None of these works survives, and small-scale copies made in later times convey little of their original majesty. He may have worked personally on the Parthenon's architectural sculpture, which undoubtedly involved a large number of masters, but equally he may have simply been a very able supervisor. We can therefore know little for certain about his artistic style. Nevertheless, Pheidias has come to be associated with the Parthenon style, which is often synonymous with the "Pheidian

style." The term conveys an ideal that was not merely artistic but also philosophical: The idealized faces and proportions of the Athenians elevate them above the uncivilized world in which they operate. They share the calmness of the gods, who are aware of, yet aloof from, human affairs as they fulfill their cosmic roles.

Given the prominence of the Parthenon, it is hardly surprising that the Pheidian style should have dominated Athenian sculpture until the end of the fifth century BCE and beyond, even though large-scale sculptural enterprises gradually dwindled with the onset of the Peloponnesian War. The style is clear in one of the last of these projects, a balustrade built around the small Temple of Athena Nike on the Akropolis in about 410–407 BCE (see fig. 5.50). Like the Parthenon frieze, it shows a festive procession, but the participants are not Athenians but winged personifications of Victory (**Nike**, plural **Nikai**). One Nike is taking off her sandals,

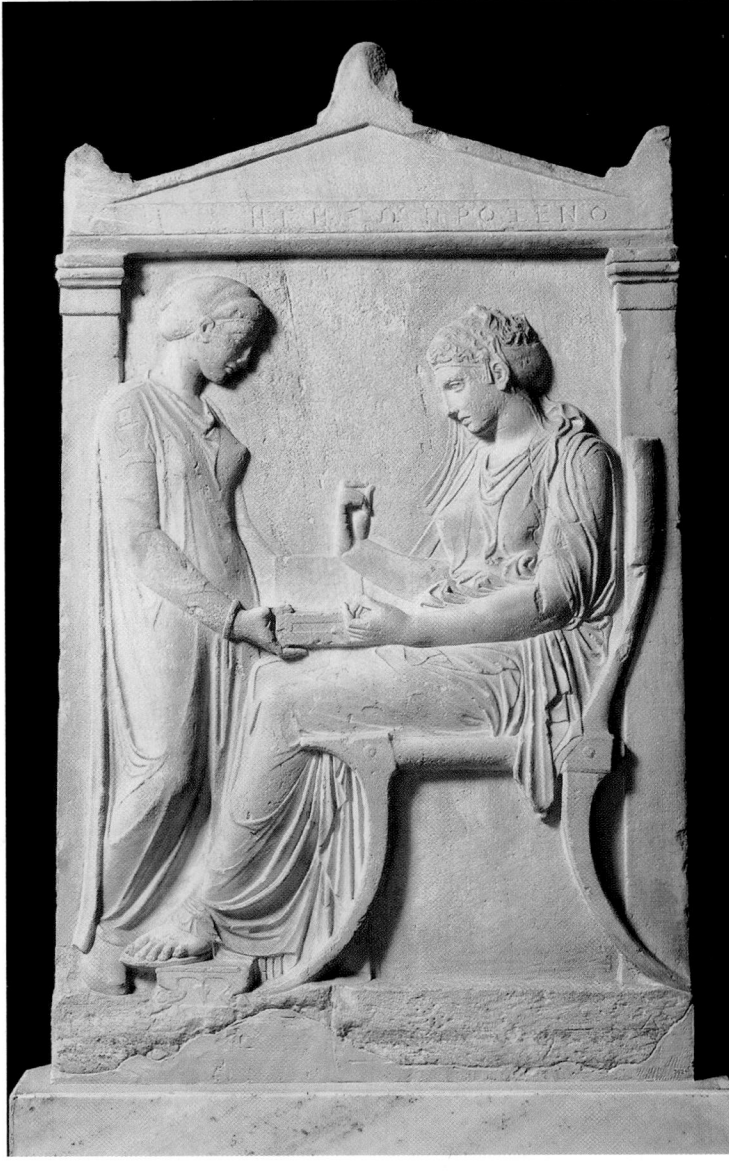

5.48 *Grave Stele of Hegeso*. ca. 410–400 BCE. Marble, height 59" (150 cm). National Archaeological Museum, Athens

indicating that she is about to step on holy ground (fig. **5.47**). Her wings keep her stable, so that she performs this normally awkward act with elegance and ease. The Pheidian style is most evident in the deeply cut folds of her "wet look" garments, which cling to her body and fall in deep swags between her legs.

On the *Grave Stele of Hegeso* (fig. **5.48**), also from the last years of the fifth century BCE, the Pheidian style is again recognizable in the drapery, but also in the smooth planes of the idealized faces, and the quiet mood of the scene. The artist represented the deceased woman seated on an elegant chair, in a simple domestic scene that became standard for funerary markers for young women, whose realm was almost exclusively within the home. She has picked a piece of jewelry from a box held by a girl servant and seems to contemplate it. The delicacy of the carving is especially clear in the forms farthest away from a viewer, such as the servant's left arm, or the veil behind Hegeso's right shoulder. Here, the relief merges with the background, strengthening the illusion that the background is empty space rather than a solid surface. This stele is a fine example of a type of memorial that Athenian sculptors produced in large numbers from about 425 BCE onward, perhaps following a relaxation of earlier sumptuary laws that had curbed expenditure on funerary commemoration. Their export must have helped to spread the Pheidian style throughout the Greek world.

THE PROPYLAIA In the year of the Parthenon's dedication, 437 BCE, Perikles commissioned another costly project: the monumental gate at the western end of the Akropolis, called the Propylaia (see fig. 5.38). Mnesikles was the architect in charge, and he completed the main section in five years; the remainder was abandoned with the onset of the Peloponnesian War in 431 BCE. He designed the entire structure in marble, and incorporated refinements similar to those in the Parthenon. In fact, Mnesikles cleverly adapted elements of traditional temple design to a totally different task, and to a site that rose steeply and irregularly. Conceived on two levels, the design transforms a rough passage among rocks into a magnificent entrance to the sacred precinct. Only the eastern porch (or façade) is in fair condition today. It resembles a Classical Doric temple façade, except for the wide opening between the third and fourth columns, which allowed traffic to pass onto the Akropolis; this feature is common in Ionian architecture. Placed along this central passageway through the Propylaia were two rows of slender Ionic columns, echoing the Ionic columns in the Parthenon. Flanking the western porch (fig. **5.49**) were two wings, of unequal size because of constraints imposed by the terrain (figs. 5.38 and 5.39). The larger one to the north contained a picture gallery (**pinakotheke**), the first known instance of a public room specially designed for the display of paintings. The southern wing may have held a library.

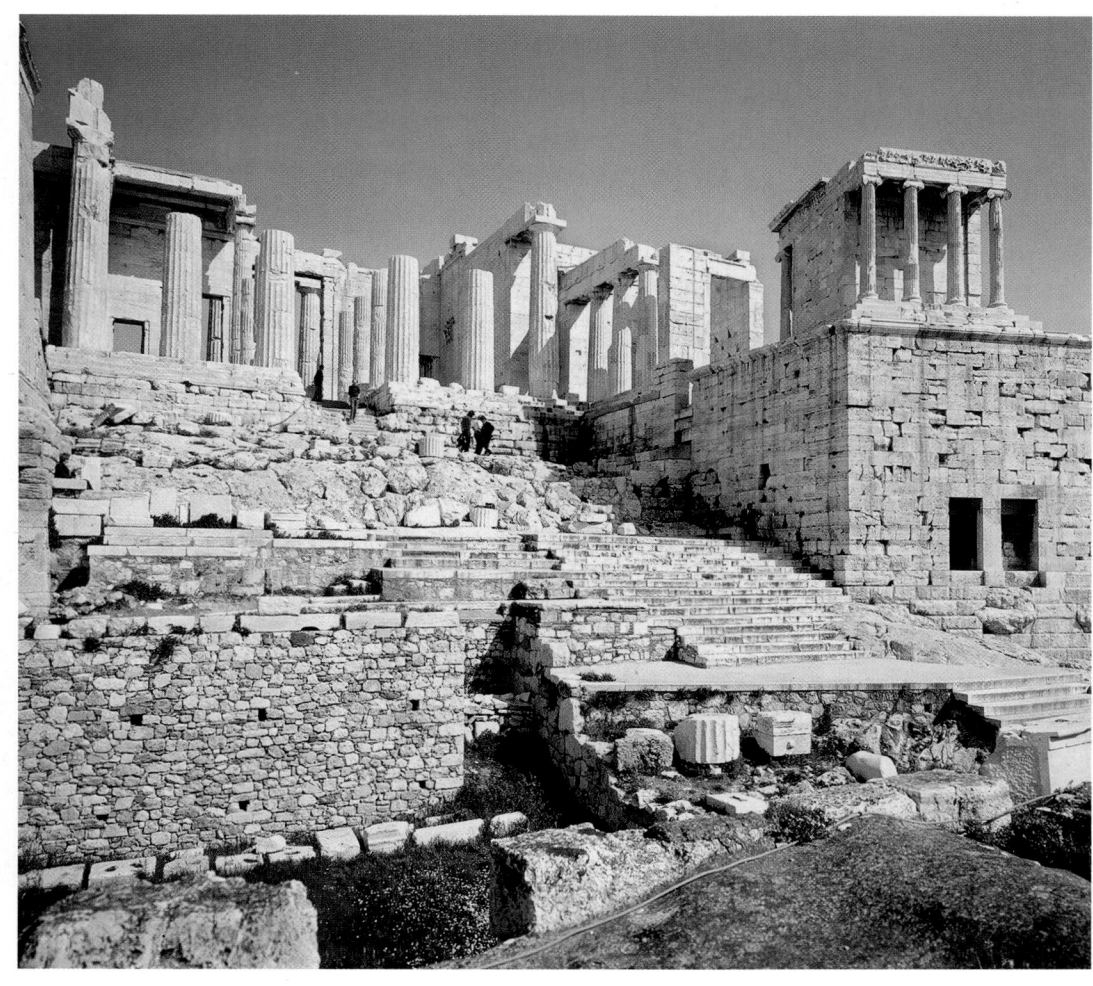

5.49 Mnesikles. The Propylaia, 437–432 BCE (view from west). Akropolis, Athens

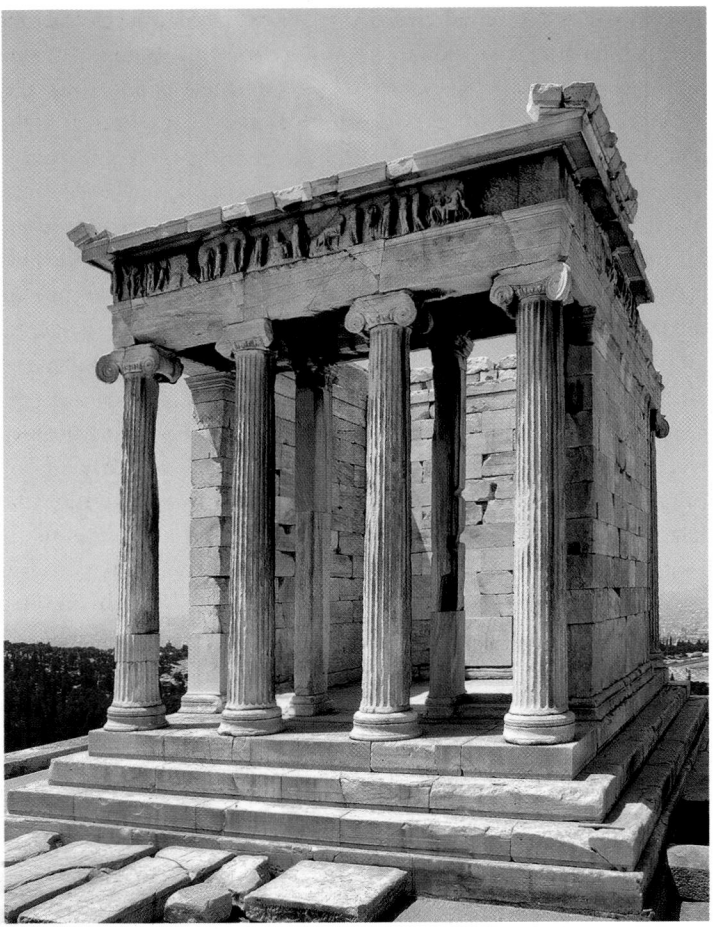

5.50 Temple of Athena Nike. 427–424 BCE (view from east). Akropolis, Athens

THE TEMPLE OF ATHENA NIKE The architects who designed the Parthenon and the Propylaia incorporated Ionic elements into essentially Doric buildings for a reason that may have had as much to do with politics as with design. In pre-Classical times, the only Ionic structures on the Greek mainland were small treasuries, like the Siphnian Treasury (fig. 5.20), which eastern Greek states erected at Delphi in their regional styles. When Athenian architects used the Ionic style, Perikles may have been making a deliberate symbolic gesture, uniting the disparate regions of Greece in an international style. The Akropolis, in fact, houses the finest surviving examples of Ionic architecture. One is the small Temple of Athena Nike, to the south of the Propylaia (fig. **5.50**). Kallikrates may have designed it 20 years earlier to celebrate the Athenian victory over the Persians, but building probably only occurred between 427 and 424 BCE. The decorative quality of the Ionic style, with finer proportions than those found in the Doric style, made it a natural choice for the jewel-like building. Standing on a projecting bastion, it was the first structure to greet a visitor to the Akropolis.

THE ERECHTHEION A second, larger Ionic temple stood alongside the Parthenon. The Erechtheion was built between 421 and 405 BCE, and was probably another of Mnesikles' projects (fig. **5.51** and plan in fig. 5.39). As with the Propylaia, the architect had to deal with difficult terrain: Not only did the site slope, but it already accommodated various shrines associated with the mythical founding of Athens that could not be moved. Beneath it, for instance, was the spot where, so Athenians believed, Poseidon and Athena competed for custody of Athens. In addition to the olive tree that Athena gave the city in the contest, the temple enclosed a saltwater pool that supposedly sprang up where Poseidon threw his trident. The architect therefore designed the Erechtheion to serve several religious functions simultaneously. Its highly irregular plan included four rooms, as well as a basement on the western side. The main, eastern room was dedicated to Athena Polias (Athena as the City Goddess) and contained the old cult image, an amorphous piece of olive wood that was the most sacred cult object in Athens; the western room was sacred to Poseidon. Another room held a cult of King Erechtheus, who promoted the worship of Athena and for whom the building is named.

Instead of a west façade, the Erechtheion has two porches attached to its flanks. A very large one dedicated to Poseidon faces north and served as the main entrance, while a smaller one juts out toward the Parthenon. The latter is the famous Porch of the Maidens (see fig. 5.51), so named because six caryatids, instead

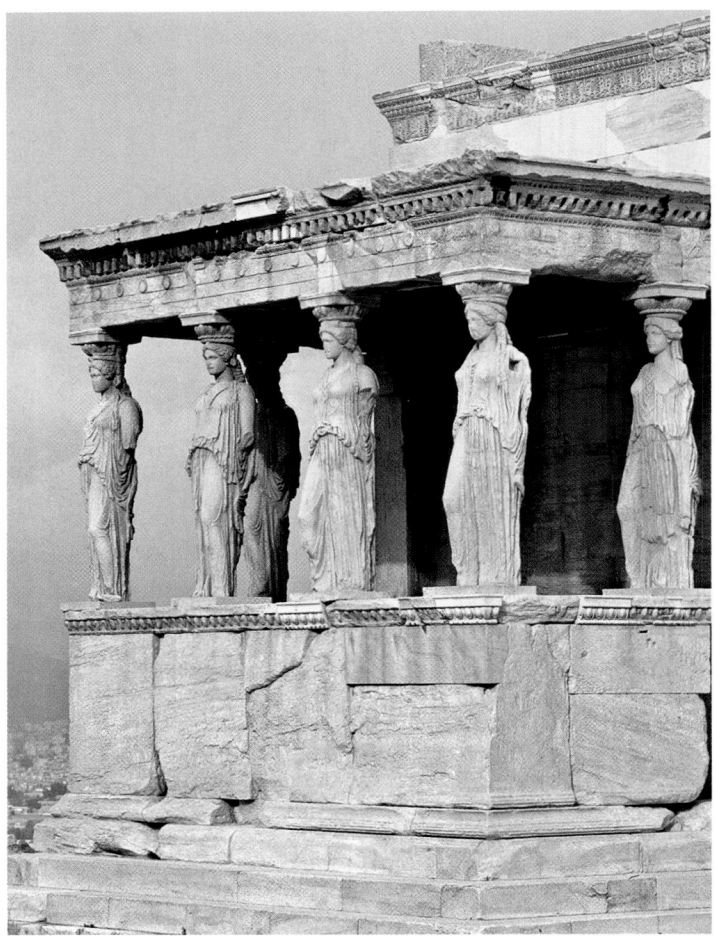

5.51 The Erechtheion. 421–405 BCE (view from the southeast). Akropolis, Athens

of columns, support its roof on a high parapet. The Roman architect Vitruvius wrote that these figural columns represented the women of Caryae, a city-state in the Peloponnese that formed an alliance with the Persians in the Persian Wars. When the war was over, the triumphant Greeks killed the men of Caryae, and took the women as slaves, forcing them nonetheless to retain their fine clothing and other marks of their former status as visible reminders of their shame. Thus, Vitruvius continues, architects designed images of these women to bear the burden of their state's dishonor in perpetuity. Vitruvius' explanation for the origin of caryatids is inconsistent with the fact that they appear on the Siphnian Treasury well before the Persian Wars (see fig. 5.20); but it may reveal the special significance of caryatids for Athenians after the war. Even beyond the caryatids, the Erechtheion was a highly decorative temple. Its pediments remained bare, perhaps for lack of funds at the end of the Peloponnesian War, and little survives of the sculptural frieze. However, the carving on the bases and capitals of the columns, and on the frames of doorways and windows, is extraordinarily delicate and rich. Indeed, according to stone inscriptions detailing construction expenses for the building, it cost more than the temple's figural sculpture.

Although the Akropolis buildings arose over the course of several decades, Perikles clearly intended them as a programmatic unit. The solid, stately forms of the Doric Parthenon and Propylaia complemented the lighter, more decorative style of the Temple of Athena Nike and Erechtheion, and together they honored Athens' protective goddess, and expressed the ideals and grandeur of the city-state and its place in the wider Greek world.

THE LATE CLASSICAL PERIOD

By the end of the fifth century BCE, Athens' supremacy was on the wane. Conflict between Athens and the Peloponnesian cities of Corinth and Sparta, which had been smoldering since about 460 BCE, gradually escalated into the great Peloponnesian War in 431. By the time this ended in 404, Athens had lost. During the following century, the Greek city-states were constantly at odds with one another. In 338 BCE, Philip II, who had acceded to power in the kingdom of Macedon, to the north, exploited their disunity by invading Greece, and decisively defeated the Athenians and Thebans at the Battle of Chaironeia. The change in Greece's fortune finds its reflection in the art and architecture of the time, as artists and architects start to move away from traditional forms and subjects.

Late Classical Architecture: Civic and Sacred

Two notable changes occurred in monumental architecture in the late fifth and fourth centuries BCE. One was a shift in emphasis: As well as constructing temples, architects explored a range of other building types. Many of these—stoas, meeting houses for the governing council, and the like—had long existed, but now took on grander form. The other was the development of a new style: the Corinthian.

THE MAUSOLEUM AT HALIKARNASSOS In Halikarnassos (present-day Bodrum, in southwest Turkey; see map 5.1), the tendency toward monumentalization resulted in a vast tomb for Mausolos, who ruled Caria from 377 to 353 BCE as satrap for the Persians. His wife and sister, Artemisia, commissioned Pytheos of Priene to design the sepulcher to commemorate Mausolos as hero-founder of Halikarnassos. Such was its renown in antiquity that the ancients counted it among the seven wonders of the ancient world and by Roman imperial times its title, the Mausoleum, was used to describe any monumental tomb. It stood reasonably intact until the thirteenth century CE, when an earthquake brought down the upper sections. Then, in the late fifteenth and early sixteenth centuries, the Knights of St. John used the site as a source of squared stone to refortify their castle. In 1857, the British archaeologist Charles Newton removed many sculptural fragments to the British Museum. Danish excavations continue to yield information at the site. When coupled with literary evidence, archaeological data permits reconstructions, though none has met with universal approval (see www.myartslab.com). One hypothesis appears in figure **5.52**. The tomb was rectangular in plan, and soared 140 feet high in at

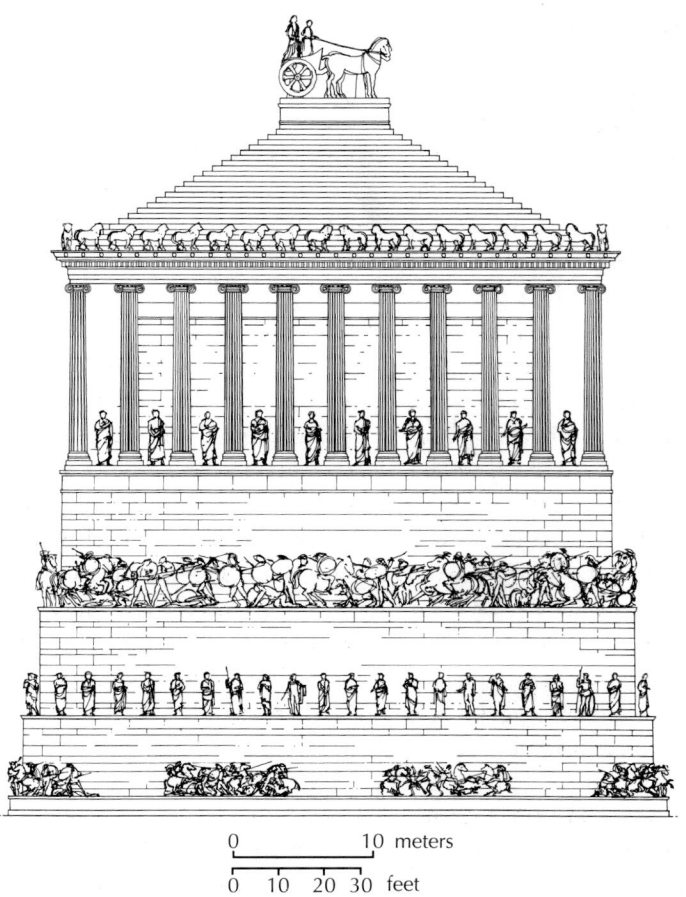

5.52 Reconstruction drawing of the Mausoleum at Halikarnassos. ca. 359–351 BCE (from H. Colvin)

0   10 meters
0   10   20 30   feet

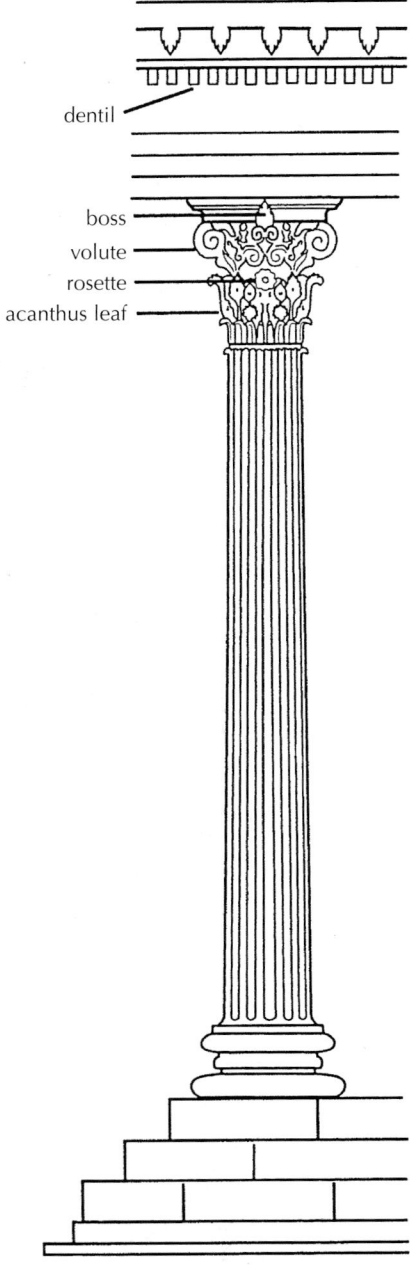

dentil

boss
volute
rosette
acanthus leaf

5.53 Corinthian style in elevation

CORINTHIAN CAPITAL The other major change in architecture that took place in the late fifth century BCE was the development of the **Corinthian capital** (fig. **5.53**) as an elaborate substitute for the Ionic. Its shape is an inverted bell covered with the curly shoots and leaves of an acanthus plant, which seem to sprout from the top of the column shaft. Writing about four centuries later in Italy, Vitruvius ascribed its invention to the metalworker Kallimachos. At first, Greek builders only used Corinthian capitals in temple interiors, perhaps because of the conservative nature of Greek architecture, or because of the perceived sanctity of its vegetal forms. It was not until the second century BCE that Corinthian columns appeared on the exteriors of buildings. The capital in figure **5.54** belongs to a circular shrine, or tholos at Epidauros designed by Polykleitos the Younger. The circular form of the shrine is further evidence of the preoccupation with new types of building, and its elaborate interior continues the tradition, begun with the Parthenon, of stressing the articulation of interior space.

Late Classical Sculpture

The Pheidian style, with its apparent confidence in the transcendence of the Athenian city-state, did not survive Athens' devastating defeat in the Peloponnesian War. At the end of the fifth century, a shift in mood is perceptible in sculpture, which seems to reflect a different—and less optimistic—view of man's place in the universe.

Scholars attempt to match surviving sculptures with fourth-century BCE sculptors named in literary sources. Among these is Skopas of Paros. According to the Roman writer Pliny the Elder, he was one of four masters chosen to work on the Mausoleum of Halikarnassos, and art historians recognize his dynamic style in some parts of a frieze from the tomb depicting the battle of the Greeks and the Amazons. His greatest fame, though, derives from

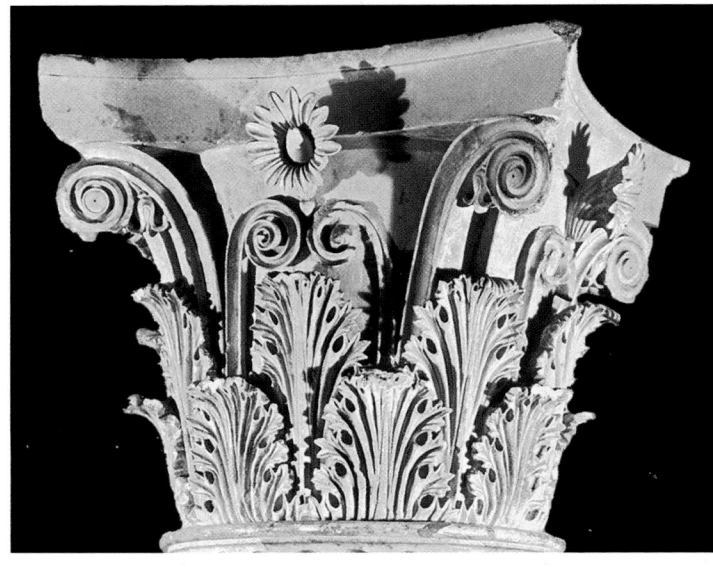

5.54 Polykleitos the Younger. Corinthian capital, from tholos at Epidauros. ca. 350 BCE. Museum, Epidauros, Greece

least three sections, covered with sculpture: A high podium, an Ionic colonnade, and a pyramidal roof, where steps climbed to a platform supporting a statue of Mausolos or one of his ancestors in a chariot.

The Mausoleum combined the monumental tomb-building tradition of the region, Lycia, with a Greek peristyle and sculpture, and an Egyptian pyramid. The grouping of these elements in a single monument is evidence of a growing diversity in architecture. It may also have had a propagandistic function: It may have expressed Carian supremacy in the region and the symbiosis of Greek and non-Greek civilizations that might be achieved through founding a Carian empire headed by Halikarnassos.

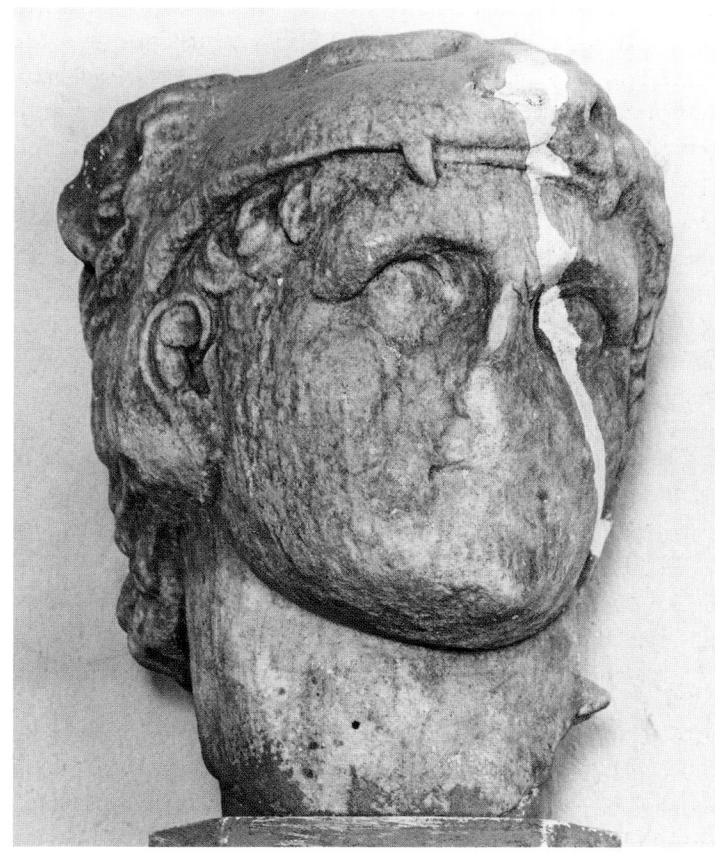

5.55 Head of Herakles or Telephos, from west pediment of Temple of Athena Alea, Tegea. ca. 340 BCE. Marble, height 12½" (31.75 cm). Stolen from the Archaeological Museum, Tegea

the way he infused emotion into the faces he sculpted. A fragmentary head from a pediment of the Temple of Athena Alea at Tegea of about 340 BCE is either by Skopas, or an artist deeply influenced by his work (fig. **5.55**). A lion skin covering the head identifies it as either Herakles or his son Telephos. The smooth planes and fleshy treatment of the face are characteristic of Classical art, as seen on the Parthenon. What is new, however, is how the sculptor cut the marble away sharply over the eyes toward the bridge of the nose to create a dark shadow. At the outer edge, the eyelid bulges to overhang the eye. This simple change charges the face with a depth of emotion not seen before. The slightly parted lips and the sharp turn of the head enhance the effect.

PRAXITELES If the Greeks were less confident of their place in the world in the Late Classical period, they were also less certain of their relationship to fate and the gods. This is reflected in the work of Praxiteles, who was at work at roughly the same time as Skopas. Choosing to work in marble rather than bronze, he executed several statues of divinities. Where fifth-century BCE artists had stressed the gods' majesty, Praxiteles gave them a youthful sensuousness that suggests their willful capriciousness toward humans. His most famous work is a sculpture of Aphrodite, dating to about 340–330 BCE (fig. **5.56**). Pliny records that the people of Kos commissioned a cult statue of Aphrodite from

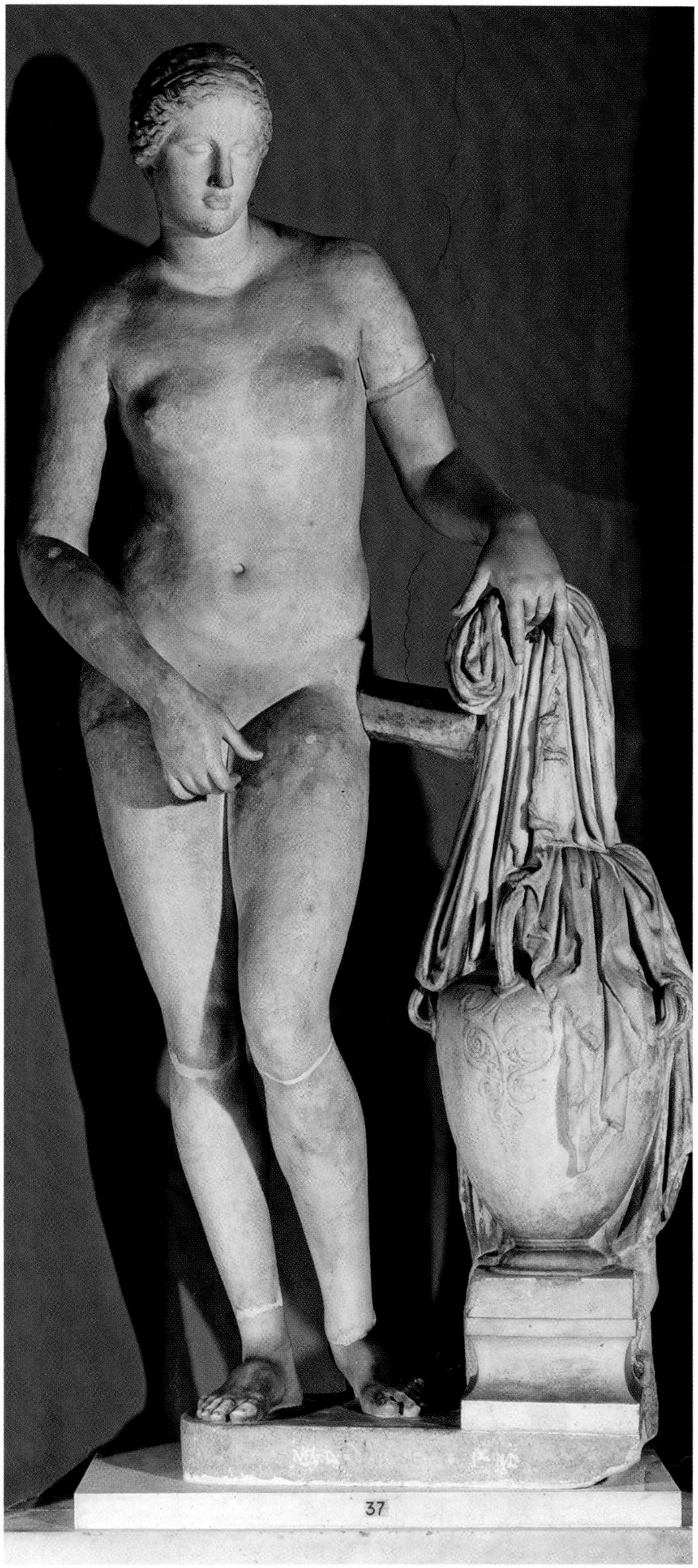

5.56 *Aphrodite of Knidos.* Roman copy after an original of ca. 340–330 BCE by Praxiteles. Marble, height 6'8" (2 m). Musei Vaticani, Rome

Praxiteles, but rejected the nude statue he offered them in favor of a draped version. But the inhabitants of Knidos purchased the nude statue, and profited from the risk: Her fame spread fast, and visitors came to the island from far and wide to see her. (See www.myartslab.com.) Perhaps it was her nudity that drew so much attention: She was the first nude monumental statue of a goddess in the Greek world. Yet even if artists had previously reserved female nudity principally for representations of slaves or courtesans, the clinging drapery of the fifth century BCE had exposed almost as much of the female anatomy as it concealed. Her appeal may have resided just as much in the blatant eroticism of the image. A viewer catches Aphrodite either as she is about to bathe or as she is rising from her bath. With her right hand, she covers her nudity in a gesture of modesty, while grasping for a robe with her left. Her head is slightly turned, so she does not engage a viewer's gaze directly, but a viewer is made complicit with the sculpture, willingly or not, by having inappropriately witnessed her in her nudity. Perhaps, in her capriciousness, Aphrodite intended to be surprised as she bathed; the uncertainty for a viewer augments the erotic quality of the image. By some accounts, the Knidians displayed Praxiteles' sculpture in a circular shrine with entrances at front and back, so visitors could view the cult statue from all sides. A viewer's role is more complex here than in the Classical period: The sculpture invites physical and emotional engagement, not merely respect.

Praxiteles' Aphrodite is known to us only through Roman copies. In this respect, a group representing Hermes holding the infant Dionysos poses complicated questions (fig. **5.57**). The Roman writer Pausanias mentions seeing such a statue by Praxiteles in the Temple of Hera at Olympia, where this marble was found in 1877. It is of such high quality that art historians have long regarded it as a late work by Praxiteles himself. Now, however, most scholars believe it to be a fine copy of the first century BCE because of the strut support and unfinished back; analysis of the tool marks on the surface of the marble support this date, as do the sandals, which are distinctly Roman in style. Still, the group has all the characteristics of Praxitelean sculpture. Hermes is more slender in proportion than Polykleitos' *Doryphoros* (see fig. 5.33), and the chiastic pose is so exaggerated as to have become a fully relaxed and languid curve of the torso. The anatomy, so clearly defined on the *Doryphoros*, blurs to suggest a youthful sensuousness rather than athletic prowess. The surface treatment of the marble is masterful, contrasting highly polished skin with rough, almost expressionistic hair. The group has a humorous quality typical of Praxiteles' work as well: The messenger god originally dangled a bunch of grapes in front of Dionysos, whose attempts to reach for them foreshadow his eventual role as the god of wine. Yet, depending upon a viewer's mood (or worldview), Hermes' distant gaze may also hold a callous disregard for the child's efforts.

LYSIPPOS A third great name in fourth-century BCE sculpture is Lysippos, who had an extremely long career. He may have begun sculpting as early as about 370 BCE and continued almost to the end of the century. Known from Roman copies, his *Apoxyomenos* (a youth scraping oil from his skin with a strigil) dates to about 330 BCE (fig. **5.58**) and is in dialogue with Polykleitos' *Doryphoros* (see fig. 5.33). Lysippos preferred more slender proportions for his athlete, calculating the length of the head as one-eighth of the body's length, rather than one-seventh as Polykleitos had. (See

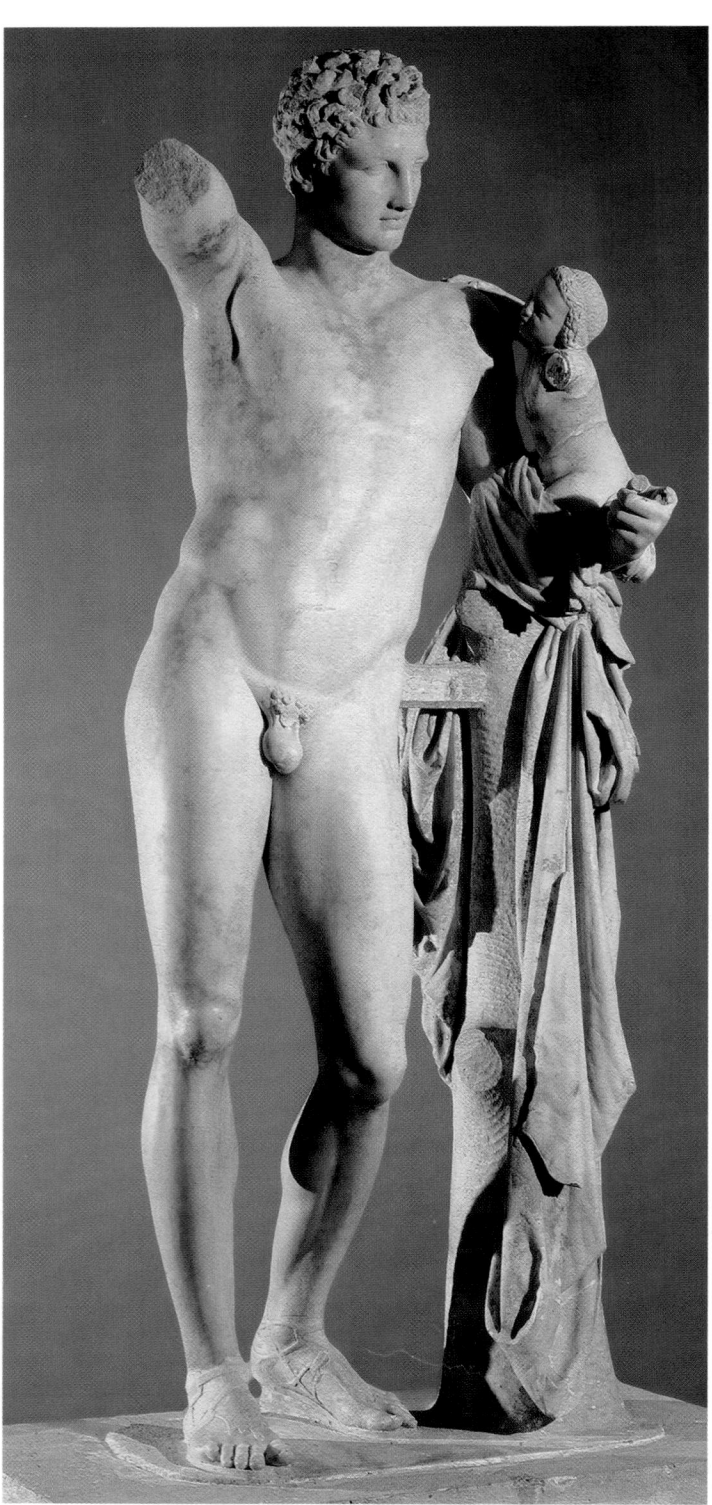

5.57 *Hermes*. Roman copy after an original of ca. 320–310 BCE by Praxiteles. Marble, height 7'1" (2.16 m). Archaeological Museum, Olympia

www.myartslab.com.) The *Apoxyomenos* leans further back into his chiastic pose, too—a sign of Praxiteles' influence—and the diagonal line of the free leg suggests freedom of movement. Most innovative, however, is the positioning of the athlete's arms. The outstretched arm reaches forward into a viewer's space. Since a frontal view foreshortens the arm, it entices a viewer to move around the sculpture to understand the full range of the action;

like Praxiteles, Lysippos breaks the primacy of the frontal view for a standing figure. The athlete's left arm bends around to meet the right at chest height, so the sculpture deliberately contains space within its composition. Lysippos challenges the stark opposition between sculpture and its environment; the two begin to merge. This device is symptomatic of a new interest in illusionism in the Late Classical and Hellenistic ages.

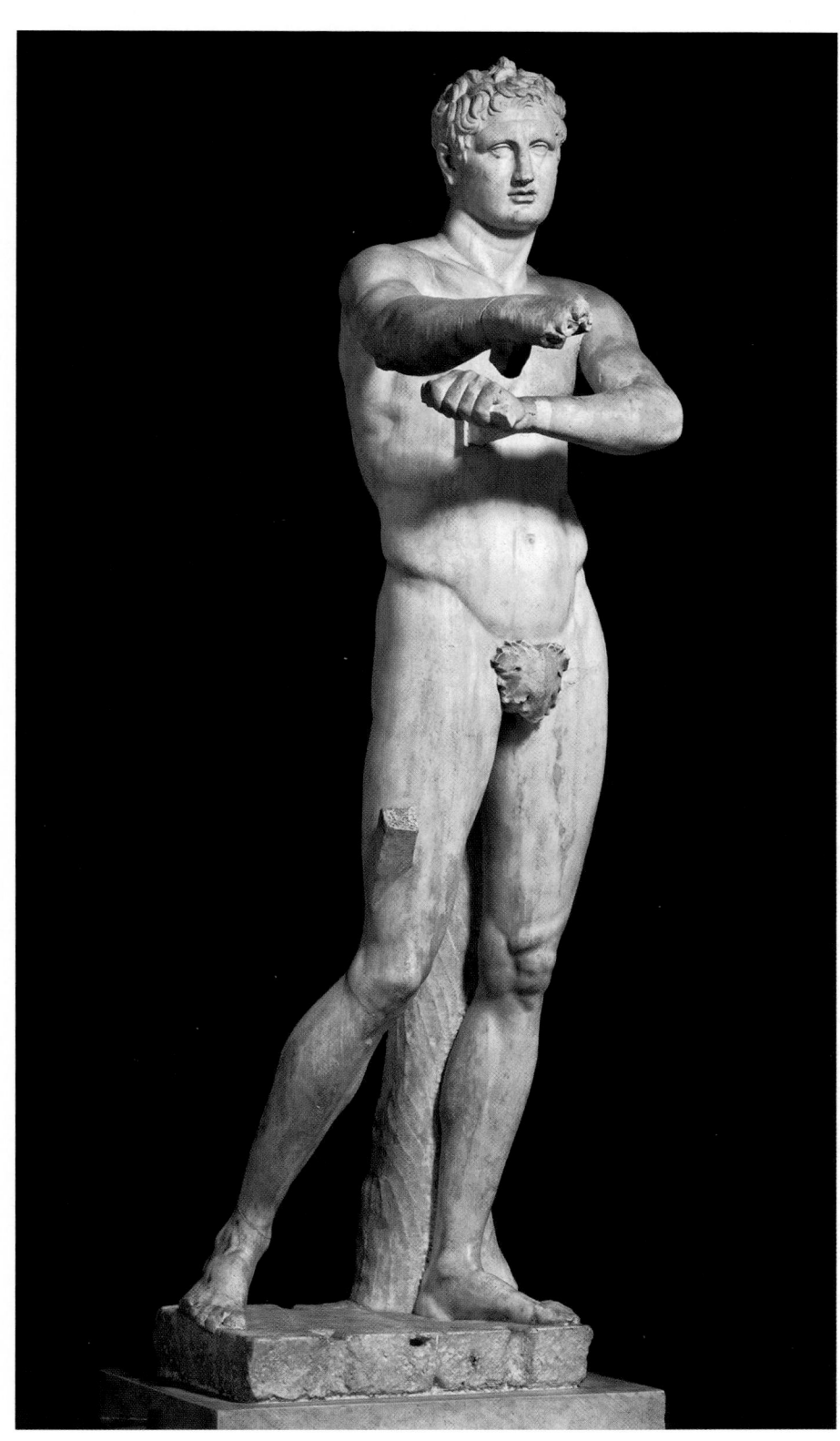

5.58 *Apoxyomenos* (*Scraper*). Roman marble copy, probably after a bronze original of ca. 330 BCE by Lysippos. Height 6'9" (2.1 m). Musei Vaticani, Rome

Painting in the Late Classical Age

Written sources name some of the famous painters of the Classical age, and reveal a good deal about how painting evolved, but they rarely include details of what it actually looked like. The great age of Greek painting began early in the Classical period with Polygnotos of Thasos and his collaborator, Mikon of Athens, who both worked as sculptors as well. Polygnotos was known for paintings depicting the aftermath of the Trojan War in Delphi, and mythological paintings coupled with a depiction of the Battle of Marathon decorating the Stoa Poikile (Painted Stoa) in the Athenian agora (see fig. 5.37). He introduced several innovations in painting, including the depiction of emotion and character, which became as central to Classical painting as they were to sculpture. He was also first to depict women in transparent drapery, and to forgo the notion of a single ground-line, placing figures instead at varying levels in a landscape setting.

The placement of figures at different levels of terrain seems to have influenced a contemporary vase painter, known today as the Niobid Painter. His name vase (the vase for which scholars name him) is a calyx krater (a wine-mixing bowl), which shows the outcome of Niobe's foolish boast that she had more—and more beautiful—children than Leto, mother of Apollo and Artemis: The sibling gods of hunting shoot down Niobe's sons and daughters (fig. **5.59**). Each of the figures has his or her own ground-line, which undulates to suggest a rocky landscape. Artemis and Apollo stand above two of their victims, who are sprawled over boulders, but we should probably understand the terrain to recede into the distance.

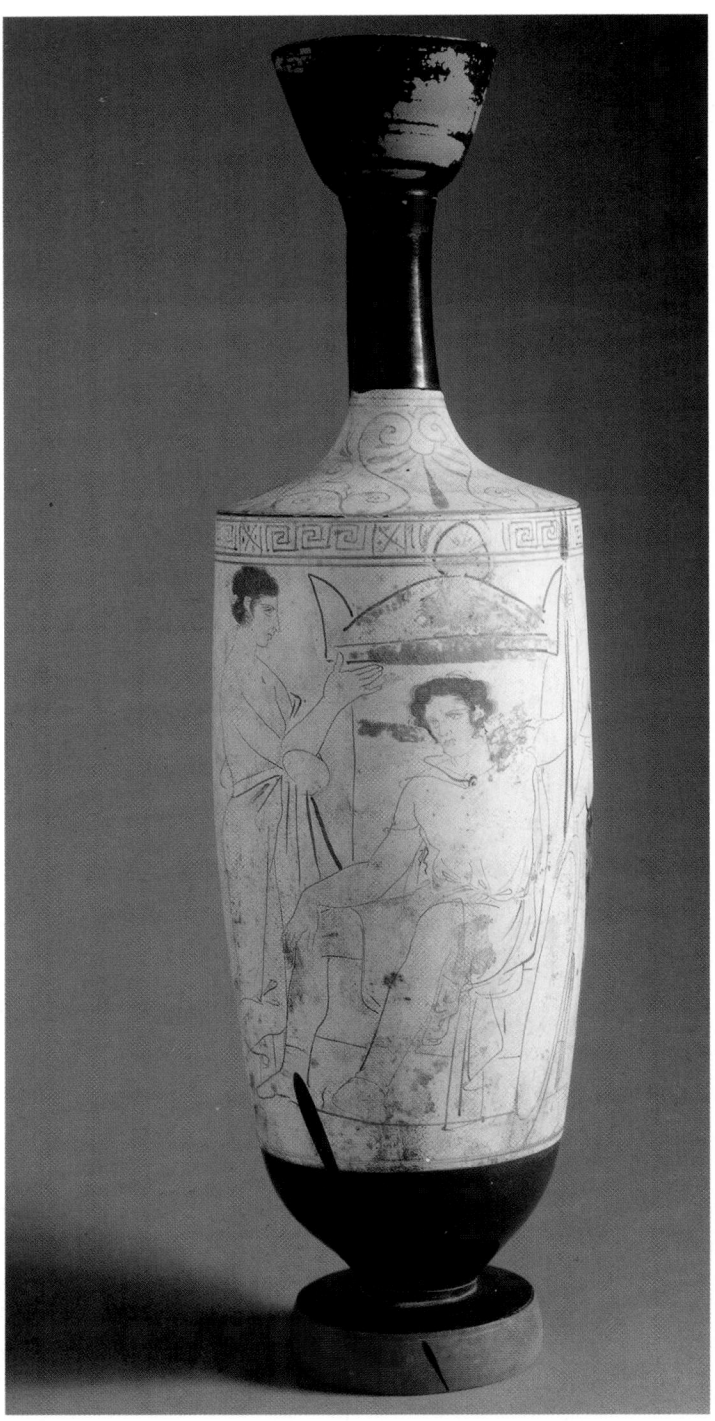

5.60 Reed Painter. White-ground lekythos. ca. 425–400 BCE. National Archaeological Museum, Athens

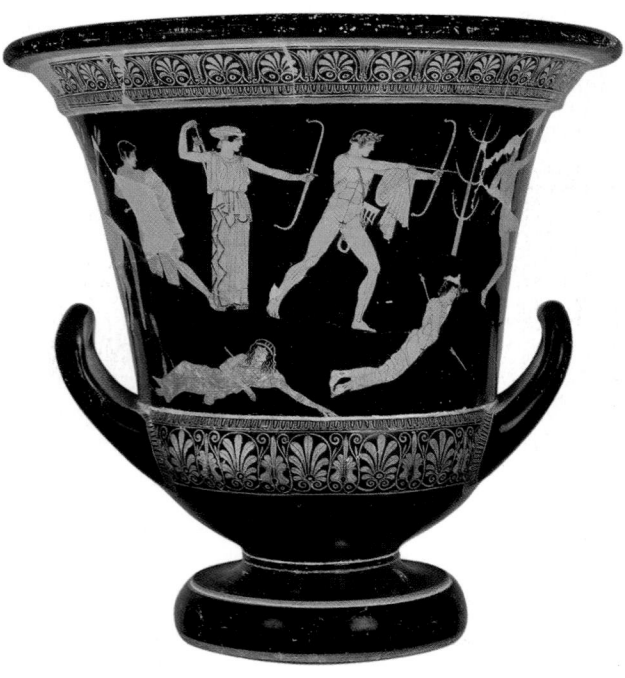

5.59 Niobid Painter. Red-figured calyx krater, from Orvieto. ca. 460–450 BCE. Musée du Louvre, Paris

Significant technical differences separated wall painting from red-figured vase painting. Much closer to wall painting was a technique reserved almost exclusively for the vases Greeks deposited with burials: **white-ground** vase painting. Artists working in this technique painted a range of colors onto a white slip background, and favored a type of oil flask used in funerary rituals, known as a **lekythos**. On a lekythos from the last quarter of the fifth century BCE, attributed to the Reed Painter (fig. **5.60**), a disconsolate young man sits on the steps of a tomb. A woman on the right holds his helmet, while a second man stands to the left with one arm raised in a gesture of farewell. Black outlines define the scene, filled with washes of vivid color. Some blue still survives on parts of the tomb and the seated man's cloak, and brown in the figures' hair, but most of the colors have long vanished, since fugitive paints sufficed for a vessel that did not have to withstand prolonged or repeated use. The freedom of the technique allowed the painter to explore foreshortening and depth, and to achieve a remarkably expressionistic effect with a few fluid lines. The deceased man's deep-set brooding eyes give some indication of the emotion painters could capture. Despite the artistic advantages of the white-ground technique, from the mid-fifth century BCE on monumental painting gradually eclipsed vase painting, though in some cases vase painters tried to reproduce large-scale compositions.

THE AGE OF ALEXANDER AND THE HELLENISTIC PERIOD

In 336 BCE, Philip II of Macedon died, and his kingdom passed to his son Alexander. Alexander the Great is one of the romantic figures of history, renowned for his military genius and personal charm. He embarked upon a great campaign of conquest, overcoming Egypt and the Persians, then continuing on to Mesopotamia and present-day Afghanistan. In 323 BCE, having founded over 70 cities, he died at the age of 33. His conquests changed the face of the Greek world dramatically, expanding it into unknown spheres, creating new political alignments, and breaking down cultural boundaries (see map 5.2).

The years following Alexander's death were fraught with struggles between members of his family and his generals, as each tried to establish himself as his sole successor; none succeeded. By about 275 BCE, Alexander's lands had coalesced into three main kingdoms, which would dominate the Mediterranean until the Romans gradually assumed control. Ptolemy founded a dynasty in Egypt that reigned until Octavian (later the Roman emperor Augustus) defeated Cleopatra VII in 31 BCE. In the east, the Seleucid family captured Babylon in 312 BCE. From Syria they ruled a kingdom which, at its largest, extended from present-day western Turkey to Afghanistan. They lost control of a small pocket of territory around Pergamon to the Attalids, who bequeathed their city to the Romans in 133 BCE. In 64 BCE, the Seleucid kingdom came under Roman control. Most coveted was Alexander's ancestral Macedon, which the Antigonids controlled until the Roman conquest in 168 BCE. Within these kingdoms, powerful cities grew—among them, Alexandria, Antioch, and

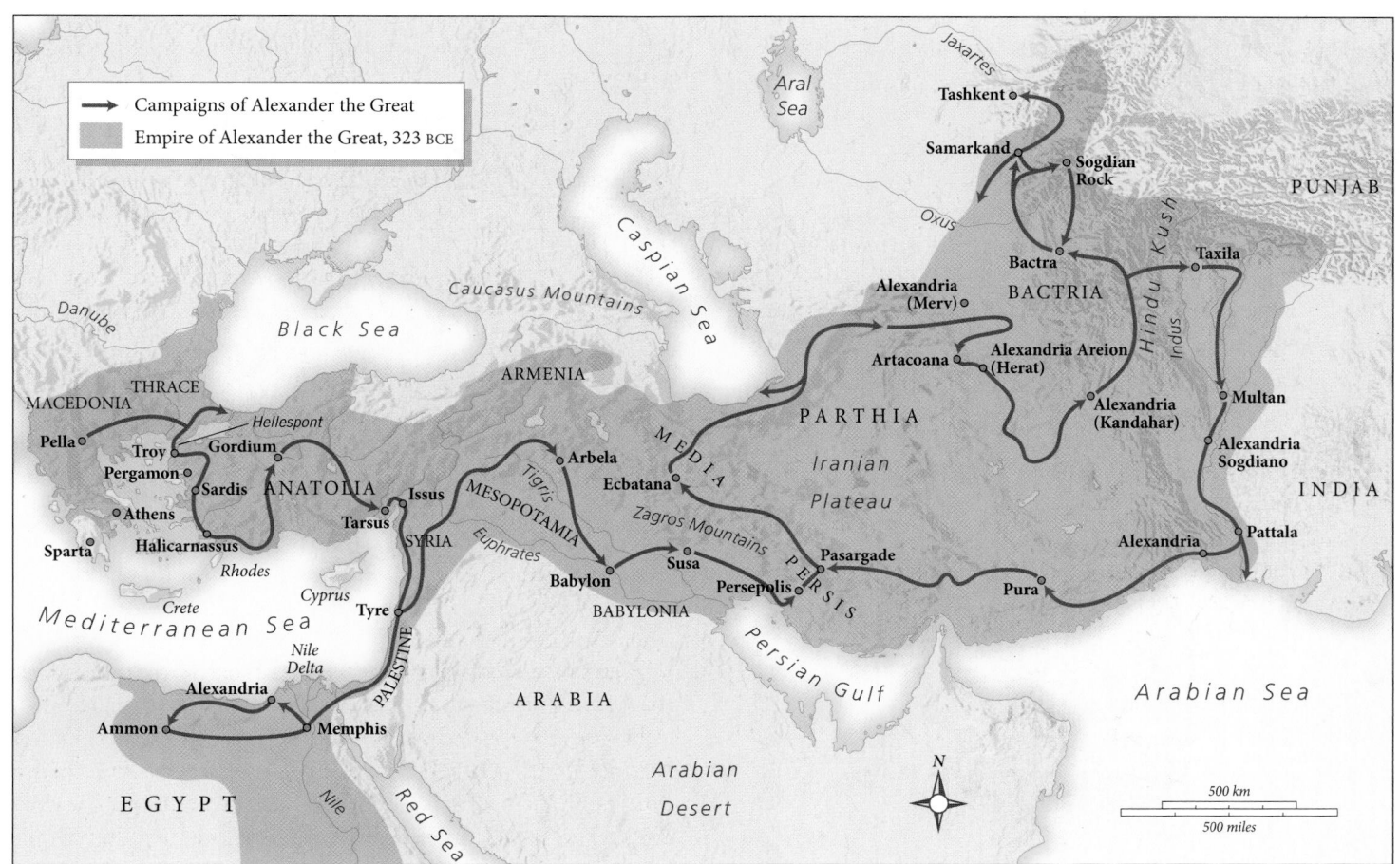

Map 5.2 Hellenistic Greece

Pergamon—with teeming populations drawn from all over the new Greek world. They vied for cultural preeminence, and art played a large part in the rivalry. Scholars call the period from the death of Alexander until Roman rule the Hellenistic period, and Hellenistic culture was radically different from that of Classical times. The expansion of Greek dominance meant that Greek cultural institutions prevailed over a vast territory; those institutions commingled with the strong cultural traditions of the indigenous peoples. The result was a rich and diverse society, in which an individual's identity was more complex than before: the kings of Pergamon, for instance, were not Greek but strove for Greekness and identified themselves as Greek. All the same, over a wide region, people were united by a common cultural vocabulary, known as a *koine* (Greek for "common thing"). The art of the time reflects this richness: diverse styles coexisted, and artists drew inspiration from indigenous forms as well as the Greek heritage.

Architecture: The Scholarly Tradition and Theatricality

Within the cultural centers of the Hellenistic world, academies emerged, which fostered avid debate among scholars in a range of fields. They engaged, among other things, in a close analysis of the arts, and developed canons by which they could judge works of literature, art, and architecture. In architecture, this led, predictably, to a heightened interest in systems of proportions, recorded in architectural treatises by practitioners of the day. Vitruvius asserts that the leading protagonist in this movement was Pytheos of Priene, one of the architects of the Mausoleum at Halikarnassos (see fig. 5.52). Like most, his treatise does not survive, but Vitruvius notes that he was dismissive of the Doric style because problems with the spacing of corner triglyphs made it impossible to impose the style without compromise. Pytheos worked instead in the Ionic style (in which the volutes of corner capitals could be angled), as seen in his temple to Athena at Priene, dedicated in 334 BCE (fig. **5.61**).

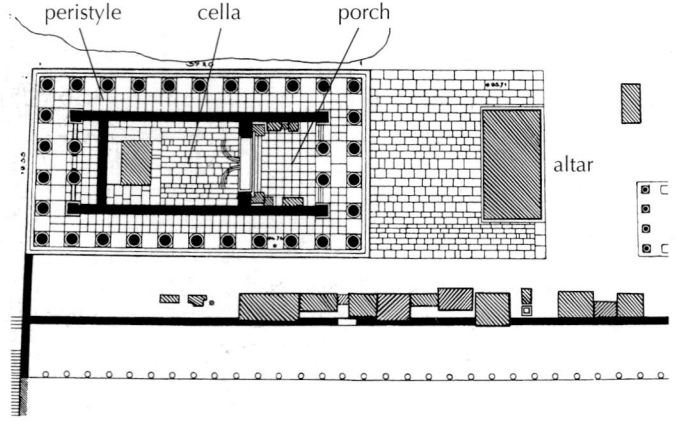

5.61 Plan of Pytheos. Temple of Athena, Priene. 334 BCE

The temple's colonnade had 6 columns by 11, and a grid of squares, each 6 by 6 Attic feet (the Attic foot is slightly longer than the English foot), that dictated the proportions of all of its elements. Proportions controlled the elevation as well: For instance, the columns were 43 feet high and the entablature was 7 feet high—a total of 50 feet, half the external length of the cella. Unlike the Parthenon and other Classical temples, there were no deviations from the rule, and no refinements. The temple is a work of the intellect, the product of a didactic tradition, rather than a compromise between theory and practice. In fact, Vitruvius faults Pytheos precisely for his inability to differentiate between the two.

While this scholarly tradition flourished, the relaxation of architectural guidelines and the combination of architectural types that had occurred in the Late Classical period heralded another development. This was a penchant for dramatic siting, impressive vistas, and surprise revelations. Scholars have termed this movement "theatricality," and it balanced and complemented the scholarly tradition. As the glory of Athens declined, the Athenians and other Greeks came to think of themselves less as members of a city-state and more as individuals; architecture, in turn, began to cater more and more to personal experience, often manipulating visitors toward a meaningful revelation.

THE TEMPLE OF APOLLO, DIDYMA Begun in about 300 BCE and still unfinished by the end of the Roman period, the Temple of Apollo at Didyma is a good example of architectural theatricality (figs. **5.62** and **5.63**). Its ground plan and design appear to have been established by the renowned architects Paionios of Ephesos and Daphnis of Miletos, on the site and at the scale of an Archaic temple destroyed by the Persians in 494 BCE.

From the outside, the temple appeared similar to other large-scale dipteral Ionic buildings of the area. A visitor would naturally expect the interior to repeat the format of canonical Greek temples such as the Parthenon; but, in fact, the architects constantly defied these expectations, leading visitors instead to dramatic vistas, perhaps intending to heighten their religious experience. Although the temple appeared to be accessible from all sides, its seven massive steps were on a divine, not a mortal scale, and far too high to climb comfortably. Instead, visitors climbed a set of shallower steps at the front, and entered the porch between its vast columns, set to mimic the grove of sacred trees around the building. As expected, an opening led to the cella—but this cella stood approximately 5 feet off the ground, so access was impossible. From this raised threshold, scholars believe, the oracular priestess may have uttered her prophecies to those standing below in the porch. The path further into the building led to the right or left of the threshold, where dark barrel-vaulted tunnels led downward. For a Greek visitor, a barrel-vaulted tunnel evoked a dark interior such as a cave. Yet these passages did not lead to a covered cella, but a vast open courtyard drenched with bright sunshine: A revelation, it must have seemed.

At the end of the courtyard was the shrine itself, a small Ionic building dedicated to Apollo. Near the shrine were sacred laurel bushes and a spring of holy water. Turning back from the shrine, a visitor faced another astonishing sight: A wide, steep staircase dwarfed the tunnels through which he or she had entered the courtyard, and led up to a pair of towering **engaged** Corinthian columns (joined to the wall). These may have signaled that the room that lay beyond them was the priestess' innermost sanctuary. We know little of the goings-on inside Greek temples, yet the processional quality of this staircase and the large scale of the courtyard suggest that large crowds of worshipers could have gathered there to witness ritual ceremonies. Also unknown is the function of small staircases leading off from the sanctuary and up to the roof over the colonnades. Building inscriptions describe them as "labyrinths," and the ceiling above them is

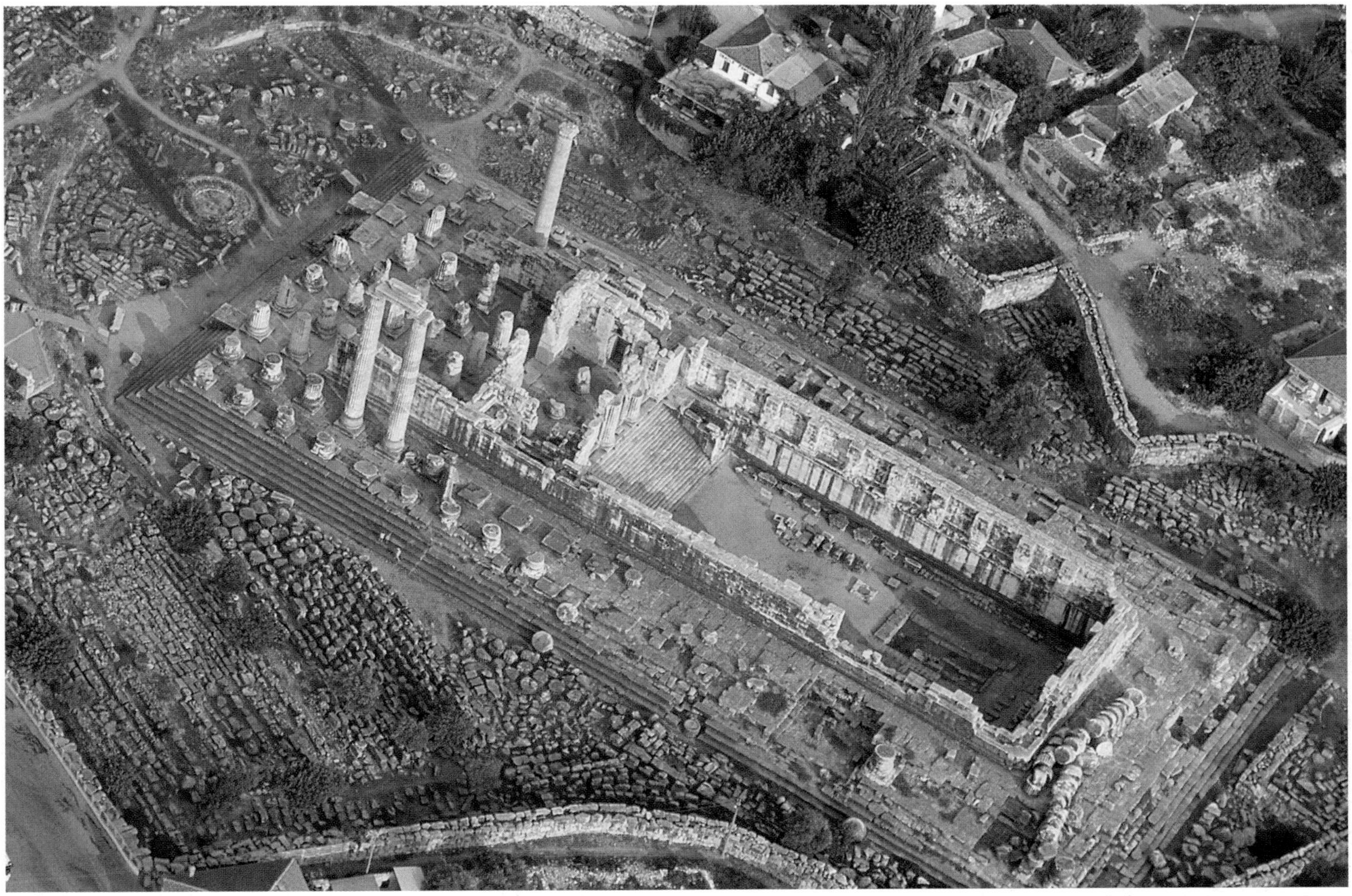

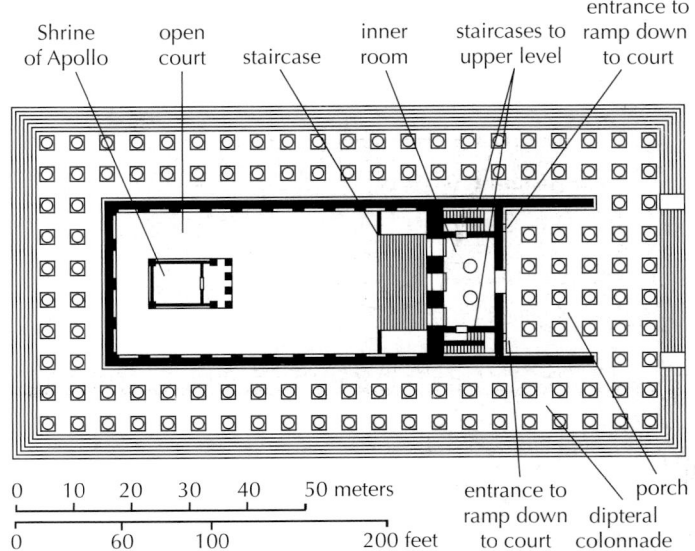

5.62   Paionios of Ephesos and Daphnis of Miletos. Temple of Apollo, Didyma, Turkey. Begun 313 BCE

5.63   Plan of Temple of Apollo, Didyma, Turkey

Shrine of Apollo   open court   staircase   inner room   staircases to upper level   entrance to ramp down to court

entrance to ramp down to court   porch dipteral colonnade

0   10   20   30   40   50 meters
0   60   100   200 feet

carved with a brightly painted meander pattern (see fig. 5.3), the Egyptian hieroglyphic sign for a maze. They may have provided maintenance workers with access to the roof, but they may equally have accommodated revelatory dramas in honor of Apollo.

As a whole, the temple's design manipulated visitors along unexpected paths, and offered constant surprises. Yet the temple is remarkable for another reason besides. Inside the courtyard, archaeologists unexpectedly discovered diagrams incised (so lightly that they are visible only under a strong raking light) upon its walls. These etchings are scale drawings for aspects of the building's design, ranging from capital decoration to column entasis. They provide a rare insight into the design process in Greek building. They suggest that architects drew a building's design onto its surfaces as it rose, and workers then polished them off as they finished those surfaces. This temple's incompletion preserved the design drawings in place.

City Planning

Early Greek cities such as Athens grew organically, transforming gradually from small settlements into larger urban developments. Streets were typically winding, and building blocks were irregular. From the seventh century BCE onward, colonization offered Greeks an opportunity to conceive cities as a whole, and to assess different types of city planning, while from the Late Classical period, philosophers debated the structure of ideal cities. Hippodamos of Miletos was the first to write a treatise on city design, advocating grid planning—that is, laying out city streets in intersecting horizontals and verticals. In the mid-fifth century BCE, he designed the Piraeus, near Athens, as a grid, and the pattern is still used in many Western cities today. The design offered many advantages: For an architect, it provided regularity; for colonists, it simplified the distribution of allotments; and for inhabitants, it meant a new ease of orientation. When the inhabitants of Priene relocated their city to avoid flooding, in approximately 350 BCE, they opted for the efficiency of a grid plan (fig. 5.64). As the model demonstrates, the city planners applied the grid to the sloping terrain uncompromisingly. On some longitudinal axes, they inserted staircases to climb straight, steep inclines. Useful for pedestrians, the stairs must have been impassable by wheeled vehicles. Though perhaps a misjudgment, this may equally have been a form of traffic control.

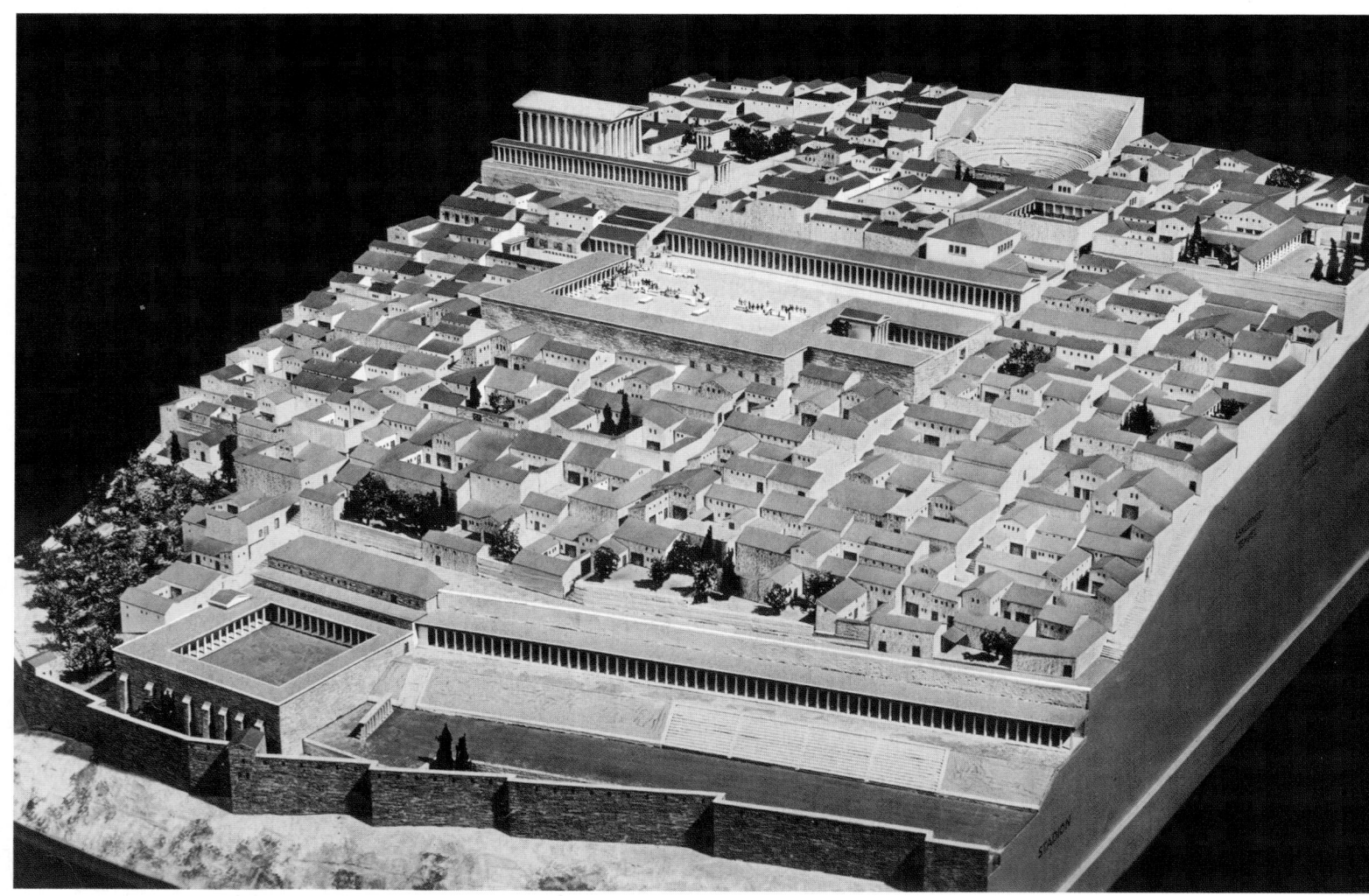

5.64   Model of the city of Priene. 4th century BCE and later. Staatliche Museen, Berlin

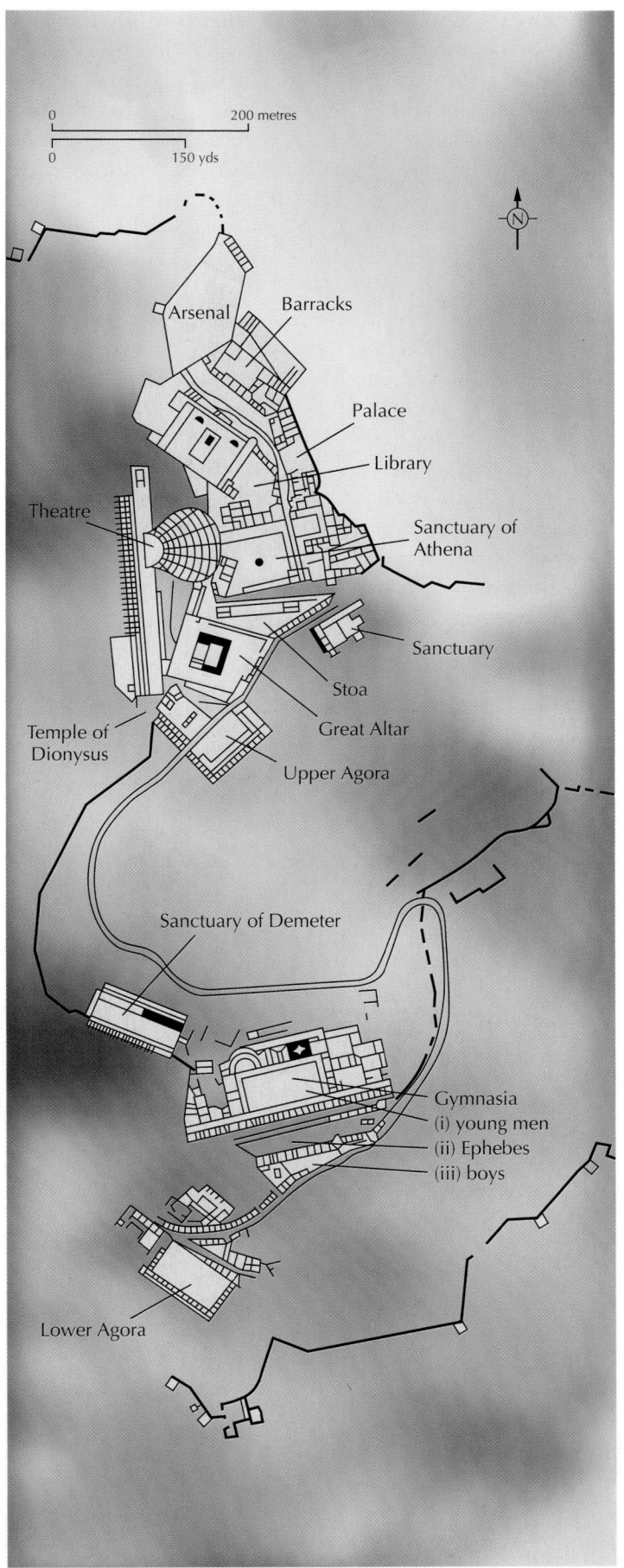

5.65   Plan of Pergamon, Turkey. ca. 2nd century BCE

PERGAMON: A THEATRICAL PLAN A visitor to the city of Pergamon would have had a dramatically different experience. There, in the early second century BCE, King Eumenes II and his architects eschewed a grid as they planned an expansion of the city (fig. **5.65**). Residential areas lay mainly on the plain of the Kaikos River; nearby was the towering Akropolis. The new design exploited the dramatic rise in terrain from one to the other, apparently assigning symbolic meaning to the ascent as well. On the lower levels were amenities of everyday life, such as the agora. As the road climbed the southern slope of the Akropolis, it passed through vaulted entrance tunnels to emerge at three *gymnasia* (schools); the first was for boys, the second for ephebes (adolescents aged 15–17), and the third and highest for young men. Farther up the road were sanctuaries to Hera and Demeter.

The road followed the terrain, snaking past an earlier agora, now chiefly used for legal and political purposes, to the Akropolis proper, where Eumenes II, or perhaps his successor Attalos II, dedicated a magnificent altar court to Zeus (see fig. 5.72). Further up and to the east was a shrine for the hero cult, a **heroön**. A long portico temporarily obscured any view of the journey's great crescendo; passing through it, a visitor entered the sanctuary of Athena, patron goddess of Pergamon, where the city's oldest temple stood, alongside Eumenes' celebrated library, with an over-life-size marble version of Pheidias' *Athena Parthenos* (see fig. 5.41). This sanctuary marked the privileged place of learning in Pergamene culture. On its own, the temple was not remarkable. Yet it acquired meaning from the symbolic journey required to reach it. From the sanctuary, a visitor could look out over the steep **cavea** (or seating area) of the Theater of Dionysos across the plain's breathtaking panorama. Beyond the sanctuary, to the northeast, were the royal residence and barracks for the guard. Like the sanctuary, the residence offered magnificent views of the river and the receding countryside, and cool breezes blowing through the valley and up to the Akropolis must have provided relief from the fierce summer heat. At every turn, the city's designer considered a visitor's experience. The impressive vistas and sudden surprises are hallmarks of Hellenistic theatricality.

THE THEATER AT EPIDAUROS Within these cities, architects continued the Late Classical trend toward formalizing a variety of types of architecture. Given the propensity for theatricality, it is no surprise that they paid close attention to theater buildings. Theaters had long been part of the religious landscape of Greek cities, since Greeks gathered in their communities for the choral performances and plays that were central to festivals of Dionysos. The basic prerequisites for a theater were a hillside, on which an audience could sit (the cavea), and a level area for the performance (the **orchestra**). In the Late Classical and Hellenistic periods, however, theaters became more formalized as their essential components took on architectural form.

In the sanctuary of the healing god Asklepios at Epidauros on the Peloponnese, a magnificent stone theater was constructed in

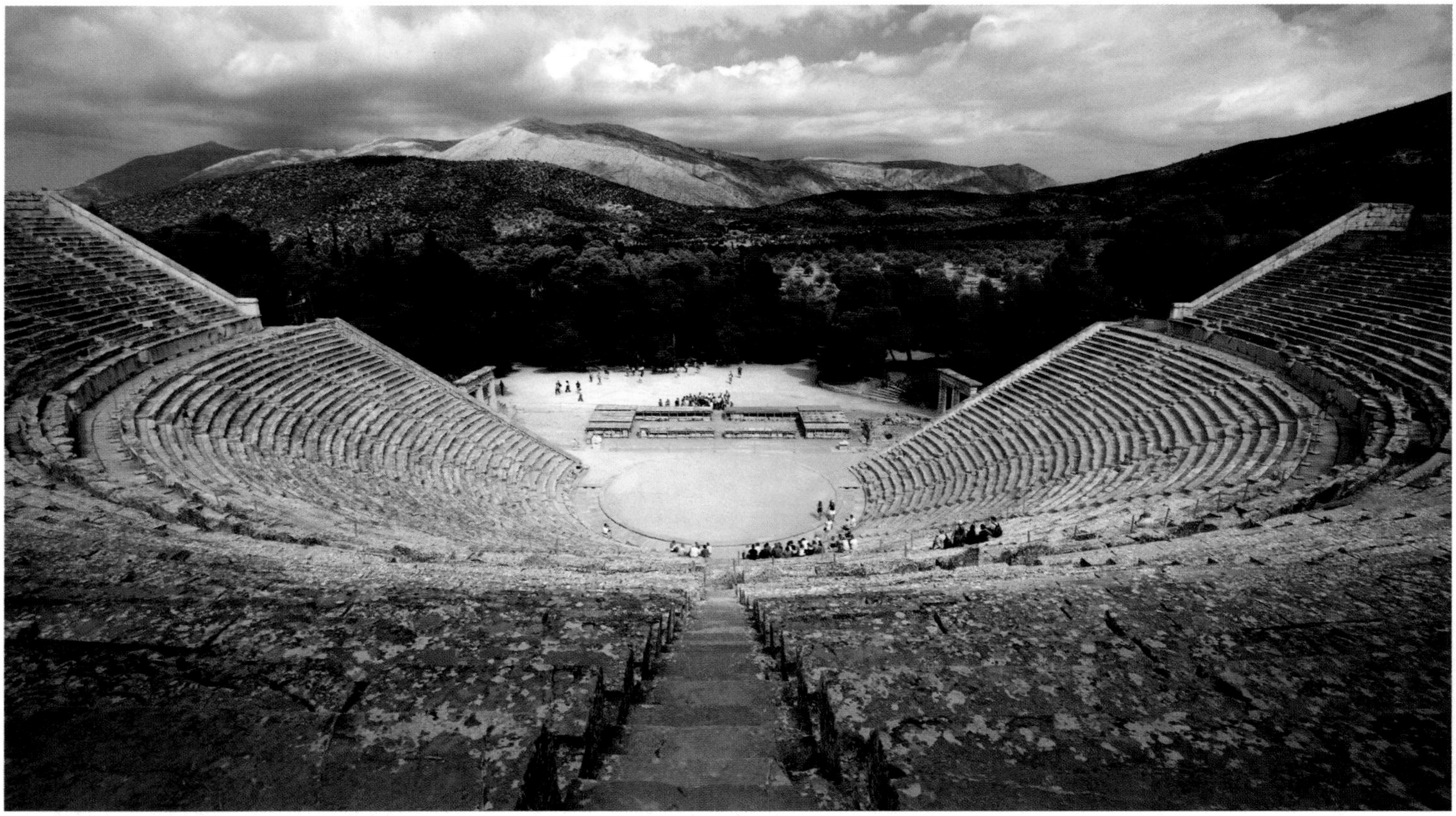

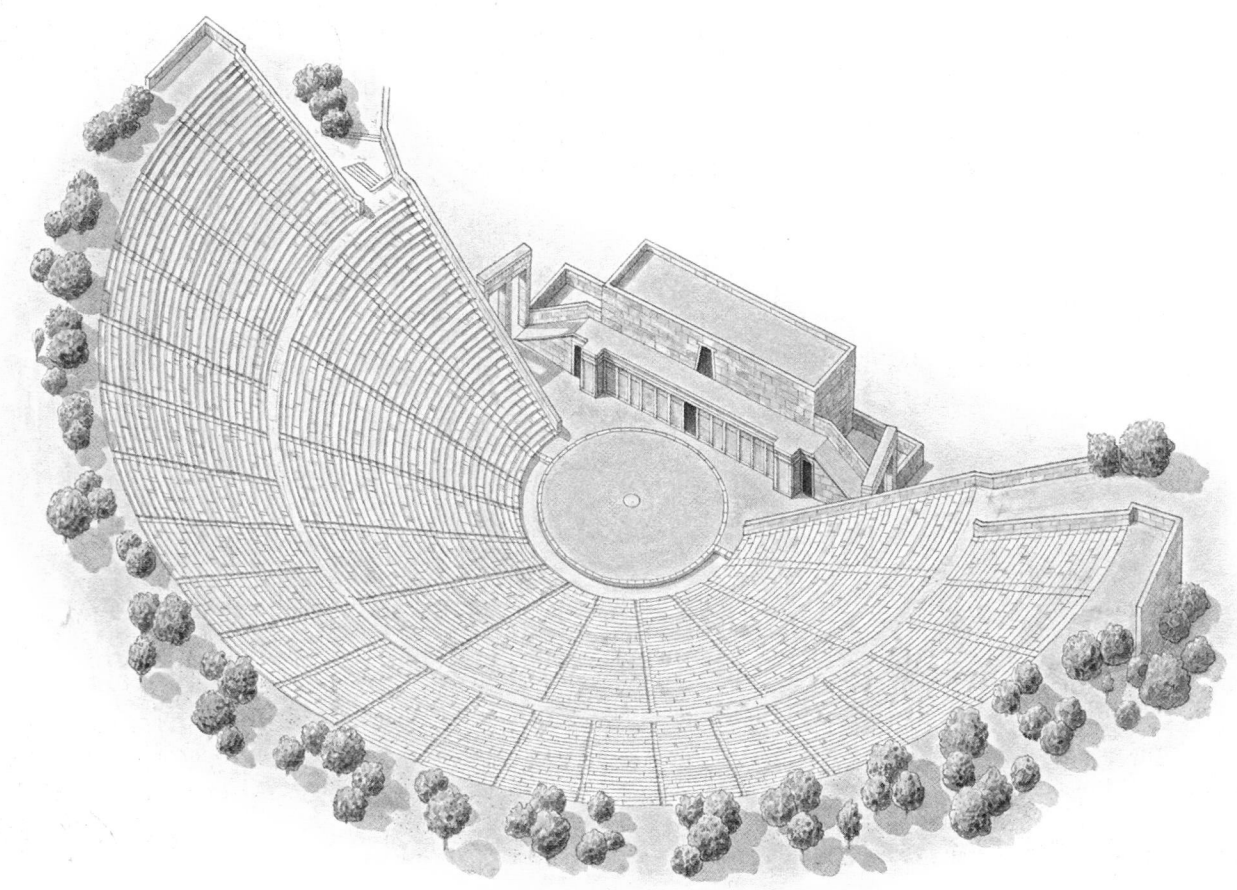

5.66 Theater, Epidauros. Early 3rd to 2nd centuries BCE

5.67 Plan of the theater, Epidauros (after Picard-Cambridge) the early third century BCE; its upper tier was completed in the second century BCE (figs. **5.66** and **5.67**). Row upon row of stone seats lined the sloping hillside, covering slightly more than a semicircle. To facilitate the audience's circulation, the architect grouped the seats in wedgelike sections (**cunei**), separated by staircases; a wide horizontal corridor divides the upper and lower sections. Actors performed in the level circle at the center, with a stage building (**skene**) behind as a backdrop, containing utility rooms for storage and dressing. Because it was open to the sky, no roof supports obstructed the audience's view of the performance, and many of the seats offered spectacular vistas across the landscape as well. Yet perhaps the most astonishing feature of the theater is its acoustics, which visitors can still experience: Its funnel shape carries the slightest whisper up to the highest points of the auditorium. This form is familiar to theatergoers today, a testament to its success.

THE PHAROS AT ALEXANDRIA In Alexandria, on the northwest coast of the Nile Delta, a vast and innovative lighthouse was a testament to the city's cosmopolitan nature and the vitality of shipping and commerce throughout the Hellenistic Mediterranean (fig. **5.68**). Alexander the Great founded the city to a grid design by Dinocrites of Rhodes, but the famed lighthouse, or Pharos, was not begun until the reign of Ptolemy I, in ca. 279 BCE, and was completed under his son, Ptolemy II Philadelphos. Some sources attribute it to an architect named Sostratus. The building has long collapsed, but a French team has recently recovered some of its blocks in underwater excavations. Together with mosaic depictions and medieval descriptions, archaeological evidence suggests a building with a square, slightly tapering base, an octagonal central drum, and a tholos-like element, crowned by a huge bronze statue at the dizzying height of about 400 feet. Ancient sources describe a fire at the summit,

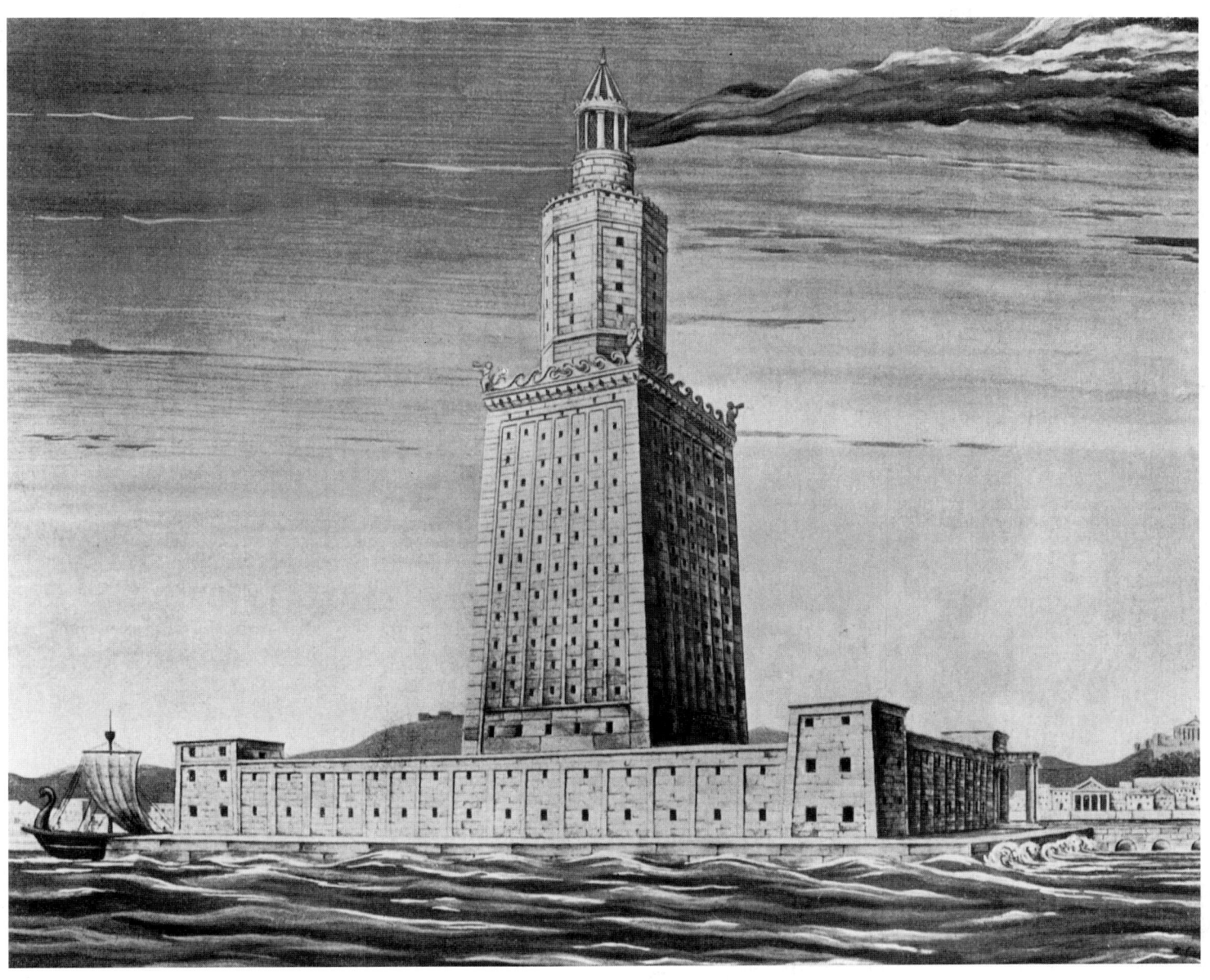

5.68 Alexandria (Egypt), Pharos (lighthouse) completed under Ptolemy II Philadelphos 280–79 BCE, height over 394 ft (120 m); one of the Seven Wonders of the World

and an annular corridor circled up through the tower, wide enough for mules to climb to the top with fuel—a type of petroleum called naphtha, perhaps, that is found in ponds. Yet archaeologists are uncertain how to reconcile a fire with a stone tholos, which would have cracked if exposed to intense heat. The building became an icon for the city. Its monumentality earned it a place among the seven wonders of the ancient world, and it was widely imitated by other cities.

Hellenistic Sculpture: Expression and Movement

Hellenistic sculptors also responded to the cultural changes of the Hellenistc world. Fourth-century BCE sculptors had explored the portrayal of emotion and three-dimensional movement, and their Hellenistic successors made further radical strides in these directions. Both resulted in heightened drama and viewer involvement. That said, one can make only broad generalizations about Hellenistic sculpture, as it is notoriously difficult to date and to attribute to a firm place of origin. Often it is style alone that leads scholars to ascribe a sculpture to this period, and even that is not always straightforward: Although there is good evidence of a dialogue between sculptors, they were working throughout a vast territory where numerous local influences were at play, making the body of material much less homogeneous than Classical sculpture.

PORTRAITURE A chief development in sculpture in this period was portraiture. If Archaic artists depicted individuals at all, they represented them with the all-purpose figures of kouroi and

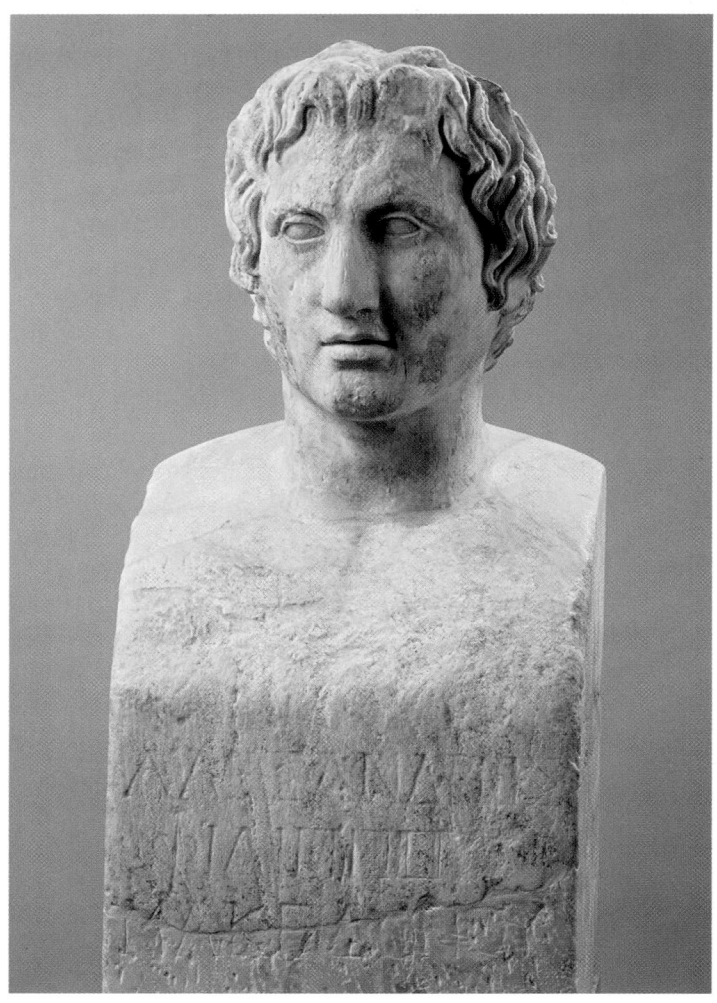

5.69 Lysippos. Portrait of Alexander the Great, the "Azara Herm." Roman copy after an original of the late 4th century BCE. Marble, height 27" (68 cm). Musée du Louvre, Paris

korai. Individual likenesses were unknown in art of the Classical period, which sought a timeless ideal. A copy of a famous sculpture of Perikles dating from about 425 BCE, for instance, differs from the idealized youths of the Parthenon frieze only in that the Perikles wears a beard and a helmet. Later, in the mid-fourth century BCE, portraiture became a major branch of Greek sculpture, and it continued to flourish in Hellenistic times. One of the catalysts for this change was Alexander the Great himself. Recognizing the power of a consistent visual image, he retained Lysippos as the exclusive creator of his sculpted portraits. No surviving original preserves Lysippos' touch, but scholars consider the so-called "Azara Herm" to be relatively faithful to its model (fig. **5.69**). To be sure, the face has an idealized quality: Its planes are smooth, especially around the brow. Yet individuality emerges in the unruly hair, raised at the front in Alexander the Great's characteristic cowlick (or *anastole*), and in the twist of the head, which removes the portrait from a timeless realm and animates it

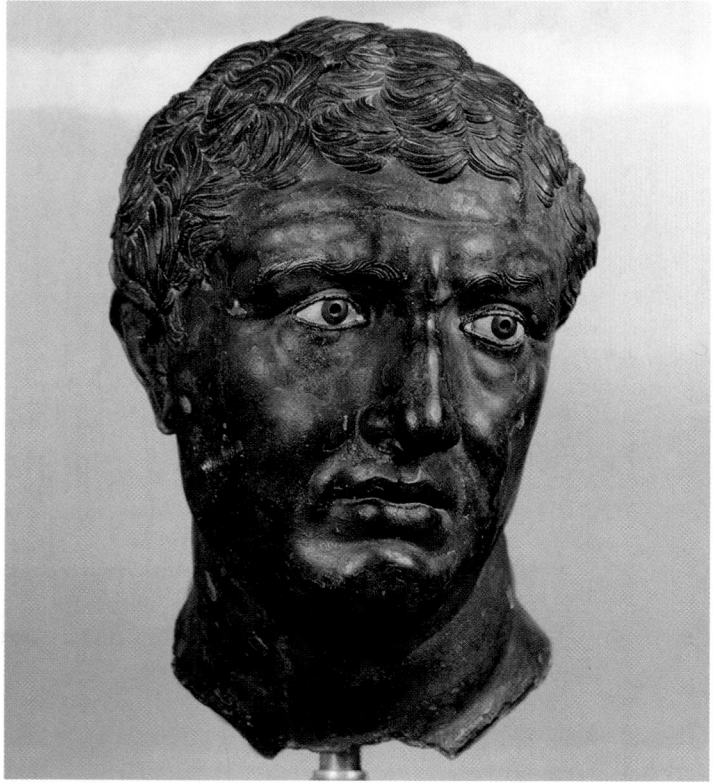

5.70 *Portrait Head*, from Delos. ca. 80 BCE. Bronze, height 12¾" (32.4 cm). National Archaeological Museum, Athens. Ministry of Culture Archaeological Receipts Fund. 14612

with action. Moreover, Alexander does not engage with a viewer, but has a distant gaze. These characteristics would become emblematic of Alexander, and Hellenistic and Roman generals would adopt them as attributes in their own portraiture. With this image, the individual came to inhabit the sculpture, and portraiture began to flourish as a genre.

As with so many Greek sculptures, original Hellenistic portraits are extremely rare. One is an early first-century BCE bronze head from Delos (fig. 5.70), which may portray a trader: The island of Delos was a lively trading port, and many merchants there became extremely wealthy. Unlike the Romans, the Greeks did not isolate an individual's personality in portrait busts, but considered it to animate the full body. Thus this head is just a fragment of a full-length statue. The artist fused the heroic qualities of Alexander's likeness—the whimsical turn of the head, for instance, and the full head of hair—with modeled surfaces. The fleshy features, the uncertain mouth, and the furrowed brows capture an individual likeness. If they also suggest character traits, it is hard to read them with any precision at such a cultural distance.

Like architects, Hellenistic sculptors engaged their audience in the experience of their work, and favored dramatic subjects infused with emotion. The *Dying Trumpeter*, preserved in a Roman copy (fig. 5.71), probably belonged on one of two statue bases found in the Sanctuary of Athena on the Akropolis of Pergamon, and commemorated Attalos I's defeat of the Gauls in about 233 BCE. Gone is the Classical tradition of referring to the enemy through mythological analogy (see figs. 5.35 and 5.44). Instead, the sculptor specifically identifies the enemy as a Gaul through his bushy hair and moustache, and by the torque, or braided gold band, that he wears around his neck. Gone, too, is any suggestion of the inferiority of the vanquished. The Gaul dies nobly, sinking quietly to the ground or struggling to prop himself up, as blood pours from a wound in his chest. His body is powerful, his strength palpable. He faces his agonies alone, mindless of any viewer. A viewer, in turn, is drawn in by the privateness of the moment, and drawn around the sculpture by the pyramidal composition and the foreshortening witnessed from every angle. The *Dying Trumpeter* was probably one sculpture in a group, but the victor, always present in Classical battle scenes, was absent. The monument celebrates the conqueror's valor by exalting the enemy he overcame; the greater the enemy, the greater the victory. Pliny records a famous sculpture by Epigonos of a trumpet player, and this Roman copy may reflect that work.

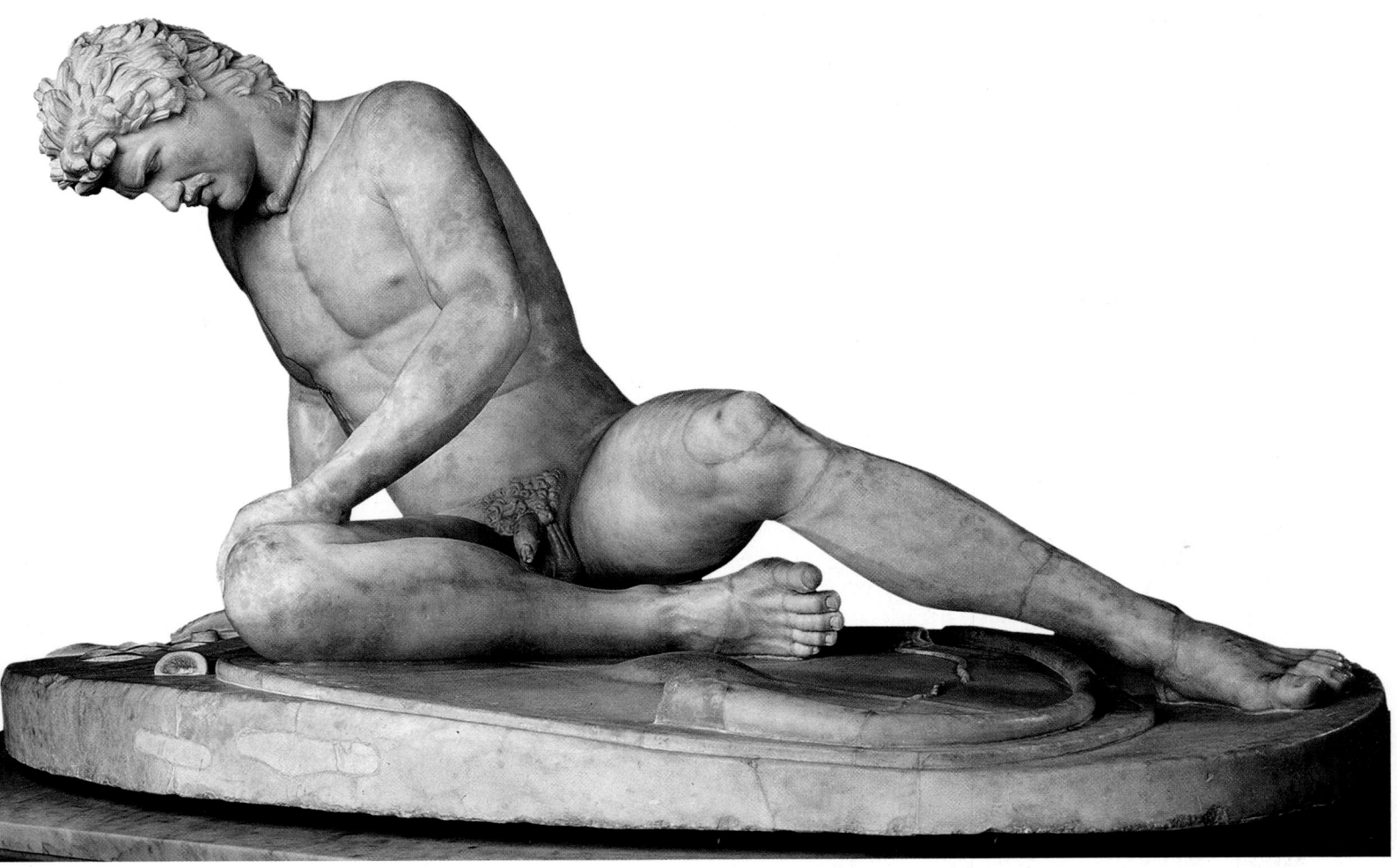

5.71   Epigonos of Pergamon (?). *Dying Trumpeter*. Perhaps a Roman copy after a bronze original of ca. 230–220 BCE, from Pergamon, Turkey. Marble, life-size. Museo Capitolino, Rome

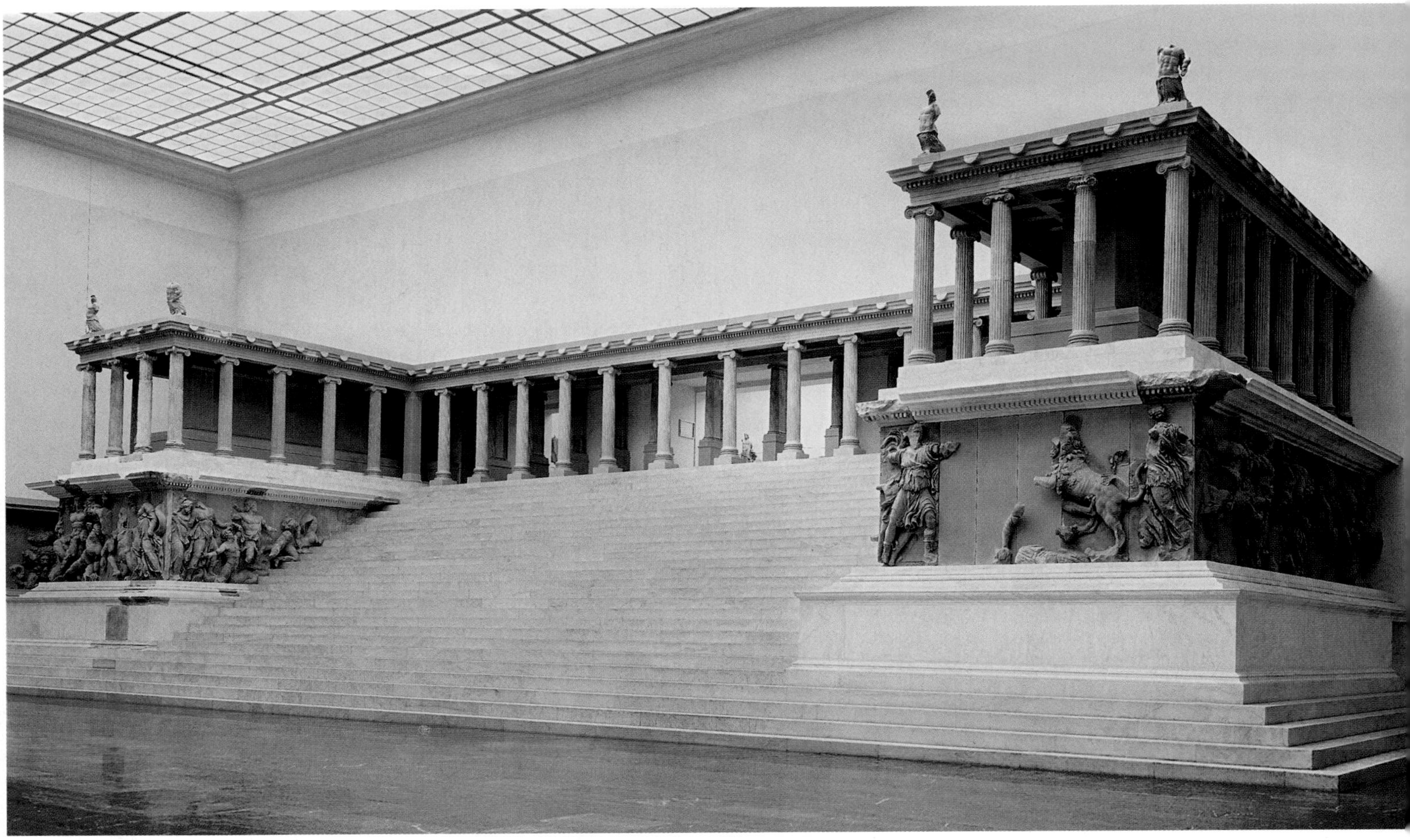

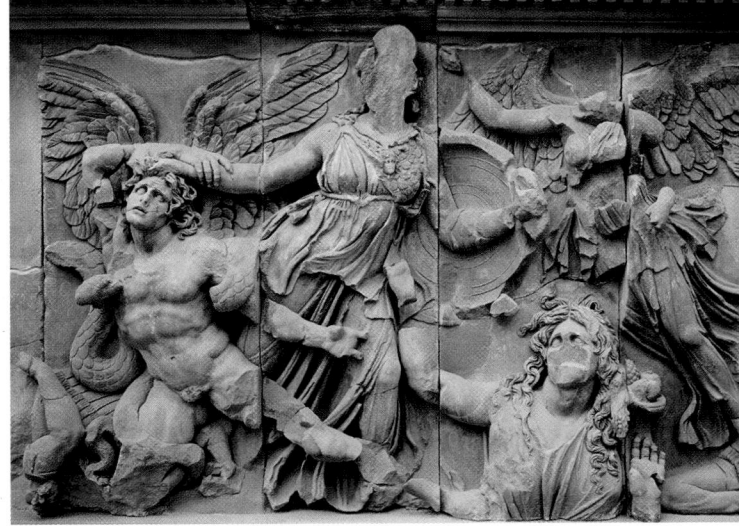

5.72 West front of Great Altar of Zeus at Pergamon (restored). Staatliche Museen zu Berlin, Preussischer Kulturbesitz, Antikensammlung

DRAMATIC VICTORY MONUMENTS Sculptures decorating the Great Altar of Zeus at Pergamon exemplify the highly emotional, dramatic style at its height (figs. **5.72** and **5.73**). The monument dates to the second quarter of the second century BCE, when Eumenes II, or Attalos II, built it to commemorate territorial victories over Pontos and Bithynia and the establishment of a grand victory festival, the *Nikephoria*. The altar stood high on a podium within a large rectangular enclosure defined by an Ionic colonnade. A wide staircase at the front provided access. The altar and its enclosure, which both go by the name of the Great Altar, stood on a terrace on the Pergamene Akropolis. A German team excavated the monument from 1878 to 1886, and its entire west front, with the great flight of stairs leading to its entrance, has been reconstructed in Berlin (see fig. 5.72). The vast enclosure belongs to a long Ionian tradition of massive altars, but this is by far the most elaborate extant example. Its boldest feature is a frieze encircling the base, which extends over 400 feet in length and over 7 feet in height. Its subject, the Battle of the Gods and Giants, was a familiar theme in architectural sculpture. Here, as before, it worked allegorically, symbolizing Eumenes' victories. Never before, however, had artists treated the subject so extensively or so dramatically. About 84 figures crowd the composition, interspersed with numerous animals. This was no mean feat: The designer must have relied upon research by scholars

5.73 *Athena and Alkyoneus*, from east side of Great Frieze of the Great Altar of Zeus at Pergamon, second quarter of the 2nd century BCE. Marble, height 7'6" (2.29 m). Staatliche Museen zu Berlin, Preussischer Kulturbesitz, Antikensammlung

working in the Pergamene library (such as Krates of Mallos, a renowned Stoic theoretician and literary critic) to identify protagonists for this great battle. The scholars may also have assisted

J. J. Winckelmann and the Apollo Belvedere

Despite the best efforts of contemporary art historians, many assessments of art today are deeply informed by a notion of beauty rooted in Greek **Classicism**. This bias has been present through the ages since antiquity; but its abiding power is also the legacy of a pioneering German antiquarian, Johann Joachim Winckelmann, who is often called the father of art history. Born in Stendal in Prussia in 1717, Winckelmann studied in Halle and Jena before becoming librarian for Count Heinrich von Bünau near Dresden. It was in von Bünau's library that he gained an education in the visual arts, which led to his first publication, *Reflections on the Imitation of Greek Works of Art in Painting and Sculpture*, in 1755. In that same year he moved to Rome, and was soon appointed librarian and advisor to Cardinal Alessandro Albani. In 1764, after the publication of his seminal *History of Art of Antiquity*, he became papal antiquary and director of antiquities in Rome. *Unpublished Antiquities*, of 1767, was his last work before his rather ignominious death a year later at the hands of a petty criminal.

The impact of his published works has been enormous. He was first, for instance, to determine that most Greek sculptures (which he often conflated with their Roman copies) represented not historical figures but mythological characters. Even more significant was his contention that Greek art captured an ideal beauty that transcended nature. He established a model for the development of art that divided art history into periods that coincided with political events. The Older Style was the precursor to the High or Sublime Style. Next came the Beautiful Style, and finally the Style of the Imitators. In ancient art, these correspond to the Archaic, fifth-century BCE Classical, Late Classical, and Hellenistic and Roman periods. This progression from rise to eventual decline still lies at the heart of most studies of art history, regardless of the era. When it came to assigning works of art to these phases, Winckelmann was, in a sense, trapped by his own scheme. Reluctant to allot works he admired to the "decline" phase of Hellenistic and Roman art, he often dated sculptures much too early; such was the case with the *Laocoön* (see *The Art Historian's Lens,* page 183), which he placed in the fourth century BCE, and the *Apollo Belvedere*, which he considered a Greek original.

The *Apollo Belvedere* first came to light again in the fifteenth century CE, and quickly made its way into the collection of Pope Julius II. It represents the god in an open pose, with his left arm outstretched, perhaps to hold a bow. Winckelmann was one of many antiquarians to be profoundly moved by the statue. Combined in its form he perceived both power and desirability, and he penned a rhapsodic description of it that is tinged with eroticizing overtones. "I forget all else at the sight of this miracle of art," he wrote. "My breast seems to enlarge and swell with reverence." Few scholars share his enthusiasm for the piece today. Its significance for art historians resides more in its modern reception—the role it played for admiring Renaissance artists, for instance—than in its place in ancient culture. As for its date, most scholars now identify it as a second-century CE copy or interpretation of a Greek original; the latter is sometimes attributed to Leochares, who worked at the end of the fourth century BCE.

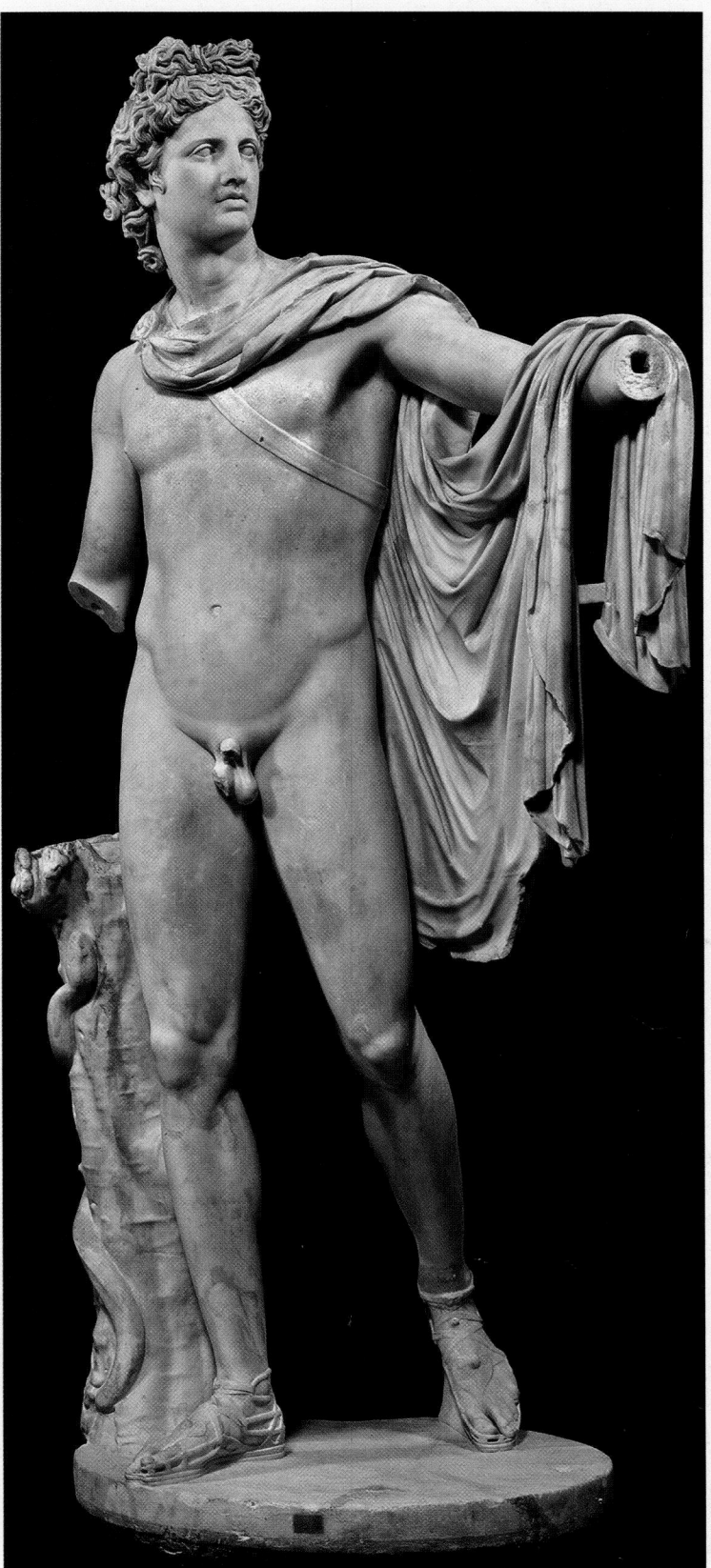

Apollo Belvedere. Roman marble copy, probably of a Greek original of the late 4th century BCE. Height 7'4" (2.3 m). Musei Vaticani, Rome

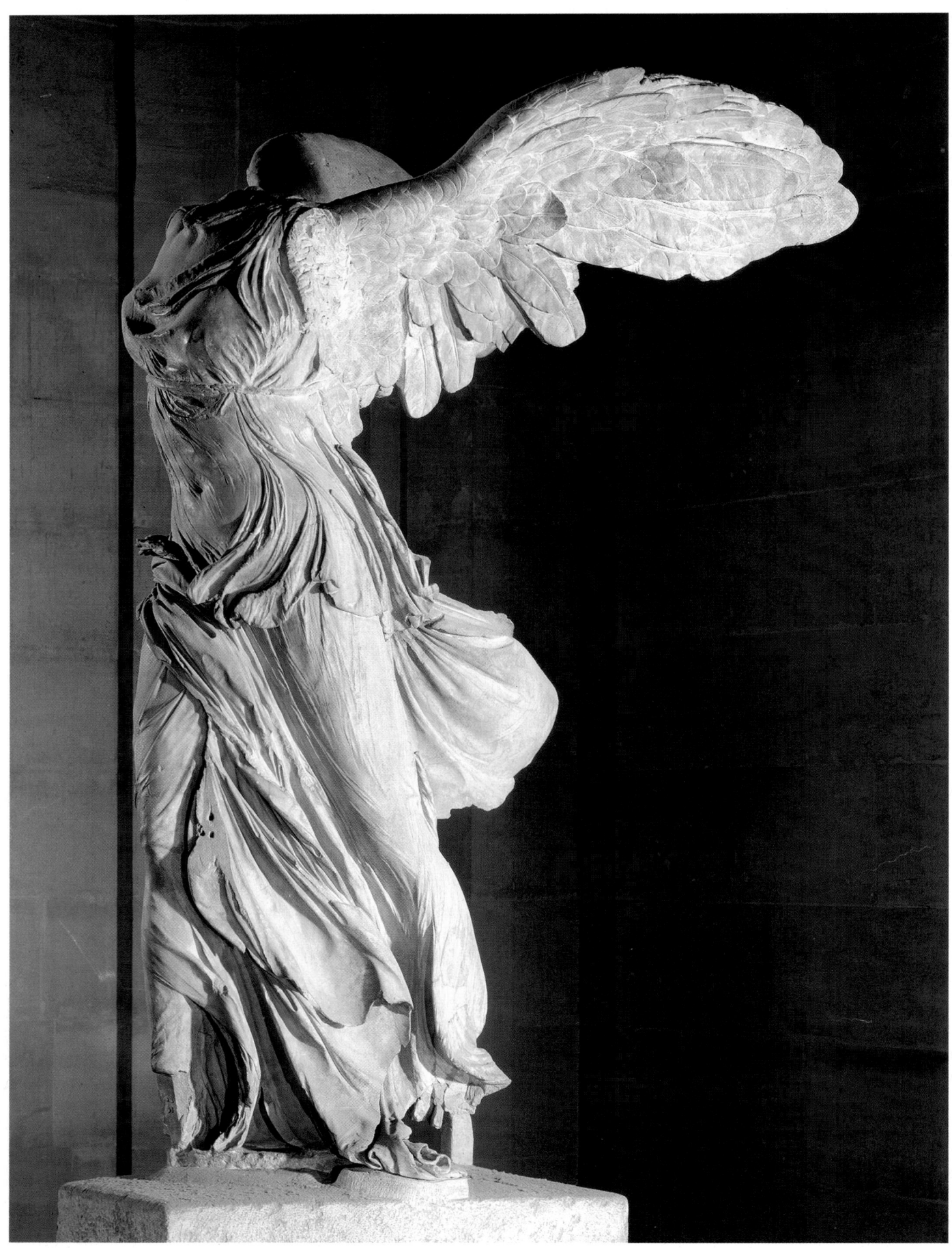

5.74 Pythokritos of Rhodes (?). *Nike of Samothrace*. ca. 190 BCE. Marble, height 8' (2.44 m). Musée du Louvre, Paris with creating a balanced and resonant composition, for despite the chaotic appearance of the mêlée, guiding principles lurk behind it. Modern scholars still struggle to understand these principles fully, even with the help of inscriptions naming some of the gods on the molding in the entablature and giants on the base molding. On the eastern frieze, facing the sanctuary's great propylon and the rising sun, were the Olympian gods. The most prominent position belonged to Athena. On the south, drenched in sun, were heavenly lights such as Helios; on the shadowy north were divinities of the night. Deities of the earth and sea were on the west. Compositional parallels unified the four sides. The frieze is direct evidence of the Hellenistic scholarly tradition at work.

On the other hand, it is also deeply imbued with Hellenistic theatricality. Sculptors carved the figures so deeply, and undercut them in places so forcefully, that they are almost in the round. The high relief creates a vivid interplay of light and dark, and on the staircase, the figures seem to spill out onto the steps and climb alongside an ascending visitor. Muscular bodies rush at each other, overlapping and entwining (see fig. 5.73). The giants' snaky extremities twist and curl, echoed in their deeply drilled tendrils of ropelike hair. Wings beat and garments blow furiously in the wind or twist around those they robe, not to reveal the anatomy beneath but to create motion; they have a life of their own and their texture contrasts with the smoothness of the giants' flesh. The giants' emotion is palpable: They agonize in the torment of their defeat, their brows creased in pain, their eyes deep-set in an exaggerated style reminiscent of Skopas. A writhing motion pervades the entire design, and links the figures in a single continuous rhythm. This rhythm, and the quiet Classicism of the gods' faces, so starkly opposed to the giants' faces, create a unity that keeps the violence of the struggle from exploding its architectural frame—but only just. For the first time in the long tradition of its depiction, a viewer has a visceral sense of what a terrible cosmic crisis this battle would be.

The weight and solidity of the great gigantomachy make it a fitting frieze for its place on the building's platform. A second, lighter frieze encircled the inside of the colonnade, and may be slightly later. This frieze portrays the life of Telephos, son of Herakles and legendary founder of Mysia, the region of Pergamon.

Though an altar first and foremost, the Great Altar of Zeus also commemorates Eumenes' victory. Its magnificence underscores the precariousness of the Hellenistic world, and the importance of conquest to a ruler's image. Dramatic location and style combine in another victory monument of the early second century BCE, the *Nike of Samothrace* (fig. **5.74**). The sculpture probably celebrates the naval victories—*nike* means "victory"—of Eudamos, an admiral in command of the fleet at Rhodes, over Antiochos the Great and the Seleucid forces in 190 BCE. The Rhodian marble of the sculpture's base, and evidence from inscriptions, suggest that the sculpture comes from Rhodes, and may be the work of the renowned artist Pythokritos from that island. The victory goddess seems to be landing on the prow of a ship, as if to bestow a crown of victory upon Eudamos. Alternatively, she could be about to take flight. Her massive wings soar out behind her, stretching the limits of the marble's tensile strength. The lift of the wings makes the whole statue appear weightless, despite the great mass of stone: In a new variant of the chiastic stance, neither leg holds the body's full weight. The wings and the drapery give the sculpture its energy. The drapery swirls around the goddess's body, exposing her anatomy and stressing the sensuous curves of her form. Yet it has its own function as well: Its swirling motion suggests the headwind she struggles against, which, in turn, balances the rushing forward thrust of her arrival. The drapery creates the environment around the figure.

This sculpture is a rare instance of a monument coming to light, in 1863, in its original location—in the Sanctuary of the Great Gods at Samothrace, where it must have been a dedication. The stone prow stood high on a terrace overlooking the theater and the sea, within a pool of water that must have reflected the Nike's white marble forms. The pool was raised above a second water basin filled with rocks, to evoke a coastline.

PLAYFULNESS IN SCULPTURE Scholars use the term **baroque** to describe the extreme emotions, extravagant gestures, and theatrical locations that characterize the Great Altar of Zeus and the *Nike of Samothrace*. Art historians first used the word to describe seventeenth-century CE art, but the scholars of Hellenistic art borrowed it on recognizing similarities between the two styles. With its dramatic qualities, the Hellenistic baroque style has tended to eclipse the many other contemporary movements in sculpture. One of these is a penchant for works of a light-hearted and sometimes faintly erotic quality. These appear to be a reaction to the weightiness of the baroque style, and sometimes they have an element of parody to them, suggesting that the sculptor hoped to reduce the grand themes of the classical and baroque styles to a comical level. Scholars describe these works somewhat inadequately by the term **Rococo**, which they also borrow from scholarship on later European art. Some of them represent amorous interactions between divine or semidivine and human figures. In the example shown here, dating to about 100 BCE, Aphrodite wields a slipper to fend off the advances of a lecherous Pan, the half-man, half-goat god of the forests (fig. **5.75**). Eros hovers mischievously between them. With her sensuous roundness and her modest hand gesture, the goddess recalls Praxiteles' bathing *Aphrodite of Knidos* (see fig. 5.56). Here, the erotic possibilities that Praxiteles dangled provocatively in the air are unambiguously answered, and by a humorously undesirable partner. Rather than grasping for her drapery to preserve her dignity, the majestic Aphrodite is reduced to grabbing a slipper in self-defense. This sculpture is another rare example of a Greek original found in the location in which it was used in antiquity. Archaeologists unearthed it in the clubhouse of a group of merchants from Berytus (Beirut) on Delos. Still, it is unclear whether the sculptural group was a cult image or a decorative piece.

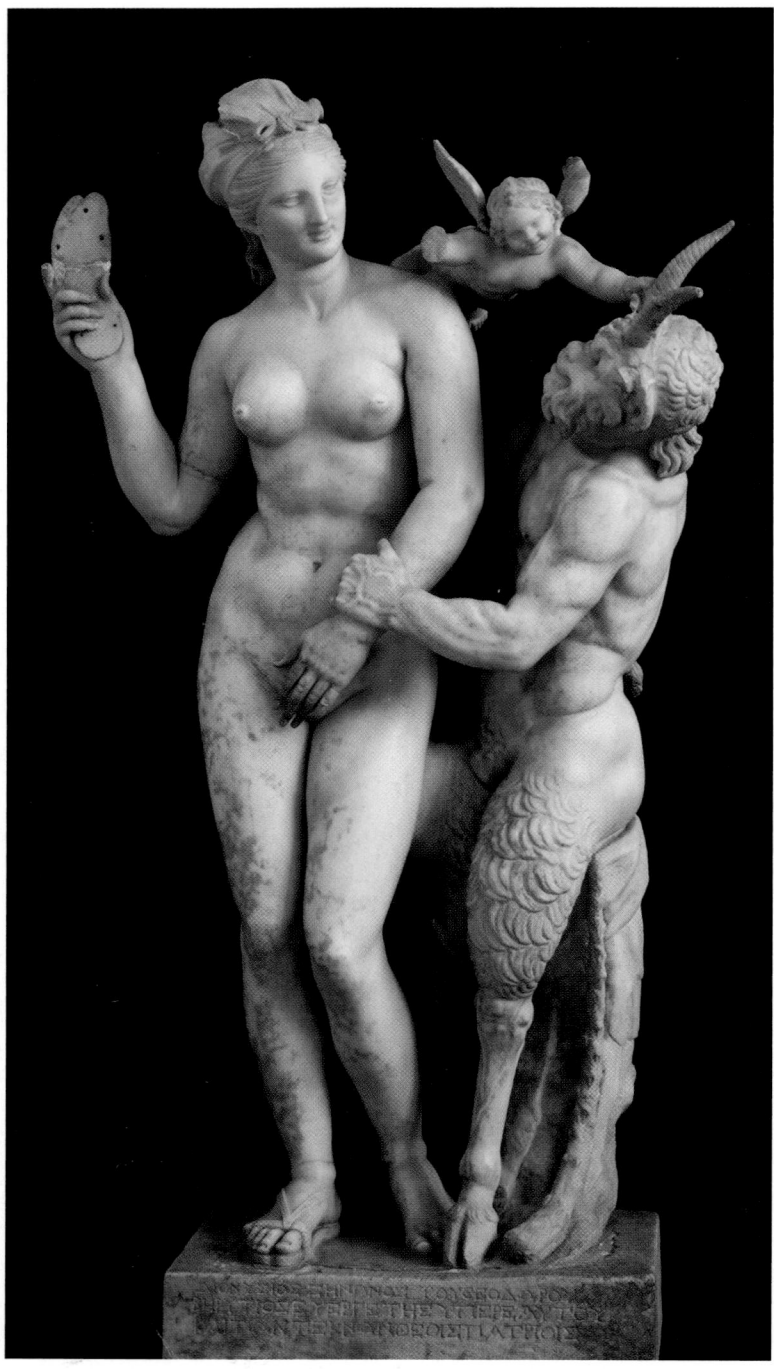

Wrinkles cover her face, and the skin on her exposed shoulder and chest sags with age. She wears a buckled tunic, which identifies her as a member of an affluent social class. Other sculptures of this kind focus on the ravaging effects of a rustic life on the poor—an old shepherdess, for instance; yet in this sculpture, the artist explores drunkenness and old age. With her wine jar and her garment slipping from her shoulder, she may even be in ironic dialogue with figures of Aphrodite with her water vessel (see fig. 5.56). Without further insights into the cultural context for the image, it is hard to know if the sculptor intended to offer a sympathetic view of his subject, exalting her nobility, or to engage in hard social commentary.

5.75 *Aphrodite, Pan, and Eros*. ca. 100 BCE. Marble, height 51" (132 cm). National Archaeological Museum, Athens

HELLENISTIC REALISM Scholars sometimes group these light-hearted sculptures together with a series of works depicting unidealized and realistic everyday life. Their genre is known as Hellenistic realism, and a sculpture of a drunken old woman illustrates it well (fig. **5.76**). Known from Roman copies, this piece has at times been ascribed to Myron of Thebes, who may have worked at Pergamon. The evidence is slim, and the figure may fit better with the cultural context of Alexandria, where realism seems to have been particularly prevalent. The woman crouches on the ground, clasping a wine bottle, her head flung far back.

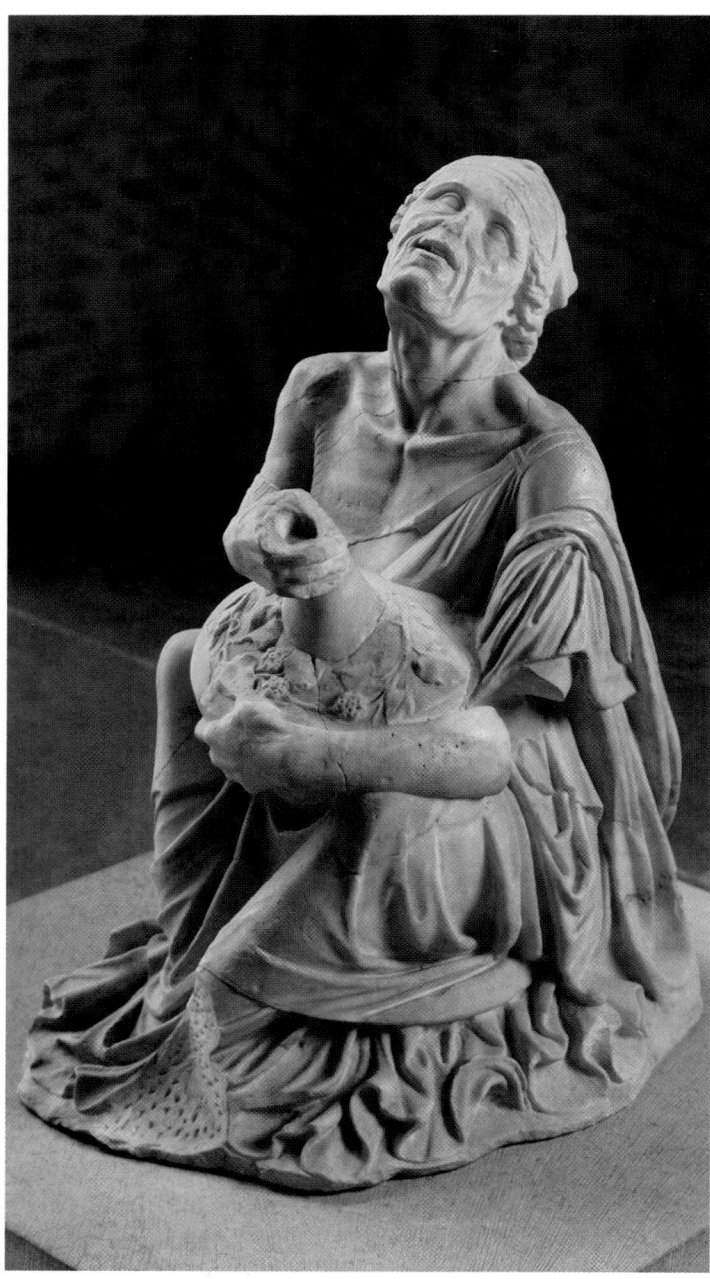

5.76 *Drunken Old Woman*. Roman copy of an original of the late 3rd or late 2nd century BCE. Marble, height 36" (92 cm). Staatliche Antikensammlungen und Glyptothek, Munich

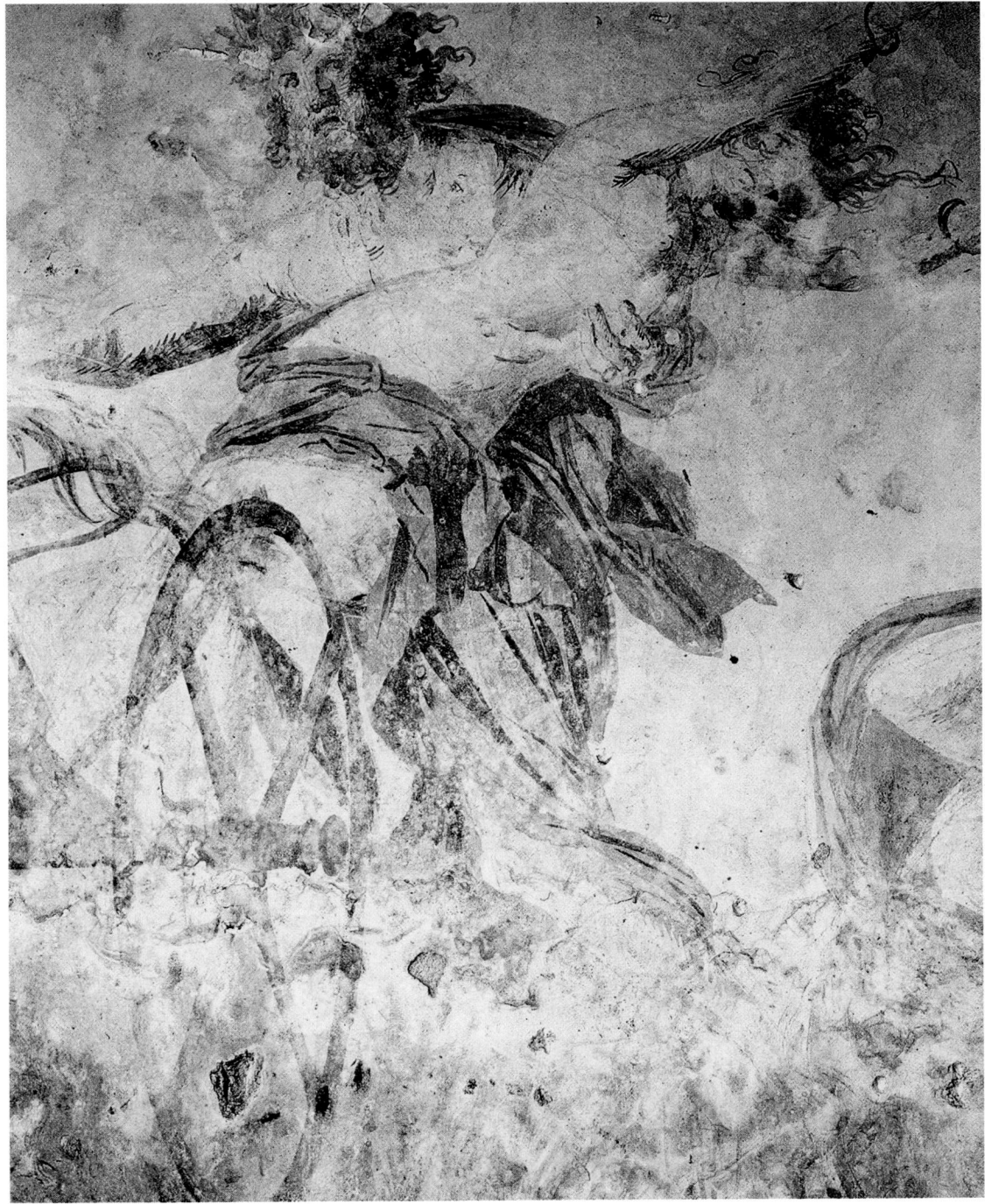

5.77 *The Abduction of Persephone*, Tomb I, Vergina, Macedonia (detail). ca. 340–330 BCE

Hellenistic Painting

It was in the fourth century BCE that Greek wall painting came into its own. Pliny names a number of leading painters, but no surviving work can be attributed to them to give proof of his words. (See www.myartslab.com.) All the same, paintings are preserved in Macedonian tombs, several of which have recently come—and keep coming—to light in northern Greece (in the region of Macedonia). These tombs are of great importance because they contain the only surviving relatively complete Greek wall paintings, and offer a tantalizing glimpse of what painters

could accomplish. The section shown here (fig. **5.77**) comes from a small tomb at Vergina, dating to about 340–330 BCE. The subject, the abduction of Persephone, is appropriate to the funereal setting. Pluto, ruler of the underworld, carries away Persephone to be his queen. Thanks to Zeus' intervention, Persephone would be allowed to return to the world of the living for six months of every year. Here, the artist has chosen the moment when Pluto seizes Persephone into his speeding chariot, her handmaiden rearing back in fright and horror. This is the most harrowing moment, before Persephone knows that Zeus will find a compromise, when

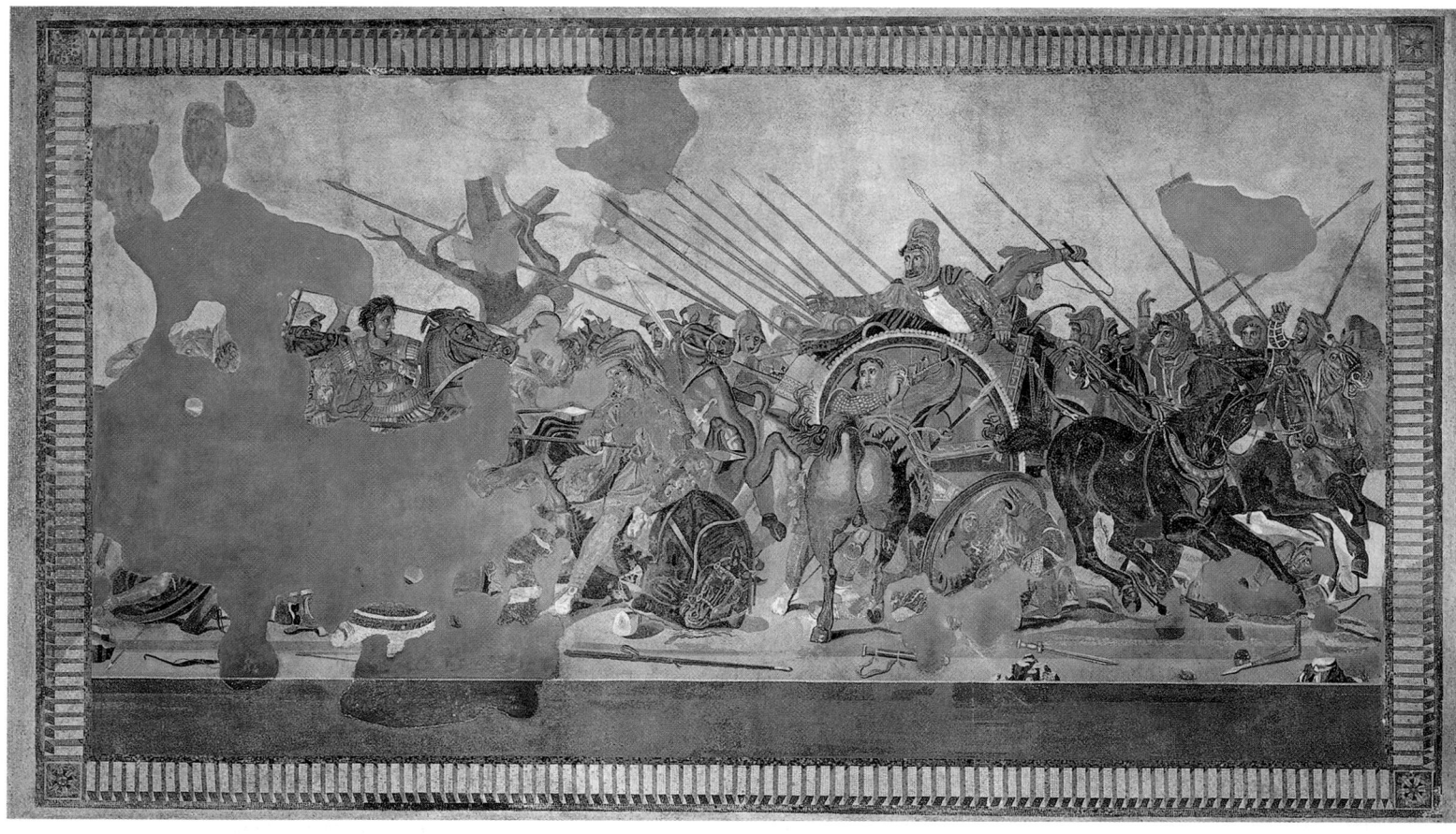

5.78 *The Battle of Issos* or *Battle of Alexander and the Persians*. Mosaic copy from Pompeii of a Hellenistic painting of ca. 315 BCE. ca. 100 BCE. 8'11" × 16'9½" (2.7 × 5.1 m). Museo Archaeologico Nazionale, Naples

her futile struggle seems the only possible escape from the underworld. The painting captures all of the myth's drama. Persephone flings her body backward, while the chariot rushes onward with her captor; their bodies cross as a sign of conflict. The chariot plunges toward a viewer, its wheel sharply foreshortened. Masterful brushwork animates the scene. With swift flourishes, the artist sends hair and drapery flying, and lends plasticity to the garments. Hatchwork rounds out the bodies' flesh, as on the arms and shoulders. The colors are brilliant washes, with shading for texture. Literary sources attribute the discovery of **shading** (the modulation of volume by means of contrasting light and shade), known as skiagraphia, to a painter named Apollodorus, who used the technique perhaps as early as the fifth century BCE. They also associate **spatial perspective** (rendering recession of space) with Agatharchos and the art of stage scenery during the heyday of Athenian drama. The exploration and perfection of both devices during the course of the fourth century BCE illustrate the fascination with illusionism at this time.

Roman copies and imitations may also provide a general impression of Greek wall painting. According to Pliny, at the end of the fourth century BCE, Philoxenos of Eretria painted Alexander the Great's victory over Darius III at Issos. This is the subject of a large and masterful floor mosaic from a Pompeian house of about 100 BCE (fig. **5.78**), which could be a copy of Philoxenos' painting. Yet a female painter named Helen, from Alexandria, also painted the subject, and most scholars believe the mosaic copies her work. It depicts Darius and the fleeing Persians on the right and, in the badly damaged left-hand portion, the figure of Alexander. The mosaic follows a four-color scheme (yellow, red, black, and white) that is known to have been widely used in the late fourth century BCE. (See www.myartslab.com.) The crowding, the air of frantic excitement, the powerfully modeled and foreshortened forms, and the precise shadows also place the scene in the fourth century BCE, as does the minimal treatment of landscape, suggested by a single barren tree to the left of center.

The abundance of surviving Greek art from a period of over seven centuries is a testimony to great intellectual fervor and political change. Devastating wars with their own and neighboring peoples continually shaped Greek culture and art. In the course of those centuries, Greek art changed almost unrecognizably. From the abstract forms of the Geometric period, it transformed itself into the myriad styles of the Hellenistic period. To be sure, the quest for naturalism in sculpture and painting was a driving force in this change. Yet that quest in art was merely part of a more pervasive philosophical outlook, which led to a fascination with proportions and with scholarly analysis of the arts. If the Persian and Peloponnesian Wars, and the Macedonian conquests took their toll, they also fueled the urge to express emotion in the visual arts, and to appeal to an individual's personal experience of the world.

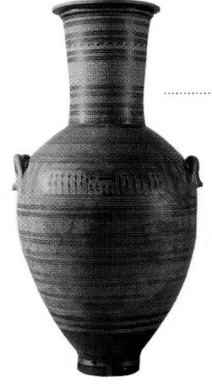

ca. 750 BCE *Dipylon Vase*

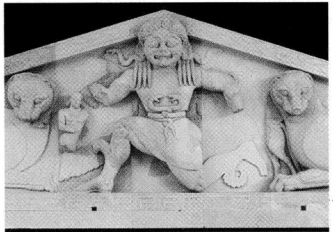

600 BCE Temple of Artemis, Corfu

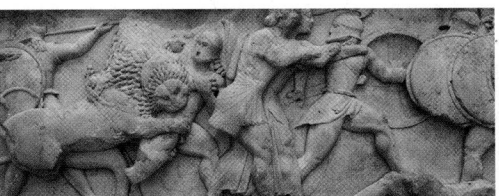

ca. 525 BCE Siphnian Treasury at Delphi

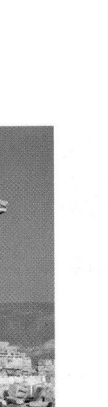

ca. 480 BCE *Kritios Boy*

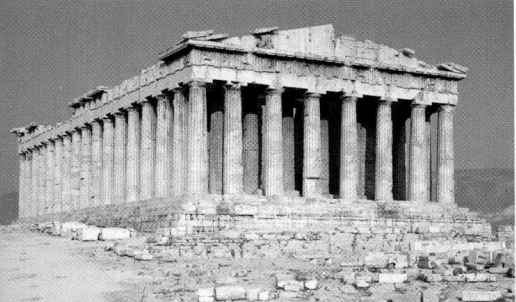

ca. 447 BCE Perikles orders the construction of the Parthenon

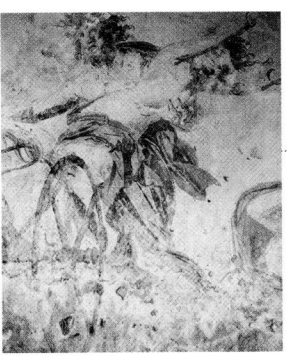

340–330 BCE *The Abduction of Persephone* at Vergina

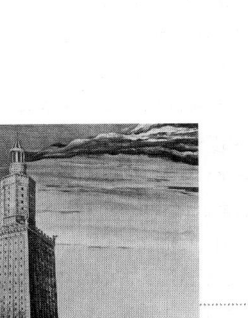

ca. 279 BCE Ptolemy I commissions the Pharos at Alexandria

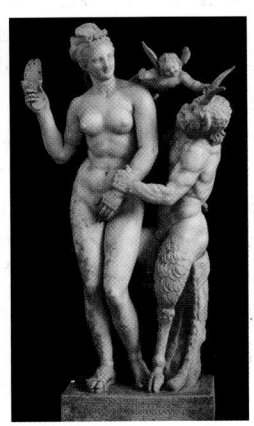

ca. 100 BCE *Aphrodite, Pan, and Eros*

Greek Art

800 BCE

◀ ca. 8th century BCE Homer writes *The Iliad* and *The Odyssey*
◀ 776 BCE First Olympic Games

700 BCE

◀ mid-7th century BCE Black-figured vase-painting technique develops
◀ ca. 650 BCE Greeks establish trading posts in Egypt
◀ 7th century BCE Doric and Ionic styles develop

600 BCE

500 BCE

ca. 518 BCE Construction of the Persian palace at Persepolis begins
◀ ca. 500 BCE Red-figured vase-painting technique becomes prevalent in Athens
490 BCE Greeks defeat the Persians at the Battle of Marathon
478 BCE Greek city-states found the Delian League against the Persians
458 BCE Aeschylus writes the *Oresteia* trilogy
◀ 431–404 BCE Peloponnesian War

400 BCE

◀ 387 BCE Plato founds the Academy in Athens

◀ 338 BCE Philip II of Macedon invades Greece
336–323 BCE Reign of Alexander the Great

300 BCE

200 BCE

◀ 168 BCE Romans conquer Macedon

100 BCE

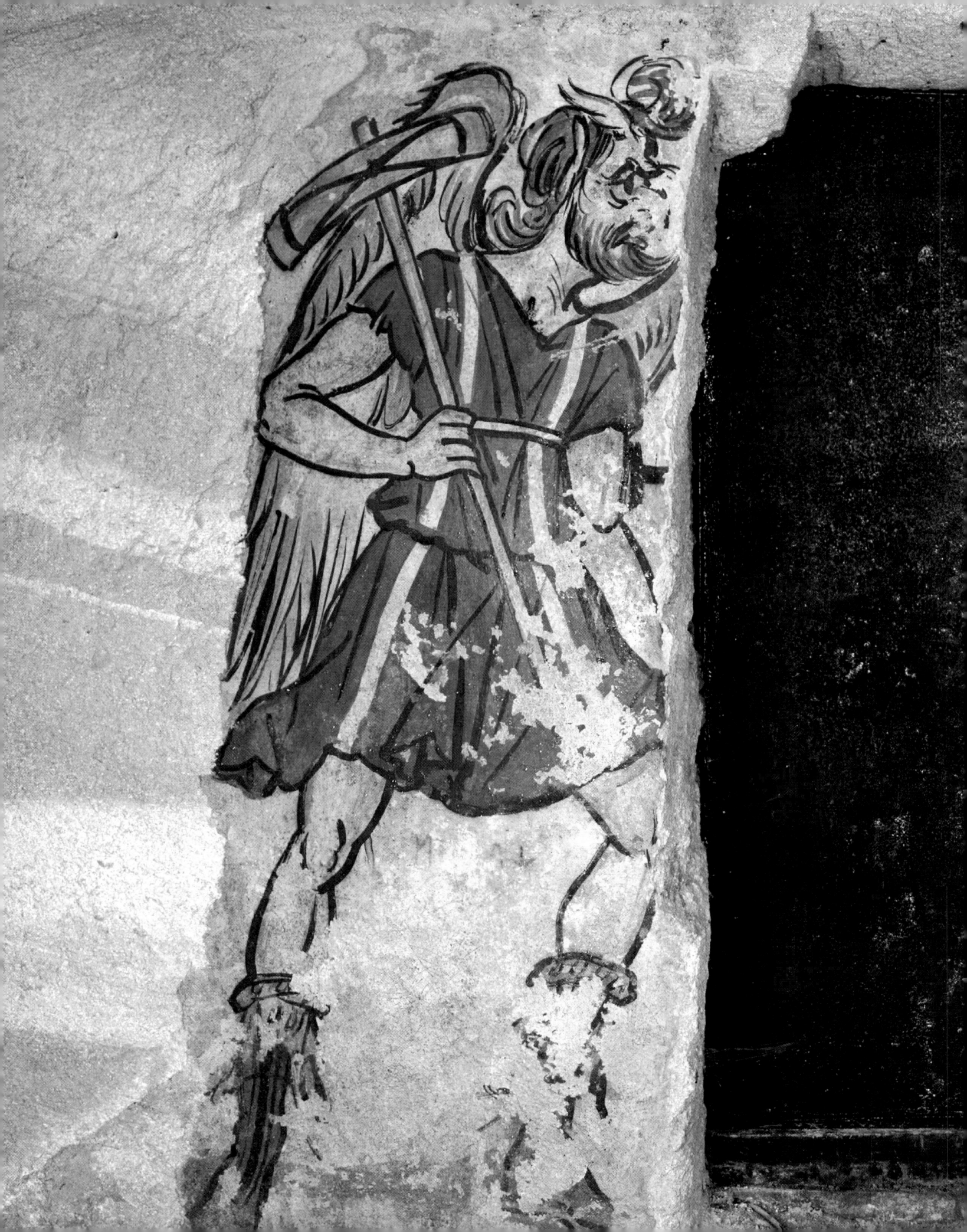

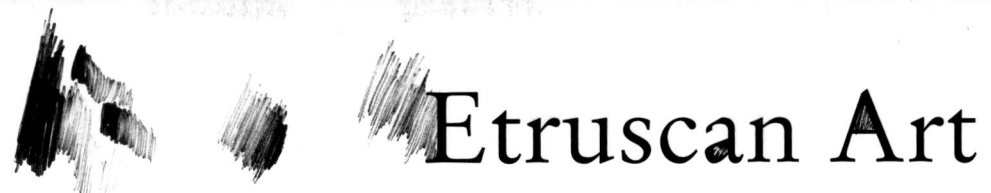

CHAPTER 6

Etruscan Art

ARLY ETRUSCAN CULTURE, KNOWN AS VILLANOVAN, APPEARED ON the Italian peninsula in the tenth century BCE. Who the Etruscans were remains a mystery; even in antiquity, writers disputed their origins. The Greek historian Herodotus believed that they had left their homeland of Lydia in Asia Minor in about 1200 BCE, and settled in what are now the Italian

regions of Tuscany, Umbria, and Lazio (map **6.1**). Recent DNA sampling may support his view. Others claimed they were indigenous. Wherever they came from, the Etruscans had strong cultural links with Asia Minor and the ancient Near East. In fact, their visual culture is a rich blend of distinctly Etruscan traits with influences from the East and from Greece. Since Greek citystates had established colonies in Italy from the eighth century BCE, contact between the two cultures was inevitable. The close relationship between Etruscan and Greek art forms has led scholars to define the stylistic periods of Etruscan art with terms that are similar to those used for Greece. Toward the end of the eighth century BCE the Etruscans began to use the Greek alphabet, and this makes it possible to read their inscriptions, which survive in the thousands; but since their language is unrelated to any other, we cannot always understand their meaning.

The Etruscans reached the height of their power in the seventh and sixth centuries BCE, coinciding with the Archaic period in Greece. They amassed great wealth from mining metals, and their cities rivaled those of the Greeks; their fleet dominated the western Mediterranean and protected a vast commercial network that competed with the Greeks and Phoenicians; and their territory extended from the lower Po Valley in the north to Naples in the south. But, like the Greeks, the Etruscans never formed a unified

Detail of figure 6.6, Charun from the Tomb of the Anina Family

nation. They remained a loose federation of individual city-states, united by a common language and religion, but given to conflict and slow to unite against a common enemy. This may have been one cause of their gradual downfall. In 474 BCE, the Etruscans' archrival, Syracuse, defeated the Etruscan fleet. And during the later fifth and fourth centuries BCE, one Etruscan city after another fell to the Romans. By 270 BCE, all the Etruscan citystates had lost their independence to Rome, although if we are to judge by the splendor of their tombs during this period of political struggle, many still prospered.

The bulk of our knowledge about Etruscan culture comes from art, and especially from their monumental tombs. These structures provide information about Etruscan building practices, and artists often painted them with scenes that reveal a glimpse of Etruscan life. Objects found within them attest to the Etruscans' reputation as fine sculptors and metalworkers. Large numbers of painted vases from Athens have also come to light in tombs, demonstrating the Etruscans' close trade ties with Greece.

FUNERARY ART

As with burials elsewhere in prehistoric Europe, early burials on the Italian peninsula were modest. The living either buried the deceased in shallow graves or cremated them, and placed the ashes, in a pottery vessel or cinerary urn, in a simple pit.

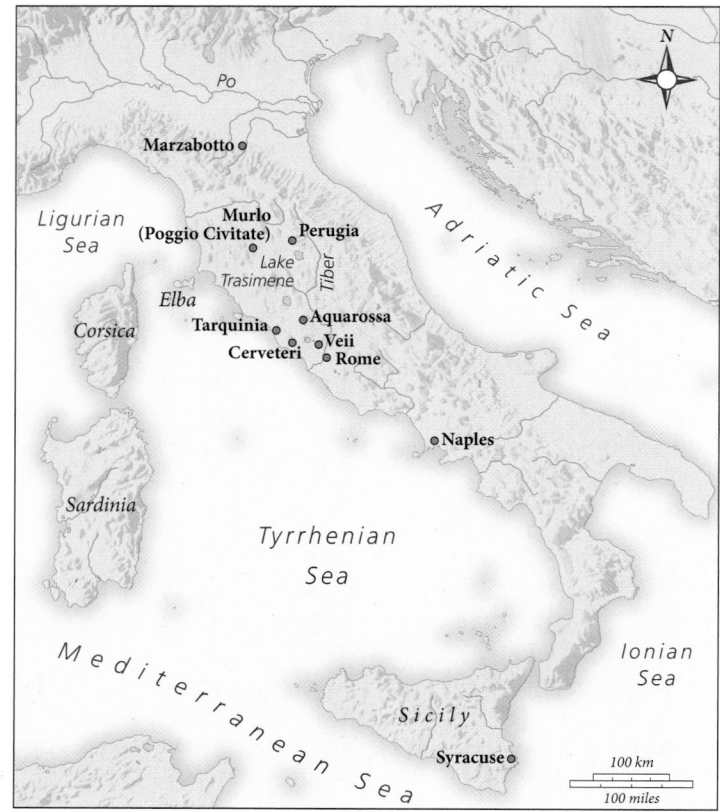

Map 6.1   Italian Peninsula in Etruscan times

Sometimes they buried offerings with the dead—weapons for men, and jewelry and weaving implements for women. Early in the seventh century BCE, as Etruscans began to bury their dead in family groups, funerary customs for men and women became more elaborate, and the tombs of the wealthy gradually transformed into monumental structures.

Tombs and Their Contents

Named for the amateur archaeologists who excavated it, the Regolini-Galassi Tomb at Cerveteri is an early example of this more elaborate burial practice, dating to the so-called Orientalizing phase of the mid-seventh century BCE, when Etruscan arts show a marked influence from Eastern motifs. Etruscans formed tombs in the shape of mounds called **tumuli**, which were grouped together outside the living spaces of Etruscan towns to create a city of the dead, or necropolis. In this example, builders roofed the long dromos (plural, dromoi) or pathway leading into the tomb with corbeled vaults built of horizontal, overlapping courses of stone blocks, similar to the casemates at Tiryns (see fig. 4.20). Among the grave goods was a spectacular fibula (fig. **6.1**). A fibula resembled a brooch or a

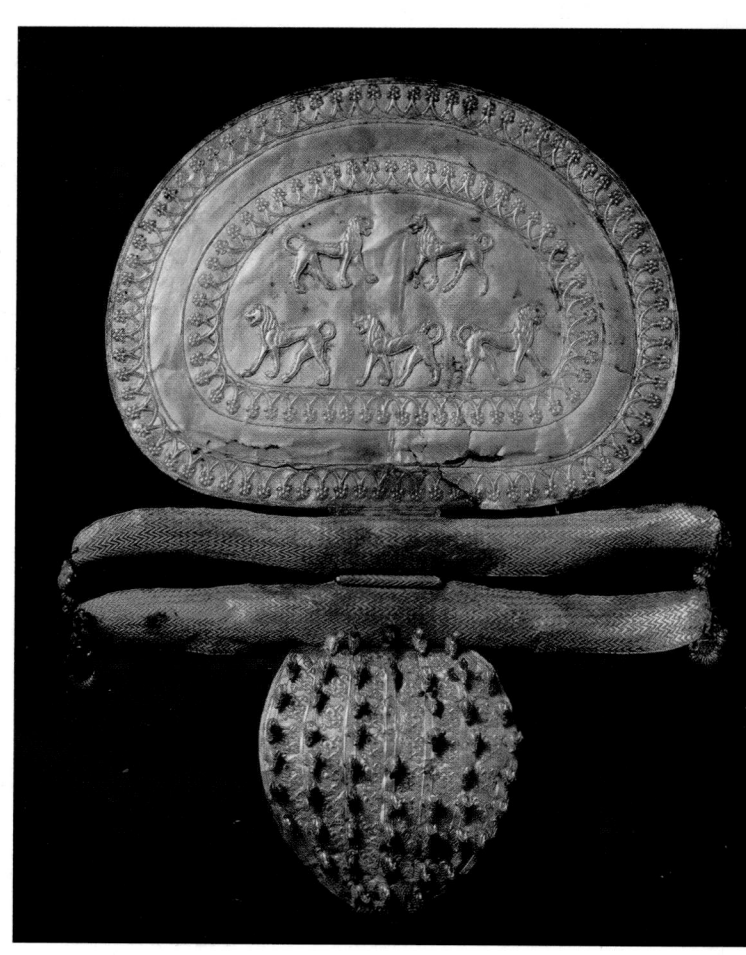

6.1   Fibula, from Regolini-Galassi Tomb, Cerveteri. ca. 670–650 BCE. Gold, length 11½" (29.2cm). Musei Vaticani, Museo Gregoriano Etrusco, Città del Vaticano, Rome

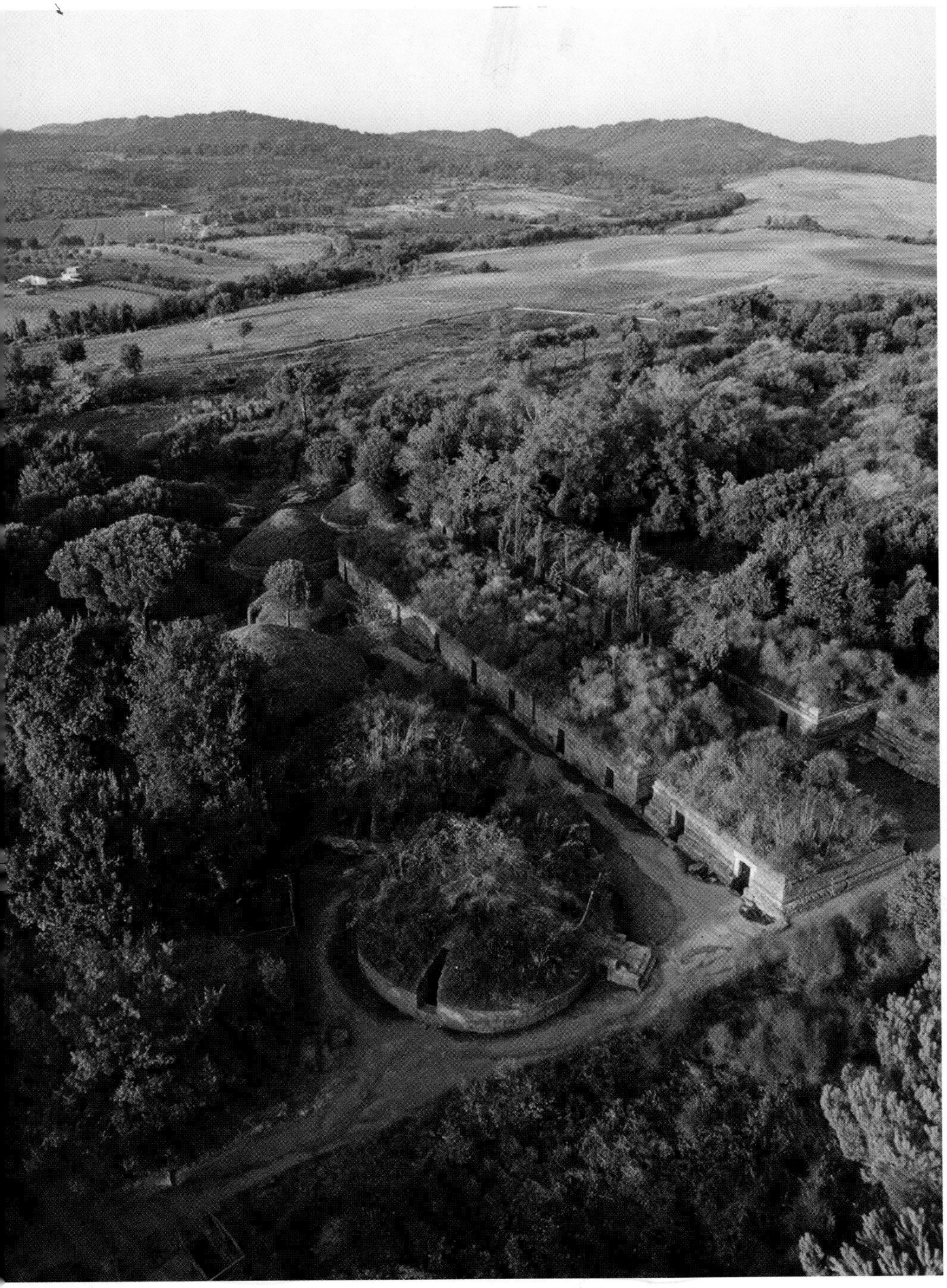

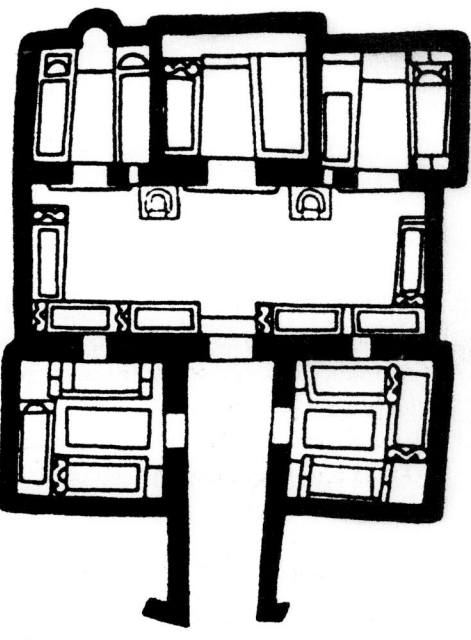

6.3 Plan of Tomb of the Shields and Chairs, Cerveteri. ca. 550–500 BCE

decorative safety pin, and often served to hold a garment together at the neck. At 11½ inches in length, this magnificent example is a *tour de force* of the goldsmith's art (see *Materials and Techniques*, page 169), and justifies the fame Etruscan goldsmiths enjoyed in antiquity. Covering the lower leaflike portion are 55 gold ducks in the round. On the upper portion, shaped like a three-quarter-moon, repoussé work defines pacing lions, whose profile pose and erect stance may derive from Phoenician precedents. Indeed, though the workmanship is probably Etruscan, the animal motifs suggest familiarity with the artworks of Near Eastern cultures (see fig. 2.10). Also buried in tombs of this time were precious objects imported from the ancient Near East, such as ivories.

The Regolini-Galassi Tomb is but one of many tumulus tombs built at necropoleis near Cerveteri over the course of several centuries until about 100 BCE (fig. 6.2). The local stone is a soft volcanic rock known as *tuff*, which is easy to cut and hardens after prolonged exposure to the air. Those who created the tumuli excavated into bedrock, cutting away a path and burial chambers. They used excavated stone to build a circular retaining wall around the chambers, and piled up soil above it. Often several dromoi led to independent networks of chambers within a single mound. The layout of the burial chambers varies (fig. 6.3), and scholars have supposed that these dwellings of the dead mimicked contemporary houses, often complete with chairs or beds carved

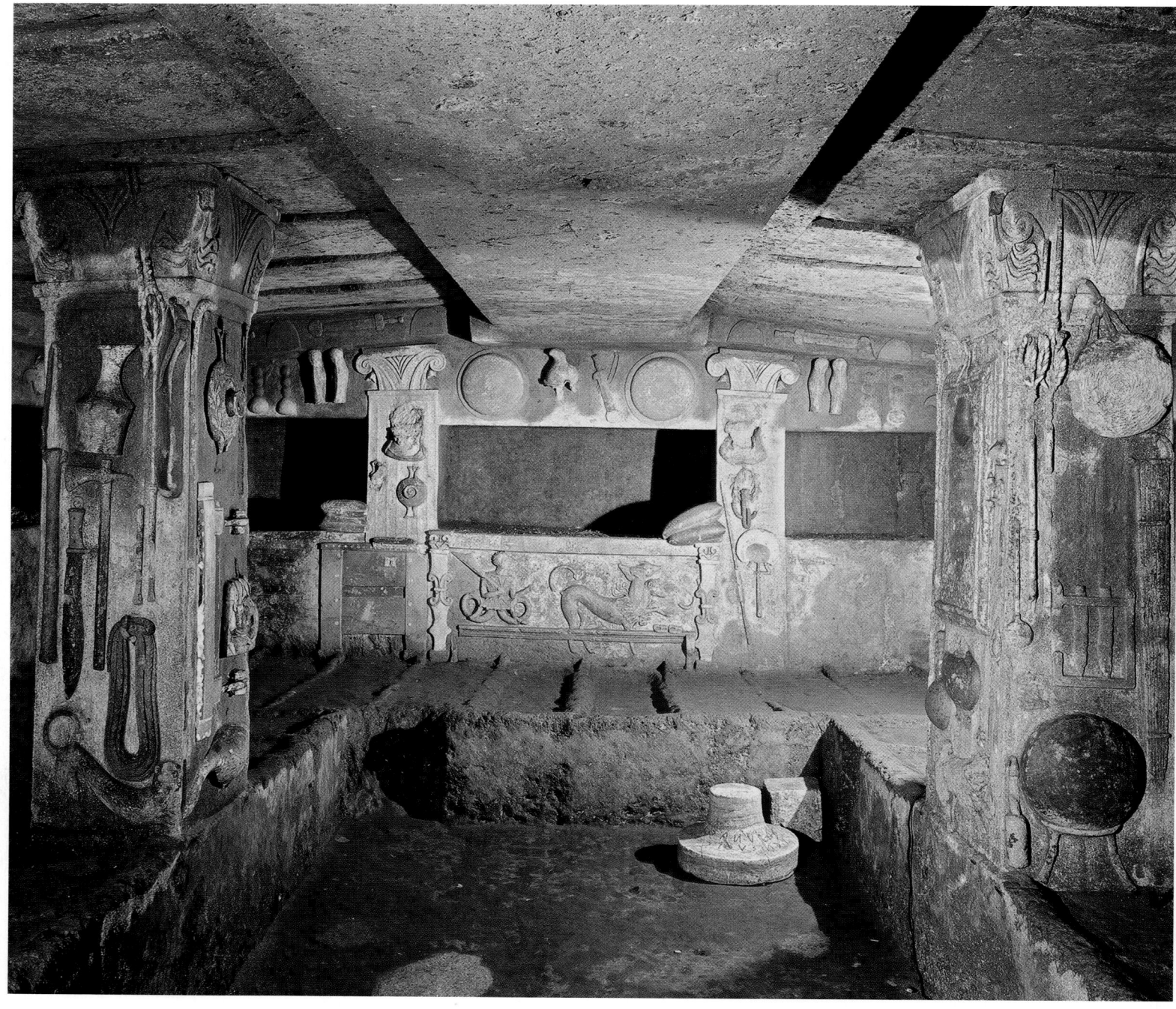

6.4 Burial chamber, Tomb of the Reliefs, Cerveteri. 3rd century BCE

out of the rock as furnishing. This may be true, but it is hard to confirm given the scant evidence for Etruscan residences. In a late example, the Tomb of the Reliefs at Cerveteri, an artist applied everything the dead might want in the afterlife onto the walls in stucco (fig. **6.4**). Reproductions of weapons, armor, household implements, and domestic animals cover the piers and the walls between the niches. Two damaged busts may have represented the dead or underworld deities. The concept of burying items that would be of service in the afterlife is reminiscent of Egyptian funerary practice, though replicas of actual items differ markedly between the two cultures.

Farther north, at Tarquinia, tombs consist of chambers sunk into the earth with a steep underground dromos. Vibrant paintings cover the walls, executed while the plaster was wet. At one end of the low chamber in the Tomb of Hunting and Fishing is a marine panorama, dating to about 530–520 BCE (fig. **6.5**) during the Archaic period. In the vast expanse of water and sky, fishermen cast lines from a boat, as brightly colored dolphins leap through the waves. A figure on a rocky promontory aims his slingshot at large birds in bright red, blue, and yellow that swoop through the sky. Unlike Greek landscape scenes, where humans dominate their surroundings, here the figures are just one part of

Etruscan Gold-Working

Early in their history, the Etruscans became talented metalworkers, with special proficiency in gold-working. The goldsmith responsible for the fibula in figure 6.1 was a master of two complex techniques: filigree and granulation.

Filigree is the art of soldering fine gold wires—singly or twisted together into a rope—onto a gold background. The goldsmith used this process to outline the ornamental decoration and two-dimensional animals on the fibula's surface. Etruscan artists were so expert that they could even create openwork designs independent of a backplate.

Granulation describes the process of soldering tiny gold balls or grains onto a background. Skilled Etruscan artists worked with grains as small as ½₅₀", using them to decorate large areas, or to define linear or geometric patterns. Alternatively, they might employ them in conjunction with embossed designs, or in a mass to create a silhouette against the background. Finally, they might cover the background with grains, leaving a design in silhouette.

Mastery of granulation was lost in early medieval Europe, as tastes changed and different gold-working techniques came to be preferred. Goldsmiths use various methods today, but scholars do not know how Etruscan artists prepared the grains. They may have placed fragments of gold in a crucible, separating them with charcoal. When heated, the gold would melt into separate balls. Goldsmiths would then remove the charcoal that kept the balls apart. Alternatively, they may have poured molten gold into water from a height, to ensure that tiny grains would form into small balls. When the liquid metal reached the water, it would cool into solid form. For all but the simplest designs (which were applied straight to the background), the artist probably arranged the grains in a design engraved on a stone or metal plate, and lowered a piece of adhesive-covered papyrus or leather, fixed to the end of a tube, over the design, to pick up the grains. They could then be treated with solder and transferred to the gold backplate.

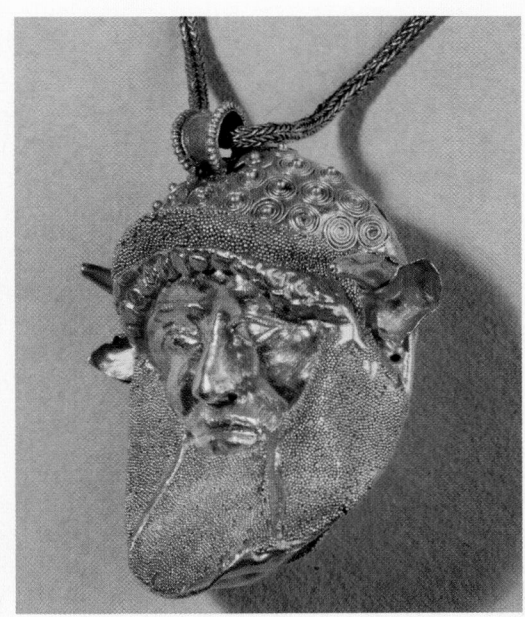

Pendant representing the head of Acheloos, decorated with granulation. 6th century BCE. Musée du Louvre, Paris

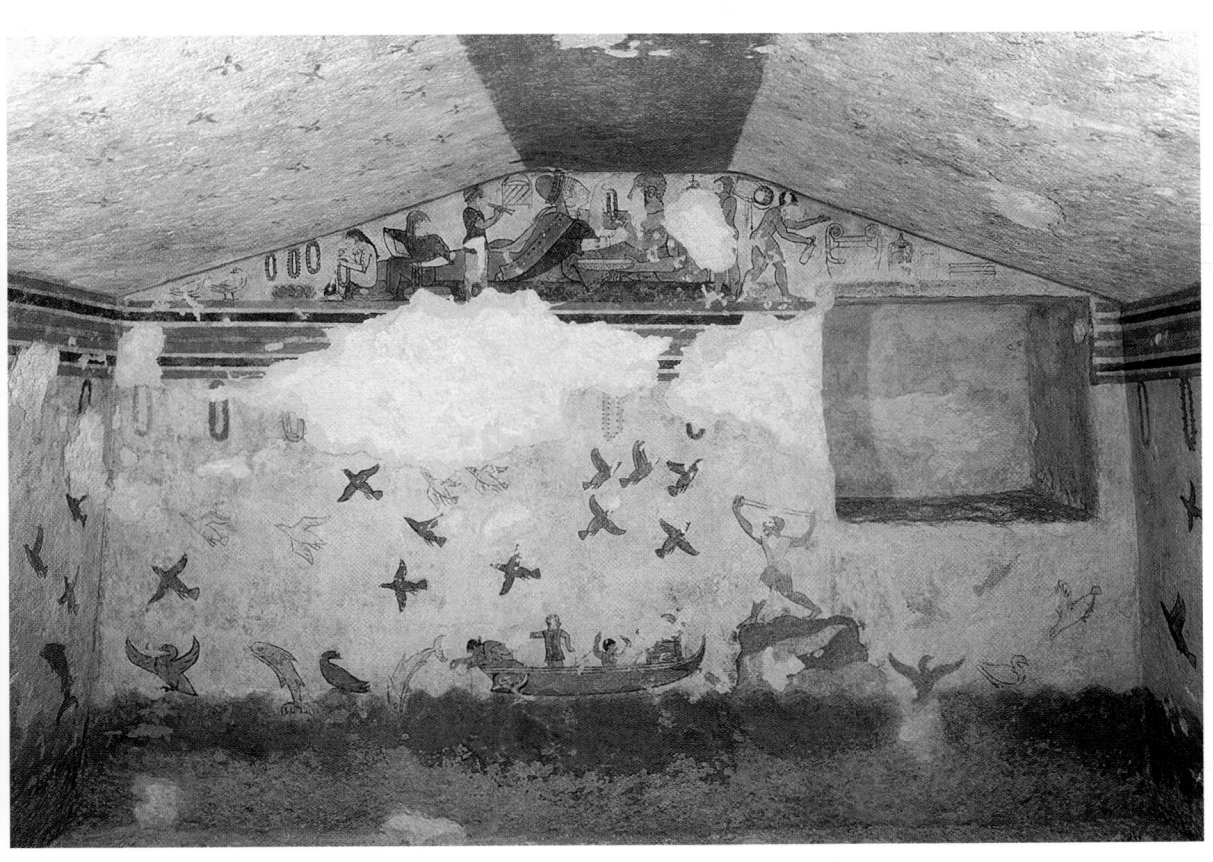

6.5 Tomb of Hunting and Fishing, Tarquinia. ca. 530–520 BCE

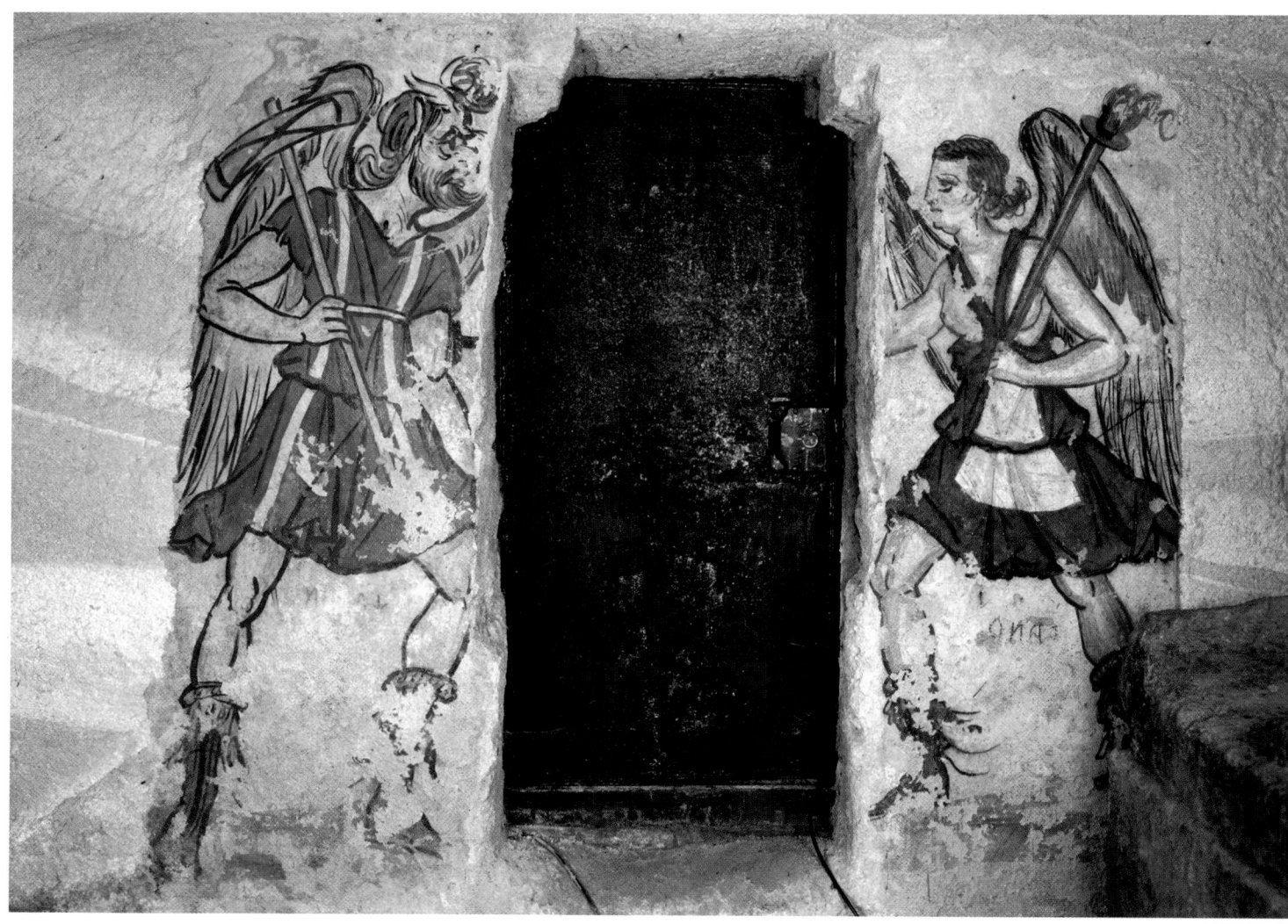

6.6   Charun and Vanth from the Tomb of the Anina Family, Tarquinia. 3rd century BCE

a larger scheme. The exuberance of the colors and gestures, too, is characteristically Etruscan. All the same, here as in most tombs, the treatment of drapery and anatomy reveals that developing Greek painting influenced Etruscan tomb painters.

The artist seems to have conceived of the scene as a view from a tent or hut, defined by wide bands of color at cornice level and roofed with a light tapestry. Hanging from the cornice are festive garlands of the kind probably used during funerary rituals. In many tombs, images of animals fill the **gable**—leopards, sometimes, or fantastic hybrids—perhaps used as guardian figures to ward off evil. Above the fishing scene, a man and woman recline together at a banquet, where musicians entertain them and servants attend to their needs. One draws wine from a large mixing bowl, or krater, while another makes wreaths. In contrast to Greek drinking parties (symposia), which were reserved for men and courtesans, Etruscan banquet scenes include respectable women reclining alongside men. Banquet paintings appear frequently in Etruscan tombs; athletic games were another common subject, as were scenes that focused on musicians and dancers.

The purpose of these paintings is hard to determine. They may record and perpetuate activities the deceased once enjoyed, or depict rituals observed at the funeral (the games, in fact, are probably the forerunners of Roman gladiatorial contests). Or, like Egyptian tomb paintings, they may have served as provisions for the afterlife of the deceased. At the heart of the problem of interpretation lies our general ignorance about Etruscan beliefs concerning death and the afterlife. Roman writers describe them as a highly religious people, and their priests are known to have read meaning into the flight of birds in different sectors of the sky; beyond that, as enigmatic as they are, these paintings actually constitute a large part of our evidence for understanding Etruscan beliefs. In a few tombs, paintings seem to reflect Greek myths, but these images merely compound the problem, since we cannot be sure that the Etruscans intended the same meaning as Greek artists.

However we interpret these Archaic and Classical images, it is clear that a distinct change in the content of tomb paintings begins in the Late Classical period during the fourth century BCE. An overwhelming sense of sadness replaces the energetic mood of the foregoing periods. The exuberant **palette** of the earlier phases, with its bright reds and yellows, gives way to a somber range of darker colors. At this time, funerary images often depict processions taking the deceased to a world of the dead, or they are set in a shadowy underworld. In the Tomb of the Anina Family at Tarquinia, dating to about the end of the fourth century BCE, two winged demons flank a door to another world (fig. **6.6**). A hook-nosed male demon Charun, on the left, is the soul's guide to the underworld. He holds the hammer with which he will open the door, while Vanth, a female demon on the right, bears a torch to light the darkness. It is possible that the gloomy subjects reflected difficult times, as they coincide with the Roman conquest and subordination of Etruscan cities.

Containers used for the remains of the dead manifest similar changes. In the Orientalizing period, the pottery urns traditionally used for ashes gradually took on human characteristics (fig. **6.7**). The lid became a head, perhaps intended to represent the deceased, and body markings appeared on the vessel itself. Hair and jewelry may have been attached where holes appear in the terra-cotta surface. Sometimes the urn was placed on a sort of throne in the tomb, which may have indicated a high status for the deceased.

In Cerveteri, two monumental sarcophagi of the Archaic period have come to light, molded in terra cotta in two separate halves. One of them, dating to about 520 BCE, is shown here (fig. **6.8**). The artist shaped the lid to resemble a couch, and reclining side by side on top are full-length sculptures of a man and woman, presumably a married couple. A wineskin (a soft canteen made from an animal skin) cushions the woman's left elbow, and the man has his arm around her shoulders. Both figures once held

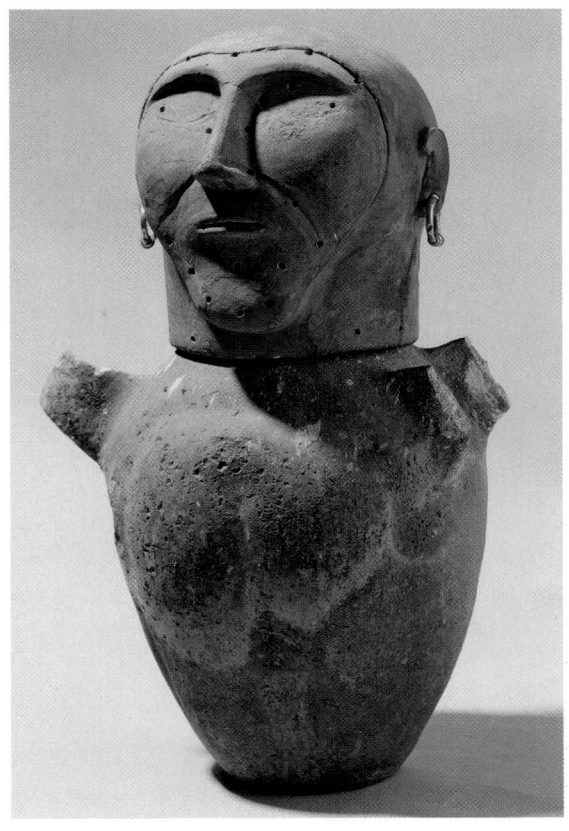

6.7   Human-headed cinerary urn. ca. 675–650 BCE. Terra cotta, height 25½" (64.7 cm). Museo Etrusco, Chiusi, Italy

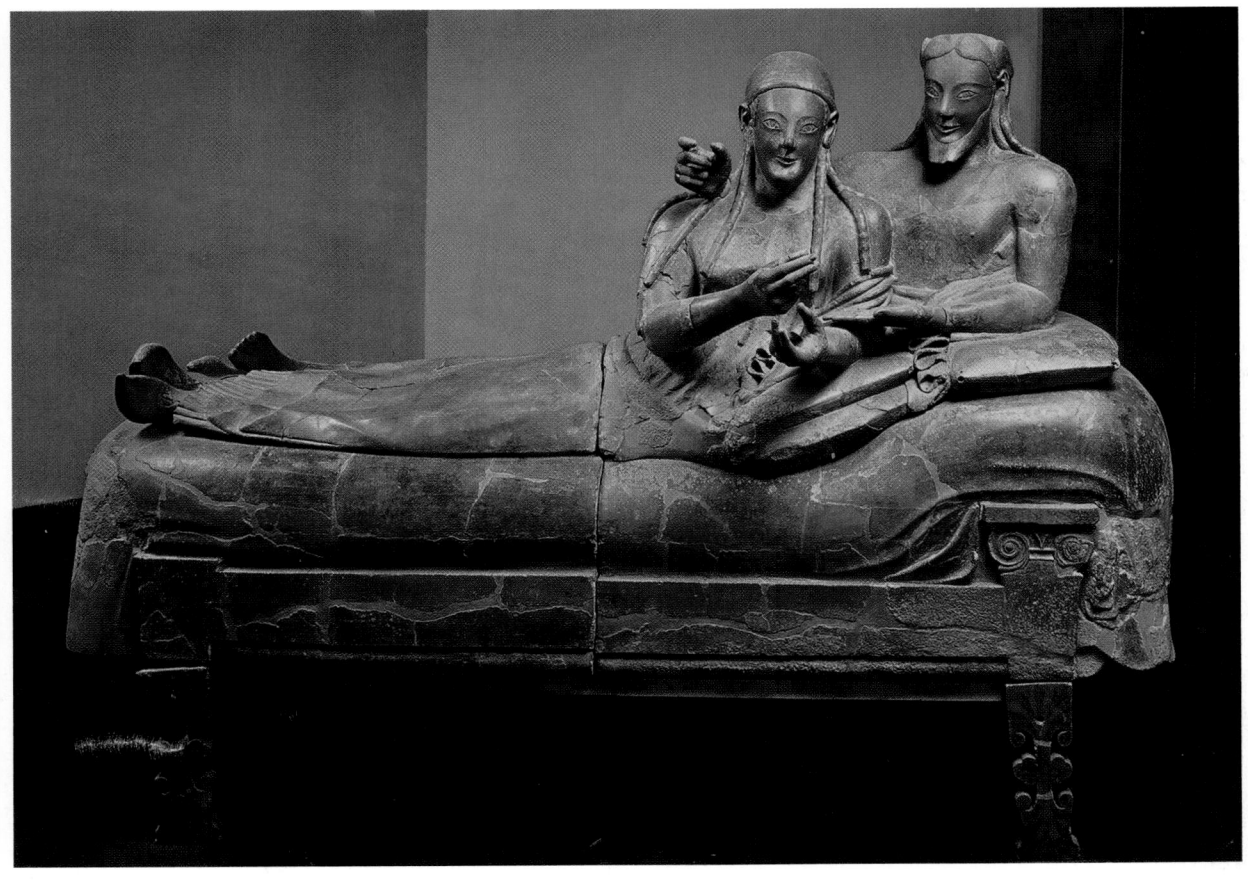

6.8   Sarcophagus, from Cerveteri. ca. 520 BCE. Terra cotta, length 6'7" (2 m). Museo Nazionale di Villa Giulia, Rome

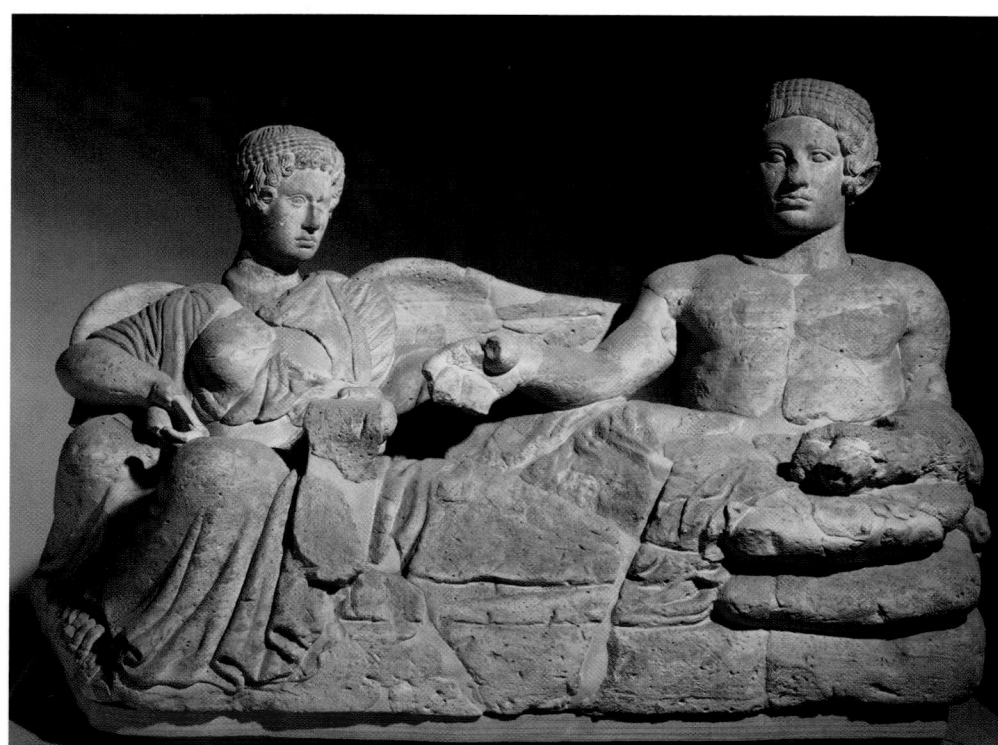

6.9 *Youth and Female Demon*. Cinerary container. Early 4th century BCE. Stone (*pietra fetida*), length 47" (119.4 cm). Museo Archaeologico Nazionale, Florence

out objects in their hands—a cup or an **alabastron** (a perfume container), perhaps, or an egg, symbol of eternity. Despite the abstract forms and rigid poses of the Archaic style, the soft material allows the sculptor to model rounded forms and capture an extraordinary directness and vivacity. The artist painted the entire work in bright colors, which conservators have revealed more clearly in a recent cleaning.

The change in mood, from optimistic to somber, that characterizes tomb paintings between the fifth and fourth centuries BCE also becomes apparent if we compare the sarcophagus in figure 6.8 with a cinerary container made of soft stone soon after 400 BCE (fig. **6.9**). At one end reclines a young man wearing his mantle pulled down around his waist, in the Etruscan style. As in wall paintings of this period, a woman sits at the foot of the couch. Yet she is not his wife. Her wings identify her as a demon from the world of the dead, and the scroll in her left hand may record his fate. The two figures set at either end of the couch create a balanced composition, but their separation marks a new mood of

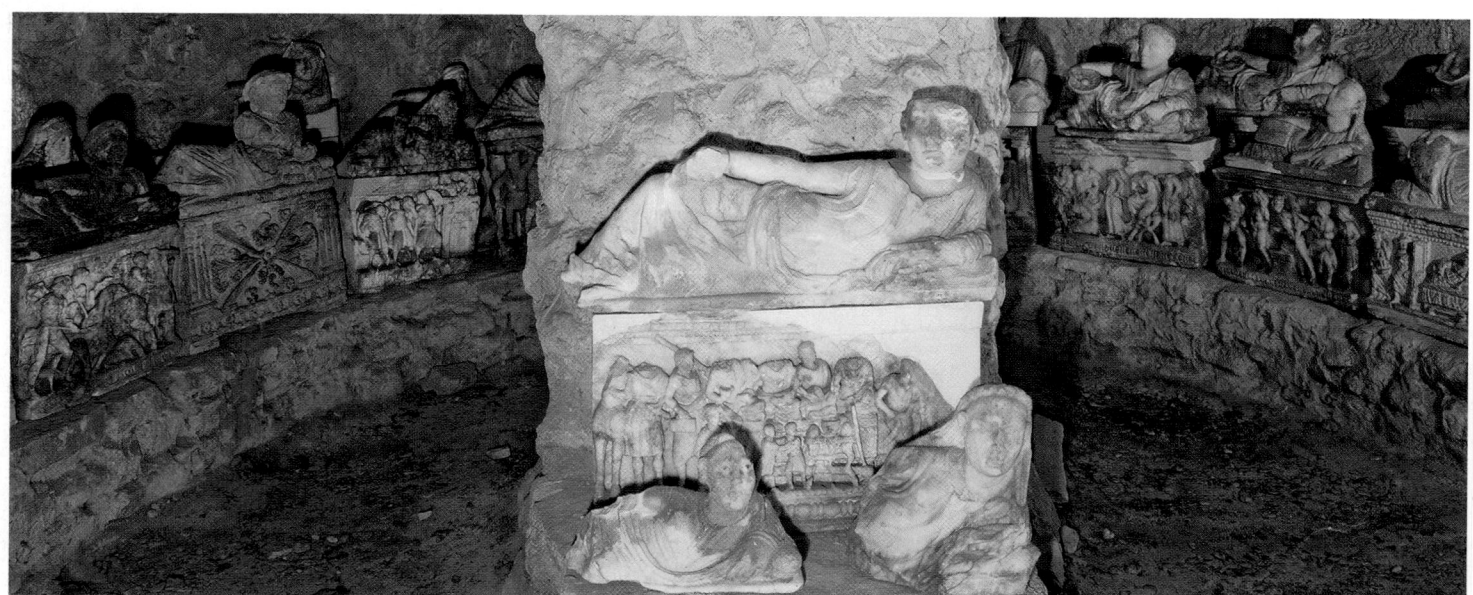

6.10　Funerary urns in the Inghirami Tomb, Volterra. Hellenistic period, ca. 2nd century BCE

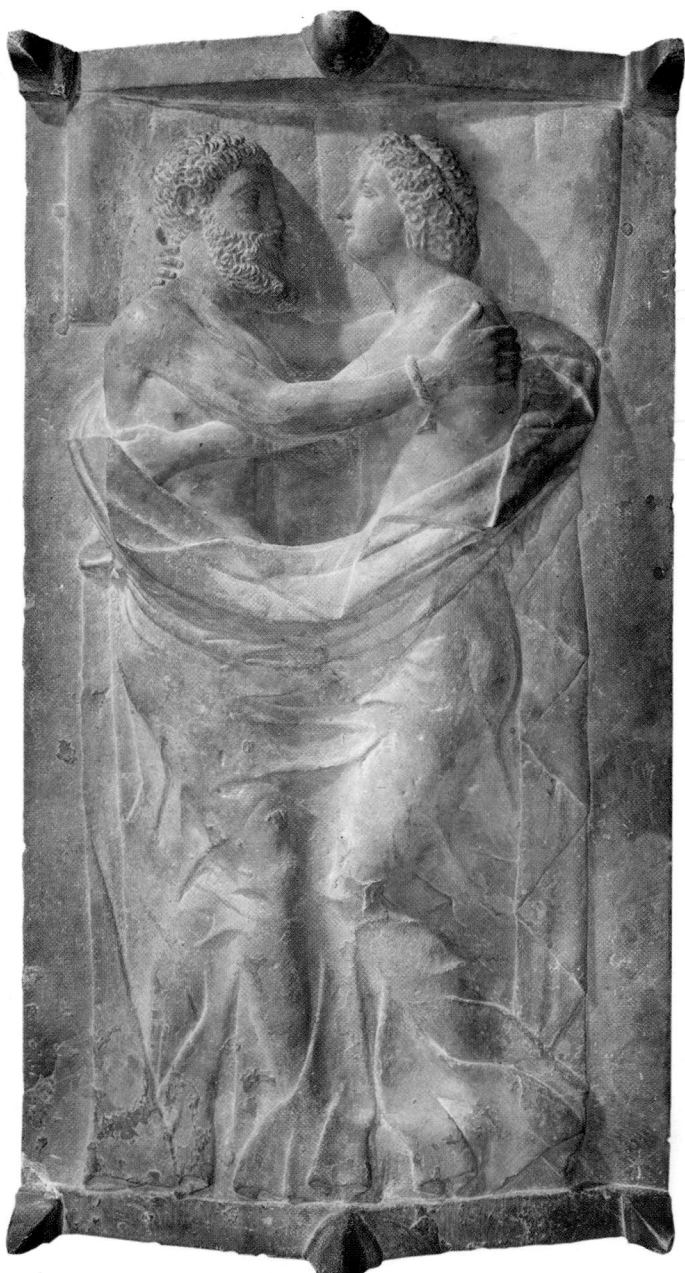

6.11 Sarcophagus lid of Larth Tetnies and Thanchvil Tarnai. ca. 350–300 BCE. Marble, length 7' (2.13 m). Museum of Fine Arts, Boston. Gift of Mrs. Gardner Brewer, 86.145 a-b

ARCHITECTURE

According to Roman writers, the Etruscans were masters of engineering, town planning, and surveying. Almost certainly, the Romans learned from them, especially in water management (drainage systems and aqueducts) and bridge building. Exactly *what* they learned is hard to determine, however. Since it was built predominantly of wood or mud brick, relatively little Etruscan and early Roman architecture survives. Additionally, many Etruscan towns lie beneath existing Italian towns, and any permanent materials employed in their construction have often been reused.

Etruscan cities generally sat on hilltops close to a navigable river or the sea. From the seventh century BCE on, in some places the inhabitants added massive defensive walls. A late example of civic architecture survives in the city of Perugia, where sections of a fortification wall and some of its gates still stand. The best-known of these is the Porta Marzia (Gate of Mars) of the second century BCE, the upper portion of which the Renaissance architect Antonio da Sangallo encased in a later wall (fig. **6.12**). The gate is an early example of a voussoir arch, built out of a series of truncated wedge-shaped stones called **voussoirs** set in a semicircle against a wooden framework, which was removed after construction. Once the voussoirs were in place, they were remarkably strong; any downward thrust from above (the weight of the wall over the void, for instance) merely strengthened their bond by pressing them more tightly against one another. Above the arch, and separated from one another by engaged pilasters, sculpted figures of Tinia (the Etruscan equivalent of Zeus or Jupiter) and his sons (equivalent to Castor and Pollux) with their horses look out over a balustrade. The arch is visual evidence of the confluence of

melancholy associated with death, which each individual must face alone. Still, wealthy Etruscans continued to bury their dead together in family tombs, and the familial context for cinerary urns like this one must have gone some way toward mitigating the isolation of death (fig. **6.10**). Moreover, while cinerary urns of this kind were typical, usually with a single figure reclining on the lid, a few grand sarcophagi survive. On the lid of one are carved a man and woman in a tender embrace, lying under a sheet as if in their marital bed (fig. **6.11**). The coiffures and beard reflect Greek fashion, and the sides of the chest feature battle scenes influenced by Greek iconography, yet the finished product is definitively Etruscan.

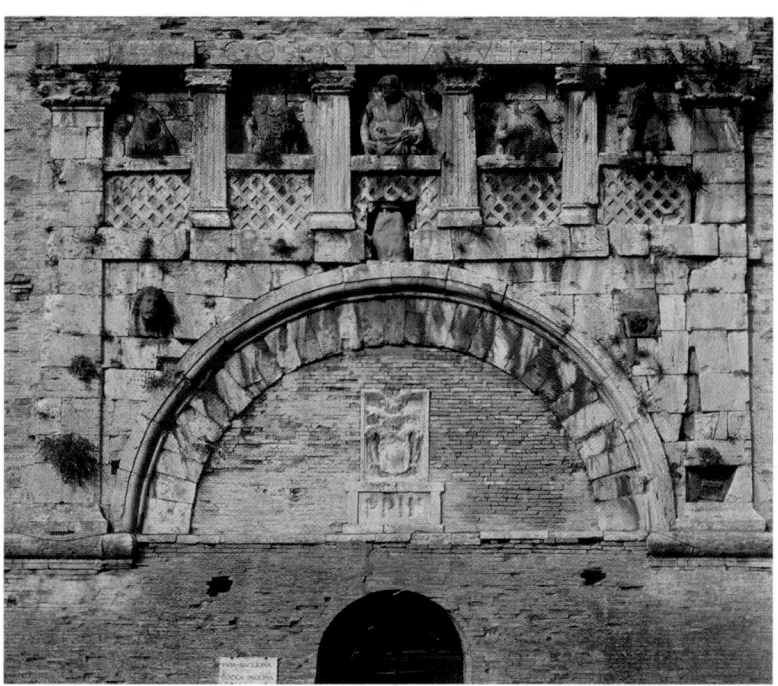

6.12 Porta Marzia, Perugia. 2nd century BCE

cultures so prevalent in the Mediterranean in the last centuries before the Common Era.

City Planning

The hilltops of Etruria did not lend themselves to grid planning, yet there is good evidence at sites like Marzabotto that when the Etruscans colonized the flatlands of the Po Valley in northern Italy, from the sixth century BCE on, they laid out newly founded cities as a network of streets. These centered on the intersection of two main thoroughfares, one running north–south (known in Latin as the *cardo*) and one running east–west (the *decumanus*). The resulting four quarters could be further subdivided or expanded, according to need. This system seems consistent with religious beliefs that led the Etruscans to divide the sky into regions according to the points of the compass. The Romans also adopted it for the new colonies they founded throughout Italy, Western Europe, and North Africa, and for military camps.

Little survives of the houses that composed Etruscan towns. Unlike tombs, they were built with a packed-earth technique (**pisé**) similar to wattle and daub or adobe, with only the base made of stone. Even these stone footprints are hard to discern, since the hilltops favored by the Etruscans have been inhabited more or less continually since their days. In a few places, however, archaeologists have unearthed the remains of monumental building complexes that may have been palaces or large villas. An especially fine example existed at Poggio Civitate (present-day Murlo) in the sixth century BCE, where numerous rooms framed a large central courtyard (fig. 6.13). This kind of architecture is conceptually linked to typically Roman **atrium** houses (see fig. 7.50). In order to protect the wooden fabric of their monumental buildings, Etruscans nailed terra-cotta revetment plaques over exposed parts of beams. A mid-sixth-century BCE monumental residential building at Acquarossa yielded a fine set of molded and painted

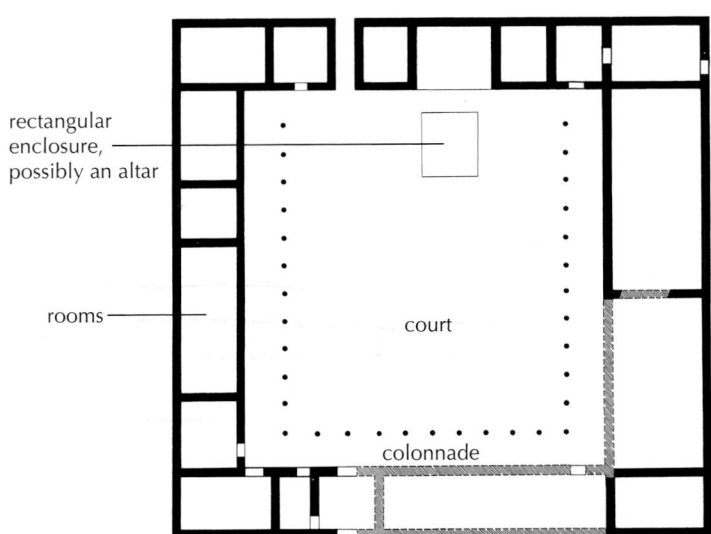

6.13 Plan of residential complex, Murlo (Poggio Civitate). 6th century BCE

revetments. One of them shows a banquet scene, with diners on couches amid musicians (fig. 6.14), and others depicted Herakles accomplishing his labors. With their bright colors, the revetments enlivened the building, but they may also have aligned the elite property owners with the Greek hero.

Etruscans built their temples of mud brick and wood, so once again only the stone foundations survive. Early temples consisted of little more than modest rectangular cellas (rooms for holding cult figures). Later temples seem to have fallen heavily under the influence of the innovative design of the massive Temple of Jupiter Optimus Maximus on the Capitoline Hill in Rome (see fig. 7.1). As a result, they are characterized by a tall base, or podium, with steps only on the front (fig. 6.15). The steps lead to a deep porch with rows of columns, and to the cella beyond,

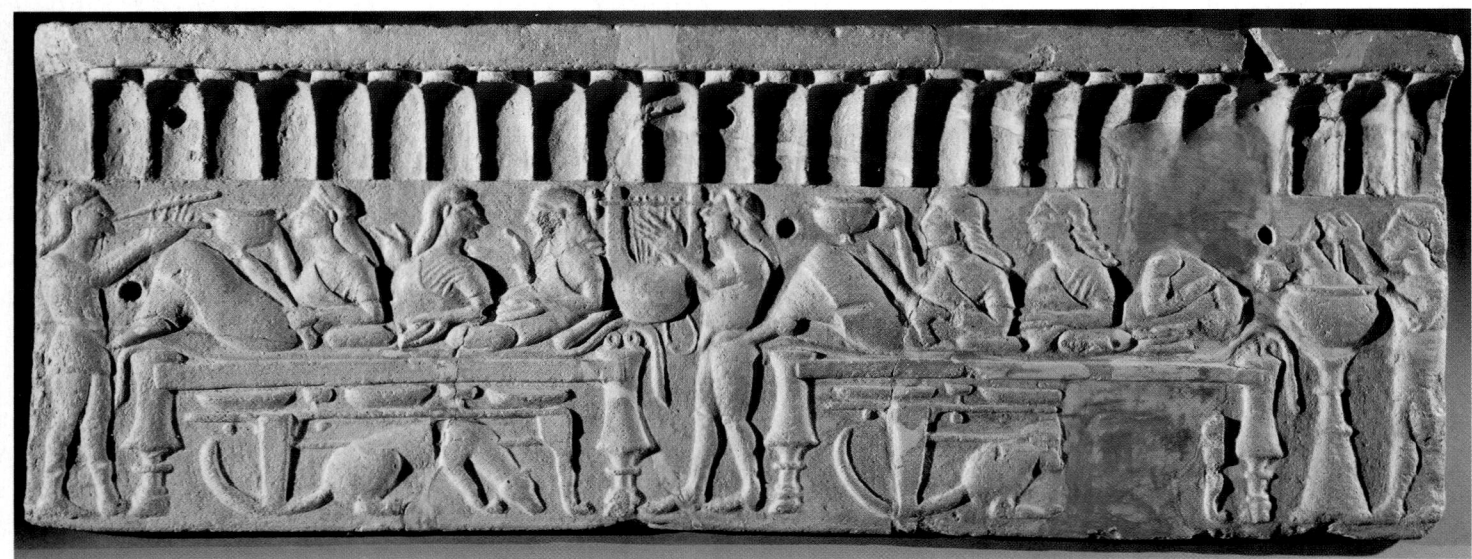

6.14 Revetment plaque, from Acquarossa. ca. 575–550 BCE. Painted terra cotta, height 8.3" (21 cm). Museo Archeologico Nazionale, Viterbo

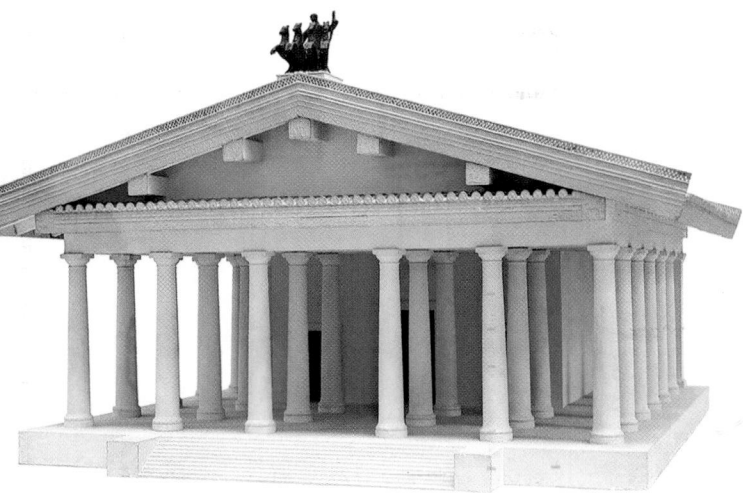

6.15 Reconstruction of an Etruscan temple, as described by Vitruvius. Museo delle Antichità Etrusche e Italiche, Università di Roma "La Sapienza"

which was often subdivided into three compartments. The terra-cotta tile roof hung well over the walls in wide eaves, to protect the mud bricks from rain, and terra-cotta revetments sheathed the beams.

SCULPTURE

As with their Greek counterparts, Etruscan temples were highly ornate, but where Greeks used marble to adorn their temples, Etruscans had little access to this material. The decoration on Etruscan temples usually consisted of the brightly painted terra-cotta revetments that protected the architrave and the edges of the roof. After about 400 BCE, Etruscan artists sometimes designed large-scale terra-cotta groups to fill the pediment above the porch. The most dramatic use of sculpture, however, was on the ridgepole—the horizontal beam at the crest of a gabled roof. Terra-cotta figures at this height depicted not only single figures but narratives.

Dynamism in Terra Cotta and Bronze

One of the most famous surviving temple sculptures comes from Veii, a site some 14 miles (22 km) north of Rome. Both Roman texts and archaeological evidence indicate that Veii was an important sculptural center by the end of the sixth century BCE.

The late sixth-century BCE temple at Veii was probably devoted to the Etruscan gods Menrva, Aritimi, and Turan. Four life-size terra-cotta statues crowned the ridge of the roof. (Similar examples appear in the reconstruction model, see fig. 6.15.) They formed a dynamic and interactive group representing the contest of Hercle (equivalent to Hercules) and Aplu (Apollo) for the sacred hind (female deer) in the presence of other deities. The best-preserved of the figures is Aplu (fig. **6.16**). He wears a mantle with curved hem later known to Romans as a toga. The drapery falls across his form in ornamental patterns and exposes his

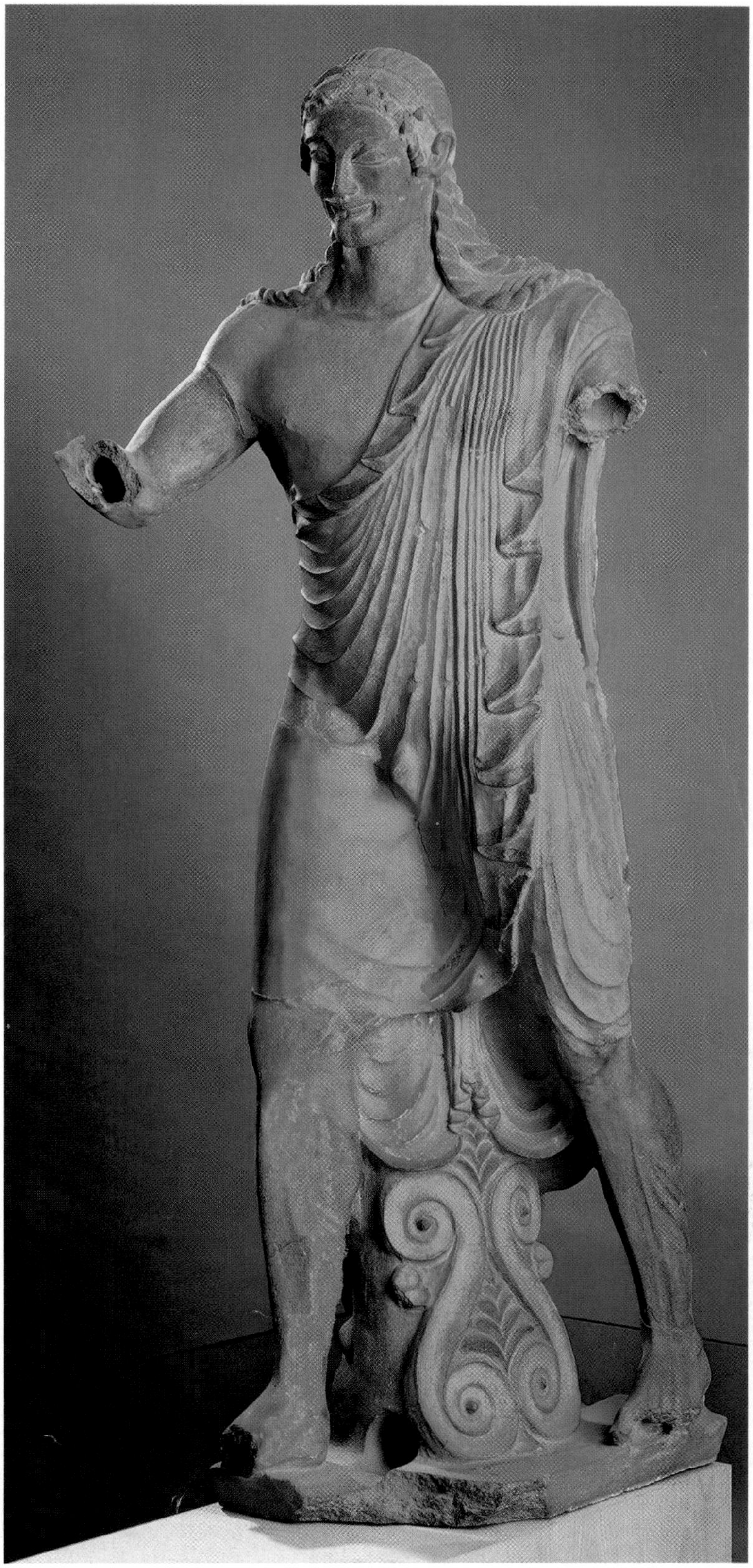

6.16 Vulca of Veii (?). *Aplu (Apollo)*, from Veii. ca. 510 BCE. Terra cotta, height 5'9" (1.75 m). Museo Nazionale di Villa Giulia, Rome

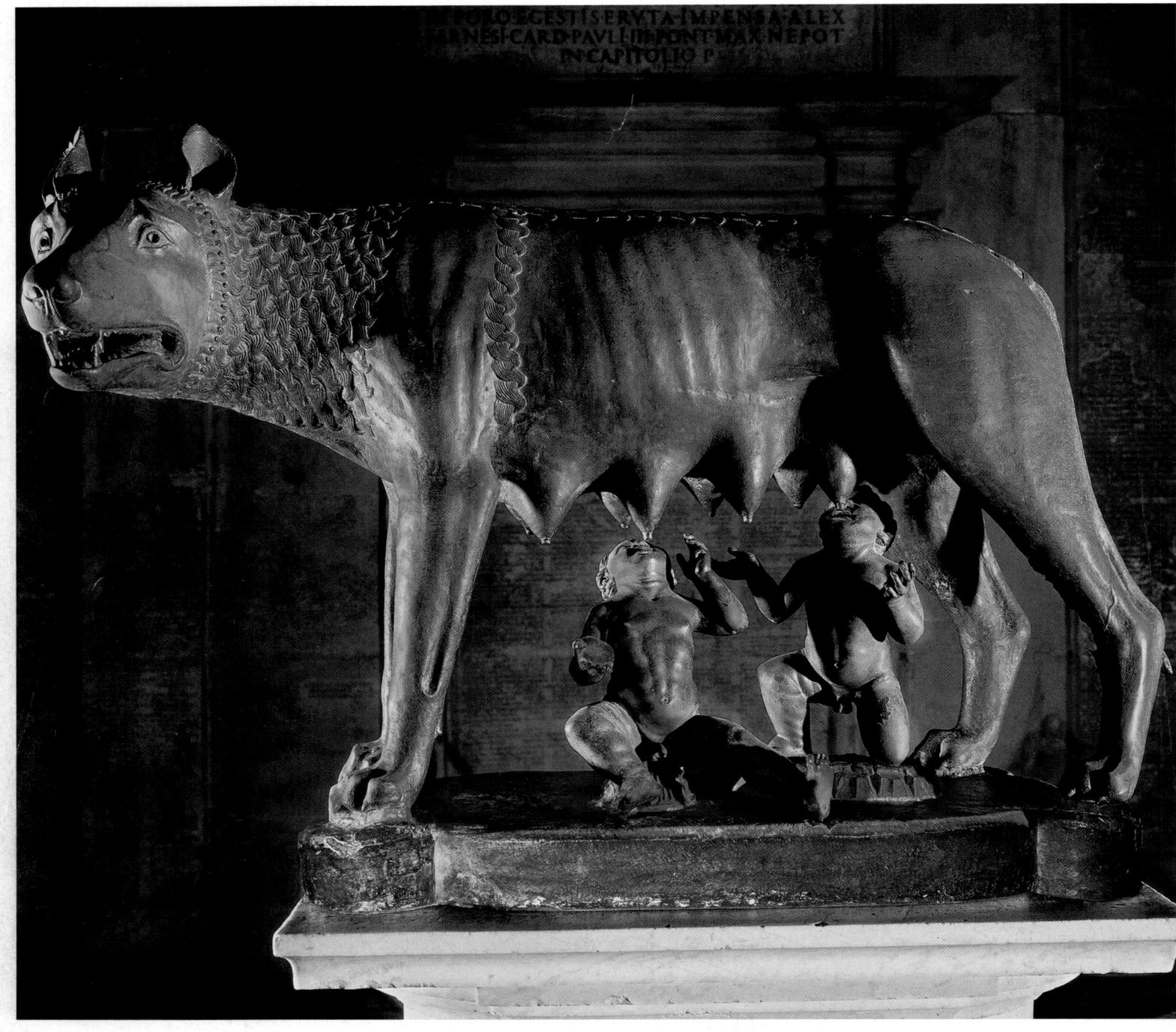

6.17 *She-Wolf*. ca. 500 BCE. Bronze, height 33½" (85 cm). Museo Capitolino, Rome

massive body, with its sinewy, muscular legs. The stylistic similarity to contemporary Greek kouroi and korai signals the influence Greek sculpture must have had on the Etruscans. Yet this god moves in a hurried, purposeful stride that has no equivalent in free-standing Greek statues of the same date. Rendered in terra cotta, which allowed the sculptor greater freedom than stone to experiment with poses, this is a purely Etruscan energy. These sculptures have been attributed to a famous Etruscan sculptor, Vulca of Veii, celebrated in Latin literary sources.

Etruscan sculptors also demonstrated extraordinary skill as bronze-casters. One of the most renowned works of Etruscan sculpture is the bronze *She-Wolf* now housed in the Capitoline Museums in Rome (fig. **6.17**). Its most likely date is the fifth century BCE, and, judging by its workmanship, it is probably by the hand of an Etruscan artist. The stylized, patterned treatment of the wolf's mane and hackles sets off the bold but smoothly modeled muscularity of her body, tensed for attack. Simple lines augment her power: The straight back and neck contrast with the sharp turn of the head toward a viewer, highlighting her ferocity. So polished is the metal's surface that it almost seems wet; her fangs seem to glisten. The early history and subject matter of this statue is unknown. However, evidence suggests that it was highly valued in later antiquity, particularly by the Romans. According to Roman legend, the twin brothers Romulus and Remus, descendants of refugees from Troy in Asia Minor, founded Rome in 753/52 BCE. Abandoned as babies, they were nourished by a she-wolf in the wild. Romans may have seen in this Etruscan bronze a representation of their legendary mother wolf. In fact, the early fourth-century CE emperor Maxentius built a grand palace in Rome, where, in a large **exedra** (alcove) framed by a walkway, archaeologists found a statue base with fittings that exactly match the footprints of the she-wolf. A later sculptor—probably Antonio Polaiuolo—added the twins Romulus and Remus beneath her between 1471 and 1473, to resemble Roman coin images of the lactating she-wolf with the babies.

The Etruscan concern with images of the dead might lead us to expect an early interest in portraiture. Yet the features of funerary images such as those in figures 6.8 and 6.9 are stylized rather than individualized. Not until a century later, toward 300 BCE, did individual likenesses begin to appear in Etruscan sculpture. Greek portraiture may have influenced the change, but terra cotta, the material of so much Etruscan sculpture, lent itself to easy modeling of distinctive facial features and a sensitive treatment of flesh, and must have facilitated the development of the genre. The artist individualized an example from Cerveteri by giving it protruding

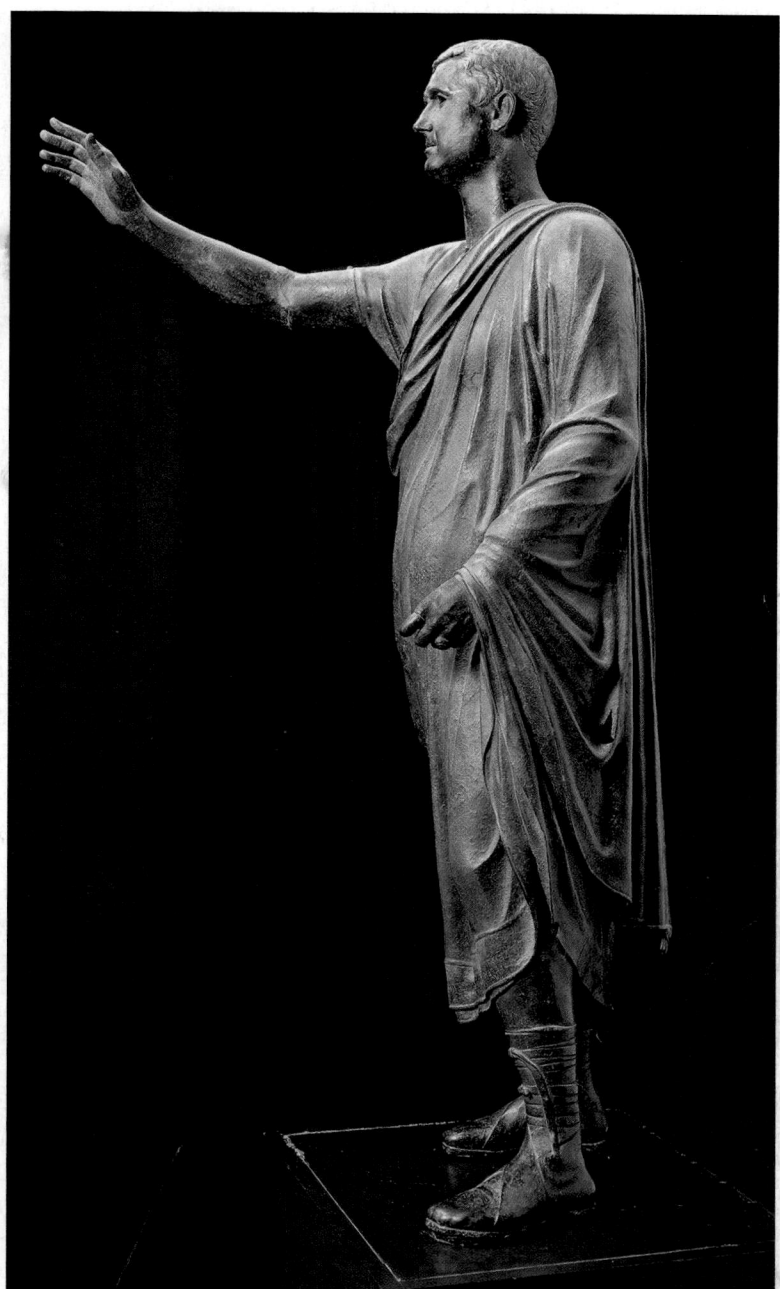

6.19 *L'Arringatore (the Orator)*. Early 1st century BCE. Bronze, height 5'11" (2.80 m). Museo Archaeologico Nazionale, Florence

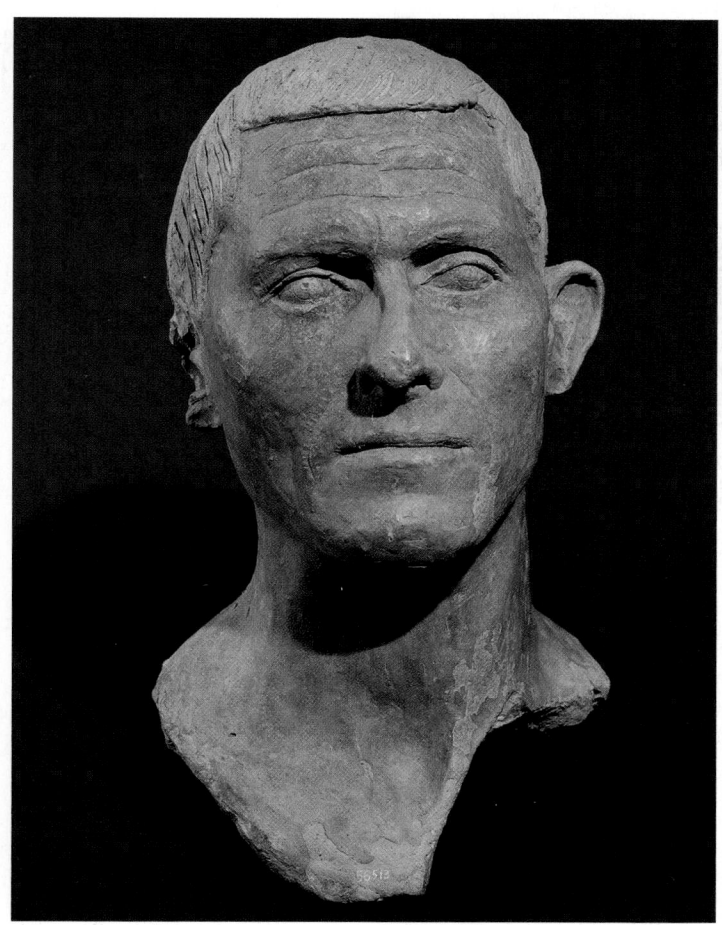

6.18 *Portrait of a Man*, from Manganello. 1st century BCE. Terra cotta, height 12" (30.5 cm). Museo Nazionale di Villa Giulia, Rome

ears, a crooked nose, and blond hair. Many Etruscan portraits, like this one, come from votive deposits, where Etruscans left them as offerings to the gods (fig. **6.18**).

Etruscan artists also produced fine portraits in bronze. A life-size sculpture of an orator known today as *L'Arringatore (the Orator)* shows how impressive their full-length sculptures were (fig. **6.19**). Most scholars place this sculpture in the early years of the first century BCE. It comes from Lake Trasimene, in the central Etruscan territory, and bears an Etruscan inscription that includes the name Aule Meteli (*Aulus Metellus* in Latin), presumably the name of the person it represents. The inscription shows that the workmanship is Etruscan, yet the high boots mark the

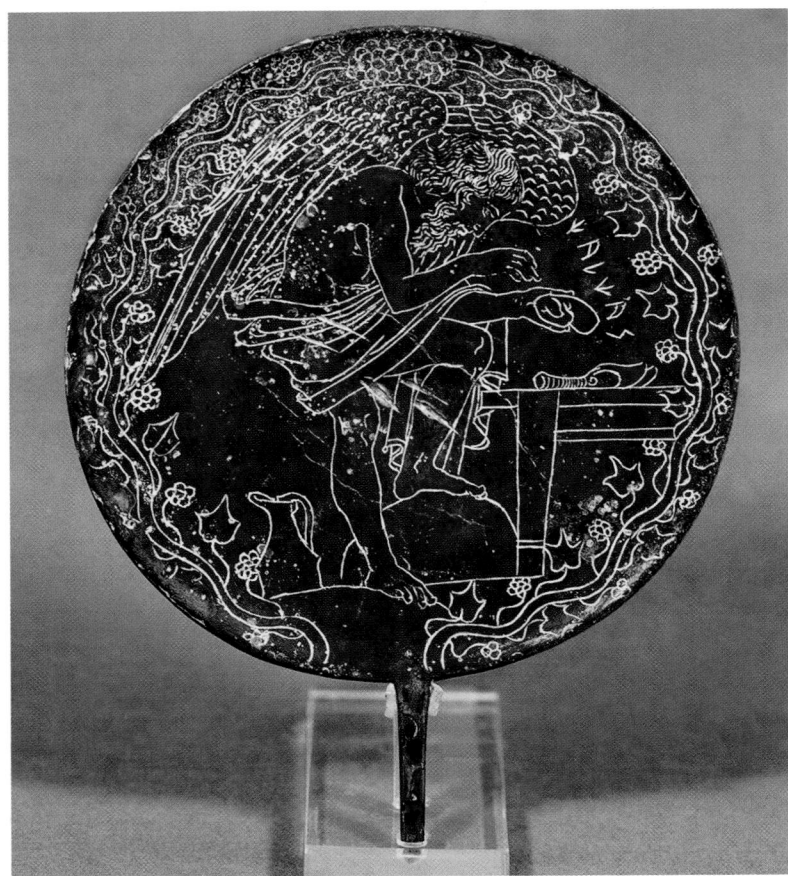

6.20 Engraved back of a mirror. ca. 400 BCE. Bronze, diameter 6" (15.3 cm).
Musei Vaticani, Museo Gregoriano Etrusco, Città del Vaticano, Rome

subject as Roman, or at least an official appointed by the Romans. The raised arm, a gesture that denotes both address and salutation, is common to hundreds of Roman statues. The sculpture raises questions about the roles of artist and patron in the conquered Etruscan territories. The high quality of the casting and finishing of Etruscan bronze works bears out their fame as metalworkers. Their skill is hardly surprising in a land whose wealth was founded on the exploitation of copper, iron, and silver deposits.

From the sixth century BCE on, Etruscans produced large numbers of bronze statuettes, mirrors, and other objects for domestic use and for export. They often engraved the backs of mirrors with scenes from Etruscan versions of Greek myths devoted to the loves of the gods. Such amorous subjects were appropriate for objects used for self-admiration. The design on the back of a mirror created soon after 400 BCE (fig. **6.20**) is of a different genre, and shows how the Etruscans adapted Greek traditions to their own ends. Within an undulating wreath of vines stands a winged old man, one foot raised upon a rock. An inscription identifies him as the seer Chalchas, an Etruscan version of the Greek figure known from Homer's *Iliad*. Yet this is the full extent of the borrowing, for the wings make the figure entirely Etruscan, and he is engaged in haruspicy, a pursuit that was central to Etruscan ritual: He is gazing intently at the liver of a sacrificial animal, searching for omens or portents. The Etruscans believed

that signs in the natural world, such as thunderstorms or, as we have seen, the flight of birds, or even the entrails of sacrificed animals, expressed the will of the gods. In fact, they viewed the liver as a sort of microcosm, divided into sections that corresponded to the 16 regions of the sky. By reading natural signs, those priests who were skilled in the arts of augury, as this practice was also called, could determine whether the gods approved or disapproved of their acts. These priests enjoyed great prestige and power, and they continued to thrive long after the Romans had subordinated Etruscan culture. The Romans themselves consulted them before any major public or private event. As the Roman philosopher and statesman Seneca wrote: "This is the difference between us and the Etruscans…Since they attribute everything to divine agency, they are of the opinion that things do not reveal the future because they have occurred, but that they occur because they are meant to reveal the future." Mirrors, too, were valued for their ability to reveal the future, which is probably why the artist represented this scene here.

Etruscan artists and architects show immense skill and versatility when working in many different mediums. Their work is a true product of the Mediterranean crossroads. Their Greek counterparts exerted some influence on them, and they exchanged inspiration with the Romans. Still, Etruscan works stand distinctly apart.

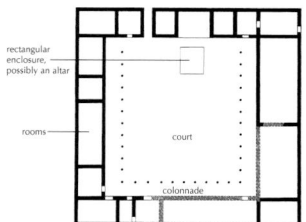

6th century BCE Monumental building complex at Murlo

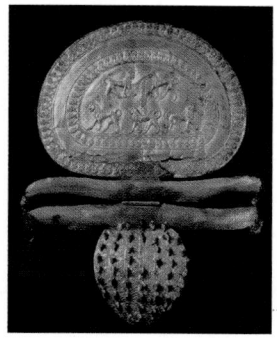

ca. 670–650 BCE Regolini-Galassi gold fibula

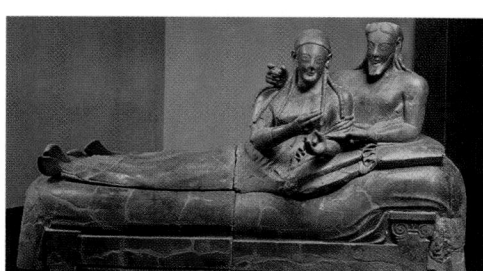

ca. 520 BCE Etruscan terra-cotta sarcophagus from Cerveteri

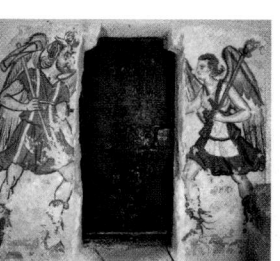

ca. 500 BCE The Capitoline *She-Wolf*

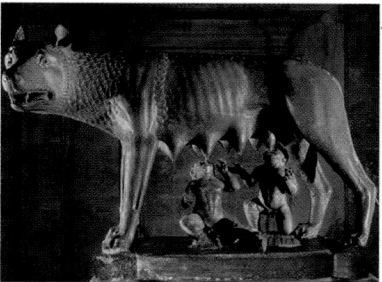

...nd of 4th century BCE Tomb of ...he Anina Family at Tarquinia

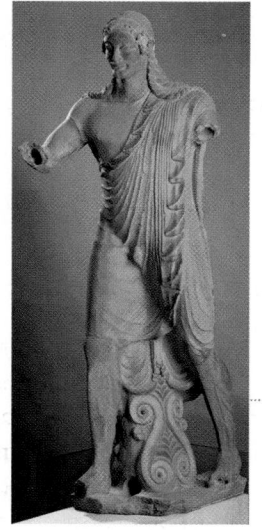

ca. 400 BCE *Aplu* (*Apollo*) of Veii

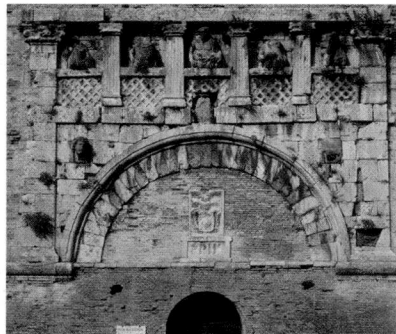

2nd century BCE The Porta Marzia in Perugia

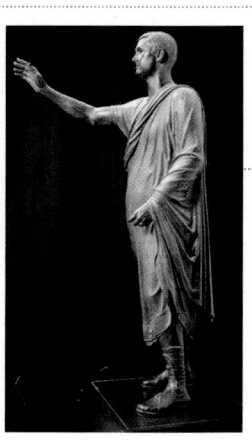

ca. 100 BCE *L'Arringatore* (*the Orator*)

Etruscan Art

1000 BCE

◄ ca. 1000 BCE Etruscan culture appears on the Italian peninsula

900 BCE

800 BCE

ca. 750 BCE Greek sculptural group, *Man and Centaur*, possibly from Olympia

700 BCE

mid-7th century BCE Black-figured vase-painting technique develops in Athens

ca. 668–627 BCE Assyrian construction of the North Palace of Ashurbanipal

600 BCE

◄ ca. 600s–500s BCE The height of Etruscan power

ca. 575 BCE Babylonians construct the Ishtar Gate

500 BCE

◄ 500s BCE Etruscans begin colonizing the flatlands south of Rome

◄ ca. 480–336 BCE Classical period in Greece

447–432 BCE Construction of the Parthenon in Athens

400 BCE

◄ ca. 396 BCE The Romans besiege and conquer Veii

ca. 380–330 BCE The Mausoleum at Halikarnassos

◄ 331 BCE Alexander the Great defeats the Persians

300 BCE

ca. 300 BCE Construction begins on the Temple of Apollo at Didyma

◄ 270 BCE All Etruscan city-states had lost their independence to Rome

200 BCE

ca. 175 BCE Great Altar of Zeus at Pergamon

100 BCE

ca. 80 BCE Greek portrait head from Delos

0

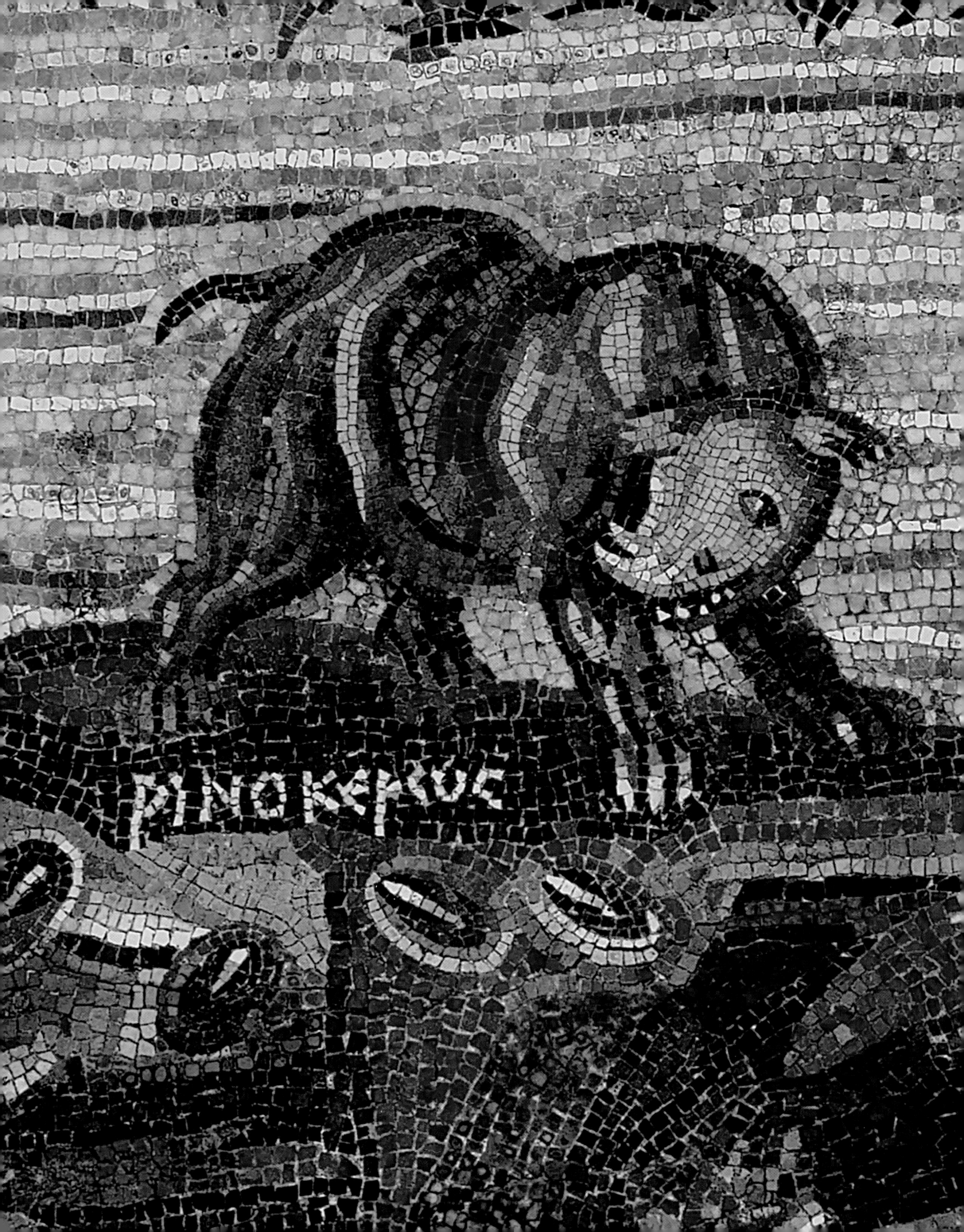

RINOKEPVE

CHAPTER 7

Roman Art

O F ALL THE CIVILIZATIONS OF THE ANCIENT WORLD, THE MOST accessible to modern scholars is that of ancient Rome. Romans built countless monuments throughout their empire, many of which are extraordinarily well preserved. A vast literary legacy, ranging from poetry and histories to inscriptions that recorded everyday events, also reveals

a great deal about Roman culture. Yet few questions are more difficult to address than "What is Roman art?"

Rome was a significant power in the Mediterranean from the fifth century BCE until the fourth century CE. At the Empire's height, its borders stretched from present-day Morocco to Iran, and from Egypt to Scotland (map 7.1). Greece was a relatively early addition to Roman territory, and much of Roman public art draws heavily on Greek styles, both Classical and Hellenistic. In the nineteenth and early twentieth centuries, influenced by early art historians like Winckelmann (see *The Art Historian's Lens*, page 157), art connoisseurs exalted Greek Classicism as the height of stylistic achievement, and considered Roman art derivative, the last chapter, so to speak, of Greek art history. This view changed radically in the ensuing years, especially as pure connoisseurship (an assessment of quality and authenticity) began to yield to other branches of art history. Scholars now focus, for instance, on the roles of a work of art in its social and political contexts. Yet regardless of how one assesses Roman artists for drawing on Greek styles, these were by no means the only styles at play in the Roman world. Works of art created in the provinces or for the nonelite have their own style, as do those of late antiquity. There were also phases of distinct "Egyptianizing" in Rome.

Detail of figure 7.15, *Nile Mosaic*, from Sanctuary of Fortuna Primigenia

Roman art was the art of both Republic and Empire, the art of a small city that became a vast empire. It was created by Roman artists, but not exclusively; the greatest architect of Trajan's time may have been from Damascus. Perhaps the most useful way to think of Roman art is to see it as an art of **syncretism**—an art that brings diverse elements together to produce something entirely new, with a powerful message-bearing potential. Syncretism was a profoundly Roman attitude, and was probably the secret to Rome's extraordinarily successful expansion. From the very start, Roman society was unusually tolerant of non-Roman traditions, as long as they did not undermine the state. Romans did not, on the whole, subordinate the populations of newly conquered regions, eventually according many the rights of citizenship and receiving non-Roman gods hospitably in the capital. This Roman propensity for integrating other cultures led to a remarkably diverse world.

EARLY ROME AND THE REPUBLIC

According to Roman legend, Romulus founded the city of Rome in 753/52 BCE, in the region known as Latium, on a site near the Tiber River. The sons of Mars and Rhea Silvia, who later became a Vestal Virgin, Romulus and his twin, Remus, were abandoned at birth, and raised by a she-wolf (see fig. 6.17). Yet archaeological

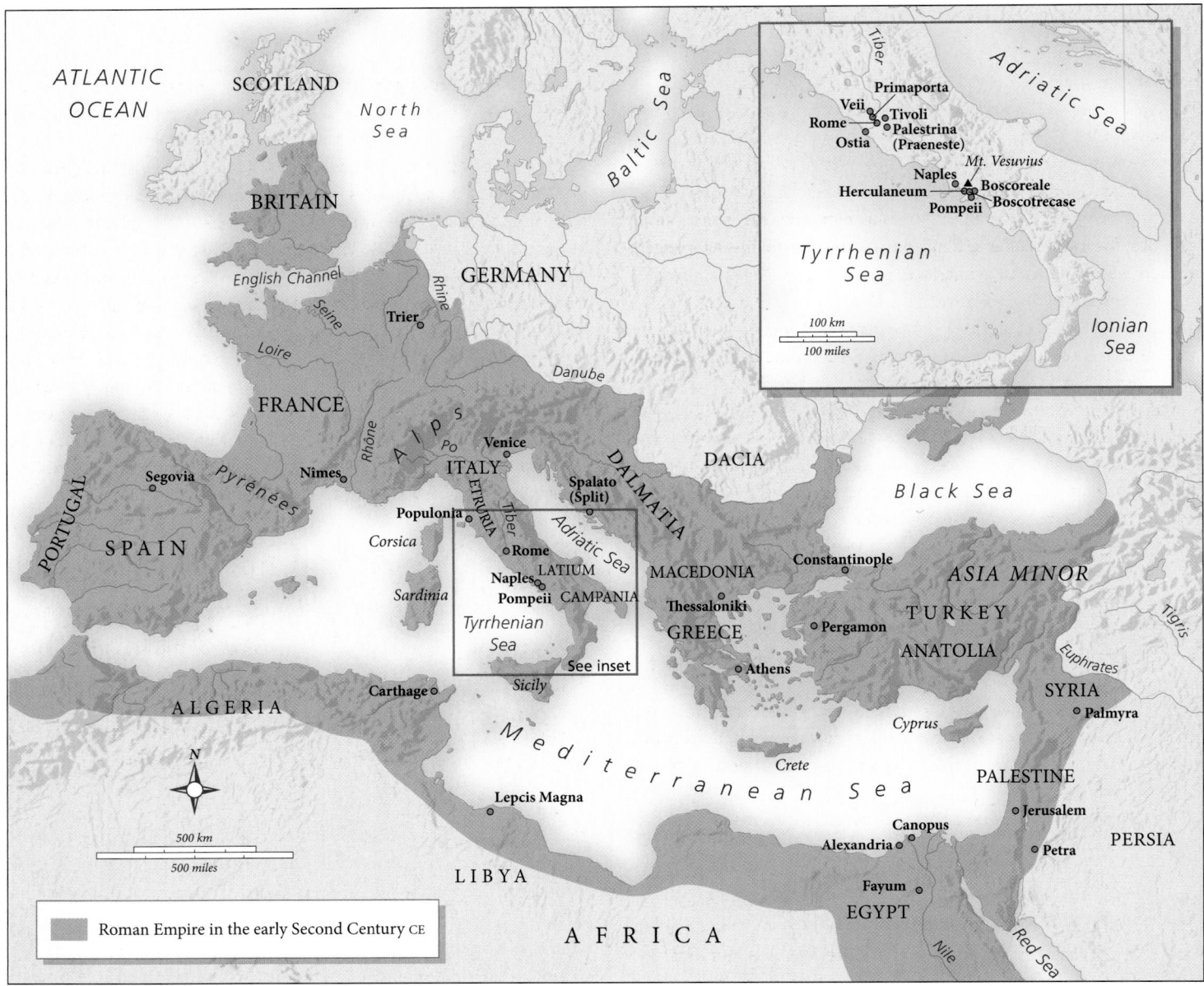

Map 7.1   Roman Empire in the early 2nd century CE

evidence shows that people had actually lived on the site since about 1000 BCE. From the eighth to the sixth centuries BCE, a series of kings built the first defensive wall around the settlement, drained and filled the swampy plain of the Forum, and built a vast temple on the Capitoline Hill, making an urban center out of what had been little more than a group of villages. The kings established many of Rome's lasting institutions, such as priesthoods and techniques of warfare. In about 509 BCE, the Roman elite expelled the last king, and gradually established a republic, with an unwritten constitution.

Under the Republic, a group of elected magistrates managed the affairs of the growing state. Two consuls headed them, and a Senate served as an advisory council. Popular uprisings led to greater rights and representation for the nonelite over the next 200 years. Rome gained most of its territorial empire during the course of the republic. First Rome and its allies, the Latin League,

destroyed the southern Etruscan city of Veii in 396 BCE. The Gauls, from the north, sacked Rome in 390 BCE, but this seems only to have spurred Rome on to greater conquest. By 275 BCE, Rome controlled all of Italy, including the Greek colonies of the south. Three Punic (from the Latin for "Phoenician") Wars against the North African city of Carthage ended with the decisive razing of Carthage in 146 BCE, and during the second century BCE all of Greece and Asia Minor also came under Roman control. Yet despite its successes, from about 133 BCE to 31 BCE, the Late Republic was in turmoil. Factional politics, mob violence, assassination, and competition among aristocratic families led to the breakdown of the constitution and to civil war. Julius Caesar became perpetual dictator in 46 BCE, a position that other senators were unable to tolerate. Two years later, they assassinated him.

During the course of the Republic, magistrates commissioned works of architecture and sculpture to embellish the city as well

Recognizing Copies: The Case of the Laocoön

In one of the most powerful passages of *The Aeneid*, Vergil describes the punishment of Laocoön, who, according to legend, was a priest at the time of the Trojan War. He warned the Trojans against accepting the wooden horse, the famous gift that hid invading Greeks within. The goddess Minerva, on the side of the Greeks, punished Laocoön by sending two giant serpents to devour him and his sons. Vergil describes the twin snakes gliding out of the sea to the altar where Laocoön was conducting a sacrifice, strangling him in their terrible coils, turning sacrificer into sacrificed. (See www.myartslab.com.)

In January 1506, a sculptural group depicting Laocoön and his sons writhing in the coils of snakes was unearthed on the Esquiline Hill in Rome. Renaissance humanists immediately hailed the group as an original Greek sculpture describing this brutal scene. It was, they thought, a sculpture that Pliny the Elder praised in his *Natural History* (completed in 77 CE). Pliny believed the Laocoön group that stood in Titus' palace to be the work of three sculptors from Rhodes: Hagesandros, Polydorus, and Athenodorus. Within a year of its rediscovery, the group had become the property of Pope Julius II, who installed it in his sculpture gallery, the Belvedere Courtyard in the Vatican. The sculpture quickly became a focus for contemporary artists, who both used it as a model and struggled to restore Laocoön's missing right arm (now bent behind him in what art historians consider the correct position). Its instant fame derived in part from the tidy convergence of the rediscovered sculpture with ancient literary sources: The masterpiece represented a dramatic moment in Rome's greatest epic and was described by a reputable Roman author.

The Laocoön group caught the rapt attention of the eighteenth-century art historian J. J. Winckelmann (see *The Art Historian's Lens*, page 157). He recognized a powerful tension between the subjects' agonizing death throes and a viewer's pleasure at the work's extraordinary quality. Such was his admiration that he could only see the piece as a Classical work, and dated it to the fourth century BCE; any later and it would be Hellenistic, a period that he characterized as a time of artistic decline. So began a wide debate on not only the date of the sculpture, but also its originality. For many scholars, the writhing agony of the Trojan priest and his sons bears all the hallmarks of the Hellenistic baroque style, as seen in the gigantomachy (the war between gods and giants) of the Great Altar of Zeus at Pergamon (see figs. 5.72 and 5.73). A masterpiece of the Hellenistic style, it should accordingly date to the third or second century BCE. On the other hand, evidence from inscriptions links the three artists named by Pliny to sculptors at work in the mid-first century BCE, making the sculpture considerably later and removing it from the apogee of the Hellenistic age. Yet there are cases of artists' names being passed down through several generations, and it is not at all clear that the group is in fact the sculpture Pliny admired.

Pliny specified that Laocoön was sculpted from a single piece of marble, and this sculpture is not; even more telling is the fact that a slab of Carrara marble—which was not exploited until the reign of Augustus (r. 27 BCE–14 CE)—is incorporated into the altar at the back. Is the sculpture then an early imperial work? Or is this much-lauded masterpiece a Roman copy of a Hellenistic work? If so, does that reduce its status? As if this were not debate enough, one contention takes Laocoön out of the realm of antiquity altogether, and identifies it instead as a Renaissance work by none other than Michelangelo. Evidence cited includes a pen study by the artist depicting a male torso resembling Laocoön's, dating to 1501. At this point, all that can be said with certainty about Laocoön is that the tidy picture imagined by sixteenth-century admirers has become considerably murkier.

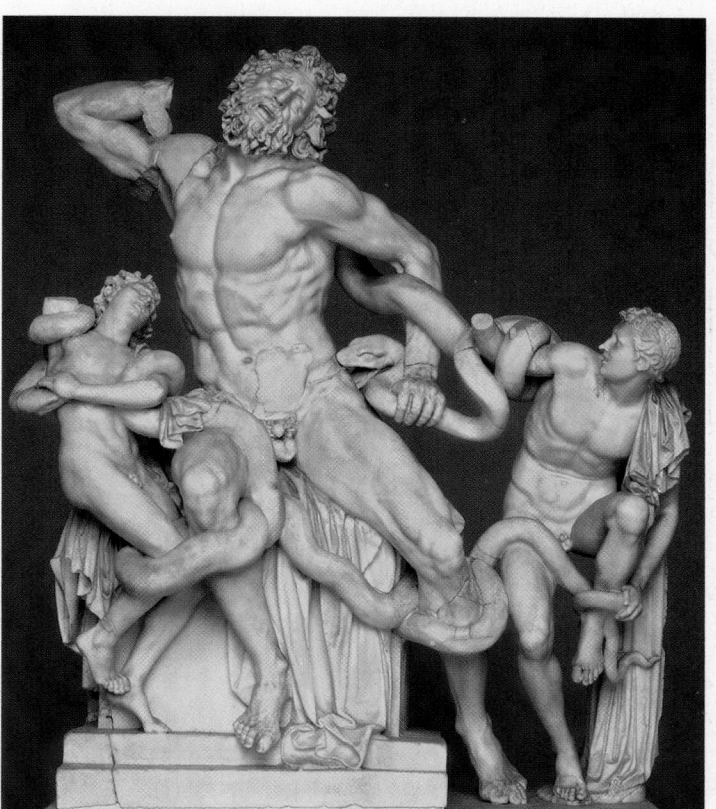

Laocoön, 1st century CE. Marble, height 7' (2.1 m). Musei Vaticani, Museo Pio Clementino, Cortile Ottagono, Città del Vaticano, Rome

---

as to enhance their own careers. Roman conquests abroad brought new artistic forms to the city, especially from Greece, which merged with Italic (i.e., typical of people of the Italian peninsula) forms to create a Roman artistic vocabulary, and the development of new building technologies such as concrete strongly influenced architectural designs.

NEW DIRECTIONS IN ARCHITECTURE

Roman architecture has had a more lasting impact on Western building through the ages than any other ancient tradition. It is an architecture of power, mediated through the solidity of its forms, and through the experience of those forms. Roman builders were indebted to Greek traditions, especially in their use of the Doric, Ionic, and Corinthian styles, yet these traditions inspired buildings that were decidedly Roman.

THE DEVELOPMENT OF FORMS The Temple of Jupiter Optimus Maximus on the Capitoline Hill was the first truly monumental building of Rome (fig. **7.1**). Romans worshiped a wide range of gods, some of them indigenous, but many others adopted from other cultures; in fact, their pantheon of state gods was roughly equivalent to the Greek pantheon. The Capitoline temple honored the chief god, Jupiter, roughly equivalent to the Greek Zeus. Its construction began under two sixth-century BCE kings, Tarquinius the Ancient and Tarquinius the Proud, but it was one of Rome's first consuls who actually dedicated the finished temple. Its scale was unprecedented on the Italian peninsula, evoking the massive Ionic temples of eastern Greece (see fig. 5.12). It stood on a high masonry platform, with steps leading up to the façade. Six wooden columns marked the front, and six columns flanked each side. Two rows of columns supported the roof over a deep porch. An Etruscan artist, Vulca of Veii, crafted a vast terra-cotta acroterion for the peak of the pediment, representing Jupiter in a four-horse chariot. A triple cella with walls of wood-framed mud brick accommodated cult statues of Jupiter, Juno, and Minerva, and recent excavations suggest that two additional rooms were arranged across the rear, accessed from the lateral colonnades. The rectilinear forms, the use of columns, and a gabled roof echo Greek design; yet the high podium and the emphatic frontal

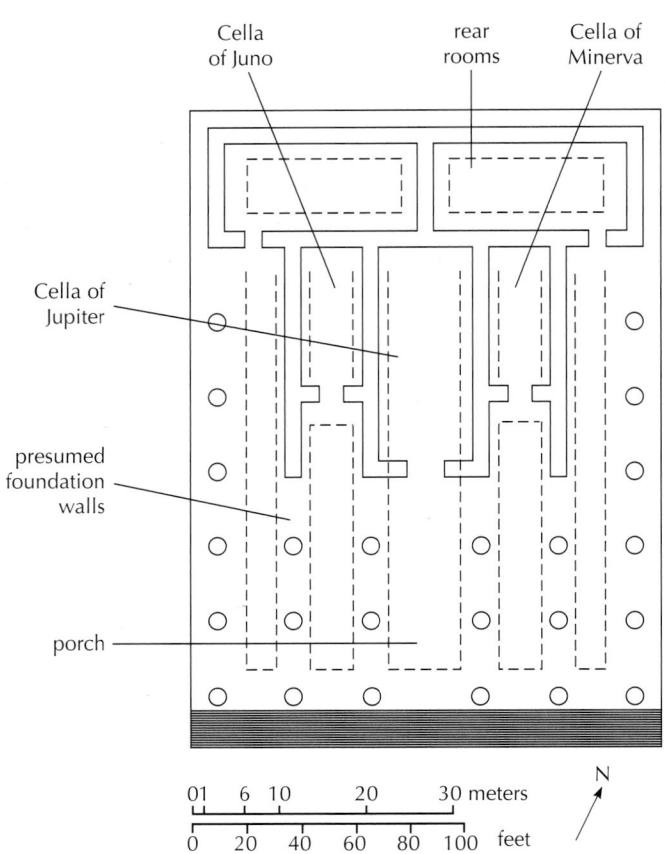

7.1 Restored plan of Temple of Jupiter Optimus Maximus, Capitoline Hill, Rome. Dedicated ca. 509 BCE

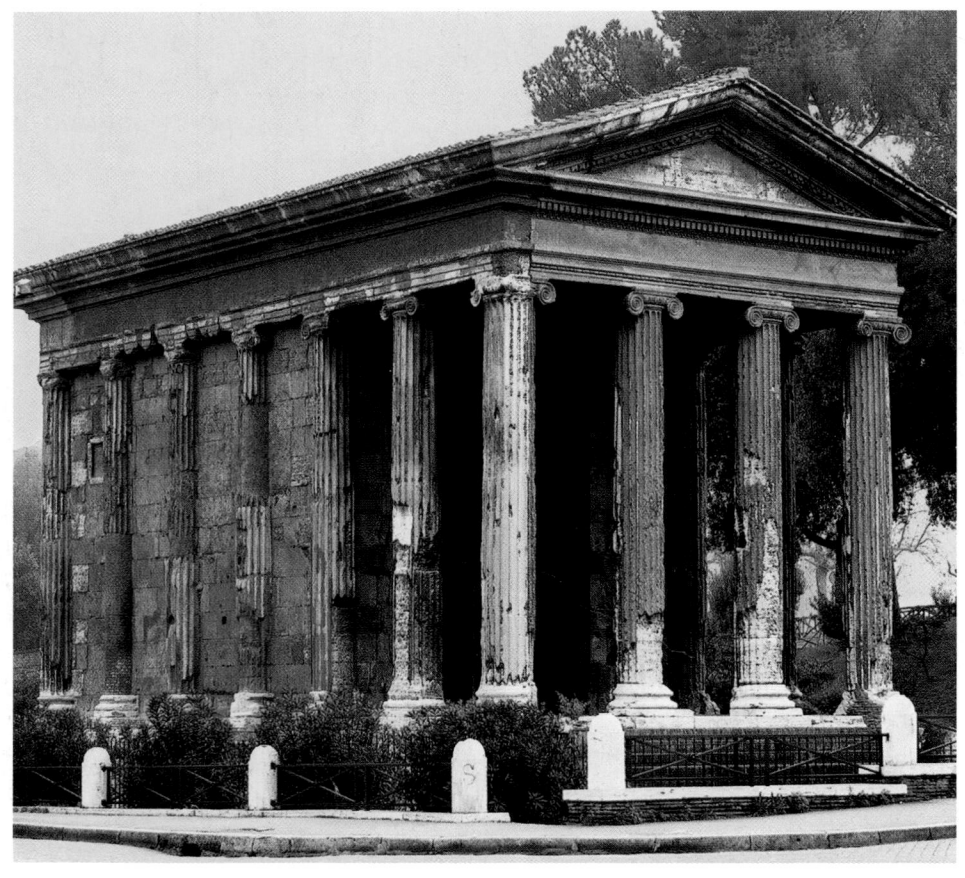

7.2 Temple of Portunus, Rome. ca. 80–70 BCE

access set it apart. Scholars call these features Etrusco-Italic, and they characterize most Roman temples in centuries to come.

Although the practice of borrowing Greek forms began early in the Republic, it was particularly marked during the period of Rome's conquest of Greece, when architects used Greek building materials as well as essential building forms. After celebrating a triumph over Macedonia in 146 BCE, the general Metellus commissioned Rome's first all-marble temple and hired a Greek architect, Hermodorus, for the job. It no longer survives, but was probably close in form to the remarkably well-preserved temple to the harbor-god Portunus near the Tiber (fig. **7.2**). Dating from 80 to 70 BCE, the temple is in the Italic style: It stands on a podium, and engaged lateral columns (instead of a true peristyle)

emphasize the frontal approach. All the same, the Ionic columns have the slender proportions of Classical Greek temples, and a white marble stucco covering their travertine and tufa shafts, bases, and capitals deliberately evoked the translucent marbles of Greek architecture.

Roman architects quickly combined the rectilinear designs of Greek architecture with the curved form of the arch (fig. 7.3). An arch could be a free-standing monument in its own right, or be applied to a building, often to frame an entrance. To construct arches, builders assembled wedge-shaped voussoirs, as seen in the Etruscan Porta Marzia at Perugia (see fig. 6.12). These arches are extremely strong, in contrast to corbeled arches (see fig. 4.21). Voussoir arches were not a Roman or an Etruscan invention: Near

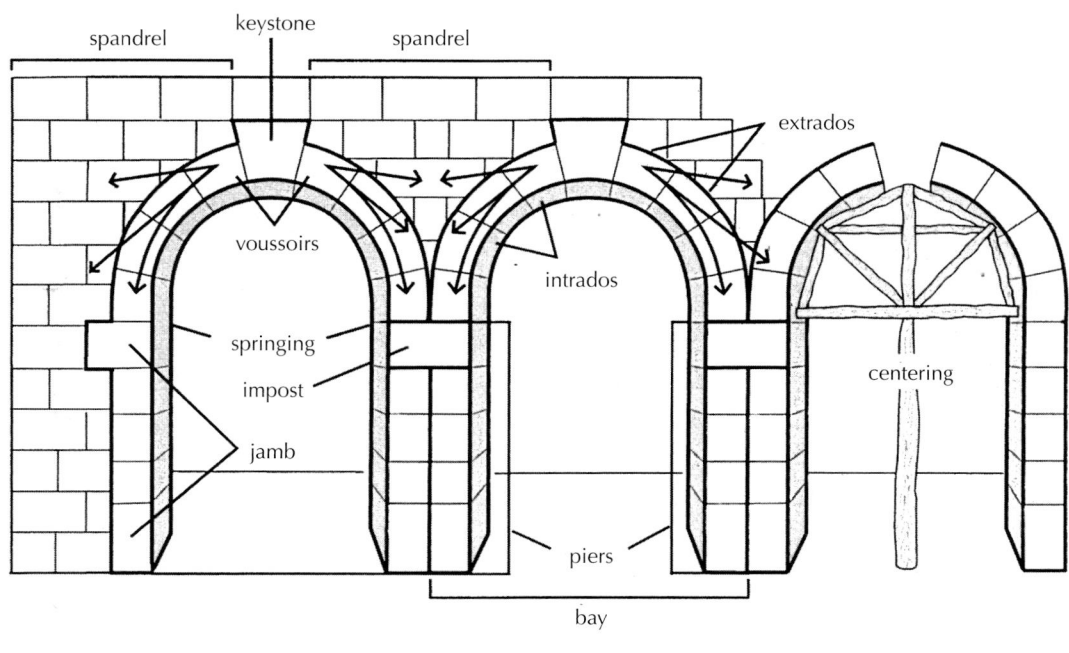

round arch

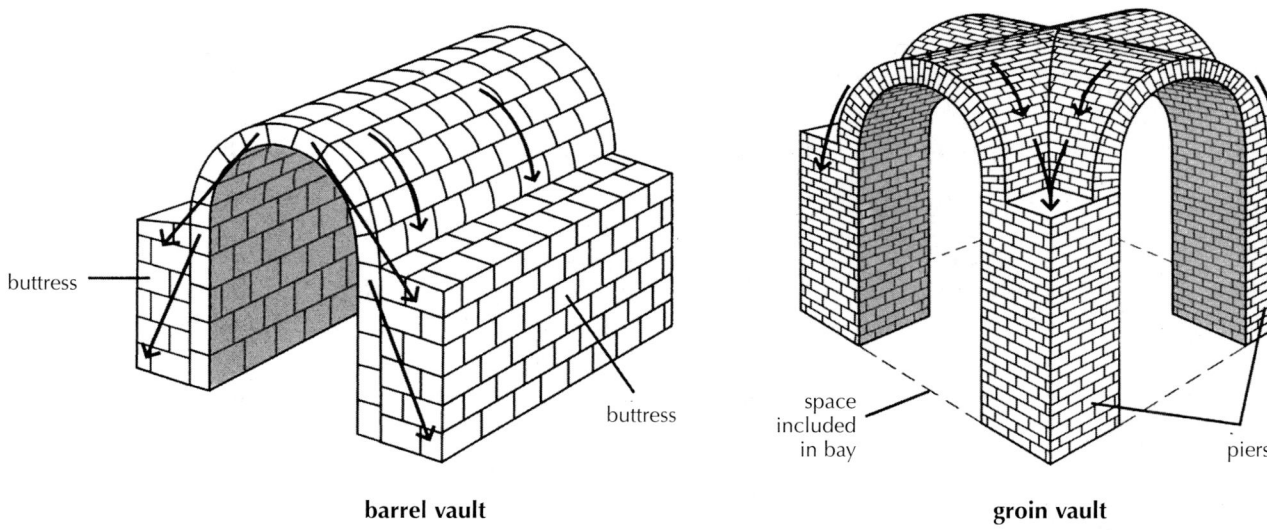

barrel vault   **groin vault**

7.3   Arch, barrel vault, and groin vault

Eastern architects used them in ziggurat foundations and in city gates, and Egyptian builders employed them, as well as their extension, the **barrel vault**, as early as about 1250 BCE, mainly in underground tombs and utilitarian buildings, rather than for monumental public buildings; Greeks architects constructed underground structures or simple gateways with arches. The Romans, however, put them to widespread use in public architecture, making them one of the hallmarks of Roman building.

THE CONCRETE REVOLUTION It was the development of concrete, however, that was a catalyst for the most dramatic changes in Roman architecture. Concrete is a mixture of mortar and pieces of aggregate such as tufa, limestone, or brick. At first, Roman architects used it as fill, between walls or in podiums. Yet on adding *pozzolana* sand to the mortar, they discovered a material of remarkable durability—which would even cure (or set) under water—and they used it with growing confidence from the second century BCE onward. Despite its strength, it was not attractive to the eye, and builders concealed it with cosmetic facings of stone, brick, and plaster, which changed with the passing years and therefore provide archaeologists with an invaluable tool for dating Roman buildings. The advantages of concrete were quickly evident: It was strong and inexpensive, and could be worked by relatively unskilled laborers. It was also extraordinarily adaptable. By constructing wooden frameworks into which they poured the concrete, builders could mold it to shapes that would have been impossible or prohibitively time-consuming to make using cut stone, wood, or mud brick. In terms of design, the history of Roman architecture is a dialogue between the traditional rectilinear forms of Greek and early Italic post-and-lintel traditions (construction using vertical posts to support vertical elements) on the one hand, and the freedoms afforded by this malleable material on the other.

Two quite different Republican structures demonstrate concrete's advantages. A building of the second century BCE, long identified as the Porticus Aemilia, but almost certainly the Navalia, or ship shed for the Roman fleet, is the earliest known building in Rome constructed entirely of concrete. Its dimensions were simply staggering: It stretched 1,600 Roman feet (a little shorter than modern feet) along the Tiber and was 300 feet deep. As the partial reconstruction in figure **7.4** illustrates, the architects took advantage of the new material to create a remarkably open interior space. Soaring barrel vaults roofed 50 transverse corridors, built in four rising sections to accommodate the sloping terrain. Arches pierced the walls supporting the vaults, so that air could circulate freely. Roman sailors could pull the ships into these spaces for easy maintenance in the winter months.

East of Rome, in the Apennine foothills, the town of Palestrina (ancient Praeneste) is home to another masterpiece of concrete construction (figs. **7.5** and **7.6**). The spectacular sanctuary to the goddess Fortuna Primigenia, dated to the late second century BCE, was an oracular center where priests interpreted divine will by drawing lots. Architects used concrete to mold structures over the entire surface of the hillside and to craft spaces

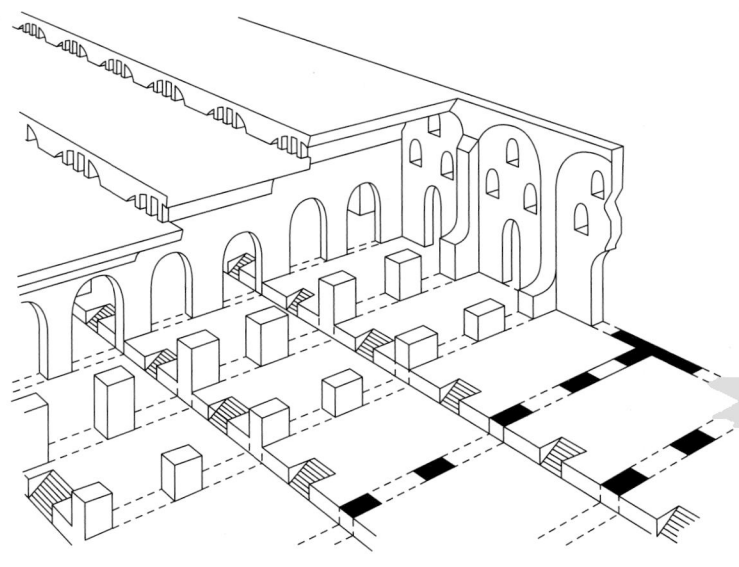

7.4 Navalia, Rome. First half of the 2nd century BCE. Partial reconstruction drawing

that controlled and heightened a visitor's experience. The sanctuary ascended in seven levels. At the bottom stood an early temple, a **basilica** (see page 225), and a senate house. The upper terraces rose in a grand crescendo around a central axis, established by a series of statue niches and staircases. A visitor climbed lateral staircases to the third terrace, where steep ramps, roofed with sloping barrel vaults, led upward. A bright shaft of daylight beckoned from the end of the ramp, where an open landing provided the first of several stunning views across the countryside.

On the fourth level, colonnaded exedrae (semicircular recesses) framed the altars. Barrel vaults roofed the colonnades, inscribing a half-circle both horizontally and vertically (**annular** barrel vaults). Their curved forms animate the straight lines, since columns set in a semicircle shift their relationship to the environment with every step a visitor takes. A wide central staircase leads upward to the next level. After the confinement of the ramps, its steps were exposed, engendering a sense of vulnerability in the visitor. On this level, shops probably sold souvenirs and votive objects. Standing on this terrace, a visitor was directly above the voids of the barrel vaults below, evidence of the architects' confidence in the structure. The next terrace was a huge open court, with double colonnades on three sides. The visitor climbed to a small theater topped by a double annular colonnade. Here religious performances took place against the magnificent backdrop of the countryside beyond, and in full sight of Fortuna, the goddess whose circular temple crowned the complex. Its diminutive size drew grandeur from the vast scale of the whole—all accomplished with concrete. The hugely versatile material plays easily with the landscape, transforming nature to heighten a visitor's religious experience.

The first century BCE was a turning point in the use of architecture for political purposes. One of the most magnificent buildings of this time was the vast theater complex of Pompey, which would remain Rome's most important theater throughout antiquity.

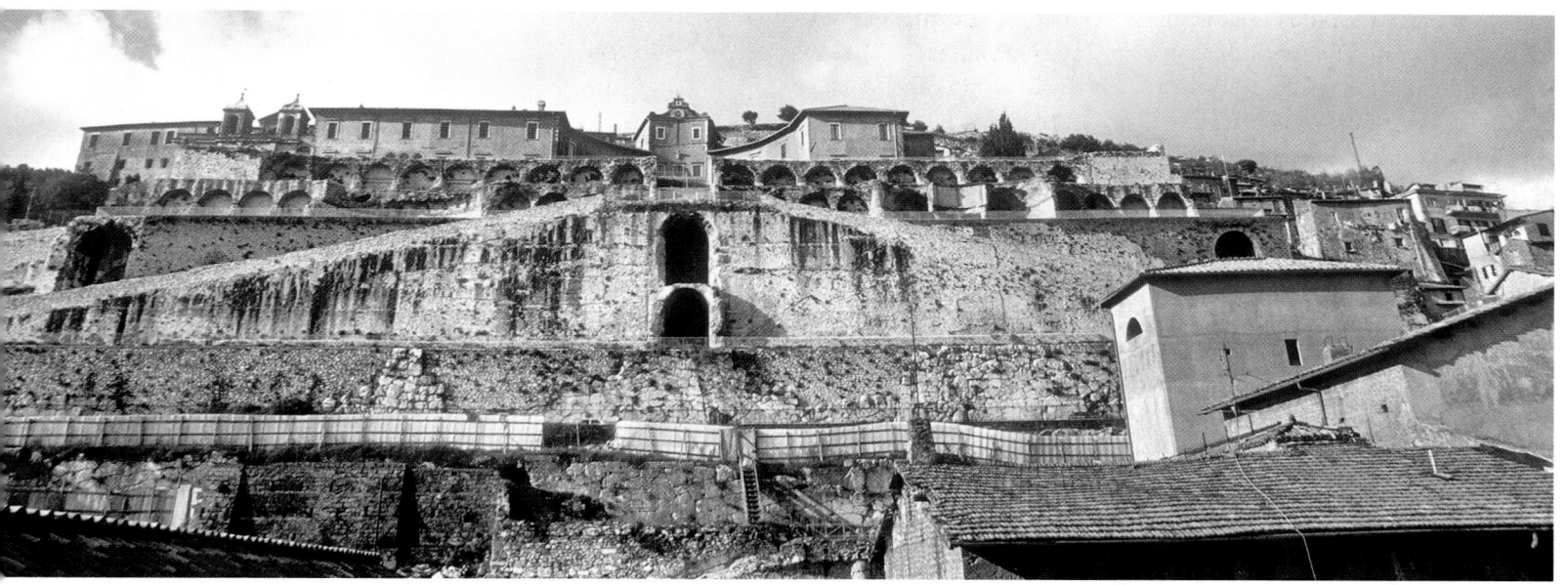

7.5 Sanctuary of Fortuna Primigenia, Praeneste (Palestrina). Late 2nd century BCE

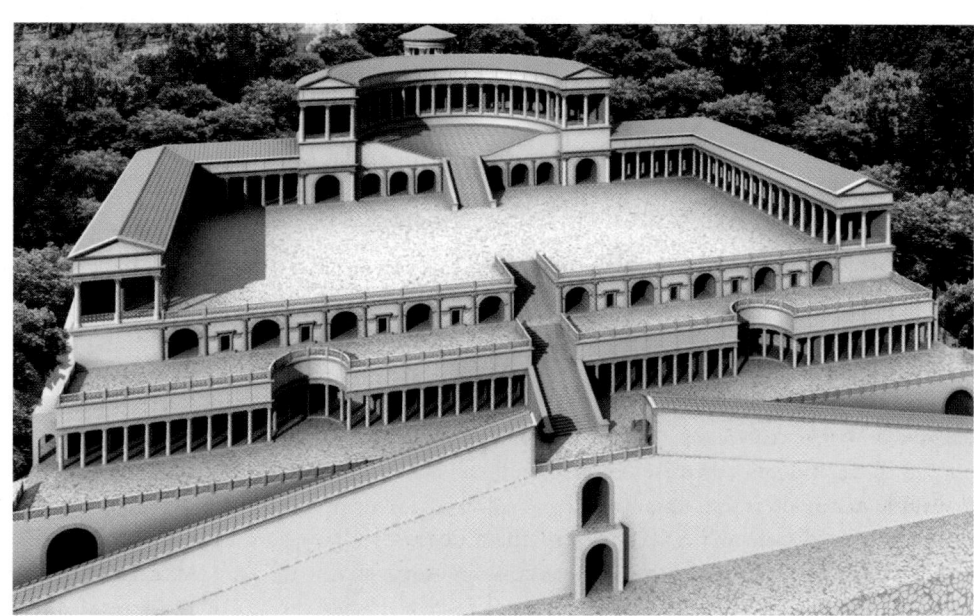

7.6 Reconstruction of Sanctuary of Fortuna Primigenia, Praeneste

Like Julius Caesar after him, Pompey (active in Roman politics in the 70s and 60s BCE) maneuvered his way into a position of sole authority in Rome and used architecture to express and justify his aconstitutional power. To commemorate his conquests, he conceived of a theater on the Field of Mars, just outside the northern city boundary, dedicated to his patron goddess Venus Victrix (the Conqueror) (fig. **7.7**). Later buildings on the site incorporate traces of its superstructure, and the street plan still reflects its curved form. Moreover, its ground plan is inscribed on an ancient marble map of the city, carved in the early third century CE, and new excavations may uncover more of its vaulted substructure. The reconstruction in figure 7.7 is therefore provisional, a combination of archaeological evidence and conjecture; it is likely to change as new evidence emerges. In some respects, Pompey's theater resembled its Greek forebears, with sloping banks of seats in a semicircular arrangement, a ground-level **orchestra** area, and a raised stage for scenery. In other ways, however, it was radically different. It was not, for instance, nestled into a preexisting hillside. Instead, the architect created an artificial slope out of concrete, rising on radially disposed barrel vaults, which buttressed one another for a strong structure. Concrete, in other words, gave the designer freedom to build independent of the landscape. The curved cavea (seating area), moreover, was a true half-circle, rather than the extended half-circle of Greek theaters. At the summit of the cavea were three shrines and a temple dedicated to Venus. The curved façade held statues personifying the nations Pompey had subdued. Beyond the theater, and adjoining it behind the stage building, porticoes defined a vast garden, where Romans could admire valuable works of art, such as sculptures, paintings, and tapestries, many of which had been brought from Greece. These public gardens were Pompey's gift to the people of Rome—an implicit way of winning political favor.

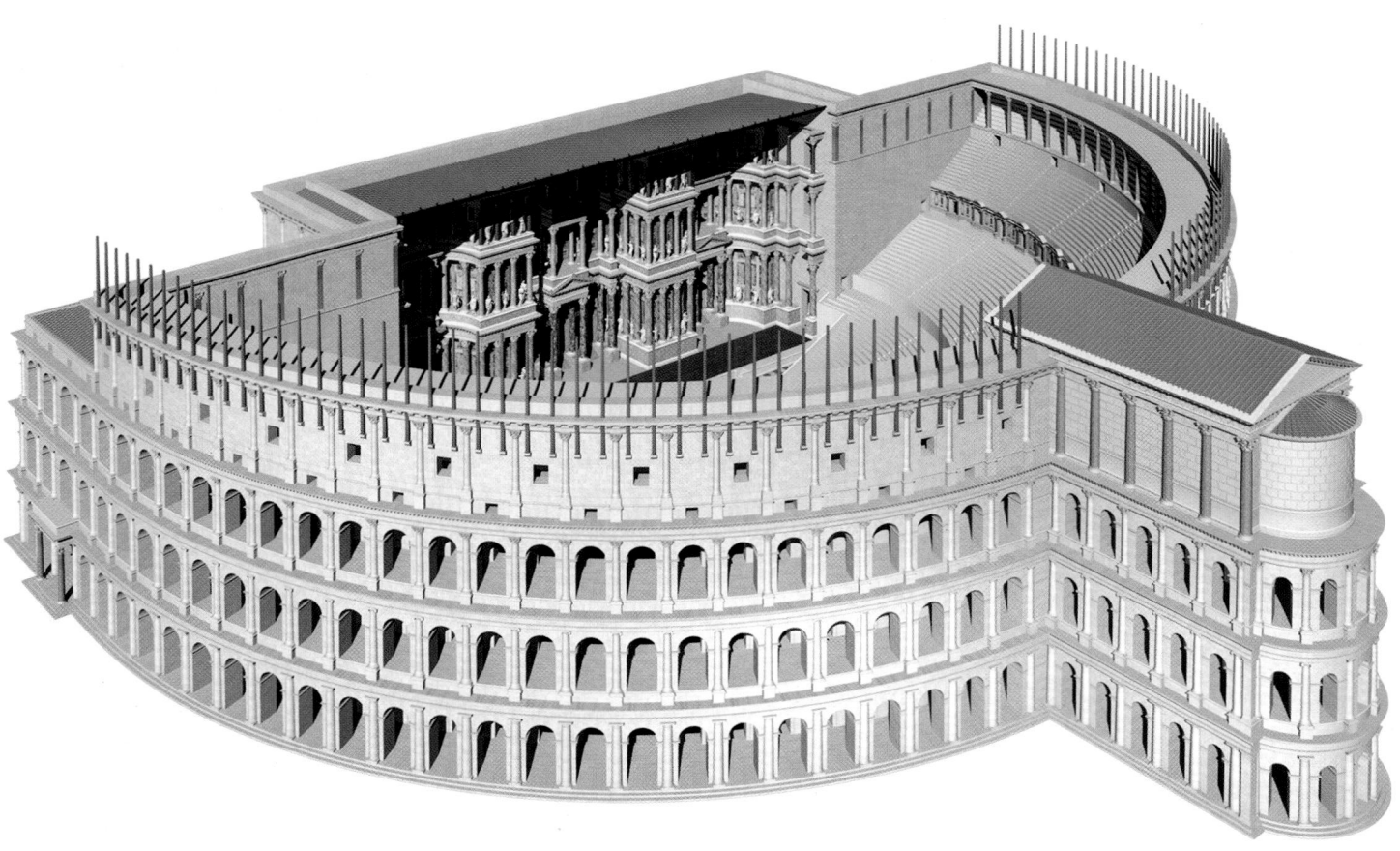

7.7 Theater complex of Pompey, Rome. Dedicated in 55 BCE. Provisional reconstruction by James E. Packer and John Burge

Pompey's theater complex dwarfed the smaller, scattered buildings that individual magistrates had commissioned up to that point. It was also Rome's first permanent theater. As in Greece, plays were an essential component of religious ceremonies, and Romans had always constructed the buildings that accommodated them out of wood, assembling them for the occasion and then dismantling them. In fact, some elite Romans spoke out against the construction of permanent theaters—ostensibly on moral grounds, but also because they were places for the nonelite to meet. Pompey circumvented such objections by describing his theater as a mere appendage to the temple of Venus at its summit, and in building the complex he set the precedent for the great forum project of Julius Caesar, and the imperial fora that would follow (see page 196).

Sculpture

FREE-STANDING SCULPTURE In early Rome, as elsewhere in Italy, sculptors worked primarily in terra cotta and in bronze. Countless terra-cotta votive objects survive from sanctuaries, where visitors dedicated them in hope of divine favor. The gradual conquest of Greece in the second century BCE had led to a fascination with Greek works of art, which flooded into Rome as booty. So intense was the fascination, in fact, that in the late first century BCE, the poet Horace commented ironically, "Greece, having been conquered, conquered her wild conqueror, and brought the arts into rustic Latium." Paraded through the streets

of Rome as part of the triumphal procession, the works of art ended their journey by decorating public spaces, such as the theater complex of Pompey (see fig. 7.7).

These glistening bronze and marble works provoked reaction. For most, it seems, they were a welcome sign of Rome's cultural advance, more visually pleasing than indigenous sculptures in terra cotta. Elite Romans assembled magnificent collections of Greek art in their homes; through their display they could give visual expression to their erudition. The Villa of the Papyri in Herculaneum, a city built on the slopes of Vesuvius in southwest Italy, preserved an extensive collection *in situ* when the volcano erupted. The villa and its collection are partially reconstructed in the Getty Museum in Malibu, California. When Greek originals were not available, copyists provided alternatives in the styles of known Greek artists. (See *Materials and Techniques*, page 193, and *The Art Historian's Lens*, page 183.) A series of letters from Cicero, a lawyer and writer of the mid-first century BCE, to his friend Atticus in Athens shows the process at work: he asks Atticus to send him sculptures to decorate the various parts of his villa. (See *Primary Source*, page 192.) The stylistic borrowings also had a bold political dimension, showing that Rome had bested the great cultures of Greece.

RELIEF SCULPTURE A few strident voices spoke out against the invasion of Greek art. Most vociferous was Cato ("The Moralist"), for whom traditional Roman art forms symbolized the staunch moral and religious values that had led to, and justified,

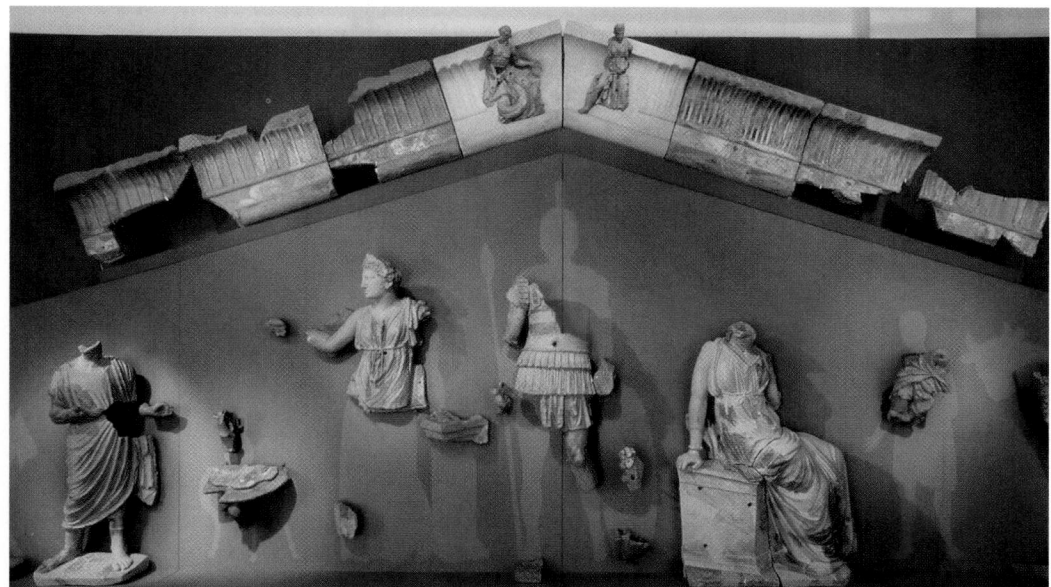

Rome's political ascent. A set of magnificent terra-cotta pediment sculptures discovered on Via di San Gregorio in Rome during sewer repairs in 1878 gives an impression of the art form he was intent on defending (figs. **7.8** and **7.9**). The subject of the pediment appears to be a *suovetaurilia*, a sacrifice of a pig, a sheep, and a bull. The larger-scale figures probably represent divinities—perhaps Mars in the center, with breastplate and spear, and two flanking goddesses. Smaller figures include a male in a toga, perhaps the presiding magistrate; a male in tunic and mantle; and several *victimarii* (attendants to the sacrificial animals). The artists sculpted the figures in such high relief that they are almost fully in the round, and applied them to a smooth background, painted black; they protrude emphatically toward the top, in order to be legible from below. As in Egypt, color conventions distinguish the female figures, with their cream skin tones, from the deeper red males.

The pediment may have belonged to a temple to Mars on the Caelian Hill. Scholars date it to the third quarter of the second century BCE, which places it at the height of Greek influence in Rome. This is clearly evident in Mars' Hellenistic breastplate, the **classicizing** treatment of the drapery and faces, and the musculature. All the same, the material and technique are distinctly Italic, and the refined modeling and high polish demonstrate how striking terra-cotta works could be.

Sometimes Roman sculpture commemorated specific events, as it did in the ancient Near East (see figs. 2.12 and 2.19). Classical Greek sculptors disguised historical events in mythical clothing— a combat of Lapiths and Centaurs, for instance, or Greeks and Amazons (see figs. 5.35, and 5.44)—and this convention broke down only slightly in the Classical period. The Romans, by contrast, represented actual events, developing a form of sculpture known as historical relief—although many were not historically accurate. The reliefs shown in figure **7.10**, sometimes called the

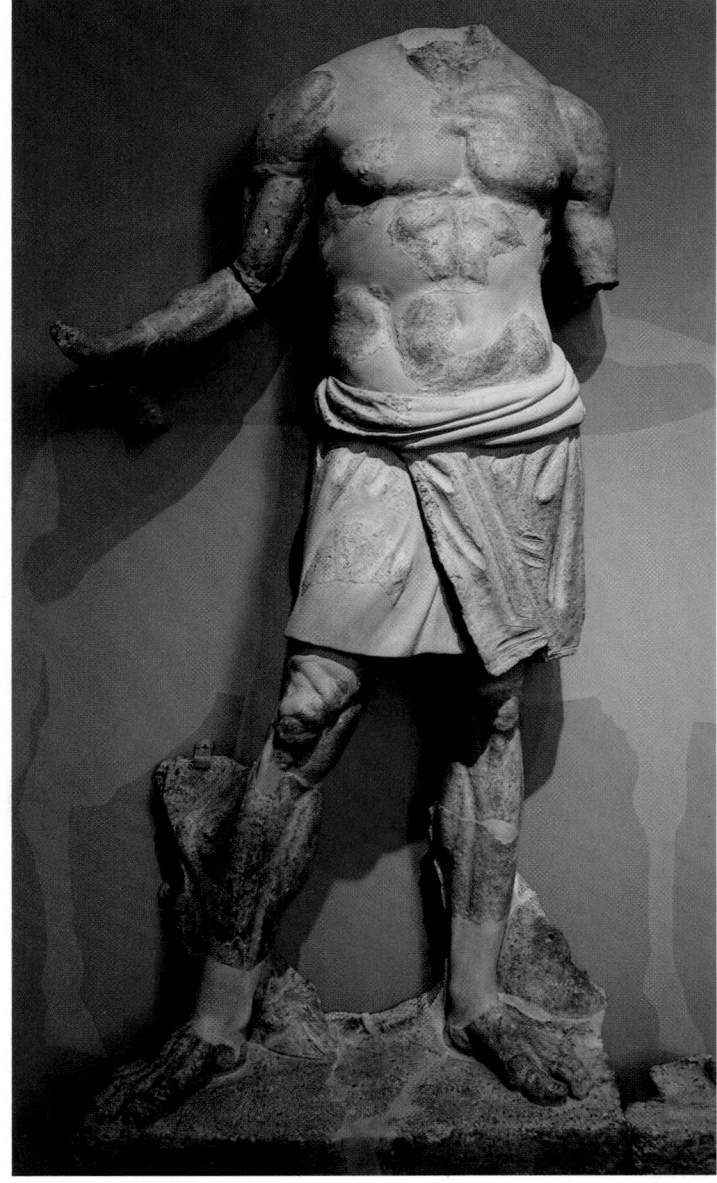

7.9 Victimarius from the Via di San Gregorio pediment.
Painted terra cotta, height 41½" (106 cm). Museo Capitolino, Rome

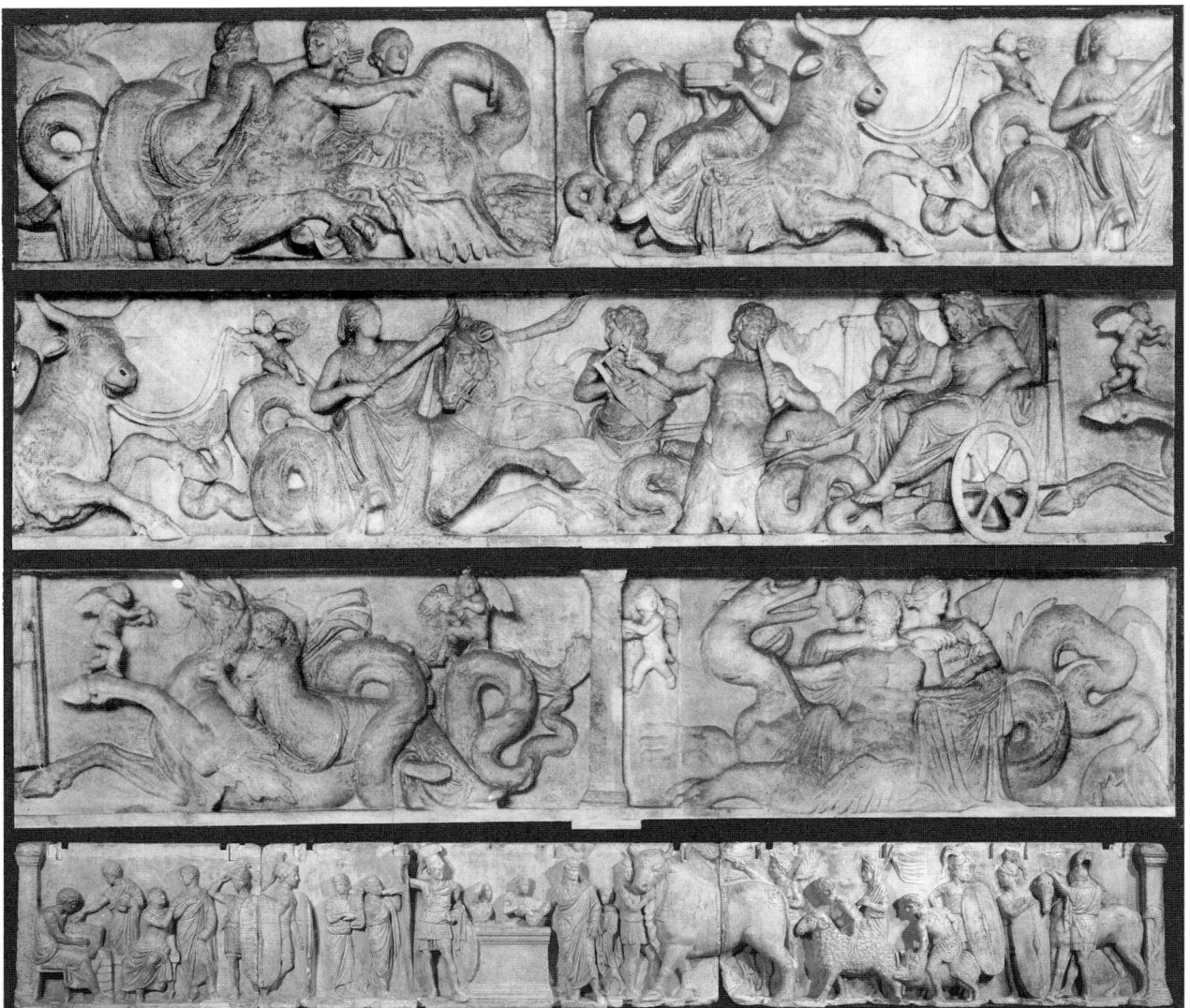

7.10 Sculptural reliefs from statue base, showing sea thiasos and census, from the so-called Altar of Domitius Ahenobarbus or Base of Marcus Antonius. Late 2nd to early 1st century BCE. Marble. Musée du Louvre, Paris, and Glyptothek, Staatliche Antikensammlungen, Munich

Base of Marcus Antonius, probably decorated a base for a statuary group, which scholars place near the route used for triumphal processions through Rome. One long section shows a census, a ceremony during which individuals recorded their property holdings with the state to qualify for military service (which was a prerequisite for public office). On the left side, soldiers and civilians line up to be entered into the census. Two large figures flanking an altar represent a statue of Mars, god of war, and the officiating censor, who probably commissioned the monument. Attendants escort a bull, a sheep, and a pig for sacrifice at an altar, marking the closing ceremony of the census.

On the same monument, the remaining reliefs depict a marine thiasos (procession) for the marriage of the sea-god Neptune and a sea-nymph, Amphitrite. But these reliefs are in an entirely different style. The swirling motion of the marriage procession and its Hellenistic forms contrast dramatically with the static composition of the census relief and the stocky proportions of its figures. Moreover, the panels are carved from different types of marble. Scholars suppose that the sea-thiasos sections were not original to this context, but that a triumphant general brought them back as spoils from Greece to grace a triumphal monument—proof, as it were, of his conquest. By contrast, artists carved the census relief in Rome to complement the thiasos. Together, the reliefs may represent the patron's military and political achievements.

PORTRAIT SCULPTURE Literary sources reveal that the Senate and People (the governing bodies of the Republic) of Rome honored political or military figures by putting their statues on public display, often in the Roman Forum, the civic heart of the city (see page 196). The custom began in the early Republic and continued until the end of the Empire. Many of the early portraits were bronze and were melted down in later years for coinage or weaponry. A magnificent bronze male head dating to the late first century BCE, a mere fragment of a full-length figure, gives a tantalizing sense of how these statues once looked (fig. **7.11**). Sixteenth-century antiquarians dubbed it "Brutus," after the founder and first consul of the Republic. Strong features characterize the over-life-size portrait: a solid neck, a square jaw accentuated by a short beard, high cheekbones, and a firm brow. The image derives its power not from classical idealization or the

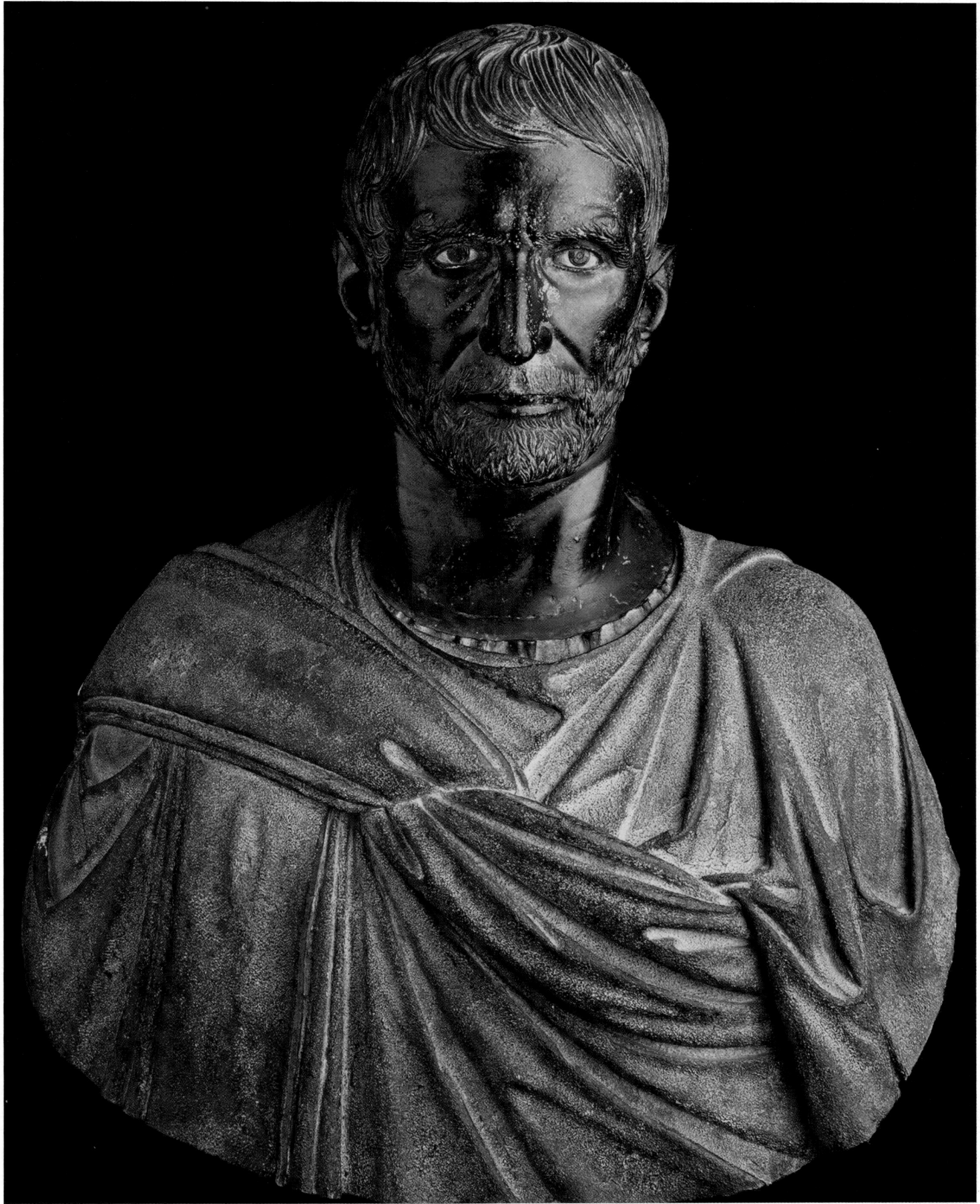

7.11   *"Brutus."* Late 1st-century BCE head, modern bust. Bronze, slightly over-life-size. Museo del Palazzo dei Conservatori, Rome

Cicero (106–43 BCE)

Letters to Atticus I. 9–10 (67 BCE, Rome)

Marcus Tullius Cicero was a leading politician and orator in Rome during the turbulent days of the late Republic. He is known through his extensive writings, which include orations, rhetorical and philosophical treatises, and letters. Like many other Roman statesmen, he filled his many houses and villas with works of Greek art, either original or copied. Atticus was his childhood friend, who maintained communication with Cicero after moving to Athens and served as his purchasing agent for works of art.

IX

Cicero to Atticus, Greeting

Your letters are much too few and far between, considering that it is much easier for you to find someone coming to Rome than for me to find anyone going to Athens. Besides, you can be surer that I am at Rome than I can be that you are in Athens. The shortness of this letter is due to my doubts as to your whereabouts. Not knowing for certain where you are, I don't want private correspondence to fall into a stranger's hands.

I am awaiting impatiently the statues of Megaric marble and those of Hermes, which you mentioned in your letter. Don't hesitate to send anything else of the same kind that you have, if it is fit for my Academy. My purse is long enough. This is my little weakness; and what I want especially are those that are fit for a Gymnasium. Lentulus promises his ships. Please bestir yourself about it. Thyillus asks you, or rather has got me to ask you, for some books on the ritual of the Eumolpidae.

Source: *Cicero, Letters to Atticus*, 3 vols., tr. E.O. Winstedt (1912–18)

stylized qualities of, for instance, the portrait of an Akkadian ruler (see fig. 2.11), but from the creases and furrows that record a life of engagement. The slight downward turn of the head may indicate that it once belonged to an equestrian portrait, originally displayed raised above a viewer.

The majority of Republican portraits were stone and date to the end of the second century and the first century BCE. Most represent men at an advanced age (fig. **7.12**). Wrinkles cover their faces, etching deep crags into their cheeks and brows. Artists played up distinguishing marks—like warts, a hooked nose, or a receding hairline—rather than smoothing over them. In the example illustrated here, remnants of a veil suggest that the subject was represented as a priest. Although there is no way of knowing what the sitter looked like, the images appear realistic, so that scholars term the style **veristic**, from the Latin *verus*, meaning "true." Cultures construct different ideals, and to Romans, responsibility and experience came with seniority. Military service was a prerequisite for office, and most magistracies had minimum-age requirements. An image marked by age therefore conveyed the necessary qualities for winning votes for political office, and the veristic style became the hallmark of Late Republican portraiture.

Where the impetus to produce likenesses came from is a mystery that scholars have struggled to solve. For some, its roots lie in an Italic practice of storing ancestral masks in the home to provide a visual genealogy—in this society, a good pedigree was a reliable steppingstone to political success. Polybius, a Greek historian of the mid-second century BCE, recounts that before burying a family member, living relatives would wear these ancestral masks in a funerary procession, parading the family's history in front of bystanders. (See *Primary Source*, page 194.) Other scholars trace it to a Greek custom of placing votive statues of athletes and other important individuals in sacred precincts, and indeed some Roman portraits were executed in Greek styles.

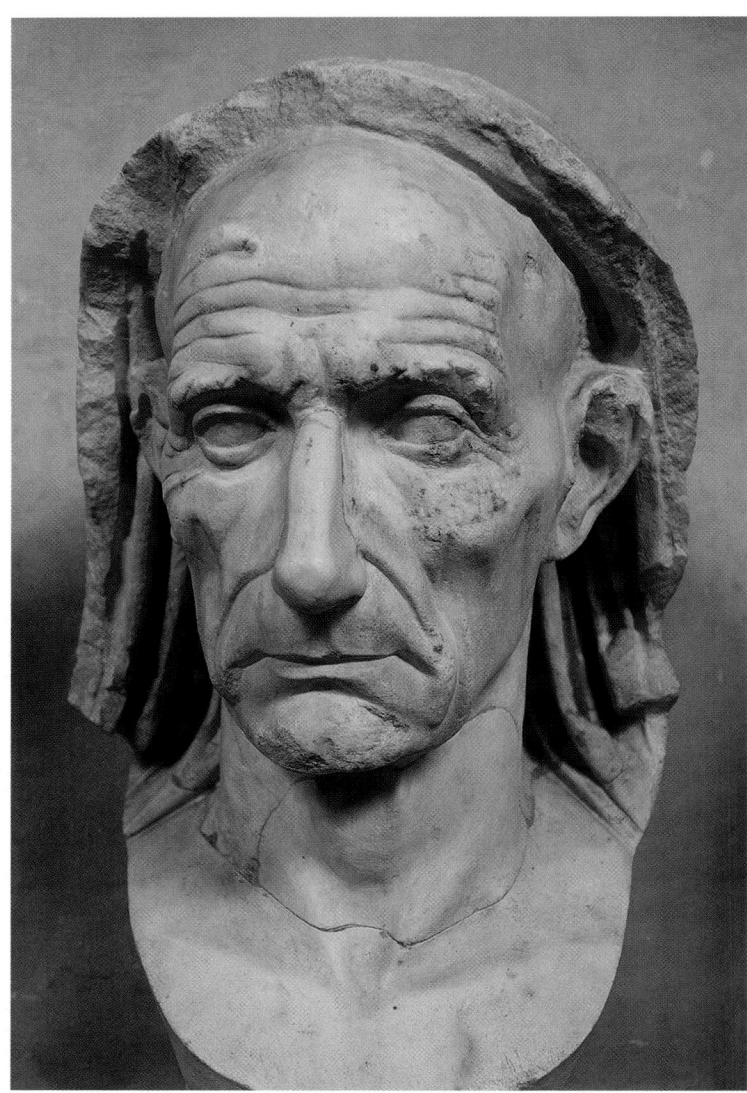

7.12 Veristic male portrait. Early 1st century BCE. Marble, life-size. Musei Vaticani, Rome

Copying Greek Sculptures

In order to satisfy a growing demand for Greek sculptures, artists set up copying workshops in Athens and Rome, where they produced copies of famous "masterpieces." Some of these copies may have been relatively close replicas of the originals; others were adaptations, where the copyist's own creativity came freely into play. Given the paucity of surviving Greek originals, it is often difficult for scholars to determine the appearance of the original, and thus to distinguish replica from adaptation. One clue to recognizing a marble copy (whether a true replica or a free adaptation) of a bronze original is to look for the use of struts to strengthen the stone, since marble has a different tensile strength from bronze (see the tree trunk and the strut at the hip in fig. 5.33).

Scholars have long believed that Roman copyists used a pointing machine (a duplicating device that takes one to one measurements), similar to a kind that was used in the early nineteenth century, but evidence from unfinished sculptures now suggests a different technique using calipers, known as triangulation. By establishing three points on the model, and the same three points on a new block of stone, an artist can calculate and transfer any other point on the model sculpture to a new place on the copy. The sculptor takes measurements from each of the three points on the original to a fourth new point, and, using those measurements, makes arcs with the calipers from each of the three points on the new block of stone. Where the arcs intersect is the fourth point (see fig. 4) on the copy. In order to alter the scale from original to copy, the artist simply multiplies or divides the measurements. Having taken a number of points in this way, the sculptor uses a chisel to cut away the stone between the points. The accuracy of the resultant copy depends upon how many points the sculptor takes.

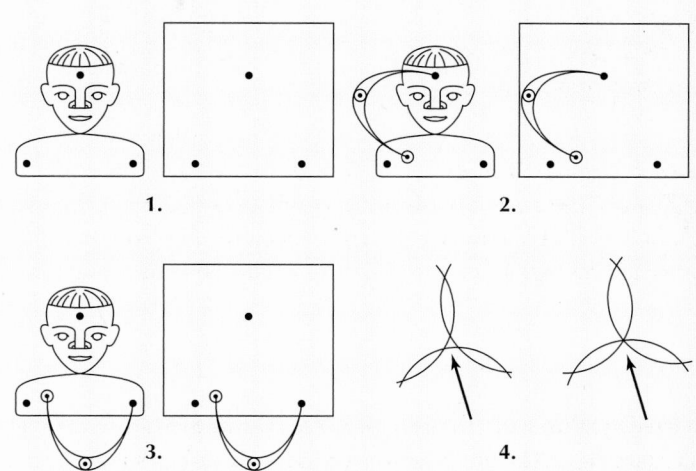

The triangulation process

Aspiring politicians probably commissioned many of these Republican portraits, but scholars can rarely give a name to the individuals portrayed. Inscriptions identifying the subject are scarce, and the coin portraits that help to identify later public figures only appear from the mid-first century BCE on. By contrast, we can readily identify individuals represented in a related class of monument. In the Late Republican and Augustan periods, emancipated slaves commissioned group portraits in relief, which they mounted on roadside funerary monuments (fig. **7.13**). Usually, a long rectangular frame surrounds shoulder-length truncated busts of the subjects. The very fact that the ex-slaves are depicted visually reflects their freed status; other visual cues reinforce it, such as a ring, either painted or carved on a man's hand, or the joined right hands of a man and woman, symbolizing marriage, which was not legal among slaves. An inscription records their names and status. In this example, the freed slaves' one-time owner appears in the center of the relief.

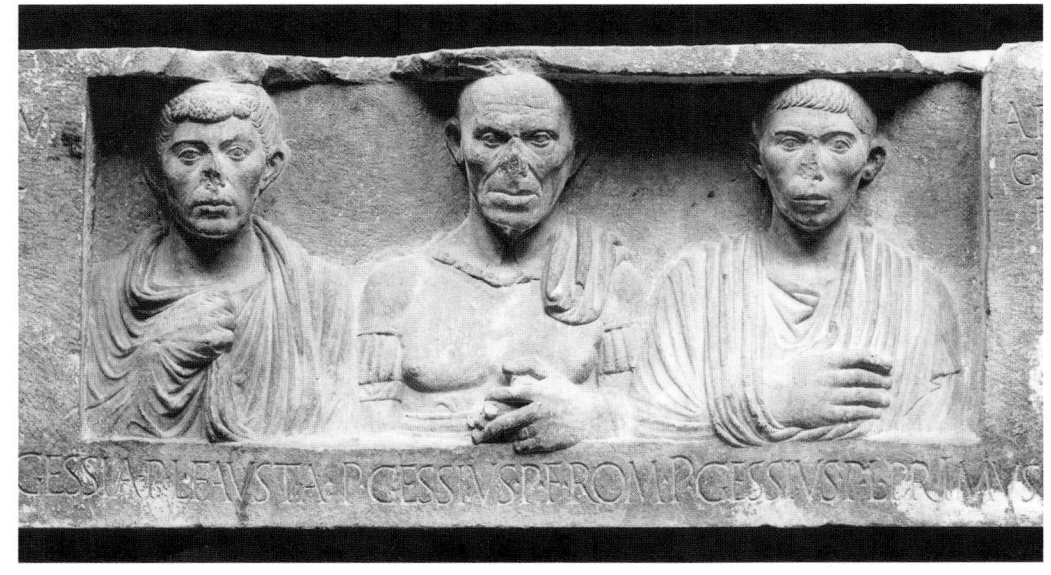

7.13 Funerary relief of the Gessii. ca. 50 BCE. Marble, 25⁹⁄₁₆ × 80½ × 13⅜" (65 × 204.5 × 34 cm). Museum of Fine Arts, Boston, Archibald Cary Coolidge Fund. 37.100

Polybius (ca. 200–ca. 118 BCE)

Histories, from Book VI

Polybius was a Greek historian active during the Roman conquest of his homeland. His Histories *recount the rise of Rome from the third century BCE to the destruction of Corinth in 146 BCE. In Book VI he considers cultural and other factors explaining Rome's success.*

Whenever any illustrious man dies ... they place the image of the departed in the most conspicuous position in the house, enclosed in a wooden shrine. This image is a mask reproducing with remarkable fidelity both the features and complexion of the deceased. On the occasion of public sacrifices they display these images, and decorate them with much care, and when any distinguished member of the family dies they take them to the funeral, putting them on men who seem to them to bear the closest resemblance to the original in stature and carriage. These representatives wear togas, with a purple border if the deceased was a consul or praetor, whole purple if he was a censor, and embroidered with gold if he had celebrated a triumph or achieved anything similar. They all ride in chariots preceded by the fasces, axes, and other insignia ... and when they arrive at the rostra they all seat themselves in a row on ivory chairs. There could not easily be a more ennobling spectacle for a young man who aspires to fame and virtue. For who would not be inspired by the sight of the images of men renowned for their excellence, all together and as if alive and breathing? ... By this means, by this constant renewal of the good report of brave men, the celebrity of those who performed noble deeds is rendered immortal.... But the most important result is that young men are thus inspired to endure every suffering for the public welfare in the hope of winning the glory that attends on brave men.

Source: *Polybius: The Histories*, Vol. 3, tr. W.R. Paton (Cambridge, MA: Harvard University Press, 1923)

Painting and Mosaic

Lamentably few free-standing portraits come from known archaeological contexts. Romans appear to have displayed them in tombs as well as in homes and public places. Tombs were more than just lodging places for the dead. They were the focus of routine funerary rituals, and during the course of the Republic they became stages for displaying the feats of ancestors in order to elevate family status. Paintings, both inside and out, served this purpose well.

A tomb on the Esquiline Hill in Rome yielded a fragmentary painting of the late fourth or early third century BCE, depicting scenes from a conflict between the Romans and a neighboring tribe, the Samnites (fig. **7.14**). A label identifies a toga-clad figure on the upper right as Quintus Fabius, a renowned general who may have been the tomb's owner. He holds out a spear to a figure identified as Fannius on the left, who wears golden greaves and loincloth. Behind Fannius is a crenelated city wall, and in the lower registers are scenes of battle and parlay. The labels suggest that the images record specific events, relating the subject matter to the relief sculptures discussed previously. Literary sources state that Roman generals also made a practice of commissioning panel paintings of their military achievements, which they displayed in triumphal processions before installing them in a public building such as a temple.

As well as ornamenting walls with narrative paintings, Roman artists also decorated floors with mosaics. They fitted together minute colored stones called **tesserae** to create a pattern or a figured image. An extraordinary example survives from an apsidal room opening onto the forum at Praeneste (Palestrina) (fig. **7.15**; see figs. **7.5** and **7.6**), probably dating to the end of the second century BCE. The mosaic is a large visual map of Egypt, perhaps inspired by an Alexandrian work. The Nile dominates. In the foreground is Alexandria, with its monumental buildings, lush vegetation, and cosmopolitan lifestyle. A vignette at the lower right may show a Roman general's visit to Egypt. The mosaicist

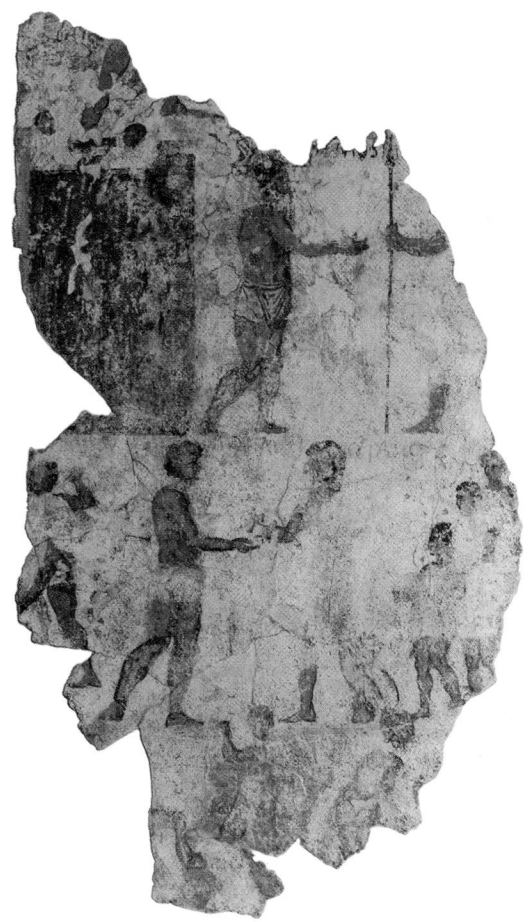

7.14 Esquiline tomb painting. Late 4th or early 3rd century BCE. Painted on plaster, 34½ × 17¾" (87.6 × 45 cm). Museo Montemartini, Rome

depicted different buildings from different perspectives to accommodate a viewer's movement across the floor, and suggested recession by placing distant scenes at the top of the mosaic: the river winds away into the distance toward Ethiopia where hunters

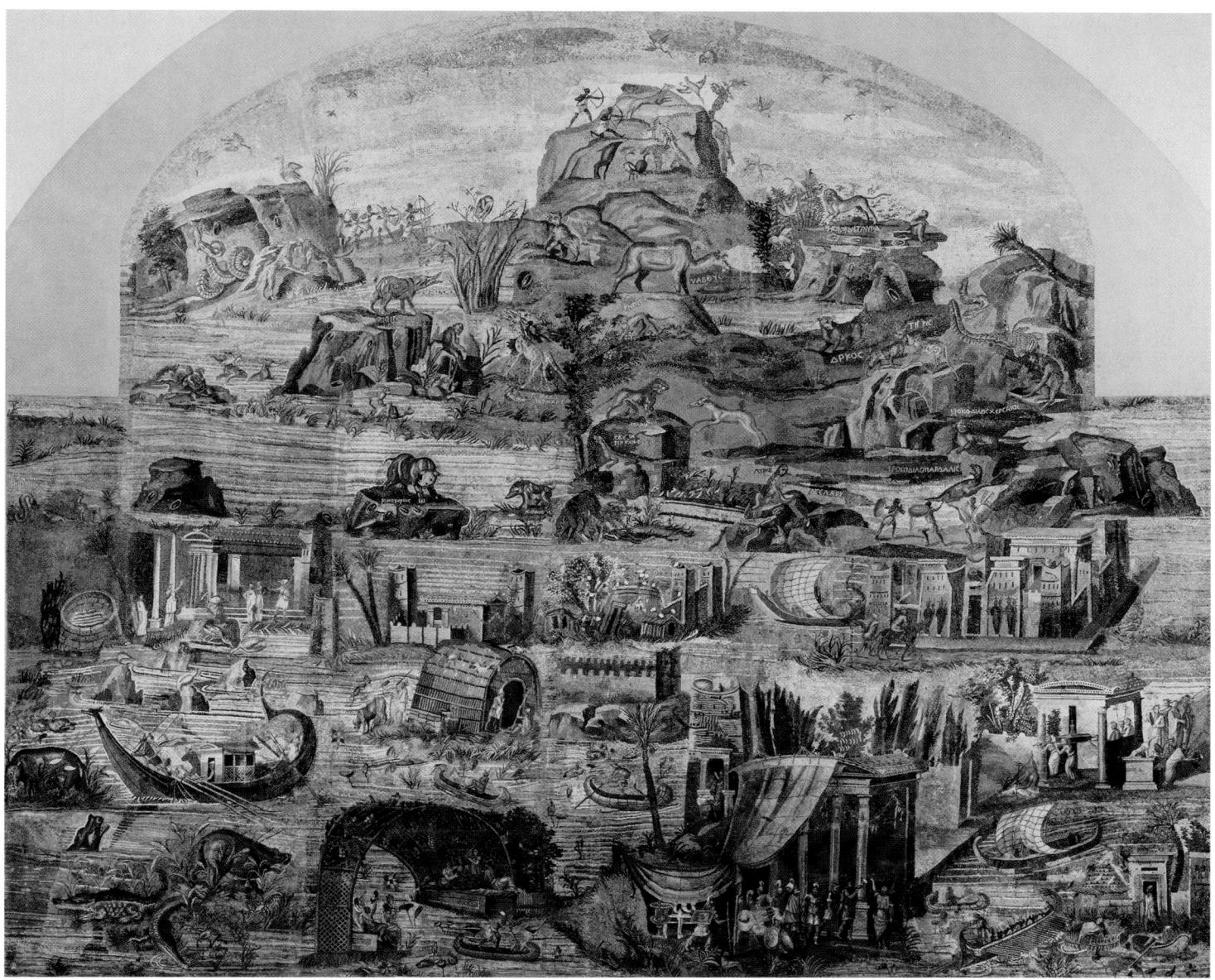

7.15 *Nile Mosaic*, from Sanctuary of Fortuna Primigenia, Praeneste (Palestrina). First century BCE. Height approx. 16' (4.88 m), width approx. 20' (6.10 m). Museo Archaeologico Nazionale, Palestrina

pursue wild animals—such as crocodiles and hippopotami—labeled with Greek names. Colors also become less vibrant in the faraway scenes, a device known as **atmospheric perspective**. Remarkable for its fine execution and the richness of its colors, the mosaic is a testament to a fascination with far-off lands during a phase of Rome's rapid expansion.

THE EARLY EMPIRE

The last century of the Republic witnessed a gradual breakdown of order in Rome, as ambitious men vied for sole authority in the city. Julius Caesar's assassination on the Ides of March of 44 BCE was a last-ditch effort to safeguard the constitution. His heir, Octavian, took revenge on the principal assassins, Brutus and Cassius, and then eliminated his own rival for power, Mark

Antony, who had made an alliance with the Egyptian queen Cleopatra. In 27 BCE, the Senate named Octavian as Augustus Caesar, and he became *princeps*, or first citizen. History recognizes him as the first Roman emperor. The arts flourished in the Augustan age. Artists took a new interest in classicism, while Virgil penned *The Aeneid* as a Latin response to Homer's epics, and Horace and Ovid wrote poetry of lasting renown.

The birth of the Roman Empire brought a period of greater stability to the Mediterranean region than had previously been known. Roman domination continued to spread, and at its largest extent, in the time of Trajan (98–117 CE), the Empire stretched through most of Europe, as far north as northern England, through much of the Middle East including Armenia and Assyria, and throughout coastal North Africa. Romanization spread through these regions. Roman institutions—political, social, and religious—mingled with indigenous ones, leading to a degree of homogenization through much of the Roman world. Increasingly, the emperor and his family became the principal patrons of public art and architecture in Rome. Often, their public monuments stressed the legitimacy of the imperial family.

Architecture

THE IMPERIAL FORA During the Republic, the Roman Forum was the bustling center of civic life (figs. **7.16** and **7.17**). It was there, in markets and basilicas, that people shopped and attended court cases and schools. The Senate deliberated in the Forum's Senate House, and temples to the state gods housed cult statues as well as the state treasury. Gladiators fought in the open space in the center of the Forum, where temporary wooden bleachers were erected for spectators. The Forum continued to accommodate many essential Roman functions during the Empire, but some moved to new imperial complexes. Pompey's theater complex was the first of a series of huge urban interventions through which Rome's autocrats curried favor with the populace. Julius Caesar and Augustus each commissioned a forum, separate from but close to the Roman Forum, establishing a tradition that Vespasian, Domitian, and Trajan followed. As the plan in figure 7.17 reveals, these fora were closely connected to each other topographically and drew significance from their proximity. A visitor entered the Forum of Augustus directly from that of his divinized ancestor Caesar, cementing the connection through physical experience. Augustus' Forum was a large open plaza with porticoes lining the long sides. At the end of the plaza was a temple to Mars the Avenger, which Augustus had vowed to erect after Caesar's assassination. When compared with the free forms of the Sanctuary of Fortuna Primigenia at Praeneste, this complex is overwhelmingly rectilinear and Classically inspired, as was most Augustan architecture. This deliberate choice evoked the pinnacle of Greek achievement in fifth-century BCE Athens, and the pervasive use of marble, available from newly opened quarries at Carrara, underlined the effect. Sculpture filled the Forum. The porticoes housed full-length, labeled portraits of great men from Rome's legendary past and recent history, suggesting a link between the past and the Augustan present. In the attic (upper level) of the porticoes, engaged caryatids (supporting columns in the shape of draped female figures) flanked shields decorated with heads of Jupiter Ammon (god of the Sahara, sometimes described as Alexander the Great's father). The carved women replicated the figures on the south porch of the Erechtheion on the Athenian Akropolis (see fig. 5.51), where Augustus' architects were engaged in restoration work. Many of the rituals once accommodated by Rome's historic buildings such as the Temple of Capitoline Jupiter now moved to Augustus' Forum, and by diverting these state activities to an arena associated with his name, Augustus placed himself explicitly at the head of Roman public life.

The largest of all the imperial fora was Trajan's, financed with the spoils of his wars against the Dacians. Reconstructions of the complex give a sense of its former magnificence (fig. **7.18**). Located alongside Augustus' Forum, it adapted many of that

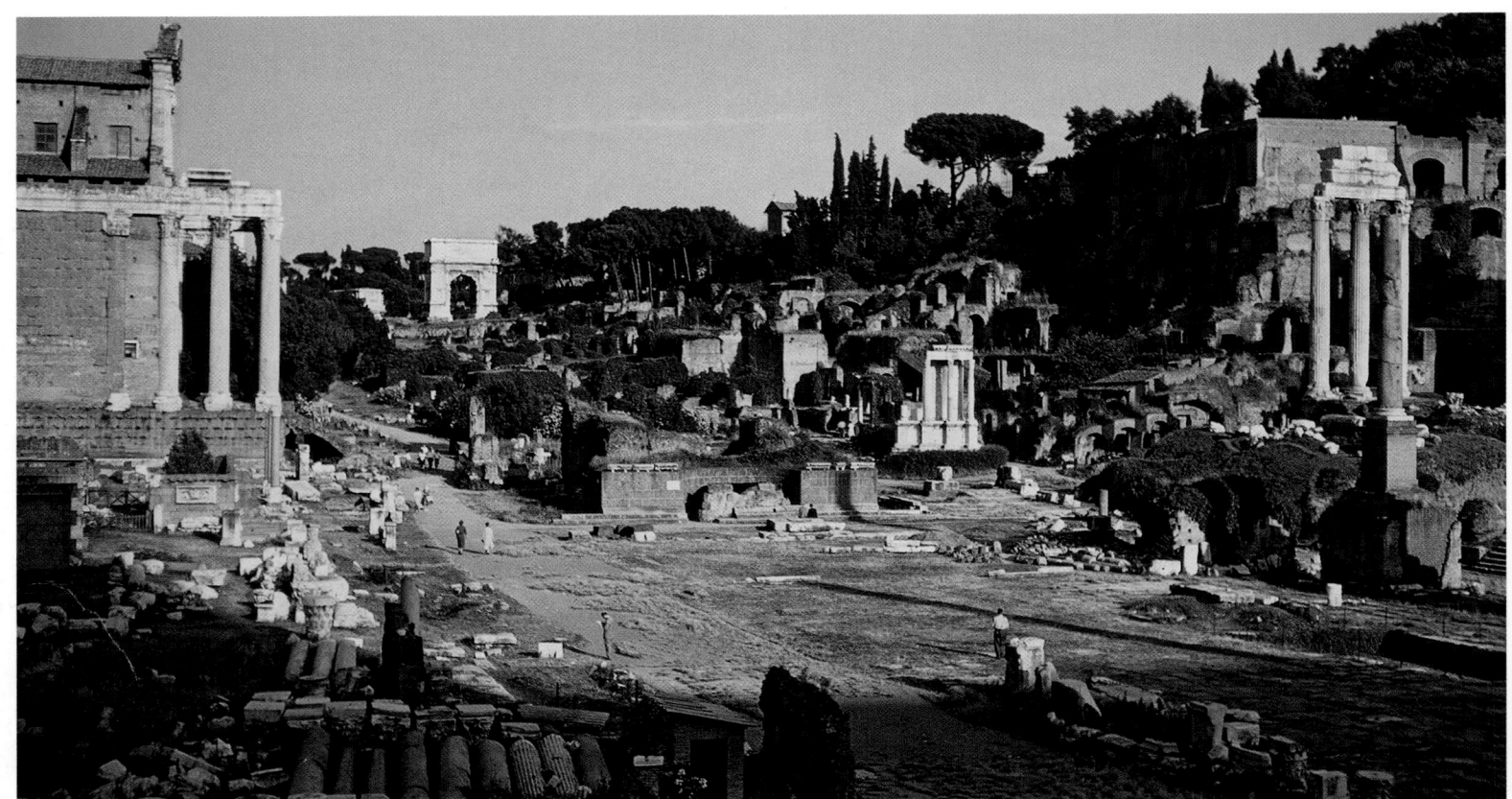

7.16 View of the Forum in Rome

7.17 Plan of the Fora, Rome

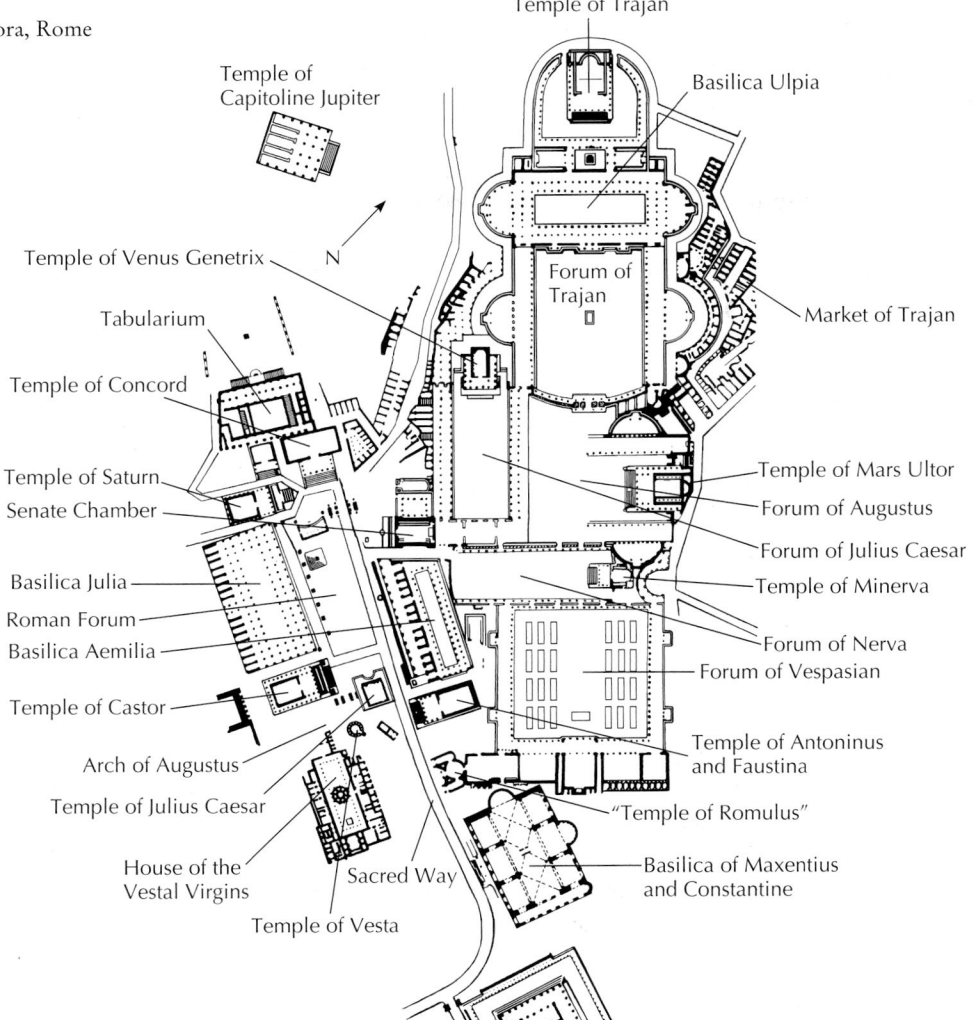

Temple of Trajan

Temple of Capitoline Jupiter

Basilica Ulpia

Temple of Venus Genetrix

N

Forum of Trajan

Tabularium

Market of Trajan

Temple of Concord

Temple of Saturn

Senate Chamber

Temple of Mars Ultor

Forum of Augustus

Forum of Julius Caesar

Basilica Julia

Roman Forum

Temple of Minerva

Basilica Aemilia

Forum of Nerva

Temple of Castor

Forum of Vespasian

Arch of Augustus

Temple of Julius Caesar

Temple of Antoninus and Faustina

House of the Vestal Virgins

Sacred Way

"Temple of Romulus"

Temple of Vesta

Basilica of Maxentius and Constantine

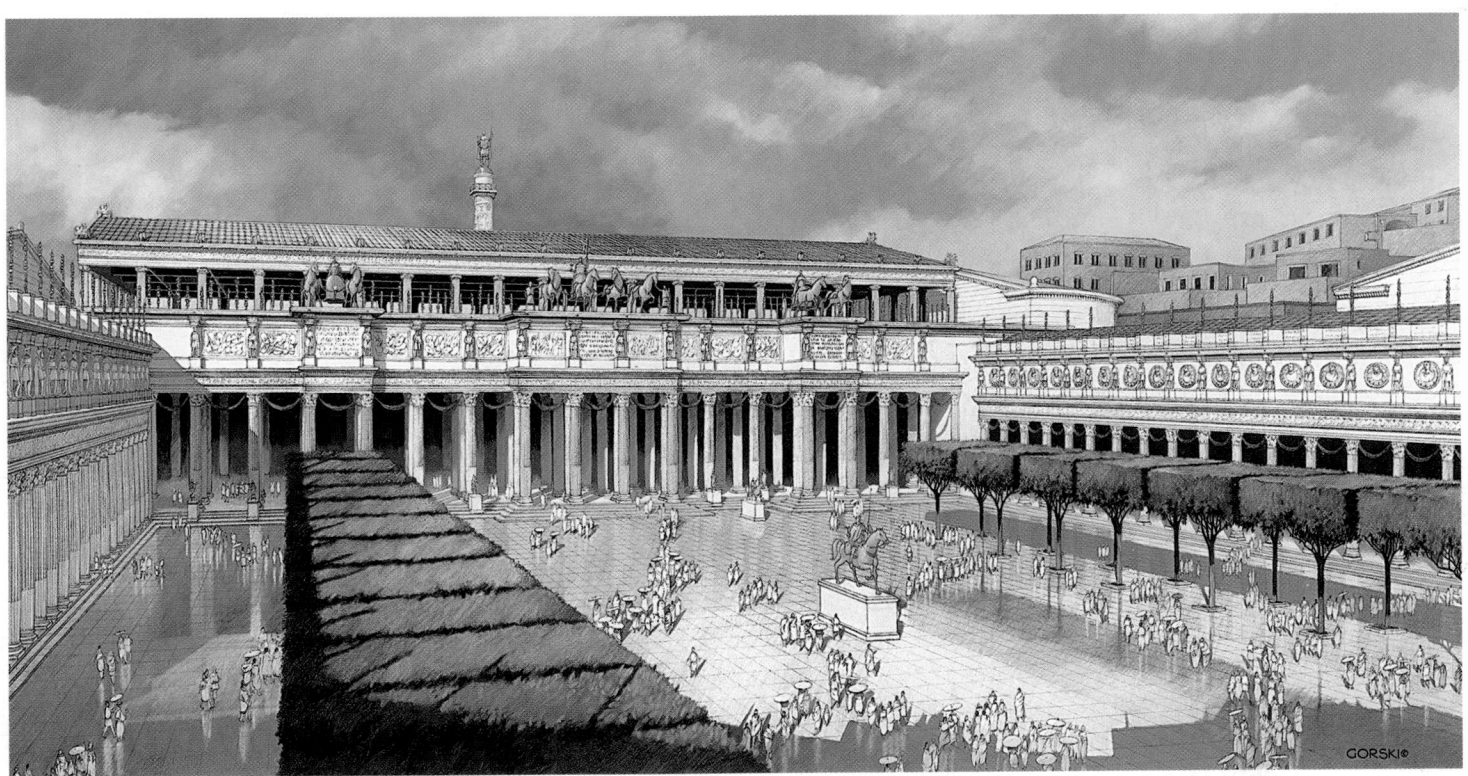

7.18 Forum of Trajan, Rome. Restored view by Gilbert Gorski

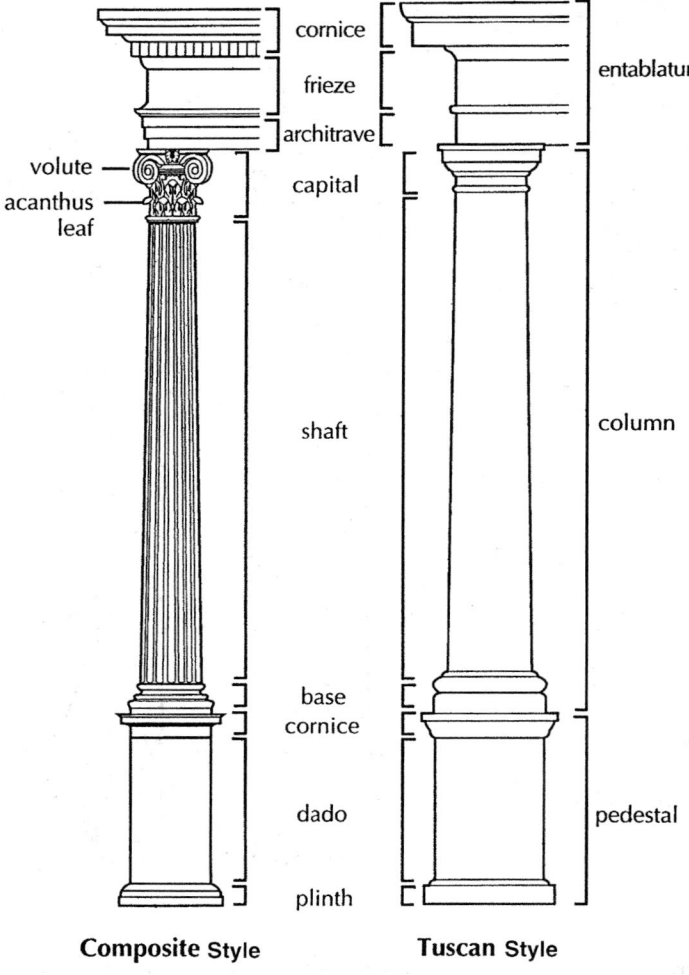

volute —
acanthus leaf —

cornice
frieze
architrave
capital

shaft

base
cornice

dado

plinth

Composite Style

entablature

column

pedestal

Tuscan Style

7.19   Tuscan and composite styles

THE COLOSSEUM Tuscan columns frequently appear in a decorative capacity on entertainment buildings. Vespasian was the first to construct a permanent amphitheater for the gladiatorial games and mock sea battles that were so central to Roman entertainment and to Rome's penal system (figs. **7.20**, **7.21**, and **7.22**). Putting on shows for the populace was a crucial form of favor-gaining benefaction, and the audience assembled for diversion but also to see their emperor and to receive the free handouts that he would make on these occasions. Vespasian died before completing the Colosseum, and his son Titus inaugurated it in 80 CE with over 100 days of games, at a cost of over 9,000 animal lives.

In terms of sheer mass, the Colosseum was one of the largest single buildings anywhere: It stood 159 feet high, 616 feet 9 inches long, and 511 feet 11 inches wide, and held well over 50,000 spectators. Concrete—faced with travertine—was the secret of its success. In plan, 80 radial barrel-vaulted wedges ringed an oval arena. Each barrel vault buttressed the next, making the ring remarkably stable (see fig. 7.22). The wedges sloped down from the outside to the ringside to support seating, as in Pompey's theater, and the architects accommodated countless stairways and corridors within the wedges to ensure the smooth flow of traffic between the entrances and the seating areas and the arena. During the performances, Romans took their seats strictly according to social rank, and the distinctive clothing of each order visually set off one

forum's features to new effect. In place of the caryatids in the portico attics, for instance, were statues of captive Dacians carved from exotic marbles. Beyond a basilica at the far end, two libraries and a temple defined a small courtyard, where Trajan's Column stood (see figs. 7.39 and 7.40). The Forum's message is clear: The Dacian Wars brought Rome great financial benefit. As in many societies, the ruling elite hoped to dispel the starker realities of war through visual propaganda.

The change in patronage from magistrates to emperor is one of the major developments in architecture during the Empire. Another is the invention of the **composite capital**. To the building styles that they borrowed from Greece, Roman architects added two more (fig. **7.19**). One was the **Tuscan style**, which resembled the Doric style except that the shaft stood on a base. This style was in use throughout the Roman period. The composite capital was an imperial phenomenon: Architects used it as a substitute for the Ionic capital on secular buildings, especially from the reign of the first Flavian emperor, Vespasian (69–79 CE). It combined the volutes of an Ionic capital with the acanthus leaves of the Corinthian capital, to rich decorative effect.

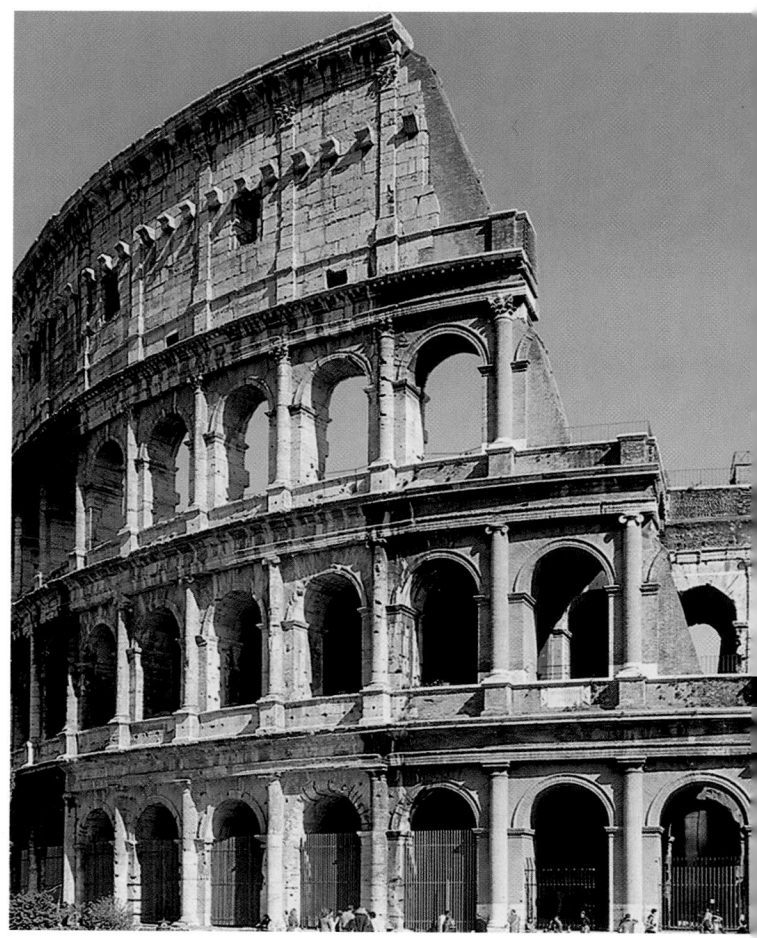

7.20   Exterior of Colosseum

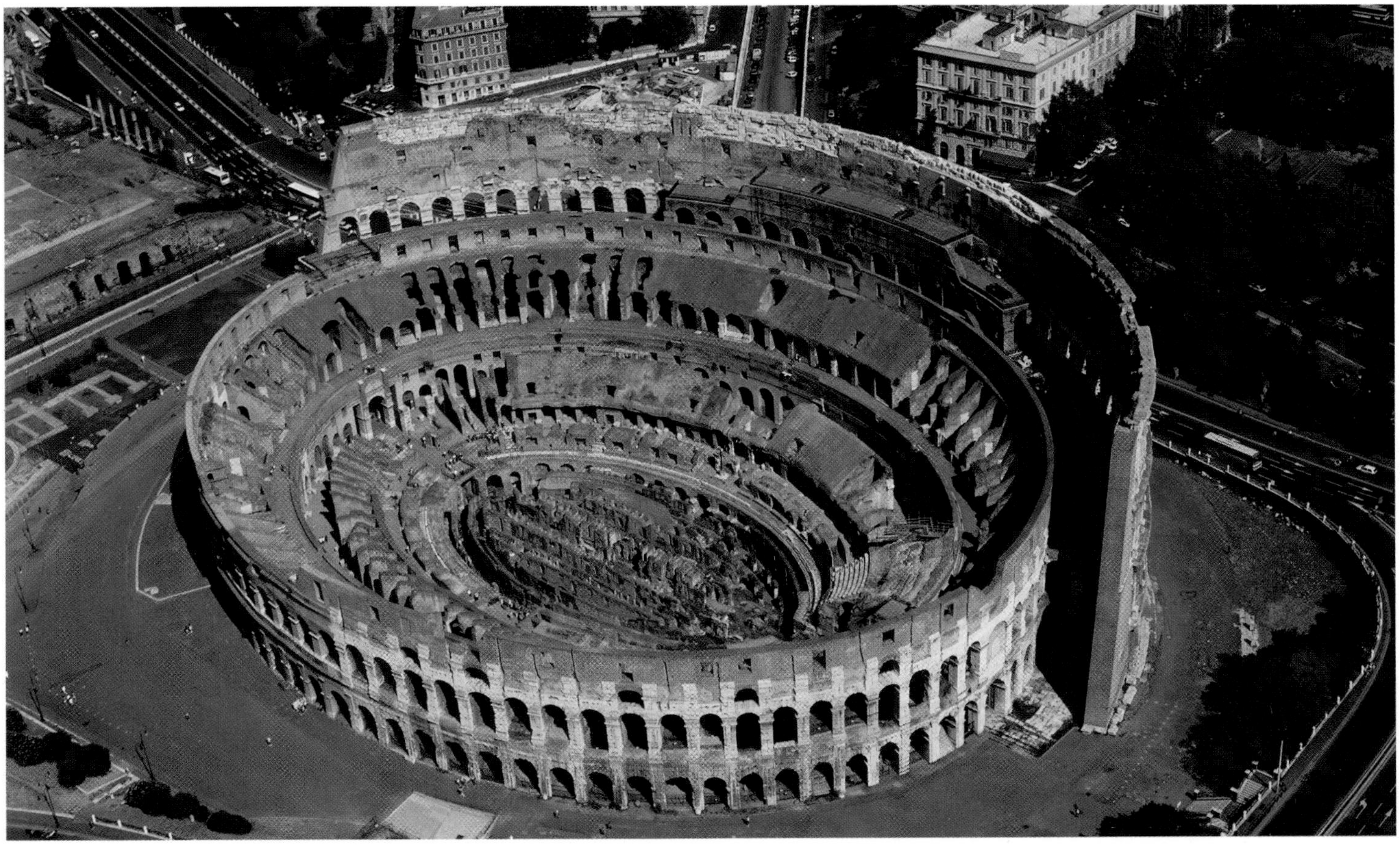

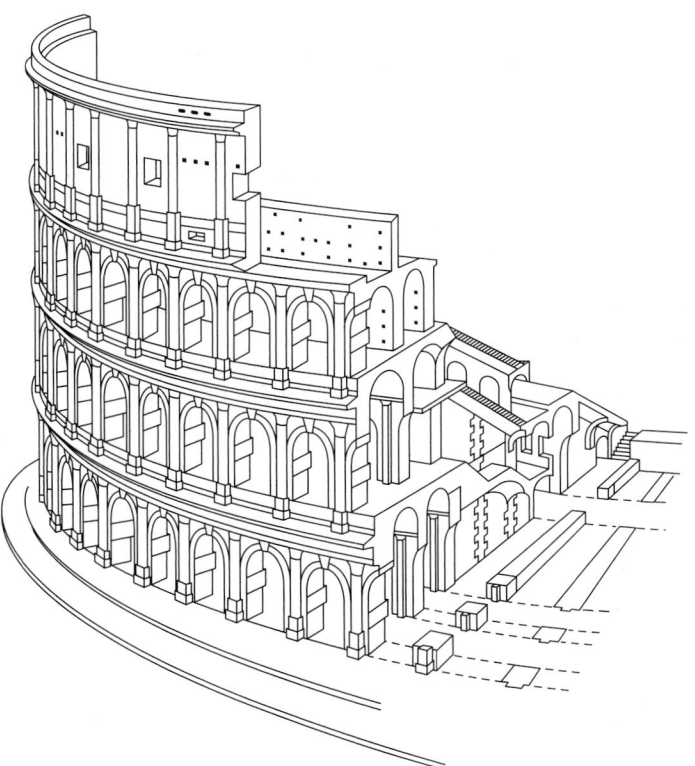

7.21 Colosseum, Rome. 72–80 CE

7.22 Sectional view of Colosseum

group from another. On the hottest days, sailors stationed nearby rigged a *velarium*, huge canvas sheets, over the seating areas to provide shade. Dignified and monumental, the exterior reflects the structure's interior organization. Eighty arched entrances led into the building, framed with engaged Tuscan columns. On the second story, Ionic columns framed a second set of arches, and on the third are engaged Corinthian columns. Engaged Corinthian pilasters embellish the wall on the fourth.

THE PANTHEON But of all the masterpieces Roman architects accomplished with concrete, the Pantheon is perhaps the most remarkable (fig. **7.23**). Augustus' right-hand man, Agrippa, built the first Pantheon on the site. Its name suggests that he intended it as a temple to all the gods. This was a Hellenistic concept, and it included living and deceased members of the ruling family among the gods. When a fire destroyed this temple in 80 CE, Domitian built a reconstruction, which perished after a lightning strike. The Pantheon we see today, which has a substantially different design, is probably the work of Trajan's architect, perhaps Apollodorus. The temple was completed in Hadrian's reign, and as an act of piety, Hadrian left Agrippa's name in the inscription (see *The Art Historian's Lens*, page 202). It owes its status as one of the best-preserved temples of Rome to its transformation into a church in the early seventh century CE. All the same, its surroundings have changed sufficiently through the ages to alter a visitor's experience of it quite profoundly.

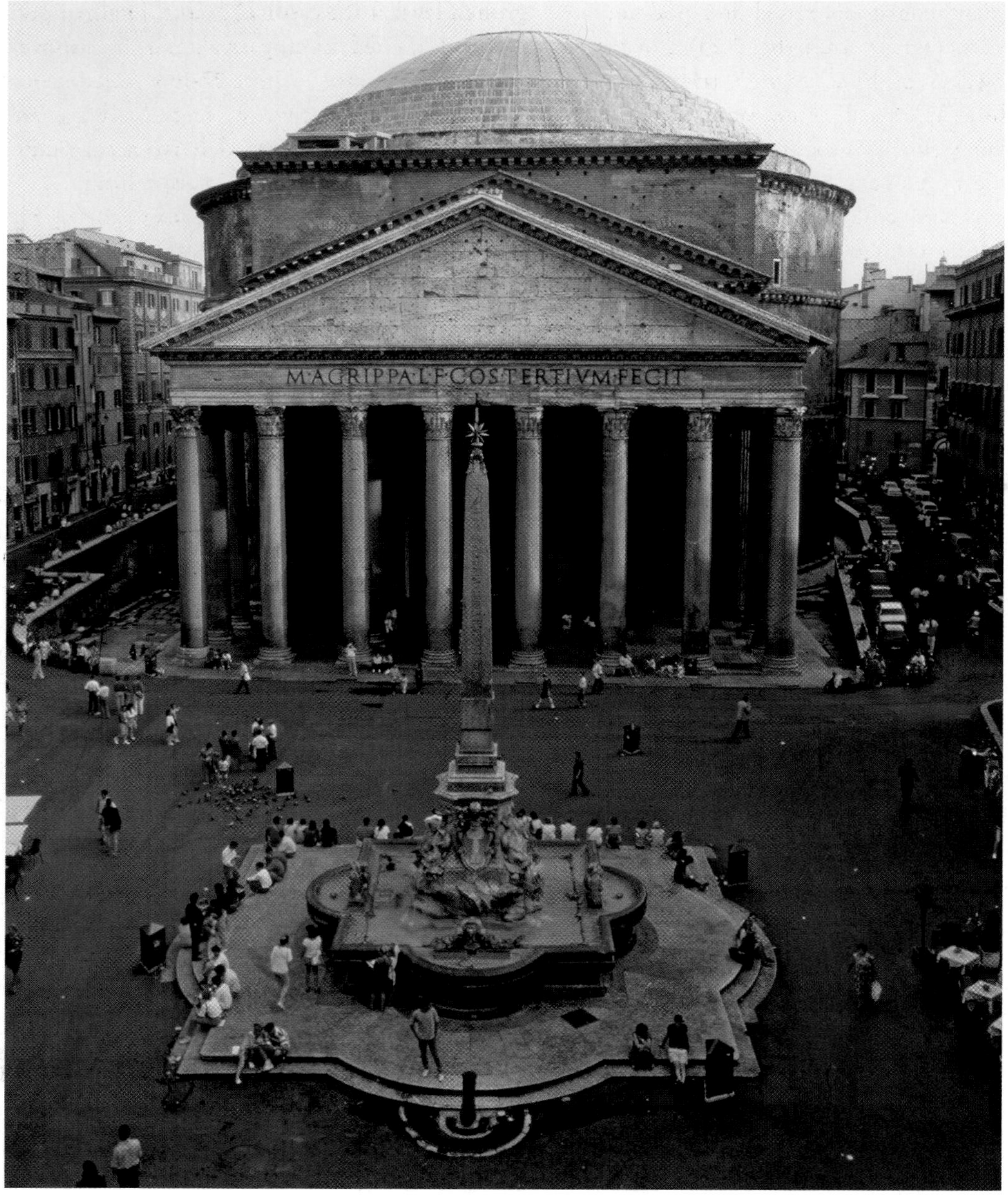

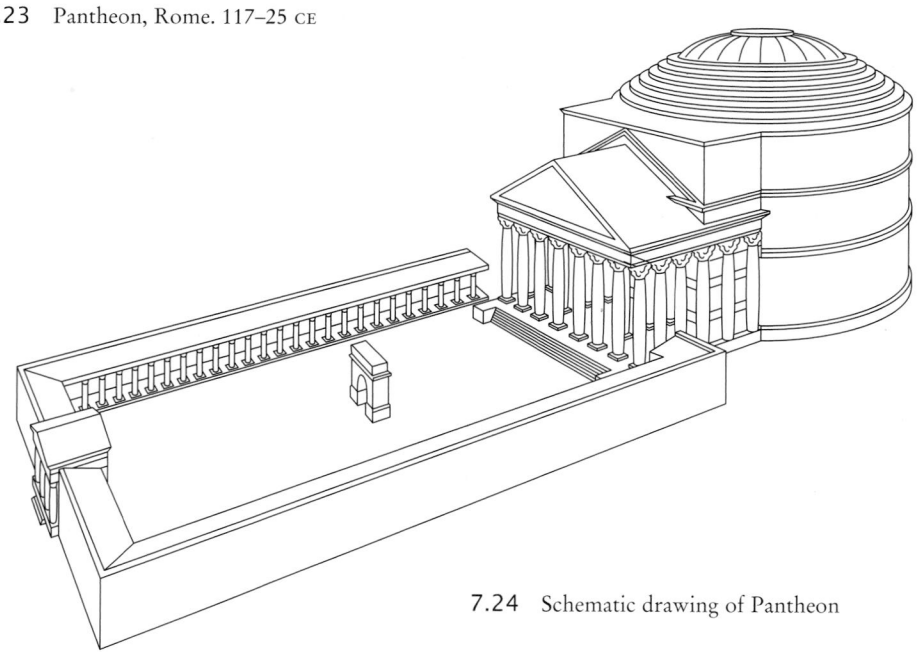

7.23　Pantheon, Rome. 117–25 CE

7.24　Schematic drawing of Pantheon

In Roman times, the Pantheon stood, raised on a podium, at the south end of a large rectangular court (fig. **7.24**). Porticoes framed the three remaining sides of the court and extended on the south up to the sides of the temple's pedimented porch, hiding the temple's circular drum from view. A visitor approaching the temple's broad octastyle façade would have been struck by the forest of massive monolithic gray and pink granite columns soaring upward; but in most other respects, the temple's form would have been familiar, evoking an expectation of a rectangular cella beyond the huge bronze doors, and a large cult statue. Yet a surprise was in store. On stepping across the threshold (figs. **7.25** and **7.26**), a visitor faced a vast circular hall, with seven large niches at ground level at the cardinal points. Engaged pilasters and bronze grilles decorated an attic level, and high above soared an enormous **dome**, pierced with a 27-foot hole, or **oculus**, open to the sky. Through the oculus came a glowing shaft of light, slicing through the shadows from high overhead. Dome and drum are of equal height, and the total interior height, 143 feet, is also the dome's diameter (fig. **7.27**). For many ancient viewers, the resultant sphere would have symbolized eternity and perfection, and the dome's surface, once emblazoned with bronze rosettes in its **coffers** (recessed panels), must have evoked a starry night sky.

For a visitor entering the cella, there was no obvious cue to point out where to go, except toward the light at the center. In

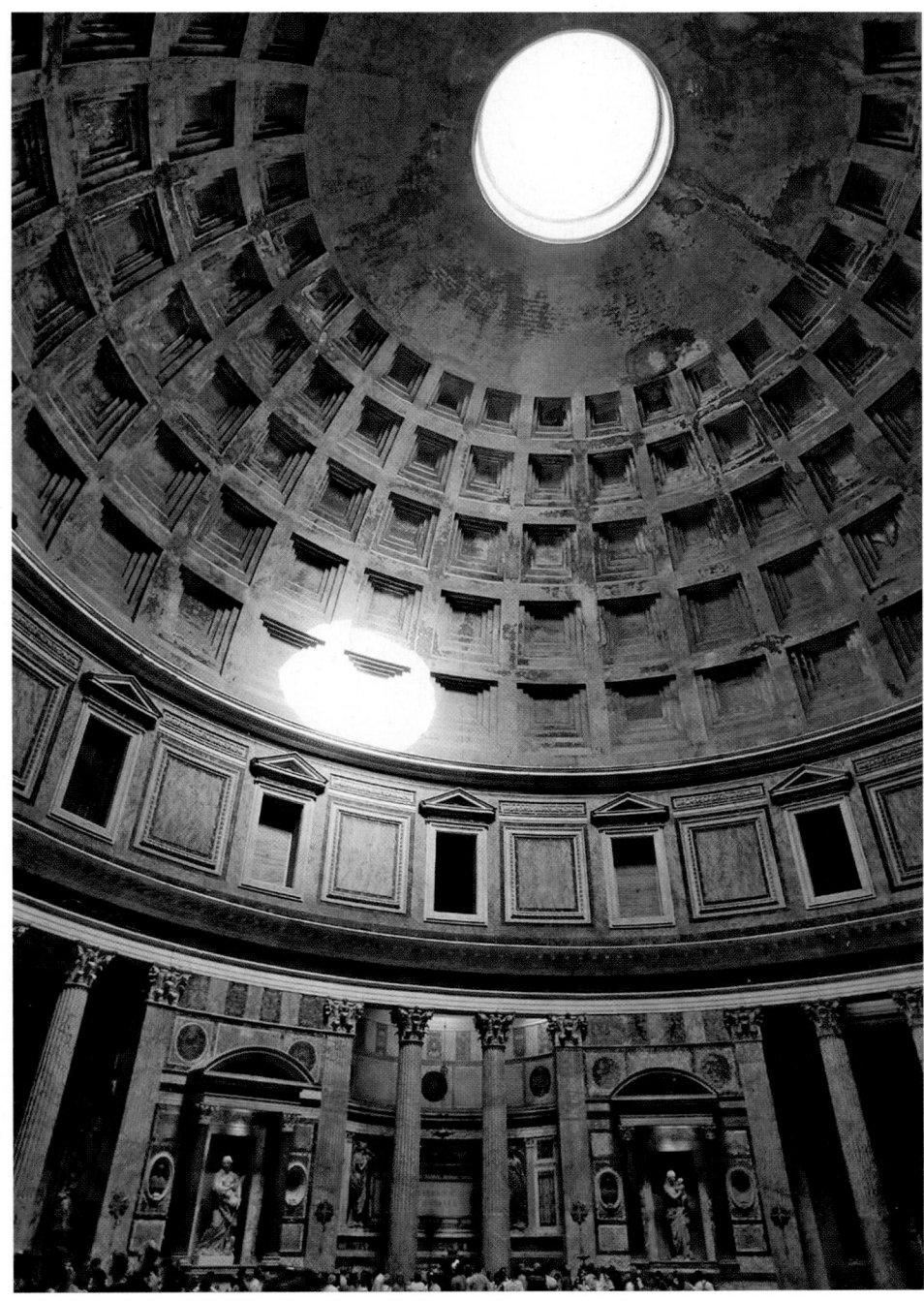

7.25 Interior of Pantheon

7.26 Plan of Pantheon

Two Pantheon Problems

Until the early twentieth century, most scholars believed that the existing Pantheon was an Augustan building, partially because its inscription attributes it to Agrippa, Augustus' right-hand man. In 1936–38, archaeologist Herbert Bloch produced a masterly analysis of Roman brick-stamps—stamps that manufacturers impressed on bricks while they were wet. Often, these incorporated the names of consuls, especially in the second century CE, which allows scholars to date bricks to a span of years, and sometimes even to a precise year. Bloch's assessment of bricks used in the Pantheon led him to confirm what archaeologists had begun to suspect on the basis of excavations: that the Pantheon was not Agrippa's temple but a later rebuilding of it. Bloch assigned it to the reign of Hadrian. However, Lise Hetland's new reading of the Pantheon brick-stamps stresses the presence of Trajanic bricks in early stages of the temple's construction. This suggests that building began in Trajan's reign, and ended under Hadrian. The Pantheon may be the work of Apollodorus, designer of Trajan's Forum, who also constructed an imperial bath building with similar design features. If true, as many believe, this redating will engender new interpretations of the building's significance and new assessments of the emperors' respective building programs.

Since the fifteenth century, architects studying the Pantheon have struggled with a paradox: Despite the building's profound impact on Western architecture from the moment of its construction, irregularities in its design suggest that it is seriously flawed. These irregularities include an inexplicable second pediment, above and behind the first; the fact that the exterior cornices are at different levels on circular drum and porch; and unaccountable misalignments in the floor plan. To explain these irregularities, scholars initially concluded that the present building is the result of several different building campaigns—a theory that Bloch's brick analysis roundly disproved.

In 1987, while doodling on a napkin over a beer at a pub, three British scholars, Paul Davies, David Hemsoll and Mark Wilson Jones, recognized that if the 40-foot column shafts of the Pantheon's porch were replaced with 50-foot shafts, the irregularities would disappear. The taller shafts would raise the pediment to the level of the "ghost" pediment; the cornices would align around the entire building; and because the shafts would be thicker, the imperfections in the floor plan would be resolved. Gray and pink granite shafts come from Aswan in Egypt. Fifty-foot shafts are relatively rare; in the event that they were—for instance—lost at sea, 40-foot replacements would have been more readily available to keep construction on schedule. The British scholars' contention—which is now widely accepted—is that an unforeseen circumstance forced the builders to deviate from the design mid-construction. One of the most admired buildings of antiquity, in other words, is probably a brilliant compromise between design and necessity.

fact, the dome's coffers only make sense perspectively from directly beneath the oculus. Once a visitor reached the center, molded space and applied decoration combined to provide a stunning effect. Beginning in the Renaissance, scholars have found fault with the Pantheon's architect for neglecting to align the ribs between the dome coffers with the pilasters in the attic zone and the ground-floor columns. The design is not without logic: a void or a row of coffers aligns exactly over each central intercolumniation (space between columns) on the ground floor. All the same,

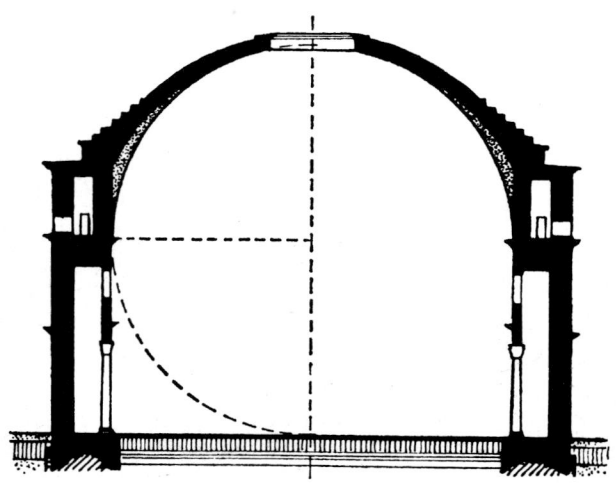

7.27   Transverse section of Pantheon

the absence of a systemic network of continuous vertical lines between top and bottom means that, visually speaking, the dome is not anchored. The optical effect is that it hovers unfettered above the visitor—who feels, paradoxically, both sheltered and exposed. The dome seems to be in perpetual motion, spinning overhead in the same way as the heavens it imitates. An all-but-imperceptible rise in the floor at the center exaggerates this sensation, which can incite an unnerving feeling similar to vertigo. A visitor's instinct, in response, is to take refuge in the safety of the curved wall. The building is all experience, and photographs do it no justice. This is the place, so literary sources relate, where Hadrian preferred to hold court, greeting foreign embassies and adjudicating disputes here. The temple's form cast the emperor in an authoritative position as controller of his revolving universe. He must have appeared like a divine revelation before his guests, who were already awed and completely manipulated by the building that enclosed them.

The Pantheon is the extraordinary result of an increased confidence in the potential and strength of concrete. The architect calibrated the aggregate as the building rose, from travertine to tufa, then brick, and finally pumice, to reduce its weight. The dome's weight is concentrated on eight wide pillars between the interior alcoves, rather than resting uniformly on the drum (the circular cella wall) (see fig. 7.26). The alcoves, in turn, with their screens of columns, visually reduce the solidity of the walls, and colored marbles on the interior surfaces add energy to the whole.

As in Trajan's Forum, the marbles were symbolic. They underlined the vast reach of imperial authority, assuming trade with or control over Egypt (gray and rose-pink granite, porphyry), Phrygia (Phrygian purple and white stone), the island of Teos (Lucullan red and black stone), and Chemtou in Tunisia (Numidian yellow stone).

HADRIAN'S VILLA AT TIVOLI As well as commissioning public architecture, emperors also built magnificent residences for themselves. From the start of the Empire, the emperor's principal home was on the Palatine Hill in Rome (from which the term "palace" derives). Yet, like many members of the elite, he had several properties, many of which were outside of Rome. The most famous is the Villa of Hadrian at Tibur (present-day Tivoli). Built on the site of a Republican villa, this residence was a vast sprawling complex of buildings, some or all of which Hadrian may have designed himself. The villa's forms appear to follow the natural line of the landscape, but in fact massive earthworks rearranged the terrain to accommodate the architecture and to allow for impressive vistas, cool retreats, and surprise revelations. Water was a common feature, in pools and running channels, adding sound and motion, reflecting light, and offering coolness in the summer heat. Throughout the villa were mosaics, paintings, and sculptures. The emperor may have collected some of these works of art during his extensive travels, especially in Egypt and Greece. A desire to evoke the far-flung regions of the Empire may also have inspired some of the buildings: A fourth-century CE biographer claims that Hadrian "built up his villa at Tibur in an extraordinary way, applying to parts of it the renowned names of provinces and places, such as the Lyceum, the Academy, the *prytaneum*, the Canopus, the *Poecile*, and Tempe. And so as to omit nothing, he even fashioned 'infernal regions.'" This statement has led modern scholars to give fanciful names to many parts of the villa. Few of them are based on archaeological evidence, and they lead visitors to faulty conclusions about the buildings' functions. The canal shown in figure **7.28** has long been known as the Canopus, after a town in Egypt. Only recently have scholars proposed more neutral terms for the villa's components, in this case the "Scenic Canal."

Portrait Sculpture

By the time Augustus had effectively become emperor, he was no more than 36. With its stress on maturity, the veristic portrait style so characteristic of the Republic might have served to underline his unusual, not to say aconstitutional, status in Rome. Perhaps as a consequence, Augustus turned instead to a more Hellenizing style. Portraits made right up to his death in his late

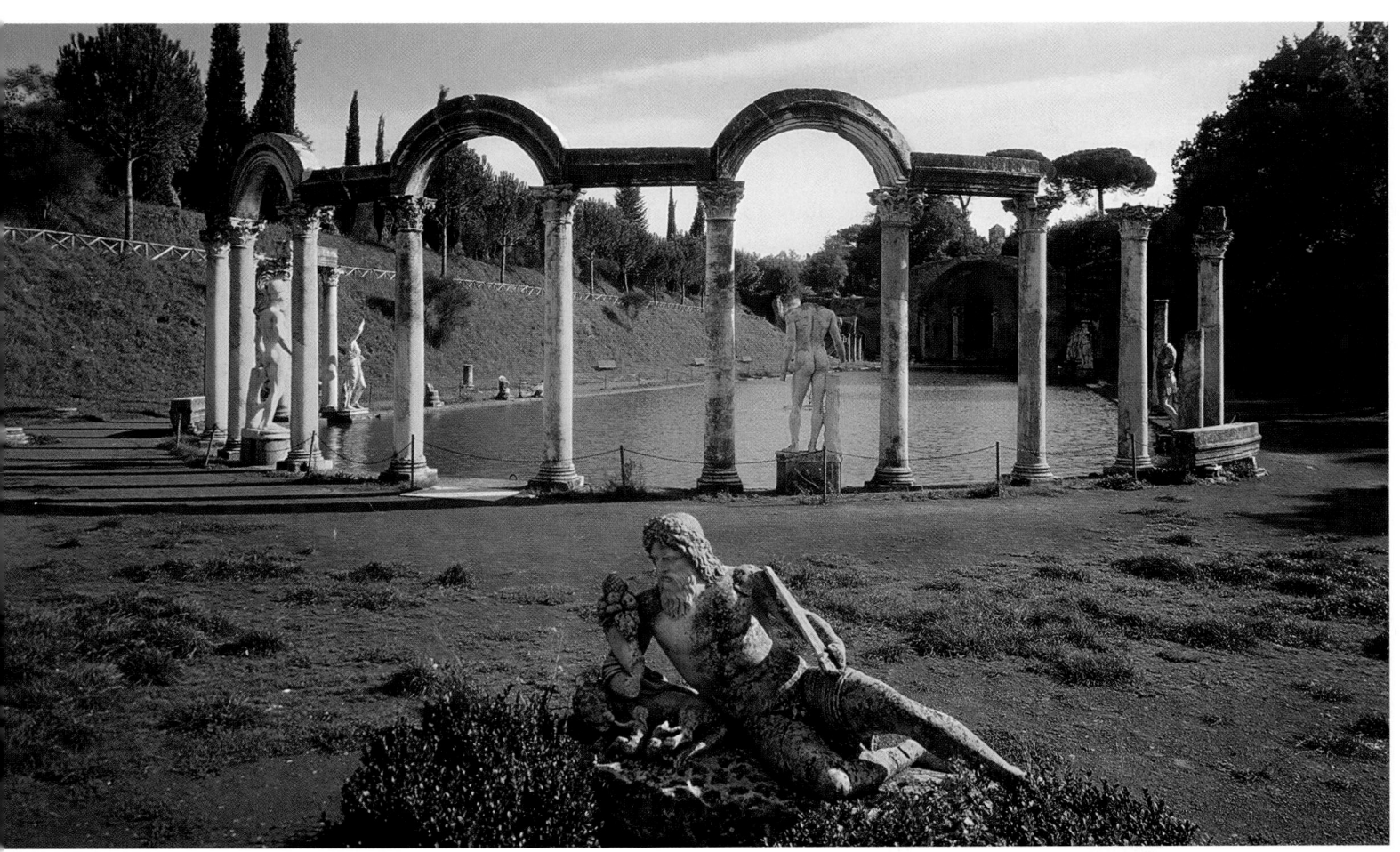

7.28 Scenic Canal, Hadrian's Villa, Tivoli. ca. 130–38 CE

seventies depict him as an ageless youth, as seen in a statue discovered in the house of his wife Livia at Primaporta (fig. **7.29**). The emperor appears in battledress with his arm raised in a gesture of address. The portrait seems to combine a series of references to previous works of art and historical events in order to strengthen Augustus' claim to authority.

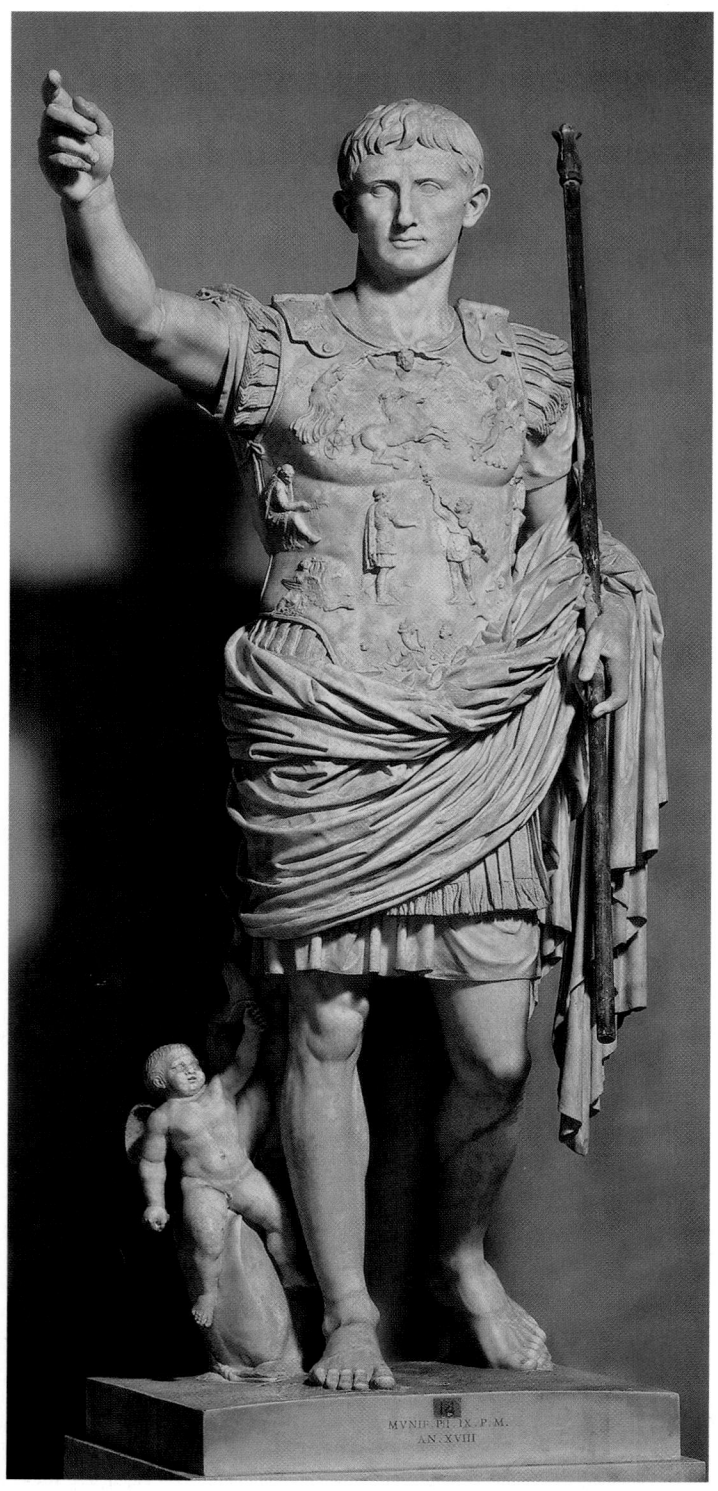

7.29 *Augustus of Primaporta.* Possibly Roman copy of a statue of ca. 20 CE. Marble, height 6'8" (2.03 m). Musei Vaticani, Braccio Nuovo, Rome

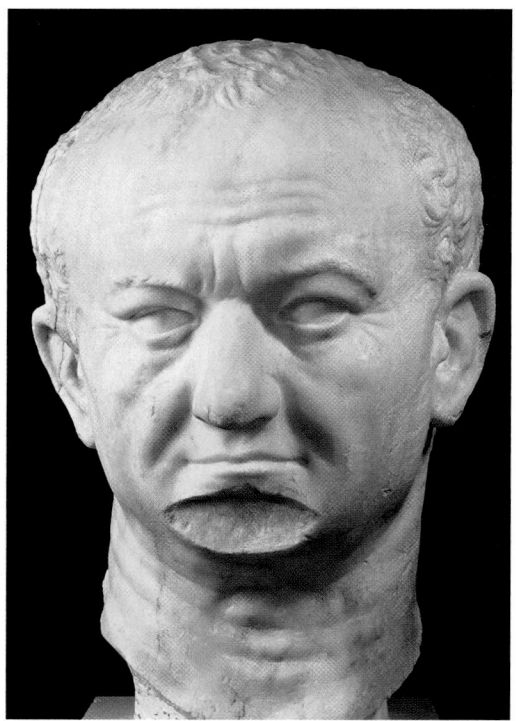

7.30 *Portrait of Vespasian.* ca. 75 CE. Marble, life-size. Museo Nazionale Romano, Rome

The chiastic stance, and the smooth features of Augustus' face, are so reminiscent of Polykleitos' *Doryphoros* (see fig. 5.33) that scholars assume that Augustus turned deliberately to this well-known image. There was good reason for this kind of imitation: The Classical Greek style evoked the apogee of Athenian culture, casting Augustan Rome as Greece's successor (and conqueror) in cultural supremacy. Even Augustus' hair is similar to that of the *Doryphoros*—except, that is, at the front, where the locks part slightly over the center of the brow, a subtle reference to Alexander the Great, another youthful general, whose cowlick was such a distinctive feature of his portraits (see fig. 5.69).

Next to Augustus' right ankle, a cupid playfully rides a dolphin, serving as a strut to strengthen the marble. Most Romans would have recognized that Cupid, or Eros, the son of Venus, symbolized Augustus' claim of descent from the goddess of love through his Trojan ancestor Aeneas. The dolphin evoked the sea, and specifically the site off the coast of Actium where Augustus had prevailed over Mark Antony and Cleopatra in a celebrated naval battle in 31 BCE. By associating Augustus with historical or divine figures, these references projected an image of earthly and divinely ordained power, thereby elevating the emperor above other politicians.

The iconography of Augustus' breastplate serves a similar purpose by calling attention to an important event in 20 BCE, when the Parthians returned standards that they had captured, to Roman shame, in 53 BCE. A figure usually identified as Tiberius, Augustus' eventual successor, or the god Mars, accepts the standards from a Parthian soldier, possibly King Phraates IV. Celestial gods and terrestrial personifications frame the scene, giving the event a cosmic and eternal significance. This diplomatic victory took on momentous proportions in Augustan propaganda. The scene suggests that the portrait dates to about 19 BCE. The emperor is barefoot, which usually denotes divine status. Later in the Roman period, or in the Eastern Empire, emperors might be depicted as gods while still alive, but with Caesar's legacy still fresh in Roman minds, it is unlikely that Augustus would have been so presumptuous. Some scholars therefore conclude that the statue is a posthumous copy of a bronze original dating to about 20 BCE.

The *Primaporta Augustus* offers a good example of a tendency in Roman art to express a message through references to earlier works. Naturally, not all Romans would have understood all the references in any given work, but the frequency of visual "quotations" suggests that Romans, like many other ancient peoples, were extremely visually astute. In fact, the history of Roman portraiture, as with many other branches of Roman art, is one of constant association with, and negation of (or conscious turning away from), past images. In their portraits, Augustus' dynastic successors, for instance, look very much like the first emperor from whom they drew their authority, even though they were rarely (or at best distantly) related by blood. But then, with the emperor Vespasian, founder of the Flavian dynasty, there was a return to a more veristic style of portrait (fig. **7.30**). Scholars reason that this maneuver was part of a deliberate attempt to restore social order when he came into power in 69 CE, after a year of civil war. A soldier by background, Vespasian justified his authority through his military success, and appealed to the rank and file through this harshly matter-of-fact image. However,

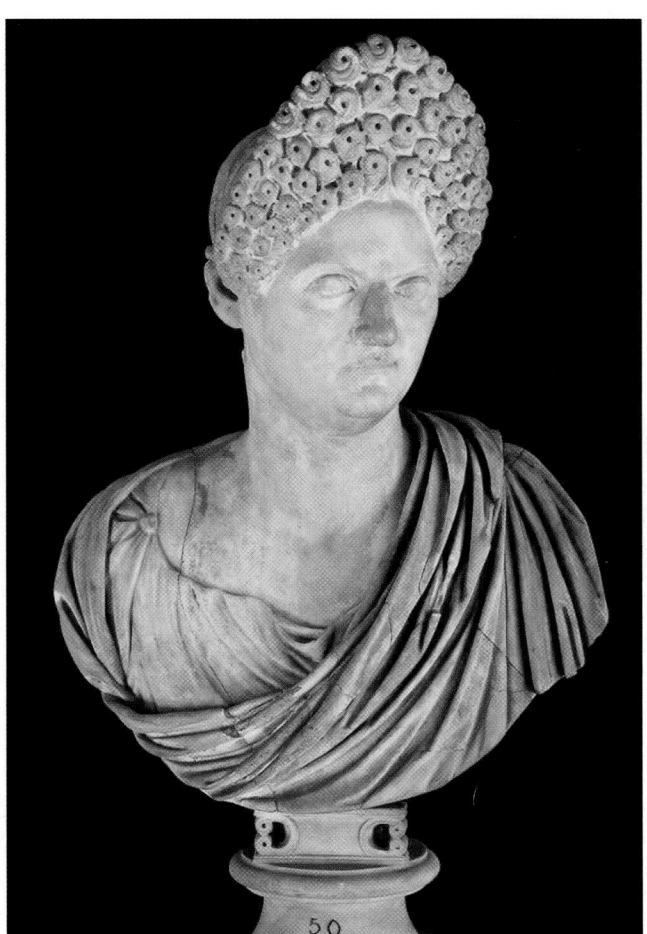

7.32 *Portrait of Domitia Longina*. Late 1st century CE. Marble, height 24" (60.8 cm). Courtesy of San Antonio Museum of Art, San Antonio, Texas. Gift of Gilbert M. Denman, Jr.

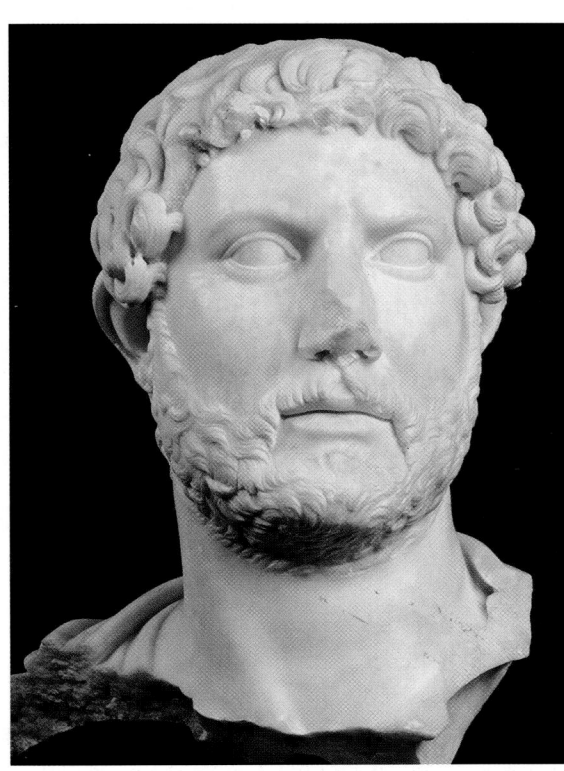

7.31 *Portrait of Hadrian*. After 117 CE. Marble, height 16.7" (42.5 cm). Museo Nazionale Romano, Rome

several years later, Hadrian's portraits revived the classicism associated with Augustus, taking the Greek style even further. Nicknamed "The Greekling" by the ancients for his admiration of Greek culture, he adopted the full beard that was characteristic of Greek philosophers (fig. **7.31**); ancient reports that he was trying to conceal scars from acne are unlikely to be true. It was in his reign that sculptors began to carve the pupils and irises of eyes, rather than painting them.

Imperial portraits survive in great multitudes. They fall into a number of types, suggesting that there was a master portrait, often executed for a specific occasion, which sculptors would copy for dissemination within and outside of Rome; other sculptors would copy these copies, in turn, leading to a ripple effect around the empire. Thousands of portraits of nonimperial subjects also survive. Scholars can rarely identify them, but date them on the basis of similarities with members of the imperial family. When dealing with female portraits, hairstyles are especially useful since they change relatively rapidly. Livia's simple coiffure, with a roll, or *nodus*, at the front is a far cry from the towering hairstyle of Domitia Longina, wife of Domitian, one of Vespasian's sons (fig. **7.32**). Built around a framework (often of wicker), her coiffure was a masterpiece in itself, and its representation in

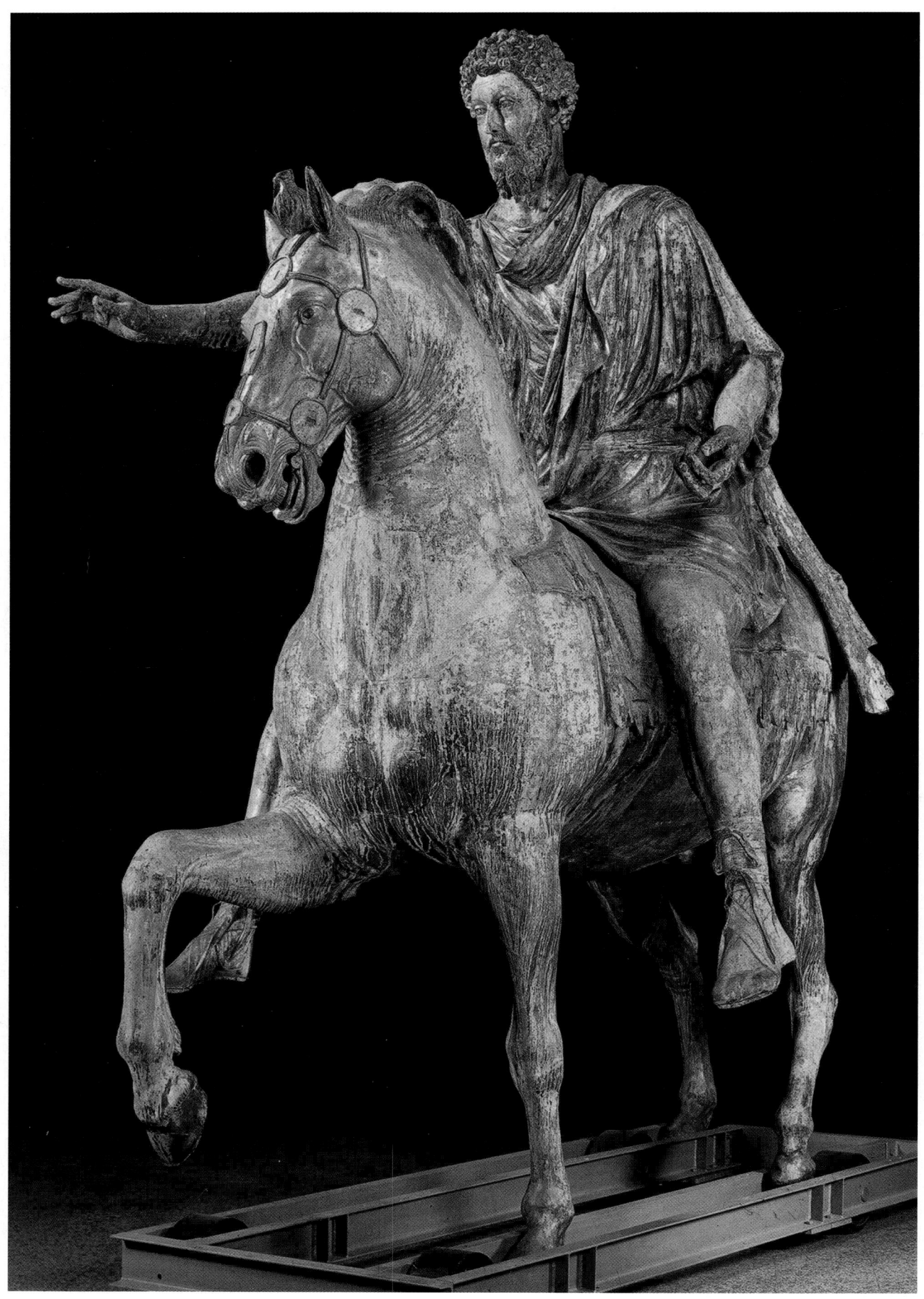

7.33 *Equestrian Statue of Marcus Aurelius.* 161–80 CE. Bronze, over-life-size. Museo del Palazzo dei Conservatori, Rome sculpture reflected her status, as well as affording the sculptor an opportunity to explore contrasts of texture between skin and hair, and to drill deep into the marble for a strong play of light and shadow.

Beginning in the second half of the second century CE, Roman portraits gradually take on a more abstract quality. This is perceptible in a spectacular gilded bronze portrait of Marcus Aurelius, which was spared the melting pot in the medieval period because Christians misidentified the subject as Constantine the Great, champion of Christianity (fig. 7.33). With one arm outstretched in a gesture of mercy, the emperor sits calmly astride a spirited horse, whose raised front leg once rested on a conquered barbarian. As in the portrait of Hadrian and the vast majority of second- and third-century CE male portraits, Marcus Aurelius is bearded. He was interested in philosophy, and his Stoic musings still survive as the "Meditations." Sculpture of the time reflects such abstract concerns. For example, his eyelids fall in languid fashion over his pupils, lending them a remote quality.

Relief Sculpture

The Republican practice of commissioning narrative reliefs to record specific events continued well into the Empire. The reliefs were mounted on public buildings and monuments, such as the *Ara Pacis Augustae*, or Altar of Augustan Peace, as well as commemorative columns and arches.

THE *ARA PACIS AUGUSTAE* ALTAR OF AUGUSTAN PEACE   The Senate and People of Rome vowed the *Ara Pacis Augustae* (fig. 7.34) in 13 BCE when Augustus returned safely from Spain and Gaul, and it was dedicated in 9 BCE. It stood inside a marble enclosure, which was open to the sky and richly sculpted over its entire surface. On east and west sides, flanking two entrances, relief panels represent allegorical figures, or personifications, and figures from Rome's legendary past. On the west end, a fragmentary panel shows a she-wolf suckling the infants Romulus and Remus, under the watchful eyes of the shepherd

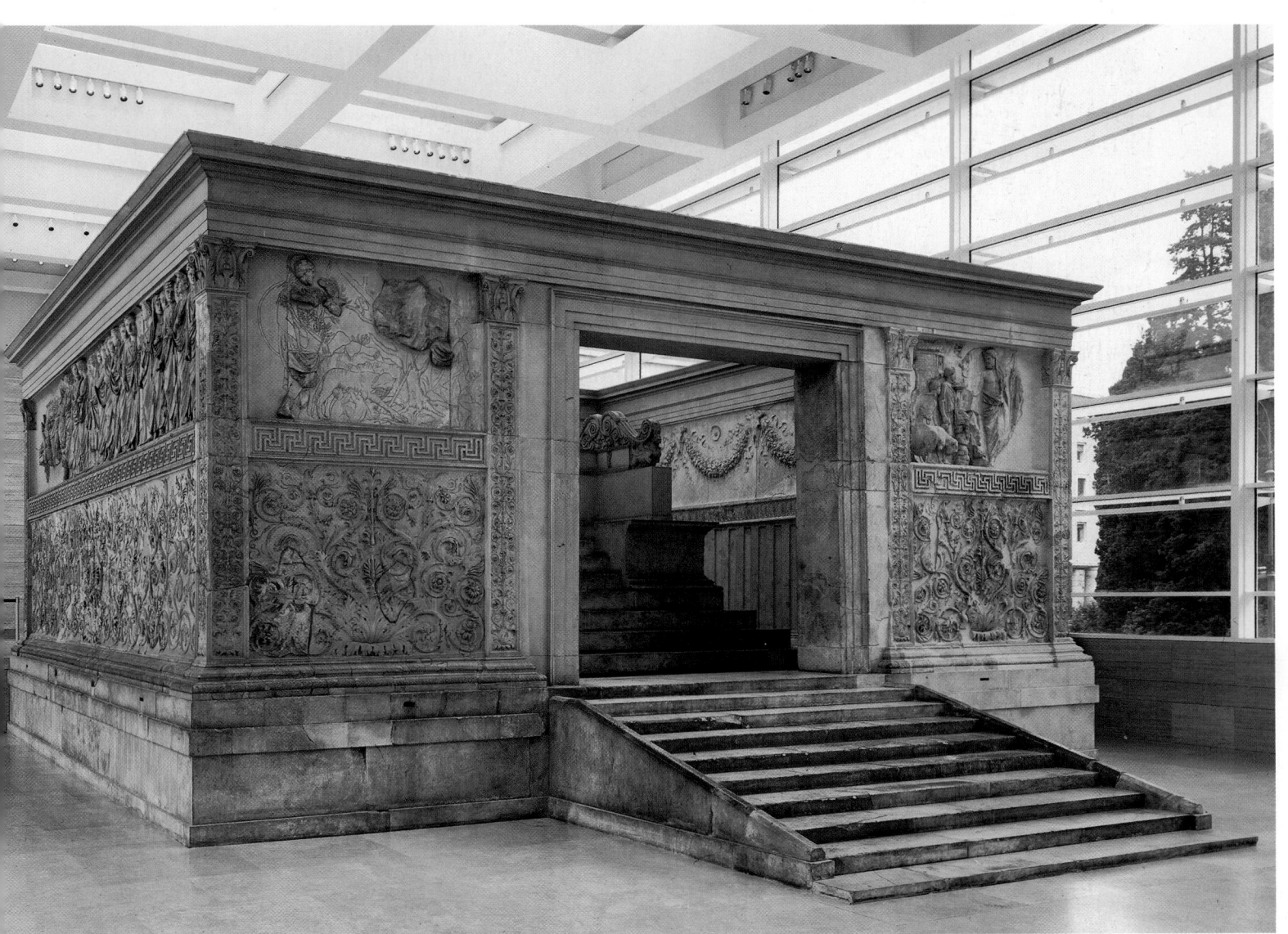

7.34   West façade of *Ara Pacis Augustae*. 13–9 BCE. Marble, width of altar approx. 35' (10.7 m). Museum of the Ara Pacis, Rome

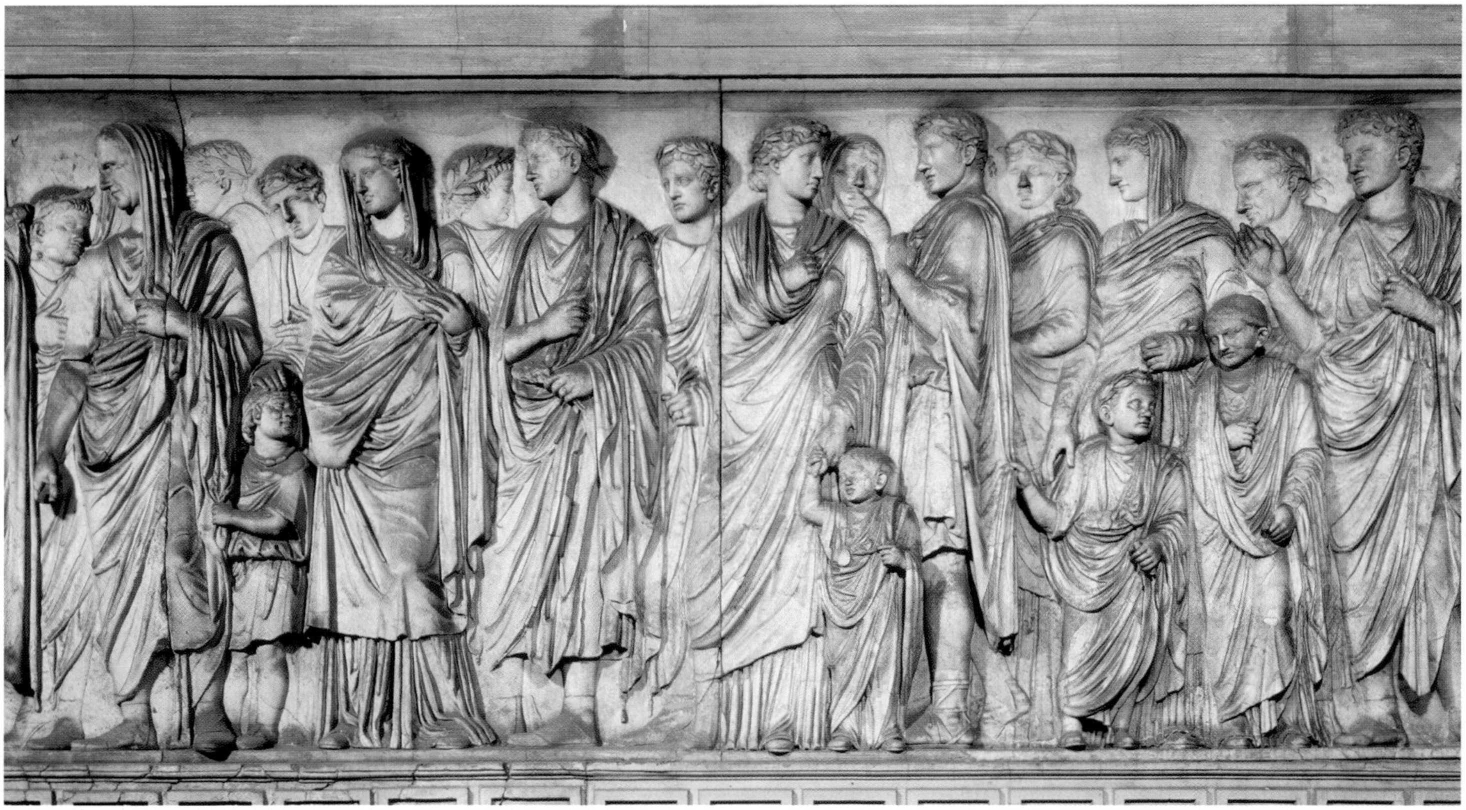

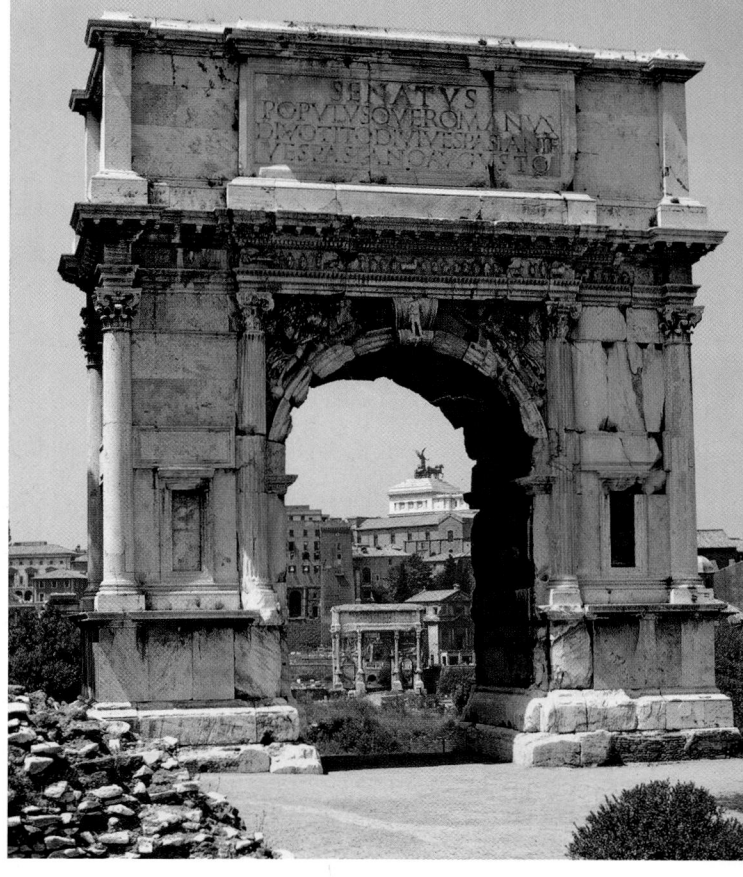

7.35 Imperial Procession south frieze, *Ara Pacis Augustae*. 13–9 BCE. Marble, height 5'3" (1.6 m). Rome

Faustulus, who discovered and adopted them. In a second relief, Aeneas (or perhaps, according to a recent interpretation, Numa, second king of Rome) makes a sacrifice at an altar of roughly hewn stones. At the east end, a relief depicting the goddess Roma seated on her weapons balances a panel with a female figure (the goddess Venus or Ceres, perhaps, or Peace, Italia, or Mother Earth) embodying the notion of peace. Together, the panels express the message of peace that Augustus was intent on promoting, in contrast with the bleakness of the preceding civil wars. The same message was implicit in the acanthus relief that encircles the enclosure in a lower register. Vegetation unfurls in rich abundance, populated with small creatures such as lizards and frogs.

On north and south sides, the upper register contains continuous procession friezes that portray members of the imperial family interspersed with the college of priests and senators (fig. **7.35**). The friezes record a particular event on the day of the altar's dedication. A large gap in the relief falls exactly on Augustus, whose action remains unidentified. Still, the friezes are significant for a number of reasons. In their superficial resemblance to the Greek Parthenon frieze (see figs. 5.45 and 5.46), they bear witness, once again, to a preference for Greek styles in the Augustan age. They also include a number of women from the imperial family, including Livia, and small children. Their inclusion probably denotes the importance of dynasty, as well as referring to moral legislation Augustus enacted to curb adultery and promote childbirth among the elite.

7.36 Arch of Titus, Rome. ca. 81 CE. Marble

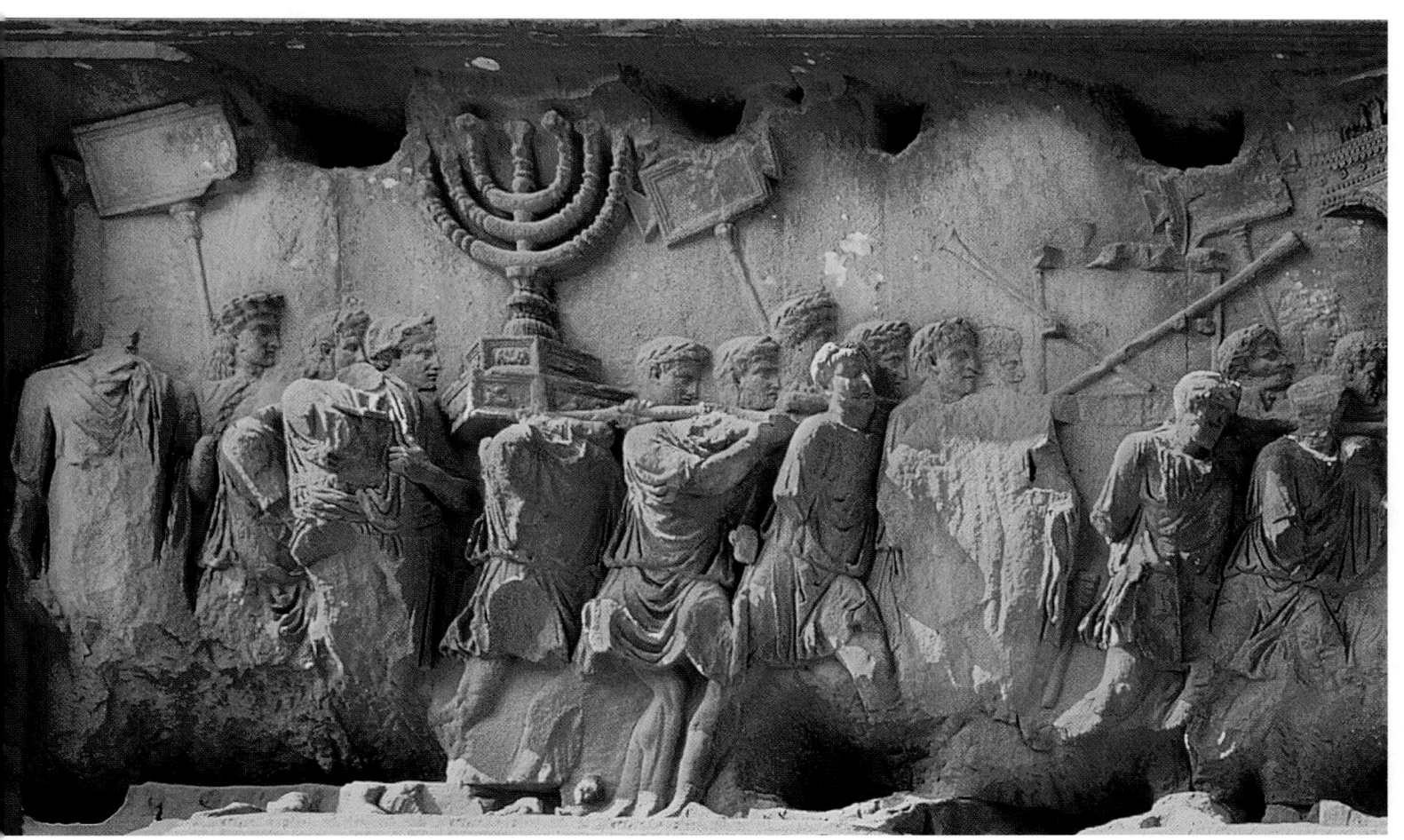

7.37   Relief in bay of Arch of Titus, showing procession of spoils from the Temple in Jerusalem. ca. 81 CE. Marble, height 7'10" (2.39 m)

THE ARCH OF TITUS   Reliefs also decorated free-standing arches. Members of the elite first erected arches during the Republic, though no early examples survive. During the Empire, many arches celebrated triumphs, but they also served as commemorative monuments for the dead. Their enduring impact on Western architecture is readily understandable: As with free-standing columns, their chief *raison d'être* was to express a visual message. Often they stood at or near an entrance to a public area, and framed the transition, or **liminal space** (from *limen*, Latin for "threshold"), between one place and another. Many societies consider liminal spaces unsettling and in need of protection; the lamassu of Mesopotamia, one might note, guarded doorways (see fig. 2.18). The Arch of Titus, son and successor of Vespasian, stands at the far eastern end of the Roman Forum. It is the earliest surviving free-standing arch in Rome, though much of it is the product of architect Giuseppe Valadier's restoration from 1822 to 1824 (fig. **7.36**). It may have been a triumphal monument, but given that its inscription and a small relief panel describe Titus as a god, it is more likely that it commemorates his apotheosis (or divinization) after his death in 81 CE. Its principal sculptural relief panels are within the bay, and both refer to the triumph after the destruction of the Second Temple in Jerusalem in 70 CE. In one

of them, soldiers carry booty through the streets, including a seven-branched menorah (a Jewish candelabra) and other sacred furniture looted from the Temple (fig. 7.37). The panel marks an important move toward spatial illusionism. Two ranks of figures appear, carved in different levels of relief. The background figures are in such shallow relief that they seem to fade into the distance. The procession breaks away abruptly at the sides, so that it appears to continue beyond a viewer's line of sight. On the right, it disappears through a triumphal arch, placed at an angle to the background so that only the nearer half emerges in relief, giving the illusion of spatial depth. The panel even bulges out slightly at the center, so that it seems to turn right in front of a viewer standing inside the arch's bay, making the viewer a part of the action. In the other panel, Titus rides in a triumphal chariot, high above a teeming crowd, signified through differing levels of relief (fig. **7.38**). The horses appear in profile, but the chariot is frontal, giving the illusion that the procession is approaching a viewer before turning sharply. Behind the emperor, a personification of victory crowns him for his success. Additional personifications—Honor and Virtue, perhaps, or Roma—accompany the chariot. Their presence, and the absence of Vespasian, whom the Jewish historian Josephus places in the scene, sound a cautionary note for those who

Josephus (37/8–ca. 100 CE)

The Jewish War, from Book VII

The Jewish soldier and historian Josephus Flavius was born Joseph Ben Matthias in Jerusalem. He was named commander of Galilee during the uprising of 66–70 CE against the Romans in the reign of Nero. After surrendering, he won the favor of the general Titus Flavius Sabinus Vespasian and took the name Flavius as his own. Josephus moved to Rome, where he wrote an account of the war (75–79 CE) and Antiquities of the Jews (93 CE). The following passage from his history of the rebellion describes the triumphal procession into Rome following the Sack of Jerusalem in 70 CE, which is depicted on the Arch of Titus (figs. 7.38 and 7.39).

I t is impossible to give a worthy description of the great number of splendid sights and of the magnificence which occurred in every conceivable form, be it works of art, varieties of wealth, or natural objects of great rarity. For almost all the wondrous and expensive objects which had ever been collected, piece by piece, from one land and another, by prosperous men—all this, being brought together for exhibition on a single day, gave a true indication of the greatness of the Roman Empire. For a vast amount of silver and gold and ivory, wrought into every sort of form, was to be seen, giving not so much the impression of being borne along in a procession as, one might say, of flowing by like a river. Woven tapestries were carried along, some dyed purple and of great rarity, others having varied representations of living figures embroidered on them with great exactness, the handiwork of Babylonians. Transparent stones, some set into gold crowns, some displayed in other ways, were borne by in such great numbers that the conception which we had formed of their rarity seemed pointless. Images of the Roman gods, of wondrous size and made with no inconsiderable workmanship, were also exhibited, and of these there was not one which was not made of some expensive material. ...

The rest of the spoils were borne along in random heaps. The most interesting of all were the spoils seized from the temple of Jerusalem: a gold table weighing many talents, and a lampstand, also made of gold, which was made in a form different from that which we usually employ. For there was a central shaft fastened to the base; then spandrels extended from this in an arrangement which rather resembled the shape of a trident, and on the end of each of these spandrels a lamp was forged. There were seven of these, emphasizing the honor accorded to the number seven among the Jews. The law of the Jews was borne along after these as the last of the spoils. In the next section a good many images of Victory were paraded by. The workmanship of all of these was in ivory and gold. Vespasian drove along behind these and Titus followed him; Domitian rode beside them, dressed in a dazzling fashion and riding a horse which was worth seeing.

Source: J.J. Pollitt, *The Art in Rome, c. 753 B.C.–A.D. 337: Sources and Documents* (NJ: Cambridge University Press, 1983)

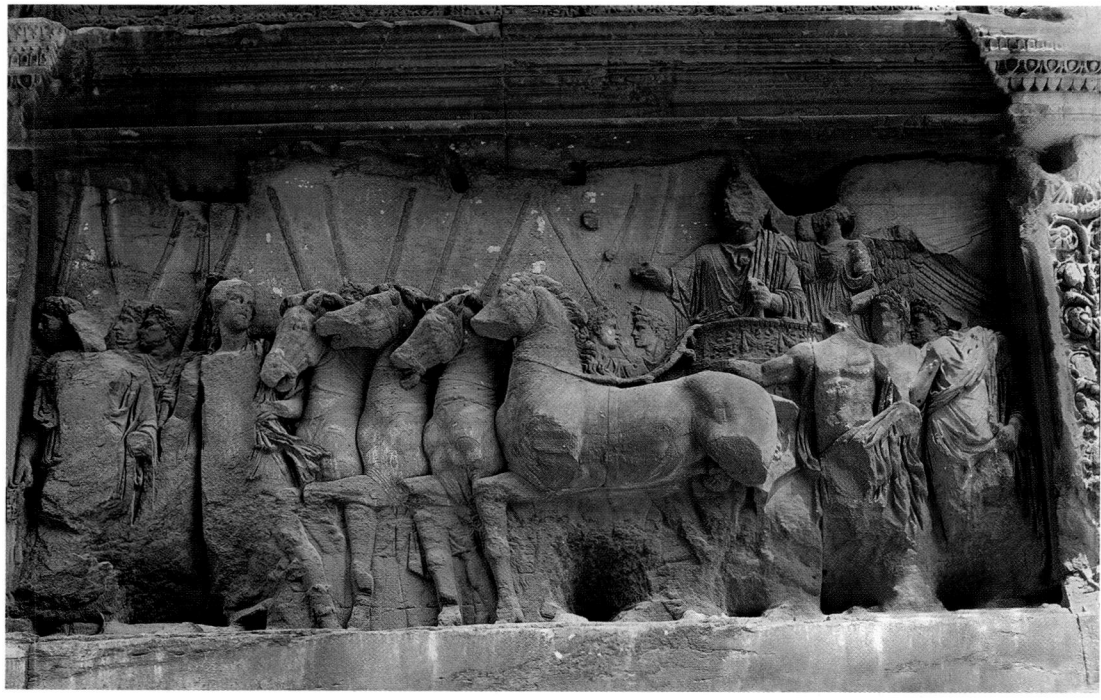

7.38 Relief in bay of Arch of Titus, showing Titus riding in triumph

would read Roman visual narratives as accurate accounts of historical events. (See *Primary Source*, above.) Artists constructed these narratives to express a version of events that served the patron's ideology.

THE COLUMN OF TRAJAN The exploration of space and narrative strategies comes into full bloom in the Column of Trajan (fig. **7.39**), erected between 106 and 113 CE in a small court to the west of Trajan's Forum (see figs. 7.17 and 7.18). Soaring about 150

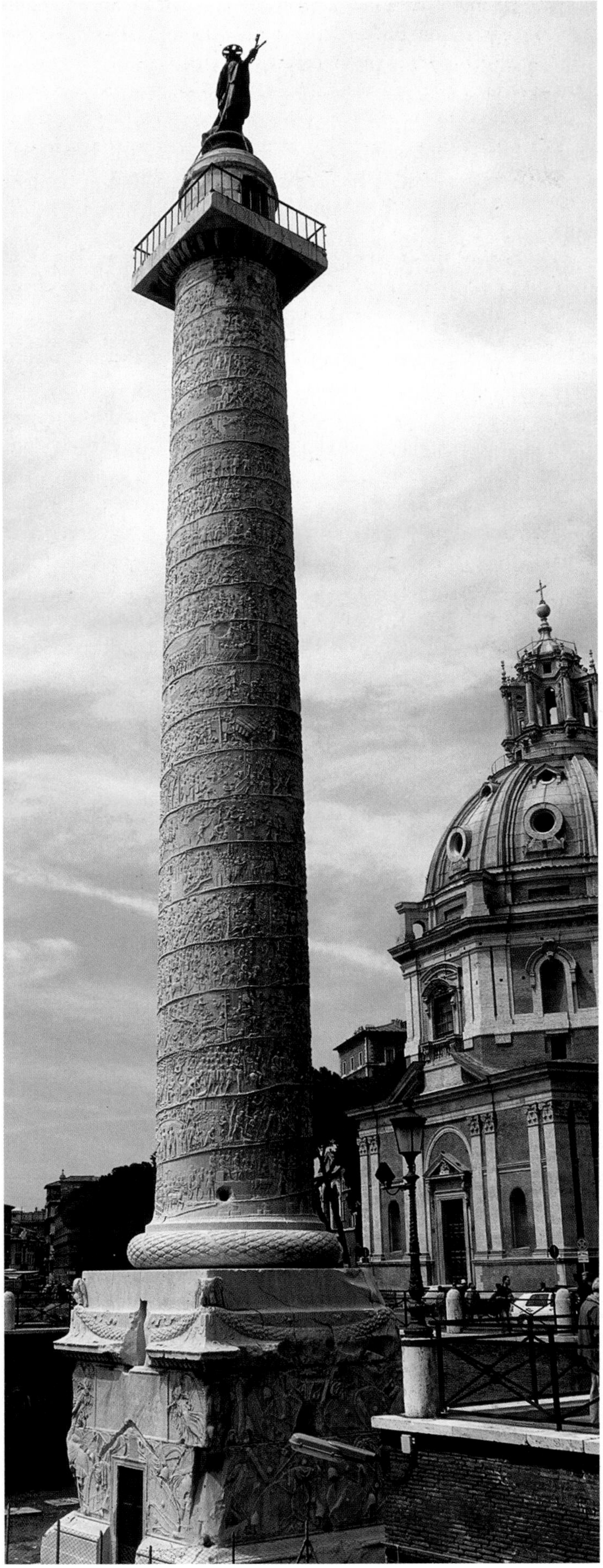

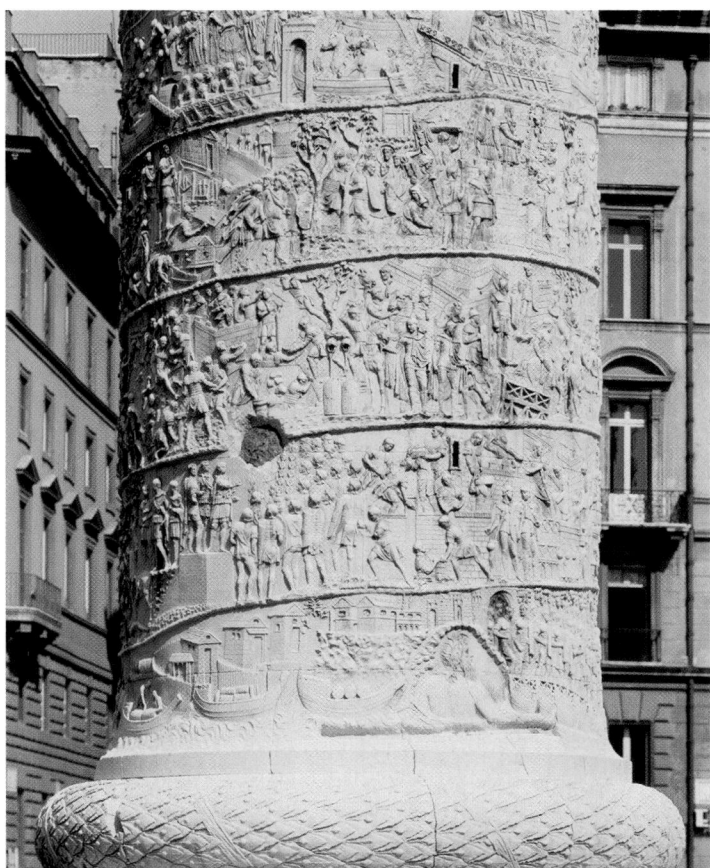

7.40 Lower portion of Column of Trajan, Rome. 106–13 CE. Marble, height of relief band approx. 50" (127 cm)

Roman feet high, this supported a gilded statue of the emperor, lost in medieval times. Winding through the interior of its shaft was a spiral staircase leading to a viewing platform, from which a visitor could look out over Trajan's extraordinary building complex. Free-standing columns had been used as commemorative monuments in Greece from Hellenistic times, but the sheer scale of Trajan's Column, usually credited as the work of Apollodorus, along with its role as **belvedere** (or viewing station), makes it nothing short of a world wonder. However, art historians have tended to focus not on the engineering feat the column represents, but on the 656-foot-long continuous narrative relief that winds around its shaft in a counterclockwise direction, celebrating the emperor's victorious campaigns against the people of Dacia (in present-day Romania).

The narrative begins with the Roman army's crossing of the Danube to reach Dacian territory (fig. **7.40**). The river appears as a large personification. To the left are riverboats loaded with supplies and a Roman town on a rocky bank. The second band shows Trajan speaking to his soldiers, and soldiers building fortifications. In the third, soldiers construct a garrison camp and bridge as the cavalry sets out on a reconnaissance mission; and in the

7.39 Column of Trajan, Rome. 106–13 CE. Marble, height 125' (38 m)

fourth, foot soldiers cross a stream while, to the right, the emperor addresses his troops in front of a Dacian fortress. These scenes are a fair sampling of events shown on the column. Among the more than 150 episodes, combat occurs only rarely. The geographic, logistic, and political aspects of the campaign receive more attention, much as they do in Julius Caesar's literary account of his conquest of Gaul.

Individual scenes are not distinctly separate from one another. Sculptors placed trees and buildings in such a way as to suggest divisions, but the scenes still merge into a continuous whole, with important protagonists, such as Trajan, appearing multiple times. Thus, they preserved visual continuity without sacrificing the coherence of each scene. Although Assyrian and Egyptian artists created visual narratives of military conquests, this relief is by far the most ambitious composition so far in terms of the number of figures and the density of the narrative, and understanding it is a complicated matter. Continuous illustrated **rotuli** (scrolls) are a likely inspiration for the composition, if such things existed before the column's construction.

Also problematic is the fact that in order to follow the narrative sequence, a viewer has to keep turning around the column, head inclined upward. Above the fourth or fifth turn, details become hard to make out with the naked eye, even if the addition of paint made the sculpture more vivid. It might have been possible to view the upper spirals from balconies on surrounding buildings in antiquity, but the format would still have required an encircling motion. These problems have led scholars to propose viewing strategies. They have long noted that the relief is formulaic; that is, the sculptors repeated a fairly limited number of stock scenes again and again. These include, for instance, sacrifice scenes, the emperor addressing his troops, or soldiers constructing forts and dismantling enemy cities. Though these are not identical, they are similar enough to be recognized at a distance, which helps make the upper spirals more legible. The designer may also have aligned important and representative scenes on the cardinal axes of the column, so that a viewer could grasp an abbreviated version of the whole from a single standpoint. Yet there is always the possibility that the designer intended viewers to have to turn around the column in order to read its narrative. The column's base would serve as a burial chamber for Trajan's ashes after his death in 117 CE, and an encircling motion would be entirely consistent with a widespread Roman funerary ritual known as the *decursio*, in which visitors to a tomb walked around it to protect the dead buried within, to keep harmful spirits in the grave, and to pay perpetual homage to the deceased.

THE COLUMN BASE OF ANTONINUS PIUS The point at which the classicizing phase of Roman sculpture, still so evident on the Column of Trajan, starts to yield to the more abstract style of late antiquity—with its less naturalistic, more linear treatment

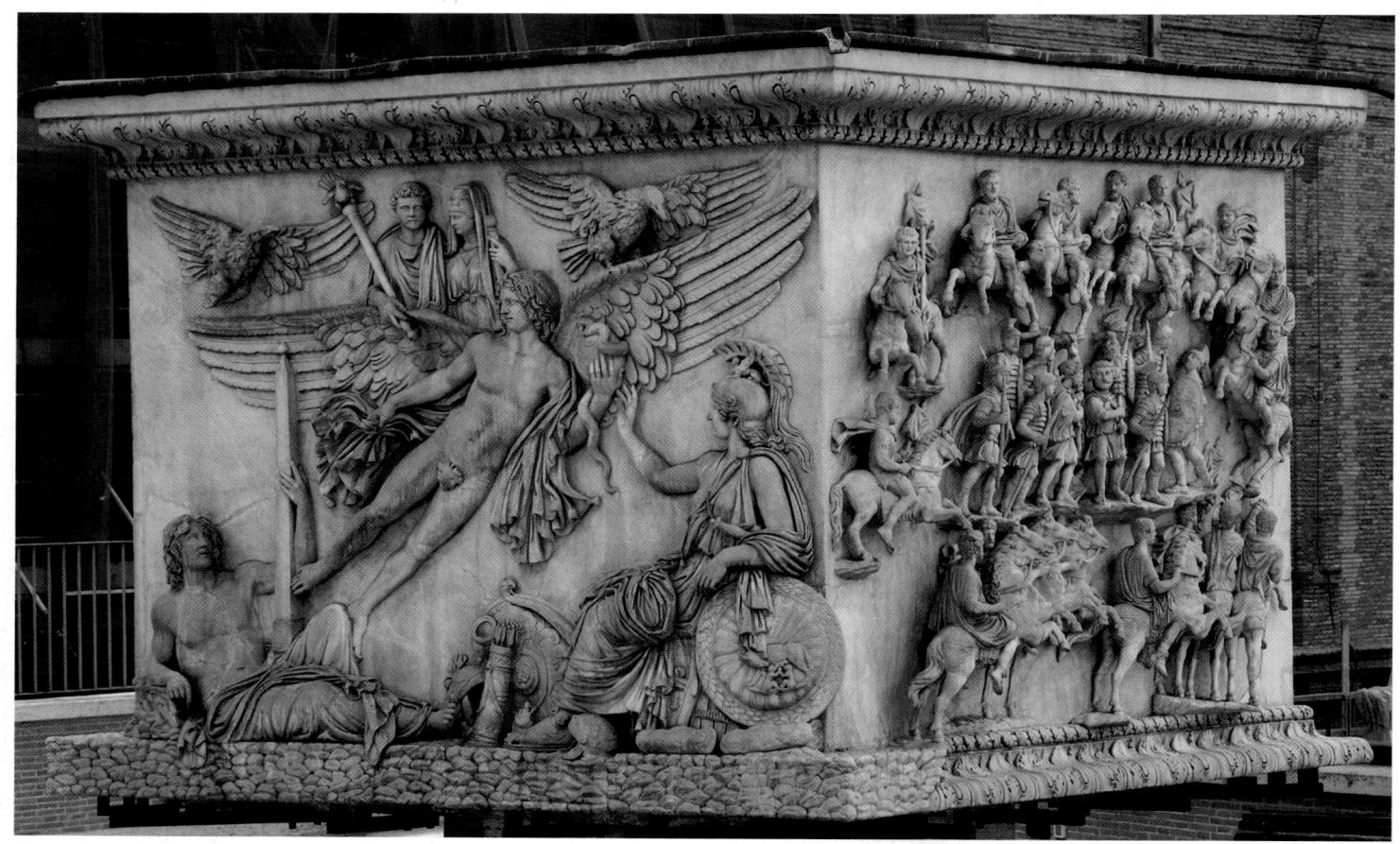

7.41   Column base of Antoninus Pius and Faustina. "Apotheosis" and "*decursio*" reliefs. ca. 161 CE. Marble. Musei Vaticani, Rome

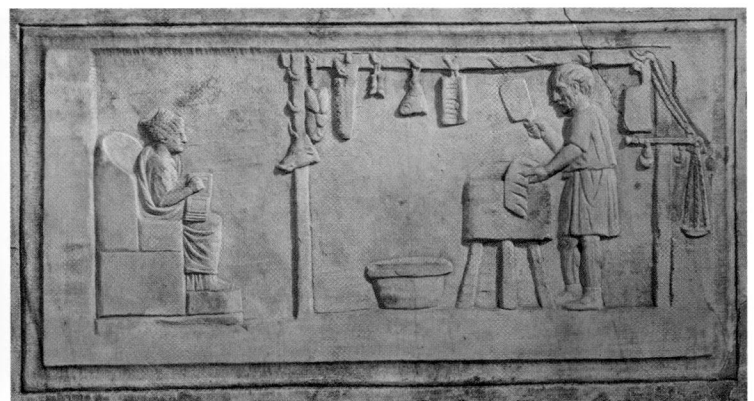

7.42 Funerary relief of a butcher and a woman. Mid-2nd century CE. Marble, 13½× 26½" (34.5 × 67.3 cm). Staatliche Kunstsammlungen, Dresden

of the body—is a matter of some debate. A critical shift may have taken place with the column base of Antoninus Pius and his wife, Faustina the Elder. Antoninus died in 161 CE. His successors, Marcus Aurelius and Lucius Verus, erected a 50-foot porphyry column in his honor, surmounted by his statue. Its white marble base is all that survives. One side bears an inscription. On another is an apotheosis scene, where a winged figure bears the emperor and his wife to the heavens, while personifications of the Field of Mars (where the cremation took place) and Rome look on (fig. **7.41**). The figures have lithe, Classical proportions, and idealized faces, with smooth, even planes and ageless features. On the two remaining sides of the base, Roman cavalrymen ride in a counterclockwise circle around a group of infantrymen, in nearly identical scenes that probably represent the *decursio* around the funeral pyre. The sculptural style of these scenes is unlike the apotheosis scene. The soldiers have stocky, squat proportions, and the action unfolds in a bird's-eye perspective, while the soldiers are viewed

from the side. Both of these factors find parallels in sculpture commissioned in the provinces and in nonelite circles. Figure **7.42** shows a nonelite style, in a funerary relief commemorating a butcher and a woman. The image has a flatness that is different from the illusionistic treatment of space on the panels of the Arch of Titus (see figs. 7.37 and 7.38) The figures are stocky, and the butcher's head is large in proportion to his body. The artist's priority was probably legibility: The patron would have mounted the panel on the façade of a tomb, so that viewers could see it from a distance. The linear treatment of the image and the boldness of the forms served this goal well. The introduction of these qualities into imperial commissions in Rome signals a change in the way state art expressed messages.

Art and Architecture in the Provinces

The spread of Rome's authority over a wide geographical reach had a profound impact on artistic and architectural production in those areas. As Rome's political and cultural institutions reached the provinces, so did the architectural and artistic forms that accommodated them. Sometimes provincial monuments are all but indistinguishable from those in the city of Rome; but more often the syncretism of Roman forms and indigenous styles and materials led to works that were at once recognizably Roman and yet distinctive to their locale.

The principal written sources on the provinces tend to be works by Romans. For this reason, it is hard to assess how provincial peoples reacted to Roman rule. But it certainly brought them some benefits. For instance, Roman engineers had mastered the art of moving water efficiently, and the new aqueducts that sprang up in urban centers around the Empire must have improved local standards of living immeasurably. A striking aqueduct still stands at Segovia in Spain, dating to the first or early second century CE (fig. **7.43**). It brought water from Riofrío, about

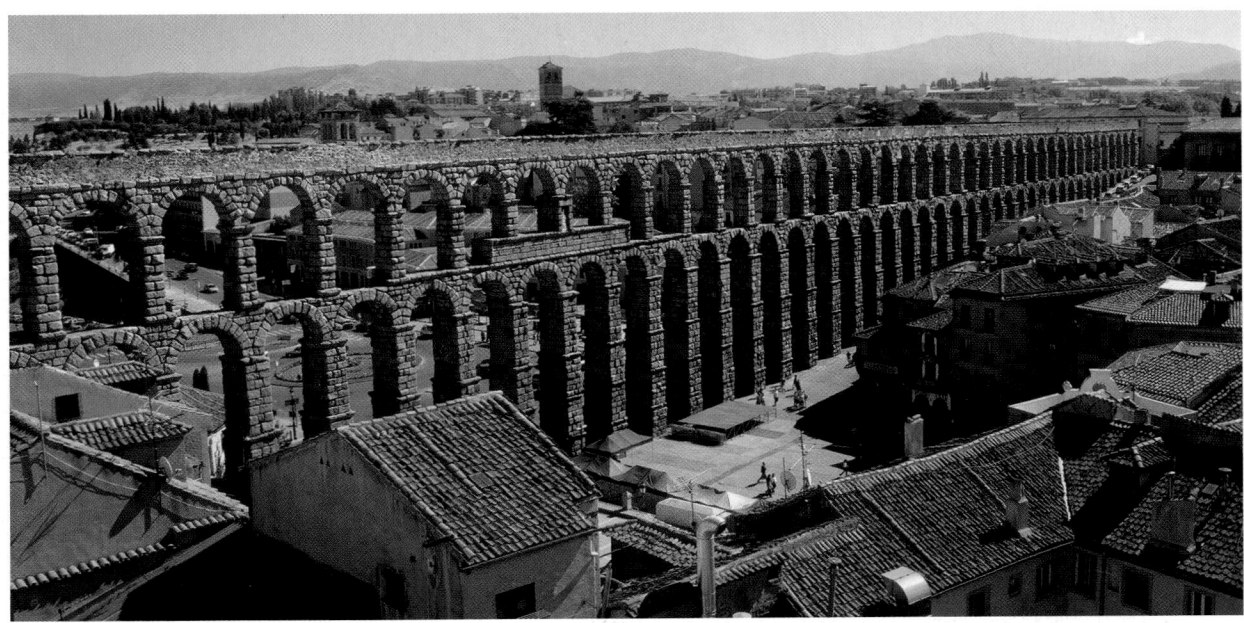

7.43 Aqueduct, Segovia. 1st or early 2nd century CE

10½ miles (17 km) away, flowing for most of its length through an underground channel. Approaching the town, however, architects built a massive bridge stretching 2,666 feet long and up to 98 feet high to span a valley. One hundred and eighteen arches support the water channel, superimposed in two registers at the highest point. Like most provincial builders, the architects used a local stone, in this case granite, which they assembled without mortar and left unfinished to give it an air of strength. Despite the obvious practical advantages the aqueduct provided, the design also illustrates how Roman architecture could effect dominion. The arches—such a quintessentially Roman form—march relentlessly across the terrain, symbolically conquering it with their step. Even the act of moving water was a conquest of a kind, a conquest of Nature.

THE MAISON CARÉE, NÎMES Romans carried their way of life with them across the Empire, constructing theaters and amphitheaters in a Roman style, and temples to accommodate their rituals. A well-preserved temple (fig. 7.44) known as the Maison Carrée (Square House) survives in the French town of Nîmes (ancient Nemausus). Typically Roman, it stands on a high podium, with a frontal staircase. Six Corinthian columns across the front lead into a deep porch and to the cella; engaged columns decorate the cella's exterior walls. Reconstructing an inscription

in bronze letters on its architrave from the evidence of dowel holes, scholars long thought the temple to have been dedicated to Rome and Augustus during the Augustan age. Acanthus scrolls in the frieze appeared to be reminiscent of the *Ara Pacis*, and the masonry style showed similarities to that of the Temple of Mars the Avenger in Augustus' Forum. Indeed, scholars once considered the temple evidence for traveling workshops. Recent research has cast doubt on this view, though, and illustrates the danger that historians may construct the very history they are looking for by interpreting evidence to fit preconceived theories. As it turns out, the dowel holes could support any number of different inscriptions; and the **module** (construction measure) employed throughout the building only came into use under Trajan. The building could be a temple dedicated to Trajan's wife, Plotina, as attested in literary sources.

EL KHASNEH, PETRA In some cases, the syncretism of indigenous building traditions with Roman styles resulted in powerful new effects. This appears to be the case with the extraordinary rock-cut façade known as El Khasneh, or the Treasury, at the site of Petra in present-day Jordan (fig. 7.45). This façade is the first sight to greet a visitor who wanders through the long, twisting gorge known as the Siq, leading to the town center. The Nabataeans, a nomadic people who settled this area before the

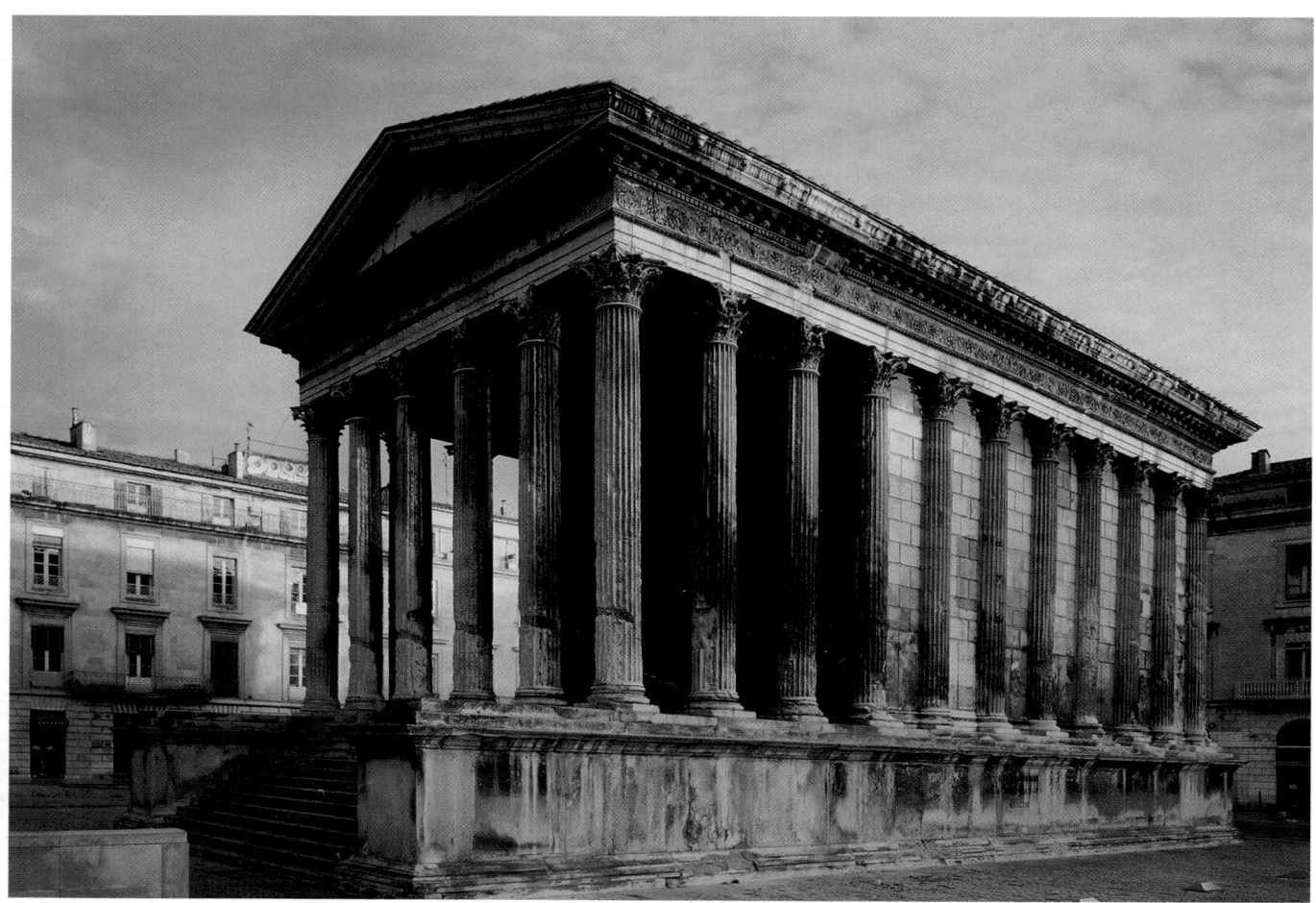

7.44 Maison Carrée, Nîmes. Early 2nd century CE (?)

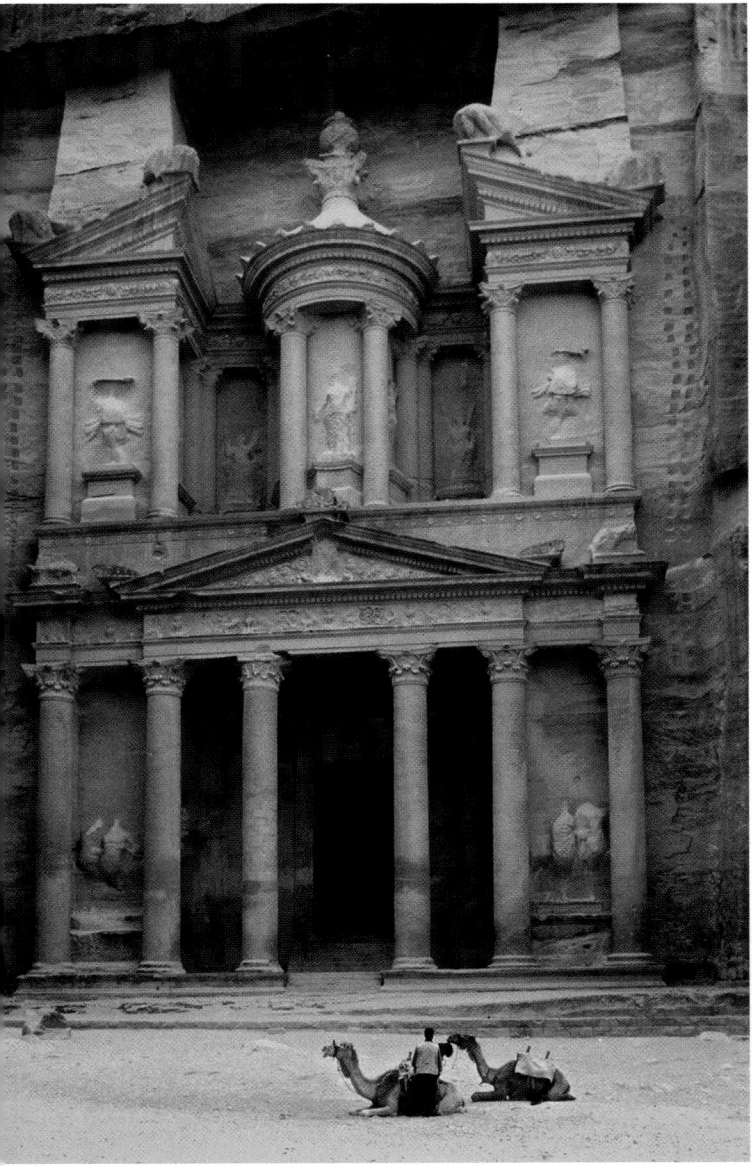

7.45 El Khasneh, Petra, Jordan. Probably early 2nd century CE

playful treatment of once-structural elements became popular in the provinces and in Rome in the second century CE, and scholars sometimes describe it as a "baroque" phase, for its similarities to Italian Baroque architecture. The monument's function may have changed for Roman usage as well: Relief sculptures between the columns seem to represent figures from the cult of Isis, suggesting that it was a temple. In some cases, inscriptions and other written documents indicate who commissioned monuments in the provinces; the patron might be local, a Roman official, or even the emperor himself. More often, as in this case, there is no such evidence, which makes it hard to determine meaning in a particular choice of design.

SCULPTURE AND PAINTING Sculpture in the Roman provinces also has a distinctive look—the result, generally, of a merging of different traditions. A limestone funerary relief from Palmyra in Syria from the second half of the second century CE (fig. **7.46**) once sealed the opening to a burial within a characteristically Palmyrene monument, a tower tomb. An Aramaic inscription identifies the subject as Tibnan, an elite woman, who holds a small child in one arm. The language bespeaks her origin, and the strict frontality, large staring eyes, and local dress and headband set her apart from elite women of Rome (see fig. 7.32). All the same, the portrait has distinctly Roman qualities: Tibnan

Romans took control in 106 CE, buried their wealthy dead in tombs cut out of the pink sandstone cliffs, and some have seen El Khasneh as one of their monuments. Most now agree, however, that it belongs to the Trajanic or Hadrianic period. Carved from the living rock, the monument resembles a temple façade, with six columns beneath an architrave decorated with floral designs and a pediment. In a second story, lateral columns support the angles of a broken pediment. Between them is a tholos with a conical roof, surmounted by an ornamental finial. In modern times, locals imagined that pirates had stored their treasure in the finial, lending the monument its name; bullet holes show how they tried to knock it down. The façade is a striking amalgamation of a Nabataean concept with Roman decorative features—the Corinthian column capitals, for instance, and the vegetal designs. The architectural elements are not structural, and this allows for a freedom and quality of fantasy in the design, not unlike the fantasy vistas of Second Style wall paintings (see page 221). This

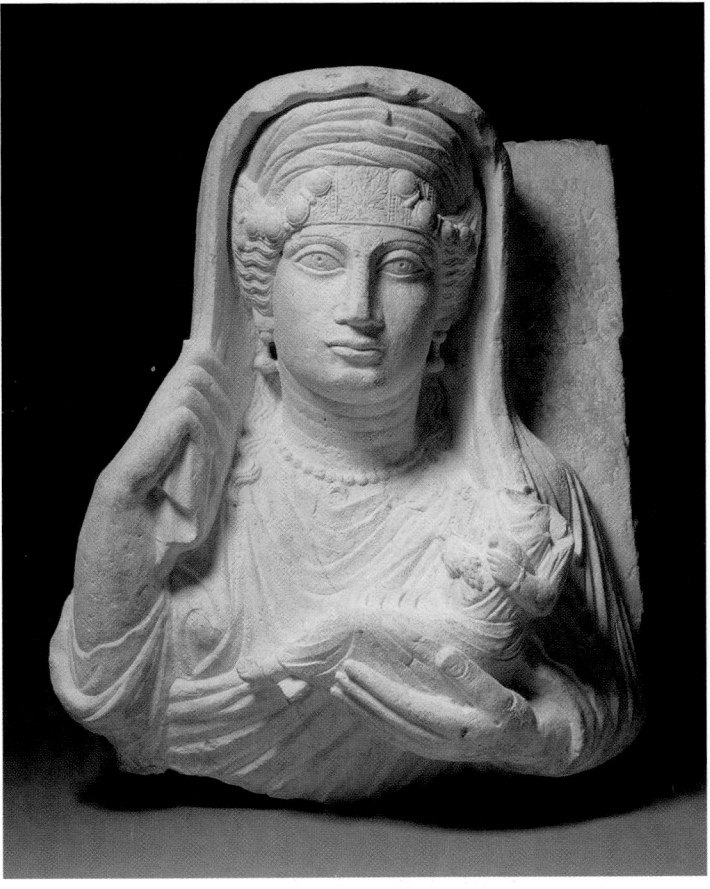

7.46 Funerary relief of Tibnan, from Palmyra, Syria. ca. 150–200 CE. Painted limestone. Musée du Louvre, Paris

raises her right hand, for instance, to hold her veil, in a Roman gesture that signified chastity (or *pudicitia*, defined as loyalty to one's husband) (see fig. 7.13). The portrait neatly encapsulates the dual identity of this provincial woman, who is both Palmyrene and Roman.

The largest body of painting to survive from the Roman world is wall painting (see page 218). Yet the sands of Fayum, in Lower Egypt, preserved a magnificent group of painted portraits, once attached over the faces of embalmed, mummified corpses (fig. 7.47). The earliest of them appear to date from the second century

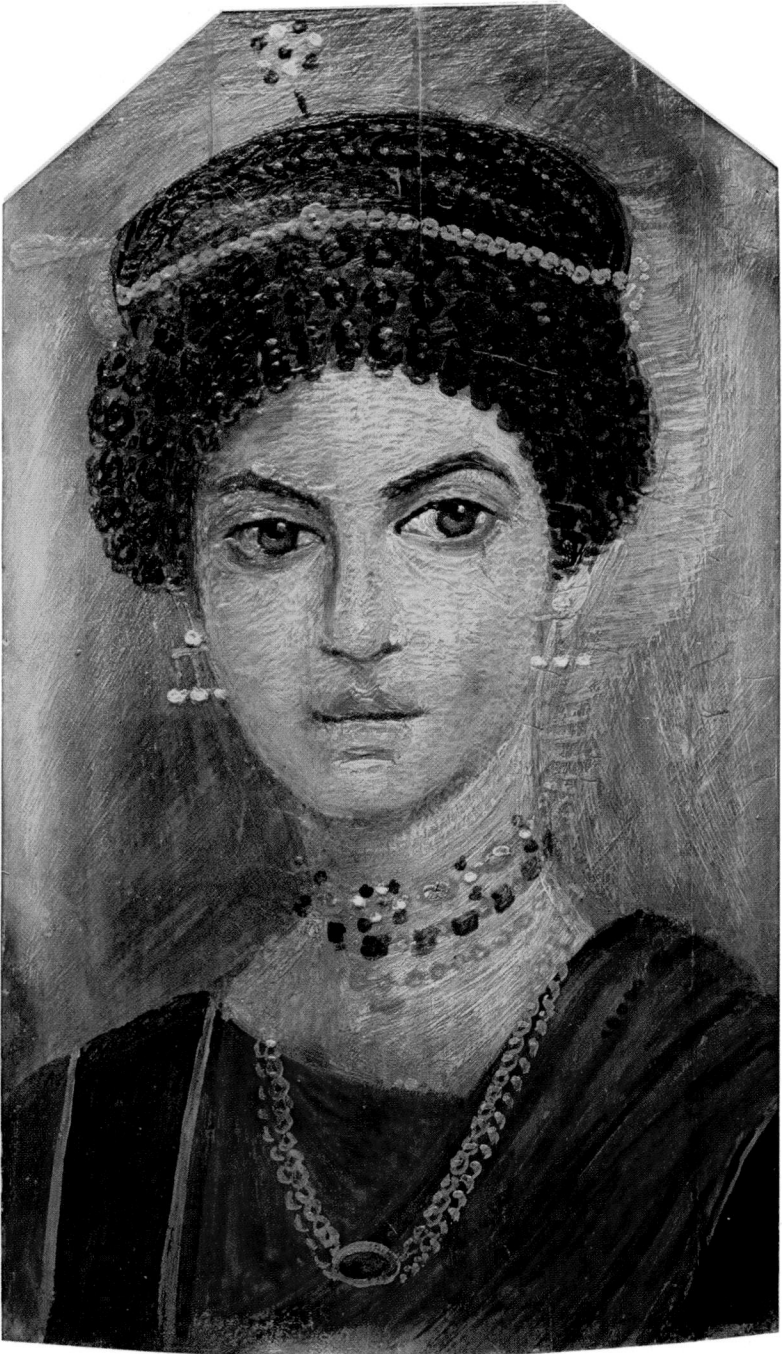

7.47 *Portrait of a Woman*, from Hawara in the Fayum, Lower Egypt. ca. 110–30 CE. Encaustic on wooden panel. Royal Museum of Scotland. © Trustees of the National Museum of Scotland

CE. Artists painted them on wooden panels in the **encaustic** technique, which involves suspending pigments in hot wax. The mixture can be opaque and creamy, like oil paint, or thin and translucent. The medium is extremely durable, and the panels retain an extraordinary freshness; the wax also gives them a lustrous vitality. The quality of the portraits varies dramatically. At their best, they have a haunting immediacy, largely the result of the need to work quickly before the hot wax set. The woman pictured here wears a crimson tunic and a wealth of jewelry. Rows of black circles denote the ringlets of her hair, bound with a golden diadem. Her appearance is Roman, yet the portrait itself speaks of her local identity, since she was buried in the Egyptian, not the Roman, fashion. As a result, these portraits belong rightly in the history of both Roman art and Egyptian art.

Domestic Art and Architecture

The Romans are one of the few ancient peoples to have left abundant evidence of domestic architecture and its decoration. This is largely due to the catastrophic eruption of Vesuvius in 79 CE, which left the nearby cities of Pompeii and Herculaneum buried under a thick blanket of ash and lava. When excavations began in Pompeii in the eighteenth century, archaeologists discovered a city frozen in time. Utensils and remnants of furniture were still in place in houses, inns, and bath buildings, allowing historians to reconstruct the rituals of daily life in extraordinary detail.

POMPEII AND HERCULANEUM In its early days, the Oscans inhabited Pompeii. Another early Italic tribe, the Samnites, took control in the late fifth century BCE, and the city's monumentalization began under their aegis, and under the influence of nearby Greek cities. After the Social War of 90–89 BCE, the Roman dictator Sulla refounded Pompeii as a Roman colony. Like other colonies, which took their design from Roman army camps, Pompeii had two main streets, the *cardo* and the *decumanus* (fig. **7.48**). At their intersection stood the forum, the civic heart of the city, near which the Pompeiians built the principal temples and two theaters. Interspersed among surrounding streets were houses and the other buildings that accommodated everyday Roman life: baths for daily bathing and socializing, taverns and fast-food kitchens, launderers with their great vats of urine for washing clothes, and brothels. A state-of-the-art amphitheater on the outskirts of the city, which was a prototype for the Colosseum, provided gladiatorial entertainments, and outside the city gates the wealthy buried their dead in monumental tombs. In the Augustan period, an aqueduct brought fresh water to the public fountains that flowed continuously throughout the city. Water flushed the basalt-paved streets to keep them clean, and raised steppingstones allowed pedestrians to cross from sidewalk to sidewalk without getting wet.

The unusually good state of preservation of the houses of Pompeii and Herculaneum means that they dominate scholarly discussion, as they will here; yet such was the durability of Roman domestic construction that houses survive elsewhere as

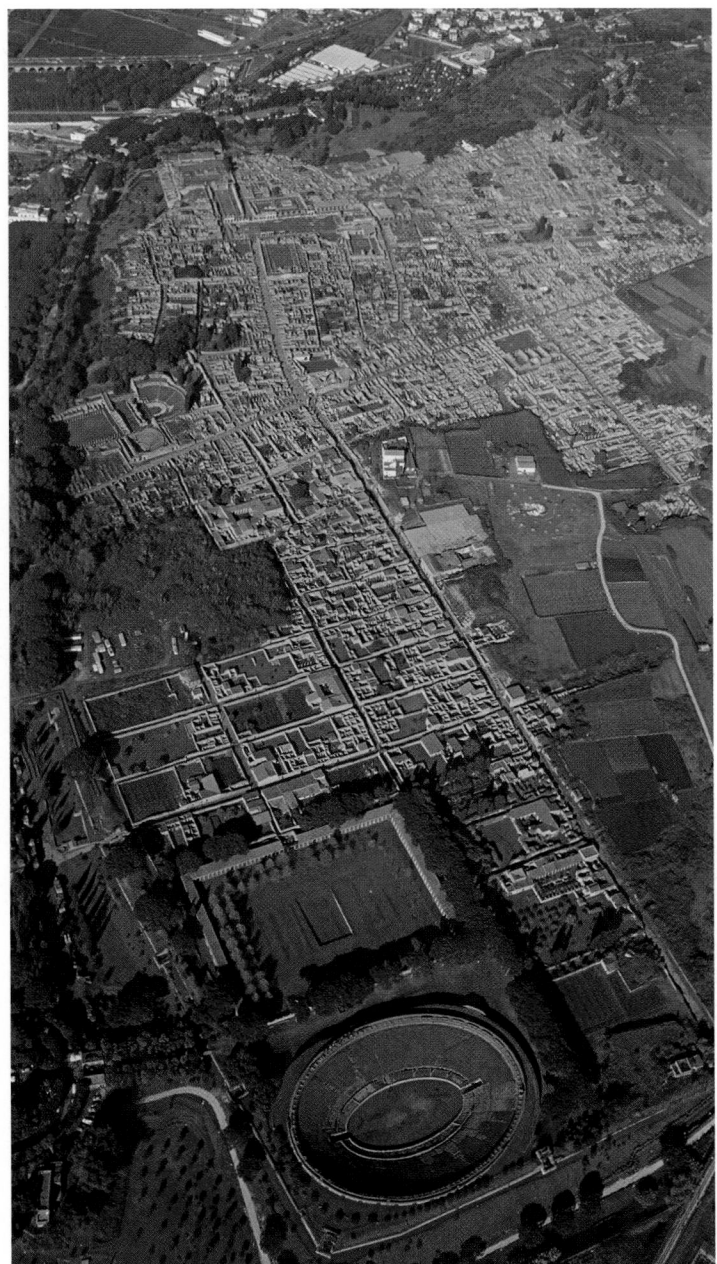

7.48 Aerial view of Pompeii

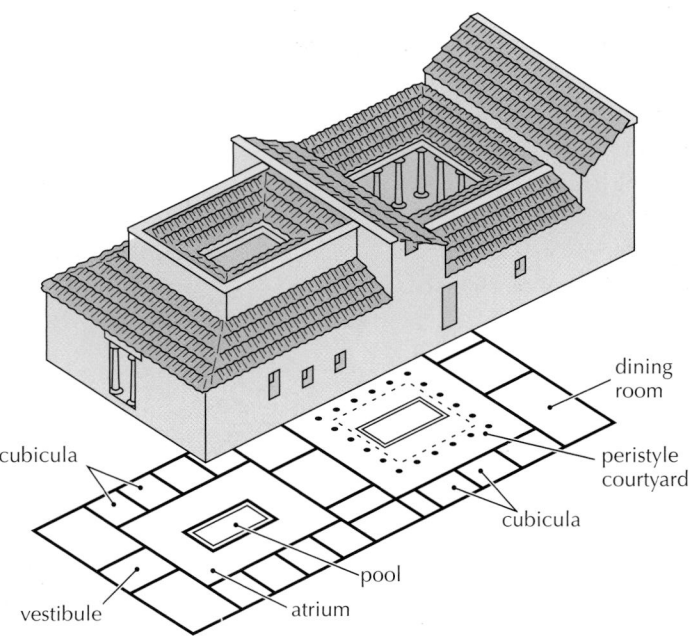

7.49 Reconstruction of Pompeiian house

cubicula
peristyle
courtyard
dining
room
cubicula
vestibule
pool
atrium

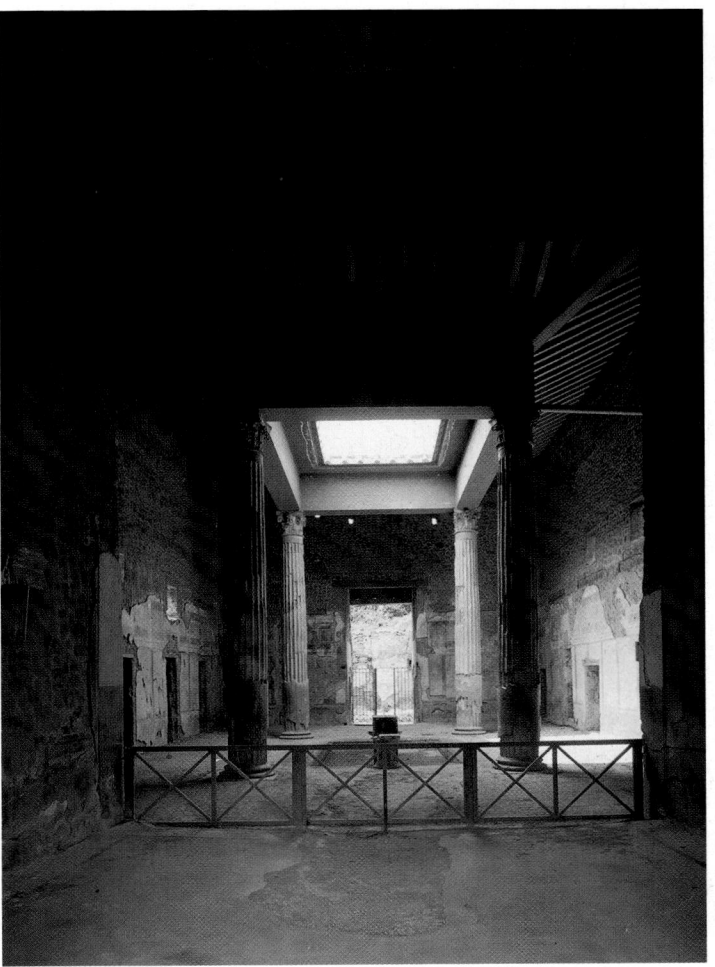

7.50 Atrium of the House of the Silver Wedding, Pompeii. 2nd century BCE–79 CE

well, as far afield as Morocco and Jordan, and although Roman houses have many common qualities, they also differ from one region to the next, to cater, for instance, to local climates. One should be cautious, therefore, about conceiving of a "typical" Roman house.

Scholars describe elite Roman houses by their Latin name, **domus**, known from Vitruvius and other ancient writing (fig. 7.49). (See www.myartslab.com.) Its most distinctive feature is an atrium, a square or oblong central hall lit by an opening in the roof, answered by a shallow pool, or **impluvium**, in the ground to collect rainwater. The airy quality of the atrium confers an element of grandeur upon the house, visible here in the House of the Silver Wedding (fig. **7.50**), and by tradition it was where Romans kept portraits of ancestors. Other rooms, such as bedrooms

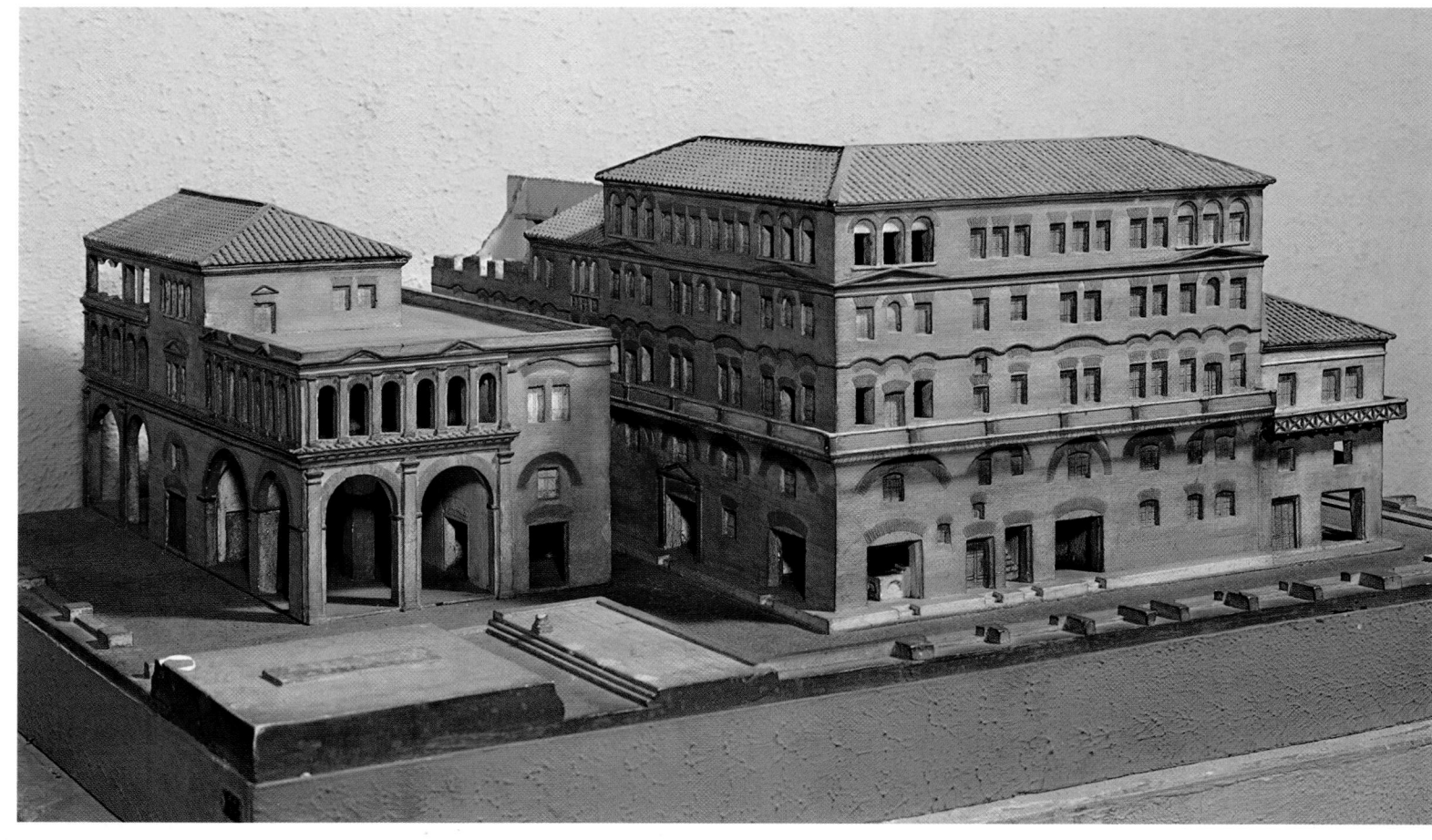

7.51 Model of apartment block

(**cubicula**), group around the atrium, which often leads to a *tablinum*, a reception room, where the family kept its archives. Beyond the tablinum, a colonnade (the *peristyle*) surrounds a garden, where the owner could display sculpture and take fresh air. There might be additional rooms at the back of the house. The chief light source was the atrium and the peristyle; walls facing the street did not typically have windows, but one should not be misled into believing that these houses were therefore particularly private. Romans routinely used rooms flanking the entryway as shops, and the front door often stood open. At the heart of Roman society was a client–patron relationship, and clients routinely visited their patrons in their homes, in a morning ritual known as the *salutatio*. The householder also conducted business in his home, even in the bedrooms. A visitor's access to the different parts of the house depended on his relationship with the owner, who would greet most visitors in the large central rooms.

In any given region of the Empire, there were huge discrepancies between the houses of the rich and the dwellings of the poor. Abandoned in the Middle Ages, Rome's port city, Ostia, preserves many examples of high-occupancy dwellings, known as **insulae** (literally "islands") (fig. **7.51**). An **insula** was generally a substantial concrete-and-brick building (or chain of buildings) around a small central court, with many features of a present-day apartment block. On the ground floor, shops and taverns opened to the street; above lived numerous families in cramped quarters. Some insulae had as many as five stories, with balconies above the second floor. Wealthy property owners often made a handsome income from these buildings.

MAU'S FOUR STYLES OF PAINTING Compared with Greek painting, Roman domestic painting—mostly wall painting—survives in great abundance. It comes mainly from Pompeii and Herculaneum, and also from Rome and its environs, and it dates mostly to a span of less than 200 years, from the end of the second century BCE to the late first century CE. Given the public character of a domus, these paintings were more than mere decoration: They also testified to a family's wealth and status.

Basing his analysis partly on Vitruvius' discussion of painting, the late nineteenth-century German art historian August Mau distinguished four styles of Roman wall painting (fig. **7.52**), which are useful as general guidelines. (See www.myartslab.com.) In the First Style, dating to the late second century BCE, artists used paint and stucco to imitate expensive colored marble paneling. Starting about 100 BCE, Second Style painters sought to open up the flat expanse of the wall by including architectural features and figures. In a room in the Villa of the Mysteries just outside Pompeii, dating from about 60 to 50 BCE, the lower part of the wall (the **dado**) and the upper section above the cornice level are painted in rich mottled colors to resemble exotic stone (fig. **7.53**). Figures interact as if on a narrow ledge set against a deep

August Mau (1840–1909 produced what remains the scheme that underpins all stylistic analysis of Pompeian decor: he divided the wall painting into four 'Styles,' each representing a phase in the chronology of Pompeian painting, from the second century BCE to the final eruption in 79 CE.

7.52 August Mau's Four Styles of Pompeiian wall painting

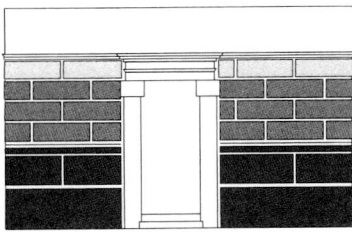

1. 'The First, or Incrustation, style': the wall is painted (and moulded in stucco) to imitate masonry blocks, no figured scenes. Second century BCE.

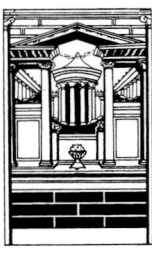

2. 'The Second, or Architectural, style': characteristically featuring illusionistic architectural vistas. c.100—15 BCE.

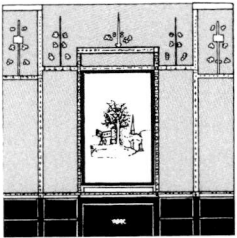

3. 'The Third, or Ornate, style': the vistas here give way to a delicate decorative scheme, concentrating on formal ornament. c.15 BCE.—50 CE.

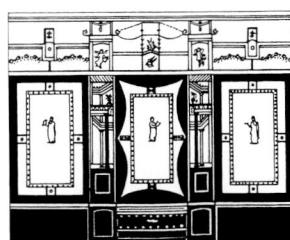

4. 'The Fourth, or Intricate, style': a more extravagant painterly style, parading the whole range of decorative idioms. c.50 CE.

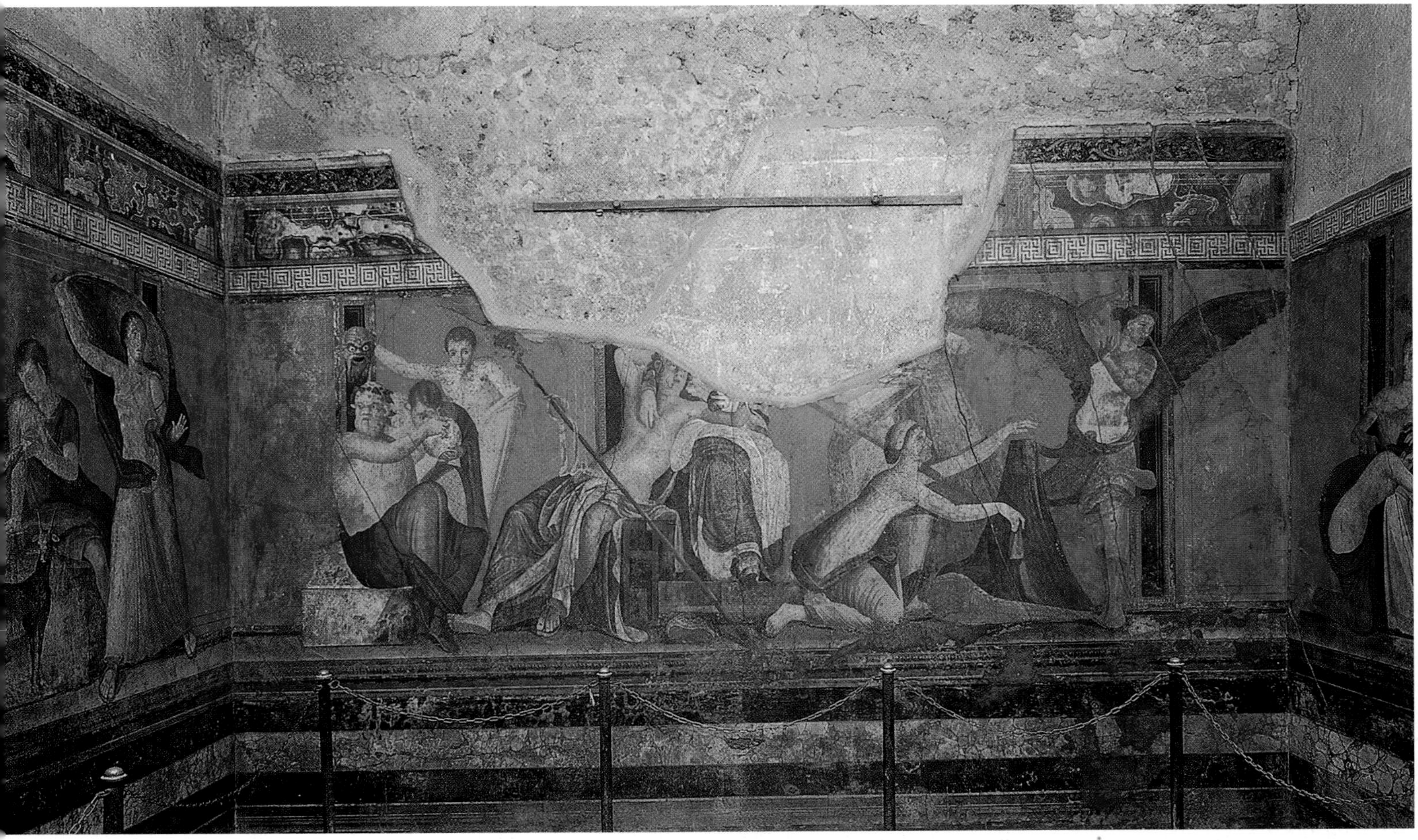

7.53 *Scenes of Dionysiac Mystery Cult,* from the Villa of the Mysteries, Pompeii. Second Style wall painting. ca. 60–50 BCE

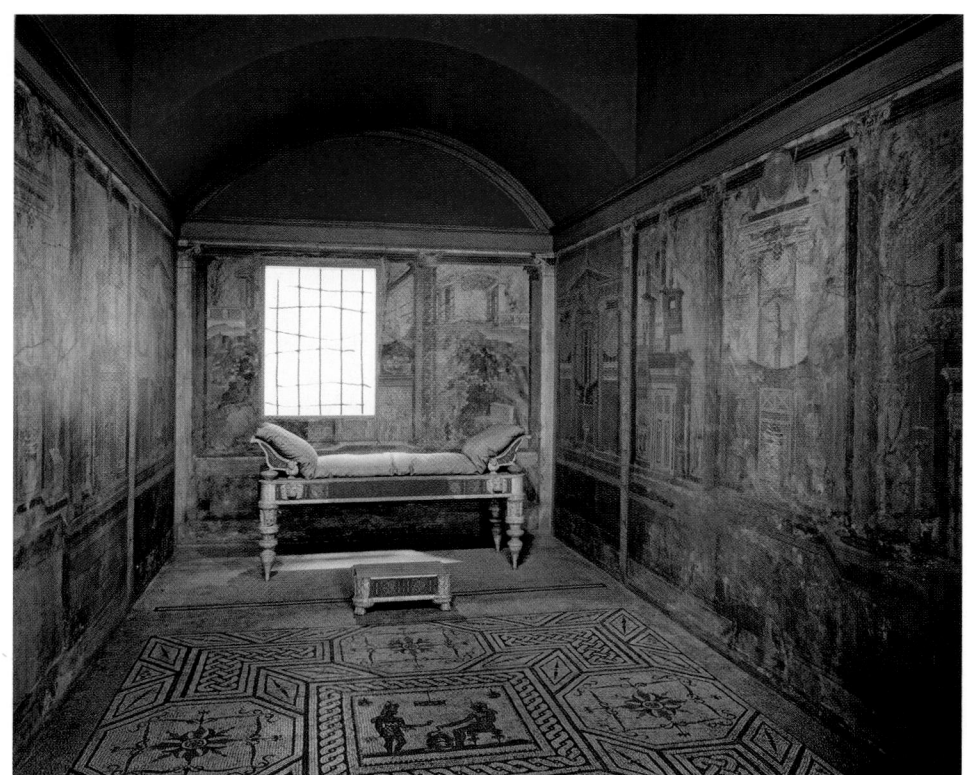

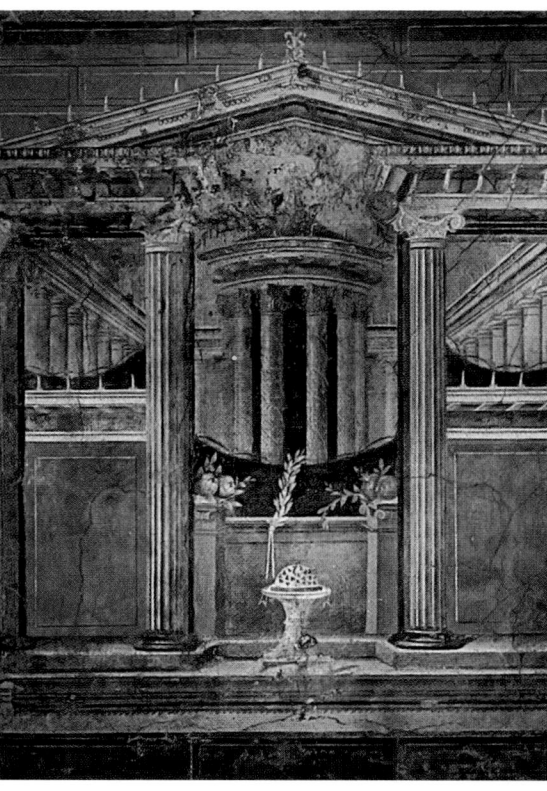

7.54 Second Style wall painting, from the Villa of Publius Fannius Synistor at Boscoreale, near Pompeii. Mid-1st century BCE. Fresco on lime plaster, 8'8½" × 19'7⅛" × 10'11½" (2.65 × 5.84 × 3.34 m). Metropolitan Museum of Art, New York, Rogers Fund, 1903 (03.14.13)

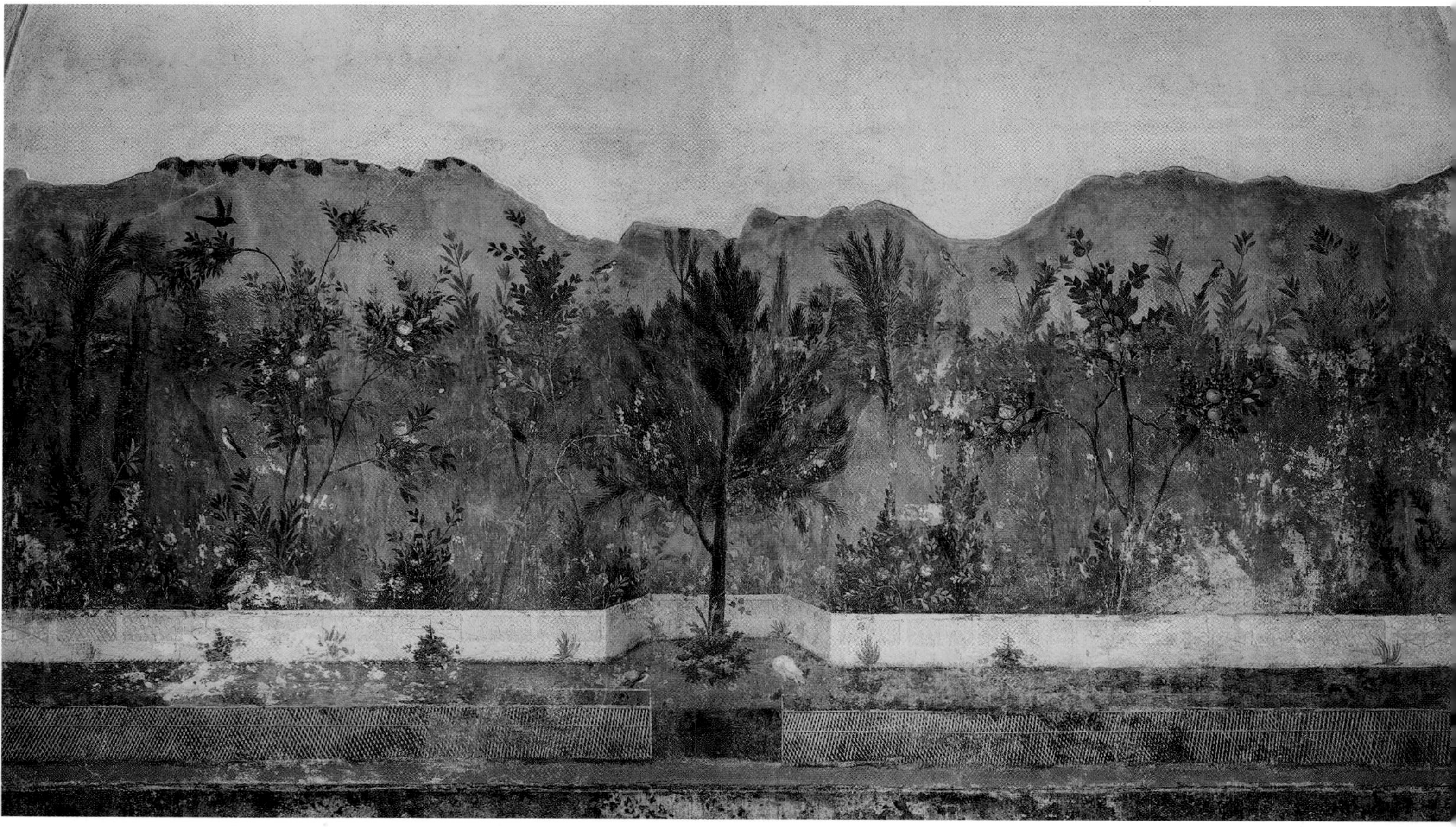

7.55 Second Style wall painting of garden, from the Villa of Livia at Primaporta. ca. 20 BCE. Museo delle Terme, Rome red background, articulated by upright strips of black resembling stylized columns. They are engaged in rites associated with the Dionysiac mysteries, one of the so-called mystery religions originating in Greece. The scene may represent an initiation into womanhood or marriage, in the presence of Dionysos and Ariadne with a train of satyrs. The solidity of the near-life-size figures, the bold modeling of their bodies, and their calm but varied poses lend a quiet power and vivid drama to the room.

In some cases, Second Style artists employed architectural vistas to open the wall into a fantasy realm, suggesting another world beyond the room. This movement may reflect architectural backdrops in contemporaneous theaters. In an example from the Villa of Publius Fannius Synistor at Boscoreale, near Pompeii, now reconstructed in the Metropolitan Museum of Art in New York (fig. **7.54**), there is a foreground of architectural features: A painted parapet wall runs around the lower part of the surface, and resting on it are columns, which support a cornice. Receding away from the foreground, in a range of different perspectives, stoas and tholoi and scenic gazebos mingle with

one another in a maze of architectural fantasy, flooded with light to convey a sense of open space. A viewer struggles to disentangle the structures from one other; their size and spatial relationships are hard to determine. The world of the painting is a world inaccessible to those who view it, hovering out of reach. In the Villa of Livia at Primaporta, the garden beyond the trellis fence and low wall is an idyll of nature, filled with flowers, fruit trees, and birds (fig. **7.55**). Although its lushness beckons, this fantasy garden is only for looking. Here the artist employed atmospheric perspective: Plants and animals become less distinct as they recede into the background.

The Third Style dominated wall decoration from about 20 BCE until at least the middle of the first century CE. In this phase, artists abandoned illusionism in favor of solid planes of intense colors like black and red, which they often articulated with attenuated architectural features and imitation panel paintings. The Fourth Style, which prevailed at the time of Vesuvius' eruption, was the most intricate of the four, uniting aspects of all three preceding styles to create an extravagant effect. The Ixion Room in the House of the Vettii (fig. **7.56**) combines imitation

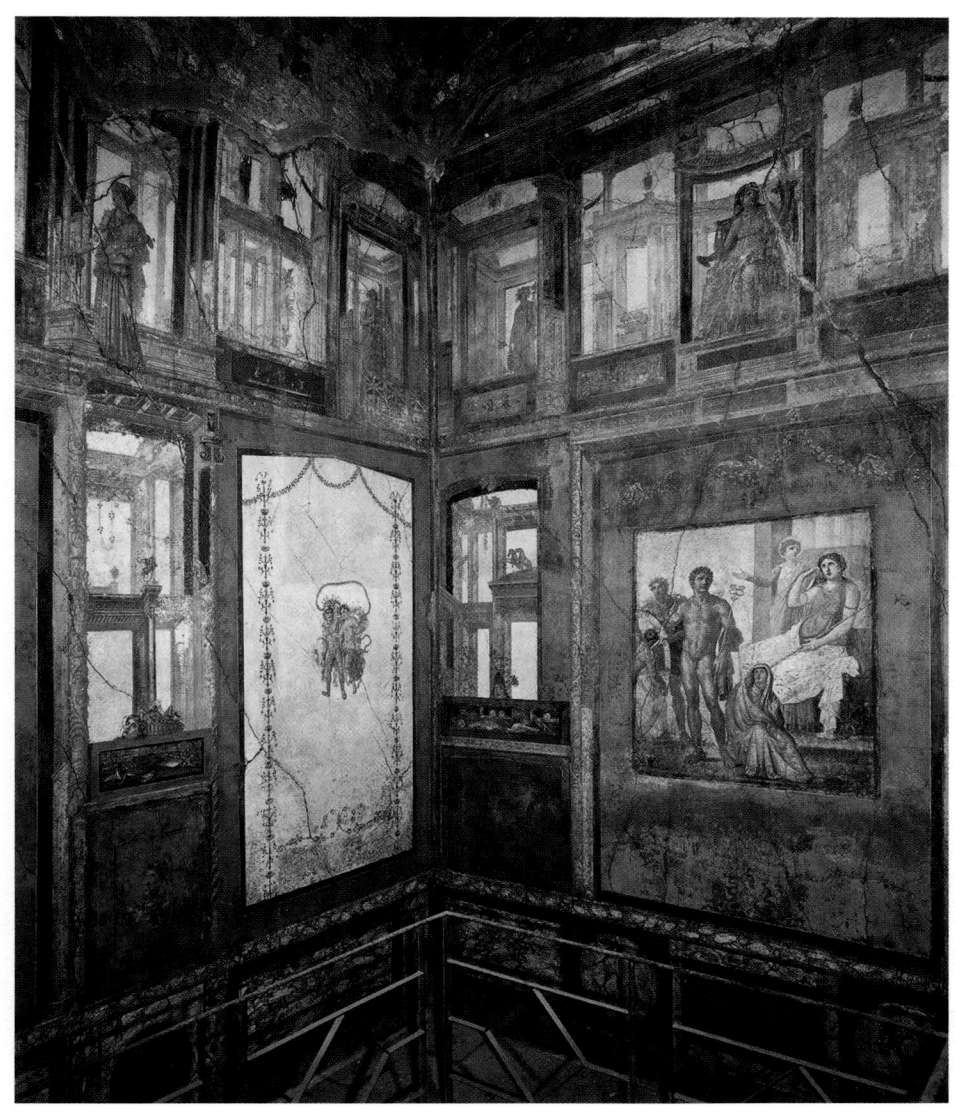

7.56 Fourth Style wall painting, Ixion Room, House of the Vettii, Pompeii. 63–79 CE

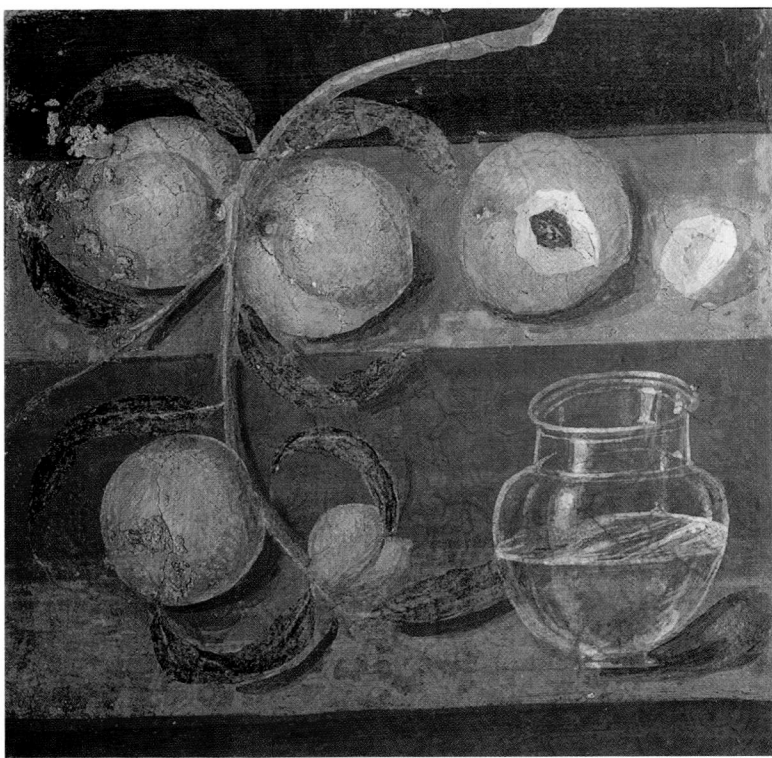

7.57 Still-life painting of peaches and water jar, from Herculaneum. ca. 50 CE. Museo Archeologico Nazionale, Naples

marble paneling, framed mythological scenes resembling panel pictures set into the wall, and fantastic architectural vistas receding into space.

Within these Fourth Style designs, the artist might insert **still life** panels, which usually took the form of **trompe-l'oeil** (intended to trick the eye) niches or cupboards, with objects on shelves. A twenty-first-century viewer finds little unusual about this, yet these are the only visual studies of mundane, inanimate objects until the early modern period. The driving force in these paintings was not a narrative, as in many Roman paintings, but a close analysis of life. The example illustrated here depicts green peaches and a jar half-filled with water (fig. **7.57**). Touches of white paint capture the effect of light playing on the surface of the jar and the water within. Shadows fall in different directions around the peaches, suggesting that the artist was more interested in forging a spatial relationship between the peaches and their surroundings than in indicating a single light source. It is possible, too, that the painting reflects the shadow's movement as the artist worked.

As in the Ixion Room in the House of the Vettii (see fig. 7.56), many Roman paintings depicted Greek themes. The few painters' names on record show that at least some of them were of Greek origin. There are also sufficient cases of paintings (or elements of paintings) closely resembling one another to indicate that artists used copybooks; in some cases, they may have been working from a Greek original, adapting the image to their own purposes. The *Alexander Mosaic* in the House of the Faun is a possible instance of an artist copying a famous Greek painting, albeit into a different medium (see fig. 5.78). Given the scarcity of Greek mural paintings, however, it is rarely possible to demonstrate a clear connection between Greek original and Roman copy. Given the evident innovation in Roman painting, there is no reason to suppose that Roman artists were not capable of creating their own compositions and narratives when they chose. In recent years, scholarship has become less preoccupied with tracing Greek influences, and more focused on ways in which painting ensembles affected experience or dictated movement through a house, and expressed the owner's status. In fact, a genre of ancient literature known as *ekphrasis* is a learned exposition on a real or imagined painting. (See www.myartslab.com.) On the basis of these writings, scholars believe that homeowners sometimes conceived paintings as conversation pieces for their guests, who might discuss them as they dined. A painting program, then, takes on a new level of importance for what it might disclose about the patron's erudition, status, or aspirations.

THE LATE EMPIRE

During Marcus Aurelius' reign, incursions at the Empire's German and Danubian borders were a constant threat. His son Commodus succeeded him in 180 CE, and was assassinated in 192 CE. The imperial administration then hit an all-time low when, in 193 CE, the throne was auctioned off to the highest bidder. After a brief respite under the Severan dynasty, Rome entered a half-century of civil war, when a succession of emperors came to power and quickly fell through violence. Diocletian (r. 284–305 CE) finally restored imperial authority. His approach was to impose rigid order on all aspects of civil as well as military life. Recognizing the emperor's vulnerability, he also chose to divide authority among four rulers, known as the tetrarchs. Two were senior emperors, the Augusti; and two juniors, the Caesars. Terms of power were to be limited, and the Caesars were to succeed the Augusti. The tetrarchy dissolved in the early fourth century CE, and Constantine the Great, the first emperor to embrace Christianity, rose to power, overcoming his chief rival, Maxentius, at the Battle of the Milvian Bridge in Rome in 312 CE. Art forms are distinctly abstract in late antiquity, and scholars sometimes associate the change with the militaristic mood of the time. Sculptural forms are less naturalistic than before, and architects focus on simple but powerful geometric shapes.

Architecture

By the Late Empire, architects in Rome had more or less abandoned the straightforward use of post-and-lintel construction. Their interests appear to have focused instead on exploring the interior spaces that concrete made possible. Column, architrave, and pediment took on decorative roles, superimposed on brick-and-concrete cores.

Painted Stone in Greece and Rome

For many people, the prevailing image of Greek and Roman architecture and sculpture is white marble. There is good reason for this: As ancient works emerge from the ground, white is the dominant color. White columns still gleam majestically against the blues skies of lands once Greek or Roman, and white sculptures line the halls of European and American museums. Moreover, architects and sculptors such as Michelangelo drew their inspiration from these colorless pieces, and their pristine classicizing works have helped to perpetuate the impression.

Yet art historians have long noted traces of paint on Greek and Roman works of all kinds. As early as 1812, when German archaeologists unearthed the pedimental sculptures from the Temple of Aphaia at Aegina (see fig. 5.22), vestiges of paint fueled a lasting debate about color on ancient stone. Initially, attention focused on architecture, but with the discovery of the portrait of Augustus from Primaporta in 1863 (see fig. 7.29), scholars intensified their analysis of sculpture as well. Still, as the debate gained strength between the twentieth-century world wars, researchers discovered that their labors encountered ideological and aesthetic resistance.

In recent decades, researchers have profited from advances in technology to attempt convincing reconstructions of well-known ancient works as they might once have appeared, including two examples shown here: an archer from Aegina and a portrait of the Roman emperor Caligula. They use improved ultraviolet light techniques (first pioneered by P. de la Coste-Messelière to examine the frieze of the Treasury of the Siphnians at Delphi, see fig. 5.21), and analysis by raking light and microscope to find traces of paint that are invisible to the naked eye. Other techniques include X-ray diffractometry and infrared spectography, which identify specific organic and mineral compounds. From these analyses, and from literary evidence such as the writings of Pliny the Elder, Vinzenz Brinkmann and others conclude that ancient artists employed a rich array of pigments that sometimes originated far from their use. Among them were cinnabar for red (from Istria and Andalusia), widely available ocher for yellow, azurite for blue (from Sinai as well as Italy and Spain), green malachite (from Laurion, near Athens), and arsenic for a luminous yellow and orange (from Anatolia). To make black paint, they collected smoke from burning bones or green wood. Artists also added gold and silver leaf to their sculptures. Recent analyses indicate that ancient artists often used strong, vibrant colors, a far cry from the muted tones that archaeologists first envisioned.

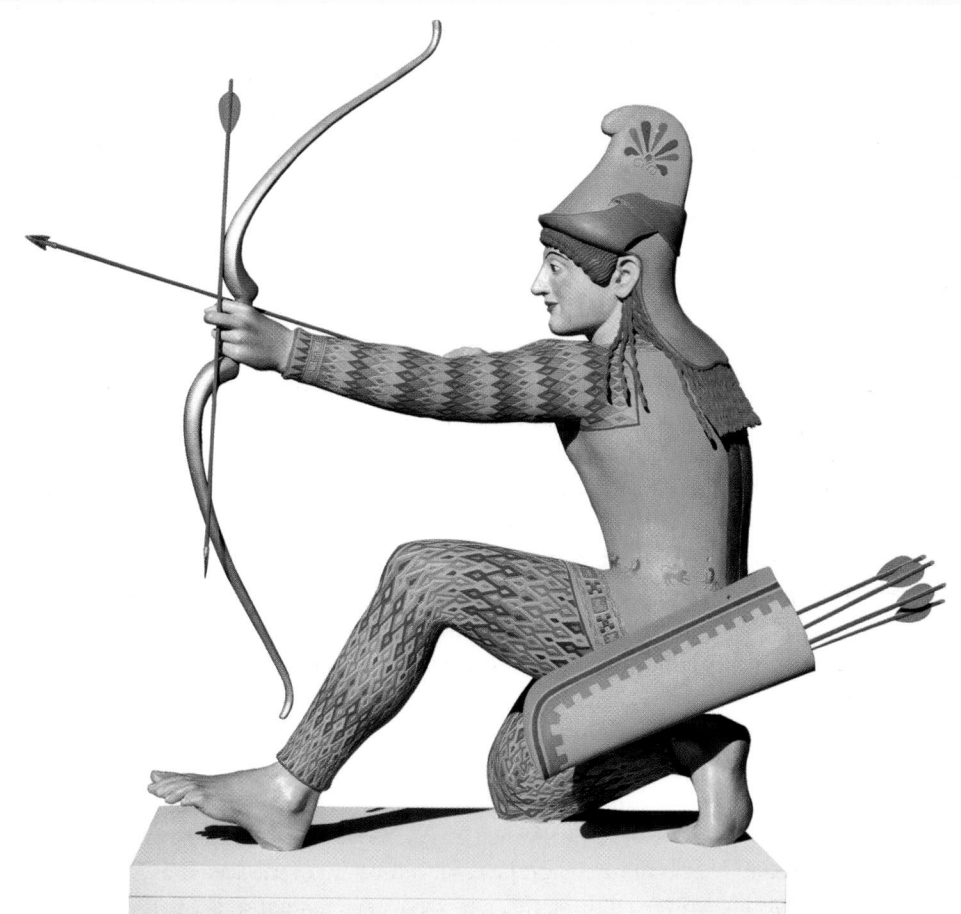

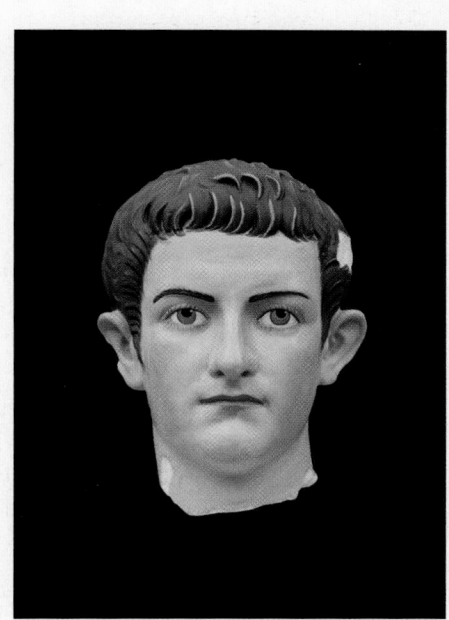

Head of Caligula, color reconstruction

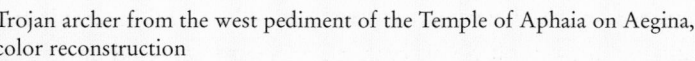

Trojan archer from the west pediment of the Temple of Aphaia on Aegina, color reconstruction

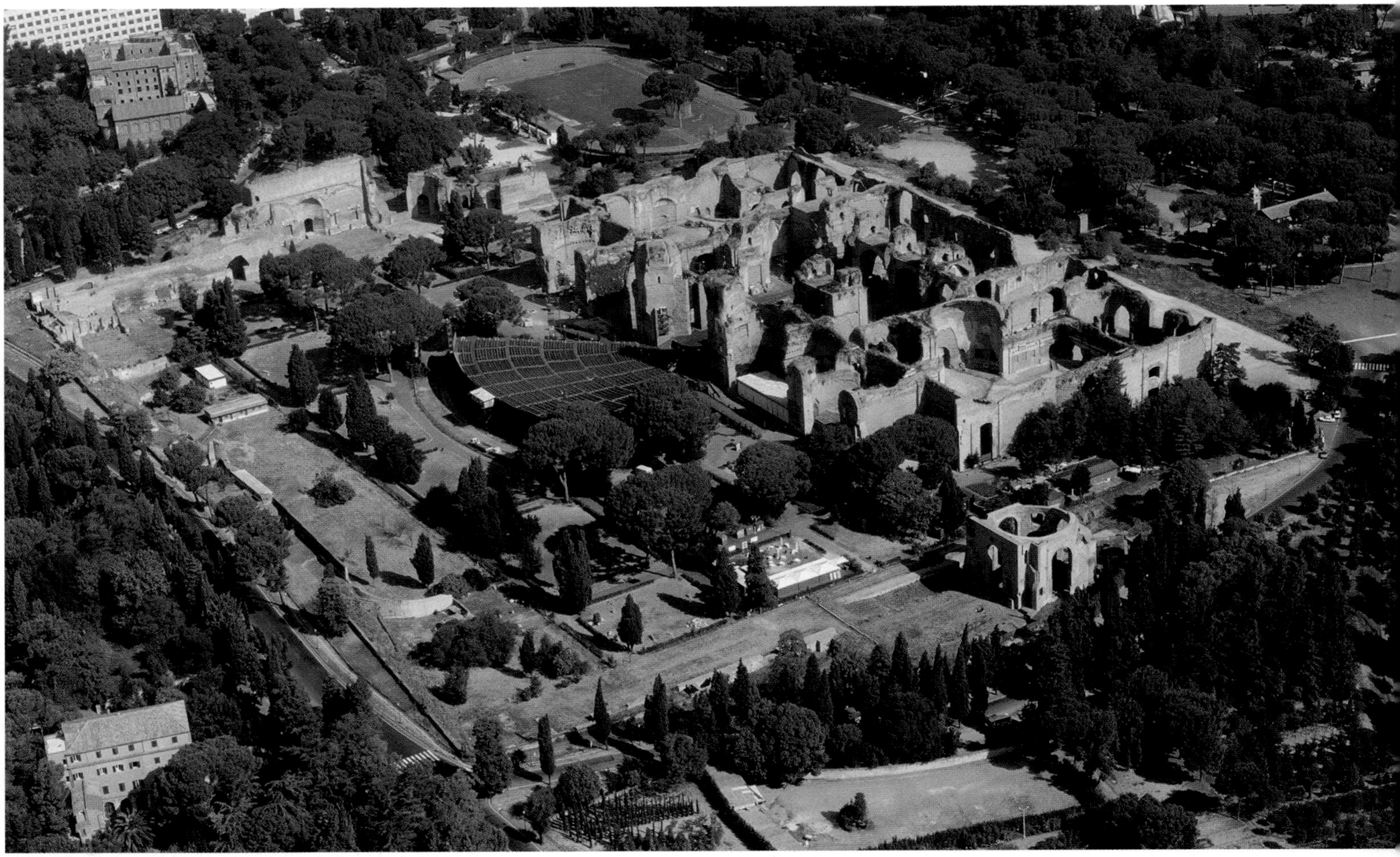

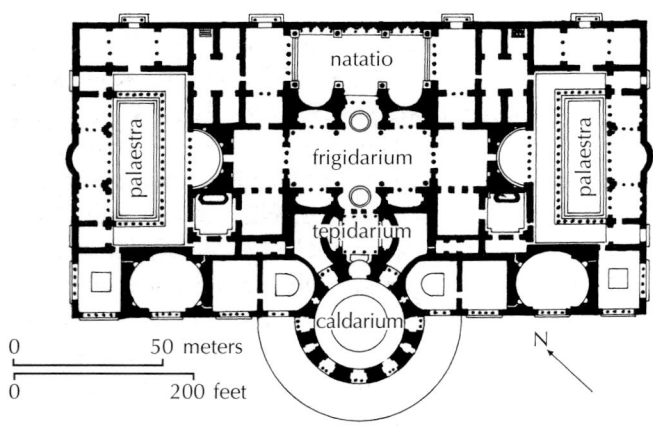

7.58 Baths of Caracalla, Rome. ca. 211–16 CE

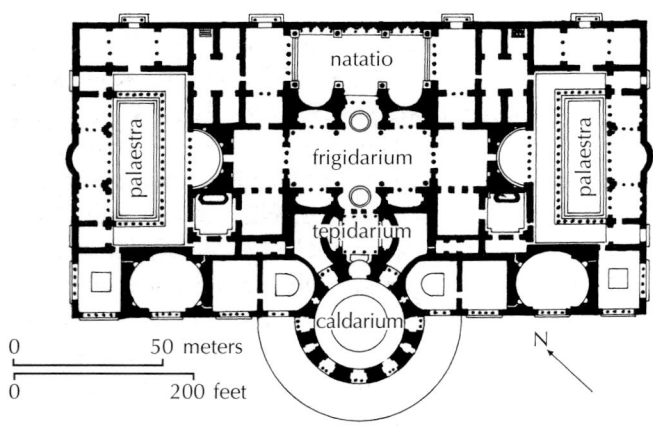

7.59 Plan of Baths of Caracalla

THE BATHS OF CARACALLA Imperial bath buildings demonstrate the new Late Empire architectural interests very clearly. By the beginning of the third century CE, public baths were a long-established tradition in Roman life. Emperors had routinely embellished the city with baths as an act of benefaction. Romans who did not own private baths expected to bathe publicly most days, but the baths served other functions as well. They became a place of social interaction, where Romans conducted business and the wealthy flaunted troops of slaves. The Baths of Caracalla, built between 211 and 216 CE, were the most extensive and lavish of their kind (figs. **7.58** and **7.59**). Set within a rectangular perimeter wall, they included the essential bathing facilities, arranged in a standardized layout: a cold room (*frigidarium*), a circular hot room (*caldarium*), and a warm room (*tepidarium*), as well as a vast swimming pool (*natatio*), changing rooms (*apodyteria*), and exercise areas (*palaestrae*). Lecture halls, libraries, and temples made for a multifaceted experience within its walls. Engineers had long mastered the technology for heating the warm rooms: They raised the floors on brick piers, and directed hot air from a furnace into the open space below. This is known as a *hypocaust* system. The sheer scale of Caracalla's complex must have been astounding: The principal block of buildings measured an immense 656 by 374 feet. Three vast groin vaults roofed the largest room, the frigidarium. Luscious marble panels revetted the walls, and sculptures animated the halls.

THE BASILICA OF MAXENTIUS When Maxentius commissioned a vast basilica for the center of Rome, the architects looked to the massive uninterrupted spaces of bath buildings for

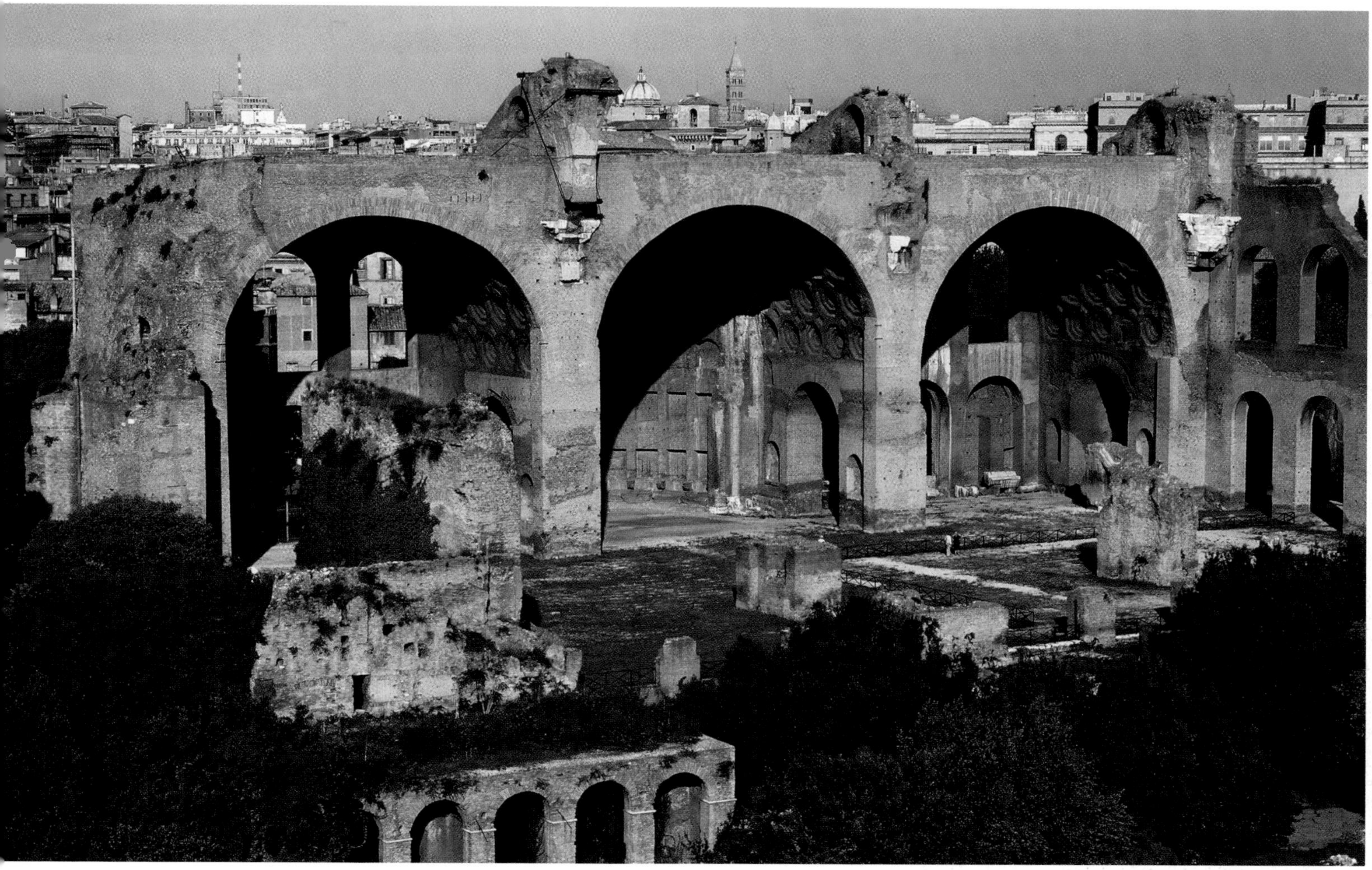

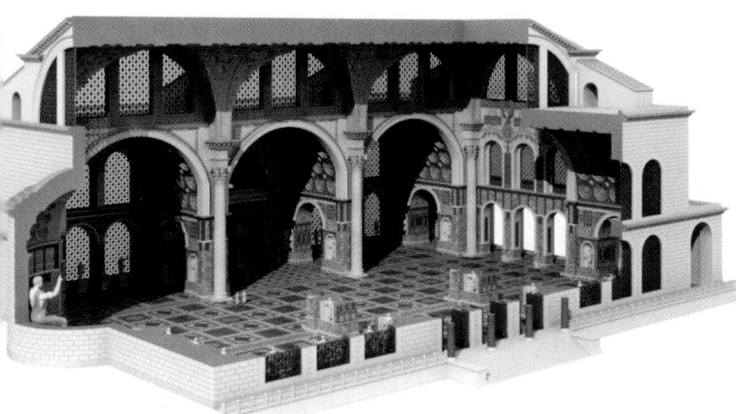

7.60 Basilica of Maxentius, renamed Basilica of Constantine, Rome. ca. 307 CE

7.61 Basilica of Maxentius, renamed Basilica of Constantine. Reconstruction (after Huelsen)

inspiration. Basilicas (from the Greek *basileus*, meaning "king") had a long history in Rome. Since the Republic, they had served as civic halls, and they became a standard feature of Roman towns. One of their chief functions was to provide a dignified setting for the courts of law that dispensed justice in the name of the emperor. Vitruvius prescribed principles for their placement and proportions, but in practice they never conformed to a single type and varied from region to region. The Basilica of Maxentius (figs. **7.60** and **7.61**) was built on an even grander scale than the Baths of Caracalla and was probably the largest roofed interior in Rome. It had three **aisles**, of which only the north one still stands. Transverse barrel vaults covered the lateral aisles, and the wider, taller central aisle or nave was covered with three massive groin vaults. Since a groin vault concentrates its weight and thrust at the four corners (see fig. 7.3), the architect could pierce the nave's upper walls with a large **clerestory** (window in the topmost wall zone). As a result, the interior of the basilica must have had a light and airy quality. The building had two entrances, each faced by an **apse**: through a transverse vestibule at the east end, and through a stepped doorway on the south, leading from the Roman Forum. On overcoming Maxentius, Constantine expropriated the basilica. He gave it his own name, and placed his colossal portrait in the western apse (see fig. 7.68). Expropriations of this kind were not uncommon in Rome, and show how critical it was to have a physical presence in the city.

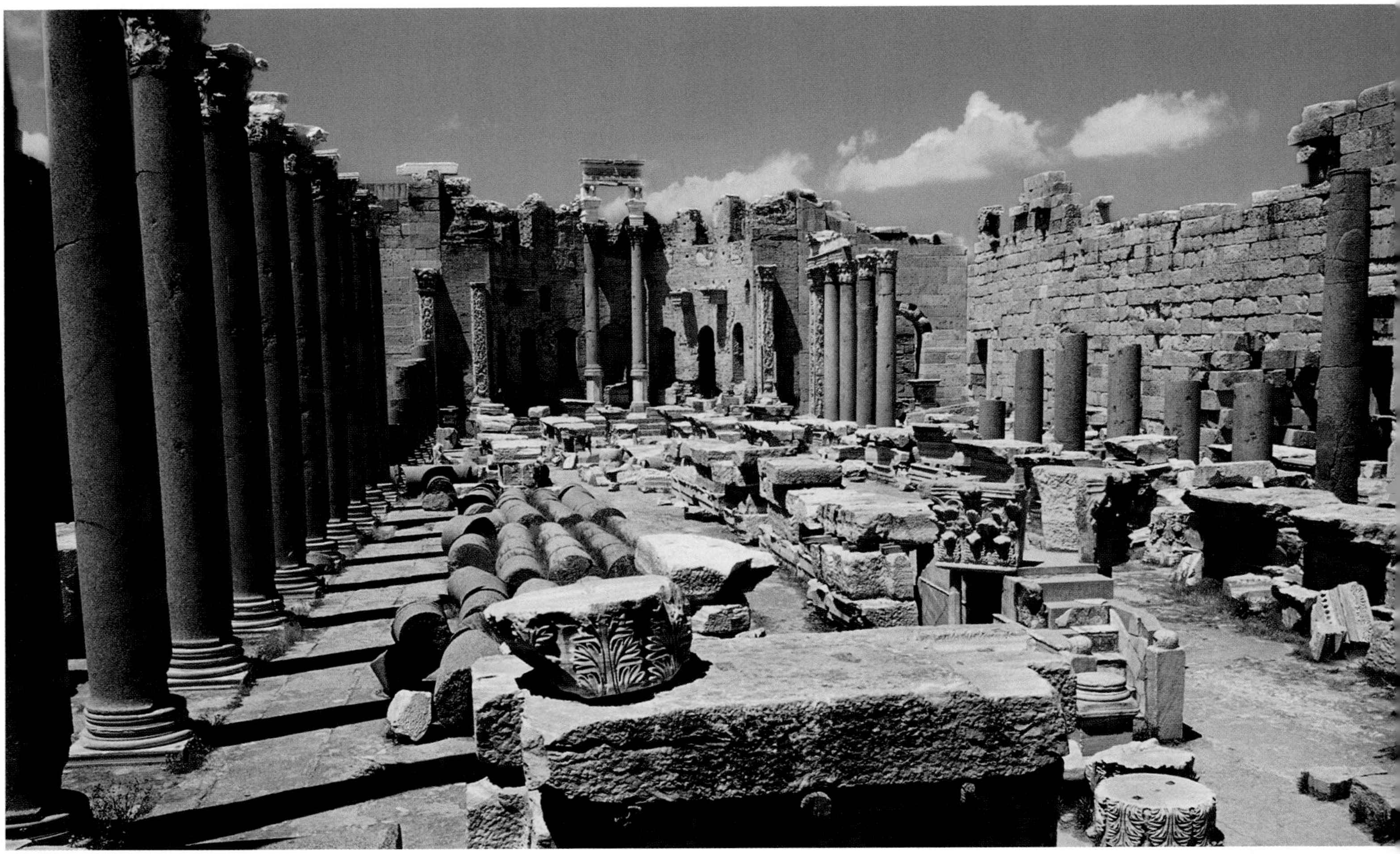

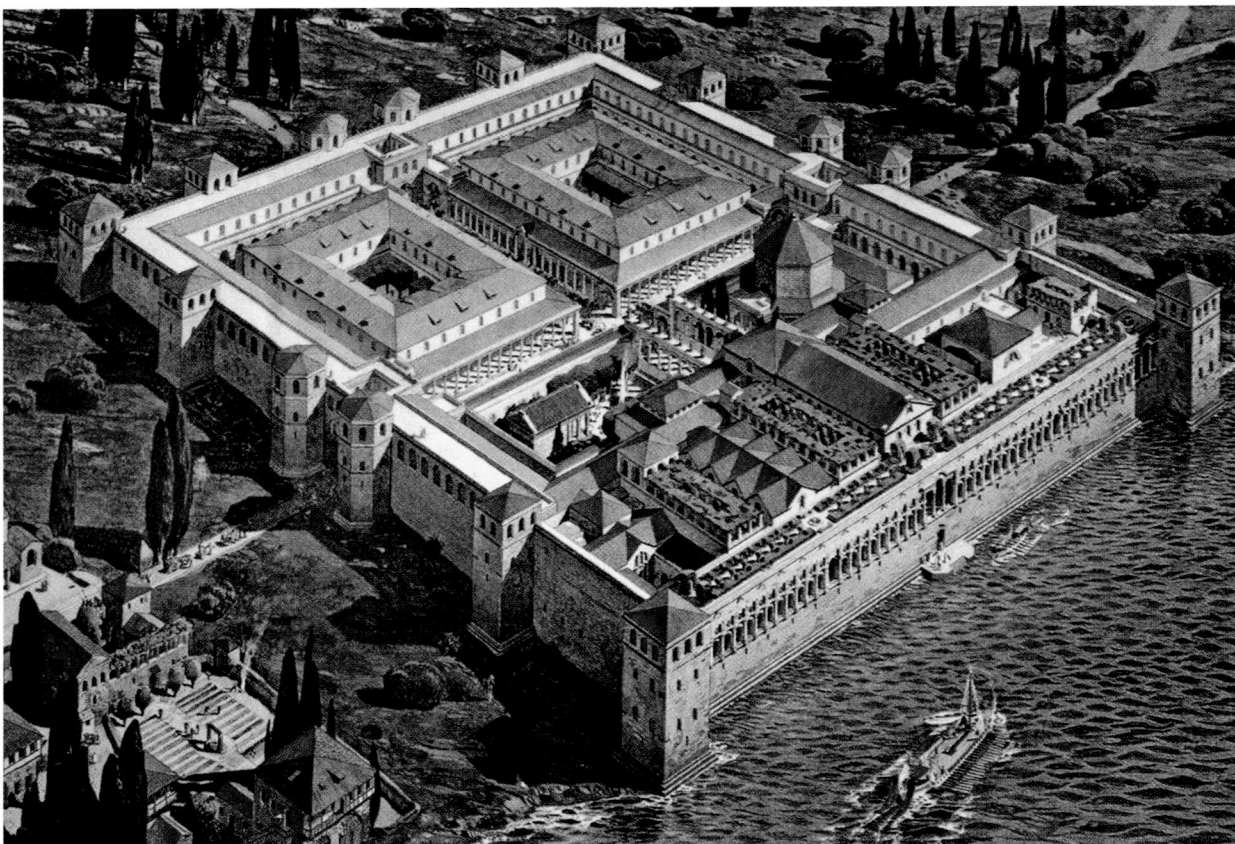

7.62 Basilica, Lepcis Magna, Libya. Early 3rd century CE

7.63 Palace of Diocletian, Spalato (Split), Croatia. Restored view. ca. 300 CE

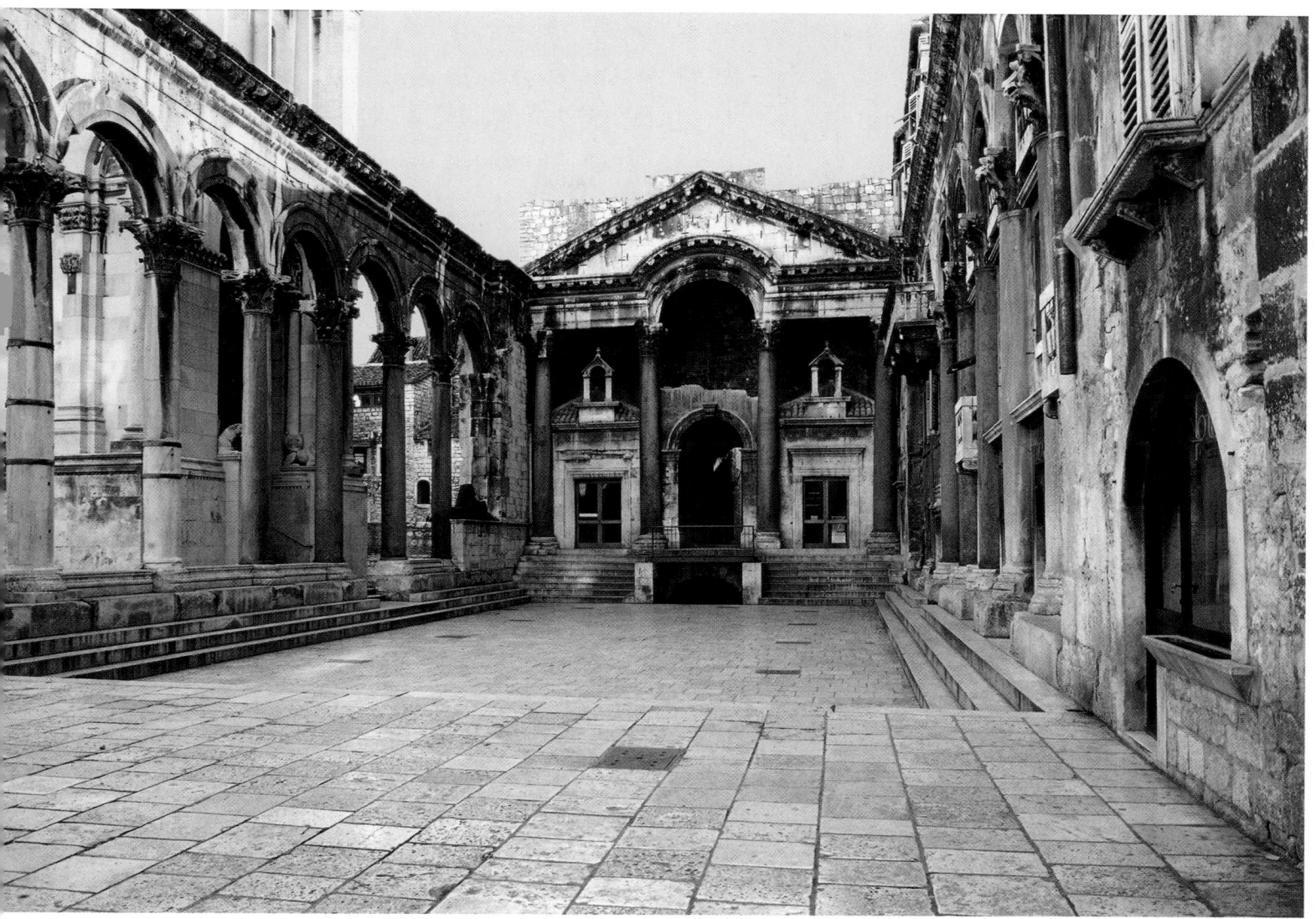

7.64 Peristyle, Palace of Diocletian

Architecture in the Provinces

By the early second century CE, Roman emperors were no longer exclusively from Italy; Trajan came from Spain and Septimius Severus was from North Africa. Both emperors embellished their native cities with new construction. Severus' home, Lepcis Magna, in present-day Libya, remains remarkably well preserved. The emperor was responsible for a grand new forum there, and a magnificent basilica with a long central aisle closed by an apse at either end (fig. 7.62). Colonnades in two stories provide access to the side aisles, which were lower than the nave to permit clerestory windows in the upper part of the wall. The wooden ceiling has long since perished.

DIOCLETIAN'S PALACE, SPLIT Developments in Roman architecture after Diocletian came to power appear to go hand-in-hand with the profound changes he made to society. This is clear in his palace at Split (ancient Spalato, in Croatia) overlooking the Adriatic Sea, which he commissioned for his abdication in 305 CE (figs. 7.63 and 7.64). Although intended as a residence, it is essentially a military fort, with defensive walls, gates, and towers. As in a military camp, two intersecting colonnaded streets stretched between the gates and divided the rectangular space within the walls, measuring about 650 by 500 feet, into four blocks. The street from the main gate led to a sunken peristyle court. Columns on two sides support **arcuated** (arched) lintels, used only sporadically since the early Empire and popular in late antiquity. They direct a visitor's gaze to the far end of the court, where an arcuated lintel set between the two central columns within a pediment creates a frame. It was here that the former emperor made public appearances. Behind this grand entrance was a vestibule, opening onto the audience hall. To the left of the peristyle court stood a large octagonal mausoleum, now used as a cathedral. Loosely based upon the Pantheon (see figs. 7.23–7.27), this type of imperial mausoleum would be one of the prototypes for Christian **martyria**, burial places of martyred saints. To the right of the court Diocletian dedicated a small temple to Jupiter, his patron god. The topographical relationship between mausoleum and temple implied an equivalency between emperor and god.

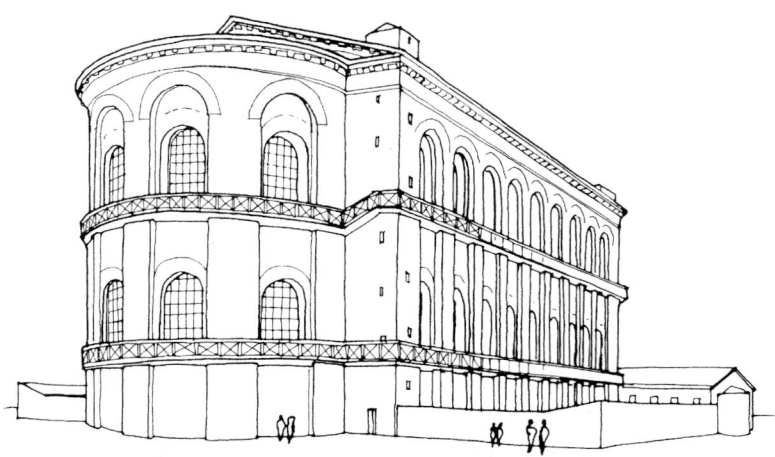

7.65 Basilica of Constantius Chlorus, Trier, Germany. Early 4th century CE

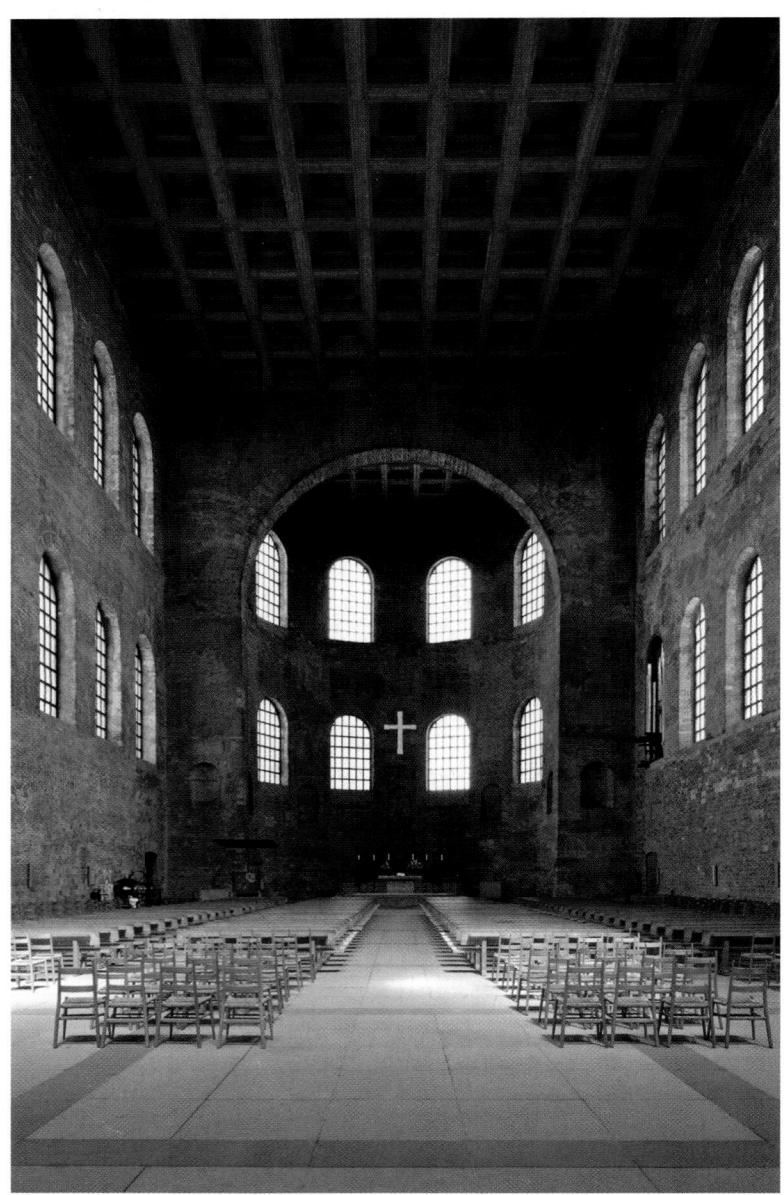

7.66 Interior of Basilica of Constantius Chlorus

THE BASILICA OF CONSTANTIUS, TRIER When Diocletian divided authority between the tetrarchs, each of them established a capital in a different region of the empire and embellished it with appropriate grandeur. Constantius Chlorus, father of Constantine the Great, made his seat at Trier, in present-day Germany. There he constructed a basilica, which now functions as a church (figs. **7.65** and **7.66**). In its design, Classical forms have dissolved entirely, leaving vast abstract expanses of solid and void. Elongated arches break the great mass of its walls, and serve as visual buttresses to frame the windows, beneath which were balconies. As vast as the interior was, the architect aspired to achieving an illusion of even greater dimensions. The windows in the apse are significantly smaller than those in the side walls, and the apse ceiling is lower than the ceiling over the main hall. Both devices make it appear that the apse recedes farther into the distance than it does. Not only did this make the building appear grander, but the apse was where the emperor—or his image—would hold sway, and the altered dimensions would have made him appear significantly larger than life. The vocabulary of Roman building had changed, in other words, but it remained an architecture of power.

Portrait Sculpture

During the tetrarchy, portraiture took on a radically abstract quality. Two porphyry sculptural groups now immured in the Basilica of San Marco in Venice were probably originally mounted on columns (fig. **7.67**). Each group shows two tetrarchs in elaborate military dress, with bird-headed sword hilts and flat Pannonian caps that probably represent the powerful Illyrian officer class from which they came. The figures are all but indistinguishable from one another (except that in each group, one is bearded, the other close-shaven). Their proportions are squat and nonnaturalistic, their facial features abstract rather than individualized. The portraits suggest that authority resides in the office of emperor, not in the individual who holds the office. The sameness of the portraits underlines the tetrarchs' equality, while their close embrace stresses unanimity and solidarity. The choice of material speaks volumes too: Porphyry, a hard Egyptian stone of deep purple color, had long been reserved for imperial use.

The severe abstraction abates only a little under Constantine, whose portraitist combined it with an Augustan classicism to create the colossal head of figure **7.68**. The head is one fragment of a vast seated portrait that once occupied an apse in the basilica Constantine expropriated from Maxentius (see figs. 7.60 and 7.61). The head alone is 8 feet tall, and its dominant feature is the disproportionately large and deeply carved eyes. Combined with the stiff frontality of the face, they give the image an iconic quality. Some scholars associate changes like these with the spirituality of the later Empire, exemplified by Constantine's adherence to Christianity. Perhaps the eyes gaze at something beyond this world; perhaps they are a window to the soul. At the same time, a soft modeling to the cheeks and mouth renders the portrait more naturalistic than its tetrarchic predecessors. Moreover, the

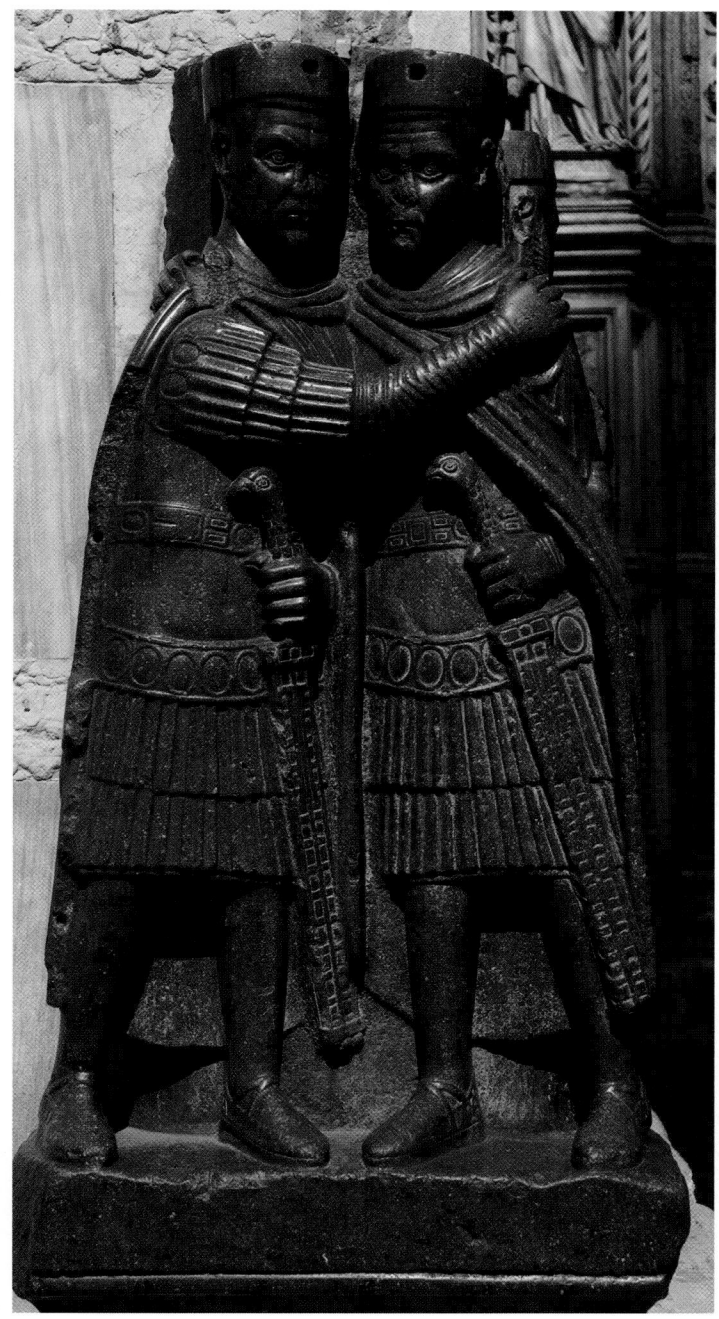

7.67 Portrait group of the tetrarchs. ca. 305 CE. Porphyry, height 51" (129.5 cm). Basilica of San Marco, Venice

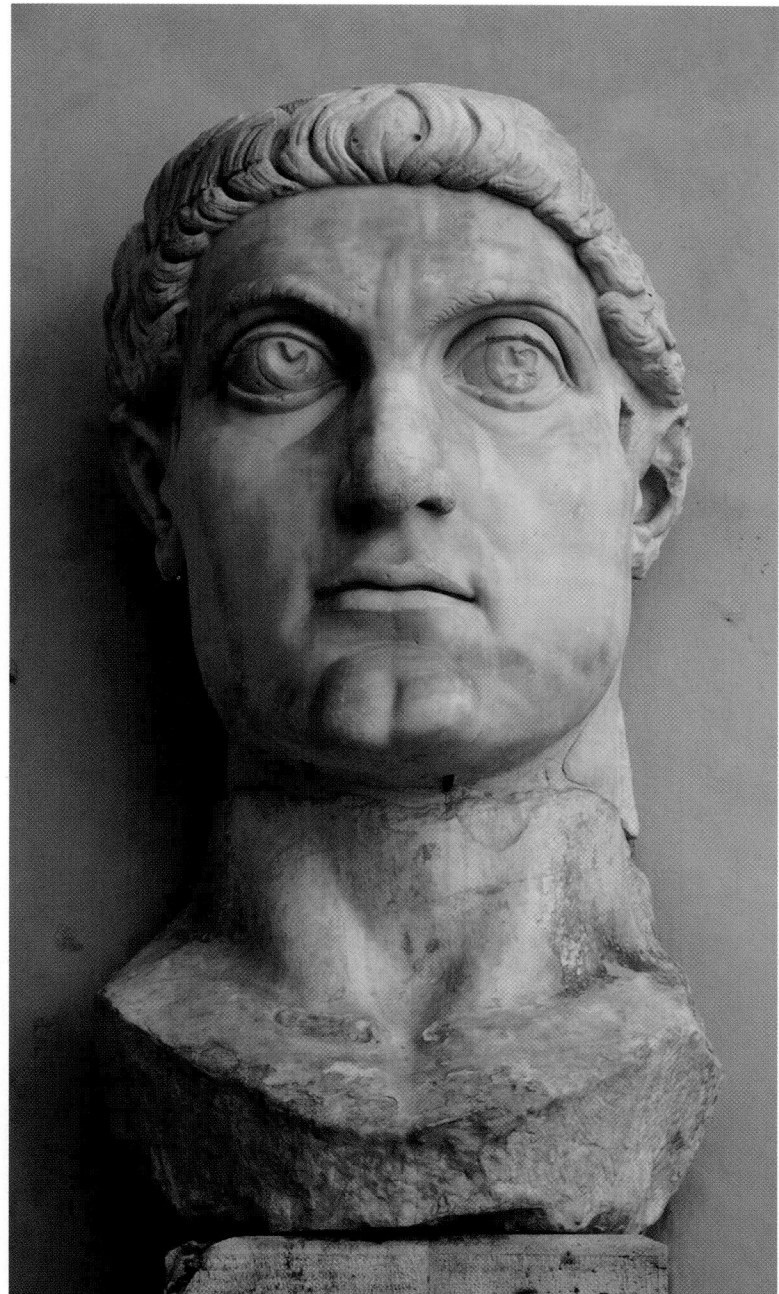

7.68 *Portrait of Constantine the Great.* Early 4th century CE. Marble, height 8' (2.4 m). Museo del Palazzo dei Conservatori, Rome

full cap of hair, and the absence of a beard, appear to be direct references to Trajan and Augustus, great emperors of the past whose achievements still gave the office its authority.

Relief Sculpture

The second century CE witnessed a shift in Roman funerary customs. Inhumation gradually took the place of cremation for all but the imperial family. This led to a demand for marble sarcophagi in place of cinerary urns, and sculptors decorated them with a profusion of designs, which they passed from shop to shop,

probably in pattern books of some kind. Preferences changed over time. For example, under Marcus Aurelius, patrons favored battle sarcophagi. In the third century CE, biographical and historical scenes preserved aspects of the deceased's life. Most popular were scenes taken from Greek mythology. Their purpose may have been to glorify the deceased through analogy to the legendary heroes of the past; they may equally have expressed the owner's erudition. Figure **7.69** illustrates a moment from the myth of Meleager. In Homer's account, Meleager saved Calydon from a ferocious boar, which Artemis had sent to ravage his father's land; he then died in a battle over its pelt. For the Romans, Meleager

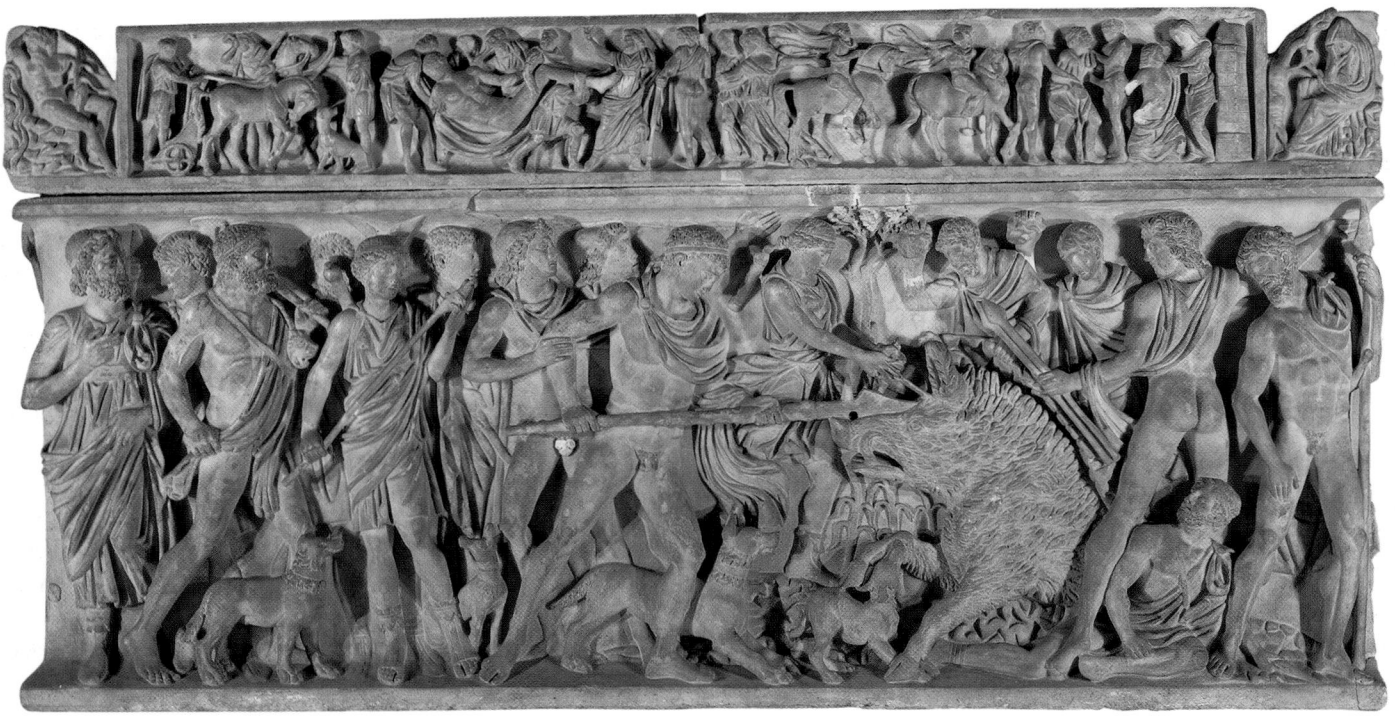

7.69 *Meleager Sarcophagus*. ca. 180 CE. Marble. Galleria Doria Pamphilj, Rome

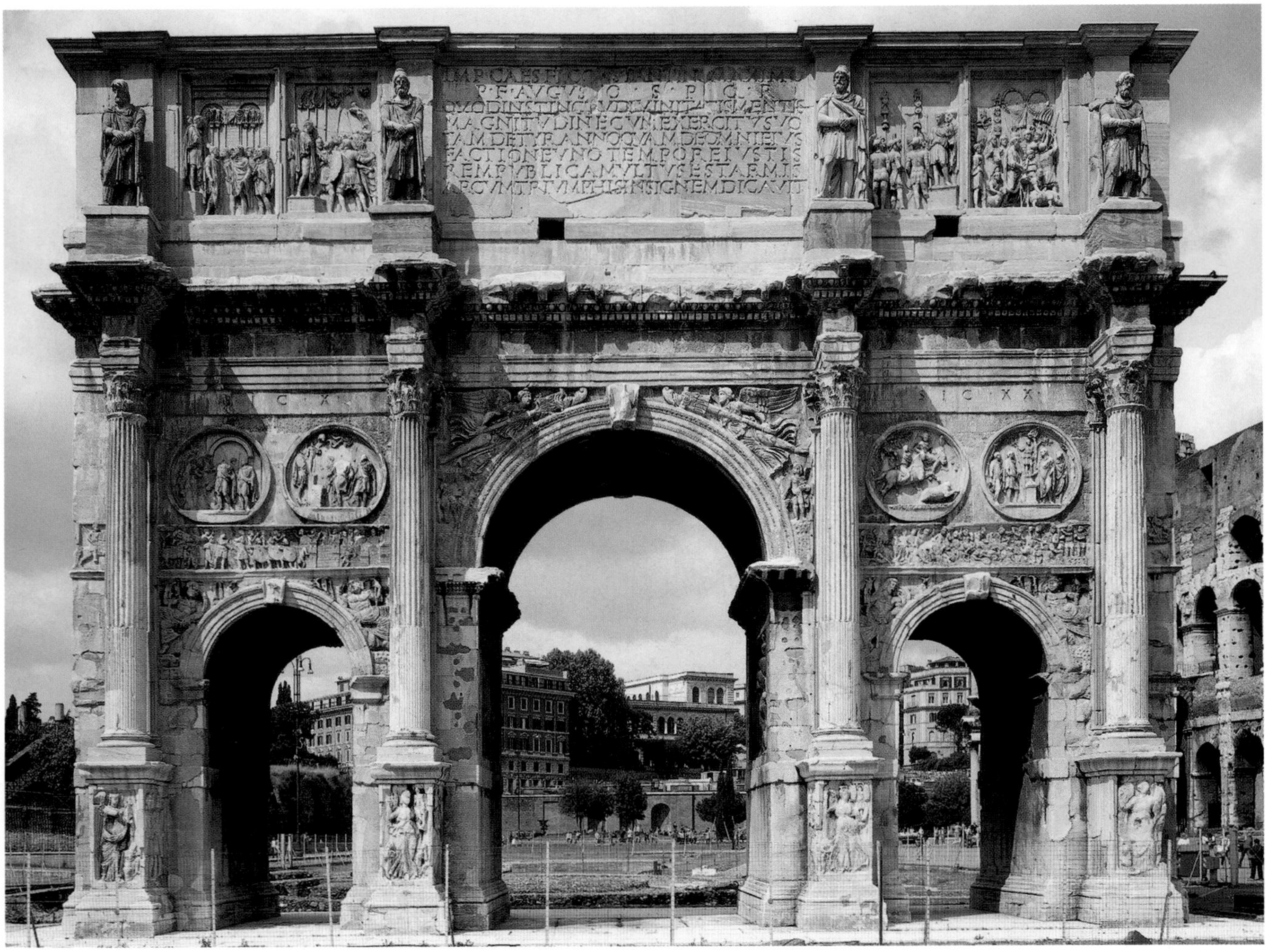

7.70 Arch of Constantine, Rome. 312–15 CE

was an example of noble *virtus*, or manly prowess. For his heroism and death in the service of his city, he earned immortality. The relief's style owes much to Greek sculpture, but crowding the entire surface with figures (known as *horror vacui*) is an entirely Roman practice.

THE ARCH OF CONSTANTINE In 315 CE, the Senate and People of Rome dedicated a triple-bayed arch to Constantine near the Colosseum to celebrate his ten-year anniversary and his conquest of Maxentius (fig. **7.70**). It is one of the largest imperial arches, but what makes it unusual is that so little of the sculptural relief on its surface was specifically designed for this monument (fig. **7.71**). The free-standing Dacian captives on the attic (upper portion) probably originated in Trajan's Forum, as did the Great Trajanic Frieze on the ends of the attic and inside the central bay. Eight hunting and sacrifice tondi above the lateral bays once belonged to a Hadrianic monument, and eight Aurelian panels on the attic may have decorated an arch to Marcus Aurelius. When the arch was constructed, sculptors recarved the heads of earlier emperors to resemble Constantine and his coemperor, Licinius. A modern restoration replaced some of them with heads of Trajan.

Scholars describe sculptural and architectural borrowings of this kind by the modern term **spolia**, from the Latin *spolium*, meaning "hide stripped from an animal," a term primarily used for spoils taken in war. No ancient testimony acknowledges or explains the practice, and the spolia raise all manner of questions—such as how Romans perceived the stripping of one monument in favor of another, and what became of the original monument if it was still standing. In a renowned assault on late antique sculpture in the 1950s, art historian Bernard Berenson condemned the use of spolia as evidence of a pervasive artistic decline in the period, which he attributed to a mass exodus of artists from a city on the brink of destruction. Other scholars, assuming that Romans recognized style differences, see the spolia as part of a legitimation ideology, expressing qualities of "emperorness." By leaning on "good" rulers of the past, Constantine may have hoped to harness the reputations that they had earned during their lifetimes, as well as the nostalgic idealization that had

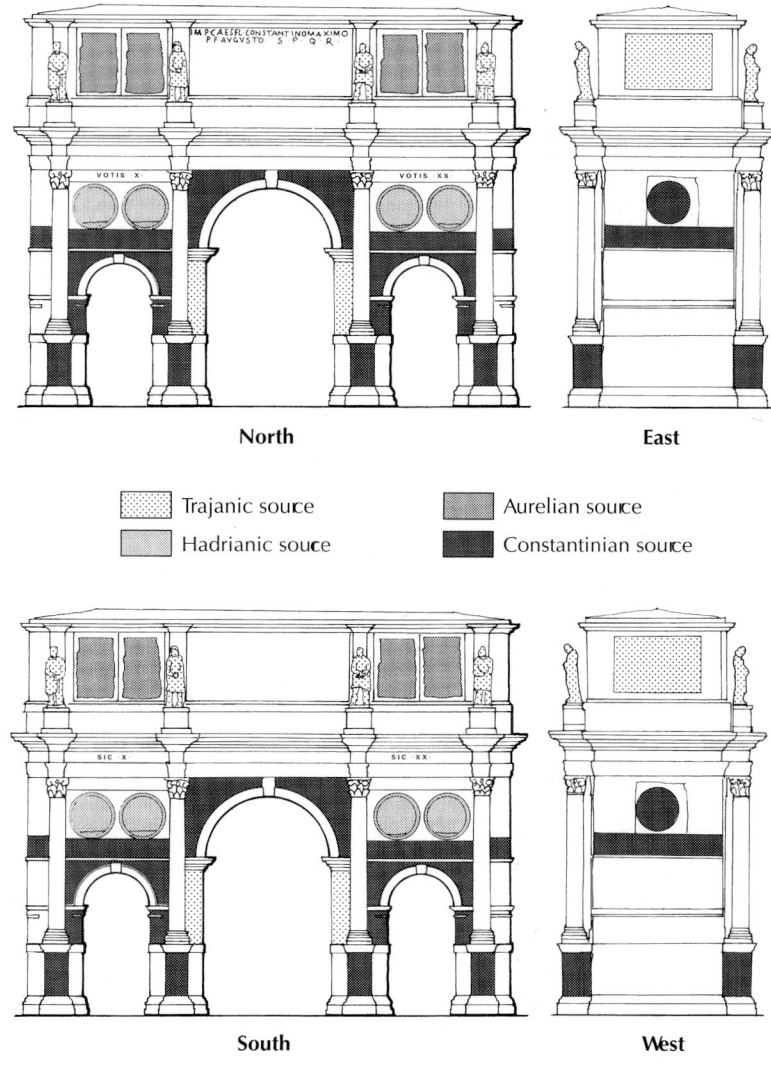

North   **East**

Trajanic source   Aurelian source
Hadrianic source   Constantinian source

South   **West**

7.71   Schematic drawing of Arch of Constantine showing reused sculpture

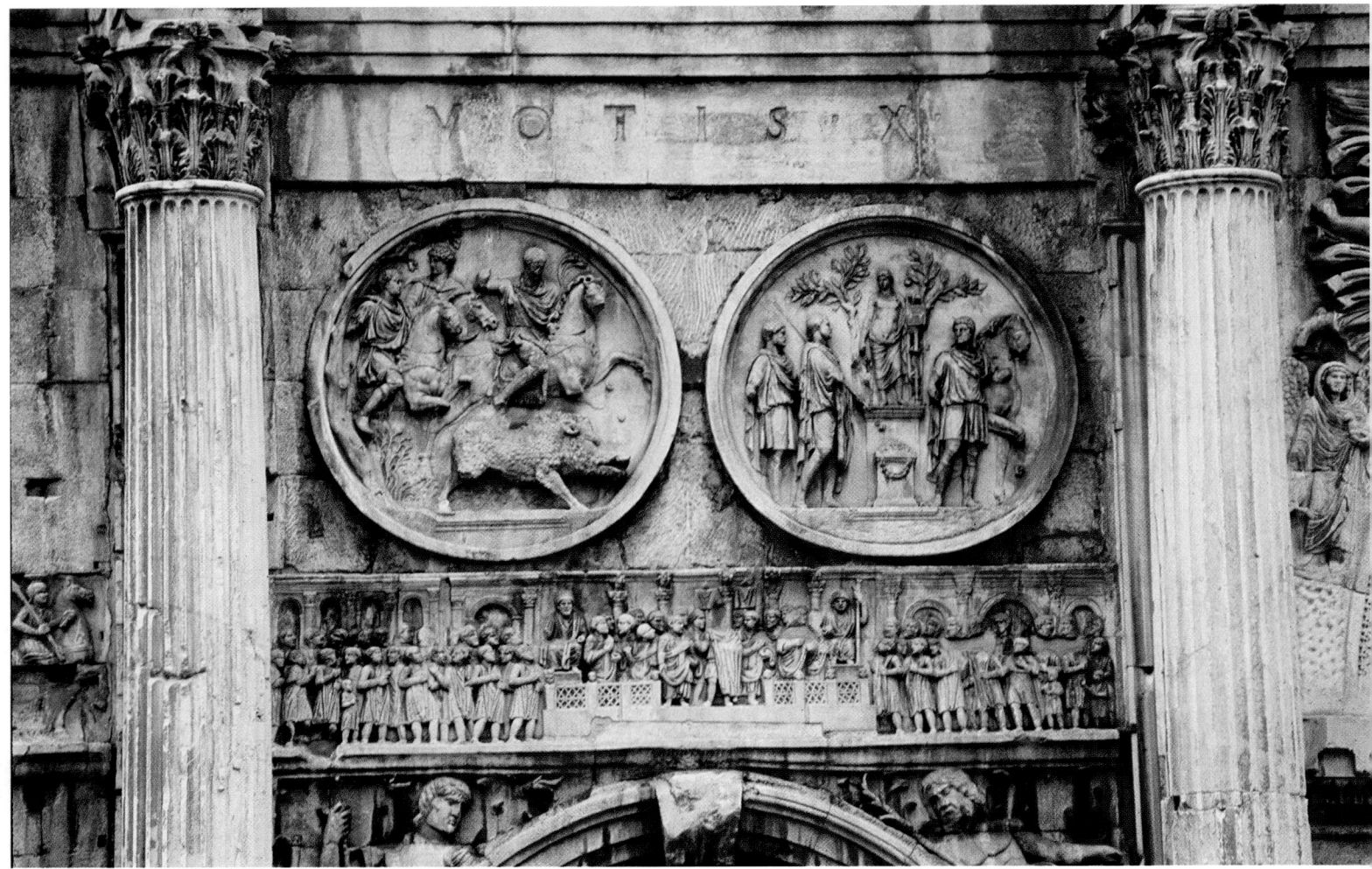

7.72 Constantinian relief from Arch of Constantine

accrued to those reputations through the intervening years. Constantine had reason to legitimize his authority: Maxentius had been a formidable opponent, with his efforts to reposition Rome at the Empire's center through a policy of revivalism. Moreover, as the first openly Christian emperor, Constantine risked alienating a pagan Senate. If this interpretation is correct, it is not dissimilar from readings of the Republican statue base, partly made up of Greek reliefs, as seen in figure 7.10.

To complement the borrowed pieces, Constantinian artists carved bases for the columns that flank the bays, a continuous relief to encircle the arch above the lateral bays, and roundels for the sides of the arch. One scene depicts Constantine addressing the Senate and people of Rome from the speaker's platform, or **rostrum**, in the Forum, after entering Rome in 312 CE (fig. **7.72**). Figures crowd the scene. Their heads are disproportionately large, their bodies stocky, and their poses unnaturally rigid. Lines carved on the flat surface render anatomical details in place of modeling. The artist eschewed devices used on the Arch of Titus panels to give an illusion of depth; a second row of heads arranged above the first indicates recession (see figs. 7.37 and 7.38). Berenson judged the Constantinian reliefs just as harshly as the act of spoliation. Yet their abstract quality makes them unusually

legible from a distance, which is how viewers would have seen them. A careful order governs the composition, with the frontal emperor occupying the center; other figures turn and focus attention on him. Buildings in the background are sufficiently distinct to make the setting recognizable even today as the Roman Forum. The artists privileged the reliefs' message-bearing potential over illusionism or naturalism.

During the course of about a millennium, Rome grew from a small city to the capital of a massive, culturally diverse empire. Those years witnessed huge developments in architecture, due as much to changes in technology as to political motivations. Post-and-lintel construction combined with free forms made possible by concrete, and then dissolved in favor of new abstract concepts of space. In the provinces, architecture brought some improvements in standards of living, but also helped to secure Roman control, exerting a constant Roman presence far from the center of administration. Sculpture and painting abounded within public and private buildings. Often sculpture carried a strong political message, its style chosen to best reinforce its content. As with architecture, an abstract style came to dominate sculpture in late antiquity, due perhaps to a change in concepts of rulership and an increased spirituality.

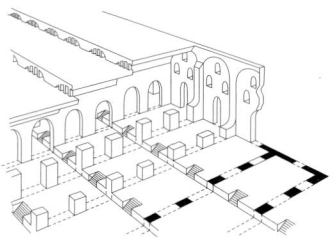

200–150 BCE Navalia in Rome, earliest known building constructed entirely of concrete

Roman Art

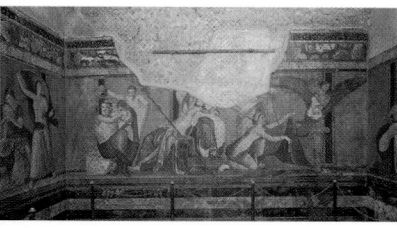

ca. 60–50 BCE Paintings from the Villa of the Mysteries, outside Pompeii

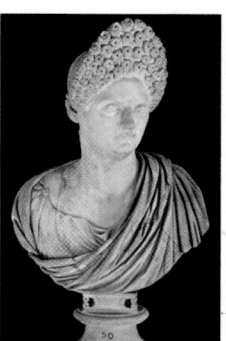

late 1st century CE Portrait of Domitia Longina

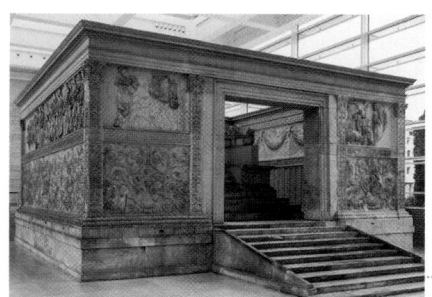

13–9 BCE Dedication of the *Ara Pacis Augustae*, the Altar of Augustan Peace

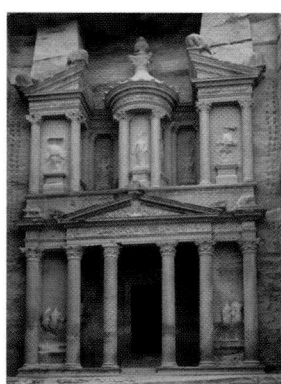

early 100s CE El Khasneh in Petra, Jordan

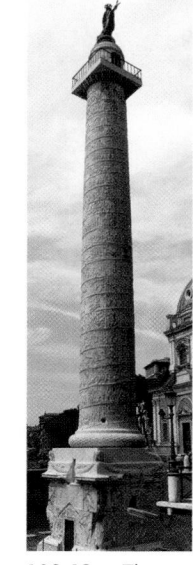

106–13 CE The Column of Trajan is erected in Rome

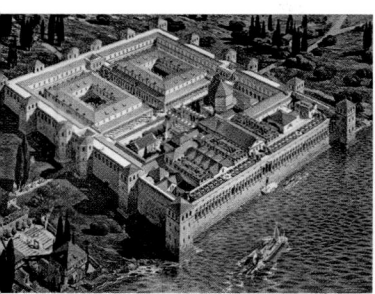

300 CE Diocletian builds his palace palato, Croatia

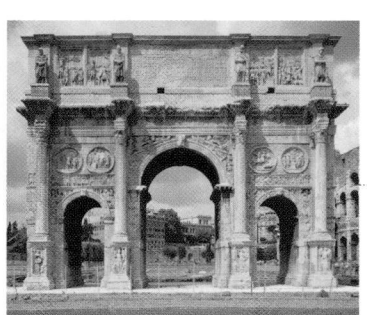

315 CE Dedication of the Arch of Constantine in Rome

1000 BCE

◄ ca. 1000 BCE Earliest inhabitants of Rome

500 BCE

◄ ca. 509 BCE Elite Romans turn against the monarchy, expelling the last king

····· ca. 447 BCE Perikles orders the construction of the Parthenon

400 BCE

····· 340–330 BCE *The Abduction of Persephone* tomb painting at Vergina

····· ca. 279 BCE Ptolemy I commissions the Pharos at Alexandria

300 BCE

◄ by 275 BCE Rome controls all of Italy

200 BCE

100 BCE

◄ 106 BCE Birth of the Roman orator and statesman Cicero

◄ 100s BCE Rome controls Greece and Asia Minor

◄ 46–44 BCE Julius Caesar becomes perpetual dictator of Rome and is assassinated

◄ 27 BCE The Roman Senate names Octavian Augustus Caesar

0

◄ 19 BCE The poet Vergil dies, leaving *The Aeneid* unfinished

◄ 23/24–79 CE Pliny the Elder; wrote *Natural History*

◄ 79 CE Vesuvius erupts

100 CE

····· 100s CE The earliest painted portraits from the Fayum, Lower Egypt

200 CE

····· 242–72 CE Shapur I's Sassanian palace at Ctesiphon

◄ ca. 284 CE Diocletian establishes the tetrarchy

300 CE

400 CE

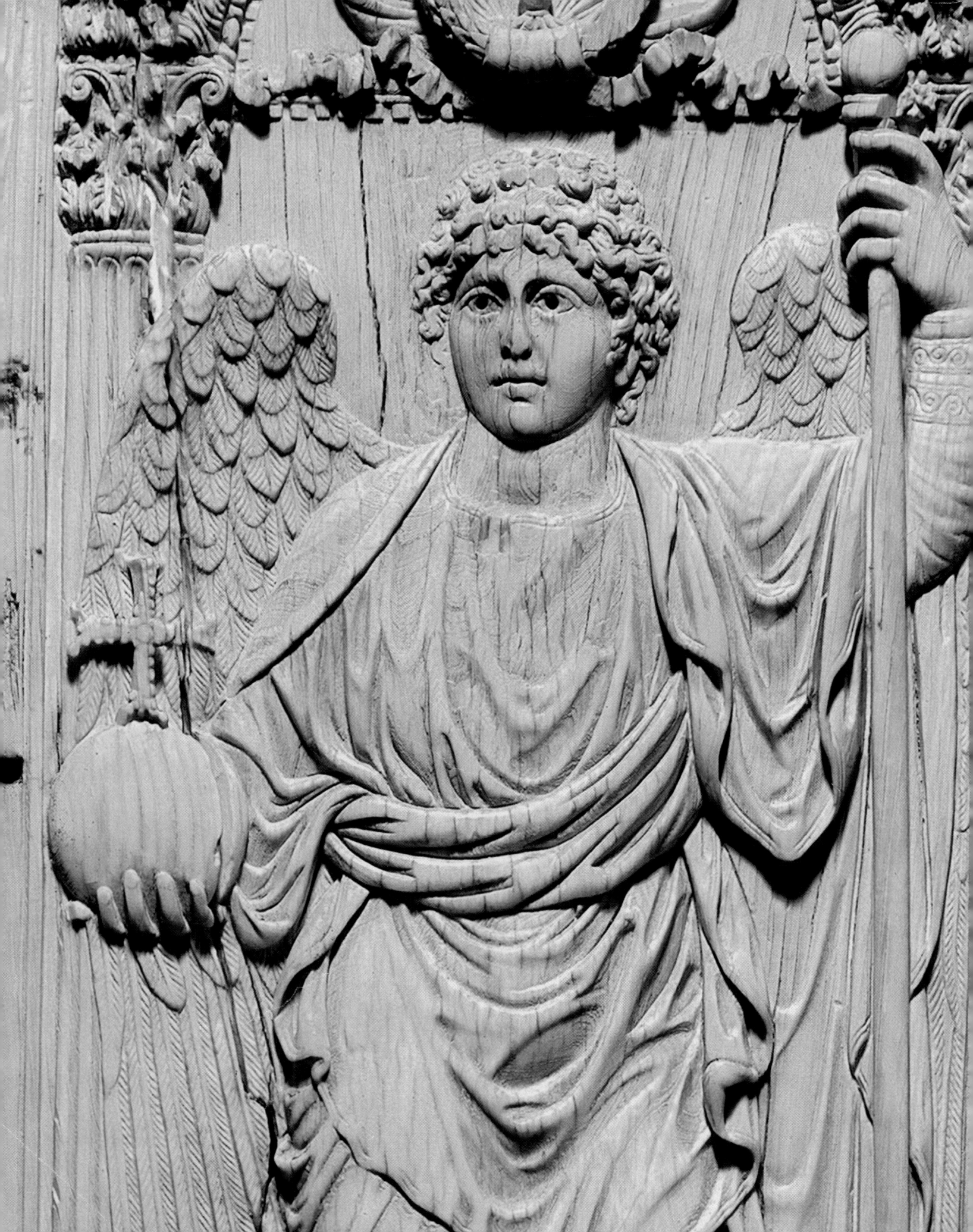

CHAPTER 8

Early Jewish, Early Christian, and Byzantine Art

THE LATE ROMAN EMPIRE WAS HOME TO A VAST MELTING POT OF creeds—including the ancient faith of Judaism, as well as Christianity, Mithraism, Manichaeism, and Gnosticism, to name a few. These competing faiths shared several features, including an emphasis on divine revelation through a chief prophet or messiah and the hope of salvation. Of

these religions, Christianity became the most widespread and influential. The art, principally Jewish and Christian, discussed in this chapter reflects the importance of these religions at a time when Roman authority waned. The unified political structure that Rome had created began to break apart by the fourth century ce, with the result that separate imperial centers were established for the Western Empire and its eastern counterpart, called the Byzantine Empire, each of which developed distinctive forms of art.

The Jews of the Late Roman Empire were a Semitic people descended from the ancient Hebrews. The Hebrew people—their tradition recounts—arrived in Canaan on the eastern shores of the Mediterranean from Egypt around the thirteenth century BCE, as a result of a long journey chronicled in the Hebrew Bible, the so-called Old Testament. They established themselves as a United Kingdom of Israel a generation or so before 1000 BCE, when Jerusalem was made the capital under King David, and it was shortly afterward that King Solomon built a Temple there. The area was subsequently ruled by a series of foreign occupiers, including Babylonians, Assyrians, Persians, Greeks (under Alexander the Great), and, most significantly for our studies, Romans, who under General Pompey conquered Israel in 63 BCE. The Romans referred to this land as Palestine.

Christianity was centered on the life and teaching of Jesus of Nazareth, who himself as well as many of his followers came from the ranks of the Jews. The religion spread from Palestine, first to Greek-speaking communities, notably to Alexandria, in Egypt, then reached the Latin-speaking world by the end of the second century CE. The Gospels of Matthew, Mark, Luke, and John, our principal source of information about Jesus' life, were probably written in the late first century CE, some decades after Jesus' death. The Gospels present him as a historical person and as the Son of God and Messiah, or the "Anointed One." The eloquence and significance of Christ's teachings, the miracles attributed to him, and his innate goodness were considered signs of his divinity. The Roman authorities, viewing Jesus' teaching as subversive, had him arrested, tried, and ultimately punished and executed by crucifixion. As the faith spread, the Romans believed Christians threatened the status quo, and intermittently persecuted them. Still, by 300 CE, nearly one-third of Rome was Christian, though the new faith had little standing until it gained the support of the Emperor Constantine the Great.

Constantine was battling his fellow tetrarch, Maxentius, for control of the Western Empire. According to his biographer, Bishop Eusebius of Caeserea, Constantine claimed to have seen a sign in the sky in the form of the monogram of Christ, formed by the Chi Rho, the first letters of Christ's name in Greek, and to have had a dream in which Christ himself assured him of his victory over Maxentius, which took place in 312 CE at the Milvian

Detail of figure 8.33, *The Archangel Michael*. Leaf of a diptych

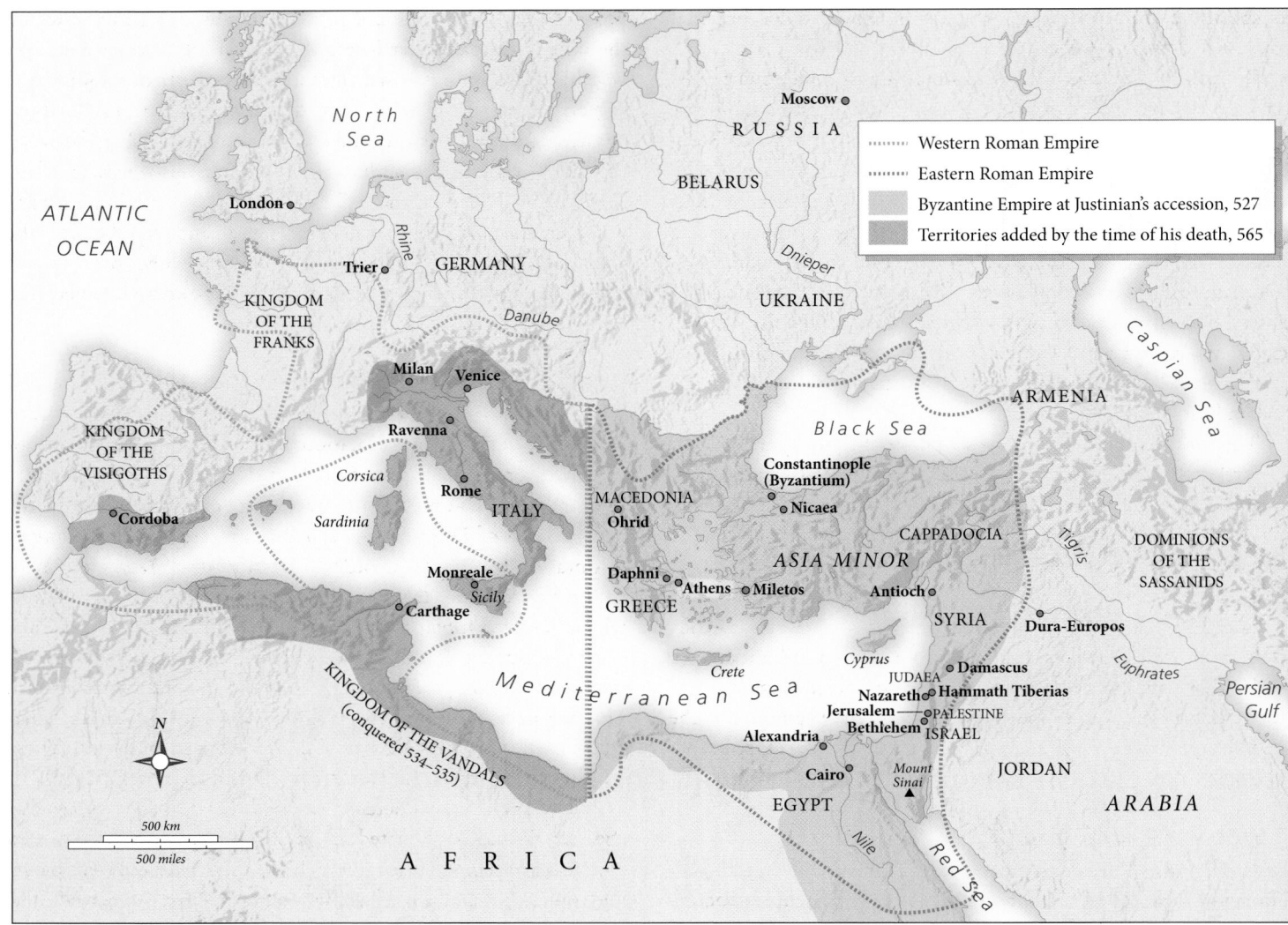

North
Sea

ATLANTIC
OCEAN

RUSSIA

BELARUS

London ○

Trier ○   GERMANY

KINGDOM
OF THE
FRANKS

Rhine

Danube

Dnieper

UKRAINE

Caspian
Sea

Milan ○   Venice ○

Ravenna ○

KINGDOM
OF THE
VISIGOTHS

Corsica

Rome ○   ITALY

Sardinia

Cordoba ○

Monreale ○

Carthage ○   Sicily

KINGDOM OF THE VANDALS
(conquered 534–535)

N

500 km

500 miles

MACEDONIA
Ohrid ○

Daphni ○
Athens ○   Miletos ○
GREECE

Crete

Mediterranean Sea

Alexandria ○

Cairo ○

EGYPT

Nile

Black Sea

Constantinople
(Byzantium) ○
○ Nicaea

ASIA MINOR

CAPPADOCIA

Antioch ○

SYRIA

Cyprus

JUDAEA   ○ Damascus
Nazareth ○   ○ Hammath Tiberias
Jerusalem ○———○ PALESTINE
Bethlehem ○   ISRAEL

Mount
Sinai ▲

Red Sea

ARMENIA

Tigris

DOMINIONS
OF THE
SASSANIDS

Dura-Europos ○

Euphrates

Persian
Gulf

JORDAN

ARABIA

Moscow ○

.... Western Roman Empire
.... Eastern Roman Empire
▢ Byzantine Empire at Justinian's accession, 527
▢ Territories added by the time of his death, 565

AFRICA

Map 8.1   Eastern and Western Roman Empires

Bridge in Rome. This is the triumph commemorated by the Arch of Constantine (see fig. 7.70). After having consolidated imperial power, Constantine promoted Christianity throughout the Empire. He began building important religious structures and convening Church councils. He claimed that his political authority was granted by God, and placed himself at the head of the Church as well as of the state. His choice to accept and promote Christianity was a turning point in history, as it resulted in the union of Christianity with the legacy of the Roman Empire. The character of the Middle Ages—and thus of the rest of European history—depended directly on Constantine's decision.

Constantine also decided to build a new capital for the Roman Empire at the strategically located Greek town of Byzantium, which was renamed Constantinople (present-day Istanbul). Constantine certainly did not anticipate it, but within a century of this event, Rome had divided into two halves: an Eastern Empire, of which Constantinople was the capital, and a Western Empire centered at Rome (see map **8.1**). Imperial might and wealth were concentrated in Constantinople, enriching and protecting the Eastern Empire. In the West, imperial authority was less effective in the face of new challenges, as non-Roman groups first invaded

and then settled. The two empires grew apart, in their institutions and in the practice of their common faith.

Into the vacuum of power left by the decline of imperial institutions in the West stepped the Bishop of Rome. Deriving his authority from St. Peter, the Pope, as the Bishop of Rome became known, claimed to be the head of the universal Christian Church, although his Eastern counterpart, the patriarch of Constantinople, disputed this claim. Differences in doctrine and **liturgy** continued to develop until eventually the division of Christendom into a Western or Catholic Church and an Eastern or Orthodox Church became all but final. The Great Schism, or final break, between the two churches occurred in the eleventh century.

The religious separation of East and West profoundly affected the development of Christian art in the Late Roman Empire. "Early Christian" does not, strictly speaking, designate a style. It refers, rather, to any work of art produced by or for Christians during the time prior to the splitting off of the Eastern Church from the Western Church: that is, roughly during the first five centuries after the birth of Jesus. "Byzantine," on the other hand, designates not only the art of the Eastern Roman Empire but also its specific culture and style, which was linked to the imperial court of Constantinople.

Both Early Christian and Byzantine, and to some extent early Jewish, art have their origins in Rome, and at various moments classical style is preserved or revived. But the art forms of Early Christian art differ from those of the Greek and Roman world. Whereas the ancients expressed the physical presence of their gods in naturalistic sculpture and paintings, Early Christian artists explored a different vision. In the service of their new faith, they concentrated on symbolic representation, using physical means to express a spiritual essence. Early Christian art refined the increasingly stylized and abstracted art forms of the Late Roman Empire into a visual language that could express both profoundly spiritual and unmistakably secular power.

This culture of Christianity—shaped by Rome, by migrations of northern European peoples, and by Christian faith and institutions—lasted a thousand years. Later historians, looking back from the Renaissance, when Roman forms were deliberately being revived, called this civilization medieval; they saw the Middle Ages as an epoch between themselves and the ancient world. (The term "medieval" is derived from the Latin *medium aevum*, and is thus a synonym for the Middle Ages.) The chronological limits of the Middle Ages are somewhat fluid, but for many historians, the victory of Constantine the Great in 312 marks the beginning of the Middle Ages, while the Renaissance in the 1400s marks its end.

EARLY JEWISH ART

The art of a variety of religions and by a range of peoples continued to be produced during the Late Roman Empire. Indeed, the relationships among these various religious arts make clear that none of them was produced in a vacuum and that each affected the others. Of particular interest is Jewish art, both as a subject worthy of study in its own right and because its development is acutely intertwined with that of Christian art, establishing connections nearly as profound as are the relationships between the two religions themselves. The artistic influences, perhaps better-termed "dependencies," between the two religions go both ways: Each seems to have been interested in and stimulated by the artistic production of the other. At the same time, both Jewish and Christian art developed within an environment where the dominant artistic force was clearly Roman.

DURA-EUROPOS SYNAGOGUE Discoveries in Palestine and other neighboring regions within the last century have forced scholars to revise their estimation of the quantity and quality of Jewish art produced in antiquity. Central to this reevaluation was the fortuitous and remarkable discovery of a synagogue in the Syrian town of Dura-Europos, a Roman outpost on the upper Euphrates. In 256 CE, in order to protect itself from imminent attack by Persians, the town strengthened its protective walls, which involved filling in some adjacent streets in order to form a defensive bunker. Buried as a result, and thus preserved, were a number of buildings, including a shrine to Mithras (worshiped in Zoroastrianism, the ancient religion of Persia), a Jewish synagogue, and a house that was used for Christian rituals. These buildings were excavated in the late 1920s and early 1930s.

The bench-lined sanctuary of the Dura-Europos synagogue (fig. **8.1**) would have seated about 120 people. It was decorated with painted ceiling tiles and with four registers of **tempera** paintings on its walls, more than half of which have survived. The mural paintings illustrate episodes from the Hebrew Bible, including scenes featuring Moses and other patriarchs and

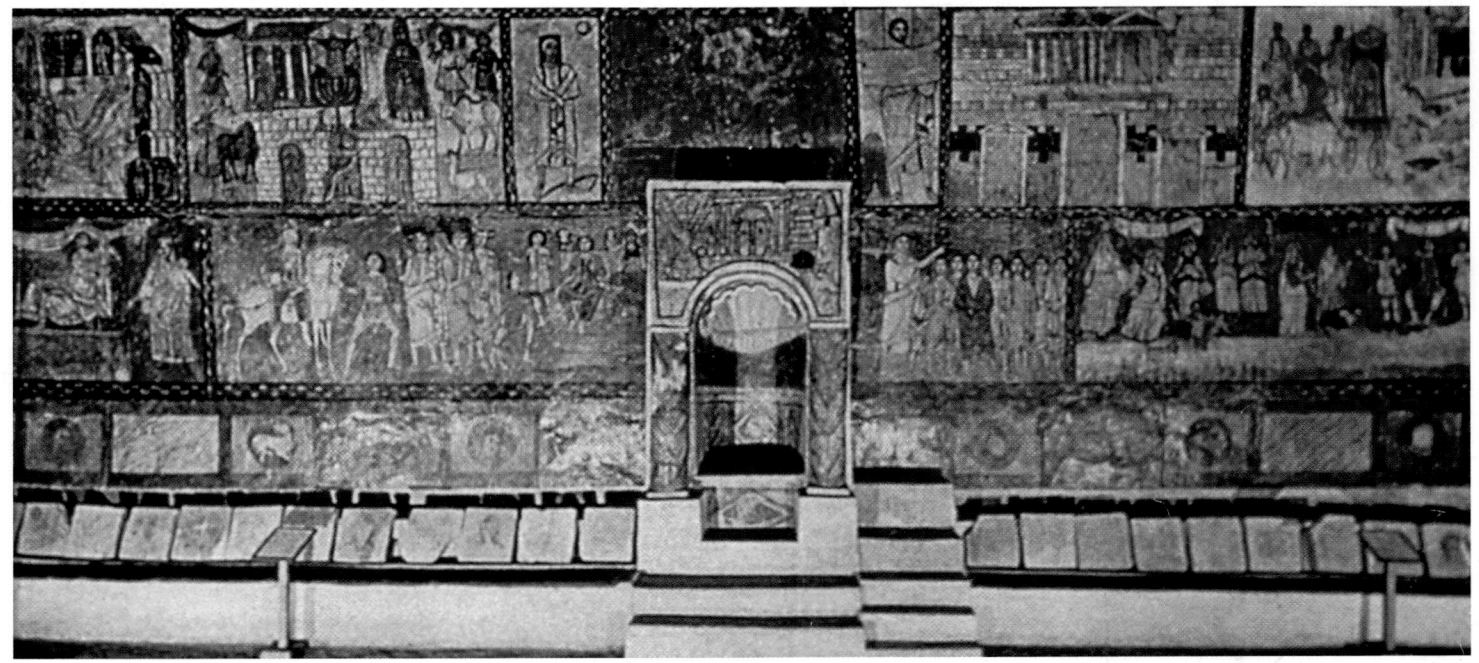

8.1   West wall of sanctuary of synagogue, Dura-Europos, Syria. 245–46 CE. Tempera on plaster. Reconstructed in the National Museum, Damascus, Syria

prophets. The synagogue was rebuilt or refurbished in 245 and 246, just a decade before the defenses against Persian attack were raised; as such, it was virtually new when buried. A niche in the center of the Jerusalem-facing west wall housed a shrine for the Torah, the **parchment** scroll containing the first five books of the Hebrew Bible. The shrine is decorated with a representation of a temple and a menorah, the seven-branched candelabrum that was housed in the Second Temple in Jerusalem, the center of Jewish worship and ritual for centuries, which was destroyed by the Romans in 70 CE (see page 209 and fig. 7.37). The message—one confirmed by writings by rabbis, those Jewish religious leaders and teachers who became increasingly important after the first century CE—is that the synagogues in which Jews practice their religion are to be equated with the Temple in Jerusalem. Indeed, the synagogue was the place where many rituals, for example, the blowing of the ram's horn (the *shofar*), historically practiced in the Temple, came to be performed. Prayers offered in the synagogue substituted for sacrifices that originally took place in the Temple.

The Dura-Europos paintings were created in a space that served a ritual function, where the practice of the liturgy, a body of rites prescribed for public worship, was consistent and alive. To some extent, the decoration of this synagogue provides both a setting for, and a reflection of, ceremonial performance by the local community. In addition to wall murals, ritual objects, and other decorations, the sounds of prayer and the aroma of incense embellished the synagogue and accentuated the sense of a charged space created for the enactment of the liturgy.

Previous to the discovery of the Dura-Europos wall paintings, it had traditionally been assumed that Jews rarely produced art, a notion based on the biblical proscription against making graven images as described in the Second Commandment (Exodus 20:4–6; Deuteronomy 5:8–10: "You shall not make to you any graven image, or any likeness of any thing that is in heaven above, or that is in the earth beneath....You shall not bow down yourself to them, nor serve them"). While the Dura-Europos paintings are the most extensive figural body of early Jewish art to survive, early writings by rabbis specifically mention the existence of mural programs in third-century CE Palestine and, as we shall see, synagogue decorations survive there in some number. Representations of God do not appear in Jewish contexts, and it is here that we should understand the significance of the edict against the production of graven images. The Second Commandment was not an injunction against representation, but rather, more specifically against making idols.

Although the Dura-Europos wall paintings would not have been unique in their own time, the lack of surviving comparable material makes any attempt to see a systematic program of images far from secure, and some scholars claim that there was in fact none. One suggestion is that the scenes could have been used by

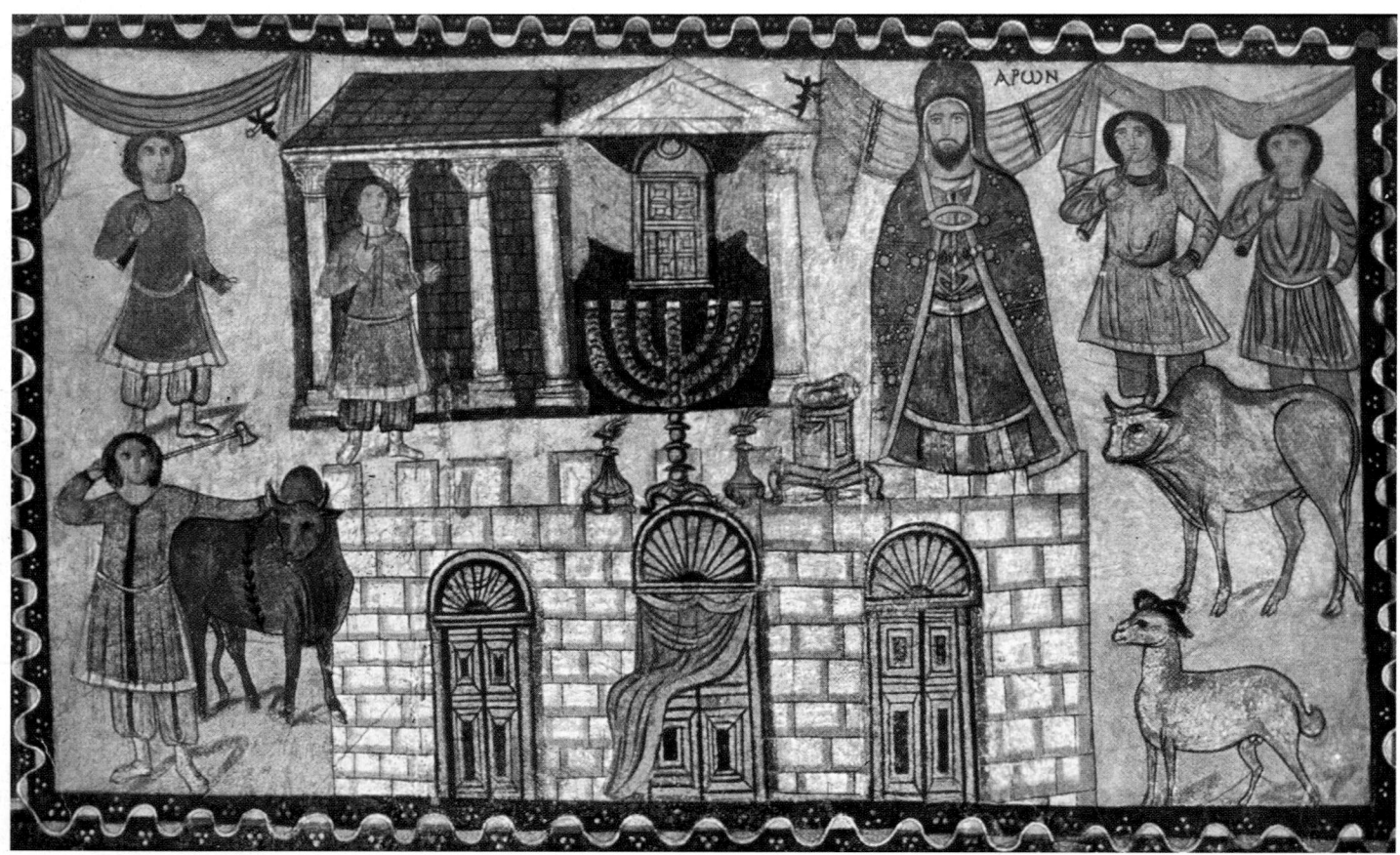

8.2　*Consecration of the Tabernacle and Its Priests*, detail of west wall of sanctuary of synagogue, Dura-Europos, Syria. Tempera on plaster, 4'8¼" × 7'8¼" (1.4 × 2.3 m)

preachers as illustrations for their sermons, turning from one to the other as appropriate. However, others have argued that the scenes selected for illustration emphasize the Lord's special covenant with the chosen people of Israel; still others have noted the concentration of scenes, for example those in which Moses and the prophets Elijah and Ezekiel figure, that offer the promise of revival in both a personal and a messianic sense. This message of redemption is reinforced by the identification of the synagogue with the Temple in Jerusalem.

The Dura-Europos west-wall panel of the *Consecration of the Tabernacle* (fig. **8.2**) illustrates details mentioned in the Hebrew Bible, in various chapters of Exodus and in Numbers 7:89–8:2, which chronicle the creation and consecration of a portable tent used during the Israelites' Exodus from Egypt and that housed the Ark of the Covenant, the chest in which Moses placed the tablets containing the Ten Commandments, the foundation of Jewish law that God delivered to him on the journey from Egypt. The Tabernacle, described in the Bible as tentlike and composed of poles and goat's-hair curtains, is here a Roman temple (see figs. 7.2 and 7.44) surrounded by a defensive wall pierced by three portals. It is not clear whether the permanent building represented here, rather than the portable tent described in the Bible, is a result of scriptural interpretation, or whether it perhaps reflects concern on the part of the population of a frontier town for security and defense; it might also replicate a pictorial source relied upon by the artist.

The golden menorah (described in Exodus 25:31–40) is placed in front of the temple and below the Ark of the Covenant, which bears a strong resemblance to the Dura-Europos Torah-shrine niche. The attendant and the red heifer in the lower left-hand corner are derived from Roman scenes of animal sacrifice; hence, they show remnants of foreshortening that are not found among the other figures. Other echoes of Roman painting appear in the perspective view of the altar table next to the figure of Aaron, the first Jewish high priest, whose name, interestingly, is inscribed in Greek. Most of the rest of the scenes reveal little interest in either light or space in the Roman sense. The spatial sequence of objects and people is conveyed by other means. The menorah, the two incense burners on either side of it, the altar, and Aaron are to be seen as behind, rather than on top of, the wall in vertical perspective. Their size, however, is based on their importance, not on their position in space. Aaron, as the main figure, is not only larger than the attendants but also more abstract. Because of its ritual meaning, his costume is shown in detail, at the cost of the body underneath. The attendants, on the other hand, show some mobility and three-dimensional form. Their garments, surprisingly, are Persian, a sign of the mixture of civilizations and the melting-pot conditions in this border area. In terms of style, the synagogue paintings should be seen in the context of the developing abstraction of later Roman art (see figs. 7.67 and 7.72).

The west-wall mural, then, combines a variety of elements that suggest that the ritual being performed is timeless and recurring. The mural depicts an event of great religious importance: the consecration of the Tabernacle and its priests. We can read the details—animals, human beings, buildings, cult objects—without trouble, but their relationship to one another is not clear. There is no action, no story, only an assembly of forms and figures, which, however, the synagogue members would have been able to link together.

HAMMATH TIBERIAS SYNAGOGUE In addition to wall paintings and liturgical objects, a number of synagogues, particularly in Palestine, were decorated with floor mosaics. The fourth-century mosaic floor of a synagogue at Hammath Tiberias (fig. **8.3**) on the shore of the Sea of Galilee contains motifs that are typical of synagogue pavements, including a wheel with the signs of the zodiac between its spokes and in the center a representation of Helios, the Greek sun-god, bearing a staff and globe, with rays emanating from his head and riding a quadriga, a two-wheeled chariot drawn by four horses. Scholars have debated this reliance on the art of another culture for sources of imagery; some see it as a formal borrowing without overt concern for meaning, while

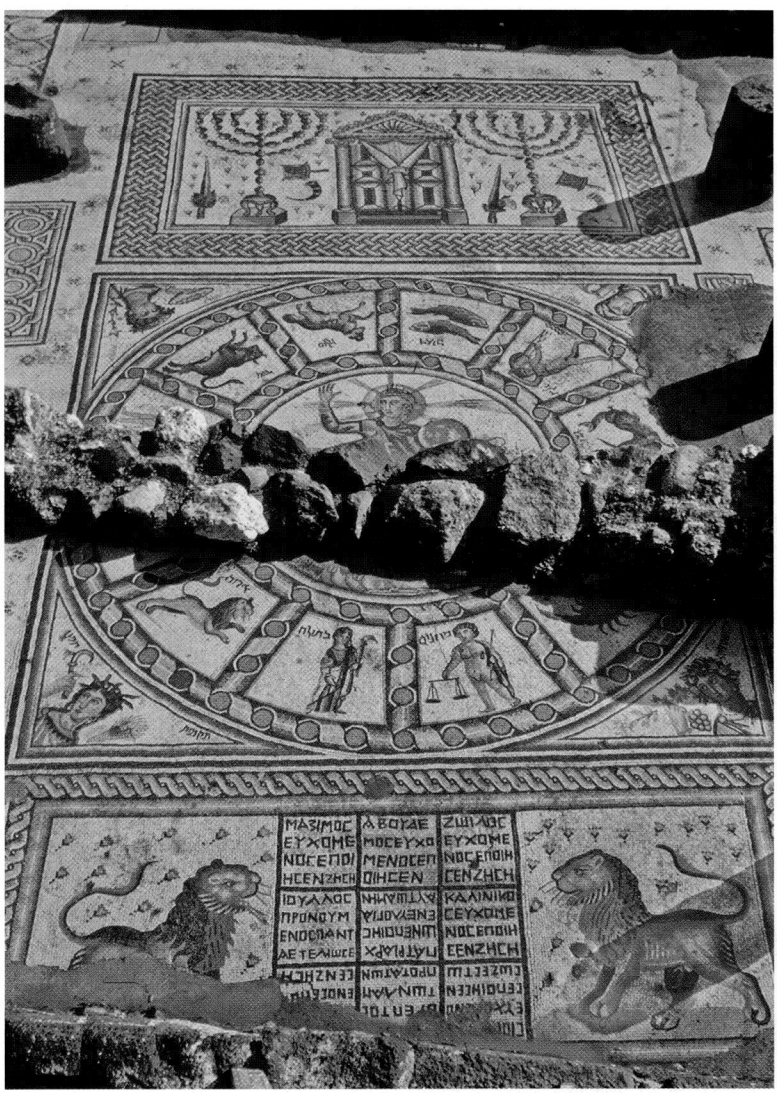

8.3 Floor mosaic, synagogue, Hammath Tiberias, Israel. 4th century CE

others recognize a desire to transfer the authority of traditional pagan images to a new context.

In the corners between the circle of the zodiac and the square frame that encloses it are representations of the seasons, while below the zodiac panel, two lions flank an inscription in Greek that praises the synagogue's builders and describes the donation of precious metals to the synagogue, referred to as a "holy place." A number of Palestinian synagogue mosaics took the zodiac as their central feature: This might be related to the Jews' sense of themselves as distinctive in part because of their use of a calendar different from those of other peoples. The zodiac undoubtedly refers as well to God's creation of the universe.

Represented above the zodiac is a Torah shrine, framed by menorahs and other ritual objects, including incense shovels and the *shofar*, as well as a tied bundle of palm, willow, and myrtle branches (the *lulav*) and citrons (*etrogs*), used in the harvest festival, all elements from the liturgy. The mosaic of the ark and menorah panel was placed facing Jerusalem, in front of the raised podium where the actual Torah shrine was located. The mosaic at Hammath Tiberias creates and unifies sacred time and sacred space.

The mosaic's style of representation is reminiscent of Roman mosaic work (see fig. 7.15). The figures' modeling is subtle and shadows suggest solid, if squat, bodies. Some scholars have cited the fact that the nude figures of Libra and Gemini are uncircumcised as evidence for the Jewish resistance to making images, suggesting that the artists responsible for these works were Gentiles. But at other sites inscriptions identify the mosaicists as Jewish, and it is more probable, given the long history of the representation of the zodiac, that this detail reflects pictorial sources rather than any comment, conscious or otherwise, by the makers of the mosaic.

The Hebrew and Greek used in the mosaic—and there are inscriptions in Aramaic (a Semitic language) as well—reflect the fact that multiple traditions are at work here. Indeed, although the images at Hammath Tiberias and at Dura-Europos have special relevance to Jewish history, beliefs, and rituals, many reflect Graeco-Roman content, even if it was Judaized in accordance with the special concerns and needs of the communities the images served. A similar pattern is also evident in the development of the earliest Christian art.

EARLY CHRISTIAN ART

Christian Art before Constantine

We do not know when or where the first Christian works of art were produced. None of the surviving paintings or sculptures can be dated to earlier than about 200 CE. In fact, we know little about Christian art before the reign of Constantine the Great. This is hardly accidental. It is in Rome that we have the greatest concentration of the earliest surviving works, yet before Constantine, Rome was not the center of the faith. Older and larger Christian communities existed in the great cities of North Africa and the Near East, such as Alexandria and Antioch, but we only have hints of what Christian places of worship there and in centers such as Syria and Palestine might have looked like.

THE ART OF THE CATACOMBS The painted decoration of the Roman **catacombs**, underground burial places, is the only sizable body of material we have from which to study the earliest Christian art. The burial rite and the safeguarding of the tomb were of vital concern to early Christians, whose faith rested on salvation, the hope of eternal life in paradise. As such, paintings in catacombs tell us a good deal about the spirit of the communities that commissioned them.

The ceiling of one of the more elaborate chambers in the catacomb of Santissimi Pietro e Marcellino in Rome (fig. **8.4**) is decorated in a style that is at once formal and uncomplicated. Fixed borders control the overall organization; a central medallion or circle contains the figure of a shepherd, who is flanked by sheep and carries a lamb across his shoulders. The circle is connected to four **lunettes** (semicircular spaces), and in the four corners are single figures with outstretched, raised arms. The style of painting reflects Roman murals, both in the landscape settings and in the use of linear devices to divide the scenes into compartments (see figs. 7.55 and 7.56). But the representations seem sketchier, less grounded in natural observation than their Roman relatives. The differences are partly due to the nature of the subterranean spaces, their use, and their meaning.

Catacombs would have been used only occasionally beyond the actual circumstance of burial, perhaps for a commemorative celebration. This is probably one reason why the wall paintings do not show much detail and care of execution. One imagines as well that artists of the first rank would have chosen more salubrious locations in which to work. Another reason for the sketchiness of these paintings is that their primary value is symbolic. Consistent with the biblical prohibition against image making, as specified in the Second Commandment, Christ is generally not represented in the catacombs, except by metaphor. The shepherd with a sheep on his shoulder is a potent allusion to Christ, since in a number of biblical accounts Christ refers to himself as the Good Shepherd, concerned for the well-being of his flock and willing to sacrifice himself in order to guarantee the salvation of those who follow him (Luke 15:4–6; John 10:1–18). This Good Shepherd metaphor also builds on references in the Hebrew Bible, as in Psalm 23:

> The Lord is my shepherd; I shall not want.
> He makes me to lie down in green pastures:
> he leads me beside the still waters.
> He restores my soul…
> Surely goodness and mercy shall follow me
> all the days of my life:
> and I will dwell in the house of the Lord for ever.

This correlation between New Testament and Hebrew Bible reflects the fact that many of the converts to the new faith were Jewish.

The Life of Jesus

Events in the life of Jesus, from his birth through his ascension to Heaven, are traditionally grouped in cycles, each with numerous episodes. The scenes most frequently depicted in European art are presented here.

Incarnation Cycle and The Childhood of Jesus

These episodes concern Jesus' conception, birth, infancy, and youth.

Annunciation The archangel Gabriel tells Mary that she will bear God's son. The Holy Spirit, shown usually as a dove, represents the Incarnation, the miraculous conception.

Visitation The pregnant Mary visits her older cousin Elizabeth, who is to bear John the Baptist and who is the first to recognize the divine nature of the baby Mary is carrying.

Nativity At the birth of Jesus, the Holy Family—Mary, his foster father, Joseph, and the Christ Child—is usually depicted in a stable or, in Byzantine representations, in a cave.

Annunciation to the Shepherds and Adoration of the Shepherds An angel announces the birth of Jesus to shepherds in the field at night. The shepherds then go to the birthplace to pay homage to the child.

Adoration of the Magi The Magi, wise men from the East (called the Three Kings in the Middle Ages), follow a bright star for 12 days until they find the Holy Family and present their gifts to Jesus.

Presentation in the Temple Mary and Joseph take the infant Jesus to the Temple in Jerusalem, where Simeon, a devout man, and Anna, a prophetess, foresee Jesus' messianic mission (his mission as Savior) and martyr's death.

Massacre of the Innocents and Flight into Egypt King Herod orders all male children under the age of two in and around Bethlehem to be killed in order to preclude his being murdered by a rival newborn king spoken of in a prophecy. The Holy Family flees to Egypt.

Public Ministry Cycle

These accounts of Jesus' public career include his gathering of disciples, his preaching, and the performance of miracles.

Baptism John the Baptist baptizes Jesus in the Jordan River, recognizing his incarnation as the Son of God. This marks the beginning of Jesus' ministry.

Calling of Matthew The tax collector Matthew becomes Jesus' first disciple (apostle) when Jesus calls to him, "Follow me."

Jesus Walking on the Water During a storm, Jesus walks on the water of the Sea of Galilee to reach his apostles in a boat.

Raising of Lazarus Jesus brings his friend Lazarus back to life four days after his death and burial.

Delivery of the Keys to Peter Jesus names the apostle Peter as his successor by giving him the "keys" to the Kingdom of Heaven.

Transfiguration As Jesus' closest disciples watch, God transforms Jesus into a dazzling vision and proclaims him to be his own son.

Cleansing the Temple Jesus clears the Temple in Jerusalem of money-changers and animal traders.

Passion Cycle

The Passion (from passio, Latin for "suffering") cycle relates Jesus' death, resurrection from the dead, and ascension to heaven.

Entry into Jerusalem Welcomed by crowds as the Messiah, Jesus triumphantly rides an ass into the city of Jerusalem.

Last Supper At the Passover seder, Jesus tells his disciples of his impending death and lays the foundation for the Christian rite of the Eucharist: the taking of bread and wine in remembrance of Christ. (Strictly speaking, Jesus is called Jesus until he leaves his earthly physical form, after which he is called Christ.)

Jesus Washing the Disciples' Feet Following the Last Supper, Jesus washes the feet of his disciples to demonstrate humility.

Agony in the Garden In Gethsemane, the disciples sleep while Jesus wrestles with his mortal dread of suffering and dying.

Betrayal (Arrest) The disciple Judas Iscariot takes money to identify Jesus to Roman soldiers. Jesus is arrested.

Denial of Peter As Jesus predicted, Peter, waiting outside the high priest's palace, denies knowing Jesus three times as Jesus is being questioned by the high priest Caiaphas.

Jesus before Pilate Jesus is questioned by the Roman governor Pontius Pilate regarding whether or not he calls himself King of the Jews. Jesus does not answer. Pilate reluctantly condemns him.

Flagellation (Scourging) Jesus is whipped by Roman soldiers.

Jesus Crowned with Thorns (The Mocking of Christ) Pilate's soldiers mock Jesus by dressing him in robes, crowning him with thorns, and calling him King of the Jews.

Carrying of the Cross (Road to Calvary) Jesus carries the wooden Cross on which he will be executed from Pilate's house to the hill of Golgotha, which means "the place of the skull."

Crucifixion Jesus is nailed to the Cross by his hands and feet, and dies after great physical suffering.

Descent from the Cross (Deposition) Jesus' followers lower his body from the Cross and wrap it for burial. Also present are the Virgin Mary, the apostle John, and, in some accounts, Mary Magdalen.

Lamentation (*Pietà* or *Vesperbild*) The grief-stricken followers gather around Jesus' body. In the *Pietà*, his body lies in the lap of the Virgin.

Entombment The Virgin Mary and others place the wrapped body in a sarcophagus, or rock tomb.

Descent into Limbo (Harrowing of Hell or Anastasis in the Orthodox Church) Christ descends to Hell, or Limbo, to free deserving souls who have not heard the Christian message—the prophets of the Hebrew Bible, the kings of Israel, and Adam and Eve.

Resurrection Christ rises from the dead on the third day after his entombment.

The Marys at the Tomb As terrified soldiers look on, Christ's female followers (the Virgin Mary, Mary Magdalen, and Mary, mother of the apostle James the Greater) discover the empty tomb.

Noli Me Tangere, Supper at Emmaus, and the Doubting of Thomas In three episodes during the 40 days between his resurrection and ascent into Heaven, Christ tells Mary Magdalen not to touch him (*Noli me tangere*), shares a supper with his disciples at Emmaus, and invites the apostle Thomas to touch the lance wound in his side.

Ascension As his disciples watch, Christ is taken into Heaven from the Mount of Olives.

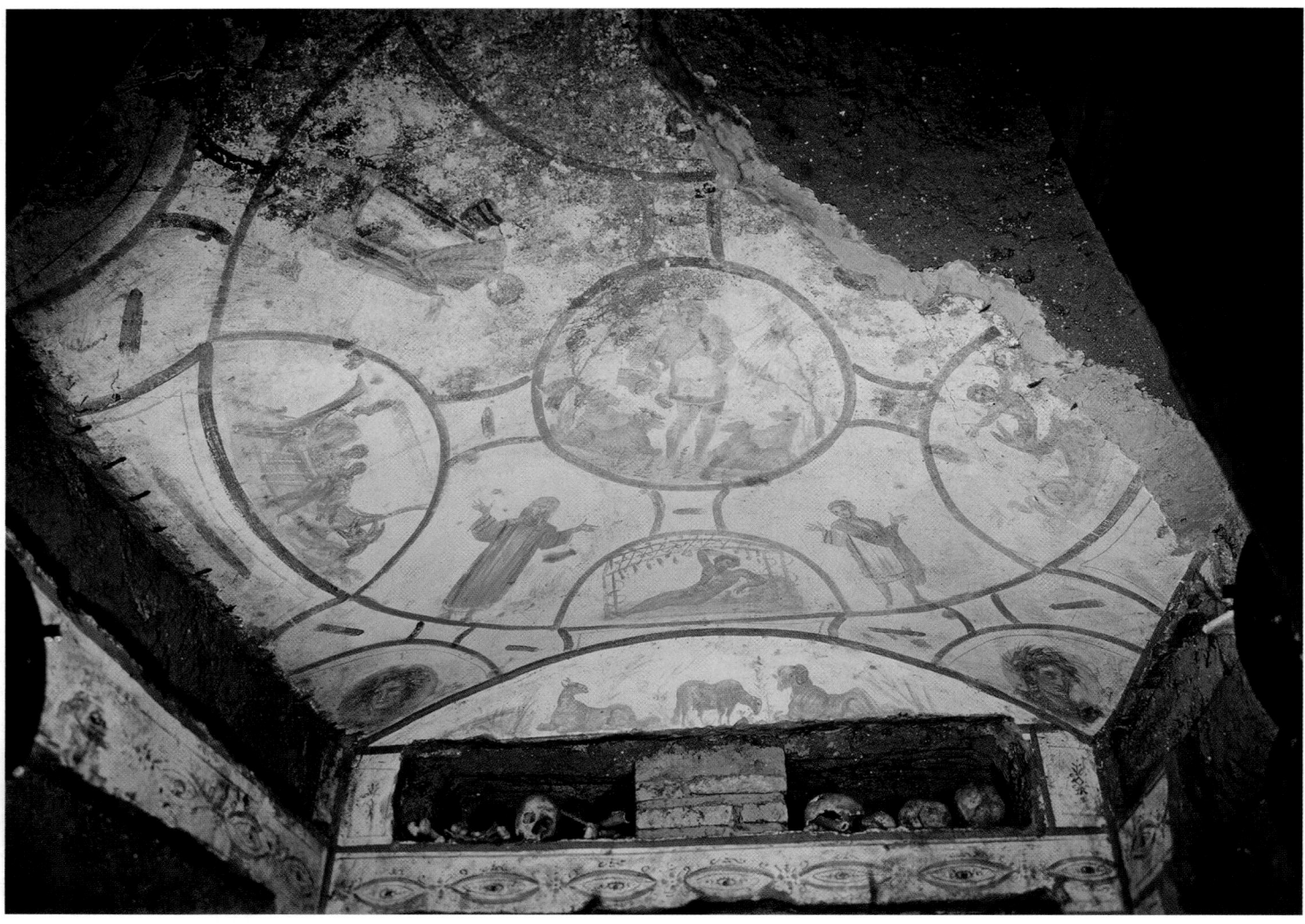

8.4 Painted ceiling, Catacomb of Santissimi Pietro e Marcellino, Rome, Italy. 4th century CE

The four lunettes around the Good Shepherd form a cycle dedicated to the Hebrew prophet Jonah. (See *Informing Art*, page 273.) Here, too, the symbolic references to Christian beliefs about Christ are clear: Just as it is a principle of faith that Jonah spent three days within the belly of the whale, so Christ is supposed to have spent three days in the tomb, and just as Jonah was released with unharmed body, so Christ was resurrected from his tomb in physical wholeness. Indeed, in Matthew 12:40 Christ compares himself to Jonah. Recent converts would probably have felt comfortable knowing that didactic aspects of their old faith could find a sympathetic response in the new religion. Jonah's story is presented as a **prefiguration** (foreseeing) of events in Christ's life, thus assigning the Hebrew Bible story the role of prophecy and the Christian Bible one of its fulfillment. As Christian thinkers increasingly analyzed the prophetic relationship of the Hebrew Bible to the Christian one, they developed a virtual system of concordances, called **typology**, that was to have far-reaching significance.

The painted ceiling in the Santissimi Pietro e Marcellino catacomb also borrows imagery from classical sources. The Good Shepherd himself is a reminder of pagan symbols of charity in the form of ancient sculptures of men carrying sacrificial animals on their shoulders. The posture of Jonah, reclining under the gourd bush, benefiting from God's beneficence, derives from Roman pagan mythological representations of Endymion, a youth so beautiful that he was rewarded with eternal sleep. So, as with their Jewish counterparts, former practitioners of pagan religions who had converted to Christianity would also have been familiar with some of the images and ideas expressed in Early Christian art.

Both the Good Shepherd and Jonah are associated with messages of comfort, reminding us that Early Christian art developed during the turmoil of Rome's decline, a time of political, social, and economic instability. The allure of the new religion must have been profound indeed, suggesting that things of this world were of less significance than those of a future world, which offered the hope of eternal peace. The four standing figures between the lunettes are **orants** (worshipers), represented in what had long been the standard pose of prayer, signifying the virtues of faith and piety that make personal salvation possible.

One might question the extent to which the Christian use of pagan and Jewish subjects had a political agenda. After all, on some level, to borrow forms from other cultures and religions and to use them for new purposes are acts of appropriation. By adopting forms used by an older, more established culture, Christians expressed their ambition to dominate that culture—indeed, to supplant it. Such appropriation becomes more systematic as the new religion of Christianity becomes increasingly powerful.

SCULPTURE Sculpture seems to have played a secondary role in Early Christian art. The biblical prohibition on graven images was thought to apply with particular force to large cult statues, idols worshiped in pagan temples. In order to avoid the taint of idolatry, therefore, Christian sculpture had to shun life-size representations of the human figure. Sculpture thus developed in an antimonumental direction: away from the spatial depth, naturalism, and massive scale of Graeco-Roman sculpture and toward shallow, small-scale forms and lacelike surface decoration.

The earliest works of Christian sculpture are sarcophagi, stone coffins, which from the middle of the third century on were produced for the more important members of the Church. They evolved from the pagan examples that had replaced cinerary urns in Roman society around the time of Hadrian. Before Constantine, their decoration consisted mostly of a repertory of familiar themes from the catacombs. Examples of these can be seen on the marble sarcophagus of the mid-third century from Santa Maria Antiqua in Rome (fig. **8.5**). On the left are scenes featuring Jonah: the ship, the sea monster, and the reclining prophet. Jonah's well-chiseled anatomy and the elegance of his pose remind us of the classical sources that must have served as a model for the artist. So, too, the Good Shepherd, though stylized, reminds of us of classical statuary in that he is able to distribute

weight well enough to manage with some comfort the burden of the sheep he carries. Again, the orant in the center, with hands upraised in prayer, is a subject we have seen in catacomb painting. The seated figure holding a scroll derives from antique representations of writers or philosophers and is another of the metaphoric references to Christ, in this case to his role as teacher. On the right is a scene of baptism. The figure being baptized may be Christ himself. If so, this might indicate an increased movement toward narrative, since baptism was an event in the life of Jesus (see *Informing Art*, page 241), and a willingness to represent him directly. On the other hand, the figure appears to be generic, nonindividualized, virtually childlike in its proportions. This generic representation could be a result of both a fear of making an idolatrous image and an interest in expressing the more essential nature of the scene, from which a portrait of the person of Christ would detract.

THE HOUSE CHURCH Although we have little archaeological evidence of the places where Early Christians gathered, literary accounts, including biblical references, suggest that Christians met regularly to celebrate their shared belief in Christ as the Son of God and Savior and to observe some type of Eucharist, or spiritual union, with him by the partaking of consecrated bread and wine (representing Christ's flesh and blood) in remembrance of the Last Supper, at which Jesus and his disciples enjoyed a final communal meal. Such gatherings of Christians probably originally took place in private homes, which were only later replaced by public spaces designed specifically for Christian worship. This situation is perhaps to be expected, both because

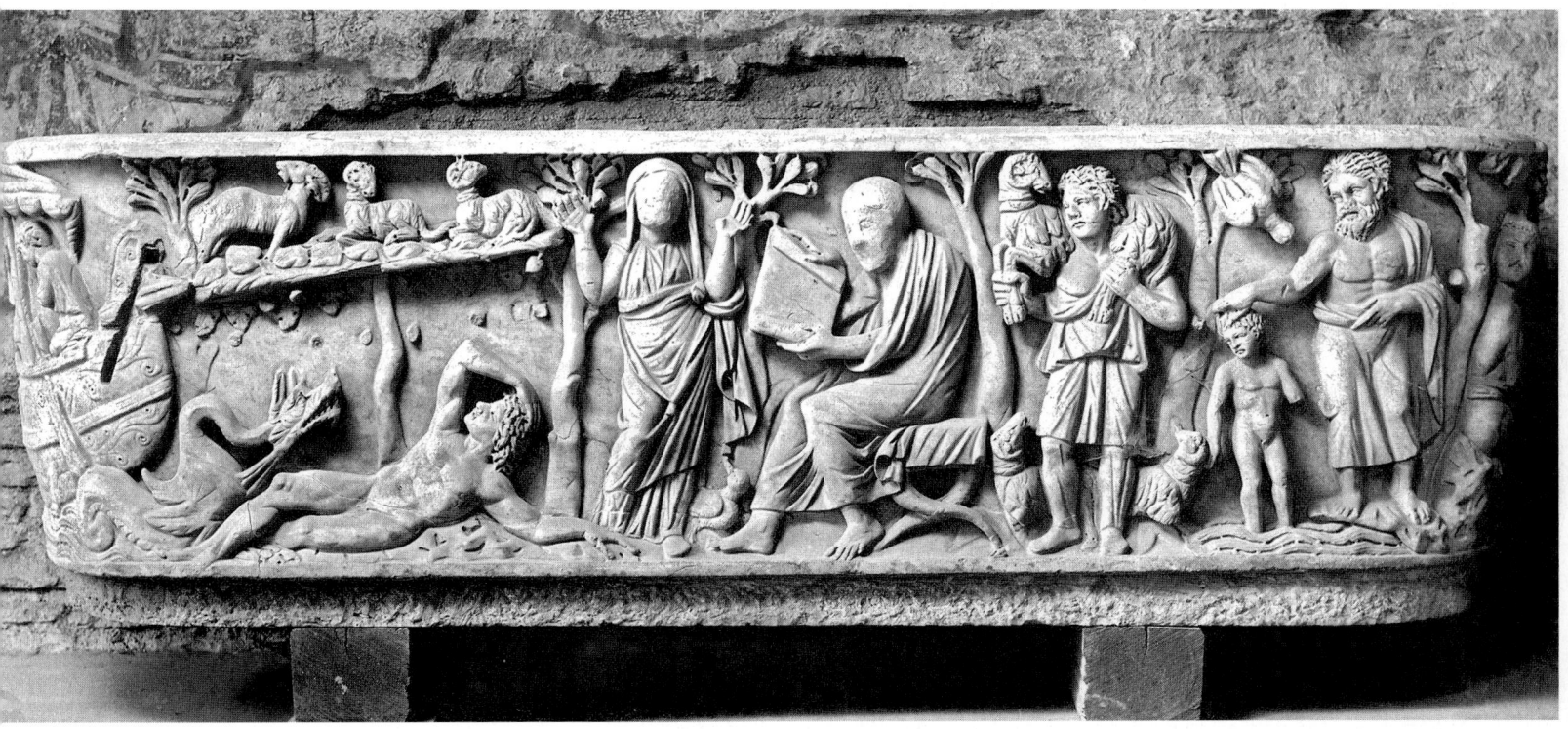

8.5   Sarcophagus, Santa Maria Antiqua, Rome, Italy. ca. 270 CE. Marble, 1'11¼" × 7'2" (0.85 × 2.2 m)

The Book of the Popes (Liber Pontificalis)

From the Life of Pope Sylvester I

This text is an official history of the Roman papacy from St. Peter (died ca. 64 CE) to the twelfth century. Its biographies of the early popes were compiled from archival documents. What follows, for example, is a list of gifts to Old St. Peter's by Emperor Constantine in the time of Pope Sylvester I (314–335 CE). Lavish imperial donations such as these set a standard that subsequent popes and other prelates continued to match.

Constantine Augustus built the basilica of blessed Peter, the apostle, and laid there the coffin with the body of the holy Peter; the coffin itself he enclosed on all sides with bronze. Above he set porphyry columns for adornment and other spiral columns which he brought from Greece. He made a vaulted apse in the basilica, gleaming with gold, and over the body of the blessed Peter, above the bronze which enclosed it, he set a cross of purest gold. He gave also 4 brass candlesticks, 10 feet in height, overlaid with silver, with figures in silver of the acts of the apostles, 3 golden chalices, 20 silver chalices, 2 golden pitchers, 5 silver pitchers, a golden paten with a turret of purest gold and a dove, a golden crown before the body, that is a chandelier, with 50 dolphins, 32 silver lamps in the basilica, with dolphins, for the right of the basilica 30 silver lamps, the altar itself of silver overlaid with gold, adorned on every side with gems, 400 in number, a censer of purest gold adorned on every side with jewels.

Source: Caecilia Davis-Weyer, *Early Medieval Art 300-1150* (Upper Saddle River, NJ: Prentice Hall, 1st ed., 1971)

Christianity was something of an underground religion and because other religions also seem to have used private houses as gathering places; for instance, the Villa of the Mysteries in Pompeii (see fig. 7.53).

The same defensive barrier that preserved the Dura-Europos synagogue (see page 237) also buried what must have been a traditional Christian meeting place. The house is in most ways a typical two-story Roman domus. A large room opened onto the atrium and would have served as a community assembly room, while another space, judging by a font that takes up an entire wall of the room (fig. **8.6**), was apparently reserved for baptism, the rite whereby Christians are initiated into the religion by virtue of being sprinkled or immersed in water. The font is covered by a stone canopy, and frescoed scenes decorate the lunette on the end wall under the canopy and also the side walls. Some of the subjects represented are familiar: In the lunette is a Good Shepherd balancing a sheep on his shoulders with his flock before him, and, at the bottom left, now barely visible, are figures of Adam and Eve. Represented on the side wall are three women holding candles who proceed toward a stone sarcophagus. This scene represents the three Marys at the Tomb (see *Informing Art*, page 241), who, when approaching the tomb of Christ (as described in Matthew 28:1–10), meet an angel who tells them that the tomb is empty because the entombed Christ has risen.

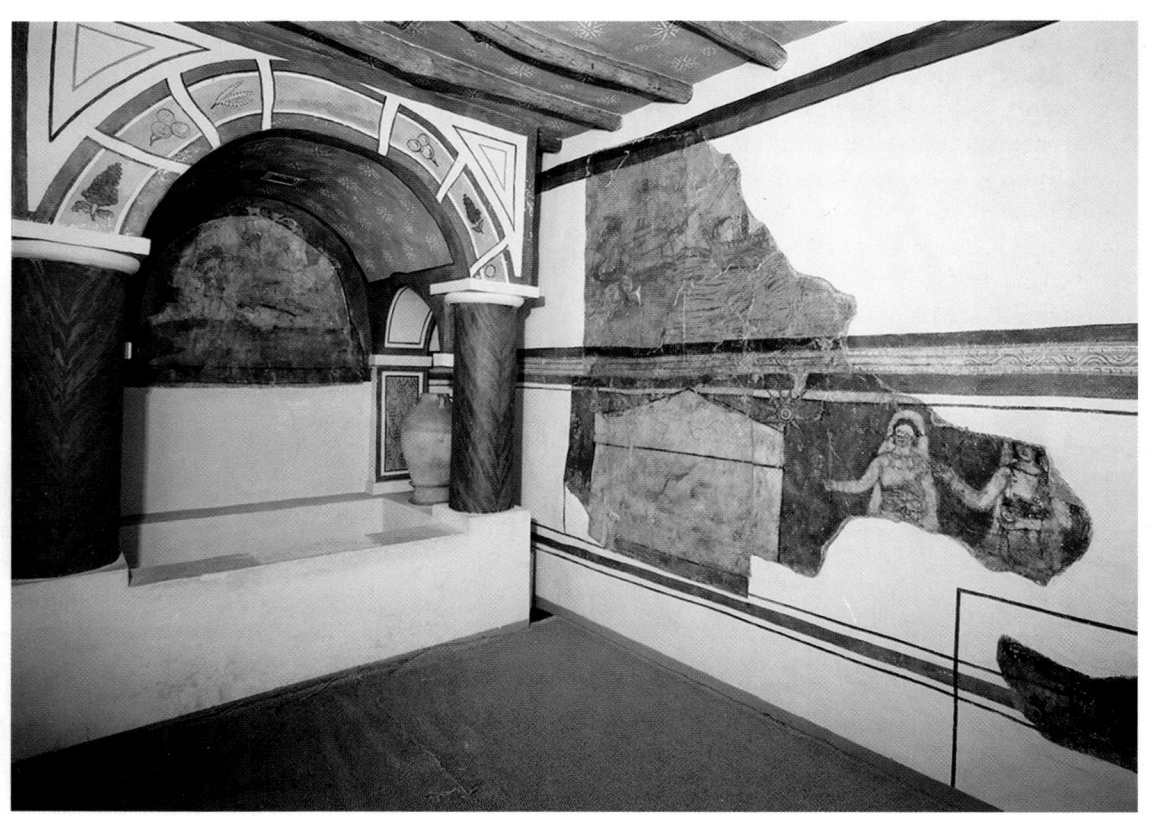

8.6 Model of the Baptistery, the Christian Meeting House (*domus ecclesiae*) at Dura-Europos, Syria. Before 256 CE. Yale University Art Gallery, New Haven, CT

The representations on the wall of the Dura-Europos house can be connected with those found in Early Christian catacombs and on sarcophagi through shared imagery, such as the depictions of the Good Shepherd and Adam and Eve. Such images indicate a general concern with issues of death and retribution, resurrection and salvation. The inclusion here of Adam and Eve reminds the viewer of the Original Sin, committed by Adam and passed from one generation to the next, from which humankind will be redeemed as a result of Christ's sacrificial death and his resurrection, which the scene of the Marys visiting his empty tomb emphasizes. The association of these funerary subjects with baptism was a logical pairing for Christians, who view baptism as a rebirth into the new faith, just as they see physical death as a rebirth into everlasting life. Even when artists were experimenting with how best to depict entirely new subject matter, those responsible for its creation, whether artists or patrons, applied an overwhelming conceptual consistency to Christian art during the first several centuries of the Christian era. This was perhaps a result of the new religion's need for didactic representations that could be readily understood.

Christians in other areas of the Empire also used the type of the *domus ecclesiae*, or **house church**, seen at Dura-Europos. In Rome itself we know of 25 private houses—and undoubtedly there were more—reserved as places of Christian worship, although most of them were destroyed by the later building of churches on their sites.

Christian Art after Official Recognition of Christianity

The building of churches on the sites of what once were private houses used for Christian worship reflects a change in the status of Christianity during the fourth century from an alternative religion to an official religion endorsed by the emperor Constantine. Almost overnight, an impressive architectural setting had to be created for the new official faith, so that the Church might be visible to all. Constantine himself devoted the full resources of his office to this task. Within a few years, an astonishing number of large, imperially sponsored churches arose, not only in Rome but also in Constantinople, in the Holy Land, and at other important sites.

THE CHRISTIAN BASILICA The most important Constantinian church structures were a type of basilica, and this form provided the basic model for the development of church architecture in Western Europe. The Early Christian basilica owes its essential features to imperial basilicas, such as the Basilica Ulpia (see fig. 7.17). As with the imperial basilicas, it is characterized by a long **nave** flanked by side aisles and lit by clerestory windows in the upper part of the wall, with an apse (though only at one end) and a **trussed** wooden roof. The Roman basilica was a suitable model since it combined the spacious interior needed to accommodate a large number of people with (perhaps most important) imperial associations that proclaimed the privileged

status of Christianity. As the largely civil functions of the Roman basilica were quite different from its new uses as a house of worship, the Roman-style basilica had to be redesigned to acknowledge these changes. Therefore, the longitudinal plan of the basilica was given a new focus: the altar placed in front of the semicircular apse, normally at the eastern end of the nave. The significance of the altar's placement in the east, where the sun rises, reminds us that Christian art, like that of Judaism (see page 240), inherited many divine attributes from other religions. In this case, Christ shares an imagery with the Roman god Apollo, in his manifestation as sun-god.

The greatest Constantinian church was Old St. Peter's Basilica in Rome (figs. **8.7** and **8.8**). It was torn down and replaced by the

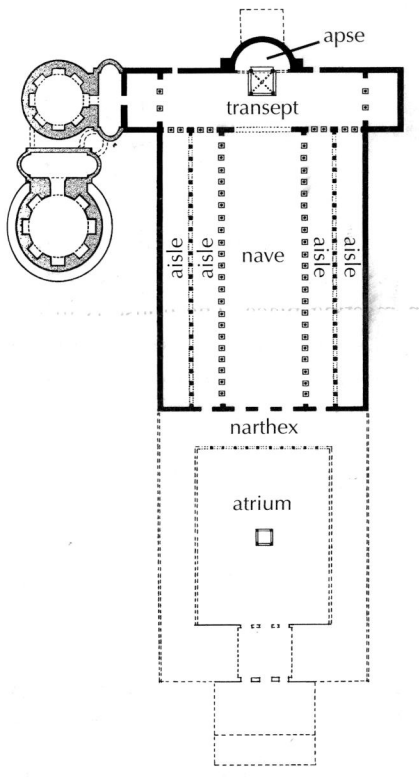

8.7   Plan of Old St. Peter's, Rome, Italy. ca. 324–400 CE (after Frazer)

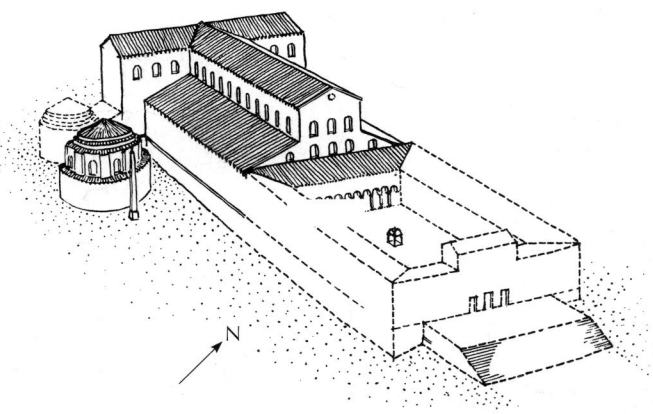

8.8   Reconstruction of Old St. Peter's, Rome, Italy, as it appeared ca. 400 CE (after Krautheimer)

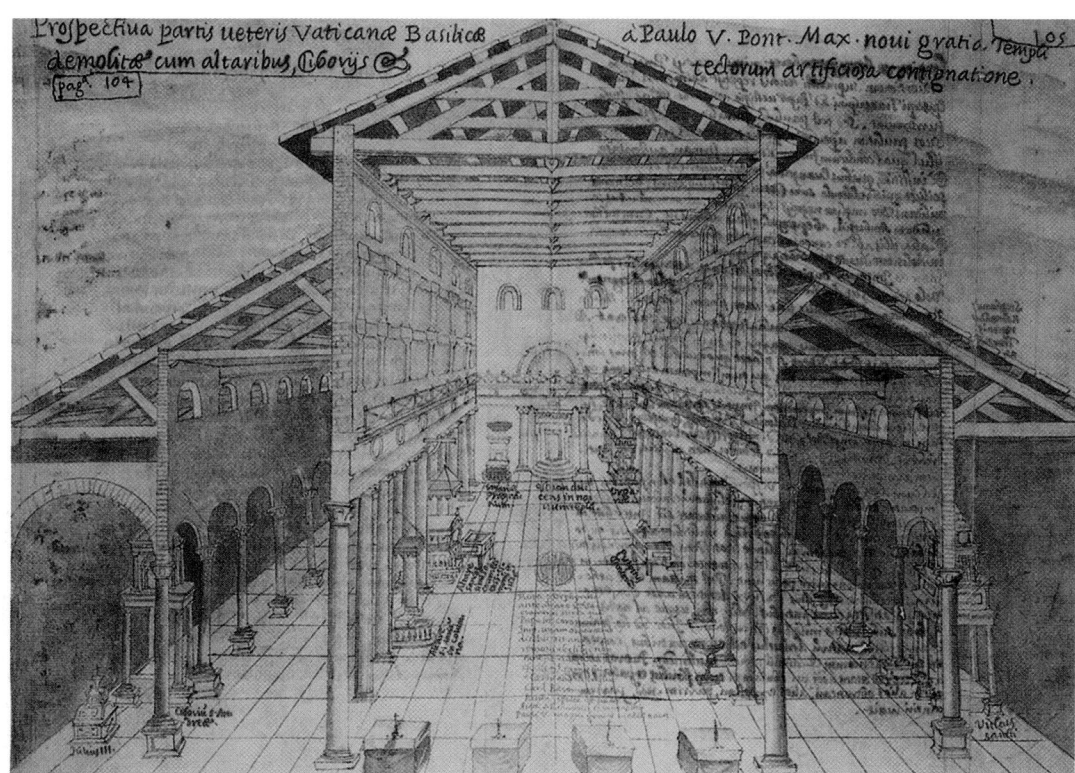

Prospectiua partis ueteris Vaticanæ Basilicæ demolitæ cum altaribus, Ciborijs ② [pag. 104]

a Paulo V. Pont. Max. noui gratia Templi tectorum artificiosa compaginatione.

8.9 Jacopo Grimaldi, *Interior of Old St. Peter's, Rome*. Drawing, 1619. MS: Barbarini Lat. 2733, fols. 104v–105r. Vatican Library, Rome, Italy

present St. Peter's Basilica, in the Vatican, during the sixteenth and seventeenth centuries, but its appearance is preserved in a seventeenth-century album of copies of earlier drawings (fig. **8.9**), and there are literary descriptions as well. Together these sources give us a clear idea of the original plan for the church. Begun as early as 319 and finished by 329, Old St. Peter's was built on the Vatican Hill next to a pagan burial ground. It stood directly over the grave of St. Peter, which was marked by a shrine covered with a **baldacchino**, a canopy that designates a place of honor. As such, Old St. Peter's served as the apostle's martyrium, a building that housed sacred relics or the remains of a holy person. The location of St. Peter's burial spot was the focus of the church, and due to site restrictions, its apse was at the west end of the church, an unusual feature. Rituals were conducted from a portable altar placed before the shrine, using gold and silver implements donated by the emperor himself. (See *Primary Source*, page 244.)

To enter the church, the congregation first crossed a colonnaded court, the **atrium**, which was added toward the end of the fourth century; this feature derived from the Roman basilica. Congregants then passed through the **narthex**, an entrance hall, into the church itself. The steady rhythm of the nave colonnade would have pulled them toward the **triumphal arch** that separates the nave from the apse, which it also serves to frame. The shrine stood at the junction of the nave and the **transept**, a separate space placed perpendicular to the nave and aisles. Spaces at the end of the transept, marked off by columns, might have served to prepare items used during church rites and to hold offerings brought by the faithful.

The main focus of Christian liturgy was, and is, the Mass, which includes the sacrament of Communion, the symbolic reenactment on the altar of Jesus' sacrifice. The Early Christian basilica encouraged attention to the altar, making it the focal point of the church by placing it opposite the entrance and at the end of a long nave. Even beyond this general emphasis on the altar, Old St. Peter's gave special prominence to the altar zone through its special, additional function as a martyrium.

Although today we think of the practice of religion as an open one, in the early Church only those who had proven themselves Christians could witness the complete performance of the liturgy. It was through baptism that catechumens, those receiving instruction in preparation for their initiation into the new religion, became full-fledged Christians. Before baptism, they could hear, but not see, parts of the Mass. Even today, Christians refer to this as the "mystery" of the Mass.

CENTRAL-PLAN STRUCTURES Buildings of round or polygonal shape capped by a dome entered the tradition of Christian architecture in Constantine's time. Roman emperors had built similar structures to serve as monumental tombs or mausoleums, such as the one Diocletian had built for himself at his palace at Spalato (see fig. 7.63). Not surprisingly, therefore, the Early Christian central-plan building was often associated with funerary functions, as was Santa Costanza, in Rome, the mausoleum of Constantine's daughter Constantia (figs. **8.10** and **8.11**). Built over a catacomb, it was originally attached to the now-ruined basilican church of Sant'Agnese fuori le mura (St. Agnes Outside the Walls). The focus of the building is on the central space, illuminated by clerestory windows, over which rises a dome supported by twelve pairs of columns. Four of the arches of this colonnade stand slightly higher than the others and suggest a

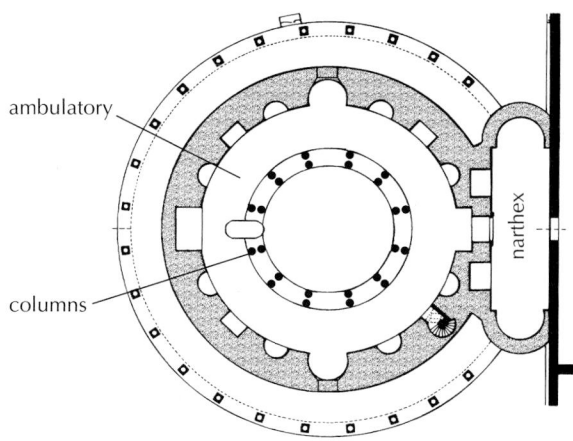

8.10 Plan of Santa Costanza, Rome, Italy. ca. 350 CE

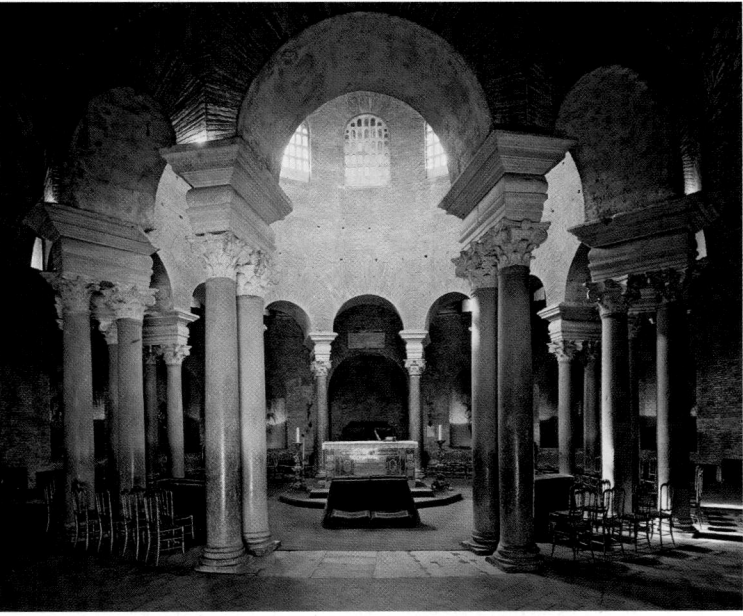

8.11 Interior (view through ambulatory into rotunda) of Santa Costanza, Rome, Italy

cross inscribed within a circle. The significance of the cross in a funerary context results from its association with Christ, who, though martyred on a cross, rose victorious over death. The Cross was meaningful to all Christians but particularly to the family of Constantine, whose personal conversion was a result of his vision of the Cross, which had signaled his victory at the Battle of the Milvian Bridge in 312. The sarcophagus of Constantia was originally placed under the eastern, more-elevated arch. Encircling the building is an **ambulatory**, a ring-shaped aisle, covered by a barrel vault (see fig. 7.3).

Central-plan and basilican structures are not as different as they might first appear. In fact, a **section** of a central-plan building parallels a section of a basilican church in that both have a high central space with a clerestory flanked by a lower aisle. While the basilica plan stretches this form so that emphasis is on the end of the building, the central plan, as seen in Santa Costanza, spins the section on axis, accentuating the center. You can see this clearly by comparing figures 8.9 and 8.11.

MERGING THE BASILICAN AND CENTRAL PLANS Since Constantine continued to follow Roman imperial traditions even as he accepted the tenets of Christianity, it is not surprising that when he supported the construction of buildings in the Holy Land to mark places significant in the life of Jesus, he chose plans based on Roman imperial building types, thus accentuating his ambitions for his new religion. The basilican Church of the Holy Sepulcher (fig. 8.12), in Jerusalem, marked the location where St. Helena, mother of Constantine, had found the True Cross (that is, the cross on which Jesus was crucified as opposed to those crosses on which the thieves who were sentenced to death along with Christ were crucified). Beyond the basilica was the Rotunda of the Anastasis (Greek for "resurrection"), built over the tomb where Christ's body is reputed to have lain for the three days before his resurrection. Although the Constantinian building was subsequently destroyed and later rebuilt in a somewhat different form, this aisled basilica included a **gallery**, a second story placed over the side aisles of a church, increasing the space available for the throngs of pilgrims who flocked to key sites. The apse was ringed with twelve columns, which Eusebius, Constantine's confidant and biographer, equated with Jesus' twelve apostles. (See *Informing Art*, page 273.) In the Anastasis rotunda, too, there would have been a gallery, but in all other ways this rotunda has the same silhouette as Santa Costanza. Both have ambulatories formed by columns arranged around a domed central space, although unlike Santa Costanza's masonry dome, the dome of the Anastasis rotunda was probably made of wood. The similarity of form is not surprising. Both were products of the benefaction of the imperial family and both served funereal functions. As such, their roots in imperial mausoleums are appropriate, even as their forms become conveyors of new meaning. The Church of the Holy Sepulcher complex shares with Old St. Peter's a desire to combine the congregational aspects of a Roman basilica with a martyrium in a monument that eulogizes the deceased whom it commemorates—Christ himself.

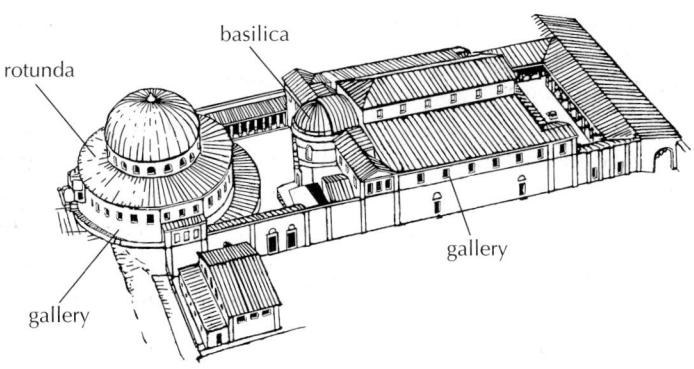

8.12 Reconstruction of Church of the Holy Sepulcher, Jerusalem, Israel, as it appeared ca. 350 CE (after Conant)

Mosaics

Mosaics—designs composed of small pieces of colored material set in plaster or mortar—had been used by the Sumerians as early as the third millennium BCE to decorate architectural surfaces. The Hellenistic Greeks used pebbles and the Romans, using small cubes of marble called tesserae, had refined the technique to the point that it could be used to copy paintings, as seen in The Battle of Alexander (see fig. 5.78). Although most Roman mosaics were for floors, the Romans also produced wall mosaics, but these were usually reserved for special purposes, for example in fountain rooms or outdoor spaces where fresco would be vulnerable to deterioration.

The extensive and complex wall mosaics of Early Christian art are essentially without precedent. The color scale of Roman mosaics, although rich in gradations, lacked brilliance, since it was limited to the kinds of colored marble found in nature. Early Christian mosaics, by contrast, consist of tesserae made of colored glass, which the Romans had known but never fully exploited. Glass tesserae offered colors, including gold, of far greater range and intensity than marble tesserae. Moreover, the shiny, somewhat irregular faces of glass tesserae, each set slightly askew from its neighbor, act as tiny reflectors, so that the overall effect is like a glittering, immaterial screen rather than a solid, continuous surface. All these qualities made glass mosaic the ideal material for the new architectural aesthetic of Early Christian basilicas.

Glass for tesserae was made by combining sand, soda or potash, and lime with metallic oxides, which determined the resultant hues. Hardened sheets of glass were marked off and cut into tesserae of approximately cubic shape. For gold mosaics, gold leaf was placed on a sheet of glass, then glass, still in liquid form, was applied over it and heat applied to bond the glass layers, effectively embedding the gold leaf within glass.

The mosaic process was labor-intensive, not only to create the design, but also to set the tesserae. Hundreds of thousands of tesserae were needed to cover a church interior, and setting them required skill and training. The process typically began by applying multiple layers of plaster (about 3 inches thick in all) to a wall. Recent investigations have shown that mosaics were generally prepared *in situ*. A drawing was done directly on the surface to be decorated, which was then painted in order to create a guide for the design. Red was used in areas that were to be covered with gold, since red added richness to the gold ground.

Tesserae were then laid into still-fresh plaster, which was sufficiently soft so that at least half the surface of the tesserae could be submerged; a secure attachment was thus guaranteed. The process required deliberate planning, since only the section of wall that could be finished in a day, roughly the time it would take for plaster to dry, would receive the final coat of plaster into which the tesserae were set.

Some medieval treatises distinguish between *pictores imaginarii* (mosaic painters) and *musearii* (mosaic workers), suggesting a hierarchy in the division of labor. Under any circumstances, mosaic production was a costly enterprise; it has been estimated that it was at least four times more expensive than wall painting. Clearly the aesthetic advantages of mosaics, as well as their durability, were thought sufficient to justify the expense.

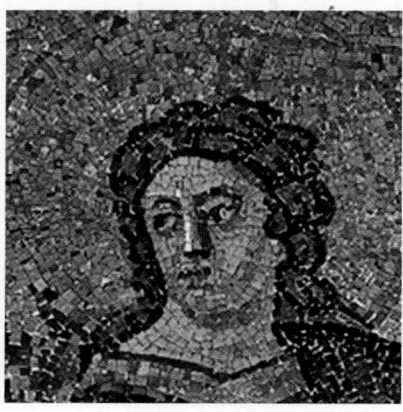

Detail of *Good Shepherd*, figure 8.15

ARCHITECTURAL DECORATION: WALL MOSAICS The rapid growth of large-scale Christian architecture had a revolutionary effect on Early Christian pictorial art. All of a sudden, huge wall surfaces had to be covered with images worthy of their monumental framework. Out of this need emerged a new art form, the Early Christian wall mosaic, which to a large extent replaced the older and cheaper medium of mural painting. (See *Materials and Techniques*, above.) The challenge of inventing a body of Christian imagery produced an extraordinary creative outpouring. Large pictorial cycles of subjects selected from the Hebrew and Christian Bibles were spread over the nave walls, the triumphal arch, and the apse. These cycles must have drawn on sources that reflected the whole range of Graeco-Roman painting as well as artistic traditions that had developed in the Christian communities of North Africa and the Near East.

Decoration of fourth-century churches is largely fragmentary or known only from literary accounts; it is in fifth-century churches that we can see the full development of mosaic-decorated Christian structures. During the fifth century, the Late Empire was threatened at all its borders by migrating tribes. Even the capital of the Western Empire at Rome was vulnerable. So the emperor Honorius moved it north, first to Milan, and when that city was besieged in 402, to Ravenna on the Adriatic coast, thought to be more easily defensible than inland sites.

The Mausoleum of Galla Placidia (fig. **8.13**) was named after Honorius' sister (who ruled the Empire as regent) because it was believed that she was buried there, though it is likely that it was begun as a chapel dedicated to the martyr St. Lawrence. Its central plan takes the form of a **Greek cross**, that is, a cross with arms of equal length. The exterior brick walls of the building, although perhaps originally covered, were always much simpler than the rich

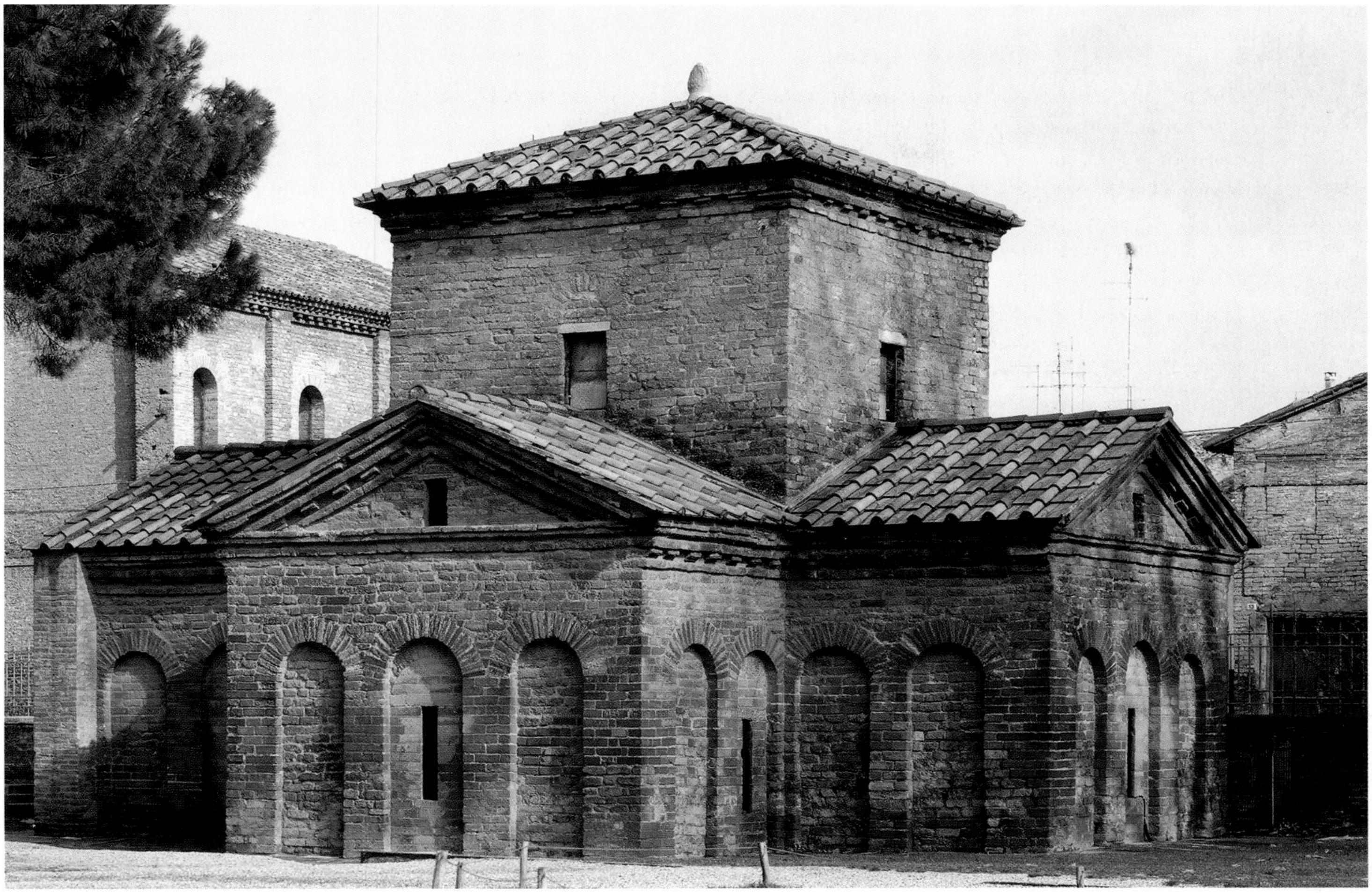

8.13   Mausoleum of Galla Placidia, Ravenna, Italy. 425–50 CE

interior (fig. **8.14**). Having left the everyday world behind, a visitor would encounter a shimmering realm of light and color where precious marble surfaces and glittering mosaics evoke the spiritual splendor of the Kingdom of God. To some extent, the building is analogous to the ideal Christian, simple in external body and glorious in inner spirit, an analogy certainly not missed by early Christians.

The barrel vaults and dome of the Mausoleum of Galla Placidia are covered with luxurious leaflike decoration and fields of stars. Above the vaults, apostles flank a pair of doves and fountains, symbolic of souls drinking from the waters of Paradise. In one lunette, St. Lawrence is shown beside the flame-racked grill on which he was martyred. A cabinet holding books, identified as the four Gospels, reminds us that Lawrence was martyred for refusing to surrender the riches of the Church, here represented as books, to the Roman authorities. That books would be equated with treasure is perhaps not surprising, for, as we shall see, they were luxurious objects that played a vital function within the Church. The books also remind us that Christians referred to themselves as people of the Book, a designation they shared with the earlier Hebrew and later Muslim faiths.

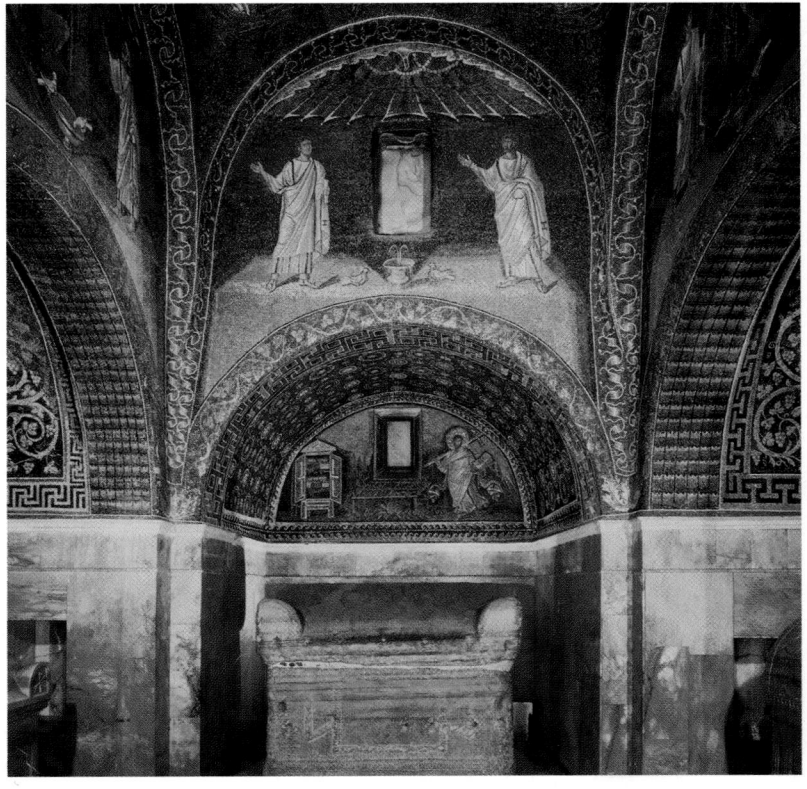

8.14   Interior of Mausoleum of Galla Placidia, Ravenna, Italy

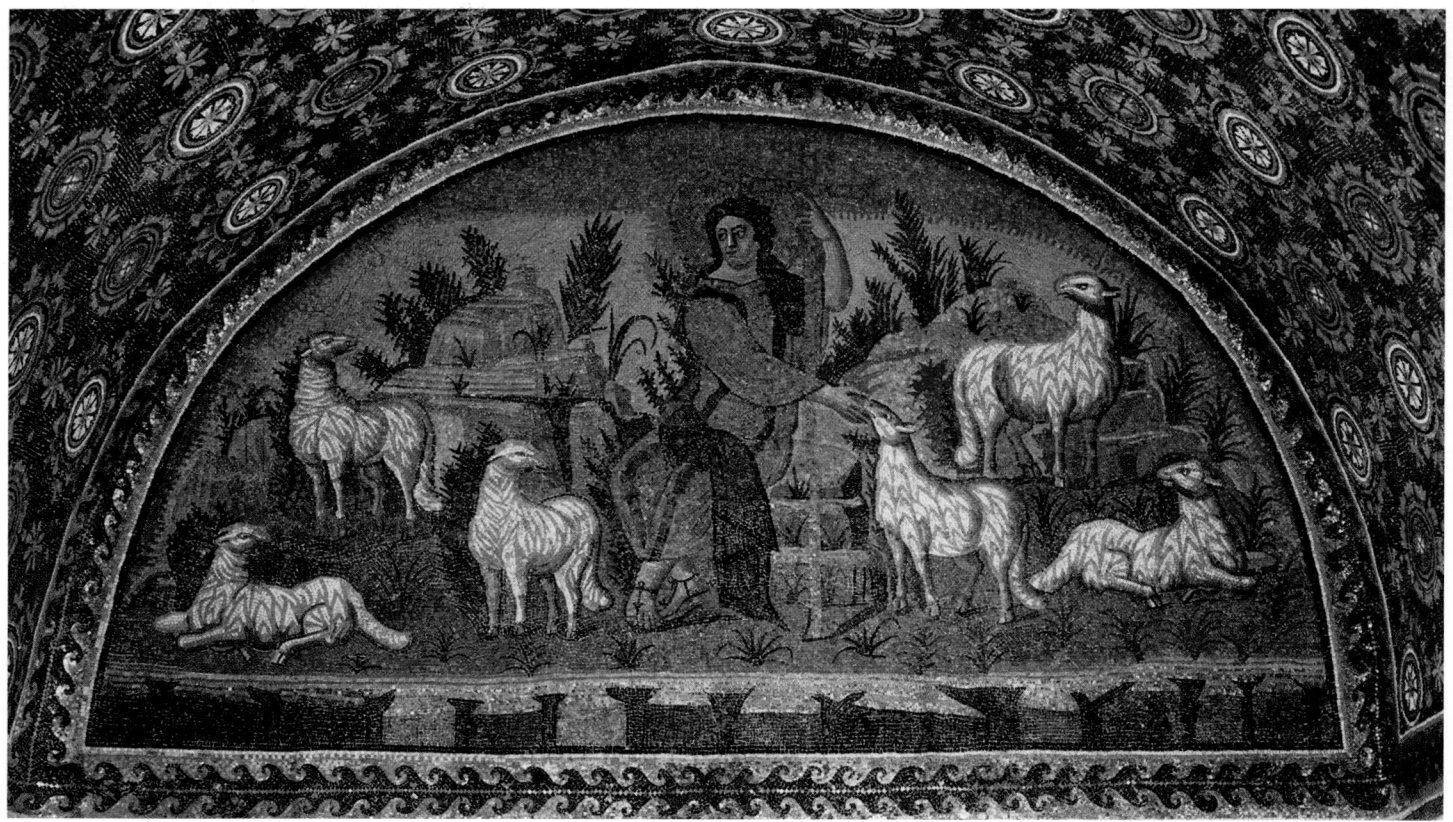

8.15 *Good Shepherd*, Mausoleum of Galla Placidia, Ravenna, Italy. Mosaic

Another lunette contains a mosaic of the Good Shepherd seated in a fully realized landscape (fig. **8.15**), expanding the central subject of so many catacomb paintings with its more elaborate and formal treatment. Here, the Good Shepherd is a young man with many attributes adopted from imperial art. His halo comes from representations of the emperor as sun-king, and his gold robes and purple scarf are traditional signifiers of royal stature. These attributes are appropriate to a commission by the imperial family, but equally significant is the way formal features further the message, and perhaps here there is a paradox. While Christ, with realistically modeled face, flowing hair and garments, sits comfortably in a lush landscape with a sky-blue background, the prevalence of gold denies naturalism to the scene. The paradox is that Christ is at once human, imperial, and of this world, and yet also beyond it, existing within a glimmering ethereal realm of which he is a natural part. Roman mural painting used illusionistic devices to suggest a reality beyond the surface of the wall (see figs. 7.54 and 7.55), whereas Early Christian mosaics used the glitter of gold tesserae to create a luminous realm filled with celestial beings, symbols, or narrative action. Thus, Early Christian mosaics transform the illusionistic tradition of ancient painting with the new Christian message.

The basilica of Santa Maria Maggiore in Rome (fig. **8.16**), built between 432 and 440, was the first church dedicated to Mary, begun only a year after she was declared the *Theotokos* (Greek for "the bearer of god") by the Council of Ephesus. The apse is a later replacement, but the general outline of the original building and

much of the mosaic decoration survive. These mosaics include the triumphal arch decoration and more than half of the 42 mosaic panels that were placed above the classically inspired entablature of the nave colonnade. Pilasters and colonettes framed these panels. Sadly, much of this architectural decoration is now missing. An enthroned Virgin in the original apse was framed by the triumphal arch, which contains stories from Jesus' infancy—an appropriate introduction to Mary, because of her involvement in those episodes.

The panels above the nave colonnade illustrate scenes from the Hebrew Bible. They combine narration with a concern for structured symmetry. For instance, in the left half of *The Parting of Lot and Abraham* (fig. **8.17**), Abraham, his son Isaac, and the rest of his family depart for the land of Canaan. On the right, Lot and his clan, including his two small daughters, turn toward the city of Sodom. The artist who designed this scene from Genesis 13 faced the same task as the ancient Roman sculptors of the Column of Trajan (see fig. 7.39): He needed to condense complex actions into a form that could be read at a distance. In fact, he employed many of the same shorthand devices, such as the formulas for house, tree, and city, and the device of showing a crowd of people as a cluster of heads, rather like a bunch of grapes.

In the Trajanic reliefs, these devices were used only to the extent that they allowed the artist to portray actual historical events. The mosaics in Santa Maria Maggiore, by contrast, depict the history of human salvation, beginning with scenes from the Hebrew Bible along the nave and ending with the life of Jesus as

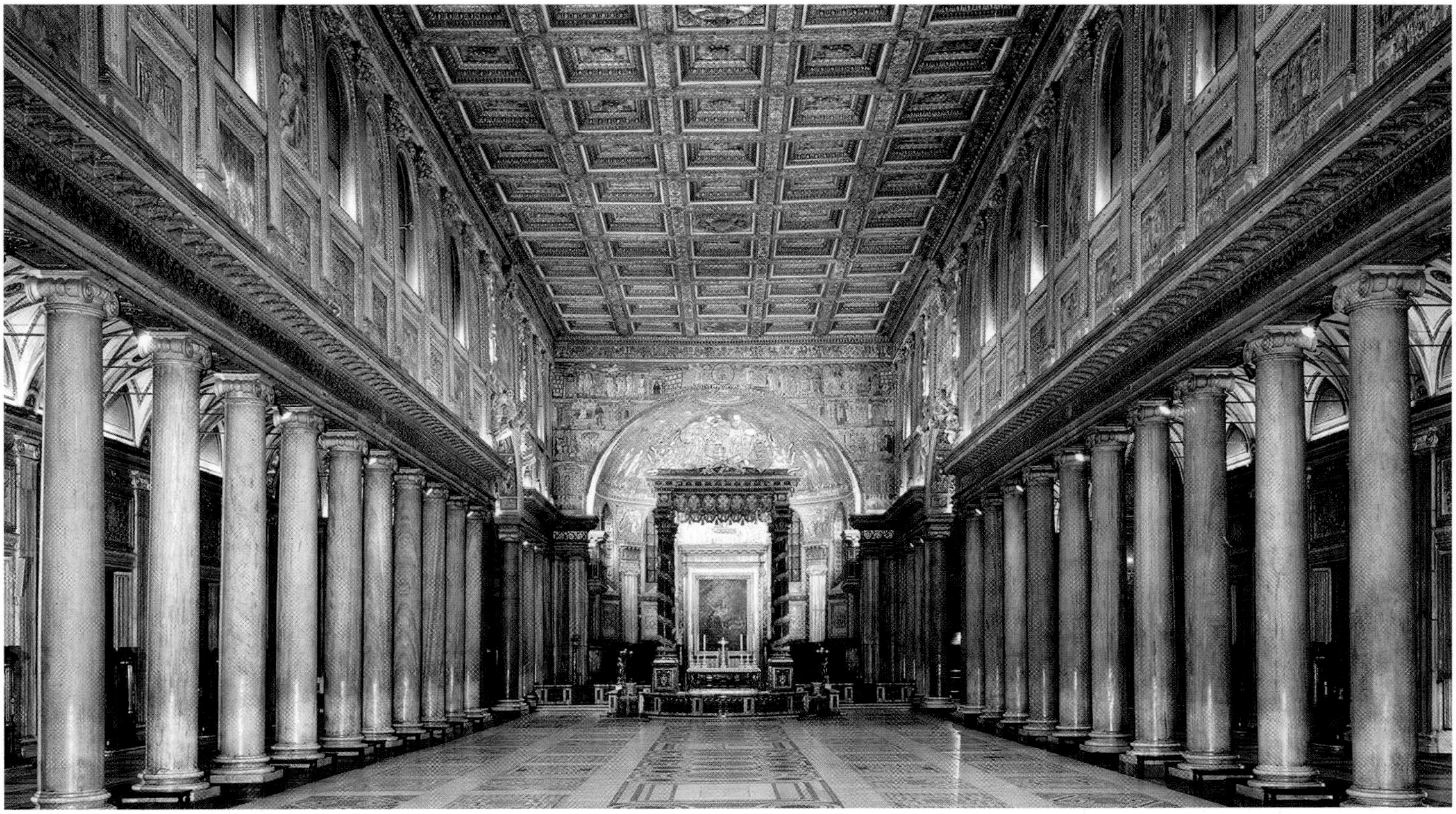

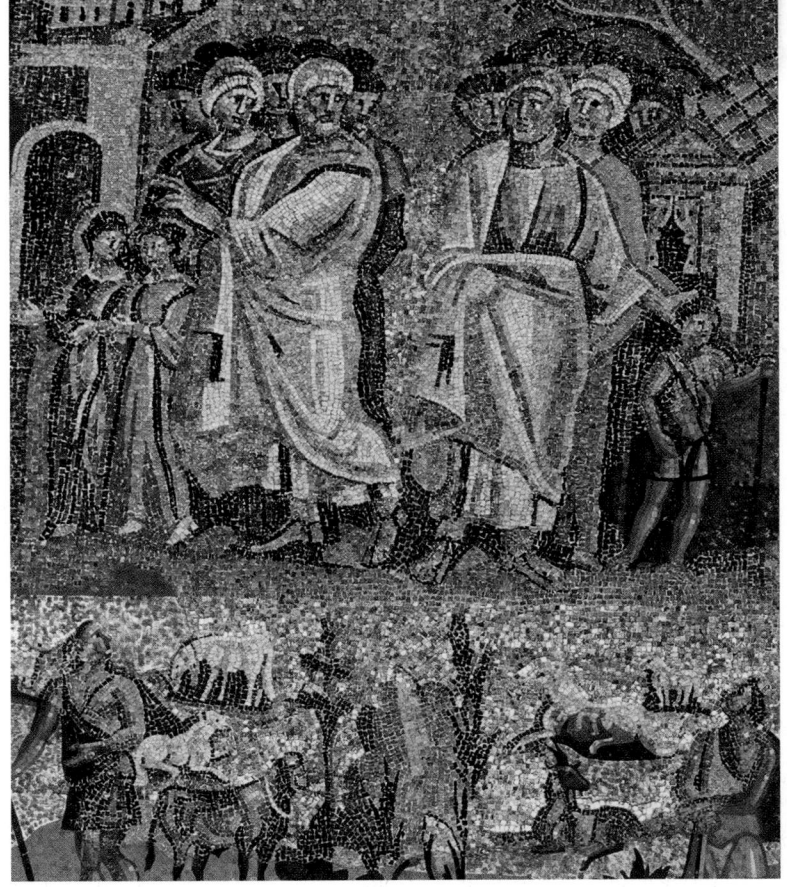

8.16 Interior of Santa Maria Maggiore, Rome, Italy. ca. 432–40 CE

the Messiah on the triumphal arch. For those who read the Bible literally, the scheme is not only a historical cycle but also a symbolic program that presents a higher reality—the Word of God. Hence, the artist was not concerned with the details of historical narrative. Glances and gestures were more important than realistic movement or three-dimensional form. In *The Parting of Lot and Abraham*, the symmetrical composition, with its gap in the center, makes clear the significance of this parting: Abraham represents the way of righteousness, while Sodom, which was destroyed by the Lord, signifies the way of evil. Beneath *The Parting of Lot and Abraham* is a classically inspired but thoroughly transformed landscape, its shepherds placed on a green ground, while their sheep, as if on little islands, float in gold surroundings.

What were the visual sources of the mosaic compositions at Santa Maria Maggiore and other churches like it? These were certainly not the first depictions of scenes from the Bible. For certain subjects, such as the Last Supper, models could have been found among the catacomb murals, but others, such as the story of Joshua, may have come from illustrated manuscripts, to which, since they were portable, art historians have assigned an important role as models.

8.17 *The Parting of Lot and Abraham* and *Shepherds in a Landscape*, Santa Maria Maggiore, Rome, Italy. Mosaic

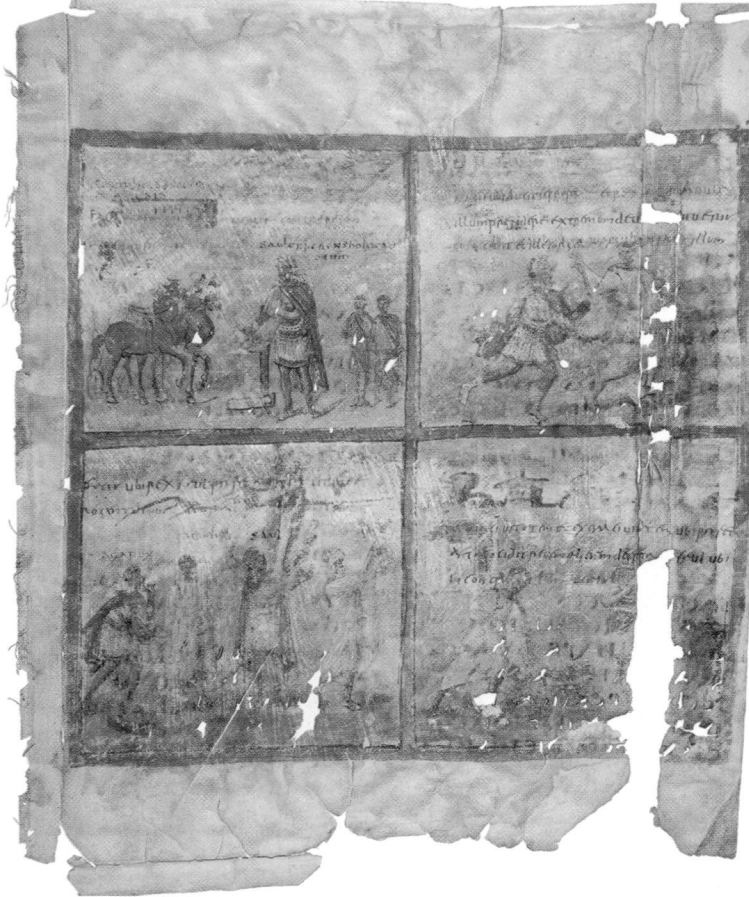

8.18 Scenes from the Book of Kings, from the *Quedlinburg Itala*.
ca. 425–450 CE. Tempera on vellum, 12 × 18" (30.5 × 45.8 cm).
Staatliche Bibliothek, Berlin

ILLUSTRATED BOOKS Because Christianity, like Judaism, was based on the Word of God as revealed in the Bible, early Christians sponsored duplication of sacred texts on a large scale. What did the earliest Bible illustrations look like? Since books are frail things, we have only indirect evidence of their history in the ancient world. This begins in Egypt with scrolls made from the papyrus plant, which is like paper but more brittle (see page 77; fig. 3.41). Papyrus scrolls were produced throughout antiquity. Not until the second century BCE, in late Hellenistic times, did better materials become available. These were parchment (bleached animal hide) and **vellum** (a type of parchment noted for its fineness), both of which last far longer than papyrus. They were strong enough to be creased without breaking and thus made possible the kind of bound book we know today, technically called a codex, which appeared sometime in the late first century CE.

Between the second and the fourth centuries CE, the vellum codex gradually replaced the papyrus roll. This change had an important effect on book illustration. Scroll illustrations seem to have been mostly line drawings, since layers of pigment would soon have cracked and come off during rolling and unrolling. Although parchment and vellum were less fragile than papyrus,

they too were fragile mediums. Nevertheless, the codex permitted the use of rich colors, including gold. Hence it could make book illustration—or, as we usually say, **manuscript illumination**—the small-scale counterpart of murals, mosaics, and panel pictures. Some questions are still unanswered. When, where, and how quickly did book illumination develop? Were most of the subjects biblical, mythological, or historical? How much of a carryover was there from scroll to codex?

One of the earliest surviving books that illustrate the Bible is an early fifth-century fragment, the so-called *Quedlinburg Itala* (fig. **8.18**). The fragment is from an illustrated Book of Kings (one of the 39 books of the Hebrew Bible) that has been calculated to have originally contained some 60 illustrations, each image probably comprising multiple scenes. On the **folio** (manuscript leaf) reproduced here, four scenes depict Saul's meeting with Samuel after the defeat of Amalekites (I Samuel 15:13–33); each scene is framed so as to accentuate the overall unity of the composition. The misty landscape, architectural elements, and sky-blue and pink background recall the antique Roman tradition of atmospheric illusionism of the sort we met in Roman painting (see fig. 7.55).

Visible under the flaking paint in this badly damaged fragment are written instructions to the artist, part of which read, "You make the prophet speaking facing King Saul sacrificing." Apparently the artist was left free to interpret pictorially these written instructions, suggesting the lack of an illustrated model.

Particularly intriguing is the fact that the artist of the Quedlinburg fragment worked together in a Roman **scriptorium**

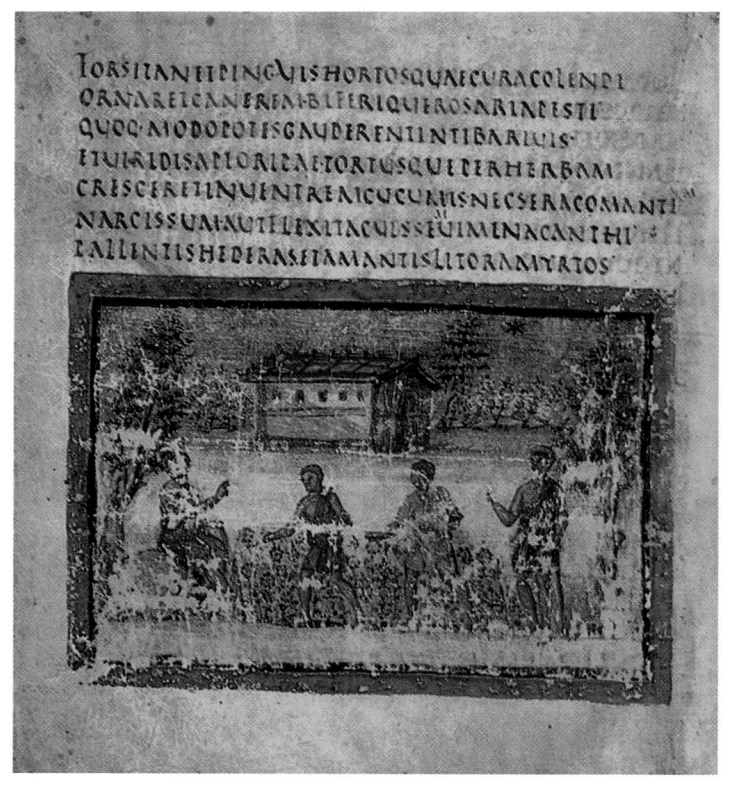

8.19 Miniature from the *Vatican Vergil*. Early 5th century CE.
Tempera on vellum, 8⅝ × 7¼" (21.9 × 19.6 cm).
Biblioteca Apostolica Vaticana, Rome

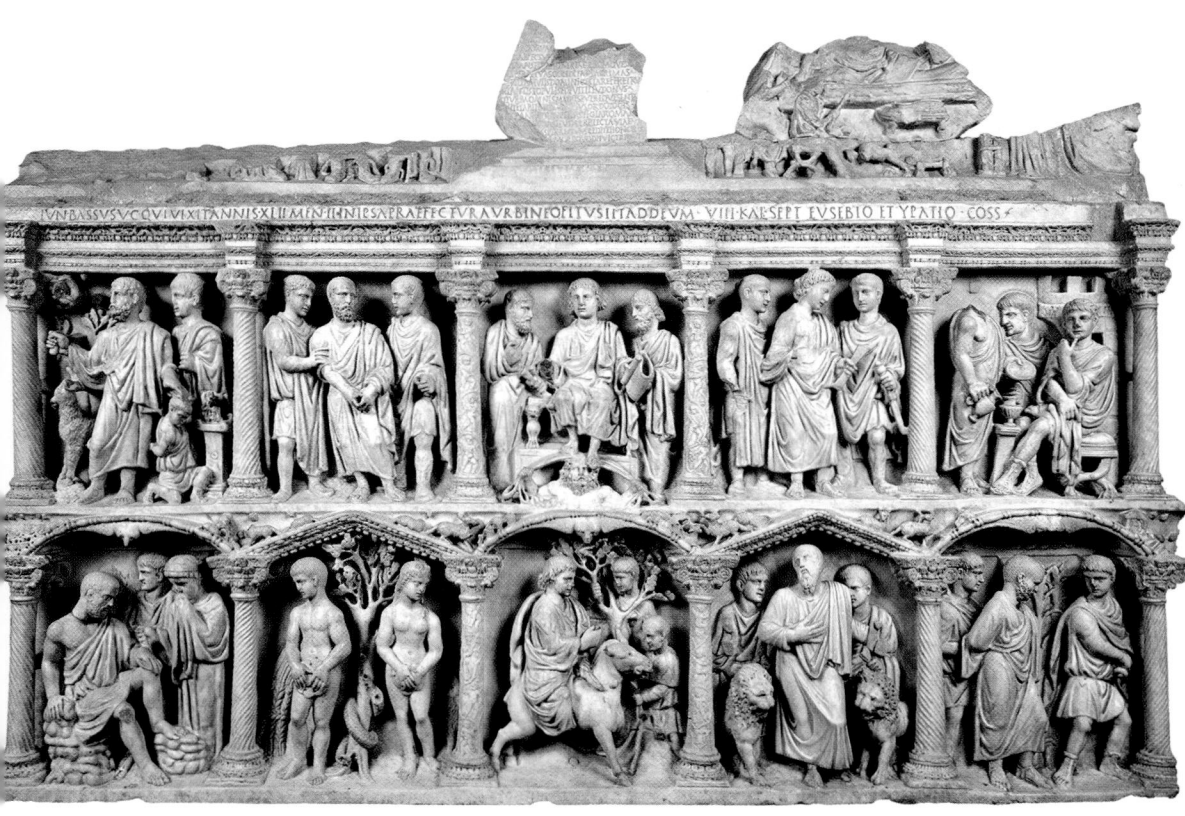

8.20 *Sarcophagus of Junius Bassus*. ca. 359 CE. Marble, 3'10½" × 8' (1.2 × 2.4 m). Museo Storico del Capitolino di San Pietro, Rome

(a workshop for copying and illustrating manuscripts) with an artist who illustrated the first-century BCE Roman pagan poet Vergil's *Aeneid* and *Georgics* in the so-called *Vatican Vergil*, named after the collection in which it is housed today (fig. **8.19**). We might well ask if this is evidence of non-Christian artists working for Christian patrons and to what extent pagan motifs might have been carried over to Christian subjects.

Like the *Quedlinburg Itala*, the *Vatican Vergil* reflects the Roman tradition of illusionism and is closely linked in style to the mosaics of the contemporaneous Santa Maria Maggiore. The picture, separated from the rest of the page by a heavy frame, is like a window, and in the landscape—similar to that in the *Quedlinburg Itala* in being set off by the pink and blue sky—we find the remains of deep space, **perspective**, and the play of light and shade. The illustration is balanced by beautifully executed letters, which hover over the page like a curtain.

Perhaps it is not accidental that the illusionism in both the *Quedlinburg Itala* and the *Vatican Vergil* reminds us so much of the art of Rome during its glory days, nor that so many architectural features of the contemporaneous Santa Maria Maggiore are so classicizing. All of these works were produced in Rome just when that city was under direct threat; the emphasis on Rome's historic splendor might well have proven comforting during difficult times. However, the political reality was far removed from the lofty ambitions of artists and patrons. Rome was sacked by the Visigoths in 410 and, as noted, the capital of the Western Empire was moved farther north, settling first in Milan, then finally in Ravenna.

SCULPTURE As we have seen, the increase in standing of Christianity had a profound effect on artistic production, moving Christian art from a modest and private sphere to a public and official arena. As Early Christian architecture and its decoration began to demonstrate increasing monumentality as a result of its dependence on Roman imperial traditions, so too Early Christian sculpture became more impressive. This is apparent in a fine Early Christian stone coffin, the *Sarcophagus of Junius Bassus* (fig. **8.20**).

The richly carved sarcophagus was made for a prefect of Rome who died in 359 at age 42 and who, an inscription tells us, had been "newly baptized." The front, divided by columns into ten compartments, contains scenes from the Hebrew Bible and the Christian one, also called the New Testament. In the upper register we see (from left to right) the Sacrifice of Isaac, St. Peter Taken Prisoner, Christ Enthroned Between Sts. Peter and Paul, and Jesus before Pontius Pilate (this last scene composed of two compartments). In the lower register are the Suffering of Job, the Temptation of Adam and Eve, Jesus' Entry into Jerusalem, Daniel in the Lions' Den, and St. Paul Led to His Martyrdom.

Clearly the status of Christianity has changed when a major state official proclaims, both in inscription and through representation, his belief in Christianity. The depictions of Peter and Paul, the veritable official saints of the city of Rome—each is commemorated by a major basilica in the city—can be related to Junius Bassus' role as a high-ranking government official. Authoritative as well is Christ's place in the central scenes of each register. In the top register, Christ is enthroned with his feet treading on a personification of Coelus, the Roman pagan god of the heavens, as he dispenses the law to his disciples. Thus, Christ appropriates one of the emperor's formal privileges, as lawgiver, a role that Junius Bassus as prefect would have exercised on the emperor's behalf. Below this compartment, Christ enters Jerusalem in triumph. As compared to the earliest Christian representations, such as the Santa Maria Antiqua sarcophagus, Christ is now depicted directly, not through allusion alone, and his imperial nature is thereby accentuated. Daniel in the Lions' Den, the Sacrifice of Isaac, and Adam and Eve are subjects that appeared in earlier representations in catacombs. Daniel's salvation is a type for Christ, as well as for all Christians who hope for divine salvation; Abraham's willingness to sacrifice his beloved son Isaac parallels God's sacrifice on the Cross of his son, Jesus Christ; the fact that God spares Isaac speaks of salvation by Divine Grace; Adam and Eve refer to the Original Sin that led to Christ's sacrificial death and his resurrection. Thus, old methods of explication are combined with new manifestations of Christianity's important role in society, particularly by stressing Christ's imperial nature.

The style of the sarcophagus also relies on imperial convention. This is most evident in the elements of classicism that are expressed, such as the placement within deep, space-filled niches of figures that recall the dignity of Greek and Roman sculpture. Other classicizing features include the way that the figures seem capable of distributing weight, the draperies that reveal the bodies beneath them, and the narrative clarity. However, beneath this veneer of classicism we recognize doll-like bodies with large heads and a passive air in scenes that would otherwise seem to call for dramatic action. It is as if the events and figures are no longer intended to tell their own story but to call to mind a larger symbolic meaning that unites them.

The reliance on classicizing forms on the *Sarcophagus of Junius Bassus* reminds us that Early Christian art appears throughout the Mediterranean basin in what we think of as the classical world. During the first five centuries after Jesus' death, the art of the entire area was more or less unified in content and style. Increasing political and religious divisions in the region, however, began to affect artistic production so that it is appropriate to recognize the appearance, or, perhaps better stated, the growth of another branch of Christian art that we label Byzantine.

BYZANTINE ART

Early Byzantine Art

There is no clear-cut geographical or chronological line between Early Christian and Byzantine art. West Roman and East Roman—or, as some scholars prefer to call them, Western and Eastern Christian—traits are difficult to separate before the sixth century. Until that time, both geographical areas contributed to the development of Early Christian art. As the Western Empire declined, however, cultural leadership tended to shift to the Eastern Empire. This process was completed during the reign of Justinian, who ruled the Eastern Empire from 527 to 565. Under the patronage of Justinian, Constantinople became the artistic as

well as the political capital of the Empire. Justinian himself was a man of strongly Latin orientation, and he almost succeeded in reuniting Constantine's domain. The monuments he sponsored have a grandeur that justifies the claim that his era was a Golden Age, as some have labeled it.

The political and religious differences between East and West became an artistic division as well. In Western Europe, Celtic and Germanic peoples inherited the civilization of Late Antiquity, of which Early Christian art had been a part, but they then transformed it radically. The East, in contrast, experienced no such break. Late Antiquity lived on in the Byzantine Empire, although Greek and other eastern Mediterranean elements came increasingly to the fore at the expense of the Roman heritage. Even so, a sense of tradition played a central role in the development of Byzantine art.

ARCHITECTURE AND ITS DECORATION Ironically, the greatest number of Early Byzantine monuments survives today not in Constantinople, where much has been destroyed, but on Italian soil, in Ravenna. That town, as we have seen, had become the capital of the West Roman emperors at the beginning of the fifth century. At the end of the century it was taken by Theodoric, king of the Ostrogoths, whose tastes were patterned after those of Constantinople, where he had lived for an extended period. The Ostrogothic rule of Ravenna ended in 540, when the Byzantine general Belisarius conquered the city for Justinian. Ravenna then became an exarchate, or provincial capital, the main stronghold of Byzantine rule in Italy. Thus, Ravenna serves as a kind of microcosm of the transformation and divisions of the later Roman Empire.

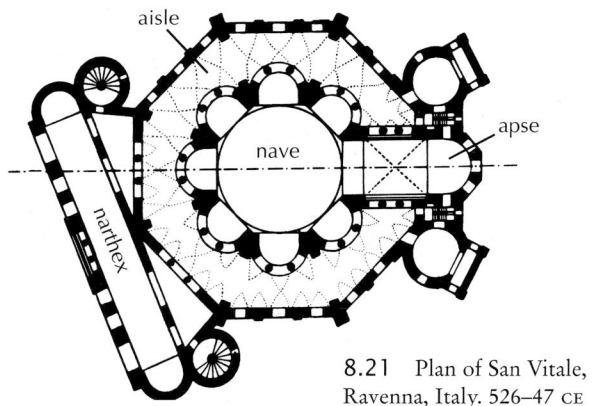

8.21   Plan of San Vitale, Ravenna, Italy. 526–47 CE

8.22   Section of San Vitale, Ravenna, Italy

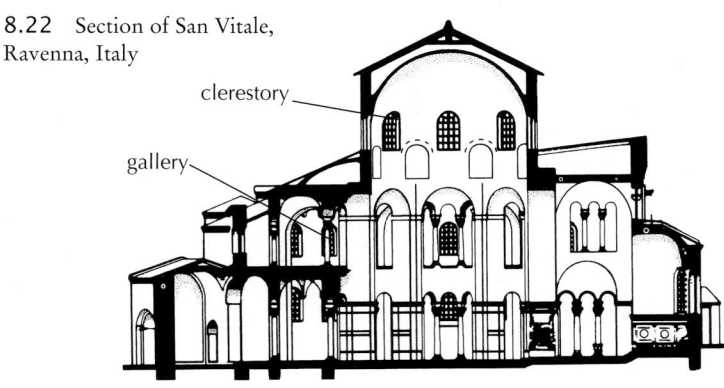

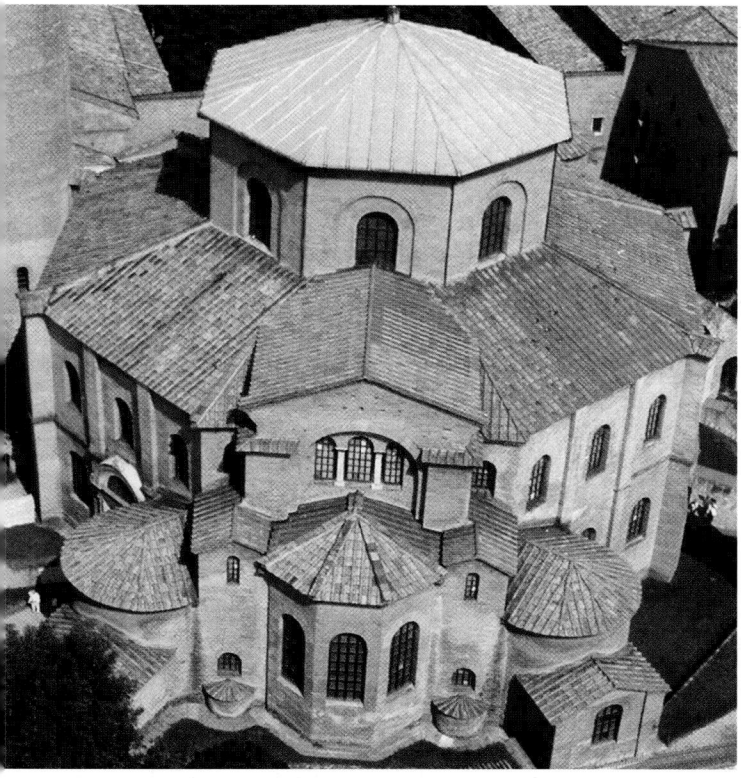

8.23 Exterior of San Vitale, Ravenna, Italy

The most important building of the Early Byzantine period, begun in 526 under Ostrogothic rule, was the church of San Vitale. Built chiefly during the 540s and completed in 547, it represents a Byzantine building of a type derived mainly from Constantinople. The octagonal plan with a circular core ringed by an ambulatory (figs. **8.21**, **8.22** and **8.23**) is a descendant of the mausoleum of Santa Costanza in Rome (see fig. 8.10), but other aspects of the building show the influence of the Eastern Empire, where domed churches of various kinds had been built during the previous century. Compared to Santa Costanza, San Vitale is both larger in scale and significantly richer in spatial effect (fig. **8.24**). In particular, below the clerestory, the nave wall turns into a series of semicircular niches that penetrate the ambulatory and link that surrounding aisle to the nave in a new and intricate way. The movement around the center space is thus enlivened so that the decorated surfaces seem to pulsate. The aisle itself has a second story, the galleries, which may have been reserved for women. This reflects a practice in a number of Eastern religions, including some forms of Judaism, where it is current even today. Large windows on every level are made possible by a new economy in the construction of the vaulting—hollow clay tubes allowing for a lighter structure—and the interior is flooded with light.

The plan of San Vitale shows only remnants of the longitudinal axis of the Early Christian basilica: toward the east, a

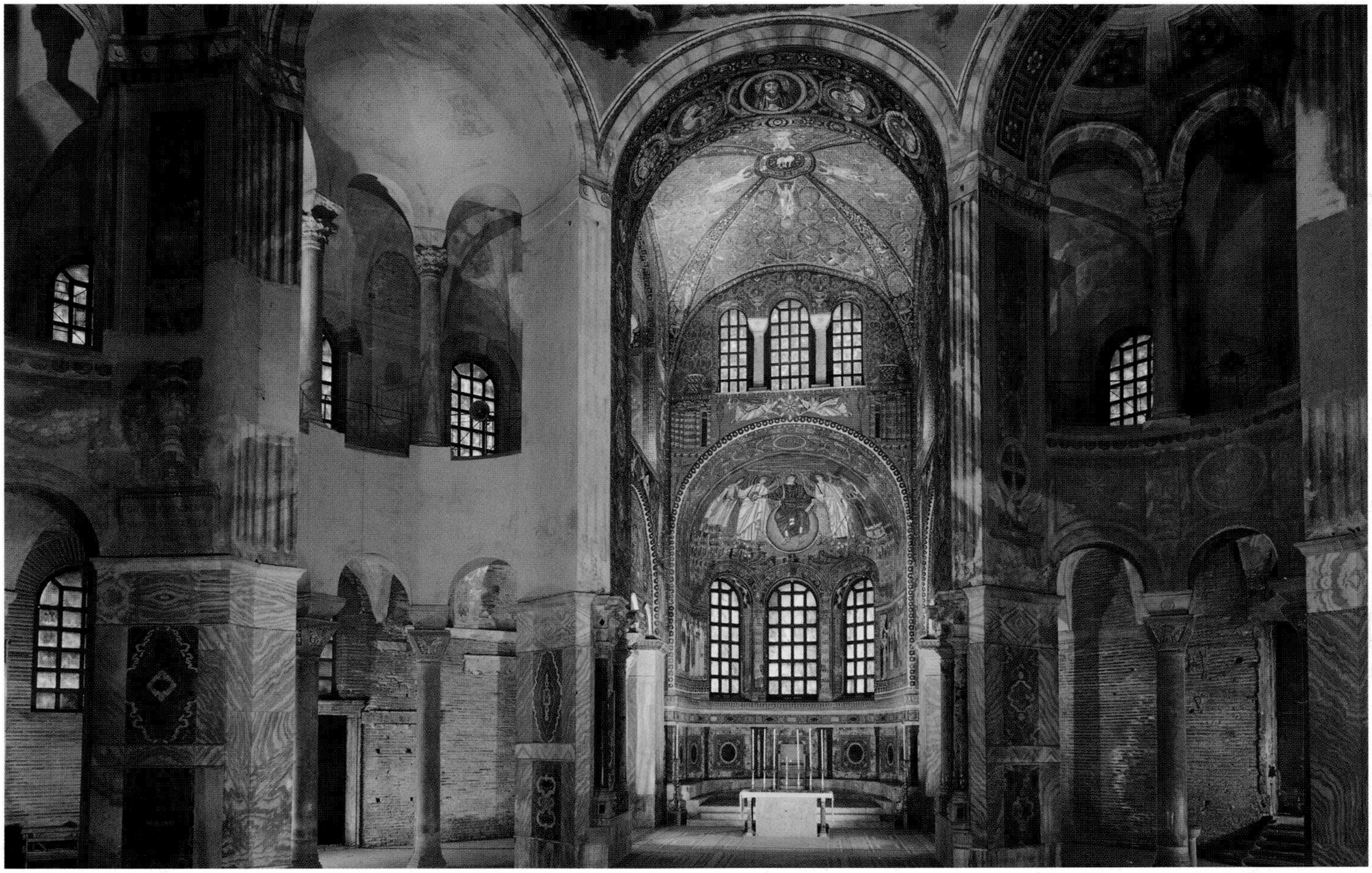

8.24 Interior (view toward the apse) of San Vitale, Ravenna, Italy

cross-vaulted compartment for the altar, backed by an apse; and on the other side, a narthex. How did it happen that the East favored a type of church building (as distinct from mausoleums) so different from the basilica and—from the Western point of view—so ill-adapted to Christian ritual? After all, had not the design of the basilica been backed by the authority of Constantine himself? Scholars have suggested a number of reasons, practical, religious, and political, including the particular needs of the Eastern liturgy that would have been practiced in Ravenna. All of them may be relevant. In any event, from the time of Justinian, domed, central-plan churches dominated the world of Orthodox Christianity as thoroughly as the basilican plan dominated the architecture of the medieval West.

At San Vitale the odd, nonsymmetrical placement of the narthex, which has never been fully explained, might be a key to helping us understand how the building functioned. Some have

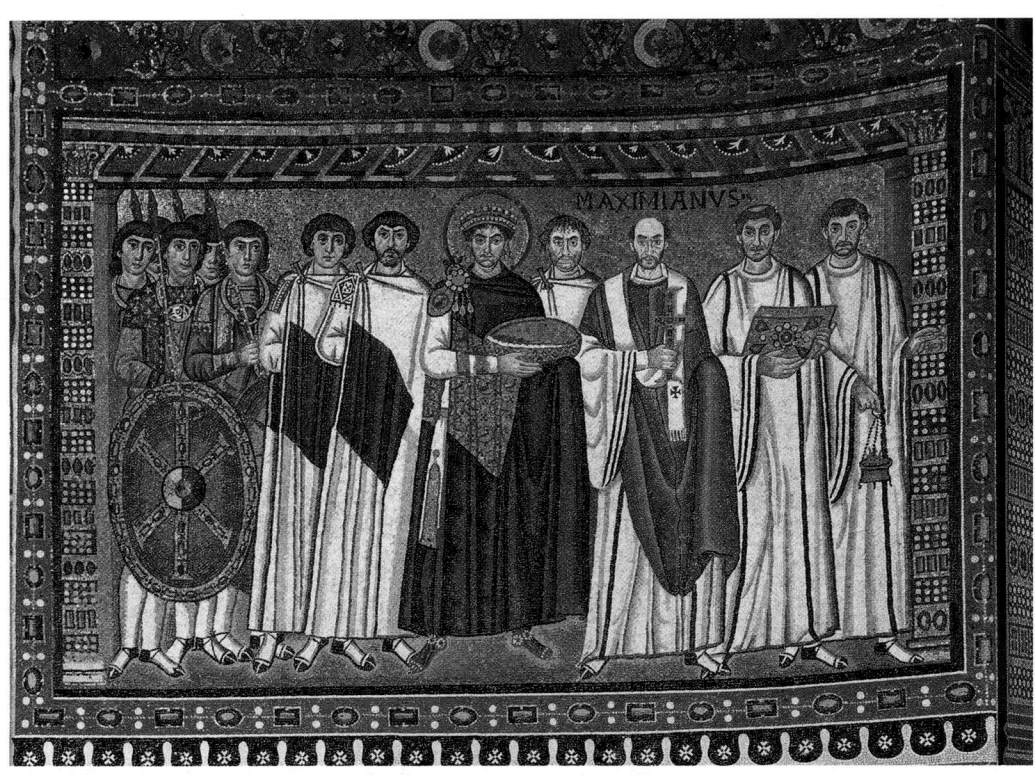

8.25 *Emperor Justinian and His Attendants*, San Vitale, Ravenna, Italy. ca. 547 CE. Mosaic

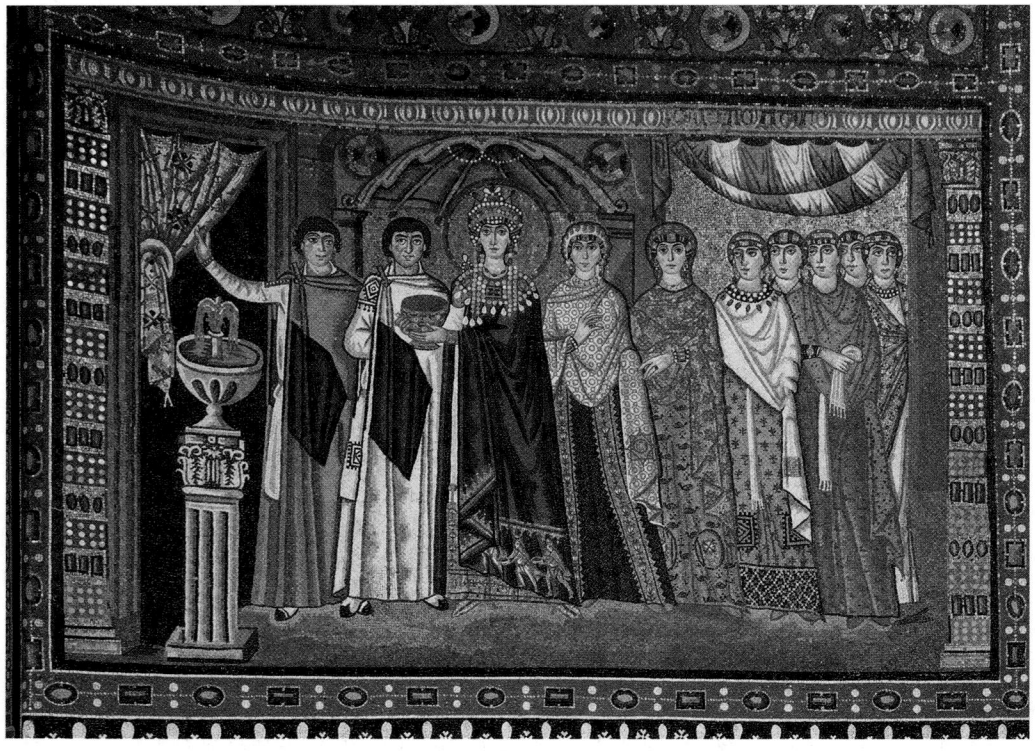

8.26 *Empress Theodora and Her Attendants*, San Vitale, Ravenna, Italy. ca. 547 CE. Mosaic

suggested that the narthex is turned to be parallel to an atrium, the axis of which was determined by site limitations. Others see it as a conscious design feature that accentuates the transition between the exterior and interior of the church. Whatever the reason, in order to enter the building, visitors were forced to change axis, shifting to the right or left in order to align themselves with the main apse. The alteration of the journey into the building is unsettling, almost disorienting, an effect heightened by passing from the lighted area of the narthex to the shaded ambulatory, and then into the high and luminous domed center space. The passage from physical to spiritual realms so essential to worship is manifest as a separation between the external world and the internal space of the building.

The complexity of the architecture of the interior is matched by its lavish decoration. San Vitale's link with the Byzantine court can be seen in two prominent mosaics flanking the altar (figs. **8.25** and **8.26**). They depict Justinian and his empress, Theodora, accompanied by officials, the local clergy, and ladies-in-waiting,

about to enter the church, as if it were a palace chapel. In these large panels, the design of which most likely came from an imperial workshop, we find an ideal of beauty that is very different from the squat, large-headed figures we met in the art of the fourth and fifth centuries. These figures are tall and slim, with tiny feet and small almond-shaped faces dominated by huge eyes. They seem capable only of making ceremonial gestures and displaying magnificent costumes. There is no hint of movement or change. The dimensions of time and earthly space, suggested by a green ground, give way to an eternal present in the form of a golden otherworldly setting. Hence, the solemn, frontal images seem to belong as much to a celestial court as to a secular one. The quality of soaring slenderness that endows the figures with an air of mute exaltation is shared by the mysterious interior space of San Vitale, which these figures inhabit.

The union of political and spiritual authority expressed in these mosaics reflects the "divine kingship" of the Byzantine emperor and honors the royal couple as donors of the church. It is as though the mosaic figures are in fact participating in the liturgy, even though the empress and emperor are actually thousands of miles away. The embroidery on the hem of Theodora's mantle shows the three Magi carrying their gifts to Mary and the newborn King, and like them the imperial couple bring offerings. Justinian brings bread and Theodora a chalice, undoubtedly references to the Eucharist and Jesus' sacrifice of his own flesh and blood to redeem humanity. The emperor is flanked by 12 companions, the imperial equivalent of the 12 apostles. Moreover, Justinian is portrayed in a manner that recalls Constantine, that first Christian emperor: The shield with Christ's monogram equates Justinian's conquest of Ravenna with the divinely inspired Constantinian triumph at the Milvian Bridge that ultimately led to the founding of Constantinople, the court to which Justinian was heir.

Among the surviving monuments of Justinian's reign in Constantinople, the most important by far is Hagia Sophia (Church of Holy Wisdom) (figs. **8.27** and **8.28**). The first church on that site was commissioned by Constantine but was destroyed

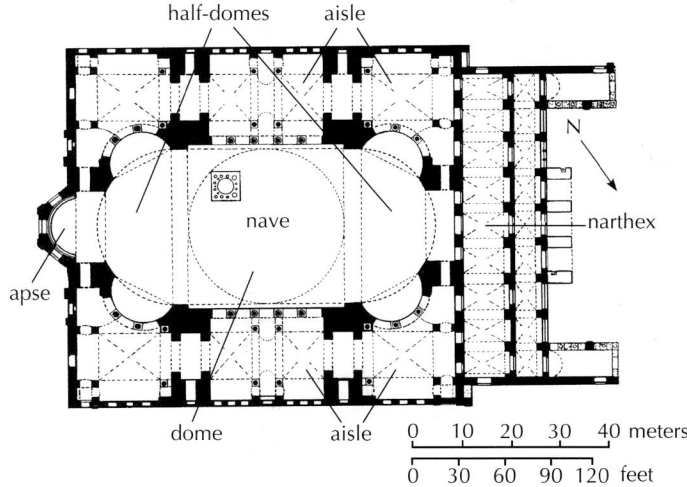

8.27 Plan of Anthemius of Tralles and Isidorus of Miletus. Hagia Sophia, Istanbul, Turkey. 532–37 CE (after V. Sybel)

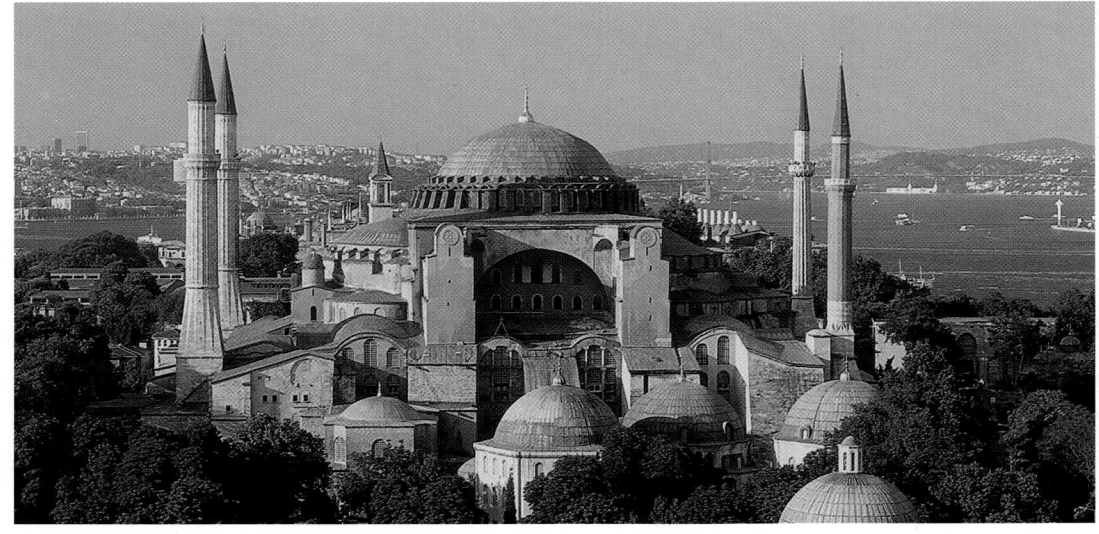

8.28 Exterior of Hagia Sophia, Istanbul, Turkey

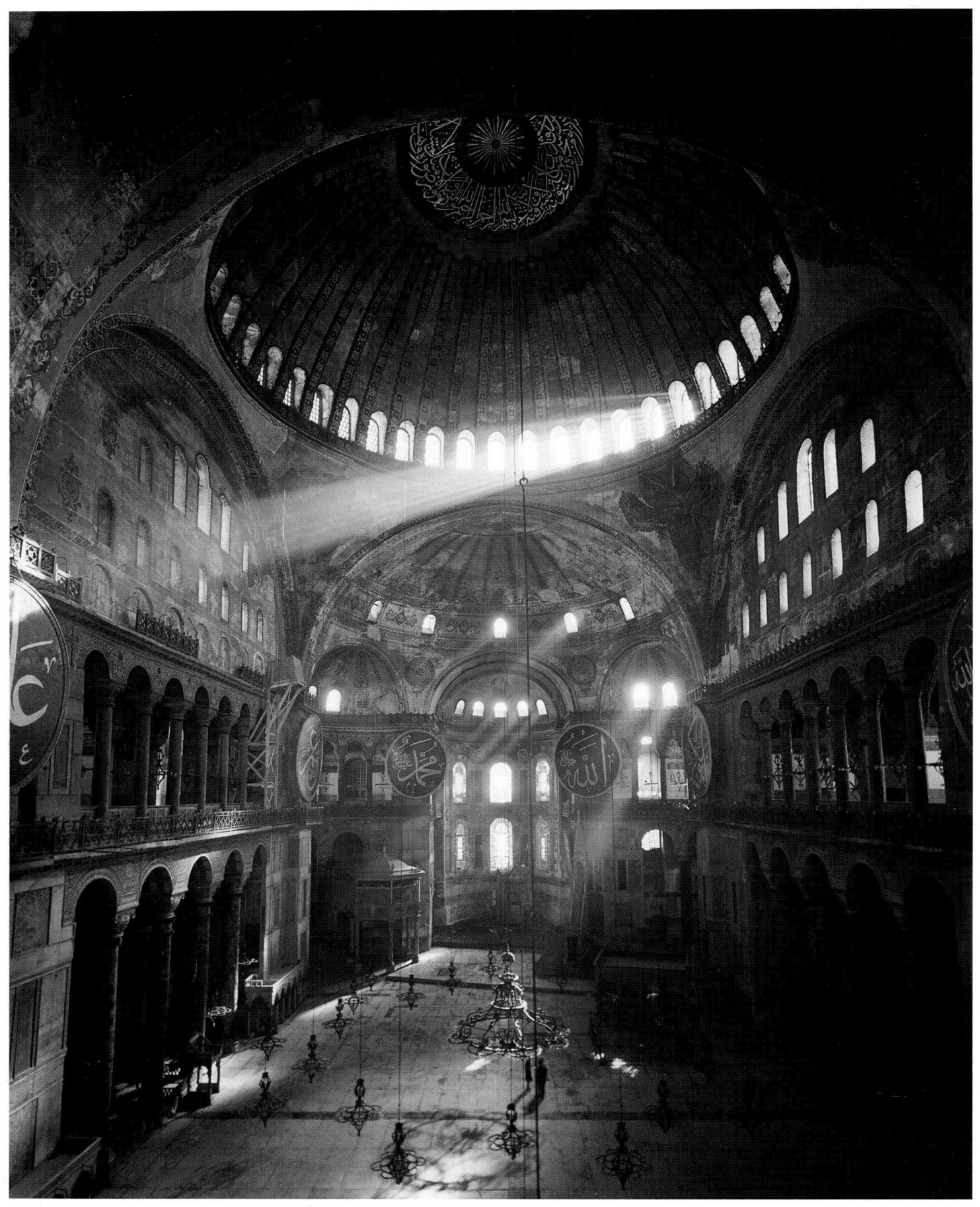

8.29   Interior of Hagia Sophia, Istanbul, Turkey

in 532 during rioting that almost deposed Justinian, who immediately rebuilt the church, a sign of the continuity of his imperial authority. Completed in only five years, Hagia Sophia achieved such fame that the names of the architects, too, were remembered: Anthemius of Tralles, an expert in geometry and the theory of statics and kinetics; and Isidorus of Miletus, who taught physics and wrote on vaulting techniques. The dome collapsed in the earthquake of 558, and a new, taller one was built from a design by Isidorus' nephew. After the Turkish conquest in 1453, the church became a **mosque**. The Turks added four **minarets** and extra buttresses to the exterior at that time (see fig. 8.28), as well as large medallions with Islamic invocations on the interior (fig. **8.29**). In the twentieth century, after the building was turned into a museum, some of the mosaic decoration that had been largely hidden under whitewash was uncovered.

Hagia Sophia has the longitudinal axis of an Early Christian basilica, but the central feature of the nave is a vast, squarish space crowned by a huge dome (see fig. 8.27). At either end are half-domes, so that the nave takes the form of a great ellipse. Attached to the half-domes are semicircular apses with open **arcades** (a series of arches) similar to those in San Vitale. One might say, then, that the dome of Hagia Sophia has been placed over a central space and, at the same time, inserted between the two halves of a divided central-plan church. The dome rests on four arches that carry its weight to the **piers**, large, upright architectural supports, at the corners of the square. Thus, the brilliant gold-mosaic walls below these arches, pierced with windows, have no weight-bearing function at all and act as mere curtains. The transition from the square formed by the arches to the circular rim of the dome is achieved by spherical triangles called **pendentives** (fig. **8.30**). Hence, we speak of the entire unit as a dome on pendentives. This device, along with a new technique for building domes using thin bricks embedded in mortar, permits the construction of taller, lighter, and more economical domes than the older method of placing the dome on a round or polygonal base as, for example, in the Pantheon in Rome (see fig. 7.24).

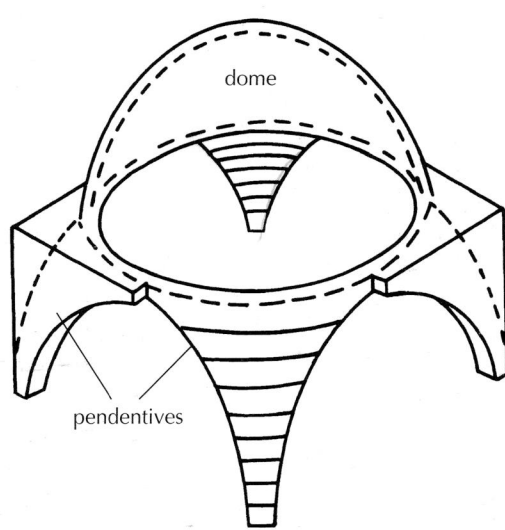

8.30 Dome on pendentives

Where or when the dome on pendentives was invented we do not know. Hagia Sophia is the earliest example we have of its use on a monumental scale, and it had a lasting impact. It became a basic feature of Byzantine architecture and, later, of Western architecture as well. Given the audacity of Hagia Sophia's design, it is not surprising that its architects were not described as builders, but rather as theoretical scientists, renowned for their knowledge of mathematics and physics. Its massive exterior, firmly planted upon the earth like a great mound, rises by stages to a height of 184 feet—41 feet taller than the Pantheon—and therefore its dome, though its diameter is somewhat smaller (112 feet), stands out far more boldly in its urban setting.

Once we are inside Hagia Sophia (see fig. 8.29), all sense of weight disappears. Nothing remains but a space that inflates, like so many sails, the apses, the pendentives, and the dome itself. The first dome, the one that fell in 558, was less steep than the present one, and one imagines that the sense of swelling form and heaving surface would originally have been even more intense than it is today. Here, the architectural aesthetic we saw taking shape in Early Christian architecture has achieved a new, magnificent dimension. Even more than before, light plays a key role. The dome seems to float—"like the radiant heavens," according to a contemporary description—because it rests upon a closely spaced row of windows; light, both real and reflected, virtually separates the dome from the arches on which it rests. So many openings pierce the nave walls that the effect is akin to the transparency of lace curtains. The golden glitter of the mosaics must have completed the "illusion of unreality." Its purpose is clear. As Procopius, the court historian to Justinian, wrote: "Whenever one enters this church to pray, he understands at once that it is not by any human power or skill, but by the influence of God, that this work has been so finely turned. And so his mind is lifted up toward God and exalted, feeling that He cannot be far away, but must especially love to dwell in this place that He has chosen." (See *Primary Source*, page 260.) We can sense the new aesthetic even in ornamental details such as moldings and capitals (fig. **8.31**). The scrolls, acanthus leaves, and similar decorations are motifs derived from classical architecture, but their effect here is radically different. The heavily patterned butterfly-marble facing of the piers denies their substantiality, and instead of actively cushioning the impact of heavy weight on the shaft of the column, the capital has become like an openwork basket of starched lace, the delicate surface pattern of which belies the strength and solidity of the stone. The contrast between the decoration of these structural members and their weight-bearing function accentuates the viewer's disorientation, an effect that would only have been increased if the interior of the building were viewed from aisle or gallery. In fact, it is from there that most congregants would have experienced the building during religious services, with no opportunity to take in or understand the entire structure.

The guiding principle of Graeco-Roman architecture had been to express a balance of opposing forces, rather like the balance within the contrapposto of a Classical statue. The result was a muscular display of active and passive members. In comparison,

Procopius of Caesarea (Sixth Century)

From Buildings

Procopius was a historian during the reign of Emperor Justinian. He wrote an entire book (ca. 550 CE) about the fortifications, aqueducts, churches, and other public buildings constructed by Justinian throughout the Byzantine Empire. The book begins with the greatest of these, Hagia Sophia (see figs. 8.27–8.31).

The emperor, disregarding all considerations of expense, raised craftsmen from the whole world. It was Anthemius of Tralles, the most learned man in the discipline called engineering, that ministered to the emperor's zeal by regulating the work of the builders and preparing in advance designs of what was going to be built. He had as partner another engineer called Isidore, a native of Miletus.

So the church has been made a spectacle of great beauty, stupendous to those who see it and altogether incredible to those who hear of it. It subtly combines its mass with the harmony of its proportions, having neither any excess nor any deficiency, inasmuch as it is more pompous than ordinary [buildings] and considerably more decorous than those which are huge beyond measure; and it abounds exceedingly in gleaming sunlight. You might say that the [interior] space is not illuminated by the sun from the outside, but that the radiance is generated within, so great an abundance of light bathes this shrine all round....Above the arches the construction rises in a circle. Rising above this circle is an enormous spherical dome which makes the building exceptionally beautiful. It seems not to be founded on solid masonry, but to be suspended from heaven by that golden chain and so covers the space. All of these elements, marvelously fitted together in mid-air, suspended from one another and reposing only on the parts adjacent to them, produce a unified and most remarkable harmony in the work, and yet do not allow the spectators to rest their gaze upon any one of them for a length of time, but each detail readily draws and attracts the eye to itself. Thus the vision constantly shifts round, and the beholders are quite unable to select any particular element which they might admire more than all the others. No matter how much they concentrate their attention on this side and that, and examine everything with contracted eyebrows, they are unable to understand the craftsmanship and always depart from there amazed by the perplexing spectacle.

Source: Cyril Mango, *The Art of the Byzantine Empire, 312-1453: Sources and Documents* (Upper Saddle River, NJ: Prentice Hall, 1st ed., 1972)

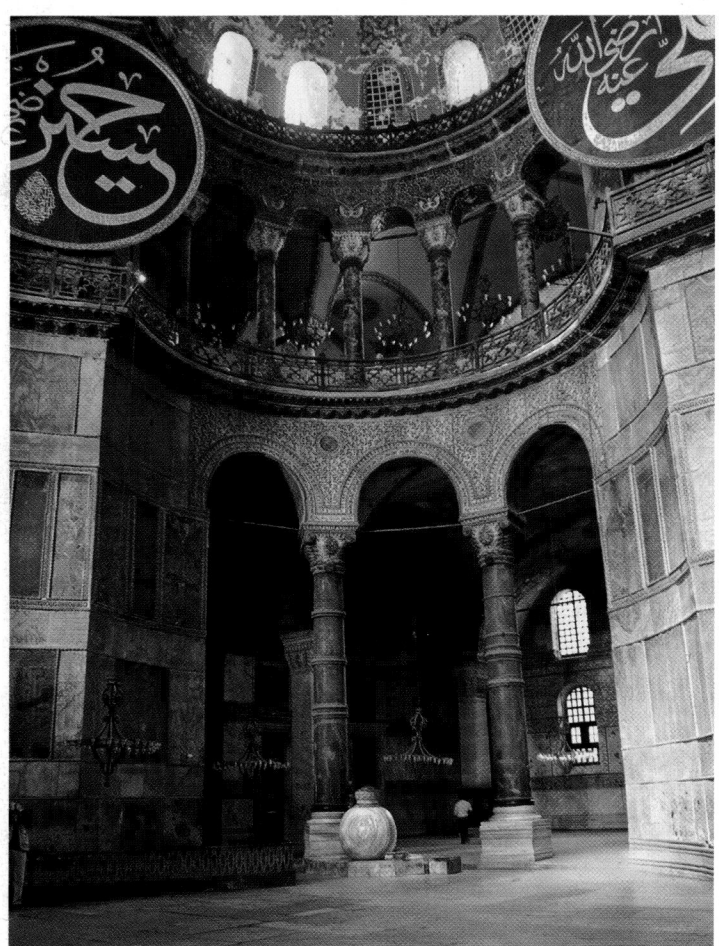

8.31　Arcade and capitals, Hagia Sophia, Istanbul, Turkey

the material structure of Byzantine architecture, and to some extent of Early Christian architecture as well, is subservient to the creation of immaterial space. Walls and vaults seem like weightless shells, their actual thickness and solidity hidden rather than emphasized. And the glitter of the mosaics must have completed the illusion of unreality, fitting the spirit of these interiors to perfection.

SCULPTURE Beyond architectural decorations and some sarcophagi, Early Byzantine sculpture consists mainly of reliefs in ivory and silver, which survive in considerable numbers. Vestiges of classicism are apparent in the beautifully carved ivory diptych of *Justinian as Conqueror*, which celebrates the emperor's victories in Italy, North Africa, and Asia (fig. **8.32**). The subject restates in Christian terms the allegorical scene on the breastplate of the *Augustus of Primaporta* (see fig. 7.29). The figure of Victory appears twice: above the emperor, to his right, and as a statuette held by the Roman officer at the left, who was no doubt mirrored in the missing panel at the right. Scythians, Indians, even lions and elephants, representing the lands conquered by Justinian, offer gifts and pay homage, while a figure personifying the Earth supports Justinian's foot to signify the emperor's dominion over the entire world. His role as triumphant general and ruler of the Empire is blessed from Heaven (note the sun, moon, and star) by Christ, whose image is in a medallion carried by two heraldically arranged angels. The large head and bulging features of Justinian brim with the same energy as his charging steed. He is a far cry from the calm philosopher portrayed on the *Equestrian Statue of Marcus Aurelius* (see fig. 7.33) from which the image is derived.

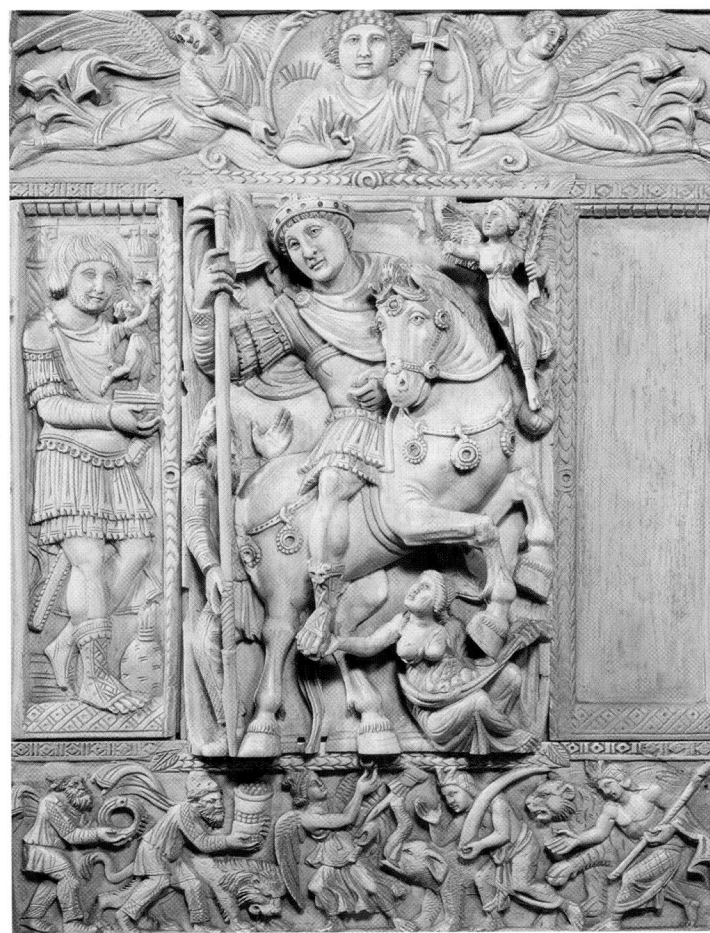

8.32 *Justinian as Conqueror*. ca. 525–50 CE. Ivory,
13½ × 10½" (34.2 × 26.8 cm). Musée du Louvre, Paris

An ivory relief showing the archangel Michael (fig. **8.33**), also from the time of Justinian, looks back to earlier classical ivories. It may have been paired with a missing panel showing Justinian, who, it has been suggested, commissioned it. The inscription above has the prayer "Receive these gifts, and having learned the cause…," which would probably have continued on the missing leaf with a plea to forgive the owner's sins, apparently a reference to the emperor's humility. In any event, this ivory must have been done around 520–30 by an imperial workshop in Constantinople.

The majestic archangel is a descendant of the winged Victories of Graeco-Roman art, down to the rich drapery revealing lithe limbs (see fig. 5.47), and recalls the Victories on the plaque of *Justinian as Conqueror* (see fig. 8.32). Here, classicism has become an eloquent vehicle for Christian content. The power the angel heralds is not of this world, nor does he inhabit an earthly space. The niche he occupies has lost all three-dimensional reality. The angel's relationship to its architectural setting is purely symbolic and ornamental, so that, given the position of the feet on the steps, he seems to hover rather than stand. From the ankles down he seems to be situated between the columns, while his arms and wings are in front of them. It is this disembodied quality, conveyed through harmonious forms, that makes the archangel Michael's presence so compelling. The paradox of a believable

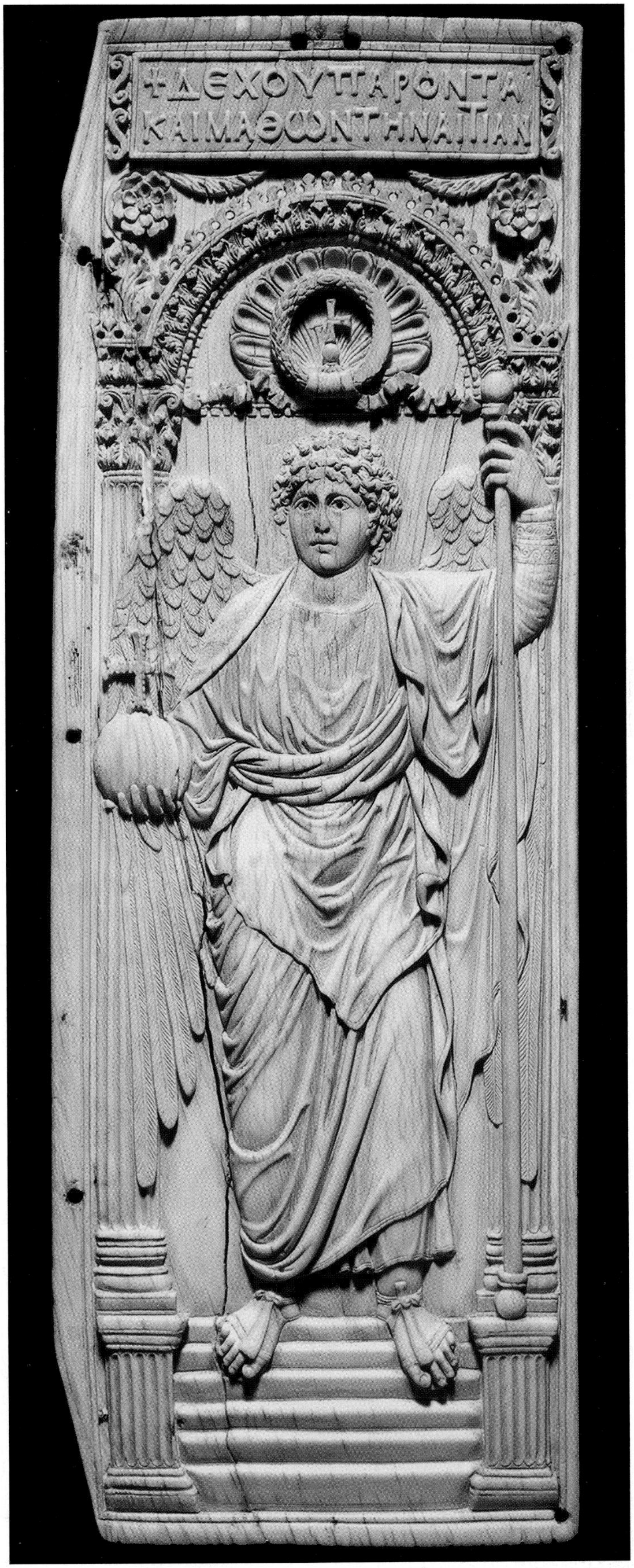

8.33 *The Archangel Michael*. Leaf of a diptych. Early 6th century CE.
Ivory, 17 × 5½" (43.3 × 14 cm). The British Museum, London

figure represented naturalistically but existing within an ambiguous, indeed impossible, setting connects this work with other products of Justinian's court, such as those buildings where solid structures serve to create ephemeral spaces.

ILLUSTRATED BOOKS Illustrated books of the Early Byzantine period also contain echoes of Graeco-Roman style adapted to religious narrative. The most important example, the *Vienna Genesis* (fig. **8.34**), containing a Greek text of the first book of the Bible, has a richness similar to the mosaics we have seen. White highlights and fluttering drapery that clings to the bodies animate the scene. The book was written in silver (now tarnished black) and decorated with brilliantly colored miniatures on dyed-purple vellum, that color being reserved for the imperial court. Although some scholars have suggested that an imperial scriptorium in Constantinople produced the manuscript, recent research points to Syria as the more likely source because there are parallels to manuscripts produced there, as well as some Syrian mosaics.

Our page shows a number of scenes from the story of Jacob. In the center foreground, Jacob wrestles with the angel and then receives his blessing. Hence, the picture does not show just a single event but a whole sequence. The scenes take place along a U-shaped path, so that progression in space becomes progression in time. This method, known as **continuous narration**, goes back as far as ancient Egypt and Mesopotamia. Its appearance in

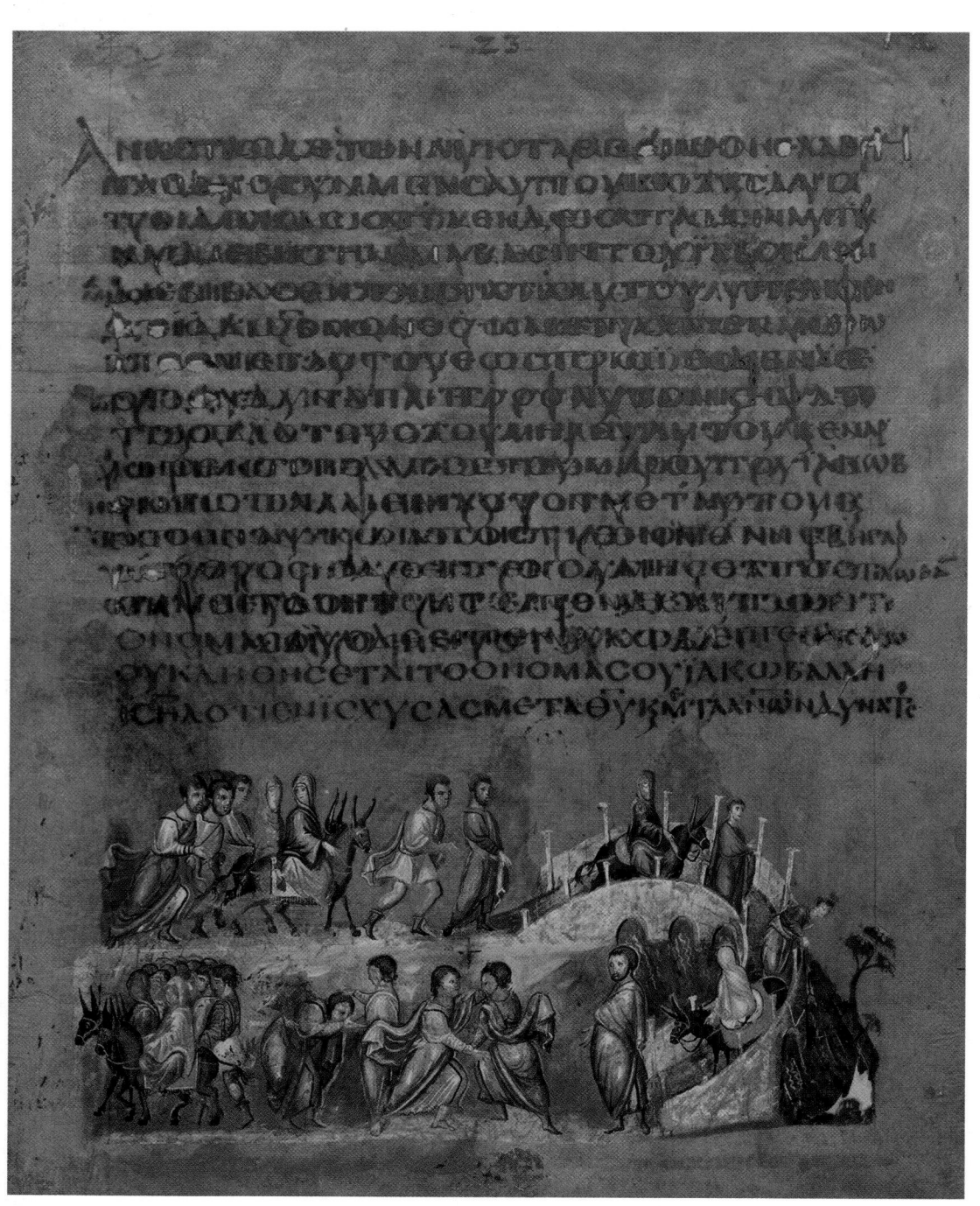

8.34 *Jacob Wrestling the Angel*, from the *Vienna Genesis*. Early 6th century CE. Tempera and silver on dyed vellum, 13¼ × 9½" (33.6 × 24.1 cm). Österreichische Nationalbibliothek, Vienna

miniatures such as this may reflect earlier illustrations made in scroll rather than book form, although this hypothesis has been contested. The picture certainly looks like a frieze turned back upon itself. For manuscript illustration, continuous narrative makes the most economical use of space. The painter can pack a maximum number of scenes into a small area, and the picture can be read like lines of text as a running account, rather than as a window that requires a frame.

ICONS The religious **icon** (from the Greek word *eikon*, meaning "image") provided another focus for representation at the time of Justinian. Icons generally took Christ, the Enthroned Madonna, or saints as their principal subjects, and were objects of personal as well as public veneration. From the beginning they were considered portraits, for such pictures had developed in Early Christian times out of Graeco-Roman portrait panels. The issue that they might be considered idols led to arguments about their appropriateness and their power. (See *Primary Source*, page 266.) These discussions related to the contemporaneous debates on the dual nature of Christ as God and man, at once both spiritual and physical—debates that Byzantine emperors had no qualms about joining. One of the chief arguments in favor of image production was the claim that Christ had appeared with the Virgin to St. Luke and permitted him to paint their portrait together, and that other portraits of Christ or of the Virgin had miraculously appeared on earth by divine command. These "true" sacred images were considered to have been the sources for the later ones made by human artists, permitting a chain of copies and copies of copies, which has often made it difficult for art historians to date them.

Icons functioned as living images to instruct and inspire the worshiper. (See www.myartslab.com.) Because the actual figure— be it Christ, Mary, a saint, or an angel—was thought to reside in the image, icons were believed to be able to intercede on behalf of the faithful. They were reputed to have miraculous healing properties, and some were carried into battle or placed over city gates, effectively offering totemic protection to their communities. Describing an icon of the archangel Michael, the sixth-century poet Agathias writes: "The wax remarkably has represented the invisible....The viewer can directly venerate the archangel [and] trembles as if in his actual presence. The eyes encourage deep thoughts; through art and its colors the innermost prayer of the viewer is passed to the image."

Little is known about the origins of icons, since most early examples were intentionally destroyed by those who believed they led to idolatry; hence icons are scarce. The irony of this is particularly poignant, since early icons were painted in encaustic, the medium in which pigment is suspended in hot wax, chosen for its durability.

Many of the surviving early examples come from the Monastery of St. Catherine at Mount Sinai in Egypt. Monasteries, such as that at Mount Sinai, were heirs to a tradition that had developed in Egypt in the second and third centuries, whereby people withdrew from society and its material temptations to devote themselves to prayer and contemplation. Although many of these early ascetics lived alone as hermits, increasingly they gathered together to live in monasteries, communities governed by a series of regulations, called the Rule. (See www.myartslab.com.) The Rule that was followed determined the type, or Order, of the monastic community. By the fifth century, monasticism had spread north into Italy, across the Continent, and throughout western Britain and Ireland.

The isolated desert location of Sinai and its remove from the material world aided the survival of numerous objects there. An icon of Christ (fig. **8.35**), generally dated to sometime in the sixth century but with later repainting, is magnificent for its freshness of color and vibrancy of brushstroke. Its link with

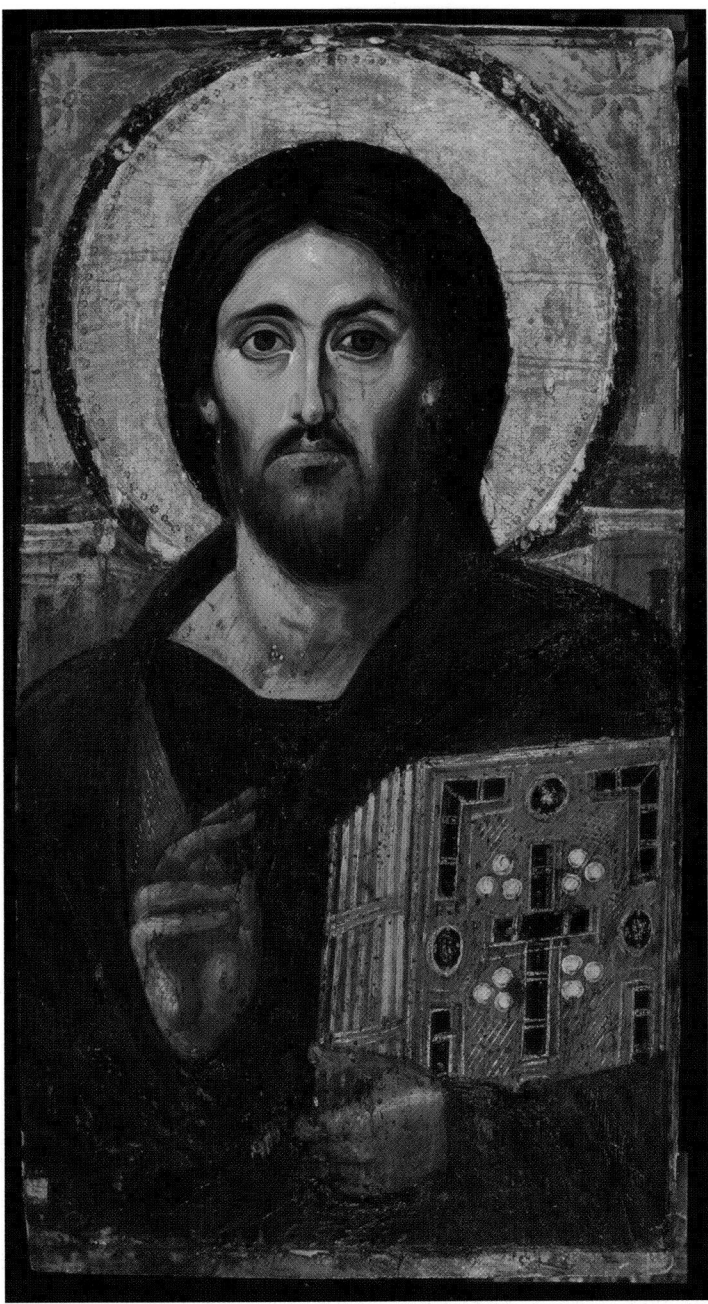

8.35 *Christ*, Monastery of St. Catherine, Mount Sinai, Egypt. 6th century CE. Encaustic on panel, 34 × 17⅞" (84 × 45.5 cm)

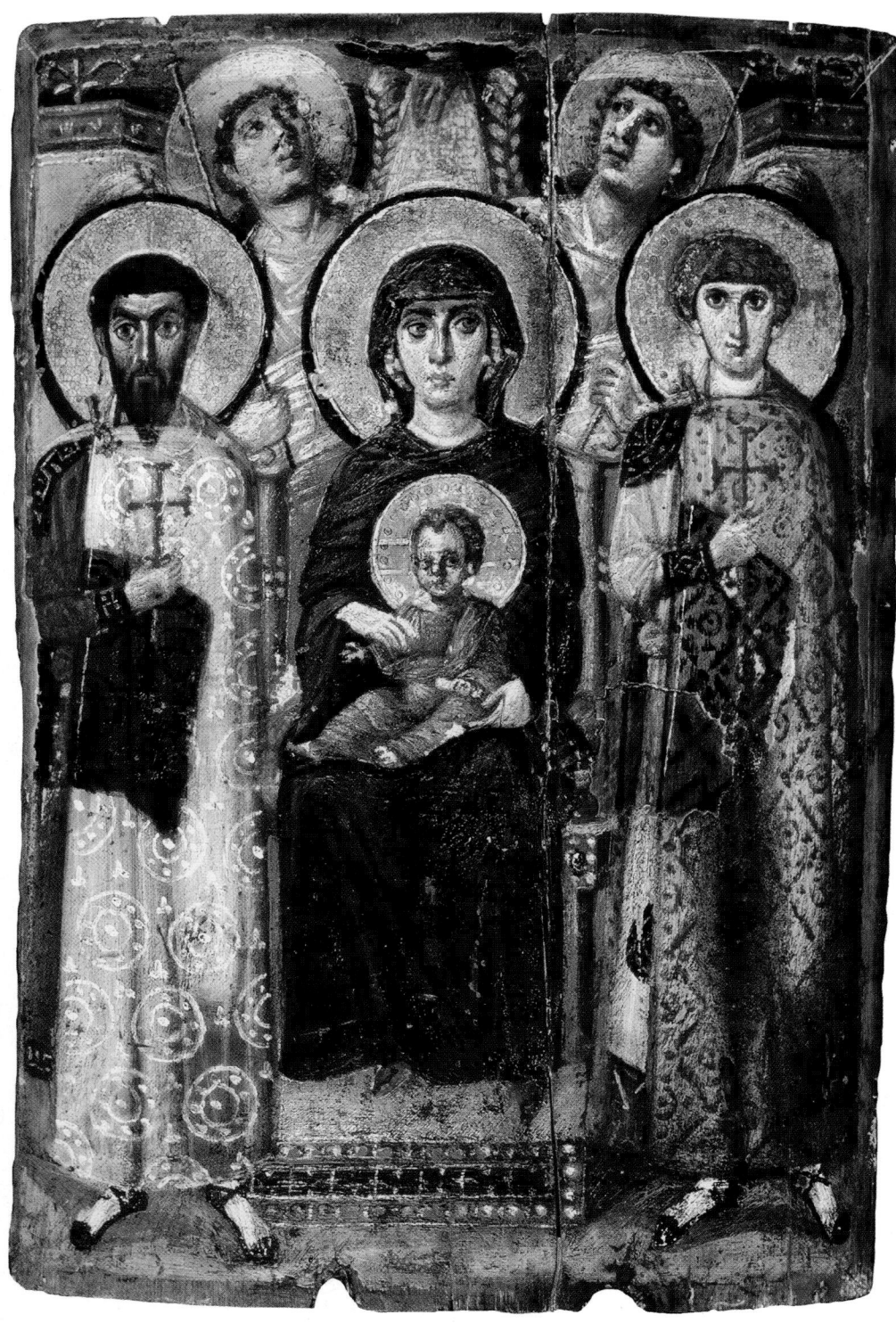

8.36 *Virgin and Child Enthroned Between Saints and Angels*, Monastery of St. Catherine, Mount Sinai, Egypt. Late 6th century CE. Encaustic on panel, 27 × 19⅜" (68.5 × 49.2 cm)

Graeco-Roman portraiture is clear not only from the use of encaustic but also from the gradations of light and shade in Christ's face and on his neck, reminiscent of the treatment of the woman in our Roman Fayum portrait, also in encaustic (see fig. 7.47). The combination of a frontal, unflinching gaze, establishing a direct bond with the viewer, with the lively and lifelike modeling of the face suggests the kind of dichotomy between spiritual and physical that we have seen in so much Early Byzantine art. That dichotomy is accentuated here by the enormous gold halo

hovering over an architectural background. It is as if the walls retreat into the background in response to the halo and in order to allow space for Christ.

The *Virgin and Child Enthroned Between Saints and Angels* icon (fig. 8.36), also from the Monastery of St. Catherine at Mount Sinai, is striking for the variety of styles used to represent the different figure types. The Virgin and Christ are large, their modeled faces help convey with some delicacy their solidity, while the two warrior saints, probably Theodore on the left and

George (or Demetrios) on the right, recall the stiff figures that accompany Justinian in San Vitale (see fig. 8.25). Typically for early icons, however, their heads are too large for their doll-like bodies. Behind are two almost ethereal angels looking skyward; both resemble Roman representations. It is typical of the conservative icon tradition that an artist would remain faithful to his varied sources in order to preserve the likenesses of the holy figures; yet it is also possible that different styles in the same work are considered appropriate for the differing religious roles the portrayed personages play. For example, the Virgin's pose signals that for the Byzantines the Madonna was the regal mother, the *Theotokos*, while the stiff formality of the soldier saints is appropriate to represent stalwart defenders of the faith.

The Iconoclastic Controversy

After the time of Justinian, the development of Byzantine art—not only painting but sculpture and architecture as well—was disrupted by the so-called Iconoclastic Controversy. The conflict, which began with an edict promulgated by the Byzantine emperor Leo III in 726 prohibiting religious images, raged for more than 100 years between two hostile groups. The image destroyers, Iconoclasts, led by the emperor and supported mainly in the eastern provinces, insisted on a literal interpretation of the biblical ban against graven images because their use led to idolatry. They wanted to restrict religious art to abstract symbols and plant or animal forms. Their opponents, the Iconophiles, were led by the monks and were particularly centered in the western provinces, where the imperial edict remained ineffective for the most part. The strongest argument in favor of icons was Neo-Platonic: Because Christ and his image are inseparable, the honor given to the image is transferred to him. (See *Primary Source*, page 266.)

The roots of the argument go very deep. Theologically, they involved the basic issue of the relationship of the human and the divine in the person of Christ. Moreover, some people resented that, for many, icons had come to replace the Eucharist as the focus of lay devotion. Socially and politically, the conflict was a power struggle between Church and State, which in theory were united in the figure of the emperor. The conflict came during a low point in Byzantine power, when the Empire had been greatly reduced in size by the rise of Islam. **Iconoclasm**, it was argued, was justified by Leo's victories over the Arabs, who were themselves, ironically, iconoclasts. The controversy caused an irreparable break between Catholicism and the Orthodox faith, although the two churches remained officially united until 1054, when the pope excommunicated the Eastern patriarch for heresy.

If the edict barring images had been enforced throughout the Empire, it might well have dealt Byzantine religious art a fatal blow. It did succeed in greatly reducing the production of sacred images, but it failed to wipe it out entirely, so there was a fairly rapid recovery after the victory of the Iconophiles in 843. The *Khludov Psalter* (fig. **8.37**) was produced soon after that date, perhaps in Constantinople and for use in Hagia Sophia. A **psalter** contains the Book of Psalms from the Hebrew Bible. The Psalms, traditionally believed to have been written by King David, are sacred songs or hymns. The illustration in figure 8.37 accompanies Psalm 69, a plea by the psalmist for salvation from his tormentors. The illustrations not only make the case for why images should be permitted, they also liken the Iconoclasts, identified by inscription, with the crucifiers of Jesus, whose vinegar-soaked sponge is equated with the implements used to whitewash icons.

Middle Byzantine Art

While we know little for certain about how the Byzantine artistic tradition managed to survive from the early eighth to the mid-ninth century, Iconoclasm seems to have brought about a renewed interest in secular art, which was not affected by the ban. This may help to explain the astonishing appearance of antique motifs in the art of the Middle Byzantine period, sometimes referred to as the Second Golden Age. Hence, there was a fairly rapid recovery after the victory of the Iconophiles. A revival of Byzantine

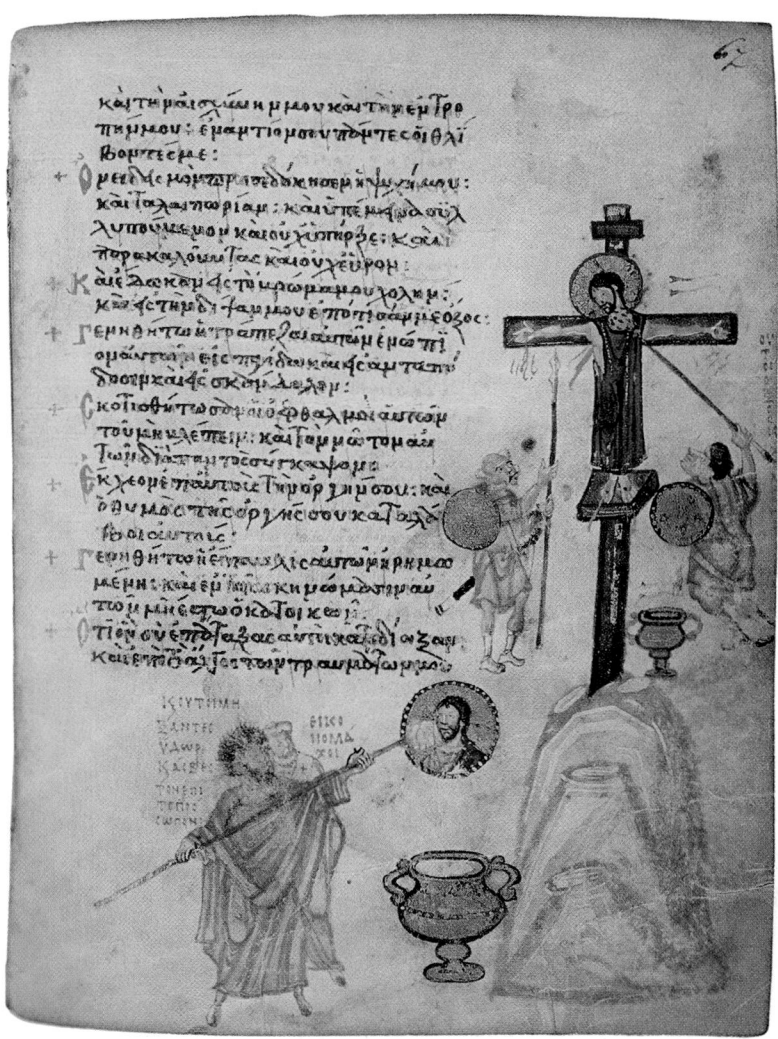

8.37 *The Crucifixion and Iconoclasts*, from the *Khludov Psalter*. After 843 CE. Tempera on vellum, 7¾ × 6" (19.5 × 15 cm). State Historical Museum, Moscow

St. Theodore the Studite
(759–826 CE)

From Second and Third Refutations of the Iconoclasts

Theodore of the Stoudios monastery in Constantinople was a principal defender of icons against the Iconoclasts. St. Theodore refuted their charges of idolatry by examining how an image is and is not identical to its prototype (the person portrayed). Some of his arguments reflect the Neo-Platonic theory expounded by Plotinus that the sense-world is related to the divine by emanation.

Every image has a relation to its archetype; the natural image has a natural relation, while the artificial image has an artificial relation. The natural image is identical both in essence and in likeness with that of which it bears the imprint: thus Christ is identical with His Father in respect to divinity, but identical with His mother in respect to humanity. The artificial image is the same as its archetype in likeness, but different in essence, like Christ and His icon.

Therefore there is an artificial image of Christ, to whom the image has its relation.

If every body is inseparably followed by its own shadow, and no one in his right mind could say that a body is shadowless, but rather we can see in the body the shadow which follows, and in the shadow the body which precedes: thus no one could say that Christ is imageless, if indeed He has a body with its characteristic form, but rather we can see in Christ His image existing by implication and in the image Christ plainly visible as its prototype.

By its potential existence even before its artistic production we can always see the image in Christ; just as, for example, we can see the shadow always potentially accompanying the body, even if it is not given form by the radiation of light. In this manner it is not unreasonable to reckon Christ and His image among things which are simultaneous.

If, therefore, Christ cannot exist unless His image exists in potential, and if, before the image is produced artistically, it subsists always in the prototype: then the veneration of Christ is destroyed by anyone who does not admit that His image is also venerated in Him.

Source: *On the Holy Icons*, tr. Catherine P. Roth. (Crestwood, NY: St. Vladimir's Seminary Press, 1981)

---

artistic traditions, as well as of classical learning and literature, followed the years of Iconoclasm and lasted from the late ninth to the eleventh century. This revival, spearheaded by Emperor Basil I the Macedonian, was underscored by the reopening of the university in Constantinople.

ILLUSTRATED BOOKS An example of the antique revival is the *Joshua Roll* (fig. **8.38**), illustrated in Constantinople in the middle of the tenth century. Some art historians have seen these illustrations of the Hebrew Bible hero Joshua's victories in the Holy Land as alluding to recent Byzantine military successes against the Muslims there. But there are problems correlating the historical events with the date of the manuscript based on stylistic criteria. It is possible that the manuscript projects aspirations more than it reflects accomplishments. That the manuscript takes the form of a scroll, an archaic type of manuscript that had been replaced by the codex a full eight centuries earlier (see page 252), is remarkable. Whether or not scholars who argue that the manuscript is an accurate copy of an earlier scroll are correct, the drawn rather than painted style and the elegantly disposed figures in

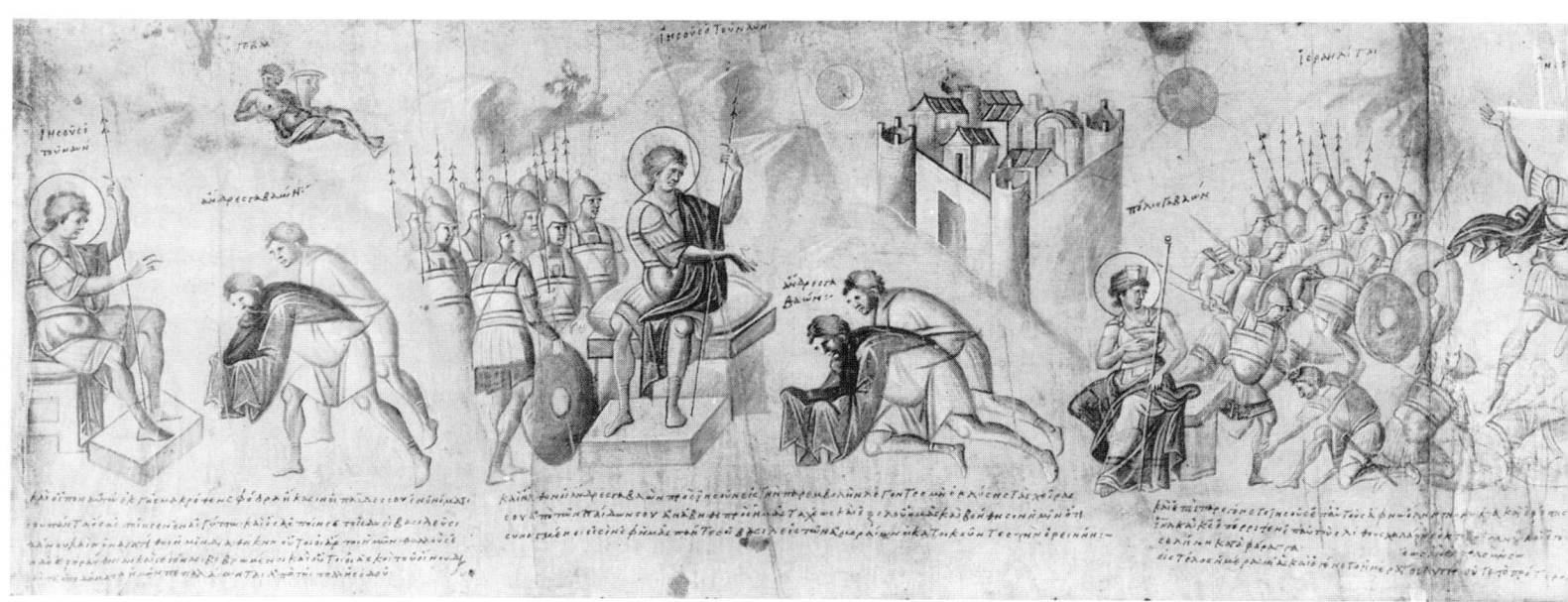

8.38 Page with *Joshua and the Emissaries from Gibeon*, from the *Joshua Roll*. ca. 950 CE. Tempera on vellum, height 12¼" (31 cm). Biblioteca Apostolica Vaticana, Rome. (Cod. Palat. grec. 431)

landscapes and against cityscapes give us some idea of what antique examples must have looked like. That such an obsolete, indeed impractical, vehicle as the scroll, whether an original or a copy, was chosen for such a lavish enterprise illustrates why scholars have referred to this period as a renaissance, or rebirth, crediting much of its vigor to Constantine VII, who ruled in the tenth century. Emperor in name only for most of his life, he devoted his energies instead to art and scholarship.

David Composing the Psalms (fig. **8.39**) is one of eight full-page scenes in the mid-tenth-century *Paris Psalter*. Illustrating David's life, these scenes introduce the Psalms, which, as stated above, David was thought to have composed. Not only do we find a landscape that recalls Roman murals (see fig. 7.55), but the figures, too, clearly derive from Roman models. David himself

could well be mistaken for Orpheus charming the beasts with his music. His companions are even more surprising, since they are allegorical figures that have nothing to do with the Bible. The young woman next to David is the personification of Melody, the one coyly hiding behind a pillar is the mountain nymph Echo, and the male figure with a tree trunk personifies the mountains of Bethlehem.

Once again style promotes meaning in the way consciously classical forms herald the revival of image making after the Iconoclastic Controversy. But despite the presence of revivalist aspects, the late date of the picture is evident from certain qualities of style, such as the crowded composition of space-consuming figures and the abstract zigzag pattern of the drapery covering Melody's legs. In truth, one might well ask to what extent and

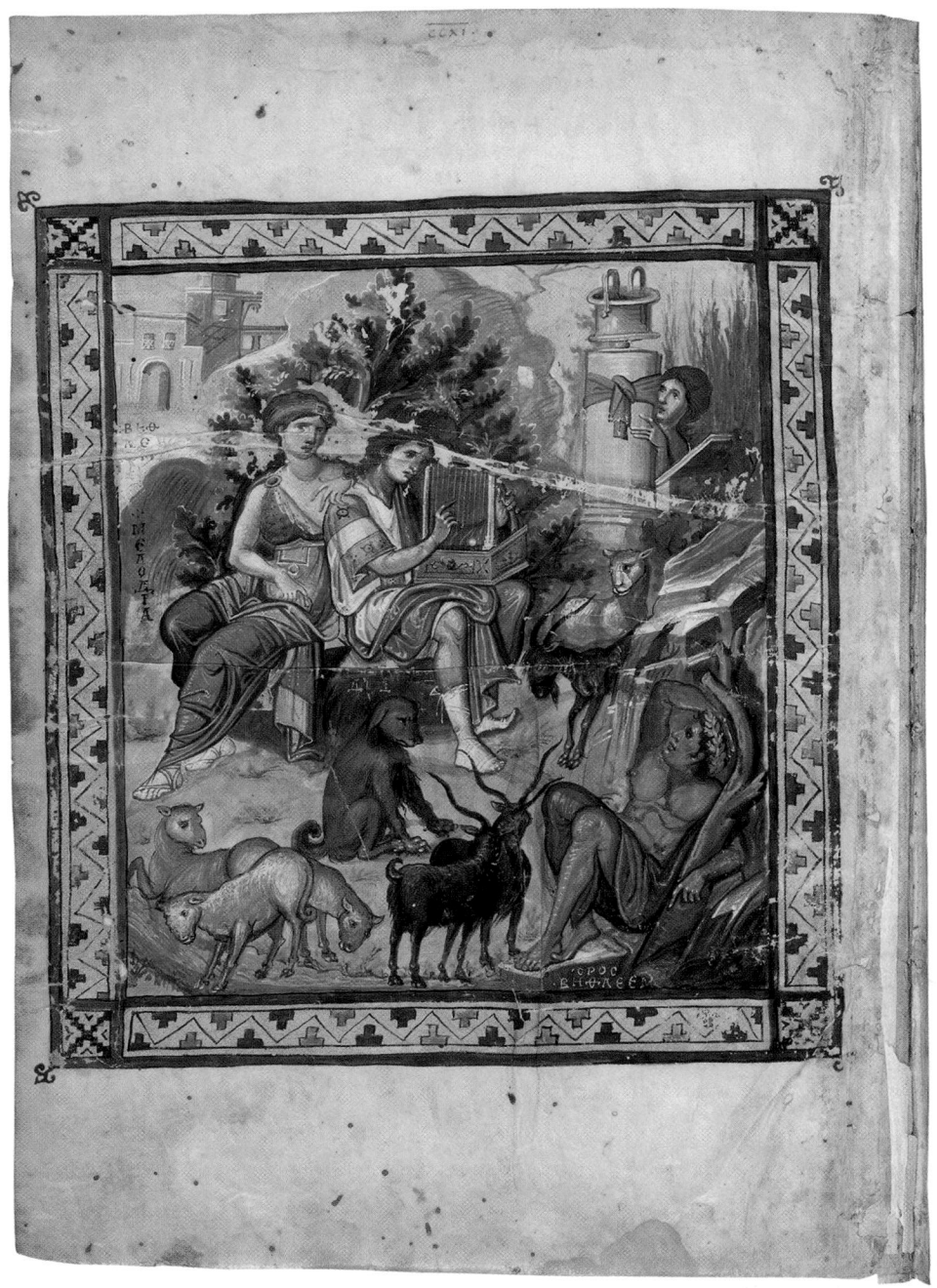

8.39 *David Composing the Psalms*, from the *Paris Psalter*. ca. 950 CE. Tempera on vellum, 14⅛ × 10¼" (36 × 26 cm). Bibliothèque Nationale, Paris

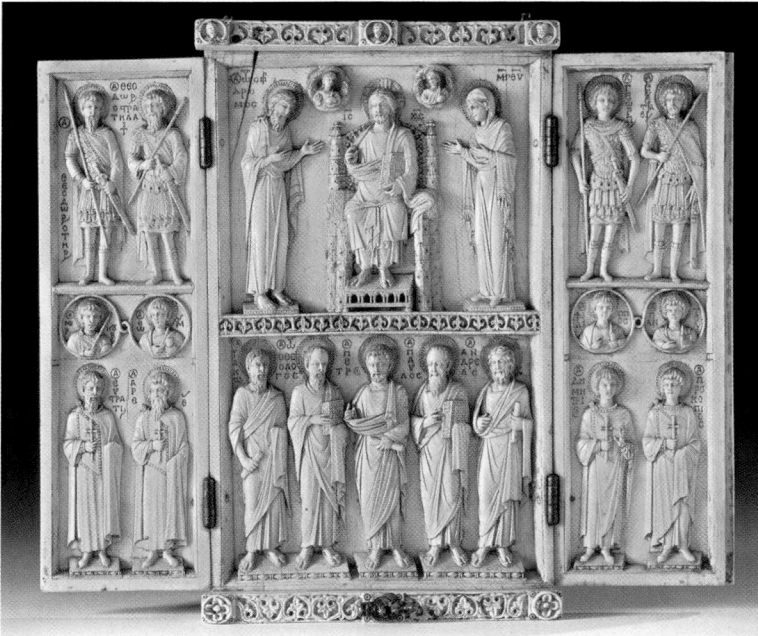

8.40 *Harbaville Triptych*. Late 10th century CE. Ivory,
9½ × 11" (24.1 × 28 cm). Musée du Louvre, Paris

how, despite Iconoclasm, antique methods and forms survived—
that is, how much of what we see is the result of continuities
rather than revivals.

SCULPTURE Monumental sculpture, as we saw earlier, largely
disappeared from the fifth century on. In Byzantine art, large-
scale statuary died out with the last imperial portraits, and stone
carving was confined almost entirely to architectural ornament.
But small-scale reliefs, especially in ivory and metal, continued to
be produced in large numbers with a variety of content, style, and
purpose. The *Harbaville Triptych* (fig. **8.40**), named after a recent
owner, is a portable shrine in ivory with two hinged wings of the
kind a high official might carry for his private worship while traveling; despite its monumental presence, it is less than 10 inches
high. This triptych, and others like it, serve as a vehicle for private
devotion, establishing a parallel between the act of prayer on the
part of viewers with the role of the saints who pray for them. In
the upper half of the center panel we see Christ Enthroned.
Flanking him are John the Baptist and the Virgin, who plead for
divine mercy on behalf of humanity. This scene, the so-called
deësis, was a theme of relatively recent Byzantine invention.
Below are five apostles arranged in strictly frontal view. Only in
the upper tier of each wing of the triptych is this formula relaxed.
There, we find an echo of classical contrapposto in the poses of
the military saints in the top registers of the lateral panels. It is
possible that we are looking at a continuity of the approach we
saw in the early *Virgin and Child Enthroned between Saints and
Angels* icon from Mount Sinai (see fig. 8.36), whereby different
figure types require different representational modes. Here, the
active poses of the military saints contrast with the elegant
restraint of the other holy figures, whereas in the Mount Sinai

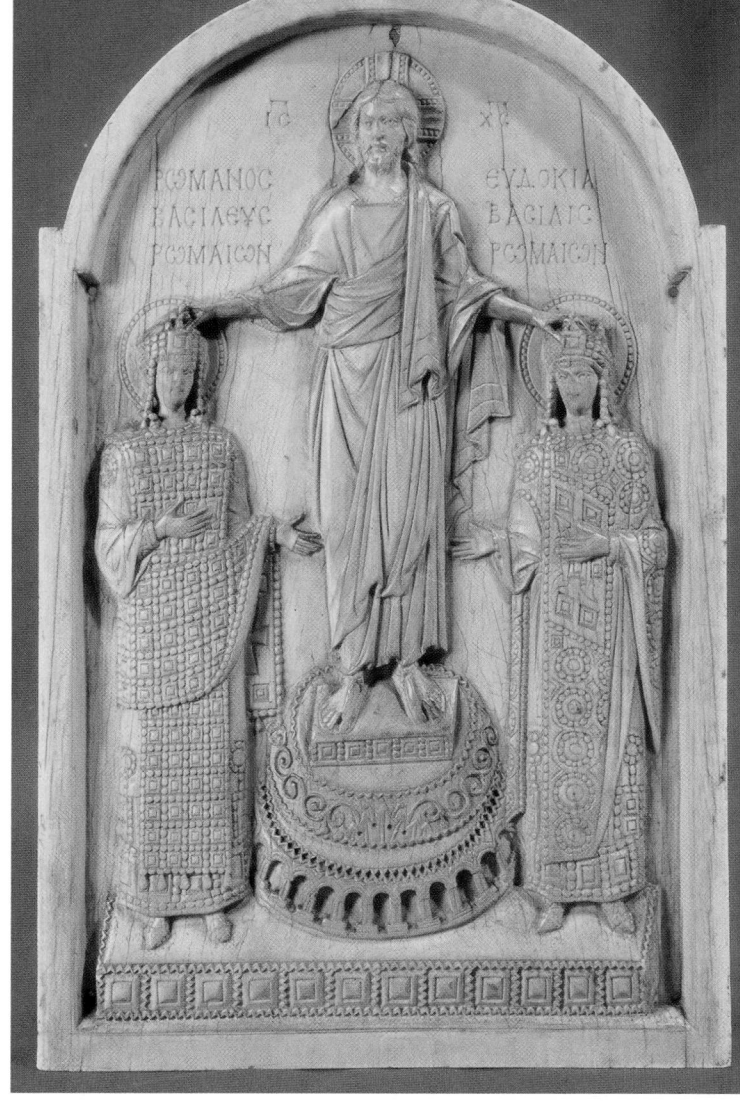

8.41 *Christ Crowning Romanos and Eudokia* ("Romanos Ivory").
945–49 CE. Ivory, 9¾ × 6⅛" (24.6 × 15.5 cm). Cabinet des Médailles,
Bibliothèque Nationale, Paris

icon the angels have the active poses and the military saints
are static.

Refinement and control also mark the attitude of the figures
on the ivory of *Christ Crowning Romanos and Eudokia* (fig. **8.41**),
where the authority of the two haloed figures is confirmed by
their divine election as emperor and empress. Once again there is
some stylistic opposition, perhaps even tension: The body-revealing drapery of Christ contrasts with the stiff, patterned garments
of the imperial figures; the ample space that surrounds Christ
contrasts with the ambiguous space between the flanking figures
and the elevated podium on which Christ stands. Unequivocal,
however, as with the *Justinian as Conqueror* ivory (see fig. 8.32),
is the message of a relationship between a pious emperor and his
god, beneficial to both parties. The imperial couple's elevated relationship to Christ recalls that of John the Baptist and Mary on the
Harbaville Triptych (see fig. 8.40).

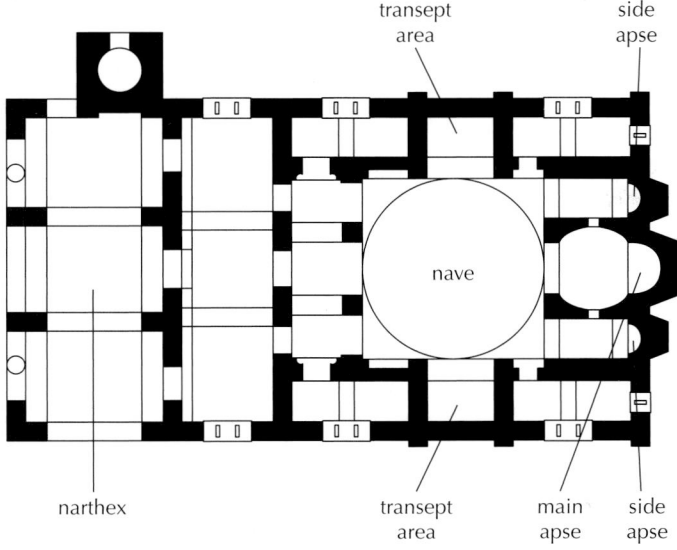

transept area · side apse

nave

narthex · transept area · main apse · side apse

8.42 Plan of Church of the Dormition, Daphni, Greece. 11th century CE

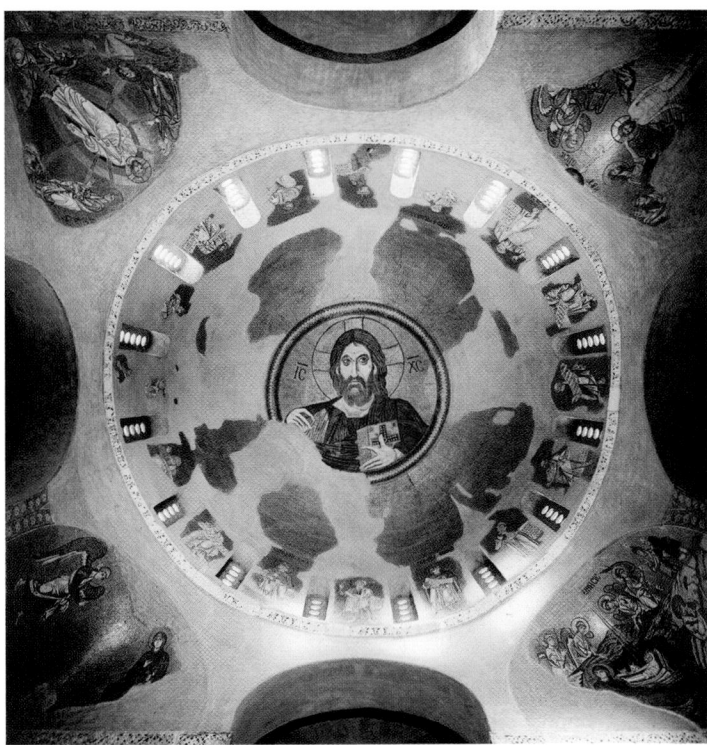

8.44 *Christ Pantocrator*, Church of the Dormition, Daphni, Greece. Dome mosaics

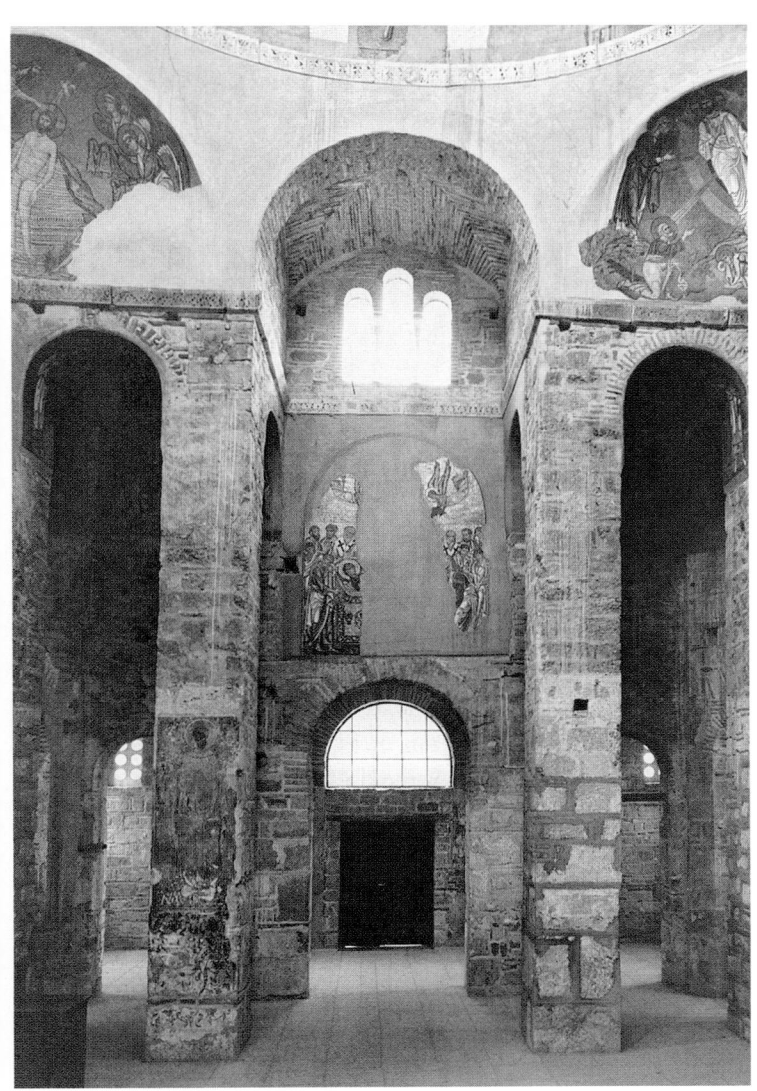

8.43 Interior (facing west) of Church of the Dormition, Daphni, Greece

ARCHITECTURE AND ITS DECORATION Byzantine architecture never produced another structure to match the scale of Hagia Sophia. The churches built after the Iconoclastic Controversy were initially modest in scale and usually monastic, perhaps reflecting the fact that monks had been important in arguing against Iconoclasm; later monasteries erected in Constantinople under imperial patronage were much larger and served social purposes as schools and hospitals. Monasticism dominated the practice of Christianity, and in monastic churches liturgy, ritual, and symbolism were combined in a dynamic manner. The monastic Church of the Dormition at Daphni, near Athens in Greece, follows the usual Middle Byzantine plan of a Greek cross contained within a square, but with a narthex added on one side and an apse on the other (fig. **8.42**). The central feature is a dome on a cylinder, or drum. The drum raises the dome high above the rest of the building and demonstrates a preference for elongated proportions (fig. **8.43**). The impact of this verticality, however, strikes us fully only when we enter the church. The tall, narrow compartments produce both an unusually active space, with abrupt changes of light and shade, and a sense almost of compression. This feeling is dramatically relieved as we raise our glance toward the luminous pool of space beneath the dome, which draws us around and upward (fig. **8.44**). The suspended dome of Hagia Sophia is clearly the conceptual precedent for this form.

The mosaics inside the church at Daphni are some of the finest works of the Second Golden Age. They show a dignity and gravity that merges harmoniously with the spiritualized ideal of

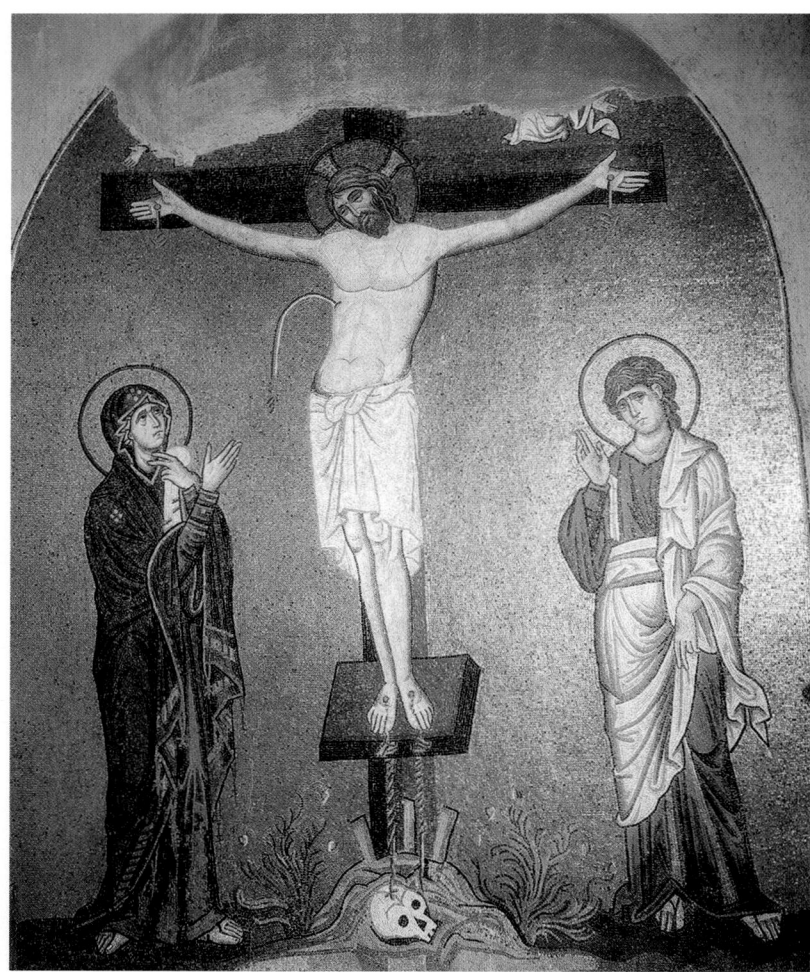

8.45 *The Crucifixion*, Church of the Dormition, Daphni, Greece. Mosaic

human beauty we encountered in the art of Justinian's reign. For instance, the classical qualities of *The Crucifixion* mosaic (fig. **8.45**), on the east wall of the north transept arm of the church, are deeply felt, yet they are also completely Christian. There is no attempt to create a realistic spatial setting, but the composition has a balance and clarity that are truly monumental. The heroic nudity of Christ and the statuesque dignity of the two flanking figures make them seem extraordinarily organic and graceful compared to the stiff poses in the Justinian and Theodora mosaics at San Vitale (see figs. 8.25 and 8.26).

This new interest in depicting the crucified Christ, that is, the Christ of the Passion, seems more emotional than physical. In the Daphni *Crucifixion* mosaic, Christ is flanked by the Virgin and St. John. The gestures and facial expressions of all three figures convey a restrained and noble suffering. We cannot say when and where this human interpretation of the Savior first appeared, but it seems to have developed in the wake of the Iconoclastic Controversy. There are, to be sure, a few earlier examples of it, but none of them appeals to the emotions of the viewer so powerfully as the Daphni *Crucifixion*. To have introduced this compassionate view of Christ into sacred depiction was perhaps the greatest achievement of Middle Byzantine art. Early Christian

art lacked this quality entirely. It stressed the Savior's divine wisdom and power rather than his sacrificial death. Hence, Early Christian artists depicted the Crucifixion only rarely and without pathos, though with a similar simplicity.

Alongside the new emphasis on the Christ of the Passion, the Second Golden Age gave importance to the image of Christ Pantocrator, an oversize, awesome (though heavily restored) mosaic image of which stares down from the center of the dome at Daphni against a gold background (see fig. 8.44). The Pantocrator is Christ as both Judge and Ruler of the Universe, the All-Holder who contains everything. The type descends from images of the bearded Zeus. The bearded face of Jesus first appears during the sixth century, and we have already seen an early example in the icon from Mount Sinai (see fig. 8.35). Once again, tradition and innovation mark Middle Byzantine achievements.

These two mosaic images are part of a larger comprehensive program that served a special spiritual function. (See www.myartslab.com.) Otto Demus, writing in 1948, felicitously described Middle Byzantine churches such as the one at Daphni as a cosmos, the dome representing the heavens, while the vaults and the **squinches**, those devices, similar to pendentives, used to cut the corners of the square space below to make a transition to the cylinder above, signify the Holy Land (see figs. 8.43 and 8.44). The walls and supports below form the earthly world. Thus, there is a hierarchy of level, increasing verticality being equated with degrees of holiness, a sense of which is reinforced by the physical experience of the building's upward spiral pull. The beholder is on the lowest level; the saints are on the walls and supports (visible in fig. 8.43); events in the life of Jesus that took place in the Holy Land, including the Annunciation, Nativity, Baptism, and Transfiguration, are on the vaults and squinches (figs. 8.43 and 8.44 show the Annunciation in the lower left squinch, while the other scenes move around in a counterclockwise direction); and the Pantocrator is in the dome above (see fig. 8.44). Taken together, these representations illustrate the Orthodox belief in the Incarnation as the redemption of Original Sin and the triumph over death.

The movement around the building to witness the Christological cycle, which depicts the events of Christ's life, makes viewers, in effect, symbolic pilgrims to the Holy Land and is combined with a vertical momentum, a virtual personal journey Heavenward. The impression is quite different from the experience of viewers in a Western basilica, even if both attempt to define a spiritual journey through architectural means and in aesthetic terms. In both, passage through space is a means to a goal, but when Orthodox (Eastern) and Catholic (Western) churches are compared, the manner and direction of movement is very different indeed. The decoration at Daphni, magnificent as it is, survives only in fragmentary state. The Venetians desecrated the church in 1207 and in the 1890s earthquake damage was severe. As a result of these vicissitudes, the mosaics were heavily restored and the marble revetment that covered the walls is now missing, the exposed stone and brick giving the building a too-sturdy

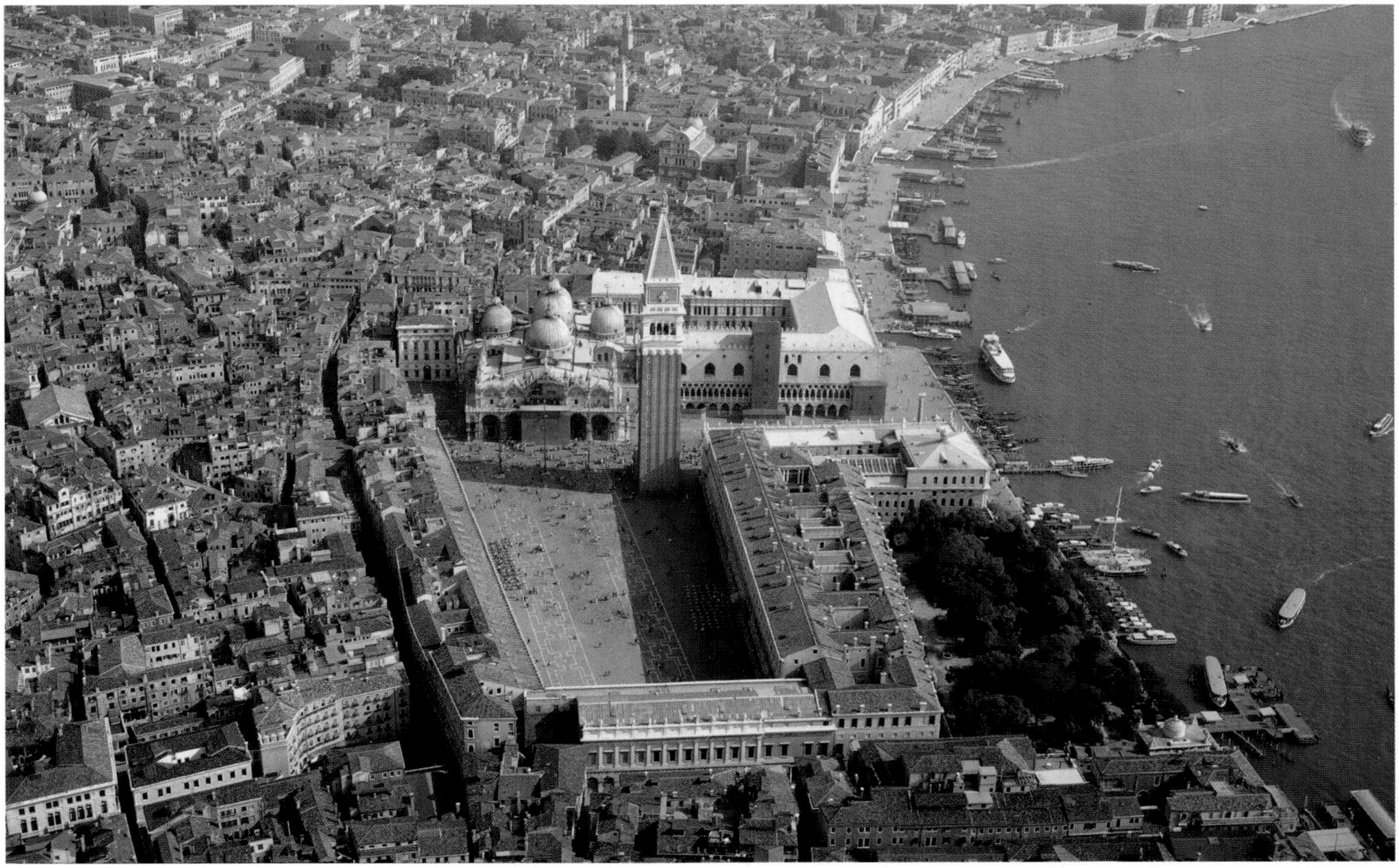

8.46 Aerial view of St. Mark's, Venice, Italy. Begun 1063 CE

aspect. Also missing, since Daphni lacks the monastic community that was responsible for its creation—today it is a museum—is the experiential quality of chanting clergy, burning incense, and glittering liturgical objects of precious metals.

The largest and most lavishly decorated church of the period that still survives is St. Mark's in Venice (figs. **8.46** and **8.47**), begun in 1063, only nine years after the official schism between the Western and Eastern churches. Venice was a province of Ravenna and for some time, thus, a Byzantine dependency. The Church of St. Mark's was both a palace chapel for the Venetian rulers and a **cathedral** (a bishop's church, so named because it houses the bishop's throne, or *cathedra* in Latin). The church was so extensive, employing five domes in place of Daphni's single dome, that the Classical system used at Daphni had to be expanded here. The present structure replaced two earlier churches of the same name on the site; it is modeled on the Church of the Holy Apostles in Constantinople, which had been rebuilt by Justinian after the riot of 532 and was later destroyed. The Venetians had long been under Byzantine rule, and they remained artistically dependent on the East for many years after they had become politically and commercially powerful in their

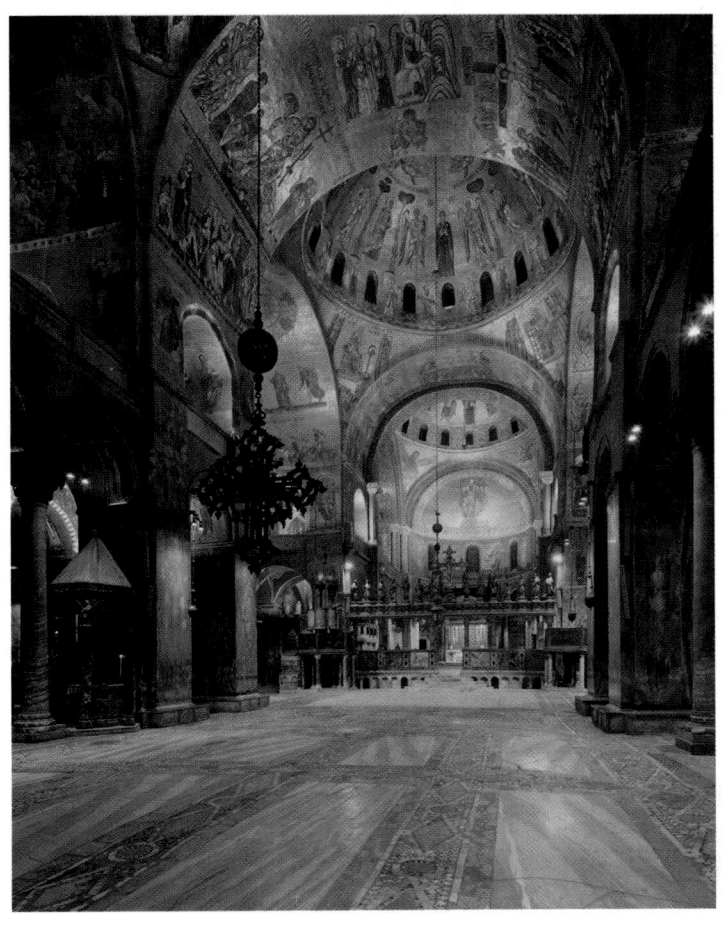

8.47 Interior of St. Mark's, Venice, Italy

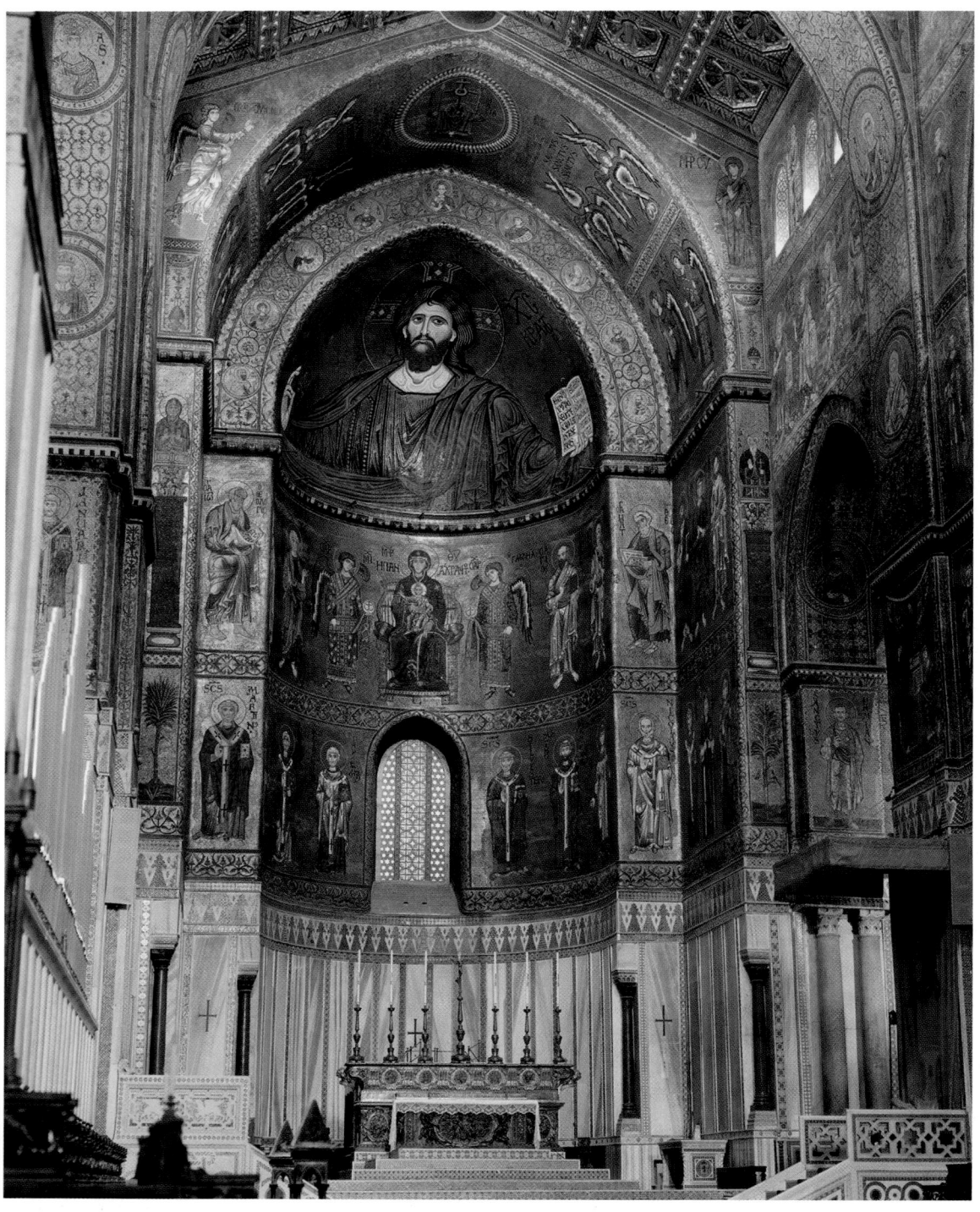

own right. Their wish to emulate Byzantium, and Constantinople in particular, is evidence of the great sway that culture and city still held.

At St. Mark's the Greek-cross plan is emphasized, since each arm of the cross has a dome of its own. These domes are not raised on drums. Instead, they are encased in bulbous wooden helmets covered by gilt copper sheeting and topped by ornate **lanterns** (small structures often used to admit light into the enclosed spaces below), so that the domes appear taller and more visible at a distance. (They make a splendid landmark for seafarers.) The spacious interior shows that St. Mark's was meant for the people

of a large city rather than a small monastic community such as at Daphni.

The Byzantine manner, transmitted to Italy, became known as the "Greek style." Sometimes it was carried by models from Constantinople, but most often it was brought directly by visiting Byzantine artists. At St. Mark's, Byzantine artists and the locals trained by them executed the mosaics. The "Greek style" also appears in a number of magnificent churches and monasteries in Sicily, a former Byzantine holding that was taken from the Muslims by the Normans in 1091 and then united with southern Italy. The Norman kings considered themselves the equals of the

Biblical and Celestial Beings

Much of Western art refers to biblical persons and celestial beings. Their names appear in titles of paintings and sculpture and in discussions of subject matter. The following is a brief guide to some of the most commonly encountered persons and beings in Christian art.

Patriarchs Literally, patriarchs are the male heads of families, or rulers of tribes. The Hebrew Bible patriarchs are Abraham, Isaac, Jacob, and Jacob's 12 sons. The word *patriarch* may also refer to the bishops of the five chief bishoprics of Christendom: Alexandria, Antioch, Constantinople, Jerusalem, and Rome.

Prophets In Christian art, the word *prophets* usually refers to the Hebrew Bible figures whose writings were seen to foretell the coming of Christ. The so-called major prophets are Isaiah, Jeremiah, and Ezekiel. The minor prophets are Hosea, Joel, Amos, Obadiah, Jonah, Micah, Nahum, Habakkuk, Zephaniah, Haggai, Zechariah, and Malachi.

Trinity Central to Christian belief is the doctrine of the *Trinity* which states that One God exists in Three Persons: Father, Son (Jesus Christ), and Holy Spirit. The Holy Spirit is often represented as a dove.

Holy Family The infant Jesus, his mother Mary (also called the Virgin or the Virgin Mary), and his foster father, Joseph, constitute the *Holy Family*. Sometimes Mary's mother, St. Anne, appears with them.

John the Baptist The precursor of Jesus Christ, John the Baptist is regarded by Christians as the last prophet before the coming of the Messiah in the person of Jesus. John baptized his followers in the name of the coming Messiah; he recognized Jesus as that Messiah when he saw the Holy Spirit descend on Jesus when he came to John to be baptized. John the Baptist is not the same person as John the Evangelist, one the the 12 apostles.

Evangelists There are four: Matthew, Mark, Luke, and John—each an author of one of the Gospels. Matthew and John were among Jesus' 12 apostles. Mark and Luke wrote in the second half of the first century CE.

Apostles/Disciples The apostles are the 12 disciples of Jesus Christ. He asked them to convert the "nations" to his faith. They are Peter (Simon Peter), Andrew, James the Greater, John, Philip, Bartholomew, Matthew, Thomas, James the Less, Jude (or Thaddaeus), Simon the Canaanite, and Judas Iscariot. After Judas betrayed Jesus, his place was taken by Matthias. St. Paul (though not a disciple) is also considered an apostle.

Angels and Archangels Beings of a spiritual nature, angels are spoken of in the Hebrew and Christian Bibles as having been created by God to be heavenly messengers between God and human beings, heaven, and earth. Mentioned first by the apostle Paul, archangels, unlike angels, have names: Michael, Gabriel, and Raphael. In all, there are seven archangels in the Christian tradition.

Saints Persons are declared saints only after death. The pope acknowledges sainthood by canonization, a process based on meeting rigid criteria of authentic miracles and beatitude, or blessed character. At the same time, the pope ordains a public cult of the new saint throughout the Catholic Church. A similar process is followed in the Orthodox Church.

Martyrs Originally, the word *martyr* (from the Greek meaning "witness") referred to each of the apostles. Later, it signified those persecuted for their faith. Still later, the term was reserved for those who died in the name of Christ.

Byzantine emperors and proved it by calling in teams of mosaicists from Constantinople to decorate their splendid religious buildings. The mosaics at the cathedral of Monreale (fig. **8.48**), are the last examples to be executed in Sicily in a thoroughly Byzantine style, although the selection and distribution of their subjects are largely Western. The wall surfaces these mosaics covered are vast; the largest to be decorated in this technique. The art historian John Lowden has claimed that 100 million individual tesserae would have been needed to create the more than 1½ acres of mosaics at Monreale. The artists adapted their figure types and subjects to a Western building and Western subjects. Certainly masterful is the way the Pantocrator of a Byzantine domed church now controls the space of the apse and the way registers of figures lining the walls define, indeed clarify in a very un-Byzantine way, the basilica form. Even if the composition is unlike that of Byzantine churches of the period in Greece and Constantinople, it does parallel the arrangement of figures on some Middle Byzantine icons and ivories, such as the *Harbaville Triptych* (see fig. 8.40). Christ's open book contains the text "I am the light of the world…" in Greek on one page and in Latin on the other, the schism in language being united through art.

Late Byzantine Art

In 1204, Byzantium suffered an almost fatal defeat when the armies of the Fourth Crusade, instead of warring against the Turks, captured and sacked the city of Constantinople. For more than 50 years, the core of the Eastern Empire remained in Western hands. Byzantium, however, survived this catastrophe. In 1261, it regained its independence, which lasted until the Turkish conquest in 1453. The fourteenth century saw a last flowering of Byzantine painting under a series of enlightened rulers.

ICONS The Crusades decisively changed the course of Byzantine art through bringing it into contact with the West. The impact is apparent in the *Madonna Enthroned* (fig. **8.49**), which unites elements of East and West, so that its authorship has been much debated. Because icons were objects of veneration, and because they embodied sacredness, they had to conform to strict rules, with fixed patterns repeated over and over again. As a result, most icons are noteworthy more for exacting craftsmanship than artistic inventiveness. Although painted at the end of the thirteenth century, our example reflects a much earlier type

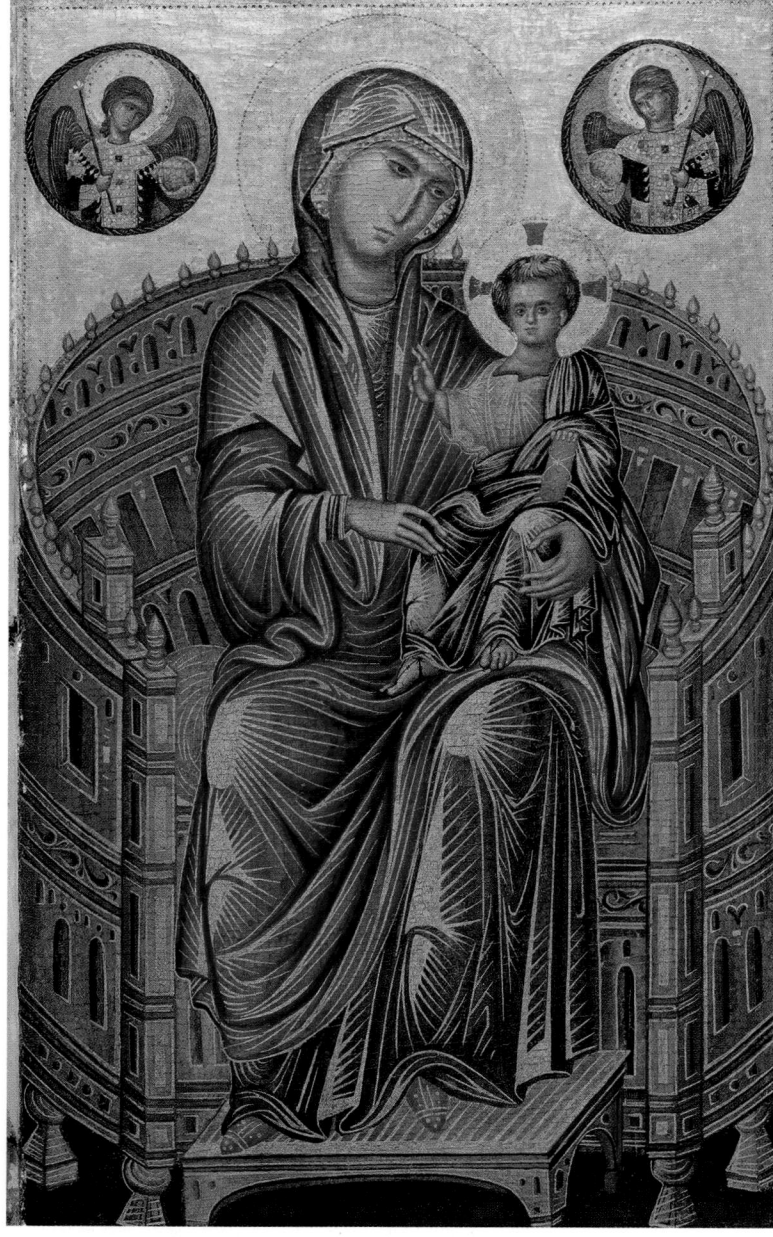

8.49 *Madonna Enthroned.* Late 13th century CE. Tempera on panel, 32⅛ × 19⅜" (81.9 × 49.3 cm). National Gallery of Art, Washington, D.C. Andrew Mellon Collection. 1937.1.1

(see fig. 8.36). There are echoes of the Middle Byzantine style in the graceful pose, the play of drapery folds, and the tender melancholy of the Virgin's face. But these elements have become abstract, reflecting a new taste and style in Late Byzantine art. The highlights on the drapery that resemble sunbursts are not a new development, yet they seem more rigid and stylized than in Middle Byzantine examples. Faces are carefully modeled with gentle highlights and suave shading. The linear treatment of drapery in combination with the soft shading of hands and faces continues the long-established Byzantine pattern of having naturalistic and antinaturalistic aspects play off each other in the same work.

The total effect is neither flat nor spatial, but transparent—so that the shapes look as if they are lit from behind. Indeed, the gold background and highlights are so brilliant that even the shadows never seem wholly opaque. This all-pervading radiance, we will recall, first appears in Early Christian mosaics (see fig. 8.17). Panels such as the *Madonna Enthroned* may therefore be viewed as the aesthetic equivalent of mosaics and not simply as the descendants of the panel-painting tradition. In fact, some of the most precious Byzantine icons are miniature mosaics attached to panels, and our artist may have been trained as a mosaicist rather than as a painter.

Although many details relate this icon to Byzantine works, particularly from Constantinople, some scholars claim that it was produced by a Western artist in emulation of Byzantine painting. For example, the manner in which the Enthroned Virgin presents the Christ Child is Byzantine, while the blessing gesture of Christ is Western. The red background of the angels in medallions is another feature found in the West rather than in Byzantium. An origin in Cyprus, then ruled by the French, has been suggested, but where this work was painted remains an open question. The controversy is heightened by the fact that the icon was subjected to a very heavy restoration before it arrived at the National Gallery in Washington, D.C. Whatever its origin, the *Madonna Enthroned* points to a profound shift in the relationship between the two traditions: After 600 years of borrowing from Byzantium, Western art has begun to contribute something in return.

An icon from Ohrid, in Macedonia, though probably made in Constantinople, illustrates a type distinct from those we have seen previously in that it relates a narrative event, the Annunciation to the Virgin of her imminent role as Mother of God (fig. **8.50**). The increased interest in narrative subjects for icons might derive from the elaborate decorative programs in Middle Byzantine churches. This icon is bilateral (or two-sided). On the other side, the Virgin Mary, to whom the church at Ohrid was dedicated, is represented holding her son. Such icons were probably meant to be mounted on a pole, both for processions and for placement within churches, where worshipers would have been able to view both sides.

The gold background heightens the tension of the spatial relationship established between the archangel Gabriel and the Virgin. The former both cuts through space and slides across it, while the latter seems boxed in by the canopy that frames and encloses her. In the sharpness of their folds, Gabriel's garments appear almost metallic. These contrast with the dark robes of the Virgin. One can imagine how moved a viewer might have been by personal contact with this imposing icon, which measures more than 3 feet high.

MOSAICS AND MURAL PAINTING The finest surviving cycles of Late Byzantine mosaics and paintings are found in Istanbul's Kariye Camii, the former Church of the Savior in the Chora Monastery. (*Kariye* is the Turkish adaptation of the ancient Greek word *chora*, which refers to the countryside, that is, outside the city walls; *camii* denotes a mosque, to which the building

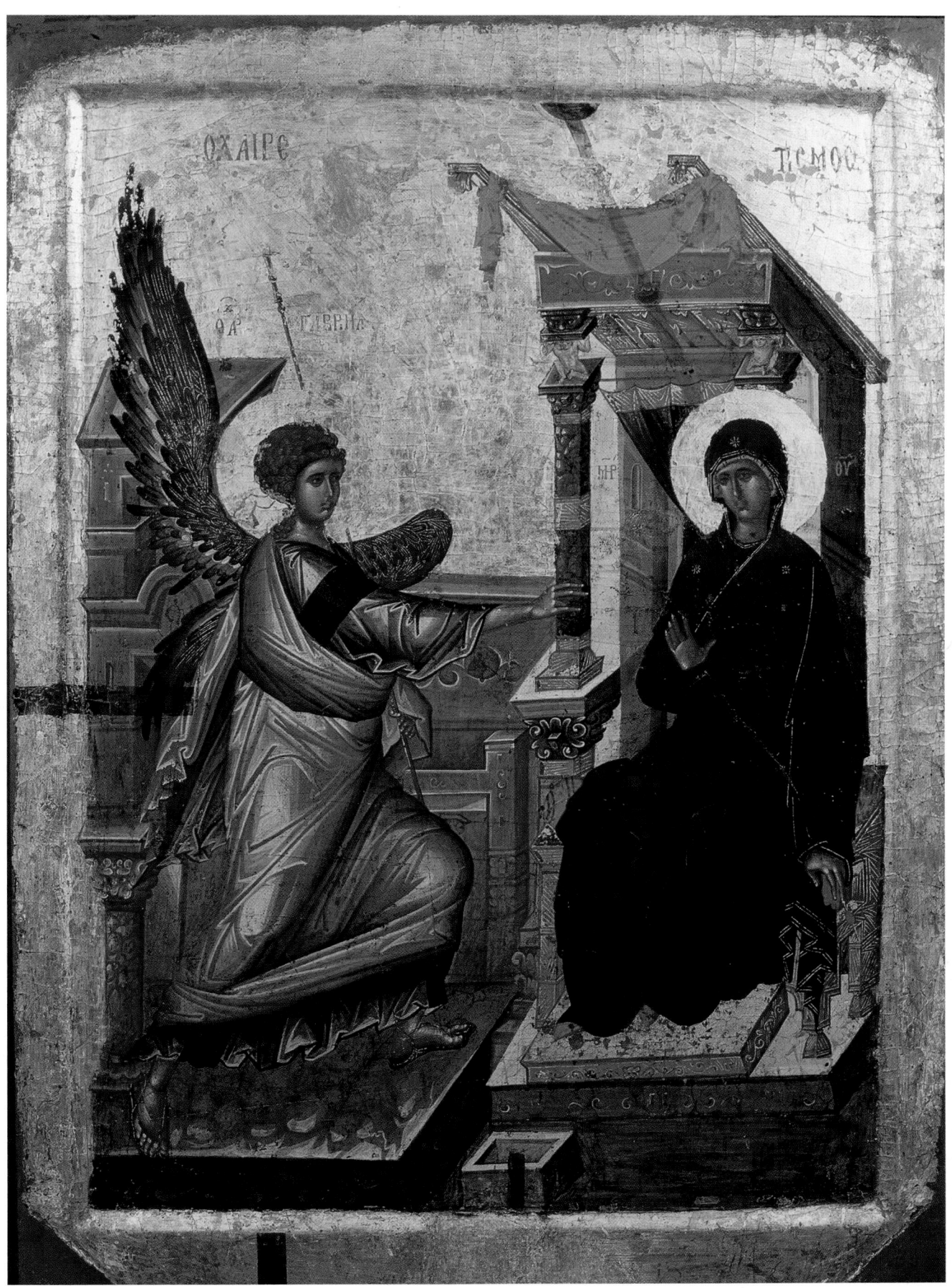

8.50 *Annunciation to the Virgin*, from Church of the Virgin Peribleptos, Ohrid, Macedonia. Early 14th century CE. Tempera on panel, 36⅝ × 26¾" (93 × 68 cm). Icon Gallery, Ohrid, Macedonia

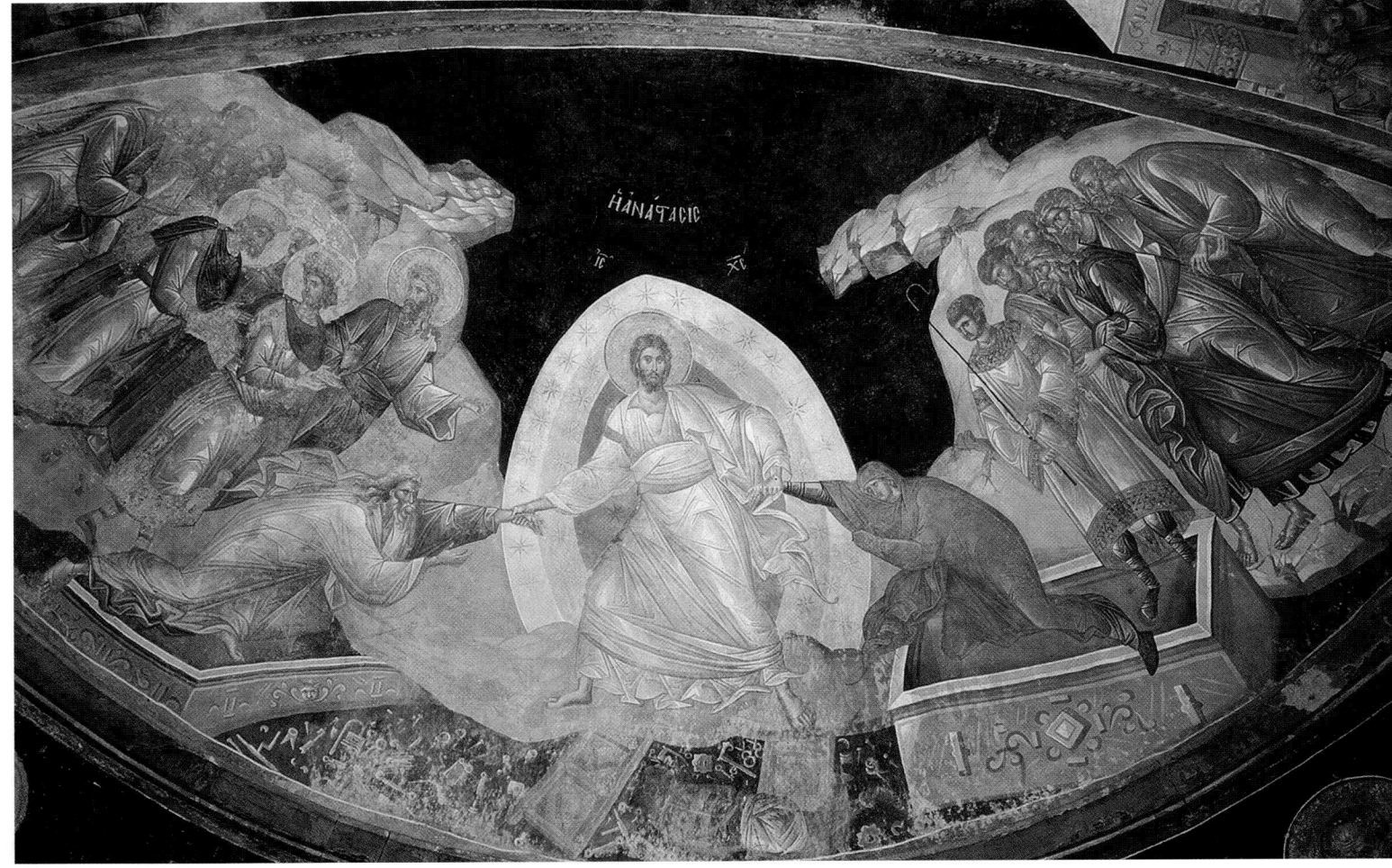

8.51   *Anastasis*, Kariye Camii (Church of the Savior in the Chora monastery), Istanbul, Turkey. ca. 1310–20 CE. Fresco

was converted after the Turkish conquest, although the site is now a museum.) These particular mosaics and paintings represent the climax of the humanism that emerged in Middle Byzantine art. Theodore Metochites, a scholar and poet who was prime minister to the emperor Andronicus II, restored the church and paid for its decoration at the beginning of the fourteenth century.

The wall paintings in the mortuary chapel attached to Kariye Camii are especially impressive. Some have suggested that because of the Empire's greatly reduced resources, murals often took the place of mosaics, but at Kariye Camii they exist on an even footing and may even have been designed by the same artist. The main scene depicts the traditional Byzantine image of the Anastasis (fig. **8.51**), the event just before the Resurrection, which Western Christians call the Descent into Limbo or the Harrowing of Hell, clearly a fitting subject for the funerary setting. Surrounded by a **mandorla**, a radiant almond shape, Christ has vanquished Satan and battered down the gates of Hell. (Note the bound Satan at his

feet, in the midst of a profusion of hardware; the two kings to the left are David and Solomon.) The central group of Christ raising Adam and Eve from the dead has tremendous dramatic force; Christ moves with extraordinary physical energy, tearing Adam and Eve from their graves, so that they appear to fly through the air—a magnificently expressive image of divine triumph.

Such dynamism had been unknown in the Early Byzantine tradition, although the emotional force of Middle Byzantine painting might well have prepared the way for the vivacity of the Kariye Camii representations. Coming in the fourteenth century, this Late Byzantine style shows that 800 years after Justinian, when the Anastasis first appeared as a subject, Byzantine art still had all its creative powers. Thus, despite the diverse uses it served, its long chronological spread, and the different cultures and wide geographic areas it spanned, Byzantine art continued to preserve long-established traditions. Indeed, its durability verges on the immutable.

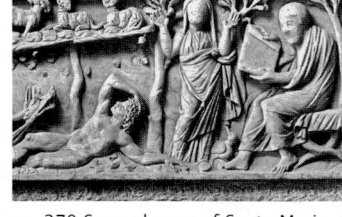

ca. 270 Sarcophagus of Santa Maria Antiqua

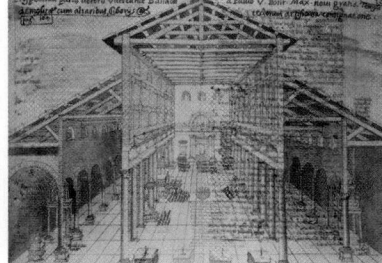

319-29 Old St. Peter's

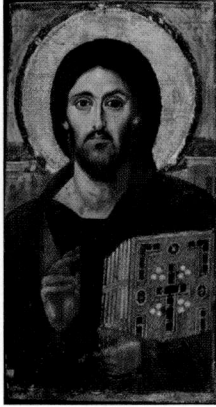

early 6th century
Icon of Christ from Mount Sinai

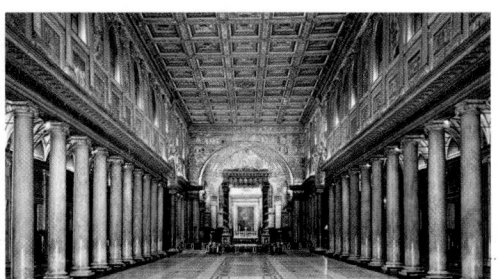

ca. 432-40 Santa Maria Maggiore

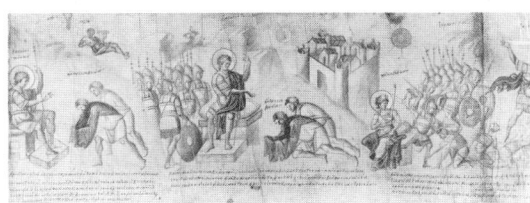

ca. 950 *Joshua Roll*

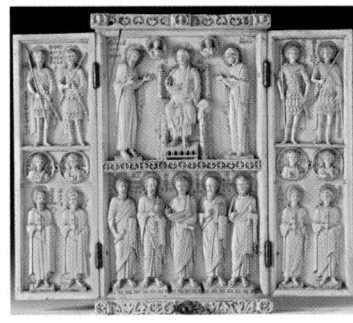

late 10th century
Harbaville Triptych

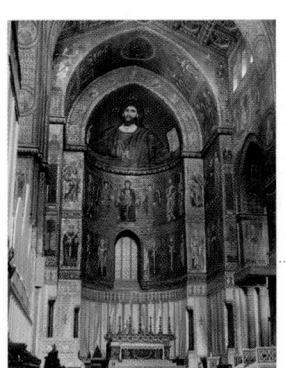

ca. 1180-90 Apse mosaic of Monreale

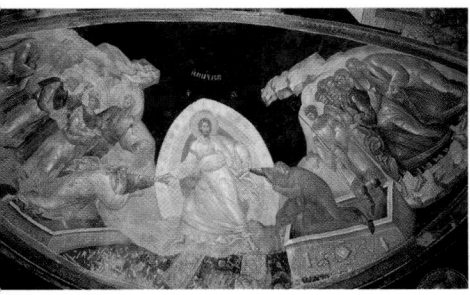

a. 1310-20 Kariye Camii *Anastasis*

Early Jewish, Early Christian, and Byzantine Art

200

◄ 256 Dura-Europus falls to Persians
    260-272 *Shapur I Triumphing over the Roman Emperors Philip the Arab and Valerian*, Naksh-i-Rustam, Iran
    ca.300 Palace of Diocletian, Split, Croatia

300

◄ 312 Constantine the Great's victory over Maxentius at the Milvian Bridge
    312-15 Arch of Constantine, Rome

◄ 330 Constantinople becomes the capital of the Roman Empire

400

◄ 395 Roman Empire divided into Eastern and Western halves

500

◄ 540 Byzantine general Belisarius conquers Ravenna for Justinian

600

700

◄ 726-843 Iconoclastic Controversy

800

900

1000

◄ 1054 Schism of Orthodox (Eastern) and Roman Catholic (Western) churches

1100

1200

1300

1400

◄ 1454 Turks capture Constantinople

1500

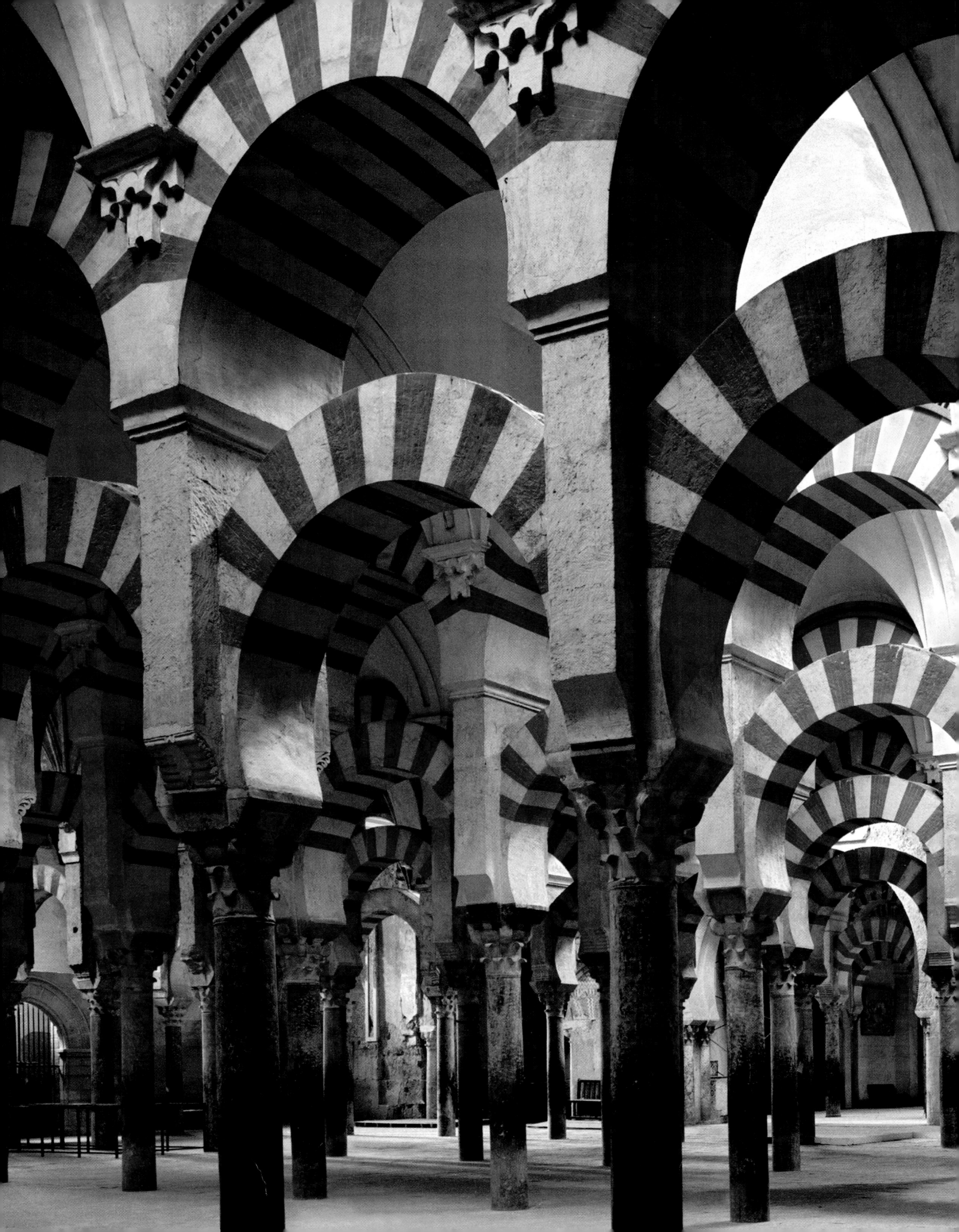

CHAPTER 9

Islamic Art

THE RELIGION KNOWN AS ISLAM TOOK FORM IN THE EARLY SEVENTH century on the Arabian peninsula (see *Informing Art*, page 283). A scant 30 years after the death of its founder, the Prophet Muhammad (also known as the Messenger), in 632, Arab warriors had carried the new faith into much of today's Middle East. A century after the death of the

Prophet, Islam had spread across Africa into Spain in the west, and into the Indus valley and Central Asia in the east (map **9.1**). The original Arab adherents of Islam were eventually augmented by Berbers, Visigoths, Turks, and Persians. The cultural complexity of today's Islamic world existed almost from the beginning. As this phenomenal expansion took place, the inevitable clashing and combining of old cultures with the new religion gave birth to what was to become a vibrant tradition of Islamic art.

Examining the formation of Islamic art gives us an intriguing look at the phenomenon of syncretism in art history, the process whereby a new artistic tradition emerges as a creative combination of previously existing artistic ideas under the impetus of a new ideology. Just as the first Christian art developed out of a mixture of various preexisting classical and Near Eastern artistic ideas adapted to serve the needs of religious and then princely patrons (see Chapter 8), so the new Islamic art first took form as a series of appropriations of preexisting traditions from other cultures molded into a new synthesis, in the service both of the new Islamic religion and Islamic princes.

The vast geographical and chronological scope of Islamic art means that it cannot be encompassed in simple definitions. Islam, the religion, is a significant element in Islamic culture, but Islamic art is far more than a religious art; it encompasses secular elements

Detail of figure 9.8, Interior of prayer hall, Great Mosque of Córdoba, Spain

and elements frowned upon, if not actually forbidden, by some Islamic theologians. As with all art, Islamic art encompasses and reflects the consistencies and contradictions of the society and culture that give it life.

With all of its individual styles of time and place, and with the various sectarian differences within Islam, Islamic art nonetheless has certain unifying themes. The first of these is reverence for the Word—the Qur'an—and for the language of the Word—Arabic—as reflected in the art of beautiful writing. From the angular, horizontal **kufic** alphabet of early Islam (fig. **9.1**) to complex cursive styles developed in later times, Islamic art, both secular and religious, shows a remarkable affinity for the written word, be it scripture or secular narrative poetry (see *Primary Source*, page 281). A second theme is the development of artistic expression independent of the human figure. Given the mistrust of figural images in many Islamic religious traditions, we see in Islamic art sophisticated and complex vocabularies of vegetal, floral, and geometric designs used in conjunction with beautiful writing. A third theme is the equality of genres. To understand and appreciate Islamic art we need to discard the notion of the primacy of (figural) painting and (figural) sculpture in the European tradition. In the Islamic world, the arts of ceramics, metalware, weaving, and carving in precious materials rank with other mediums in an artistic spectrum devoid of the formal hierarchy that in the West led to a distinction between "fine arts" and "decorative arts." In this sense, looking at Islamic art can be both enlightening and liberating.

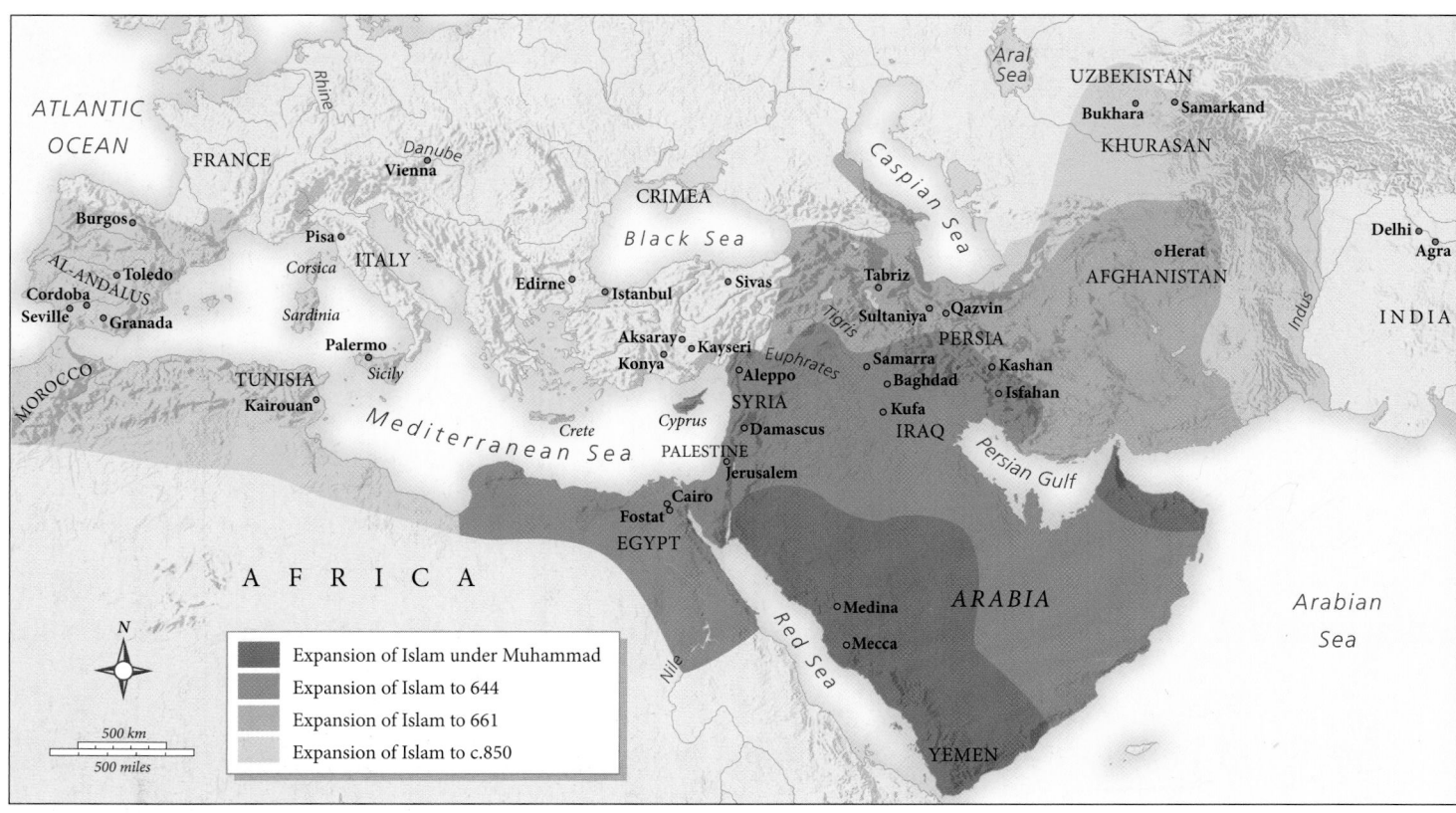

Map 9.1 The Expansion of Islam to 850

THE FORMATION OF ISLAMIC ART

Islamic art first took shape as a series of appropriations of pre-existing Graeco-Roman, Byzantine Christian, and Sasanian (see page 45) forms. These were molded into a new synthesis to serve the needs of the new Islamic religion and the desires and political goals of Islamic princes. The appropriation and adaptation of preexisting forms in the service of the emerging Islamic culture is particularly apparent in architecture.

Religious Architecture

The new religion required certain types of distinctive buildings, such as a place for community prayers that was visually identified with the new faith. The new Islamic rulers needed dwellings appropriate to their power and wealth. Eventually, the faith would also require commemorative buildings that memorialized great rulers, holy men, or historic events. As such, Islamic architecture came to develop a rich variety of forms and genres, and a distinctive repertoire of decoration that became emblematic of the faith itself.

DOME OF THE ROCK The earliest major Islamic building to have survived into our time, the Dome of the Rock in Jerusalem (fig. **9.2**), is a case in point. After the Arabian cities of Mecca and Medina, Jerusalem was the holiest Islamic site. For the first Muslims, the Temple Mount in Jerusalem marked the place where

God tested Ibrahim's faith by demanding the sacrifice of his first-born son Ismail. From the same site, according to later Islamic legend, the Prophet was taken by Gabriel on a *mi'raj* (spiritual journey) to experience both Heaven and Hell, Muhammad being the only mortal allowed to see these places before death.

It is far from a coincidence that the Dome of the Rock is built on Mount Moriah in Jerusalem, a place that was originally the site of the First (Solomon's) and Second (Herod's) Temples, the geographic center of the Jewish faith (see page 235). It is also far from a coincidence that the domed silhouette and ringlike plan of the Dome of the Rock (fig. **9.3**) echo the form of the sixth-century Byzantine shrine of the Holy Sepulcher (see fig. 8.12), marking the burial place of Jesus, just a few hundred yards to the west. The Dome of the Rock was constructed by artists and craftspeople, many of whom were undoubtedly local Christians or new converts to Islam, probably under orders from the Muslim caliph (from the Arabic *khalifa*, meaning "successor") Abd al-Malik sometime around the year 690. Erected on a holy place that was also one of the highest points in the city, it eloquently proclaimed that Jerusalem was under the control of Islam.

A closer look at the building shows both the nature of early Islamic syncretism and the impact of the Messenger's views on the visual arts. The ground plan of the building (see fig. 9.3), with its two ambulatories around the central bare rock, ideal for organizing visits of large numbers of pilgrims to the shrine, recalls not only the Holy Sepulcher but also central-plan domed churches from early Christian times (see fig. 8.10). Just to the south of the

Muhammad Ibn Mahmud Al-Amuli (Iran, 14th Century)

From *Nafâ'is al-Funûn* (The Beauty of Knowledge)

Countless Islamic adages and anecdotes testify to the importance and beauty of elegant writing, the only art form to which Islamic theologians gave their unqualified approval. Al-Amuli's encyclopedic treatise on knowledge cites the Qur'an in praising the art of beautiful writing as the fulfillment of God's will, bringing respect and honor to the practitioner.

The art of writing is an honourable one and a soul-nurturing accomplishment; as a manual attainment it is always elegant, and enjoys general approval; it is respected in every land; it rises to eminence and wins the confidence of every class; being always held to be of high rank and dignity, oppression cannot touch it, and it is held in remembrance in every country, and every wall is adorned by its hand. Honour enough for it in this connexion is that the Lord of Lords, whose names are hallowed in His incontrovertible Revelation, swore—"By the pen, and what they write" (Qur. lxviii.1), and He spake these words: "Recite! Thy Lord is the most generous, who hath taught by means of the pen, Hath taught man what he knew not" (Qur. xcvi. 3–5).

It is honour and exaltation enough for the writing pen
For ever, that it was by the pen that God swore.

The Prophet (peace be upon him!) said: "Beauty of handwriting is incumbent upon you, for it is one of the keys of man's daily bread." A wise man has said: "Writing is a spiritual geometry, wrought by a material instrument."

Source: Sir Thomas W. Arnold, *Painting in Islam: A Study of the Place of Pictorial Art in Muslim Culture* (NY: Dover, 1965)

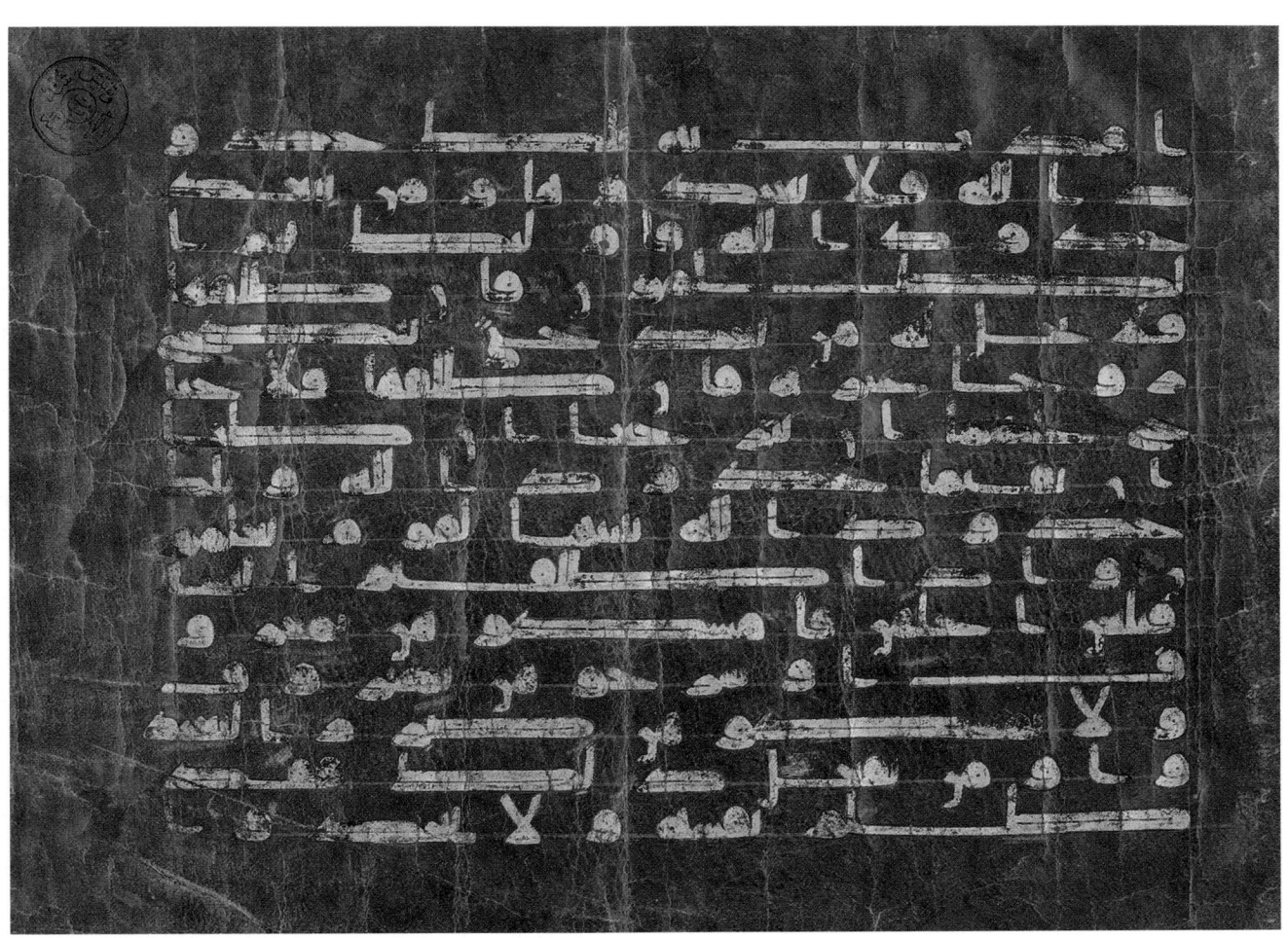

9.1   Page with kufic script from an Abbasid Qur'an, probably from Tunisia. 9th century. Ink, color, gold, and silver on dyed blue vellum, 11¼ × 14¾" (28.6 × 37.5 cm). Harvard Art Museum, Arthur M. Sackler Museum. Harvard University Museums, Cambridge, MA, Francis Burr Memorial Fund, 1967.23

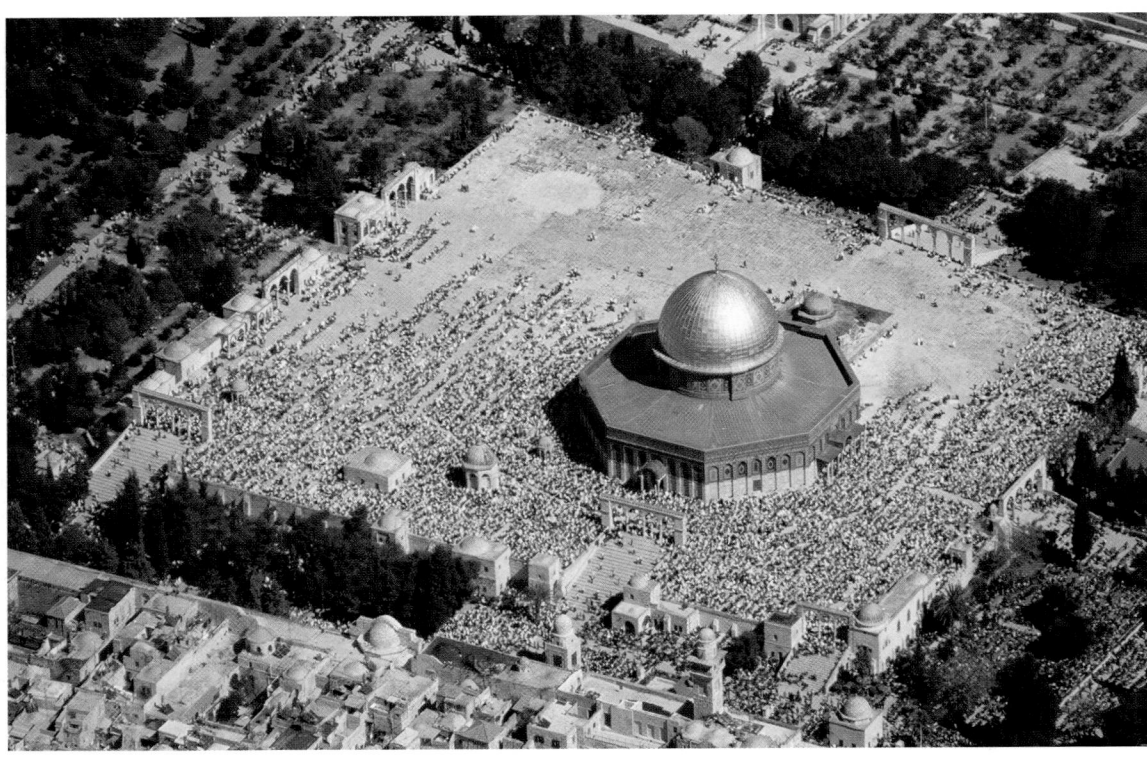

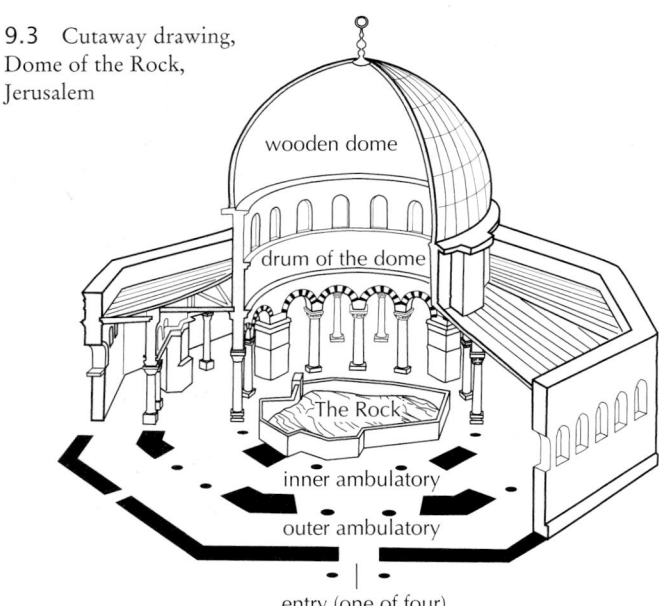

9.3 Cutaway drawing, Dome of the Rock, Jerusalem

wooden dome

drum of the dome

The Rock

inner ambulatory

outer ambulatory

entry (one of four)

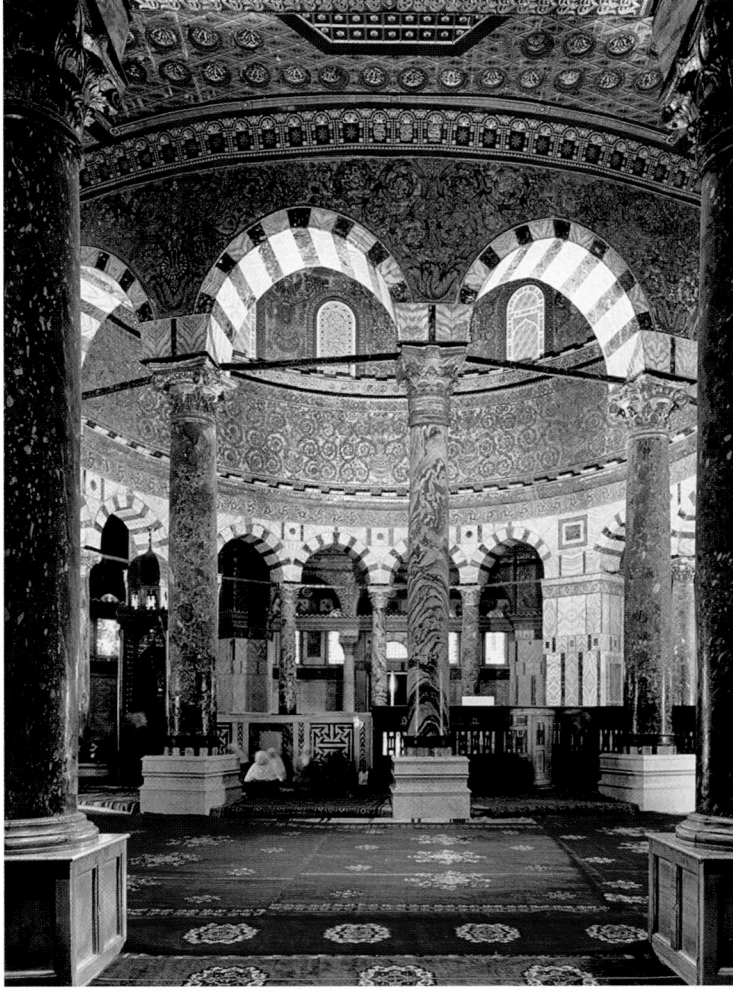

Dome of the Rock, providing a place for prayer directly next to the shrine, was an equally venerable and revered Islamic structure, the communal prayer hall known today as the al-Aqsa Mosque. The dome of the shrine itself was a well-established symbol for the vault of heaven, especially appropriate given the ultimate goal of the Messenger's mystical and spiritual journey. The columns and capitals, recycled from Classical monuments, convey an impression of tradition and permanence, wealth and power, to Muslim and non-Muslim alike.

The original mosaic decoration (fig. **9.4**) consisted of Arabic script, repeating geometric motifs, and highly stylized vegetal and

9.4 Interior, Dome of the Rock, Jerusalem

Islam and Its Messenger

Islam (an Arabic word denoting submission to God's will) is the predominant religion of a vast area of the world extending across Africa, Europe, and Asia, with many different ethnicities, cultures, languages, and forms of social and political organization. Muslims (those who submit) believe that Muhammad (ca. 570–632), an orphaned member of a major tribal group from the city of Mecca in the western Arabian peninsula, was chosen by God (in Arabic, Allah) to serve as God's Messenger, or Prophet, to humanity. Muhammad is said to have received the Word of God as a series of poetical recitations (in Arabic, Qur'an), brought to him by the archangel Jibra'il (Gabriel). Muhammad memorized and recited these poetic verses, and taught them to his followers. Organized into *sura* (chapters) and finally written down after the death of Muhammad in 632, these prayers, stories, exhortations, and commandments constitute the Qur'an, Islam's sacred book. The Qur'an, together with official collections of *hadith* (remembrances) of the exemplary life of Muhammad as the Messenger, form the basis of Islamic religious practice and law.

While the Prophet quickly gained adherents, those in power in Mecca were threatened by the challenges the new faith posed to their political and economic power, and in 622 he was forced to leave Mecca with a few of his followers, moving to the city of Medina some 190 miles (300 km) to the north. Muhammad's community, in constant conflict with the Meccans to the south, continued to grow, and more revelations were received. The Prophet's house in Medina, constructed in the form of an open square, became the prototype for countless mosques in subsequent centuries.

Islam was defined by Muhammad as the culmination of a prophetic tradition that began with God's covenant with Ibrahim (Abraham). The Qur'an prominently mentions many of the major figures of the Hebrew Bible, such as Ibrahim, Musa (Moses), and Sulayman (Solomon), as well as the prophet 'Isa (Jesus) and his mother, Maryam (Mary). Islamic belief is fundamentally very simple: To become a Muslim, one repeats with conviction the phrase, "There is no God but God; Muhammad is the Messenger of God." This Affirmation of Faith is the first of the so-called Five Pillars of Islam. The others are prayer (the five daily prayers and the major weekly prayer at noon on Friday, the Muslim Day of Congregation), fasting (abstention from food and drink during daylight hours during the lunar month of Ramadan), pilgrimage (in Arabic, hajj, a journey to Mecca during the lunar month of Dhu'l Hijja), and charity (institutionalized as a formal system of tithing, intended to benefit the sick and needy of the Islamic community).

In addition, Islam proclaimed three other tenets that were to have a major impact on art. The first was the protected status of the "People of the Book"—Jews and Christians—in Muslim society, as ordained by God in the Qur'an. The second, based on several anecdotes from the Prophet's life, is a profound mistrust of certain images—pictures and statues of humans and animals—as potentially idolatrous, a point of view Islam shares with Judaism, and which has occasionally influenced the history of Christian art as well. The third, held in common with Judaism and contrasting markedly with the Christianity of that time, was a high regard for literacy and the individual's reading and study of Scripture, coupled through most of Islamic history with a reverence for the written alphabet—in the case of Islam, the Arabic alphabet, which in early Islam used an angular form of script known as kufic (see fig. 9.1). The beauty of the script, with its contrasting thin and thick lines, written from right to left in an almost rhythmic visual cadence, was deemed appropriate for the poetic words of God himself. These three factors, taken in the general context of Islamic belief and early Islamic political history, were to have a profound effect on the molding of the Islamic artistic tradition.

---

floral elements. Eventually, these design elements would form a distinctively Islamic repertoire of decoration. One was Arabic script used in the many religious inscriptions. Two others were a vocabulary of scrolling vines, leaves, and flowers distantly based on nature, and a range of repeating geometric patterns. Both the natural elements and the geometric patterns were staples of late Classical and Sasanian art. A fourth set of motifs consisted of jewels and jeweled objects, symbols of royalty. But in marked contrast to the Graeco-Roman and Christian religious art traditions, nowhere in the Dome of the Rock do the forms of humans or animals appear. The inscriptions in the Dome of the Rock, taken from the Qur'an, were carefully chosen to underline the importance of the building itself, its symbolic location in a city holy to Jews and Christians as well as Muslims, and its place within a religion and society that saw itself as the culmination of the two earlier scriptural traditions, and which afforded tolerance and acceptance of both Christians and Jews.

THE HYPOSTYLE MOSQUE Of the Five Pillars of Islam, the religious duty of prayer proved the most important in the development of Islamic architecture. In major cities such as Damascus, the Arab Umayyad caliphs of early Islam either built or converted from preexisting structures the first great buildings for Muslim public worship called **mosques** in English (from the Arabic *masjid*, meaning "place of prostration"). These first mosques, designed to contain the entire male population of a city during the noon prayer on Friday, recall the form of the Messenger's house in Medina, with a rectangular courtyard, usually surrounded by covered arcades, and a larger hypostyle (many-columned) hall on the **qibla**, the side facing Mecca. The architecture emphasized the equality of all Muslims before God and the absence in Islam of an ordained clergy: There is little axiality in the early Arab mosques—no long straight pathway leading to an architectural focus visible throughout the structure. With prayer occurring directly between each worshiper and God, and no ordained clergy or canonized saints to provide intercession, the interior space of the early mosque was essentially determined by practicality, not by ceremony. Thus, there was no place for music or processions; many doors were placed for maximum convenience of the daily coming and going of worshipers; and a

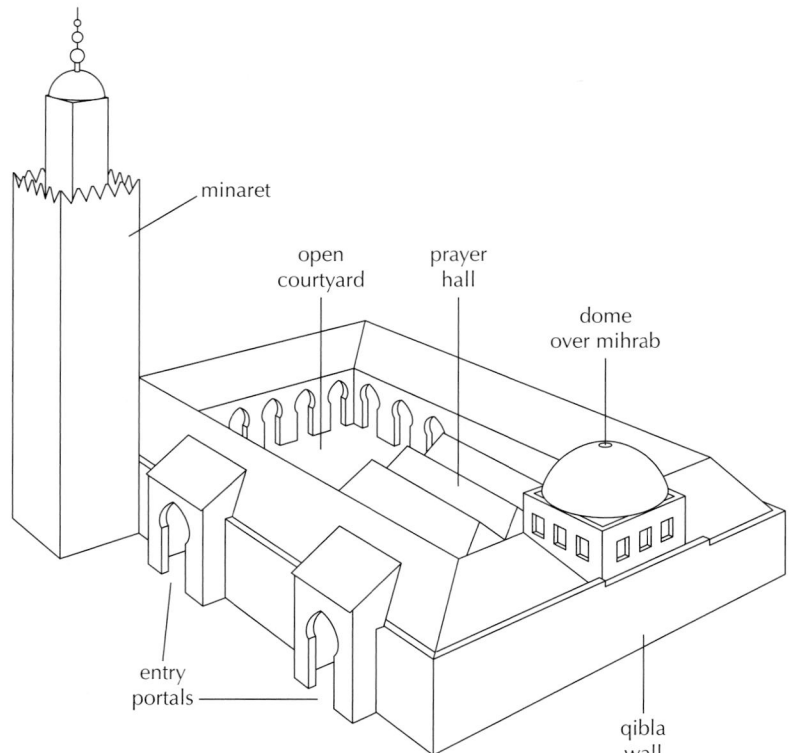

9.5 Schematic drawing of a generic Arab hypostyle mosque

large centralized or axial space, so important for the drama of the Christian Mass, was deemed unnecessary. A simple **minbar** (pulpit) served for the delivery of sermons after the Friday noon prayer, and an empty **mihrab** (niche) in the qibla wall was added to indicate the direction of Mecca (fig. **9.5**). Mats of grass or rushes, and later woolen carpets, often covered the floors. These provided a clean place for the standing, bowing, kneeling, and prostration, with the brief touching of the forehead to the ground, while reciting prayers, that constitute the essence of Islamic worship. Oil lamps provided illumination for the dawn and late evening prayers. Pools or fountains in the courtyard allowed for the ceremonial washing of hands and feet required before prayers. In later times, a tower, known in English as a **minaret**, advertised the presence of the mosque and served as a place from which to broadcast the call to prayer given five times a day by a *muezzin*, an individual usually selected for the beauty and power of his voice. And in some mosques a small platform called a **dikka** provided a place for the muezzin to chant prayers aloud.

Secular Architecture

The advent of Islam did not mean the end of secular art in the Middle East. The early Islamic princely patrons, Arabs from the Umayyad ruling house, in addition to establishing the canonical form of the Islamic house of prayer, were also quickly seduced by the splendor of Sasanian and Graeco-Roman princely art. Although their urban palaces have not survived, they also constructed luxurious and secluded palaces out in the desert, away from the metropolitan centers, and some of these have been rediscovered in relatively recent times. In addition to walled residences for ruler and courtiers in the traditional hollow square form of the

Roman military encampment, the Umayyads built large and sumptuous bathhouses with halls for entertainment, often lavishly furnished with mosaic floors in a Late Roman style and decorated with pictorial and sculptural images of luxury. Among the subjects depicted were the royal hunt, court musicians (fig. 9.6), the enjoyment of Roman-style baths, dancing courtesans, scenes from everyday life, and images of ancient derivation denoting

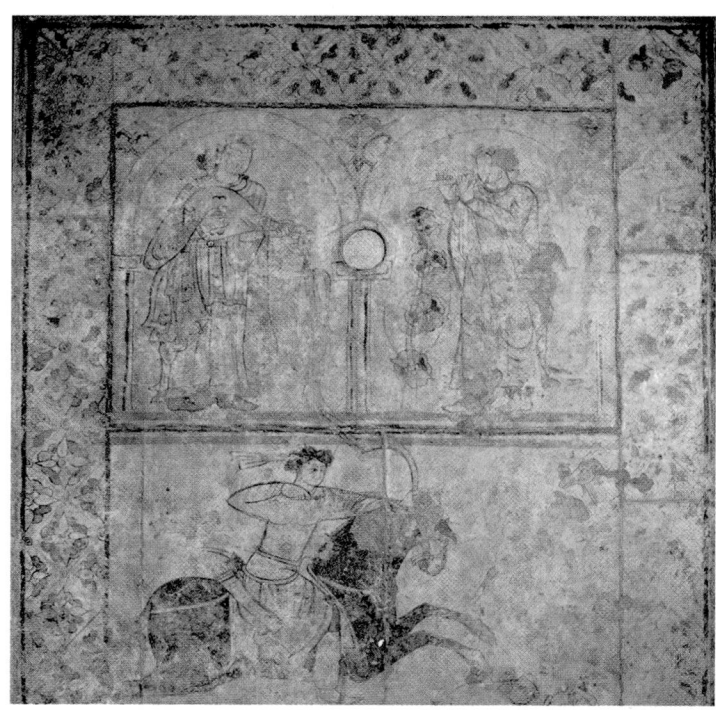

9.6 Floor fresco depicting two court musicians and a mounted hunter, from Qasr al-Hayr (West). ca. 730. National Museum, Damascus

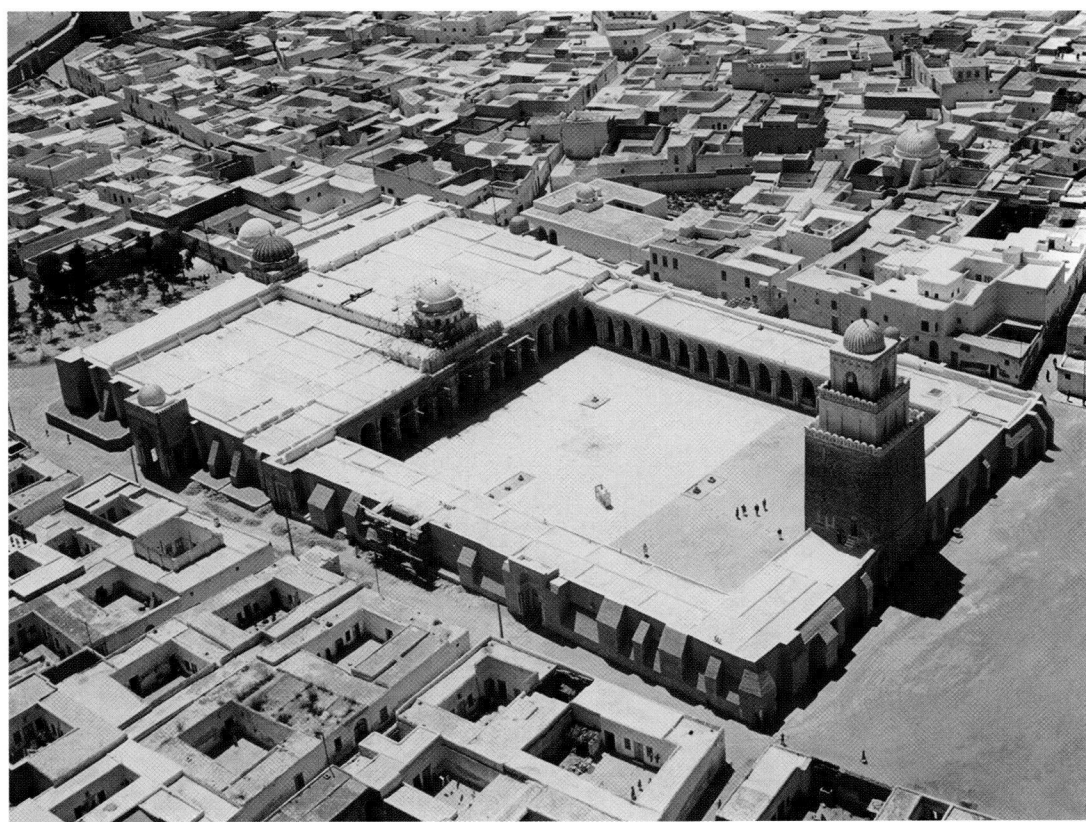

fertility, sexuality, and kingly prowess. The puritanical demands of religion thus immediately came into conflict with the age-old symbols of royal wealth, luxury, and entertainment. So great was the embedded power of the artistic imagery of kingship in the Middle East that it quickly made an impact on the material culture of the new Islamic ruling elite.

THE DEVELOPMENT OF ISLAMIC STYLE

By 750, the Umayyad dynasty based in Roman Syria had been supplanted by the Abbasid dynasty centered in Mesopotamia. Here the new caliphs built their capital, called Baghdad, on the Tigris River, and later a vast palace city to the north of Baghdad at Samarra. The original Round City of Baghdad, the site of which lies under the present-day city, was largely abandoned and destroyed long before the Mongols sacked the city in 1258, but its powerful memory lived on in Arabic poetry and prose literature. Samarra's impressive mud-brick ruins still stretch for miles along the Tigris. Under Abbasid rule, the building of mosques in newly conquered areas proceeded apace across the now-extensive Islamic Empire.

Religious Architecture

Chief among the new structures were the large Abbasid congregational mosques that both practically and symbolically served as religious gathering places for prayers, sermons, and religious education. Large examples, many now in ruins, were built all over Iraq, and in Egypt and elsewhere. An archetypal example is the largely ninth-century congregational mosque at Kairouan, a city in what is now Tunisia established under the Abbasids.

GREAT MOSQUE OF KAIROUAN Based like all major Arab mosques on the house of the Prophet in Medina and the four-square Mediterranean courtyard house, examples of which today still surround the structure, the Great Mosque of Kairouan consists of a rectangular courtyard surrounded by covered halls, a large hypostyle prayer hall, and a towering minaret (fig. **9.7**). Two domes mark the area: in front of the mihrab and in the middle of the prayer hall facing the court. This aside, the multitude of entrances on three sides of the building, conceived to facilitate entry and exit for the five daily prayers, free the building from the domination of a central axis for processions of clergy; it is thus the very opposite of the Early Christian basilican church, organized for priestly and theatrical ritual. The simplicity of the mosque reflects the simplicity of Islamic prayer. The mosque's lack of both axiality and uninterrupted interior space stems from the essential lack of hierarchy among worshipers. Each worshiper prays directly to God using a simple ritual formula usually completed in a few minutes. Artistic attention was lavished on the mihrab, of carved marble and ceramic tiles, and the minbar, elaborately carved of Indian teak. In the Kairouan mosque, a carved wooden screen, primarily a product of security rather than ritual needs, encloses a small area near the mihrab called the **maqsura**, where the ruler could pray alone.

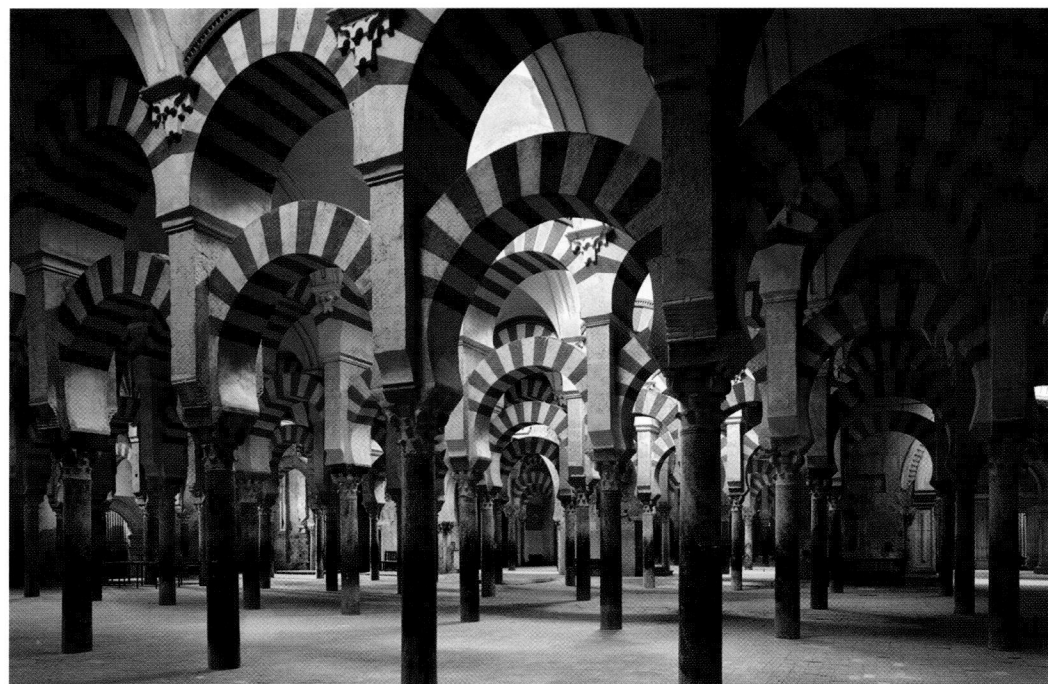

9.8 Interior of prayer hall, Great Mosque of Córdoba, Spain

GREAT MOSQUE OF CÓRDOBA Even farther to the west, in southern Spain, where the sole surviving prince of the exterminated Umayyad house founded an independent state after 750, a brilliant center of Islamic culture developed in the city of Córdoba, in al-Andalus (now Andalusia). By the tenth century, the Great Mosque of Córdoba, after a series of embellishments and enlargements, had become one of the most beautiful Islamic houses of worship. A typical Arab hypostyle hall, the interior of the Córdoba mosque became after several expansions a virtual forest of columns (fig. **9.8**). Its characteristic "horseshoe" arcades are composed of arches using alternating red and white voussoirs, and include the additional element of one set of arches superimposed above another on elongated imposts. This creates an impression of almost limitless space—this space is, however, composed of relatively small architectural elements repeated again and again. Compared with a Christian structure like Hagia Sophia (see figs. 8.27 and 8.29) or Old St. Peter's (see figs. 8.7 and 8.9), Córdoba has an equally large interior area, but there is no centralized space for the sacred theater of the Christian rite. The mosque interior, including the maqsura area around the mihrab, was lavishly decorated with mosaic and carved stone. Tenth-century marble grilles (fig. **9.9**) on the qibla wall present early examples of what we sometimes call **geometric arabesque**: The artist carves out of marble what is essentially a single straplike line that intertwines, creating a characteristic openwork screen of stars and polygons. In the beauty of such artistic geometry many Muslims see a reflection of God's creative hand in the universe.

In addition to providing a community prayer hall, the large Islamic mosques such as the Great Mosque of Córdoba also often incorporated schools and universities, public baths, hospitals and medical schools, soup kitchens for the poor, hostels for travelers and merchants, public clocks (knowing the correct time was

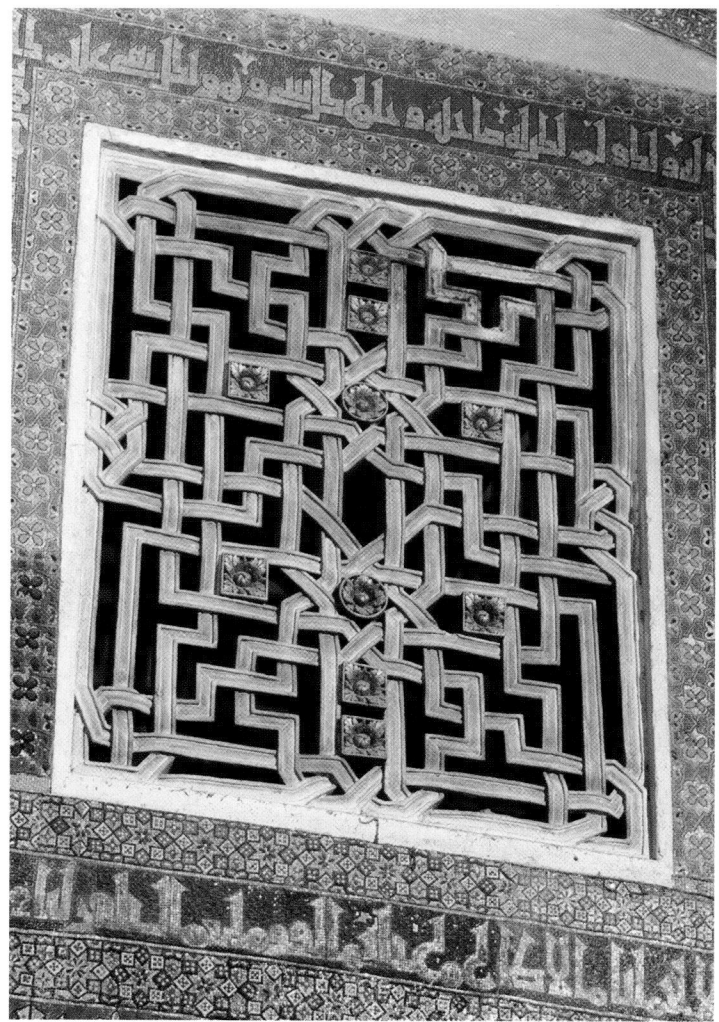

9.9 Carved stone grille on qibla wall of Great Mosque of Córdoba. Mid-10th century

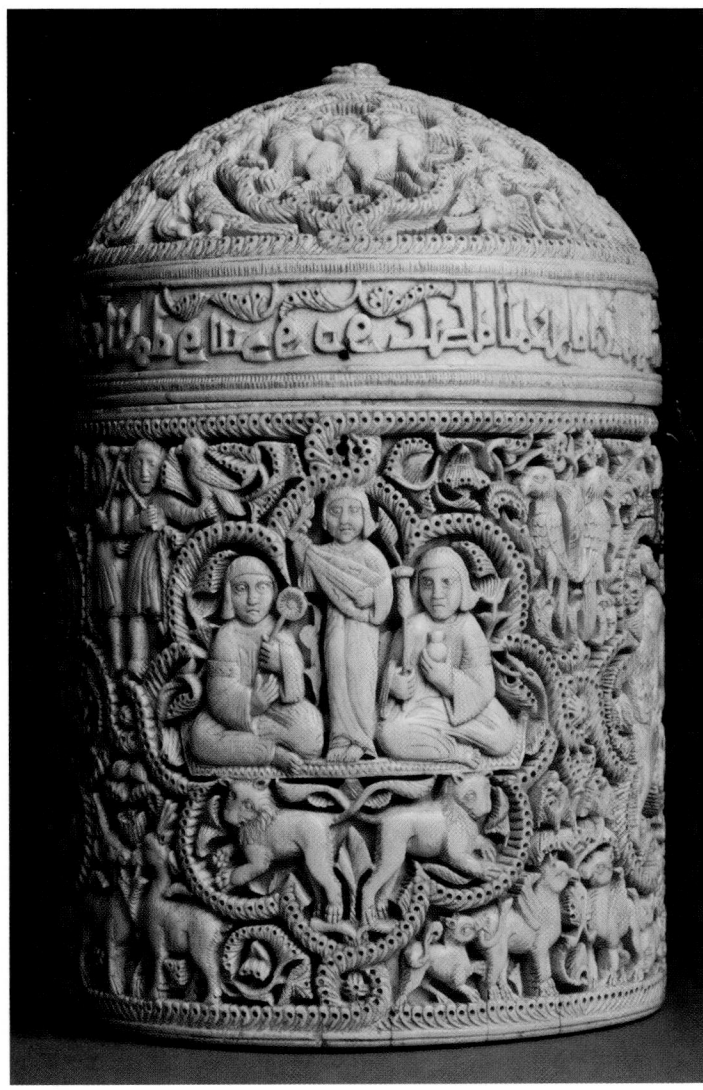

9.10 Ivory casket of al-Mughira, from Córdoba. ca. 960. Height 6" (15 cm), diameter 3" (8 cm). Musée du Louvre, Paris, Inv. 4068

essential for the variable timing of the five daily prayers), public toilets, and fountains serving as the public water supply for the immediate area. Endowments known as *waqf*, based on the income from rental properties, supported the many functions of mosques. Waqfs were also established for social-service institutions and for shrines that were founded independently of mosques. Artistic votive gifts made to such institutions, such as Qur'an manuscripts, lamps, beautiful wooden furniture, carpets, and other objects, were in theory protected in perpetuity, becoming part of the waqf itself. As a consequence, such institutions often became great magnets for works of art, accumulating over time important libraries and collections of beautiful furnishings.

Luxury Arts

On the outskirts of Córdoba, the Umayyads built another huge Islamic palace city known as Medina al-Zahra. A ruin today, the palace complex once included royal workshops for luxury objects such as silk textiles and carved ivory, used as symbols of royal wealth and power and given as royal ceremonial gifts. A small, domed **pyxis** (ivory box) made there for a tenth-century Umayyad prince (fig. **9.10**) incorporates in its decoration a microcosm of Islamic royal imagery and symbolism, including depictions of falconry and hunting, sports, and court musicians, set amid lush carved vegetal ornament and a kufic inscription frieze. Such lavish objects had a symbolic importance far beyond their practical use as containers for jewelry or cosmetics. Their complex, many-layered iconography and their importance and symbolism as royal gifts continue to be studied today.

In the eleventh century, Berber armies serving the Almoravid dynasty from North Africa razed Medina al-Zahra to its foundations, although they and their successors, the Almohads, also built significant monuments in the Maghreb (present-day Morocco and northwestern Africa) and in al-Andalus. But the growing and continual pressure of Christian reconquest from the north saw a dramatic decline in Muslim power in Spain. By the fourteenth century, the Almohad capital of Seville had fallen to the Christian kings of Spain, and Muslims working under Christian rule, known as *Mudejares,* continued Islamic artistic traditions under Christian patronage. (See *The Art Historian's Lens*, page 290.)

ISLAMIC ART AND THE PERSIAN INHERITANCE

In the central and western Islamic lands, from Spain to the western Mediterranean littoral, Islamic arts developed within the geography and culture of the Graeco-Roman tradition; in the east, however, the situation was in many respects quite different. In Mesopotamia and Iran, the Arab Muslim conquerors encountered the cultural sphere of the Sasanians, the heirs to over 1,000 years of Persian civilization with an impressive tradition of art and architecture. This tradition included royal imagery of ceremonial pomp, warfare, and the royal sport of hunting (see fig. 2.20), as well as large and impressive palace buildings.

Architecture

In the eastern Islamic world, following pre-Islamic architectural practice, brick rather than stone was the most common masonry construction material. In place of cylindrical columns, massive brick piers often provided vertical structural support in buildings, and heavy vaults rather than tiled wooden-beam roofs were often chosen to cover interior spaces. Islamic architecture in Mesopotamia, Iran, and Central Asia reflects the available materials, earlier cultural traditions, and even the climate of those regions in distinctive ways. It also provides a curious blending of secular and religious buildings; just as the open arcaded courtyard helps to define both mosque and palace in the Islamic west, another form, known as the iwan, came to define both royal and religious structures in the east.

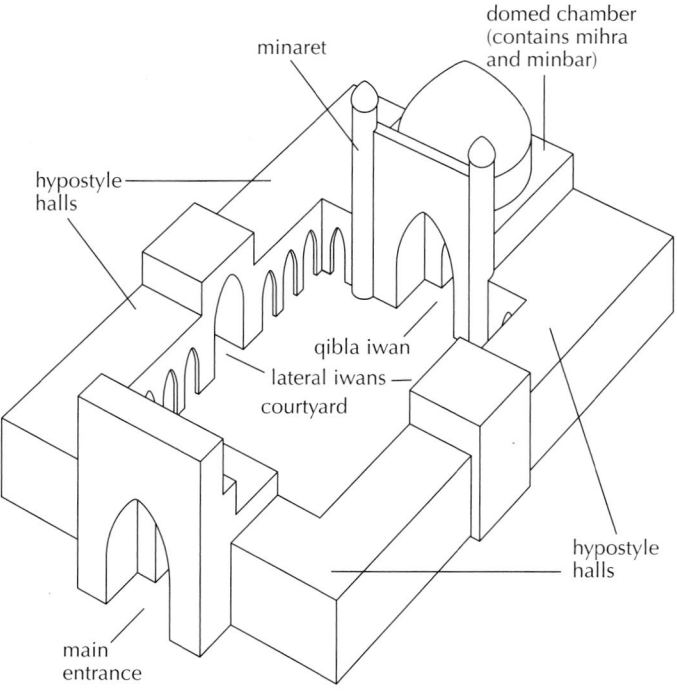

9.11 Schematic drawing of a generic Persian four-iwan mosque

THE FOUR-IWAN MOSQUE One of the first large vaulted brick structures with one open side, known as an iwan, was constructed by the Sasanian ruler Shapur I as an audience hall for his royal palace at Ctesiphon in Mesopotamia (see fig. 2.32).

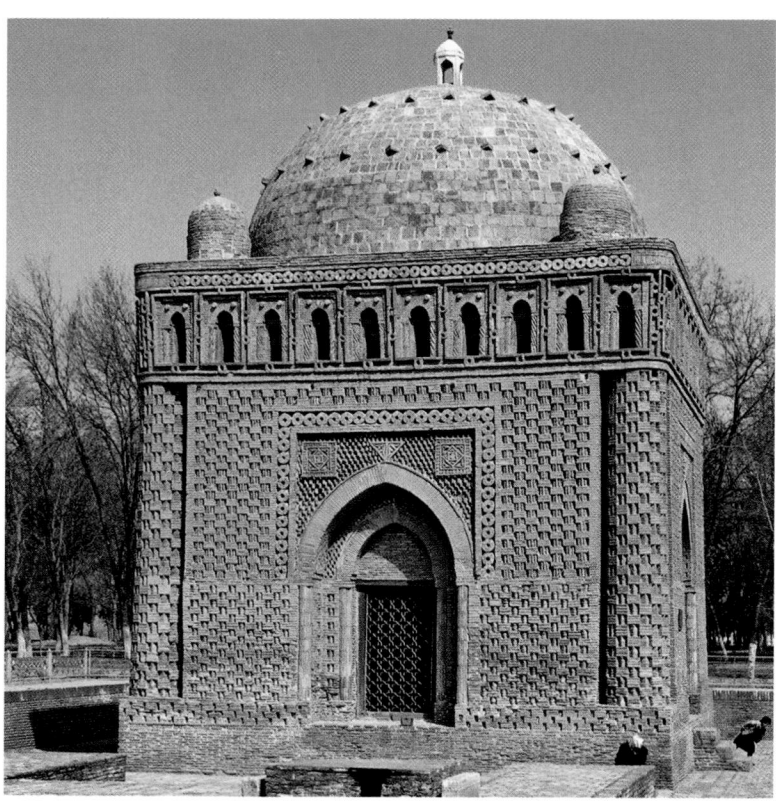

9.12 Tomb of the Samanids, Bukhara, Uzbekistan. ca. 901

The form seems originally to have symbolized royal authority in Iran, and under Islam it was eventually incorporated into a new type of prayer structure, the four-iwan mosque, by placing one massive brick recess in the middle of each of the sides of the rectangular courtyard (fig. **9.11**). From the twelfth century onward, the four-iwan courtyard was a standard feature of both mosques and religious schools of a type known as the *madrasa* throughout Iran and Islamic Central Asia. In most of Iran, as in Mesopotamia, brick was the preferred building material, and the vaults of Iranian mosques were supported by heavy brick piers.

TOMB OF THE SAMANIDS In the aftermath of the Arab conquest of Iran, the Persian cultural tradition gradually reasserted itself in many ways. One of the earliest surviving Islamic dynastic tombs was built in the early tenth century for the Persian Samanid dynasty in Bukhara, an eastern city beyond the Oxus River, today in Uzbekistan (fig. **9.12**). This small cubic structure is in basic concept a hemispherical dome on four massive piers, evidently derived in part from the form of a Sasanian fire temple used for Zoroastrian worship. The dome is supported on the square chamber by means of four squinches in the corners, while the readily available and relatively humble material of brick is used to brilliant effect, with various surface textures recalling woven reeds, kufic inscriptions, and what look like engaged columns in the corners. While the Messenger had opposed all shrines and the prominent tomb structures of kings and saints, which he viewed as suggestive of polytheism or idolatry, the symbolism associated with dynastic kingship and the veneration of major religious figures in Islam meant that tombs and shrines were to figure prominently in the history of architecture throughout the Islamic world.

Figural Art Forms in Iran

The Iranian part of the Islamic world had inherited a rich tradition of material culture, and the successive rulers of Iran, whether themselves Arab, Persian, Turkish, or Mongol in ancestry, fell under the seductive spell of the Persian heritage, which they combined with their Islamic beliefs and traditions. From the prosperous cities of tenth- and eleventh-century Iran there have survived beautiful ceramic wares decorated with maxims, good wishes, and prayers in beautiful calligraphy with figural and vegetal decoration, as well as some exceptional silk textiles and metal objects. The Seljuk Turkish invaders, who ruled Iran from the mid-eleventh century onward, not only built great mosques and tomb structures, but also ruled over a prosperous urban culture that among other things produced one of the richest known traditions of decorated ceramics. Using figural images of all kinds in a multitude of sophisticated techniques, including the use of a metallic pigment known as **luster** fired over the glaze and polychrome enamel decoration known as **mina'i**, these ceramic wares incorporated for middle-class patrons a very diverse repertoire of scenes from Persian romances and mythology, themes from Sufism (the Islamic mystical religious tradition), and the now-familiar Islamic

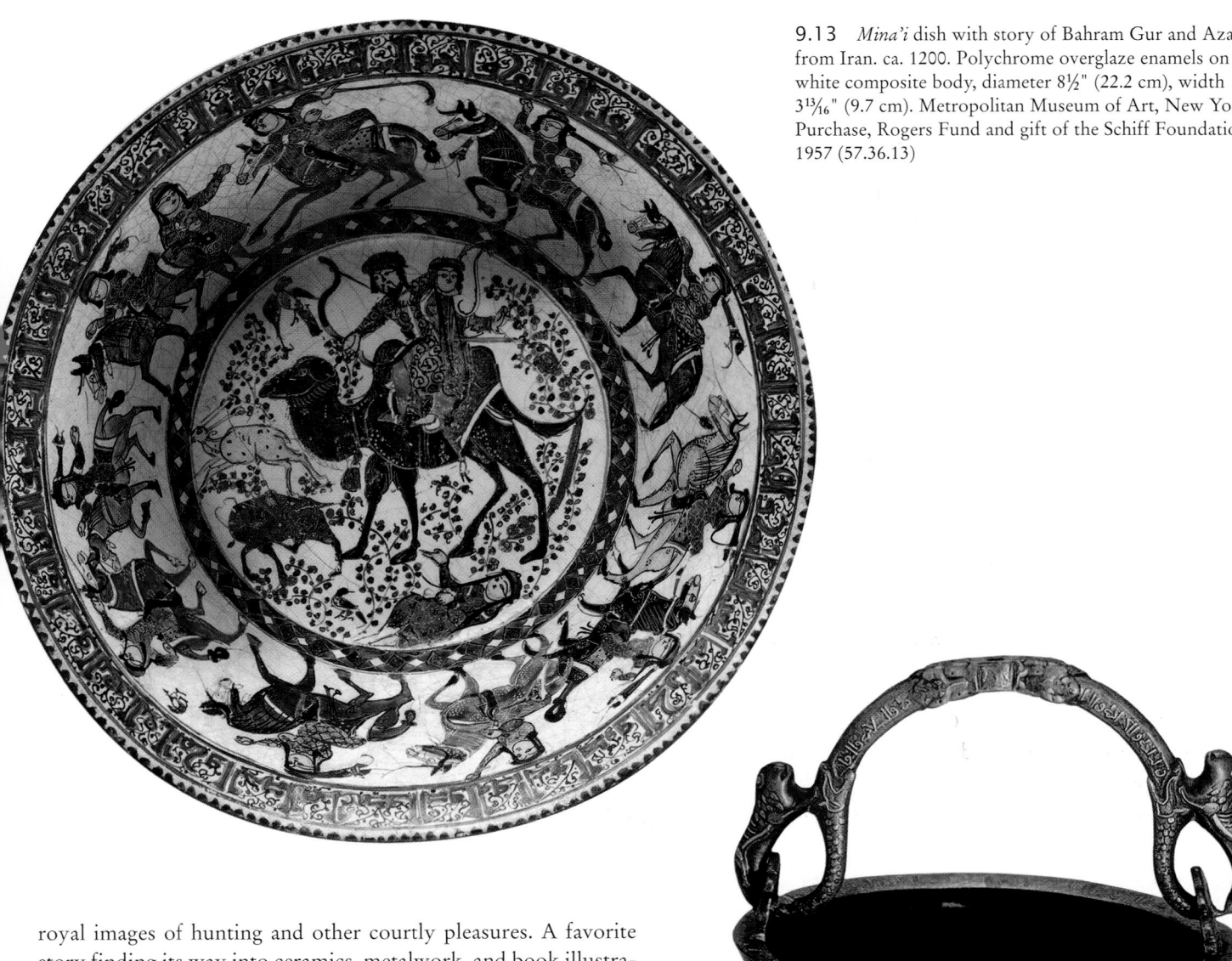

9.13 *Mina'i* dish with story of Bahram Gur and Azadeh, from Iran. ca. 1200. Polychrome overglaze enamels on white composite body, diameter 8½" (22.2 cm), width 3¹³⁄₁₆" (9.7 cm). Metropolitan Museum of Art, New York. Purchase, Rogers Fund and gift of the Schiff Foundation, 1957 (57.36.13)

royal images of hunting and other courtly pleasures. A favorite story finding its way into ceramics, metalwork, and book illustration was that of the royal hunter Bahram Gur and his skeptical girlfriend, the harpist Azadeh. A mina'i plate shows two episodes of continuous narrative, with Azadeh on the camel with her royal lover, and then pushed off the beast after making a remark belittling the hero's marksmanship (fig. **9.13**).

Also noteworthy was the practice of inlaying precious metals into brass or bronze, often incorporating human and animal images. This art form apparently began in Khurasan (formerly the northeastern part of Iran) in the twelfth century and gradually found its way west into upper Mesopotamia by the early thirteenth century. The full repertoire of royal themes is represented in these opulent objects, in which on occasion even the letters of the inscriptions themselves take on human forms (fig. **9.14**). Also created under the Iranian Seljuks were stucco relief sculptures incorporating the human figure. To what do we owe this burst of figural art in seeming contradiction to strict Islamic practice? Practical rather than dogmatic, Iranians under the Seljuks apparently believed that figural images did not necessarily have to be identified with polytheism or idolatry, but could usefully serve both secular and religious purposes without morally corrupting the viewer.

9.14 Muhammad ibn abd al-Wahid (caster) and Masud ibn Ahmad al-Naqqash (inlayer). Cast bronze alloy bucket, inlaid with silver and copper, from Herat. 1163 CE. The State Hermitage Museum, St. Petersburg, Inv. no. IR 2268

Spanish Islamic Art and Europe in the Middle Ages

In 711, the combined Arab and Berber forces of the Muslim commander Tariq ibn Ziyad crossed over the Straits of Gibraltar. By 716, most of Spain was in Muslim hands. Under the rule of the Umayyad dynasty (751–1017), Córdoba became the capital of a prosperous, tolerant, and powerful Muslim kingdom in Spain, in which Christians and Jews played important roles in cultural life. During the eleventh and twelfth centuries, in the aftermath of the fall of the Umayyads, successive Berber invasions from North Africa, first by the Almoravids and then the Almohads, brought new Muslim dynastic patrons into Spain, who oversaw splendid new artistic production. But they also suffered a series of military defeats at the hands of the strengthening Christian powers in the north. Of the several small Islamic kingdoms that formed in the twilight of Muslim rule in Spain, one in particular, that of the Nasrids, ruling in Granada from 1230 to 1492, saw a last glorious flowering of the arts before its defeat by the Castilians and Aragonese united under Ferdinand and Isabella.

The dominant Muslim style in the arts of southern Spain affected artistic production of non-Muslims in many complex ways. From the tenth through the twelfth centuries, in the hardscrabble mountainside principalities of the Christian north, builders built small churches and monasteries in the **mozarab** style, using the horseshoe arches, alternating colored voussoirs, and mosaics of colored stone they had seen in the Muslim south. At the same time, in the northern monasteries, artist-monks illustrated manuscripts of the *Commentaries on the Apocalypse* of Beatus of Liebana with paintings that also reflected the dominant Muslim style. Beyond the Pyrenees, along the medieval pilgrimage roads into France, aspects of the Muslim style even influenced French Romanesque art; the twelfth-century wooden doors of Le Puy Cathedral in France bore an elaborate kufic inscription in Arabic: *mashallah*—"may God protect this place."

After the Christian reconquest of central southern Spain gained momentum in the last part of the thirteenth century, artisans among the conquered Muslim peoples living under Christian rule, known as Mudejares, working under Catholic patrons, continued to produce works of art—buildings, carpets, ceramic wares, and ivories among them—in the Muslim style. The greatest monument of Mudejar art is the fourteenth-century Alcazar or royal palace of King Pedro of Castile in Seville, the style of which is remarkably similar to that of the Alhambra (see fig. 9.27), then being built in nearby Granada. Also noteworthy are the surviving Mudejar synagogues of Córdoba, Granada, and Toledo; with its Hebrew inscriptions intermingling with those in Arabic, the decoration of the Toledan synagogue of Samuel Halevy Abulafia, popularly known as El Tránsito (ca. 1360), follows the Muslim style closely. It appears to demonstrate that important elements of the Arabic-speaking Jewish population of Spain at the time felt themselves fully invested in the dominant artistic culture.

Nationalistic European scholars once preferred to ignore or to deprecate this intermingling of cultures in medieval Spain, but recent scholarship and exhibitions have brought about renewed interest in the Spanish Muslim impact on Europe and in the nature of the flowering of Christian and Jewish culture during the period of *convivencia* (living together) in medieval Muslim Spain. The final expulsion of Muslims and Jews from Spain by the ethnic cleansing of Ferdinand and Isabella in the early sixteenth century brought most of this productive symbiosis to an unhappy end.

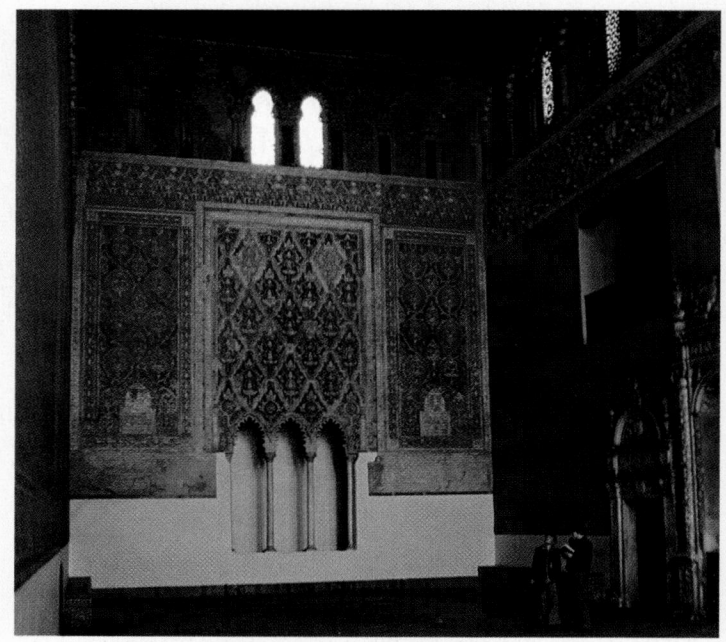

Interior, Transito Synagogue, ca. 1360. Toledo, Spain

THE CLASSICAL AGE

In the center of the Islamic world, in what some scholars term its classical age (roughly 800–1250), the power and influence of Mesopotamia gradually waned with the decline of the Abbasid caliphate. In 969, the Fatimids, a North African Arab dynasty claiming descent from the Messenger's daughter Fatima, conquered Fostat, the Abbasids' major city in Egypt, and founded as their new capital the nearby city of Cairo. The Fatimids were Shi'ites—Muslims who believed that only descendants of Muhammad could legitimately lead the Islamic community. They took their name from the term *shi'at'Ali* ("the party of Ali"), Muhammad's son-in-law, husband of Fatima, and father of the Prophet's grandsons Hasan and Husein. Shi'ite Muslims themselves were divided into several major and many minor sects, all of which opposed the basic political tenets of Sunni, or orthodox, Islam, where having the blood of the Messenger was not a prerequisite for holding political power.

The rise of the Fatimids in the tenth century coincided with a gradual weakening of Abbasid power and a decline in the caliphate authority, based in Baghdad. By the eleventh century, the Seljuk Turks had moved westward out of Central Asia to gain

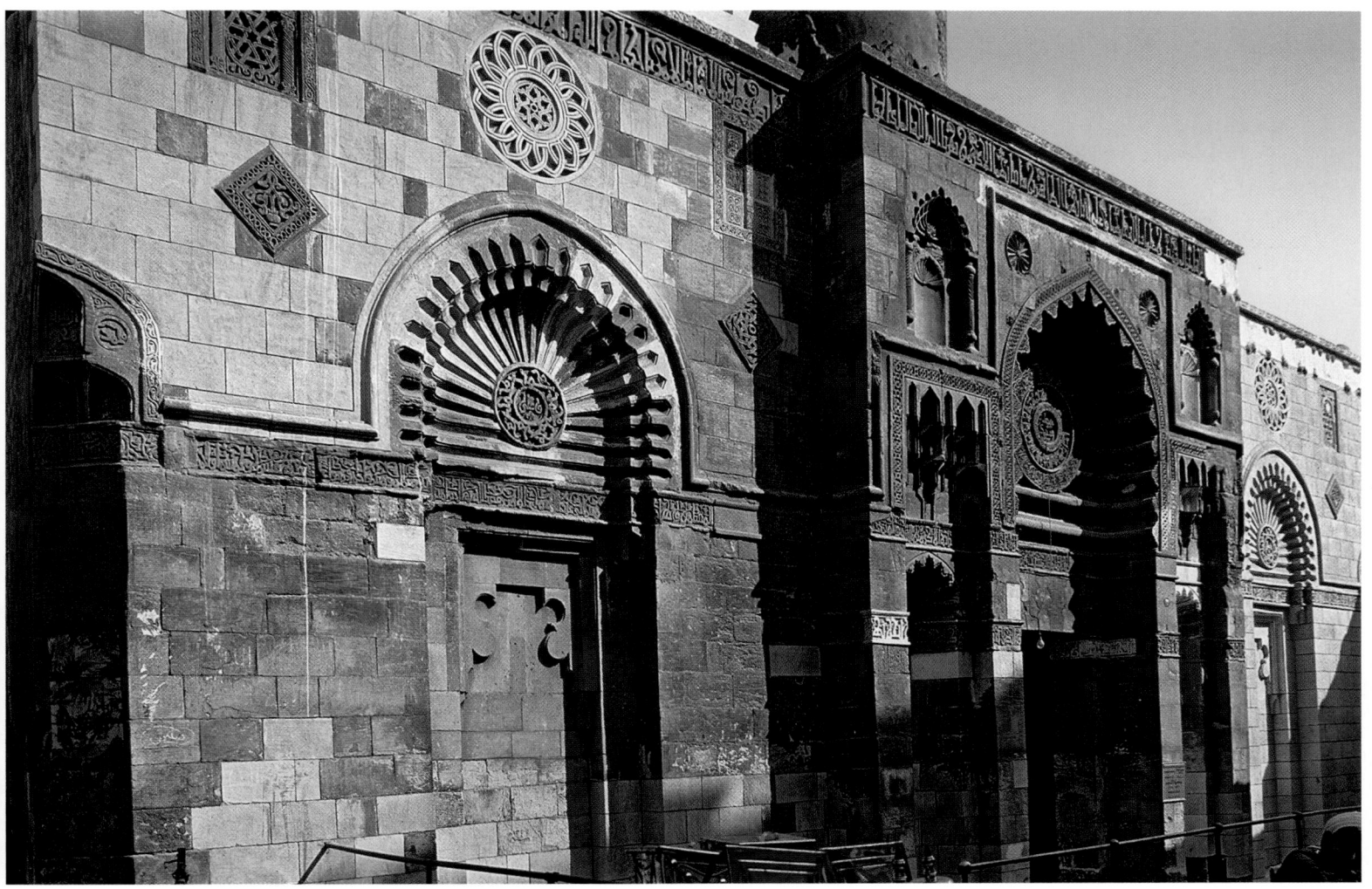

9.15   The al-Aqmar Mmosque, Cairo. ca. 1026

control first in Iran and then in northern Mesopotamia and Asia Minor; around the same time, in 1099, the Norman warriors of the First Crusade captured Jerusalem. The Seljuks were Sunni Muslims; they fostered arts of all kinds and supported Sunni doctrine with the founding of many madrasa colleges for the teaching of Sunni law. In the late twelfth century, another Sunni dynasty, the Ayyubids, drove the Christians out of Jerusalem, and for a brief time also oversaw important developments in the arts.

The Fatimid Artistic Impact

Under the Fatimids, Egypt experienced a major artistic revival. The eleventh-century city walls of Cairo, incorporating the latest cutting-edge military technology, were constructed with stone stripped from the outer parts of the pyramids in nearby Giza. Two great urban palaces, decorated with figural images of music making, dancing, hunting, and royal ritual, were constructed within the city, and elaborate parades and ceremonial processions proclaimed the dynasty's power. Not one but two congregational mosques were constructed in Cairo under Fatimid rule, and smaller mosques served individual neighborhoods of

the city, which by the twelfth century had expanded beyond its original walls.

AL-AQMAR MOSQUE   Among the most beautiful of the Fatimid mosques in Cairo is the small mosque known as al-Aqmar (fig. **9.15**), built by a Fatimid noble. It was skillfully constructed on an irregular plot of land, with its off-axis façade corresponding to the original street. In addition to the carved stone, Arabic inscriptions, and ornamental niches, we see to either side of the main portal a developed form of **muqarnas**, the distinctive geometric, almost crystalline faceted decoration, composed of small nichelike forms, that eventually became an iconic form of Islamic decoration from the Atlantic to beyond the Oxus.

TEXTILES AND IVORIES   Under the Fatimids, a thriving maritime commerce between Egypt and Italy left its mark in the form of Islamic artistic influence on twelfth-century Italian architecture in port cities such as Palermo, Salerno, Amalfi, and Pisa. In addition, preexisting traditions of weaving, mostly carried on by indigenous Coptic Christians, continued to flourish alongside the production of new textiles incorporating silk imported from Iran

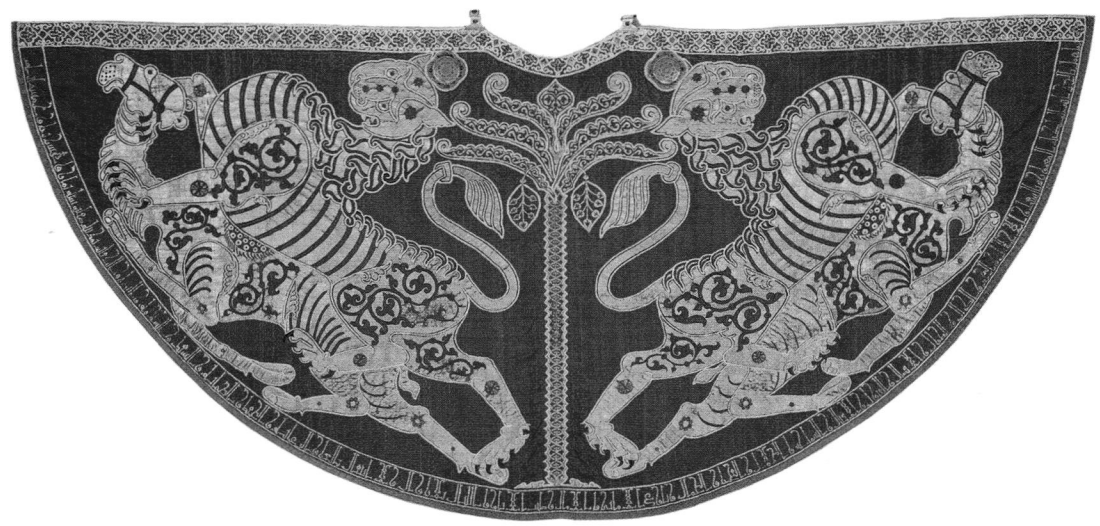

9.16   Cloak of Roger II of Sicily. 12th century. Red silk embroidered with silk and pearls, diameter 11'3" (3.42 m). Made in Palermo for the coronation of Roger II in 1133–34. Kunsthistoriches Museum, Vienna

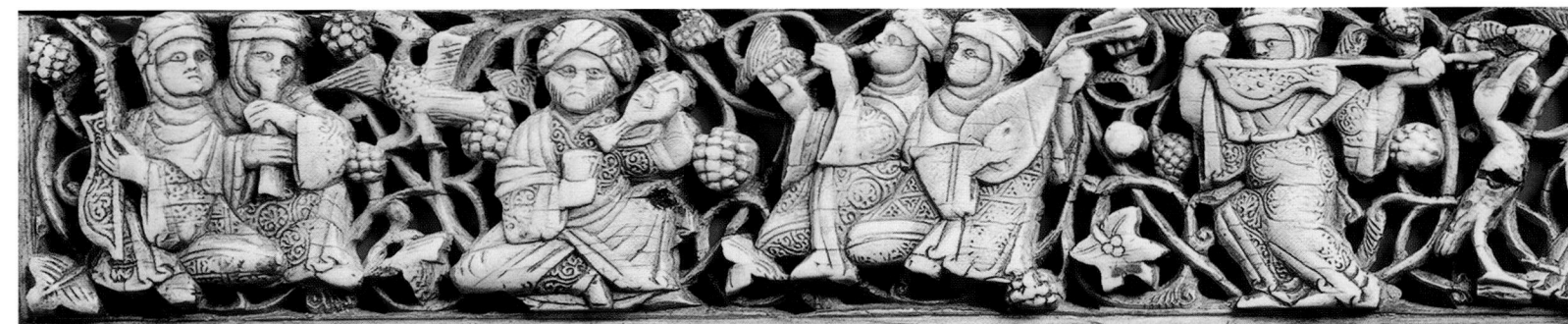

9.17   Detail of carved ivory frame with court scenes, from Egypt. 12th century. 17¾ × 14⅓" (44.9 × 36.5 cm). Staatliche Museen Preussischer Kulturbesitz, Museum für Islamische Kunst, Berlin, I.6375

or China. In the twelfth century, Muslim artisans working in Palermo in Sicily, newly conquered by the Normans, created the elaborate embroidered cape of King Roger II (r. 1095–1154), with inscriptions in Arabic praising the Catholic ruler (fig. **9.16**). It was used for many centuries in Habsburg coronations. Along with remarkable luster-painted ceramics, textiles, rock crystal, and glassware, Fatimid artists produced carved ivory objects significant both for their beauty and for the insights they provide into Fatimid court life. One of these, an ivory frame now in Berlin (fig. **9.17**), shows a multitude of energetic figures engaged in dancing, music making, hunting, wrestling, and drinking what can only be supposed to be wine, whose prohibition in the Qur'an did not preclude its use or depiction in the private customs and art of Islamic palaces.

The Ayyubids and the Seljuk Turks of Asia Minor

It was during the Seljuk Turkish rule over central and northern Palestine, in 1099, that European warriors of the First Crusade captured Jerusalem, which remained briefly in Christian hands until its recapture in 1187 by the Ayyubid sultan Salah ad-Din, known in the West as Saladin. The period of the Crusades was to last until the fourteenth century, when all but the last vestiges of crusader kingdoms disappeared from the eastern Mediterranean. Artistic cross-fertilization between Catholic Europe and the Muslim Middle East developed extensively during the entire period, and persisted long after the crusaders departed. The Ayyubids, a Kurdish dynasty originating in northern Syria, reconquered greater Syria and Egypt for Sunni Islam in the twelfth century, and their brief reign, ending in the mid-thirteenth century, produced a remarkable record of accomplishment in architecture and the arts. Ayyubid military architecture, such as the citadels of Aleppo and Cairo, embodied the latest military technology, and was to inspire many a European castle constructed in the Romanesque and Gothic eras. Under the Ayyubids, the arts of inlaid metalwork, ceramics, and enameled glassware also flourished.

To the east, in the twilight of the dynasty's glory, the ancient Abbasid capital of Baghdad experienced by the early thirteenth

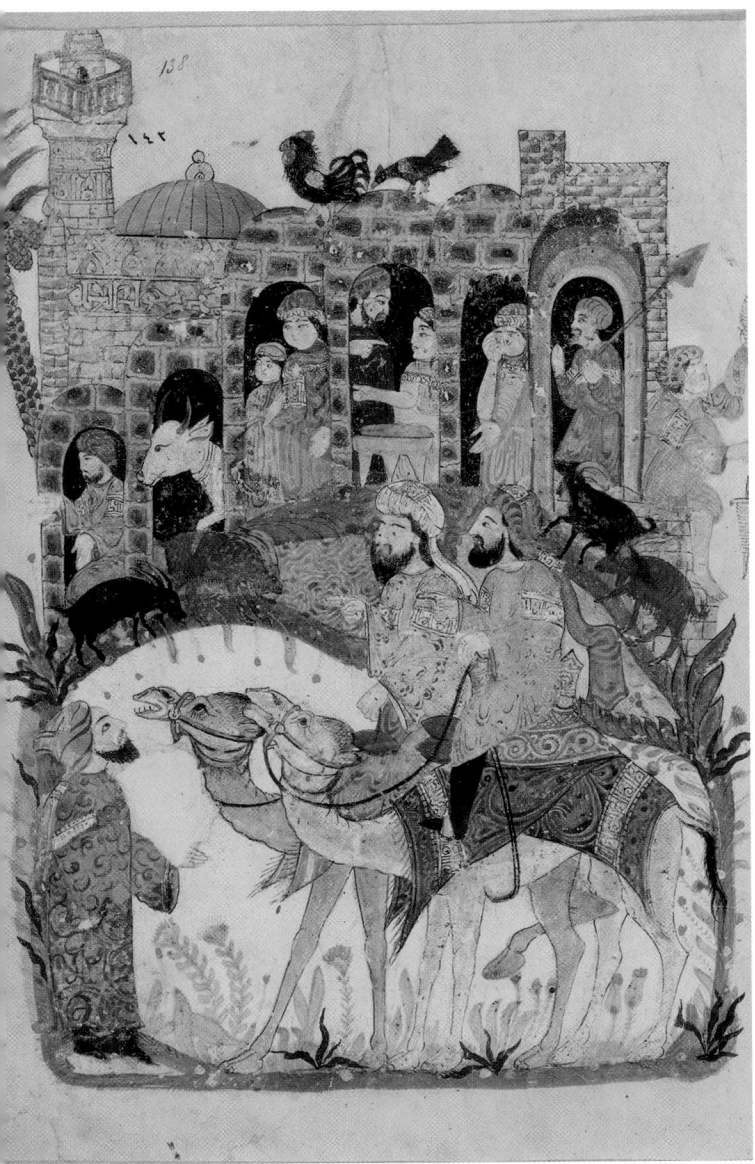

THE CARAVANSARAY The largest buildings constructed by the Seljuks in Asia Minor are a type of fortified wayside inn known in Turkish as **han** and in the West as **caravansaray**. Built at regular intervals along the main caravan routes linking the cities of Asia Minor, these buildings usually consisted of an outer court and a vaulted inner hall. The outer court had stables for pack animals, baths for travelers, a small mosque, and a kitchen. The inner hall, where goods could be stored and travelers slept, often had a tall dome on squinches, the pyramidal exterior of which could be seen along the highway from a great distance. The largest and most handsome of the Asia Minor hans, the Sultan Han, built between the cities of Konya and Aksaray around 1229 by Sultan Alaeddin Keykubad, has beautifully carved doorways leading into the courtyard and vaulted hall, and evidently employed in its construction the services of both local and Syrian stone carvers. A similar structure was built by the same ruler on the Kayseri-Sivas road and also called the Sultan Han (fig. **9.19**); dozens of others are still today found in Turkey. They facilitated commerce throughout Asia Minor, where beautifully constructed and elaborately decorated mosques, madrasas, and palaces were built throughout the twelfth and thirteenth centuries.

9.18 Yahya ibn Mahmud al-Wasiti, *Scene in an Arab Village*, illustration from a *Maqamat* manuscript. ca. 1237. Opaque watercolors on paper, 13¾ × 10¼" (34.8 × 26 cm). Bibliothèque Nationale, Paris. MS. arabe 5847, folio 138r

century a revival in the arts of the book. Such artists as Yahya ibn Mahmud al-Wasiti produced miniature paintings remarkable for their humor, observations of everyday life, and insights into human foibles, here seen illustrating a *Maqamat* manuscript (fig. **9.18**). (*Maqamat* means "stories" and this manuscript contains 50 short stories.)

To the north, the Seljuk Turks had finally entered the Asia Minor heartland of the Byzantine Empire after 1071. In the following 200 years, with the full participation of the artists of both the Muslim and the Christian communities in the prosperous urban centers of Asia Minor, art and architecture flourished under what were known as the Seljuks of Rum (Rome). Craftspeople and artists from Iran, as well as from Syria and Egypt, served the lavish patronage of the Seljuk sultans.

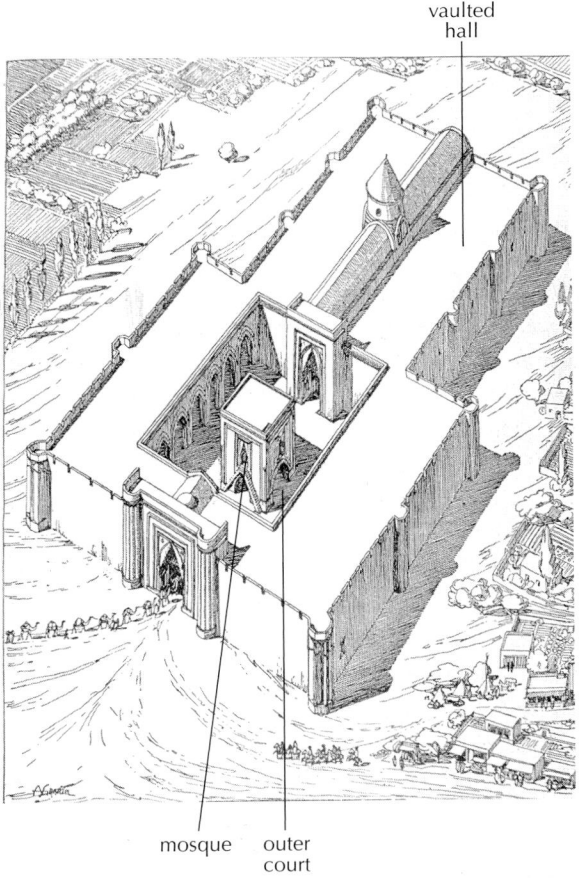

9.19 Sultan Han, Kayseri-Sivas road, Turkey. ca. 1236. Drawing by Albert Gabriel

LATER CLASSICAL ART AND ARCHITECTURE

By the second decade of the thirteenth century, reports began to arrive in the Islamic lands of Central Asia, Iran, Egypt, Syria, and Asia Minor of an ominous power rising in the east. The eventual triumph of the Mongol successors of Genghis Khan brought devastation to much of the Islamic world east of the Mediterranean. Some areas, such as Asia Minor, emerged relatively unscathed. Others, such as the Central Asian city of Bukhara (sacked and burned in 1220) and the Abbasid capital of Baghdad (sacked and destroyed in 1258), suffered untold losses in architectural monuments and artistic goods, as well as the even more serious destruction of infrastructure, such as irrigation canals, roads, and social services. However, by the end of the thirteenth century,

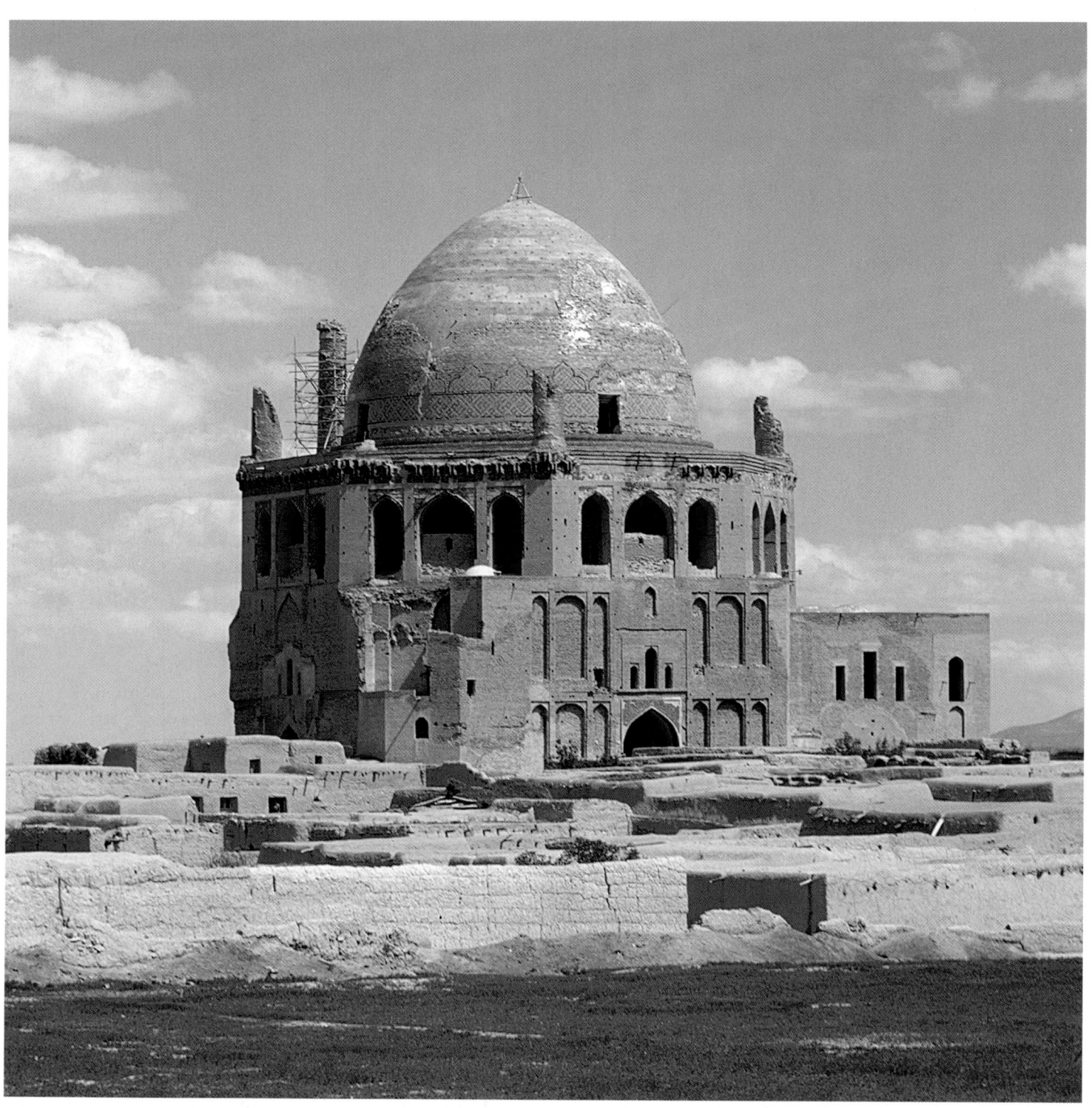

9.20   Tomb of Oljeytu, Sultaniya, Iran. ca. 1314

the western Mongol rulers, known as Il-Khans, had converted to Islam, and their patronage and that of their successors brought about in Iran and its surrounding areas yet another period of artistic flowering, in which artists in western Asia were exposed to new artistic inspiration from China, flowing west through the Mongol domains on what historians now call the Silk Road, a 5,000-mile (8,000-km) network of caravan routes from Honan (present-day Luoyang) through the Islamic world to Europe.

Mongol rule in Central Asia and Iran was short-lived, but the artistic legacy of the Mongols continued under the Timurids, who by the late fourteenth century had established their empire in the former Mongol lands and produced a brilliant court tradition, the legacy of which was eventually felt from the eastern Mediterranean to central India. Far to the west and south, after 1260, Sunni Mamluks in Syria and Egypt, inheritors of the Fatimid Shi'ite capital of Cairo, set about their own symbolic appropriation of the land, with a new architecture of tall domes and complex minarets, and an artistic economy that mixed the Turkic (of the people who originated in central Asia and migrated to northern, central and western Eurasia, including the Anatolian peninsula) tastes of the ruling class with indigenous Egyptian traditions. Trade between Cairo and Italy was brisk, and Mamluk artistic production sometimes even reflected the commercial attractiveness of Mamluk goods in Europe.

Mongol Patronage

In the realms of art and architecture, the Mongols built on what had come before them. The legacy of later Arab book illustration, which had flowered in Iraq in the decades before the Mongol sack of Baghdad in 1258, lived on in elements of the emergent Iranian tradition of miniature painting that began in the first half of the fourteenth century under Mongol patronage in their capital of Tabriz in northwest Iran. Artists in Tabriz produced paintings in a new style that incorporated aspects of Chinese brush painting and Chinese landscape. In other Mongol centers, Chinese motifs and raw materials contributed to a revival of silk weaving, and preexisting traditions of inlaid metalwork and luster-painted ceramics developed in new directions. Like almost all foreigners who had conquered Iran from the time of Alexander the Great, the Mongol rulers quickly became "Persianized," commissioning illustrated manuscripts of the Persian national epic, the *Shah-nameh* or "Book of Kings," and building four-iwan brick mosques and high-domed tomb structures in the Persian style. The nature of Mongol patronage in Iran can be seen in the tomb structure built by the Il-Khan Oljeytu (r. 1304–1317). The son of a Sunni father and a Christian mother, Oljeytu founded a new capital in Sultaniya, bringing artists and builders from all over his realms to embellish it. At the center of his capital stands a huge structure with a massive pointed dome covered with turquoise blue tiles, the royal mausoleum of Oljeytu (fig. 9.20). With its painted interior decoration of carved and painted stucco (fig. 9.21) and elaborate tile decoration, it is unprecedented in size and scale for an Islamic shrine or tomb. This great domed building in

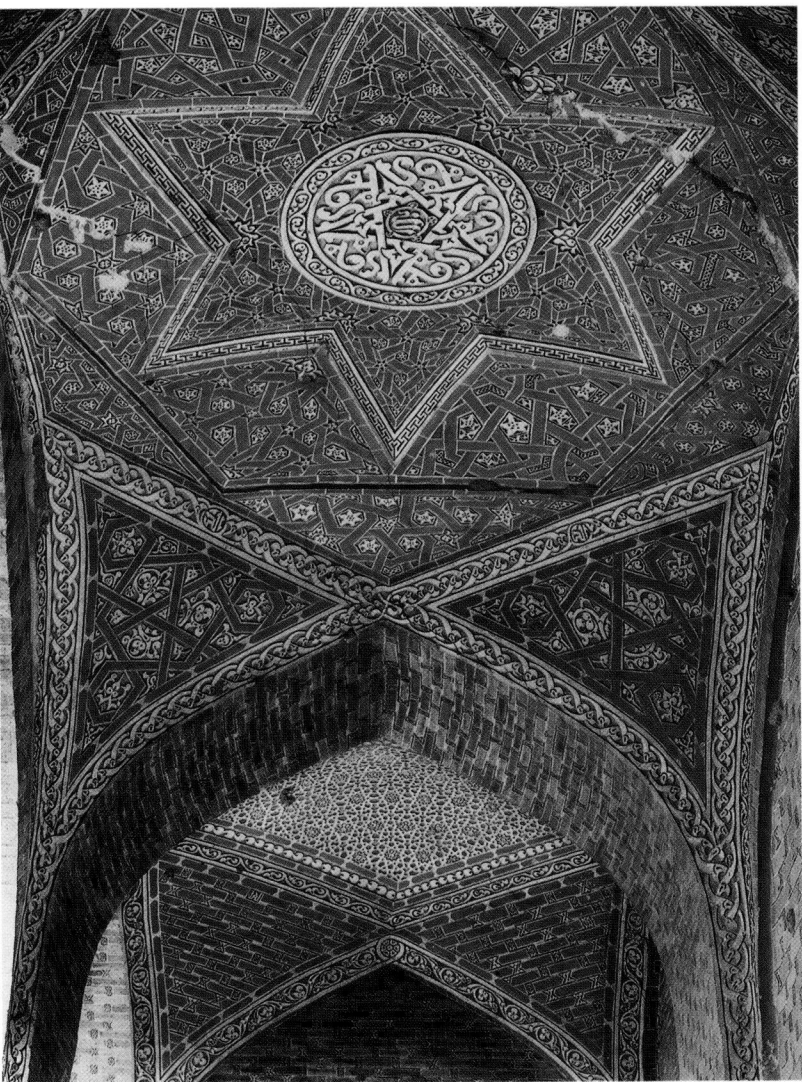

9.21 Interior, Tomb of Oljeytu, Iran. By permission of Hans and Sonia Seherr-Thoss

Sultaniya represents the grandiose artistic aspirations of the Il-Khans, as well as their enlightened patronage of artistic innovation within preexisting Persian traditions.

Timurid Patronage

After the death of the last ruler of the short-lived Il-Khan dynasty in 1337, Iran and Islamic Central Asia broke up into smaller principalities, one of which, that of the Jalayrid dynasty, kept the tradition of Mongol painting alive in Tabriz and Baghdad. By the late fourteenth century, another Turko-Mongol power had risen beyond the Oxus, this time under the rule of the strategic genius Timur (r. ca. 1370–1405), known in the West as Tamerlane.

ARCHITECTURE AND ITS DECORATION In his capital city of Samarkand, Timur built in the 1390s a gigantic congregational mosque, the largest four-iwan mosque in the Iranian tradition, and his palace of Aq Saray in his nearby birthplace was built

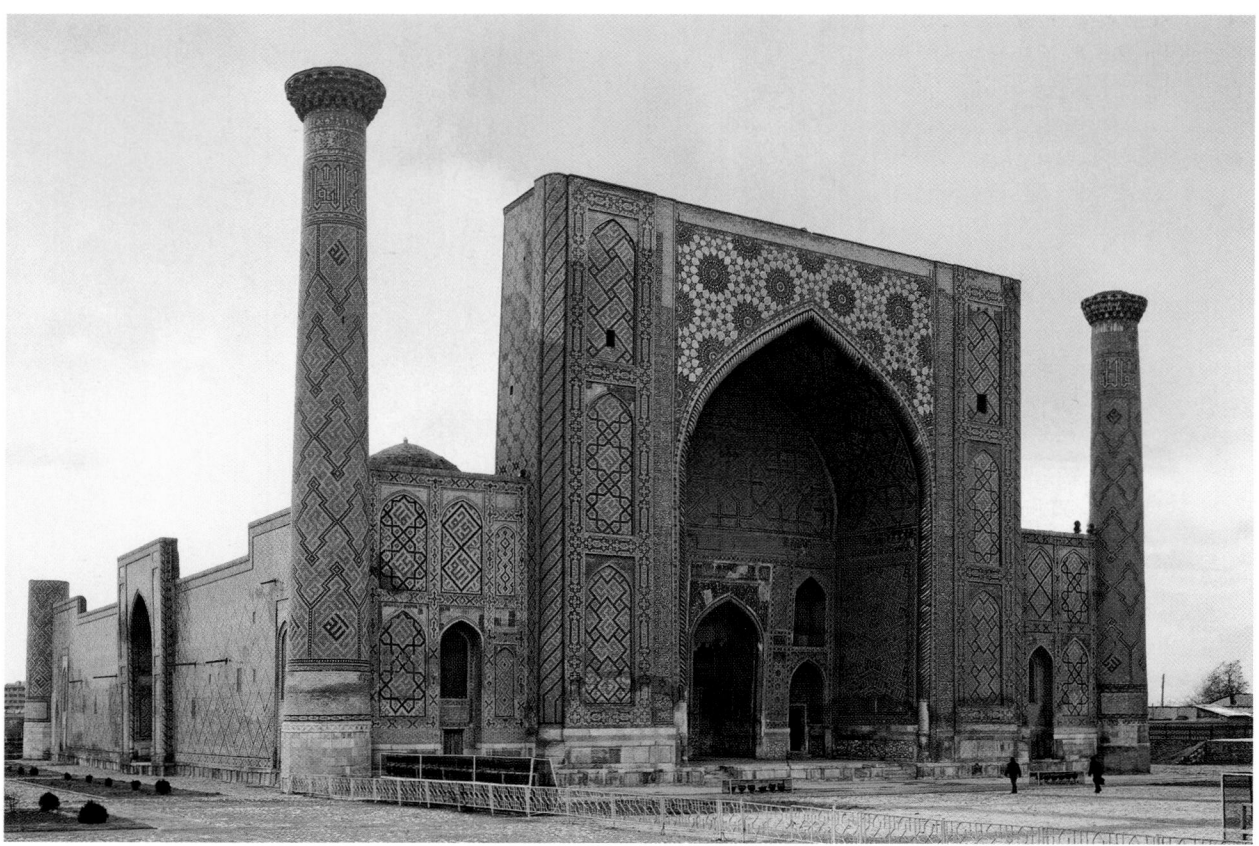

on an equally gargantuan scale. The artistic aspirations of the Timurid dynasty reached their climax in the fifteenth century. At Herat, which became the main capital under the rule of Timur's son Shah Rukh (r. 1405–1447), Timur's grandson Baysunghur founded a royal library—in fact, a royal design studio—that, in addition to producing beautiful books decorated with illuminations, miniature paintings, and calligraphy, served as a central source of designs for many other artistic mediums, drawing on the artistic legacy of the Jalayrids as well as the arts of China and Central Asia.

To the north in Samarkand, in present-day Uzbekistan, another of Timur's grandsons, Ulugh Beg, founded (ca. 1420) a major astronomical observatory as well as one of the most important Timurid madrasa colleges (fig. 9.22). Ulugh Beg's college has a massive iwan before its main portal and two cylindrical minarets. Elaborate, carefully constructed mosaics of colored tiles in geometric and vegetal patterns lavishly decorate the entire façade. Ceramic building decoration in Central Asia under the Timurids and their immediate predecessors developed a rich variety and complexity equaled but never surpassed in the subsequent history of art in the region of Iran.

BOOK ILLUSTRATION It was in Herat, in the twilight of the Timurid dynasty at the end of the fifteenth century, that the long and complex history of Persian book painting saw one of its most glorious chapters. In the 1480s and 1490s, the great master Behzad and his colleagues brought about a series of refinements in Islamic painting that have become legendary. Behzad himself had not

only a sensitivity to the lyrical and heroic themes of Persian poetic texts, but a keen eye for the world around him. In many of his paintings made to illustrate verse texts, such as this illustration from a manuscript of the *Bostan* (*Poetic Garden*) of Sa'di, it is the everyday heart of Herat that we see so masterfully depicted (fig. **9.23**). In a scene outside a mosque, the high point of view allows us to look into the courtyard, while at the doorway a rich man encounters a beggar, and another man washes at a fountain. Behzad's spatial and narrative clarity, overlapping elements in ingenious ways to give a sense of three dimensions while portraying all of his protagonists in the same scale, brings a new power to these small paintings, the small size of which does not restrict their generous pictorial space, complex settings, and large cast of characters.

Mamluk Patronage

In the central Islamic lands, only one power had successfully repulsed the Mongol invasions of the thirteenth century. When the last Ayyubid ruler of Egypt died in 1250, his wife married her husband's leading general, a Mamluk, or slave soldier, of Kipchak Turkish origin named Baybars, who became ruler in 1260. That year, at the Battle of Ain Jalut (in what is now northern Israel), a Mamluk army defeated the Il-Khan's Mongol troops. As a result, Egypt and much of Syria remained free of Mongol rule under the various Mamluk dynasties, which ruled from Cairo and Damascus, from 1250 until the conquest of Cairo by the Ottoman Turks in 1517.

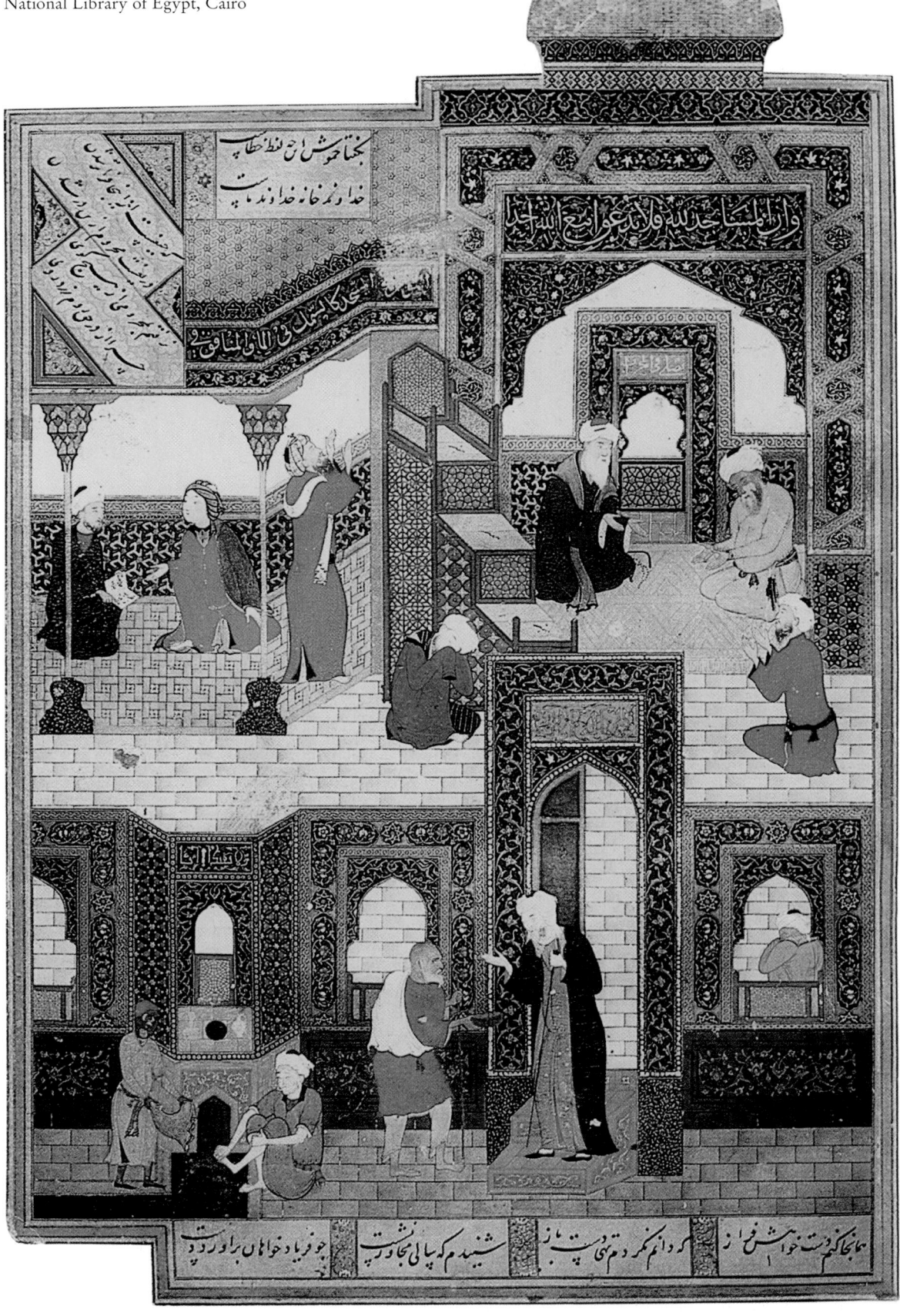

9.23 Behzad, *A Poor Man Refused Admittance to a Mosque*, from a manuscript of the *Bostan* of Sa'di, from Herat. 1486 CE. Opaque watercolors, ink, and gold on paper, 12 × 8½" (30.5 × 21.5 cm). General Egyptian Book Organization, Cairo, Adab Farsi 908. National Library of Egypt, Cairo

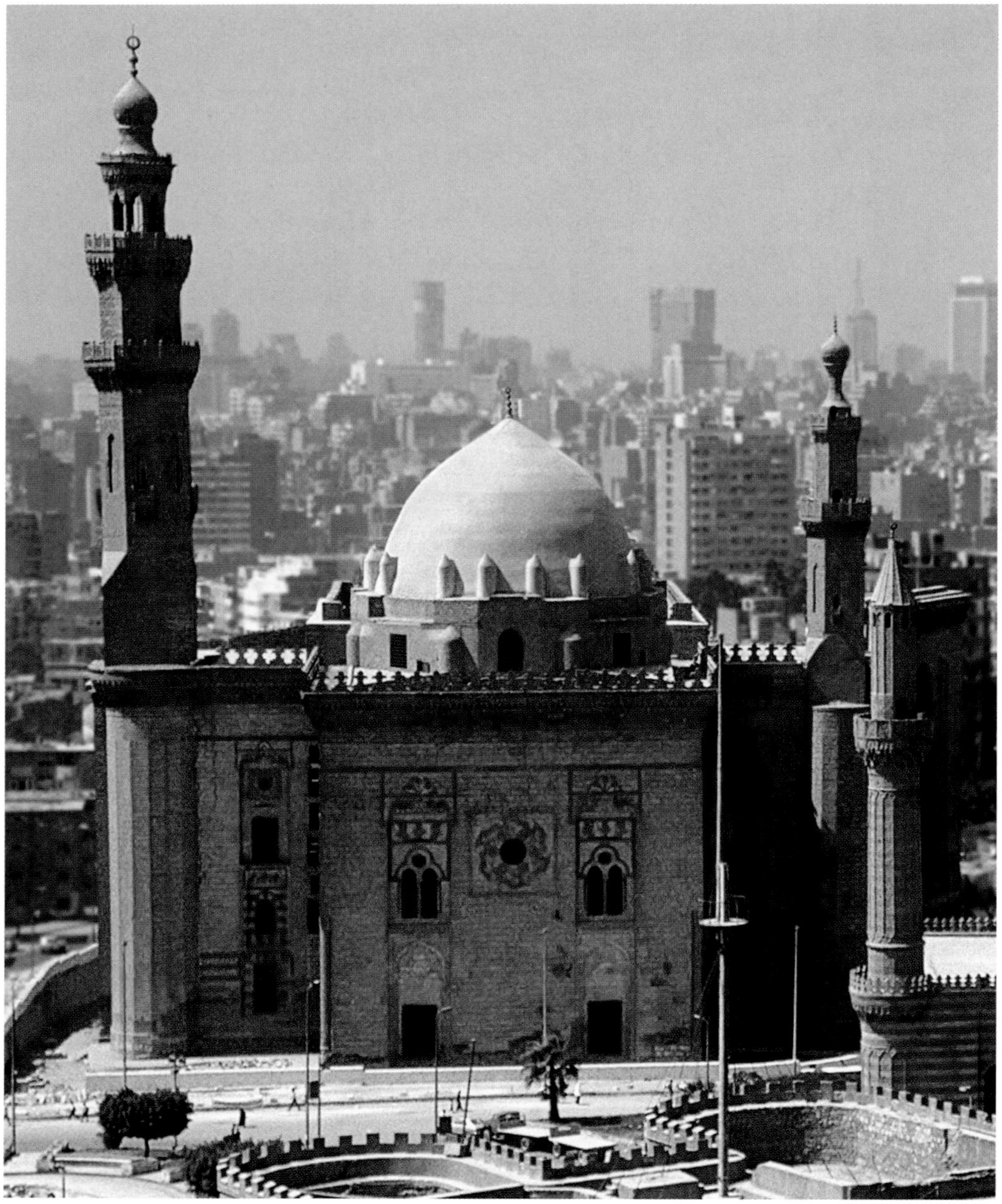

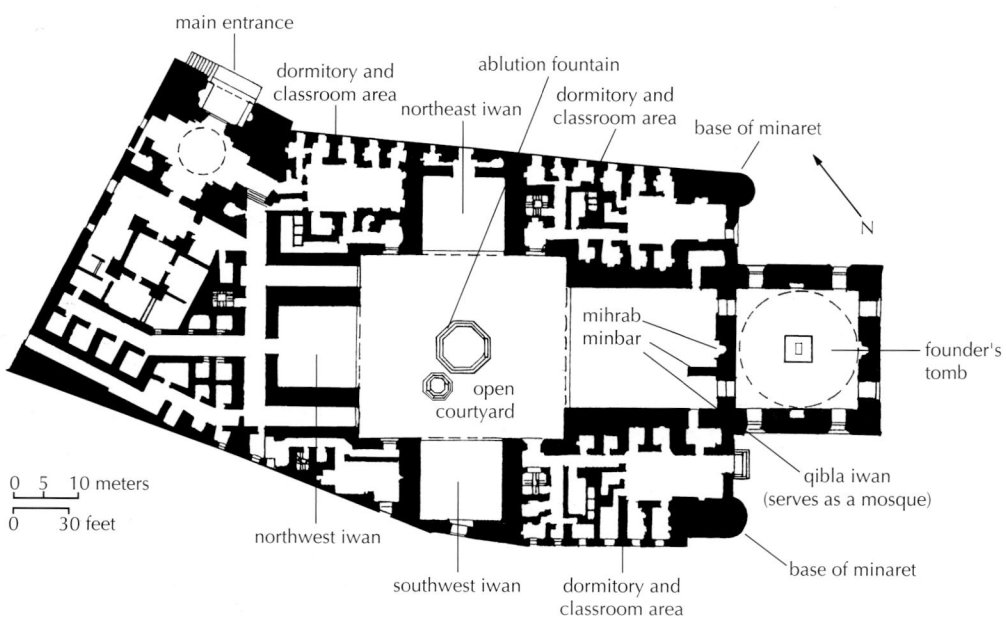

9.24 Complex of Sultan Hasan, Cairo, Egypt. ca. 1354–61

main entrance

dormitory and classroom area

ablution fountain

northeast iwan

dormitory and classroom area

base of minaret

N

mihrab
minbar

founder's tomb

open courtyard

qibla iwan (serves as a mosque)

0 5 10 meters

0 30 feet

base of minaret

northwest iwan

southwest iwan

dormitory and classroom area

9.25 Plan of the complex of Sultan Hasan, Cairo

ARCHITECTURE It is easy to see an evolutionary progression from the art of Egypt in Fatimid and then Ayyubid times into the Mamluk reign. Mamluk patronage was at times quite lavish, and most of the artistic character of today's Cairo comes from the Mamluk period. Working within the confines of often irregularly shaped plots of urban land in the crowded Egyptian metropolis, builders under Mamluk patronage created mosques, madrasas, tombs, and a distinctive combination of public libraries and water fountains. These works are characterized by a new style of elaborately decorated high domes, complex multibalconied minarets, and lavish decoration incorporating both carving and multicolored marble mosaic paneling. As Sunni Muslims living in the shadow of the Shi'ite Fatimid past, the Turkish-speaking Mamluks, often unable to speak or write Arabic, not only built mosques, but also a very large number of madrasas, or institutions of higher education, to serve the local populace.

The largest and most impressive of these is the madrasa and tomb of Sultan Hasan (fig. **9.24**). It was constructed between 1354 and 1361 by the otherwise undistinguished Mamluk sultan Nasir ad-Din al-Hasan, into whose state coffers had flowed a torrent of riches as a result of the high mortality of the mid-century outbreak of Black Death, which left many large estates without heirs. Designed as four separate colleges within one building (fig. **9.25**), each devoted to one of the four major schools of Islamic jurisprudence, the mammoth structure houses a mosque in the qibla iwan of its huge four-iwan courtyard, as well as classrooms, dormitory rooms, and, on the south side behind the qibla wall, the gigantic domed tomb of Sultan Hasan himself. Decorated with varicolored marble mosaic paneling, with spectacular carved portals, bronze doors inlaid with silver and gold, and furnishings such as a marble minbar and muezzin platform and a walnut Qur'an lectern inlaid with ebony and ivory, the madrasa and tomb of Sultan Hasan show the artistic aspirations of the Mamluks to be equal to those of their Mongol rivals to the northeast in size, expense, and beauty. Right down to the Ottoman conquest in 1517, Mamluk patrons in Egypt and Syria continued to produce a large number of beautiful buildings, including the famous tombs that today crowd Cairo's Northern Cemetery.

ENAMELED GLASS, METALWORK, AND CARPETS
Mamluk patronage in Syria and Egypt also inherited a tradition of enameled glass that had begun under the Ayyubids. By the early fourteenth century, Mamluk glass vessels enameled with bright colors had become world-famous. Various Mamluk nobles commissioned glass oil lamps destined to be hung in their tombs and mosques, and artists incorporated the patrons' blazons, or coats of arms, in the decoration (fig. **9.26**). Under the Mamluks, by around 1300, the art of inlaying silver and gold into bronze and brass had also reached its apogee in Islamic art. In later Mamluk times, from the fifteenth century onward, the Mamluk realms saw the production of spectacular carpets that were exported to Europe, where, like the enameled glass, they were highly prized. (See *Materials and Techniques*, page 301.)

Nasrid Patronage: The Alhambra

By the mid-fourteenth century, most of Muslim al-Andalus had fallen to the Christian reconquest; Seville and Córdoba were part of the Castilian domains, and only the mountain kingdom of Granada in the south in the shadow of the Sierra Nevada remained under Muslim control, ruled by the Nasrid dynasty. On a flat hill towering over the city of Granada, the Nasrid monarchs built a palace known to them as al-Qasr al-Hamra (The Red Palace), and to history as the Alhambra. Originally conceived, as most Islamic palaces were, as a series of pavilions and smaller buildings constructed around one or more garden courtyards, the Alhambra incorporated metaphors for Paradise on earth. The inscriptions on its walls, some of which were written by one of the great Arab poets of the time, form a hymn of praise to the palace itself. Although what remains today is only a small fragment of the original palace, the rest having been consumed by a mammoth Renaissance palace and an equally huge Franciscan monastery, the most beautiful of the Alhambra's surviving courtyards, known as the Court of the Lions, gives us a vivid picture of

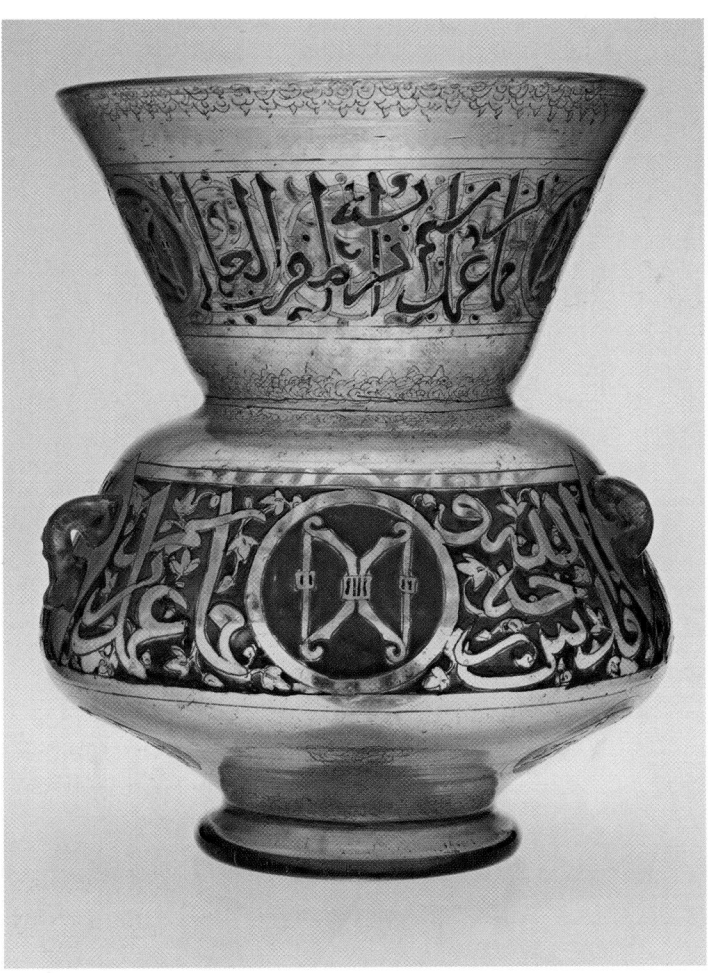

9.26   Mosque lamp with blazon, from Cairo. ca. 1285. Enameled, stained, and gilded glass, height 10⅓" (26.2 cm), width 8¼" (21 cm). Metropolitan Museum of Art, New York. Gift of J. Pierpont Morgan. 1919 17.190.985

PRIMARY SOURCE

The Ottoman Sultan Selim II (1524–1574)

An Order from the Imperial Court

By spring 1572 the building of the sultan's mosque in Edirne was well under way. From the royal palace, the sultan took a very close interest in the progress of affairs, an approach that seems to have bordered on micromanagement. He even dictated what inscriptions were to be placed in what locations in the building.

To the Architect in Chief:

For the inscriptions that are currently needed for my noble mosque in Edirne that I have ordered to be built, you have requested the services of the calligrapher Molla Hasan. Now this individual has been retained and dispatched for the above-mentioned business. I have ordered that, upon receipt and by fulfillment of this order, you show him the places in the noble mosque where he will prepare suitable and appropriate inscriptions, whether they be executed on tiles, or be simple painted inscriptions.

Conveyed though the Chief Tile-Maker

The 8th of Muharrem, 980 (May 21, 1572)

Source: Ahmed Refik, *Mimar Sinan*, tr. Walter Denny (Istanbul: Kanaat Kutuphanesi, 1931)

the elegance, beauty, and luxury of the Nasrid court (fig. **9.27**). In the center of the court, a large stone basin carried on the backs of twelve lions holds a playing fountain, the pressurized water coming from the distant mountains. From the basin, four water channels reflecting the four rivers of Paradise carry the water into four pavilions on the sides of the courtyard. In its elaborately carved stucco, once vividly polychromed, and in its delicate and elaborate muqarnas and intricate inscriptions carried on slender multiple or single columns, the richly textured and almost gravity-defying architecture of the Alhambra creates an awesome impression. The Alhambra was to influence artistic consciousness for centuries to come, finding heirs in both sixteenth-century Morocco and in nineteenth-century Europe and the United States.

THE THREE LATE EMPIRES

In later Islamic times, three large empires formed major centers of Islamic artistic accomplishment: the Ottoman, the Safavid, and the Mughal. At the end of the thirteenth century, in a corner of Asia Minor just a dozen or so miles from the Byzantine capital of Constantinople, a vassal of the declining Seljuk sultanate named Osman (r. ca. 1281–1324) established a tiny frontier principality hosting warriors eager to expand the realms of Islam at the expense of the Christians. From this seed grew a mighty empire, which by the mid-sixteenth century had almost turned the Mediterranean into a Turkish lake, ruling from Cairo to the outskirts of Vienna, and from Algiers to northwestern Iran. It lasted until 1922. At the beginning of the sixteenth century, five decades

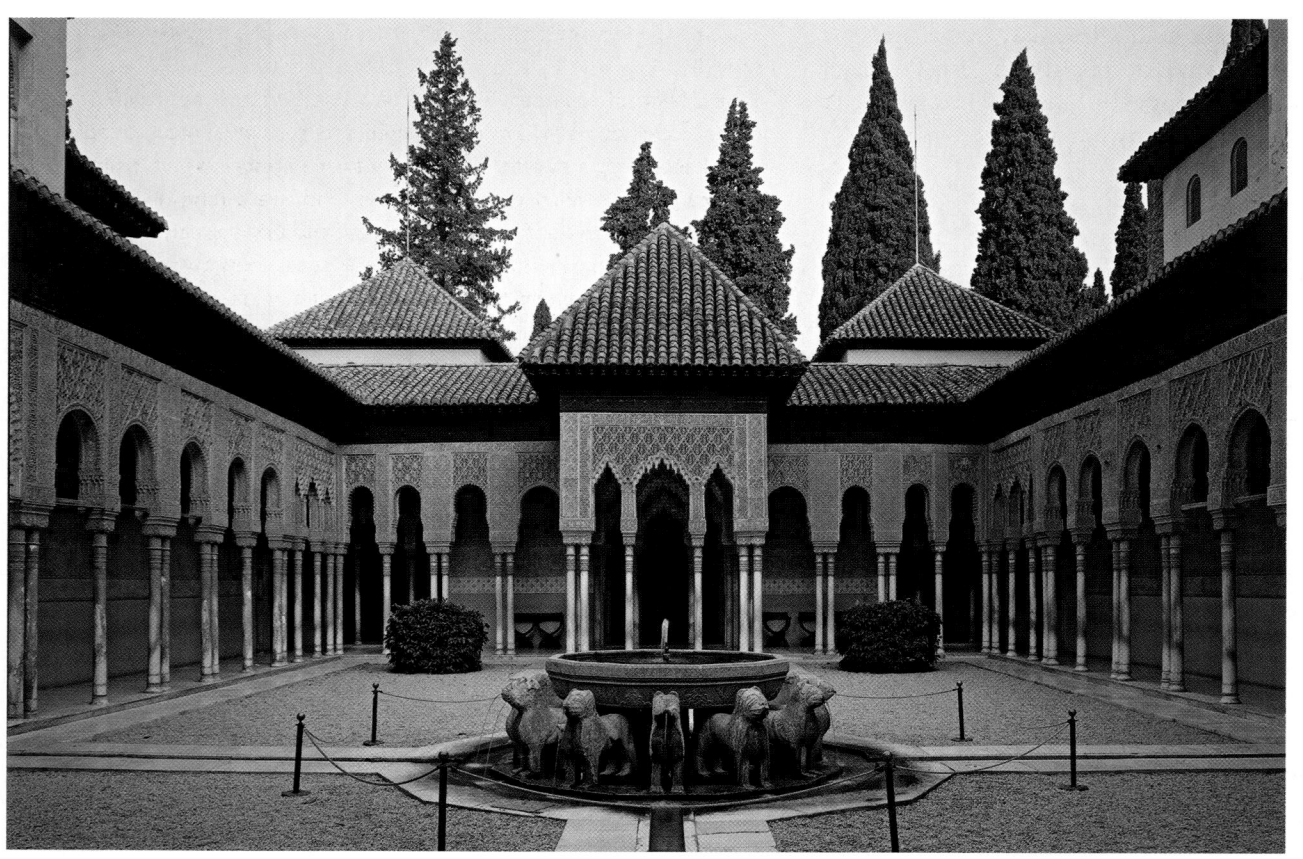

9.27 Court of the Lions, Alhambra, Granada, Spain. Mid-14th century

The Oriental Carpet

No artistic product of the Islamic world is better known outside its original home than the pile carpet, popularly called the oriental carpet. Carpets are heavy textiles meant to be used essentially in the form in which they leave the weaver's loom. That is, they are not cut or tailored, and they are usually woven as complete artistic works, not as goods sold by the yard. Their uses vary extensively from floor coverings to architectural decorations, from cushions and bolsters to bags and sacks of all sizes and shapes, and from animal trappings to religious objects (prayer rugs that provide a clean place for Muslim prayer). They can be used as secular or religious wall decoration. Carpet weaving is a deeply embedded art in the culture of many Islamic societies. It is a part of the socialization of young women, who form the bulk of Islamic artist-weavers. It is found not only in nomadic encampments and villages, but also in urban commercial weaving establishments and, in former times, in special workshops that functioned directly under court patronage in Islamic lands.

There are several different techniques for weaving Islamic carpets, but the best-known is the **pile carpet**, in which row after horizontal row of individual knots of colored wool are tied on vertical pairs of **warp** yarns, and each row of knots is then beaten in place by a beater, a tool that resembles a combination of a comb and a hammer, and subsequently locked in place by the passing of one or more horizontal **weft** yarns. The ends of each knot protrude vertically on the upper, or "right," side of the carpet, giving it a thick pile surface, at once highly reactive to light, conducive to rich color effects, and providing excellent insulation from cold floors or the earthen ground of a nomad's tent.

The carpet form probably arose originally among pre-Islamic nomadic peoples in Central Asia. The bulk of surviving early Islamic carpets, thought to have been woven from the thirteenth through fifteenth centuries, show connections in both design and technique to a nomadic past. In the fifteenth century, the so-called carpet design

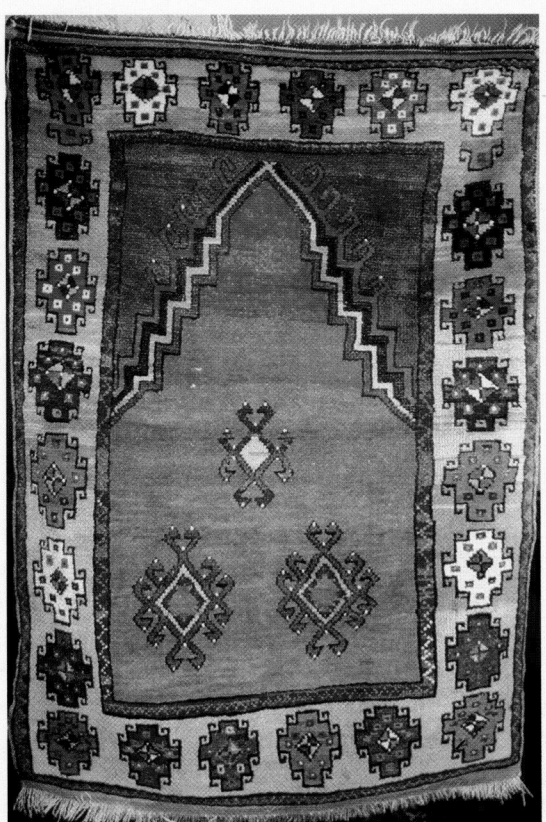

Village carpet in geometric design, Konya area, Turkey. 18th or 19th century. Private collection. Courtesy of Gerard Paquin

revolution led to the production of Islamic carpets in designs that were created by court artists, and then translated into instructions for carpet weavers. These carpets were often used by royalty or given as gifts to royalty.

The design of a carpet, like that of a picture made on an ink-jet printer, is created out of a grid of colored dots consisting of small individual knots of colored wool that when viewed together form a design. Some carpets are fairly coarse in weave, and use a long pile; such carpets tend to use bold geometric designs and brilliant colors. Other carpets, such as those produced after designs by court or commercial artists, may use a much finer weave (in extreme cases, more than 2,000 knots in a square inch) and a short pile to reproduce curvilinear ornamental designs, calligraphy, or even depictions of humans and animals (see fig. 9.32) in large carpets. The symbolism of carpets may be extremely complex, varying from totemic designs of tribal significance to figural designs with arcane religious or secular meanings.

Exported to Europe since the fourteenth century, Islamic pile carpets have historically formed an East–West cultural bridge. In Europe, they not only decorated the palaces of the nobility and the houses of wealthy urban merchants, but were also used in churches, religious shrines, and as part of both secular and religious ceremonies. Islamic carpets, as prized works of art and signs of status and wealth, were frequently depicted in European paintings (see figs. 14.14, 14.21, and 20.36). Carpet weaving continues to flourish in the Middle East today. Demand for Islamic carpets in both East and West has actually increased in the late twentieth and early twenty-first centuries.

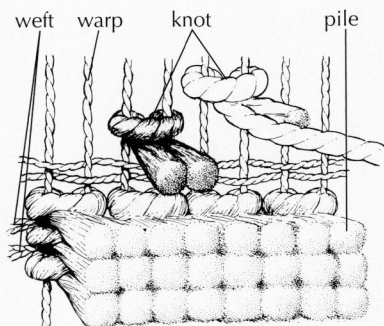

weft   warp   knot   pile

Rows of individual knots, tied over two vertical warps, are tied, cut, and tightly hammered in place and locked in by a pair of horizontal wefts

The symmetrical knotting structure used in many Turkish and Transcaucasian carpets after the Ottomans had conquered Constantinople and made it their capital, a charismatic Shi'ite warrior from northwestern Iran, the Safavid prince Ismail (r. 1501–1524), founded another great empire. In its successive capitals of Tabriz, Qazvin, and Isfahan, the Safavid state was to bring many genres of art to new levels of accomplishment within the Islamic world. Until the middle of the eighteenth century, the Safavids remained major rivals of the Ottomans, and their distinctive styles in architecture, book painting, and the applied arts of carpets and textiles influenced their neighbors to both west and east. In 1526, a Turkish prince from Central Asia named Babur (r. 1526–1530) invaded northern India. After a series of reverses and recoveries, Babur's grandson Akbar the Great (r. 1556–1605) firmly established the Mughal dynasty in the subcontinent. Through the next century and a half, the fabled palaces and monuments of the Mughal capital cities of Delhi, Agra, and Fatehpur Sikri, visited by Muslim and European travelers alike, became a byword throughout the world for the beauty, luxury, and opulence of the Islamic arts.

The Ottomans in Europe and Asia

At first there was little to distinguish what became known as the Ottoman Empire (in Italy, Osman was known as "Ottomano") from more than a dozen other small Islamic states that filled the vacuum left by the collapsing Seljuk power in Asia Minor. But, by

1357, the Ottomans had crossed the Dardanelles, a narrow strait between Europe and Asia, into the Balkans, and eventually by 1453 they had claimed the elusive prize of Constantinople itself, the second Rome and capital of Eastern Christianity. In this, their capital city, popularly renamed Istanbul, and in their summer and military capital of Edirne, 120 miles (190 km) farther west into Europe, the Ottomans used their enormous economic power to patronize art and architecture on an unprecedented scale.

ARCHITECTURE To their Topkapi Palace in Istanbul flocked artists from Iran, Egypt, the Balkans, and even from western Europe, while in the sixteenth century the architect known to posterity as Sinan the Great presided over an architectural establishment that saw the erection of hundreds of bridges, hans, madrasas, palaces, baths, markets, and mosques. The great imperial mosques of the Ottomans paid homage to the traditional Arab mosque by incorporating an atriumlike arcaded courtyard into their design. However, the vast interior space and daring engineering of Justinian's Hagia Sophia (see figs. 8.28 and 8.29), in combination with their own well-developed traditions, provoked an architectural response that made Ottoman mosques, often built in climates with extensive rainfall and winter snows, vastly different from mosques of the Arab or Iranian traditions. In 1572, Sinan built for Sultan Selim II (r. 1566–1574) in Edirne a huge imperial mosque that the architect considered his masterpiece

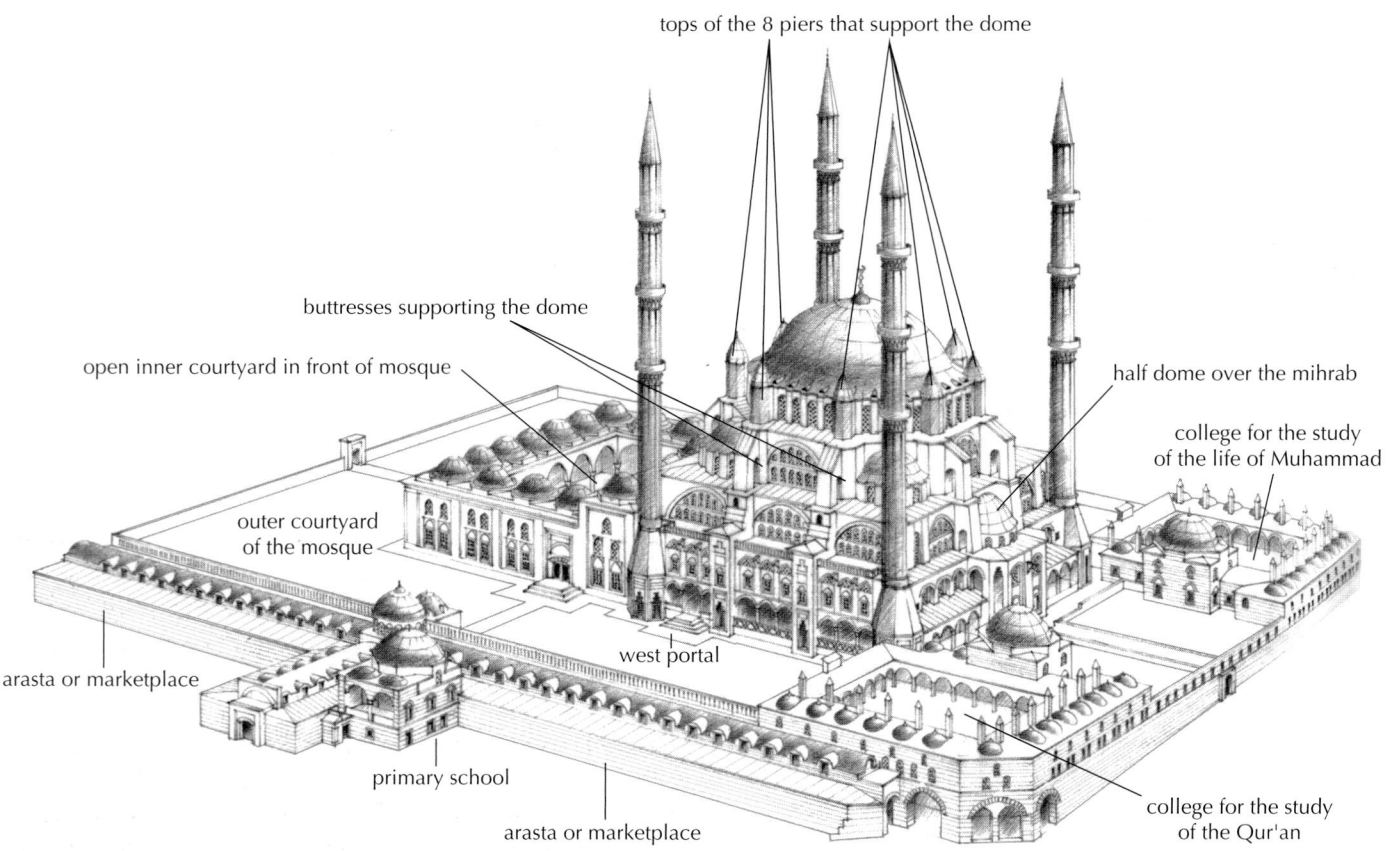

tops of the 8 piers that support the dome

buttresses supporting the dome

open inner courtyard in front of mosque

half dome over the mihrab

college for the study of the life of Muhammad

outer courtyard of the mosque

arasta or marketplace

west portal

primary school

arasta or marketplace

college for the study of the Qur'an

9.28 Sinan the Great. Cutaway of the Mosque of Selim II (Selimiye), Edirne, Turkey. 1569–74

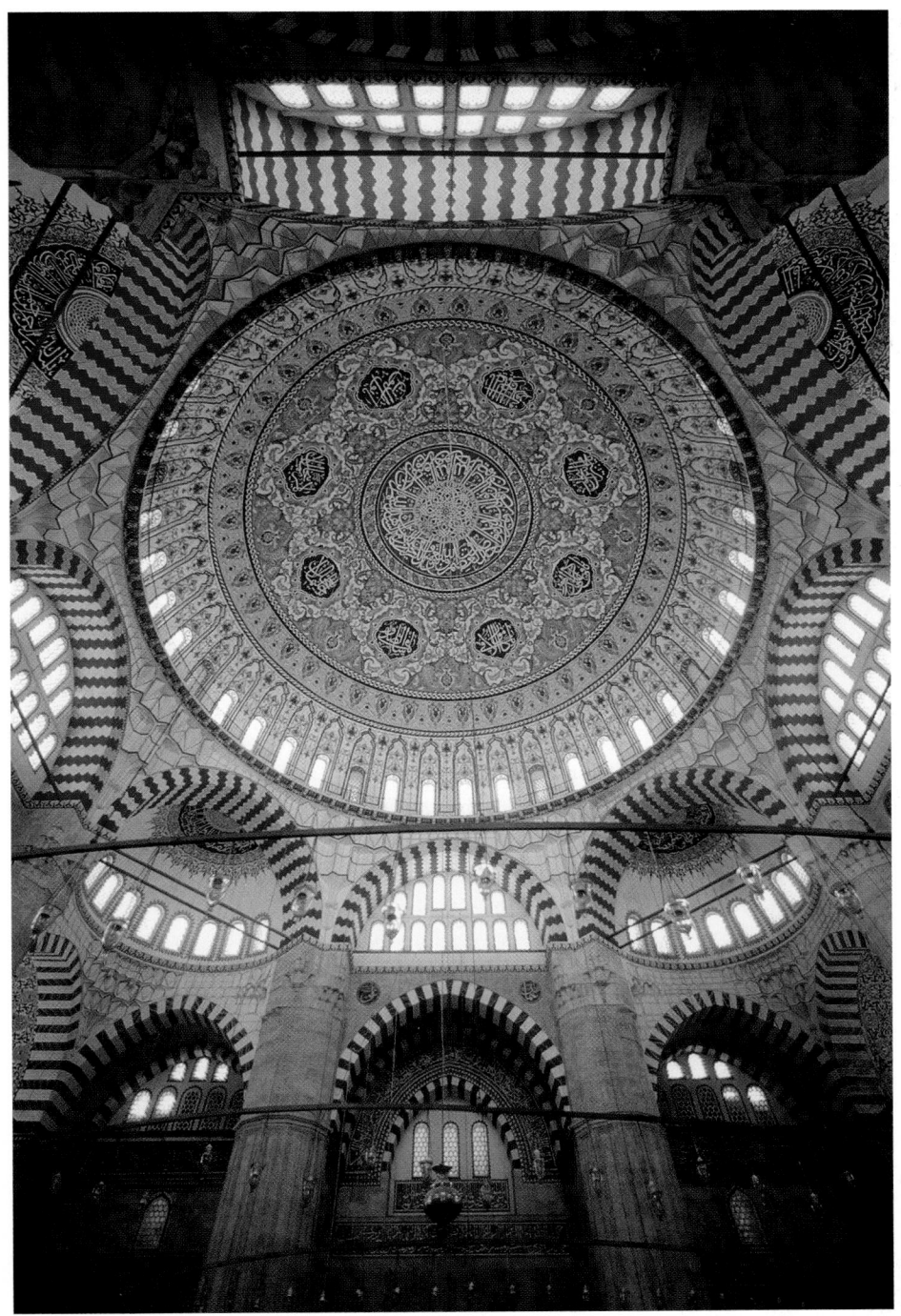

(fig. **9.28**). The courtyard with surrounding arcades and central fountain recalls the typical Arab mosque plan, but the huge lead-covered dome and the four pencil-thin triple-balconied minarets proclaim the Ottoman architectural style, while the vast interior, with its eight huge piers supporting a dome almost 197 feet high and over 108 feet in diameter, shows a unified and clearly delineated space (fig. **9.29**) that is completely different both from the Arab hypostyle mosque with its fragmented space, and from the Hagia Sophia with its mysterious structural and spatial ambiguity. In Sinan's work, the structural components—the muscles and sinews, as it were—rather than being hidden, are a primary source of the buildings' visual appeal. The Ottomans preferred an austere exterior of bare whitish stone contrasting with the dark-gray lead sheets used for waterproofing the domes and semidomes of their structures, while the interiors frequently incorporated beautiful polychrome tiles with designs of strikingly naturalistic flowers. (See *Primary Source*, page 300.)

THE OTTOMAN COURT STYLE By 1500, the Ottomans, like the Timurids before them, had developed a royal design studio, called the "house of design," that served as the central focus of royal artistic patronage. It reached its zenith under the patronage of Süleyman I, "The Magnificent" (r. 1520–1566), his son Selim II (r. 1566–1574), and his grandson Murad III (r. 1576–1595).

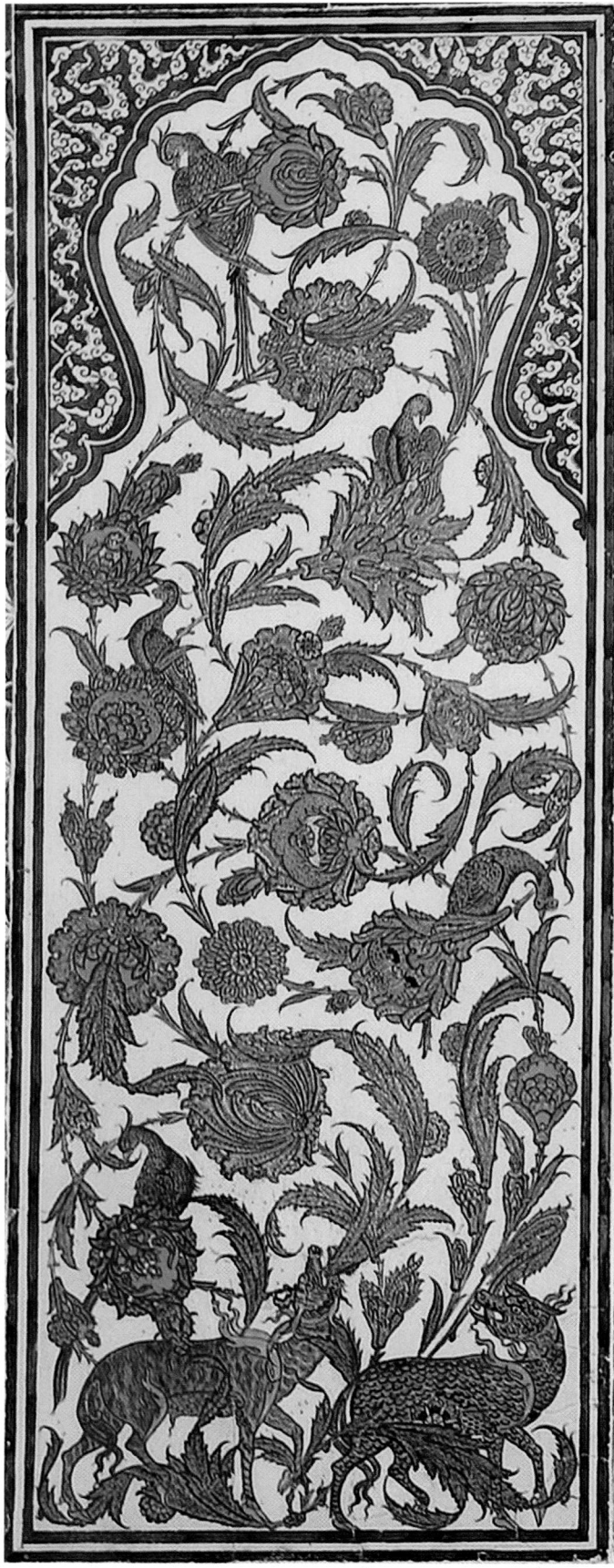

9.30 Shah Kulu (?). Tile painted in hatayi style with saz design. ca. 1525–50. Cobalt and turquoise underglaze painting on composite fritware body covered with white slip, 50 × 19" (127 × 48.5 cm). Topkapı Palace Museum, Istanbul

Among the many artistic innovations to emerge from this complex of artists working in almost every conceivable medium and genre is a style of ornament called by some **saz**, taking its name from a legendary enchanted forest, and by others **hatayi**—that is, "from Cathay," or "China." Created in part by an émigré artist from Tabriz named Shah Kulu, who was head of the Ottoman royal studio by the mid-sixteenth century, the style is typified by energetic and graceful compositions of curved leaves and complex floral palmettes linked by vines that appear to overlap and penetrate each other, sometimes embellished with birds or strange antelopelike creatures. The saz or hatayi style is found in ceramic wares, manuscript illuminations, carpets, silk textiles, freehand drawings executed for the albums of royal collectors, and some remarkable blue and turquoise paintings on tile, probably from the hand of Shah Kulu himself (fig. **9.30**). Ottoman ceramics and silks were exported in large quantities to Russia and Europe, where along with the much-prized carpets from Asia Minor they were quickly absorbed into European material culture.

The Safavid Period in Iran

Shortly after 1500, Ismail, a charismatic prince descended from a family of venerated Shi'ite clerics in northwestern Persia, declared himself the Safavid shah (or king) of Iran. Quickly overrunning much of the formerly Timurid domains, the young ruler established his capital in the city of Tabriz in northwestern Iran, formerly the capital of two provincial Turkmen dynasties (a Turkic people who occupied parts of Central Asia), precariously close to the eastern reaches of the Sunni Ottoman Empire. There, under Ismail (r. 1501–1523) and his successor Tahmasp (r. 1524–1576), who in 1548 moved his capital to the strategically more secure Qazvin to the east, the arts flourished.

BOOK ILLUSTRATION AND CARPETS: TABRIZ Early in the sixteenth century, the aged painter Behzad was brought from the east to Tabriz, where his influence, combined with the indigenous Turkmen painting style of pre-Safavid times, brought about a remarkable artistic synthesis. In the hands of one of the great geniuses of Islamic art, the Turkmen-born artist Sultan-Muhammad—it was not uncommon for artists in royal ateliers to incorporate honorifics like shah (king), sultan (ruler), or aqa (noble) into their names—the new Safavid style of miniature painting reached fresh heights in expressiveness as well as technique. One of the painter's most appealing creations is an illustration painted with opaque watercolors on paper in Tabriz around 1529 for a royal manuscript of a *divan*, or collection of poems, by the fourteenth-century poet Hafiz, utilizing the theme of heavenly and earthly intoxication, a favorite motif of mystical Persian poetry (fig. **9.31**). A group of elderly professors from a religious college are shown in various stages of disorderly intoxication, accompanied by servants, some fawning and others apparently terrified, while a group of strangely attired and caricatured musicians provides background music. On the roof of the building angels join in the revelry, while on the balcony the pie-eyed poet

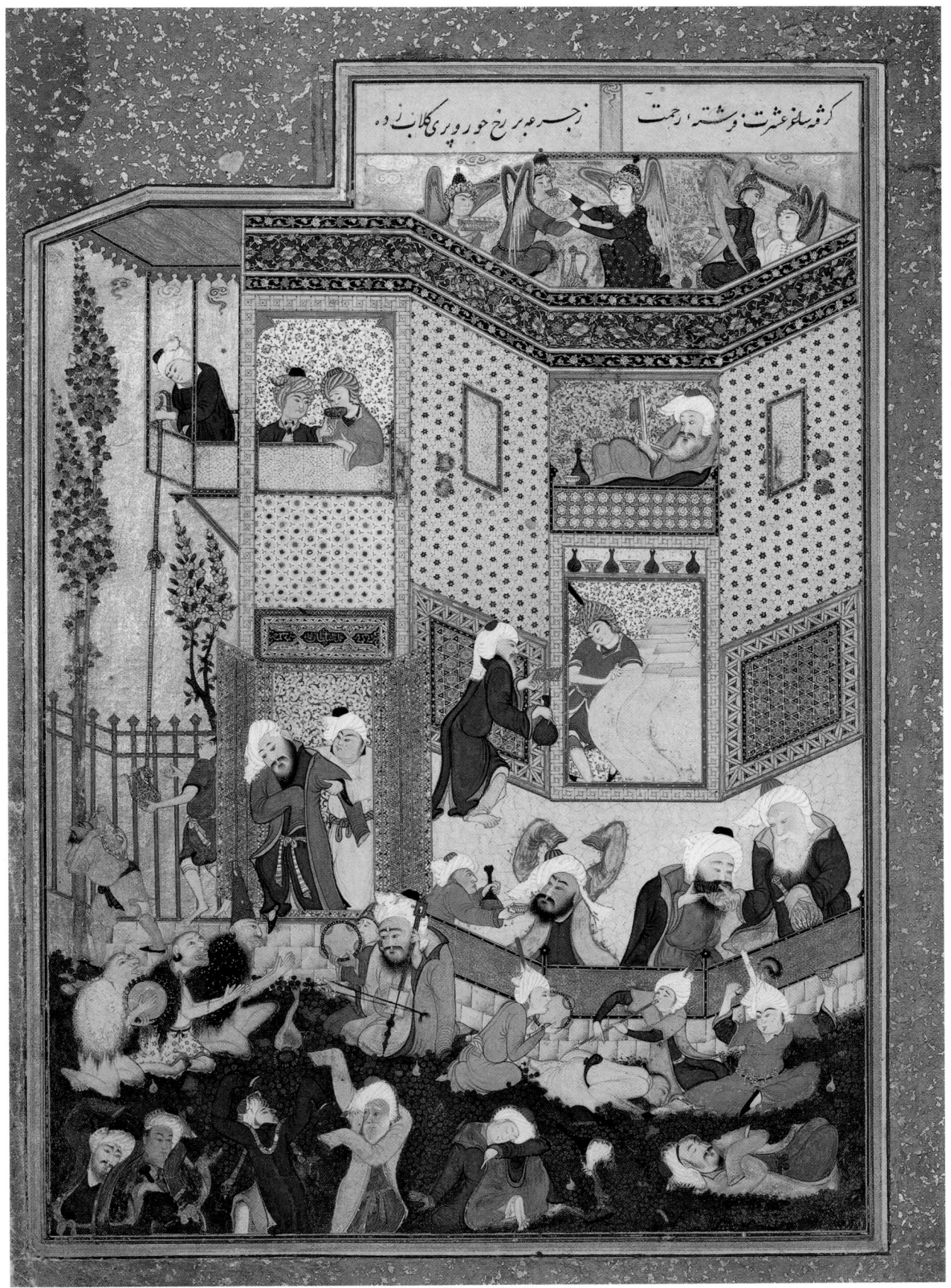

9.31 Folio from the *Divan* of Hafiz, *Allegory of worldly and Otherworldly Drunkenness*. Islamic, Iran Tabriz, Illustrated Manuscript. Safavid period (1501–1722), Shah Tahmasp (1524–76), ca. 1526–27. Opaque watercolors, ink, and gold on paper, 11⅜ × 8½" (28.9 × 21.6 cm). Promised Gift of Mr. and Mrs. Stuart Cary Welch Jr. Partially owned by Metropolitan Museum of Art, New York, and the Arthur Sackler Museum, Harvard University, 1988 (1988 430)

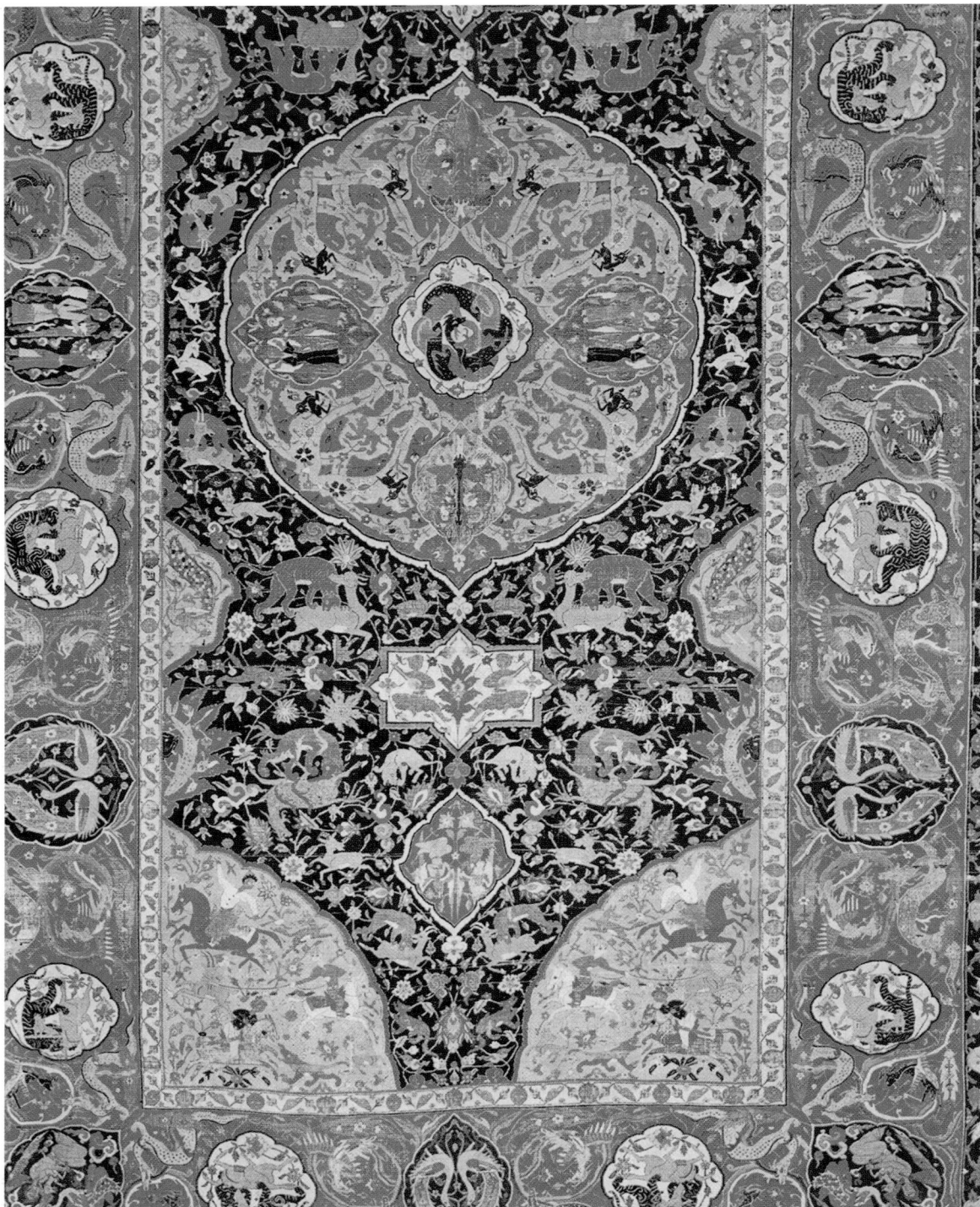

9.32 Detail of the Sanguszko figural-design carpet, from Iran. ca. 1575–1600. Wool pile knotted on cotton warp and weft, entire carpet 19'8" × 10'8" (6.4 × 3.3 m). Private collection

himself struggles to write his poem. Using an incredibly fine brushstroke, and a thick white application of paint to create the textures of the white silk Safavid turbans, with their characteristic colored batonlike ornaments sticking out the top, Sultan-Muhammad has created a work that reminds us that Islamic civilization is no stranger to humor or to the enjoyment of a good time, both metaphorically and literally.

The new style in book painting, with its brilliant colors, expressive faces, and great variety of body types, often set in a landscape filled with flowers or in a lavish architectural setting,

was immediately transferable to other mediums. A carpet woven somewhere in the Safavid domains in the second half of the sixteenth century shows the application of the figural style of miniature painting to a symbolically complex composition of royal and heavenly motifs (fig. 9.32). It incorporates the royal hunt, the enjoyment of wine in a paradiselike setting, and a host of birds and animals. These forms are subject to a complex layering of symbolism, often intermingling the sacred and the profane, that reflects the strong role of Sufi mysticism in Safavid culture, as well as an age-old Persian love of wine, poetry, and beautiful possessions.

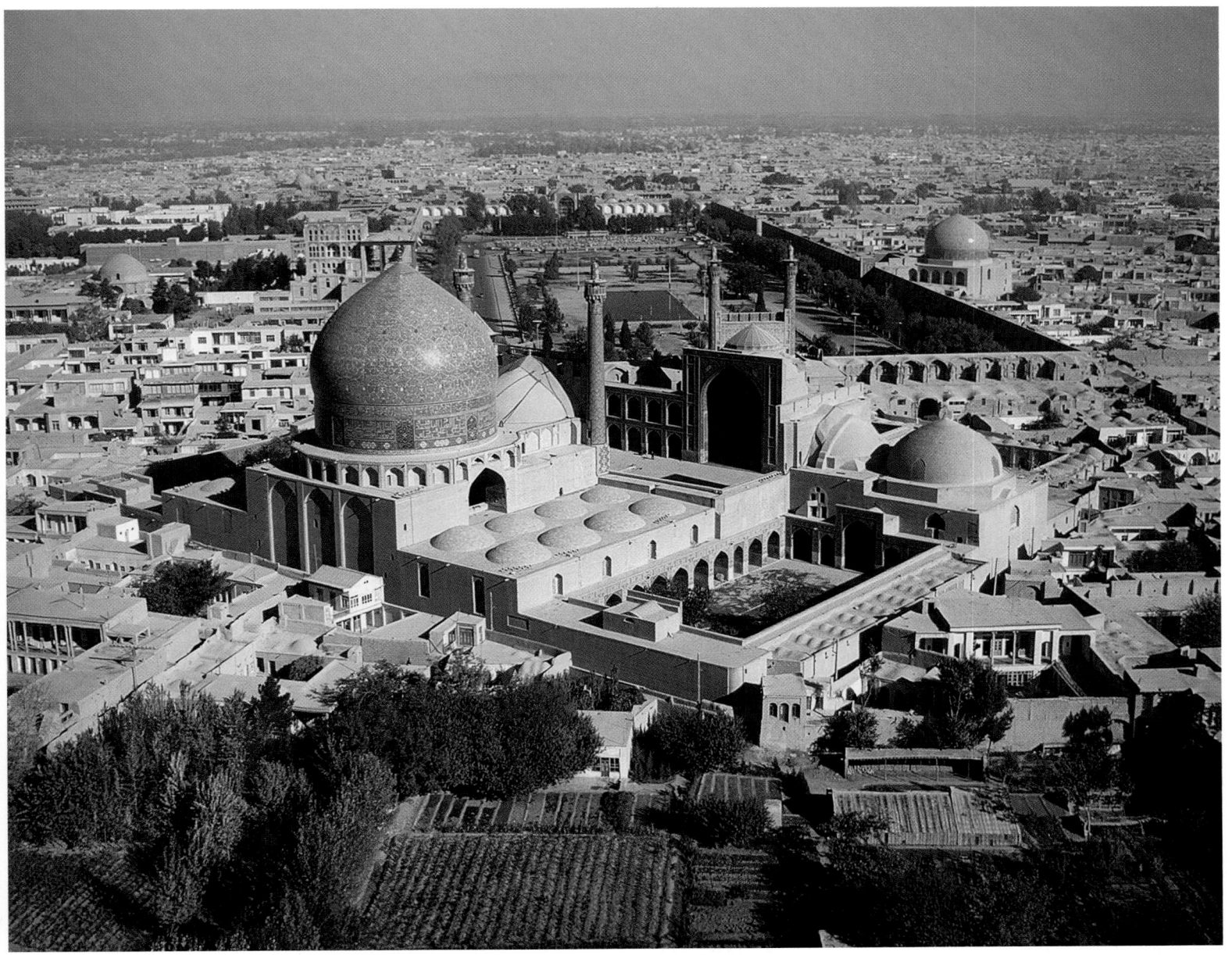

9.33 Aerial view of the Royal Mosque of Shah Abbas I (Masjid-i Shah), Isfahan, Iran. 1611–16

ARCHITECTURE: THE PLANNED CITY OF ISFAHAN By the beginning of the seventeenth century, the Safavid capital had been moved once again to the old city of Isfahan in the Persian heartland. There, the energetic and powerful Abbas I (r. 1588–1629) laid out to the south of the original city a new city with large public spaces and broad avenues, with palaces for the nobility and a quarter for Armenian Christian merchants. The splendor and prosperity of this new Isfahan drew commerce and travelers from all over the world, and the luxury goods sold in its bazaars, from silks and ceramics to metalware and carpets, together with the beauty of its gardens and the richness of its inhabitants, led to a famous Persian adage: "Isfahan is half the world." At one end of a huge open square known as the **maidan**, itself oriented with the North Star, Shah Abbas built his Royal

Mosque (fig. **9.33**). Because the qibla lies to the southwest, facing Mecca, the mosque has to be at an entirely different orientation than the maidan. An ingenious 45-degree turn beyond the main portal deftly accomplishes a directional accommodation, leading into the huge open courtyard of the mosque, with its enormous domed chamber behind the qibla iwan, and all visible surfaces completely covered in brilliantly colored tiles.

The shops that line the sides of the maidan all contributed rents to the waqf or endowment of the mosque, and in the middle of the west side of the maidan, Shah Abbas built a palace from the balcony of which he could watch processions and sporting events in the square itself. The rest of the new city of Isfahan consisted in large part of spacious gardens surrounding the pavilionlike palaces of the Safavid nobility.

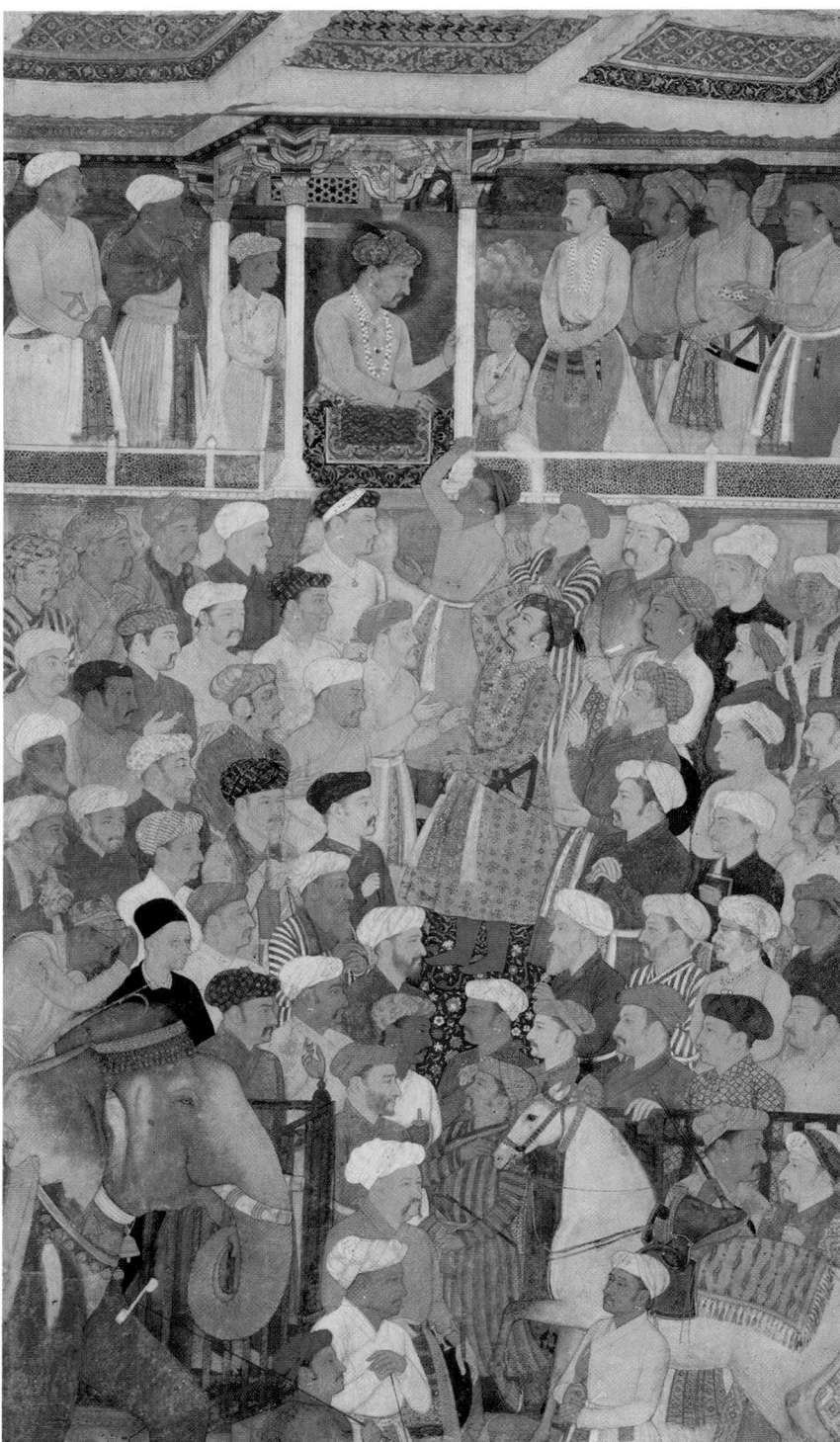

9.34 Manohar and Abul Hasan
Ceremonial Audience of Jahangir, from a
Jahangir-nama manuscript, northern India.
ca. 1620. Opaque watercolors and ink on paper,
13¾ × 7⅞" (35 × 20 cm). Museum of Fine Arts,
Boston. Frances Bartlett Donation of 1912 and
Picture Fund. Photograph © 2006 Museum of
Fine Arts, Boston, 14654

The Mughal Period in India

In 1526, Babur, who claimed descent from the Mongol Timur
(hence the dynastic name "Mughal"), defeated a combined army
of Hindu princedoms in northern India to establish the Mughal
dynasty in the subcontinent. Although India had had an Islamic
presence in Delhi since around 1200, the Mughal Empire was to
bring a new flowering of Islamic art and architecture to the
subcontinent. Centered in the capital cities of Agra, Delhi, and
Fatehpur-Sikri, the scene of building and the production of works
of art on a mammoth scale, the Mughal style built on an artistic
combination of Central Asian, Safavid Persian, and indigenous
Hindu art and culture. Under Babur's grandson Akbar the Great
(r. 1556–1605), himself an unusually capable and charismatic ruler,
the style took on its distinctive form. Akbar was a remarkably tolerant ruler, fascinated by Hinduism, interested in Persian poetry
and art, and a patron of one of the major Indian Sufi orders.
Under his patronage a royal studio of Persian and native painters

Abd Al-Hamid Lahori (d. 1654)

From *Padshah Nama (Book of the Emperor)*

Abd al-Hamid Lahori was official court historian to Shah Jahan, who built the Taj Mahal as a monument to the memory of his beloved wife Mumtaz Mahal. The Padshah Nama was written in three volumes, each corresponding to a decade in Shah Jahan's reign. Before he could finish the third volume, Lahori was taken ill, and the work was completed by his younger colleague Muhammad Waris in 1657. This excerpt is from a much longer discussion of the building of the monument, together with an elaborate description of the tomb itself, the outbuildings, and the surrounding gardens.

At the beginning of the fifth year of the exalted accession (January, 1632), the excavation was started for the laying of the foundation of this sublime edifice, which is situated overlooking the Jumna river flowing adjacent to the north. And when the spade-wielders with robust arms and hands strong as steel, had with unceasing effort excavated down to the water-table, the ingenious masons and architects of astonishing achievements most firmly built its foundation with stone and mortar up to the level of the ground.

And on top of this foundation there was raised a kind of platform of brick and mortar in one solid block, measuring 374 cubits long by 140 wide and 16 high, to serve as the plinth of this exalted mausoleum—which evokes a vision of the heavenly gardens of Rizwan and epitomizes, as it were, the holy abodes of Paradise.

And from all parts of the empire, there were assembled great numbers of skilled stonecutters, lapidaries, and inlayers, each an expert in his art, who commenced work along with other craftsmen. In the middle of this platform plinth—which ranks [in magnificence] with the heavenly Throne of God—there was constructed another solid and level platform. In the center of the second platform, the building of this heaven-lofty and Paradise-like mausoleum was constructed on the plan of a Baghdadi octagon, 70 cubits in diameter, on a base plinth one cubit in height.

Situated in the exact center of the building, the domed hall over the sepulcher of that recipient of divine grace has been finished with white marble within and without. From the floor to the curvature, the hall under the dome is octagonal in shape, with a diameter of 22 cubits. The curvature is ornamented with *muqarnas* motifs, while from the cornice to the inner summit of the dome, which is at a height of 32 yards from the floor of the building, there are arranged marble slabs cut in a geometric molded pattern.

Source: W. E. Begley and Z. A. Desai, *Taj Mahal: The Illumined Tomb* (Cambridge, MA: Aga Kahn Program for Islamic Architecture, 1989)

blended their traditions to form a new style of miniature painting. In addition, Central Asian, Persian, and local builders and craftspeople blended their architectural styles and techniques to create a new Mughal style in architecture.

In a sense, the Mughal art of India revels in extremes—the largest and the smallest of Islamic miniature paintings, the largest but also the most finely woven small Islamic carpets, the most spectacular of all Islamic tomb structures, and the most extravagant Islamic jewelry and fanciful hardstone carving are all to be found here.

BOOK ILLUSTRATION A miniature painting in opaque watercolors on paper of a *darbar*, or ceremonial audience, given by the Mughal emperor Jahangir (r. 1605–1627), probably completed around 1620 by the court artists Manohar and Abul Hasan, shows the characteristics of the Mughal style (fig. **9.34**). The Mughals liked realistic pictures of current events; and almost every individual in the crowd can be identified by comparison with individual portraits made around the same time. Along with this specificity, extended to the visiting black-clad European monk and even to the smiling elephant, is a love of opulent detail, while space is created in the time-honored Islamic fashion by the use of a high point of view and an overlapping technique.

DECORATIVE ARTS A different side of Mughal art is seen in a wine cup fashioned from translucent white jade (fig. **9.35**) for the emperor Shah Jahan (r. 1628–1657). The delicately petaled

blossom that forms the bowl of the cup gently tapers to the handle in the form of a bearded mountain goat from Kashmir. Despite the hardness of the stone, which had to be shaped by grinding for

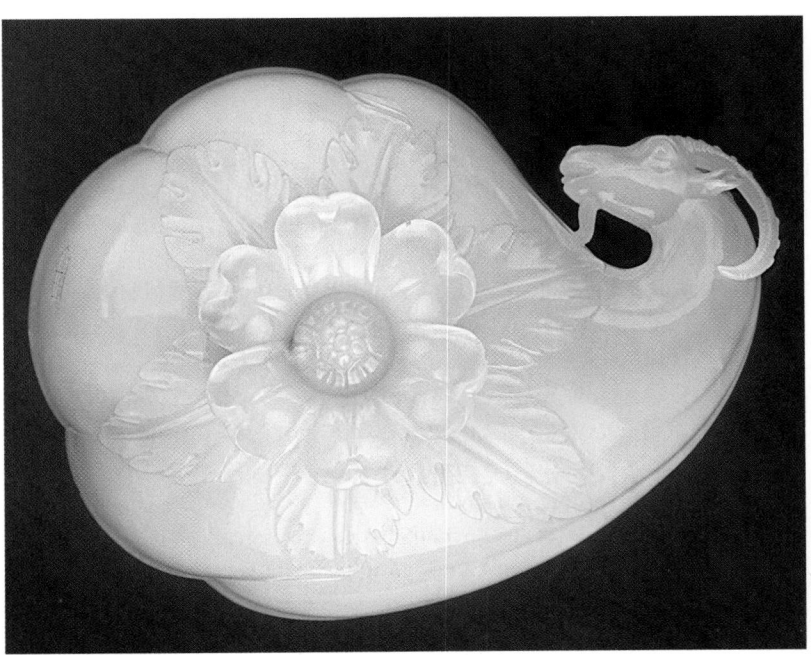

9.35 Wine cup of Shah Jahan, from northern India. Mid-17th century. White jade, 2¼ × 6¾" (5.7 × 17.14 cm). Victoria & Albert Museum, London

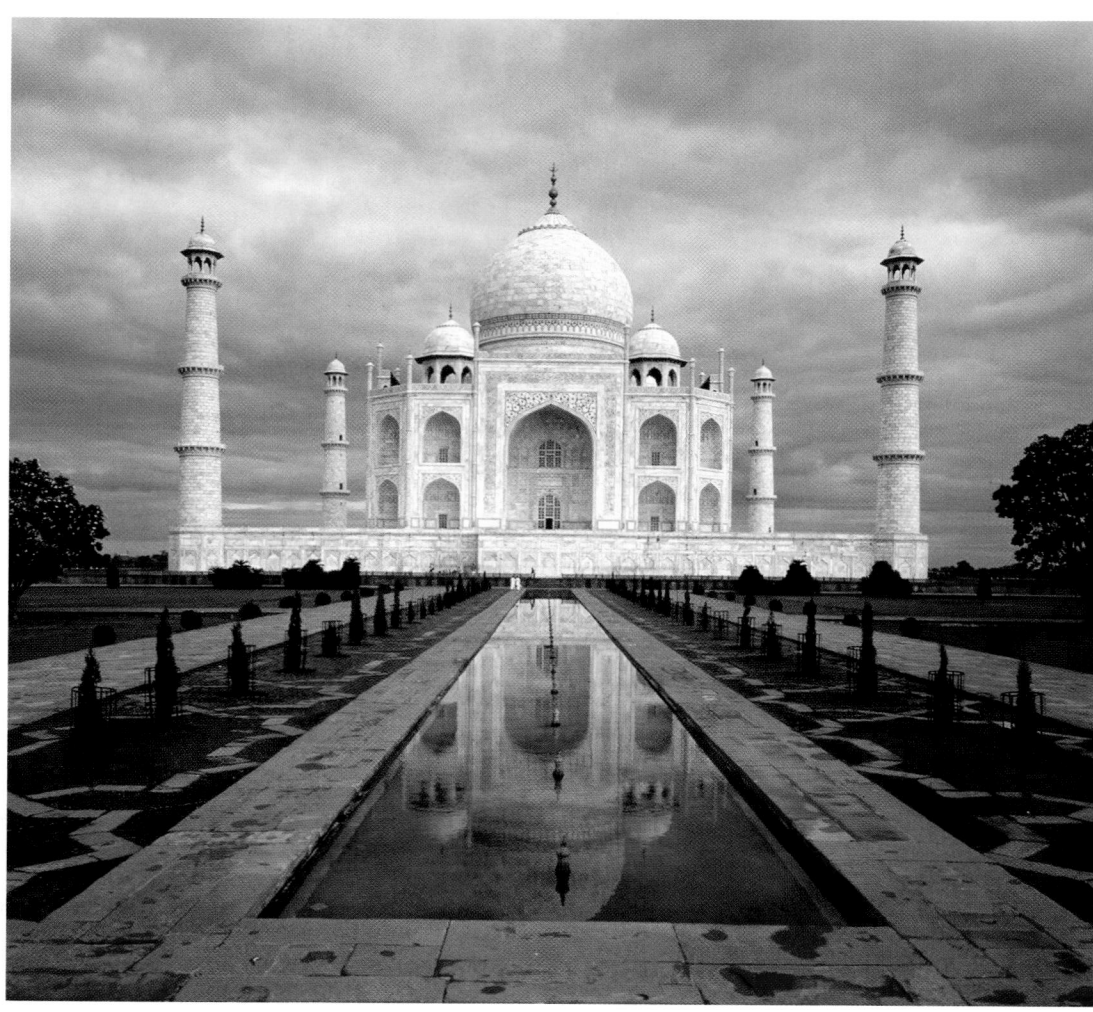

hundreds of hours, the finished product has the freshness of a flower itself. The same attention to botanical realism can be seen in floral decoration in many Mughal mediums, from textiles and carpets to carved and inlaid marble.

ARCHITECTURE: TAJ MAHAL The most famous of all Mughal works is doubtless the Taj Mahal, a royal tomb in Agra completed around 1650 and commissioned by Shah Jahan in memory of his deceased wife Mumtaz Mahal (fig. **9.36**). The building has the ground plan of a Timurid garden kiosk or palace from Central Asia, while the central dome recalls that of the Royal Mosque of Isfahan. (See *Primary Source*, page 309.) The snowy-white marble is lavishly inlaid with colored semiprecious stones in the form of flowers, vines, and beautiful cursive inscriptions. Set at one end of an elaborate quadripartite formal garden with four axial pools in the Persian style, the Taj Mahal is far more than a royal tomb or a dynastic monument. The inscriptions evoke the metaphor of the gardens of Paradise that are promised to devout believers in the Qur'an, and the domed building is a self-conscious evocation of the throne of God, re-created in an earthly version of divine Paradise.

CONTINUITY AND CHANGE IN ISLAMIC ART

In the eighteenth and nineteenth centuries, the great traditions of Islamic art continued through tumultuous periods of change. Economic decline led to a diminution in the royal patronage that had produced some of the most spectacular works of earlier periods, but stylistic traditions in every major area of the Islamic world continued to live on, despite political and economic dislocation, European colonialism, and the increasing use of factory-made goods in everyday life. Art of all kinds in a huge variety of mediums flourishes throughout the Islamic world in many countries today, largely ignored even by specialists in Islamic art because they have been trained to look at the works of earlier periods. Slowly, through encounters with new mediums and genres, with the pervasive American-European tradition of the later twentieth century, and through reencounters with their own historical past, Muslim artists are creating new traditions that seek to express what almost every artistic tradition has always embodied in almost every time—new creativity in the context of a rich and meaningful past.

Islamic Art

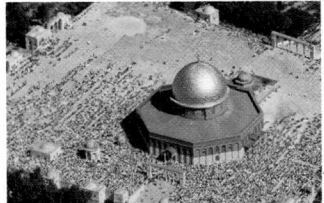

ca. 690 Construction of the
Dome of the Rock in Jerusalem

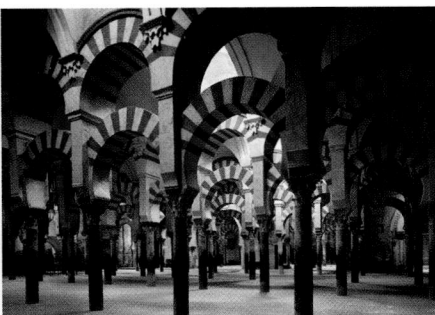

700 Construction begins on Great Mosque
at Córdoba, Spain

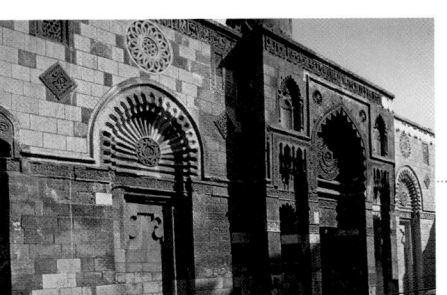

ca. 1026 Construction of al-Aqmar mosque, Cairo

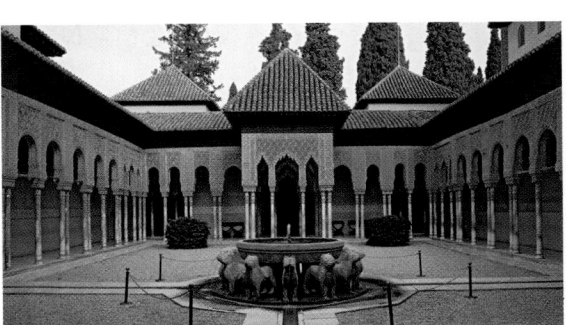

1354–91 Court of the Lions, Alhambra

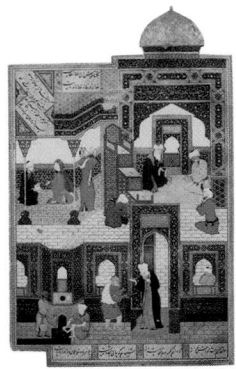

1486 Behzad's illustrations
for the *Bostan*

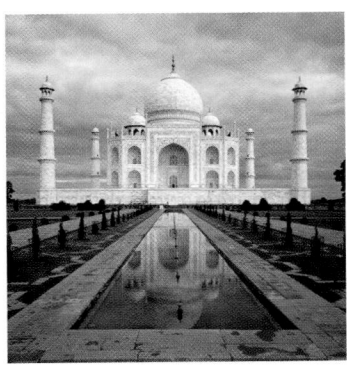

ca. 1650 Completion of Taj Mahal
in Agra, India

Early 900s Islamic tombs
built in Bukhara for Persian
Samanid dynasty

600

700

800

900

1000

1100

1200

1300

1400

1500

1600

1700

◄ 632 Death of the Prophet Muhammad

◄ by 700s Islam reaches Spain and Central Asia

◄ 750 Abbasid dynasty supplants Umayyad dynasty

········· ca. 950 *Joshua Roll*
◄ 962 Otto I crowned Holy Roman Emperor
◄ 969 Cairo founded as the capital of the Fatimids

◄ mid-1000s Seljuk Turkish invaders begin rule

◄ 1099 First Crusade warriors capture Jerusalem

········· 1180-90 Apse mosaic of Monreale

◄ 1258 Mongols sack and destroy Baghdad
◄ by end of 1200s Western Mongol rulers converted
to Islam
◄ by 1300s Almohad capital of Seville falls to kings
of Castile
········· ca. 1310-20 Keriye Camii *Anastasis*
◄ mid-1300s Most of Muslim al-Andalus fallen to
Christian Reconquest

◄ 1453 Ottomans claim Constantinople as their
capital

◄ 1501 Prince Ismail founds Safavid Empire in Iran

◄ 1556-1605 Akbar the Great rules Mughal India

◄ 1616 Death of English playwright William
Shakespeare

311

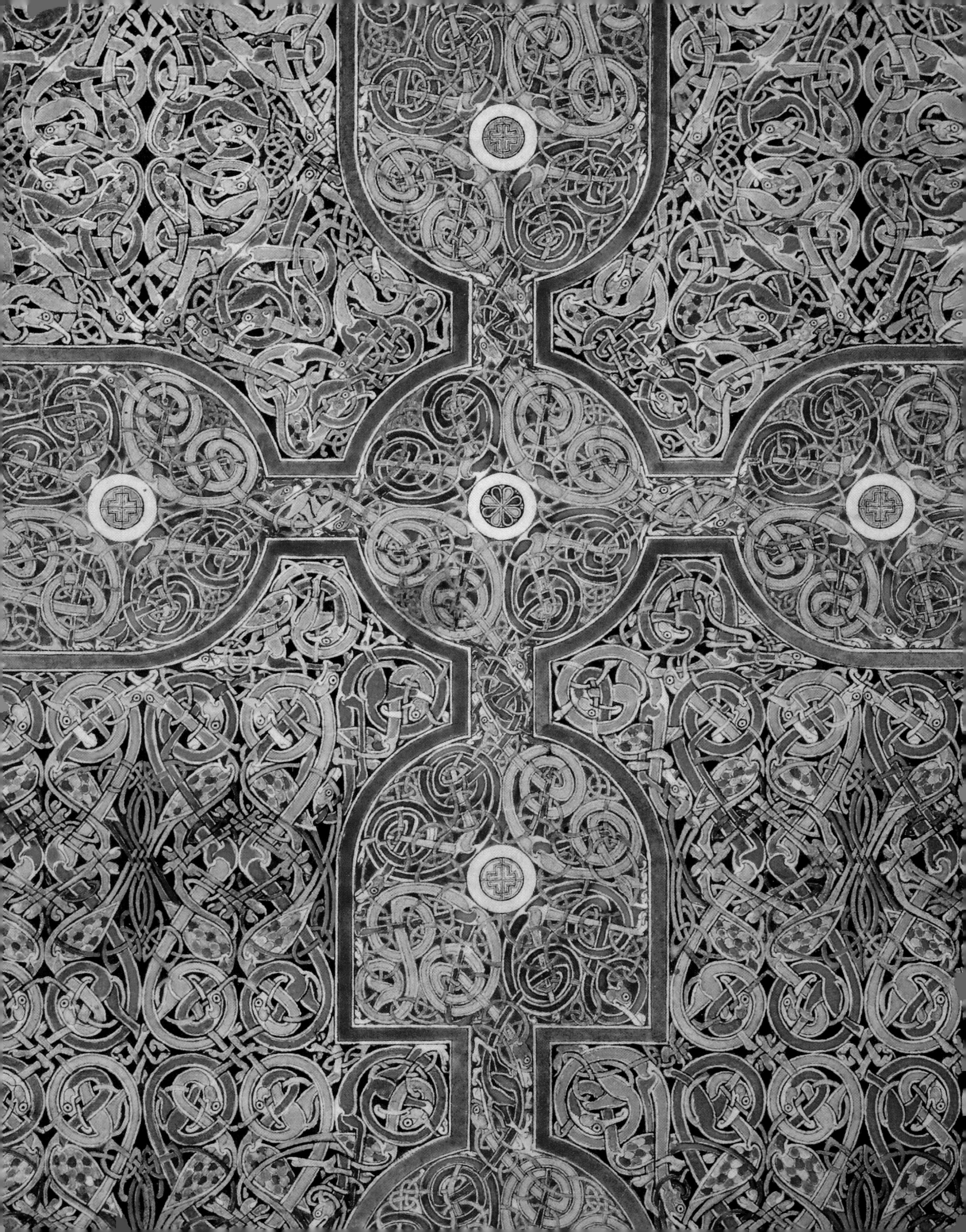

Early Medieval Art

THE TERM EARLY MEDIEVAL IS SOMETHING OF A CATCHALL PHRASE used to describe the art of a number of cultures and a variety of regions in western Europe after the Fall of Rome (476 CE) until the eleventh century (map **10.1**). Significant in Rome's demise was the power asserted by migrating Germanic peoples (including Franks, Visigoths, Ostrogoths, and

Saxons), who moved into and through Europe and eventually established permanent settlements both north of the Alps and in Italy, Spain, and southern France. These were clearly tumultuous times, as invaders clashed and eventually mixed with local inhabitants, including the Celts, the descendants of the Iron Age peoples of Europe. ("Celt" is a confusing term, since it is also used to define tribal groups who occupied Britain and Ireland between the fifth and twelfth centuries.) As the invaders established permanent settlements, they adopted many customs traditional to the areas they inhabited. Overlaid on this mix of customs were Roman traditions, including those of Christianity, which in many cases had been adopted by indigenous local tribes when they were conquered by Rome.

The allure of Christianity—for both its spiritual message and for the structure it imposed on a fragmented society in times of turmoil—once again proved momentous. Conversion from pagan worship, however, was now less an individual decision (as it had been in the Early Christian period) than a social one. Often, when a tribal leader decided to convert to Christianity, his subjects converted with him, virtually en masse, as occurred in Reims on Christmas Day in 496, when 3,000 Franks were baptized along with Clovis, their king.

The Church emerged as a force vitally important for European unification; even so, loyalty to family and clan continued to govern social and political alliances. Strong chiefs assumed leadership and established tribal allegiances and methods of exchange, both economic and political, that would eventually result in the development throughout western Europe of a system of political organization known as feudalism. These social and political alignments eventually led to a succession of ruling dynasties governed by strong leaders who were able to increase the areas under their dominion. These dynasties (principally the Carolingian and Ottonian) were ambitious to reestablish a centralized authority, absent in Europe after the Fall of Rome. The attempt to provide a stable political structure was based, if not in the reality of the Roman Empire, then at least in the ideals embodied in its legacy.

The art that resulted from this cultural interchange is a vibrant and vital mix. Artistic methods, materials, and traditions, introduced by migration, were combined with those that predominated in the regions where tribes settled. Much of this art is marked by elaborate patterns of interlocking and interwoven designs that decorate sumptuous objects of personal adornment, reflecting their owners' social position. Eventually the Church assumed increasing importance in commissioning works of art, and there was a shift of emphasis in the types of objects produced. The Church built and decorated many houses of worship and established a large number of monastic communities. Within the monasteries, scriptoria made elaborately decorated books, which

Detail of figure 10.5, Cross page, from the Lindisfarne Gospels

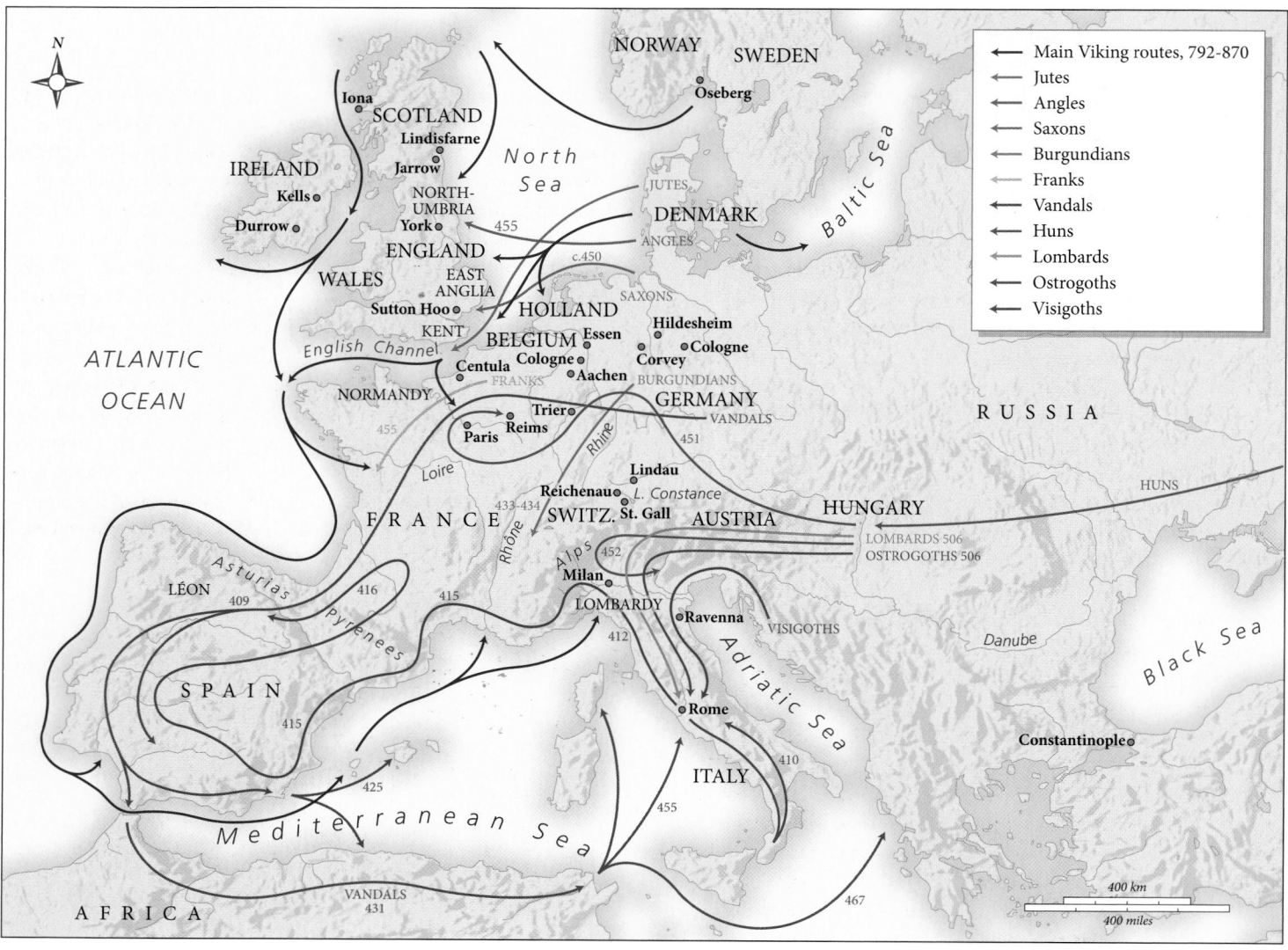

Map 10.1   Europe in the early Middle Ages

were sent off with missionaries as aids in their efforts to convert and educate.

Carolingian and Ottonian artists expressed the imperial ambitions of their leaders by building churches and designing architectural complexes that consciously emulated Rome. Roman-derived Early Christian basilicas served as models for a large number of buildings north of the Alps. Court-related artists also produced copies of ancient books. And three-dimensional sculpture, an art form virtually abandoned after the Fall of Rome, once again attracted the attention of artists and their patrons. Thus, out of an amalgam of diverse and conflicting forces, and as new social and cultural entities developed, an art emerged that is as varied as it is exciting.

ANGLO-SAXON ART

The widespread migrations of peoples transformed Europe. In 376, the Huns, who had advanced beyond the Black Sea from Central Asia, became a serious threat to Europe. They pushed the Germanic Visigoths westward into the Roman Empire from the Danube. Then in 451, under Attila (d. 453), they invaded Gaul, present-day France and Germany, and its resident Celts. Also in the fifth century, the Angles and Saxons from today's Denmark and northern Germany invaded the British Isles, which had been colonized for centuries by Celts. Many of these Germanic tribes developed into virtual kingdoms: the Visigoths in Spain, the Burgundians and Franks in Gaul, the Ostrogoths and Lombards in Italy. The Vikings controlled Scandinavia and ventured afar, a result of their might as sailors.

The Germanic peoples brought with them art forms that were portable: weaving, metalwork, jewelry, and woodcarvings. Artistic production in these mediums required training and skill of execution, and metalwork in particular had intrinsic value, since it was often made of gold or silver and inlaid with precious stones. Metalworkers had high social status, a measure of the respect accorded to their labor and to the value of the objects they produced. (See *Materials and Techniques*, page 315.) In some Germanic folk legends, metalworkers have abilities so remarkable that they are described as magical. Numerous small-scale objects

Metalwork

Metal was a precious commodity in the Middle Ages. Even in the ancient world, patterns of interchange and colonization can be related to exploration for desirable metals: For example, the Greek settlements in Italy and Roman settlements in Spain were a result of a desire for metals. Popular metals employed in the early Middle Ages included gold, silver, copper, iron, and bronze. The many ways that metals could be worked was undoubtedly one of their most compelling features. They could be flattened, drawn thin, or made into an open-work design of filigree, lacy decoration made from intertwined wires. They could also be cast, engraved, punched, stamped, and decorated with colored stones, glass, or enamels.

The large gold buckle from the Sutton Hoo ship burial (see fig. 10.1) contains nearly a pound of gold, although it is only one of many gold pieces found in the burial site. That so much early medieval metalwork from grave sites is gold reflects the value attached to the metal. In addition, gold is not harmed by contact with either earth or water (whereas silver and other metals are subject to progressive destruction when exposed to the elements). Although gold had been obtained in Europe through mining since Roman times, the most common method of acquiring it was by collecting nuggets or small grains from rivers and streams (called placer or alluvial gold). The Rhine, Tiber, Po, Rhone, and Garonne rivers, along which the Germanic tribes settled, were major sources of this type of gold, which medieval writers refer to as "sand" gold.

Sutton Hoo's gold buckle is decorated with granulation, beads of gold bonded to the surface, as well as **inlaid niello**, the dark material that is set into incisions in the metal surface and that sets off the intricate interlace designs composed of lines and dots. Niello is a sulfur alloy of silver, copper, or lead that, when heated, fuses with the metal that surrounds it, in this case gold, and produces a nearly black substance. The shiny dark niello serves to emphasize the brilliance of the gold and to accentuate the details of the intricate patterns.

A medieval treatise written by a monk named Theophilus in Germany in the early twelfth century contains instructions for polishing inlaid niello. First, smooth the niello with a soft stone dampened with saliva; then, using a piece of limewood, rub it with a powder of ground soft stone and saliva. After that, as Theophilus explains:

> For a very long time, lightly rub the niello with this piece of wood and the powder, continually adding spittle so that it remains moist, until it becomes bright all over. Then take some wax from the hollow of your ear, and, when you have wiped the niello dry with a fine linen cloth, you smear this all over it and rub lightly with a goatskin or deerskin until it becomes completely bright.

—Theophilus, *De diversis artibus*, tr. C. R. Dodwell as *Theophilus: The Various Arts* (London: Nelson, 1961)

The Sutton Hoo purse lid (see fig. 10.3) and hinged clasps (see fig. 10.2) are also notable for their *cloisonné* decoration. Cloisonné is an ancient technique, used as early as the second millennium BCE in the eastern Mediterranean. Individual metal strips, or *cloisons* (French for "partitions"), are attached on edge to a baseplate as little walls to form cells that enclose glass or gems. For the Sutton Hoo jewelry, red garnets are used extensively. In fact, the Sutton Hoo jewelry includes more than 4,000 individual garnets. Colored glass, often arranged in checkered patterns, is also used in these pieces; on the main field of the hinged clasps, *cloisons* enclose colored glass to form a step pattern, which enhances the overall decorative effect.

Many of the decorative devices and materials employed in Anglo-Saxon metalwork were later used by Irish metalworkers. A spectacular example is the *Tara Brooch*, an accidental find made by a child playing by the seashore in County Meath, Ireland, in 1850. The brooch is a kind of stickpin used to join two pieces of a garment together. An incredible amount of decoration—including spirals, bird, animal, and human heads, and interlace patterns—is compressed on a piece of jewelry of just over 3½ inches in diameter. Panels of gold filigree, consisting of fine soldered wire, are combined on the back of the brooch with silver plaques with inlaid spiral designs in copper. A braided wire attachment was possibly a safety chain.

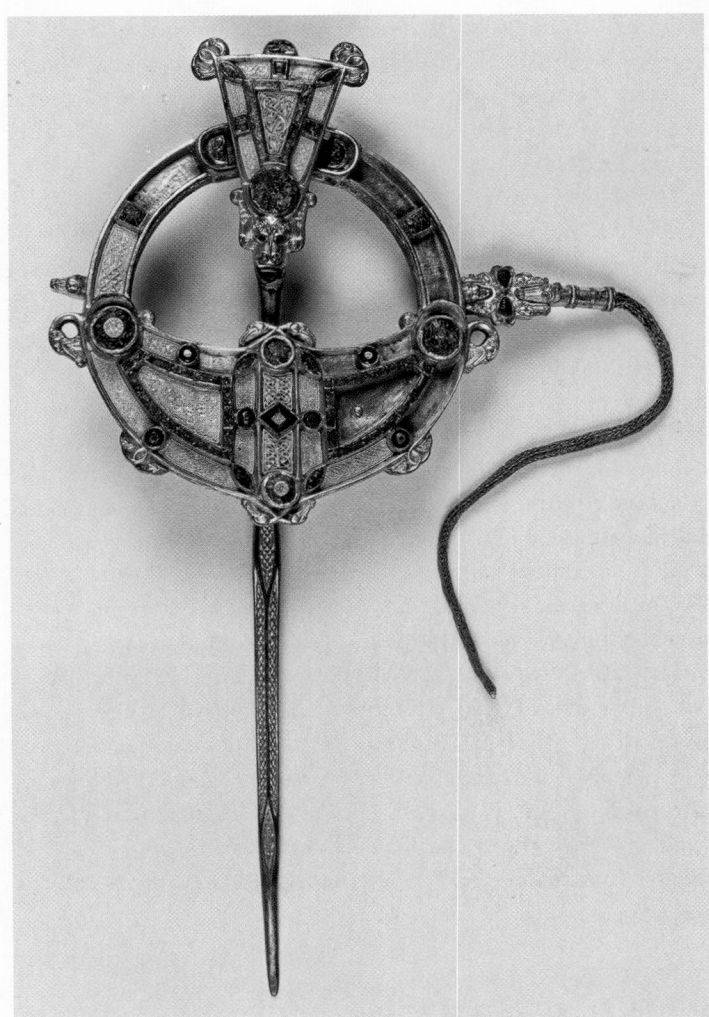

Tara Brooch, from Bettystown, County Meath, Ireland. 8th century. Gilt, bronze, glass, and enamel, diameter 3⅝" (8.7 cm). National Museum of Ireland, Dublin reflect the vitality of artistic forms produced by these migrating peoples, demonstrating an aesthetic that is quite different from the tradition that derives from Greece and Rome, yet equally rich in myth and imagery.

The Animal Style

The artistic tradition of the Germanic peoples, referred to by some scholars as the **animal style** because of its heavy use of stylized animal-like forms, merged with the intricate ornamental metal-work of the Celts, producing a unique combination of abstract and organic shapes, of formal discipline and imaginative freedom.

SHIP BURIAL, SUTTON HOO, ENGLAND An Anglo-Saxon ship burial in England follows the age-old tradition of burying important people with their personal effects. This custom may reflect a concern for the afterlife or it may simply be a way to honor the dead, but undoubtedly a correlation was understood between a sea voyage and the journey to an eternal resting place. The ship burial at Sutton Hoo (*hoo* is Anglo-Saxon for "head-land" or "promontory"), discovered in 1939 in one of 18 burial mounds on the site, is of a seventh-century Anglian king (gener-ally thought to be King Raedwald, who died around 625). The ship, one of two buried on the site, was over 90 feet long and 14 feet in the beam and was hauled more than a third of a mile from the sea. Military gear, silver and enamelware, official royal regalia, gold coins, and objects of personal adornment are all part of the entombment. Since no trace of a body was originally found in the ship, some claimed that the burial was a **cenotaph**, a memorial monument to honor a person buried elsewhere; it was also argued that the highly acidic soil could have destroyed any evidence of human remains. More recent analysis suggests that the presence of phosphate residuals, particularly along the keel of the ship, could indicate biological remains. Even if that claim is correct, it would not necessarily prove that those remains were human, since ani-mals were buried in other mounds at Sutton Hoo; the practice of

burying items that were part of a funeral feast could also produce phosphatic residue.

The Anglo-Saxon poem *Beowulf*, so concerned with displays of royal responsibility and obligation, includes a description of a ship fitted out for a funeral that is reminiscent of the Sutton Hoo burial. The funeral is that of Beowulf's father, King Scyld:

> A ring-whorled prow rode in the harbour,
> ice-clad, outbound, a craft for a prince.
> They stretched their beloved lord in his boat,
> laid out by the mast, amidships,
> the great ring-giver. Far-fetched treasures
> were piled upon him, and precious gear.
> I never heard before of a ship so well furbished
> with battle tackle, bladed weapons
> and coats of mail. The massed treasure
> was loaded on top of him: it would travel far
> on out into the ocean's sway.

Translated by Seamus Heaney, *Beowulf. A New Verse Translation*
(NY: Farrar, Straus, & Giroux, 2000)

Although *Beowulf* describes events that predate the Sutton Hoo find by at least a century, the poem was probably not composed until a century or more after that burial. So, while *Beowulf* should not be taken as a documentary account, it does suggest a royal context for the Sutton Hoo site.

Intricate animal-style design covers a large gold buckle from Sutton Hoo (fig. **10.1**). Two interlaced biting snakes decorate the stud to which the tongue of the buckle is attached. That stud is in turn affixed to a plaque with intertwined serpents and eagle heads covering virtually every available space. It has been traditional for scholars to refer to the need to decorate all surfaces as an expres-sion of *horror vacui*, a fear of empty space. But this designation imposes our contemporary values on a culture alien to them. Unlike the Greeks and Romans, who used spatial illusionism to animate their art, Germanic and Celtic artists used intricate patterns to

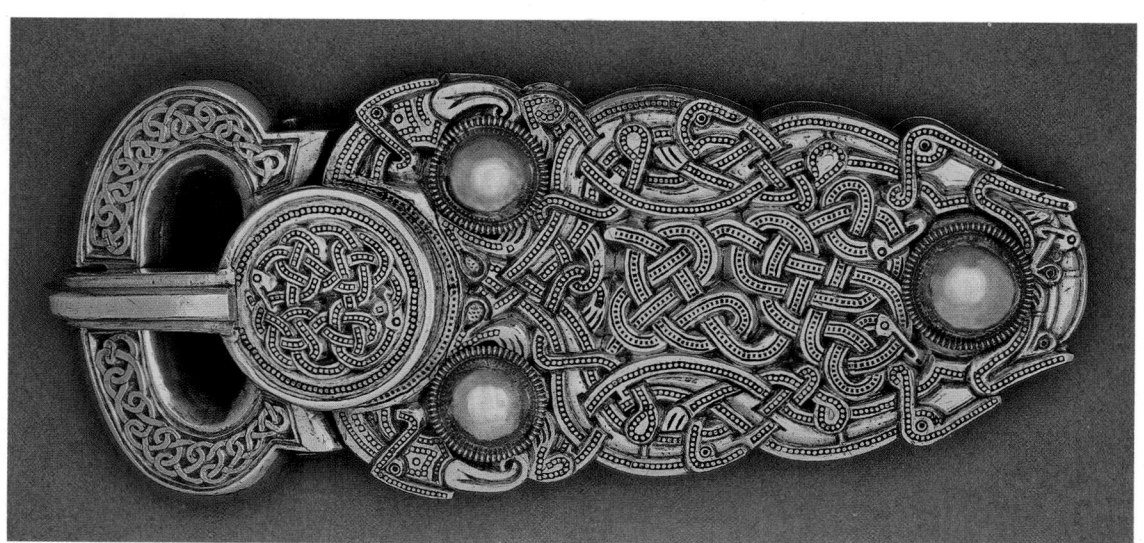

10.1 Gold buckle, from the Sutton Hoo ship burial. First half of 7th century. Gold, length 5¼" (13.4 cm). The British Museum, London. Courtesy of the Trustees

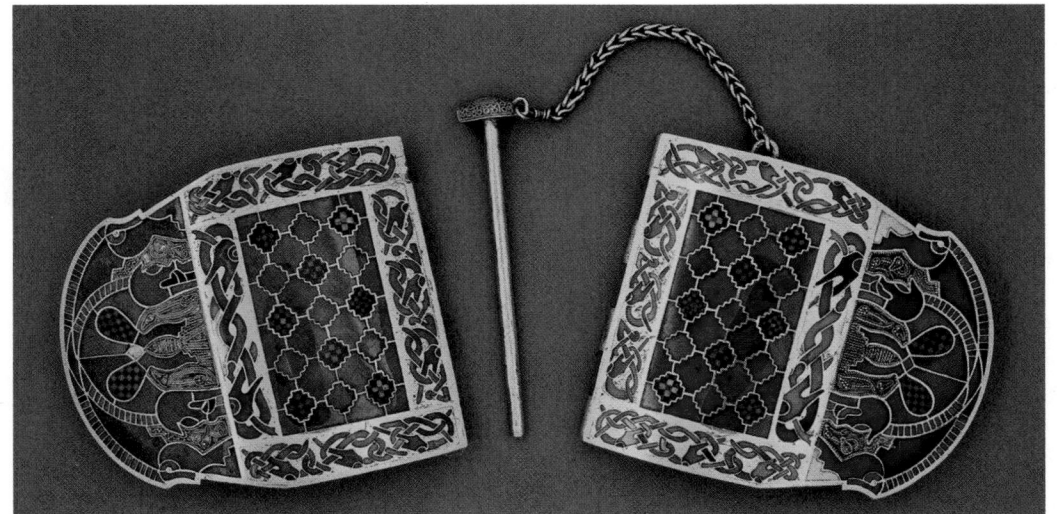

enliven the surface of their precious objects. Although the designs can seem confusing and claustrophobic to us, there is a consistent and intentional tightness in the way the patterns hold together.

A pair of hinged clasps (fig. 10.2) from the burial also contains intertwined serpents, here functioning as framing devices for a diagonally oriented checkerboard field of garnets and glass set in gold. At the end of each clasp is a curved plaque on which crouch boars back to back. So tightly integrated into the design are these animals that it is difficult to decide if the plaque curves to allow for the representation of the boars or if the animals' backs hunch in response to the shape of the clasp.

A gold, enamel, and garnet purse cover (fig. 10.3) was also found at Sutton Hoo. The three hinges at the top of the purse attached to leather straps suspended from the belt that was held together by the gold buckle illustrated in fig. 10.1. The purse itself was probably a leather pouch, the whole arrangement reminiscent of the sporran that Scots wear in front of their kilts. Its original ivory or bone background does not survive and has been replaced. Each of four pairs of symmetrical motifs has its own distinctive character, an indication that they were assembled from different sources. One, the standing man between facing animals in the lower row, has a very long history indeed. We first saw him in

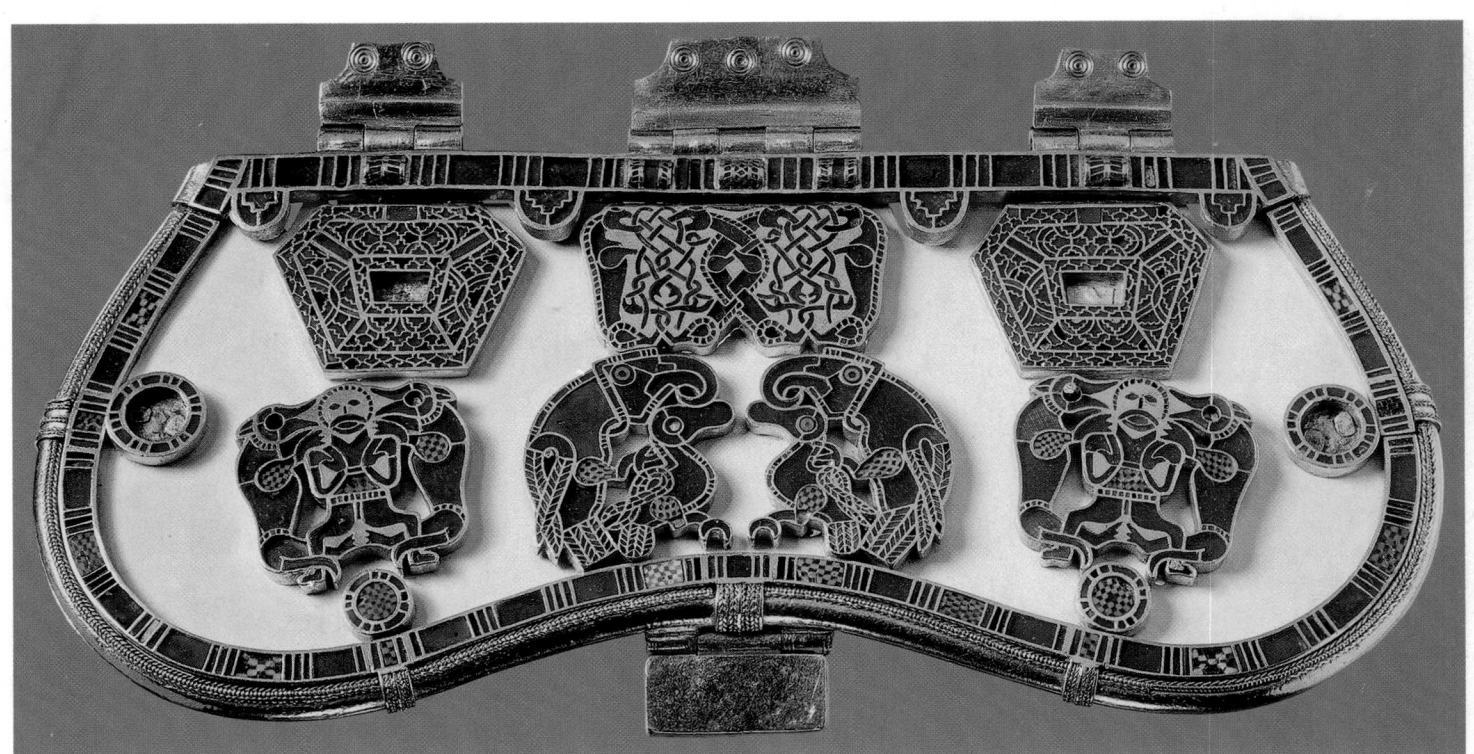

10.3 Purse cover, from the Sutton Hoo ship burial. First half of 7th century. Gold with garnets and enamels, length 8" (20.3 cm). The British Museum, London. Courtesy of the Trustees

Mesopotamian art more than 3,200 years earlier (see fig. 2.9). The upper design, at the center, is of more recent origin. It consists of fighting animals whose tails, legs, and jaws are elongated into bands that form a complex interweaving pattern. The fourth design, on the top left and right, uses interlacing bands as an ornamental device. The combination of these bands with the animal style, as shown here, seems to have been invented not long before our purse cover was made.

The Sutton Hoo objects are significant for the way they illustrate the transmission of motifs and techniques through the migration of various peoples. They show evidence of cultural interchange with Germanic peoples, combined with evidence of Scandinavian roots, but there are other noteworthy connections as well. King Raedwald was reputed to have made offerings to Christ, as well as to his ancestral pagan gods. A number of the objects discovered at Sutton Hoo make specific reference to Christianity, including silver bowls decorated with a cross, undoubtedly the result of trade with the Mediterranean. There is also a set of spoons inscribed with the names of Saul and Paul, perhaps a reference to Christian conversion (Saul changed his name to Paul on his conversion). Is it too much to wonder, as some scholars have done, if the crosses inscribed in the glass checkerboards on the Sutton Hoo clasps (see fig. 10.2) are a conscious reference to the new religion? These clasps were sewn onto two parts of a garment, probably held together at the shoulders, as is suggested by their curvature. Although executed in the patterns of Anglo-Saxon style, they take the form of fasteners very like those seen in Roman gear; for example, the shoulder attachments of the breastplate of the *Augustus of Primaporta* (see fig. 7.29). In fact, Roman and Byzantine articles accompany other objects of local manufacture that copy imperial forms in the Sutton Hoo graves. This has been cited as evidence that the chieftain buried or commemorated there consciously presented himself as a Roman ruler.

The chief medium of the animal style was clearly metalwork. Such articles, small, durable, and often of exquisitely refined craftsmanship, were eagerly sought after, which accounts for the rapid diffusion of the animal-style repertoire of forms. These forms spread not only geographically but also from one material to another, migrating from metal into wood, stone, and even paint. They were used to convey a variety of messages, some clearly pagan and others Christian.

HIBERNO-SAXON ART

During the early Middle Ages, the Irish (called Hibernians after the Roman name for Ireland, Hibernia) came to be the spiritual and cultural leaders of western Europe. Since the Irish had never been part of the Roman Empire, the missionaries who carried Christianity to them from England in the fifth century found a Celtic society that was barbarian by Roman standards. The Irish readily accepted Christianity, bringing them into contact with Mediterranean civilization. However, because the institutional framework of the Roman Church was essentially urban, it did not suit the rural Irish way of life. Irish Christians preferred to follow the example of the desert saints of Egypt and the Near East, who had sought spiritual perfection in the solitude of the wilderness, where groups of them founded the earliest monasteries (see page 263). Thus, Irish monasteries were established in isolated, secluded areas, even on islands off the mainland, and such places required complete self-sufficiency.

Manuscripts

Irish monasteries soon became centers of learning and the arts, with much energy spent copying literary and religious texts. They also sent monks abroad to preach to nonbelievers and to found monasteries in northern Britain and Europe, from present-day France to Austria. Each monastery's scriptorium became an artistic center. Although pictures illustrating biblical events held little

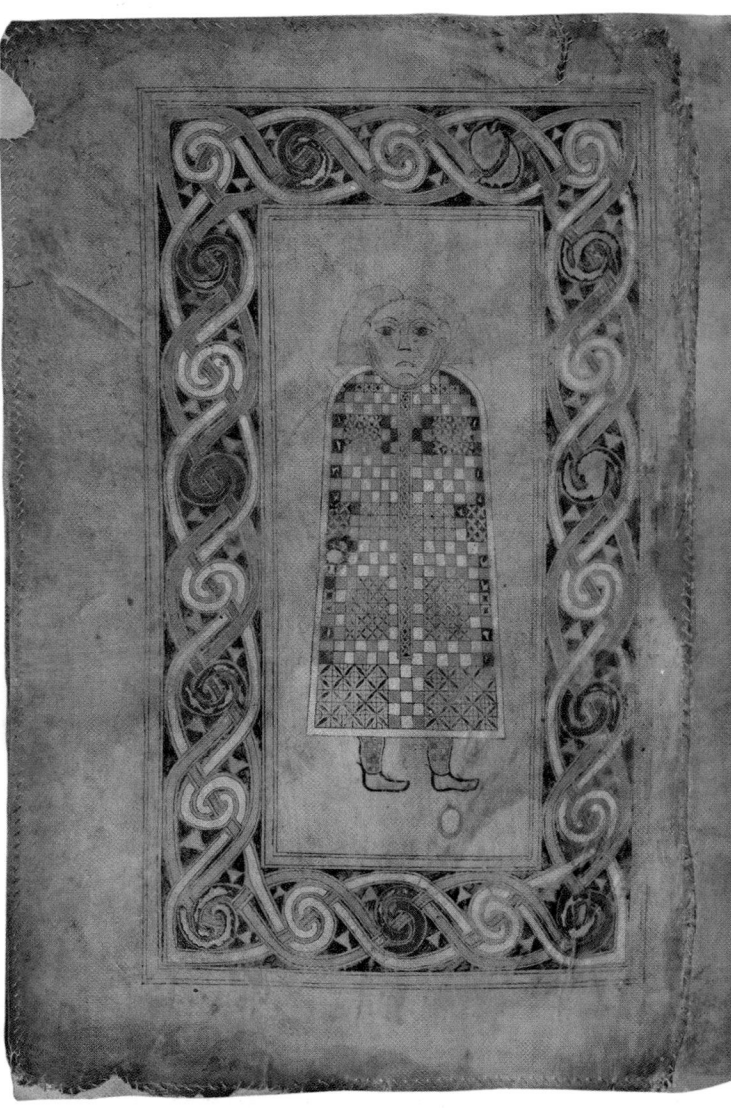

10.4 *Symbol of St. Matthew*, from the *Book of Durrow*. ca. 680. Tempera on vellum, 9⅝ × 6⅛" (24.7 × 15.7 cm). Trinity College, Dublin

interest for the Irish monks, they devoted great efforts to decorative embellishment. The finest of these manuscripts belong to the Hiberno-Saxon style—a style that combines Christian with Celtic and Germanic elements, and that flourished in the monasteries of Ireland as well as those founded by Irish monks in Saxon England. These Irish monks helped speed the conversion to Christianity in Europe north of the Alps. Throughout Europe, they made the monastery a cultural center and thus influenced medieval civilization for several hundred years.

In order to spread the message concerning Christ, the Kingdom of God, and salvation—called the Gospel—the Irish monasteries had to produce large numbers of copies of the Bible and other Christian books by hand. Every manuscript copy was looked upon as a sacred object containing the Word of God, and its beauty needed to reflect the importance of its contents. Each of the four books of the Gospel, which were credited to the evangelists Matthew, Mark, Luke, and John, was prefaced by a representation of the book's author or an animal that functioned as his symbol. These symbols were assigned to the evangelists by early commentators, including St. Jerome (342–420), who was responsible for the first translation of the Bible into Latin. Although the tradition of assigning specific symbols was at first far from codified, eventually the symbols came to be systematically associated with the evangelists as follows: the man or angel with St. Matthew, the lion with St. Mark, the ox with St. Luke, and the eagle with St. John. These beasts were described in the Book of Ezekiel (1:5–14) in the Hebrew Bible and in the Apocalypse of St. John the Evangelist (4:6–8) in the Christian one.

The illustration of the symbol of St. Matthew in the *Book of Durrow* (fig. **10.4**) shows how ornamental pattern can animate a figure even while accentuating its surface decoration. The body of the figure, composed of framed sections of a checkerboard pattern, recalls the ornamental quality of the Sutton Hoo clasps (see fig. **10.2**). The addition of a head, which confronts us directly, and feet, turned to the side, transform the decorative motifs into a human figure. Active, elaborate patterns, previously seen in metalwork, are here employed to demonstrate that St. Matthew's message is precious. Irish scribes and artists were revered for their abilities and achievements. A medieval account relates how, after his death, an Irish scribe's hands were preserved as relics capable of performing miracles.

THE *LINDISFARNE GOSPELS* Thanks to a later **colophon** (a note at the end of a manuscript), we know a great deal about the origin of the *Lindisfarne Gospels*, produced in Northumbria, England, including the name of the translator (Aldred) and of the scribe (Bishop Eadfrith), who presumably painted the illuminations as well. (See *Primary Source*, page 320.) Given the high regard in which Irish scribes and artists were held, it is not surprising that a bishop is credited with writing and decorating this manuscript. In Irish monasteries monks were divided into three categories: juniors (pupils and novice monks), working brothers (engaged in manual labor), and seniors (the most experienced monks, who were responsible for copying sacred books).

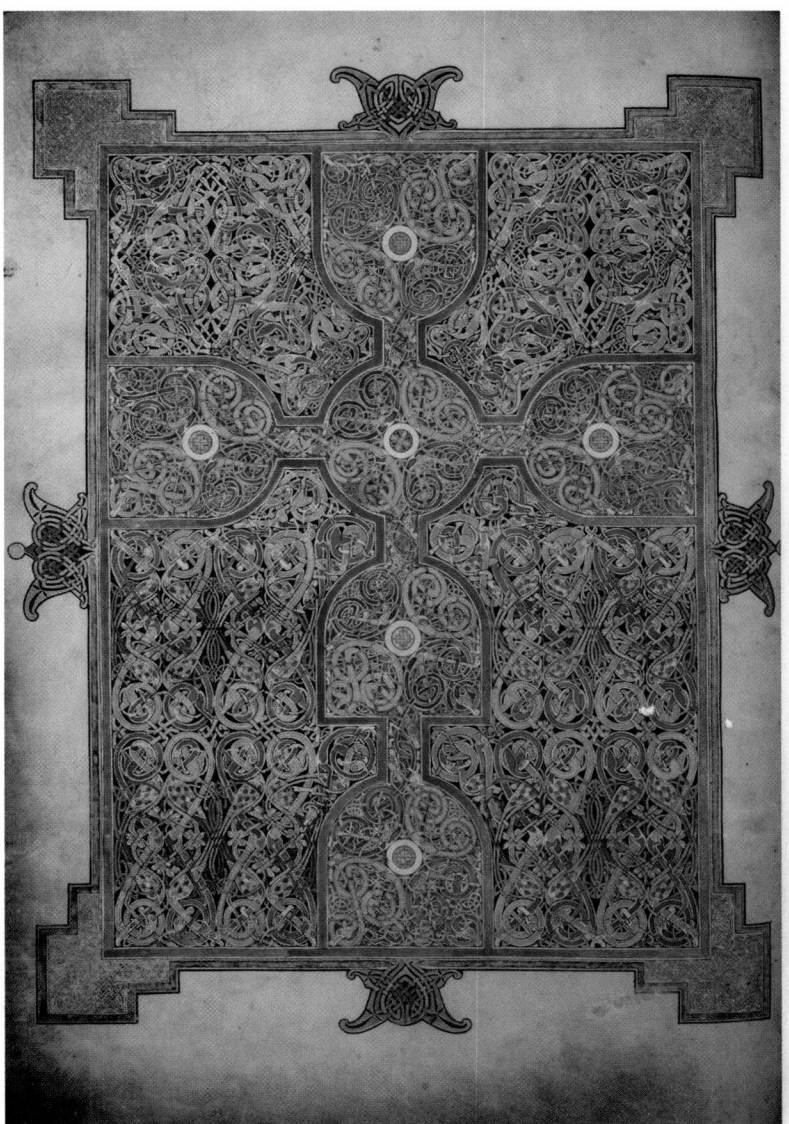

10.5 Cross page, from the *Lindisfarne Gospels*. ca. 700. Tempera on vellum, 13½ × 9¼" (34.3 × 23.5 cm). The British Library, London

The Cross page (fig. **10.5** and see page 312) is a creation of breathtaking complexity. Working with the precision of a jeweler, the **miniaturist** (the illuminator of the manuscript) poured into the geometric frame animal interlace so dense and yet so full of movement that the fighting beasts on the Sutton Hoo purse cover (see fig. 10.3) seem simple in comparison. In order to achieve this effect, the artist had to work within a severe discipline as though he were following specific rules. The smallest motifs and the largest patterns were worked out in advance of painting. Ruler and compass were used to mark the page with a network of grid lines and with points, both drawn and pricked. In applying paint, the artist followed his drawing exactly. No mark is allowed to interfere with either the rigid balance of individual features or the overall design. The scholar Françoise Henry has suggested that artists conceived of their work as "a sort of sacred riddle" composed of abstract forms to be sorted out and deciphered. Organic

Lindisfarne Gospels

Colophon

Colophons are notes written at the end of some manuscripts recording who wrote them, when, for whom, etc. The colophon at the end of the Lindisfarne Gospels (ca. 700 CE) was written some 250 years after the text, but most scholars believe that its information is accurate. It names the scribe, the binder, the maker of the metal ornaments on the binding, and the author of the English translation of the Latin text, but no painter. The painting seems to have been done by Eadfrith, the scribe.

Eadfrith, Bishop of the Lindisfarne Church, originally wrote this book, for God and for Saint Cuthbert and ... for all the saints whose relics are in the Island. And Ethelwald, Bishop of the Lindisfarne islanders, impressed it on the outside and covered it—as he well knew how to do. And Billfrith, the anchorite, forged the ornaments which are on it on the outside and adorned it with gold and with gems and also with gilded-over silver—pure metal. And Aldred, unworthy and most miserable priest, glossed it in English between the lines with the help of God and Saint Cuthbert.

Source: Cotton MS Nero, D. IV. The British Library

---

and geometric shapes had to be kept separate. Within the animal compartments, every line had to turn out to be part of an animal's body. Other rules concerned symmetry, mirror-image effects, and repetitions of shapes and colors. Only by intense observation can we enter into the spirit of this mazelike world. It is as if these biting and clawing monsters are subdued by the power of the Cross,

10.6 *St. Matthew*, from the *Lindisfarne Gospels*. ca. 700. Tempera on vellum, 13½ × 9¼" (34.3 × 23.5 cm). The British Library, London (MS Cotton Nero D.4)

converted to Christian purpose just as were the Celtic tribes themselves.

Several factors came together to foster the development of the Hiberno-Saxon style: the isolation of the Irish, the sophistication of their scriptoria in the secluded monastic environments, and the zealous desire to spread the word of Christianity. In time and with more contact with the Continent—Rome in particular—Hiberno-Saxon art reflected new influences. The illustration of Matthew in the *Lindisfarne Gospels* (fig. **10.6**) is striking by comparison with the Matthew from the *Book of Durrow* (see fig. 10.4), made only a generation or two earlier. In the *Lindisfarne Gospels*, Matthew studies his text intently, and the artist suggests a sense of space by turning the figure and the bench on an angle to indicate depth, whereas in the *Book of Durrow*, the saint stares out frontally at the reader with his hands at his sides. There are no other figures in the *Book of Durrow* image, whereas the tied-back curtain in the Lindisfarne manuscript reveals an unidentified figure, whom some identify as Christ holding the Christian Bible and others, more convincingly, as Moses holding the Hebrew Bible. The latter identification is more compelling because the contrast between the open book of the Gospel writer and the closed book of the other figure correlates with distinctions between the two Testaments that were often made in the Middle Ages. Also, whereas Matthew in the *Book of Durrow* wears a costume of flat patterns, the Lindisfarne Matthew wears clothes marked by folds; a dark undergarment is distinguished from a lighter toga, suggesting a pliant material that responds to the body beneath it.

How do we explain this change? We know that in the seventh and eighth centuries the Irish had increased contact with Rome and came to adopt Roman liturgical practices. For example, the abbot of the monastery of Jarrow, near Lindisfarne, is reported to have returned from Rome at the end of the seventh century with a host of manuscripts. Artists at Jarrow probably used the illuminations in these manuscripts as models. The illustration of the prophet Ezra restoring the Bible from the *Codex Amiatinus* (fig. **10.7**), produced at Jarrow, is undoubtedly an adaptation of Roman illuminations available at the monastery. The artist depicts the book cupboard (reminiscent of the one in the St. Lawrence lunette from Galla Placidia [see fig. 8.14]), table, bench,

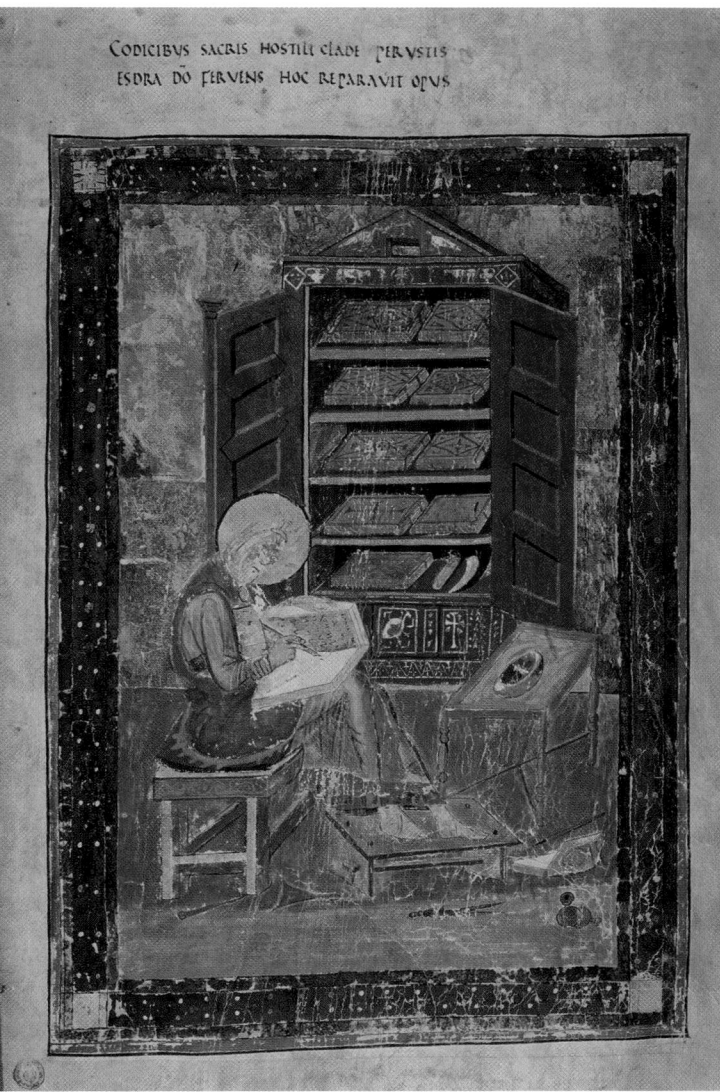

10.7 *Ezra Restoring the Bible*, from the *Codex Amiatinus*. Early 8th century. Tempera on vellum, 20 × 13½" (50.5 × 34.3 cm). Biblioteca Medicea Laurenziana, Florence

and footstool by using oblique angles, which convey a sense of perspective, as if the objects recede into depth. Likewise, the shading in the drapery and the shadow of the inkwell on the floor promote a sense of depth. The artist also used color blending (evident on Ezra's garments and on his hands, face, and feet) to model form. Notice, in particular, how Ezra's cushion seems to have been depressed by the weight of his body, lending further substance to the prophet's figure.

Some have suggested that Eadfrith, the illustrator of the Lindisfarne Matthew (see fig. 10.6), referred to the same Roman manuscript that inspired the Ezra artist, who produced a more faithful interpretation of it. Indeed, identical poses and parallel features such as the bench are too conspicuous to be ignored. However, Eadfrith was eager, or perhaps felt required, to maintain some Hiberno-Saxon traditional devices: Unlike the Ezra artist, he decorated the bench with multiple patterns, and suggested depth in the drapery by juxtaposing near-complementary colors,

playing off the reddish folds against the greenish cloth. Eadfrith employed the same rigid outline, geometric decoration, and flat planes of color that he used for the manuscript's nonfigural pages (see fig. 10.5). Much as the Ezra page allows us to appreciate what antique manuscripts that no longer survive might have looked like, the Lindisfarne page is both more striking and more dramatic. As the *Lindisfarne Gospels* document a process of synthesis between northern and Mediterranean elements, it helps us appreciate the remarkable contribution to European art made by migration styles and the skill of Hiberno-Saxon artists.

THE *BOOK OF KELLS* The Hiberno-Saxon manuscript style reached its climax a hundred years after the *Lindisfarne Gospels* in the *Book of Kells*, the most elaborate codex of Celtic art. It was probably made, or at least begun, at the end of the eighth or the beginning of the ninth century at the monastery on the island of Iona, off the western coast of Scotland, which had been founded by Irish monks in the sixth century. The book's name derives from the Irish monastery of Kells, where the manuscript was housed from the late ninth century until the seventeenth century. Its many pages reflect a wide array of influences from the Mediterranean to the English Channel.

The Chi Rho Iota monogram page illustrates Christ's initials, *XPI*, in Greek (fig. **10.8**). Alongside them appear the words *Christi autem generatio*, or "now this is how the birth of Christ came about," heralding the beginning of the Book of Matthew (1:18), in which the birth of Jesus is celebrated. The Chi Rho Iota page has much the same swirling design as the Cross page from the *Lindisfarne Gospels*, and a viewer can also see parallels to contemporary jewelry, such as the *Tara Brooch* (see *Materials and Techniques*, page 315). The relationship between manuscript illumination and precious metalwork is far from accidental, evidenced by the display of both on altars and their being housed in church treasuries. During a period when literacy was rare and class-based, the book was a symbol of authority and dominance, an object that must have mystified many people as much as it elucidated matters for others.

On the Chi Rho Iota page, the rigid geometry of the Lindisfarne Cross page and the *Tara Brooch* has been relaxed somewhat, and for the first time images of humans are incorporated into the design. The very top of the X-shaped Chi sprouts a recognizable face, while along its shaft are three angels with wings. And in a touch of enchanting fantasy, the tendril-like P-shaped Rho ends in a human head that has been hypothesized to be a representation of Christ. More surprising still is the introduction of the natural world. Nearly hidden in the ornamentation, as if playing a game of hide-and-seek, are cats and mice, butterflies, even otters catching fish. No doubt they performed a symbolic function for medieval readers, even if the meaning is no longer apparent to us. The richness and intricacy of the illustration compels concentration, establishing a direct connection between the viewer and the image in much the same way as does the fixed, direct gaze of the holy figure in an Early Byzantine icon (see fig. 8.35). In each work, icon and manuscript illumination,

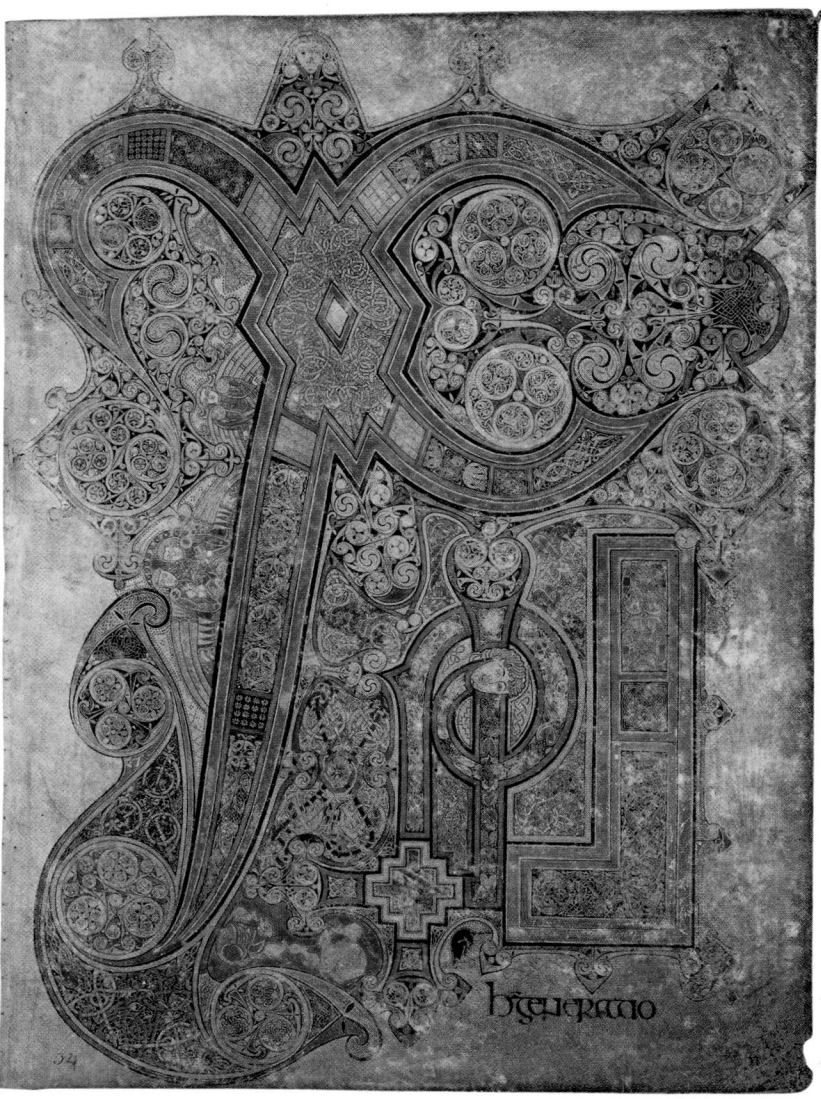

10.8 Chi Rho Iota page, from the Book of Matthew (1:18), from the *Book of Kells*. ca. 800. Ink and pigments on vellum, 13 × 9½" (33 × 24.1 cm). Trinity College Library, Dublin

the power of the image is so strong that the viewer virtually enters into its realm, forgetting the world outside its frame.

VIKING ART

It was not only in Hiberno-Saxon art that the animal style showed its power to adapt to a variety of materials and forms of expression. The inhabitants of Scandinavia (Norway, Sweden, and Denmark) had lived out of the Roman orbit, although they shared many beliefs and practices with their Germanic brethren and neighbors. In fact, the animal style flourished in Scandinavia long beyond the Germanic-Nordic migrations in the region, longer than it did anywhere else. These northern people are often labeled Vikings, though the term is a misleading one, since it derives from the Old Norse *Vinkingr*, which means sea pirate or raider; thus, these people were really only "Vikings" when they went "*a-viking*" out of their own coastal waters, to England or Russia, for instance. By the eighth century, Nordic sailors increasingly wandered around the shores of Europe, both trading with and attacking the local populations. This sometimes led to permanent settlements, such as occurred in Iceland in the ninth century and Greenland in the tenth, and when a colony was established in northwestern France. Even today, the French region is called Normandy and its inhabitants are referred to as Normans in recognition of its settlement by Norsemen (or "North Men").

SHIP BURIAL, OSEBERG, NORWAY It is in Scandinavia that the origins for burying important people in ships, such as at Sutton Hoo, can be found; this is also where the practice seems to have continued longer than elsewhere. A buried Viking ship of the early ninth century, found at Oseberg, in southern Norway, is more than 75 feet long; the boat was not a raiding vessel, but rather a pleasure craft, used for sailing in calm waters (fig. 10.9). Two women, placed on beds in a burial chamber, were interred within the ship, which also included oars, a ramp, an elaborately carved cart, sleds, and the skeletons of at least ten horses. Grave robbers stole whatever jewelry and metalwork, which is presumed to have been significant, that accompanied the deceased in the buried vessel.

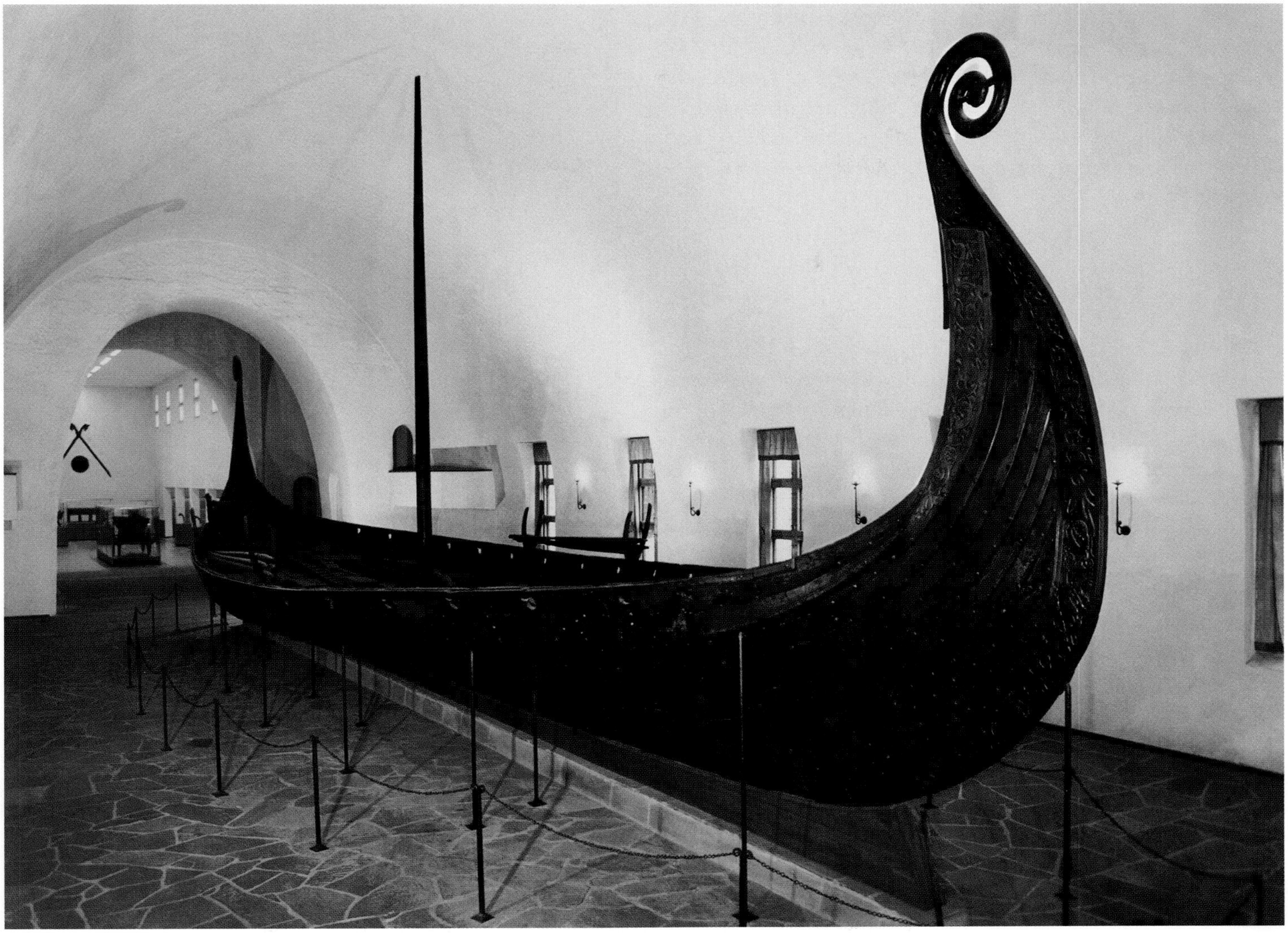

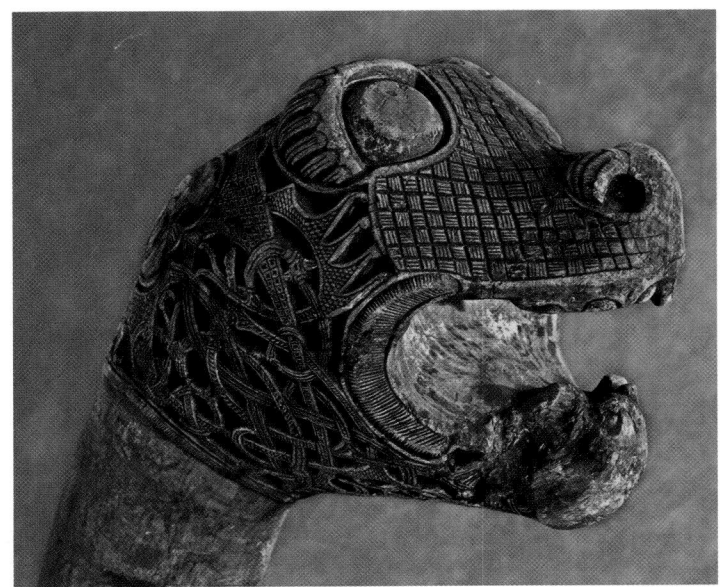

10.9 Burial ship, from Oseberg, Norway. ca. 834. Wood, length 75'6" (23 m). Vikingskiphuset, Universitets Oldsaksamling, Oslo, Norway

The prow and stern of the ship end in wavelike spirals, and the prow terminates in a serpent's head. If we recall the passage in *Beowulf* cited above (see page 316), we realize that the "ring-whorled prow" of the poem undoubtedly describes the spiral ornament of a boat such as the one from Oseberg. The body of the ship is framed at bow and stern by bands of carved reliefs in which biting and clawing animals are intertwined in an intricate and strangely orderly procession. Five wooden posts decorated with snarling monsters looking like mythical sea dragons were found in the buried ship. Their actual function is not known, although suggestions include the possibility that they were carried in processions or used for cult functions. The head on one of the posts (fig. 10.10) displays all the characteristics of the animal style and is surprisingly realistic, as are such details as the teeth, gums, and nostrils. Interlacing and geometric patterns cover the head, with deep undercutting and rounded forms accentuating these surface designs. Although the origins of the patterns employed here are found within Germanic and Anglo-Saxon motifs, they have been forcefully adapted to fit the animal head's dynamic curving forms. Scientific studies using dendrochronology

10.10 *Animal Head*, from the Oseberg burial ship. ca. 834. Wood, height approx. 5" (12.7 cm). Vikingskiphuset, Universitets Oldsaksamling, Oslo (the analysis of the growth rings of trees or wooden objects) date the Oseberg ship burial to 834. One of the women buried at Oseberg is often identified as Queen Asa, wife of Gudröd the Magnificent (ca. 780–820), because it is assumed that only a royal personage would have had the resources to commission objects of such richness, but recent scholarship questions the royal nature of the burial.

CAROLINGIAN ART

During the late eighth century, a new empire developed out of the collection of tribes and kingdoms that dominated northern continental Europe. This empire, which united most of Europe from the North Sea to Spain and as far south as Lombardy in northern Italy, was founded by Charlemagne, who ruled as king of the Franks from 768 to 814. Pope Leo III bestowed on him the title of emperor of Rome in Old St. Peter's basilica on Christmas Day in the year 800, pronouncing him successor to Constantine, the first Christian emperor. Although Charlemagne was able to resist the pope's attempts to assert his authority over the newly created Catholic Empire, there was now an interdependence of spiritual and political authority, of Church and State, that would define the history of western Europe for many centuries.

The emperors were crowned in Rome, but they did not live there. Charlemagne built his capital at the center of his power, in Aachen (Aix-la-Chapelle), located in what is now Germany and close to France, Belgium, and the Netherlands. The period dominated by Charlemagne and his successors, roughly from 768 to 877, is labeled Carolingian (derived from Charlemagne's Latin name, *Carolus Magnus*, meaning "Charles the Great"). Among Charlemagne's goals were to better the administration of his realm and the teaching of Christian truths. He summoned the best minds to his court, including Alcuin of York, the most learned scholar of the day, to restore ancient Roman learning and to establish a system of schools at every cathedral and monastery. The emperor took an active hand in this renewal, which went well beyond a mere interest in old books to include political objectives. He modeled his rule after the Roman Empire under Constantine and Justinian—rather than their pagan predecessors—and proclaimed a *renovatio imperii romani*, a "renewal of imperial Rome," his efforts being aided by the pope who had crowned him Holy Roman Emperor. The artists working for Charlemagne and other Carolingian rulers consciously sought to emulate Rome; by combining their admiration for antiquity with native northern European features, they produced original works of art of the highest quality.

Sculpture

A bronze *Equestrian Statue of a Carolingian Ruler* (fig. **10.11**), once thought to be of Charlemagne himself but now generally said to be of his grandson Charles the Bald, conveys the political objectives of the Carolingian dynasty. The ruler, wearing imperial

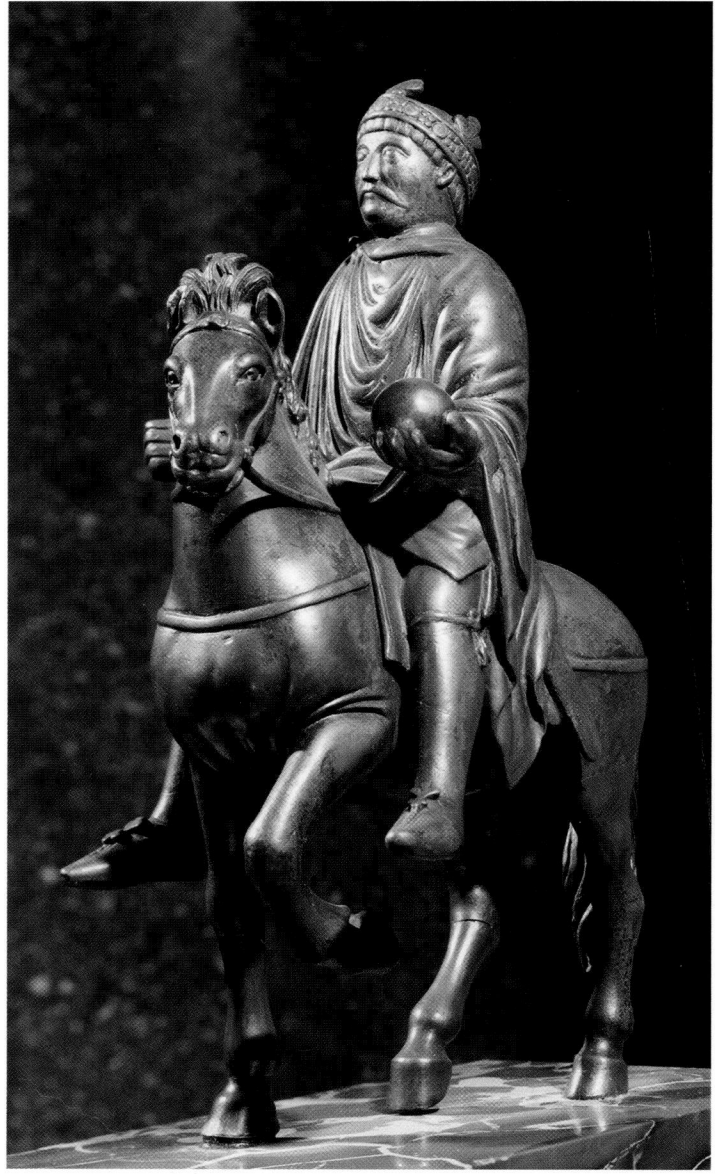

10.11   *Equestrian Statue of a Carolingian Ruler* (Charles the Bald?). 9th century. Bronze, height 9½" (24.4 cm). Musée du Louvre, Paris

robes, sits as triumphantly on his steed as if he were on a throne. In his hand is an orb signifying his domination of the world. The statue is probably modeled on a now lost antique Roman equestrian statue of Theodoric, which Charlemagne had brought from Ravenna for the courtyard of his imperial palace. There are other possible sources, including a bronze equestrian statue of Marcus Aurelius (see fig. 7.33), once mistakenly thought to represent Constantine, the first Christian emperor, and thus also an appropriate model for the ambitious Charlemagne and his successors.

The Carolingian statue is not a slavish copy of its antique model. It is simpler and less cluttered with detail than the statue of Marcus Aurelius for instance. What is important is that it communicates the significant message that the Carolingian rulers were heirs to the Roman imperial throne. What is most striking is the difference in size: Marcus Aurelius stands more than 11 feet high, while the Carolingian figure does not reach 10 inches. Yet the diminutive statue expresses as much majesty and dignity as the more monumental example. Given the metalwork tradition of the Franks, the miniaturization is not only appropriate, but might in itself suggest value. Unfortunately, we do not know the audience for the work or how it was used, though its smallness could relate to portability.

Illuminated Books

Charlemagne's interest in promoting learning and culture required the production of large numbers of books by his scriptoria. He established an "academy" at his court and encouraged the collecting and copying of many works of ancient Roman literature. In fact, the oldest surviving texts of many classical Latin authors are found in Carolingian manuscripts that were long considered of Roman origin. This very page is printed in letters

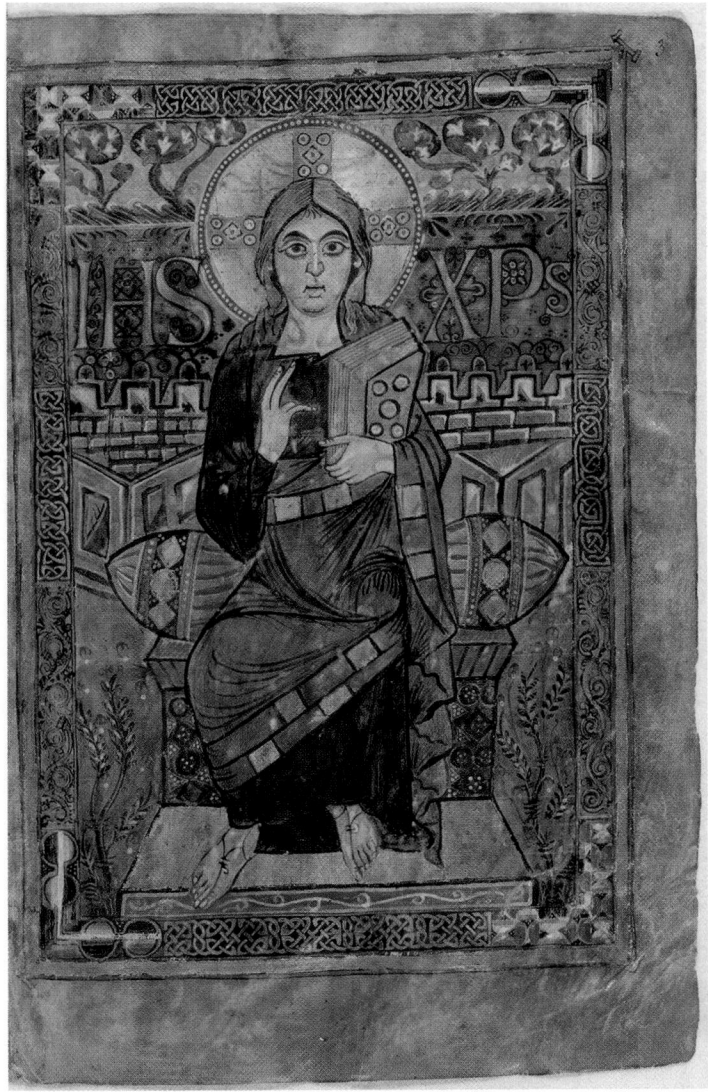

10.12 *Christ Enthroned*, from the *Godescalc Gospels* (*Lectionary*). 781–83. Tempera on vellum, 12⅝ × 8¼" (32.4 × 21.2 cm). Bibliothèque Nationale, Paris

the shapes of which derive from the script in Carolingian manuscripts. The fact that these letters are known today as "Roman" rather than Carolingian is a result of the confusion about the manuscripts' origins.

THE *GODESCALC GOSPELS* One of the earliest manuscripts created in Charlemagne's scriptoria is the *Godescalc Gospels*, named after the monk who signed his name to the book; it is generally thought to reflect manuscripts and objects that Charlemagne brought back with him from Rome. The manuscript's most compelling image is of a monumental Enthroned Christ (fig. **10.12**), whose large staring eyes communicate directly with the viewer. His purple garments denote imperial stature. (Purple was the color of royalty in the Roman world.) The concentration on imperial imagery reflects Charlemagne's personal ambitions, which were to be realized about 20 years later, when he received the title of Holy Roman Emperor in 800. Hard lines and swirling patterns around the knees suggest where drapery falls over the body, and white lines on the hands, neck, and face indicate highlights. It is as if the artist is attempting to emulate Roman modeling, but does so in a Northern manner, by using linear patterns.

Christ sits within an enclosed garden, a motif reminiscent of Roman painting (see fig. 7.55), but transformed here into flat decorative elements, almost like the designs on a carpet. The outlined letters of Christ's name and the frame, composed of interlace patterns, are reminiscent of metalwork (see figs. 10.1–10.3) and Hiberno-Saxon illuminations (see figs. 10.4–10.6). A great painter has fused the heritage of Rome with the decorative devices traditionally employed by northern European artists.

This manuscript includes a dedicatory poem commemorating the baptism of Charlemagne's sons by Pope Hadrian in Rome in 781. By bringing his sons to Rome to be baptized, Charlemagne effectively acknowledged the authority of the pope in ecclesiastical matters, although this was often disputed by later rulers. In turn, the pope placed himself and all of Western Christianity under the protection of the emperor.

THE *GOSPEL BOOK OF CHARLEMAGNE* The *Gospel Book of Charlemagne* (also known as the *Coronation Gospels* because later German emperors swore on this book during their coronations) is said to have been found in Charlemagne's tomb and is thought to have been produced at his court. Looking at the page with St. Matthew (fig. **10.13**), we can hardly believe that such a work could have been executed in northern Europe and less than a generation after the *Godescalc Gospels*. Were it not for the large golden halo, the evangelist might almost be mistaken for a Roman portrait in the naturalness and solidity with which he inhabits the landscape setting. The artist shows himself fully conversant with the Roman tradition of painting, from the modeling of the forms, the shading of face, hands, and feet, and the body-revealing drapery, to the acanthus ornament on the wide frame, which makes the picture seem like a window. Since the manner of painting is so clearly Mediterranean, some claim that the artist must have come from Byzantium or Italy.

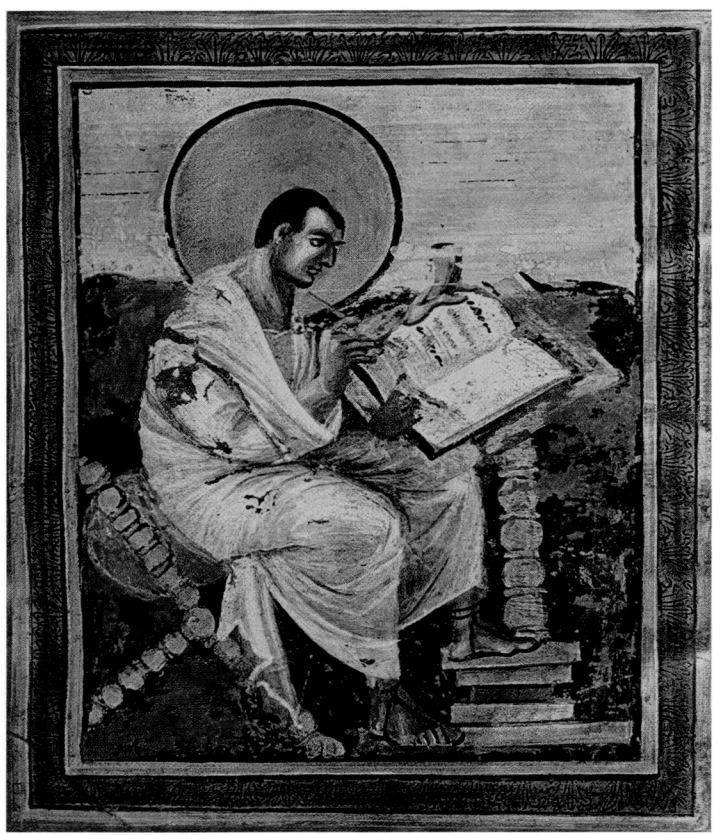

10.13 *St. Matthew*, from the *Gospel Book of Charlemagne* (*Coronation Gospels*). ca. 800–10. Ink and colors on vellum, 13 × 10" (33 × 25.4 cm). Kunsthistorisches Museum, Vienna

THE *GOSPEL BOOK OF ARCHBISHOP EBBO OF REIMS*
Less reflective of classical models, but equally reliant on them, is a miniature painted some three decades later for the *Gospel Book of Archbishop Ebbo of Reims* (fig. **10.14**). The subject is once again St. Matthew, and the pose is similar to that in the *Gospel Book of Charlemagne*, but this picture is filled with a vibrant energy that sets everything in motion. The thickly painted drapery swirls about the figure, the hills heave upward, and the architecture and vegetation seem tossed about by a whirlwind. Even the acanthus pattern on the frame assumes a strange, flamelike character. The evangelist has been transformed from a Roman author setting down his thoughts into a man seized with the frenzy of divine inspiration, a vehicle for recording the Word of God. The way the artist communicates this energy, particularly through the expressive use of flickering line, employing his brush as if it were a pen, recalls the endless interlaced movement in the ornamentation of Hiberno-Saxon manuscripts (see figs. 10.5 and 10.8).

THE *UTRECHT PSALTER*
The imperial scriptorium at Reims responsible for the *Ebbo Gospels* also produced perhaps the most extraordinary of all Carolingian manuscripts, the *Utrecht Psalter* (fig. **10.15**), where energetic form is expressed with remarkable pen drawings. That the artist has followed a much older model is indicated by the architectural and landscape settings of the

scenes, which recall the Column of Trajan (see fig. 7.40). Another indication is the use of Roman capital lettering, which had gone out of general use several centuries before. The rhythmic quality of the draftsmanship, however, gives these sketches an expressive unity that could not have been present in earlier pictures. Without this rhythmic quality, the drawings of the *Utrecht Psalter* would carry little conviction, for the poetic language of the Psalms does not lend itself to illustration in the same way as the narrative portions of the Bible. Perhaps, as some scholars have suggested, we can attribute the drawn rather than painted style to the influence of an antique scroll (see fig. 8.38 and page 266) that no longer survives.

The artist represented the Psalms by taking each phrase literally and then visualizing it in some way. Thus, the top of our page illustrates, "Let them bring me unto thy holy hill, and to thy tabernacles" (Psalms 43:3). Toward the bottom of the page, we see the Lord reclining on a bed, flanked by pleading angels. The image is based on the words "Awake, why sleepest thou, Oh Lord?" (Psalms 44:23). On the left, the faithful crouch before the Temple ("for ... our belly cleaveth unto the earth" [Psalms 44:25]), and at the city gate in the foreground they are killed ("as sheep for the slaughter" [Psalms 44:22]). In the hands of a less imaginative

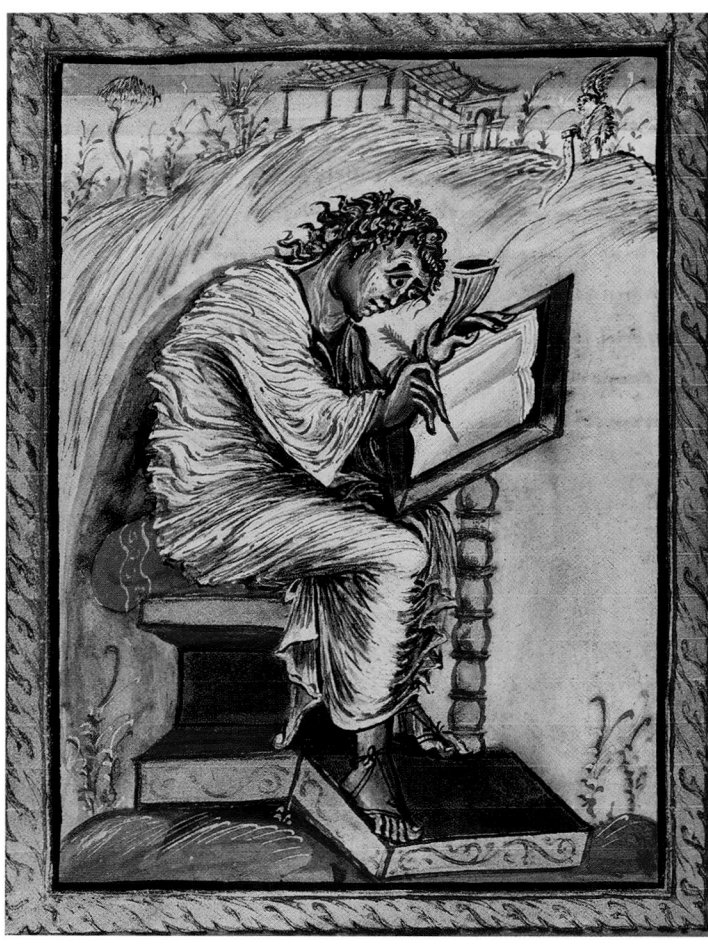

10.14 *St. Matthew*, from the *Gospel Book of Archbishop Ebbo of Reims*. ca. 816–35. Ink and colors on vellum, 10¼ × 8¾" (26 × 22.2 cm). Bibliothèque Municipale, Épernay, France

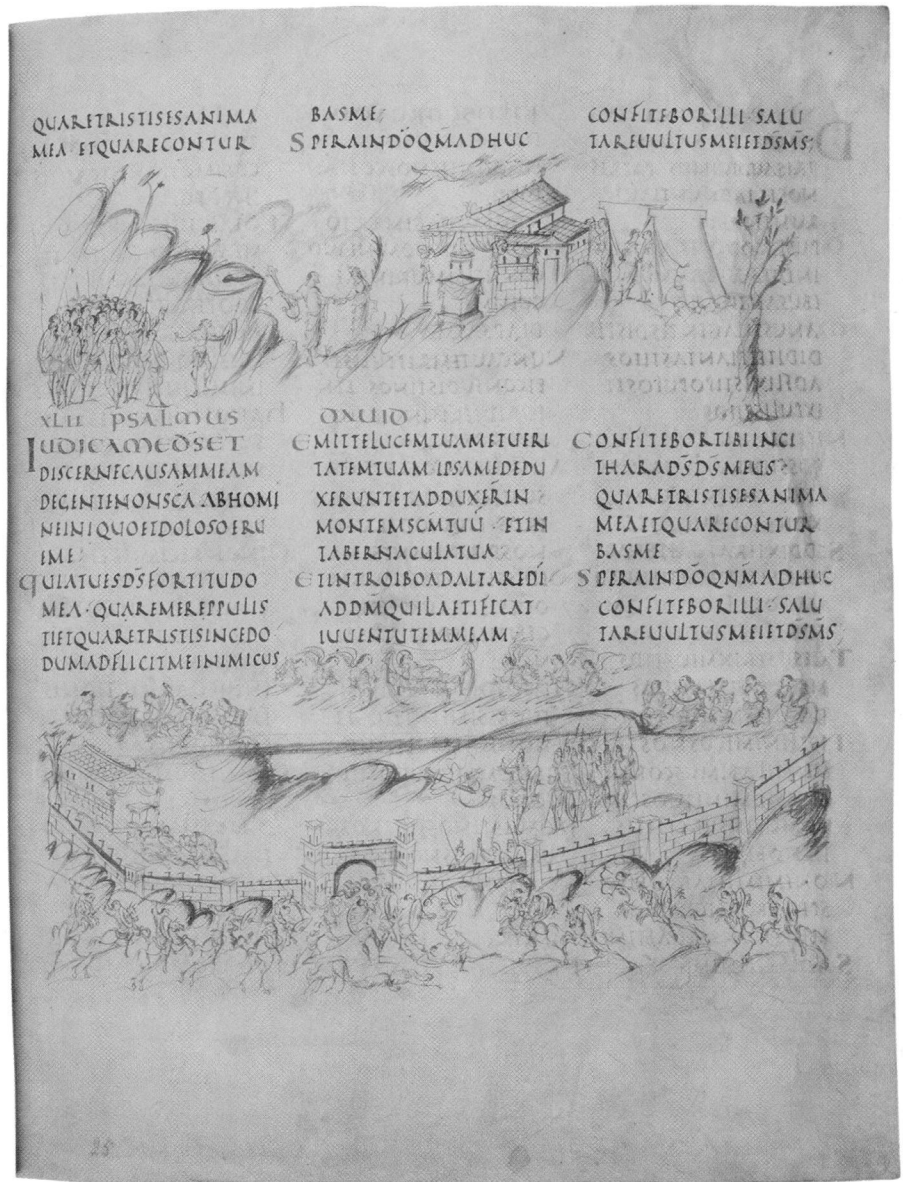

QUARETRISTISESANIMA   BASME   CONFITEBORILIII SALU
MEA ETQUARECONTUR   SPERAINDOQMADHUC   TAREUULTUSMEIEEDSMS·

XLII PSALMUS   OXUID   CONFITEBORTIBIINCI
IUDICAMEDSET   CMITTELUCEMIUAMETUERI IHARADSDSMEUS·
DISCERNECAUSAMMEAM   TATEMIUAM LPSAMEDEDU   QUARETRISTISESANIMA
DICENTIENONSCA ABHOMI XERUNTETADDUXERIN   MEAETQUARECONTUR
NEINIQUOETDOLOSOERU   MONTEMSCMTUU ETIN   BASME
IME   TABERNACULATUA   SPERAINDOQNMADHUC
QUIATUESDSFORTITUDO   CIINTROIBOADALTARIDI   CONFITEBORILIII SALU
MEA·QUAREMEREPPULIS   ADDMQUILAETIFICAT   TAREUULTUSMEIEEDSMS·
TIETQUARETRISTISINCEDO IUUENTUTEMMEAM
DUMADFLLCITMEINIMICUS

10.15 Illustrations to Psalms 43 and 44, from the *Utrecht Psalter*. ca. 820–32. Ink on vellum, 13 × 9⅞" (33 × 25 cm). University Library, Utrecht, the Netherlands (MS 32, fol. 25r and 26r)

artist, this procedure could well have turned into a tiresome game; instead, it has the force of great drama. The wonderfully rhythmic and energetic quality of the draftsmanship renders these sketches both coherent and affecting.

The literal approach to illustrating the Psalms in the *Utrecht Psalter* has a conceptual parallel in the lucidity with which the letters and words are delineated. This is a manuscript designed to be read; indeed, one needs to do so in order to be able to interpret the scenes represented. This is very different from our experience with Hiberno-Saxon manuscripts such as the *Book of Kells* (see fig. 10.8). There, letters and words seem to mystify, rather than clarify; it is as if the power of the word is unrelated to its legibility. Comparison of the two manuscripts underscores how Western Europe had been transformed from an oral to a written culture, in part a result of Charlemagne's ambitions and policies.

THE *LINDAU GOSPELS* COVER   The Reims style (see figs. 10.14 and 10.15) is also apparent in the reliefs on the front cover of the *Lindau Gospels* (fig. **10.16**), dating from the third quarter of the ninth century, in the expressive, near-frenetic figures that float around the image of the crucified Christ. Given the Carolingian investment in preserving and embellishing the written word, the cover was a fittingly sumptuous protection for a book. The clusters of semiprecious stones are not mounted directly on the gold ground but raised on clawed feet or arcaded **turrets** (towerlike projections), so that light can penetrate from beneath to bring out their full brilliance. The raised stones also protect the delicate figures in repoussé, produced from relatively thin gold sheets, when the book is opened flat. Christ betrays no hint of pain or death. He seems to stand rather than to hang, his arms spread out in a solemn gesture.

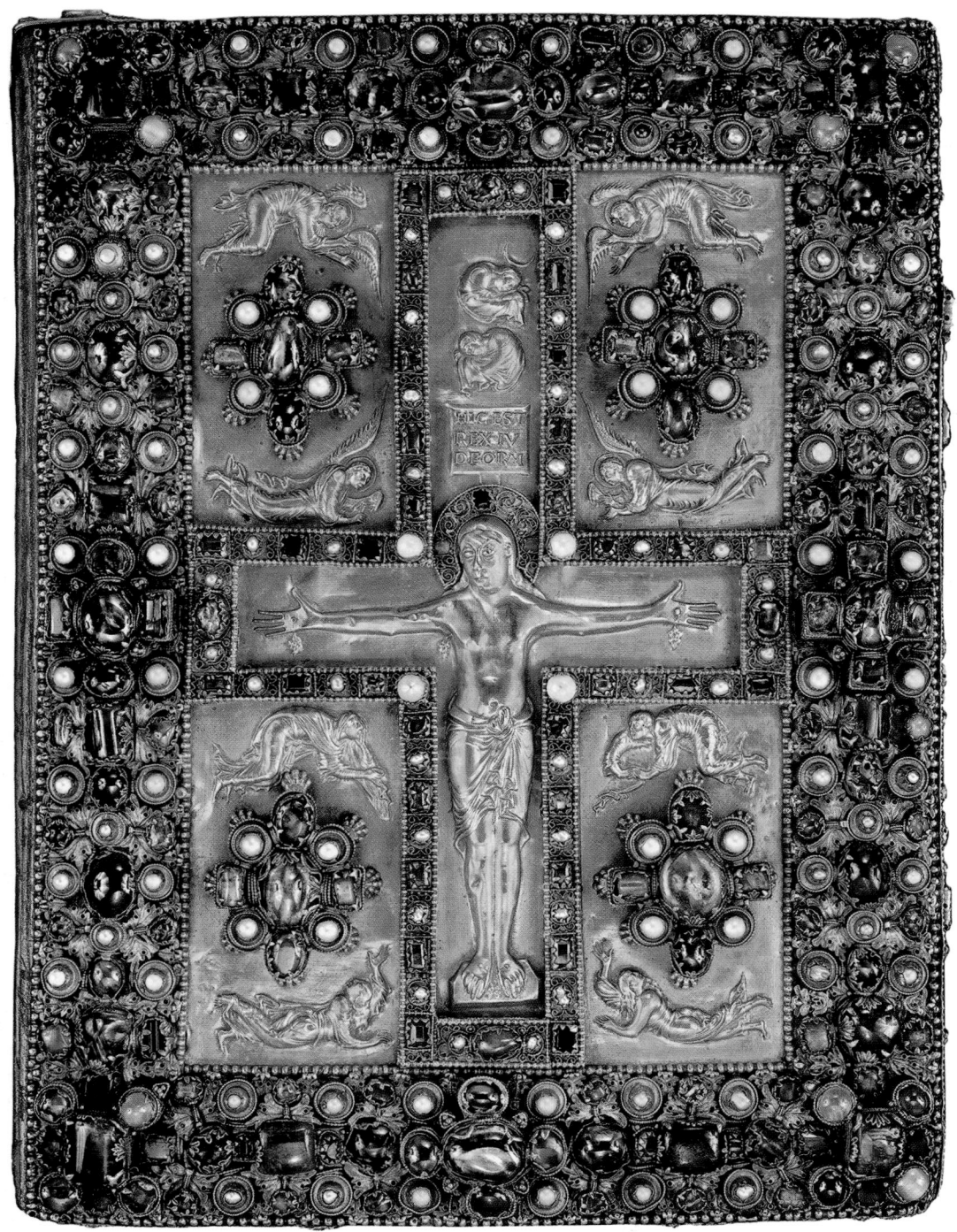

10.16 Front cover of binding, *Lindau Gospels*. ca. 870. Gold and jewels, 13¾ × 10½" (35 × 26.7 cm). The Pierpont Morgan Library, New York

Architecture

Although relatively few Carolingian buildings survive, excavations demonstrate a significant increase in building activity during the Carolingian period, a reflection of the security and prosperity that Charlemagne established at the beginning of his reign and that continued for some time. As was the case with his painters, Charlemagne's architects sought to revive the splendor of the Roman Empire, which they did by erecting buildings whose models were largely from Rome and Ravenna, both of which Charlemagne visited. While Rome had been the capital of the Empire, Ravenna had been a Christian imperial outpost, and thus a worthy prototype for what Charlemagne hoped to create in his own land.

PALACE CHAPEL OF CHARLEMAGNE, AACHEN Toward the end of the eighth century, Charlemagne erected his imperial palace at Aachen. Prior to this time, Charlemagne's court had

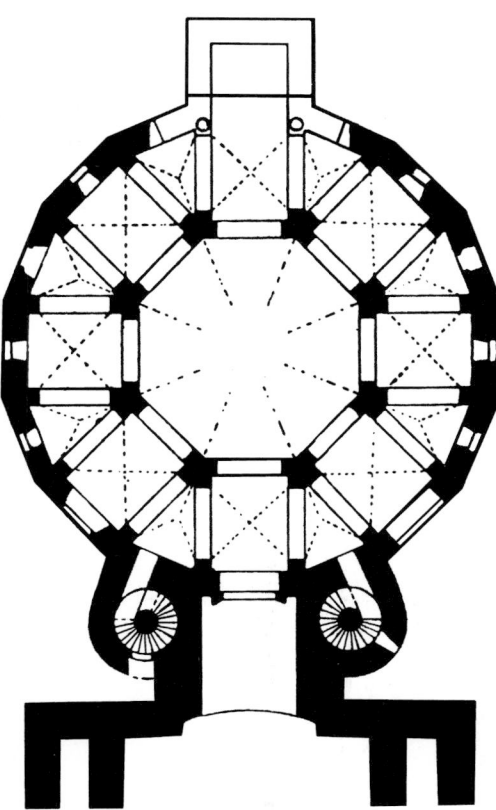

10.17 Odo of Metz. Plan of Palace Chapel of Charlemagne, Aachen, Germany. 792–805

been itinerant, moving from place to place as the political situation required. Now, to signify Charlemagne's position as a Christian ruler, architects modeled his palace complex on Constantine's Lateran Palace in Rome. Charlemagne's palace included a basilica, called the Royal Hall, which was linked to the Palace Chapel. The plan for the latter (fig. 10.17) was probably inspired by the church of San Vitale in Ravenna, which the emperor saw first hand (see figs. 8.21–8.24). The building (fig. 10.18) was designed by Odo of Metz, probably the earliest architect north of the Alps known to us by name. Einhard, Charlemagne's trusted advisor and biographer, supervised the project.

The debt to San Vitale is especially clear in cross section (fig. 10.19; compare fig. 8.22). The chapel design is by no means a mere

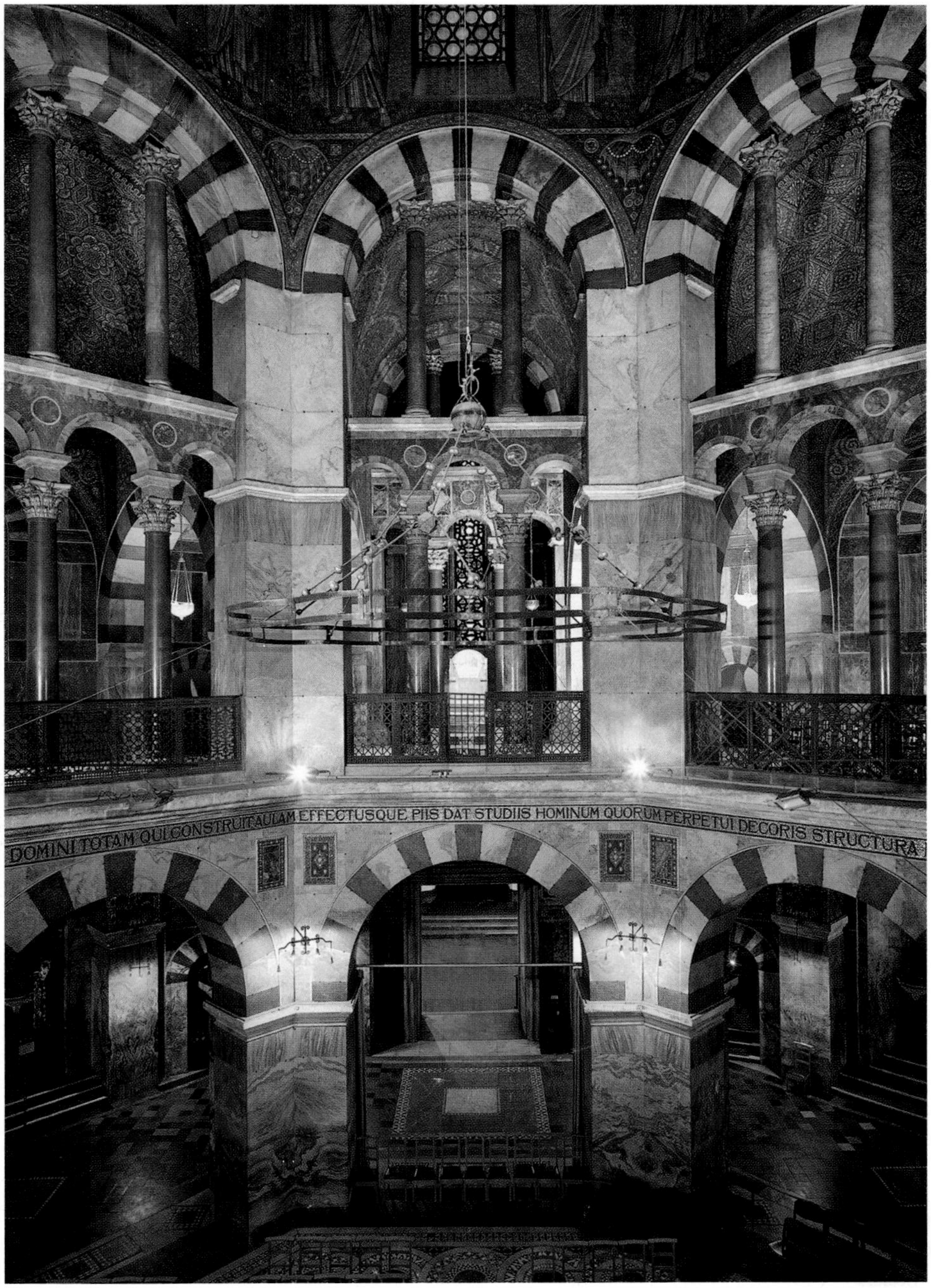

10.18 Odo of Metz. Interior of the Palace Chapel of Charlemagne, Aachen, Germany

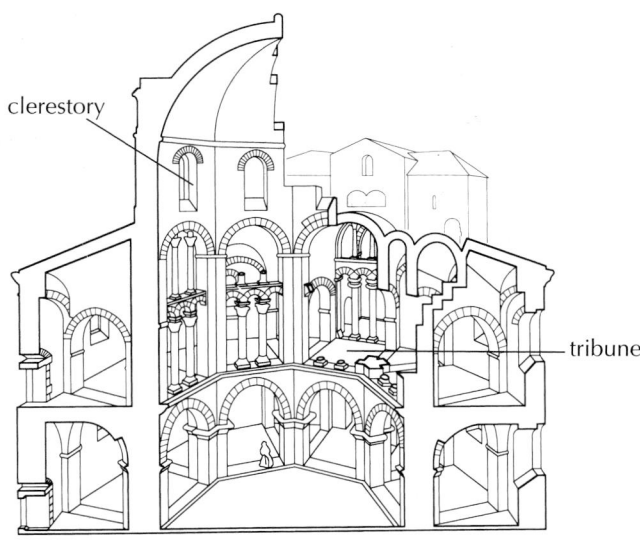

clerestory

tribune

10.19 Odo of Metz. Section of the Palace Chapel of Charlemagne, Aachen, Germany (after Kubach)

ABBEY CHURCH OF SAINT-RIQUIER An even more elaborate westwork formed part of one of the greatest basilican churches of Carolingian times: the Abbey church of Saint-Riquier at the monastery of Centula in northeastern France. (An **abbey** is a religious community headed by an abbot, or, in the case of a women's community, an abbess.) The monastery was rebuilt in 790 by Abbot Angilbert, a poet and scholar of Charlemagne's court. The present church was largely built in the fifteenth and sixteenth centuries, but we know the Carolingian design from descriptions, drawings, and prints, such as the **engraving** reproduced here (fig. **10.20**). The monastery included not only the abbey church, dedicated to Saint-Riquier, but also two chapels, one dedicated to St. Mary, the other to St. Benedict, founder of the Benedictine order, whose Rule the monks followed. (See *Primary Source*, page 331.)

Benedict of Nursia established his order in 529 when he founded a monastery in Monte Cassino, south of Rome. Benedict's Rule required monks to labor, study, and pray, providing for both the sound administration of the monastery and the

echo of San Vitale but a vigorous reinterpretation of it. Piers and vaults are impressively massive by comparison, while the geometric clarity of the spatial units is very different from the fluid space of the earlier structure. To construct such a building on northern soil was a difficult undertaking. Columns and bronze gratings were imported from Italy, and expert stonemasons must have been hard to find. The columns are placed within the arches of the upper story, where they are structurally unnecessary, but where they accentuate a sense of support and create opportunities to offer Roman details. San Vitale had been designed to be ambiguous, to produce an otherworldly interior space. Aachen, by comparison, is sturdy and sober. The soft, bulging curvilinear forms of San Vitale's arcades are here replaced with clear-cut piers, which make manifest their ability to support the heavy weight of Aachen's dome, while the San Vitale dome seems light and to hover above the interior space of the building.

Equally important is Odo's scheme for the western entrance, now largely obscured by later additions and rebuilding. At San Vitale, the entrance consists of a broad, semidetached narthex with twin stair turrets, placed at an odd angle to the main axis of the church. At Aachen, these elements are molded into a tall, compact unit, in line with the main axis and attached to the chapel itself. This monumental structure, known as a **westwork** (from the German *Westwerk*), makes one of its first appearances here.

Charlemagne placed his throne in the **tribune** (the gallery of the westwork), behind the great opening above the entrance. From here, the emperor could emerge to show himself to those assembled in the atrium below. The throne faced an altar dedicated to Christ, who seemed to bless the emperor from above in the dome mosaic. Thus, although contemporary documents say very little about its function, the westwork seems to have served initially as a royal compartment or chapel.

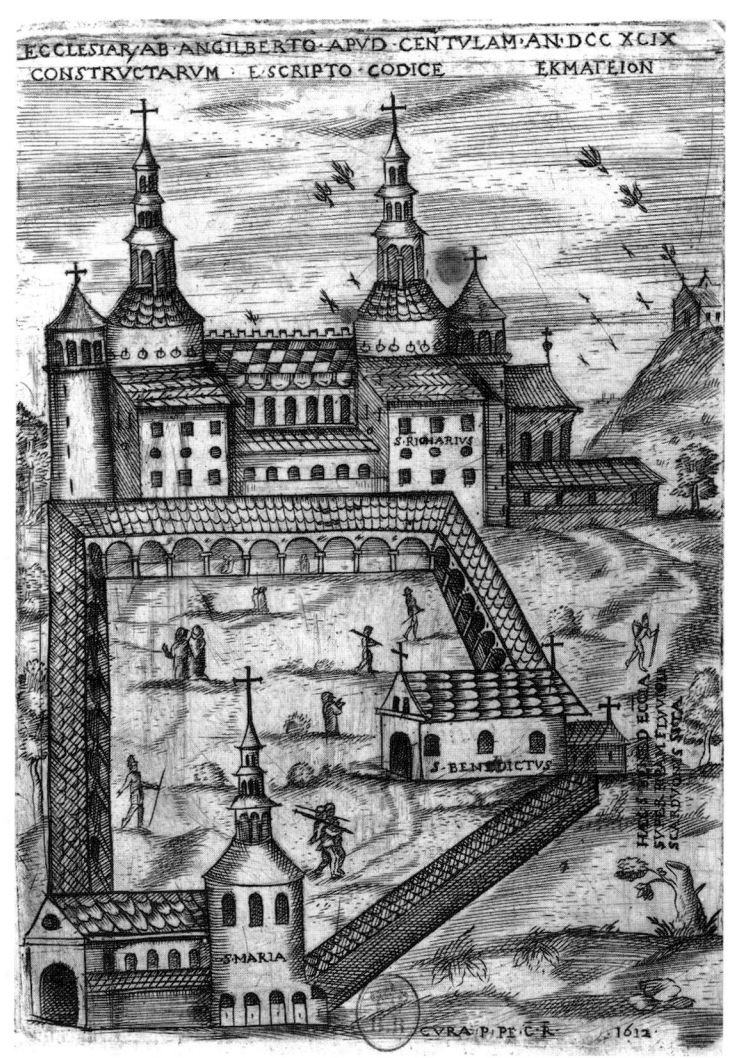

10.20 Abbey church of Saint-Riquier, monastery of Centula, France. Dedicated ca. 790. A 1673 engraving after a 1612 view by Petau, from an 11th-century manuscript illumination. Bibliothèque Nationale, Paris

PRIMARY SOURCE

Hariulf (ca. 1060–1143)

From *History of the Monastery of Saint-Riquier*

Hariulf was a monk at Saint-Riquier until 1105, when he became abbot of St. Peter's at Oudenbourg in Belgium.

The church dedicated to the Savior and St. Richarius ... was among all other churches of its time the most famous. ... The eastern tower is close to the sepulcher of St. Richarius. ... The western tower is especially dedicated to the Savior. ...

If one surveys the place, one sees that the largest church, that of St. Richarius, lies to the north. The second, somewhat smaller one, which has been built in honor of our Lady on this side of the river, lies to the south. The third one, the smallest, lies to the east. The cloisters of the monks are laid out in a triangular fashion, one roof extending from St. Richarius' to St. Mary's, one from St. Mary's to St. Benedict's and one from St. Benedict's to St. Richarius'. ... The monastery is so arranged that, according to the rule laid down by St. Benedict, all arts and all necessary labors can be executed within its walls. The river flows through it, and turns the mill of the brothers.

Source: Caecilia Davis-Weyer, *Early Medieval Art 300–1150* (Upper Saddle River, NJ: Prentice Hall, 1st ed., 1971).

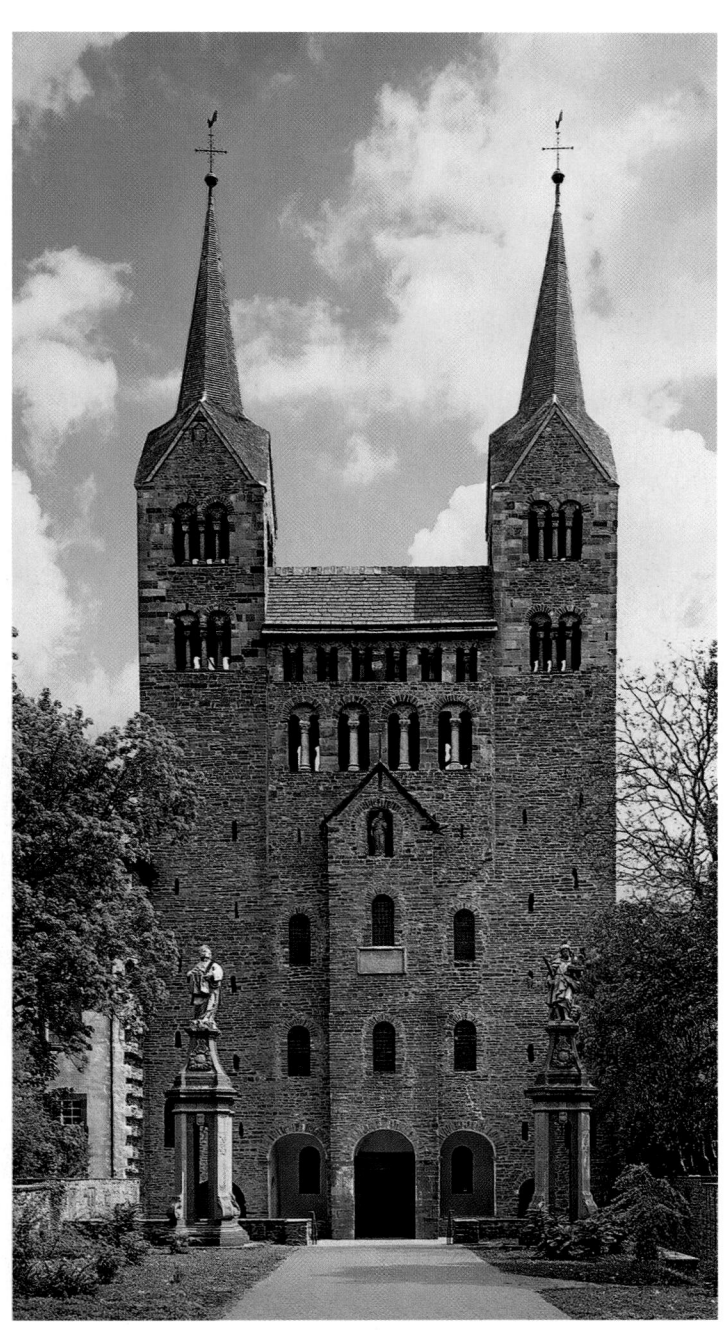

10.21 Westwork, abbey church, with later additions. Corvey, Germany. Late 9th century

spiritual needs of individual monks. (See www.myartslab.com.) By the ninth century, largely due to support from Charlemagne, Benedict's requirements for monastic life had been accepted by monasteries across Europe. Charlemagne recognized that the orderliness of the Rule was consistent with his own goal to provide stability through a sound, working system of governance, both civil and religious.

The three buildings of the monastery at Centula are connected by a covered walkway, forming a triangular **cloister** (an open court surrounded by a covered arcaded walk, used for meditation, study, and exercise). This shape has symbolic significance, reflecting this particular monastery's dedication to the Holy Trinity. The plan of Saint-Riquier reads as a traditional basilica, with a central nave flanked by side aisles and terminating in a transept and apse. In fact, Charlemagne sent to Rome for drawings and measurements of traditional basilicas to guide his local builders. In elevation, however, Saint-Riquier's multiple towers provide vertical accents that are very different from the longitudinal silhouette of Early Christian basilicas, such as Old St. Peter's (see fig. 8.8).

The westwork of Saint-Riquier balanced the visual weight of the transept and east end of the church; it also provided additional room for the liturgical needs of a large community, which numbered some 300 monks, 100 novices, and numerous staff (see www.myartslab.com). Twenty-five relics related to Christ were displayed in the westwork entrance, and above that was an upper chapel dedicated to the Savior. On feast days, and in particular at Easter, the community positioned itself here for the beginning of an elaborate processional liturgy. (See *Primary Source*, page 332.) Thus, to some extent the westwork functioned as a separate commemorative building, the conceptual equivalent of the Early Christian mausoleum and martyrium, but now attached to a basilican church.

ABBEY CHURCH, CORVEY Saint-Riquier was widely imitated in other Carolingian monastery churches. The best-preserved example is the abbey church at Corvey (fig. **10.21**), built in 873–85. Except for the upper stories, which date from around 1146, the westwork retains much of its original appearance. It is impressive not only because of its height but also because of its expansive surfaces, which emphasize the clear geometry and powerful masses of the exterior. The westwork provided a suitably

St. Angilbert (ca. 750–814)

From *Customary for the Different Devotions*

Angilbert, a member of Charlemagne's court, became lay abbot of Saint-Riquier in 781 and sponsored the monastery's rebuilding. His description reveals how the resident monks moved from one part of the basilica to another while chanting the devotions prescribed in the Rule of St. Benedict.

When the brethren have sung Vespers and Matins at the altar of the Savior, then one choir should descend on the side of the holy Resurrection, the other one on the side of the holy Ascension, and having prayed there the processions should in the same fashion as before move singing toward the altars of St. John and St. Martin. After having prayed they should enter from both sides through the arches in the middle of the church and pray at the holy Passion. From there they should go to the altar of St. Richarius. After praying they should divide themselves again as before and go to the altars of St. Stephen and St. Lawrence and from there go singing and praying to the altar of the Holy Cross. Thence they should go again to the altar of St. Maurice and through the long gallery to the church of St. Benedict.

Source: Caecilia Davis-Weyer, *Early Medieval Art 300–1150* (Englewood Cliffs, NJ: Prentice Hall, 1st ed., 1971)

regal entrance, which may well be its greatest significance. But it had functional benefits too. At Corvey, musical notation scratched on the walls of the gallery reminds us that the boys' choir would have been positioned here, its voices spreading upward as well as throughout the church.

PLAN OF A MONASTERY, ST. GALL The importance of monasteries in the culture of the early medieval period and their close link with the imperial court are evident in the plan for a monastery at St. Gall in Switzerland (fig. **10.22**). The plan exists in a large, unique drawing on five sheets of parchment sewn together

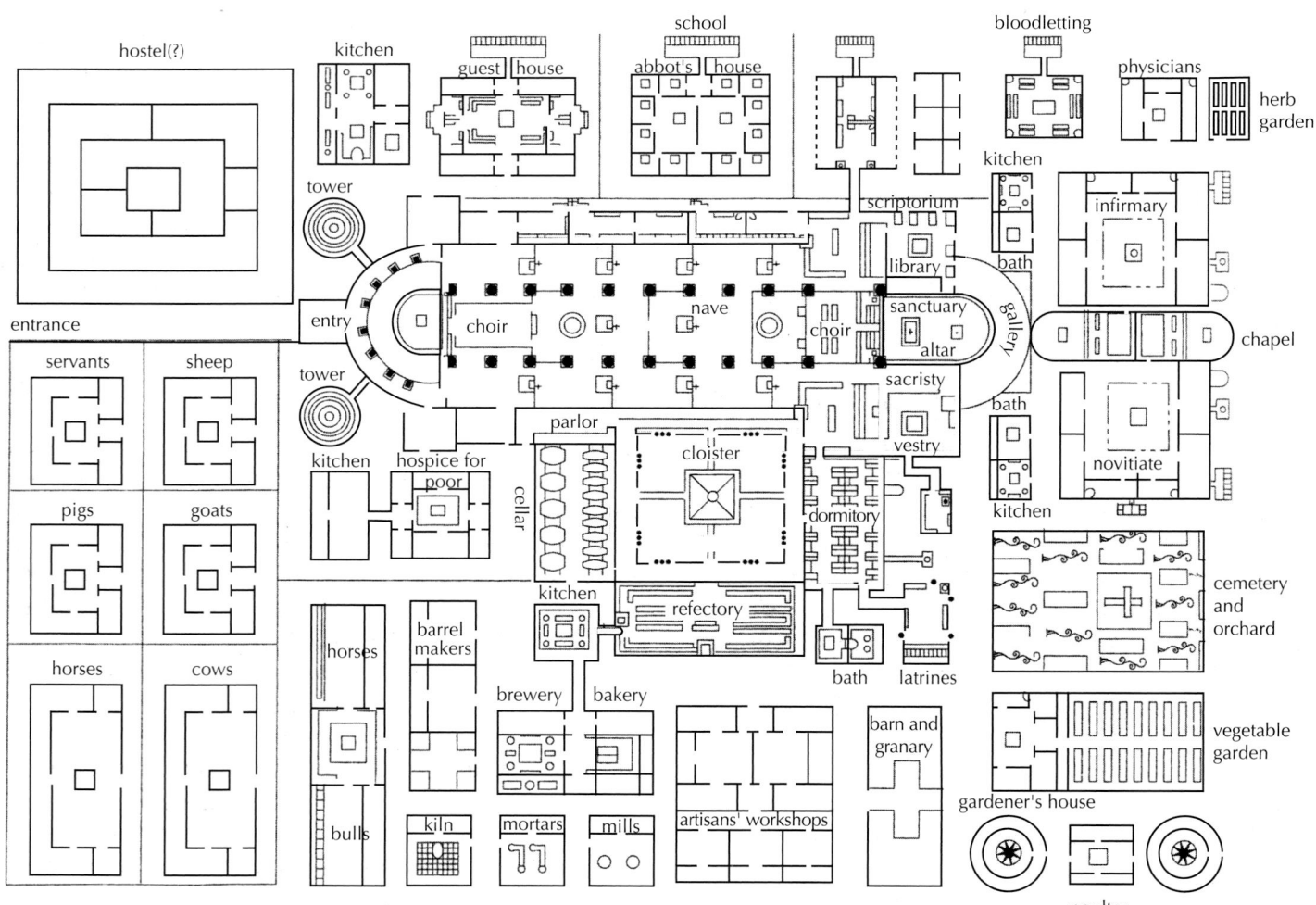

10.22 Plan of a monastery. Redrawn, with inscriptions translated into English from the Latin, from the original of ca. 820. Red ink on parchment, 28 × 44⅛" (71.1 × 112.1 cm). Stiftsbibliothek, St. Gall, Switzerland

and is preserved in the chapter library at St. Gall. This drawing was sent by Abbot Haito of Reichenau to Gozbert, the abbot of St. Gall, for "you to study only," as an aid to him in rebuilding his monastery. We may therefore regard it as a model or ideal plan, to be modified to meet local needs.

The monastery plan shows a complex, self-contained unit filling a rectangle about 500 by 700 feet and providing a logical arrangement of buildings based on their function. From the west end of the monastery, the main entrance path passes between stables and a hostelry toward a gate. This admits the visitor to a colonnaded semicircular portico (porch) flanked by two round towers forming a westwork that would have loomed above the low outer buildings. The plan emphasizes the church as the center of the monastic community. This church is a traditional basilica (see figs. 8.7–8.9), with an apse at each end. The nave and aisles, which contain many other altars, do not form a single continuous space but are subdivided into compartments by screens. There are numerous entrances: two beside the western apse, others on the north and south flanks.

This arrangement reflects the functions of a monastery church, which was designed for the liturgical needs of the monks rather than for a lay congregation. Adjoining the church to the south is an arcaded cloister, around which are grouped the monks' dormitory (on the east side), a refectory (dining hall) and kitchen (on the south side), and a cellar. The three large buildings north of the church are a guesthouse, a school, and the abbot's house. To the east are an infirmary, a chapel, and quarters for novices (new members of the community), the cemetery (marked by a large cross), a garden, and coops for chickens and geese. On the south side are workshops, barns, and other service buildings.

The St. Gall plan was laid out using a module (standard unit). This module, expressed as parts or multiples of 2½ feet, can be found throughout the plan, from the division of the church to the length of the cemetery plots. The imposition of a module on the plan of St. Gall is a tangible manifestation both of the administrative orderliness and stability so sought after by Charlemagne and of the aims of monasticism, as defined by St. Benedict of Nursia's Rule.

Unfortunately, political stability proved elusive. Upon the death of Charlemagne's son, Louis I, in 840, a bitter battle arose among Louis's sons for the empire built by their grandfather. The brothers eventually signed a treaty in 843 dividing the empire into western, central, and eastern parts: Charles the Bald became the West Frankish King, founding the French Carolingian dynasty in what became modern France; Louis the German became the East Frankish King, ruling an area roughly equivalent to that of present-day Germany; and Lothair I became the Holy Roman Emperor, ruling the middle area running from the Netherlands down to Italy. The distribution of the Carolingian domain among Louis's heirs weakened the empire, brought a halt to Carolingian cultural efforts, and eventually exposed continental Europe to attack by the Muslims from the south, the Slavs and Magyars from the east, and the Vikings from the north. As stated earlier, the Vikings invaded northwestern France and, through a land

grant from Charles the Bald, occupied the area now known as Normandy.

Although political stability ultimately eluded Charlemagne's heirs, the artists of the Carolingian period were able to create an enduring art that combined the northern reliance on decoration—on surface, pattern, and line—with the Mediterranean concern for solidity and monumentality. Carolingian art was to serve as a worthy model for emulation by artists and patrons when the revival of Charlemagne's vision of a united and stable Europe reappeared during the next centuries.

OTTONIAN ART

When the last East Frankish monarch died in 911, the center of political power moved to the eastern portion of the former Carolingian Empire, in an area roughly equivalent to present-day Germany, under German kings of Saxon descent. Beginning with Henry I, these kings pushed back invaders, reestablished an effective central government, improved trade and the economy, and began a new dynasty, called Ottonian after its three principal rulers: Otto I, Otto II, and Otto III. During the Ottonian period, which lasted from 919 to 1024, Germany was the leading nation of Europe politically and artistically. In both realms, German achievements began as revivals of Carolingian traditions but soon developed an original character.

The greatest of the Ottonian kings, Otto I, revived the imperial ambitions of Charlemagne. After marrying the widow of a Lombard king in 951, he extended his rule over most of what is now northern Italy. Then, in 962, he was crowned emperor by Pope John XII, whom the emperor later deposed for conspiring against him, insisting on the imperial right to designate future popes.

Architecture

Among the most pressing concerns of the Ottonian emperors was the reform of the Church, which had become corrupt and mismanaged. They did this by establishing closer alliances with the papacy and by fostering monastic reforms, which they supported by sponsoring many new religious buildings. The renewal of impressive building programs effectively revived the architectural ambitions of their Carolingian predecessors, while at the same time conveying and furthering the Ottonians' aspirations to restore the imperial glory of Christian Rome.

NUNNERY CHURCH OF ST. CYRIAKUS, GERNRODE One of the best-preserved Ottonian churches was built in 961 for the nunnery, or convent, at Gernrode (fig. **10.23**), founded by Gero, margrave (military governor) under Otto I. The church was dedicated to St. Cyriakus and used the basic form of the Early Christian basilica (see figs. 8.7–8.9), which had also dominated architectural planning during the Carolingian period. However, the architect of St. Cyriakus raised the apse above the level of the rest of the church to make room for a half-buried basement chapel, or **crypt**, a feature not present in the Early Christian basilica. Such crypts with ambulatories, usually housing the venerated tomb of a saint, had been introduced into Western church architecture during Carolingian times. Moreover, at St. Cyriakus, a gallery has been inserted between the nave arcade and the clerestory. A series of columns and piers divide the gallery in such a way that the piers of the gallery are positioned over the piers of the nave arcade. This provides a series of repeated vertical accents, effectively dividing the building into vertical sections.

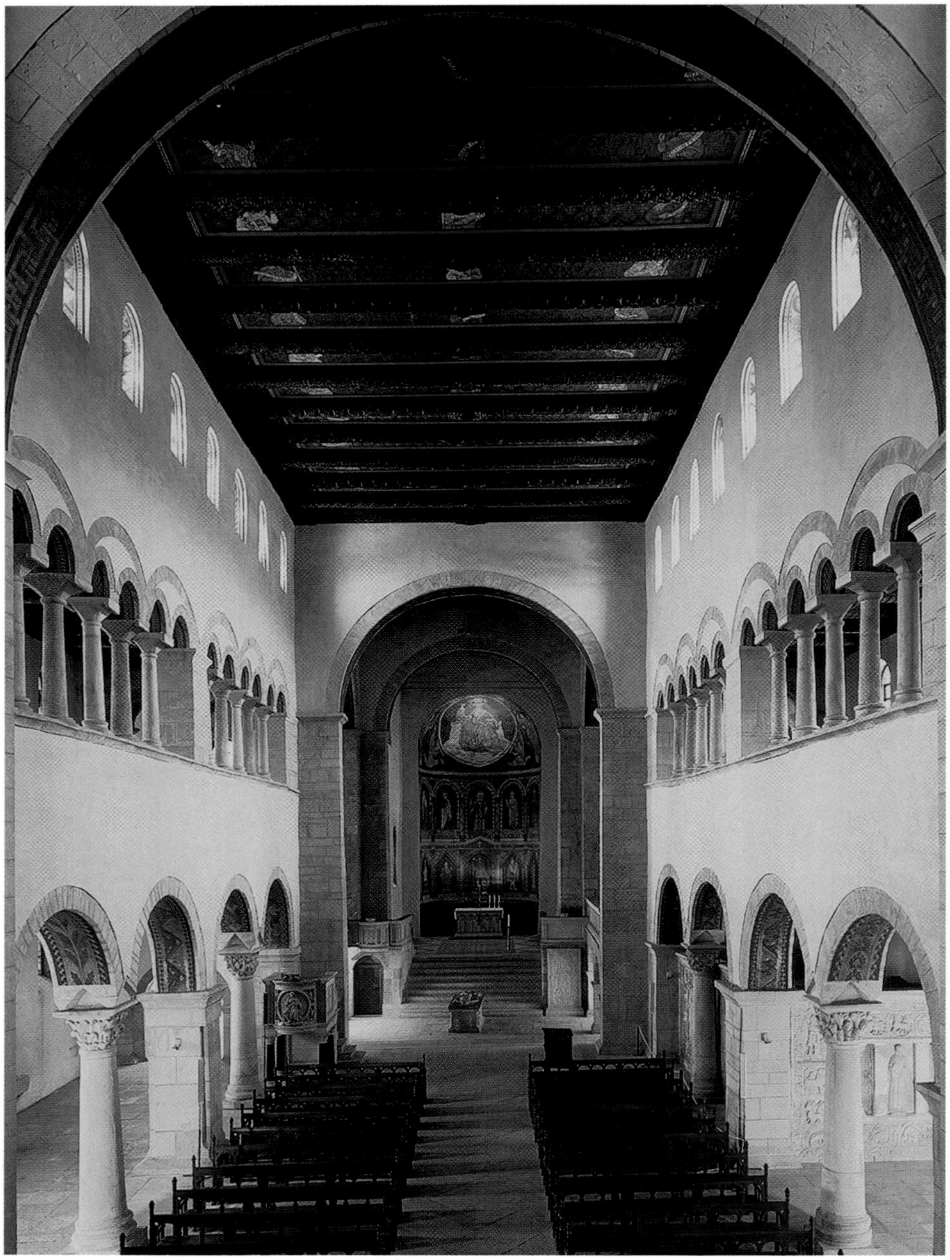

This emphasis on verticality is different from the overwhelming effect of horizontality that characterizes Early Christian buildings, and indicates a trend that will be significant in the later development of medieval architecture. Neither the origin nor the intended function of the gallery is clear. Some scholars have noted

similarities to galleried Byzantine churches, such as two fifth-century examples in Salonika in Greece. It is possible that the gallery at St. Cyriakus contained altars, as was the case in the galleried westworks of Carolingian churches, such as at Corvey (see fig. 10.21).

ST. MICHAEL'S AT HILDESHEIM The most ambitious patron of architecture and art in the Ottonian age was Bernward, who became bishop of Hildesheim after having been court chaplain. Bernward was also tutor of Otto III during the regency of his mother, Empress Theophano, wife of Otto II and a Byzantine princess in her own right. Bernward's chief monument is the Benedictine abbey church of St. Michael's at Hildesheim. The plan of this monastic church (fig. **10.24**) derives from that of Saint-Riquier at Centula (see fig. 10.20). With its two choirs and

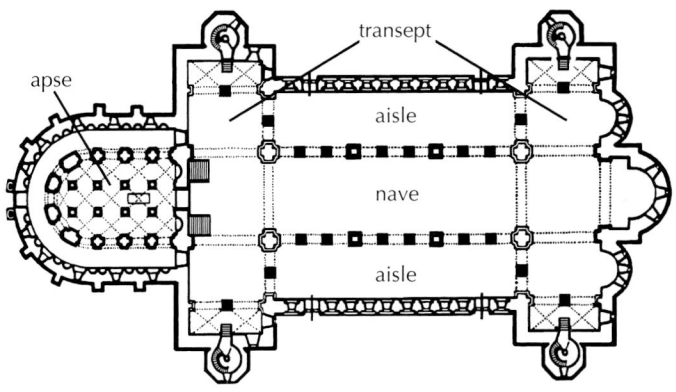

10.24 Reconstructed plan, abbey church of St. Michael's, Hildesheim, Germany. 1001–33 (after Beseler)

turrets at the end of each transept (fig. **10.25**; see also fig. 10.24). But the supports of the nave arcade, instead of being uniform, consist of pairs of columns separated by square piers (fig. **10.26**). This alternating system divides the arcade into three equal units, each with three openings. These units are equal in length to the width of the transepts, which are similarly divided into three compartments.

Thus, as in the St. Gall plan, a modular system governs the division of spaces. The module can also be seen on the exterior of the building, which reads as a series of cubes arranged by stacking. The first and third units correspond with the entrances, thus echoing the axis of the transepts. Moreover, since the aisles and nave are unusually wide in relation to their length, the architect's intention must have been to achieve a harmonious balance between the longitudinal and horizontal axes throughout the structure.

St. Michael's was severely damaged during World War II, but the restored interior retains the majestic feel of the original design. Frescoes originally decorated the great expanse of wall space between the arcade and clerestory, paralleling the arrangement of

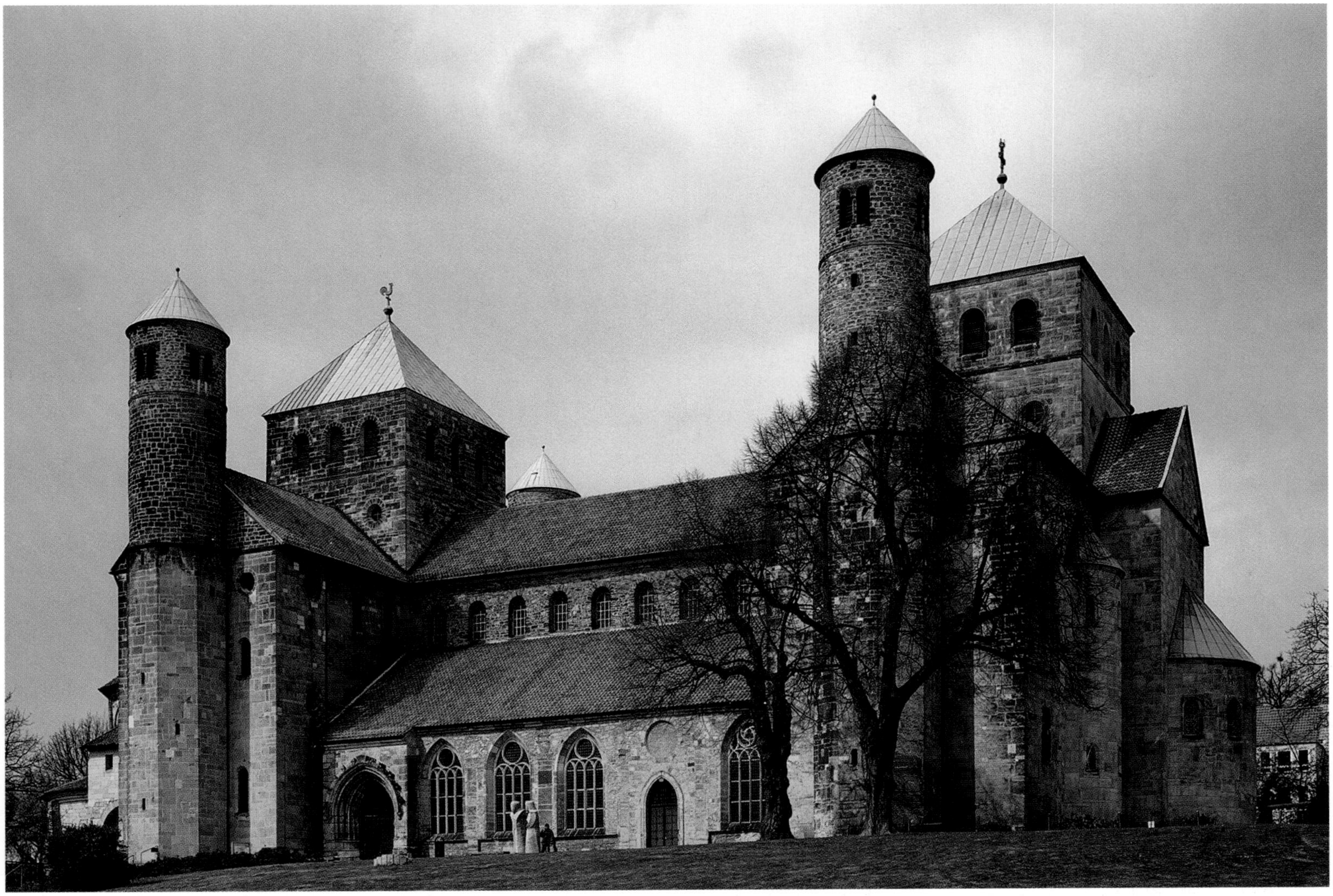

side entrances, it also recalls the monastery church of the St. Gall plan (see fig. 10.22). However, in St. Michael's the symmetry is carried much further. There are two identical transepts, each with a tower, where the transept and the nave cross, and a pair of stair

10.25 Exterior, abbey church of St. Michael's, Hildesheim, Germany

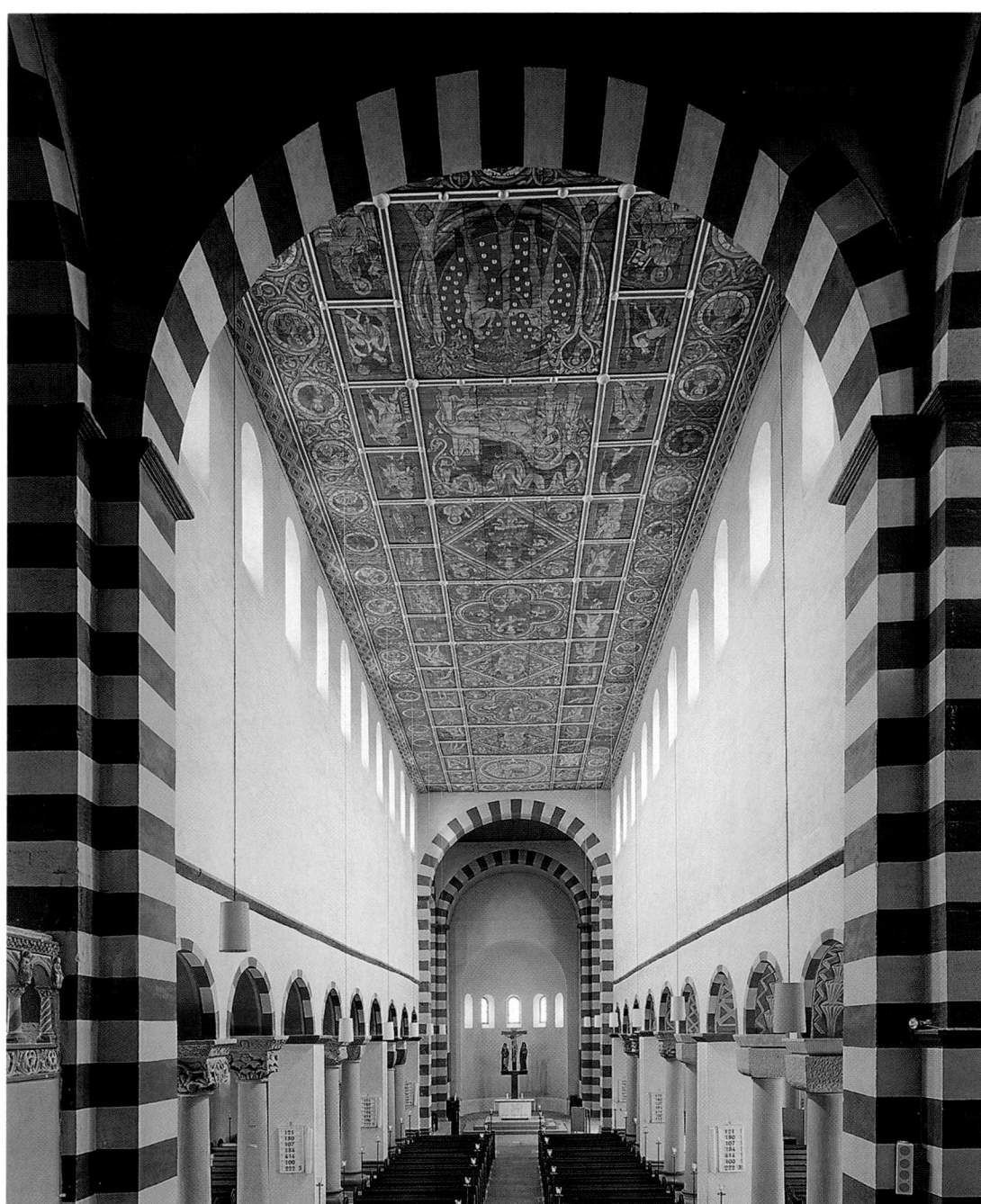

mosaics in Early Christian basilicas such as Santa Maria Maggiore (see fig. 8.16). (The capitals of the columns date from the twelfth century; the painted wooden ceiling from the thirteenth.) The western choir is especially interesting. As at Gernrode (see fig. 10.23), there is a raised crypt. Monks could enter the crypt (apparently a special sanctuary for relics of the saint) from both the transept and the west. Arched openings pierced the walls and linked the crypt with the U-shaped ambulatory wrapped around it. The ambulatory must originally have been visible from above ground, where it enriched the exterior of the choir, since there were windows in its outer wall. The design of St. Michael's is distinguished by the crypt's large scale and its careful integration with the rest of the building.

Metalwork

The Ottonian emperors' reliance on church authority to strengthen their own governmental rule encouraged them not only to build new churches but also to provide sumptuous works of art to decorate them. The works they and their cohorts sponsored were richly appointed and executed in expensive, often precious materials.

BRONZE DOORS OF BISHOP BERNWARD, HILDESHEIM

For St. Michael's at Hildesheim, Bernward commissioned a pair of extensively sculptured bronze doors (figs. **10.27** and **10.28**) that were finished in 1015, the year the crypt was consecrated.

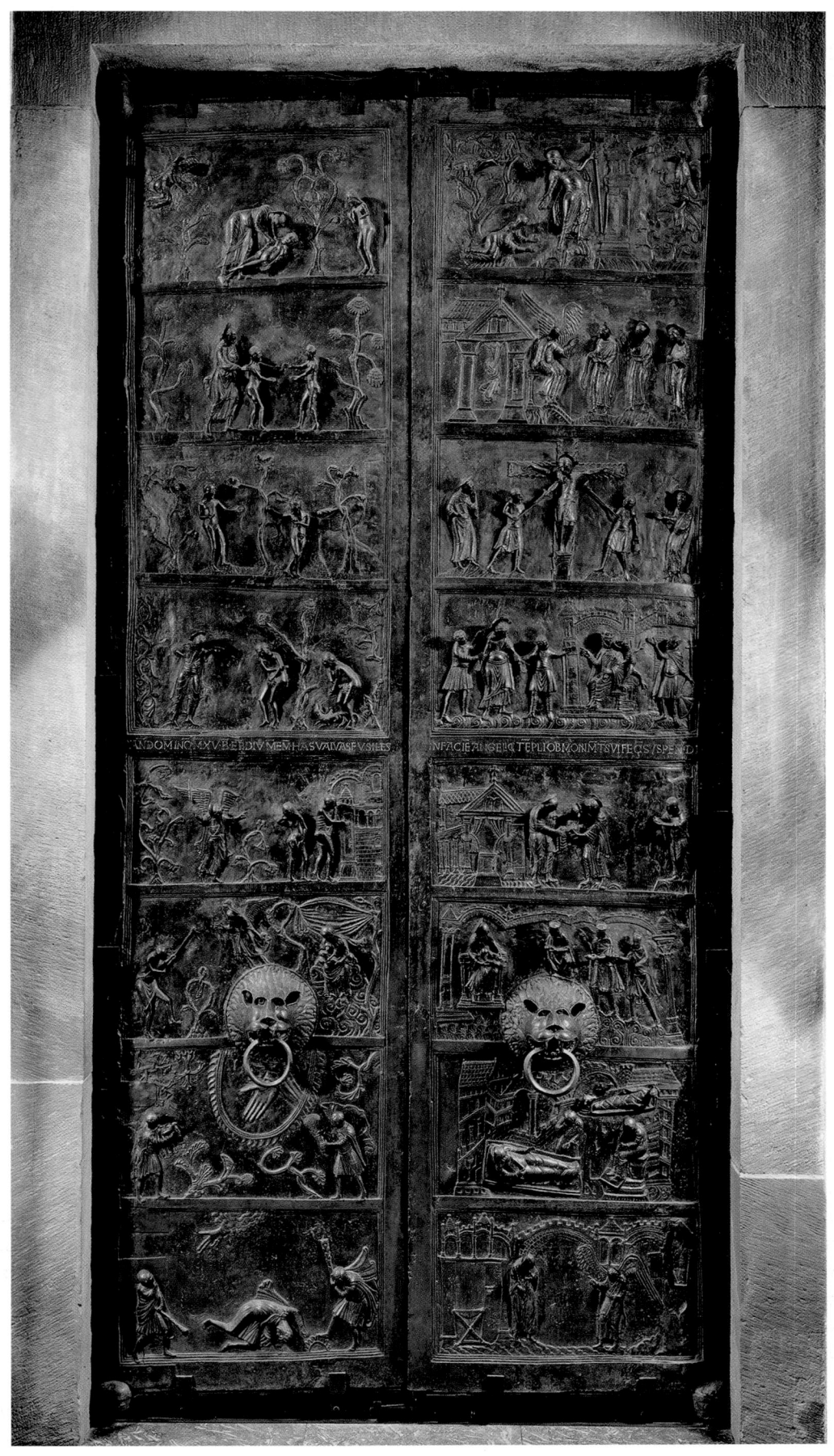

10.27 Doors of Bishop Bernward, Hildesheim cathedral (originally made for abbey church of St. Michael's, Hildesheim), Germany. 1015. Bronze, height approx. 16' (4.8 m)

Old Testament	Comparison of themes	New Testament
Formation of Eve	Paradise Lost and then Paradise Gained	Noli Me Tangere
Eve Presented to Adam	Salutations	The Three Marys at the Tomb
Temptation and Fall	Tree of Knowledge (sin) vs. Tree of Life (The Cross, Salvation)	The Crucifixion
Accusation and Judgment of Adam and Eve	Judgment	Judgment of Jesus by Pilate
Expulsion from Paradise	Separation from God vs. Reunion with God	Presentation of Jesus in Temple
Adam and Eve Working	Firstborn Sons of Eve (Cain) and Mary (Jesus); Poverty vs. Wealth	Adoration of the Magi
Offerings by Cain (grain) and Abel (lamb)	Abel's Sacrificial Lamb vs. Jesus, Lamb of God	The Nativity
Cain Slaying Abel	Despair, Sin, Murder vs. Hope and Everlasting Life	The Annunciation

According to his biographer, Thangmar of Heidelberg, Bernward excelled in the arts and "distinguished himself remarkably in the science of metalwork and the whole art of building." So, he must have been closely involved in the project. The idea for the doors may have come to him as a result of his visit to Rome, where he would have seen ancient Roman (and perhaps Byzantine) doors of bronze and wood. He would also certainly have been aware of the bronze doors that Charlemagne had commissioned for his palace chapel at Aachen.

The doors at Hildesheim are considered by many scholars to be the first monumental sculptures created by the lost-wax process (see page 128) since antiquity. Each door was cast as one piece and measures over 16 feet in height. They are also the first doors since the Early Christian period to have been decorated with stories. Our detail (fig. **10.29**) shows God accusing and judging Adam and Eve after the Temptation and Fall, when they have committed the Original Sin of eating the forbidden fruit in the Garden of Eden. Below it, in inlaid letters notable for their classical Roman character, is part of an inscription, with the date and Bernward's name. This inscription was added around 1035, when the doors were moved from the monastery of St. Michael and

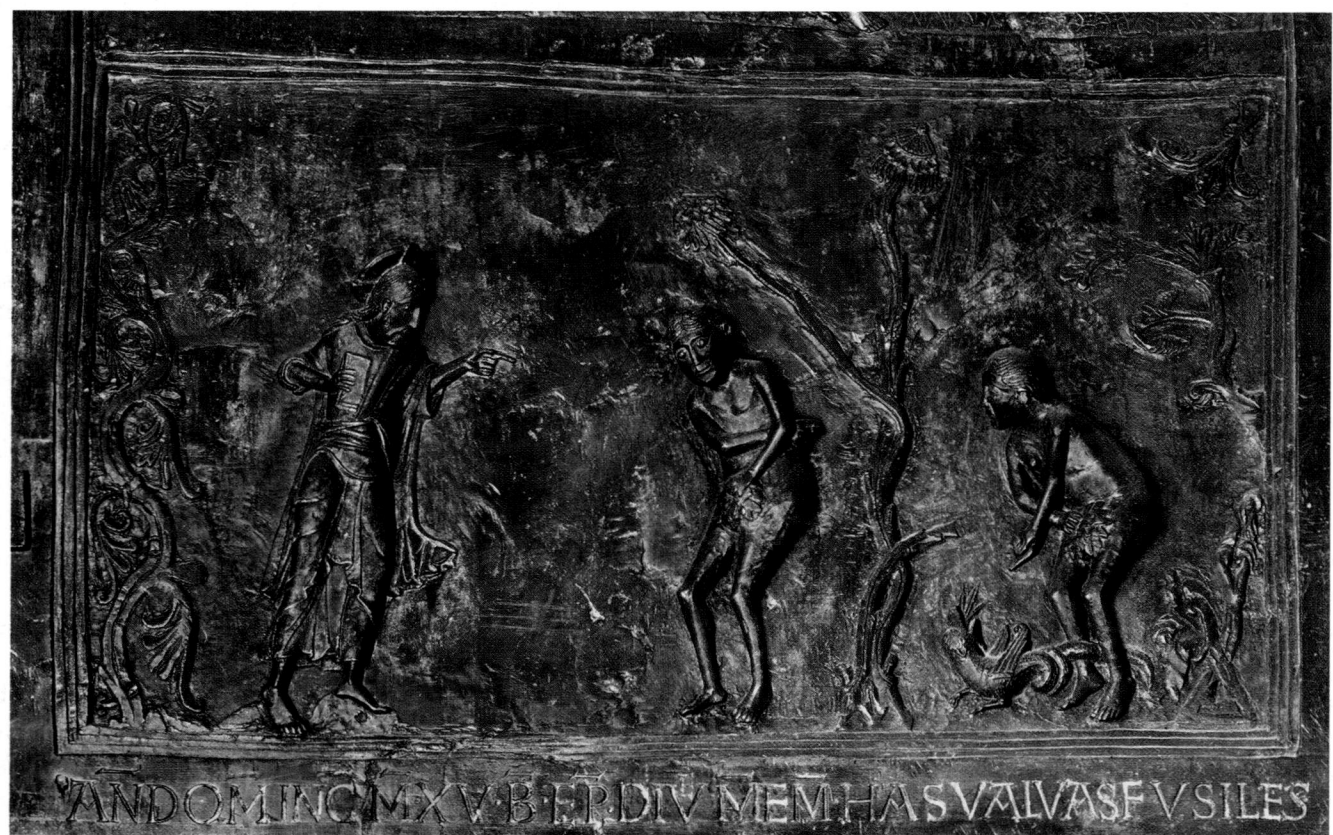

10.29 *Accusation and Judgment of Adam and Eve*, from the Doors of Bishop Bernward, Hildesheim, Germany. Bronze, approx. 23 × 43" (58.3 × 109.3 cm)

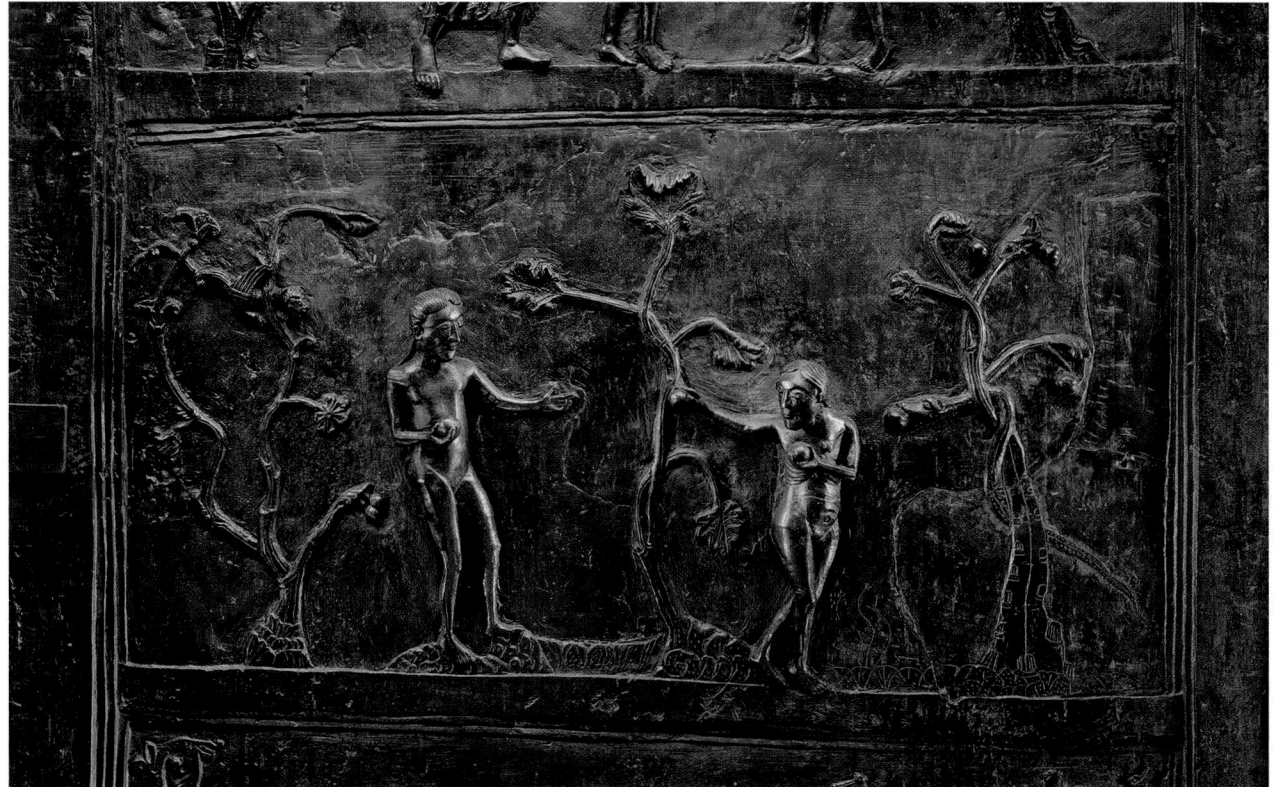

10.30 *Temptation and Fall*, from the Doors of Bishop Bernward, Hildesheim, Germany. Bronze, approx. 23 × 43" (58.3 × 109.3 cm)

attached to the westwork of Hildesheim cathedral, where they would have been seen by a larger public than in the monastic setting of St. Michael's. The new, more prominent setting indicates how valued they were in their own time.

The composition most likely derives from a manuscript illumination, since there are very similar scenes in medieval Bibles. Yet this is no mere imitation. The story is conveyed with splendid directness and expressive force. The accusing finger of the Lord, seen against a great void, is the focal point of the drama. It points to a cringing Adam, who passes the blame to Eve, who in turn passes it to the serpent at her feet. The trees and landscape elements are in relatively low relief and remain sketchy, which encourages them to be read as background elements, while the figures, though of awkward proportions, project forward so that the heads are three-dimensional.

The subjects on the left door are taken from the Hebrew Bible and those on the right from the New Testament (see fig. 10.28). The Hebrew Bible stories are presented chronologically from top to bottom, while the New Testament scenes move in reverse order, from bottom to top, suggesting the Christian message is uplifting. When read as horizontal pairs, the panels deliver a message of the origin and redemption of sin through a system of typology, whereby the Hebrew Bible stories prefigure New Testament ones. For example, the *Temptation and Fall* (fig. 10.30) is opposite the *Crucifixion*. In the center of the left panel is the tree whose fruit led to the Original Sin; in the center of the right panel is the cross on which Jesus was crucified, which medieval

Christians believed was made from the wood of the tree from Eden and was therefore the instrument for redemption from the sin of that original act. Compositional similarities between the two scenes stress their typological relationship: In the left panel Adam and Eve's hands, which flank the cross-shaped tree, establish a visual parallel to the spears the soldiers use to pierce Christ's body on the right panel.

Eve plays a particularly significant role on the doors; in fact, the narrative begins with her formation, not with the creation of Adam, as might be expected, since according to the Bible Adam's creation antecedes Eve's. In the *Temptation and Fall*, Eve's attitude and gesture parallel those of the serpent at the right, who, like Eve, offers an apple. This makes explicit Eve's role as seductive agent, accentuated by the way she holds the apple so closely to her chest that it almost appears as if she were grasping her breast rather than the fruit. With this gesture Eve's guilt in humankind's exile from Paradise is emphasized and her sexuality underscored.

While Early Christian writers had considered Eve responsible for the Original Sin, during the Ottonian period references to her guilt multiply and become more vigorous. This might have been as a result of efforts by Bishop Bernward and others to reform the morality of the clergy in an attempt to restore the vow of celibacy to priests and monks, some of whom were known to cohabit with wives and children in their monasteries. Thus, the burden of clerical immorality is, in effect, assigned to Eve, the first woman and the first seductress.

Ivories and Manuscripts: Conveyors of Imperial Grandeur

The right of the Ottonian monarchs to call themselves Roman emperors was challenged by Byzantine rulers, who continued to claim that title as their own even though the division of the Roman Empire into Eastern and Western empires was complete by the end of the fourth century. When Otto II married the Byzantine princess Theophano, he was able to use the full title of Holy Roman Emperor with impunity. While early Ottonian illuminators faithfully replicated features of Carolingian manuscripts, later Ottonian manuscripts, as well as ivories, blend Carolingian and Byzantine elements into a new style of extraordinary scope and power. Byzantine artists working for the court provided an impetus to find new ways of presenting both religious and imperial images. Ottonian manuscripts indicate an increasing interest on the part of artists and patrons in narrative cycles of Jesus' life, which is the period's most important contribution to the field of **iconography** (the study of the use and meaning of images in art).

CHRIST BLESSING OTTO II AND THEOPHANO An ivory of *Christ Blessing Emperor Otto II and Empress Theophano* (fig. **10.31**) commemorated their coronation, presenting it as divinely sanctioned. In style, the ivory is similar to the Byzantine ivory of *Christ Crowning Romanos and Eudokia* (see fig. 8.41), carved a generation or so earlier. The composition of both works is identical: A long-haired, bearded Christ (identified by a halo inscribed with a cross) is elevated in the center of each panel and anoints the empress and emperor, who flank him. In both ivories, the imperial costumes are composed of similar elaborate geometric surface decorations. This similarity suggests that the Otto II ivory is an eastern import, as does the inscription, which seems to be the work of a Greek using both Greek and Latin letters. However, because Otto's costume is not accurate for a Byzantine ruler's coronation, and because the inscription tells us that the donor—who huddles in front of Otto's stool and grasps the leg of the larger stool that supports Christ—was an Ottonian bishop who lived in Italy, it is more likely that the ivory was produced within Ottonian lands in Italy. No matter where this work was produced, it demonstrates the interest of the Ottonian court in importing Byzantine style as well as actual objects, thus establishing on another level a connection to the art of the Mediterranean. Here again, the king is presented as the Holy Roman Emperor, a divinely ordained ruler.

THE *GOSPEL BOOK OF OTTO III* Produced for the son of Otto II and Theophano, the *Gospel Book of Otto III* communicates an imperial grandeur equal to that of the coronation ivory of his parents. In figure **10.32** the emperor displays the imperial regalia—a crown, an eagle scepter, and a cross-inscribed orb—while his throne is decorated with imperial lions. Representatives of the two domains that he controls—the military and the ecclesiastical—flank him, reminiscent of Justinian's placement in the center of the same domains in the San Vitale mosaic (see fig. 8.25). On the facing folio, the four geographical parts of the realm—Slavinia, Germania, Gallia, and Roma—offer homage. Their stances recall traditional representations of the Magi offering gifts to Christ, such as the scene decorating Theodora's robe in the mosaic at San Vitale in Ravenna (see fig. 8.26).

The manuscript is dated to around 1000, not long after Otto III was crowned king of Germany at Aachen in 986 and Holy Roman Emperor at Rome in 993. The way Otto is represented

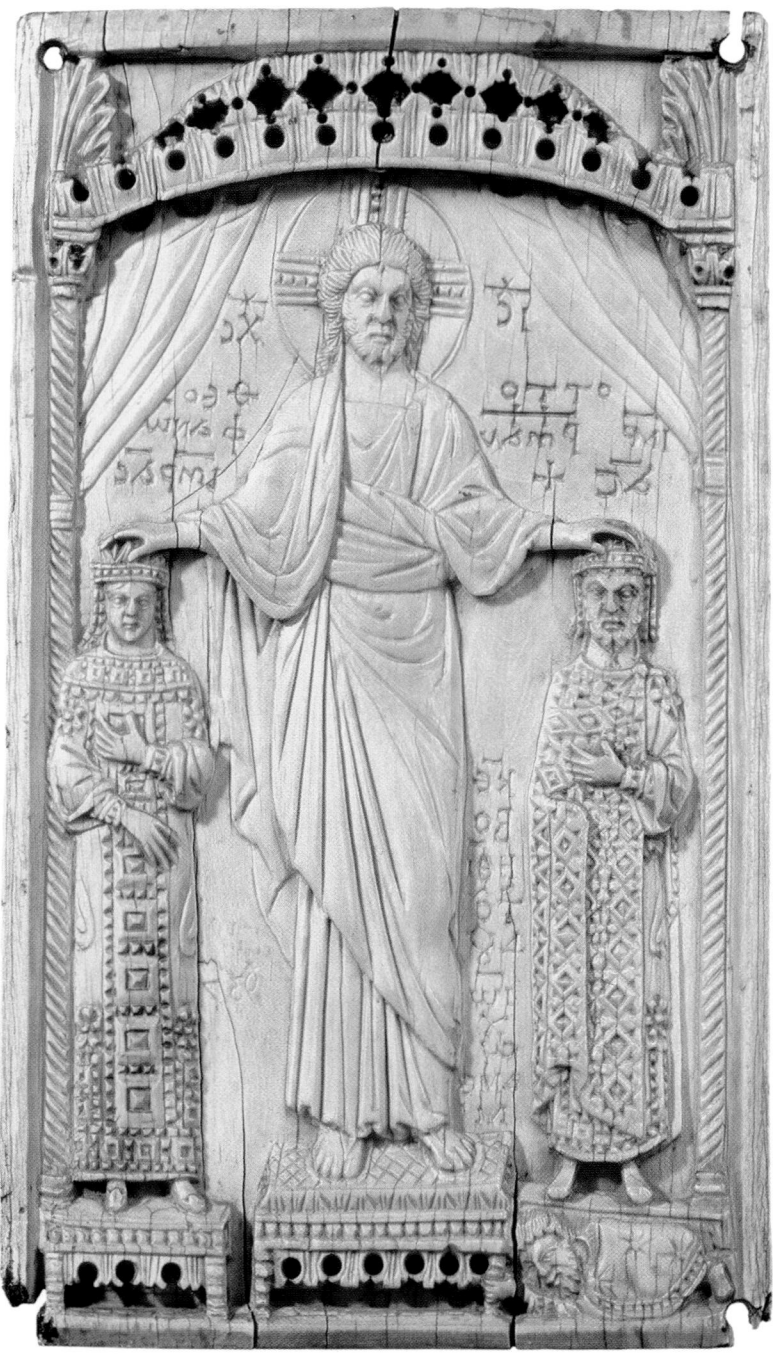

10.31 *Christ Blessing Emperor Otto II and Empress Theophano*. 982–83. Ivory, 7⅛ × 4" (18.3 × 10.3 cm). Musée du Moyen Âge (Cluny), Paris

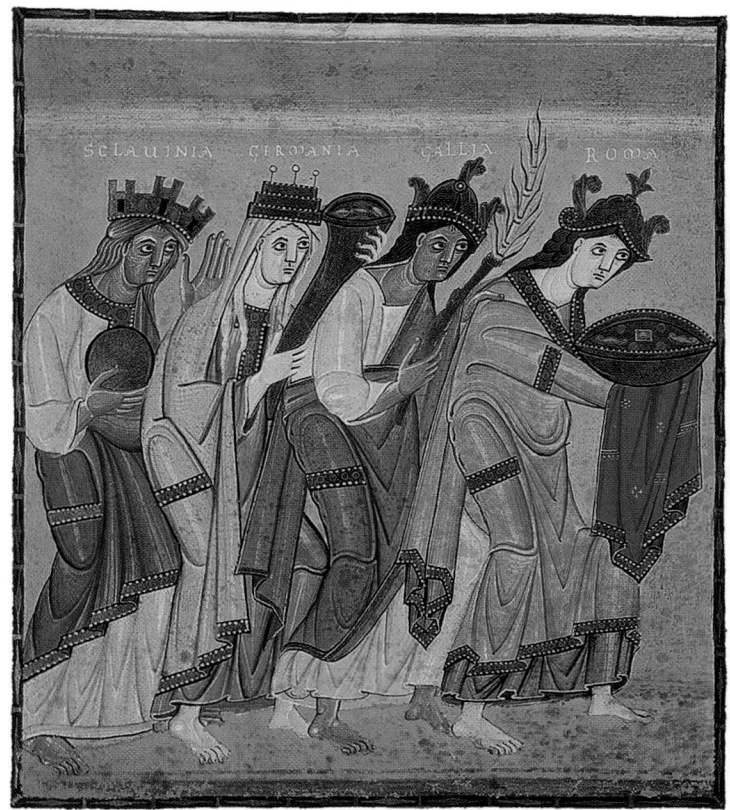
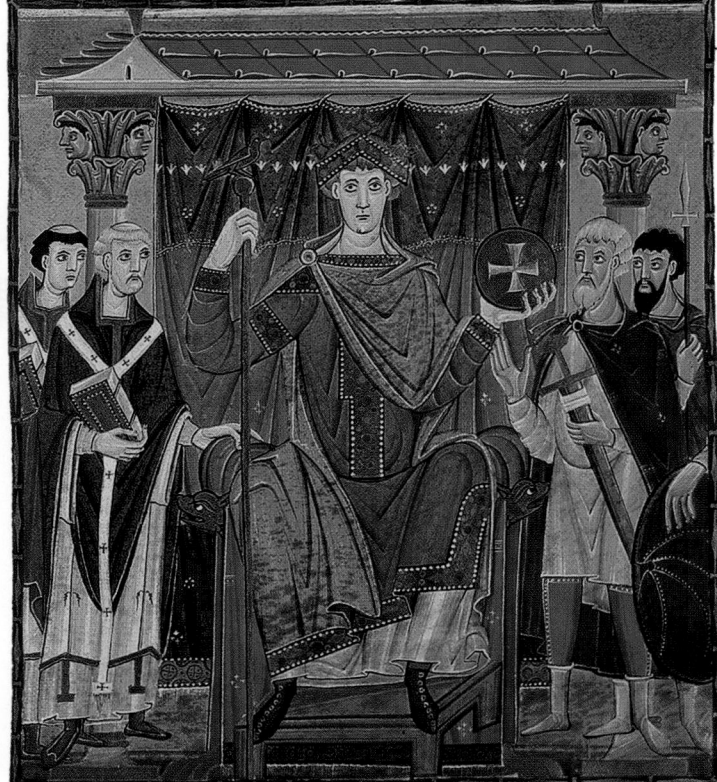

10.32   *Otto III Receiving the Homage of the Four Parts of the Empire*
and *Otto III Between Church and State*, from the *Gospel Book of Otto III*.
ca. 997–1000. Tempera on vellum, each folio 13 × 9⅜" (33 × 23.8 cm).
Staatsbibliothek, Munich

visually in the manuscript thus parallels historical facts. He is
presented here as the rightful and worthy heir to Roman and
Byzantine emperors as well as to Charlemagne, and his imperial
dignity is enhanced by association with Christ, a reversal of the
practice in Early Christian depictions, where Christ is ennobled
in the fashion of a Roman emperor. The soft pastel hues of the
background recall the illusionism of Graeco-Roman landscapes
and the *Quedlinburg Itala* fragment (see fig. 8.18). Such a style
shows that the artist was probably aware of Roman, as well as
Byzantine, manners of representation.

The *Gospel Book of Otto III* contains one of the most extensive sets of illustrations of the life of Christ. The scene of *Jesus
Washing the Feet of St. Peter* (fig. **10.33**) once again contains strong
echoes of ancient painting, transmitted through Byzantine art.
The architectural frame around Jesus is a late descendant of the
kind of architectural perspectives we saw in Roman wall painting
(see figs. 7.54 and 7.56), and the intense gold background reminds
us of Byzantine painting and mosaics, which the Ottonian artist
has put to new use. What was an architectural vista in the mural

10.33   *Jesus Washing the Feet of St. Peter*, from the *Gospel Book of
Otto III*. ca. 997–1000. Tempera on vellum, 13 × 9⅜" (33 × 23.8 cm).
Staatsbibliothek, Munich

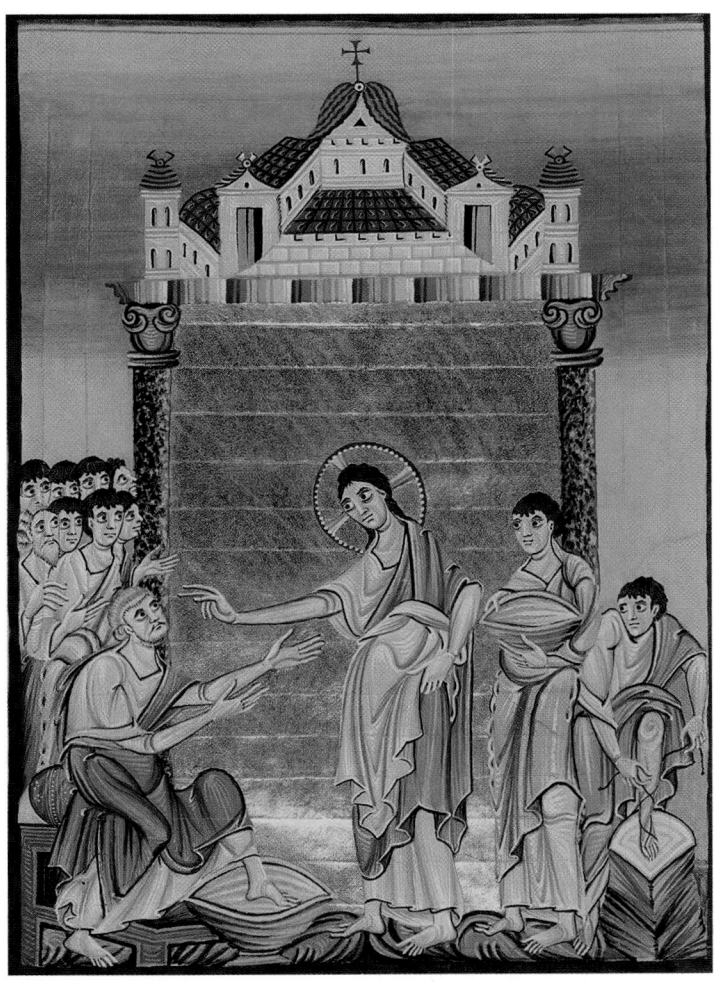

from Boscoreale (see fig. 7.54) now becomes the Heavenly City, the House of the Lord, filled with golden celestial space in contrast with the atmospheric earthly space outside.

The figures have also been transformed. In ancient art, this composition, in which a standing figure extends an arm to a seated supplicating figure and is watched by bystanders and assisted by others, was used to depict a doctor treating a patient. Here, though, the emphasis has shifted from physical to spiritual action. Not only do glances and gestures convey this new kind of action, but so too does scale. Jesus and his apostle Peter, the most animated figures, are larger than the rest, and Jesus' "active" arm is longer than his "passive" one. And the eight apostles, who are compressed into a tiny space and merely watch, have less physical substance than the fanlike Early Christian crowd from which this grouping derives (see fig. 8.17). The blending of Classical and Byzantine elements results in a new style of expressive abstraction.

A miniature showing St. Luke from the *Gospel Book of Otto III* (fig. **10.34**) is a symbolic image of overwhelming grandeur despite its small size. Unlike depictions of evangelists in Carolingian manuscripts (see figs. 10.13 and 10.14), here St. Luke is not shown writing. Instead, his Gospel lies completed on his lap. The evangelist seems to be as much a part of the mystical scene as he is its presenter. Enthroned on two rainbows, Luke holds aloft an awesome cluster of clouds from which tongues of light radiate in every direction. Within it we see his symbol, the ox, surrounded by five Hebrew prophets and an outer circle of angels. At the bottom, two lambs drink the life-giving waters that spring from beneath his feet. The key to the design is in the inscription: *Fonte patrum ductas bos agnis elicit undas* ("From the source of the fathers, the ox brings forth a flow of water for the lambs"). The Ottonian artist has truly "illuminated" the meaning of this terse phrase.

Sculpture

Large-scale and free-standing sculpture was rare in the early Middle Ages, in part because of the lingering fear of idol worship and because the general interest in producing portable objects virtually precluded its production. However, during the Ottonian period the scale of sculpture increased (witness Bernward's doors for St. Michael's at Hildesheim), and even many small-scale works demonstrate an imposing monumentality.

THE *GERO CRUCIFIX* The *Gero Crucifix* (fig. 10.35), named for Archbishop Gero of Cologne, who commissioned it around 970, is an example of a large-scale work—it is in fact life-size—with a monumental presence, indicative of the major transformation that Ottonian sculptors were able to achieve even when dealing with traditional subjects. How this happens is evident if we compare the *Gero Crucifix* with the Christ on the cover of the *Lindau Gospels* (see fig. 10.16). The two works are separated by little more than 100 years but show marked contrast. The *Gero Crucifix* presents a sculptural image that is new to Western art, since for the first time a dead Christ is represented on the Cross. Made of painted and gilded oak, it is carved in powerfully rounded forms. Particularly striking is the forward bulge of the heavy body, which emphasizes the physical strain on the arms and shoulders, making the pain seem almost unbearable. The face, with its deeply incised, angular features, is a mask of agony from which all life has fled. The image is filled with deep feeling for Christ's suffering.

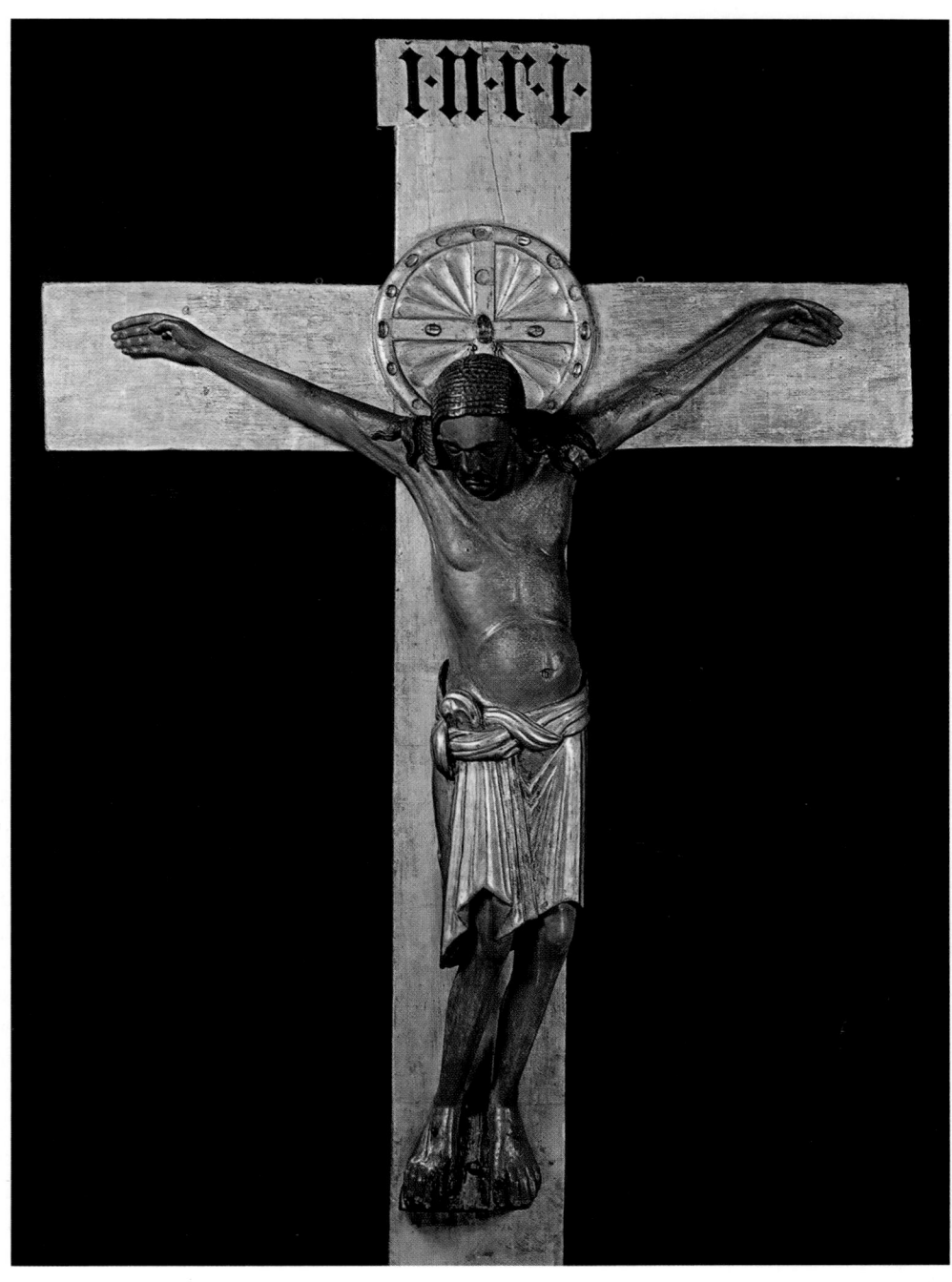

10.35 *Gero Crucifix*. ca. 970. Painted and gilded wood, height 6'2" (1.88 m). Cologne cathedral, Germany

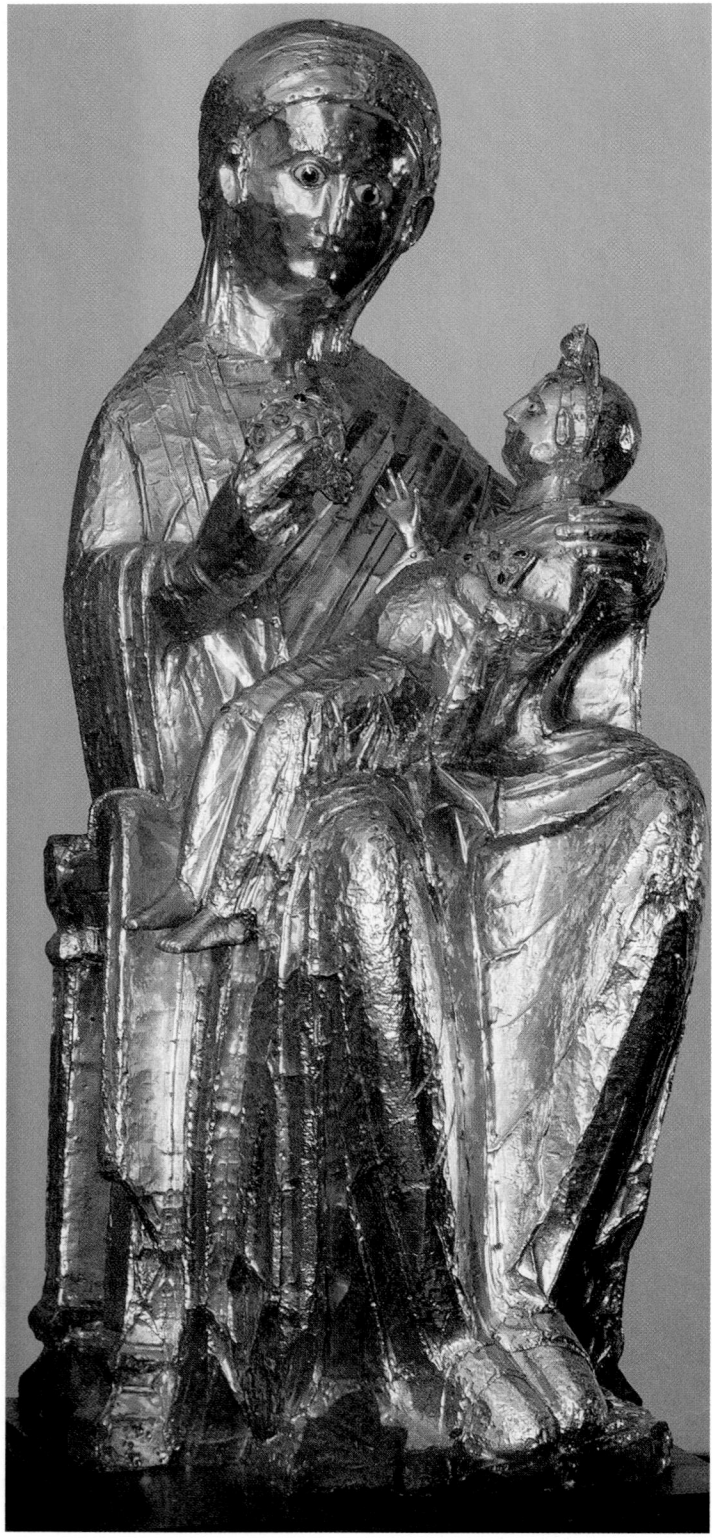

10.36 *Virgin of Essen*. ca. 980. Gold over wood, enamel, filigree, and gems, height 29½" (75.6 cm). Cathedral Treasury, Essen, Germany

How did the Ottonian sculptor arrive at this bold conception? The *Gero Crucifix* was clearly influenced by Middle Byzantine art, which had created the compassionate view of Christ on the Cross in other mediums (see fig. 8.45). Yet, that source alone is not enough to explain the results. It remained for the Ottonian artist to translate the Byzantine image into large-scale sculptural terms and to replace its gentle pathos with expressive realism. Even though there were some clerics who rekindled the deep-rooted fear of idolatry, they could not restrain the newly found emphasis on the humanity of Christ or the increasing interest in relics, which were, after all, three-dimensional objects. In fact, there is a space in the back of the head of the Gero Christ to hold the Host (the bread or wafer taken during that part of the Mass referred to as Communion), transforming the sculpture into a **reliquary** (a container to enshrine holy remnants or relics).

THE *VIRGIN OF ESSEN* The *Virgin of Essen* (fig. **10.36**), given to the Cathedral of Essen around 980 by Abbess Matilda, grand-daughter of Otto I, was almost certainly designed as a reliquary, although that is hard to establish definitively since the sculpture's original wooden core does not survive. All that is left is the exterior covering of gold sheets. Matilda also donated two—and possibly three—gold, enamel, and jeweled crosses to the cathedral. This rich treasure, glittering on candlelit altars, would have made an impressive display and signaled the church's patronage by a member of the imperial family. The *Virgin of Essen* is one of the earliest free-standing sculptures of the Virgin Mary. The golden apple Mary holds symbolizes her typological status as the new Eve; thus, the sculpture is related conceptually to the message on Bernward's bronze doors (see fig. 10.27).

Despite the tender, almost doll-like figures of Mary and Christ, the *Virgin of Essen* has a commanding presence. This is due to Mary's frontal pose, her large staring eyes, and the brilliance of the gold, which is enhanced by the gems, enamels, and filigree that decorate the apple and Christ's book and halo. Linear details, such as drapery folds, and facial features are suppressed to place emphasis on the figure's corporeality. Thus, although employing some early medieval metalwork materials and techniques that stretch back to the Anglo-Saxon period and to still-earlier traditions as well, the Essen Madonna has moved away from the traditional Germanic concentration on line and surface effect. Despite her small size—less than 2½ feet high—the simplification of form and the concentration on abstract shapes result in a marked movement toward monumentality, which also characterized the *Gero Crucifix*. These works herald new aesthetic aims that will dominate eleventh-century sculpture throughout western Europe.

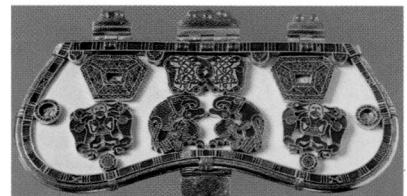
ca. 624 Ship burial at Sutton Hoo, England

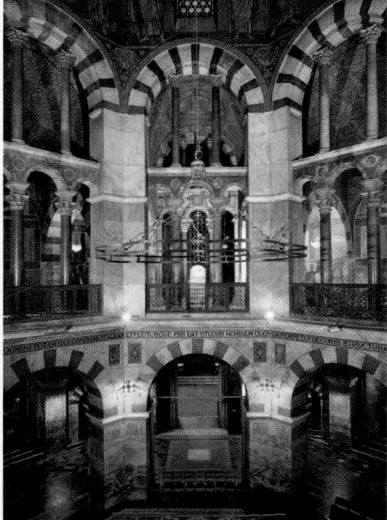
792–805 Palace Chapel of Charlemagne, Aachen

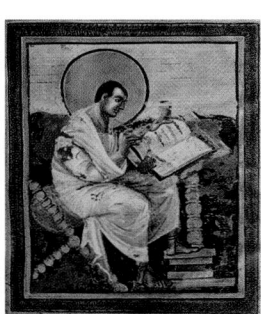
ca. 800–10 *Gospel Book of Charlemagne* (*Coronation Gospels*)

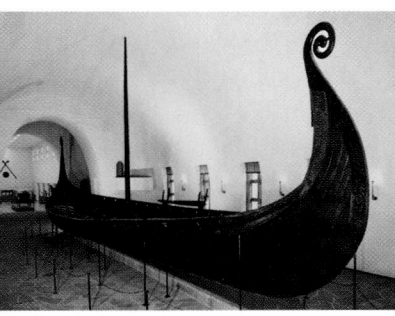
. 834 Oseberg ship burial

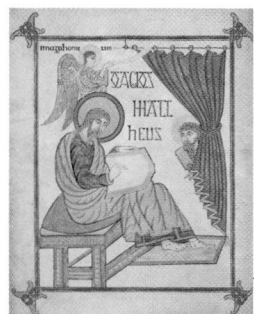
ca. 700 *Lindisfarne Gospels*

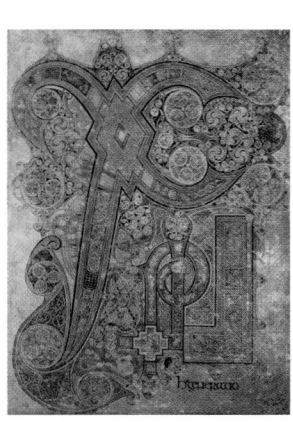
ca. 800 *Book of Kells*

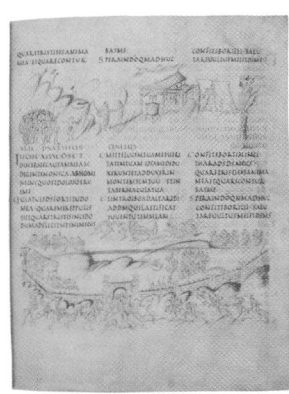
ca 820–32 *Utrecht Psalter*

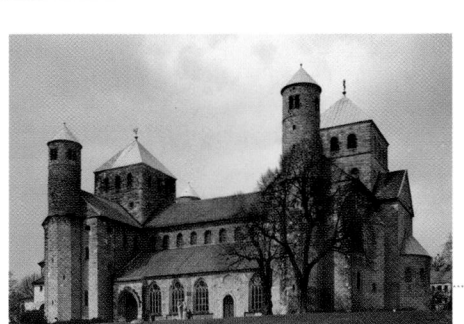
1001–33 St. Michael's, Hildesheim

Early Medieval Art

400

◄ 5th century Angles and Saxons invade the British Isles
◄ 451 Attila the Hun invades Europe

◄ 476 Fall of Rome

500

········ 532–37 Hagia Sophia, Istanbul

◄ ca. 570 Birth of the Prophet Muhammad in Mecca

600

········ ca. 690 Dome of the Rock, Jerusalem

700

◄ 726–843 Iconoclastic Controversy

········ 785 Great Mosque, Córdoba

800

◄ 843 Charlemagne's three grandsons divide his empire

900

········ 950 *Paris Psalter*
◄ 962 Otto I crowned Holy Roman Emperor

1000

1100

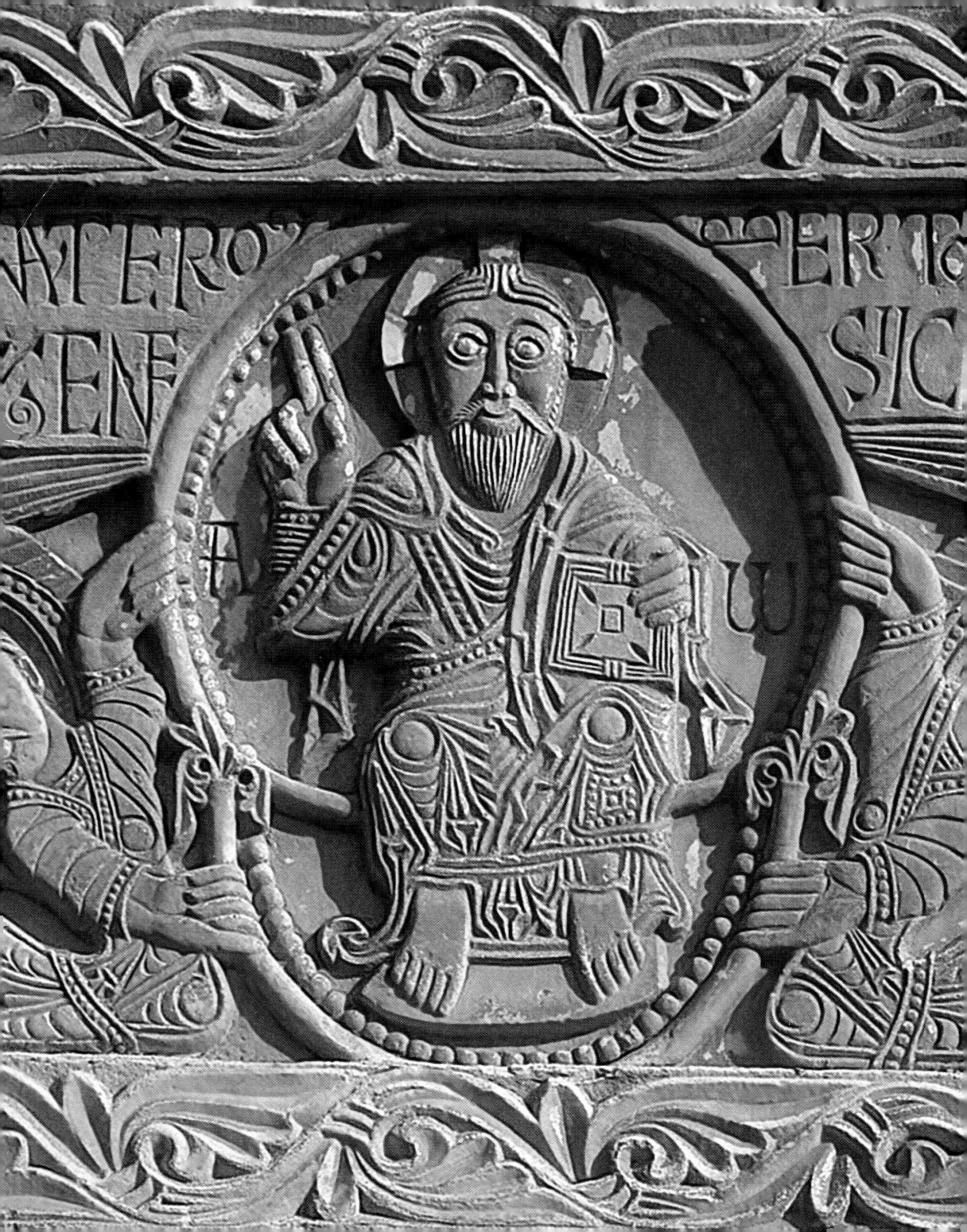

Romanesque Art

ROMANESQUE MEANS, LITERALLY, "IN THE ROMAN MANNER." WE USE this stylistic term today to identify the art of much of the eleventh and twelfth centuries. The borrowing of details or specific features from the antique past does not distinguish Romanesque art from the art of other post-Classical periods, for the artists of these periods also relied heavily on Rome

for their formal and expressive languages. However, in Romanesque art, the aesthetic integrity and grandeur of the Roman model survive in a more vital and compelling form than in previous periods. Yet Rome was not the period's only inspiration: Romanesque artists tapped sources in Carolingian and Ottonian art, and were influenced by Early Christian, Byzantine, Celtic-Germanic, and Islamic traditions as well.

While Carolingian and Ottonian art developed principally in response to the patronage of the royal courts, Romanesque art sprang up all over western Europe at about the same time and in a variety of regional styles that are nevertheless closely related. What welded this variety into a coherent style was not any single force but several factors.

For one thing, Christianity was close to triumphing everywhere in Europe. The Vikings, still largely pagan in the ninth and tenth centuries when their raids terrorized the British Isles and the Continent, had finally entered the Catholic fold, not only in Normandy but in Scandinavia as well. Meanwhile, in 1031, the caliphate of Córdoba had broken up into many small Muslim states, opening the way for Christian conquest of the Iberian peninsula.

Another factor was the growing spirit of religious enthusiasm. The year 1000—the millennium—had come and gone without the

apocalyptic end of the world that many had predicted from their reading of the book of Revelation in the Bible. Chapter 20 of this New Testament book, written about 50 years after Jesus' death, prophesizes that the Second Coming, when Christ will return to earth and end the world as we know it, would occur after 1,000 years. Many people, fearing the end of days, reacted to the approach of the year 1000 with terror and to its smooth passing with great relief and, in some quarters, a heightened spirituality. This was demonstrated by the large number of people making pilgrimages to sacred sites, by repeated Christian Crusades against the Muslims in the Holy Land, and by an increase in the number and size of monasteries.

A general growth in population and an increase in prosperity during the Romanesque period are also significant, as was the reopening of the Mediterranean trade routes by the navies of Venice, Genoa, Amalfi, Pisa, and Rimini. The revival of trade and travel linked Europe commercially and culturally, stimulating the flowering of urban life.

At the end of the early medieval period, Europe was still largely an agricultural society. A decentralized political and social system, known today as feudalism, had begun to develop, mainly in France and Germany, where it had deep historical roots. In this system, landowning lords granted some of their property to knights (originally, these were cavalry officers). In return for these fiefs, or feuds, as the land parcels were called, the knights gave military and other service to their lords, to whom they were

Detail of figure 11.2, Lintel of west portal, church of
Saint-Genis-des-Fontaines, France

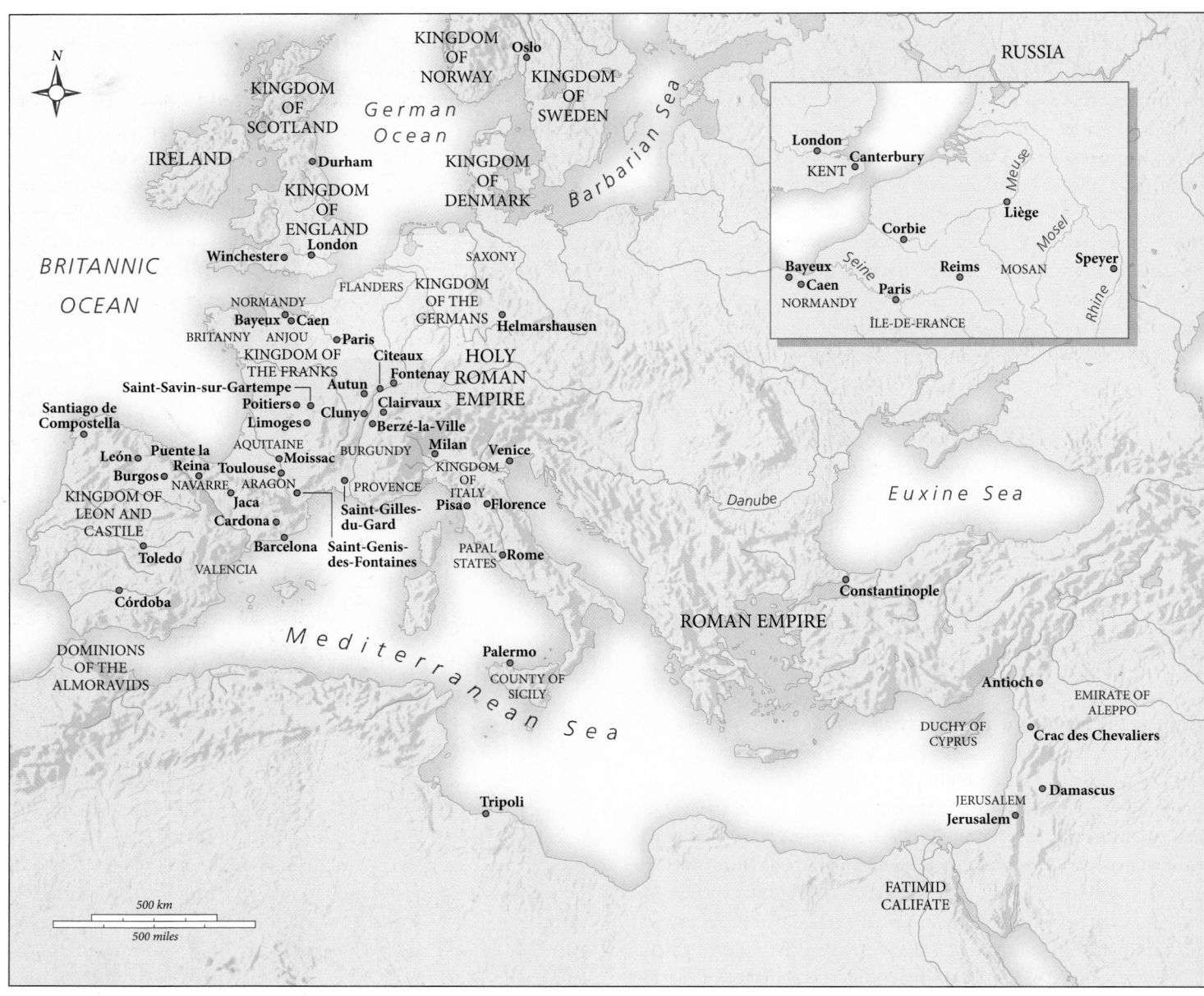

Map 11.1   Europe in the Romanesque period

linked through a complex system of personal bonds—termed vassalage—that extended all the way to the king. A large class of generally downtrodden, virtually powerless peasants (serfs) worked the land itself. Towns that had shrunk in size during the migrations and invasions of the early Middle Ages—Rome, for instance, with about 1 million people in 300, fell to less than 50,000 at one point, and some smaller cities were deserted altogether—started to regain their former importance. New towns sprang up everywhere, achieving independence via charters that enumerated a town's privileges and immunities in return for a feudal lord's guarantee of protection.

These social changes were made possible by technological advances in agriculture, such as improved milling machinery and better iron plows that dug deeper furrows. For the first time since the Fall of Rome, farmers could grow more food than they needed for themselves. In many ways, then, western Europe between 1050 and 1200 became a great deal more "Roman-esque" than it had been since the sixth century. It recaptured some of the trade patterns, the urban quality, and the military strength of ancient imperial times. Despite Charlemagne's attempt to unify Europe, there was no central political authority, for Europe was still divided into small units ruled by powerful families. Even the king of France controlled not much more than the area around Paris. However, some monasteries came to rival the wealth and power of kings, and the central spiritual authority of the pope acted as a unifying force throughout Europe. In 1095, Pope Urban II called for the First Crusade to liberate the Holy Land from Muslim rule and to aid the Byzantine emperor against the advancing Turks. The army of crusaders was far larger than any secular ruler could have raised for the purpose.

This brief historical account underscores the number of institutions, organizations, and systems that helped to create European stability. Monasticism, feudalism, urbanism, commerce, pilgrimage, crusade, papacy, and the royal court all played their roles by setting in motion internationalizing forces that affected the transmission of artistic forms. Population growth and an increase in the number of new settlements stimulated building activity, much of it for religious, i.e., Christian use. The development of better tools, such as saws to cut stone, resulted in improved masonry techniques. Many new constructions were made of well-cut, straight-edged blocks of stone and were monumental, built on a scale that rivaled the achievements of Rome. Heavy walls created solid and durable structures that conveyed a sense of enclosure and security, and the stone vaults covering these buildings enhanced their stability. These vaults, as well as the proliferation of architectural sculpture, consciously emulated the Roman manner of construction and design. Embellishing churches and monasteries with reliquaries and other adornments, including illuminated manuscripts, provided for the needs of both the local population and pilgrims.

FIRST EXPRESSIONS OF ROMANESQUE STYLE

Although Romanesque art quickly spread throughout Europe, its first appearances occur in a zone running from Lombardy in Italy through southern France and into northern Spain, into the region of Catalonia. Stone-vaulted buildings decorated with wall arcades and architectural sculpture, which are characteristic features of this early phase, survive in great numbers in these regions.

Architecture

The most striking feature of Romanesque art is the amazing increase in building activity. An eleventh-century monk, Raoul Glaber, conveys the enthusiasm for building that characterizes the period:

> Just before the third year after the millennium, throughout the whole world, but most especially in Italy and Gaul, men began to reconstruct churches. … But it seemed as though each Christian community were aiming to surpass all others in the splendor of construction. It was as if the whole world were shaking itself free, shrugging off the burden of the past, and cladding itself everywhere in a white mantle of churches.
>
> J. France, *The Five Books of the Histories* (Oxford, 1989)

These churches were not only more numerous than those of the early Middle Ages, they were also larger, more richly ornamented, and more "Roman-looking." Their naves had stone vaults instead of wooden roofs, and their exteriors were decorated with both architectural ornament and sculpture. Romanesque monuments of the first importance are distributed over an area that might well have represented the Catholic world: from northern Spain to the Rhineland, from the Scottish–English border to central Italy.

CHURCH OF SANT VINCENÇ, CARDONA An excellent example of an early phase of Romanesque architecture is the collegiate church of Sant Vincenç (fig. **11.1**), built within the walled confines of the castle at Cardona on the southern flank of the Catalan Pyrenees. The church, begun in 1029 and consecrated in 1040, is straightforward both in plan and in elevation. A barrel-vaulted nave creates a continuous space marked off by transverse arches into units of space called **bays**. The domed bay

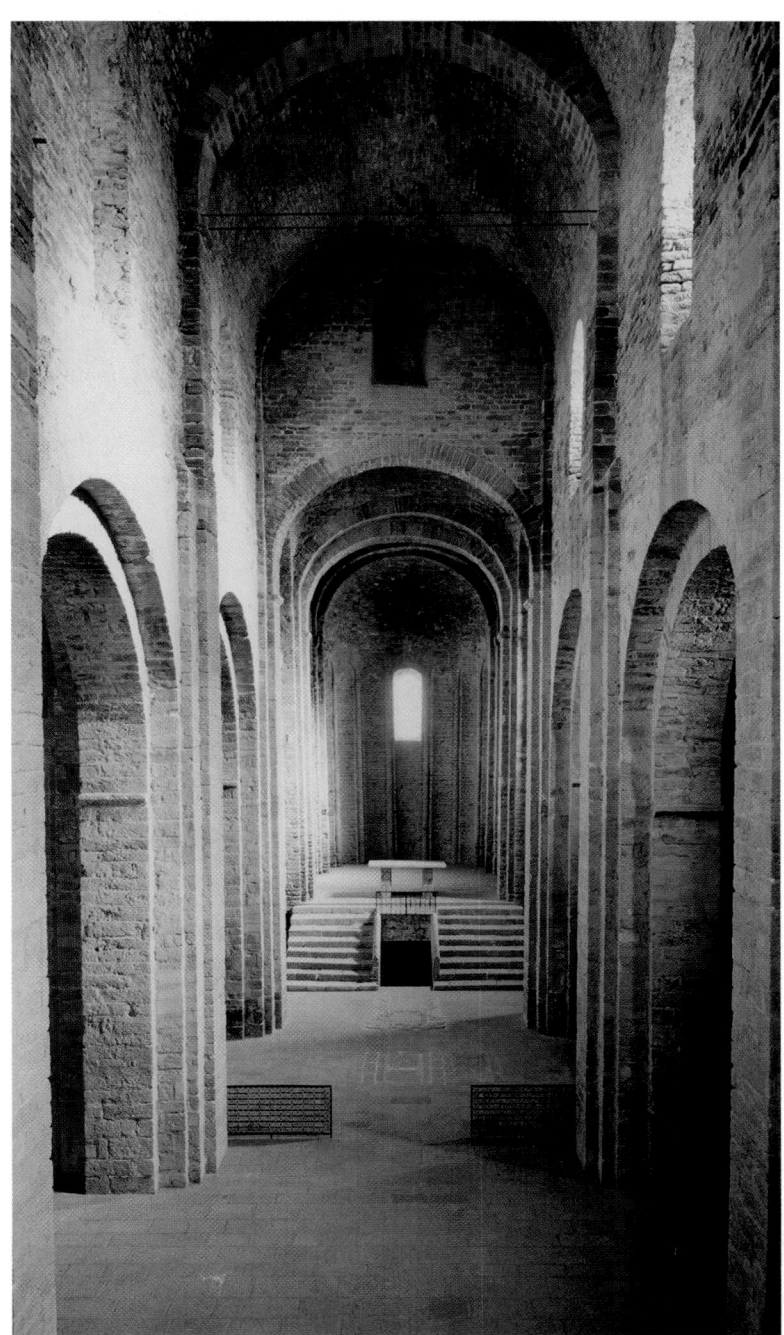

11.1   Nave and choir (looking east), church of Sant Vincenç, Cardona, Spain. ca. 1029–1040

in front of the **chancel** (the part of the church containing the altar and seats for the clergy) focuses attention on the ceremonial heart of the church. Blind niches in the chancel walls establish a rhythmic variety that is accentuated in the nave by the staggered cadence of massive **compound piers**, solid masonry supports with rectangular projections attached to their four faces. The projections reflect the different structural elements that combine to support the building. One projection rises the full height of the nave to support the transverse arch, another forms the arch that extends across the side aisle, and two others connect to the arches of the nave arcade. Clearly the architectural effort at Sant Vincenç required detailed, systematic planning. Vaulting the nave to eliminate the fire hazard of a wooden roof was not only a practical necessity, it also challenged architects to make the House of the Lord grander.

Sant Vincenç's vertical integration of piers and vault is undoubtedly derived from the desire to unify the elevation in early medieval buildings, for example the Carolingian chapel at Aachen (see fig. 10.18) and the Ottonian church at Gernrode (see fig. 10.23). However, the wall planes of the Ottonian church appear flat by comparison to the angular surfaces of Sant Vincenç, where the clarity of articulation endows the building with a heightened sense of unity and **harmony**. The compound pier is, in fact, a major architectural innovation of the Romanesque

period. Limited light and robust stone construction create an interior at once sheltering and inspiring; the sober arrangement of simple yet powerful forms is masterfully realized.

Monumental Stone Sculpture

The revival of monumental stone sculpture in the Romanesque era is as significant as the architectural achievements of the period. Free-standing statues had all but disappeared from Western art after the fifth century, and stone relief survived only as architectural ornament or surface decoration, while three-dimensional sculpture was rare. Thus, the only sculptural tradition that continued through the early medieval period was that of sculpture-in-miniature: small reliefs and occasional statuettes in metal or ivory. In works such as the bronze doors of Bishop Bernward (see fig. 10.27), Ottonian art had enlarged the small scale of this tradition but had not changed its spirit. Moreover, its truly large-scale sculptural efforts, such as the *Gero Crucifix* (see fig. 10.35), were limited almost entirely to wood.

LINTEL AT SAINT-GENIS-DES-FONTAINES The marble lintel at Saint-Genis-des-Fontaines, on the French side of the Pyrenees, is dated by inscription to between 1020 and 1021 (fig. **11.2**). It spans the doorway of the church and is one of the

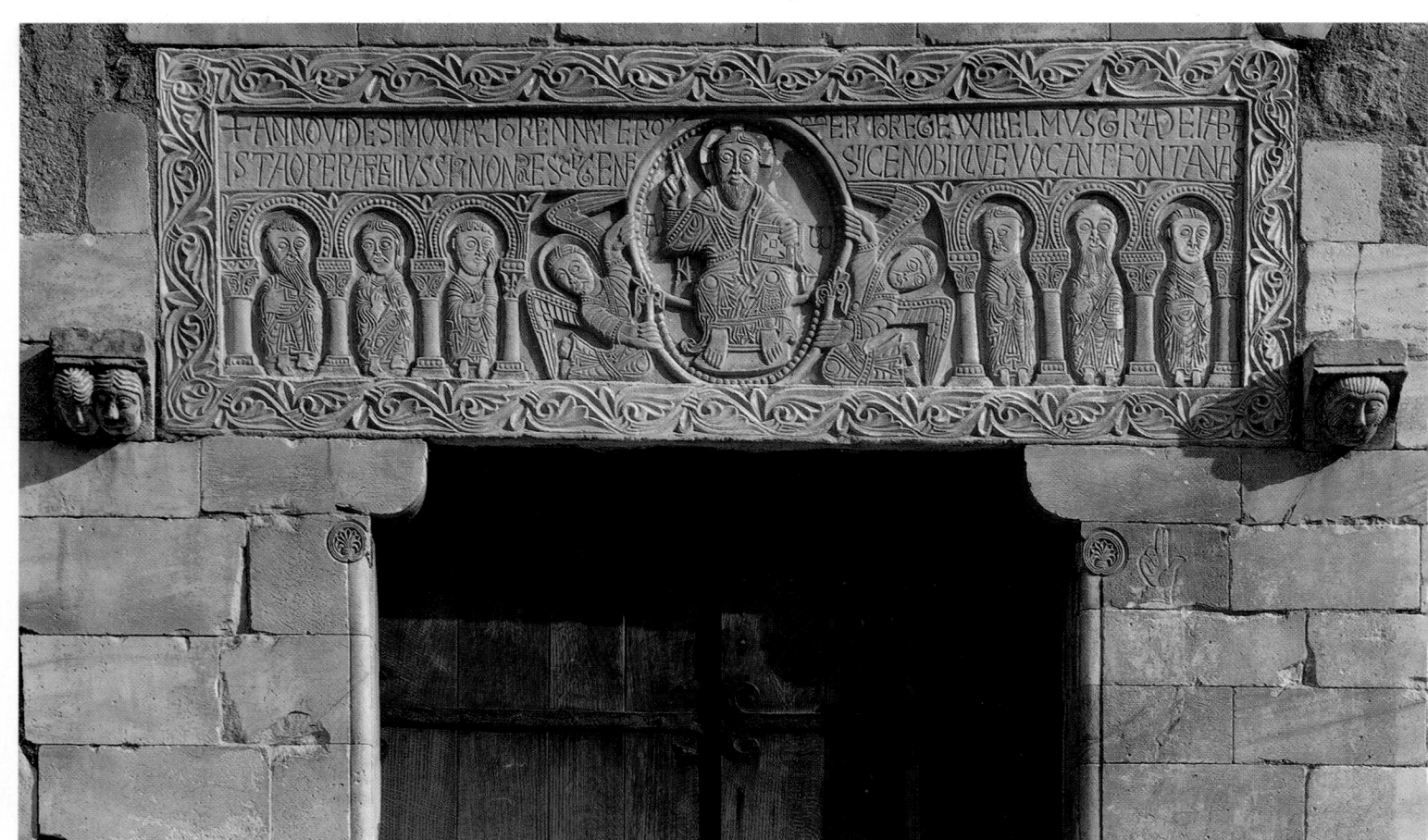

11.2   Lintel of west portal, church of Saint-Genis-des-Fontaines, France. 1020–21. Approx. 2 × 7' (61 cm × 2.1 m)

earliest examples of Romanesque figurative sculpture. The inscription gives the names of the leaders of two stabilizing institutions of the period, "Rotberto Rege" (King Robert) and "Willelmus Aba" (Abbot William), the former a feudal lord and the latter the leader of a monastery. The central motif, Christ in Majesty supported by angels, is flanked by six apostles; each apostle holds a book and stands under an arcade. Christ's mandorla is formed by two intersecting circles. One symbolizes the earth and the other heaven, the two realms over which he presides.

The Saint-Genis lintel is modest in size, only about 2 feet high by 7 feet long. The reliance on line to indicate facial features, drapery folds, and ornamental decoration is reminiscent of early medieval manuscript illuminations and reaches as far back as the Hiberno-Saxon period (see fig. 10.6). The carving, with flat surfaces marked by incision, resembles the decorative arts, particularly ivory and metalwork. This can be verified by comparing some of the patterns (for example, the beading around the arches) with metalwork techniques (see fig. 10.1). The correlation explains where carvers might have found their sources of inspiration after centuries during which stone sculpture had been virtually abandoned.

Although the figures are rendered with individualized hairstyles and facial features and with a variety of gestures, they are clearly stylized. Each is contained by the frame around him in such a way that it is difficult to decide if the figures are governed by their frames or if the arches swell in response to the figures. The equilibrium between frame and figure parallels the harmonious balance between structure and decoration that characterizes early Romanesque buildings such as Sant Vincenç at Cardona.

MATURE ROMANESQUE

Early Romanesque experiments in sturdy construction, which relied on the skills of masons and sculptors, led to buildings that employed both more sculpture and increasingly sophisticated vaulting techniques. Sculptural decoration was arranged into complicated and didactic iconographic programs. Romanesque architecture and sculpture continue to convey messages of security and spirituality, employing a consistent aesthetic approach that is also visible in the manuscripts and metalwork produced during the period. As Romanesque art developed, it spread throughout Europe, becoming a pan-European art.

Pilgrimage Churches and Their Art

Among the most significant social phenomena of eleventh- and twelfth-century Europe was the increased ability of people of all classes to travel. While some journeys were made as a result of expanded trade, others, such as a crusade or pilgrimage, were ostensibly for religious purposes. Individual pilgrims made journeys to holy places for different reasons, but most shared the hope that they would find special powers or dispensations as a result of their journey. Pilgrimage was not a Romanesque

invention. As early as the late fourth century, Egeria, a Spanish pilgrim to Jerusalem, chronicled her visit to the locations central to Christ's life, among them the church of the Holy Sepulcher (see fig. 8.12). Special, often miraculous, powers associated with these holy sites were transferred to relics, those body parts of holy persons or objects that had come in contact with Christ, his close followers, or other holy figures, particularly his mother, the Virgin Mary.

Partly due to the Muslim conquest of the Holy Land, travel there was difficult during the Middle Ages. This led, on the one hand, to a zeal for crusade and, on the other, to a veneration of places within Europe that had important relics or that had been the site of special events. Rome, in particular, became a popular pilgrimage site, beneficiary of the aura of sanctity surrounding SS. Peter and Paul, both of whom lived and were buried there (see page 246). So did Santiago de Compostela on the Iberian peninsula. Cultural anthropologists have attempted to account for the incredible popularity and significance of pilgrimage to the medieval world as well as to our own. They explain that when pilgrims embark on their journey they enter a special transitional, or liminal, zone where social norms and hierarchies are replaced with a sense of shared experience. This creates a temporary condition of community, in which people of disparate backgrounds and social levels can communicate as equals. The buildings and objects pilgrims saw and experienced fostered this sense of community. The pilgrimage and the churches associated with it also provided opportunities for pilgrims to experience spiritual fulfillment through the journey itself, which demonstrated their piety both to themselves and to the world, and through the experience of beautiful and moving buildings and the objects they contained.

SANTIAGO DE COMPOSTELA The tomb of St. James at Santiago de Compostela in northwest Spain marked the most westerly point of Christian Europe. According to tradition, the apostle James (or Santiago in Spanish) had preached Christianity on the Iberian peninsula. After returning to the Holy Land, he was martyred there and his body was returned to Spain under dramatic circumstances. Reports of the tomb's miraculous power attracted large numbers of pilgrims from all over Europe. Many had to brave a difficult sea journey or an exhausting crossing of the Pyrenees mountains in order to reach the apostle's tomb at Compostela. (See *Primary Source*, page 352.) During the twelfth century as many as tens of thousands of people might have made the journey in a single year. The difficulty of the journey added to its allure. Since much of Spain was under Muslim control, pilgrims considered the trip to Santiago equivalent to a journey to the Muslim-held Holy Land.

The cathedral at Santiago de Compostela had much to offer those brave hearts sufficiently fortunate to reach their goal. The plan (fig. **11.3**) includes side aisles that run uninterruptedly around the church and form an ambulatory around the apse. Visitors used these aisles to circumambulate the space, even when the religious offices were being celebrated in the nave and **crossing**. **Apsidioles**, or small apselike chapels, arranged along the

The Pilgrim's Guide

From *Pilgrim's Guide to Santiago de Compostela*

The Pilgrim's Guide, *written around 1130, gives a vivid account of the routes to Santiago de Compostela and what was to be met along them by pilgrims traveling to the shrine of the apostle James there (see map 11.2, page 354). It also provides interesting information on the personnel in charge of the construction of the shrine at the cathedral.*

There are four roads which, leading to Santiago, converge into one near Puente la Reina [see fig. 11.8], in Spanish territory. One goes through St-Gilles [see fig. 11.31], Montpellier, Toulouse [see fig. 11.7] and [the pass of] Somport; another passes through Notre-Dame of Le Puy and Ste-Foy at Conques and Saint-Pierre at Moissac [see figs. 11.12–11.16]; another proceeds through Ste-Marie-Madeleine of Vézelay, St-Léonard of the Limousin and the city of Périgueux; another goes by St-Martin of Tours to St-Hilaire of Poitiers, St-Jean-d'Angély, St-Eutrope of Saintes and the city of Bordeaux. ...

After that are the Landes of the Bordelais, a three-days' journey, exhausting to be sure. This is a country devoid of all good things, lacking in bread, wine, meat, fish, water and springs, sparse in towns, flat, sandy but abundant, however, in honey, millet, panic-grass and pigs. If, however, by chance you cross it in summer, take care to guard your face from the enormous insects, commonly called *guespe* [wasps] or *tauones* [horseflies], which are most abundant there; and if you do not watch carefully where you put your feet, you will slip rapidly up to your knees in the quicksand that abounds there. ...

After this valley is found the land of Navarre, which abounds in bread and wine, milk and cattle. The Navarrese and Basques are held to be exactly alike....This is a barbarous race unlike all other races in customs and in character, full of malice, swarthy in colour, evil of face, depraved, perverse, perfidious, empty of faith and corrupt, libidinous, drunken, experienced in all violence, ferocious and wild, dishonest and reprobate, impious and harsh, cruel and contentious, unversed in anything good, well-trained in all vices and iniquities. ...

Source: *Pilgrim's Guide to Santiago de Compostela: A Critical Edition*, II, ed. and tr. Paula Gerson, Annie Shaver Crandell, Alison Stones and Jeanne Krochalis (London: Harvey Miller Publishers, 1998)

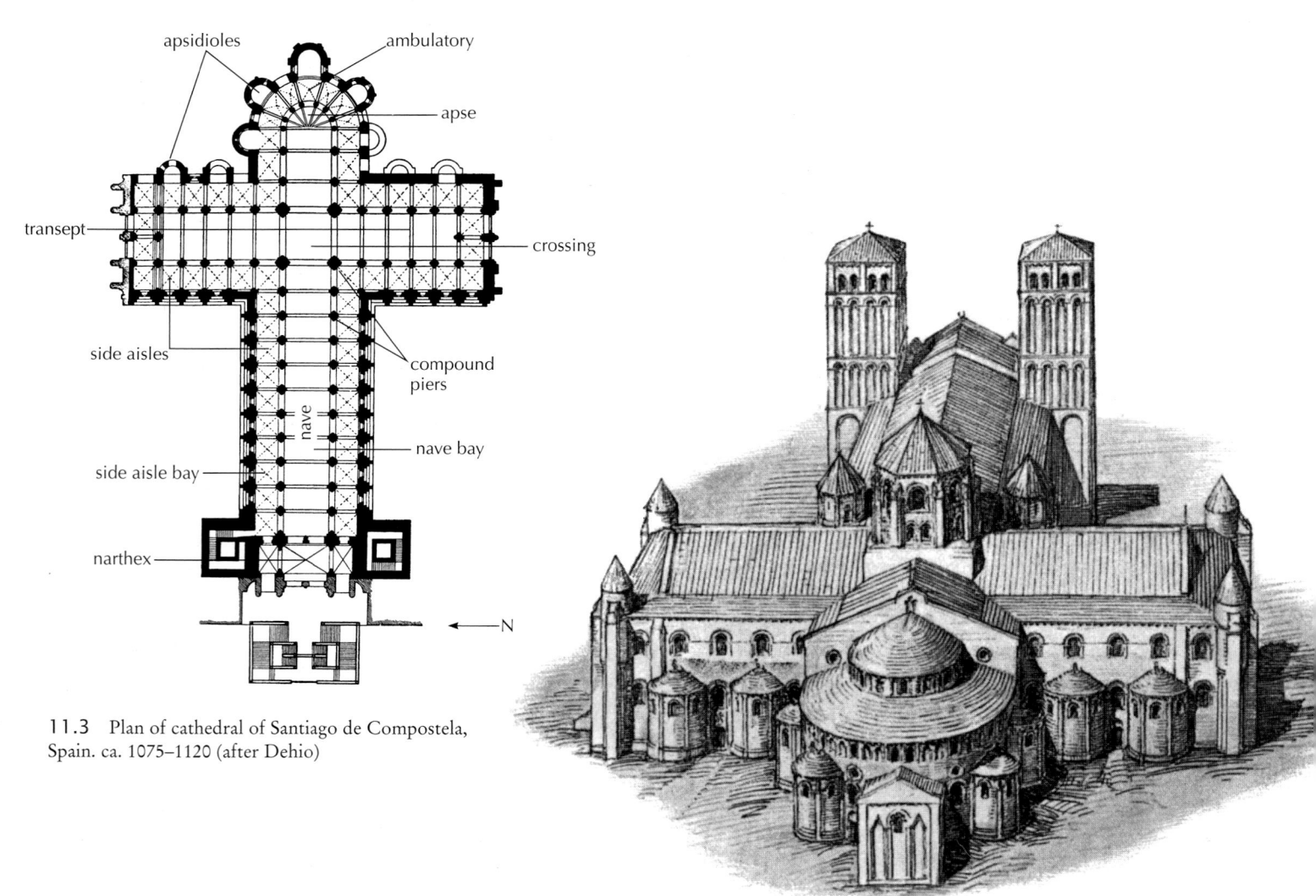

11.3   Plan of cathedral of Santiago de Compostela, Spain. ca. 1075–1120 (after Dehio)

11.4   Reconstruction of cathedral of Santiago de Compostela (after Conant)

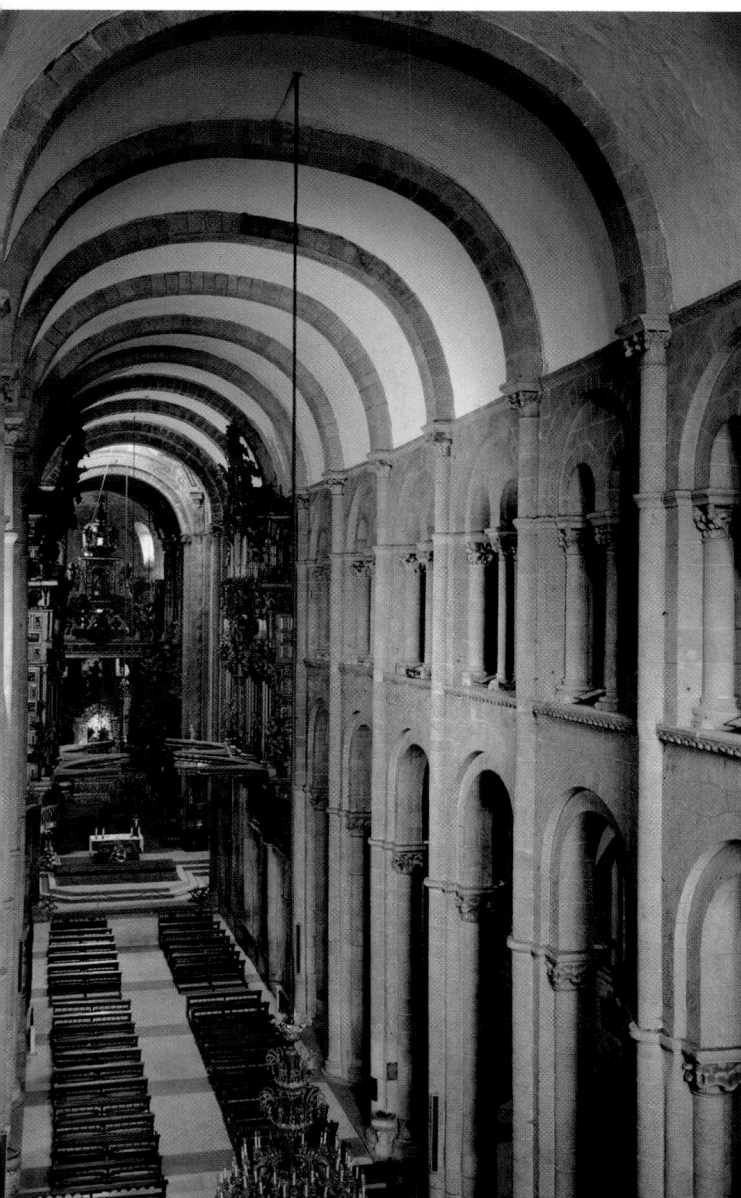

11.5 Nave of cathedral of Santiago de Compostela

the road from Le Puy), and Saint-Sernin at Toulouse (on the road from Saint-Gilles-du-Gard). (See map 11.2.)

The plan of Santiago de Compostela (see fig. 11.3) is composed of multiple modular units. It recalls the system of architectural composition based on additive components that was employed during the early Middle Ages (see page 333). The bays of the nave and the transept are half the size of the square crossing, and the square bays of the side aisles are in turn a quarter the size of the crossing and thus half the size of the nave bays. As at Sant Vincenç at Cardona (see fig. 11.1), the building's elevation (see fig. 11.5) mirrors the clarity of its plan. The four **colonnettes**, small detached columns, of the compound piers reflect the building's structural elements. However, overall there is less wall surface in the Santiago de Compostela nave, and colonnettes, used in place of Sant Vincenç's rectangular attachments to the compound piers (see pages 349–50), more richly articulate the nave elevation.

So as not to weaken the barrel vaults at their **springing**, where they would need the most support, Santiago de Compostela was built without a clerestory. Since a vault becomes more difficult to sustain the farther it is from the ground, every resource had to be mined to enable the nave to be as tall as possible. The galleries built over the inner aisles counterbalance the lateral pressure of the nave vault. Inside the nave, vaults, arches, engaged colonnettes, and pilasters are all firmly knit together into a coherent order that recaptures the vocabulary and syntax of ancient Roman architecture to a remarkable degree. Diffused light, subtle and atmospheric, filters into the nave through the side aisles and the galleries above. What function the galleries served is much debated. Conceivably they provided overflow space for the large numbers of pilgrims who visited the church, particularly on feast days, and indeed the famous *Pilgrim's Guide*, written around 1130, mentions the presence of altars in the galleries. But the galleries also provide for an elegantly elaborated interior, as the *Pilgrim's Guide* also makes clear:

> In truth, in this church no fissure or fault is found; it is admirably constructed, grand, spacious, bright, of proper magnitude, harmonious in width, length and height, of admirable and ineffable workmanship, built in two storys, just like a royal palace. For indeed, whoever visits the naves of the gallery, if he goes up sad, after having seen the perfect beauty of this temple, he will be made happy and joyful.

Pilgrim's Guide to Santiago de Compostela: A Critical Edition, II, ed. and tr. Paula Gerson, Annie Shaver Crandell, Alison Stones, and Jeanne Krochalis (London: Harvey Miller Publishers, 1998)

The synthesis of emotional and spiritual response described in the *Pilgrim's Guide* results from the Romanesque builders' ability to fuse structure and aesthetics. In another section of his book, the *Guide*'s author notes with admiration the quality of the stonework, as "hard as marble." By using a simile that compares the stone used to build the cathedral with the quintessential building material of the Classical past, he clearly expresses a fact that

eastern walls of the transepts and around the apse, provided multiple opportunities to display the relics that pilgrims had come to venerate (fig. **11.4**). As pilgrims approached the nave from the west entrance and walked through the building, they were conscious of marching step by step toward their goals in the apses, altars, and reliquaries at the east end of the church (fig. **11.5**).

Passage through the cathedral was thus a microcosm of the longer journey the pilgrims had taken on the open road, and as such Santiago de Compostela might readily be called a **pilgrimage plan** church. A group of great churches of varying sizes and details, using the same pilgrimage plan, were built along the roads leading to Compostela. Major churches built to this plan are situated on each of the four main roads leading through France: Saint-Martin at Tours (on the road from Paris), Saint-Martial at Limoges (on the road from Vézelay), Sainte-Foy at Conques (on

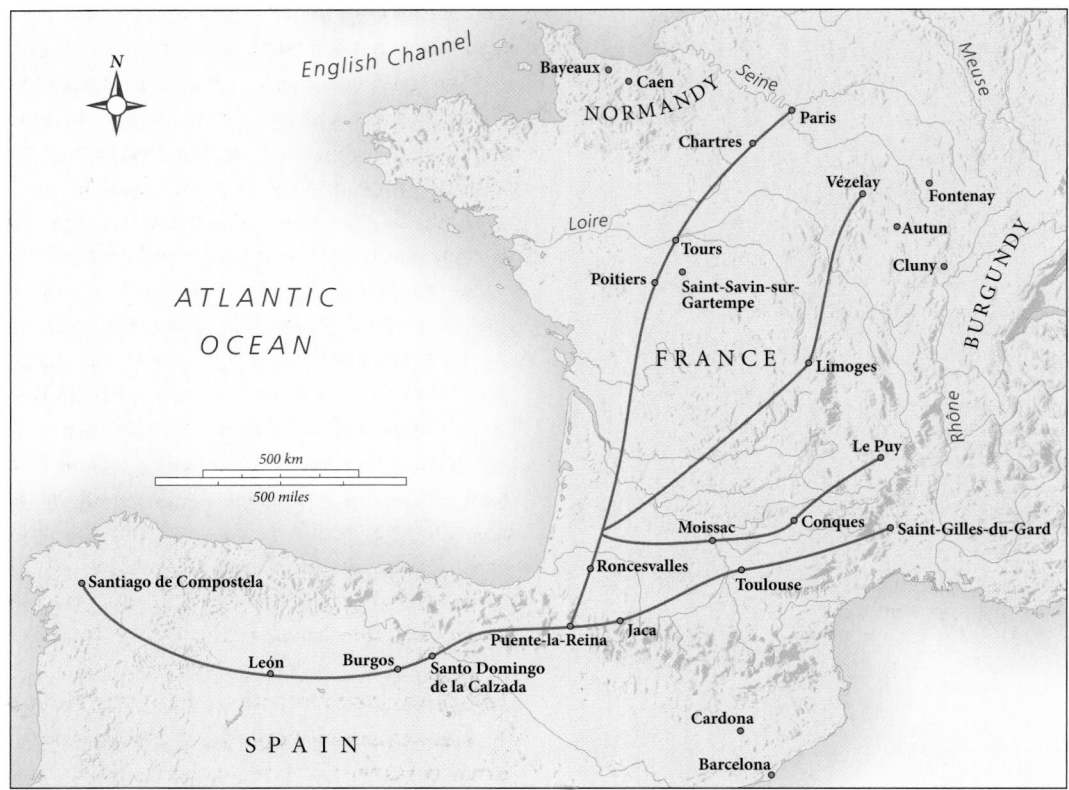

Map 11.2   The Pilgrimage routes to Santiago de Compostela

viewers today can still appreciate—that in both detail and execution Santiago de Compostela emulates the nobility and dignity of Roman architecture.

RELIQUARIES   A twelfth-century casket, today in the Metropolitan Museum of Art in New York (fig. **11.6**), is typical of the kinds of decorated reliquaries that pilgrims saw on their journeys to Compostela and Rome. This one was probably made in Limoges, a major stop on the road to Compostela and a center of enamel production, where there was a large church built according to the pilgrimage plan. The material and the bold areas of flat color, evident in both the foliage and the symbols of the four evangelists, relate this work to the tradition of migration and early medieval metalwork (see fig. 10.3). The method of manufacture is **champlevé**, which was derived from the cloisonné technique (see page 315). Instead of cells formed from thin strips of metal attached to a support, as with cloisonné, the metal surface is gouged out to create compartments that contain the colored

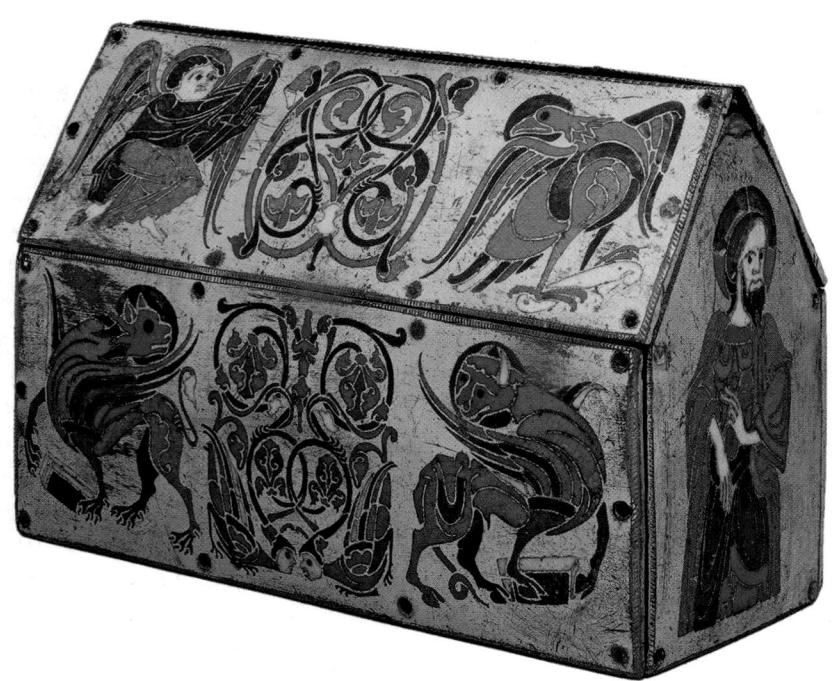

11.6   Reliquary casket with symbols of the four Evangelists. ca. 1150. Champlevé enamel on gilt copper, 4⅞ × 7⁷/₁₆ × 3⅜" (12.4 × 18.9 × 8.5 cm). Metropolitan Museum of Art, New York. Gift of J. Pierpont Morgan, 1917 (17.190.685-687, 695, 710–11)

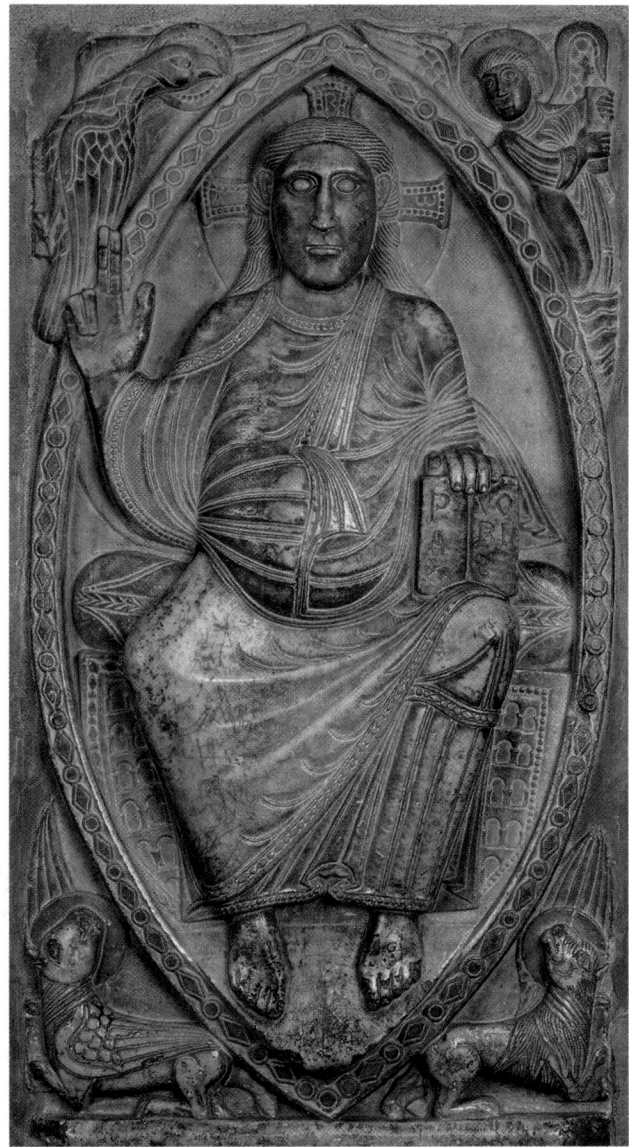

11.7 *Christ in Majesty* (*Maiestas Domini*), Saint-Sernin, Toulouse, France. ca. 1096. Marble, height 50" (127 cm)

enamel. The preciousness of the enamel on the gilt copper of our reliquary and its lavish decoration suit its exceptional and holy contents, thought to be relics of St. Martial, identified by inscription on the other side of the box, since the reliquary comes from a church dedicated to him in Champagnat, about 60 miles (96 km) from Limoges.

MONUMENTAL SCULPTURE Many of the churches along the pilgrimage route had elaborate sculptural programs decorating their interiors and portals. A series of large marble plaques, currently placed in the ambulatory of Saint-Sernin in Toulouse, located on the pilgrimage route that cuts across southern France (see map 11.2), dates to the years immediately preceding 1100. Six of these plaques depict angels and apostles, while one represents a seated Christ, the *Christ in Majesty* (fig. **11.7**). Although their original location is not certain, the plaques most likely decorated

the zone around the altar and shrine of St. Sernin, thus embellishing an area deemed particularly holy by pilgrims.

The shallow relief and many decorative effects of the Christ plaque recall earlier metalwork and ivory objects (see figs. 10.16 and 10.31). The extensive use of double lines, some creating raised sections, some impressed ones, enhances the figure's volumetric presence. The treatment also brings to mind manuscript illumination, particularly Carolingian and Ottonian examples, but also Byzantine ones. In the arrangement of the figure, the play of linear drapery folds, and the variety of ornamental devices, we are not far from the Christ of the *Godescalc Gospels* (see fig. 10.12), which was in Saint-Sernin during the Middle Ages.

The figure of Christ, somewhat more than half life-size, was not meant to be viewed exclusively at close range. Its impressive bulk and weight make it prominent even from a considerable distance. This emphasis on volume hints at what may have been the main inspiration behind the revival of large-scale sculpture: A stone-carved image, being solid and three-dimensional, is far more "real" than a painted one.

SECULAR STRUCTURES ALONG THE PILGRIMAGE ROAD

A complex infrastructure was needed to service an enterprise as extensive as the pilgrimage to Compostela. Establishments such as hospices and hospitals provided for the needs of pilgrims. Improved roads and bridges were of particular importance, and a number of Spanish monarchs of the eleventh and twelfth centuries took their construction as essential goals, both to support pilgrims coming to Spain and to encourage closer relationships abroad, particularly with France. Such connections aimed to strengthen Christian foundations in Spain, a reaction to the Muslim presence in the Iberian peninsula. Holy stature was often credited to people who built and maintained the actual roads on which pilgrims trekked, as was the case with Santo Domingo de la Calzada (literally "of the paved road" or "roadway"), who built, in addition to a pilgrims' hostel and hospital, a long bridge over the Oja River and who maintained the roads around the town that came to be named after him.

THE BRIDGE AT PUENTE LA REINA Almost a week before arriving in the town of Santo Domingo de la Calzada, pilgrims would have crossed a large, stately bridge in the town of Puente la Reina (fig. **11.8**). The town's name derives from that mid-twelfth-century bridge (*puente* in Spanish), around which a settlement developed. Seven round-headed arches, only six of which survive today, formed the original bridge. The largest, central arch and the flanking arches, which decrease in span, fall on large pillars that are buttressed by wedge-shaped cutwaters, designed to break the current. Open arches fill the **spandrels**, the areas between the curves of two adjoining arches, and serve at once the physical function of lightening the weight of the bridge and the visual function of establishing, along with the arches of the bridge itself, a stepped rhythm that accentuates the structure's purpose to facilitate passage. The bridge is 350 feet long and nearly 10 feet wide, while its central arch spans 65 feet, a daring achievement for

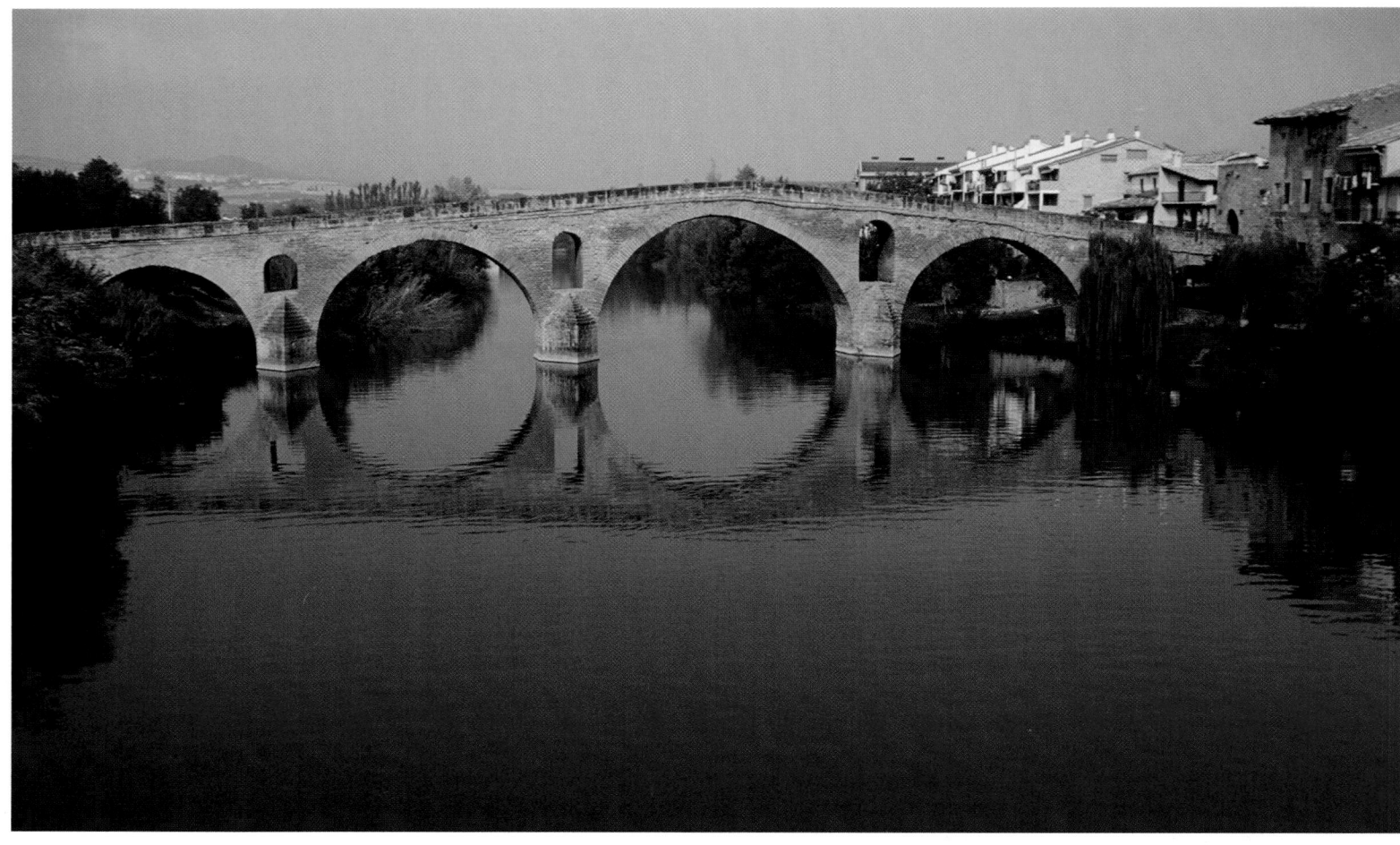

11.8 Bridge over the Arga River, Puente la Reina, Spain. 11th century

the period and one that helps account for its fame. A little chapel in the center of the bridge was destroyed in the nineteenth century and around the same time towers at each end were razed, though one was reconstructed in the middle of the last century. The bridge was undoubtedly the result of royal patronage, as is reflected by its name (*reina* means queen in Spanish), although which queen commissioned it is an unresolved question. Even though crossing the bridge at Puente la Reina would have required payment of a toll, or a charge to cross it, the *Pilgrim's Guide* makes clear the benefits accrued from avoiding ferrymen, infamous for the exorbitant prices they charged as well as for their treachery:

> Upon leaving this country, the way of Saint James crosses two rivers which ... can not be crossed without a barque [boat]— may their boatmen be utterly damned! For, although the rivers are quite narrow, nevertheless, they are in the habit of getting one *nummus* [coin] from every person, poor as well as rich, whom they ferry across, and for a beast four, which they undeservedly extort. ... When you get in, be careful not to fall into the water by accident. ... If the boat is overladen with too many people, it will soon be in peril. Many times also, after receiving the money, the ferrymen take on such a throng of pilgrims that the boat tips over, and the pilgrims are killed in the water. Thereupon the ferrymen rejoice wickedly after seizing the spoils from the dead.

> *Pilgrim's Guide to Santiago de Compostela:*
> *A Critical Edition*, II
> ed. and tr. Paula Gerson, Annie Shaver Crandell,
> Alison Stones, and Jeanne Krochalis
> (London: Harvey Miller Publishers, 1998)

Cluniac Architecture and Sculpture

During the time when the sculptural decoration of Saint-Sernin was executed, the church was under the auspices of monks from the great Benedictine monastery of Cluny. Cluny was responsible for a network of dependencies; its "daughter" houses, spread across Europe, numbered more than 1,400, including a number of monasteries located on the pilgrimage road that served the needs of pilgrims. The Cluniac order's influence and growth were remarkable. The order could determine papal elections and call for crusades against the Muslims. The rise and spread of various monastic orders was significant for the development of Romanesque art, but none was more important than Cluny.

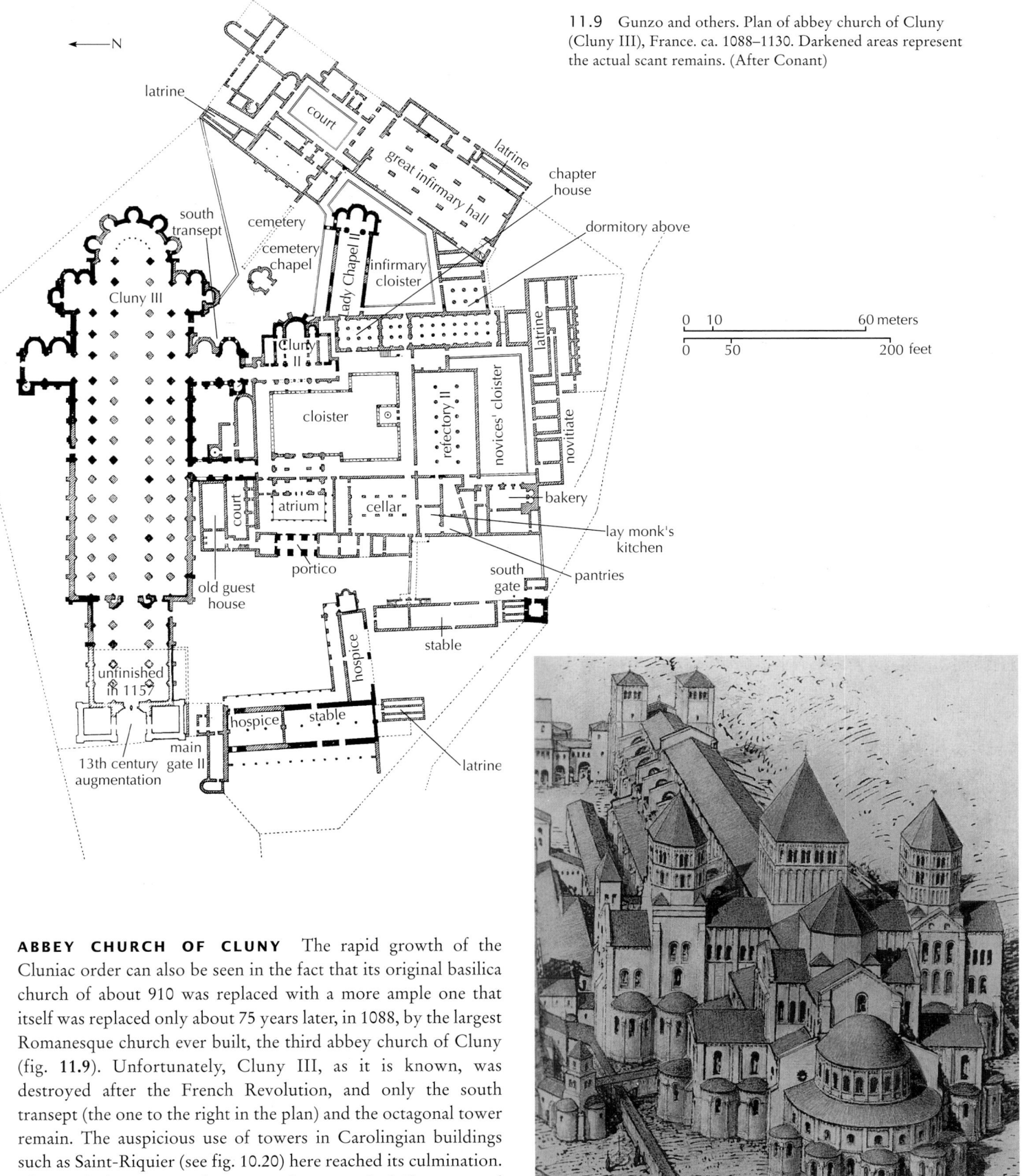

latrine

court

great infirmary hall

latrine

chapter house

11.9 Gunzo and others. Plan of abbey church of Cluny (Cluny III), France. ca. 1088–1130. Darkened areas represent the actual scant remains. (After Conant)

south transept

cemetery

cemetery chapel

Lady Chapel II

infirmary cloister

dormitory above

Cluny III

Cluny II

latrine

cloister

refectory II

novices' cloister

novitiate

0 10   60 meters
0   50   200 feet

atrium

cellar

bakery

court

lay monk's kitchen

old guest house

portico

south gate

pantries

stable

hospice

unfinished in 1157

hospice   stable

13th century augmentation

main gate II

latrine

ABBEY CHURCH OF CLUNY The rapid growth of the Cluniac order can also be seen in the fact that its original basilica church of about 910 was replaced with a more ample one that itself was replaced only about 75 years later, in 1088, by the largest Romanesque church ever built, the third abbey church of Cluny (fig. **11.9**). Unfortunately, Cluny III, as it is known, was destroyed after the French Revolution, and only the south transept (the one to the right in the plan) and the octagonal tower remain. The auspicious use of towers in Carolingian buildings such as Saint-Riquier (see fig. 10.20) here reached its culmination. The apsidioles, apses, and towers at the east end of Cluny created a monumental gathering of ever-higher forms. Individual elements functioned together in built harmony (fig. **11.10**); the south transept with octagonal tower at its crossing is on the left in this reconstruction.

11.10 Reconstruction of abbey church of Cluny (Cluny III), from east (after Conant)

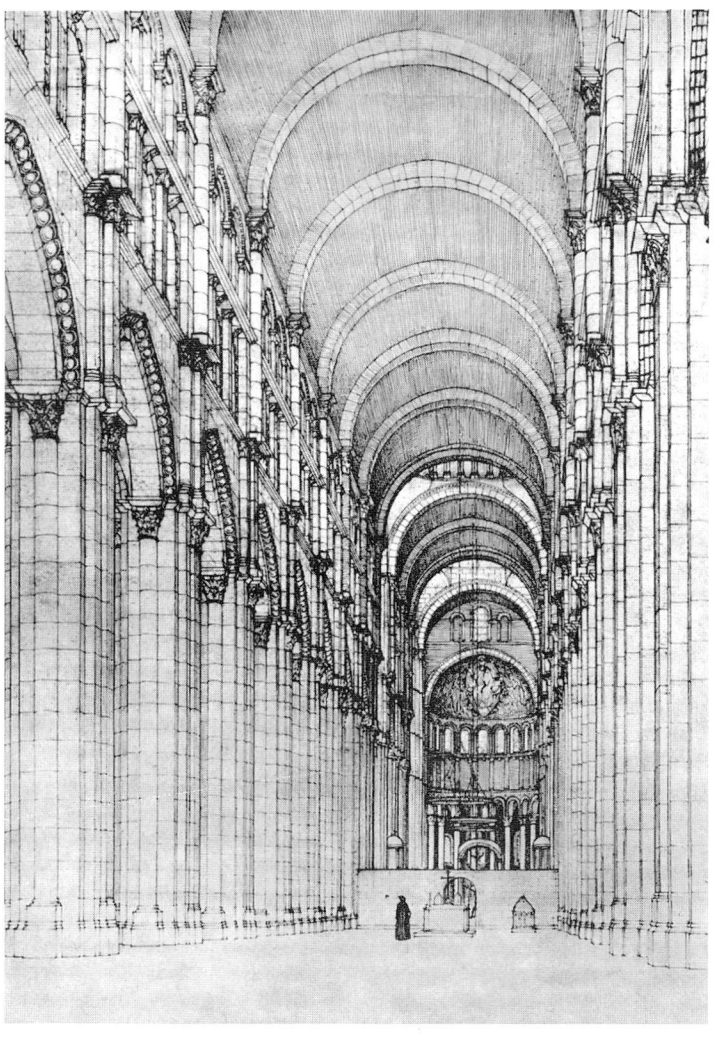

11.11   Reconstruction of abbey church of Cluny (Cluny III), nave and interior (after Conant)

The proportions of Cluny III were based on ratios of "perfect" numbers and on musical harmonies, reminding us of the importance of music in the medieval Church. Monks chanted their prayers eight times a day and Gunzo, one of the architects of Cluny III, was noted for his musicianship. A benefit of stone-vaulted buildings was their acoustic resonance; this feature might well have encouraged the widespread use of stone vaulting or at least made the heavy financial investment acceptable to the community. Even today, it is a moving experience to hear Gregorian chants sung beneath the vaults of a Romanesque church.

The interior of Cluny III (fig. **11.11**) was as elegant as it was huge, its vaults reaching 100 feet. Below the clerestory, and in place of a gallery, was a **triforium**, the series of three-arched openings (one series per bay); the triforium, which is closed to the outside of the building, creates a space within the wall, barely sufficient to allow passage, that lightens it both physically and visually. The clerestory and triforium are connected by pilaster strips with Corinthian capitals, reminiscent of Roman architectural decoration. What is not Roman is the use of slightly pointed arches in the nave arcade, a device thought to derive from contact with Islamic culture (see fig. 9.12). By eliminating the center part of the rounded arch, which responds the most to the pull of gravity, the two halves of a pointed arch brace each other. Because the pointed arch exerts less outward pressure than the semicircular arch, not only can it be made steeper, but the walls can be pierced (with windows and triforium arcades) and thus made lighter.

MONASTERY OF MOISSAC The priory of Saint-Pierre at Moissac, located on the pilgrimage road close to Toulouse and also under the direction of Cluny, was another important center of Romanesque art. The cloister, adjacent to the church and

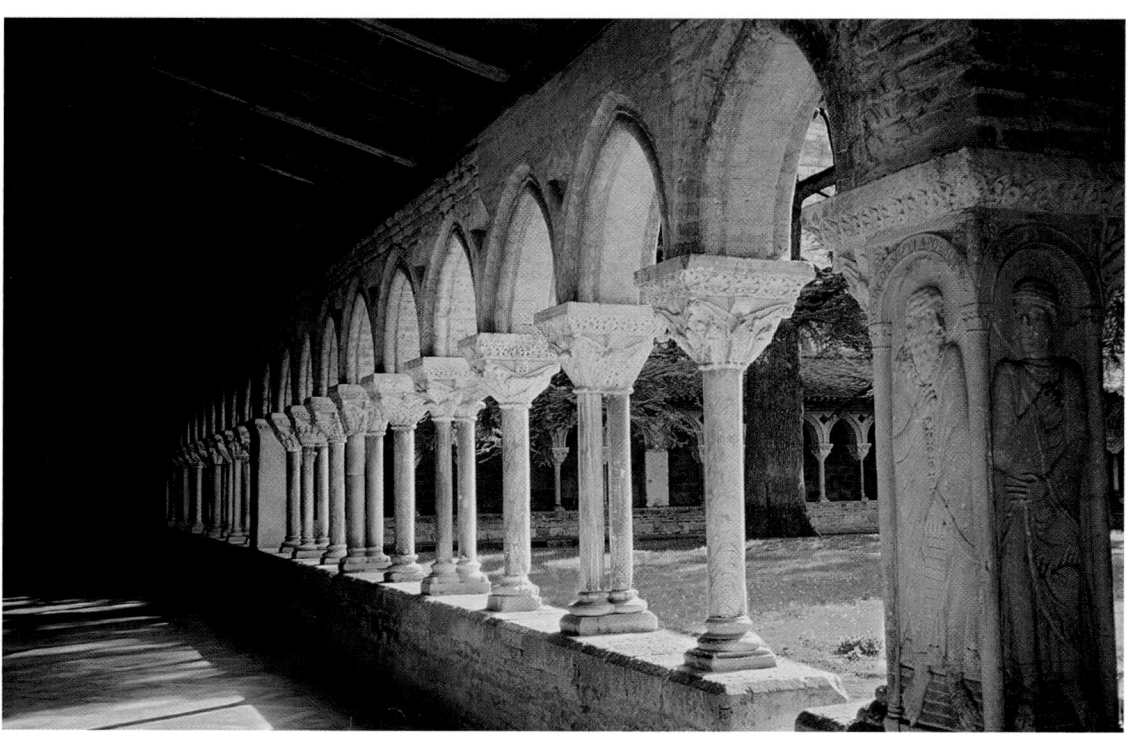

11.12   Cloister, priory of Saint-Pierre, Moissac, France. ca. 1100

St. Bernard of Clairvaux (1090–1153)

From *Apologia to Abbot William of Saint-Thierry*

Bernard of Clairvaux was a member of the Cistercians, an ascetic order founded in the eleventh century in opposition to the increasing opulence of the Benedictines. His letter to the Benedictine abbot William of Saint-Thierry of around 1127 denounces all monastic luxury, especially the presence of art in cloisters. Like many others, Bernard believed that monks were spiritually superior to the "carnal" layfolk and so should not need material inducements to devotion.

As a monk, I put to monks the same question that a pagan used to criticize other pagans: "Tell me, priests," he said, "what is gold doing in the holy place?" I, however, say … "Tell me, poor men, if indeed you are poor men, what is gold doing in the holy place?" For certainly bishops have one kind of business, and monks another. We [monks] know that since they [bishops] are responsible for both the wise and the foolish, they stimulate the devotion of a carnal people with material ornaments because they cannot do so with spiritual ones. But we who have withdrawn from the people, we who have left behind all that is precious and beautiful in this world for the sake of Christ, we who regard as dung all things shining in beauty, soothing in sound, agreeable in fragrance, sweet in taste, pleasant in touch—in short, all material pleasures— … whose devotion, I ask, do we strive to excite in all this? …

Does not avarice, which is in the service of idols, cause all this? Money is sown with such skill that it may be multiplied. … The very sight of these costly but wonderful illusions inflames men more to give than to pray. In this way wealth is derived from wealth. Eyes are fixed on relics covered with gold and purses are opened. The thoroughly beautiful image of some male or female saint is exhibited and that saint is believed to be the more holy the more highly colored the image is. People rush to kiss it, they are invited to donate, and they admire the beautiful more than they venerate the sacred. … What do you think is being sought in all this? The compunction of penitents, or the astonishment of those who gaze at it? O vanity of vanities! The Church is radiant in its walls and destitute in its poor. It serves the eyes of the rich at the expense of the poor. It dresses its stone in gold and it abandons its children naked. The curious find that which may delight them, but those in need do not find that which should sustain them.

But apart from this, in the cloisters, before the eyes of the brothers while they read—what is that ridiculous monstrosity doing, an amazing kind of deformed beauty and yet a beautiful deformity? What are the filthy apes doing there? The fierce lions? The monstrous centaurs? The creatures, part man and part beast? The striped tigers? The fighting soldiers? The hunters blowing horns? You may see many bodies under one head, and conversely many heads on one body. On one side the tail of a serpent is seen on a quadruped, on the other side the head of a quadruped is on the body of a fish. Over there an animal has a horse for the front half and a goat for the back; here a creature which is horned in front is equine behind. In short, everywhere so plentiful and astonishing a variety of contradictory forms is seen that one would rather read in the marble than in books, and spend the whole day wondering at every single one of them than in meditating on the law of God. Good God! If one is not ashamed of the absurdity, why is one not at least troubled at the expense?

Source: Conrad Rudolph, *The "Things of Greater Importance": Bernard of Clairvaux's Apologia and the Medieval Attitude Toward Art* (Philadelphia: University of Pennsylvania Press, 1990)

reserved for the use of its monks, was formed by four covered passageways arranged around an open garden (fig. **11.12**). Protected from the elements, the monks could practice their spiritual exercises here; they used the zone for a variety of other functions as well. The cloister was central to monastic life and physically occupied a central position within the monastic complex, as is seen in the St. Gall and Cluny plans. Seventy-six sculptured capitals decorate this private zone. While they include representations of Bible stories, many are decorated with foliage, birds, animals, and monstrous creatures.

Although the Romanesque period is far removed chronologically from the Early Christian aversion to image making, even during this period there were those who objected to the corrupting power of visual representation. One of them was St. Bernard of Clairvaux, a member of the Cistercian order, a reform movement created around 1100 in part as a reaction to the increasing economic and political successes of Cluny and in order to provide a monastic life more in keeping with St. Benedict's rules (see pages 330–31). In truth, it is hard to correlate the worldly achievements of a monastery such as that at Moissac or at Cluny—the wealth they acquired and the political clout they exercised—with the values to which monks traditionally aspired, which were based on the renunciation of earthly pleasures in favor of the pursuit of spiritual ideals. The pictorial representation of Christian themes was often justified by a famous saying: *Quod legentibus scriptura, hoc idiotis … pictura.* Translated freely, this means that painting conveys the Word of God to the unlettered. Although St. Bernard did not object specifically to the teaching role of art, he had little use for church decoration and would surely have disapproved of the Moissac cloister's excesses, which were clearly meant to appeal to the eye as well as the spirit. In a letter of 1127 to Abbot William of Saint-Thierry concerning the decoration of churches, St. Bernard condemned art made for contemplation by monks. (See *Primary Source*, above.)

If the Moissac monks had a profusion of sculpture to engage them, so too did pilgrims and layfolk visiting the monastery's church. Its elaborately sculptured portal (fig. **11.13**) was executed almost a generation after the cloister was finished. It displays the parts of a typical Romanesque portal (fig. **11.14**). Christ in Majesty takes center stage in the **tympanum**, the lunette above the lintel of the portal. He is shown during his Second Coming, when he returns to Earth after the apocalyptic end of days, as described in the book of Revelation (4:1–8), in order to judge mortals as saved or damned. In accordance with the biblical

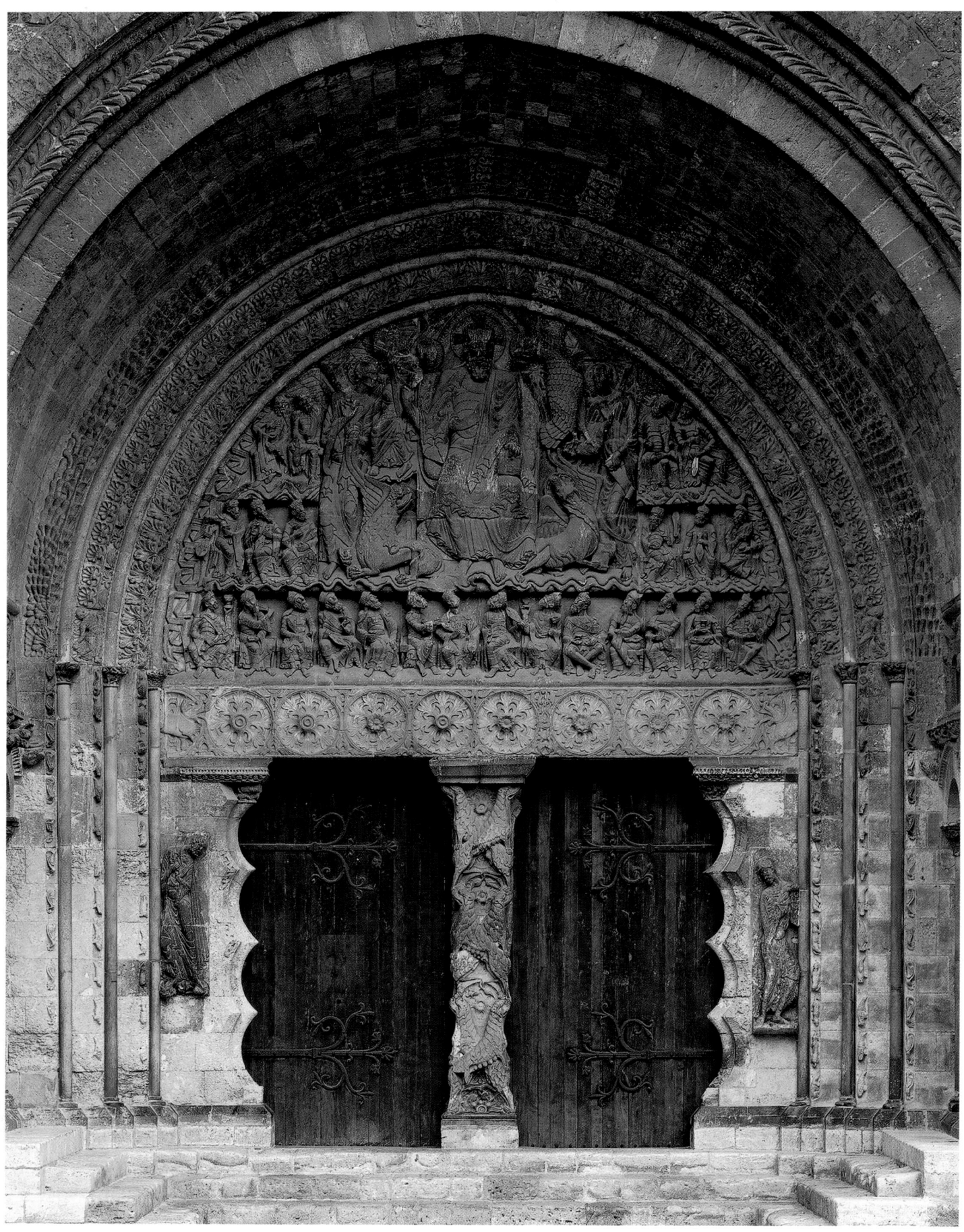

11.13 South portal with *Second Coming of Christ* on tympanum, church of Saint-Pierre, Moissac. ca. 1115–30

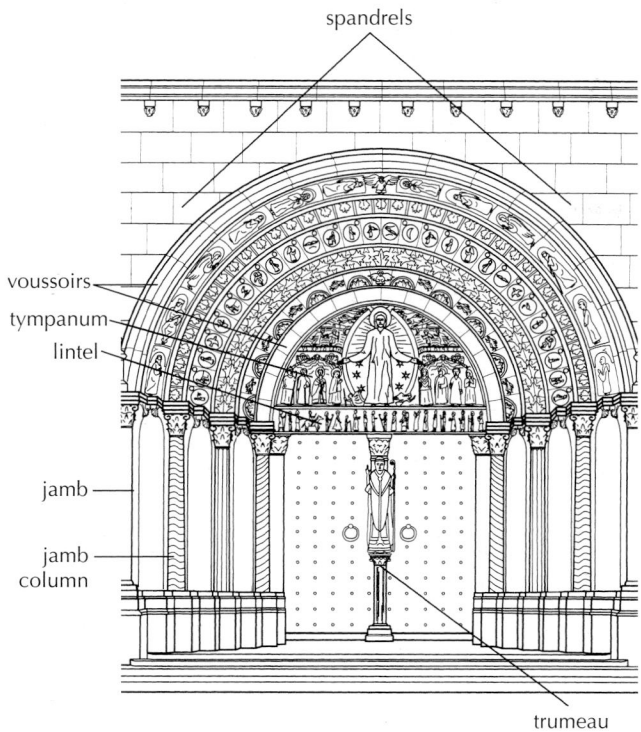

11.14 Romanesque portal ensemble

spandrels

voussoirs

tympanum

lintel

jamb

jamb column

trumeau

---

turns his head toward the interior of the church as he unfurls his scroll. The crossed lions that form a symmetrical zigzag on the face of the trumeau "animate" the shaft the same way the interlacing beasts of Irish miniatures (from which they are descended) enliven the spaces they inhabit.

We can trace the crossed lions through textiles to Persian metalwork, although not in this towerlike formation. Ultimately they descend from the heraldic animals of ancient Near Eastern art (see fig. 2.9). Yet we cannot account for their presence at Moissac in terms of their effectiveness as ornament alone. They belong to an extensive family of savage or monstrous creatures in Romanesque art that retain their demoniacal vitality even as they are forced to perform a supporting function. Their purpose is thus not only decorative but expressive; they embody dark forces that have been domesticated into guardian figures or banished to a position that holds them fixed for all eternity, however much they may snarl in protest. One medieval bishop argued that seeing animals sculpted in churches would so terrify parishioners that they would be encouraged to refrain from sinful deeds.

account, Christ is attended by four beasts, which accompany two angels and 24 elders, while wavy lines beneath their feet represent "the sea of glass like crystal." The elders, relatively small compared with the other figures, and many of them gesticulating, can barely contain their excitement in the face of the remarkable vision. Abstraction and activity characterize the style of carving, in which quivering lines, borders of meandering ribbon patterns, and fluttering drapery offset a hierarchy of scale and pose. The use of abstraction in the service of religious zeal has parallels in earlier medieval art, for example the manuscript illuminations of the *Ebbo Gospel Book* (see fig. 10.14) and the *Utrecht Psalter* (see fig. 10.15). At Moissac, however, the presentation is on a monumental, public scale.

Other parts of the Moissac portal are also treated sculpturally. Both the **trumeau** (the center post supporting the lintel) and the jambs (the sides of the doorway) have scalloped outlines (see fig. 11.13), modeled on a popular Islamic device. By borrowing forms from the art of Islam at Moissac and other churches, Christians were expressing their admiration and regard for Arab artistic achievements. At the same time, such acts of appropriation could also express the Christian ambition to dominate the Muslim enemy. The pilgrimage to Santiago was a similar manifestation of anti-Islamic feeling.

The scalloped outlines framing the doorway activate and dramatize the experience of entering the church. Human and animal forms are treated with flexibility. For instance, the spidery prophet on the side of the trumeau seems perfectly adapted to his precarious perch, even as he struggles to free himself from the stone (fig. **11.15**). With legs crossed in a graceful movement, he

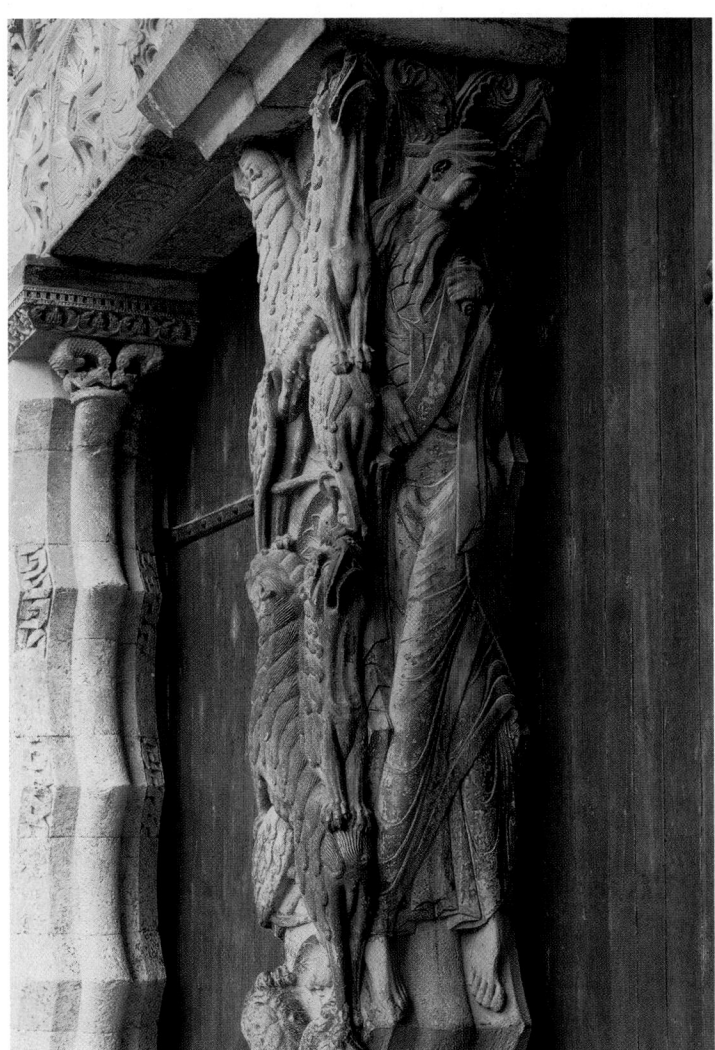

11.15 Trumeau and jambs, south portal, church of Saint-Pierre, Moissac

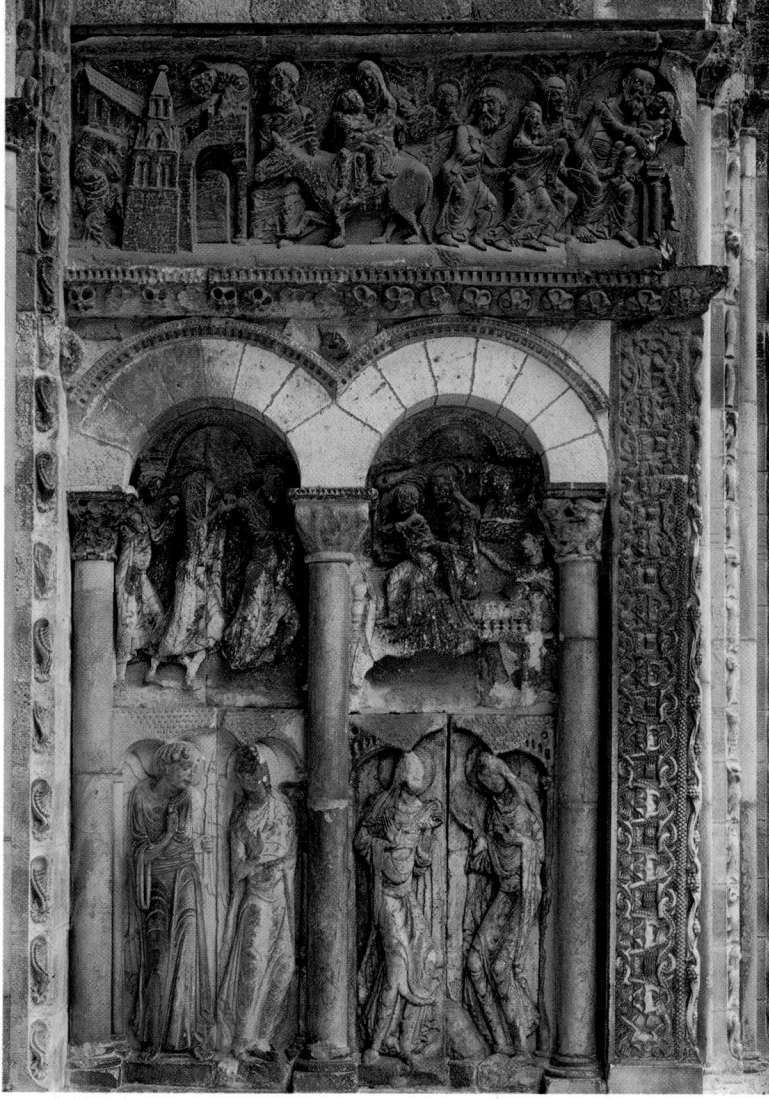

11.16   East flank, south portal, church of Saint-Pierre, Moissac

church. The journey into the church became a veritable rite of passage, transformative both physically and spiritually.

CATHEDRAL OF SAINT-LAZARE, AUTUN Close to Cluny and dependent on it was the cathedral of Saint-Lazare at Autun. The tympanum of its west portal (fig. **11.17**) represents the Last Judgment, the most awe-inspiring scene in Christian art. This scene depicts Christ after his Second Coming as he separates those who will be eternally saved from those who are damned. His figure, much larger than any other, dominates the tympanum. The sculptor, Gislebertus, whose signature appears immediately under the feet of Christ in the center of the tympanum, treats the subject with extraordinary force. Gislebertus is only one of a number of Romanesque sculptors with distinct artistic personalities who are known to us by name. His style is sufficiently individual to enable scholars to posit convincingly that he trained at Cluny before his elevation to master's rank at Autun.

On the left side of the tympanum, apostles observe the weighing of souls, which takes place on the right side. Four angels in the corners sound the trumpets of the Apocalypse. At the bottom, the dead rise from their graves, trembling with fear; some are already beset by snakes or gripped by huge, clawlike hands. Above, their fate quite literally hangs in the balance, with devils yanking at one end of the scales and angels at the other. The saved souls cling like children to the angels for protection before their ascent to the heavenly Jerusalem (far left), while the condemned, seized by grinning devils, are cast into the mouth of Hell (far right). These nightmarish devils are human in general outline, but they have birdlike legs, furry thighs, tails, pointed ears, and savage mouths. The hierarchical, abstract, and patterned representation of Christ conveys his formidable power more effectively than any naturalistic image could. No visitor who had "read in the marble" (to quote St. Bernard of Clairvaux) could fail to enter the church in a chastened spirit.

The Last Judgment, with its emphasis on retribution, was a standard subject for the tympana of Romanesque churches. It was probably chosen because some medieval justice was dispensed in front of the church portal, *ante ecclesium*. Thus, actual judicial proceedings paralleled the divine judgment represented here. Trial was by ordeal, whereby the accused established innocence only by withstanding grueling physical tests. The ordeals must, in reality, have been as terrifying as the scenes depicted on the tympanum.

The outer **archivolt** (a molded band forming an arch) surrounding the west tympanum on Autun's cathedral is composed of medallions containing calendar scenes, comprised, in typical medieval fashion, of the signs of the zodiac and the corresponding labors of the months. The calendar serves to place the fearsome events of the Last Judgment within cosmological time, that is, within the physical realm that all of us occupy on earth.

The north portal of the cathedral was dismantled in the eighteenth century but Gislebertus's *Eve* (fig. **11.18**), a fragment of the lintel, survives in the Musée Rolin. It demonstrates the master's incredibly expressive range. The relief was balanced on the other

A deep porch with lavishly sculptured lateral ends frames the Moissac portal. Within an arcade on the east flank (fig. **11.16**), we see, on the lower left, the Annunciation to the Virgin, and to the right, the Visitation (when Mary visits her cousin Elizabeth, mother of John the Baptist, to announce that she is pregnant), and the Adoration of the Magi in the top two panels under the arches. (The angel of the Annunciation is a modern replacement.) Other events from the early life of Jesus are on the frieze above. All of the figures have the same thin limbs and eloquent gestures as the prophet on the trumeau. On the west flank, not illustrated here, is a representation of the vice of *luxuria* (lust), presented as antithetical to the virtue of the Virgin Mary. The juxtaposition recalls the pairing during the early Middle Ages of Eve's sinfulness with Mary's purity (see fig. 10.27). The messages at Moissac are patently didactic, meant both to command and to enlighten. When visitors on the pilgrim road faced the deep portal of the church they were virtually surrounded by the sculptural program, and this intensified the liminal experience of crossing into the

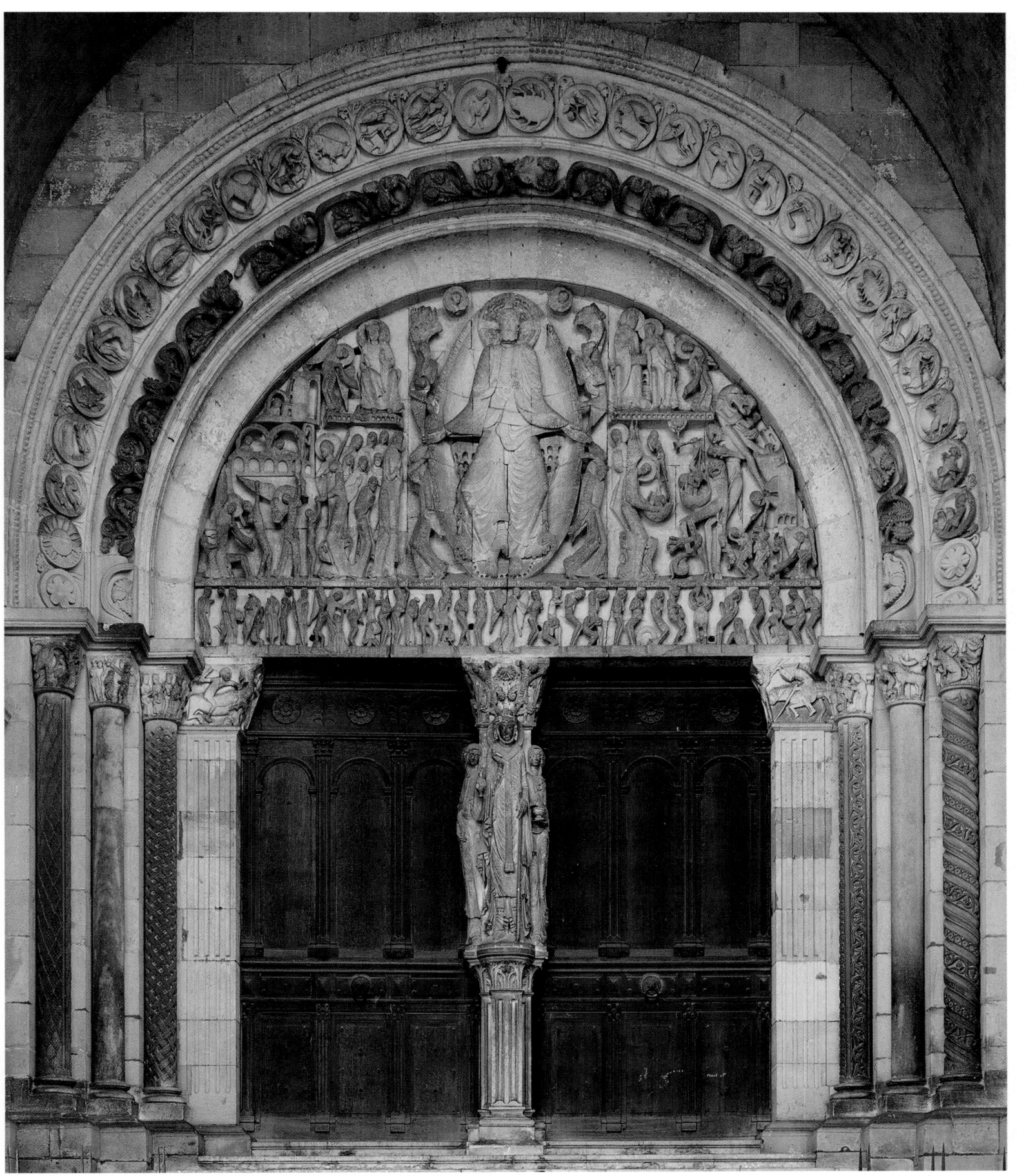

11.17 West portal, with *Last Judgment* by Gislebertus on tympanum, cathedral of Saint-Lazare, Autun, France. ca. 1120–35

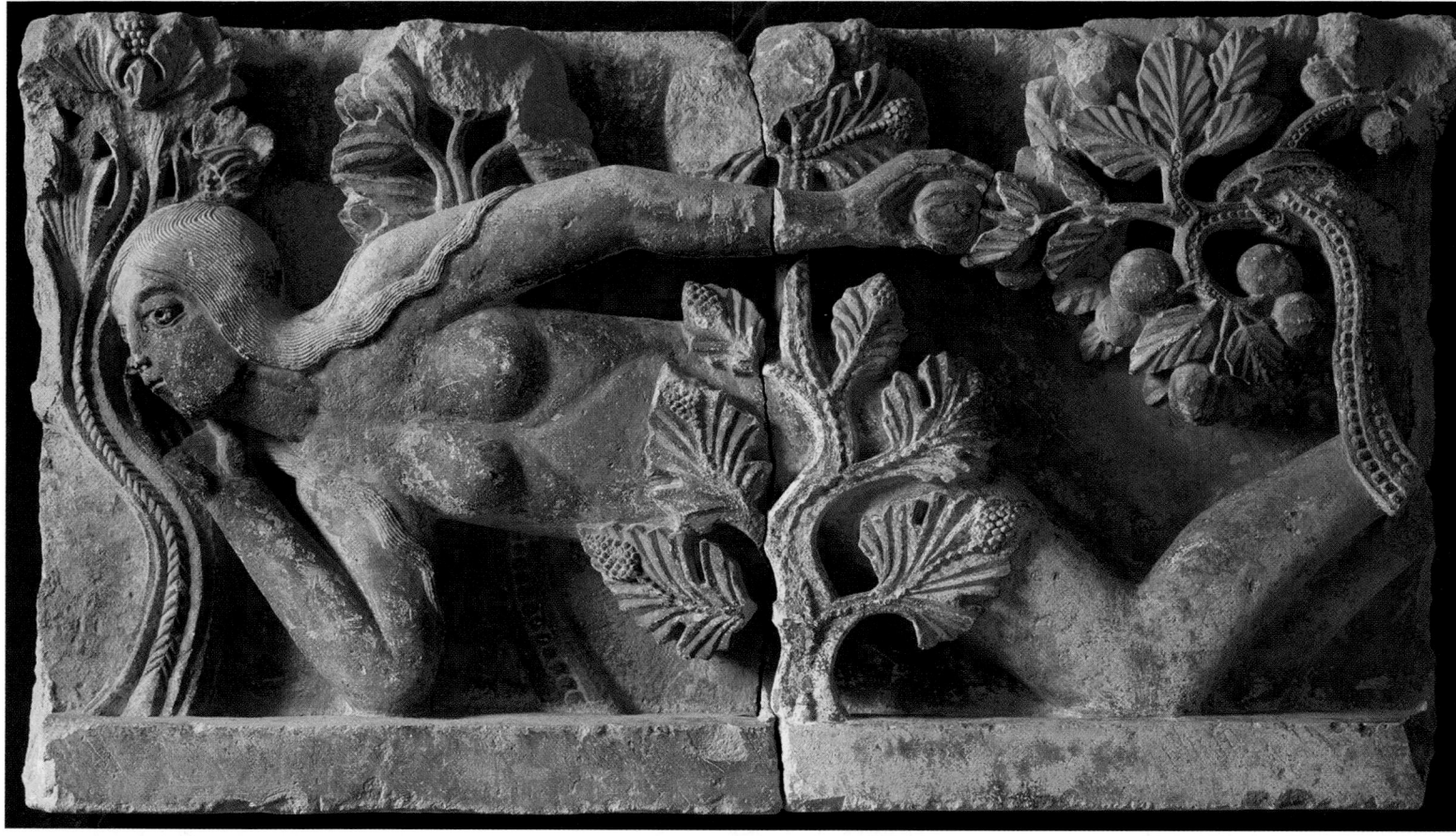

11.18 Gislebertus, *Eve*, right half of lintel, north portal, from cathedral of Saint-Lazare, Autun, France. 1120–32. 28½ × 51" (72.4 × 129.5 cm). Musée Rolin, Autun

side of the lintel by a representation of Adam. Once again the choice of subjects undoubtedly relates to the portal's liturgical function, since public penitential rites took place in front of the north portal. Adam and Eve's sin—the original one, after all—was mentioned in the penitential liturgy, in which sinners, seeking forgiveness for their transgressions, participated. In the relief, Eve's delicate gestures of grasping the fruit and touching her cheek as if in contemplation result in a beguiling, sensual silhouette. Her posture is not merely the consequence of the narrow horizontal space she occupies; rather, her pose emulates a slithering earthbound serpent, so she is temptress as well as tempted. As we saw on the bronze doors of Bishop Bernward at Hildesheim (see fig. 10.27), in medieval eyes Eve symbolized the base enchantments embodied by all worldly women.

SARCOPHAGUS OF DOÑA SANCHA A different view of women can be seen in the stone sarcophagus created around 1120 to house the remains of Doña Sancha, a princess of the kingdom of Aragon in northern Spain. Aragon had strong ties to Cluny; about 50 years before Sancha's sarcophagus was carved, her brother, King Sancho Ramírez, undertook a Cluniac reform of the monasteries in his kingdom. This was part of his efforts to strengthen Christian foundations in Spain, a reaction to the Muslim presence on the Iberian peninsula.

At the center of one side of the sarcophagus (fig. **11.19**), two angels support a nude figure in a mandorla, representing the soul of the deceased being lifted to Heaven, an appropriate subject for a funerary monument. On the left, three clerics under an arch perform a Mass for the dead, and on the right, two women, probably Sancha's sisters, stand under an arch and flank the enthroned princess. The arrangement in this right panel, which proclaims the dignity and importance of the larger central figure of Sancha, relies on an antique tradition, seen, for example, on the fourth-century *Sarcophagus of Junius Bassus* (see fig. 8.20).

On the other side of the sarcophagus are three mounted figures, each under an arch. Two armed horsemen confront each other, while the third straddles a lion and grasps its open jaws with his hands. The most compelling interpretation of the confronted horsemen identifies them as combatants in the struggle between good and evil, a common subject in Christian art. The lion rider in the right arcade has variously been identified as the long-haired Samson or the youthful David, both Hebrew Bible prototypes for the Christian struggle against evil.

Sancha was a key figure in her kingdom at a time when the Aragonese kings were fighting to conquer Spain from the Muslims, who then held sway over much of the Iberian peninsula. That scenes of battle, even ones that can be symbolically or allegorically interpreted, were considered appropriate for the

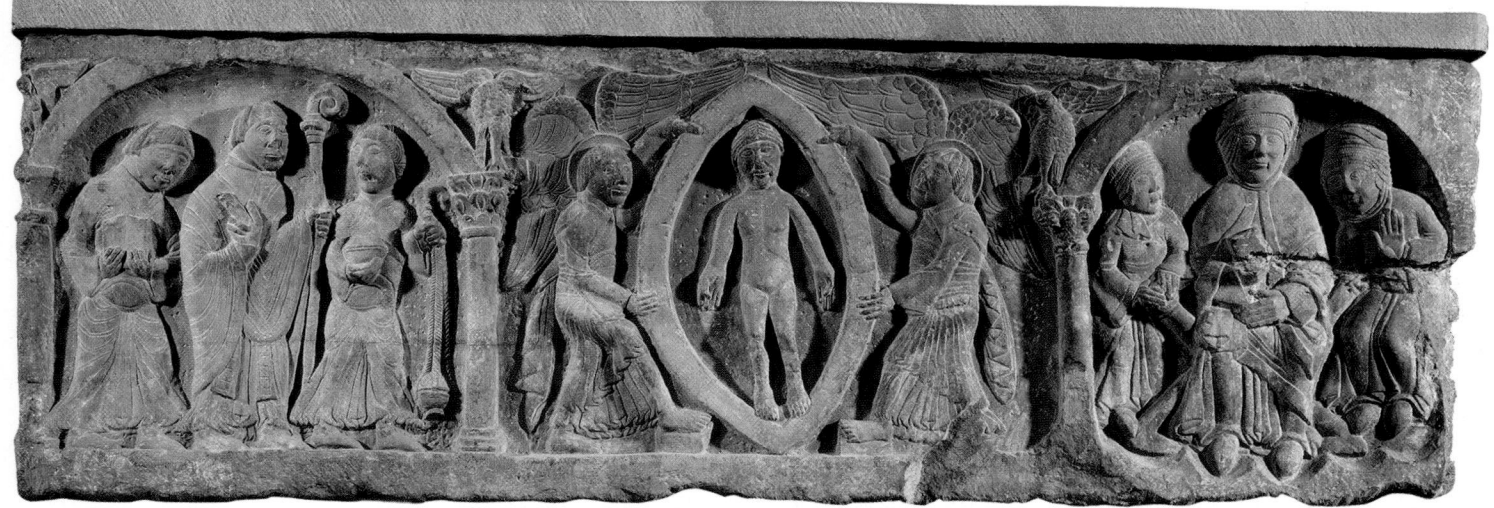

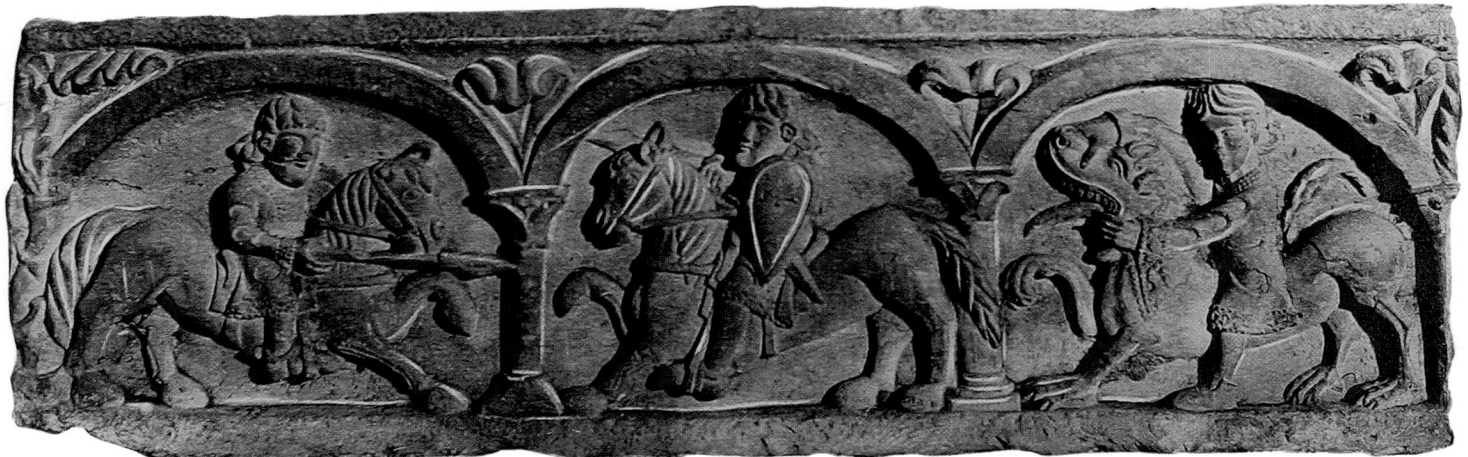

11.19   *Sarcophagus of Doña Sancha*, front and back sides. ca. 1120. Stone, 25.8 × 78.74" (65 × 200 cm). Monastério de las Benedictinas, Jaca, Spain

sarcophagus of a woman is a mark of the culture of Romanesque Spain, which one scholar has called "a society organized for war." Many legends sprang up about women's roles in the defense of territories newly conquered from Muslims by Christian warriors. The pressing need for settlement and permanent organization required women to engage actively in the acquisition and exchange of land and other properties at a time when their men were away on military campaigns. If Sancha were an isolated instance of a woman of power enjoying special prestige, it would not add much to our knowledge of the Romanesque period. But, in fact, women in eleventh- and twelfth-century Spain played an inordinately important role in the formation of political structures, and as commissioners of works of art.

The triumphal aspirations represented on Sancha's sarcophagus are balanced by the sensitive depiction of the soul, whose tender expression suggests hope as well as anxiety, common human responses when contemplating death. Notice how the center group is the only one not covered by an arch, a strategy that emphasizes a sense of upward thrust and hence suggests a heavenly journey.

Cluniac Wall Painting

Because the destruction of Cluny's buildings resulted in the loss of its wall paintings, we can best appreciate what these might have looked like by examining allied monuments. A good one for this purpose is the priory of Berzé-la-Ville.

THE BERZÉ-LA-VILLE APSE The early twelfth-century priory of Berzé-la-Ville, just a few miles southeast of Cluny, was built as a retreat for Cluny's abbot, and the apse paintings in its chapel (fig. **11.20**) emulate those in the church of the mother house. Christ in Majesty occupies the center of the composition, surrounded by the apostles. The elongated faces and the graceful manner in which drapery is pulled across limbs impart delicacy and elegance to the images; patterns of rhythmic concentric lines and bright highlights indicate the multiple folds in the cloth. Although these devices ultimately derive from Byzantine sources, such as the *Paris Psalter* (see fig. 8.39), the path by which they were acquired was indirect, coming from Byzantine art in Italy, not Constantinople. The library at Cluny was rich in

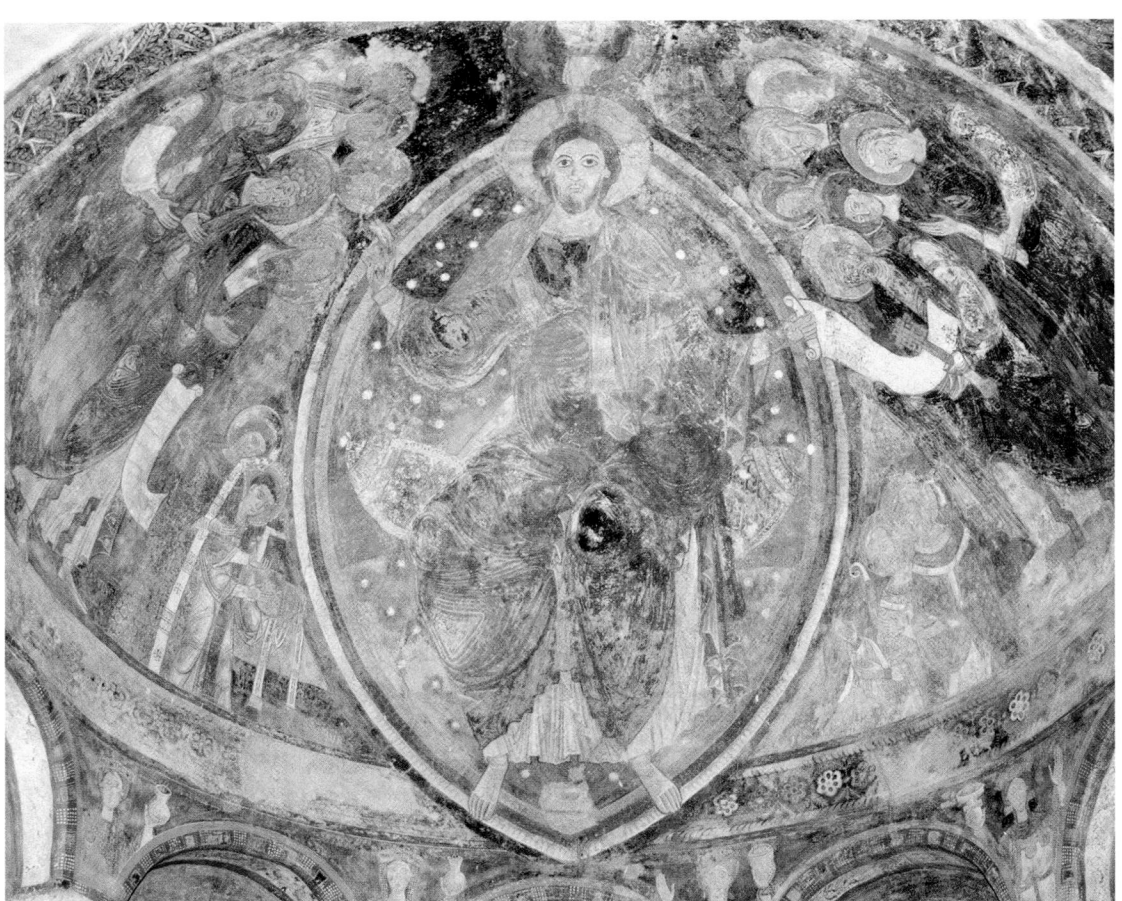

Italo-Byzantine manuscripts, and Cluniac manuscript illumination also favors this style.

Cistercian Architecture and Art

As we have seen, Cluny's very success made it the subject of criticism, particularly by the Cistercians, whose mother house was at Cîteaux in Burgundy. In addition to prayer, the Cistercians devoted themselves to hard work, which helped guarantee their own great success. Sound economic planning, skill in agriculture and husbandry, and wealthy benefactors furthered their cause. At a time of rising urban growth, the serenity of the isolated sites of their monasteries must also have been attractive. The Cistercian order and its style spread across Europe, and by the end of the twelfth century the Cistercians controlled nearly 700 monasteries. Cistercian architecture in its simplicity contrasts markedly with the architecture of the Cluniac order.

ABBEY CHURCH AT FONTENAY The abbey church at Fontenay, not far from Cîteaux, was begun in 1139, a generation after St. Bernard founded a monastery there. It is the best-preserved Cistercian church built in the first half of the twelfth century. Fontenay exemplifies the Cistercian reliance on simple and unadorned forms in contrast to the opulence promulgated by Cluny. In its orderliness, the plan of simple geometric shapes (fig. **11.21**) builds on monastic schemes dating as far back as

the St. Gall drawing (see fig. 10.22). By comparison to the expansive plan of Cluny (see fig. 11.9), where the huge abbey church dominated a sprawling complex, Fontenay is precise, a pure and tightly controlled equilibrium balancing all of its constituent parts.

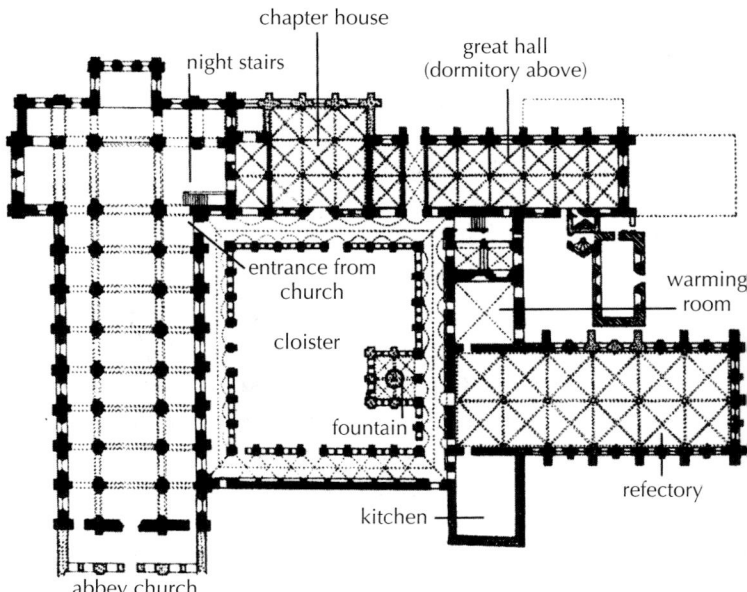

11.21   Plan of Fontenay Abbey, France. Begun in 1139

Other Benedictine Architecture and Wall Painting

The Benedictine abbey church of Saint-Savin-sur-Gartempe is of a type known as a **hall church** (fig. **11.23**). The nave vault lacks transverse arches, since its weight rests directly on the nave arcade, which is supported by a majestic set of columns. The nave is fairly well lit, for the two aisles are carried almost to the same height as the nave, and their outer walls have generous windows.

Although Saint-Savin-sur-Gartempe has a luxurious sculptural program and a rich doorway, the hall church was designed particularly to offer a continuous surface for murals. *The Building of the Tower of Babel* (fig. **11.24**) is part of an extensive cycle of scenes from the Hebrew Bible on the vault. It is an intensely dramatic design, crowded with strenuous action. God himself, on the far left, participates directly in the narrative, addressing the

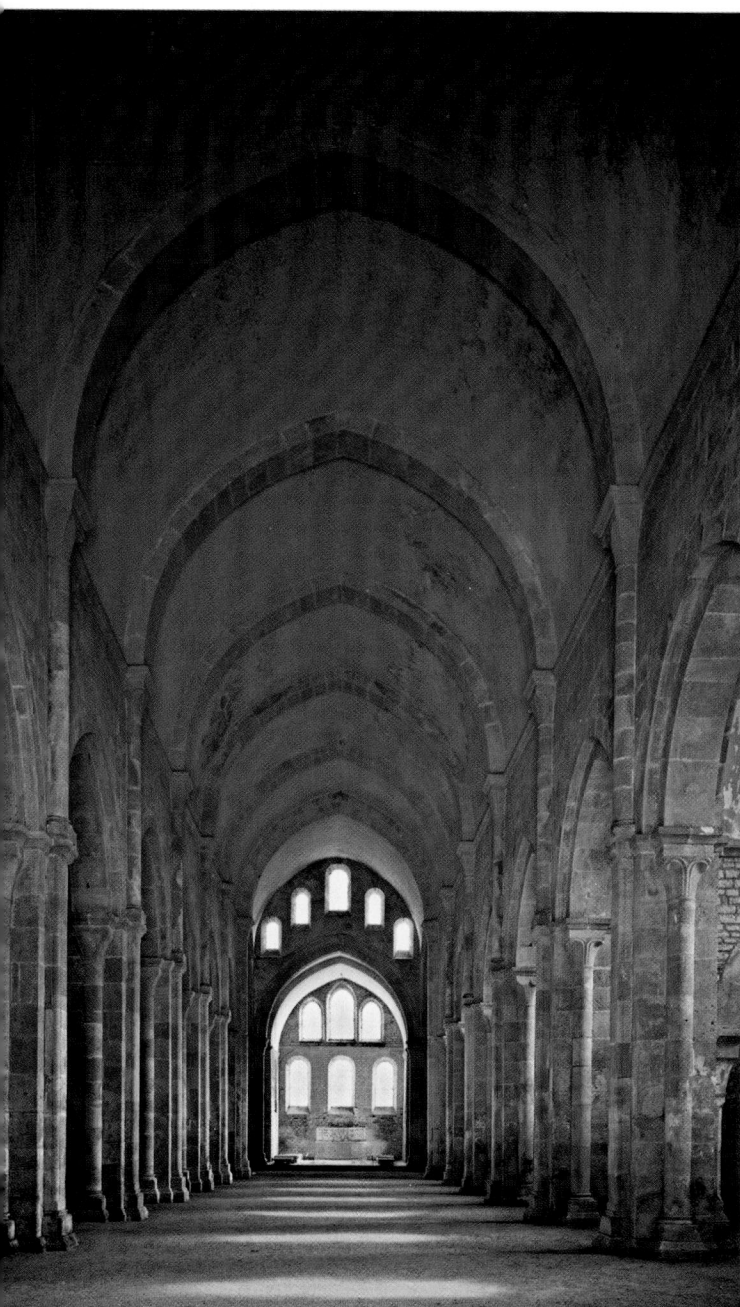

11.22   Nave of the abbey church, Fontenay. 1139–47

The east end of the church is unembellished by apses, and no towers were planned. Since Cistercians permitted neither sculpture nor wall painting, the interior of the church (fig. **11.22**) lacks applied decoration. Clerestory and gallery are suppressed. However, in their own terms, the clean lines of the pointed transverse arches that define the nave and openings into the side aisles, and the pattern of unframed windows, create an elegant refinement. The simple forms are at once graceful and moving. Once again, the church serves as a safe, tranquil, and spiritual refuge from worldly burdens, although different in effect from the protective enclosures that other Romanesque churches offer (see figs. 11.1 and 11.5).

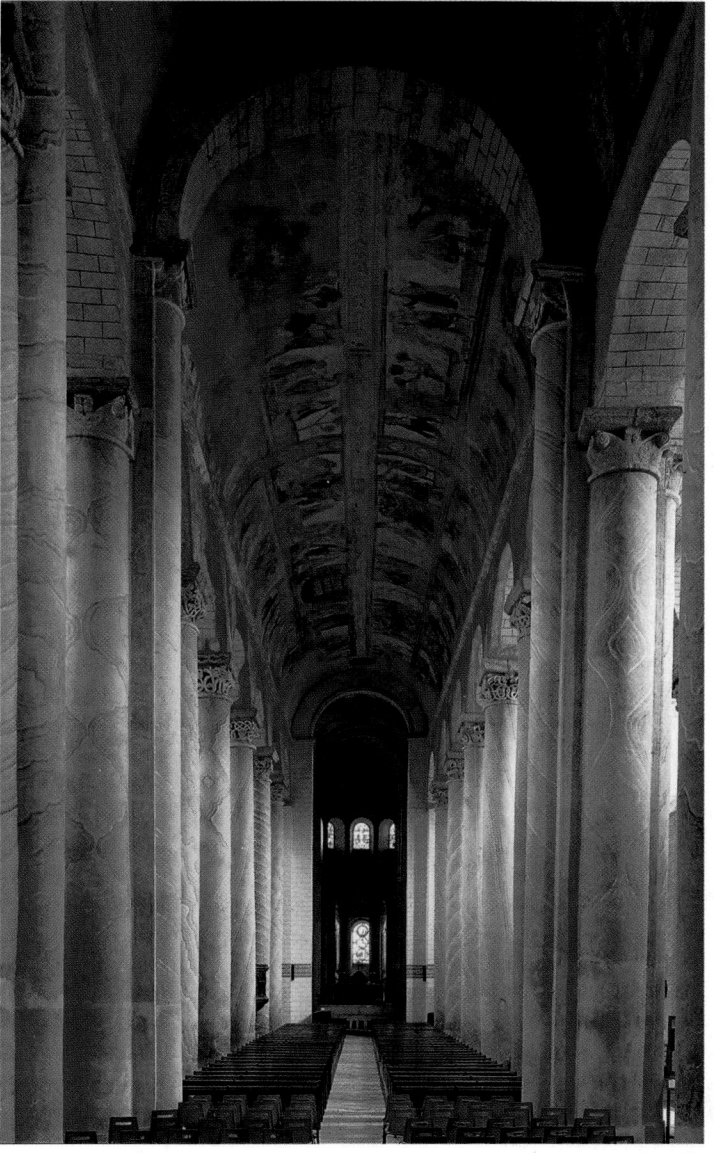

11.23   Choir, ca. 1060–75, and nave, ca. 1095–1115, of abbey church of Saint-Savin-sur-Gartempe, France

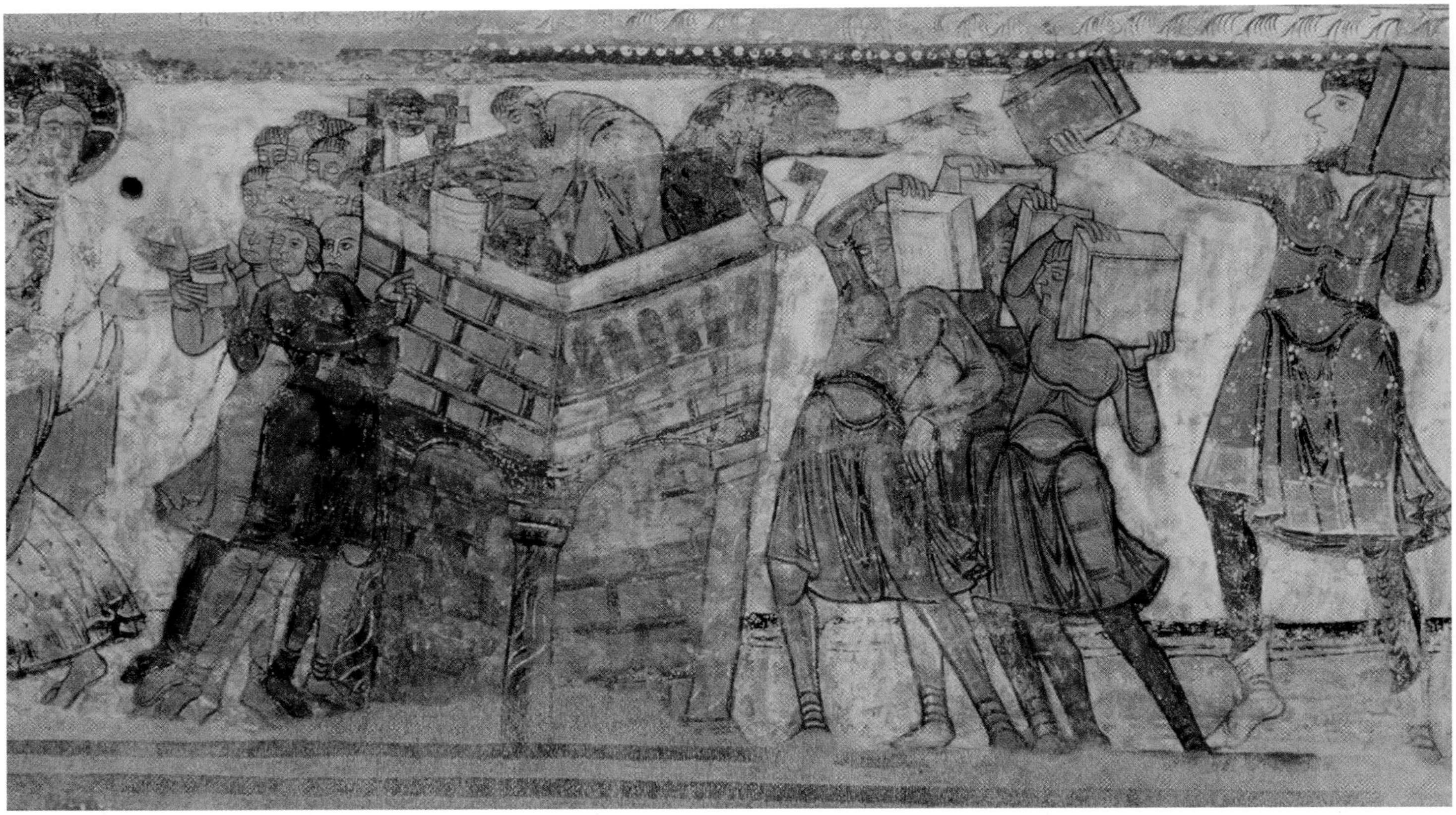

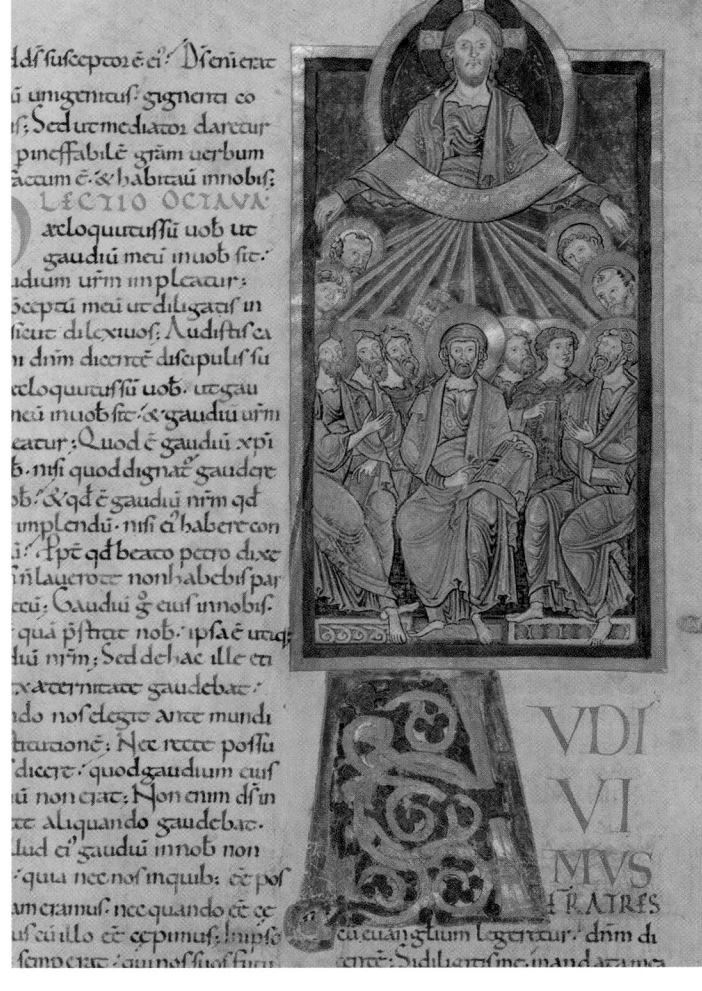

11.24 *The Building of the Tower of Babel.* Early 12th century. Detail of painting on the nave vault, Saint-Savin-sur-Gartempe, France

builders of the huge structure. He is counterbalanced, on the right, by the giant Nimrod, leader of the project, who frantically hands blocks of stone to the masons atop the tower. The entire scene becomes a great test of strength between God and mortals. The heavy, dark contours and the emphatic gestures make the composition easy to read from the floor below. Elsewhere in the church the viewer can see Christian biblical scenes and scenes from the lives of local saints. Although paintings in Romanesque churches were not necessarily the norm, they were common features. Many frescoes no longer exist as a result of restoration programs. (See *The Art Historian's Lens*, page 369.)

Book Illustration

As in the early Middle Ages, manuscript production in the Romanesque period continued to be largely the responsibility of monastic scriptoria under the supervision of monks. Manuscripts produced by Cluniac scriptoria are stylistically similar to wall paintings in Cluniac churches and often express concerns remarkably akin to those of the period's architects and sculptors. Those

11.25 *Pentecost*, from the *Cluny Lectionary*. Early 12th century. Tempera on vellum, 9 × 5" (22.9 × 12.7 cm). Bibliothèque Nationale, Paris

Preserving and Restoring Architecture

The conservation and the preservation of any work of art are delicate tasks. In the case of architecture, the issues to be considered are particularly acute since, in addition to aesthetic criteria, restorers must take into account a building's function. What does one do, for example, with a building originally built to satisfy functions that are no longer relevant? Such is the question with medieval castles and palaces, as well as with churches located in areas where population shifts have reduced the size of their parishes. Should these buildings be retrofitted for new uses, even if that transforms their original character?

The restoration of Romanesque buildings poses some special problems. In many regions of Europe, virtually every village has its own Romanesque church, but diocesan and governmental institutions have difficulty in obtaining the funds to preserve them. Moreover, Romanesque architecture is characterized by its great variety. Thus, a one-size-fits-all approach to restoration, which might be efficient on a practical level, only erases the essential distinctions that give the Romanesque its exceptional quality.

Art historian C. Edson Armi has written penetratingly about recent restorations of Romanesque churches in the Burgundy region of France.* Although the French Restoration Service has a long tradition of intervening to save historic buildings, it does not have the resources to maintain all needy monuments. Increasingly, it has had to focus on simply reacting to severe problems, often when it is too late to correct them. Additionally, the service has a pattern of applying a universal, rather than a specific, approach to the restoration of buildings. In the mid-twentieth century, it was fashionable to clean the surfaces of Romanesque churches within an inch of their lives, and restorers indiscriminately removed any surface coverings—sometimes including original ones—to expose underlying stone or brick. It was thought that by exposing the original materials and structure, the building's true expressive nature would be revealed.

By late in the twentieth century, the pendulum had swung the other way, and the norm was to plaster both interior and exterior surfaces of Romanesque churches—in some cases, the same ones that had been completely stripped only a generation or so earlier. While it is true that during the Middle Ages the surfaces of buildings, whether of brick or stone, were often covered with plaster, this was not always the case. Armi demonstrates how recent interventions have covered up valuable evidence of original materials and structure, information that would help an architectural historian "appreciate large issues like the concept, process and history of a building." Since Armi has shown that a mason's techniques are as distinctive as a painter's or a sculptor's, the lost information could well be key to placing a building in its art historical context. Armi proposes early preservation programs to prevent the need for severe reconstructions that are often based more on conjecture than on fact. Before undertaking any project, he would require modern restorers to acquire a sound understanding of the historical and architectural situation of individual buildings and regions. He proposes that review committees participate in decisions about the restoration of important buildings. Armi has been guided by standards established at the 1964 Venice International Congress of Architects and Technicians of Historic Monuments, which require that whatever is done to a building must demonstrate "respect for original material and authentic documents ... and must stop at the point where conjecture begins." Any restorations "must be distinguishable from the original so that restoration does not falsify the artistic or historic evidence." We also need to ask to what extent one should accept or reject previous changes to buildings. Is it always important to get back to the hypothetical origin of a building, or is it appropriate to consider buildings as entities that change over time? Is there an ideal moment that restorers should aim to preserve? When is it proper to remove a later addition to a building and when should that addition be preserved? A case in point is the Early Christian basilica of Santa Maria Maggiore (see page 250). The original fifth-century apse was destroyed when a new one was added in 1290; during the next 35 years, leading artists of the day decorated it with magnificent mosaics. Certainly, in this case, to restore the building to its fifth-century state would produce a loss much greater than any advantage obtained by re-creating original forms.

*C. Edson Armi, "Report on the Destruction of Romanesque Architecture in Burgundy," *Journal of the Society of Architectural Historians*, vol. 55, 1996, pages 300–327.

---

produced in Cistercian scriptoria are particularly inventive, often based on the observation of daily life. Many manuscripts produced at Cîteaux show strong English influence, and some were perhaps executed by English illuminators. Although a great variety of styles characterize Romanesque manuscripts, the interrelationship of monastic communities accounts for some consistency in manuscript production across various regions during the period. Some manuscripts produced in northern France, Belgium, and southern England are so closely related in style that at times we cannot be sure on which side of the English Channel a given manuscript was produced.

THE *CLUNY LECTIONARY* *Pentecost* (fig. 11.25), an illumination from the *Cluny Lectionary*, represents the descent of the Holy Spirit on the apostles after the Resurrection of Christ. As in the apse fresco at Berzé-la-Ville (see fig. 11.20), a viewer sees highlighted drapery tautly drawn across limbs. Other stylistic features also recall Byzantine devices. The delicate, classicizing faces of some of the prophets evoke Middle Byzantine painting (see figs. 8.38 and 8.39), and the other faces with long mustaches falling over ample beards recall the Byzantine manner of representing saints and prophets (see fig. 8.40). Even Christ at the top of the folio is presented in his typical Byzantine role as Pantocrator. The apostle distinguished by his central placement is Peter, the same saint who receives the scroll from Christ in the Berzé-la-Ville apse painting. Since Cluny was dedicated to St. Peter, it was only logical to stress his importance, but there is a political message here as well. Cluny's foundation charter states that the monastery was answerable only to Rome and the pope, heir to Peter's throne, and not to any king or emperor. This special privilege assured Cluny enormous power and ultimately its success too.

THE *CODEX COLBERTINUS* The illustration of St. Matthew from the *Codex Colbertinus* (fig. **11.26**) is similar in concept and

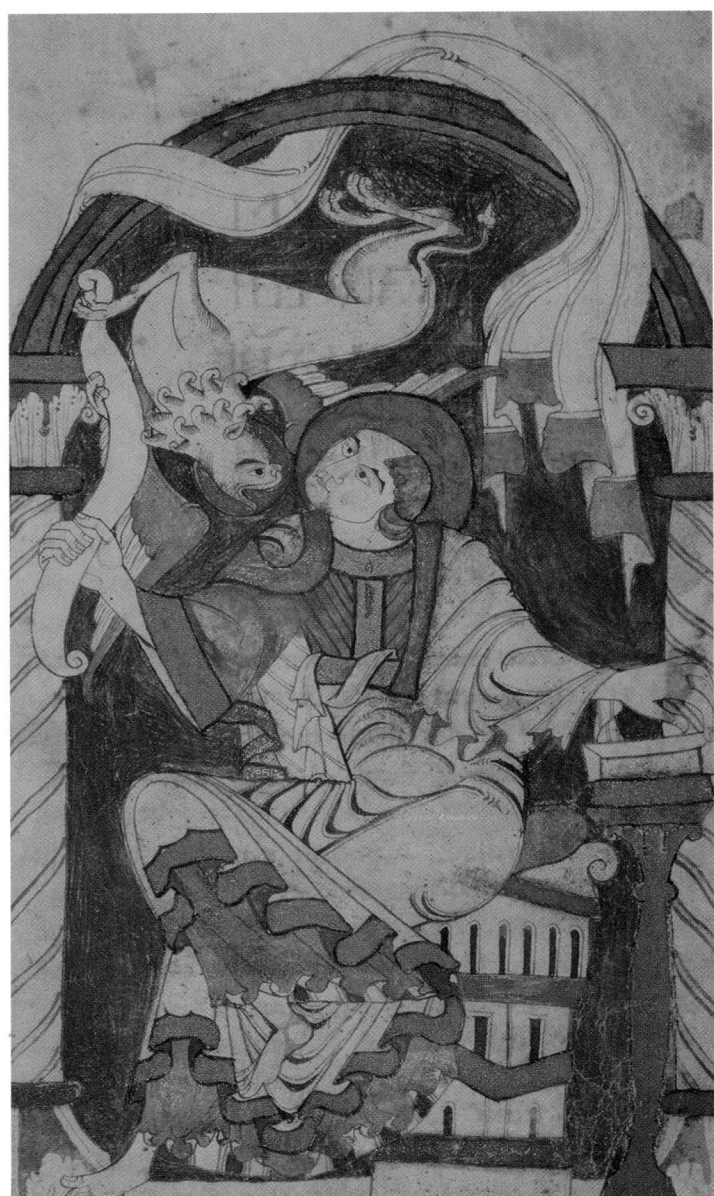

11.27   *St. Mark*, from a Gospel book produced at the abbey at Corbie. Early 12th century. Tempera on vellum, 10¾ × 7⅞" (27.3 × 20 cm). Bibliothèque Municipale, Amiens, France

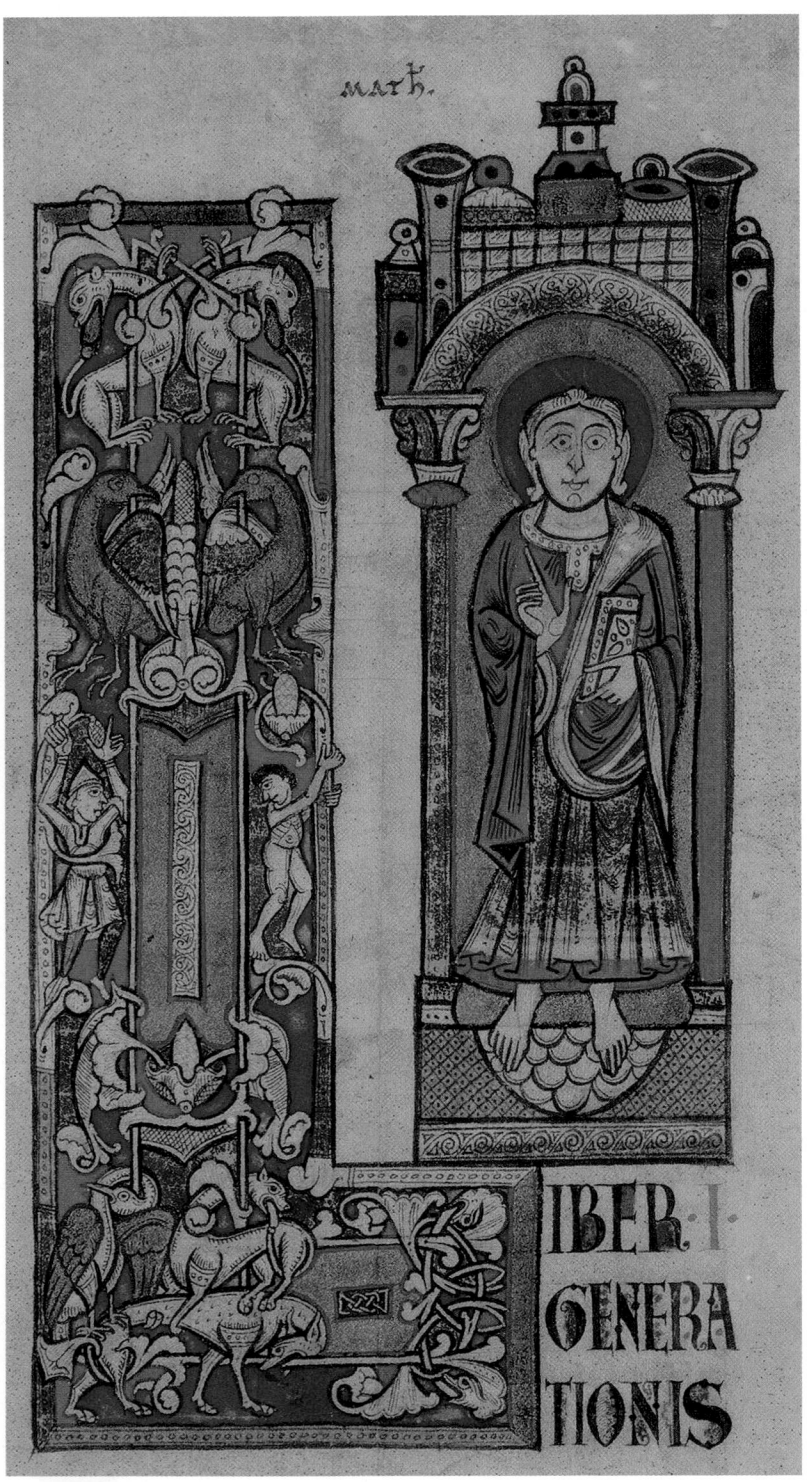

11.26   *St. Matthew*, from the *Codex Colbertinus*. ca. 1100. Tempera on vellum, 7½ × 4" (19 × 10.16 cm). Bibliothèque Nationale, Paris

pose to a number of Romanesque carvings, particularly the pier reliefs from the Moissac cloister (see fig. 11.12). The manuscript was made at that monastery, or nearby, just when sculptors were at work in the cloister. Matthew appears at the beginning of his Gospel, next to an embellished letter "L," the first letter of *Liber*, meaning "book." Figures, animals, foliage, and decorative patterns conform to the shape of the letter, recalling the way Romanesque sculptured figures correspond to their frames (see fig. 11.2).

In contrast to the small, freely disposed figures and animals in the initial, the figure of Matthew confronts us directly. Although he fills the available space of the architectural setting, a number of features deny his solidity. The heavy outlines and bold colors are reminiscent of enamelwork (see fig. 11.6) and, in combination with a variety of juxtaposed patterns, serve to flatten the image. These devices demonstrate to what extent forms popular during the early Middle Ages remained vital.

THE CORBIE GOSPEL BOOK In its monumentality, the image of St. Mark from an early twelfth-century Gospel book produced at Corbie (fig. **11.27**) can also be likened to Romanesque sculpture. The active pose and zigzag composition bear comparison with the prophet on the Moissac trumeau (see fig. 11.15). The twisting movement of the lines, not only in the figure of St. Mark but also in the winged lion, the scroll, and the curtain, also recalls Carolingian miniatures of the Reims School, such as the *Ebbo Gospel Book* (see fig. 10.14).

This resemblance helps us see the differences between them as well. In the Romanesque manuscript, every trace of classical illusionism has disappeared. The fluid modeling of the Reims School, with its suggestion of light and space, has been replaced here by firm contours filled in with bright, solid colors. As a result, the three-dimensional aspects of the picture are reduced to overlapping planes. Yet by sacrificing the last remnants of modeling in terms of light and shade, the Romanesque artist has given his work a clarity and precision that had not been possible in Carolingian or Ottonian times. Here, the representational, the symbolic, and the decorative elements of the design are fully integrated.

GREGORY'S *MORALIA IN JOB* Although in principle, given the concern about elaborate decoration by St. Bernard and others, Cistercian manuscripts were to be decorated only with nonfigurative initials of single colors, in actuality a number of beautiful and fascinating manuscripts were produced for the order. It is not easy to explain why an exception was made for this genre of art. It might simply have been because official statutes against the decoration of manuscripts were not established until 1134. (Some scholars claim these statutes date from 1152.) Pope Gregory's *Moralia in Job*, produced in 1111 at Cîteaux, is a charming example (fig. **11.28**). The manuscript contains decorated initials, depicting some of the monastery's daily activities, including the initial "I," formed by a tree, which a lay brother and a monk work together to fell. The bright, flat colors and patterned foliage of the tree contrast with seemingly naturalistic details. The monk's garment, his bunched trousers, and the dagger suspended on his belt convey the workaday quality of monastic life. The scene correlates with the accompanying text and reflects Cistercian monastic values. The monk depicted here is engaged in hard manual labor, as required by the Benedictine Rule. His tattered garments highlight the Cistercians' humility and their avoidance of luxury, a reaction to the perceived perversion of Benedictine values by other monks, including those at Cluny. In the second half of the twelfth century, with few exceptions, Cistercian manuscripts received only very simple decorations, apparently as a result of the statutes prohibiting elaborate adornments.

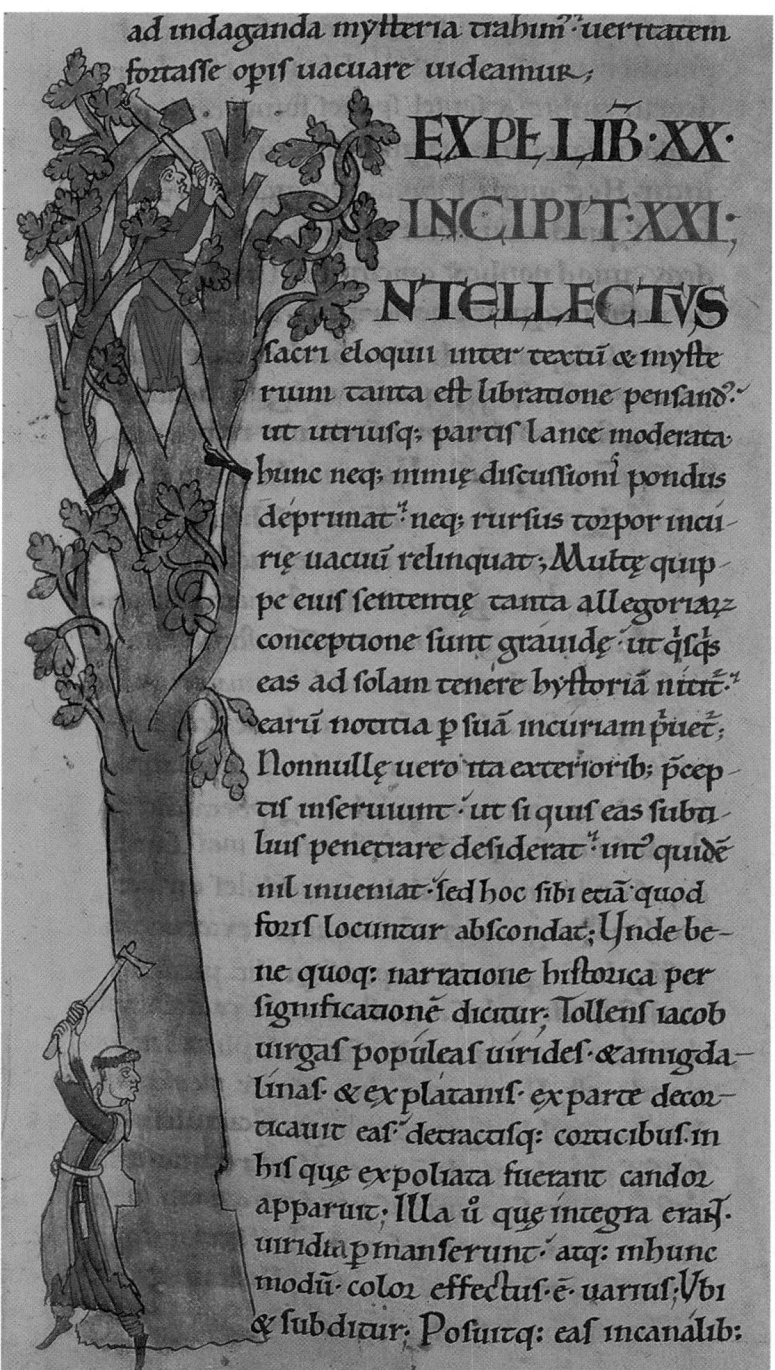

11.28 Initial "I," from Gregory the Great's *Moralia in Job*. 1111. Tempera on vellum, 21 × 6" (53.34 × 15.24 cm). Bibliothèque Municipale, Dijon, France

GOSPEL BOOK OF ABBOT WEDRICUS The style of the miniature of St. John from the *Gospel Book of Abbot Wedricus* (fig. **11.29**) has been linked with both northern France and England, and its linear draftsmanship was influenced by Byzantine art. Note the ropelike loops of drapery, the origin of which can be traced to such works as the *Crucifixion* at Daphni (see fig. 8.45) and, even further back, to the *Archangel Michael* ivory (see fig. 8.33). At the same time, the energetic rhythm

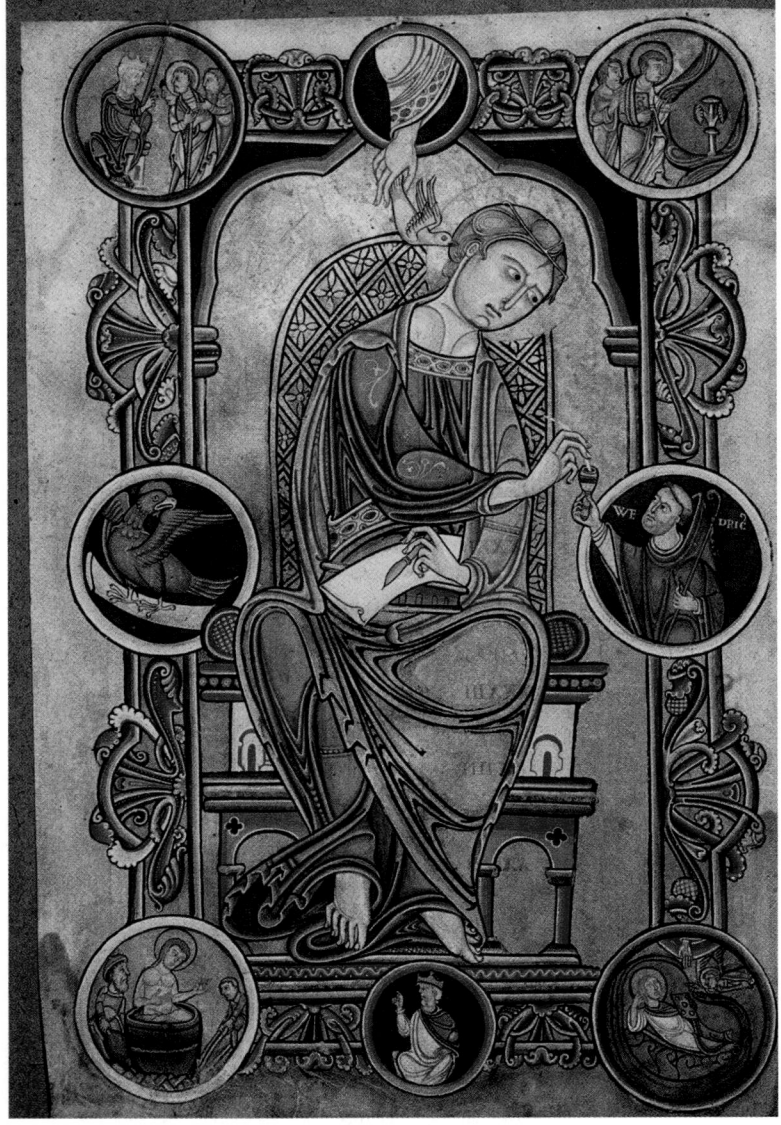

11.29 *St. John the Evangelist*, from the *Gospel Book of Abbot Wedricus.* ca. 1147. Tempera on vellum, 14 × 9½" (35.5 × 24.1 cm). Société Archéologique et Historique, Avesnes-sur-Helpe, France

unifying the composition in the Corbie style (see fig. 11.27) has not been lost entirely. The controlled dynamics of every contour, both in the main figure and in the frame, unite the varied elements of the composition. This quality of line betrays its ultimate source: the Celtic-Germanic heritage.

If we compare the Abbot Wedricus miniature of St. John with the Cross page of the *Lindisfarne Gospels* (see fig. 10.5), we see how much the interlacing patterns of the early Middle Ages have contributed to the design of the St. John page. The drapery folds and the clusters of floral ornament have an impulsive yet disciplined liveliness that echoes the intertwined snakelike monsters of the animal style (even though the foliage is derived from the classical acanthus), and the human figures are based on Carolingian and Byzantine models. The unity of the page is conveyed not only by the forms but by the content as well. St. John inhabits the

frame so thoroughly that we could not remove him from it without cutting off his ink supply (offered by the donor of the manuscript, Abbot Wedricus), his source of inspiration (the dove of the Holy Spirit in the hand of God), or his symbol (the eagle), all located in medallions on the page borders. The other medallions, less closely linked with the main figure, show scenes from the life of St. John.

OTHER REGIONAL VARIANTS OF ROMANESQUE STYLE

Although consistent aesthetic aims expressed across mediums link the art of diverse areas of Europe during the Romanesque period, a variety of regional approaches can also be identified. These distinct approaches appear in regions of what is now France as well as in other parts of Europe, such as Tuscany in Italy, the Meuse Valley, Germany, and England. Regional variety in Romanesque art reflects the political conditions of eleventh- and twelfth-century western Europe, which was governed by a feudal, though loose, alliance of princes and dukes. Language differences also help account for regional diversity. For example, even within France a number of languages were spoken, among them the *langue d'oc*, the language of southwestern France, and the *langue d'oil*, the language of the center and north. Different regions had different artistic sources available to artists and patrons. In Germany and other parts of northern Europe, Ottonian art provided compelling models, while in Italy and southern France, where antique survivals were numerous, artists borrowed and transformed Roman forms in order to realize Romanesque aesthetic aims. In England, which through conquest had become the domain of Norman dukes in 1066, the artwork of French Normandy provided models.

Western France: Poitou

A so-called school of sculptural decoration appears during the Romanesque period in the region known as Poitou, part of the duchy of Aquitaine in southwestern France. A notable example is Notre-Dame-la-Grande in Poitiers, seat of the lords of Aquitaine.

NOTRE-DAME-LA-GRANDE, POITIERS The broad screenlike façade of Notre-Dame-la-Grande (fig. **11.30**) offers an expanded field for sculptural decoration. Elaborately bordered arcades house large seated or standing figures. Below them, a wide band of relief carving stretches across the façade. The Fall of Adam and Eve appears with scenes from the life of Mary, including the Annunciation and Nativity, once again juxtaposing Eve and Mary (see pages 344 and 362). Next to the representation of Adam and Eve, an inscription identifies an enthroned figure as Nebuchadnezzar, the king of Babylon mentioned in the Hebrew Bible. The *Play of Adam*—a twelfth-century medieval drama of a type that was traditionally performed in churches—probably served as the source for the choice and arrangement of figures at

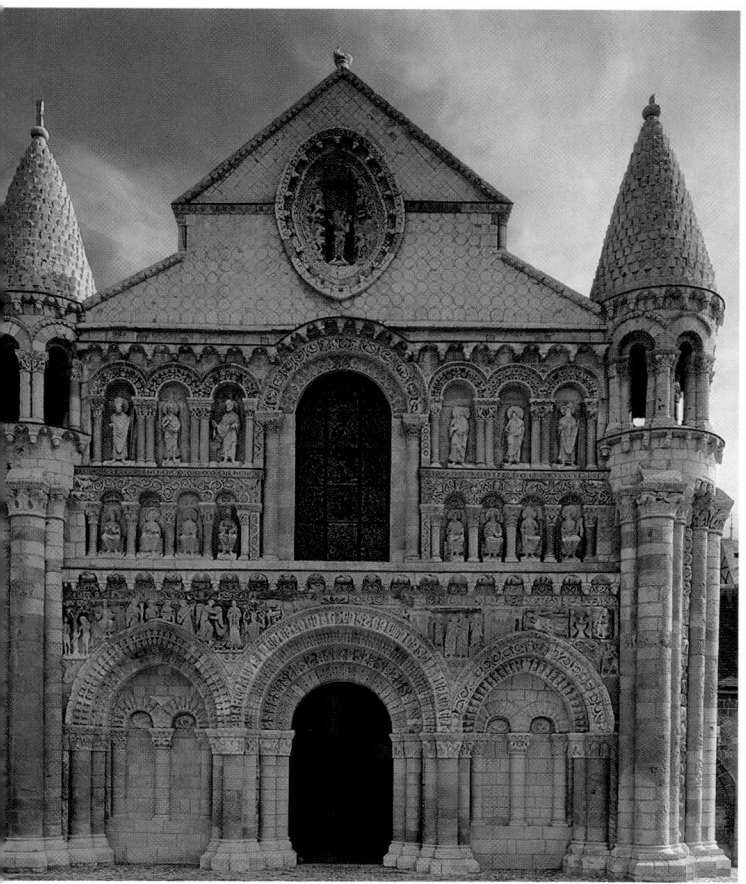

11.30 West façade, Notre-Dame-la-Grande, Poitiers, France. Early 12th century

Notre-Dame-la-Grande. Beside Nebuchadnezzar, centered above the arch on the left of the portal, there are four figures carrying either scrolls or books on which are inscribed lines from the Adam play, in which Adam and Eve figure prominently and Nebuchadnezzar is also mentioned.

Essential to the rich sculptural effect is the deeply recessed doorway, without tympanum but framed by a series of arches with multiple archivolts. The conical helmets of the towers nearly match the height of the **gable** (the triangular wall section at the top of the façade), which rises above the actual level of the roof behind it. The gable contains a representation of Christ with angels, their height in the composition denoting their heavenly place. The sculptural program spread out over this entire area is a visual exposition of Christian doctrine intended as a feast for the eyes as well as the mind.

Southeastern France: Provence

In the French region of Provence, south of Burgundy, Romanesque art benefitted from its proximity to Italy. The name Provence derives from its ancient designation as a *provincia romana* in recognition of its close political and cultural connections to Rome; even today vestiges of Roman art and architecture abound in the region, such as the Maison Carrée in Nîmes (see fig. 7.44).

SAINT-GILLES-DU-GARD The façade of the abbey church of Saint-Gilles-du-Gard (fig. **11.31**), like Notre-Dame-la-Grande in Poitiers, screens the church. Both churches were major stops on

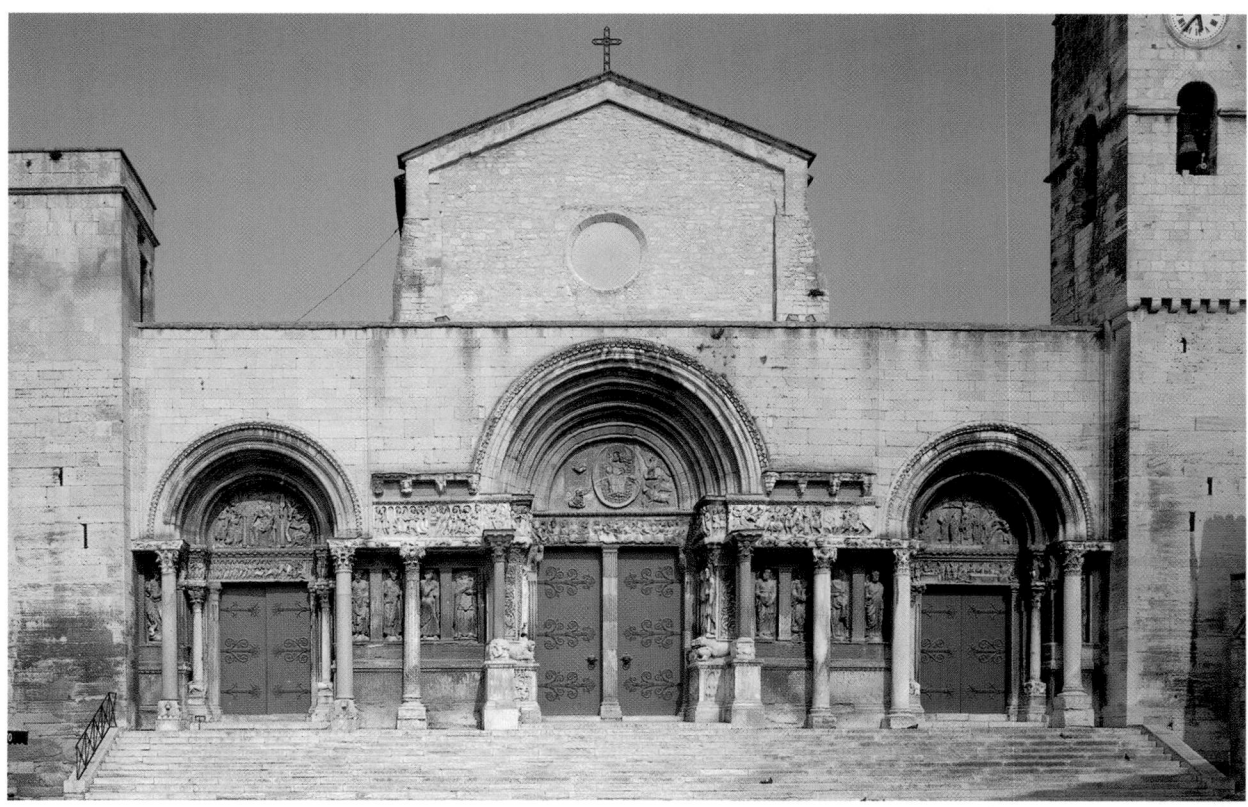

11.31 West façade, Saint-Gilles-du-Gard, France. Mid-12th century

the pilgrimage road to Santiago de Compostela (see map 11.2). The façade of Saint-Gilles has suffered some later rearrangements and the original probably displayed a more consistent horizontality, with continuous friezes, lintels, cornices, and bases, instead of the staggered ones that we see today. Scholars have claimed that inspiration for Saint-Gilles-du-Gard's façade, composed of three arches, can be found in the screenlike stage sets (see fig. 7.7) of Roman theaters and in the Roman triumphal arch (see fig. 7.71), connecting ancient triumphal imagery with the important liminal function of entering the church. Given contemporary concerns for Christian victory, in particular the struggle to conquer the Muslims, the formal association between the façade and a Roman triumphal monument must have seemed particularly fitting here, since the town of Saint-Gilles on the Rhône River estuary was a principal site of embarkation for the Holy Land by French crusaders led by the counts of Toulouse, among whose possessions Saint-Gilles-du-Gard figured. Moreover, the military orders of the Knights of the Temple (the Templars), and the Knights of St. John of Jerusalem (the Hospitalers), which were founded to protect pilgrimage routes and sites in the Holy Land, had their primary commanderies (districts or estates administered by a commander of an order of knights) in the West at Saint-Gilles. The depiction of Jesus' triumphal entry into Jerusalem, which appears on the lintel supporting the left tympanum, would undoubtedly have had special meaning for contemporary viewers.

The Holy Land

Many consider the Holy Land a virtual French province during much of the eleventh and twelfth centuries, largely as a result of crusader activity there. The history of the Crusades is a complex one and the motives of crusaders diverse. Some went for what one early twelfth-century priest described as "superficial reasons," that is, for the excitement of foreign travel and for financial gain, while others undertook it as a form of penance or out of deeply felt religious piety, seeking to free the places where Christ lived, taught, and died from the Muslims who had occupied them. The First Crusade, mobilized by Pope Urban II in 1095, managed to claim Jerusalem after three years, but later crusades were generally disastrous. The Second Crusade (1147–49), which was preached by St. Bernard of Clairvaux after the fall of Edessa to the Turks, succeeded only in capturing Lisbon from the Arabs, while the Third Crusade, begun in 1189, failed to reconquer Jerusalem from the sultan Saladin, who had taken it two years earlier. The Fourth (and final major) Crusade did little to hinder the advance of Islam; its sole result was the taking of Constantinople by crusaders in 1204, one of the most ignominious events in church history.

CRAC DES CHEVALIERS To defend territories conquered during the First Crusade, French crusaders erected a significant number of castles in the Holy Land. Among the best-preserved of these is in northern Syria, the Crac des Chevaliers (the name derives from the Syrian word for fortress and the French word for

knight) (fig. **11.32**). The Crac des Chevaliers guards the Homs Pass, an important commercial corridor, and rises more than 2,000 feet above the fertile pastures of the Orantes Valley. In 1110, the Franks, under Raymond IV of Saint-Gilles, count of Toulouse and subsequently count of Tripoli, occupied the site of what had been a small eleventh-century Arab fort, which was then rebuilt and expanded, and later, in 1142, given to the Hospitalers. The castle sits on a natural outcrop of rock, whose sharp drop protected it on the north, east, and west. The first Christian castle took the form of a trapezoidal precinct enclosed by curtain walls with salient (projecting) rectangular towers. These towers were later converted to rounded ones because they provided better sight lines for defense in time of siege; and an outer enclosure, also composed of curtain walls and rounded projections, in some places more than 25 feet thick, was added. Much of this happened as a result of major earthquake damage in 1170. Battered (sloping) walls, difficult to scale, were added to the inner precinct. Defenses also included slits for archers and **crenelations**, notched battlements at the top of the walls that shielded warriors while allowing them to release their weapons. Projecting from the walls are **machicolations**, providing an enclosed area supported by a row of arches and containing openings through which soldiers could drop rocks on attackers. An aqueduct brought water from the summit of a nearby mountain, filling cisterns and a reservoir built between the inner and outer walls that also served as a defense. It has been estimated that in time of siege the Crac would have been able to stock provisions for five years.

While a major function of the Crac des Chevaliers was clearly defense, it also served as a point of departure for incursions into neighboring territory and to establish control over the large fertile valley below and the trade routes that crossed it. Castles were the center of authority over the local population: in the case of the Crac, a largely Muslim one. The castle proclaimed the rite of rule of the overlord and as such upheld the structure of feudal society and the relationship between lord and vassal. Castles were viewed as symbols of power, and in the later Middle Ages architectural features such as crenelations, that had been developed for defensive purposes were applied to palaces where their original function was no longer required.

While some scholars have seen the Crac des Chevaliers and other crusader castles in the Holy Land as providing the opportunity for military engineers to invent and develop new systems of defense, particularly against siege warfare, which were then exported to western Europe, others have stressed the possibility that crusaders were influenced by Muslim and Byzantine castles, both of which they would have encountered in the Holy Land. Building activity by the crusaders was not limited to defensive structures, however. Indeed, a number of Romanesque churches, many of them pilgrimage sites, such as the Holy Sepulcher in Jerusalem (see fig. 8.12) and a church dedicated to the Nativity in Bethlehem, were built or reconstructed during the period, and these buildings, like the Crac des Chevaliers, provide evidence of a continued syncretism in the region. Romanesque castles share the same aesthetic concerns as Romanesque churches and other

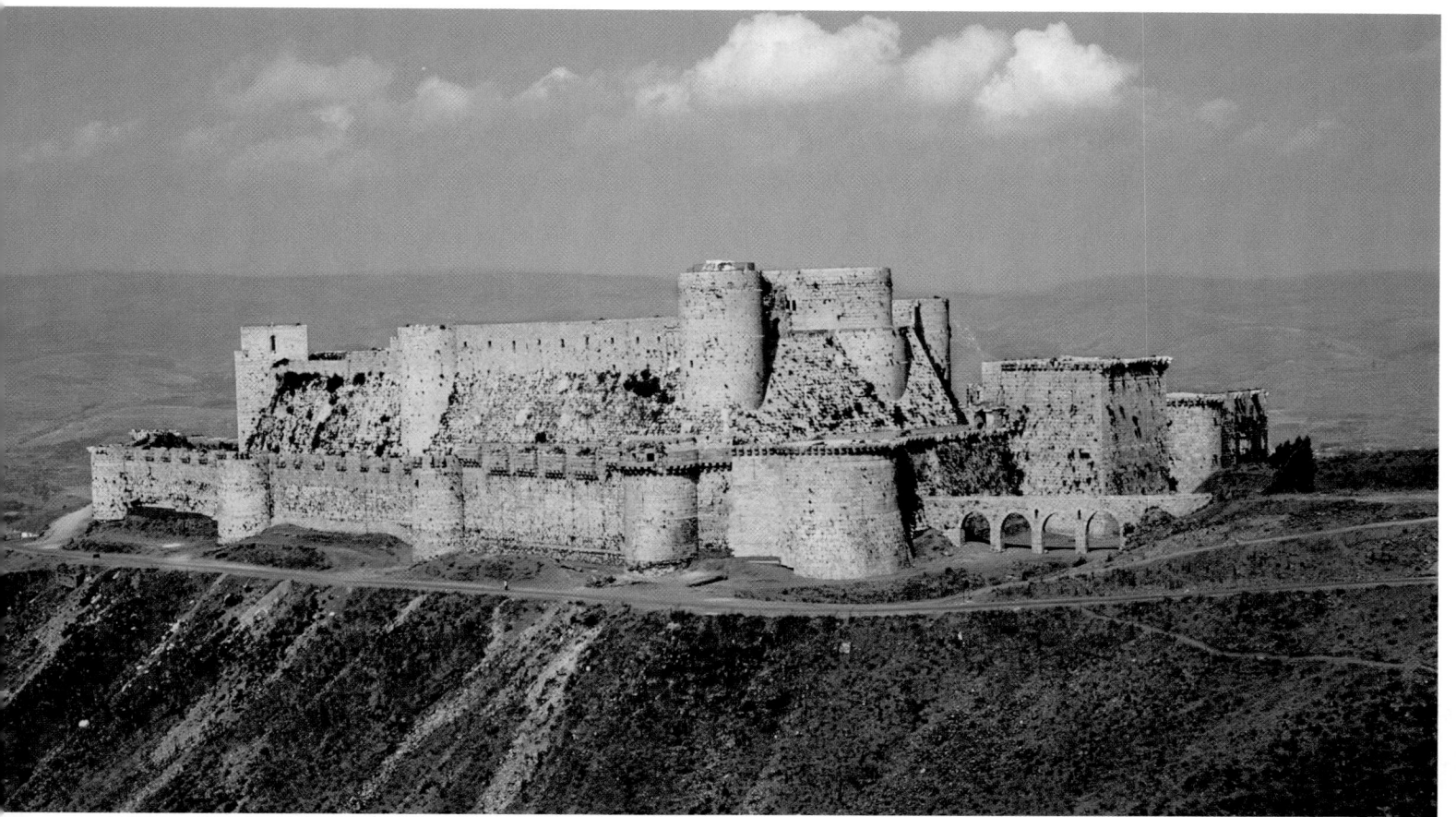

11.32 Crac des Chevaliers, Homs Pass, Syria. 12th century with later additions

buildings, and use the same system of solid stone walls, arches, and vaults. The rhythmic arrangement of curved and straight walls and the repeated patterns of wall openings suggest that similar concerns for design and proportionality were at play.

In 1271, the Crac des Chevaliers fell to the Muslims, and the chapel, which the Christians had erected within the inner precinct, was converted into a mosque. At the same time, the southern square tower, visible at the right of figure 11.32, and the round projection to the left of the aqueduct were reconstructed, since it was from the less easily defensible south that the Muslims had attacked.

Tuscany

During the Romanesque period, Tuscany, a region in northwestern Italy divided into several independent city-states, the chief of which were Pisa, Florence, Prato, and Livorno, continued to deploy what were basically Early Christian architectural forms. However, they added decorative features inspired by Roman architecture.

PISA CATHEDRAL The most famous monument of the Italian Romanesque owes its fame to an accident. Because of poor foundations, the Leaning Tower of Pisa in Tuscany, designed by the sculptor Bonanno Pisano (active 1174–86), began to tilt even

before it was completed (fig. **11.33**). This type of free-standing tower, or **campanile**, appears in Italy as early as the ninth or tenth century. The tradition of the detached campanile remained so strong in Italy that towers hardly ever became an integral part of the church itself. The complex at Pisa includes a church and a circular, domed baptistery to the west. The ensemble of buildings, built on an open site north of the city, reflects the wealth and pride of the city-republic of Pisa after its naval victory over the Muslims at Palermo in 1062.

The Pisa baptistery was begun in 1153 by Diotisalvi but everything above the arcaded first level was reworked a century later. Throughout the Middle Ages, Tuscany remained conscious of its antique heritage. The idea of a separate baptistery relies on Early Christian precedents. The round form of the Pisa one and its original cone vault also reflect the structure of the Rotunda of the Anastasis in Jerusalem (see fig. 8.12). The comparison would undoubtedly have been comprehensible to Pisans, whose seamen profited by carrying pilgrims and crusaders to the Holy Land. Once again, the opportunity for increased trade and travel, the lure of pilgrimage, and the ongoing struggle against the Muslims in Iberia and the eastern Mediterranean were decisive forces in shaping Romanesque monuments.

The basic plan of Pisa cathedral is that of an Early Christian basilica, but it has been transformed into a **Latin cross** (where three arms are of equal length and one is longer) by the addition

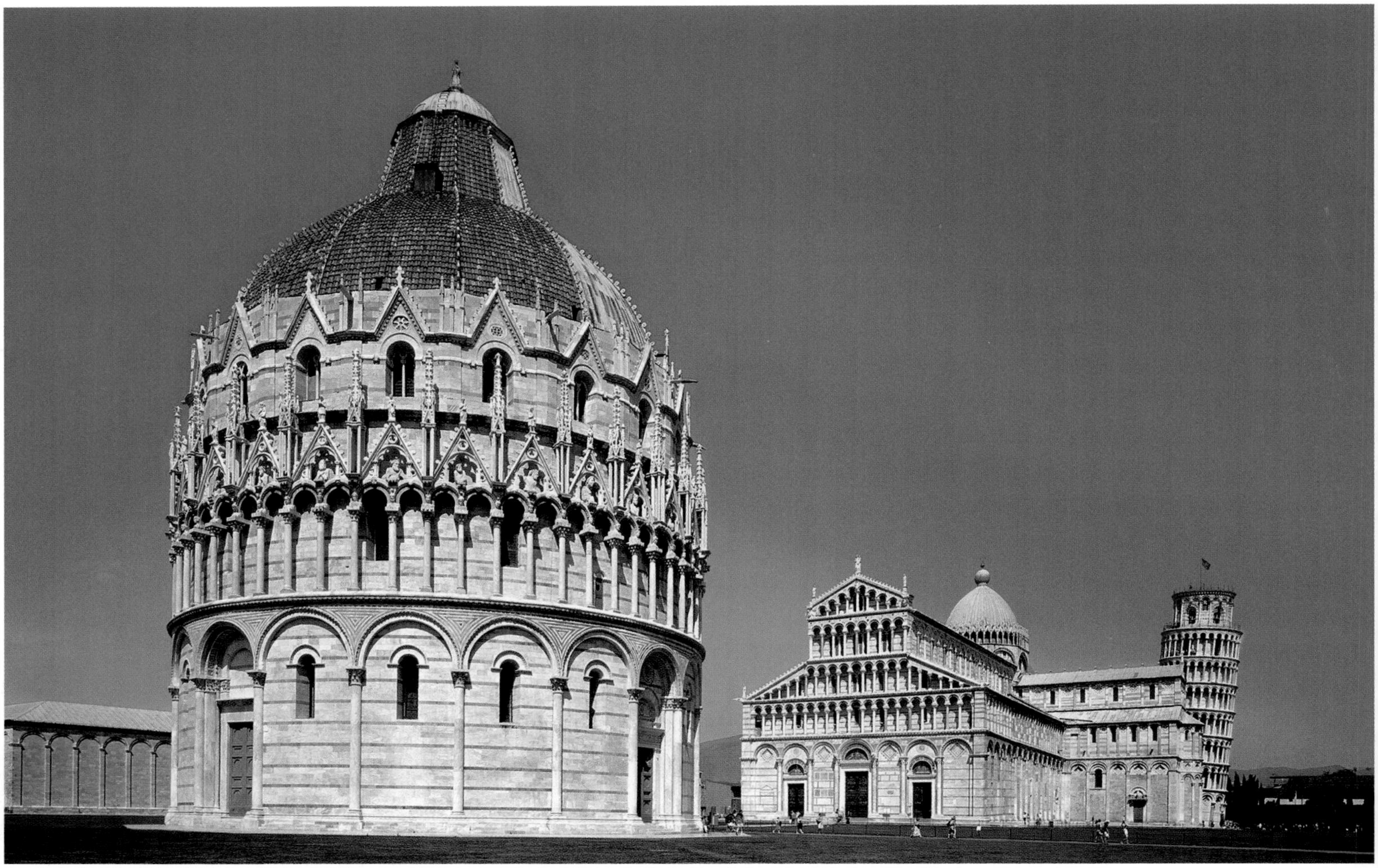

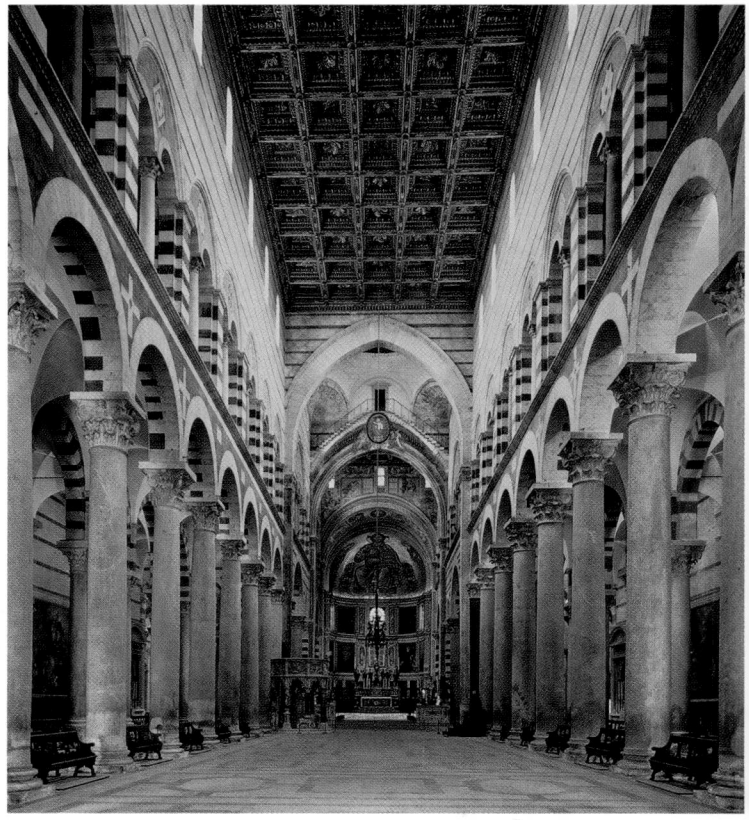

11.33 Baptistery, cathedral, and campanile (view from the west), Pisa, Italy. 1053–1272

of transept arms that resemble small basilicas with apses of their own. A dome marks the crossing. The rest of the church has a wooden roof, except for the aisles (four in the nave, two in the transept arms), which have **groin vaults**, formed when two barrel vaults intersect. The interior (fig. **11.34**) has somewhat taller proportions than an Early Christian basilica, because there are galleries over the aisles as well as a clerestory. Yet the classical columns supporting the nave and aisle arcades still recall types that would fit comfortably in an Early Christian basilica (see fig. 8.9).

A deliberate revival of the antique Roman style in Tuscan architecture was the use of a multicolored marble "skin" on the exteriors of churches. Little of this inlay is left today on the ancient monuments of Rome because much of it was literally "lifted" to decorate later buildings. However, the interior of the

11.34 Interior, Pisa cathedral

Pantheon still gives us some idea of what this must have looked like. Pisa cathedral and its companion buildings are covered in white marble inlaid with horizontal stripes and ornamental patterns in dark-green marble. This decorative scheme is combined with blind arcades and galleries. The result is a richness very different from austere Early Christian exteriors.

BAPTISTERY OF SAN GIOVANNI, FLORENCE In Florence, which was to outstrip Pisa commercially and artistically, the greatest achievement of the Tuscan Romanesque is the baptistery of San Giovanni (fig. **11.35**) opposite the cathedral (see fig. 13.10). It is a domed, octagonal building of impressive size, begun in the middle of the eleventh century. The eight sides of the building continue a long tradition in baptistery design and symbolically allude to rebirth: The world began on the eighth day

following the Creation, and Christ was resurrected on the eighth day of the Passion. The green-and-white marble paneling is typical of the Florentine Romanesque in its severely geometric lines. The triple arches of the second-story blind arcades, with their triumphal-arch design, are extraordinarily classical in proportion and detail.

SAN MINIATO AL MONTE, FLORENCE The magnificent site of the Benedictine monastery of San Miniato al Monte overlooking the city of Florence reflects that establishment's grandeur during the Middle Ages. The church is dedicated to St. Minias, Florence's first Christian martyr, a third-century hermit who was beheaded by the Romans. It is said that, after his martyrdom, St. Minias gathered his head and proceeded to the cave where he had lived and died; subsequently a church was built on site. The

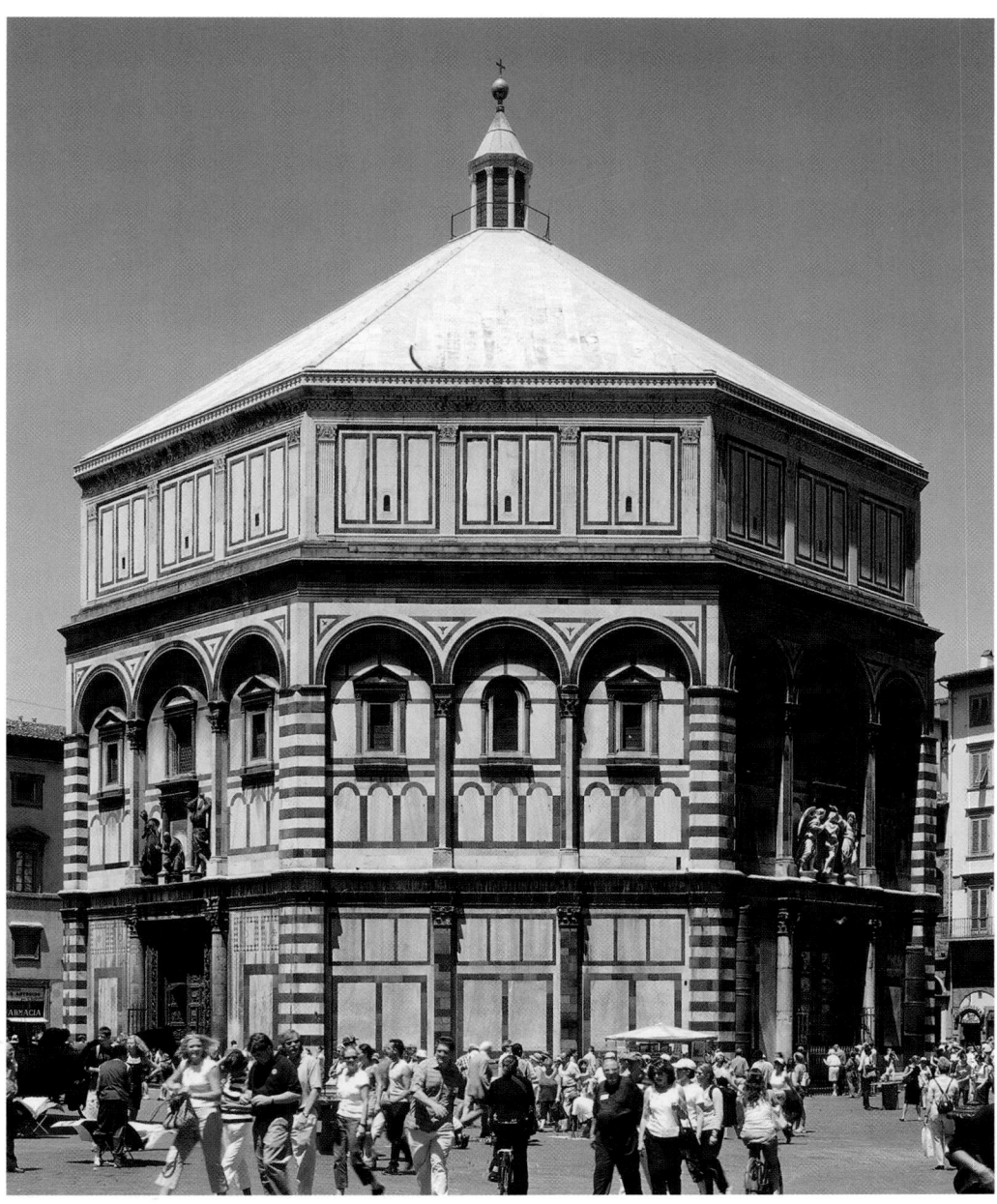

11.35 Baptistery of San Giovanni, Florence, Italy. ca. 1060–1150

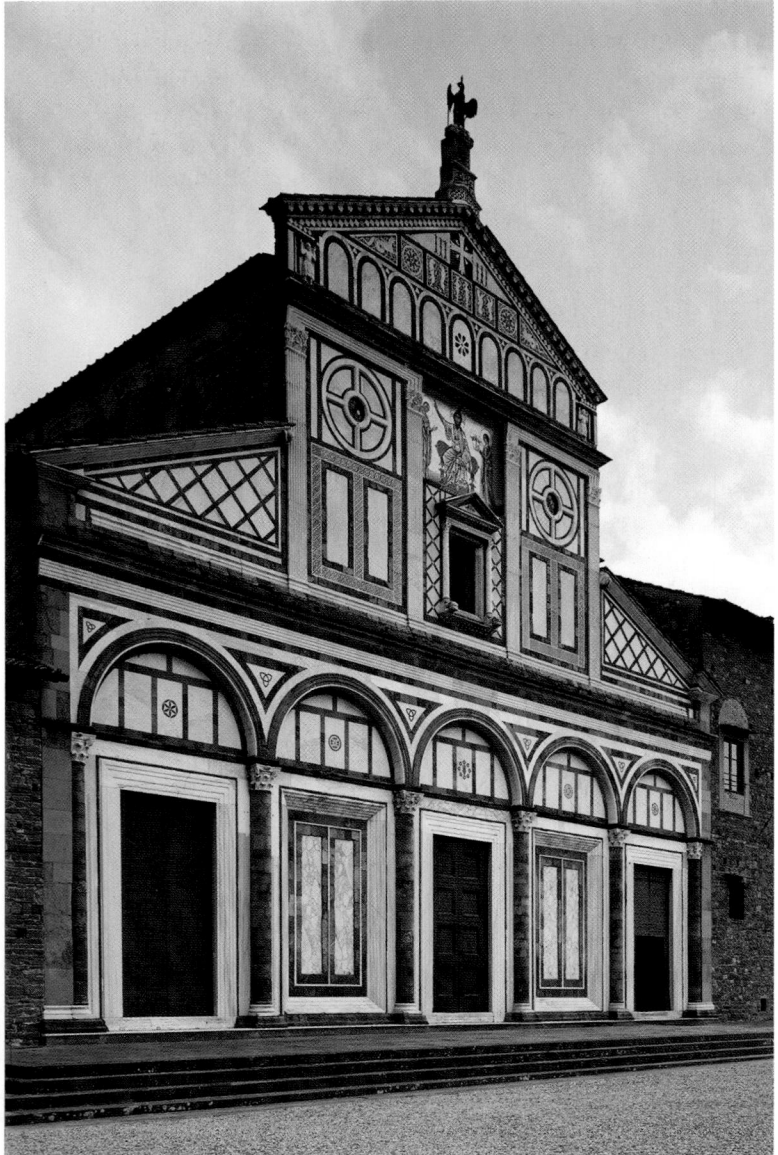

11.36 Façade, San Miniato al Monte, Florence, Italy. 1062–1150

Germany

In Germany, the traditions of the Holy Roman Empire functioned as filters for the revival of Roman forms. As a result, German Romanesque architecture, centered in the Rhineland, relied for its organization and formal vocabulary on buildings patronized by Carolingian and Ottonian rulers.

SPEYER CATHEDRAL The cathedral of Speyer, which contained tombs of Holy Roman emperors, was consecrated in 1061. It included a timber-roof nave (fig. 11.37), not unlike those of Carolingian and Ottonian buildings. A major rebuilding of the cathedral in 1080 added groin vaults to the nave (fig. 11.38), providing a solution to a problem that had limited Romanesque builders: While the barrel vault used in the churches we have previously examined offered an aesthetically pleasing, acoustically resonant, and fire-resistant space, it limited the amount of light that could enter the nave. The problem was that the weakest part of the vault, the springing (the point where the arch rises from its support) was precisely the point where clerestory windows were needed. There had been exceptional buildings that included clerestories, such as Sant Vincenç at Cardona (see fig. 11.1) and the abbey church at Cluny (see fig. 11.11). But Sant Vincenç's

gabled façade of the church (fig. 11.36) coincides with the shape of the wooden-roofed and aisled basilica. As with the baptistery of San Giovanni, and begun only a few years after it, geometric precision governs the arrangement of the façade's green-and-white marble covering. Although the treatment of surface and the materials employed are distinctive to Tuscany, the organization of elements compares with Romanesque arrangements elsewhere. The individual, additive units decorating Florentine Romanesque buildings also parallel the compartmentalized bays in pilgrimage churches (see fig. 11.5) and the way French Romanesque portals (see figs. 11.13, 11.30, 11.31) are composed of individual units that maintain their identities though functioning in unison. Roman elements employed in conscious revival—here the use of marble and the repeated arches that rest on columns topped with Corinthian capitals—unite many of these Romanesque works as well.

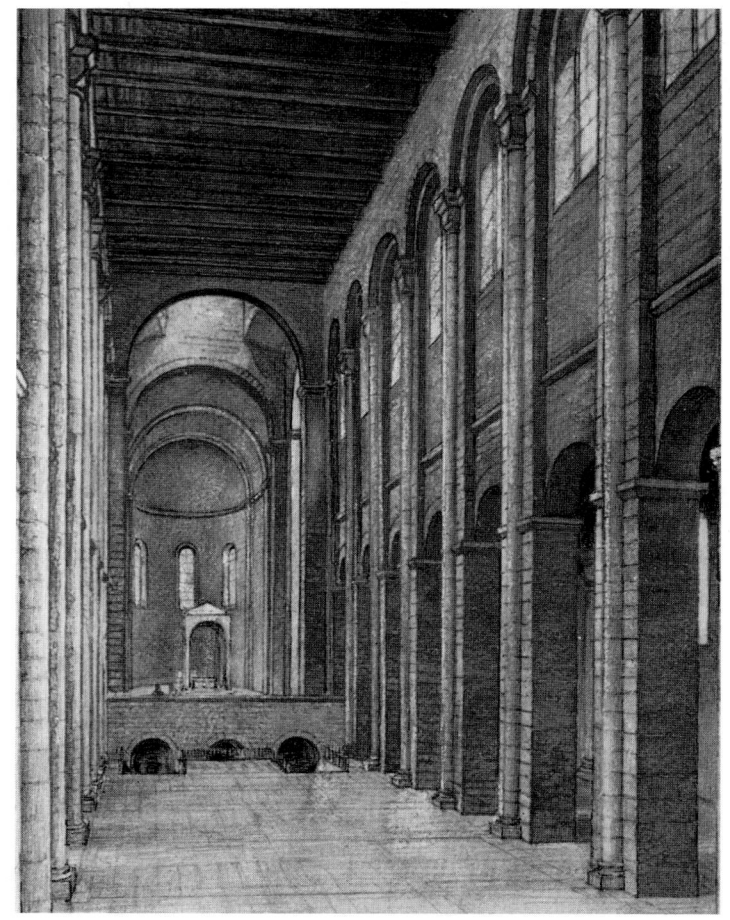

11.37 Reconstruction of interior of Speyer cathedral, Germany. ca. 1030–61 (after Conant)

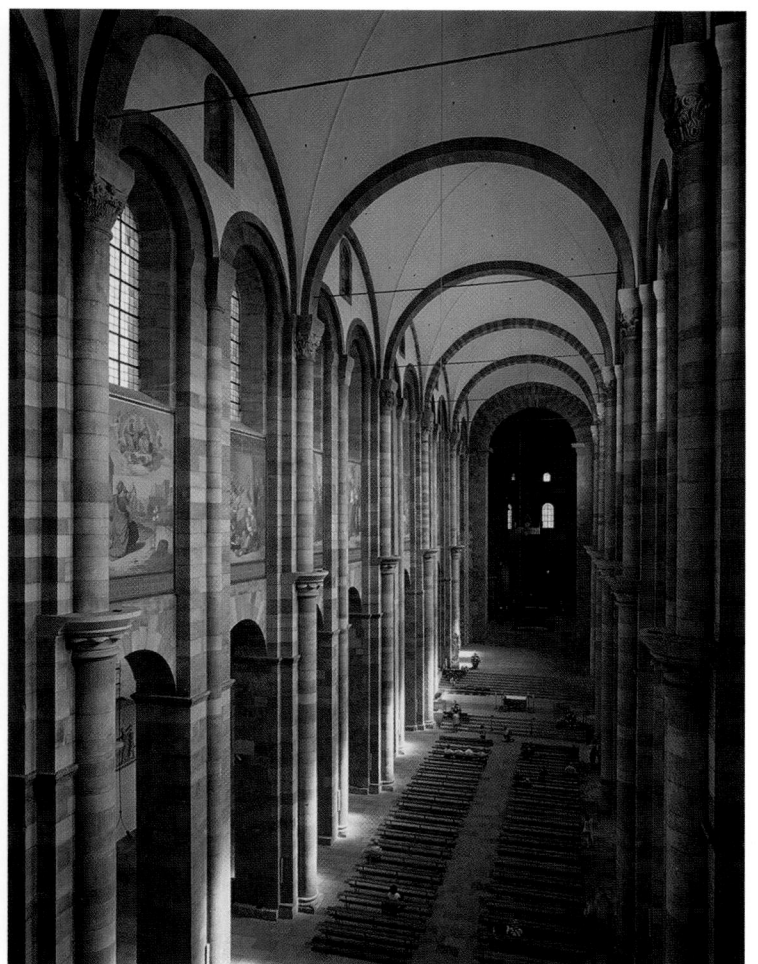

11.38 Interior, Speyer cathedral. ca. 1030–61; vaulted ca. 1080–1106

vaults. The use of these compound piers aligns Speyer with Romanesque buildings of other regions (see figs. 11.1, 11.5, and 11.22). The alternating support system establishes a rhythm that must have struck a familiar chord in Germany. It had appeared in the Ottonian buildings of Gernrode (see fig. 10.23) and Hildesheim (see fig. 10.26), although in these buildings such a system was purely aesthetic.

The Meuse Valley: Mosan Style

An important group of Romanesque sculptors, who excelled in metalwork, operated in the valley of the Meuse River, which runs from northeastern France into present-day Belgium and Holland. This region had been the home of the classicizing Reims style in Carolingian times (see figs. 10.14, 10.15, and 10.16), and during the Romanesque period an awareness of classical sources again pervades its art, called Mosan. Abbot Hellinus of Liège commissioned a bronze baptismal font for the church of Notre-Dame-aux-Fonts in Liège (fig. **11.39**). The generally accepted attribution to Renier of Huy, the earliest Mosan artist whose name we know, is largely circumstantial. The font, completed in 1118 and today in the church of Saint-Barthélemy, is a remarkable achievement: Cast in one piece, it is over 2 feet high and 3½ feet in diameter. The vessel rested on 12 oxen, like Solomon's basin in the Temple at Jerusalem as described in the first book of Kings in the Hebrew Bible: "And he made the molten sea ... It stood upon twelve oxen ... and all their hinder parts were inward." Christian writers described Solomon's basin as a prototype for the baptismal font and the 12 oxen as precursors of the apostles.

windows are limited in number and scale, and at Cluny it was necessary to employ a series of devices, including pointed arches and enlarged buttresses, to provide adequate support for the high barrel vault.

The builders of Speyer cathedral solved this problem with the groin vault. (See *Materials and Techniques*, page 380.) The groin vault, which had been used so effectively by the Romans, efficiently channeled thrust onto four corner points. This allowed for open space under each arch, which could be used for window openings without diminishing the strength of the vault. The erection of groin vaults in the nave of Speyer cathedral was accompanied by an enlargement of its clerestory windows. Romanesque builders knew the technology of groin-vault construction and had previously employed groin vaults to cover lower spaces, in side aisles and in crypts, as at Pisa (see fig. 11.34), but apparently they found them daunting to build on a large scale. Speyer represents a genuine breakthrough in building technology: The scale is so great that it dwarfs every other church of the period.

The individual groin-vaulted bays at Speyer form a chain of compartmentalized units of space. Each groin vault comprises two bays of the original nave. Colonnettes attached to alternate piers articulate the distribution of weight necessary to support the

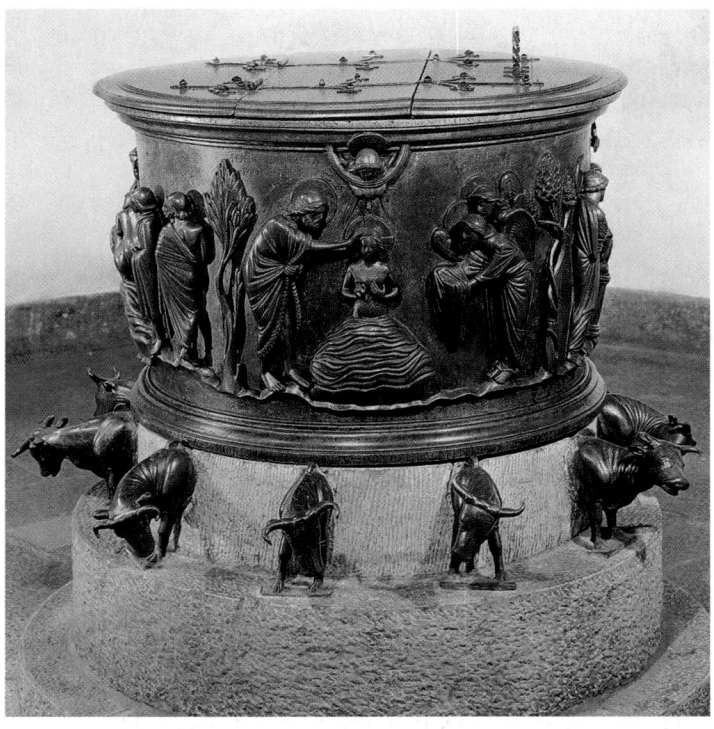

11.39 Renier of Huy. Baptismal Font. 1107–18. Bronze, height 25" (63.5 cm). Saint-Barthélemy, Liège, Belgium

Vaulting

Vaulting is a technique for covering buildings that is based on the principles of arcuation, that is, construction that uses the arch form (a). Although vaulting was used in Mesopotamia, Egypt, and Greece, it was the Etruscans and Romans who first exploited the vault for expressive and aesthetic purposes (see page 186). While most early medieval buildings were covered with timber-beam roofs, during the Romanesque period stone vaulting became the dominant roofing type. Its reintroduction in the eleventh century was a major component of the revival of Roman artistic forms during the Romanesque period. Although Roman vaults were principally made of concrete, medieval vaults were usually made either of rubble or masonry, bound with mortar.

The erection of stone vaults in medieval buildings required enormous effort and great expense, but the benefits were numerous. These included fire resistance, particularly important for buildings illuminated by candles and for tall structures that attracted lightning. The history of medieval buildings is largely a history of fires. Widespread attacks by Vikings, Magyars from Hungary, and Muslims also made stronger buildings desirable. In addition, stone vaulting provides excellent acoustics, a significant consideration for churches in which the liturgy was chanted. No less important than these practical benefits were the aesthetic ones: Vaulted buildings appear dignified and monumental, and they provide an unambiguous sense of enclosure. There are many types of vaults: barrel, quadrant, groin, ribbed, and the dome.

The barrel vault, essentially an arch projected in depth, is the most basic form (b). This was the first type exploited by medieval builders because it lent itself to covering rectangular basilicas. Unfortunately, the barrel vault creates dark spaces, since opening up the nave walls with clerestory windows weakens the vault at its most vulnerable point, the springing. It is here, at the base of the arch, that the force of gravity, which is channeled through the arch, results in lateral forces pushing sideways. This outward thrust needs to be contained, usually by building thick walls to buttress the vault.

In Romanesque churches with wide side aisles, architects were faced with the problem of transferring the thrust of the barrel vault across the side aisles to the outer walls. They were able to do this by vaulting the galleries over the aisles with **quadrant vaults** (half-barrel vaults), which buttress the barrel vault of the nave. These buildings were also dark, with light entering only from windows at the ends of the barrel vaults and in the side walls, filtered through aisle and gallery before reaching the nave.

The introduction of the groin vault provided for more luminous structures that required less building material; thus, buildings became lighter in both senses of the word. A groin vault is formed when two barrel vaults intersect (c); the thrust of each vault is countered by the vault running perpendicular to it. (The term "groin" refers to the junction where the vaults intersect.) Thrust is thus channeled to four corner points, allowing for windows or other openings in the wall under each of the intersecting arches.

The **ribbed vault**, introduced at Durham cathedral, was probably invented as a decorative device (d); only later did architects and masons come to appreciate its structural advantages. Larger stones are placed on the groins of the vault to form diagonal arches. These function as a fixed scaffold to support the vault's curved panels, called **webs**, which essentially fill the spaces between the ribs. Ribbed vaults were easier to construct and required less centering (see below) than unribbed vaults; their webs could be built of lighter material, since the ribbed groins channeled the major lateral thrust more efficiently.

Romanesque masons also employed the dome, which is essentially an arch rotated on axis to form a vault (e). In Romanesque churches, domes cover centralized buildings or mark significant elements, for example the area where the transept crosses the nave. Vaults are not easy to construct and Romanesque vaults were heavy: Often more than a foot thick, each could weigh several tons. Arcuation is a dynamic system, with all its elements interlocked; as a result, the vault is stable only when it is complete. During construction it needs to be supported by a wooden framework, called a **centering**. Once the vault is built and the buttresses are in place, the vault becomes self-supporting and the centering can be removed. The widespread use of the vault and its progressive refinement during the Romanesque period represent significant achievements, which were crucial for the continued development of medieval building, particularly during the Gothic period.

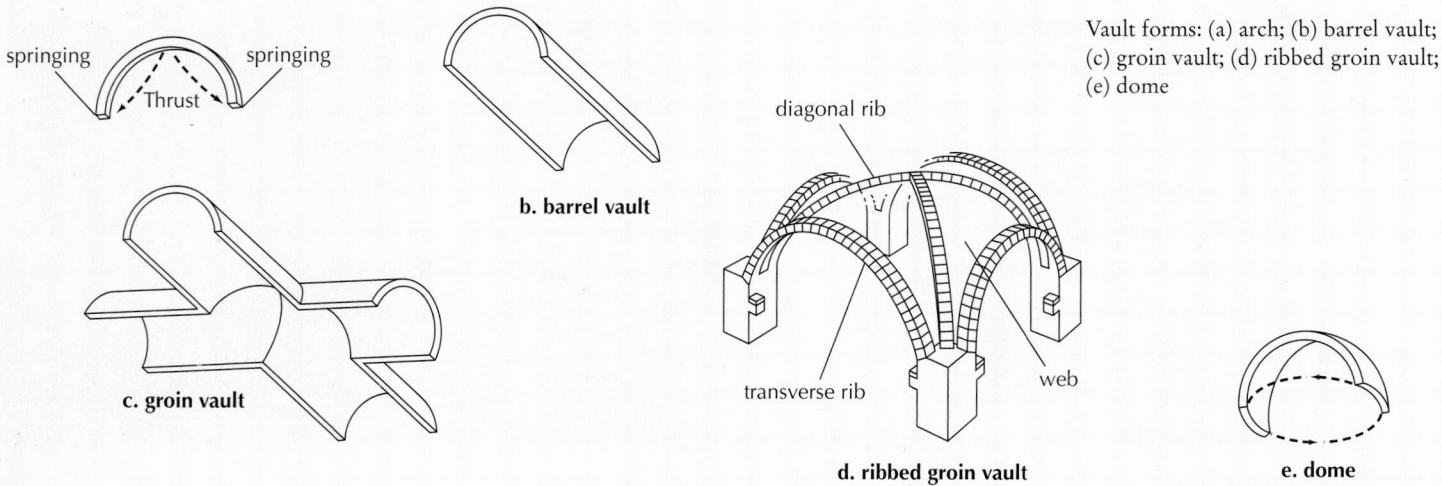

springing   springing
Thrust

b. barrel vault

c. groin vault

Vault forms: (a) arch; (b) barrel vault;
(c) groin vault; (d) ribbed groin vault;
(e) dome

diagonal rib

transverse rib   web

d. ribbed groin vault

e. dome

The reliefs are about the same height as those on the bronze doors of Bishop Bernward at Hildesheim (see fig. 10.27). Instead of the rough expressive power of the Ottonian panels, however, the viewer sees a harmonious balance of design, a subtle control of the sculptured surfaces, and an understanding of organic structure that are surprisingly classical for a medieval work. The figure seen from the back (beyond the tree on the left), with its graceful movement and Greek-looking drapery, might almost be taken for a work from antiquity. Renier also expressed his interest in antique form through the use of bronze, rejecting the monumentality implicit in stone sculpture. The strong northern European metalwork tradition now serves to convey classical values, so alien to early medieval metalworkers who had previously dominated the art of this area.

The Romanesque antique revival in the Mosan region has a special character, quite different from the abstract, decorative qualities that characterize the work of other regions, so demonstrating that while Romanesque art shares a common interest in reviving classical forms, there was great variety in the ways that classicism was expressed. The Liège font and other Mosan sculptures are carved in high relief or are fully three-dimensional, with convincing anatomical details and proportions. Yet, the concern of Mosan sculptors was not so much for naturalism as for an idealism that here produces classicizing forms.

Normandy and England

Farther north, Christianity was strongly supported by the Norman dukes and barons, former Vikings who had turned Normandy into a powerful feudal domain that included the allegiance of abbots and bishops as vassals in return for grants of land. Duke William II of Normandy actively promoted monastic reform and founded numerous abbeys. Normandy soon became a cultural center of international importance. When William invaded Anglo-Saxon England in 1066 and became king there, England became politically allied to northern France. For that reason Norman and English art of the Romanesque period share many stylistic traits.

THE BAYEUX TAPESTRY The complex relationship between the Normans and the English is hinted at in the *Bayeux Tapestry* (figs. **11.40** and **11.41**), important both as a historical record and as a work of art. In actuality it is not a tapestry at all, since it is not woven, but rather an embroidered linen frieze 230 feet long. The 50 surviving scenes record the events, culminating in 1066, when William the Conqueror crossed the English Channel to claim the throne of England upon the death of King Edward the Confessor. According to the narrative of the "tapestry," Harold, an Anglo-Saxon earl, had retracted his oath of fealty to William in order to

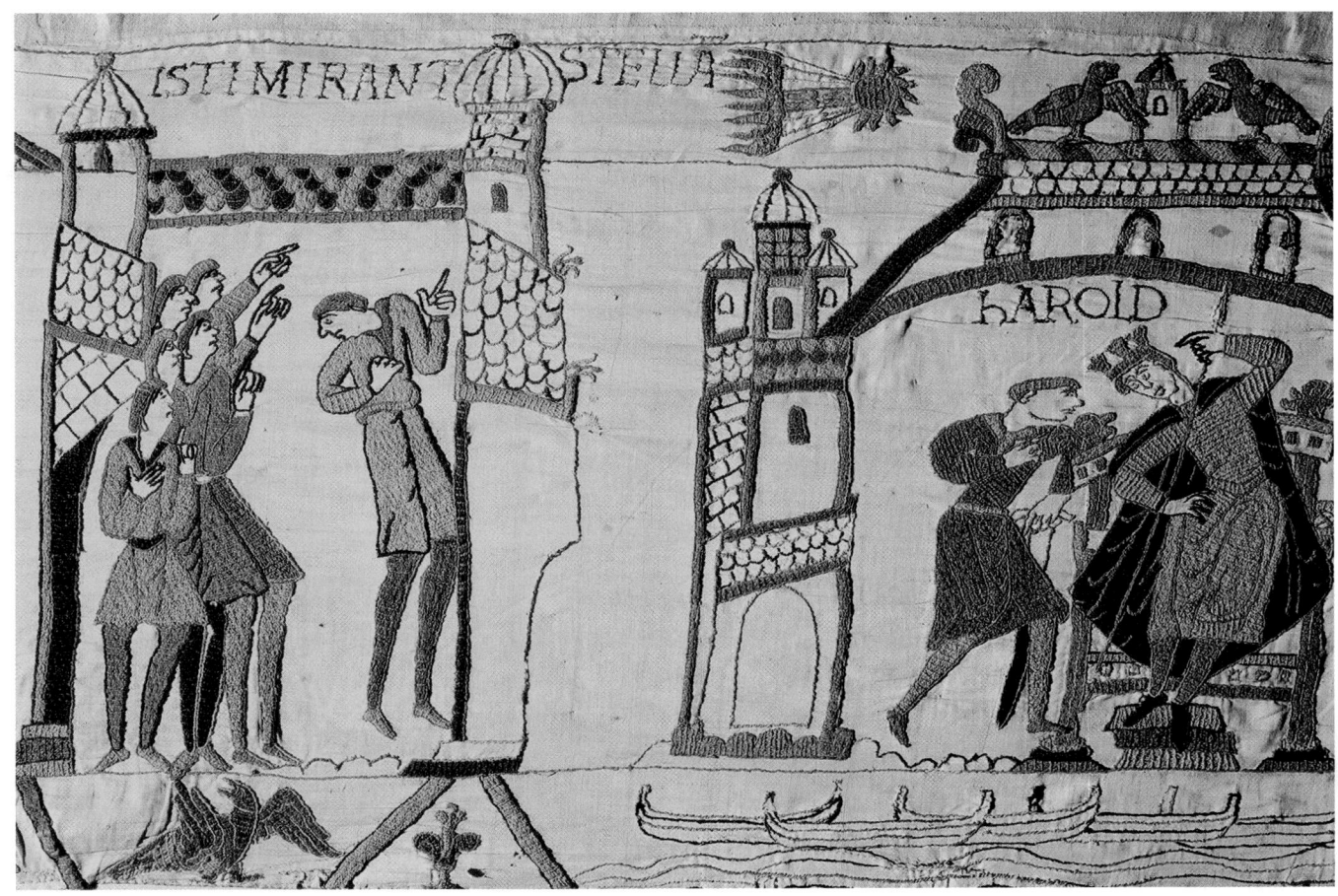

11.40 *Crowds Gaze in Awe at a Comet as Harold Is Told of an Omen*, detail of the *Bayeux Tapestry*. ca. 1066–83. Wool embroidery on linen, height 20" (50.7 cm). Centre Guillaume le Conquérant, Bayeux, France

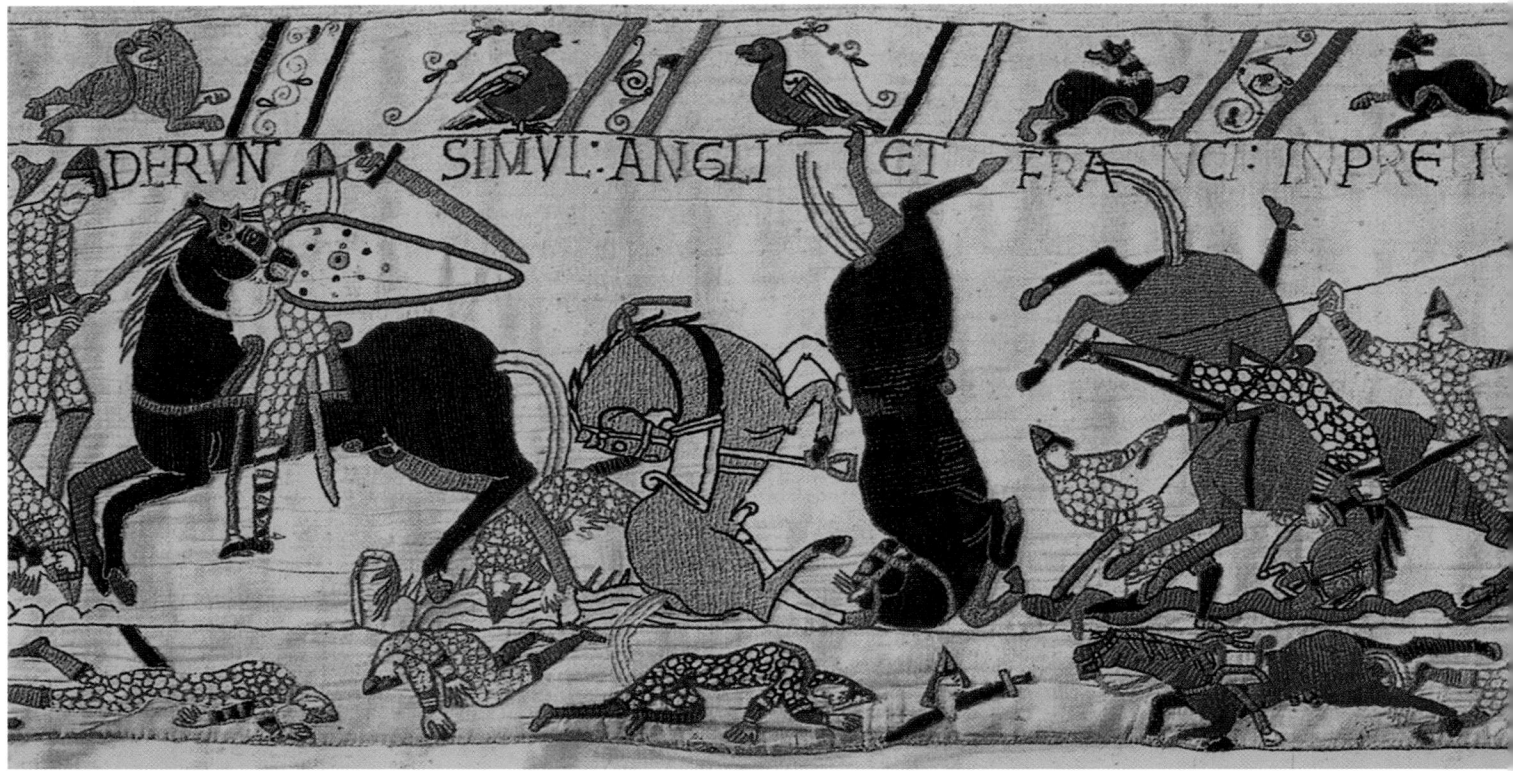

11.41 *The Battle of Hastings*, detail of the *Bayeux Tapestry*. Wool embroidery on linen, height 20" (50.7 cm). Centre Guillaume le Conquérant, Bayeux, France

accept the throne offered him by the English nobles. William retaliated by invading England, and his Norman troops vanquished the English as Harold fell in battle. Since a Norman patron presumably commissioned the work, the story is told from the conquerors' perspective, yet its manufacture has generally been credited to English needlewomen, justly famous during the Middle Ages for their skill.

The *Bayeux Tapestry* exhibits the same monumentality and interest in narrative that we saw in the illuminations of the *Gospel Book of Abbot Wedricus* (see fig. 11.29), which, as noted, is a manuscript linked to both Normandy and England. The Bayeux designer has integrated narrative and ornament with complete ease. Two border strips frame the main frieze; while some of the images in these margins are decorative, others offer a commentary on the continuous narrative. In one scene (see fig. 11.40), an aide announces to a recently crowned Harold the appearance of an amazing natural phenomenon, represented in the upper border as a spinning star leaving its fiery trail. The inscription *ISTI MIRANT STELLA* ("These men marvel at the star") records the brilliant apparition of Halley's Comet in 1066, during the days immediately following Harold's coronation. To the medieval viewer, the prophetic significance of the natural event would have been clear, especially when viewed after the fact. Beneath Harold, ghostly boats await the Normans, who are preparing to cross the English Channel. The scene foreshadows the violent events to come.

Although the *Bayeux Tapestry* does not use the pictorial devices of classical painting, such as foreshortening and overlapping (see

fig. 5.78), it presents a vivid and detailed account of warfare in the eleventh century as well as a hint of the Normans' abilities as builders of fortresslike castles. The massed forms of the Graeco-Roman scene are replaced by a new kind of individualism that makes each figure a potential hero, whether by force or by cunning. Note how the soldier who has fallen from the horse with its hind legs in the air is, in turn, toppling his foe by yanking at the saddle girth of his mount. The kinship with the Corbie Gospel book manuscript (see fig. 11.27) is noticeable in the lively somersaults of the horses, so like the pose of the lion in the miniature. In the Middle Ages, the religious and secular spheres were not sharply distinguished from each other, and as such the same pictorial devices were employed in both. The energy and linear clarity of the *Bayeux Tapestry* and the Corbie Gospel book remind the viewer of the monumental figures of Romanesque sculpture.

DURHAM CATHEDRAL Norman architecture is responsible for a great breakthrough in structural engineering, which took place in England, where King William made donations to build in a Norman style. Durham cathedral, begun in 1093, is among the largest churches of medieval Europe (fig. **11.42**): Its nave is wider than that of Santiago de Compostela, and its overall length (400 feet) is also greater. The nave may have been designed to be vaulted from the start. The vault over its eastern end had been completed by 1107, in a remarkably short space of time, and the rest of the nave was vaulted by 1130 (fig. **11.43**).

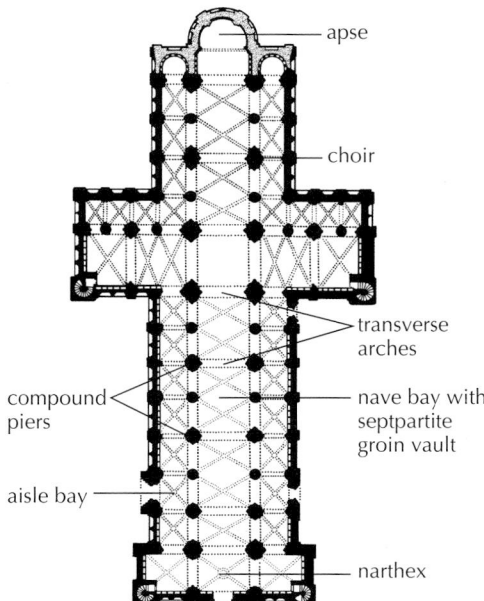

11.42 Plan of Durham cathedral, England. 1093–1130 (after Conant)

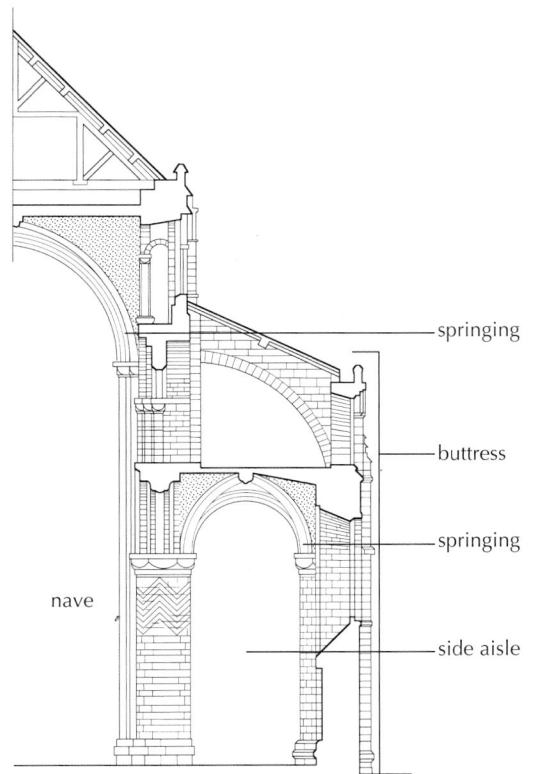

11.44 Transverse section of Durham cathedral (after Acland)

This vault is of great interest. As the earliest systematic use of a **ribbed groin vault** over a three-story nave, it marks a basic advance beyond Speyer. Looking at the plan (see fig. 11.42), we see that the aisles consist of the usual almost-square groin-vaulted compartments. The bays of the nave, separated by strong transverse

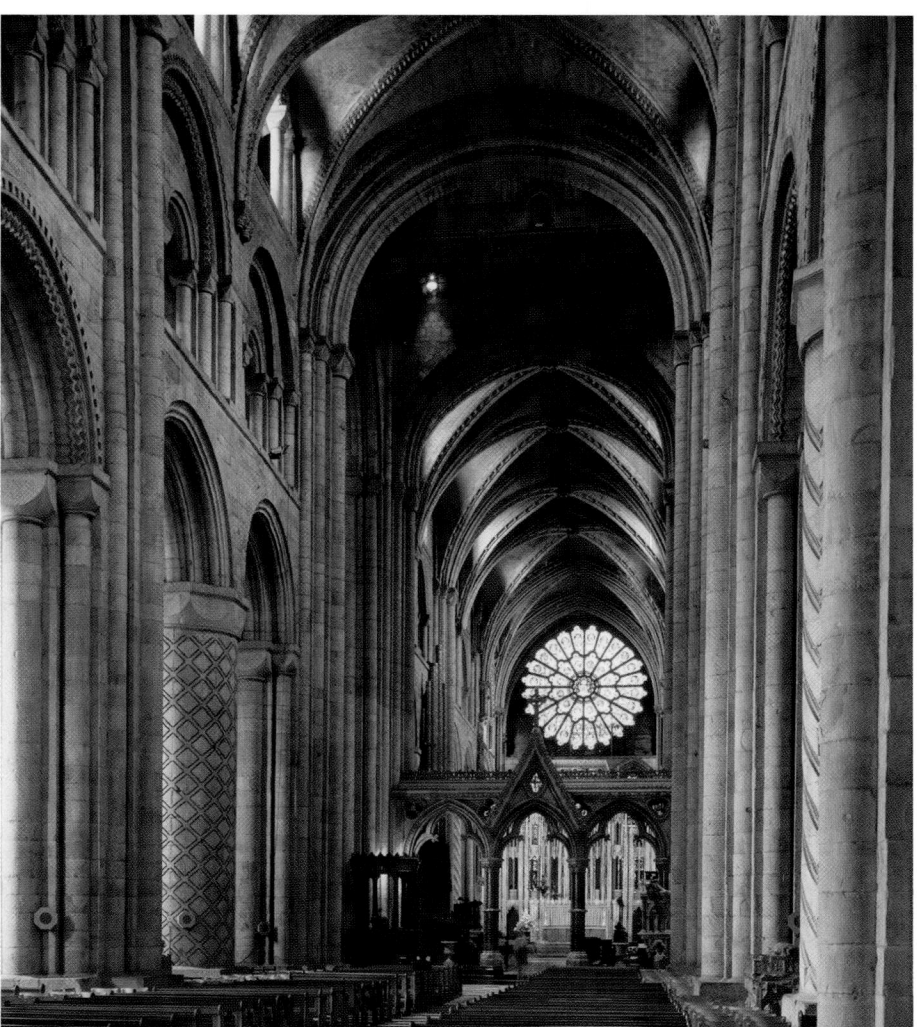

11.43 Nave (looking east), Durham cathedral

arches, are oblong and also groin-vaulted, so that the ribs of each bay form a double-X design. Each vault of the nave is thus divided into seven sections. These vaults are referred to as **septpartite** (or seven-part) groin vaults. Since the nave bays are twice as long as the aisle bays, transverse arches occur only at the odd-numbered piers of the nave arcade (see fig. 11.43). The piers therefore alternate in size. Unlike Speyer cathedral (see fig. 11.38), where a colonnette was added to every other nave pier to strengthen it, at Durham the odd-numbered piers are intrinsically different from the even-numbered ones. The odd-numbered ones are larger and compound, with bundles of column and pilaster shafts attached to a square or oblong core, while the even-numbered ones are thinner and cylindrical.

The outward thrust and weight of the whole vault are concentrated at six securely anchored points on the gallery level from which the ribs spring. The ribs were needed to provide a stable skeleton for the groin vault, and the curved surfaces between them were filled in with masonry of a minimal thickness. Thus, both weight and thrust were reduced, and carried downward to the outer wall of the aisles by buttresses (fig. **11.44**). This flexible system resulted in more efficient vault erection and greater economy of construction. We do not know whether this ingenious scheme was actually invented at Durham, but it could not have been devised much earlier, for it is still in an experimental stage. While the transverse arches at the crossing are round, those to the west of it are slightly pointed, indicating an ongoing search for improvements.

The ribbed groin-vault system had other advantages. From an aesthetic standpoint, the nave at Durham is among the finest in all Romanesque architecture. The sturdiness of the alternating piers makes a splendid contrast to the dramatically lit, sail-like surfaces of the vault. This relatively lightweight, flexible system permits broad expanses of great height to be covered with fireproof vaulting and yet retain the ample lighting of a clerestory. Durham exhibits great structural strength; even so, the decoration incised in its round piers, each different from the others, and the pattern established by the vault ribs hark back to the Anglo-Saxon love of decoration and interest in surface pattern (see figs. 10.1–10.3).

SAINT-ÉTIENNE, CAEN The abbey church of Saint-Étienne at Caen (fig. **11.45**) was founded by William the Conqueror a year or two after his invasion of England in 1066, but it took over 100 years to complete. Over this period of time the fruits of Durham cathedral's ribbed groin-vault system matured. The west façade (fig. **11.46**) offers a striking contrast with Notre-Dame-la-Grande in Poitiers (see fig. 11.30) and other Romanesque façades (see figs. 11.13, 11.17, and 11.31). The westwork proclaims this an imperial church. Its closest ancestors are Carolingian churches, such as the abbey church at Corvey (see fig. 10.21), built under royal patronage. Like them, it has a minimum of decoration. Four huge buttresses divide the front of the church into three vertical sections. The thrust upward continues in the two towers, the height of which would be impressive even without the tall helmets, which

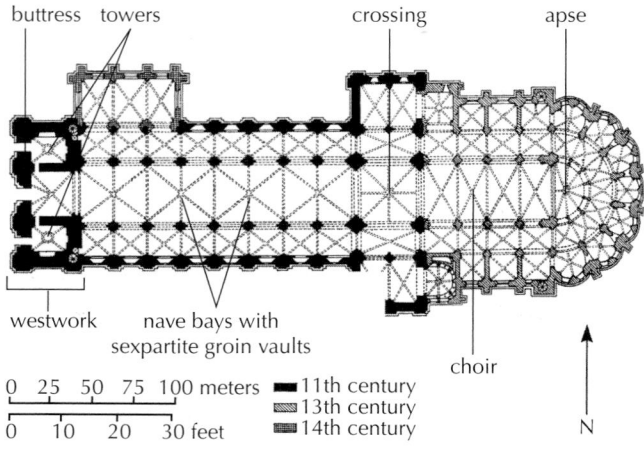

11.45 Plan of abbey church of Saint-Étienne, Caen, France. Begun 1068

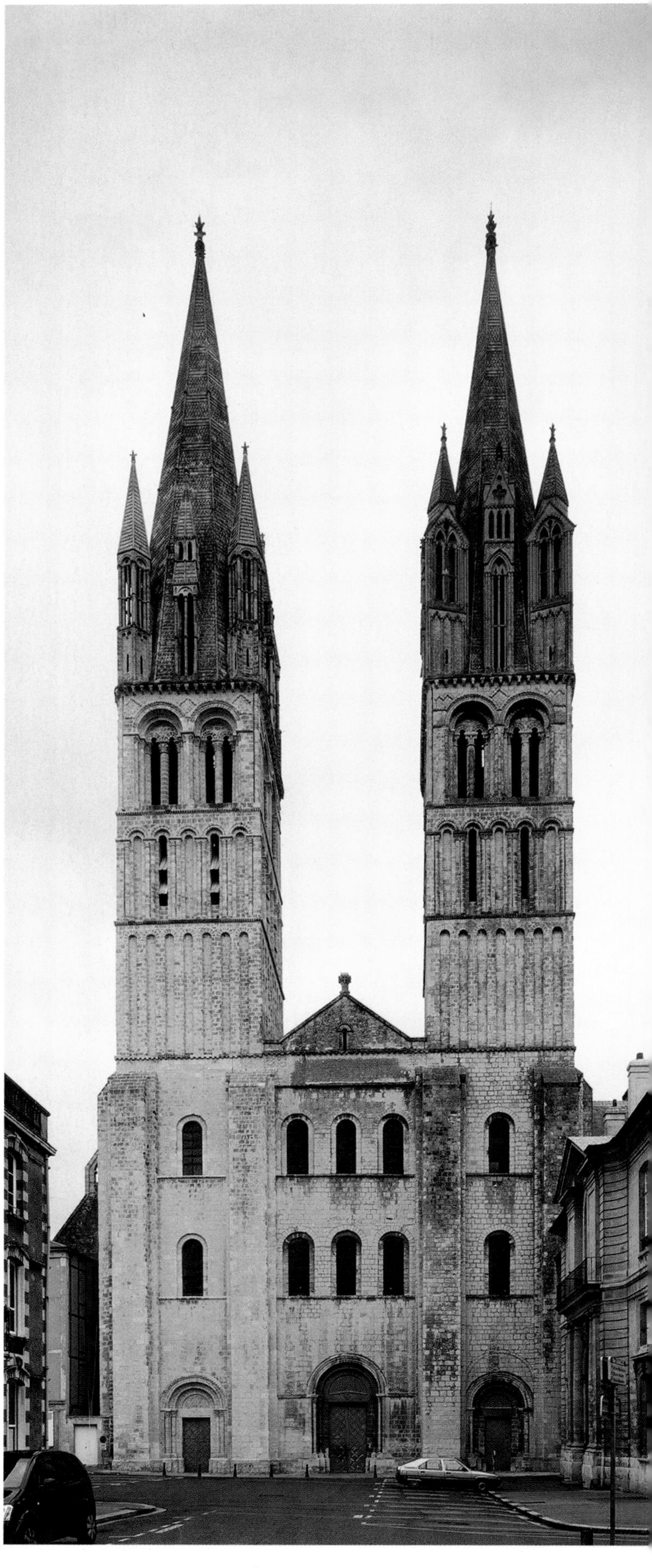

11.46 West façade of Saint-Étienne, Caen, France

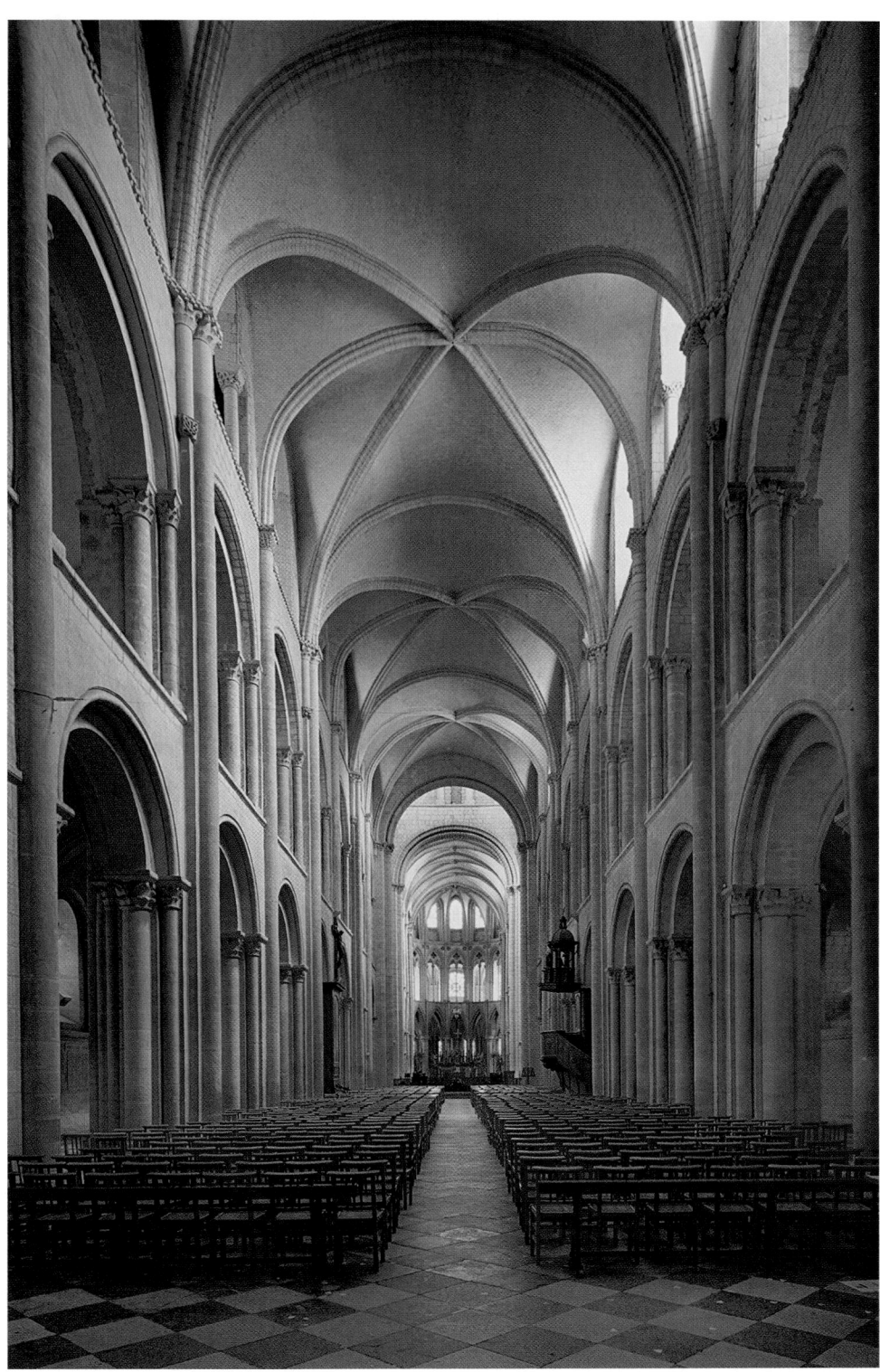

are later additions. Saint-Étienne is cool and composed, encouraging viewers to appreciate its refined proportions, a feature shared with many other Romanesque buildings.

In the interior of Saint-Étienne (fig. **11.47**), the nave was originally planned to have a wooden ceiling, as well as galleries and a clerestory. After the experience of Durham, however, it became possible in the early twelfth century to build a groined nave vault, with only slight changes in the wall design. The bays of the nave here are approximately square (see fig. 11.45), whereas at Durham they were oblong. Therefore, the double-X rib pattern could be replaced by a single X with an additional transverse rib, which produced a **sexpartite** groin vault, with six sections instead of seven. These vaults are no longer separated by heavy transverse arches but instead by simple ribs. The resulting reduction in weight also gives a stronger sense of continuity to the nave vault as a whole and produces a less emphatic alternation of piers. Compared with Durham, the nave of Saint-Étienne has an airy lightness.

THE PARADOXICAL MEANING OF ROMANESQUE

The improved economic conditions and political stability of Europe, outlined at the beginning of this chapter, had their rewards in the secure structures built in the twelfth century. However, the architecture's defensive qualities also suggest a paradox: As much as the stalwart, powerfully built buildings express a newfound confidence, they also reveal lingering apprehension. The terrifying Last Judgment scenes (see fig. 11.17) and other Romanesque visions of monsters and diabolical beings attest to this anxiety. A folio of the *Winchester Psalter* (fig. **11.48**), produced in England during the middle of the twelfth century, depicts a large Hell mouth: The heavy arched jaws of the devil's head contain monstrous forms devouring sinners of all classes.

The inscription, written in Anglo-Norman French, translates as: "Here is Hell and the angels who lock the doors." The heavy walls and repeated enclosures that govern so much Romanesque sculpture and architecture have their counterpart in this representation. The frame, with its serene cadence of heavily outlined decorations, encloses and controls the frightening image.

The manuscript was commissioned by Henry of Blois, bishop of Winchester, who had been a monk at Cluny and collected antique sculpture and Byzantine paintings on his journeys to Rome. The *Winchester Psalter* exemplifies how international artistic forces functioned during the Romanesque period to help create a vision expressive of the hopes and fears of a society yearning for protection from dark elements. It is instructive that, in the end, assistance from a heavenly being—the angel who locks the Hell-mouth door—is required to contain the potent forces of evil.

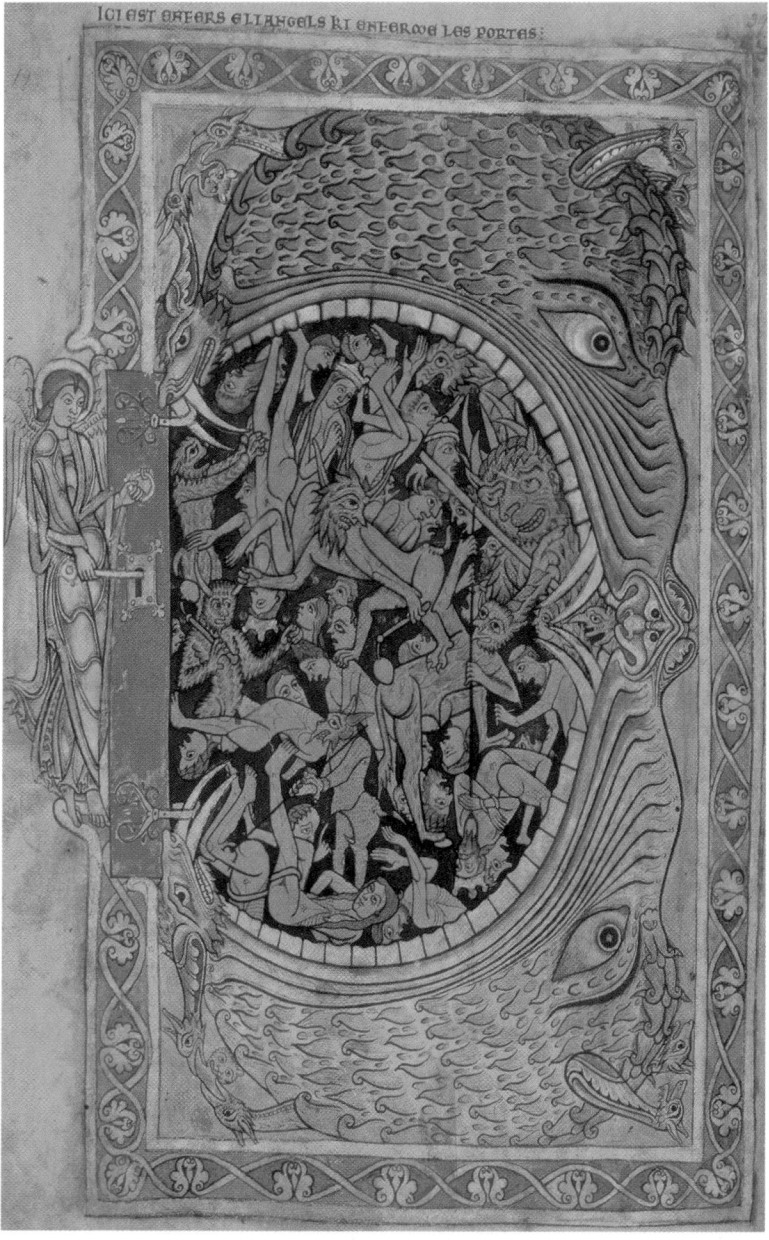

11.48 *Mouth of Hell*, from the *Winchester Psalter*. From Winchester, England. ca. 1150. Tempera on vellum, 12¾ × 9" (32.5 × 23 cm). The British Library, London (MS Cotton Nero D.4)

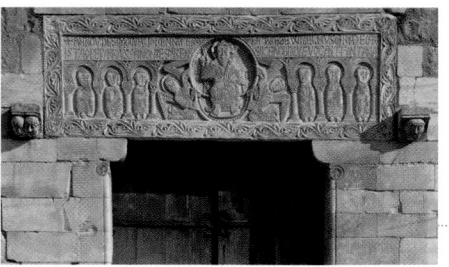

1020–21 Lintel from Saint-Genis-des-Fontaines

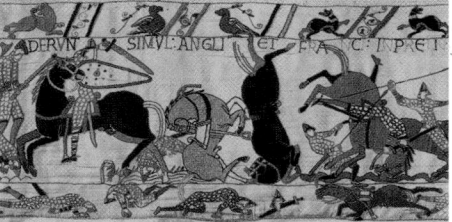

1040 Consecration of church of Sant Vincenç in Cardona

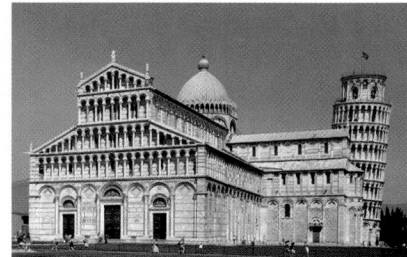

1063 Pisa cathedral begun

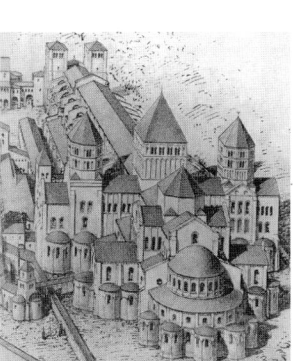

1066–83 *Bayeux Tapestry*

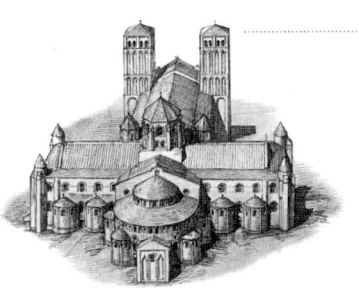

ca. 1075–1120 Cathedral of Santiago de Compostela

1088 Cluny III begun

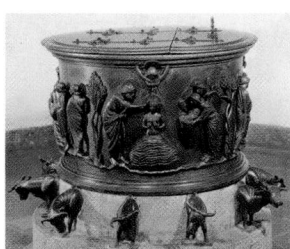

1107–18 Baptismal font at Liège

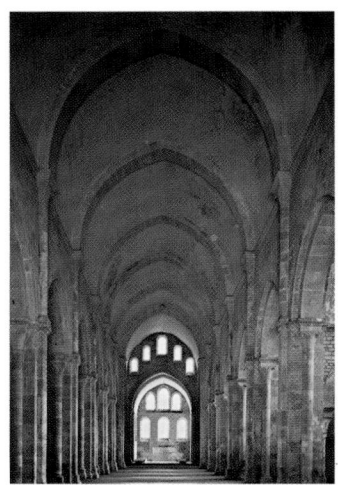

1139–47 Abbey church at Fontenay

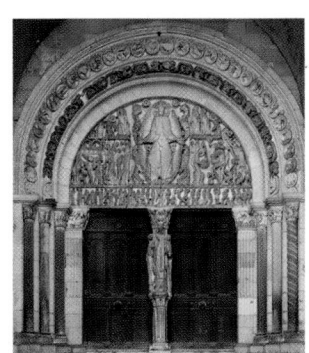

1120–35 West portal, cathedral of Saint-Lazare, Autun

1000

1025

ca. 1026 Al-Aqmar Mosque in Cairo

1033 Church of St. Michael's, Hildesheim finished

1050

1063 St. Mark's in Venice begun

◄ 1066 Battle of Hastings

1075

◄ 1099 Warriors of First Crusade capture Jerusalem

1100

◄ 1115-1120 Nave of Saint-Étienne at Caen vaulted

◄ ca.1127 Apologia of St. Bernard of Clairvaux
◄ ca.1130 Pilgrim's Guide
1133–34 Cloak of Roger II of Sicily

1125

◄ ca.1150 Winchester Psalter

1150

1175

1180–90 Mosaics of cathedral of Monreale

1200

◄ 1204 Crusaders take Constantinople

1225

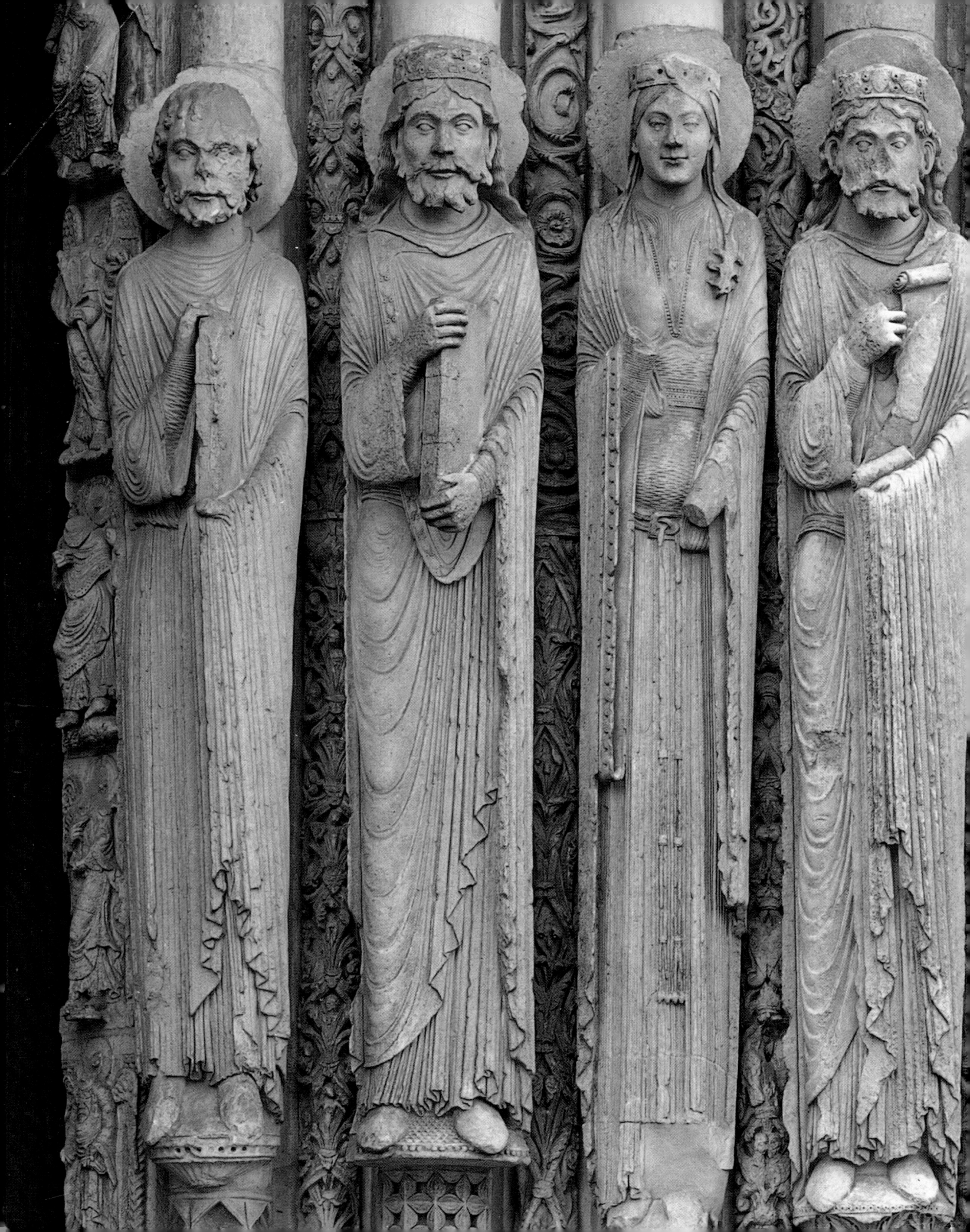

Gothic Art

THE GOTHIC ERA UNFOLDED IN A PROCESS OF GEOGRAPHIC expansion, its rapid growth demonstrating its broad visual and expressive appeal. At the start, about 1140, the area in which Gothic art was produced was small indeed. It included only the province known as the Île-de-France (Paris and vicinity), the royal domain of the French

kings (see map 12.1). A hundred years later, most of western Europe, from Sicily to Norway, had adopted the Gothic style, with only a few Romanesque pockets left here and there. By 1400, however, the Gothic area had begun to shrink. It no longer included Italy, and by 1550 it had disappeared almost entirely, except in England. The Gothic layer, then, has a rather complicated shape. Its depth ranges from close to 400 years in some places to only 150 in others.

The term **Gothic** was used in the sixteenth century to describe a style of buildings thought to have descended from the Goths, those tribes that occupied northern Europe during the early Middle Ages. Although the ancestry of the style is not as direct as these early writers claimed, they were accurate about its geography, since the style is most recognizable north of the Alps. As Gothic art spread from the Île-de-France to the rest of the country and then through all of Europe, it was referred to as *opus modernum* (modern work) or *opus francigenum* (French work). These designations are significant, because they tell us that in its own time the style was viewed as innovative and as having its origins in France. In the course of the thirteenth century, the new style gradually lost its imported flavor, and regional variety began to reassert itself.

Detail of figure 12.6, Jamb statues, west portal of cathedral of Notre-Dame, Chartres

For a century—from about 1150 to 1250, during the Age of the Great Cathedrals—architecture played the dominant role in the formation of a coherent Gothic style. In addition to religious buildings, secular architecture—including castles, palaces, and civic buildings, such as hospitals—also flourished during the Gothic period. Gothic sculpture was at first severely architectural in spirit but became more independent after 1200. Late Gothic architecture and sculpture strive for more pictorial effects.

Artistic developments roughly parallel what was happening in the political arena, for the Gothic was a distinctive period not only artistically but politically as well. Aided by technological advances including cannon and iron crossbow design, princes and kings were able to conquer increasingly large territories, which were administered for them by vassals, who in turn collected taxes to support armies and navies. In France, the Capetian line at first ruled only the fertile territory of the Île-de-France, but by 1300 it had added much of the land previously held by the count of Flanders, as well as Bourges, Tours, and Amiens—all of which were to become the sites of important Gothic cathedrals—and the central provinces of the Auvergne and the southern provinces of Languedoc. King Philip Augustus, who reigned from 1180 to 1223, was able to quadruple the size of the royal domain and, at the same time, concentrate authority in the figure of the king. The French kings also acquired Normandy from England. This gave rise to the conflicting claims over the kingship of France known as the Hundred Years' War (1339–1453), which consolidated a

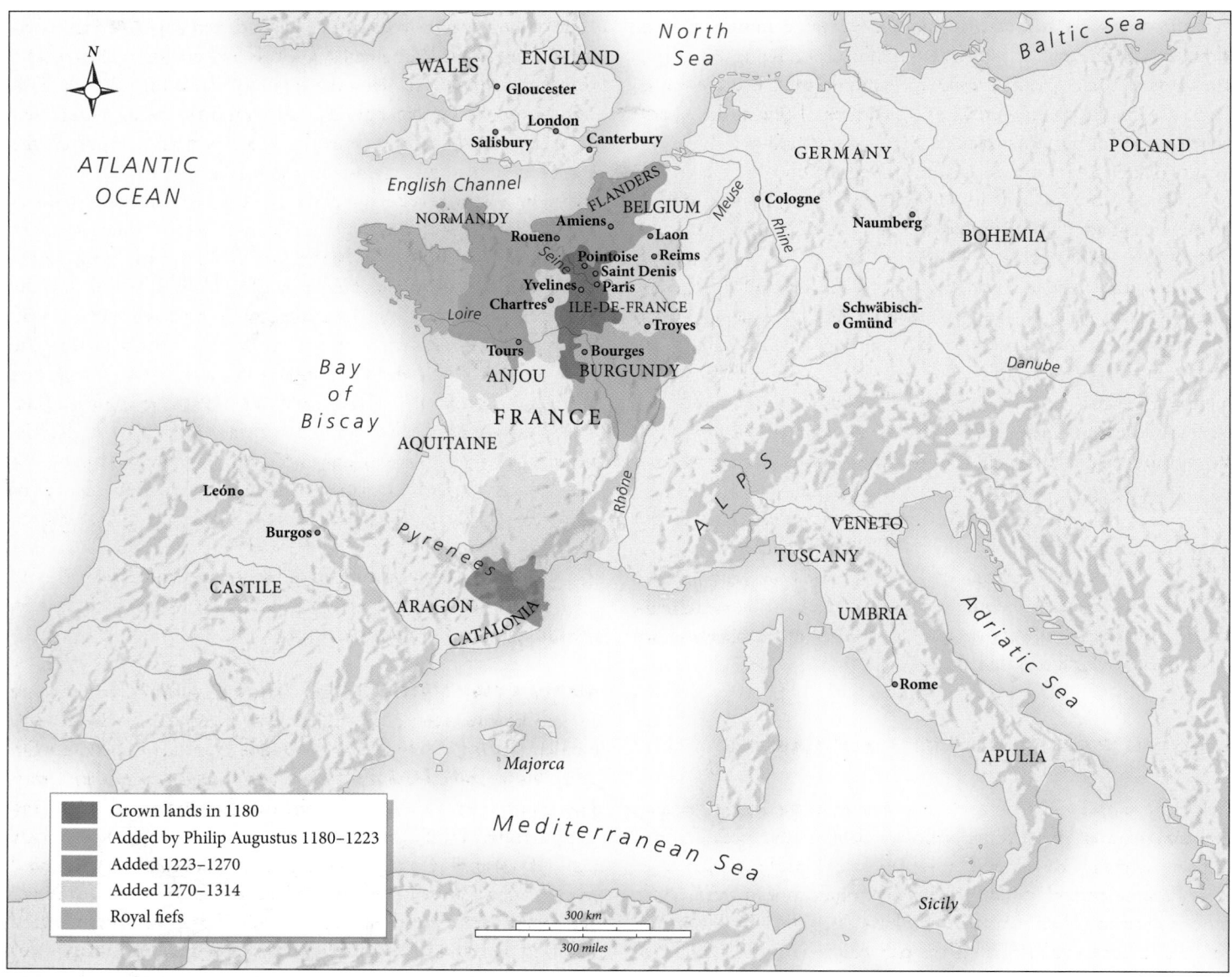

Map 12.1 Europe in the Gothic period

growing sense of nationalism on both sides of the English Channel. While much Gothic art seems to develop in a logical manner, the Hundred Years' War, with its shifting alliances and threats to economic and social stability, interrupted the production of art in some areas of Europe.

Germany remained a collection of independent city-states ruled by electors, who were responsible for, among other things, choosing kings. The powers of German kings were therefore severely limited. Supported by shifting alliances with the papacy, the kings of France and England emerged as the leading powers at the expense of the Germans in the early thirteenth century, which was generally a time of peace and prosperity. After 1290, however, the balance of power broke down.

The growth of urban centers and the increasing importance of cathedrals, the seats of bishops, are formative features of the Gothic period. In the century before the death of King Louis IX in 1270, there were 80 cathedrals built in France, many of them

new foundations. Universities developed out of cathedral schools as the principal centers of learning, thus taking on the role previously played by monasteries. Universities provided instruction in theology, philosophy, law, and medicine, those areas of study deemed necessary for *universitas litterarum* (universal learning). At the same time, literature written in the vernacular (as opposed to Latin) began to emerge, making it accessible to a broader public. It was during the thirteenth century that French became an official state language. Romanesque art had been predominantly a rural and monastic art, while Gothic art, by contrast, was increasingly cosmopolitan.

Urban growth was both the result and cause of economic, social, and demographic changes. Agriculture became more efficient, with increased acreage under cultivation, and surplus production provided commodities for sale and purchase. This produced, in turn, a money economy based on investment, profit, and trade, in place of barter. Money rather than personal services now directed social interchange, and the increased amount of it in circulation produced a veritable middle class, living in cities, which were the centers of trade and commerce. Once out from under the feudal yoke, merchants and artists of this middle class were free to form **guilds** to control the production and distribution of goods and services. A general and significant increase in population also spurred urban growth. Roughly 42 million people occupied Europe around the year 1000; by 1300, the population had reached about 73 million.

During the thirteenth century, Western European Christianity found in St. Thomas Aquinas its greatest intellect since St. Augustine and St. Jerome some 850 years earlier. Aquinas, an Italian theologian, studied in Cologne and taught in Paris. His method of argument, called **scholasticism**, used reason to understand and explain faith. Scholasticism had a profound effect on European thought; its harmonization of rationalism and spirituality effectively sanctioned the systematic study of all natural phenomena as expressions of divine truths. Gothic builders shared qualities with the Scholastics. They brought the logic and clarity of engineering principles to bear on revelation, using physical forces to create a concord of spiritual experiences in much the same way the Scholastics used elucidation and clarification to build their well-constructed arguments.

EARLY GOTHIC ART IN FRANCE

It is not clear why Gothic art first appeared in the Île-de-France, the area around Paris. Some scholars believe that because this region had not developed a strong local style during the Romanesque period, it was particularly open to innovation and influence from other areas. Others have suggested that it was a result of a concerted effort on the part of the kings of France to aggrandize themselves, since it was here that their domains were located. Certainly the Île-de-France is fortuitously positioned, near the center of France and thus accessible to the south and west, where major sculptural programs flourished during the Romanesque period, and adjacent to Normandy, where many structural innovations, including the ribbed groin vault, had been introduced to France.

Saint-Denis: Suger and the Beginnings of Gothic Architecture

The study of Gothic art begins with an examination of the rebuilding of the royal abbey church of Saint-Denis just outside the city of Paris. The rebuilding of this historic church was undertaken between 1137 and 1144 by its abbot, Suger. His ambitious building program was designed to emphasize the relationship between Saint-Denis and the French monarchy. The kings of France, who belonged to the Capetian line, in practice had less power than the nobles who, in theory, were their vassals. The only area the king ruled directly was the Île-de-France, and even there his authority was often challenged. Not until the early twelfth

century did royal power begin to expand, and Suger, as chief advisor to King Louis VI, helped shape this process. It was Suger who forged the alliance between the monarchy and the Church. This union brought the bishops of France (and the cities under their authority) to the king's side; the king, in turn, supported the papacy in its struggle against the German emperors.

Suger also engaged in spiritual politics. By giving the monarchy religious significance and glorifying it as the strong right arm of justice, he sought to rally the nation behind the king. Saint-Denis was a key element in his plan. The church, founded in the late eighth century, enjoyed a dual prestige. It was the shrine of St. Denis, the Apostle of France and its patron saint, as well as the chief memorial of the Carolingian dynasty from which the Capetians drew their authority. Both Charlemagne and his father, Pepin, were consecrated as kings at Saint-Denis. It was also the burial place of the kings Charles Martel, Pepin, and Charles the Bald. Suger aspired to make the abbey the spiritual center of France, a pilgrimage church to outshine all others and to provide a focal point for religious as well as patriotic emotion. To achieve this goal, the old structure had to be rebuilt and enlarged. The great abbot himself wrote two accounts of the church and its rebuilding. (See *Primary Source*, page 393.)

AMBULATORY AND CHOIR The ambulatory and radiating chapels surrounding the arcaded apse (figs. **12.1** and **12.2**) are familiar elements from the Romanesque pilgrimage choir (see fig. 11.3), but at Saint-Denis they have been integrated in a new way. The choir is as rationally planned and constructed as in any Romanesque church, yet the entire plan is held together by a new kind of geometric order (see fig. 12.1). Seven nearly identical wedge-shaped units fan out from the center of the apse. Instead of being in separate apsidioles, the chapels merge to form, in effect, a second ambulatory. We experience this double ambulatory not as a series of individual compartments but as a continuous space, the shape of which is outlined by the network of slender arches, ribs, and columns that sustains the vaults. Ribbed groin vaulting based on the pointed arch is used throughout. By this date, the pointed arch (which can be "stretched" to reach any desired height regardless of the width of its base) has become an essential part of the ribbed groin vault, which is no longer restricted to square or near-square compartments. It has a new flexibility that allows it to cover areas of almost any shape, such as the trapezoids and pentagons of this ambulatory.

What most distinguishes the interior of Saint-Denis (see fig. 12.2) from earlier church interiors is its lightness, in both senses of the word. The architectural forms seem graceful, almost weightless, compared to the massive solidity of Romanesque architecture. The fluid spaciousness of Saint-Denis' choir results from its slim columns, whose use was made possible by the relative lightness of the vaults they needed to support. In addition, the windows are so large that they no longer give the impression of being openings cut into a wall but, in effect, translucent walls, consisting of stained glass. What makes this abundance of light possible are heavy buttresses that jut out between the chapels to

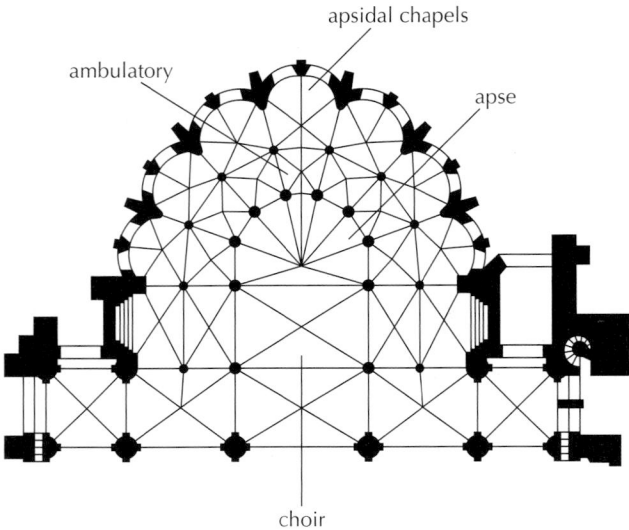

12.1 Plan of the choir and ambulatory, abbey church of Saint-Denis, France. 1140–44 (Peter Kidson)

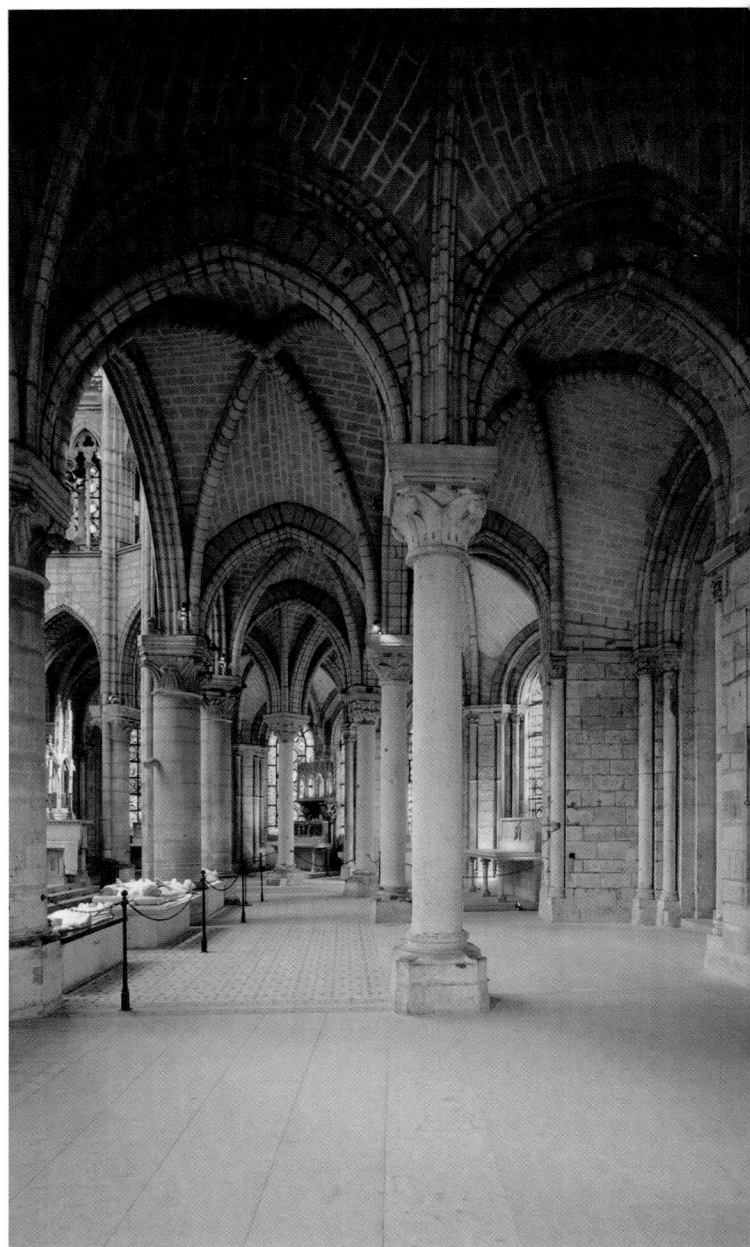

12.2 Ambulatory of abbey church of Saint-Denis

contain the outward pressure of the vaults. In the plan (see fig. 12.1), they look like stubby arrows pointing toward the center of the apse. No wonder, then, that the interior appears so airy, since the heaviest parts of the structural skeleton are relegated to the exterior. The impression would be even more striking if we could see all of Suger's choir, for the upper part of the apse, rising above the double ambulatory, had very large, tall windows. Unfortunately, later transformations of the building destroyed the choir's original effect.

In describing Suger's ambulatory and choir, we have also described the essentials of Gothic architecture. Yet none of the elements that makes up its design is really new. The pilgrimage choir plan, the pointed arch, and the ribbed groin vault can be found in regional schools of the French and Anglo-Norman Romanesque. However, their combination in the same building was of such importance to Suger that—as he himself tells us—he brought together artisans from many different regions for Saint-Denis. We must not conclude from this, however, that Gothic architecture was merely a synthesis of Romanesque traits. If we did, we would be hard pressed to explain the new spirit, particularly the quest for luminosity, that strikes us so forcibly at Saint-Denis. Suger's account of the rebuilding of his church stresses luminosity as the highest value achieved in the new structure. Thus, Suger suggests, the "miraculous" light that floods the choir through the "most sacred" stained-glass windows becomes the Light Divine, a revelation of the spirit of God. Suger also claims that harmony, the perfect relationship among parts in terms of mathematical proportions or ratios, is the source of all beauty, since it exemplifies the laws by which divine reason made the universe.

This symbolic interpretation of light and numerical harmony was well established in Christian thought long before Suger's time. It derived from the writings of a sixth-century Greek theologian who, in the Middle Ages, was mistakenly believed to have been Dionysius the Areopagite, an Athenian disciple of St. Paul, who is mentioned in the New Testament book of Acts. In France, the writer Dionysius was identified with St. Denis, since the saint's name in Latin is Dionysius. Not surprisingly, Suger attached great authority to the writings of Dionysius, which were available to him in the library at Saint-Denis; Dionysian light-and-number symbolism particularly appealed to him

At the heart of Suger's mystical intent for Saint-Denis was the belief that the material realm is the steppingstone for spiritual contemplation and thus that dark, jewel-like light filtering through the church's stained-glass windows would transport the viewer to "some strange region of the universe which neither exists entirely in the slime of earth nor entirely in the purity of

Suger of Saint-Denis (1081–1151)

From *On the Consecration of the Church of Saint-Denis* and *On What Was Done Under His Administration*

Abbot Suger left two accounts of his rebuilding of the abbey church of Saint-Denis. He justifies his enlargement of the Carolingian building with reference to its overcrowding on religious holidays. After rebuilding the west end of the Carolingian church, he destroyed its eastern apse and built a much larger, more elaborate choir over the old crypt. Saint-Denis was a Benedictine abbey, though its church was open to layfolk and attracted them in large numbers. The ostentatious embellishment of the church was the type of material display deplored by St. Bernard of Clairvaux (see page 359). Suger's descriptions of Saint-Denis suggest a sensuous love of precious materials, but also a belief that contemplation of these materials could lead the worshiper to a state of heightened spiritual awareness. Like the Byzantine rationale for icons, the notion of "anagogical" transportation to another dimension is indebted to Neo-Platonism.

Through a fortunate circumstance—the number of the faithful growing and frequently gathering to seek the intercession of the Saints—the [old] basilica had come to suffer grave inconveniences. Often on feast days, completely filled, it disgorged through all its doors the excess of the crowds as they moved in opposite directions, and the outward pressure of the foremost ones not only prevented those attempting to enter from entering but also expelled those who had already entered. At times you could see that no one among the countless thousands of people because of their very density could move a foot; that no one, because of their very congestion, could [do] anything but stand like a marble statue, stay benumbed or, as a last resort, scream. The distress of the women was so great and so intolerable that you could see how they cried out horribly, how several of them, lifted by the pious assistance of men above the heads of the crowd, marched forward as though upon a pavement; and how many others, gasping with their last breath, panted in the cloisters of the brethren to the despair of everyone ...

Moreover, it was cunningly provided that—through the upper columns and central arches which were to be placed upon the lower ones built in the crypt—the central nave of the old [church] should be equalized, by means of geometrical and arithmetical instruments, with the central nave of the new addition; and, likewise, that the dimensions of the old side-aisles should be equalized with the dimensions of the new side-aisles, except for that elegant and praiseworthy extension, in [the form of] a circular string of chapels, by virtue of which the whole [church] would shine with the wonderful and uninterrupted light of most luminous windows, pervading the interior beauty. ...

We insisted that the adorable, life-giving cross should be adorned. Therefore we searched around everywhere by ourselves and by our agents for an abundance of precious pearls and gems. One merry but notable miracle which the Lord granted us in this connection we do not wish to pass over. For when I was in difficulty for want of gems and could not sufficiently provide myself with more (for their scarcity makes them very expensive): then, lo and behold, [monks] from three abbeys of two Orders—that is, from Cîteaux and another abbey of the [Cistercian] Order, and from Fontevrault offered us for sale an abundance of gems such as we had not hoped to find in ten years, hyacinths, sapphires, rubies, emeralds, topazes. ...

Often we contemplate these different ornaments both new and old. When the loveliness of the many-colored gems has called me away from external cares, and worthy meditation has induced me to reflect, transferring that which is material to that which is immaterial, on the diversity of the sacred virtues: then it seems to me that I see myself dwelling, as it were, in some strange region of the universe which neither exists entirely in the slime of the earth nor entirely in the purity of Heaven; and that, by the grace of God, I can be transported from this inferior to that higher world in an anagogical manner.

We [also] caused to be painted, by the exquisite hands of many masters from different regions, a splendid variety of new windows.

Source: *Abbott Suger on the Abbey Church of Saint-Denis and Its Art Treasures*, ed. and tr. Erwin Panofsky (Princeton, NJ: Princeton University Press, 1946)

Heaven." The success of the choir design at Saint-Denis, therefore, derives not only from its architectural qualities but also from its extraordinary psychological impact. Visitors, it seems, were overwhelmed by both, and within a few decades the new style had spread far beyond the Île-de-France.

SUGER AND THE MEDIEVAL ARCHITECT Although Suger was not an architect, there is no contradiction between his lack of professional training and his claim of responsibility for the technical advances and resultant style of "his" new church. In the twelfth century, the term "architect" had a very different meaning from what it does today. To the medieval mind, the overall leader of the project could be considered its architect. Even God, as creator of the universe, was sometimes represented as an architect employing builders' tools. After all, the function of a church is not merely to enclose a maximum of space with a minimum of material, but also to embody and convey religious ideas. For the master who built the choir of Saint-Denis, the technical problems of vaulting must have been inseparable from issues of form and meaning. The design includes elements that express function without actually performing it. An example is the slender column shafts (**responds**) that seem to transfer the weight of the vaults to the church floor.

In order to know what concepts to convey, the medieval builder needed the guidance of religious authority. At a minimum, such guidance might be a simple directive to follow some established model. Suger, however, took a more active role, proposing objectives to which his master masons must have been singularly responsive. Close collaboration between patron and architect or master builder had of course occurred before—between Perikles and Pheidias, for example (see pages 136–39)—just as it does today.

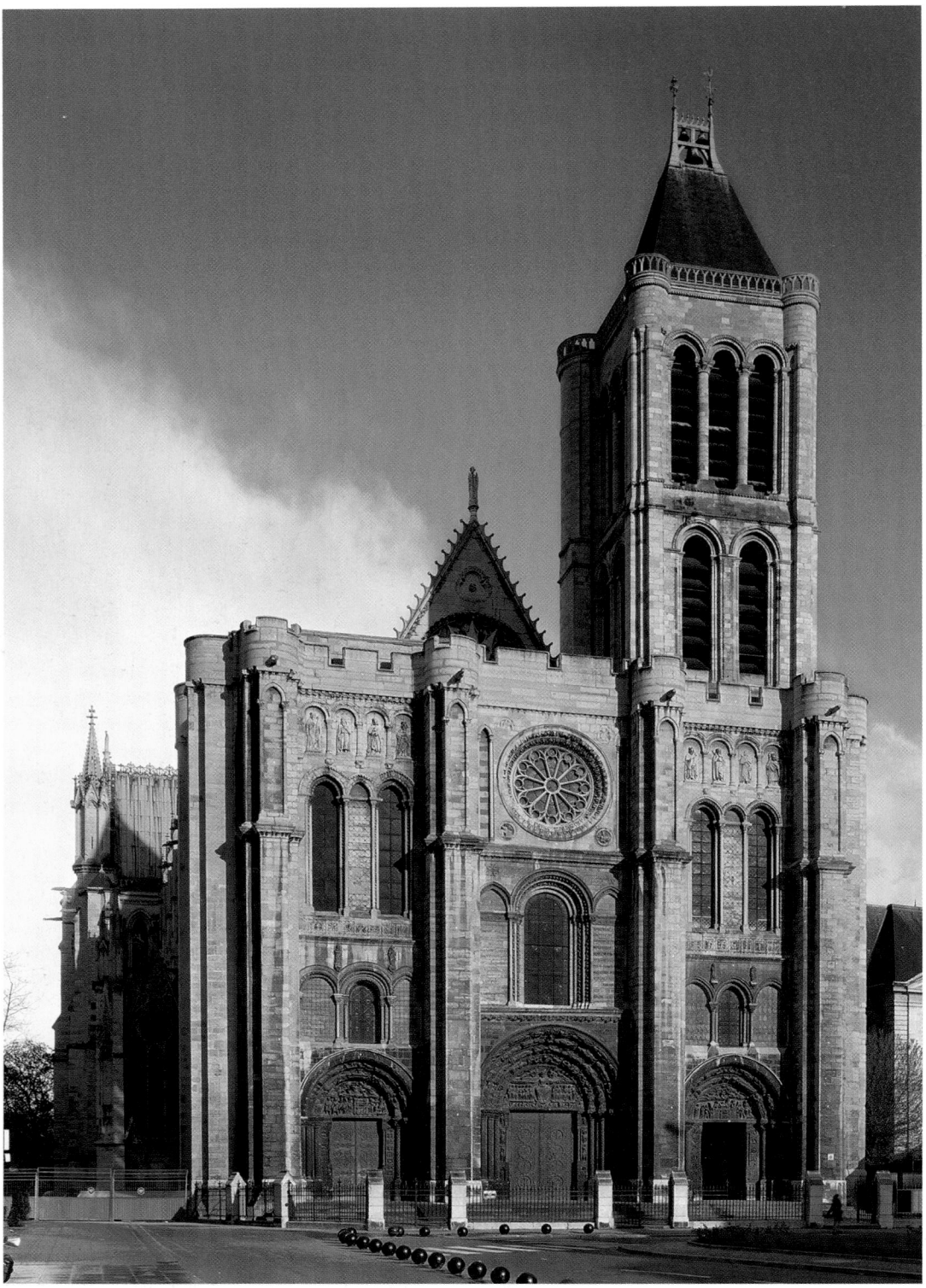

12.3 West façade of abbey church of Saint-Denis. ca. 1137–40

CONSTRUCTING SAINT-DENIS Building Saint-Denis was an expensive and complex task that required the combined resources of Church and State. Suger used stone from quarries near Pontoise for the ambulatory columns and lumber from the forest of Yvelines for the roof. Both had to be transported by land and river, which was a slow and costly process. The master builder probably employed several hundred stonemasons and two or three times that many laborers. Advances in technology spurred by warfare made possible improved construction techniques that were essential for building the new rib vaults. Especially important were better cranes powered by windlasses, treadwheels that used counterweights, and double pulleys for greater efficiency.

These devices could be put up and taken down with ease, allowing for lighter scaffolding suspended from the wall instead of resting on the ground.

WEST FAÇADE Although Abbot Suger planned to rebuild all of Saint-Denis, the only part of the church that he saw completed, other than the ambulatory and choir, was the west façade. Its overall design (fig. **12.3**) derived from Norman Romanesque façades. A comparison between Saint-Denis and Saint-Étienne at Caen (see fig. 11.46) reveals a number of shared basic features. These include the pier buttresses that reinforce the corners of the towers and divide the façade vertically into three main parts, the placement of the portals, and the three-story arrangement. However, Saint-Denis's three portals are far larger and more richly carved than those at Saint-Étienne or any other Norman Romanesque church. From this we can conjecture that Abbot Suger attached considerable importance to the sculptural decoration of Saint-Denis, although his account of the church does not discuss it at length.

The rich sculptural decoration included carved tympana, archivolts, and jambs. The arrangement recalls the façades of southwestern France (see fig. 11.13) and the carved portals of Burgundy (see fig. 11.17). These correlations corroborate Suger's claim that his workforce included artists from many regions. Unhappily, the trumeau figure of St. Denis and the statue-columns of the jambs were removed in 1770 and 1771, when the central portal was enlarged. A few years later, during the French Revolution, a mob attacked the heads of the remaining figures and melted down the metal doors. As a result of these ravages and a series of clumsy restorations undertaken during the eighteenth and nineteenth centuries, we can gain only a general view of Suger's ideas about the role of sculpture at Saint-Denis. To envision what the west portal originally looked like we have to turn to the cathedral of Chartres, where some of the Saint-Denis sculptors subsequently worked.

Chartres Cathedral

Toward 1145 the bishop of the town of Chartres, who was a friend of Abbot Suger and shared many of his ideas, began to rebuild a cathedral in the new style, dedicated to Notre-Dame ("Our Lady," the Virgin Mary). Fifty years later a fire destroyed all but the eastern crypt and the west façade. (See www.myarts lab.com.) Our discussion of Chartres is divided into two sections: First we will discuss the west façade and later in the chapter that portion of the cathedral rebuilt after the fire of 1194.

WEST FAÇADE The surviving west façade (fig. **12.4**), in many ways reminiscent of Saint-Denis, is divided into units of two and three and is a model of clarity. Yet, because construction proceeded in stages and was never entirely finished, the harmony of the result is evolutionary rather than systematic. For example, the two west towers, though similar, are by no means identical. Moreover, their **spires**, the tall towers with tapering roofs, are

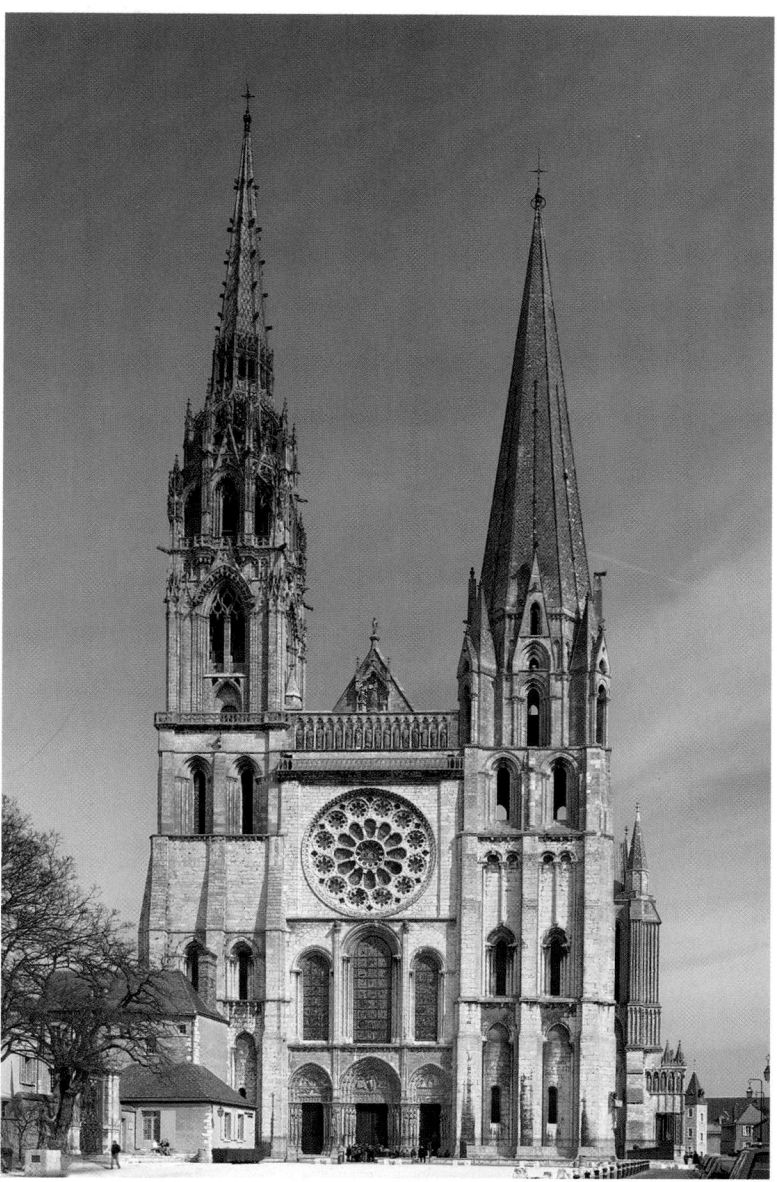

12.4 West façade of cathedral of Notre-Dame, Chartres, France. ca. 1145–1220. (Left spire is from 16th century)

very different: That on the left in figure 12.4 dates from the early sixteenth century, nearly 300 years later than its mate.

To judge from old drawings of Saint-Denis, the Chartres jambs (figs. **12.5** and **12.6**) are so similar to those of the original Saint-Denis portals that the same sculptors must have worked on both buildings. Tall figures attached to columns flanked the doorways of both churches. Figures had appeared on the jambs or trumeaux of Romanesque portals (see figs. 11.13 and 11.15), but they were reliefs carved from the masonry of the doorway. The Chartres jamb figures, in contrast, are essentially statues, each with its own axis. They could, in theory at least, be detached from their supports. This is a development of truly revolutionary importance and could apparently be made only by borrowing the cylindrical shape of the column for the human figure. That the figures are round gives them a corporeal presence, and their heads

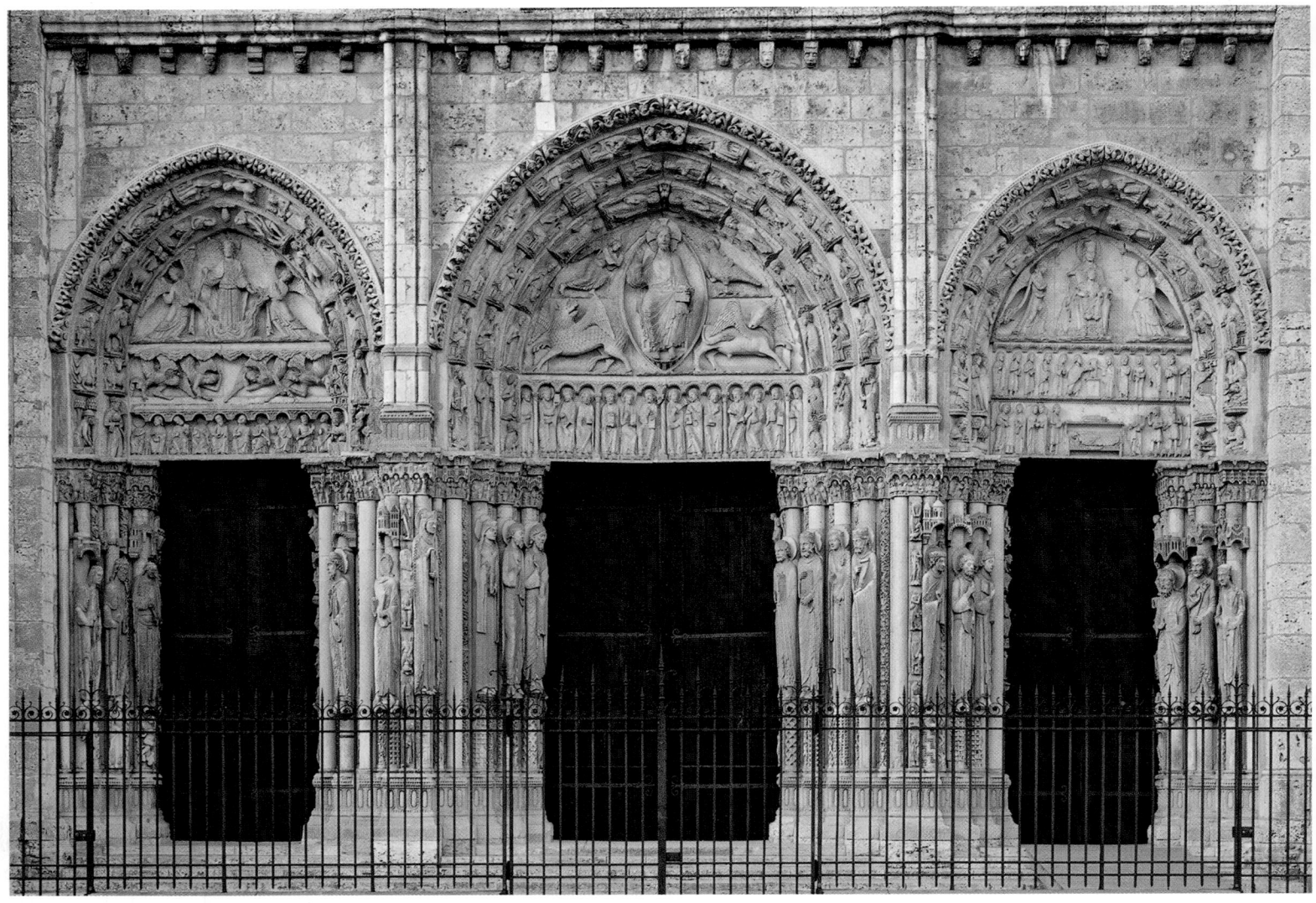

12.5   West portal (Royal Portal) of cathedral of Notre-Dame, Chartres. ca. 1145–50

show a gentle, human quality that indicates a naturalistic trend in Gothic sculpture, quite different from the apparent aims of Romanesque sculptors to accentuate stylization.

On the west portal of Chartres naturalism appears as if in reaction against the fantastic and demoniacal aspects of Romanesque art, a response that may be seen in the solemn spirit of the figures and their increased physical bulk. This is apparent by comparing the Christ of Chartres's center tympanum (see fig. 12.5) with his counterpart in the tympanum at Moissac (see fig. 11.13). It also appears in the visual and thematic unity underlying the entire sculptural program at Chartres. While an understanding of the subtler aspects of this program requires a knowledge of the theology that would have been taught by leading scholars of the day at the Chartres cathedral school, its main elements can be readily understood.

The jamb statues form a continuous sequence linking all three portals (see fig. 12.5). Together they represent the prophets, kings, and queens of the Hebrew Bible. Their purpose is to acclaim the rulers of France as their spiritual descendants, and to stress the harmony of spiritual and secular rule, of priests (or bishops) and kings—ideals previously put forward by Abbot Suger. Above the main doorway, symbols of the four evangelists flank Christ in Majesty. The apostles are below, while the 24 elders (see page 361) occupy the two outer archivolts. Although the components are similar to those of the Moissac tympanum, the effect at Chartres is calm and comforting whereas at Moissac the effect is dramatic and unsettling. The right-hand tympanum at Chartres shows Christ's Incarnation: the Birth, the Presentation in the Temple, and the infant Christ Child on the lap of the Virgin, who symbolizes the Church. The design achieves compositional and thematic unity by elevating Christ in the center of each register: on the manger, on an altar, and on the lap of his mother. In the surrounding archivolts, representations of the liberal arts as human wisdom pay homage to the divine wisdom of Christ. Finally, in the left-hand tympanum, we see the timeless Heavenly Christ (or perhaps the Christ of the Ascension) framed by the ever-repeating cycle of the year: the signs of the zodiac and their earthly counterparts, the labors of the 12 months.

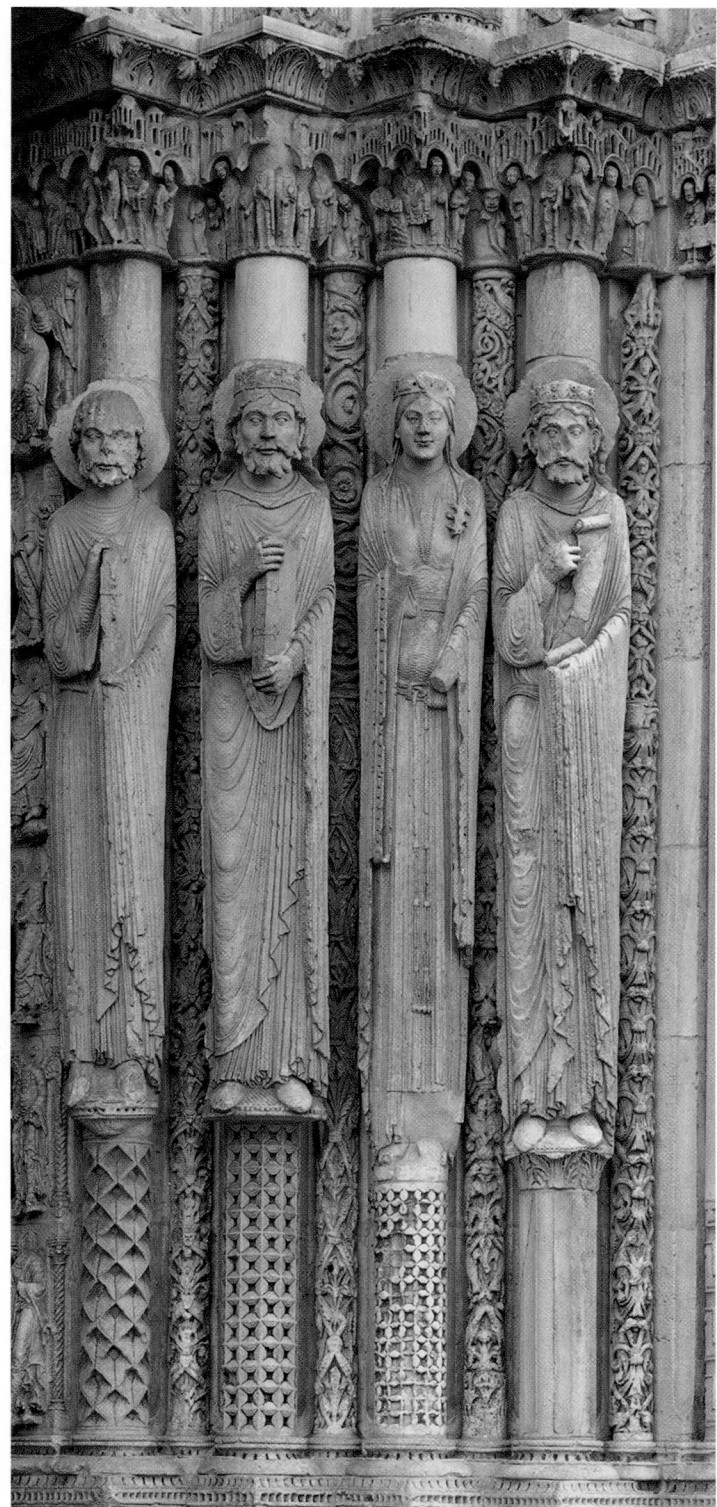

12.6 Jamb statues, west portal of cathedral of Notre-Dame, Chartres

Laon Cathedral

Because the mid-twelfth-century church that stood behind the west façade of Chartres cathedral was destroyed by fire in 1194, we must turn to the cathedral of Notre-Dame at Laon to appreciate an Early Gothic interior. This cathedral was begun just before 1160.

NAVE The interior elevation of Laon cathedral (fig. **12.7**) includes a nave arcade, gallery, triforium, and clerestory, all features found in Romanesque architecture but never together in the same building. The stacking of four levels is a Gothic innovation and lightens the weight of the walls. The elevation develops logically and harmoniously: The single opening of the nave arcade is doubled in the gallery, then triple arches follow in the triforium, while a broad clerestory window balances the single nave arcade opening that began the vertical sequence. The rhythmical arrangement articulates a heightened sense of verticality, while the multiple openings allow increased light to enter the nave, directly from the clerestory and indirectly through galleries and side aisles.

Sexpartite nave vaults over squarish bays at Laon continue the kind of structural experimentation begun by the Norman Romanesque builders of Saint-Étienne at Caen (see fig. 11.47) and Durham cathedral (see fig. 11.43). Laon uses the pointed ribbed vaults, pioneered in the western bays of the nave at Durham, throughout the building. Alternating bundles of shafts rising

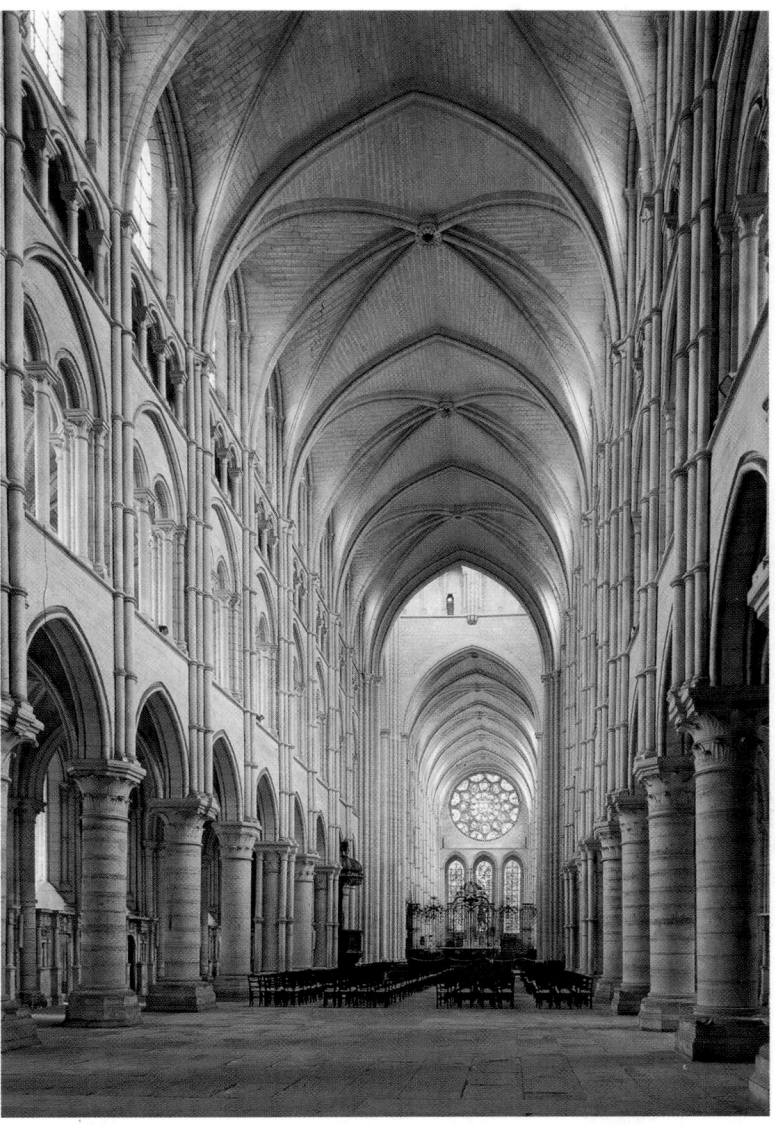

12.7 Nave of cathedral of Notre-Dame, Laon, France. ca. 1160–1210

along the wall reflect the nature of the sexpartite vaults above: Clusters of five colonnettes indicate where transverse arches cross the nave, while three colonnettes adorn the intermediate piers. Although the system develops from Romanesque building practice (see pages 350 and 353), the elements seem more delicate in the Gothic building. By contrast, Romanesque interiors such as Santiago de Compostela (see fig. 11.5) and Durham cathedral (see fig. 11.43) emphasize the great effort required to support the weight of the vaults.

Some scholars see a change in program at Laon as revealing the evolving objectives of this cathedral's designers. At the east end of the nave, where the building work began, clustered shafts were added to piers as well as to the wall. In the later, more westerly nave bays, the round piers are plain. Instead of the staggered rhythm created by the earlier alternating pier arrangement, the change produced a more flowing effect. However, the tradeoff for the increased uniformity of the new arrangement was a loss of structural explicitness. For other scholars, the shafts attached to the Laon nave piers mark a liturgical division in the building, the site of a screen separating the choir occupied by clerics from the spaces used by the lay congregation. Gothic churches, like earlier religious buildings (see page 238), were settings for devotions and backdrops for the performance of the liturgy; as such, they framed the movements and words sung in processions and practiced in sacramental rites.

Cathedral of Notre-Dame in Paris

The plan of the cathedral in Notre-Dame at Paris is recorded as having been begun in 1163, only a few years after Notre-Dame at

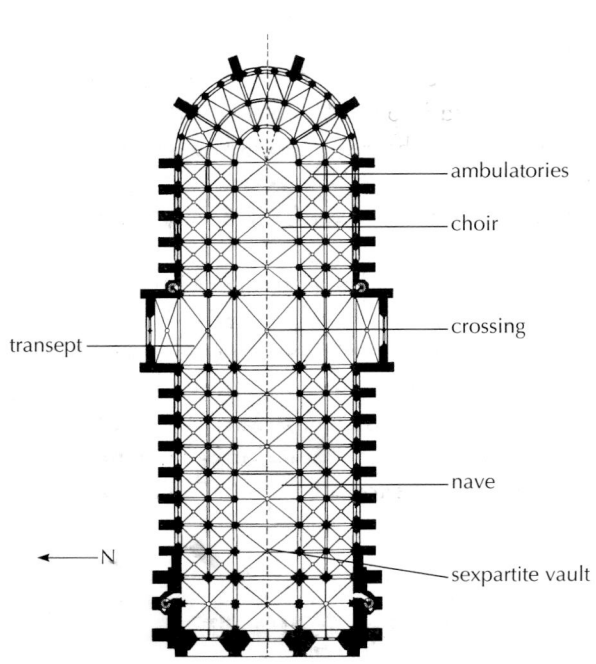

ambulatories

choir

crossing

transept

nave

sexpartite vault

N

12.8   Plan of cathedral of Notre-Dame, Paris. ca. 1155–ca. 1250

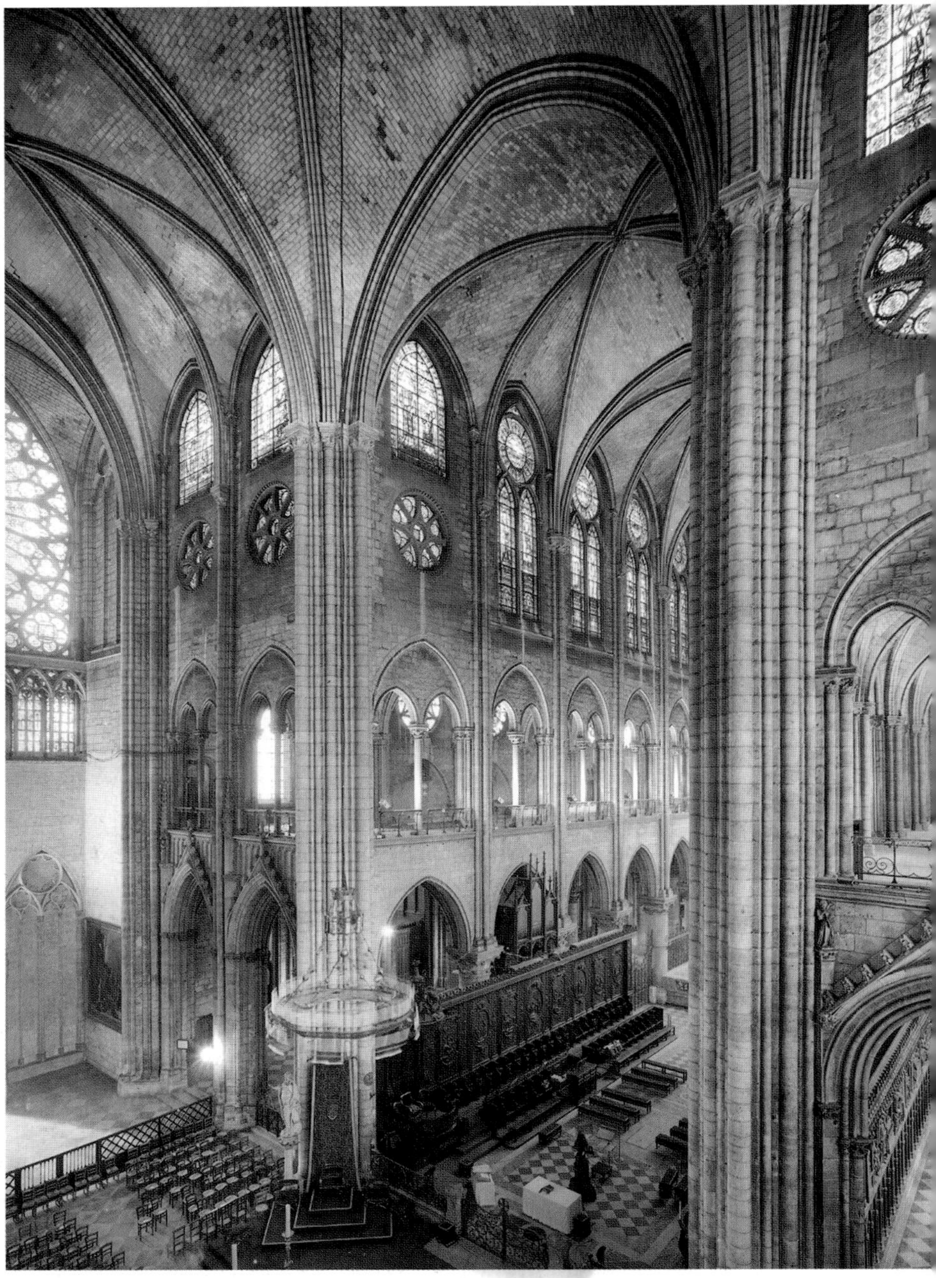

12.9   Nave of cathedral of Notre-Dame, Paris

oculi were inserted in place of the arcaded triforium. Stylish as this change might have been when the building was begun, a thirteenth-century reconstruction completely eliminated the triforium in order to enlarge the clerestory windows. Because a few bays were returned to their original four-part elevation in a nineteenth-century restoration, we can compare the original and the remodeled elevations (fig. 12.9). The design change reveals a continuing desire to reduce wall surface and increase the amount of light entering the building. The large clerestory windows and the light and slender forms produce nave walls that seem amazingly thin. This creates an effect of weightlessness.

Like uniformity in the plan, the vertical emphasis of the interior is a clear Gothic trait. It depends not only on the actual proportions of the nave, but also on a constant and repeated accentuation of upward momentum and the apparent ease with which a sense of height is attained.

WEST FAÇADE The most monumental aspect of the exterior of Notre-Dame in Paris is its west façade (fig. 12.10). This retains its original appearance, except for the sculpture, which was badly damaged during the French Revolution and is largely restored. All of its details are integrated into a coherent whole. Here, the meaning of Suger's emphasis on harmony, geometric order, and proportion is even more evident than at Saint-Denis itself and the result goes well beyond the achievement of Chartres cathedral's west portal.

This formal discipline is also apparent in the placement of the sculpture, which no longer shows the spontaneous growth typical of the Romanesque. Instead, it has been assigned a precise role within the architectural framework. At the same time, the cubic solidity of the façade has been moderated by lacelike arcades and window perforations, which break down the continuity of the wall surfaces so that the total effect is of a weightless openwork screen.

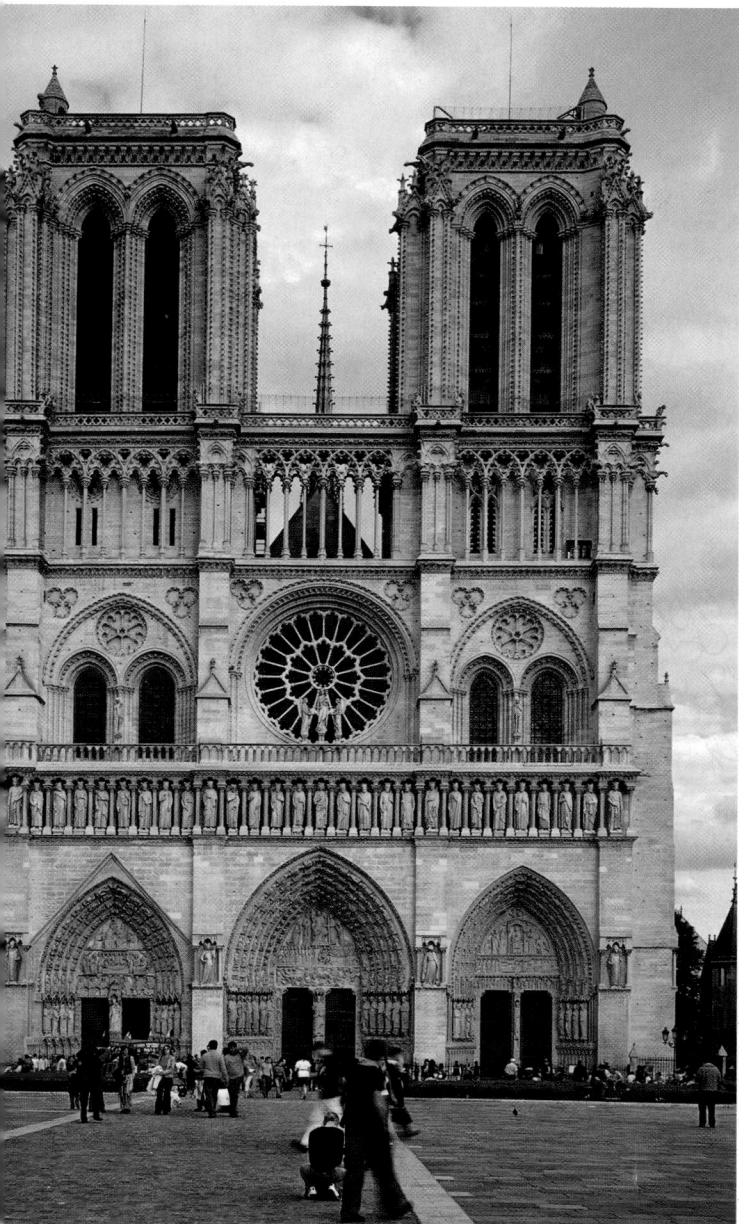

12.10   West façade of cathedral of Notre-Dame, Paris. ca. 1200–50

HIGH GOTHIC ART IN FRANCE

The political and economic stability of France during the thirteenth century encouraged the continued growth of cities, an ideal context for producing monumental architecture. Some art historians have seen the attempts to integrate structure and design in Early Gothic art as a series of experiments that were resolved during the High Gothic period. This is undoubtedly true to some extent, but the art of the thirteenth century also demonstrates an interest in pursuing refinements that synthesize engineering and aesthetics. Thus, High Gothic art is as much a continuation of Early Gothic experiments as it is their culmination. It is during this time that the names of architects, who previously had been largely anonymous, proliferate, a reflection of the value placed on their achievements and of an increasing interest in personal identity. This concern for the individual also reflects a changing class structure in which those engaged in trade and commerce become more independent.

Laon, although there is evidence that it might actually have been started as early as the mid-1150s. Notre-Dame, Paris is extraordinarily compact and achieves a unity not present in either Romanesque buildings or earlier Gothic ones (fig. 12.8).

NAVE The transept of the church barely exceeds the width of the façade, perhaps a result of the cathedral's site adjacency to the Seine River, which might not have allowed for a boldly projecting transept. As at Saint-Denis (see fig. 12.1), the double ambulatory of the choir continues directly into the aisles, but there are no radiating chapels. This stress on uniformity in the plan finds a parallel in the treatment of the elevation; despite the use of sexpartite vaults, there is no alternating system of supports. As at Laon (see fig. 12.7), the Paris elevation was originally four-part, though

The Rebuilding of Chartres Cathedral

The rebuilding of Chartres cathedral after the fire of 1194 marks the next step in the development of Gothic architecture. The new building was largely completed within an astonishingly brief span of 26 years. Its crypt houses Chartres's most important possession: remnants of a tunic said to have been worn by the Virgin Mary, to whom the cathedral is dedicated, at the time of Jesus' nativity. The relic, which miraculously survived the great fire of 1194, had drawn pilgrims from all over Europe.

The fire also spared the west façade and portals, and the decision to conserve these architectural features—which, at the time of the fire, were nearly 50 years old and certainly out of fashion—is worth noting. After initial despair at the damage wrought by the fire, civic and ecclesiastical authorities animated their followers by interpreting the event as an expression of the will of

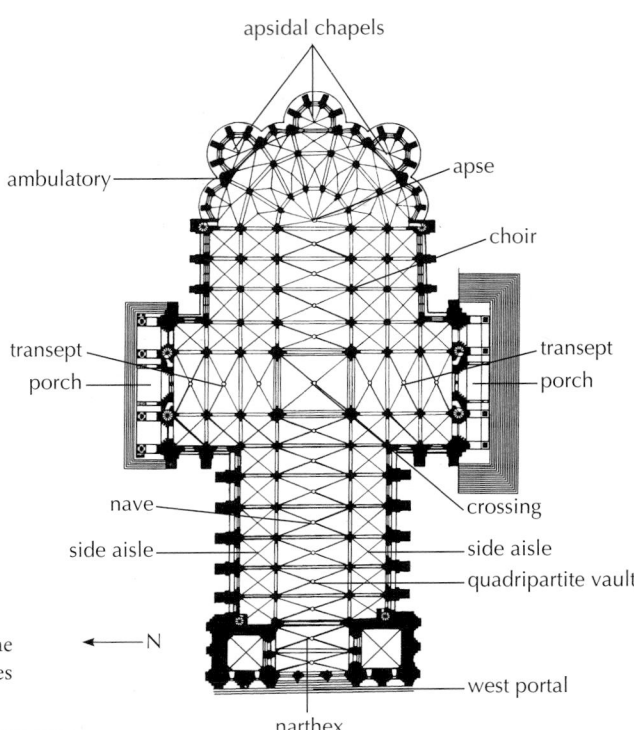

12.11   Plan of cathedral of Notre-Dame (as rebuilt after 1194), Chartres

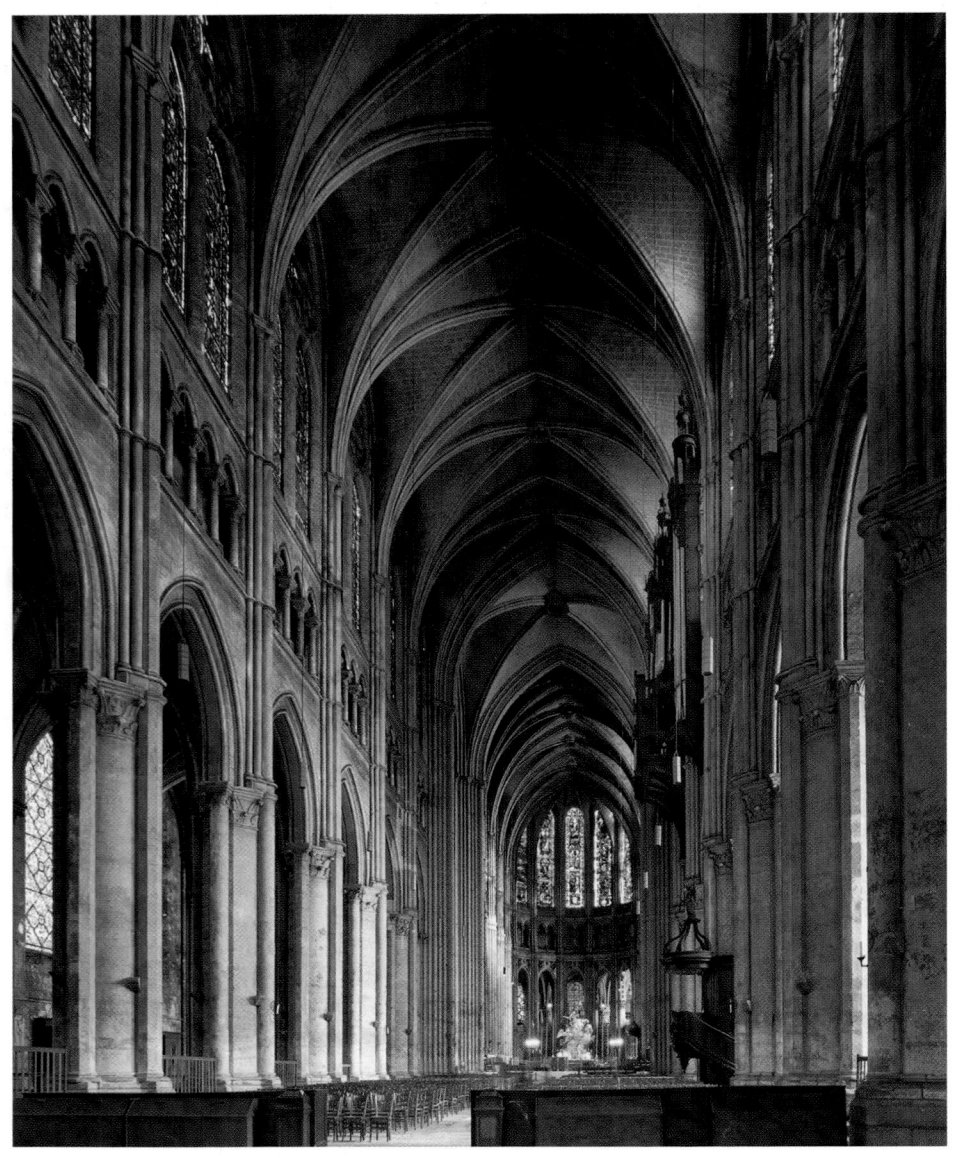

12.12   Nave and choir of cathedral of Notre-Dame, Chartres. ca. 1194–1220

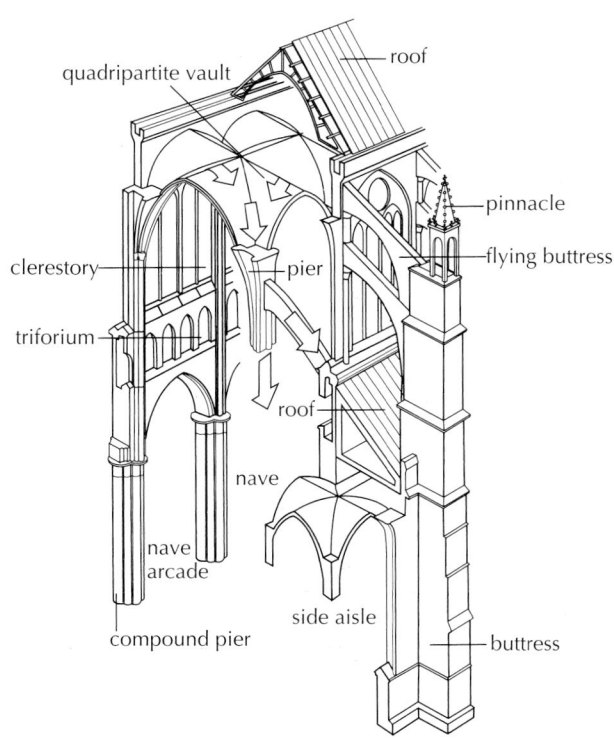

12.13　Axonometric projection of a High Gothic cathedral (after Acland)

Labels: quadripartite vault, roof, pinnacle, flying buttress, clerestory, pier, triforium, roof, nave, nave arcade, compound pier, side aisle, buttress

the Virgin herself that a new and more glorious cathedral be built. Since the west end of the church, like the famous relic of the Virgin, had also been spared, it too was treated as a relic worthy of preservation. Recognizing the divine plan in what otherwise would have been disheartening circumstances helped fuel enthusiasm for rebuilding and accounts for the rapid pace of construction.

To provide room for large numbers of visitors without disturbing worshipers, there is a wide aisle running the length of the nave and around the transept (fig. 12.11). It is joined at the choir by a second aisle, forming an ambulatory that connects the apsidal chapels. Worshipers entered the building through the old

west portal and passed through a relatively low narthex. It would have taken some time for their eyes to adjust to the darkness of the interior. Even the noise of daily life would have been shut out, and sounds within the building would have been at first eerily muffled. Once worshipers had recovered from this disorienting effect, they would have become aware of a glimmering light, which guided them into the cavernous church. The transition, both subtle and profound, accentuated the significance of entering the church. As with entries into Romanesque and Byzantine churches (see pages 256–57 and 362), a liminal, or transitional, zone signaled that visitors had left the temporal world behind. Patrons, designers, and builders of a religious edifice had again found meaningful physical forms to encourage and sustain powerful spiritual experiences.

NAVE Designed a generation after Notre-Dame in Paris, the rebuilt nave of Chartres cathedral (fig. **12.12**) is the first fully developed example of the mature, or High, Gothic. Several features distinguish this style. By eliminating the gallery, the designers of Chartres imposed a three-part elevation on the wall (fig. **12.13**). Romanesque builders had used tripartite wall divisions (see figs. 11.11, 11.43, and 11.47), but the Chartres solution diminishes horizontality and treats the wall surface as a coherent vertical unit. (It was in an attempt to rival High Gothic buildings such as Chartres that the Early Gothic nave wall of Notre-Dame in Paris was reconfigured into a three-part elevation from its original Early Gothic four-part form [see fig. 12.9].) Shafts attached to the piers at Chartres stress the continuity of the vertical lines and guide our eye upward to the vaults, which appear as diaphanous webs stretched across the slender ribs. Quadripartite, or four-part, vaults now replace the sexpartite vaults of Early Gothic buildings (fig. **12.14**). Quadripartite vaults cover rectangular bays and, as a result, the builders no longer needed to worry about an alternating system of supports. The quickened rhythm of shorter, rectangular bays intensifies the perceived pace of propulsion down the nave. The openings of the pointed nave arcade are taller and narrower than before, and the clerestory is larger so that it is the same height as the nave arcade. Because there are so few walls, the vast interior space appears at first to lack clear boundaries.

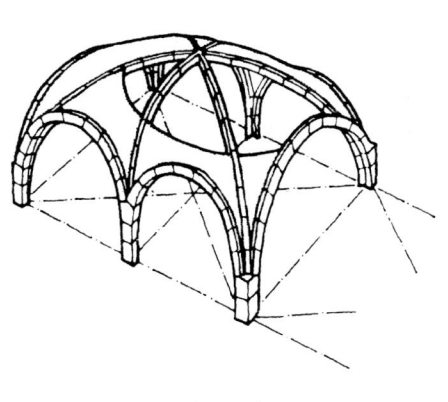

sexpartite vault

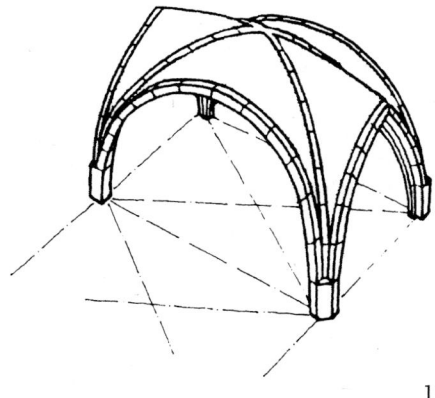

quadripartite vault

12.14　(a) Sexpartite vaulting and (b) quadripartite vaulting

Theophilus Presbyter (12th century)

De diversis artibus, from Book II: "The Art of the Worker in Glass"

"Theophilus" may have been the pseudonym of Roger of Helmarshausen, a Benedictine monk and metalworker. Metalwork is the subject of the third book of this treatise, following books on painting and stained glass. Theophilus' text, written in the twelfth century, is the first in the Western tradition to give a practitioner's account of the technology of art production.

Chapter 17: *Laying Out Windows*

When you want to lay out glass windows, first make yourself a smooth flat wooden board. Then take a piece of chalk, scrape it with a knife all over the board, sprinkle water on it everywhere, and rub it all over with a cloth. When it has dried, take the measurements of one section in a window, and draw it on the board with a rule and compasses. Draw as many figures as you wish, first with [a point made of] lead or tin, then with red or black pigment, making all the lines carefully, because, when you have painted the glass, you will have to fit together the shadows and highlights in accordance with [the design on] the board. Then arrange the different kinds of robes and designate the color of each with a mark in its proper place; and indicate the color of anything else you want to paint with a letter.

After this, take a lead pot and in it put chalk ground with water. Make yourself two or three brushes out of hair from the tail of a marten, badger, squirrel, or cat or from the mane of a donkey. Now take a piece of glass of whatever kind you have chosen, but larger on all sides than the place in which it is to be set, and lay it on the ground for that place. Then you will see the drawing on the board through the intervening glass, and, following it, draw the outlines only on the glass with chalk.

Chapter 18: *Glass Cutting*

Next heat on the fireplace an iron cutting tool, which should be thin everywhere except at the end, where it should be thicker. When the thicker part is red-hot, apply it to the glass that you want to cut, and soon there will appear the beginning of a crack. If the glass is hard [and does not crack at once], wet it with saliva on your finger in the place where you had applied the tool. It will immediately split and, as soon as it has, draw the tool along the line you want to cut and the split will follow.

Source: Theophilus, *On Divers Arts: The Foremost Medieval Treatise on Painting, Glassmaking, and Metalwork*, tr. John G. Hawthorne and Cyril Stanley Smith (NY: Dover Publications, 1979)

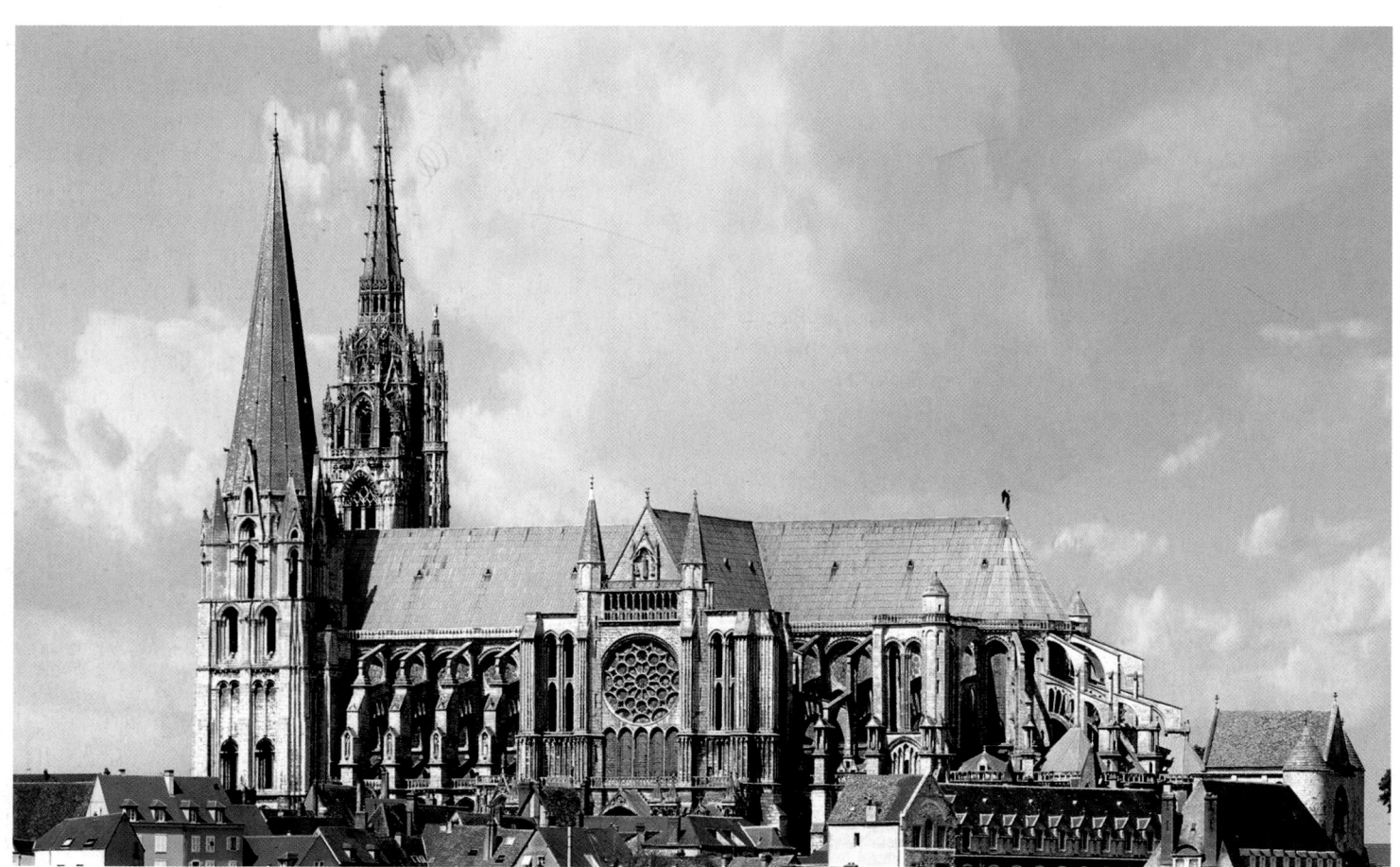

12.15 Cathedral of Notre-Dame, Chartres (from the south)

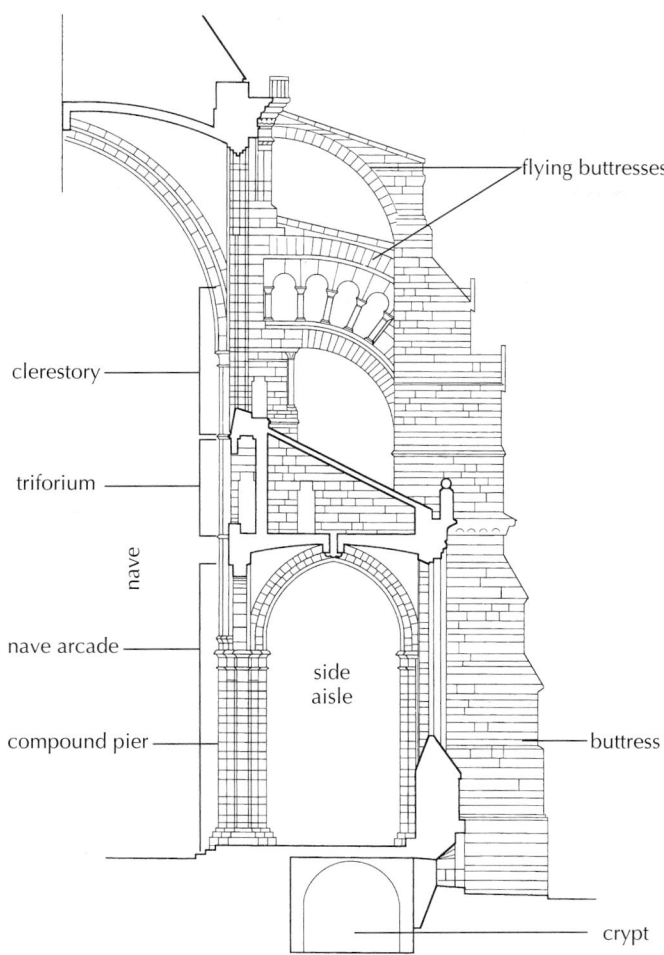

12.16 Transverse section of cathedral of Notre-Dame, Chartres (after Acland)

them together to form walls, both outer and inner. The intermediate space was filled with mortar and rough stones, a task which the less skilled roughmasons performed. The inner and outer walls were connected by tie-courses of finished freestone, which gave added strength to the walls.

STAINED GLASS Alone among all major Gothic cathedrals, Chartres still retains most of its more than 180 original stained-glass windows (fig. **12.17**). The magic of the jewel-like light from the clerestory is unforgettable to anyone who has experienced it. The windows admit far less light than one might expect. They act mainly as diffusing filters that change the quality of daylight, giving it the poetic and symbolic values so highly praised by Abbot Suger. The sensation of ethereal light dissolves the physical solidity of the church and, hence, the distinction between the temporal and the divine realms. This "miraculous light" creates the intensely mystical experience that lies at the heart of Gothic spirituality.

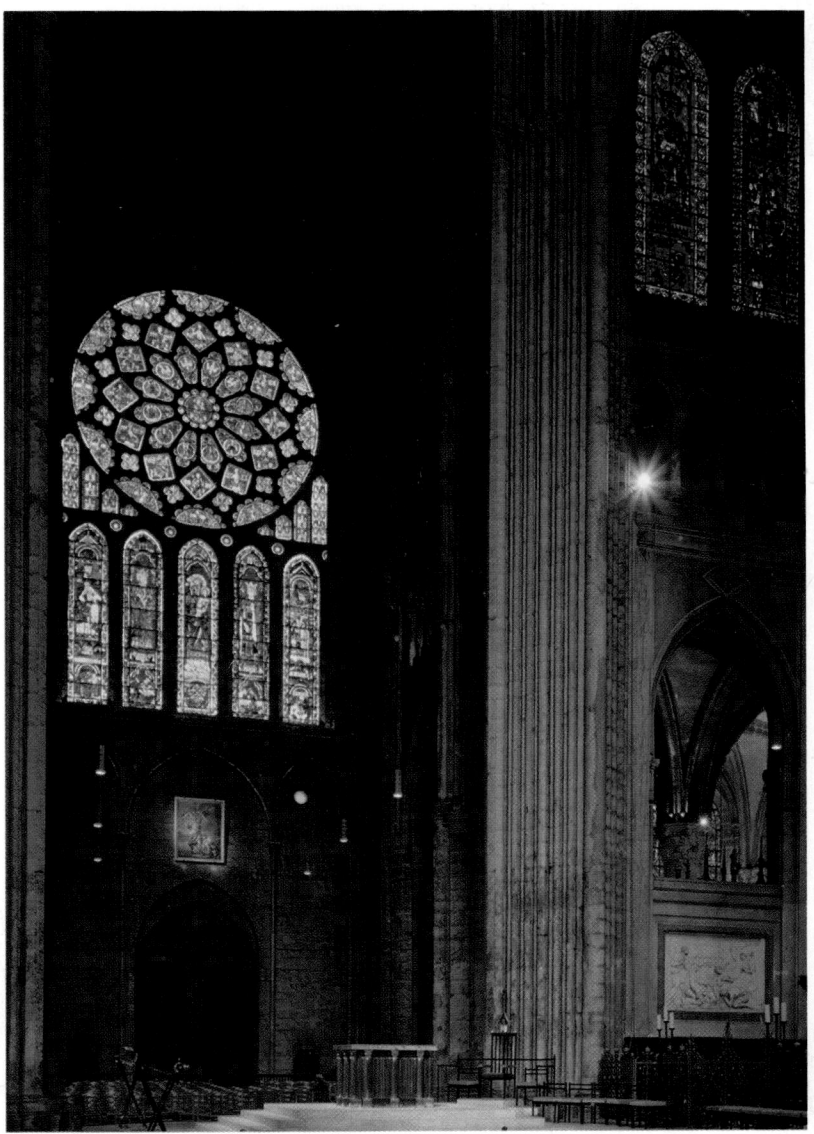

12.17 North transept of cathedral of Notre-Dame, Chartres

BUTTRESSES In Chartres, as in Suger's choir at Saint-Denis, the buttresses (the heavy bones of the structural skeleton) are visible only outside the building (figs. **12.15** and **12.16**). The plan (see fig. 12.11) shows them as massive blocks of masonry that stick out from the building. Above the aisles, these piers turn into **flying buttresses**—arched bridges that reach upward to the critical spots between the clerestory windows where the outward thrust of the nave vault is concentrated (see fig. 12.16). The flying buttresses were also designed to resist the considerable wind pressure on the high-pitched roof. This method of anchoring vaults, so characteristic of Gothic architecture, certainly owed its origin to functional considerations, but the flying buttress is also an integral aesthetic and expressive feature of the building. Its shape could emphasize both verticality and support (in addition to actually providing it) in a variety of ways, according to the designer's sense of style.

The masonry techniques involved in constructing cathedrals required both brute labor and skill. Freemasons, those who worked in freestone, which has a uniform texture and can be chiseled without breaking, carved the individual blocks and set

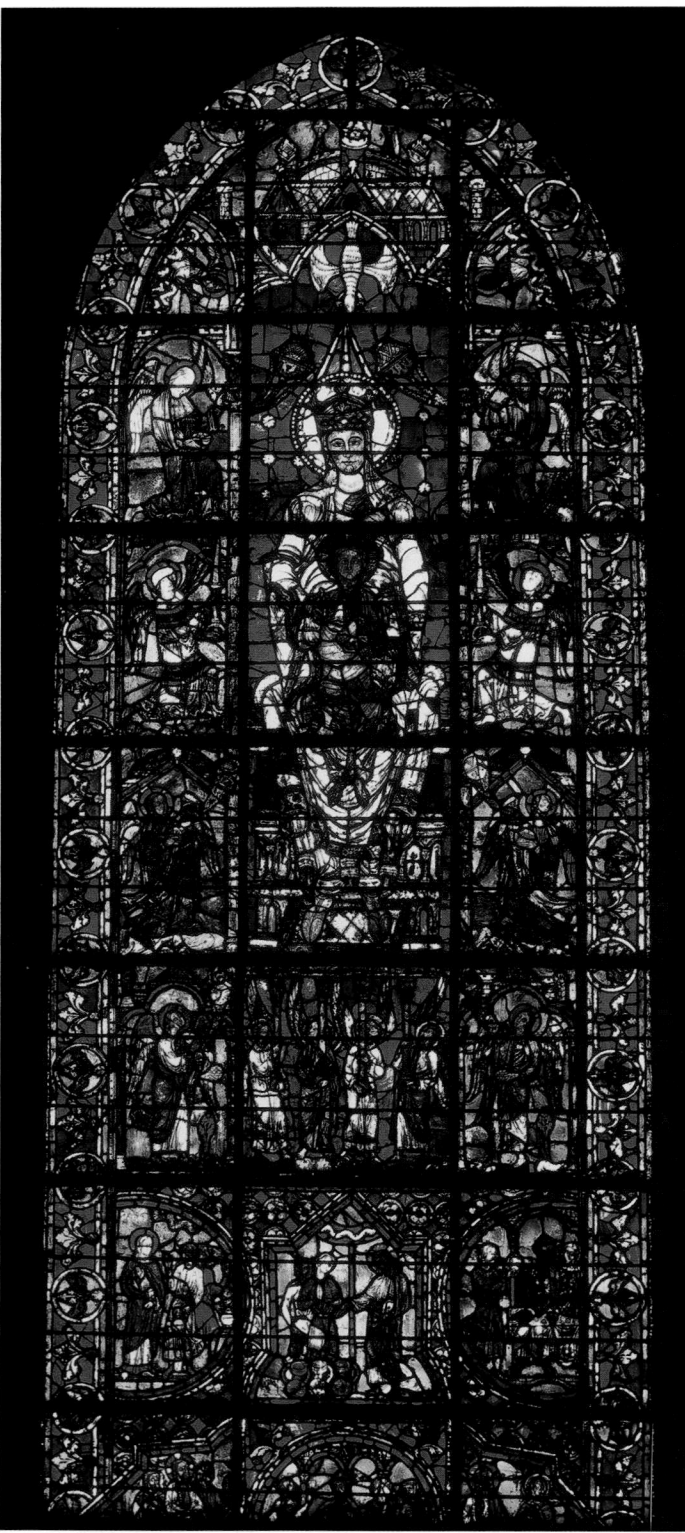

12.18 *Notre Dame de la Belle Verrière*, cathedral of Notre-Dame, Chartres. ca. 1170 (framing panels are 13th century). Stained-glass window, height approx. 14' (4.27 m)

The majestic *Notre Dame de la Belle Verrière* (literally, "Our Lady of the Beautiful Window") at Chartres (fig. **12.18**) appears as a weightless form hovering effortlessly in indeterminate space. This window, the only one apart from those of the west façade to survive the 1194 fire, consists of hundreds of small pieces of tinted glass held together by strips of lead. Methods of medieval glass-making limited the maximum size of these pieces, so the design could not simply be "painted on glass." Rather, the window was painted *with* glass. It was assembled much like a mosaic or a jig-saw puzzle, out of odd-shaped fragments cut to fit the contours of the shapes. (See *Primary Source*, page 402.) This process encourages an abstract, ornamental style, which tends to resist any attempt at three-dimensional effects. Only in the hands of a great master could the maze of lead strips lead to such monumental forms. (See *Materials and Techniques*, page 405.)

Given the way stained glass accentuates pattern and decorative effect, it is not surprising that it was so popular during the Middle Ages. Its brilliant surfaces are like the flat stones and enamel-work so highly prized in earlier periods (see fig. 10.2); enamel is in fact a kind of glass. The intensity with which the viewer engages with the image parallels the direct connection between viewer and object evident in much of the art of the earlier Middle Ages. Worthy comparisons with *Notre Dame de la Belle Verrière* are the Byzantine mosaics from the church of the Dormition at Daphni (see figs. 8.44 and 8.45) for the way they command our attention and communicate directly with a viewer. Both use otherworldly light to convey spiritual messages: on the one hand, filtered through stained glass, and on the other, reflected off gold-glass mosaics.

The stained-glass workers who filled the windows of the great Gothic cathedrals also had to face difficulties arising from the enormous scale of their work. The task required a degree of orderly planning that had no precedent in medieval painting. Only architects and stonemasons knew how to deal with this problem, and it was their methods that the stained-glass workers borrowed in mapping out their own designs. Gothic architectural design relied on a system of geometric relationships to establish numerical harmony; the same rules could be used to control the design of stained-glass windows or even an individual figure. (See *The Art Historian's Lens*, page 406.)

The drawings in a notebook compiled about 1240 by Villard de Honnecourt, who traveled widely and documented the major buildings he examined, provide some insight into this procedure. (See www.myartslab.com.) What we see in his *Wheel of Fortune* (fig. **12.19**) is not the final version of the design but the system of circles and triangles on which the artist based the image. It illustrates the fundamental importance of such geometric schemes.

TRANSEPTS AND THEIR SCULPTURE Each of the transept arms of Chartres cathedral has three deeply recessed and lavishly decorated portals, five **lancets** (tall, narrow windows crowned by a sharply pointed arch), and an immense **rose window**, the large medallion of glass in the center of the façade (see figs. 12.15 and 12.17). The walls of these north and south façades have little solidity; they are so heavily pierced as to be nearly skeletal. On the earlier west façade, which holds the main entrance to the cathedral, the rose window, which was added after the 1194 fire, is composed of a grouping of holes cut out of the solid wall (see fig. 12.4). By comparison, thin membranes hold the glass of the north

Stained Glass

Colored glass was not new in the thirteenth century, when it was used to spectacular effect in the windows of Gothic churches. It can be traced back more than 3,000 years to Egypt, and abundant evidence indicates that the Romans employed thin translucent sheets of glass in their buildings. Literary accounts, supported by some surviving examples, also describe colored glass in Early Christian, Byzantine, Muslim, and early medieval buildings.

In the twelfth-century artist's handbook *De diversis artibus*, the monk Theophilus Presbyter described in great detail the technique for making stained glass (see *Primary Source*, page 402). It required a molten mixture of silica (basically sand), potash (to lower the temperature at which silica melts), and lime (a stabilizer), plus the addition of metal oxides to color or "stain" the glass: The addition of cobalt oxide resulted in blue glass, copper oxide in red, and manganese oxide in purple. The glassworker heated the mixture in a wood-fired furnace and either poured it into molds to cool or shaped it by blowing air through a tube to form the soft glass mixture into an oval ball or cylinder, which he then cut open and flattened.

On a wooden board that had previously been covered with chalk, a designer created a drawing the same size as the window to be filled. Individual pieces of colored glass were cut with hot iron rods to fit the drawing and then arranged on it. Finer details, such as facial features and drapery folds, were then painted on with lead oxides, and the glass was placed in a wood-fired kiln to fuse the painted-on designs with the glass. Individual glass pieces were fitted together into malleable lead strips called **cames**. To permanently hold the composition in place, it was attached to an iron frame secured within the window opening. In the early twelfth century, the iron frame formed a grid of squares of about 2 feet on each side (see fig. 12.18). By the thirteenth century, glaziers employed complicated shapes, including circles, lozenges, and quatrefoils, to create increasingly complex designs (see fig. 12.32).

Stained-glass production was a costly, time-consuming, and labor-intensive activity with a marked division of labor. The artisans who made the glass supported the work of the glaziers who designed and produced the windows.

Although stained glass appears throughout Europe (see fig. 12.47), the most significant achievements in glass were made in northern Europe. To produce stained glass required abundant wood, both for firing the furnaces and kilns and for making potash, and it was in the north where there were sufficient forests to support a glassmaking industry. It was also in the north where the value of light entering a building could best be appreciated.

The effect of multicolored refracted light playing off surfaces and across spaces virtually transforms Gothic buildings. Glaziers needed to consider how individual windows could harmoniously relate to the buildings that enframed them and to a larger iconographic and aesthetic program. At Chartres, for example, blue glass predominates in the north transept rose window, while red, which admits less light, predominates in the southern rose window. Since southern light is much stronger than northern, the effect of the two roses is balanced in relation to the amount of natural light entering the building. Stained glass also provided the means to relate stories and images and to imbue them with metaphoric form. The thirteenth-century writer William Durandus of Mende, in his *Rationale divinorum officiorum*, wrote that "the windows of the church are the Holy Scriptures, which expel the wind and the rain, that is all things hurtful, but transmit the light of the true Sun, that is God, into the hearts of the faithful," while St. Bernard of Clairvaux (see page 359) explained that light could pass through glass without damaging it, just as the word of God had penetrated the womb of the Virgin Mary without violating it.

By the late thirteenth century, the preference for colored glass had diminished and large areas of clear glass dominate church construction (see fig. 12.34). Where figures are employed, they remain quite vividly colored, but are isolated within large expanses of grayish **grisaille glass**, with yellow-stained glass used to represent architectural frames around the figures. This paler glass allows light to illuminate more fully the increasingly complex architectural details of later Gothic architecture.

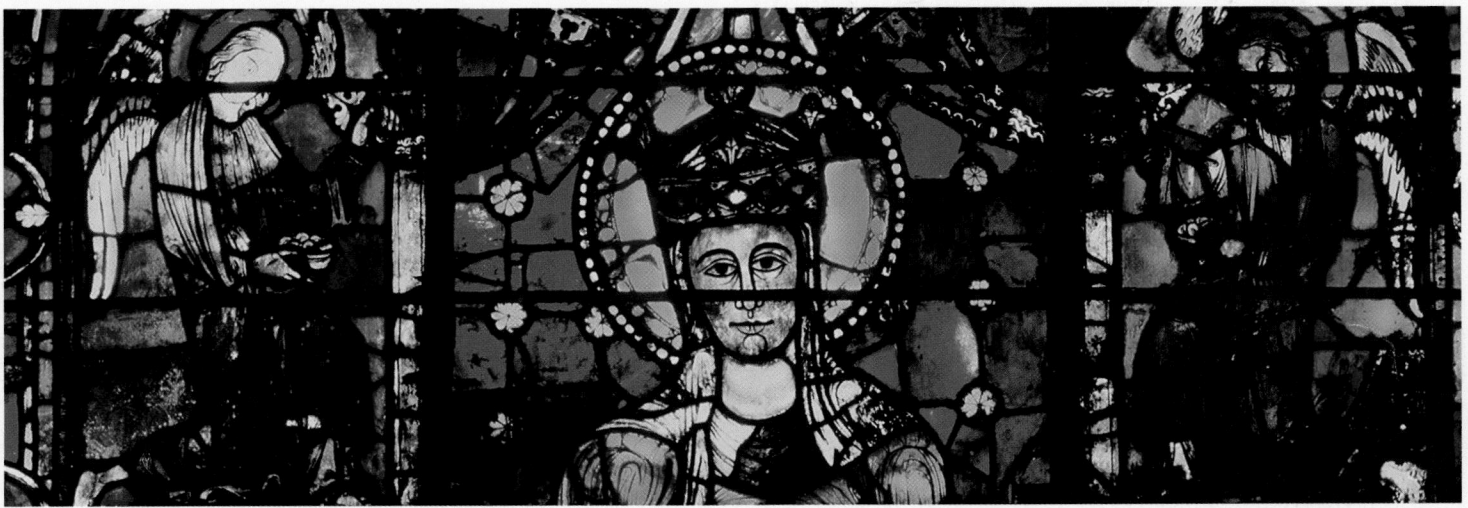

Detail from *Notre Dame de la Belle Verrière*, cathedral of Notre-Dame, Chartres. ca. 1170

Modules and Proportions

Just as musicologists have tried to reconstruct original performance practice during the Middle Ages, so too architectural historians have tried to find the underlying systems that govern the design and construction of medieval buildings, so that they can understand the methods and intentions of medieval builders. How medieval architects and masons decided on the measurements and patterns they employed is a fascinating topic that has been explored by architectural historians since the nineteenth century. Few medieval documents explain how individual architects went about establishing the specific relationships they used, so scholars have to measure buildings and analyze those measurements in order to decipher the systems that were used to design them. The task is not always easy. The medieval yardstick was not the same in all regions, as it was the responsibility of local authorities to control measurement; so, for example, a specific measure in Paris was often different from the measure used in another French town.

The most basic method of establishing a proportional order in building was to either multiply or to divide a unit of measure, a system employed in the ninth century in the St. Gall monastery plan (see fig. 10.22), and in later buildings, such as the cathedral of Santiago de Compostela (see fig. 11.3), where the square at the crossing of the nave is halved to determine the size of the nave bays and quartered for aisle bays. Medieval architects also employed more complicated proportional schemes. For example, by taking the diagonal of a square and rotating it, a designer could produce a rectangle with a consistent proportional relationship based on the square root of 2 (1.414); that is, the proportion of the shorter side of the rectangle to its longer side is 1:1.414. This proportional system had been used throughout antiquity, appearing: for example, in Vitruvius' writings (see www.myartslab.com). The design tools an architect would have needed to produce shapes using these proportions were simply a right angle, a measuring rod, and a compass or a string, which could be used to rotate diagonals and thus form arches.

Art historians have also attempted to understand the philosophical and symbolic significance of medieval systems of measurements. In his analysis of the Gothic cathedral, Otto von Simson described how St. Augustine—whose fifth-century writings were of singular importance throughout the Middle Ages—saw modulation as producing a whole and perfect system that, in effect, reflects the order of the universe. Augustine relies on the biblical description (Wisdom of Solomon 11:21) of an omnipotent God who "hast ordered all things in measure, and number, and weight." For Augustine, the employment of ratios in art, as well as in music, not only produces beauty but also allows us to appreciate the divine order. Architectural historians have demonstrated that figures from Platonic geometry, including the pentagon, the equilateral triangle, and the square, were also understood and employed by medieval builders. For Plato, these shapes were associated with the elements that form the cosmos. Thus, once again, medieval architects found a physical system that expressed the perfection and wholeness of the universe.

Since the plans and elevations of Gothic cathedrals were viewed as mirrors of divine truths, these buildings can be appreciated as a union of engineering and theology, structure and meaning. Undoubtedly, for the medieval mind, the mathematics needed to plan medieval buildings and the symbolism of the proportions and geometry employed were inseparable.

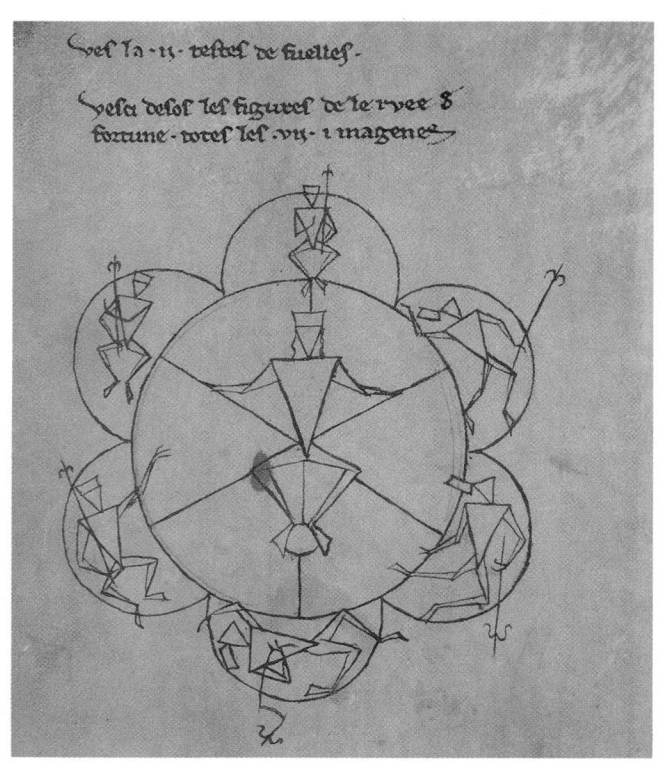

rose in place. Art historians use the terms **plate tracery** and **bar tracery** to describe the different methods of composition employed here. With plate tracery the windows seem to be cut through solid stone walls, while in bar tracery, slender pieces of stone frame and hold in the colored glass. The bar tracery of the transept roses creates intricate decorative patterns and permits an increased amount of glass in relation to frame or wall surface.

The north transept (fig. **12.20**) is devoted to the Virgin Mary. She had already appeared over the right portal of the west façade in her traditional role as the Mother of God seated on the Throne of Divine Wisdom (see fig. 12.5). Her new prominence reflects the growing importance of the cult of the Virgin, which the Church had actively promoted since the Romanesque period. The growth of Mariology, as it is known, was linked to a new emphasis on divine love, embraced by the faithful as part of a more human view of Christianity that increased in popularity during the Gothic era. The cult of the Virgin at Chartres developed special meaning about 1204, when the cathedral received the head of her

12.19   Villard de Honnecourt, *Wheel of Fortune*. ca. 1240. Ink on vellum. Bibliothèque Nationale, Paris

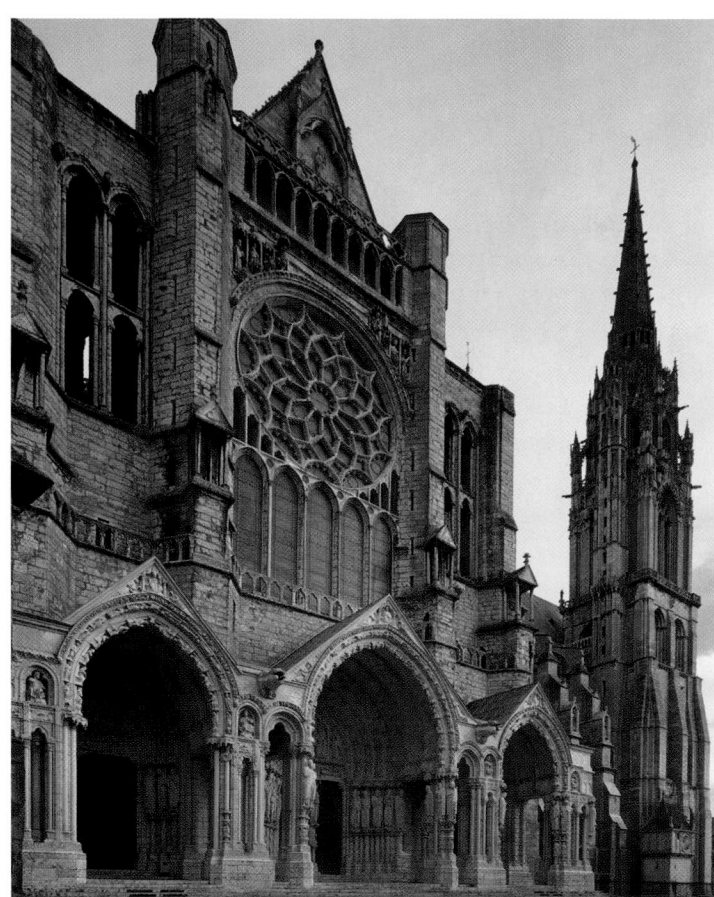

12.20 Portals, north transept of cathedral of Notre-Dame, Chartres. ca. 1204–30

mother, St. Anne, as a relic. This relic, in combination with the tunic of the Virgin that had miraculously survived the fire of a decade earlier, gave Chartres exceptional status among those devoted to Mary.

The north tympanum of about 1210 depicts events associated with the Feast of the Assumption, when Mary was transported to Heaven (fig. 12.21). These events are the Death (Dormition), Assumption, and Coronation of the Virgin, which, along with the Annunciation, became the most frequently portrayed subjects relating to her life. They rely on theological interpretations that identify Mary with the Church as the Bride of Christ and the Gateway to Heaven, in addition to her traditional role as divine intercessor. She becomes not only Christ's companion, but also his queen. Unlike earlier representations, many of which rely on Byzantine examples, these are of Western invention. The figures have a monumentality never found before in medieval sculpture. Moreover, the treatment is so pictorial that the scenes are independent of the architectural setting into which they are crammed.

Whereas the *Coronation of the Virgin* represents a relatively early phase of High Gothic sculpture, the jamb statues of the transept portals show a discernible evolution, even among themselves since they were carved at different times. The relationship

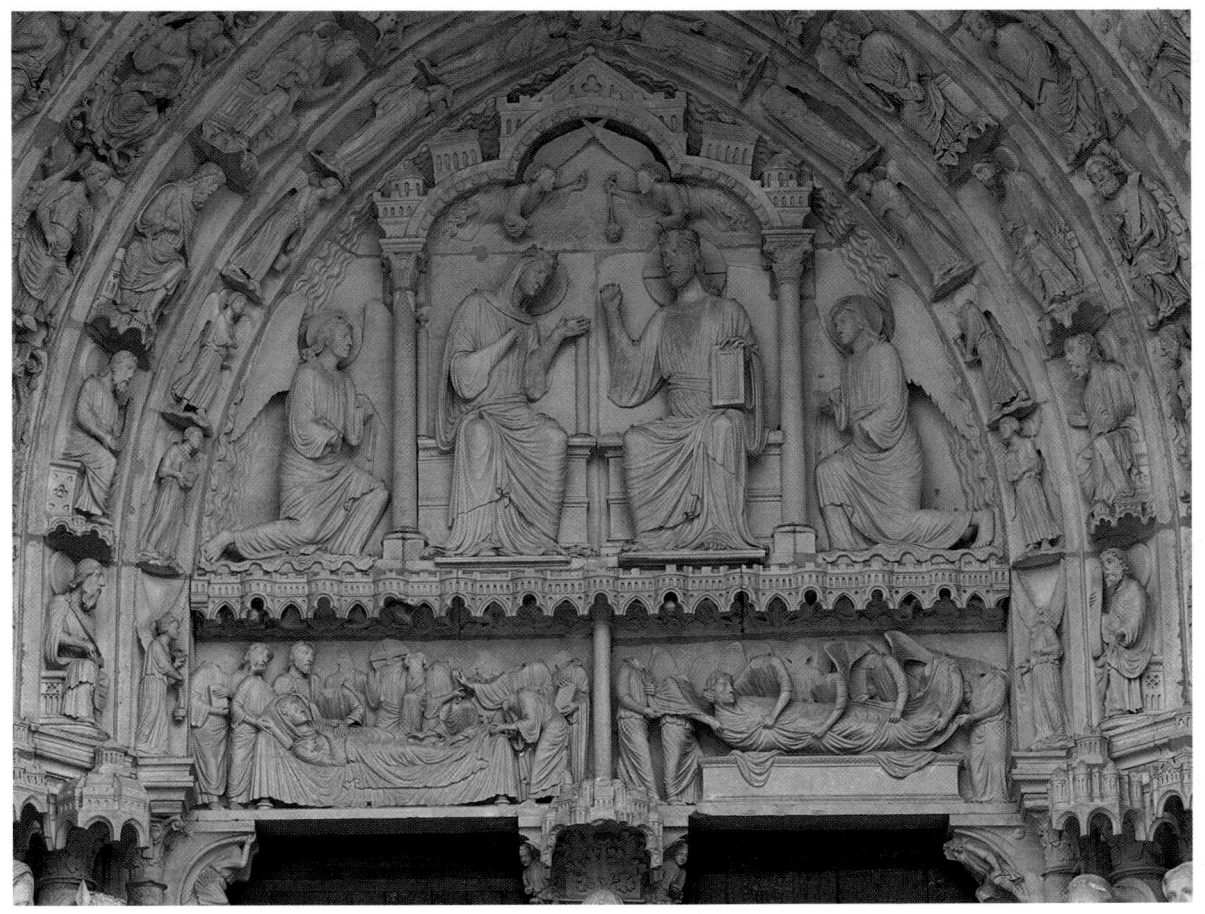

12.21 *Coronation of the Virgin* (tympanum), *Dormition* and *Assumption of the Virgin* (lintel), north portal of cathedral of Notre-Dame, Chartres. ca. 1210

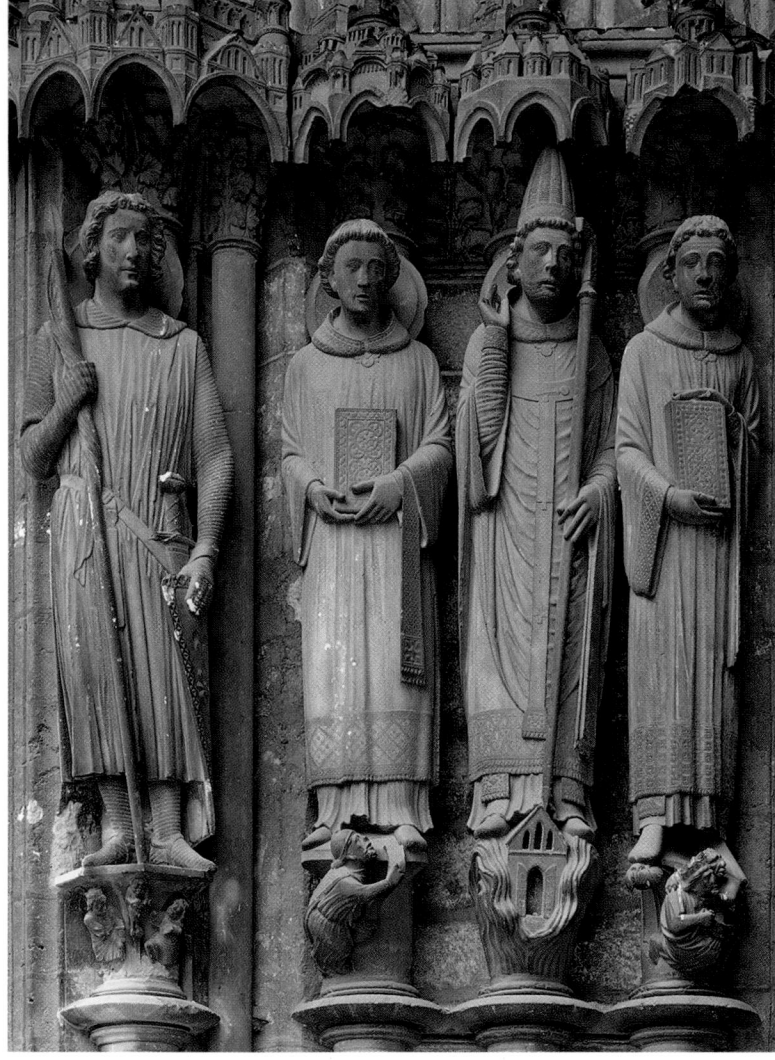

12.22 Jamb statues, south transept portal of cathedral of Notre-Dame, Chartres. ca. 1215–20. Left-most figure (St. Theodore) ca. 1230

between statue and column begins to dissolve. The columns are quite literally put in the shade by the greater width of the figures, by the strongly projecting canopies, and by the elaborately carved bases of the statues.

A good instance of this early dissolution of the relationship between statues and columns is seen on one of the south transept portal jambs (fig. **12.22**). The three saints on the right (Lawrence, Clement, and Stephen) still echo the cylindrical shape of Early Gothic jamb statues (see fig. 12.6), though the heads are no longer strictly in line with the central axis of the body. By comparison, the knight on the left, St. Theodore, who was carved about ten or fifteen years later, stands at ease, in a semblance of classical *contrapposto*. His feet rest on a horizontal platform, rather than on a sloping shelf as before, and the axis of his body, instead of being straight, describes a slight but perceptible S-curve. Even more surprising is the wealth of carefully observed detail in his weapons and in the texture of his tunic and chain mail. Above all, there is the organic structure of the body. Not since imperial Roman times (see fig. 7.29) have we seen a figure that so convincingly

suggests the organic structure of a human body. Yet the most impressive quality of the St. Theodore statue is not its naturalism but the sense of serenity and balance that it conveys. This ideal portrait of the Christian soldier, dressed as a contemporary warrior, expresses the spirit of the crusades in its most elevated form.

Amiens Cathedral

The High Gothic style defined at Chartres reaches its climax a generation later in the interior of Amiens cathedral (figs. **12.23** and **12.24**). Amiens was begun in 1220, two years after a fire destroyed an earlier cathedral on the site and while Chartres was still under construction; the nave was vaulted by 1236 and work on the choir continued for another 25 years. It is significant that we know the names of the cathedral's architects, Robert de Luzarches, Thomas de Cormont, and his son Renaud de Cormont, since it indicates the heightened social status of Gothic builders.

NAVE The breathtaking height of the nave (fig. 12.24) is the dominant achievement both technically and aesthetically at Amiens. We can see clearly the relatively swift and continuous progression toward verticality in French Gothic cathedral architecture by comparing the nave elevations of the Early Gothic cathedral of Notre-Dame in Paris and the High Gothic cathedrals of Chartres and Amiens (fig. **12.25**). The height of the Amiens nave arcade, greatly increased in proportion to the rest of the wall, creates a soaring effect; it alone is almost as high (70 feet) as the entire four-story elevation of Laon (78 feet). The complete nave rises 140 feet above the ground, while that at Chartres measures "only" 118 feet from floor to vault. Moreover, the width of the Amiens nave is narrower in proportion to its height; at Paris, the ratio of nave width to height is 1:2.2 and at Chartres 1:2.4, while at Amiens it is 1:3. Thus, the effect of soaring verticality increased in direct proportion to the apparent narrowing of the nave. There is also increased vertical integration through the use of shafts that rise directly through the capitals of the piers. Moreover, the triforium and clerestory are connected visually by means of a central colonnette, so that the entire wall above the nave arcade is pulled together vertically. At Amiens, the vaults are as taut and thin as membranes; skeletal construction is carried to its virtual limits.

Reims Cathedral

We can trace the same emphasis on verticality and translucency in the development of the High Gothic façade. The one at Reims cathedral makes an instructive contrast with Notre-Dame in Paris, even though it was designed only about 30 years later. Reims, as the coronation cathedral of the kings of France, was closely linked to Paris, where the kings held court. The two share many elements, including broad transepts that extend out from the body of the church only slightly, but they have been reshaped into very different ensembles (fig. **12.26**).

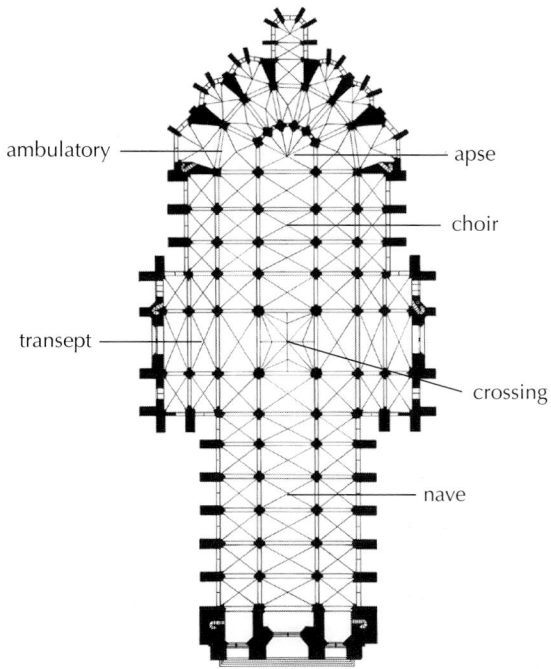

12.23 Robert de Luzarches, Thomas de Cormont, and Renaud de Cormont. Plan of cathedral of Notre-Dame, Amiens. Begun 1220

ambulatory

apse

choir

transept

crossing

nave

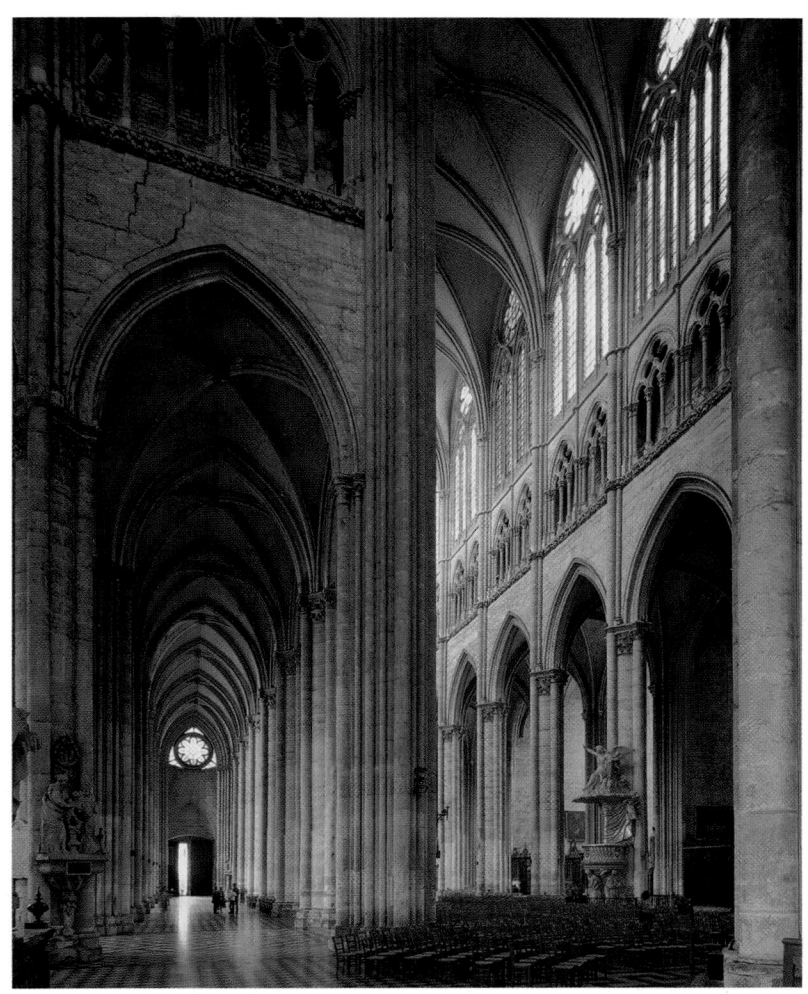

12.24 Nave and side aisle of cathedral of Notre-Dame, Amiens

12.25 Comparison of nave elevations in same scale (after Grodecki)

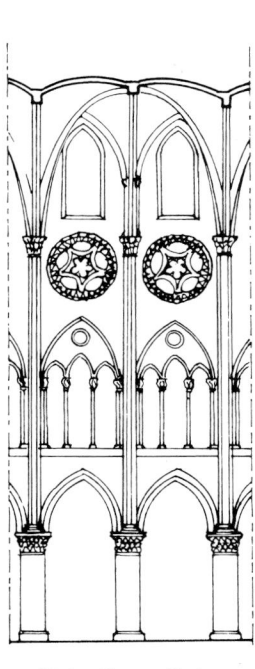

Notre-Dame, Paris

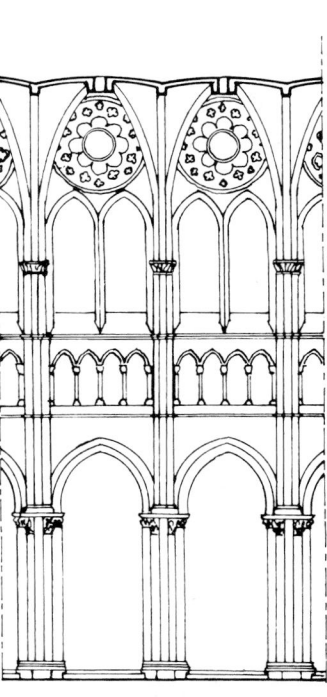

Chartres Cathedral

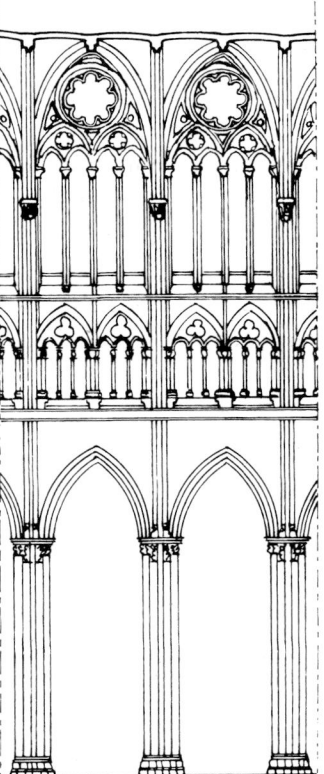

Amiens Cathedral

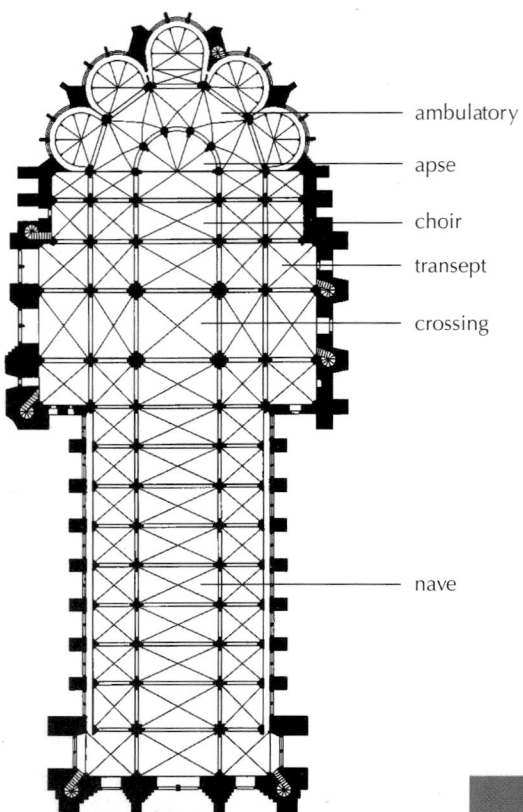

ambulatory

apse

choir

transept

crossing

nave

12.26 Plan of cathedral of Notre-Dame, Reims. ca. 1225–90

WEST FAÇADE The portals on the west façade of Reims cathedral (fig. **12.27**), instead of being recessed as in Paris (see fig. 12.10), project forward as gabled porches, with windows in place of tympana above the doorways. The gallery of royal statues, which in Paris forms a horizontal band between the first and second stories, has been raised in Reims until it merges with the third-story arcade. Every detail except the rose window has become taller and narrower than before. **Pinnacles** (small pointed elements capping piers, buttresses, and other architectural forms) everywhere accentuate restless upward movement. The sculptural decoration, by far the most lavish of its kind, no longer remains in clearly marked-off zones, but has now spread to so many new perches, not only on the façade but on the flanks of the edifice as well, that the exterior begins to look like a dovecote for statues.

WEST PORTAL SCULPTURE The jamb figures at Reims are not in their original positions because some sculptures were moved between the west façade and the transept portals. As a result, continuity of style and program is difficult to assess. However, we can study here individual sculptures of distinctive style and high quality. Gothic classicism (see page 408) reached

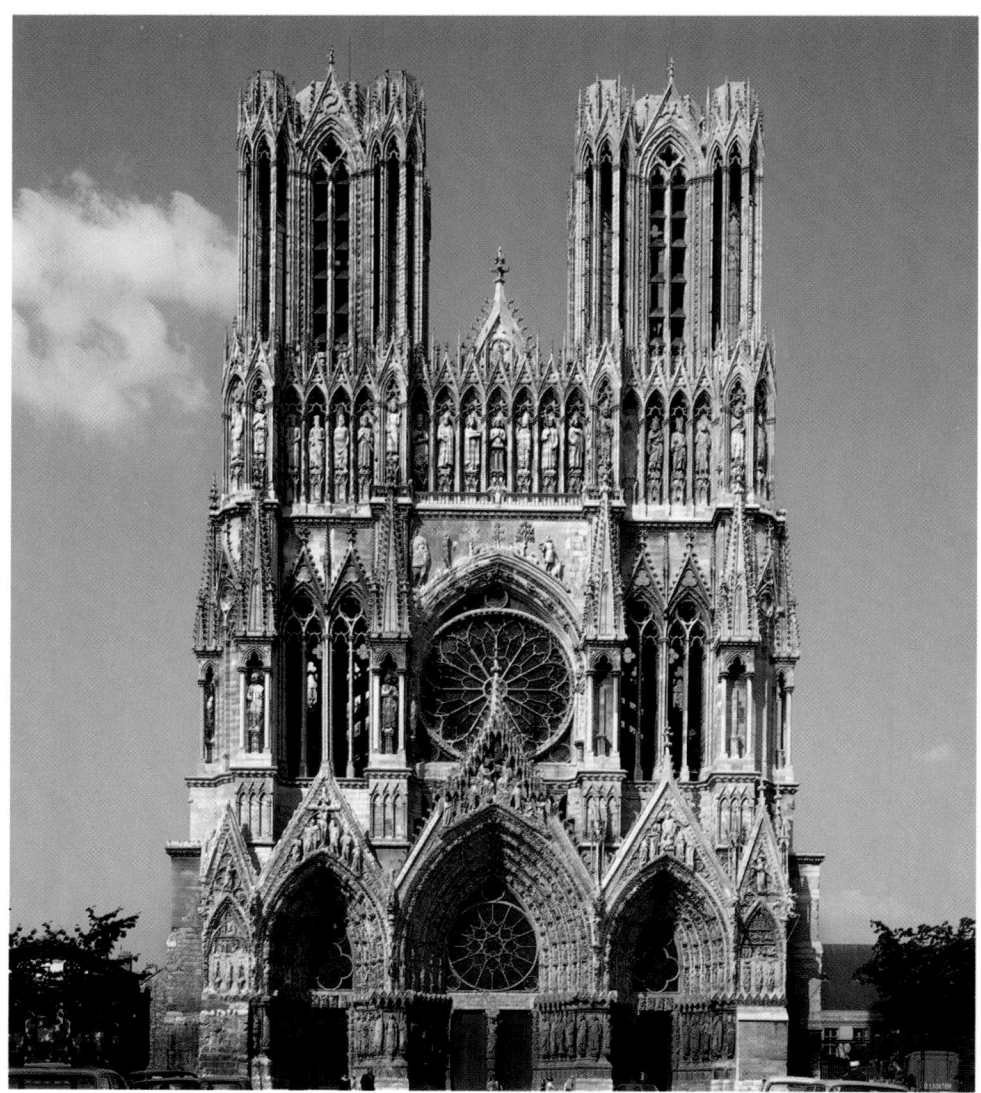

12.27 Cathedral of Notre-Dame, Reims (from the west)

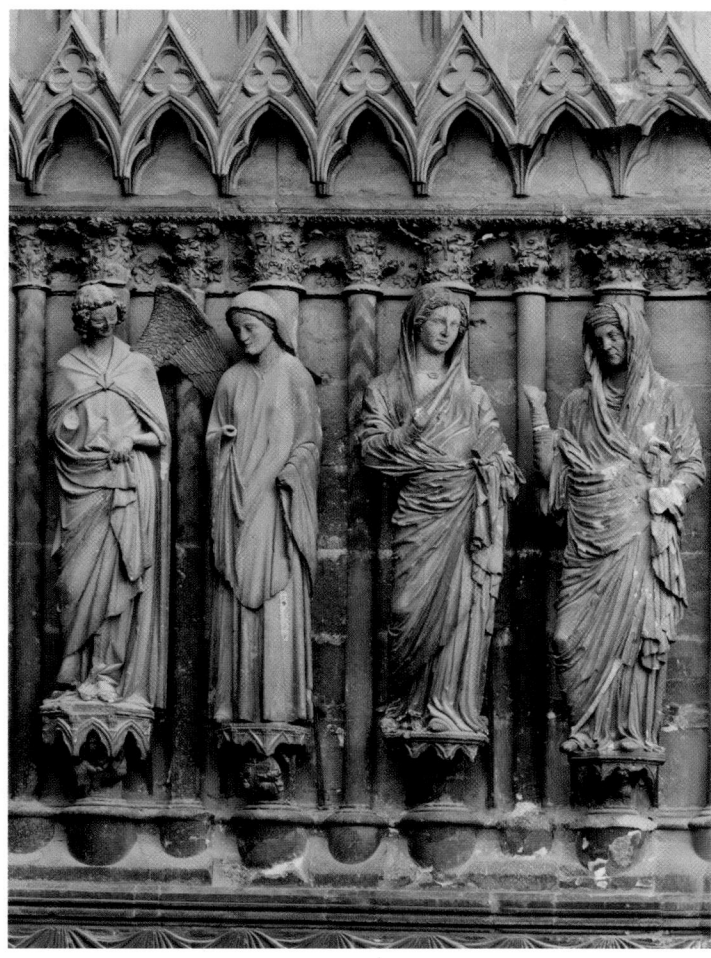

12.28 *Annunciation* and *Visitation*, west portal of cathedral of Notre-Dame, Reims. ca. 1230–65

Roman presence in Reims, and excavations during the last century established that the first cathedral on the site was built over Roman baths. That Roman models might have been available to the Reims sculptors is thus a real possibility.

Because of the vast scale and time frame of the sculptural program at Reims (and at other cathedrals as well), it was necessary to employ a variety of sculptors working in distinct styles. Two of these styles, both clearly different from the classicism of the *Visitation*, appear in the *Annunciation* group (see fig. 12.28, the two figures on the left). The difference in style within a single group derives from the fact that the angel Gabriel and the Virgin were not originally intended as a pair, but were only later installed next to each other. The Virgin, from between 1240 and 1245, has a rigidly vertical axis, and her garments form straight, tubular folds meeting at sharp angles. This severe style was probably developed about 1220 by the sculptors of the west portals of Notre-Dame in Paris; from there, it traveled to Reims as well as Amiens. The angel, in contrast, is remarkably graceful and was carved at least a decade later than the Virgin of the *Annunciation*, between 1255 and 1265. Features such as the tiny, round face framed by curly locks, the emphatic smile, the strong S-curve of the slender body, and the rich drapery of this "elegant style" spread far and wide during the following decades. In fact, the style soon became the standard formula for Gothic sculpture. Its effect will be seen for many years to come, not only in France but also abroad.

RELIEF SCULPTURE A mature example of the elegant style is the group of *Melchizedek and Abraham* (fig. **12.29**), carved shortly after the middle of the thirteenth century, for the interior west wall of Reims cathedral. These sculptures were probably

its climax in some of these Reims statues. The most famous of them is the *Visitation* group (fig. **12.28**, the two figures on the right), which was carved between 1230 and 1233. It depicts the Virgin Mary announcing the news of her pregnancy to her cousin Elizabeth.

For a pair of jamb figures to enact a narrative scene such as this would have been inconceivable in Early Gothic sculpture, where individual figures remained isolated, even within unified programs. That the *Visitation* figures are now free to interact shows how far the column has receded into the background. The S-curve, resulting from the pronounced contrapposto, is much more obvious here than in the St. Theodore from Chartres (see fig. 12.22) and dominates both the side and front views of the figures. The figures gesture at each other as they communicate across the space that separates them, an engagement with open space that recalls the more active role taken on by space in High Gothic architecture, too.

Horizontal folds of cloth pulled across the women's abdomens emphasize the physical bulk of their bodies. Mary and Elizabeth remind us so strongly of ancient Roman matrons that we might wonder if the artist was inspired by large-scale Roman sculpture (compare fig. 7.35). A surviving gate attests to an earlier

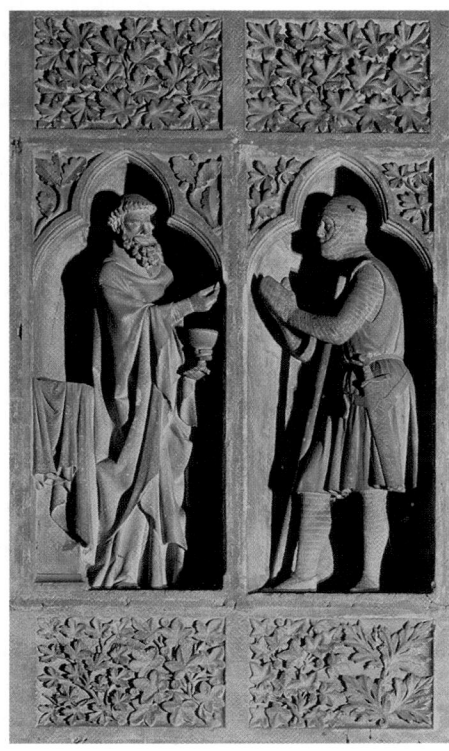

12.29 *Melchizedek and Abraham*, interior west wall of cathedral of Notre-Dame, Reims. ca. 1260–70

conceived in relation to the royal coronation ceremonies held in the cathedral. Abraham and Melchizedek were chosen as subjects because, as described in Genesis 14:18–20 in the Hebrew Bible, they are sacred leaders. The meaning relayed here expands on ideas expressed in the jamb statues of Chartres cathedral's west façade, where parallels are drawn between biblical royalty and the kings and queens of France (see page 396). The Reims scene emphasizes that earthly power is conferred through and in the service of the Church and that the archbishop of Reims, who anointed new kings, bestowed on them the lawful rite to rule as sovereign Christian monarchs. Abraham's costume, that of a medieval knight, would undoubtedly have encouraged the thirteenth-century viewer to draw parallels with the reigning monarch.

The carving of the figures recalls the vigorous realism of the St. Theodore at Chartres (see fig. 12.22) in the attention the sculptor invested in his garments and trappings. Melchizedek, however, shows clearly his proximity to the angel of the Reims *Annunciation* (see fig. 12.28) in his even more elaborately curled hair and beard, and the ample draperies that nearly swallow his body among the play of folds. Deep recesses and sharply projecting ridges show a new awareness of the effects of light and shadow that are as pictorial as they are sculptural. This pictorialism is also apparent in the way the figures interact, despite being placed in deep niches. The realism of the figures is heightened by the foliage that occupies the framing elements around them, representing specific and recognizable plants, which include oak and fig leaves as well as acorns.

References to the increasing realism of Gothic sculpture need qualification, since Gothic realism was never systematic. Rather, it was a realism of particulars, focused on specific details rather than on overall structure. Its most characteristic products are not only the classically oriented jamb statues and tympanum compositions of the early and mid-thirteenth century, but also small-scale carvings, such as the *Labors of the Months* and the *Signs of the Zodiac* in **quatrefoil** (four-lobed) frames on the façade of Amiens cathedral (fig. 12.30). The same subjects appear on Romanesque (see page 362) and Early Gothic portals (see page 396), but at Amiens they demonstrate a delightful observation of everyday life. The sculptor was clever in arranging individual scenes within the decorative quatrefoils, a shape difficult to master compositionally.

The High Gothic cathedrals of France represent a concentrated effort rarely seen before or since. The huge cost of these truly national monuments was borne by donations and taxes collected from all over the country and from all classes of society. These cathedrals express the merging of religious and patriotic fervor that had been Abbot Suger's goal. However, the great expense and forced taxation required to construct these buildings did produce vehement objections. In 1233, for example, construction of Reims cathedral was suspended as a result of civil unrest directed against the cathedral authorities and was not resumed for

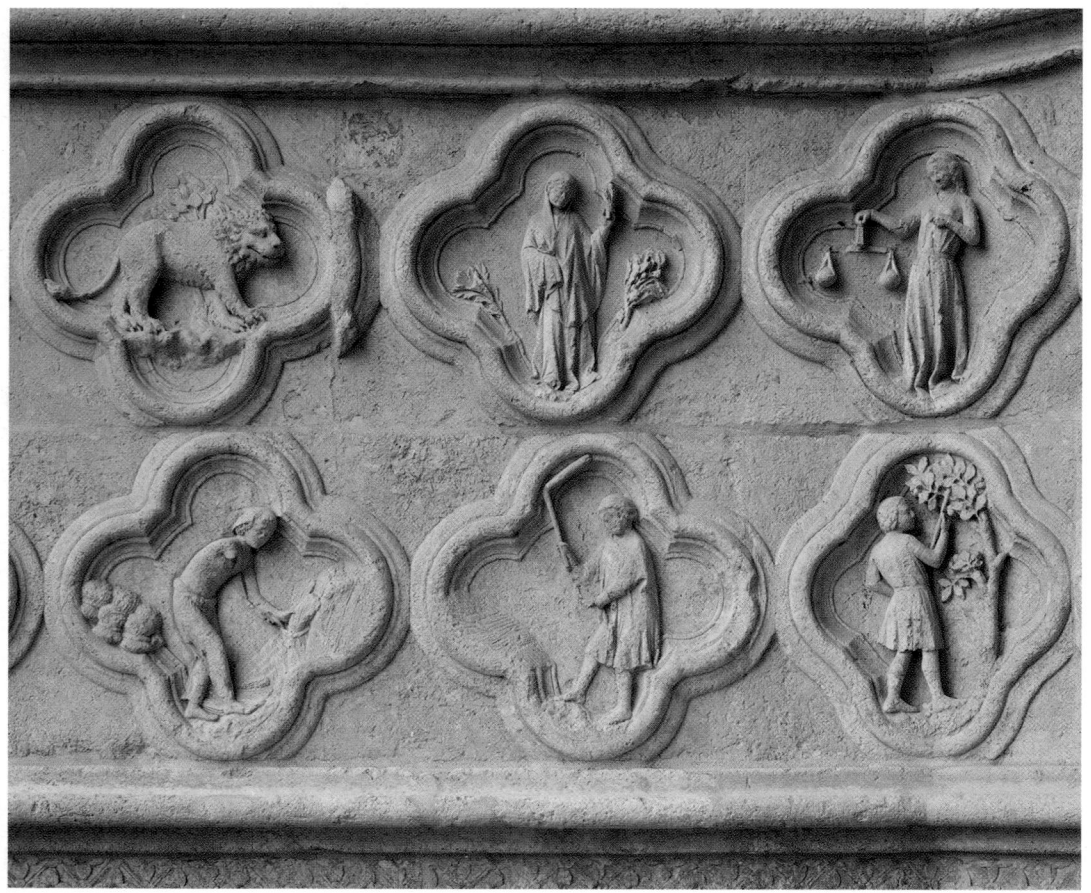

12.30 *Signs of the Zodiac* (Leo, Virgo, and Libra) and *Labors of the Months* (July, August, and September), west façade of Amiens cathedral. ca. 1220–30

three years. This cessation of building activity helps explain the variety of styles at Reims. By the middle of the thirteenth century the wave of enthusiasm for large-scale projects had passed its peak. Work on the vast structures now proceeded at a slower pace. New projects were fewer and generally far less ambitious. As a result, the highly organized teams of masons and sculptors that had formed at the sites of the great cathedrals during the preceding decades gradually broke up into smaller units.

RAYONNANT OR COURT STYLE

One of those who still had the will and means to build on an impressive scale during the mid-thirteenth century was King Louis IX (known as St. Louis following his canonization in 1297, fewer than 30 years after his death). Under the king's governance and as a result of a treaty with the English that resulted in French control of Normandy, the map of Louis's possessions began to take on the shape of present-day France. The increasing importance of the monarchy and the rising importance of Paris, where the court was located, is reflected in the degree to which Louis was able to define a court style, manifest as an appreciation of visual elegance and material luxury, which was favored as well by the upper echelons of aristocratic society. Our sense of Paris as an artistic center effectively begins under St. Louis.

Sainte-Chapelle

St. Louis's mark on the stylistic evolution of Gothic is most dramatically seen in his court chapel, called the Sainte-Chapelle, which was designed by 1241 and completed within seven years (fig. 12.31). The two-story building comprises a ground floor, a relatively low chapel for court officials, and an upper floor to which the royal family had direct access from their quarters in the palace. In essence, the building is a type of palatine chapel for which Charlemagne's building at Aachen (see fig. 10.18) serves as an early prototype.

The impetus for the building was provided by Louis's acquisition from his cousin, the emperor of Constantinople, of the Crown of Thorns and other relics of Christ's Passion, including a part of the True Cross, the iron lance, the sponge, and a nail. Such sacred relics required a glorious space for their display. Rich colors, elaborate patterns, and extensive amounts of gold, largely restored in the nineteenth century, cover the Sainte-Chapelle's walls, vaults, and other structural members (fig. 12.32). This decoration complements the stained glass that constitutes most of the surface of the chapel. The stained-glass windows concentrate on historical and biblical scenes that prefigure the sacred kingship of French monarchs. Above the altar, an elevated shrine, destined to frame the sacred relics, was left open at the back so that filtered light would bathe the venerated objects on display. The delicate glass cage of the building, jewel-like in the intensity of the colored light that enters it, functions in effect as a monumental reliquary. The tall, thin lancets accentuate verticality to such a degree that

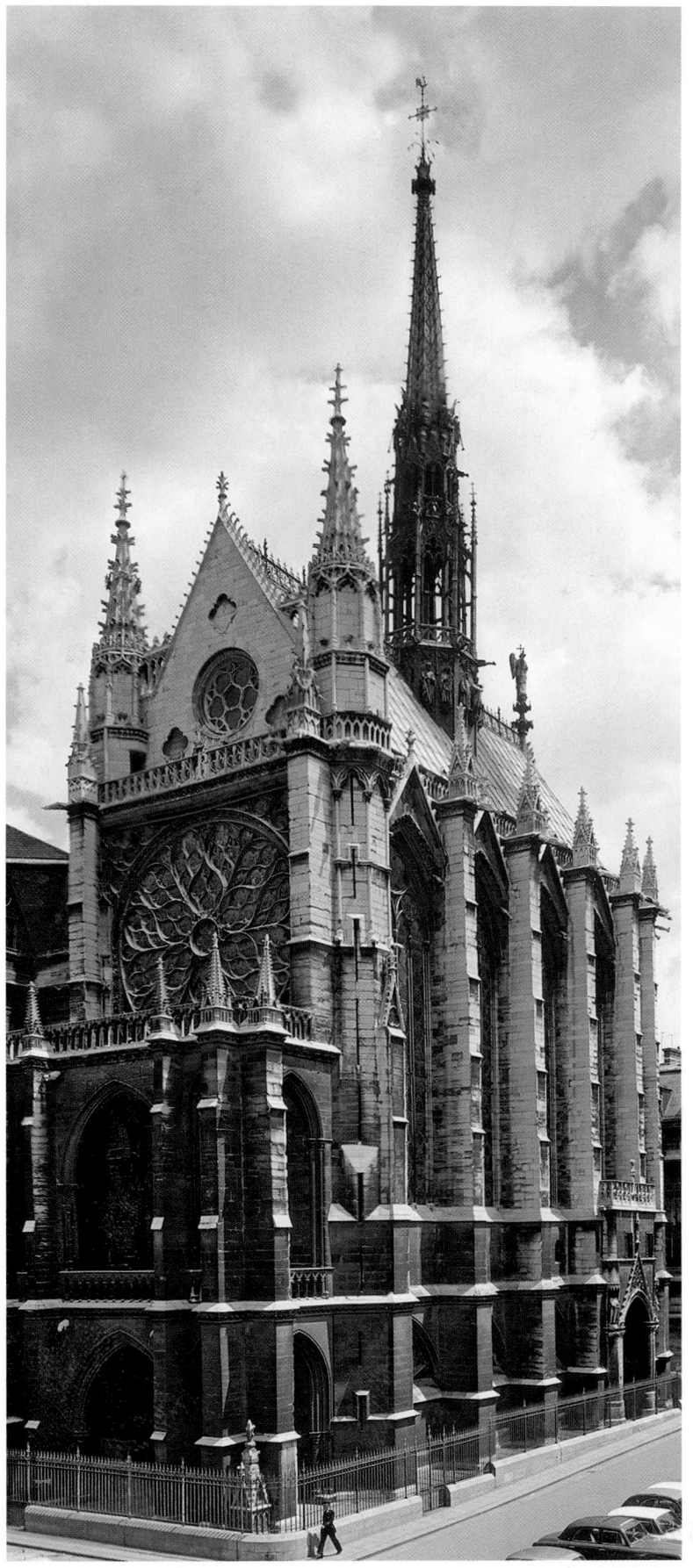

12.31 Sainte-Chapelle, Paris (from the southwest). 1241–48. (Rose window, late 15th century)

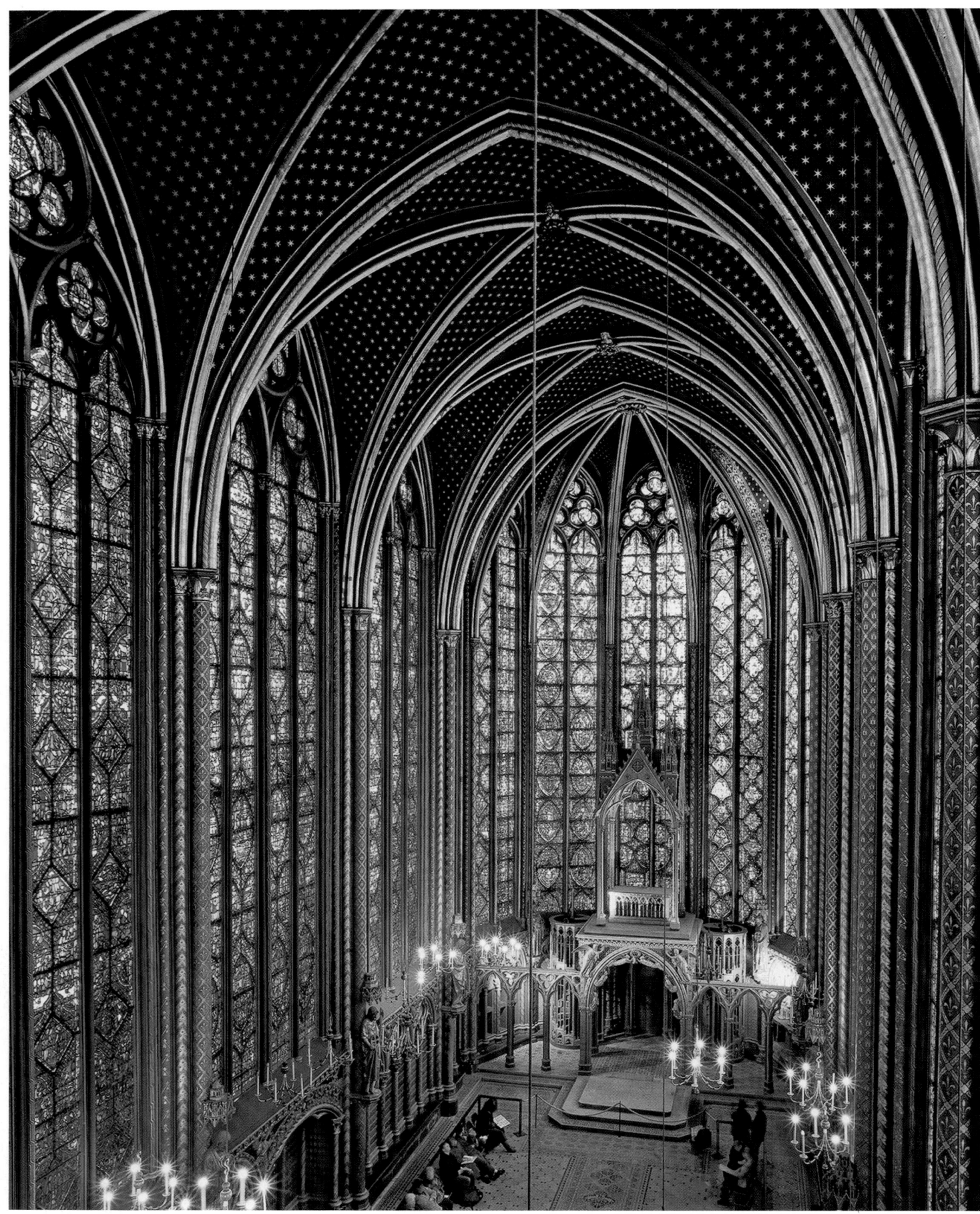

12.32　Interior of upper chapel, Sainte-Chapelle, Paris

the building conveys a sense of monumentality comparable to any cathedral despite its diminutive scale. On entering, a viewer is virtually immersed in its aura of light, different from any normal experience of the physical world. Thus, as with Hagia Sophia (see pages 257–60), spirituality is made manifest through the materiality of architecture and its decoration.

The Sainte-Chapelle's exterior buttresses are relatively modest in scale, given the great amount of glass and the large size of the windows in proportion to the walls (see fig. 12.31). By keeping the buttresses close to the building, the builders kept to a minimum the shadows cast across the windows. In order to withstand the physical forces usually contained by more prominent buttresses, two horizontal iron chains passing across the chapel's windows reinforce the structure, a remarkably effective solution to the structural and aesthetic problems the builders faced.

This phase of Gothic is often referred to as **rayonnant**, from the French *rayonner*, "to radiate light." The term derives from the prevalence of raylike bar tracery in buildings of the period, which originally appeared in rose windows and later began to appear throughout entire churches. The style, closely associated with the court, spread through the French royal domain and then through much of Europe.

Saint-Urbain in Troyes

Saint-Urbain in Troyes (figs. **12.33** and **12.34**), built during the later years of the thirteenth century, was commissioned by Pope Urban IV (r. 1261–1264) to mark his birthplace and was dedicated to his patron saint. By eliminating the triforium and simplifying the plan, the designer created a delicate glass cage of only two stories; the slightly larger upper one is virtually all glass, much of it clear. The delicate tracery of the choir windows, which begin only 10 feet above the floor, emphasizes the effect of a screen dematerialized by light. Flying buttresses so thin as to be hardly noticeable support the building. The same spiny elegance characterizes the architectural ornament: Gables are fully detached from the window walls they are designed to support. The delicacy of Saint-Urbain leaves no doubt that the heroic age of the Gothic

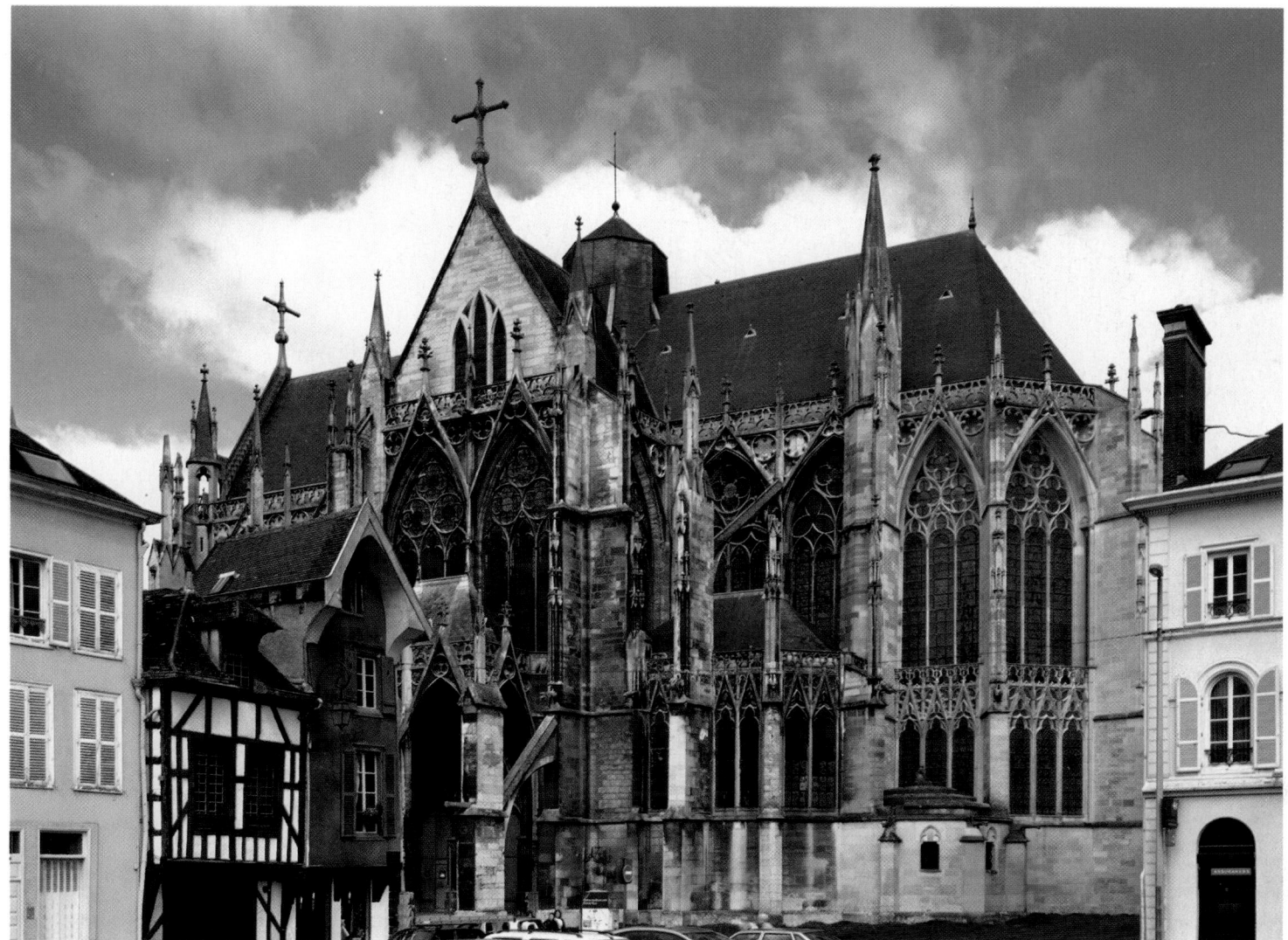

12.33 Saint-Urbain, Troyes, France. Begun 1262

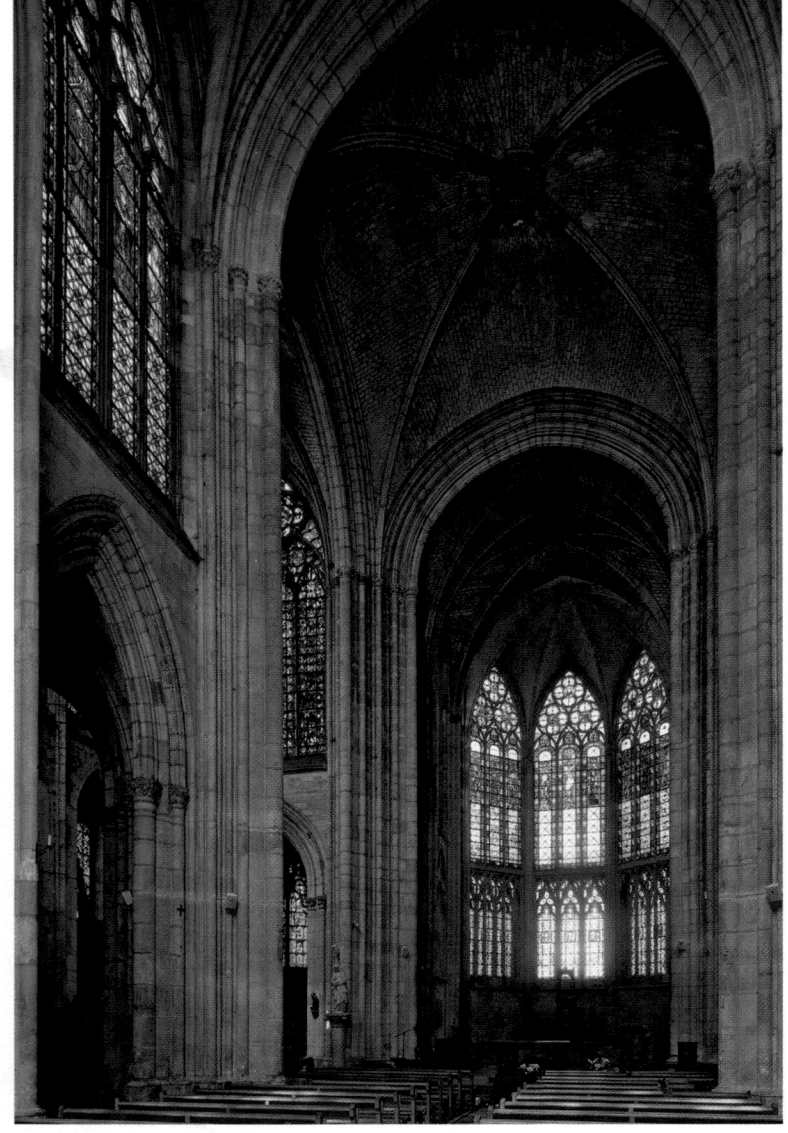

12.34 Interior of Saint-Urbain, Troyes, France

style is past. Refinement of detail, rather than monumentality, is now the chief concern.

Manuscript Illumination

Some authors have been concerned that the term "rayonnant" is appropriate only for architecture. Recognizing that there were also major achievements in the pictorial arts within Louis IX's court and in the upper echelons of aristocratic society, they prefer the term **court style**, which they use synonymously with rayonnant to define the art of this time. In fact, there are many connections between the building arts and the elaborate devotional works with exquisite miniatures produced for the personal enjoyment and education of the royal family and for others who were literate and could afford them. These products of French manuscript workshops disseminated the refined taste that made the court art of Paris the standard for all Europe.

PSALTER OF BLANCHE OF CASTILE A psalter executed around 1230 for Blanche of Castile, mother of King Louis IX, shows these connections. The psalter (fig. **12.35**) was probably made during the period when Blanche served as regent (1226–34) for Louis, who had inherited the throne at age 12 and could not reign in his own right for another six years. The range and intensity of colors (particularly of red and blue), the heavy outlines, and the placement of scenes within geometric shapes—here interlocked circles and semicircles—recall the treatment and arrangement of stained glass seen, for example, behind the shrine at Sainte-Chapelle (see fig. 12.32). The polished gold background of the illuminated page creates a dazzling display, not unlike the effect of light transmitted through glass or reflected from the metal surface of a reliquary.

BIBLE MORALISÉE A new type of bible, the moralized Bible (*Bible moralisée*), was first produced in Paris in the early thirteenth century, also for Blanche of Castile. It included biblical scenes and a short biblical text and moralizing commentary, both

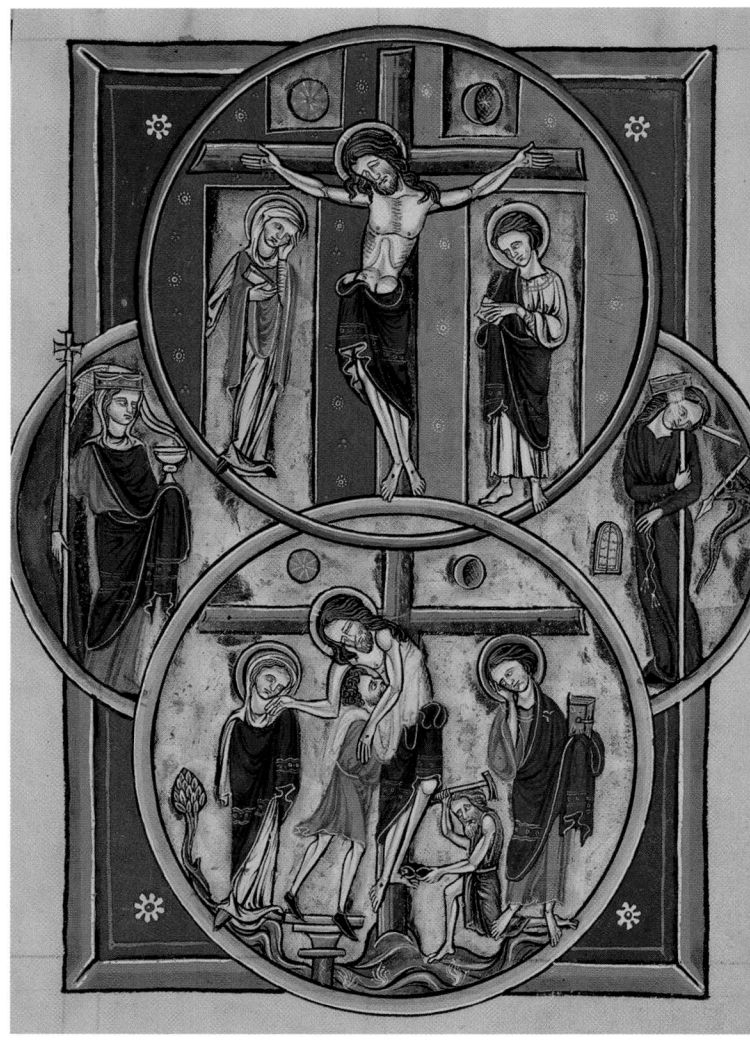

12.35 *Crucifixion* and *Deposition*, from the *Psalter of Blanche of Castile*. ca. 1230. Ink, tempera, and gold leaf on vellum, 7¾ × 6" (19.9 × 15.4 cm). Bibliothèque de l'Arsenal, Paris. Res ms 1186

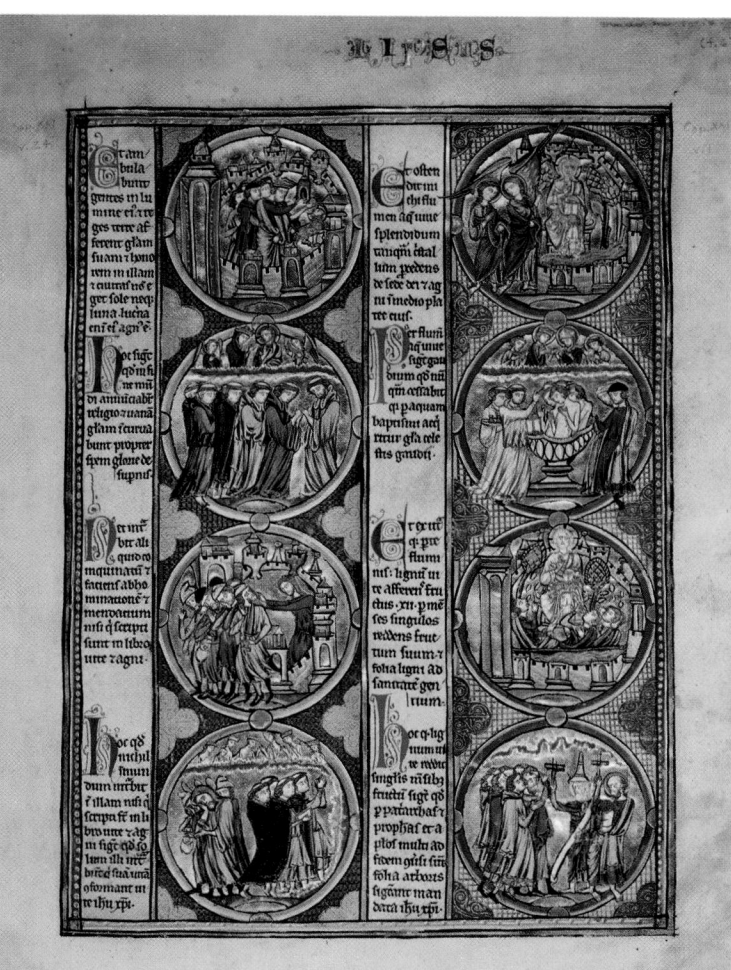

12.36 *Scenes from the Apocalypse*, from a *Bible moralisée*. ca. 1225–35. Ink, tempera, and gold leaf on vellum, 15 × 10½" (38 × 26.6 cm). Pierpont Morgan Library, New York

Sainte-Chapelle (see fig. 12.32) offer a particularly clear parallel. The spaces around the roundels in the manuscript abound with flourishes and checkerboard or diaper patterns of repeated diamonds, analogous to the decoration surrounding the scenes in the Sainte-Chapelle windows.

PSALTER OF ST. LOUIS Perhaps the closest parallel between painting and architectural form is the *Psalter of St. Louis*, which was executed in the 1260s (fig. **12.37**). The folio reproduced here illustrates the same Genesis scene of Abraham and Melchizedek as is represented on the interior of Reims cathedral (see fig. 12.29). Abraham and his troops wear crusader armor, establishing an association between contemporary struggles to free Christian lands and heroic biblical events. Louis was an eager warrior for Christianity who organized and participated in two crusades, in 1254 and 1270, the latter being the occasion of his death in Tunisia. The gold background and the banks of clouds

visual and textual, either in Latin or French, intended to make the biblical accounts more relevant to contemporary viewers. The form demonstrates a will to instruct, and the use of the vernacular French suggests its use by nonclerical persons. It is not surprising, given the didactic quality of the moralized Bible, that its creation in Paris is coeval with the emergence there of the university as an institution. The manuscript illustrated here (fig. **12.36**) is a few years later than the original one and divided between the cathedral of Toledo, in Spain, and the Pierpont Morgan Library, in New York, and originally comprised nearly 3,000 illustrated pages.

These bibles were made for the personal use of the kings and queens of France and perhaps for other high-ranking persons as well. They were intended both as precious objects and guides for good conduct, treating important issues of the time, such as heresy, sex, and the behavior of rulers. The moralizing tone of these instructional guides is very much in keeping with the character and accomplishments of the pious and compassionate King Louis, guided by Blanche, his powerful and involved mother. The scenes on the page shown here are arranged in vertically stacked roundels, and once again the tall and narrow windows of the

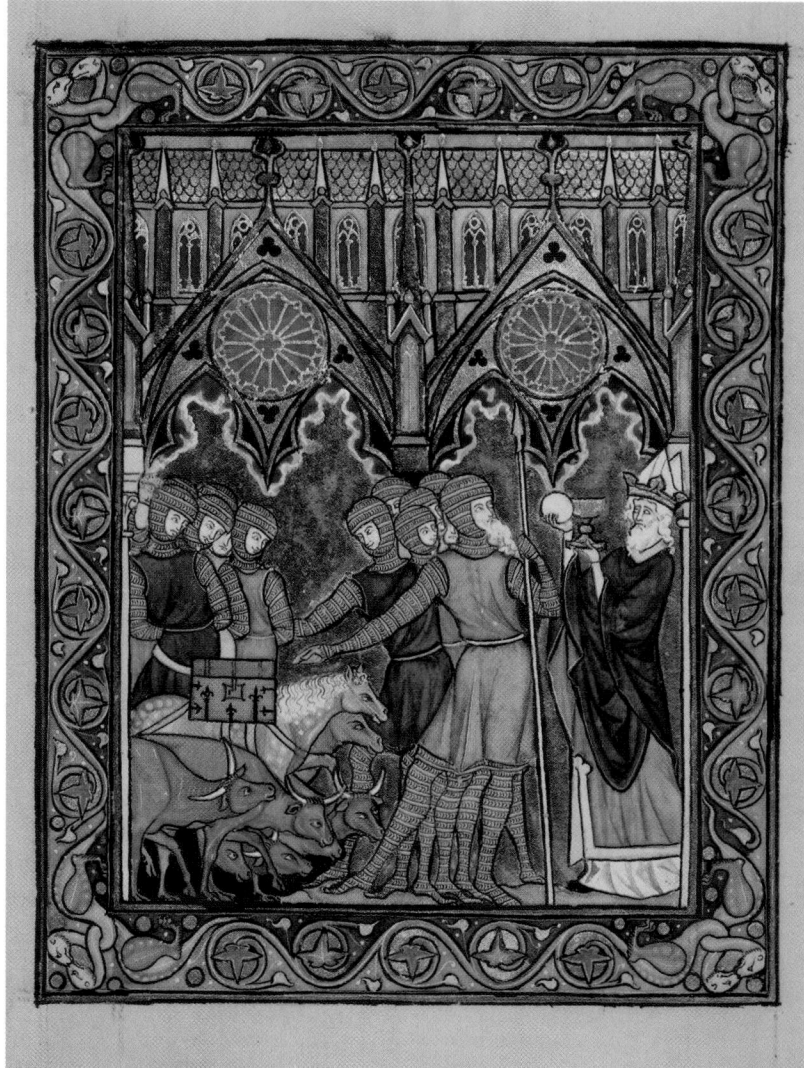

12.37 *Melchizedek and Abraham*, from the *Psalter of St. Louis*. 1253–70. Ink, tempera, and gold leaf on vellum, 5 × 3½" (13.6 × 8.9 cm). Bibliothèque Nationale, Paris

that waft around the arcades, hovering like incense in a church, accentuate the sacral aspects of the representation.

The manuscript's painted architecture is modeled directly on the Sainte-Chapelle (see fig. 12.31). The illustration also recalls the canopies above the heads of jamb statues at Chartres (see fig. 12.22) and the arched twin niches that enclose the Reims relief of Abraham and Melchizedek (see fig. 12.29). Against the two-dimensional background of the page, the figures stand out in relief by their smooth and skillful modeling. The outer contours are defined by heavy, dark lines, once again like the lead strips in stained-glass windows. The figures themselves display all the features of the elegant style seen in Gothic sculpture: graceful gestures, swaying poses, smiling faces, and neatly waved hair. (Compare the *Annunciation* angel in fig. 12.28 and *Melchizedek and Abraham* in fig. 12.29.) This miniature thus exemplifies the refined taste of the court art of Paris.

LATE GOTHIC ART IN FRANCE

Although Late Gothic art builds on earlier achievements, during this period artists felt free to deviate from previous patterns of development. Builders showed increased concern for unity of plan, but they also employed curvilinear and elaborate decorative forms that often showed little concern for the clarity of structure so important in earlier Gothic works. Elaborate arrangements of overlapping and pierced planes produced complex visual displays. Late Gothic manuscripts and sculptures are also highly decorated and are rich in surface treatment, accentuating their precious qualities.

Manuscript Illumination

A notably broader audience for books was stimulated by the Fourth Lateran Council, which met in Rome in 1215 and aimed to increase general Christian education. Until the thirteenth century, illuminated manuscripts had been produced in monastic scriptoria. Now, along with many other activities that were once the special preserve of the clergy, manuscript production shifted to urban workshops organized by laypeople, the ancestors of the publishing houses of today. Here again, the workshops of sculptors and stained-glass painters may have set the pattern. Paris was renowned as a center of manuscript production, and it is possible even today to identify the streets on which the workshops were clustered.

PRAYER BOOK OF PHILIP IV THE FAIR Some of these new, secular illuminators are known to us by name. Among them is Master Honoré of Paris, who in 1296 painted the miniatures in the *Prayer Book of Philip IV the Fair* (fig. **12.38**), commissioned by the grandson of Louis IX and designed for use in the Sainte-Chapelle. Master Honoré was a well-remunerated artist: in 1292, he paid higher taxes than any other member of the Paris guild of miniature painters. (The guild was an association of

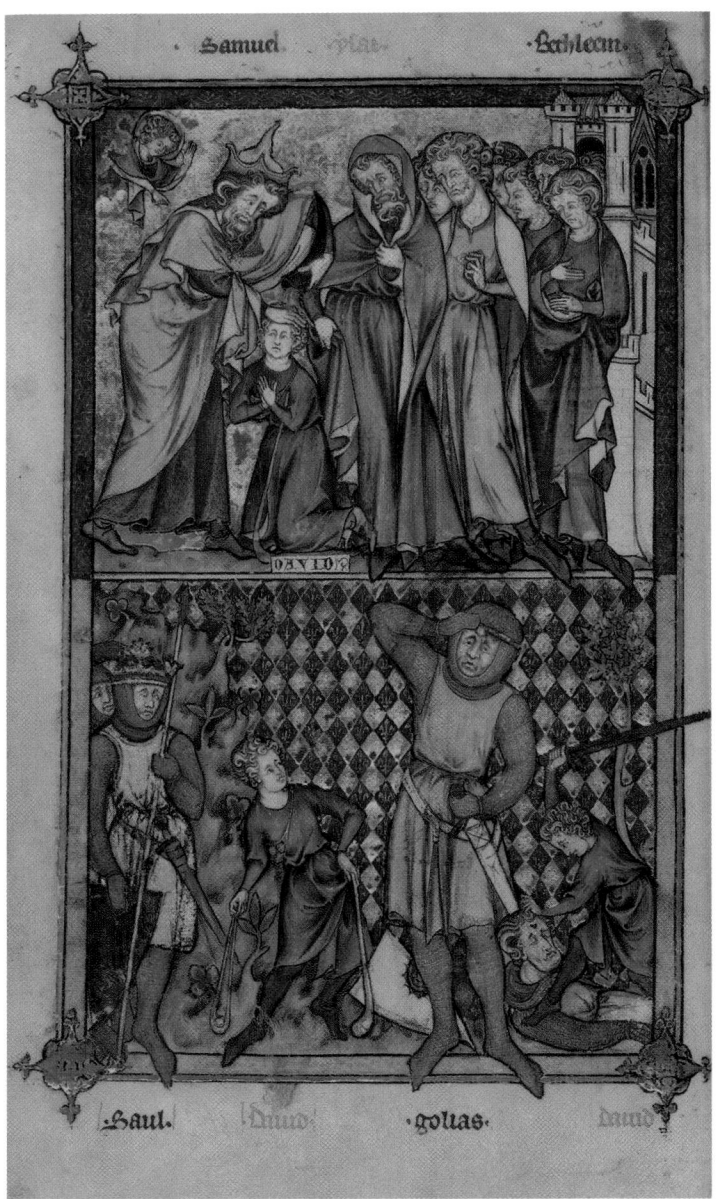

12.38 Master Honoré, *David and Goliath*, from the *Prayer Book of Philip IV the Fair*. 1296. Ink and tempera on vellum, 7⅞ × 4⅞" (20.2 × 12.5 cm). Bibliothèque Nationale, Paris

craftsmen engaged in a particular trade, formed to maintain standards and protect common interests.) The University of Paris commissioned his workshop to produce illuminated copies of ecclesiastical law. Our illustration shows him working in a style derived from the *Psalter of St. Louis* (see fig. 12.37). Here, however, the framework no longer dominates the composition. The figures have become larger and their relieflike modeling more pronounced, an effect achieved through gentle shifts of color and modulated white highlights, quite different from the flat planes of color so characteristic of earlier manuscripts. The figures, though active and engaging, do not appear to stand comfortably, since their turned-down feet are flattened against the page. However, the figures are allowed to overlap the frame, which helps to detach them from the flat pattern of the background and

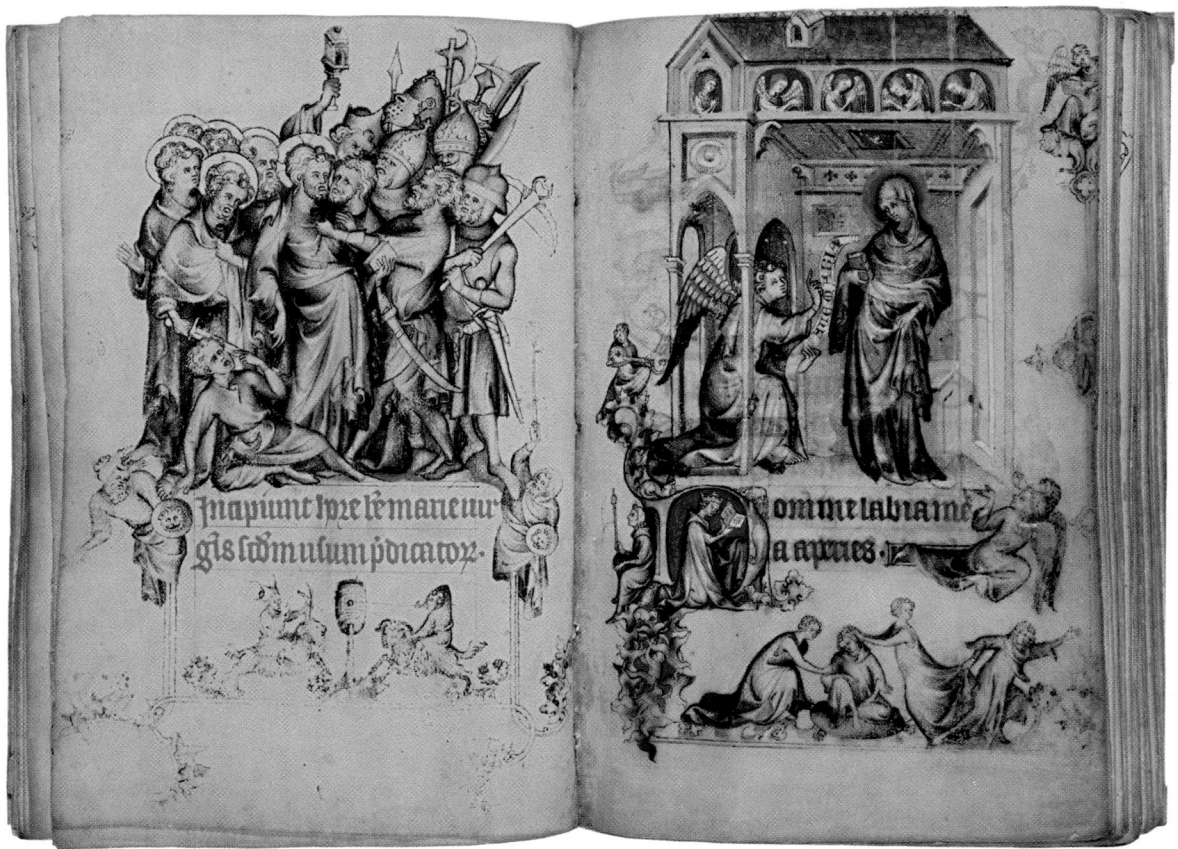

12.39 Jean Pucelle, *The Betrayal of Christ* (folio 15 verso) and *Annunciation* (folio 16 recto), from the *Hours of Jeanne d'Évreux*. 1324–28. Grisaille and tempera on vellum, each page 3½ × 2⁷⁄₁₆" (8.9 × 6.2 cm). (Shown larger than actual size.) Metropolitan Museum of Art, New York. The Cloisters Collection, Purchase, 1954 (54.1.2)

thus introduces a certain, though very limited, depth into the picture. The implication of space helps further the storytelling quality of the representation. In the lower scene, David and Goliath each appear twice; in an expressive detail, Goliath, as if in distress, brings his hand to his forehead even before David has released his shot.

HOURS OF JEANNE D'ÉVREUX The interest in depicting sculptural figures was further developed by the illuminator Jean Pucelle in a prayer book—called a **book of hours**—illuminated in Paris between 1324 and 1328 for Jeanne d'Évreux, queen of France (fig. **12.39**) and probably a gift from her husband, the king. A book of hours was used for private prayer and contained the devotions for the seven canonical hours of the day as well as liturgy for local saints; often a calendar was also included. The book, only 3½ inches high, is jewel-like, fitting for the private use of a queen. The *Annunciation* is represented on the right-hand page and the *Betrayal of Jesus* on the left. The style of the figures recalls Master Honoré (see fig. 12.38), but the delicate **grisaille** (painting in gray) adds a soft roundness to the forms, the enhanced shading conveying a heightened sense of relief. This is not Pucelle's only contribution: The architectural interior reveals

a spatial recession previously unknown in northern European painting. In the *Annunciation*, Gabriel kneels in an anteroom, while angels appear in the windows of an attic, from which the dove of the Holy Spirit descends.

In representing this new pictorial space, Jean Pucelle had to take into account the special needs of a manuscript page. The Virgin's chamber does not fill the entire picture surface. It is as though it were an airy cage floating on the blank background (note the supporting angel on the right), like the rest of the ornamental framework, so that the entire page forms a harmonious unit. Many of the details are peripheral to the religious purpose of the manuscript. The kneeling queen inside the initial D is surely meant to be Jeanne d'Évreux at her prayers; it is as if her intense devotions have produced a tangible vision of the Annunciation. The identity of the man with the staff next to her is unclear, although he appears to be a courtier listening to the lute player perched on the tendril above him. The combination of scenes is a commentary on experiences that become real even if they lack physical substance: Music is at once actual and ephemeral, as is Jeanne's religious vision.

Other enchanting **vignettes** (small decorative or ornamental designs or scenes) fill the page. A rabbit peers from its burrow beneath the girl on the left, and in the foliage leading up to the initial we find a monkey and a squirrel. These fanciful marginal designs—or **drôleries**—are a common feature of Northern Gothic manuscripts. They originated more than a century before Jean Pucelle in the regions along the English Channel. From there they quickly spread to Paris and the other centers of Gothic art. Their subjects include a wide range of motifs: fantasy, fable, and grotesque humor, as well as scenes of everyday life, which appear side by side with religious themes. The essence of drôlerie is its playfulness. In this special domain, the artist enjoys an almost unlimited freedom—comparable to a jester's—which accounts for the wide appeal of drôleries during the later Middle Ages.

The seeming innocence of Pucelle's drôleries nevertheless hides a serious purpose, which is particularly evident in the example at the bottom of the right-hand page, a type of illustration referred to as a **bas-de-page** (French for "bottom of the page"). The four figures are playing a game of tag called Froggy in the Middle, a reference to the *Betrayal of Jesus* on the opposite page. Below the latter scene, two knights on goats joust at a barrel. This image not only mocks courtly chivalry but also refers to Jesus as a "scapegoat," and to the spear that pierced his side at the Crucifixion. The scapegoat refers to the Hebrew Bible description (Leviticus 16) of a goat that would bear the blame for all the sins and transgressions of the people, a fitting parallel to Christ's suffering and redemptive death.

LE DIT DU LION (THE ENCHANTED GARDEN) The

nature of manuscript production (see page 418) in independent lay workshops and the increasing use of the vernacular (see pages 390 and 417) resulted in the introduction of new modes of expression and subjects of interest to a secular audience. An instructive example is one of the first true European landscapes created to illustrate a passage of the poem *Le Dit du Lion* (fig. **12.40**) by Guillaume de Machaut of around 1350. The *Dit* (literally "spoken") indicates that it was not meant to be sung; the French poem describes an enchanted garden seen by a lover who is visiting an adjacent castle. The scene accurately illustrates several verses of the poem including the delightful lines:

> To make their pleasing melody
> Birds are sitting in a tree
> One, two, five, and even six I see.

The cool colors, flickering highlights, and charmingly depicted details of flora and fauna convey a sense of carefully observed nature and a feeling for illusionistic space.

Guillaume de Machaut, the first composer of polyphonic music whom we know by name, seems to have personally supervised the production of manuscripts of his works, which included, in addition to poetry, both sacred and secular music. This reflects the important role books played during this period, that is, when they were becoming accessible to a broader public. Machaut's interest in how his works were presented indicates pride and self-awareness on the part of a writer and musician to parallel what we have already seen of Gothic artists and architects (see page 399).

Sculpture

Portal sculpture, the principal interest of the Early and High Gothic periods, is of relatively little consequence during the Late Gothic period. Single figures, carved in the round, many of them cult figures, are now fully detached from any architectural setting. As the individual's importance in society increased, so individual sculpted figures became more prominent. Sculptors' guilds were now well established. Two guild masters, appointed by the king, guaranteed that sculptors would fulfill the statutes that governed their corporation. In addition to stone carving, sculptors produced a significant number of precious objects in metal and ivory.

VIRGIN OF JEANNE D'ÉVREUX Pucelle's Virgin of the

Annunciation (see fig. 12.39), with its poised elegance, has a remarkable counterpart in the silver-gilt statue that the same patron offered to the abbey of Saint-Denis in 1339 (fig. **12.41**). The elegance and refinement of the *Virgin of Jeanne d'Évreux* reminds us that metalwork—so significant during the earlier Middle Ages—continued to be a valued medium. Even during the Early Gothic period, Abbot Suger made clear the funds that patrons were willing to invest in reliquaries, shrines, altar embellishments, and liturgical vessels: It has been calculated that the reliquary designed for the Crown of Thorns cost more than twice the construction expenses of the Sainte-Chapelle, which was built to house it.

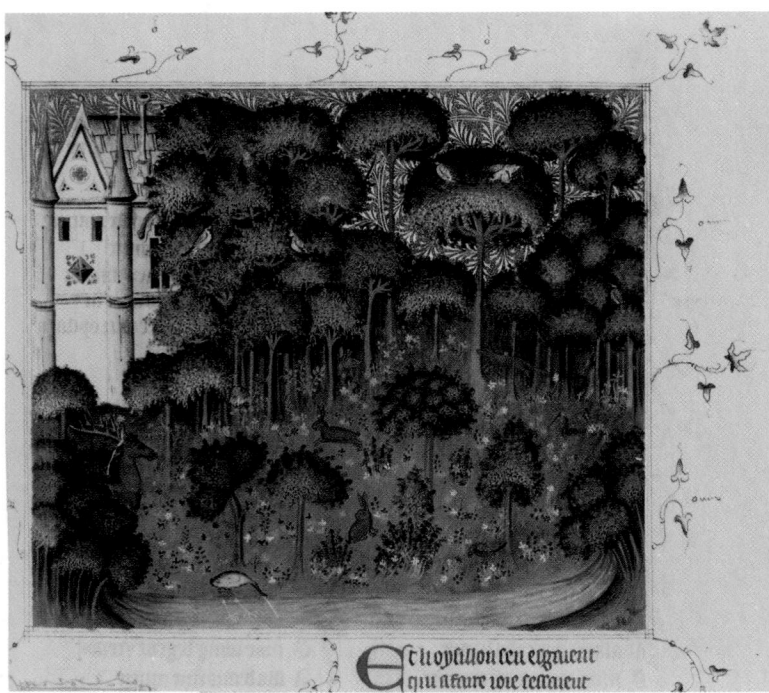

12.40 Guillaume de Machaut. *The Enchanted Garden*, from *Le Dit du Lion*. 1350–55. Ink, tempera, and gold leaf on vellum, 11⅘ × 8¼" (30 × 21 cm). Bibliothèque Nationale, Paris

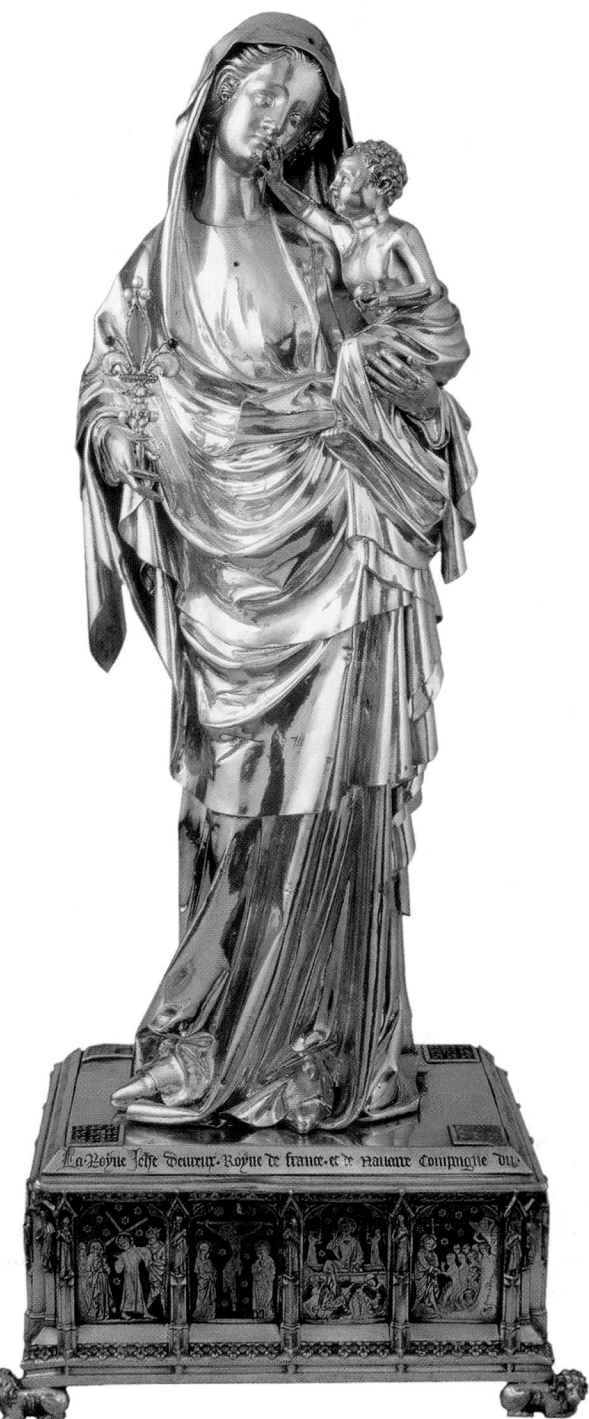

12.41 *Virgin of Jeanne d'Évreux*. 1339. Silver gilt and enamel, height 27½" (68 cm). Musée du Louvre, Paris (Inv MR342; MR419)

In the *Virgin of Jeanne d'Évreux*, the graceful sway of the Virgin's body is counterbalanced by the harmonious way in which the drapery's vertical folds and soft curves play off each other. The Christ Child touches his mother's lips in a gesture both delicate and intimate. The inscription on the base of the statue recording the royal gift and the *fleur-de-lis*, symbol of French royalty, held by the Virgin, associate her royal stature with that of the donor.

VIRGIN OF PARIS   In another early fourteenth-century sculpture of the Virgin, we see how traces of classicism increasingly disappear from Gothic sculpture, while elegance becomes a virtual end in itself. Thus, the human figure of the *Virgin of Paris* (fig. **12.42**) in Notre-Dame cathedral is now strangely abstract. It consists largely of hollows, and the projections are so reduced

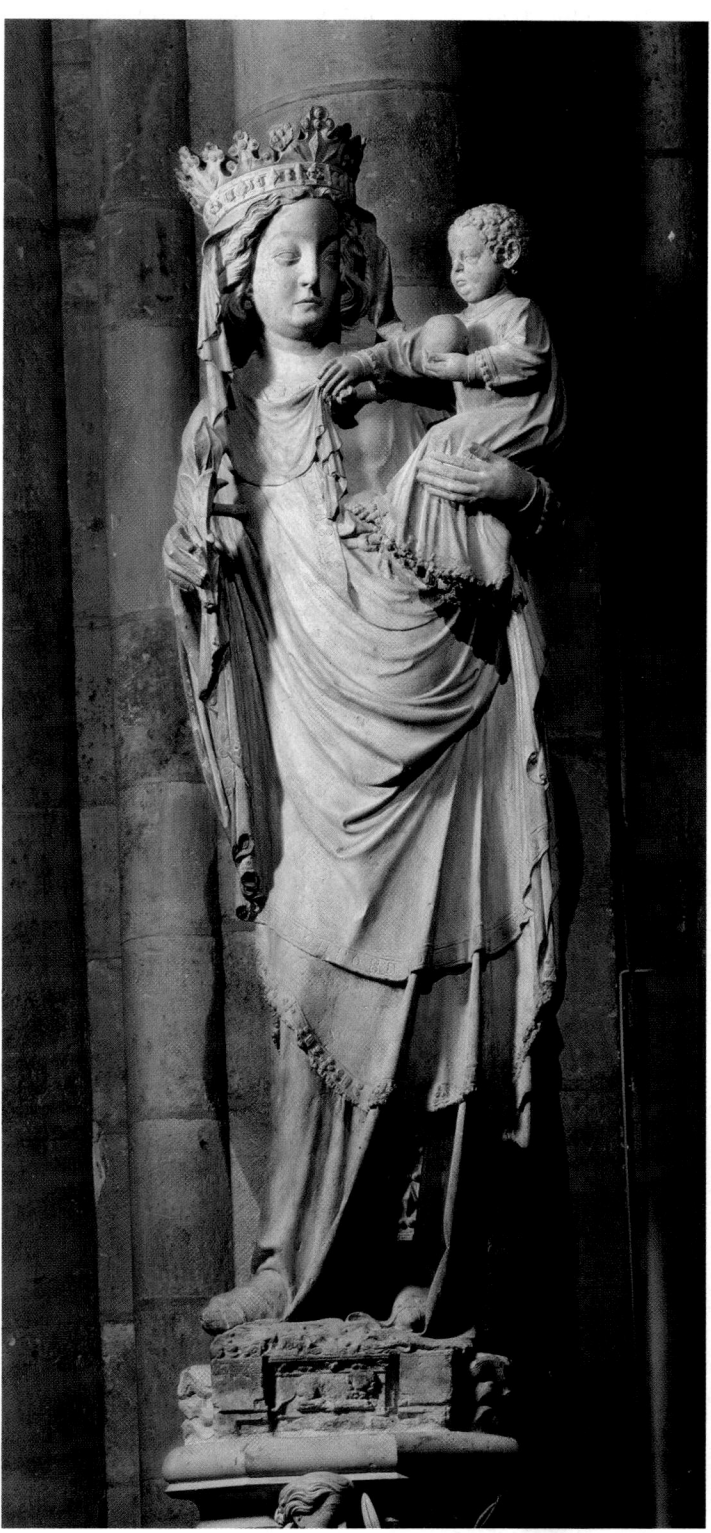

12.42 *Virgin of Paris*. Early 14th century. Stone. Cathedral of Notre-Dame, Paris

that a viewer sees them as lines rather than volumes. The statue is quite literally disembodied—its swaying stance bears little relation to Classical *contrapposto*, since it no longer supports the figure. Compared to such unearthly grace, the angel of the Reims *Annunciation* (see fig. 12.28) seems solid indeed; yet it contains the seed of the very qualities expressed so strikingly in the *Virgin of Paris*. Earlier instances of Gothic naturalism (see page 412), which focused on particulars, survive here as a kind of intimate realism in which the infant Christ is no longer a Savior-in-miniature facing the viewer but, rather, a human child playing with his mother's veil.

The elegant manner of this new style was encouraged by the royal court of France and thus had special authority. It is this graceful expressive quality, not realism or classicism, that is the essence of Gothic art. These Late Gothic sculptures might lack the epic quality of Early Gothic sculpture, but they are still impressive and relate to Late Gothic art in other mediums, such as ivory, as we shall now see.

SIEGE OF THE CASTLE OF LOVE The *Virgin of Jeanne d'Évreux* and the *Virgin of Paris* were made for a sophisticated audience that valued elegant and luxurious objects. These patrons also commissioned secular articles for their own use, many of which were made by the same artists who created religious images. Objects, in precious materials such as ivory, were often decorated with scenes from the romantic courtly literature that was popular at the time. These stories were recounted by troubadours, whose favorite subjects were the sweetness and the bitterness of love. The *Siege of the Castle of Love* (fig. **12.43**) is depicted on a fourteenth-century ivory mirror back, which originally held a polished metal disk on its other side. Knights, some on horseback, attack a castle inhabited by women. However, by conscious design the battle lacks intensity, since the equestrian at the left is more concerned with the women in the castle, who toss roses at their attackers, than he is with the combat taking place in front of him. At the upper right, a knight scales the castle walls, helped up by a lady within it. On the other side, a soldier climbs a tree in order to surrender his sword to a woman armed with roses.

The scene depicted is remarkably close to the thirteenth-century poem *Roman de la Rose* (*Romance of the Rose*), written in vernacular French by Guillaume de Lorris and Jean de Meung, in which a knight and his colleagues assault the Castle of Love. The fairy-tale quality of the ivory reflects the images in the poem, which describe a dream sequence. The story is an allegory, with the castle symbolizing women and the attack upon it a form of courtship. Thus, even if the battle represented here is a mock one, all parties have something to gain from it.

The courtly subject with women as its focus is clearly appropriate for a mirror, since it is put to use in the cause of female personal adornment. Small mirrors like this were carried by their owners, some suspended from belts. It was only in the twelfth century that cosmetics were reintroduced to western Europe. Although they had been in common use in antiquity, they had fallen out of use after the fall of Rome. Crusaders helped reestablish the habit of applying cosmetics as a result of their contact with the eastern Mediterranean, where the custom had continued from antiquity.

This ivory was made in Paris, where a guild of makers of ivory combs and mirrors is documented at this time. Both the function and subject of the mirror back suggest a social context in which the reading of romances and the appreciation of luxury objects are linked. Some years later, though still within the fourteenth century, the account book of a French duke records his purchase from a Parisian dealer of an ivory mirror and six wooden candlesticks "so that he could read romances." The production of luxury ivories trails off after the middle of the fourteenth century, a result of the economic turmoil precipitated by the Hundred Years' War.

Architecture: The Flamboyant Phase

Although the beginnings of the Late, or Flamboyant, phase of Gothic architecture go back to the late thirteenth century, during the Hundred Years' War (1337–1453) artistic production diminished significantly. Hence, we do not meet any full-fledged examples of Flamboyant art until the early fifteenth century. **Flamboyant**, literally meaning "flamelike" in French, refers to the undulating curves and reverse curves that are a main feature of Late Gothic bar tracery. Structurally, Flamboyant Gothic shows few significant developments of its own.

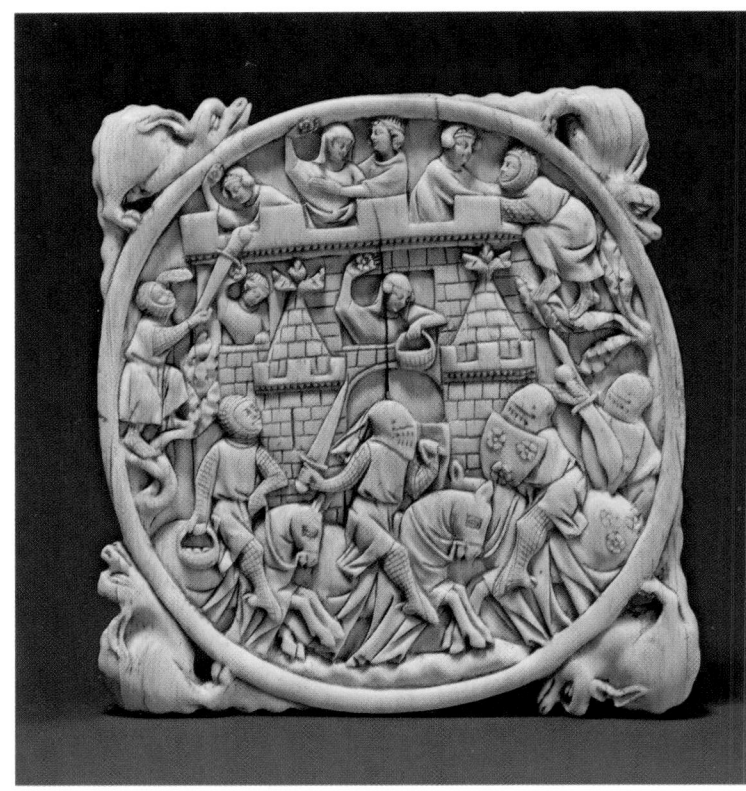

12.43 *Siege of the Castle of Love.* Back of a mirror. ca. 1320–50. Ivory, 4½ × 4¼ × ½" (11.5 × 10.9 × 1.27 cm). Seattle Art Museum. Donald E. Frederick Memorial Collection (49.37)

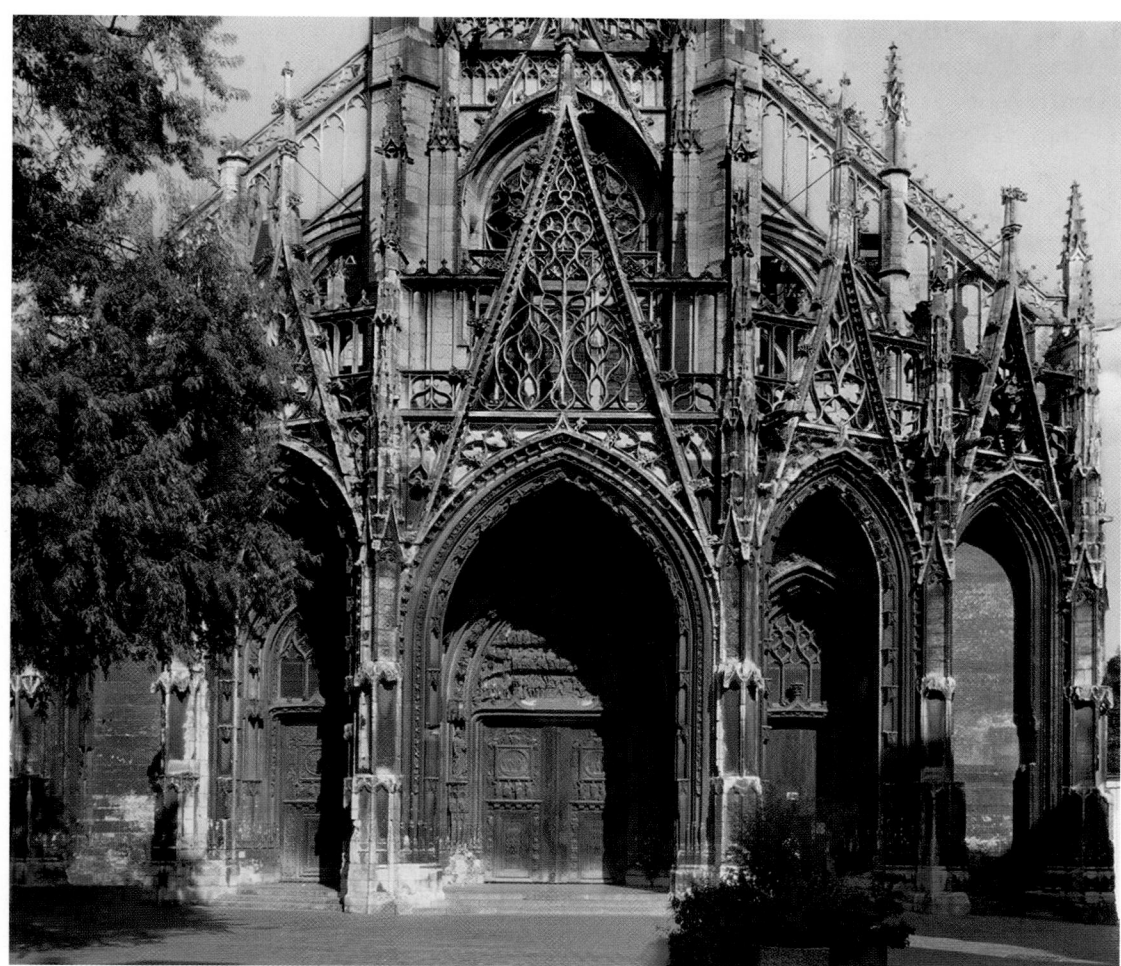

12.44 Pierre Robin and Ambroise Harel. West façade of Saint-Maclou, Rouen, France. 1434–90

SAINT-MACLOU IN ROUEN What distinguishes Saint-Maclou at Rouen (fig. **12.44**) from Saint-Urbain at Troyes (see fig. 12.33) is the profusion of its ornament, which clearly announces the Flamboyant style. The church was designed by Pierre Robin in 1434; Ambroise Harel directed the workshop from 1467 to 1480, during which time a substantial portion of the west façade was built, although it was not completed until around 1490. The façade curves back on either side, allowing the central portal to project outward, establishing a hierarchy of forms, which variations in height accentuate.

Harel covered Saint-Maclou's structural skeleton with a web of decoration so dense and fanciful as almost to hide it completely. To locate the bones of the building within this picturesque tangle of lines becomes a fascinating game of hide-and-seek. Even a careful examination of the building's exterior does not help to decipher its interior arrangement. Repeated motifs, such as the pointed gable, appear both to emerge from the building and to soar above it. It is through the central gable, rather than above it, that the rose window appears. The gable, previously an element of enclosure (see figs. 12.20 and 12.27), is now so eaten into by shimmering tracery that it has become a purely decorative form used to create a lively if unsettling effect. The activation of architectural forms through spatial means is comparable to the interest in volume and depth exhibited by Late Gothic sculptors and painters.

THE SPREAD OF GOTHIC ART

The refined royal French style of the Paris region was enthusiastically received abroad, where it was adapted to a variety of local conditions. In fact, the Gothic monuments of England and Germany have become objects of such intense national pride since the early nineteenth century that Gothic has been claimed as a native style in both countries. A number of factors contributed to the rapid spread of Gothic art. Among them were the skill of French architects and stone carvers and the prestige of French centers of learning, such as the cathedral School of Chartres and the University of Paris. Still, one wonders whether any of these explanations really go to the heart of the matter. The basic reason for the spread of Gothic art was undoubtedly the persuasive power of the style itself. It kindled the imagination and aroused religious feeling even among people far removed from the cultural climate of the Île-de-France.

Spain

During the Romanesque period, Spanish artists had adopted the French manner of building and decoration in part to disassociate themselves from—and indeed to express their supremacy over—the Muslims with whom they shared the Iberian peninsula. This identification of French style with Christian conquest encouraged the reception of the Gothic style in Spain during the thirteenth century, when numerous Christian victories (principal among them the battle at Navas de Tolosa in 1212) drove the Muslims farther and farther south.

LEÓN   The cathedral of Santa María in León (figs. **12.45** and **12.46**), a city with a long history as a royal capital, recalls French High Gothic buildings associated with the monarchy, especially Reims cathedral, the French coronation church. The east end of León, with its ambulatory and five radiating chapels, is particularly similar to the arrangement at Reims (see fig. 12.26), so much so that, although the specific identification of León's architect has been questioned, there has never been any doubt that he was French, nor that he knew the cathedral at Reims intimately. This reliance on a French model indicates a time lag, since León was not begun until the 1240s, some 30 years after Reims. León's elevation (fig. **12.47**) is more up-to-date, and its tall, thin clerestory lancets recall the Sainte-Chapelle (see fig. 12.32), completed in the same decade in which León was begun.

The association of León with French royal buildings is significant at this time. In 1230, Ferdinand III united the kingdoms of

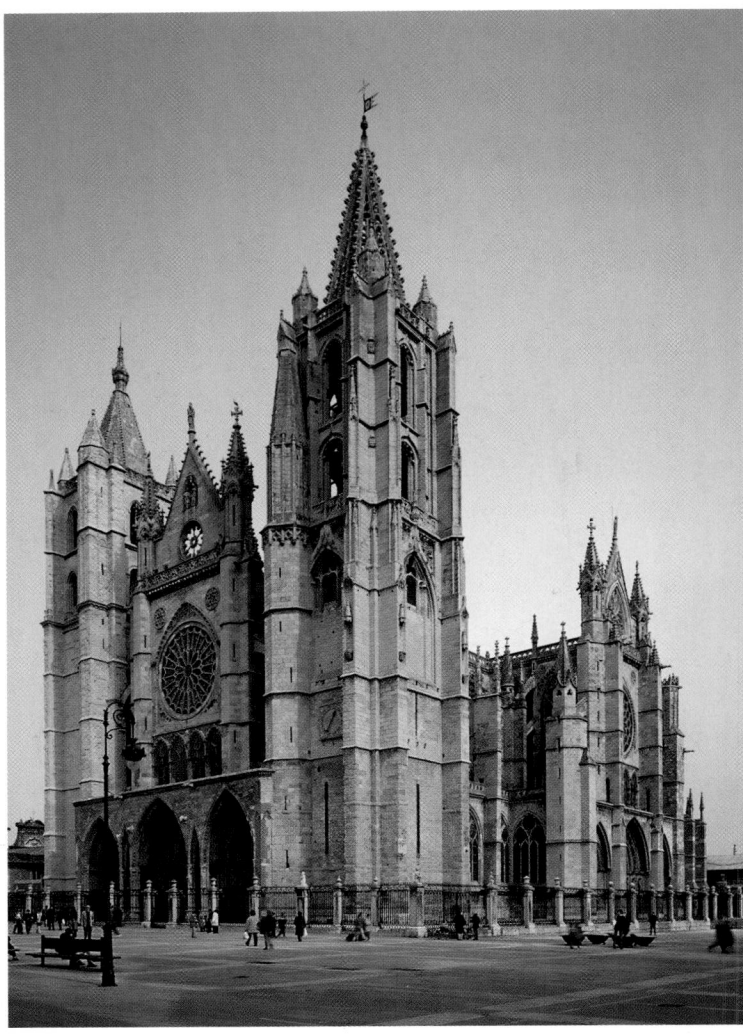

12.46   Exterior of cathedral of Santa María, León, Spain

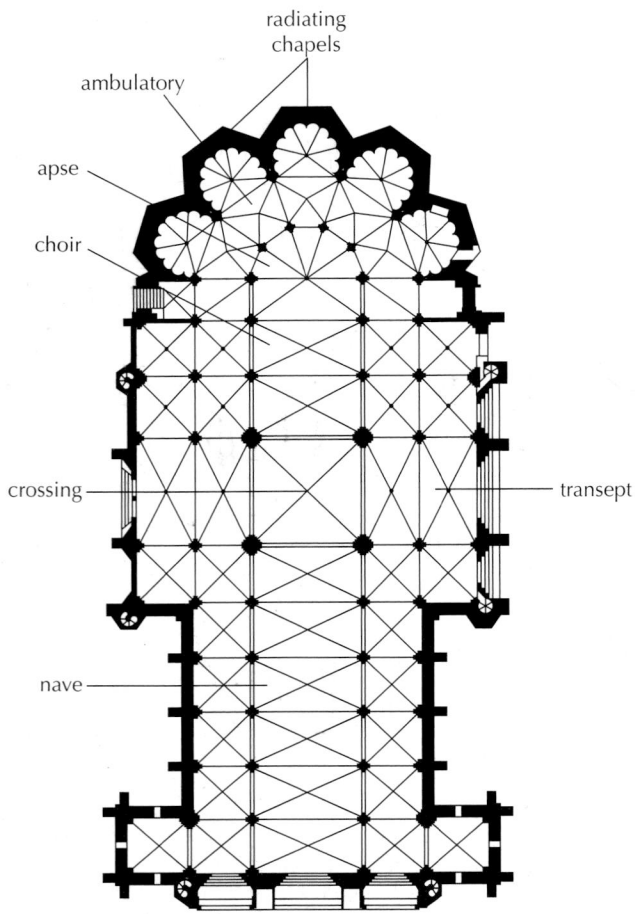

12.45   Plan of cathedral of Santa María, León, Spain. Begun 1240s (drawing by Giroux after De los Rios)

León and Castile. Despite this, royal attentions continued to favor Burgos, capital of Castile, which had earlier been declared "mother and head" of all churches in the kingdom and where a Gothic cathedral in the French style was begun in 1221. The Leónese promoted their city's historic rank as royal capital, more venerable than Burgos, through the building program of their new cathedral.

Although many of the jamb figures of the cathedral of Santa María at León have been rearranged from their original locations, the sculptors' reliance on the French High Gothic manner of carving is clear. The figure of Simeon, the New Testament seer who recognized the infant Jesus as Redeemer (fig. **12.48**), carved in the last decades of the thirteenth century and placed on the right portal of the west façade, recalls sculptures from Reims (see figs. 12.28 and 12.29) in the elegant elongation of the body, the complicated and crisp folds of drapery, and the thick, wavy beard.

León is only one of a number of Spanish Gothic cathedrals that look to France for their inspiration. Toledo and Burgos, both cities with claims to royal status, also created buildings to designs that relied on French models and employed architects who

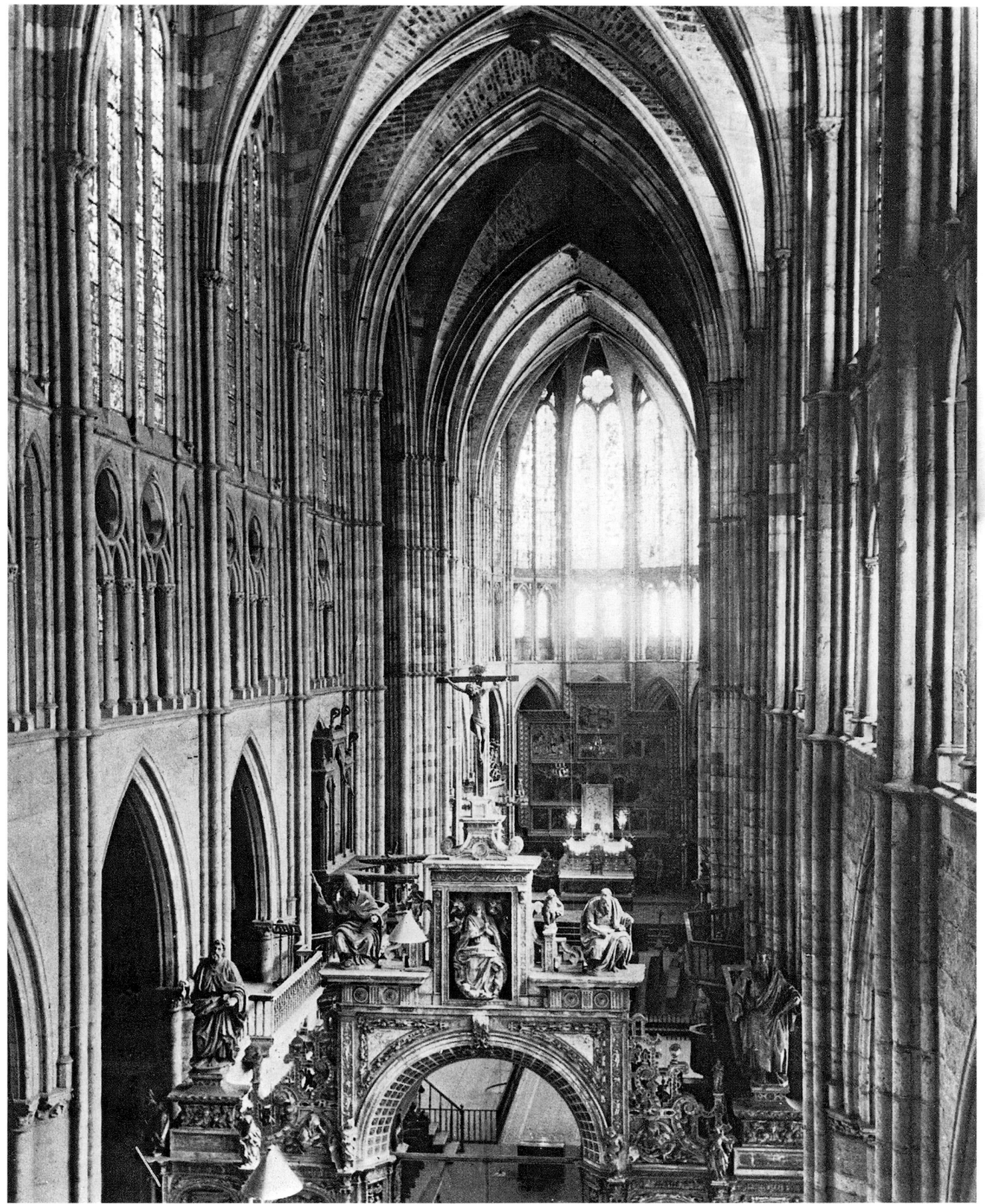

12.47   Interior of cathedral of Santa María, León, Spain

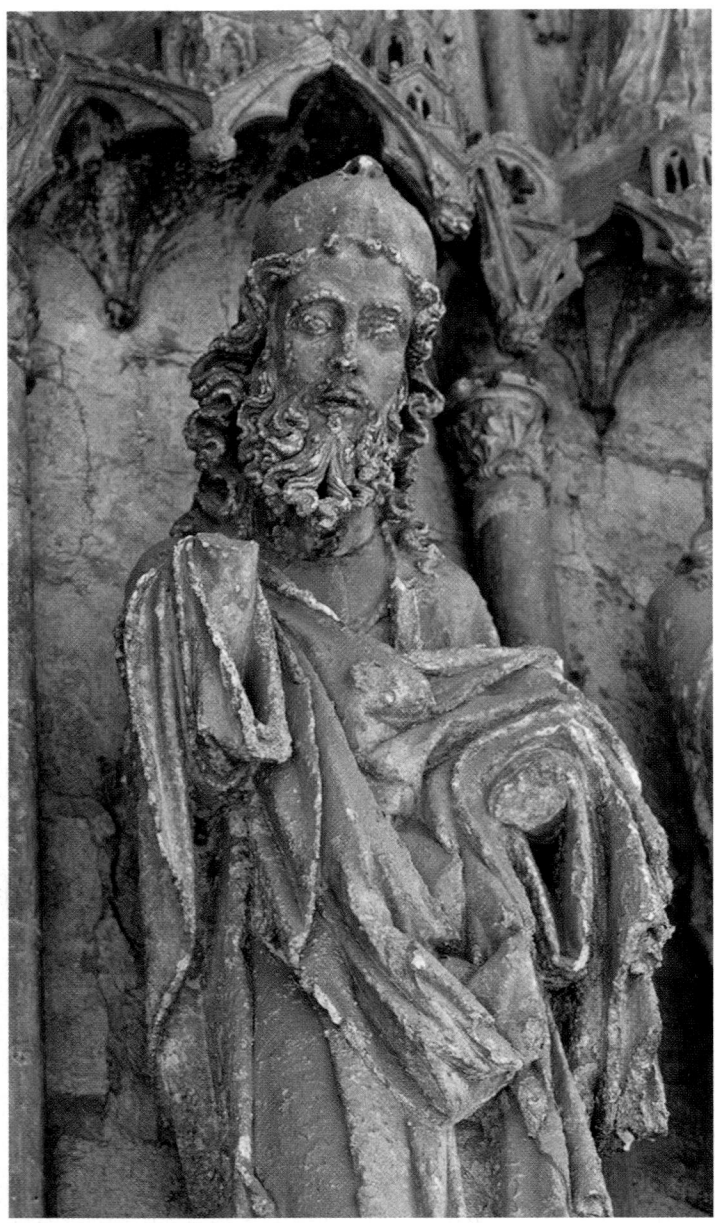

12.48 *Simeon*, jamb statue, south portal of west façade, cathedral of Santa Maria, León. ca. 1280–1300

dominated the second quarter of the thirteenth century. Although there was a great deal of building during those decades, it consisted mostly of additions to existing Anglo-Norman structures. Many English cathedrals begun during the Romanesque period had remained unfinished; they were now completed or enlarged. As a result, we find few churches that are designed entirely in the Early English style.

SALISBURY CATHEDRAL The exception to the trend of multiple periods and styles in a single English Gothic church is Salisbury cathedral, begun in 1220, the same year as Amiens cathedral. One sees immediately how different the exterior of Salisbury (fig. **12.49**) is from French Gothic churches (see figs. 12.10, 12.20, and 12.27) and how futile it would be to judge it by the same standards. Compactness and verticality have given way to a long, low, sprawling look. (The crossing tower, which provides a dramatic unifying accent, was built a century later than the rest and is much taller than originally planned.) Since height is not the main goal, flying buttresses are used only as an afterthought, not as integral design elements. The west façade is treated like a screen wall, wider than the church itself and divided into horizontal bands of ornament and statuary. The towers have shrunk to stubby turrets (small towers). The plan (fig. **12.50**), with its double transept, retains the segmented quality of the Romanesque, while the square east end derives from Cistercian architecture (see fig. 11.21).

As we enter the nave (fig. **12.51**), we recognize many elements familiar to us from French interiors of the time, such as Chartres cathedral (see fig. 12.12). However, the English interpretation produces a very different effect. As on the façade, horizontal divisions dominate at the expense of the vertical. Hence, we experience the nave wall not as a succession of vertical bays but as a series of arches and supports. These supports, carved of dark stone, stand out against the rest of the interior. This method of stressing their special function is one of the hallmarks of the Early English style. The use of bands of color also emphasizes horizontality.

Another distinctive feature is the steep curve of the nave vault. The ribs rise all the way from the triforium level. As a result, the clerestory gives the impression of being tucked away among the vaults. At Durham cathedral, more than a century earlier, the same treatment had been a technical necessity (see figs. 11.43 and 11.44). Now, it has become a matter of style, in keeping with the character of English Early Gothic as a whole. This character might be described as conservative in the positive sense: It accepts the French form but tones down its revolutionary aspects to maintain a strong sense of continuity with the Anglo-Norman past. In fact, French elements were integrated with a structure that was still based on thick walls with passages much like that found in Durham cathedral. The contrast between the bold upward thrust of the fourteenth-century crossing tower at Salisbury and the leisurely horizontal progression throughout the rest of this thirteenth-century cathedral suggests that English Gothic had developed in a new direction during the intervening 100 years.

undoubtedly came from France. Thus, the royal origins of the Gothic style were clearly not forgotten, even when the style was exported from France more than 100 years after its original appearance there.

England

England was especially receptive to the new style, which developed there as the influence of Gothic forms from the Île-de-France melded with Anglo-Norman Romanesque features. A French architect who rebuilt the choir of Canterbury cathedral introduced the French Gothic manner to England in 1175. Within less than 50 years, English Gothic developed a well-defined character of its own, known as the **Early English style**, which

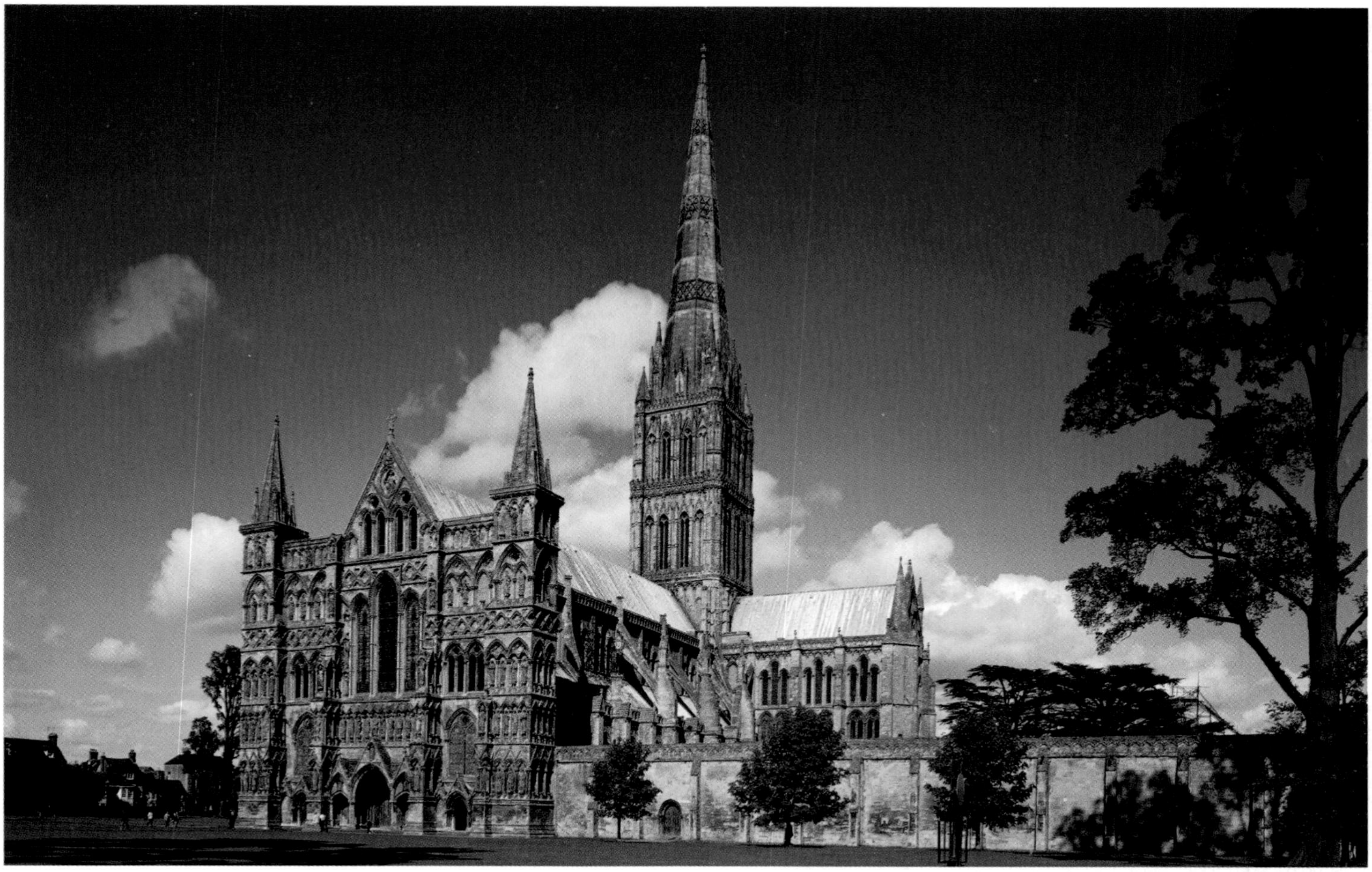

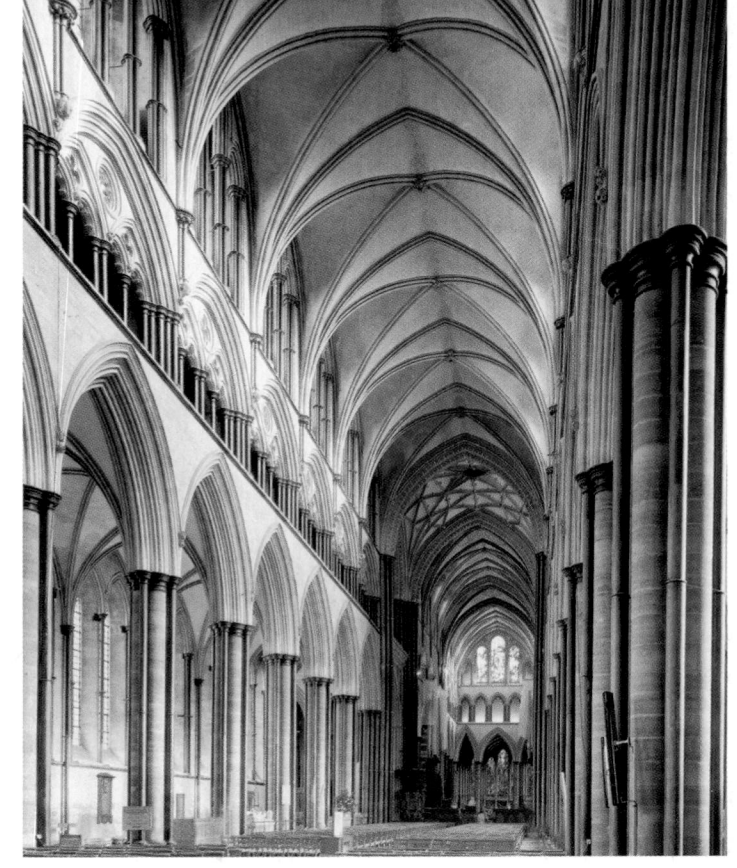

12.49 Salisbury cathedral (from the southwest) (spire ca. 1320–30)

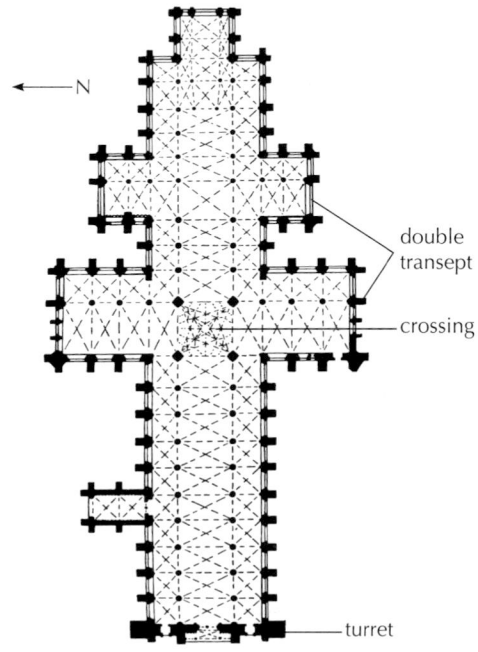

12.50 Plan of Salisbury cathedral, England. 1220–65

12.51 Nave of Salisbury cathedral

GLOUCESTER CATHEDRAL The change in the English Gothic becomes very clear if we compare the interior of Salisbury with the choir of Gloucester cathedral, built in the second quarter of the fourteenth century (fig. **12.52**). Gloucester is an outstanding example of English Late Gothic, also called the **Perpendicular Gothic style**. The name certainly fits, since we now find a dominant vertical accent that was absent in the English Early Gothic style. Vertical continuity is most evident at Gloucester in the responds that run in an unbroken line from the floor to the vault. In this respect, Perpendicular Gothic is much closer to French sources, but it includes so many uniquely English features that it would look out of place on the Continent. The repetition of small uniform tracery panels recalls the bands of statuary on the west façade at Salisbury (see fig. 12.49). The square end repeats the apses of earlier English churches, and the upward curve of the vault is as steep as in the nave of Salisbury (see fig. 12.51).

The ribs of the vaults, on the other hand, have taken on a new role. They have been multiplied until they form an ornamental network that screens the boundaries between the bays, with the result that the entire vault looks like one continuous surface. The ceiling reads as a canopy fluttering above the interior. This effect, in turn, emphasizes the unity of the interior space. Such elaboration of the classic four-part vault is characteristic of the Flamboyant style on the Continent as well (see pages 422–23), but the English started it earlier and carried it much further.

WESTMINSTER HALL The Perpendicular Gothic vaults of Gloucester and the taste for ornate and decorative forms that they represent have a parallel in wooden construction in England. Wood is obviously more fragile than stone and, given the prevalence of fires during the Middle Ages, few monumental wooden structures survive. The timber roof of Westminster Hall in London (fig. **12.53**) is exceptional. The oak ceiling covers what was the great hall of the principal London residence of English monarchs during the Middle Ages; most of the palace was destroyed by fire in 1834 and on the site the Houses of Parliament, still officially referred to as the Palace of Westminster, was subsequently built.

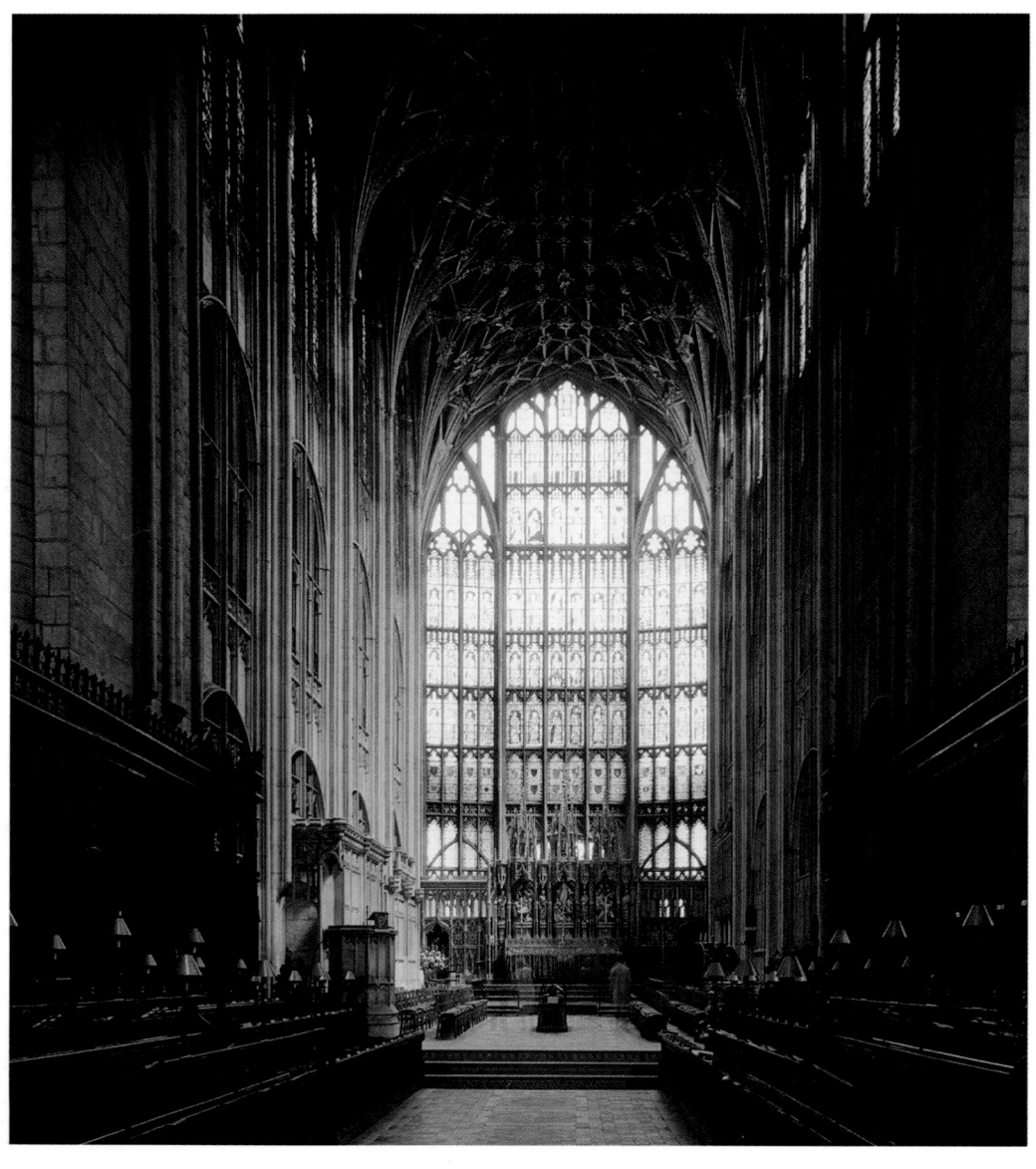

12.52   Choir of Gloucester cathedral, England. 1332–57

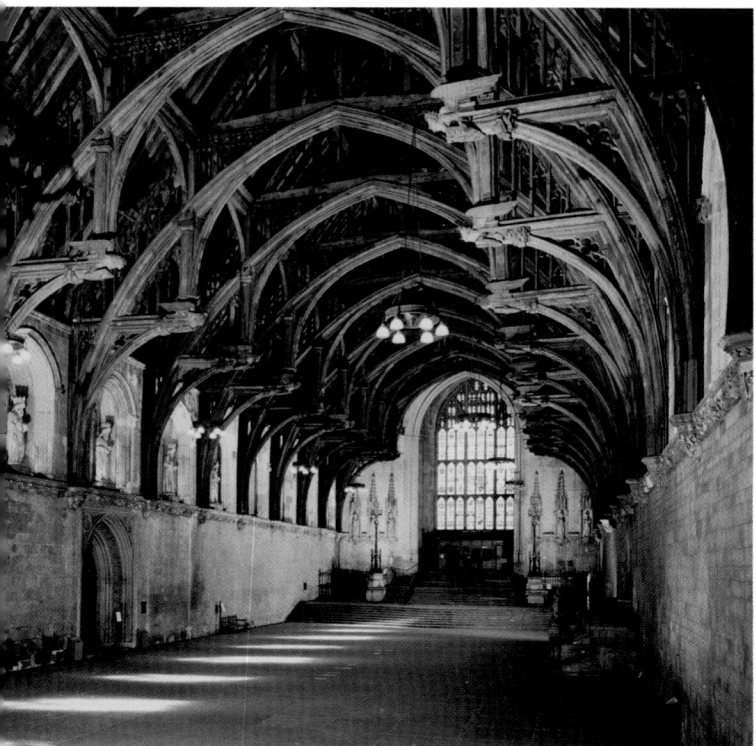

12.53   Henry Yevele and Hugh Herland. Interior and wooden roof of Westminster Hall, London. 1390s

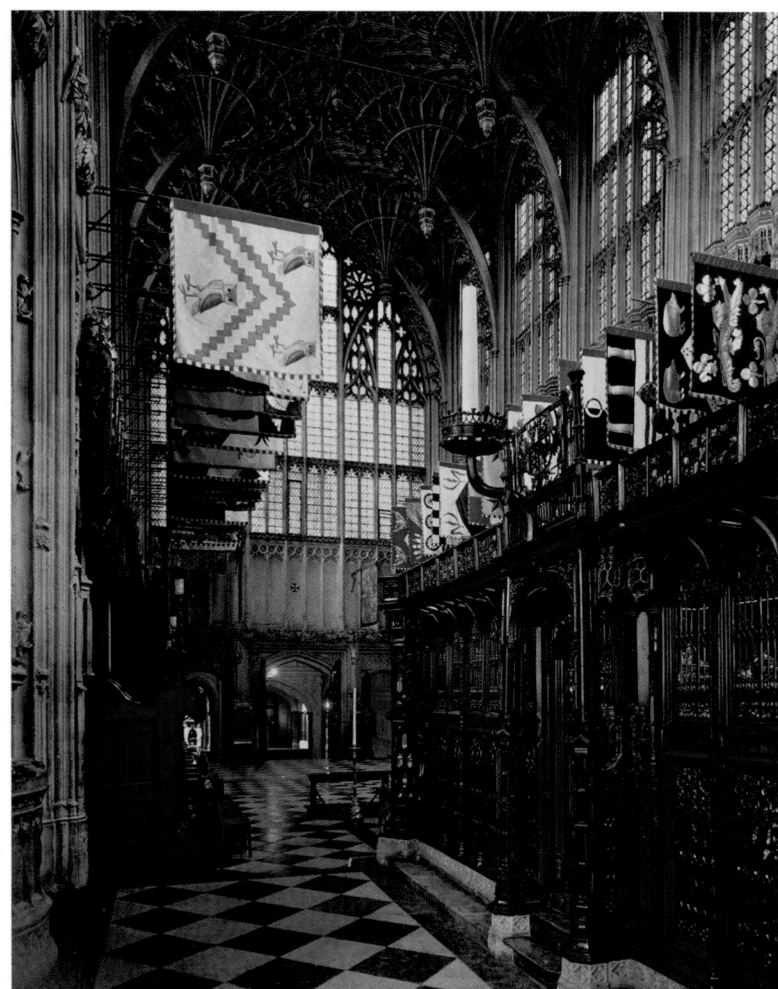

12.54   Chapel of Henry VII, Westminster Abbey, London. 1503–19

Westminster Hall, originally constructed in 1097 in the Norman Romanesque style, contained a central space flanked by side aisles marked with wooden posts. When the current roof was added between 1395 and 1396 by the master mason Henry Yevele and the master carpenter Hugh Herland, the old posts were removed so that the vast space, more than 235 feet long, 67 feet wide, and 90 feet high, is roofed without floor supports, covering a space half as large again as any hall previously built in England. Major structural elements are found in the hammer beams, which stick out horizontally from the wall and are carved with flying angels, and the arches that are supported on stone brackets decorated with heraldic designs. As is true with vaulted Gothic buildings (see fig. 12.13), each design constituent of the roof supports additional elements in a complex and intricate system based on interdependence, so that, for example, the hammer beams resist horizontal thrust while the arches channel vertical force to the masonry walls. The weight of the roof is indeed considerable, calculated at approximately 660 tons. The walls, belonging to the original Romanesque building, were reinforced on the exterior with flying buttresses at the time the timber ceiling was added. Admittedly, some of the elements, such as the profusion of Perpendicular tracery, serve more of a decorative than a structural function, but they too relate to the development in the fourteenth century of large, heavily decorated, stone-vaulted spaces free of interior supports (see fig. 12.52); as with those buildings, the integration of engineering and aesthetics at Westminster Hall is a remarkable achievement. Secular and religious buildings thus express similar aesthetic aims.

CHAPEL OF HENRY VII The Perpendicular Gothic style reaches its climax in the amazing hanging vault of Henry VII's Chapel at Westminster Abbey, built in the early years of the sixteenth century (fig. **12.54**). With its lanternlike knobs hanging from conical "fans," this chapel merges ribs and tracery patterns in a dazzling display of architectural pageantry. The complex vault patterns are unrelated to the structure of either the walls or the vaults themselves. Like the decorative features of Saint-Maclou in Rouen (see fig. 12.44), elaborate motifs obscure rather than clarify the architecture.

QUEEN MARY PSALTER As with Gothic architecture in England, manuscript illumination also shows an ambiguous relationship to French models. Some features are remarkably akin to those in French works, while others seem more concerned with continuing traditional English forms and manner of representation. The *Queen Mary Psalter* (fig. **12.55**) contains about 1,000 separate images, including biblical scenes, illustrations of saints' lives, and hunting scenes. The folio illustrating *Jesus Teaching in the Temple* combines two types of painting, which appear throughout the manuscript. The main scene is a full-color illumination, with a

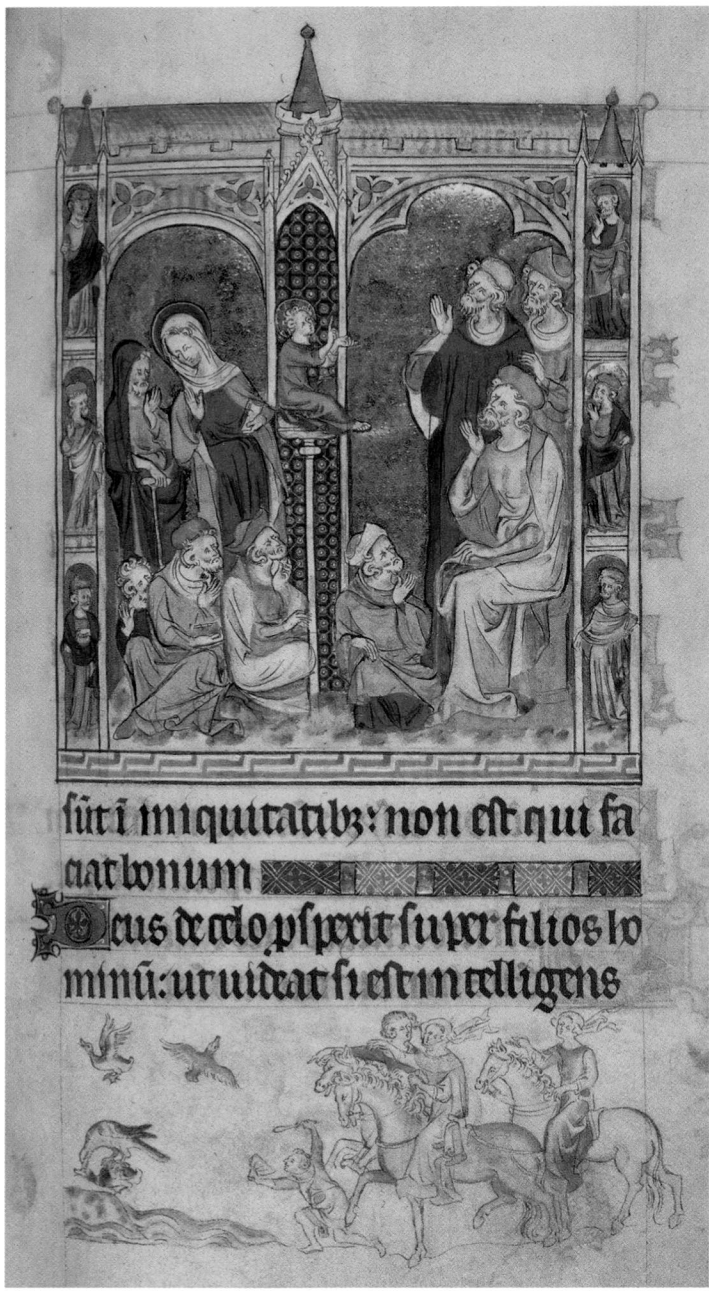

The bas-de-page represents an elegant equestrian couple out hawking. A female attendant on horseback and a boy servant on foot accompany them. The lively scene, taken from the daily life of the nobility, is filled with naturalistic details, from the falcon attacking a duck at the lower left, to the way the male rider engages his female companion, both of them pointing at the hunt scene in front of them. Their forward movement is propelled by the active, wavelike lines of the horses' manes and the servant's gestures. In the main scene, line also conveys meaning with sensitivity and precision. The soft lines of hair and cloth that frame the face of the Virgin Mary contrast strongly with the sharply curved lines of the hair and beards of the Jews gathered in the Temple to hear her son teach.

The iconographic connection between the vignette in the bottom margin and the biblical scene is not clear. What *is* clear is that scenes from the courtly world are interwoven, or at least coexist, with biblical history, as they did in French manuscripts of the same period. In the English manuscript, however, the marginal illustrations are serial; they continue from one page to the next, just as the cycle of biblical events does. It is not known for whom this manuscript was made, although there is general agreement that it must have been produced between about 1310 and 1320 and, given its splendor, must have been a royal commission. The most convincing theory posits that King Edward II (r. 1307–1327) commissioned the book for his queen, Isabella of France. The name by which the manuscript is known today results from the fact that it was given to Queen Mary Tudor in the sixteenth century.

Germany

In Germany, Gothic architecture took root a good deal more slowly than in England. Until the mid-thirteenth century, the Romanesque tradition, with its persistent Ottonian elements, remained dominant, despite the growing acceptance of Early Gothic features. From about 1250 on, however, the High Gothic of the Île-de-France had a strong impact on the Rhineland. Cologne cathedral (begun in 1248) is an ambitious attempt to carry the full-fledged French system beyond the stage of Amiens. However, it was not completed until modern times. Nor were any others like it ever built. While some German sculptors relied on French models, others pursued a more independent course, unlike German architects. German Gothic sculptures are sometimes dramatic, sometimes poignant, and sometimes lifelike, but they always express deep, if sometimes restrained, emotion.

HEILIGENKREUZ IN SCHWÄBISH-GMÜND Especially characteristic of German Gothic is the hall church, or **Hallenkirche**. This type of church, with aisles and nave of the same height, stems from Romanesque architecture (see fig. 11.23). Although also found in France, it was in Germany that its possibilities were explored fully. Heiligenkreuz (Holy Cross) in Schwäbish-Gmünd (fig. **12.56**) is one of many examples from central Germany. Heinrich Parler the Elder began Heiligenkreuz

12.55 *Jesus Teaching in the Temple* and *Hunting Scene*, from the *Queen Mary Psalter*. ca. 1310–20. Ink, tempera, and gold leaf on vellum, 7 × 4½" (17.9 × 11.5 cm). The British Library, London. By permission of the British Library

decorative gold background and an architectural framework, while the bas-de-page is a tinted drawing. Despite the differences in technique, both scenes (and all the others in the manuscript) were created by a single artist, a remarkable achievement, particularly since this artist produced at least two other fully decorated books. Although scholars have suggested a general reliance on a French manner in the arrangement of the scenes, in the graceful, courtly sway of the figure, and in the inclusion of bas-de-page illustrations, the style of painting is more closely related to older English models. It is almost purely linear and there is very little evidence of shading.

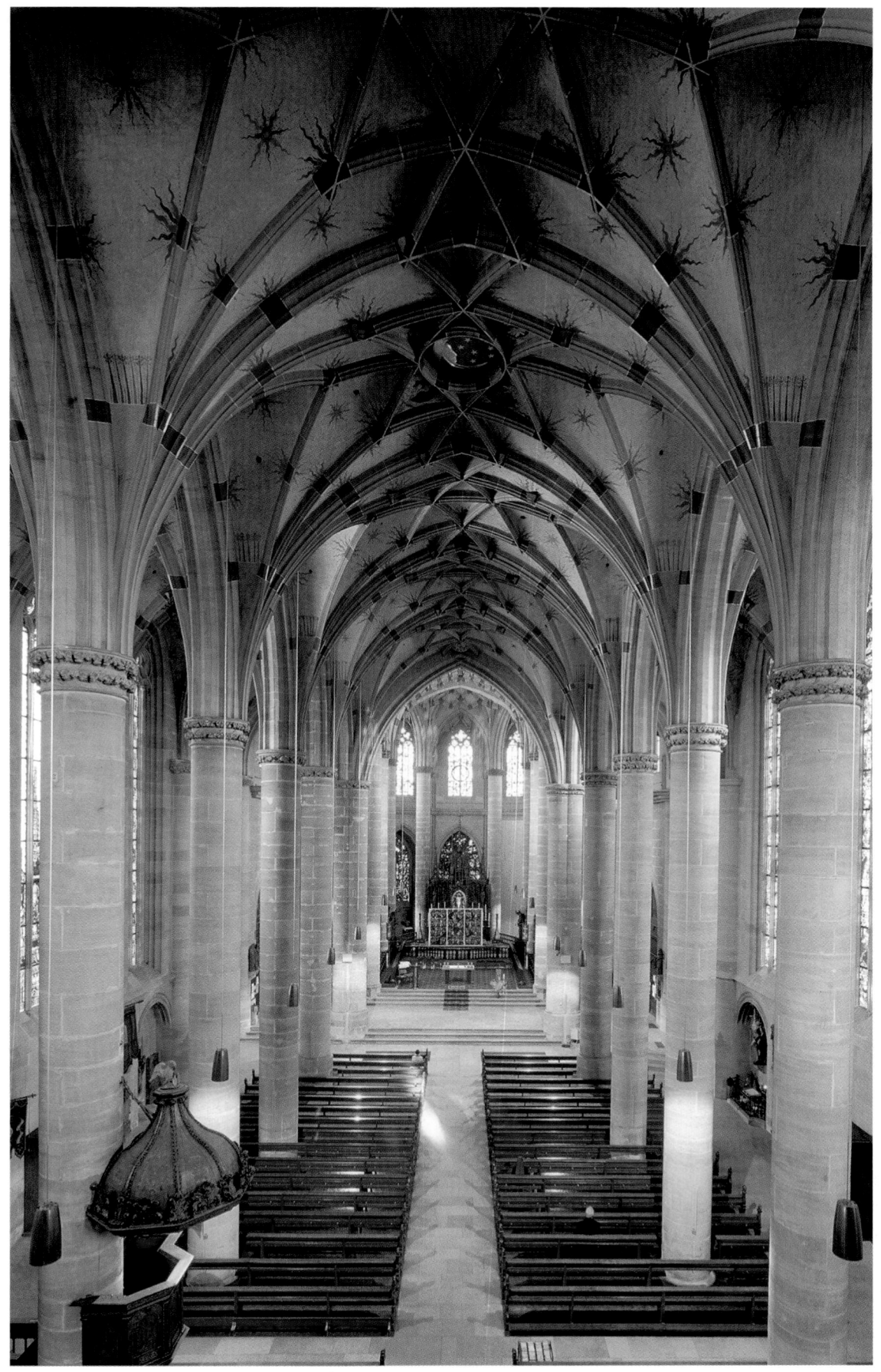

12.56   Heinrich Parler the Elder and Peter Parler (?). Nave and choir of Heiligenkreuz,
Schwäbish-Gmünd, Germany. Begun 1317

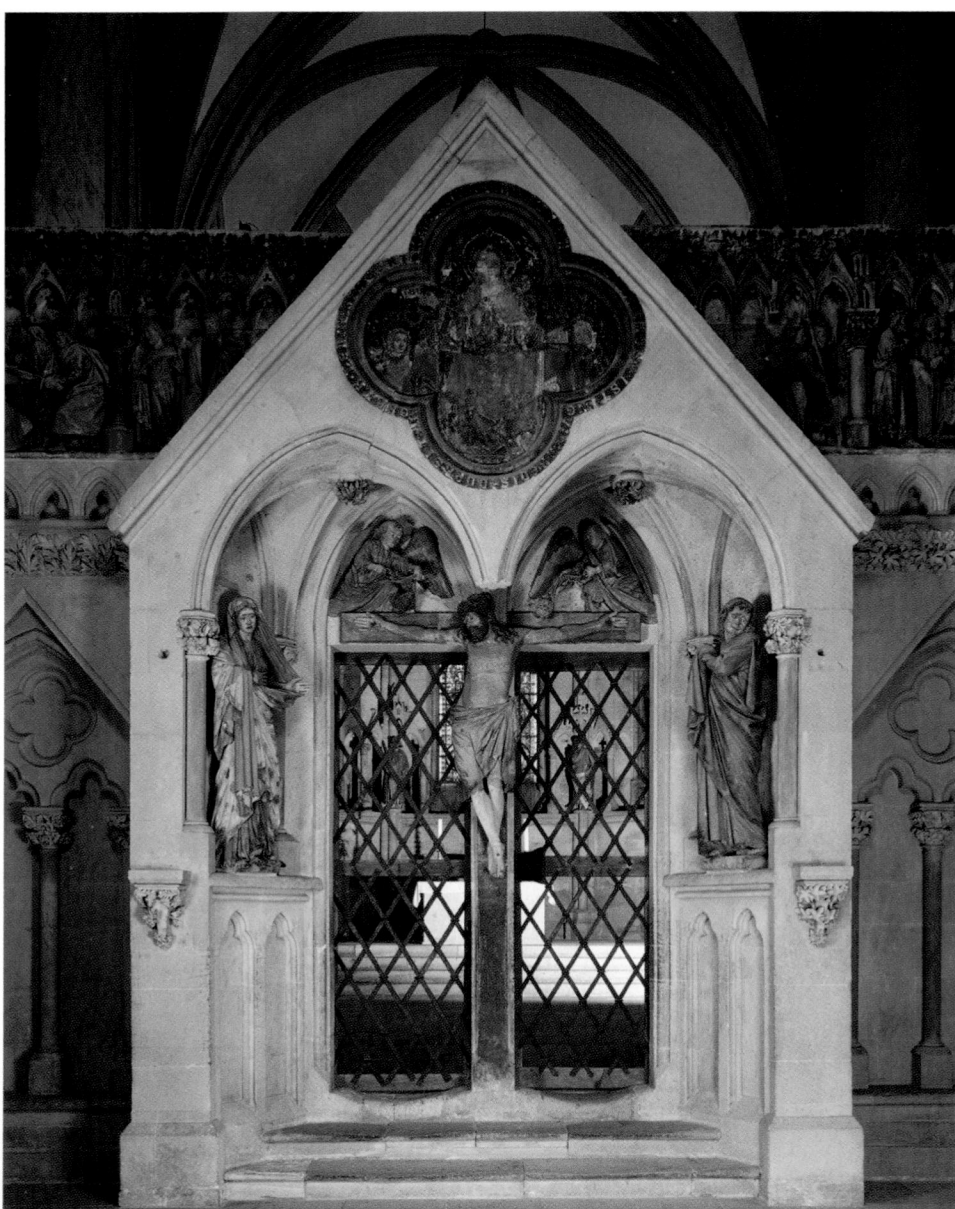

12.57 Naumburg Master. *Crucifixion*, on the choir screen, and the *Virgin* and *John the Evangelist*, Naumburg cathedral, Germany. ca. 1255. Stone

in 1317, although it was perhaps his son Peter who was responsible for the enlarged choir of 1351. (Heinrich had at least two other sons, two grandsons, and a great-grandson who were also architects.) The space has a fluidity and expansiveness that enfolds us as if we were standing under a huge canopy, reminiscent of the effect at Gloucester cathedral (see fig. 12.52). There is no clear sense of direction to guide us. And the unbroken lines of the pillars, formed by bundles of shafts that diverge as they turn into lacy ribs covering the vaults, seem to echo the continuous movement that we feel in the space itself.

NAUMBURG CATHEDRAL The growth of Gothic sculpture in Germany can be easily traced. From the 1220s on, German masters who had been trained in the sculpture workshops of the French cathedrals brought the new style back home. Because German architecture at that time was still mainly Romanesque, however, large statuary cycles like those at Chartres and Reims

were not produced on façades, where they would have looked out of place. As a result, German Gothic sculpture tended to be less closely linked with its architectural setting. In fact, the finest work was often done for the interiors of churches.

This independence permitted a greater expressive freedom than in France. It is strikingly evident in the work of the Naumburg Master, whose best-known work is the series of statues and reliefs made around 1255 for Naumburg cathedral. The *Crucifixion* (fig. 12.57) forms the center of the choir screen; flanking it are statues of the Virgin and John the Evangelist. Enclosed by a deep, gabled porch, the three figures frame the opening that links the nave with the sanctuary. Rather than placing the group above the screen, as was usual, the sculptor brought the subject down to earth physically and emotionally. The suffering of Jesus thus becomes a human reality through the emphasis on the weight and volume of his body. Mary and John, pleading with the viewer, convey their grief more eloquently than ever before.

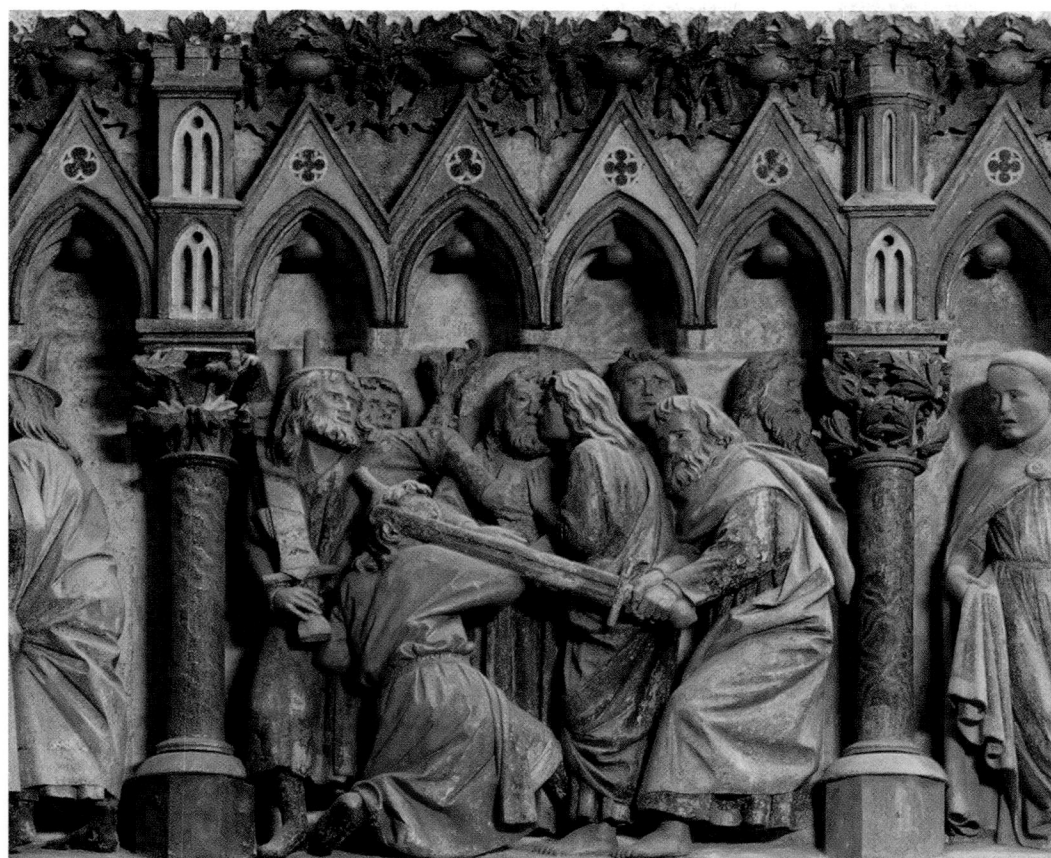

12.58 Naumburg Master.
The Kiss of Judas, on the choir screen,
Naumburg cathedral. ca. 1255. Stone

The pathos of these figures is heroic and dramatic compared with the quiet lyricism of the Reims *Visitation* (see fig. 12.28). If the classical High Gothic sculpture of France can be compared with the calm restraint of Pheidias (see fig. 5.43), the Naumburg Master embodies the temperamental counterpart of the strained physicality demonstrated in Hellenistic art (see fig. 5.71).

The same intensity dominates the Passion scenes, such as *The Kiss of Judas* (fig. **12.58**), with its strong contrast between the meekness of Jesus and the violence of the sword-wielding St. Peter. Attached to the responds inside the choir are life-size statues of 12 nobles associated with the founding of the eleventh-century cathedral. The sculptures were made at a time when Bishop Dietrich II of Naumburg was attempting to raise funds to build a new choir for the cathedral. By highlighting the original building's generous benefactors, the bishop encouraged parishioners to support the new building campaign, to join the ranks of the cathedral's munificent sponsors. These men and women were not of the artist's own time—to him they were only names in a chronicle. Yet the pair *Ekkehard and Uta* (fig. **12.59**) are as individual and realistic as if they had been portrayed from life. The gestures of their hands, the handling of their drapery, and their fixed gazes communicate human qualities with great subtlety. Their individuality and specificity remind us that the concern for the personal identity of individuals signaled important social

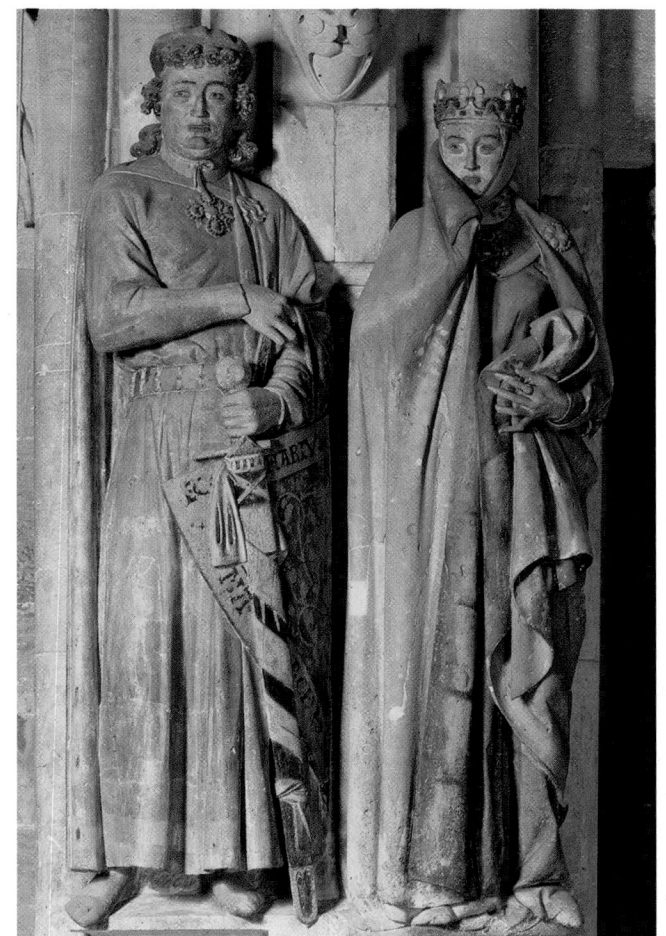

12.59 *Ekkehard and Uta*, Naumburg cathedral. ca. 1249–55. Stone

changes during the Gothic period. The trend toward realism is not unique here and is reminiscent of what occurred at Reims cathedral (see figs. 12.28 and 12.29). The inclusion of historical figures within a sacred space is unusual, and it is perhaps the fact that the persons represented were long dead that made them appropriate for representation here.

The paint that is still visible on Naumburg's interior sculpture helps us appreciate how Gothic sculpture might have looked originally. Gothic interiors, as can be seen in the restored Sainte-Chapelle, were elaborately painted. Exterior sculpture was also painted, but that paint rarely survives today.

ROETTGEN PIETÀ Gothic sculpture, as we have come to know it so far, reflects a desire to give a greater emotional appeal to traditional themes of Christian art. Toward the end of the thirteenth century, this tendency gave rise to a new kind of religious image. (See www.myartslab.com.) Originally designed for private devotion, it is often referred to by the German term **Andachtsbild** (contemplation image), since Germany played the leading part in its development. The most widespread type was a representation of the Virgin grieving over the dead Christ. It is called a **Pietà** after an Italian word derived from the Latin *pietas*, the root word for both "pity" and "piety." No such scene occurs in the scriptural accounts of the Passion. We do not know where or when the Pietà was invented, but it portrays one of the Seven Sorrows of the Virgin. It thus forms a tragic counterpart to the motif of the Madonna and Child, one of her Seven Joys.

The *Roettgen Pietà* (fig. **12.60**) is carved of wood and vividly painted. Like most such groups, this large cult statue was meant to be placed on an altar. The style, like the subject, expresses the emotional fervor of lay religiosity, which emphasized a personal relationship with God as part of the tide of mysticism that swept over fourteenth-century Europe. Realism here is purely a means to enhance the work's impact. The faces convey unbearable pain and grief; the wounds are exaggerated grotesquely; and the bodies and limbs are puppetlike in their thinness and rigidity. The purpose of the work is clearly to arouse so overwhelming a sense of horror and pity that the faithful will share in Christ's suffering and identify with the grief-stricken Mother of God. The ultimate goal of this emotional bond is a spiritual transformation that grasps the central mystery of God in human form through compassion (meaning "to suffer with").

At first glance, the *Roettgen Pietà* would seem to have little in common with the *Virgin of Paris* (see fig. 12.42), which dates from the same period. Yet they share a lean, "deflated" quality of form and exert a strong emotional appeal to a viewer. Both features characterize the art of northern Europe from the late thirteenth to the mid-fourteenth century. Only after 1350 do we again find an interest in weight and volume, coupled with a renewed desire to explore tangible reality as part of a change in religious outlook.

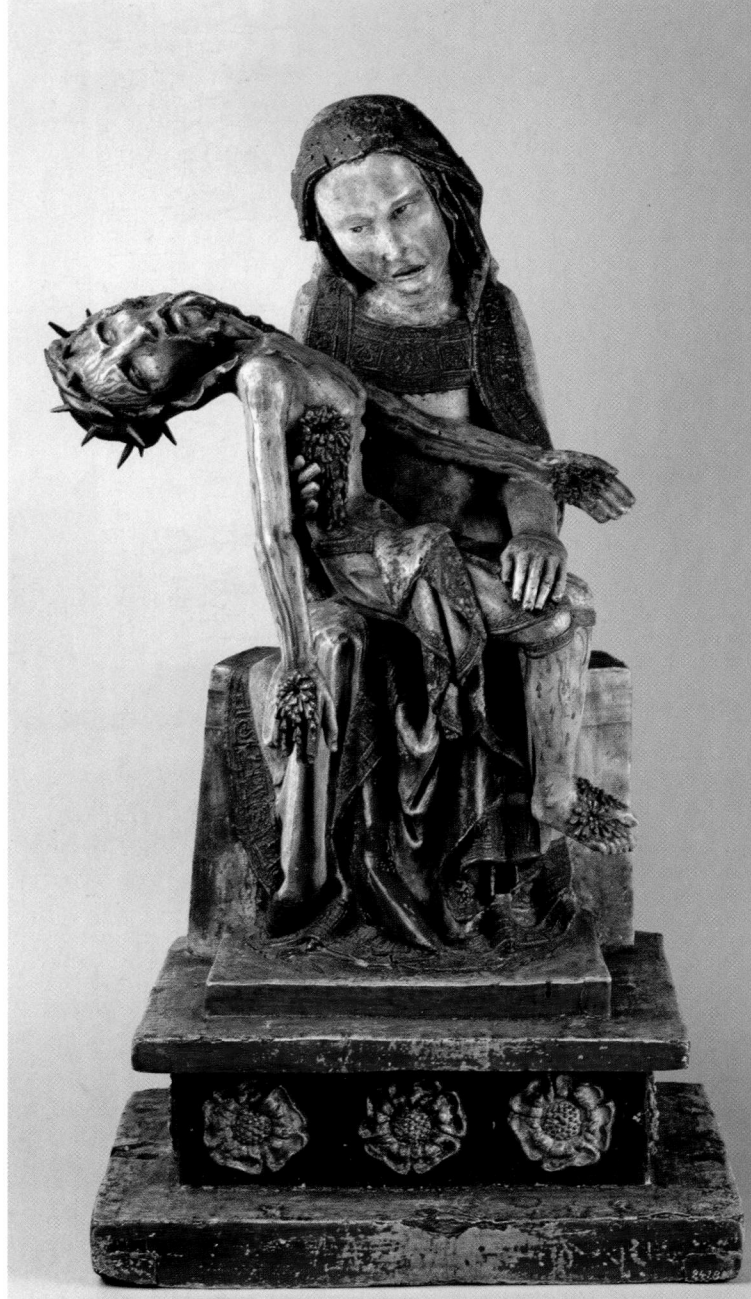

12.60 *Roettgen Pietà.* Early 14th century. Wood, height 34½" (87.5 cm). Rheinisches Landesmuseum, Bonn

The growing concern for the individual that is expressed in much of the Gothic art we have studied so far develops most fully in Italy and becomes the central focus of Gothic experiments there. Indeed, the Gothic achievements in Italy are of such consequence in their own right and for the later development of Western art that they have been assigned their own chapter in this book, which follows.

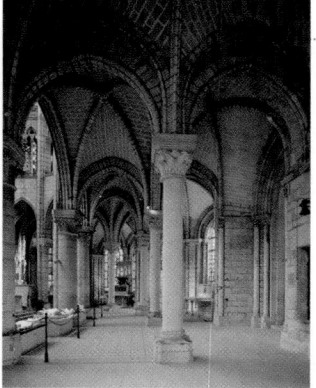
1137 Rebuilding of abbey church of Saint-Denis begun

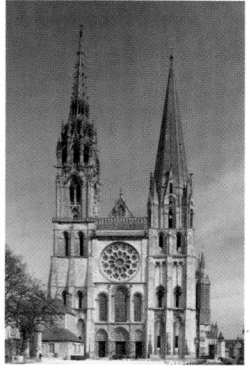
1163 Cathedral of Notre-Dame at Paris begun

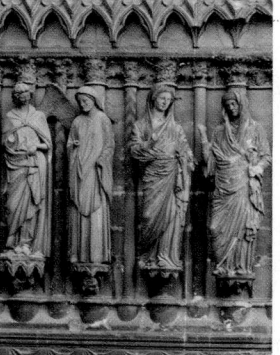
1230-65 *Annunciation* and *Visitation*, cathedral of Notre-Dame at Reims

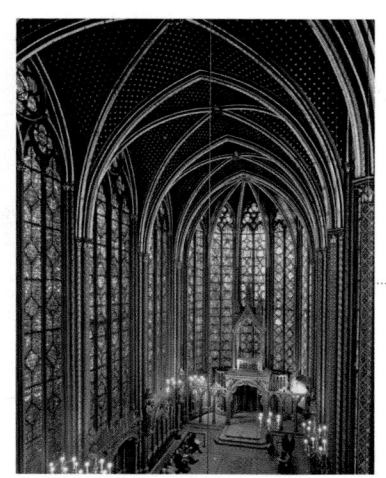
1241-48 Sainte-Chapelle in Paris

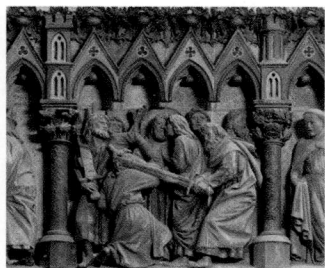
ca. 1255 Naumburg cathedral sculptures

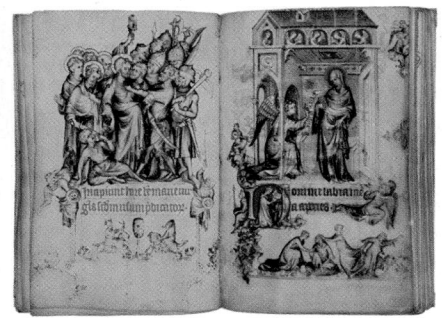
1324-28 *Hours of Jeanne d'Evreux*

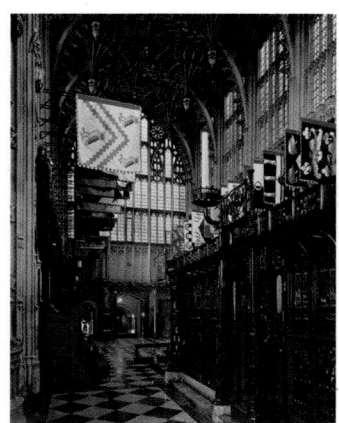
1503-19 Chapel of Henry VII, Westminster Abbey in London

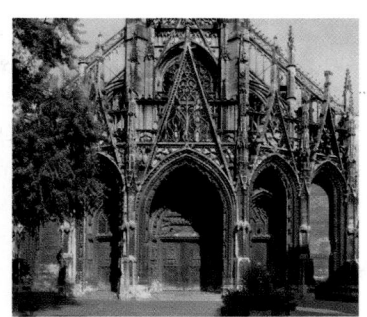
1434-90 Saint-Maclou in Rouen designed

Gothic Art

1100

◄ 1122 Suger becomes Abbott of Saint-Denis

ca. 1139-47 Abbey church at Fontenay

1150

ca. 1150 *Winchester Psalter*

◄ 1180-1223 Reign of French king Philip August

◄ 1194 Fire destroys much of cathedral of Notre-Dame at Chartres

1200

◄ 1230 King Ferdinand III unites kingdoms of León and Castile

1250

◄ 1252 Thomas Aquinas begins teaching in Paris

◄ 1270 Death of French king Louis IX (St. Louis)

1300

◄ 1332-57 Choir of Gloucester cathedral.

◄ 1337-1453 Hundred Years' War between England and France

◄ 1339 Virgin of Jeanne d'Évreux given to Saint-Denis.

1350

◄ 1350-55 Guillaume de Machaut's Le Dit de Lion.

ca. 1354-61 Complex of Sultan Husan in Cairo

ca. mid-14th century Court of the Lions, Alhambra in Granada

◄ 1395-96 Westminster Hall roofed

1400

◄ 1434-90 Saint-Maclou in Rouen

1450

1500

◄ 1503-19 Chapel of Henry VII in Westminster Abbey

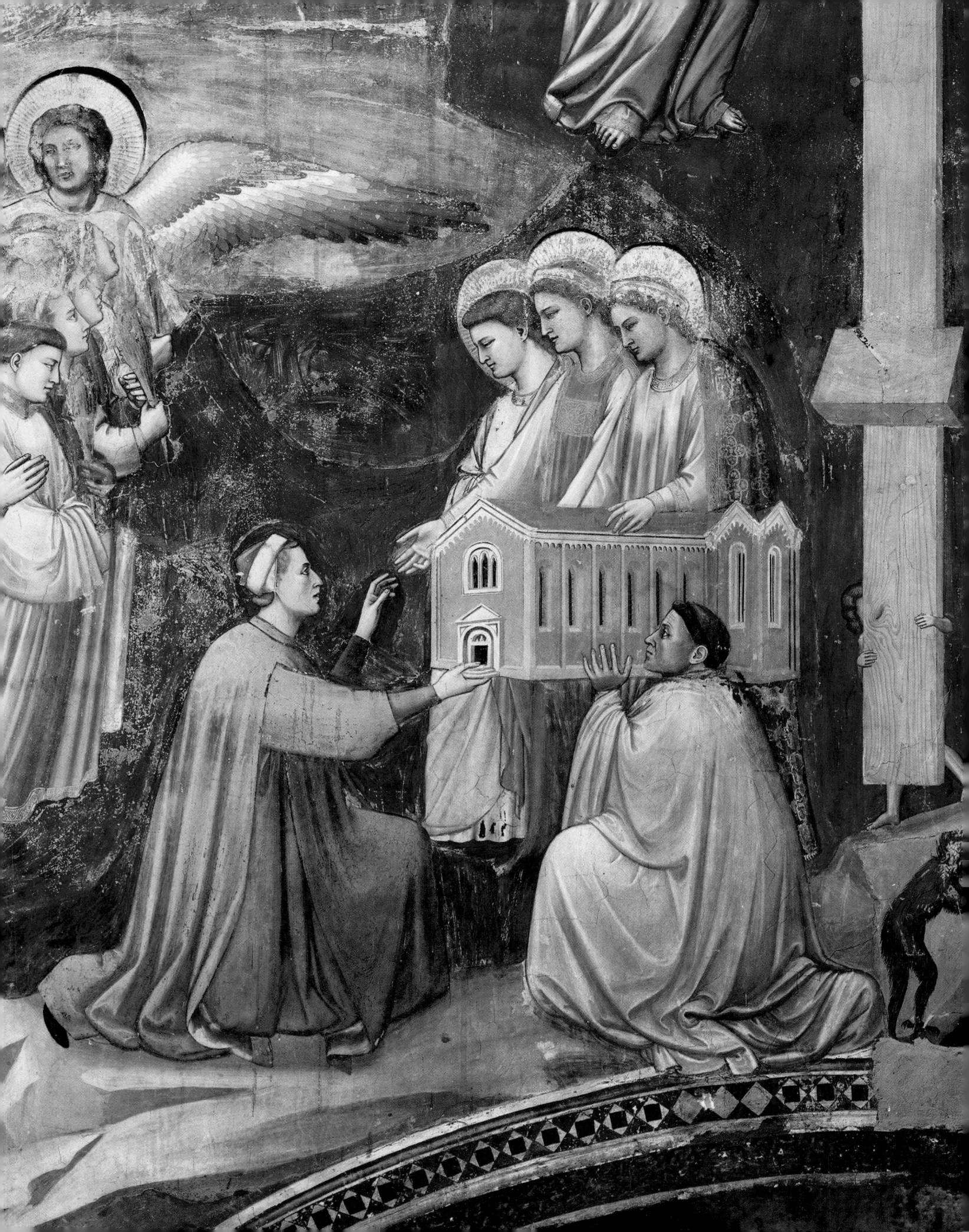

CHAPTER 13

Art in Thirteenth- and Fourteenth-Century Italy

T HE MAP OF THE ITALIAN PENINSULA (MAP 13.1) HINTS AT THE forces that shaped life and art there in the thirteenth and fourteenth centuries. Although the Alps separate the peninsula from the rest of Europe, branches of the Mediterranean Sea surround it, providing access by water to the rest of the world. As the heart of the Roman Empire, the

peninsula abounded in the physical remains of Rome. Italy was also the center of the Catholic Church for much of the Middle Ages, bringing church officials and ambassadors from Europe to its cities. The culture formed by this geography was distinctive and cosmopolitan.

The length of the coastline encouraged trade by sea, while Italy's location made it a natural link between Europe and Africa and Asia. Coastal cities, such as Pisa, Genoa and Venice, controlled these important trade routes. Italian vessels carried goods from as far away as Constantinople and the Baltics to its cities. Merchants traveled over land, too, even reaching the court of the Great Khan in China.

This geography had profound effects on Italian society. In the absence of a strong central authority, the cities controlled the regions around them, so that there was no single political unit called Italy. Unlike many other parts of Europe, political power lay not in the hands of the hereditary aristocracy, but in the hands of urban elites. Monarchs controlled only a few regions: Lombardy in the north and Naples in the south. Instead, the wealthiest and most influential cities, including Florence and Siena, were organized as representative republics, with political offices held by mercantile oligarchs. As a check on inherited

power, some cities even excluded the landed aristocracy from participating in their political processes.

The larger powers of Europe, especially the two international institutions of the Holy Roman Empire and the papacy, often interfered in Italian politics, though sometimes from a distance. The emperors usually remained north of the Alps, though they claimed to control portions of Italy. The papacy left Italy for southern France in the fourteenth century, underscoring the power and influence of the French king. The prestige of the French monarchy enhanced the appeal of the **Gothic** style of building born near Paris and its related pictorial innovations, which artists in Italy adapted to their traditions.

The context in which Italian artists developed their skills differed from the rest of Europe. Throughout the Middle Ages, Roman and Early Christian art served as an inspiration for Italian architects and sculptors, as is visible in such works as the **cathedral** of Pisa (see fig. 11.33). In the mid-thirteenth century, the Holy Roman emperor Frederick II (1194–1250), who lived for a time in southern Italy, deliberately revived imperial Roman style to express his own political ambitions as heir to the Roman Empire. The other empire, Byzantium, kept a presence throughout Italy, too—through mosaics at Ravenna, Sicily, and Venice, and through the circulation of artists and **icons** such as the *Madonna Enthroned* (see fig. 8.49). A further element added to the vocabulary of Italian artists was the French Gothic style, created in the Paris region and introduced through the travels of artists and patrons.

Detail of figure 13.18, the Last Judgment Giotto, showing Enrico Scrovegni Offering the Chapel. Interior of Arena (Scrovegni) Chapel, Padua.

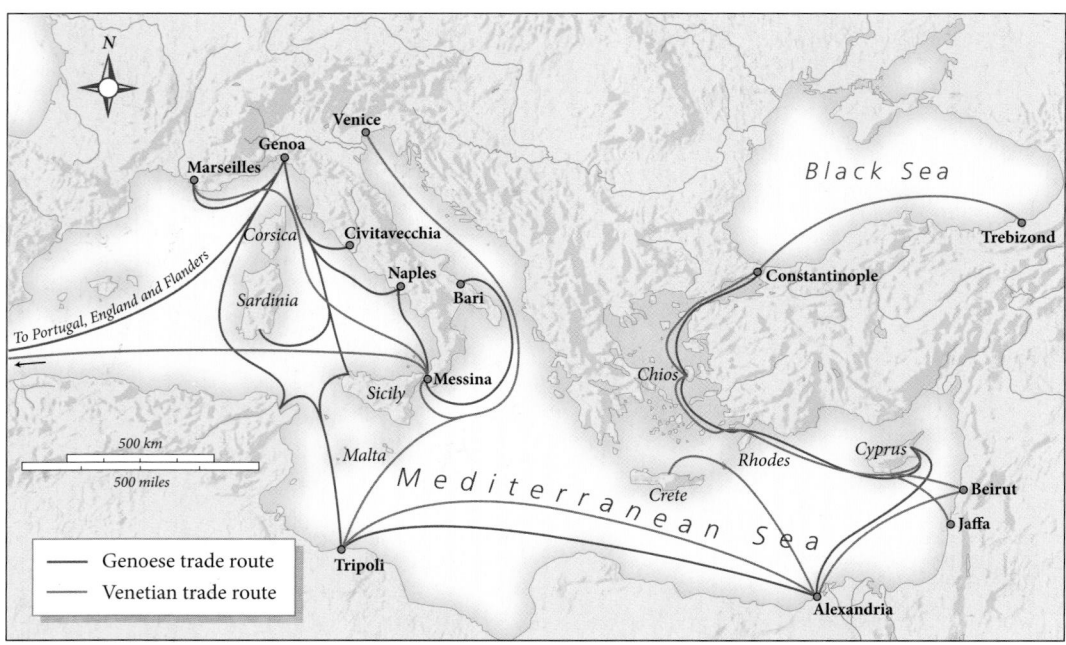

Map 13.1   The Italian Peninsula's key sea trade-routes

One of those travelers, the poet churchman, and scholar Francesco Petrarch, exemplifies another aspect of fourteenth-century Italian culture: a growing interest in the creative works of individuals. Petrarch and his contemporaries Dante Alighieri and Giovanni Boccaccio belong to a generation of thinkers and writers who turned to the study of ancient works of literature, history, and art to seek out beautiful and correct forms. Petrarch also sought to improve the quality of written Latin, and thereby to emulate the works of the Roman authors Vergil and Cicero. This study of ancient thought and art led to a search for moral clarity and models of behavior, a mode of inquiry that came to be known as **humanism**. Humanists valued the works of the ancients, both in the literary and the visual arts, and they looked to the classical past for solutions to modern problems. They particularly admired Roman writers who championed civic and personal virtues, such as service to the state and stoicism in times of trouble. Humanists considered Roman forms the most authoritative and, therefore, the most worthy of imitation, though Greek texts and ideas were also admired.

The study of the art of Rome and Greece would profoundly change the culture and the art of Europe by encouraging artists to look at nature carefully and to consider the human experience as a valid subject for art. These trends found encouragement in the ideals and theology of late medieval groups, such as the Dominicans, who valued classical learning, and the Franciscans, whose founder saw God in the beauty of nature. These bodies, called mendicants because they originally supported themselves from alms, became an important stimulus to thirteenth- and fourteenth-century patronage.

THE GROWTH OF THE MENDICANT ORDERS AND THE VISUAL ARTS IN ITALY

The two major mendicant groups were the Franciscans and the Dominicans. They established international "orders," as many monastic groups had done in the Middle Ages, although their missions differed from those of traditional monks. Both orders were founded to minister to the lay populations in the rapidly expanding cities; they did not retreat from the world, but engaged with it. Each order of friars (brothers) built churches in the cities so that sermons could be preached to crowds of people. The Dominicans, founded by Dominic de Guzmán in 1216, were especially concerned with combating heresy. The Franciscan order, founded by Francis of Assisi in 1209, worked in the cities to bring deeper spirituality and comfort to the poor. Taking vows of poverty, Franciscans were committed to teaching the laity and to encouraging them to pursue spiritual growth. Toward this goal, they told stories and used images to explain and affirm the teachings of the Church. Characteristically, Franciscans urged the faithful to visualize events such as the Nativity in tangible ways, including setting up Nativity scenes (crèches) in churches as an aid to devotion. Both orders played important roles in late medieval religious and artistic life, though the Franciscans held a special place in Italy since their founder was a native son.

The Franciscans at Assisi and Florence

The charismatic Francis died in 1226 and was named a saint two years later. His home town and burial place was the site of a huge

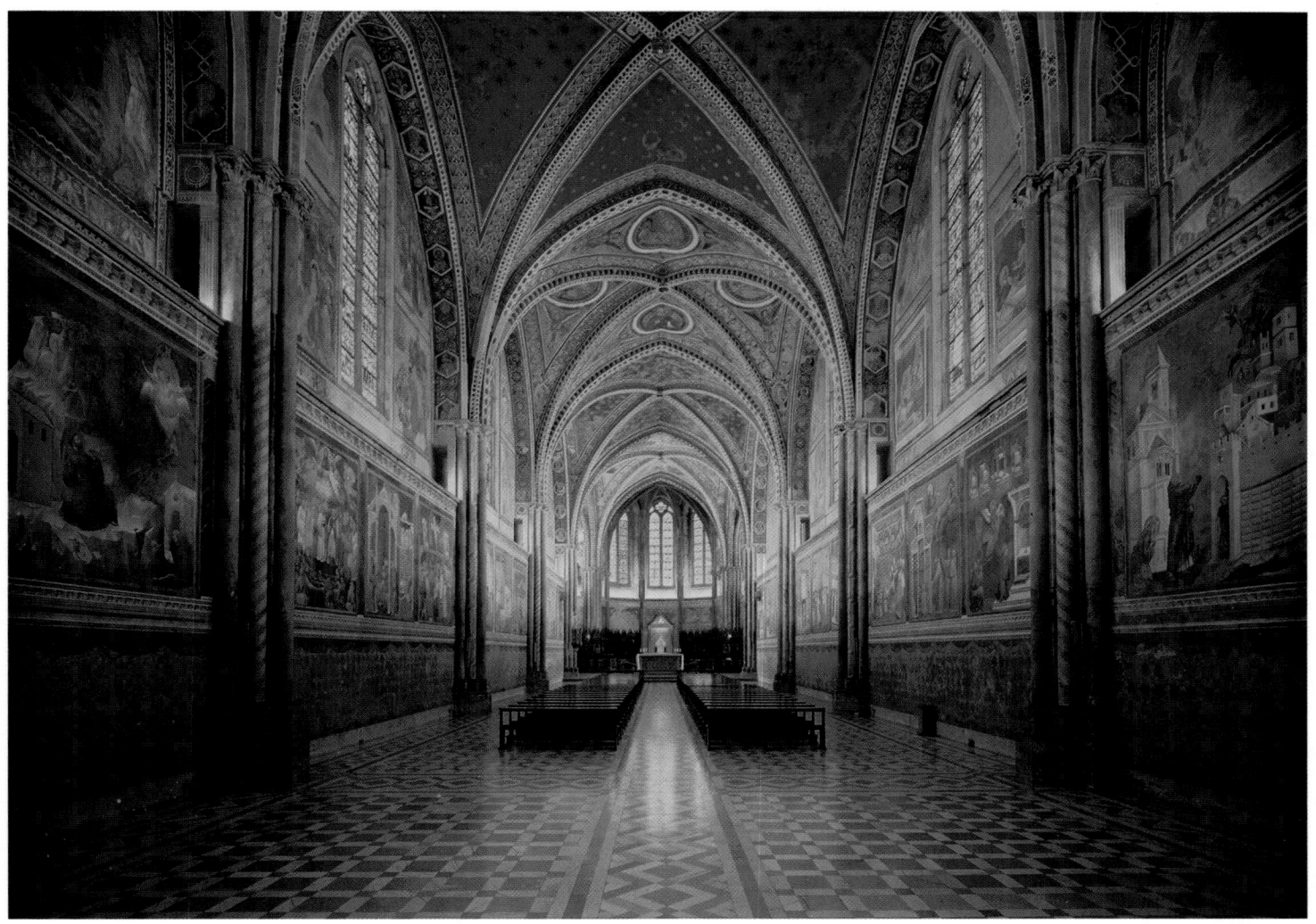

13.1   Interior of Upper Church, Basilica of San Francesco, Assisi. Begun 1228; consecrated 1253

church built in his honor. The pope sponsored its construction, which began shortly after Francis's canonization in 1228; the church was consecrated in 1253. Because it held the body of the popular saint, it was built as a large, multistoried structure in order to accommodate the numerous pilgrims it attracted. Most pilgrims would first encounter the large hall of the Upper Church, before descending to a church below. The Upper Church (fig. **13.1**) consists of a single long **nave,** or central hall, where crowds could gather. Whereas French churches of the same period reduced wall surfaces in their naves in favor of large stained-glass windows and complex vertical supports, as is the case at Chartres (see fig. 12.12), San Francesco at Assisi has relatively small windows and large expanses of wall surface. As in the northern churches, at San Francesco a brick **vault,** supported by Gothic pointed **arches,** covers the nave. Yet San Francesco is neither as high nor as spatially complex as French Gothic churches. The elimination of lower side **aisles** along the length of the nave simplifies the space and makes the walls more prominent. These wall surfaces became a magnet for artists, especially below the windows in the nave of the Upper Church. Their paintings were executed in the fresco technique, which Italian artists had

used throughout the Middle Ages. (See *Materials and Techniques,* page 441.)

The scale of the painting program at Assisi required teams of artists drawn from all over Italy and the work took many years to complete. From the 1270s through the early fourteenth century, papal sponsorship brought together artists from Rome, Siena, Florence, and elsewhere. Assisi became a laboratory for the development and dissemination of fourteenth-century Italian art. The frescoes flanking the nave windows depict biblical scenes from the book of Genesis and the life of Christ. But the most visible frescoes in the nave were painted below the windows; these depict the life and achievements of Francis himself.

The artists responsible for the St. Francis cycle had to devise images that conveyed both the events of Francis's life and their significance to Christian history. The events chosen for depiction came from biographies of Francis's life composed by his followers. One important theme found in these texts is the saint's veneration of nature as a manifestation of divine workmanship. The scene *St. Francis Preaching to the Birds* (fig. **13.2**) expresses this theme and Francis's attitude that all creatures are connected. The fresco depicts Francis in his brown habit standing in a landscape

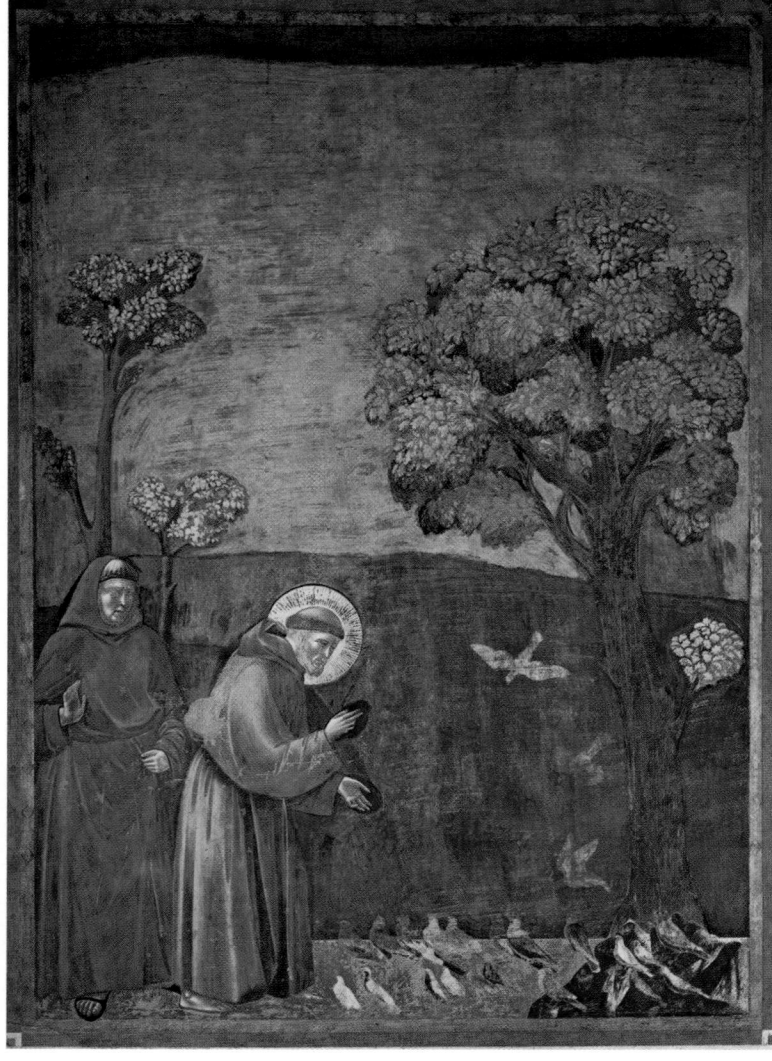

13.2 Anonymous. *St. Francis Preaching to the Birds*, from Basilica of San Francesco, Assisi. Begun 1290 (?). Fresco

documentary evidence is lacking, and the opinions of connoisseurs vary. Some prefer to assign these frescoes to an anonymous master, or masters, named either after the paintings at Assisi or subgroups among them. Since many painters worked in the same space, they competed with and influenced each other, thus affecting the future direction of Italian art.

Franciscan women served God within the walls of their convents, through their vocations as nuns, and their prayers for their neighbors. Like the friars, these women devoted themselves to poverty and simplicity, and their convents and churches were often less wealthy than many of the masculine institutions. Franciscan nuns belonged to the branch of the order founded by Francis's associate, St. Clare, who was canonized in 1255. The thirteenth-

and speaking to a flock of birds. To the astonished eyes of his companion, Francis appears to be able to communicate with the birds, who gather at his feet to listen.

The artist sets the scene outdoors by framing the figures with trees and painting the background blue. A narrow shelf of earth creates a platform on which the bulky figures stand. Francis and his companion are rendered naturalistically, as the artist describes light washing over their forms to suggest their mass and weight. Francis's figure becomes the focal point of the image, through his central position, the halo around his head, and his downward glance. His body language—the bent-over stance, the movement of his hands—express his intense engagement with the birds as representatives of nature. The simplicity of the composition makes the fresco easily legible and memorable.

The identities of the artists responsible for the frescoes in the nave of San Francesco are uncertain and controversial. One of the artists mentioned as a primary designer and painter is the Roman Pietro Cavallini; another is the Florentine Giotto di Bondone. But

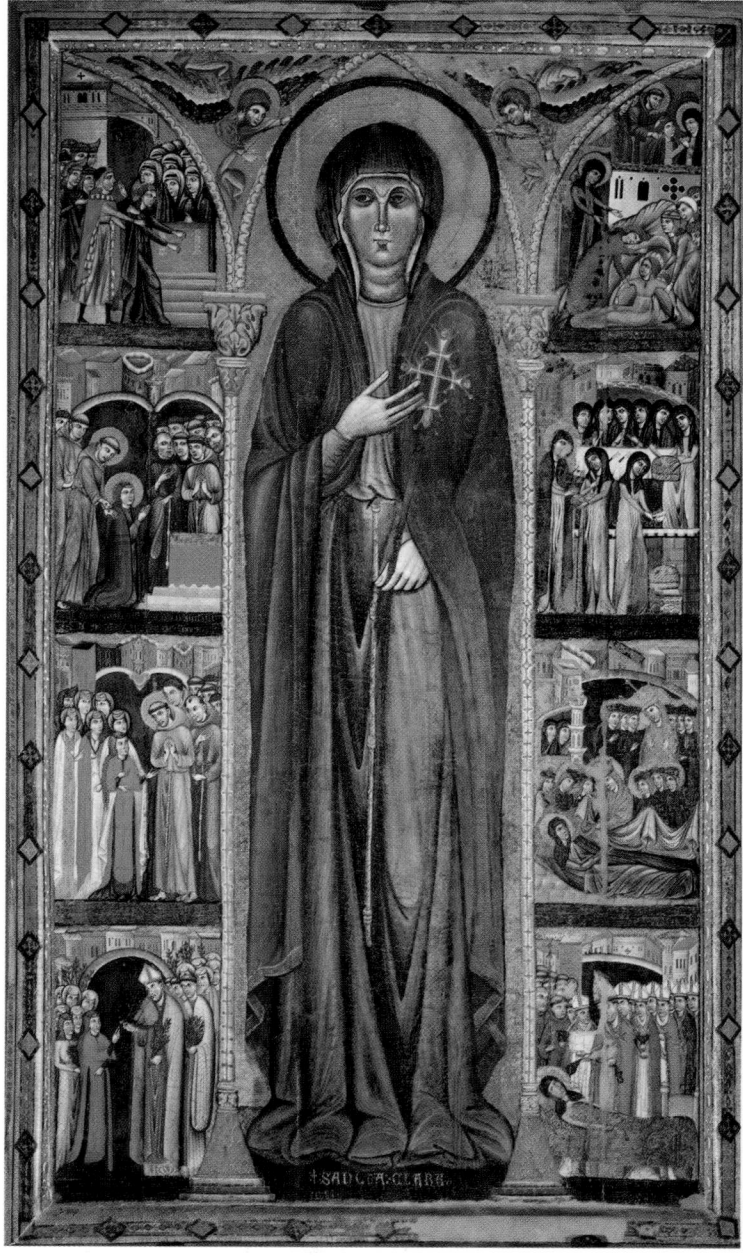

13.3 *Altarpiece of St. Clare.* ca. 1280. Tempera on panel, 9 × 5'6" (2.73 × 1.65 m). Convent of Santa Chiara, Assisi

Fresco Painting and Conservation

Fresco is a technique for applying paint to walls that results in an image that is both durable and brilliant. Frescoed surfaces are built up in layers: Over the rough wall goes a layer of rough lime-based plaster called *arriccio*. The artist then draws preliminary sketches onto this layer of plaster. Because they are done in red, these sketches are called *sinopie* (an Italian word derived from ancient Sinope, in Asia Minor, which was famous as a source of red-colored pigment). Then a finer plaster called *intonaco* is applied in areas just large enough to provide for a day's worth of painting—the *giornata* (from *giorno*, the Italian word for "day"). While the plaster is still wet, the artist applies pigments suspended in lime water. As the plaster dries, the pigments bind to it, creating a *buon fresco*, or "true fresco." Plaster dries in a day, which is why only the amount of wet plaster that can be painted during that time can be applied. The work has to be done on a scaffold, so it is carried out from top to bottom, usually in horizontal strips about 4 to 6 feet long. As each horizontal level is completed, the scaffolding is lowered for the next level. To prevent chemical interactions with the lime of the plaster, some colors have to be applied *a secco* or dry; many details of images are applied this way as well. *Fresco secco* does not bond to the plaster as surely as *buon fresco* does, so it tends to flake off over time. Consequently, some frescoes have subsequently been touched up with tempera paints.

Although durability is the key reason for painting in fresco, over the centuries wars and floods have caused damage. Modern conservators have developed techniques for removing frescoes from walls and installing them elsewhere. After the Arno River flooded in 1966, many Florentine frescoes were rescued in this way, not only preserving the artworks but greatly adding to the knowledge and technology required for this task. When a fresco is removed, series of cuts are made around the image. Then, a supporting canvaslike material is applied to the frescoed surface with a water-soluble glue. The surface to which the canvaslike material has been glued can then be pulled off gently and transferred to a new support to be hung elsewhere, after which the canvas can be removed. Such removals have exposed many *sinopie*, such as the one shown here. The fresco, attributed to Francesco Traini

(see fig. 13.30), was badly damaged by fire in 1944 and had to be detached from the wall in order to save what was left of it. This procedure revealed the plaster underneath, on which the composition had been sketched out. These drawings, of the same size as the fresco itself, are much freer-looking in style than the actual fresco. They often reveal the artist's personal style more directly than the painted version, which was carried out with the aid of assistants.

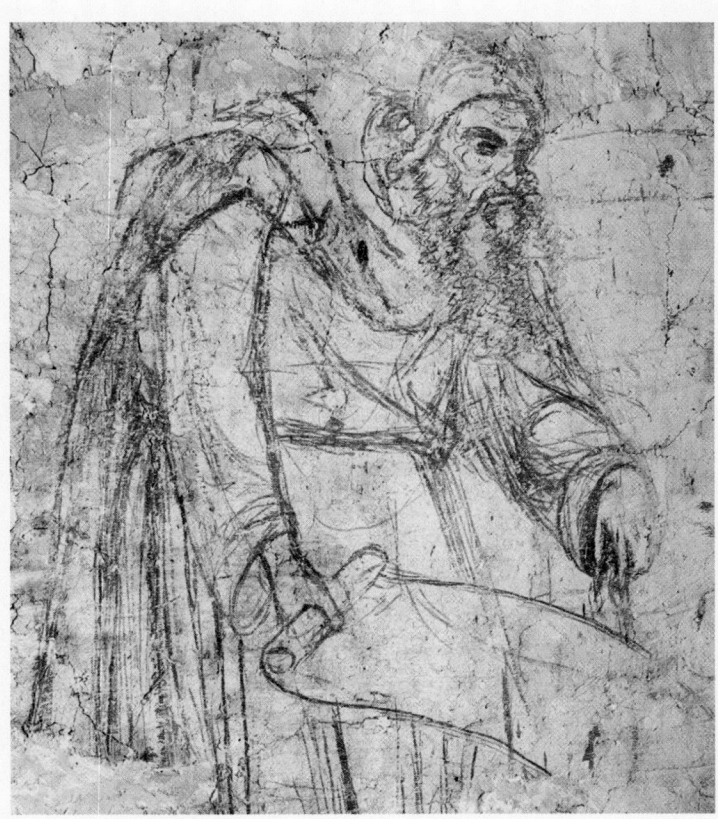

Anonymous (Francesco Traini?). Sinopia drawing for *The Triumph of Death* (detail). Camposanto, Pisa

century convent in Assisi dedicated to St. Clare does not boast a large fresco cycle but preserves a painted panel (fig. **13.3**) intended to sit on an **altar** (an **altarpiece**). A tall rectangle of wood covered with egg-based **tempera** paints, it was executed around 1280. It is dominated by the figure of St. Clare, dressed in the habit of her order, standing frontally and holding the staff of an abbess. The image does not portray her specific features as a portrait would, but represents her as a saintly figure of authority, whose large staring eyes and frontal posture have roots in Byzantine art. Alongside the saint eight tiny narratives convey stories about her life, death, and miracles. These **vignettes** relate her commitment to her vocation, her obedience to Francis and the Church, and her service to her fellow nuns. The narratives make little pretense at three-dimensional form or spatial structure, keeping the focus on the figures and their actions the better to tell the story.

Churches and Their Furnishings in Urban Centers

Franciscan churches began to appear all over Italy as the friars ministered to the spiritual lives of city dwellers. A characteristic example in Florence is the church of Santa Croce (Holy Cross), begun around 1295 (figs. **13.4** and **13.5**). The architect was probably the Tuscan sculptor Arnolfo di Cambio. Like San Francesco in Assisi, Santa Croce shares some features with Gothic churches in northern Europe, but it differs from them too. Its form is a **basilica** (a standard church plan including nave, side aisles, and apse), though the eastern end, where the high altar and many chapels are located, terminates in mostly rectilinear forms. Only the **apse** (or projecting niche), where the altar stands, is polygonal. This simplified design for the most sacred spaces in the

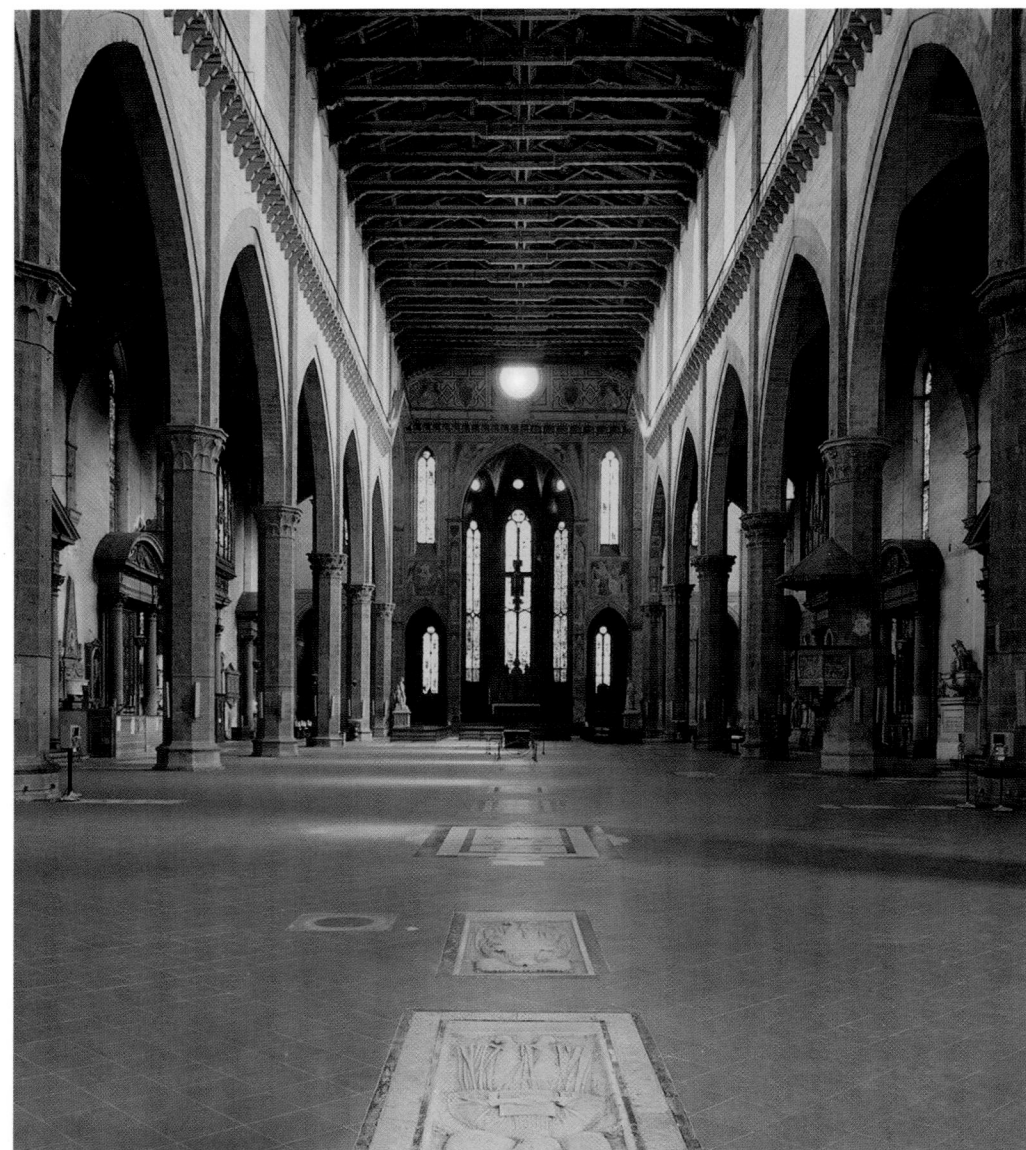

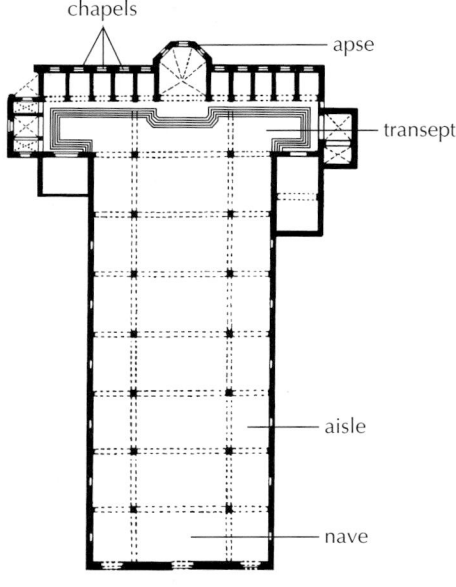

13.4 Arnolfo di Cambio (?). Nave and choir of Santa Croce, Florence. Begun ca. 1295

13.5 Plan of Santa Croce

church probably comes from monastic churches, especially of the reform-minded Cistercian order; for example, the plan of Fontenay Abbey (see fig. 11.21). The nave's proportions are broad and expansive rather than vertical. The nave **arcade** uses a Gothic pointed arch, while vertical moldings pull the eye up to the ceiling. Where in a French Gothic church, however, such moldings would support a vaulted ceiling, at Santa Croce wooden **trusses** (beams or rafters joined together) span the nave. The only vaults are at the apse and several chapels at the ends of the **transept**, the perpendicular space between the nave and the apse.

As the stone vaults of San Francesco in Assisi, the order's mother church, indicate that the friars were not averse to such structures, the choice of a wooden roof at Santa Croce may need explanation. This preference perhaps originates in a Tuscan tradition, as the great **Romanesque** cathedral of nearby Pisa (fig. 11.34) also has a wooden roof. Santa Croce's broad nave with high arches is also reminiscent of Early Christian churches (see fig. 8.9), so the choice may also spring from a desire to evoke the

simplicity of Early Christian basilicas and thus link Franciscan poverty with the traditions of the early Church. A vaulted nave would have been much more expensive.

Santa Croce served the growing population of Florence by providing room for elite burials in its aisles and chapels. The church's wide spaces also held large crowds so they could hear the friars' sermons.

Pulpits in Pisan Churches

For reading Scripture at services and for preaching, churchmen often commissioned monumental pulpits with narrative or symbolic images carved onto them. Several monumental pulpits were made by members of a family of sculptors who worked in Pisa, including Nicola Pisano (ca. 1220/25–1284) and his son Giovanni Pisano (1265–1314). Though the two men worked at various sites throughout Italy, they executed important pulpits for the cathedral and baptistery at Pisa.

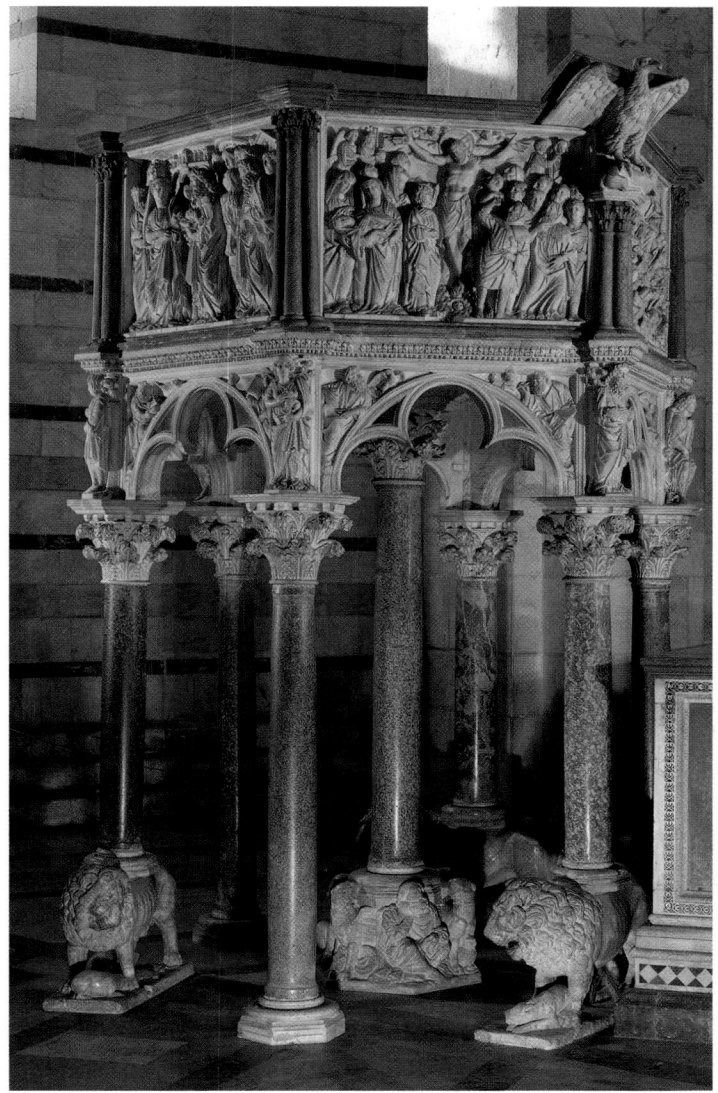

13.6   Nicola Pisano. Pulpit. 1259–60. Marble, height 15' (4.6 m). Baptistery, Pisa

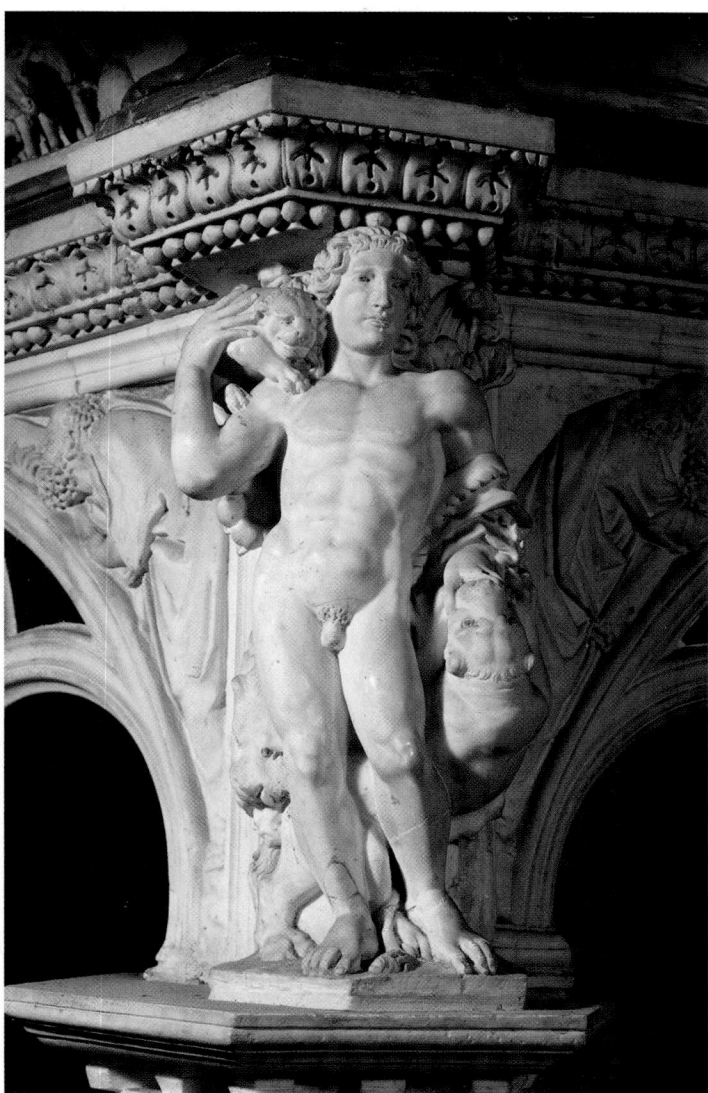

13.7   Nicola Pisano. *Fortitude*, detail of pulpit

For the Pisan baptistery, Nicola Pisano and his workshop carved a hexagonal marble pulpit finished around 1260 (fig. **13.6**). Rising to about 15 feet high, so the assembly could see and hear the speaker, the six sides of the pulpit rest on colored marble columns supporting classically inspired **capitals**. Above the capitals, carved into leaf shapes, small figures symbolizing the virtues stand between cusped arches, while figures of the prophets sit in the **spandrels** (the areas above the curves) of these arches. Surprisingly, one of these figures (fig. **13.7**) is a male nude with a lion cub on his shoulder and a lion skin over his arm. His form and the lion skin should identify him as the Greek hero Herakles (Hercules in Latin). Some scholars, however, have interpreted these same details to identify him as Daniel, the biblical hero whose faith allowed him to survive the lion's den. In either case, in the program of the pulpit, he stands for the Christian virtue of Fortitude. His anatomy, his proportions, and his stance are probably the product of Nicola Pisano's study of Roman and Early Christian sculpture. The figure's heroic nudity and his posture, with the

weight balanced on one leg to suggest movement, seem to be inspired by ancient models. Pisano had worked for Frederick II in southern Italy and at Rome, but his deep knowledge of ancient art may also derive from study of Roman artifacts in Pisa.

Nicola's study of the Roman past informs many other elements in his pulpit, including the narratives he carved for the six rectangular sides of the pulpit itself. These scenes from the life of Christ are carved in **relief**, so they project from the background. The Nativity scene in figure **13.8** is a densely crowded composition that combines the Annunciation with the Birth of Christ. The relief is treated as a shallow box filled with solid convex shapes in the manner of Roman **sarcophagi** (carved stone coffins), which Pisa's monumental cemetery preserved in good numbers. The Virgin has the dignity and bearing of a Roman matron. Pisano also knew Byzantine images of the Nativity, for the recumbent figure of the Virgin reflects that tradition. As the largest and most central figure, the reclining Virgin overpowers all the other elements in the composition. Around her, the details of

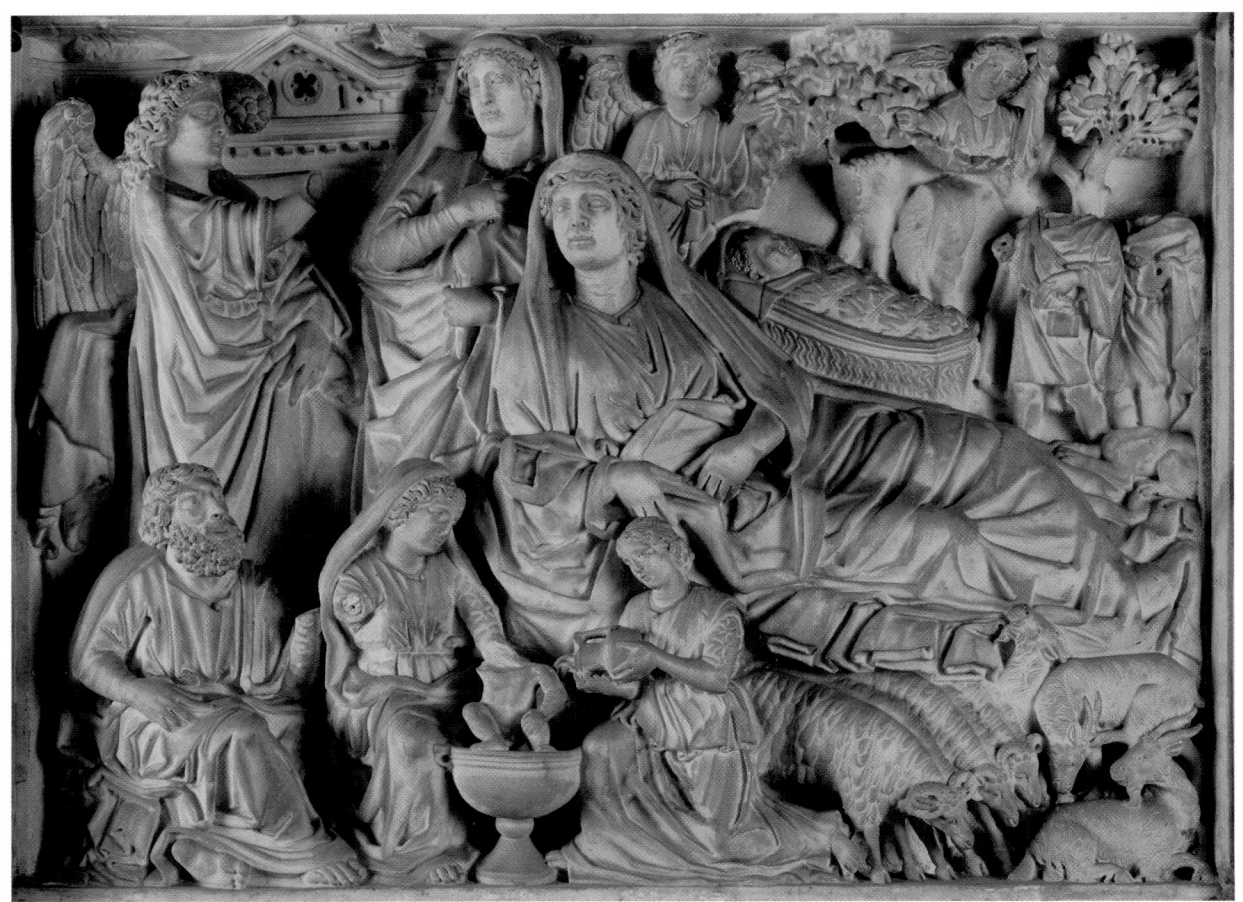

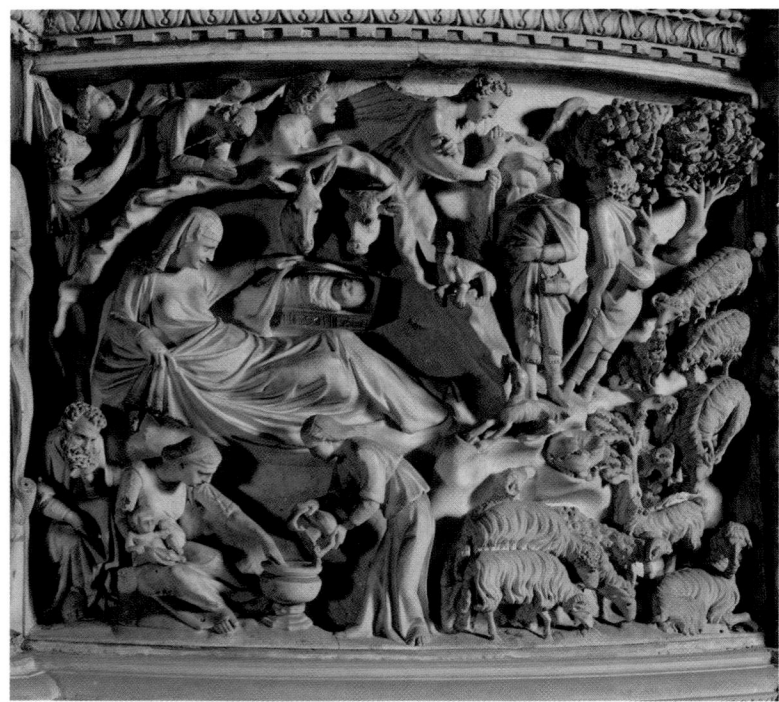

13.9 Giovanni Pisano, *Nativity*, detail of pulpit. 1302–10. Marble. Pisa cathedral

the narrative or setting, such as the midwives washing the child and Joseph's wondering gaze at the events, give the relief a human touch. Using forms inspired by both Byzantine and Roman models, Nicola uses broad figures, wrapped in **classicizing** draperies, to endow the scene with gravity and moral weight.

When his son Giovanni Pisano carved a pulpit about 50 years later for the cathedral of Pisa, he chose a different emphasis. Though executed at the same size and using the same material, his relief of the Nativity from the cathedral pulpit (fig. **13.9**) makes a strong contrast to his father's earlier work. Depicting the Nativity and the Annunciation to the shepherds, Giovanni dwells on the landscape and animal elements: Sheep and trees fill the right edge of the composition, while the Nativity itself takes place in a shallow cave in the Byzantine tradition. The Virgin still dominates the composition, but she is no longer a dignified matron staring out of the image. Instead, she is a young mother whose gaze and tender attention focus on her newborn child. Her proportions are elongated rather than sturdy. Rather than echoing Roman or Classical models, Giovanni has clearly studied contemporary French works to bring elegance and a detailed observation of nature to the image. Giovanni's swaying figures move more comfortably in the space they occupy. Where Nicola's *Nativity* is dominated by convex, bulging masses, Giovanni's appears to be made up of cavities and shadows. The play of lights and darks in Giovanni's relief exhibits a dynamic quality that contrasts with the serene calm of his father's work.

Expanding Florence Cathedral

The building and adornment of Pisa's cathedral complex were a civic as well as a religious duty for the town's citizens. As Italian cities grew and prospered, their religious centers grew with them. East of Pisa, along the Arno River, the increasing wealth of Florence inspired that town to undertake major projects for its cathedral and baptistery in order to compete with its neighbors. One of Nicola Pisano's students, Arnolfo di Cambio (ca. 1245–1302), was chosen to design a new cathedral for Florence to replace a smaller church that stood on the site. The cathedral was begun in 1296 (figs. **13.10**, **13.11**, and **13.12**). The project took the skills and energy of several generations, and the plan was modified more than once. For example, in 1357 Francesco Talenti (active 1325–1369) took over the project and dramatically extended the building to the east. By 1367, a committee of artists consulted by the overseers of the construction decided to cover the eastern zone with a high **dome**. The west façade and other portals continued to be adorned with sculpture throughout the **Renaissance** period, but the marble cladding on the building was not completed until the nineteenth century. Florence's Duomo (dome) was intended to be a grand structure that would not only serve as the spiritual center of the city, but as a statement of its wealth and importance.

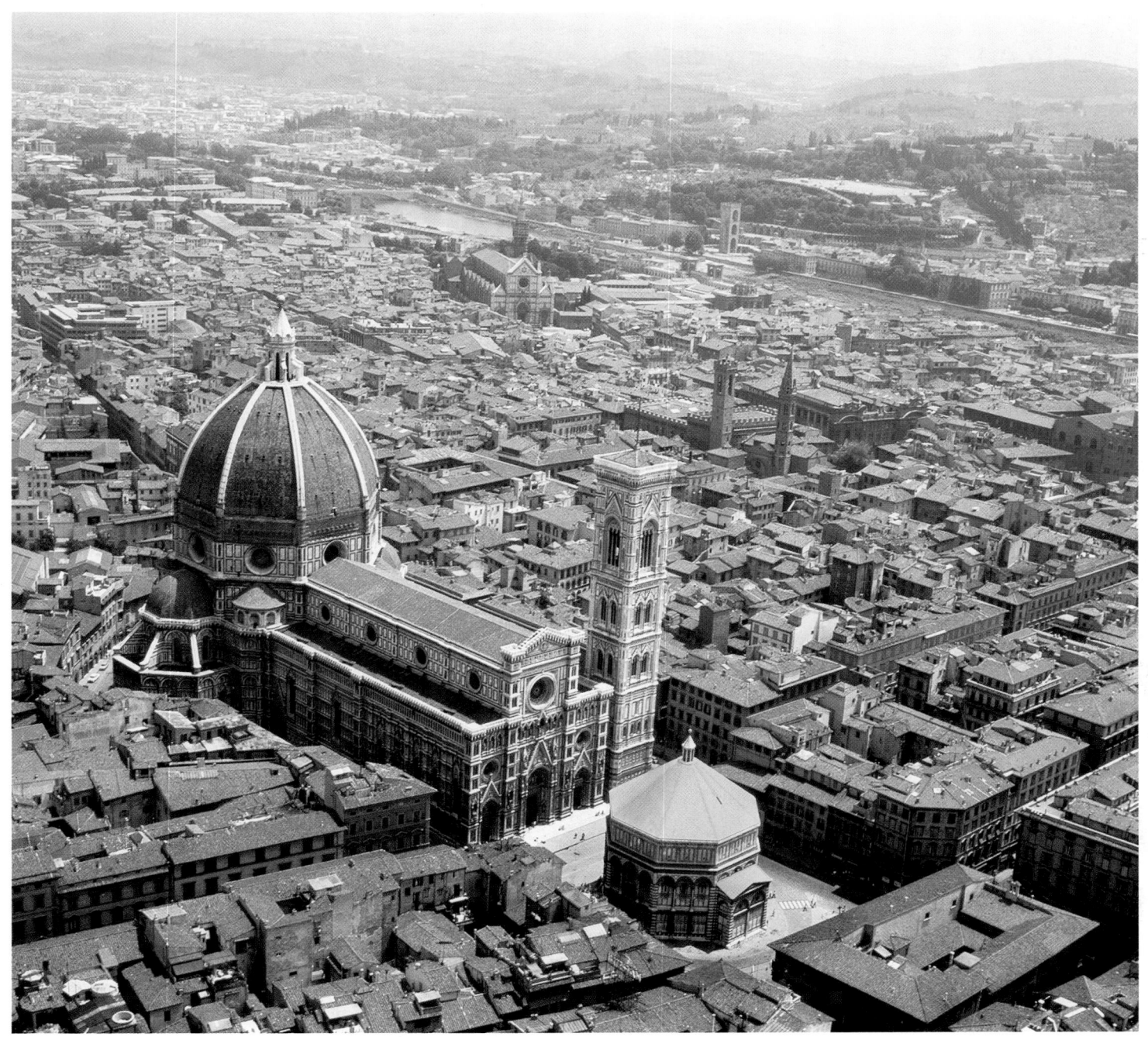

13.10   Florence cathedral and baptistery seen from the air. Cathedral begun 1296

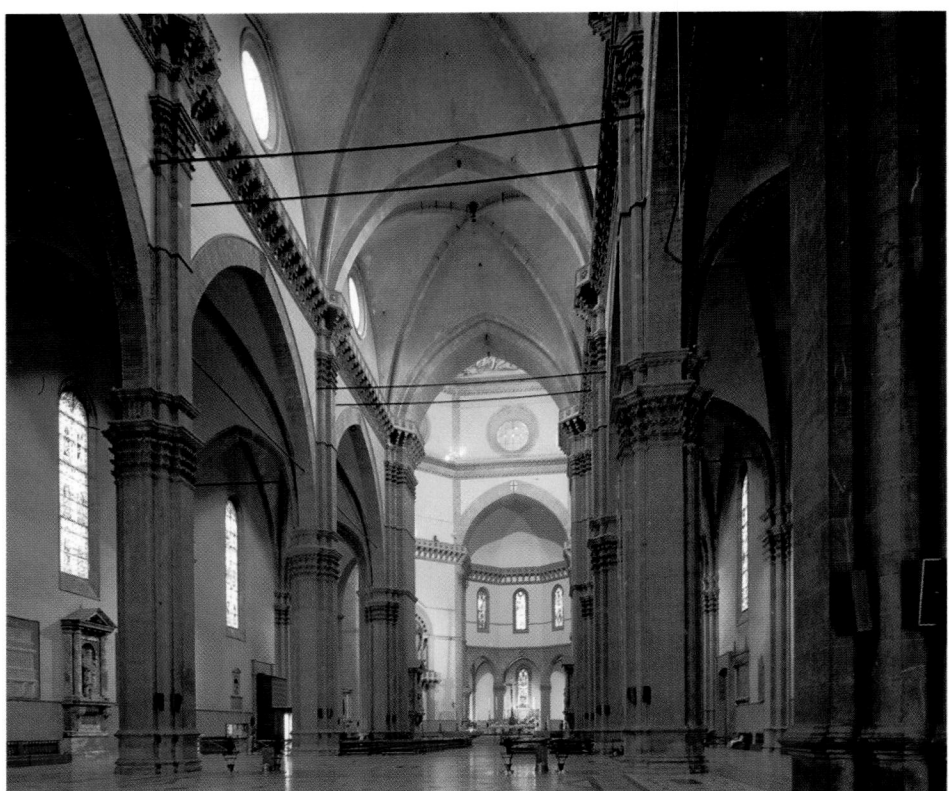

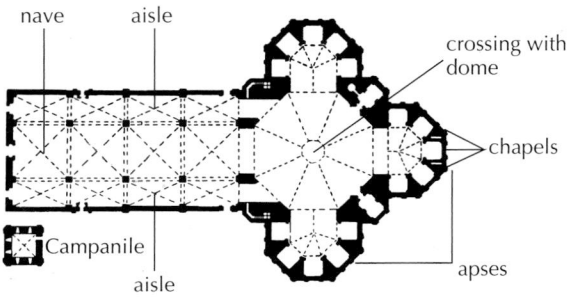

13.12 Plan of Florence cathedral and campanile

Arnolfo's original design provided for a large basilica with a high arcade and broad proportions that differs sharply from contemporary Gothic structures in France, even as it employs some of the technology of French Gothic. High pointed arches in the nave arcade rest on **piers** (vertical supports) articulated with leaf-shaped capitals. Flat moldings rise to the **clerestory** level, above the arcade. Windows in the clerestory and aisles are relatively small, leaving much more wall surface than in French cathedrals. Although the original plan called for a trussed wooden roof like the one at Santa Croce, by the mid-fourteenth century the plan had been altered to include **ribbed groin vaults** (stone vaults comprised of four sections with reinforcing along their edges), a detail closer to the northern Gothic taste. The later plans enlarged the eastern zone to terminate in three faceted arms which meet to form an octagonal space (the **crossing**) that would be covered by a dome. (This design appears in the fresco in fig. 13.31.) While this project included **flying buttresses** like French Gothic churches, these were never built. The scale of the proposed dome presented engineering difficulties that were not solved until the early fifteenth century. Instead of tall western towers incorporated into the façade, which was the norm in Gothic France, the cathedral has a **campanile** (bell tower) as a separate structure in the Italian tradition. The campanile is the work of the Florentine painter Giotto and his successors. If Florence's cathedral has Gothic elements in its vaults and arches, these foreign forms are tempered by local traditions.

Opposite the cathedral's west front stands the venerable baptistery of Florence, built in the eleventh century on much older foundations, which the Florentines believed to be Roman; they saw the glory of their own past in the structure's age. St. John the Baptist is a patron saint of the city of Florence; newborns became citizens of Florence by being baptized in this structure. The baptistery was the site of important artistic projects throughout the Renaissance. In 1330, its overseers commissioned another sculptor from Pisa, Andrea Pisano (ca. 1295–1348; no relation to Nicola or Giovanni) to cast a new pair of bronze doors for the baptistery. These were finished and installed in 1336 (fig. **13.13**). Cast of bronze and gilded, the project required 28 separate panels across the two panels of the door. They mostly represent scenes from the life of John the Baptist. Each vignette is framed by a Gothic **quatrefoil**, such as those found on the exteriors of French cathedrals. Yet within most of the four-lobed frames, Andrea provides a projecting ledge to support the figures and the landscape or architectural backgrounds. The relief showing the Baptism of Christ demonstrates Andrea's clear compositional technique:

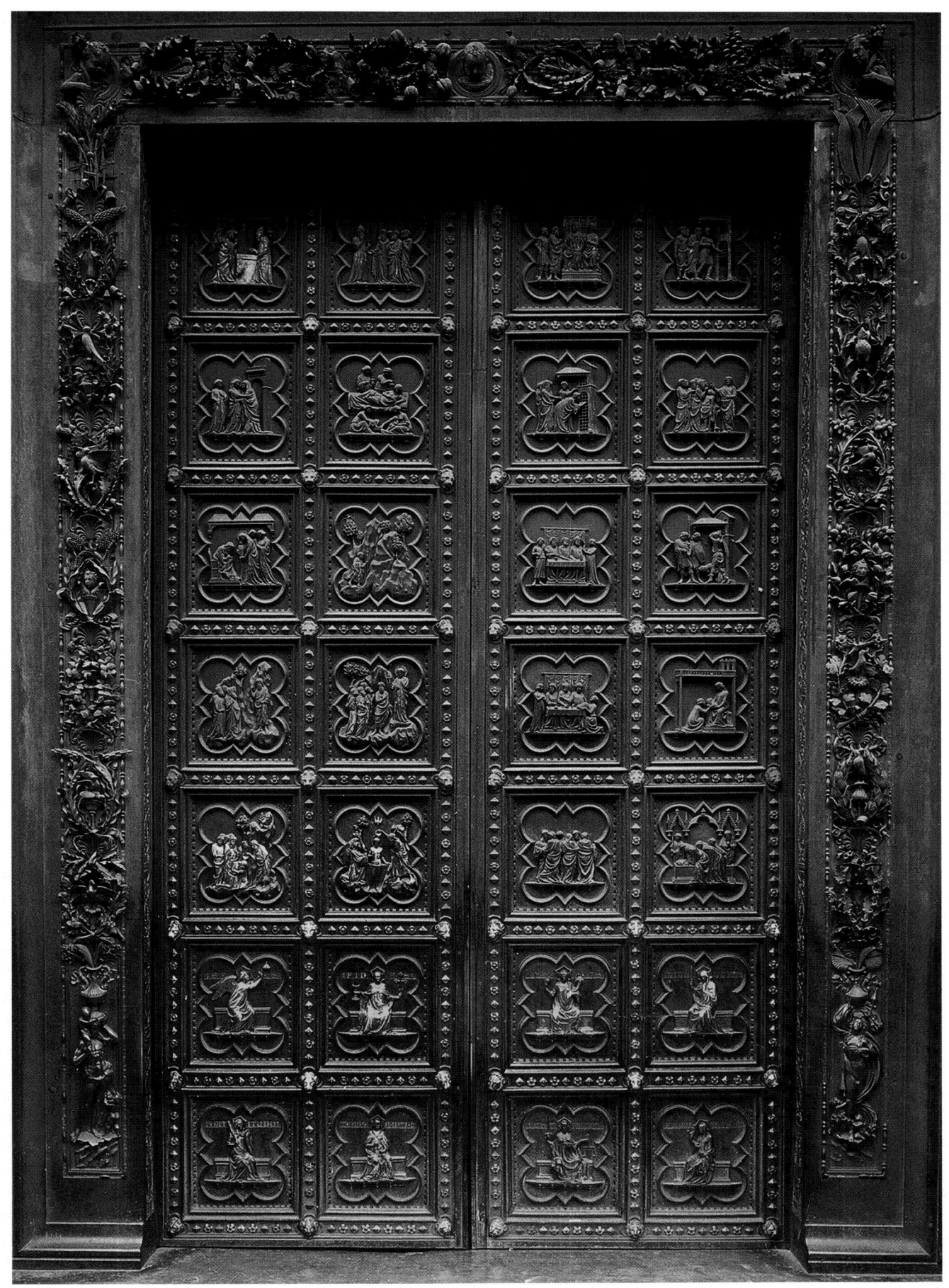

13.13   Andrea Pisano. South doors, baptistery of San Giovanni, Florence. 1330–36. Gilt bronze

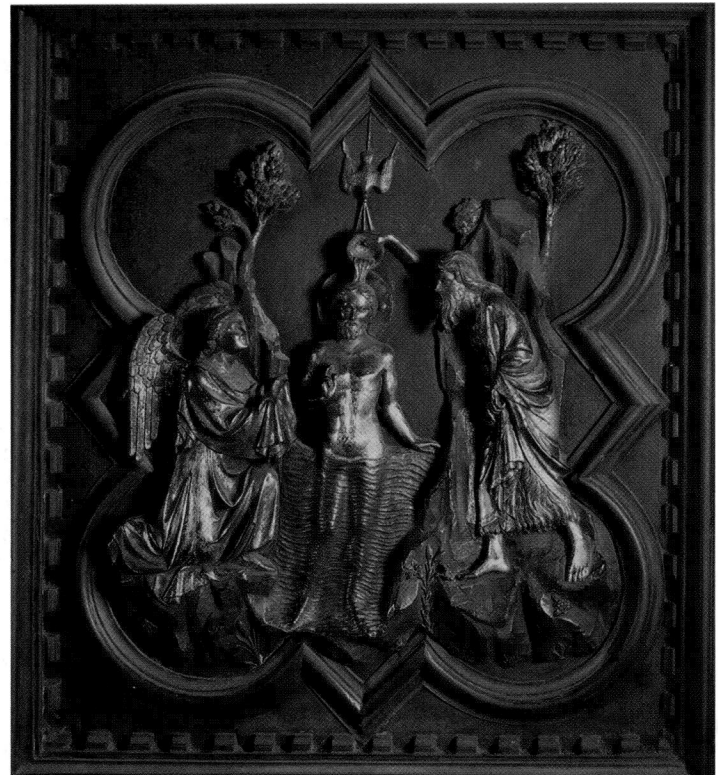

13.14 Andrea Pisano, *The Baptism of Christ*, from the south doors, baptistery of San Giovanni, Florence. 1330–36. Gilt bronze

Similar to fortified castles in the region, the Palazzo boasts thick stone walls, heavy **battlements** (defensive parapets), and a tall tower. Few windows pierce the walls of the lowest level, whose stones are left rough and uneven (or **rusticated**) to create the appearance of greater strength. The two upper stories display smoother masonry and more elegant pointed windows. The tower serves not only as a symbol of civic pride, but as a defensive structure. It sits slightly off-center for two reasons: This part of the building rests on the foundations of an earlier tower, and its position makes it visible from a main street in the city. Boasting the highest civic tower in the city, the Palazzo della Signoria dominated the skyline of Florence and expressed the power of the communal good over powerful individual families.

Christ stands at the center, framed by John on the right in the act of baptism and an angelic witness on the left (fig. **13.14**). The dove symbolizing the Holy Spirit appears above Christ's head. The emphasis is on the key figures, with little detail to distract from the main narrative; only a few small elements suggest the landscape context of the Jordan River. If the beautiful torso of Christ in the river recalls the Fortitude figure from Nicola Pisano's Pisa Baptistery, the simplicity of the landscape and composition recall the frescoes at Assisi.

Building for the City Government: The Palazzo della Signoria

While the citizens of Florence were building the huge cathedral, the political faction that supported the papacy instead of the Holy Roman Empire consolidated its power in the city. The pro-papal party (the Guelphs) was largely composed of wealthier merchants who sought to contain the dynastic ambitions of aristocratic families who supported the emperor (the Ghibellines). The pro-papal group commissioned a large structure to house their governing council and to serve as the symbol of the political independence of the city. They probably chose Arnolfo di Cambio to design the Palazzo della Signoria (fig. **13.15**). It was begun in 1298 and completed in 1310, though it has been subject to later expansion and remodeling. It became known as the Palazzo Vecchio (or old palace) during the sixteenth century, when the ruling Medici family moved to another palace.

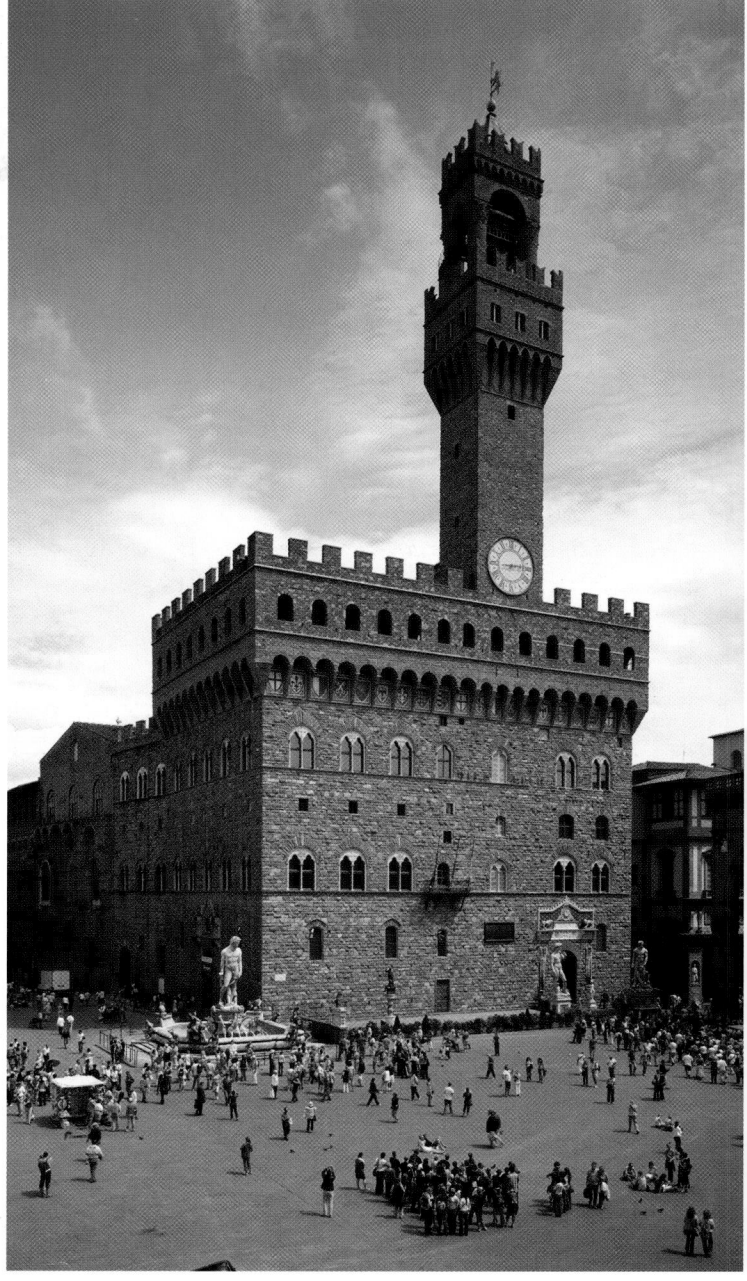

13.15 Palazzo della Signoria (Palazzo Vecchio), Florence. Begun 1298

PAINTING IN TUSCANY

As with other art forms in the thirteenth century, Italian painting's stylistic beginnings are different from those of the rest of Europe, although they shared traits and ideas. Italy's ties to the Roman past and the Byzantine present would inspire Italian painters to render forms in naturalistic and monumental images. Throughout the Middle Ages, Byzantine mosaics and murals were visible to Italian artists. Venice had long-standing trading ties with the Byzantine Empire, while the crusades of the twelfth and thirteenth centuries had brought Italy in even closer contact with Byzantium, including the diversion of the Fourth Crusade in 1204 to Constantinople itself.

One result of the short-lived occupation of Constantinople by western Europeans, from 1204 to 1261, was an infusion of Byzantine art forms and artists into Italy, which had a momentous effect on the development of Italian art in the thirteenth century. Later observers of the rapid changes that occurred in Italian painting from 1200 to 1550 described the starting point of these changes as the "Greek manner," by which they meant Byzantine art. Writing in the sixteenth century, the biographer and artist Giorgio Vasari reported that in the mid-thirteenth century, "Some Greek painters were summoned to Florence by the government of the city for no other purpose than the revival of painting in their midst, since that art was not so much debased as altogether lost." Vasari assumes that medieval Italian painting was all but nonexistent and attributes to Byzantine art great influence over the development of Italian art in the thirteenth century. Italian artists were able to absorb the Byzantine tradition far more thoroughly at this time than ever before. When Gothic style from northern Europe began to influence artists working in this Byzantinizing tradition, a revolutionary synthesis of the two was accomplished by a generation of innovative and productive painters in Tuscan cities.

Cimabue and Giotto

One such artist was Cimabue of Florence (ca. 1250–after 1300), whom Vasari claimed had been apprenticed to a Greek painter. His presence has also been noted in Assisi, Rome, and Pisa. In the 1280s, he painted a large panel depicting the Madonna Enthroned (fig. **13.16**), or Madonna in Majesty (Maestà), to sit on an altar in the church of Santa Trinità in Florence; the large scale of the altarpiece—it is more than 12 feet high—made it the devotional focus of the church. Its composition recalls Byzantine icons, such as the *Madonna Enthroned* (see fig. 8.49), but its scale and verticality are closer to the *Altarpiece of St. Clare* (fig. 13.3) and similar thirteenth-century altarpieces than to Byzantine prototypes. Mary and her son occupy a heavy golden throne, flanked by rows of angels on either side. Hebrew Bible prophets holding scrolls appear below, as if forming a foundation for Mary's throne; the relationship between the Hebrew Bible and the New Testament is an important theme in Christian art. The Virgin's towering scale and the brilliant blue of her gown against

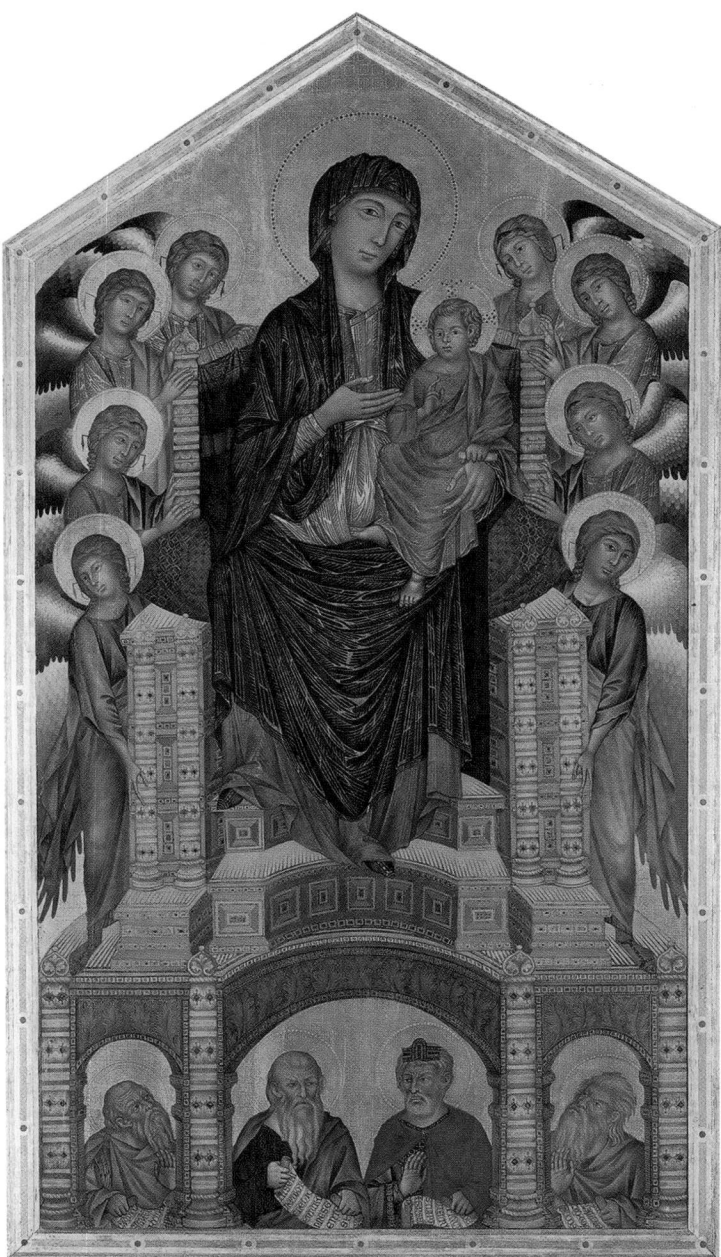

13.16 Cimabue, *Madonna Enthroned*. ca. 1280–90. Tempera on panel, 12'7½" × 7'4" (3.9 × 2.2 m). Galleria degli Uffizi, Florence

the gold-leaf background draw a viewer's eye to her; with her gesture she emphasizes the presence of her son. Like Byzantine painters, Cimabue uses linear gold elements to enhance her dignity, but in his hands the network of gold lines follows the line of her body instead of creating abstract patterns. The severe design and solemn expression are appropriate to the monumental scale of the painting.

Later artists in Renaissance Italy, such as Lorenzo Ghiberti (see Chapter 15) and Giorgio Vasari (see Chapter 16) claimed that Cimabue was the teacher of Giotto di Bondone (ca. 1267–1336/37), one of the key figures in the history of art. If so, Giotto may have learned from him the "Greek Manner" in which Cimabue worked. Some scholars believe that Giotto also worked movement from light into dark, so that the figures appear to be three-dimensional forms.

The throne exhibits some features of contemporary Italian architecture, such as the high pointed arches, though Giotto uses them to create a nichelike structure. This encloses the Madonna on three sides, setting her apart from the gold background, and defines the space that she inhabits. Giotto further suggests space by placing angels kneeling before the throne and by the overlapping figures of saints, who seem to stand behind one another on a level surface. The throne's lavish ornamentation includes a feature that is especially interesting: the colored marble surfaces of the base and of the quatrefoil within the **gable**. Such illusionistic stone textures had been highly developed by ancient painters (see fig. 7.56), and their appearance here is evidence that Giotto was familiar with whatever ancient murals could still be seen in medieval Rome.

THE ARENA CHAPEL IN PADUA Giotto's innovative ideas about light and space were accompanied by a gift for storytelling. Although scholars are not certain that he was among the artists who painted the nave frescoes at Assisi, his fresco cycles share formal and narrative characteristics with those images (see fig.

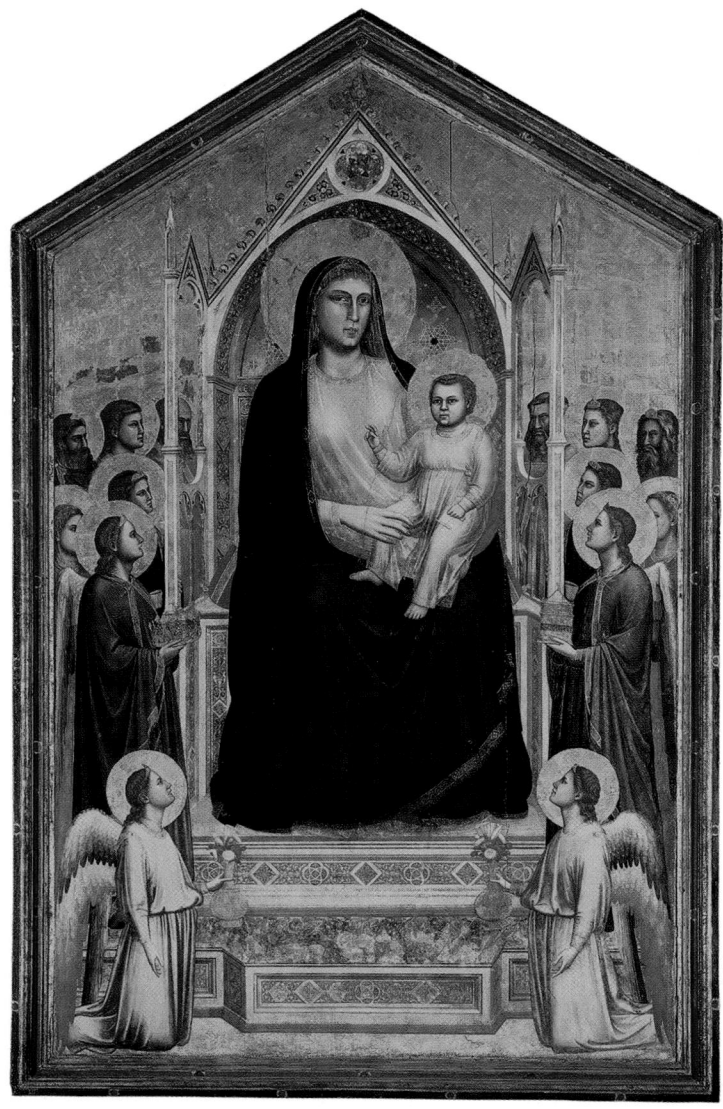

13.17 Giotto, *Madonna Enthroned.* ca. 1310. Tempera on panel, 10'8" × 6'8" (3.3 × 2 m). Galleria degli Uffizi, Florence

at Assisi, while documents tell us that Giotto worked in Rome where examples of both ancient and Early Christian art were available for artists to study. Equally important, however, was the influence of the Pisani—Nicolo and Giovanni—with their blend of **classicism** and Gothic **naturalism** to express strong emotional content. (See figs. 13.8 and 13.9.)

We can see Giotto's relationship to, but difference from, Cimabue in a tall altarpiece showing the Madonna Enthroned, which he painted around 1310 for the church of All Saints (Ognissanti) in Florence (fig. **13.17**). Like Cimabue's Santa Trinità Madonna, Giotto depicts the Queen of Heaven and her son enthroned among holy figures against a gold background. The Virgin's deep blue robe and huge scale bring a viewer's eye directly to her and to the Christ Child in her lap. All the other figures gaze at them, both signaling and heightening their importance. Unlike Cimabue, Giotto models the figures in light, so that they appear to be solid, sculptural forms. Where Cimabue turns light into a network of golden lines, Giotto achieves a gradual

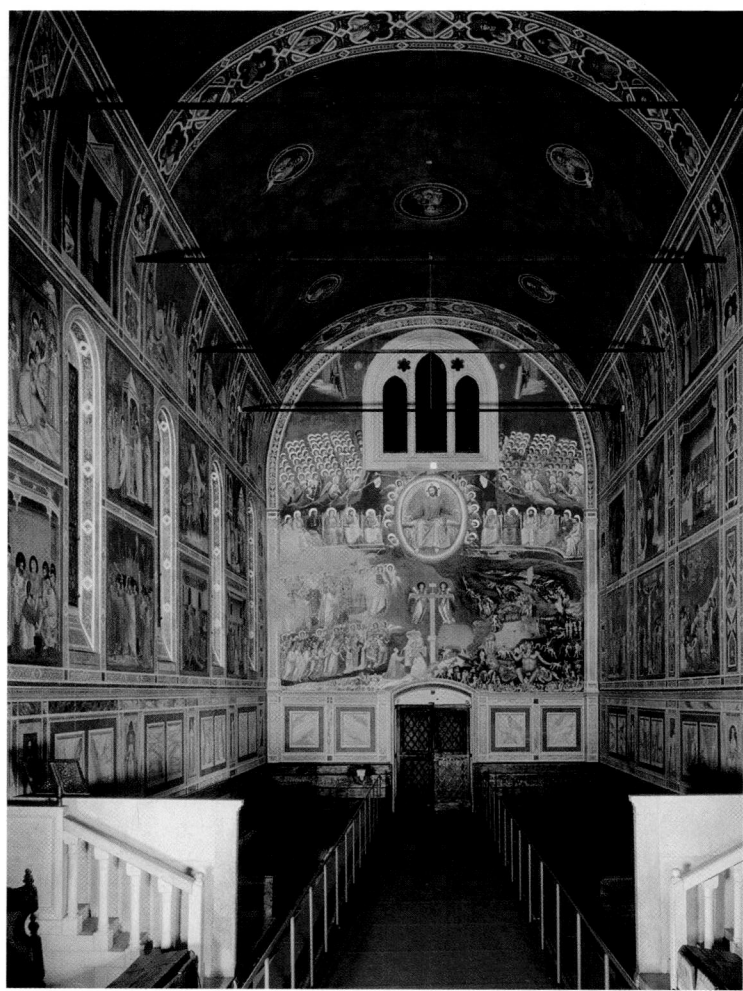

13.18 Interior of Arena (Scrovegni) Chapel, Padua. 1305–06

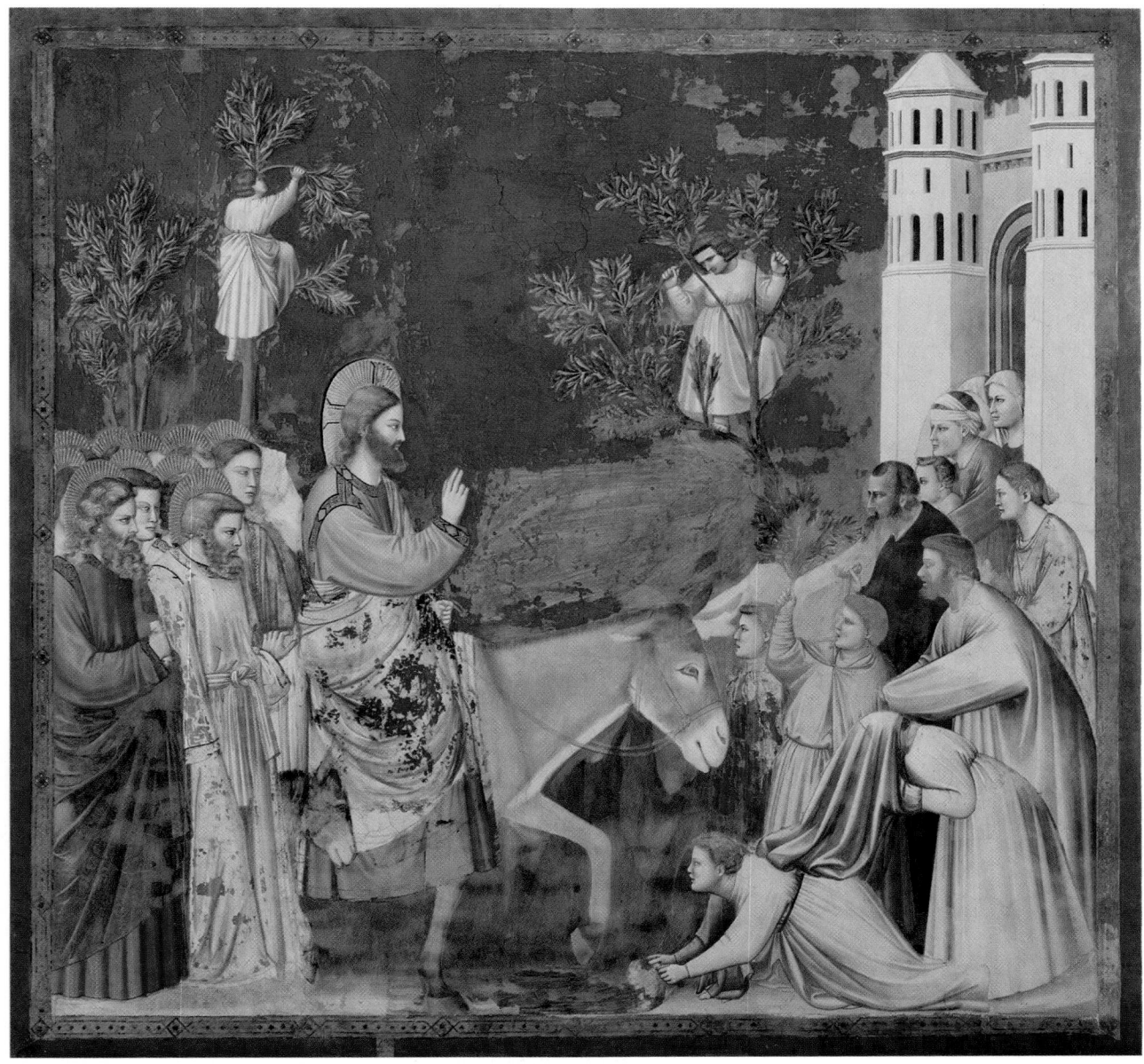

13.19 Giotto, *Christ Entering Jerusalem*, Arena (Scrovegni) Chapel, Padua. 1305–06. Fresco

13.2). Of Giotto's surviving murals, those in the Arena, or Scrovegni, Chapel in Padua, painted in 1305 and 1306, are wonderfully preserved and recently restored. It is known variously as the Arena Chapel because the site once housed a Roman arena, and the Scrovegni Chapel because it was built by Enrico Scrovegni, a Paduan banker, next to his palace, where he intended it to serve as his burial chapel. Dedicated to "Our Lady of Charity", the structure is a one-room hall covered with a **barrel vault** (fig. **13.18**).

Giotto and his assistants painted the whole chapel from floor to ceiling in the fresco technique. A blue field with gold stars symbolic of Heaven dominates the barrel vault, below which the walls are divided into three **registers** or horizontal rows. Each register contains rectangular fields for narrative scenes representing the lives of the Virgin and Christ. The Annunciation appears at the altar end of the room; this represents the archangel Gabriel

announcing to Mary that she has been chosen to bear the son of God. The theme commemorates the Incarnation of Christ and marks the beginning of the plan of Salvation, according to Catholic belief. At the other end of the chapel, Giotto depicted the Last Judgment (the events predicted for the end of time). At the foot of the Last Judgment, Giotto has included the figure of the donor, Enrico Scrovegni, offering his chapel to the Virgin and angels (see page 436). Along the length of the wall, the top register depicts stories of the early life of Mary and her parents; the center register focuses on stories of Christ's life and miracles; and the lowest register depicts his Passion, Death, and Resurrection. Below the narratives, the walls resemble marble panels interspersed with reliefs, but everything is painted.

One scene in the middle register, *Christ Entering Jerusalem*, depicts the event commemorated by Christians on Palm Sunday (fig. **13.19**). The Gospels report that the citizens welcomed

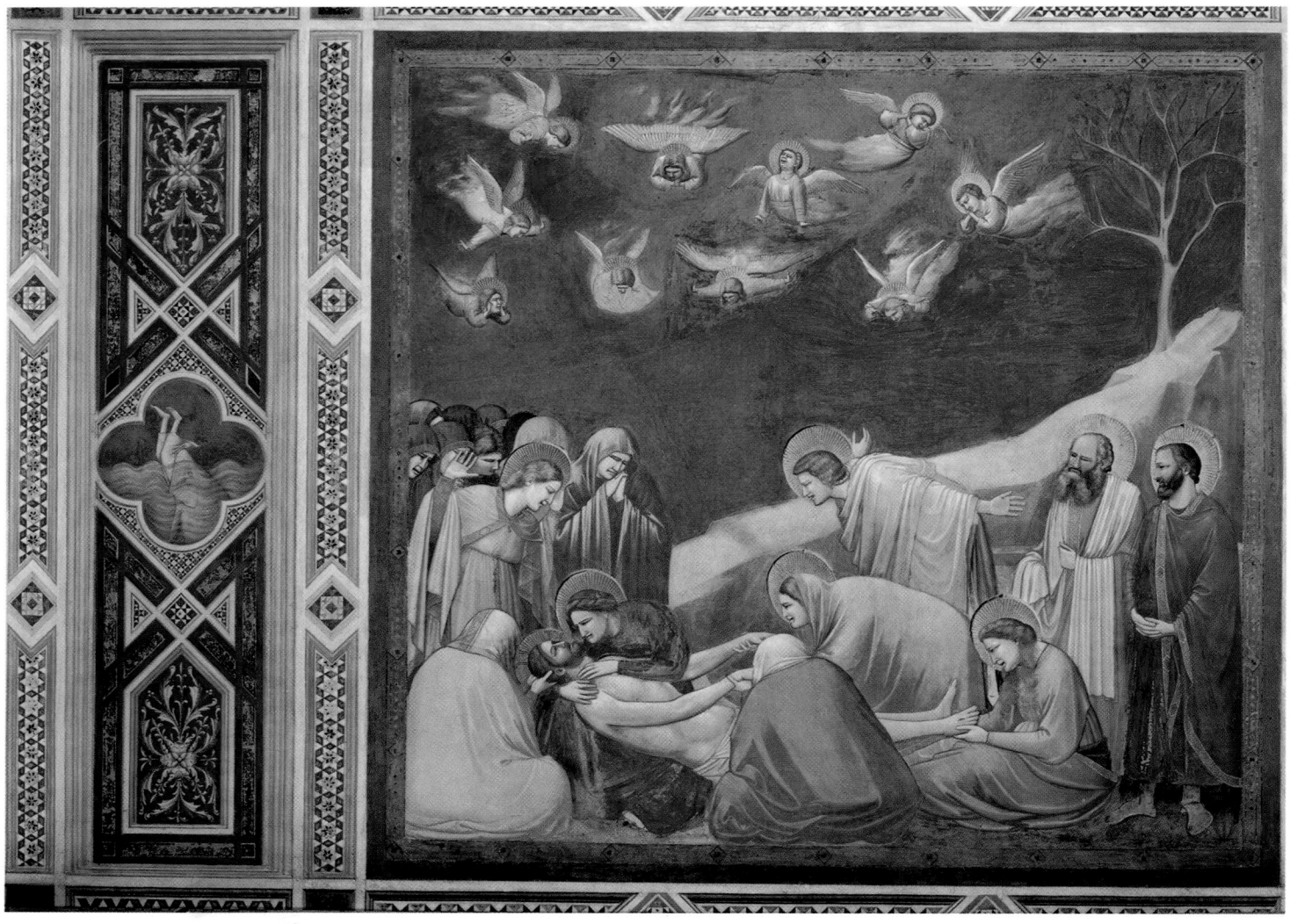

13.20 Giotto, *The Lamentation*, Arena (Scrovegni) Chapel, Padua. 1305–06. Fresco

Jesus with palm fronds and cheers as he entered Jerusalem riding a donkey; Christ's arrival on a humble mount fulfilled a Hebrew Bible prophecy. Giotto places the entire scene in the foreground of his image, which brings the events very close to a viewer. Furthermore, Giotto gives his forms such a strong three-dimensional quality that they almost seem as solid as sculpture. The rounded forms create the illusion of space in which the actors exist.

Giotto deliberately leaves the setting spare for this event, except for the trees in which children climb and the city gate on the right. His large simple forms, strong grouping of figures, and the limited depth of his stage give his scenes a remarkable spatial coherence. The massed verticals of the block of apostles on the left contrast with the upward slope of the crowd welcoming Jesus on the right; but Jesus, alone in the center, bridges the gap between the two groups. His isolation and dignity, even as he rides the donkey toward the city where he will die, give the painting a solemn air.

Giotto's skill at perfectly matching composition and meaning may also be seen in the scenes on the lowest register, which focus on the Passion. A viewer gazing at these frescoes sees them straight on, so the painter organizes the scenes to exploit that relationship. One of the most memorable of these paintings depicts the Lamentation, the moment of last farewell between Jesus and his mother and friends (fig. **13.20**). Although this event does not appear in the Gospels, by the end of the Middle Ages versions of this theme had appeared in both Byzantine and in Western medieval art.

The tragic mood of this Lamentation, found also in religious texts of the era, is created by the formal rhythm of the design as well as by the gestures and expressions of the participants. The low center of gravity and the hunched figures convey the somber quality of the scene, as do the cool colors and bare sky. With extraordinary boldness, Giotto sets off the frozen grief of the human mourners against the frantic movement of the weeping angels among the clouds. It is as if the figures on the ground are restrained by their obligation to maintain the stability of the composition, while the angels, small and weightless as birds, are able to move—and feel—freely.

Once again, the simple setting heightens the impact of the drama. The descending slope of the hill acts as a unifying element that directs attention toward the heads of Christ and the Virgin, which are the focal point of the scene. Even the tree has a twin function. Its barrenness and isolation suggest that all of nature shares in the sorrow over Christ's death. Yet it also carries a more precise symbolic message: It refers to the Tree of Knowledge, which the sin of Adam and Eve had caused to wither and which was to be restored to life through Christ's sacrificial death.

Giotto's frescoes in the Arena Chapel established his fame among his contemporaries. In the *Divine Comedy*, written around 1315, the great Italian poet Dante Alighieri mentions the rising reputation of the young Florentine: "Once Cimabue thought to hold the field as painter, Giotto now is all the rage, dimming the luster of the other's fame." (See www.myartslab.com.) Giotto continued to work in Florence for 30 years after completing the chapel frescoes, in 1334 being named the architect of Florence cathedral, for which he designed the campanile (see figs. 13.10 and 13.12). His influence over the next generation was inescapable and was felt by artists all over Italy.

Siena: Devotion to Mary in Works by Duccio and Simone

Giotto's slightly older contemporary Duccio di Buoninsegna of Siena (ca. 1255–before 1319) directed another busy and influential workshop in the neighboring Tuscan city of Siena. The city of Siena competed with Florence on a number of fronts—military, economic, and cultural—and fostered a distinct identity and visual tradition. Its wealth came from agriculture and trade. After a key military victory against Florence in 1260, Siena took the Virgin Mary as its protector and patron. The Sienese chose a representative form of government—a republic—directed by the *Nove* (the Nine), who were chosen from the elite merchants of the city. By the end of the thirteenth century, this government had taken up the project of building a town hall (fig. **13.21**), the Palazzo Pubblico, as an expression of their city's wealth and status.

Begun by 1298, the Palazzo Pubblico served not only to house the city government, but to frame a public space, the Piazza del

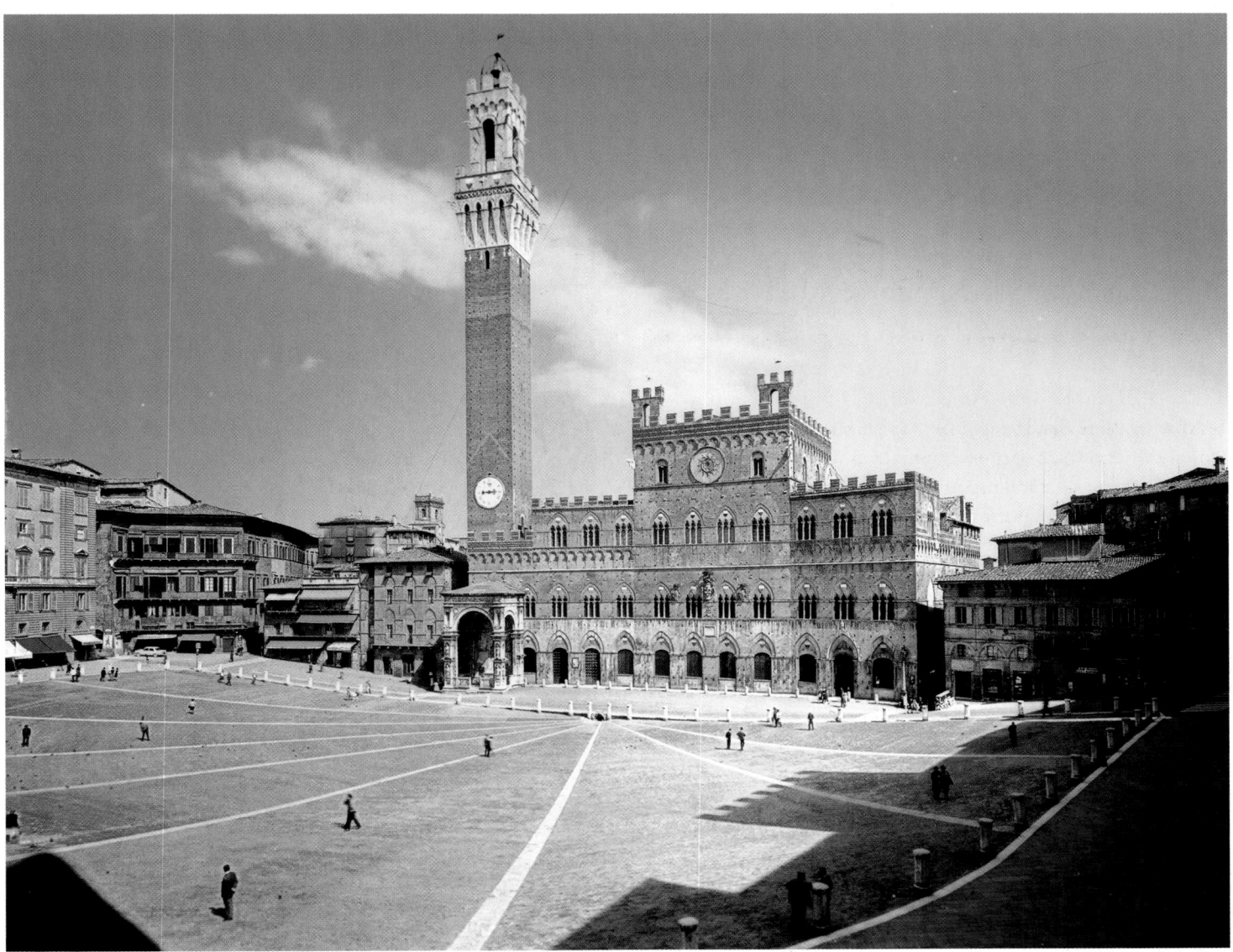

13.21 Palazzo Pubblico, Siena. Begun ca. 1298

PRIMARY SOURCE

Agnolo di Tura del Grasso

From his *Chronicle*

Duccio's Maestà *(see fig. 13.22) stood on the main altar of Siena cathedral until 1506, when it was removed to the transept. It was sawed apart in 1771, and some panels were acquired subsequently by museums in Europe and the United States. This local history of about 1350 describes the civic celebration that accompanied the installation of the altarpiece in 1311.*

These paintings [the *Maestà*] were executed by master Duccio, son of Nicolò, painter of Siena, the finest artist to be found anywhere at his time. He painted the altarpiece in the house of the Muciatti outside the gate toward Stalloreggi in the suburb of Laterino. On the 9th of June [1311], at midday, the Sienese carried the altarpiece in great devotion to the cathedral in a procession, which included Bishop Roger of Casole, the entire clergy of the cathedral, all monks and nuns of the city, and the Nine Gentlemen [Nove] and officials of the city such as the podestà and the captain, and all the people. One by one the worthiest, with lighted candles in their hands, took their places near the altarpiece. Behind them came women and children with great devotion. They accompanied the painting up to the cathedral, walking in procession around the Campo, while all the bells rang joyfully. All the shops were closed out of devotion, all through Siena many alms were given to the poor with many speeches and prayers to God and to his Holy Mother, that she might help to preserve and increase the peace and well being of the city and its jurisdiction, as she was the advocate and protection of said city, and deliver it from all danger and wickedness directed against it. In this way the said altarpiece was taken into the cathedral and placed on the main altar. The altarpiece is painted on the back with scenes from the Old Testament and the Passion of Jesus Christ and in front with the Virgin Mary and her Son in her arms and many saints at the sides, the whole decorated with fine gold. The altarpiece cost 3000 gold florins.

Source: Teresa G. Frisch, *Gothic Art 1140–c 1450* (Englewood Cliffs, NJ: Prentice Hall, 1971)

Campo, where the city's economic, political, religious, and social life was played out. Both the timing and the character of the Palazzo Pubblico point to the city's rivalry with Florence, which was then building the Palazzo della Signoria. Built of brick and stone, Siena's Palazzo Pubblico rises to three stories and supports a tower, as does Florence's Palazzo. It also terminates in castlelike battlements at the roofline. But it has many more windows and other openings, and a more ornamental and elegant façade. The tower, not completed until the 1340s, is intentionally taller than that of the Palazzo della Signoria.

The city also concerned itself with adorning its cathedral, dedicated to the Virgin. For the high altar of the cathedral the directors of the cathedral works hired Duccio to paint a large altarpiece, called the *Maestà* as it depicts the Virgin and Child in Majesty (fig. **13.22**). Commissioned in 1308, the *Maestà* was installed in the cathedral in 1311 amidst processions and celebrations in the city. (See *Primary Source*, above, and *The Art Historian's Lens*, page 455.) Duccio's signature at the base of the throne expresses his pride in the work: "Holy Mother of God, be the cause of peace to Siena, and of life to Duccio because he has painted you thus."

Painted in tempera, Duccio's image measures approximately 7 by 13 feet without its architectural frame and many subsidiary elements. It takes the shape of a **polyptych**, or multipaneled work. The regal figures of the Virgin and Child in the *Maestà* sit on a complex throne draped in golden cloth. The Virgin is by far the largest and most impressive figure in this assembly, swathed in the rich blue reserved for her by contemporary practice. Surrounding her is a carefully balanced arrangement of saints and angels, each bearing a golden halo. In the front row kneel Siena's other patron saints, all gesturing and gazing at her. The Virgin may seem much like Cimabue's (see fig. 13.16) which Duccio probably knew, as both originated in the Greek manner.

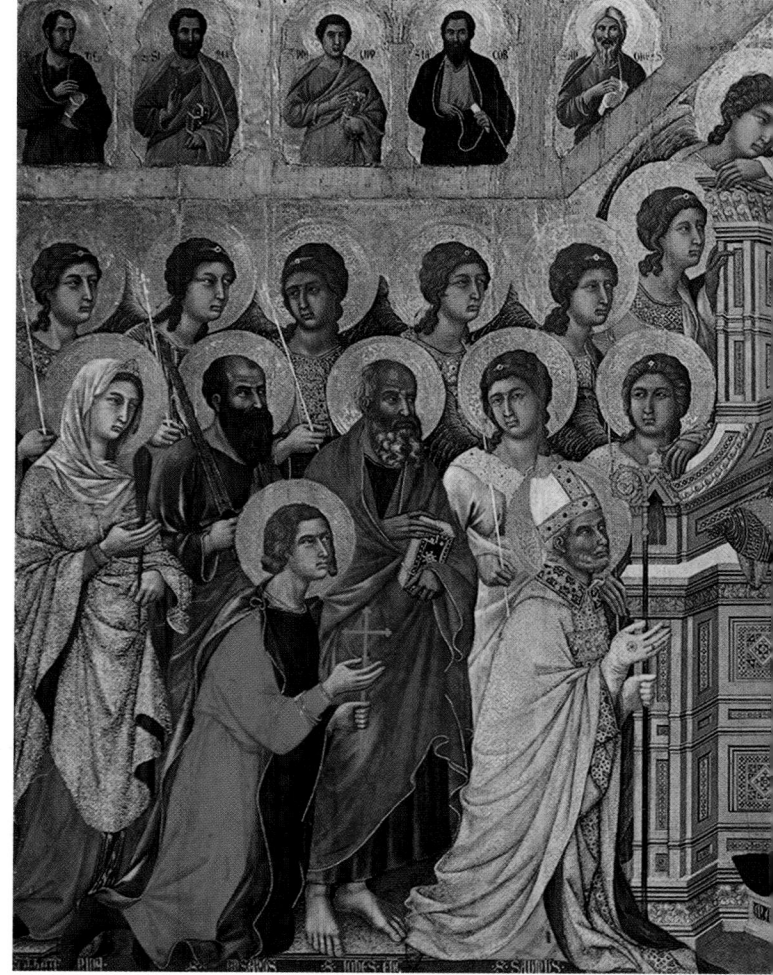

Duccio, however, relaxes the rigid, angular draperies of that tradition so that they give way to an undulating softness. The bodies, faces, and hands of the many figures seem to swell with three-dimensional life as the painter explores the fall of light on their

The Social Work of Images

The report of the celebrations held in Siena when Duccio's *Maestà* was installed in the city's cathedral attests to the importance of this painting for the entire community. It was a source of pride for the citizens of Siena, but also a powerful embodiment of the Virgin's protection of the city. Although modern audiences expect to find and react to works of art hanging in museums, art historians have demonstrated that art served different purposes in late medieval Europe. Few in the West today believe that a work of art can influence events or change lives. But in fourteenth-century Europe, people thought about images in much more active terms. Art could be a path to the sacred or a helper in times of trouble.

During a drought in 1354, for example, the city fathers of Florence paraded a miracle-working image of the Virgin from the village of Impruneta through the city in hopes of improving the weather. People with illness or health problems venerated a fresco of the Annunciation in the church of the Santissima Annunziata in Florence; they gave gifts to the image in hopes of respite from their problems. When the plague came to Florence, artists were commissioned to paint scenes depicting St. Sebastian and other saints who were considered protectors against this deadly disease.

Images were also called upon for help outside the sacred space of the church. Continuing a tradition begun in the fourteenth century, street corners in Italy are often adorned with images of the Virgin, to whom passersby may pray or show respect. Candles may be lit or gifts offered to such images in hopes of the Virgin's assistance. Art historians are also studying how works of art functioned among late medieval populations to forge bonds among social groups and encourage group identity. For example, outside the confines of monasteries, groups of citizens formed social organizations that were dedicated to a patron saint, whose image would be an important element of the group's identity.

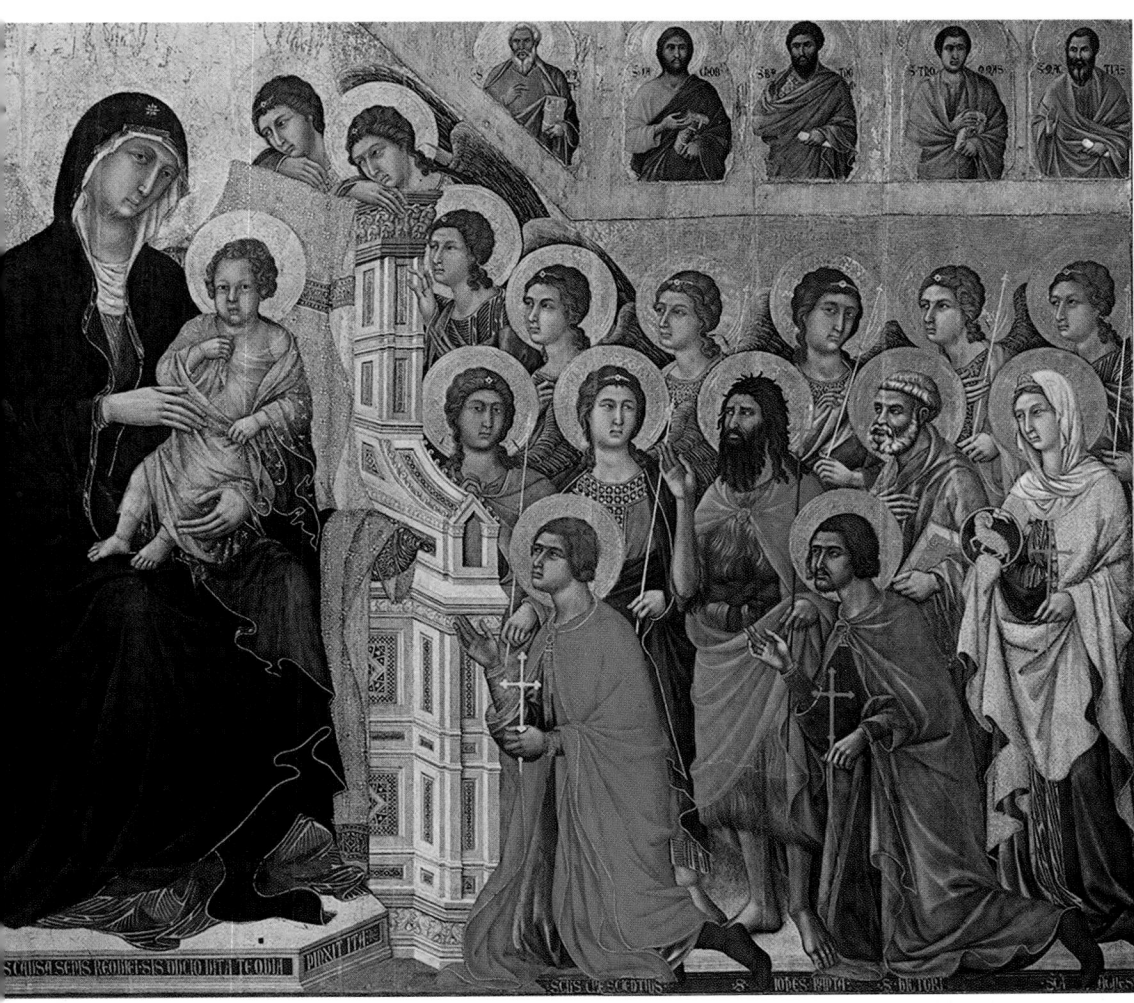

13.22 Duccio, *Madonna Enthroned*, center of the *Maestà Altar*. 1308–11. Tempera on panel, height 6'10½" (2.1 m). Museo dell'Opera del Duomo, Siena

forms. Byzantine painting preserved aspects of ancient illusionism, which inspired Duccio to a profound degree. Nonetheless, Duccio's work also reflects contemporary Gothic sensibilities in the fluidity of the drapery, the appealing naturalness of the figures, and the glances by which the figures communicate with each other. An important source of this Gothic influence was probably Giovanni Pisano, who worked in Siena from 1285 to 1295 as the sculptor-architect in charge of the cathedral façade.

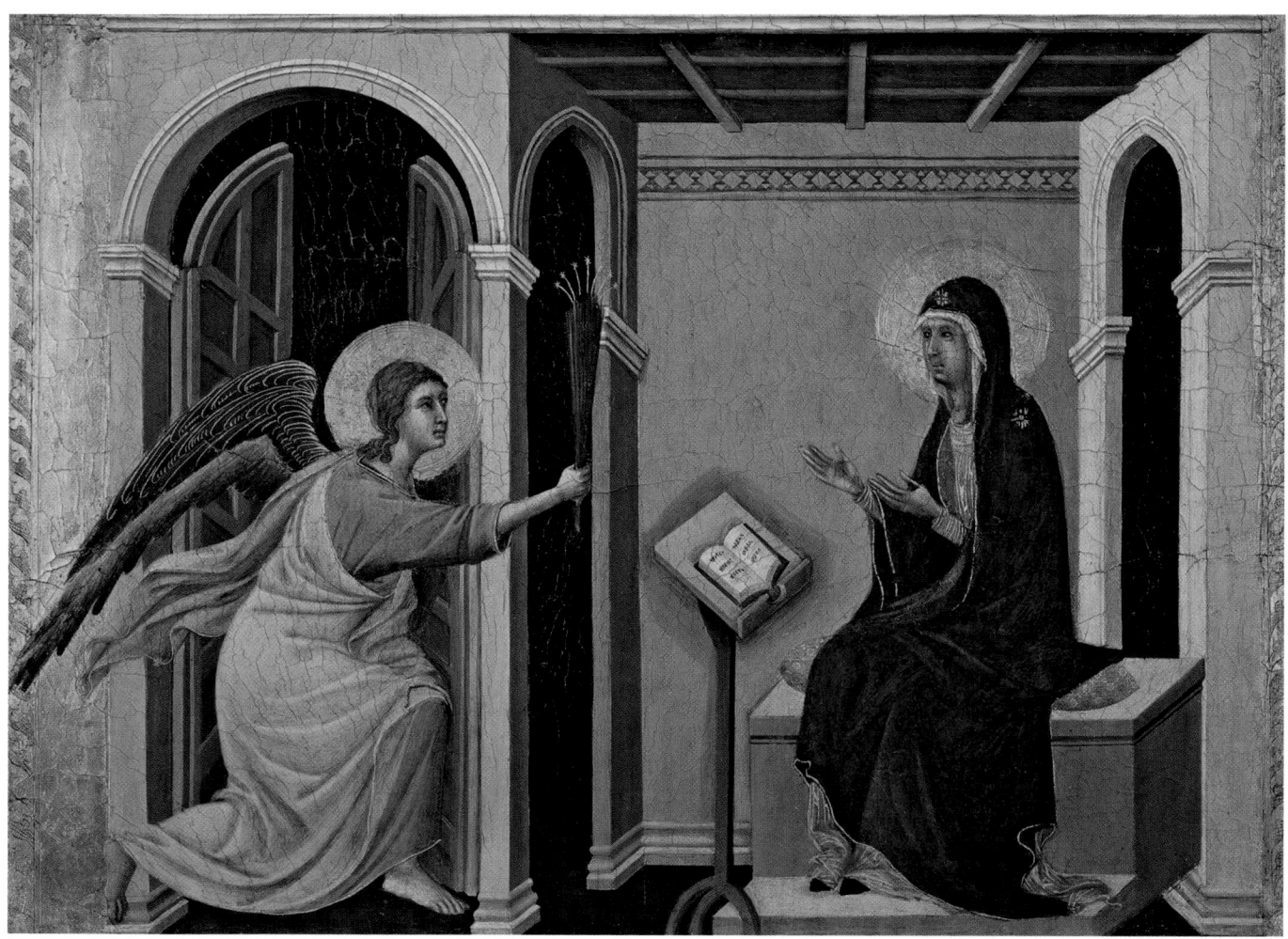

13.23 Duccio, *Annunciation of the Death of the Virgin*, from the *Maestà Altar*. Museo dell'Opera del Duomo, Siena

Some evidence hints that Duccio may have traveled to Paris, where he would have encountered French Gothic style directly.

In addition to the principal scene, the *Maestà* included on its front and back numerous small scenes from the lives of Christ and the Virgin. In these panels, Duccio's synthesis of Gothic and Byzantine elements exploits a new kind of picture space and, with it, a new treatment of narrative. The *Annunciation of the Death of the Virgin* (fig. **13.23**), which originally stood above the main image on the front of the altarpiece, represents two figures enclosed by an architectural interior; Duccio implies space for the figures to inhabit by representing walls and ceiling beams as receding into depth (called **foreshortening**). His architecture integrates the figures within the drama. In a parallel scene to the Annunciation (see fig. 13.25, for comparison), this panel depicts the archangel Gabriel returning to the mature Virgin to warn her of her impending death. The architecture places the two figures in the same uncluttered room, but enframes them separately. Despite sharing the space, each figure is isolated. Duccio's innovative use of architecture to enhance the narrative of his paintings inspired his younger French contemporary, Jean Pucelle, who adapted this composition for the *Annunciation* in the *Hours of Jeanne d'Evreux* (see fig. 12.39).

The architecture keeps its space-creating function even in the outdoor scenes on the back of the *Maestà*, such as in *Christ Entering Jerusalem* (fig. **13.24**), a theme that Giotto had treated only a few years before in Padua. Where Giotto places Christ at the center of two groups of people, Duccio places him closer to the apostles and on one side of the composition. He conveys the diagonal movement into depth not by the figures, who have the same scale throughout, but by the walls on either side of the road leading to the city, by the gate that frames the crowd welcoming Christ, and by the buildings in the background. Where Giotto reduces his treatment of the theme to a few figures and a bare backdrop, Duccio includes not only detailed architectural elements, some of which resemble contemporary Tuscan buildings, but also many figures, including one peering at the crowd in the streets from a first-floor window. Duccio gives a viewer a more complete description of the event than Giotto, whose work stresses the doctrinal and psychological import of the moment. The goals of the two painters differ, and so do the formal means they use to achieve them.

Duccio trained the next generation of painters in Siena. One distinguished disciple was Simone Martini (ca. 1284–1344), who also worked in Assisi but spent the last years of his life in

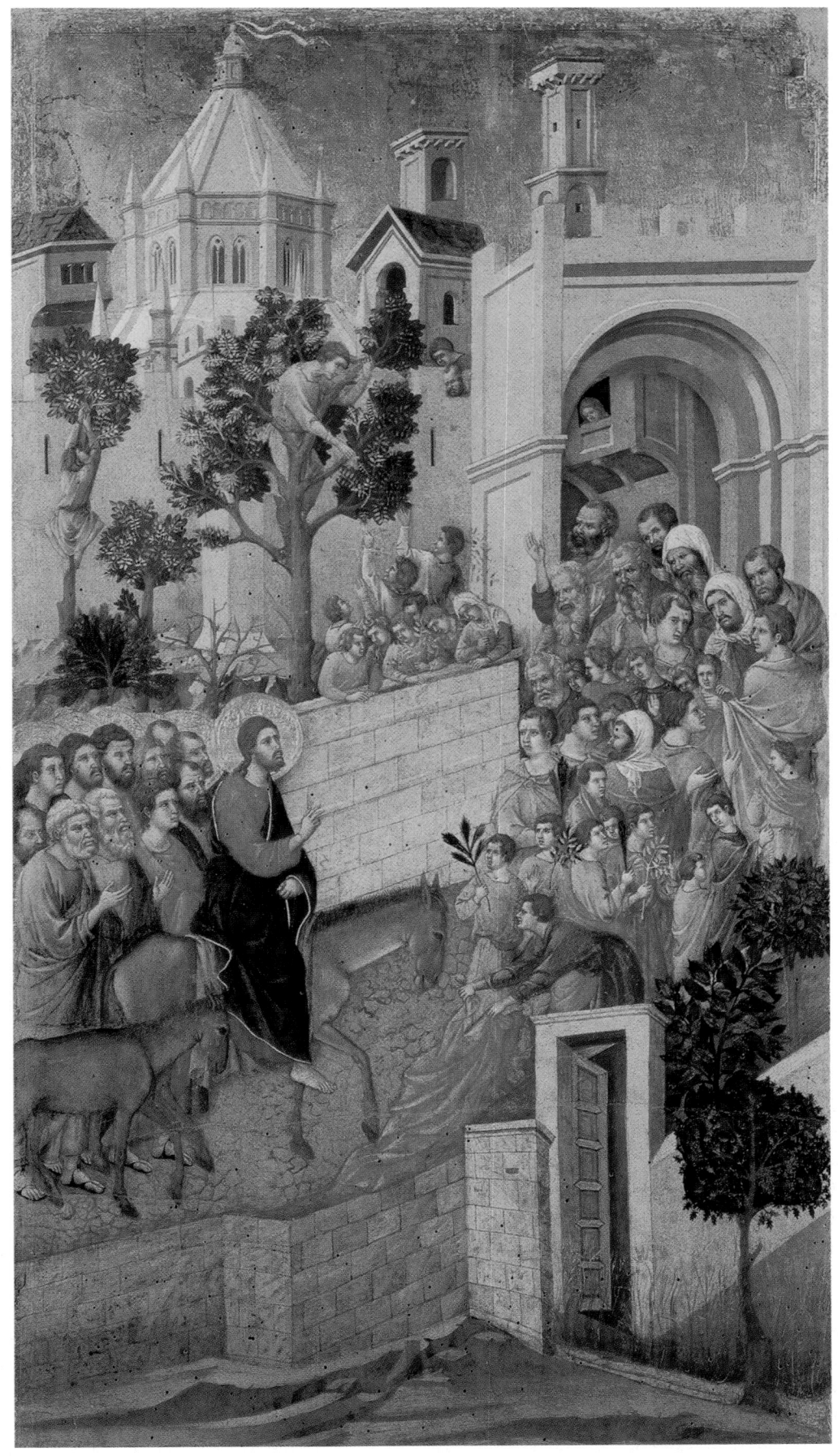

13.24 Duccio, *Christ Entering Jerusalem*, from the back of the *Maestà Altar*. 1308–11.
Tempera on panel, 40½ × 21⅛" (103 × 53.7 cm). Museo dell'Opera del Duomo, Siena

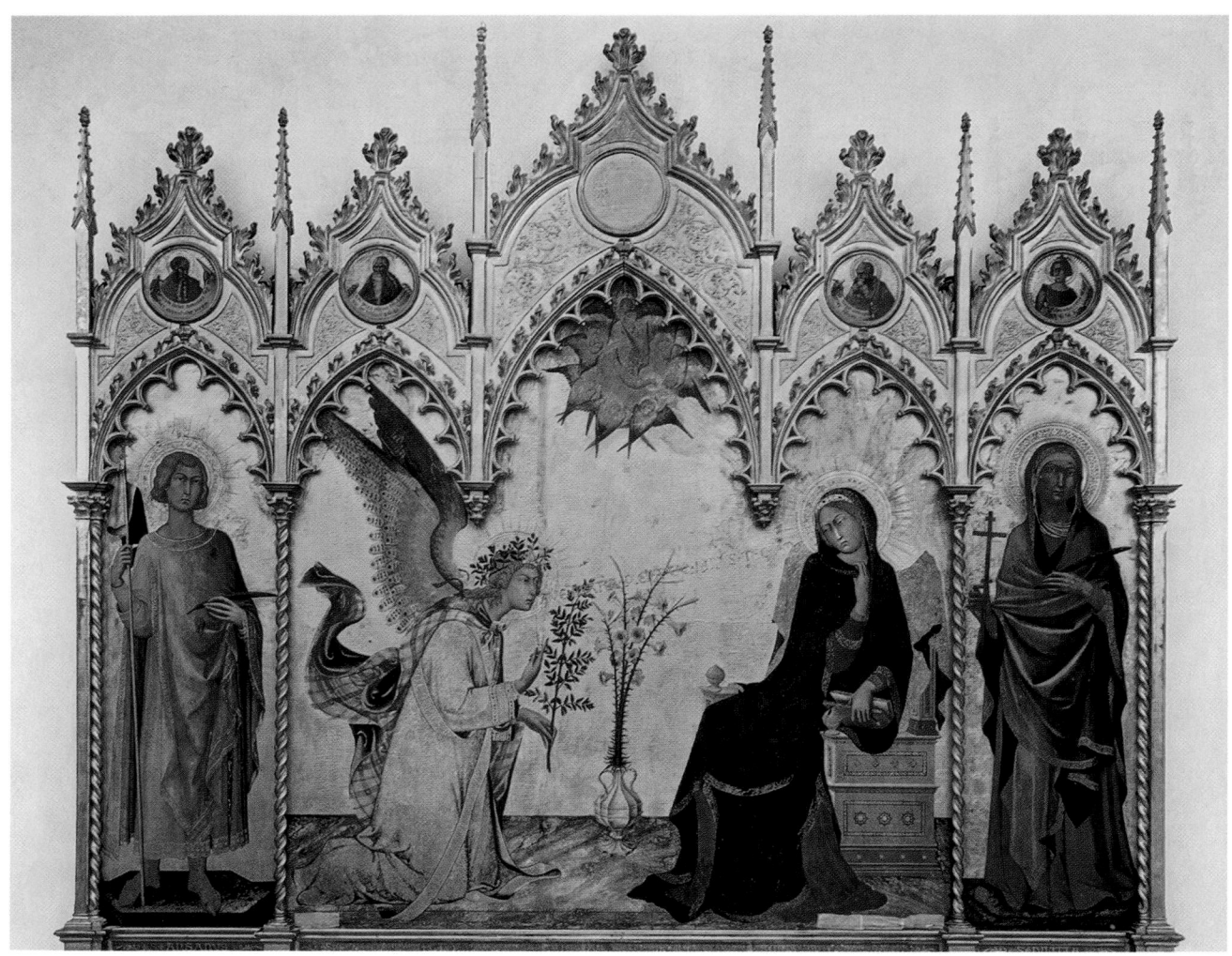

13.25   Simone Martini, *Annunciation*. ca. 1330. Tempera on panel, 10' × 8'9" (3 × 2.7 m). Galleria degli Uffizi, Florence

Avignon, the town in southern France that served as the residence of the popes during most of the fourteenth century. In 1333, the directors of Siena cathedral commissioned Simone to make another altarpiece to complement Duccio's *Maestà*. His *Annunciation* (fig. **13.25**) in its restored cusped and gilded frame hints at what has been lost in the dismemberment of Duccio's *Maestà*, which had a complex Gothic frame. Simone's altarpiece, in the form of a **triptych** or three-part structure, depicts the Annunciation flanked by two local saints set against a brilliant gold ground. To connect her visually to the *Maestà*, Simone's Virgin sits in a similar cloth-covered throne and wears similar garments.

In Simone's picture, the angel Gabriel approaches Mary from the left to pronounce the words *"Ave Maria gratia plena Dominus tecum"* ("Hail Mary, full of grace, the Lord is with you"). These words are familiar to believers as a popular prayer. Simone renders the words in relief on the surface of this painting, covering them in the same gold leaf that transforms the scene into a heavenly vision. Details like the marble floor, the lilies symbolic of purity, and the sumptuous garment worn by the angel add to the richness of the image. Simone adds an element of doubt to the narrative, as the Virgin responds to her visitor with surprise and

pulls away from him. The dove of the Holy Spirit flies toward her in anticipation of her momentous acceptance of her role as the mother of Jesus, thereby beginning the process of Salvation. Like Giotto, Simone has reduced the narrative to its simplest terms, but like Duccio, his figures have a lyrical elegance that lifts them out of the ordinary and into the realm of the spiritual.

Pietro and Ambrogio Lorenzetti

Another altarpiece commissioned for the cathedral at Siena takes a more down-to-earth approach to representing the life of the Virgin. This is the *Birth of the Virgin* (fig. **13.26**) painted in 1342 by Pietro Lorenzetti (active ca. 1306–1348). Pietro and his brother Ambrogio (active ca. 1317–1348), learned their craft in Siena in Duccio's workshop, though their work also shows the influence of Giotto. Pietro has been linked to work at Assisi, and Ambrogio enrolled in the painters' **guild** of Florence in the 1330s. Like Simone's, Pietro's altarpiece is a triptych, though it has lost its original frame. In this triptych, Pietro has related the painted architecture to the real architecture of the frame so closely that the two are seen as a single system. Moreover, the vaulted room

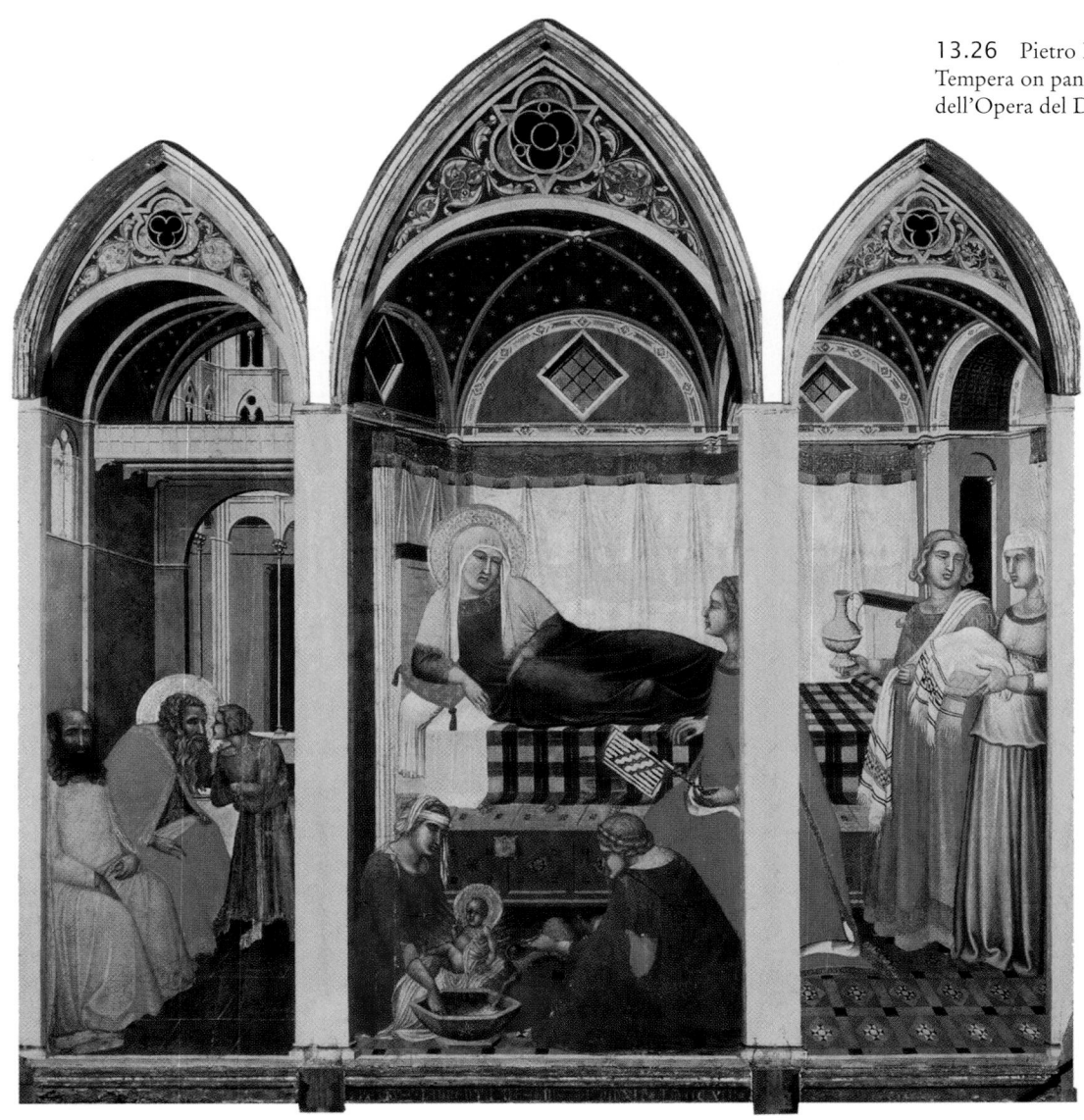

where the birth takes place occupies two panels and continues unbroken behind the column that divides the center from the right wing. The left wing represents a small chamber which opens onto a Gothic façade. Pietro's achievement of spatial illusion here is the outcome of a development that began three decades earlier in the work of Giotto and Duccio. Pietro treats the painting surface like a transparent window *through* which—not *on* which—a viewer experiences a space comparable to the real world. Pietro uses the architecture in his painting to carve out boxes of space that his figures appear to inhabit, but he is also inspired by Giotto's technique of giving his figures such mass and weight that they seem to create their own space. His innovation served the narrative and liturgical needs of Siena cathedral by depicting another key moment in the life of the Virgin, her birth, which was also an important feast day in the Church. St. Anne rests in her childbed, while midwives attend the newborn Virgin and other women tend to the mother. The figure of the midwife pouring water for the baby's bath seems to derive from the figure seen from the back in Giotto's *Lamentation* (see fig. 13.20). The father, Joachim, waits for a report of the birth outside the room.

GOOD AND BAD GOVERNMENT Pietro's brother, Ambrogio Lorenzetti, combined these same influences in a major project for the Palazzo Pubblico, executed between 1338 and 1340. The ruling Council of Nine commissioned several local artists to adorn the building, including Simone Martini. For their council room, they hired Ambrogio to paint an **allegory**, or moralizing narrative, contrasting good and bad government. In the room where the council deliberated, these frescoes aimed to inspire its members to achieve good government. Although the negative example of the effects of Bad Government has been severely damaged, the frescoes that depict the positive example of Good Government are remarkably well preserved (fig. **13.27**). On the short wall of the room, Ambrogio depicted the *Allegory of Good Government* as an assembly of figures personifying virtues who flank the large enthroned figure of the Common Good. To the left, another enthroned figure personifies Justice, who is inspired by Wisdom. Below the virtues stand 24 members of the Sienese judiciary under the guidance of the personification of Concord.

On the long wall, the fresco of *Good Government in the City* (fig. **13.28**) bears an inscription praising Justice and the many

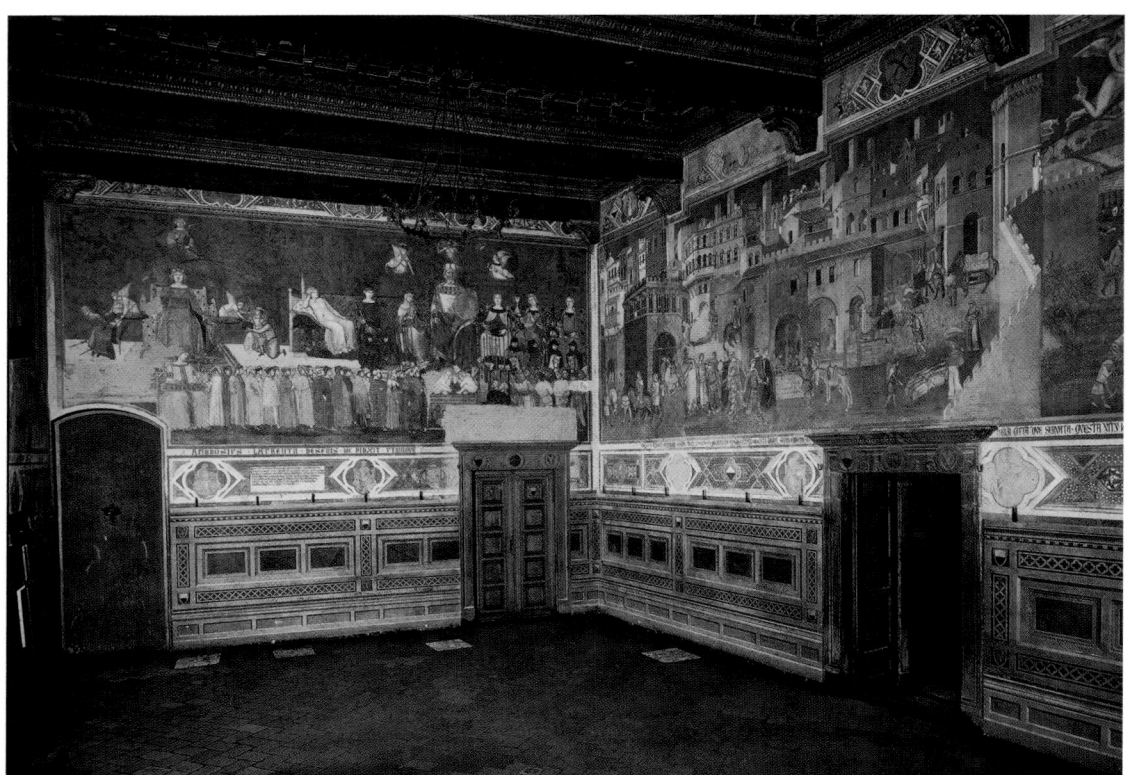

13.27 Ambrogio Lorenzetti, *Allegory of Good Government* (left). *Good Government in the City* (right), and portion of *Good Government in the Country* (far right), Sala della Pace, Palazzo Pubblico, Siena. 1338–40. Fresco

benefits that derive from her. (See *Primary Source*, page 461.) In this fresco, Ambrogio renders an architectural portrait of Siena. To show the life of a well-ordered city-state, the artist fills the streets and houses with activity. Within the city, merchants do business, teachers conduct classes, buildings go up, and the streets teem with people. On the right, outside the city walls, *Good*

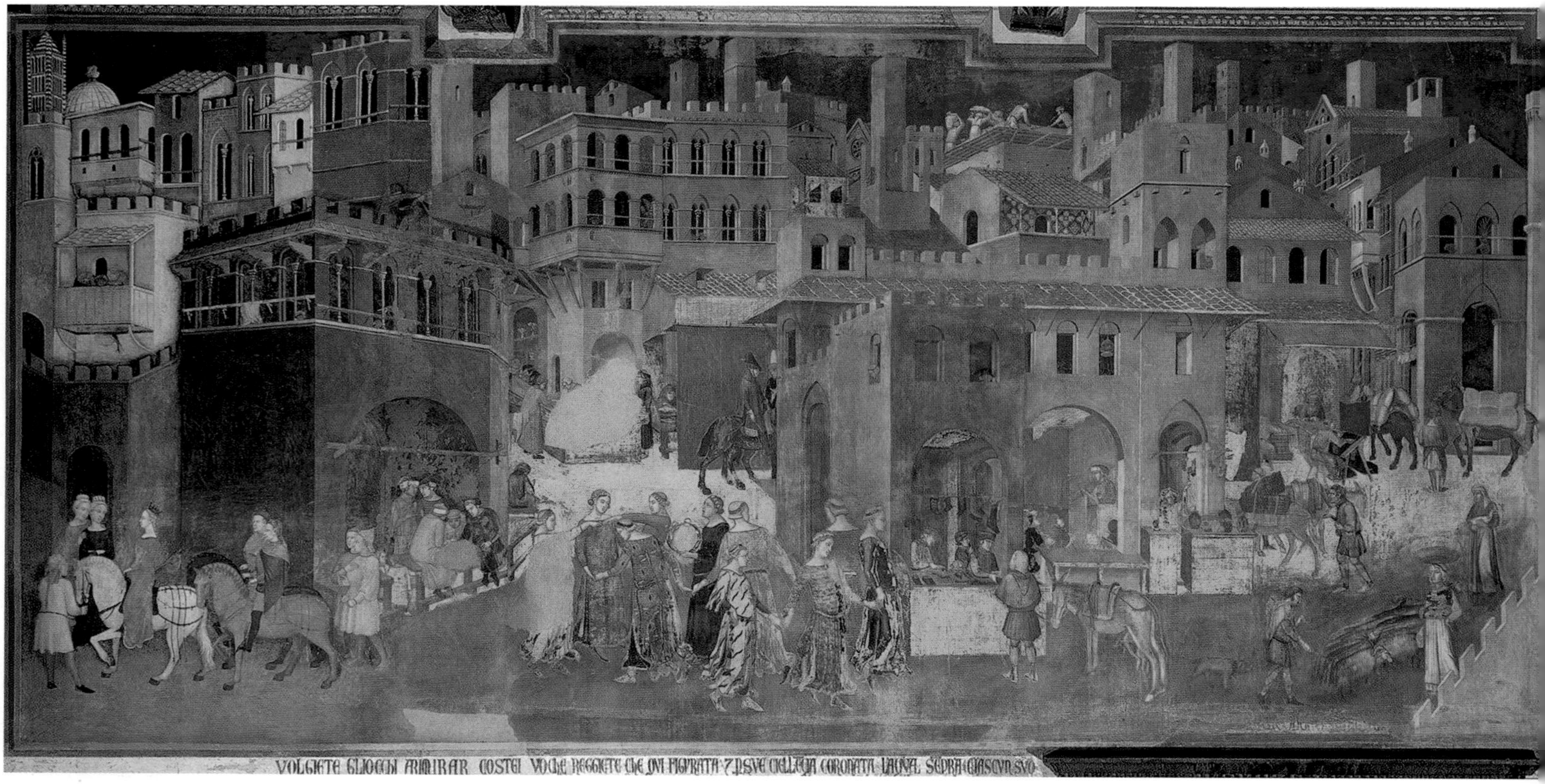

13.28 Ambrogio Lorenzetti, *Good Government in the City*

Inscriptions on the Frescoes in the Palazzo Pubblico, Siena

The first inscription is painted in a strip below the fresco of Good Government (see figs. 13.27 and 13.28), which is dated between 1338 and 1340. The second is held by the personification of Security, who hovers over the landscape in figure 13.29.

Turn your eyes to behold her,
you who are governing, [Justice] who is portrayed here,
crowned on account of her excellence,
who always renders to everyone his due.
Look how many goods derive from her
and how sweet and peaceful is that life

of the city where is preserved
this virtue who outshines any other.
She guards and defends
those who honor her, and nourishes and feeds them.
From her light is born
Requiting those who do good
and giving due punishment to the wicked.

Without fear every man may travel freely
and each may till and sow,
so long as this commune
shall maintain this lady [Justice] sovereign,
for she has stripped the wicked of all power.

Source: Randolph Starn and Loren Partridge, *Arts of Power: Three Halls of State in Italy, 1300–1600* (Berkeley: University of California Press, 1992)

Government in the Country provides a view of the Sienese farmland, fringed by distant mountains (fig. **13.29**) and overseen by a personification of Security. It is a true landscape—the first since ancient Roman times (see fig. 7.55). It represents a sweeping view of the orderly hillside: vineyards, farms, and pastures result from a fruitful nature possessed by well-governed humans. Ambrogio observes the peasants at their seasonal labors, which support the life within the city, even as the countryside is safe for travelers, merchants, and pleasure-seekers.

Artists and Patrons in Times of Crisis

Ambrogio's ideal vision of the city and its surroundings reveals how the citizens of Siena imagined their government and their city at a moment of peace and prosperity. The first three decades of the fourteenth century in Siena, as in Florence, were a period of political stability and economic expansion, as well as of great artistic achievement. In the 1340s, however, both cities suffered a series of catastrophes whose effects were to be felt for many years.

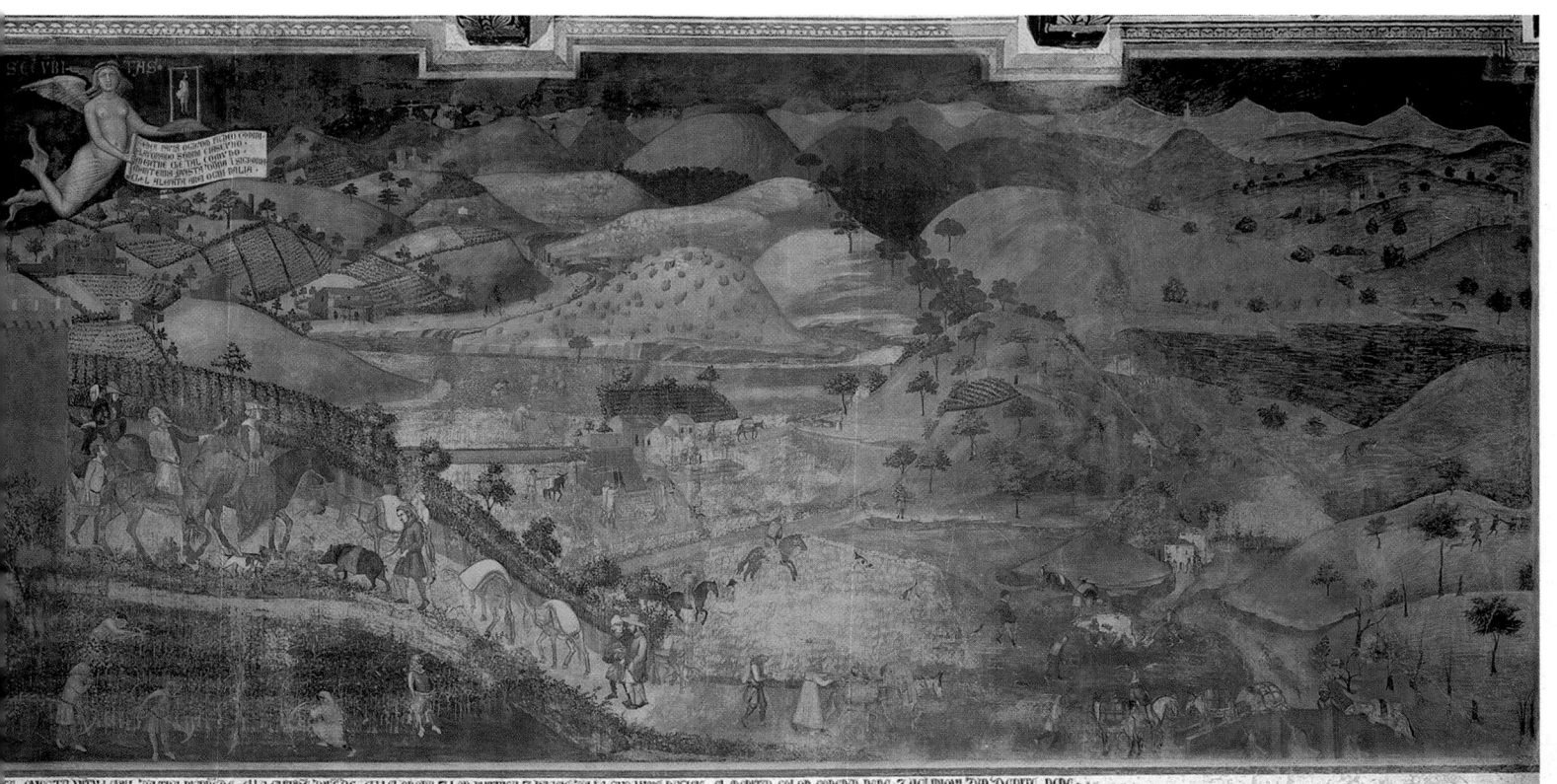

13.29 Ambrogio Lorenzetti, *Good Government in the Country*

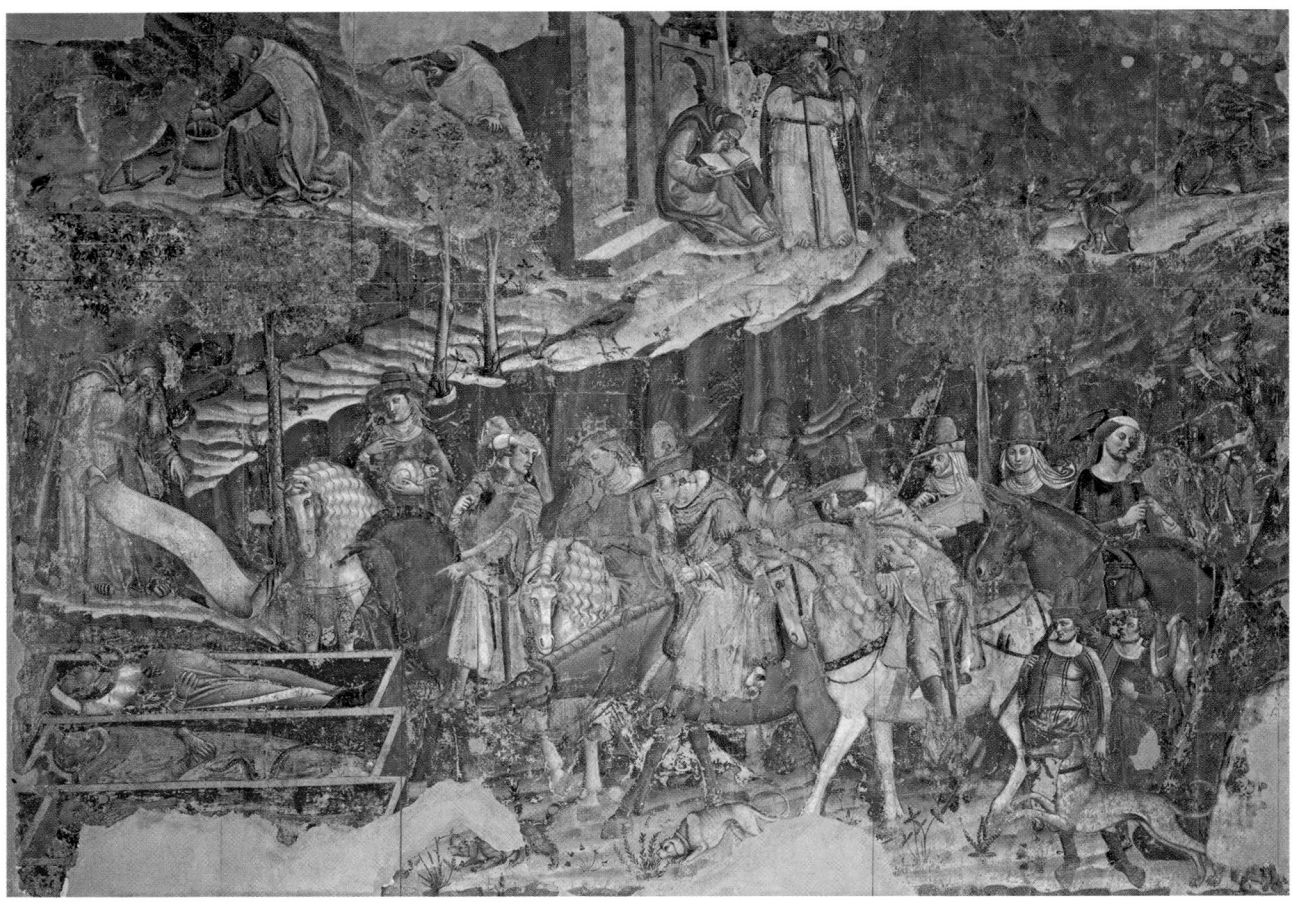

13.30 Anonymous (Francesco Traini ?), *The Triumph of Death* (detail), Camposanto, Pisa. ca. 1325–50. Fresco

Constant warfare pushed scores of banks and merchants into bankruptcy, internal upheavals shook governments, and there were repeated crop failures and famine. Then, in 1348, the pandemic of bubonic plague—the Black Death—that spread throughout Europe wiped out more than half the population of the two cities (see map **13.2**). Flea-infested rats swarmed into cities from the barren countryside in search of food and so spread the disease. Popular reactions to these events were mixed. Many people saw them as signs of divine wrath, warnings to a sinful humanity to forgo the pleasures of this earth. In such people, the Black Death intensified an interest in religion and the promise of heavenly rewards. To others, such as the merry company who entertain each other by telling stories in the Florentine humanist Giovanni Boccaccio's (1313–1375) book the *Decameron*, finished around 1353, the fear of death intensified the desire to enjoy life while there was still time. (See www.myartslab.com.)

Late medieval people were regularly confronted with the inevitability and power of death. A series of frescoes painted on the walls of the Camposanto, the monumental cemetery building next to Pisa cathedral, offers a variety of responses to death. Because of its somber message, these frescoes were once dated after the outbreak of the plague, but recent research has pushed the date closer to the 1330s. The painter is not known, though some scholars attribute the work to a Pisan artist named Francesco Traini (documented ca. 1321–1363). The huge fresco

cycle, which was damaged in 1944 as a result of bombings in World War II, included a powerful *Last Judgment* and an image called *The Triumph of Death*, which asserts that death comes to all, rich or poor, saint or sinner. In a particularly dramatic detail (fig. **13.30**), the elegantly costumed men and women on horseback have suddenly come upon three decaying corpses in open coffins. Even the animals are terrified by the sight and smell of rotting flesh. The hermit St. Macarius, having renounced all earthly pleasures, points out the lesson of the scene. His scroll reads: "If your mind be well aware, keeping here your view attentive, your vainglory will be vanquished and you will see pride eliminated. And, again, you will realize this if you observe that which is written." As the hermits in the hills above make clear, the way to salvation is through renunciation of the world in favor of the spiritual life. The artist's style recalls the realism of Ambrogio Lorenzetti, although the forms are harsher and more expressive.

It is likely that the Lorenzetti brothers perished in the Black Death of 1348–49, along with thousands of other people throughout Tuscany. Scholars have studied the impact of the plague on artists and patrons of works of art in the second half of the fourteenth century to determine its effect on style and subject matter. We can assume that many painters died, so the number of artists probably diminished. Documentary research reveals that the number of endowed chapels, tombs, and funeral masses rose as people worried about their mortality. Many such burials and endowments were made in mendicant churches, such as the Franciscan Santa Croce and the Dominican Santa Maria Novella in Florence.

At Santa Maria Novella, a Florentine merchant named Buonamico Guidalotti, who died in 1355, provided funds in his will for a new chapterhouse for the Dominican community in which he could be buried. The chapel served as a meeting room for the friars and as such was painted with frescoes expressing the role of Dominicans in the struggle for salvation. A fresco on one of the walls of the Guidalotti Chapel, painted by Andrea Bonaiuti (also known as Andrea da Firenze, active 1346–1379) between 1365 and 1367, depicts the actions of Dominicans to assure the access of the faithful to Heaven, hence its title: *The Way of Salvation* (fig. **13.31**). In the lower section of the fresco, spiritual and temporal leaders gather before a representation of the then-unfinished cathedral of Florence. The fresco depicts a model of the church rather than its actual state of construction. Groups of Dominicans preach to the laity and convert heretics amidst black and white dogs (a punning reference to the order—the *Domini canes*, or the dogs of the Lord). On the upper right, some heedless aristocrats enjoy the pleasures of the senses, while at the center, a Dominican shows the more spiritually minded the path to Heaven, whose gate is guarded by St. Peter. Andrea's fresco reveals the influence both of Ambrogio Lorenzetti's *Allegory of Good Government* (see fig. 13.27) and the fresco on the walls of the cemetery near Pisa cathedral (see fig. 13.30). Nonetheless, the fresco's symmetry and the sense of order reveal a didactic function: It seeks legibility rather than illusion, and serenity rather than emotion.

Florence, however, did not complete its cathedral in the fourteenth century, and it was not to enjoy the calm atmosphere portrayed in Andrea's fresco. The plague returned in 1363, the political elite clashed with the papacy, and an uprising among the working classes created social and economic turmoil. The wealthier classes restored their power in 1381. Florence overcame these disasters to flourish in the fifteenth century as a center of economic energy, political astuteness, and cultural leadership. As the fifteenth century began, a new generation of Florentine artists would look to the art of Giotto and his contemporaries in their search for new forms of visual expression.

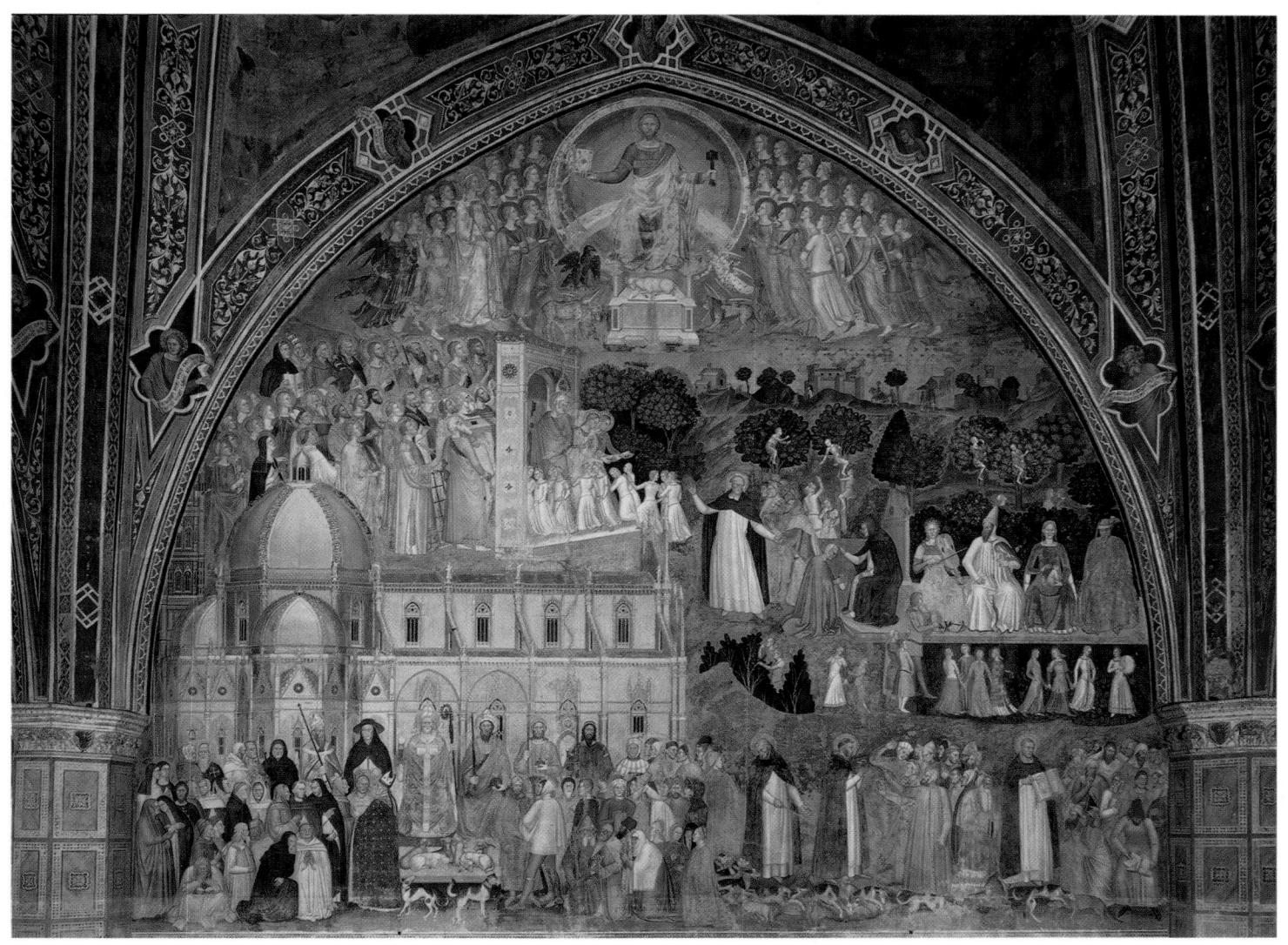

13.31 Andrea da Firenze, *The Way of Salvation*, Guidalotti Chapel, Santa Maria Novella, Florence. 1365–67. Fresco, width 38' (11.6 m)

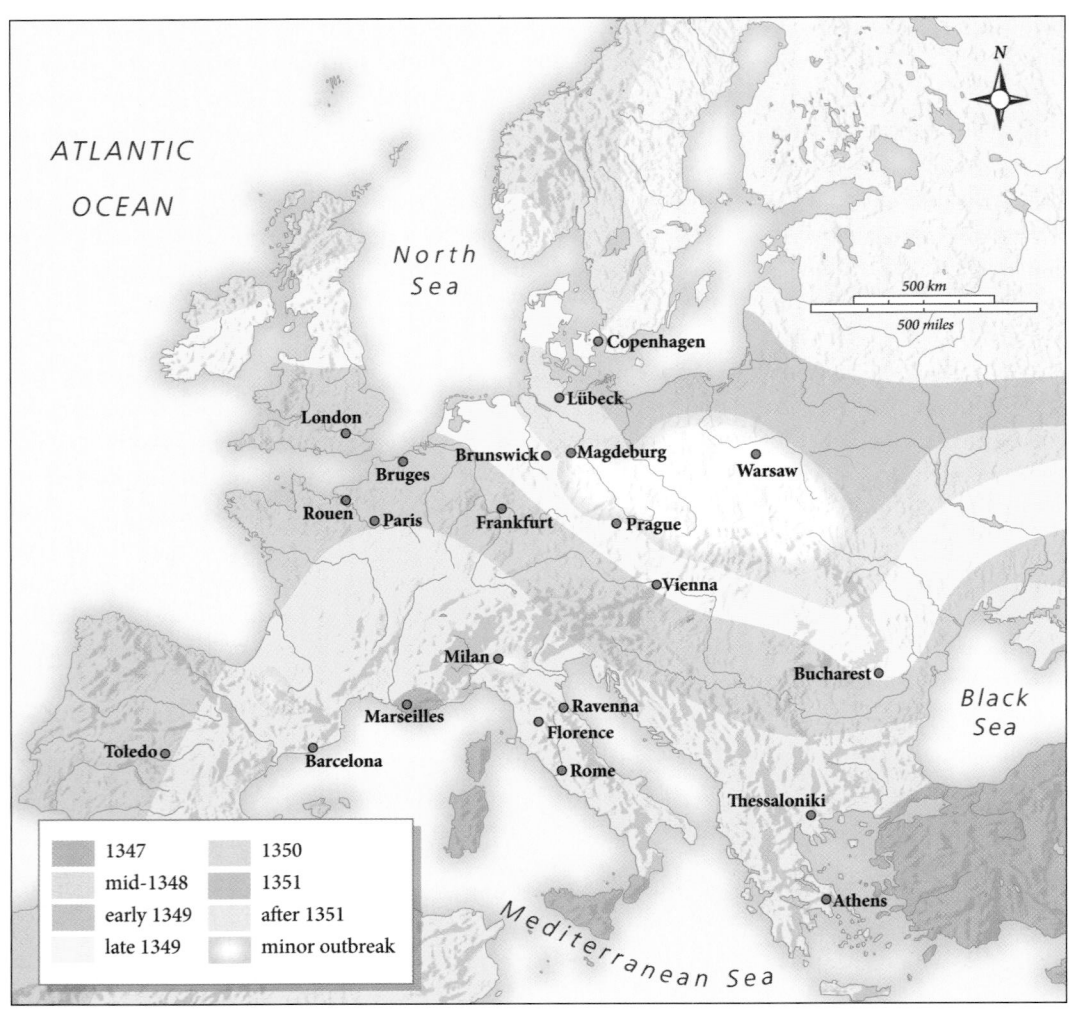

Map 13.2 The Bubonic Plague spreads across Europe, 1347–1351

ATLANTIC OCEAN

North Sea

Copenhagen
Lübeck
London
Brunswick · Magdeburg
Bruges · Warsaw
Rouen · Paris
Frankfurt · Prague
Vienna
Milan
Bucharest
Black Sea
Marseilles · Ravenna
Florence
Toledo · Barcelona
Rome
Thessaloniki
Mediterranean Sea
Athens

500 km
500 miles

N

1347		1350	
mid-1348		1351	
early 1349		after 1351	
late 1349		minor outbreak	

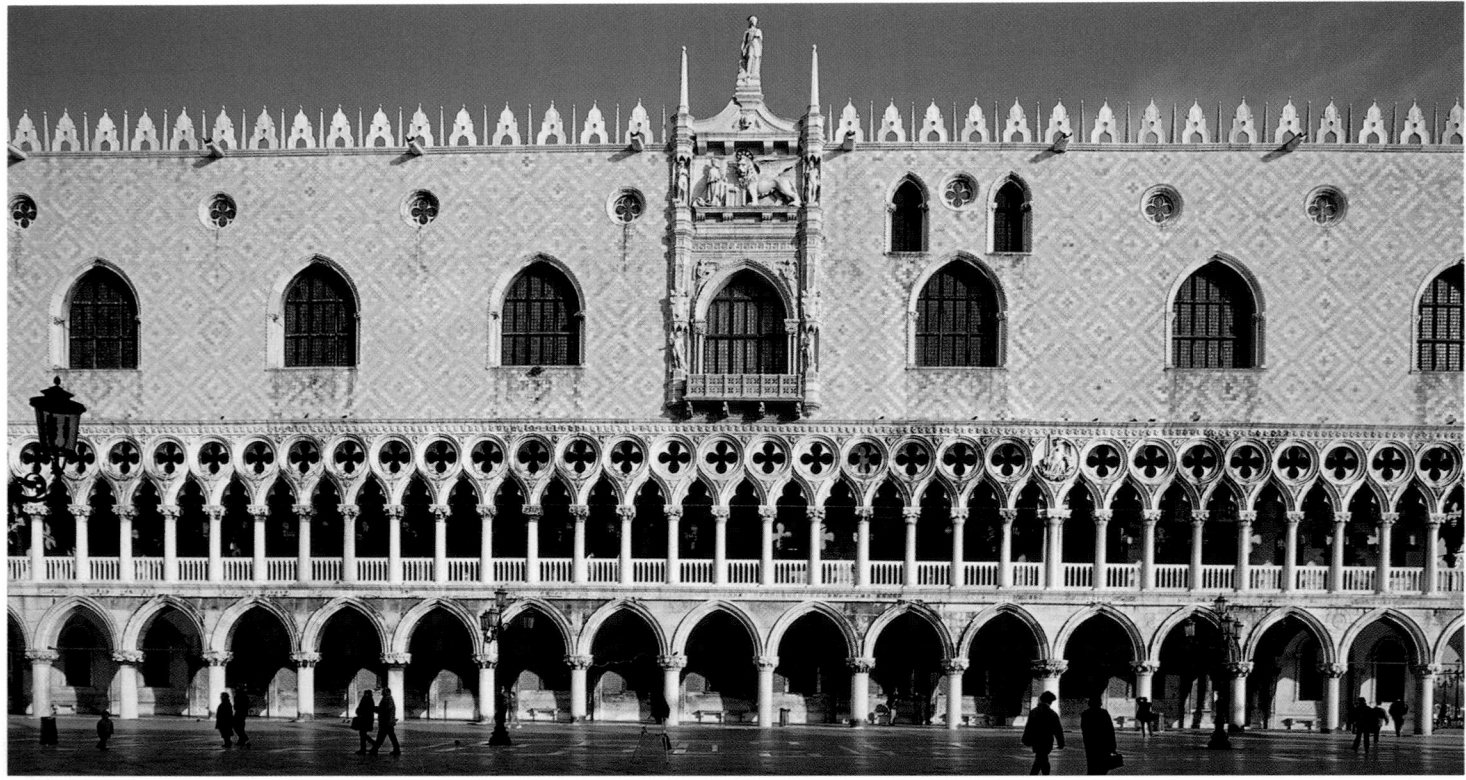

13.32 Doge's Palace, Venice. Begun 1340

NORTHERN ITALY

Political struggles did not disturb Venice in the fourteenth century. Unlike Florence, which was riven by warring factions, the city enjoyed political stability. Since 1297, it had closed off membership in the merchant oligarchy that participated in government, and the city's leader (the Doge) was elected from this group. This created a stable social climate, so neither Venetian palaces nor their communal buildings required the defensive architecture seen in Florentine structures such as the Palazzo della Signoria (see fig. 13.15). A somewhat different atmosphere existed in Milan, west of Venice in Lombardy, where a monarchical government lay in the hands of a single family with great dynastic ambitions. In Lombardy, the main political and cultural connections were with northern Europe, which had important results for the type and the style of art produced there.

Venice: Political Stability and Sumptuous Architecture

The differing political situations in Florence and Venice affected palace design. Whereas the Florentine palace was solid and impenetrable, the Venetian equivalent is airy and open, full of windows and arcades that are anything but defensible. Venetian architects borrowed from Gothic, Byzantine, and Islamic precedents in an elegant display of the city's wealth and security. When a larger meeting space was needed for the Great Council, the city decided to enlarge the Doge's Palace near St. Mark's cathedral in 1340 (fig. 13.32). Work continued here until the mid-fifteenth century. In contrast to the fortresslike Palazzo della Signoria in Florence, the Doge's Palace is open at the base, the weight of its upper stories resting on two stories of pointed arcades. The lower arcade provides a covered passageway around the building, the upper a balcony. The lavish moldings and the quatrefoils of the arcades give the structure an ornamentality accented by the doubling of the rhythm in the upper arcade. The walls of the structure are ornamented with stonework in a diamond pattern, making them both visually lighter and more ornate.

Milan: The Visconti Family and Northern Influences

Lombardy had a different political structure and a closer relationship with Gothic France, which found expression in its visual arts. The Visconti family had acquired great wealth from the products of this richly agricultural region. Besides controlling Lombardy, the Visconti positioned themselves among the great families of Europe through marriage ties to members of the Italian and European nobility. By 1395, Giangaleazzo Visconti had been named duke of Milan, had married the daughter of the king of France, and had wed his daughter to the French king's brother, Louis, duke of Orleans.

The authoritarian nature of Visconti rule in Milan may be seen in the tomb of Giangaleazzo's uncle Bernabò Visconti (fig. 13.33).

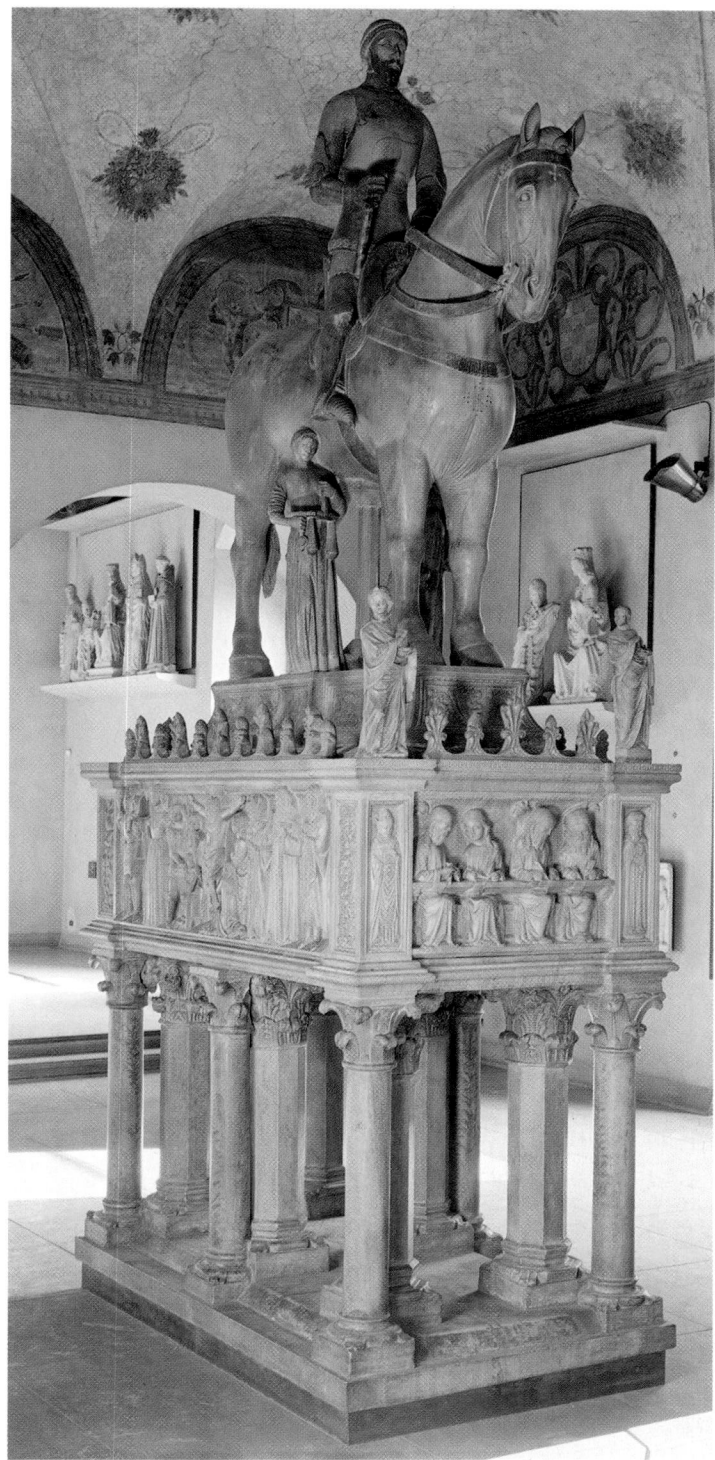

13.33   Tomb of Bernabò Visconti. Before 1363. Marble, 19'8" (6 m). Castello Sforzesco, Milan

Completed around 1363, perhaps by the local sculptor Bonino da Campione (active ca. 1357–1397), the marble structure includes a sarcophagus that supports a sculpted figure of Bernabò on horseback. Though now in a museum, Bernabò's equestrian monument originally stood over the altar of a church in Milan. The figure stands rather than sits on the horse, forcefully commanding the space over the high altar. The idea of the equestrian image of a ruler goes back to antiquity, with the *Equestrian Statue of Marcus Aurelius* (see fig. 7.33) visible in Rome throughout the Middle Ages.

The ruling aristocracy of Europe claimed for themselves the prerogative of equestrian imagery. In this sculpture, Bernabò is rigid and formal in his bearing; originally the figure was covered with silver and gold leaf to further enhance its impressiveness. Yet the treatment of the horse, with its sensitive proportions and realistically observed anatomy, points to a Lombard interest in the natural depiction of form, which may be a result of contact with contemporary French art.

Bernabò's nephew, who deposed him to claim power, used the visual arts as part of his own campaign to be named duke of Milan. Giangaleazzo Visconti encouraged the construction of a new cathedral in Milan in 1386 and commissioned expensive illuminated manuscripts like his French peers. His **Book of Hours** was begun around 1395 by Giovannino dei Grassi (active ca. 1380–1398) and features numerous personal representations and references to the duke. The page in figure **13.34** begins one of the Psalms with an illuminated initial "D" wherein King David appears. David is both the author of the text and a good biblical

exemplar of a ruler. An unfurling ribbon ornamented with the French *fleur-de-lis* forms the "D"; shields at the corners bear the Visconti emblem of the viper. Below the text appears a portrait of Giangaleazzo in the profile arrangement that was familiar from ancient coins. Although the portrait is naturalistic, it is set into an undulating frame that supports the rays of the sun, another Visconti emblem. Around the portrait Giovannino has painted images of stags and a hunting dog, paying great attention to the accurate rendering of these natural forms. Such flashes of realism amidst the splendor of the page reflect both the patrons and the artist's contribution to the developing International Gothic style. Commissioning such lavish books was an expression of the status and power that Giangaleazzo attempted to wield. His ambition to bring most of northern Italy under his control would profoundly affect the arts in Tuscany in the early fifteenth century.

Starting from the local traditions of Italy and the inspiration of Byzantine and French Gothic style, Italian artists of the thirteenth and fourteenth centuries created works of art with pronounced elements of naturalism and featuring increasingly complex imagery. Their accomplishments provided a foundation for the artists of the subsequent century in Italy and the rest of Europe.

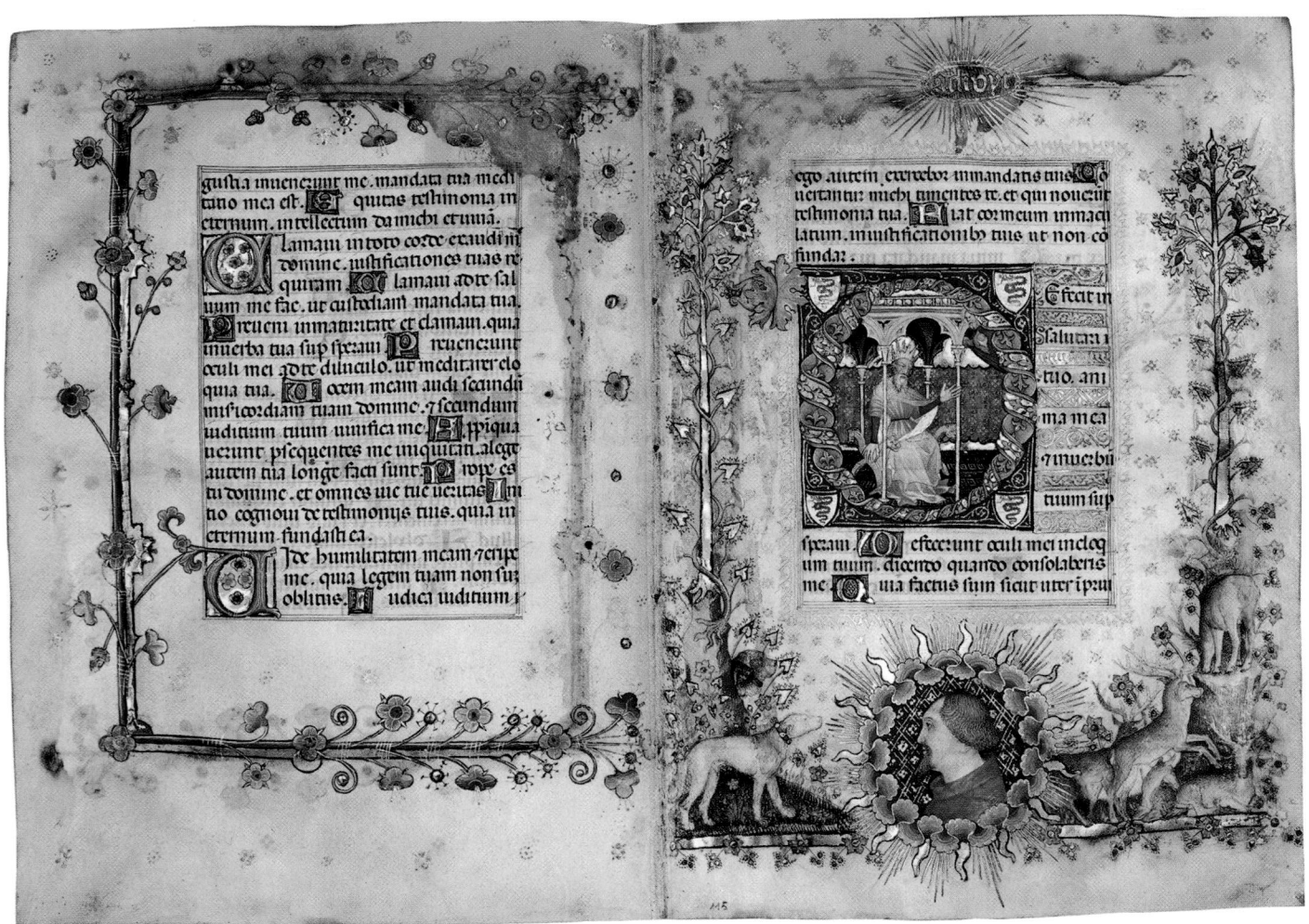

13.34 Giovannino dei Grassi, *Hours of Giangaleazzo Visconti*. ca. 1395. Tempera and gold on parchment, 9¾ × 6⅞" (24.7 × 17.5 cm). Banco Rari, Biblioteca Nazionale, 397 folio 115/H, Florence

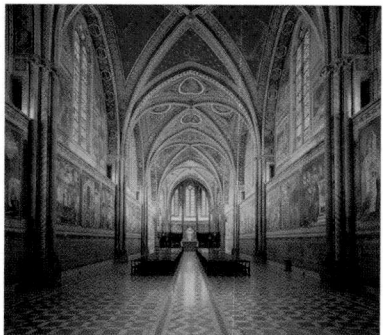

1228 Work begins on San Francesco,
Assisi

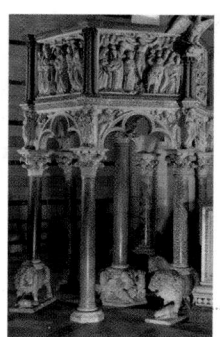

1260 Nicola Pisano's
Pisa pulpit

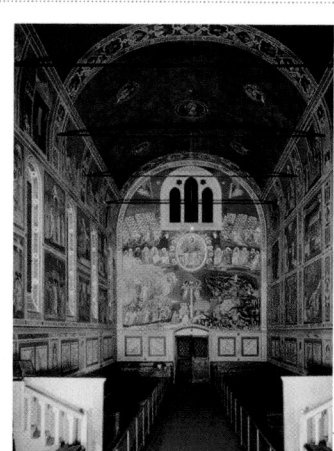

1298 Palazzo della Signoria
begun in Florence

1305 Giotto's Arena Chapel frescoes

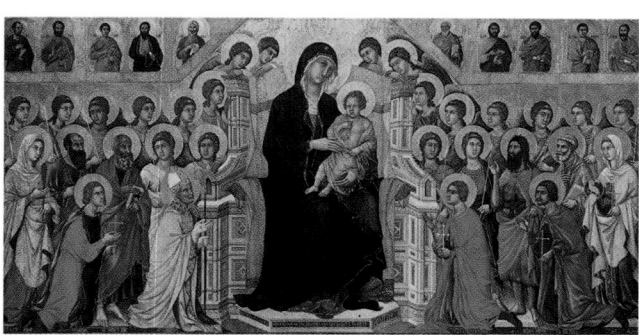

1311 Duccio's *Maestà* completed in Siena

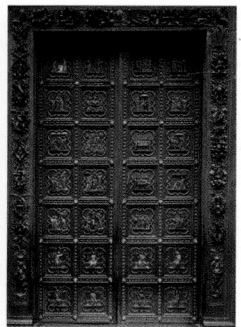

1330 Doors of baptistery
of Florence

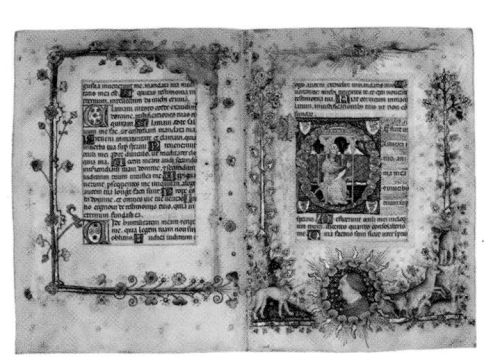

1395 *Hours of Giangaleazzo Visconti*

Art in Thirteenth- and Fourteenth-Century Italy

1200

1225

1250

1275

1300

1325

1350

1375

1400

◄ *1204 Europeans in Fourth Crusade conquer Constantinople*

◄ *1234 Canonization of Dominic de Guzmán*

◄ *1250 Death of Emperor Frederick II*

1262 Saint-Urbain at Troyes begun

◄ *1271–95 Marco Polo travels to China*

1295 Prayer Book of Philip the Fair
◄ *1297 Venetian oligarchy closes ranks*

◄ 1305–78 Papacy in Avignon, France

1310 *Queen Mary Psalter*
ca. 1314 Tomb of Oljeytu, Sultaniya, Iran

1339 *Virgin* of Jeanne d'Évreux
◄ 1347–48 Black Death ravages Europe
1351 Peter Parler adds choir to church of Heiligenkreuz, Schwäbisch-Gmünd, Germany

◄ *1378 Wool workers (Ciompi) revolt in Florence*

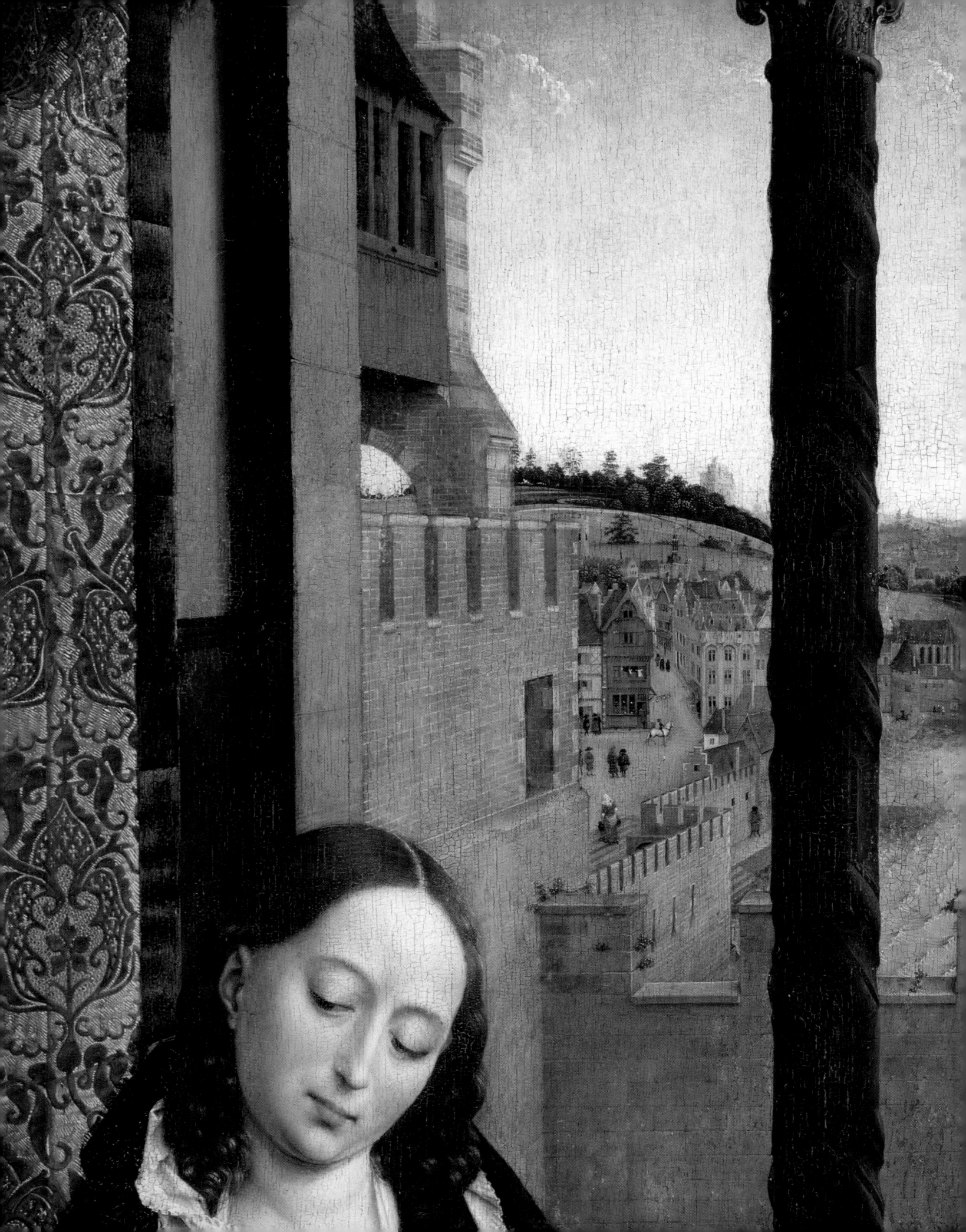

CHAPTER 14

Artistic Innovations in Fifteenth-Century Northern Europe

THE GREAT CATHEDRALS OF EUROPE'S GOTHIC ERA—THE PRODUCTS of collaboration among church officials, rulers, and the laity—were mostly completed by 1400. As monuments of Christian faith, they exemplify the medieval outlook. But cathedrals are also monuments of cities, where major social and economic changes would set the stage for the

modern world. As the fourteenth century came to an end, the medieval agrarian economy was giving way to an economy based on manufacturing and trade, activities that took place in urban centers. A social shift accompanied this economic change. Many city dwellers belonged to the middle classes, whose upper ranks enjoyed literacy, leisure, and disposable income. With these advantages, the middle classes gained greater social and cultural influence than they had wielded in the Middle Ages, when the clergy and aristocracy had dominated. This transformation had a profound effect on European culture, including the development of the visual arts.

Cities such as Paris, London, Prague, Bruges, Barcelona, and Basel were home to artisans, dayworkers, and merchants as well as aristocrats. Urban economies based more on money and wages than landed wealth required bankers, lawyers, and entrepreneurs. Investors seeking new products and markets encouraged technological innovations, such as the printing press, an invention with sweeping consequences. Some cities specialized in manufacturing specific goods, such as tapestries, or working in specific materials, such as metalworking (map **14.1**). The raw materials for such products came from mines or farms from all over Europe, as well as Asia and Africa, following organized trade routes. Trade put more liquid wealth into the hands of merchants and artisans, who

were emboldened to seek more autonomy from the traditional aristocracy, who sought to maintain the feudal status quo.

Two of the most far-reaching changes concerned increased literacy and changes in religious expression. In the fourteenth century, the pope left Rome for Avignon, France, where his successors resided until 1378. On the papacy's return to Rome, however, a faction remained in France and elected their own pope. This created a schism in the Church that only ended in 1417. But the damage to the integrity of the papacy had already been done. Such scandals undermined confidence in the institutional Church, leading many laypeople to turn to religious movements that encouraged them to read sacred texts on their own, to meditate on Scripture, and to seek a personal relationship with God. One such movement was called the Modern Devotion, but mendicant friars and other clerics also encouraged this new lay piety. Although the Church was not wholly comfortable with this phenomenon, the persuasiveness of the preachers supporting it spread the new outlook. These religious impulses and increasing literacy fueled a demand for books in vernacular (local) languages, including translations of Scripture. The printing press made books more available, further stimulating the development and spread of knowledge.

Books and the ideas within them spread easily in an era when political changes brought significant changes to northern Europe whose boundaries now began to resemble those of present-day European nations. The Hundred Years' War between France and

Detail of figure 14.16, Rogier van der Weyden, *St. Luke Drawing the Virgin*

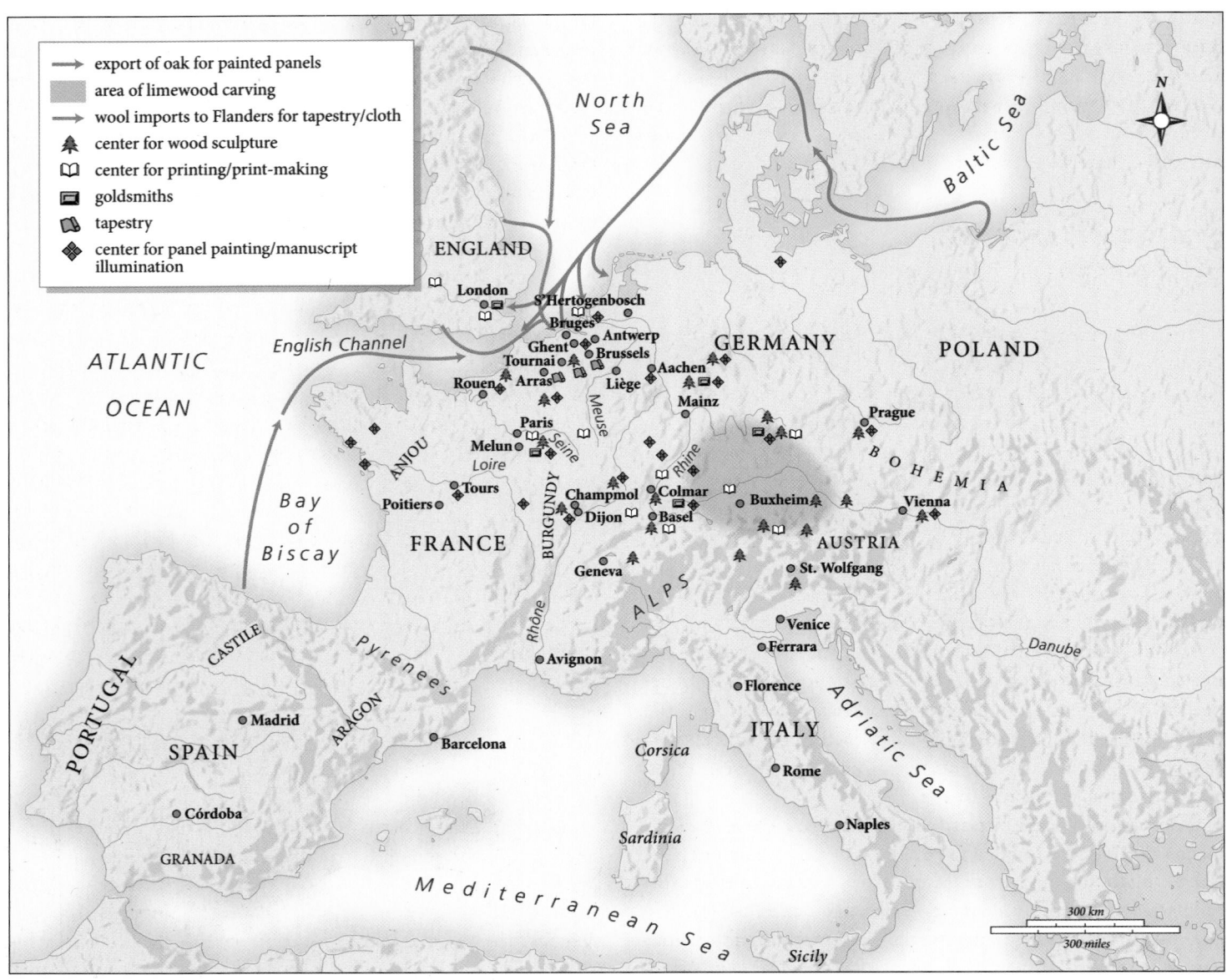

Map 14.1   Craft and manufacturing specialties in Northern Europe in the Early Modern period

England finally ended in 1453. This allowed the French monarchy to recover, but civil war kept England politically unstable until late in the fifteenth century. French kings, however, had to contend with their Burgundian cousins, who controlled the trading hub of northern Europe: the rich lands of Flanders in the southern Netherlands (present-day Belgium) and the northern Netherlands (present-day Holland). Indeed, Duke Philip the Good of Burgundy (r. 1419–1467) was one of the most powerful men of the century.

Duke Philip's son, Charles, wanted to create his own kingdom out of the regions he inherited, a matter on which he unsuccessfully petitioned the Holy Roman emperor. The emperor had nominal control of much of Central Europe, but local rulers within this region often flouted his authority. On the Iberian peninsula, the marriage between Queen Isabella of Castile and King Ferdinand of Aragon created a unified Spanish kingdom that became increasingly powerful. Competition among the

regions of Europe for trade routes led to the voyages of Christopher Columbus, which would enrich the Spanish crown and bring European culture to another hemisphere.

A new style of visual art that stressed naturalism accompanied these political and social changes. As in the medieval era, aristocrats and churchmen continued to commission works, but the new ranks of society—bureaucrats and merchants—also became art patrons. For the merchants and middle-class patrons in urban centers, painters made images in a new medium with a new character. Using oil paints, artists in the Netherlands made paintings that still astonish viewers today by their close approximation to optical reality. By midcentury, this strongly naturalistic style became the dominant visual language of northern Europe, attracting patrons from all classes and many countries.

This transition was gradual and by no means universal. Faced with a growing middle class, the traditional aristocracy attempted to maintain their privileges and status. Among the aristocratic courts of France, the Holy Roman Empire, England, and the Burgundian Netherlands, many of which were linked by treaty or marriage, a preference emerged for a highly refined form of Gothic art, which has been termed International Gothic. Yet within these courtly images were the seeds of the heightened naturalism that would blossom in the fifteenth century.

COURTLY ART: THE INTERNATIONAL GOTHIC

As the fourteenth century came to an end, aristocratic patrons throughout Europe indulged a taste for objects made of sumptuous materials with elegant forms, based on the Gothic style. The latter had been born in France and was linked with the powerful French monarchy, so its latest manifestation owed a great deal to the forms and traditions of France. Cosmopolitan courts such as Avignon and Paris attracted artists from many regions and allowed them to exchange ideas. These circumstances produced the style historians call the International Gothic. The artists of the International Gothic also adapted some elements from fourteenth-century Italy, including devices to imply spatial settings borrowed from Duccio and Pietro Lorenzetti, and certain themes and compositions, such as aristocrats enjoying the countryside (see figs. 13.30 and 13.31). The chronological limits of this style are somewhat fluid, as some objects ascribed to the International Gothic date from the mid-fourteenth century, whereas others may date as late as the mid-fifteenth.

International Gothic artists came from Italy, France, Flanders, Germany, Spain, Bohemia, Austria, England, and elsewhere. They produced works of exquisite craftsmanship, with sometimes very complex iconographies, out of expensive materials for elite patrons. In making these objects, artists followed Gothic principles, which used geometric patterns to impose order on natural forms to idealize them (as we saw for example in fig. 12.19, in the work of Villard de Honnecourt), but they added details directly observed from nature, too. Many scholars see the detailed naturalism that appears in the International Gothic as a key stimulus for the more thoroughgoing naturalism of the early Flemish painters and their followers in the fifteenth century.

Sculpture for the French Royal Family

The French royal family was among the most active patrons of the International Gothic. King Charles V had three brothers, all of whom were active patrons of the arts. The youngest of them, Philip the Bold, became duke of Burgundy in 1363; then he added the title of count of Flanders through his marriage to Margaret of Mâle. Through these territorial acquisitions, the dukes of Burgundy became powerbrokers in the military and economic struggles of the fifteenth century. Works of art helped further Philip's status, providing an important example for his successors.

In his domain of Burgundy, Duke Philip the Bold established a Carthusian monastery, the Chartreuse de Champmol, outside

Dijon. Although the monastery was almost completely destroyed in the late eighteenth century during the anti-aristocratic riots of the French Revolution, some parts of the building survive. For the construction of this monastery, which Philip intended to serve as his family mausoleum, he assembled a team of artists, many of them from the Netherlands. Chief among them was the sculptor Claus Sluter (ca. 1360–1406) who came from Brussels. Remnants of Sluter's work at the Chartreuse de Champmol include tombs, portal sculptures and other sculptural projects.

THE WELL OF MOSES AT THE CHARTREUSE DE CHAMPMOL The most emblematic among those of the International Gothic style is *The Well of Moses* (fig. **14.1**). At one time, this hexagonal well, surrounded by statues of Hebrew Bible prophets, was topped by a life-size Calvary scene with Christ on the Cross flanked by his mother and saints. This served as a visual expression of the fulfillment by the New Testament of the Hebrew Bible. With the loss of most of the Calvary scene, however, it is the six figures of Hebrew Bible prophets on the base who must represent Sluter's achievement for us. Supported on a narrow console and framed by slim colonnettes. The majestic Moses wears a long flowing beard and drapery that envelops his body like an ample shell. The swelling forms of the prophets seem to reach out

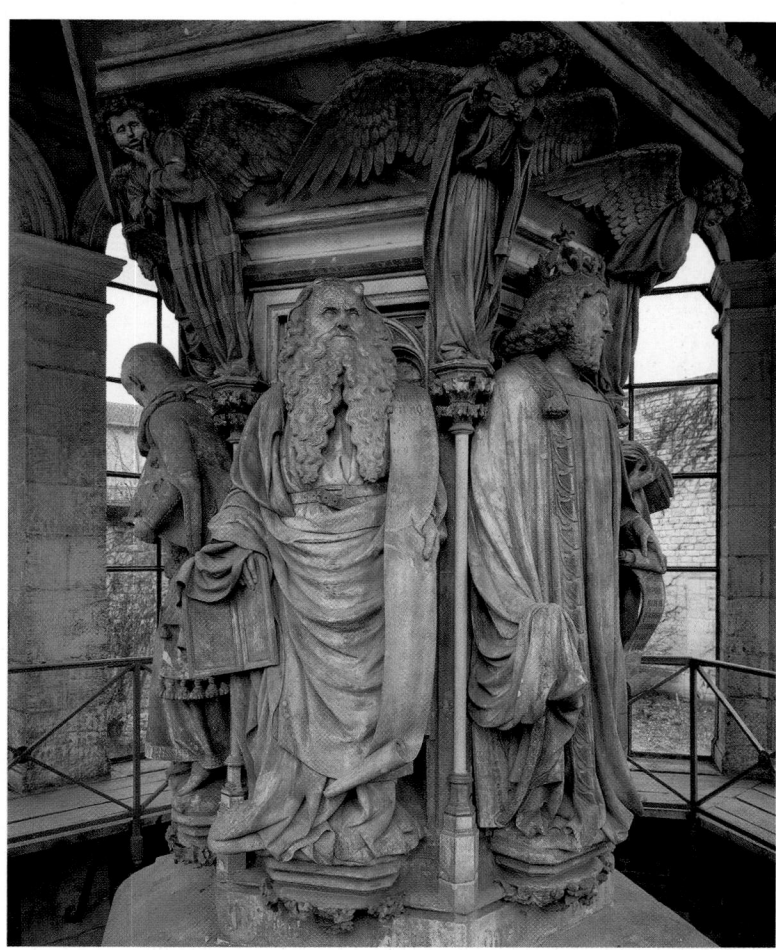

14.1 Claus Sluter, *The Well of Moses*, Chartreuse de Champmol, France. 1395–1406. Stone, height of figures approx. 6' (1.8 m)

into the surrounding space to interact directly with a viewer. Each prophet carries a scroll with texts that predict the death of Christ, and each bears an attribute that identifies him. To Moses' right stands King David, wearing the crown and robe of monarchy. The intense, staring Moses bears a pair of horns to identify him; this detail arose from a mistranslation of the Hebrew word for "ray" during the early Christian period. The horns describe Moses, holding the tablets of the Ten Commandments, after his encounter with God on Sinai. The lifelike feeling created by Moses' size and naturalistic rendering must have been greatly enhanced by the colors added to the stone by the painter Jean Malouel; these have now largely disappeared. Sluter gave one of the prophets a pair of bronze spectacles to further the connection to the real world. This attachment to the specific distinguishes Sluter's naturalistic style from that of the earlier period and is one of the hallmarks of the International Gothic.

THE ALTARPIECE AT THE CHARTREUSE DE CHAMPMOL
In addition to sculptural projects for the Chartreuse de Champmol, Duke Philip commissioned an altarpiece for its

church that was executed between 1394 and 1399. The ensemble included an elaborately carved relief for the central section by Jacques de Baerze (showing the Adoration of the Magi, the Crucifixion, and the Entombment) and wings by the Flemish painter Melchior Broederlam (ca. 1355–1410) (fig. 14.2). (Their complex shape results from the format of the central section.) Each panel of these wings depicts two scenes from the infancy of Christ: The left wing depicts the Annunciation and the Visitation (when the pregnant Virgin visited her cousin Elizabeth, who was herself expecting John the Baptist); the right, the presentation of the infant Christ to the rabbi Simeon in the Temple and the flight of the holy family from Bethlehem into Egypt to escape the persecution of Herod. The painter uses landscape and architectural elements to define the narratives and to fill in available spaces. Broederlam arranges the architecture so a viewer can see inside, as if into a doll's house; the spatial arrangements, however, derive from Duccio and the Lorenzetti (see figs. 13.23 and 13.26). Details of the landscape are out of scale with the figures, yet the panels convey a strong feeling of depth thanks to the subtlety of the modeling. The softly rounded shapes and the dark, velvety

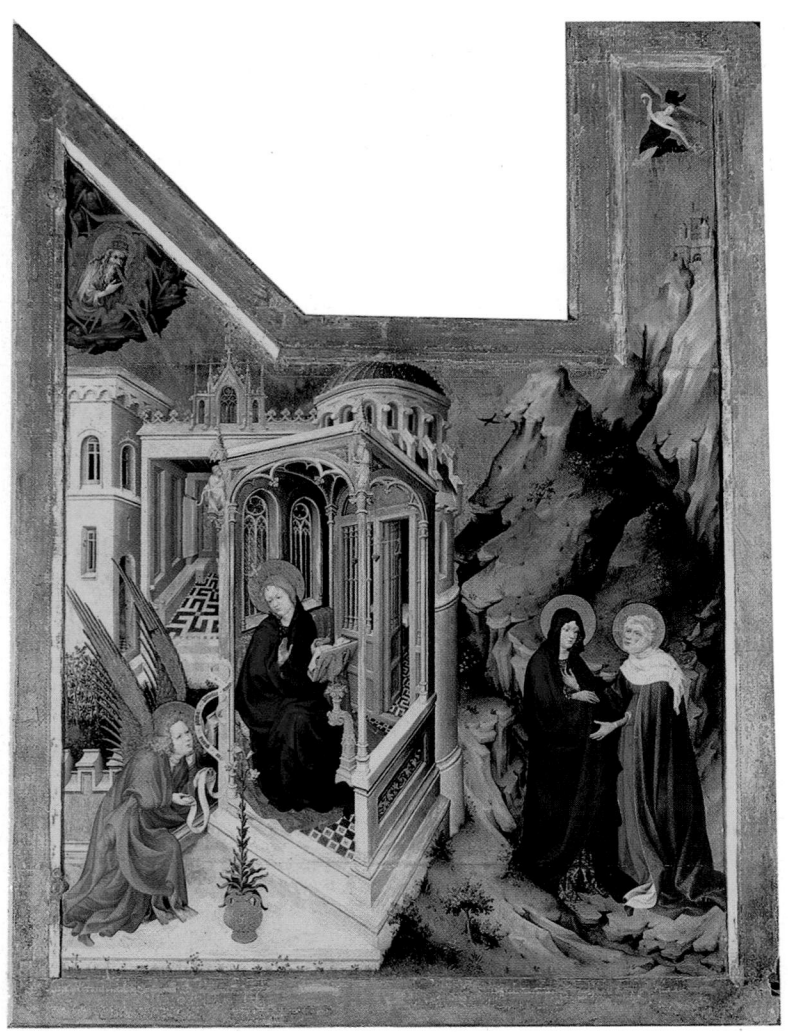 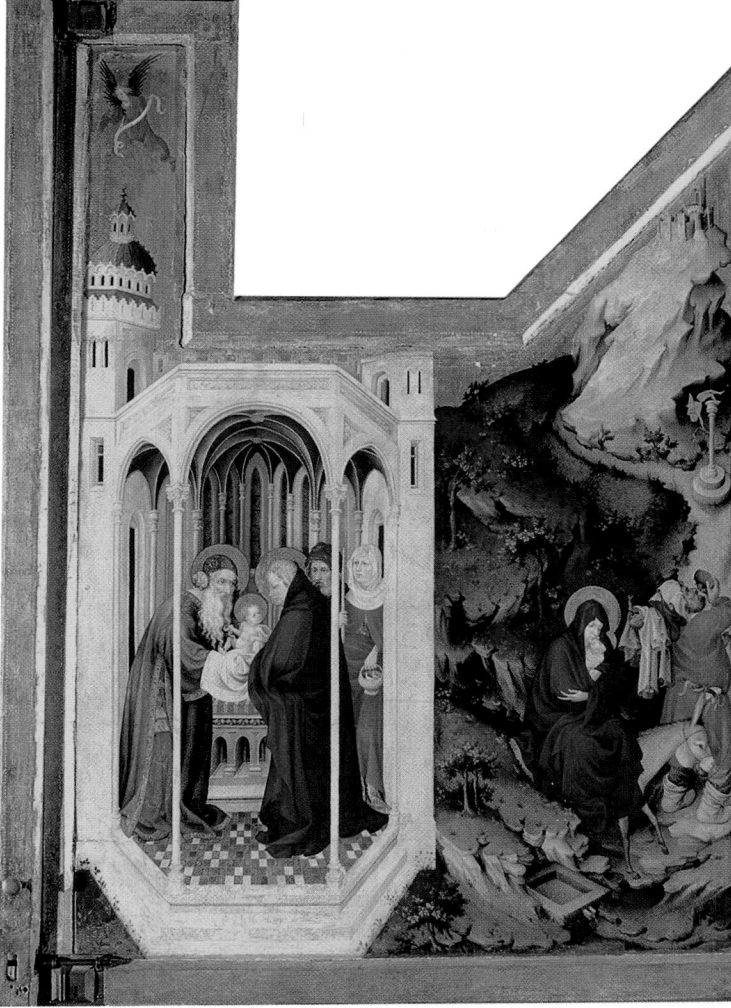

14.2 Melchior Broederlam, *Infancy of Christ* panels, wings of the altarpiece of the Chartreuse de Champmol. 1394–99.
Tempera on panel, each 65 × 49¼" (167 × 125 cm). Musée des Beaux-Arts, Dijon, France

shadows create the illusion of weight, as do the ample, loosely draped garments, reminiscent of the sculpture of Sluter.

Broederlam's panels display another feature of the International Gothic style: the realistic depiction of small details. Observing nature in detail was certainly not new; similar realism may be seen in some Gothic sculpture (see fig. 12.28) and among some drôleries (small designs, often of fables or scenes from everyday life) in the margins of manuscripts such as the *Hours of Jeanne d'Évreux* (fig. 12.39). In Broederlam's Annunciation panel, such realism is evident in the carefully rendered foliage and flowers of the enclosed garden behind Gabriel at the left. In the right-hand panel, touches of naturalistic detail include the delightful donkey, the tiny fountain at its feet, and the rustic figure of St. Joseph, who looks like a simple peasant in contrast with the delicate, aristocratic beauty of the Virgin. These painstaking touches give Broederlam's work the flavor of an enlarged miniature rather than of a large-scale painting, even though the panels are more than 5 feet tall. But they do more than merely endow the image with small flashes of realism: They contribute to its meaning. In the left-hand panel, for example, the lily signifies Mary's virginity, as does the enclosed garden next to her, which is inspired by a metaphor from the biblical Song of Songs: "A garden enclosed is my sister, my spouse; a spring shut up, a fountain sealed." Even the architecture contributes to the meaning. The contrasting Romanesque and Gothic buildings stand for the Hebrew Bible and New Testament respectively. Broederlam both enchants and instructs in this painting.

Illuminated Manuscripts: Books of Hours

Broederlam's work in these painted altarpiece wings reflects the influence of manuscript illuminations, which had been an important medium in northern Europe throughout the Middle Ages. The French court prized these expensive, custom-made objects. Philip the Bold's older brother, Jean, duke of Berry in central France, commissioned many of these sumptuous books, amassing a huge collection in his lifetime.

The luxurious book of hours known as *Les Très Riches Heures du Duc de Berry* (*The Very Rich Hours of the Duke of Berry*), is one of the most famous of the duke's books and a prime example of the International Gothic style. The artists responsible for it were Pol de Limbourg and his two brothers, Herman and Jean. They were introduced to the court by their uncle, Jean Malouel, the painter who had applied the colors to Sluter's *The Well of Moses*, and came to share an appointment as court painters to the duke, reflecting the high regard they enjoyed. One or more of the brothers must have visited Italy, for their work includes numerous motifs and whole compositions borrowed from the artists of Tuscany and Lombardy.

The Limbourg Brothers began the *Très Riches Heures* about 1413 and left it unfinished when they died in 1416, probably of the plague. As a result, some pages were completed long after their deaths. The most famous pages in the book are devoted to the calendar and depict human activities and the cycle of nature.

Such image cycles, originally consisting of 12 single figures each performing an appropriate seasonal activity, were an established tradition in medieval art. In this manuscript, the calendar pages depict aristocrats and peasants in detailed and elegant images in activities appropriate to the month represented.

The page for January, for example (fig. **14.3**), shows a scene of feasting, a traditional choice for the cold winter months. But the Limbourgs flatter their patron by depicting the duke himself at the table, seated before a large fireplace, whose wicker screen serves to frame him. Wearing a fur cap and embroidered blue garment, Duke Jean sits beneath a wall hanging adorned with his coat of arms and swans, his personal emblem. Before him, a feast is laid out on golden plates and sumptuous vessels. He discourses with a clergyman seated near him, while expensively dressed courtiers

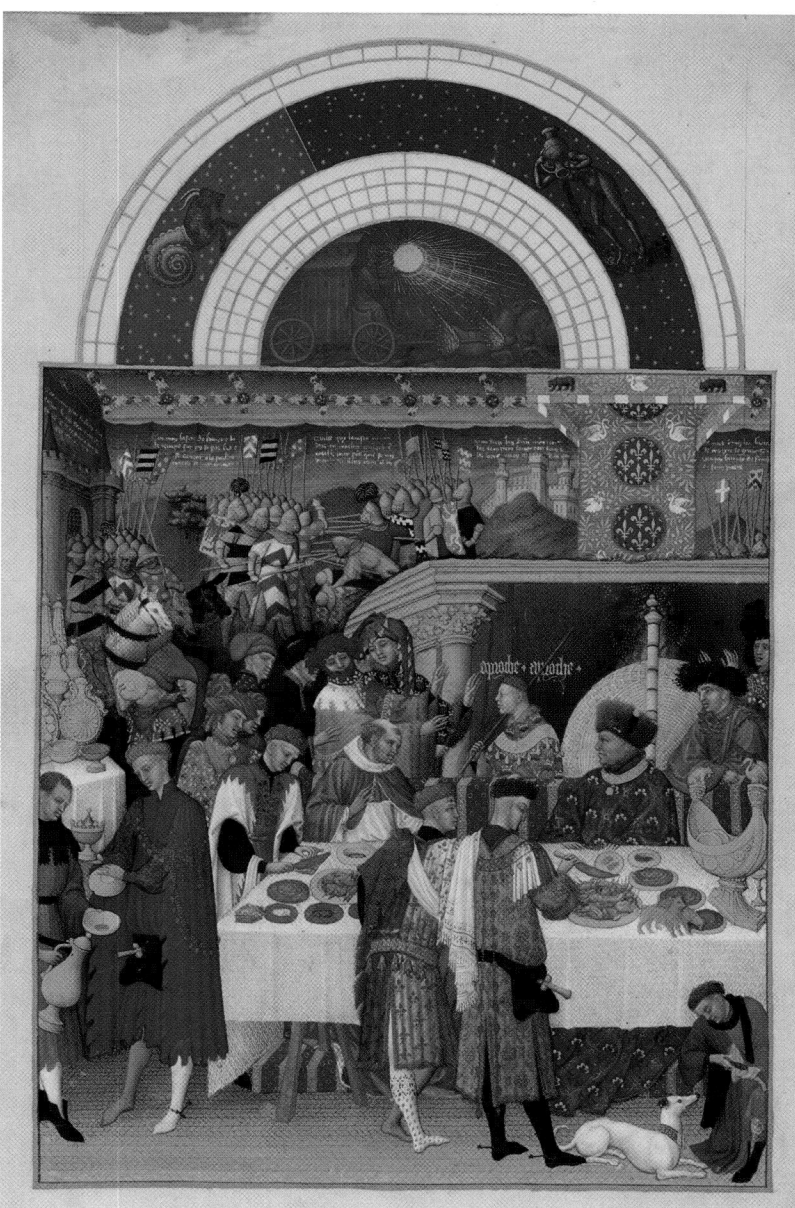

14.3 Limbourg Brothers. January page, *Les Très Riches Heures du Duc de Berry*. 1413–16. 8⅞ × 5⅜" (22.5 × 13.7 cm). Musée Condé, Chantilly, France

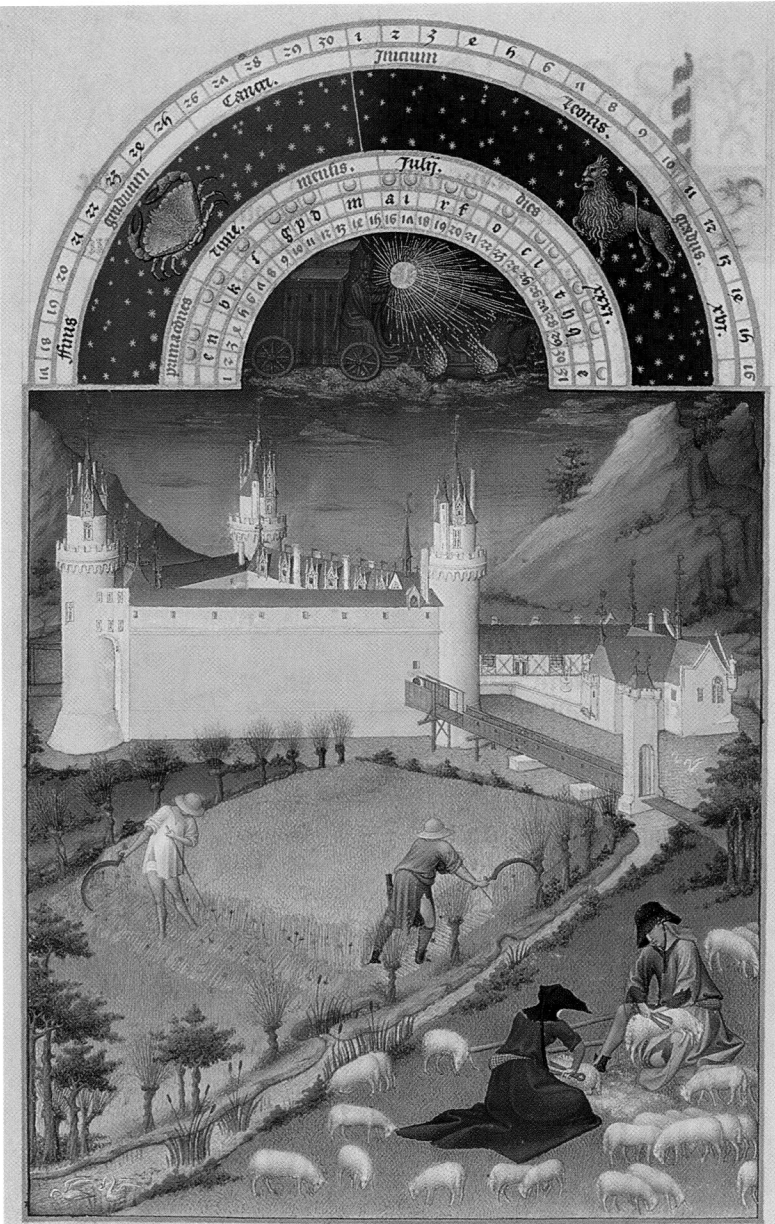

14.4 Limbourg Brothers. July page, *Les Très Riches Heures du Duc de Berry.* 1413–16. 8⅞ × 5⅜" (22.5 × 13.7 cm). Musée Condé, Chantilly, France

wait on the duke or warm themselves at the fire. Painted tapestries hang on the wall next to and above the mantel. Using brilliant colors, the artists reproduce the table setting, the items on the menu, the patterns in the draperies, even the texture of the floor covering. Such detailed observation records the pleasures of the winter season for the duke, who could literally see himself in the page.

The chronological elements above the interior scene on this page are unfinished, but they are complete in another page of the book for the summer season. The calendar page for July (fig. **14.4**) notes the passage of time in several ways: A semicircular section at the top marks the days numerically and includes the astrological signs for the month. Below this, the labor of the month is performed, as peasants harvest wheat and shear sheep in the fields, beneath a precisely rendered castle, Jean de Berry's Chateau du Clain (Poitiers), now destroyed but well documented. The page depicts the orderly harvesting of a fruitful earth by the peaceful peasantry for the eyes of the man who owns the castle. This idealized view of the social order of feudalism is achieved by combining the portrait of the castle and naturalistic details of the sheep or the scythes with an artificial space that rises up the picture plane rather than receding into depth. The carefully crafted composition links the three major zones into triangular elements that fit together like a jigsaw puzzle. The jewel-like color and splashes of gold leaf in the calendar zone contribute to the sumptuous effect of the page. The prestige of the patron and the sheer innovation of the images, especially on the calendar pages, in the *Très Riches Heures* inspired many later copies.

Bohemia and England

Other courts and regions in Europe shared the French taste for the International Gothic. In Central Europe, the city of Prague, the capital of Bohemia, became a major cosmopolitan center thanks to Emperor Charles IV (1316–1378). Charles was educated in Paris at the court of the French king Charles IV, whose daughter he married and in whose honor he changed his name from Wenceslaus. After returning to Prague and succeeding his father as king of Bohemia, Charles was named Holy Roman emperor by the German Electors at Aachen in 1349 and crowned as such in Rome in 1355.

Charles wanted to make Prague a center of learning, and in 1348 he established a university modeled on the one in Paris. It soon attracted many of the best minds in Europe. He also became a patron of the arts and founded a guild for artists. In addition to encouraging local talent, Charles brought artists from all over Europe to his city. In his castle of Karlstein, just outside of Prague, he built a chapel dedicated to the Holy Cross that

imitated Louis IX's Sainte Chapelle (fig. 12.32). Instead of stained glass, however, the walls of this chapel were covered in paintings done by Master Theodoric, the first head of the painters' guild of Prague. The paintings were executed between 1357 and 1367.

St. Matthew and the Angel (fig. **14.5**) comes from this project. As one of the authors of the Gospels, Matthew holds a book while an angel whispers in his ear. A long-standing medieval tradition assigned symbols to each of the four Evangelists, in Matthew's case an angel. Master Theodoric makes the angel an active participant in the work of the saint. Matthew himself is rendered as a three-dimensional figure, whose blue garment falls across his body in softly modeled folds of drapery. This style probably derives from Theodoric's study of Italian artists, either in his native Austria or Prague.

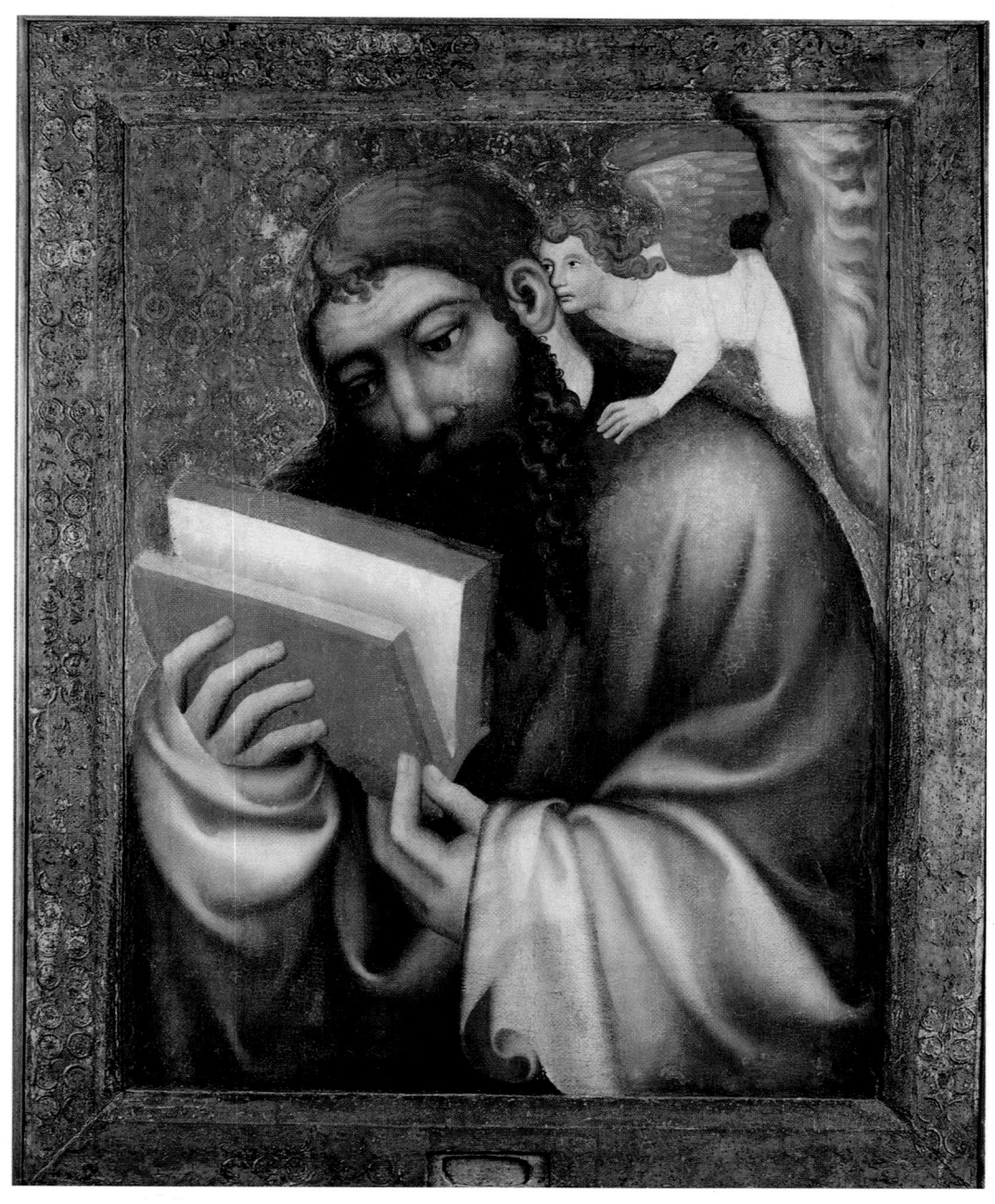

14.5 Master Theodoric, *St. Matthew and the Angel*. ca. 1360–65. Panel, 45¼ × 37" (1.15 × 0.93 m). National Gallery, Prague

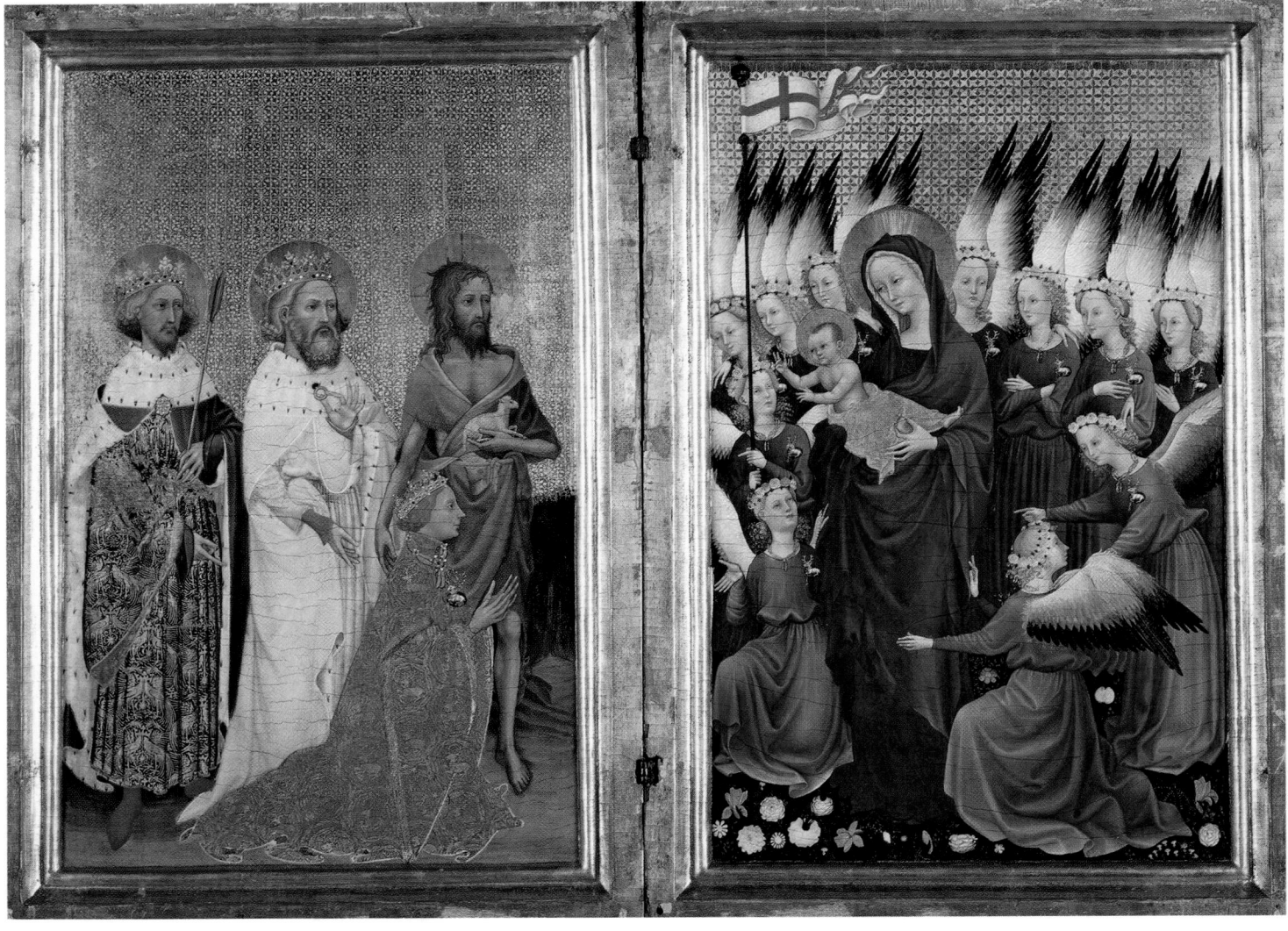

14.6 *The Wilton Diptych*. ca. 1400. Panel, 20⅞ × 14⅝" (53 × 37 cm). National Gallery of Art, London

In a pattern typical among late medieval dynasties, the emperor Charles IV's daughter, Anne of Bohemia, married the English king Richard II in 1382. Richard, who ruled from 1377 to 1399, is the figure depicted in a painting called (for the collector who once owned it) *The Wilton Diptych* (fig. 14.6). A **diptych** is a double panel that opens on a hinge at the center like a book. This diptych represents King Richard II kneeling before his patron saints to venerate the Virgin Mary and her Child. The gazes of the figures connect across the panels as they stare at the Virgin and Child, who playfully reaches out toward the king. Angels accompany the elegant figure of the Virgin, who appears like a queen surrounded by her palace guard, yet because the angels wear badges with emblems of Richard himself, it is his guard that surrounds her. The sumptuous colors and tall weightless figures stand in an eternal setting defined by a beautifully tooled gold background. Yet the drapery worn by the angels is modeled in the same natural light as Master Theodoric's *St. Matthew*. Scholars are still debating whether the unidentified artist who achieved this combination of Gothic otherworldliness and natural observation came from France, England, Bohemia, or somewhere else.

URBAN CENTERS AND THE NEW ART

Many of the artists whom the patrons in the courts preferred for their projects came from the cities of the southern Netherlands: Bruges, Brussels, Ghent, and Tournai. These were centers of international commerce in whose streets many languages could be heard as merchants from all over Europe gathered to do business. They were very jealous of their status as independent entities with special privileges to govern themselves, set trade tariffs, and establish militias. Their claims for independence often clashed with the desires of aristocratic overlords to tax and control their inhabitants. Buildings like the Town Hall of Bruges (fig. 14.7), built between 1376 and 1402, were designed to provide a setting for town councils and to serve as symbols of the independence and privileges the cities claimed. The Town Hall is one of the earliest such structures in northern Europe. Set on a major town square, it looks like an ecclesiastical structure, with its high gabled roof, traceried windows, and vaulted interior. The façade emu-lates Gothic churches, too, with its many sculpted figures depicting not saints, but the local rulers, the counts of Flanders.

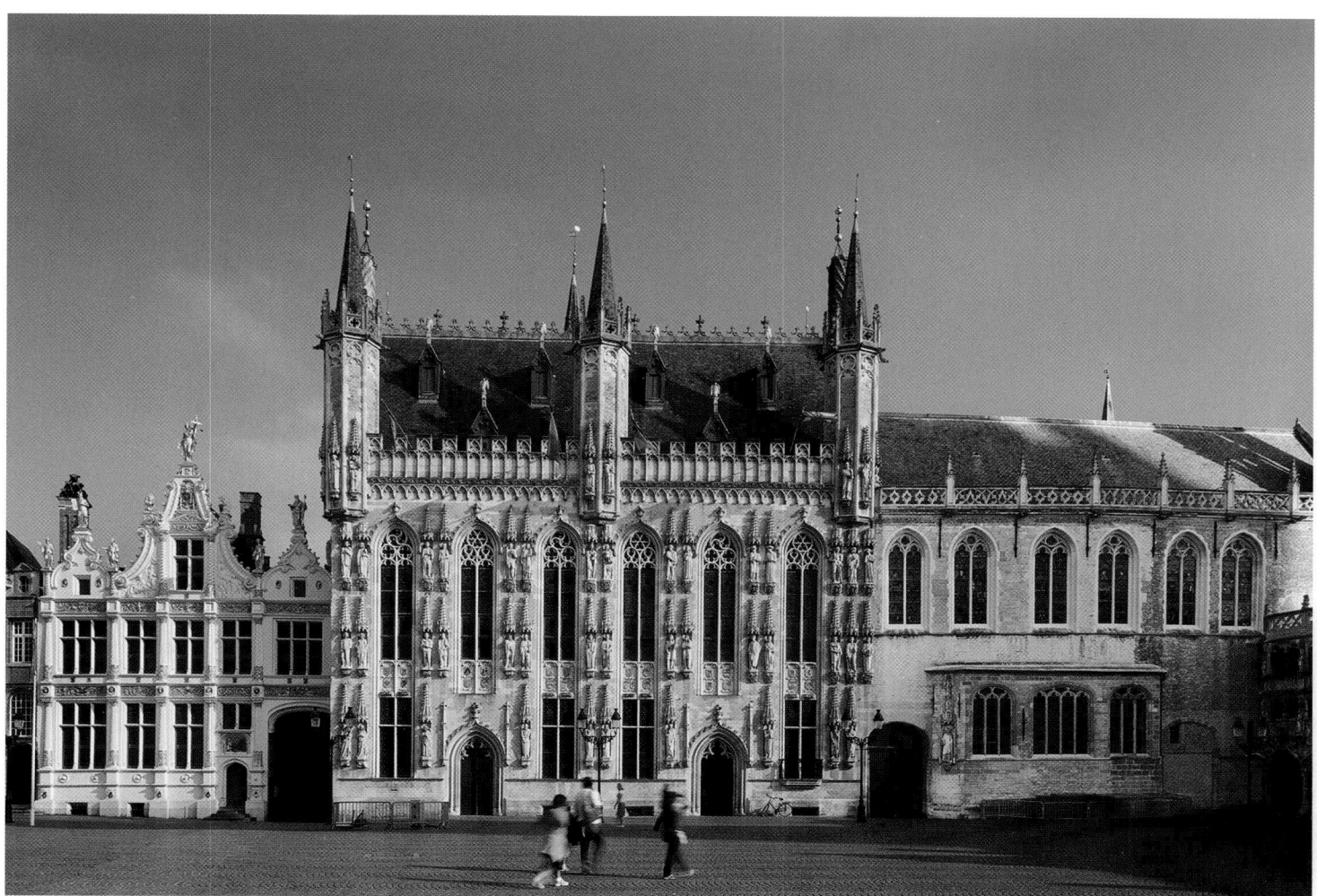

14.7   Façade of Bruges Town Hall. Begun 1376

(The building was damaged during the French Revolution, and the statues on the façade today are modern.) While the interior of the structure functioned as a council hall for self-rule and issuing judgments, the exterior sculpture expressed the nominal rule of the counts of Flanders.

It is in the cities of Flanders that the beginnings of an artistic revolution may be seen. Working either for courts or for citizens, artists began to make images in oil paint that represent sacred figures as if they existed in the natural world, giving tangible form to spiritual concepts.

Robert Campin in Tournai

An early pioneer of this naturalistic revolution is Robert Campin (1378–1444), the foremost painter in Tournai, an important trade center in southwestern Belgium. Campin ran a busy workshop, from which several other successful painters emerged, including Rogier van der Weyden.

THE MÉRODE TRIPTYCH The most famous work attributed to Campin is the *Mérode Triptych* (fig. **14.8**), dated on the basis of style to around 1425. The name derives from an early owner of

the painting, but the subject of the central panel is the Annunciation, frequently depicted in earlier Christian art. Typically, those earlier representations of the Annunciation set the event in an ecclesiastical building (see fig. 14.2) or other sacred space (see fig. 13.25), but Campin places the Virgin and the angel Gabriel in what appears to be the main room of a bourgeois house, complete with open shutters, well-used fireplace, and cushioned bench. Despite the supernatural events, a viewer has the sense of actually looking through the surface of the panel into a world that mimics reality. Campin uses several devices to create this effect. He fits the objects and figures into boxes of space aligned with the parts of the triptych. Sometimes the fit isn't comfortable, but he renders details in such a way as to make every object as concrete as possible in its shape, size, color, and texture. He also paints two kinds of light. One is of a diffused kind that creates soft shadows and delicate gradations of brightness; the other is more direct and enters through the two round windows, casting shadows on the wall. Campin's color scheme, with its muted tonality, unifies all three panels; his bright colors have richness and depth, and he achieves smooth transitions from lights into darks. These effects were made possible by the use of oil. (See *Materials and Techniques*, page 479.) Although medieval artists

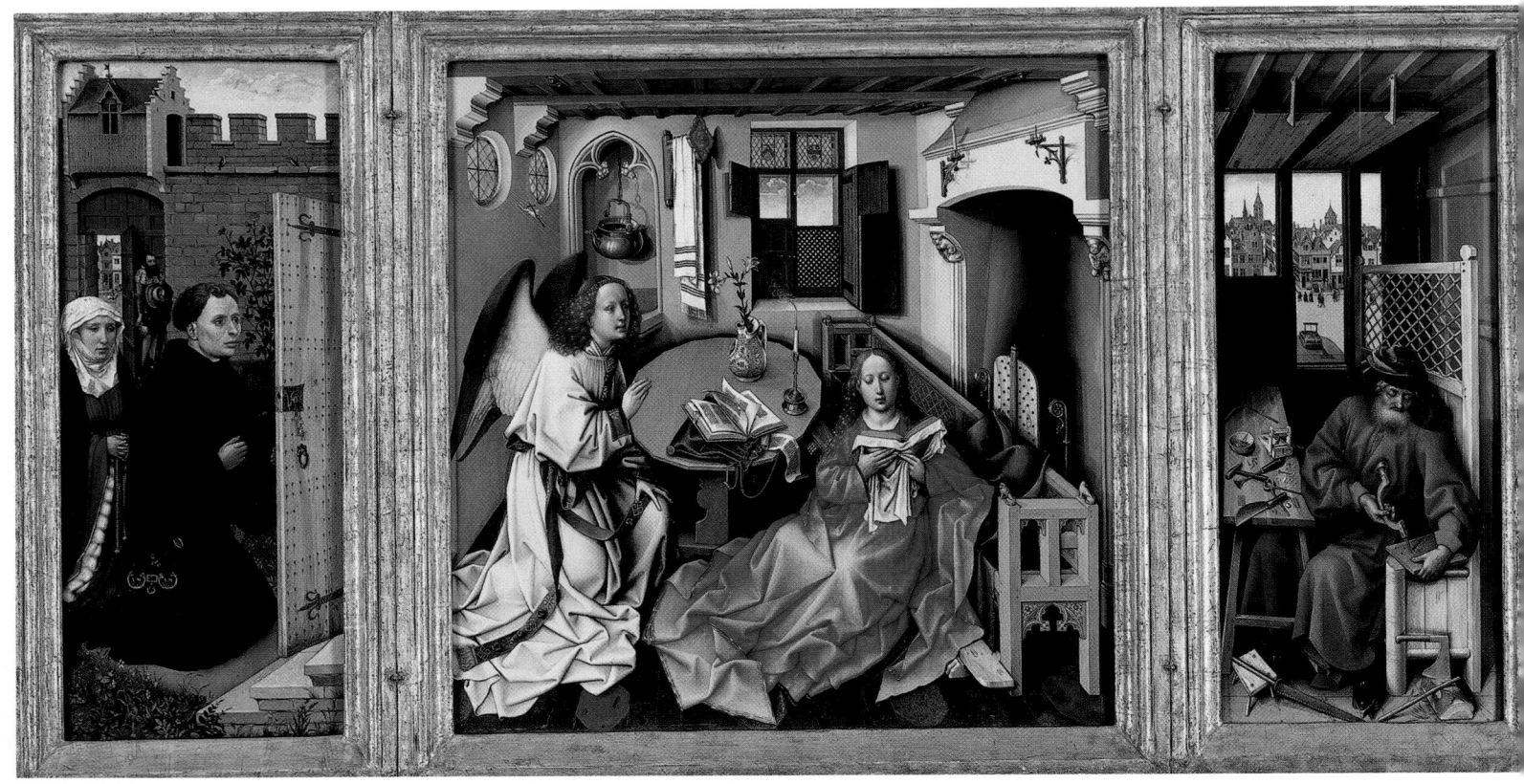

14.8 Robert Campin and workshop. *Mérode Triptych*. ca. 1425–30. Oil on oak, center panel 25¼ × 24⅞" (64.1 × 63.2 cm), each wing approx. 25⅜ × 10⅞" (64.5 × 27.4 cm). Metropolitan Museum of Art, New York, The Cloisters Collection, 1956. 56.70a-c

had knowledge of oil paint, Campin and his contemporaries expanded its possibilities for painting on panels. Its use allowed him to create a much more thorough illusion of reality than the flashes of natural detail seen in the work of court artists.

Campin was no court painter but a townsman who catered to the tastes of fellow citizens, such as the two donors shown here piously kneeling outside the Virgin's chamber. A coat of arms painted in the window of the central panel points to a family of merchants who had settled in Tournai by 1427. Obviously they were wealthy enough to commission this triptych, probably for their own dwelling, as it is too small for installation in a public church. Perhaps it was this function that inspired the artist to break with tradition in the picture. This Annunciation takes place in a fully equipped domestic interior with figures that are rendered as real people, with mass and weight. The drapery of their garments falls in deep folds, anchoring the figures to the floor, as in the sculpture of Claus Sluter (see fig. 14.1). Gabriel adopts a not-quite-kneeling, not-quite-standing position as he raises his right hand to speak. Mary's red dress draws attention to her as she sits on the floor, book in hand. Between them, a table supports another book, a vase of lilies, and a candle. Above and behind Gabriel, the tiny figure of a baby holding a cross, who must be Christ, floats downward toward Mary. In the left wing panel, the donors kneel in a garden, as though looking through the open door to witness this event. The whole effect is of time frozen: Something important is about to happen. Where Simone Martini

had rendered Gabriel and the Virgin as slim, weightless figures set against an eternal gold ground (see fig. 13.25), Campin depicts their substantial bodies in a recognizably earthly setting for the eyes of the donor couple. They see the event taking place in their world, not in Heaven.

The right wing panel depicts Joseph, the carpenter, at work, though just what he is making is debatable. Scholars have identified the mysterious boxlike object on the window ledge as a mousetrap, an object that the Christian theologian St. Augustine used metaphorically to explain God's plan for salvation when he said, "The Cross of the Lord was the devil's mousetrap." The mousetrap could be a visual cue to the reason for Christ's incarnation, which is about to occur in the central panel. Equally puzzling is the object in Joseph's hand, identified by some as a fire screen (like the one in the central panel) and by others as part of a press through which grapes are forced to make wine (which would refer to the wine used in the sacrament of the Eucharist).

Such carefully chosen details have persuaded many scholars that Campin used these forms as symbols to convey spiritual messages. We have seen some of these symbols before: The flowers, for example, are associated with the Virgin as emblems of her purity and other virtues; they appeared in Simone Martini's Annunciation (see fig. 13.25). Interpreting other details, such as the smoking candle next to the vase of lilies, has been more difficult. Its glowing wick and the curl of smoke indicate that it has just been extinguished. To explain why a candle had been lit

Panel Painting in Tempera and Oil

In the fourteenth and fifteenth centuries, painters worked with liquid pigments on wooden panels. The type of wood used varied from region to region, though oak panels were preferred in northern Europe because they could be sawn into thin planks to serve as supports for the paint. Pine, fruitwoods, and poplar were also used. Once the panels had been formed, and often inserted into a frame by a carpenter, the flat surface would be covered with a film of gesso (a type of fine plaster) to create a smooth surface for the image. Often an underdrawing would be laid onto the gesso as a guide for the painter or his assistants.

For pigments, artists used oxides, plants, minerals, or semiprecious stones. They ground these materials into powders that had to be mixed with some sort of liquid medium to bind them to the panel. The basic medium of medieval panel painting had been tempera, in which the finely ground pigments were mixed ("tempered") with diluted egg yolk. This produced a thin, tough, quick-drying coat that was well suited to the medieval taste for high-keyed flat color surfaces. However, in tempera the different tones on the panel could not be blended smoothly, and the progression of values necessary for three-dimensional effects was difficult to achieve.

While medieval artists had used oil-based paints for special purposes, such as coating stone surfaces or painting on metal, artists like Jan van Eyck and Robert Campin in Flanders exploited it for panel paintings. Oil, a viscous, slow-drying medium, can produce a variety of effects, from thin, translucent films (called **glazes**) to a thick layer of creamy, heavy-bodied paint (called **impasto**). The tones can also yield a continuous scale of hues, including rich, velvety dark shades. Oil painting offers another advantage over egg tempera, **encaustic**, and fresco: It allows artists to change their minds and rework their paintings. As the use of oil paints spread across Europe, some artists adopted a mixed technique, using tempera for the base layers and covering these with oil glazes. Although pigments continued to be mixed with tempera for some time, oil has been the painter's basic medium until very recently.

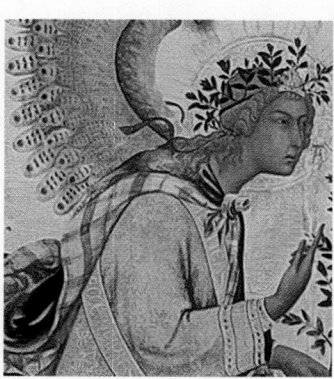
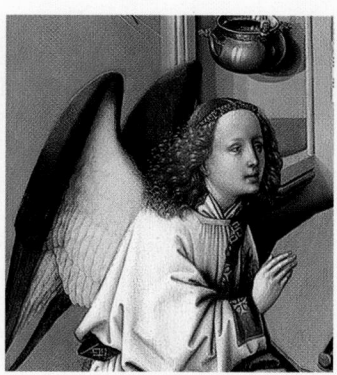

Simone Martini's image of the angel Gabriel is painted in tempera, which dries quickly; consequently, the layers of paint do not blend, and individual strokes of the brush are visible on the surface.

Campin's Gabriel is painted with oil, which dries slowly and is translucent. Each layer of color merges with the one below it to create a mirrorlike finish.

on a sunny day, and what had snuffed out its flame, scholars have pointed to the arrival of Christ on a beam of light coming through the round window: In theological terms, the arrival of the true light (Christ) extinguishes the mundane one.

The appearance in Campin's picture of so many carefully delineated objects suggests that these details constitute a symbolic program, which either the artist or the patron conceived. Theologians or scholars may have provided Campin with the more learned aspects of the symbolism, but it was the artist who found the means to express these complex ideas in symbolic terms using forms observed in the visible world. Modern scholars also debate the reasons why Campin and his contemporaries wanted to record the world with such fidelity. Some have argued that philosophies about nature and the natural world had changed, along with religious practices. Others have suggested that pragmatic merchants demanded directly observed renderings of things they could see.

The Annunciation certainly has liturgical and theological import, but it is also a story about the conception of a child. The couple on the left kneel devoutly before the image of these events. From their perspective, the triptych may be an expression of their own desire for children or their reverence for the Holy Family as a model for their own. Such personalized approaches to holy figures and sacred dramas enlivened religious life at the end of the Middle Ages. Believers were encouraged in sermons, Passion plays, and written texts to visualize the sacred in terms they could understand and to meditate on events from Christ's life in order to increase their empathy and devotion. Although monks and nuns had long practiced such contemplation, the religious movement called the Modern Devotion helped to spread these ideas among the laity. New texts, such as the *Imitation of Christ* by Thomas à Kempis, provided guidance for laypeople wishing to emulate Christ. Artists like Campin may have been responding to the call to see the physical world as a mirror of divine truths and to create moving and pious images of sacred events occurring in everyday environments.

Jan van Eyck in Bruges

The visual revolution achieved in paintings such as the *Mérode Triptych* was recognized and admired not only by patrons in Flanders but also by patrons in Italy. Italian observers provide the earliest external assessments of the Flemish innovators. They recognized that the technical achievement of oil painting contributed to the striking naturalism and evocation of religious feeling in Flemish painting, and they credited the "invention" of oil painting to Jan van Eyck (1390–1441). (See www.myartslab.com.) As a result, his is one of the more famous names of fifteenth-century art, and he is a figure about whom we know a good deal.

Jan worked first for the count of Holland and then for the reigning duke of Burgundy, Philip the Good, from 1425 until his death in Bruges in 1441. Both a townsman and a court painter, Jan was highly esteemed by Philip the Good, who occasionally sent him on diplomatic errands. Unusual for his time, he signed and dated several surviving pictures, which has allowed historians to identify his artistic output and to assign unsigned works to him based on the signed ones.

THE *GHENT ALTARPIECE* The *Ghent Altarpiece* is one of the most famous of early Flemish paintings. From the moment it was installed in a chapel of the cathedral of St. John in Ghent (see fig. 14.12), it began to draw a crowd. Albrecht Dürer visited it in 1520, and much later artists like the nineteenth-century French painter Ingres drew inspiration from it. An inscription on the now-lost frame identified Jan van Eyck as the artist who finished this multipaneled altarpiece in May 1432 and alluded to the collaboration of his older brother, Hubert, who died in 1426. The basic form of this complex altarpiece is a triptych (consisting of three hinged panels), but here each of the three units consists of four panels. Since the wings are also painted on both sides, the altarpiece contains a total of 20 images of various shapes and sizes. Discontinuities among the many panels suggest alterations took place as the work progressed. It appears that Jan took over a number of panels left unfinished by Hubert, completed them, added some of his own, and assembled the whole at the request of the wealthy donor, Jodicus Vijd. Vijd's portrait with that of his wife, Elizabeth Borluut, appears on the outer panels of the altar when the triptych is closed (fig. **14.9**).

Their portraits appear on the lower tier with two other figures, each in a separate niche framed by painted Gothic tracery. Next to

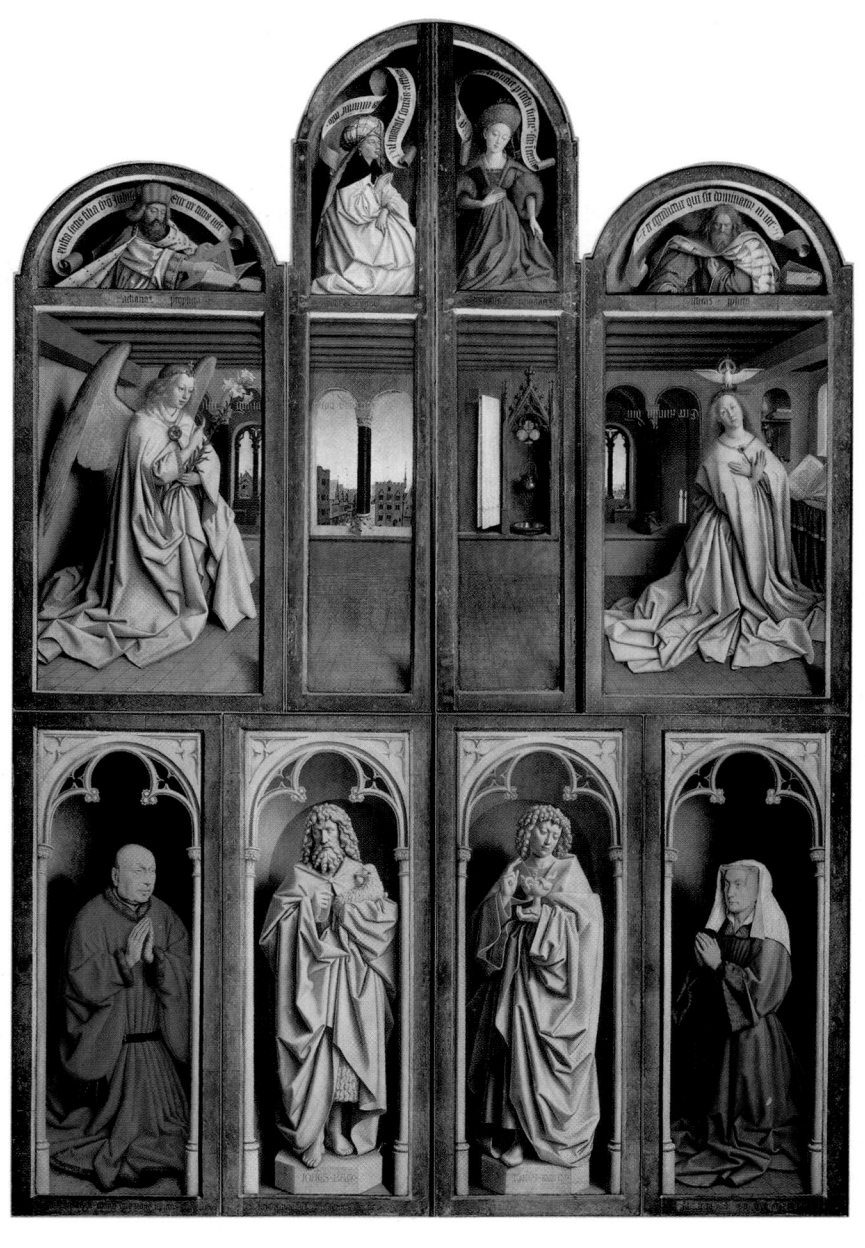

14.9 Hubert and Jan van Eyck, *Ghent Altarpiece* (closed), Church of St. Bavo, Ghent, Belgium. Completed 1432. Oil on panel, 11'5" × 7'6" (3.4 × 2.25 m)

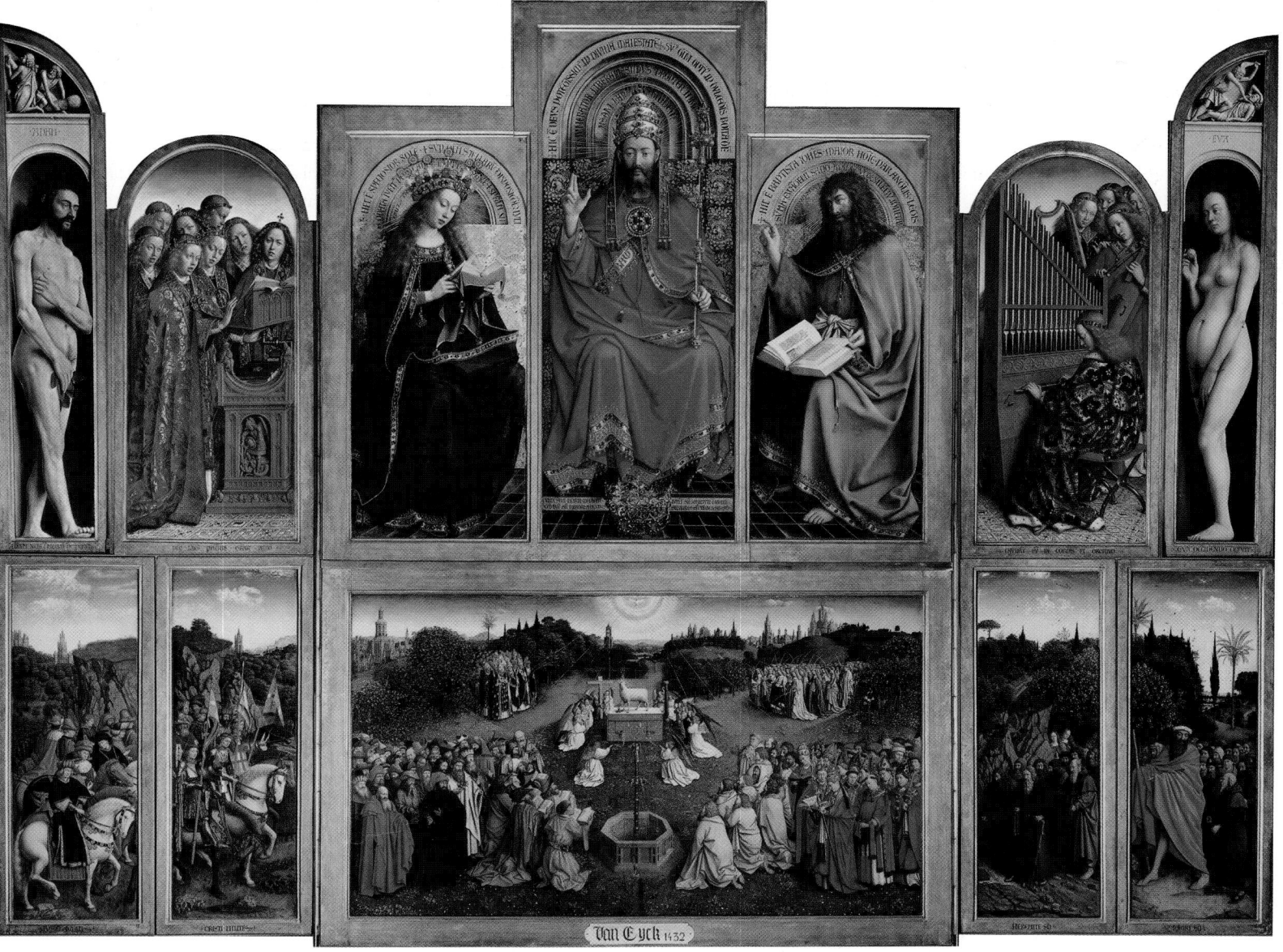

14.10 Hubert and Jan van Eyck, *Ghent Altarpiece* (open). 11'5"× 15'1" (3.4 × 4.5 m)

the donors are John the Baptist and John the Evangelist, the patrons of the cathedral, painted in **grisaille** (a monochrome; in this case to imitate the grayish color of statues). The upper tier has two pairs of panels of different width. The artist has made a virtue of this awkward necessity by combining all four into one interior, whose foreshortened timber ceiling crosses all four panels. In addition to the continuous space, Jan heightens the illusion by painting shadows on the floor of the Virgin's chamber as if they were cast by the frames of the panels. Prophets and sibyls occupy an upper story, their prophecies written in Gothic script in scrolls above their heads. In such altarpieces, the wings stayed closed except on Sundays, specific feast days, and when other liturgically important moments required them to be opened.

When the wings are opened (fig. **14.10**) the viewer sees a detailed rendering of a celestial assembly: Across the bottom tier, groups of figures converge on a central image of an altar, upon which stands a haloed Lamb. This assembly includes angels, apostles, popes, theologians, virgin martyrs, hermits, pilgrims, knights, and judges (including, possibly, a reference to Jan's employer, Duke Philip the Good). A verdant landscape provides the setting for this mystic Mass, with towers of numerous churches in the skyline. Above this earthly paradise reigns an imposing Court of Heaven, with the Lord in a bright red robe at the center. Flanking him are Mary and John the Baptist. To the left and right, choirs of angels sing and play musical instruments. At the outer edges of this upper tier stand Adam and Eve, rendered as nudes in shallow niches, below grisaille images of Abel and Cain. The almost life-size nudes are portrayed with careful attention to their anatomy and caressed by a delicate play of light and shade (fig. **14.11**).

The figures' poses are comparable to those in Gothic manuscripts, but here the artist breathes life into the forms by rendering

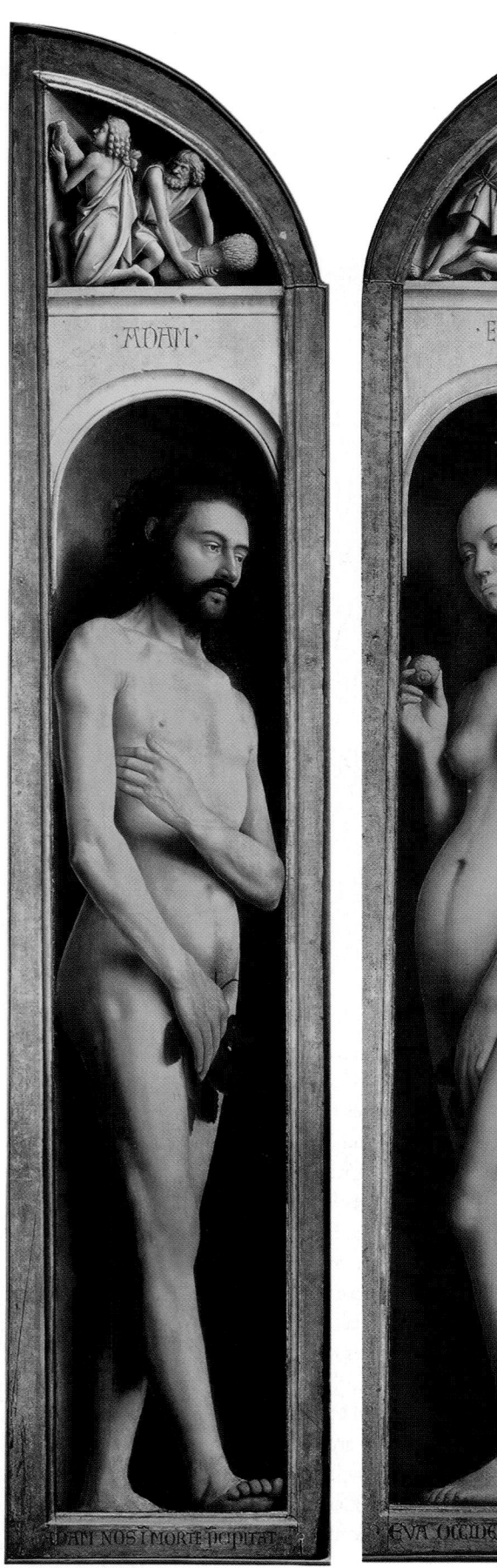
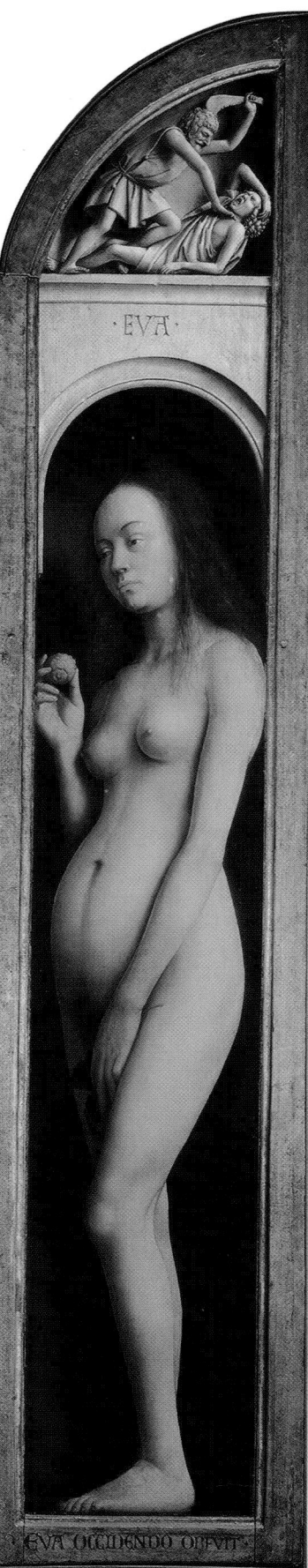

14.11 Hubert and Jan van Eyck, *Adam and Eve*, detail of *Ghent Altarpiece*. Left and right wings

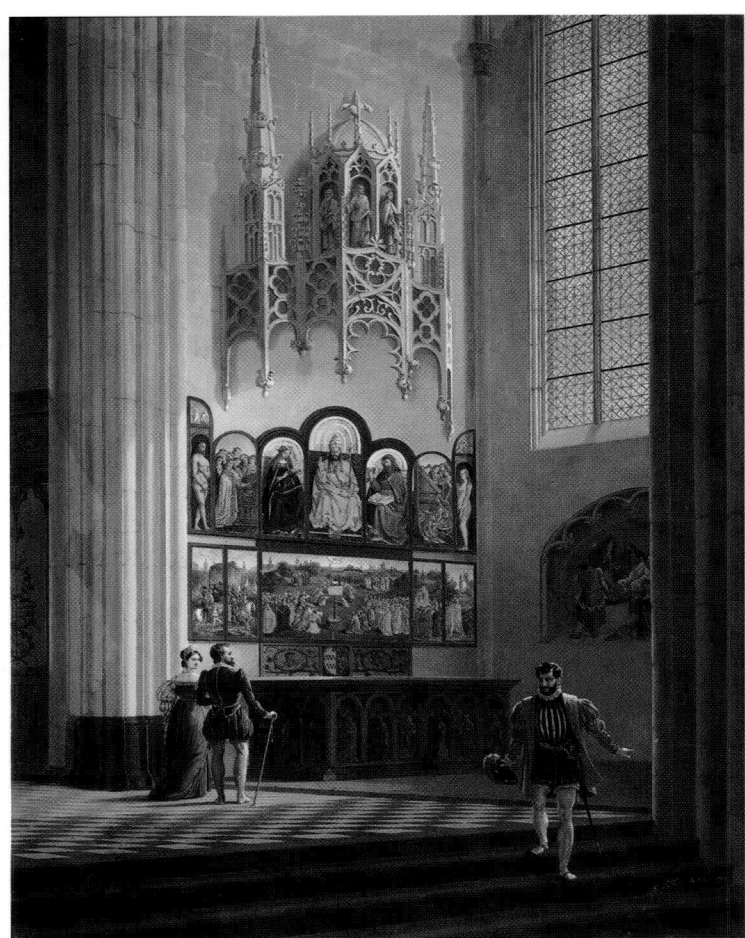

14.12 Painting of *Ghent Altarpiece* in chapel. Rijksmuseum, Amsterdam

the textures and colors of the bodies with great accuracy. Seeing this work on the altar of the Vijd Chapel in Ghent cathedral (fig. **14.12**), a viewer could not fail to be impressed by the scale and setting of the painting. The tone and majesty of this ensemble are very different from the domestic intimacy of the *Mérode Triptych*. The function of the altarpiece is to elucidate the **liturgy** performed in front of it. When open, its subject is the Mass itself, here shown in a paradisiacal setting. The number of books represented and the many erudite inscriptions celebrating Christian learning suggest that a cleric or theologian may have advised Jan in developing the program. But Jan accomplished the difficult task of bringing the disparate panels together and welding them into an imposing and memorable experience.

Jan's work is large in scale but full of naturally observed details and glowing color. His technique of building up color in layers of glazes results in highly saturated hues, while the slow, methodical application of paint blends brushstrokes to a mirrorlike finish. Jan offers a glimpse into Heaven to stimulate devotion. If, as some scholars believe, the whole altarpiece was set into a Gothic architectural frame, one meaning of the image becomes the importance of the Church itself as an institution and as a pathway to salvation.

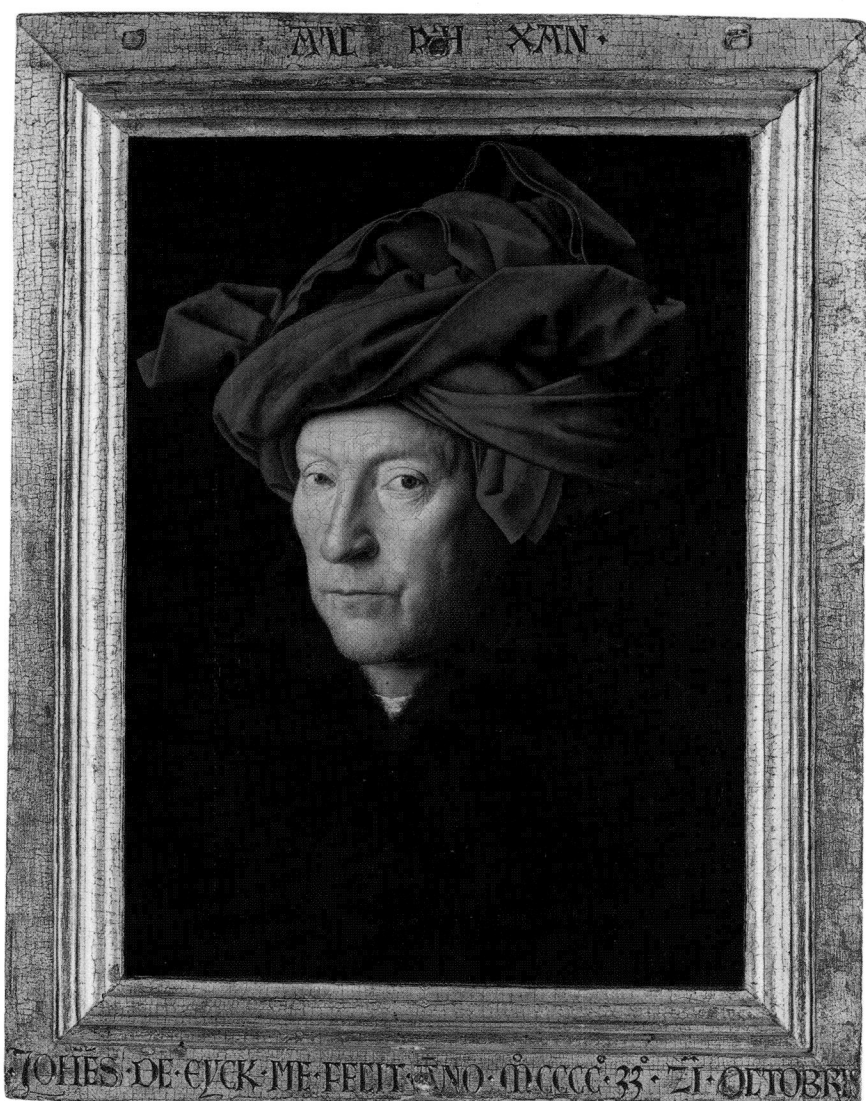

14.13 Jan van Eyck, *Man in a Red Turban (Self-Portrait?)*. 1433. Oil on panel, 13⅛ × 10¼" (33 × 25.8 cm). The National Gallery, London

SECULAR IMAGES Jan van Eyck also made purely secular paintings, fulfilling the commissions of the court and of the middle-class citizens of Flemish towns. One example is Jan's *Man in a Red Turban* (fig. **14.13**), signed and dated 1433, which represents a middle-aged man in a three-quarters pose whose face is framed by his dramatic headgear. Warm light bathes the distinctive face emerging from the dark background of this painting and reveals every detail of shape and texture with almost microscopic precision. The artist does not explore the sitter's personality, yet the man gazes out of the picture to make eye contact with the viewer. This innovation, and the slight strain about the eyes which may come from gazing into a mirror, suggests that the painting may be a self-portrait. The self-consciousness that such a project demands may relate to the text painted on the frame: An inscription reads *"ALS ICH KAN"* ("As I can" or "As best I can"). This motto appears on other works by Jan, too, perhaps challenging other artists to do better, for he has done all he can. Though transposed into Greek letters, the phrase is Flemish; this implies that Jan saw himself in competition with the ancients as well as with his contemporaries. Whatever his reason may have been, we can read the motto as another sign of Jan's self-consciousness about his work as an artist and his place in history.

The next example demonstrates that Jan van Eyck's signatures complicate the task of interpreting his work. One of the most studied and yet still mysterious of his surviving images represents a man and a woman standing in a richly furnished room, equipped with a brass chandelier, a mirror, and a canopied bed (fig. **14.14**). Jan signed the painting, not on the frame, as he did in many of his other paintings, but within the panel itself. Above the painted mirror in a formal script, the translated signature reads, "Jan van Eyck was here, 1434." The features of the man, if not the lady, are specific enough to be a portrait, and the image is unusual enough that scholars have been able to use later documents to identify the subject as Giovanni Arnolfini, an Italian merchant living in Bruges. For many years, scholars believed that his companion should be identified as Giovanna Cenami, Arnolfini's wife; recent research, however, makes this doubtful, as that marriage took place much later than 1434.

Whatever their names, the painted couple appear in the main room of a fifteenth-century house that is somewhat more

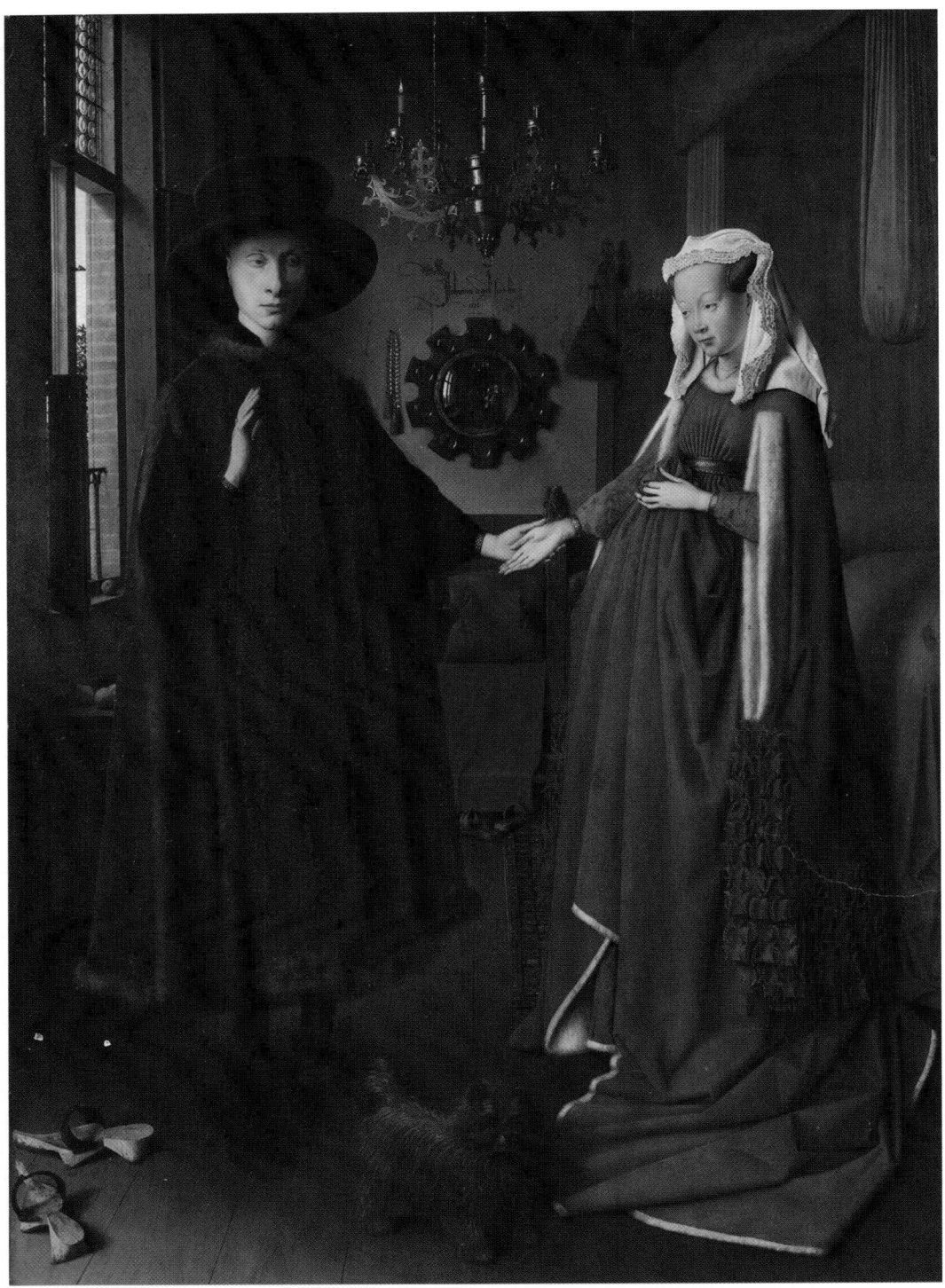

14.14 Jan van Eyck, *The "Arnolfini Portrait."* 1434. Oil on panel, 33 × 22½" (83.7 × 57 cm). The National Gallery, London

expensively furnished than the room in the *Mérode Triptych.* The two join hands, with the man raising his right hand as if in a solemn oath, seemingly quite alone in the room. In the mirror behind them, however, is the reflection of two men. Because the signature appears right above the mirror, many scholars believe that one of these men must be Jan van Eyck himself, perhaps the figure wearing the red headdress. The combination of the signature, with its flourishes and phrasing, and the image of the men in

the mirror suggests to some that Jan is acting as a witness to whatever is occurring in the room.

Traditionally, scholars have argued that this panel represents either the wedding or the engagement of the couple shown, either of which would have required a legal and financial contract between their two families. By this reading, the painting commemorates the union of the couple. If so, the second man in the mirror may be the bride's father, who would have made the

Cyriacus of Ancona (1449)

Rogier van der Weyden probably visited Italy, and sources reveal that he made several paintings for prominent Italian patrons, including the Este family of Ferrara. One of Rogier's most discussed images in Italy drew the praise of Cyriacus of Ancona, a humanist and diplomat who had traveled widely in the service of Italian princes.

After that famous man from Bruges, Johannes the glory of painting [i.e., Jan van Eyck], Roger in Brussels is considered the outstanding painter of our time. By the hand of this most excellent painter is a magnificently wrought picture which the illustrious prince Lionello of Este showed me in Ferrara on July 8, 1449. In it one sees our first progenitors, and in a most pious image the ordeal of the Deposition of the God-Incarnate, with a large crowd of men and women standing about in deep mourning. All this is admirably depicted with what I would call divine rather than human art. There you could see those faces come alive and breathe which he wanted to show as living, and likewise the deceased as dead, and in particular, many garments, multicolored soldiers' cloaks, clothes prodigiously enhanced by purple and gold, pearls, precious stones, and everything else you would think to have been produced not by the artifice of human hands but by all-bearing nature itself.

Source: *Northern Renaissance Art 1400-1600: Sources and Documents*, ed. Wolfgang Stechow (Evanston, IL: Northwestern University Press, 1989)

contract for the marriage of his daughter. The woman's gesture to lift her heavy gown may suggest her wish for children, and the bed behind her may suggest the consummation of the marriage. Another recent interpretation sees the image as a commemoration of a wife who died giving birth, which might explain her generalized features and the carved figure of St. Margaret, to whom pregnant women prayed for safe delivery.

Given the scene's secular nature, scholars have debated whether the realistic touches serve simply as an accurate record of an event and its domestic setting, or whether those details carry more symbolic weight. The couple may have taken off their shoes as a matter of custom, or the artist may want to imply that they are standing on "holy ground." (This symbol has its origins in stories of Moses removing his sandals at the burning bush on Mount Sinai; that is, in the presence of God.) The little dog may be a beloved pet, like those in the January page of the *Très Riches Heures* (see fig. 14.3), or it could be an emblem of fidelity. (*Fides* is Latin for faithfulness, the origin of the traditional dog name, Fido.) The other furnishings of the room suggest other questions. Here is yet another candle (in the chandelier) burning in broad daylight, but no holy figure is present as in the *Mérode Triptych*. Pieces of fruit on the window sill may be expressions of the couple's wealth, or refer to the temptation of Adam and Eve. Tiny images of Christ's Passion and Resurrection in the small medallions that surround the mirror sound the only unambiguously religious note in the picture. Scholars are still investigating the function and patronage of this image as they are now much less certain about the meaning of the image than they used to be. Jan van Eyck's carefully crafted image incites much scholarly fascination, just as his work garnered much praise from his employer, the duke of Burgundy.

Rogier van der Weyden in Brussels

His status as a court painter exempted Jan van Eyck from the restrictions that governed other artists in Flemish towns. Regulations for the training of artists and the market for works of art came from the guilds, professional organizations of artists established to protect the interests of their members. Aspiring artists learned their trade as apprentices in the workshop of a certified master. After a fixed period, an apprentice became a journeyman (or dayworker) who could then hire out his services to others but not open his own shop. Journeymen often traveled to learn from artists other than their master. Becoming a master required completing a "masterpiece" that was evaluated by the leaders of the guild. Guilds not only controlled training but limited competition from artists outside their towns, investigated disputes among members, and saw to the social and economic needs of members, such as providing for burials, pensions, and the care of widows. Guilds were both economic and social institutions, assuring the quality of their products and seeing to the well-being of their members.

One illustrious graduate of the guild system was Rogier van der Weyden (1399/1400–1464), a painter who trained with Robert Campin in Tournai, and who certainly knew the work of Jan van Eyck. By 1435, Rogier had established a flourishing workshop in Brussels which took commissions from as far away as Italy and Spain. Perhaps his most influential work is the *Descent from the Cross* (fig. **14.15**), which dates from about 1435. The crossbowmen's guild of Louvain (near Brussels) commissioned it as the center of an altarpiece for a church there. In this work, Rogier depicted the moment when Christ's followers lower his body from the Cross; the mourners crowd into a shallow box of space. Rogier modeled the forms carefully to suggest sculptural presence, and included enough detail to show every nuance of texture.

Rogier's goal is to increase the expressive content of his pictures. He emphasizes the emotional impact of the scene on its participants. Their faces and postures express the grief of the figures. John the Evangelist on the left and Mary Magdalen on the right are bowed in pain. The Virgin's swoon echoes the pose and expression of her son. Rogier depicts her intense pain and grief in order to inspire the same compassion in a viewer. He has staged his scene in a shallow niche or shrine, not against a landscape. This bold device focuses a viewer's attention on the foreground and allows the artist to mold the figures into a coherent group. Furthermore, the emphasis on the body of Christ at the center of the composition refers to the celebration of the Eucharist, which takes place before the altarpiece during the Mass. Rogier could

14.15 Rogier van der Weyden, *Descent from the Cross*. ca. 1435. Oil on panel, 7'2⅝" × 8'7⅛" (2.2 × 2.6 m). Museo del Prado, Madrid

find precedents for these grief-stricken gestures and faces in earlier sculpture; these figures share the strong emotion of the mourners on the Naumburg choir screen (see fig. 12.57) or the Virgin in the *Roettgen Pietà* (see fig. 12.60). Rogier's memorable painting inspired many copies, in both painting and sculpture.

The heightened emotion with which Rogier imbues his works was noted and admired by the Italian diplomat Cyriacus of Ancona, who saw another painting by Rogier on this theme in 1449. (See *Primary Source*, page 485.) This commentator singled out the naturalism in Rogier's work, as he admired the figures who seemed to come alive in Rogier's painting. Other Italian scholars remarked on Flemish painting's naturalism and piety as well. Viewers in Flanders would have brought their own interest in meditating on the sacrifice of Christ to their experience of Rogier's painting.

Rogier's depiction of *St. Luke Drawing the Virgin*, dated between 1435 and 1440 (fig. **14.16**), reveals his debt to earlier Flemish artists. The figure of Mary nursing her son in this image shows the continuing influence of Campin, while the composition is based on a work by Jan van Eyck. In contrast to the *Descent from the Cross*, here Rogier creates a deep landscape that moves into the distance. The figures inhabit a room that opens onto a

garden protected by fortifications. A man and a woman peer over these battlements toward a busy Flemish city in the distance, where shopkeepers open for the day and citizens walk the street.

The painting represents St. Luke the Evangelist in a different role, as the portrayer of the Virgin and Christ Child. A Byzantine tradition explained that the Madonna appeared miraculously to Luke, so that he could take her portrait. This legend helped to account for numerous miraculous images of the Madonna in the later Middle Ages. Rogier depicts Luke drawing the features of the Virgin in **silverpoint** (a drawing technique using a stylus of silver scraped across prepared paper) as she appears before him. (Such drawings were the starting point for most paintings of the period.) Because of this story, St. Luke became the patron of painters' guilds throughout Europe. Later documents describe a painting like this one in the chapel of the Brussels Guild of St. Luke. Since this image depicts the making of an image, Rogier's painting may be a self-conscious statement about the dignity of painting and painters. It was copied numerous times in the fifteenth century, even by Rogier's own workshop. In recent years, scholars have been studying such paintings with new scientific tools that examine the techniques used by the artists. (See *The Art Historian's Lens*, page 488.)

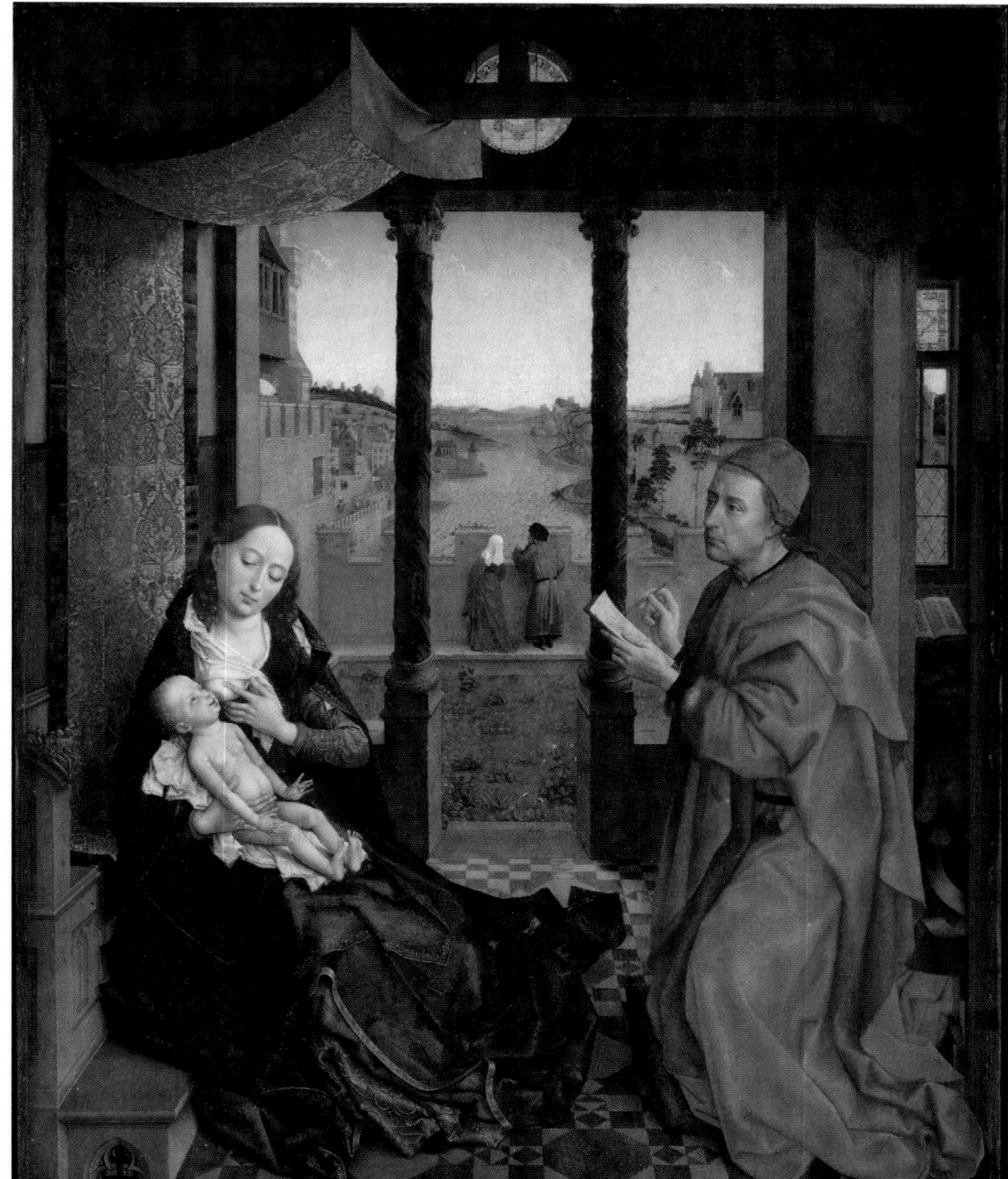

14.16 Rogier van der Weyden, *St. Luke Drawing the Virgin*. ca. 1435–40. Oil and tempera on panel, 54⅛ × 43⅝" (1.38 × 1.11 m). Museum of Fine Arts, Boston. Gift of Mr. and Mrs. Henry Lee Higginson, 1893. Photograph © 2006, Museum of Fine Arts, Boston. 93.153

LATE FIFTEENTH-CENTURY ART IN THE NETHERLANDS

The paintings of Robert Campin, Jan van Eyck, and Rogier van der Weyden offered powerful examples for other artists to follow, in the Netherlands and beyond. In the later fifteenth century, court patrons continued to prefer objects made of expensive materials, particularly gold. They also commissioned illuminated manuscripts and tapestries. At the same time, patronage by the merchant class continued to grow, and painters found work in commissions from the middle classes. Nonetheless, the medium of painting gained in prestige as the century wore on, attracting interest and patronage in aristocratic circles. Despite the increasing market for paintings, large-scale sculpture continued to find a market in the fifteenth-century Netherlands, though little has survived the ravages of war, social and religious upheavals, and changes of taste. Even rarer are survivals of objects made in precious metals, as the very valuable raw material was easily recycled when money was scarce.

Aristocratic Tastes for Precious Objects, Personal Books, and Tapestries

Aristocratic patrons commissioned small-scale precious objects throughout the fifteenth century. One, whose brilliance makes us mourn the loss of others, is the *Statuette of Charles the Bold*, preserved in the treasury of the cathedral of Liège in eastern Belgium

Scientific and Technical Study of Paintings

Investigative tools used in the contemporary scientific study of materials are providing new information about the practices of artists in the past. The very materiality of works of art makes them appropriate for the same sort of study as archaeological discoveries. Chemical analysis of paints and pigments is providing information on the recipes for making paints that artists used. This information can be used to examine workshop practices, to establish authenticity of given objects, and to suggest methods of conservation.

Modern scholars use a variety of techniques to investigate paintings. **X-radiographic** imaging penetrates painted surfaces and produces a photographic analysis of the use of lead in the painting process. Because lead white was used to lighten pigments, x-radiographs allow an investigator to examine how an artist modeled forms with lighter colors. X-radiographs also reveal details about an artist's brushwork or changes made as the painting progressed. Another technique uses **infrared light**, which can see through painted surfaces to distinguish dark marks on the white ground of a panel. Aided by special infrared cameras (a technique called **infrared reflectography**), analysts can photograph the underdrawings and initial paint layers below painted surfaces; computers match these photos to produce images of the preparatory layers of the painting. This information is invaluable for studying the creative process. It has also aided in determining which of the many versions of Rogier's *St. Luke Drawing the Virgin* (see fig. 14.16) was executed first.

Because many Renaissance panels are painted on wood, scholars have been able to determine the age of a particular panel from the number of tree rings in it, using a technique known as *dendrochronology*. The number of tree rings in a panel is then compared to a database of tree rings that have been dated to define the time when the tree was probably cut down. This can then provide additional evidence for dating the painting. Such evidence has caused some scholars to date Bosch's *The Garden of Earthly Delights* (see fig. 14.22) to around 1480. Similar techniques have revealed the composition of the limestone used in Gothic sculpture and the chemical makeup of ancient bronzes.

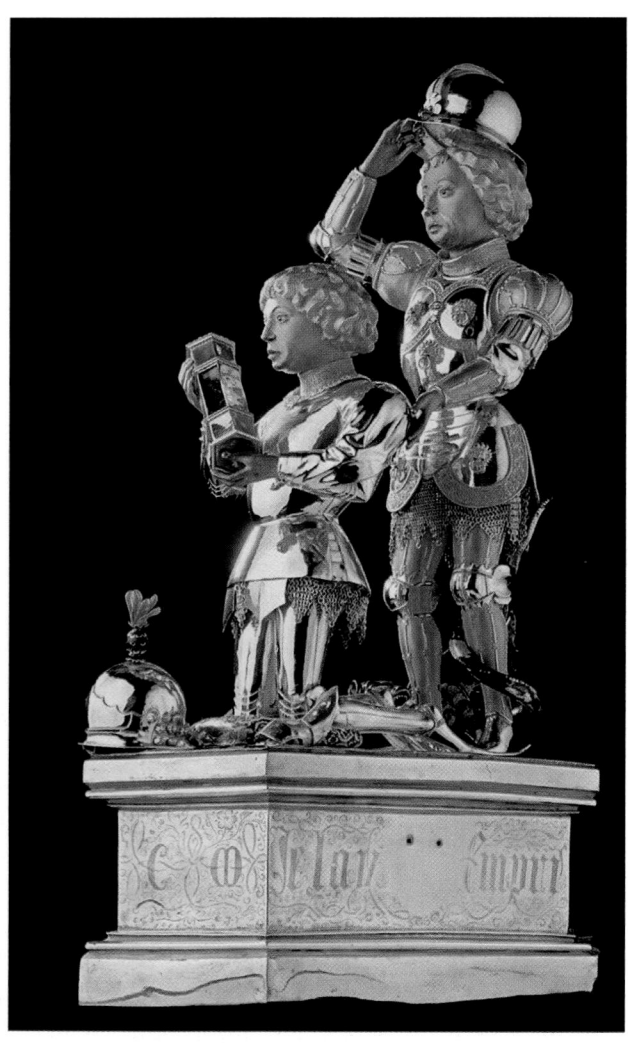

14.17 Gerard Loyet, *Statuette of Charles the Bold*. ca. 1471. 21 × 12½ × 7" (53 × 32 × 17.5 cm). Cathedral treasury, Liège

(fig. **14.17**). Duke Charles the Bold of Burgundy commissioned the goldsmith Gerard Loyet (before 1442–1500) to make this figure; he then gave it to the cathedral in Liège in 1471, perhaps to assert his control over that rebellious city. Made of gold and silver gilt with enamel details, the 21-inch-high statuette represents Duke Charles holding a reliquary; behind him stands St. George, Charles's favorite patron saint, who lifts his helmet in greeting. The duke is dressed in armor, kneeling on a pillow to make his offering. The object demonstrates Loyet's skill and the prestige of such objects in the Burgundian court. The composition derives from a painting by Jan van Eyck, and so reflects the rising status of panel painters as creative innovators.

The taste of the court also ran to expensive books. Despite the introduction of the printing press (see pages 499–502), among the traditional elites, the manuscript book—custom-made to celebrate the purchaser's status and interests—retained its appeal. Books of hours, in which prayers were organized into cycles according to the hours of the day, appealed especially to women. A striking example of a complex and lavish illuminated book is the *Hours of Mary of Burgundy*, which includes the coat of arms of Mary, daughter of Charles the Bold and last duchess of Burgundy, evidence that she owned the book before her death in 1482.

Mary herself may be the woman depicted in figure **14.18**. In this full-page miniature, the anonymous artist (named after this book of hours) depicts an elegantly dressed young woman reading from a book of hours similar to the *Hours of Mary of Burgundy*. Her costume and surroundings indicate her status: Golden brocades, transparent veils, jewelry, and flowers surround her, and a little dog rests on her lap. She sits in a private chapel, whose windows open onto a view of a light-filled Gothic church. Through the window the viewer sees the Virgin Mary with her child seated in the sanctuary, surrounded by angels. To the right

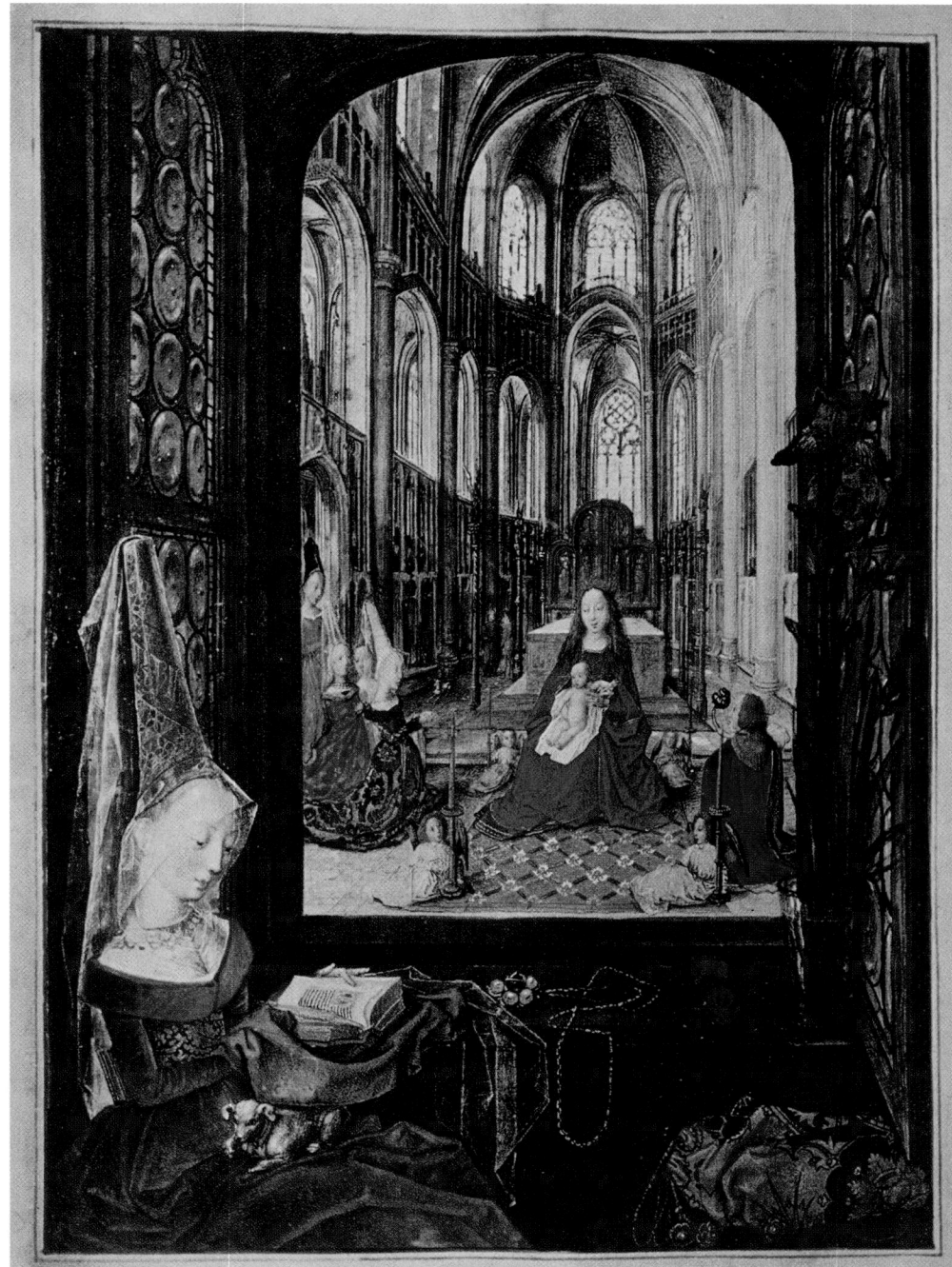

14.18 Mary of Burgundy Painter, page with *Mary at Her Devotions*, from the *Hours of Mary of Burgundy*. ca. 1480 (before 1482). Colors and ink on parchment, 7½ × 5¼" (19.1 × 13.3 cm). Österreichisches Nationalbibliothek, Vienna. E 28.560-C, Cod. 1857. fol. 14v

of these sacred figures kneels a group of noble women, whose access to the child and his mother may be what the woman in the foreground prays for.

The artist creates a picture within a picture here, as the glimpse into the church is completely framed by the architecture of the lady's chapel. Earlier manuscript artists (like the Limbourg Brothers) usually put floral or other decorative motifs in the border and created a spatial context only for the main image. This artist, however, treats the border as a spatial entity in its own right that links the border and the main image. The artist takes care to record the tactile and sensuous quality of the dog's fur, the transparency of the glass vase, and the reflective qualities of the pearls on the ledge. The manuscript page has the impact of a painted panel.

The court was also the key market for the flourishing industry in tapestries. Major workshops practiced in Brussels, Tournai, and Arras; the latter city's name became synonymous with the art form. Woven with colored threads of wool or silk, tapestries were popular with the courtly class or their peers in the Church. The tapestry fragment of *Penelope Weaving* (fig. **14.19**), for example, was part of a series of "Famous Women" commissioned by the bishop of Tournai around 1480. The image depicts the wife of Odysseus (or Ulysses) working at a loom. According to Homer's *Odyssey*, Penelope fended off her numerous suitors with her weaving; she insisted she would not marry again until she had completed her work, which she unwove every evening. Although a figure from the classical past, Penelope is dressed in the costume

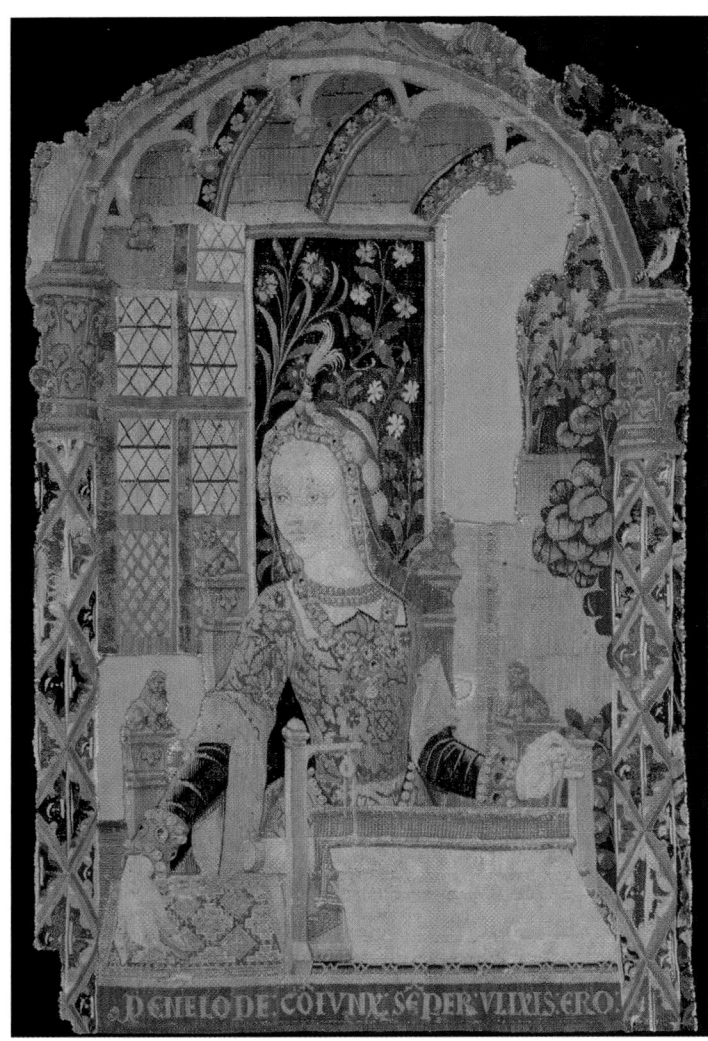

of a fifteenth-century lady. The influence of paintings is apparent in the suggestion of space, the detailed treatment of her gems and garment, and in the figure. On the wall behind Penelope hangs a tapestry within the tapestry, in a two-dimensional pattern of repeated floral forms called *millefleurs*, one of the best-selling designs for tapestry in the fifteenth century. The court of Burgundy shared their Italian contemporaries' interest in stories of the ancients as exemplars for the present, but they envisioned them in familiar, not historic terms. The naturalism of the Flemish painters provided a language for the tapestry weavers to satisfy courtly taste.

Panel Paintings in the Southern Netherlands

While the court collected precious objects, illuminated manuscripts, and tapestries, the middle-class demand for panel paintings continued to grow. International businessmen invested their money and their reputations in commissioning paintings from Flemish artists like Hugo van der Goes (ca. 1440–1482). Having served as dean of the painters' guild of Ghent, Hugo entered a monastery near Brussels as a lay brother in 1475. He continued to paint there until his death in 1482. His best-known work is the huge altarpiece commissioned around 1474 by an agent of the

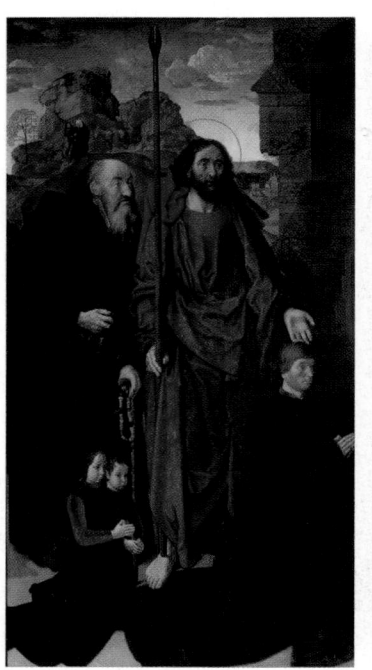
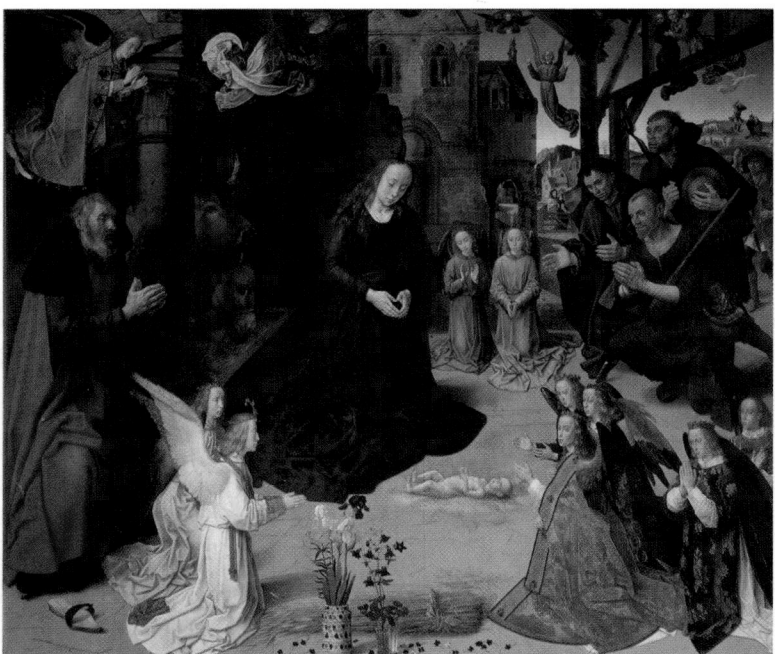
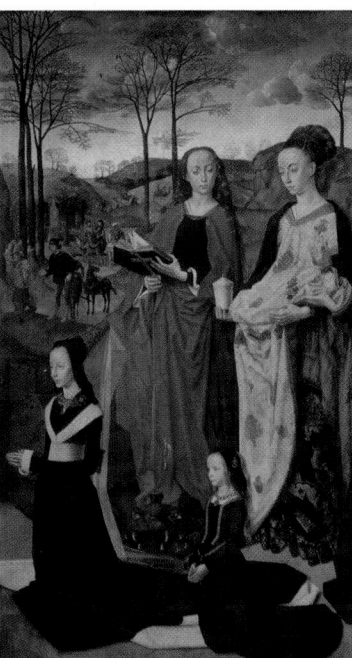

14.20 Hugo van der Goes, *The Portinari Altarpiece* (open). ca. 1474–76. Tempera and oil on panel, center 8'3½"× 10' (2.5 × 3.1 m), wings each 8'3½"× 4'7½" (2.5 × 1.4 m). Galleria degli Uffizi, Florence

Medici bank in Bruges, who shipped it to Florence (fig. **14.20**). The 10-foot-wide central panel represents the Virgin, St. Joseph, and shepherds adoring the newborn Christ Child in Bethlehem. In the wings, members of the donor family, including Tommaso Portinari, his wife, Maria Maddelena Baroncelli, and their children, kneel to face the central image. A spacious landscape unites all three wings as a continuous space, with the bare trees and December sky suggesting not the Holy Land but Flanders itself. Objects in the distance have turned the blue of the atmosphere; this use of **atmospheric perspective** (a technique that recognizes the loss of color in distant objects) infuses the panel with a cool tonality. Hugo filled this setting with figures and objects rendered with precise detail in deeply saturated colors.

Despite Hugo's realistic renderings of both landscape and figures, the image contains numerous contradictions for expressive effect. Figures vary greatly in scale: The angels and kneeling members of the Portinari family are dwarfed by the other figures; the patron saints in the wings are the same size as Joseph, the Virgin Mary, and the shepherds of the Nativity in the center panel. These shifts of scale undermine the pictorial space that the artist has provided for his figures. Another contrast occurs between the raucous intrusion of the shepherds and the ritual solemnity of all the other figures. These fieldhands gaze in breathless wonder at the newborn Christ Child, who is the focus of all the figures ranged around him. Mary, however, sits at the physical center of the

composition. Such deliberate contrasts between the pictorial and psychological focal points, between the scale of the historical and the contemporary figures, and between the static and kinetic postures of the figures contribute to the unsettling effect of the work.

The background is populated with narratives that support the main theme. Behind the figures in the left-hand panel, Mary and Joseph travel toward Bethlehem. Behind the saints on the right, the Magi progress toward the center. And in the center, angels flicker across the surface, lit by both natural and supernatural light. Strategically placed at the front of the picture is a beautiful **still life** of flowers and a sheaf of wheat. As with so many other realistic details in Flemish paintings, these have been interpreted symbolically. The wheat refers to the bread of the Eucharist and the flowers to the Virgin. Portinari brought the triptych to Florence in 1483 and installed it in the family chapel attached to the hospital of Sant' Egidio. There it proclaimed the taste, wealth, and piety of the donor. Judging from their imitation of it, Italian painters who saw the work there especially admired its naturalism and its unidealized representation of the shepherds.

Triptychs were often intended for liturgical spaces. For more domestic spaces, patrons wanted smaller objects. For example, the young up-and-coming citizen of Bruges Martin van Nieuwenhove commissioned a diptych from Hans Memling in 1487 (fig. **14.21**). Born in Germany (ca. 1435–1494), Memling worked in Bruges, where his refined style, based on Rogier and

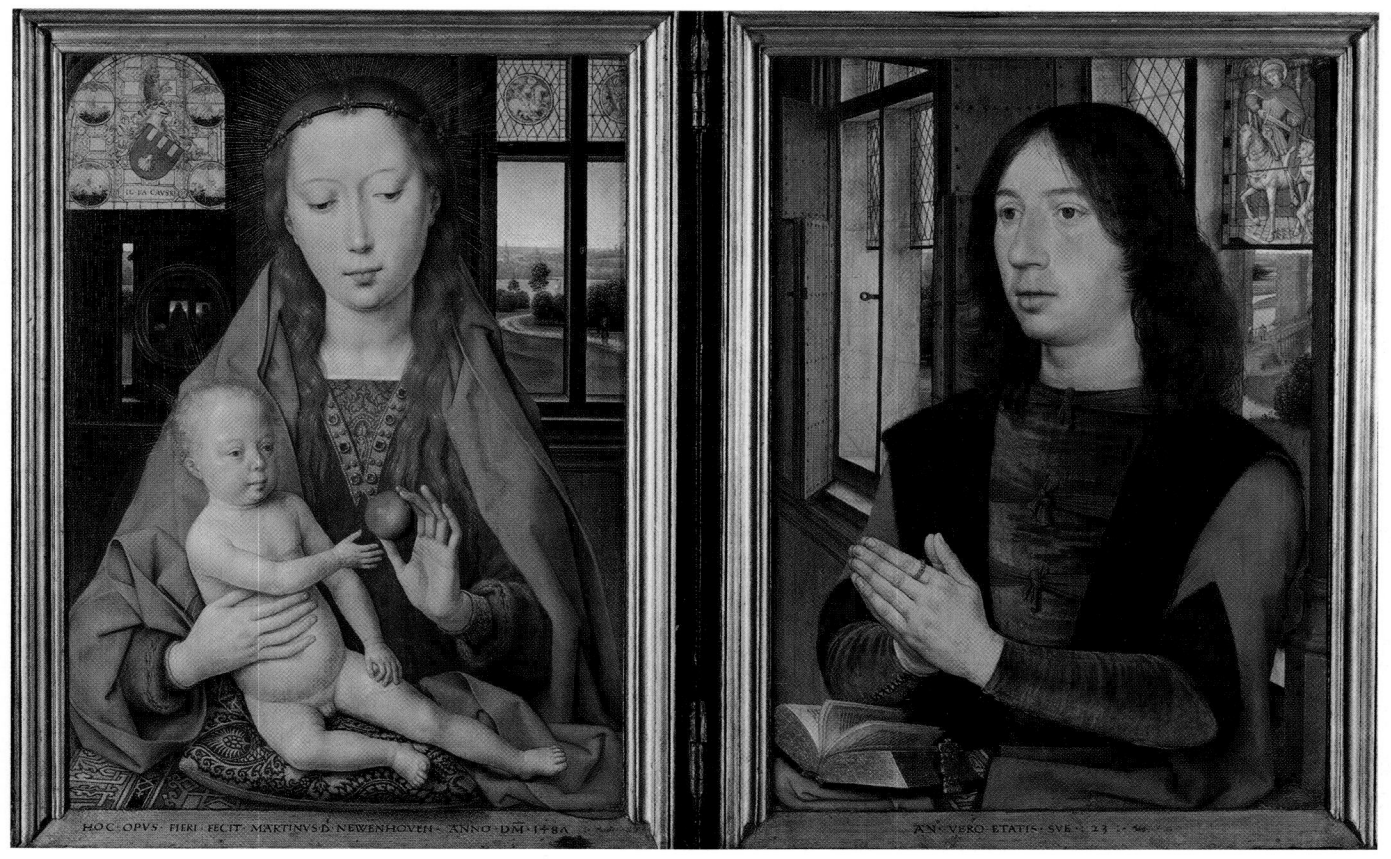

14.21 Hans Memling, *Madonna and Child*, left-hand wing of *Diptych of Martin van Nieuwenhove*. 1487. Panel, 17⅜ × 13" (44 × 33 cm). Hans Memling Museum, Musea Brugge, Sint-Jans Hospital, Bruges

Jan van Eyck, brought him commissions from patrons from all over Europe. Italians in Bruges especially preferred his workshop, as did local patricians like Van Nieuwenhove. An inscription on the frame of his diptych identifies the patron and gives his age, while his stylish garment and gilt-edged prayer book express his social status. Behind him a piece of stained glass represents his patron saint, Martin. The young man focuses his gaze on the left-hand panel, where an image of the Virgin and Child appears. Martin's family coat of arms in the window behind them implies that the Virgin and Child are visiting him in his own home. The reflection in the mirror further expresses this conceit: the artist has included the reflections of both the Virgin and young man appearing in the same space. Memling has borrowed the concave mirror Jan van Eyck used in *The "Arnolfini Portrait"* (see fig. 14.14) to unite the two halves of the diptych.

Memling's image demonstrates a new trend in portraiture: In addition to rendering the features, he creates a believable setting for the figure. This contrasts to the inky blackness behind the figure in Jan van Eyck's *Man in a Red Turban* (see fig. 14.13). Access to the divine remains a preoccupation for otherwise worldly men; in this light-filled room, Martin kneels in permanent prayer, so that the image becomes an expression of his devotion. But this object also served as a piece of self-promotion, as the many personal references to the patron display his self-assurance and social status.

The Northern Netherlands

The innovations of the early fifteenth-century painters quickly spread to the northern Netherlands (present-day Holland), the origin of one of the most famous paintings from the era, Hieronymus Bosch's *The Garden of Earthly Delights* (fig. **14.22**). Bosch (ca. 1450–1516) came from a family of painters. He spent his life in the town of 's Hertogenbosch, the seat of a ducal residence, from which his name derives. His patrons included the duke of Burgundy, whose grandson, King Philip II of Spain, owned numerous Bosch paintings in the sixteenth century; it was in Philip's collection that Fray José de Sigüenza encountered Bosch's painting. (See *Primary Source*, page 494.) Sigüenza's account has been an important document for interpreting this complex and surprising painting, whose subject and meaning have been vigorously debated.

Divided into three panels, *The Garden of Earthly Delights* represents humans in the natural world. A continuous landscape unites the three sections; the high horizon and atmospheric perspective imply a deep vista of the earth from an omniscient vantage point. Shades of green create an undulating topography marked by thickets of trees and bodies of water. Throughout, small creatures both human and nonhuman swarm, while strange rock formations and other objects appear at intervals. As Sigüenza says, the left-hand wing appears to represent the Garden of Eden,

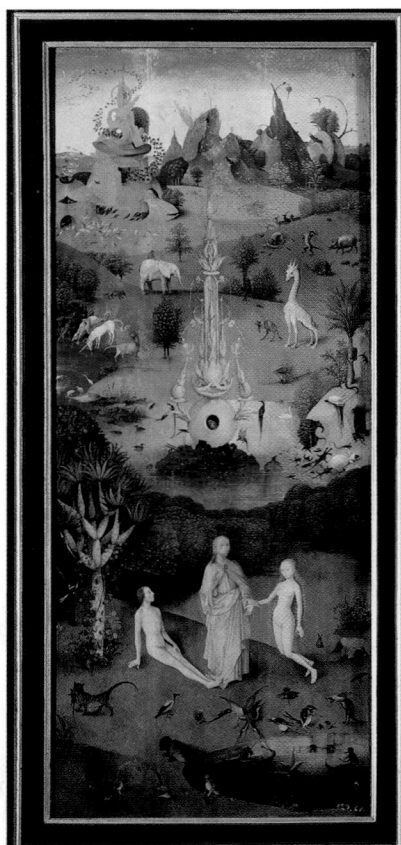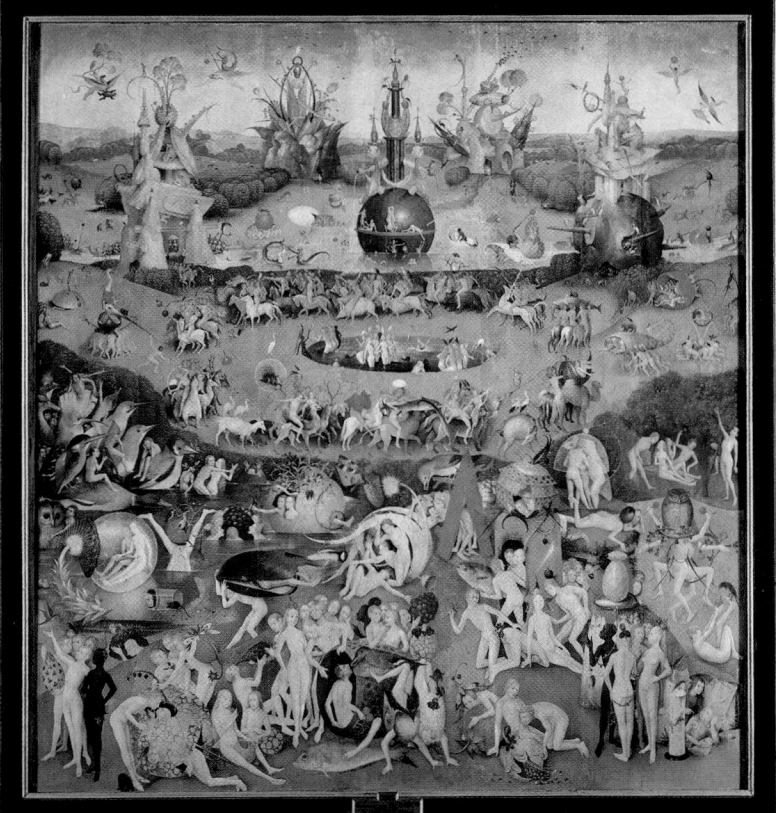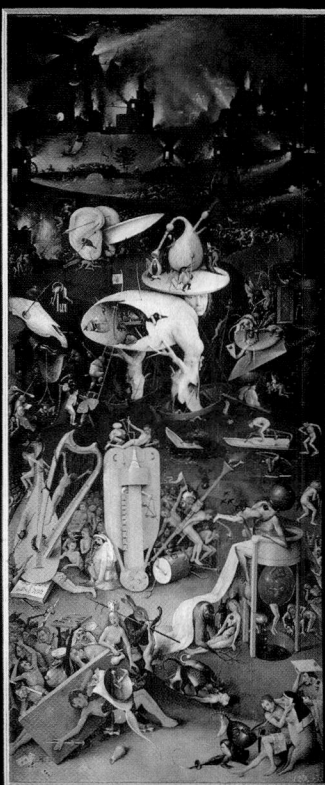

14.22 Hieronymus Bosch, *The Garden of Earthly Delights*. ca. 1480–1515. Oil on panel, center 7'2½"× 6'4½" (2.19 × 1.95 m), each wing 7'2½"× 3'2" (2.19 × 0.96 m). Museo del Prado, Madrid

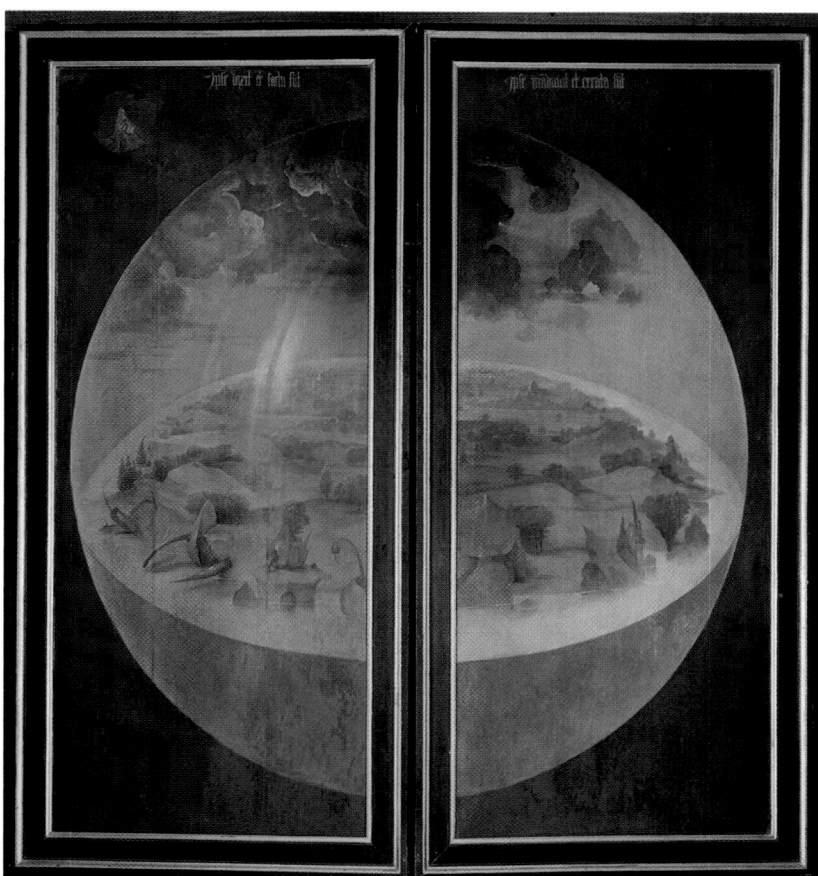

14.23 Hieronymus Bosch, *The Garden of Earthly Delights* (outer wings closed). ca. 1480–1515. Oil on panel, each wing 7'2½" × 3'2" (2.19 × 0.96 m). Museo del Prado, Madrid

where the Lord introduces Adam to the newly created Eve. This airy landscape is filled with animals, including such exotic creatures as an elephant and a giraffe; it also includes strange hybrid monsters. The central panel reveals a world inhabited by tiny humans who frolic among giant fruits, birds, and other creatures. In the middle ground, men parade around a circular basin on the backs of all sorts of beasts. Many of the humans interact with huge birds, fruits, flowers, or marine animals. The right-hand wing depicts an infernal zone, which may be Hell, where strange hybrid creatures torment the tiny humans with punishments appropriate to their sins. When the triptych is closed (fig. **14.23**), its outer wings depict a crystal globe with an image of the earth emerging from the waters, with God watching over the events from above. An inscription from Psalm 33 says: "For he spoke and it came to pass; he commanded it and it stood forth." Some see this image as the third day of creation, others identify it as the flood of Noah.

Despite its triptych format, this is not a traditional altarpiece but a secular work. It belonged to Count Henry III of Nassau, in whose palace in Brussels it was reported to be in 1517, though recent research suggests Bosch could have painted it as early as 1480. Many scholars place it ca. 1500–1505 and assume that Henry of Nassau commissioned it. Scholars have studied many different aspects of Bosch's painting in an effort to find the key to its meaning. Some have looked at the numerous visual references to verbal puns and proverbs. One theory holds that it represents

the time of Noah, as shown by the image of a flood on the exterior; another that the many swarming nudes express the views of a heretical group that promoted free love; yet another that the infernal landscape in the right-hand wing demonstrates a moralizing condemnation of carnal sin.

These interpretations suggest that Bosch was a pessimist sermonizing about the depravity of humankind. This is certainly the way that José de Sigüenza described it, although his text also suggests several "allegories or metaphors" embedded in the painting. Yet the image itself is beautifully painted and as seductive as the sirens in the pool in the middle of the central panel. There is an innocence, even a poetic beauty, in this panorama of human activity that suggests something other than outright condemnation of the acts so carefully depicted. This ambivalence has fueled numerous interpretations, including a recent proposal that the image depicts an alternative view of history in which the Original Sin of Adam and Eve does not happen, and therefore humans continue to live in a state of innocence.

Another interpretation of this painting links it to the practice of alchemy as an allegory of redemption. The many strangely shaped rocks and fountains refer to the tools and vessels used in this medieval science. Bosch married an apothecary's daughter, so his use of the visual symbols of that science has a strong historical basis. If we consider its secular function and the interests of his educated patron, however, Bosch's painting seems to warn its audience against too much concern for sensual pleasures in the world.

Fray José de Sigüenza (1544?–1606)

From *The History of the Order of St. Jerome*

The works of Hieronymus Bosch were collected by the Spanish king Philip II (r. 1556–1598) and were displayed in his Escorial Palace near Madrid, where Sigüenza was the librarian. The interpretation of Bosch's work was as difficult then as it is today and caused just as much disagreement. This passage is Sigüenza's attempt to interpret the painting that we call The Garden of Earthly Delights *(see fig. 14.22).*

Among these German and Flemish pictures...there are distributed throughout the house many by a certain Geronimo Bosch. Of him I want to speak at somewhat greater length for various reasons: first, because his great inventiveness merits it; second, because they are commonly called the absurdities of Geronimo Bosque by people who observe little in what they look at; and third, because I think that these people consider them without reason as being tainted by heresy....

The difference that, to my mind, exists between the pictures of this man and those of all others is that the others try to paint man as he appears on the outside, while he alone had the audacity to paint him as he is on the inside....

The...painting has as its basic theme and subject a flower and the fruit of [a] type that we call strawberries.... In order for one to understand his idea, I will expound upon it in the same order in which he has organized it. Between two pictures is one large painting, with two doors that close over it. In the first of the panels he painted the Creation of Man, showing how God put him in paradise, a delightful place...and how He commands him as a test of his obedience and faith not to eat from the tree, and how later the devil deceived him in the form of a serpent. He eats and, trespassing God's rule, is exiled from that wondrous place and deprived of the high dignity for which he was created.... This is [shown] with a thousand fantasies and observations that serve as warnings....

In the large painting that follows he painted the pursuits of man after he was exiled from paradise and placed in this world, and he shows him searching after the glory that is like hay or straw, like a plant without fruit, which one knows will be cast into the oven the next day...and thus uncovers the life, the activities, and the thoughts of these sons of sin and wrath, who, having forgotten the commands of God...strive for and undertake the glory of the flesh....

In this painting we find, as if alive and vivid, an infinite number of passages from the scriptures that touch upon the evil ways of man...many allegories or metaphors that present them in the guise of tame, wild, fierce, lazy, sagacious, cruel, and bloodthirsty beasts of burden and riding animals.... Here is also demonstrated the transmigration of souls that Pythagoras, Plato, and other poets...displayed in the attempt to show us the bad customs, habits, dress, disposition, or sinister shades with which the souls of miserable men clothe themselves—that through pride they are transformed into lions; by vengefulness into tigers; through lust into mules, horses, and pigs; by tyranny into fish; by vanity into peacocks; by slyness and craft into foxes; by gluttony into apes and wolves; by callousness and evil into asses; by stupidity into sheep; because of rashness into goats....

One can reap great profit by observing himself thus portrayed true to life from the inside....And he would also see in the last panel the miserable end and goal of his pains, efforts, and preoccupations, and how...the brief joys are transformed into eternal wrath, with no hope or grace.

REGIONAL RESPONSES TO THE EARLY NETHERLANDISH STYLE

Artists in many regions of Europe responded to the formal and technical achievements of the generation of Robert Campin and Jan van Eyck. Local traditions and tastes influenced these regional responses, but patrons found the naturalism of the new style useful for their religious and social purposes. Many regions of Europe, among them France, Spain, and Central Europe, therefore produced their own variations on this style.

France

The geographic proximity, trade routes, linguistic links, and political relationships between the Burgundian Netherlands and France helped to spread the innovations in technique and style throughout France. Artists either traveled to Flemish cities or developed their own brand of naturalism in imitation of the effects that Rogier van der Weyden or Hugo van der Goes had achieved (see figs. 14.15 and 14.20). Still, French art has its own distinctive characteristics. In the first half of the fifteenth century, the troubles of the Hundred Years' War limited expenditure on art. Citizens of the war-torn cities commissioned very little, but members of the Church and court continued earlier forms of patronage.

After establishing his rule at the close of the Hundred Years' War, King Charles VII of France appointed Jean Fouquet (ca. 1420–1481) of Tours as his court painter. Both a book illuminator and a panel painter, Fouquet traveled to Italy around 1445, where he learned some of the innovations of contemporary Italian art (see Chapter 15). His work, however, owes much to the Netherlandish style in technique, color, and approach. Charles VII's treasurer, Étienne Chevalier, commissioned Fouquet around 1450 to paint a diptych representing himself and his patron saint, Stephen, in proximity to the Virgin and Child, the so-called *Melun Diptych* (figs. **14.24** and **14.25**). Like his Flemish contemporaries, Fouquet records the specific physiognomy of the patron in his fur-lined garment. The head of the saint, who carries a book and a stone (which refers to his martyrdom), seems as individual as that of the donor.

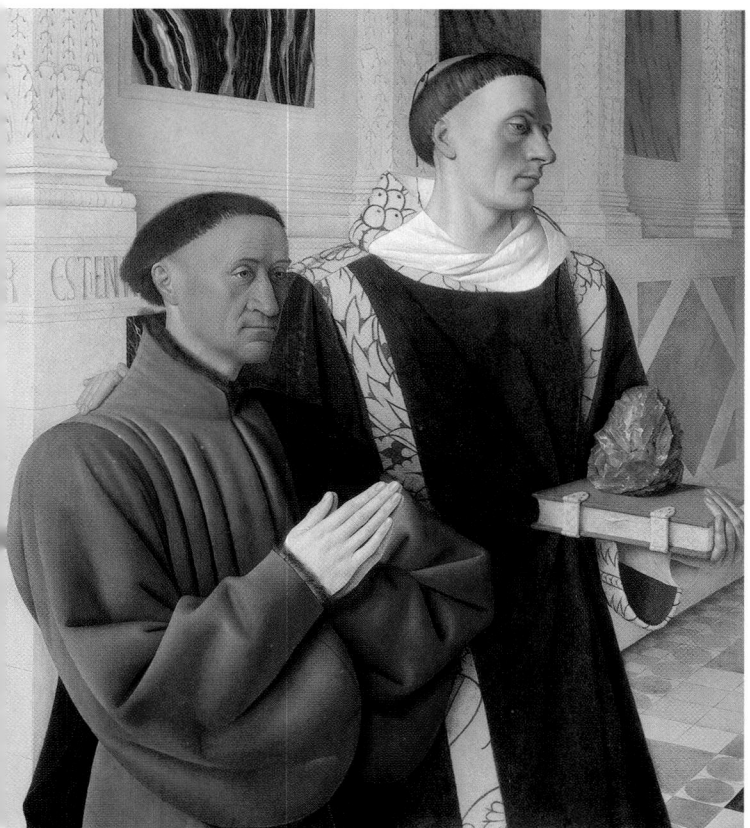

14.24 Jean Fouquet, *Étienne Chevalier and St. Stephen*, left wing of
the *Melun Diptych*. ca. 1450. Oil on panel, 36½ × 33½" (92.7 × 85 cm).
Staatliche Museen zu Berlin, Gemäldegalerie

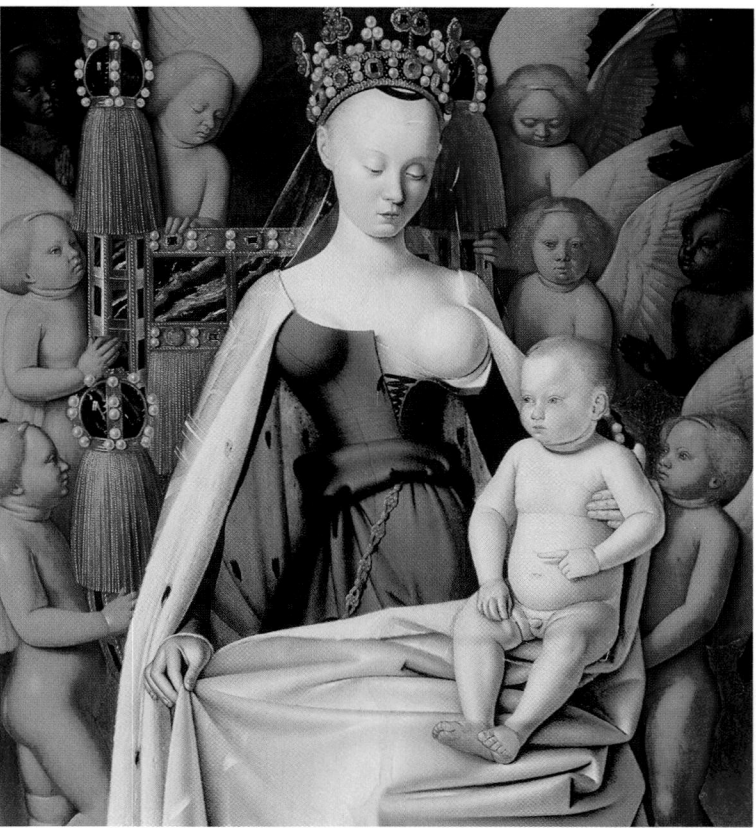

14.25 Jean Fouquet, *Madonna and Child*, right wing of the *Melun
Diptych*. ca. 1450. Oil on panel, 36⅝ × 33½" (94.5 × 85.5 cm).
Koninklijk Museum Voor Schone Kunsten, Antwerpen Belgie
(Musée Royal des Beaux-Arts, Antwerp, Belgium)

They stand in a room with marbled floors and marble panels
on the walls, framed by antique-inspired pilasters that recede
to suggest space. The two men gaze across the frame toward
an image of the enthroned Virgin and Child. According to an
old tradition, the Madonna is also a portrait: of Agnès Sorel,
Charles VII's mistress. If so, the panel presents an image of
courtly beauty, as befits the Queen of Heaven, seen wearing a
crown amid a choir of angels. Fouquet deliberately contrasts the
earthly and divine realms. The deep space in the left panel differs
strikingly from that on the right, organized as a rising triangle,
with the cool colors of the Virgin and Child set against the vivid
reds and blues of the angels. In contrast to his Flemish counterparts, Fouquet is not interested in suggesting specific textures,
and he subordinates details to the overall design. He does not
appeal to the emotions. His images are geometrically ordered and
rational rather than expressive.

Spain

Netherlandish naturalism reverberated strongly on the Iberian
peninsula in the fifteenth century. Artists traveled between
Flanders and Spain, and trade, diplomacy, and a dynastic marriage
brought the united kingdoms of Castile and Aragon into increasingly close contact with Flanders. These contacts were echoed in

the works of art imported into Spain from Flanders and in works
of art produced in Spain by local artists.

A powerful example of the Spanish interpretation of Flemish
naturalism is the *Pietà* painted in 1490 by Bartolomé Bermejo (ca.
1440–1500) for a deacon of the cathedral of Barcelona (fig. **14.26**).
Bermejo was born in Córdoba, but he worked in many regions of
Spain, and may have been trained in Bruges. His *Pietà* sets the
image of the Virgin grieving for her dead son in a dark and atmospheric landscape dominated by an empty cross. Instead of the
historical mourners called for by the narrative, and included by
Giotto in his fresco in Padua (see fig. 13.20), Mary and Christ are
flanked by St. Jerome to a viewer's left (the lion is his attribute)
and a portrait of the deacon to the right. This removes the theme
from a strict narrative context and makes the painting function as
an image of devotion similar to the *Roettgen Pietà* (see fig. 12.60),
though the precise detail of the figures and the landscape derive
from Flemish models. In contrast to the cool rationality of
Fouquet, Bermejo's work is highly emotional and expressive.

Central Europe

Linked by trade and political ties to the Netherlands, artists and
patrons in Central Europe were also receptive to the new style,
especially in cities along the Rhine (see map 14.1). One such artist,

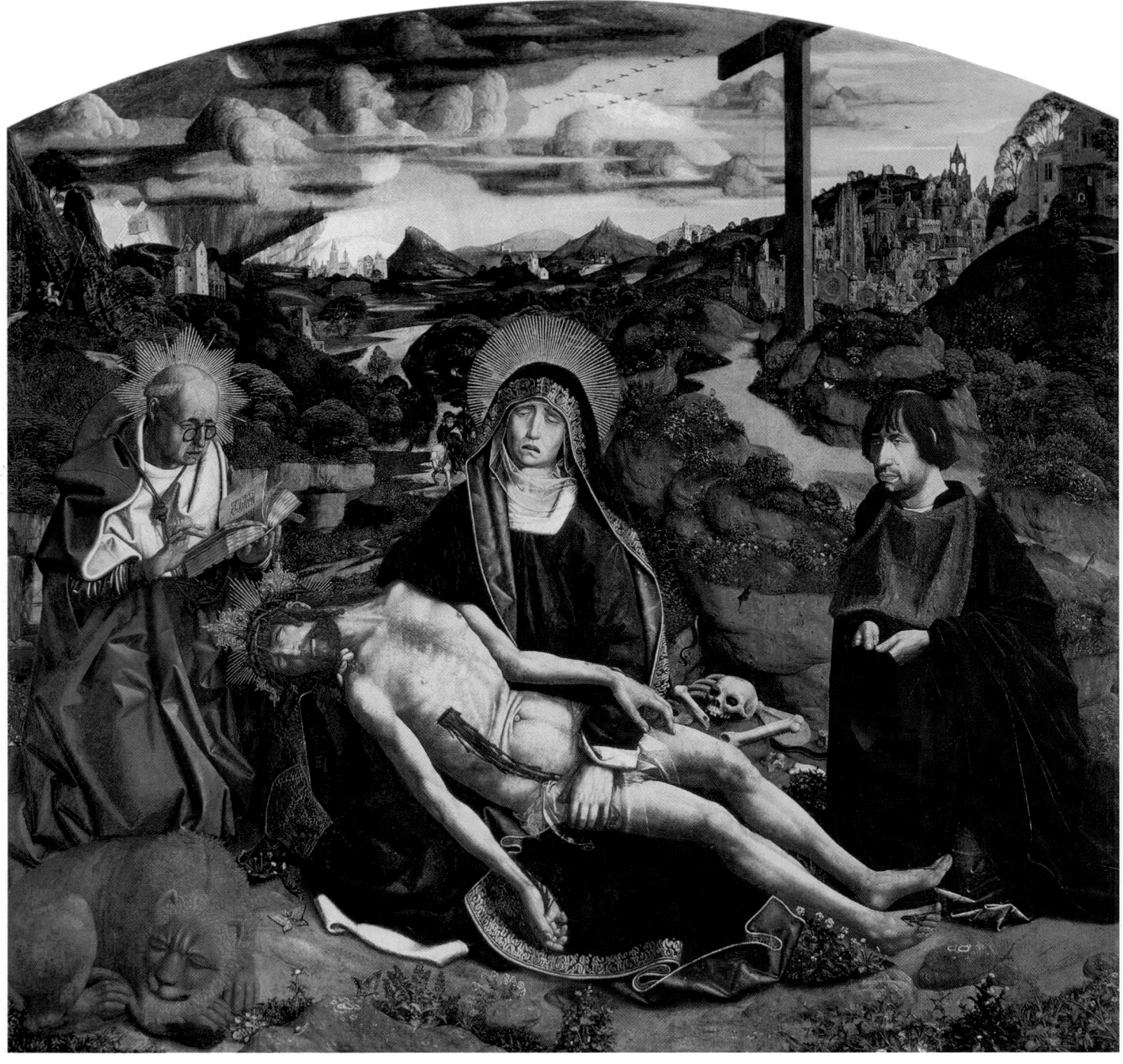

14.26 Bartolomé Bermejo, *Pietà*, cathedral, Barcelona. 1490. Panel, 74⅜ × 68⅞" (189 × 175 cm) including frame

Conrad Witz (1400/10–1445/46) became a citizen of Basel, Switzerland, and a master in the city's guild of painters at just the moment that the Church's Council of Basel concluded. This council, or synod, had met from 1431 to 1434 to debate whether the pope alone or councils of bishops had the right to determine doctrine. These controversial issues inform the paintings Witz made in 1444 for the bishop of Geneva, which were destined for the cathedral of St. Peter.

The panels represent scenes from the life of St. Peter, *The Miraculous Draught of Fishes* (fig. 14.27) depicts Christ calling St. Peter to walk across the Sea of Galilee to join him. The solidly modeled figure of Christ dominates the right-hand side of the composition, in part because his red garment contrasts vividly with the green tones of the painting. St. Peter appears twice, once in the boat among other apostles, who are called to be "fishers of men," and again sinking into the waters upon which Christ seems to float. The technique and style owe much to the Flemings, but Witz devotes his attention to the landscape. In place of the Sea of Galilee, Witz substitutes Lake Geneva, emphasizing local topography, such as the distinctive mountain above Christ's head. He accurately depicts every reflection on the water, so that we can see the bottom of the lake in the foreground and a variety of textures

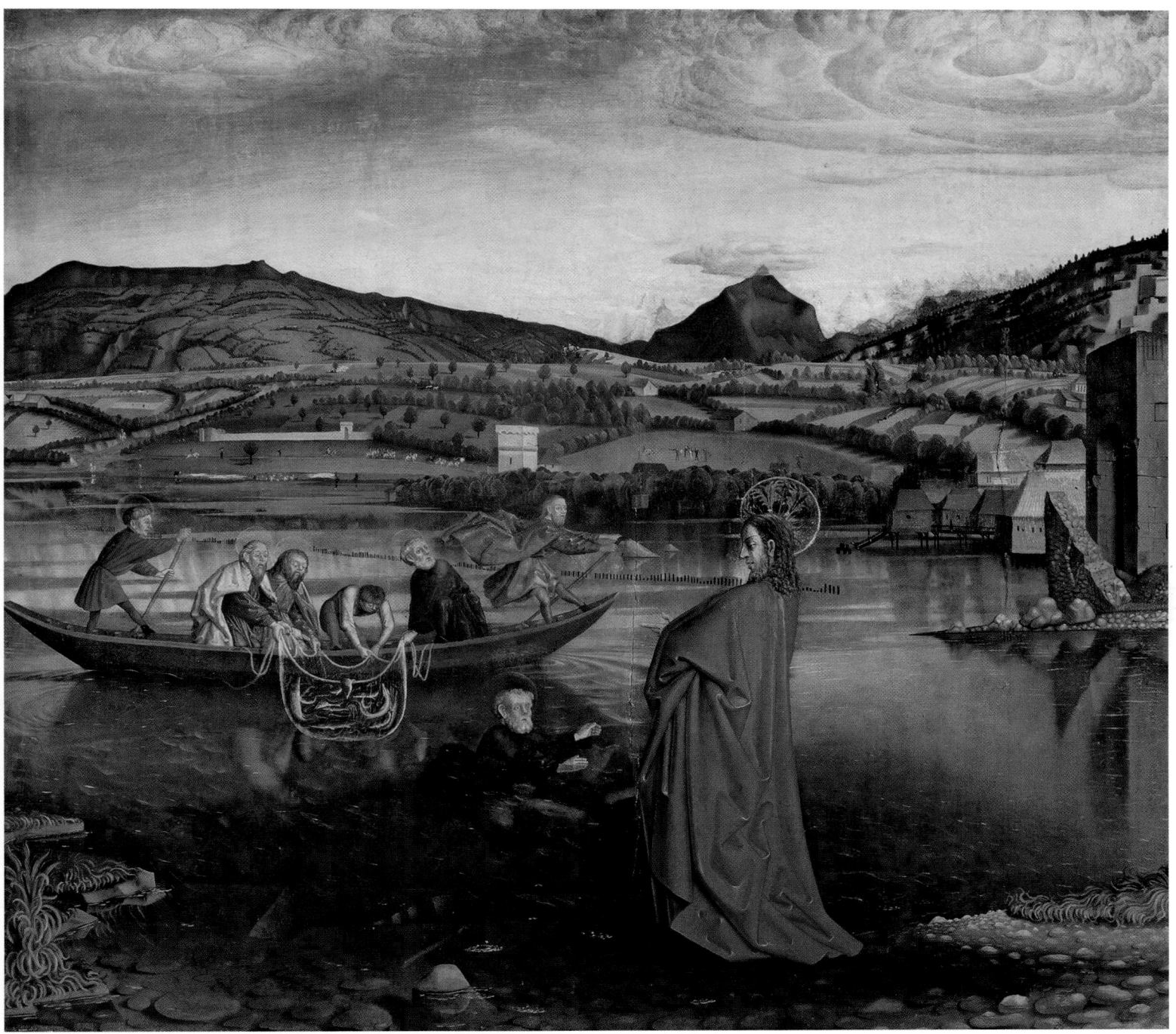

14.27 Conrad Witz, *The Miraculous Draught of Fishes*. 1444. Oil on wood of fir tree, 51 × 61" (132 × 154 cm). Musée d'Art et d'Histoire, Geneva, Switzerland. 1843.11

on the water's surface in the background. Witz places the events of the historical past in the setting of the present. Peter's sinking into the water, suggesting his need for assistance, may be evidence of the bishop's support for the council's role in advising the pope.

AN ALTARPIECE IN ITS ORIGINAL SETTING Witz's panels were originally the wings of an altarpiece, many of which had sculptures as their central element, or **corpus**. In German-speaking regions, altarpieces were usually made of wood, often large and intricately carved. Protestant reformers in the sixteenth century destroyed many sculpted religious images, so surviving

examples are relatively rare. The *St. Wolfgang Altarpiece* (fig. **14.28**) by the Tyrolean sculptor and painter Michael Pacher (ca. 1435–1498) is impressive both because of its scale and because it remains in its original setting.

The surviving contract between the abbot who commissioned it and the painter specifies both the subject matter and the quality of the materials and workmanship. (See *Primary Source*, page 499.) This was the normal pattern for contracts given to artists for expensive projects in the period.

Much as Jan van Eyck did in the *Ghent Altarpiece*, Pacher creates a vision of Heaven: The corpus depicts the coronation of the

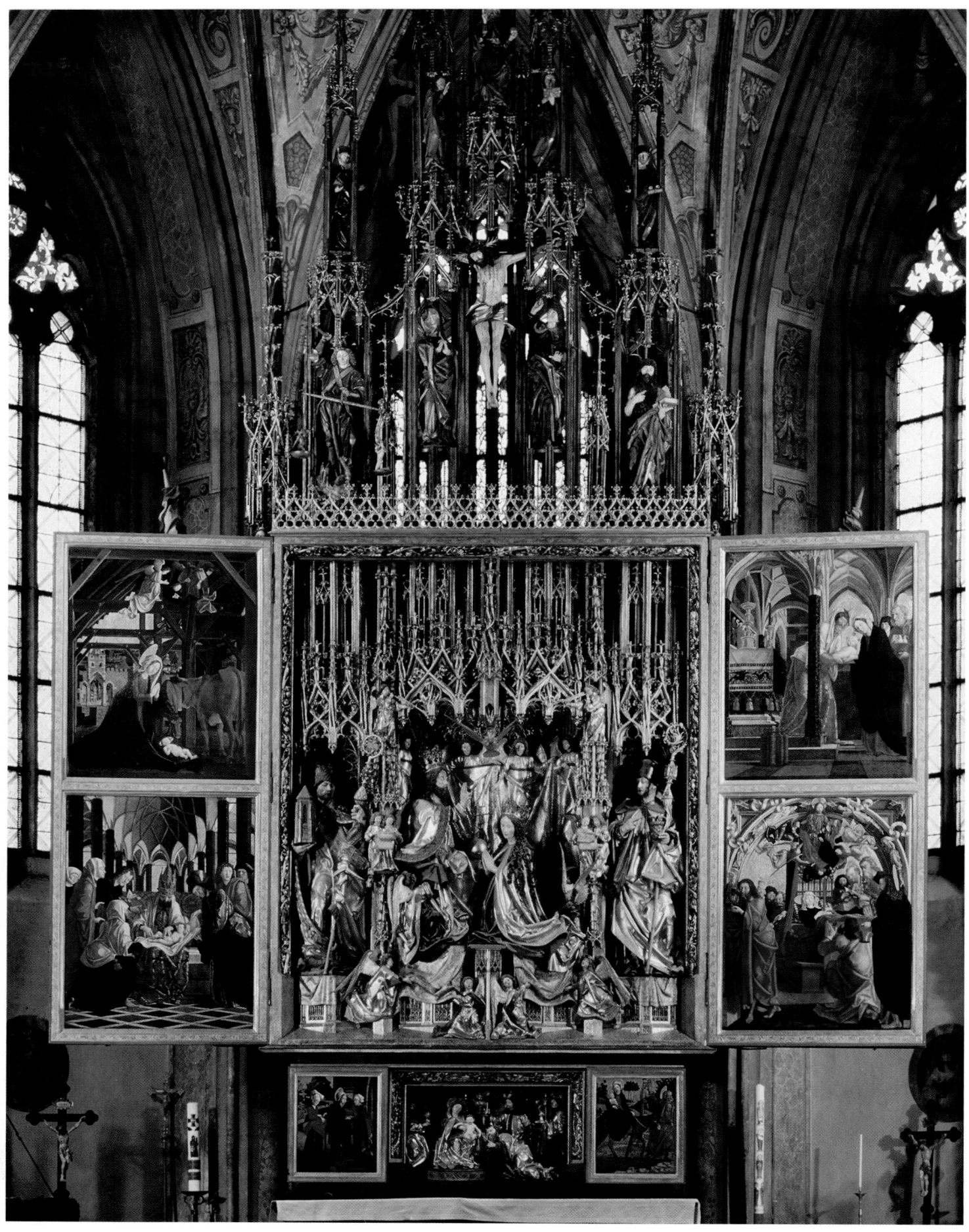

From the Contract for the St. Wolfgang Altarpiece

It took Michael Pacher 11 years (1471–81) to complete this elaborate altarpiece for the pilgrimage church of St. Wolfgang. The altarpiece is still in its original location.

Here is recorded the pact and contract concerning the altar at St. Wolfgang, concluded between the very Reverend, Reverend Benedict, Abbot of Mondsee and of his monastery there, and Master Michael, painter of Bruneck, on St. Lucy's day of the year 1471.

ITEM, it is first to be recorded that the altar shall be made conforming to the elevation and design which the painter has brought to us at Mondsee, and to its exact measurements.

ITEM, the predella shrine shall be guilded on the inside and it shall show Mary seated with the Christ Child, Joseph, and the Three Kings with their gifts; and if these should not completely fill the predella shrine he shall make more figures or armored men, all gilt.

ITEM, the main shrine shall show the Coronation of Mary with angels and gilt drapery—the most precious and the best he can make.

ITEM, on one side St. Wolfgang with mitre, crozier, church, and hatchet; on the other St. Benedict with cap, crozier, and a tumbler, entirely gilded and silvered where needed.

ITEM, to the sides of the altar shall stand St. Florian and St. George, fine armored men, silvered and gilded where needed.

ITEM, the inner wings of the altar shall be provided with good paintings, the panels gilded and equipped with gables and pinnacles, representing four subjects, one each....

ITEM, the outer wings—when the altar is closed—shall be done with good pigments and with gold added to the colors; the subject from the life of St. Wolfgang....

ITEM, at St. Wolfgang, while he completes and sets up the altar, we shall provide his meals and drink, and also the iron work necessary for setting up the altar, as well as help with loading wherever necessary.

ITEM, the contract is made for the sum of one thousand two hundred Hungarian guilders or ducats....

ITEM, if the altar is either not worth this sum or of higher value, and there should be some difference of opinion between us, both parties shall appoint equal numbers of experts to decide the matter.

Source: *Northern Renaissance Art 1400-1600: Sources and Documents*, ed. Wolfgang Stechow (Evanston, IL: Northwestern University Press, 1989)

Virgin as Queen of Heaven flanked by the patron saints of the monastery. Carved of soft wood that permits the sculptor to create deep folds and sharp edges, the lavishly gilt and colored forms make a dazzling spectacle as they emerge from the shadows under Flamboyant Gothic canopies. The figures and setting in the central panel seem to melt into a pattern of twisting lines that permits only the heads to stand out as separate elements.

The complexity and surface ornamentation that dominate the corpus contrast with the paintings of scenes from the life of the Virgin on the interior of the wings. Here, the artist represents large figures, strongly modeled by clear light, and he suggests a deep space for them. He takes a viewer's vantage point into account, so that the upper panels are represented as if seen from below. This kind of **perspective** must have been inspired by developments in contemporary Italian painting. Pacher almost certainly crossed the Alps and visited northern Italy, where some of his works were commissioned and where he had learned to use the Italians' new technique for projecting space. (Compare his perspective to Mantegna's in fig. 15.49.) This type of perspective appears only in the wings, however, where scenes from the historical past are set into spaces that look like the Austrian present. The interior of the temple where the circumcision takes place, for example, has a vault much like ones in Late Gothic churches. Pacher makes the historical scenes in the wings much more down to earth than the spectacle of Heaven in the center.

14.28   Michael Pacher, *St. Wolfgang Altarpiece*, church of St. Wolfgang, Austria. 1471–81. Carved wood, figures about life-size; wings, oil on panel

PRINTING AND THE GRAPHIC ARTS

Along with the new techniques of painting, fifteenth-century Europe saw the development of a new medium: printmaking. The invention of movable type and the printed page would have enormous consequences for Western civilization. Tradition has credited Johann Gutenberg (ca. 1397–1468) with inventing movable type, but the roots of printing actually lie in the ancient Near East 5,000 years ago. The Sumerians were the earliest "printers," for their relief impressions on clay, from stone seals, were carved with both pictures and inscriptions (fig. 2.10). From Mesopotamia the use of seals spread to India and eventually to China. The Chinese applied ink to their seals in order to impress them on wood or silk, and in the second century CE they invented paper. By the ninth century they were printing pictures and books from wooden blocks carved in relief, and 200 years later, they developed movable type. Some of the products of Chinese printing may have reached the medieval West—perhaps through Islamic intermediaries.

The technique for manufacturing paper came to Europe from contact with Islamic regions, though it gained ground as a cheap alternative to parchment only very slowly. While printing on wood blocks was known in the late Middle Ages, it was used solely for ornamental patterns on cloth. All the more astonishing, then, is the sudden development, over the course of a mere century, of a printing technology capable of producing editions of several hundred copies of relatively inexpensive books. The new technology spread quickly across Europe, spawning the new industry of bookmaking. Printed books were far less expensive than handmade volumes, but they were useless to those who

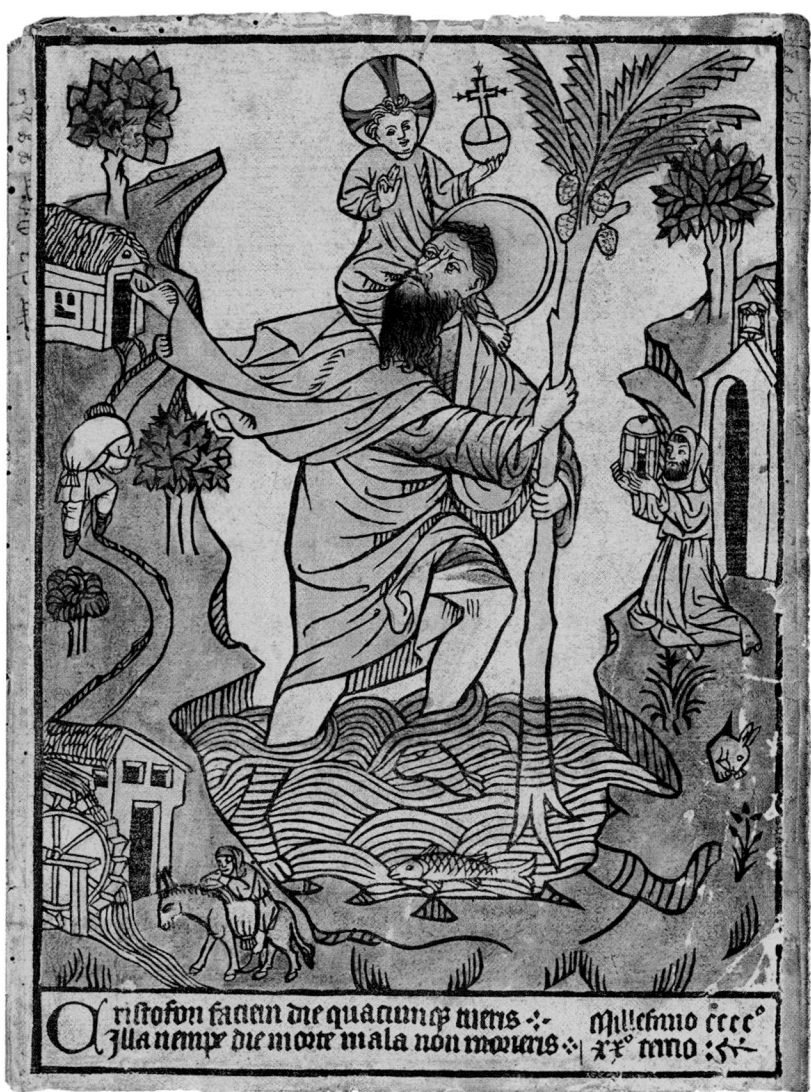

14.29 *Buxheim St. Christopher.* 1423. Handcolored woodcut, 11⅜ × 8⅛" (28.8 × 20.6 cm). John Rylands University Library. The John Rylands University Library of Manchester

could not read. Literacy began to rise among the lower classes, a consequence that would have a profound effect on Western civilization. To compete with illuminated manuscripts, printed books included printed images, which were often handcolored to imitate the more expensive manuscripts. Ultimately, the printed book almost completely replaced the illuminated manuscript.

The pictorial and literary aspects of printing were closely linked from the start. The practice of inking pictorial designs carved on wooden blocks and then printing those designs on paper began in Europe late in the fourteenth century. Early surviving examples of such prints, called **woodcuts**, come from France, the Netherlands, and Germany. Painters or sculptors probably furnished the designs, but specialists did the actual carving of the wood blocks. (For the various techniques of printing, for pictures as well as books, see *Materials and Techniques*, page 501.)

An early dated example of a woodcut is the *Buxheim St. Christopher* (fig. **14.29**), so called because it came from a monastery in that south German town. This single sheet, hand-colored woodcut bears the date 1423 and a prayer to the saint;

woodcuts combining image and text like this on a single block were sometimes assembled into popular picture books called **block books**. Simple, heavy lines define the forms in the print, including the fall of the garment around the figures and the contours of objects. Thinner lines in parallel rows—called **hatching**—denote shadows or textures of objects, but the composition is strictly two-dimensional, as the landscape forms rise along the picture plane to surround the figures. According to legend, Christopher, patron saint of travelers, was a giant who ferried people across a river; he was surprised one day by the weight of a child, who turned out to be Christ.

The forms in the *Buxheim St. Christopher* owe a great deal to Late Gothic style, but the audience for prints were not the aristocrats of the Middle Ages. Fifteenth-century woodcuts were popular art. A single wood block yielded thousands of copies, to be sold for pennies apiece, so that for the first time in history almost anyone could own pictures. A detail from a Flemish Annunciation panel of about 1435 in figure **14.30** reveals one use to which people put such prints: A print much like the *Buxheim St. Christopher* is pinned on a wall in a middle-class household.

Printmaking

Printmaking is a technique for making multiple copies of the same image. In the fifteenth century, most prints used dark black ink on paper (though some are printed on parchment). Printmakers used one of several techniques to make these images; the two broad categories are **relief** prints (in which the lines to be printed are raised from the block) and **intaglio** (in which the lines to be printed are cut into a plate). Designs (and text) will print as reversed images as they are transferred to the paper by the force of a press. By 1500, printing technology allowed for the reproduction of pictures by several methods, all developed at the same time as the printing of type.

Woodcut

In a woodcut, the design is cut into a wood block so that raised ridges will print. The thinner the ridges are, the more difficult they are to carve, so specialists took over this phase of the work. Early woodcuts often include inscriptions, but to carve lines of text backward in relief on a wooden block must have been risky—a single slip could ruin an entire page. It is little wonder, then, that printers soon had the idea of putting each letter on its own small block. Wooden movable type carved by hand worked well for large letters but not for small ones, and the technique proved cumbersome for printing long texts such as the Bible. By 1450, this problem had been solved through the introduction of metal type cast from molds, and the stage was set for book production as it was practiced until the late twentieth century. Because the text was carved in relief, it became apparent that accompanying pictures should be carved in relief as well, so that an entire page could be printed with one run of the press over the **matrix**—or form—which held all the information to be printed.

Engraving

The technique of engraving—embellishing metal surfaces with incised pictures—had developed in classical antiquity (see fig. 6.20) and continued to be practiced throughout the Middle Ages (see fig. 11.7). Goldsmiths and designers of armor, in particular, were experts in incising designs on metal surfaces. These skills allowed goldsmiths to engrave a plate that could serve as the matrix for a paper print. Because the lines themselves were incised into the plate, more linear information could be included in the design. In an engraving, lines are V-shaped grooves cut with a special tool, called a **burin**, into a metal plate—usually copper, which is relatively soft and easy to work with. Ink is forced into the grooves made by the burin, the plate is wiped clean of excess ink, and a damp sheet of paper is placed on top of the inked plate; the force of a press transfers the ink—and the design—to the paper.

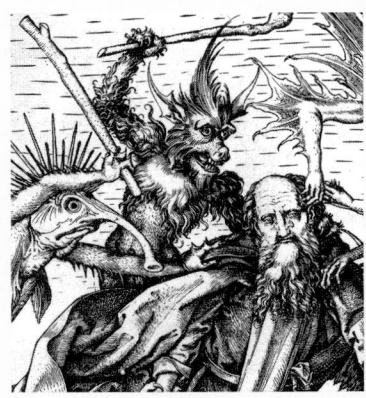

Detail of Schongauer's *The Temptation of St. Anthony*. See fig. 14.31

From the start, **engravings** (images taken from incised plates) appealed to a smaller and more sophisticated public. The oldest surviving examples, from about 1430, already show the influence of Flemish painters. Early engravers were usually trained as goldsmiths, but their prints reflect local painting styles. Their forms are systematically modeled with fine hatched lines and are often convincingly foreshortened. Distinctive styles appear even in the earliest engravings, and engravers often included initials and dates in their prints. Consequently, many engravers of the late fifteenth century are known to us by name.

Printing Centers in Colmar and Basel

Martin Schongauer of Colmar, then in Germany (ca. 1435/50 –1491) learned the goldsmith's craft from his father, but he became a printmaker and a painter. He studied the paintings of Rogier van der Weyden, which probably influenced the style of

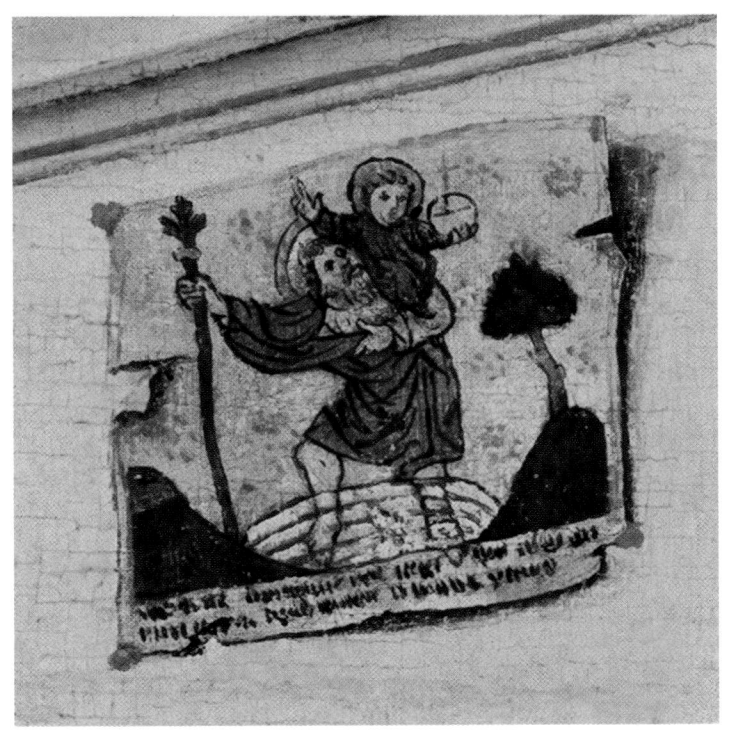

14.30 Jacques Daret, woodcut of St. Christopher, *Annunciation* (detail). ca. 1435. Musée Royaux d'Art et d'Histoire, Brussels, Belgium

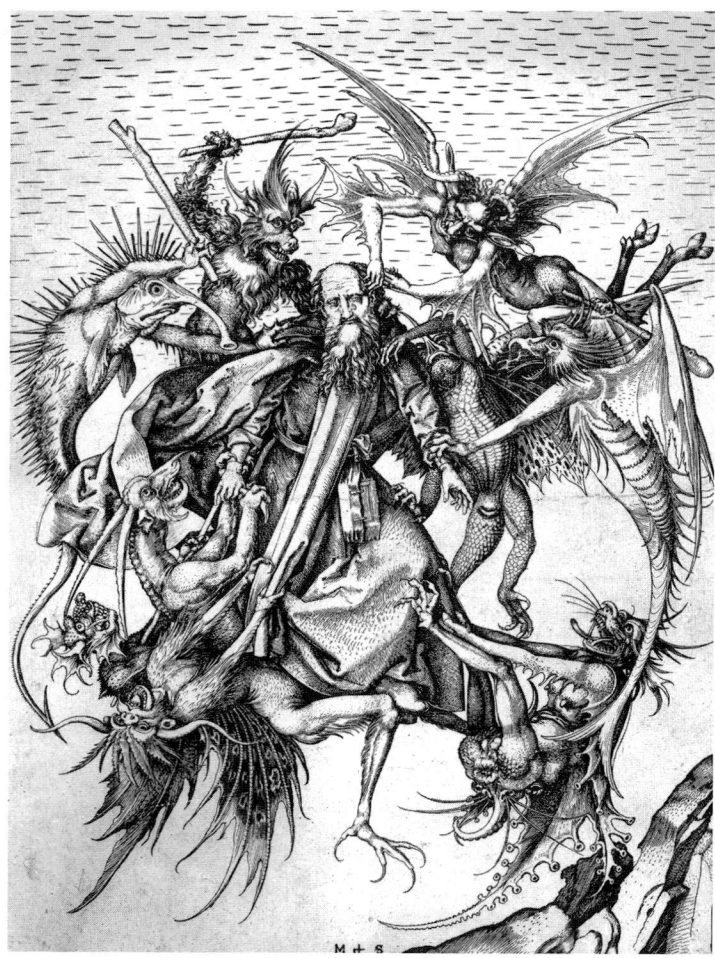

14.31 Martin Schongauer, *The Temptation of St. Anthony*. ca. 1480–90. Engraving, 11½ × 8⅝" (29.2 × 21.8 cm). Metropolitan Museum of Art, New York, Rogers Fund, 1920

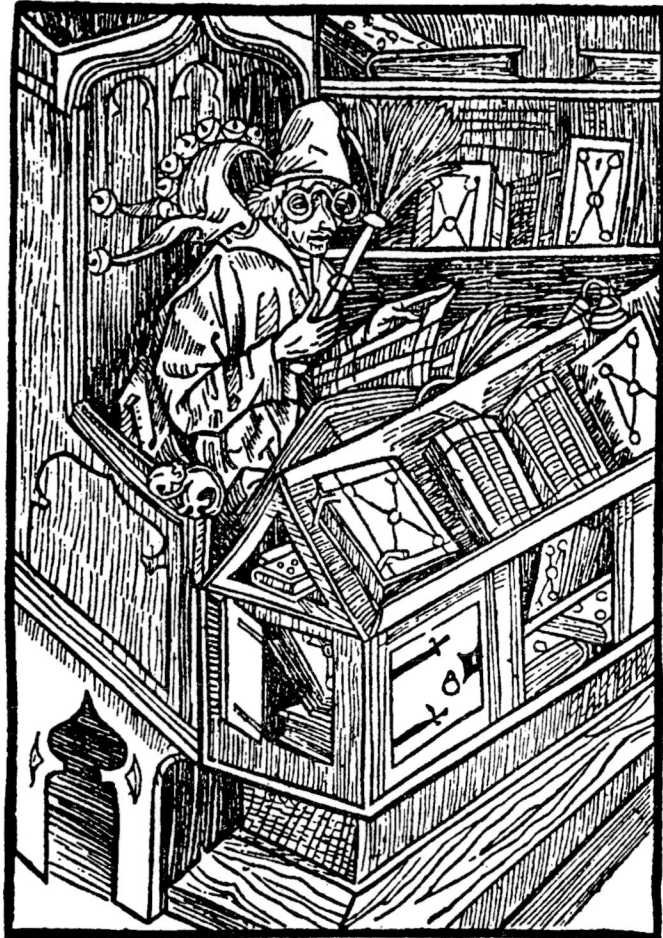

14.32 *Scholar in Study*, woodcut from Sebastian Brant's *Ship of Fools* (Basel, 1494)

his engravings. Their complex designs, spatial depth, and rich textures make them competitors to panel paintings. Some artists found inspiration in them for large-scale pictures. They were also copied by other printmakers. *The Temptation of St. Anthony* (fig. **14.31**) is one of Schongauer's most famous works—known and admired in sixteenth-century Italy. The print represents the climax of St. Anthony's resistance to the Devil. Unable to tempt him to sin, the Devil sent demons to torment him. Varying the type of mark he made on the plate, Schongauer displays a wide range of tonal values and a rhythmic quality of line, and he approximates a wide range of textures—spiky, scaly, leathery, furry—to enhance the expressive impact of the image.

Since the time of Conrad Witz, the Swiss city of Basel had embraced the new technology for printing books to become a major center for publishing. There, a group of reform-minded intellectuals and authors contributed texts for publication, which graphic artists illustrated with woodcuts. One of the best sellers of the period was a satirical text by Sebastian Brant called the *Ship of Fools*, published in Basel in 1494. Brant's text poked fun at many of the ills he perceived in his society, which, as the title implies, he characterized as a boat piloted by Folly. One important theme his

text addresses is contemporary dissatisfaction with the Church. This tide of anticlerical feeling was already rising when Luther's critique of the Church was posted in 1517 in Wittenberg (see page 634). But Brant's satirical eye also fell on his own peers, as the woodcut in figure **14.32** reveals. The image depicts a scholar in his study surrounded by books, but rather than read them, he holds a duster to clean them. The man's costume, including a hood with bells on it, identifies him as a fool. Compared with the *Buxheim St. Christopher*, the unnamed artist who produced this woodcut increases the density of hatching that implies texture and volume and attempts a spatial context for the forms. The practice of coloring prints fell by the wayside as the medium developed its own aesthetic and appeal.

As a period of cultural flowering and great innovation, from the complex naturalistic imagery in the paintings of Campin and Jan van Eyck to the dynamism of the new technology of printing, we could consider the fifteenth century in northern Europe a renaissance. That term is usually linked to this century, but not to this region: Another version of naturalistic representation was developing at the same time in Italy, to which we shall turn in the next chapter.

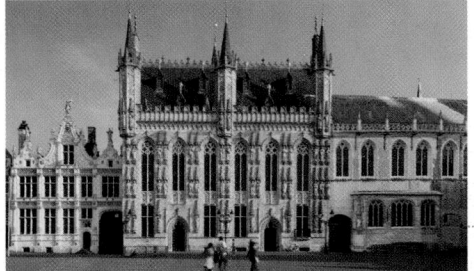
1376 Bruges Town Hall begun

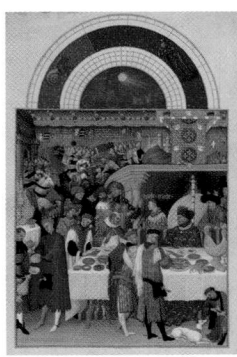
1416 *Très Riches Heures du Duc de Berry* left incomplete at death of Limbourg Brothers

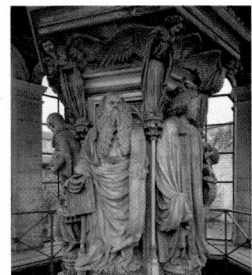
1395 Sluter begins *The Well of Moses*

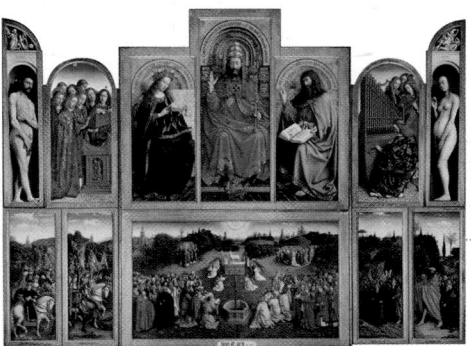
1432 *Ghent Altarpiece* installed in cathedral of Ghent

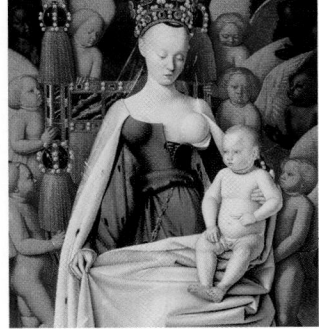
1450 Jean Fouquet's *Mélun Diptych*

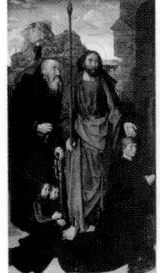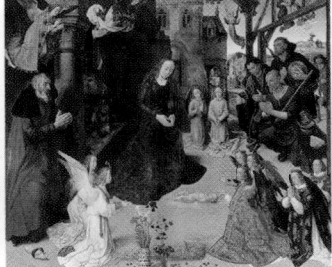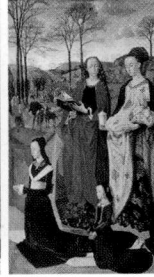
1483 *Portinari Altarpiece* arrives in Florence

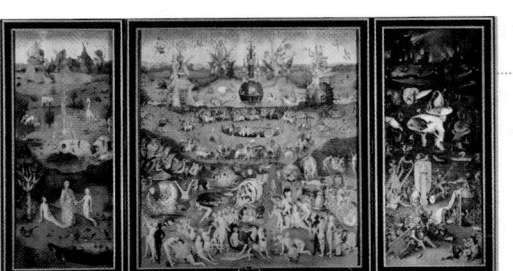
ca. 1505 Hieronymus Bosch's *The Garden of Earthly Delights*

Artistic Innovations in Fifteenth-Century Northern Europe

1360

1380

◀ 1378 Pope returns from Avignon to Rome

◀ 1384 Philip the Bold, duke of Burgundy inherits Flanders

········ 1395 *Hours of Giangaleozzo Visconti*

◀ 1377–99 King Richard II rules England

1400

◀ 1415 Battle of Agincourt

◀ 1419–67 Philip the Good duke of Burgundy

1420

········ 1434 West façade of Saint-Maclou, Rouen begun

1440

◀ 1453 End of the Hundred Years' War between England and France
ca. 1455 Gutenberg prints Bible in Mainz, Germany
1455–87 Wars of the Roses in England

1460

◀ 1477 Marriage of Mary of Burgundy to Maximilian of Hapsburg

1480

◀ 1494 Charles VIII of France invades Italy

1500

········ 1503 Lady Chapel of Henry VII begun at Westminster Abbey, London

1520

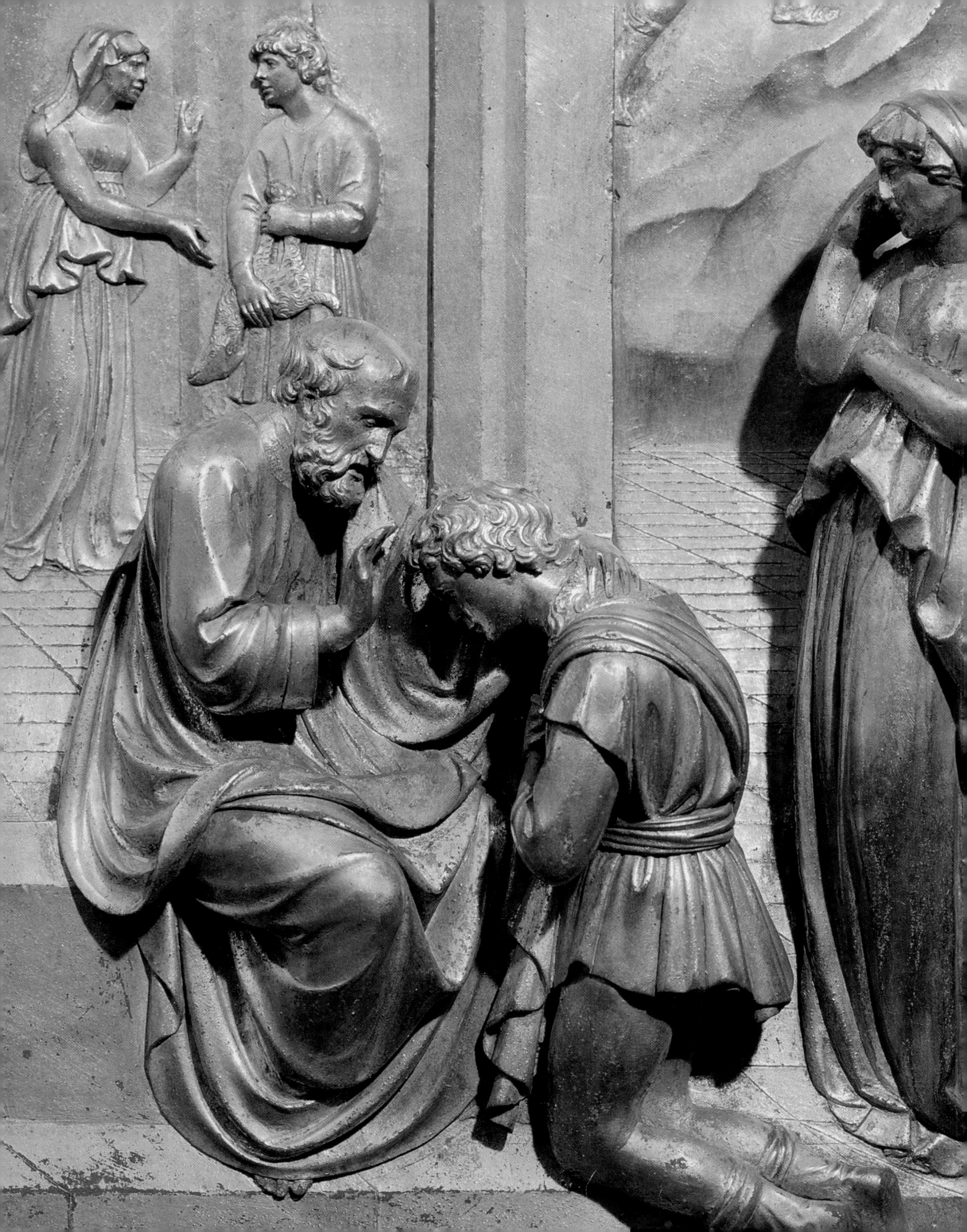

The Early Renaissance in Fifteenth-Century Italy

NEITHER A SCHOLAR WRITING A HISTORY OF FRANCE IN THIRTEENTH-century Paris nor a notary writing a contract in fourteenth-century Bruges could have imagined that he was living in a "middle" age; he only knew that his age followed the eras of the past. But intellectuals in fifteenth-century Italy thought of themselves as living in a *new* age, one that was

distinct from the immediate past. This consciousness of historical difference separates the thinkers of the fifteenth and sixteenth centuries from their medieval forebears. These thinkers devalued the post-Roman, or medieval world, and believed they could improve their culture by reviving the best features of antiquity, that is, Roman and Greek culture. Their efforts, beginning in the fifteenth century in Italy, sparked a cultural flowering of great significance for the history of Europe.

First called the *rinascimento*, Italian for "rebirth," the period came to be known by its French name, the Renaissance. Its original users defined it as the rebirth of classical learning, literature, and art. Modern historians have divided the Italian Renaissance into stages: an early phase in the fifteenth century, the High Renaissance denoting a period of exceptional achievement, and the Late Renaissance, which is primarily a chronological term. Neither the definition of the Renaissance as the revival of classical forms nor the chronological limits apply easily outside of Italy, but the broader definition of a Renaissance as a cultural or artistic renewal has come to apply elsewhere. In northern Europe, as we have seen in Chapter 14, scholars and artists did not have the same dedication to reviving the ancients, though they did study the past. More significant was an economic and

cultural expansion that resulted in far-reaching technical and cultural achievements.

The causes of the cultural flowering in Italy are complex, as events, people, ideas, and social shifts came together in a revolution that produced many of the characteristics of modern European civilization. For this reason, some scholars refer to this era as the "early modern period." This cultural shift was fundamentally an intellectual one. The followers of the fourteenth-century author Petrarch began to study texts from Greece and Rome both for their moral content and their style. They committed themselves to the *studia humanitatis*—the study of human works, emphasizing rhetoric, literature, history, and moral philosophy. The roots of humanist education lay in the medieval university, which prized theology, but in the Renaissance humanism aimed to create knowledge for practical use in the world—for lawyers, bureaucrats, politicians, diplomats, and merchants.

Humanist scrutiny of ancient texts not only deepened knowledge of Latin authors, but also stimulated the study of the great Greek thinkers such as Aristotle, Plato, Euclid, and Ptolemy. Humanists' analytical approach and empirical observations inspired new thinking in many fields, including mathematics and natural science. Studying history taught the importance of individuals acting in the world to assure their personal fame, yet also encouraged educated people to serve the common good by participating in civic life. Humanist educational ideas spread quickly throughout Italy, aided by the introduction into Italy of

Detail of figure 15.17, Lorenzo Ghiberti, *The Story of Jacob and Esau*, panel of the *Gates of Paradise*

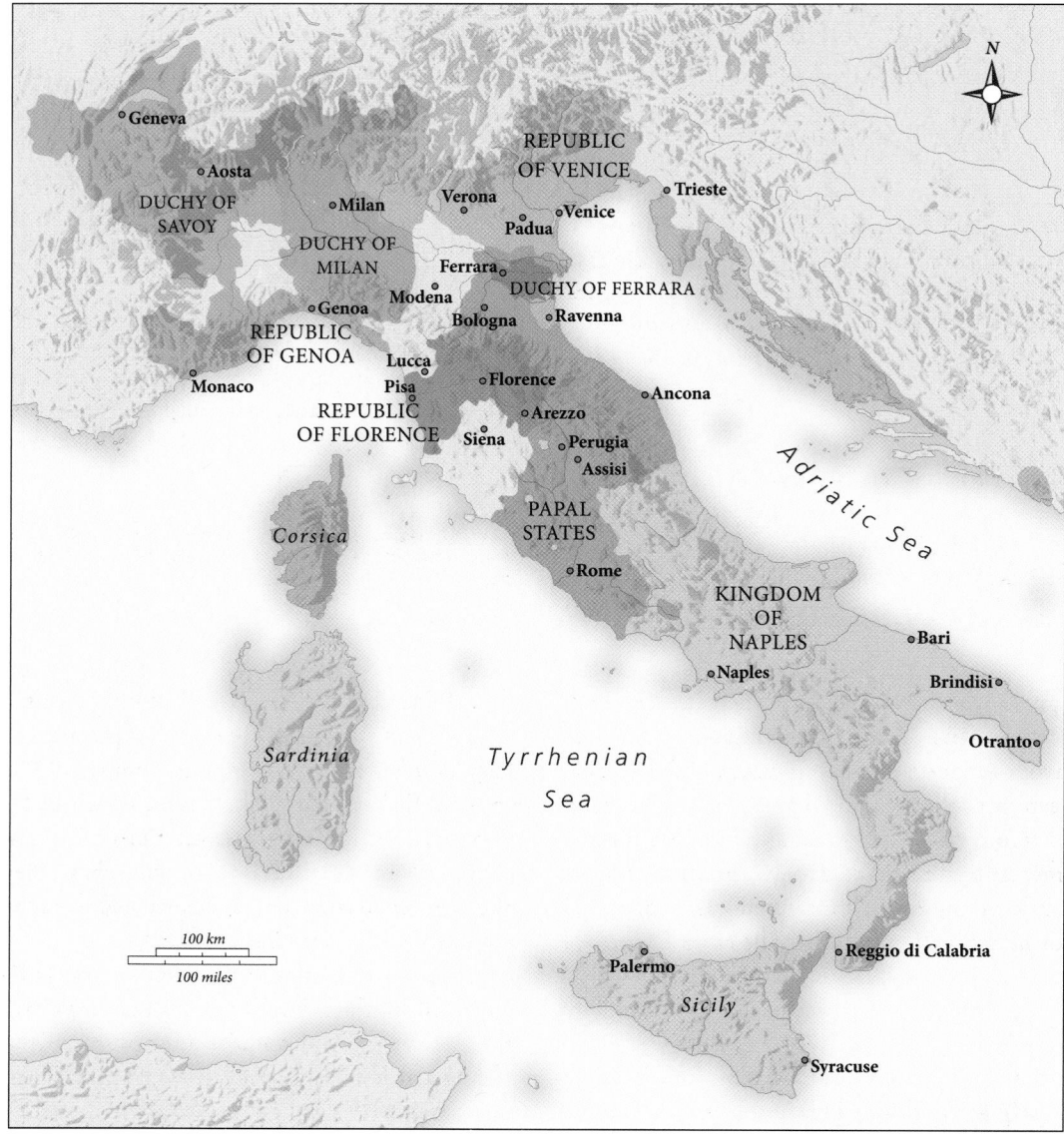

Map 15.1 Political units of the Italian Peninsula in the fifteenth century

the printing press in 1464, which made books more widely available. Governing parties throughout Italy, whether princes, popes, or elected councils, used humanists in their bureaucracies and courts to conduct their business.

Humanist ideas affected artists as well as the patrons who hired them. As humanists studied ancient texts, artists studied ancient artworks, not just to imitate details or motifs, but to understand the principles by which ancient buildings were designed and ancient sculptures achieved their naturalism. Renaissance artists took up the ancient ideal of rivaling nature in their art and brought their practical skills to this intellectual aim. They devised techniques such as perspective and mastered new technologies like oil painting and printmaking to further their goal of reproducing the natural world and to spread their ideas.

Artists employed these ideas and techniques to make art that served spiritual and dynastic functions for their patrons. Medieval

institutions—religious orders, guilds, and the Church—commissioned church buildings, architectural sculpture, wall paintings, altar furnishings, and other objects as they had in earlier centuries, though secular patronage increased. The artists earned personal glory along the way, so that by the end of the century the status of the artist had changed. Through much of the Middle Ages, the social and economic position of artists in society was comparable to that of any other artisan. They were respected for the skill of their hands, but not considered intellectuals. Many artists in fifteenth-century Italy behaved like intellectuals, investigating the past and solving problems scientifically, so the status of the artist rose as a result.

During this period, there was still no single political entity called Italy. Regions of different size and political organization competed with each other economically and often on the battlefield (map 15.1). The Kingdom of Naples in the south was a

In Praise of the City of Florence (ca. 1403–4) by Leonardo Bruni

Though born in Arezzo, Leonardo Bruni (1370–1444) moved to Florence to take up law and humanistic studies. His mentor, Coluccio Salutati, was the chancellor of Florence, to which post Bruni succeeded in 1406. An ardent student of classical literature, he modeled his own writings on those of Greek and Roman authors. He wrote this panegyric to Florence after the death of Giangaleazzo Visconti, which ended the threat to the city from Milan.

Therefore, what ornament does this city lack? What category of endeavor is not fully worthy of praises and grandeur? What about the quality of the forebears? Why are they not the descendants of the Roman people? What about glory? Florence has done and daily continues to do great deeds of honor and virtue both at home and abroad. What about the splendor of the architecture, the buildings, the cleanliness, the wealth, the great population, the healthfulness and pleasantness of the site? What more can a city desire? Nothing at all. What, therefore, should we say now? What remains to be done? Nothing other than to venerate God on account of His great beneficence and to offer our prayers to God. Therefore, our Almighty and Everlasting God, in whose churches and at whose altars your Florentines worship most devoutly; and you, Most Holy Mother, to whom this city has erected a great temple of fine and glimmering marble, where you are at once mother and purest virgin tending your most sweet son; and you, John the Baptist, whom this city has adopted as its patron saint—all of you, defend this most beautiful and distinguished city from every adversity and from every evil.

Source: "Panegyric to the City of Florence," tr. Benjamin G. Kohl in *The Earthly Republic: Italian Humanists on Government and Society* (Philadelphia: University of Pennsylvania Press, 1978)

monarchy. Dukes, princes, and despots carved up northern Italy into city-states, including Milan, Mantua, and Urbino. The pope returned to Rome from Avignon to reclaim control of the Papal States which had been lost when the papacy moved to France in 1305. And the major trading cities of Venice and Florence formed republics, where mercantile elites controlled political power. Though the cultural flowering we call the Renaissance occurred throughout Italy, for many modern scholars the city of Florence was its birthplace.

FLORENCE IN THE FIFTEENTH CENTURY

One reason for the prominence of Florence in histories of the Renaissance is that many early humanists were Florentines who patriotically praised their hometown. Florence was an important manufacturing center, a key center for trade, and a major center for international banking, whose wealth and social dynamism attracted talented individuals. Instead of hereditary aristocrats, bankers and merchants controlled the government. Groups of merchants and artisans banded together in guilds (economic and social organizations) to strengthen their positions. The governing council, called the Signoria, consisted of officials elected from members of the guilds and prominent mercantile families. The government was a republic, a word that for Florentines signaled their identity as the heirs of the ancient Roman Republic.

Florentine politicians, such as Coluccio Salutati and Leonardo Bruni, successive chancellors to the Signoria, gave eloquent voice to Florentine aspirations. Urging the city to defy the duke of Milan as he threatened to invade in 1401–02, Salutati called on the city's Roman history as a model to follow. After this threat had passed, Leonardo Bruni declared that Florence had been able to defy Milan because of her republican institutions, her cultural achievements, and the origins of her people. In his *In Praise of the City of Florence* (1403–04), he compared Florence's virtues to those of fifth-century BCE Athens, which had defied the invading Persians. Yet he also praised Florentine piety and devotion, expressed in the building of churches. (See *Primary Source*, above.) Renaissance humanists wished to reconcile the lessons of antiquity with their Christian faith.

Bruni's words may explain why practical Florentines invested so much of their wealth in cultural activity. The Signoria and subsidiary groups commissioned numerous public projects to beautify and improve their city (map 15.2, page 517). It was not only individuals and families who sponsored public projects, so too did merchant guilds, which held competitions among artists for their commissions. The successful accomplishment of projects of great visibility enhanced the prestige of sponsoring individuals and groups and drew artists to the city. Many native sons (daughters were forbidden entry to most guilds, so few women became artists) became sculptors, painters, and goldsmiths. In this climate of humanism, innovation, and display, the Renaissance in Florence opens with a competition.

The Baptistery Competition

Andrea Pisano's bronze doors for the baptistery (see fig. 13.13), completed in 1360, were an impressive example of Florentine taste and piety. Their success inspired the overseers of the works at the baptistery, the Guild of Wool Merchants, to open another competition for a second set of bronze doors. They asked each entrant to make a design on the theme of the Sacrifice of Isaac, while retaining the Gothic quatrefoil shape from Andrea Pisano's first doors for the baptistery (see fig. 13.14). Competing artistsall had to include the same figures and were given the same materials. Seven artists made trial reliefs for this competition,

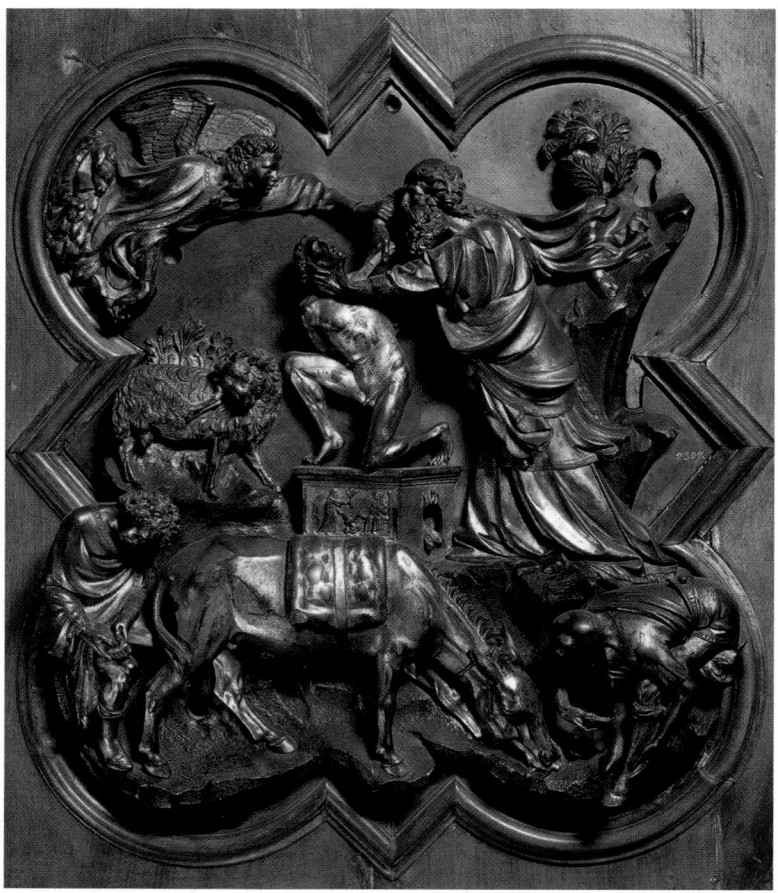

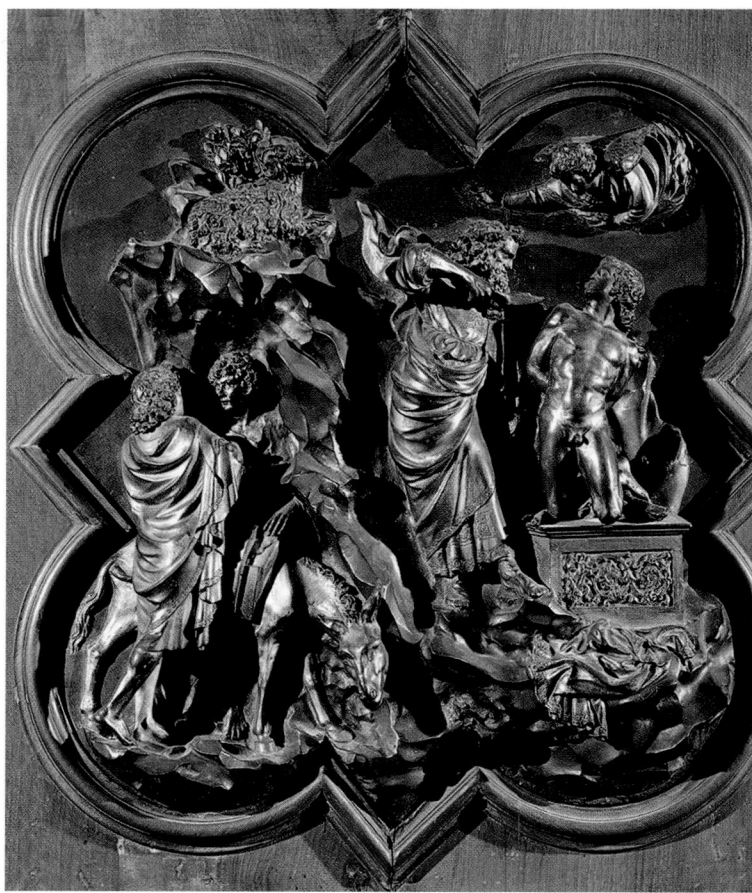

15.1 Filippo Brunelleschi, *The Sacrifice of Isaac*. 1401–03.
Panel, gilt bronze relief, 21 × 17" (53.3 × 43.2 cm).
Museo Nazionale del Bargello, Florence

15.2 Lorenzo Ghiberti, *The Sacrifice of Isaac*. 1401–03.
Panel, gilt bronze relief, 21 × 17" (53.3 × 43.2 cm).
Museo Nazionale del Bargello, Florence

though only two of them survive. One is by Filippo Brunelleschi (1377–1446) (fig. **15.1**); the other is by Lorenzo Ghiberti (1381–1455), whom the guild ultimately chose to execute the second doors of the baptistery (fig. **15.2**). Ghiberti left a description of the competition and his acclaim as the victor in his *Commentaries*, written late in his life. (See *Primary Source*, page 509.)

The subject the artists were assigned, from the book of Genesis, recounts how God ordered Abraham to sacrifice his only son; obediently, Abraham led Isaac to an altar on a mountain and lifted his knife to slaughter him when an angel halted the sacrifice. Although Isaac is a figure for Christ in Christian theology, this is also the story of a chosen people avoiding doom through divine intervention, an issue about which Florentines felt strongly in 1402. For the artists, the challenge was to fill the four lobes of the quatrefoil, yet at the same time to convey the narrative succinctly and naturalistically. In his trial relief, Brunelleschi organized the forms to focus on the dynamic figure of Abraham whose arm, lifted to strike Isaac, is grasped by the angel rushing in from the left. Isaac struggles as his father grabs his neck, contorting his posture and increasing the drama. The ram who replaces him as the sacrifice stands next to the altar. Subsidiary figures of shepherds and a donkey fill the lower portions of the quatrefoil;

though their postures are complex (one of them based on an ancient work of art), they do not contribute much to the main theme. Brunelleschi gives his figures great naturalism, and the composition great drama.

Ghiberti's relief reveals the strength of his composition, his skill at rendering the human form, and his observation of natural details. Ghiberti solved the problem of the quatrefoil field by placing narrative details in the margins and the focal point at the center. Thus, the ram on the mountain appears in the upper left and the foreshortened angel on the right. At the center, Abraham gestures dramatically as he moves to sacrifice his son, bound and naked on an altar. Isaac twists to face the spectator, his beautifully formed torso contrasting with the drapery worn by his father. He does not struggle, but seems heroically to accept his fate. A wedge of mountain keeps other figures away from the main scene. Ghiberti's design successfully combines movement, focus, and narrative. At the same time, his interest in the lyrical patterning of the International Gothic tempers the brutality of the scene. Abraham's drapery falls in cascades similar to those of the figure of Moses in Sluter's *The Well of Moses* (see fig. 14.1). In addition to the design, Ghiberti's entry demonstrated a technical finesse that may have persuaded the judges to select him: Unlike Brunelleschi, he cast his entry in one piece.

Lorenzo Ghiberti
(ca. 1381–1455)

The Commentaries, from Book 2

Ghiberti's incomplete Commentaries *is an important early document of art history. The first book consists largely of extracts from Pliny and Vitruvius; the second is about art in Italy in the thirteenth and four-teenth centuries and ends with an account of Ghiberti's own work (see fig. 15.2).*

Whereas all gifts of fortune are given and as easily taken back, but disciplines attached to the mind never fail, but remain fixed to the very end ... I give greatest and infinite thanks to my parents, who ... were careful to teach me the art, and the one that cannot be tried without the discipline of letters. ... Whereas therefore through parents' care and the learning of rules I have gone far in the subject of letters or learning in philology, and love the writing of commentaries. I have furnished my mind with these possessions, of which the final fruit is this, not to need any property or riches, and most of all to desire nothing. ... I have tried to inquire how nature proceeds ... and how I can get near her, how things seen reach the eye and how the power of vision works, and how visual ... works, and how visual things move, and how the theory of sculpture and paint-ing ought to be pursued.

In my youth, in the year of Our Lord 1400, I left Florence because of both the bad air and the bad state of the country. ... My mind was largely directed to painting. ... Nevertheless ... I was written to by my friends how the board of the temple of St. John the Baptist was sending for well-versed masters, of whom they wanted to see a test piece. A great many very well qualified masters came through all the lands of Italy to put themselves to this test. ... Each one was given four bronze plates. As the demonstration, the board of the temple wanted each one to make a scene ... [of] the sacrifice of Isaac. ... These tests were to be carried out in a year. ... The competitors were ...: Filippo di ser Brunellesco, Simone da Colle, Niccolo D'Arezzo, Jacopo della Quercia from Siena, Francesco da Valdambrino, Nicolo Lamberti. ... The palm of victory was conceded to me by all the expects and by all those who took the test with me. The glory was conceded to me universally, without exception. Everyone felt I had gone beyond the others in that time, without a single exception, with a great consultation and examination by learned men.

... The judges were thirty-four, counting those of the city and the surrounding areas: the endorsement in my favor of the victory was given by all, and the by the consuls and board and the whole body of the merchants guild, which has the temple of St. John the Baptist in its charge. It was ... determined that I should do this bronze door for this temple, and I executed it with great diligence. And this is the first work; with the frame around it, it added up to about twenty-two thousand florins.

Source: Creighton Gilbert, ed., *Italian Art 1400–1500: Sources and Documents* (Evanston, IL: Northwestern University Press, 1992)

The casting of the doors kept Ghiberti's workshop busy for 20 years. Many of the most sought-after artists of the next generation spent time there, as he completed the doors. The competition between these two artists sets the stage for developments in both architecture and sculpture in Florence during the first half of the fifteenth century.

Architecture and Antiquity in Florence

Although he may have lost the competition for the baptistery doors, Filippo Brunelleschi is a crucial figure for Renaissance art, especially in architecture. While he continued to work in sculp-ture, his study of ancient buildings drew him to solving architec-tural problems. After losing the competition for the doors, Brunelleschi went to Rome with his friend the sculptor Donatello. There he studied ancient structures and reportedly took exact measurements of them. His discovery of linear per-spective (discussed later in this chapter) may well have grown out of his search for an accurate way of recording the appearance of those ancient buildings. He brought his study of ancient buildings to the service of design problems at the Florentine Duomo, at other churches and chapels in Florence, and other structures. Other architects working in Florence took inspiration from his example, among them Leon Battista Alberti. His treatises on both painting and architecture helped to spread Brunelleschi's innovations.

BRUNELLESCHI AND THE DOME OF FLORENCE CATHEDRAL Between 1417 and 1419, Brunelleschi again com-peted with Ghiberti, this time for the job of building the dome for Florence cathedral (fig. **15.3**). The dome had been planned half a century earlier, so at this stage only details could be changed, and its vast size posed a problem of construction. Brunelleschi's pro-posals were the fruit of his study of Gothic, Roman, Byzantine, and maybe even Persian buildings, but the building of the dome was as much a feat of engineering as of style. (See *Materials and Techniques*, page 512.) The project occupied him for most of the rest of his life, and it would come to symbolize Florentine inventiveness, piety, ambition, and skill.

Soaring hundreds of feet above street level, the dome dwarfs all other structures in Florence. Resting visually on the smaller semidomes that surround the cathedral's eastern end, the ribs of the dome rise upward dramatically, terminating in a marble cupola or lantern. Brunelleschi designed this lantern to tie the eight exterior ribs together, but it also marks the crescendo of that upward movement. When the cathedral was dedicated on March 25, 1436, the city rejoiced. Florence had demonstrated its devotion to the Virgin Mary, as well as its ambition to overawe

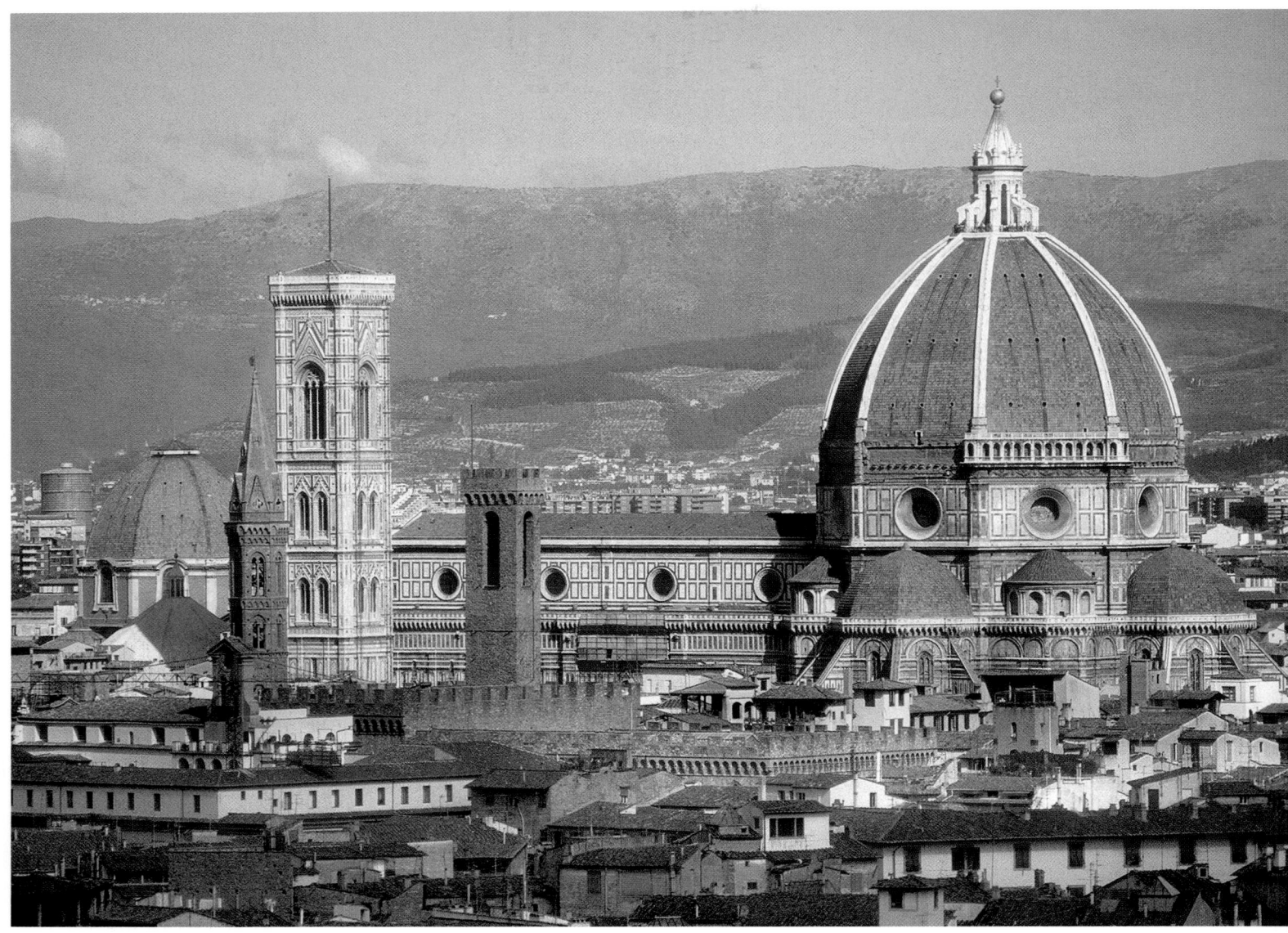

15.3 Filippo Brunelleschi. Dome of Florence cathedral (Santa Maria del Fiore). 1420–36. Height 100' (35.5 m), diameter 459' (140 m)

its neighbors culturally. Florentines were justifiably proud that a native son had so cleverly accomplished what previous generations had failed to do. Brunelleschi's forms would influence architecture far beyond Tuscany.

BRUNELLESCHI'S *OSPEDALE DEGLI INNOCENTI* The work at the Duomo came under the purview of the wool merchants' guild, but another guild in Florence sponsored a different sort of public project for the city, intended to address a social problem. The Guild of Silk Manufacturers and Goldsmiths hired Brunelleschi to design a hospital for abandoned children near the church of the Santissima Annunziata. In 1421, construction began on the Ospedale degli Innocenti (Hospital of the Innocents), although building continued long after Brunelleschi's death. The façade of the hospital (fig. **15.4**) consists of a covered walkway, or **loggia**, defined by an arcade raised slightly above ground level. A strong horizontal molding sits above the arcade, and above that is a simple arrangement of **pedimented** windows.

In designing this hospital, Brunelleschi revived the architectural forms of the ancients, as seen in the columns, their capitals, the arches, and the entablatures. Doing so demanded that he work within rigid rules. Unlike a medieval column (see, for example, the colonnettes in the nave of San Francesco in Assisi, fig. 13.1), a Classical column is strictly defined; its details and proportions can vary only within narrow limits. Unlike any other arch (horseshoe, pointed, and so forth), the Classical round arch has only one possible shape: a semicircle. The Classical **architrave**, profiles, and ornaments must all follow similarly strict rules. This is not to say that Classical forms are completely inflexible. But the discipline of the Greek orders, which can be felt even in the most original Roman buildings, demands regularity and discourages arbitrary departures from the norm. Using such "standardized" forms, Brunelleschi designed the façade of this hospital as a series of blocks of space of the same size, defined by the **bays** of the arcade. Each bay establishes a square of space that is covered by a dome resting on **pendentives** (fig. **15.5**). Transverse arches divide the

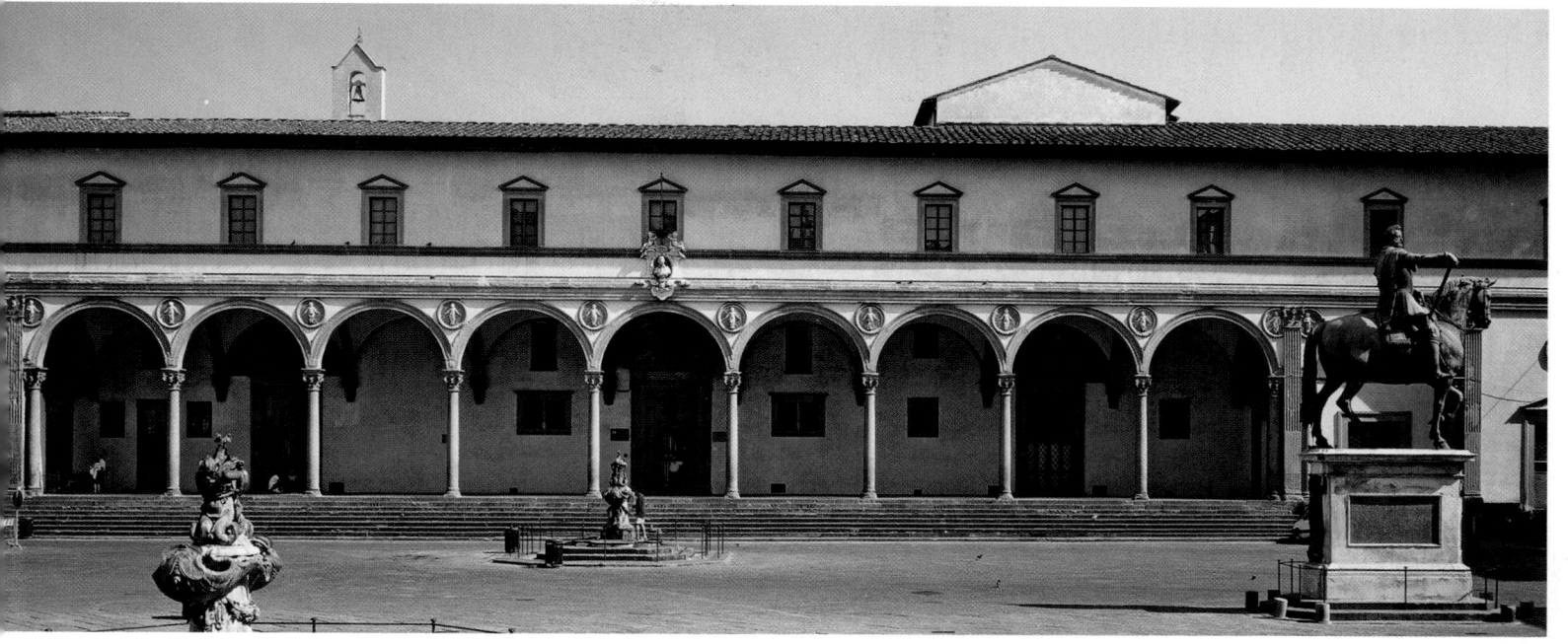

15.4 Filippo Brunelleschi. Ospedale degli Innocenti (Hospital of the Innocents), Florence. Begun 1421

domes inside the arcade. Using contrasting colors of stone, Brunelleschi emphasizes the edges of these units of space without disrupting their rhythmic sequence.

One other principle accounts for the balanced nature of the design. For Brunelleschi, the secret of good architecture lay in choosing the "right" proportions—that is, proportional ratios

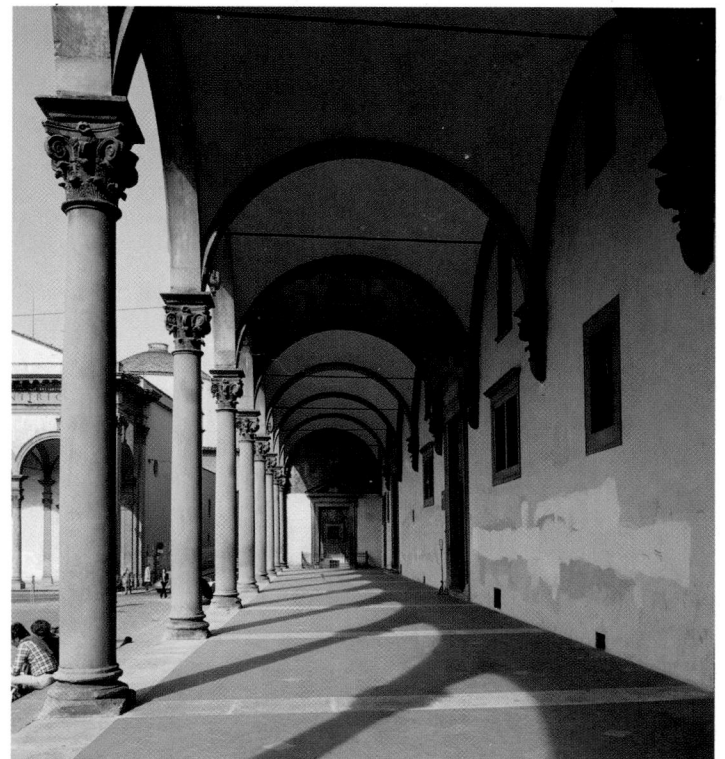

15.5 View under arcade of Ospedale degli Innocenti, Florence

expressed in simple whole numbers—for all the major measurements of a building. For example, the entablature over the columns sits at twice the height of a column for a ratio of 2:1. The ancients had possessed this secret, he believed, and he tried to discover it when he measured their monuments. What he found, and exactly how he applied it, is uncertain, but his knowledge may have been passed to Leon Battista Alberti. In his *Treatise on Architecture*, Alberti argues that the mathematical ratios that determine musical harmony must also govern architecture, for they recur throughout the universe and thus are divine in origin. (See *Primary Source*, page 514.) Similar ideas, derived from the theories of the Greek philosopher Pythagoras, had been current during the Middle Ages, but they had never before been expressed so directly and simply. At the Innocenti, Brunelleschi used ratios to dictate relationships: The windows are centered between the columns, the intervals between columns equal the height of the columns, the span between the columns is the distance from the column to the wall. Proportion locks the composition into a balanced whole. The arcade, with its beautifully proportioned columns supporting arches, made of a dark local sandstone called *pietra serena* (literally, "peaceful stone"), gives the façade a graceful rhythm.

Above the spandrels of the arches, terra-cotta reliefs in later roundels from the della Robbia workshop depict babies, the "innocents" for whom the structure was named. Brunelleschi's Innocenti not only served Florence's poor, it defined a public square. This loggia establishes one side of a piazza perpendicular to the church of the Santissima Annunziata; later, the façades of other buildings formed the remaining limits of the square. Such public spaces were used for social, religious, and political functions, and by echoing the design of the Roman Forum, they expressed the Florentine sense of themselves as the heirs to Rome.

Brunelleschi's Dome

As the basic dimensions and plans for the cathedral of Florence had been established in the fourteenth century, Brunelleschi first determined to lift the dome on a drum above the level of the nave. He proposed to build the dome in two separate shells, which was a method more common in Islamic than Italian architecture, especially in Persia. Compare the fourteenth-century tomb of the Il-Khan Oljeytu in Sultaniya (see fig. 9.20). These two shells were supported by a series of ribs, eight of them visible on the exterior but others hidden; the vertical ribs were themselves linked by rows of horizontal ribs, a system which may have been inspired by the coffered dome of the Pantheon (see fig. 7.25). Both the use of ribs and the pointed profile reflect Gothic practice. The dual shells of the dome lighten the whole mass since their walls are thin relative to their size. Brunelleschi's herringbone-pattern brickwork serves both to resist cracks caused by settling and to lessen the weight as the courses of brick get thinner as they rise.

Along with these design features, Brunelleschi proposed innovations in the construction process. The traditional practice had been to construct a wooden centering across the span of the dome to support it during construction, but this required huge pieces of timber. To avoid this, Brunelleschi designed a new system by which temporary scaffolding was cantilevered out from the walls of the drum, thereby reducing the size and amount of timber needed during building. And

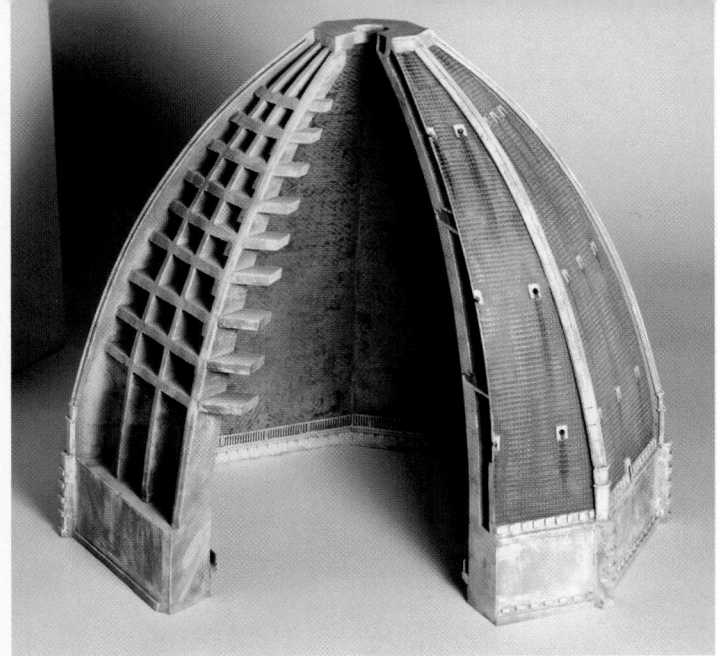

Model of some of the structural features of Brunelleschi's dome

instead of having building materials carried up on ramps to the required level, he designed new hoisting machines. Brunelleschi's entire scheme reflects a bold, analytical mind that was willing to discard conventional solutions if better ones could be devised.

In the revival of classical forms, Renaissance architecture found a standard vocabulary. The theory of harmonious proportions gave it a syntax that had been mostly absent from medieval architecture. Similarly, the revival of classical forms and proportions enabled Brunelleschi to transform the architectural "vernacular" of his region into a stable, precise, and coherent system. Brunelleschi's achievement placed architecture on a firm footing and applied the lessons of classical antiquity for modern Christian ends. Furthermore, his study of the ancients and his practical application of classical geometric proportions probably stimulated his discovery of a system for rendering forms in three dimensions. This technique became known as linear or **scientific perspective**. (See *Materials and Techniques*, page 516.)

BRUNELLESCHI AT SAN LORENZO Brunelleschi's skills also brought him to the notice of private patrons. Early in the fifteenth century, the up-and-coming Medici family began a project to rebuild their parish church. In 1419, Giovanni di Bicci de' Medici commissioned Brunelleschi to add a sacristy to the Romanesque church of San Lorenzo. The sacristy serves two purposes; it provides a liturgical space in which the priest prepares himself for the ritual of the Mass, but Giovanni also intended it as a funerary chapel. Because a later generation of Medici commissioned a sacristy on the opposite side of the church, Brunelleschi's chapel, completed by 1429, became known as the Old Sacristy.

The chapel (fig. **15.6**) consists of a square room oriented toward a niche with an altar. Brunelleschi covered this rectilinear

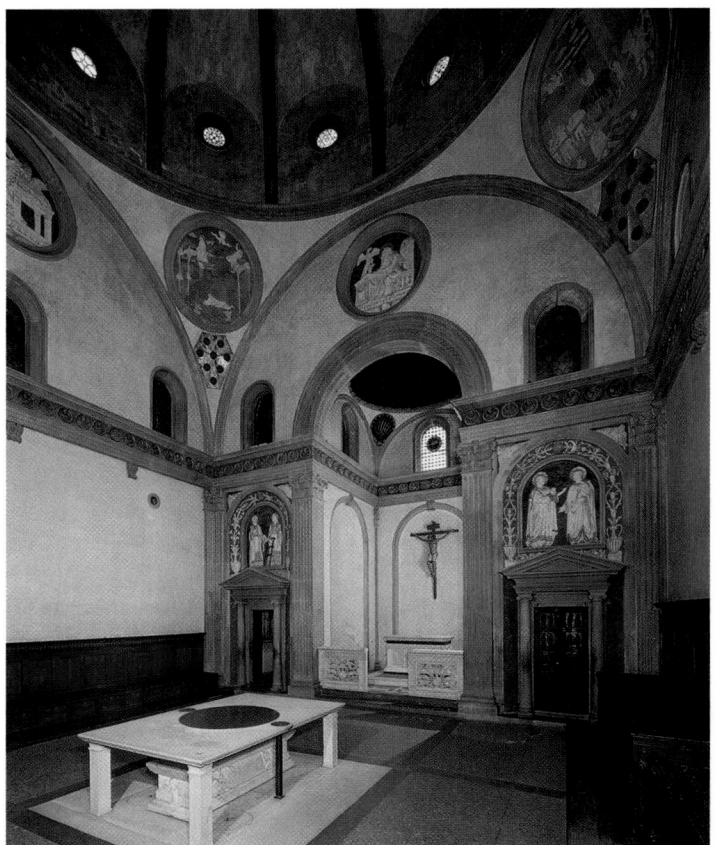

15.6 Filippo Brunelleschi, Old Sacristy, church of San Lorenzo, Florence. 1421–28

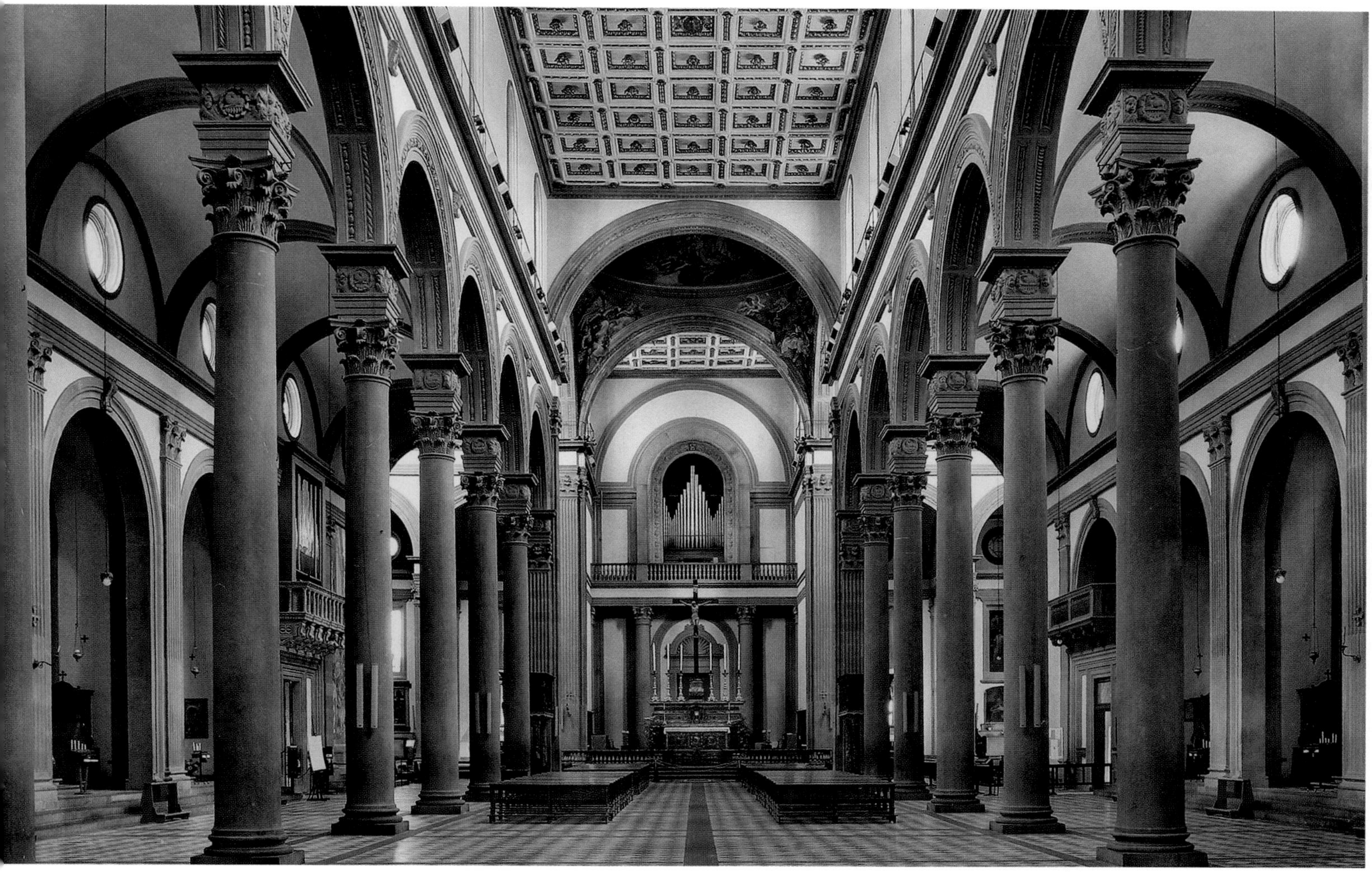

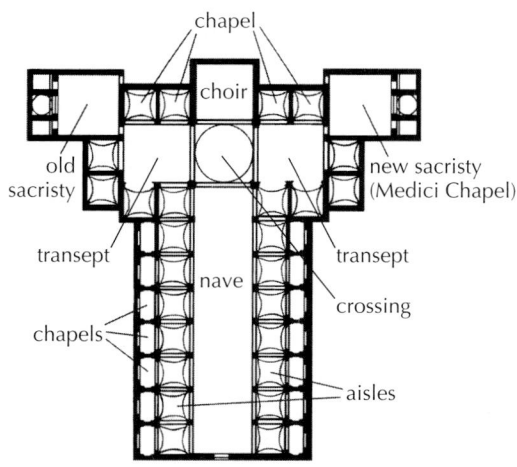

15.7 Filippo Brunelleschi. Nave of church of San Lorenzo, Florence. ca. 1421–69

space with a dome resting on triangular pendentives, uniting the circular form of a dome with a square. In plan, the square inscribes the circle. These two forms were thought ideal by ancient architects like Vitruvius, and thus by Brunelleschi and contemporary humanists. Proportion is also important here; Brunelleschi uses a 2:1 measure to determine the height of the architrave as well as further subdivisions of wall and space (such as the height of the doors that flank the altar). He marked these divisions, and in fact all the points where walls and other structural elements meet, with stone moldings that contrast with the wall. The result is a room that seems at once light and stable, spacious and harmonious, and that melds Christian function with forms inspired by antiquity.

The family was so pleased with his plans for this sacristy that they asked Brunelleschi to develop a new design for the entire church. Brunelleschi's work began in the 1420s, but construction proceeded in fits and starts; the nave was not completed until 1469, more than 20 years after the architect's death. (The exterior remains unfinished to this day.) Nevertheless, the building in its present form is essentially what Brunelleschi had envisioned about 1420, and it represents the first full statement of his architectural aims (figs. **15.7** and **15.8**).

15.8 Plan of church of San Lorenzo

If the sacristy offered a new and exciting solution to issues of space and structure, the plan of the church itself seems at first glance to be more conventional. The plan shows it to be a basilica form, with nave and aisles; it terminates in a square east end and

Leon Battista Alberti on what makes a building beautiful

From the *Ten Books on Architecture* (1452)

Alberti composed his treatise on architecture after studying the treatise by the Roman architect Vitruvius. Originally written in Latin, his treatise prescribes the best way to design and build buildings and was intended for both practicing architects and for their patrons. This passage argues that the key to good building is something Alberti called concinnitus, *which means something like consonance or harmony.*

When you make judgments on beauty, you do not follow mere fancy, but the workings of a reasoning faculty that is inborn in the mind…Within the form and figure of a building there resides some natural excellence and perfection that excites the mind and is immediately recognized by it. I myself believe that form, dignity, grace and other such qualities depend on it, and as soon as anything is removed or altered these qualities are themselves weakened and perish …

From this we may conclude … that the three principal components of that whole theory into which we inquire are number, what we might call outline, and position. But arising from the composition and connection of these three is a further quality in which beauty shines full face: our term for this is *concinnitas*, which we say is nourished with every grace and splendor. It is the task and aim of *concinnitas* to compose parts that are quite separate from each other by their nature, according to some precise rule, so that they correspond to one another in appearance. That is why when the mind is reached by way of sight or sound, or any other means, *concinnitas* is instantly recognized …

Let us conclude as follows. Beauty is a form of sympathy and consonance of the parts within a body, according to definite number, outline and position, as dictated by *concinnitas*, the absolute and fundamental rule in nature. This is the main object of the art of building, and the source of her dignity, charm, authority and worth.

Source: Leon Battista Alberti, *On the Art of Building in Ten Books*, tr. Joseph Rykwert, Neil Leach and Robert Tavernor (Cambridge, MA: The MIT Press, 1988)

limits ornament as in some Cistercian churches (see fig. 11.21). San Lorenzo's unvaulted nave and transept recall Franciscan churches like Santa Croce (see fig. 13.4). Brunelleschi was constrained by the just completed sacristy and the preexisting church. But a new emphasis on symmetry and regularity distinguishes his design for San Lorenzo, accompanied by architectural elements inspired by the past and organized by attention to proportion. The ground plan demonstrates Brunelleschi's technique of composing with units of space in regular square blocks, so that each bay of the nave is twice as wide as its side aisles, and the crossing and choir are each four times the size of each bay of the aisle.

Inside, static order has replaced the flowing spatial movement of Gothic church interiors, such as Chartres (see fig. 12.12). From the portal, a viewer can clearly see the entire structure, almost as if looking at a demonstration of scientific perspective. The effect recalls the "old-fashioned" Tuscan Romanesque, as seen at Pisa cathedral (see fig. 11.34), as well as Early Christian basilicas like Santa Maria Maggiore in Rome (see fig. 8.16). To Brunelleschi, these monuments exemplified the church architecture of antiquity. They inspired his use of round arches and columns, rather than piers, in the nave arcade. Yet these earlier buildings lack the lightness and clarity of San Lorenzo; their columns are larger and more closely spaced, so that they tend to screen off the aisles from the nave. Only the **blind arcade** on the exterior of the Florentine baptistery is as graceful in its proportions as San Lorenzo's, but it has no supporting function (see fig. 11.35). Since the Baptistery was thought to have once been a classical temple, it was an appropriate source of inspiration for Brunelleschi and for the new generation of Medici patrons.

Brunelleschi's innovations in construction techniques, in designing spaces, and in using the architectural vocabulary of antiquity made his work very influential. Some of the next generation of architects, such as Michelozzo (see page 533) trained with him. He was also a friend and correspondent of Leon Battista Alberti (1404–1472), a Florentine humanist, scholar and author; his treatise *On Painting* (which is dedicated to Brunelleschi, refers to "our dear friend" Donatello, and praises Masaccio), completed ca. 1435, helped to spread Brunelleschi's formula for perspective and the author's own ideas about what good painting required. During a stay at the court of Ferrara in 1438, Alberti was asked to restore Vitruvius' treatise on architecture, then known in various manuscripts. Upon his return to Rome five years later, he began a systematic study of the monuments of ancient Rome that led to the *Ten Books on Architecture* (finished 1452 and published 1485)—the first book of its kind since Vitruvius' treatise, on which it is modeled. (See *Primary Source*, above.) Alberti's ideas about architecture had roots in his study of the past, but his emphasis and prescriptions for proportion owe something to Brunelleschi, too. Alberti's writings helped to spread Florentine innovations through Italy and increased the prestige of Florentine artists as well. It brought him important commissions as an architect.

ALBERTI AT SANTA MARIA NOVELLA Few of Brunelleschi's buildings were completed in his lifetime, so we do not know what he would have done with their façades. In fact, few of the major churches of Florence had their façades completed in the Renaissance. (Neither Santa Croce nor the Duomo had complete façades until the nineteenth century; San Lorenzo still has no façade.) One important church in Florence that did have its façade completed, however, is Santa Maria Novella. The exterior of this Dominican church, built largely between 1278 and 1350, had been left unfinished above the row of polychromed Gothic niches with their Gothic portals.

Repairing and improving a church was an act of piety—motivation enough for a neighbor of Santa Maria Novella, the

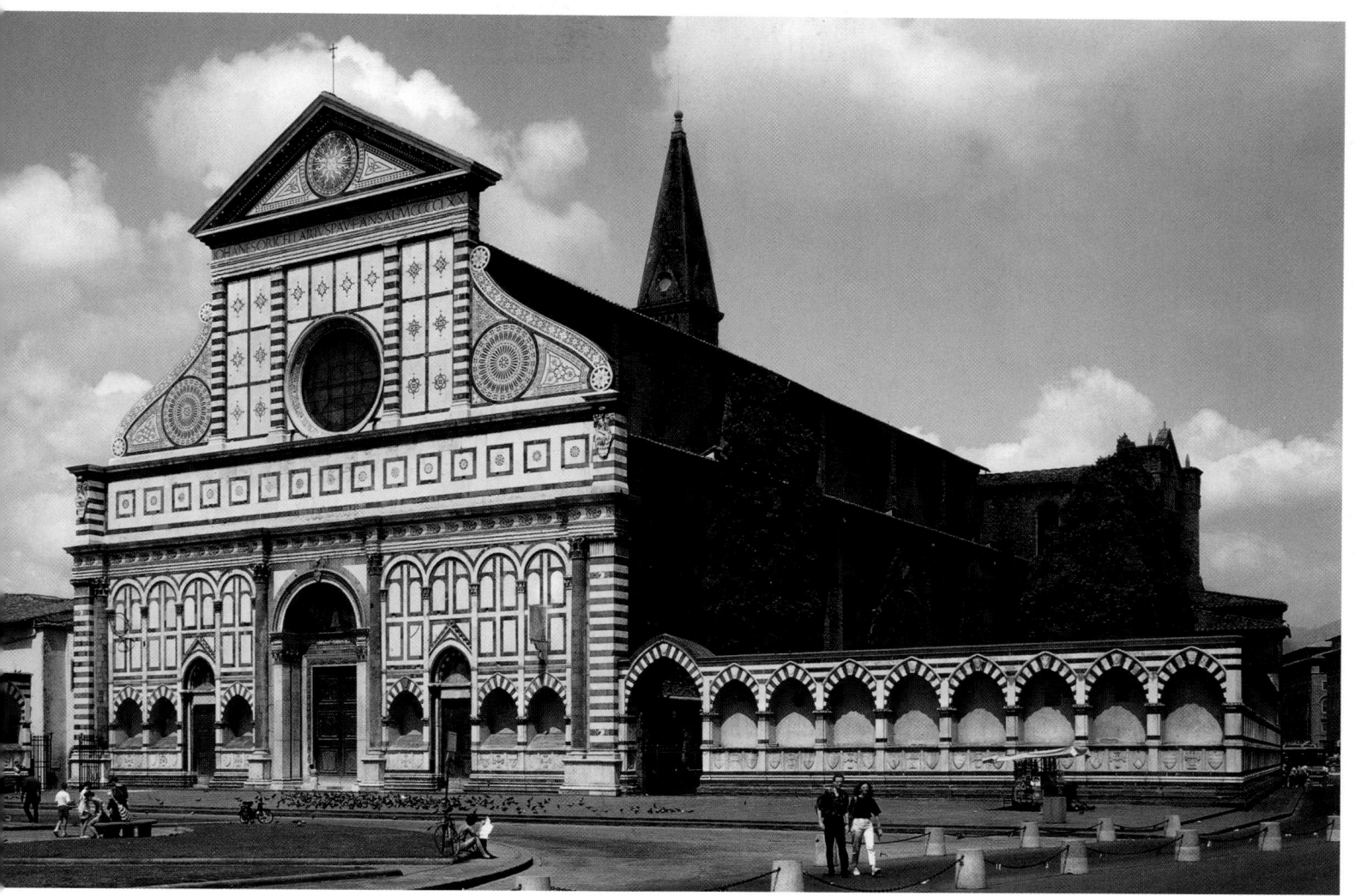

15.9 Leon Battista Alberti. Façade of Santa Maria Novella, Florence. 1458–70

wealthy Giovanni Rucellai, to have this façade completed around 1458 (fig. **15.9**). Rucellai paid Leon Battista Alberti to design and install a marble façade. Multicolored marble façades were traditional in Tuscany. Alberti's models for this project included the cathedral (see fig. 15.3) and other churches in Florence, including the baptistery (see fig. 11.35) and San Miniato al Monte (see fig. 11.36), from which the emphatic arcades may derive.

Other than the doorways and giant round oculus, which were fixed, Alberti's façade masks its relationship to the rest of the church. As he chose not to let the internal structure of the church (with its nave higher than the side aisles) limit him, the architect could use a system of squares to design the façade. Three main squares divide the façade. Two on the lower story flank the extraordinarily classicizing main portal; likewise, the "temple" atop the frieze fits within a square. Mathematical ratios lock these squares into relationships with the whole façade and with the other elements of the composition. Alberti's use of graceful scrolls to bridge the gap between the temple and the frieze was truly innovative and was to prove extremely influential (see fig. 17.23). It also helps to disguise the loose fit of the façade with the

main body of the church by hiding the clerestory. Just below the pediment on the frieze level of the "temple," Alberti includes an inscription that credits Giovanni Rucellai for bringing the work to completion. It is the patron, not the artist, who gains the glory for the work.

Alberti built other influential buildings outside Florence (see page 546). He and Brunelleschi laid the foundations for later architects to design buildings based on their principles of emulating antiquity and designing with an eye to harmonious proportions.

Ancient Inspirations in Florentine Sculpture

While work continued on the baptistery doors and the dome of Florence cathedral, another competition played out nearby at Or San Michele. Begun in 1337, this structure served both as a granary and a shrine holding a locally venerated image of the Virgin and Child. The guilds of Florence oversaw the building, with each one taking responsibility for filling a niche on the exterior with sculpture. In 1406, the city set a deadline to complete the work

Perspective

One of the genuinely transformative inventions of the Renaissance was linear, or scientific, perspective, sometimes called one-point or center-point perspective. The system is a geometric procedure for projecting the illusion of space onto a two-dimensional surface. Its central feature is the **vanishing point**, a single point toward which any set of parallel lines will seem to converge. If these lines are perpendicular to the picture plane, their vanishing point will be on the horizon. (Such lines are called **orthogonals**.) To further clarify the space, lines parallel to the picture plane, called **transversals** (not shown), are laid in at regular intervals, derived geometrically.

Brunelleschi is said to have developed this tool, but artists had been experimenting since antiquity with techniques to create the illusion of depth on a flat surface. At Pompeii, wall painters sometimes used color to suggest deep space (see fig. 7.55), a technique known as atmospheric or aerial perspective. This method recognizes the eye's inability to perceive color at great distances, and that specific colors become light blue or gray at the horizon line. In addition, the forms themselves often become less clear. (See the lower section of fig. 14.10.) Artists also adjusted spatial elements according to how the forms looked to them, sometimes with excellent results, as in Van Eyck's *The "Arnolfini Portrait"* (see fig. 14.14).

In Early Renaissance Italy, scientific perspective systemized the projection of space using mathematics and geometry, overturning the intuitive perspective practices of the past. This "scientific" approach to making images (whether paintings, prints, drawings, or reliefs) became an argument for upgrading the fine arts to become one of the liberal arts. In 1435, Brunelleschi's discovery was described in *On Painting* by Leon Battista Alberti, the first Renaissance treatise on painting. It remains a standard element of drawing instruction to this day.

One advantage of this technique is that the artist can adjust the perspectival system to take account of the presence of a spectator. The method presupposes that a beholder's eye occupies a fixed point in space, so that a perspective picture dictates where the viewer must stand to see it properly. Thus the artist who knows in advance that the image will be seen from above or below, rather than at ordinary eye level, can make the perspective construction correspond to these conditions. (See, for example, fig. 15.55.) Sometimes, however, these vantage points are so abnormal (as when a viewer is looking up at an image on the ceiling) that the design must be foreshortened to an extreme degree. In such cases, the artist may create an "ideal beholder" for the image, regardless of a spectator's actual viewpoint.

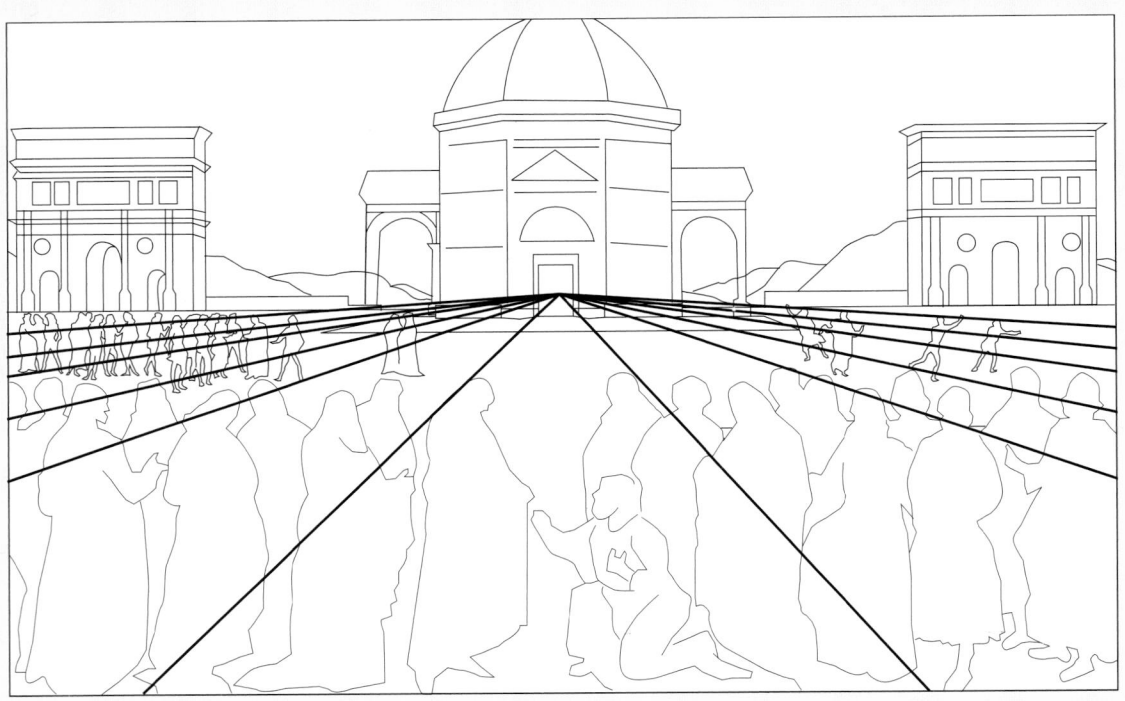

Perspective image with *Delivery of the Keys* (see fig. 15.55)

within ten years. In the decades that followed, the guilds and the sculptors they commissioned competed intensely to create impressive statues of their patron saints. The major guilds commissioned Lorenzo Ghiberti to execute several statues for Or San Michele, while some younger sculptors won commissions from less powerful guilds.

NANNI DI BANCO The Guild of Wood and Stone Carvers hired one of its members, Nanni di Banco (ca. 1380–1421), to fill its niche at Or San Michele with an image of the Four Crowned Saints, called the *Quattro Coronati* (fig. **15.10**). Carved between 1409 and 1416/17, these figures represent four Christian sculptors who were executed for refusing to carve a pagan statue ordered by

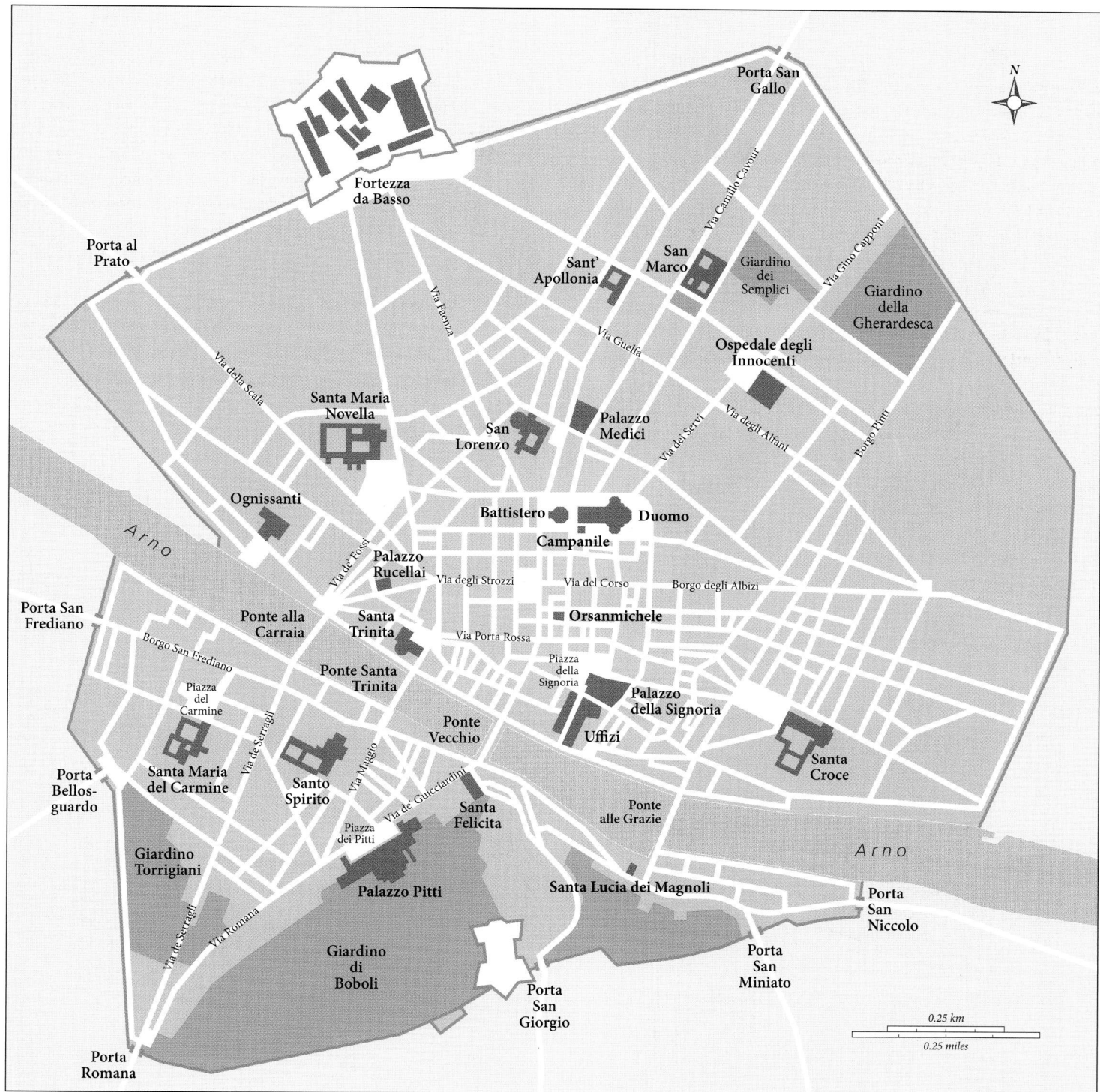

Map 15.2 Key monuments in Renaissance Florence

the Roman emperor Diocletian. The life-size saints stand in a Gothic niche as if discussing their impending fate. Their bodies seem to spill out of the confines of the niche, draped as they are in the heavy folds of their togas. These garments and the heads of the second and third of the *Coronati* directly recall Roman portrait sculpture of the first century CE (see fig. 7.35). It is as if Nanni were situating the martyrs in their historical moment. His

figures emulate Roman verism and monumentality. The relief below the saints represents a sculptor, stonecutters, and a mason at work, both explaining the story of the martyrs and advertising the skills of the patrons who commissioned the work. This double function occurs often in the statues designed for the niches on Or San Michele, reflecting the building's double origin in commerce and piety.

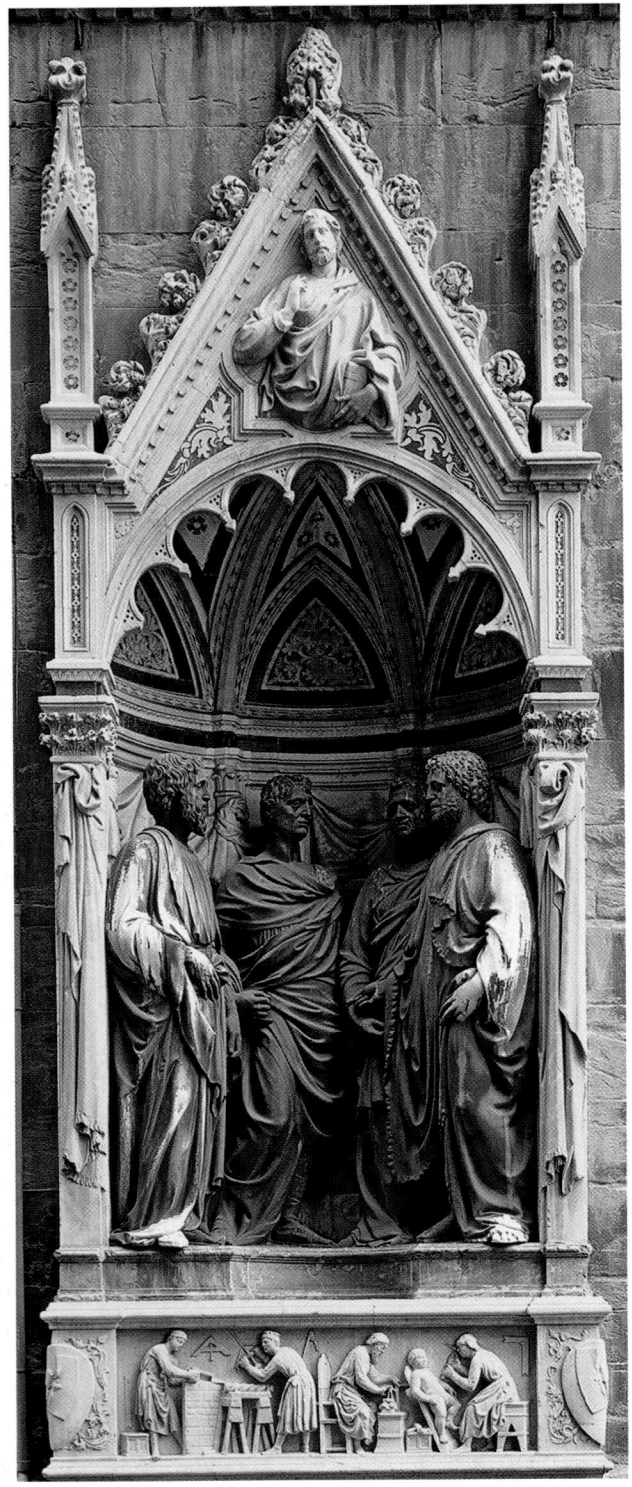

15.10 Nanni di Banco, *Quattro Coronati* (*Four Saints*).
ca. 1409–16/17. Marble, 6' (1.83 m). Museo di Or San Michele,
Florence

DONATELLO AT OR SAN MICHELE One of Ghiberti's former assistants, the young Donatello (1389–1466) executed several
statues for Or San Michele. The linen weavers' guild turned to
him to fill its niche with a figure probably completed in 1413 (fig.
15.11). Their patron, St. Mark, stands almost 8 feet high, but that
is only one of the features that makes him so imposing. His large,

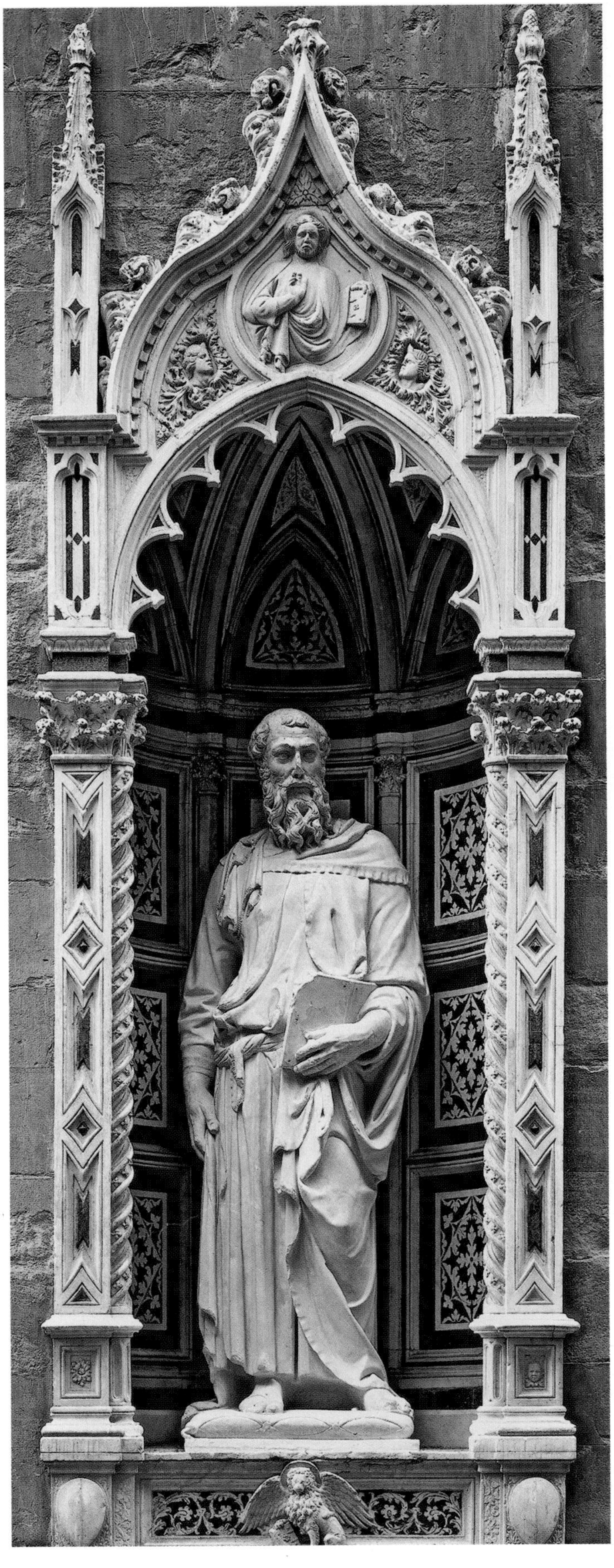

15.11 Donatello, *St. Mark*. ca. 1411–13. Marble, 7'9" (2.4 m).
Museo di Or San Michele, Florence

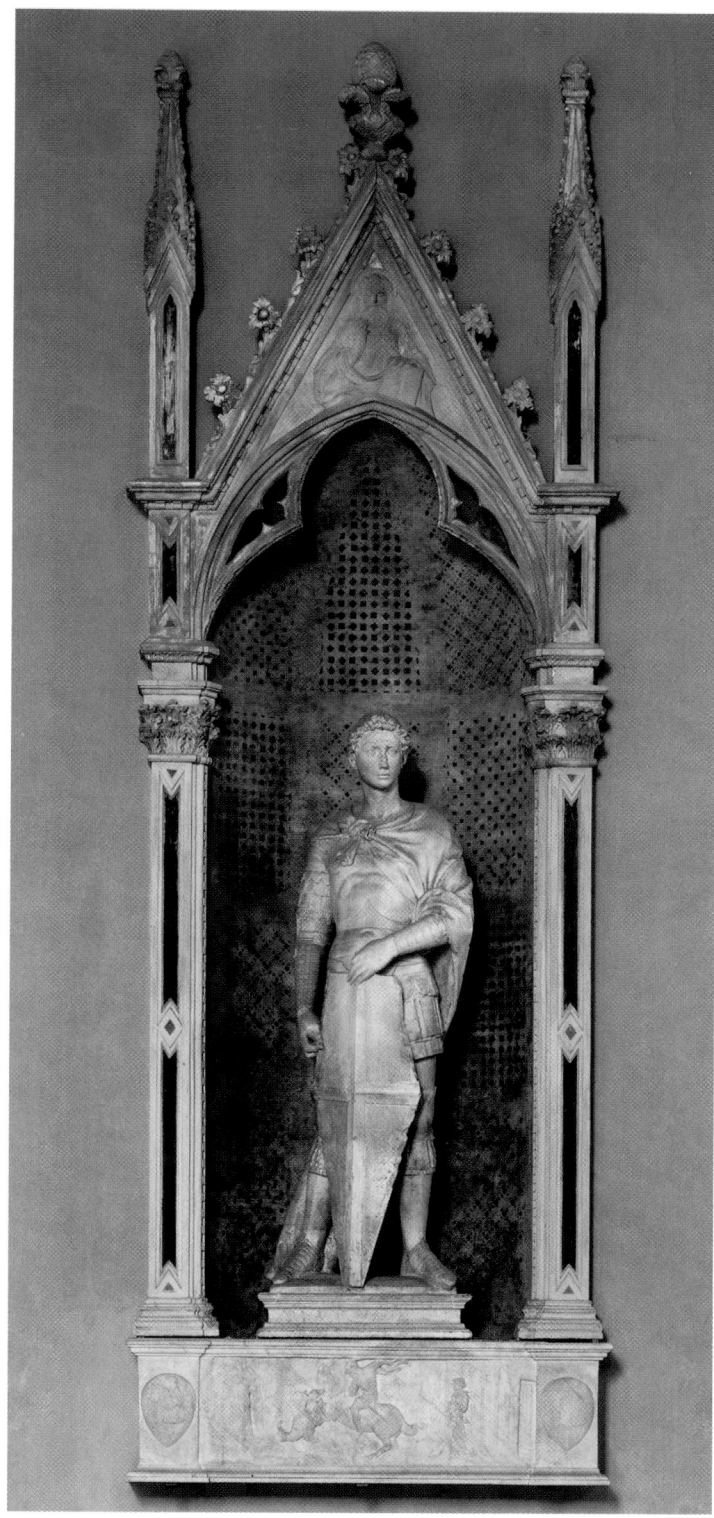

15.12 Donatello, *St. George*, from Or San Michele, Florence. ca. 1410–20. Marble, height of statue 6'10" (2.1 m). Relief 15¼ × 47¼" (39 × 120 cm). Museo Nazionale del Bargello, Florence

Donatello treats the human body as an articulated structure, capable of movement, and its drapery as a separate element that is based on the shapes underneath rather than on patterns and shapes imposed from outside. Following classical precedents such as the *Doryphoros*, Donatello carefully balances the composition, so the elements on the left (as a viewer sees it) stress the vertical and the static, while those on the right emphasize the diagonal and kinetic. St. Mark's deeply carved eyes and undulating beard give him a powerful personality, while the mass of drapery reminds the viewer of the linen weavers' products. This work reflects Donatello's deep understanding of the principles that guided the artists of antiquity and his commitment to them. *St. Mark* reveals what Donatello learned from studying ancient works of sculpture: an emphasis on naturalistic form, the independence of body and drapery, a balanced but contrasting composition, the potential for movement, and psychological presence.

Donatello finished his *St. George* (fig. **15.12**) for the Guild of Armorers around 1417. The niche is so shallow that the figure seems poised to step out of it. Although dressed in armor, he appears able to move his limbs easily. His stance, with the weight placed on the forward leg, suggests he is ready for combat. Originally, he held a real sword or lance in his right hand, and he wore a real helmet, effectively showcasing the guild's wares. The controlled energy of his body is reflected in his eyes, which seem to scan the horizon for the enemy. St. George is portrayed as a Christian soldier, spiritually akin to the *St. Theodore* at Chartres (see fig. 12.22) and to other figures of chivalry.

Below the niche a relief panel shows the hero's best-known exploit, the slaying of a dragon. The woman on the right is the princess whom he had come to free. Here, Donatello devised a new kind of shallow relief (called **schiacciato**, meaning "flattened-out"), yet he created an illusion of almost infinite depth. In this relief, the landscape behind the figures consists of delicate surface modulations that catch light from varying angles. Every tiny ripple has a descriptive power that is greater than its real depth. The sculptor's chisel, like a painter's brush, becomes a tool for creating shades of light and dark. The energetic figure of the saint on horseback, battling the dragon in the foreground, protrudes from this atmospheric background, while the princess watches. The whole work becomes an image of watchfulness and preparedness for danger.

DONATELLO AT WORK IN SIENA, PADUA, AND FLORENCE Donatello's innovations in Florence soon became known elsewhere in Italy, leading to commissions in other cities, such as Siena and Padua. His career was long and productive making him the most influential sculptor of fifteenth-century Italy. It is worth pausing here to consider the range of his activities from the 1420s until the 1460s, as there is such variety, invention and power in his art.

Donatello's early career may have begun in Ghiberti's workshop, but he ultimately competed with his mentor both at Or San Michele and in Siena. In 1416, Lorenzo Ghiberti was one of a group of artists hired to execute a new baptismal font for that

powerful hands grip a book (his Gospel). His body stands in a pose Donatello learned from studying the art of the ancients: One leg is flexed while the other holds the body's weight in a **contrapposto** stance (see fig. 5.33). St. Mark's drapery falls in deep folds to reveal and emphasize his posture.

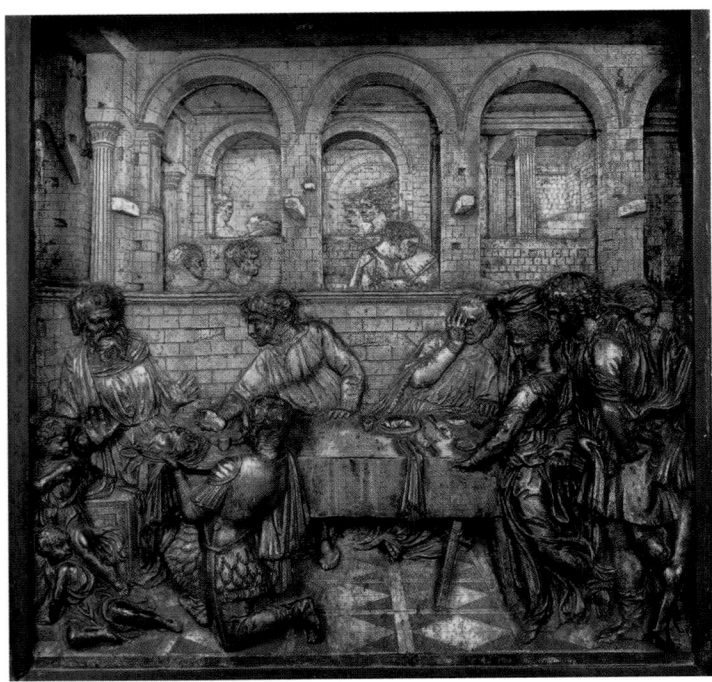

15.13 Donatello, *The Feast of Herod*, Siena cathedral. ca. 1425. Gilt bronze, 23½" (59.7 cm) square

city's baptistery, San Giovanni. Donatello took over one of the relief panels for the sides of the hexagonal basin in 1423. He finished *The Feast of Herod* (fig. **15.13**) by 1427. The relief represents the story of John the Baptist's martyrdom; Salome, the stepdaughter of King Herod, requested the head of the saint as a reward for performing a dance. Donatello combines many stages in the narrative into one space. The focus of the drama—the executioner presenting the head of St. John the Baptist to Herod—is far to the left, while the dancing Salome and most of the spectators are massed on the right. Yet the center is empty. Donatello created this gaping hole to add to the impact of the shocking sight, bolstered by the witnesses' gestures and expressions. Moreover, the centrifugal movement of the figures suggests that the picture space does not end within the panel but continues in every direction. The frame thus becomes a window through which is seen a segment of deepening space. The arched openings within the panel frame additional segments of the same reality, luring the viewer farther into the space.

This architecture, with its round arches and fluted columns and pilasters, reflects the designs of Donatello's friend and colleague Filippo Brunelleschi. More importantly, *The Feast of Herod* is an example of a picture space using Brunelleschi's linear

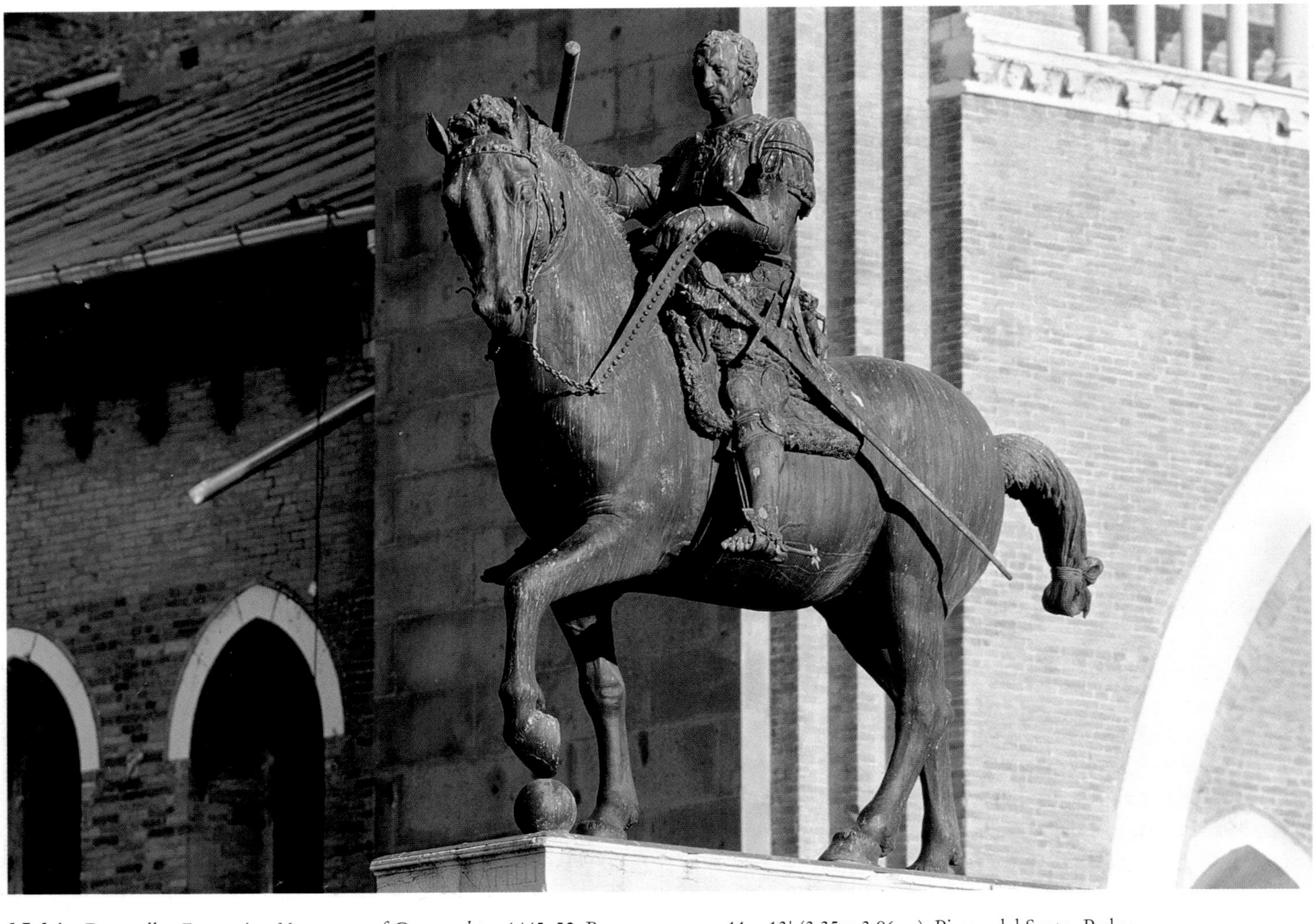

15.14 Donatello, *Equestrian Monument of Gattamelata*. 1445–50. Bronze, approx. 11 × 13' (3.35 × 3.96 m). Piazza del Santo, Padua

perspective. A series of arches set at different depths provides the setting for different figures and moments in the biblical story: In the background, we see the servant carrying the head of the Baptist, which he then presents to Herod in the foreground. Donatello used perspective to organize the action as a continuous narrative, unfolding through space as well as time.

Donatello's successes in Tuscany led to a commission from the Republic of Venice in 1443. The commander of the Venetian armies, Erasmo da Narni (nicknamed "Gattamelata"), had recently died, and Venice sought to honor him with a statue. To this end, Donatello produced his largest free-standing work in bronze: the *Equestrian Monument of Gattamelata* (fig. **15.14**), which still stands in its original position on a tall pedestal near the church of St. Anthony in Padua. Having visited Rome, Donatello certainly knew the tradition of equestrian statues exemplified by that of Marcus Aurelius (see fig. 7.33). The work also reflects the medieval tradition seen in the monument to Bernabò Visconti in Milan (fig. 13.33). Like the *Equestrian Statue of Marcus Aurelius*, the *Gattamelata* is impressive in scale and creates a sense of balance and dignity. The horse, a heavy-set animal fit to carry a man in full armor, is so large that the rider must dominate it by force of personality rather than by size. Like the Visconti work, it belongs to a tradition of representations of military leaders on horseback as funerary monuments. In his vivid portrait of a general, Donatello reenergizes this tradition by the carefully realistic depiction of the armor and fittings, and his powerful characterization of Gattamelata's features.

Despite these "foreign" commissions, Donatello spent most of his career in Florence, where he produced works for the Duomo, the Palazzo della Signoria and for important families like the Medici. For the latter's palace, he apparently executed a bronze *David* (see fig. 15.33), which will be discussed below. In addition to projects in bronze, Donatello worked in less expensive mediums. Although the circumstances of its commission are unclear, Donatello carved a powerful *Mary Magdalen* sometime in mid-century. Rather than marble or bronze, this life-size figure (fig. **15.15**) was carved in poplar wood, then painted and gilded. Our earliest reference to this object dates from around 1500 and describes it as being displayed in the baptistery, although there has been much speculation about its origins and date. Late medieval enhancements of Mary of Magdala's biography reported that she spent the last years of her life in the desert as a hermit in penitence. In his image of her, Donatello carves the soft wood into complex textures to render her rough garment and her hair, and to give her figure a gaunt, emaciated look. Her limbs and face are painted the ruddy color of someone who lives in the desert, while her hair was originally gilded. The artist is less interested in ancient forms here than he is in expressive naturalism.

Even though the date for this figure is uncertain, many scholars see the *Magdalen* as a work of Donatello's old age, and thus in its spiritual intensity they see a change of mood for the artist. In any case, the *Magdalen* demonstrates Donatello's range as a sculptor, as he explores the expressive possibilities of another sculpted medium. He worked in wood, marble, bronze, and terra

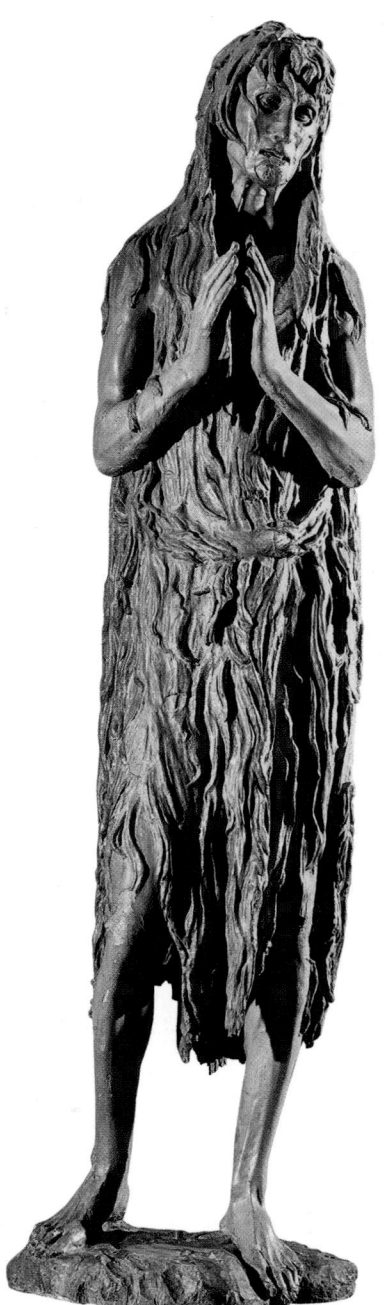

15.15   Donatello, *Mary Magdalen*. ca. 1430–50. Polychrome and gold on wood, height 6'1" (1.85 m). Museo dell'Opera del Duomo, Florence

cotta, leaving a prodigious amount of sculpture behind when he died in 1466.

GHIBERTI AND LATER FLORENTINE SCULPTURE

Donatello's contemporary Lorenzo Ghiberti's work on the bronze doors for the baptistery continued, with the assistance of numerous other artists, until their completion in 1424. This set of doors so impressed the Guild of Wool Merchants, which oversaw the building, that it commissioned him to execute a second pair. These doors, begun in 1425 but not completed until 1452, were ultimately installed in the east entry of the baptistery, facing the

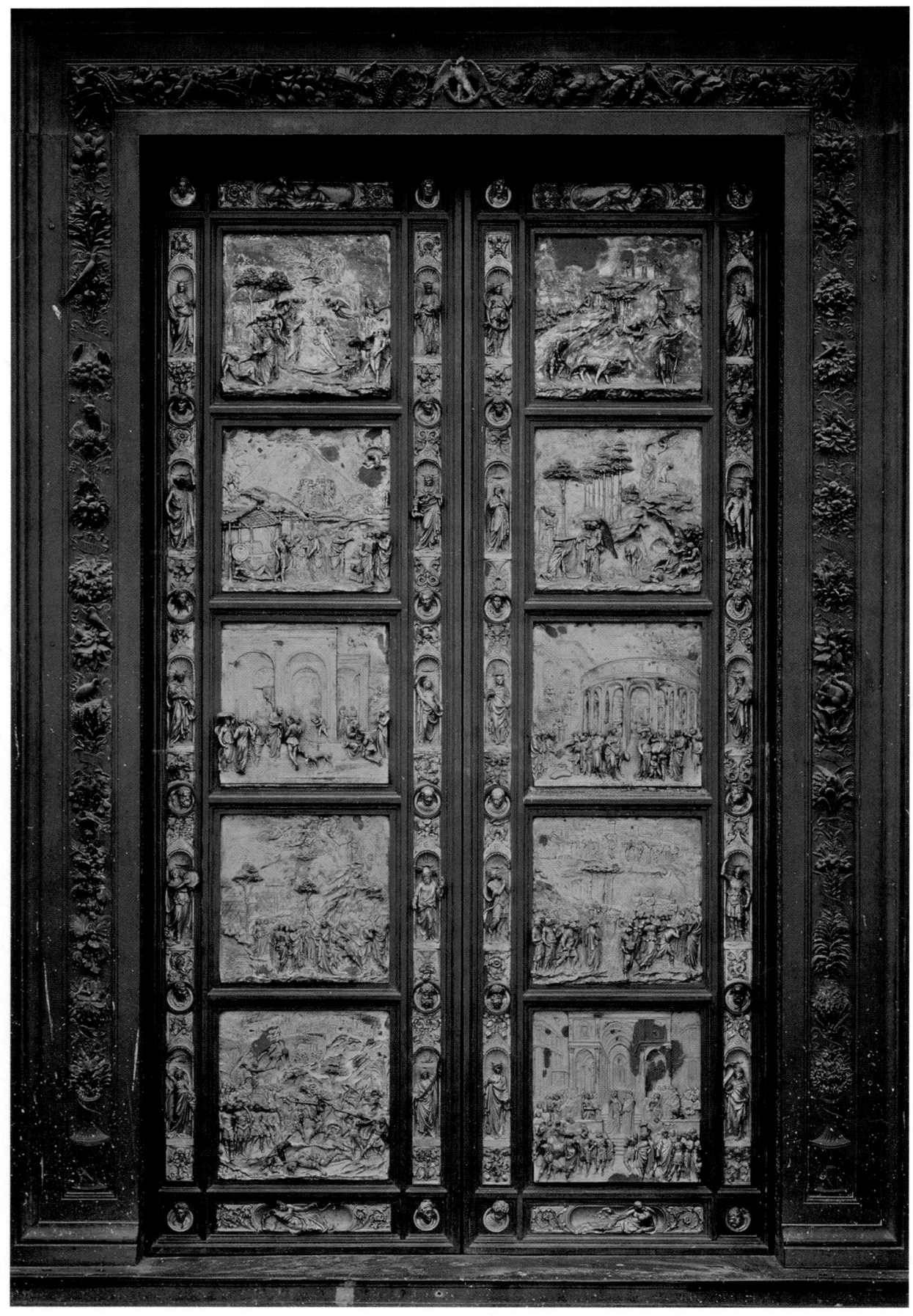

15.16 Lorenzo Ghiberti, *Gates of Paradise*, east doors of the Baptistery of San Giovanni, Florence. 1425–52. Gilt bronze, height 15' (4.57 m)

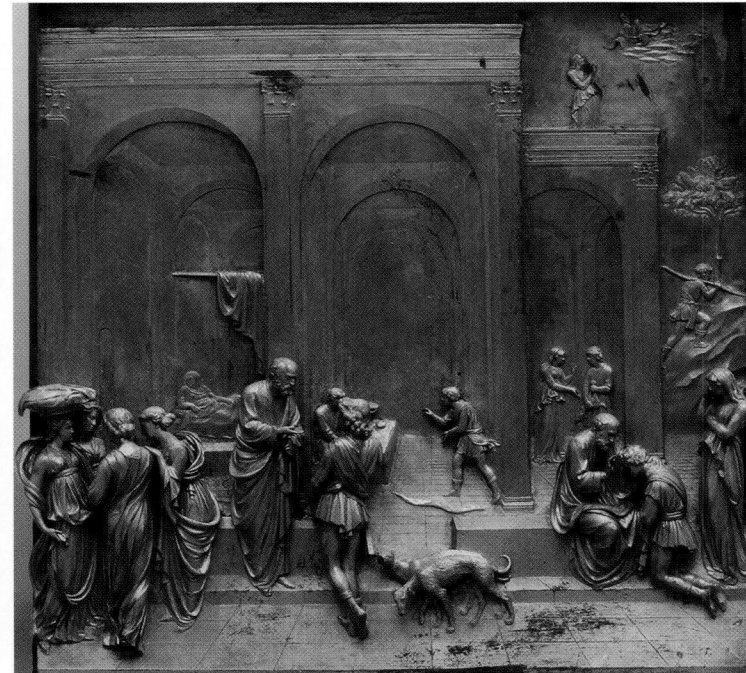

15.17 Lorenzo Ghiberti, *The Story of Jacob and Esau*, panel of the *Gates of Paradise*, Baptistery of San Giovanni, Florence. ca. 1435. Gilt bronze, 31¼" (79.5 cm) square

cathedral; this area is called the Paradise, so the doors were termed the *Gates of Paradise* (fig. 15.16), a witticism that reportedly originated with Michelangelo. Where the earlier doors by Andrea Pisano and Ghiberti each bore 28 small panels in quatrefoils, these two doors each contain five large panels in simple square frames, creating a larger field for each image. These panels depict scenes from the Hebrew Bible, completing the program of all three doors: One door is devoted to the life of John the Baptist, one to the life of Christ, and one to the Hebrew Bible. Two humanists may have planned the program for the later doors: Ambrogio Traversari (1386–1439) and the chancellor, Leonardo Bruni. The latter prescribed that the doors should be both significant and splendid. To achieve splendor, Ghiberti completely gilded the masterfully crafted bronze reliefs and framed the panels with figures of prophets in niches, portrait heads in roundels, and foliate decorations. Significance was achieved through the selection of themes and the legibility of the narratives.

In designing these reliefs, Ghiberti drew on the new devices for pictorial imagery he and his rivals had pioneered, including the *schiacciato* relief devised by Donatello for the *St. George* at Or San Michele and the linear perspective developed by Brunelleschi. The graceful proportions, elegant stances, and fluid drapery of the figures bespeak Ghiberti's allegiance to the International Gothic style. The hint of depth seen in *The Sacrifice of Isaac* (see fig. 15.2) has grown in *The Story of Jacob and Esau* (fig. 15.17) into a deeper space defined by the arches of a building planned to accommodate the figures as they appear and reappear throughout the structure in a continuous narrative. The relief tells the story of Isaac mistakenly blessing his younger son, Jacob, instead of the elder, Esau.

The blind Isaac sends Esau off to hunt on the left, but confers his blessing on the disguised Jacob on the right. Isaac's effective preference to the younger Jacob over the older Esau foreshadowed Christianity replacing Judaism for medieval theologians. Ghiberti's spacious hall is a fine example of Early Renaissance architectural design.

A HUMANIST'S TOMB Tomb sculpture was another important form in fifteenth-century Florence. On the death of its illustrious chancellor Leonardo Bruni, the city of Florence honored him with a monument installed in Santa Croce (fig. 15.18). This humanist and statesman had played a vital part in the city's affairs since the

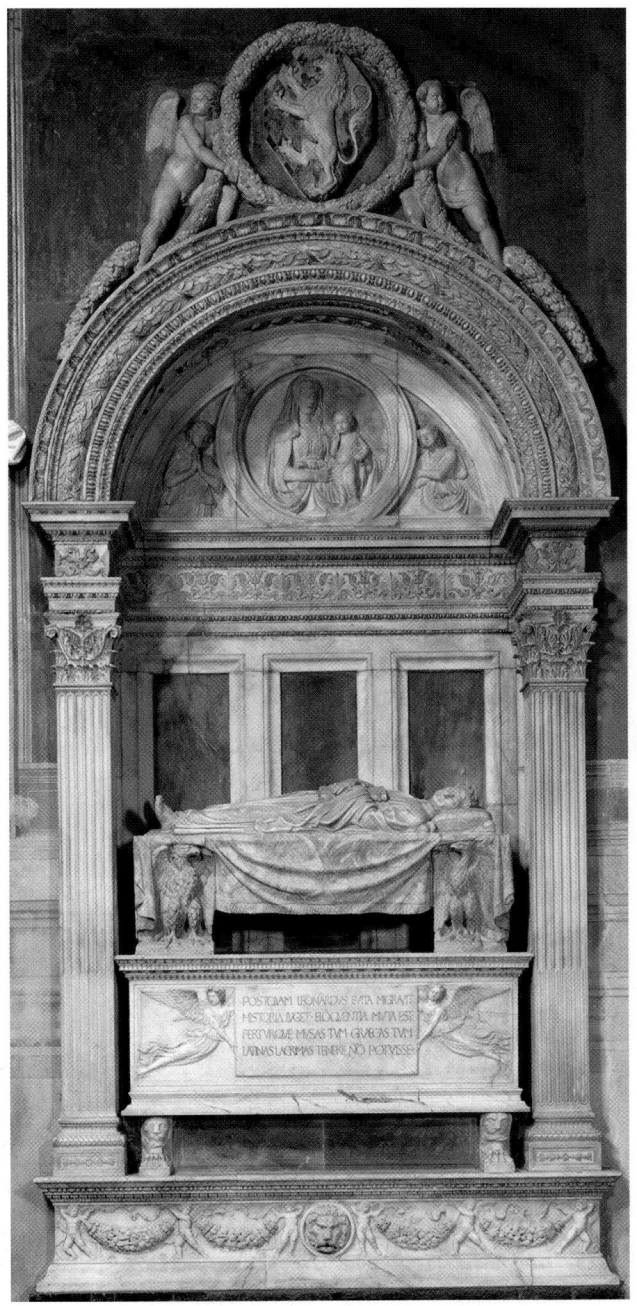

15.18 Bernardo Rossellino, *Tomb of Leonardo Bruni*, Santa Croce, Florence. ca. 1445–50. Marble, height to top of arch 20' (6.1 m)

beginning of the century; when he died in 1444, he received a grand funeral "in the manner of the ancients." Bernardo Rossellino (1409–1464), a sculptor from the countryside around Florence, executed the tomb. Since Bruni had been born in Arezzo, his native town probably contributed to the project and perhaps favored Rossellino, another former resident, for the commission.

Bruni's contributions to the city as politician, historian, and literary figure forged Florentines' notion of themselves as the heirs to Roman culture, so Rossellino's design paid homage to this theme. His effigy lies on a bier supported by Roman eagles, his head wreathed in laurel and his right hand resting on a book (perhaps his own *History of Florence*). On the sarcophagus, two figures with wings hold an eloquent inscription. The only religious element appears in the **lunette**, where the Madonna and Child look down at the effigy from a roundel. Above the arch, a heraldic lion appears in a wreath supported by angels. This symbol of Florence associates Bruni with the city he served and links Florence to his goal of reviving Roman virtues.

LATER SCULPTURE AT OR SAN MICHELE Although many of the guilds had filled their niches by 1430, more sculptural commissions were given at Or San Michele in the second half of the century. Not all groups active in commissioning works of art could afford the expense of bronze or marble; some guilds installed terra-cotta roundels in the façade above the niches. The leading sculptor in this medium was Luca della Robbia (1400–1482), a student of Nanni di Banco, who executed a medallion of the Virgin and Child for the Guild of Doctors and Apothecaries around 1465 (fig. **15.19**). Luca covered the earth-colored clay with enamel-like glazes to mask the surface and

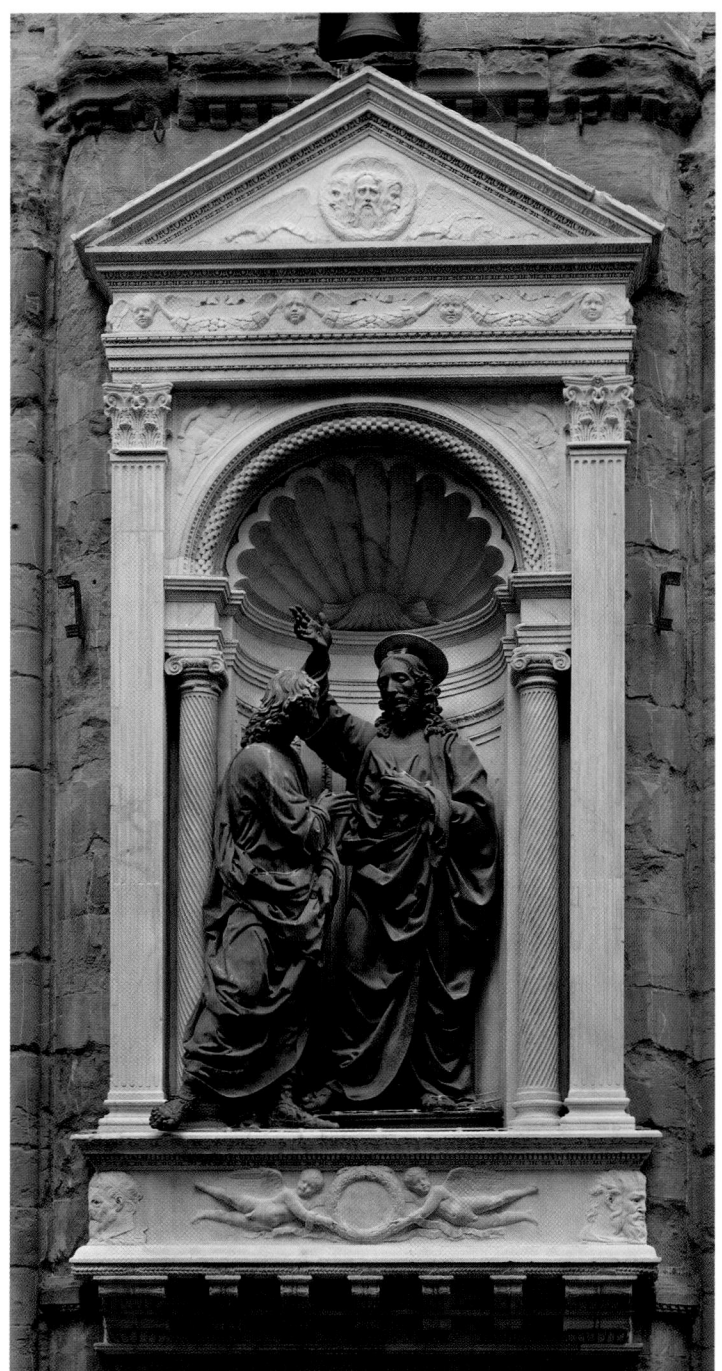

15.20 Andrea del Verrocchio, *The Incredulity of Thomas.* 1467–83. Bronze, height of Christ 7'6½" (2.28 m), Thomas 6'6¾" (2 m). Or San Michele, Florence (copy in niche)

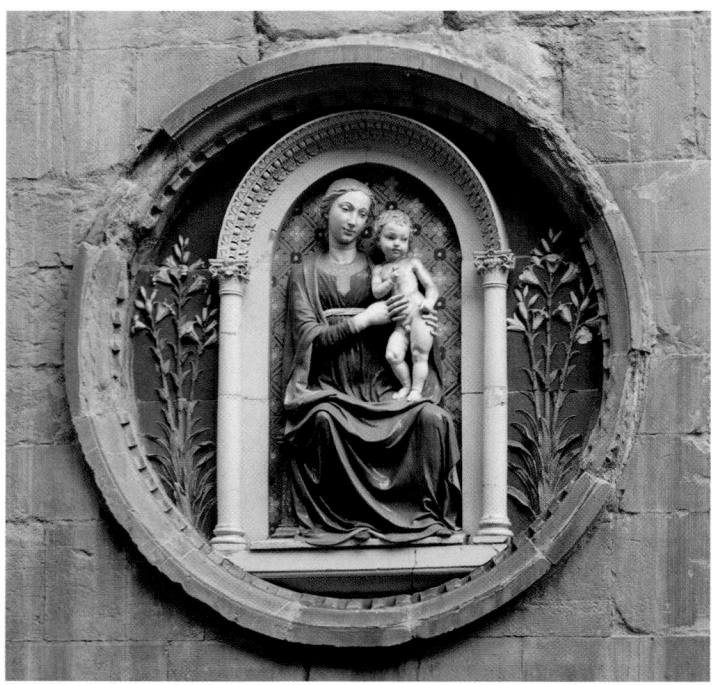

15.19 Luca della Robbia, *Madonna and Child.* ca. 1465. Glazed terra cotta. Or San Michele, Florence

protect it from the weather. This relief depicts the Virgin and Child beneath a Brunelleschian arch, flanked by lilies. The blue background highlights the flowers and the architectural forms. Mother and child form a compact group, their heads echoing each other, as they look downward to make eye contact with a viewer passing by. Such inexpensive substitutes for marble and bronze carvings attracted many customers and the della Robbia workshop became a factory, turning out scores of small Madonna reliefs still visible throughout Florence.

Patronage Studies

Seeing a work of art in a museum, a modern viewer may not be aware of its original function or context, nor of the circumstances that brought it into creation. Many art historians find that an important way to investigate these circumstances is to focus on the patronage of art. Such studies may include finding evidence in documents indicating who paid the artist for the work; considering what role the patron may have had in determining style or subject matter; evaluating the relationship between the artist and the patron; and drawing conclusions about what the patron wanted the work of art to do.

Relationships between patron and artist in the Renaissance varied greatly. In princely courts, an artist could be considered a member of the household staff, with many rather mundane tasks to do, or an esteemed member of the prince's circle, with special status and prestige. In urban centers, artists may have interacted with patrons on a more socially equal level, but the person buying the work of art still had a great deal to say about the finished product. In gifts made to churches, patrons might want their portraits painted into the work of art or their coat of arms prominently displayed to remind a viewer of the identity of the donor, a practice that was widespread by the end of the Middle Ages. The system of patronage in Italy was part of a larger social network. In Florence, the great families of a neighborhood were often the major patrons of large projects for the entire neighborhood (for example, the Medici at San Lorenzo and the Rucellai at Santa Maria Novella). Other families or groups often allied themselves with the great families for political, social, or commercial reasons. In some cases, this resulted in works of art that represented or made reference to the great families. Artists favored by the major patrons could gain other clients among the followers of those patrons. The investigation of these issues has enhanced our understanding of the way works of art functioned in their time.

Later interventions at Or San Michele brought other changes. Sometime after 1462, a sculpture by Donatello was removed and its niche reassigned to the judges of the merchants' guild. This group, responsible for adjudicating commercial cases, hired Andrea del Verrocchio (1435–1488) to fill the niche with an image reflecting their activities, using a theme traditionally associated with justice. The architecture of the niche remained as Donatello had designed it, so Verrocchio executed the figures of *The Incredulity of Thomas* (fig. **15.20**) without backs to squeeze them into the shallow space. The bronze figures stand close together, as the apostle Thomas seeks proof of the miracle of the Resurrection by probing the wound in Christ's side. Verrocchio was a painter as well as a sculptor, and this sculpture shares with contemporary paintings an interest in textures, the play of light and dark in massive drapery folds, and illusionism. The niche can barely contain the oversized figures, so Thomas's foot projects beyond the limits of the frame, linking passersby to the scene. His body twists into the composition, leading a viewer to the gentle features of Christ. The eloquent poses and bold exchange of gestures between Christ and Thomas convey the drama of the scene. Verrocchio lets the active drapery, with its deep folds, suggest the calm of Christ and the disturbance in Thomas's mind. Michelangelo admired the *The Incredulity of Thomas* for the beauty of the figures; and Leonardo da Vinci learned directly from Verrocchio, as his teacher, to create figures whose actions express the passions of the mind.

Sculpture in Florence took many forms, though it was often commissioned in association with buildings. Doors, niches, baptismal fonts, and altars were all adorned with sculpture in relief or with figural works of a scale and impressiveness that almost brings them to life. Materials ranged from less expensive terra cotta to gilded bronze. Renaissance sculptors' study of the ancients and interest in naturalism inspired their increasingly realistic and psychologically charged imagery.

Painting in Florentine Churches and Chapels

Well-funded guilds oversaw the sculptural adornment of public buildings like the baptistery and Or San Michele, and great families often sponsored building programs in churches. Many of the elite families of Florence, having patronage rights in chapels, commissioned paintings rather than sculpture. (See *The Art Historian's Lens*, above.) The stimulus of such fresco and panel commissions led to many innovations in the art of painting. The achievements of the sculptors in realizing vivid sacred characters on the niches of Or San Michele and the tools for projecting space provided by Brunelleschi inspired new directions in Renaissance painting.

GENTILE DA FABRIANO Patrons commissioned chapels in mendicant and parish churches, such as the Gothic church of Santa Trinità. Here the sacristy was endowed by the Strozzi, one of the wealthiest families in Florence. To complete the program, Palla Strozzi hired Gentile da Fabriano to paint the altarpiece, *The Adoration of the Magi*, which Gentile signed and dated in 1423 (fig. **15.21**). Gentile (ca. 1385–1427) worked throughout northern Italy in a style informed by the International Gothic. The lavish, triple-arched gilt frame of the altarpiece, with a **predella** (the base of the altarpiece) and gable figures, encloses a single scene in the central panel: the visit of the Magi to Bethlehem to acknowledge the newborn Jesus as king. A cavalcade of richly dressed courtiers, as well as horses, dogs, and exotic animals (monkeys, leopards, and camels), fills the front plane of the picture as the three kings advance to venerate the child, who sits in his mother's lap to the left. Behind the stable and rock formations that define the frontal plane, the landscape winds upward into the arches of the frame. In those distant vistas appear the Magi wending their way to Bethlehem; towns and castles mark their route. So despite the

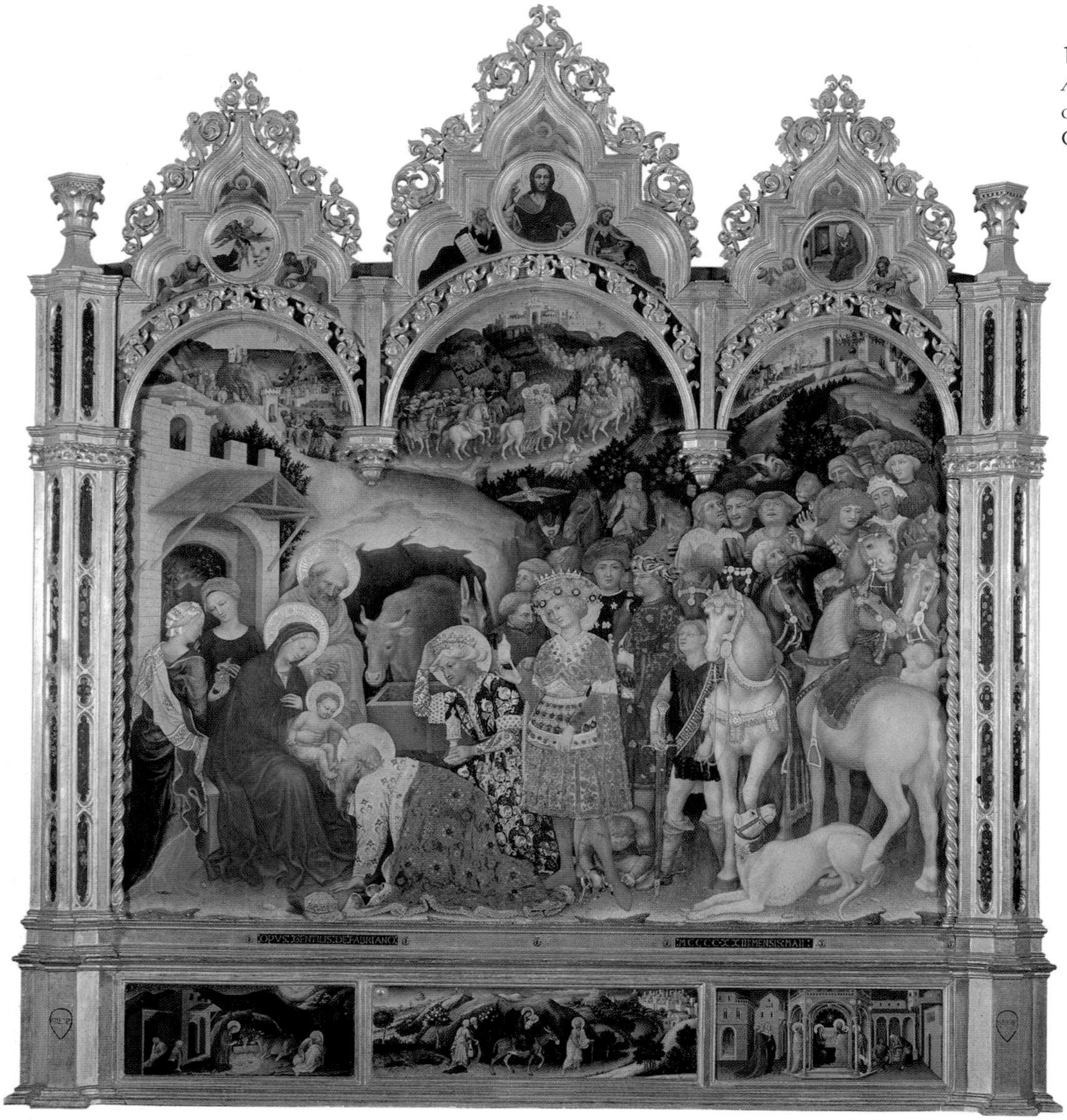

15.21   Gentile da Fabriano,
Adoration of the Magi. 1423. Tempera
on panel, 9'10" × 9'3" (3 × 2.82 m).
Galleria degli Uffizi, Florence

apparently unified landscape, several episodes of the narrative
appear in the center panel. Other moments in the story—the
Nativity, the Flight into Egypt, the Presentation in the Temple—
appear in the predella. Small images in the gable above the center
panel preface the story with images of the Annunciation.

Gentile's altarpiece imagines the events of the Magi's visit in
courtly and sumptuous terms. Not only is the image full of elegant
figures, garbed in brilliant brocades and surrounded by colorful
retainers, but the panel also shines with gold leaf and tooled surfaces. (The haloes of the Virgin and St. Joseph bear pseudo-kufic

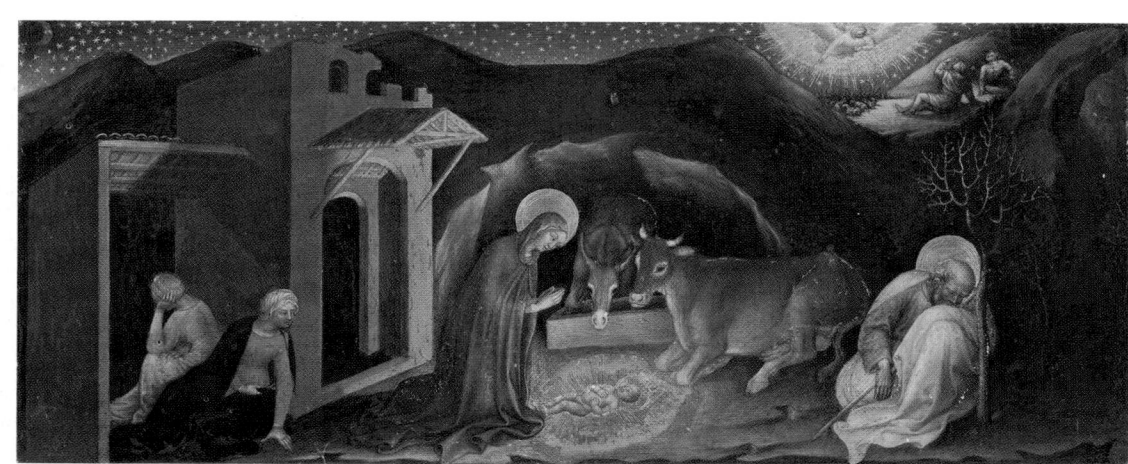

15.22   Gentile da Fabriano,
The Nativity, detail of *Adoration
of the Magi* predella. 1423.
Tempera on panel, 12¼ × 29½"
(31 × 75 cm)

inscriptions, attesting to Gentile's contact with Islamic works, probably in Venice.) The kings, also given halos, stand not only for the international acknowledgement of Christ's divinity, but for the three ages of man: youth, middle age, and old age. The artist crowds the space, and the festive pageant almost overwhelms the Holy Family with its profusion of men and beasts, including some marvelously rendered horses. Despite this crowding, a golden light unites the whole image, illuminating the bodies of the animals, the faces of the humans, and parts of the landscape. These forms are softly modeled to suggest volume for the figures and to counteract the strong flattening effect of the gold. The predella scene of the Nativity (fig. **15.22**) demonstrates this aspect of Gentile's art further, as it stresses the function of light over line to delineate the forms. What is more, the source for the light that models the figures and the shed in the predella is the mystical light emanating from the Christ Child himself. Gentile's picture reveals his awareness of light as a carrier of meaning.

MASACCIO AT SANTA MARIA NOVELLA Gentile's refined style made him very popular among aristocratic patrons throughout Italy, but it was his approach to light that would strongly influence younger painters. One such was Masaccio (Tommaso di Ser Giovanni di Mone Cassai, 1401–1428). Leon Battista Alberti, a contemporary of Massacio, celebrated the young painter's work in his treatise "On Painting," finished around 1435. Vasari noted that many sixteenth-century artists admired Masaccio, but nonetheless, in the 1560s, he covered up one of Masaccio's most famous works in Santa Maria Novella (fig. **15.23**) when he remodeled the church. Ultimately, this action probably saved Masaccio's work, but much about its commissioning and meaning remains obscure.

Because the fresco originally stood above a tomb slab for the Lenzi family, many scholars have concluded that they commissioned Masaccio to paint the fresco depicting the Holy Trinity in the company of the Virgin, St. John the Evangelist, and the two donors. The lowest section depicts a skeleton lying on a sarcophagus. An inscription (in Italian) reads, "What I once was, you are; what I am, you will become." The large scale, balanced composition, and sculptural volume of the figures in this painting have their origins in the art of Giotto (see figs. 13.17–13.20). But although Giotto was a starting point for Masaccio, in Giotto's work, body and drapery form a single unit, whereas Masaccio's figures, like Donatello's, are "clothed nudes," whose drapery falls in response to the body underneath.

The setting reveals the artist's awareness of Brunelleschi's new architecture and of his system of perspective. (See *Materials and Techniques*, page 516.) The tall pilasters next to the painted columns recall the pilasters Brunelleschi designed for the Old Sacristy, as do the simple moldings that define the arch and the entablature of this fictive chapel. Masaccio's use of perspective gives the spectator all the data needed to measure the depth of this painted interior, to draw its plan, and to envision the structure in three dimensions. This barrel-vaulted chamber is not a shallow niche, but a deep space in which the figures can move freely. The

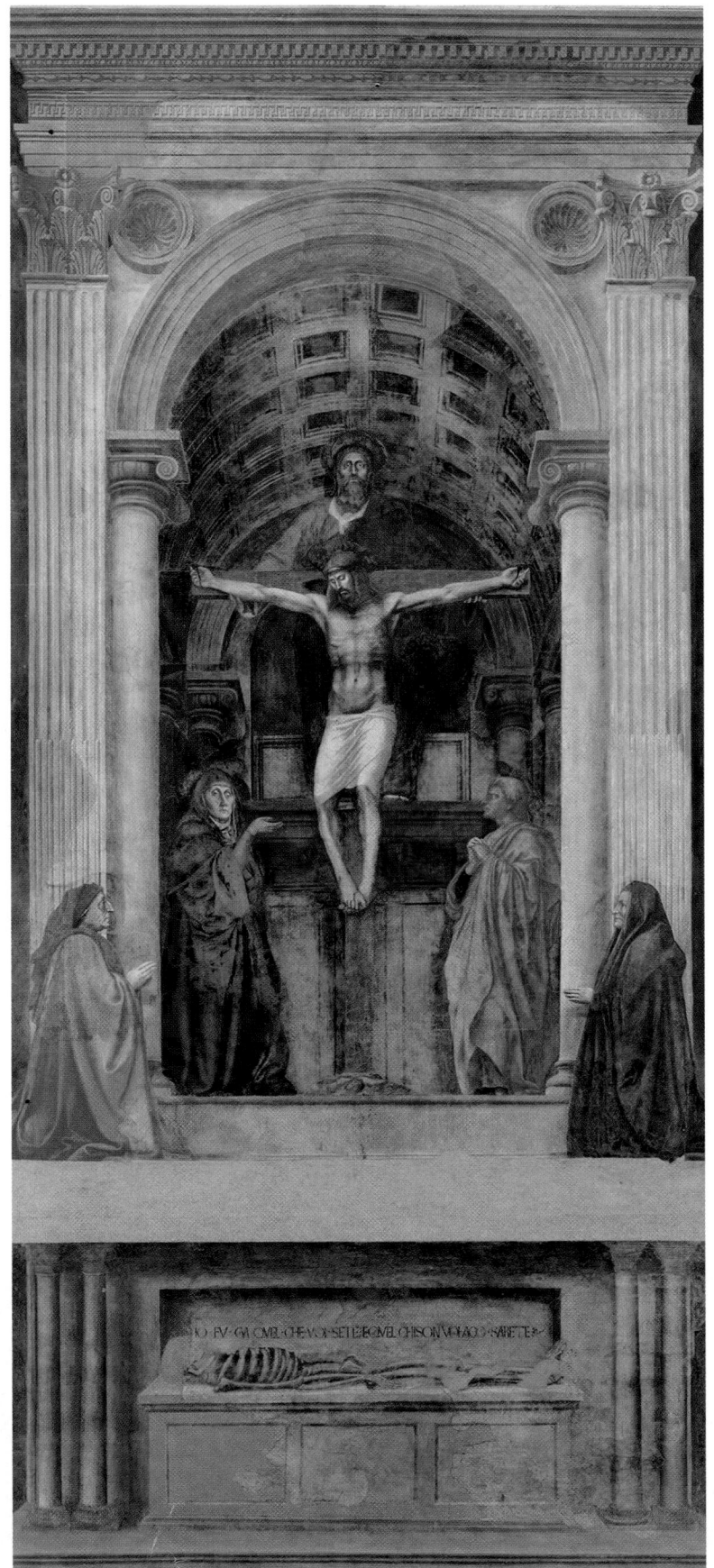

15.23 Masaccio, *The Holy Trinity with the Virgin, St. John, and Two Donors*. ca. 1425. Fresco, detached from wall, 21'10⅝ × 10'4¾" (6.67 × 3.17 m). Santa Maria Novella, Florence

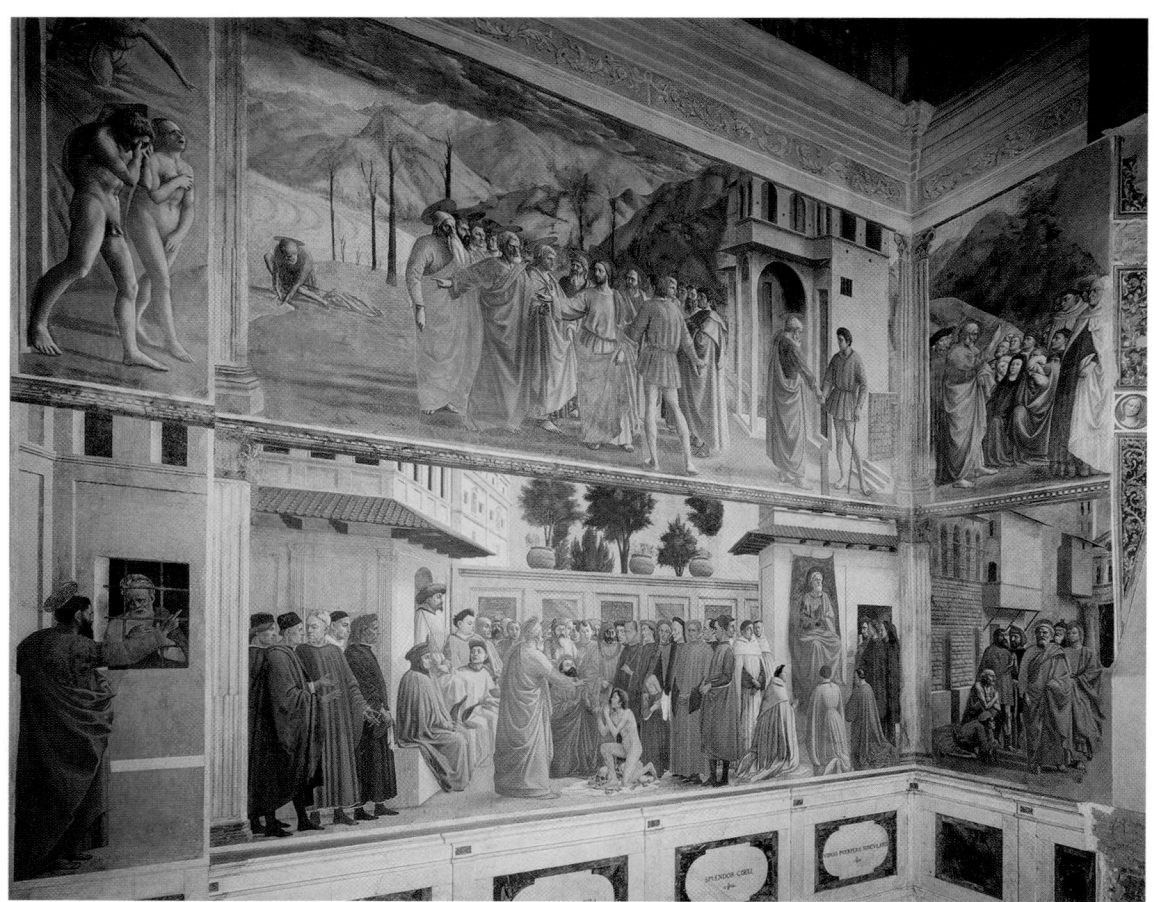

15.24 Left wall of Brancacci Chapel, Florence, with frescoes by Masaccio and others, Santa Maria del Carmine, Florence

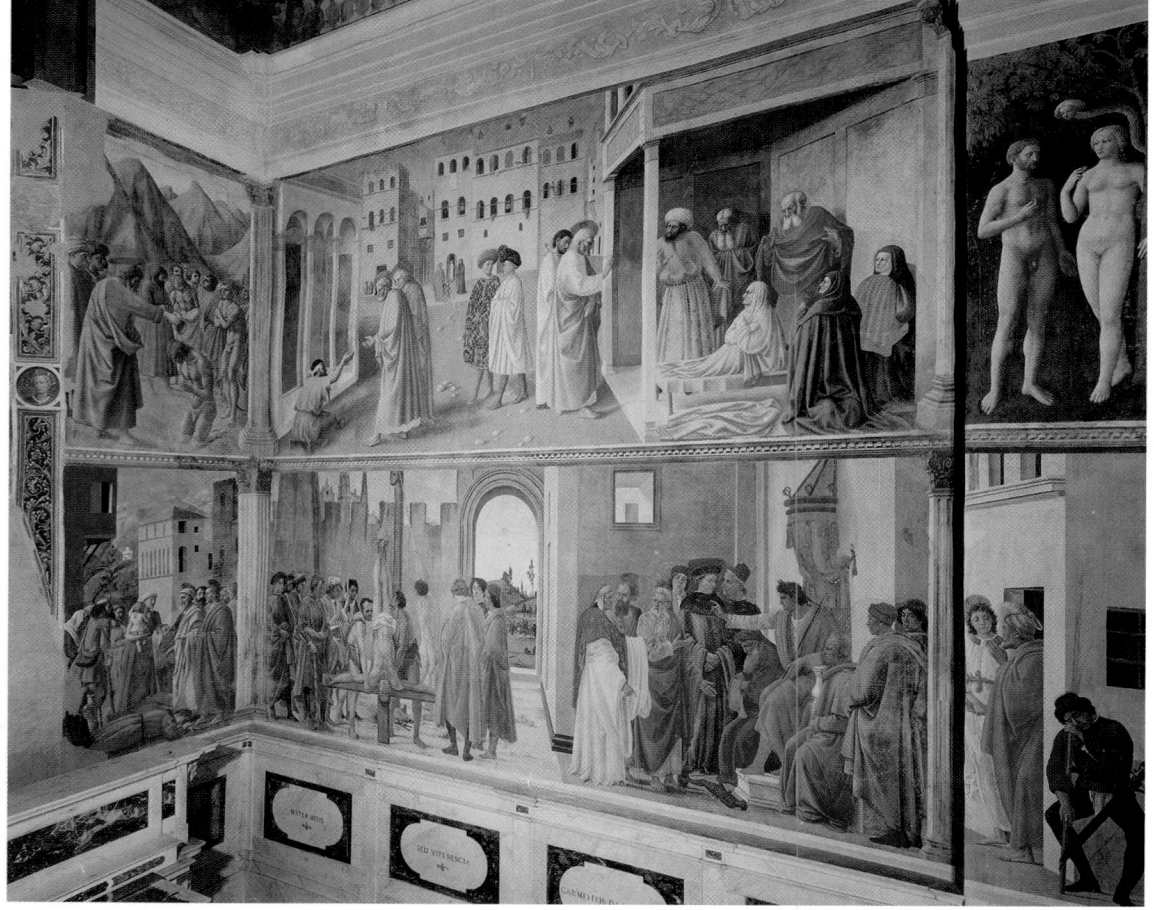

15.25 Right wall of Brancacci Chapel, Florence, with frescoes by Masaccio, Masolino, and Filippino Lippi, Santa Maria del Carmine, Florence

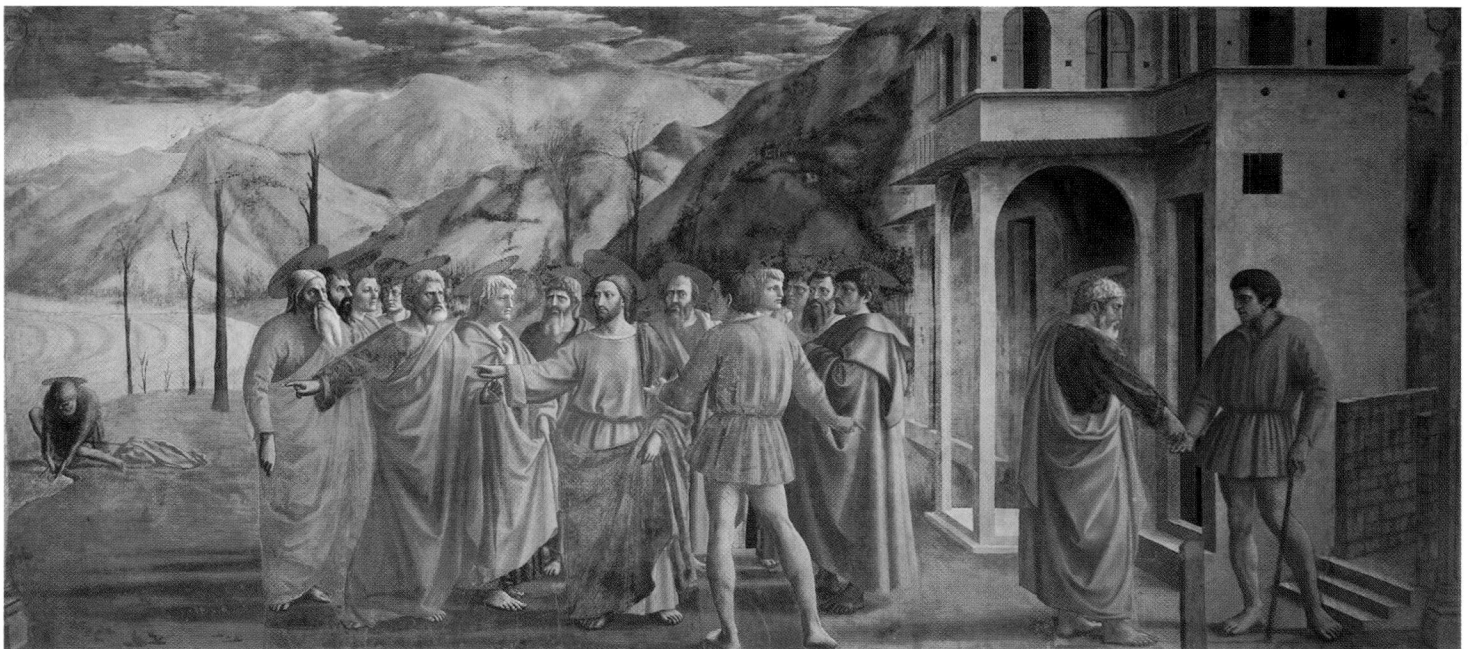

15.26   Masaccio, *The Tribute Money*. ca. 1425. Fresco, 8'1" × 19'7" (1.87 × 1.57 m). Brancacci Chapel, Florence

picture space is independent of the figures; they inhabit the space, but they do not create it. Masaccio used Brunelleschi's invention to create an illusion of space where none exists.

All the lines perpendicular to the picture plane converge toward a point below the foot of the Cross, on the platform that supports the kneeling donors. To see the fresco correctly, we must face this point, which is at an eye level somewhat more than 5 feet above the floor of the church. The figures within the chamber are 5 feet tall, slightly less than life-size, while the donors, who are closer to the viewer, are fully life-size. The framework therefore is "life-size," too, since it is directly behind the donors. The chapel that opens out behind them seems to belong to the same scale: It moves backward into space, covered by a barrel vault. That vault is subdivided by square **coffers**, an echo of the dome of the Pantheon (see fig. 7.25). The space seems measurable, palpable. However, the position of God the Father is puzzling. His arms support the Cross, close to the front plane, while his feet rest on a ledge attached to a wall. It is difficult to measure the distance to the ledge; if it is against the back wall, then the figure of God destroys the spatial effect. But why should the laws of perspective constrain God? Another possibility is that Masaccio intended to locate the ledge directly behind the Cross, as we can tell by the strong shadow that St. John casts on the wall below.

God the Father holds his son while the dove of the Holy Spirit is a further link between them. Masaccio further expresses the theme of the Trinity by the triangular composition that begins with the donors and rises to the halo of God. Color balances the composition, too, as opposing reds and blues unite in the garment worn by God. The whole scene has a tragic air, made more solemn by the calm gesture of the Virgin, as she points to the Crucifixion, and by the understated grief of St. John the Evangelist. The reality

of death but promise of resurrection is an appropriate theme for a funerary commemoration.

THE BRANCACCI CHAPEL If we are uncertain about the identity of the donors for the *Trinity* fresco, we do know who paid for the largest group of Masaccio's surviving works. To fulfill a bequest from his uncle Pietro, Felice Brancacci, a wealthy silk merchant and sometime ambassador, underwrote the frescoes in the Brancacci Chapel in Santa Maria del Carmine (figs. **15.24** and **15.25**). The frescoes depict the life of St. Peter. Work began in the chapel around 1425, when Masaccio collaborated with a slightly older painter named Masolino (1383–ca. 1440). The project was left incomplete when both artists were called away to work on other commissions. Masaccio went to Rome, where he died in 1428. The chapel remained unfinished until the Florentine painter Filippino Lippi (1457/58–1504) finally completed the lower tier on either side in the 1480s. These frescoes transform the space of the chapel into a display of narratives from Scripture.

The most famous of the frescoes is *The Tribute Money* by Masaccio, located in the upper tier (fig. **15.26**). It depicts the story told in the Gospel of Matthew (17:24–27) as a continuous narrative. In the center, Christ instructs Peter to catch a fish, whose mouth will contain money for the tax collector. On the far left, in the distance, Peter takes the coin from the fish's mouth, and on the right he gives it to the tax collector. Masaccio uses perspective to create a deep space for the narrative and to link the painting's space to the space of a viewer, Masaccio models the forms in the picture with light that seems to have its source in the real window of the chapel. He also uses atmospheric perspective in the subtle tones of the landscape to make the forms somewhat hazy, seen as well in the *Ghent Altarpiece* by Hubert and Jan van Eyck (see fig.

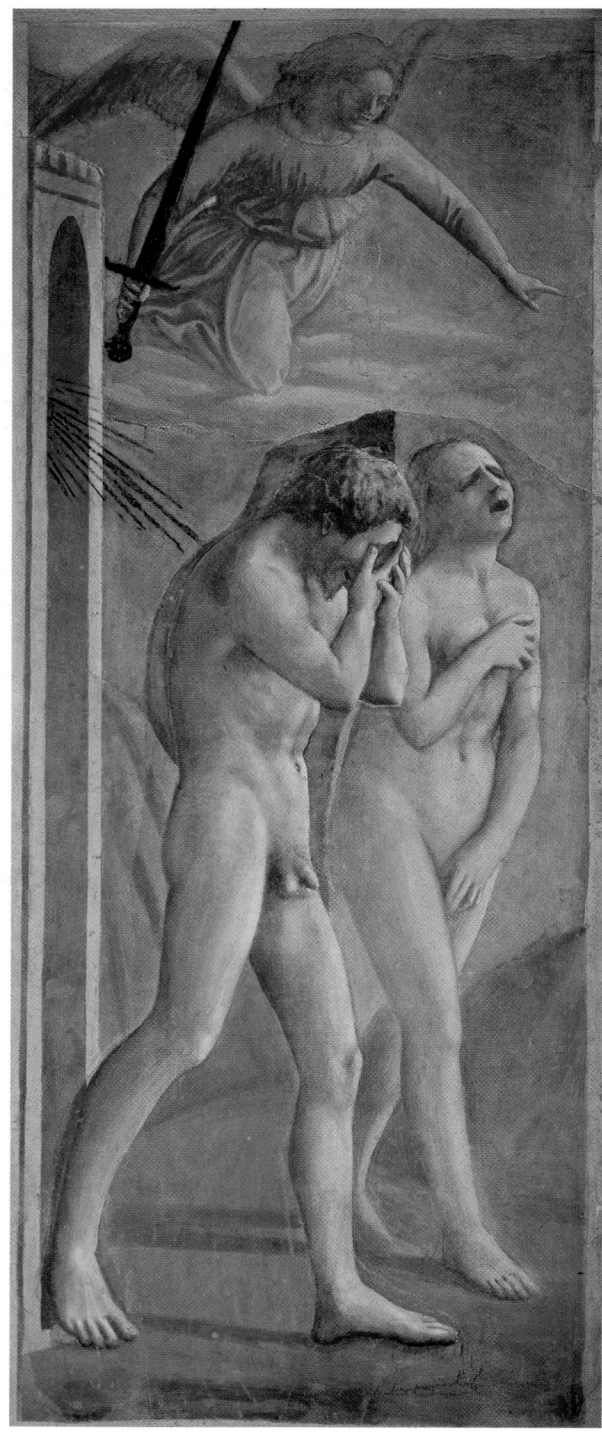

15.27 Masaccio, *The Expulsion from Paradise*. ca. 1425. Fresco, 7'1¼" × 10'35½" (214 × 90 cm). Brancacci Chapel, Florence

inspired by Donatello. Fine vertical lines scratched in the plaster establish the axis of each figure from the head to the heel of the engaged leg. In accord with this dignified approach, the figures seem rather static. Instead of employing violent physical movement, Masaccio's figures here convey the narrative by their intense glances and a few strong gestures.

In *The Expulsion from Paradise* just to the left (fig. **15.27**), however, Masaccio shows the human body in motion. The tall, narrow format of this fresco leaves little room for a spatial setting. The gate of Paradise is barely indicated, and in the background are a few shadowy, barren slopes. Yet the soft, atmospheric modeling, and especially the boldly foreshortened angel, convey a sense of unlimited space. Masaccio's grief-stricken Adam and Eve are striking representations of the beauty and power of the nude human form.

In contrast to the fluid grace of Gentile da Fabriano's painting (see figs. 15.21 and 15.22), Masaccio's paintings represent a less beautiful reality. However, at the Brancacci Chapel and elsewhere, Masaccio worked alongside Masolino, who had been strongly influenced by Gentile. The two painters worked well together and even collaborated on some of the frescoes. (The head of Christ in *The Tribute Money* may be by Masolino.) Nowhere is the contrast between the two artists' styles more striking than in *The Temptation* by Masolino (visible in the upper right of fig. 15.25). Where Masolino's figures of Adam and Eve are serenely beautiful nudes bathed in a diffuse natural light, Masaccio's express powerful emotion through their sheer physicality. Before he could finish the Brancacci Chapel, Masaccio left for Rome to work on another commission; he died there at a very young age, but his work stimulated other painters to experiment with perspectival space.

Florentine Painters in the Age of the Medici

Florentine politics played a role in delaying the completion of the Brancacci Chapel. The patron, Felice Brancacci, was the son-in-law of Palla Strozzi and part of a political faction that drove Cosimo de' Medici into exile in 1433. When Cosimo returned to Florence in 1434, he expelled both the Strozzi and the Brancacci from the city. The Medici family consolidated their power to become the most powerful family in Florence, a position they maintained until 1494.

Across four generations, Medici men were active in government and in business, while Medici women contributed to the social and religious life of the city. The family's wealth came from their mercantile and banking interests and the wise political alliances they struck both within Florence and in other Italian centers. As bankers to the pope, the Medici became leaders in the Florentine pro-papal party, and ultimately became the *de facto* rulers of the city.

Their fortunes had been made at the end of the fourteenth century by the shrewd investments of Giovanni di Bicci de' Medici (1360–1429). His son Cosimo (1389–1464) was involved in the factional disputes of the 1430s, resulting in his exile from the city

14.10). The effect also recalls the setting used a decade earlier in Donatello's small relief of St. George (see fig. 15.12).

The figures in *The Tribute Money*, even more than those in the *Trinity* fresco, show Masaccio's ability to merge the weight and volume of Giotto's figures with the new functional view of body and drapery. The organization of the central group surrounding Christ seems to draw from Nanni di Banco's *Quattro Coronati* (see fig. 15.10), yet their balanced contrapposto poses may be in 1433. But in 1434 his party triumphed, and Cosimo returned as the leader of the Florentine government. Cosimo's sons Piero (1416–1469) and Giovanni (1421–1463) followed their father's example; and Piero's son, Lorenzo, called "The Magnificent" (1449–1492), became one of the most celebrated and well-connected men of the century. In addition to creating links to other prominent families in Florence and beyond, the Medici family promoted the literary and educational innovations of Florentine humanists, and actively used works of art to express their political and social status. This period of Medici domination saw the continued development of the stylistic innovations of the early fifteenth century along with new themes in art. Painters working in Florence from the 1430s to the 1460s were profoundly affected by the achievements of Masaccio and Donatello, Brunelleschi's antiquity-inspired architecture, and the drive toward greater naturalism. In addition, this generation of painters became very proficient at the technique of linear perspective. Their works executed for religious settings throughout the city treat sacred figures with a new reality.

FRA ANGELICO AT SAN MARCO With the support of Cosimo de' Medici, the Dominicans built a second convent for their friars in Florence in 1436. Among the members of this community was a talented painter from the Florentine countryside, Fra (Brother) Giovanni da Fiesole, called Fra Angelico (ca. 1400–1455). For this new community, Angelico painted altarpieces, books, and many frescoes in the friars' living quarters. His *Annunciation* fresco, executed between 1440 and 1445, is placed prominently at the entry to the dormitory (fig. **15.28**). Angelico sets the angel and Mary into a vaulted space very similar to the real architecture of the convent, itself inspired by Brunelleschi. A perspectival scheme defines the space, although the figures are too large to stand comfortably in it. The Virgin and the angel Gabriel glance at each other across the space; they humbly fold their hands, expressing their submission to divine will. The forms are graceful, and the overall scene is spare, rather than extravagant. The colors are pale, the composition has been pared to the minimum, and the light bathes all the forms in a soft glow. Angelico's composition has the simplicity and spatial sophistication of Masaccio (see fig. 15.26), with figures that are as graceful as Gentile da Fabriano's (see fig. 15.21). An inscription at the base of the fresco calls on the friars who pass by to say an Ave Maria. The fresco enhanced their life of prayer and contemplation, as was the goal of such imagery in religious communities.

CASTAGNO AT SANT'APOLLONIA Florence was home to many convents of women whose residents also wished to adorn their establishments. Unlike Fra Angelico, however, few nuns had the opportunity to train as painters to do the work themselves. Thus, professional painters like Andrea del Castagno (ca. 1423–1457) were hired to provide convent spaces with appropriate imagery. For the Benedictine convent of Sant'Apollonia,

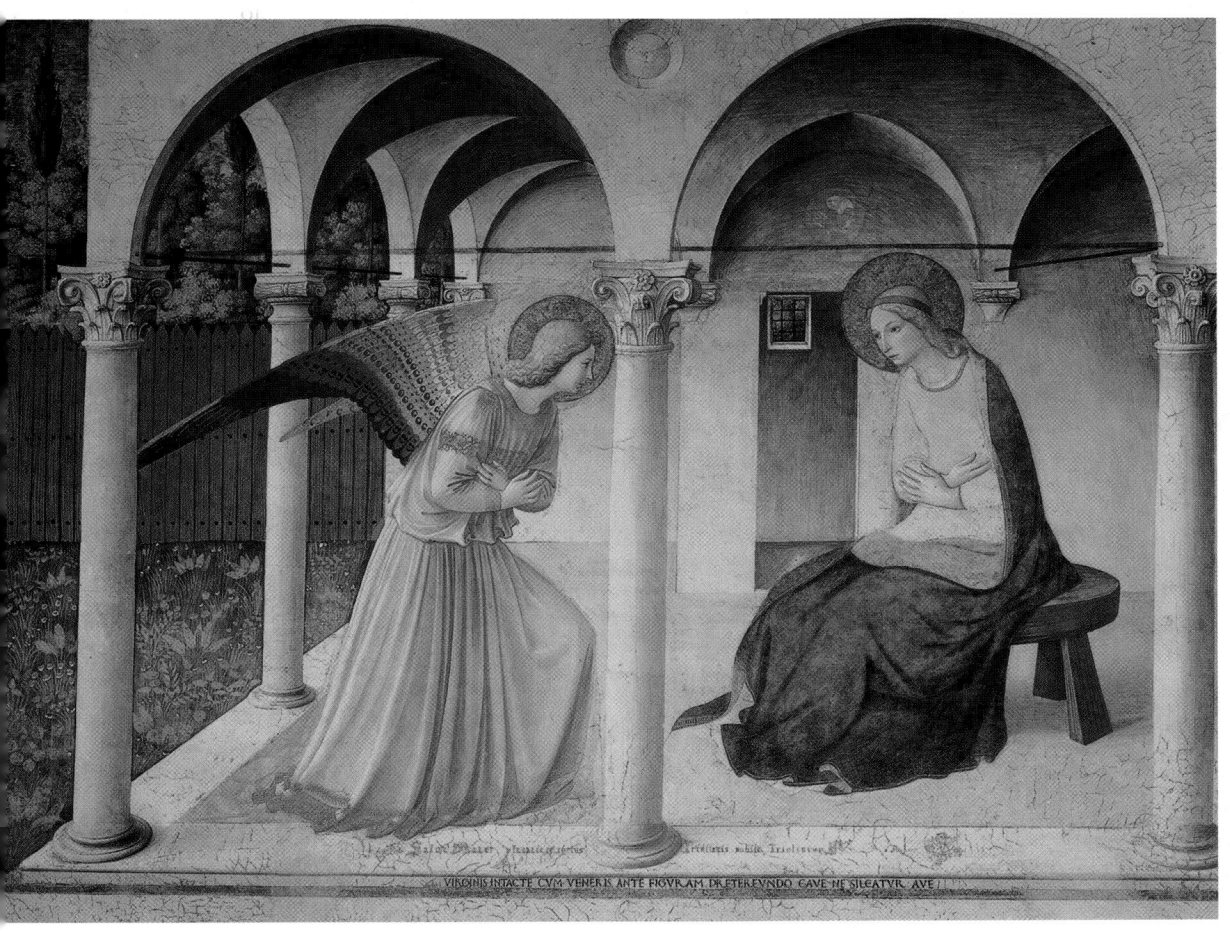

15.28 Fra Angelico, *Annunciation*. ca. 1440–45. Fresco, 7'1" × 10'6" (2.1 × 3.2 m). Museo di San Marco, Florence

Castagno painted his most famous fresco, *The Last Supper* (fig. **15.29**) around 1447. This fresco is the best preserved of a series he painted in the refectory (dining hall) of the convent. The image depicts the events of Holy Thursday, when Jesus and his apostles gather to dine, and Jesus reveals that he will be betrayed. Castagno sets the event in a richly paneled alcove framed by classicizing pilasters and other antique decorative elements. By skillfully using perspective, Castagno creates a stagelike space for the event. Strong contrasts of light and dark define sculpturally imagined figures seated around the table. As in medieval representations of the subject, Judas sits alone on the near side of the table. The symmetry of the architecture, emphasized by the colorful inlays, imposes a similar order among the figures and threatens to imprison them. There is little communication among the apostles—only a glance here, a gesture there—so that a brooding silence hovers over the scene. Breaking with the demands of tradition and perspective, Castagno used a daring device to disrupt the symmetry and focus on the drama of the scene. Five of the six marble panels on the wall behind the table are filled with subdued colored marble, but above the heads of St. Peter, Judas, and Jesus, the marble's veining is so garish and explosive that a bolt of lightning seems to descend on Judas' head to focus attention on these key figures. This theme often adorned Florentine refectories as the monks or nuns imitated Christ and the apostles as they dined. The sisters who dined in front of this fresco could see in it examples to follow and to avoid.

DOMENICO VENEZIANO AT SANTA LUCIA DEI MAGNOLI

Religious imagery adorned the altars of parish churches to instruct the laity. An important shift occurred in the design of altar panels in the 1440s, perhaps at the hands of Fra Angelico, that was soon adopted by many painters. Earlier altarpieces, like Gentile's *Adoration of the Magi* (see fig. 15.21), were complex ensembles with elaborately carved frames, but the newer altarpieces emphasized gilded carpentry less and geometric clarity more. For the main altar of the church of Santa Lucia dei Magnoli in Florence, Domenico Veneziano (ca. 1410–1461) executed the *Madonna and Child with Saints* around 1445 (fig. **15.30**). As his name suggests, Domenico was from Venice; he came to Florence in search of work in 1439. A letter he addressed to the son of Cosimo de' Medici in 1438 reveals that he knew about the commissions being awarded there (see *Primary Source*, page 534), while his work shows that he had studied Florentine artists. The altarpiece he painted for Santa Lucia depicts an enthroned Madonna and Child framed by architecture and surrounded by saints, including Zenobius, a patron saint of Florence, and Lucy, an early Christian martyr, who holds a dish containing her eyes.

The theme of the central Madonna surrounded by saints and sometimes angels is often termed a *sacra conversazione* (sacred conversation), which suggests that the image is not a narrative, but a glimpse of a heavenly court peopled by dignified and decorous courtiers. Domenico imagines this gathering in a light-filled loggia articulated with pink and green marble. The architecture is clear and convincing, yet the space it defines is an ideal one elevated above the everyday world. Domenico may have modeled this space on Masaccio's *Holy Trinity* fresco (see fig. 15.23), for his St. John (second from left) looks at us while pointing toward the Madonna, repeating the glance and gesture of Masaccio's Virgin. Domenico's perspective setting is worthy of Masaccio's, although his architectural forms have Gothic proportions and arches. The slim, sinewy bodies of the male saints, with their highly individualized, expressive faces, show Donatello's influence (see fig. 15.12).

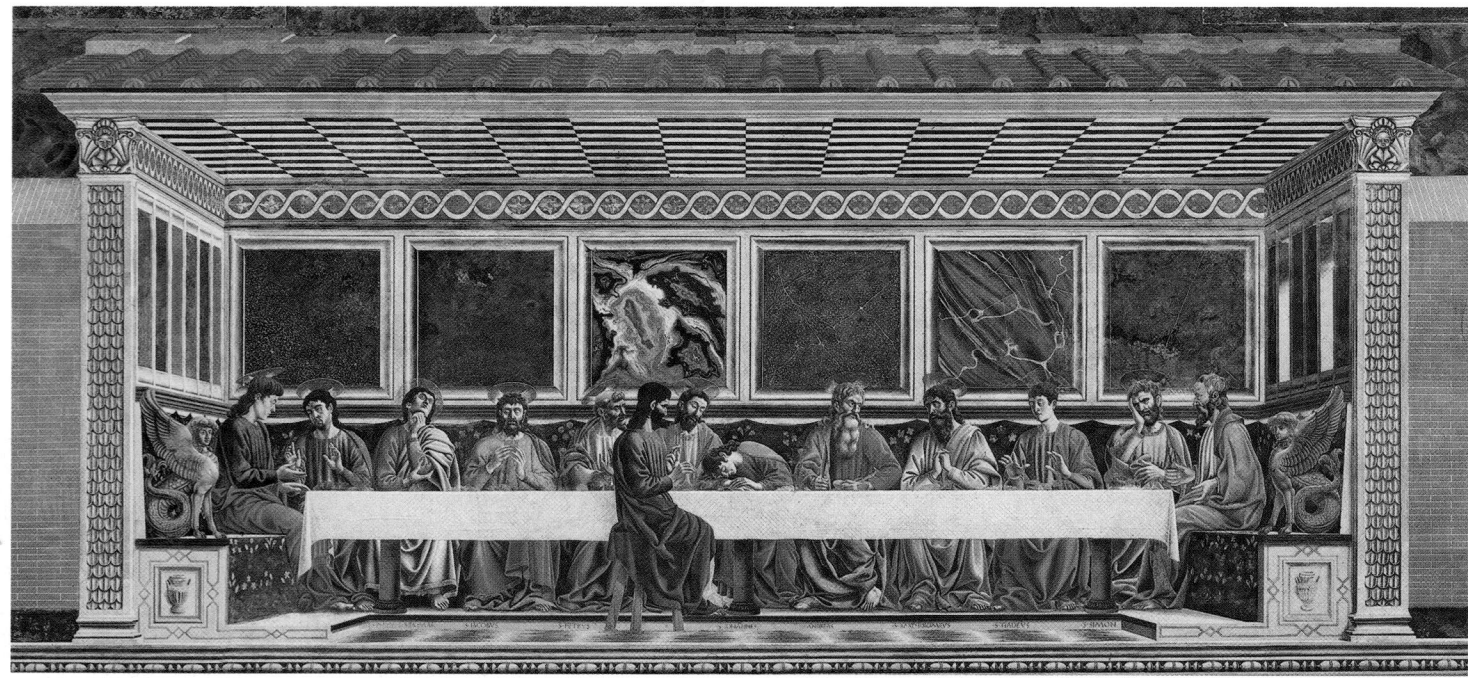

15.29 Andrea del Castagno, *The Last Supper*. ca. 1445–50. Fresco. Sant'Apollonia, Florence

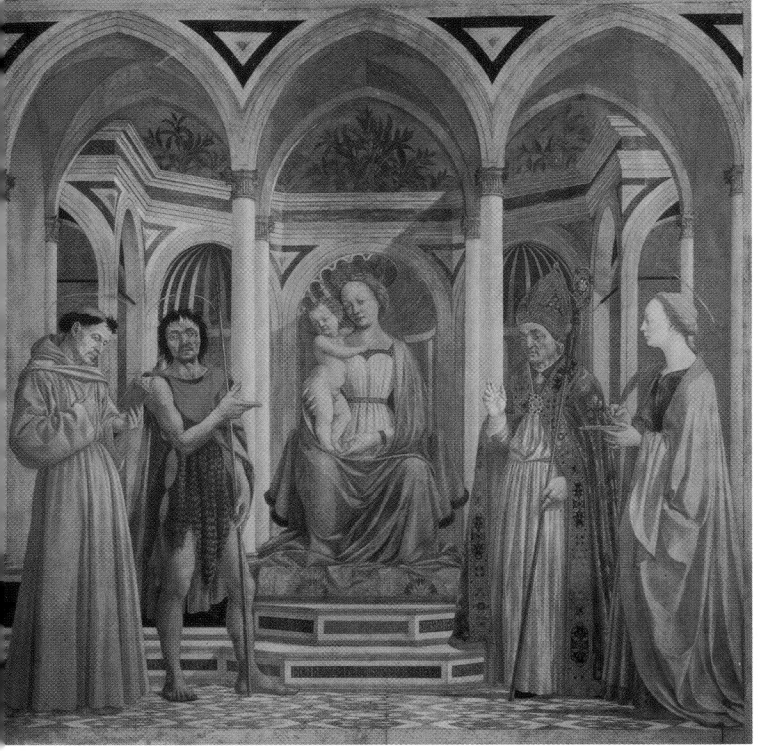

15.30 Domenico Veneziano, *Madonna and Child with Saints.* ca. 1445. Tempera on panel, 6'10" × 7' (2.08 × 2.13 m). Galleria degli Uffizi, Florence

inspiration for younger sculptors like Pollaiuolo. Painters tacked between the grave simplicity of Masaccio and the idealized elegance of Gentile da Fabriano to find the right language to depict imagery drawn from the ancient world. Architects such as Michelozzo built family homes endowed with great dignity by their use of classical forms.

Palace Architecture

As their status rose in Florence, the Medici required a more lavish palace to house them and accommodate political and diplomatic functions. Nevertheless, Cosimo de' Medici turned down a design by Brunelleschi for this project, perhaps because he found it ostentatious. The commission went instead to a younger architect, Michelozzo di Bartolomeo (1396–1472), who had worked as a sculptor with both Ghiberti and Donatello. His design (fig. **15.31**) recalls the fortresslike Florentine palaces of old; it may have been this conservatism that appealed to Cosimo. (The windows on the ground floor were added by Michelangelo in 1516–17, and the whole was extended by the Riccardi family in the seventeenth century.)

Domenico treats color as an integral part of his work. This *sacra conversazione* is as noteworthy for its **palette** as for its composition. The blond tonality—its harmony of pink, light green, and white set off by spots of red, blue, and yellow—reconciles the brightness of Gothic panel painting with natural light and perspectival space. The sunlight streams in from the right, as revealed by the cast shadow behind the Madonna. The surfaces reflect the light so strongly that even the shadowed areas glow with color. Color, light, and space come together in this painting to make a heavenly vision in which the faithful may take comfort.

DOMESTIC LIFE: PALACES, FURNISHINGS, AND PAINTINGS IN MEDICEAN FLORENCE

Patrons like Giovanni Rucellai or Cosimo de' Medici asked artists to create works of art for their homes as well as for their churches. As family fortunes rose, palaces needed building or remodeling to provide an appropriate setting for family life and civic display. Furnishings within the home had to express the status of the family. Sculptures and paintings of new sorts, such as **cassone** paintings (see page 537), proclaimed the alliances between families. Works of art depicted new subjects, many of them inspired by antique art, which reflected the humanist educations of both artists and patrons. In sculpture, the long-lived Donatello was an

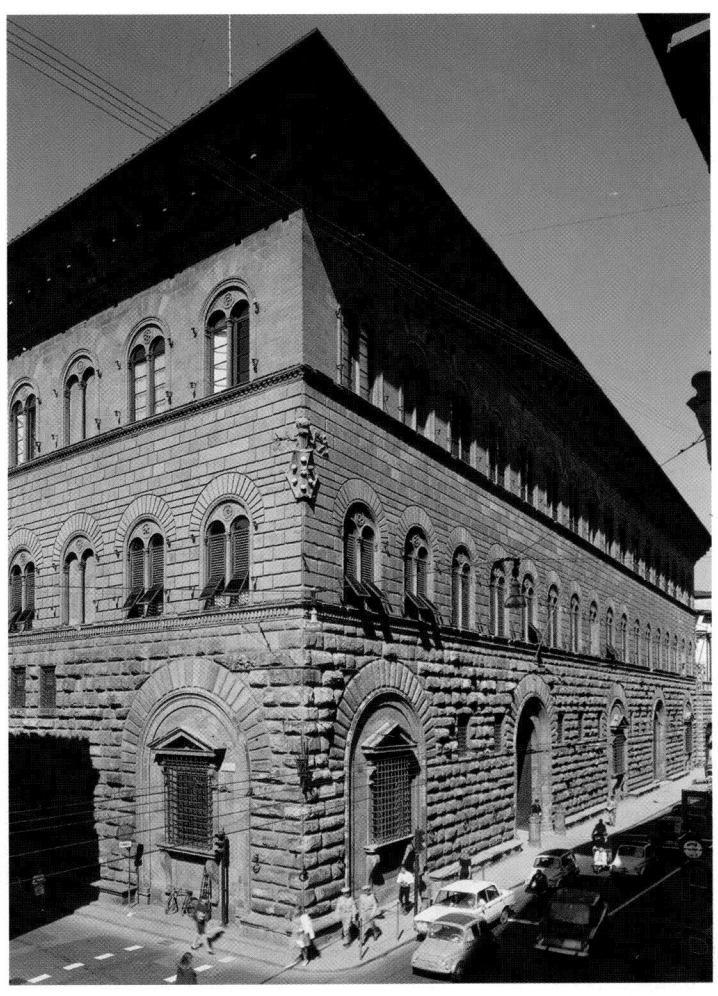

15.31 Michelozzo di Bartolomeo. Palazzo Medici-Riccardi, Florence. Begun 1444

Domenico Veneziano Solicits Work

The Venetian painter wrote to Piero de' Medici in 1438 requesting that he be considered for a commission that the family was about to award. The letter reveals Domenico's knowledge of the work to be done, and his arguments for why he should do it.

To the honorable and generous man Piero di Cosimo de' Medici of Florence. …

Honorable and generous sir. After the due salutations. I inform you that by God's grace I am well. And I wish to see you well and happy. Many, many times I have asked about you. … [A]nd having first learned where you were, I would have written to you for my comfort and duty. Considering that my low condition does not deserve to write to your nobility, only the perfect and good love I have for you and all your people gives me the daring to write, considering how duty-bound I am to do so.

Just now I have heard that Cosimo [Piero's father] has decided to have an altarpiece made, in other words painted, and wants a magnificent work, which pleases me very much. And it would please me more if through your generosity I could paint it. And if that happens, I am in hopes with God's help to do marvelous things, although there are good masters like Fra Filippo [Lippi] and Fra Giovanni [Angelico] who have much work to do. Fra Filippo in particular has a panel going to Santo Spirito which he won't finish in five years working day and night, it's so big. But however that may be, my great good will to serve you makes me presume to offer myself. And in case I should do less well than anyone at all, I wish to be obligated to any merited punishment, and to provide any test sample needed, doing honor to everyone. And if the work were so large that Cosimo decided to give it to several masters, or else more to one than to another, I beg you as far as a servant may beg a master that you may be pleased to enlist your strength favorably and helpfully to me in arranging that I may have some little part of it … and I promise you my work will bring you honor. …

By your most faithful servant Domenico da Veneziano painter, commending himself to you, in Perugia, 1438, first of April.

Source: Creighton Gilbert, ed., *Italian Art 1400-1500: Sources and Documents* (Evanston, IL: Northwestern University Press, 1992)

Michelozzo borrowed the rustication from the Palazzo della Signoria (see fig. 13.15), but he lightened the forms significantly. The three stories form a graded sequence: The lowest features

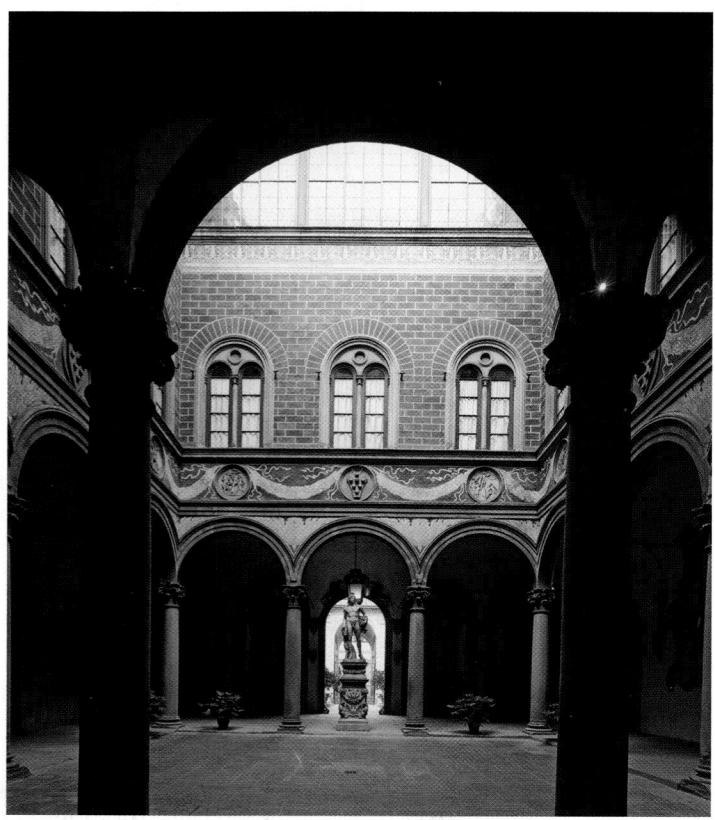

15.32 Michelozzo di Bartolomeo. Courtyard of Palazzo Medici-Riccardi

rough-hewn, "rusticated" masonry; the second has smooth-surfaced blocks; and the third has an unbroken surface. The building seems heavier on the bottom and lighter above. On top of the structure rests, like a lid, a strongly projecting cornice of the sort found on Roman temples. Inside, the spaces of the palace open to a central courtyard defined by an arcade resting on Brunelleschian classicizing columns (fig. 15.32). The arcade supports a frieze with carved medallions featuring symbols favored by the Medici (the seven balls are on the Medici coat of arms) and **sgraffito ornament** (incised decorative designs). The double-lancet windows of the façade reappear here. The effect of the whole is to provide a splendid setting for Medici affairs: familial, social, commercial, and governmental. Thus, the large courtyard that dominates the interior is ceremonial as well as practical.

DONATELLO'S *DAVID* One of the most debated works of the Renaissance, Donatello's bronze *David* (fig. 15.33), once stood on a high pedestal in the courtyard of the Medici palace. The *David* may be the first free-standing, life-size nude statue made since antiquity. The sheer expense of casting a whole figure of this sort in bronze, and with gilt parts, required a patron with the wealth of the Medici to pay for it. Using the lost-wax method of casting (see *Materials and Techniques*, page 128), Donatello composed the figure to be seen from every side, as the contrapposto stance and high finish of the work demand that a viewer walk around it.

Both the date of the *David* and its interpretation have sparked controversy. The evidence for its date is unclear; the only firm documentation places it in the Medici palace by 1469; scholars have proposed dates from the 1420s to 1460s. Much in the figure is difficult to square with the biblical story. The young David stands with his left foot atop the severed head of the giant accentuate his nudity. David wields Goliath's sword, which is too large for him, and his gaze seems impassive when we consider the terror he has just confronted.

One key to the meaning of the *David* may be an inscription once written on its base that identified David as the defender of the fatherland: Since David had been venerated as a patron of the city, the Medici chose to appropriate this symbol of Florentine civic virtue and install it in their residence. (Donatello had earlier sculpted a marble image of David that stood in the Palazzo della Signoria, so even the choice of sculptor may be significant.) But scholars have debated the specific associations of the statue: one proposal is that the *David* celebrates a particular Florentine military victory, or perhaps a Medici political victory; another proposal is that it represents Florentine vigilance, or is a symbol of republican victory over tyranny. At the same time, its presence in the Medici palace may turn it into a symbol of dynastic power. All of this is made more complicated by the figure's youth and nudity. Our understanding of how fifteenth-century Florentines viewed the sculpture is still developing.

HERCULEAN IMAGES The Medici family appear to have made a habit of borrowing Florentine civic imagery for their palace. Sometime around 1475, Antonio del Pollaiuolo (1431–1498) executed the *Hercules and Antaeus* (fig. **15.34**) for the family. Unlike

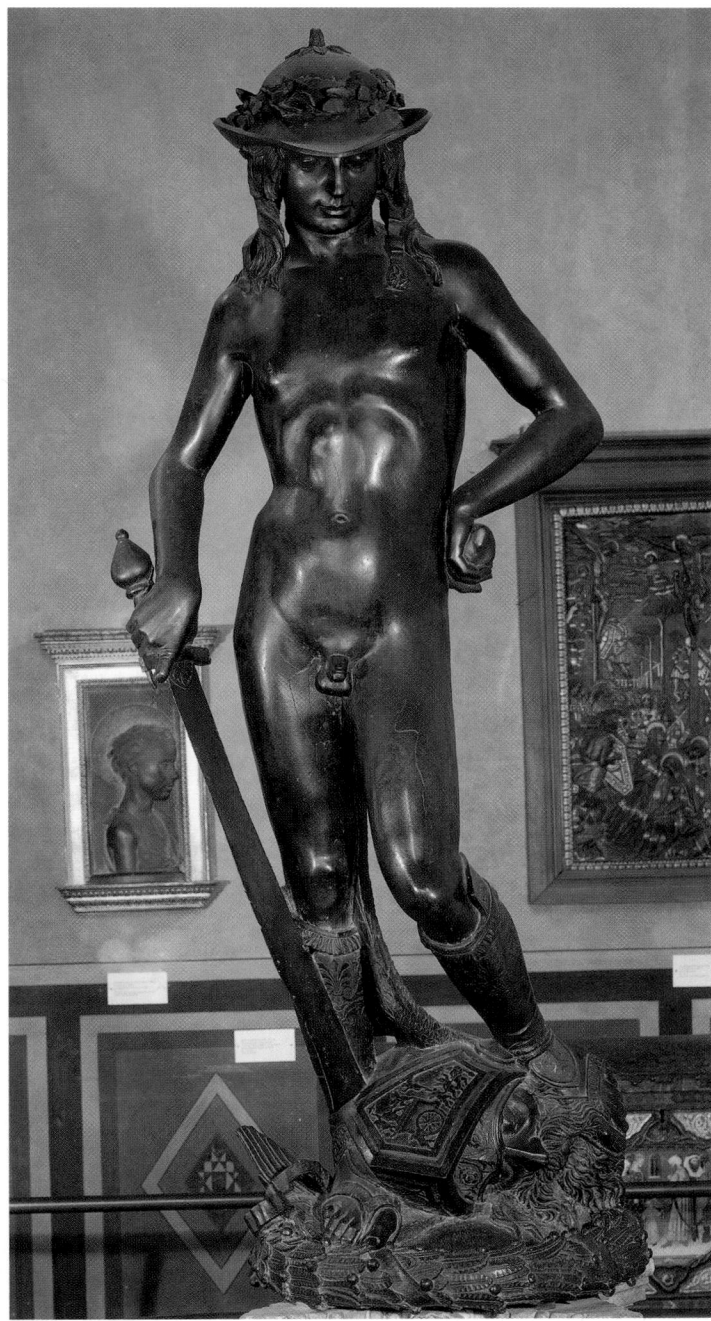

15.33   Donatello, *David*. ca. 1420s–60s. Bronze, height 5'2¼" (1.58 m). Museo Nazionale del Bargello, Florence

Goliath, whom he has miraculously defeated. Nonetheless, Donatello depicts the already victorious David still holding the stone that bought Goliath down. Most untraditionally, he also depicts David nude, which may be intended to suggest his status as a hero in the ancient mode. But instead of depicting him as a full-grown youth like the athletes of Greece, Donatello chose to model an adolescent boy with a softly sensuous torso, like Isaac in Ghiberti's competition panel (see fig. 15.2). The *David*'s contrapposto alludes to ancient sources, but it also gives the nude youth a languid pose, which some critics have seen as sexually suggestive. The broad-brimmed hat and knee-high boots seem to

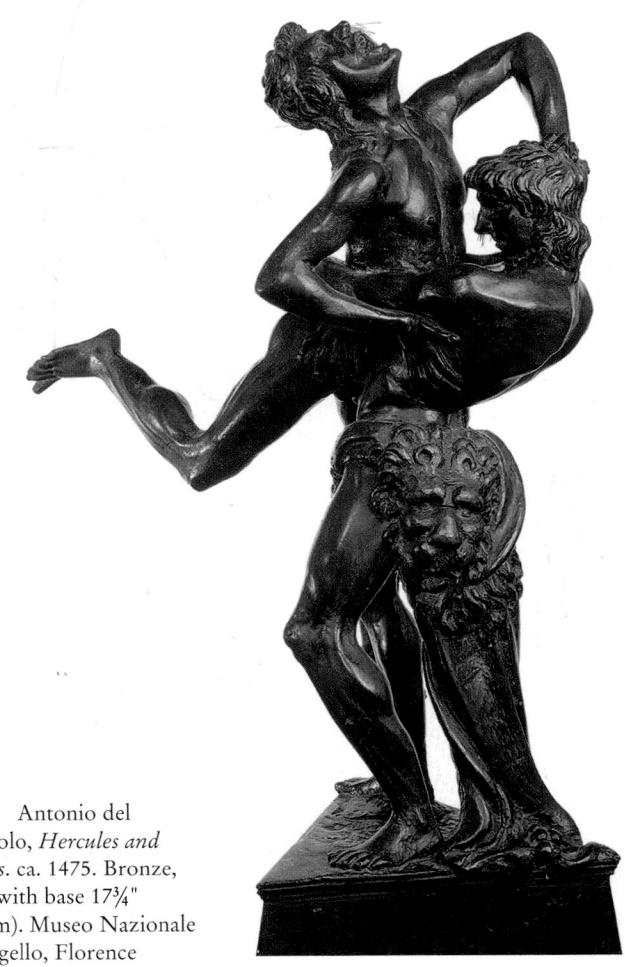

15.34   Antonio del Pollaiuolo, *Hercules and Antaeus*. ca. 1475. Bronze, height with base 17¾" (45.8 cm). Museo Nazionale del Bargello, Florence

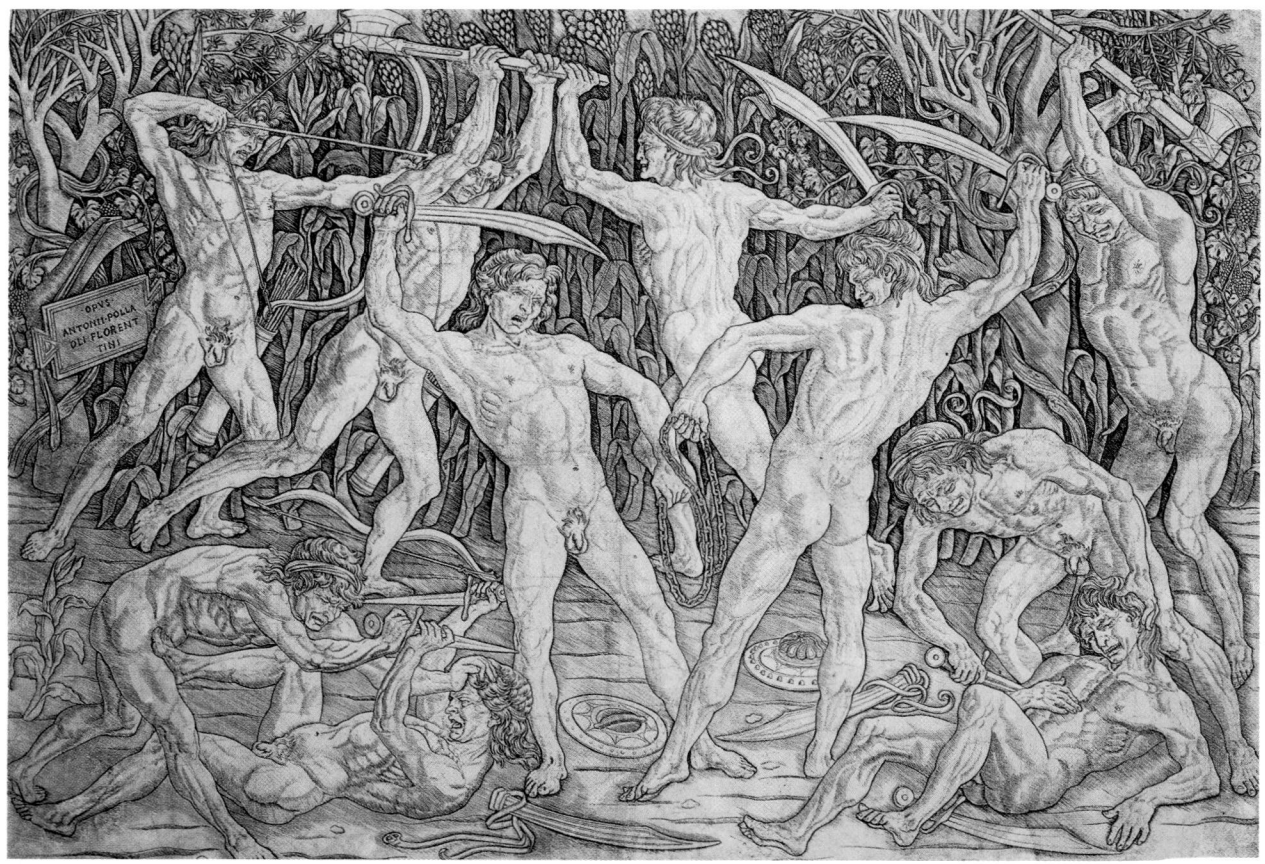

15.35   Antonio del Pollaiuolo, *Battle of the Nudes*. ca. 1465–70. Engraving, 15⅛" × 23¼" (38.3 × 59 cm). Cincinnati Art Museum, Ohio. Bequest of Herbert Greer French. 1943.118

the *David*, this is a table statue, only about 18 inches high, but it has the visual impact of a much larger object. It represents Hercules—another patron of Florence—battling Antaeus, the son of an earth goddess. Antaeus gains strength from contact with the earth, so Hercules must lift him off the ground to defeat him. Pollaiuolo had been trained as a goldsmith and metalworker, probably in the Ghiberti workshop, but was deeply impressed by the work of Donatello and Andrea del Castagno, as well as by ancient art. All these sources influence the distinctive style of the statuette.

To create a free-standing group of two struggling figures, even on a small scale, was a daring idea. There is no precedent for this design among earlier statuary groups, whether from antiquity or the Renaissance. Even bolder is the centrifugal force of the composition. Limbs seem to move outward in every direction, so the viewer must examine the statuette from all sides. Despite its violent action, the group is in perfect balance. To stress the central axis, Pollaiuolo in effect grafted the upper part of Antaeus onto the lower part of Hercules as he lifts him in a stranglehold. Pollaiuolo was a painter and engraver as well as a bronze sculptor, and we know that about 1465 he did a closely related painting of Hercules and Antaeus for the Medici.

Few of Pollaiuolo's paintings have survived, and only one engraving, the *Battle of the Nudes* (fig. **15.35**). The latter is one of Pollaiuolo's most elaborate designs. Its subject is not known, though it may derive from an ancient text. One purpose the engraving serves is to display the artist's mastery of the nude body in action and thus to advertise his skill. This may account for the prominent signature in the print; he signs it *"Opus Antonii Pollaioli Florentini"* ("The work of Antonio Pollaiuolo of Florence"). In 1465–70, when the print must have been produced, depicting the nude in action was still a novel problem, which Pollaiuolo explored in his paintings, sculptures, and prints. He realized that a full understanding of movement demanded a detailed knowledge of anatomy, down to the last muscle and sinew. These naked men look almost as if their skin has been stripped off to reveal the play of muscles underneath. So, to a lesser extent, do the two figures of Pollaiuolo's statuette *Hercules and Antaeus*.

Paintings for Palaces

The interiors of patrician palaces served not only as private quarters and settings for family life, but as public spaces where family members performed civic roles. A visitor would find paintings and perhaps sculptures, many on religious subjects, in these buildings. Indeed, early in the fifteenth century, one of the leading clerics of Tuscany urged that religious images be displayed in private homes. In a treatise written in 1403, Cardinal Giovanni Dominici counseled that images of Christ, Mary, and saints in the home would encourage children to emulate those holy figures. (See *Primary Source*, page 539.)

Patrician homes also showcased **cassoni** (sing. cassone), carved or painted chests for storing valuables. The product of collaboration between skilled carpenters, woodworkers, and painters, such chests were usually decorated, sometimes with military imagery, like the one in figure **15.36**, which bears the arms of the Strozzi family. This chest probably came from the busy workshop of Apollonio di Giovanni (1414–1465) and Marco del Buono Giamberti (1402–1489). Its front panel depicts the conquest of Trebizond (a town on the Black Sea) by Turkish forces in 1461; as a result, Venetian traders were expelled and Florence increased its influence in the Mediterranean. The busy composition features small figures battling in front of a city wall; their armor is gilded to create a sumptuous surface. Antique-inspired scrolls flank the narrative, while the heavy lid and base shine with gold.

Cassoni were also adorned with scenes from mythology, history, and romance. Pairs of cassoni were usually given to a bride on her wedding; they mark the union of two families, and thus reflect family status as much as nuptial concerns. Edifying or learned stories on cassoni often derived from studies of ancient authors such as Plutarch, Ovid, or Vergil. Thus, cassone panels displayed a family's wealth, their learning and interest in humanism, sometimes their patriotism, and very often lessons for a bride to take with her to her new home.

Another type of domestic decoration was the circular painting, or **tondo**, which was something of a Florentine specialty. Many of the leading painters of the middle and later decades of the fifteenth century produced tondi, including Fra Filippo Lippi

(ca. 1406–1469), to whom has been attributed the *Madonna and Child with the Birth of the Virgin* (fig. **15.37**). The Florentine banker Lionardo Bartolini Salimbeni may have commissioned this panel to commemorate a birth in his family. Lippi presents the Madonna and infant Jesus as an exemplary mother and child. Fra Filippo's youthful Mary has a slender elegance and gentle sweetness that may derive from Fra Angelico's work (see fig. 15.28), although his figures and setting are more complicated and ornate. The curly edge of the Virgin's headdress and the curved folds of her mantle streaming to the left, which accentuate her turn to the right, add a lyrical quality to her figure. The child Jesus picks seeds out of a pomegranate, an emblem of eternal life. At the same time, the seeds may also symbolize fertility, since the secondary theme here is St. Anne giving birth to the Virgin.

Behind the Virgin is a stagelike scene that is surprisingly cluttered, created by a perspective scheme with several vanishing points. In the background to the left is a domestic interior showing the Virgin's birth, with St. Anne in childbed. To the right is the meeting of St. Anne and her husband, St. Joachim at the Golden Gate of Jerusalem, after an angel had appeared to them separately and promised them a child. In contrast to all other depictions of this legend, the event in this painting is presented as if it were taking place before the entrance to a private house.

Lippi could have learned to use this kind of continuous narrative from reliefs by Donatello and Ghiberti: Compare *The Feast of Herod* (see fig. 15.13) and *The Story of Jacob and Esau* (see fig. 15.17), which incorporate similarly complex spaces to tell their stories. Lippi quotes from Ghiberti's relief in this tondo in the figure of the maidservant to the right of the Virgin. After Masaccio's

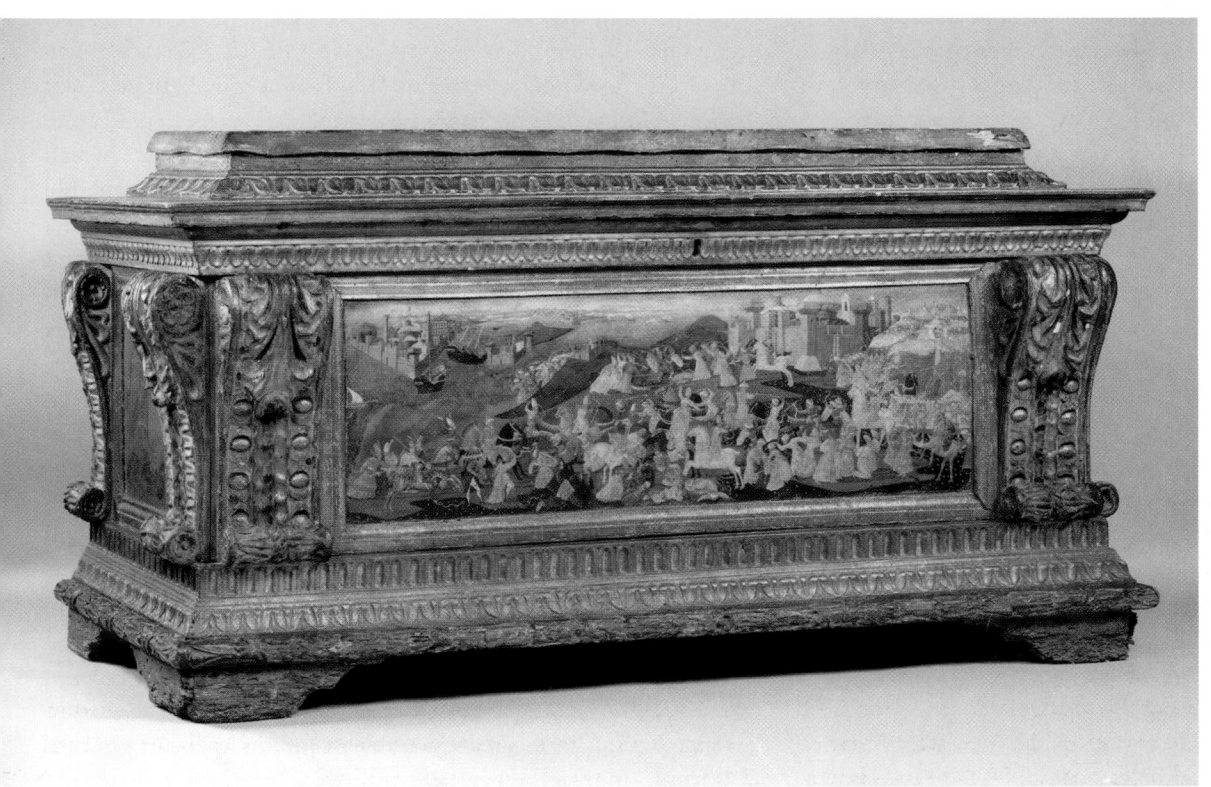

15.36 Marco del Buono Giamberti and Apollonio di Giovanni di Tomaso. Cassone with the Conquest of Trebizond. ca. 1461–65. Tempera, gold, and silver on wood, 39½ × 77 × 32⅞" (100.3 × 195.6 × 83.5 cm). Metropolitan Museum of Art, New York. John Stewart Kennedy Fund, 1914 (14.39)

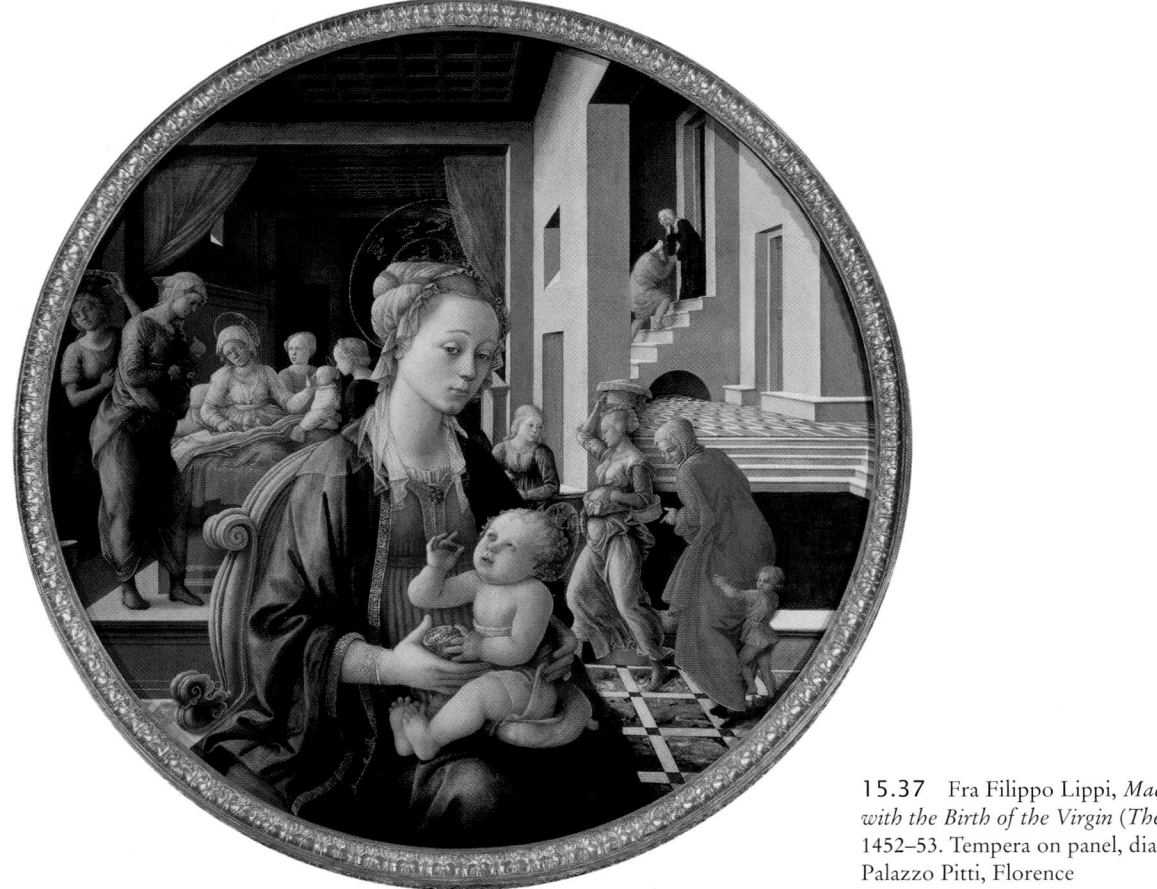

15.37 Fra Filippo Lippi, *Madonna and Child with the Birth of the Virgin* (*The Bartolini Tondo*). 1452–53. Tempera on panel, diameter 53" (134.6 cm). Palazzo Pitti, Florence

death, the age, experience, and prestige of Donatello and Ghiberti gave them an authority unmatched by any other painter active at the time. Their influence, and that of the Flemish masters, on Fra Filippo's outlook was of great importance, since he played a vital role in setting the course of Florentine painting during the second half of the century.

UCCELLO'S *BATTLE OF SAN ROMANO* The same family linked to Lippi's tondo commissioned a set of wall paintings with a fascinating history. The Florentine artist Paolo Uccello (1397–1475) painted the *Battle of San Romano* (fig. **15.38**) as one of three panels depicting a battle between Florence and Lucca in 1432. Florence's victory in this battle was one of the factors that led to Cosimo de' Medici's consolidation of power. Uccello depicts the charge of the Florentine forces led by Cosimo's ally, Niccolò da Tolentino, the man on the white horse wielding a general's baton at the center of the painting. Because of the importance of this subject to the Medici, scholars long believed that they commissioned this painting. The series was identified as one described as hanging in Lorenzo de' Medici's bedroom in a document of 1492. Recent research, however, shows that it was Lionardo Bartolini Salimbeni, who was a member of the governing council of Florence during the battle, who commissioned Uccello to paint these panels for his town house in Florence around 1438. After his death, Lorenzo de' Medici sought to

obtain them, first by purchase and, when that failed, by force. The sons of the original owner filed a lawsuit for their return. These circumstances suggest the importance of the paintings for both families.

Uccello's painting seems to record a ceremony rather than a war, as the plastic shapes of the figures and horses march across a grid consisting of discarded weapons and pieces of armor. These objects form the orthogonals of a perspective scheme that is neatly arranged to include a fallen soldier. A thick hedge of bushes defines this foreground plane, beyond which appears a landscape that rises up the picture plane rather than receding deeply into space. Spots of brilliant color and a lavish use of gold reinforce the surface pattern, which would have been more brilliant originally, as some of the armor is covered in silver foil that has now tarnished. Such splendid surfaces remind us of the paintings of Gentile da Fabriano (see fig. 15.21). Uccello's work owes much to International Gothic displays of lavish materials and flashes of natural observation, with the added element of perspectival renderings of forms and space.

MYTHOLOGIES FOR MEDICI PALACES In addition to acquiring paintings in Florence through commission, purchase, or force, the Medici had numerous contacts with northern Europe, not only through diplomatic exchanges, but through their banking business. Medici agents in Bruges sent many works of art to Florence, as inventories confirm. In this, the Medici behaved as

Giovanni Dominici Urges Parents to Put Religious Images in Their Homes

Florentine by birth, Dominici entered the Dominican order, where he became involved with reform. Among his writings was the Regola del governo di cura familiare *(Rule for the Management of Family Care) of 1403, from which this excerpt is taken.*

Part IV [on the management of children]. In the first consideration, which is to bring them up for God ... you should observe five little rules. ... The first is to have paintings in the house, of holy little boys or young virgins, in which your child when still in swaddling clothes may delight, as being like himself, and may be seized upon by the like thing, with actions and signs attractive to infancy. And as I say for painting, so I say of sculptures. The Virgin Mary is good to have, with the child on her arm, and the little bird or the pomegranate in his fist. A good figure would be Jesus suckling, Jesus sleeping on his mother's lap, Jesus standing politely before her, Jesus making a hem and the mother sewing that hem. In the same way he may mirror himself in the holy Baptist, dressed in camel skin, a small boy entering the desert, playing with birds, sucking on the sweet leaves, sleeping on the ground. It would do no harm if he saw Jesus and the Baptist, the little Jesus and the Evangelist grouped together, and the murdered innocents, so that fear of arms and armed men would come over him. And so too little girls should be brought up in the sight of the eleven thousand virgins, discussing, fighting and praying. I would like them to see Agnes with the fat lamb, Cecilia crowned with roses, Elizabeth with many roses, Catherine on the wheel, with other figures that would give them love of virginity with their mothers' milk, desire for Christ, hatred of sins, disgust at vanity, shrinking from bad companions, and a beginning, through considering the saints, of contemplating the supreme saint of saints. ... I warn you if you have paintings in your house for this purpose, avoid frames of gold and silver, lest they become more idolatrous than faithful, since, if they see more candles lit and more hats removed and more kneeling to figures that are gilded and adorned with precious stones than to the old smoky ones, they will only learn to revere gold and jewels, and not the figures, or rather, the truths represented by those figures.

Source: Creighton Gilbert, ed., *Italian Art 1400–1500: Sources and Documents* (Evanston, IL: Northwestern University Press, 1992)

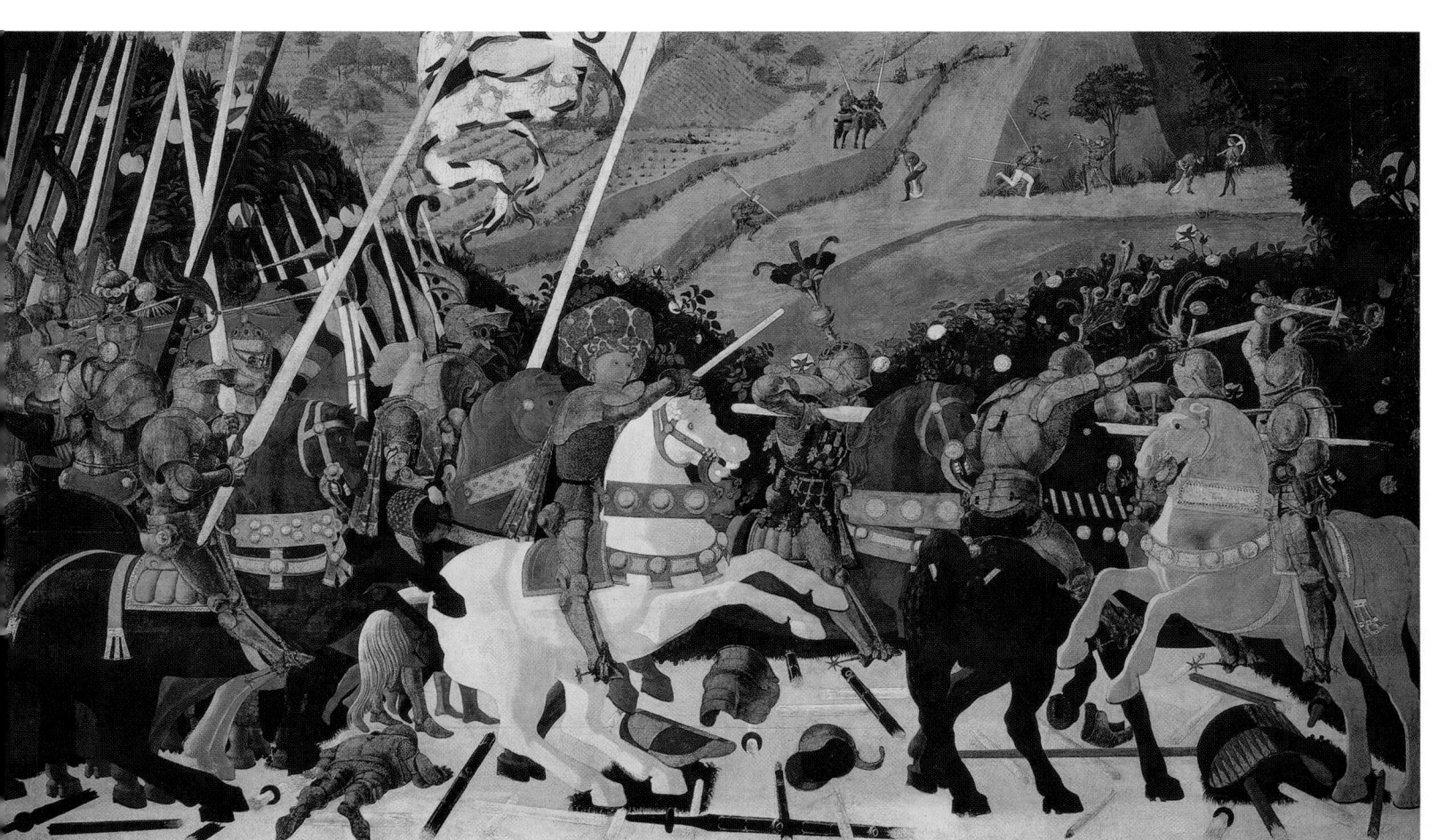

15.38   Paolo Uccello, *Battle of San Romano.* ca. 1438. Tempera and silver foil on wood panel, 6' × 10'5¾" (1.8 × 3.2 m). The National Gallery, London.

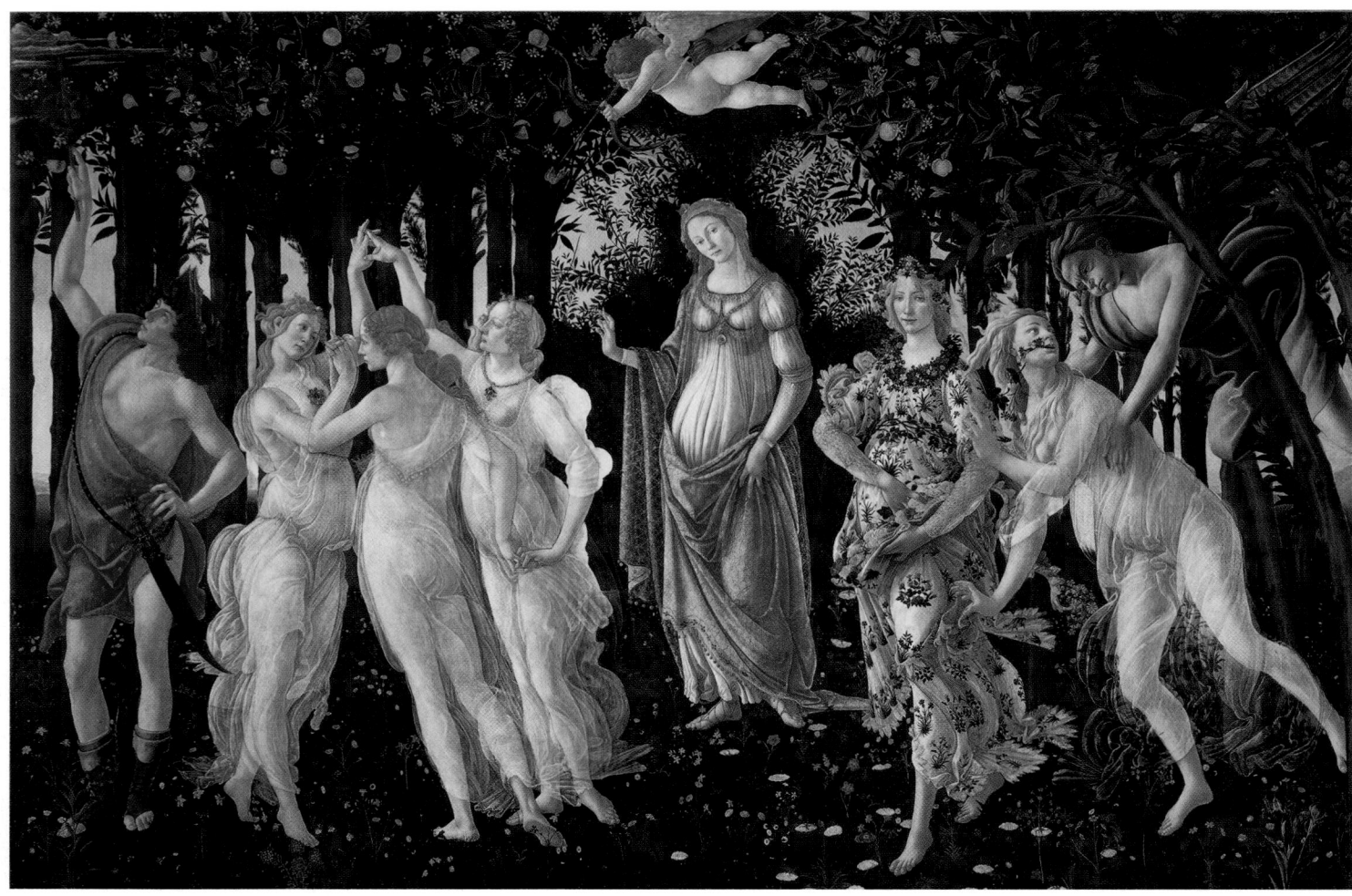

15.39 Sandro Botticelli, *Primavera*. ca. 1482. Tempera on panel, 6'8" × 10'4" (2.03 × 3.15 m). Galleria degli Uffizi, Florence

did many of the ruling families of Italy, for Flemish art was widely admired in places as disparate as Naples, Venice, Ferrara, Urbino, and Milan. Through such acquisitions, the Medici palace was filled with panel paintings and tapestries from the North. These objects made a profound impression on Florentine artists like Paolo Uccello, Filippo Lippi, Domenico Ghirlandaio, and the young Sandro Botticelli.

Botticelli (1445–1510), who had trained with Fra Filippo Lippi, became one of the favorite painters of the Medici circle—the group of nobles, scholars, and poets surrounding Lorenzo the Magnificent, the head of the Medici family and, for all practical purposes, the real ruler of the city from 1469 until 1492. The *Primavera* (*Spring*) (fig. **15.39**) was probably painted for a cousin who grew up in the household of Lorenzo the Magnificent. This work, and two others on the theme of love, may have been commissioned for the young man's wedding, which took place in 1482, the date often proposed for the painting.

Scholars have proposed numerous interpretations of this image. The painting depicts Venus in her sacred grove, with Eros flying overhead. Her companions, the Three Graces and Hermes (the Roman god Mercury), stand on the left; to the right, the wind-god Zephyr reaches for the nymph Chloris, whom he

then transforms into Flora, the goddess of flowers. One interpretation links the *Primavera* to the writings of the Neo-Platonist philosopher Marsilio Ficino (1433–1499), who was widely read and admired at the Medici court. Ficino assigned to Venus the virtues (or graces) desirable in women. With her modest garment and gentle gestures, Venus is the reigning divinity in this fertile garden. At left, Mercury keeps clouds away, while Flora embodies fertility. Other readings of the *Primavera* see it as an allegory about the immortality of the soul (drawing a parallel between the story of Chloris and the Rape of Persephone). Since the painting was made in connection with a wedding, it may be a celebration of marriage and fertility, as the dense thicket of orange trees and carpet of flowers seem to suggest.

Often paired with the *Primavera* in the public imagination is Botticelli's most famous image, *The Birth of Venus* (fig. **15.40**), which also once hung in a Medici villa. It may have been painted several years later, however. In this painting, too, the central figure in the composition is Venus, though here she floats slowly toward the shore, where a flower-clad woman waits to enfold her in a flowered robe. Her movement is aided by Zephyr accompanied by Chloris (Flora). Unlike the *Primavera*, here the space behind the figures seems to open out into the distance, with the

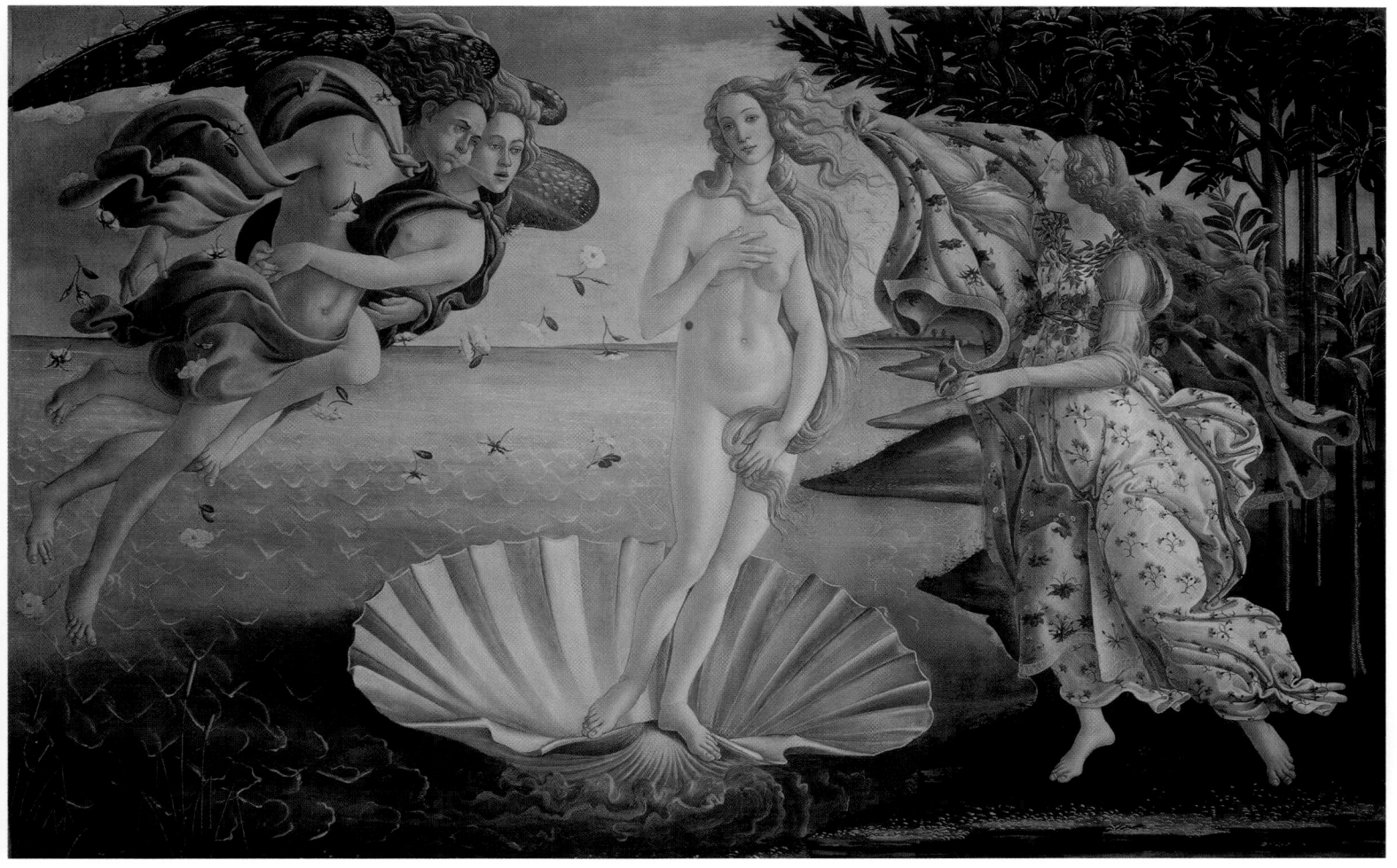

15.40   Sandro Botticelli, *The Birth of Venus*. ca. 1485. Tempera on panel, 5'8⅞" × 9'1⅞" (1.8 × 2.8 m). Galleria degli Uffizi, Florence

sky and water creating a light, cool tonality for the painting. In the figures, though, the shallow modeling and emphasis on outline produce an effect of low relief rather than of solid, three-dimensional shapes. The bodies seem to be drained of all weight, so that they float even when they touch the ground.

These ethereal figures re-create ancient forms. Botticelli's figure of *Venus* depends on a variant of the *Aphrodite of Knidas* by Praxiteles (see fig. 5.56). The subject itself seems related to the Homeric *Hymn to Aphrodite*, which begins: "I shall sing of beautiful Aphrodite…who is obeyed by the flowery sea-girt land of Cyprus, whither soft Zephyr and the breeze wafted her in soft foam over the waves. Gently the golden-filleted Horae received her, and clad her in divine garments." Still, no single literary source accounts for the pictorial conception. It may owe something to Ovid and the poet Poliziano, who was, like Botticelli, a member of the Medici circle. But again, the thinking of Marsilio Ficino may play a role here. Among the Neo-Platonists, Venus appears in two guises, a celestial Venus and a mundane Venus; the former was a source of divine love, the latter of physical love. *The Birth of Venus* may be an allegory of the origin of the celestial Venus for an audience attuned to the nuances of Neo-Platonic philosophy. The elegant forms and high finish of the painting,

combined with the erudite subject matter based on ancient thought, exemplify the taste of the Medici court.

Portraiture

Images of history, of contemporary events, or of ancient myths demonstrate the increasing interest in secular themes in the art of the Renaissance. Another genre of image in great demand was the portrait. In addition to dynastic images for kings, or monuments to war heroes, the second half of the fifteenth century saw the spread of portraits of merchants, brides, and artists.

The idea of recording specific likenesses was inspired by the fifteenth century's increasing awareness of the individual, but also by the study of Roman art, where portraits abound. Artists were already making donor portraits like Masaccio's *Trinity* fresco (see fig. 15.23), funerary monuments like Bruni's tomb (fig. 15.18), and commemorations of public figures like Donatello's *Gattamelata* (fig. 15.14), but new forms of portraiture developed in the fifteenth century.

The Florentine painter Domenico Ghirlandaio (1449–1494) inserted portraits of his patrons and their families into the many fresco cycles he painted, but he also made portraits as stand-alone

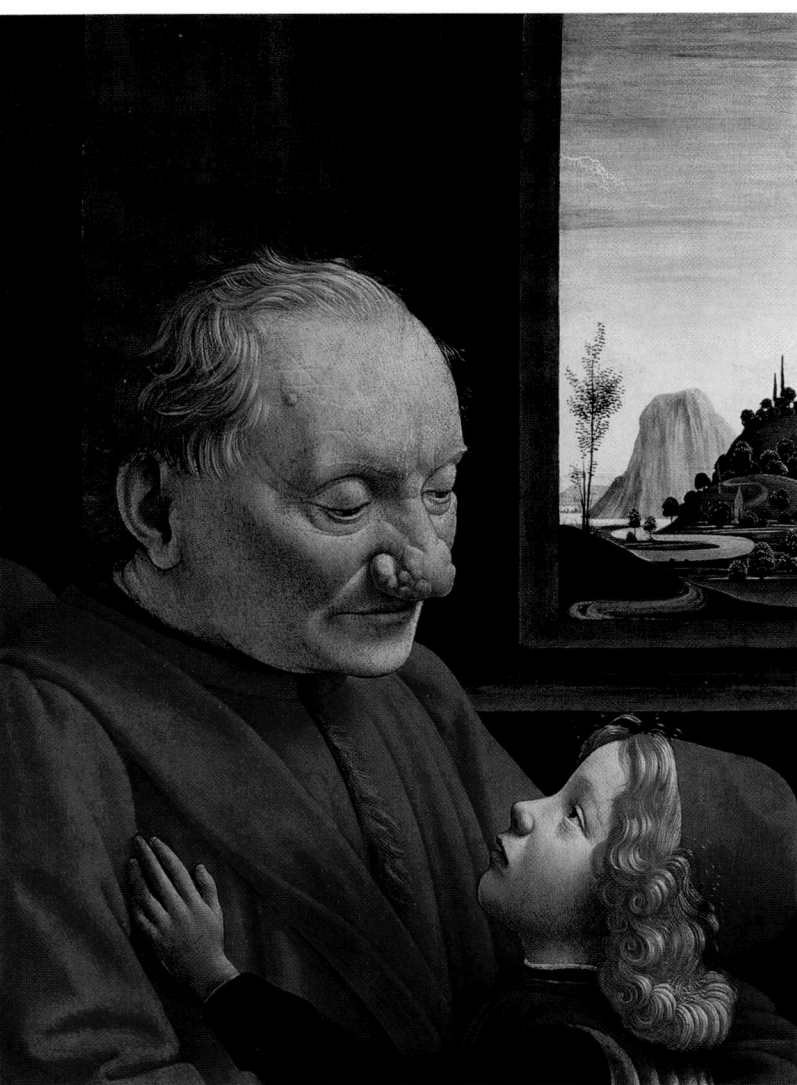

15.41 Domenico Ghirlandaio,
An Old Man and a Young Boy.
ca. 1480. Tempera and oil on wood
panel, 24⅛ × 18" (61.2 × 45.4 cm).
Musée du Louvre, Paris

paintings. Florentine artists before Ghirlandaio, as he himself did too, produced profile portraits in emulation of Roman coins. But around 1480, both Ghirlandaio and his younger colleague Botticelli began to adopt the three-quarter view (the sitter half turned toward the viewer, between profile and frontal gaze) in their portraits, and the practice soon became widespread. Both profile and three-quarter views appear in Ghirlandaio's most touching individual portrait, *An Old Man and a Young Boy* (fig. **15.41**), usually dated to around 1480. Despite the very specific physiognomy of the old man, whose nose has been disfigured by rosacea (a skin disorder), the sitters and their relationship to each other are unknown. Their intimate gestures suggest that they represent two generations of one family; if so, the painting depicts the continuity of the family line. Leon Battista Alberti defined the function of portraits as being "to make the absent present," which may be the case with this image; it appears to be based on a drawing taken at the time of the old man's death. The connection between generations depicted in this family group may be more symbolic than real. Even though the textures are somewhat generalized and the composition geometrically ordered, Ghirlandaio's attention to detail may reflect his acquaintance with

Netherlandish art. The landscape view through the window that breaks up the picture plane was also a northern European idea (see fig. 14.21). But the most important contribution was the three-quarter view of the human face, which had been used in Flanders since the 1420s.

Portraits in three dimensions enjoyed a certain vogue in the fifteenth century, too, especially among the wealthiest families. The Medici commissioned numerous family likenesses for their palaces and for their friends, but they preferred the **portrait bust**, a shoulder-length sculptural likeness. This form was most likely to draw parallels between themselves and Roman families who owned numerous busts of their ancestors (see fig. 7.12). The Florentine busts celebrated the living, however, not the dead, and were made of marble, bronze, or terra cotta by some of the leading sculptors of the century. Piero de' Medici and his wife, Lucrezia Tornabuoni, were recorded in such busts, as were their sons, Giuliano and Lorenzo de' Medici. The format was used for portraits of both men and women, including that shown in figure **15.42**. Dated to around 1475–80, this marble bust by Verrocchio depicts a young woman holding a bouquet. It is unusual in showing the sitter in half-length, which gives the artist room to render her

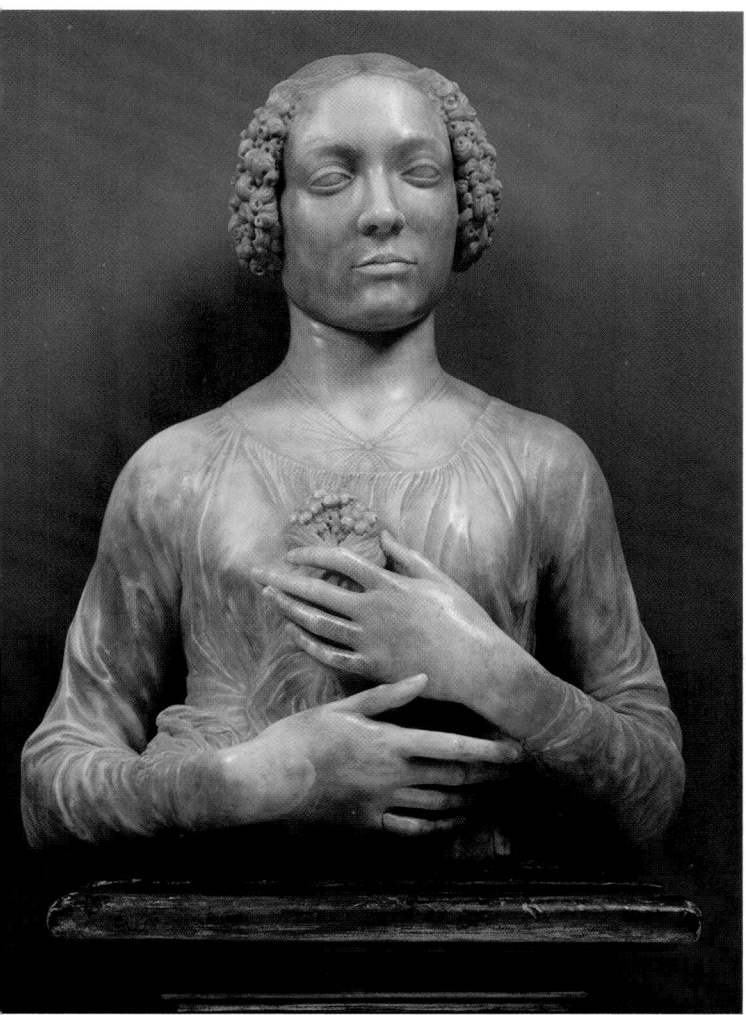

15.42 Andrea del Verrocchio, *Lady with a Bunch of Flowers*. ca. 1475. Marble, height 23²/₃" (60 cm). Museo Nazionale del Bargello, Florence

Savonarola, who attacked the "cult of paganism" and the materialism he saw in Florentine culture. Savonarola's exhortations to repentance and his strong criticism of corruption, not only in Florence but in the church hierarchy, made him many enemies, and he was executed in 1498. As the fifteenth century came to an end, Florence was battling for its life against the stronger powers of the papacy, Spain, and France.

RENAISSANCE ART THROUGHOUT ITALY, 1450–1500

Artists from all over Italy and well beyond found in the innovations being explored in Florence a stimulus for their own work, though they responded to the new styles in individual ways. Additionally, patrons throughout Italy saw the advantages of expressing their authority through visual and textual references to antiquity. By midcentury, linear perspective was in widespread use, and Florentine techniques for rendering form through light were being practiced by many artists. Piero della Francesca blended his own fascination with mathematics, the ancient world, and Flemish painting to create a personal style that found favor in several Italian courts. The Florentine humanist and architect Leon Battista Alberti designed influential buildings in northern Italy, including one for the marquis of Mantua, who had also attracted the services of the painter-archaeologist Andrea Mantegna. The city of Venice commissioned Florentine artists, such as Andrea del Verrocchio, for major projects, but local traditions in architecture and painting remained strong. Venetian painters like Giovanni Bellini developed an influential school that rivaled the Florentine style. As the papacy regained its control in Rome, Perugino and Luca Signorelli created projects designed to celebrate papal power.

Piero della Francesca in Central Italy

One of the most distinctive and original artists of the second half of the fifteenth century was Piero della Francesca (ca. 1420–1492), who visited Florence while training with Domenico Veneziano (see fig. 15.30). Piero came from Borgo San Sepolcro in southeastern Tuscany, where he completed some of his earliest commissions. He worked for patrons in Tuscany, Rimini, and Ferrara, and executed several important works for Federico da Montefeltro, a *condottiere* (mercenary general) turned ruler of Urbino (southeast of Tuscany) around 1470. Piero's early training with Domenico Veneziano may be seen in his use of color, while his experience of Masaccio is apparent in the solidity and simplicity of his forms and the solemn character of his compositions. The early fifteenth-century systemization of perspective was critical for Piero, who became such an expert at mathematically determining perspective and at rendering figures in space that he wrote a treatise about it. It is likely that Piero made contact with Leon Battista Alberti, with whom he shared patrons, as well as an interest in art theory.

expressive hands. Her hair is arranged fashionably, though her garment is simple. Verrocchio manipulates the marble to distinguish textural effects of hair, eyebrows, flowers, and the transparent undergarment buttoned at her neck. The slight tilt of her head and the placement of her hands give the figure movement and grace. Although speculation about her identity has suggested a connection to Lorenzo de' Medici, the identity of the lady in this lyrical portrait remains unknown.

The court around Lorenzo the Magnificent was learned, ambitious, and very cultivated. Lorenzo was the patron of numerous humanists, philosophers, poets, and artists, including the young Michelangelo. Yet this brilliant court did not outlast Lorenzo's death in 1492. His heir, Piero de' Medici, did not share his father's diplomatic gifts. What is more, he faced an increasingly unstable economy (the bank failed in 1494) and invading armies from France and Spain. Piero's inept handling of these crises encouraged an uprising in Florence in 1494, which expelled the Medici faction and sought to restore republican government. The power vacuum was filled for a time by the Dominican friar Girolamo

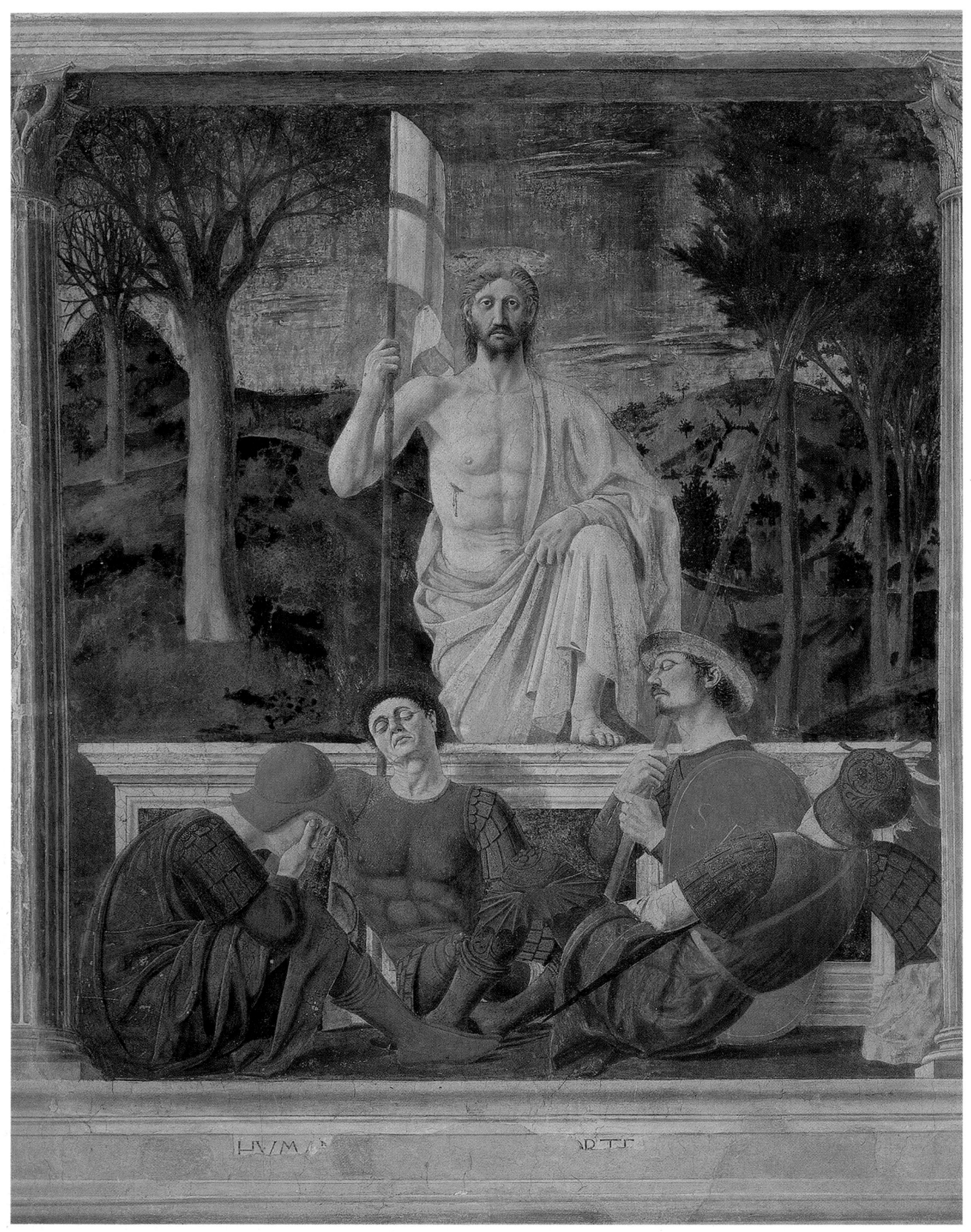

15.43 Piero della Francesca, *Resurrection*. ca. 1463. Fresco, 7'5" × 6'6½" (2.25 × 1.99 m). Palazzo Comunale, Borgo San Sepolcro

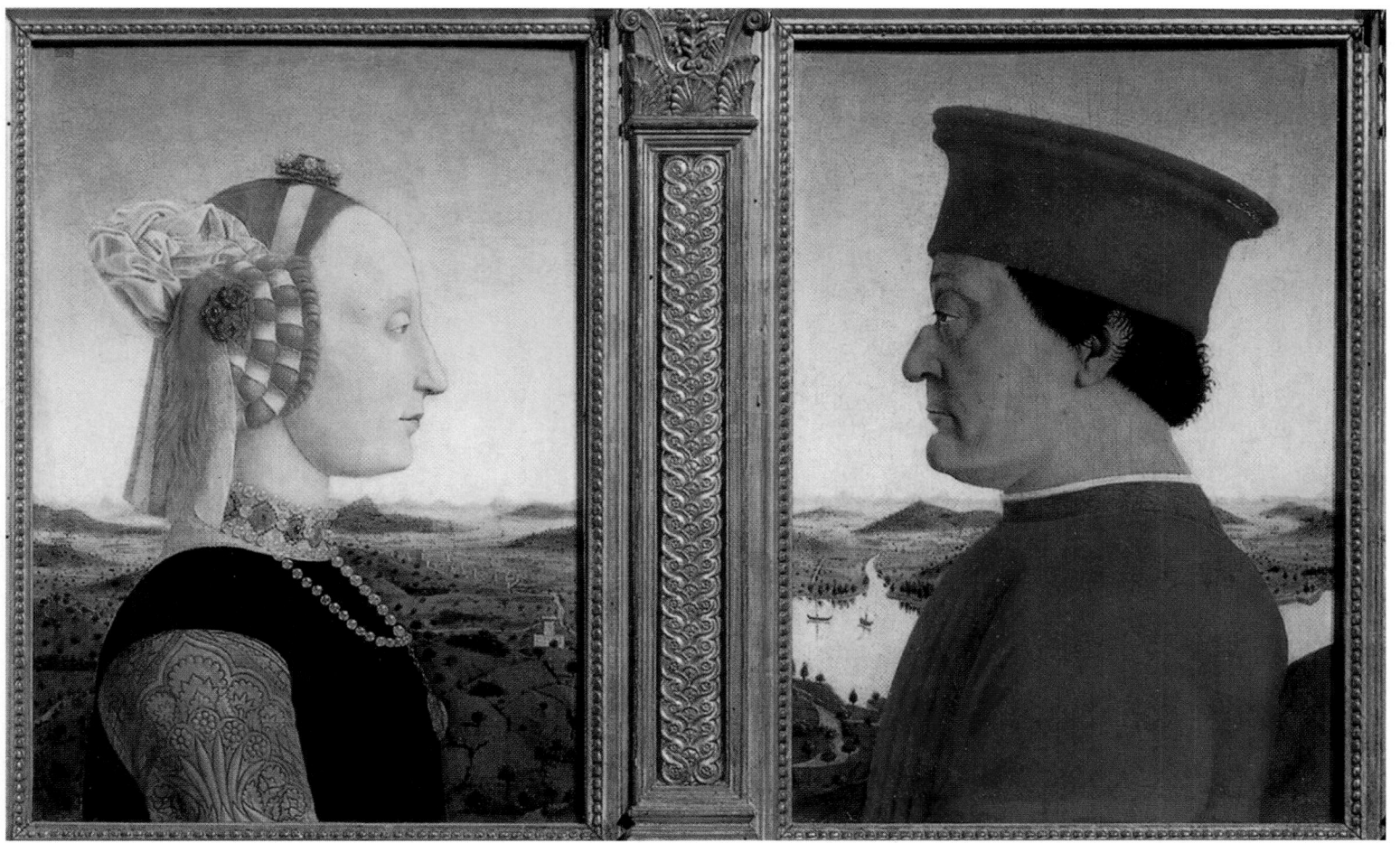

15.44 Piero della Francesca, *Double Portrait of Battista Sforza and Federico da Montefeltro*. ca. 1474. Oil and tempera on panel, each panel 18½ × 13" (47 × 33 cm). Galleria degli Uffizi, Florence

A work that Piero made for his hometown reflects this combination of influences on his art. The city of Borgo San Sepolcro commissioned him to paint a fresco for its Palazzo Comunale, probably around 1460. Befitting the name of the town, which means the "Holy Sepulcher," Piero's theme is Christ Resurrected stepping out of his tomb (fig. **15.43**). The figure of Christ dominates the composition: His frontality and the triangular composition may derive from works like the *Trinity* fresco by Masaccio (see fig. 15.23), but the light of sunrise and the pale colors reflect the art of Domenico Veneziano. The contrast offered by the dead trees on the left and the living ones on the right adds to the theme of resurrection. Piero pays special attention to the arrangement of the Roman soldiers asleep in front of the sepulcher; they are variations on a theme of bodies in space. The spectator must look up to see the glorified body of Christ, so perfect in his anatomy and so serene in his aspect as he triumphs over death. Columns, soldiers, and tomb are all rendered as if seen from below, displaying Piero's mastery of perspective.

Piero's art brought him to the attention of the cultivated Duke Federico da Montefeltro, who attracted artists from all over Europe to his court at Urbino. There, Piero came into contact, and perhaps competition, with artists not only from Italy but also from Spain and Flanders. From them, Piero learned the new technique of painting with oil glazes and became an early practitioner of this technique in central Italy. Piero's quiet, spatially complex paintings were thus enriched with more brilliant colors and surface textures in the style of Flemish art. Piero painted a double portrait of the duke and duchess (fig. **15.44**) about 1474. This painting demonstrates Piero's mastery of spatial representation and clarity of form by using the rich hues and varied textures made possible by oil painting. The diptych portrays both the duke and his wife in profile facing each other in front of a deep, continuous landscape. Presented in a complex gilded frame, the diptych appears much larger and monumental than it really is. Federico, whose face had been disfigured in a tournament, shows his good side. He is depicted on the reverse of his portrait in ducal garb, suggesting a date for the painting after 1474. His wife, Battista, had been dead for two years by then, six months after providing him with a son and heir. Piero gives her the place of honor to the viewer's left. Her pale features are framed by her complicated hairstyle and her gems and brocades. A shadow falls over the landscape behind her, while the landscape behind her husband is lighter and busier. The rigid profiles placed against the low horizon and deep landscape give the figures an unapproachable and monumental appearance. Piero's balanced and spacious composition results in an image of calm authority and triumph.

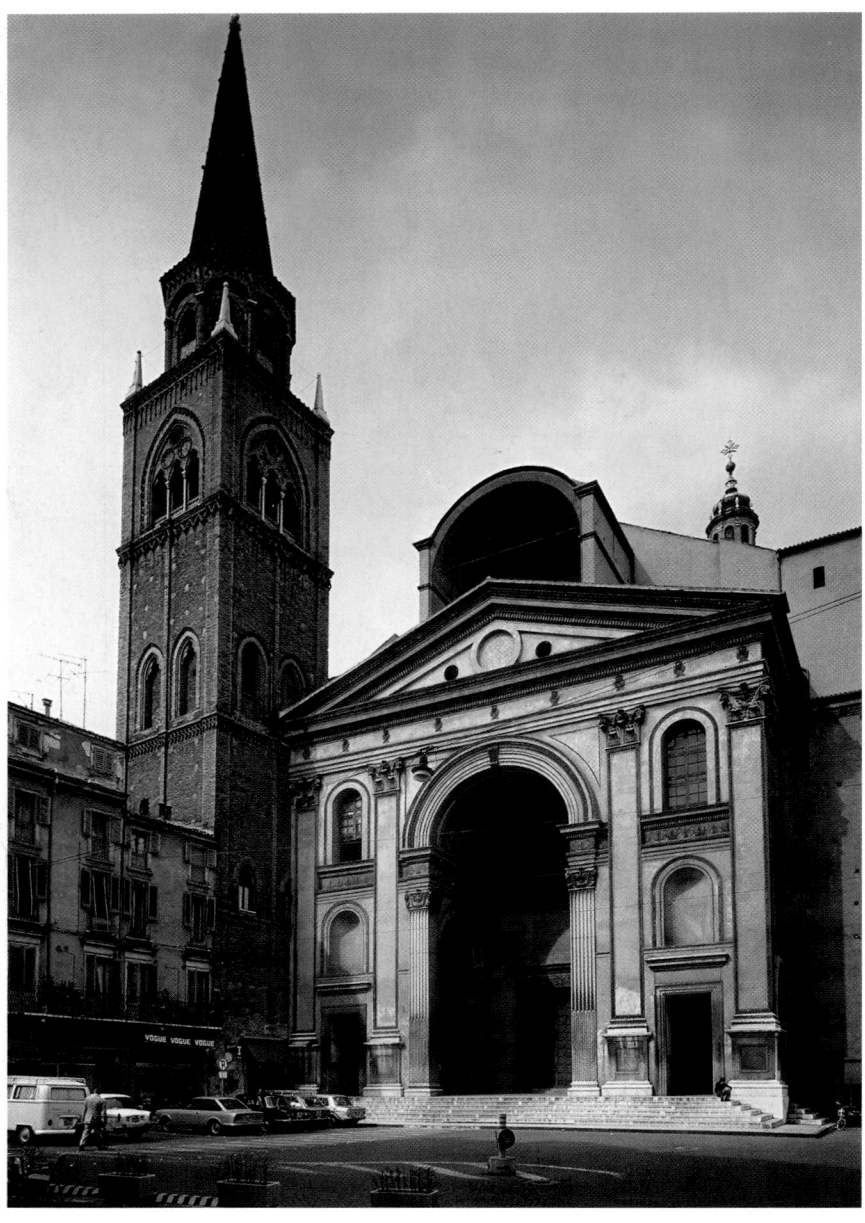

15.45 Leon Battista Alberti. Church of Sant'Andrea, Mantua. Designed 1470

Alberti and Mantegna in Mantua

Duke Federigo was a relative newcomer to power in Urbino, but Mantua, in the northern Po Valley, had been dominated for more than a century by the Gonzaga family. They created a brilliant court, peopled with humanists, educators, and artists. Marquis Ludovico Gonzaga had married a German princess, Barbara of Brandenburg, and the court was very cosmopolitan. Works such as the *Ten Books on Architecture* (ca. 1452) brought Leon Battista Alberti great prominence and the Gonzaga lured him to their service.

In 1470, Alberti had designed the church of Sant'Andrea in Mantua, his last work (fig. **15.45**). The majestic façade expresses Alberti's ultimate goal of merging classical temple forms with the traditional basilican church. Here, he interweaves a triumphal arch motif, now with a huge recessed center niche to serve as the portal, with a classical temple front. To keep the two competing forms in equilibrium, he uses flat pilasters that stress the primacy of the wall surface. Two sizes of pilaster achieve this balance: The smaller pilasters support the arch over the huge central niche, and the larger ones support the unbroken architrave and the strongly outlined pediment. The larger pilasters form what is known as a **colossal order**, meaning that it is more than one story high. These tall pilasters balance the horizontal and vertical elements of the design.

To further unify the façade, Alberti inscribed the entire design within a square, even though it made the façade much lower than the height of the nave. (The effect of the west wall protruding above the pediment appears more disturbing in photographs than from street level, where it can hardly be seen.) While the façade is distinct from the main body of the structure, it offers a "preview" of the interior, where the same colossal order, the same proportions, and the same triumphal-arch motif reappear on the walls of the nave (fig. **15.46**). Unlike the façade of Santa Maria Novella (see fig. 15.9), Alberti announced the interior elevation on the exterior.

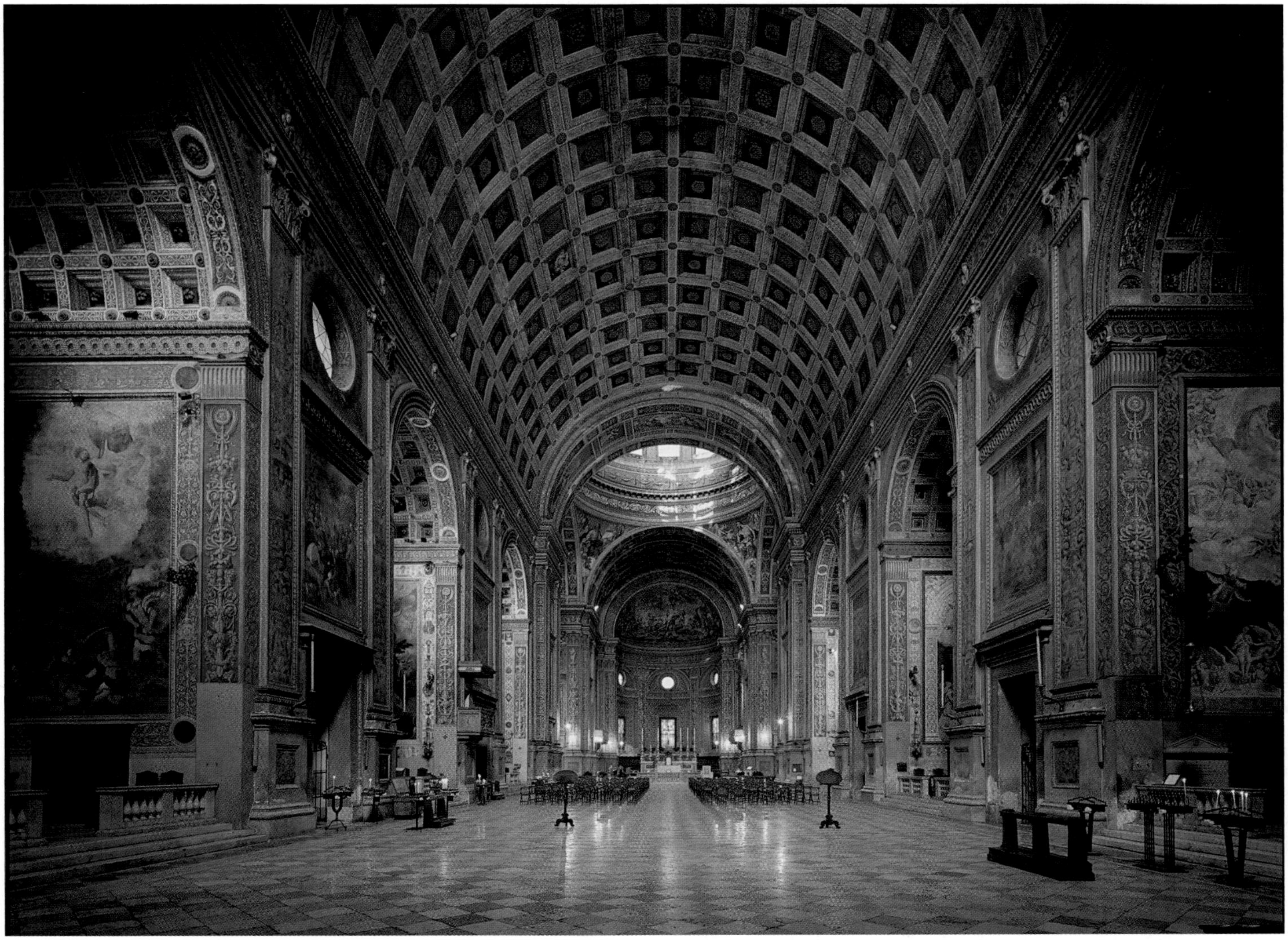

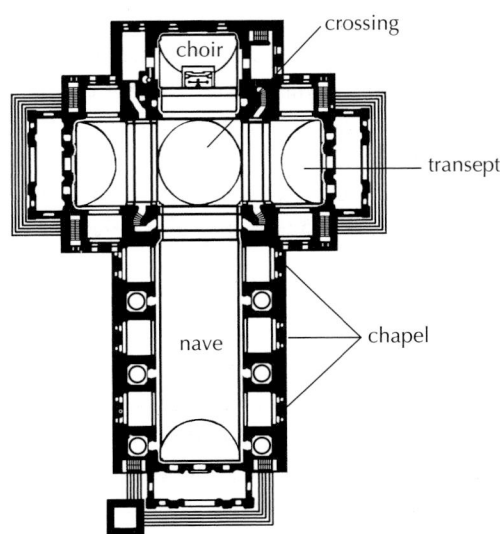

15.46 Leon Battista Alberti. Interior of church of Sant'Andrea, Mantua

15.47 Plan of Sant'Andrea (transept, dome, and choir are later additions)

Compared with Brunelleschi's San Lorenzo (see fig. 15.8), the plan (fig. **15.47**) is extraordinarily compact. Had the church been completed as planned, the difference would be even more marked. Alberti's design had no transept, dome, or choir—all of these were added in the mid-eighteenth century; he planned only a nave ending in an apse. Following the example of the Basilica of Constantine (see figs. 7.60 and 7.61), Alberti replaced the aisles with alternating large and small vaulted chapels and eliminated the clerestory. The colossal pilasters and the arches of the large chapels support a coffered barrel vault of impressive size. (The nave is as wide as the façade.) Here, Alberti has drawn upon his study of the massive vaulted halls in ancient Roman baths and basilicas, but he interprets these models freely to create a structure that can truly be called a "Christian temple." Such a synthesis of ancient forms and Christian functions was a primary goal of fifteenth-century humanists and their patrician sponsors. Alberti's accomplishment of this goal at Sant'Andrea would inspire many other architects to do the same.

The humanist court at Mantua played host for many years to one of the most intellectually inclined artists of the century,

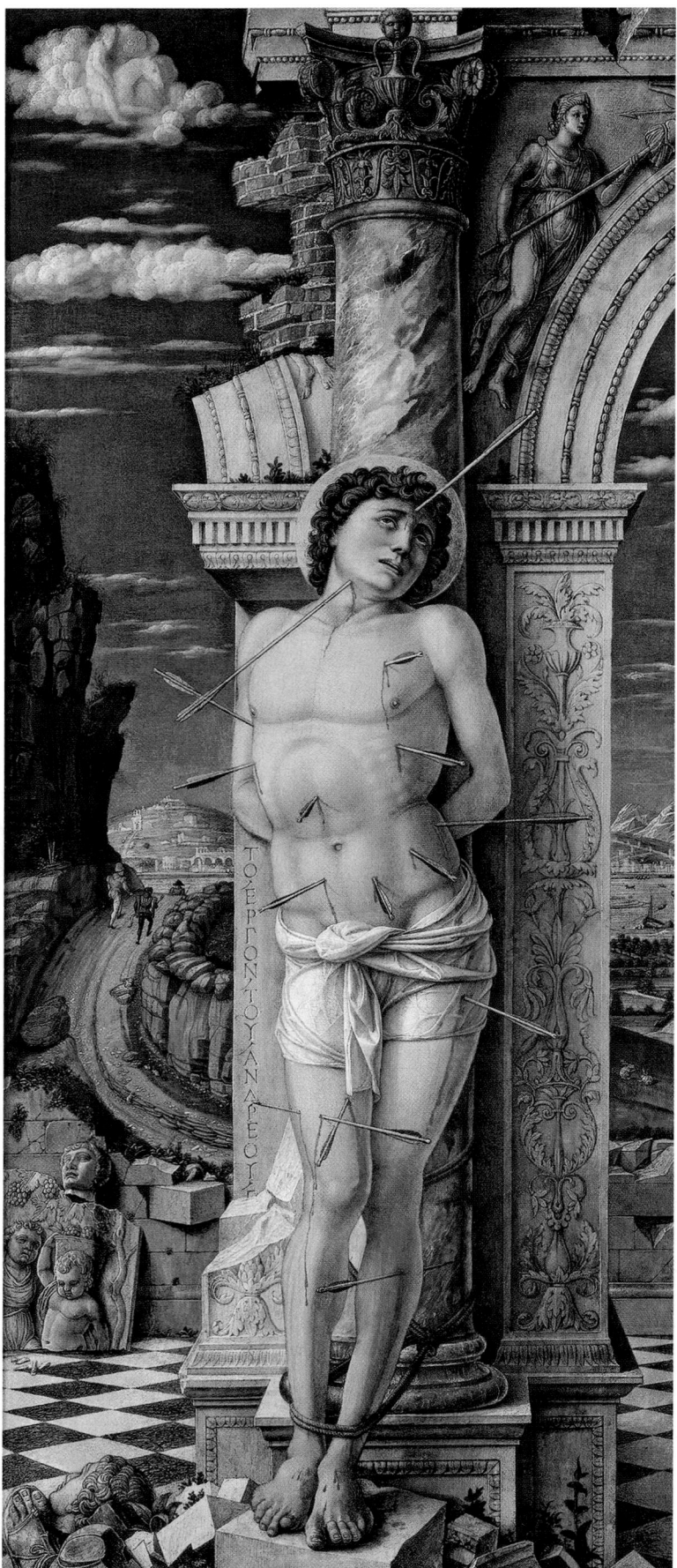

15.48 Andrea Mantegna, *St. Sebastian*. ca. 1450s. Tempera on panel, 26¾ × 11⅞" (68 × 30.6 cm). Kunsthistorisches Museum, Vienna

Andrea del Mantegna (1431–1506). Trained in Padua, but aware of artistic currents in Venice, Florence, and Rome and brother-in-law to Giovanni Bellini, Mantegna became court painter to the Gonzaga in 1460, a position he held until his death at age 75. His interests as a painter, humanist, and archaeologist can be seen in the panel depicting *St. Sebastian* (fig. **15.48**), probably painted in the 1450s. Sebastian was an early Christian martyr who was condemned to be executed by archers. (He recovered from these wounds, which may explain why he was invoked so often against the plague.) Mantegna depicts the anatomically precise and carefully proportioned body of the saint tied to a classical column. These forms are crisply drawn and modeled to resemble sculpture. Architectural and sculptural classical ruins lie at his feet and behind him, and next to him, on the left, is the artist's signature in Greek. A road leads into the distance, traversed by the archers who have just shot the saint; through this device, Mantegna lets the perspectively constructed space denote the passage of time. Beyond these men appears an atmospheric landscape and a deep-blue sky dotted with soft white clouds. The scene is bathed in warm late-afternoon sunlight, which creates a melancholy mood. The light-filled landscape in the background indicates Mantegna's awareness of Flemish paintings, which had reached Florence as well as Venice by 1450, where Mantegna would have encountered them.

Mantegna's patron for the *St. Sebastian* is unknown, but as a court painter, he served the marquis of Mantua. For the marquis' palace in Mantua, he painted a room that has come to be called the *Camera Picta*, or painted room (fig. **15.49**). This was a multipurpose vaulted room—sometimes bedroom, sometimes reception hall—which Mantegna finished in 1474. On the walls he painted portraits of the Gonzaga family, their retainers, their children, and their possessions. The room celebrates the marquis's brilliant court, his dynastic accomplishments, and his wealth, in a witty display that became an attraction for visiting humanists, politicians, artists, and princes. In such ways, princes used art to improve their social and political positions. The *Camera Picta* also celebrates Mantegna's skill and brought him fame among his contemporaries.

Mantegna used the actual architecture of the room—the **corbels** supporting the vaults, the mantel over the fireplace—to create an illusionistic glimpse of the Gonzaga family at home. Trompe-l'oeil pilasters serve as window frames through which a viewer sees members of the family out-of-doors; the figures of Ludovico and his son Francesco, recently made a cardinal, are observed by servants with a horse and dogs on the other side of the main door. In addition to the specific features of the people and the naturalism of the details, Mantegna's mastery of perspective allows him to connect the painted world to the real world of the spectator. The centerpiece of this illusion occurs at the crown of the vault (fig. **15.50**), where Mantegna paints a fictive oculus through which a spectator sees the sky. Framing this window is a foreshortened balustrade on which little *putti* (small boys) climb and over which court ladies peer. Mantegna uses many devices to create illusions in this room, including drapery that appears to be

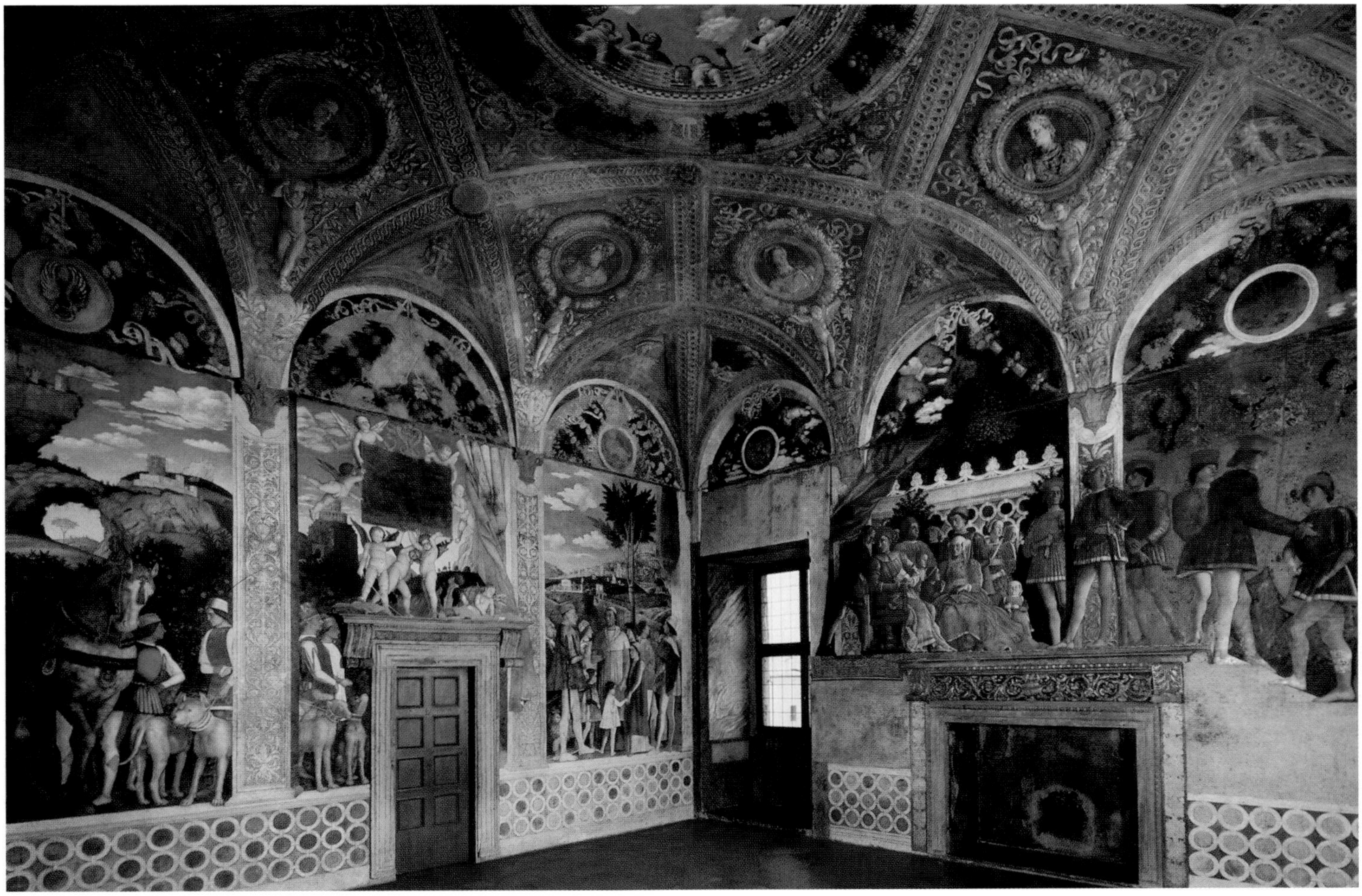

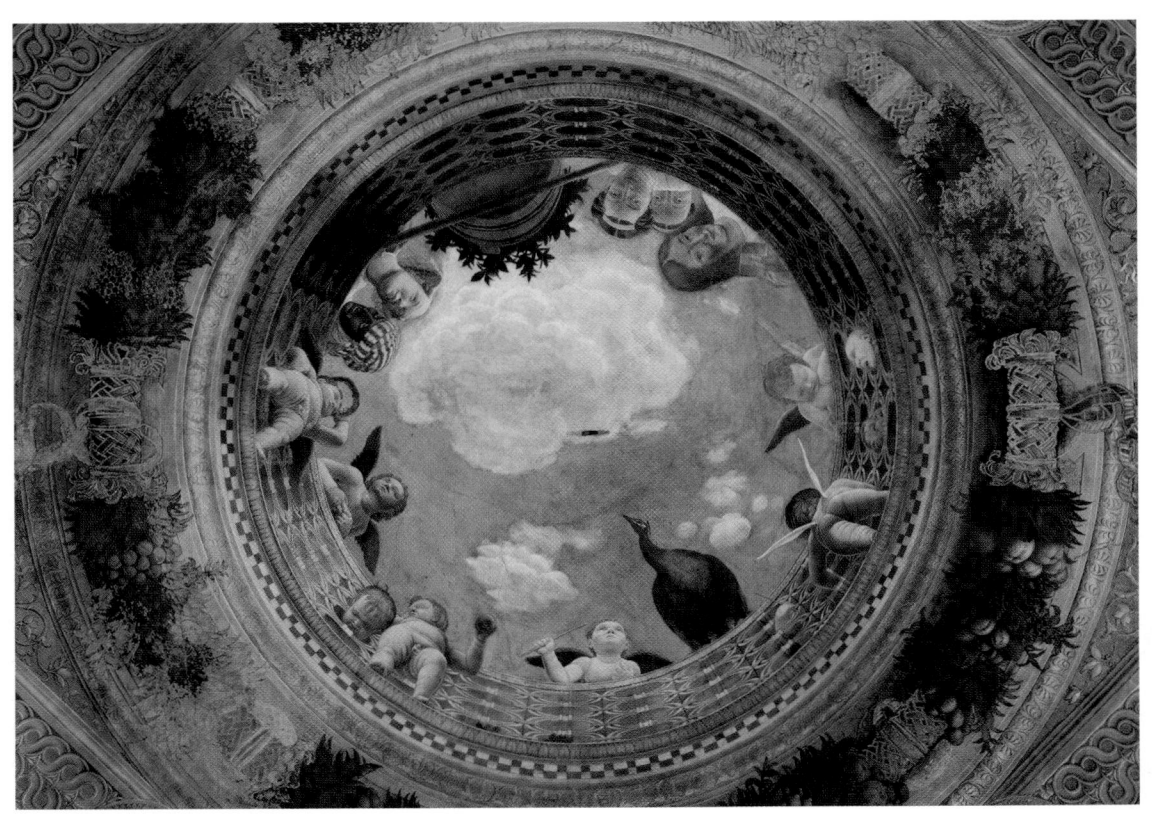

15.49 Andrea Mantegna, *Camera Picta*. 1465–74. Fresco. Ducal Palace, Mantua

15.50 Andrea Mantegna, *Camera Picta*, detail of ceiling

fluttering in the outside breeze and trompe l'oeil reliefs of Roman emperors on the vaults. Above the mantel, Ludovico appears again, this time in a more formal setting, surrounded by family and courtiers. The brilliance of the court is wonderfully captured by Mantegna's splendid paintings.

Venice

While it extended control over its neighbors, Venice maintained a stable republican government throughout the fifteenth century. Protected from outsiders by its lagoon, it was ruled by a merchant aristocracy so firmly established that there was little internal conflict and the Doge's Palace (see fig. 13.32) could forgo any fortifications. Similarly, the houses of Venetian patricians were not required to serve as fortresses, with the result that they developed into graceful, ornate structures. The Ca' d'Oro (fig. **15.51**) was built beginning in 1421 for Marino Contarini, whose family had long prospered from trade. To assert his status, Contarini spared no expense on his dwelling on the Grand Canal. It received its name ("house of gold") from the lavish gold leaf that once adorned the façade.

The design in part reflects the different functions of the building. The ground floor was used as a shipping center and warehouse, while the second story is devoted mainly to a large reception hall, with several smaller rooms to the right. Private quarters are found mainly on the upper floor. The intersecting ribs of arches form a delicate latticework on the façade, which combine with the brilliant colors and the use of gold to express the family's wealth, position, and ambition.

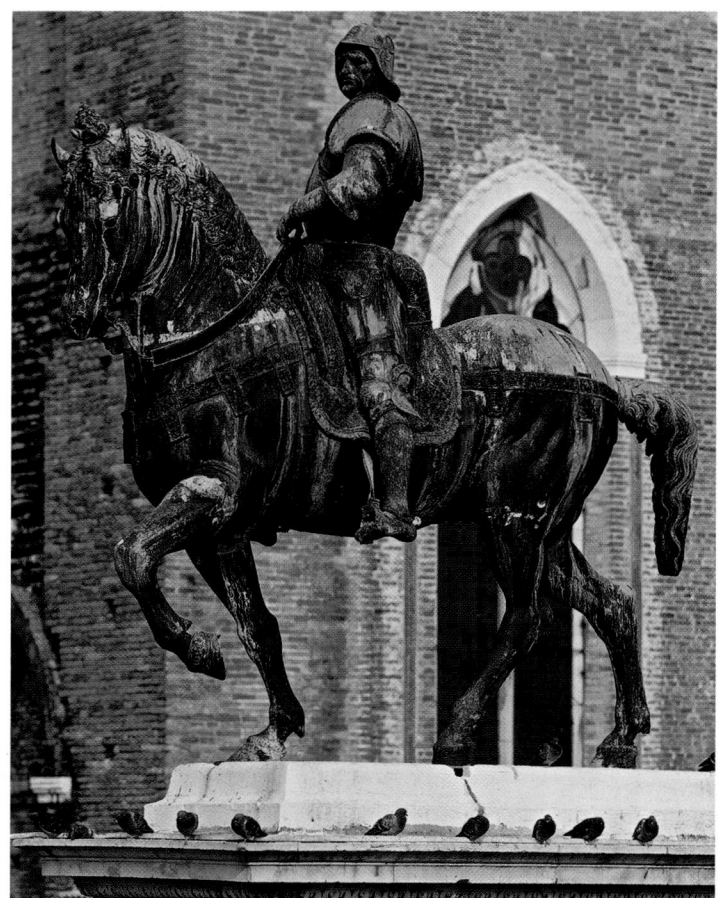

15.52   Andrea del Verrocchio, *Equestrian Monument of Colleoni.* ca. 1483–88. Bronze, height 13' (3.9 m). Campo Santissimi Giovanni e Paolo, Venice

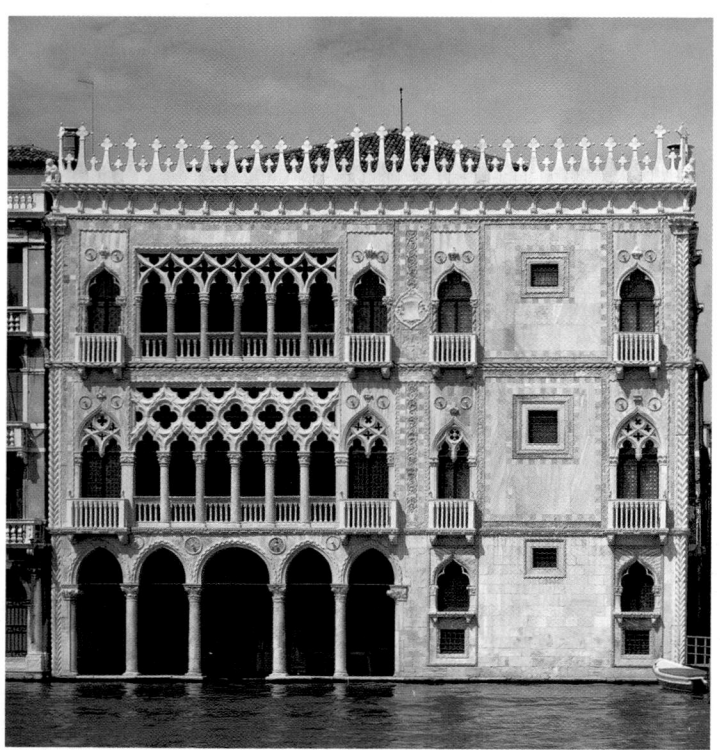

15.51   Ca' d'Oro, Venice. 1421–40

ECHOES OF DONATELLO'S *GATTAMELATA*   Local Venetian traditions gave way slowly to the revival of interest in ancient art coming from Florence. Several Florentine artists, including Donatello and Andrea del Castagno, were called to Venice to execute important commissions. Flemish painting was admired and collected in Venice, which as a center for international trade housed colonies of merchants from northern Europe. By the end of the century, Venice had also adopted the new techniques and references to ancient art as useful tools for expressing itself. A good example of this is the commission given by the republic to Verrocchio to execute a large bronze equestrian statue commemorating a Venetian army commander, the *condottiere* Bartolommeo Colleoni (fig. **15.52**). Colleoni had requested such a statue in his will, in which he also left a large fortune to the city-state. Colleoni obviously knew the Gattamelata statue (see fig. 15.14) by Donatello, and wanted the same honor for himself. Verrocchio likely viewed Donatello's work as the model for his statue, yet he did more than simply imitate it, bringing his painter's skills to the rendering of the textures and details of the monument.

Colleoni's horse is graceful and spirited; its thin hide reveals veins, muscles, and sinews, in contrast to the rigid surfaces of the armored figure bestriding it. Since the horse is also smaller in relation to its rider than in the Gattamelata statue, Colleoni looms in the saddle as the very image of forceful dominance. Legs straight, one shoulder thrust forward, he surveys the scene before him with the same concentration we saw in Donatello's *St. George* (see fig. 15.12). Like Donatello's work, the Colleoni statue reminds a viewer of the contributions its subject made to his city.

BELLINI AND OIL PAINTING In addition to the revival of Roman forms, the traditions of Venice were further enhanced late in the fifteenth century by an exploration of the new medium of oil painting. A crucial intermediary in introducing this technique to Venice was probably Antonello da Messina, a painter from southern Italy who may have traveled to Flanders to learn it; he is documented in Venice in the 1470s. In the work of Giovanni Bellini (ca. 1430–1507), Mantegna's brother-in-law and a member of a family of painters, the technique of painting in oil pioneered by the Flemish is combined with Florentine spatial systems and Venetian light and color.

Bellini's *St. Francis in the Desert* (fig. 15.53), dating from about 1480, displays the artist's synthesis of these elements to create a wholly original image. In this painting, St. Francis has just stepped out of his hermit's cell, fitted out with a desk under an arbor. He has left his wooden sandals behind and looks up ecstatically to the sky. Some scholars believe the painting shows Francis receiving the stigmata (the wounds of Christ) on the Feast of the Holy Cross in 1224, when a crucified seraph reportedly appeared to him on Mount La Verna, in Tuscany. Others have argued that the scene "illustrates" the *Hymn of the Sun*, which Francis composed the next year, after his annual fast at a hermitage near his hometown of Assisi. Whichever narrative moment is depicted, the painting expresses Franciscan ideals. For St. Francis, "Brother Sun, who gives the day…and…is beautiful and radiant with great

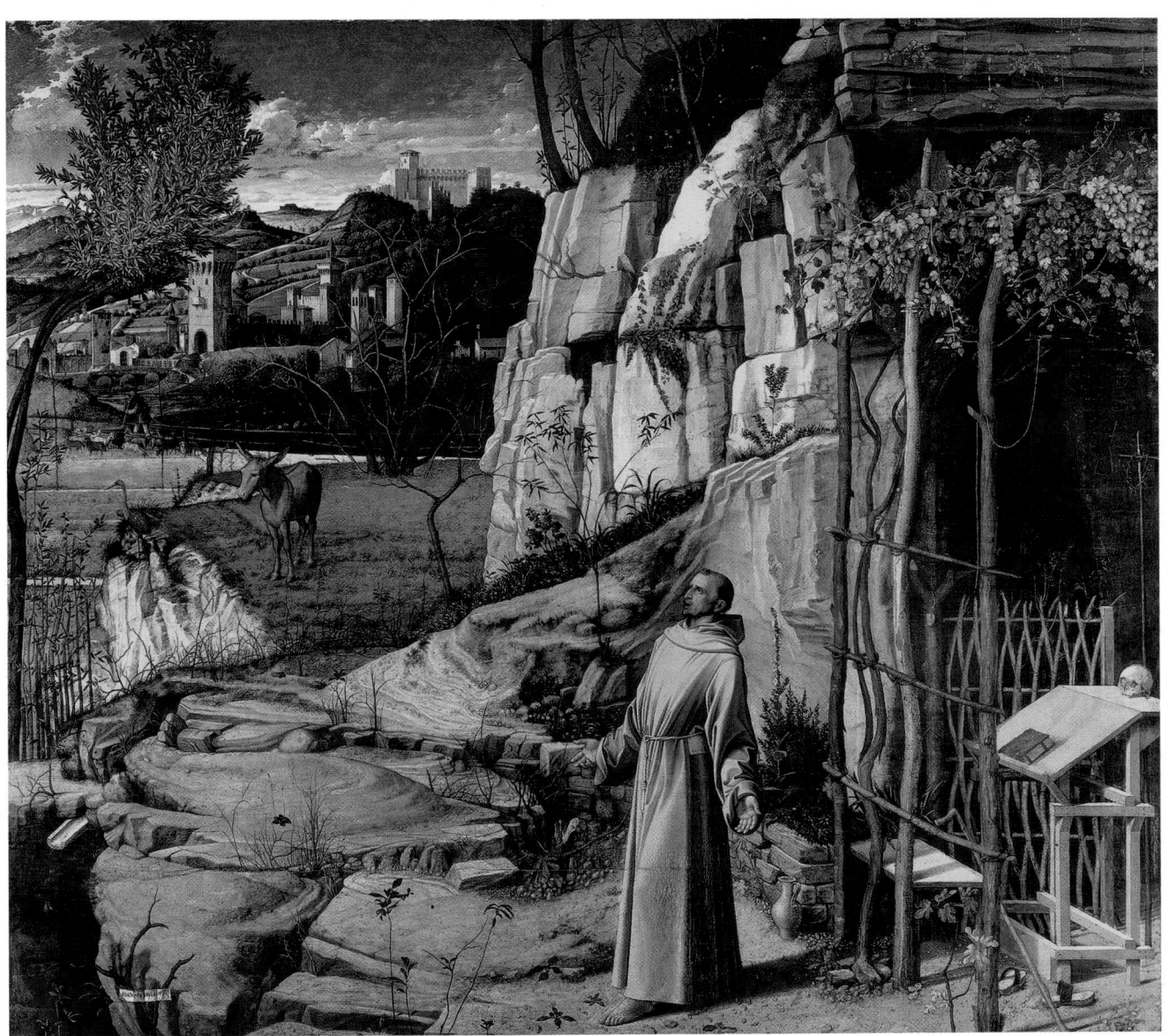

15.53   Giovanni Bellini, *St. Francis in the Desert*. ca. 1480. Tempera and oil on poplar panel (cradled), 49 × 57⅞" (124.4 × 141.9 cm). The Frick Collection, New York

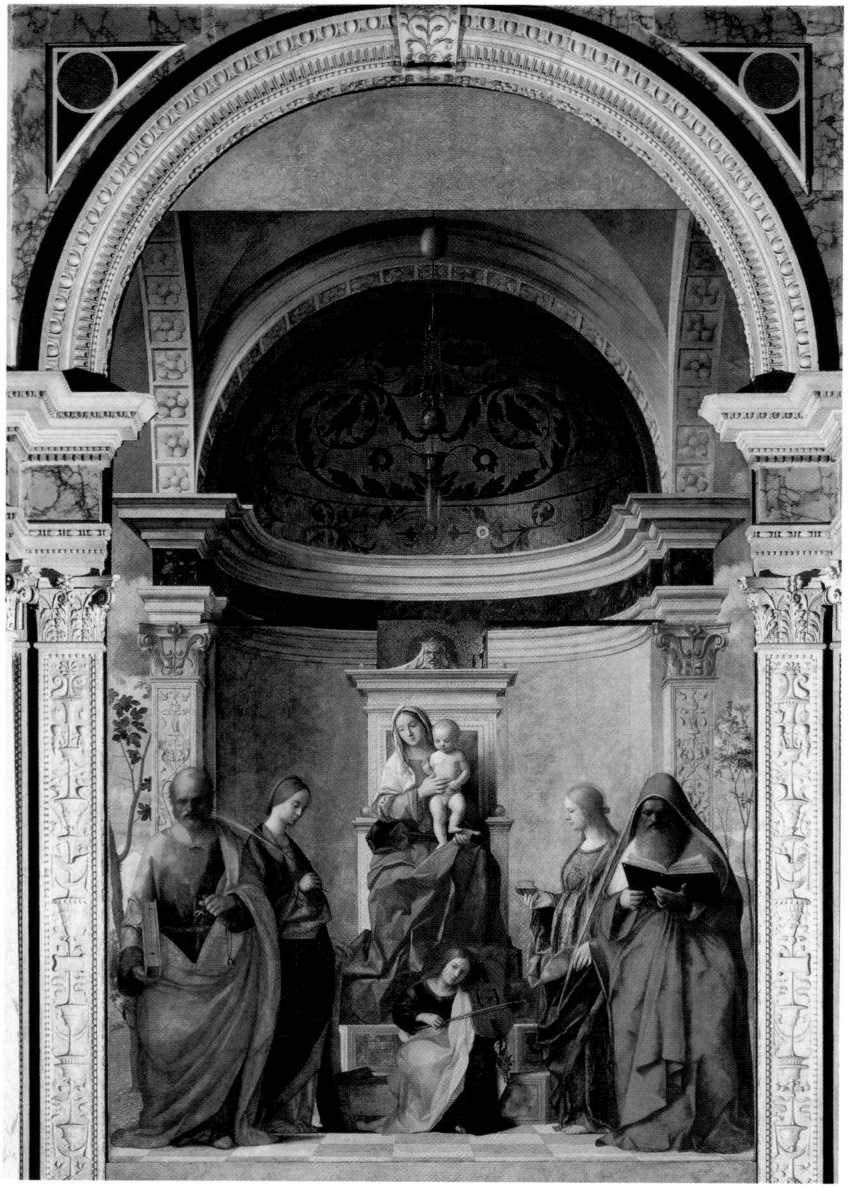

15.54 Giovanni Bellini, *Madonna and Saints*. 1505. Oil on panel, 16'5⅛" × 7'9" (5 × 2.4 m). San Zaccaria, Venice

splendor," was a symbol of the Lord. What he sees in the painting is not the sun itself, which is obscured by a cloud, but God revealed as the light divine. This miraculous light is so intense that it illuminates the entire scene.

In the background is a magnificent expanse of Italian countryside. St. Francis is so small compared to the landscape setting that he seems almost incidental. Yet his mystic rapture before the beauty of the visible world guides a viewer's response to the vista, which is ample and intimate at the same time. St. Francis believed that God created nature for the benefit of humanity. Bellini uses the tools of the Renaissance artist to re-create a vision of natural beauty. In this deep space, derived using the rules of perspective, he depicts detailed textures and forms to populate the landscape. Some of these forms may express Franciscan values. For Francis, the road to salvation lay in the ascetic life of the hermit, symbolized by the cave. The donkey may stand for St. Francis himself, who referred to his body as Brother Ass, which must be disciplined. The other animals—heron, bittern, and rabbit—are,

like monks, solitary creatures in Christian lore. Yet Bellini's soft colors and glowing light infuse the painting with a warmth that makes such a solitary life not only bearable, but enviable.

As the foremost artist of Venice, Bellini produced a number of altarpieces of the *sacra conversazione* type. The last known and most monumental is the *Madonna and Saints* (fig. **15.54**), done in 1505 for the Benedictine convent of San Zaccaria. Here, the Queen of Heaven is raised up on a throne with her Child, while SS. Peter, Catherine, Lucy, and Jerome stand before her. The placement of the female saints may reflect the interests of the nuns for whom the altarpiece was made. (When the painting was fitted with its present frame a decade later, it was cut at the sides, and a piece, since removed, was added at the top.) Compared with Domenico Veneziano's *sacra conversazione* of 60 years earlier (see fig. 15.30), the setting is simpler but even more impressive. Instead of a Gothic canopy, the saints are gathered below a semidome covered with mosaic in the Venetian medieval tradition (see fig. 8.47). It is as if the celestial assembly is taking place in Venice itself. Bellini's figures are comfortably inserted into the apse in a stable pyramid composition. The structure is obviously not a real church, for its sides are open and the scene is flooded with sunlight.

What distinguishes this altar from earlier Florentine examples is not only the spaciousness of the design but its calm, meditative mood. Here, the figures seem isolated and deep in thought. The silence is enhanced by the way the artist has bathed the scene in a delicate haze. There are no harsh contrasts. Light and shadow blend in almost imperceptible gradations, and colors glow with a new richness. Bellini creates a glimpse of a heavenly court peopled by ideal figures in an ideal space.

Rome and the Papal States

Long neglected during the papal exile in Avignon (see page 469), Rome once more became a major artistic center in the late fifteenth century. As the papacy regained power on Italian soil, the popes began to beautify both the Vatican and the surrounding city. They also reasserted their power as temporal lords over Rome and the Papal States. These popes believed that the monuments of Christian Rome should outshine those of the pagan past. To achieve this goal, they called many artists from Florence and the surrounding areas to Rome in the fifteenth century, including Leon Battista Alberti, Gentile da Fabriano, Masaccio, Fra Angelico, Piero della Francesca, and Sandro Botticelli. Like the other courts of Italy, the papacy saw the value of spending money on adorning both ecclesiastical and domestic structures.

THE SISTINE CHAPEL Pope Sixtus IV della Rovere (r. 1471–1484) sponsored several important projects in the last quarter of the century. One of these was the building at the Vatican of a new chapel for the pope, called the Sistine Chapel after Sixtus IV. Around 1481–82, Sixtus commissioned a cycle of frescoes for the walls of the chapel depicting events from the life of Moses (on the left wall) and Christ (on the right wall), representing the Hebrew Bible and New Testament. To execute them, he hired most of the key painters from central Italy, among them Botticelli, Ghirlandaio, and Pietro Vanucci, called Perugino (ca. 1450–1523). Born near Perugia in Umbria (the region southeast of Tuscany), Perugino maintained close ties with Florence. He completed the Sistine Chapel fresco *The Delivery of the Keys* (fig. **15.55**) in 1482.

The gravely symmetrical design conveys the special importance of the subject in this particular setting: The authority of St. Peter as the first pope, as well as of all those who followed him, rests on his having received the keys to the Kingdom of Heaven from Christ himself. The figures have the crackling drapery and idealized features of Verrocchio (see fig. 15.20) in whose workshop Perugino spent some time. Along with the other apostles, a number of bystanders with highly individualized features witness the solemn event.

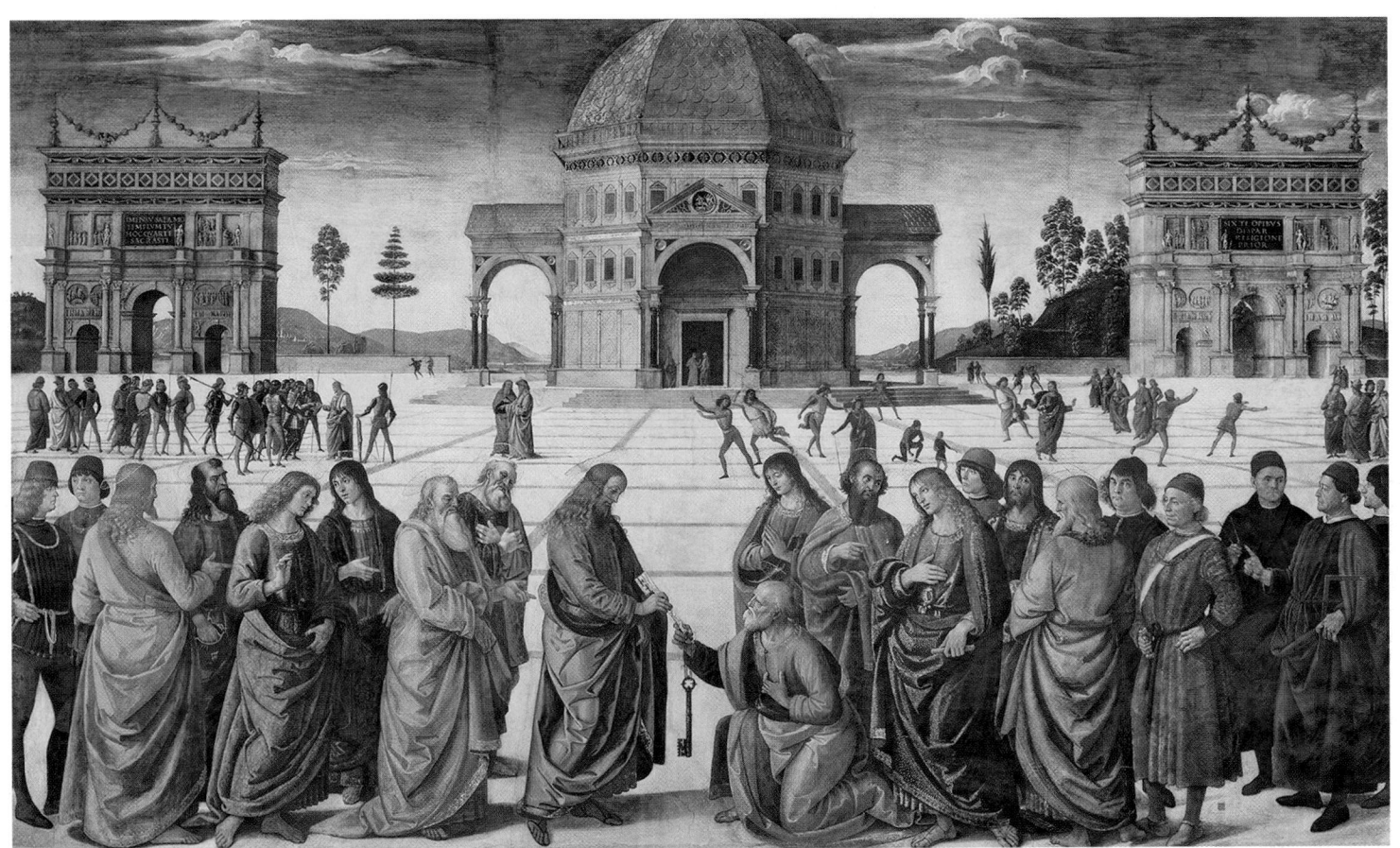

15.55   Pietro Perugino, *The Delivery of the Keys*. 1482. Fresco, 11'5½" × 18'8½" (3.5 × 5.7 m). Sistine Chapel, Vatican Palace, Rome

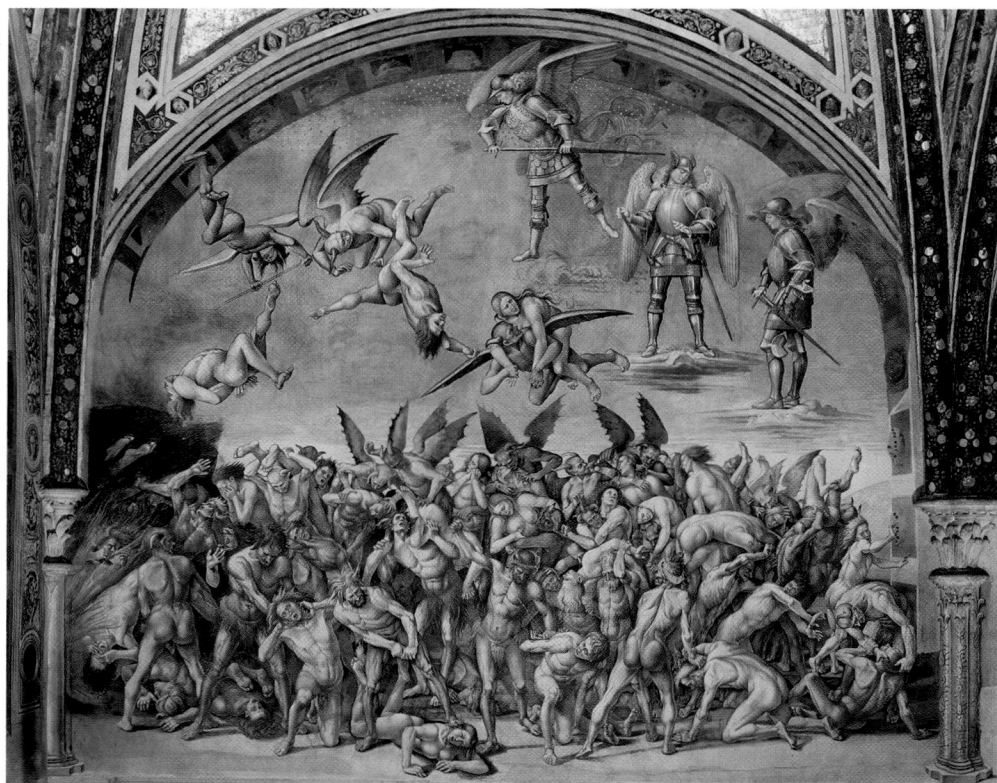

15.56 Luca Signorelli, *The Damned Cast into Hell*. 1499–1500. Fresco, width approx. 23' (7 m). San Brizio Chapel, Orvieto

In the vast expanse of the background, two further narratives appear: To the left, in the middle distance, is the story of the tribute money; to the right, the attempted stoning of Christ. The inscriptions on the two Roman triumphal arches (modeled on the Arch of Constantine; see fig. 7.70) favorably compare Sixtus IV to Solomon, who built the Temple of Jerusalem. These arches flank a domed structure seemingly inspired by the ideal church of Alberti's *Treatise on Architecture*. Also Albertian is the mathematically exact perspective, which lends the view its spatial clarity. The symmetry and clear space of the image express the character of the rule of Sixtus IV, not only in spiritual but also in temporal terms.

SIGNORELLI AND THE CHAPEL OF SAN BRIZIO Sixtus's claims over the Papal States were taken up by his successor, Alexander VI, who pursued temporal power with armies as well as spiritual weapons. Such activities drew the censure of other Christians, both in Italy and elsewhere, fueling the anticlerical feelings of the next century. The city of Orvieto in Umbria had shown great allegiance to the papacy, and in return, the pope adorned the chapel of San Brizio in the city's cathedral with a series of frescoes beginning in 1499. The commission for the project went to Luca Signorelli (1445/50–1523), a Tuscan painter who had studied with Piero della Francesca. The theme chosen for the frescoes is the end of the world, as predicted in the book of Revelation, and further elaborated by St. Augustine, Thomas Aquinas, and Dante, as well as the fifteenth-century Dominican preacher Vincent Ferrer. One of the most memorable of these frescoes is *The Damned Cast into Hell* (fig. **15.56**). Signorelli

envisions the scene as a mass of bodies pressed forcefully downward to be tormented by devils and licked by the flames of Hell, while the archangel Michael oversees the punishment. Inspired by the muscular forms of Pollaiuolo, Signorelli uses the nude body as an expressive instrument: The damned twist and turn, their bodies expressing the torments they face. The chaotic composition and compressed space contrasts strikingly with the rational calm of Perugino's *The Delivery of the Keys* (see fig. 15.55). Signorelli's frightening image of the end of time was painted as the year 1500 approached, a date which many believed would signal the end of days.

The late 1490s were a time of great uncertainty in Italy. The Medici were expelled from Florence; the French invaded in 1494; the plague returned to ravage cities; and the Turks continued their incursions into Europe. (The Turks had crushed the Christian forces at Lepanto, Greece, in 1499, a defeat that would be avenged in a second, more famous battle at the same site in 1571.) Fears that the "end of days" were coming were fanned by the sermons of Savonarola and other preachers.

By this time, however, the artists and patrons of Italy lived in a much different world. Despite Savonarola's charges of "paganism" in late fifteenth-century Italy, the revival of ancient thought and art was there to stay. Under the influence of the ancients and their humanist contemporaries, the artists of Renaissance Italy had transformed the look and design of buildings, the scale and significance of sculpture, and the forms and techniques of painting. They developed new means to render the world in their images, using perspective and naturalism, and created works of art that united ancient forms with contemporary content.

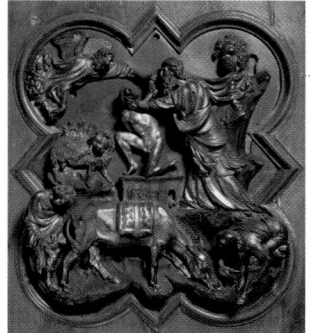

1401 Brunelleschi's and
Ghiberti's competition panels
for northern doors of the
Baptistery of Florence

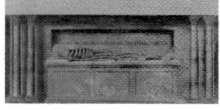

ca. 1425 Masaccio's
Trinity fresco in Santa
Maria Novella

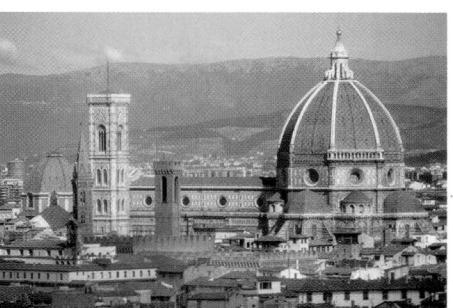

1436 Dedication of the Florentine cathedral
with Brunelleschi's dome

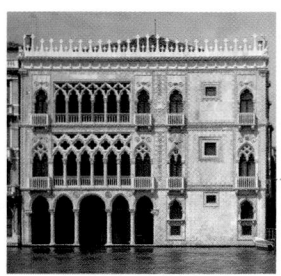

1440 Completion of Ca' d'Oro
in Venice

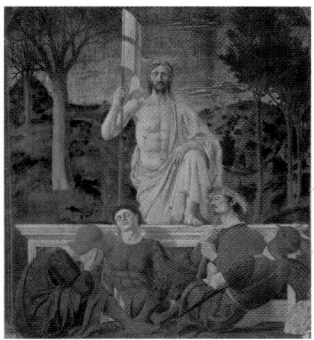

ca. 1463 Piero della Francesca
Resurrection

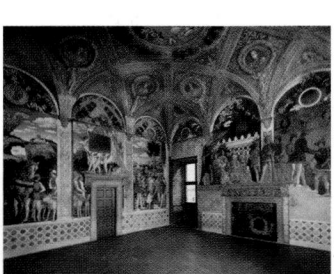

1474 Completion of Mantegna's
Camera Picta in Mantua

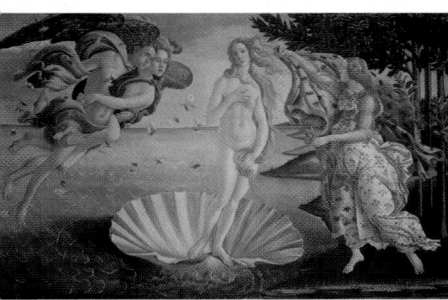

ca. 1485 Botticelli's *Birth of Venus*

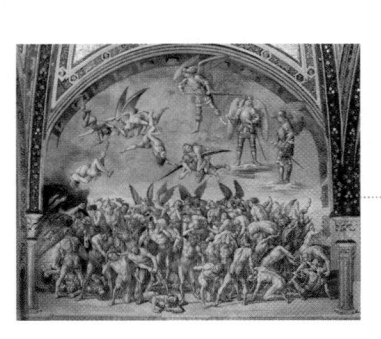

1499 Signorelli's *Damned
Cast into Hell*

The Early Renaissance in Fifteenth-Century Italy

1400

◄ 1402 Giangaleozzo Visconti dies, ending threat
to Florence

1410

1416 *Très Riches Heures of Jean de Berry* by the
Limbourg Brothers

1420

◄ 1420 Papacy returns to Rome from Avignon

1430

1432 Jan van Eyck's *Ghent Altarpiece*

1440

◄ 1439 Council of Florence attempts to reunite
Roman and Byzantine churches

1450

◄ 1452 Leon Battista Alberti completes his Treatise
on Architecture
◄ 1453 Constantinople falls to the Ottoman Turks

1460

◄ 1466 Leonardo da Vinci enters Verrocchio's
workshop

1470

◄ 1469 Lorenzo de' Medici ascends to power in
Florence
1471 *Statuette of Charles the Bold* by Loyet

1480

1482 Hugo van der Goes' *Portinari Altarpiece*
arrives in Florence

◄ 1488 Michelangelo in workshop of Ghirlandaio

1490

◄ 1492 Columbus sails west
◄ 1494 Medici expelled from Florence

1500

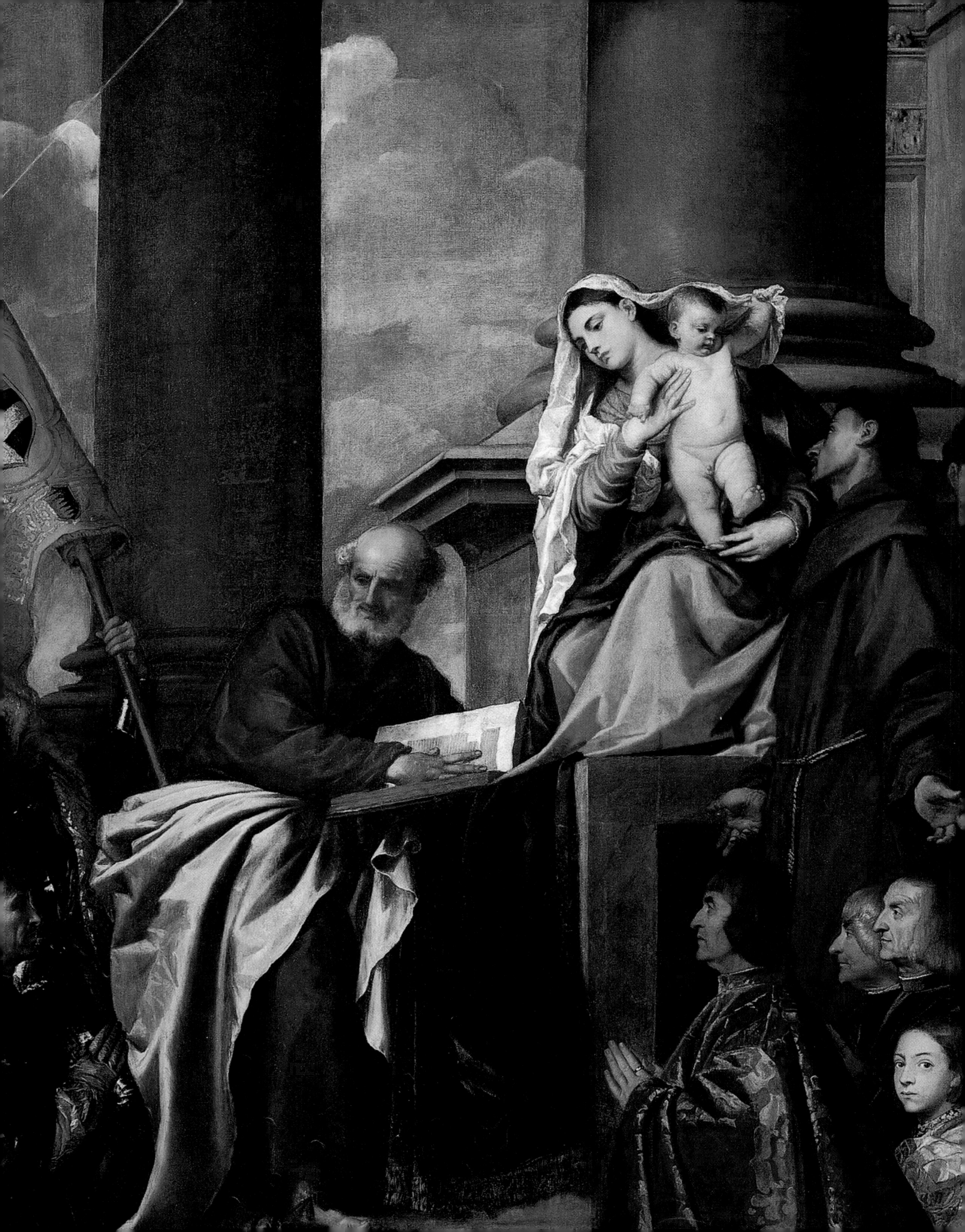

CHAPTER 16

The High Renaissance in Italy, 1495–1520

OOKING BACK AT THE ARTISTS OF THE FIFTEENTH CENTURY, THE artist and art historian Giorgio Vasari wrote in 1550, "Truly great was the advancement conferred on the arts of architecture, painting, and sculpture by those excellent masters." From Vasari's perspective, the earlier generation had provided the groundwork that enabled sixteenth-century artists to

"surpass the age of the ancients." Later artists and critics agreed with Vasari's judgment that the artists who worked in the decades just before and after 1500 attained a perfection in their art worthy of admiration and emulation.

For Vasari, the artists of this generation were paragons of their profession. Following Vasari, artists and art teachers of subsequent centuries have used the works of this 25-year period between 1495 and 1520, known as the High Renaissance, as a benchmark against which to measure their own. Yet the idea of a "High" Renaissance presupposes that it follows something "lower," which seems an odd way to characterize the Italian art of the inventive and dynamic fifteenth century. For this and other reasons, this terminology has been reconsidered in the past few decades. Nonetheless, however we label it, this brief period saw the creation of what are still some of the most revered works of European art. These were created by the most celebrated names in the history of art, as chronicled in Vasari's *The Lives of the Most Eminent Painters, Sculptors and Architects of Italy*. Vasari's book placed the biography of the artist at the center of the study of art, and his *Lives* became a model for art-historical writing. Indeed, the celebrity of artists is a distinctive characteristic of the early sixteenth century.

Leonardo, Bramante, Michelangelo, Raphael, Giorgione, and Titian were all sought after in early sixteenth-century Italy, and the two who lived beyond 1520, Michelangelo and Titian, were internationally celebrated during their lifetimes. This fame was part of a wholesale change in the status of artists that had been occurring gradually during the course of the fifteenth century and which gained strength with these artists. Despite the qualities of their births, or the differences in their styles and personalities, these artists were given the respect due to intellectuals and humanists. Their social status was on a par with members of the great royal courts. In some cases, they were called "genius" or "divine." Some among them were raised to the nobility.

Part of this cult of fame was owed to the patrons who commissioned this small number of gifted and ambitious men to make works of art for them. This period saw the coming together of demanding patrons—rulers, popes, princes—and innovative artists. Patrons competed for works by these artists and in so doing set the artists into competition with each other; this pattern had already begun in early fifteenth-century Florence. The artists tested their skills against each other to inspire them to produce innovations in technique and in expression. The prestige of their patrons contributed to the mystique that developed around the artists, even as the reputations of the artists enriched the prestige of the patrons.

What is truly remarkable about this group of artists is their mastery of technique in their chosen mediums and in their styles of expression. Each of these artists developed a distinctive visual

Detail of figure 16.32, Titian, *Madonna with Members of the Pesaro Family* style that grew out of the ideas of the fifteenth century, but which, through their personal vision, their awareness of intellectual trends, and their hard work, gave rise to works of art that their contemporaries claimed surpassed both nature and the ancients. Their pictorial works share certain features: an approach to the imitation of nature that idealizes forms even as they are rendered to replicate nature; understanding of and reliance on the forms of antiquity; balance and clarity in their compositions; and emotional power.

Also remarkable is that works of such authority and harmony were produced during a quarter-century of crisis and instability. During this period, Italy was threatened by the Turkish expansion from Istanbul, invaded by the French, and torn apart by internal wars. Florence saw the exile of the Medici, the rise of Girolamo Savonarola, the establishment of a republic, and the return of the Medici. Venice saw its territories stripped away by its rivals. Milan was ruled by a despot, then conquered by the French. The papacy began a program of territorial reclamation and expansion that brought it into conflict with its neighbors; the Roman Church also had to contend with the shock of a theological challenge offered by Martin Luther's critique of Catholic dogma and practice. All of Europe was astonished by reports of new lands and new peoples across the ocean, which challenged their notion of the world itself.

THE HIGH RENAISSANCE IN FLORENCE AND MILAN

Florence's reputation as a center for the arts made it a magnet for artists and patrons as the fifteenth century came to a close. The brilliance of the court around Lorenzo de' Medici came to an end with his death in 1492 and the subsequent failure of his son as the leader of the city. Many Florentines heeded the warnings of the preacher Girolamo Savonarola, who encouraged them to reform their faith and their lives; in response, they rejected the worldly culture of the Medici court. Under his influence, "pagan" texts and works of art were burned in bonfires in the Piazza della Signoria; the painter Sandro Botticelli destroyed several of his paintings at these bonfires. Yet the penitential furor that Savonarola urged did not outlive the preacher's execution in 1498. Florence restored its republican form of government, which lasted only until the next generation of Medici politicians took

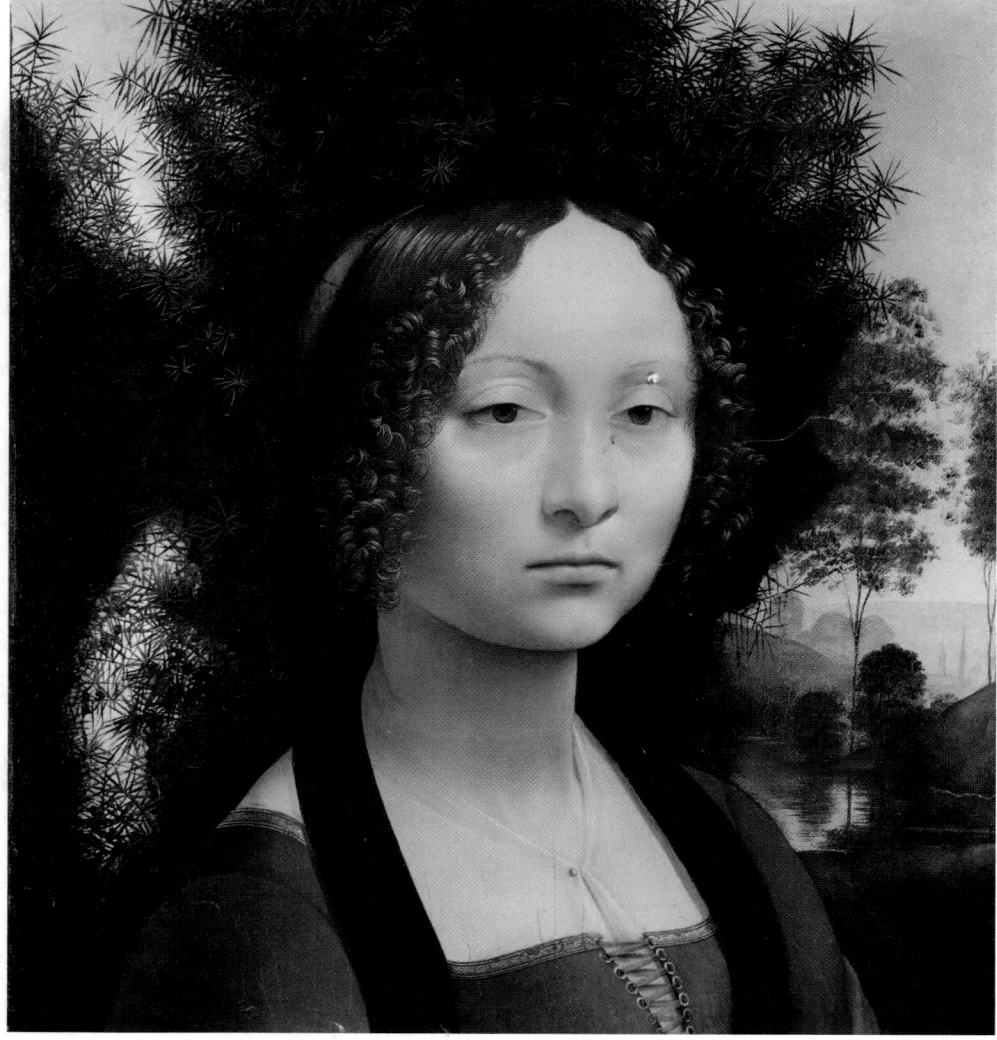

16.1 Leonardo da Vinci, *Portrait of Ginevra de' Benci*, ca. 1474–78 Oil on panel, 16¹³⁄₁₆ × 14⁹⁄₁₆" (42.7 × 37 cm). National Gallery of Art, Washington, D.C. Ailsa Mellon Bruce Fund.1967.6.1.a

back the reins of government in 1512. The political ferment seems to have inspired tremendous artistic innovation, as witnessed in the works of Leonardo da Vinci and Michelangelo Buonarotti.

Leonardo da Vinci in Florence

Leonardo da Vinci was at once a scientist, painter, sculptor, musician, architect, and engineer. Born the son of a notary in the little Tuscan town of Vinci in 1452, Leonardo trained as a painter in Florence in Verrocchio's busy workshop. He left Florence around 1482 to work for Ludovico Sforza, the duke of Milan, primarily as a military engineer and only secondarily as an artist. On Sforza's removal by the French in 1499, Leonardo made his way to Venice, Rome, and Florence, where he executed several commissions between 1503 and 1505. From 1506 through 1516 he worked in Rome and Florence and again in Milan, whose French overlord, Francis I, invited him to retire to a chateau in the Loire Valley. Leonardo died there in 1519.

During his twenties, as a student and then assistant in the workshop, Leonardo collaborated with his teacher Verrocchio before taking commissions on his own. Several works from this period remained unfinished, but one that he completed is the *Portrait of Ginevra de' Benci*, usually dated between 1474 and 1478 (fig. **16.1**). Vasari described this painting in his Life of Leonardo, and most authorities recognize it as an early work by his hand.

The sitter's identity is known, both from what Vasari says and elements of the painting itself. The young woman stands before a thick hedge of juniper, which is a pun on her name (juniper is *ginepro* in Italian); it is also a symbol of chastity. The reverse of this panel depicts another sprig of juniper and a painted scroll that says, "She adorns her beauty with virtue." The portrait was cut down in size at some point in its history, and it likely originally included the sitter's hands, in an arrangement much like that of the marble *Lady with Flowers* by Verrocchio (see fig. 15.42). Among the Florentine elite, Ginevra de' Benci was a celebrated beauty and a poet, though little of her poetry survives. She was married in 1474, and this may be the reason for the commission of the portrait.

Marriage or betrothal occasioned the painting of portraits of women, usually setting them in interiors, wearing expensive jewelry and garments, and often in profile arrangements. Leonardo breaks this mold, by setting the young woman (she was 16 when she married) out of doors in an atmospheric landscape and in a three-quarter view. Flemish portraits (see fig. 14.21) that had made their way to Florence probably inspired these choices. Flemish works definitely informed Leonardo's use of oil as the medium for his paintings. Other artists in late fifteenth-century Florence adopted these same elements, including Domenico Ghirlandaio (see fig. 15.41). What is extraordinary here is what these tools achieve in Leonardo's hands. As in Ghirlandaio's lovely portrait of an old man, we see the three-quarter pose, brilliant color, and a view of a landscape. Both artists use atmospheric perspective to suggest the lack of local color in the distant

landscape, but Leonardo's landscape is much more believable and humid-looking. He exploits the oil technique here to blend his brushstrokes very subtly so as to diminish the appearance of contour lines. His figures seem to exist only as the result of light falling on three-dimensional objects. This method of modeling is called **chiaroscuro**, the Italian word for "light and dark." Starting from a middle tone laid all over the panel, Leonardo renders deep shadows and bright highlights for his forms. Instead of standing side by side in a vacuum, forms share in a new pictorial unity created by the softening of contours in an envelope of atmosphere. These early experiments in the oil medium and the intelligence he gives to his sitter point to directions his art would take in the future.

Leonardo in Milan

Leaving behind several incomplete commissions, Leonardo left Florence for Milan in 1481, where he entered the employ of Ludovico Sforza, duke of Milan. He stayed there until 1499, working as an engineer, court artist, and military designer. As had Brunelleschi before him, Leonardo turned to analysis and research to solve a variety of problems, both artistic and scientific. He believed the world to be intelligible through mathematics, which formed the basis for his investigations. Thus, the artist must know not only the rules of perspective, but all the laws of nature. To him, the eye was the perfect means of gaining such knowledge. The extraordinary range of his inquiries can be seen in the hundreds of drawings and notes that he made and hoped one day to turn into an encyclopedic set of treatises. He was fascinated by all elements of nature: animals, water, anatomy, and the workings of the mind. How original he was as a scientist is still a matter of debate, but he pioneered modern scientific illustration, an essential tool for anatomists and biologists. His drawings, such as the *Embryo in the Womb* (fig. **16.2**), combine his own vivid observations with the analytic clarity of diagrams—or, to paraphrase Leonardo himself, sight and insight. The sheet of studies shown here is a product of his skill at rendering what he saw, and of his dispassionate recording of details both in visual terms and in his notes, written backward in mirror-writing.

Like other fifteenth-century scholars, he read ancient authorities to assist his inquiries. To prepare himself for human dissections, Leonardo read the works of the Greek physician Galen. His interest in architecture and engineering led him to the works of the Roman architect Vitruvius, whose treatise had inspired Alberti earlier in the century. A drawing from the late 1480s (fig. **16.3**) visualizes Vitruvius' notion that the human body may be used to derive the perfect geometrical forms of the circle and the square. This is a powerful image of the value that humanists and architects placed on these geometric elements, as carriers of profound meaning as well as visual forms. Like other humanists, Leonardo was interested in the place of man in the world.

His patrons consulted with Leonardo on several sorts of building and engineering projects. He seems, however, to have been less concerned with actual building than with tackling

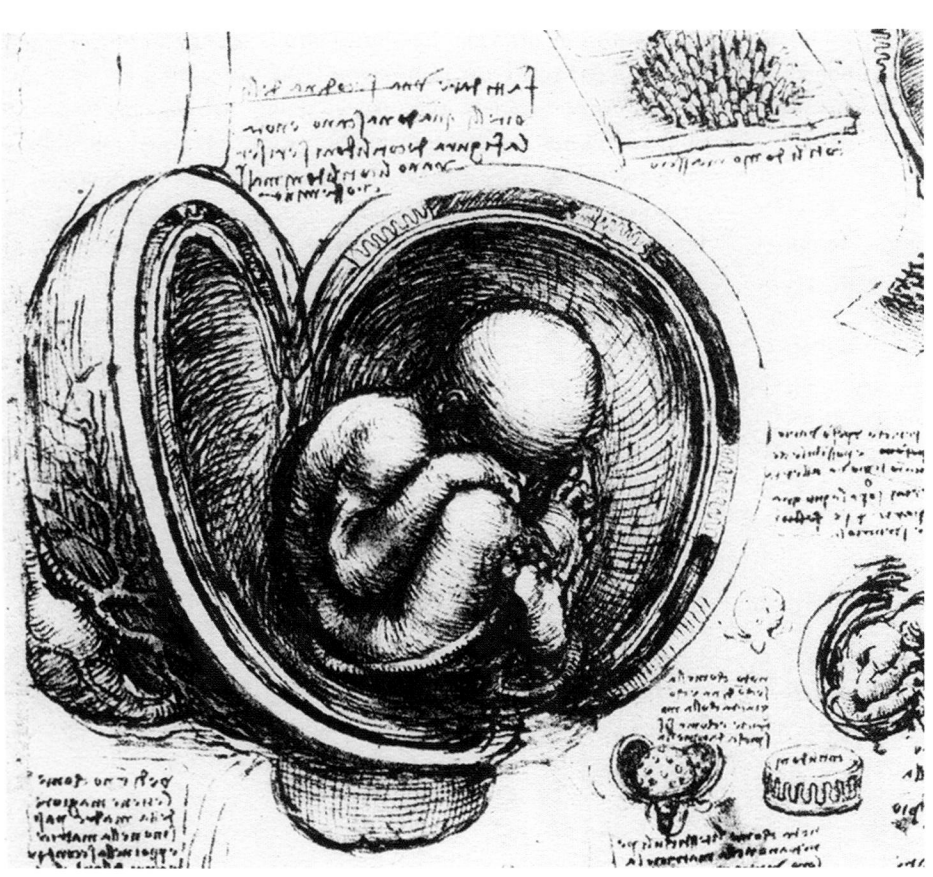

16.2 Leonardo da Vinci, *Embryo in the Womb*. ca. 1510. Pen drawing, 11⅞ × 8⅜" (30.4 × 21.5 cm). Windsor Castle, Royal Library

16.3 (BELOW LEFT) Leonardo da Vinci, *Vitruvian Man*. ca. 1487. Pen and ink, 13½ × 9½" (34.3 × 24.5 cm). Gallerie dell'Accademia, Venice

16.4 (BELOW) Leonardo da Vinci, *Project for a Church* (Ms. B). ca. 1490. Pen drawing, 9⅛ × 6¾" (23 × 17 cm). Bibliothèque de l'Arsenal, Paris

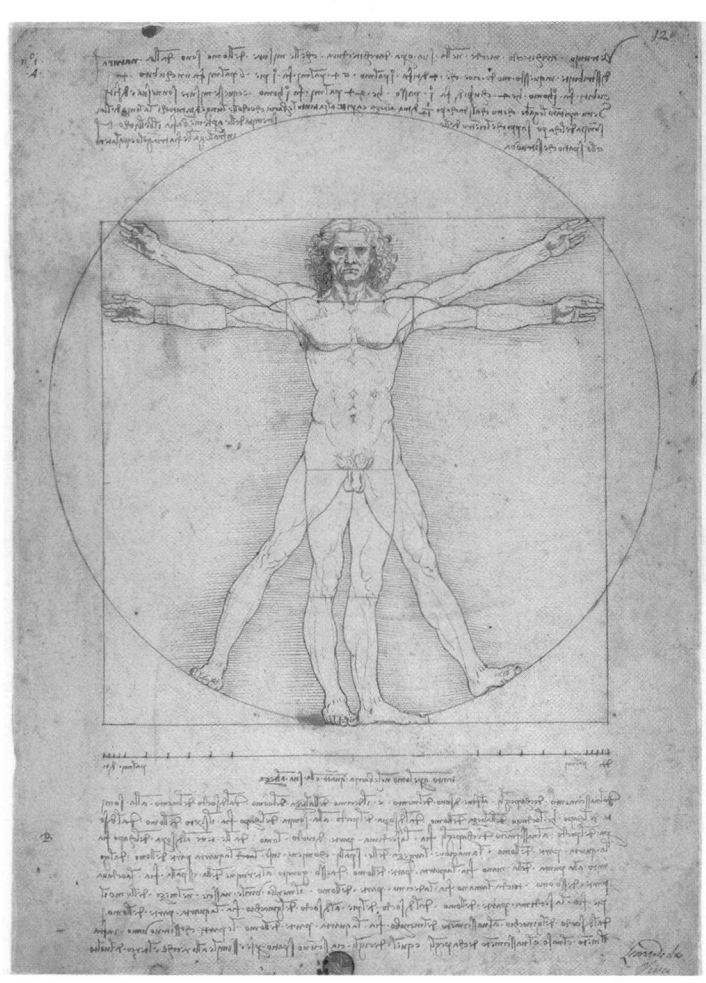

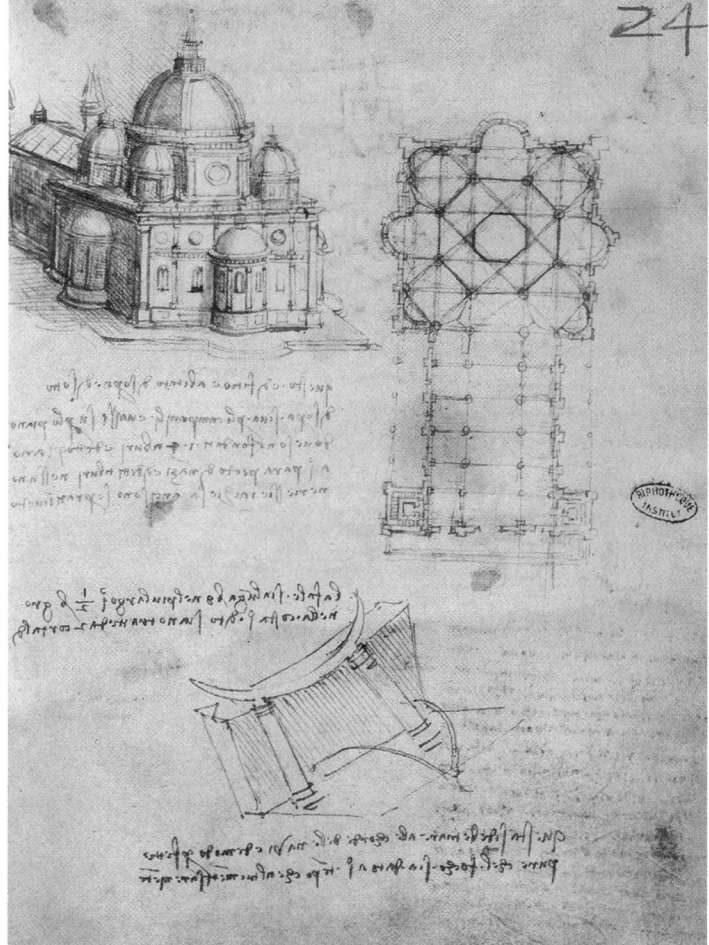

theoretical problems of structure and design. The many architectural projects still to be seen in his notebooks were intended to remain on paper. Yet these sketches, especially those of his Milanese period, reveal Leonardo's probing of the design problems faced by his forebears Brunelleschi and Alberti, as well as by his contemporaries. The domed central-plan churches of the type shown in figure **16.4** hold particular interest to architectural history. In this drawing, Leonardo imagines a union of circle and square, controlled by proportion, and articulated by classical orders. In conception, this design stands halfway between the dome of Florence cathedral and the most ambitious structure of the sixteenth century, the new basilica of St. Peter's in Rome.

Soon after arriving in Milan, Leonardo began painting *The Virgin of the Rocks* (fig. **16.5**) for a confraternity (lay brotherhood)

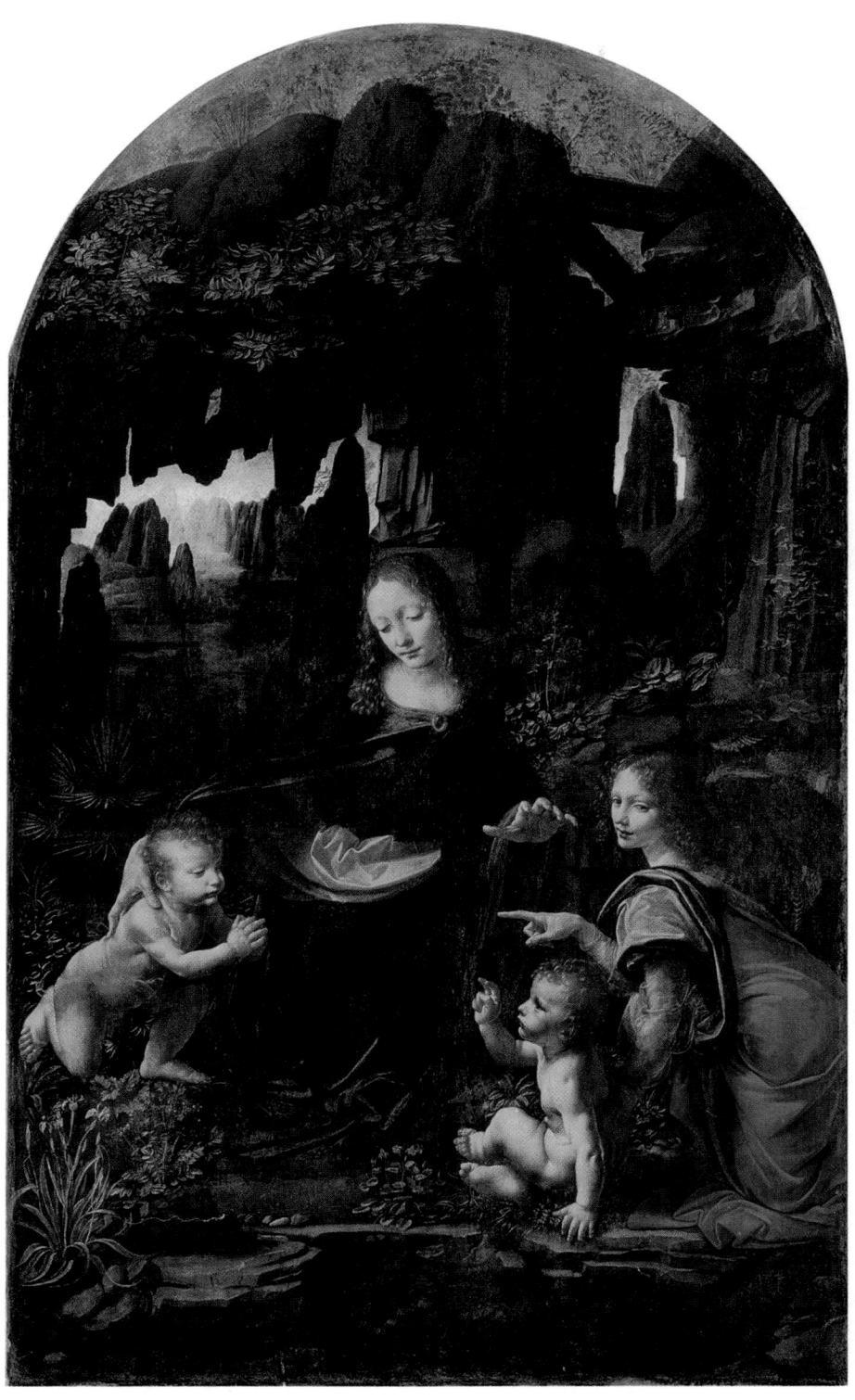

16.5   Leonardo da Vinci, *The Virgin of the Rocks*. ca. 1485. Oil on panel transferred to canvas, 6'6" × 4' (1.9 × 1.2 m). Musée du Louvre, Paris

Leonardo Da Vinci (1452–1519)

From his undated manuscripts

Leonardo, the consummate High Renaissance man, wrote on a variety of topics. The comparison of the arts, or paragone, *was a common subject in High Renaissance scholarship.*

He Who Depreciates Painting Loves Neither Philosophy nor Nature

If you despise painting, which is the sole imitator of all visible works of nature, you certainly will be despising a subtle invention which brings philosophy and subtle speculation to bear on the nature of all forms—sea and land, plants and animals, grasses and flowers—which are enveloped in shade and light. Truly painting is a science, the true-born child of nature. For painting is born of nature; to be more correct we should call it the grandchild of nature, since all visible things were brought forth by nature and these, her children, have given birth to painting. Therefore we may justly speak of it as the grandchild of nature and as related to God.

A Comparison Between Poetry and Painting

The imagination cannot visualize such beauty as is seen by the eye, because the eye receives the actual semblances or images of objects and transmits them through the sense organ to the understanding where they are judged. But the imagination never gets outside the understanding;…it reaches the memory and stops and dies there if the imagined object is not of great beauty; thus poetry is born in the mind or rather in the imagination of the poet who, because he describes the same things as the painter, claims to be the painter's

equal! … The object of the imagination does not come from without but is born in the darkness of the mind's eye. What a difference between forming a mental image of such light in the darkness of the mind's eye and actually perceiving it outside the darkness!

If you, poet, had to represent a murderous battle you would have to describe the air obscured and darkened by fumes from frightful and deadly engines mixed with thick clouds of dust polluting the atmosphere, and the panicky flight of wretches fearful of horrible death. In that case the painter will be your superior, because your pen will be worn out before you can fully describe what the painter can demonstrate forthwith by the aid of his science, and your tongue will be parched with thirst and your body overcome by sleep and hunger before you can describe with words what a painter is able to show you in an instant.

Of the Sculptor and Painter

The sculptor's art requires more physical exertion than the painter's, that is to say, his work is mechanical and entails less mental effort. Compared with painting, there is little scientific research; for the sculptor's work consists in only taking off and the painter's in always putting on. The sculptor is always taking off from the same material, while the painter is always putting on a variety of materials. The sculptor gives all his attention to the lines that circumscribe the material which he is carving, and the painter studies these same lines, but he has besides to study the shade and light, the color and the foreshortening. With respect to these the sculptor is helped throughout by nature, which supplies the shade and light and the perspective. While the painter has to acquire these by dint of his ingenuity and has himself to play the part of nature, the sculptor always finds them ready made.

Source: *The Literary Works of Leonardo da Vinci*, ed. Jean Paul Richter (London: Phaidon Press, 1975)

dedicated to the Immaculate Conception, which maintained a chapel in San Francesco Grande in Milan. (Completion of the project was delayed because it became the subject of a dispute with the patrons.) The subject—the infant St. John adoring Jesus in the presence of the Virgin—enjoyed a certain popularity in Florence in the late fifteenth century. Speculation on the early life of Jesus and his cousin, the Baptist, led to stories about their meeting as children. Franciscan preachers encouraged believers to meditate on the "human" side of Jesus' life and stories like this were the result. Such tales report the young Baptist spending his life as a hermit; because of this, artists represented him wearing a hair shirt. Leonardo imagines this meeting almost as a vision of Christ appearing to the infant Baptist in the wilderness. The young Baptist kneels on the left and looks toward Jesus, who blesses him. The Virgin Mary is the link between the two boys, as she protectively reaches for the Baptist with one hand and holds the other open-palmed over her son. An angel with a billowing red cloak steadies Jesus and points toward the Baptist, while looking out at the viewer.

The scene is mysterious in many ways. The secluded rocky setting, the pool in the foreground, and the carefully rendered plant life suggest symbolic meanings, but scholars are still debating the details. The figures emerge from the semidarkness of the grotto, enveloped in a moist atmosphere that delicately veils their forms. This fine haze, called **sfumato** (smokiness), lends an unusual warmth and intimacy to the scene. The light draws attention to the finely realized bodies of the children and the beautiful heads of the Virgin and the angel. Leonardo arranges the figures into a pyramid of form, with the figures establishing a solid geometric shape in space which has the Virgin's head at the apex. As a result, the composition is stable and balanced, but the gestures lead the eye back and forth to suggest the relationships among the figures. The selective light, quiet mood, and tender gestures create a remote, dreamlike quality, and make the picture seem a poetic vision rather than an image of reality.

Leonardo had much to say about the relationship between poetry and painting. He thought sight was the superior sense and that painters were better equipped to represent what the eye could

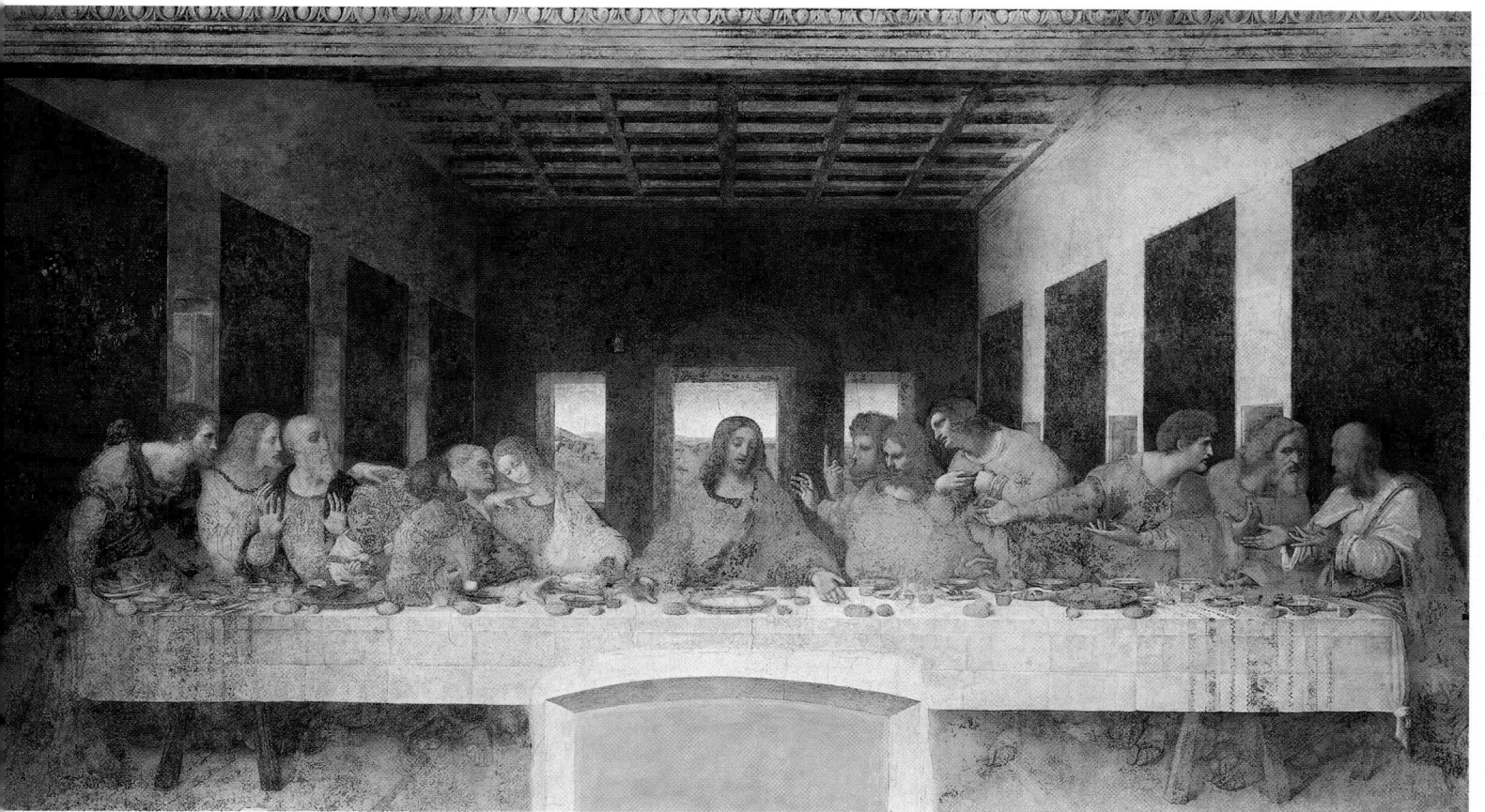

16.6   Leonardo da Vinci, *The Last Supper*. ca. 1495–98. Tempera wall mural, 15'2" × 28'10" (4.6 × 8.8 m). Santa Maria delle Grazie, Milan

see or imagine. His notebooks include many comments on the *paragone*, or comparison, between painting and poetry. This competition between art forms was rooted in the Roman poet Horace's statement that poetry is like painting ("*ut pictura poesis*"), which artists of the High Renaissance reinterpreted to mean that painting and poetry seek similar effects. (See *Primary Source*, page 562.) Leonardo's musings on the rivalry between poetry and painting extended to that between painting and sculpture. He argued that painting was superior to sculpture primarily because it provided the possibility for creating the sort of illusionary spaces and textures seen in *The Virgin of the Rocks*. Additionally, the painter could dress elegantly for his work, and not subject himself to the clouds of dust or the brute force needed to make sculpture. Not all of his contemporaries agreed. Michelangelo, for one, defended the art of sculpture as superior to painting, precisely because it created fully three-dimensional forms while painting merely created illusions.

Leonardo's skill at creating such illusions and his experimental approach to achieving them is apparent in *The Last Supper* (fig. 16.6), executed between 1495 and 1498. Leonardo's patron, Duke Ludovico, commissioned him to decorate the refectory (dining hall) of the Dominican monastery of Santa Maria delle Grazie, which housed the duke's family chapel. The resulting painting became instantly famous and was copied numerous times by other artists, but a modern viewer can only imagine its original

splendor, despite the painting's recent restoration. Dissatisfied with the limitations of the traditional fresco technique, Leonardo experimented with an oil-tempera medium on dry plaster that did not adhere well to the wall in the humidity of Milan. What is more, the quality of the painting has been diminished by renovations and damage done to the wall. Yet what remains is more than adequate to account for its tremendous impact.

The theme of the Last Supper was conventional for monastic refectories, as a comparison with Castagno's *The Last Supper* (see fig. 15.29), painted half a century before, reveals. Monks or nuns dined in silence before images of the apostles and Christ at table. Like Castagno, Leonardo creates a spatial setting that seems like an annex to the real interior of the room, though deeper and more atmospheric than the earlier fresco. The central vanishing point of the perspective system is located behind the head of Jesus in the exact middle of the fresco; it thus becomes charged with symbolic significance. Equally symbolic is the opening in the wall behind Jesus: It acts as the architectural equivalent of a halo. Rather than Castagno's explosion of marble veining or an artificial disk of gold, Leonardo lets natural light enframe Jesus. All elements of the picture—light, composition, colors, setting—focus the attention on Jesus.

He has presumably just spoken the fateful words, "One of you shall betray me." The disciples ask, "Lord, is it I?" The apostles who flank Jesus do not merely react to these words. Rather,

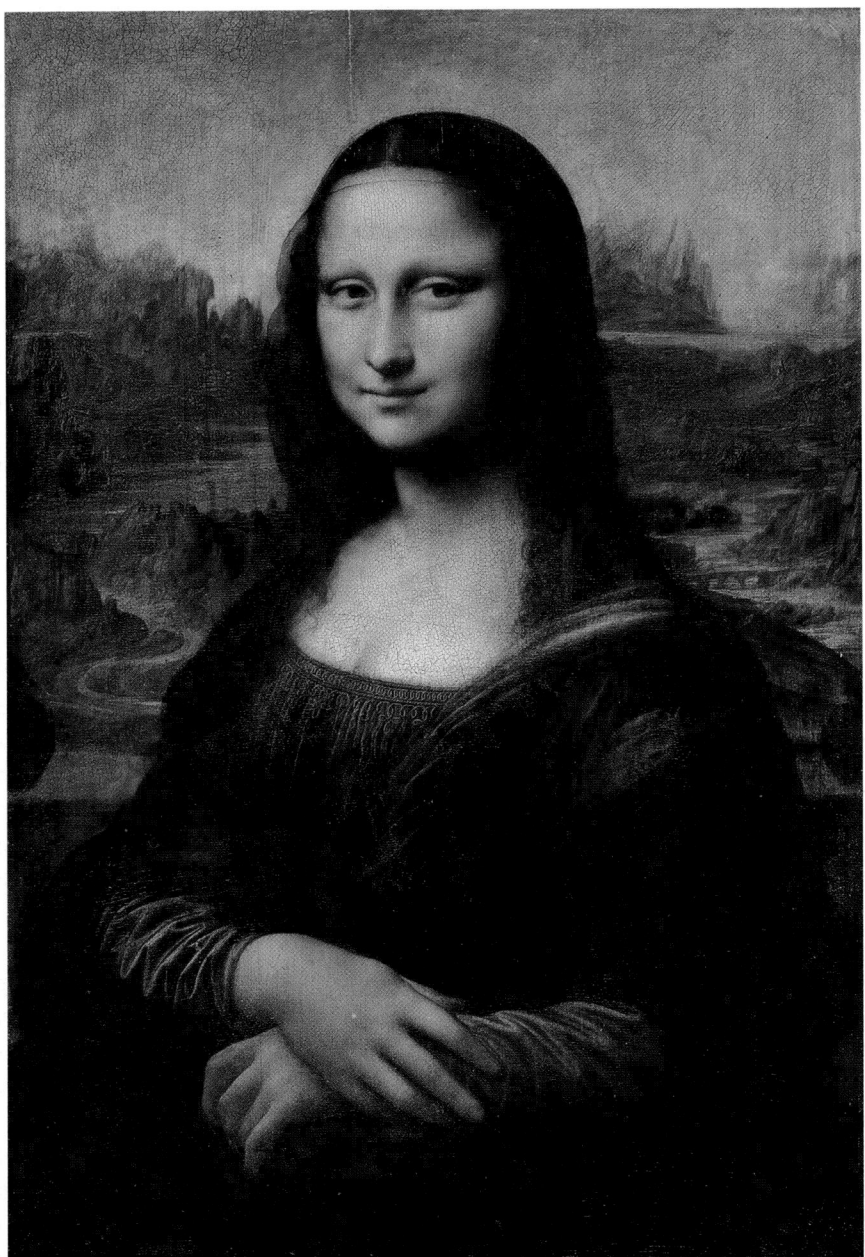

16.7 Leonardo da Vinci, *Mona Lisa*. ca. 1503–05. Oil on panel, 30¼ × 21" (77 × 53.5 cm). Musée du Louvre, Paris

each reveals his own personality, his own relationship to Jesus. In the group to his right, Peter impulsively grabs a knife; next to him John seems lost in thought; and Judas (the figure leaning on the table in the group to Jesus' right) recoils from Jesus into shadow. Leonardo has carefully calculated each pose and expression so that the drama unfolds across the picture plane. The figures exemplify what the artist wrote in one of his notebooks—that the highest and most difficult aim of painting is to depict "the intention of man's soul" through gestures and movements of the limbs.

But to view this scene as just one moment in a psychological drama does not do justice to Leonardo's aims, which went well beyond a literal rendering of the biblical narrative. He clearly wanted to condense his subject, both physically (by the compact, monumental grouping of the figures) and spiritually (by presenting many levels of meaning at one time). Thus, Jesus' gesture is one both of submission to the divine will and of offering. His calm presence at the center of the table suggests that, in addition to the drama of the announcement, Jesus also institutes the Eucharist, in which bread and wine become his body and blood. Such multiple meanings would serve as spiritual food for the Dominican friars who lived in the presence of this image.

Leonardo Back in Florence and Elsewhere

In 1499, the duchy of Milan fell to the French, so Leonardo returned to Florence after brief trips to Mantua and Venice. He must have found the political climate very different from what he remembered. Florentines had become unhappy with the rule of Lorenzo de' Medici's son, Piero, and had expelled the Medici;

until their return in 1512, the city was a republic again. For a while, Leonardo seems to have been active mainly as an engineer and surveyor. Then, in 1503, the city commissioned him to do a mural for the council chamber of the Palazzo della Signoria, which he abandoned in 1506 and returned to Milan.

THE *MONA LISA* While working on the mural, Leonardo also painted the portrait of a woman, whom Vasari identified as Lisa Gherardini, wife of Francesco del Giocondo, the so-called *Mona Lisa* (fig. **16.7**). (Because of her husband's name, the French call her "La Gioconda.") Much recent research has tended to confirm this identity. If it is indeed the Lady Lisa (Mona is a contraction of Madonna), who married in 1495 at age 16, she was about 25 when the portrait was made. For reasons that are now unclear, Leonardo kept this painting, possibly continuing to work on it. After his death in France, the portrait entered the collection of King Francis I. From the royal collection, it became a key possession of the Musée du Louvre. To some extent its fame is a product of its ownership.

But the *Mona Lisa* is also famous for its formal qualities. We may be able to see them more clearly in comparison to his earlier portrait of Ginevra de' Benci (see fig. 16.1). Both paintings break with the fifteenth-century tradition of depicting young women in profile. Leonardo depicts both of these young women in three-quarter poses against landscape backgrounds. He also depicts the women in simple garments, without the jewels and brocades that adorned most brides, to concentrate on their features. As he had originally done with Ginevra, Leonardo represents Mona Lisa at half-length, so that her hands are included in the image. The whole composition thus forms a stable pyramid. Compared to Ginevra, however, Mona Lisa seems a creature of a different order. Leonardo renders the subtle movement of light washing over her figure to draw attention to her features. Having mastered the oil technique, he builds the forms from layers of glazes so thin that the panel appears to glow with a gentle light from within, despite the dirty varnish that now obscures the painting. Mona Lisa sits before an evocative landscape, whose mountainous elements emerge from a cool sfumato backdrop, while the rivers and bridges winding through it echo the highlights on her drapery; the landscape envelops her, where for Ginevra it seems a mere backdrop. The beautifully observed details of Mona Lisa's high brow and crossed hands give her as much character as her famous smile. Vasari helped to spread the fame of the painting, for he claimed the portrait exemplified "how faithfully art can imitate nature." (See www.myartslab.com.) This skill, for Vasari, was the root of Leonardo's genius. For later generations, the *Mona Lisa* has served as the consummate example of his art.

ROME RESURGENT

By the end of the fifteenth century, the papacy had firmly reestablished itself in Rome. Along with their spiritual control of the Church, the popes reasserted political and military control over the Papal States in the area around Rome. Rebuilding the city was an expression of the papal intentions to rule there, as Sixtus IV had demonstrated with his building of the Sistine Chapel, among other projects. Alexander VI, who became pope in 1492, used his papacy to enlarge papal domains through the marriages of his daughter, Lucrezia Borgia, and through the military exploits undertaken by his son Cesare Borgia. He also made the papal court the peer of any princely court in Italy. On Alexander's death, the new pope Julius II (r. 1503–1513) made his aim the physical renewal of Rome, hoping that it would rival the glory of the ancient city. He invested vast sums in large-scale projects involving architecture, sculpture, and painting, and he called on numerous artists to work for him. The ancient city's Roman and medieval monuments inspired a variety of projects in the Renaissance city (map **16.1**). Under Julius, Rome became the crucible of the High Renaissance.

Bramante in Rome

The most important architect in Julius's Rome was Donato Bramante (1444–1514). A native of Urbino, he began his career as a fresco painter. Influenced by Piero della Francesca and Andrea Mantegna, Bramante became skilled at rendering architectural settings in correct perspective. Leonardo may also have had some influence on Bramante, as the two were colleagues at the court of Milan. Bramante's architectural works take Brunelleschi and Alberti as their main points of departure.

After Milan fell to the French in 1499, Bramante went to Rome, where he experienced Roman buildings first hand. There, the Spanish-born pope Alexander VI had begun the process of enlarging and enhancing papal holdings, in which endeavor he had the support of the powerful Spanish monarchs, Ferdinand and Isabella. The Spanish rulers commissioned Bramante around 1500 to build a structure to mark the supposed site of St. Peter's crucifixion, attached to the church of San Pietro in Montorio (fig. **16.8**). Because of its powerful evocation of Roman circular temples, it was called the Tempietto, or "little temple." This structure serves as a **martyrium**, a special chapel associated with a martyr.

In early Christian Rome, such structures were often centralized in plan. Bramante, however, seems as much inspired by the precepts of Alberti and the experiments of Leonardo as he is by the experience of Rome itself. A contemporary, Sebastiano Serlio, recorded Bramante's design in an architectural treatise that was published in the 1540s. According to this plan, Bramante intended to surround the Tempietto by a circular, colonnaded courtyard that would entirely respond to the structure. This conception was as bold and novel as the design of the chapel itself (fig. **16.9**), for not only does the chapel's colonnade dictate the courtyard's colonnade, the walls of the courtyard open into concave niches that echo the façade of the chapel.

This façade, with its three-step platform and use of the plain Tuscan Doric order, recalls Roman temple architecture more directly than does any fifteenth-century building (see fig. 7.23). Moreover, the entire design is based on the **module** of the

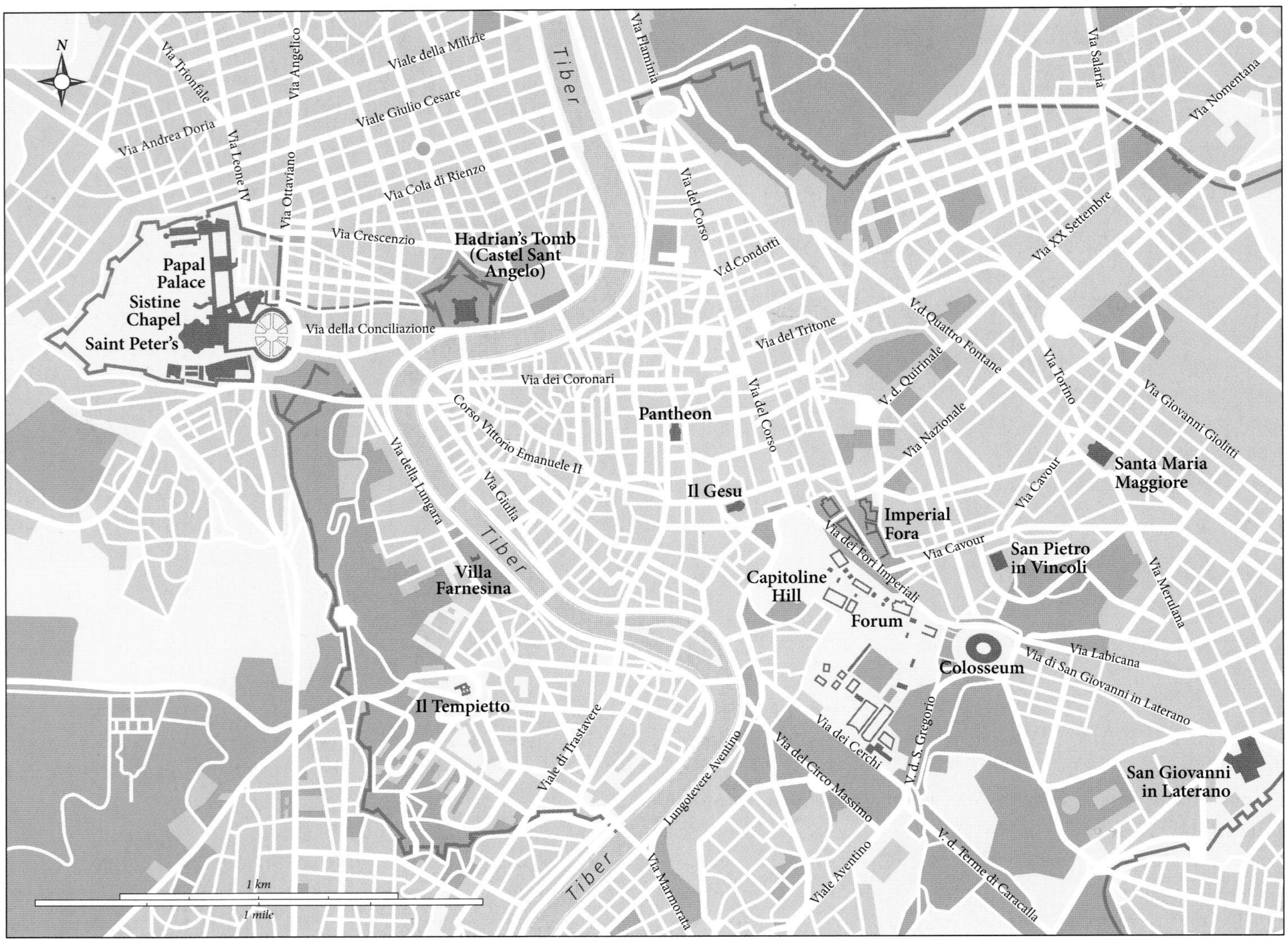

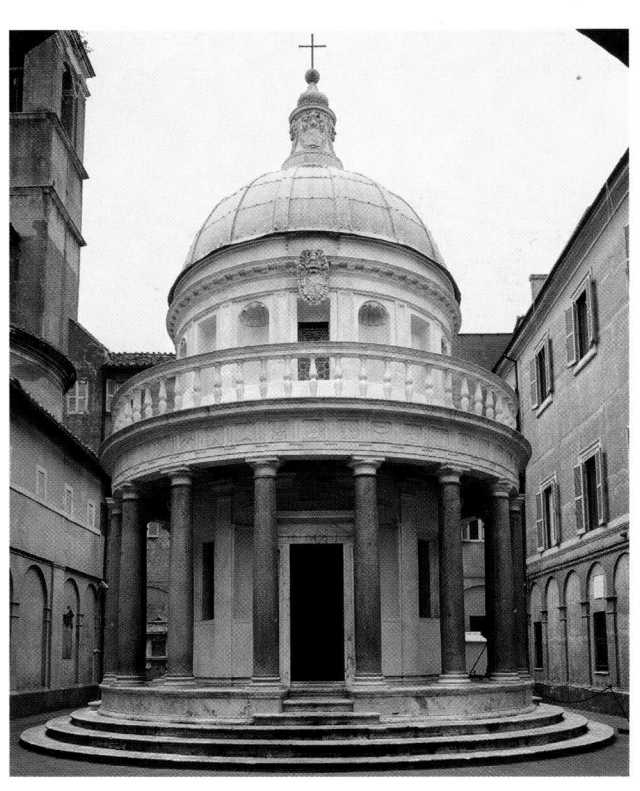

Map 16.1   Renaissance and earlier monuments in Rome

columns: For example, the distance between the columns is four times their diameter, and they are placed two diameters from the wall. This insistent logic follows the rules of temple design established by Vitruvius. Equally striking is Bramante's use of the "sculptured wall" in the Tempietto itself and the courtyard, as shown in the plan. Deeply recessed niches in the upper story are counterbalanced by the convex shape of the dome and by strongly projecting moldings and **cornices**. As a result, the Tempietto has a monumentality that belies its modest size. The building, including the sculptural decoration in the metopes and frieze around the base, is a brilliant example of papal propaganda. The Tempietto proclaims Christ and the popes (considered the successors of St. Peter) as the direct heirs of Rome. Bramante used the language of ancient Rome to express the claims of the modern pope. The publication of the design by Serlio helped spread the specific elements

16.8   Donato Bramante. Tempietto, San Pietro in Montorio, Rome. 1502–11

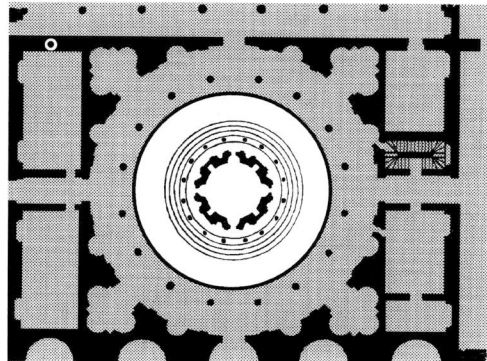

16.9 Plan of Bramante's Tempietto (after Serlio, in *Regole generali di architettura*)

and the underlying design concepts of this building, and it became a very influential structure.

Such work brought Bramante to the notice of Alexander VI's successor, Julius II. The nephew of Sixtus IV, Giuliano delle Rovere, as Pope Julius II, had great ambitions for the Church and for Rome. He used art and artists as tools in his goal of restoring papal authority over Christendom. This is nowhere more evident than in Julius's decision to replace the Constantinian basilica of St. Peter's (see fig. 8.8), which was in poor condition, with a church so magnificent that it would overshadow all the monuments of imperial Rome. He gave the commission to Bramante and laid the cornerstone for the project in 1506. Because of later changes, we know Bramante's original design mostly from a plan (fig. **16.10**) and from the medal commemorating the start of the building campaign (fig. **16.11**), which shows the exterior in general terms. These reveal the innovative approach that Bramante took in this project, which was grand both in scale and in conception.

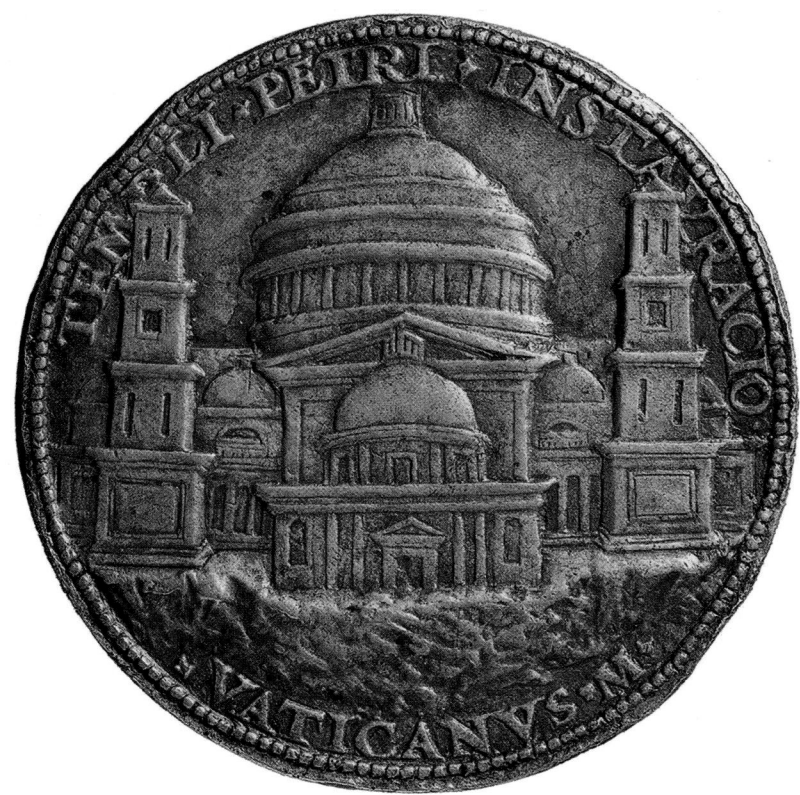

16.11 Cristoforo Foppa Caradosso. Bronze medal showing Bramante's design for St. Peter's. 1506. The British Museum, London

The plan and commemorative medal indicate that Bramante envisioned a huge round dome, similar to the Pantheon's, to crown the crossing of the barrel-vaulted arms of a Greek cross, that is, a cross with four arms the same length. Four lesser domes, each surmounting a chapel that echoes the main space, and tall corner towers were planned around the central dome. As Alberti prescribed and Leonardo proposed, Bramante's plan is based on the circle and the square. Not only had the ancients revered these perfect forms, Bramante's contemporaries saw them as appropriate symbols for the Christian empire that Julius planned. Bramante envisioned four identical façades dominated by classical forms: domes, half-domes, colonnades, and pediments. The principal dome would have been encircled by a colonnade as well. The whole façade would have been a unified, symmetrical sculptural form, united by proportion and the interplay of geometric elements.

But this logical interlocking of forms would have been accompanied by the structure's huge scale, for Julius's church was intended to be more than 500 feet long. Such a monumental undertaking required vast sums of money, and the construction of St. Peter's progressed so slowly that in 1514, when Bramante died, only the four crossing piers had been built. For the next three decades the project was carried on by other architects, who altered his design in a number of ways. A new and decisive phase in the history of St. Peter's began in 1546, when Michelangelo

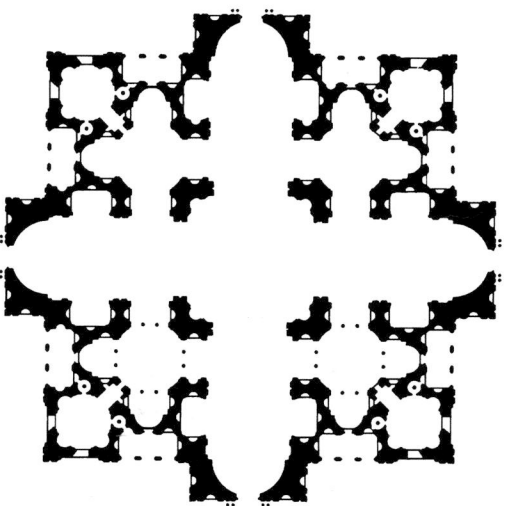

16.10 Donato Bramante. Original plan for St. Peter's, Rome. 1506 (after Geymuller)

Michelangelo Interprets the Vatican Pietà

The Pietà *for Cardinal Jean de Villiers de la Groslaye, now in St. Peter's, helped to establish Michelangelo's reputation as a sculptor. In his* Life of Michelangelo Buonarotti, *first published in 1553, Michelangelo's friend and biographer, Ascanio Condivi, quotes the sculptor explaining features of the work.*

A little later on, the Cardinal of Saint-Denis … commissioned him to make from one piece of marble that marvelous statue of Our Lady … [she] is positioned seated on the rock, in which the cross was sunk, with her dead Son on her lap, and of such and so rare a beauty, that no one sees her without being inwardly moved to pity. An image truly worthy of the humanity which belongs properly to the Son of God and to such a mother; although there are some who make the reproach that the mother is shown as too young, in relation to her Son. But when I was discussing this with Michelangelo one day, he replied to me: "Don't you know that chaste women remain far fresher than those who are not chaste? So much more the Virgin, in whom never has the least lascivious desire ever arisen that might alter her body. Moreover, let me add this, that besides such freshness and flower of youth being maintained in her in this natural way it may be believed to have been assisted by divine power to prove to the world the virginity and perpetual purity of the mother. This was not necessary in the Son; rather completely the opposite; because to show that, as He did, the Son of God took a truly human body, and was subjected to all that an ordinary man endures, except sin, there was no need for the divine to hold back the human, but to leave it to its order and course, so that the time of life He showed was exactly what it was. Consequently you are not to wonder if for these reasons I have made the most Holy Virgin, mother of God, far younger in comparison with her Son than her age would ordinarily require, and that I left the Son at his own age."

This reflection would be worthy of any theologian. … When he made this work, Michelangelo would have been 24 or 25 years old. He acquired great fame and reputation from this effort, and indeed it was already everyone's opinion that he had not only surpassed all his contemporaries, and those who came before him, but that he also contended with the ancients.

Source: *Michelangelo, Life, Letters and Poetry*, ed. and tr. George Bull (Oxford: Oxford University Press, 1987)

took charge. It was then altered again in the seventeenth century. Nevertheless, Bramante's original plan for St. Peter's was to put Roman imperial and Early Christian forms at the service of a Renaissance pope's spiritual and temporal ambitions.

Michelangelo in Rome and Florence

Julius's ambitions were also the spur for one of the crucial figures in the history of art, Michelangelo di Lodovico Buonarroti Simoni (1475–1564). Acclaimed by his contemporaries, admired by his successors, and hailed as "divine" by Vasari, Michelangelo is one of the most influential and imitated artists in history. Gifted, driven, he has become the archetype of the genius, whose intellect and talents enabled him to work in many mediums; he was a sculptor, architect, painter, and poet. Pope Julius encouraged him in his ambition to outdo the artists of antiquity, by giving him opportunities to produce some of his most inspired and famous works.

Unlike Leonardo, for whom painting was the noblest of the arts because it embraced every visible aspect of the world, Michelangelo was a sculptor to the core. More specifically, he was a carver of marble statues. The limitations of sculpture, which Leonardo condemned as mechanical, unimaginative, and dirty, were virtues in Michelangelo's eyes. Only the "liberation" of real, three-dimensional bodies from recalcitrant matter could satisfy Michelangelo. Painting, for him, should imitate the roundness of sculptured forms. Architecture, too, ought to share the organic qualities of the human figure.

Michelangelo's belief in the human image as the supreme vehicle of artistic expression gave him a sense of kinship with ancient sculptors, more so than with other Renaissance practitioners. Among Italian masters, he nonetheless admired Giotto, Masaccio, and Donatello more than his contemporaries. Although his family came from the nobility, and therefore initially opposed his desire to become an artist, Michelangelo was apprenticed to Ghirlandaio, from whom he learned painting techniques. He came to the attention of Lorenzo de' Medici, who invited him to study the antique statues in the garden of one of the Medici houses. The overseer of this collection, Bertoldo di Giovanni (ca. 1420–1491), a pupil of Donatello, may have taught Michelangelo the rudiments of sculpture. From the beginning, however, Michelangelo was a carver rather than a modeler. He rarely worked in clay, except for sketches; he preferred harder materials, especially marble, which he shaped with his chisel.

The young artist's mind was decisively shaped by the cultural climate of Florence during the 1480s and 1490s, even though the troubled times led him to flee the city for Rome in 1496. Lorenzo de' Medici's death in 1492 put an end to the intellectual atmosphere that he had fostered. The subsequent expulsion of the Medici, and the rise to power of the fiery preacher Girolamo Savonarola, brought calls for a spiritual awakening and a rejection of "paganism" and materialism. Both the Neo-Platonism of Marsilio Ficino and the religious reforms of Savonarola affected Michelangelo profoundly. Just as he conceived his statues as human bodies released from their marble prisons, so he saw the body as the earthly prison of the soul—noble perhaps, but a prison nonetheless. This dualism of body and spirit endows his figures with extraordinary pathos. Although outwardly calm, they seem stirred by an overwhelming psychic energy that finds no release in physical action.

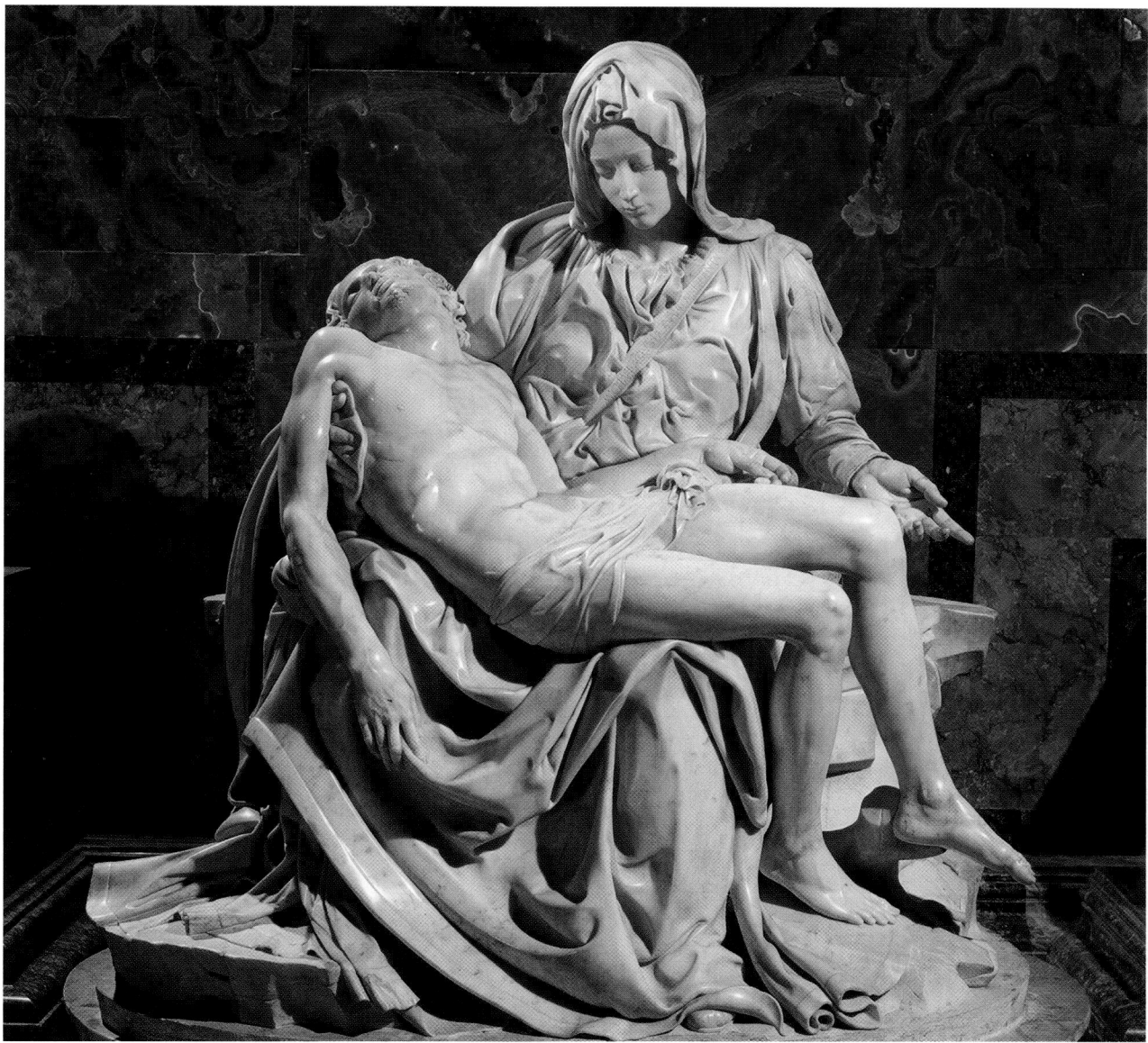

16.12   Michelangelo, *Pietà*. ca. 1498. Marble, height 68½" (173.9 cm). St. Peter's, Rome

PIETÀ   Having left Florence after the exile of the Medici, Michelangelo worked in Bologna and then Rome, where a French cardinal commissioned him in 1498 to carve a Pietà for his tomb chapel close to St. Peter's (fig. **16.12**). In the contract, Michelangelo promised to carve "the most beautiful work of marble in Rome." The subject of the Pietà was more familiar in northern Europe than in Italy, appearing in such works as the *Roettgen Pietà* (see fig. 12.60), although the theme of the Virgin's lamentation for her dead son had appeared in works such as Giotto's Arena Chapel frescoes (see fig. 13.20). Michelangelo, however, imagines the farewell between mother and son as a calm and transcendent moment rather than a tortured or hopeless one. The composition is stable; the over-large figure of the Virgin with her deeply carved robe easily supports the weight of her dead son.

The Virgin seems far too young to be holding her grown son, so in addition to the Pietà, the image echoes the theme of the Madonna and Child. Michelangelo himself intended her youth to express her perpetual virginity, according to his friend and biographer, Ascanio Condivi. (See *Primary Source*, page 568.) Michelangelo doesn't merely tell a story, he offers viewers the opportunity to contemplate the central mystery of Christian faith—Christ as God in human form who sacrificed himself to redeem Original Sin—with the same serenity as Mary herself. When the *Pietà* was first displayed in 1499, some controversy surrounded its authorship; Michelangelo put it to rest by carving his name on the Virgin's sash. The inscription proudly asserts his authorship and his origin in Florence. At 24, his fame was assured.

DAVID   When this project was completed, Michelangelo returned to Florence, which had reestablished a republican form of government. There, in 1501, directors of the works for Florence cathedral commissioned him to execute a figure to be installed on one of the buttresses of the façade. The 18-foot-high block of marble for this project had been partly carved by an earlier sculptor, but Michelangelo accepted the challenge to create something memorable from it. The result was the gigantic figure of the *David* (fig. **16.13**). When it was completed in 1504, a committee of civic leaders and artists decided instead to put it in front of the Palazzo della Signoria, the seat of the Florentine government. They placed a circlet of gilt bronze leaves around the statue's hips and put a gilt bronze wreath on David's head. The city of Florence claimed the figure as an emblem of its own republican virtues.

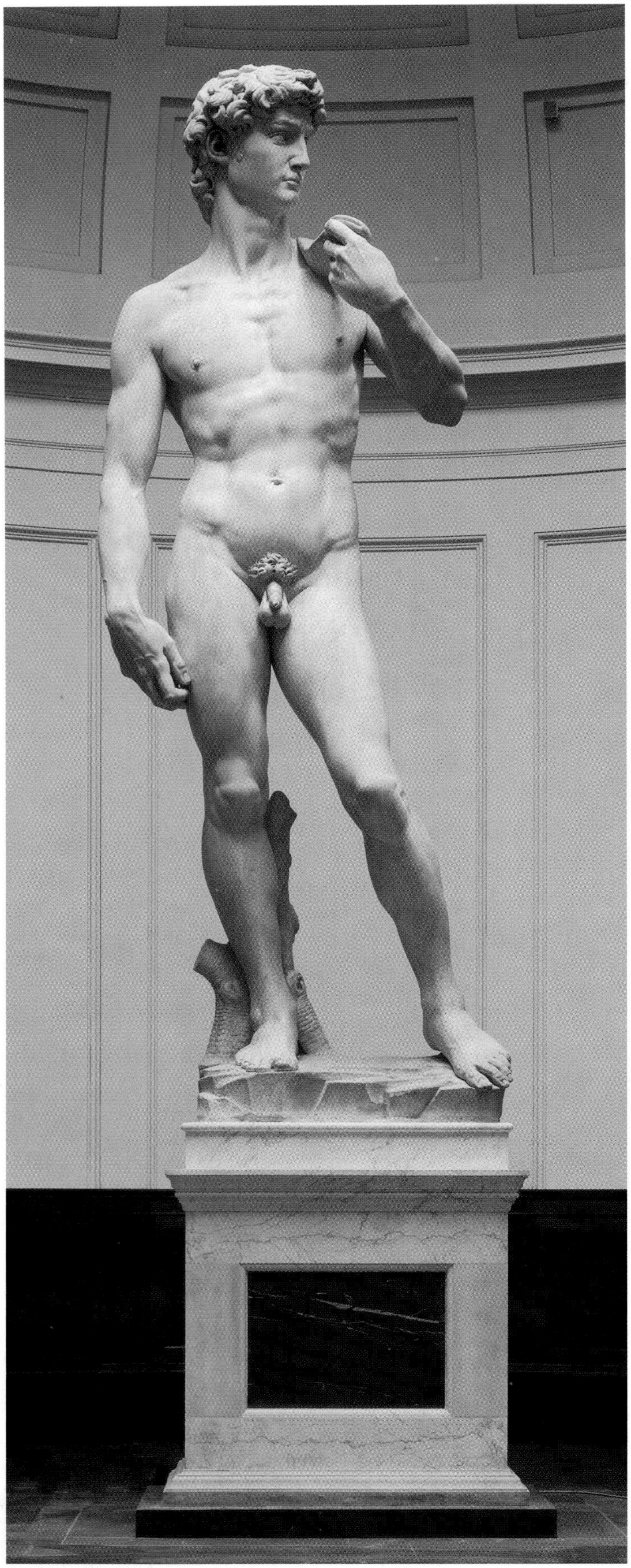

Michelangelo treated the biblical figure not as a victorious hero, but as the ever-vigilant guardian of the city. Unlike Donatello in his bronze *David* for the Medici (see fig. 15.33), Michelangelo omits the head of Goliath; instead David nervously fingers a slingshot, as his eyes focus on an opponent in the distance. Although both Donatello and Michelangelo rendered David as a nude, the style of the later sculpture proclaims an ideal very different from the wiry slenderness of Donatello's youth. Michelangelo had just spent several years in Rome, where he had been deeply impressed with the emotion-charged, muscular bodies of Hellenistic sculpture, which were being avidly collected there. (See *The Art Historian's Lens*, page 157.) Their heroic scale, their superhuman beauty and power, and the swelling volume of

16.13 Michelangelo, *David*. 1501–04. Marble, height 17'⅛" (5.22 m). Galleria dell'Accademia, Florence

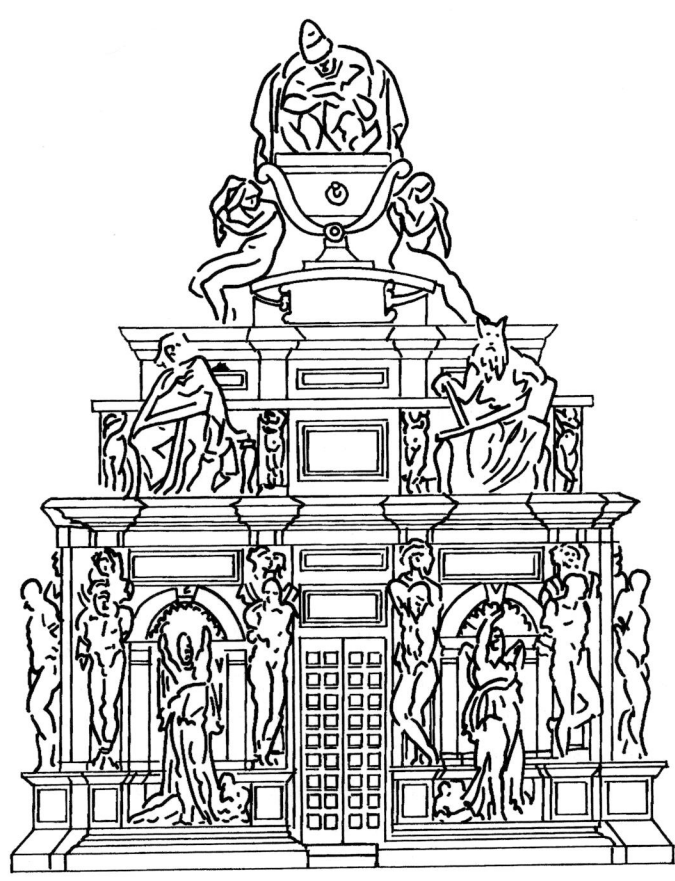

16.14 Reconstruction of Michelangelo's plan (ca. 1505) of the Tomb of Pope Julius II (after Tolnay)

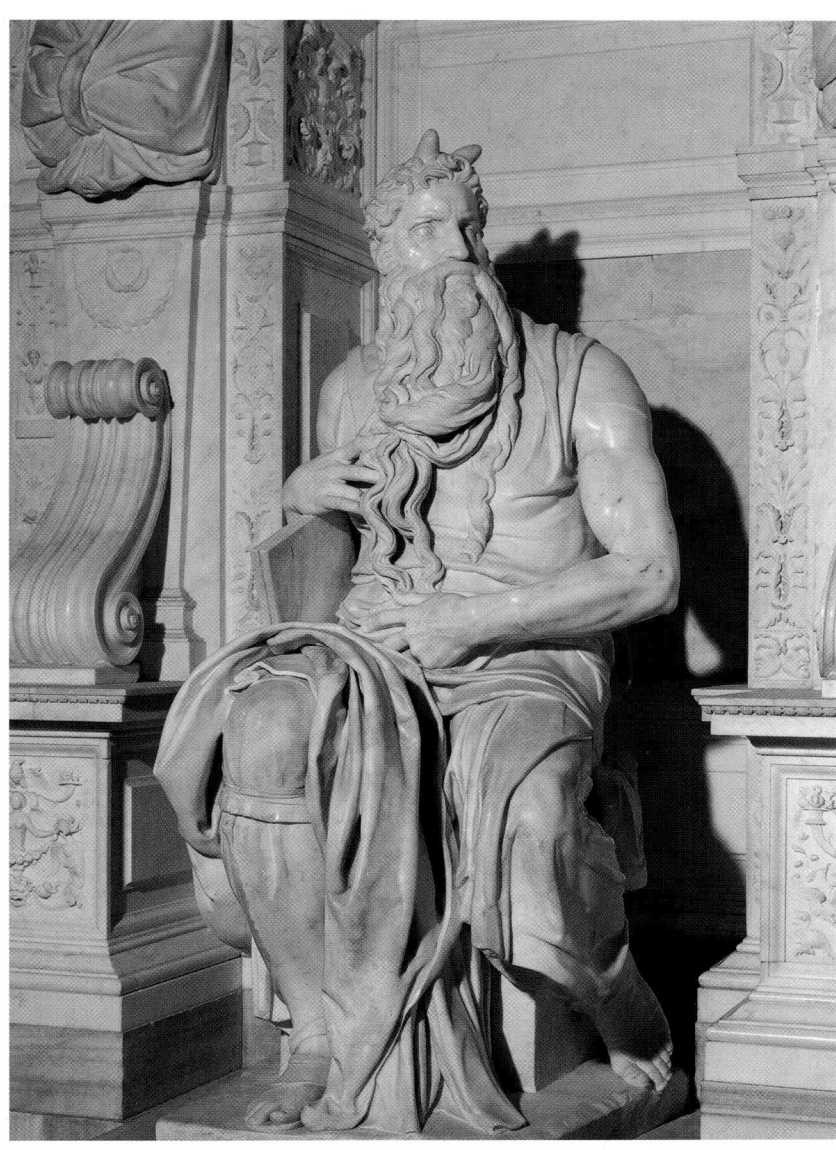

16.15 Michelangelo, *Moses*. ca. 1513–15. Marble, height 7'8½" (2.35 m). San Pietro in Vincoli, Rome

their forms became part of Michelangelo's own style and, through him, of Renaissance art in general. In the *David*, Michelangelo competes with antiquity on equal terms and replaces its authority with his own. But instead of the emotionally wrought figures he saw in Hellenistic works, Michelangelo crafted the *David* to be at once calm and tense, active yet static, full of the potential for movement rather than its actual expression.

Michelangelo in the Service of Pope Julius II

The ambition to create powerful works of art is a hallmark of Michelangelo's career. It is seen again in the project he undertook for the Tomb of Julius II, planned for the new St. Peter's. The commission was given in 1505, but Julius interrupted it, then died in 1513, leaving the project incomplete. His heirs negotiated with Michelangelo over the next 30 years to produce a reduced version of the original plan. The initial plan, reconstructed in figure **16.14**, combined sculpture and architecture into a grand statement of the glory of the pope. Julius's sarcophagus was to sit at the apex of this architectural mass, intended in the first plan to enclose a burial chamber.

On lower levels of the structure Michelangelo planned a figure of St. Paul and one of the Hebrew Bible hero, Moses (fig. **16.15**). This figure was completed about ten years later. The *Moses*, meant to be seen from below, has the awesome force Vasari called *terribilità*—a concept similar to the "sublime" (see page 790). It strikes fear in a viewer from its sheer force. His pose, both watchful and meditative, suggests a man capable of wise leadership as well as towering wrath. Moses has just received the Ten Commandments, which he holds close to his massive torso. The horns, a traditional attribute based on a mistranslation of the Hebrew word for "ray" in the Vulgate (Latin Bible), which is also seen in Sluter's *The Well of Moses* (see fig. 14.1), signify the divine favor bestowed on Moses, whose face shone after he came down from Mount Sinai (Exodus 34). Michelangelo planned other figures for the project, including bound men, whose meaning is still obscure, as well as personifications of the active and contemplative life. Some of these, including the *Moses*, were assembled into the monument

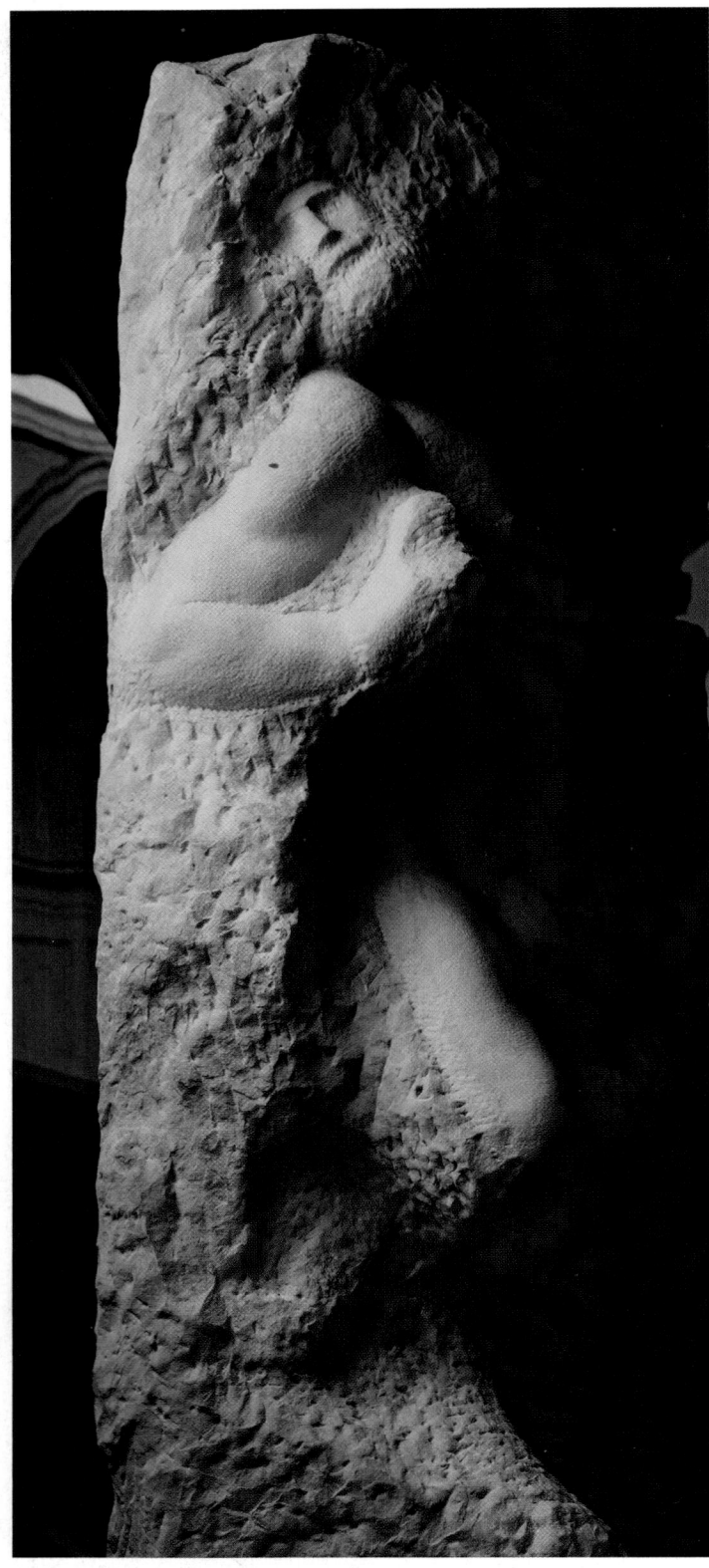

16.16 Michelangelo, *Awakening Prisoner*. ca. 1525. Marble, height 8'11" (2.7 m). Galleria dell'Accademia, Florence

for Julius installed in the church of San Pietro in Vincoli in Rome, on a scale much reduced from the initial plan.

One later figure for the tomb, the unfinished *Awakening Prisoner* (fig. **16.16**), provides invaluable insights into Michelangelo's artistic personality and working methods. For

him, the making of a work of art was both joyous and painful, full of surprises, and not mechanical in any way. It appears that he started the process of carving a statue by trying to perceive a figure in the block as it came to him from the quarry. (At times he may even have visualized figures while picking out his material on the spot.) He may have believed that he could see "signs of life" within the marble—a knee or an elbow pressing against the surface. This attitude is expressed in one of his most famous sonnets, written around 1540:

> Not even the best of artists has any conception
> That a single marble block does not contain
> within its excess, and *that* is only attained
> by the hand that obeys the intellect.

Source: James Saslow's translation, from *The Poetry of Michelangelo* (New Haven, CT: Yale University Press, 1991), page 302

To get a firmer grip on the dimly felt image that he believed was inside the stone, Michelangelo made numerous drawings, and sometimes small models in wax or clay, before daring to assault the marble itself. His practice was to draw the main view on the front of the block. Once he started carving, every stroke of the chisel would commit him more and more to a specific conception of the figure hidden in the block. The marble would permit him to free the figure only if his guess about its shape was correct. Sometimes the stone refused to give up some essential part of the figure within it, and he left the work unfinished. Michelangelo himself may have appreciated the expressive qualities of incomplete works. Although he abandoned *Awakening Prisoner* for other reasons, every gesture seems to record the struggle for liberation of the figure.

Pope Julius interrupted Michelangelo's work on the tomb at an early stage. The pope's decision to enlarge St. Peter's, a commission he gave to Bramante in 1506, altered his patronage priorities, and this so angered Michelangelo that he left Rome. Two years later, the pope half-forced, half-coaxed him to return to paint frescoes on the ceiling of the Sistine Chapel in the Vatican.

FRESCOES FOR THE SISTINE CHAPEL CEILING The Sistine Chapel takes its name from Pope Sixtus IV, Julius's uncle, who had it built and adorned between 1477 and 1482. Driven by his desire to resume work on the tomb, Michelangelo finished the ceiling in only four years, between May 1508 and November 1512 (fig. **16.17**). In this brief period of intense creation in a medium that he never felt was his own, Michelangelo produced a work of truly epochal importance.

The ceiling is a shallow barrel vault interrupted over the windows by the triangular spandrels that support it. Michelangelo treated this surface as a single entity, with hundreds of figures distributed rhythmically within a painted architectural framework. Several different themes intersect throughout this complex structure (fig. **16.18**). In the center, subdivided by ten illusionistic

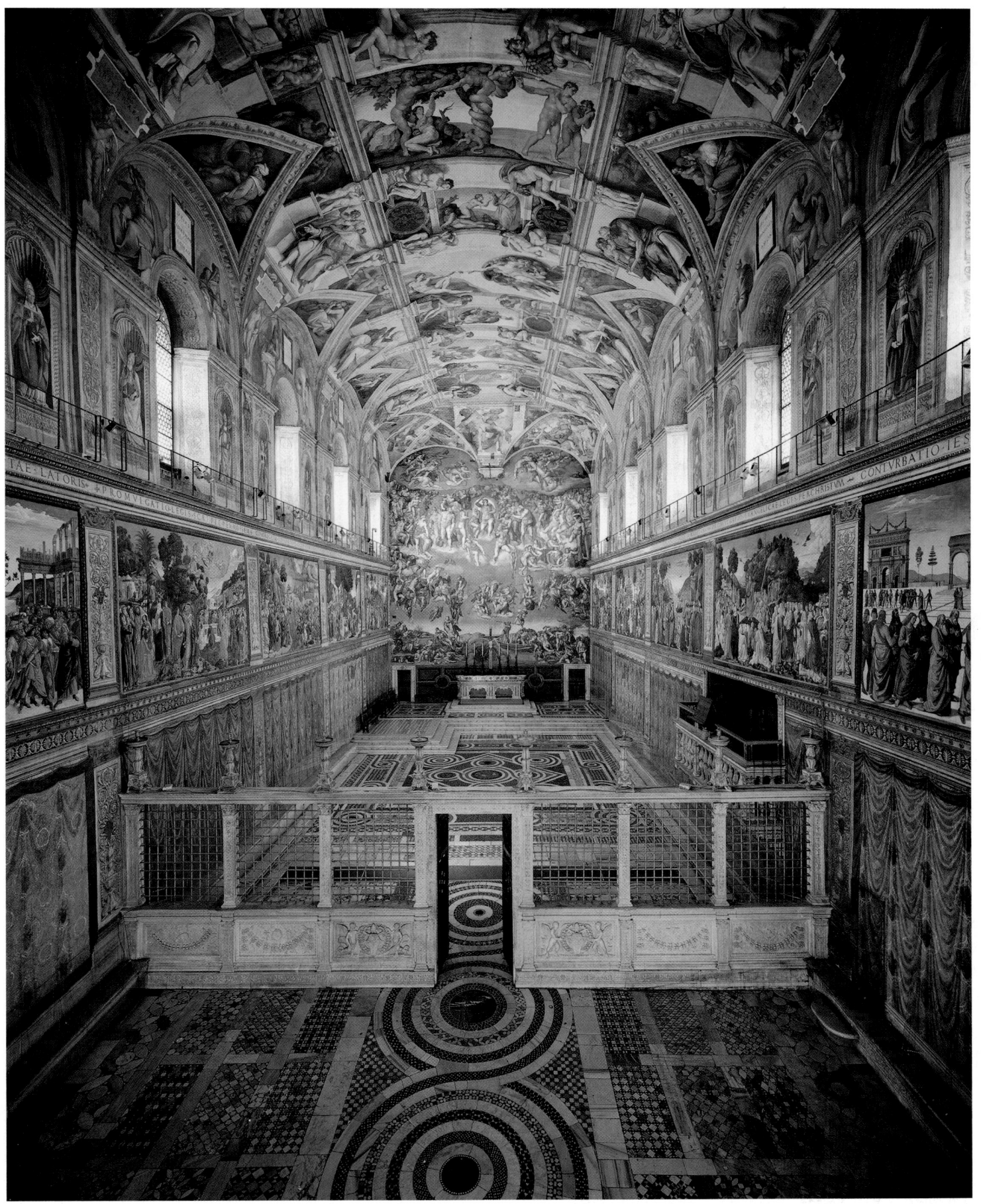

16.17 Interior of the Sistine Chapel showing Michelangelo's ceiling fresco, Vatican, Rome

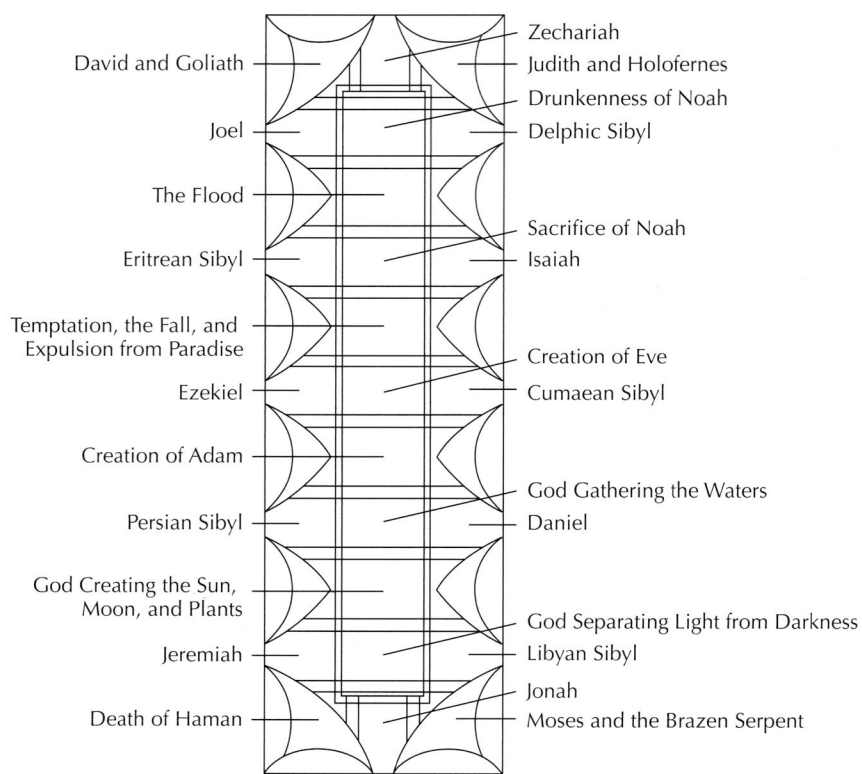

16.18 Diagram of subjects in Sistine Chapel, Vatican, Rome

David and Goliath
Joel
The Flood
Eritrean Sibyl
Temptation, the Fall, and Expulsion from Paradise
Ezekiel
Creation of Adam
Persian Sibyl
God Creating the Sun, Moon, and Plants
Jeremiah
Death of Haman

Zechariah
Judith and Holofernes
Drunkenness of Noah
Delphic Sibyl
Sacrifice of Noah
Isaiah
Creation of Eve
Cumaean Sibyl
God Gathering the Waters
Daniel
God Separating Light from Darkness
Libyan Sibyl
Jonah
Moses and the Brazen Serpent

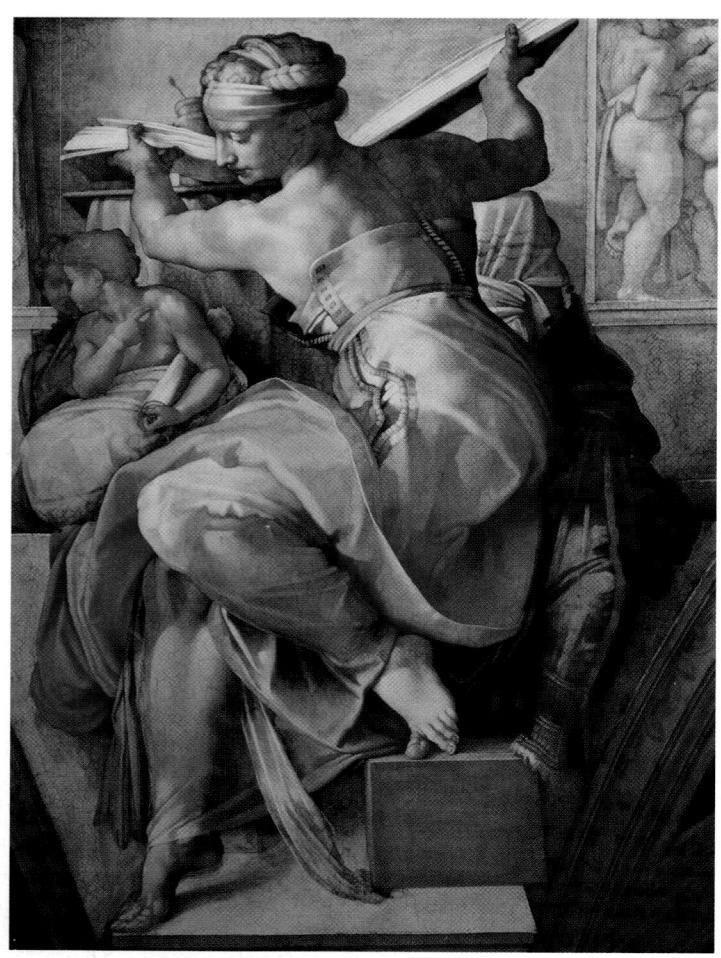

16.19 Libyan Sibyl portion of the Sistine Chapel ceiling

transverse arches, are nine scenes from the book of Genesis, from the Creation of the World (at the altar end) to the Drunkenness of Noah (near the entry door); large figures of prophets and sibyls flank these narratives. In the triangular spandrels sit the ancestors of Christ, who also appear in the lunettes flanking the windows. Further narrative scenes occur at the corner pendentives, focusing on the Hebrew Bible heroes and prophets who **prefigured** Christ. Scholars are still debating the theological import of the whole program and whether Michelangelo consulted with advisors in the development of the themes. While the Creation and Fall of Man occur at the center of the ceiling, the prophets and ancestors predict the salvation of humanity in Christ. Except for the architecture, these themes are expressed almost entirely by the human figure.

The Sistine Chapel ceiling swarms with figures, most of them in the sort of restless posture seen in the *Moses*. For example, as seen in figure **16.19**, the Libyan Sibyl (a sibyl was a pagan prophetess, in whose prophecies Christians saw evidence for the coming of Christ) barely sits on her throne, but twists backward to close her book. Her muscular forms derive from Michelangelo's life drawings of young men. (See *Materials and Techniques*, page 575.) These figures also stem from Michelangelo's deep study of ancient sculpture, which he hoped to surpass. Since the cleaning of the frescoes in the 1980s, scholars have come to appreciate the brilliance of Michelangelo's colors, and the pairing of complementary colors he used in the draperies. (See *The Art Historian's Lens*, page 578.)

A similar energy pervades the center narratives. *The Fall of Man* and *The Expulsion from the Garden of Eden* (fig. **16.20**) show

Drawings

Medieval artists had used the technique of drawing to record monuments they had seen or to preserve compositions for future use. These drawings were usually made with pen and ink on parchment. During the Renaissance, the increasing availability of paper expanded the uses of drawings and encouraged artists to use a variety of mediums in making them.

Pen and ink on paper were used most often, as the liquid ink could be transferred to the paper by means of a sharp quill pen or stylus. Sometimes the forms drawn with ink were further elaborated with a wash (usually diluted ink) applied with a brush. Some artists preferred to work with liquid mediums and thin brushes to render all the forms.

Artists also drew on the relatively rough surface of paper using charcoal or chalk. These naturally occurring materials are both dry and crumbly enough to leave traces when the artist applies them to the paper. The lines they leave can be thick or thin, rendered with carefully descriptive marks or with quick evocative strokes. Artists could smudge these soft mediums to soften contours and fill in shadows, or to produce parallel lines called hatching to describe shadows. See, for example, the variety of strokes Michelangelo used to make the red chalk study for the Libyan Sibyl on the Sistine Chapel ceiling.

More difficult to master was the technique of silverpoint. This entailed using a metal stylus to leave marks on a surface. Silver was the most prized metal for this technique, though lead was also used. Mistakes could not be undone, so it took great skill to work in silverpoint. To make silver leave traces on paper, the paper had to be stiffened up by coating it with a mixture of finely ground bone and size (a gluelike substance). Such coatings were sometimes tinted. When the silver stylus is applied, thin delicate lines are left behind that darken with age.

Renaissance artists also expanded the uses of drawings. Apprentices learned how to render forms using drawings; artists worked out solutions to visual problems with drawings. Drawings were also used to enable artists to negotiate contracts and to record finished works as a kind of diary or model book.

Artists also made **cartoons**, or full-scale patterns, for larger works such as frescoes or tapestries (see fig. 16.26). Transferring designs from drawings onto larger surfaces could be achieved in a number of ways. A grid could be placed over the design to serve as a guide for replicating the image on a larger scale. Or cartoons for frescoes could

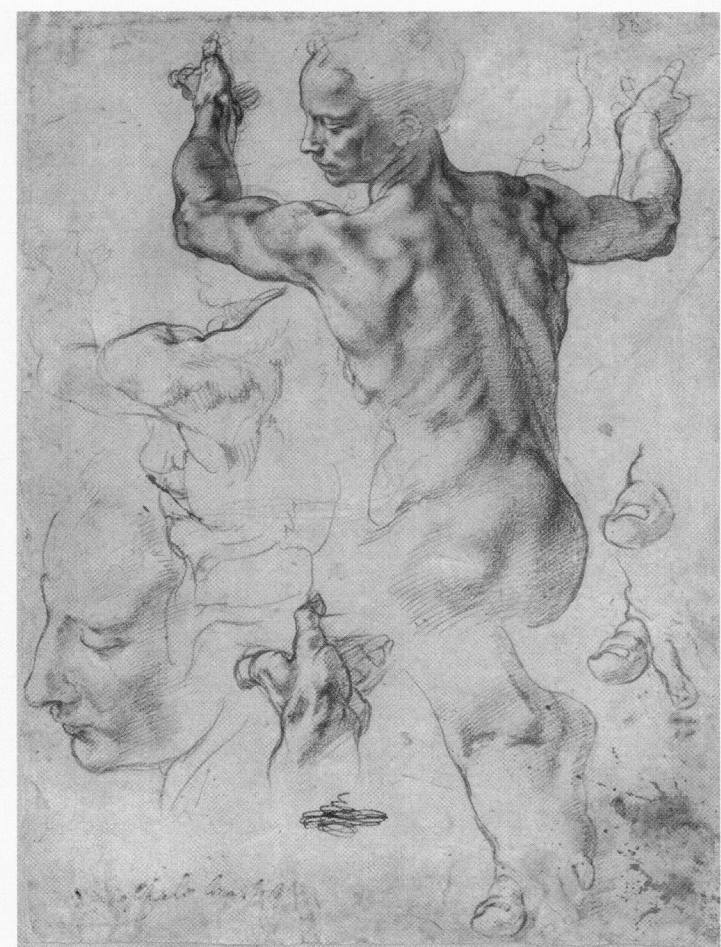

Michelangelo Buonarroti, *Studies for the Libyan Sibyl*. 1508–12. Red chalk, 11⅜ × 8⁷⁄₁₆" (28.9 × 21.4 cm). Metropolitan Museum of Art, New York. Joseph Pulitzer Bequest, 1924 (24.197.2)

be pricked along the main lines of the design; through these tiny holes a powder was forced to reproduce the design on the wall. This is called **pouncing**.

In the sixteenth century, drawings became prized in their own right and were collected by artists, patrons, and connoisseurs. The drawing was thought to reveal something that a finished work could not: the artist's process, the artist's personality, and ultimately, the artist's genius.

the bold, intense hues and expressive body language that characterize the whole ceiling. Michelangelo's figures are full of life, acting out their epic roles in sparse landscape settings. To the left of the Tree of Knowledge, Adam and Eve form a spiral composition as they reach toward the forbidden fruit, while the composition of *The Expulsion from the Garden of Eden* is particularly close to Masaccio's (see fig. 15.27) in its intense drama. The nude youths (*ignudi*) flanking the main sections of the ceiling play an important visual role in Michelangelo's design. They are found at regular intervals, forming a kind of chain linking the narratives. Yet their meaning remains uncertain. Some scholars have proposed

that they represent the world of pagan antiquity. Others have debated whether they are angels or images of human souls. They hold acorns, a reference to the pope's family name, delle Rovere (*rovere* means "oak"). The *ignudi* also support bronze medallions that look like trophies, reminding the viewer of Julius's military campaigns throughout Italy.

The most memorable of the center narratives is *The Creation of Adam* (fig. **16.21**). The fresco depicts not the physical molding of Adam's body, but the passage to him of the divine spark—the soul. The expressive composition conveys a profound conception of the relationship between God and humankind. Michelangelo's

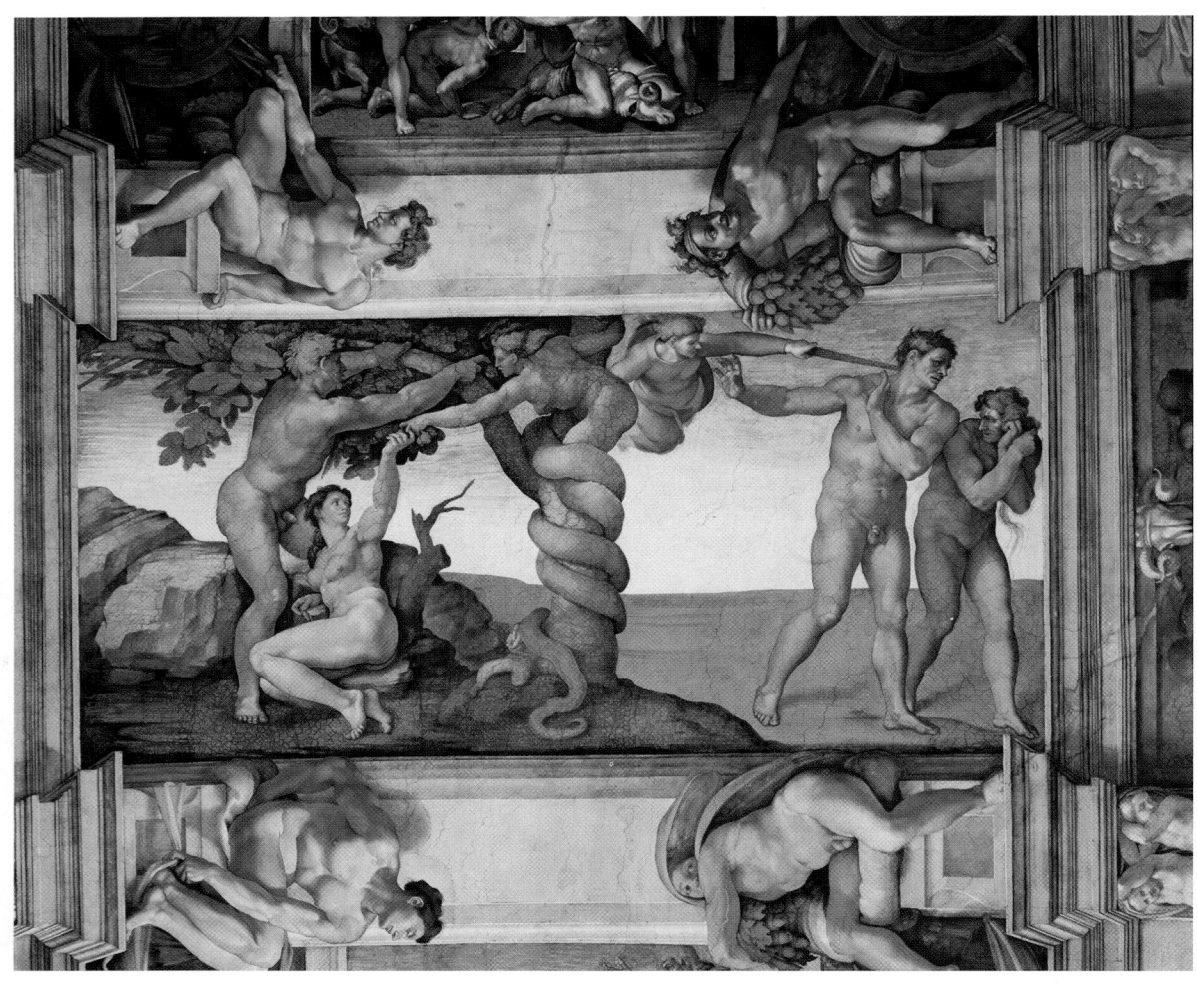

16.20   Michelangelo, *The Fall of Man* and *The Expulsion from the Garden of Eden*. 1508–12.
From the Sistine Chapel ceiling, Vatican, Rome.

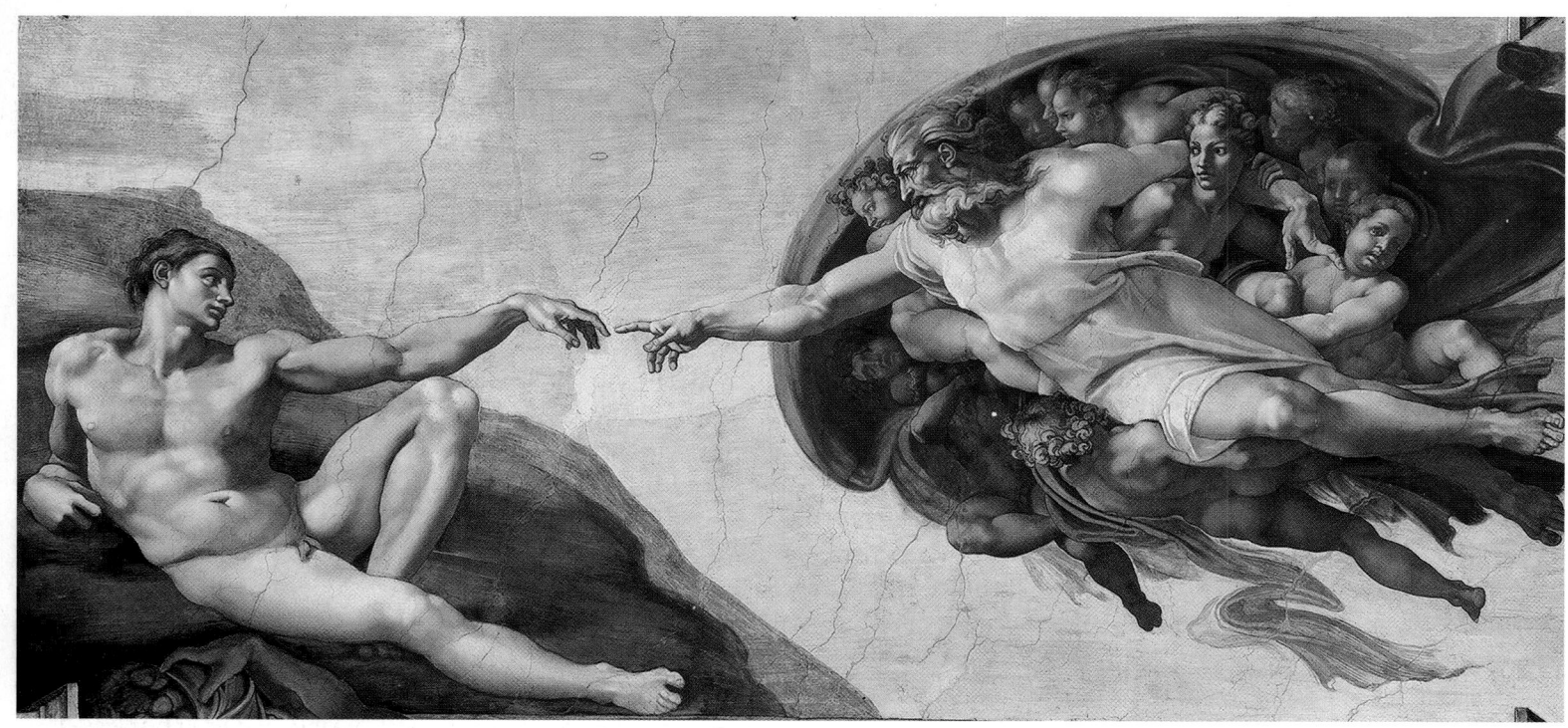

16.21   Michelangelo, *The Creation of Adam*. 1508–12. Portion of the Sistine Chapel ceiling design contrasts the earthbound Adam, who has been likened to an awakening river-god, with the dynamic figure of God rushing through the sky. Adam gazes not only toward his Creator, he also looks toward the figures in the shelter of God's left arm. The identity of these figures has been vigorously debated: The female may be Eve, awaiting her creation in the next panel; another proposal is that she may be Mary, with Jesus at her knee, foreordained to redeem fallen humanity. The entire image has come to be seen as the perfect expression of Michelangelo's view of his own artistic creativity.

After the death of Julius II in 1513, Michelangelo returned to his work on the pope's tomb. But when Leo X (the son of Lorenzo de' Medici) acceded to the papacy, he sent Michelangelo back to Florence, to work on projects for the Medici family, which had been restored to power. There, his style developed and changed, until his eventual return to Rome in the 1530s.

Raphael in Florence and Rome

If Michelangelo represents the solitary genius, Raphael of Urbino (Raffaello Sanzio, 1483–1520) belongs to the opposite type: the artist as a man of the world. The contrast between them was clear to their contemporaries, and both enjoyed great fame. Vasari's book, with its championing of Michelangelo, helped to inspire later generations' veneration of Michelangelo over Raphael, in part because of the two men's biographies. Where Michelangelo's dramatic conflicts with his art and with his patrons made a good narrative, Raphael's career seems too much a success story, his work too marked by effortless grace, to match the tragic heroism of Michelangelo. Raphael's gifts were in his technical brilliance, his intelligent approach to composing pictures, and his dialogue with the other artists of his time. He is the central painter of the High Renaissance. During his relatively brief career he created the largest body of Renaissance pictorial work outside of Titian's, one that is notable for its variety and power. He also oversaw a lively and large workshop, from which many artists of the next generation emerged, effectively putting his stamp on the whole period.

RAPHAEL'S EARLY MADONNAS Raphael had a genius for synthesis that enabled him to merge the qualities of Leonardo and Michelangelo. His art is lyrical and dramatic, pictorially rich and sculpturally solid. These qualities are already present in the Madonnas he painted in Florence (1504–08) after his apprenticeship with Perugino. The meditative calm of the so-called *La Belle Jardinière* (*Beautiful Gardener*) (fig. **16.22**) still reflects the style of his teacher; the forms are, however, more ample and the chiaroscuro expertly rendered. The young Jesus and John the Baptist have perfect little bodies, posed in graceful postures to interact with each other and the Virgin. For this image, Raphael reworks a composition by Leonardo, but he replaces the enigmatic gestures in *The Virgin of the Rocks* with a gentle, rhythmic interplay. Raphael substitutes for Leonardo's intricate grouping a stable pyramid whose severity is relieved by Mary's billowing cape. Equally striking is the carefully observed landscape, whose

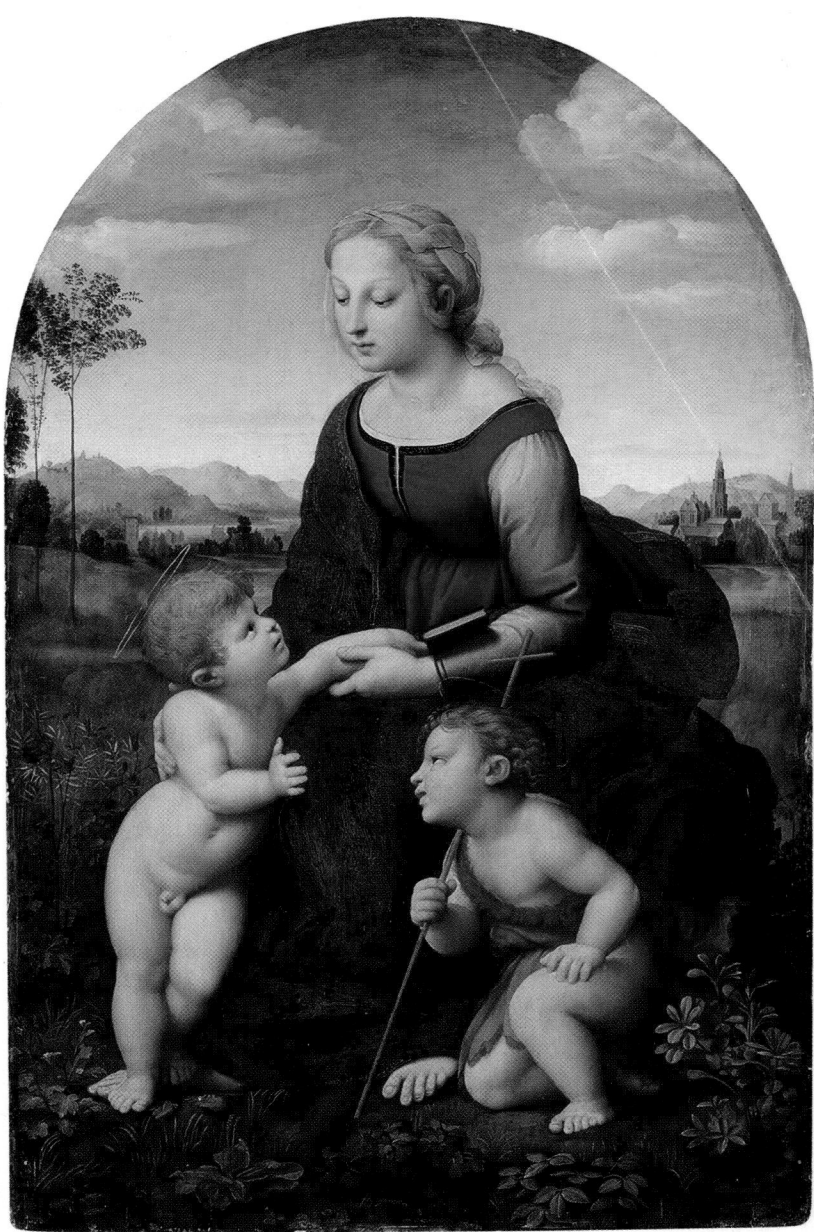

16.22   Raphael, *La Belle Jardinière*. 1507. Oil on panel, 48 × 31½" (122 × 80 cm). Musée du Louvre, Paris

bright light and natural beauty provide an appropriate setting for the figure group.

One of the reasons *La Belle Jardinière* looks different from *The Virgin of the Rocks* (see fig. 16.5), to which it is otherwise so clearly indebted, is Michelangelo's influence, which is seen in the figural composition. The full force of this influence can be felt only in Raphael's Roman works, however. In 1508, at the time Michelangelo began to paint the Sistine Chapel ceiling, Julius II summoned Raphael from Florence at the suggestion of Bramante, who also came from Urbino. At first, Raphael mined ideas he had developed under his teacher Perugino, but Rome utterly transformed him as an artist, just as it had Bramante, and he underwent an astonishing growth.

Cleaning and Restoring Works of Art

One of the most controversial topics in contemporary art history is whether and how to clean venerable but soiled works of art. Heated exchanges, accusations, and lawsuits regularly accompany cleaning and restoration projects. Cleaning means just that—removing soot, grime, pollutants, and sometimes layers of varnish or other protective materials earlier generations of owners put on a work. Restoration may involve replacing missing elements in a work to suggest to a viewer what an object looked like on its completion. Both processes are hotly debated today.

Many of the most famous images from the Renaissance have been at the center of these controversies: Giotto's Arena Chapel, Masaccio's Brancacci Chapel, Leonardo's *Last Supper*, Michelangelo's frescoes at the Sistine Chapel, and Michelangelo's *David*. Questions arise because of the jarring outcomes that can result from cleaning projects. For example, when the Sistine Chapel ceiling was cleaned in the 1980s, critics complained that the process removed the top layer of the paint, leaving only "garish" underpainting. Michelangelo's reputation as a colorist has been permanently changed by the cleaning of the ceiling frescoes.

The techniques of cleaning vary according to the medium and condition of the work, but conservators try to use the least damaging solvents possible, and they document every step they take. Work can be very slow, as in the case of *The Last Supper*. The project took 20 years, as cleaners had to contend with the work of earlier "restorers," who had filled in missing sections of the image with new paint.

Current cleaning removed overpaints, and filled in missing areas with removable water-based pigment. Restorers today are careful to add only materials that can be removed without damaging the original object.

Museums routinely clean objects in their care to conserve them. Major museums keep large conservation laboratories staffed by art historians, chemists, and artists to treat works of art. Often the impetus and funding for such projects comes when an object is requested for an important exhibition. In the case of the Sistine Chapel ceiling, a corporation underwrote the cleaning of the ceiling in exchange for the rights to make a film about the process. Philanthropic and corporate donors have supported many recent cleaning projects.

The *David* offers a good example of why objects need cleaning. The statue stood in the Piazza della Signoria for almost four centuries, subjected to pollutants and humidity, until it was removed to the Galleria dell'Accademia in Florence in 1873. (A copy now stands in the Piazza.) In 2003, a cleaning program was undertaken, again amidst protests: Critics wanted a minimally invasive dry cleaning (like a careful dusting), but the curators used a distilled water, clay, and cellulose paste to draw pollutants out of the marble. Mineral spirits (solvents) were used to remove wax on the marble.

Perhaps the one object from the High Renaissance most in need of cleaning today—but unlikely to receive it—is Leonardo's *Mona Lisa*. The current directors of the Louvre have said that no such cleaning is planned.

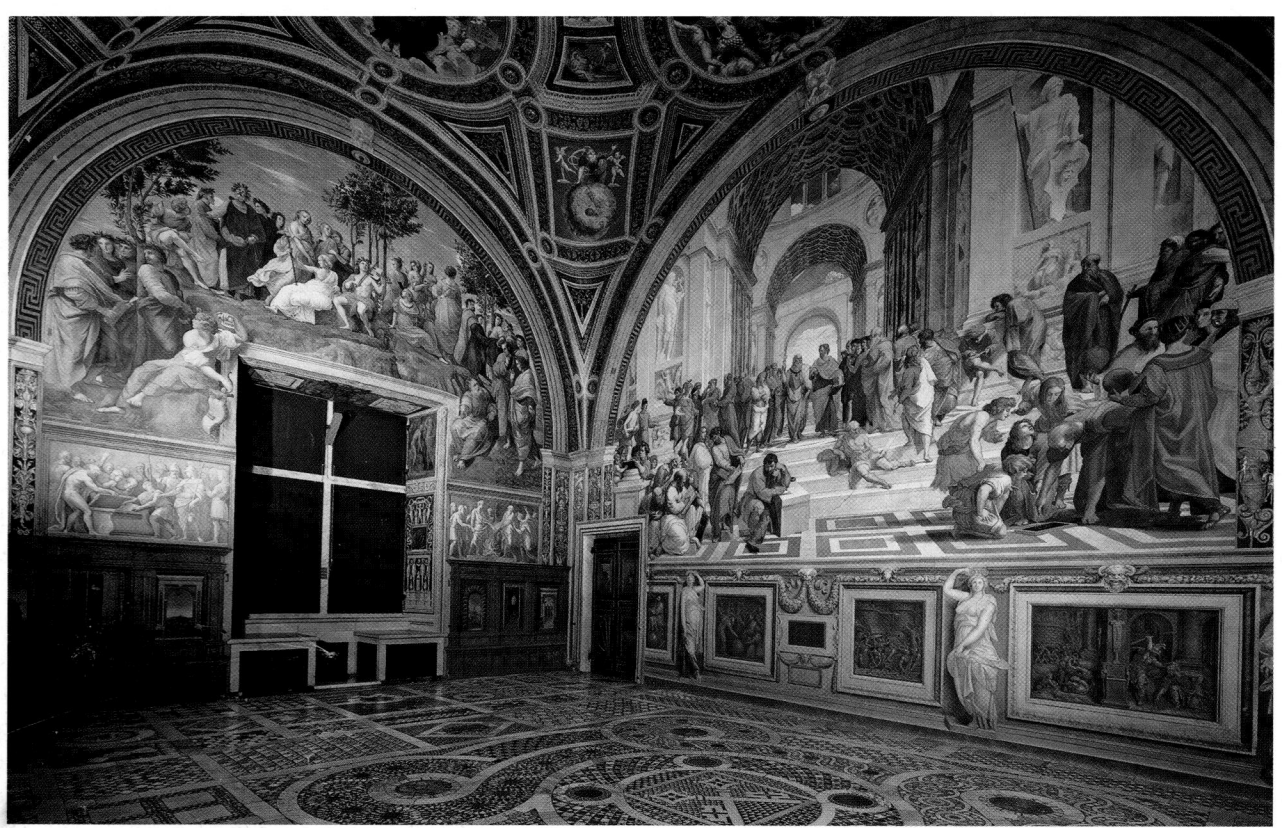

16.23 Raphael. Frescoes of the Stanza della Segnatura, Vatican Palace, Rome. 1508–11

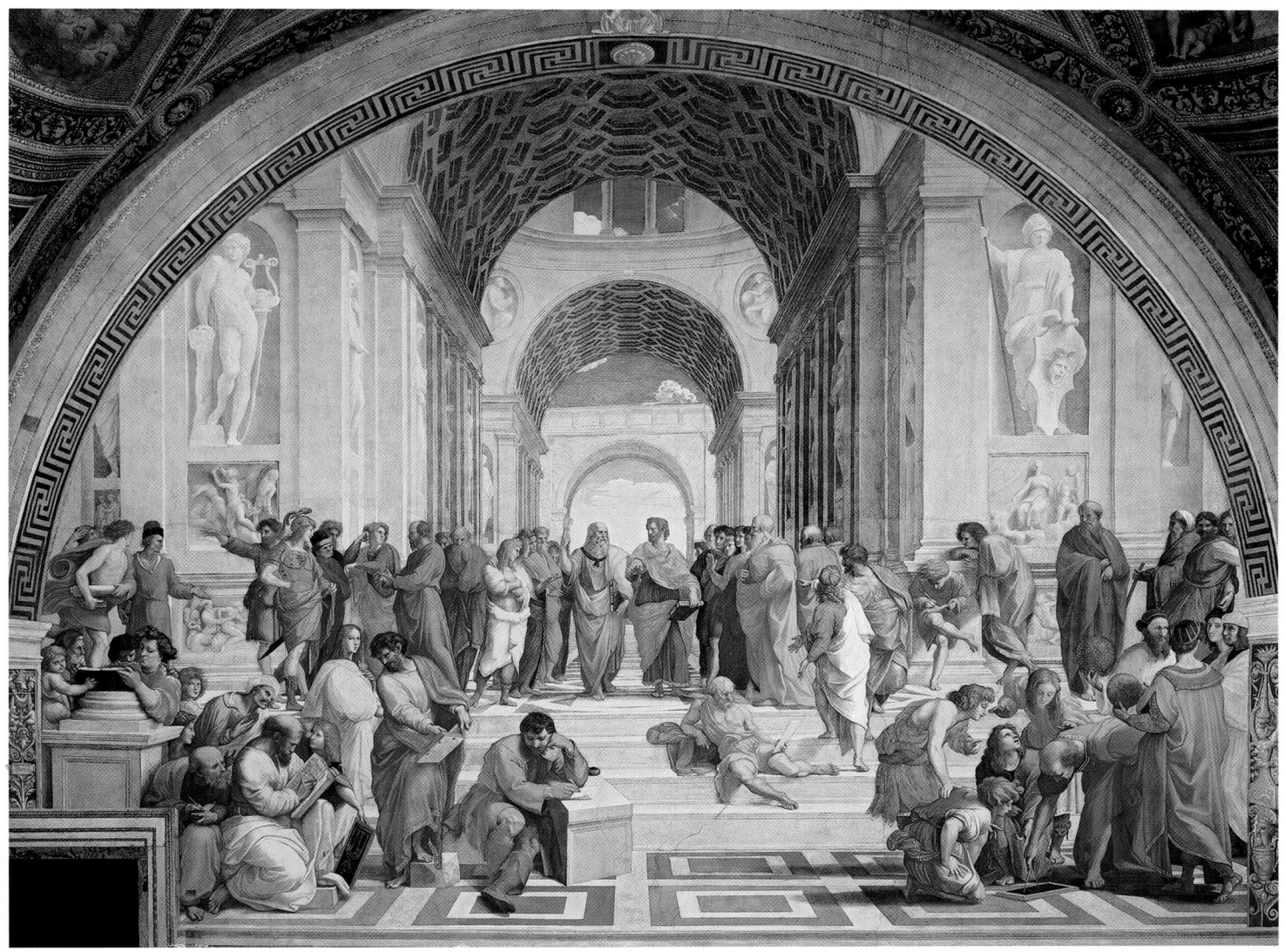

16.24 Raphael, *The School of Athens*, Stanza della Segnatura, Vatican Palace, Rome. 1508–11. Fresco

FRESCOES FOR THE STANZA DELLA SEGNATURA The results can be seen in the Stanza della Segnatura (fig. **16.23**), the first in a series of rooms which Julius commissioned him to decorate at the Vatican Palace. The frescoes painted by Raphael in this room show an almost endless fertility in the creation of daring narrative compositions. The "Room of the Signature," as it is translated, derives its name from its later function as the place where papal bulls (documents) were signed, though originally it housed Julius II's personal library. Beginning in 1508, Raphael painted a cycle of frescoes on its walls and ceiling that refer to the four domains of learning: theology, philosophy, law, and the arts. In general, the Stanza represents a summation of High Renaissance humanism, for it attempts to represent the unity of knowledge in one grand scheme. Raphael probably had a team of scholars and theologians as advisors, yet the design is his alone.

To represent these subjects, Raphael depicted figures from history and mythology in illusionistic spaces. For the arts, for example, the space above and flanking a window depicts Parnassus, the sacred mountain of Apollo. The god appears playing a lyre in a grove of laurel trees surrounded by the Nine Muses and great poets from antiquity down to the artist's own time. Dante stands on the left, near the blind Homer, Petrarch stands to the right, while Sappho appears to lean on the window frame at lower left. Her figure and that of the poet opposite her connect the painted Parnassus with the space of the room. Raphael uses the same illusionistic device that Mantegna exploited in the *Camera Picta* in Mantua (see fig. 15.49). The painting reflects the papal court's dream of a Golden Age under Julius II, in which the Vatican Hill would become the new Parnassus.

Of all the frescoes in the Stanza della Segnatura, *The School of Athens* (fig. **16.24**) has long been acknowledged as Raphael's masterpiece and the embodiment of the classical spirit of the High Renaissance. The title was only assigned later, and the subject of the painting has been much debated. The fresco seems to represent a group of famous Greek philosophers gathered around Plato and Aristotle, each in a characteristic pose or activity. Raphael may have already studied parts of the Sistine Chapel ceiling, then nearing completion: He owes to Michelangelo the expressive energy, the physical power, and dramatic grouping of his figures. Yet he has not simply borrowed Michelangelo's gestures and poses. He has absorbed them into his own style and thus given them a different meaning. Body and spirit, action and emotion are balanced harmoniously, and all members of this great assembly play their roles with magnificent, purposeful clarity.

The conception of *The School of Athens* suggests the spirit of Leonardo's *The Last Supper* (see fig. 16.6), as Raphael organizes his figures into groups like Leonardo's. He further distinguishes the relationships among individuals and groups, and links them in a formal rhythm. (The artist worked out the poses in a series of drawings, many made from life.) Also in the spirit of Leonardo is the symmetrical design, as well as the interdependence of the figures and their architectural setting. Like Leonardo's work, an opening in the building serves as a frame for the key figures. But Raphael's building plays a greater role in the composition than the hall does in *The Last Supper*. With its lofty dome, barrel vault, and colossal statuary, it is classical in spirit, yet Christian in meaning. Inspired by Bramante, who, Vasari informs us, helped Raphael with the architecture, the building seems like an advance view of the new St. Peter's, then being constructed. Capacious, luxurious, overpowering, the building is more inspired by Roman structures, such as the Basilica of Maxentius and Constantine (see fig. 7.60), than by anything Greek. Yet two illusionistically rendered sculptures of Greek divinities preside over this gathering of learned men of the Greek past: Apollo, patron of the arts with his lyre to the left, and Athena, in her guise as Minerva, goddess of wisdom, on the right.

The program of *The School of Athens* reflects the most learned humanism of the day, which commentators are still elucidating. Since Vasari's time, historians have attempted to identify the figures inhabiting this imposing space. At center stage, Plato (whose face resembles Leonardo's) holds his book about cosmology and numerology, *Timaeus*, which provided the basis for much of the Neo-Platonism that came to pervade Christianity. To Plato's left (a viewer's right), his pupil Aristotle grasps a volume of his *Ethics*, which, like his science, is grounded in what is knowable in the material world. The tomes explain why Plato is pointing rhetorically to the heavens, Aristotle to the earth. The figures represent the two most important Greek philosophers, whose approaches, although seemingly opposite, were deemed complementary by many Renaissance humanists. In this composition, the two schools of philosophy come together.

Some believe that Raphael organized his array of philosophers to reflect the two camps: the idealists and the empiricists. To Plato's right is his mentor, Socrates, who addresses a group of disciples by counting out his arguments on his fingers. Standing before the steps are figures representing mathematics and physics (the lower branches of philosophy that are the gateway to higher knowledge). Here appears the bearded Pythagoras, for whom the truth of all things is to be found in numbers. The diagrams and sums on the tablets at his feet symbolize the importance of number in philosophy. On the other side of the same plane, Raphael

borrowed the features of Bramante for the head of Euclid, seen drawing or measuring two overlapping triangles with a pair of compasses in the foreground to the lower right. Behind him, two men holding globes may represent Zoroaster the astronomer and Ptolemy the geographer. Vasari tells us that the man wearing a black hat behind these scientists is a self-portrait of Raphael, who places himself in the Aristotelian camp.

Despite the competition between them, Raphael added Michelangelo at the last minute (as revealed by his insertion of a layer of fresh plaster or *intonaco* on which to paint the new figure), whom he has cast as Heraclitus, a sixth-century BCE philosopher, shown deep in thought sitting on the steps in the Platonic camp. (Heraclitus was often paired with Diogenes the Cynic, shown here lying at the feet of Plato and Aristotle.) Scholars have remarked that this figure is not only a portrait of the sculptor, but is rendered in the style of the figures on the nearby Sistine Chapel ceiling. The inclusion of so many artists among, as well as in the guise of, famous philosophers is testimony to their recently acquired—and hard-won—status as members of the learned community.

PAPAL AND PRIVATE COMMISSIONS After Julius II died in 1513, Raphael was hired by his successor, Leo X, who ordered

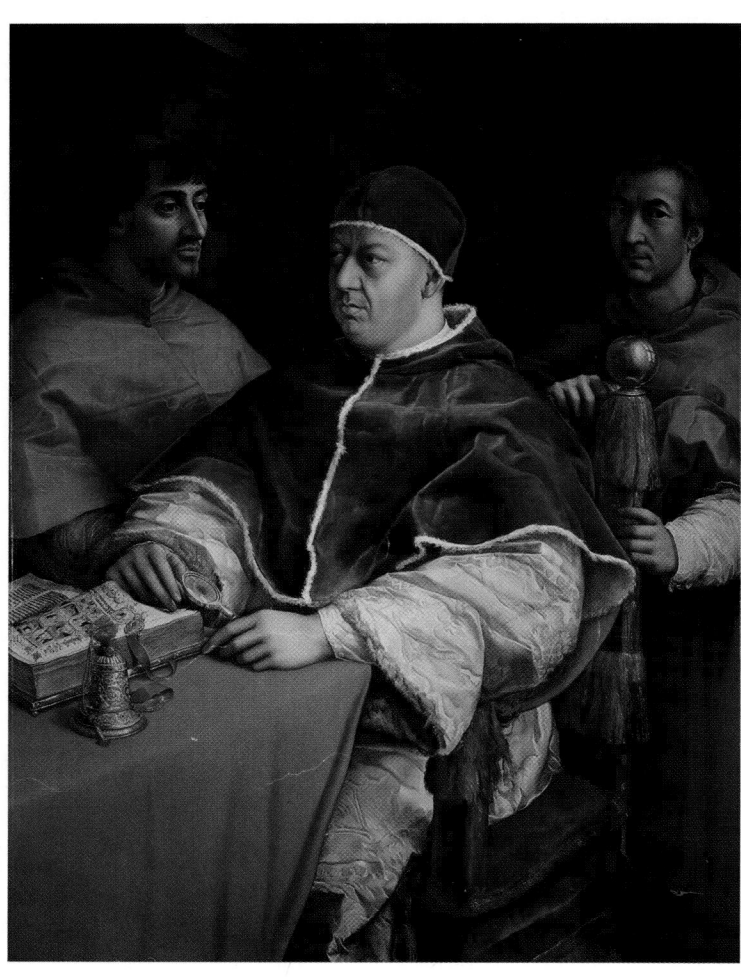

16.25 Raphael, *Portrait of Pope Leo X with Cardinals Giulio de' Medici and Luigi de' Rossi.* ca. 1517. Oil on panel, 60⅝ × 46⅞" (154 × 119 cm). Galleria degli Uffizi, Florence

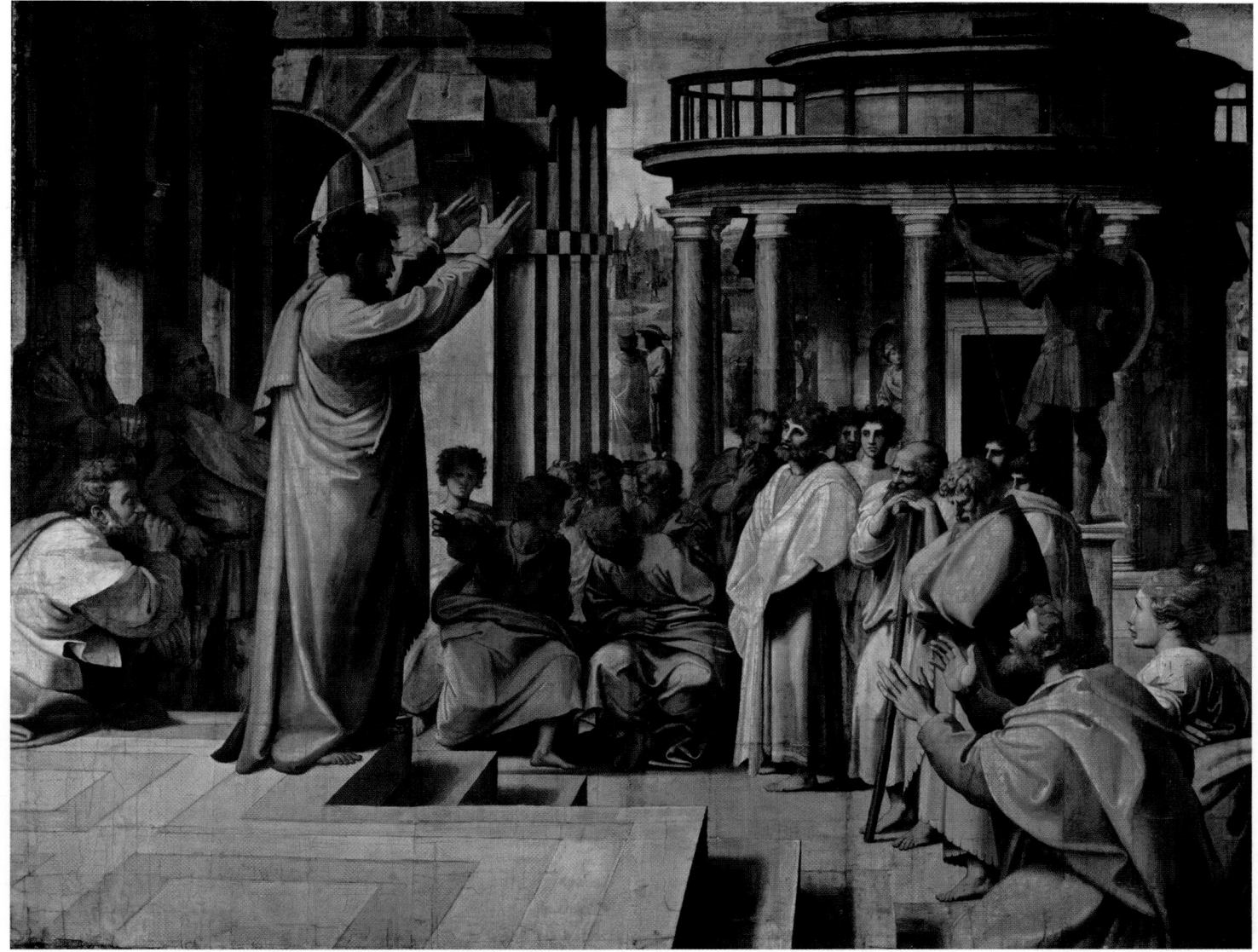

16.26   Raphael, *St. Paul Preaching at Athens*. 1515–16. Cartoon, gouache on paper, 11'3" × 14'6" (3.4 × 4.4 m). Victoria & Albert Museum, London

him to finish painting the papal apartments. The pope also sat for portraits. In the *Portrait of Pope Leo X with Cardinals Giulio de' Medici and Luigi de' Rossi* (fig. **16.25**), painted about 1517, Raphael did little to improve the heavy-jowled features of the pope, or the faces of his associates. (Giulio de' Medici, on the left, became pope himself in 1523, as Clement VII.) The three men are gathered around a table, on which rests a beautifully worked bell and an illuminated manuscript. Rather than a spiritual being or a warrior, the pope is represented as a collector and connoisseur, shown examining a precious object. The textures of the brocades and fur-lined garment only add to the sensual experience. Light enters this space from a window on the right whose shape is reflected in the brass ball of the chair's finial, a reference to the Medici coat of arms. This meditation on the sense of sight owes a debt to Netherlandish art. Leo sent the portrait to Florence to serve as his stand-in during wedding festivities for his Medici cousins there.

Raphael's work clearly pleased the new pope. After Bramante's death in 1514, Raphael was named the architect of St. Peter's and subsequently superintendent of antiquities in Rome. In 1516, Pope Leo X sent Michelangelo to Florence to work at San Lorenzo, leaving Raphael as the leading artist in Rome. He was flooded with commissions, and of necessity depended increasingly on his growing workshop.

In 1515–16, the pope commissioned Raphael to design a set of tapestries on the theme of the Acts of the Apostles for the Sistine Chapel. The commission placed him in direct competition with Michelangelo; consequently, Raphael designed and executed the ten huge cartoons (see *Materials and Techniques*, page 575) for this series with great care and enthusiasm. Because the cartoons were sent to Flanders to be woven, they helped to spread High Renaissance ideas from Italy to northern Europe. One of the most influential of these cartoons is *St. Paul Preaching at Athens* (fig. **16.26**), which demonstrates Raphael's synthesizing genius.

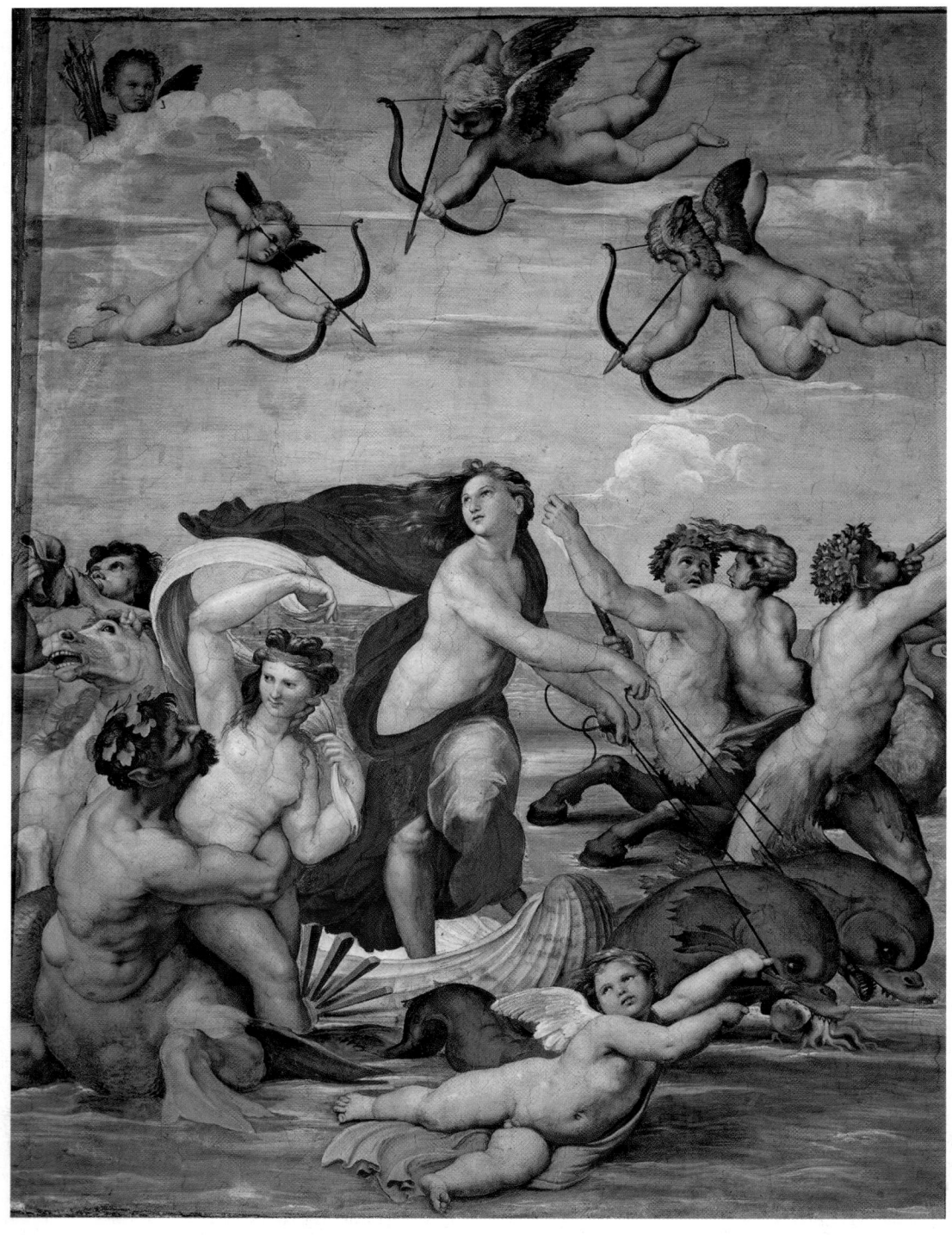

16.27   Raphael, *Galatea*, Villa Farnesina, Rome. ca. 1513. Fresco, 9'8⅛" × 7'4" (3 × 2.2 m)

For the imposing figure of St. Paul, Raphael has adapted the severity and simplicity of Masaccio's Brancacci Chapel frescoes (see figs. 15.24–15.27). The power of the saint's words is expressed not only by his gestures, but by the responses of the voluminously clad audience. Bramante inspires the architecture that defines the space; the plain Tuscan order of the columns in the round temple in the background recalls the Tempietto (see fig. 16.8). Instead of allowing the eye to wander deeply into the distance, Raphael limits the space to a foreground plane, into which a viewer is invited by the steps in the foreground. The simplicity

and grandeur of the conception conveys the narrative in bold, clear terms that are only enhanced by the large scale of the figures.

Other patrons in Rome also engaged Raphael's busy workshop; the powerful Sienese banker Agostino Chigi hired Raphael to adorn his new villa in Rome, now called the Villa Farnesina after a later owner. The building served as the setting for Chigi's interests: in the antique, in conspicuous display, and in love. Throughout the villa he commissioned frescoes on themes from the pagan past. For this setting, Raphael painted the *Galatea* around 1513 (fig. **16.27**). The beautiful nymph Galatea,

PRIMARY SOURCE

On Raphael's Death

Raphael died in Rome in April of 1520. In a letter to Isabella d'Este, the duchess of Mantua, the humanist Pandolfo Pico della Mirandola tells her about the artist's death and the reaction of Rome to his loss.

... now I shall inform you of ... the death of Raphael of Urbino, who died last night, that is, on Good Friday, leaving this court in the greatest and most universal distress because of the loss of hope for the very great things one expected of him that would have given glory to our time. And indeed it is said about this that he gave promise for everything great, through what one could already see of his works and through the grander ones he had begun. ... Here one speaks of nothing else but of the death of this good man, who at thirty-three years of age has finished his first life; his second one, however, that of fame which is not subject to time and death, will be eternal, both through his works and through the men of learning that will write in his praise.

Source: Konrad Oberhuber, *Raphael. The Paintings* (Munich and New York: Prestel, 1999)

vainly pursued by the giant Polyphemus, belongs to Greek mythology, known to the Renaissance through the verses of Ovid. Raphael's *Galatea* celebrates the sensuality of the pagan spirit as if it were a living force. Although the composition of the nude female riding a seashell recalls Botticelli's *The Birth of Venus* (see fig. 15.40), a painting Raphael may have known in Florence, the resemblance only serves to emphasize their profound differences. Raphael's figures are vigorously sculptural and arranged in a dynamic spiral movement around the twisting Galatea. In Botticelli's picture, the movement is not generated by the figures but imposed on them by the decorative, linear design that places all the figures on the same plane. Like Michelangelo, Raphael uses the arrangement of figures, rather than any detailed perspective scheme, to call up an illusion of space and to create a vortex of movement.

Raphael's statuesque, full-bodied figures suggest his careful study of ancient Roman sculpture which, like Michelangelo, he wanted to surpass. An even more direct example of his use of antique sources is his design for the engraving of *The Judgment of Paris* by Marcantonio Raimondi, executed about 1520 (fig. **16.28**). Collectors increasingly desired to own Raphael's drawings, so he used the skills of the engraver to record and to spread his designs. Raphael based this one on a Roman sarcophagus panel, which he has interpreted rather than copied. The engraving depicts the Judgment of Paris witnessed by the Olympian gods in heaven and a group of river-gods on the lower right. The statuesque figures are firmly defined in the engravings through the strong contours and chiaroscuro, and they occupy a frontal plane across the images. In images like this, Raphael translated the art of antiquity for generations of artists to come.

Raphael's life was cut short in 1520, when he died after a brief illness. Roman society mourned him bitterly, according to the reports of witnesses. (See *Primary Source*, above.) Befitting the new status assigned to artists, he was buried in the Pantheon. Significantly, many of the leading artists of the next generation emerged from Raphael's workshop and took his style as their point of departure.

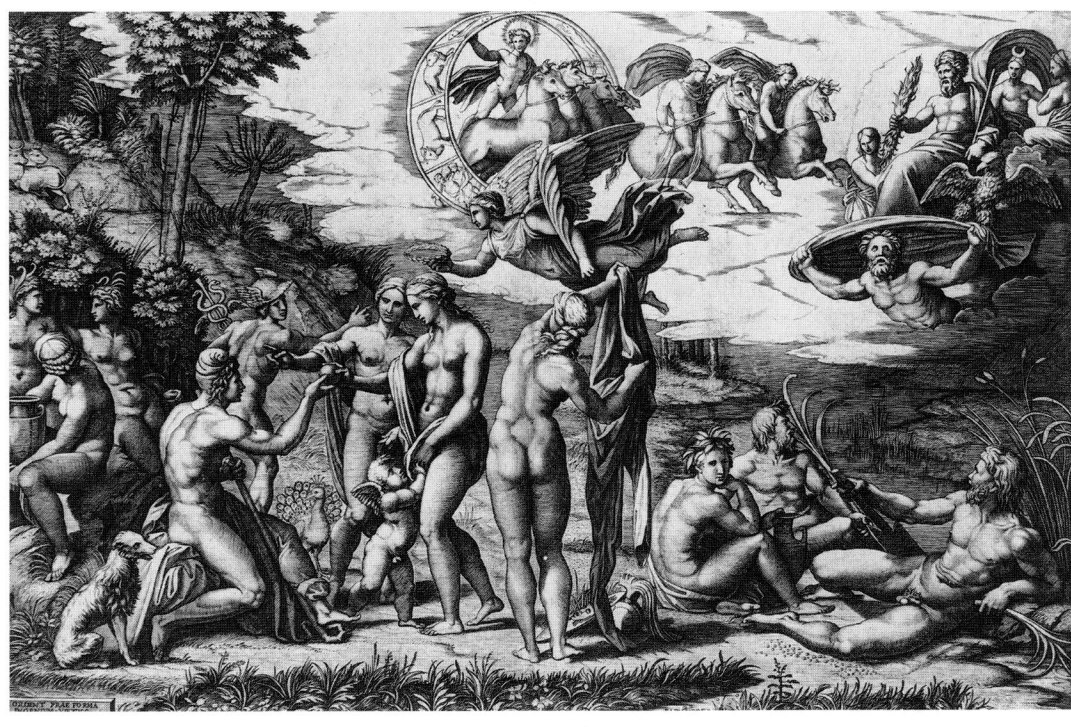

16.28 Marcantonio Raimondi, after Raphael, *The Judgment of Paris*. ca. 1510–20. Engraving, $11^7/_{16} \times 17^3/_{16}$" (29.1 × 43.7 cm). Metropolitan Museum of Art, New York. Rogers Fund, 1919. (19.74.1)

VENICE

As Rome became the center of an imperial papal style of art, Venice endured the enmity of its neighbors and the dismantling of its northern Italian empire. Having gradually expanded its influence over northeastern Italy, in 1509 the Republic of Venice faced a threat from the League of Cambrai, an international military alliance aimed against it. Yet, by 1529, Venice had outlasted this menace to its power and reclaimed most of its lost territory. Resisting the invasions of Europe by the Turks, Venice's navy fought determinedly in the eastern Mediterranean to hold off this threat. In the midst of this turmoil, artists in Venice built on the traditions of the fifteenth century and the innovations of Giovanni Bellini to create a distinct visual language. Two artists in particular, Giorgione and Titian, created new subjects, approaches to images, and techniques.

Giorgione

Giorgione da Castelfranco (1478–1510) left the orbit of Giovanni Bellini (see figs. 15.53 and 15.54) to create some of the most mysterious and beguiling paintings of the Renaissance. Although he painted some religious works, he seems to have specialized in smaller-scale paintings on secular themes for the homes of wealthy collectors. His death at a young age, probably from the plague, left the field open for his young colleague, Titian, who worked in his shop for some time. Some of the works traditionally ascribed to Giorgione have, in fact, been argued for Titian in recent years. Many of his works defy attempts to interpret them.

This is the case with Giorgione's *The Tempest* (fig. **16.29**). Documents record the picture in the collection of the patrician Gabriele Vendramin, one of Venice's greatest patrons of the arts. Scholars have offered many possible explanations of this image, which depicts a stormy landscape inhabited by a male figure on the left and a nursing mother on the right. The male has been identified as a shepherd, a warrior, or an angel; the nude woman has been identified as Eve, as Hagar, as Venus, or Nature herself. The figures, and thus any narrative content, remain enigmatic. In fact, Giorgione's landscape seems to provide the key to interpretation. With its verdant setting and humid atmosphere, the scene is like an enchanted idyll, a dream of pastoral beauty soon to be swept away, as the fury of a summer thunderstorm lights the sky. While the painting is very similar in mood to that conjured by the *Arcadia* of Jacopo Sannazaro, a poem about unrequited love that was popular in Giorgione's day, even such parallels do not account for all the details in the image. Scholars have argued that *The Tempest* initiates what was to become an important new tradition in art, the making of pictorial equivalents to poetry or *poesie*, as contemporaries called them: atmospheric images that set a mood rather than convey a story. Nonetheless, what the original audience may have read into the image continues to perplex modern viewers.

A similar problem confronts the viewer of the so-called *Fête Champêtre* or *Pastoral Concert* (fig. **16.30**). The picture has been on display in the Louvre in Paris since the nineteenth century, where it arrived from the French royal collection. It depicts a group of young people gathered in a lush landscape to make music when a shepherd and his flock come upon them. Attempts to find a narrative subject to attach to this image have proven fruitless: No single literary source seems to account for it. Most puzzling are the nude women, one of whom is about to play a recorder, while another takes water from a fountain. One proposal identifies them as the Muses, ancient female divinities who inspire the arts. The forms are rendered in a soft chiaroscuro technique so that they emerge from the atmospheric landscape as soft round shapes. The landscape moves from dark to light to dark passages, receding into the atmospheric distance. There is some evidence that the young Titian may have intervened in this work. Instead of telling a story, the painting seems designed to evoke a mood.

Vasari criticized Giorgione for not making drawings as part of his process of painting. (See www.myartslab.com.) Steeped in the Florentine tradition of Leonardo, Michelangelo, and Raphael, Vasari argued that drawing, or *disegno* was fundamental to good painting. The Venetians, however, valued light and color above all else to create their sensual images. Vasari dismissed this as mere *colore*, which he argued was secondary to the process of drawing. The resulting competition between *disegno* and *colore* provided

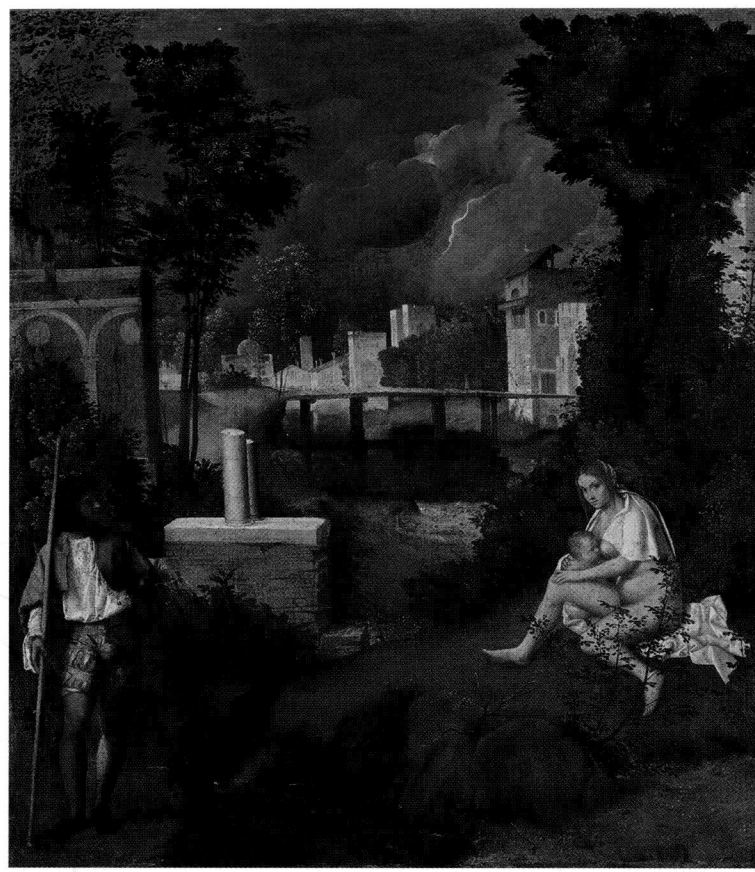

16.29 Giorgione, *The Tempest*. ca. 1505. Oil on canvas, 31¼ × 28¾" (79.5 × 73 cm). Galleria dell'Accademia, Venice

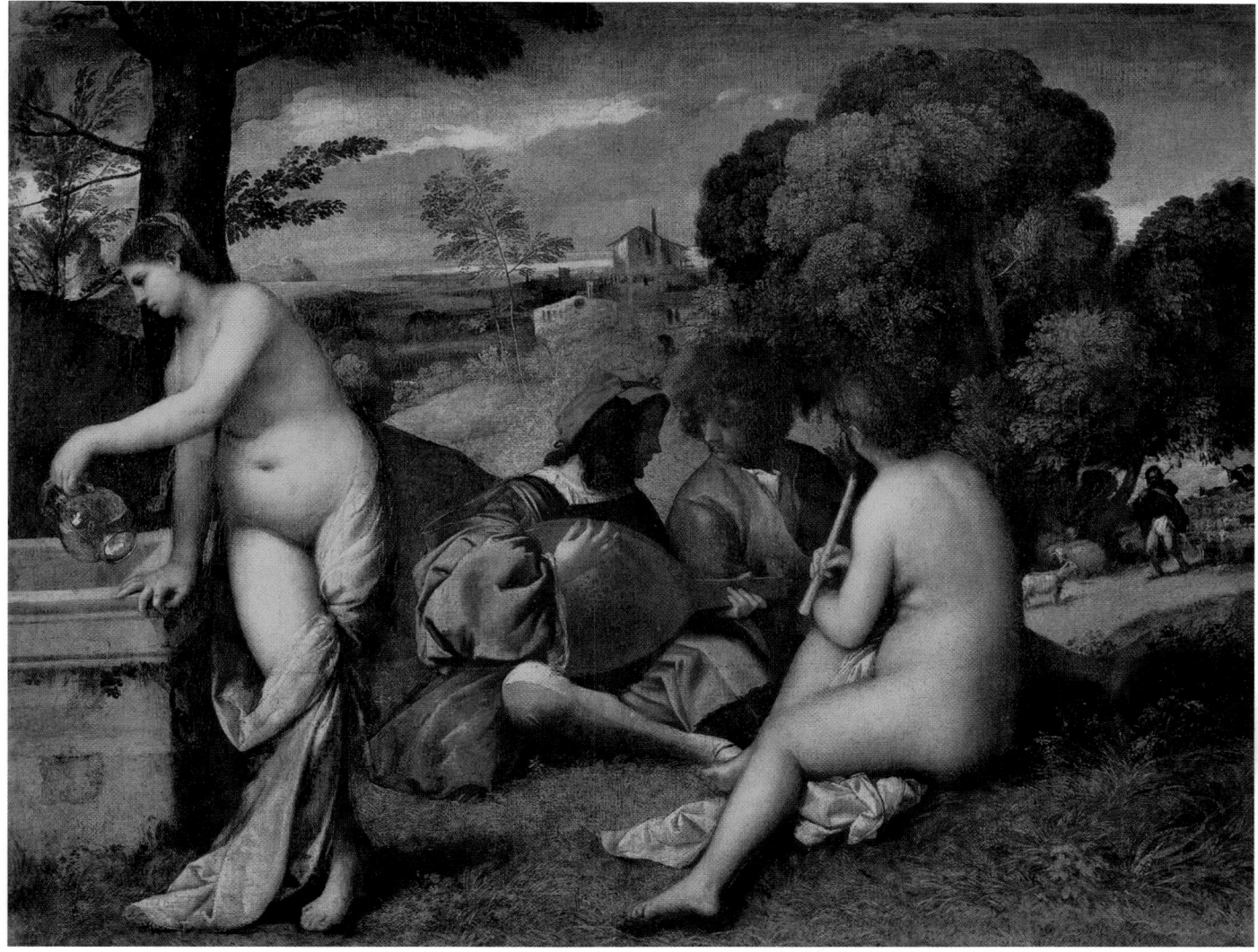

16.30 Giorgione (and Titian?), *Fête Champêtre* (*Pastoral Concert*). ca. 1509–10. Oil on canvas, 43¼ × 54⅜" (105 × 136.5 cm). Musée du Louvre, Paris

the grounds for criticizing or praising paintings well beyond the sixteenth century.

Titian

Giorgione died before he could fully explore the sensuous, lyrical world he had created in the *Fête Champêtre*. This task was taken up by Titian (Tiziano Vecellio, 1488/90–1576), who trained with Bellini and then with Giorgione and even repainted some of their works. Titian would dominate Venetian painting for the next half-century. Throughout his long life, he earned commissions from the most illustrious patrons in Europe; he trained many of the most important Venetian artists of the next century.

Titian's interpretation of the legacy of Giorgione may be seen in the *Bacchanal* (fig. **16.31**), commissioned around 1518 by Alfonso d'Este, the duke of Ferrara, for his Camerino d'Alabastro (Little Room of Alabaster). In this painting Titian attempted to remake a Roman painting known only from descriptions by the Roman author Philostratus. The theme is the effect of a river of wine on the inhabitants of the island of Andros. Titian depicts a crowd of figures in various stages of undress hoisting jugs of wine and generally misbehaving. The painting thus competes with both antique art and literature. Titian's landscape, rich in contrasts of cool and warm tones, has all the poetry of Giorgione, but the figures are of another breed. Active and muscular, they move with a joyous freedom that recalls Raphael's *Galatea* (see fig. 16.27).

By this time, many of Michelangelo's and Raphael's compositions had been engraved; it was from these reproductions that Titian became familiar with the Roman High Renaissance. At least one figure, the man bending over to fill his jug in the river, may be copied from Michelangelo. A number of the figures in his *Bacchanal* also reflect the influence of classical art. Titian's approach to antiquity, however, is very different from Raphael's. He visualizes the realm of ancient myths as part of the natural world, inhabited not by animated statues but by beings of flesh and blood. The nude young woman who has passed out in the lower right corner is posed in such a way as to show off her beautiful young body for the viewer's pleasure. The figures of the

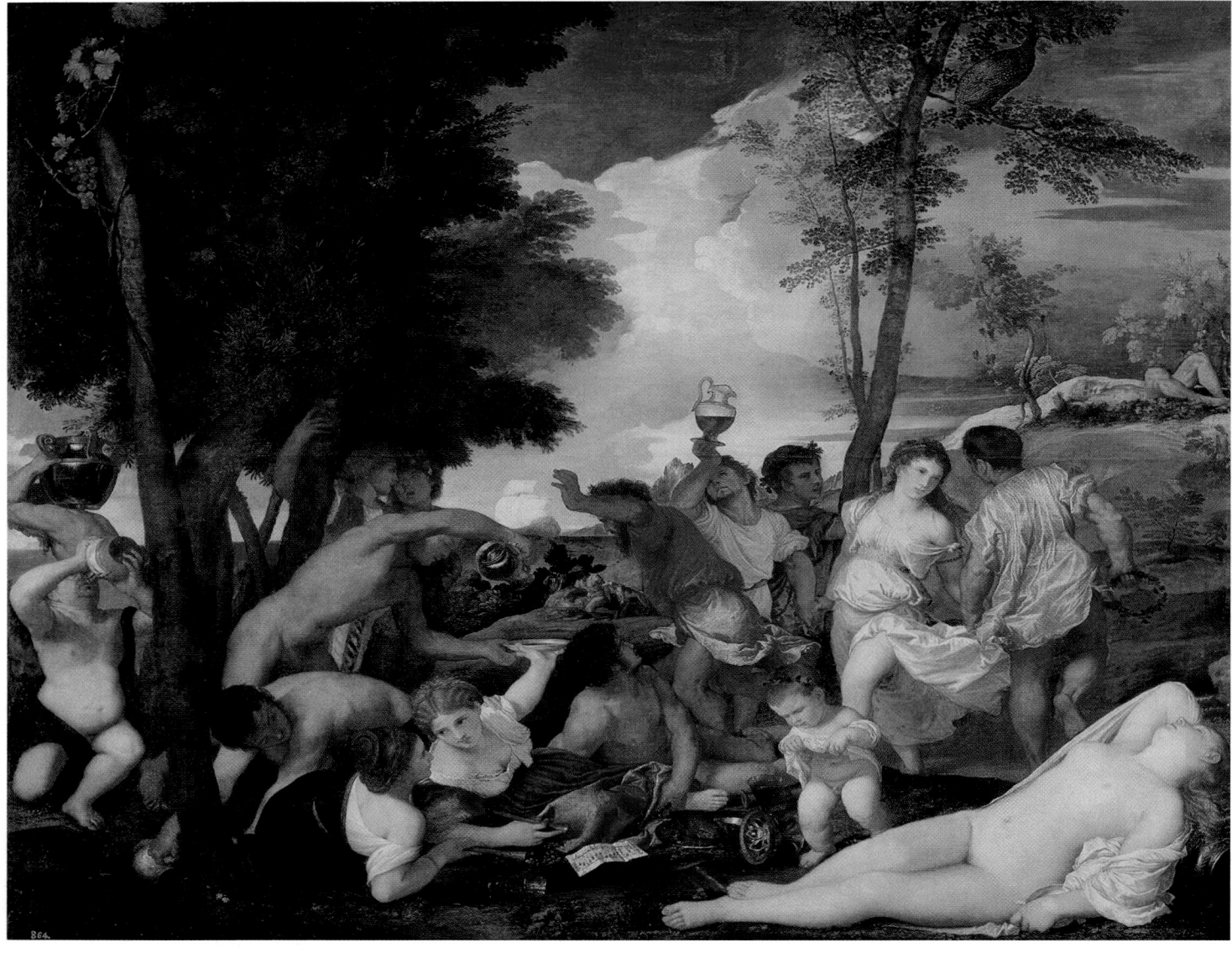

16.31 Titian, *Bacchanal*. ca. 1518. Oil on canvas, 5'8⅝" × 6'4" (1.7 × 1.9 m). Museo del Prado, Madrid

Bacchanal are idealized just enough to persuade us that they belong to a long-lost Golden Age. They invite us to share their blissful state in a way that makes the *Galatea* seem cold and remote by comparison.

Titian's ability to transform older traditions can also be seen in his *Madonna with Members of the Pesaro Family* (fig. **16.32**), commissioned in 1519 and installed in 1526 on the altar of the Immaculate Conception of the Franciscan church of Santa Maria Gloriosa dei Frari. Here, he takes a *sacra conversazione* in the tradition of Domenico Veneziano and Giovanni Bellini (see figs. 15.30 and 15.54) and reimagines both the composition and the figures. He sets the Virgin and Child at the apex of a triangular arrangement of figures, but replaces the familiar frontal view with an oblique one that is far more active. The infant Jesus is as natural as the child in the *Bacchanal*, pudgy and innocently playing with his mother's veil. More solemnly, the Virgin and St. Peter turn to the donor, Jacopo Pesaro, seen kneeling in devotion at the left. On the other side are the donor's brothers and sons with SS. Francis and Anthony of Padua.

Titian places the Virgin's throne on the steps of a monumental church. The huge columns, which are the key to the setting, represent the gateway to Heaven, traditionally identified with Mary herself; the painting celebrates her as the Immaculate Conception, who was born without Original Sin. Because the view is diagonal, open sky and clouds fill most of the background. Except for the kneeling donors, every figure seems to move. The officer with the flag bearing the coats of arms of Pesaro and of Pope Alexander VI seems ready to lead a charge up the steps. He is probably

16.32 Titian, *Madonna with Members of the Pesaro Family*. 1526. Oil on canvas, 16' × 8'10" (4.9 × 2.7 m). Santa Maria Gloriosa dei Frari, Venice

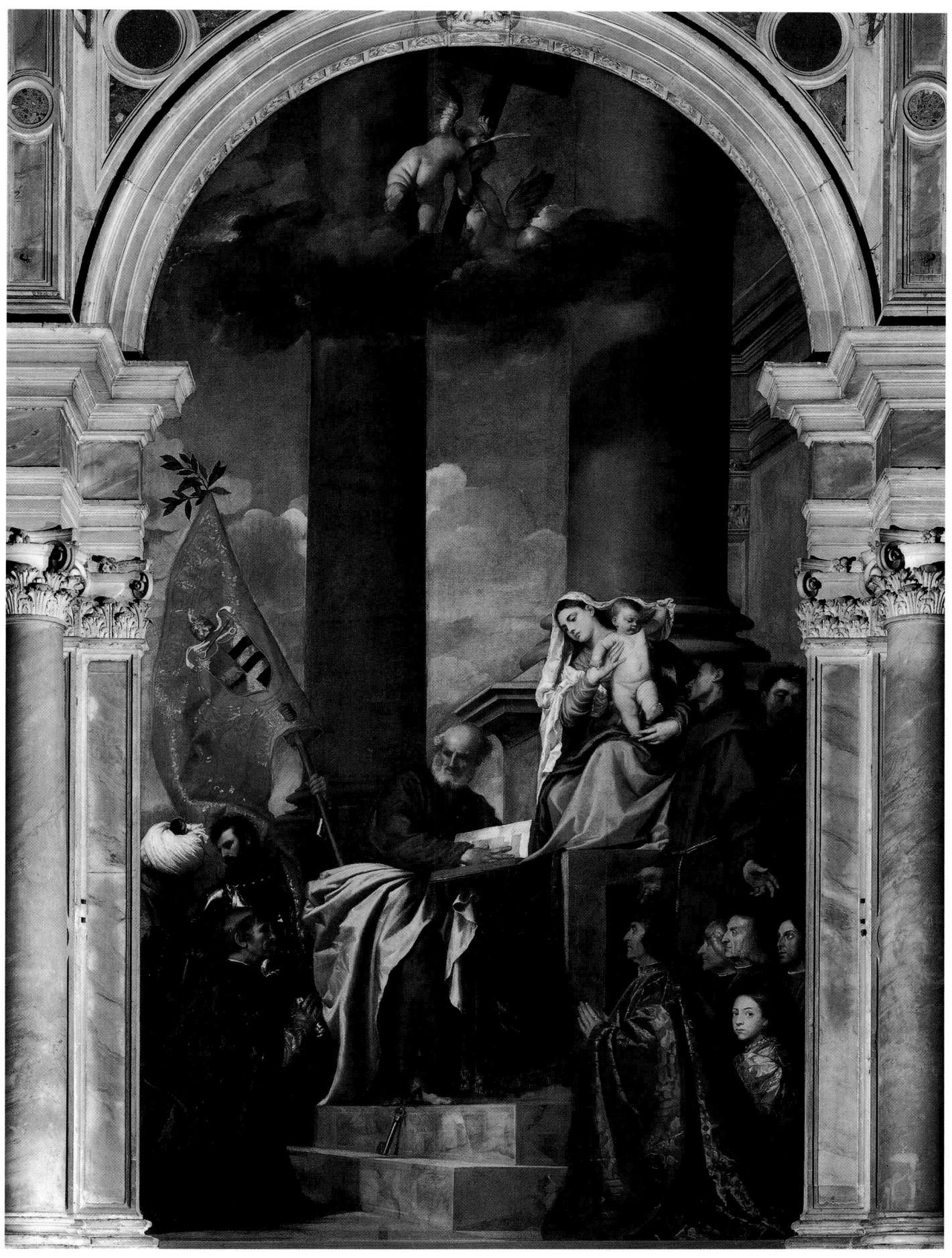

St. Maurice, namesake of the battle at Santa Mauro. There, the papal fleet commanded by Pesaro, bishop of Paphos, and the Venetian navy, under his cousin Benedetto Pesaro, defeated the Turks in 1502—note the turbaned figure beside him. St. Peter, identified by the key near his foot, represents the Catholic Church victorious over Islam and, as Pesaro's patron saint, acts as his intercessor with the Madonna. The design remains harmoniously self-contained, despite the strong drama. Brilliant sunlight makes every color and texture sparkle, in keeping with the joyous spirit of the altar. The only hint of tragedy is the cross held by the two little angels. Hidden by clouds from the participants in the *sacra conversazione*, it adds a note of poignancy to the scene.

After Raphael's death, Titian became the most sought-after portraitist of the age. His immense gifts, evident in the donors' portraits in the *Pesaro Madonna*, are equally striking in the *Man with a Blue Sleeve* (fig. 16.33). Titian places his sitter against a nonspecific backdrop behind a stone parapet, on which his initials ("T. V." for Tiziano Vecellio) appear. This is an arrangement pioneered by Flemish painters. The man turns to look at a viewer, making eye contact. His self-confident air is expressed not only by his cool glance, but also by the commanding presence of the man's projecting arm, which appears to reach out into a viewer's space. The man also wears a fur robe: His garment indicates his elite social status. Titian records the textures of hair, cloth, and stone with great fidelity, all the while wrapping his figure in an atmospheric space through his use of chiaroscuro. The identity of the sitter is not known, but Titian attempts to record his personality as well as his appearance. An early tradition identified the man as the poet Ariosto; another hypothesis identifies him as a Venetian patrician for whose family Titian worked; yet another would claim this as a self-portrait. In any case, Titian's links to Bellini and to Giorgione shine through in this image.

Titian's career was to last long into the sixteenth century. His art is based on nature, whose likeness he records with great skill. He endows his figures with grace and personality, and wraps them in atmospheric light. Titian's gift for compositions using naturalistic forms inspired by the ancient world make him a true representative of the High Renaissance.

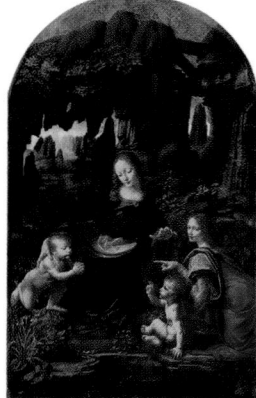

ca. 1485 Leonardo in Milan begins *The Virgin of the Rocks*

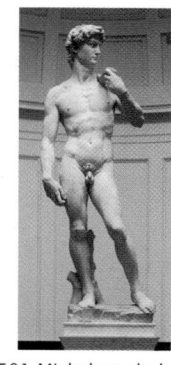

1501 Michelangelo begins work on the *David*

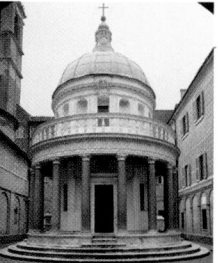

1502-11 Bramante's Tempietto

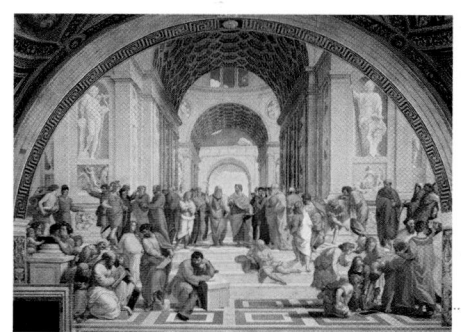

1508-11 Raphael's *The School of Athens*

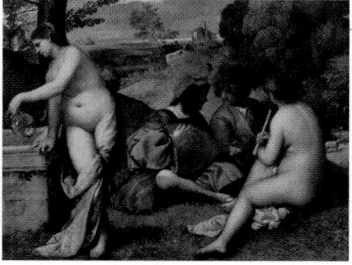

ca. 1509-10 Giorgione's *Fête Champêtre*

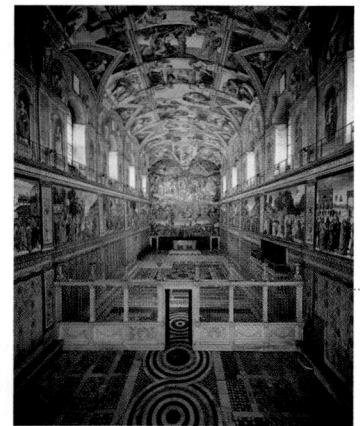

1512 Michelangelo's Sistine Chapel ceiling completed

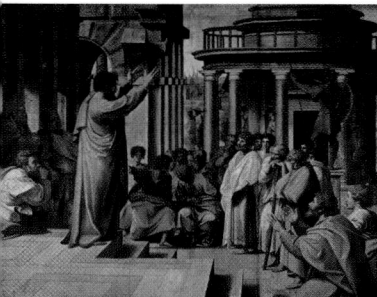

1515 Raphael's cartoon for tapestry of *St. Paul Preaching at Athens*

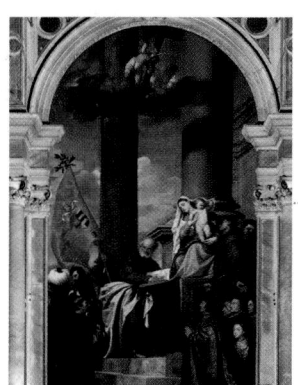

1526 Titian's *Madonna with Members of the Pesaro Family*

The High Renaissance in Italy, 1495–1520

1480

1490

◀ 1492 Death of Lorenzo de' Medici

◀ 1494 *Ship of Fools* published in Basel

◀ 1498 Execution of Savonarola in Florence

1500

◀ 1503 Pope Julius II assumes papal throne

1505 Giovanni Bellini's *Madonna and Saints*

◀ 1509 League of Cambrai formed against Venice

1510

◀ 1512 Florentine Republic dismantled; Medici return
◀ 1513 Leo X pope

◀ 1517 Luther posts his *Ninety-five Theses*, sparking the Reformation

◀ 1519 Leonardo dies in France

1520

◀ 1521 Hernán Cortés conquers Mexico for Spain

1530

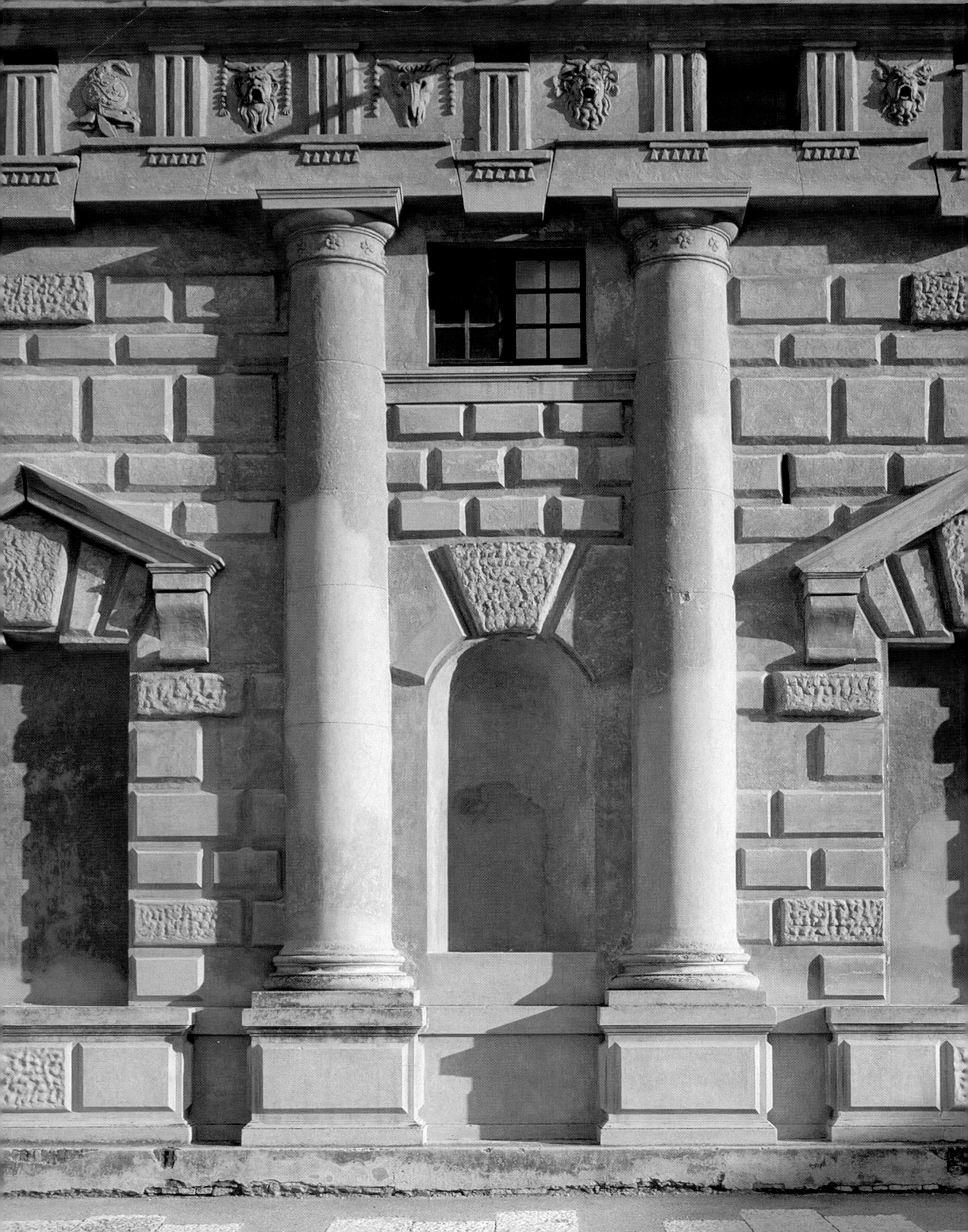

CHAPTER 17

The Late Renaissance and Mannerism in Sixteenth-Century Italy

FROM THE MOMENT THAT MARTIN LUTHER POSTED HIS CHALLENGE to the Roman Catholic Church in Wittenberg in 1517, the political and cultural landscape of Europe began to change. Europe's ostensible religious unity was fractured as entire regions left the Catholic fold. The great powers of France, Spain, and Germany warred with each other on the Italian

peninsula, even as the Turkish expansion into Europe threatened all. The spiritual challenge of the Reformation and the rise of powerful courts affected Italian artists in this period by changing the climate in which they worked and the nature of their patronage. No single style dominated the sixteenth century in Italy, though all the artists working in what is conventionally called the Late Renaissance were profoundly affected by the achievements of the High Renaissance.

The authority of the generation of the High Renaissance would both challenge and nourish later generations of artists. In the works of Leonardo, Raphael, Bramante, and Giorgione, younger artists could observe their elders' skillful rendering of chiaroscuro, perspective, and sfumato, as well as the elder generation's veneration of antiquity. The new generations imitated their technical expertise, their compositions, and their themes. At the same time, the artists of the High Renaissance continued to seek new ways to solve visual problems. Indeed, two of the key figures of the older generation lived to transform their styles: Michelangelo was active until 1564, and Titian until 1576.

The notion of the artist as an especially creative figure was passed on to later generations, yet much had changed. International interventions in Italy came to a head in 1527 when Rome itself was invaded and sacked by imperial troops of the

Habsburgs; three years later, Charles V was crowned Holy Roman emperor in Bologna. His presence in Italy had important repercussions: In 1530, he overthrew the reestablished Republic of Florence and restored the Medici to power. Cosimo I de' Medici became duke of Florence in 1537 and grand duke of Tuscany in 1569. Charles also promoted the rule of the Gonzaga of Mantua and awarded a knighthood to Titian. He and his successors became avid patrons of Titian, spreading the influence and prestige of Italian Renaissance style throughout Europe.

The Protestant movement spread quickly through northern Europe, as Luther, Zwingli, Calvin, and other theologians rejected papal authority and redefined Christian doctrine. Some of the reformers urged their followers to destroy religious images as idolatrous, leading to widespread destruction of images, stained glass, and other religious art. Italy itself, home of the Roman Catholic Church, resisted the new faiths. Nonetheless, through the first half of the sixteenth century, pressures for reform within the Catholic Church grew. The Roman Church had traditionally approved the role of images as tools for teaching and for encouraging piety, and through the efforts of reformers, this was now affirmed as official Church policy. (See www.myartslab.com.) But with its authority threatened by the Protestant Reformation, the Catholic Church asserted even more control over the content and style of images to assure doctrinal correctness. As it sought to define itself against the Protestant Reformation, religious imagery became increasingly standardized.

Detail of figure 17.24, Giulio Romano. Courtyard of the Palazzo del Te

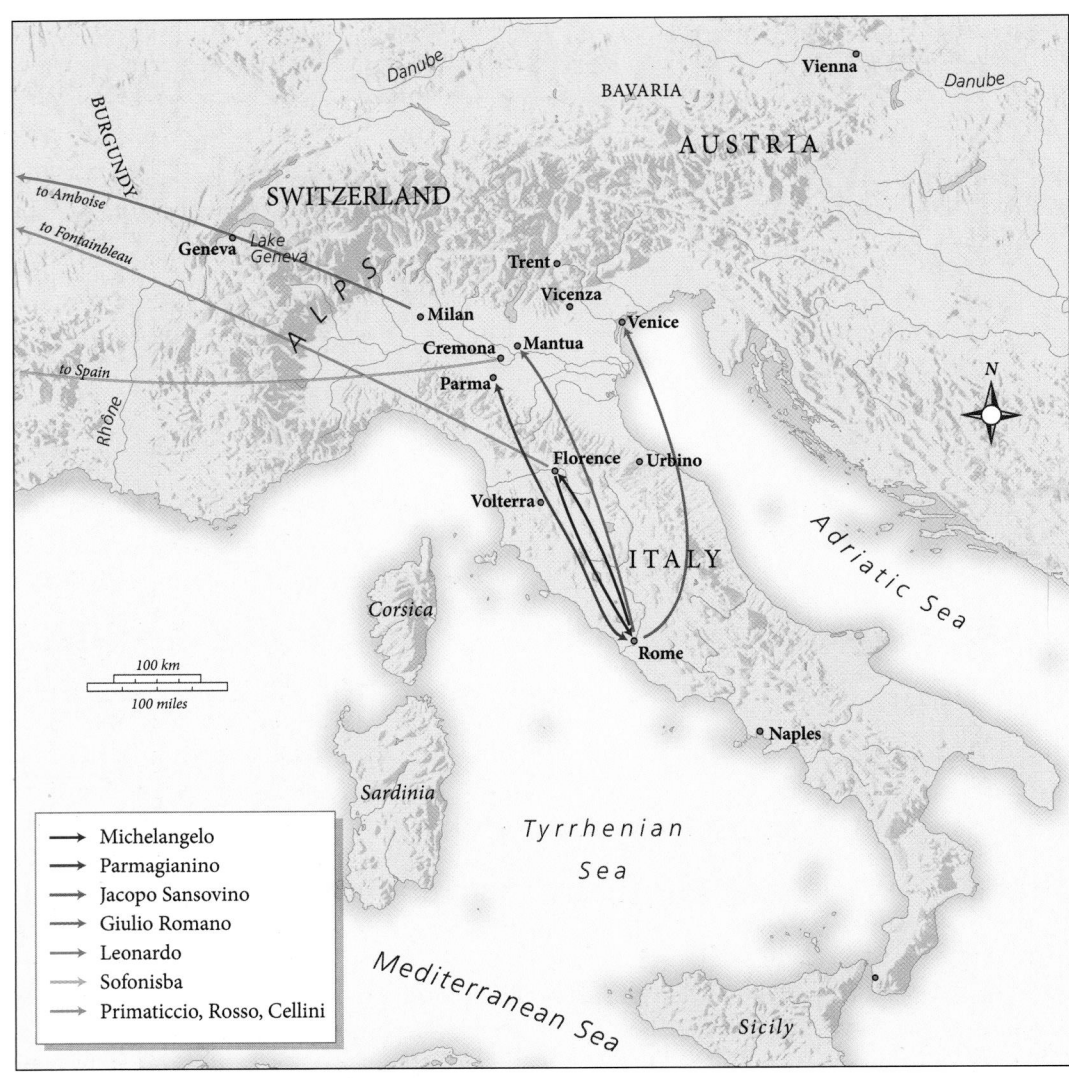

Map 17.1   Travels of some artists in sixteenth-century Italy

Artists responded to all these phenomena. The Sack of Rome in 1527 scattered Roman-based artists throughout Italy and Europe (map **17.1**). Commissions came mostly from the princely courts, so artists' works reflected the taste and concerns of this powerful elite. The connections among the courts helped to spread a new style, usually labeled Mannerist, which lasted through much of the century. The style was typically used for paintings and sculptures, though some works of architecture exhibit Mannerist tendencies.

The term derived from the word *maniera*, meaning manner or style, which was used approvingly by contemporaries. Building on the achievements of Raphael and Michelangelo, above all, artists of the 1520s and later developed a style that emphasized technical virtuosity, erudite subject matter, beautiful figures, and deliberately complex compositions that would appeal to sophisticated tastes. Mannerism became a style of utmost refinement, which emphasized grace, variety, and virtuoso display instead of clarity and unity. Mannerist artists self-consciously explored new definitions of beauty: Rather than repeat ancient forms, they experimented with proportions, ideal figure types, and unusual compositions. Like the artists of the High Renaissance, they aimed for originality and personal expression, which they considered their due as privileged creators.

Just what Mannerism represented continues to spark debate. Some have argued that it signified a decline, because it rejected the standards of the High Renaissance. (These critics, of course, prefer the "classical" works of the High Renaissance.) But the reasons that artists rejected the stability, assurance, and ideal forms of the High Renaissance are not well understood. Perhaps the new generation was attempting to define itself as different from its elders. Or, Mannerism may be seen as an expression of cultural crisis. Some scholars relate it to the spiritual crises brought on by the Reformation and the Catholic Counter-Reformation, while others see Mannerism as the product of an elite class's identity and taste. Even as scholars debate its origins and meanings, it is clear that Mannerism's earliest products appear in Florence in the 1520s, which was very different from the Florence of 1505.

LATE RENAISSANCE FLORENCE: THE CHURCH, THE COURT, AND MANNERISM

Under Medici rule, from 1512 to 1527, Florentine artists absorbed the innovations of the High Renaissance. Pope Leo X sent Michelangelo from Rome to Florence to work on projects for the Medici. The artistic descendants of Raphael came to the city as

well. Having contributed so much to the development of the Early and High Renaissance, Florentine artists now developed a new style that seems to reject the serenity and confidence of High Renaissance art. Using the techniques of naturalism, chiaroscuro, and figural composition learned from Leonardo, Michelangelo, and Raphael, this generation of artists made images that are less balanced and more expressive than those of the earlier generation. In works of the 1520s, a group of Florentine artists created images of deep spiritual power in this new style. This spiritual resurgence may be a reaction to the challenges of the Reformation, or it may be due to the legacy of the fiery preacher Savonarola, who had preached repentance in Florence in the 1490s.

Florentine Religious Painting in the 1520s

An early expression of the new style appears in *The Descent from the Cross* (fig. **17.1**) by Rosso Fiorentino (1495–1540), whose style is very idiosyncratic. A religious society of flagellants, Catholics whose penitential rituals included whipping themselves to express penitence, hired Rosso to paint this altarpiece in 1521. The Company of the Cross of the Day in the Tuscan city of Volterra chose the theme of the lowering of the body of Christ from the Cross, the subject of Rogier van der Weyden's painting of 1438 (see fig. 14.15). To reference the name of the sponsoring group, Rosso has given a great deal of emphasis to the Cross itself. While the composition looks back in part to Early Renaissance art, such as Masaccio's *Trinity* fresco (see fig. 15.23), the composition is much less stable than the triangle used by Masaccio. Instead of moving slowly and carefully back into space, the forms all appear on the same plane. The muscular bodies of the agitated figures recall Michelangelo, but the draperies have brittle, sharp-edged planes. The low horizon line sets the figures against a dark sky, creating a disquieting effect. The colors are not primaries but sharply contrasting, and the brilliant light seems to fall on the bodies irrationally. Unlike the orderly calm and deep space of Leonardo's *The Last Supper* (see fig. 16.6), Rosso creates an unstable composition within a compressed space staffed by figures that move frantically to lower the body of Christ. Only Christ's figure appears serene in the midst of this emotionally charged image. The Mannerist rejection of High Renaissance ideals allows Rosso to create in *The Descent from the Cross* a work that was especially appropriate to the piety of the confraternity members who commissioned it. Rosso himself left central Italy after the Sack of Rome in 1527 by Charles V, ultimately being lured to France to work for Francis I at his palace of Fontainebleau (see map 17.1 and Chapter 18).

Rosso's friend and contemporary Jacopo da Pontormo (1494–1556) developed his own version of the Mannerist style. The Capponi family hired Pontormo to transform their family chapel in the church of Santa Felicita in Florence (fig. **17.2**). The architecture of the chapel, built around 1420, is Brunelleschian in its simplicity, consisting of a dome over a square room, as in the Old Sacristy at San Lorenzo (see fig. 15.6). When Ludovico di Gino Capponi acquired its patronage in 1525, to be used as

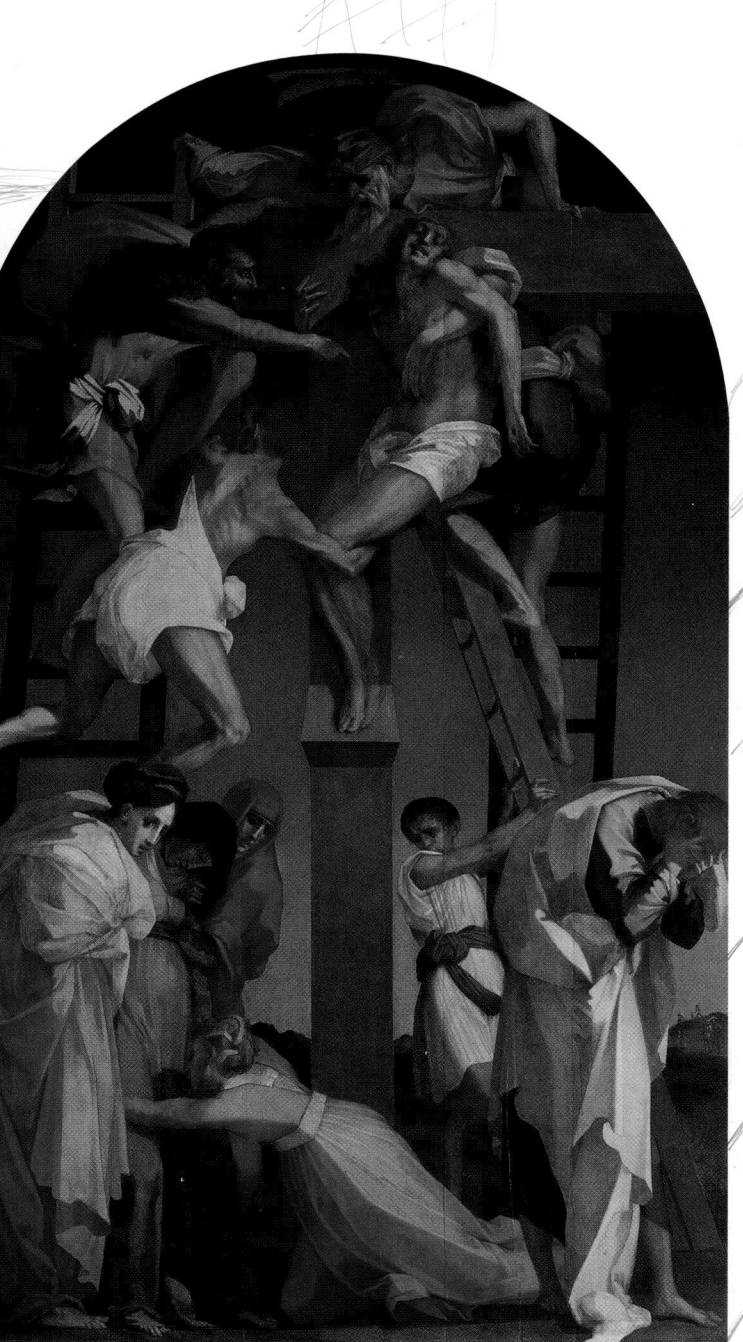

17.1 Rosso Fiorentino, *The Descent from the Cross.* 1521. Oil on panel, 13' × 6'6" (4 × 2 m). Commissioned for the Chapel of the Compagnia della Croce di Giorno in the church of San Francisco in Volterra. Pinacoteca Comunale, Volterra

may have been inspired by the colors of the Sistine Chapel ceiling (see fig. 16.19). Although they seem to act together, the mourners are lost in a grief too personal to share with one another. In this hushed atmosphere, anguish is transformed into a lyrical expression of exquisite sensitivity. The entire scene is as haunted as Pontormo's self-portrait just to the right of the swooning Madonna. The body of Christ is held up for a viewer, much as the host is during the Mass, the image conveying to believers a sense of the tragic scale of Christ's sacrifice, which the Eucharist reenacts. Originally, the dome above the altarpiece depicted God the Father, to whom the body would be offered. Pontormo may have rejected the values of the High Renaissance, but he endows this image with deeply felt emotion.

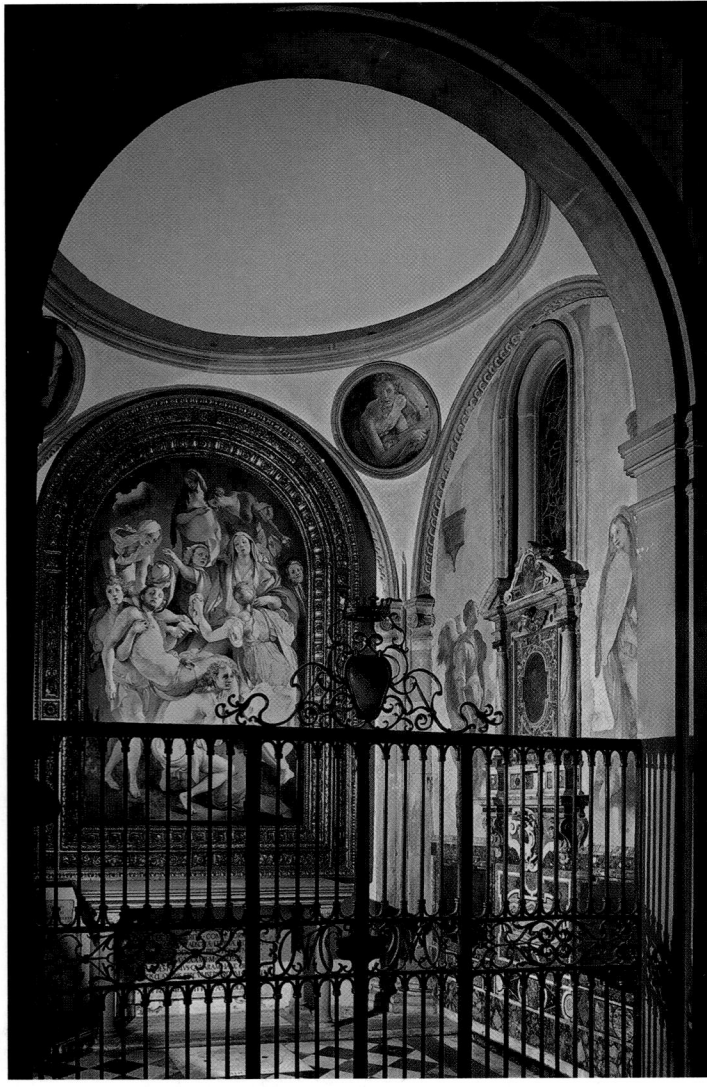

17.2 Capponi Chapel, Santa Felicità, Florence. Built by Filippo Brunelleschi, 1419–23. Paintings by Pontormo, 1525–28

a funerary chapel, he changed its dedication to the Pietà. He commissioned Pontormo to paint the altarpiece (fig. **17.3**) and frescoes on the walls and dome. The altarpiece, completed by 1528, remains in its original location in the chapel.

Pontormo's painting contrasts sharply with Rosso's *The Descent from the Cross*. It lacks a cross or any other indications of a specific narrative, so its subject is unclear, although the chapel's dedication points to the Pietà. The Virgin swoons as two androgynous figures hold up the body of Christ for a viewer's contemplation. Unlike Rosso's elongated forms, Pontormo's figures display an ideal beauty and sculptural solidity inspired by Michelangelo, yet Pontormo has squeezed them into an implausibly confined space.

In Pontormo's painting, everything is subordinated to the play of graceful rhythms created by the tightly interlocking forms. The colors are desaturated: pale blues, pinks, oranges, and greens that

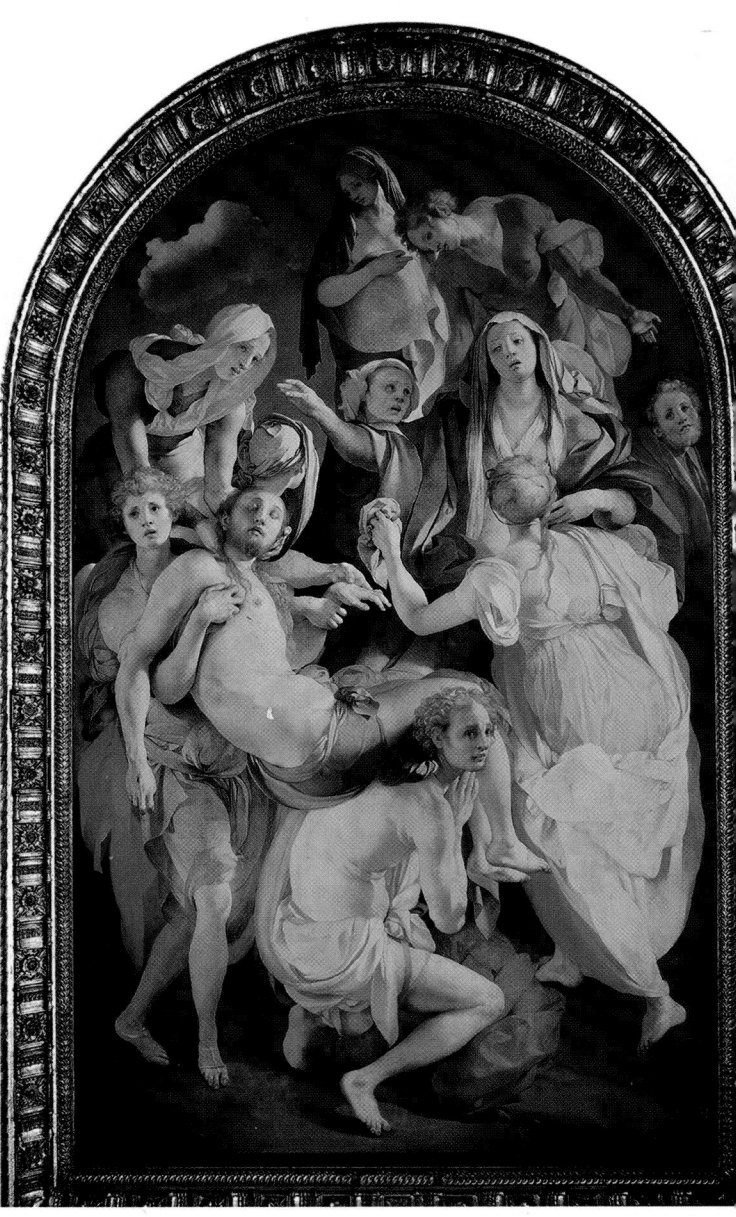

17.3 Jacopo da Pontormo, *Pietà*. ca. 1526–28. Oil on panel, 10'3" × 6'4" (3.1 × 1.9 m). Santa Felicita, Florence

The Medici in Florence: From Dynasty to Duchy

In the chaos after the Sack of Rome of 1527, the Medici were again ousted from Florence and the Republic of Florence was reinstated. But the restoration of relations between the pope and the Holy Roman emperor allowed the Medici to return to power by 1530. The Medici pope Clement VII (r. 1523–1534) promoted his family's interests, and worked to enhance their power as the rulers of Florence. Although he was an ardent republican, Michelangelo was continually employed by this court, executing works intended to glorify the Medici dynasty in Florence.

THE NEW SACRISTY OF SAN LORENZO Michelangelo's activities centered on the Medici church of San Lorenzo. A century after Brunelleschi's design for the sacristy of this church (see fig. 15.6), which held the tombs of an earlier generation of Medici,

Pope Leo X decided to build a matching structure, the New Sacristy. It was to house the tombs of Leo X's father, Lorenzo the Magnificent, Lorenzo's brother Giuliano, and two younger members of the family, also named Lorenzo and Giuliano. Aided by numerous assistants, Michelangelo worked on the project from 1519 to 1534 and managed to complete the architecture and two of the tombs, those for the later Lorenzo and Giuliano (fig. **17.4**); these tombs are nearly mirror images of each other. Michelangelo conceived of the New Sacristy as an architectural-sculptural ensemble.

Michelangelo's chapel starts from Brunelleschi's design for a square space covered by a dome, though he inserted another story above the architrave and below the supports for the dome. This gives the chapel greater verticality and brings in more light. The wall scheme also follows Brunelleschi, although the *pietra serena* pilasters and entablatures are bolder and taller than Brunelleschi's. Between the pilasters Michelangelo inserted blind windows

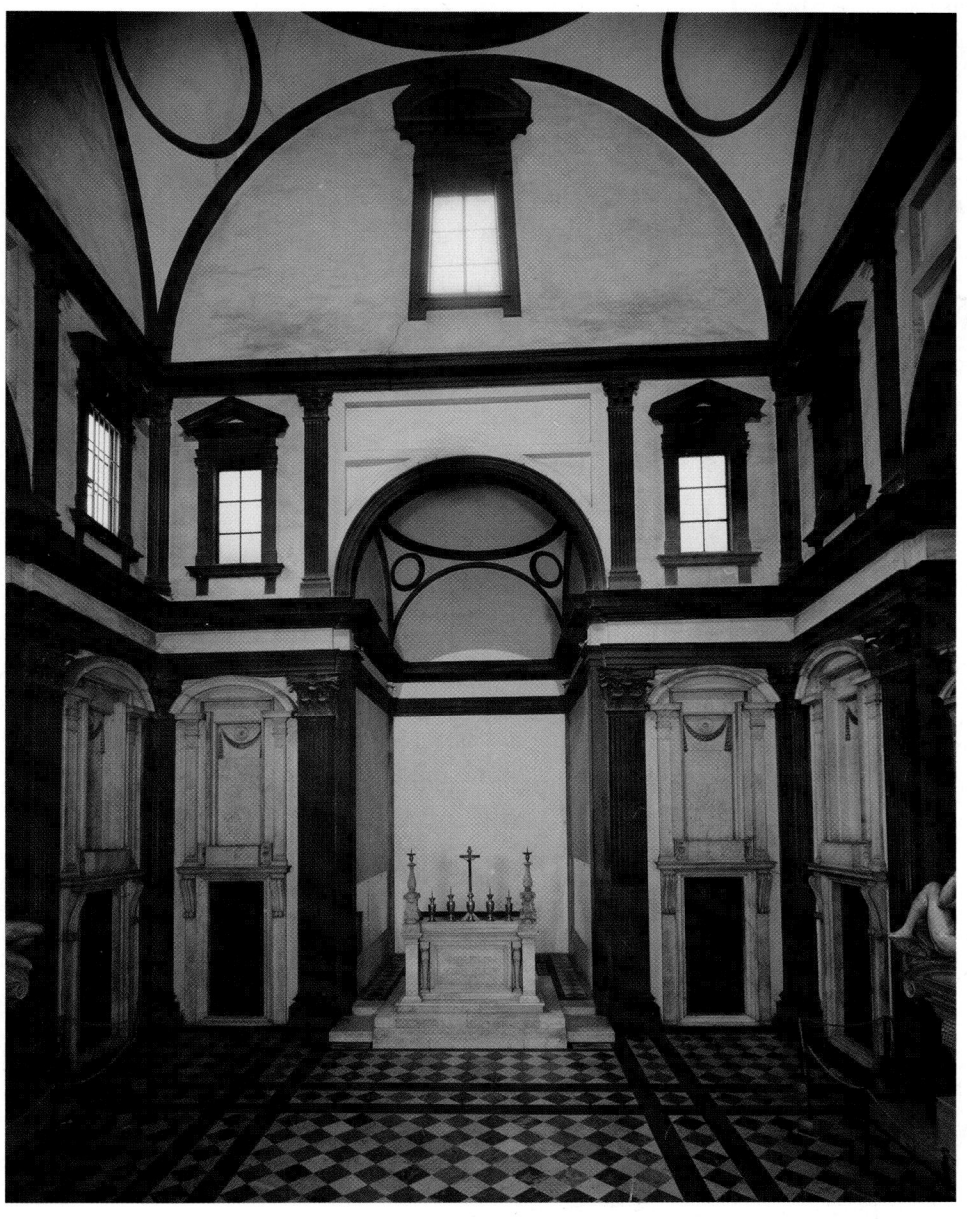

17.4 Michelangelo, New Sacristy, San Lorenzo, Florence. 1519–34

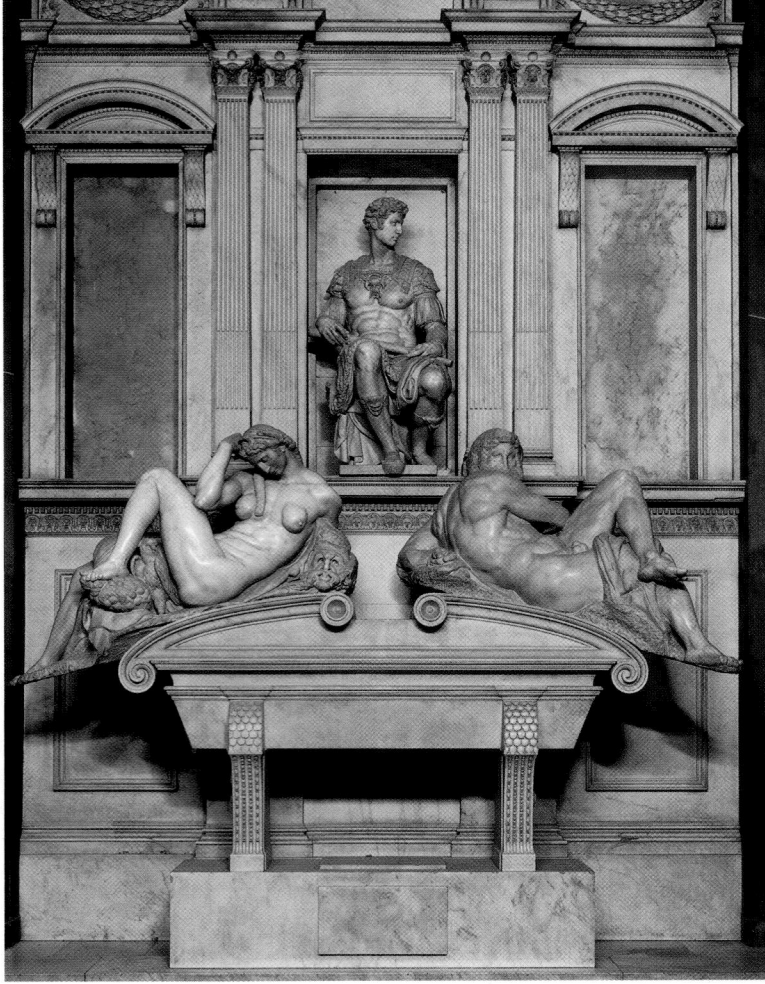

17.5 Michelangelo. Tomb of Giuliano de' Medici. 1519–34. Marble, height of central figure 5'11" (1.81 m). New Sacristy, San Lorenzo, Florence

of verticals and horizontals hold the triangle of statues in place; their slender, sharp-edged forms contrast with the roundness and weight of the sculpture.

The design shows some kinship with such Early Renaissance tombs as Rossellino's tomb for Leonardo Bruni (see fig. 15.18), but the differences are marked. There is no outright Christian imagery, no inscription, and the effigy has been replaced by two allegorical figures—Day on the right and Night on the left. Some lines penned on one of Michelangelo's drawings suggest what these figures mean: "Day and Night speak, and say: We with our swift course have brought the Duke Giuliano to death….It is only just that the Duke takes revenge [for] he has taken the light from us; and with his closed eyes has locked ours shut, which no longer shine on earth." The reclining figures, themselves derived from ancient river-gods, contrast in mood: Day, whose face was left deliberately unfinished, seems to brood, while Night appears restless. Giuliano, the ideal image of the prince, wears classical military garb and bears no resemblance to the deceased. ("A thousand years from now, nobody will know what he looked like,"

topped by curved pediments. Such features activate the wall, leaving little blank surface; Michelangelo treated the walls themselves as sculptural forms in a way Brunelleschi never did.

The New Sacristy is the only one of the artist's works in which the statues remain in the setting originally intended for them, although their exact placement remains problematic. Michelangelo's plans for the Medici tombs underwent many changes while the work was under way. Other figures and reliefs for the project were designed but never executed. The present state of the Medici tombs can hardly be what Michelangelo ultimately intended, as the process was halted when the artist permanently left Florence for Rome in 1534.

The tomb of Giuliano (fig. **17.5**) remains an imposing visual unit, composed of a sarcophagus structure supporting two sculpted nudes above which sits an armored figure, all framed by Michelangelo's inventive reimagining of Classical architecture. The central niche seems barely to accommodate the seated figure; paired pilasters flank the figure and support an entablature that breaks over them. The curving pediments over the blank windows on either side echo the shape of the sarcophagus below. A network

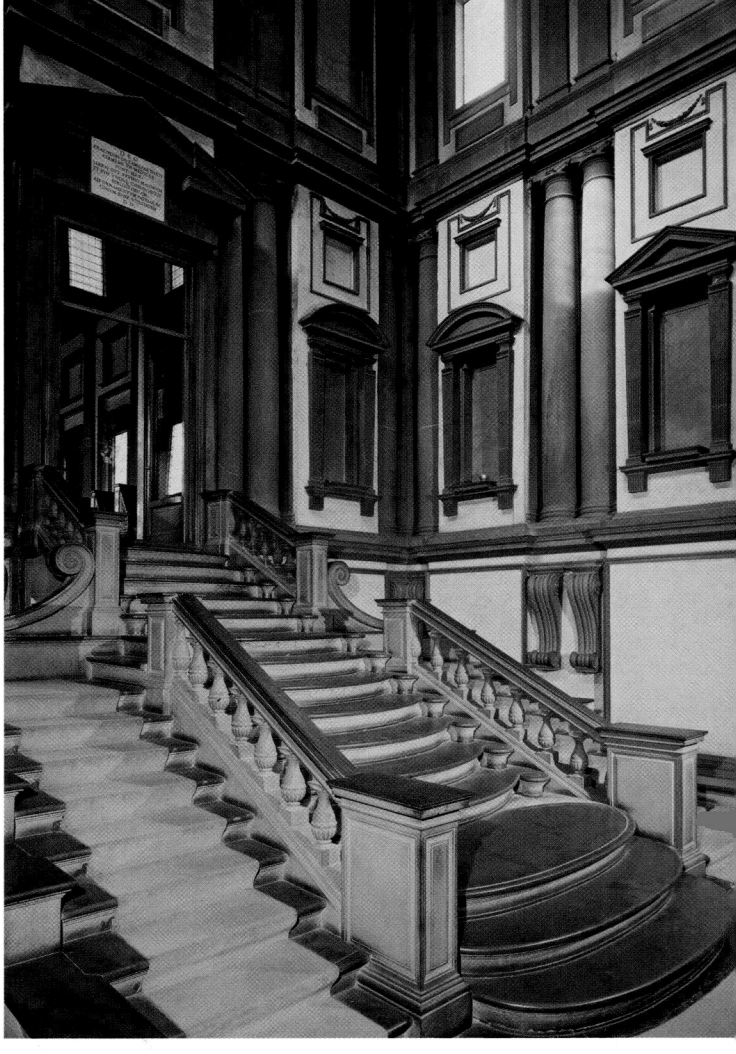

17.6 Michelangelo and Bartolommeo Ammanati. Vestibule of the Laurentian Library, Florence. Begun 1523; stairway designed 1558–59

Michelangelo is said to have remarked.) His beautifully proportioned figure seems ready for action, as he fidgets with his baton. His gaze was to be directed at the never-completed tomb of Lorenzo the Magnificent. Instead of a commemorative monument that looks retrospectively at the accomplishments of the deceased, the tomb of Giuliano and the New Sacristy as a whole were to express the triumph of the Medici family over time.

Michelangelo's reimagining of Brunelleschi at the New Sacristy inspired Vasari to write that "all artists are under a great and permanent obligation to Michelangelo, seeing that he broke the bonds and chains that had previously confined them to the creation of traditional forms." However, Michelangelo's full powers as a creator of architectural forms are only really displayed for the first time in the vestibule to the Laurentian Library, which adjoins San Lorenzo.

THE LAURENTIAN LIBRARY Clement VII commissioned this library (fig. **17.6**) in 1523 to house, for the public, the huge collection of books and manuscripts belonging to the Medici family. Such projects display the Medici beneficence to the city and their encouragement of learning. The Laurentian Library is a long narrow hall that is preceded by the imposing vestibule, begun in 1523 but not completed until much later.

Judged by the standards of Bramante or Vitruvius, everything in the vestibule is wrong. The pediment above the door is broken. The pilasters defining the blank niches taper downward, and the columns belong to no recognizable order. The scroll brackets sustain nothing. Most paradoxical of all are the recessed columns. This feature flies in the face of convention. In the classical post-and-lintel system, the columns (or pilasters) and entablature must

project from the wall in order to stress their separate identities, as they do in the Roman Temple of Portunus (see fig. 7.2). Michelangelo dared to defy the classical system by inserting columns into the wall. In the confined space of the entryway, the columns give the wall a monumental dignity without intruding into the vestibule. The grand staircase, designed later by Michelangelo and built by Bartolommeo Ammanati, activates the space through its cascading forms.

THE UFFIZI, PALAZZO PITTI AND BOBOLI GARDENS
In concentrating their patronage at San Lorenzo, this generation of Medici followed the patterns of the fifteenth century. But the Medici dukes were not content to live in the Palazzo Medici built by Michelozzo. The family of Cosimo I de' Medici moved into the Palazzo della Signoria in the center of the city in 1540 (see fig. 13.15). Where earlier generations of Medici rulers separated their private residence from the seat of government, the new Medici dukes did what they could to unite them. Consequently, they had the interior of the former town hall remodeled to create a residential space, and they built new areas for both court and government.

To this end, Cosimo I de' Medici commissioned a new building to house the bureaucracies of his court in 1559. This project was assigned to Giorgio Vasari (1511–1574), the painter, historian, and architect. The building of the Uffizi, finished around 1580, consists of two long wings that face each other across a narrow court and are linked at one end by a loggia (fig. **17.7**). Situated between the Palazzo della Signoria and the Arno River, it served to restructure both the city space and the widely dispersed Florentine ministries. Numerous windows and architectural moldings enliven the façades. Colonnades interrupted by piers at

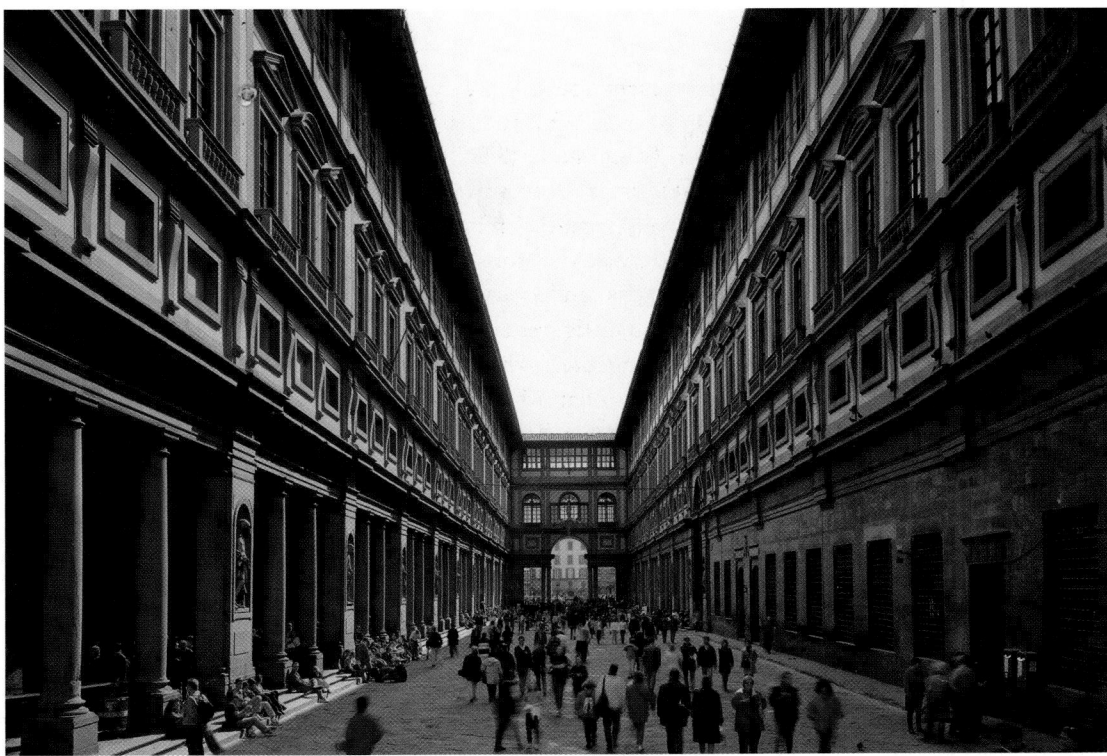

17.7 Giorgio Vasari.
Courtyard of Uffizi,
Florence. Begun 1560

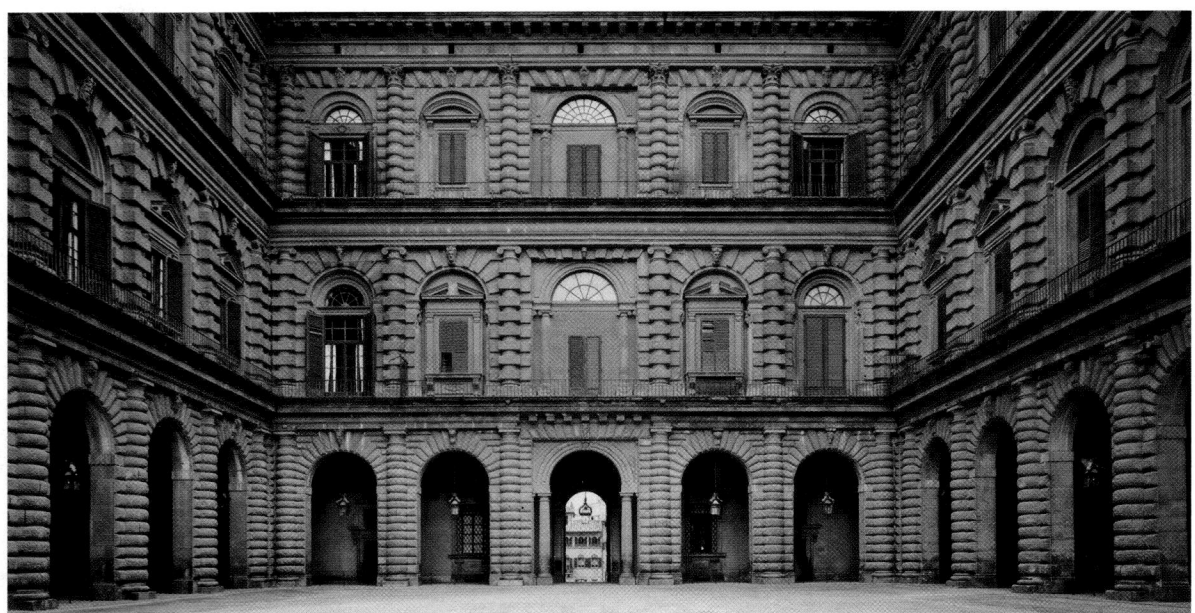

regular intervals define the long façade at left; these units define spaces allotted for different bureaucracies. Although strongly marked by Michelangelo's architecture at San Lorenzo, the courtyard also makes reference to the Roman Forum and thus links Cosimo to Roman emperors.

In their search for appropriate settings for the court, the Medici acquired the Palazzo Pitti, across the Arno River from the Uffizi, which had been built in the fifteenth century. The sculptor Bartolommeo Ammanati (1511–1592) enlarged the fifteenth-century palazzo with a courtyard between 1558 and 1570 (fig. **17.8**). Like Michelozzo's Medici palace (see fig. 15.32), this courtyard enframes a space that is both utilitarian and ceremonial; but where the fifteenth-century palace seems ornate and delicate, this courtyard has a fortresslike character. The three-story scheme of superimposed orders, derived from the Roman Colosseum (fig. 7.20), has been overlaid with an extravagant pattern of rustication that "imprisons" the columns and reduces them to a passive role, despite the display of muscularity. The creative combination of a classical vocabulary with the unorthodox treatment of the rustication creates a raw expression of power. The Palazzo Pitti functions today as a museum displaying many of the works collected by the Medici family.

In addition to the new palace, the ducal family purchased a large area around it that they transformed into a carefully

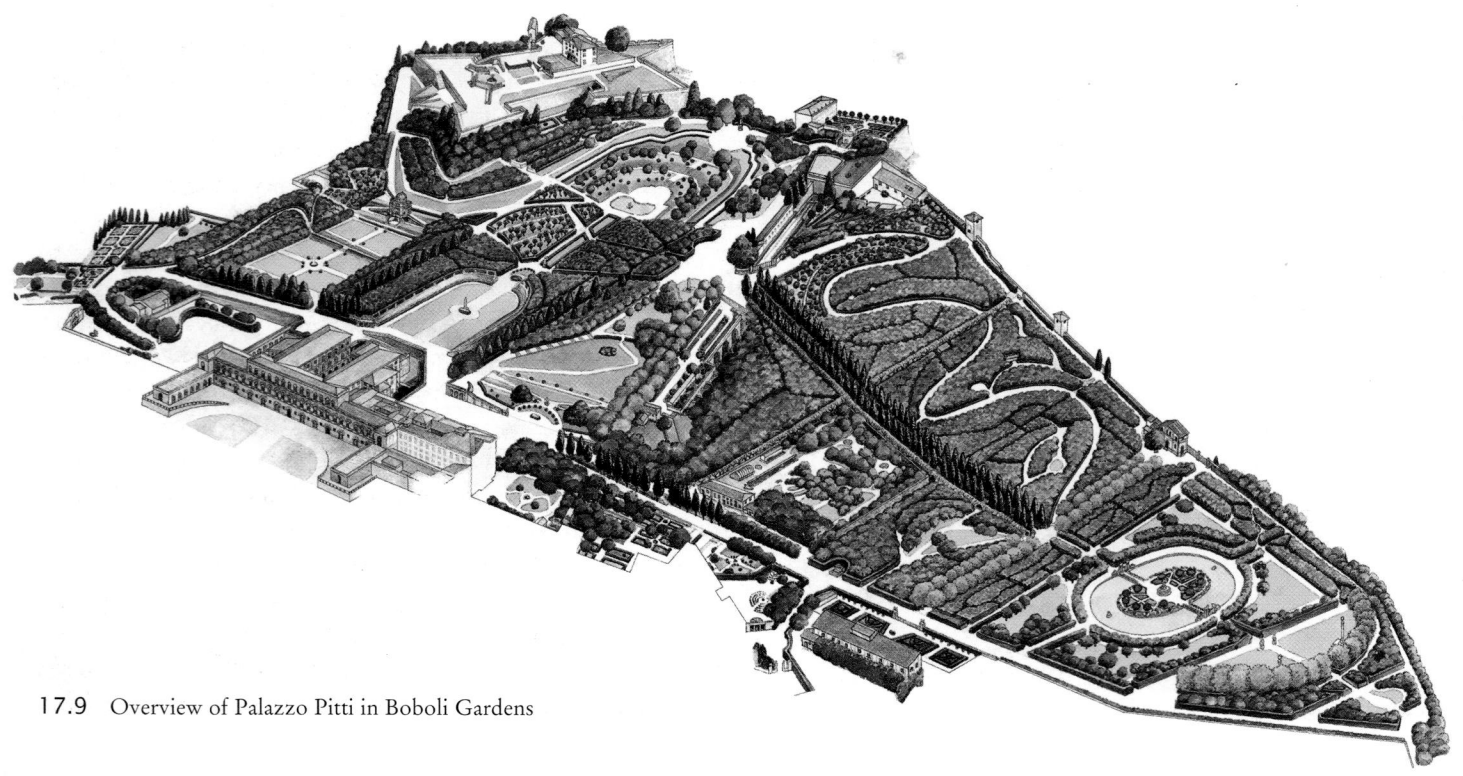

17.9 Overview of Palazzo Pitti in Boboli Gardens

landscaped park, called the Boboli Gardens (fig. **17.9**). Begun around 1549, this continued to grow and change down to the nineteenth century. The architect Nicolo Triboli (1500–1550) laid out the original plan; he imposed a regular geometry on an uneven site, including long walkways lined by foliage, fountains and pools of water, and artificial grottoes. Later in the century, other artists, including Vasari and Ammanati, adjusted and altered the design. The dukes commissioned numerous sculptures for the gardens, too, often of mythological beings or Greek gods. The gardens provided scenic vistas for the residents of the palace, but also a grand stage setting for ducal events.

PORTRAITURE AND ALLEGORY The Medici court had refined tastes and a good sense of how to use the visual arts to express their new status. As in the fifteenth century, the new generation of Medici patrons used portraiture as a means to this end. The *Portrait of Eleanora of Toledo and Her Son Giovanni de' Medici* (fig. **17.10**) by Agnolo Bronzino (1503–1572) exemplifies a new type of court portrait. This is a highly idealized painting of the wife of Cosimo I, who actually had blond hair (here darkened) and whose features have been perfected in the portrait. The portrait presents her as an ideal of beauty, just as her husband was admired for his virile good looks and courage.

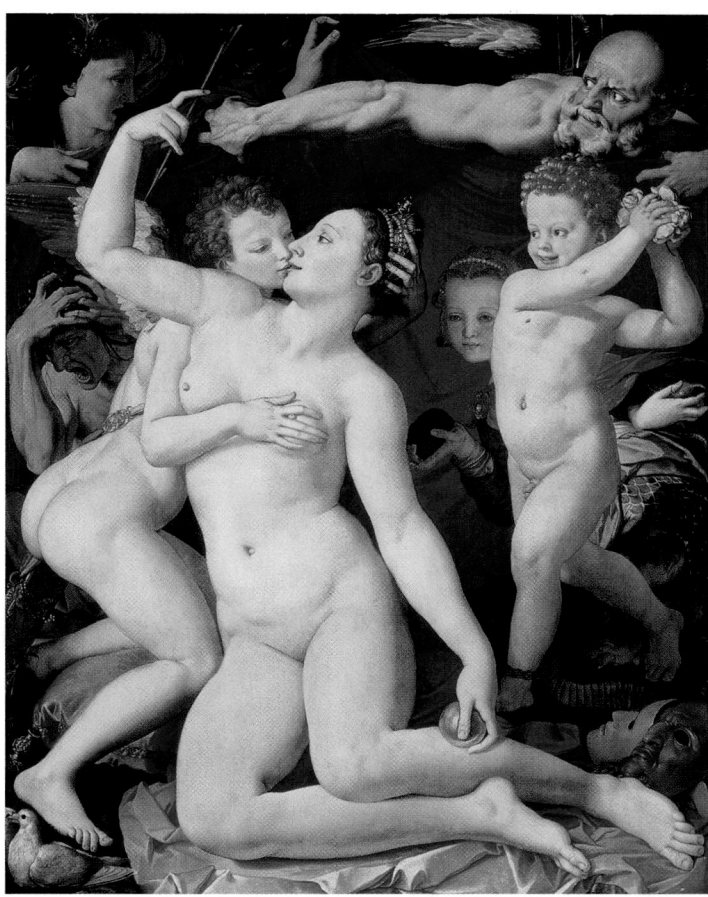

17.11 Agnolo Bronzino, *Allegory of Venus.* ca. 1546. Oil on panel, 57½ × 45⅝" (146.1 × 116.2 cm). The National Gallery, London

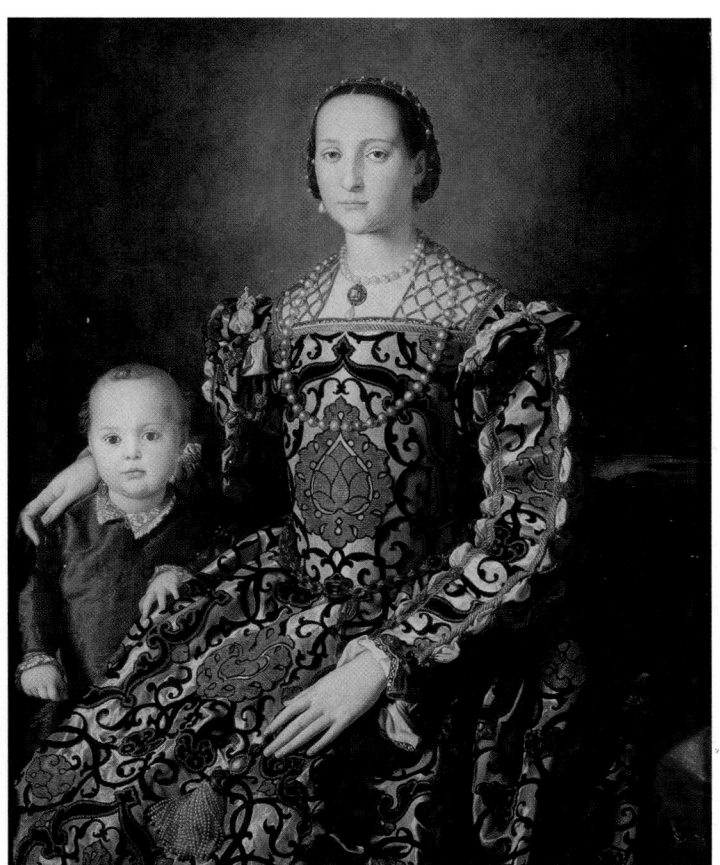

17.10 Agnolo Bronzino, *Portrait of Eleanora of Toledo and Her Son Giovanni de' Medici.* ca. 1550. Oil on panel, 45¼ × 37¾" (115 × 96 cm). Galleria degli Uffizi, Florence

An important message of the work is the continuity of the Medici dynasty, as Eleanora's arm enframes the male heir, Giovanni (born in 1543), who, however, would not outlive her. (She bore 11 children, including eight sons, before her death from tuberculosis in 1562 at about the age of 43.) This dynastic message is delivered by means of the formality of the portrait, with its frozen poses and aloof glances. Eleanora sits rigidly, with her arm resting on her silent, staring child; she wears a complicated brocaded dress and jewelry that demonstrates her wealth and status. Bronzino depicts the pair almost like a Madonna and Child, subtly comparing Eleanora to the Virgin: This reference may account for the lightening of the blue background around Eleanora's face that suggests a halo. The image contains a complex set of allusions as flattering as the improvements to her looks. Bronzino's painting describes the sitter as a member of an exalted social class, not as an individual personality. This kind of formal, distant, and allusive court portrait quickly became the ideal of court portraiture throughout Europe. (See, for example, fig. 18.26.)

Bronzino was Eleanora's preferred painter and held a court appointment. His passion for drawing and his gift for poetry came together in many of his works. Nowhere is this better seen than in his *Allegory of Venus* (fig. **17.11**), which Duke Cosimo presented to Francis I of France. From these different sources,

Benvenuto Cellini (1500–1571)

From *The Autobiography*

The Florentine sculptor wrote his autobiography between 1558 and 1566. Cellini's book retells the story of his early life, training, and artistic triumphs. It was not published until the eighteenth century. This excerpt focuses on the design and reception of the saltcellar of Francis I (see fig. 17.12). Cellini took the advice of several courtiers in approaching the project, but ultimately made his own decision about what to render in the model.

I made an oval shape the size of more than half an arm's length—in fact, almost two thirds of an arm's length—and on it, as if to show the Sea embracing the Land, I placed two nicely executed figures larger than a palm in size, seated with their legs intertwined in the same fashion as certain long-branched arms of the sea can be seen running into the land; and in the hand of the male figure of the Sea I placed a lavishly wrought ship, within which a great deal of salt could easily and well be accommodated; underneath this figure I placed four seahorses, and in the hand of this figure of the Sea I placed his

Trident. The Land I had represented as a woman whose beautiful figure was as full of as much loveliness and grace as I was able and knew how to produce, in whose hand I had placed a rich and lavishly decorated temple which rested upon the ground, and she was leaning on it with her hand; I had created the temple in order to hold the Pepper. I had placed a Horn of Plenty adorned with all the beautiful things I knew to exist in the world. Under this goddess and in the part that portrayed the earth, I had arranged all the most beautiful animals that the earth produces. Under the part devoted to the sea god I represented all the beautiful kinds of fishes and small snails that tiny space could contain; in the widest part of the oval space I created many extremely rich decorations. ... I uncovered the model [before the King], and, amazed, the King said: "This is something a hundred times more divine than anything I might have imagined. This is a magnificent piece of work by this man. He should never stop working." Then he turned to me with an expression full of delight, and told me that this was a work that pleased him enormously and that he wanted me to execute it in gold.

Source: Benvenuto Cellini, *My Life (Vita)*, tr. Julia Conaway Bondanella and Peter Bondanella (NY: Oxford University Press, 2002)

Bronzino creates a complex allegory whose meanings art historians are still probing.

Into a narrow plane close to the surface of the painting, Bronzino crowds a number of figures who have been identified only tentatively: The bald Father Time tears back the curtain from Fraud, the figure in the upper left-hand corner, to reveal Venus and Cupid in an incestuous embrace, much to the delight of the child Folly, who is armed with roses, and to the dismay of a figure tearing his hair, who has been identified as either Jealousy or Pain; on the right, Pleasure, half woman and half snake, offers a honeycomb. The moral of Bronzino's image may be that folly and pleasure blind one to the jealousy and fraud of sensual love, which time reveals.

With its extreme stylization, Bronzino's painting proclaims a refined erotic ideal that reduces passion to a genteel exchange of gestures between figures as polished and rigid as marble. The literary quality of the allegory reflects Bronzino's skill as a poet. The complexity of the conceit matches the complexity of the composition; the high quality of the technique matches the cleverness of the content. In Bronzino, the Medici found an artist whose technical virtuosity, complex imagery, and inventive compositions perfectly accorded with their taste and exemplify the Mannerist style. Cosimo's gift of a painting of such erudite imagery and accomplished technique to the king of France demonstrated his realm's achievements in the literary and visual arts.

Such complex and learned treatments occur also in the work of Benvenuto Cellini (1500–1571), a Florentine goldsmith and sculptor who owes much of his fame to his colorful autobiography. His gold saltcellar (fig. **17.12**), made for the same king, Francis I, between 1540 and 1543, is his only important work in precious metal to survive. The main function of this lavish object

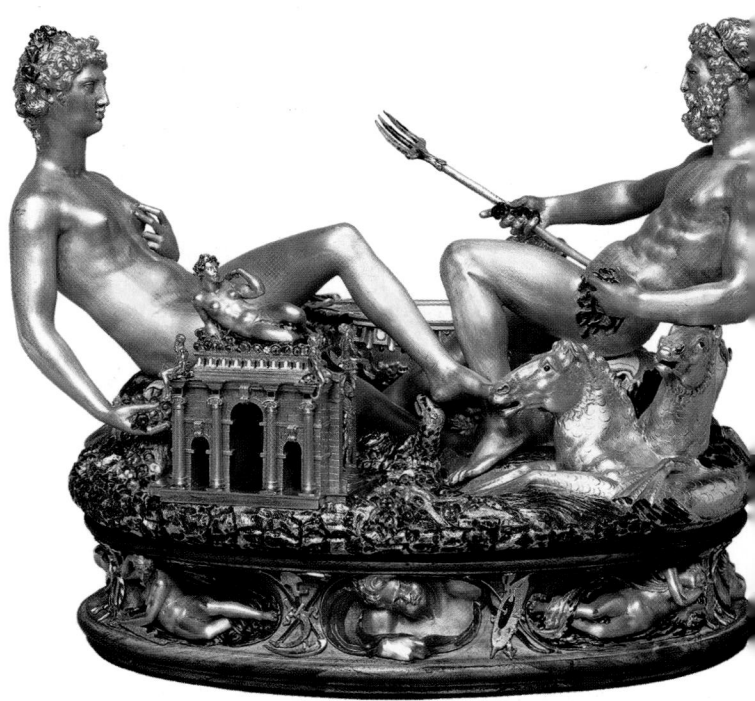

17.12   Benvenuto Cellini. Saltcellar of Francis I. 1540–43. Gold with enamel, 10¼ × 13⅛" (26 × 33.3 cm). Kunsthistorisches Museum, Vienna

is clearly as a conversation piece. Because salt comes from the sea and pepper from the earth, the boat-shaped salt container is protected by Neptune. The pepper, in a tiny triumphal arch, is watched over by a personification of Earth who, in another context, might be the god's consort Amphitrite. On the base are figures representing the four seasons and the four parts of the day. Such references remind the viewer of the Medici tombs, as does the figure personifying Earth. Cellini wants to impress with his ingenuity and skill. In his autobiography (see *Primary Source*, page 600), he explained how he came to design the model for the saltcellar and its **iconography**. He had imagined the figure of the Earth as "a woman whose beautiful figure was as full of as much loveliness and grace as I was able and knew how to produce." In true Mannerist fashion, the allegorical significance of the design is simply a pretext for this display of virtuosity. Cellini then modestly reports the reaction of Francis I to his design: "This is a magnificent piece of work by this man. He should never stop working."

THE ACCADEMIA DEL DISEGNO One of the aims of the duke was to promote the arts in Tuscany, a goal shared by Giorgio Vasari, who had dedicated his collection of biographies, first published in 1550, to Cosimo I. Cosimo sponsored the establishment of the Accademia del Disegno (Academy of Design) in 1563, intended to improve the training of artists and to enhance the status of the arts. Bronzino and Giorgio Vasari were founding members. Training in the academy stressed drawing and the study of the human figure, which was deepened not only by life drawing but also by dissections. Both nature and the ancients were esteemed, and the art of Michelangelo was held to be the highest achievement of the moderns. The academy emphasized the study of history and literature as well as the skills of the artist. The specifically Tuscan emphasis on drawing (*disegno*) reflected the allegiances of the founders, who stressed art as an intellectual activity, not mere craft.

To the academy came Jean Bologne (1529–1608), a gifted sculptor from Douai in northern France, who had encountered Italian styles at the court of Francis I. He found employment at the ducal court and, under the Italianized name of Giovanni Bologna, became the most important sculptor in Florence during the last third of the sixteenth century. To demonstrate his skill, he chose to sculpt what seemed to him a most difficult feat: three contrasting figures united in a single action. When creating the group, Bologna had no specific theme in mind, but when it was finished a member of the Florentine academy proposed the title *The Rape of the Sabine Woman* (fig. **17.13**), which the artist accepted. The duke admired the work so much he had it installed near the Palazzo della Signoria.

The subject proposed was drawn from the legends of ancient Rome. According to the story, the city's founders, an adventurous band of men from across the sea, tried in vain to find wives among their neighbors, the Sabines. Finally, they resorted to a trick. Having invited the entire Sabine tribe into Rome for a festival, they attacked them, took the women away by force, and thus

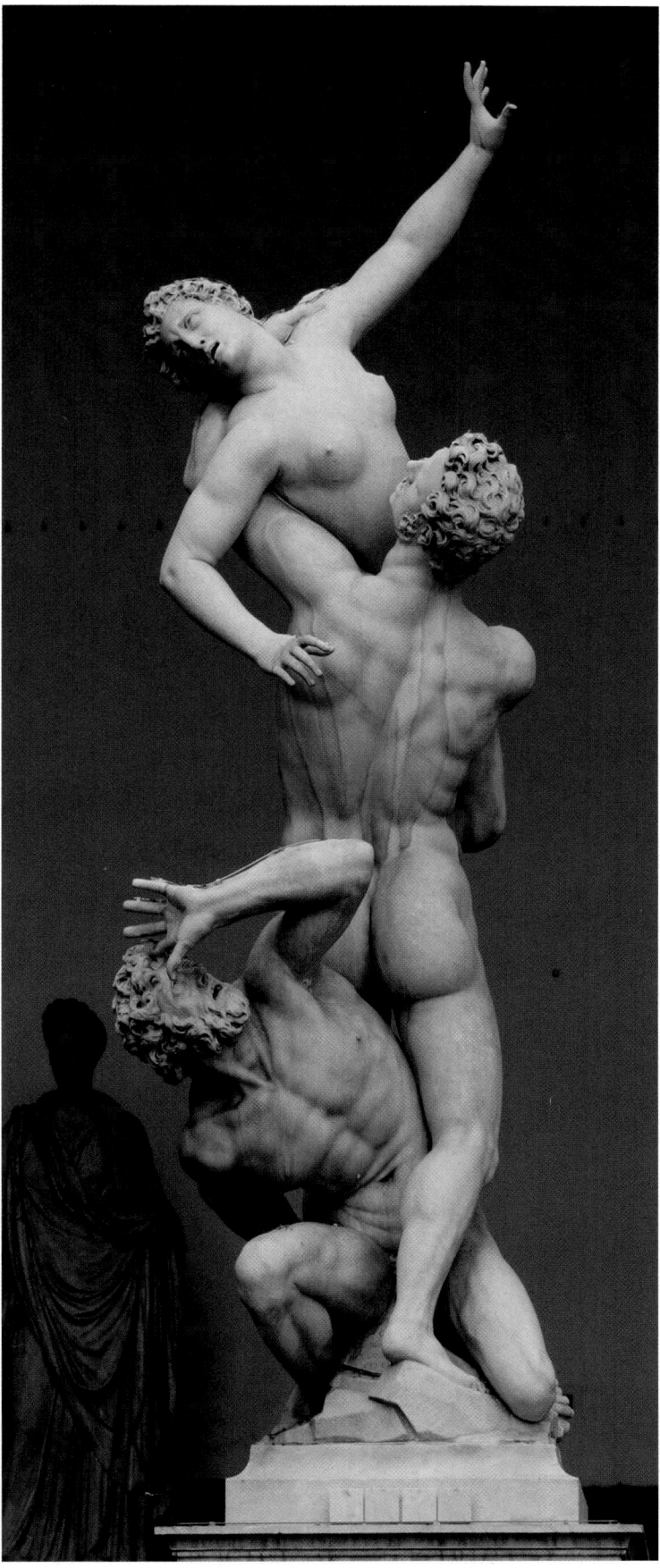

17.13 Giovanni Bologna, *The Rape of the Sabine Woman*. Completed 1583. Marble, height 13'6" (4.1 m). Loggia dei Lanzi, Florence

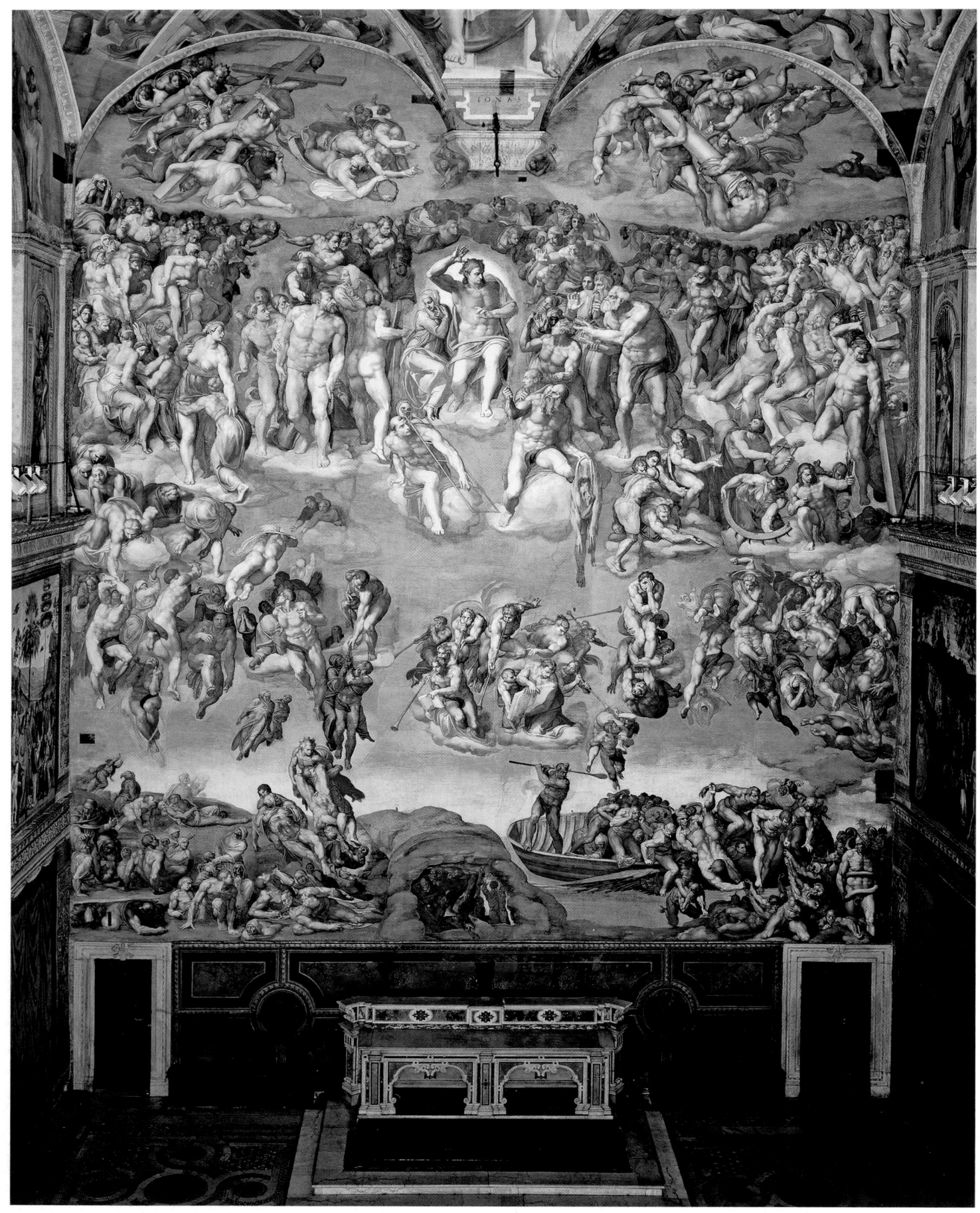

17.14 Michelangelo, *The Last Judgment*. 1534–41. Fresco. Sistine Chapel, Vatican City

Michelangelo the Poet

Michelangelo's prodigious creativity was manifested in many different art forms: sculpture, painting, architecture, and poetry. Allusive and dense with imagery, his poems do not explain his works in visual mediums, but they do sometimes treat parallel themes. This poem uses metaphors that appear visually in the Sistine Chapel's The Last Judgment. *It was a gift to his friend and reported lover Tommaso Cavalieri, a Roman nobleman.*

The smith when forging iron uses fire
to match the beauty shaped within his mind;
and fire alone will help the artist find

a way so to transmute base metal higher
to turn it gold; the phoenix seeks its pyre
to be reborn; just so I leave mankind
but hope to rise resplendent, new refined,
with souls whom death and time will never tire.
And this transforming fire good fortune brings
by burning out my life to make me new
although among the dead I then be counted.
True to its element the fire wings
its way to heaven, and to me is true
by taking me aloft where love is mounted.

Source: Michelangelo Buonarotti, *Life, Letters and Poetry*, ed. and tr. G. Bull (Oxford: Oxford University Press, 1987)

---

ensured the future of their race. Bologna's sculpture sanitizes what is an act of raw power and violence as the figures spiral upward in carefully rehearsed movements. Bologna wished to display his virtuosity and saw his task only in formal terms: to carve in marble, on a massive scale, a sculptural composition that was to be seen from all sides. The contrast between form and content that the Mannerist tendency encouraged could not be clearer.

ROME REFORMED

While the Medici were consolidating their power in Florence, in Rome, popes Julius II and Leo X sought to join their religious authority with secular power. Naturally, conflicts arose between the papacy and the princes of Europe: The contest between the papacy and the Holy Roman Empire resulted in the Sack of Rome in 1527 by Habsburg troops. Pope Leo X's cousin Clement VII fled, and much destruction ensued. Despite this shock to both the dignity of the city and the papacy, Clement ultimately crowned Charles V as emperor, and returned, once again, to his project of promoting the Medici family. When Clement died in 1534, the cardinals turned to a reform-minded member of a distinguished Roman family to restore the papacy's reputation and power. They chose Alessandro Farnese, a childhood friend of Leo X who had been educated in the palace of Lorenzo the Magnificent. As Pope Paul III, he encouraged Charles V's efforts to bring German princes back to the Roman Church, while at the same time trying to reassure Charles's enemy, Francis I, that Germany would not overpower France.

Paul III was very concerned by the spiritual crisis presented by the Reformation. Martin Luther had challenged both the doctrine and the authority of the Church, and his reformed version of Christianity had taken wide hold in northern Europe (see Chapter 18). To respond to the challenge of the Protestant Reformation, Paul III called the Council of Trent, which began its work in 1545 and issued its regulations in 1564. The council reaffirmed traditional Catholic doctrine and recommended reforms of liturgy, Church practices, and works of art. (See www.myartslab.com.)

The Catholic Church's most far-reaching and powerful weapon for combating what it considered heresy was the Inquisition, established in Italy in 1562 to investigate unapproved or suspect religious activities. Those found guilty of engaging in such heresies (deviations from religious orthodoxy) could be imprisoned or executed. To further control the spread of unorthodoxy, the Church compiled an Index of Prohibited Books in 1557. Texts by suspect authors or on subjects deemed unhealthful could be seized or denied publication.

Michelangelo in Rome

Like his predecessors, Paul III saw the value in commissioning large-scale projects from the leading artists of his day. Thus, he recalled Michelangelo to Rome to execute several key projects for him. Rome remained Michelangelo's home for the rest of his life. The new mood after the Sack of 1527 and during the Catholic Reformation may be reflected in the subject chosen for a major project in the Sistine Chapel. Beginning in 1534, Michelangelo painted for Paul III a powerful vision of The Last Judgment (fig. **17.14**). It took six years to complete the fresco, which was unveiled in 1541.

To represent the theme of the Last Judgment (Matthew 24:29–31) on the altar wall of the Sistine Chapel, Michelangelo had to remove not only the fifteenth-century frescoes commissioned by Sixtus IV but also parts of his own ceiling program in the upper lunettes. Traditional representations such as Giotto's at the Arena Chapel in Padua (see fig. 13.18) depict Hell as a place of physical torment. In envisioning his fresco, Michelangelo must have looked partly to Luca Signorelli's work at Orvieto Cathedral (see fig. 15.56), with its vigorous muscular nudes. Michelangelo replaces physical torments with spiritual agony expressed through violent contortions of the human body within a turbulent atmosphere. As angelic trumpeters signal the end of time, the figure of Christ sits at the fulcrum of a wheel of action: As he raises his arm, the dead rise from the earth at the lower left to yearn toward Heaven where the assembly of saints crowds about him. The damned plunge from Heaven toward Charon,

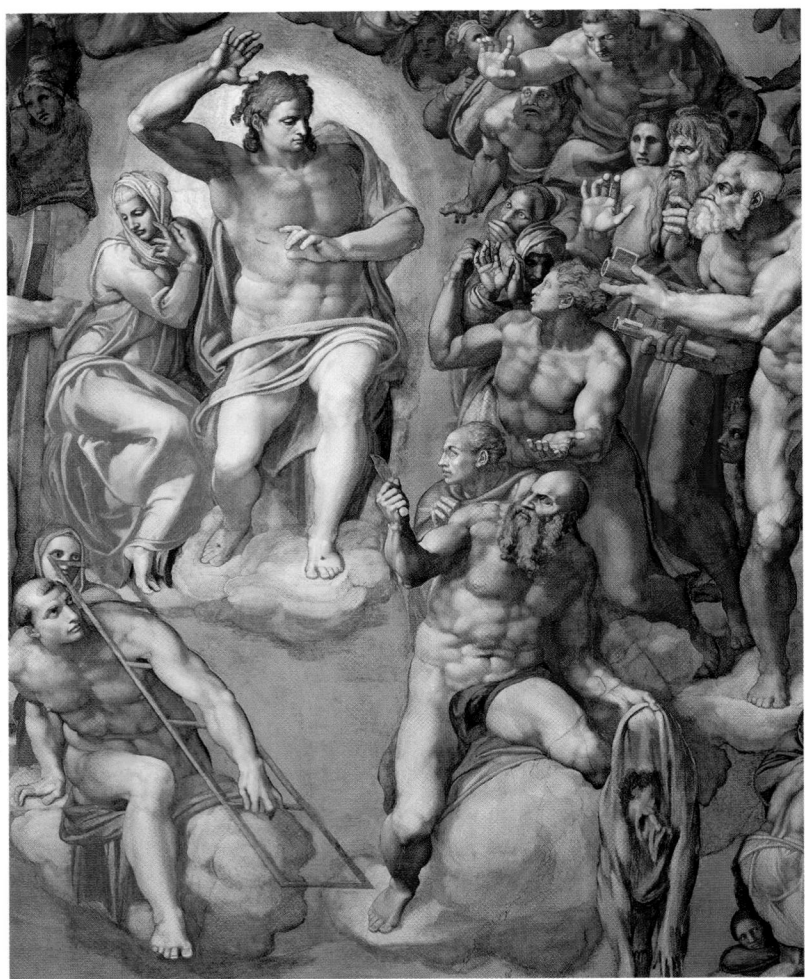

parallel ideas and metaphors may be seen in a poem he composed around 1532. (See *Primary Source*, page 603.)

These concerns also appear in a new version of the *Pietà*, begun around 1546 (fig. **17.16**). Here Michelangelo used his own features again, this time for the hooded figure—probably Nicodemus, who holds the broken body of Christ. He intended this sculptural group for his own tomb. By casting himself as a disciple tending the body of Christ, Michelangelo gives form to a conception of personal, unmediated access to the divine. The Catholic Church may have found such an idea threatening during the Catholic Reformation, when the authority of the Roman Church was being reaffirmed as Protestantism spread throughout Europe. For whatever reason, Michelangelo smashed the statue in 1555, and left it unfinished. Compared with his 1499 *Pietà*

17.15 Michelangelo, *The Last Judgment* (detail, with self-portrait)

who ferries them to the underworld. (Some contemporary viewers complained about the inclusion of a pagan character in a sacred subject.) Throughout the fresco, human figures bend, twist, climb, fall, or gaze at Christ, their forms almost superhuman in their muscular power. The nudity of the figures, which expresses Michelangelo's belief in the sanctity of the human body, disturbed his contemporaries, and shortly after he died in 1564 one of his assistants was commissioned to add bits of clothing to the fresco to mask the nudity. The fresco was cleaned in 1994, bringing out the brilliant colors, the compressed space, and dramatic composition. These features link the work to the Mannerist style, though Michelangelo defies such labels.

That the fresco expresses Michelangelo's personal vision of the end of days is suggested by one detail: Straddling a cloud just below the Lord is the apostle Bartholomew, holding a human skin to represent his martyrdom by flaying (fig. **17.15**). The face on that skin, however, is not the saint's, but Michelangelo's. In this grim self-portrait, so well hidden that it was recognized only in modern times, the artist represents himself as unworthy to be resurrected in the flesh, which is a key theme of the image. Already in his sixties, Michelangelo frequently meditated on death and salvation in his poetry as well as in his art of the period. Some

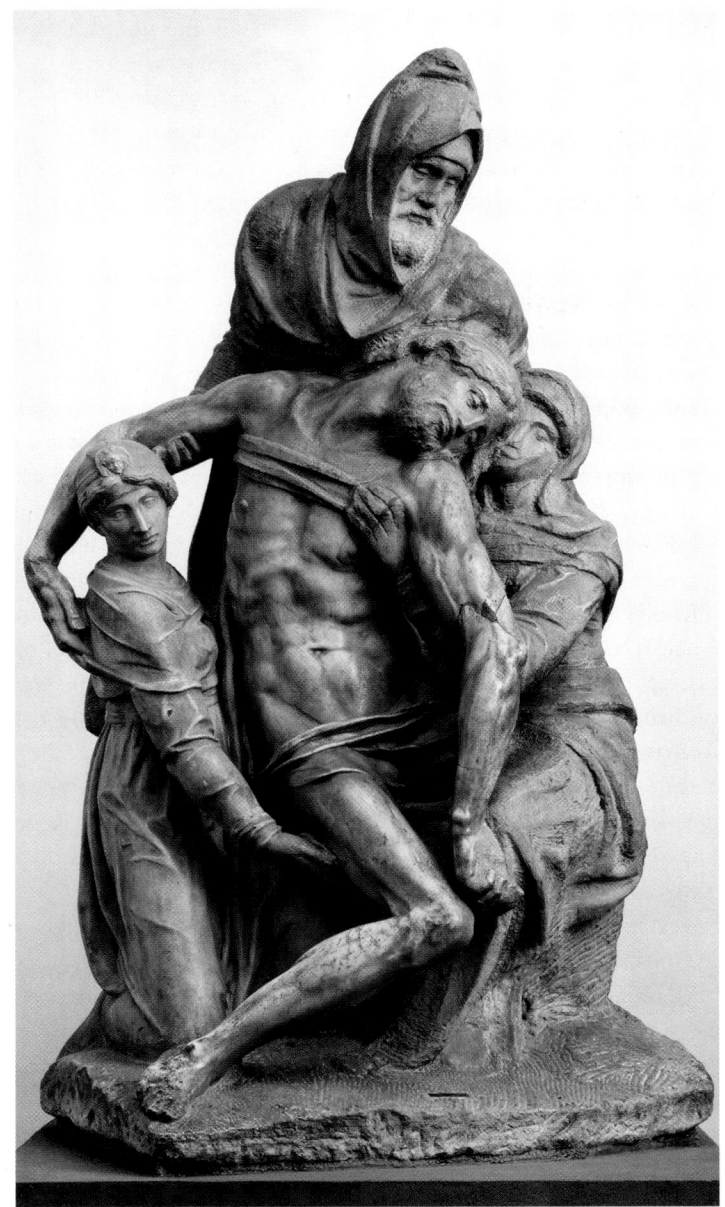

17.16 Michelangelo, *Pietà*. ca. 1546. Marble, height 7'8" (2.34 m). Museo del Opera del Duomo, Florence

(see fig. 16.12), this work is more expressive than conventionally beautiful, as though the ideals of his youth had been replaced by a greater seriousness of spiritual purpose. Many of Michelangelo's last sculptures remained unfinished as his efforts turned to architecture.

RESHAPING THE CAMPIDOGLIO While in Rome during the last 30 years of his life, Michelangelo's main pursuit was architecture. Among his activities were several public works projects. In 1537–39, he received the most ambitious commission of his career: to reshape the Campidoglio, the top of Rome's Capitoline Hill, into a piazza and frame it with a monumental architectural ensemble worthy of the site, which once had been the symbolic center of the ancient city. This was an opportunity to plan on a grand scale. Pope Paul III worked with the civilian authorities in Rome (the Conservators) to renovate this site and made Michelangelo its designer. Although not completed until long after his death, the project was carried out essentially as Michelangelo designed it. The Campidoglio has since served as a model for many other civic centers. Pope Paul III transferred the equestrian monument of Marcus Aurelius (see fig. 7.33) from the Lateran Palace to the Campidoglio and had it installed on a base that Michelangelo designed. Placed at the top of a gently rising oval mound that defines the space, the statue became the focal point of the entire scheme. (The sculpture was recently removed to an interior space to protect it.) Since the sculpted figure was thought to represent Constantine, the first Roman emperor to promote Christianity and the source of the papacy's claim to temporal power, by placing it at the center of the seat of secular government, the pope asserted papal authority in civic affairs.

Palace façades define three sides of the piazza. An engraving based on Michelangelo's design (fig. **17.17**), conveys the effect, albeit imperfectly, of the space created by the façades. The print shows the symmetry of the scheme and the sense of progression along the main axis toward the Senators' Palace, opposite the staircase that gives entry to the piazza. However, the shape of the piazza is not a rectangle but a trapezoid, a peculiarity dictated by the site. The Senators' Palace and the Conservators' Palace on the right were older buildings that had to be preserved behind new exteriors, but they were placed at an angle of 80 instead of 90 degrees. Michelangelo turned this problem into an asset. By adding the "New Palace" on the left, which complements the Conservators' Palace in style and placement, he makes the Senators' Palace look larger than it is, so that it dominates the piazza.

The whole conception has the appearance of a stage set. All three buildings are long but relatively narrow, like a show front with little behind it. However, these are not shallow screens but three-dimensional structures (fig. **17.18**). The "New Palace" and its twin, the Conservators' Palace, combine voids and solids, horizontals and verticals with a plasticity not found in any piece of architecture since Roman antiquity. The open porticoes in each structure further link the piazza and façades, just as a courtyard is related to the arcades of a **cloister**.

The columns and beams of the porticoes are contained in a colossal order of pilasters that supports a heavy cornice topped by a balustrade. Alberti had experimented with the colossal order at Sant'Andrea in Mantua (see fig. 15.45), but Michelangelo fully exploited this device. For the Senators' Palace he used a colossal order and balustrade above a tall base, which emphasizes the massiveness of the building. The single entrance at the top of the double-ramped stairway (see fig. 17.17) seems to gather all the spatial forces set in motion by the oval mound and the flanking structures. It thus provides a dramatic climax to the piazza. Brunelleschi's design for the façade of the Innocenti in Florence (see fig. 15.4), with its slim Tuscan columns and rhythmic arcade, seems a delicate frame for a piazza compared with the mass and energy of the Campidoglio. Michelangelo's powerful example of molding urban spaces was important for subsequent city planners throughout Europe.

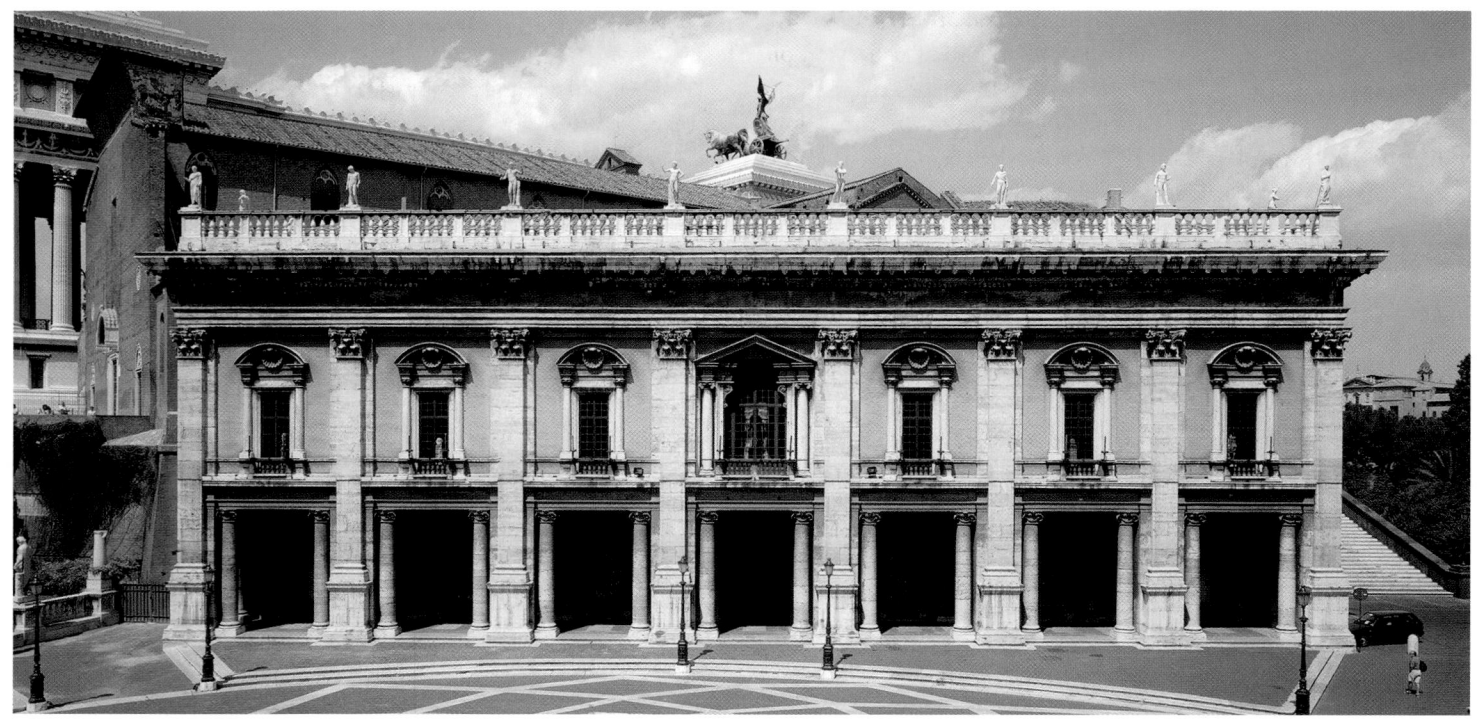

17.18   Michelangelo. Palazzo dei Conservatori, Campidoglio, Rome. Designed ca. 1545

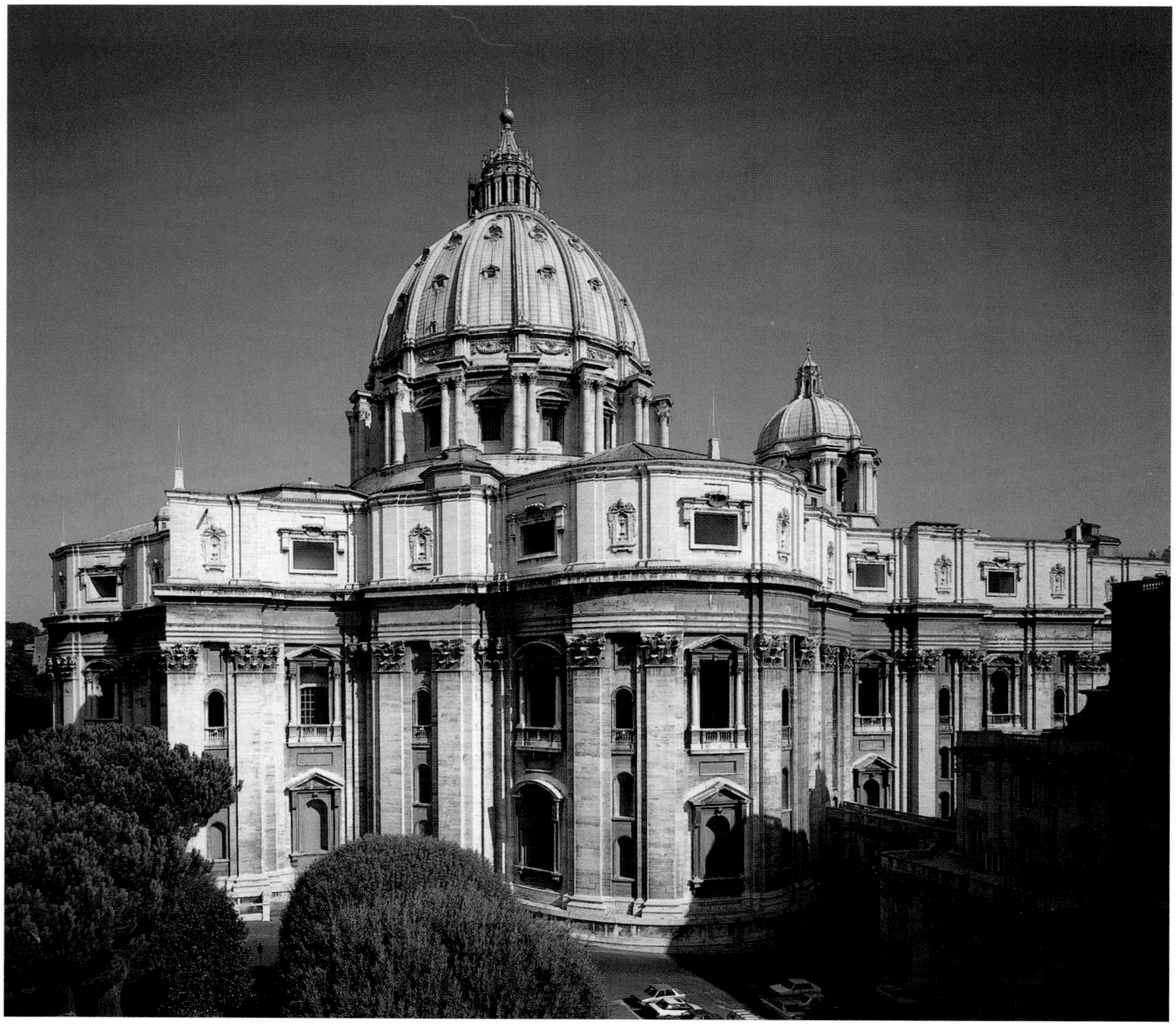

17.19   Michelangelo. St. Peter's, Rome, seen from the west. 1546–64; dome completed by Giacomo della Porta, 1590

ST. PETER'S Michelangelo used the colossal order again on the exterior of St. Peter's (fig. **17.19**). Several architects had taken on the project after Bramante's death in 1514. Michelangelo took over the design of the church in 1546 upon the death of the previous architect, Antonio da Sangallo the Younger, whose work he completely recast. Returning to a centrally focused plan, he adapted the system of the Conservators' Palace to the curving contours of the church, but with windows instead of open loggias and an attic instead of the balustrade.

Unlike Bramante's many-layered elevation (see fig. 16.11), Michelangelo uses a colossal order of pilasters to emphasize the compact body of the structure, thus setting off the dome more dramatically. The same desire for compactness and organic unity led him to simplify the interior spaces (fig. **17.20**). He brought the complex spatial sequences of Bramante's plan (see fig. 16.10) into one cross and square, held in check by the huge piers that support the central dome. He further defined its main axis by modifying the eastern apse and adding a portico to it, although this part of his design was never carried out. The dome, however, reflects

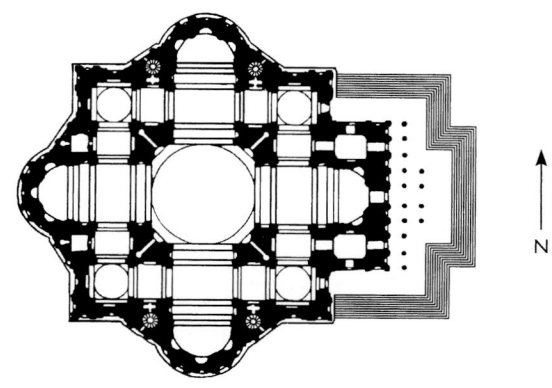

17.20   Michelangelo. Plan for St. Peter's

Michelangelo's ideas in every important respect, even though it was built after his death and has a steeper pitch than he intended.

Bramante had planned his dome as a stepped hemisphere above a narrow drum, which would have seemed to press down on the church. Michelangelo's, in contrast, has a powerful thrust that draws energy upward from the main body of the structure. Michelangelo borrowed not only the double-shell construction but also the Gothic profile from the Florence Cathedral dome (see fig. 15.3 and *Materials and Techniques*, page 512), yet the effect is very different. The smooth planes of Brunelleschi's dome give no hint of the internal stresses. Michelangelo, however, gives sculptured shape to these forces and visually links them to the rest of the building. The double columns of the high drum take up the vertical impetus of the colossal pilasters. This upward momentum continues in the ribs and the raised curve of the cupola, and then culminates in the tall lantern. The logic of this design is so persuasive that almost all domes built between 1600 and 1900 were influenced by it.

The Catholic Reformation and Il Gesù

Despite its visual logic and powerful design, Michelangelo's centralized plan at St. Peter's served as a model for few other churches in the era of the Catholic Reformation. As the Council of Trent finished its deliberations in 1564, the Church reasserted its traditions and reformed its liturgies. The council decreed that believers should see the elevation of the Host at the heart of the Mass, which was best accomplished in the long nave of a basilica with an unencumbered view of the altar. Despite its symbolic attractions, the centralized plan did not achieve this goal.

Another result of the reform movement within the Catholic Church was the establishment of new religious orders. One of the most ambitious and energetic was the Society of Jesus, or Jesuits, founded by Ignatius of Loyola and promoted by Pope Paul III. He approved the order in 1540; by 1550, the Jesuits were planning their own church, Il Gesù in Rome. Michelangelo once promised a design for this project, though he apparently never furnished it; the plan that the order adopted came from one of Michelangelo's assistants, Giacomo Vignola (1507–1573) in 1568. For Vignola's plan Giacomo della Porta (ca. 1540–1602) designed the façade. It was not completed until 1584. As the mother church of the Jesuits, its design must have been closely supervised so as to conform to the aims of the order. The Jesuits were at once intellectuals, mystics, and missionaries, whose charge was to fight heresy in Europe and spread Christianity to Asia and America. They required churches that adhered to the precepts of the Council of Trent—churches that would have impressive grand-eur while avoiding excessive ornament. Il Gesù may be seen as the architectural embodiment of the spirit of the Catholic Reformation.

Il Gesù is a compact basilica dominated by its mighty nave (fig. **17.21**). Chapels have replaced side aisles, thus assembling the congregation in one large, hall-like space directly in view of the altar. The attention of the audience is strongly directed toward altar and pulpit, as a representation of the interior shows

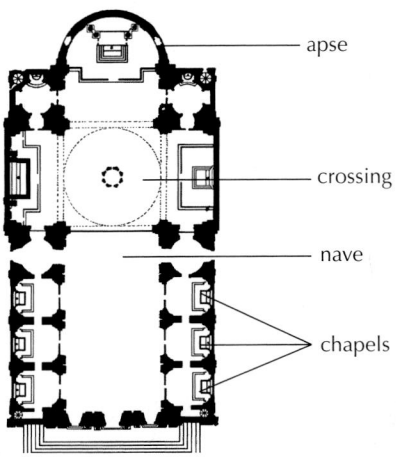

17.21   Giacomo Vignola. Plan of Il Gesù, Rome. 1568

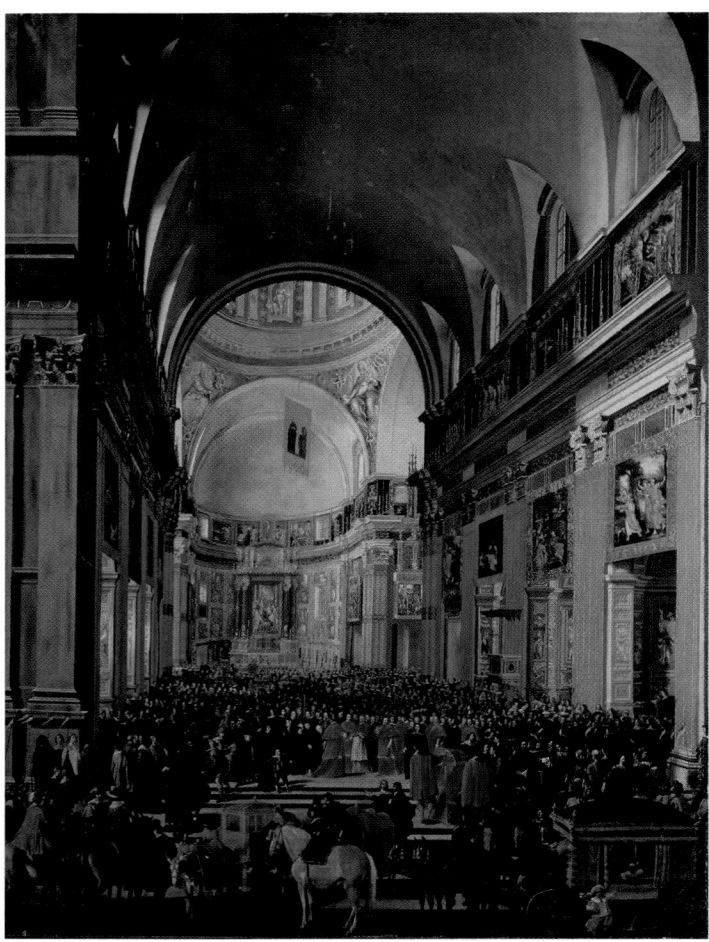

(fig. **17.22**). (The painting depicts how the church would look from the street if the center part of the façade were removed. For the later decoration of the nave vault, see fig. 19.12.) The painting also depicts a feature that the ground plan cannot show: the dramatic contrast between the dim nave and the amply lighted eastern part of the church, thanks to the large windows in the drum of the dome. Light has been consciously exploited for its expressive possibilities—a novel device, theatrical in the best sense of the term—to give Il Gesù a stronger emotional focus than we have as yet found in a church interior.

The façade by Giacomo della Porta (fig. **17.23**) is as bold as the plan. It is divided into two stories by a strongly projecting entablature that is supported by paired pilasters that clearly derive from Michelangelo, with whom Della Porta had worked. The same pattern recurs in the upper story on a somewhat smaller scale, with four instead of six pairs of supports. To bridge the difference in width and hide the roof line, Della Porta inserted two scroll-shaped buttresses. This device, taken from the façade of Santa Maria Novella in Florence by Alberti (see fig. 15.9), forms a graceful transition to the large pediment crowning the façade, which retains the classic proportions of Renaissance architecture: The height equals the width.

Della Porta has masterfully integrated all the parts of the façade into a single whole: Both stories share the same vertical rhythm, which even the horizontal members obey. (Note the way the broken entablature **responds** to the pilasters.) In turn, the

17.22 Andrea Sacchi and Jan Miel, *Urban VIII Visiting Il Gesù*. 1639–41. Oil on canvas. Galleria Nazionale d'Arte Antica, Rome

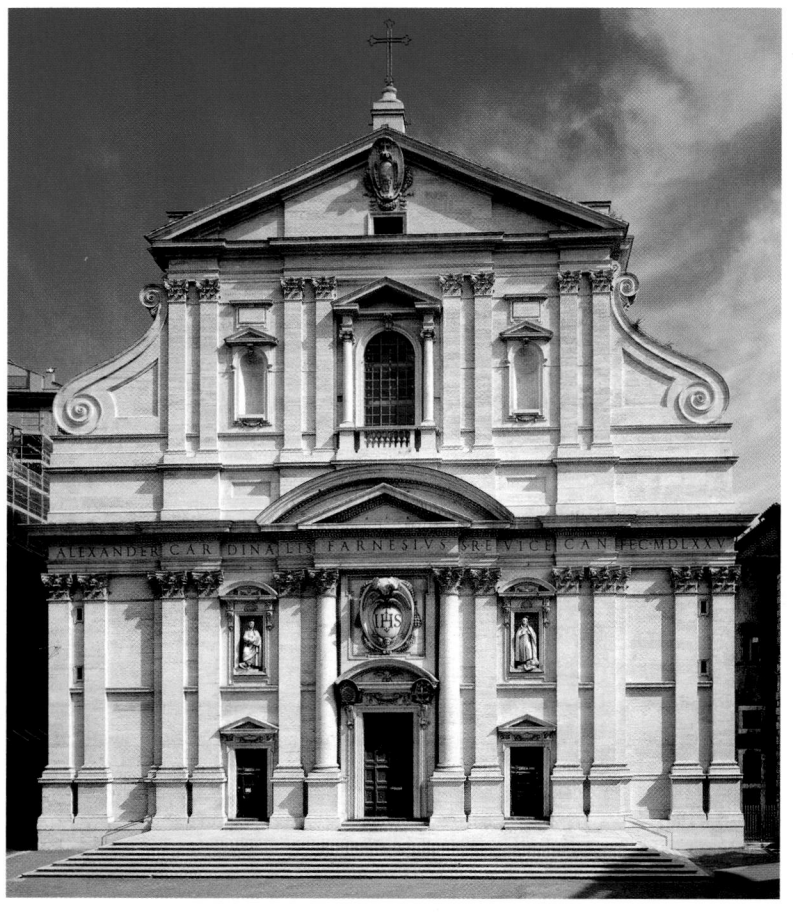

17.23 Giacomo della Porta. Façade of Il Gesù, Rome. ca. 1575–84

horizontal divisions determine the size of the vertical members, so there is no colossal order. Michelangelo inspired the sculptural treatment of the façade, which places greater emphasis on the main portal. Its double frame—two pediments resting on coupled pilasters and columns—projects beyond the rest of the façade and gives strong focus to the entire design. Not since Gothic architecture has the entrance to a church received such a dramatic concentration of features. This façade, and the freedom to add movement and plastic dimension to it, set an important precedent for church architecture by the Jesuits and others during ensuing centuries.

NORTHERN ITALY: DUCAL COURTS AND URBAN CENTERS

Northern Italy was divided into a number of principalities that were smaller than the Grand Duchy of Tuscany or the Papal States. One of the most stable of these principalities was Mantua, where the Gonzaga family retained the title of marquis into the sixteenth century. Mantua was host to major artists in the fifteenth century, including Alberti and Mantegna. The family's traditions of patronage extended to women as well as men, as Isabella d'Este, the wife of Francesco II Gonzaga, was one of the most active patrons of the early sixteenth century. Her son, Federico, became marquis in 1519, a title he held until Charles V named him duke in 1530. To impress the emperor, Federico displayed his wealth and taste expressed through the arts.

The Palazzo del Te

As part of his display, Federico II Gonzaga commissioned Giulio Romano (ca. 1499–1546) to design a villa for him outside the city itself, called the Palazzo del Te, where he could house his mistress and receive the emperor. Giulio had been Raphael's chief assistant in Rome, but came to Mantua to follow in the footsteps of Mantegna and Alberti in 1524.

He designed the Palazzo del Te as a low structure appropriate to the flat landscape. For the courtyard façade (fig. **17.24**), Giulio used a vocabulary familiar to patrons of villas and palaces, such as the rusticated blocks and the smooth Tuscan order of engaged columns that support the projecting entablature. As Michelangelo did at the Laurentian Library, Giulio subverts the conventions of traditional classical architecture. The massive keystones of the blank windows appear ready to burst the triangular lintels above them. The only true arch spans the central doorway, but a pediment surmounts it—a violation of the classical **canon**. The triglyph midway between each pair of columns "slips" downward in defiance of all logic and accepted practice, thereby creating a sense that the frieze might collapse before our eyes. In a Mannerist display, Giulio broke the rules of accepted practice as if to say that the rules did not apply to him, or to his patron.

What is merely a possibility on the exterior of the Palazzo del Te seems to be fully realized in the interior, where Giulio painted a series of rooms with illusionistic frescoes on themes drawn from antiquity. Unlike the frescoes of Raphael in Rome, these are not images of a distant and beautiful Golden Age, but vivid and dramatic expressions of power. In the Sala dei Giganti (Room of the Giants) (fig. **17.25**), Giulio painted a fresco of the gods expelling the giants from Mount Olympus as a cataclysm of falling bodies and columns. A viewer seems to see an entire temple collapsing. Figures of the winds in the upper corners of the wall appear to topple architectural elements onto the huge figures of giants, crushing them. As if witnessing the power of the new Olympian gods, a viewer feels transported into the terror

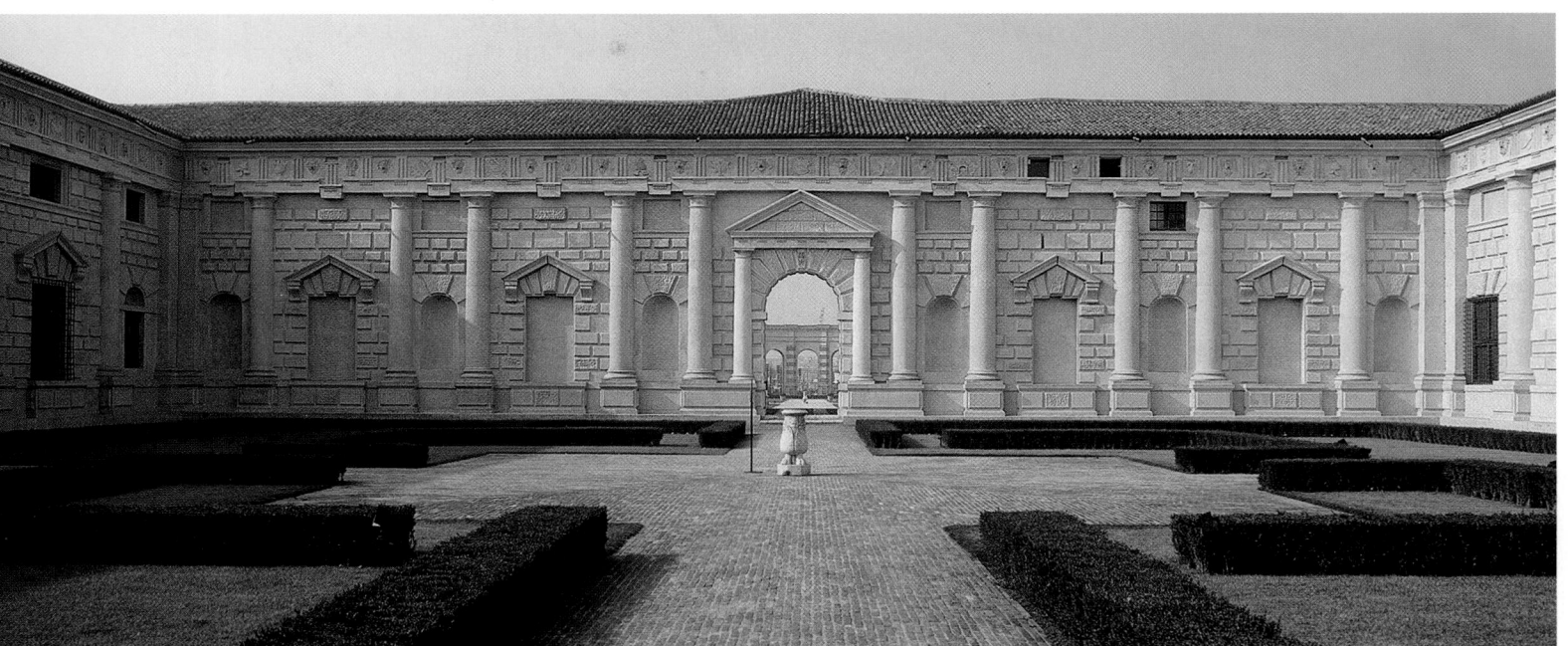

17.24   Giulio Romano. Courtyard of the Palazzo del Te, Mantua. ca. 1527–34

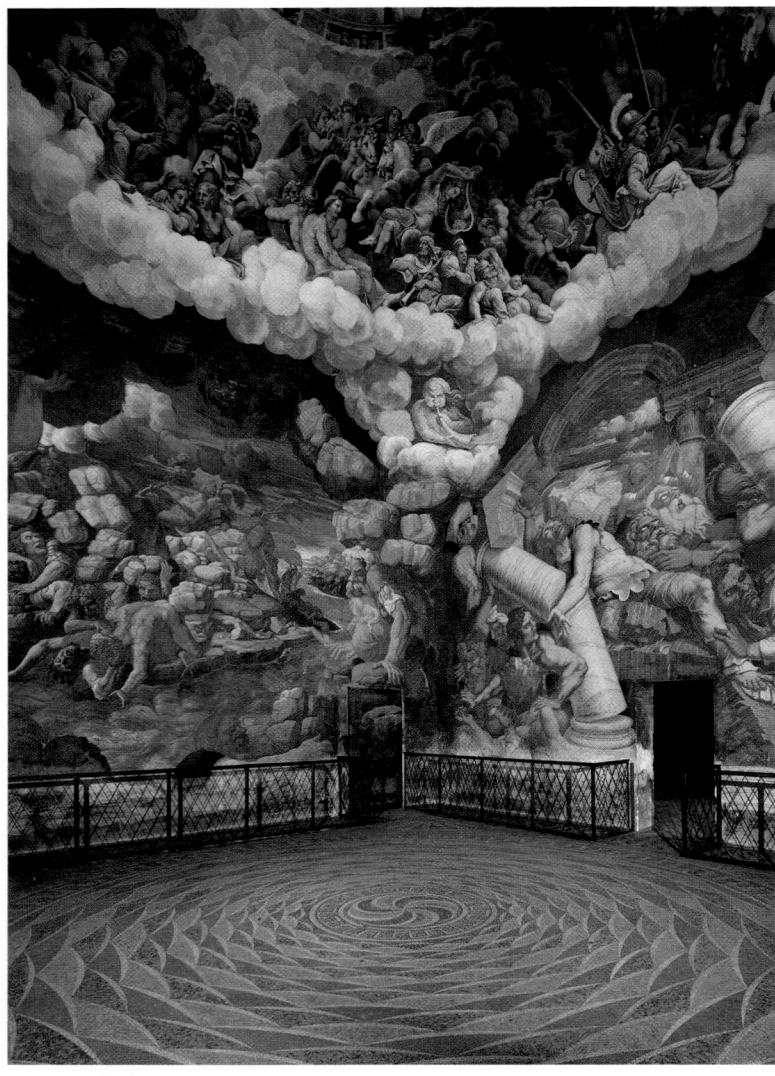

17.25 Giulio Romano, *Fall of the Giants from Mount Olympus*, from the Sala dei Giganti. ca. 1530–32. Palazzo del Te, Mantua

of the event. Of course, the duke himself was imagined as Zeus (Jupiter) in this conceit, so the whole illusion speaks to the power of Duke Federico.

This conceit was also applied to paintings for the same duke's palace in Mantua, which he commissioned from Antonio Allegri da Correggio (1489/94–1534), called Correggio, about the same time. This gifted northern Italian painter, who spent most of his brief career in Parma, absorbed the influences of Leonardo, the Venetians, Michelangelo, and Raphael into a distinctive and sensual style. Duke Federico commissioned a series of the Loves of Jupiter, among which is the *Jupiter and Io* (fig. **17.26**). As Ovid recounts, Jupiter changed his shape numerous times to seduce his lovers; here, the nymph Io, swoons in the embrace of a cloudlike Jupiter. The use of Leonardesque sfumato, combined with a Venetian sense of color and texture, produces a frank sensuality that exceeds even Titian's *Bacchanal* (see fig. 16.31). Correggio renders the vaporous form of the god with a remarkable degree of illusionism. The eroticism of the image reflects a taste shared by

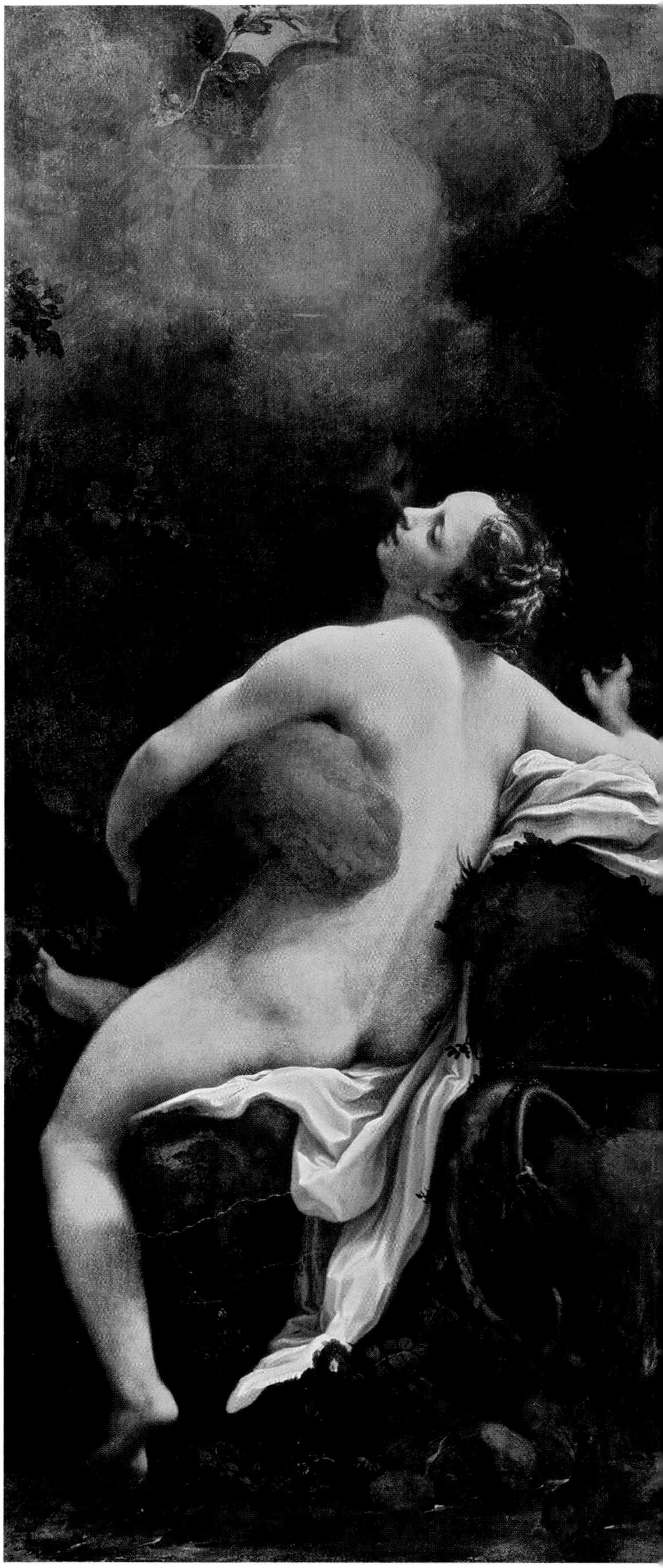

17.26 Correggio, *Jupiter and Io*. ca. 1532. Oil on canvas, 64½ × 27¾" (163.8 × 70.5 cm). Kunsthistorisches Museum, Vienna

many of the courts of Europe, visible in Bronzino's *Allegory of Venus* (see fig. 17.11) and Titian's *Rape of Europa* (see fig. 17.36).

PARMA AND CREMONA

The larger political entities in Italy aimed to swallow up the smaller ones. The Papal States expanded to include cities like Bologna and Parma, while the Duchy of Milan gobbled up the city of Cremona. Forms of art and patronage established by courts in Rome, Florence, and Milan were emulated by the citizens of these cities.

Correggio and Parmigianino in Parma

Correggio spent much of his career in the city of Parma, which had recently been absorbed into the Papal States. This new affiliation brought the city new wealth and inspired local patrons of art and architecture; more than once Correggio was the artist chosen for their projects. He put his skills to work in the dome of Parma Cathedral where he painted the fresco of *The Assumption of the Virgin* between 1522 and 1530 (fig. **17.27**). The surfaces of the dome are painted away by Correggio's illusionistic perspective. A viewer standing below the dome is transported into the heavens, as the sky opens to receive the body of the Virgin rising into the light.

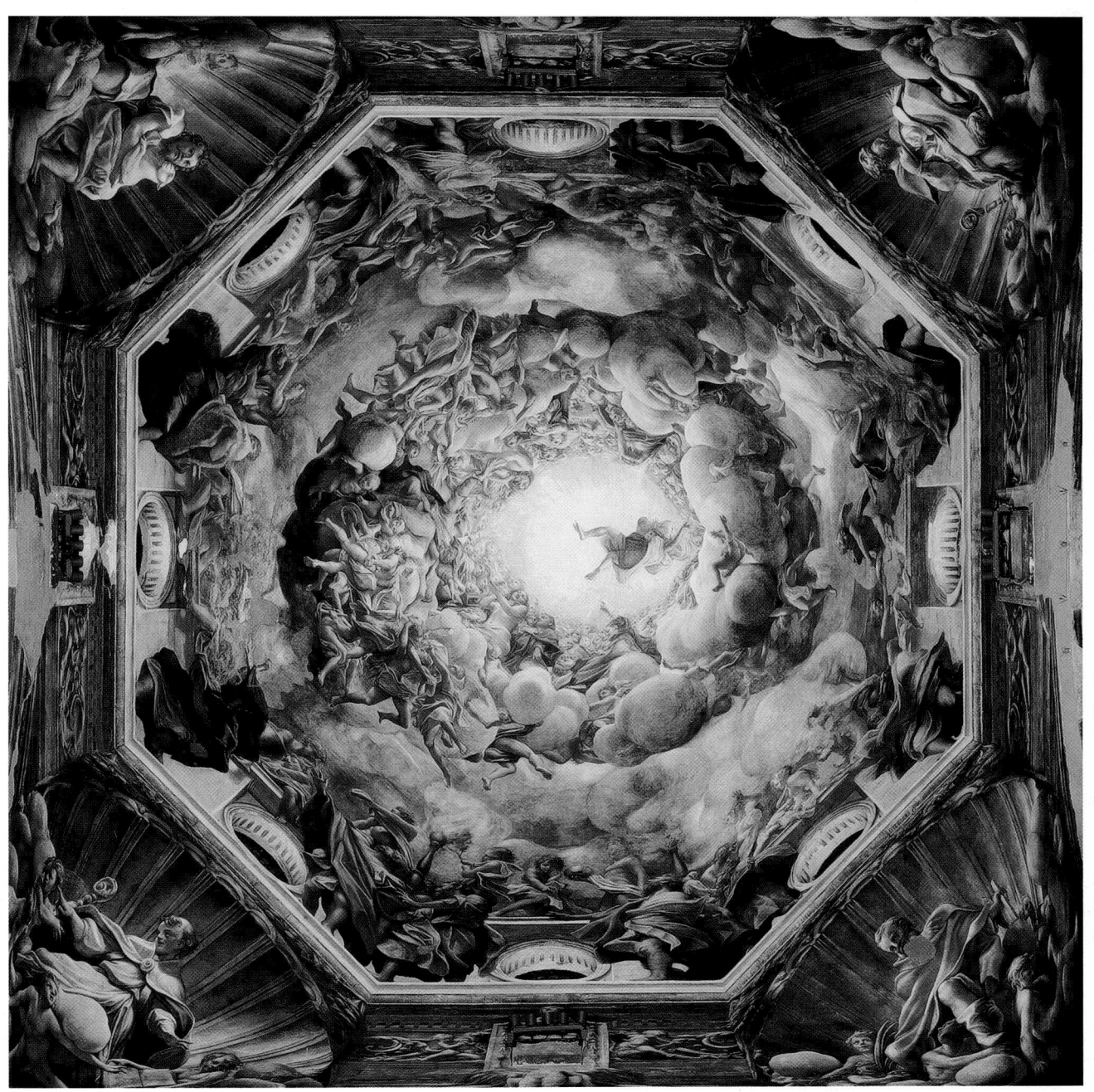

17.27 Correggio, *The Assumption of the Virgin.* ca. 1522–30. Fresco, diameter of base of dome 35'10" × 37'11" (10.93 × 11.56 m). Dome of cathedral, Parma, Italy

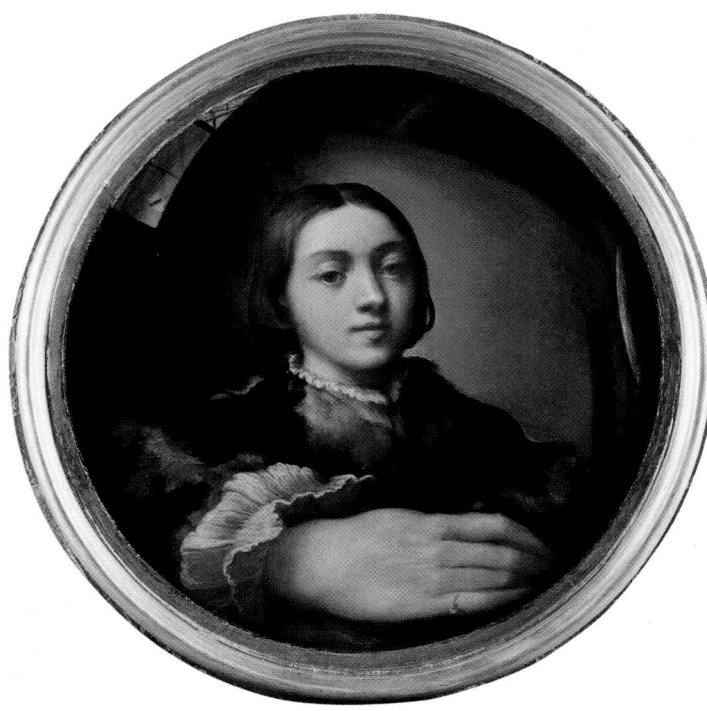

17.28 Parmigianino, *Self-Portrait*. 1524. Oil on panel, diameter 9⅝" (24.7 cm). Kunsthistorisches Museum, Vienna

Correggio here initiates a new kind of visionary representation in which Heaven and earth are joined visually and spiritually through the magic of perspective and the artist's skill. Not since Mantegna's *Camera Picta* in Mantua (see fig. 15.50) has a ceiling been so totally replaced by a painted illusion; the concept would reverberate in the works of other artists in the seventeenth century, when ceilings would disappear through illusionistic devices, as can be seen in the work of Pietro da Cortona (see fig. 19.11) and Giovanni Battista Gaulli (see fig. 19.12). Correggio also gave the figures themselves the ability to move with such exhilarating ease that the force of gravity seems not to exist for them, and they frankly delight in their weightless condition. Reflecting the influence of Titian, these are healthy, energetic beings of flesh and blood, which makes the Assumption appear that much more miraculous.

Parma was the birthplace of yet another gifted painter, Girolamo Francesco Maria Mazzola (1503–1540), known as Parmigianino. Precocious and intelligent, Parmigianino had made his reputation as a painter in Rome, Florence, and elsewhere before returning to Parma in 1530. His *Self-Portrait* (fig. 17.28), done as a demonstration piece, suggests his self-confidence. The artist's appearance is bland and well groomed. The features, painted with Raphael's smooth perfection, are veiled by a delicate sfumato. The picture records what Parmigianino saw as he gazed at his reflection in a convex mirror, including the fishbowl distortions in his hand. Parmigianino substitutes his painting for the mirror itself, even using a specially prepared convex panel. The painting demonstrates his skill at recording what the eye sees, yet at the same time it shows off his learning by a subtle allusion to the myth of Narcissus, who, according to Greek legend, looked in a pool of water and fell in love with his own reflection.

Parmigianino's skill is evident in his most famous work, *The Madonna with the Long Neck* (fig. 17.29), commissioned in 1535 by a noblewoman of Parma for a family chapel in the church of Santa Maria dei Servi. Despite his deep study of Raphael and Correggio, Parmigianino has a different ideal of beauty, which he establishes with the large amphora offered by the figure at the left. In his painting, the perfect oval of Mary's head rests on a swanlike neck, while her body swells only to taper to her feet, which mimics the shape of the amphora. By contrast, Raphael's *La Belle Jardinière* (see fig. 16.22) seems all circles and cubes, and her features are sweet rather than haughty. Nor does Parmigianino attempt to replicate Raphael's stable compositions. Here, the

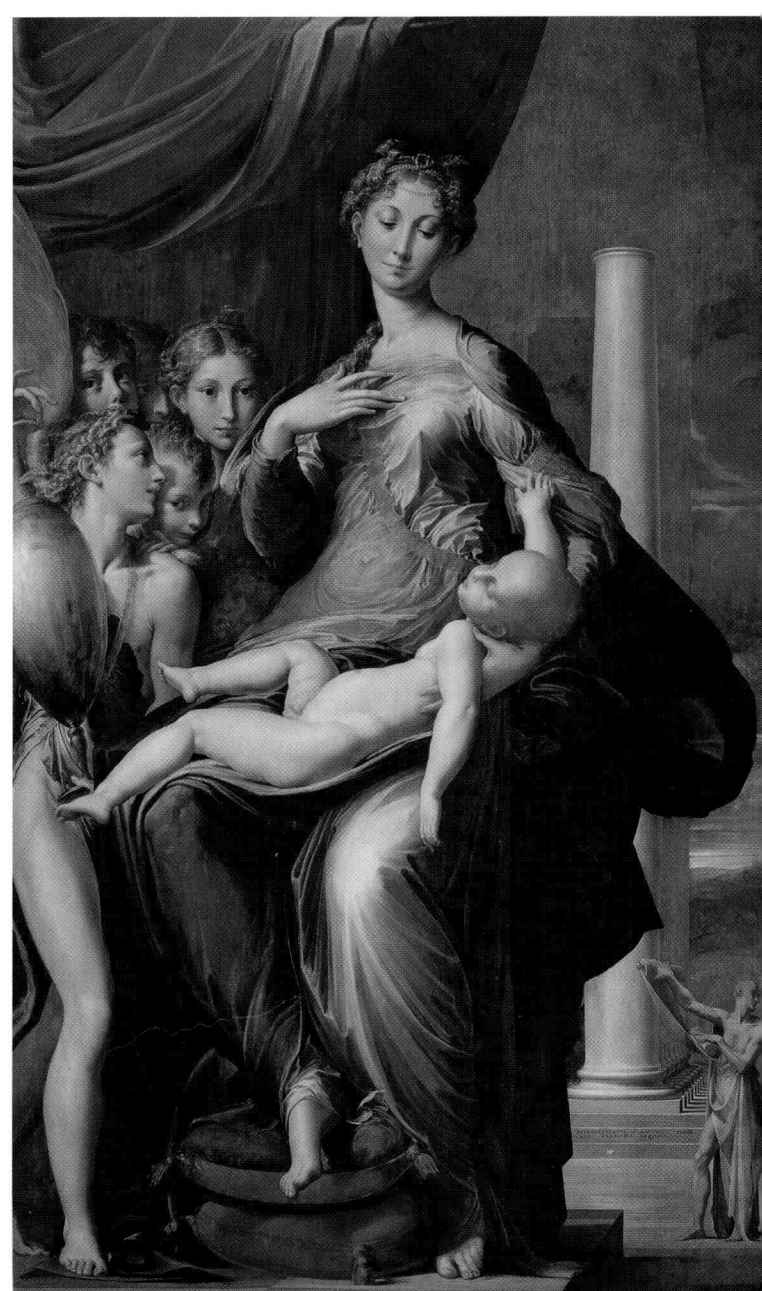

17.29 Parmigianino, *The Madonna with the Long Neck*. ca. 1535. Oil on panel, 7'1" × 4'4" (2.2 × 1.3 m). Galleria degli Uffizi, Florence

sleeping Christ Child balances precariously on the Madonna's lap, as she lifts a boneless hand to her breast. The composition is as unbalanced as the postures: heavily weighted to the left, open and distant to the right. All the figures have elongated limbs and ivory-smooth features, and the space is compressed. In typical Mannerist fashion, these elements draw attention to the artist's skill and his inversion of Raphael's ideals.

These choices may reflect the meaning of the image. The large Christ Child in his mother's lap recalls the theme of the Pietà, which implies that Jesus is already aware of his fate. Nor is the setting as arbitrary as it may seem. The gigantic column is a symbol often associated with the Madonna as the gateway to Heaven and eternal life, as well as the Immaculate Conception. At the same time it may also refer to the column on which Jesus endured the flagellation during the Passion, which the tiny figure of a prophet foretells on his scroll. *The Madonna with the Long Neck*, with its cold and memorable elegance, offers a vision of unearthly perfection.

Cremona

The Mannerist elegance that Correggio and Parmigianino achieved was but one stylistic option that artists and patrons of northern Italy could select. The work of Sofonisba Anguissola

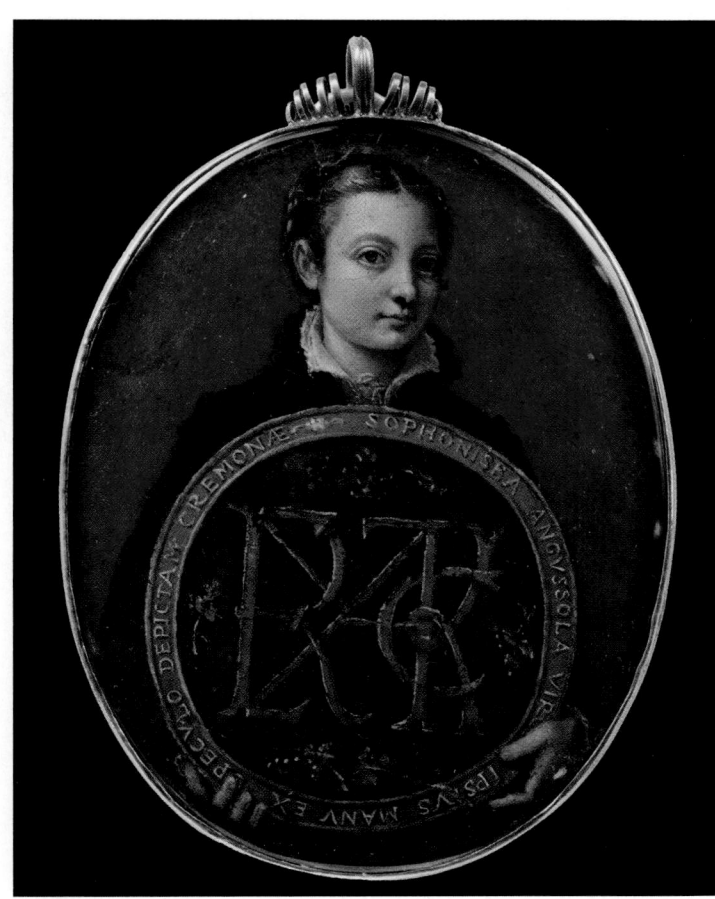

17.30 Sofonisba Anguissola, *Self-Portrait*. c. 1556. Oil on parchment, 3¼ × 2½" (8.3 × 6.4 cm). Museum of Fine Arts, Boston. Emma F. Munroe Fund, 1960. 60.155

(1532–1625) of Cremona represents a different approach. The daughter of a nobleman in that north Italian city, Sofonisba received her training in painting as a professional. This was a very unusual circumstance, as most women artists of the Renaissance learned their craft at home as the daughters of artists. Sofonisba became famous in Italy as a painter, communicating with artists all over the peninsula, including Michelangelo and Vasari. Her fame was such that Philip II of Spain hired her as his court artist. She moved to Spain in 1559 where she executed mostly portraits of imperial family members. She remained there until she married in 1573 and returned to Italy.

The reasons for her fame become clear in examining her self-portrait of about 1556 (fig. **17.30**). Executed as a miniature, the portrait was probably a gift. In the image, the 24-year-old artist represents herself staring out at the spectator wearing sober black costume and with respectably plaited hair. Sofonisba does not attempt the showy distortions that appear in Parmigianino's comparable self-portrait, done in 1524 (see fig. 17.28), preferring a straightforward naturalism to Mannerist display. She holds a medallion with a still mysterious monogram. (It may be an anagram of her father's name, although this is not certain.) Around the medallion she claims the image as a work "by her hand done with the aid of a mirror." In the miniature, Sofonisba has wittily placed her hands next to the words "by whose hand" (*ipsius manu ex*), so stressing the skill of her hands.

VENICE: THE SERENE REPUBLIC

Despite the attacks it endured at the beginning of the sixteenth century, Venice regained much of its territory and wealth by 1529. Its aristocracy reasserted its political and cultural power throughout the century, contributing to a distinctive situation for artists and for patrons. Instead of a court, Venice remained a nominal republic, controlled by ancient families, such as the Loredan, the Vendramin, and the Barbaro. In addition to religious works of art, these families commissioned works for their homes in town and for their villas in the country, so artists had a wide variety of themes to depict. The city itself expressed its status through public works projects commissioned by the civic fathers and intended to beautify the Most Serene Republic (*Serenissima*). One example of this is the refashioning of the heart of the city—the piazzetta between the cathedral of San Marco and the Canal of San Marco—with a pair of buildings in the 1530s.

Sansovino in Venice

The Council of Ten, who controlled the city, held a competition in 1535 to design a new home for the state mint (fig. **17.31**, left). They selected Jacopo Sansovino (1486–1570), a Florentine sculptor who left Rome for Venice after the Sack of Rome in 1527 and established himself as the city's chief architect. Not surprisingly, his buildings are sculptural in character. In the spirit of earlier Venetian structures such as the Ca' d'Oro (see fig. 15.51) and the

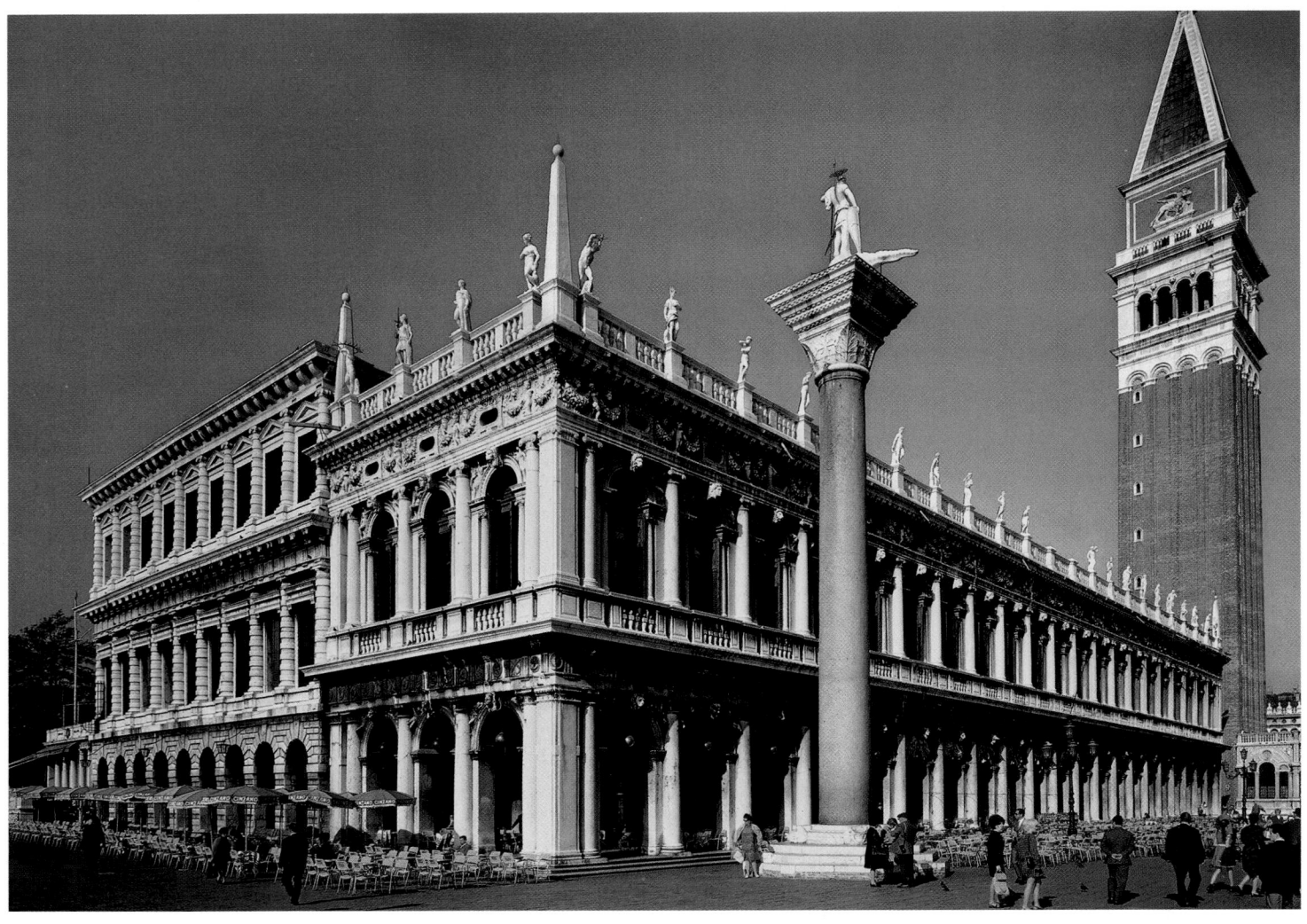

17.31 Jacopo Sansovino. Mint (left) and Library of St. Mark's, Venice. Begun ca. 1535–37

Doge's Palace (see fig. 13.32) nearby, Sansovino composed the façade to have numerous openings formed by arches and huge windows. The supporting arches and columns, however, are given greater stress by means of the rustication used throughout, which adds to the imposing effect of the building. (The top story was added around 1560.)

The Procurators of San Marco then hired Sansovino to build the Library of San Marco (see fig. 17.31, right) as a public library and repository for a rich collection of Greek and Latin manuscripts. Situated next to the mint, the library uses a much more elegant architectural vocabulary. It is a long, two-storied structure, composed as a series of arcades supporting heavy cornices. The street-level arcade is enframed by a Roman Doric order inspired by the Colosseum, while the upper story shows an elaborate treatment of the Ionic order (including triple engaged columns) surmounted by a garlanded entablature. A balustrade caps off the structure, with life-size statues over every column cluster and obelisks at each corner. The extravagant ornamentation of both structures creates an effect of opulence that proclaims the Venetian republic as a new Rome.

Andrea Palladio and Late Renaissance Architecture

Venice built many churches as well as civic buildings. The commission for San Giorgio Maggiore was awarded to one of the most influential architects of the Renaissance, Andrea Palladio (1508–1580), in 1565. Although Palladio's career centered on his native Vicenza, a town near Venice, his buildings and theoretical writings brought him international renown. Palladio believed that architecture should be governed by reason and by rules exemplified by the buildings of the ancients. He shared Leon Battista Alberti's faith in the significance of proportion. (See *Primary Source*, page 616.) The two architects differed in how they related theory to practice, however. With Alberti, the relationship had been flexible, whereas Palladio believed quite literally in practicing what he preached. This view stemmed in part from his earlier career as a stonemason and sculptor before entering the humanist circles of Count Giangiorgio Trissino of Vicenza, where he studied Vitruvius and other ancient authors and was introduced to elite patrons of the Veneto.

His first great project in Venice itself was the Benedictine church of San Giorgio Maggiore (fig. **17.32**), begun in 1565. Like his predecessors, Palladio declared that round temples are ideal because the circle is a symbol of uniformity and eternity; yet he and his patrons chose a basilican plan as the only one appropriate for Christian worship. The plan for San Giorgio Maggiore (fig. **17.33**) reflects the church's twofold purpose of serving a Benedictine monastery and a lay congregation. The main body of the church is strongly centralized—the transept is as long as the nave and a dome marks the crossing—but the longitudinal axis reasserts itself in the separate compartments for the main altar and the large choir beyond, where the monks worshiped. On the façade, Palladio wished to express the dignity of the church by using the architectural language of the ancients. He designed a flattened-out temple porch for the entrance on the grounds that "Temples ought to have ample porticos, and with larger columns than other buildings require; and it is proper that they should be great and magnificent…and built with large and beautiful proportions. They must be made of the most excellent and the most precious material, that the divinity may be honored as much as possible." To achieve this end, Palladio superimposed a tall,

narrow temple front on another low, wide one to reflect the different heights of nave and aisles in the basilica itself. The interlocking design is held together by the four gigantic columns, which function as a variant of Alberti's colossal order.

Much of Palladio's architecture consists of town houses and country villas. The Villa Rotonda (fig. **17.34**), one of Palladio's finest buildings, exemplifies his interpretation of the ancients. This country residence, built near Vicenza, beginning in 1567, for the humanist cleric Paolo Almerico, consists of a square block surmounted by a dome, with identical porches in the shape of temple fronts on all four sides. Alberti had defined the ideal church as a symmetrical, centralized design of this sort; Palladio adapted the same principles for the ideal country house. He was convinced, on the basis of his reading of Vitruvius and Pliny, that Roman private houses had porticoes like these. (Excavations have since proved him mistaken.) Palladio's use of the temple front here is more than an expression of his regard for antiquity; he considered this feature both legitimate and essential for decorum—namely, appropriateness, beauty, **harmony**, and utility—befitting the houses of "great men." This concept was embedded in the social outlook of the later sixteenth century, which required

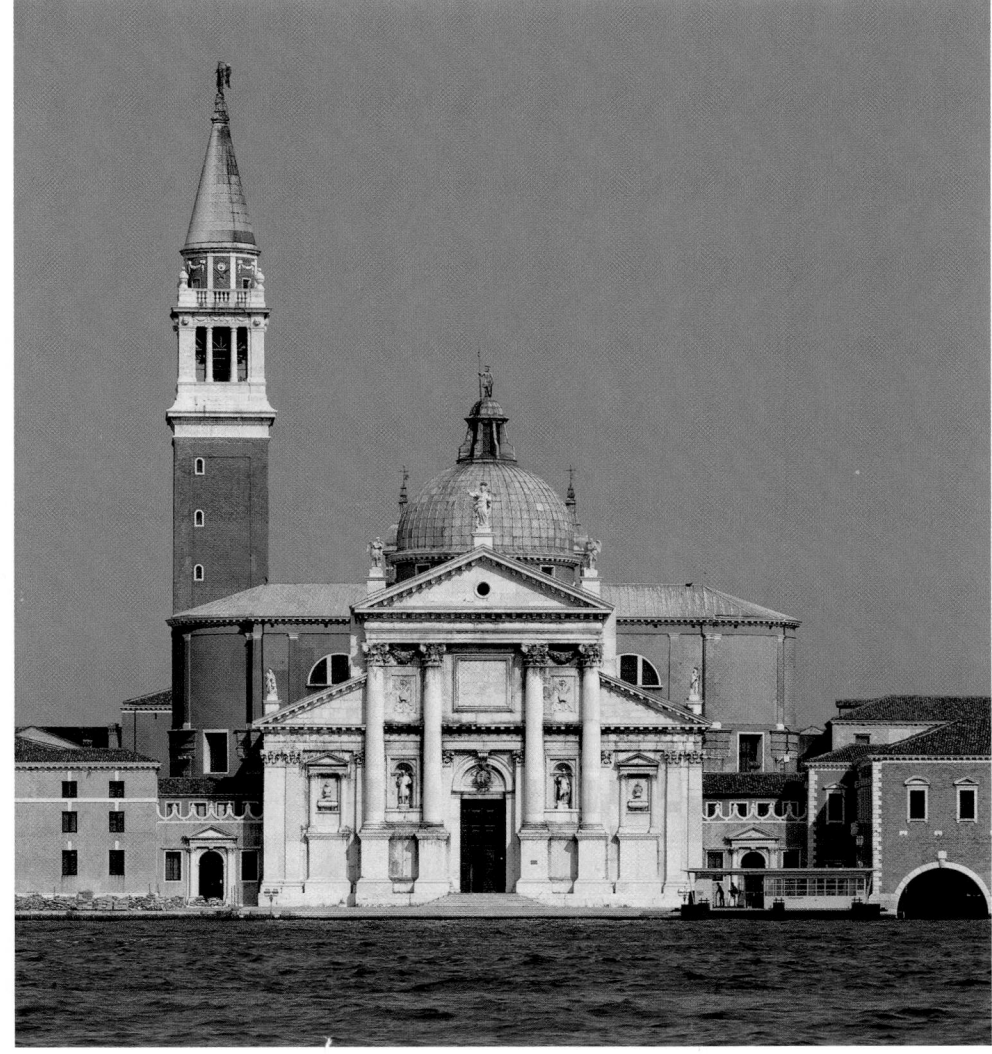

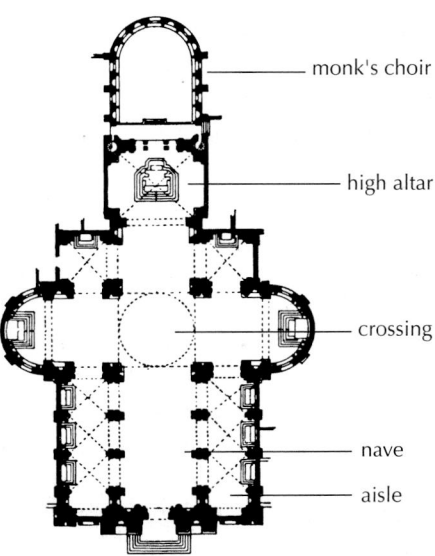

17.32   Andrea Palladio. Church of San Giorgio Maggiore, Venice. Designed 1565

17.33   Plan of Church of San Giorgio Maggiore

Andrea Palladio (1508–1580)

From *The Four Books on Architecture*

Published in 1570, Palladio's Four Books on Architecture *made an enormous impression on his European contemporaries, providing the basis for much French and English architecture of the seventeenth and eighteenth centuries.*

One must describe as suitable a house which will be appropriate to the status of the person who will have to live in it and of which the parts will correspond to the whole and to each other. But above all the architect must observe that (as Vitruvius says in Books I and VI), for great men and especially those in public office, houses with loggias and spacious, ornate halls will be required, so that those waiting to greet the master of the house or to ask him for some help or a favor can spend their time pleasantly in such spaces; similarly, smaller buildings of lesser expense and ornament will be appropriate for men of lower status. One must build in the same way for judges and lawyers … Merchants' houses should have places for storing their goods which face north and are so arranged that the owners have no fear of burglars. A building will also have decorum, if the parts correspond to the whole …

So we read that when building temples the ancients used every ingenuity to maintain decorum, which is one of the most beautiful aspects of architecture. Therefore, to maintain decorum in the shapes of our temples, we too, who have no false gods, should choose the most perfect and excellent one; and because the round form would be just that, as it alone amongst all the plans is simple, uniform, equal, strong, and capacious, let us build temples round; this form is far and away the most appropriate for them, because it is enclosed by only one boundary in which the beginning and the end … cannot be found … and since at every point the outer edge is equidistant from the center, it is perfectly adapted to demonstrate the unity, the infinite existence, the consistency and the justice of God. … recommended too are churches that are made in the shape of a cross … because … they represent, in the eyes of onlookers, that wood from which our Salvation was hung.

Source: Andrea Palladio, *The Four Books on Architecture*, tr. Robert Tavernor and Richard Schofield (Cambridge, MA: The MIT Press, 1997)

the display of great wealth and taste to assert status. Palladio's design also takes advantage of the pleasing views offered in every direction by the site. Beautifully correlated with the walls behind and the surrounding vistas, the porches of the Villa Rotonda give the structure an air of serene dignity and festive grace that is enhanced by the sculptures on the façades.

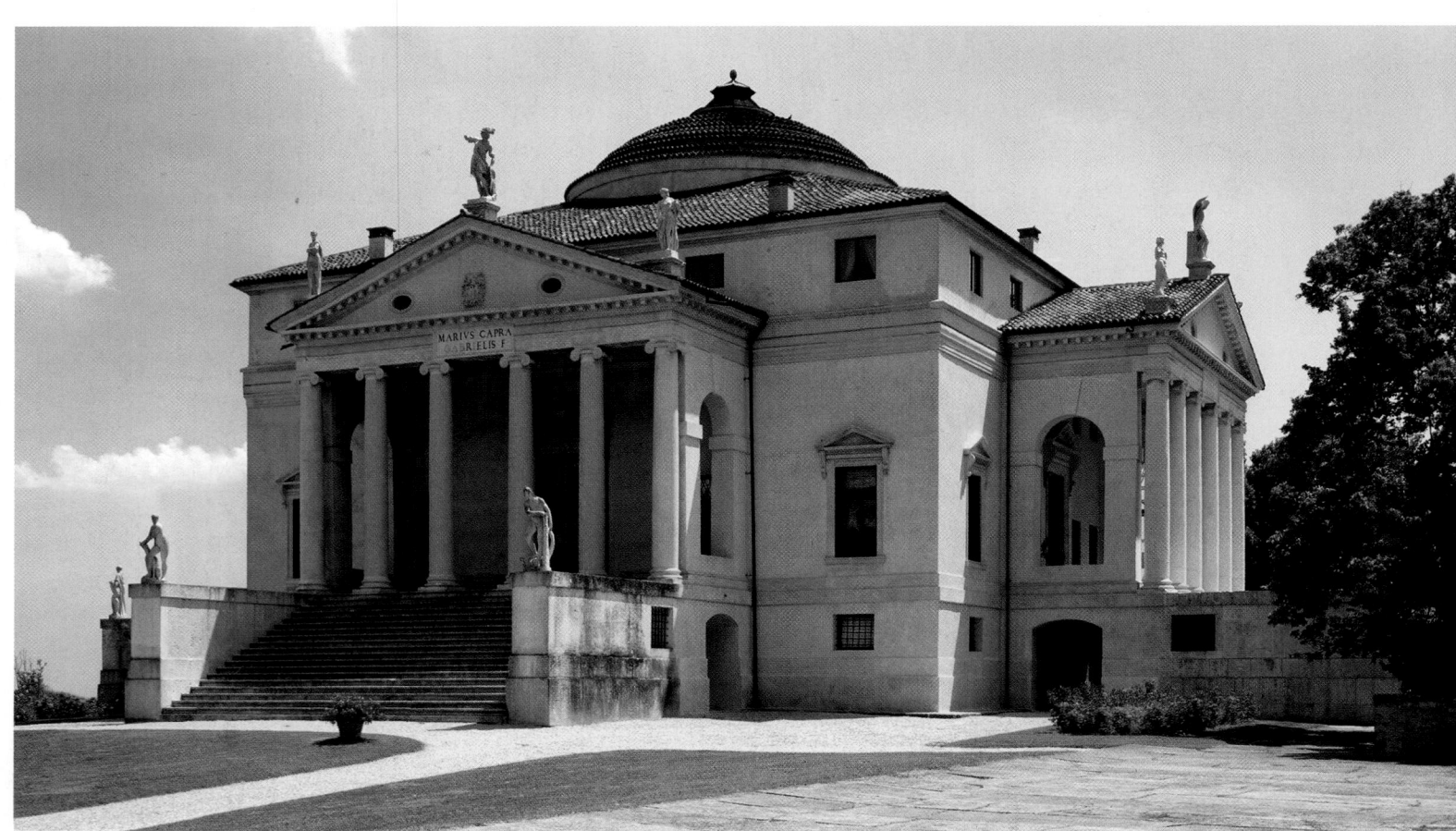

17.34   Andrea Palladio. Villa Rotonda, Vicenza. ca. 1567–70

His buildings alone would make Palladio an important figure in the history of art, but his influence extended beyond Italy, indeed beyond Europe, through his publications. Palladio's most important work in this field was his 1570 work, *The Four Books on Architecture* (excerpted in the *Primary Source*, page 616). While several architects, including Alberti, had written treatises in the fifteenth century, sixteenth-century printed books on architecture by Sebastiano Serlio and Palladio became bestsellers. Palladio's treatise was more practical than Alberti's, which may account for its great popularity among architects, and his many buildings are linked more directly with his theories. Some have claimed that Palladio designed only what was, in his view, sanctioned by ancient precedent. Indeed, the usual term for both Palladio's work and theoretical attitude is classicizing. This term denotes a conscious striving for qualities found in ancient art, although the results may not look like ancient works. Whenever later architects sought to express ideas through ancient forms, they consulted Palladio's *Four Books*. Thomas Jefferson, for instance, once referred to it as "the bible" and based several of his designs for buildings on its examples (see fig. 24.33). Such treatises, with their rules for designing beautiful buildings, formulas for correct proportion, and extensive drawings, including ground plans and elevations in woodcut, were a treasure trove for architects elsewhere in Europe and later throughout the world.

Titian

Titian (1485–1576) dominated painting in Venice throughout the sixteenth century. Like Michelangelo, he lived a long life, and he had numerous pupils to spread his ideas and techniques. His fame was such that by the 1530s his work was sought by the most elite patrons of Europe. For example, in 1538, Titian was commissioned by the duke of Urbino, Guidobaldo II della Rovere, to execute the so-called *Venus of Urbino* (fig. **17.35**). The painting, based on models by Giorgione, depicts a nude young woman lying on a bed in a well-furnished chamber. In the background, two women search in a cassone (or wedding chest) for something, perhaps for a garment. Details such as the presence of the cassone and the little dog have led some scholars to suggest that this may have been an image intended to celebrate a marriage (the dog representing faithfulness). However, the owner referred to the picture only as "the naked woman." Titian's use of color records the sensuous textures of the woman's body, which has been placed on display for a viewer whose gaze she meets. It may have been intended as an erotic image, not a classical theme.

Whether or not this is Venus, the sensuously depicted female nude became a staple product of Titian's workshop, which was supported by the patronage of other powerful men. For Phillip II of Spain (the son of Charles V), whom he met in 1548, Titian

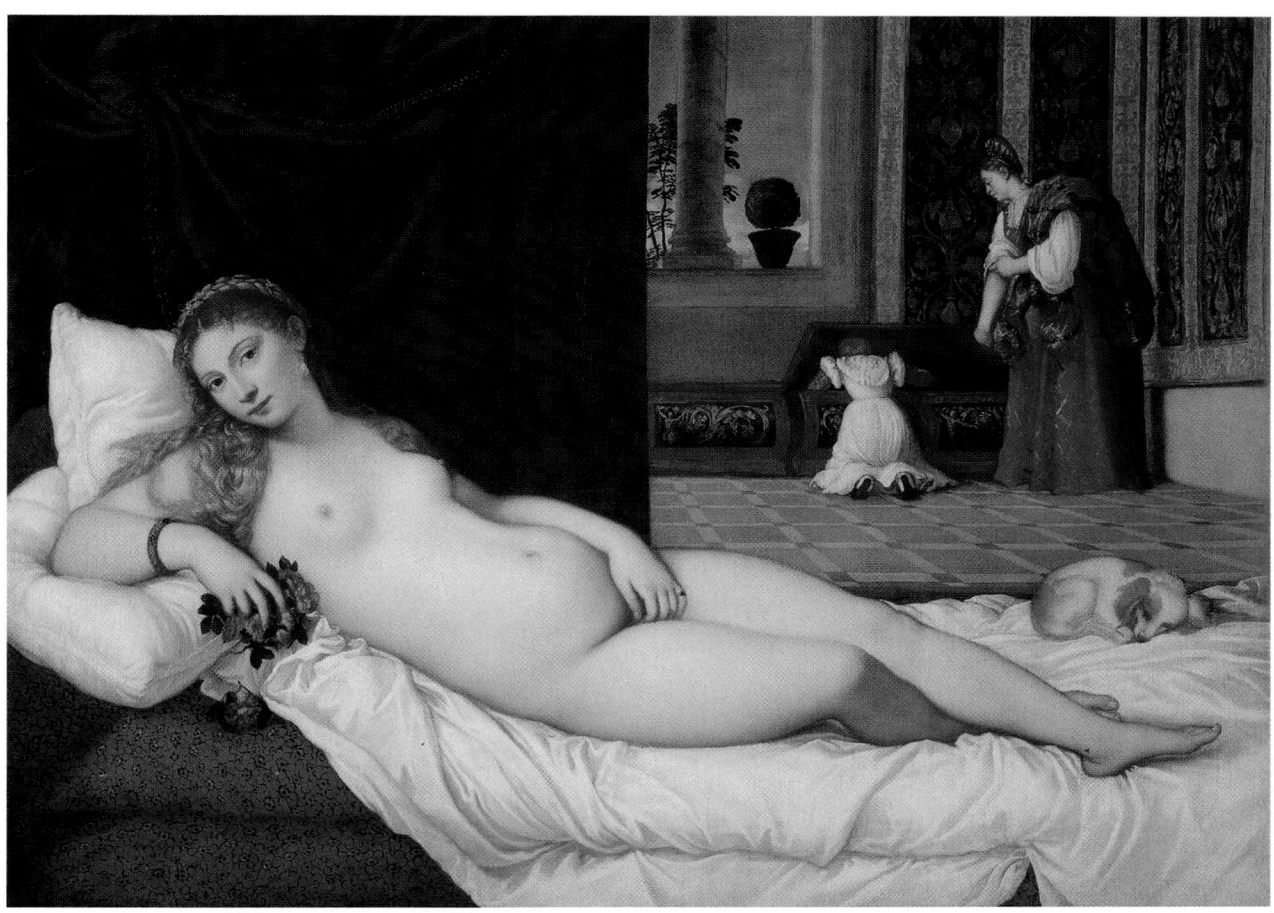

17.35 Titian, *Venus of Urbino*. ca. 1538. Oil on canvas, 47 × 65" (119 × 165 cm). Gallerie degli Uffizi, Florence

Oil on Canvas

For much of the Middle Ages and Renaissance, painters worked either directly on walls or on solid wood supports. Wood panels were formed of planks that had to be attached together, so seams are sometimes visible. While durable, wood is also heavy and susceptible to warping. In the fifteenth century, some artists both in Italy and in northern Europe painted on cloth supports, usually canvas or linen, as a less expensive substitute for wood. Canvas is also lighter, and more easily portable. Painted canvases from Flanders, called *panni dipinti*, were imported in good numbers to Italy.

In the humid climate of Venice, where neither fresco nor wood panels would easily survive, artists preferred to work on canvas supports, especially on large-scale projects. By the middle of the sixteenth century, canvas began to replace wood as the support of choice. By 1600, most patrons, who were not commissioning frescoes, preferred oil on canvas. Once the canvas itself had been stretched on a wooden framework, the artist would cover it with a gluelike material to seal the fibers. Then several priming coats would be applied and allowed to dry before painting commenced.

Working on a large scale also inspired Venetian painters to experiment with the oil medium itself. Instead of building up layers of tinted glazes over large surfaces, artists loaded the brush with more opaque color and laid it on with broad strokes. Sometimes the thick paint looked pastelike, a technique called impasto. In such cases, the surface does not have a mirrorlike smoothness, but is rough and catches the light unevenly. Titian is one of the innovators of this technique. His example was the inspiration for the painterly artists of the Baroque, including Rubens, Rembrandt, and Velázquez.

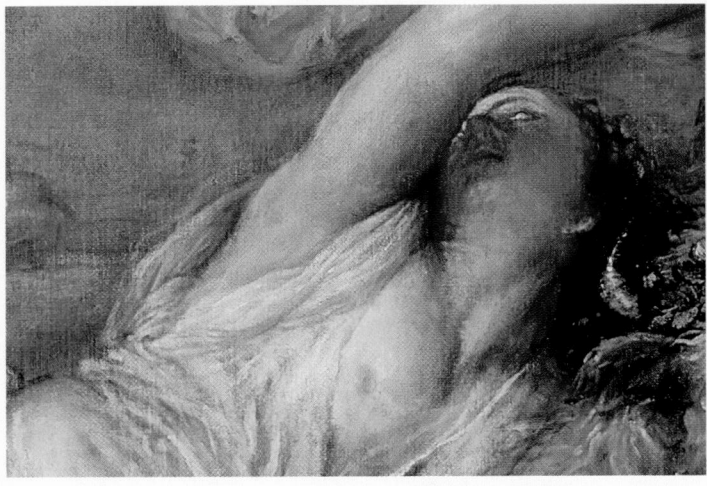

Detail of Titian, *Rape of Europa*

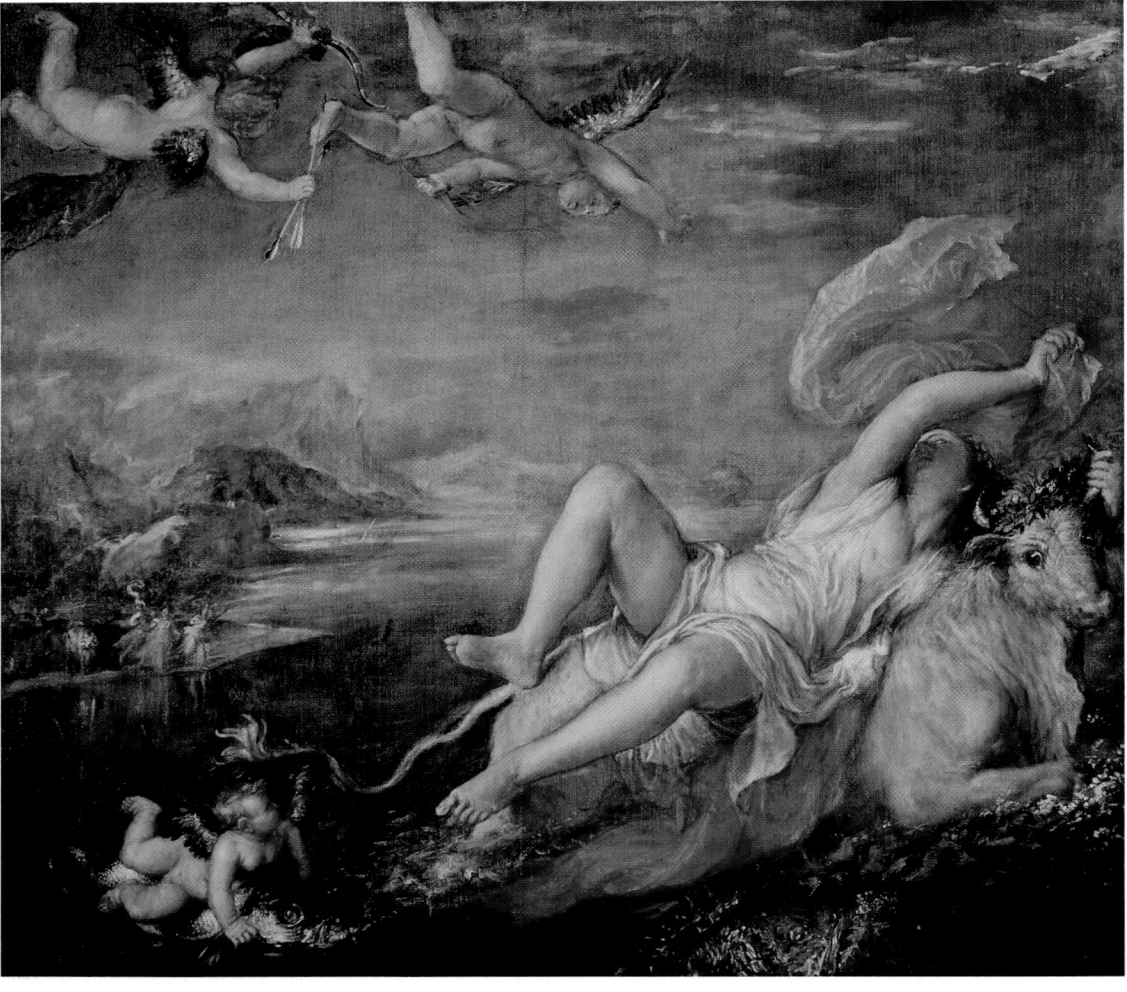

17.36 Titian, *Rape of Europa*. 1559–62. Oil on canvas, 6'1⅛" × 6'8⅔" (185 × 205 cm). Isabella Stewart Gardner Museum, Boston

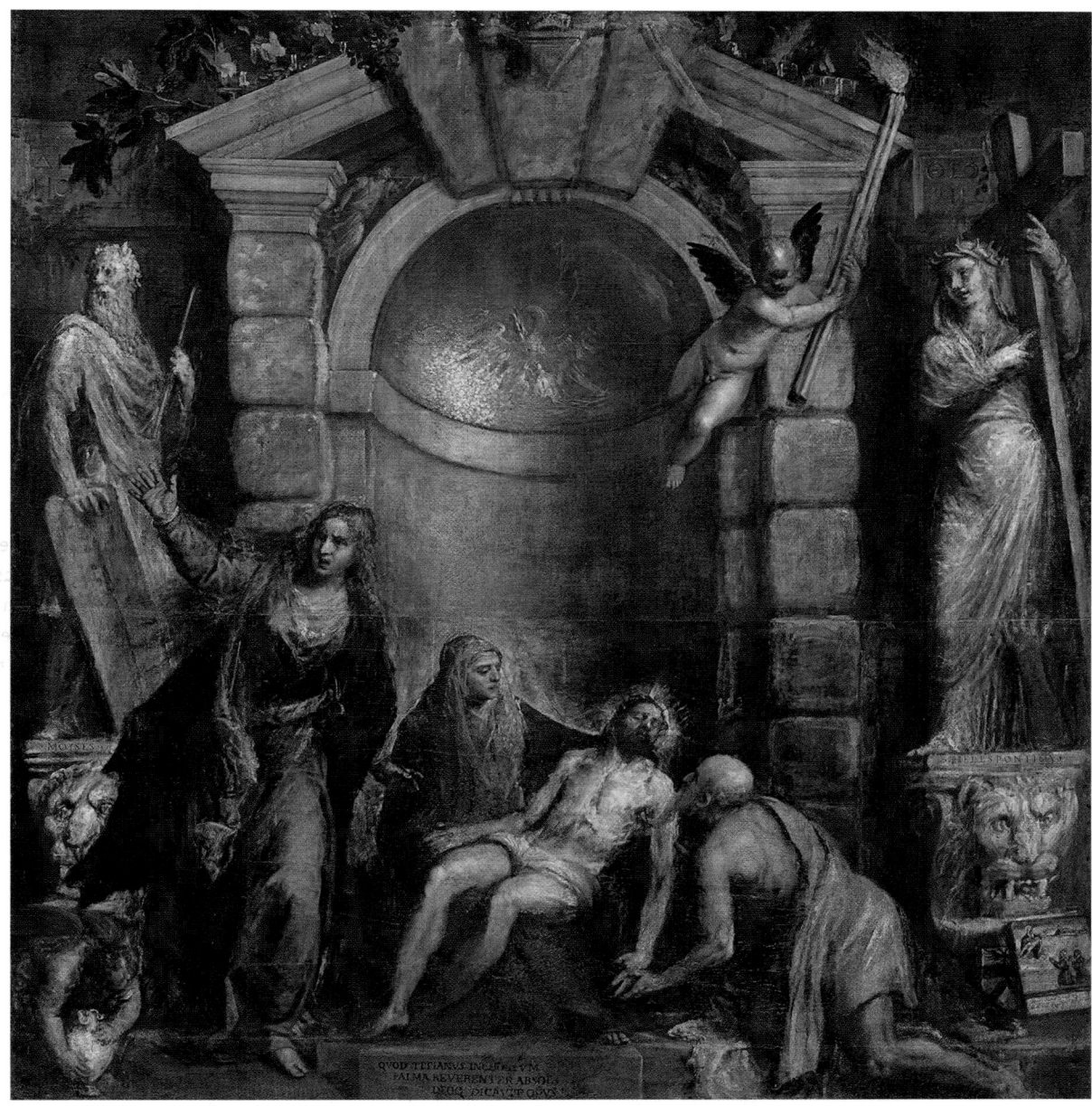

17.37 Titian, *Pietà*. ca. 1576. Canvas, 11'6" × 12'9" (3.51 × 3.89 m). Gallerie dell'Accademia, Venice

made a series of images of the Loves of Jupiter based on the Roman poet Ovid's *Metamorphoses*. There, Ovid recounted the story of the princess beguiled by Jupiter who had taken the shape of a white bull to avoid his wife's jealous gaze; this tale inspired Titian's *Rape of Europa*, finished by 1562 (fig. **17.36**). The poet says that the young woman admired the bull, whom she encountered on the seashore. When she climbed onto the beast, the god swam away with her, her veil fluttering behind her as she clung to his horn. Titian's painting takes up the story at its climax, as the bull moves away from land, leaving Europa's companions to wave ineffectually on the shore.

In Titian's painting, Europa can barely hold on to the energetic animal. Titian uses rich colors and swirling movement to heighten the sensuous forms and to create an atmospheric setting for the events. His brushwork is very free, to the point that the

forms are barely defined. This effect is enhanced by his use of the impasto technique. (See *Materials and Techniques*, page 618.) The sharp disjunction between foreground and background emphasizes the main figures' distance from land and adds drama. Such images of sensuous interaction between gods and mortals offered artists like Titian an opportunity to compete with poets. Contemporaries called these images *poesie*, just as they did the works of Giorgione (see page 584).

Titian experimented with many different forms, including prints, but his most enduring innovations were in the technique of painting on canvas. His late works demonstrate his freest brushwork. Titian intended the *Pietà* (fig. **17.37**) for his own tomb in the Franciscan church of Santa Maria Gloriosa dei Frari; incomplete at his death in 1576, it was finished by one of his students. Like Michelangelo's late *Pietà* (see fig. 17.16), Titian depicts the

From a Session of the Inquisition Tribunal in Venice of Paolo Veronese

Because of the liberal religious atmosphere of Venice, Veronese was never required to make the various changes to his painting of the Last Supper (see fig. 17.38) asked for by the tribunal of the Inquisition in this interrogation. All parties seem to have been satisfied with a mere change of title to The Feast in the House of Levi.

Today, Saturday, the 18th of the month of July, 1573, having been asked by the Holy Office to appear before the Holy Tribunal, Paolo Caliari of Verona questioned about his profession:

A: I paint and compose figures.

Q: Do you know the reason why you have been summoned?

A: No, sir.

Q: Can you imagine it?

A: I can well imagine.

Q: Say what you think the reason is.

A: According to what the Reverend Father, the Prior of the Convent of SS. Giovanni e Paolo, told me, he had been here and Your Lordships had ordered him to have painted [in the picture] a Magdalen in place of a dog. I answered him by saying I would gladly do everything necessary for my honor and for that of my painting, but that I did not understand how a figure of Magdalen would be suitable there.

Q: What picture is this of which you have spoken?

A: This is a picture of the Last Supper that Jesus Christ took with His Apostles in the house of Simon.

Q: At this Supper of Our Lord have you painted other figures?

A: Yes, milords.

Q: Tell us how many people and describe the gestures of each.

A: There is the owner of the inn, Simon; besides this figure I have made a steward, who, I imagined, had come there for his own pleasure to see how things were going at the table. There are many figures there which I cannot recall, as I painted the picture some time ago.

Q: In this Supper which you made for SS. Giovanni e Paolo what is the significance of the man whose nose is bleeding?

A: I intended to represent a servant whose nose was bleeding because of some accident.

Q: What is the significance of those armed men dressed as Germans, each with a halberd in his hand?

A: We painters take the same license the poets and the jesters take and I have represented these two halberdiers, one drinking and the other eating nearby on the stairs. They are placed there so that they might be of service because it seemed to me fitting, according to what I have been told, that the master of the house, who was great and rich, should have such servants.

Q: And that man dressed as a buffoon with a parrot on his wrist, for what purpose did you paint him on that canvas?

A: For ornament, as is customary.

Q: Who are at the table of Our Lord?

A: The Twelve Apostles.

Q: What is St. Peter, the first one, doing?

A: Carving the lamb in order to pass it to the other end of the table.

Q: What is the Apostle next to him doing?

A: He is holding a dish in order to receive what St. Peter will give him.

Q: Tell us what the one next to this one is doing.

A: He has a toothpick and cleans his teeth.

Q: Did anyone commission you to paint Germans, buffoons, and similar things in that picture?

A: No, milords, but I received the commission to decorate the picture as I saw fit. It is large and, it seemed to me, it could hold many figures.

Q: Are not the decorations which you painters are accustomed to add to paintings or pictures supposed to be suitable and proper to the subject and the principal figures or are they for pleasure—simply what comes to your imagination without any discretion or judiciousness?

A: I paint pictures as I see fit and as well as my talent permits.

Q: Does it seem fitting at the Last Supper of the Lord to paint buffoons, drunkards, Germans, dwarfs, and similar vulgarities?

A: No, milords.

Q: Do you not know that in Germany and in other places infected with heresy it is customary with various pictures full of scurrilousness and similar inventions to mock, vituperate, and scorn the things of the Holy Catholic Church in order to teach bad doctrines to foolish and ignorant people?

A: Yes, that is wrong.

After these things had been said, the judges announced that the above named Paolo would be obliged to improve and change his painting within a period of three months from the day of this admonition and that according to the opinion and decision of the Holy Tribunal all the corrections should be made at the expense of the painter and that if he did not correct the picture he would be liable to the penalties imposed by the Holy Tribunal. Thus they decreed in the best manner possible.

Source: *A Documentary History of Art*, vol. 2, ed. Elizabeth Gilmore Holt (Princeton, NJ: Princeton University Press, 1982)

body of Christ in his mother's arms as friends and followers mourn. Moses and a sibyl flank a heavily rusticated niche reminiscent of the façade of Sansovino's mint (see fig. 17.31). This large canvas owes its power not only to its large scale and dramatic composition, although these are contributing factors, but also to Titian's technique. The forms emerging from the semidarkness seem to consist wholly of light and color. The artist applies the color in thick masses of paint, yet despite this heavy impasto, the surfaces have lost every trace of material solidity. The gesture of Mary Magdalen and the sorrow in the features of the Virgin add poignancy to the scene. A kneeling figure, possibly St. Jerome, stands in for Titian himself and reaches over to touch the body of Christ in reverence. The quiet, almost resigned mood is enhanced by the painting's ethereal forms.

Titian's Legacy

Titian's creative output and reputation drew many artists to work in his workshop, but he had a tremendous influence even on those who did not. From the island of Crete (then controlled by Venice), the young Domenikos Theotokopoulos, called El Greco, came to study in Titian's shop before heading to Spain (see Chapter 18). The two leading painters in Venice after Titian, Veronese and Tintoretto, developed in different directions. Where Veronese made images that depended on early Titian works such as the *Pesaro Madonna* (see fig. 16.32) and aimed for naturalism, Tintoretto exploited the drama and fluid brushwork of Titian's later work, like the *Pietà*.

PAOLO VERONESE The paintings of Paolo Cagliari (1528–1588), called Paolo Veronese, who was born and trained in Verona, start from the naturalism inherent in Titian's style, but add an interest in details of everyday reality, as seen in animals, textiles, and foodstuffs—and in grand architectural frameworks.

In his huge canvas *The Feast in the House of Levi* (fig. **17.38**), Veronese avoids any reference to the mystical. His symmetrical composition harks back to paintings by Leonardo and Raphael, while the festive mood of the scene reflects examples by Titian of the 1520s, so that at first glance the picture looks like a High Renaissance work born 50 years too late. Veronese, however, is less interested than Leonardo in conveying spiritual or psychological depth. Originally commissioned for the refectory of a Dominican monastery, the painting depicts a sumptuous banquet, a true feast for the eyes. As with his contemporaries elsewhere in Italy, Veronese was deliberately vague about which event from the life of Jesus he originally meant to depict. He gave the painting its present title only after he had been summoned by the religious tribunal of the Inquisition on the charge of filling his picture with "buffoons, drunkards, Germans, dwarfs, and similar vulgarities" unsuited to its theme. The account of the trial shows that the tribunal thought any such representation of the Last Supper irreverent. (See *Primary Source*, page 620.) In the face of their questions, Veronese therefore settled on a different title—*The Feast in the House of Levi*—which permitted him to leave the offending incidents in place. He argued that they were no more objectionable than the nudity of Jesus and the Heavenly Host in Michelangelo's *Last Judgment*. Nevertheless, the tribunal failed to see the analogy, on the grounds that "in the Last Judgment it was not necessary to paint garments, and there is nothing in those figures that is not spiritual." Like many of his contemporaries, Veronese claimed the privilege to "paint pictures as I see fit."

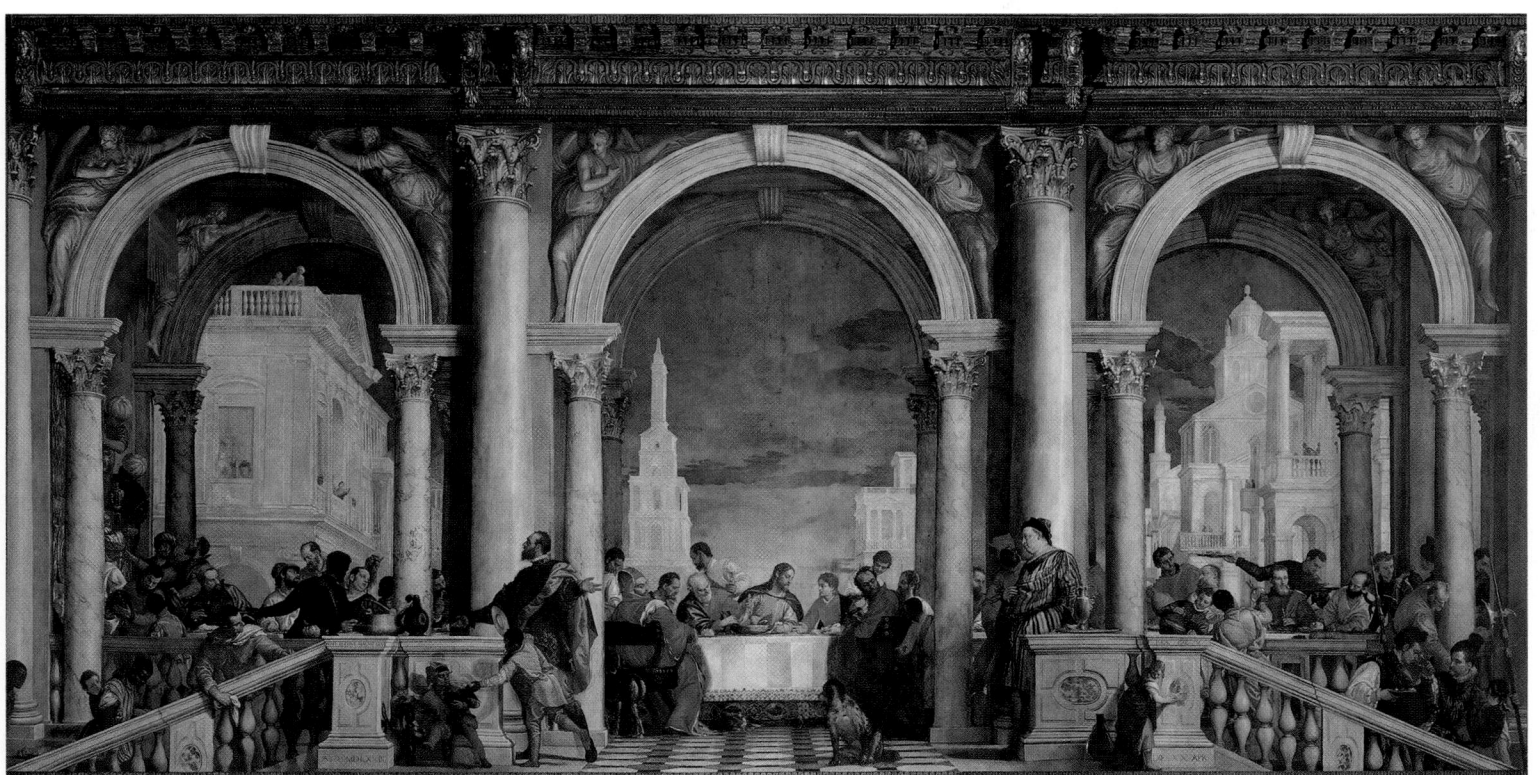

17.38 Paolo Veronese, *The Feast in the House of Levi*. 1573. Oil on canvas, 18'2" × 42' (5.5 × 12.8 m). Gallerie dell'Accademia, Venice

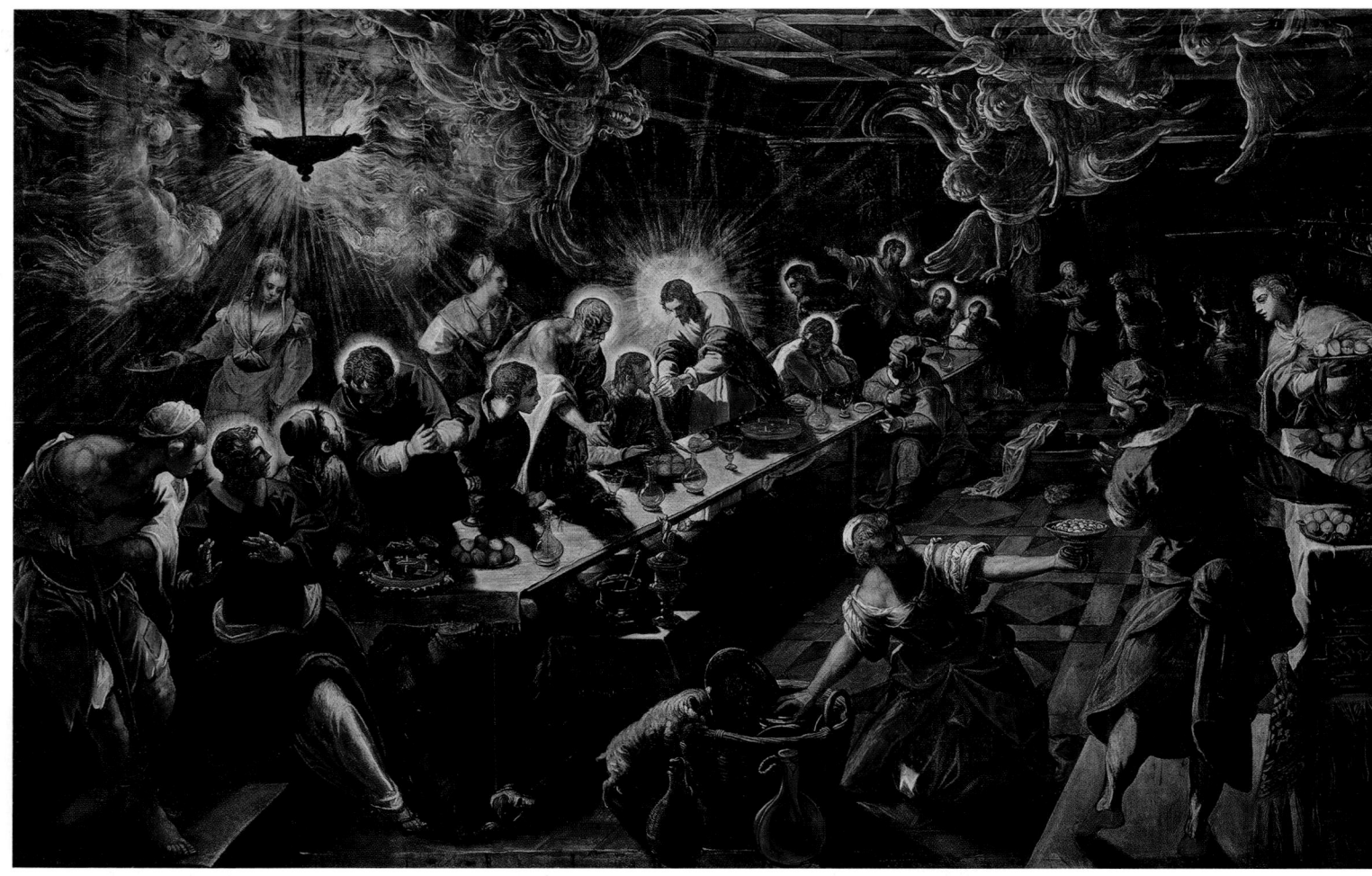

17.39 Jacopo Tintoretto, *The Last Supper*. 1594. Oil on canvas, 12' × 18'8" (3.7 × 5.7 m). San Giorgio Maggiore, Venice

TINTORETTO Jacopo Robusti (1519–1594), called Tintoretto, took a less worldly attitude. He reportedly wanted "to paint like Titian and to design like Michelangelo." He did not imitate the High Renaissance phases of those artists' careers, however, but absorbed their later styles, which are more expressive and less realistic in their effects. In a number of large-scale paintings for Venetian confraternities, groups of laypeople organized for religious activities, he assimilated the visionary effects of Titian's late paintings and the energetic compositions of the late Michelangelo. Tintoretto's final major work, *The Last Supper*, finished in 1594, is spectacular (fig. **17.39**). It seems to deny in every possible way the balance and clarity of Leonardo's version of the theme painted almost exactly a century before (see fig. 16.6), which nonetheless underlies Veronese's picture. Jesus, to be sure, is at the center of the composition, but his small figure in the middle distance is distinguished mainly by his brilliant halo. Tintoretto barely hints at the human drama of Judas' betrayal, so important to Leonardo. Judas can be seen isolated on the near side of the table across from Jesus (as Castagno had arranged him in his fresco in Sant'Apollonia, see fig. 15.29), but his role is so insignificant that he could almost be mistaken for an attendant. The table is now placed at a sharp angle to the picture plane in exaggerated perspective. This

arrangement had a purpose. Tintoretto designed it to relate the scene to the space of the **chancel** of San Giorgio Maggiore in Venice, designed by Palladio (see fig. 17.33), for which it was commissioned. When the Benedictine friars knelt at the altar rail to receive communion, they could see the scene at a less acute angle, as if the painted space continued their own.

Tintoretto gives the event an everyday setting, cluttering the scene with attendants, containers of food and drink, and domestic animals. There are also celestial attendants who converge upon Jesus as he offers his body and blood, in the form of bread and wine, to the disciples. The smoke from the blazing oil lamp miraculously turns into clouds of angels, blurring the distinction between the natural and the supernatural and turning the scene into a magnificently orchestrated vision. The artist's main concern is to make visible the miracle of the Eucharist—the Transubstantiation of earthly into divine food—in both real and symbolic terms. The central importance of this sacrament to Catholic doctrine was forcefully reasserted during the Catholic Counter-Reformation. The painting was especially appropriate for its location in San Giorgio Maggiore, which played a prominent role in the reform movement that would have broad repercussions for the arts in Europe in subsequent centuries.

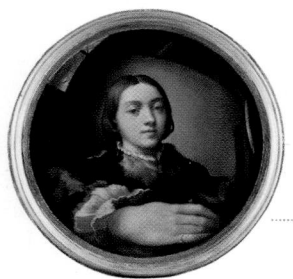

1524 Parmigianino,
Self-Portrait

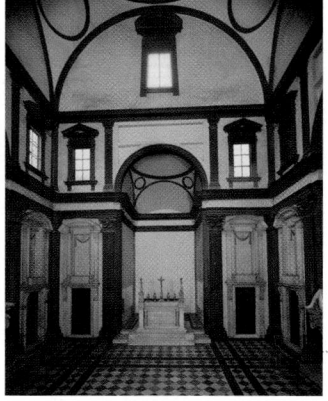

1519–34 Michelangelo's New
Sacristy at San Lorenzo in Florence

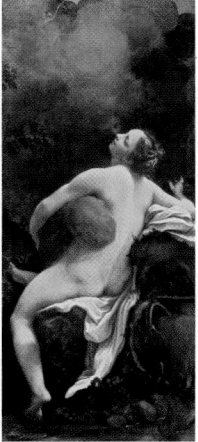

1532 Correggio,
Jupiter and Io

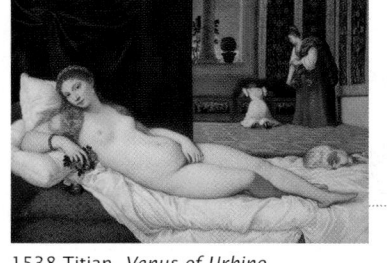

1538 Titian, *Venus of Urbino*

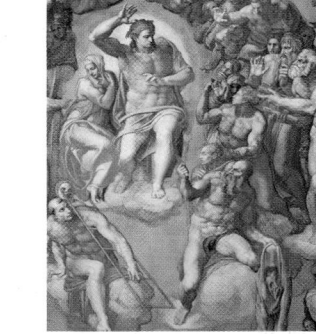

1541 Michelangelo's *Last
Judgment* in the Sistine Chapel

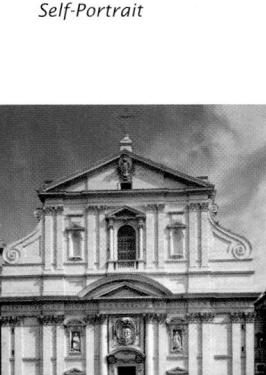

1556 Sofonisba
Anguissola,
Self-Portrait

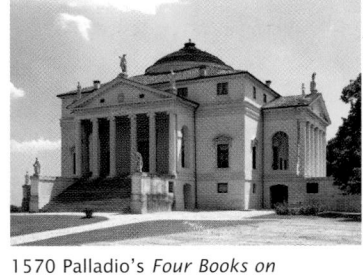

1570 Palladio's *Four Books on
Architecture* published

1575 Façade of Il Gesù in Rome

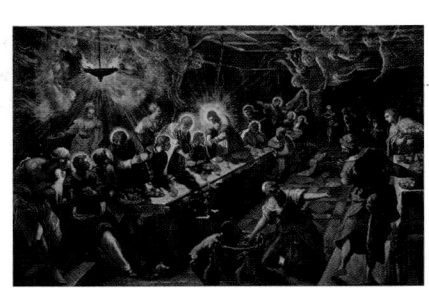

1594 Tintoretto's
Last Supper
at San Giorgio Maggiore

The Late Renaissance and Mannerism in Sixteenth-Century Italy

1500

ca. 1505 Bosch's *Garden of Earthly Delights*

1510

1520

◄ 1520 Death of Raphael
◄ 1521 Luther condemned at Diet of Worms

◄ 1527 Habsburg army sacks Rome; Giulio Romano
in Mantua

1530

◄ 1537 Cosimo I ruler in Florence

1540

◄ 1540 Ignatius of Loyola founds Society of Jesus
(Jesuits)

◄ 1545 Council of Trent opens; Catholic Reformation
begins

1550

1560

◄ 1563 Founding of Florence's Accademia del
Disegno

1570

◄ 1571 Venetian and Spanish navies defeat Turkish
fleet at Lepanto

1580

◄ 1582 Pope Gregory XIII reforms the calendar

1590

◄ 1597 Annibale Carracci in Rome

1600

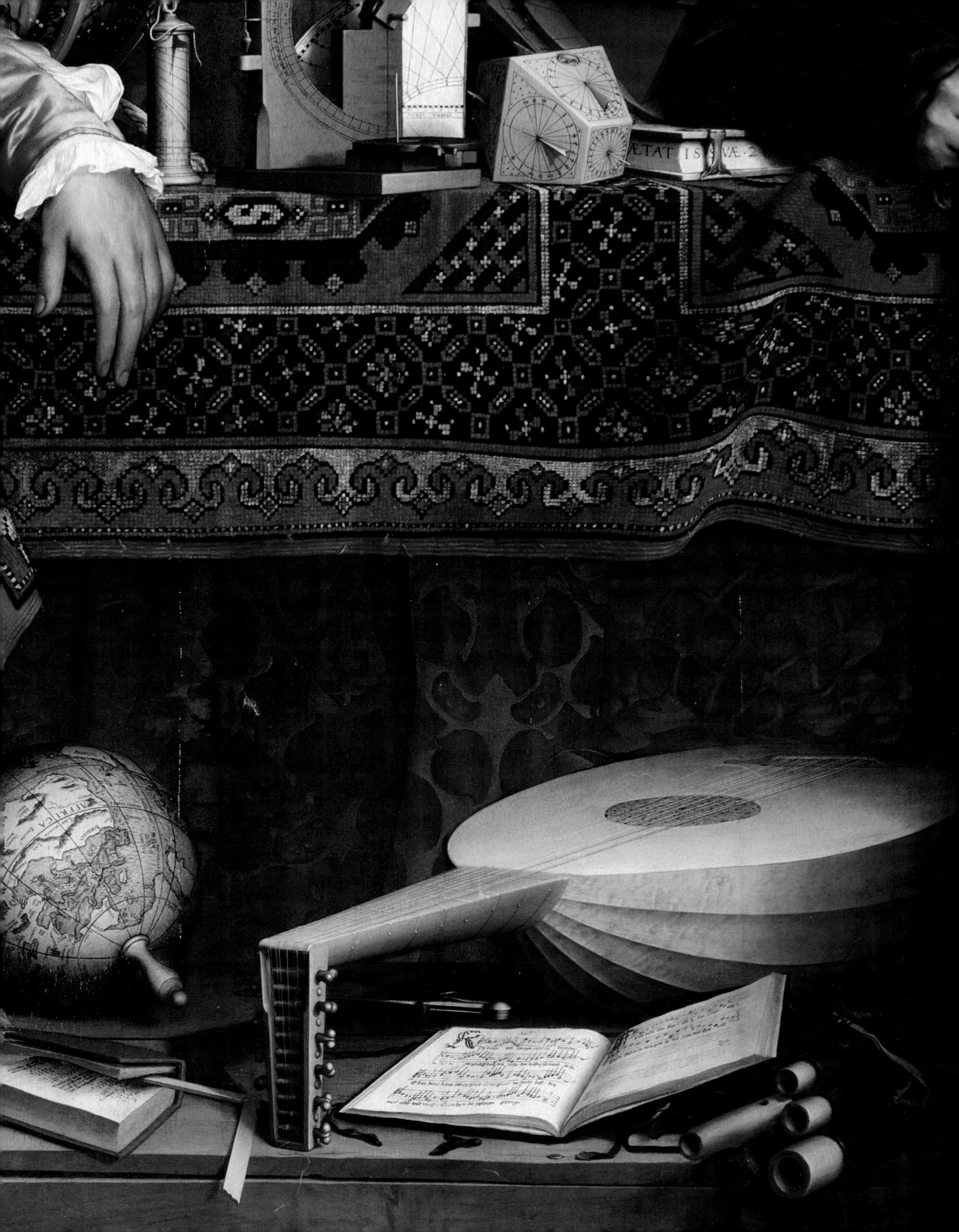

Renaissance and Reformation in Sixteenth-Century Northern Europe

MANY OF THE KEY EVENTS THAT OCCURRED DURING THE HIGH Renaissance brought important changes throughout Europe, as well as in Italy. In addition to the religious challenge of the Reformation fomented by Luther and the new cultural expressions of the Italian Renaissance, northern Europeans witnessed significant changes: the growing power

of large centralized states in France, England, Spain, and the Holy Roman Empire; the expansion of Europe's economic reach around the globe; and the rapid dissemination of new ideas and styles. As northern Europe experienced the birth pangs of the modern era, artists reconciled local traditions with these new conditions.

The challenge of the Reformation to the Roman Catholic Church would fundamentally change the map of Europe (map **18.1**). Proponents of religious reform including Luther, Ulrich Zwingli, John Calvin, and others attracted many adherents, and whole communities, cities, and even states were converted, fracturing the religious unity of Europe. Catholic Europe faced off against Protestant Europe, with great loss of life. While France and Spain remained loyal to the Roman Catholic Church, Germany, England, and the Netherlands were divided by religious sectarianism. The more radical reformed faiths deplored the Catholic tradition of religious images and relics, and encouraged the destruction of images in the areas that converted to their beliefs.

Under such conditions, artists had to find new ways to pursue their craft and new markets for their products. Those markets would continue the trends established in the fifteenth century. A growing capitalist economy brought wealth and an increasing population to the cities. Manufacturing and trade grew, especially

with the new Atlantic trade routes and colonial settlements in the Americas and Asia. Even as the cities developed in economic and social importance, increasingly authoritarian rulers asserted control over their domains.

These pressures affected the character of the arts in northern Europe. In part because of the Protestant reformers' suspicion of sculptural expression, the medium of painting increased in importance in the sixteenth century. As religious patronage waned, artists turned to secular themes, which appealed to patrons in the cities and in the courts. To compete in the open market, artists began to specialize in particular subjects or themes. The achievements of the Italian Renaissance also challenged northern artists, who absorbed Italian compositions, ideal figure types, and an admiration of antiquity. Patrons in the courts found Italian style particularly useful for expressing their power, as they built monumental palaces. Catholic rulers often used Italianate forms to affirm their faith.

FRANCE: COURTLY TASTES FOR ITALIAN FORMS

France was fertile ground for the importation of Italian ideas. French kings had been intervening in Italy for centuries, which brought them into contact with developments in Italian art and architecture. Charles VII of France had invaded Milan in 1499,

Detail of figure 18.23, Hans Holbein the Younger, *Jean de Dinteville and Georges de Selve*

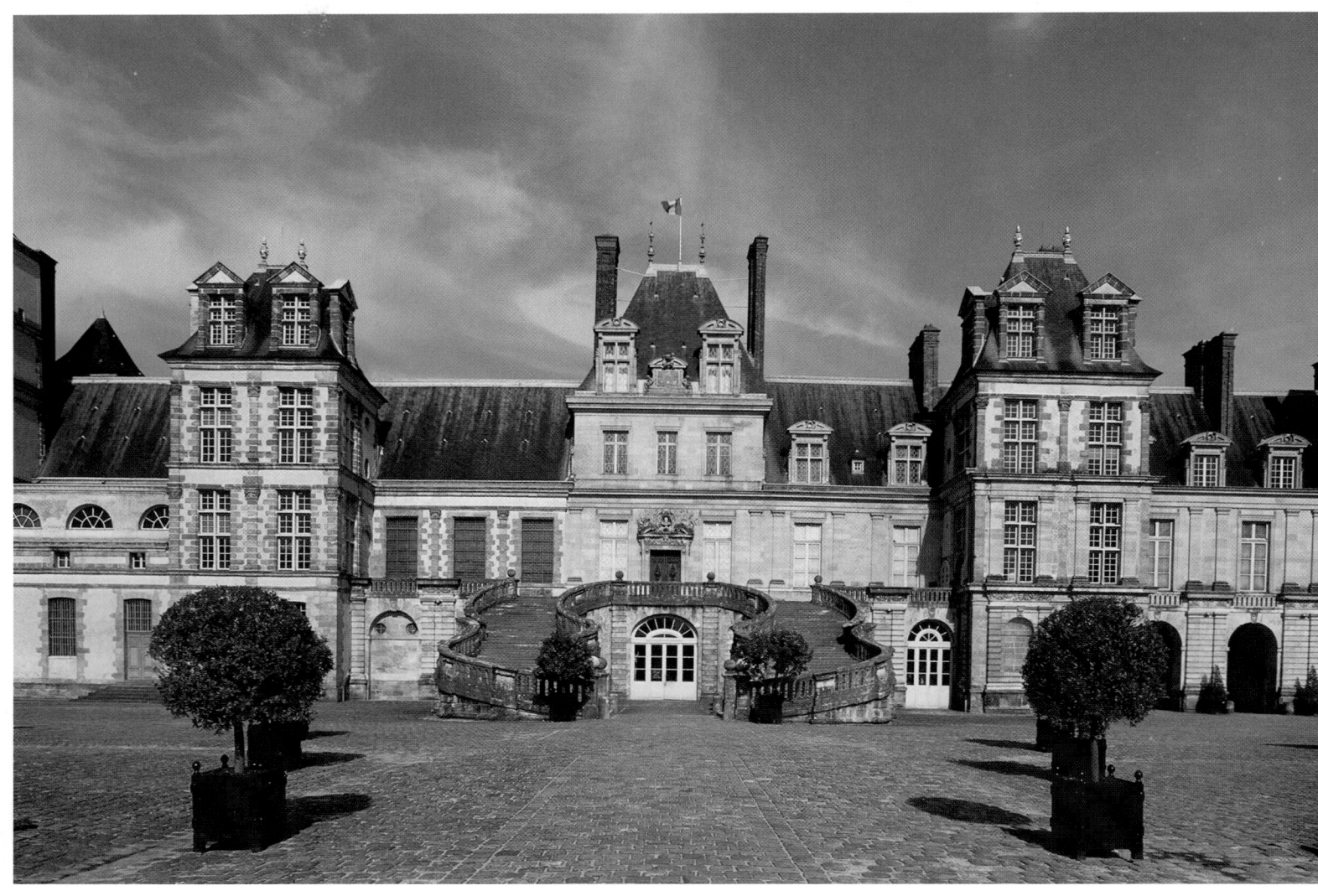

18.1 Gilles Le Breton. Cour du Cheval Blanc (Court of the White Horse), Fontainebleau. 1528–40

and his successors continued to meddle in the Italian peninsula. Francis I (r. 1515–1547) showed his admiration for Italian art by inviting Leonardo da Vinci to work for him in the Loire Valley. Leonardo had provided designs for a never-constructed chateau for the king before dying in Amboise in 1519. Francis's appreciation for Italian art and his propensity for spending money made his court a magnet for artists from Italy and elsewhere in Europe. Rosso Fiorentino, Francesco Primaticcio, Benvenuto Cellini, and others found work there. French traditions were maintained, too, as local architects interpreted Italian ideas for royal structures.

Chateaux and Palaces: Translating Italian Architecture

During the Renaissance, French castles lost their fortified aspect and became palaces for enjoying country life. The influence of Italian architectural design came into play in the design of many of these structures, especially in the chateau that Francis I built south of Paris amid the forest of Fontainebleau (fig. 18.1). In 1528,

he decided to expand the medieval hunting lodge that was once the haunt of King Louis IX. What began as a modest enlargement soon developed into a sprawling palace. The original design, much altered over the years, was largely the work of the stonemason Gilles Le Breton (d. 1553), whose father, Jean (d. 1543/44), had helped design Chambord. Fontainebleau set a fashion for French translations of Italianate architecture that was followed for nearly all French chateaux for the next 250 years.

The Cour du Cheval Blanc (Court of the White Horse) is typical of the project as a whole. The design must have evolved in an organic fashion, with new generations of patrons and architects adding to it over time. (The Italianate staircase that now dominates the courtyard was built by Jean Androuet du Cerceau in 1634.) Rectangular pavilions at regular intervals define the units of the façade. The façade employs a vocabulary from Italian architecture: pilasters mark each story, entablatures tie the whole façade together horizontally, and the lowest level uses rusticated pilasters such as those used by Sansovino at the Mint in Venice (see fig. 17.31). These elements are blended with vertical proportions, especially in the windows and along the roofline. Such

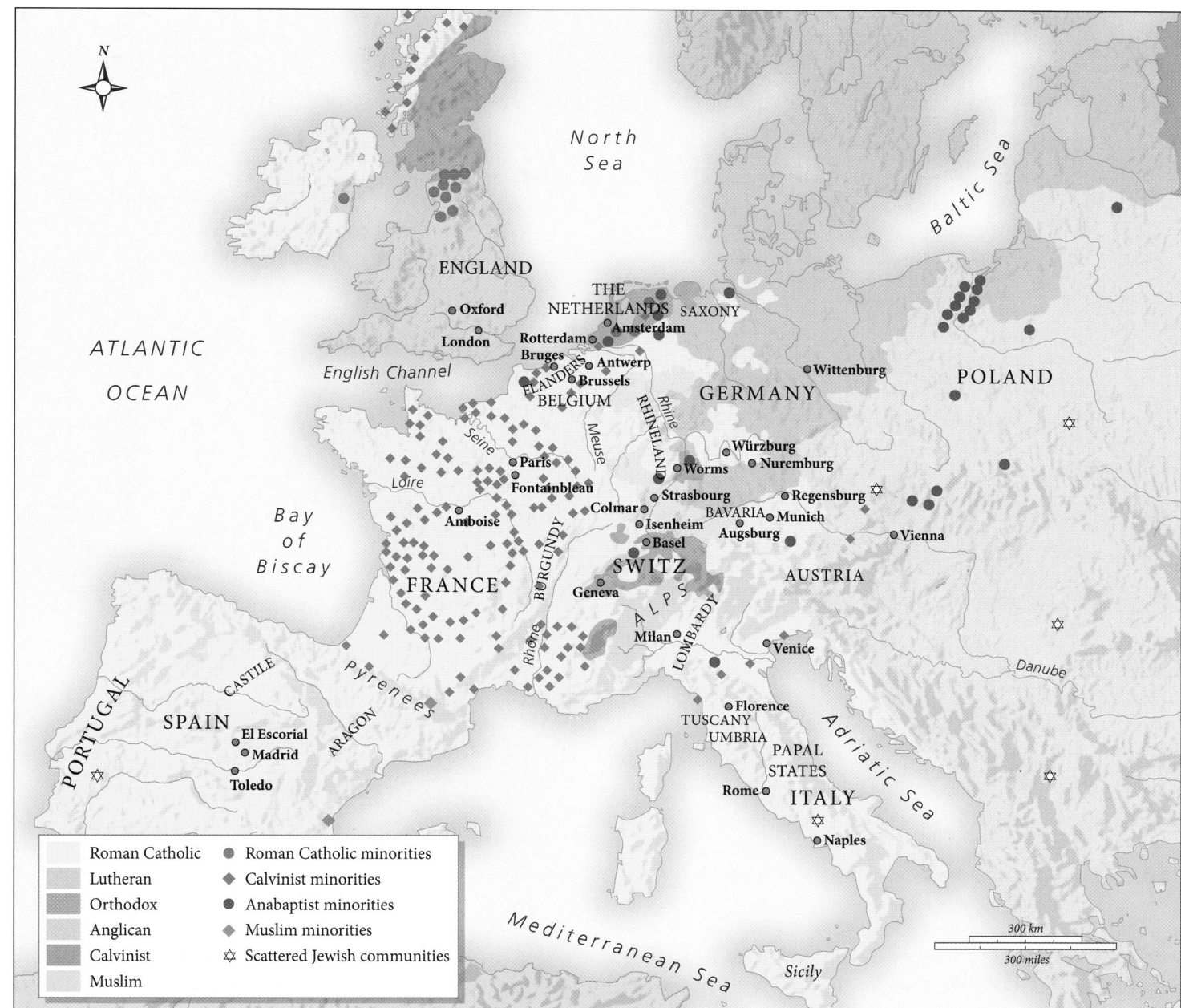

Map 18.1 Religious situation in Europe in the late sixteenth century

vertical massing of forms reflects traditional castle design and the Gothic proportions that French patrons preferred to the more horizontal Italianate models.

THE LOUVRE Despite a variety of wars and other entanglements, Francis I had a great appetite for commissioning large-scale projects. In 1546, he decided to replace the Gothic royal castle in Paris, the Louvre, with a new palace on the old site. The project had barely begun at the time of his death, but his architect, Pierre Lescot (ca. 1515–1578), continued and enlarged it under his successor, Henry II. This scheme was not completed for more than a century. Lescot built the southern half of the court's west side (fig. **18.2**) in a more thoroughly Italianate style than was seen at Fontainebleau.

The design represents a genuine synthesis of the traditional French chateau with the Italian palazzo. The superimposed classical orders, the pedimented window frames, and the arcade on the ground floor stem from Italy. Three projecting pavilions, however, have replaced the chateau turrets to interrupt the continuity of the façade. The high-pitched roof is also French. The vertical accents, and the tall, narrow windows counteract and balance the horizontal elements. The whole effect is symmetrical and well organized; it is made sumptuous by the ornate carvings of the pilasters and their capitals and the relief sculpture that covers nearly all of the wall surface of the third story. These reliefs, beautifully adapted to the architecture, are by Jean Goujon (ca. 1510–1565), a French sculptor of the mid-sixteenth century with whom Lescot often collaborated.

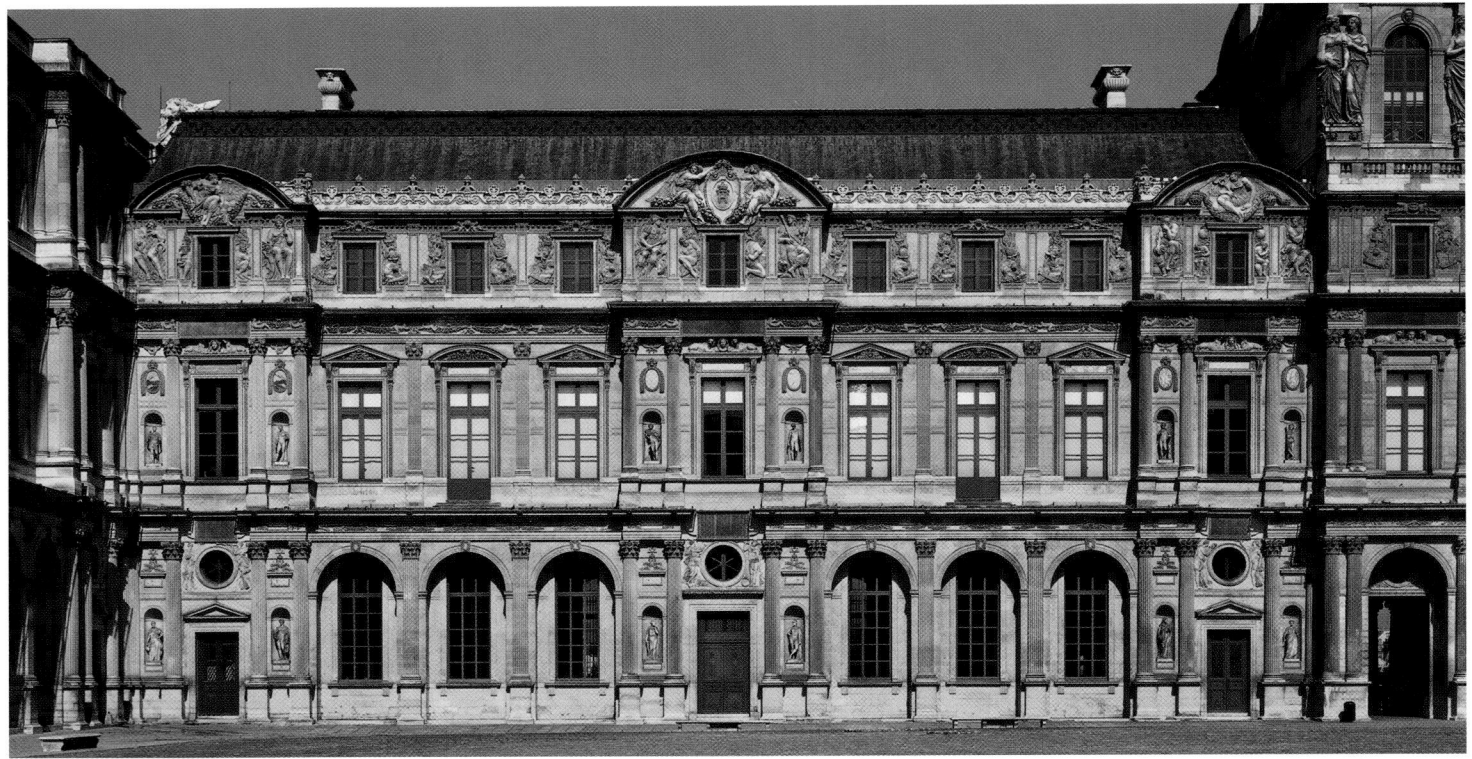

18.2 Pierre Lescot. Square Court, the Louvre, Paris. Begun 1546

Art for Castle Interiors

If the king showed a preference for Italian style, some members of the French court continued to commission works of art following the patterns established during the Middle Ages. Long after the invention of the printing press, French aristocrats continued to commission lavish books of hours and other illuminated books. French church architecture took the possibilities of the Gothic style to new heights (see fig. 12.44). Stained-glass windows remained an important medium for elite patrons, as did tapestry. The walls of their dwellings were lined with sets of these woven hangings, often depicting secular or allegorical themes. Tapestry weaving was an important industry in the Netherlands and in France. (See *Materials and Techniques*, page 629.)

A famous survival of this art form is the set of the *Unicorn Tapestries* that depict the Hunt for the Unicorn, woven around 1500 in the Southern Netherlands or northern France. *The Unicorn in Captivity* (fig. 18.3) is the culmination of a series of images describing the hunt for, death of, and resurrection of the unicorn, the mythical one-horned equine beast who could only be captured by a virgin. The theme depicts the courtly pastime of hunting, but the unicorn itself has been read as symbolizing Christ (details in the imagery suggest this) and as a secular bridegroom. This panel, which is just over 12 by 8 feet, shows the

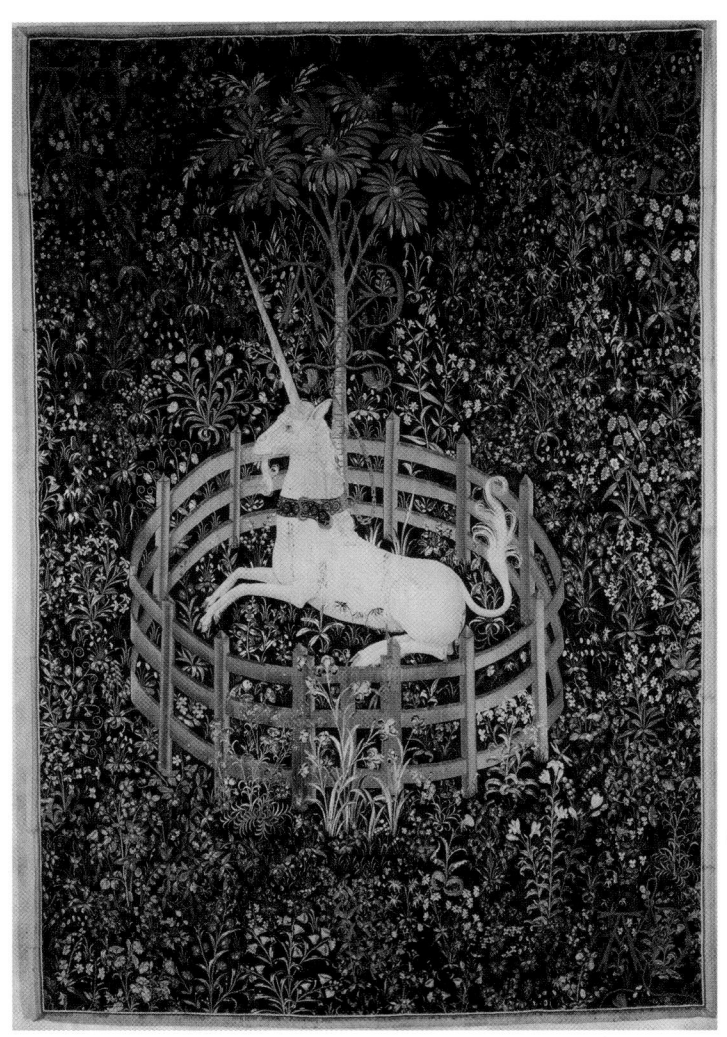

18.3 *The Unicorn in Captivity*, from the *Unicorn Tapestries*. South Netherlandish or French. ca. 1500. Wool warp, wool, silk, silver, and gilt wefts, 12'1" × 8'3" (3.68 × 2.52 m). Metropolitan Museum of Art, New York. Gift of John D. Rockefeller, Jr. 1937. 37.80.6

Making and Conserving Renaissance Tapestries

Tapestries—woven images hung on walls—were a major art form from the Middle Ages through the Baroque period. Elite patrons of Europe commissioned and purchased them to decorate the stone walls of their palaces and chateaux. In Flanders, the principal tapestry-making centers were in Arras, Tournai, and Brussels. In France, Louis XIV cemented the association of royalty with tapestry making by establishing the Royal Workshop of Gobelins in Paris, which dominated French tapestry production until the eighteenth century.

The textiles were woven on looms, such as the one pictured in the Penelope tapestry in figure 14.19. Before the weaving could begin, the patron and the master of the workshop would choose a design, which was worked up into a cartoon, a full-scale drawing for the weaver to follow.

To weave the textile, the weaver stretched supporting threads, called the warp, across the frame of a loom to the size desired. These warp threads are made of strong fibers, usually wool or linen. Colored threads of wool, silk, or spun metals are used to produce the design; these threads, called the weft, are then interwoven with the warp on the loom.

Renaissance tapestries are designated "high warp" and "low warp" according to the arrangement of the loom: The high-warp technique stretches the warp threads vertically on the loom, while the low-warp technique stretches the threads horizontally. The figure of Penelope uses a small low-warp loom, as was common in Flanders.

The weaver intertwines the horizontal threads (weft) with vertical threads (warp)

Once the warp threads are stretched on the loom, the cartoon is placed below the loom. The weaver pushes the weft threads through the warp threads, alternating colors to create the design, and then tamps the weft threads into place to form a tight weave. Because the weaver works on the back side of the tapestry as he follows the cartoon, so that different colors may be joined and threads knotted, the front (or visible side) of the tapestry reproduces the cartoon design in reverse.

Increasingly from the fifteenth century, the designs for tapestries came from painters, and as the pictorial ambitions of the painters grew, so did the techniques of the weavers to match them. The increasing illusionism in the cartoons inspired weavers to work with finer threads to make the tapestries more complex. Woven of wool, silk, and gilt threads, *The Unicorn in Captivity* (see fig. 18.3) displays tremendously detailed images of flowers, foliage, and animals. One scholar estimates that it took one hour per square inch to weave these dense designs; at this rate, a team of weavers would have been able to complete only one tapestry per year.

Conservators worked on the *Unicorn Tapestries* recently, replacing their linen backings. This made it possible to see the back of the tapestry, revealing the incredibly rich colors with which it was woven, but which have faded with the passage of time on the front. The tapestries were then immersed in purified water to be cleaned, before being allowed to dry. A new backing was then sewn into place.

---

unicorn fenced in below a pomegranate tree against a verdant background enlivened by numerous flowering plants. Specific elements such as the plants and flowers are wonderfully detailed and naturalistic, with the tapestry as a whole creating a sumptuous two-dimensional effect. The brilliant white body of the unicorn itself is the focal point at the center of the field of flowers. Details like the pomegranates—a symbol of fertility and of eternity—combine with the numerous plants and animals to suggest the theme of Christian salvation, but may also refer to marriage and procreation. Some scholars have suggested that these tapestries were created to celebrate a marriage, perhaps of the individuals whose initials (A and a backward E) intertwine in the tree branches. Despite exhaustive research, their identification remains uncertain. Tapestries continued to be an important art form in France, given an important boost by the establishment of the royal factory of Gobelins in the seventeenth century.

THE SCHOOL OF FONTAINEBLEAU Francis I's preference for Italian art is apparent throughout the chateau at Fontainebleau. The king called upon Italian artists, most of them

working in a Mannerist style, to work there, and these artists initiated the so-called School of Fontainebleau. To decorate the Gallery of Francis I, the king summoned Rosso Fiorentino from Italy (see page 593). Between 1531 and 1540, Rosso executed frescoes framed by stucco *putti*. The combination of painting and sculpted imagery inspired another Italian émigré, Francesco Primaticcio (1504–1570), who replaced Rosso as the chief designer at the royal chateau. The influence of Parmigianino is clear in Primaticcio's most important surviving work, the decorations for the room of the king's mistress, the Duchesse d'Étampes (fig. **18.4**). Primaticcio follows Rosso's general scheme of embedding paintings in a luxuriously sculptured stucco framework, which nearly swallows them. However, the figures are subtly elongated in the style of Parmigianino (see fig. 17.29). The four females in this detail have no specific allegorical significance, although their role recalls the nudes of the Sistine Chapel ceiling. These willowy figures (reminiscent of the caryatids in ancient Greek architecture) enframe paintings devoted to Alexander the Great that were executed by assistants from Primaticcio's designs.

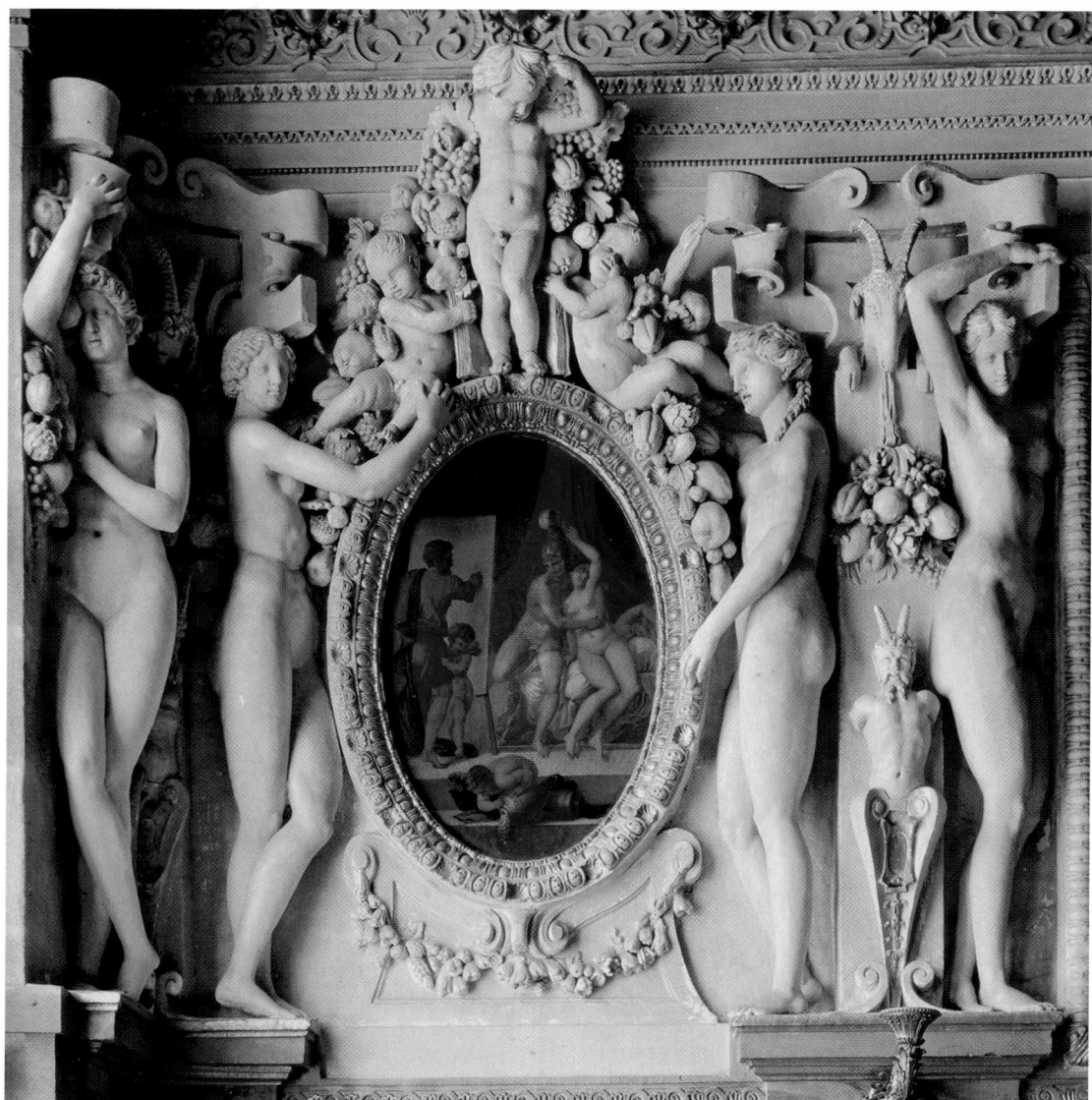

18.4 Francesco Primaticcio. Stucco figures. ca. 1541–45. Gallery of Francis I, designed for the Room of the Duchesse d'Étampes, Chateau of Fontainebleau

The scene in figure 18.4 shows Apelles painting the abduction of Campaspe by Alexander the Great. According to the story, Alexander gave his favorite concubine to the artist when he fell in love with her. Roman texts of this subject characterized this gift as a mark of Alexander's great respect for his court artist. Such mixtures of violence and eroticism appealed greatly to the courtly audience for which Primaticcio worked. The picture draws a parallel between Alexander and Francis I, and between Campaspe and the duchess, the king's mistress, who had taken Primaticcio under her protection. The artist may have seen himself in the role of Apelles.

ROYAL TOMBS AT SAINT-DENIS The presence of so many Italian artists at Fontainebleau made the chateau a laboratory of Italian style, which many French artists absorbed. For example, Germain Pilon (ca. 1535–1590) created monumental sculpture that is informed not only by the elegance of the School of Fontainebleau, but also by elements taken from ancient sculpture, the Gothic tradition, and Michelangelo. His main works are tombs,

such as the *Tomb of Henry II and Catherine de' Medici* (fig. **18.5**) commissioned by Catherine de' Medici and executed for the French royal pantheon at Saint-Denis. Primaticcio designed the architectural framework, a free-standing chapel on a platform decorated with bronze and marble reliefs. He also designed the corner figures of virtues as elegant young women. Pilon executed the sculpture. On the top of the tomb are the bronze figures of the king and queen kneeling in prayer, while inside the chapel the couple reappear as marble **gisants**, or recumbent effigies of the deceased. Gisants expressed the transient nature of the flesh, usually by showing the body in an advanced stage of decay, sometimes with vermin crawling through their open cavities. Pilon inverts this concept: Instead of portraying decaying flesh, his gisants are idealized nudes. While the likenesses of the royal couple kneeling atop the structure record their features in life, the gisants represent them as beautiful beings in death: The queen is in the pose of a classical Venus and the king is represented similarly to the dead Christ. They evoke neither horror nor pity. Instead, they have the pathos of a beauty that continues even in death.

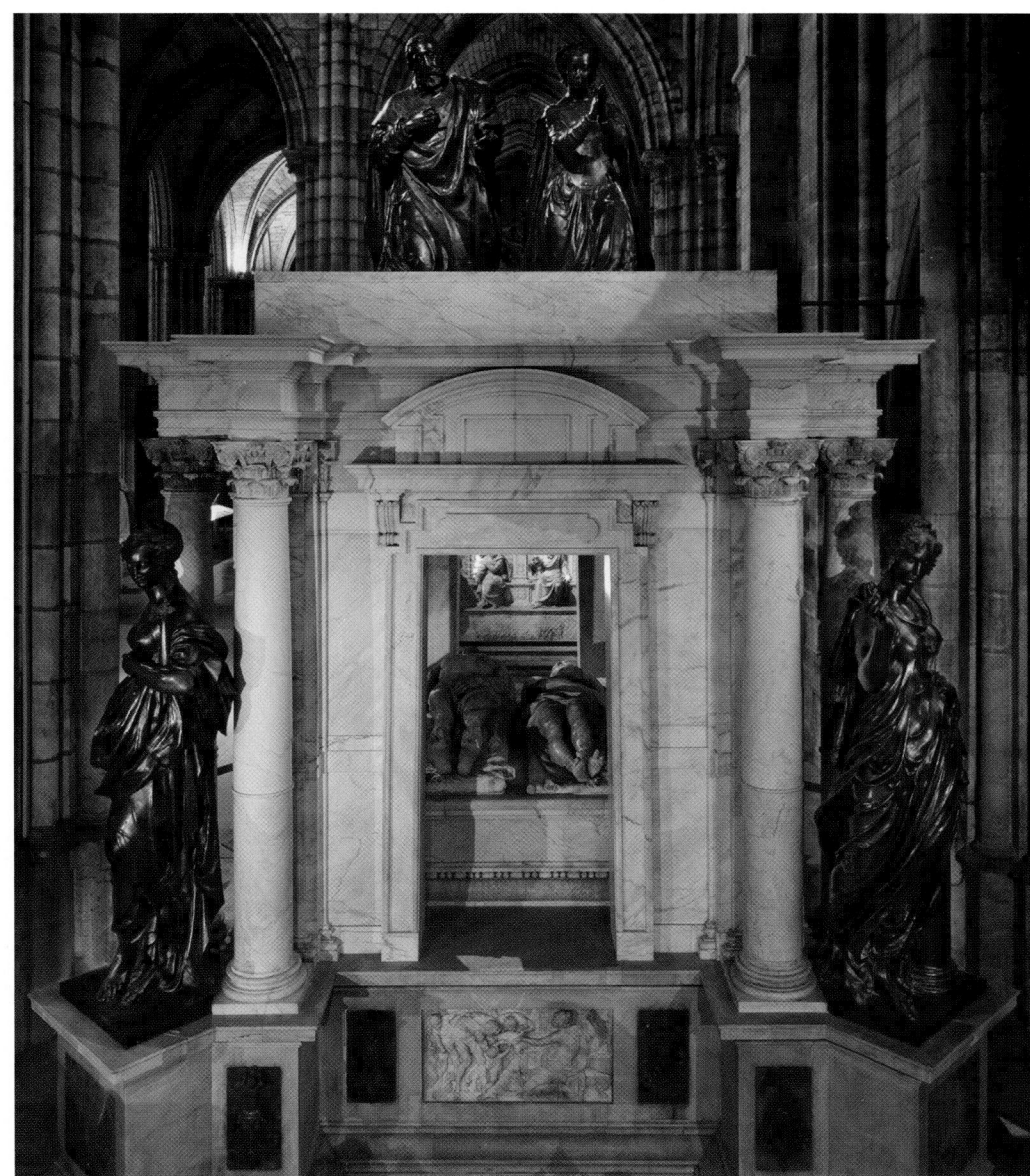

Henry II's death in 1559 left his young son—still a minor—to inherit the throne, so his widow, Catherine de' Medici, acted as regent during a troubled period. Increasing conflicts between Catholic and Protestant groups, called Huguenots, erupted into massacres and warfare between 1562 and 1598, when a policy of official toleration was announced by Henry IV.

SPAIN: GLOBAL POWER AND RELIGIOUS ORTHODOXY

Several events came together in the early sixteenth century to increase the status and influence of Spain in Europe. In 1500, Charles V was born to the son of Maximilian of Habsburg and the daughter of Ferdinand and Isabella. With this parentage, he became heir to the thrones of Spain, Aragon, and the Burgundian territories, as well as the title of Holy Roman emperor. Charles also asserted a Spanish claim to rule the Kingdom of Naples in

southern Italy. Spain was thus integrated more fully into European power struggles than it had been in previous centuries. At the same time, the colonization of the lands Columbus had claimed in the Americas brought massive wealth into Spanish hands. Charles V's efforts to promote and rule his vast holdings so exhausted him that in 1556 he divided his territory in half and abdicated in favor of his son Philip and his brother Ferdinand. Ferdinand took control of the traditional Habsburg territories in Central Europe. Reigning as king of Spain, the Netherlands, and New Spain in the Americas from 1556 to 1598, Philip inherited the problems that had bedeviled his father. Having succeeded in preventing the Turkish advance into Europe in 1571, he turned his attention to the religious upheavals that the Reformation had brought to Christian Europe. Pious and ardent in his orthodoxy, he tried to quash the rebellion of the Calvinist Northern Netherlands, and unsuccessfully attempted to invade England in 1588, when the Spanish Armada suffered a disastrous defeat in the English Channel.

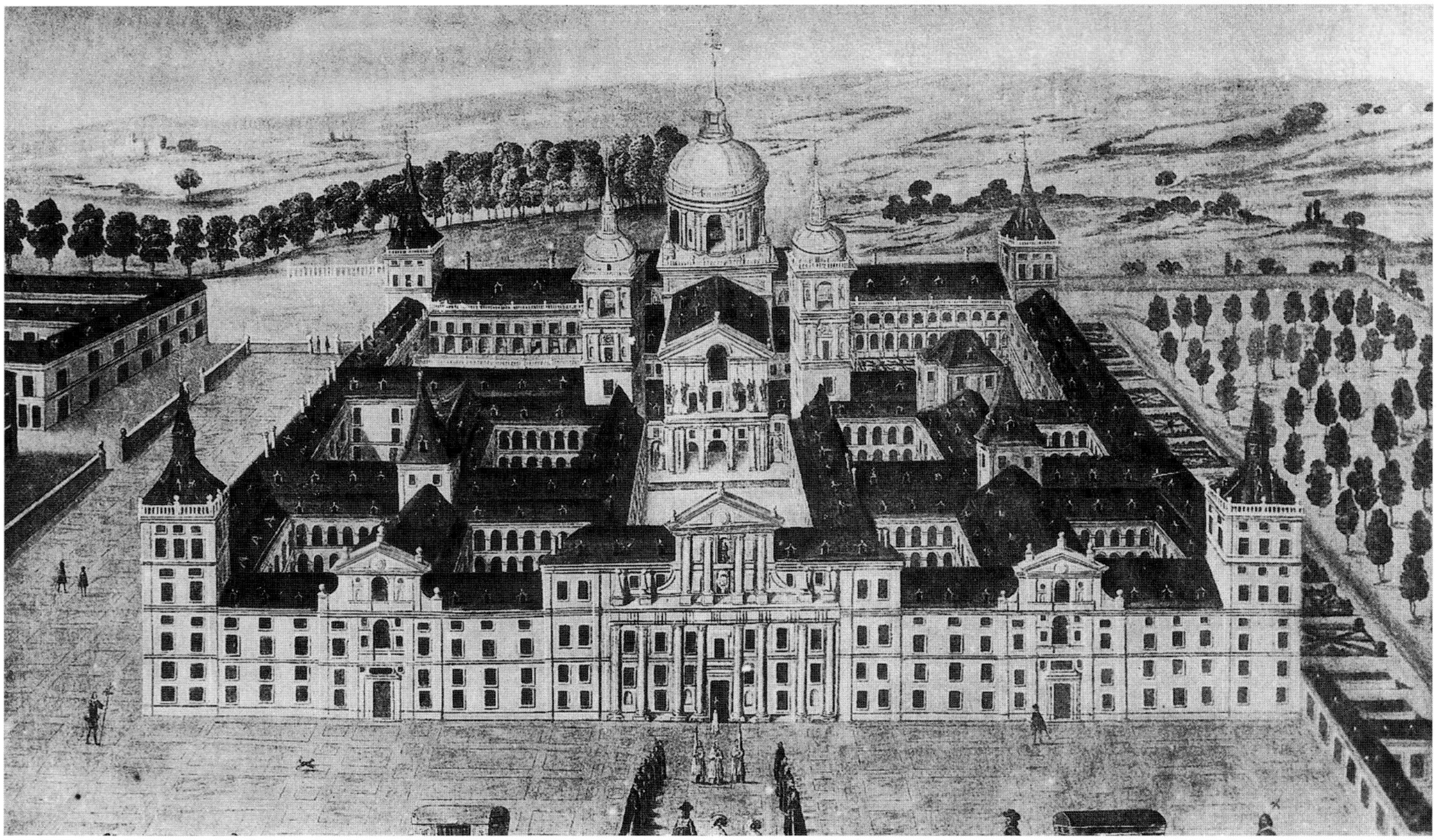

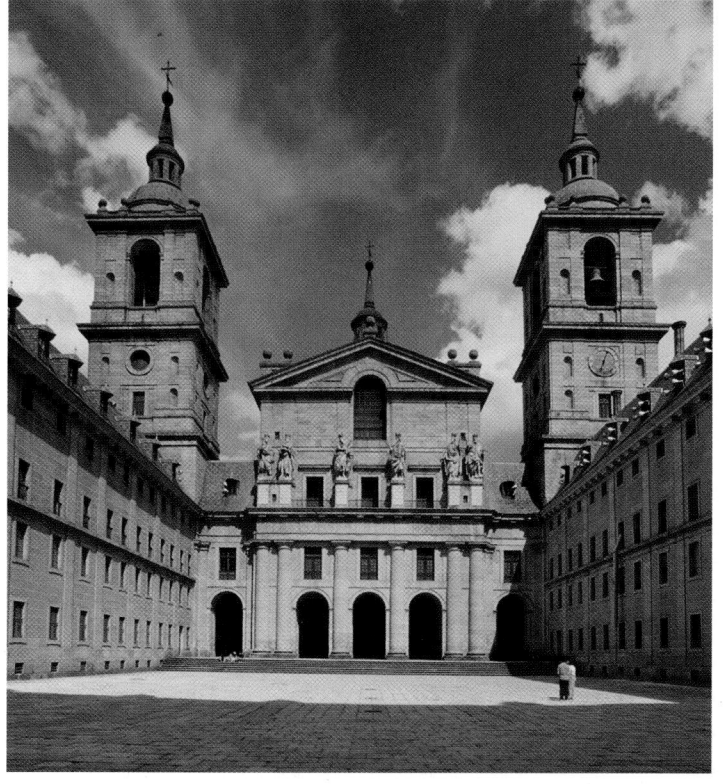

18.6   Juan Bautista de Toledo and Juan de Herrera. Escorial. Begun 1563. Near Madrid

The Escorial

Philip also inherited a taste for collecting works of art from his forebears. He invited Sophonisba Anguissola to become one of his court artists; he commissioned works from Titian and other Italian artists; he not only hired Netherlandish artists to work for him, he sought out fifteenth-century Flemish works, especially paintings by Bosch. In this effort, he acquired *The Garden of Earthly Delights* (see fig. 14.22) and many other objects, which were brought to his new palace and monastery complex outside Madrid, called the Escorial. Built to commemorate Philip's victory over the French in 1557, this massive complex (fig. **18.6**) was begun in 1563 by Juan Bautista de Toledo (d. 1567), who had worked with Michelangelo in Rome. The symmetrical massing of the buildings and the focus on the church of San Lorenzo at the center reflect Italian Renaissance models, but the scale and the simplicity of the façades were dictated by King Philip. In consultation with leading Italian architects, including Palladio and Vignola, Juan Bautista de Toledo's successor at the Escorial, Juan de Herrera, expanded the design and introduced classicizing details such as the temple fronts on the façades of the main portal and the Church of San Lorenzo (fig. **18.7**). These, however, use a very plain Doric order and the whole façade exhibits a severity and seriousness that may express Philip's commitment to the ideals of the Catholic Reformation. The complex includes a monastery and church, a palace, a seminary, a library, and a

18.7   Juan Bautista de Toledo and Juan de Herrera. Escorial, façade of main church

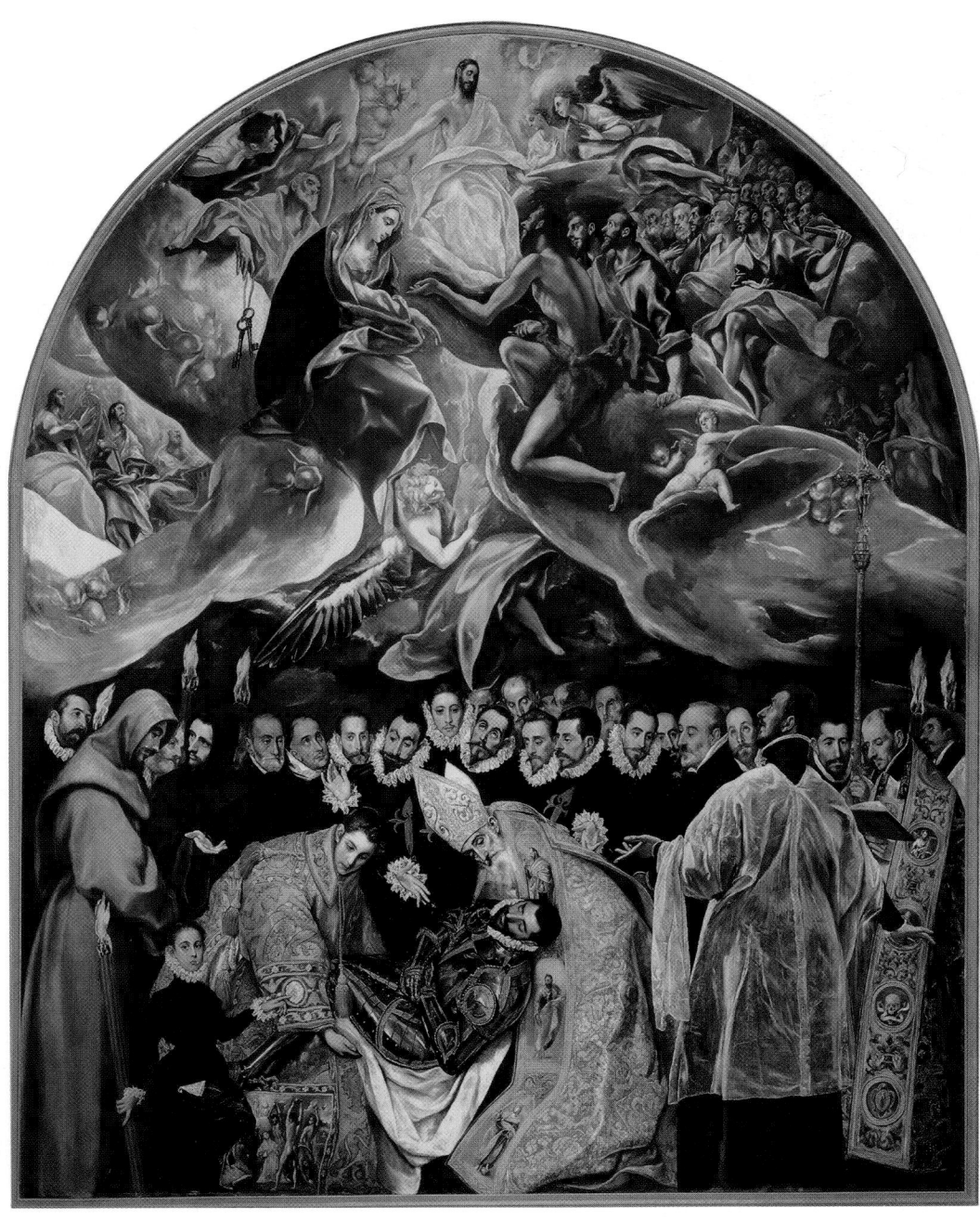

18.8 El Greco, *The Burial of Count Orgaz*. 1586. Oil on canvas, 16' × 11'10" (4.9 × 3.6 m). Santo Tomé, Toledo, Spain

burial chapel for the Spanish kings. Philip himself spent his last years here.

El Greco and Religious Painting in Spain

Philip's strong commitment to Catholic orthodoxy led him to support the work of many new orders and institutions that arose during the Catholic Reformation. The Spanish Inquisition, for example, fervently pursued the work of rooting out heresy. The Spanish-born Ignatius of Loyola's followers, the Jesuits, had a strong presence in Spain, as did the Carmelite order, whose most famous member was the nun and reformer Teresa of Ávila. Both the Jesuits and the Carmelites encouraged meditation among the faithful. Loyola wrote a treatise, *The Spiritual Exercises*, to teach believers to meditate in steps so that they might achieve visions so real that they would seem to appear before their very eyes. The

spiritual writings of Teresa of Ávila, informed by her visions, urge prayer to achieve closer union with God (see fig. 19.31).

In this atmosphere, the best-known painter of sixteenth-century Spain, Domenikos Theotokopoulos (1541–1614), called El Greco, found a home. Born on Crete, which was then under Venetian rule, he probably trained there to become an icon painter. At some point before 1568, he arrived in Venice and quickly absorbed the lessons of Titian and Tintoretto, but he also knew the art of Raphael, Michelangelo, and the Italian Mannerists. He went to Spain in 1576–77 and settled in Toledo for the rest of his life. El Greco joined the leading intellectual circles of the city, then a major center of learning, as well as the seat of Catholic reform in Spain. El Greco's painting exhibits an exalted emotionalism informed by his varied artistic sources.

Among the most impressive of El Greco's commissions is *The Burial of Count Orgaz* (fig. 18.8), executed in 1586 in the church

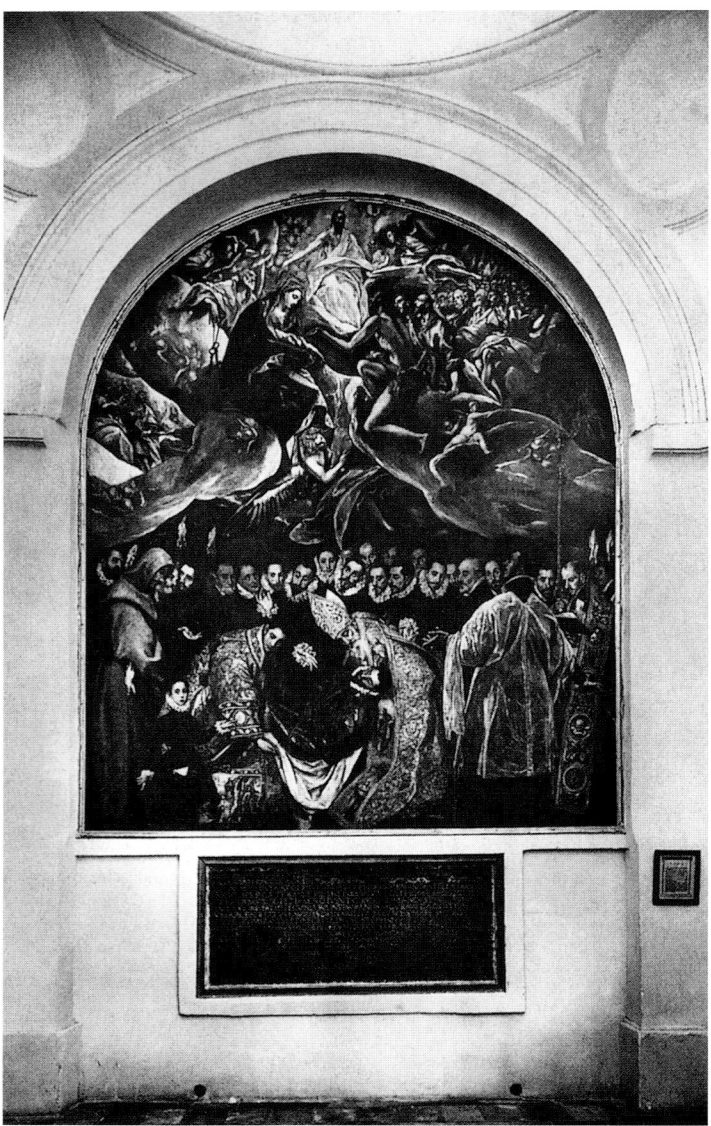

18.9 Chapel with *The Burial of Count Orgaz*. 1586. Santo Tomé, Toledo, Spain

of Santo Tomé in Toledo. The program, which was dictated in the commission, emphasizes the Roman Catholic position that good works are required to achieve salvation and that saints serve as intercessors with Heaven. This huge canvas honors a medieval benefactor so pious that St. Stephen and St. Augustine miraculously appeared at his funeral and lowered his body into its grave. Although the burial took place in 1323, El Greco presents it as a contemporary event; he even portrays many of the local nobility and clergy of his time among the attendants. The display of color and texture in the armor and vestments reflects El Greco's Venetian training. Above, the count's soul (a small, cloudlike figure like the angels in Tintoretto's *Last Supper*, see fig. 17.39) is carried to Heaven by an angel. The celestial assembly in the upper half of the picture is painted very differently from the group in the lower half: Every form—clouds, limbs, draperies—takes part in the sweeping, flamelike movement toward the figure of Christ. El Greco's compressed space, unearthly light, and weightless bodies

share stylistic features with Italian Mannerist works such as Rosso's *The Descent from the Cross* (see fig. 17.1).

Only when the work is seen in its original setting (fig. **18.9**) does its full meaning become clear. The painting fills one entire wall of its chapel, like a huge window. In the shallow space of the chapel a viewer must stand close and look sharply upward to see the upper half of the picture. The violent foreshortening is calculated to achieve an illusion of boundless space in the upper portion of the painting, while the figures in the lower foreground appear as if on a stage. The large stone plaque set into the wall also belongs to the ensemble. It represents the front of the sarcophagus into which the two saints lower the body of the count, which explains the action in the picture. A viewer, then, perceives three levels of reality. The first is the grave itself, supposedly set into the wall at eye level and closed by an actual stone slab; the second is the reenactment of the miraculous burial; and the third is the vision of celestial glory witnessed by some of the participants. This step-by-step movement into the world of the picture may be linked to meditative practices of the era. Working in steps to achieve such a vision could only be achieved through the kind of strenuous devotion and commitment to mysticism encouraged by Loyola and Teresa of Ávila. El Greco's work mirrors the intensity of such deep spiritual struggle.

CENTRAL EUROPE: THE REFORMATION AND ART

While Italy, France, and Spain adhered to the Catholic faith, elsewhere in Europe the religious and artistic situation became more volatile. In addition to Spain, Charles V had inherited the many different political units that comprised what is now Germany, Austria, Hungary, and the Czech Republic. Governing such disparate regions posed many challenges, which were passed along to Charles's brother Ferdinand when Charles stepped down as ruler in 1556. Though linked in many cases by language and cultural ties, as well as by trade, these were independent regions only nominally under control of the Holy Roman emperor. What unity they may have had suffered another blow after 1517, when religious unity was fractured by the Protestant Reformation.

In October 1517, Martin Luther, a former Augustinian friar who had become professor of theology at the University of Wittenberg, issued a public challenge to both the theology and the institutional practices of the Catholic Church. In his famous *Ninety-five Theses*, which he posted on the church door at Wittenberg Castle, Luther complained about the Catholic practice of selling indulgences—promises of redemption of sins; he argued, too, against the veneration of Mary and the saints. Most fundamental to his critique of Catholicism, Luther claimed that the Bible and natural reason were the sole bases of religious authority, and that the intervention of clerics and saints was unnecessary for salvation, which was freely given by God. It followed from this that religious authority was transferred from the pope to the individual conscience of each believer. The Catholic

Church responded by condemning Luther in 1521. But many Christians in Europe accepted his critique, which eventually fueled political instability, rebellions, and wars. Many areas of northern Germany converted to the reformed faith, while southern regions, such as Bavaria, remained Catholic. In rethinking these basic issues of faith, Luther was joined by other religious reformers (see map 18.1).

Protestant thinkers following Luther aimed to eliminate the abuses they perceived in the Catholic Church. The Swiss pastor Ulrich Zwingli wanted to reduce religion to its essentials by stressing individual access to Scripture. As a result of his literal reading of the Bible, he denounced not only the sale of indulgences, but the visual arts as well. Zwingli interpreted the Eucharist as a symbolic, rather than actual, communion of bread and wine; his theology led to a split with Luther that was never healed. What concerned the reformers above all were the twin issues of grace and free will in attaining faith and salvation. By the time of Zwingli's death at the hands of the Catholic forces in 1531, the main elements of Protestant theology had been defined. John Calvin of Geneva codified these tenets around midcentury; Calvin's vision of a moral life based on a literal reading of Scripture was to prove very influential. The spread of the reformed faiths led to decades of violence, including a Peasants' Revolt in 1525 and wars in regions that were converting to Protestantism. From 1546, German principalities fought with the emperor Charles V, until the Peace of Augsburg in 1555. By this compromise, the rulers of individual regions of Germany chose the faith for their own inhabitants. This furthered the spread of the reformed faiths, but also fostered the political divisions of the area.

The repercussions for art were equally dramatic. Luther's own attitudes toward the visual arts, expressed in his writings, veered between warning of the danger of idolatry and seeing the value of art as a tool for teaching. (See www.myartslab.com.) Some of the more radical reformers saw the many forms of medieval and Renaissance religious art as nothing short of idolatry that needed to be cleansed. Inspired by reformers' zeal, civic leaders, artisans, and workers attacked religious images in the cities. Several waves of image destruction, called **iconoclasm**, resulted in great losses of works of art from earlier periods. And as large areas of Central Europe converted to the new faiths, art forms that had been the bread and butter for artists disappeared, as churches were whitewashed and religious commissions dried up. Artists in many mediums had to find new styles, new subjects, and new markets for their work.

Humanism and the new technology of printing played a vital role in the Reformation. The humanist spirit of inquiry and respect for original texts inspired the writings of famous intellectuals and teachers, such as Desiderius Erasmus in Rotterdam, Philip Melancthon in Germany, and Thomas More in England. Published Latin texts spread new ideas all over Europe. As a result, the printing press became an important factor in both the development and the dispersion of Reformation thought. Individual access to Scripture was a fundamental tenet of the reformers, so they wanted to make available good texts of the Bible as well as translations of it into vernacular languages. Luther himself translated the Bible into German. Printed images contributed to the spread of Reformation ideas; inexpensive woodcuts satirized the Catholic hierarchy while making heroes of the reformers. Prints also illustrated the tenets of the new faiths.

Catholic Contexts: The Isenheim Altarpiece

Yet not all regions of German-speaking Europe converted to the reformed faiths, and it was not until the 1520s that the Reformation took wide hold. As such, some traditional objects were created in the sixteenth century to serve Catholic patrons. One such object is an altarpiece executed by the painter Matthias Gothart Nithart, who was known for centuries only as Grünewald (ca. 1475–1528). This nickname was given to him by a seventeenth-century author; when German artists in the modern period began searching for roots, they discovered the artist through his nickname and it has stuck. Grünewald was born in Würzburg in central Germany and worked for the archbishop of nearby Mainz. His most famous work is a transforming triptych called the *Isenheim Altarpiece*, similar in structure to the *St. Wolfgang Altarpiece* by Pacher (see fig. 14.28). It was painted between 1509–10 and 1515 for the monastery church of the Order of St. Anthony at Isenheim, in Alsace, not far from the former abbey that now houses it in the city of Colmar.

This church served the monks and the patients of the hospital attached to their monastery. The monks specialized in tending people who suffered from a disease called St. Anthony's Fire, which was a disorder caused by eating spoiled rye. This disease produced painful symptoms, including intestinal disorders, gangrenous limbs, and hallucinations. Treatment consisted mostly of soothing baths and in some cases the amputation of limbs. Grünewald's altarpiece stood on the high altar of the monastery church, where both the sick in the hospital and the monks who served them could see it. This extraordinary altarpiece encases a huge shrine carved in wood by Nicolas Hagenau around 1505. Enclosing the carved central section are nine panels organized in two sets of movable wings. These open in three stages or "views." The first of these views, when all the wings are closed, shows the Crucifixion in the center panel (fig. **18.10**). This is the view that was visible during the week. The wings depict St. Sebastian (left), who was invoked against the plague (see fig. 15.48) and St. Anthony Abbot (right), who was revered as a healer. The central image of the Crucifixion draws on the late medieval tradition of the Andachtsbild (see fig. 12.60) to emphasize the suffering of Christ and the grief of his mother. The figure of Christ, with its twisted limbs, its many wounds, its streams of blood, matches the vision of the fourteenth-century mystic St. Bridget as described in her book of *Revelations*, which had been published in a German edition in 1501–02.

Grünewald renders the body on the Cross on a heroic scale, so that it dominates the other figures and the landscape. The

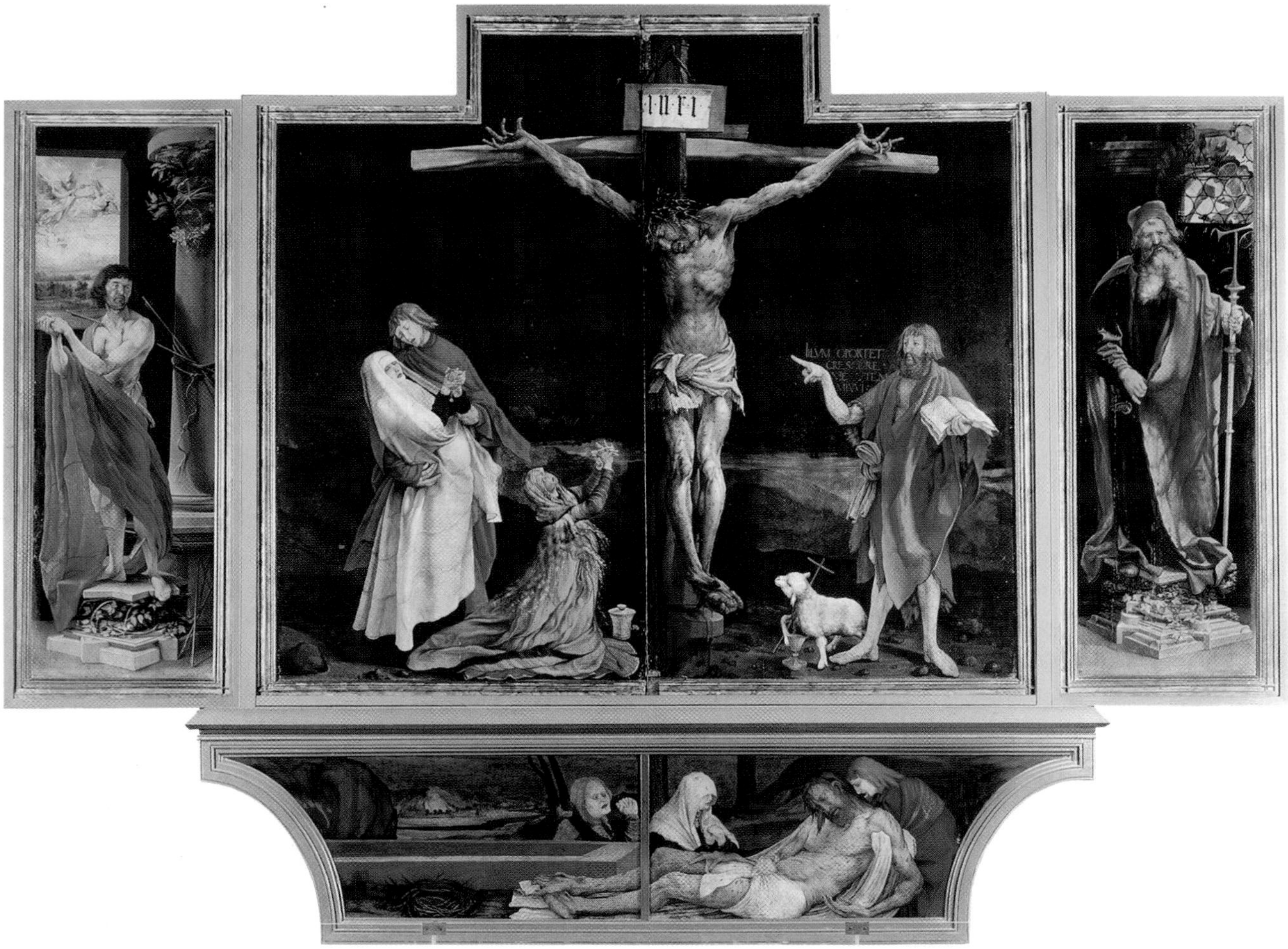

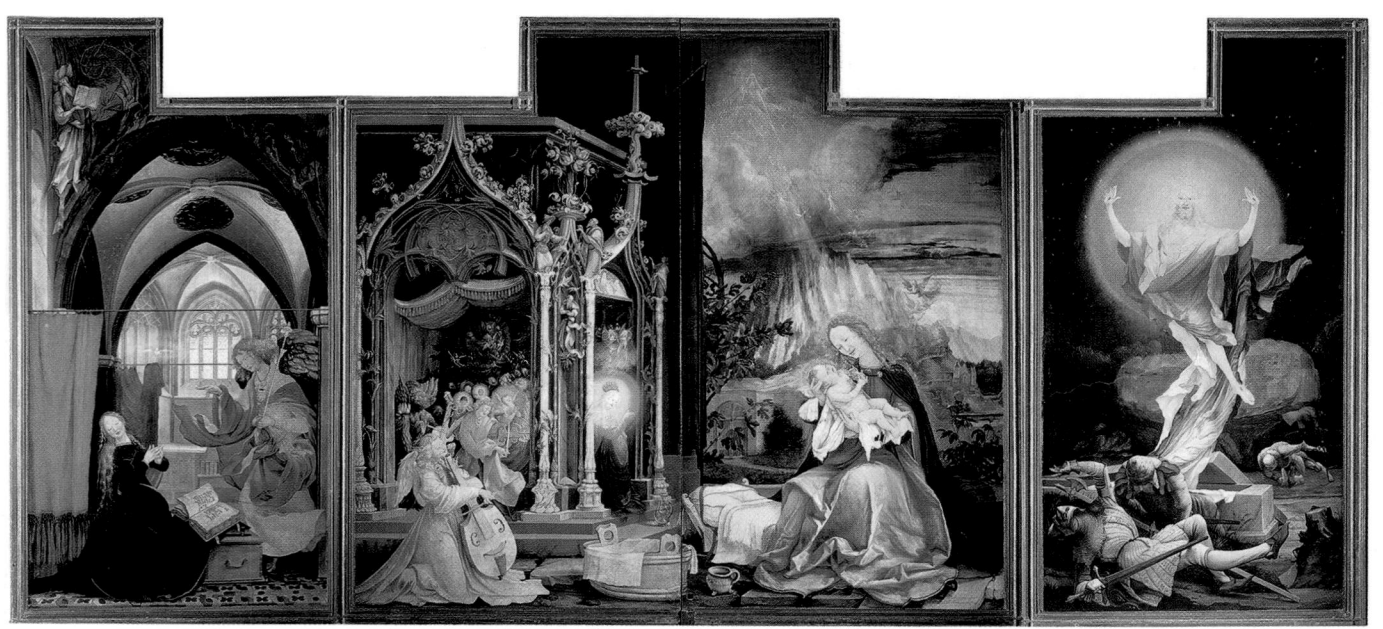

18.10 Matthias Grünewald, *St. Sebastian*; *The Crucifixion*; *St. Anthony Abbot*; predella: *Lamentation.*
Isenheim Altarpiece (closed). ca. 1509/10–15. Oil on panel, main body 9'9½" × 10'9" (2.97 × 3.28 m),
predella 2'5½" × 11'2" (0.75 × 3.4 m). Musée d'Unterlinden, Colmar, France

18.11 Matthias Grünewald, *The Annunciation*; *Madonna and Child with Angels*; *The Resurrection.*
Second view of the *Isenheim Altarpiece.* ca. 1509/10–15. Oil on panel, each wing 8'10" × 4'8"
(2.69 × 1.42 m), center panel 8'10" × 11'2½" (2.69 × 3.41 m). Musée d'Unterlinden, Colmar, France

Crucifixion, lifted from its familiar setting, becomes a lonely event silhouetted against a ghostly landscape and a blue-black sky. Despite the darkness of the landscape, an eerie light bathes the foreground figures to heighten awareness of them. On the left, Mary's white garment enfolds her as she swoons at the sight of her tortured son; the red of St. John's robe accents her paleness. Below the Cross, Mary Magdalen, identified by her ointment jar, kneels in grief to lament. On the right, John the Baptist points to the Crucified Christ with the words, "He must increase, and I must decrease," indicating the significance of Christ's sacrifice. Behind him a body of water recalls the healing power of baptism. The lamb at John's feet bleeds into a chalice, as does the lamb in the central panel of the *Ghent Altarpiece* (see fig. 14.10). The bleeding lamb is a reminder of the sacrament of the Eucharist, celebrated before the altarpiece. In the predella below, a tomb awaits the tormented body while his mother and friends bid him farewell. The predella slides apart at Christ's knees: Victims of amputation may have seen their own suffering reflected in this image.

On Sundays and feast days the outer wings were opened and the mood of the *Isenheim Altarpiece* changed dramatically (fig. 18.11). All three scenes in this second view—*The Annunciation*, the *Madonna and Child with Angels*, and *The Resurrection* (fig. 18.12)—celebrate events that are as jubilant as the Crucifixion is somber. Depicting the cycle of salvation, from the Incarnation to the Resurrection, this view of the altarpiece offered the afflicted a form of spiritual medicine while reminding them of the promise of Heaven. Throughout these panels, Grünewald depicts forms of therapy recommended for sufferers at the hospital: music, herbs, baths, and light. The contrast of the body of the dead Jesus in the predella with the Resurrected Christ in the right panel offers consolation to the dying.

Grünewald links the panels through color and composition. Reds and pinks in The Annunciation panel on the left are carried through the central panels to reach a climax with the brilliant colors surrounding the risen figure of Christ on the right. The figure of the dead Jesus held by his mother and friends in the predella adds poignancy to the figure of the child Jesus in his mother's arms in the central panel. The simple Gothic chapel in which the Annunciation takes place gives way in the next panel to a fanciful tabernacle housing choirs of angels who play stringed instruments and sing. Beneath that tabernacle appears a figure of the Virgin, crowned and glowing like a lit candle. The aureole surrounding this figure anticipates the brilliant figure of the Resurrected Christ in the right-hand panel, whose body seems to dissolve into light. The central image of the Madonna holding her child in a tender embrace gives way to a vision of Heaven, also made of pure light.

These elements lead the eye to the right panel, where the body of Christ appears to float above his stone sarcophagus. The guards set to watch the tomb are knocked senseless by the miracle. Their figures, carefully arranged in a perspectival display, contrast to the weightless and transfigured body of Christ. As he holds his hands up, the shroud falls to reveal the wounds he suffered in death,

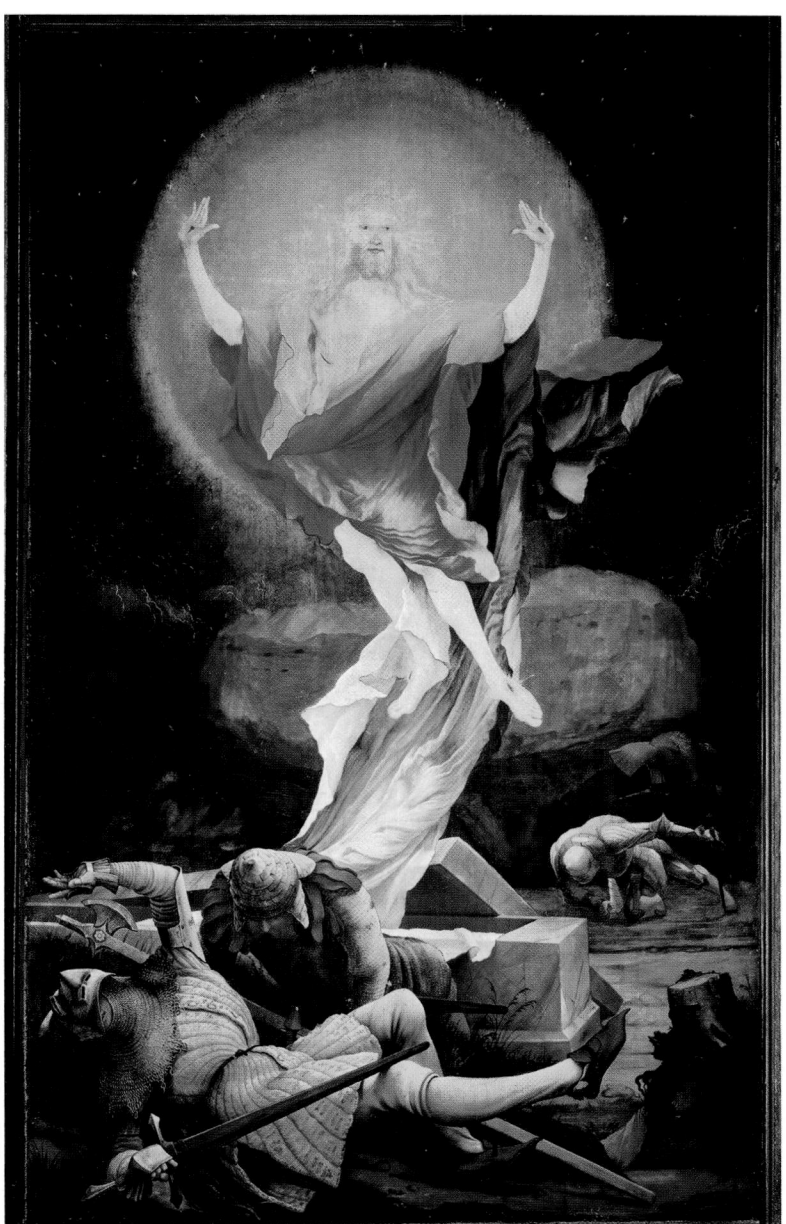

18.12 Matthias Grünewald, *The Resurrection*, from second view of the *Isenheim Altarpiece*. Musée d'Unterlinden, Colmar, France

now as brilliant as the halo that engulfs his body. This figure differs dramatically from the figure on the Cross; his body bears no scars and the proportions are closer to the Italian ideal seen in Piero della Francesca's *Resurrection* (see fig. 15.43).

Grünewald's strikingly individual approach to form is based on the traditions of the northern European Renaissance established in the fifteenth century. His oil technique, his brilliant use of color, and the detailed rendering of objects draw from that tradition, but he must have learned from the Italian Renaissance too. The low horizon lines suggest a deep space for his figures and the rendering of the tomb from which Christ rises is a study in perspective. Yet Grünewald does not try to convince the viewer of the weight and substance of his figures; his aim is to create an emotional response with the impact of a vision.

Albrecht Dürer and the Northern Renaissance

The crucial figure for the Renaissance in Germany is Grünewald's contemporary Albrecht Dürer (1471–1528). Dürer's style was formed in the tradition of northern European naturalism (which we explored in Chapter 14), but he delved deeply into the innovations and possibilities of Italian art. After training as a painter and printmaker in his native Nuremberg, Dürer traveled in northern Europe and Venice in 1494–95 before returning home to start his career. His travels not only expanded his visual repertoire, but changed his view of the world and the artist's place in it. (He returned to Italy in 1505.) Dürer adopted the ideal of the artist as a gentleman and humanistic scholar, and took the Italian view that the fine arts belonged among the liberal arts, as artists like Mantegna and Alberti had argued (see Chapter 15). By cultivating his artistic and intellectual interests, Dürer incorporated into his work an unprecedented variety of subjects and techniques. His painting technique owes much to the Flemish masters, but making copies of Italian works taught him many of the lessons of the Italian Renaissance. He was able to synthesize these traditions in his paintings and prints. As the greatest printmaker of the time, he had a wide influence on sixteenth-century art through his woodcuts and engravings, which circulated all over Europe. His prints made him famous and wealthy—so much so that he complained about the relatively poor reward he earned for his paintings.

Dürer's debt to the legacy of Jan van Eyck and Rogier van der Weyden is clear in the many drawings and watercolors he made in

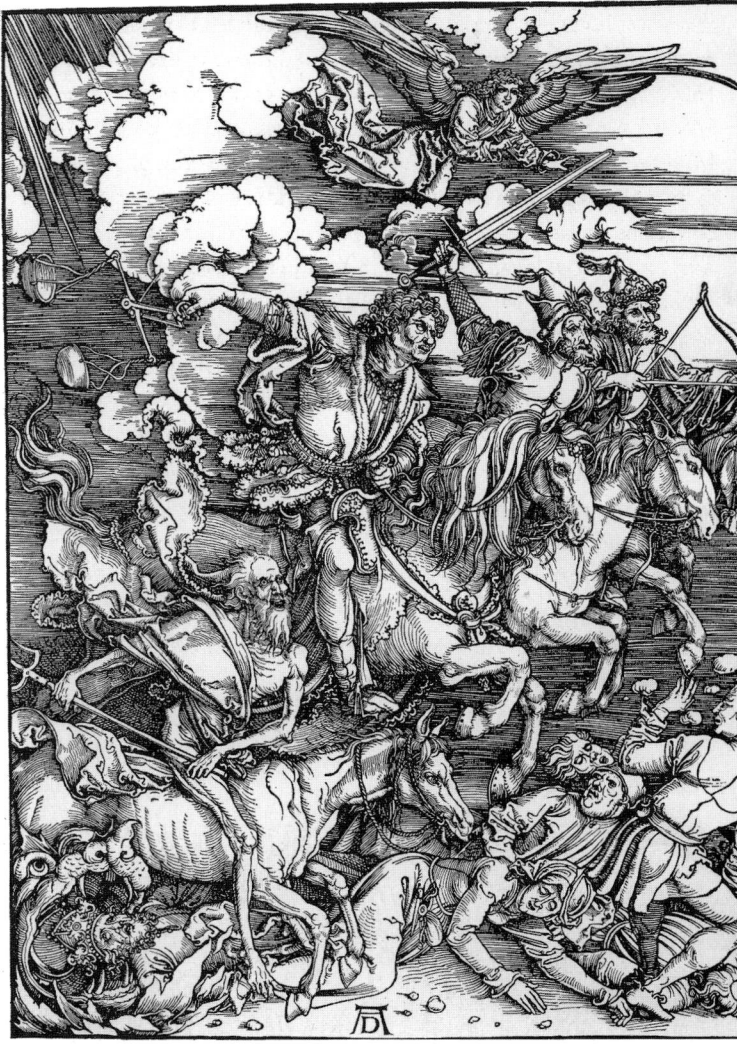

18.14 Albrecht Dürer, *The Four Horsemen of the Apocalypse*. 1498. Woodcut, 15½ × 11⅛" (39.3 × 28.3 cm). Metropolitan Museum of Art, New York. Gift of Junius S. Morgan, 1919. 19.73.209

preparation for his works. The watercolor of a hare he made in 1502 (fig. **18.13**) demonstrates the clarity of his vision and the sureness of his rendering. Dürer treated this small representative of the natural world with the dignity due to nature herself, much as Van Eyck had painted the small dog in the foreground of *The "Arnolfini Portrait"* (see fig. 14.14). Dürer uses the watercolor technique to render each hair of the fur, the curve of the ears, the sheen on the eyes. His monogram at the base of the page identifies Dürer as the creator of this image; this monogram was the signature he used on his mature prints.

Dürer's ability as a draftsman also informed his work as a printmaker. Having been trained in both woodcut and engraving, he pushed the limits of both mediums. As a mass medium, prints were not commissioned by individual patrons, but were made for the open market, so Dürer had to invest his own materials and unpaid time in these projects. This entrepreneurial spirit served him well, as his prints sold widely and quickly, in part because of

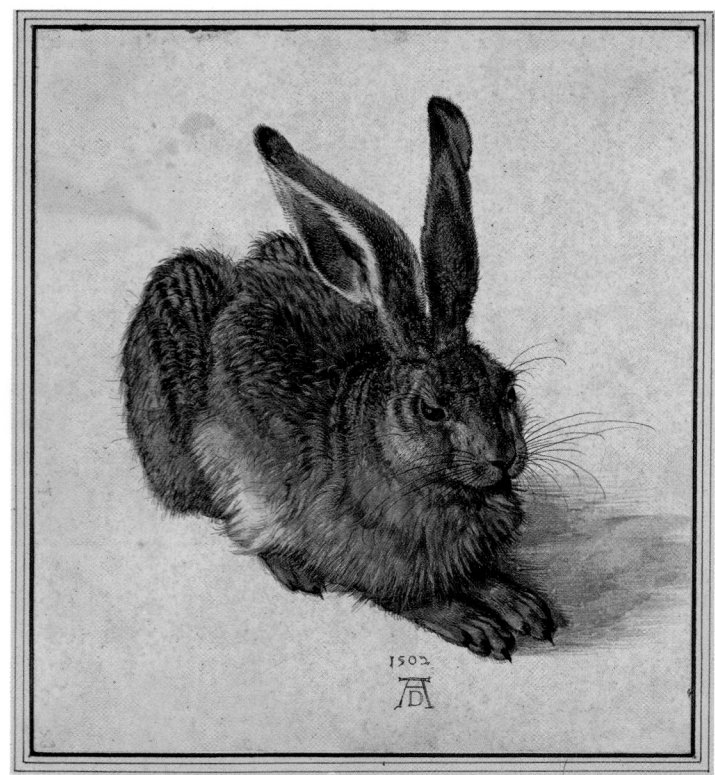

18.13 Albrecht Dürer, *Hare*. 1502. Watercolor, 9⅞ × 8⅞" (25.1 × 22.5 cm). Albertina, Vienna

his astute choice of subject matter. Signs and portents, such as the threat of invasion by the Turks and the birth of malformed animals, worried Europeans as they awaited the approach of the year 1500. As this year drew near, many people believed that the Second Coming of Christ was imminent, and prepared for the Millennium. Thus, with an eye to the market for things pertaining to popular fears about the end of time, Dürer produced a woodcut series illustrating the Apocalypse in 1498. This series was his most ambitious graphic work in the years following his return from Italy. *The Four Horsemen of the Apocalypse* (fig. **18.14**) offers the viewer a frightening visualization of the text of the book of Revelation. The image depicts War, Conquest, Famine, and Death overrunning the earth. During his trip to Italy in 1494, Dürer had encountered prints by Mantegna, which he carefully copied. He especially admired the sculptural quality Mantegna achieved in paintings such as the St. Sebastian (see fig. 15.48). The physical energy and full-bodied volume of the figures in the Apocalypse series is partly owed to Dürer's experience of Italian art, although he eliminates logical space in favor of an otherworldly flatness. Dürer has redefined his medium—the woodcut—by enriching it with the linear devices of engraving. Instead of the broad contours and occasional hatchings used to define form in earlier woodcuts, Dürer's wide range of hatching marks, varied width of lines, and strong contrasts of black and white produce ambitious pictorial effects. (Compare, for example, the *Buxheim St. Christopher* of 1423 shown in fig. 14.29). He set a standard that soon transformed the technique of woodcuts all over Europe.

Dürer's fusion of northern European and Italian traditions is apparent in his engraving entitled *Adam and Eve* of 1504 (fig. **18.15**), for which the watercolor *Hare* was a preliminary study. Here the biblical subject allows him to depict the first parents as two ideal nudes: Apollo and Venus stand in a densely wooded forest. Unlike the picturesque setting and the animals in it, Adam and Eve are not observed from life; they are constructed according to what Dürer believed to be the perfect proportions based on Vitruvius. (See www.myartslab.com.) Once again, Dürer enlarged the vocabulary of descriptive marks an engraver could use: The lines taper and swell; they intersect at varying angles; marks start and stop and dissolve into dots, called **stipples**. The result is a monochrome image with a great tonal and textural range. The animals that populate the Garden of Eden are very deliberately chosen: Scholars have interpreted the cat, rabbit, ox, and elk as symbols of the medieval theory that bodily fluids, called humors, controlled personality. The cat represents the choleric humor, quick to anger; the ox the phlegmatic humor, lethargic and slow; the elk stands for the melancholic humor, sad and serious; and the rabbit for the sanguine, energetic and sensual. In this moment before the Fall, the humors coexist in balance and the humans retain an ideal beauty. The composition itself is balanced and unified by the tonal effects. Dürer's print, which he signed prominently on the plaque by Adam's head, was enormously influential. His ideal male and female figures became models in their own right for countless other artists.

IMAGES ABOUT ARTISTRY Although best known for his prints, Dürer was also a gifted draftsman and skilled painter. One of his earliest works, a drawing made at 13, is a self-portrait that foreshadowed his fascination with his own image throughout his career. Most impressive, and very revealing, is the painted *Self-Portrait* of 1500 (fig. **18.16**). In pictorial terms, it belongs to the Flemish tradition of Jan van Eyck's *Man in a Red Turban* (see fig. 14.13), but the solemn pose and the idealization of the features have an authority not found in most portraits up to this time. Instead of a conventional three-quarter pose, Dürer places himself frontally in the composition, a pose usually reserved for images of the divine. The panel looks, in fact, like a secularized icon, for it is patterned after images of Christ. It reflects both Dürer's deep piety and the seriousness with which he viewed his mission as an artist and intellectual.

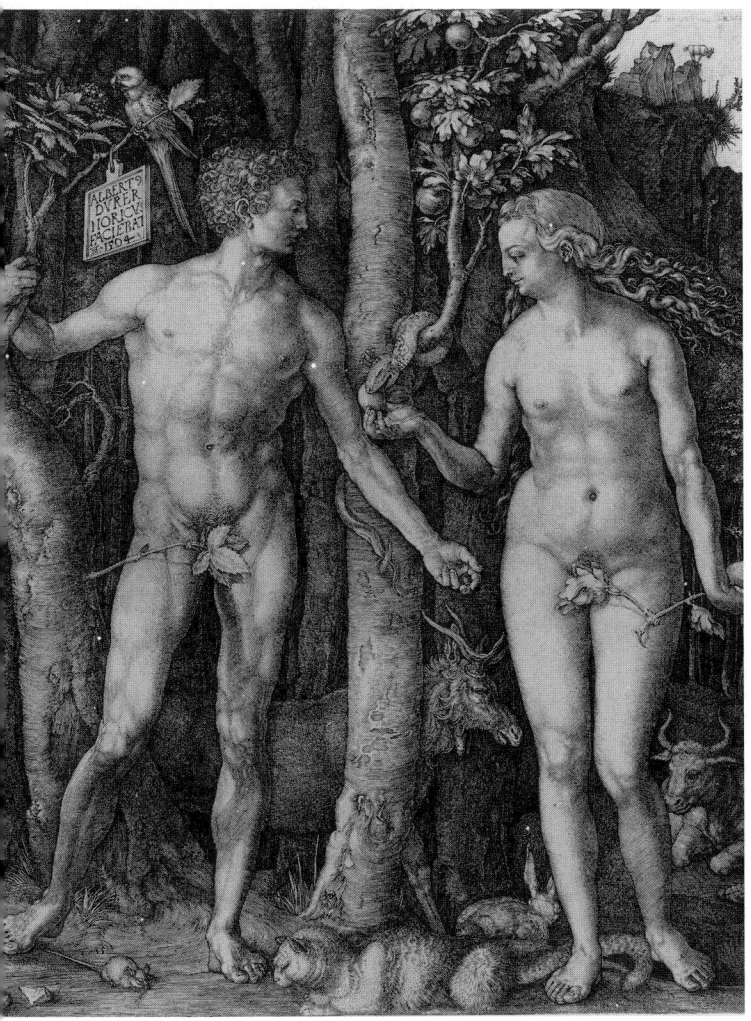

18.15   Albrecht Dürer, *Adam and Eve*. 1504. Engraving, 9⅞ × 7⅝" (25.2 × 19.4 cm). Museum of Fine Arts, Boston. Centennial gift of Landon T. Clay. 1968. 68.187

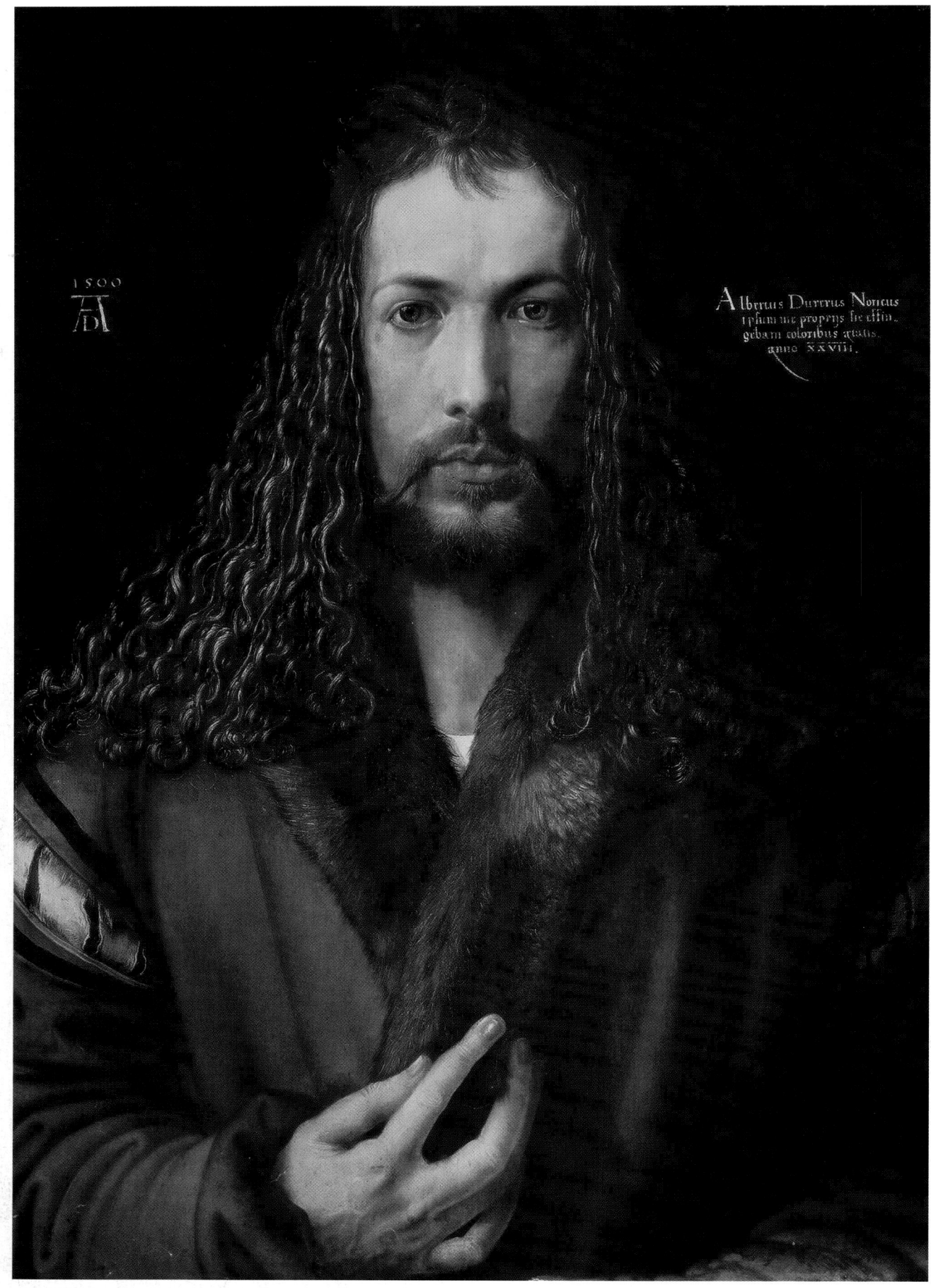

1500

AD

Albertus Durerus Noricus
ipfum me proprys sic effin.
gebam coloribus ætatis.
anno XXVIII.

18.16   Albrecht Dürer, *Self-Portrait*. 1500. Oil on panel, 26¼ × 19¼" (66.3 × 49 cm). Alte Pinakothek, Munich

Albrecht Dürer (1471–1528)

From the journal of his trip to the Netherlands, 1521

Dürer traveled to Aachen and the Netherlands in 1521 to witness the investiture of the new emperor, Charles V. He kept a diary during this journey, which offers many insights into his finances, friends, and intellectual interests. While in Antwerp he heard a false rumor that Martin Luther had been taken prisoner. In response to this news, Dürer wrote the following lament which reveals his thinking about religious issues of the moment.

On Friday before Whitsunday in the year 1521 [May 17, 1521] the news came to me in Antwerp that Martin Luther had been so treacherously taken prisoner; ... there came 10 horsemen and they treacherously carried off the pious man, betrayed into their hands, a man enlightened by the Holy Ghost, a follower of Christ and the true Christian faith. And whether he is still alive, or whether they have murdered him, which I know not, he has suffered this for the sake of Christian truth and because he rebuked the unchristian Papacy. ...

Ach, God of Heaven, pity us! O Lord Jesus Christ, pray for Thy people! ...

And if we have lost this man, who has written more clearly than any that has lived for 140 years, and to whom Thou has given such a spirit of the Gospel, we pray Thee, O Heavenly Father, that Thou wouldst again give Thy Holy Spirit to another, that he may gather Thy church anew everywhere together, that we may again live united and in Christian manner, and so, by our good works, all unbelievers as Turks, Heathen and Calicuts, may of themselves turn to us and embrace the Christian faith. ...

May every man who reads Dr. Martin Luther's books see how clear and transparent his teaching is when he sets forth the Holy Gospel. Wherefore his books are to be held in great honor and not to be burned. ... Ach, God, what might he not still have written for us in ten or twenty years? O all ye Christian men, help me to weep without ceasing for this man, inspired of God, and to pray him to send us another such enlightened man. O Erasmus of Rotterdam, where will you stand? ... O Erasmus, take your stand here, so that God himself may be your praise.

Source: Jane Campbell Hutchison, *Albrecht Dürer, a Biography* (Princeton, NJ: Princeton University Press, 1990)

The status of the artist may also be the theme of one of Dürer's most famous and puzzling prints. This is an engraving labeled *Melencolia I* (fig. **18.17**), one of a trio of prints that Dürer sold or gave away together. Dated 1514, the image represents a winged female holding a compass, surrounded by the tools of the mathematician and the artist. She holds the tools of geometry, yet is surrounded by chaos. The figure is probably a personification, though her identity is controversial: She has been identified as Melancholy, as Geometry, and as Genius. Her face in shadow, she sits in a pose long associated with melancholy, which contemporaries connected with intellectual activity and creative genius. Compare her pose to Raphael's depiction of Michelangelo as Heraclitus in *The School of Athens* (see fig. 16.24). Like Raphael, Dürer shrouds the figure's face in shadow, as though she is lost in thought. Dürer's figure thinks but cannot act, while the infant scrawling on the slate, symbolizing practical knowledge, can act but not think. Dürer appears to be making a statement here about the artistic temperament and its relationship to the melancholic humor.

Renaissance philosophers, like the Italian humanist Marsilio Ficino, viewed melancholia as the source of divine inspiration. The notion of the melancholic genius was widespread in Dürer's time. This print seems to claim for the visual artist (and perhaps for Dürer himself?) the status of divinely inspired, if melancholic, genius.

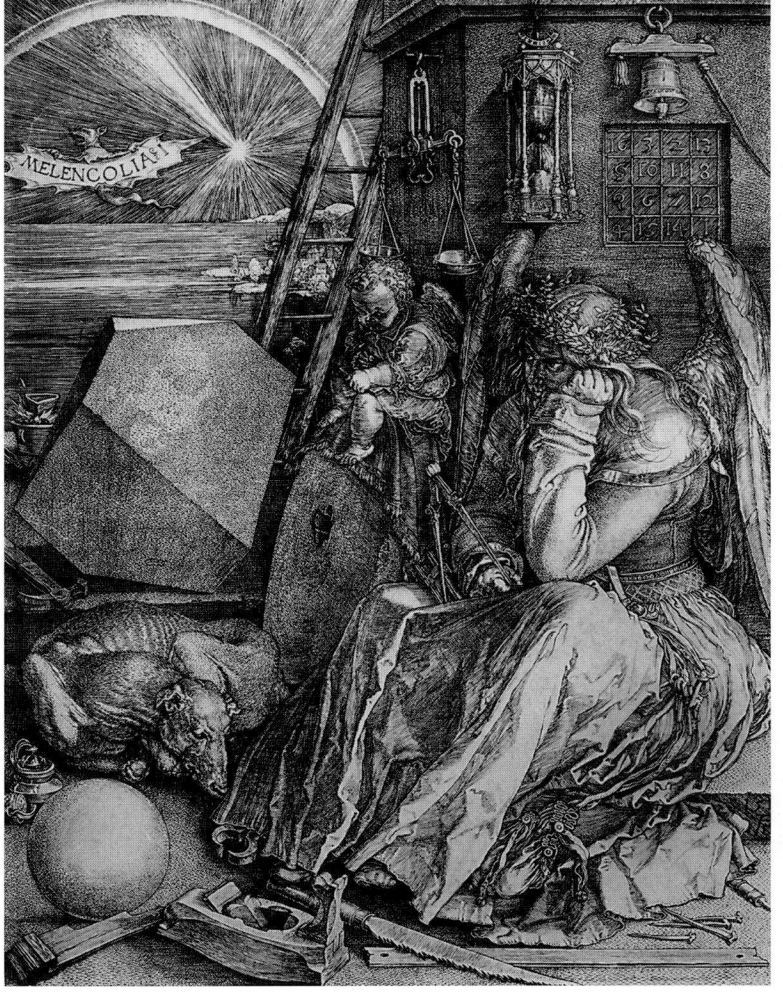

18.17   Albrecht Dürer, *Melencolia I*. 1514. Engraving, 9⅜ × 7½" (23.8 × 18.9 cm). The British Museum, London

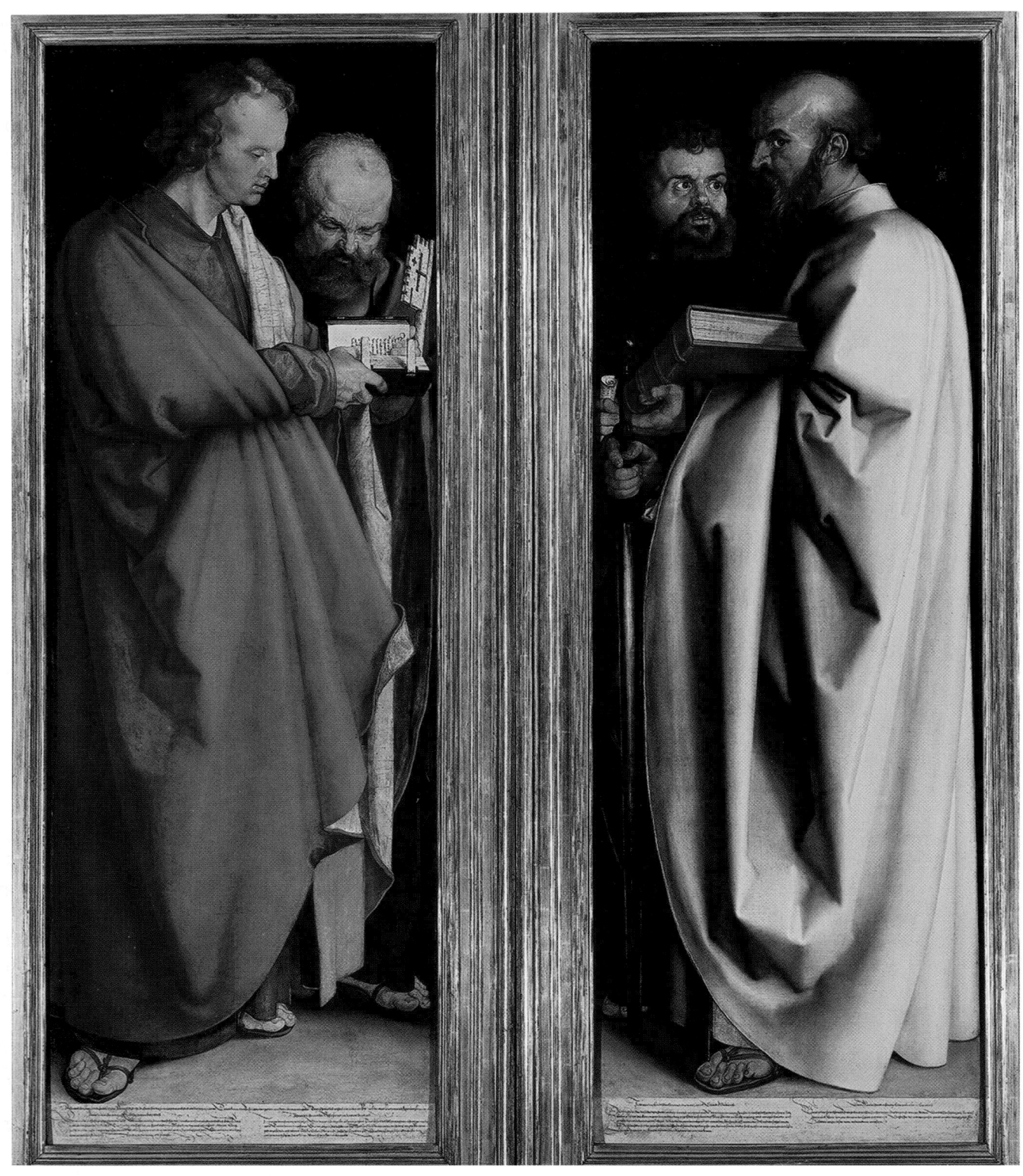

18.18 Albrecht Dürer, *The Four Apostles*. 1523–26. Oil on panel, each 7'1" × 2'6" (2.16 × 76 m). Alte Pinakothek, Munich

A REFORMATION ARTIST Dürer became an early and enthusiastic follower of Martin Luther, although, like Grünewald, he continued to work for Catholic patrons. His new faith can be sensed in the growing austerity of style and subject in his religious works after 1520, as well as in his admiration of Martin Luther, expressed in the journal he kept on a journey to the Netherlands in 1521. (See *Primary Source*, page 641.) The climax of this trend is represented by *The Four Apostles* (fig. **18.18**). These paired panels have rightly been termed Dürer's artistic testament. He presented them in 1526 to the city of Nuremberg, which had joined the Lutheran camp the year before. These four men are fundamental to Protestant doctrine. John and Paul, Luther's

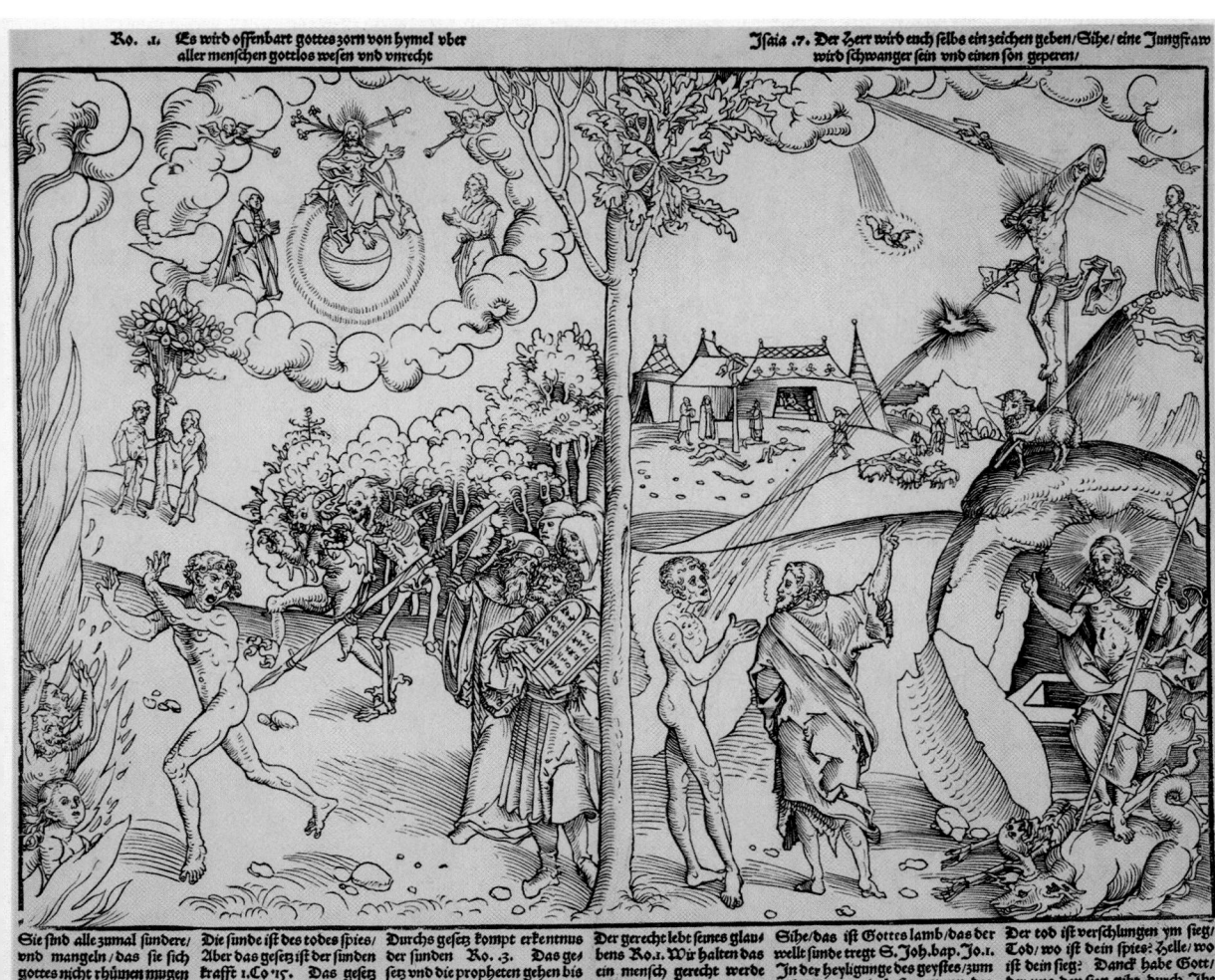

Sie sind alle zumal sündere/ vnd mangeln/das sie sich gottes nicht rhümen mugen Ro .3. | Die sünde ist des todes spies/ Aber das gesetz ist der sünden krafft 1.Co 15. Das gesetz richtet zorn an Ro .4. | Durchs gesetz kompt erkentnus der sünden Ro .3. Das gesetz vnd die propheten gehen bis auff Johannes zeit. Math. 11. | Der gerecht lebt seines glaubens Ro.1. Wir halten das ein mensch gerecht werde durch den glauben/on werg des gesetze. Ro .3. | Sihe/das ist Gottes lamb/das der wellt sünde tregt S. Joh. bap. Jo. 1. In der heyligunge des geystes/zum gehorsam/ vnd besprengung des bluts Jhesu Christi 1. Pet. .1. | Der tod ist verschlungen ym sieg/ Tod/ wo ist dein spies? Helle/ wo ist dein sieg? Danck habe Gott/ der vns den sieg gibt durch Jhe sum christü vnsern herrn 1.Cor.

favorite authors of Scripture, face one another in the foreground, with Peter and Mark behind. Quotations from their writings, inscribed below in Luther's translation, warn the city not to mistake human error and pretense for the will of God. They plead against Catholics and Protestant radicals alike. But in another, more universal sense, the figures represent the Four Temperaments and, by implication, the other cosmic quartets—the seasons, the elements, the times of day, and the ages of life. The apostles have a sculptural solidity that brings to mind Nanni di Banco's *Quattro Coronati* (see fig. 15.10). The heavily draped figures have the weight and presence of Raphael's figures in the tapestry cartoon *St. Paul Preaching at Athens* (see fig. 16.26), which Dürer probably saw on his trip to the Netherlands in 1521. Through the power of his paintings, the portable medium of prints, and his workshop, Dürer was the most influential artist of sixteenth-century Germany.

Religious and Courtly Images in the Era of Reform

The realignment of German culture and society produced by the Reformation required artists to adapt their styles and subject matter for the reformed faiths. The mass medium of prints was an important tool for spreading the tenets of the Protestant confessions. For courtly patrons, artists made images on classicizing themes, for which they used local visual traditions that emphasized detail, texture, and the natural world.

In Reformation Germany, painters had to contend with the Protestant leaders' ambivalence toward religious images. When a faith places the Word above the Image, image becomes subordinate to text; though Luther himself tolerated images (see www.myartslab.com), the works that most deliberately address Lutheran themes are often literal illustrations of texts.

LUCAS CRANACH: REFORMER AND COURT ARTIST

Lucas Cranach the Elder (1472–1553), a close friend of Martin Luther, attempted to solve the problem of casting Luther's doctrines into visual form. Cranach made numerous prints and paintings to express the tenets of the reformer. A woodcut of around 1530 entitled *An Allegory of Law and Grace* (fig. **18.19**) contrasts the difference between the fate of a Catholic and a Lutheran. The left side depicts the Catholic doctrine that the children of Adam and Eve, stained by Original Sin, must perform specific deeds according to the Law of Moses; yet when this is unsuccessful, the soul is consigned to Hell at the Last Judgment. The right side depicts Luther's position: the believer is washed in the blood of

Christ's Crucifixion, because faith in Christ alone assures salvation. Compared to Dürer's woodcuts, this image is rather simple and straightforward, without complex tonalities, illusions of space, or an emphasis on textures. Cranach makes the image as legible and accessible as the text, subordinating artistic effects to clarity.

In addition to images with Lutheran content, Cranach excelled in portraits and mythological scenes painted for aristocratic patrons, both Catholic and Protestant, in Saxony and elsewhere in Germany. In *The Judgment of Paris* (fig. **18.20**) of about 1528, Cranach retells a story from Greek mythology in which the Trojan prince Paris selects the most beautiful goddess of Olympus. He depicts Paris as a German knight clad in the fashionable armor of the nobles at the court of Saxony. The sinewy figures of the goddesses are displayed for the judgment of the prince, who confides his choice to Mercury, also dressed in armor.

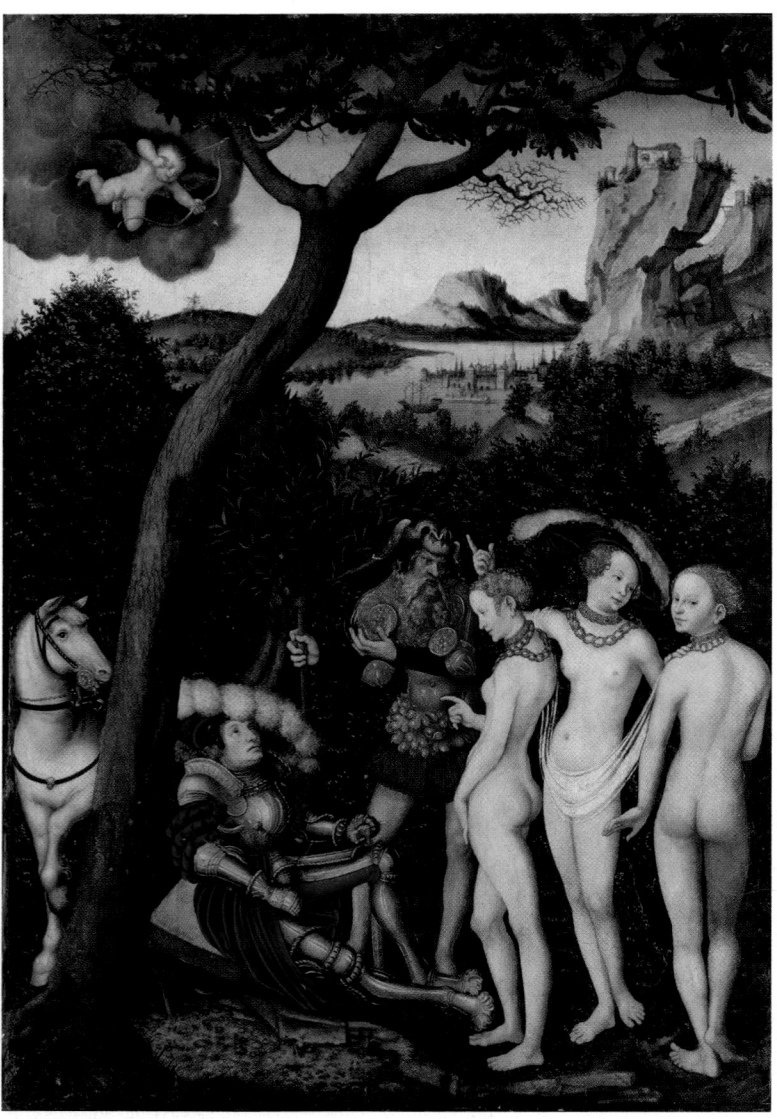

18.20 Lucas Cranach the Elder, *The Judgment of Paris*. ca. 1528. Oil on panel, 40⅛ × 28" (101.9 × 71.1 cm). Metropolitan Museum of Art, New York. Rogers Fund, 1928. 28.221

Like many of his Italian contemporaries working for aristocratic patrons, Cranach gives his classical subject an overtly erotic appeal, inviting a viewer to identify with Paris as the privileged observer of the female nudes. Yet the detailed, miniaturistic technique and the weightless bodies of the women are distinctive to Cranach. One of the most striking features here is the landscape, whose lush vegetation recalls Dürer's *Adam and Eve* (see fig. 18.15); through the thick hedge of trees in the foreground a viewer sees a distant view, featuring a body of water and a city, perhaps Troy.

ALTDORFER'S *BATTLE OF ISSOS* Both Cranach and Dürer played a critical role in the development of the Danube School of landscape painting, which appeared in southern Germany and Austria in the first half of the sixteenth century. The key figure in this school, however, was Albrecht Altdorfer (ca. 1480–1538), a slightly younger artist who spent most of his career in Bavaria. Altdorfer made prints and paintings on a variety of themes, though his primary subject is landscape, which he uses to great expressive effect. His most famous work is *The Battle of Issos* (fig. **18.21**). The painting, made in 1529, is one of a series of images depicting the exploits of historic heroes, commissioned for the Munich palace of William IV, duke of Bavaria. In a sweeping landscape, Altdorfer depicts Alexander the Great's victory over Darius of Persia, which took place in 333 BCE at Issos. This victory was the subject of a composition attributed to the Greek painter Apelles, preserved in a mosaic at Pompeii (see fig. 5.78). To make the subject clear, Altdorfer provided an explanatory text on the tablet suspended in the sky, inscriptions on the banners (probably written by the Regensburg court humanist Aventinus), and a label on Darius' fleeing chariot. The artist has tried to follow ancient descriptions of the actual number and kind of combatants in the battle and to record the geography of the Mediterranean accurately.

Altdorfer adopts an omniscient point of view, as if looking down on the action from a great height, to fit everything into the picture. From this planetary perspective, a viewer must search to find the two leaders lost in the antlike mass of their own armies. The drama of nature is more carefully elaborated than that of the human actors: One can almost feel the rotation of the globe as the sun sets in the distance and the moon rises. The curve of the earth, the drama of the clouds, the craggy mountain peaks overwhelm the mass of humanity. Such details suggest that the events portrayed have an earth-shaking importance, which was arguably the case with this historical event. However, the soldiers' armor and the fortified town in the distance are unmistakably of the sixteenth century, which encourages us to look for contemporary significance. The work was executed at the moment the Ottoman Turks were trying to invade Vienna after gaining control over much of eastern Europe. (Though the imperial forces repelled the Turks this time, they were to threaten Europe repeatedly for another 250 years.) Altdorfer's image suggests that the contemporary battle between Europeans and Turks has the same global significance as Alexander's battle with Darius.

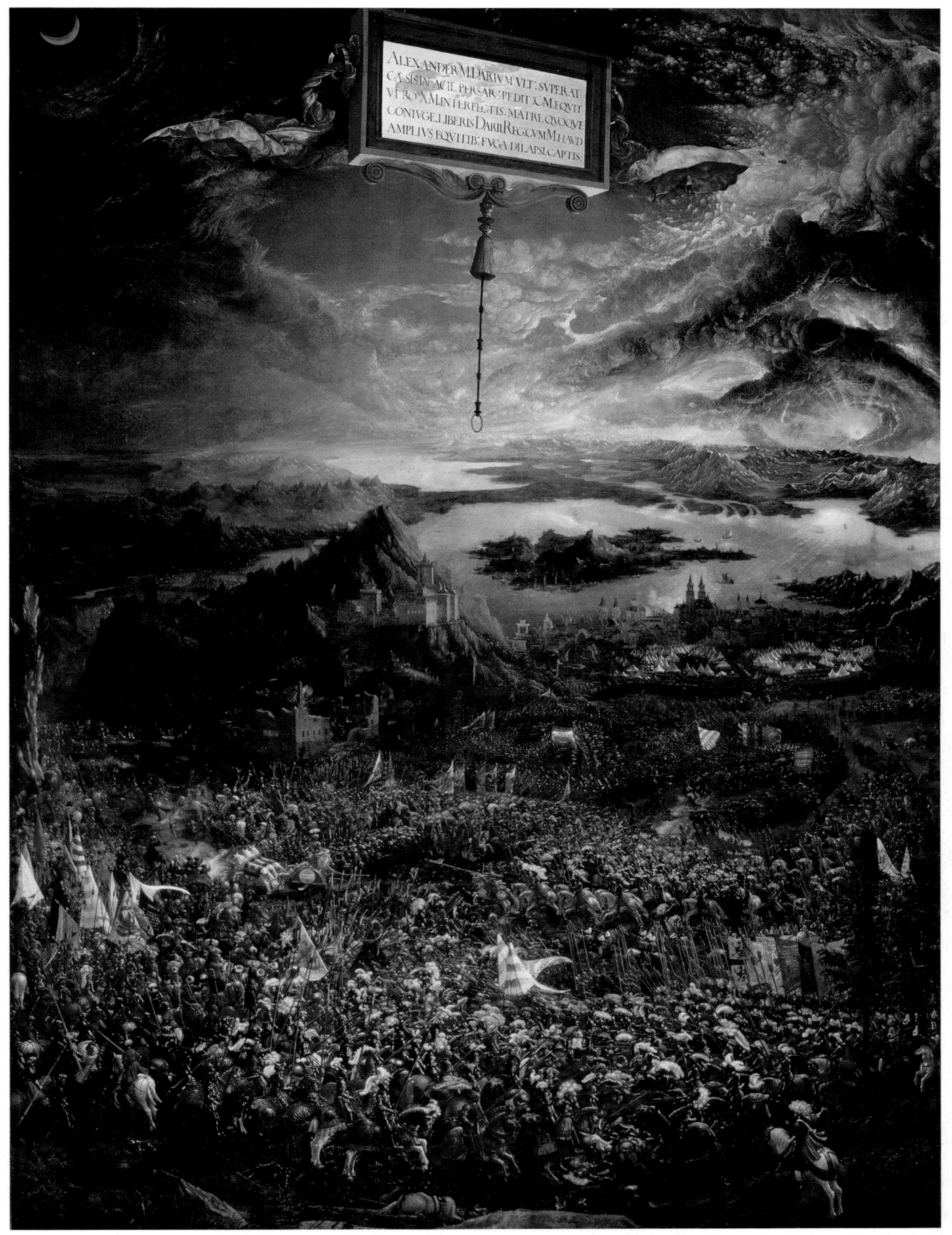

18.21 Albrecht Altdorfer, *The Battle of Issos*. 1529. Oil on panel, 62 × 47" (157.5 × 119.5 cm). Alte Pinakothek, Munich

Painting in the Cities: Humanist Themes and Religious Turmoil

Cities along the Rhine River, especially Strasbourg and Basel, were centers of commerce, publishing, and humanism. The ancient city of Strasbourg's commercial success was due to its location and its industry. Further down the Rhine, Basel had a university as well as an early printing press. It was in Basel that Sebastian Brant's *Ship of Fools* was published in 1494 (see fig. 14.32). As elsewhere, the spread of Reformation and humanist ideas to these cities profoundly affected the arts, as seen especially in the work of Hans Baldung Grien and Hans Holbein.

THE DARK SIDE OF HUMANISM: HANS BALDUNG GRIEN'S *BEWITCHED GROOM* The impact of humanism on German artists may be seen in the work of the painter and print-maker Hans Baldung Grien (1484/85–1545). This former apprentice

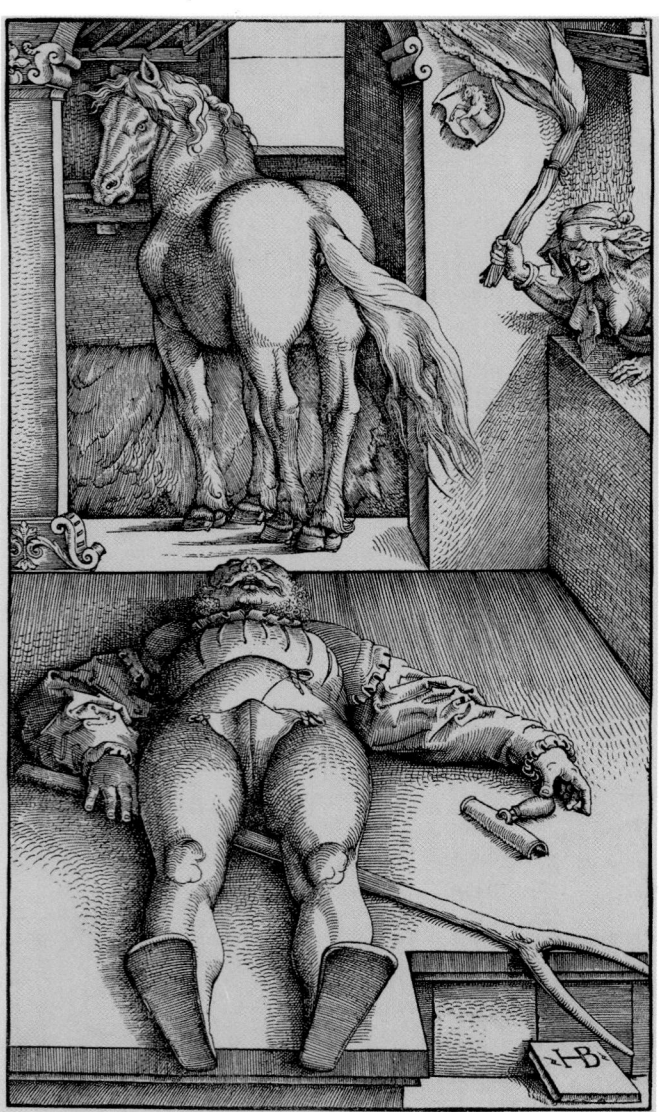

18.22 Hans Baldung Grien, *The Bewitched Groom*. ca. 1544. Woodcut on paper, 13⅓ × 7⅛" (34.2 × 20.1 cm). Art Institute of Chicago. John H. Wrenn Memorial Fund, 1937.136

of Dürer spent much of his career in Strasbourg. Although he made some religious works, Baldung Grien made numerous secular images that explore themes of witchcraft, magic, and death. A characteristic example is his woodcut usually called *The Bewitched Groom* (fig. 18.22) and dated 1544. The print depicts a man lying on the floor of a stable, a grooming tool near his hand, while a woman waving a torch leans into the space. Having spent time in Dürer's workshop, Baldung has mastered the woodcut technique and the lessons of Italian art. He uses a variety of marks to define form and to suggest textures, but he also organizes the space using perspective and foreshortening of both man and beast. He puts these skills to use in an image of the occult; most scholars see the woman with the torch as a witch, who has either stunned the man or controlled the horse to do it for her. The pitchfork beneath the groom may be her goal, as witches were reputed to use such tools to ride across the sky. Her fearsome image reflects a fear of witchcraft that took hold in Europe in the turbulent sixteenth century, even in humanist circles.

HANS HOLBEIN, FROM BASEL TO LONDON The son of a painter, Hans Holbein the Younger (1497–1543) was born and raised in Augsburg, but he initially sought to make his career in Basel. By 1520, Holbein was established there as a painter and a designer of woodcuts. He had also become a member of the humanist circle that included the writer Desiderius Erasmus (1466–1536). Yet the spread of the Reformation disrupted humanist activities in Basel. By 1525, followers of Zwingli preached the sole authority of Scripture, while more radical reformers preached that images were idols. To escape this climate, Holbein sought employment elsewhere. He had traveled to France in 1523–24, perhaps intending to offer his services to Francis I. Hoping for commissions at the court of Henry VIII, Holbein went to England in 1527, in possession of a letter from Erasmus recommending him to the humanist and royal advisor, Thomas More. In that letter, Erasmus wrote: "Here [in Basel] the arts are out in the cold." By 1528, when Holbein returned to Basel, violence had replaced rhetoric. He witnessed Protestant mobs destroying religious images, a scene Erasmus described in a letter: "Not a statue has been left in the churches or in the monasteries; all the frescoes have been whitewashed over. Everything which would burn has been set on fire, everything else hacked into little pieces. Neither value nor artistry prevailed to save anything." Holbein resolved to return to London, which he did in 1532.

Back in England, Holbein found his first patrons among merchants and diplomats, who were often also humanists. One of his largest works (fig. 18.23) depicts two ambassadors from France, Jean de Dinteville and Georges de Selve. Painted in 1533, when the English court was in turmoil because of the king's impending break with Rome, the image reflects Holbein's artistic origins and his gifts as a portraitist. The two men were friends, and Holbein represents them in full length standing in a draped room with a tall double-tiered table between them. Jean de Dinteville, on the left, wears an elaborate fur-lined tunic over his velvet garment, as well as a chain identifying him as a member of the Order of St. Michael,

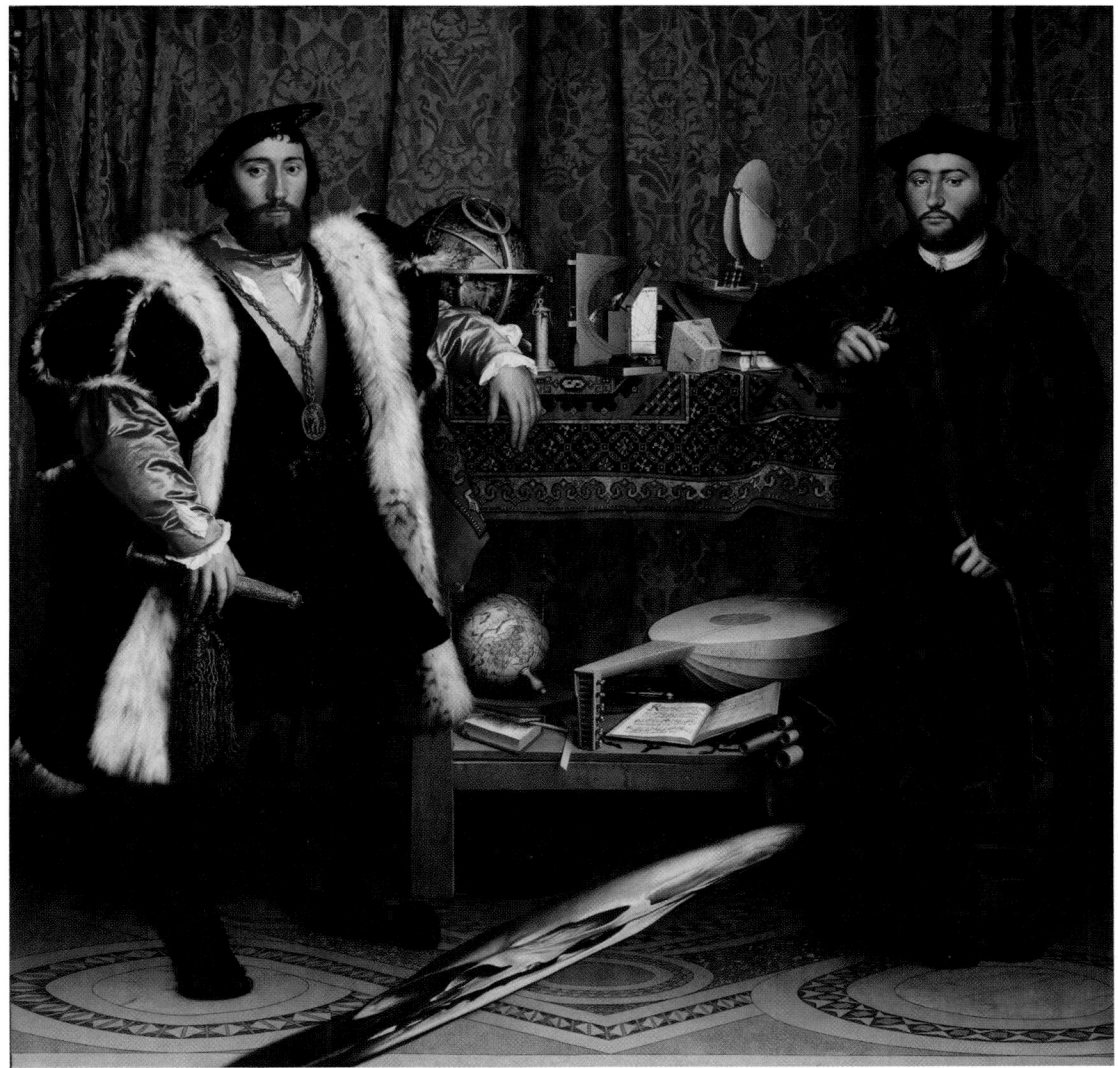

18.23 Hans Holbein the Younger, *Jean de Dinteville and Georges de Selve* ("The Ambassadors"). 1533. Oil on panel, 6'9½" × 6'10¼" (2.07 × 2.09 m). The National Gallery, London

a French chivalric order. Opposite him stands Bishop Georges de Selve, in his cleric's collar, and covered in a warm gown. He bears no weapon or baton of office, as his friend does, but rests his arm on the Bible placed on the upper tier of the table. Holbein distinguishes each man's features and social station in the portrait. His rendering of textures, surfaces, and details harks back to Jan van Eyck, as in fact the standing double portrait does (see fig. 14.14).

Nonetheless, the setting is as important as the two figures here. On the table between them, Holbein places a series of objects reflecting the interests of the two men. The bishop was a great patron of music, an enthusiasm alluded to in the presence of a lute (see page 624). The objects seem to have been chosen with care to add to the meaning of the image. Below the lute is an open book featuring hymns written by Martin Luther. The lute itself has a broken string—it is an emblem of discord. Instruments that measure time (a sundial) or that track the constellations sit on the upper tier. Two globes—a celestial globe above and a terrestrial one below—appear closer to de Dinteville. (His own town is

marked on the terrestrial globe.) These objects contrast the study of earthly and heavenly subjects, with the implication that discord and division rule the earthly sphere. Before all looms an **anamorphic** representation of a skull: It is set into a dramatically exaggerated perspective so that its form is only clearly readable from an acute angle. The skull serves as a **vanitas**, a reminder that the things of this world are fleeting. Holbein's success in recording the interests and concerns of these two men likely brought him to the notice of the rest of the court.

ENGLAND: REFORMATION AND POWER

Holbein's principal patron in England was the ambitious Henry VIII, who reigned from 1509 to 1547. Henry wanted England to be a powerbroker in the conflicts between Francis I of France and the Holy Roman emperor Charles V, although his personal

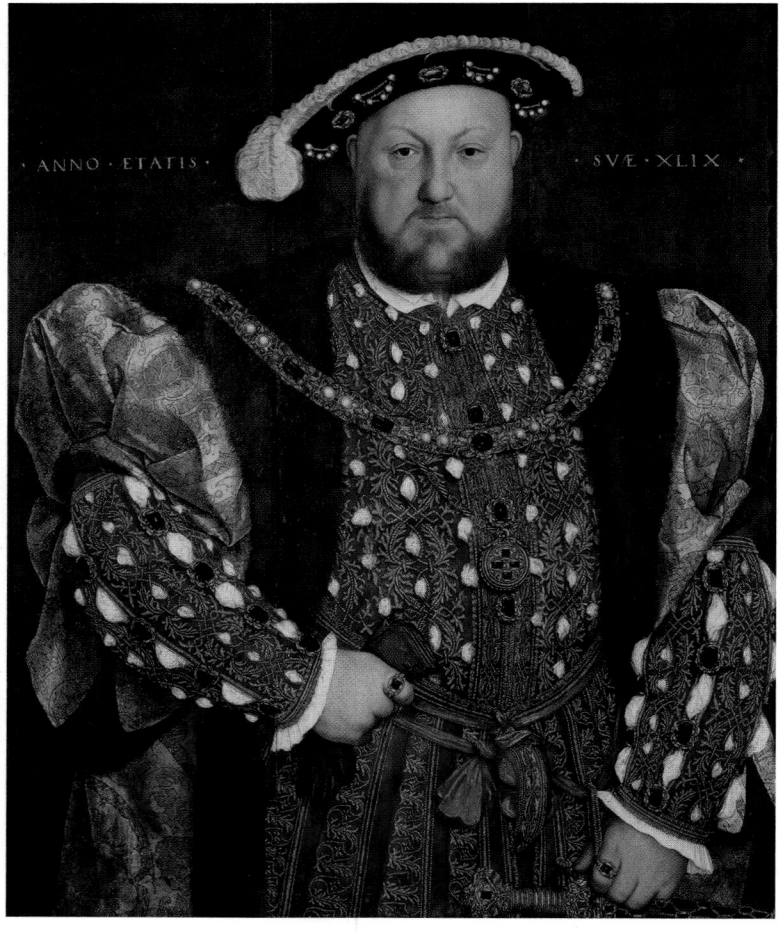

18.24 Hans Holbein the Younger, *Henry VIII*. 1540. Oil on panel, 32½ × 29" (82.6 × 74.5 cm). Galleria Nazionale d'Arte Antica, Rome

Henry's daughter Elizabeth came to the throne in 1558 at the age of 25, and through her shrewdness and luck ruled until 1603. She managed to unite a country that had been bitterly divided by religious differences, and increased the wealth and status of England through her diplomacy, her perspicacious choice of advisors and admirals, and her daring. Her most important victory was the defeat of the Spanish Armada, sent to invade England in 1588; but the Elizabethan age is also rightly famous for its music and literary arts.

The influence of Elizabethan poetry may be seen in a miniature portrait by the English painter Nicholas Hilliard (1547–1619), usually called *A Young Man Among Roses* (fig. **18.25**). Inspired by ancient **cameos** (small medallions in relief), these portable portraits on parchment were tiny keepsakes often worn as jewelry. Hilliard's style reveals the influence of Holbein in the even lighting and careful detail. However, the tall, slender proportions, elegant costume, and languorous grace may reflect the impact of Italian Mannerism, probably by way of Fontainebleau; compare the courtier's stance to that of Primaticcio's stucco figures from the French palace (see fig. 18.4). In tremendous detail on a very small scale (this miniature is just over 5 inches high), Hilliard records the costume and features of the young man and the tree and flowers that surround him. An inscription suggests that he is suffering for his love. Other details—the black and white costume, the type of rose—imply that Elizabeth herself is his beloved, inspiring speculation about the man's identity. The image may represent Robert Devereaux,

situation complicated these efforts. Married to Catherine of Aragon in 1509, 20 years later Henry was seeking to annul their union, for they had failed to produce a male heir to the throne. Thwarted in his desire by the Catholic Church, he established himself as the head of the breakaway Church of England in 1534. His desire for a male heir led Henry into a number of marriages, most of which ended either in divorce or in the execution of his wife. He had three children, who succeeded him as Edward VI, Mary I, and Elizabeth I.

Holbein had come to the notice of the king by 1536, and by 1537 was serving as the king's painter, his primary assignment being to make portraits of the king and his court. His *Henry VIII* (fig. **18.24**) of 1540 captures the supreme self-confidence of the king. He uses the rigid frontality that Dürer had chosen for his self-portrait to convey the almost divine authority of this absolute ruler. The king's physical bulk creates an overpowering sense of his ruthless, commanding personality. The portrait shares with Bronzino's *Eleanora of Toledo* (see fig. 17.10) its immobile pose, air of unapproachability, and precisely rendered costume and jewels. Holbein fashioned for Henry VIII a memorable public image of strength and power. Holbein's portraits of the king and his courtiers molded British taste in aristocratic portraiture for decades.

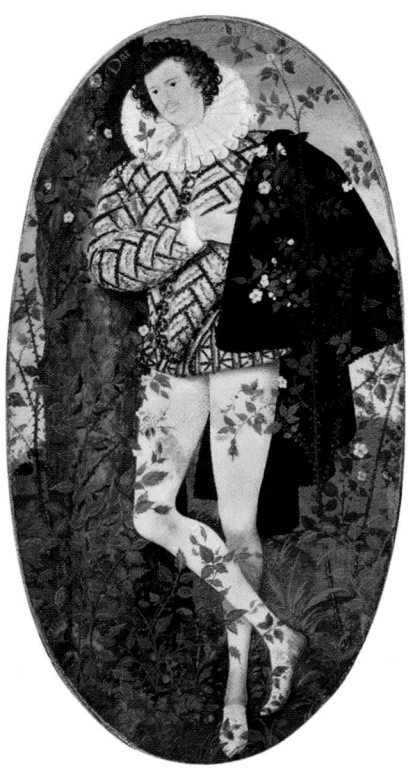

18.25 Nicholas Hilliard, *A Young Man Among Roses*. ca. 1588. Oil on parchment, 5⅜ × 2¾" (13.7 × 7 cm). Victoria & Albert Museum, London

Elizabethan Imagery

The poets and playwrights of Elizabethan England produced some of the most memorable literature in the English language. The sonnet, given authority as a poetic form by Petrarch, was used by both Edmund Spenser and William Shakespeare for their own love poetry. Spenser (ca. 1552–1599) is best known for his epic poem The Faerie Queen, an allegory in part about Elizabeth I. Though best known for his plays, William Shakespeare (1564–1616) wrote many sonnets whose imagery is as vivid as that in the paintings of Nicholas Hilliard.

Edmund Spenser, Sonnet Sixty-four, from the *Amoretti* (1595)

Coming to kiss her lips, such grace I found
Me seemed I smelt a garden of sweet flowers
That dainty odours from them threw around
For damzels fit to deck their lovers' bowers:
Her lips did smell like unto gillyflowers;
Her ruddy cheeks like unto roses red;
Her snowy brows like budded bellamours
Her lovely eyes like pinks but newly spread;
Her goodly bosom like a strawberry bed;

Her neck like to a bunch of columbines;
Her breast like lilies, ere their leaves be shed;
Her nipples like young blossomed jessamines:
Such fragrant flowers do give most odorous smell,
But her sweet odour did them all excel.

William Shakespeare, *Sonnet Eighteen*, from The Sonnets (published in 1609, though often dated to the 1590s)

Shall I compare thee to a summer's day?
Thou art more lovely and more temperate:
Rough winds do shake the darling buds of May,
And summer's lease hath all too short a date:
Sometime too hot the eye of heaven shines,
And often is his gold complexion dimmed;
And every fair from fair sometime declines,
By chance, or nature's changing course, untrimmed:
But thy eternal summer shall not fade,
Nor lose possession of that fair thou ow'st;
Nor shall Death brag thou wand'rest in his shade,
When in eternal lines to time thou grow'st.
So long as men can breathe or eyes can see,
So long lives this, and this gives life to thee.

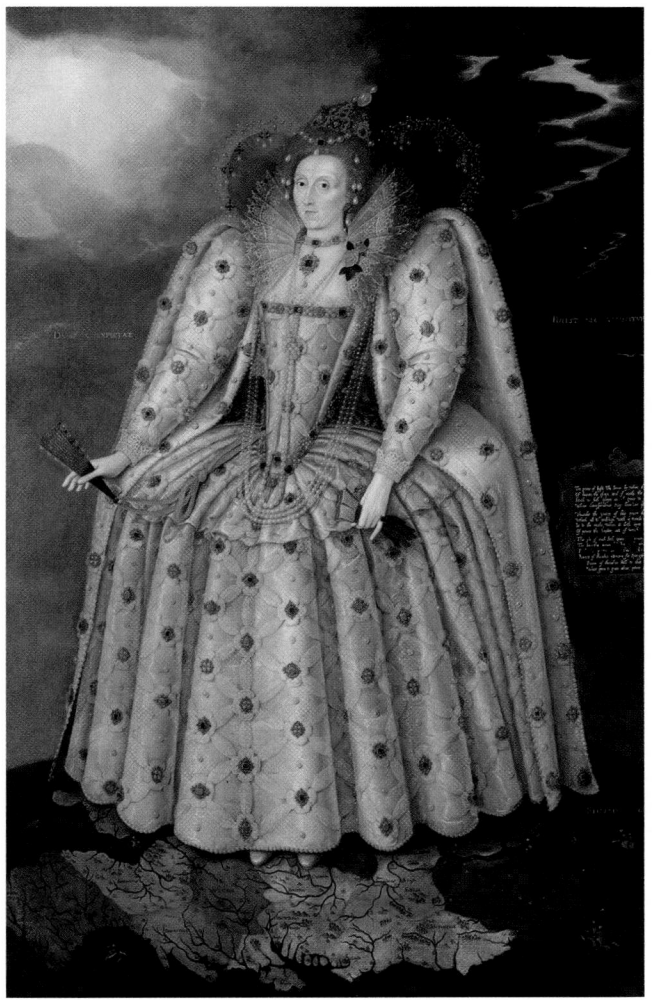

earl of Essex, Elizabeth's one-time favorite. The floral imagery and the lovesick poet are frequent motifs in Elizabethan sonnets, such as those of Edmund Spenser or William Shakespeare. Many images from the Elizabethan era carry texts or symbols that have parallels in Elizabethan court rituals and literature. (See *Primary Source*, above.)

Like her father, Henry VIII, Queen Elizabeth had a gift for managing her image. She had no Holbein in her employ to dominate the artistic life of her court, but she still managed to dictate to the many artists around her how she should be represented. She even imprisoned people for making unsanctioned images of her. A portrait by the Flemish artist Marcus Gheeraerts the Younger (fig. **18.26**) exemplifies her carefully controlled iconography. The portrait represents Elizabeth standing on a map of her realm, which she dominates by her size and frontality. Sir Henry Lee, one of Elizabeth's courtiers, probably commissioned this portrait, often called *The Ditcheley Portrait*; Ditcheley was his estate near Oxford. Elizabeth wears one of the elaborate dresses that she favored, significantly in white, the color of virginity; Elizabeth steadfastly refused to marry, claiming that she was married to England. One side of the background is dark and gloomy: A storm has just passed and the sun shines again. A fragmentary sonnet expresses thanks for a grace given. The whole image is one of supreme and serene authority.

18.26 Marcus Gheeraerts the Younger, *Portrait of Elizabeth I (The Ditcheley Portrait)*. ca. 1592. Oil on canvas, 97'11" × 5' (2.41 × 1.52 m). The National Portrait Gallery, London

THE NETHERLANDS: WORLD MARKETPLACE

Such displays of aristocratic power found less favor in the sixteenth-century Netherlands. This region, comprising present-day Holland and Belgium, had the most turbulent history of any country north of the Alps. United under Burgundian rulers in the fifteenth century, the Netherlands passed to Habsburg control through the marriage of Mary of Burgundy (see fig. 14.18) to Maximilian I. When the Reformation began, it was part of the empire under their grandson, Charles V, who also inherited the crown of Spain. Protestantism quickly gained adherents in the Northern Netherlands, and attempts to suppress the spread of reform led to a revolt there against Spanish rule that resulted in the provinces of the Northern Netherlands declaring their independence in 1579. After a bloody struggle, the Northern Provinces (present-day Holland) emerged at the end of the century as an independent state in all but name.

The Southern Provinces (roughly corresponding to present-day Belgium) remained in Spanish hands and committed to Roman Catholicism. To govern the Netherlands, both Charles V and Philip II of Spain appointed regents who established courts in the southern cities. Economic changes accompanied the momentous changes in the political and religious situation. In the Southern Netherlands, the once-thriving port of Bruges silted up and was replaced as a commercial center by Antwerp, with its deep harbor and strategic location. Antwerp became the commercial and artistic capital of the Southern Netherlands. In the Northern Netherlands the city of Amsterdam became a center of international trade.

One byproduct of the religious strife was the destruction of works of art in waves of iconoclasm, inspired by the reformers' suspicion of images. In both the Northern and Southern Netherlands, vast numbers of medieval and earlier Renaissance works of art were lost, especially religious works and sculptures, as zealous reformers confiscated or burned images they considered idolatrous. The market for sculpture in the Netherlands was effectively destroyed for the rest of the early modern period, as painting and other two-dimensional art forms came to dominate artistic production. Although some reformers allowed painted or printed images that taught the faithful about doctrine, the Catholic practice of commissioning large-scale sculptures of saints or of the Virgin to install in churches was eliminated. Artists' practices changed under these conditions; as religious commissions dried up, especially in the Northern Netherlands, artists no longer waited for patrons to hire them, but made works of art to sell in the open market instead. (See *The Art Historian's*

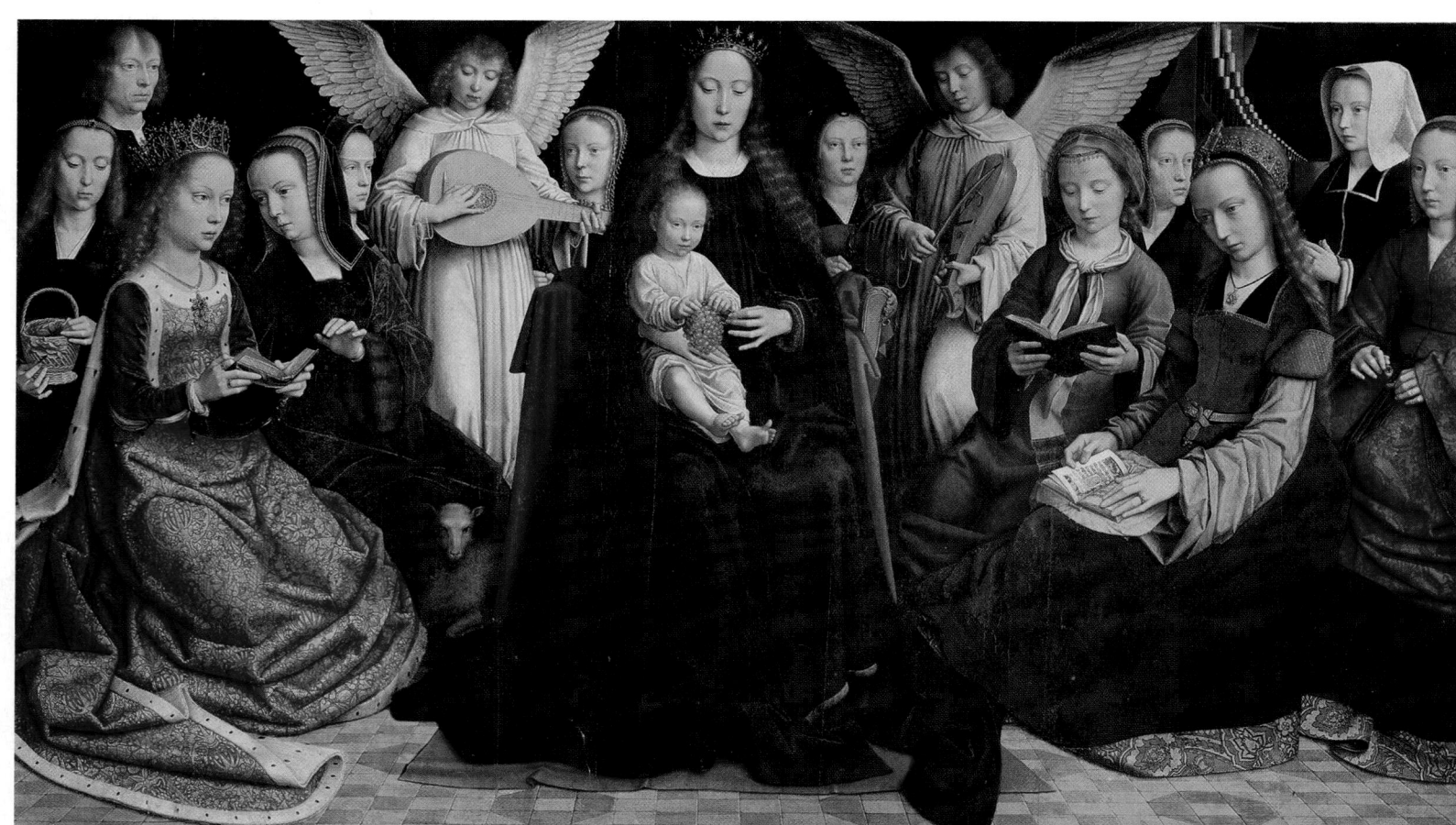

18.27 Gerard David, *Virgin Among Virgins*. 1509. Oil on panel, 46⅞ × 83½" (119 × 212 cm). Musée des Beaux-Arts, Rouen

The Economics of Art

As trade, specialization, and a money economy came to dominate northern Europe after the Middle Ages, the business of making and selling art changed. The patron–artist relationship, where a contract specified the work to be produced and the money to be paid, gave way to the modern market system, with artists beginning to make their goods for sale on the open market. In recent years, art historians have been researching and writing about this change in the economics of art, focusing on centers such as Bruges, Antwerp, Delft, Haarlem, and Amsterdam.

Scholars have used documents, such as chronicles, receipts, and contracts and the works themselves to explore the institutions that arose in response to these economic changes. The study of guilds and their regulation of the art trade illuminates one facet of the economics of art: Since the Middle Ages, these organizations had regulated the training of artists and their commercial activity and had controlled competition in their locales. The new technology of prints allowed artists to mass-produce images that were not regulated by the guilds; prints were available for purchase at trade fairs along with other commodities, sometimes by monks and nuns who sold them to support their monasteries. Dürer financed his trip from Nuremberg to Antwerp in 1521 by selling prints along the way.

By tracking the fluctuations in prices of works of art in the early modern period, scholars have been able to compare them to other commodities and to examine the impact of economic changes in the art trade on the artists themselves. Researchers have also explored the records and the physical arrangements of the marketplaces and neighborhoods where the artists displayed their work for buyers to examine and purchase them. Along with economic changes in the art trade a new player entered the art market—the dealer, who served as the middleman between the artist and the purchaser.

For art historians, an important issue is how these new economic changes and circumstances for making and selling art would affect the artworks themselves. Evidence indicates that artists and workshops standardized their production techniques, subcontracted specific elements of projects, and specialized in particular forms or subjects. The choices made for subject matter in works of art responded to economic changes, too; images such as Aertsen's *The Meat Stall* (see fig. 18.31) represent and comment on the market itself.

Lens, above.) One result was the development of new genres of art that would supplement, and eventually replace, traditional religious subjects.

To these challenges concerning subject matter and patronage should be added the challenge represented by the new Italianate style, which quickly gained favor in the courts. Responses to Italian style varied. Some artists saw no reason to change the northern European visual tradition they had inherited; some grafted Italianate decorative forms to their traditional compositions and techniques; and others dove deeply into Italian style. The latter were inspired by the example of Dürer, by works of Michelangelo and Raphael they had seen in the Netherlands, and by their own experience of Italy.

The City and the Court: David and Gossaert

The city of Bruges in the Catholic Southern Netherlands remained an important center for commerce into the sixteenth century, though much of its trade and prosperity transferred to Antwerp early in the period. Gerard David (ca. 1460–1523) carried on the distinguished tradition of Bruges painting established in the work of Van Eyck and Memling. David's workshop dominated the city to the middle of the sixteenth century. His style may be examined in a work he gave to the Carmelite nunnery in Bruges in 1509. This painting (fig. **18.27**) depicts the Virgin and Child surrounded by virgin saints; two angels serenade this assembly of women, while portraits of David and his wife, Cornelia Cnoop, appear in the corners. In traditional Flemish fashion, the forms exhibit detailed renderings of textures, layers of colors that create brilliant effects, and symbolic forms to enhance the meaning, such as the grapes held by the Christ Child and the attributes of the saints. Yet David's cool colors and soft modeling endow these figures with a calm dignity that is enhanced by the balanced composition. These silent virgins gather around the mother and son as the nuns of the convent would gather for prayer.

David worked for both individual patrons and the open market, but some of his contemporaries found employment in the aristocratic courts of the Netherlands, including Jan Gossaert (ca. 1478–1532), nicknamed "Mabuse," for his hometown of Maubeuge. His early career was spent in Antwerp, but in 1508 he accompanied Admiral Philip of Burgundy to Italy, where the Italian Renaissance and antiquity made a deep impression on him. He also worked for the regent of the Netherlands, Margaret of Austria. His paintings fuse the lessons of Italian monumentality with the detailed technique of the Netherlandish tradition.

For the castle of his patron Philip of Burgundy he made images of mythological subjects, including the *Neptune and Amphitrite* (fig. **18.28**), signed and dated by Gossaert in 1516. The painting displays the painter's fascination with antiquity and Italianate perspective, as well as his skill at rendering textures, details, and rich color, in the Netherlandish tradition. Gossaert here depicts the god and his consort as nudes, basing their postures on Dürer's 1504 *Adam and Eve* (see fig. 18.15). Gossaert endows these figures with bulky proportions that derive from his study in Rome of Hellenistic statues like the *Laocoön* (see page 183). The architecture, too, stems from ancient models, but it has a severity and a simplicity that are indebted to Bramante (see fig. 16.8). Gossaert places his figures in a templelike structure, but he gives them an impossible scale: Neptune stands as tall as the columns. Either they are ancient cult statues come to life, or a viewer witnesses an epiphany (sudden appearance) of the pagan divinities. This subject, the god of the sea, clearly reflects Admiral Philip's interests. Gossaert brings Italianate forms to the service of his Netherlandish audience in a hybrid of the two traditions.

Antwerp: Merchants, Markets, and Morality

Bruges' decline as a center for commerce occurred as Antwerp rose to prominence, which brought it new wealth and the desire for a new form of expression of that wealth. As in earlier Netherlandish cities, the town hall was the most important civic structure, and in midcentury, the city held a competition for a new design. Cornelis Floris (1514–1575), a local sculptor and architect, won the commission and began work in 1561. Floris had traveled to Italy and had studied both ancient and contemporary Italian architecture. In the design for the Antwerp town hall, he combined the precepts of Italian Renaissance architecture with northern European traditions to create the large and imposing structure (fig. **18.29**). The building uses Italian devices: The base is a rusticated arcade, like Ammanati's Palazzo Pitti (see fig. 17.8); the three stories above are articulated with Doric, Ionic, and Corinthian columns, like the Colosseum in Rome (see fig. 7.20); a central pavilion mixes sculpture and architecture, like a Roman triumphal arch (see fig. 7.70). Yet the proportions are vertical, the roofline more in keeping with Netherlandish practice, and rich carvings on the central pavilion add a focal point at the tall mass of this section of the façade. The building integrates Italian ideas differently from the way those ideas would be expressed in France or Spain (see figs. 18.2 and 18.6). Antwerp had become a global

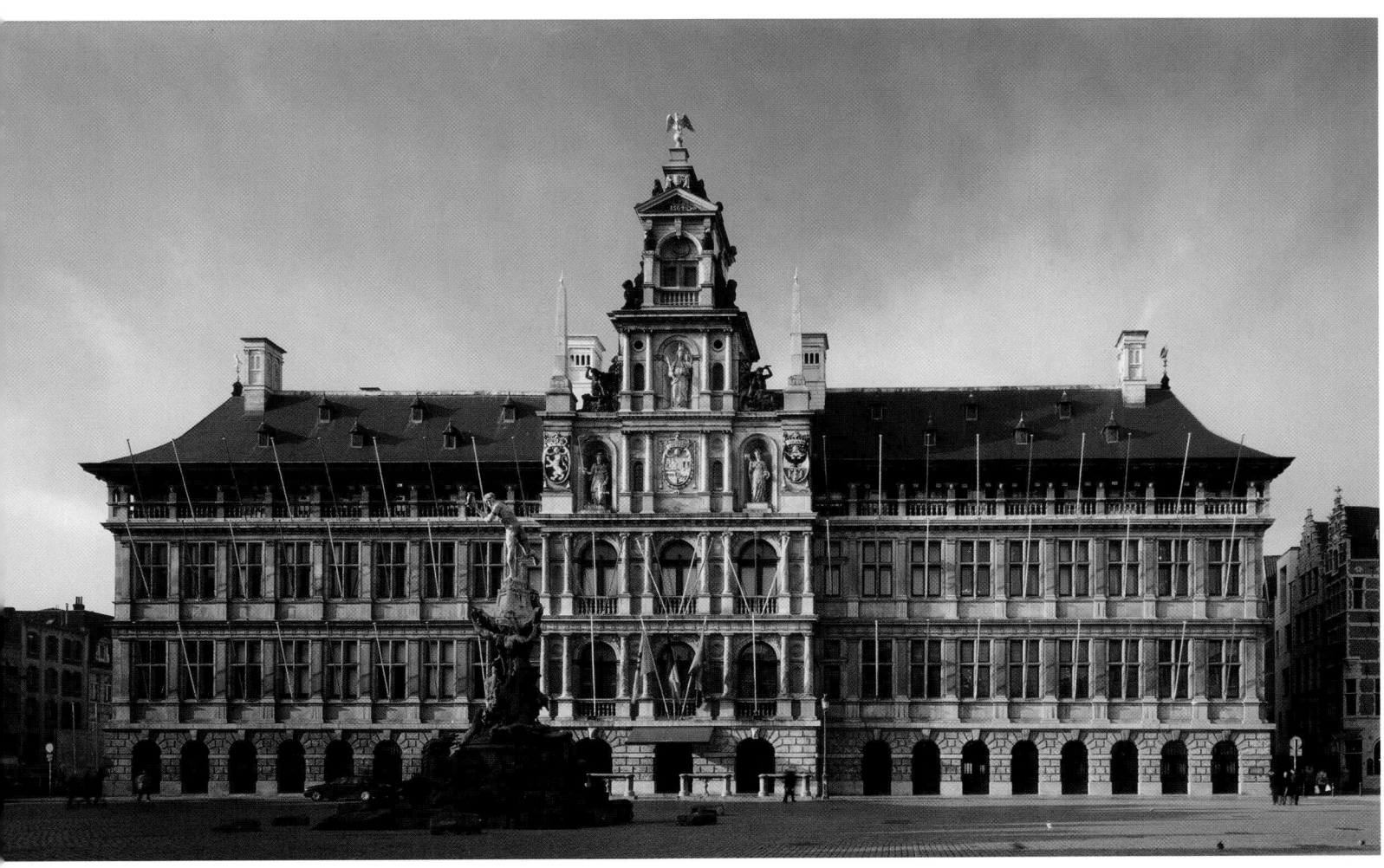

18.29 Cornelis Floris and Willem van den Broek. Town Hall, Antwerp. 1561–66

marketplace by this point, trading a variety of goods, from textiles to foodstuffs, all over the world, including the Americas and Asia. The visual arts participated in this market in a variety of ways. Tapestries were exported through Antwerp; there was a thriving market in prints; and the Plantin-Moretus Press produced editions of books that were sent all over the world. Painters in particular developed new genres of art to tap into this expanding market. Still-life, landscape, and **genre paintings** (images of daily life) had been explored by Flemish artists since the rise of the International Gothic Style and had become even more important during the fifteenth century as backdrops for religious themes. Some Antwerp artists of the sixteenth century specialized in these themes as subjects in themselves, perhaps in response to the loss of religious patronage, or maybe as a way to gain market share. These images often carry multiple meanings, at once depicting the pleasures of the world, while warning about those same pleasures.

PATINIR: THE WORLD LANDSCAPE Joachim Patinir (ca. 1480–1524) was an early specialist in landscape, whose work Dürer had seen and praised when he visited Antwerp in 1521. *The Penitence of St. Jerome* (fig. **18.30**) of about 1518 demonstrates Patinir's connection to the traditions of Flemish art while updating that tradition. He has altered the triptych form to give it curved shapes along the top; this form became the fashion for triptychs in early sixteenth-century Antwerp. The three wings of the triptych depict three different saints, with Jerome in the wilderness at the center, and John the Baptist and St. Anthony Abbot in the wings; all three were venerated as hermit saints. Their figures appear in the foreground, while the continuous landscape behind them unites all three panels. The landscape is the true subject of Patinir's work. Any narrative is completely subordinate to the deep vista of the earth, whose fields, forests, mountains, seas, and sky fill most of the panel. The human presence is very small in this landscape. Tiny figures wander through this world, while villages, cities, even ships can be distinguished in the distance.

This kind of landscape, which became very popular among European collectors in the sixteenth century, has been called a "world landscape," because of the focus on deep vistas into the distance. Like Altdorfer, Patinir uses a high viewpoint to allow for the distant view, yet he also provides a shelf of space in the foreground for the figures. Creating a smooth relationship between the foreground and the distance is of less interest to Patinir than describing the craggy blue mountains and the verdant forests. How viewers interpreted such landscapes in Patinir's time is not

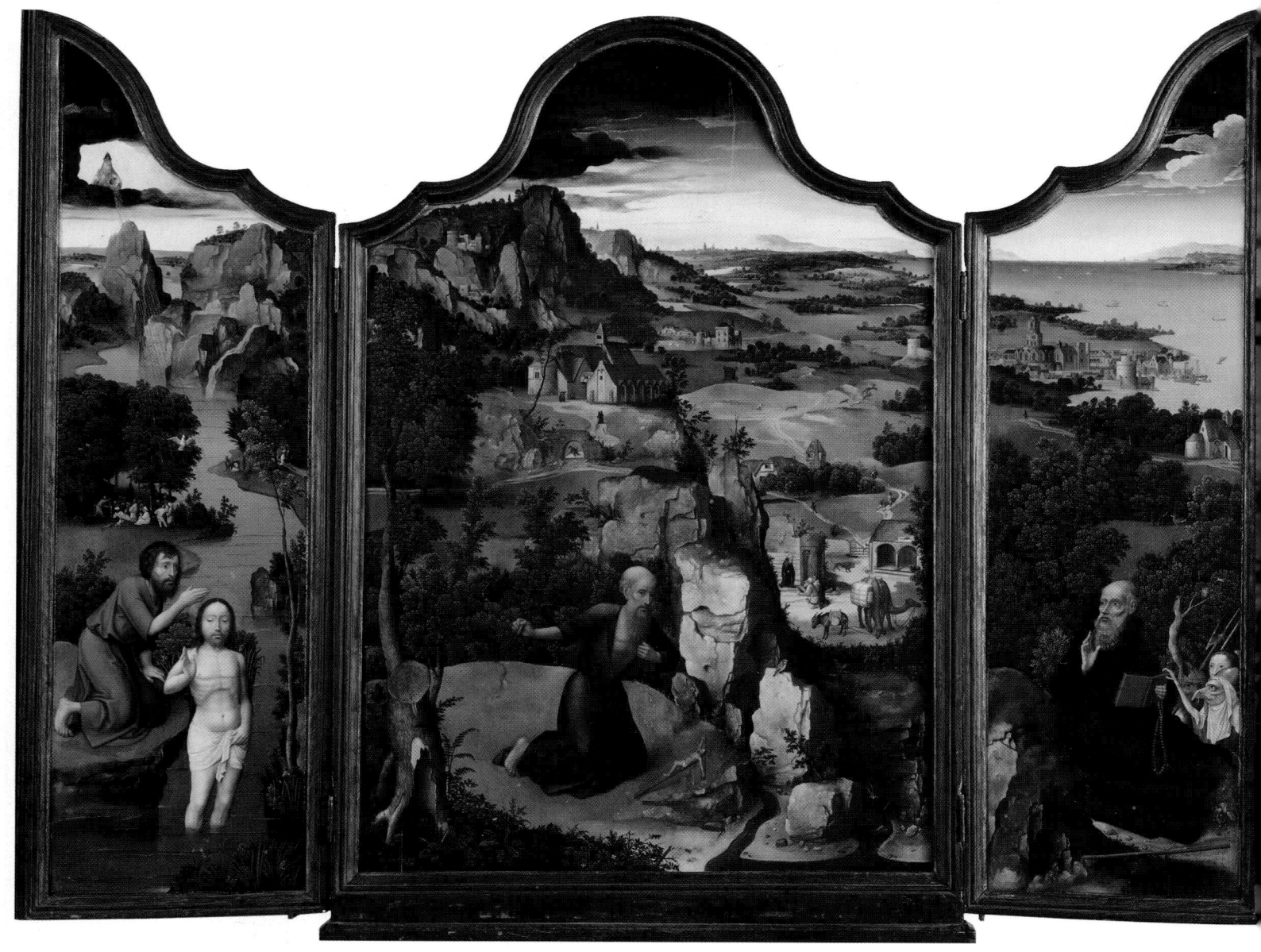

18.30 Joachim Patinir, *The Penitence of St. Jerome.* ca. 1518. Oil on panel, 47¼ × 14⅛" (120 × 36 cm). Metropolitan Museum of Art, New York. Fletcher Fund, 1936, 36.14a–c

entirely clear. On the one hand, the vista itself invites careful perusal, and viewers could study the picture and imagine the distant lands then being explored instead of traveling there themselves. At the same time, the painting has a religious subject that may have a moralizing message. Perhaps Patinir was commenting on the dangers of life in the world compared with the hermit saints' rejection of worldly things.

AERTSEN'S *THE MEAT STALL* Scholars have also ascribed a moralizing meaning to the still lifes painted by the North Netherlandish painter Pieter Aertsen (1507/08–1575). He spent his early career in Antwerp, then returned to Amsterdam in 1557, where he saw first hand the destruction of religious images by iconoclasts in 1566. *The Meat Stall* (fig. **18.31**), done in 1551 while the artist was still in Antwerp, seems at first glance to be a purely secular picture. In the foreground, we see the products for sale in a butcher's shop in overwhelming detail, with tiny human figures

in the background almost blotted out by the food. A sign to the upper right also advertises a farm for sale, so the power of the market economy is reflected in the imagery.

The still-life imagery so dominates the picture that it seems independent of the religious subject in the background. But in the distance to the left we see Mary and Jesus on the Flight into Egypt giving bread to the poor, who are ignored by the worshipers lined up for church. To the right is a tavern scene where the excesses of the senses are for sale. (Oysters were recognized as an aphrodisiac.) The eye meanders over the objects on display: some of them items of gluttony; some, like the pretzels, eaten during Lent. Some of the products may be read as Christian symbols, such as the two pairs of crossed fish signifying the Crucifixion. The two background scenes suggest different choices a viewer could make: a life of dissipation or a life of almsgiving. The foreground with its emphasis on items for sale may implicate Antwerp's principal economic activity in these choices.

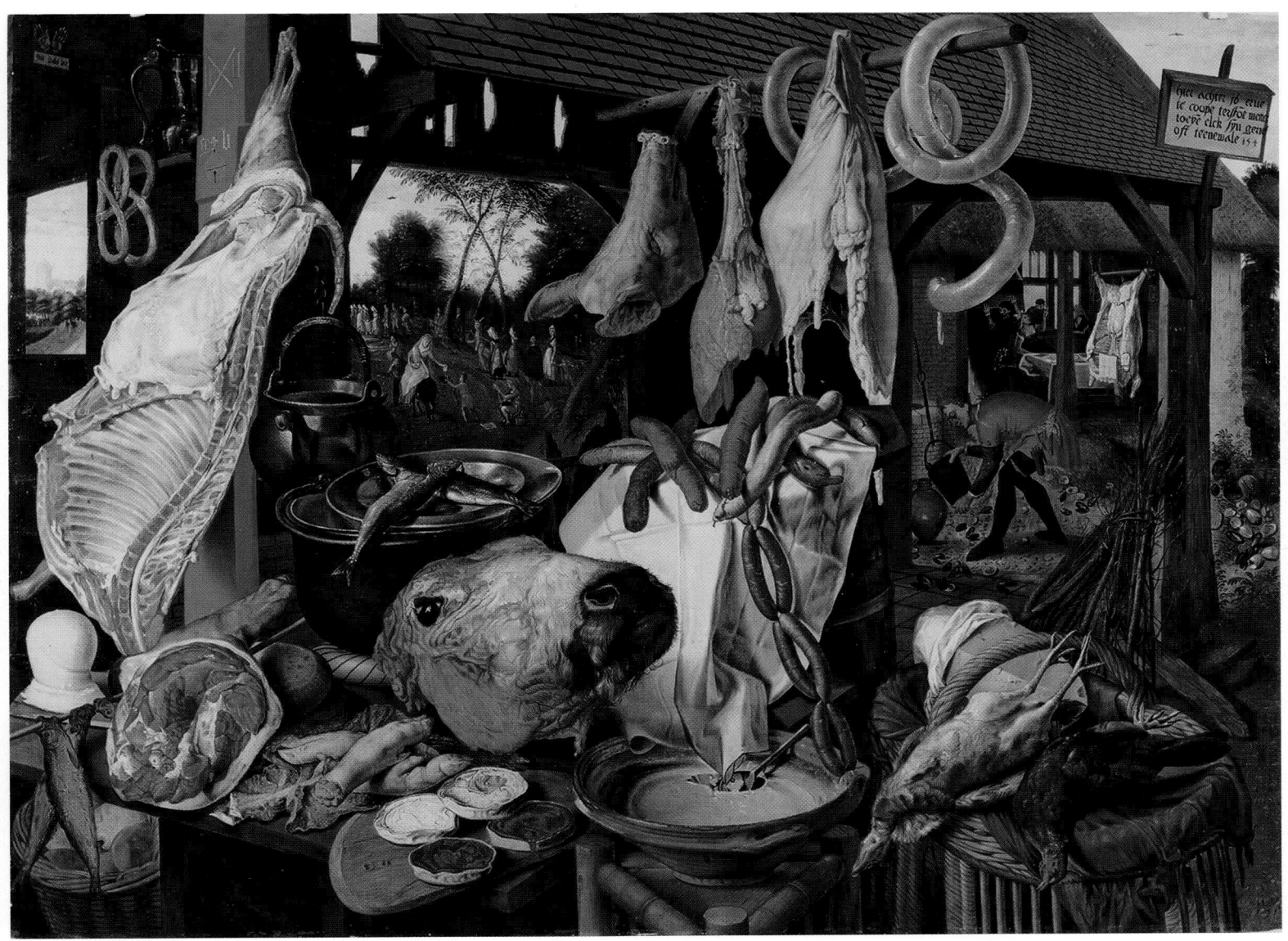

18.31 Pieter Aertsen, *The Meat Stall.* 1551. Oil on panel, 48½ × 59" (123.3 × 150 cm). University Art Collections, Uppsala University, Sweden

PIETER BRUEGEL THE ELDER Aertsen's younger contemporary and fellow Antwerp resident, Pieter Bruegel the Elder (1525/30–1569) used this same device of **inverted perspective**—putting the apparent subject of the picture in the background of many of his images. He explored landscape, peasant life, and moral allegory in his paintings. Although Bruegel spent his career in Antwerp and Brussels, he may have been born near 's-Hertogenbosch, the home of Hieronymus Bosch. Certainly Bosch's paintings impressed him deeply, and his work is similarly ambiguous in its messages. Bruegel's contemporaries admired his wit and his ability to mimic nature, though solid personal information about Bruegel is scarce.

Working as a painter and a designer of prints, he made pictures that demonstrate his interest in folk customs and the daily life of humble people. Bruegel himself was highly educated and the friend of humanists, who, with wealthy merchants, were his main clients: Urban elites collected images of the country and the people who worked the land. He also made images that many scholars have seen as offering a political commentary on the Habsburg rule over the Southern Netherlands. Members of the Habsburg court also collected his work, but during the turbulent climate of the 1560s when Philip II of Spain attempted to quash the Protestant rebellion in the Netherlands, Bruegel became fearful that his politically barbed imagery might cause trouble for his family. (See *Primary Source*, page 656.)

Like his contemporaries who followed Dürer's example, Bruegel traveled to Italy in 1552–53, visiting Rome, Naples, and Sicily. The famous monuments admired and sketched by other northern European artists, however, seem not to have interested him. He returned instead with a sheaf of magnificent landscape drawings, especially Alpine views. Out of this experience came the sweeping landscapes of Bruegel's mature style. *The Return of*

Karel van Mander Writes About Pieter Bruegel the Elder

From *The Painter's Treatise (Het Schilder Boeck)*, 1604

Van Mander's biography of Pieter Bruegel the Elder remains an important source of information about the artist, whose talent he appreciated fully.

On his journeys Bruegel did many views from nature so that it was said of him, when he traveled through the Alps, that he had swallowed all the mountains and rocks and spat them out again, after his return, on to his canvases and panels, so closely was he able to follow nature here and in her other works. ...

He did a great deal of work [in Antwerp] for a merchant, Hans Franckert, a noble and upright man, who found pleasure in Bruegel's company and met him every day. With this Franckert, Bruegel often went out into the country to see peasants at their fairs and weddings. Disguised as peasants they brought gifts like the other guests, claiming relationship or kinship with the bride or groom. Here Bruegel delighted in observing the droll behavior of the peasants, how they ate, drank, danced, capered, or made love, all of which he was well able to reproduce cleverly and pleasantly. ... He represented the peasants—men and women of the Campine and elsewhere—naturally, as they really were, betraying their boorishness in the way they walked, danced, stood still, or moved.

... An art lover in Amsterdam, Sieur Herman Pilgrims, owns a *Peasant Wedding* painted in oils, which is most beautiful. The peasants' faces and the limbs, where they are bare are yellow and brown, sunburnt; their skins are ugly, different from those of town dwellers. ...

... Many of his compositions of comical subjects, strange and full of meaning, can be seen engraved; but he made many more works of this kind in careful and beautifully finished drawings to which he had added inscriptions. But as some of them were too biting and sharp, he had them burnt by his wife when he was on his deathbed, from remorse or fear that she might get into trouble and have to answer for them.

Source: Karel van Mander, *Dutch and Flemish Painters*, tr. Constant van de Wall (Manchester, NH: Ayer Company Publishers, 1978)

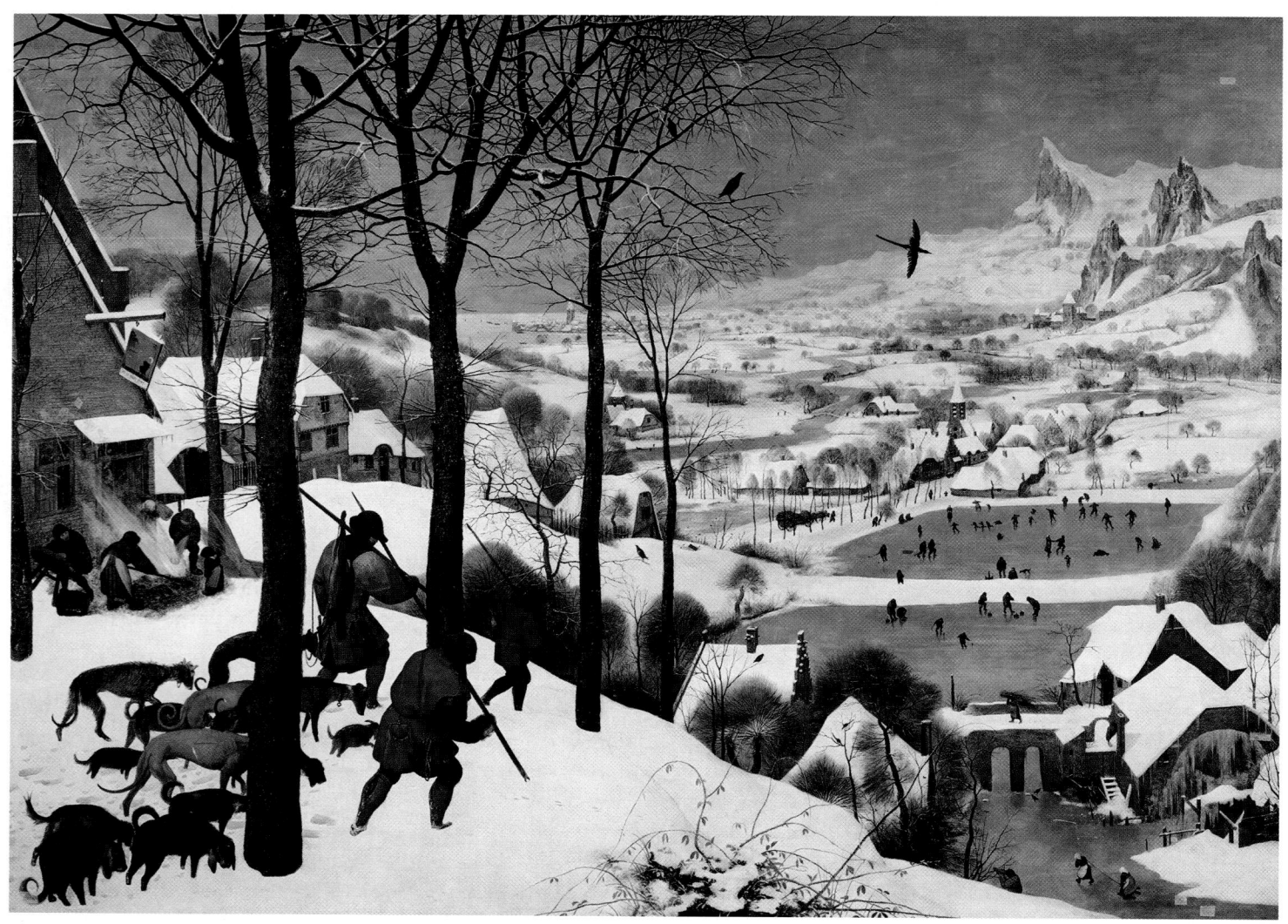

18.32 Pieter Bruegel the Elder, *The Return of the Hunters*. 1565. Oil on panel, 46½ × 63¾" (117 × 162 cm). Kunsthistorisches Museum, Vienna

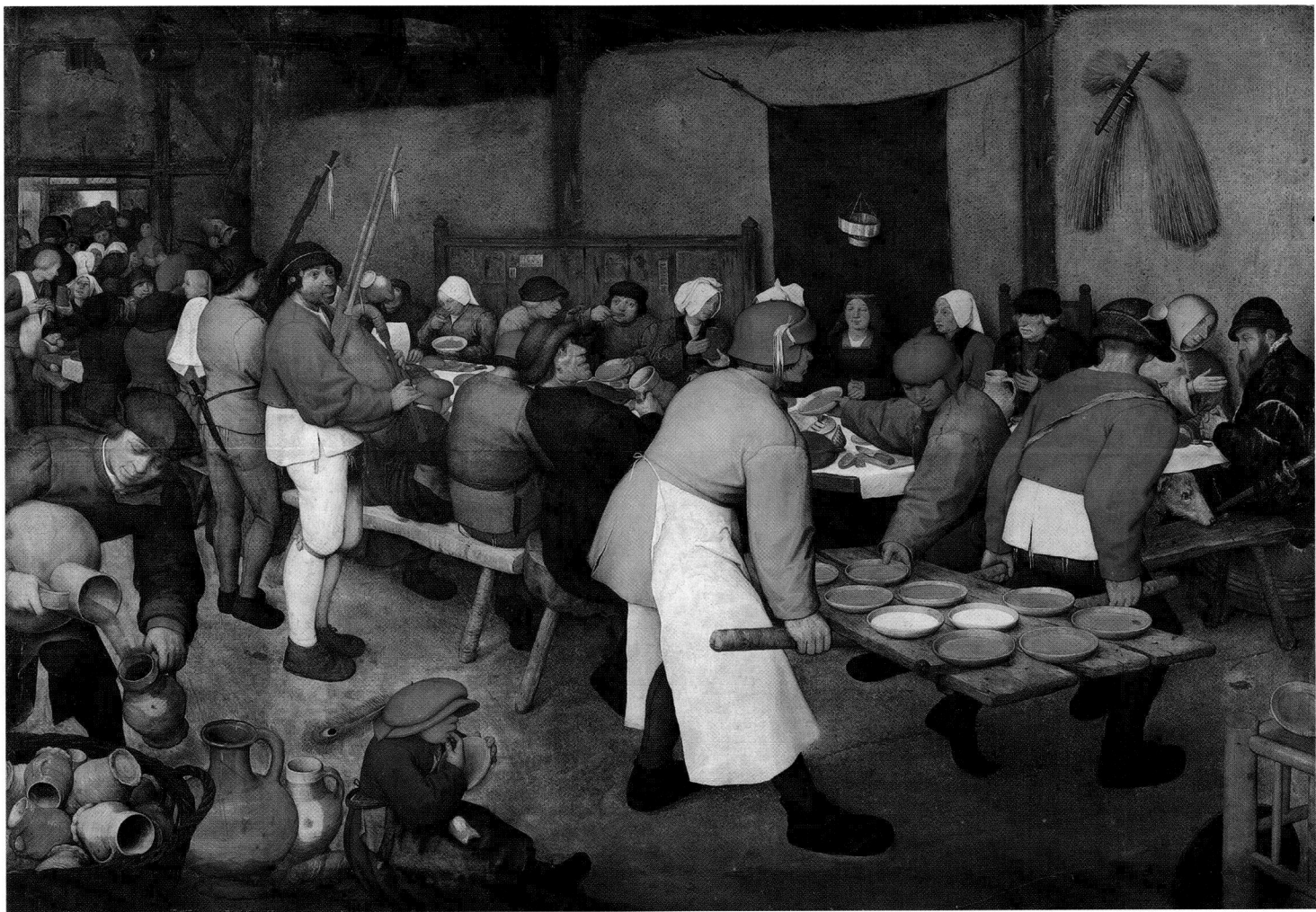

18.33 Pieter Bruegel the Elder, *Peasant Wedding*. ca. 1568. Oil on panel, 44⅞ × 64" (114 × 162.5 cm). Kunsthistorisches Museum, Vienna

the Hunters (fig. **18.32**) is one of a set of paintings depicting the months. (He often composed in series; those in this group were owned in 1565, a year after they were painted, by Niclaes Jonghelink, an Antwerp merchant.) Such scenes had their origin in medieval calendar illustrations, such as those in the *Très Riches Heures du Duc de Berry* (see fig. 14.4). In Bruegel's work, however, nature is more than a setting for human activities. It is the main subject of the picture.

Like Patinir, in *The Return of the Hunters* Bruegel provides a shelf of space in the foreground that moves precipitously into the distance toward a far horizon. In the snow-covered landscape, human and canine members of a hunting party return to their village with their skimpy catch in the gray of a northern winter. They move down a hill toward a village, where the water has frozen and become a place of recreation and where people rush to get back indoors. Human activity is fully integrated into the natural landscape in Bruegel's image.

The *Peasant Wedding* (fig. **18.33**), dated around 1568, is one of Bruegel's most memorable scenes of peasant life. His biographer, Karel van Mander, reported that Bruegel and his patron Hans

Franckert often disguised themselves as peasants and joined in their revelries so Bruegel could observe and sketch them. (See *Primary Source*, page 656.) In this painting Bruegel depicts a gathering of rustic people in a barn that has been decorated for a wedding. He has totally mastered Italian perspective, so the viewer enters a capacious room dominated by the table at which the wedding guests are gathered. The bride sits before a green curtain to distinguish her, though it is more difficult to identify the groom. Food is being distributed in the foreground, while the many empty jugs in the lower left suggest that much liquid has already been consumed. A far cry from the varieties of meats and fish depicted in Aertsen's *The Meat Stall*, the only food here is simple porridge. Bagpipers stand ready to play, but the noise level already seems high with so many figures talking amid the clattering of pottery. Bruegel's technique is as precise and detailed as that of many of his Flemish predecessors, and his figures have a weight and solidity that adds to the impression of reality.

Bruegel's images of peasants have presented challenges to art historians. Some scholars have seen Bruegel's peasant pictures as brutal caricatures of rural folk for the consumption of town

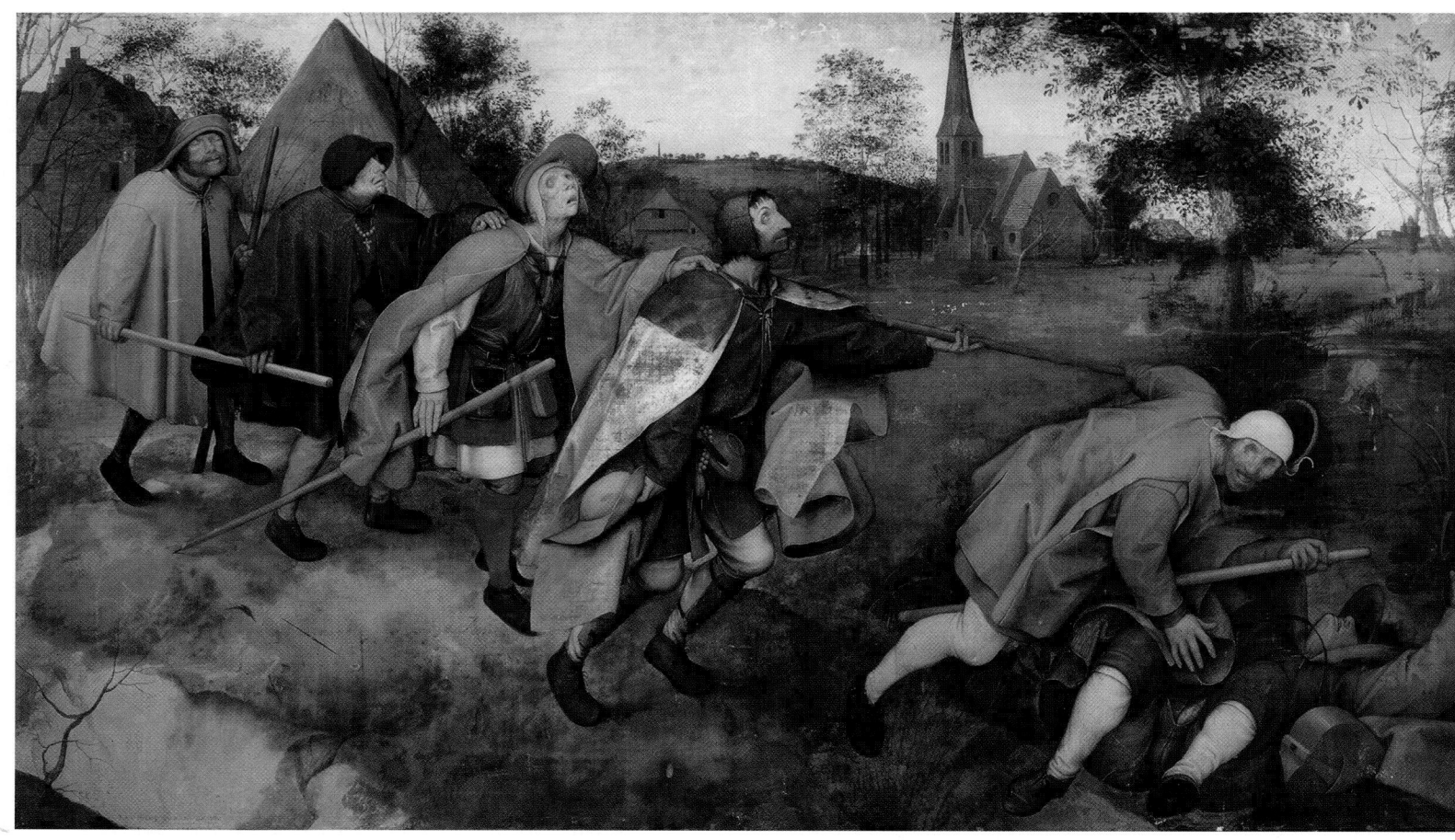

18.34 Pieter Bruegel the Elder, *The Blind Leading the Blind*. ca. 1568. Oil on panel, 34½ × 60⅝" (85 × 154 cm). Museo e Gallerie di Capodimonte, Naples

dwellers; by this reading, urbane townsfolk could use them to chuckle at the foibles of their country cousins. Still, Bruegel treats this country wedding as a serious event, and if he records the peasants' rough manners, he also records their fellowship. He treats the least of the least, like the child licking a bowl in the foreground, as worthy of observation and remembrance. For Bruegel, the common man occupies an important place in the scheme of things.

Many of Bruegel's pictures offer ambivalent lessons, some of them based on the proverbial wisdom that permeates Netherlandish literature. One of his last pictures, *The Blind Leading the Blind* (fig. **18.34**), presents just such a visual interpretation of verbal wisdom. Its source is the Gospels (Matthew 15:12–19). Jesus, speaking of the Pharisees, says, "And if the blind lead the blind, both shall fall into the ditch." This parable recurs in humanistic as well as popular literature, and it appears in at least one earlier work by Bruegel. However, the tragic depth of Bruegel's image gives urgency to the theme. He uses the detailed rendering of the Netherlandish tradition to record the infirmities

and the poverty of the blind beggars who march across this village landscape. The pose of each figure as a viewer's eye proceeds along the downward diagonal is less stable than the last one, leaving little doubt that everyone will end up in the ditch with the leader. Above the gap between the two groups, Bruegel places a village church, suggesting to some critics that the blindness is linked to the ecclesiastical establishment. But other readings are possible. For example, the church could be seen as the antidote to the men's spiritual blindness. Perhaps Bruegel found the meaning of the parable especially appropriate to his time, which was marked by religious and political fanaticism. The ambiguity of Bruegel's pictures has inspired critics and artists for centuries.

Bruegel's images offer criticism of the events of his day in a style derived from the Netherlandish past. In his time, traditional certainties about the world and man's place in it gave way to new faiths, new ideas, new political and social orders, and an expanding globe. These changes would have an important impact on subsequent centuries.

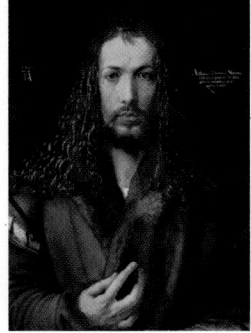

1500 Albrecht Dürer,
Self-Portrait

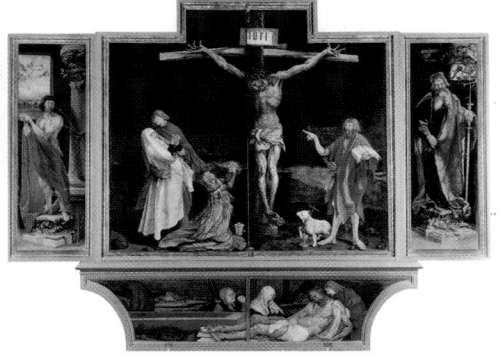

1515 Grünewald's *Isenheim
Altarpiece* completed

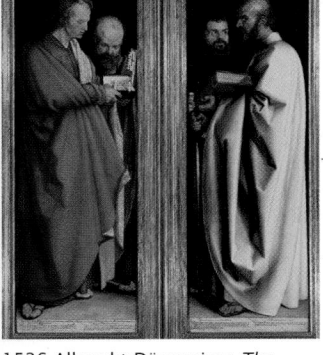

1526 Albrecht Dürer gives *The
Four Apostles* to the City of
Nuremberg

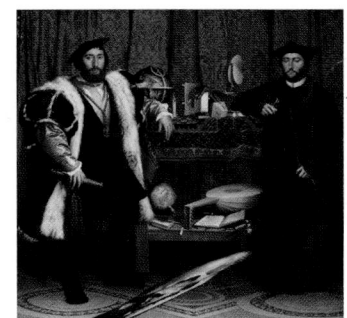

1533 Holbein's *Jean de Dinteville
and Georges de Selve* ("The
Ambassadors")

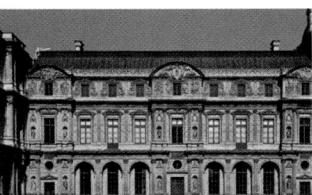

1546 Pierre Lescot, Square Court
of Louvre

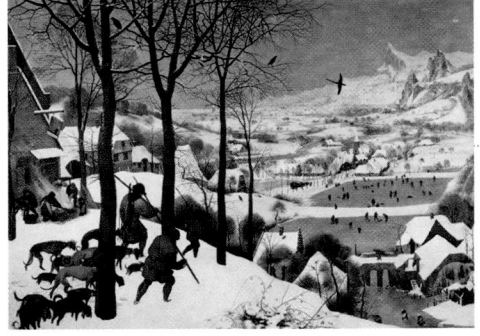

1565 Pieter Bruegel the Elder's *The Return
of the Hunters*

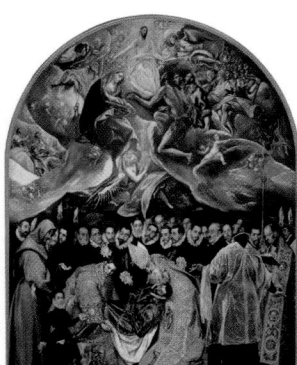

1586 El Greco, *The Burial of
Count Orgaz*

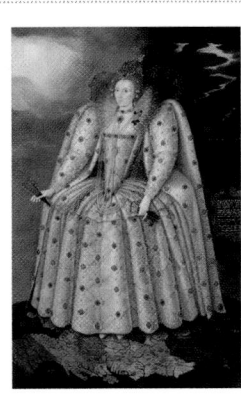

ca. 1592 *The Ditcheley
Portrait* of Elizabeth I

Renaissance and Reformation in Sixteenth-Century Northern Europe

1500

ca. 1503 Leonardo da Vinci, *Mona Lisa*

1506 Bramante's plan for new St. Peter's at the
Vatican

1510

1520

◀ 1521 Luther condemned by Catholic Church at
Diet of Worms

◀ 1525 Peasants' War ignited by Reformation
◀ 1527 Sack of Rome by German forces

1530

◀ 1534 England breaks with Roman Church
◀ 1536 John Calvin publishes the *Institutes of the
Christian Religion*

1540

ca. 1540 Cellini's saltcellar for Francis I

1550

◀ 1556 Charles V abdicates in favor of Philip II of
Spain

1560

◀ 1558 Elizabeth I accedes to English throne
◀ 1562 Wars of Religion in France
◀ 1564 Birth of William Shakespeare

1570

◀ 1573 Veronese defends his work before the
Inquisition

1580

◀ 1579 Establishment of the Dutch Republic

1583 Giovanni Bologna, *Rape of the Sabine
Woman*

◀ 1588 Philip II of Spain sends the Armada against
England

1590

1600

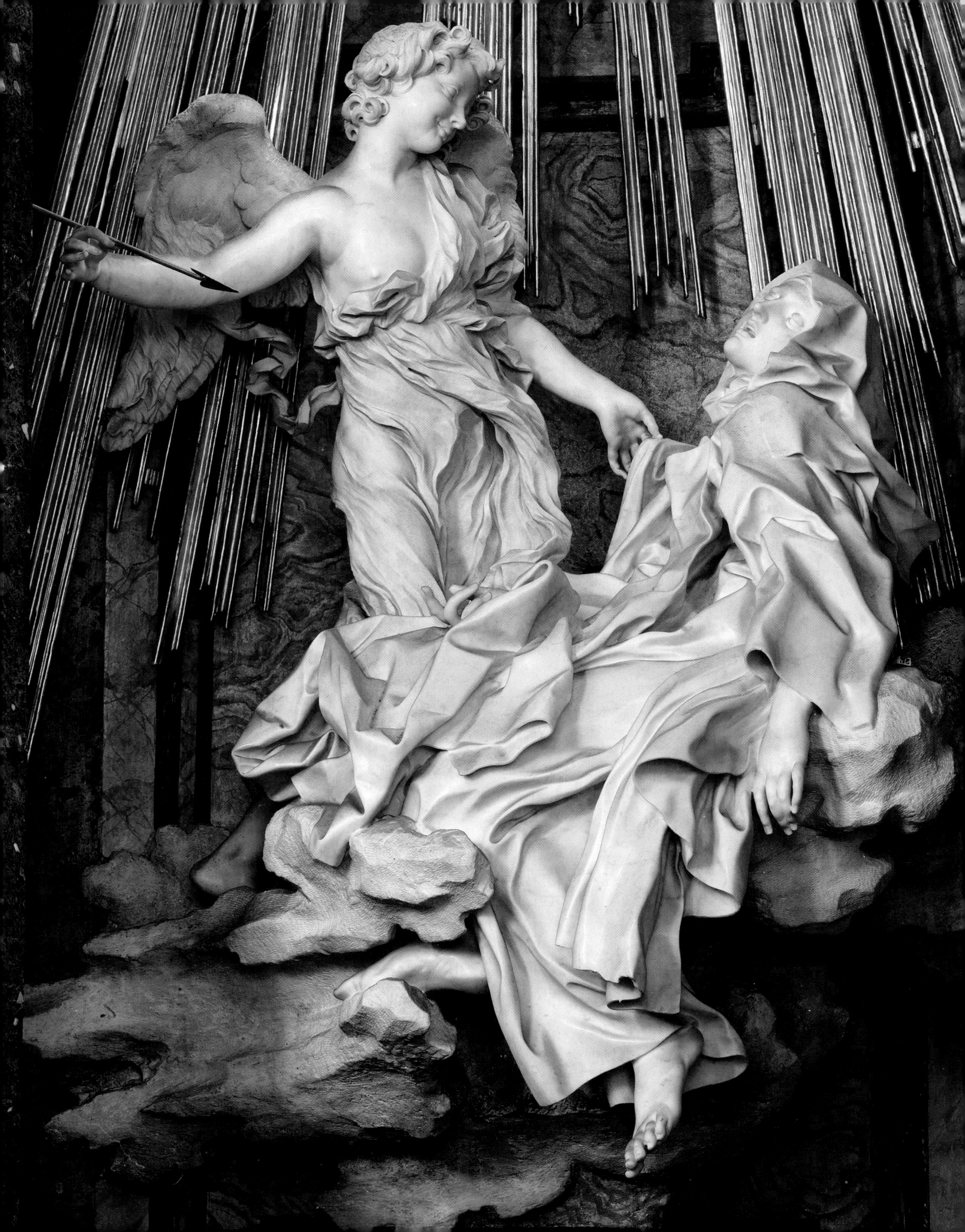

CHAPTER 19

The Baroque
in Italy and Spain

BAROQUE ART IS THE EXUBERANT, EXPRESSIVE STYLE MOST CLOSELY associated with the seventeenth century. The term itself may come from the Portuguese word *barroco*, referring to an irregular pearl; it means contorted, even grotesque, and was intended as a disparaging description of the grand, turbulent, dynamic, overwhelming style of seventeenth-century art. Art

historians remain divided over its application. Should the term Baroque only be used for the dominant style of the seventeenth century, or should it include other tendencies, such as classicism, to which it bears a complex relationship? Should the time frame also include the period 1700 to 1750, known as the **Rococo**? More important, is the Baroque distinct from both the Renaissance and the modern eras? Although a good case can be made for viewing the Baroque as the final phase of the Renaissance, we shall treat it as a distinct era. It is the beginning of the early modern period, as so many of the concerns that characterize the latter era—issues of gender, class, and sexuality—are first explored in it. The desire to evoke emotional states by appealing to the senses and to persuade, often in dramatic ways, underlies Baroque art. Some of the qualities that characterize the Baroque are grandeur, sensual richness, emotional exuberance, tension, movement, and the successful unification of the various arts.

The expansive, expressive quality of the Baroque paralleled the true expansion of European influence—geographical, political and religious—throughout the seventeenth century. The exploration of the New World that began in the sixteenth century, mobilized primarily by Spain, Portugal, and England (map **19.1**), developed in the seventeenth century into colonization, first of

the eastern coasts of North and South America, and then of Polynesia and Asia. The Dutch East India Company developed trade with the East and was headquartered in Indonesia. Jesuit missionaries traveled to Japan, China, and India, and settled in areas of North and South America. In style and spirit, the reach of the Baroque was global.

The Baroque has been called a style of persuasion, as the Catholic Church attempted to use art to speak to the faithful and to express the spirit of the Counter-Reformation. In the sixteenth century, the Church tried to halt the spread of Protestantism in Europe; by the seventeenth century, it had declared this effort a success and was celebrating its triumph. Private influential families, some of whom would later claim a pope as a member, other private patrons, and ecclesiastical orders (Jesuits, Theatines, Carmelites, and Oratorians), each built new and often large churches in Rome in the seventeenth century. And the largest building program of the Renaissance—the rebuilding of St. Peter's—would finally come to an end, its elaborate decoration profoundly reflecting the new glory of the Roman Church.

This reinvigoration of the Catholic Church began a wave of canonizations that lasted through the mid-eighteenth century. The religious heroes of the Counter-Reformation—Ignatius of Loyola, Francis Xavier (both Jesuits), Teresa of Ávila, and Filippo Neri—were named saints. (Carlo Borromeo had already been made one in 1610.) In contrast to the piety and good deeds of these reformers, the new princes of the Church were vigorous

Detail of figure 19.31, Gianlorenzo Bernini, *The Ecstasy of St. Teresa*

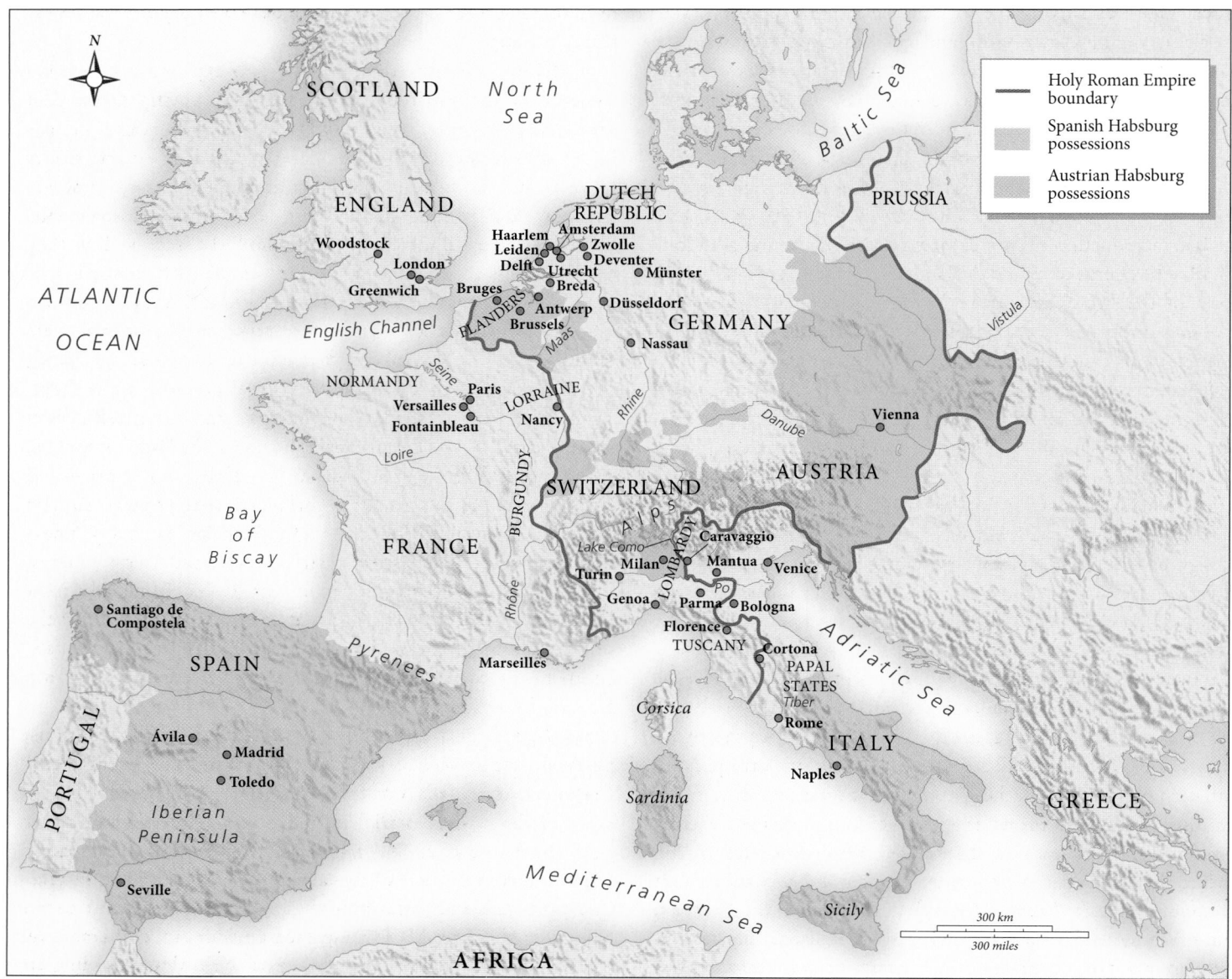

Map 19.1   Western Europe ca. 1648

patrons of the arts, both seeking glory for the Church and posthumous fame for their own families.

During the first half of the seventeenth century, Europe was torn by almost continuous warfare, which involved almost every European nation in a complex web of shifting alliances. The Thirty Years' War (1618–1648) was fueled by the ambitions of the kings of France, who sought to dominate Europe, and the Habsburgs, who ruled not only Austria and Spain but also the Southern Netherlands, Bohemia, and Hungary. Although fought largely in Germany, the war eventually engulfed nearly all of Europe. After the Treaty of Westphalia in 1648 ended the war and formally granted their freedom, the United Provinces—or the Dutch Republic as the independent Netherlands were now known—entered into a series of battles with England and France that lasted until 1679. Yet, other than in Germany, which was fragmented into over 300 little states, many in financial ruin, there

is little correlation between these rivalries and the art of the period. In fact, the seventeenth century has been called the Golden Age of Painting in France, Spain, and both the Dutch Republic and the Southern Netherlands.

The Baroque has also been identified as "the style of absolutism," reflecting the centralized state ruled by an autocrat of unlimited powers. In the latter half of the seventeenth century, Baroque palaces were built on an increasingly monumental scale to display the power and grandeur of their owners. Architecture emphasized massiveness, dramatic spaces and lighting, rich interior decoration from floor to ceiling, and luxurious materials; and it was meant as a reflection of political and economic power. Absolutism reached its climax during the reign of the French king Louis XIV in the late seventeenth century, and is seen in his palace at Versailles, with its grandiose combination of architecture, painting, decoration, and extensive gardens. But we can also associate absolutism with the Vatican, the power of the pope and his claim of authority won and reestablished through the Counter-Reformation. The power of absolutism suggests a style that will overwhelm and inspire awe in the spectator. The new style was not specifically Italian, even though it was born in Rome during the final years of the sixteenth century. Nor was it confined to religious art. Baroque elements of dramatic lighting and sweeping gestures entered the vocabulary of northern European art. The introduction of new subject matter was a vital addition. Still life, the genre scene, and the landscape quickly entered the art world of the Protestant north through etchings and paintings. Still-life paintings and landscapes were informed by the scientific observation of nature.

A recognition of the subtle relationship between Baroque art and science is essential to an understanding of the age. The complex metaphysics of the humanists, which gave everything religious meaning, was replaced by a new physics. The change began with Nicolaus Copernicus, Johannes Kepler, and Galileo Galilei, and culminated in René Descartes and Isaac Newton. Their cosmology brought scientific understanding to sensory perception. By placing the sun, not the earth (and humanity), at the center of the universe, it contradicted what our eyes (and common sense) tell us: that the sun revolves around the earth. Not only was the seventeenth century's worldview fundamentally different from the Renaissance's, but its understanding of visual reality was forever changed by the new science, thanks to advances in optical physics and physiology. These scientists knew or corresponded with each other and with the artists of their time, and their views and discoveries were known to the larger intellectual and artistic community. Newton's mathematics were known to Sir Christopher Wren and were possibly used in his rebuilding both of London and St. Paul's cathedral (see Chapter 21). Vermeer, who experimented with optical effects (see Chapter 20), would have known the developer of the microscope, Antonie van Leeuwenhoek, and the philosopher and scientist Descartes had his portrait painted by Frans Hals. Descartes postponed the publication of his own controversial work *The World* until after his death, as he had learned of Galileo's imprisonment and was also concerned for his own eternal soul, for he, too, was a Catholic and feared excommunication. Galileo's scientific and religious adversaries, the Jesuits, considered his views to be the antithesis of the Church's teachings; also opposing Galileo was Pope Urban VIII (Barberini), the same pope who envisioned a new Rome, and who was the most significant patron of Bernini. Seventeenth-century ceiling paintings, filled with astronomical and astrological figures so prominent in the Baroque, were executed to convey the all-encompassing power of the patron, who by implication controlled the very heavens above.

The rise of science also had the effect of displacing natural magic, a precursor of modern science that included both astrology and alchemy. Unlike the new science, natural magic tried to control the world through prediction and manipulation; it did so by uncovering nature's "secrets" instead of its physical laws. Yet, because it was linked to religion and morality, natural magic

lived on in popular literature and folklore well beyond the seventeenth century.

Folklore, literature, and contemporary theater became subjects for the visual arts in the Baroque, usually depicted in genre scenes—scenes from everyday life—which became popular in the seventeenth century. These genre paintings include scenes of men and women in domestic situations, eating, drinking, smoking, and playing board games and musical instruments. Sometimes they illustrate proverbs and the senses. But they should not be confused with "reality" as they are artistic inventions. The paintings are often moralizing; that is, they often warn against the very things they are depicting! Such paintings were already being executed in the sixteenth century (see fig. 18.34), but in the seventeenth century they develop into a major force, along with landscape and still-life painting, in nearly every European country—in Italy, Spain, Flanders, the Dutch Republic, and France. Paintings of foodstuffs—plain and exotic—and landscapes of rural, urban, or far-off places were popular. Turkish carpets, African elephants and lions, Brazilian parrots, Chinese Ming vases, and peoples from Africa, India, and South America can be found in seventeenth-century art. If this sounds like a list of "exotica"—that is because the exotic was a major part of the seventeenth-century experience, as people, many of them artists, began to travel to faraway places. Paintings provide us with a gateway into the Baroque world.

In the end, Baroque art was not simply the result of religious, political, intellectual, or social developments: The strengthened Catholic faith, the absolutist state, the new science, and the beginnings of the modern world combined in a volatile mixture that gave the Baroque era its fascinating variety. What ultimately unites this complex era is a reevaluation of humanity and its relation to the universe. Philosophers gave greater prominence to the human passions, which encompassed a wider range of emotions and social levels than before. The scientific revolution leading up to Newton's unified mechanics in physics responded to this same new view of humanity, which presumes a more active role for people through their ability to understand and affect the world around them. Remarkably, the early modern period remained an age of great religious faith, however divided people may have been in their loyalties. The interplay of passions, intellect, and spirituality may be seen as forming a dialogue that has never been truly resolved.

PAINTING IN ITALY

Around 1600, Rome became the fountainhead of the Baroque, as it had of the High Renaissance a century before, by attracting artists from other regions. The papacy and many of the new Church orders (Jesuits, Theatines, and Oratorians), as well as numerous private patrons from wealthy and influential families (Farnese, Barberini, and Pamphili), commissioned art on a large scale, with the aim of promoting themselves and making Rome the most beautiful city in the Christian world "for the greater glory of God and the Church." This campaign had begun as early as 1585 (indeed, we may even date this revitalization to the reign of Julius II); by the opening of the seventeenth century, Rome had attracted hosts of ambitious young artists, especially from northern Italy. It was they who created the new style.

Caravaggio and the New Style

Foremost among the young artists was the revolutionary painter Michelangelo Merisi (1571–1610), called Caravaggio after his family's hometown near Milan. After his training, begun at age 13, under a minor Milanese painter, he came to Rome in 1592 or 1593 and worked as an assistant to various artists before setting out on his own. His style of painting, his new subjects, his use of lighting, and his concept of naturalism were to change the world of painting.

According to contemporary accounts, Caravaggio painted directly on the canvas, and he worked from live models. He depicted the world he knew, so that his canvases are filled with ordinary people. They are not idealized as High Renaissance figures, nor given classical bodies, clean clothes, and perfect features. But neither are they distorted, elongated, or overtly elegant as in Mannerism. This was an entirely new

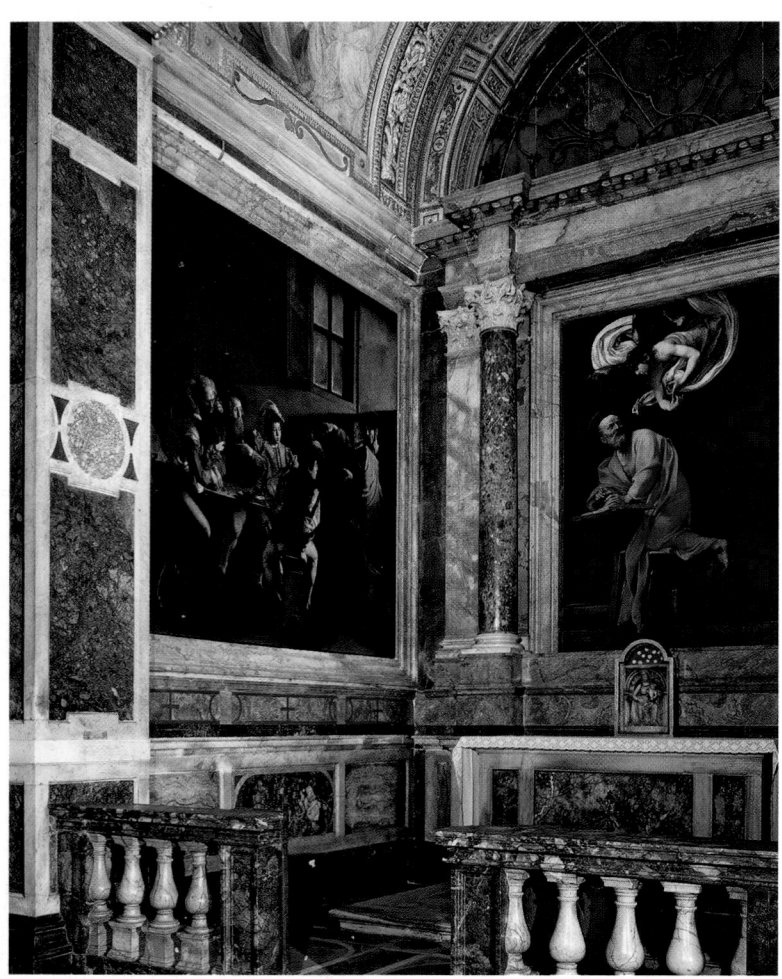

19.1   Contarelli Chapel, San Luigi dei Francesi, Rome

conception that was raw, immediate, and palpable. Caravaggio's style initiated the Baroque and caused a stir in the art world. (See www.myartslab.com.) He had numerous followers and imitators, and critics, both Italian and northern European, wrote of his work, so Caravaggio and his paintings became internationally known almost immediately.

Caravaggio's first important public commission was a series of three monumental canvases devoted to St. Matthew that he painted for the Contarelli Chapel in the church of San Luigi dei Francesi between 1599 and 1602 (fig. 19.1). This church for the French ("dei Francesi") in Rome, founded in 1518 by Cardinal Giulio de' Medici (later Pope Clement VII) and designed by Giacomo della Porta, was finished in 1589. The Chapel of St. Louis (Luigi) was endowed by the French cardinal Mathieu Contrel (Contarelli) in 1565, but the decoration was not completed at the time. More than 30 years later, Caravaggio received the commission to finish the work through the intervention of his patron, Cardinal del Monte.

As decorations, the three Contarelli paintings perform the same function that fresco cycles had in the Renaissance—each complements the others to fill out the narrative. In the chapel view, we see *St. Matthew and the Angel*, in which the tax collector Matthew turns dramatically for inspiration to the angel who dictates the gospel. The main image on the left in the chapel is *The Calling of St. Matthew* (fig. 19.2) which depicts the moment Matthew is chosen by Christ. The third canvas (on the right, but not seen here) is devoted to the saint's martyrdom.

The Calling of St. Matthew displays a naturalism that is both new and radical. Naturalism was not an end in itself for Caravaggio, but a means of conveying profoundly spiritual content. Never before have we seen a sacred subject depicted so entirely in terms of contemporary lowlife. Matthew, the well-dressed tax collector, sits with some armed men, who must be his agents, in a common, sparse room. The setting and costumes must have been very familiar to Caravaggio. Two figures approach from the right. The arrival's bare feet and simple biblical garb contrast strongly with the colorful costumes of Matthew and his companions.

Why do we sense a religious quality in this scene and not mistake it for an everyday event? What identifies one of the figures on the right as Christ, who has come to Matthew and says "Follow me"? It is surely not his halo, the only supernatural feature in the picture, which is a thin gold band that we might easily overlook. Our eyes fasten instead on his commanding gesture, borrowed from Michelangelo's Adam in *The Creation of Adam* (see fig. 16.21), which bridges the gap between the two groups of people and is echoed by Matthew, who points questioningly at himself.

The men on our left at the table seem not to be engaged in the unfolding drama, as they concentrate on the money being counted. In shadow, they are blind to the entrance of Christ—one even wears eyeglasses. Caravaggio uses the piercing light in this scene to announce Christ's presence, as Christ himself brought light: "I am the light of the world; he that followeth me shall not walk in darkness, but shall have the light of life" (John 8:12.)

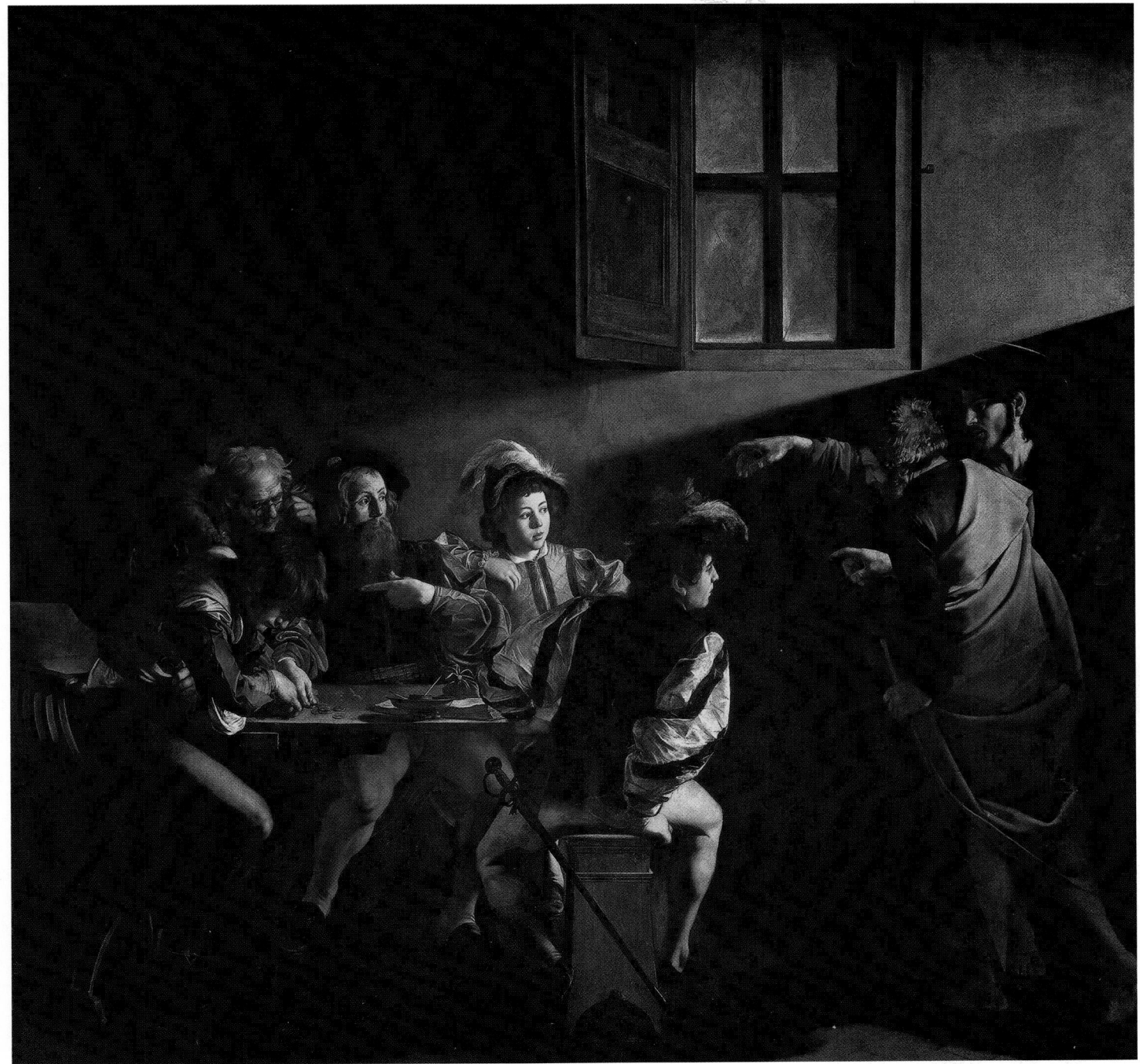

19.2 Caravaggio, *The Calling of St. Matthew*. ca. 1599–1600. Oil on canvas, 11'1" × 11'5" (3.4 × 3.5 m). Contarelli Chapel, San Luigi dei Francesi, Rome

The beam of sunlight in the darkness above Jesus is most decisive in determining the work's meaning and style. This strong beam of light against the dark background is known as a tenebristic effect, or **tenebrism**, a style that uses strong contrasts of light and dark. Caravaggio illuminates Christ's face and hand in the gloomy interior so that we see the precise *moment* of his calling to Matthew and witness a critical piece of religious history and personal conversion. Without this light, so natural yet so charged with meaning, the picture would lose its power to make us aware of the divine presence. Caravaggio gives direct expression to an attitude shared by certain saints of the Counter-Reformation: that the mysteries of faith are revealed not by speculation but through an inner experience that is open to all people.

Caravaggio's paintings have a quality of "lay Christianity" that spoke powerfully to both Catholics and Protestants. Without the painting's religious context, the men seated at the table might seem like figures in a genre scene. Indeed, Caravaggio's painting became a source for secular scenes: Fanciful costumes, with slashed sleeves and feathered berets, will appear in the works of Caravaggio's followers. Figures seen in half-length (showing only the upper half of their bodies) will also be a common element in other works by Caravaggio and his followers (see fig. 20.15).

This intense, vivid tenebrism, the cornerstone of Caravaggio's style, can be seen again in his *The Conversion of St. Paul* (fig. **19.3**). He employed it to heighten the drama and to suggest divine light at the same time. The painting is one of a pair (the other is *The Crucifixion of St. Peter*) in Santa Maria del Popolo in Rome, placed to the left and right of the rich, colorful altarpiece of *The Assumption of the Virgin* by Annibale Carracci, which Caravaggio would have seen before he executed his own work. In contrast to

that altarpiece, Caravaggio employs muted tones and a nearly black background. He uses neither color nor line (indeed, there are no known drawings by him) to better indicate the narrative. Rather, he uses light to focus, even shock a viewer. A fallen Saul (to become St. Paul at his conversion) lies on his back; we view him foreshortened, and helpless, as he is struck by the light of God. The light also reveals the flank and mane of his huge horse, which takes up most of the space. The intense raking light from an unseen source at the left is used to model forms and create textures. The figures are nearly too big for the space.

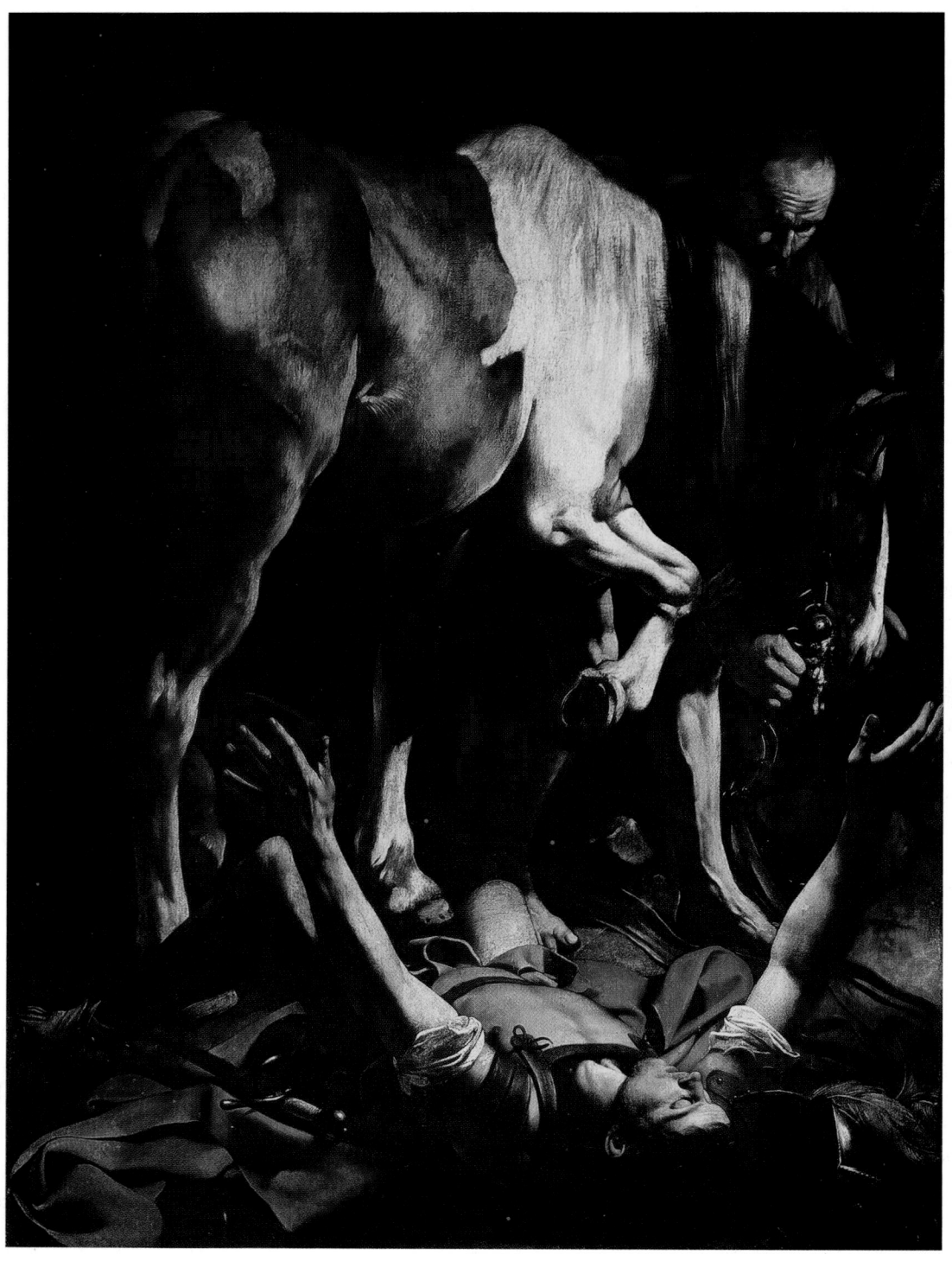

19.3 Caravaggio, *The Conversion of St. Paul.* ca. 1601. Oil on canvas, 7'6" × 5'7" (2.3 × 1.75 m). Cerasi Chapel, Santa Maria del Popolo, Rome

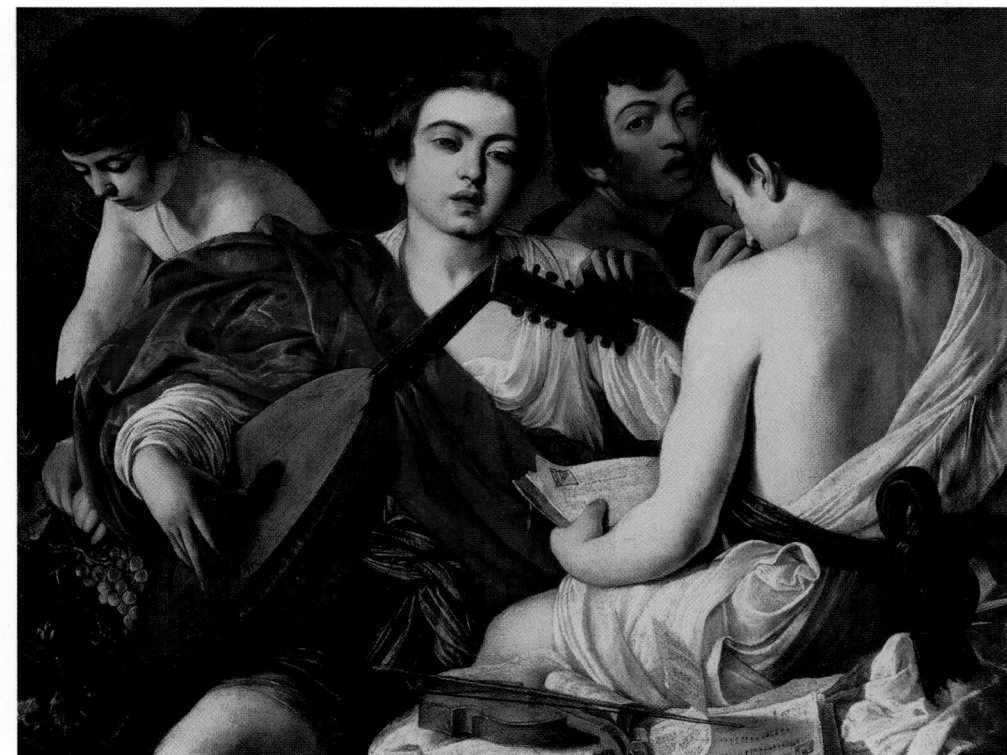

19.4 Caravaggio, *The Musicians*. ca. 1595. Oil on canvas, 36¼ × 46⅝" (92.1 × 118.4 cm). Metropolitan Museum of Art, New York. Rogers Fund, 1952. 52.81

They overwhelm us as we imagine them larger and only partly revealed by the light. The selective highlighting endows the life-size figures with a startling presence and theatricality typical of the Baroque.

Another aspect of Caravaggio's work is his focus on the sensual and erotic nature of both music and young men, who are depicted as seducing and soliciting. We see these elements in *The Musicians* (fig. **19.4**), with its four androgynous, seminude youths. Actually, it has been suggested that the painting shows two youths seen from two points of view. The musicians are half-length, but life-size; their blushed cheeks and full lips suggest erotic, sensual pleasures, enjoyed with each other and offered to a particular viewer. That viewer (the patron) was Cardinal del Monte, the influential, cultured patron and art collector, who arranged the *St. Matthew* commission for Caravaggio and who commissioned other homoerotic paintings from him. The lute, violin, horn (at back right), and the music sheets surrounding or being used by these half-draped men, and even the grapes being plucked at the left, suggest a contemporary bacchanal. The erotic undertones are part of the sensuality and passion that will be explored in the Baroque and frequently imitated in later works of art by other artists.

Highly argumentative, Caravaggio carried a sword and was often in trouble with the law for fighting. When he killed a friend in a duel over a game, Caravaggio fled Rome and spent the rest of his short life on the run. He first went to Naples, then Malta, then returned briefly to Naples. These trips account for both his work in these cities and his lasting influence there. He died traveling back to Rome, where he hoped to gain a pardon. In Italy, Caravaggio's work was praised by artists and connoisseurs—and

also criticized. Conservatives regarded Caravaggio and his work as lacking decorum: the propriety and reverence that religious subjects demanded. But many who did not like Caravaggio as a man were nevertheless influenced by his work and had to concede that his style was pervasive. The power of his style and imagery lasted into the 1630s, when it was absorbed into other Baroque tendencies.

Artemisia Gentileschi

Born in Rome, Artemisia Gentileschi (1593–ca. 1653) was the daughter of Caravaggio's friend, follower, and rival Orazio Gentileschi, and grew up in this artistic milieu. She became one of the major painters of her day and was the first woman to be admitted to the Accademia del Disegno in Florence. Nonetheless, it was difficult for a woman artist to make her way professionally. In a letter of 1649 (see *Primary Source*, page 669), she wrote that "people have cheated me" after she had submitted a drawing to a patron only to have him commission "another painter to do the painting using my work. If I were a man, I can't imagine it would have turned out this way." Her best-known subjects are biblical heroines: Bathsheba, the tragic object of King David's passion, and Judith, who saved her people by beheading Holofernes. Both themes (see fig. 20.25) were popular during the Baroque era, which delighted in erotic and violent scenes. Artemisia's frequent depictions of these women (she often portrayed herself in the lead role) suggest an ambivalence toward men that was rooted in her turbulent life. (Artemisia was raped by her teacher, Agostino Tassi [see fig. 19.10], who was tried and sentenced to banishment from Rome.)

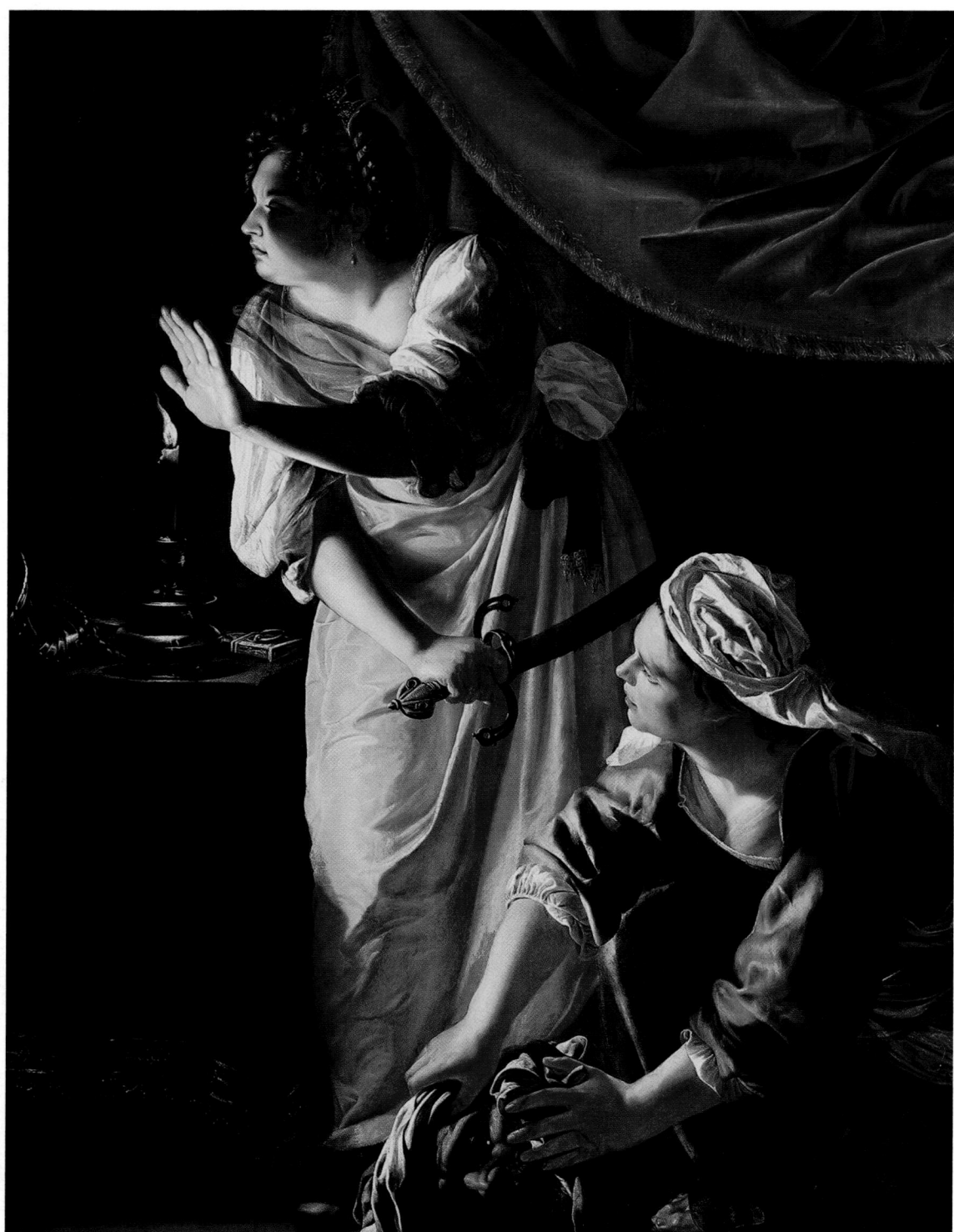

19.5 Artemisia Gentileschi, *Judith and Her Maidservant with the Head of Holofernes.* ca. 1625. Oil on Canvas, 6'½" × 4'7" (1.84 × 1.41 m). The Detroit Institute of Arts. Gift of Leslie H. Green. 52.253

Artemisia's *Judith and Her Maidservant with the Head of Holofernes* (fig. **19.5**) is a fully mature, independent, dramatic, and large work, no less powerful for its restraint. The theme is the apocryphal story of the Jewish widow Judith, who saved her people by traveling with her maid to the tent of the Assyrian general Holofernes (who was about to lead an attack on the Jews), got him drunk, and then cut off his head with his own sword. It yields parallels to the story of David and Goliath—might conquered by virtue and innocence. However, in the case of Judith slaying

Holofernes, the victor was not always seen positively, but with some suspicion since her triumph was one of deceit: Having entered his tent and offered him drink, Judith then killed her foe. The unspoken promise of sexual activity was never realized. Here, rather than the beheading itself, the artist shows the instant after. Momentarily distracted, Judith gestures theatrically as her servant stuffs Holofernes's head into a sack. The object of their attention remains hidden from view, heightening the air of suspense and intrigue. The hushed, candlelit atmosphere—tenebrism

Artemisia Gentileschi (1593–ca. 1653)

From a letter to Don Antonio Ruffo

Artemisia Gentileschi's letter of November 13, 1649 reveals the relationship of the painter to her patron and casts light on issues of originality, of price, and of working with models. Throughout, the letter discloses Artemisia's acute awareness and even contempt for those who treated her less fairly because she was a woman.

I have received a letter of October 26th, which I deeply appreciated, particularly noting how my master always concerns himself with favoring me, contrary to my merit. In it, you tell me about that gentleman who wishes to have some paintings by me, that he would like a Galatea and a Judgment of Paris, and that the Galatea should be different from the one that Your Most Illustrious Lordship owns. There was no need for you to urge me to do this, since by the grace of God and the Most Holy Virgin, they [clients] come to a woman with this kind of talent, that is, to vary the subjects in my painting; never has anyone found in my pictures any repetition of invention, not even of one hand.

As for the fact that this gentleman wishes to know the price before the work is done ... I do it most unwillingly ... I never quote a price for my works until they are done. However, since Your Most Illustrious Lordship wants me to do this, I will do what you command. Tell this gentleman that I want five hundred ducats for both; he can show them to the whole world and, should he find anyone who does not think the paintings are worth two hundred scudi more, I won't ask him to pay me the agreed price. I assure Your Most Illustrious Lordship that these are paintings with nude figures requiring very expensive female models, which is a big headache. When I find good ones they fleece me, and at other times, one must suffer [their] pettiness with the patience of Job.

As for my doing a drawing and sending it, I have made a solemn vow never to send my drawings because people have cheated me. In particular, just today I found ... that, having done a drawing of souls in Purgatory for the Bishop of St. Gata, he, in order to spend less, commissioned another painter to do the painting using my work. If I were a man, I can't imagine it would have turned out this way. ...

I must caution Your Most Illustrious Lordship that when I ask a price, I don't follow the custom in Naples, where they ask thirty and then give it for four. I am Roman, and therefore I shall act always in the Roman manner.

Source: *The Voices of Women Artists*, ed. Wendy Slatkin (Englewood Cliffs, NJ: Prentice Hall, 1993)

---

made intimate—creates a mood of mystery that conveys Judith's complex emotions with unsurpassed understanding. Gentileschi's rich palette, seen here, was to have a strong influence on painting in Naples, where she settled in 1630.

We know that, possibly for a few years (ca. 1638–40), Artemisia also worked in London where her father had been court painter to Charles I of England from 1626 to 1639. Indeed, several of her paintings were recorded in the king's inventory after his execution, and father and daughter may have worked together on a project in Greenwich. Among her most daring and creative works is *Self-Portrait as the Allegory of Painting* (fig. **19.6**), one of the most innovative self-portraits of the Baroque period.

Artemisia was able to do here what no male artist could: She depicted herself as the allegorical female figure of Painting, *La Pittura*. The dress and activity of the subject conforms to Cesare Ripa's description of *La Pittura* in his popular *Iconologia* (1593), a book of allegories and symbolic emblems for artists. There, the allegorical figure of Painting is described, in part, as a beautiful woman, with disheveled black hair, wearing a gold chain which hangs from her neck, and holding a brush in one hand and a **palette** in the other. Thus, the painting asserts Artemisia's unique role as a woman painter—representing not just herself, but all of Painting and reflecting the new, elevated status of artists.

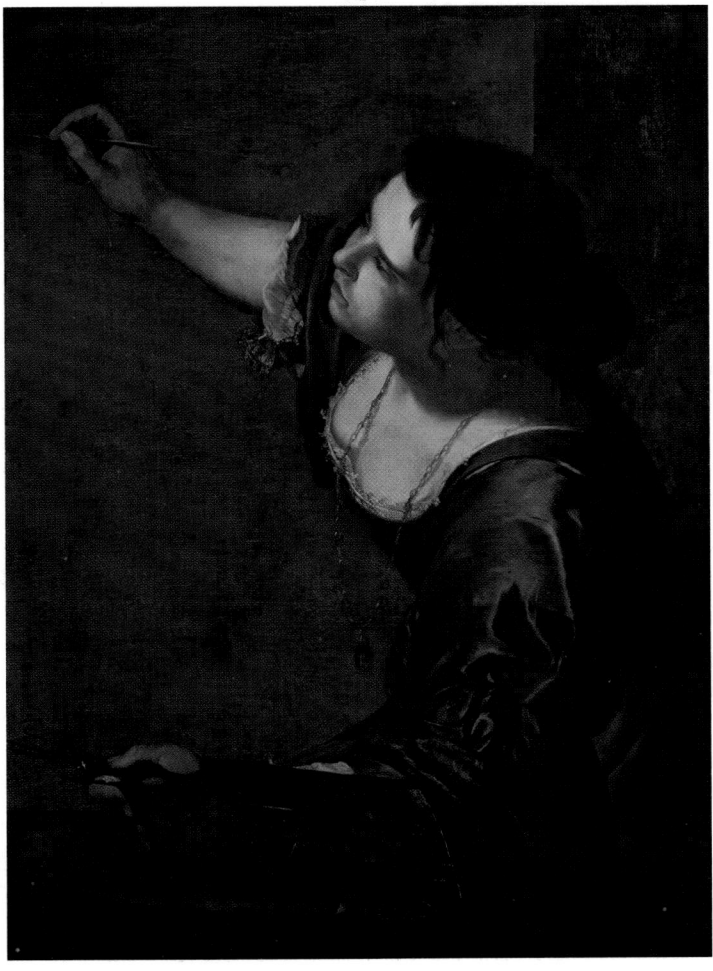

19.6 Artemisia Gentileschi, *Self-Portrait as the Allegory of Painting (La Pittura).* ca. 1638–39. Oil on canvas, 38⅞ × 29⅝" (98.6 × 75.2 cm). The Royal Collection

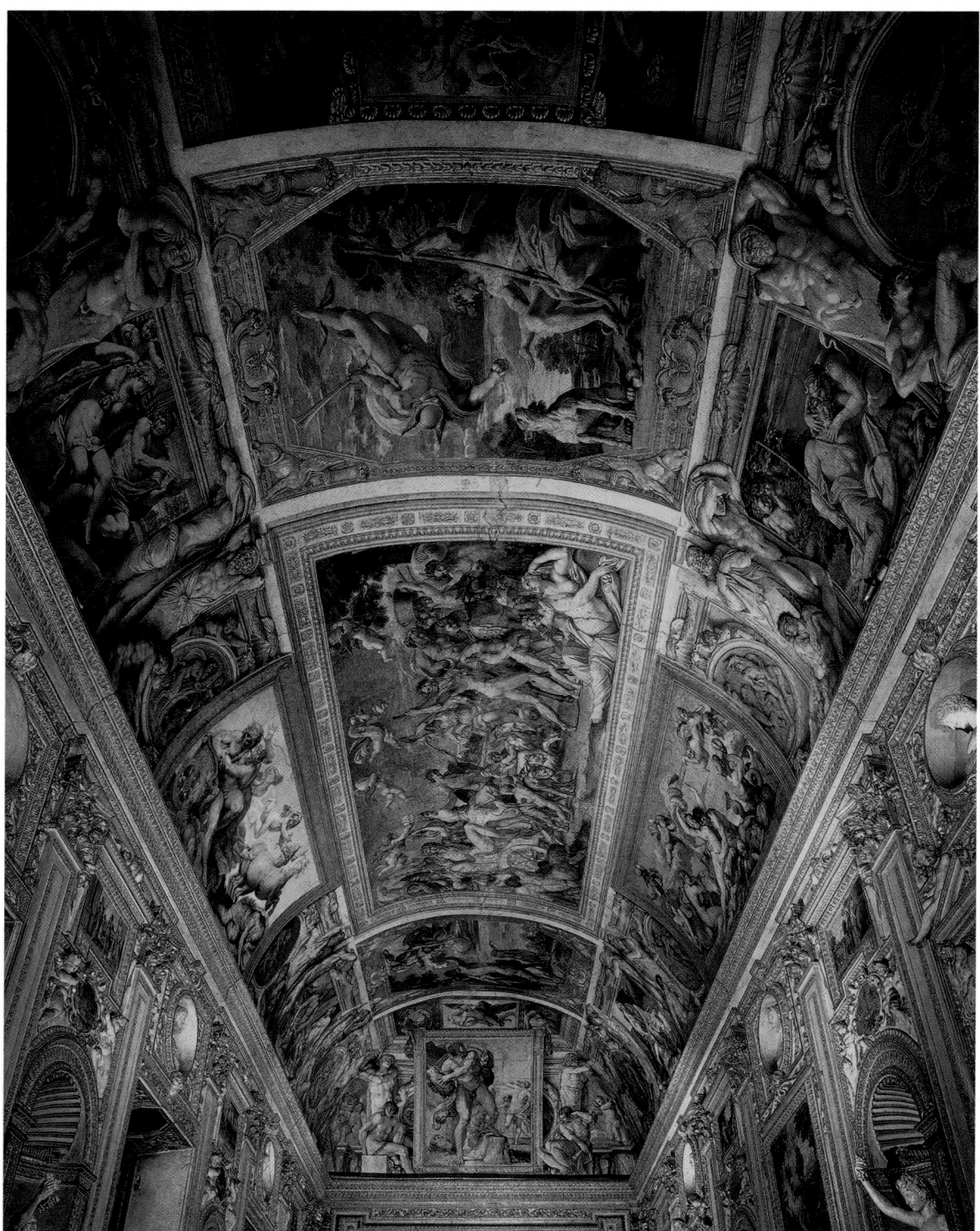

Ceiling Painting and Annibale Carracci

The conservative tastes of many Italian patrons were met by artists who were less radical than Caravaggio, and who continued a more classical tradition steeped in High Renaissance ideals. They took their lead from Annibale Carracci (1560–1609), who arrived in Rome in 1595. Annibale came from Bologna where, in the 1580s, he and two other members of his family formed an "Academy" (also see Vasari, page 601, and Goltzius, page 713) and

evolved an anti-Mannerist style based on northern Italian realism and Venetian art. He was a reformer rather than a revolutionary. Although we do not know completely what this "Academy" entailed, it seems to have incorporated drawing live models and ancient sculpture. As with Caravaggio, his experience of Roman classicism transformed his art. He, too, felt that painting must return to nature, but his approach emphasized a revival of the classics, which to him meant the art of antiquity. Annibale also sought to emulate Raphael, Michelangelo, Titian, and Correggio. In his best work, he was able to fuse these diverse elements.

Between 1597 and 1601 Annibale produced a ceiling fresco, *Loves of the Gods*, in the **gallery** of the Farnese Palace (fig. **19.7**), his most ambitious work, which soon became so famous that it ranked behind only the murals of Michelangelo and Raphael. Although we have seen ceiling painting in the Renaissance—from the fifteenth through the sixteenth centuries, with works by Mantegna, Correggio, and of course Michelangelo, whose painting of the ceiling of the Sistine Chapel would become the work against which all others would be judged—it is the Baroque period which is most associated with this form of painting.

Executed in chapels, churches, and private residences—in entranceways, hallways, and dining rooms—ceiling painting was meant to convey the power, domination, or even extravagance of the patron. One could not enter such a painted room without feeling a little awe. The styles of such works becomes increasingly extravagant from the beginning of the seventeenth century to the end and rivals even the majesty of Michelangelo. The Farnese Palace ceiling, commissioned to celebrate a family wedding, displays a humanist subject, the loves of the classical gods. As on the Sistine Chapel ceiling, the narrative scenes are surrounded by painted architecture, simulated sculpture, and nude youths, carefully foreshortened and lit from below so that they appear real. But the fresco does not rely solely on Michelangelo's masterpiece for inspiration. The main panels are presented as easel pictures, a solution adopted from Raphael. Although the ceiling is painted in fresco, these paintings are given "frames" to appear as easel paintings transported to the ceiling. This device is known as *quadri*

riportati (singular is *quadro riportato*). The ceiling "easel paintings," "medallions" and "sculpture" are painted as trompe-l'oeil. There is no regard for the spectator's point of view here. (When the viewpoint of the spectator is considered, then the artist is using "*di sotto in su*"—literally, "from below to above"; see figs. 15.50 and 17.27.) This imagery on the ceiling reflects the collection of the Farnese—paintings, medallions, sculpture—on display in the room and elsewhere. The figure of Polyphemus, hurling the stone in the "easel painting" on the short wall, is based on the *Farnese Hercules*, a Hellenistic sculpture owned by the family and displayed in the courtyard. (This same sculpture is the subject of fig. 20.14.) The ceiling is held together by an illusionistic scheme that reflects Annibale's knowledge of Correggio (see fig. 17.27) and Veronese (see fig. 17.38). Each level of reality is handled with consummate skill, and the entire ceiling has an exuberance that sets it apart from both Mannerism and High Renaissance art.

The sculptured precision of the Farnese ceiling shows us only one side of Annibale Carracci's style. Another important aspect is seen in his landscapes, such as the *Landscape with the Flight into Egypt* (fig. **19.8**). Its pastoral mood and soft light and atmosphere hark back to Giorgione and Titian (see figs. 16.29 and 16.30). The figures play a minor role here: They are as small and incidental in the manner of a northern European landscape (see fig. 18.30). The painting only hints at the biblical theme of the Flight into Egypt (there are some camels on the hillside). Indeed, the landscape would be equally suitable as a backdrop for almost any story. The old castle, the roads and fields, the flock of sheep, the ferryman with his boat—all show that this "civilized," hospitable countryside has been inhabited for a long time. Hence the figures,

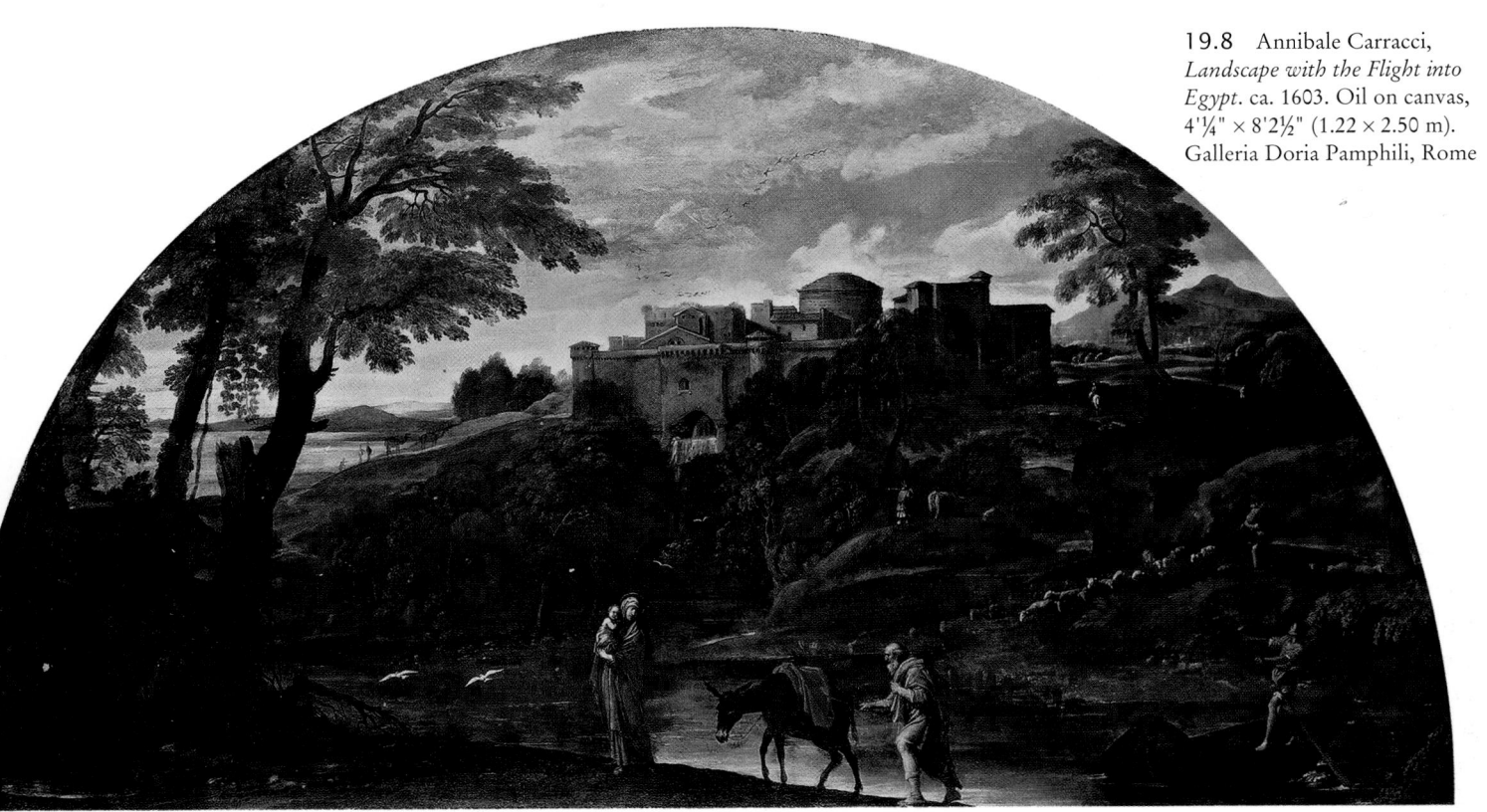

19.8 Annibale Carracci, *Landscape with the Flight into Egypt*. ca. 1603. Oil on canvas, 4'1¼" × 8'2½" (1.22 × 2.50 m). Galleria Doria Pamphili, Rome

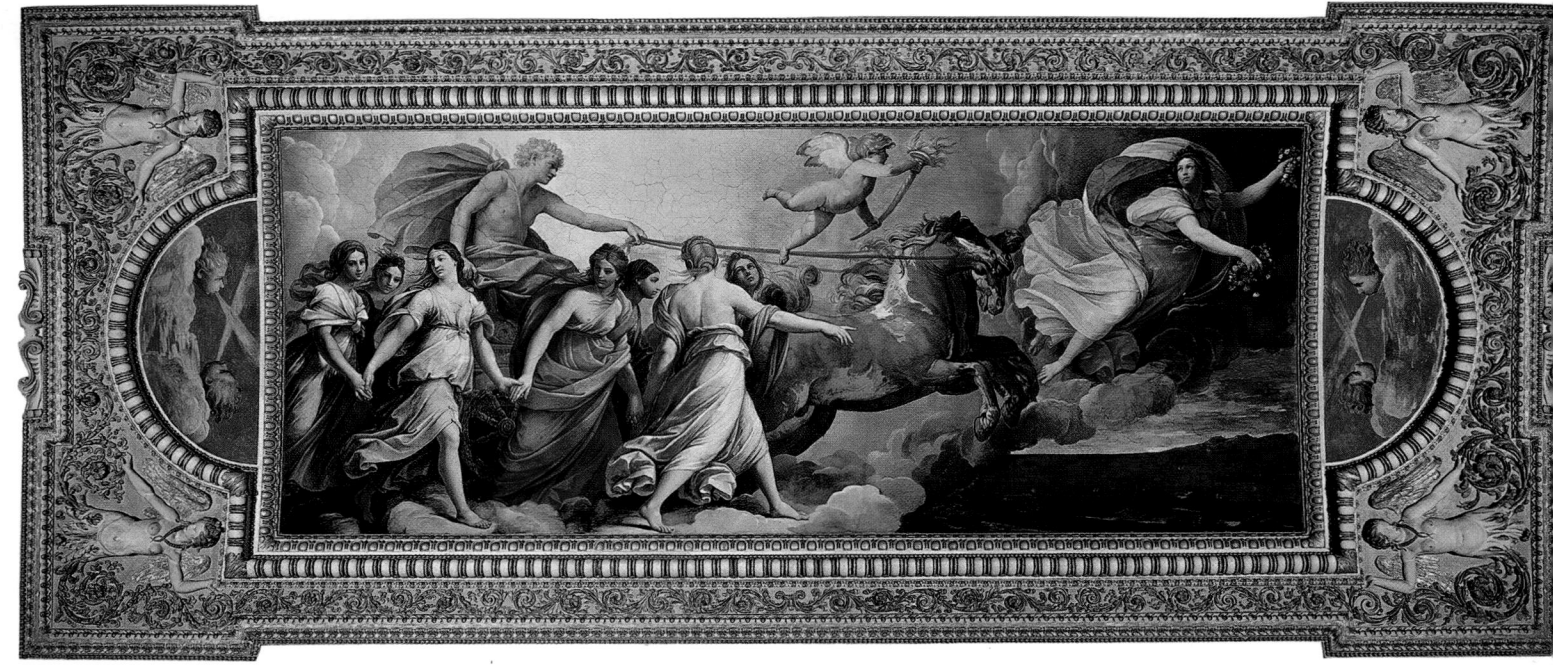

19.9 Guido Reni, *Aurora*. 1613. Ceiling fresco, approx. 9'2" × 22'11" (2.8 × 7m). Casino dell'*Aurora*, Palazzo Rospigliosi-Pallavinci, Rome

however tiny, do not appear lost or dwarfed. This firmly constructed "ideal landscape" evokes a vision of nature that is gentle yet austere, grand but not awesome.

GUIDO RENI AND GUERCINO Baroque ceilings, which began with Annibale Carracci's illusionistic ceiling for the Farnese Palace, continued in Rome with Annibale's Bolognese followers Guido Reni (1575–1642) and Giovanni Francesco Barbieri (1591–1666), called Guercino. Guercino was the leader of the Bolognese School of painting, but both he and Reni worked in Rome and executed ceilings in the second and third decades of the seventeenth century.

Annibale's Farnese Gallery seemed to offer two alternatives to them and others inspired by it. Adopting the Raphaelesque style of the mythological panels, they could arrive at a deliberate, official classicism of *quadro riportato*; or they could take their cue instead from the illusionism of the framework. Approaches varied according to personal style and the specific site. Among the earliest examples of the first alternative is Reni's *quadro riportato* ceiling fresco *Aurora* (fig. **19.9**), which shows Apollo in his chariot (the sun) led by Aurora (the dawn). Here, elegantly drawn grace becomes the pursuit of perfect beauty. The relieflike design with its glowing colors and dramatic light gives the painting an emotional force that the figures alone could never achieve. This style is called Baroque classicism to distinguish it from earlier forms of classicism.

Another *Aurora* ceiling (fig. **19.10**), painted less than ten years later by Guercino, is the very opposite of Reni's. Here (in the 1622 painting), architectural illusionistic framework (painted by Agostino Tassi), known as *quadratura*, combined with the pictorial illusionism of Correggio (see fig. 17.27) and the intense light

and color of Titian, converts the entire surface into one limitless space, in which the figures sweep past as if driven by the winds. Rather than viewing Aurora in profile as in Reni's ceiling, we are clearly positioned below, looking up, seeing the underbelly of the horses as they gallop over our heads. With this work, Guercino continued and expanded the ceiling painting tradition descended from Correggio and started what became a flood of similar visions by other artists. The dynamic fulfillment of this style became known as the High Baroque, after 1630.

PIETRO DA CORTONA AND THE BARBERINI CEILING The most overpowering of these illusionistic ceilings is the fresco by Pietro da Cortona (1596–1669) in the great hall of the Barberini Palace in Rome (fig. **19.11**). This enormous painting combines all three illusionistic systems—*quadratura* in its painted architectural framework, *quadri riportati* in the scenes on the sides, and *di sotto in su* in setting our point of view (as in our image here) to fully understand the ceiling. This work, a complex allegory, glorifies the reign of the Barberini pope Urban VIII.

The allegorical female figure of Divine Providence, its central theme, dominates the ceiling, proclaiming that the pope was chosen by her and not by political favor. Indeed, a swarm of bees (part of the Barberini coat of arms featured prominently in the ceiling) was said to have descended on the Vatican just prior to his election by the new secret ballot system in the College of Cardinals. Allegorical figures in the ceiling emphasize the pope's divine position: The Barberini bees are surrounded by the Theological Virtues, Faith, Hope, and Charity, while the papal tiara is carried by Rome and the keys of St. Peter by Religion. As in the Farnese Gallery, the ceiling area is subdivided by a painted framework that simulates architecture and sculpture, but beyond

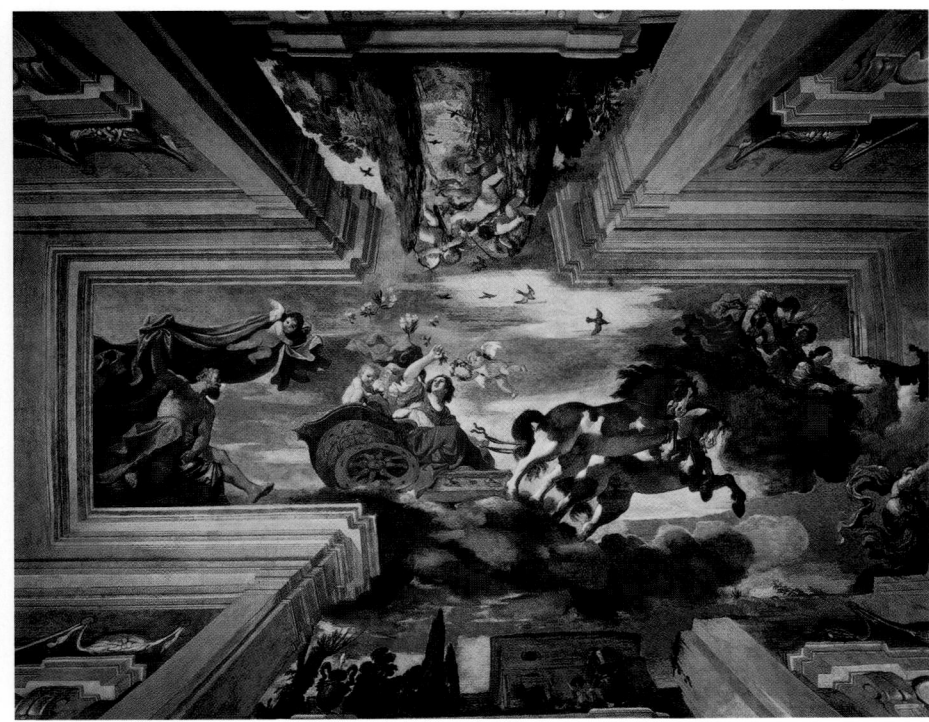

19.10 Guercino and Agostino Tassi, *Aurora*. 1621–23. Ceiling fresco. Villa Ludovisi, Rome

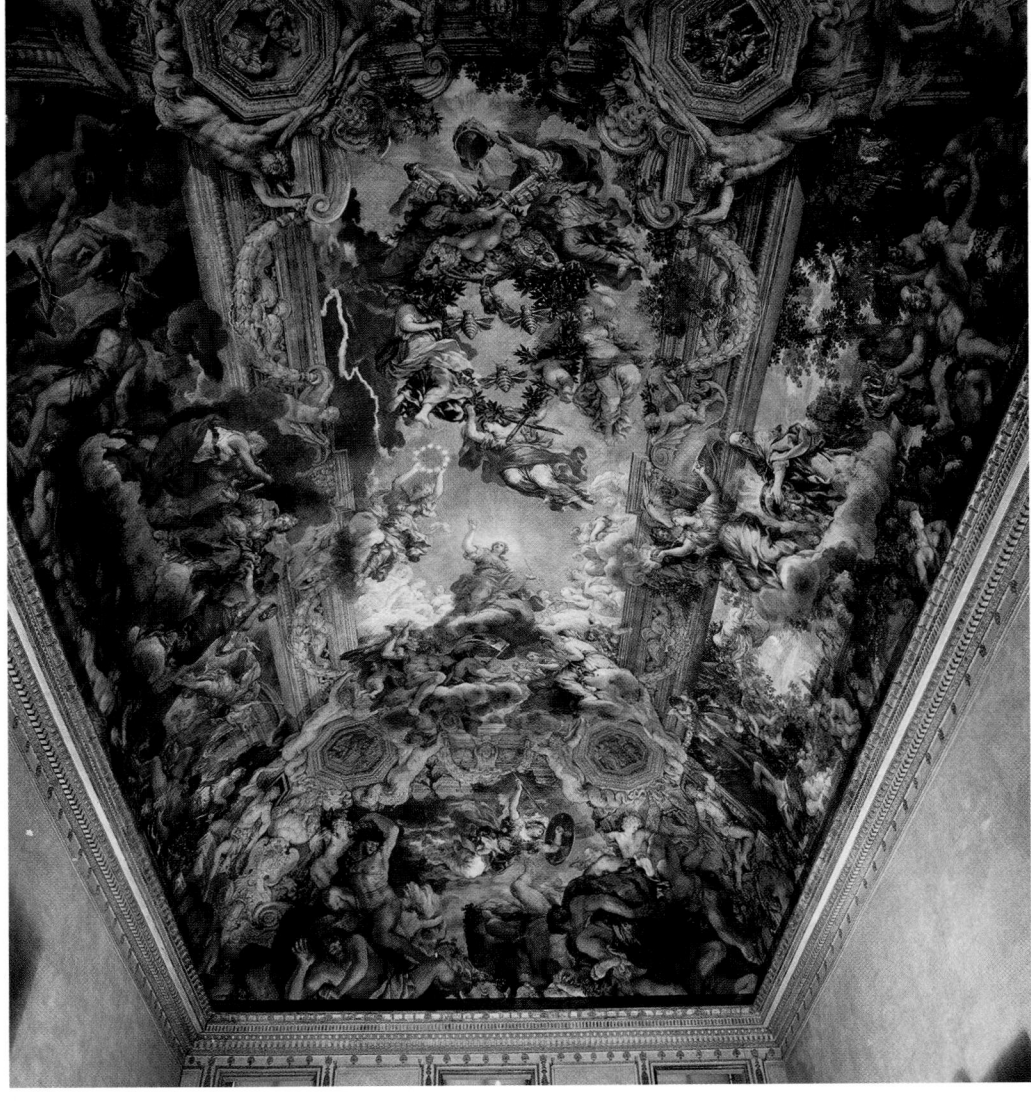

19.11 Pietro da Cortona, *Allegory of Divine Providence*. 1633–39. Ceiling fresco from intended viewpoint. Palazzo Barberini, Rome

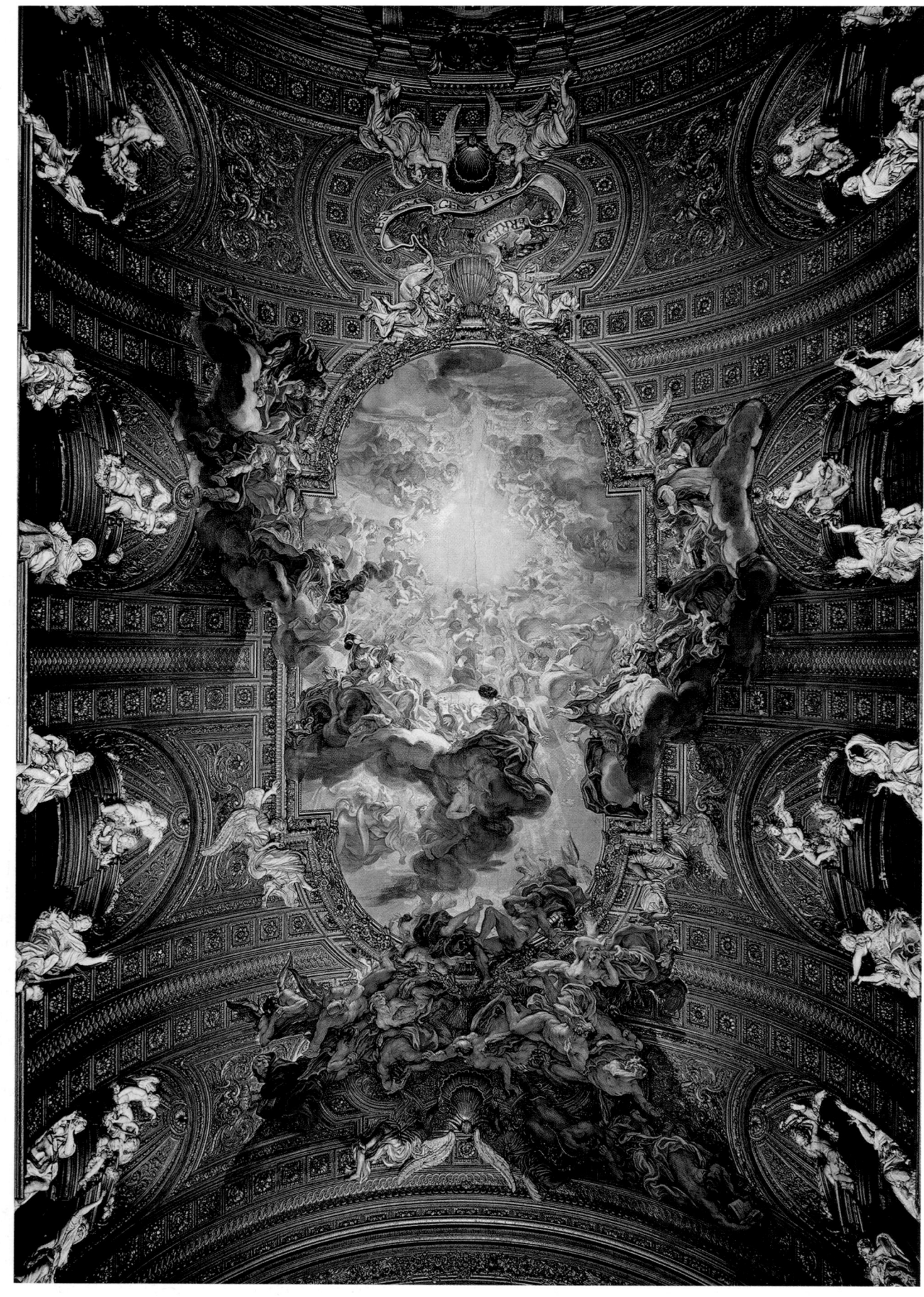

19.12   Giovanni Battista Gaulli, *Triumph of the Name of Jesus.* 1672–79. Ceiling fresco. Il Gesù, Rome it we now see the limitless sky, as in Guercino's *Aurora*. Clusters of figures, perched on clouds or soaring freely, swirl above as well as below this framework. They create a dual illusion: Some figures appear to hover inside the hall, close to us, while others recede into the distance.

Cortona's frescoes were the focal point for the rift between the High Baroque, the exaggerated, triumphal style of the age, and the Baroque classicism that grew out of the Farnese Gallery ceiling. The classicists insisted that art served a moral purpose and should observe the principles of clarity, unity, and decorum. And, supported by a tradition based on Horace's adage *ut pictura poesis* ("as is painting, so is poetry"), they maintained that painting should follow the example of tragic poetry in conveying meaning through a minimum of figures whose movements, gestures, and expressions can be easily read. Cortona, while not anti-Classical, presented the case instead for art as epic poetry, with many actors and episodes that expand on the central theme and create a magnificent effect. He was also the first to argue that art has a sensuous appeal which exists as an end in itself. Although it took place largely on a theoretical level, the debate over illusionistic ceiling painting was about more than opposing approaches to telling a story and expressing ideas in art. The core issue here lies at the very heart of the Baroque. Illusionism allowed artists to fuse separate levels of reality into a pictorial unity of such overwhelming grandeur as to sweep aside any differences between them. Despite the intensity of the controversy, in practice the two sides rarely came into conflict over easel paintings, where the differences between Cortona's and Annibale's followers were not always so clear-cut. Surprisingly, Cortona found inspiration in classical art and Raphael throughout his career. The leader of the reaction against the "excesses" of the High Baroque was neither a fresco painter nor an Italian, but a French artist living in Rome: Nicolas Poussin, who moved early on in the same antiquarian circle as Cortona but drew very different lessons from it.

GIOVANNI BATTISTA GAULLI AND IL GESÙ It is a strange fact that few ceiling frescoes were painted after Cortona finished his *Allegory of Divine Providence*. Ironically, the new style of architecture fostered by Francesco Borromini and Guarino Guarini (see pages 679–83) provided few opportunities for decoration. But, after 1670, such frescoes enjoyed a revival in older buildings which reached its peak in the interior of Il Gesù (fig. **19.12**), the mother church for the Jesuit order. At the suggestion of Gianlorenzo Bernini, the greatest sculptor-architect of the century, the commission for the ceiling frescoes went to his young protégé Giovanni Battista Gaulli (1639–1709). A talented assistant, Antonio Raggi (1624–1686), made the stucco sculpture. The program, which proved extraordinarily influential, shows Bernini and Gaulli's imaginative daring. As in the Cornaro Chapel (see fig. 19.31), the ceiling is treated as a single unit that evokes a mystical vision. The nave fresco, with its contrasts of light and dark and sharply foreshortened figures, spills dramatically over its frame, then turns into sculptured figures, combining painting, sculpture, and architecture. Here, Baroque illusionism achieves its

ultimate expression. The subject of the ceiling painting is the illuminated name of Jesus—the IHS derived from the first three letters of the Greek name of Jesus—in the center of the golden light. It is a stirring reference both to the Jesuit order, dedicated to the Name of Jesus and to the concept that Christ is the Light of the World. The impact of his light and holiness then creates the overflowing turbulence that tumbles out of the sky at the end of days and spreads the word of the Jesuit missionaries: "That at the name of Jesus, every knee should bow…" (Epistle of St. Paul to the Philippians 2:10).

ARCHITECTURE IN ITALY

The Baroque style in architecture, like that of painting, began in Rome, which was a vast construction site from the end of the sixteenth through the middle of the seventeenth century. The goals of the Counter-Reformation caused the Church to embark on a major building campaign. New churches were constructed and the new St. Peter's was finally completed. Although many of these building projects began during Renaissance, they developed distinctly different characteristics as they were completed during the Baroque. Some architects continued to use a classical vocabulary but expanded or stretched it. For instance, the idea of perfection was no longer represented by a circle, but an oval or ellipse (a new concept that was frequently the object of astronomical discussions). They incorporated domes based on Michelangelo's (see fig. 17.19) but which had a steeper profile to suggest greater drama in punctuating the sky; others designed buildings based on amorphous shapes that used classical ornamentations but not its principles.

The Completion of St. Peter's and Carlo Maderno

Carlo Maderno (ca. 1556–1629) was the most talented young architect to emerge in the midst of the vast ecclesiastical building program that commenced in Rome toward the end of the sixteenth century. In 1603, he was given the task of completing, at long last, the church of St. Peter's (fig. **19.13**). Pope Clement VIII had decided to add a nave and narthex to the west end of Michelangelo's building, thereby converting it into a basilica plan. This change, which had already been proposed by Raphael in 1514, made it possible to link St. Peter's with the Vatican Palace to the right of the church (fig. **19.14**).

Maderno's design for the façade follows the pattern established by Michelangelo for the exterior of the church. It consists of a colossal order supporting an attic, but with a dramatic emphasis on the portals. The effect can only be described as a crescendo that builds from the corners toward the center. The spacing of the supports becomes closer, the pilasters turn into columns, and the façade wall projects step by step. This quickened rhythm had been hinted at a generation earlier in Giacomo della Porta's façade for Il Gesù (see fig. 17.23). Maderno made it the dominant principle of his façade designs, not only for St. Peter's

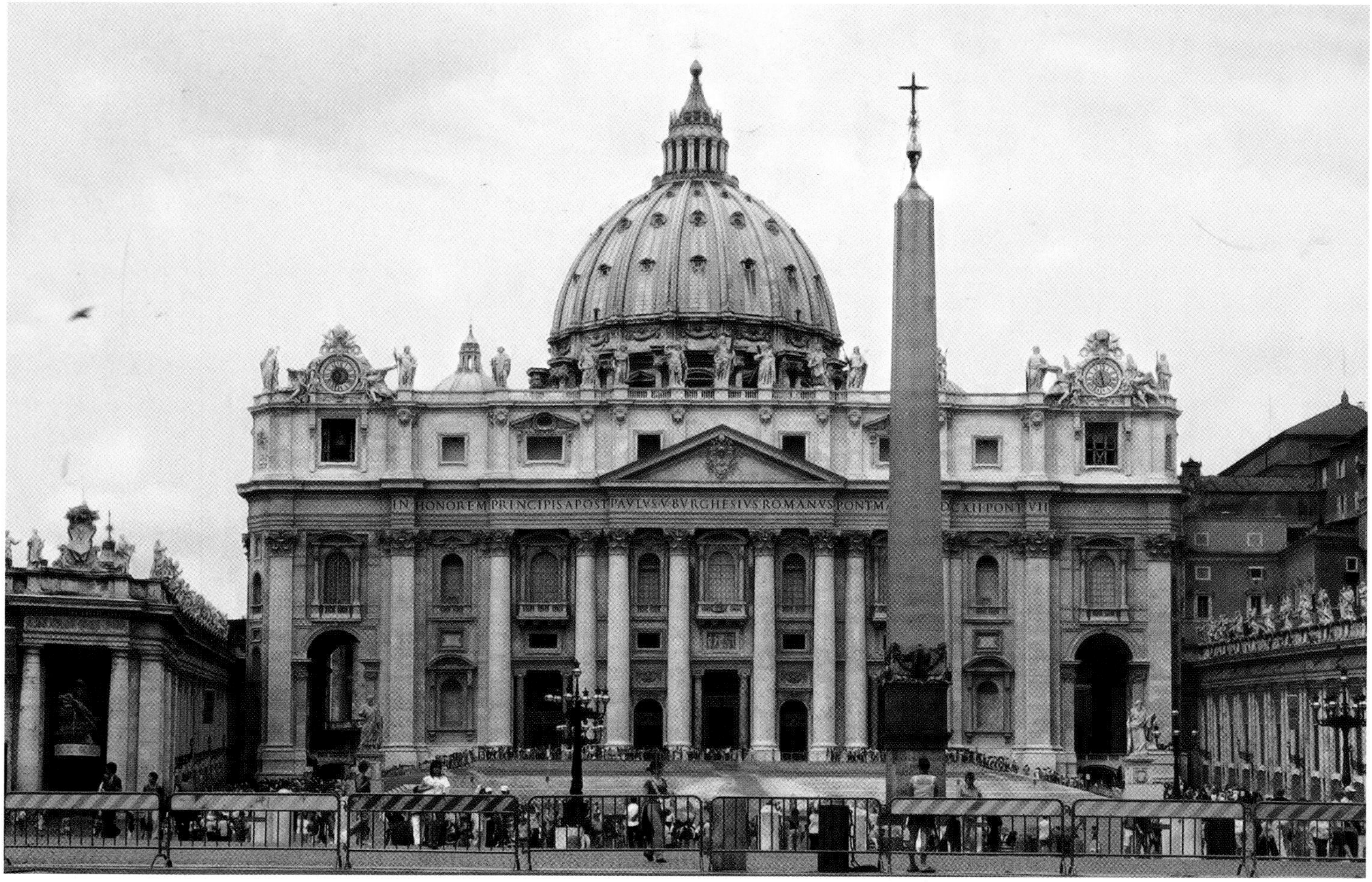

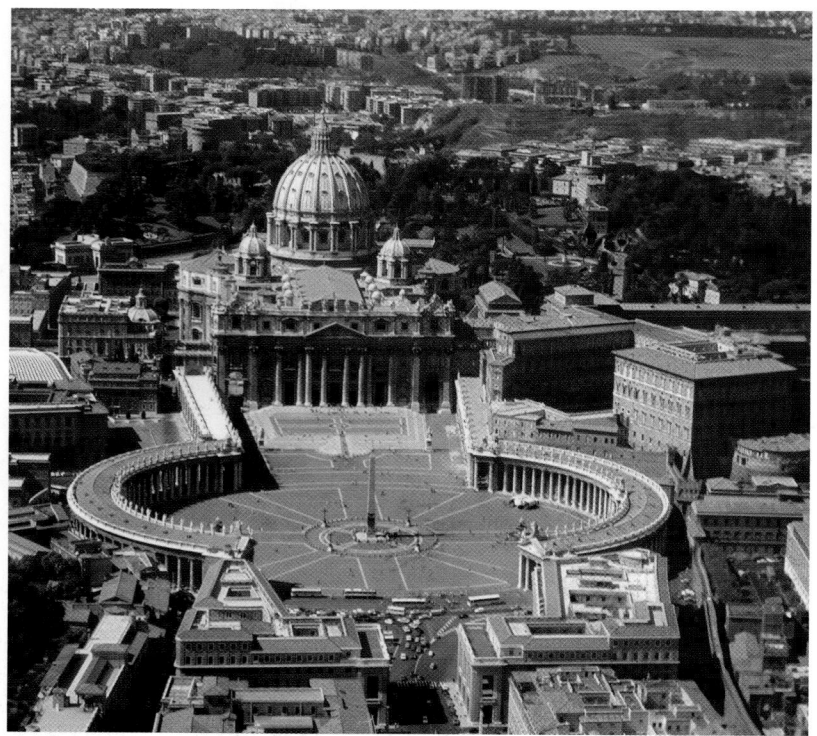

19.13 Carlo Maderno. Façade of St. Peter's, Rome. 1607–12

19.14 Aerial view of St. Peter's, Rome. Nave and façade by Carlo Maderno, 1607–12; colonnade by Gianlorenzo Bernini, designed 1657

but for smaller churches as well. In the process, he replaced the traditional concept of the church façade as one continuous wall surface, with the "façade-in-depth" becoming dynamically related to the open space before it. The possibilities of this new treatment, which derives from Michelangelo's Palazzo dei Conservatori (see fig. 17.18), were not to be exhausted until 150 years later. Recent cleaning of the façade of St. Peter's revealed it to be of a warm cream color, which emphasized its sculptural qualities.

Bernini and St. Peter's

After Maderno's death in 1629, his assistant Gianlorenzo Bernini (1598–1680) assumed the title "architect of St. Peter's." Considering himself Michelangelo's successor as both architect and sculptor, Bernini directed the building campaign and coordinated the decoration and sculpture within the church as well. Given these tasks, the enormous size of St. Peter's posed equal challenges for anyone seeking to integrate architecture and sculpture. How could its vastness be related to the human scale and given a measure of emotional warmth? Once the nave was extended following Maderno's design, Bernini realized that the vast interior needed an internal focal point. His response was to create the monumental sculptural/architectural composite form, known as the *Baldacchino* (fig. **19.15**), the "canopy" for the main altar of St. Peter's, at the very crossing of the transept and the

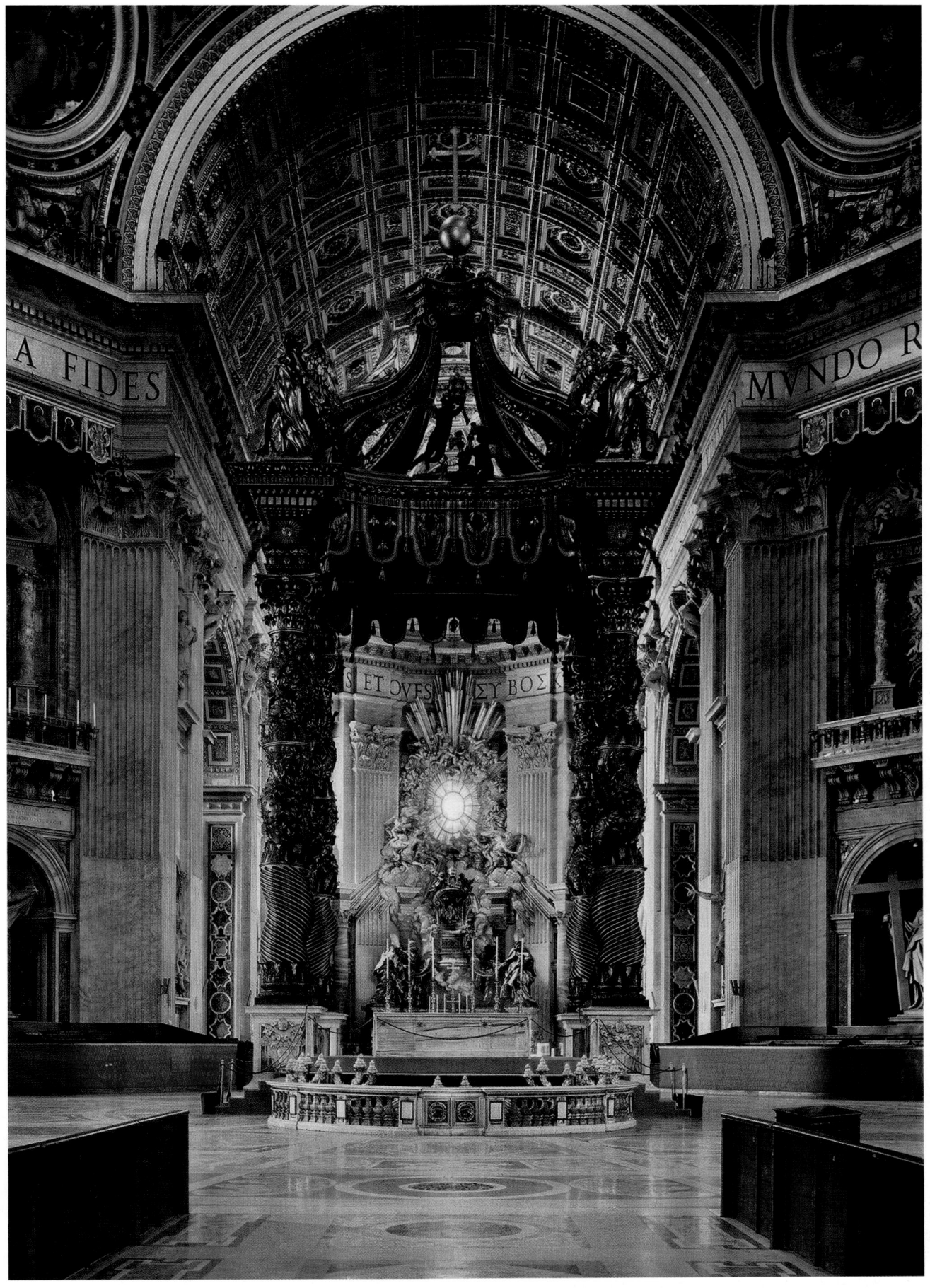

19.15 Bernini, *Baldacchino*. 1624–33. At crossing. St. Peter's, Rome nave, directly under Michelangelo's dome (see fig. 17.19) and just above the actual **crypt** of St. Peter where the pope would celebrate Mass. This nearly 100-foot piece created mostly in bronze stripped from the ancient Pantheon (see fig. 7.23) stands on four twisted columns, reminiscent of those from the original St. Peter's (and thought, too, to replicate those of Solomon's Temple). Rather than an architectural entablature mounted between the columns, Bernini inventively suggests fabric hanging between them. He used actual leaves, vines, fruits, and even lizards and cast them in bronze for the decoration. The *Baldacchino* is a splendid fusion of sculpture and architecture. At its corners are statues of angels and vigorously curved scrolls, which raise a cross above a golden orb, the symbol of the triumph of Christianity throughout the world. The entire structure is so alive with expressive energy that it may be considered as the epitome of Baroque style. In a related tribute, we see through the columns of the *Baldacchino* to the sculptural reliquary of the throne of St. Peter, the *Cathedra Petri* in the apse of the church, also designed by Bernini.

The papal insignia—the triple crown and crossed keys of St. Peter—and the coat of arms of the pope under whose patronage this structure was created—the Barberini bees of Urban VIII—are significant elements of decoration in the *Baldacchino*. These same identifiers can also be seen in Cortona's Barberini ceiling (see fig. 19.11). Bernini's *Baldacchino* honors not just the power and majesty of God, but that of his emissary on earth, the pope. Bernini's relationship with the pope was one of the most successful in the history of patronage. Indeed, upon his elevation to the papacy, Urban VIII was said to have told the artist: "It is your great good luck, Cavaliere, to see Maffeo Barberini pope; but We are even luckier in that Cavaliere Bernini lives at the time of our pontificate." (However, the artistic aims of this pope drained the papal treasury and both the pope and, by association, Bernini were blamed for the excesses after Urban's death.) As Bernini directed our attention within the church, he also (later, under the patronage of Pope Alexander VII [r. 1655–1667] orchestrated our entrance into St. Peter's. Thus, he molded the open space in front of the façade into a magnificent oval piazza that is amazingly sculptural (see fig. 19.14). This "forecourt"—an immense keyhole-shaped colossal colonnade—imposed a degree of unity on the sprawling Vatican complex, while screening off the surrounding slums. This device, which Bernini himself likened to the motherly, all-embracing arms of the Church, was not new. What *was* novel was the idea of placing it at the main entrance to a building. Also unusual was the huge scale. For sheer impressiveness, this integration of architecture and grandiose setting can be compared only with the ancient Roman sanctuary at Palestrina (see fig. 7.5). Bernini's one major failure visually of St. Peter's was his inability to execute the bell towers that were initially planned by Bramante (see fig. 16.10). He began construction, but, much to Bernini's humiliation, cracks appeared, and although these could have been the result of normal foundation settling, an inquest was convened, and the towers were dismantled. This failure would haunt him, but would provide a competitive resource for his rivals: Borromini in Italy and later Wren in England.

Architectural Components in Decoration

The huge scale, the dynamic sculptural vitality, and the ornamentation of Baroque architecture were expressed in the decorative arts as well. The 5-foot-high clock seen in figure **19.16** is made of colorful marble, lapis lazuli, black ebony, and gilt bronze, and features an oil-on-copper painting.

Clocks in the seventeenth century were not yet accurate, certainly not silent, and rarely readable at night. The novel example shown here, however, was known as an *orologio della notte* (nocturnal clock)—a clock that would be useful even at night, thanks to an innovative design by Pier Tommaso Campani (active ca. 1650– 1700). Bernini had seen a nocturnal clock on his trip to France in 1665; it was considered a true marvel. This one was made for Pope Alexander VII, a known insomniac, who requested a clock that could display the time even in darkness and run without sound. The time here is expressed in Roman

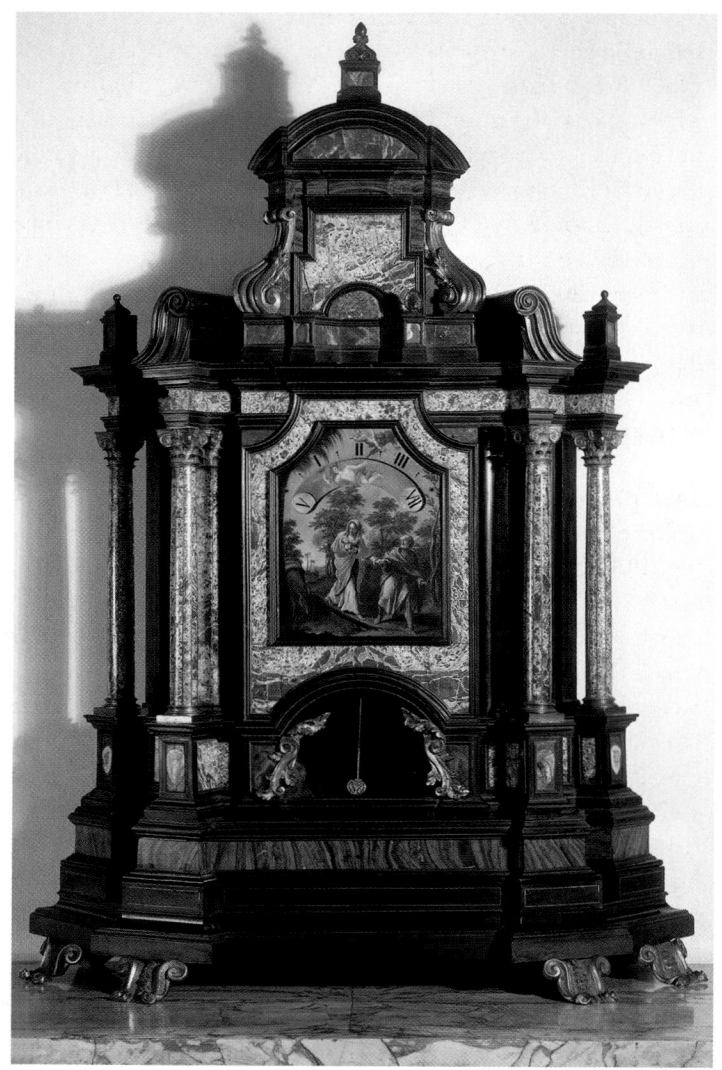

19.16 Pier Tommaso Campani and Francesco Trevisani, *Nocturnal Clock*. ca. 1680–90. Ebony and other types of hardwood, oil on copper, gilt bronze, colored stones, 63 × 45¼ × 18½" (160 × 115 × 47 cm). Pinacoteca Capitolini, Rome

numerals, pierced so that light from a hidden oil lamp could pass through them; a drum was used to quash the ticktocking sound of a pendulum.

The clock was encased in an elaborate architectural structure with paired columns and scrolled feet that resembles a tabernacle. It shows the influence of both Bernini and Borromini. The painting at its center, by Francesco Trevisani (1656–1746), is the *Flight into Egypt*. This theme is a pun on time—as time also flies. Trevisani was a well-known Roman painter, and this was no small commission. Indeed, we know that Gaulli, the painter of the ceiling of Il Gesù (see fig. 19.12), also executed paintings for such clocks.

A Baroque Alternative: Francesco Borromini

Bernini's greatest rival in architecture, Francesco Borromini (1599–1667), was a secretive and emotionally unstable artist who committed suicide. The contrast in temperament between these two architects would be evident from their works alone, even if we did not have the accounts written by their contemporaries. Bernini's church designs are dramatically simple and unified, while Borromini's structures are extravagantly complex. But where the surfaces of Bernini's interiors are extremely rich, Borromini's are surprisingly plain: They rely on the architect's phenomenal grasp of spatial geometry to achieve their spiritual effects. Bernini himself agreed with those who denounced Borromini for flagrantly disregarding the classical tradition, enshrined in Renaissance theory and practice, that architecture must reflect the proportions of the human body. Certainly, Bernini, even at the height of the Baroque, was more tied to a classical vocabulary. But perhaps his criticisms of Borromini were only an expression of all-too-human rivalries.

SAN CARLO ALLE QUATTRO FONTANE Borromini's first major project was the church of San Carlo alle Quattro Fontane (fig. **19.17**), a small structure on a difficult-to-fit corner. It is the syntax, not the vocabulary, that is new and disquieting here. The ceaseless play of concave and convex surfaces makes the entire structure seem elastic, as if pulled out of shape by pressures that no previous building could have withstood. The plan (fig. **19.18**) is a pinched oval that suggests a distended and half-melted Greek cross, yet it is a basically central-planned church. The inside of the coffered dome (fig. **19.19**), like the plan, looks "stretched": If the tension were relaxed, it would snap back to normal. Light coming from the windows, partially hidden at the base of the dome, and a honeycomb of fanciful coffers of decreasing size to create the illusion of greater height make the dome appear weightless. The symbol of the Trinity appears in the vault of the lantern in this church, built for the Trinitarians, an order dedicated to the mysteries of the Holy Trinity.

On the façade (see fig. 19.17), designed almost 30 years later, the pressures and counterpressures reach their maximum intensity. Borromini merges architecture and sculpture in a way that must have shocked Bernini. No such union had been

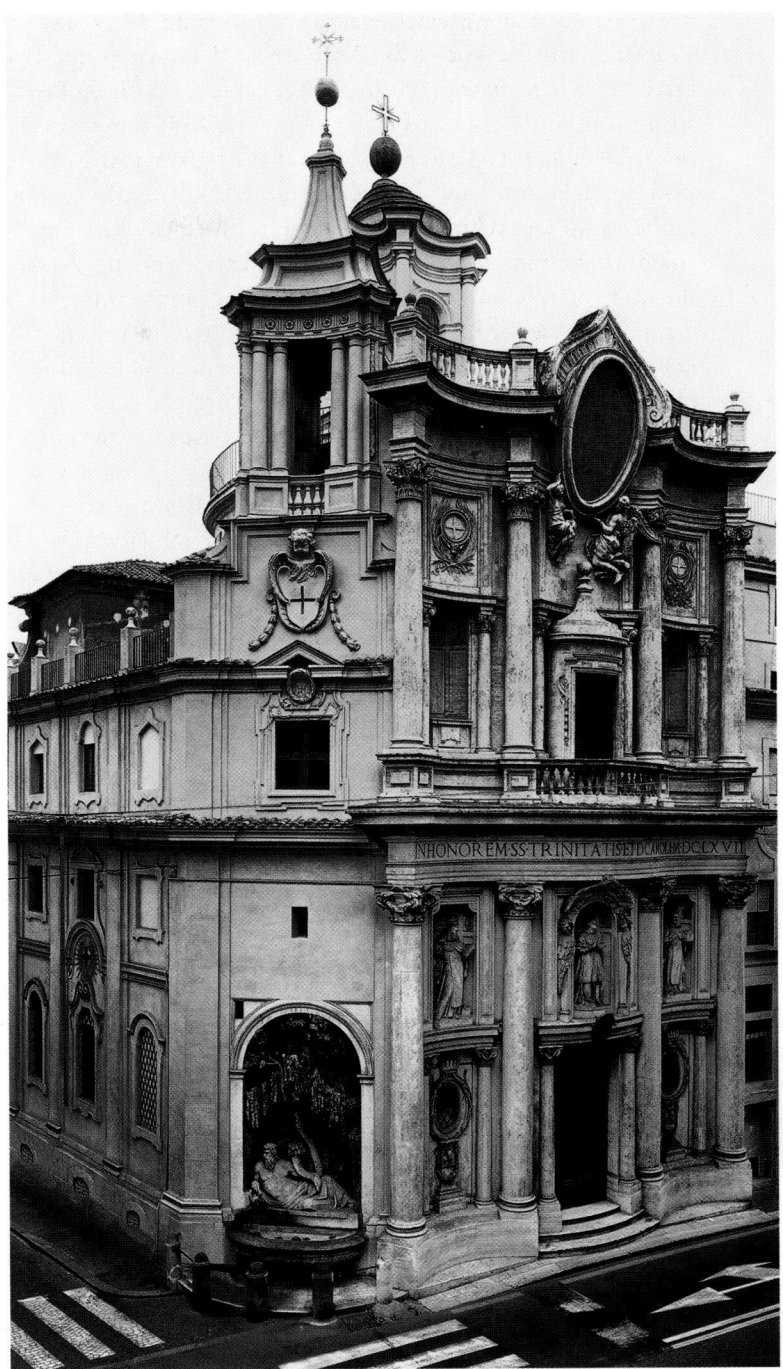

19.17 Francesco Borromini. Façade of San Carlo alle Quattro Fontane, Rome. ca. 1665–67

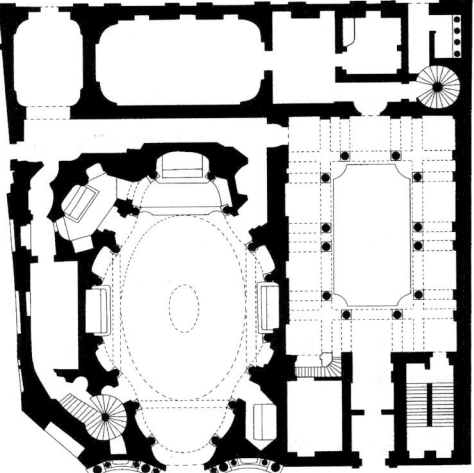

19.18 Plan of San Carlo alle Quattro Fontane. 1638–41

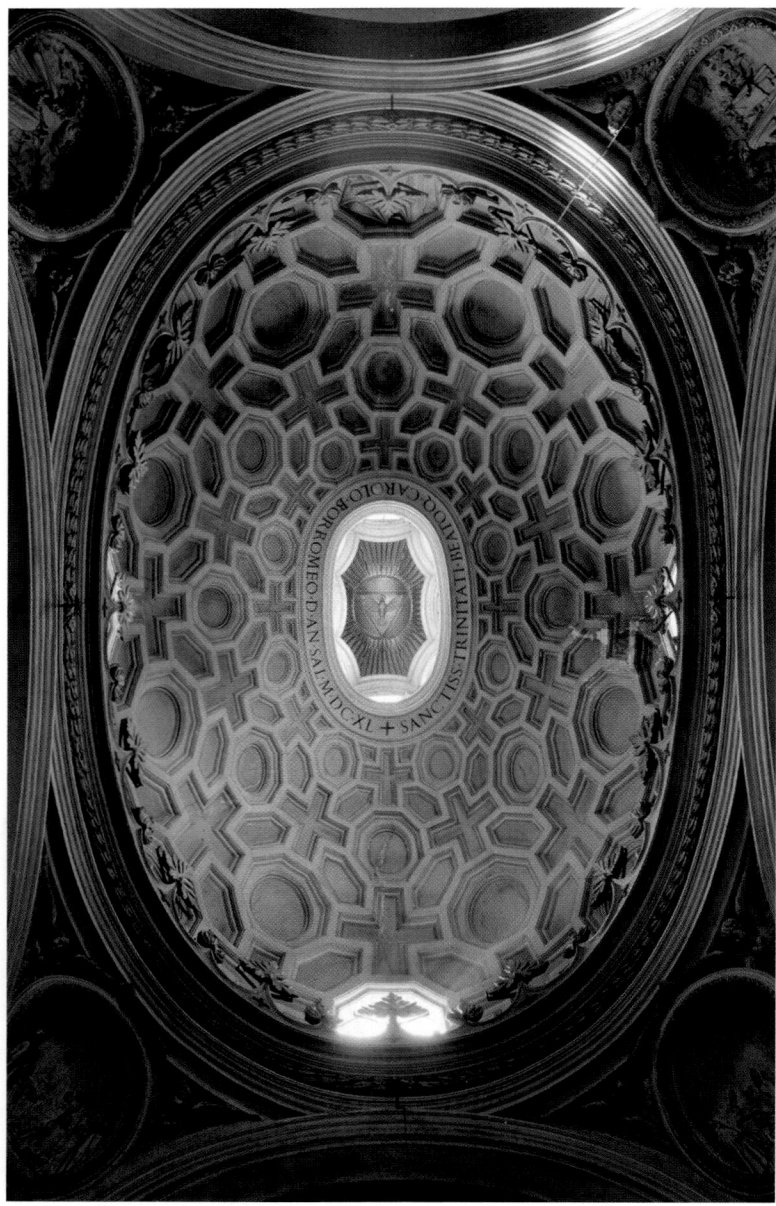

19.19 Dome of San Carlo alle Quattro Fontane. 1638–41

Borromini's church of Sant'Ivo alla Sapienza (figs. **19.20** and **19.21**) was built at the end of an existing cloister for a university, which soon became the University of Rome. It is more compact than San Carlo, but equally daring. Sant'Ivo is a small, central-plan church based on a hexagonal star. The six-pointed plan represents Sapienza (wisdom), although as the church was first built under Pope Urban VIII (Barberini) it was suggested by contemporaries that the plan represented the Barberini bee, also seen in Bernini's *Baldacchino* and Cortona's ceiling (see figs. 19.15 and 19.11). In designing this unique church, Borromini may have been thinking of octagonal structures, such as San Vitale in

attempted since Gothic art. A study of the two entablatures of fluid concave and convex turns over the bays in a mix and match fashion provides an insight into his design methods. The statues above the entrance emerge like actors entering a stage from behind a thin screen. The sculptures, interestingly enough, are by Bernini's assistant Antonio Raggi, who also worked on the ceiling of Il Gesù (see fig. 19.12). San Carlo alle Quattro Fontane established Borromini's fame. "Nothing similar," wrote the head of the religious order for which the church was built, "can be found anywhere in the world. This is attested by the foreigners who…try to procure copies of the plan. We have been asked for them by Germans, Flemings, Frenchmen, Italians, Spaniards, and even Indians." Yet the design was also described by a contemporary, no doubt because of its seeming disregard of regular geometry, as "the corruption of architecture."

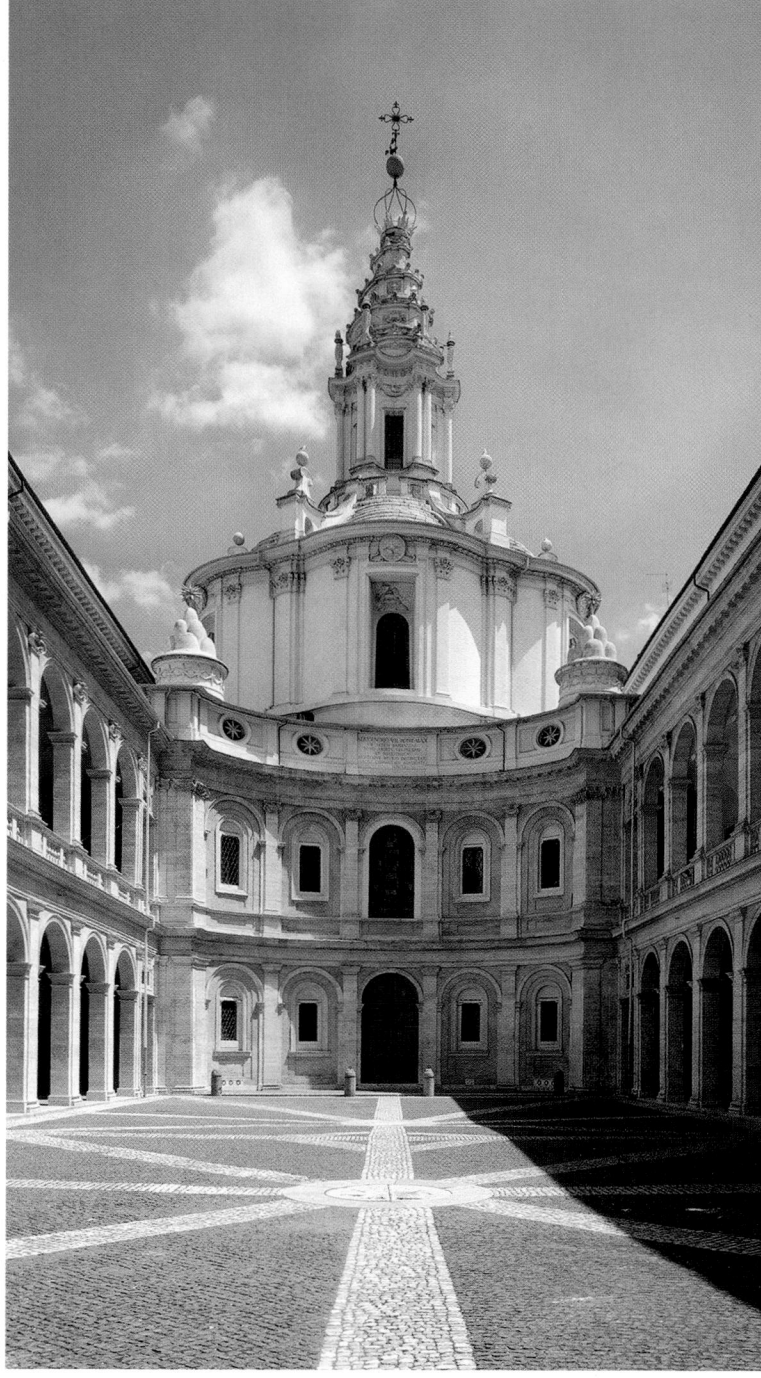

19.20 Francesco Borromini. Exterior of Sant'Ivo, Rome. Begun 1642

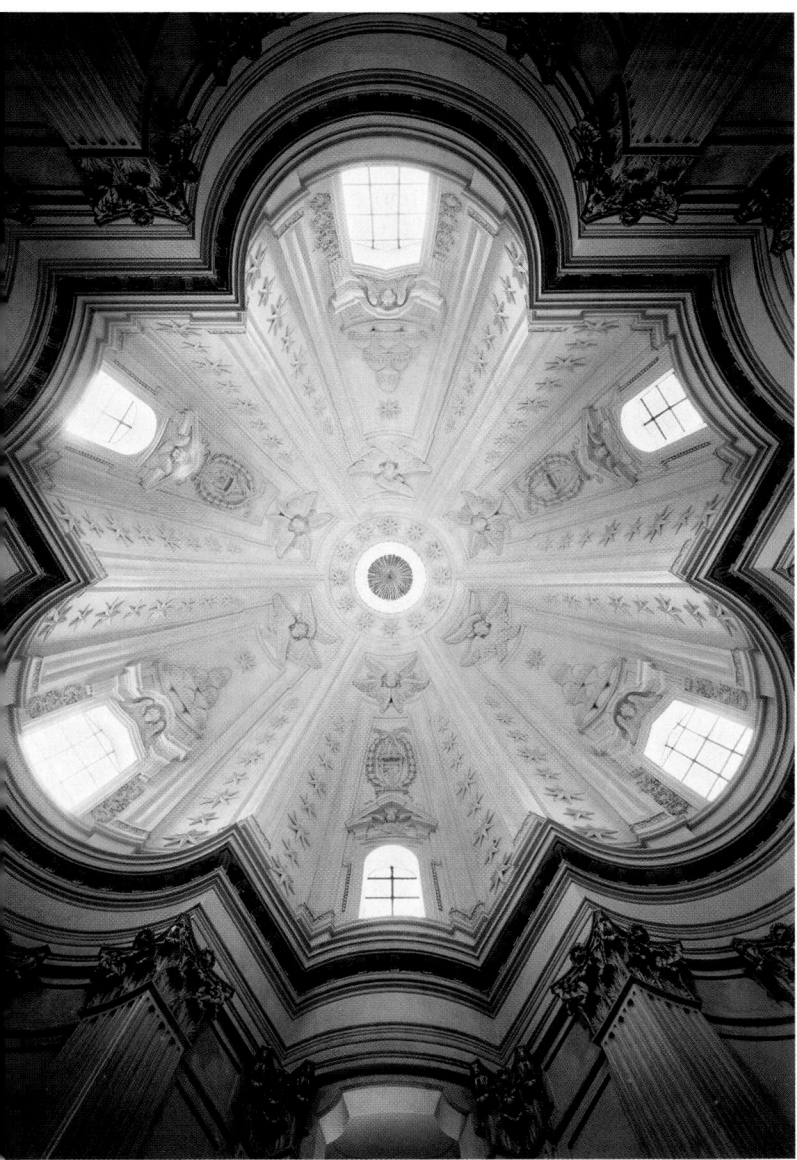

19.21   Interior view into dome of Sant'Ivo

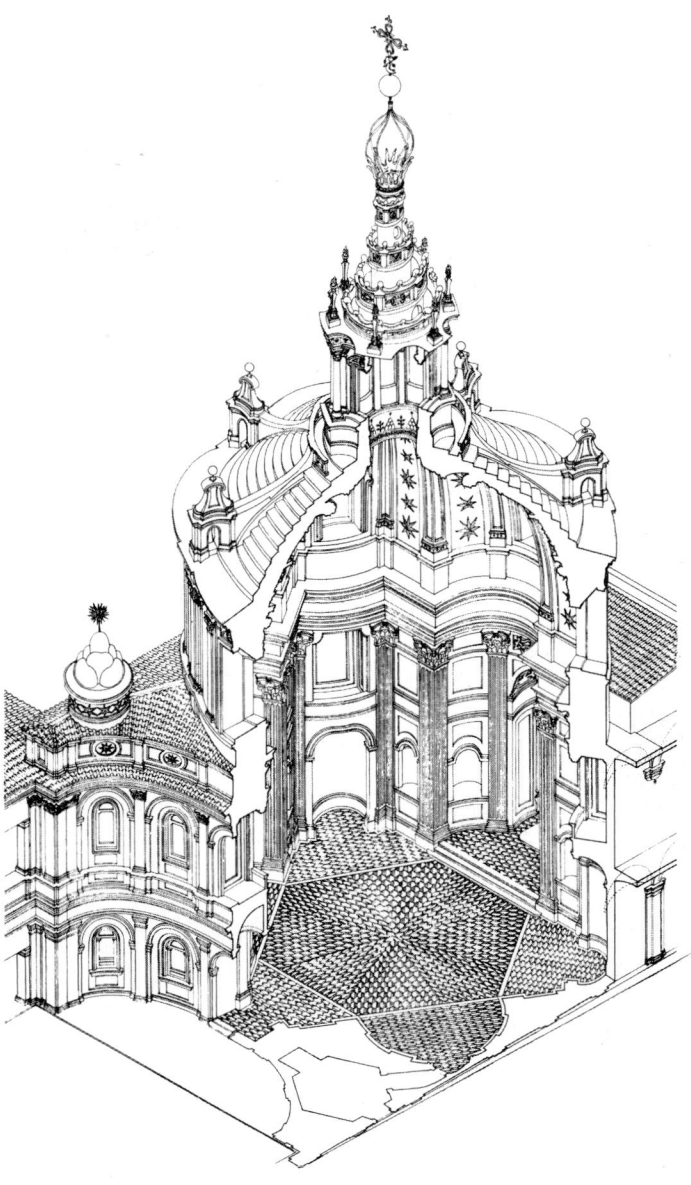

19.22   Cutaway plan of Francesco Borromini's Sant'Ivo
(from Portoghesi)

Ravenna (fig. 8.21), but the result is completely novel. Inside (fig. **19.22**), it offers a single, unified, organic experience, as the walls extend the ground plan into the vault, culminating in Borromini's unique spiral lantern. The hexagonal star pattern is continued up to the circular base of the lantern. The stars on the wall refer to the Chigi family of Pope Alexander VII, who was in power when the building was completed.

SANT'AGNESE   A third project by Borromini, the church of Sant'Agnese, is set on the Piazza Navona (fig. **19.23**), a grand ancient stadium space in which three sculptural Baroque fountains celebrate the new age. The central monument, topped by an Egyptian obelisk, is the *Four Rivers Fountain* by Bernini, and its location in front of Sant'Agnese demonstrates the rivalry between Borromini and Bernini: The latter fought for the church commission, but lost.

Sant'Agnese is of special interest as a critique of St. Peter's and each of its architects. There were two problems that Maderno had been unable to solve at St. Peter's. Although his façade forms an impressive unit with Michelangelo's dome when seen from a distance, the dome is gradually hidden by the new façade as we approach the church. It appears to "sink." Furthermore, the towers he planned for each end posed formidable structural difficulties. After Bernini's first attempt to overcome these problems failed, he proposed making the towers free-standing, but he was forced to abandon the plan when it was severely criticized. The façade of Sant'Agnese offers a brilliant solution to both of these difficulties. Borromini took over the project, which had been begun by another architect, Carlo Rainaldi (1611–1691), the year before, and completely recast it without, however, entirely abandoning the Greek-cross plan. The design is essentially a central-plan (fig. **19.24**), and the dome is

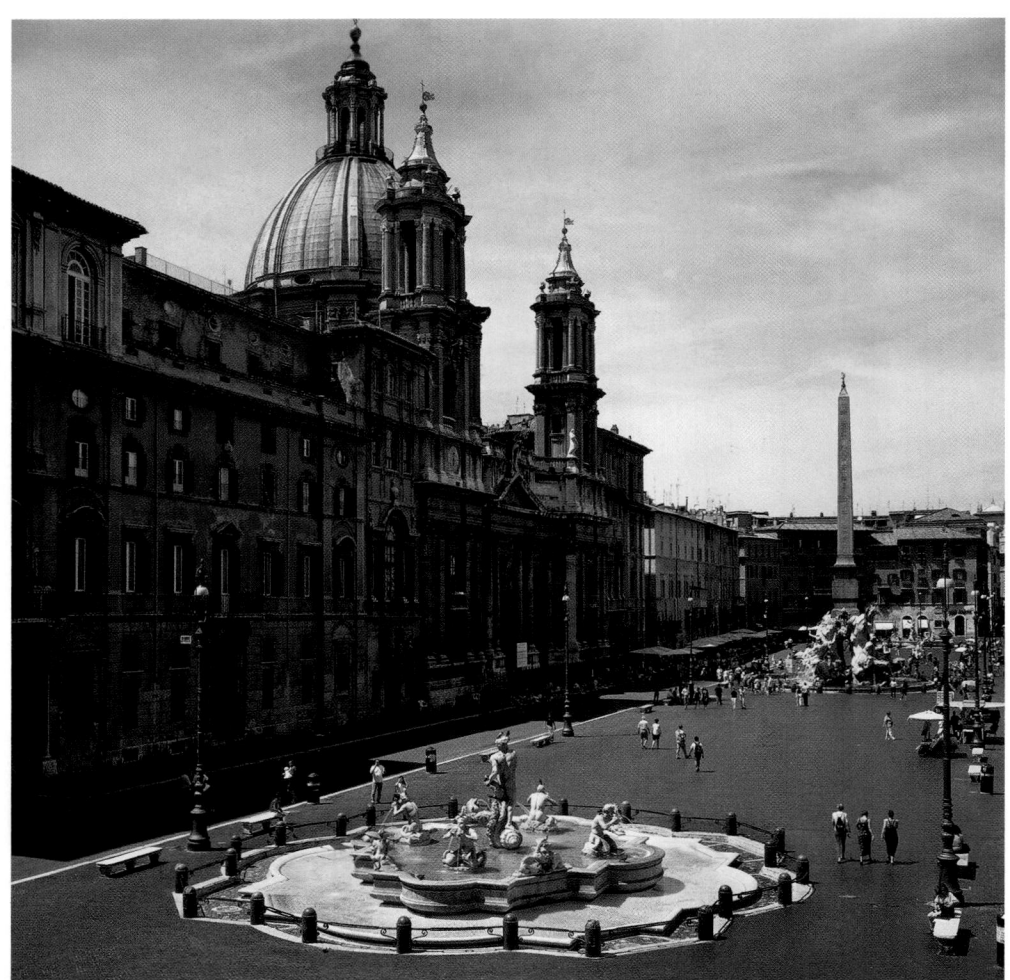

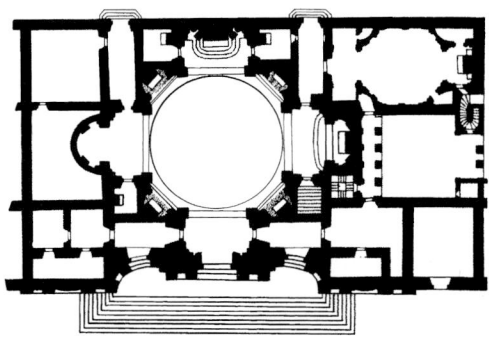

19.23 Piazza Navona, Rome, with Francesco Borromini, Sant'Agnese, center left, 1653–63, and Bernini's *Four Rivers Fountain*, center, 1648–52

19.24 Francesco Borromini. Plan of Sant'Agnese

not set back at all. The façade's lower part is adapted from the façade of St. Peter's, but it curves inward, so that the dome (a tall, slender version of Michelangelo's) functions as the upper part of the façade. As the dome is nearly at the entranceway, the problem of its apparent "sinking" is solved. The dramatic juxtaposition of concave and convex, so characteristic of Borromini, is emphasized by the two towers, which form a monumental group with the dome. Once again, Borromini joins Gothic and Renaissance features—the two-tower façade and the dome—into a remarkably elastic compound to tower over the ancient site.

The Baroque in Turin: Guarino Guarini

The new ideas introduced by Borromini were developed further not in Rome but in Turin, the capital of Piedmont, which became the creative center of Baroque architecture in Italy toward the end of the seventeenth century. In 1666, Guarino Guarini (1624–1683), Borromini's most brilliant successor, was called to Turin to work as an engineer and mathematician by Duke Carlo Emanuele II. Guarini was a Theatine priest whose genius was grounded in philosophy and mathematics. His design for the façade of the Palazzo Carignano (figs. **19.25** and **19.26**) repeats on a larger scale the undulating movement of San Carlo alle Quattro Fontane (see

fig. 19.17), using a highly individualized vocabulary. Incredibly, the exterior of the building, in the local tradition, is made almost entirely of brick, but was probably meant to be stuccoed in imitation marble.

Even more extraordinary is Guarini's dome for the Chapel of the Holy Shroud, a round structure attached to Turin cathedral (fig. **19.27**). The dome and the tall drum, with its alternating windows and niches, consists of familiar Borrominian motifs. Yet it ushers us into a realm of pure illusion completely unlike anything by the earlier architect. Here, the surface has disappeared in a

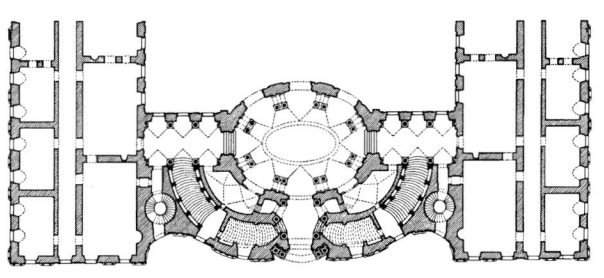

19.25 Plan of Palazzo Carignano

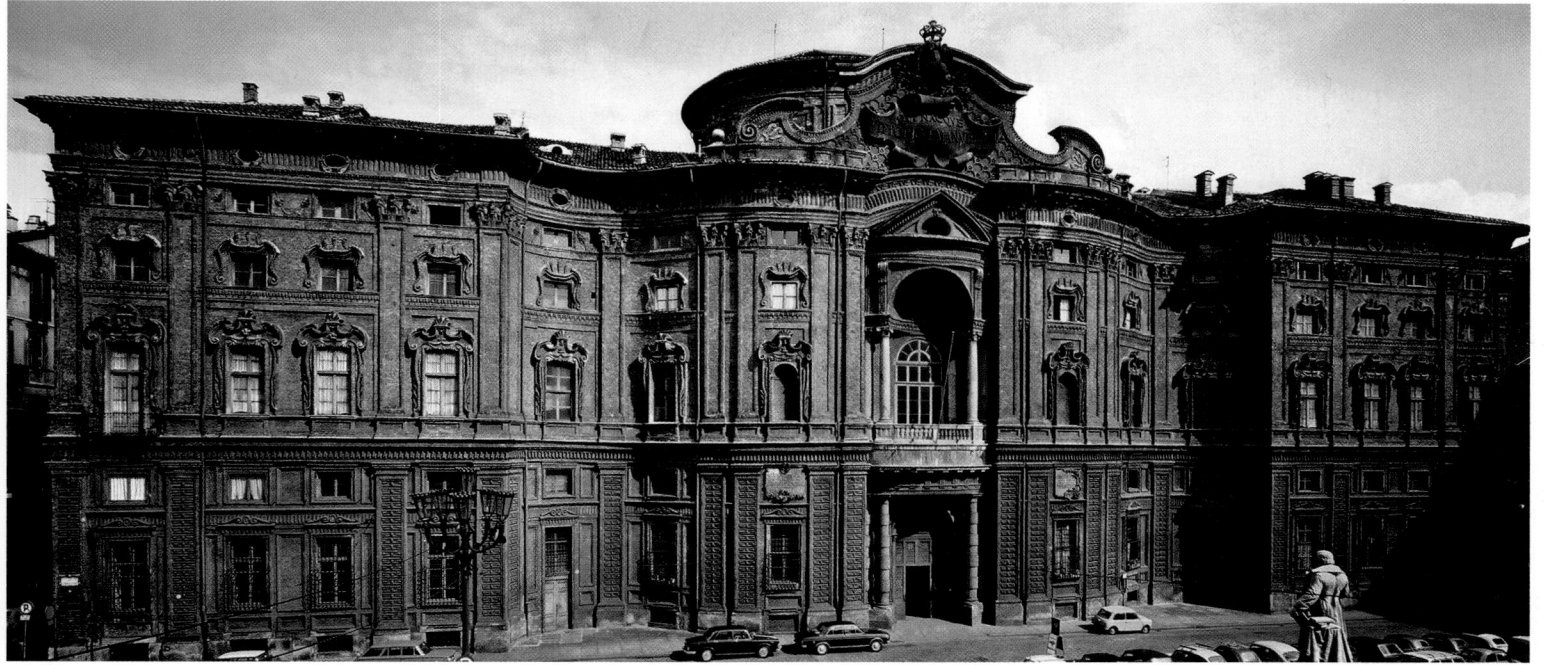

19.26   Guarino Guarini, Façade of Palazzo Carignano. Turin. Begun 1679

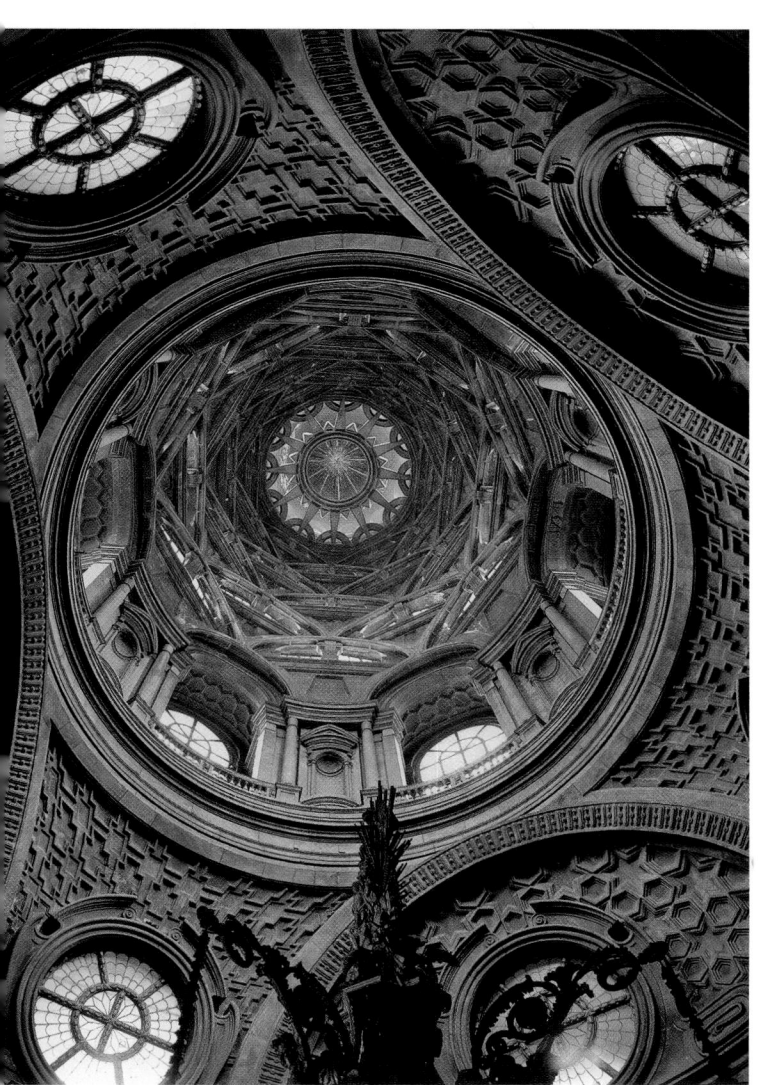

maze of ribs that is both unusual and exotic, created through the manipulation of repeated geometric forms. As a result, we find ourselves staring into a huge kaleidoscope. Above this seemingly infinite funnel of space hovers the dove of the Holy Spirit within a 12-point star inside the chapel, which holds one of the most precious relics of Christendom, the Shroud of Christ.

Guarini's dome retains the symbolic meaning of the dome of Heaven, and repeats architecturally what Correggio achieved in painting in his *Assumption of the Virgin* (see fig. 17.27). A concentric structure of alternating rings of light and shadow enhances the illusion of great depth and features brilliant light at its center; it also recalls the Passion of Christ. The objective harmony of the Renaissance has here become subjective, a compelling experience of the infinite, close to the Gothic mysticism of Abbot Suger's infinite (see page 391). If Borromini's style at times suggests a fusion of Gothic and Renaissance, Guarini takes the next step. In his writings, he contrasts the "muscular" architecture of the ancients with the effect of Gothic churches, which appear to stand only by means of some kind of miracle, and he expresses equal admiration for both. This attitude corresponds exactly to his own practice. Guarini and Borromini were obsessed with originality and were willing to break architectural rules to achieve it. By using the most advanced mathematical techniques of his day, Guarini accomplished wonders even greater than the seeming weightlessness of Gothic structures. The dome itself, for example, is on three pendentives instead of the usual four—a completely fresh approach to a traditional form.

19.27   Guarino Guarini. Dome of the Chapel of the Holy Shroud, Turin cathedral. 1668–94

The Baroque in Venice: Baldassare Longhena

The Republic of Venice commissioned a church at the head of the Grand Canal to show its gratitude to the Virgin for ending the plague of 1630—Santa Maria della Salute (fig. **19.28**; *salute* means "good health"). It was designed by Baldassare Longhena (1598–1682) in 1631 and as such may well be the first Baroque church, but it was not consecrated until 1687, after Longhena's death. It took the heart of the century to complete and rivals the masterpieces of Rome. The Salute's commission required that it be in "harmony with the site"; the structure dominates the Grand Canal and has become a focal point on the Venice skyline—unique, graceful, classical, yet ornate.

The most important aspect of the building is that its plan is that of a regular octagon whose distinctive form can be seen on its multiple façades, with a dome rising from its center. It is in the shape of a crown, referring to its dedication to the Virgin, Queen of Heaven. Each face is a double-columned triumphal arch whose columns stand on high pedestals. The entablature is joined to the drum in a series of large sculptural volutes that are both elegant and distinctive. The details—drum, double columns, and octagonal shape—all have their sources in the early Church, and in works by Bramante and Palladio, but they became the hallmark of the Baroque in Venice.

SCULPTURE IN ITALY

Baroque sculpture, like Baroque painting, was vital, energized, and dynamic, suggesting action and deep emotion. The subject matter was intended to evoke an emotional response in the viewer. Sculpture was usually life-size, but with a sense of grandeur that suggested larger-than-life figures; and many figures were indeed monumental. Deeply cut, the facial expressions and clothing caught the light and cast shadows to create not just depth but drama.

Early Baroque Sculpture: Stefano Maderno

Baroque sculpture began with the delicate naturalism of the *Santa Cecilia* (fig. **19.29**) by Stefano Maderno (ca. 1576–1636). Rather than showing his subject standing as in life, as with almost all depictions of saints, Maderno depicted her as a recumbent dead body. This fifth-century saint's body had been found, uncorrupted, just a year before, in 1599, in the church of Santa Cecilia in Trastevere. The recovery of her body prompted numerous depictions during the Baroque period of Santa Cecilia, the patron saint of music, but always showing her young, alive, engaged, and often playing a musical instrument. Here, however, she lies on her right side, on a slab of marble, her dress pulled between her knees and down to her toes as if lying on a bed rather than a morgue slab. The cut in her neck and the twisting away of her head indicate that she is dead. (Indeed, she was martyred by decapitation, but her head did not actually separate from her body.) She lies vulnerable even in her death, evoking pathos. The poignancy of Maderno's depiction of his subject is one of the characteristics of the Baroque.

The Evolution of the Baroque: Gianlorenzo Bernini

Bernini was a sculptor as well as an architect, and sculpture and architecture are never far apart in his work as we have seen in the *Baldacchino* (see fig. 19.15). He was trained by his father, Pietro Bernini (1562–1629), a sculptor who worked in Florence, Naples, and Rome, but who was also influenced by Giovanni Bologna (see fig. 17.13). Bernini's style was thus a direct outgrowth of Mannerist sculpture in many ways, but this debt alone does not explain its revolutionary qualities, which emerged early in his career.

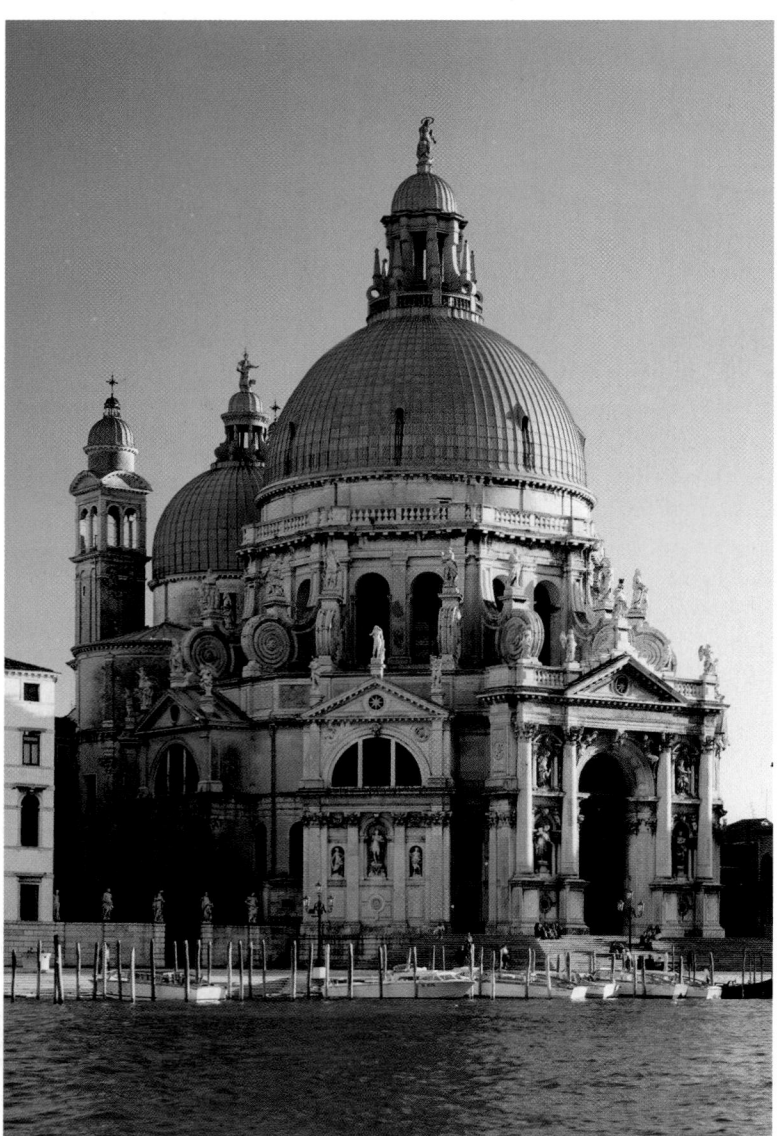

19.28   Baldassare Longhena, Santa Maria della Salute. Venice. 1631–87

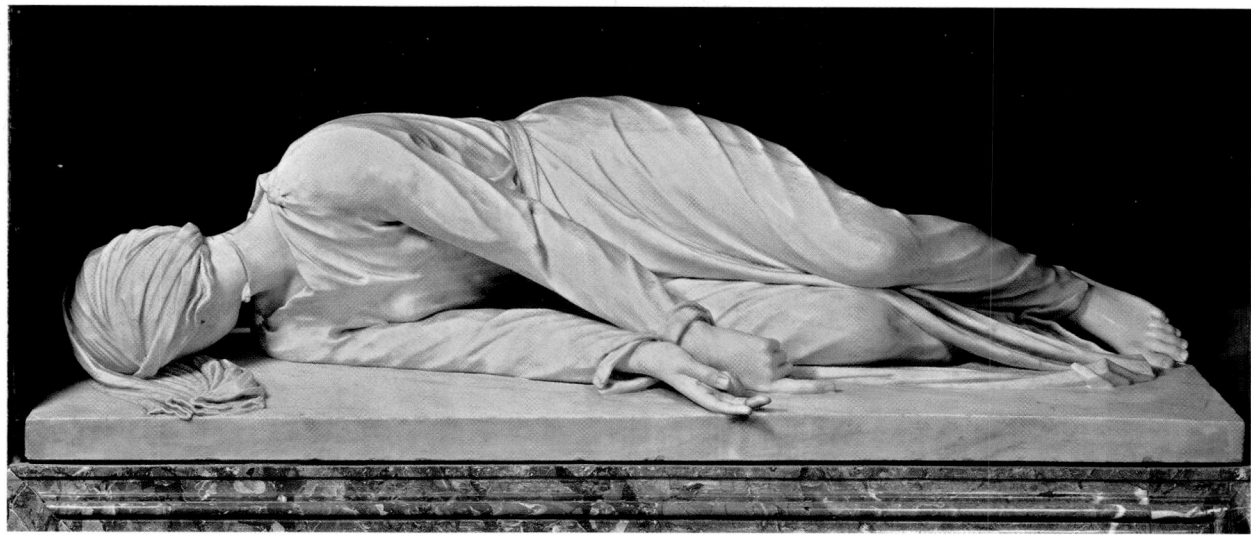

DAVID As in the colonnade for St. Peter's (see fig. 19.14), we can often see a strong relationship between Bernini's sculpture and examples from antiquity. If we compare Bernini's *David* (fig. **19.30**) with Michelangelo's (see fig. 16.13) and ask which is closer to the Pergamon frieze or the *Laocoön* (see fig. 5.73 and page 183), our vote must go to Bernini, whose sculpture shares with Hellenistic works that union of body and spirit, of motion and emotion, which Michelangelo so consciously tempers. This does not mean that Michelangelo is more classical than Bernini. It shows, rather, that the Baroque and the High Renaissance drew different lessons from ancient art.

Bernini's *David* has the fierceness of expression, movement, and dynamism of the *Laocoön*. In part, what makes it Baroque in character is the implied presence of Goliath. Unlike earlier statues of David, including Donatello's (see fig. 15.33), Bernini's is conceived not as a self-contained figure but as half of a pair, with his entire being focused on his (invisible) adversary. Bernini's *David* tells us clearly enough where he sees the enemy. Consequently, the space between David and his invisible opponent is charged with energy—it "belongs" to the statue. The intensity of his expression suggests his focused determination. It has come down to us that the *David*'s face is modeled on Bernini's own; he made this self-portrait by looking in a mirror held by his patron, Cardinal Barberini, who would become Pope Urban VIII. (See *Materials and Techniques*, page 688.)

Bernini's *David* shows us a distinctive feature of Baroque sculpture: its new, active relationship with the surrounding space. But it is meant to be seen, as is most other Baroque sculpture, from one primary point of view. Bernini presents us with "the moment" of action, not just the contemplation of the killing—as in Michelangelo's work—or the aftermath of it—as in Donatello's. Baroque sculpture often suggests a heightened vitality and energy. Because they so often present an "invisible complement" (like the

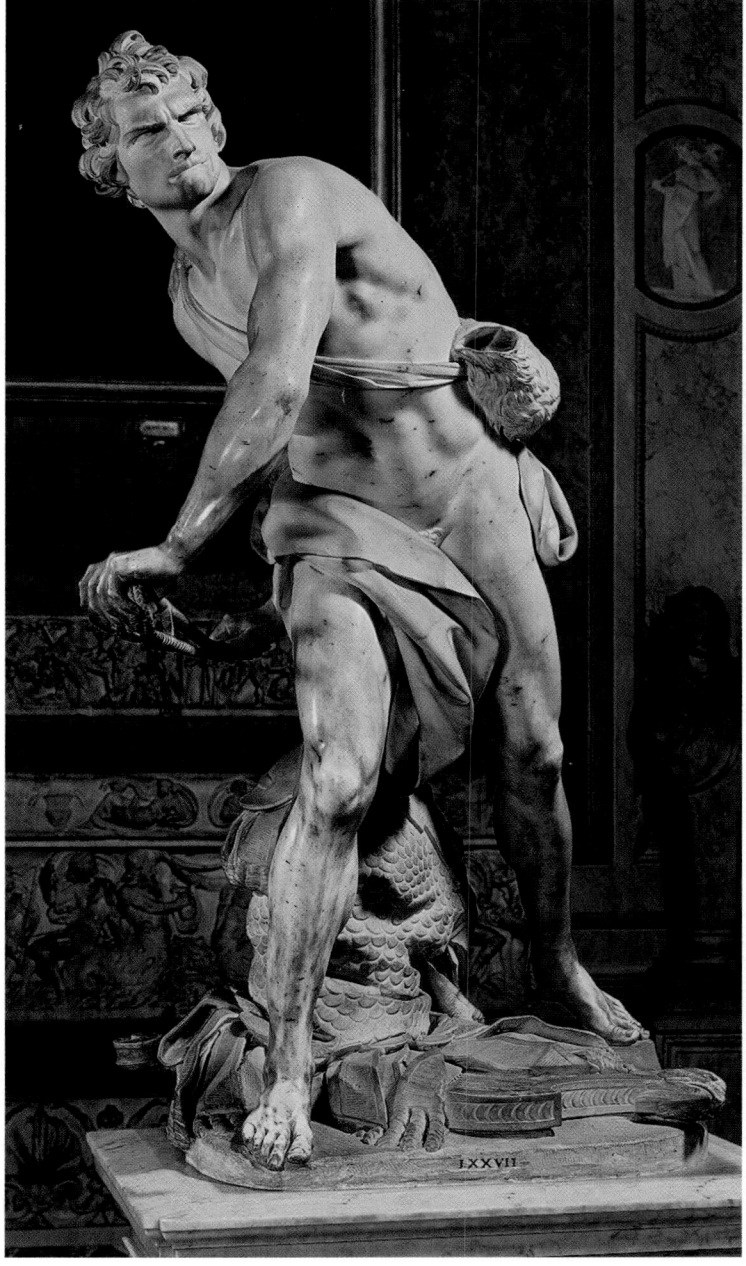

19.30 Gianlorenzo Bernini, *David*. 1623. Marble, life-size. Galleria Borghese, Rome

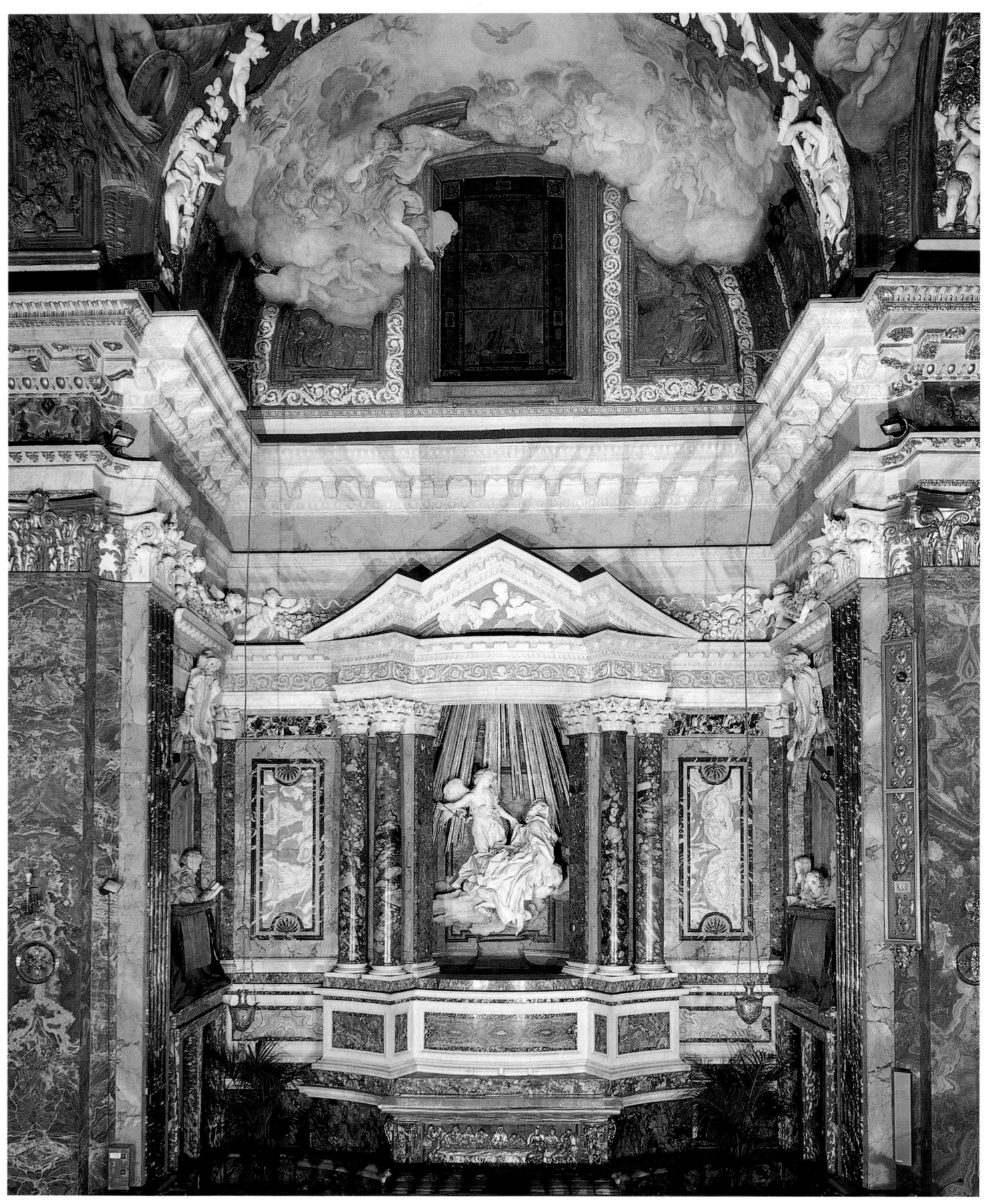

19.31 Gianlorenzo Bernini, *The Ecstasy of St. Teresa* (full chapel view). 1645–52. Marble, life-size. Cornaro Chapel, Santa Maria della Vittoria, Rome

Goliath of Bernini's *David*), Baroque statues attempt pictorial effects that were traditionally outside the realm of monumental sculpture. Such a charging of space with energy is, in fact, a key feature of Baroque art. Caravaggio had achieved it in his *The Calling of St. Matthew* with the aid of a sharply focused beam of light (see fig. 19.2). And as we have seen in Gaulli's ceiling for Il Gesù (see fig. 19.12), both painting and sculpture may be combined with architecture to form a compound dramatic illusion—one that Bernini would explore in other works.

THE CORNARO CHAPEL: *THE ECSTASY OF ST. TERESA*

Bernini had a passionate interest in the theater and was an innovative scene designer. A contemporary wrote that he "gave a public opera wherein he painted the scenes, cut the statues, invented the engines, composed the music, writ the comedy, and built the theatre." Thus he was at his best when he could merge architecture, sculpture, and painting. (See www.myartslab.com.) His masterpiece in this vein is the Cornaro Chapel in the church of Santa Maria della Vittoria, which contains *The Ecstasy of St. Teresa* (fig. 19.31 and see page 660). Teresa of Ávila (1515–1582), one of the great saints of the Counter-Reformation, and director of the Reformed Order of the Discalced ("shoeless," as shown here) Carmelites was canonized in 1622. Known for her mystical visions, she had described how an angel pierced her heart with a flaming golden arrow: "The pain was so great that I screamed aloud; but at the same time I felt such infinite sweetness that I wished the pain to last forever. It was not physical but psychic pain, although it affected the body as well to some degree. It was the sweetest caressing of the soul by God."

Bernini has made Teresa's visionary experience as sensuously real as Correggio's *Jupiter and Io* (see fig. 17.26); her arm and leg are limp and the saint's rapture is obvious. (In a different context the angel could be Cupid.) The two figures on their floating cloud, which is hollow (so Bernini could hang this group rather than fasten it to the wall), are lit from a hidden window above, so that they seem almost dematerialized. A viewer thus experiences them as a vision. The "invisible complement" here, less specific than *David*'s but equally important, is the force that carries the figures—they levitate—toward Heaven and causes the turbulence of their drapery. Its divine nature is suggested by the golden rays (gilt wood) which come from a source high above the altar. In an illusionistic fresco by Guidobaldo Abbatini (ca.1600/05–1656) on the vault of the chapel, the glory of Heaven is revealed as a dazzling burst of light from which tumble clouds of jubilant angels. This celestial explosion gives force to the thrusts of the angel's arrow and makes the ecstasy of the saint fully believable.

To complete the illusion, Bernini even provides a built-in audience for his "stage." On the sides of the chapel are balconies resembling theater boxes that contain marble relief figures depicting members of the Cornaro family, who also witness the vision. Their space and ours are the same, and thus they are part of our reality, while the saint's ecstasy, which is framed in a niche, occupies a space that is real but beyond our reach, for it is intended as a divine realm.

Finally, the ceiling fresco represents the infinite space of Heaven. We may recall that *The Burial of Count Orgaz* and its setting also form a whole that includes three levels of reality (see figs. 18.8 and 18.9). Yet there is a fundamental difference between the two chapels. El Greco's Mannerism evokes an ethereal vision in which only the stone slab of the sarcophagus is "real," in contrast to Bernini's Baroque staging, where there are several levels of reality and the distinctions between them break down. It would be easy to dismiss *The Ecstasy of St. Teresa* as a theatrical display, but Bernini was also a devout Catholic who believed that he was inspired directly by God. Like the *Spiritual Exercises* of Ignatius of Loyola, which Bernini practiced, his religious sculpture is intended to help a viewer identify with miraculous events through a vivid appeal to the senses. Theatricality in the service of faith was basic to the Counter-Reformation, which often referred to the Church as the theater of human life: It took the Baroque to bring this ideal to life.

Bernini was steeped in Renaissance humanism. Central to his sculpture is the role of gesture and expression in arousing emotion. While these devices were also important to the Renaissance, Bernini uses them with a freedom that seems anti-Classical. However, he essentially followed the concept of decorum (which also explains why his *David* is not completely nude), and he planned his effects carefully by varying them in accordance with his subject. Unlike the Frenchman Nicolas Poussin, whom he respected, Bernini did this for the sake of expressive impact rather than conceptual clarity. The approaches of the two artists were diametrically opposed. For Bernini, antiquity served as no more than a point of departure for his own inventiveness, whereas for Poussin it was a standard of comparison (see Chapter 21). It is nevertheless characteristic of the Baroque that Bernini's theories were far more orthodox than his art. Thus, he often sided with the classicists against his fellow High Baroque artists, especially Pietro da Cortona, who, like Raphael before him, also made an important contribution to architecture and was a rival to Bernini in that sphere.

A Classical Alternative: Alessandro Algardi

It is no less ironic that Cortona was the closest friend of the sculptor Alessandro Algardi (1598–1654), who is regarded as the leading classical sculptor of the Italian Baroque. His main contribution is the great marble relief *The Meeting of Pope Leo I and Attila* (fig. 19.32), done when he took over Bernini's role as principal sculptor at St. Peter's during the papacy of Innocent X. It introduces a new kind of high relief that soon became widely popular. Bernini avoided doing reliefs (when such projects were required, his studio executed them), but Algardi liked working in this more pictorial sculptural form.

The scene depicts the Huns under Attila being driven away after threatening an attack on Rome in 452, a fateful event in the early history of Christianity, when its very survival was at stake. (The actual event was very different: Leo persuaded the Huns not to attack, just as he did with the Vandals three years

Bernini's Sculptural Sketches

Small sketches in sculpture—for large-scale works of sculpture or architecture—serve as models, practice pieces, or presentation pieces for the artist to show a patron. These sculptural models are called *bozzetti* or *modelli*. *Bozzetto* (singular) means "sketch," and *bozzetti* are generally smaller and less finished than *modelli*, which may be closer to the final product, or in some other way "finished" so that a patron can see them before the completion of the project.

Artists may do several drawings as well as several *bozzetti* for a completed piece. And, indeed, Bernini did both drawings in pen and ink, in red or black chalk, or even in combinations of chalk and pen in preparation for a project, as well as making *bozzetti*. Bernini's *bozzetti* and *modelli* are made in clay (terra cotta), although the completed sculptures were executed in marble. This is not just a difference in medium, but in technique. Marble sculpture is created through a subtractive process—marble is chiseled away. But clay can be worked using both additive and subtractive methods, and we know that Bernini's work in clay was primarily additive.

We can see multiple methods and evidence of a variety of tools used by Bernini in his clay *bozzetto* of the life-size *Head of St. Jerome*, created for a full-length marble sculpture of the saint. Analysis of the clay sculpture has shown that this piece, like many others, was made from wedged clay—that is, fresh clay that is rolled, smashed, and rolled repeatedly to expel air, and then subsequently "worked." The clay is worked on by hand, using fingers (most probably the thumbs, index fingers, and middle fingers), with fingernails creating tracks, and tools that often have teeth.

The idea that the clay is worked on by the artist with his own hands—his own fingers—is a tantalizing one. Large-scale sculpture and complex sculptural and architectural projects may employ several assistants chiseling marble. But here in a *bozzetto* we may be looking at the handiwork—the very fingerprints—of the artist. Several of Bernini's *bozzetti* have been examined for fingerprints in the clay, and indeed many have been found. Of the fifteen Bernini *bozzetti* at the Fogg Art Museum (the largest single collection of his *bozzetti*), thirteen have fingerprints. Thirty-four fingerprints in total have been found and some of the same prints have been found in works executed years apart. Therefore, it is most likely that these prints are Bernini's own. He smoothed surfaces, added clay, created lines and edges with his nails, wiped and depressed the clay with his own fingers.

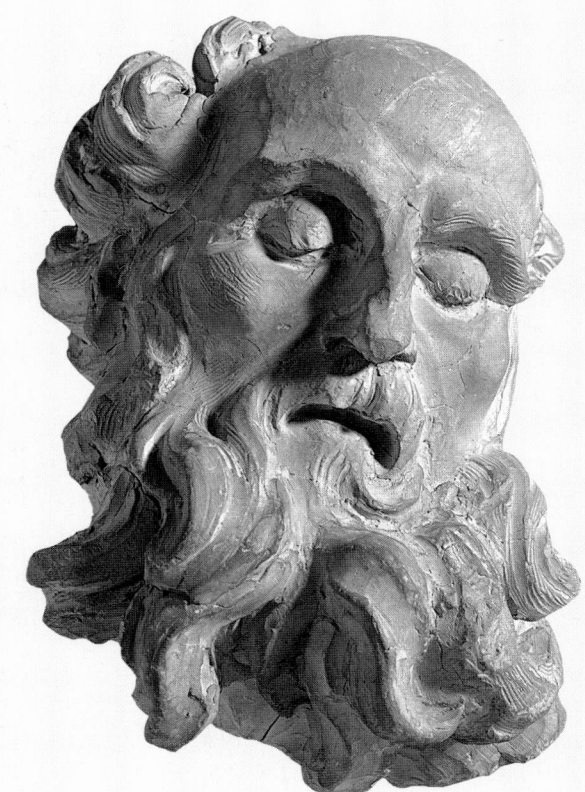

Gianlorenzo Bernini, *Head of St. Jerome*. ca. 1661. Terra cotta, height 14¼" (36.2 cm). Courtesy of the Fogg Art Museum, Harvard University Art Museum, Cambridge, MA. Alpheus Hyatt Purchasing and Friends of the Fogg Art Museum Funds, 1937.77

The *Head of St. Jerome* reveals Bernini's fingerprints, evidence of nail edging, and texturing from tined (fork-like) tools as he added more clay to represent the hair and nose. We know that the clay was hollowed out from the back, after being scooped out with fingers. As clay would be added to the face and hair, chances of cracking and breaking off increased. And we see much evidence of cracking in this *bozzetto*. It is apparent that areas were specifically smoothed over to prevent this. There is further evidence that a cloth was placed over the *Head* to keep the clay moist for continued work and to prevent further cracking.

The *Head of St. Jerome* is enormously expressive, looking tortured, with his deep-set eyes and hollow cheeks, but it is the textures in clay that make this gaunt face most memorable.

---

later. Both protagonists were on horseback, not on foot as seen here.) The subject revives a theme that is familiar to us from antiquity: the victory over barbarian forces. Now, however, it is the Church that triumphs; and the victory is spiritual rather than military.

A sculpture was commissioned since water condensation caused by its location in an old doorway of St. Peter's (and through most of the church) made paintings impossible to maintain in pristine condition. Never before had an Italian sculptor attempted such a large relief—it stands nearly 28 feet high (nearly twice the height of Ghiberti's bronze doors, see fig. 15.16).

The problems posed by translating a pictorial conception into a relief on this gigantic scale were formidable. If Algardi has not succeeded in resolving every detail, his achievement is stupendous nonetheless. By varying the depth of the carving, he nearly convinces us that the scene takes place in the same space as our own. The foreground figures are in such high relief that they seem detached from the background. They are modeled almost fully in the round. To emphasize the effect, the stage on which they are standing projects several feet beyond its surrounding niche. Thus, Attila seems to rush out toward us in fear and astonishment as he flees the vision of the two apostles defending the

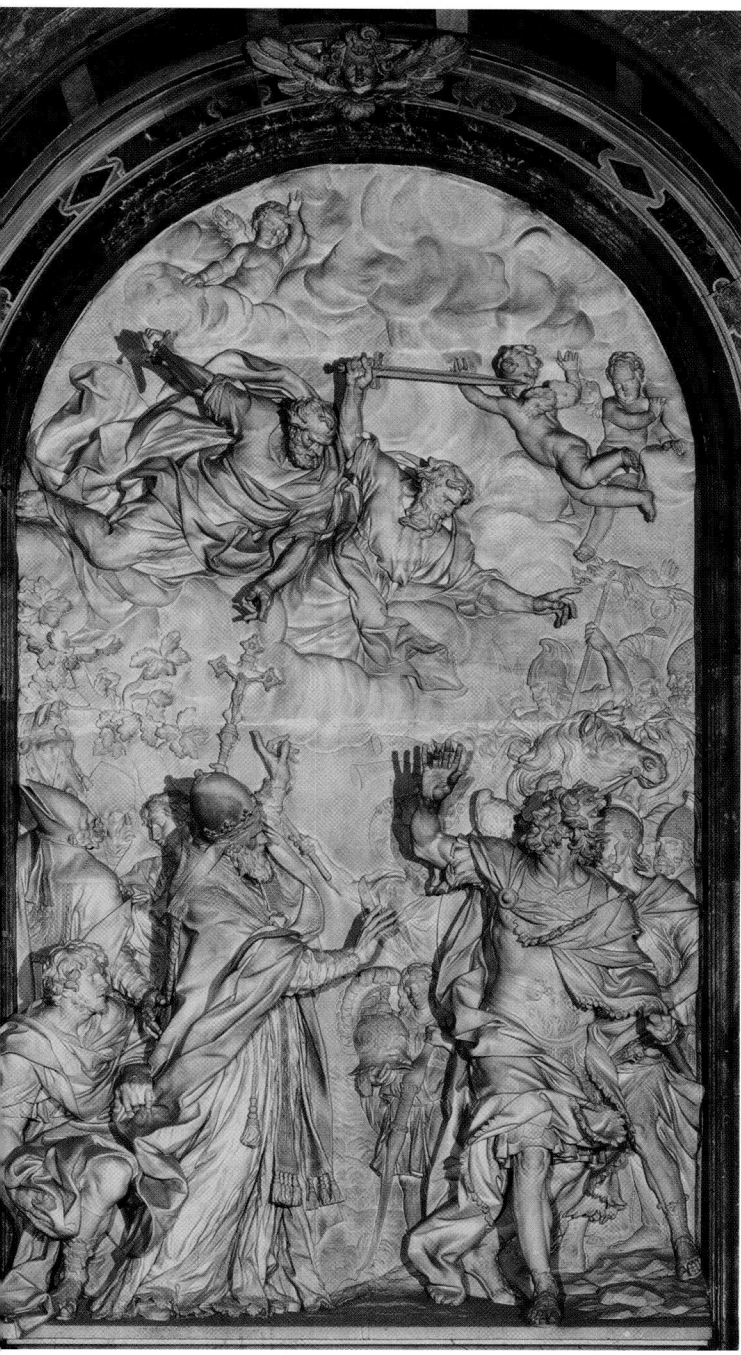

19.32 Alessandro Algardi, *The Meeting of Pope Leo I and Attila.* 1646–53. Marble, 28'1¾" × 16'2½" (8.5 × 4.9 m). St. Peter's, The Vatican, Rome

faith. The result is surprisingly persuasive in both visual and expressive terms.

Such illusionism is quintessentially Baroque. So is the intense drama, which is heightened by the twisting poses and theatrical gestures of the figures. Algardi was obviously touched by Bernini's genius. Strangely enough, the relief is partly a throwback to an *Assumption of the Virgin* of 1606–10 in Santa Maria Maggiore by Bernini's father, Pietro. Only in his observance of the three traditional levels of relief carving (low, middle, and high,

instead of continuously variable depth), his preference for frontal poses, and his restraint in dealing with the violent action can Algardi be called a classicist, and then purely in a relative sense. Clearly we must not draw the distinction between the High Baroque and Baroque classicism too sharply in sculpture, any more so than in painting.

PAINTING IN SPAIN

Spain may have been the most powerful political entity at the turn of the seventeenth century. It ruled the kingdoms of Portugal, Sicily, Naples, Milan, the North and South Netherlands, territories in North America (Florida) and South America (Chile and Argentina), the Philippines, the Canary Islands, and parts of Africa. This expansion during the sixteenth century brought it to the height of its political and economic power. Spain also produced great writers and influential saints. Indeed, the newly canonized saints of the early seventeenth century (1622)— Ignatius of Loyola, the founder of the Jesuit order, Francis Xavier, an early and influential Jesuit missionary, and Teresa of Ávila (see fig. 19.31)—were all Spanish.

Ironically, the Spanish court and most of the aristocracy held native artists in low esteem, and so preferred to employ foreign painters whenever possible. Thus, the main influences came from the Italian kingdoms and the Netherlands. Jan van Eyck visited Spain and inspired followers there, Titian worked for Charles V of Spain, and El Greco worked in Toledo from the late sixteenth into the seventeenth century; we also know that Rubens visited Spain at least twice and his work was much admired there. The patronage of the court in Madrid and its aggressive collecting, mostly by Philip IV, led to a deep appreciation of contemporary and Old Master foreign artists. The collection included works by Bosch, Raphael, Titian, Annibale, Carracci, Reni, Van Dyck, and Rubens.

Politics, art, and a common bond of loyalty to the Catholic Church connected Italy and Spain in the seventeenth century. Spain, still in the throes of the Inquisition (a medieval institution that was established separately in Spain in 1478 to enforce religious orthodoxy and revived in Italy in 1542), was staunchly conservative and unflinching; their king was titled "The Most Catholic Majesty." Spain restricted membership of the Church to only those subjects who professed their unaltering loyalty, and imprisoned, executed, or expelled those who did not, while the Vatican used its resources to bring Protestant reformers and the disaffected back to the Church. The Counter-Reformation, or Catholic Reform, began in Rome with a style—Baroque— intended to convince viewers of the dynamism and power of the Catholic Church, its patrons, and defenders. And, at the beginning of the seventeenth century, the largest city on the Italian mainland, Naples, was under the rulership of Spain, so the impact of Baroque Roman art on Neapolitan and Spanish art was profound. Spanish Baroque art was heavily influenced by the style and subject matter of Caravaggio—directly and via Naples—but had a greater starkness. Spanish naturalism may throw a harsher, stronger light on its subjects, but it is ultimately at least as sympathetic.

Spanish Still Life: Juan Sánchez Cotán

Still-life painting was unknown as a separate form until the 1590s. Spanish artists, inspired by the example of Pieter Aertsen (see fig. 18.31) and other Netherlandish painters, were the first to explore this new theme, and Spanish connoisseurs acquired vast collections of the resulting works. We see the distinctive character that Spanish artists brought to this new subject in this example (fig. **19.33**) by Juan Sánchez Cotán (1561–1627). This minor religious artist, who became a Carthusian monk, is remembered today as one of the first and most remarkable members of the Toledo school of still-life painters. Sánchez Cotán's painting has a clear order and stark simplicity, qualities that are completely controlled by the artist, who hung the vegetables with a fine string at different levels to coordinate the design—although whether the thin string would hold that full head of cabbage is a tantalizing question. Other vegetables sit on a ledge or sill. A window frames the still life: This orchestration of subject matter in direct sunlight against impenetrable darkness is the hallmark of early Spanish still-life painting. The painstaking realism in this stark setting creates a memorable image of the humble fruits and vegetables.

Although he probably used northern Italian paintings as his point of departure, Sánchez Cotán's still lifes make one think of Caravaggio, whose full impact on Spanish art, however, is not felt until considerably later. We do not know exactly how Caravaggism was transmitted. The likeliest route was through Naples, where Caravaggio had fled to safety and which was under Spanish rule.

Naples and the Impact of Caravaggio: Jusepe de Ribera

Caravaggio's main disciple in Naples was the Spaniard Jusepe de Ribera (1591–1652). Ribera settled there after having seen Caravaggio's paintings in Rome. Especially popular were Ribera's paintings of saints, prophets, and ancient beggar-philosophers. Their asceticism appealed strongly to the otherworldliness of Spanish Catholicism. Such pictures also reflected the learned humanism of the Spanish nobility, who were the artist's main patrons. Most of Ribera's figures possess a unique blend of inner strength and intensity.

His *The Club-Footed Boy* (fig. **19.34**) smiles openly and endearingly out at us, with a dimpled cheek, although we may be somewhat discomforted by his peasant dress, his begging, and his

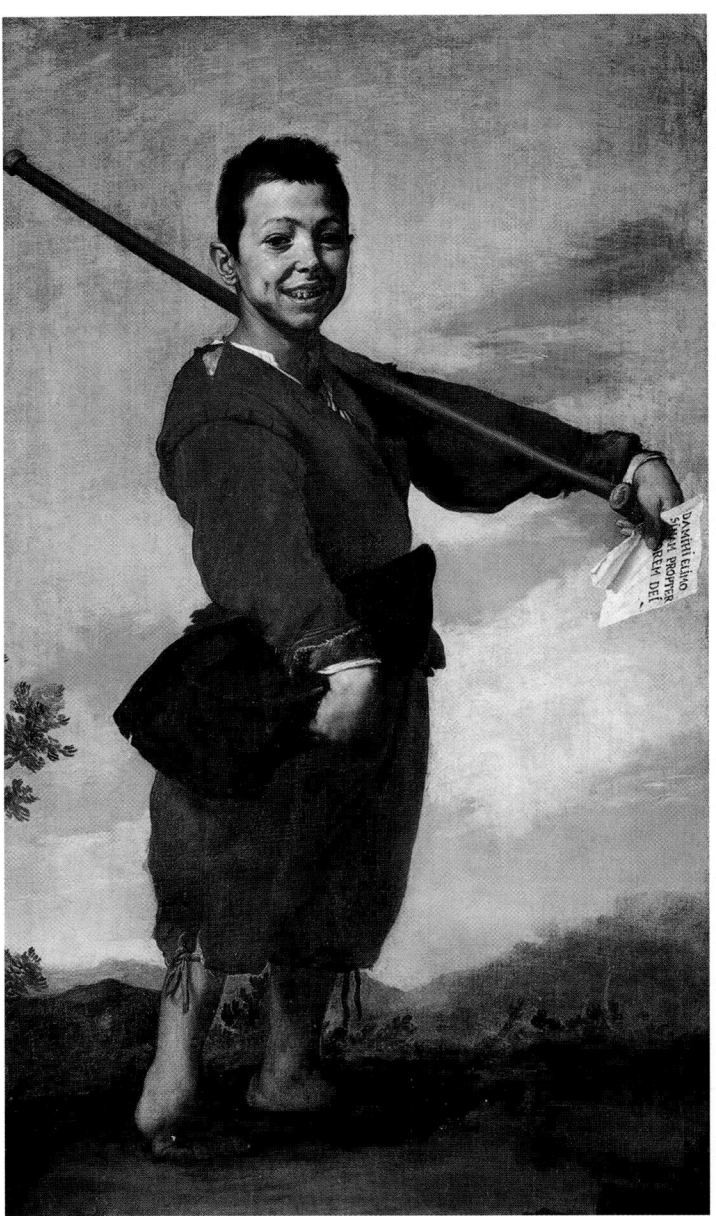

19.34   Jusepe de Ribera, *The Club-Footed Boy*. 1642. Oil on canvas, 64⅛ × 36⅝" (164 × 93 cm). Musée du Louvre, Paris

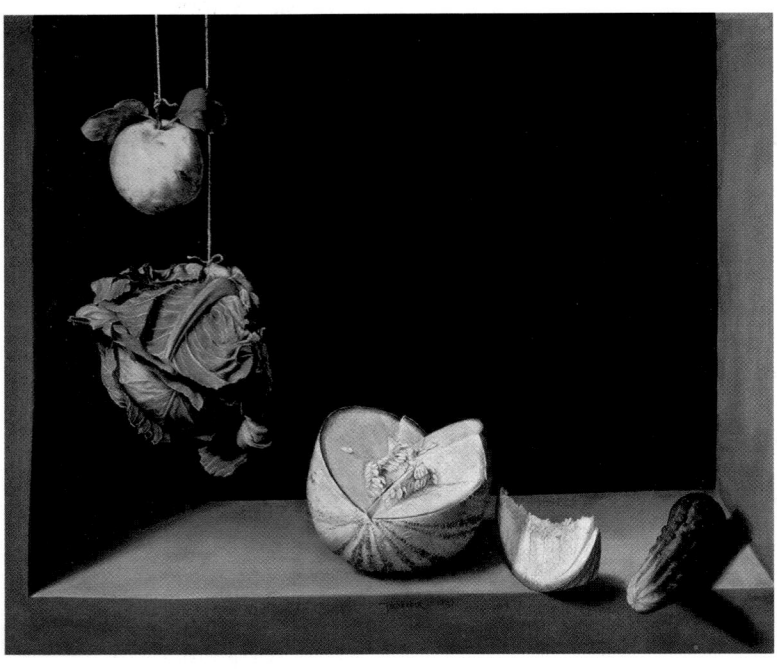

19.33   Juan Sánchez Cotán, *Quince, Cabbage, Melon, and Cucumber*. ca. 1602. Oil on canvas, 27⅛ × 33¼" (68.8 × 84.4 cm). San Diego Museum of Art. Gift of Anne R. and Amy Putnam. 1945:43

handicap. The words on the paper he holds state (in translation): "Give me alms for the love of God." This plea for charity alludes to the idea in Counter-Reformation theory that only through good works may the rich hope to attain salvation. The painting, indeed, was made for the viceroy of Naples, a wealthy collector who would have seen it as a testament to the importance of Christian charity and mercy to the poor. The boy seems almost monumental here as he stands against the broad sky with a low horizon line, like a musketeer; but instead of a weapon he holds a crutch across his shoulder. His deformed foot appears in shadow and one doesn't quite see it at first; but as the leg is lit, Ribera clearly directs our attention to it. The deformity may in fact not be a club foot but an indication of cerebral palsy. In either case, in the seventeenth century, such a deformity would have committed one to a life of begging.

Ribera executed other large paintings of beggars, of the poor, and of the blind. These were also the subjects of Pieter Bruegel the Elder (see fig. 18.34), who made prints and drawings of beggars using various crutches. As with Bruegel's works, *The Club-Footed Boy* is made with a moral purpose. The boy himself seems an embodiment of joy as he smiles, even laughs. This was considered a way for the subject to withstand misfortune, for he has the ability to dispense grace: He provides an opportunity for others to do good. Ribera's use of naturalism is a hallmark of Spanish and Neapolitan painting and etching, and it extends Caravaggio's impact. Caravaggism was felt especially in Seville, the home of the most influential Spanish Baroque painters before 1640: Diego Velázquez.

Diego Velázquez: From Seville to Court Painter

Diego Velázquez (1599–1660) painted in a Caravaggesque vein during his early years in Seville. His interests at that time centered on scenes of people eating and drinking rather than religious themes. Known as *bodegónes*, these grew out of the paintings of table-top displays brought to Spain by Flemish artists in the early seventeenth century. *The Water Carrier of Seville* (fig. **19.35**), which Velázquez painted at age 20 under the apparent influence of Ribera, already shows his genius. His powerful grasp of individual character and dignity gives this everyday scene the solemn spirit of a ritual. The scene is related to Giving Drink to the Thirsty, one of the Seven Acts of Mercy, a popular theme among Caravaggesque painters of the day. Velázquez's use of focused light and the revelation of shapes, textures, surfaces—from the glass of water to the sweat of water on the pottery jug—is extraordinary. He must have thought so, too, as he gave this painting to his sponsor, a royal chaplain from Seville, no doubt in hopes of gaining royal attention.

In the late 1620s, Velázquez was appointed court painter to Philip IV, whose reign from 1621 to 1665 was the great age of painting in Spain. Much of the credit for this must go to the duke of Olivares, who largely restored Spain's fortunes and supported an ambitious program of artistic patronage to proclaim the monarchy's greatness. Upon moving to Madrid, Velázquez

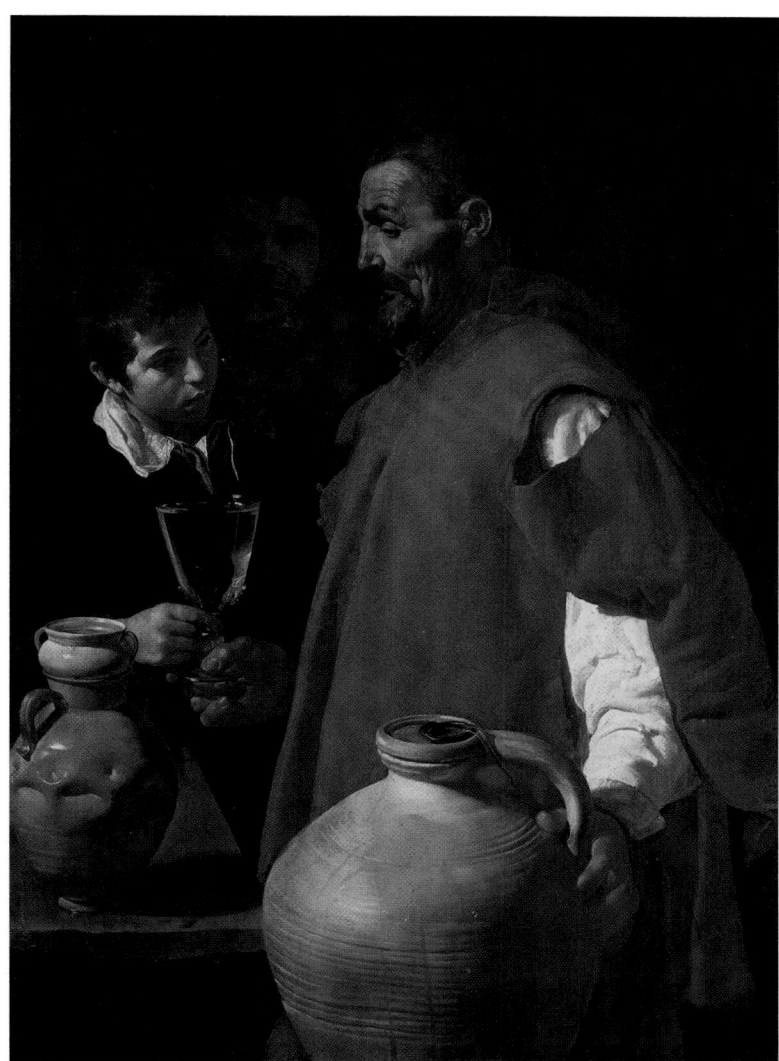

19.35   Diego Velázquez, *The Water Carrier of Seville*. ca. 1619. Oil on canvas, 41½ × 31½" (105.3 × 80 cm). Wellington Museum, London

quickly displaced the Florentines who had enjoyed the favor of Philip III and his chief minister, the duke of Lerma. A skilled courtier, the artist soon became a favorite of the king, whom he served as chamberlain. Velázquez spent most of the rest of his life in Madrid painting mainly portraits of the royal family. The earlier of these still have the strong division of light and dark and the clear outlines of his Seville period, but his work soon acquired a new fluency and richness.

SURRENDER AT BREDA   During his visit to the Spanish court on a diplomatic mission in 1628, the Flemish painter Peter Paul Rubens helped Velázquez discover the beauty of the many Titians in the king's collection. We see this most immediately in Velázquez's *Surrender at Breda* (fig. **19.36**), a dramatic and lush painting with color as rich as Titian's. It, too, would have been in the royal collection, intended as part of a series for the king's Buen Retiro Palace. The subject is an interpretation of an event in the war between the United Provinces (the Northern Netherlands) and Spain which took place in 1625, just a few years before the

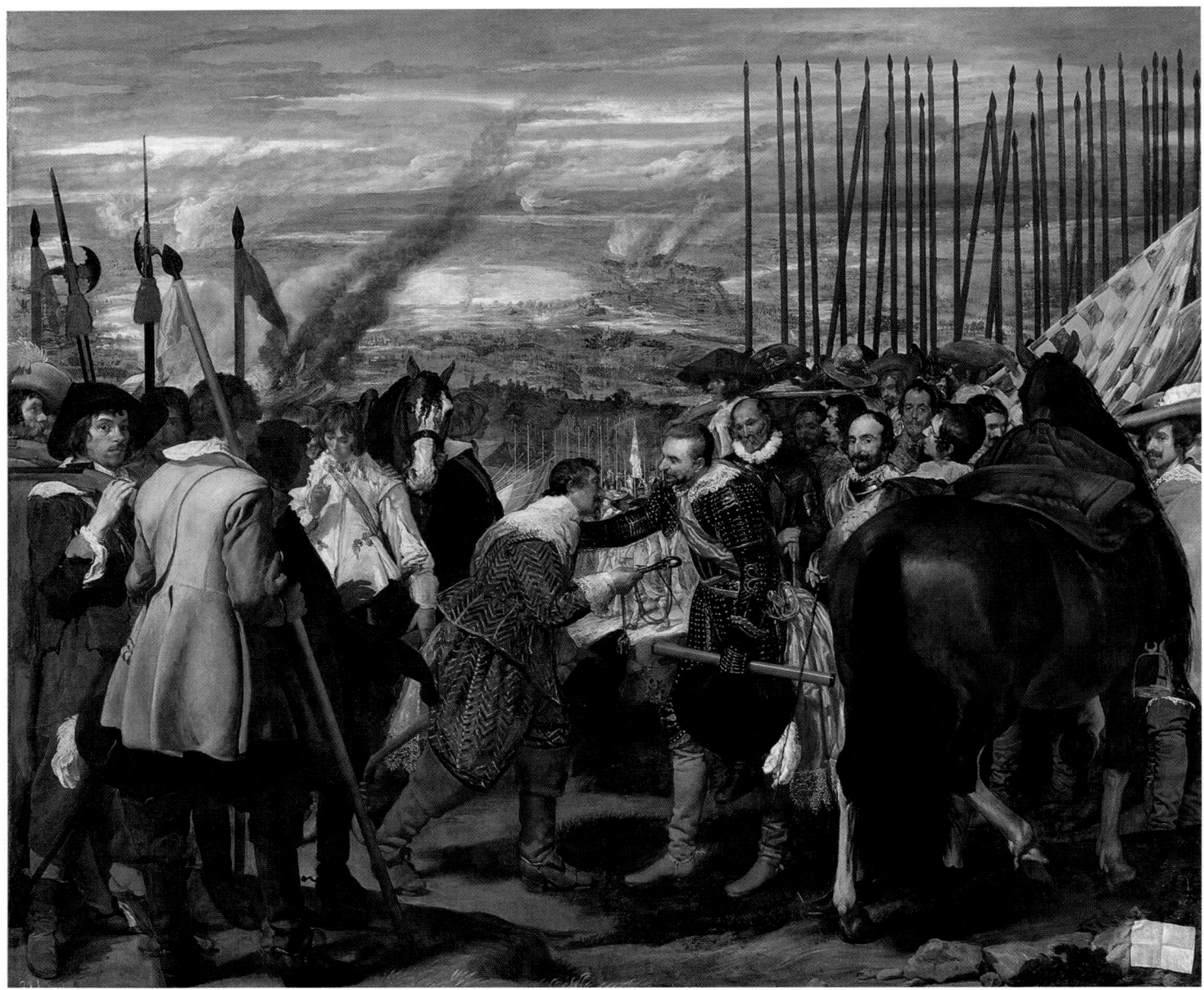

19.36 Diego Velázquez, *Surrender at Breda*. 1634–35. 10 × 12' (3.07 × 3.7 m). Museo del Prado, Madrid

painting's execution. Although the surrender did indeed occur, it certainly did not transpire in this elegant fashion. Here, the Dutch general, Justin of Nassau, on the left, bows to give the keys of the city to Spanish general, Ambrogio de Spinola, who has just gotten off his horse to meet his Dutch counterpart, even to comfort him: Note how he places his hand on the shoulder of the vanquished officer. Smoke comes from the left over the heads of the Dutch soldiers, who seem a bit dazed and forlorn, signaling the defeat of Breda. On the right are the Spanish troops who, by positioning themselves in front of the raised lances, seem to be standing more erect. Additional lances can be seen in the middle distance; one expects that the Spanish outnumbered the Dutch.

In truth, the Netherlands' revolt against Spain had ended by about 1585, with a truce in 1609, but conflicts (such as the one at Breda) continued to flare up. There were no keys to the city, and

the general probably did not get off his horse. By having the two generals confront each other not with hate but with acquiescence, Velázquez transforms a military drama into a human one. The scene Velázquez painted may in fact be derived from a contemporary play in which Spinola states: "Justin, I accept them [the keys] in full awareness of your valor; for the valor of the defeated confers fame upon the victor."

THE PORTRAIT OF JUAN DE PAREJA At court, Velázquez was famed as a portrait painter. As such, when Philip IV dispatched him to Rome in 1648 to purchase paintings and antique sculpture, he also gave permission for the artist to paint Pope Innocent X. But Velázquez's reputation seems not to have preceded him when he arrived in 1649, and he was left waiting for an interview with the pope. It was during this interlude that he

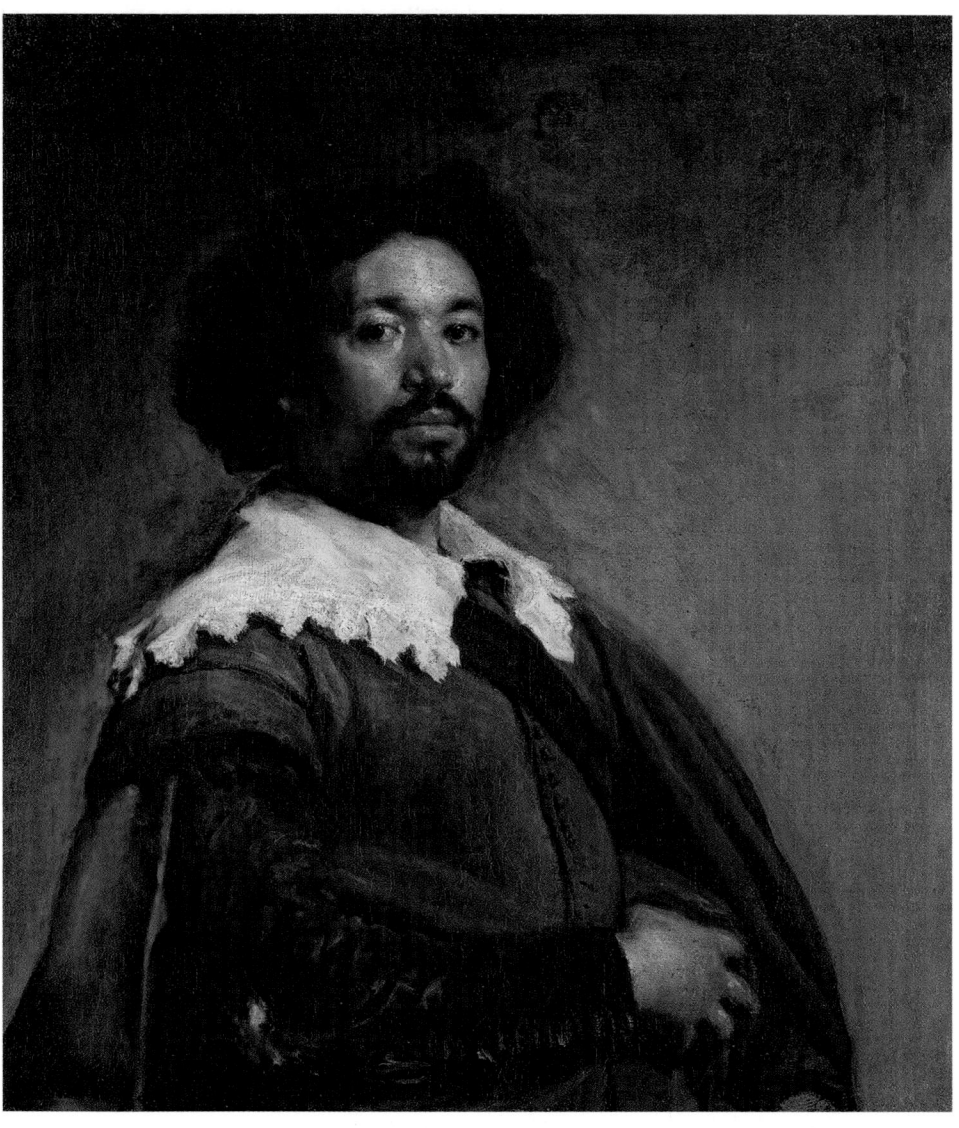

19.37 Diego Velázquez, *Juan de Pareja*. 1650. Oil on canvas, 32 × 27½" (81.3 × 69.9 cm). Metropolitan Museum of Art, New York. Purchase, Fletcher and Rogers Funds, and Bequest of Miss Adelaide Milton de Groot (1876–1967), by exchange, supplemented by gifts from Friends of the Museum, 1971. (1971.86)

painted the portrait of his Sevillian assistant and servant of Moorish descent, Juan de Pareja (ca. 1610–1670), who accompanied him to Rome and was an artist himself (fig. **19.37**). The portrait, stunningly lifelike, was acclaimed when it was exhibited at an annual art show in the Pantheon in Rome in March 1650. It was said that, of all the paintings, this one was "truth." Juan de Pareja is shown half-length, turned at a three-quarter view, but facing us—a triangular format developed by Raphael and Titian in the High Renaissance, simplifying the *Mona Lisa* (fig. 16.7), but still using it as their point of departure. As used here, the format rivets our attention to his face. The feathery lace collar, brilliantly painted, picks up the white highlights of the subject's face, creating a formidably sculptural visage. A white patch, a tear in his clothing at the elbow, reminds a viewer of his class, a device Velázquez had used earlier in *The Water Carrier of Seville*. The success of this portrait and Velázquez's sudden fame in Rome may have prompted the pope to sit for him, which he did, soon after.

THE MAIDS OF HONOR Velázquez's mature style is seen at its fullest in *The Maids of Honor* (fig. **19.38**). Both a group portrait

and a genre scene, it might be subtitled "the artist in his studio," for Velázquez depicts himself at work on a huge canvas. In the center is Princess Margarita, who has just posed for him, among her playmates and maids of honor. The faces of her parents, King Philip IV and Queen Maria Anna, appear in the mirror on the back wall. Their position also suggests a slightly different vantage point than ours, and indeed there are several viewpoints throughout the picture. In this way, the artist perhaps intended to include a viewer in the scene by implication, even though it was clearly painted for the king and hung in his summer quarters at the Alcázar Palace. Antonio Palomino, the first to discuss *The Maids of Honor*, wrote: "the name of Velázquez will live from century to century, as long as that of the most excellent and beautiful Margarita, in whose shadow his image is immortalized." Thanks to Palomino (see *Primary Source*, page 695), we know the identity of every person in the painting. Through the presence of the princess, king, and queen, the canvas commemorates Velázquez's position as royal painter and his aspiration to the Order of Santiago—a papal military order to which he gained admission only with great difficulty three years after the painting was

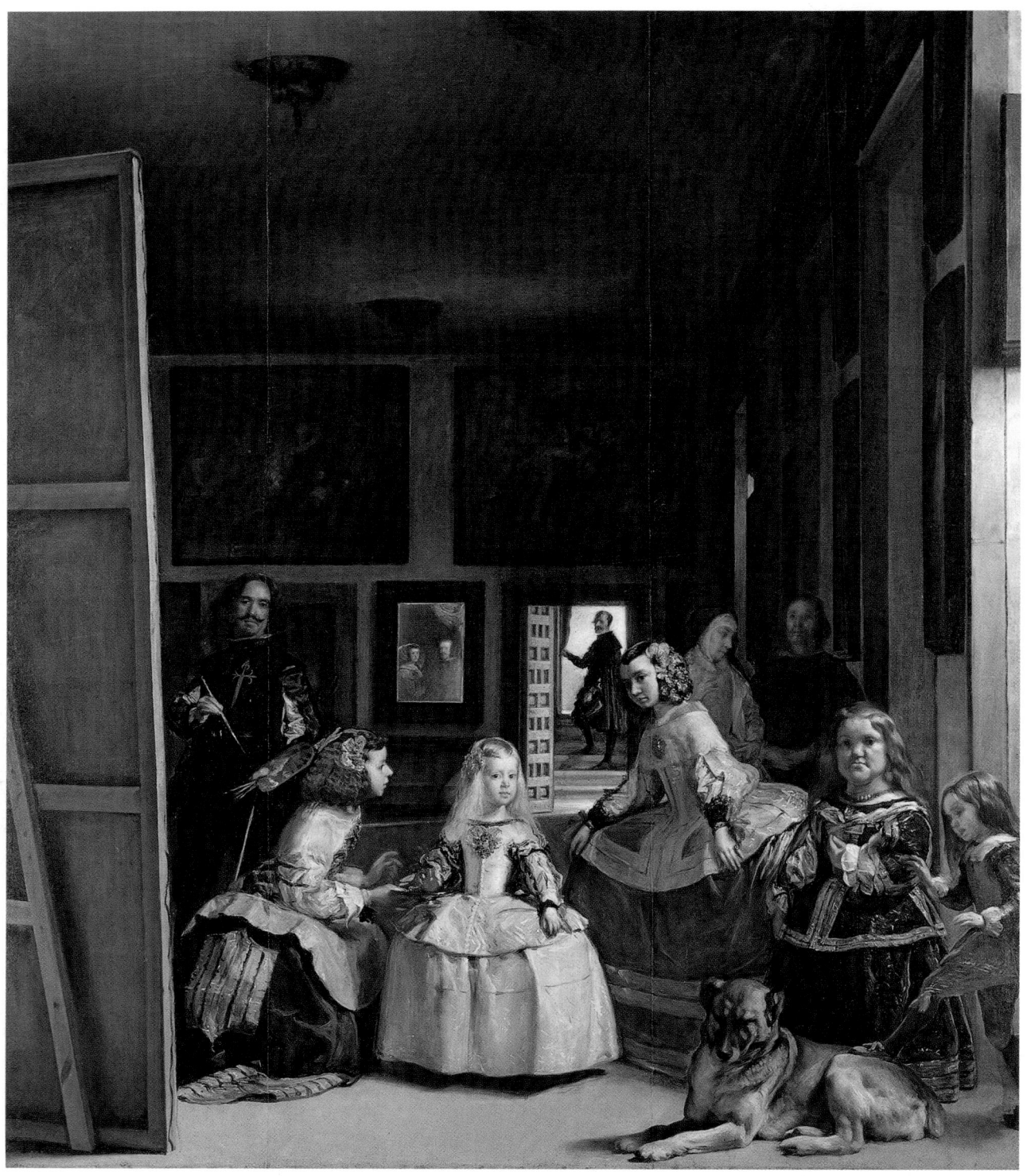

19.38 Diego Velázquez, *The Maids of Honor*. 1656. Oil on canvas, 10'5" × 9' (3.2 × 2.7 m). Museo del Prado, Madrid

executed. In the painting, he wears the red cross of the order, a detail added after his death.

Velázquez had struggled to establish his status at court. Even though the usual family investigations (almost 150 friends and relatives were interviewed) assisted his claim to nobility, the very nature of his profession worked against him. "Working with his hands" conveyed on Velázquez the very antithesis of noble status. Only by special papal dispensation was he eventually accepted into the Order of Santiago. *The Maids of Honor*, then, is an expression of personal ambition; it is a claim for both the nobility of the act of painting and that of the artist himself. The presence of the king and queen affirm his status. The Spanish court had already honored Titian and Rubens (although not in the same way); as these artists were both held in high regard, they served as models for Velázquez and continued to have a significant impact on him. The painting reveals Velázquez's fascination with light as fundamental

Antonio Palomino (1655–1726)

From *El Museo Pictórica y Escala Óptica*: On Velázquez

In 1724, Palomino wrote a biography of Spanish artists with a special focus on Velázquez, whom he revered above others. The following is a description of Velázquez's The Maids of Honor, *identifying the figures and recording comments on its reception.*

Among the marvelous pictures done by Velázquez was a large canvas with the portrait of the Empress (then the Infanta of Spain), Margarita María of Austria, as a young child. ... Kneeling at her feet is María Agustina, maid of honor of the Queen, giving her water in a small vessel. On the other side is Isabel de Velasco, also a maid of honor, who seems to be speaking. In the foreground is a dog lying down and next to it Nicolas Pertusato, a dwarf, who is stepping on it to show that it is a gentle animal in spite of its ferocious appearance. These two figures are in shadow and impart great harmony to the composition. Behind is Mari-Bárbola, a formidable-looking dwarf, and slightly farther back and in darker colors are Marcela de Ulloa, attendant to the ladies-in-waiting, and a bodyguard. On the other side is Diego Velázquez painting; he holds the palette in his left hand and a brush in his right. Around his waist he wears the key to the King's Chamber and on his breast, the Cross of the Order of Santiago that was added at His Majesty's orders after Velázquez died, because Velázquez was not a member of this Order when the picture was painted. ...

The canvas on which he is painting is large, and nothing of what he paints can be seen because only the back part is visible.

Velázquez proved his great genius because of the clever way in which he reveals the subject of what he is painting. He makes use of the mirror at the rear of the gallery to show us the reflection of our Catholic kings, Philip and Mariana. In this gallery, which is called the Room of the Prince, where he used to paint, several pictures can be seen indistinctly on the walls. These are known to be by Rubens and represent stories from Ovid's *Metamorphoses*. This gallery has several windows that are shown in perspective to make the room seem large. The light comes from the [picture's] left but enters only through the front and rear windows. ... To the left of the mirror is an open door where stands Joseph Nieto, the Queen's Marshal. He can be clearly seen in spite of the distance and poor light. Between the figures there is atmosphere. The figure painting is superior, the conception new, and in short it is impossible to overrate this painting because it is truth, not painting. Velázquez finished it in 1656. ...

The painting was highly esteemed by His Majesty and he frequently went to look at it. It was placed in the King's lower suite, in the office, along with other excellent works. In our own day, Luca Giordano was asked by Charles the Second what he thought of it and he answered, "Sir, this is the theology of Painting."

Source: *Italian & Spanish Art, 1600-1750: Sources and Documents*, ed. Robert Enggass and Jonathan Brown (Evanston, IL: Northwestern University Press, 1999)

to vision. The artist challenges us to match the mirror image against the paintings on the same wall, and against the "picture" of the man in the open doorway. Although the side lighting and strong contrasts of light and dark still suggest the influence of Caravaggio, Velázquez's technique is far subtler. The glowing colors have a Venetian richness, but the brushwork is even freer and sketchier than Titian's. Velázquez explored the optical qualities of light more fully than any other painter of his time. His aim is to represent the movement of light itself and the infinite range of its effects on form and color. For Velázquez, as for Jan Vermeer in Delft (see pages 732–33), light *creates* the visible world.

Monastic Orders and Zurbarán

Francisco de Zurbarán (1598–1664) began his professional life as a painter, as did Velázquez, in Seville, and he stands out among his contemporaries for his quiet intensity. His most important works, done for monastic orders, are filled with an ascetic piety that is uniquely Spanish. *St. Serapion* (fig. **19.39**) shows an early member of the Mercedarians (Order of Mercy) who was brutally murdered by pirates in 1240 but canonized only 100 years after this

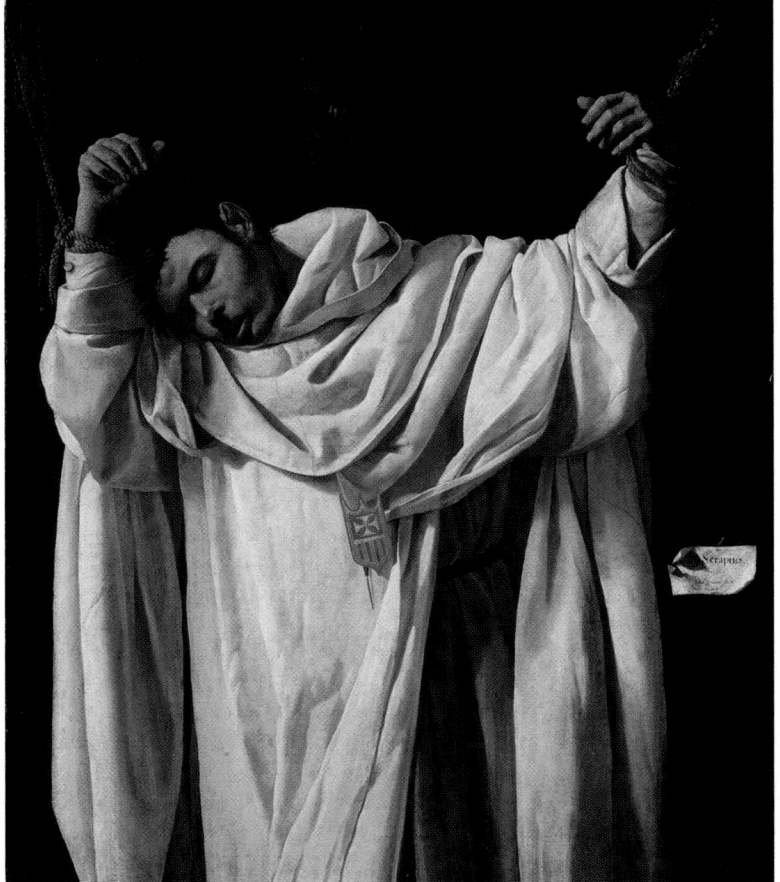

19.39 Francisco de Zurbarán, *St. Serapion*. 1628. Oil on canvas, 47½ × 41" (120.7 × 104.1 cm). Wadsworth Atheneum, Hartford, Connecticut. Ella Gallup Sumner and Mary Catlin Sumner Collection

picture was painted. The canvas was placed as a devotional image in the funerary chapel of the order, which was originally dedicated to self-sacrifice.

Zurbarán's painting reminds us of Caravaggio. Shown as a life-size, three-quarter-length figure, St. Serapion fills the picture plane: He is both a hero and a martyr. The contrast between the white habit and the dark background gives the figure a heightened visual and expressive presence, so that a viewer contemplates the slain monk with a mixture of compassion and awe. Here, pictorial purity and spiritual purity become one, and the stillness creates a reverential mood that complements the stark realism of the image. As a result, we identify with the strength of St. Serapion's faith rather than with his physical suffering. The absence of rhetorical pathos is what makes this image deeply moving.

Culmination in Devotion: Bartolomé Esteban Murillo

The work of Bartolomé Esteban Murillo (1617–1682), Zurbarán's (and, before him, Velázquez's) successor as the leading painter in Seville, is the most cosmopolitan, as well as the most accessible, of any of the Spanish Baroque artists. For that reason, he had countless followers, whose pale imitations obscure his real achievement. His many religious images, especially his depictions of the Virgin (fig. **19.40**), typified Spanish art's desire to promote the Virgin in the visual vocabulary of the seventeenth century, and they were much copied. The insistence on Virgin imagery defied the Protestant influence in much of Europe. The Immaculate Conception was controversial even among Catholics; the doctrine, promoted by Franciscans (Murillo was a lay member), says that the Virgin was conceived without Original Sin. Its detractors, led by the Dominicans, thought that she had been cleansed of sin in the womb after conception, but before birth. Paintings on this theme were used as propaganda to promote the Virgin's status so that the concept would, through art, become church dogma (accepted as true on the basis of faith); it was finally decreed as dogma in 1854. However, already in the seventeenth century there were spectacles of the "Immaculata" (processions carrying the image of the Immaculate Virgin) in Seville and papal declarations (notably by Alexander VII in 1661) that urged this change. Murillo was one of the major painters of this theme.

The haunting expressiveness of the Virgin's face and of the cherubs or angels has a gentle pathos that is more emotionally appealing than Zurbarán's austerity. This human warmth reflects a basic change in religious outlook. The Virgin's piety is shown

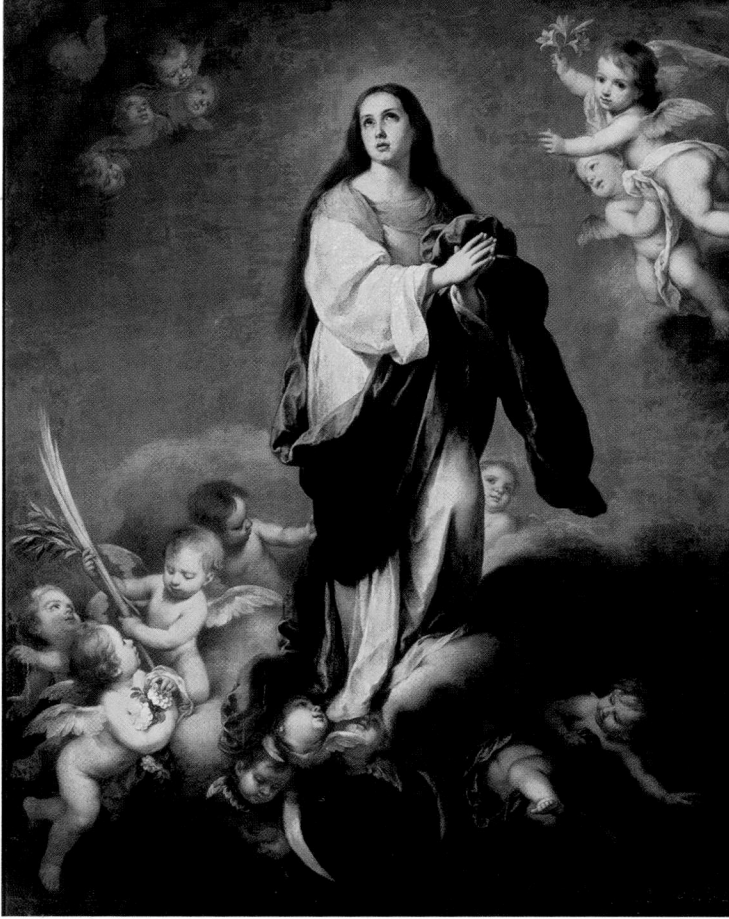

19.40 Bartolomé Esteban Murillo, *The Immaculate Conception.* ca. 1645–50. Oil on canvas, 7'8" × 6'5" (2.35 × 1.96 m). State Hermitage Museum, St. Petersburg, Russia

by her hands folded in prayer and upward glance to Heaven; she stands on a crescent moon, an attribute of the Immaculate Conception ("And there appeared a great wonder in Heaven: a woman clothed with the sun and the moon under her feet"— Revelation 12:1). The extraordinary sophistication of Murillo's brushwork and the subtlety of his color show the influence of Velázquez. Murillo succeeded so well that the vast majority of religious paintings in Spain and its South American colonies for the next 150 years were derived from his work. Although genre and still-life painting were also popular, the promotion of the Virgin in Spanish art defined Spain's Catholic and conservative art and its role in defying the Reformation of northern Europe.

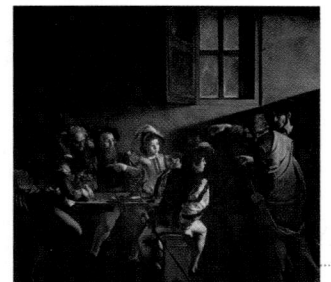

1599-1600 Caravaggio's
The Calling of St. Matthew

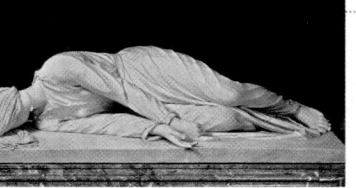

600 Maderno's *Santa Cecilia*

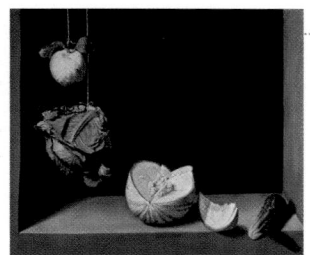

ca. 1602 Sánchez Cotán's
*Quince, Cabbage, Melon, and
Cucumber*

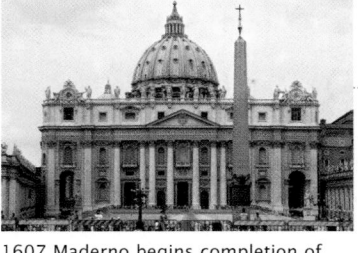

1607 Maderno begins completion of
St. Peter's Basilica

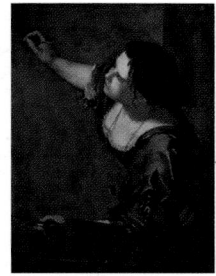

ca. 1638-39 Artemisia
Gentileschi's *Self-Portrait
as the Allegory of Painting*

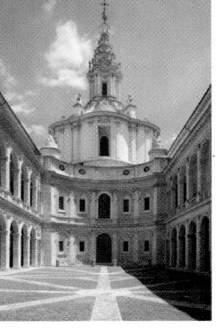

1642 Borromini's
Sant'Ivo

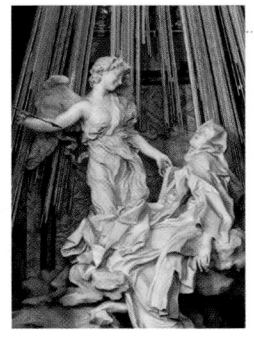

1645 Bernini's
*The Ecstasy of
St. Teresa*

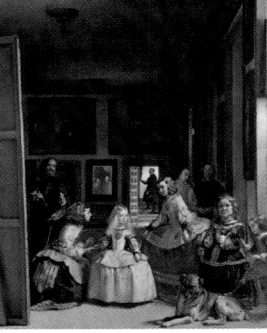

656 Velázquez's *The Maids
f Honor*

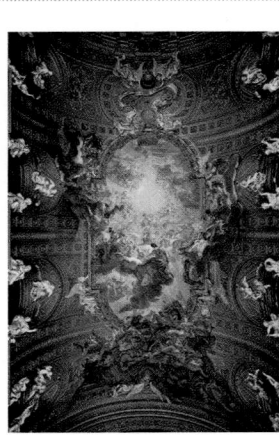

1672-79 Gaulli's *Triumph
of the Name of Jesus*

The Baroque
in Italy and Spain

1590

1600

1610

1620

1630

1640

1650

1660

1670

1680

1690

1700

◄ 1594 Tintoretto dies

◄ 1605 Miguel de Cervantes writes *Don Quixote*
◄ 1607 First opera, *L'Orfeo* by Monteverdi, performed
◄ 1609 Galileo Galilei refines astronomical telescope

◄ 1614 El Greco dies

◄ 1621 Philip IV becomes king of Spain
◄ 1622 Ignatius of Loyola, founder of the Jesuit order,
  Francis Xavier, Teresa of Ávila, and Filippo Neri, canonized
  1623 Urban VIII assumes papal throne

◄ 1633 The Inquisition forces Galileo Galilei to recant

◄ 1644 Evangelista Torricelli invents barometer
  1644 Innocent X assumes papal throne
◄ 1648 Treaty of Münster—Spain recognizes the
  Netherlands
◄ 1653 Arcangelo Corelli, master of modern violin, born
◄ 1655 Alexander VII assumes papal throne

◄ 1678 Antonio Vivaldi, composer, born

◄ 1697 Treaty of Rijswijk between Spain and France
◄ ca. 1698-1709 Bartolomeo Cristofori invents the
  modern piano

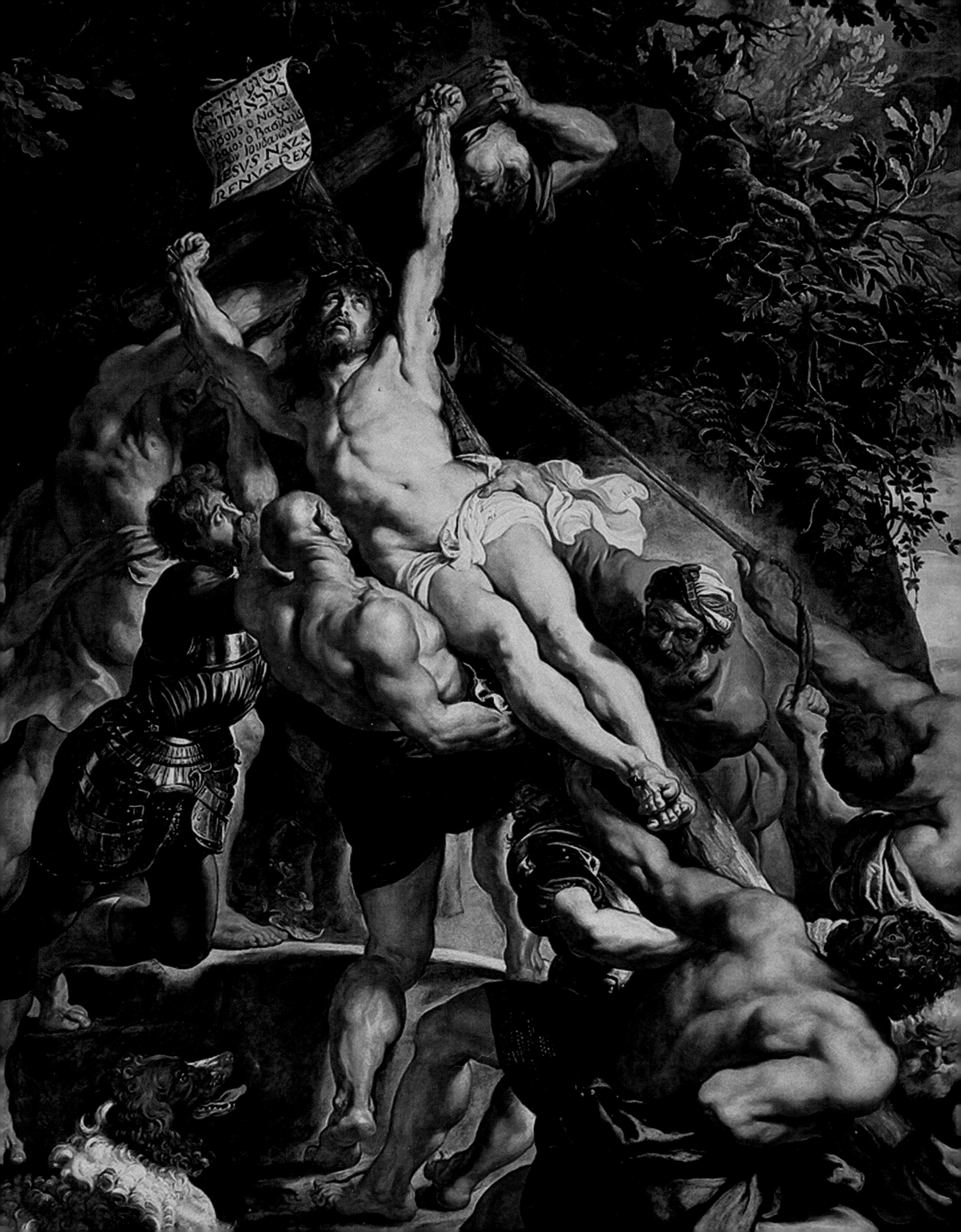

The Baroque in the Netherlands

THE SEVENTEENTH CENTURY BROUGHT A DIVISION OF THE Netherlands into two parts: the Northern Netherlands (the present-day Netherlands) and the Southern Netherlands (present-day Belgium and part of France). Each is often known by the name of its most important province: Holland (North) and Flanders (South). The Catholic Spanish Habsburgs

had ruled the Netherlands in the sixteenth century, but Philip II's repressive measures against the Protestants and his attempts to curtail their autonomy led to a rebellion that lasted 15 years. In 1581, the northern provinces of the Netherlands, led by William the Silent of Nassau of the House of Orange, declared their independence from Spain. Spain soon recovered the Southern Netherlands in 1585, and Catholicism remained the official religion. After a long struggle, the seven major provinces of the North, whose inhabitants were predominantly of the Reformed Church, became the United Provinces and gained their autonomy, which was recognized by the truce declared in 1609. Although hostilities broke out once more in 1621, the freedom of the Dutch (i.e., the people of the North) was never again seriously in doubt. Their independence was finally ratified by the Treaty of Münster, which ended the Thirty Years' War in 1648. The Dutch Republic was formally recognized by the rest of Europe as an independent state.

The division of the Netherlands had very different consequences for the respective economies, social structures, cultures, and religions of the North and the South. At the same time, throughout the seventeenth century, people crossed back and forth between the two regions, so providing some social and

cultural fluidity. After being sacked by Spanish troops in 1576, Antwerp, the leading port of the Southern Netherlands, lost half its population: Many migrated to the Northern Netherlands. The city gradually regained its position as Flanders's commercial and artistic capital, although Brussels was the seat of government. As part of the Treaty of Münster, however, the Scheldt River leading to Antwerp's harbor was closed to shipping, thus crippling trade for the next two centuries. Because Flanders continued to be ruled by Spanish regents, the Habsburgs, who viewed themselves as the defenders of the "true" (i.e., Catholic) faith, its artists relied primarily on commissions from Church and State, but the aristocracy and wealthy merchants were also important patrons.

Holland, in contrast, was proud of its hard-won freedom. Although the predominant religion was the Reformed Church, the Dutch were notable for their religious tolerance. Even Catholicism continued to flourish there, and included many artists among its ranks, while Jews found a haven from persecution. While the cultural links with Flanders remained strong, several factors encouraged the quick development of specifically Dutch artistic traditions. Unlike Flanders, where most artistic activity radiated from Antwerp, Holland had a number of local schools of painting. Besides Amsterdam, the commercial capital, there were important artists in Haarlem, Utrecht, Leiden, Delft, and other towns who established local styles. Thus, Holland produced an almost bewildering variety of masters and styles.

Detail of figure 20.1, Peter Paul Rubens, *The Raising of the Cross*

The new nation was one of merchants, farmers, and seafarers, who may formerly have earned their living from local commerce such as the fishing trade, but who now had the opportunity to have more distant adventures with the development of the famous Dutch East India Company (known as the VOC from its Dutch initials), established in 1602, and its counterpart, established in 1621, the Dutch West India Company. These companies developed trade in East Asia (China, Japan, and Indonesia) and in the Americas, bringing home exotic wares (map **20.1**, page 702), strange creatures, and fabulous flora and fauna, as well as engaging in exploration, map making, and the creation of colonial settlements. These adventures rippled though the economy: The sailors experienced them directly, but they also had a major impact on the directors and governors of the companies, who made their fortunes from these ventures. Even the townspeople who stayed home were able to purchase or at least see some of the wonders brought back from faraway places. From this time forward, the Dutch could never again be thought provincial; even those who did not travel could be considered, and would consider themselves, worldly.

As the Reformed Church was iconoclastic, Dutch artists rarely received the large-scale altarpiece commissions that were available throughout the Catholic world. While the House of Orange in The Hague and city governments and civic bodies such as militias provided a certain amount of artistic patronage, their demands were limited. As a result, private collectors became the painters' chief source of support. This was true before 1600, but the full effect of such patronage can be seen only after that date. There was no shrinkage of output. On the contrary, the public developed such an appetite for pictures that the whole country became gripped by a kind of collector's mania. During a visit to Holland in 1641, the English traveler John Evelyn noted in his diary that "tis an ordinary thing to find, a common Farmor lay out two, or 3000 pounds in this Commodity, their houses are full of them, and they vend them at their kermas'es [fairs] to very great gaines." Although it was unlikely farmers' houses were filled with paintings, or that Evelyn even visited them, there is no doubt paintings were not made only for the Church and the court. In the Northern Netherlands (as well as the Southern Netherlands), a new class of patron arose—the wealthy merchant.

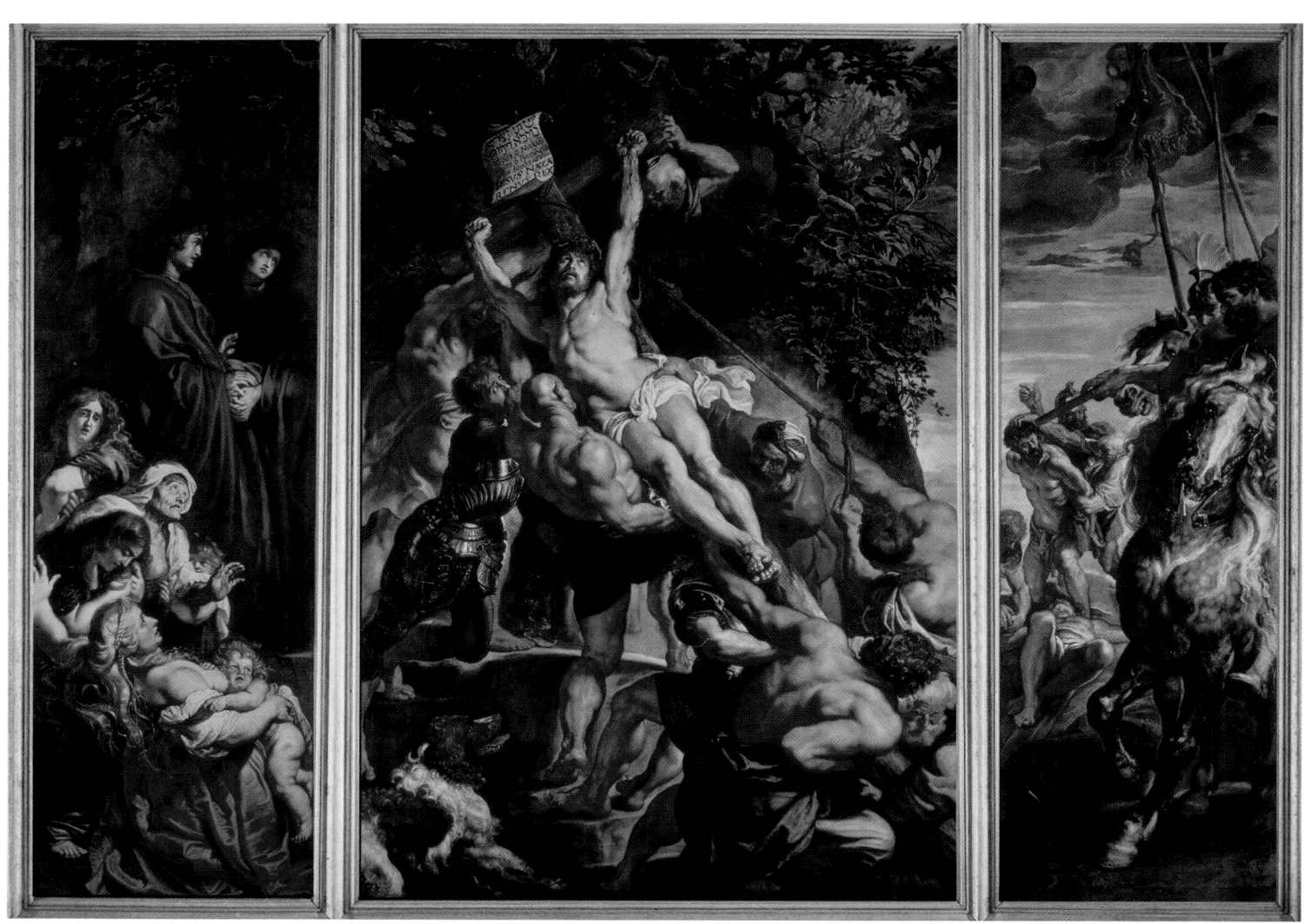

20.1   Peter Paul Rubens, *The Raising of the Cross.* 1610–11. Oil on panel, center 15'1" × 11'9⅝" (4.6 × 3.4 m), each wing 15' × 4'11" (4.57 × 1.52 m). Antwerp Cathedral, Belgium

FLANDERS

Art in seventeenth-century Flanders was defined by the art of Peter Paul Rubens. Rubens brought Flanders, really Antwerp, to international notice and the art of the Western world to Flanders. He did this through his own travels (bringing ideas back to Antwerp), his commissions, and his own extensive workshop.

Baroque art in Flanders was based on commissions. Its many churches could now, with the Truce of 1609 and hope of a sustained peace, be rebuilt and redecorated. The Habsburg archduke and archduchess, their family, and private patrons provided these commissions. Rubens's own interests were largely within the realm of painting, but his role in sculpture and sculptural decoration, architecture, costumes, and illustrated books (published by the famous Plantin Press in Antwerp) was still significant. All these art forms were directly affected by Rubens and his art.

The subjects of Flemish art, and of Rubens's paintings, were primarily religious—they were frequently large altarpieces with life-size figures, but portraits also accounted for many works. Although Rubens also executed landscapes, other artists, including Frans Snyders, Clara Peeters, Jan Davidsz. de Heem, and Jan Brueghel the Elder, frequently painted still lifes or "game pieces," sometimes in collaboration with Rubens. Rubens's one-time assistant Anthony van Dyck excelled in portraits and religious and mythological paintings, as did Jacob Jordaens, who also painted genre scenes. But all artistic efforts were influenced by Rubens.

Peter Paul Rubens and Defining the Baroque

Although the Baroque style was born in Rome, it soon became international. The great Flemish painter Peter Paul Rubens (1577–1640) played a role of unique importance in this process. He epitomized the Baroque ideal of the virtuoso artist, acting as diplomat and advisor, with an *entrée* to the courts of Europe. He was widely read and widely traveled, with a knowledge of classical literature and several languages. He was acclaimed for his intellect, and for a vitality that enabled him to unite the natural and supernatural and to attain a Baroque theatricality and drama that we have also seen in Bernini (see Chapter 19). He finished what Dürer had started 100 years earlier and Jan Gossaert had continued (see Chapter 18): the breakdown of the artistic barriers between Northern and Southern Europe. Rubens's father was a prominent Antwerp Protestant who had fled to Germany to escape Spanish persecution during the war of independence. The family had returned to Antwerp after his death, when Peter Paul was ten years old, and the boy had grown up a devout Catholic. Trained by local painters, Rubens became a master in Antwerp's Guild of St. Luke in 1598, but he only really developed a personal style when he went to Italy two years later.

During his eight years in Italy, in the art and patronage centers of Mantua, Genoa, Florence, and Rome, he absorbed the Italian tradition far more completely than had any northern European before him. He eagerly studied ancient sculpture, the masterpieces of the High Renaissance, and the work of Caravaggio and Annibale Carracci. In fact, Rubens competed on even terms with the best Italians of his day and could well have made his career in Italy: He received major commissions there for both portraits and altarpieces.

RUBENS AND THE ALTARPIECE *The Raising of the Cross* (fig. 20.1 and see page 698) was painted for the high altar of the church of St. Walburga (now destroyed). It was the first major altarpiece Rubens painted after his return to Antwerp in 1609. Its very subject (the *raising*) speaks to the dynamism of the Baroque and it shows how much he was indebted to his Italian experience. The muscular figures, modeled to show their physical power and passionate feeling, recall the antique Hellenistic sculpture that Rubens saw, drew, and collected (see *Primary Source*, page 704), and the figures from the Sistine Chapel ceiling that he also copied (fig. 20.2). These works of art served as models for his heroic figures throughout his life. He also gathered inspiration from the Farnese Gallery, while the lighting suggests Caravaggio's work (see figs. 19.1–19.4 and 19.7). The composition of the altarpiece recalls that of Rosso's *The Descent from the Cross* (see fig.

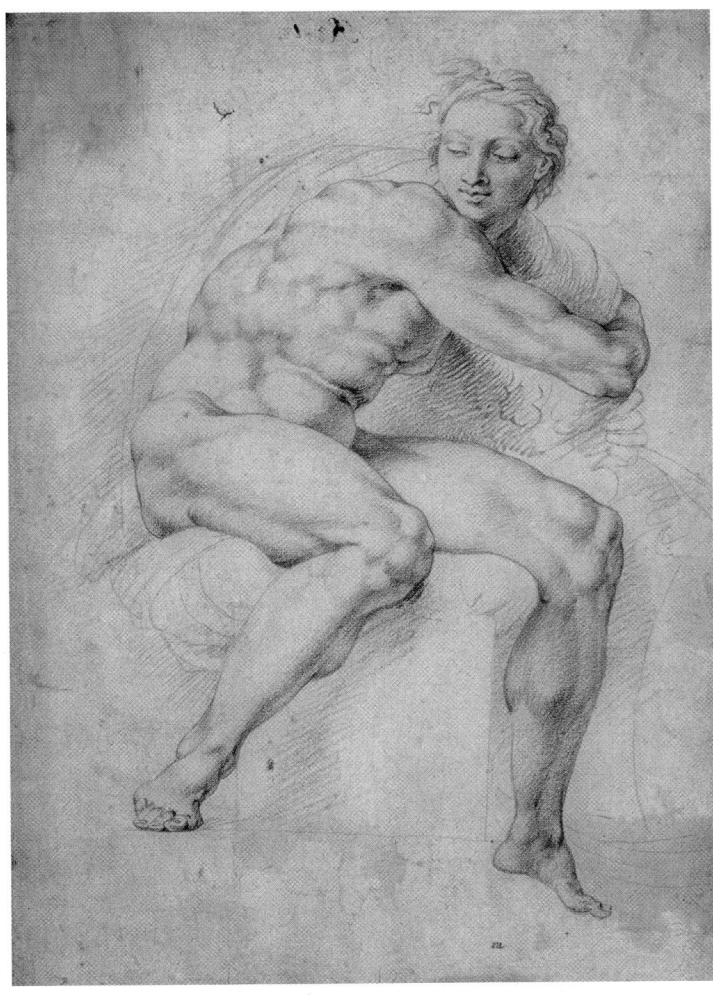

20.2 Peter Paul Rubens, *Drawing after Michelangelo's Ignudi from the Sistine Chapel Ceiling*. ca. 1601–02. Red chalk with touches of red wash, 15⅓ × 11" (38.9 × 27.8 cm). The British Museum, London

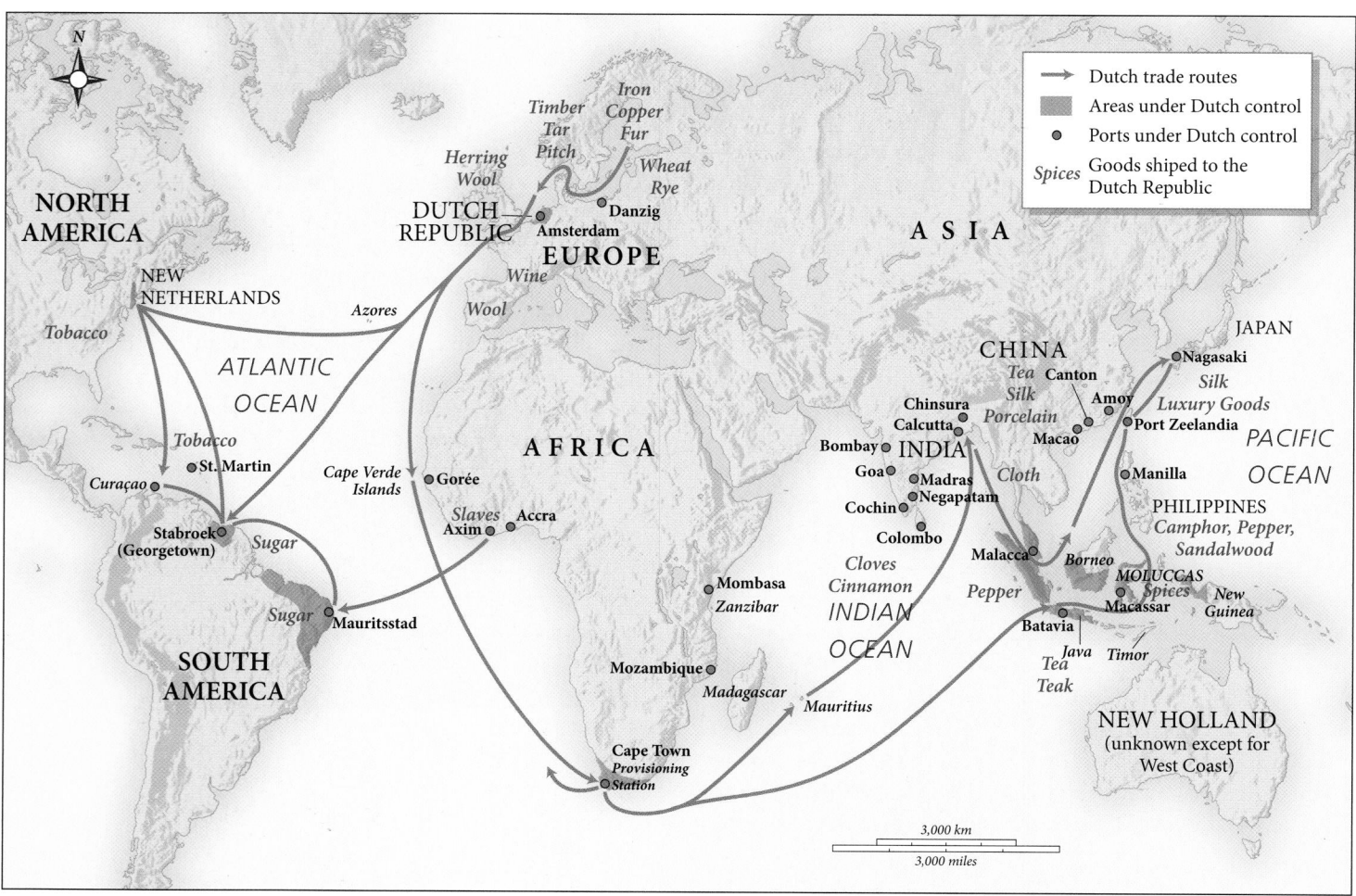

Map 20.1 Map of seventeenth-century Dutch trade routes

17.1), yet the painting is more heroic in scale and conception. Its rich color and luminosity, especially in the sky and background of the right wing, is ultimately indebted to the influence of Titian (see fig. 16.31). Thus, the altarpiece owes much of its success to Rubens's ability to combine Italian influences with Netherlandish ideas, thereby creating something entirely new. Rubens is also a Flemish realist in such details as the foliage, the armor of the soldier, and the curly-haired dog in the foreground. These varied elements are integrated into a composition of tremendous force. The unstable pyramid of bodies, swaying precariously under the strain of the dramatic action, bursts the limits of the frame in a typically Baroque way, making a viewer feel like a participant in the action.

Christ is shown parallel to the plane, so that we fully see him being raised to the crucifixion. The "raising" implies movement and action that is happening at that moment. Rubens extended the figure groups into both wings with an implied continuous landscape background. On the left are the Virgin and St. John, with horrified women; on the right are Roman soldiers; on the back of the wings (not shown here) are saints.

The altarpiece would have been 35 feet high in its final form—the main triptych was beneath a now-lost painting of God the Father, which explains Christ's heavenward imploring glance. He was surrounded by angels and a sculpted pelican (a symbol of

God's sacrifice) topped the work. The painting was placed on the high altar at the top of 19 steps, so the entire altarpiece ensemble —dramatic, powerful, and monumental—would have towered above all else.

Rubens's epic canvases define the scope and style of High Baroque painting. They possess a seemingly boundless energy and inventiveness, which, like his heroic nudes, express life at its fullest. And his portraits were equally inventive and dramatic.

RUBENS AS PORTRAITIST Rubens was one of the greatest and most influential portraitists of the seventeenth century, recording the vast wealth and stature of his often noble patrons. He painted several portraits while in Italy and maintained contacts with his Genoese patrons for years after he left. His resplendent portrait of Marchesa Brigida Spinola Doria (fig. **20.3**), a member of the ruling class of Genoese banking families, who invested in trade with Africa and the East, was painted in 1606, probably in celebration of her wedding at age 22.

Although still a large painting, it was even more monumental in the seventeenth century—perhaps 9 feet high—before being cut down on all four sides. A nineteenth-century lithograph of the painting shows that the Marchesa was originally full-length, and was shown striding from the terrace of her palazzo. She is

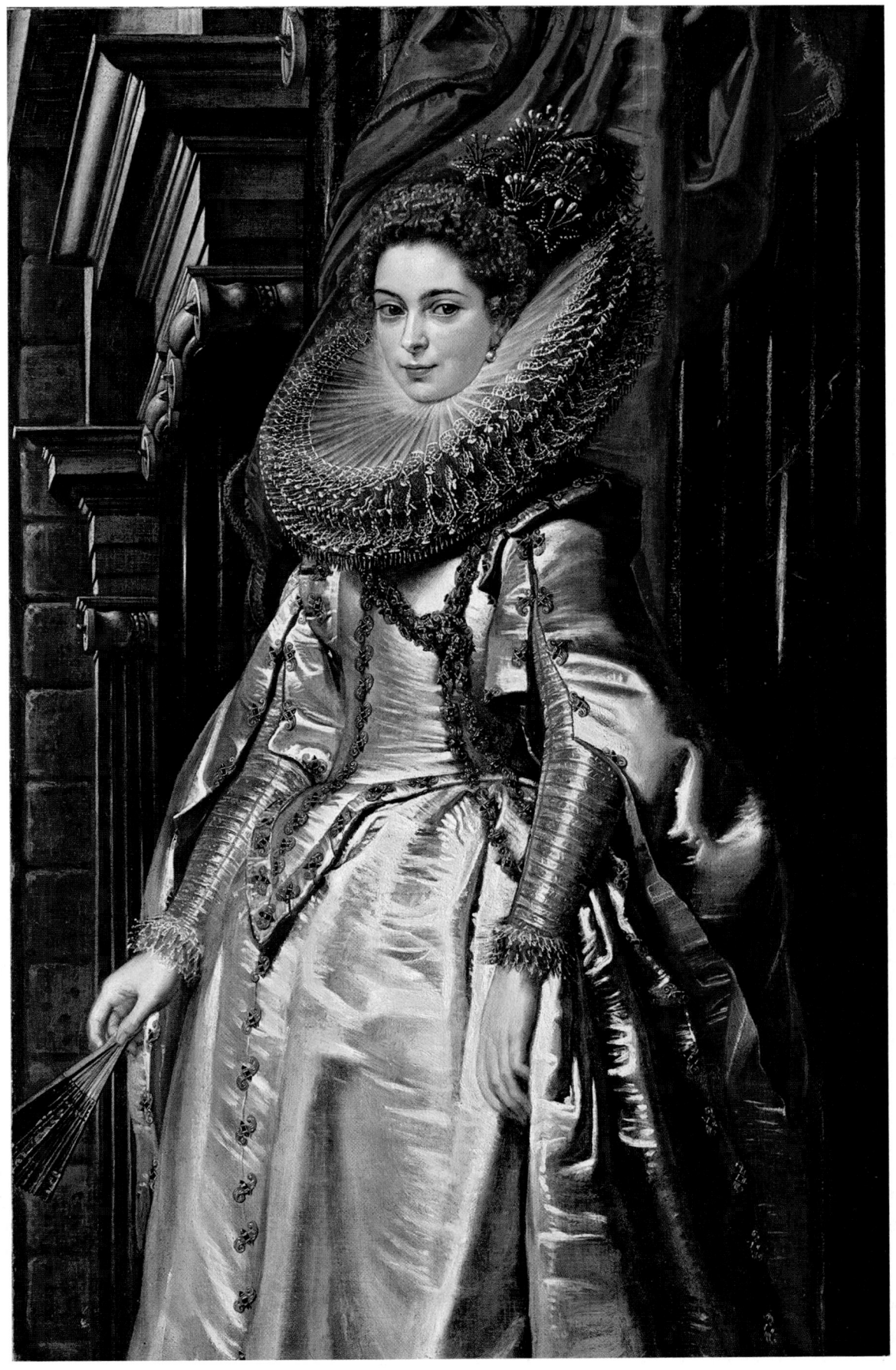

20.3   Peter Paul Rubens, *Marchesa Brigida Spinola Doria*. 1606. Oil on canvas, 5' × 3'2⅞" (152.2 × 98.7 cm).
The National Gallery of Art, Washington, D.C. Samuel H. Kress Collection. 1961.9.60.

PRIMARY SOURCE

Peter Paul Rubens (1577–1640)

From a Letter to Sir Dudley Carleton

In 1618, Rubens began a correspondence with Sir Dudley Carleton (1573–1632), the English ambassador to The Hague, in order to arrange an exchange of the Englishman's antique sculptures for his own paintings. Well-traveled and with diplomatic appointments to Paris and Venice (he was later made secretary of state), Carleton had acquired a notable collection of antique sculpture during his time in Italy (1610–15). Rubens, too, had a collection that he began to amass during his own stay in Italy (1600–1608). In his first letter, Rubens proposed an exchange for "pictures by my hand," and explains that the paintings he proposes to offer are the "flower of his stock," implying that many paintings by Rubens were not in fact executed for specific commissions but were kept by him (he lists 12 paintings in his house). The deal went through, and Rubens then had the greatest collection of antique sculpture in northern Europe, until he in turn sold part of it a few years later. In the end, 123 marbles from Carleton were exchanged for nine paintings by Rubens and three by Tintoretto, as well as a set of tapestries from Rubens's collection.

Most Excellent Sir:

By the advice of my agent, I have learned that Your Excellency is very much inclined to make some bargain with me concerning your antiquities; and it has made me hope well of this business, to see that you go about it seriously, having told him the exact price that they cost you. In regard to this, I wish to place my complete trust in your knightly word. … Your Excellency may be assured that I shall put prices on my pictures, just as if I were negotiating to sell them for cash; and in this I beg you to rely upon the word of an honest man. I find that at present I have in the house the flower of my stock, particularly some pictures which I have kept for my own enjoyment; some I have even repurchased for more than I had sold them to others. But the whole shall be at the service of Your Excellency, because I like brief negotiations, where each party gives and receives his share at once. To tell the truth, I am so burdened with commissions, both public and private, that for some years to come I cannot commit myself. Nevertheless, in case we agree as I hope, I will not fail to finish as soon as possible all those pictures that are not yet entirely completed, even though named in the list here attached. [*In the margin:* The greater part are finished.] Those that are finished I would send immediately to Your Excellency. In short, if Your Excellency will resolve to place as much trust in me as I do in you, the matter is settled. I am content to offer Your Excellency of the pictures by my hand, enumerated below, to the value of 6,000 florins, at current cash prices, for all those antiquities in Your Excellency's house, of which I have not yet seen the list, nor do I even know the number, but in everything I trust your word. Those pictures which are finished I will consign immediately to Your Excellency, and for the others that remain in my hands to finish, I will furnish good security to Your Excellency, and finish them as soon as possible. …

From Your Excellency's most affectionate servant,
Peter Paul Rubens

Antwerp, April 28, 1618

Source: *The Letters of Peter Paul Rubens*, ed. and tr. Ruth Saunders Magurn (Cambridge, MA: Harvard University Press, 1971)

---

sumptuously dressed in white satin, with a matching cape, bejeweled with a rope of gold set with gems of onyx and rubies. Her huge, multilayered ruff, typical of her time and class, frames her face, and her red hair is arranged with decorative combs of pearls and feathers. The vast flowing red cloth, which unfurls behind her, contrasts with her dress and heightens the color of her face. The diagonal movement of this drapery also suggests her forward stride. The size, full-length view, elements of movement, and color against her face are just a few of the aspects that influenced Rubens's student and assistant Anthony van Dyck (see figs. 20.7 and 20.8) in his portraits. Later stately portraits of the eighteenth and nineteenth centuries also reflect such influences.

OIL SKETCHES Rubens executed hundreds of oil sketches in preparation for his final works. They are small—small enough to hand to a patron—and represent the working art of preliminary concepts. An oil sketch for *The Raising of the Cross*, for example, suggests a less dynamic composition, changed in the final painting.

Four Studies of the Head of a Negro (fig. **20.4**) is not a sketch for any known larger piece, but we do know that Rubens used Africans in several of his paintings; studying the features and nuanced expressions of this man informed his work. It has been claimed that the four studies were done on separate occasions

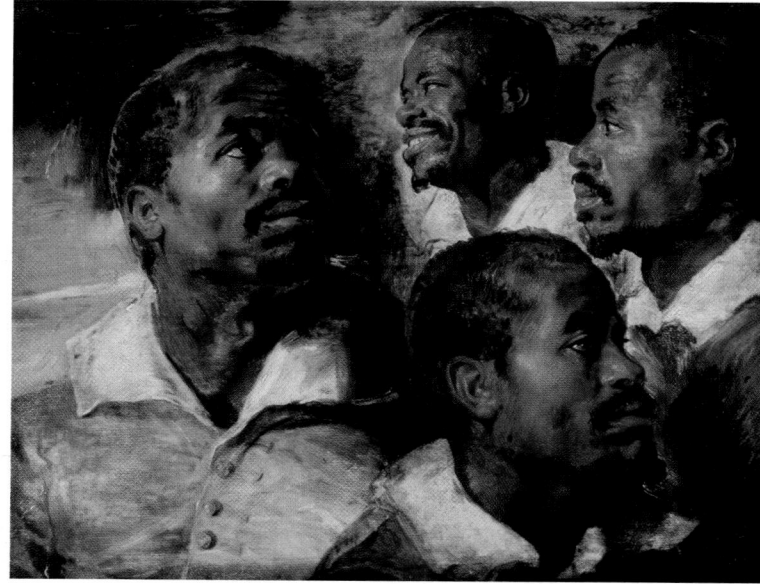

20.4   Peter Paul Rubens. *Four Studies of the Head of a Negro.* ca. 1613–15. Oil on panel transferred to canvas, 20 1/12 × 26" (51 × 66 cm). Musées Royaux des Beaux Arts de Belgique, Brussels, Belgium

over a few years, suggesting that this man was in Antwerp over an extended period—or left and returned. It is therefore likely that this African was a servant or a slave in a wealthy household. Rubens does not indicate his status; he is concerned only with his expressive sharply chiseled face.

MARIE DE' MEDICI CYCLE Rubens exhibited his virtuoso talent in portraits and monumental historical works in the 1620s with his famous cycle of paintings glorifying the career of Marie de' Medici, widow of Henry IV and mother of Louis XIII, in the Luxembourg Palace in Paris. The cycle consists of 21 paintings at least 13 feet high, with some as much as 28 feet wide. Rubens executed more than 35 sketches for these enormous paintings. Our illustration shows one episode: the young queen landing in Marseille (fig. 20.5). Rubens has turned an ordinary disembarkation into a spectacle of unparalleled splendor, combining reality and allegory. As Marie de' Medici walks down the gangplank to enter France; she has already married Henry IV by proxy in Florence, but is yet to meet her husband. Accompanied by her sister and aunt as the allegorical figure, Fame flies overhead sounding a triumphant blast on two trumpets; she is welcomed by the allegorical figure of France draped in a *fleur-de-lis* cape. Neptune and his fish-tailed crew, the Nereids, rise from the sea; having guarded the queen's journey, they rejoice at her arrival. Everything flows together here in swirling movement: Heaven and earth, history and allegory.

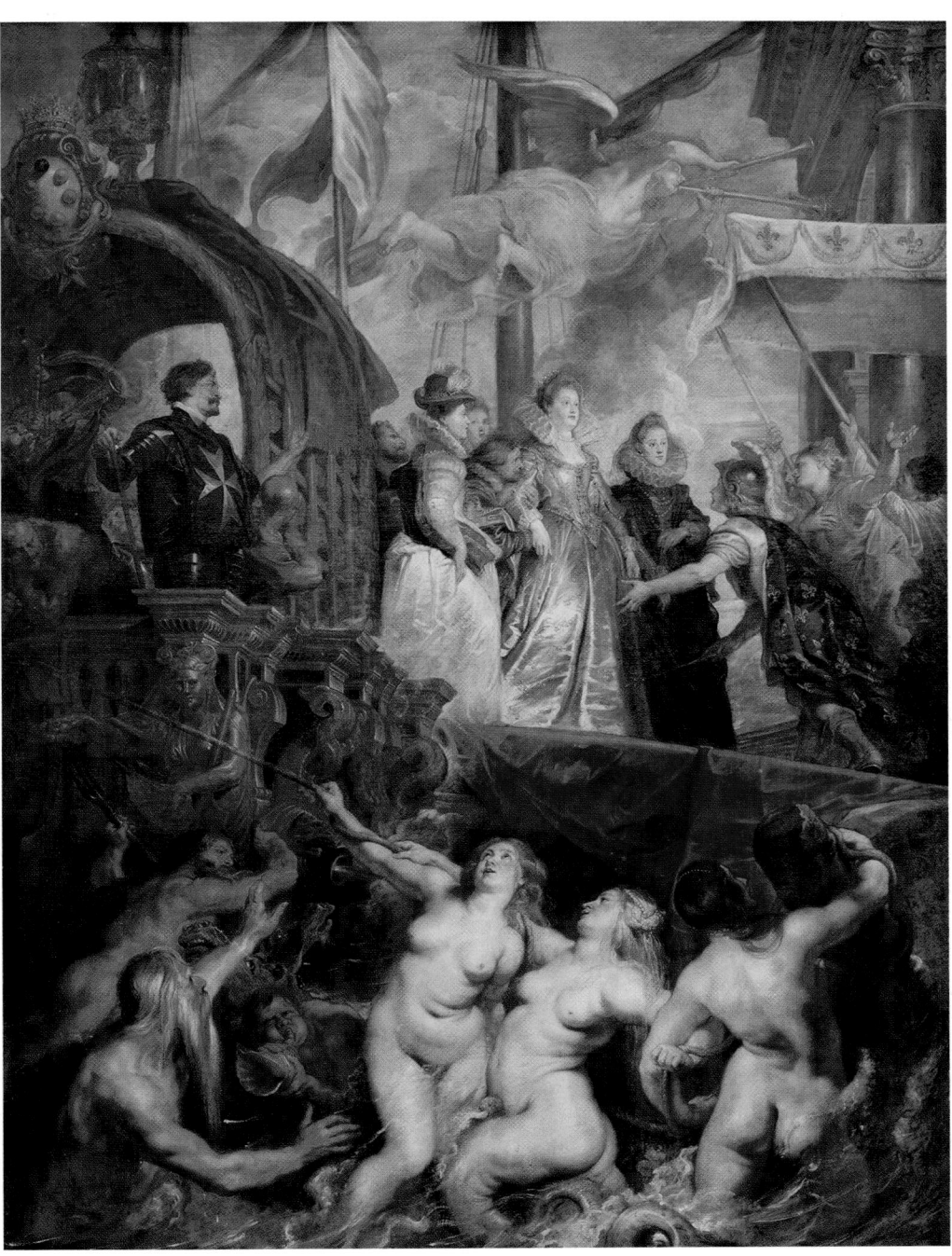

20.5 Peter Paul Rubens,
Marie de' Medici, Queen of France,
Landing in Marseilles
(November 3, 1600). 1622–25.
Oil on canvas, 12'11½" × 9'7"
(3.94 × 2.95 m).
Musée du Louvre, Paris

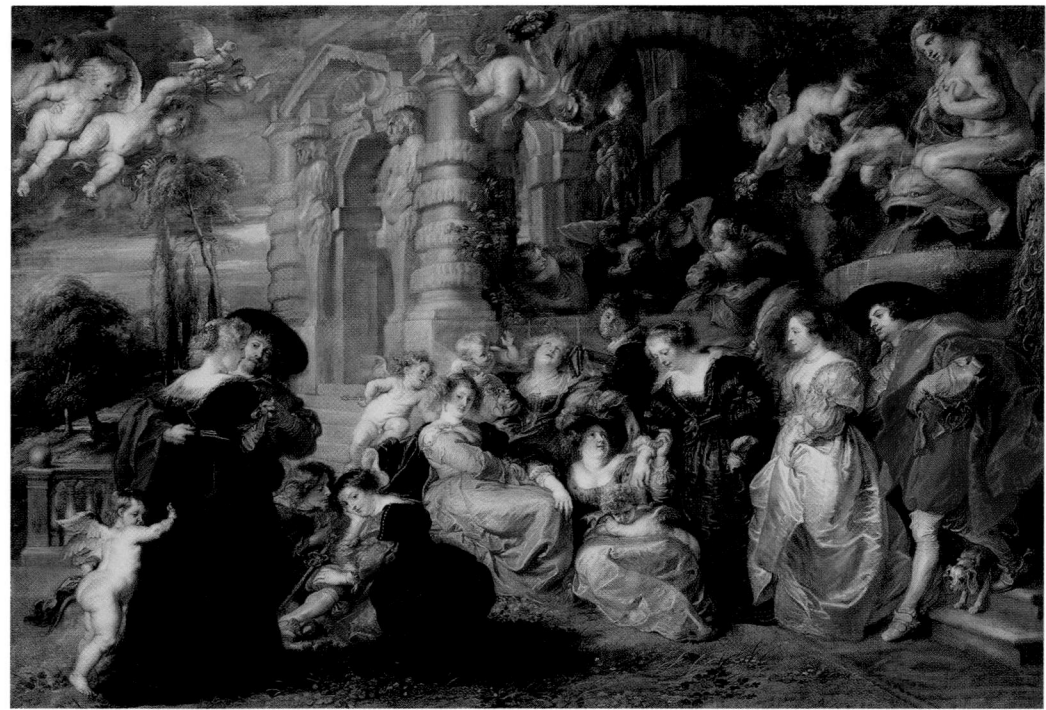

20.6   Peter Paul Rubens,
The Garden of Love. ca. 1638.
Oil on canvas, 6'6" × 9'3½"
(2 × 2.8 m). Museo del Prado, Madrid

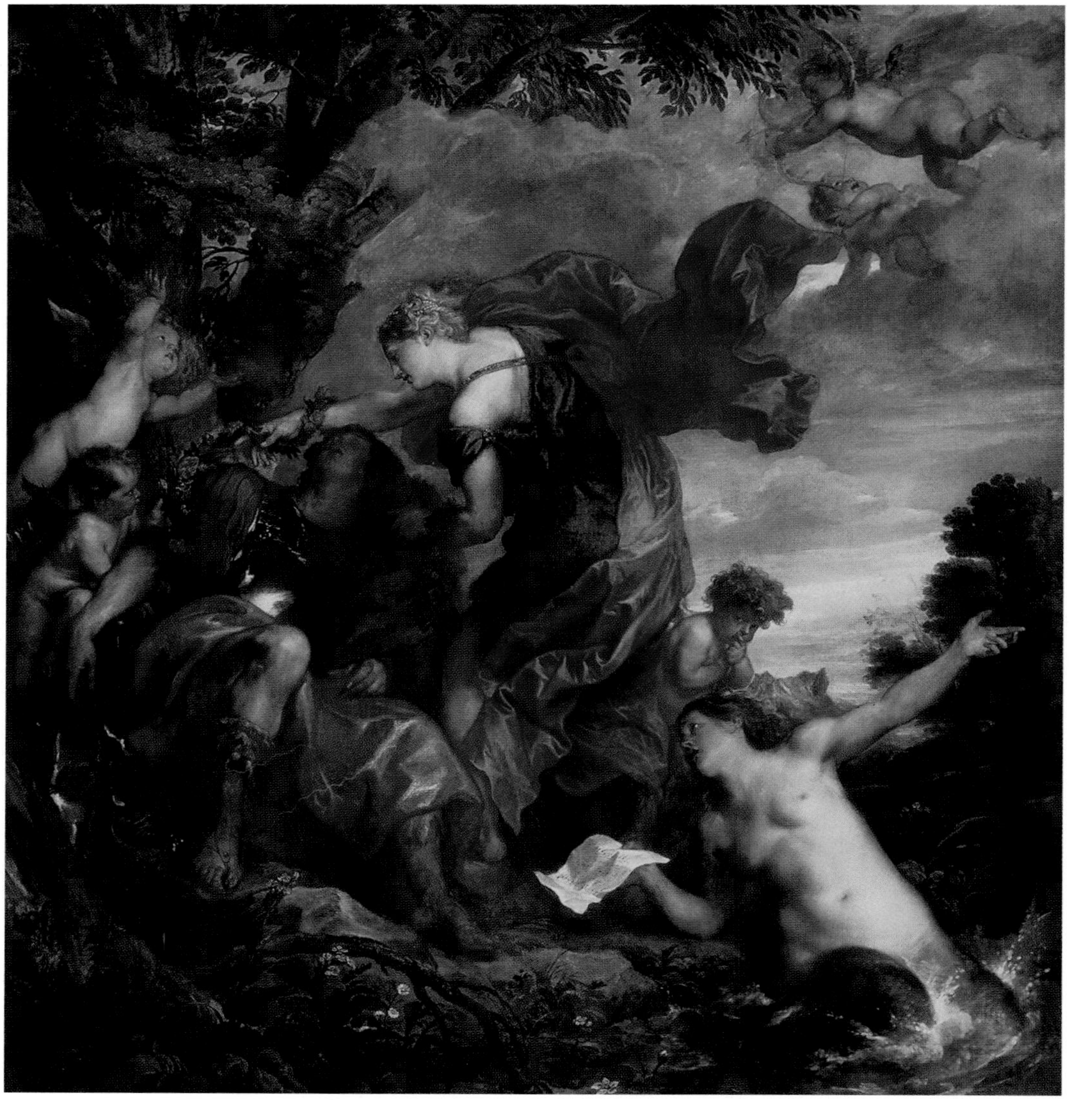

20.7   Anthony van Dyck,
Rinaldo and Armida. 1629. Oil on
canvas, 7'9" × 7'6" (2.36 × 2.24 m).
The Baltimore Museum of Art,
Baltimore, MD. The Jacob Epstein
Collection. 1951.103

RUBENS'S WORKSHOP To produce these large paintings, painting cycles, ceilings, and altarpieces, Rubens needed a large workshop; most of the Flemish artists working in the early seventeenth century studied with him at some point. They often traveled with him, worked on paintings he had begun or sketched, or began paintings for him to complete.

Rubens worked as a painter and a royal emissary. Diplomatic errands gave him entry to the royal households of the major powers, where he received numerous commissions. His duties took him to Paris, London, and Madrid—having already been to Italy—and he went to the Northern Netherlands to find an engraver for his work. He was truly an international artist.

LATE RUBENS In the 1630s, after Rubens remarried at the age of 53, his art turned inward and he made many paintings of his beautiful young wife, home, and children. He even wrote of being "at home, very contented." Rubens's *The Garden of Love* (fig. **20.6**) is a glowing tribute to life's pleasures. It shows couples, cupids, and a lifelike statue of Venus (at the upper left) in a garden in front of a building, much like Rubens's own Italianate house in Antwerp. Suggestions have been made that the male figure on the left is actually Rubens, and several of the women (mostly, the center-seated one) look like his new wife, Hélène Fourment. Certainly, the sensuality of *The Garden of Love* parallels changes in his life. This painting and the Paris *Marie de' Medici Cycle* would influence eighteenth-century Rococo painting (see page 763).

Anthony van Dyck: History and Portraiture at the English Court

Besides Rubens, only one other Flemish Baroque artist won international acclaim: Anthony van Dyck (1599–1641). He was that rarity among painters: a child prodigy. Before he was 20, he had become Rubens's most valued assistant. Like Rubens, he developed his mature style only after a stay in Italy.

As a history painter, Van Dyck was at his best in lyrical scenes of mythological love. *Rinaldo and Armida* (fig. **20.7**) is taken from Torquato Tasso's immensely popular poem about the crusades, *Jerusalem Freed* (1581), which gave rise to a new courtly ideal throughout Europe and inspired numerous operas, as well as paintings (a popular subject of Tiepolo, see page 781). Men and women at court masques played the roles of Christian Knight and Bewitching Sorceress in acting out this love-and-adventure story. Van Dyck shows the Sorceress falling in love with the Christian Knight she had intended to slay. The canvas reflects the ideals of Charles I, the English monarch for whom it was painted, and who found parallels in his own life with Tasso's epic. The English monarch, nominally a Protestant, had married the Catholic Henrietta Maria, sister of his main rival, the king of France. Charles saw himself as the virtuous ruler of a peaceful realm much like the Fortunate Isle where Armida had brought Rinaldo. (Ironically, Charles's reign ended in civil war.) The artist tells his story of ideal love in the pictorial language of Titian and Veronese,

with an expressiveness and opulence that would have been the envy of any Venetian painter. The picture was so successful that it helped Van Dyck gain an appointment to the English court two years later.

Van Dyck's fame rests mainly on the portraits he painted in London between 1632 and 1641. The *Portrait of Charles I Hunting* (fig. **20.8**) shows the king standing near a horse and two grooms in a landscape. Representing the sovereign at ease, the painting might be called a "dismounted equestrian portrait," and it is vastly different in effect from Holbein's *Portrait of Henry VIII* (see fig. 18.24). It is less rigid than a formal state portrait, but hardly less grand, for the king remains in full command of the state, which is symbolized here by the horse, which bows its head toward its master. The fluid movement of the setting complements the self-conscious elegance of the king's pose, which continues the stylized grace of Hilliard's portraits (see fig. 18.25). Charles's political position, however, was less secure than his confidence here suggests. He was beheaded by his subjects in 1649. Charles was succeeded by the puritan leader Oliver Cromwell and his followers, known as the "Roundheads" in reference to

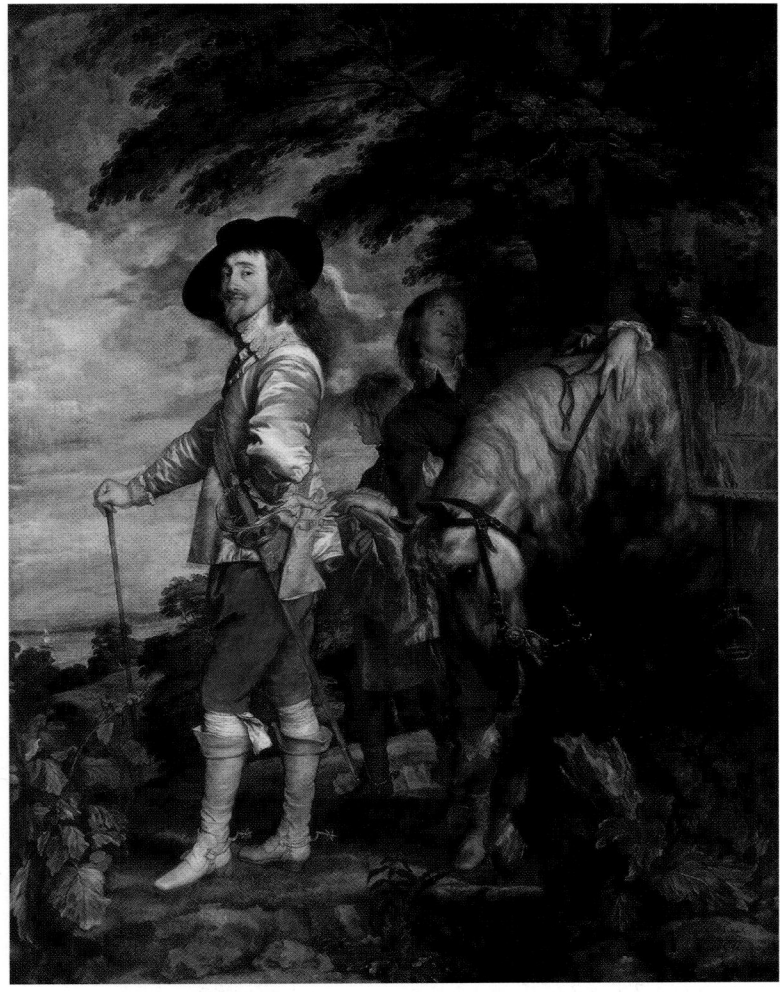

20.8 Anthony van Dyck, *Portrait of Charles I Hunting*. ca. 1635. Oil on canvas, 8'11" × 6'11½" (2.7 × 2.1 m). Musée du Louvre, Paris. Inv. 1236

their short-cropped hair. In contrast, note that in the painting Charles I's tresses drop below his shoulder in the French (Catholic) manner. However, despite Charles's execution, his son, Charles II, assumed the throne later in the period known as the Restoration.

Van Dyck has brought the court portrait up-to-date by using Rubens and Titian as his points of departure. He died eight years before the beheading of Charles I and so never had the chance to work for Charles's successors. But he created a new aristocratic portrait tradition that continued in England until the late eighteenth century and which had considerable influence on the Continent as well.

Local Flemish Art and Jacob Jordaens

Jacob Jordaens (1593–1678) was the successor to Rubens and Van Dyck as the leading artist in Flanders. Jordaens was quite prolific and is known for his paintings, drawings, watercolors, and designs for tapestries. Unlike his predecessors, he did not travel to Italy, although he received commissions from outside the country—from the Northern Netherlands, as well as from the court of Sweden and a limited one from England. Although Jordaens was never formally a student of Rubens, he was a member of his workshop, and he collaborated with the older artist, turning to him for inspiration throughout his career.

Jordaens's most characteristic subjects are mythological themes and works depicting eating and drinking such as his *The King Drinks* (fig. **20.9**), one of several versions he executed of this popular subject marking the feast of the Epiphany or Three Kings, which in Flanders is celebrated on January 6th. Traditionally, on this date friends and family gather for a large dinner where a "king" is chosen, often by lot. But in Jordaens's paintings it is always the oldest man; usually, as is the case here, the appearance of the king is based on the features of his father-in-law and former teacher, Adam van Noordt (1562–1641), although we should not suppose this work to be a family portrait. Other roles—the queen, a musician, a jester (seen at top left)—are also assigned. Jordaens shows the most exuberant moment when all toast and shout: "The King drinks!" This is a particularly rowdy scene where the physician (identified from his cap) vomits

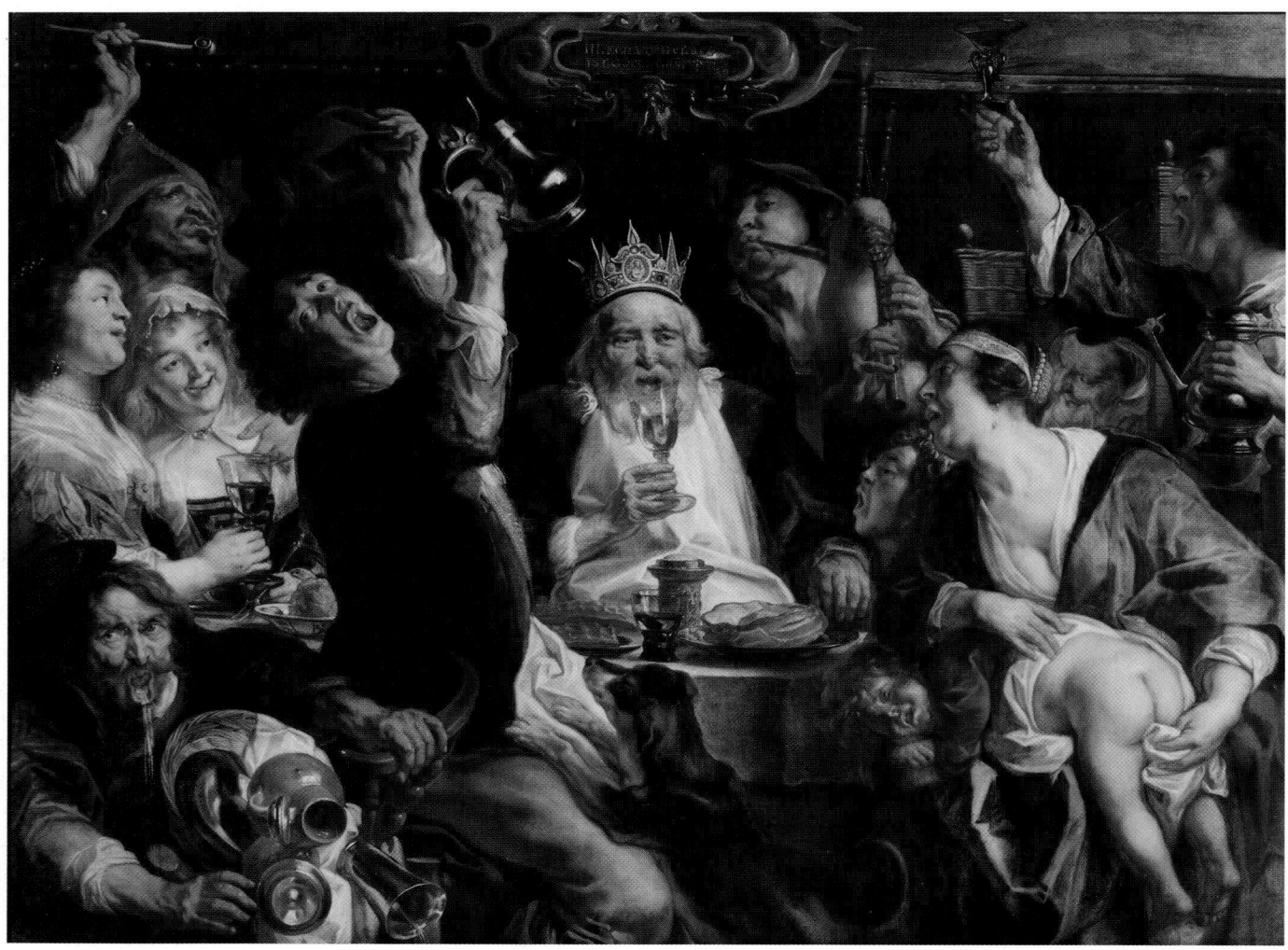

20.9   Jacob Jordaens, *The King Drinks*. 1638. Oil on canvas, 5'1⅖" × 6'10⅖" (1.56 × 2.10 m). Musées Royaux des Beaux Arts, Brussels, Belgium

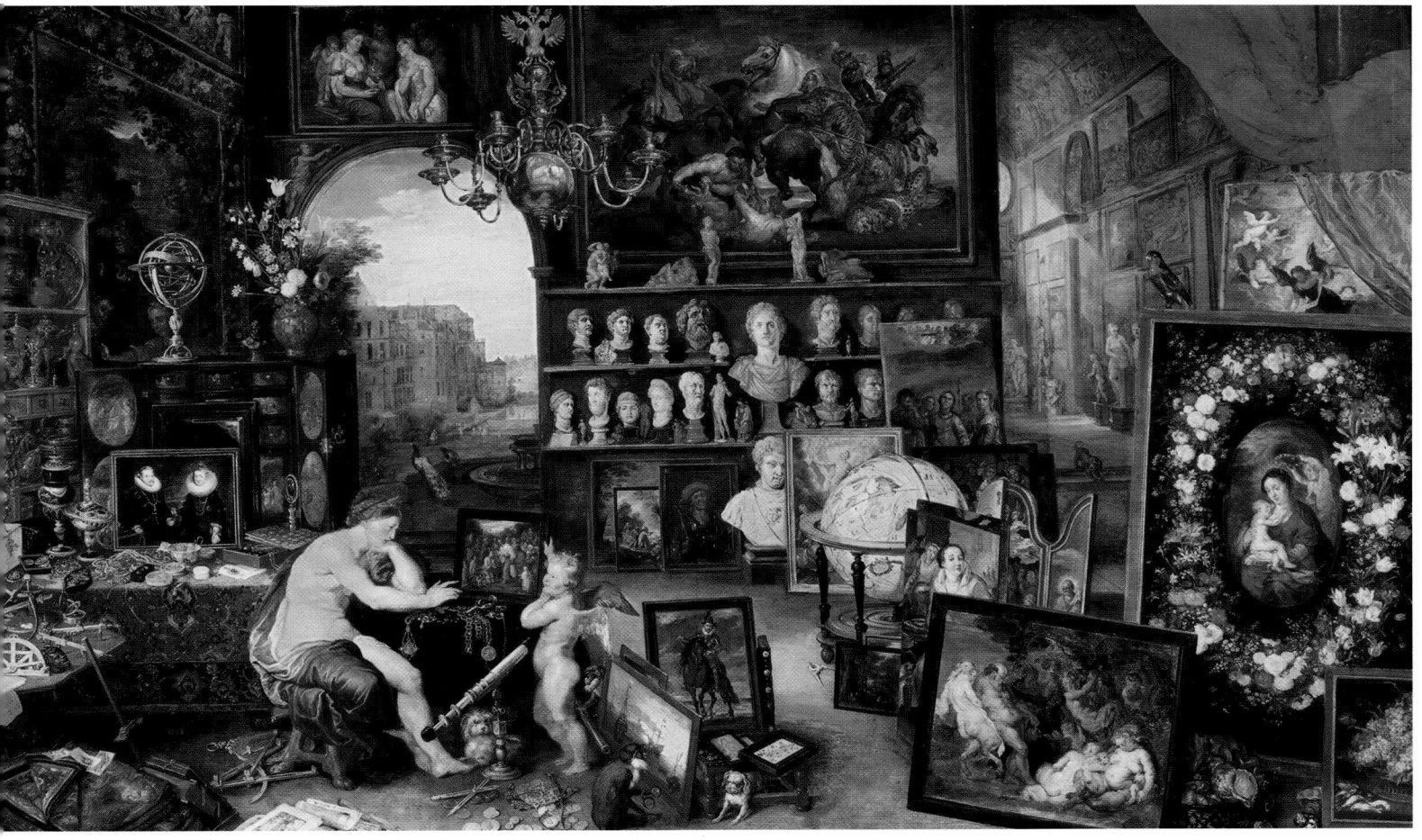

20.10 Jan Brueghel the Elder and Peter Paul Rubens, *Allegory of Sight*. 1617. Oil on panel, 25⅝ × 43" (65 × 109 cm). Museo del Prado, Madrid

on the left while a boy's bottom (not even an infant's!) is being wiped on the right—neither activity is suitable for a dinner table, but together they make a joyous painting. The painterly execution and figure types show a strong debt to Rubens, but Jordaen's figures are not idealized. There is a softness, roundness, and plainness to his life-size figures which distinguish his work. His paintings were purchased or commissioned by the newly prosperous middle class.

The Bruegel Tradition

Jan Brueghel the Elder (1568–1625) was the principal heir of the tradition of his illustrious father, Pieter Bruegel the Elder (see Chapter 18), whom he hardly knew but whose work he copied. Jan Brueghel was largely a still-life painter and one of the innovators of the "art collection" paintings that are unique to Flanders and that provide us with a view into the depth and variety of European "art collections" which developed in the princely quarters of Antwerp in the seventeenth century. These eclectic collections were known as *Kunstkammern* (literally "rooms of art") or *Wunderkammern* ("rooms of wonder"), and they give us a glimpse of the vast collections of exotica, from seashells, insects, and rare flowers to scientific instruments and paintings, that were accumulated by the aristocracy and the wealthy at that time.

His *Allegory of Sight* (fig. **20.10**) from a set of *The Five Senses* (paintings illustrating the senses of touch, smell, hearing, taste, and sight), each of the same size, executed with Rubens, shows such a *Wunder-* or *Kunstkammer*. The *Allegory of Sight*, viewed in an art gallery and appreciated only by seeing, is, of course, meant as a visual pun. The art collection seen here is that of the Habsburg archduke and archduchess (Albert and Isabella), depicted in a double portrait on the left (by Rubens), and suggests the wealth and splendor of the court. A double-headed eagle—the symbol of the Habsburgs—tops the brass chandelier. Albert and Isabella were Catholic rulers who would have associated this homage to the visible world with spiritual insight (explaining the painting of the Virgin and Child in the foreground). We obviously only glimpse part of the collection in the foreground, as the background at right indicates other rooms with more items (at left is a view of their castle outside Brussels), but the collection of paintings is prime here. We see scientific instruments (telescopes, globes), a Persian carpet (suggesting the bounty of the world), Roman portrait busts, and large and small paintings: portraits, mythological scenes, and still lifes. Some of the paintings are recognizably by

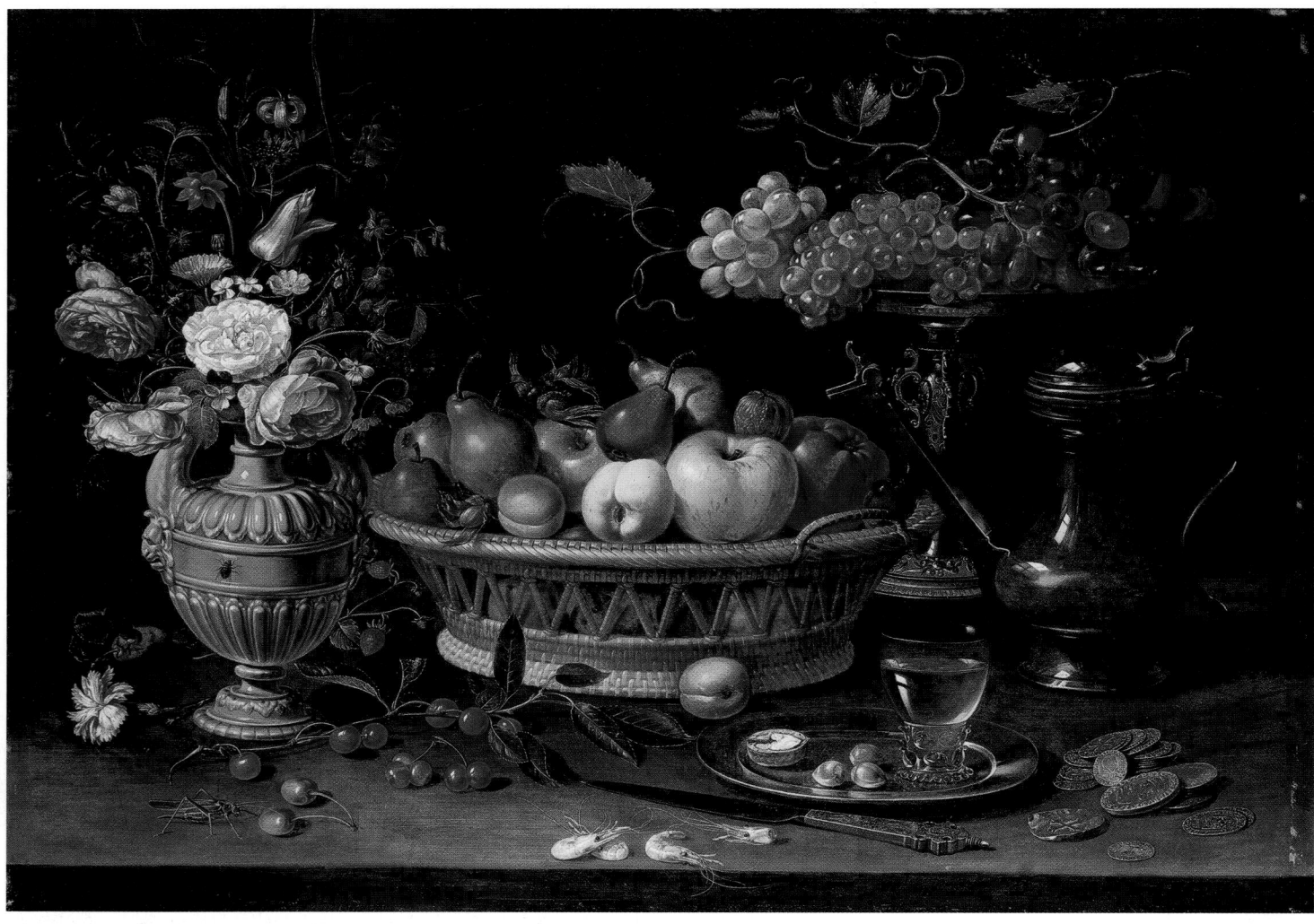

20.11   Clara Peeters, *Still Life with Fruit and Flowers*. ca. 1612. Oil on copper, 25⅕ × 35" (64 × 89 cm).
Ashmolean Museum, Oxford

Rubens and indicate his wide range—from a mythological scene featuring Silenus at the lower right to a lion and tiger hunt at the top left. The large painting seen at right showing the Virgin and Child encircled by a wreath of flowers, like the *Allegory of Sight* itself, is a collaborative effort between Brueghel and Rubens. In any collaboration, Brueghel would have begun the work, leaving areas for Rubens to fill in later, and then Brueghel would have returned to add the finishing touches. Jan Brueghel also collaborated with other artists and was a noted flower painter.

Still-Life Painting

Still-life painting in seventeenth-century Flanders took many forms—paintings of flowers, game, food, and precious objects. Even Jan Brueghel's *Allegory of Sight* enters into this realm. We usually do not know who commissioned these works and presume they were for private patrons for their homes.

The century opens with predominantly simple paintings, but by midcentury this genre has begun to explore the elaborate and dramatic explosion of objects collected at that time.

EARLY STILL LIFE: CLARA PEETERS Probably born in Antwerp, and most closely associated with that city, Clara Peeters (active 1607–ca. 1621) may have also worked in Haarlem, in the Netherlands. Her name, however, is not listed in any archival record in these cities, even though their guilds began to admit women and the number of signed works by Peeters indicate that she was a professional artist. Little is known of her life, patrons, or teachers. Nevertheless, she created some of the earliest still-life paintings. *Still Life with Fruit and Flowers* (fig. **20.11**) is an early work that combines studies of both flowers and fruit and displays several different containers, exploring a variety of textures. In the center is a basket of fruit (apples, pears, plums, apricots, and filberts), flanked on the left by a bouquet of colorful flowers (roses, a tulip—a flower relatively new to western Europe, columbine, a marigold, a cornflower, borage, wild pansies, forget-me-nots, and lilies) in a white pottery vase. On the right is a pewter wine tankard (with a reflection of Peeters) and a silver *tazza* (an Italian-made plate) holding a bunch of grapes. Also on the right is a pewter plate with a glass of white wine and some nuts. Strewn across the wooden tabletop are prawns, a carnation, a plum, cherries, a grasshopper, a strawberry, some gold and silver coins, and a knife.

Although the natural life here is plentiful, it is the coins and knife that are particularly important for both dating and determining the possible use or meaning of the painting. The coins have been dated to the reign of the Archduke Albert and Archduchess Isabella (1598–1621), and, based on the painting's style, a date of 1612 has been suggested. The knife (with its matching fork not seen here) is quite special and is of a type given as a wedding or betrothal gift. The same knife appears in several of Peeters's paintings and was probably copied from an actual one. It is inscribed in Latin with the words "fidelity" and "temperance," and is illustrated with small allegorical figures with hearts and clasped hands. Such a knife would often be inscribed with the bride's name; here, it is inscribed "Clara Peeters." Thus, it has been suggested that she painted the work in celebration of her own wedding—and that all the fruits and flowers represent the bounty and hopefulness of this event. Such paintings were frequently hung in the dining rooms of houses and complemented the meals and festivities. Many of Clara Peeters's paintings still remain in private collections today.

GAME STILL LIFE: FRANS SNYDERS A frequent collaborator with Rubens, Frans Snyders (1579–1657) studied with Pieter Brueghel the Younger (1564–1638), a son of Pieter Bruegel the Elder (see figs. 18.32–18.34) and with Jan Brueghel the Elder (see fig. 20.10). His splendid *Still Life with Dead Game, Fruits, and Vegetables in a Market* (fig. **20.12**) is the first known "gamepiece" and is a masterpiece of its kind.

Large and small items of game are for sale, but unlike the wares in Pieter Aertsen's *The Meat Stall* (fig 18.31) these animals are whole and unbutchered. The sale of game was newly regulated (as of 1613) by laws detailing hours, location (in front of town halls as shown here), and season. Anyone who followed those rules could set up a stand and give the middle class—not just the privileged nobility—a legal and easily accessible way to purchase venison and other prized game.

The artist revels in the virtuoso application of paint to create the varied textures of the game. The youth picking the old man's pocket (he is greeting us, the middle-class customer, and not paying attention to what is going on around him) and the cocks fighting in the foreground, as a cat looks on from the shadows beneath the low bench, further enliven the scene. Snyders subordinates

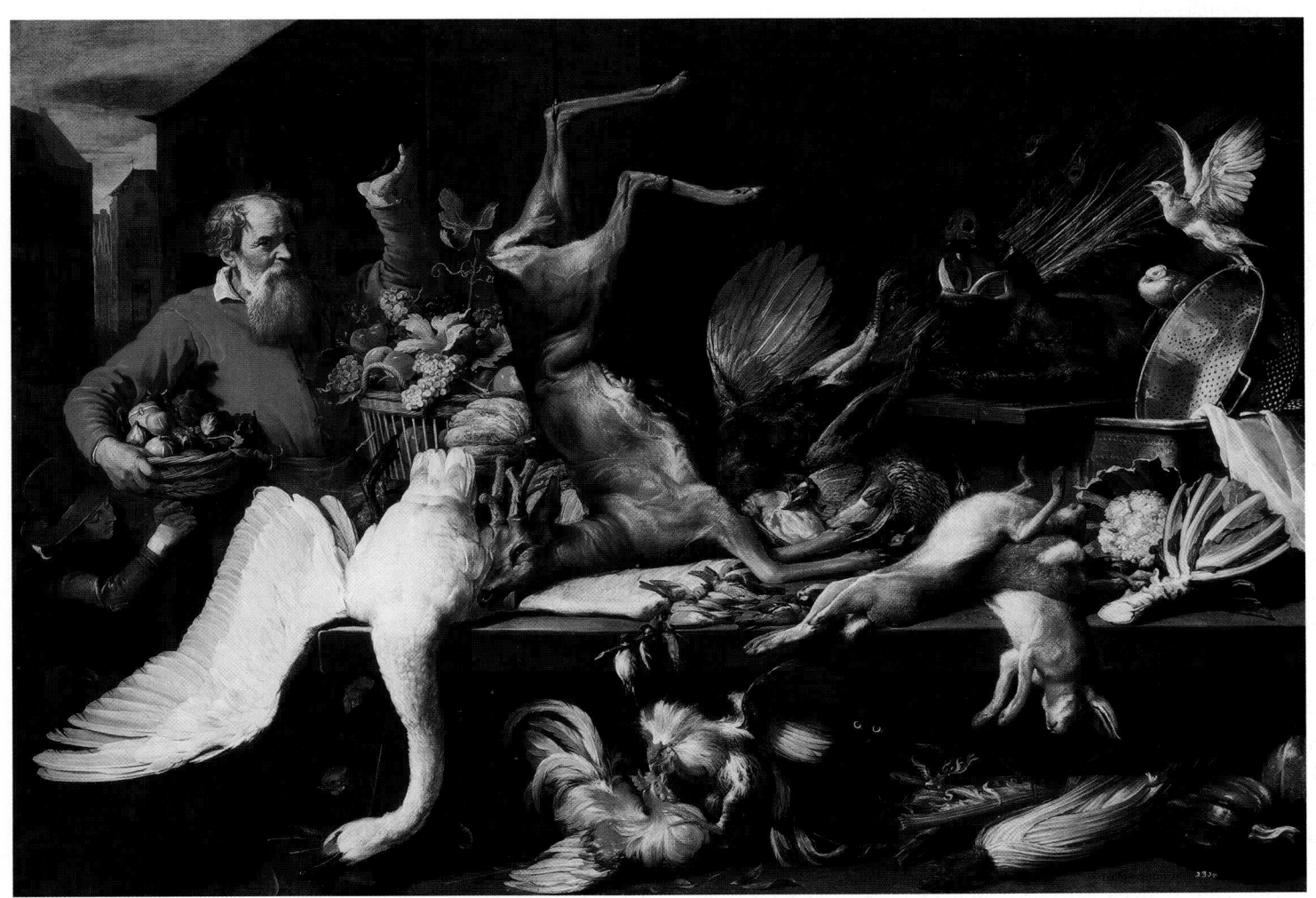

20.12 Frans Snyders, *Still Life with Dead Game, Fruits, and Vegetables in a Market*. 1614. Oil on canvas, 6'11⅞" × 10'3⅝" (2.1 × 3 m). The Art Institute of Chicago. Charles H. and Mary F. S. Worcester Fund, 1981.182

everything to the ensemble, which is characteristically Baroque in its lavishness and immediacy. The painting celebrates a time of peace and prosperity after the truce of 1609, when hunting was resumed in the replenished game preserves.

THE FLAMBOYANT STILL LIFE: JAN DAVIDSZ. DE HEEM

By midcentury, still-life paintings often presented lavish displays. These were known as **pronk** still lifes for their visual splendor, as *pronk* means "showy" or "ostentatious." This type reached its peak in the work of Jan Davidsz. de Heem (1606–1684). De Heem began his career in Holland but he soon moved to Antwerp, where he transformed the still life with his unique, flamboyant style. His *Still Life with Exotic Birds* (fig. **20.13**) is a spectacular example. He depicts sumptuous commodities—delicious food, exotic birds, and luxurious goods—from around the world (see map 20.1). The conch and nautilus shells are from the West Indies, the gray parrot is from Africa, the scarlet macaw is from Brazil, and the brilliant lobsters are probably from the New World; the Seville oranges, plums, figs, melons, oysters, gilt goblet, and silver ewer are all imported, commanding high prices in the marketplace. It is the whole world in one picture. And De Heem magnificently details the colors and textures of each of the objects.

The food is piled up on pewter platters that are unstable and suggest extravagance. Unlike in the even, horizontal compositions of Peeters (see fig. 20.11), the silver pitcher, pewter plate, Venetian glass, and gilt goblet are set in varying heights, building up to a climax with the exotic birds.

De Heem intends this display to be wondrous and theatrical, drawing back a curtain for us to see what is behind it. Even the column in the background is meant to suggest a heroic work. The result is a stunning, celebratory display that reveals the virtuosity of De Heem and defines the elements of the new style of *pronk* still life.

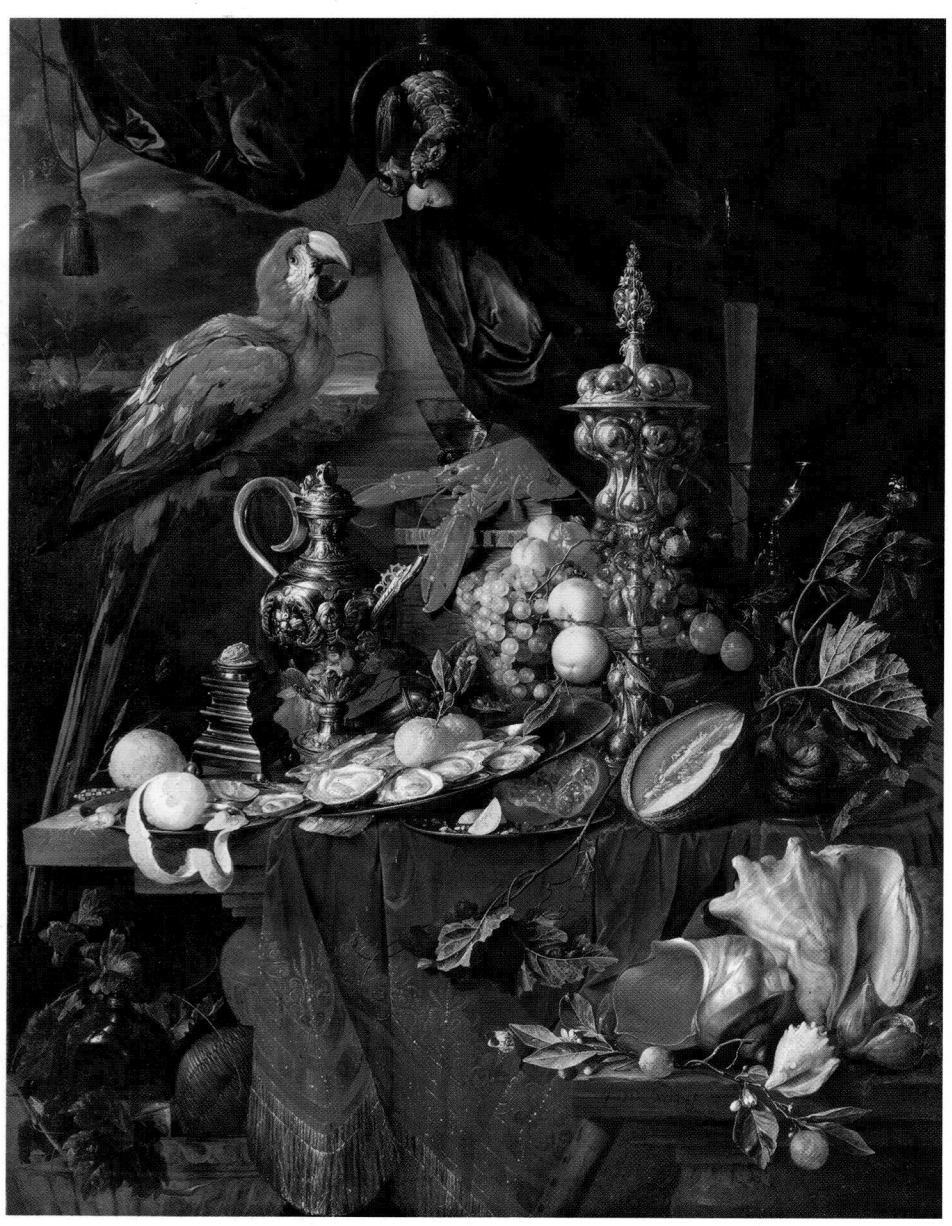

20.13 Jan Davidsz. de Heem, *Still Life with Exotic Birds*. Late 1640s. Oil on canvas, 59¼ × 45½" (150.5 × 115.5 cm). Collection of the John and Mable Ringling Museum of Art, the State Art Museum of Florida, Sarasota, Florida. Bequest of John Ringling, 1936, SN289

THE DUTCH REPUBLIC

Art in the Dutch Republic, unlike the art of Flanders, was not based largely on church or state commissions, but was one conducted primarily through private patronage and an open art market. Pictures became a commodity, and the trade in them followed the law of supply and demand. Many artists produced for the market rather than for individual patrons. Yet even the greatest masters were sometimes hard-pressed and could not fully support themselves with the money earned from their art. It was not unusual for an artist to keep an inn or run a small business on the side.

There were many artists—enough to form artistic communities—in Haarlem, Utrecht, Amsterdam, and Delft, to name but a few. Artists frequently traveled between these cities and may have known each other's work, but most artists are usually associated with only one place—Hendrick Goltzius, Frans Hals and Judith Leyster with Haarlem; Hendrick Terbrugghen with Utrecht; Rembrandt with Amsterdam; and Jan Vermeer with Delft. Some of the paintings were religious in nature, but most were not. There were individual portraits, group portraits commissioned by civic groups, landscapes, cityscapes, architectural paintings, still lifes, and genre paintings.

There were many types of paintings, and they ranged from large to small in size—small enough to hold in your hand or for ordinary people to hang on the walls of their homes.

The Haarlem Academy: Hendrick Goltzius

Like Rubens, Van Dyck, and even Jan Brueghel the Elder, many Dutch artists learned of the greatness of contemporary art in Rome and of its roots in antiquity by going there. And some, like Hendrick Goltzius (1558–1617), made numerous prints and drawings on their sojourn and brought them back for their own and others' use. Goltzius (with two other artists, Karel van Mander and Cornelis Cornelisz van Haarlem) created an "academy" in Haarlem in 1585. We know little about it, but copying from prints, from antiquity, and from each other was part of their program. The academy also produced teachers for the next generation and made the city of Haarlem a focal point for early Dutch painting, printmaking, and drawing.

The collaborative efforts of the academy seem to be limited to Goltzius's engravings of the works by his colleagues. He was a masterful engraver, whose injured hand (burned in a childhood accident) may have provided the force behind his deep curvilinear cuts in the metal. (See *Materials and Techniques*, page 501.) He also executed woodcuts and only began painting after 1600.

The engraving of the *Farnese Hercules* (fig. **20.14**) illustrates the back of the Hellenistic sculpture owned by the Farnese family, housed in their palace, and also immortalized in a painting on a ceiling there (see fig. 19.7). It is seen here in its monumental, heroic scale, being viewed by two Dutch men—probably Goltzius's two companions in Italy during his trip of 1590–91. In many ways, it is an allegory for the wide-eyed Dutch experience in Rome—awed by this city filled with ruins, architecture, and

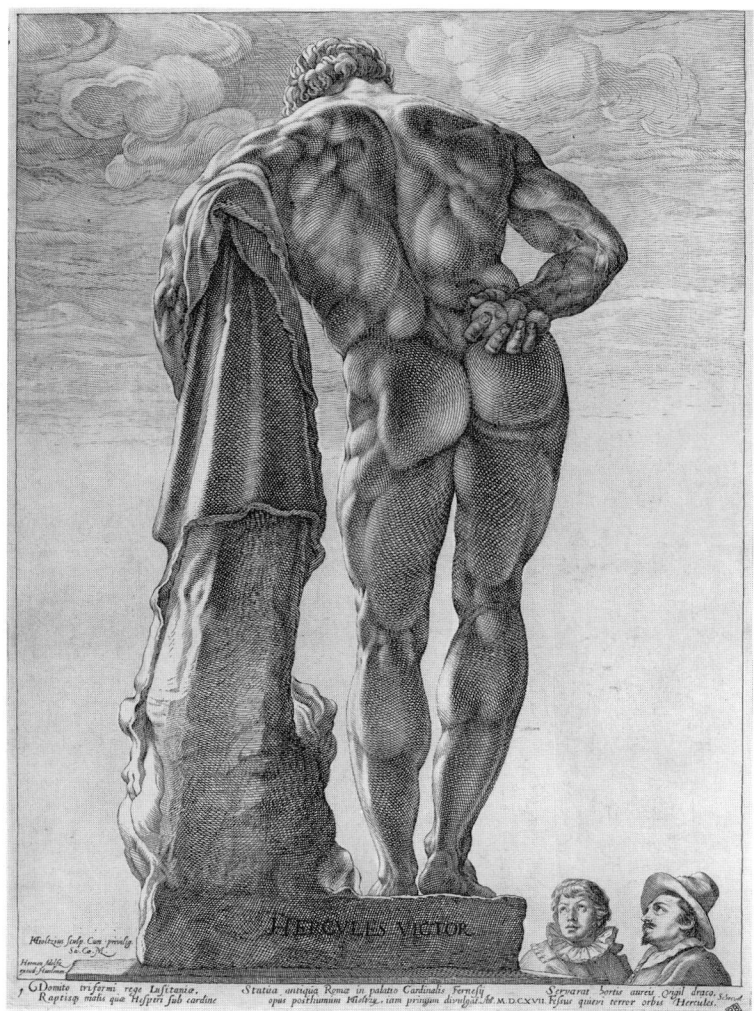

20.14 Hendrick Goltzius, *Farnese Hercules*. ca. 1597. Engraving, 16½ × 11¾" (418 × 301 cm). Metropolitan Museum of Art, New York. Gift of Henry Walters, 1917. (17.37.59)

sculpture of an ancient past. (Indeed, the Dutch would later decide to keep as ruins those buildings nearly destroyed by the Spanish so as to have their own ruins of a heroic past.) This *Hercules*, like others in the same series, is also a very large print—a Herculean effort. Goltzius's trip to Italy was taken before the appearance of Caravaggio and the Baroque, and thus it was the art of the past, rather than contemporary Italian works, that had an impact on him.

The Caravaggisti in Holland: Hendrick Terbrugghen

The Baroque style came to Holland from Antwerp through the work of Rubens, and from Rome through contact with Caravaggio's followers. Although most Dutch painters did not go to Italy, the majority of those who went in the early years of the century were from Utrecht, a town with strong Catholic traditions. One of those artists from Utrecht, Hendrick Terbrugghen (1588–1629), worked in Italy for several years and was one of the first

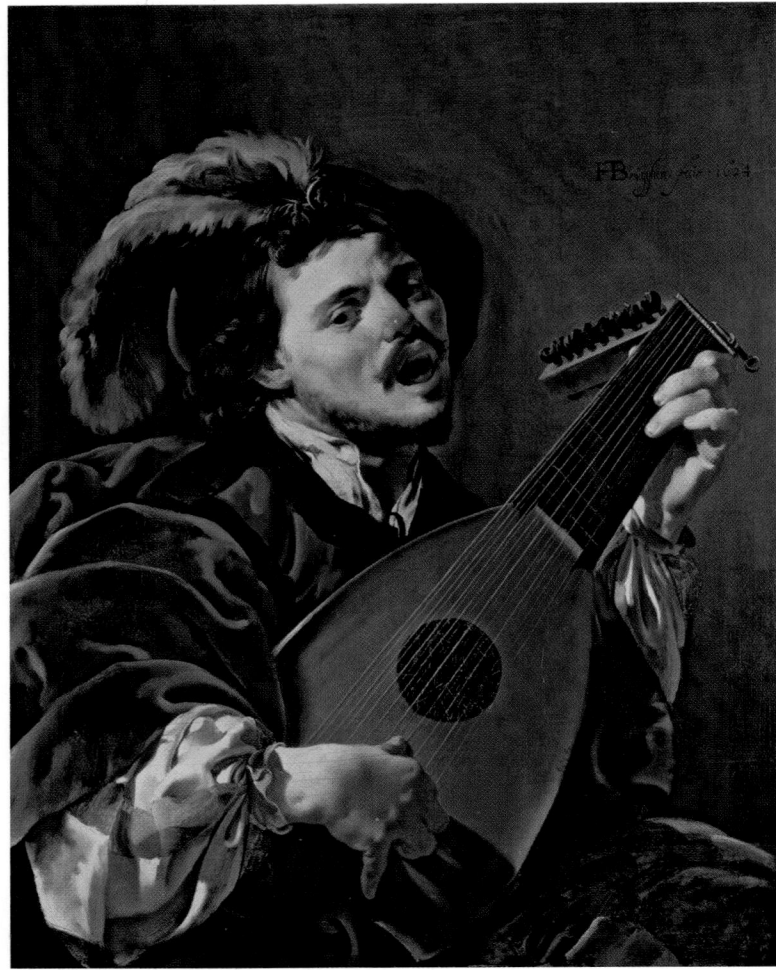

20.15 Hendrick Terbrugghen, *Singing Lute Player*. 1624. Oil on canvas, 39⅝ × 31" (100.5 × 78.7 cm). The National Gallery, London

"Caravaggisti" to return to the North. He adapted Caravaggio's style for religious paintings, but also for the single-figure genre painting. Terbrugghen's *Singing Lute Player* (fig. **20.15**) is inspired by Caravaggio's painting of the same subject, by his *Musicians* (see fig. 19.4) and by the young men in his *The Calling of St. Matthew* (see fig. 19.2), who wear slashed doublets and feathered berets. Such life-size, half-length single-figure portraits, filling the entire canvas, became common in Utrecht and grew popular elsewhere in Holland. The Utrecht School transmitted the style of Caravaggio to other Dutch masters, such as Frans Hals.

The Haarlem Community and Frans Hals

One of the first to profit from these new ideas permeating the Dutch Republic was Haarlem artist Frans Hals (ca. 1585–1666), who was born in Antwerp. Hals captured his contemporaries in both portraiture and genre painting, and he excelled at combining the two—animating his portraits and setting his subjects in somewhat relaxed or even casual stances. His genre painting, usually of single figures, portray characters that seem to be drawn from real life.

HALS AND THE CIVIC GUARD Hals's six group portraits of the Civic Guards allowed him to provide multiple enlivened, life-size portraits in single dynamic paintings. The Civic Guards, founded in the fourteenth century, were local voluntary militia groups that were instrumental in defending their cities through military service. They also had civic and religious duties, and they began having their portraits painted in the early sixteenth century. Although they had successfully defended their cities from the Spanish in the 1580s and, indeed, were proud of this accomplishment, with the truce of 1609, the Civic Guards became more like civic fraternities, with annual banquets, as seen in the *Banquet of the Officers of the St. George Civic Guard* (fig. **20.16**). The military aspects are indeed subordinated to the sense of general prosperity orchestrated in ritual. The captain in the center back wields a knife, but not as a military weapon; he is about to cut the roast. As was the custom, the colonel at the left raises his wine glass at the entrance of the standard-bearer with an unfurled banner. The highest-ranking officers are seated, while the men of lower rank and the servants stand at the back. The subjects arranged around a table laden with food on a white damask tablecloth, turn and face each other and the viewer. But 12 men around a table beg comparison with Leonardo's *The Last Supper* (see fig. 16.6). This is an undeniably secular painting, yet the event depicted is steeped in ceremony.

Although the painting vividly suggests a moment in time at an actual gathering, art historians do not believe that Hals here painted an actual event. The officers did not pose for this seating. The realism comes from the life-size scale, their gestures, the three-dimensional modeling created by paint applied "wet-in-wet" (while initial paint is still wet) with strokes of varied width and length. This modeling generated its own vibrancy, and thus the men appear as "speaking likenesses." The Civic Guard painting would become a staple in Haarlem and also in Amsterdam. Rembrandt's *The Night Watch* (see fig. 20.23) represents another form of this standard.

In Hals's painting, the black-and-white fashions offset with the red-and-white sashes nearly vibrate, creating a brilliant tableau. These men, the officers of the company, were wealthy citizens (in the case of Haarlem, they were brewers and merchants) who may have used their civic service to further their careers in government. Some even engaged Hals to execute individual portraits of themselves and family members; Hals himself became a member of the company in 1612.

A WEDDING PORTRAIT Hals's only double portrait, *Married Couple in a Garden* (fig. **20.17**), probably commemorates the wedding in 1622 of Isaac Massa (1586–1643) and his wife, Beatrix van der Laen (1592–1639). It combines the relaxed informal atmosphere of genre painting with the individual likenesses and formal attire of portraiture. This life-size couple modestly display their affection by sitting close together. Her arm is loped over his elbow, so displaying her rings (customary on the index finger); they smile broadly, their eyes twinkling, as they sit in a garden— an imaginary Garden of Love—surrounded by ivy, a symbol of steadfast love (as the ivy clings to the tree), faithfulness, and

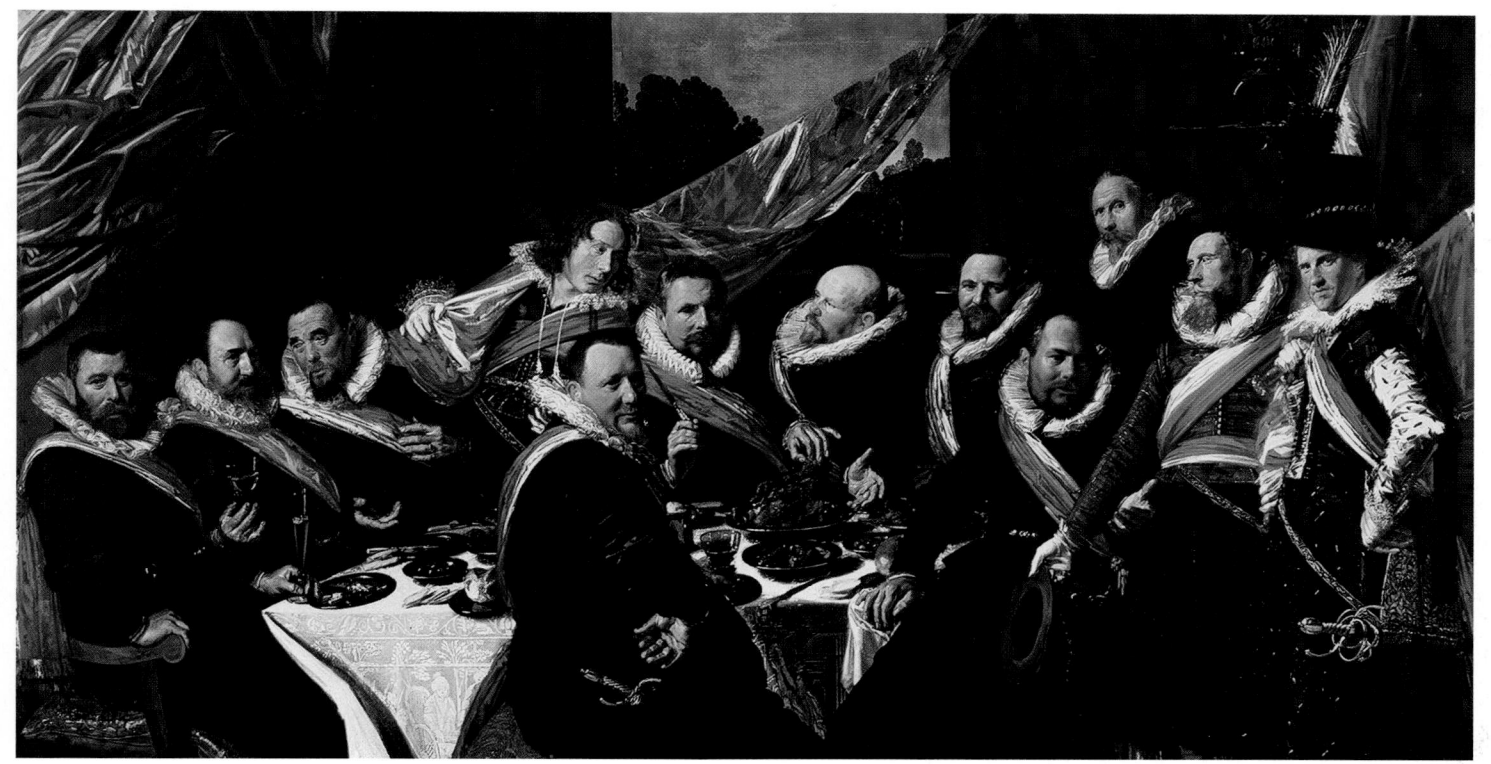

20.16 Frans Hals,
*Banquet of the Officers
of the St. George Civic
Guard.* 1616. Oil on
canvas, 5'9" × 10'7½"
(175 × 324 cm).
Frans Hals Museum,
Haarlem

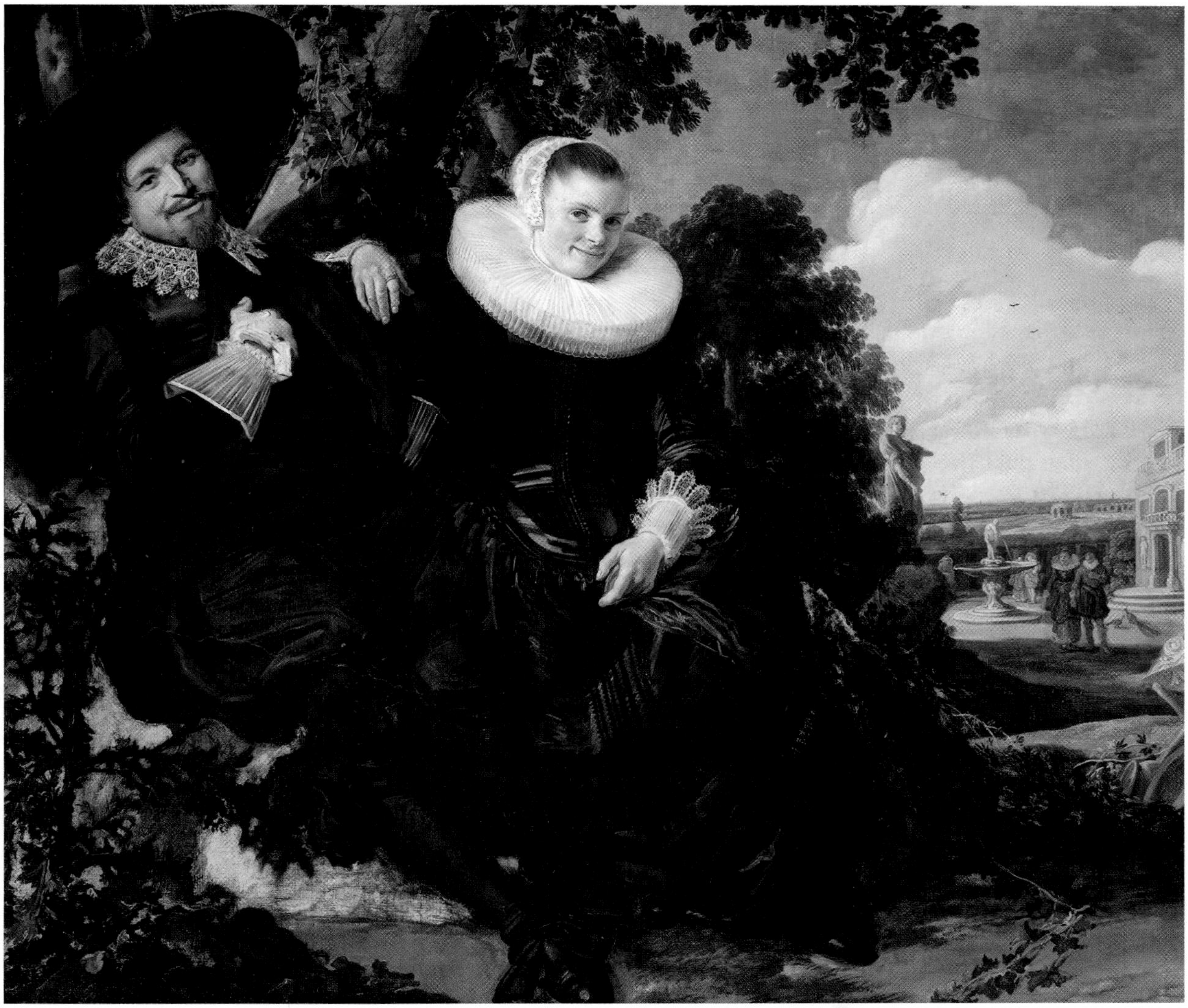

20.17 Frans Hals,
*Married Couple in a
Garden: Portrait of Isaac
Massa and Beatrix van
der Laen.* ca. 1622.
Oil on canvas. 55 × 65½"
(140 × 166.5 cm).
Rijksmuseum,
Amsterdam

fidelity. Indeed, they seem in love with each other. His right hand touches his chest (his heart) as a show of his intended affection. This painting makes a sharp contrast with Jan van Eyck's *The "Arnolfini Portrait"* (see fig. 14.14), and whether we interpret that earlier couple's presence as signaling a betrothal, wedding, or contract, we can see that the emotional tie between the Arnolfini couple was not Van Eyck's concern. This is more than a difference in personal artistic style; it is the difference between the Renaissance and the Baroque, developing over the course of 200 years. Between Van Eyck and Hals also stood Rubens, who had executed a wedding portrait of himself and his first wife that may have served as an example to Hals.

Ingeniously, Hals set the couple off-center, which adds to the spontaneity; there is also a sense that Massa, open-mouthed, is speaking to us. They wear expensive lace cuffs; his is the lace collar customary for men whereas she wears a millstone collar, with an embroidered and ribboned cap, usually worn indoors or under another hat. He wears a broad-brimmed hat in the new French fashion. Her skirt is of silk; her *vlieger* (bodice) of velvet with broad shoulders is of a kind worn only by married women, so it identifies her status.

Hals painted Massa, an important and wealthy diplomat, at least two more times as a single figure. Massa had an adventurous life: He was a geographer and a cartographer of Siberia. He traveled to Russia in 1600 and lived there for eight years, becoming fluent in the language. He was active in the fur trade and influential in establishing trade routes between the Netherlands and Russia. But his worldliness is only barely suggested in this wedding portrait set in his own garden.

HALS AND GENRE PAINTING Hals's mature style is seen in *The Jolly Toper* (fig. **20.18**), which perhaps represents an allegory of taste, one of the Five Senses, which were among the most popular themes in the seventeenth century. The painting combines Rubens's robustness with a focus on the "dramatic moment" that Hals must have derived from Caravaggesque painters in Utrecht. Everything here conveys complete spontaneity: the twinkling eyes and half-open mouth, the raised hand, the teetering wineglass, and—most important of all—the painter's quick way of setting down the forms. Hals worked in dashing brushstrokes, each so clearly visible that we can almost count the total number of "touches." Thanks to this open, split-second technique, the completed picture has the immediacy of a sketch. The impression of a race against time is, of course, deceptive. Hals undoubtedly spent hours on this life-size canvas, but he maintains the illusion of having done it all in the blink of an eye.

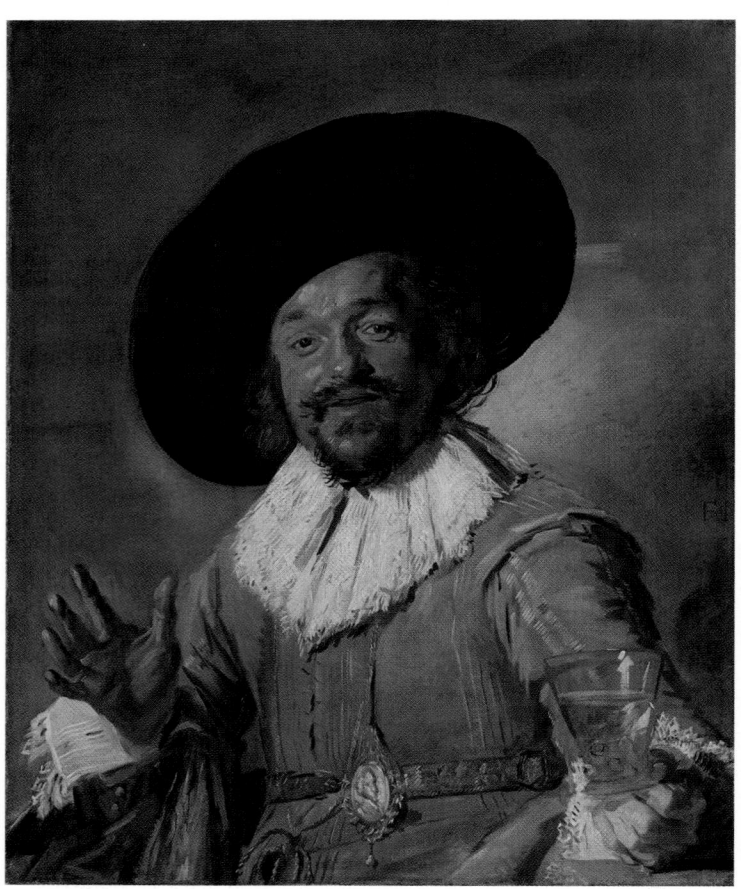

20.18 Frans Hals, *The Jolly Toper*. ca. 1628–30. Oil on canvas, 31⅞ × 26¼" (81 × 66.6 cm). Rijksmuseum, Amsterdam

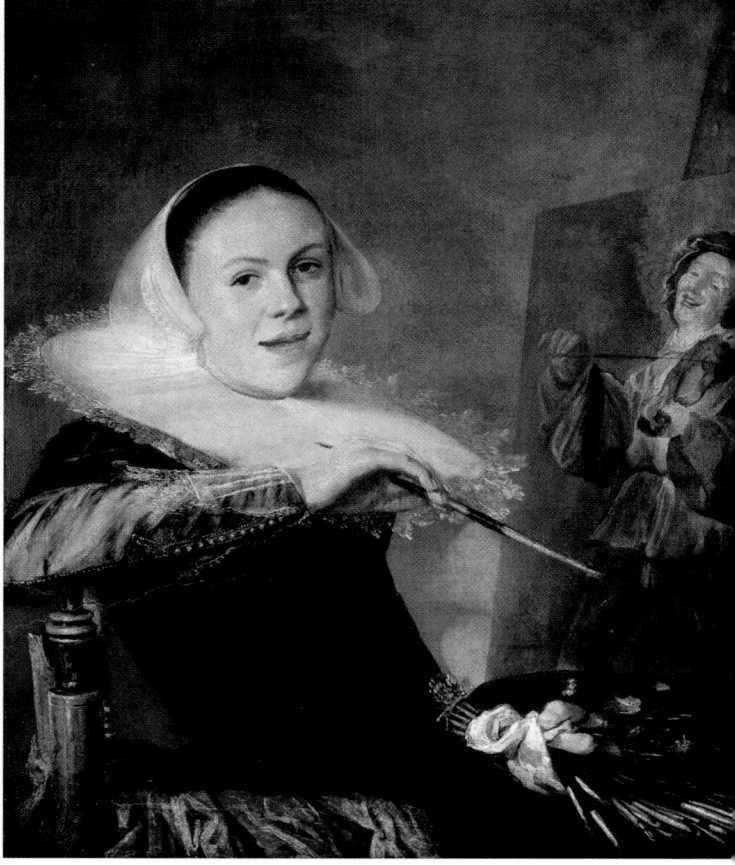

20.19 Judith Leyster, *Self-Portrait*. ca. 1633. Oil on canvas, 29⅜ × 25⅝" (72.3 × 65.3 cm). National Gallery of Art, Washington, D.C. Gift of Mr. and Mrs. Robert Woods Bliss. 1949.6.1

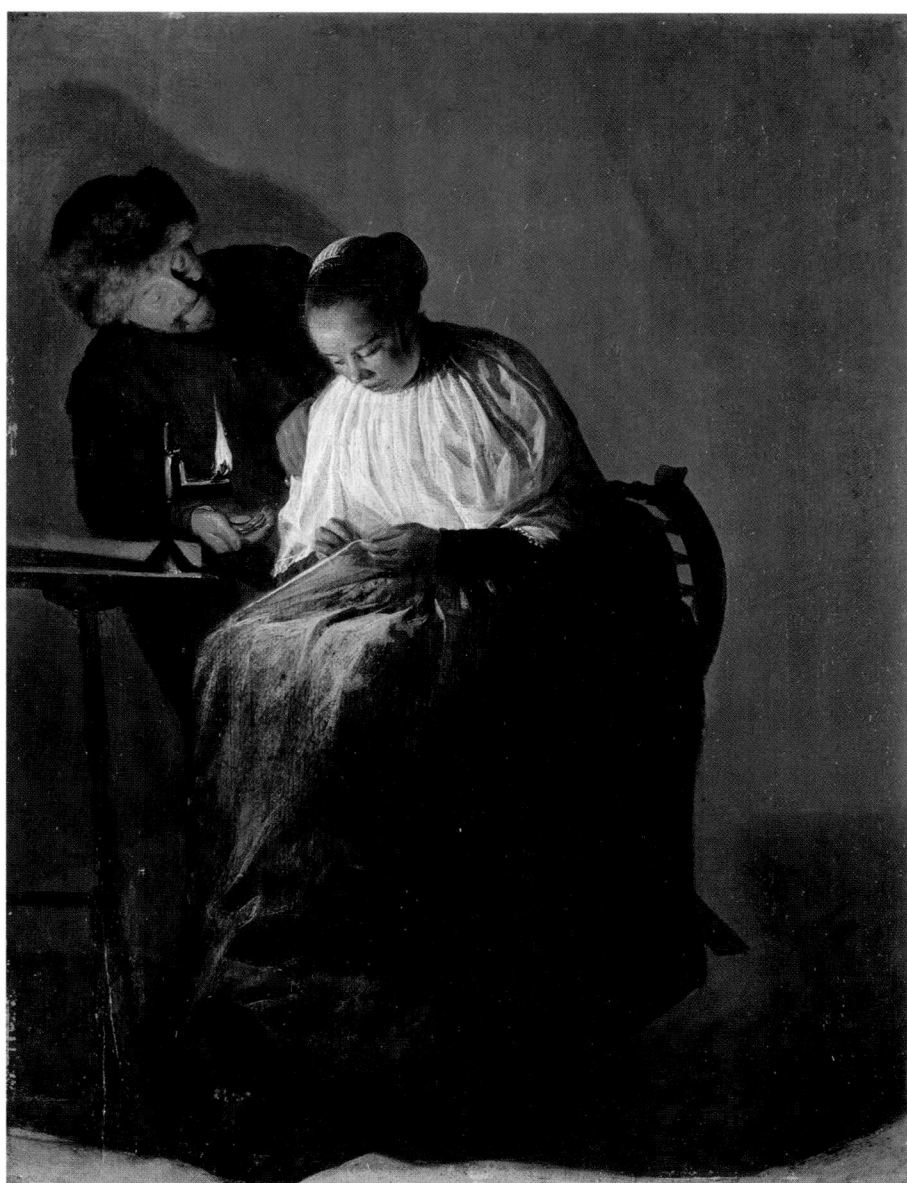

Hals, like Rembrandt van Rijn and Jan Vermeer, whom we will meet later in this chapter, is most closely identified with a period referred to as the Golden Age of Dutch Art. Individually these three artists took their northern heritage and developed from it the unique style of seventeenth-century Dutch art in Haarlem, Amsterdam, and Delft, respectively. Neither Hals, nor Rembrandt, nor Vermeer traveled to Italy.

The Next Generation in Haarlem: Judith Leyster

The most important follower of Hals was Judith Leyster (1609–1660), who was responsible for a number of works that once passed as Hals's own. She painted portraits and still lifes, but mostly genre paintings. Her *Self-Portrait* (fig. **20.19**) shows Leyster as both a portrait and genre painter, and was executed to show her mastery of both. It was probably her presentation piece to the Guild of St. Luke in Haarlem in 1633, when she became a

master and took on her own students. The painting on the easel is a detail of a popular work of hers; she uses this canvas to advertise her diverse talents. It also reveals her technical skill as she wields numerous brushes and a palette as she sits in her studio, open-mouthed, casually conversing with us. Many women artists, as Leyster does here, showed themselves painting—indicating their new professional status and their unique position. Indeed, Artemisia Gentileschi's *Self-Portrait as the Allegory of Painting* (*La Pittura*) (see fig. 19.6), executed about the same time, explores this same theme.

Leyster also explored the relationship between men and women in her work—and frequently used candlelight scenes to create mood and intimacy. Leyster's small lamplit *The Proposition* (fig. **20.20**) is one such painting. A man in a beaver hat (a foreigner) with coins in his hand approaches a woman who is diligently sewing. Is he offering to pay for her needlework? Clearly not. What are the clues to what he really wants? Leyster assigns the figures to a dark setting, whose lighting suggests intimacy. His

Authenticity and Workshops: Rubens and Rembrandt

Rubens and Rembrandt are among the many artists who ran workshops employing other artists. Anthony van Dyck, Frans Snyders, and Jan Brueghel the Elder worked with Rubens as well as independently. Frequently, paintings by Rubens will be attributed to "Rubens and Workshop." By contrast, the idea of collaboration with Rembrandt in a workshop has been slow to develop. The notion of Rembrandt as a solitary genius endured through the twentieth century and has only recently been more carefully scrutinized. Paintings found to be not wholly by Rembrandt have been "demoted" and attributed to an artist of his workshop instead. Art historians have thus begun to rethink workshop practices.

According to some art historians, Rembrandt's oeuvre (the number of paintings he produced) was almost a thousand; other historians thought he had produced a few hundred. In the 1960s, as exhibitions celebrating the 300th anniversary of his death were being organized (for 1969), it became clear that art historians had different views of who Rembrandt was and what he did. As such, in 1968, the Rembrandt Research Project was set up, establishing a team of art historians who would use scientific methods as well as connoisseurship to establish the authenticity of works attributed to Rembrandt. They would study the wood and canvas supports, date the wood (a process called dendochronology), take x-rays, use infrared photography, examine paints and ground samples, and view the paintings in raking (strong) light. The researchers made their reports and jointly issued three volumes, *The Corpus of Rembrandt Paintings*, reporting on works painted in 1625–31, 1631–34, and 1635–42; a fourth volume is devoted to self-portraits. Because of deaths and retirements, the committee's personnel has since changed, but the project continues.

Although their deliberate and scientific examinations have been incredibly useful and have provided a model for others engaged in such endeavors, their analysis of the attributions of Rembrandt works into three categories, A, B, and C, has been controversial: "A" for authentic works by Rembrandt; "B" for paintings that cannot be either accepted or rejected as authentic (the "B" category has been sarcastically labeled by some as "Bothersome"); and "C" for works rejected as inauthentic and to be attributed to others, usually to named followers of Rembrandt. What is missing from this list, of course, is the notion of collaboration—the usual workshop method we have seen in the case of Rubens. Although Rembrandt and Rubens both had active workshops over the course of their careers, art historians have chosen to view the art from these workshops differently.

---

hand touches her shoulder. Indeed, in today's jargon, she is being "hit on" by the intruder. A copy of the painting, which introduces a wine glass, points to what is missing here—any inference that the woman is interested. Such proposition paintings were in fact common, but they usually differ from this example in that they are often jovial and larger, showing women as active participants in this exchange of sex for money. Many were painted by the Utrecht Caravaggisti whose works Leyster may have known through her family's stay near Utrecht. Her painting differs markedly from these, though, as the woman does not appear interested. This intriguingly different point of view has been attributed to the fact that the artist is a woman. The painting is signed with her monogram, a conjoined "J," "L," and star, punning on her name, which means "leading star." Indeed, Leyster was referred to and celebrated during her lifetime as a "leading star" in art.

After her marriage to a fellow student of Hals's, Jan Miense Molenaer (ca. 1610–1668), the couple moved from Haarlem to Amsterdam where Leyster continued to paint, although the main body of her oeuvre was executed in Haarlem. Leyster's exploration of domestic genre painting and the poetic quality of the light in her canvases means that her work bridges the generation gap between the Caravaggisti and Jan Vermeer (see figs. 20.34 and 20.35).

Rembrandt and the Art of Amsterdam

Like Hals and Leyster, Rembrandt van Rijn (1606–1669) was influenced indirectly by Caravaggio through the Utrecht School. Rivaling Rubens as the most famous artist of his age, Rembrandt is perhaps the better-known of the two today. A painter, draftsman, and printmaker, he is equally significant in each medium. Rembrandt is known both for the intimacy and poignancy of his images which convey personal relationships and emotions (see www.myartslab.com)—an aspect seldom explored before—as well as for producing large group portraits and history pieces. He had an active workshop (see *The Art Historian's Lens*, above) for four decades and many of his followers became significant artists in his native Leiden or in Amsterdam, where he established himself.

REMBRANDT'S DRAWINGS The poignancy of his drawings can be seen in many of his studies "from life"—that is, made with the model before him. He drew in pen and ink, wash, red or black chalk, silverpoint, and combinations of these. Rembrandt's drawing of his wife, *Portrait of Saskia van Uylenburgh* (fig. **20.21**), upon their engagement, is executed in silverpoint, an unforgiving drawing tool (commonly used before the invention of the pencil) that requires precision and a sure hand, on parchment. It is clearly meant as a very special drawing to commemorate their betrothal. The inscription states (in Dutch): "This is drawn after my wife, when she was 21 years old, the third day of our betrothal, the 8th of June 1633." They were married a year later; the drawing shows a dreamy-eyed Saskia looking very much in love with the viewer (the artist). She wears a straw hat, usually associated with shepherdesses, country life, and pastoral, amorous scenes. The flowers in her hat and hands further embellish this idea. Saskia came from a well-to-do family and was the niece of Rembrandt's art dealer.

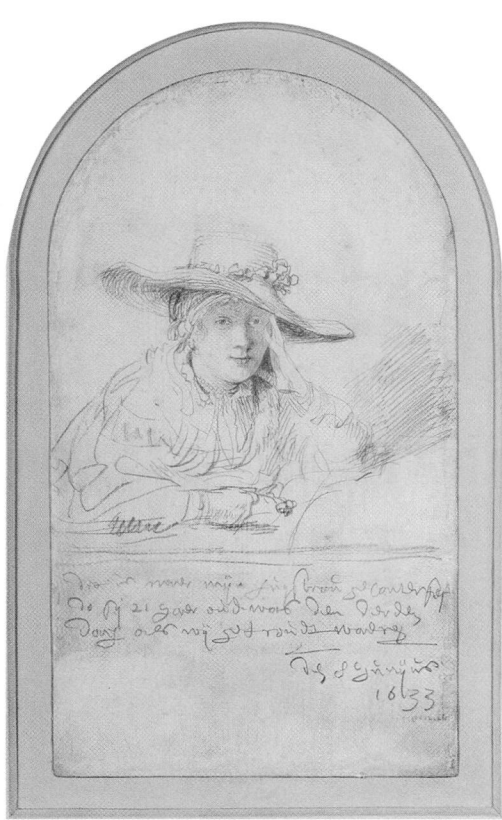

Her features appear in many of the paintings and studies for etchings he made before her death at the age of 30 in 1642.

REMBRANDT'S PAINTINGS Rembrandt's earliest paintings are small, sharply lit, and intensely realistic. Many deal with Hebrew Bible subjects, a lifelong preference on the part of the artist. (See www.myartslab.com; see also figs. 20.22 and 20.25.) They show both his greater realism and his new, more emotional attitude. Rembrandt and, indeed, many other seventeenth-century Protestants viewed the stories of the Hebrew Bible in much the same lay Christian spirit that governed Caravaggio's approach to the New Testament—as direct accounts of God's dealings with his human creations. Some of Rembrandt's biblical paintings were produced for the princely court in The Hague (despite the Reformation, the use of such images died hard), as well as for private patrons.

How strongly these stories affected him is clear in *The Blinding of Samson* (fig. **20.22**). Painted in the Baroque style he

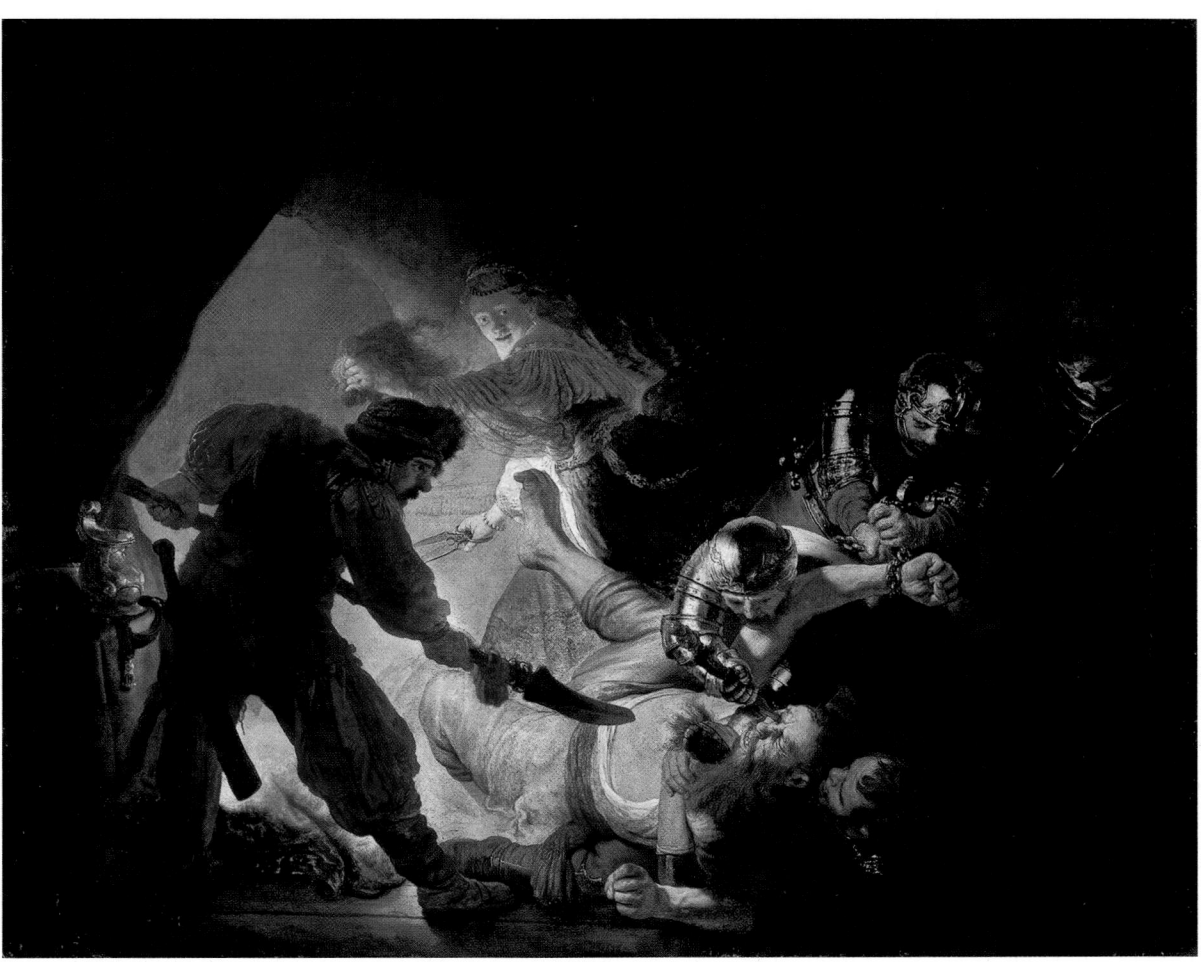

20.22 Rembrandt van Rijn, *The Blinding of Samson*. 1636. Oil on canvas, 7'9" × 9'11" (2.4 × 3 m). Städelsches Kunstinstitut und Stadtische Galerie, Frankfurt

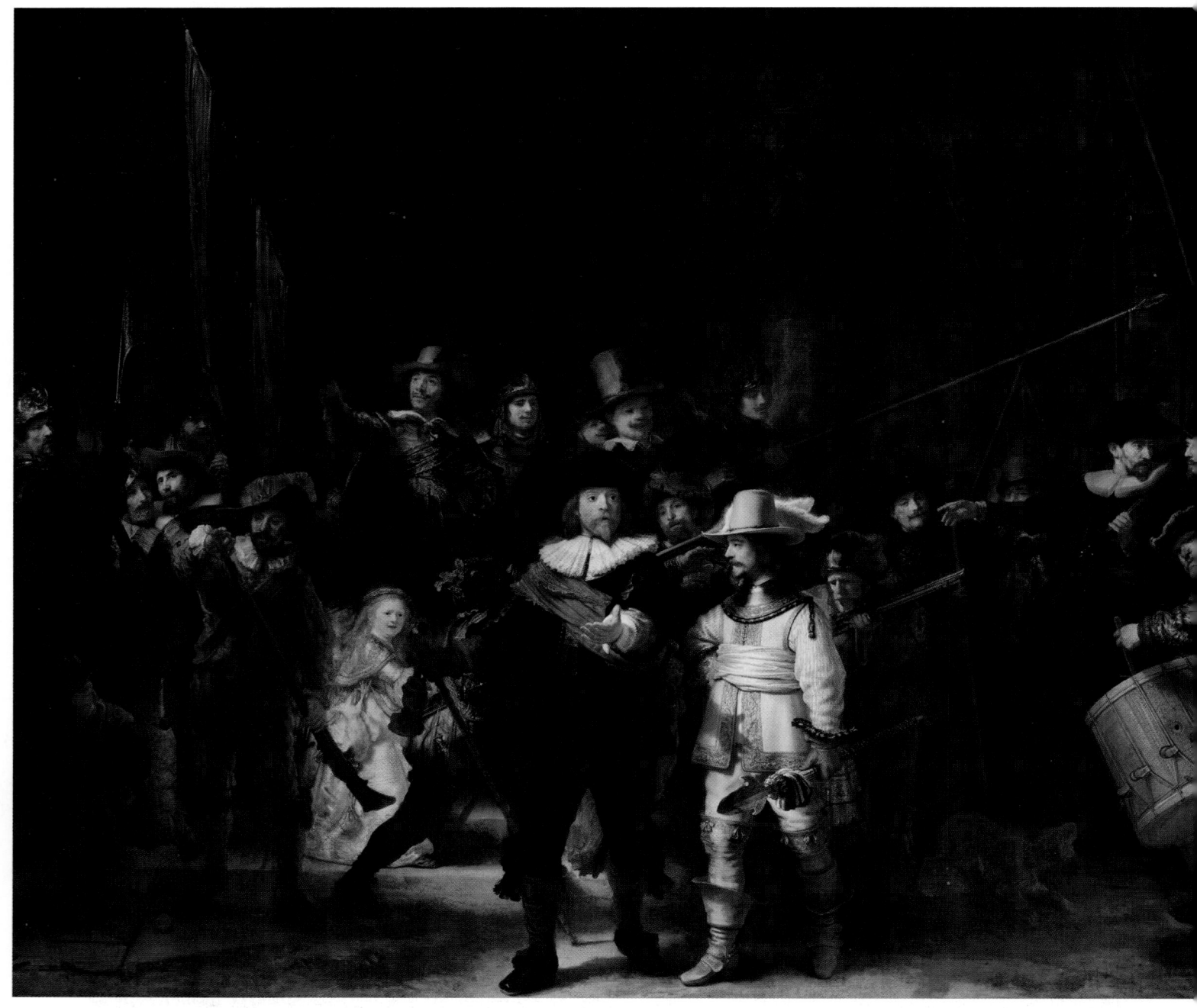

20.23 Rembrandt van Rijn, *The Night Watch* (*The Company of Captain Frans Banning Cocq*). 1642. Oil on canvas, 12'2" × 14'7" (3.8 × 4.4 m). Rijksmuseum, Amsterdam

developed in the 1630s after moving to Amsterdam, it shows Rembrandt as a master storyteller. The artist depicts the Hebrew Bible world as full of Oriental splendor and violence, and he is directly influenced by Caravaggio through the Utrecht Caravaggisti. The theatrical light pouring into the dark tent heightens the drama to the same pitch as *The Raising of the Cross* (see page 698) by Rubens, whose work Rembrandt sought to rival. But Rembrandt's decision not to travel to Italy to see the art of antiquity or the Renaissance for himself may have limited his opportunities to widen his experiences and to see contemporary art, as well. (See www.myartslab.com.) Instead, he

brought the outside world to himself. Rembrandt was an avid collector of Near Eastern objects, which often served as props in his pictures.

REMBRANDT AND THE CIVIC GUARD By the 1640s, Rembrandt had become Amsterdam's most sought-after portrait painter, and a man of considerable wealth. His famous group portrait (fig. **20.23**) known as *The Night Watch*, because of its old darkened varnish (now cleaned off), was painted in 1642. It shows a military company in the tradition of Frans Hals's Civic Guard groups (see fig. 20.16), possibly assembling for the visit of Marie de' Medici of France to Amsterdam. Although the members of the company had each contributed toward the cost of the huge canvas (originally it was much larger), Rembrandt did not give them equal weight pictorially. He wanted to avoid the mechanically regular designs of earlier group portraits—a problem only Frans Hals had solved successfully. Instead, he made the picture a virtuoso performance filled with movement and lighting, which captures the excitement of the moment and provides a unique sense of drama. The focus is on Captain Frans Banning Cocq, whose hand extends toward us and even creates a shadow across the yellow jacket of his lieutenant; other figures are plunged into shadow or hidden by overlapping. Legend has it that the people whose portraits Rembrandt had obscured were not satisfied with the painting, but there is no evidence for this claim. On the contrary, we know that the painting was much admired in its time, and Rembrandt continued to receive major public commissions in the 1650s and 1660s.

REMBRANDT AS PRINTMAKER Rembrandt's etchings show a new depth of feeling leant by the intimacy of the print medium. *The Hundred Guilder Print* (fig. **20.24**), which has been interpreted as a depiction of the entire nineteenth chapter of the Gospel of St. Matthew, combines various aspects of Christ's preachings, including the healing of the multitudes, and the gathering to him of children and those who had been forsaken. This is crystallized in the phrase which has been associated with the print from a contemporary poem: "The Son of God in a world of sorrow. …" The print is filled with pathos, revealing a humble world of bare feet and ragged clothes. The scene reveals Christ's deep compassion for the poor and outcast, who make up his audience in the print. Rembrandt had a special sympathy for the Jews, both as heirs of the biblical past and as victims of persecution, and they were often his models and also his patrons. The setting of this print suggests some corner in Amsterdam where the Jews had found a haven; they are used here to provide an "authentic" setting for Christ's teachings. Rembrandt incorporates observations of life from the drawings he made throughout his career; several of these drawings have been identified as studies for this work. Here, as in Caravaggio's *The Calling of St. Matthew* (see fig. 19.2), it is the magic of light and dark that gives the etching its spiritual significance.

The print derives its name from a story that 100 guilders was the great price paid for it at a contemporary auction. It is a

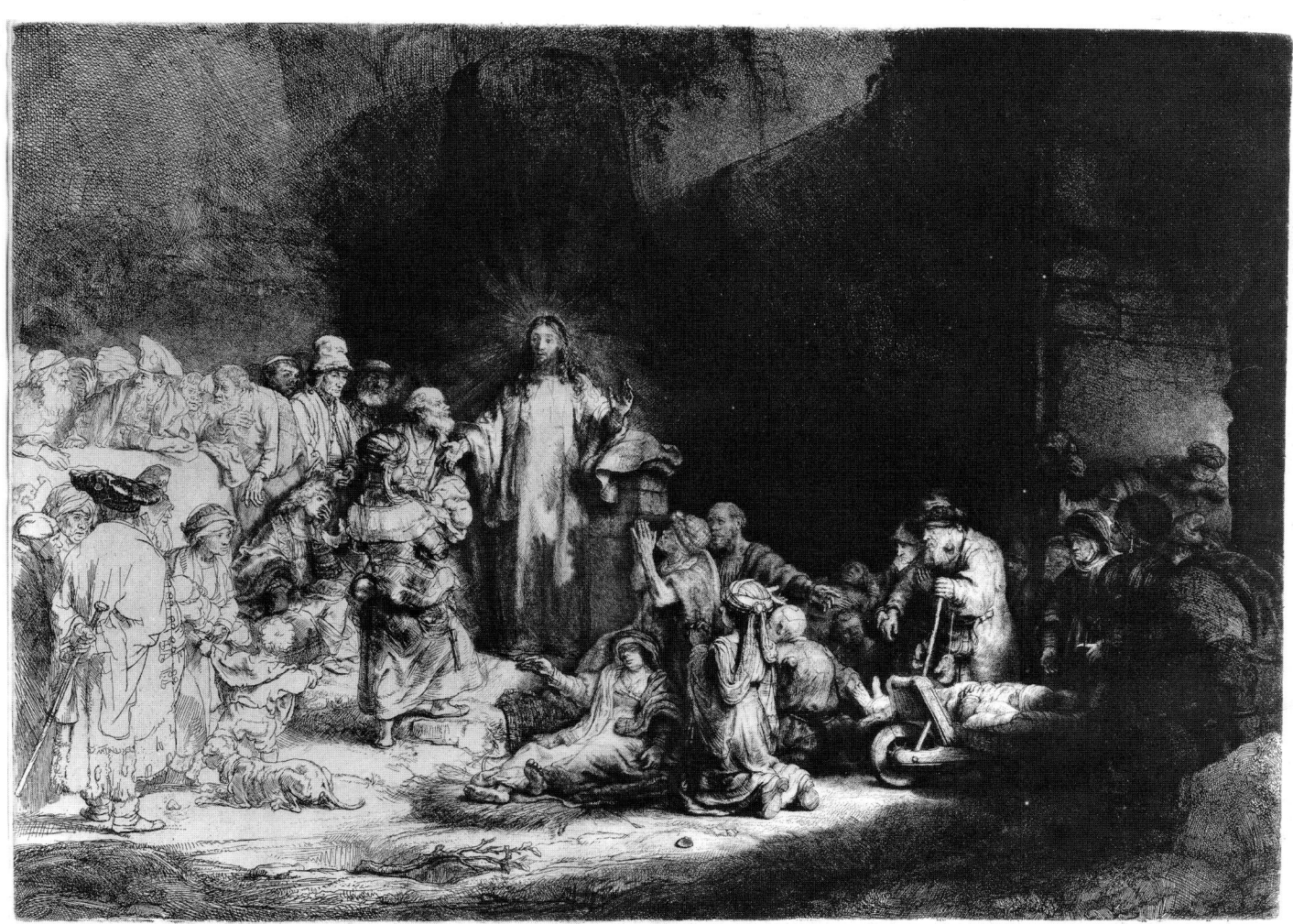

20.24   Rembrandt van Rijn, *The Hundred Guilder Print*. ca. 1647. Etching and drypoint, 11 × 12¾" (27.8 × 32.4 cm). Metropolitan Museum of Art, New York. H. O. Havemeyer Collection, Bequest of Mrs H. O. Havemeyer, 1929 (29.107.35)

Etching, Drypoint, and Selective Wiping

Etching is a form of intaglio printing. The modern technique calls for a metal plate to be cut by the artist using acid. The process begins with the metal plate initially being coated with a waxy substance. Instead of gouging grooves directly in the metal, the artist can lightly "draw" on the plate with a stylus, thereby removing the waxy coating and revealing the metal beneath. The plate is then placed in an acid bath, and the revealed metal will react with the acid, which will burn away the metal to create grooves. The plate is then removed, wiped off, and covered in ink. The excess ink is then wiped off, leaving ink only in the grooves. As with engraving, dampened paper is used to cover the plate. This is then rolled through a press. But because the acid continues to burn the metal, the etched lines may be uneven, and depending on the length of time spent in the acid bath, the grooves may be deeper. With etching, therefore, the actual creation is much like drawing (artists may even carry prepared plates with them), but the finished process also includes a component of chance.

The possibilities for creating greater tonal qualities increased with the introduction of different varieties of paper. In the seventeenth century, several printmakers, including Rembrandt, used papers ranging in quality and origin, from fine laid to a creamy, nubby oatmeal paper, to tan Chinese and Japanese papers, which seemed to make the blacks even blacker. Rembrandt also printed on vellum and even on pigskin.

The range of blacks was further extended by the use of **drypoint**. Drypoint is the process of picking out the metal on a plate with a fine, hard needle and leaving the burr, the metal filings, which will then gather up the ink. This process has the possibility of creating areas of higher black density, as in Rembrandt's *The Hundred Guilder Print* (see fig. 20.24). Drypoint is often used in combination with etching and engraving.

Another option for creating greater tonal range is not to wipe the plate completely clean. This is called **selective wiping**. It can achieve an overall dark tone, creating chiaroscuro effects. In some cases, Rembrandt seems to have hardly wiped the plate at all, keeping it mostly inked. This very selective wiping was used to create nocturnal tenebristic effects. Rembrandt's printed images created an enthusiasm for these dark etchings, and a new form of etching was developed in the late seventeenth century, called **mezzotint**. This is a process of creating many indentations in the metal so that almost the entire plate (called a "rocked" plate) will print dark and only a few areas, smoothed out by the artist, will print light. This process has recently been revived with the availability of prepared "rocked" plates.

In each of these processes, changes are possible. The initial print is called a state. In each case, after printing one example, the artist can make a change. The second printing, using the same plate or block, is called a second state. There can be many states for a single print. The block or plate is therefore quite valuable and can be used again many years later—even after the artist's death, thereby providing family members or others with income. The block or plate can be purchased, and those who make new prints can even produce new states. Sometimes the artist will deface a plate (called "striking" it) to prevent unauthorized people from using it.

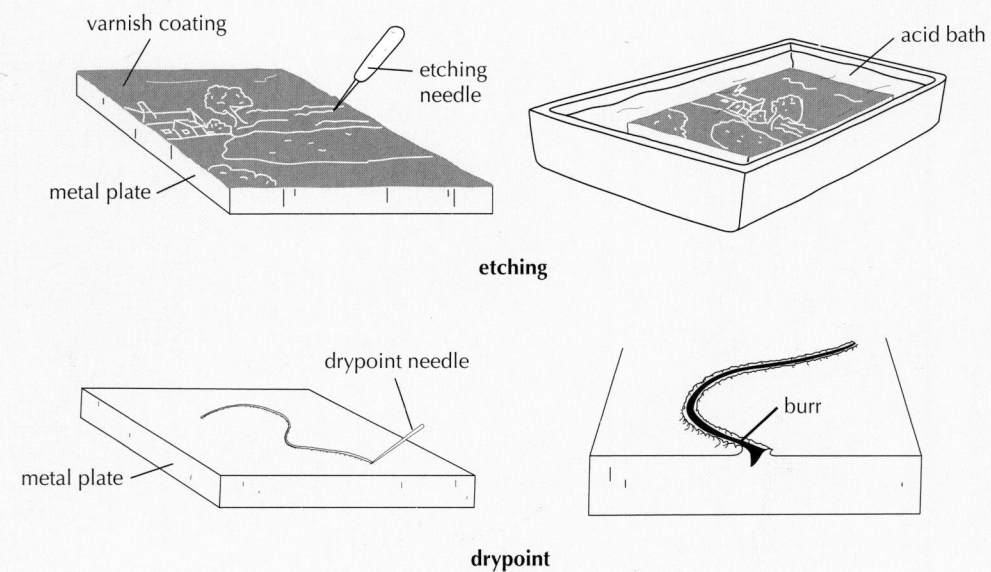

varnish coating

etching needle

metal plate

acid bath

etching

drypoint needle

metal plate

burr

drypoint

virtuoso combination of etching and drypoint (see *Materials and Techniques*, above), creating a velvety tone that can only be suggested in the reproduction here. Rembrandt's importance as a graphic artist is second only to Dürer's, although we get no more than a hint of his virtuosity from this single example.

MATURE WORK Both poignant and "from life," Rembrandt's monumental painting of *Bathsheba with King David's Letter* (fig. **20.25**) is a stunning work. We know nothing of its commissioning or later purchase. The subject of the painting, from 2 Samuel 11:2–27, would have been familiar to seventeenth-century viewers:

The biblical King David noticed the beautiful, but married, Bathsheba at her bath and summoned her. Thus began a series of events culminating in her pregnancy, the death of her husband, specifically sent to the front lines of battle to be killed, her marriage to King David, and the birth of her son who would be King Solomon. Although in the biblical account Bathsheba does not actually receive a letter, this prop became part of the visual tradition along with the attendant performing the pedicure at left.

The large nude, so close to our space, confronts us—even though she does not. Bathsheba with deep sadness and melancholy looks down at David's letter, contemplating its consequences and the loss of her own innocence. Indeed, Bathsheba, in the seventeenth century, was not considered innocent but complicit in allowing the king to see her body and therefore in betraying her marriage vows. The painting itself is not eroticized, but the sheer fleshiness and palpability of her body makes the sensual difficult to ignore. This work brings to mind the many life-size nudes by Titian (see fig. 17.35), but our painting is of a flawed human, while Titian's is that of a goddess. Rembrandt's Bathsheba is formed of flesh and light in contrast to the color of Titian's subject. Bathsheba is not at all idealized and contemporary criticism faults Rembrandt for this. "Fat swollen belly, hanging breasts, garter marks" were descriptions associated with Rembrandt's nudes. We cannot escape her disturbing reality and get lost in the narrative of the painting—as there isn't one. The work remains an icon of vulnerability.

Because Hendrickje Stoffels, Rembrandt's wife (as she was known, although they were never officially married; Saskia had died 12 years before), was also pregnant in 1654 and because she was summoned in July of that year to appear before a church committee which censured her for living in sin with Rembrandt, it has been suggested—nearly unanimously—that Bathsheba is a portrait of Hendrickje, or that Hendrickje is shown in the guise of Bathsheba. As tantalizing as this association is, there is no

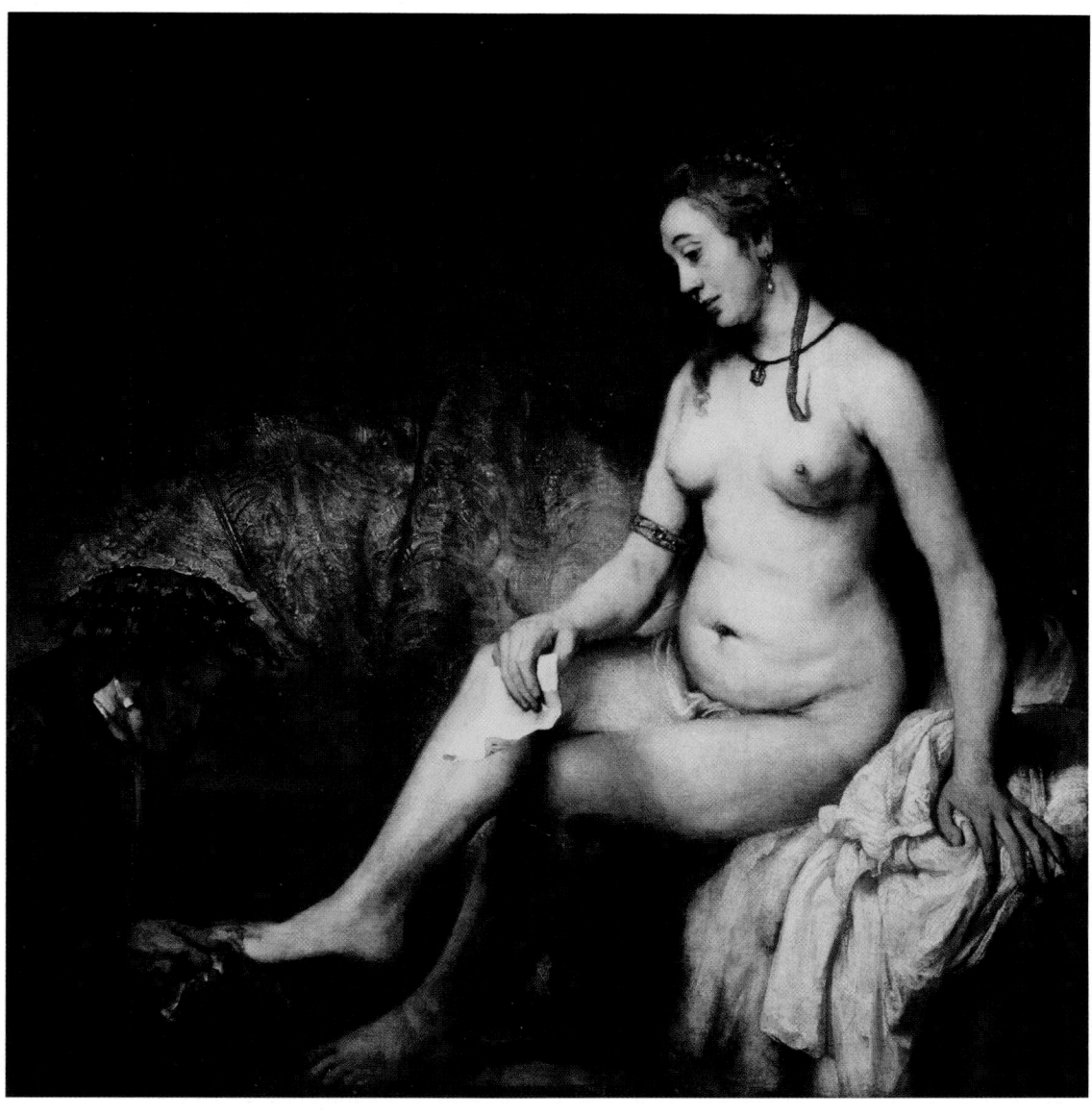

20.25   Rembrandt van Rijn, *Bathsheba with King David's Letter*. 1654. Oil on canvas, 55 1/10 × 55 1/10" (142 × 142 cm). Musée du Louvre, Paris

known image of Hendrickje, although many paintings have been called "Rembrandt's wife." But without knowing what Hendrickje looked like the connection with the *Bathsheba* is only speculation. The painting remains a poignant, powerful example of an aching drama. Creating a work of significant emotional impact was Rembrandt's forte in his mature years.

SELF-PORTRAITURE Although no likeness of Hendrickje is known, likenesses of Rembrandt are common, since he painted many self-portraits over his long career. They are experimental in the early Leiden years, theatrically disguised in the 1630s, and frank toward the end of his life. Many reasons for their execution have been suggested—as models for other paintings, as explorations of different expressions, and as possible advertisements for his craft. While our late example (fig. **20.26**) is partially indebted to frontally posed Venetian portraits, Rembrandt examines himself with a typically northern European candor. The bold pose and penetrating look bespeak a resigned but firm resolve that suggests princely nobility, which is materially underlined by his richly brocaded gold collar, fur mantle, and silver staff (sceptor?). A comparison with Holbein's *Henry VIII* (see fig. 18.24) suggests the similar concept of authority, but in the latter Holbein's interest in the detail of fabric and jewels dominates while Rembrandt uses chiaroscuro to suggest mood. There is also a marked difference in technique, as Rembrandt uses impasto, which is the layering of paints and glazes to achieve textured and atmospheric effects. Rembrandt painted several large self-portraits, including this one, toward the end of his life, and the acquisition of a "large mirror" (its breakage is documented) may have allowed him to do this.

Rembrandt and his school dominated Amsterdam. Rembrandt produced many history paintings, portraits, and etchings, and is known for his depictions of the inner person and for revealing the pathos in a scene or moment. His works are famous for their poignancy and came to represent the epitome of the Golden Age of Dutch Art.

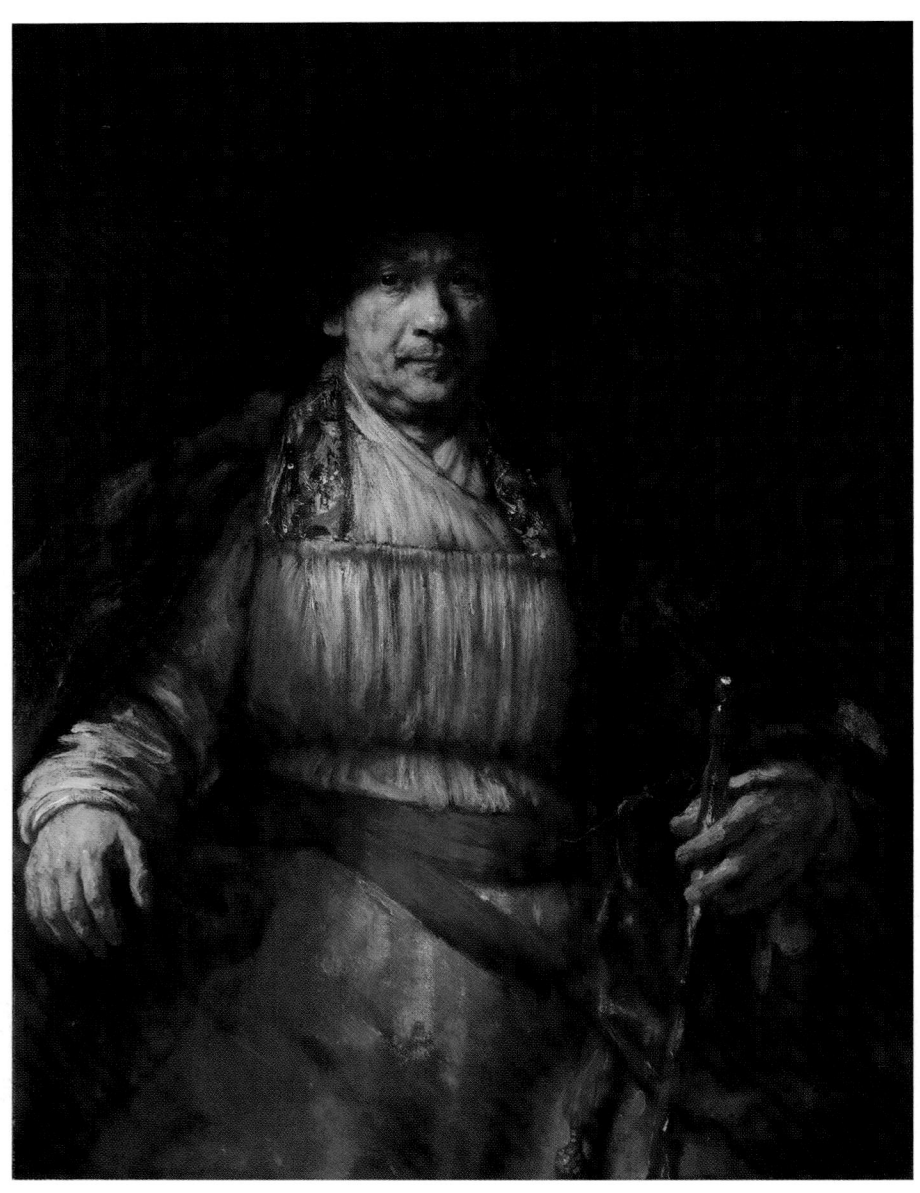

20.26 Rembrandt van Rijn, *Self-Portrait*. 1658. Oil on canvas, 52⅝ × 40⅞" (133.6 × 103.8 cm). Signed and dated on the arm of the chair at right: Rembrandt/f.1658. The Frick Collection, New York. Purchased in 1906. Acc #"06.1.97

THE MARKET: LANDSCAPE, STILL-LIFE, AND GENRE PAINTING

While Italian art was dominated by private patronage or that of the Church, art in northern Europe was largely made for the open market. Of course, portraits and group portraits, like those for the Civic Guards, were commissioned works, but a great number of paintings were also made "on spec"—that is, with the hope that they would be purchased on the open market from dealers, fairs, stores, and lotteries. We know (see *Primary Source*, page 704) that Rubens kept paintings in stock for his own use, and that these were not commissioned works. Perhaps with princely patrons in mind, Rubens painted many large works, but in Holland, paintings were often small, and featured subjects suitable for a middle-class home. Most art buyers in the Dutch Republic preferred images within their own experience: landscapes, architectural views, still lifes, and genre (everyday) scenes. These subjects, we recall, emerged in the latter half of the sixteenth century (see page 653). As the subjects became fully defined, artists began to specialize. Although this trend was not confined to Holland, Dutch painting became famous for both its volume and variety.

The richest of the newly developed "specialties" was landscape, both as a portrayal of familiar views and as an imaginative vision of nature. Landscapes—frequently with only small human figures or none at all—became a staple of seventeenth-century Dutch painting. We can see the beginnings of this in the work of Pieter Bruegel the Elder (see fig. 18.32) and in Italy as well, in such paintings as Carracci's *Landscape with the Flight into Egypt* (see fig. 19.8). But in the Netherlands, greater realism, almost a "portrait of the land," was common. A contemporary said of these landscapes: "nothing is lacking except the warmth of the sun and the movement caused by the gentle breeze."

Landscape Painting: Jan van Goyen

Jan van Goyen's (1596–1656) *Pelkus Gate Near Utrecht* (fig. 20.27), a seascape or marine painting, is the kind of landscape that enjoyed great popularity because its elements were so familiar: the distant town, with a low horizon line, under an overcast sky, seen through a moist atmosphere across an expanse of water. Van Goyen executed about a dozen paintings of this site, each featuring the fourteenth-century gate (which no longer exists). But we can see from his drawings of the site that the views are not exact, but a patchwork of reality and imaginary. The painting is characteristic of Van Goyen's ability to combine the familiar with the picturesque, creating a melancholic mood of these "nether lands," ever threatened by the sea, but also in need of it.

Like other early Dutch Baroque landscapists, Van Goyen frequently used only grays and browns, highlighted by green accents; but within this narrow range he achieved an almost infinite variety of effects. The tonal landscape style in Holland was accompanied by radically simplified compositions, and we see this effect in a monochromatic still-life painting (see fig. 20.31) of the same time. As he worked in several cities (Haarlem, Leiden, and The Hague), Van Goyen was especially influential and extremely prolific; he is credited with over 1,200 paintings and 800 drawings. His family is also evidence of the interrelationship of artists—his daughter married the genre painter Jan Steen (see page 730).

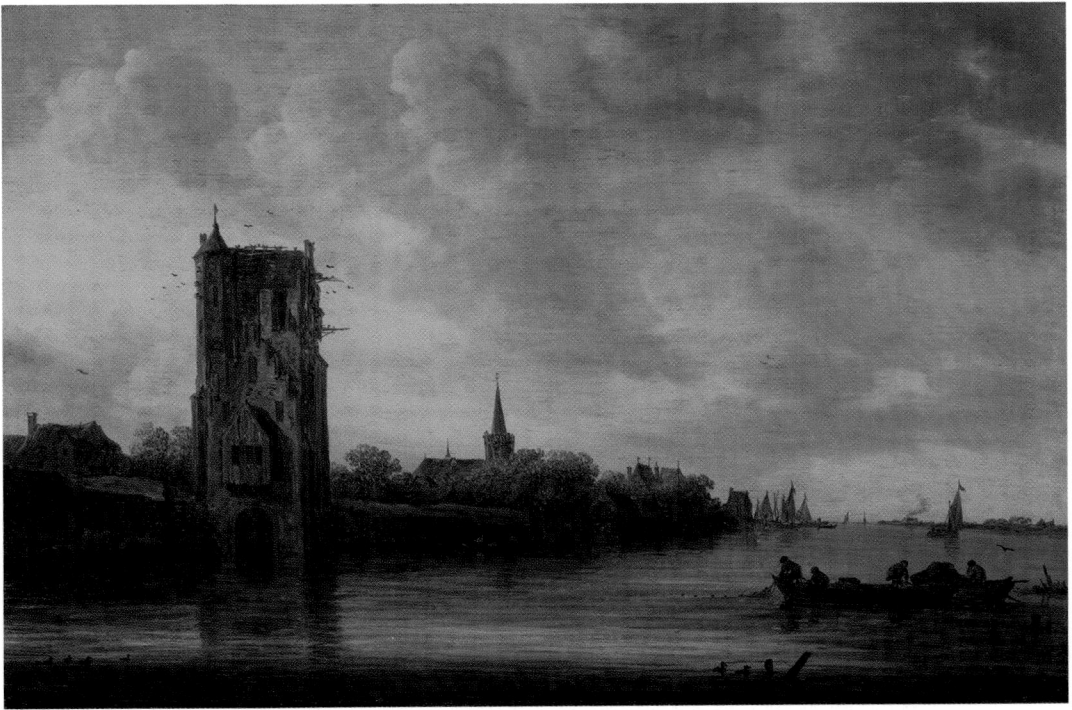

20.27 Jan van Goyen, *Pelkus Gate Near Utrecht*. 1646. Oil on wood, 14½ × 22½" (36.8 × 57.2 cm). Signed and dated (on boat): VG 1646. Metropolitan Museum of Art, New York. Gift of Francis Neilson, 1945 (45.146.3)

City Views: Jacob van Ruisdael

Identifiable city views—panoramic landscapes with their outlying countryside and picturesque sand dunes, showing Amsterdam, Haarlem, Deventer—became popular throughout the century. In the art of Jacob van Ruisdael (ca. 1628–1682), these views become testaments to the city skyline—and to the sky, which might occupy three-quarters of the painting, as it does in this painting of Haarlem (fig. **20.28**). Ruisdael did many paintings of Haarlem, known as *Haarlempjes* (little views of Haarlem). The church

spires, windmills, and ruins are all identifiable, as is the major church, the Grote Kerk (Big Church), known before the Reformation as St. Bavo (see fig. 20.30). In the foreground are the bleaching fields, where both domestic and foreign linen was washed and set out to be bleached by the sun. Haarlem water was well known for its purity and so the city was famous for its linen bleaching and beer production.

A heightened sense of drama is the core of Ruisdael's *The Jewish Cemetery* (fig. **20.29**). Natural forces dominate this wild scene, which is imaginary except for the tombs from the Jewish

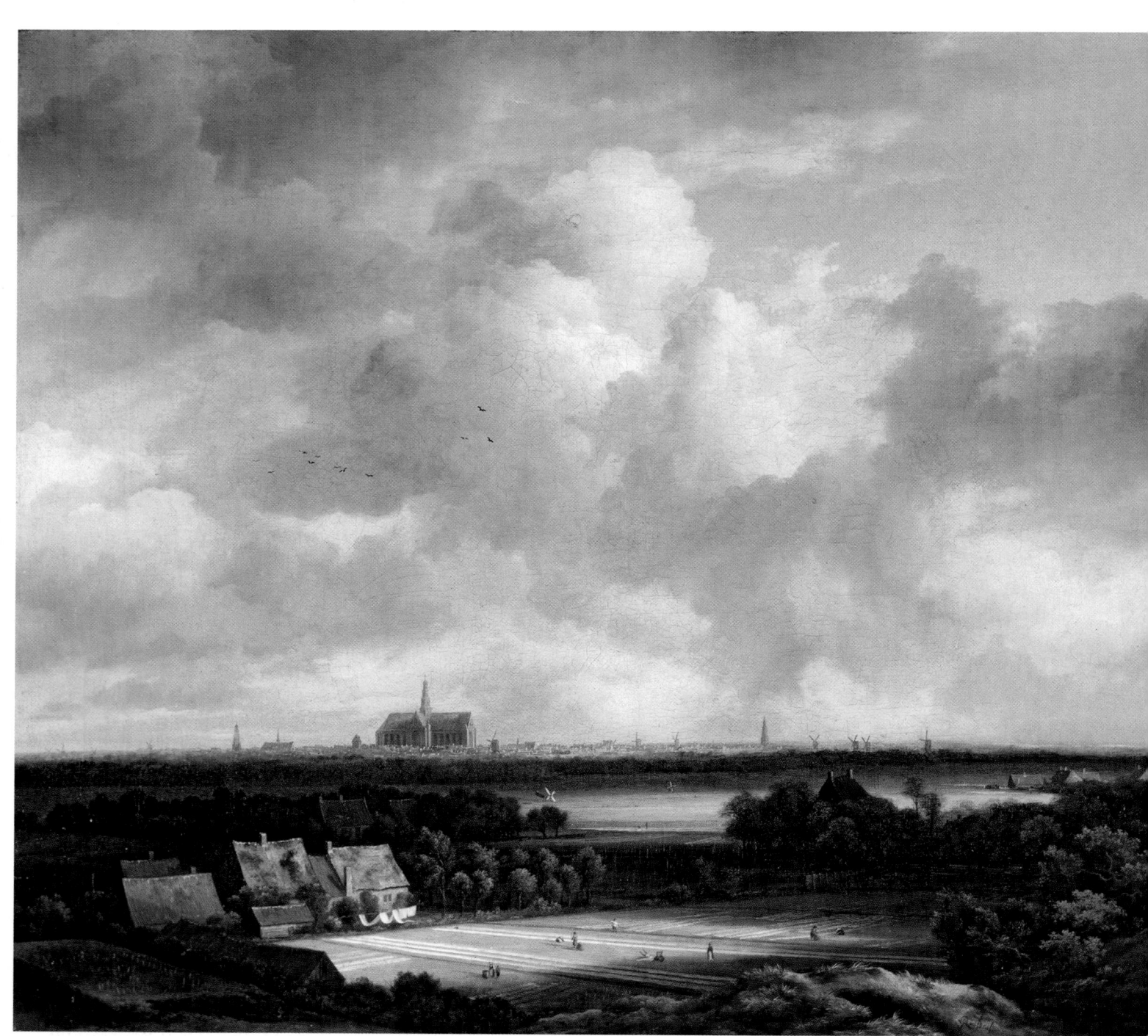

20.28   Jacob van Ruisdael, *Bleaching Grounds Near Haarlem*. ca. 1670. Oil on canvas, 21⅔ × 24½" (55.5 × 62 m). Royal Cabinet of Paintings, Mauritshuis, The Hague. Inv. 1.55

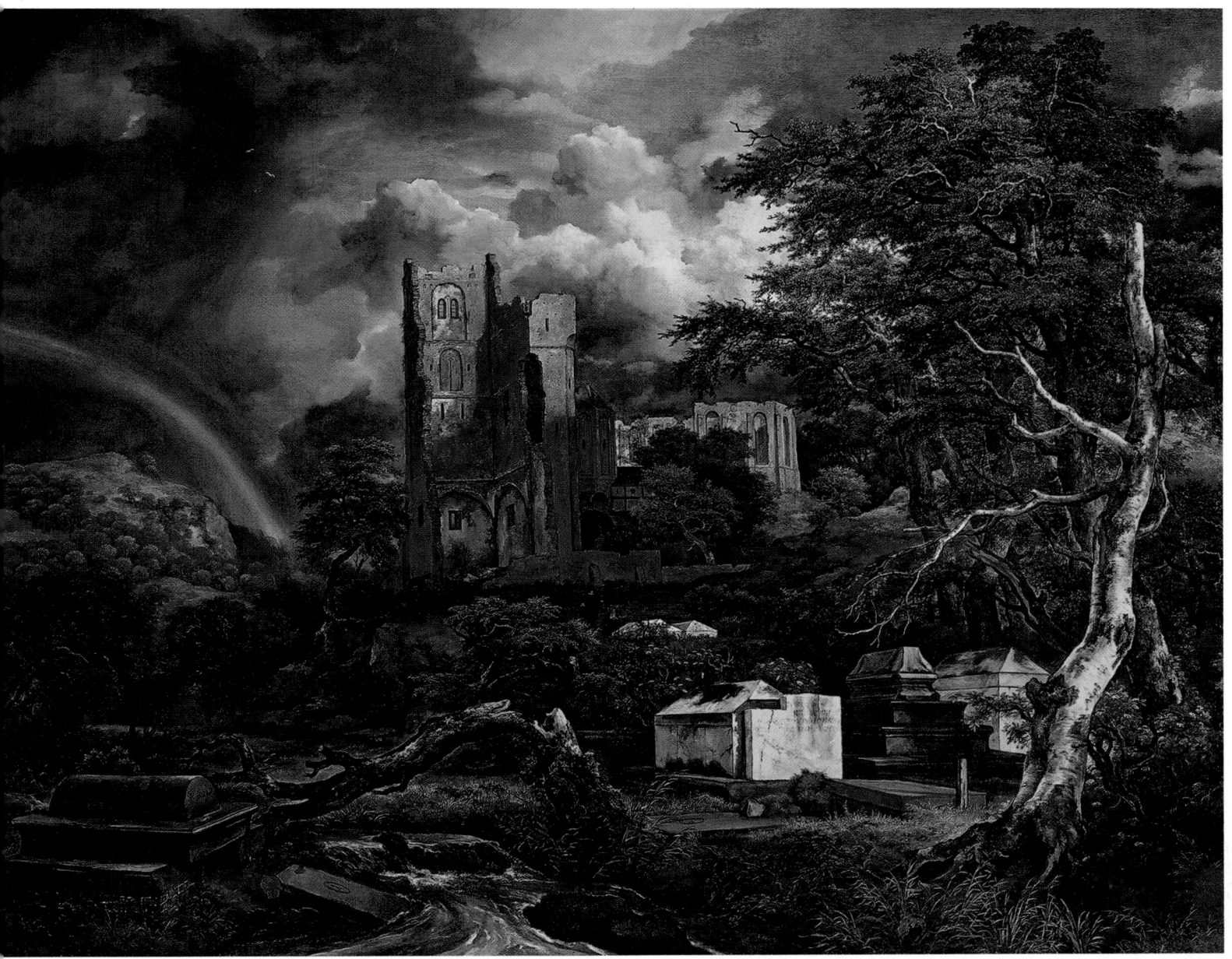

20.29 Jacob van Ruisdael, *The Jewish Cemetery*. 1655–70. Oil on canvas, 4'6" × 6'2½" (1.42 × 1.89 m).
The Detroit Institute of Arts, Detroit, MI. Gift of Julius H. Haass in memory of his brother, Dr. Ernest W. Haass. 26.3

cemetery near Amsterdam. As we have seen in Rembrandt's work (see fig. 20.24), Jews had been living in Amsterdam through the seventeenth century—some, often poor, from Germany and eastern Europe, others, often more prosperous, newly arrived from Brazil, where they went to seek refuge from the Inquisition in Spain. The cemetery, called Bet Haim (House of Life), belonged to the latter group, the Sephardic or Portuguese and Spanish Jews. Each of the tombs has been identified, and, though appearing ancient, they were all erected in the seventeenth century. Several drawings of this site by Ruisdael exist, as do prints by other artists. Jews in Amsterdam were exotic—the "other"—and this may account for the theme's popularity. Foreigners who came to Amsterdam visited and wrote about this community with curiosity and even awe.

Ruisdael adds other nonrealistic elements to his imaginary wild scene: The ruined building in the background has been identified as Egmond Abbey (Catholic), which suggests a contrast between Jews and Catholics—or perhaps a complementary relationship— since both are superseded in the Dutch Republic by the Reformed Church. Thus, the theme of death—the cemetery, the tombs, the crumbling ruins of the abbey, and the dead trees—suggests the painting is a vanitas, a memorial to the brevity of life. The term comes from the biblical book of Ecclesiastes and its phrase "vanity of vanities." It is a text on the passage of time and on mortality, just as this painting is also a visual reminder of the shortness of life. Yet the cemetery is arched by a rainbow, a sign of God's promise of redemption. *The Jewish Cemetery* inspires that awe on which the Romantics, 150 years later, based their concept of the sublime.

Architectural Painting: Pieter Saenredam

In contrast to the dramatic mood and theatrical setting of *The Jewish Cemetery*, there are many examples, in paintings, prints, and drawings, of more realistic, descriptive images of the Sephardic synagogue and many of the austere Reformed churches. The *Interior of the Choir of St. Bavo's Church at Haarlem* (fig. **20.30**), painted by Pieter Saenredam (1597–1665), one of 11 such views that he painted, is meant to serve as more than a mere record. It is, in fact, an impossible view, suggesting a greater sense of vastness in the medieval structure than actually exists. Saenredam went to great lengths to construct his paintings. First, he made both freehand sketches and measured drawings in the church. His next step was to combine the two in additional drawings. Finally, he would paint a representation of the church that utilized accurate details from his drawings but also included

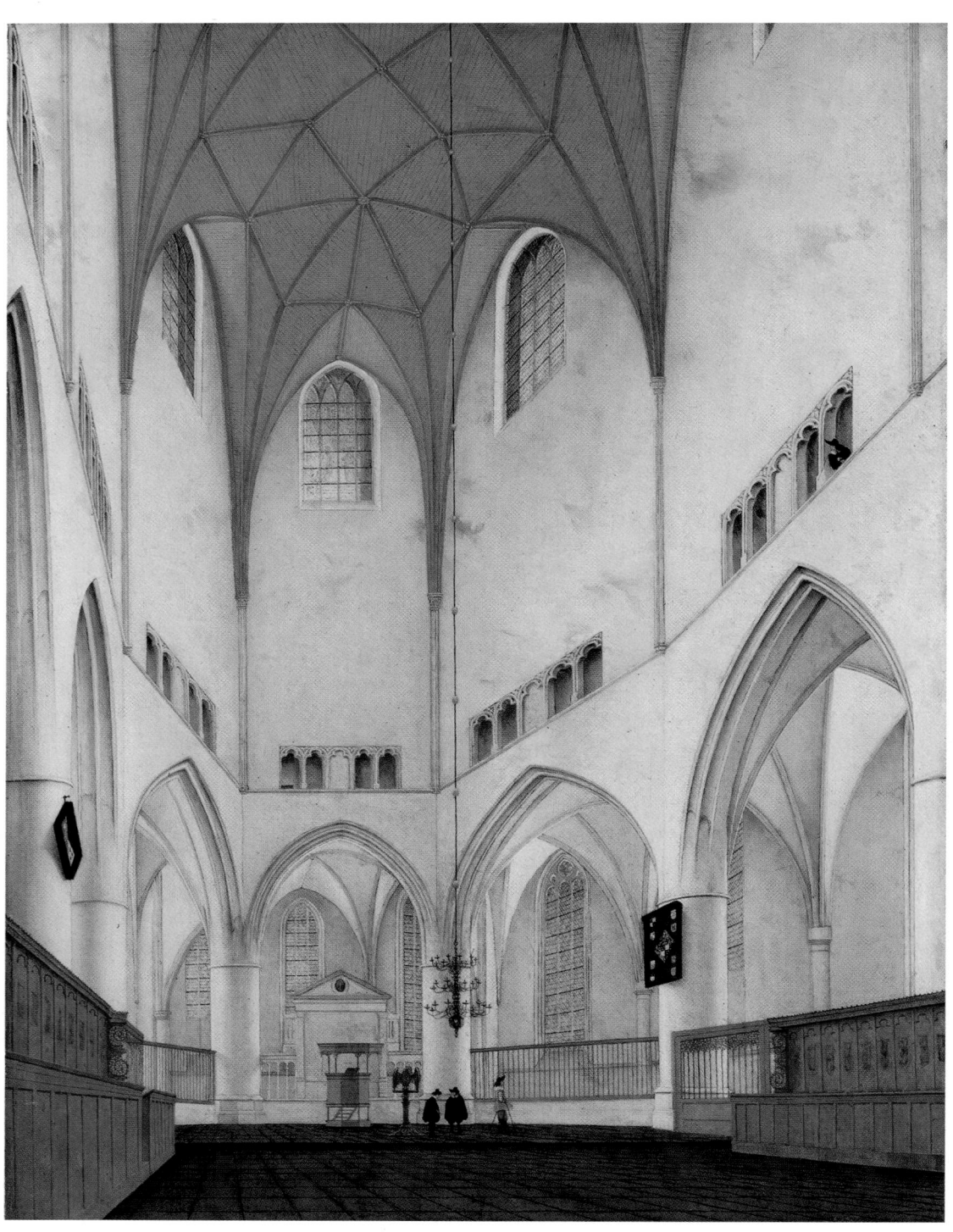

20.30 Pieter Saenredam, *Interior of the Choir of St. Bavo's Church at Haarlem*. 1660. Oil on panel, 27⅞ × 21⅝" (70.4 × 54.8 cm). Worcester Art Museum, Worcester, Massachusetts. Charlotte E. W. Buffington Fund. 1951.29

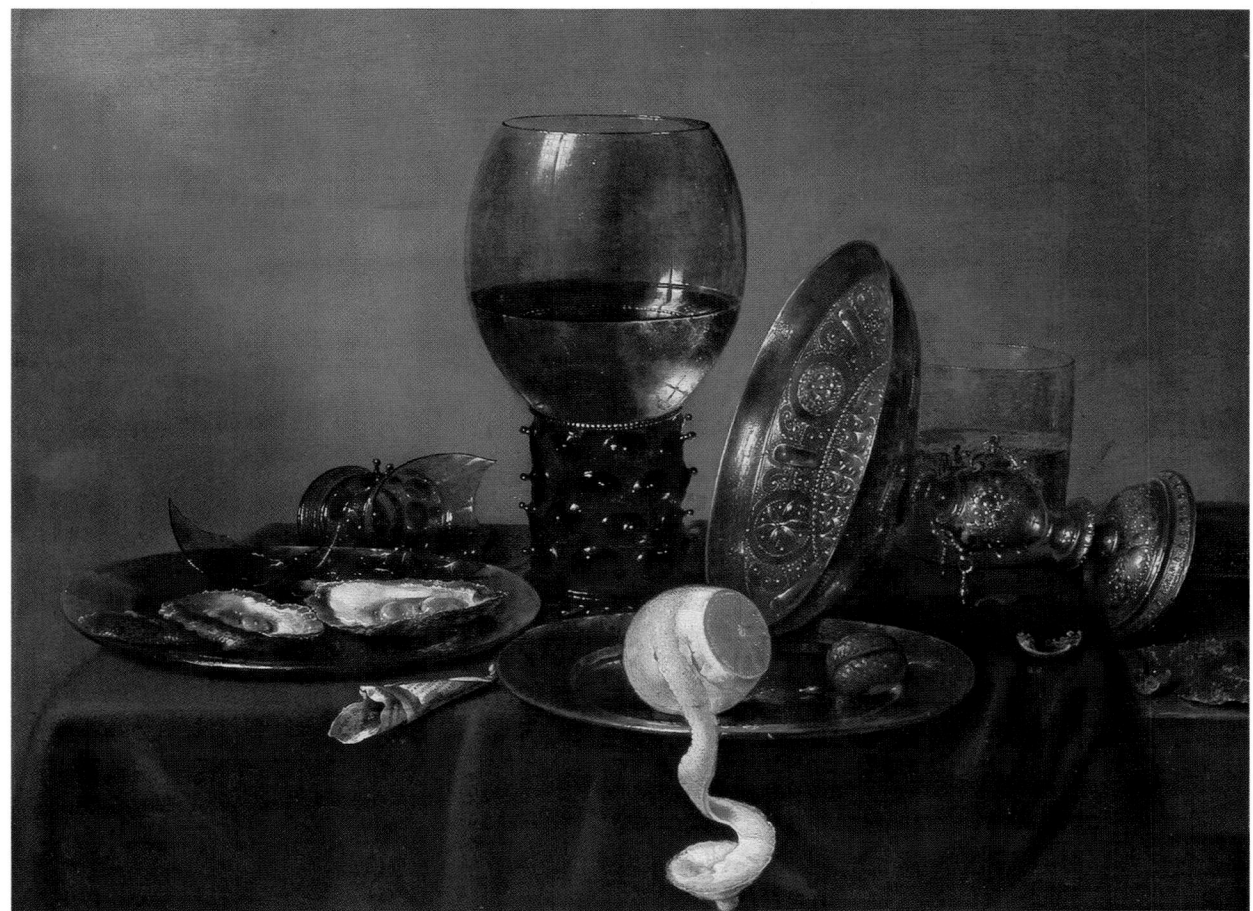

20.31 Willem Claesz, Heda. *Still Life with Oysters, a Roemer, a Lemon, and a Silver Bowl.* 1634.
Oil on panel, 16⅞ × 22⅞" (43 × 57 cm). Museum Boijmans-van Beuningen, Rotterdam, the Netherlands

exaggerated elements for effect. This is the same church that is the focus of Ruisdael's *Bleaching Grounds Near Haarlem* (see fig. 20.28). It is shown here stripped of all furnishings and white-washed under the Protestants, and it has acquired a crystalline purity that invites spiritual contemplation through the painting's quiet intensity. (Both Saenredam and Frans Hals would be buried here.) The tiny figures in the interior provide scale and often narrative. Note the fellow at right looking out of the **triforium**.

Still-life Painting: Willem Claesz. Heda

Dutch still lifes may show the remains of a meal—suggesting pleasure—and luxury objects, such as crystal goblets, glasses of different sizes, and silver dishes, chosen for their contrasting shapes, colors, and textures. Flowers, fruits, and seashells may also be shown. All are part of the world of still life. And these are not too different from the ingredients in a Flemish still life; many artists, such as Clara Peeters and Jan Davidsz. de Heem, traveled between both regions.

As seen here in his *Still Life with Oysters, a Roemer, a Lemon, and a Silver Bowl* (fig. **20.31**), the Haarlem artist Willem Claesz. Heda (1594–1680) was fascinated by surfaces and reflections—the rough edge of the lemon, the liquid, slimy quality of the oysters,

the engraving on the silver, the sparkling light on the roemer (wine glass), its multiple reflections of the window, and its *prunts* (glass drops). Heda is famous for such light effects, which are heightened by the tonal quality of the painting, which is largely monochromatic, much as in Jan van Goyen's landscape (see fig. 20.27), also of midcentury. These are in marked contrast to the colorful Flemish works of Clara Peeters and Jan Davidsz. de Heem (see figs. 20.11 and 20.13). The table is set with white wine, beer (back right), lemon, and a paper of pepper in a cone to use with the oysters, which were known to be aphrodisiacs. Yet the broken glass and overturned silver *tazza* suggest some upheaval on a narrative level. Whoever sat at this table was suddenly forced to leave the meal. The curtain that time has lowered on the scene, as it were, gives the objects a strange pathos. The unstable composition, with its signs of a hasty departure, suggests transience—a vanitas.

Flower Painting: Rachel Ruysch

The independent floral still life seems to have begun in Flanders, but it developed in both the Northern and Southern Netherlands. Rachel Ruysch (1664–1750) was one of the leading Dutch flower painters of the day, and was lauded as such in her lifetime. She had a long and prolific career and worked in Amsterdam, The Hague,

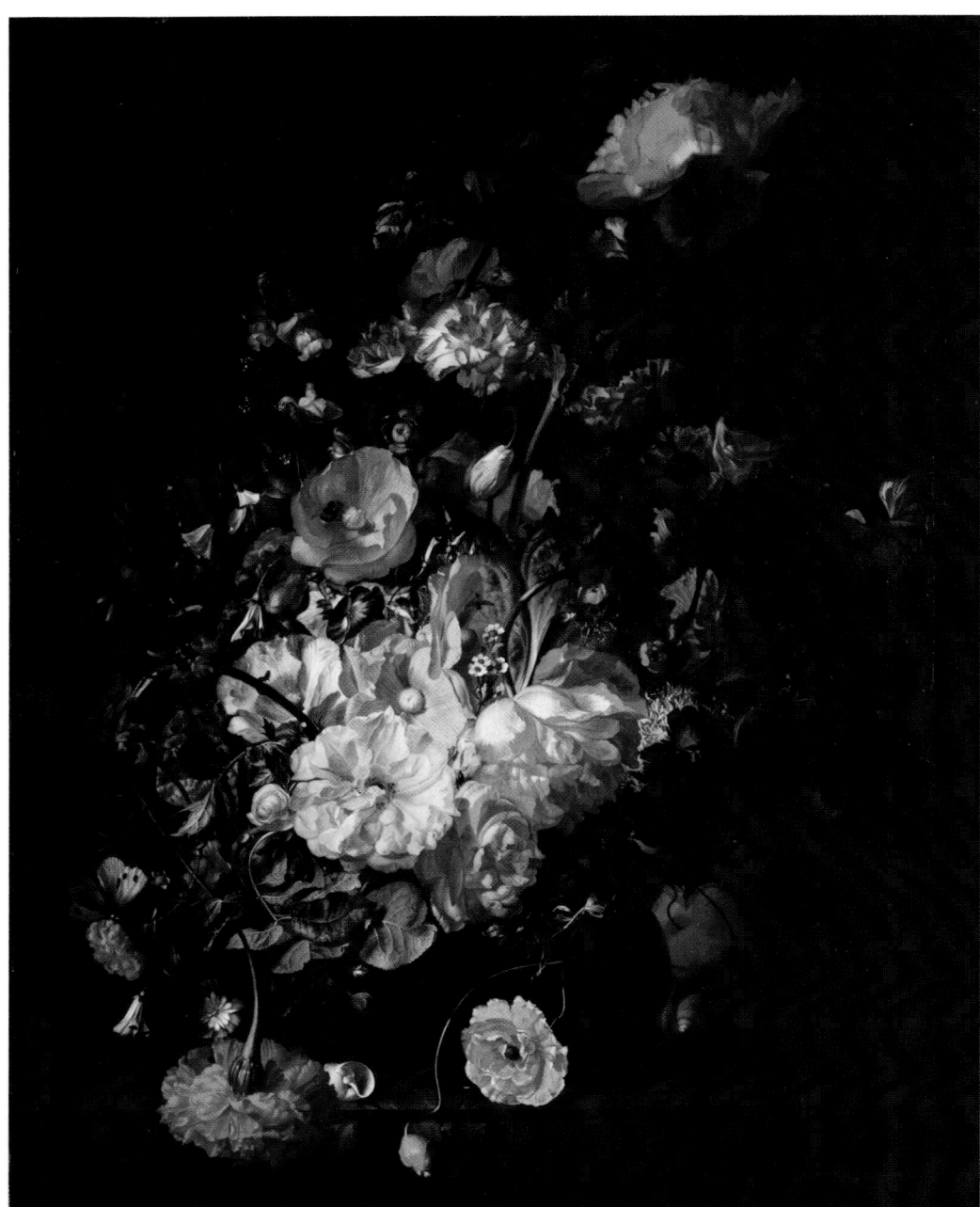

20.32 Rachel Ruysch, *Flower Still Life*. After 1700. Oil on canvas, 29¾ × 23⅞" (75.5 × 60.7 cm). The Toledo Museum of Art, Toledo, Ohio. Purchased with Funds from the Libbey Endowment, Gift of Edward Drummond Libbey. 1956.57

and Düsseldorf, where she and her husband, Juriaen Pool II (1665–1745), a portraitist, became court painters to the Elector Palatine until his death. One could say she was born to be a flower painter, as her father was a professor of anatomy and botany. Ruysch knew every blossom, every butterfly, moth, and snail that she put into a piece intimately. We know from the inclusion of flowers in earlier paintings, such as the lilies in a vase in the *Mérode Triptych* (see fig. 14.8), that flowers can have meaning beyond their beauty. The flowers in figure **20.32**, some with wild and impossibly long stems that stretch across the diagonal of the canvas, are arranged to create an extravaganza of color. Like the Heda *Still Life with Lemon and Oysters* (see fig. 20.31) with its broken glass, this still life features fallen, drooping flowers, and their near-death state again suggests a vanitas theme.

Genre Painting: Jan Steen

Many of the same themes continue to be featured in genre painting at the end of the seventeenth century, but the paintings now contain more complex narratives. Often, there are interior scenes of homes and taverns. The human figures are often no longer half-length; they are shown full length instead, even when the paintings are small, creating a further sense of intimacy. The paintings of Jan Steen, Jan Vermeer and Gerard ter Borch provide a range of subject matter, from the comical to the deeply introspective, while offering a glimpse of home, and family life, relationships, and even the fashions of the seventeenth century. A scene of both comical circumstance and family intimacy—much in the vein of Jordaens's *The King Drinks* (see fig. 20.9)—can be seen in *The Feast of St. Nicholas* (fig. **20.33**) by Jan Steen (1626–1679).

St. Nicholas has just paid his pre-Christmas visit to the household on 5 December, leaving toys, candy, and cake for the children. The little girl and boy are delighted with their presents. She holds a doll of St. John the Baptist and a bucket filled with sweets, while he plays with a golf club and ball. Everybody is jolly except their brother, on the left, who has received only a birch rod (held by the maidservant) for caning naughty children. Soon his tears will turn to joy, however: His grandmother, in the background, beckons him toward the bed, where a toy is hidden.

Steen tells the story with relish, embroidering it with many delightful details. Of all the Dutch painters of daily life, he was the sharpest and best-humored observer. To supplement his earnings, he kept an inn, which may explain his keen insight into human behavior. His sense of timing and his characterizations often remind us of Frans Hals (see figs. 20.16–20.18), while his storytelling stems from the tradition of Pieter Bruegel the Elder (see fig. 18.33). Steen was also a gifted history painter, and although portions of his work are indeed humorous, they usually convey a serious message as well. *The Feast of St. Nicholas* has just such content: The doll of St. John the Baptist is meant as a reminder of the importance of spiritual matters over worldly possessions, no matter how pleasurable the latter might be.

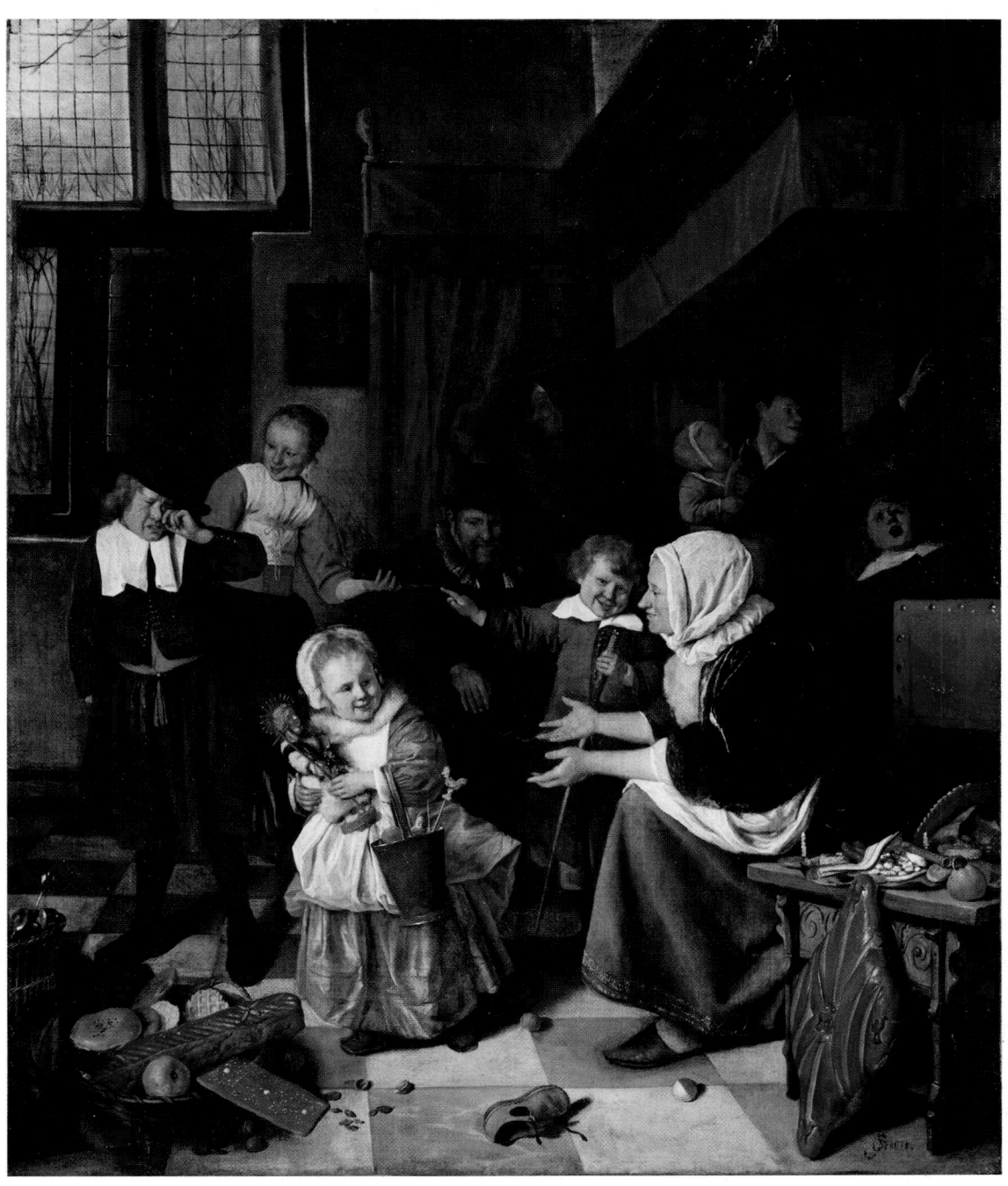

20.33   Jan Steen, *The Feast of St. Nicholas*. ca. 1660–65. Oil on canvas, 32¼ × 27¾" (82 × 70.5 cm). Rijksmuseum, Amsterdam

Intimate Genre Painting: Jan Vermeer

In the genre scenes of the Delft artist Jan Vermeer (1632–1675), by contrast, there is seldom a clear narrative. Vermeer's reputation rests on only a small number of paintings (about 35), but these are indeed quite special. Vermeer may have studied in Amsterdam and/or Utrecht, but he was certainly familiar with old and contemporary works as he, like his father, worked as an art dealer.

In an early work, *Officer and Laughing Girl* (fig. **20.34**), the figures are in a room infused by a nearly glowing light. The young woman sits beneath a large, contemporary map of the Netherlands (on its side), smiles cheerfully, and offers the man a glass of wine. We see only the silhouette of the man dressed in red, as light from the left-hand window pours in between them so that the entire painting seems to sparkle with light.

Vermeer's use of light, frequently coming from a window at the left and creating flecks of light on fabric and reflections, marks his work. To achieve these effects and create a perfectly balanced painting, he seems to have used techniques that are both old and new. Vermeer may have used a *camera obscura*, an experimental optical device (a forerunner of the photographic camera) that created an image by means of a hole for light on the inside of a dark box. The hole acts as a primitive lens and a scene from outside the box can be seen, inverted, inside it. It is not suggested here that Vermeer copied such scenes, but he may have been inspired by them. *Camera obscura* scenes have a sparkling quality, often seen in parts of Vermeer's work (as seen here in the gold threads in the woman's dress). These sparkling areas are known as "discs of confusion." The *camera obscura* was well known, and there is considerable evidence that it was used by Dutch artists. Further, Anthonie van Leeuwenhoek, the inventor of the modern microscope, lived in Delft at the same time, which suggests a local interest in practical optics.

This new way of looking is paired in Vermeer's work with an old way—a one-point perspective view with a vanishing point. It has been shown that a hole (for a pin and string) was set in a number of Vermeer's paintings to create a one-point perspective system. And indeed a vanishing point with pinhole is also observable in an x-ray. The vanishing point in this painting is set between the two figures and as such we do not focus on either one of them, but we are drawn to the space in between instead—to the very seduction of the relationship. It is the wall we focus on, with

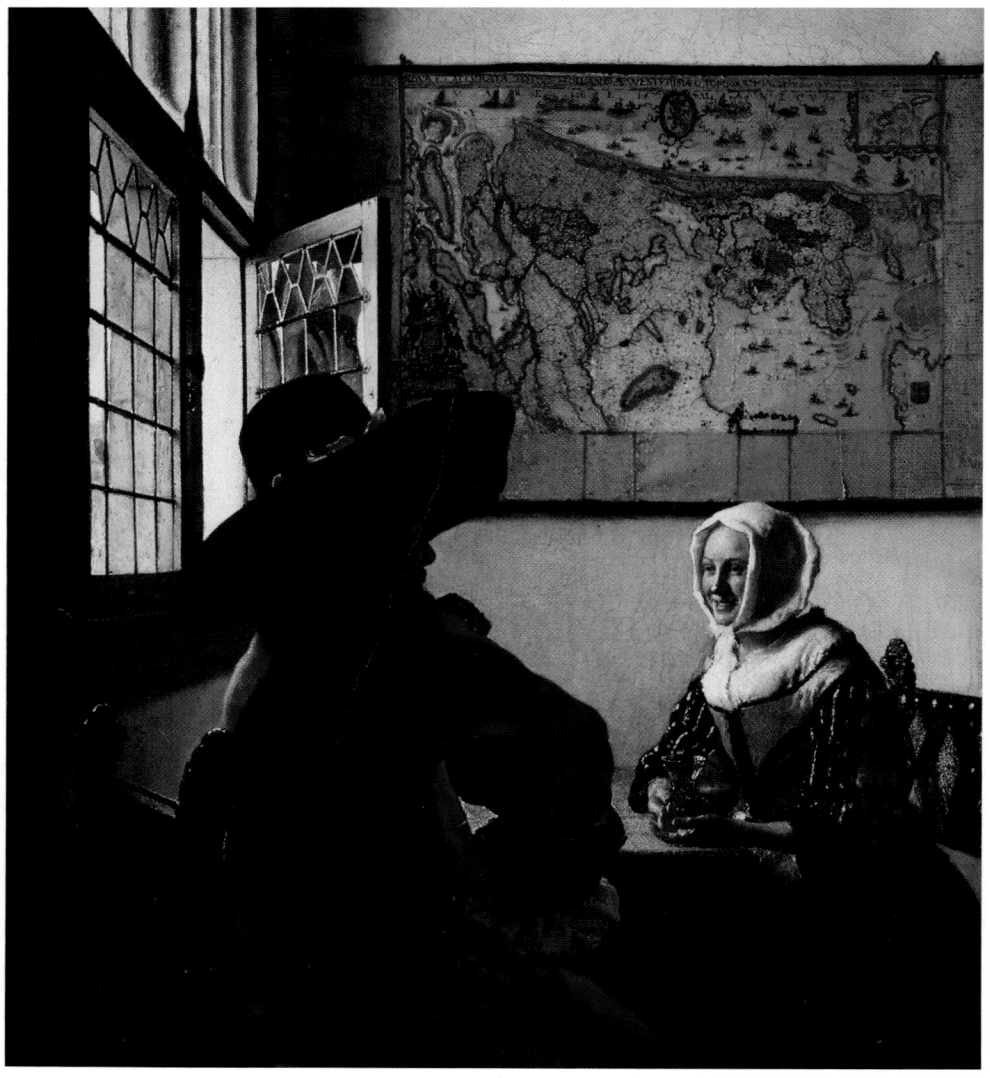

20.34 Jan Vermeer, *Officer and Laughing Girl*. ca. 1657. Oil on canvas (lined), 19⅞ × 18⅛" (50.5 × 46 cm). The Frick Collection, New York, Henry Clay Frick Bequest. 1911.1.127

20.35 Jan Vermeer,
Woman Holding a Balance.
ca. 1664. Oil on canvas,
16¾ × 15" (42.5 × 38.1 cm).
National Gallery of Art,
Washington, D.C. Widener
Collection. (1942.9.97)

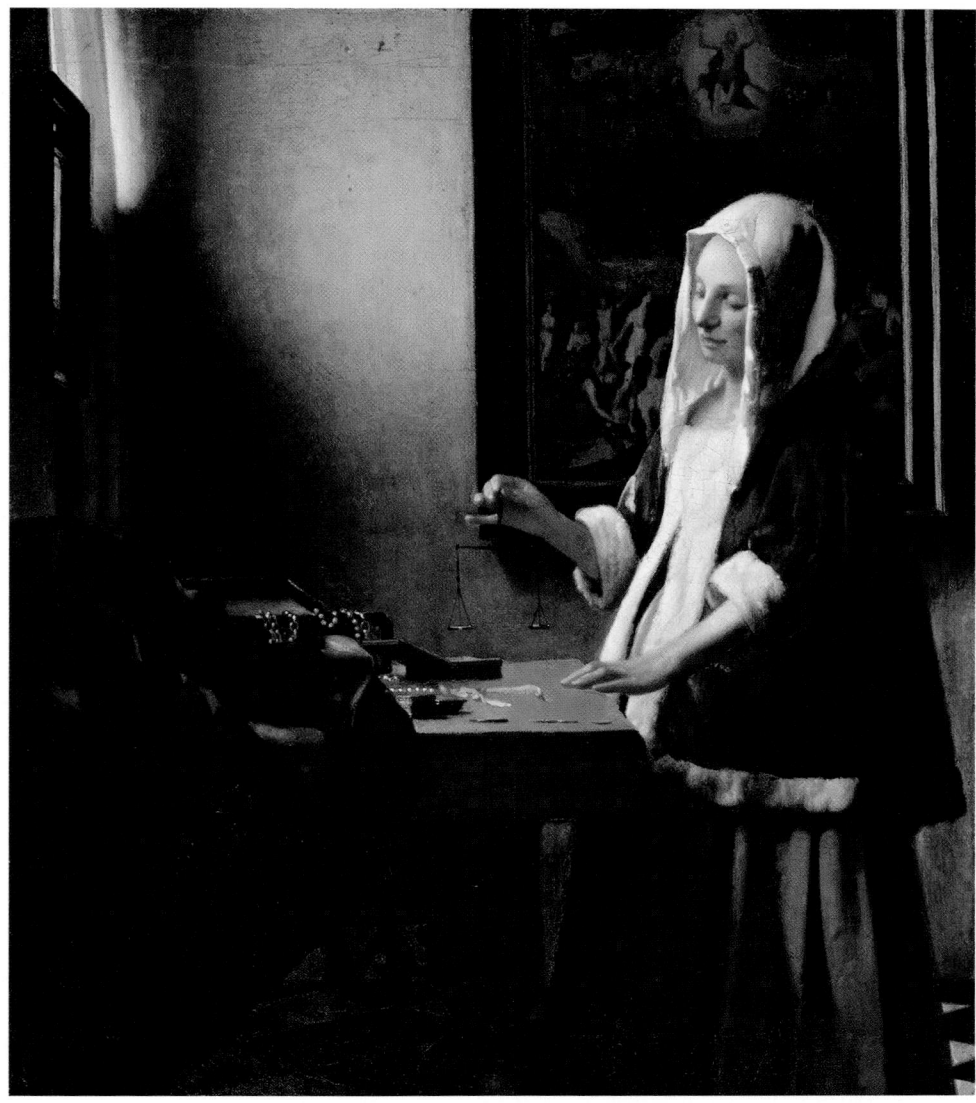

its subtle and varying tones of gray, yellow, and blue on a seemingly white surface. These are the same colors used for the map. Vermeer created an unparalleled quality of light and texture.

Vermeer is best known for his single figures, usually women, seemingly engaged in everyday tasks at private moments. They exist in a timeless "still-life" world, as if becalmed by a spell. In *Woman Holding a Balance* (fig. **20.35**), a young woman, richly dressed in the at-home wear of the day, is contemplating the balance in her hand, with strings of pearls and gold coins spread out on the table before her. The painting gives a view into such a still-life world—with a table laden with pearls and gold, paintings and fur, all magically providing an eternal, yet momentary, glance into a private world where, in fact, our view is not acknowledged. The painting in the background depicts Christ at the Last Judgment, when every soul is weighed. This may refer to the soul of the pregnant woman's unborn child, and it parallels her own activity, now contemplating the future of her unborn child. The pans of the balance were once thought to contain gold or pearls but scientific analysis of the painting indicates that they actually contain nothing, only beads of light. The painting is intensely private,

quiet, yet also highly sensual, created with optical effects that make the surface shimmer. It is the light on the pan and the pearls that we see as "discs of confusion." The vanishing point in this painting, where a hole has punctured the canvas, is just to the left of the pinky finger that holds the balance. Our eye is drawn to this spot and is fascinated by this tentative gesture. It sets the balance of all elements of the painting.

Vermeer's mastery of light's expressive qualities raises his interest in the reality of appearances to the level of poetry. He is concerned with all of light's visual and symbolic possibilities. *Woman Holding a Balance* is also testimony to the artist's faith: He was a Catholic (as was Jan Steen) living in Protestant Holland, where his religion was officially banned, although worship in private houses was tolerated.

But all of these facts somehow do not get to the magical, hypnotic, truly original nature of his paintings. We do not know Vermeer's teachers or how he developed his unique style. No painter since Jan van Eyck *saw* as intensely as Vermeer. No other painter recorded his seeing in such an exact yet somehow personal way.

Exquisite Genre Painting: Gerard ter Borch

Perhaps the most elegant—even exquisite—Dutch genre paintings were executed by Gerard ter Borch (1617–1681), who worked in the small city of Zwolle, but traveled widely both within Holland (he worked in Amsterdam and briefly in Haarlem) and Europe. He came from a family of artists but little is known of his patrons or commissions. He painted both portraits and genre scenes; both types were often small (about the size of a notebook), but the figures were full-length and attired in the height of fashion. Such is the case in the *Lady at Her Toilet* (fig. 20.36). She is, as are most of his women, dressed in satin, and Ter Borch was noted as an expert in recording this luxurious fabric. He did this by creating highly contrasting areas of light and dark, and by allowing the long satin skirts to reach the floor and buckle, creating even more shadows. The same dress is worn by another woman in a different painting by him,

and these repeated patterns suggest that Ter Borch made drawings that he could use over again. The figures stand in a seemingly contemporary, but possibly imaginary, late seventeenth-century room, with a marble, four-column fireplace, and with a canopied bed in the background. There is a Turkish-carpeted table and a page, magnificently dressed. (Pages or messengers similarly dressed also appear in paintings by other contemporary artists.) The simplicity of the room accentuates the high fashion of the woman. Her maid adjusts her dress. The mirror set in a contemporary gilt frame reflects the profile of the woman; in reality, she could not be seen from that angle. The theme of "at her toilet" can be seen in the work of Titian and Vouet (see figs. 17.35 and 21.3), and even in Rembrandt's *Bathsheba with King David's Letter* (see fig. 20.25), and the breathtaking beauty of Ter Borch's lady is reflected in all the trappings around her. The painting looks forward to the magnificence and opulence of the eighteenth century.

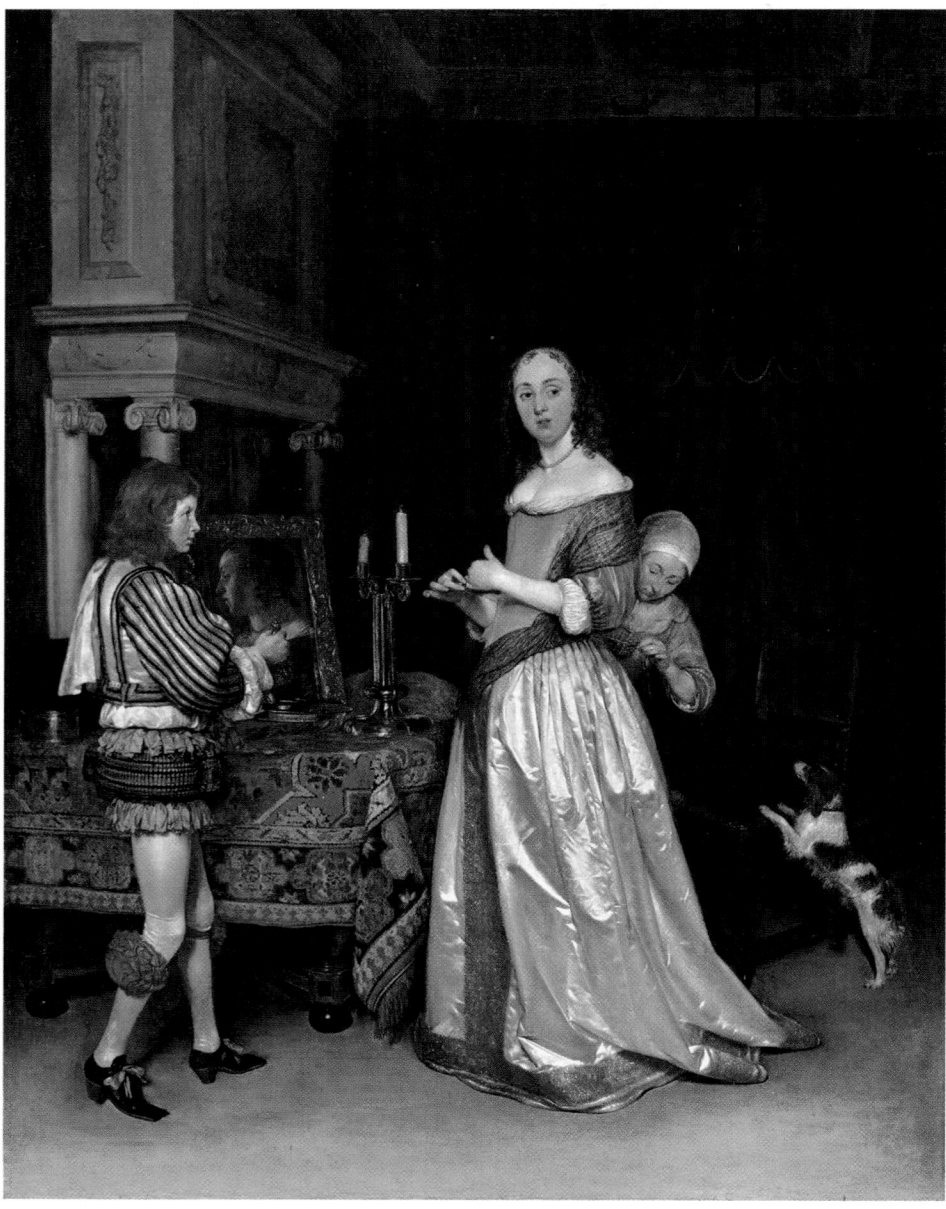

20.36 Gerard ter Borch, *Lady at Her Toilet*. ca. 1660. Oil on canvas, 30 × 23½" (76.2 × 59.7 cm). The Detroit Institute of Art, Detroit, MI. Founders Society Purchase, Eleanor Clay Ford Fund, General Membership Fund, Endowment Income Fund, and Special Activities Fund. 65.10

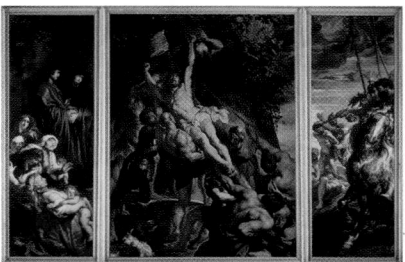
1610-11 Rubens's *The Raising of the Cross*

The Baroque in the Netherlands

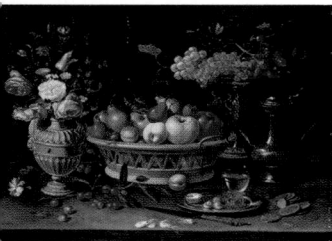
a. 1612 Clara Peeters's *Still Life with Fruit and Flowers*

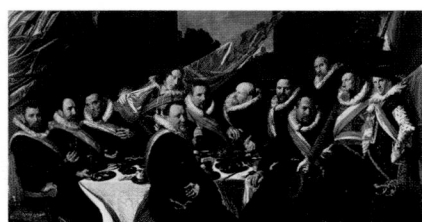
1616 Hals's *Banquet of the Officers of the St. George Civic Guard*

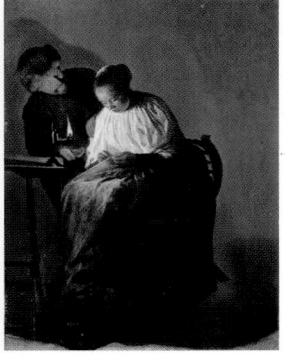
1631 Leyster's *The Proposition*

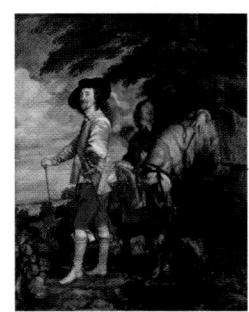
ca. 1635 Van Dyck's *Portrait of Charles I Hunting*

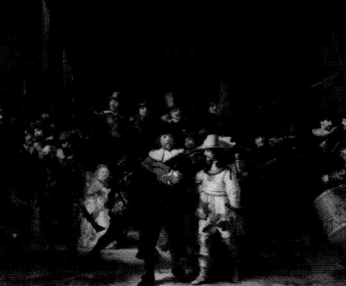
642 Rembrandt's *The Night Watch*

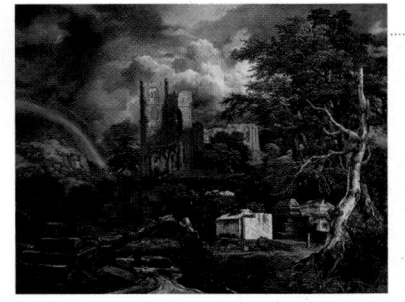
1655-70 Ruisdael's *The Jewish Cemetery*

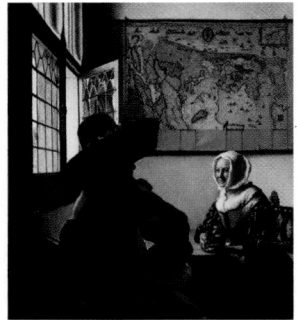
ca. 1657 Vermeer's *Officer and a Laughing Girl*

1590

1600

1610

1620

1630

1640

1650

1660

1670

1680

1597 Carracci's *Loves of the Gods*

◄ 1598 Albert and Isabella jointly rule the Spanish Netherlands

1599-1600 Caravaggio's *The Calling of St. Matthew*

◄ 1602 Dutch East India Company founded

ca. 1600 Sánchez Cotán's *Still Life with Quince, Cabbage, Melon, and Cucumber*

◄ 1626 New Amsterdam (New York City) founded by the Dutch West India Company

ca. 1638 Gentileschi's *Self-Portrait as the Allegory of Painting*

◄ 1639 Japan enforces policy of isolation from Europeans; permits a Dutch trading post

1645 Bernini's *The Ecstasy of St. Teresa*

◄ 1648 Treaty of Münster legally recognizes the Dutch Republic

1650 Velázquez's *The Maids of Honor*

◄ 1676 Anthonie van Leeuwenhoek first to record bacteria under a microscope

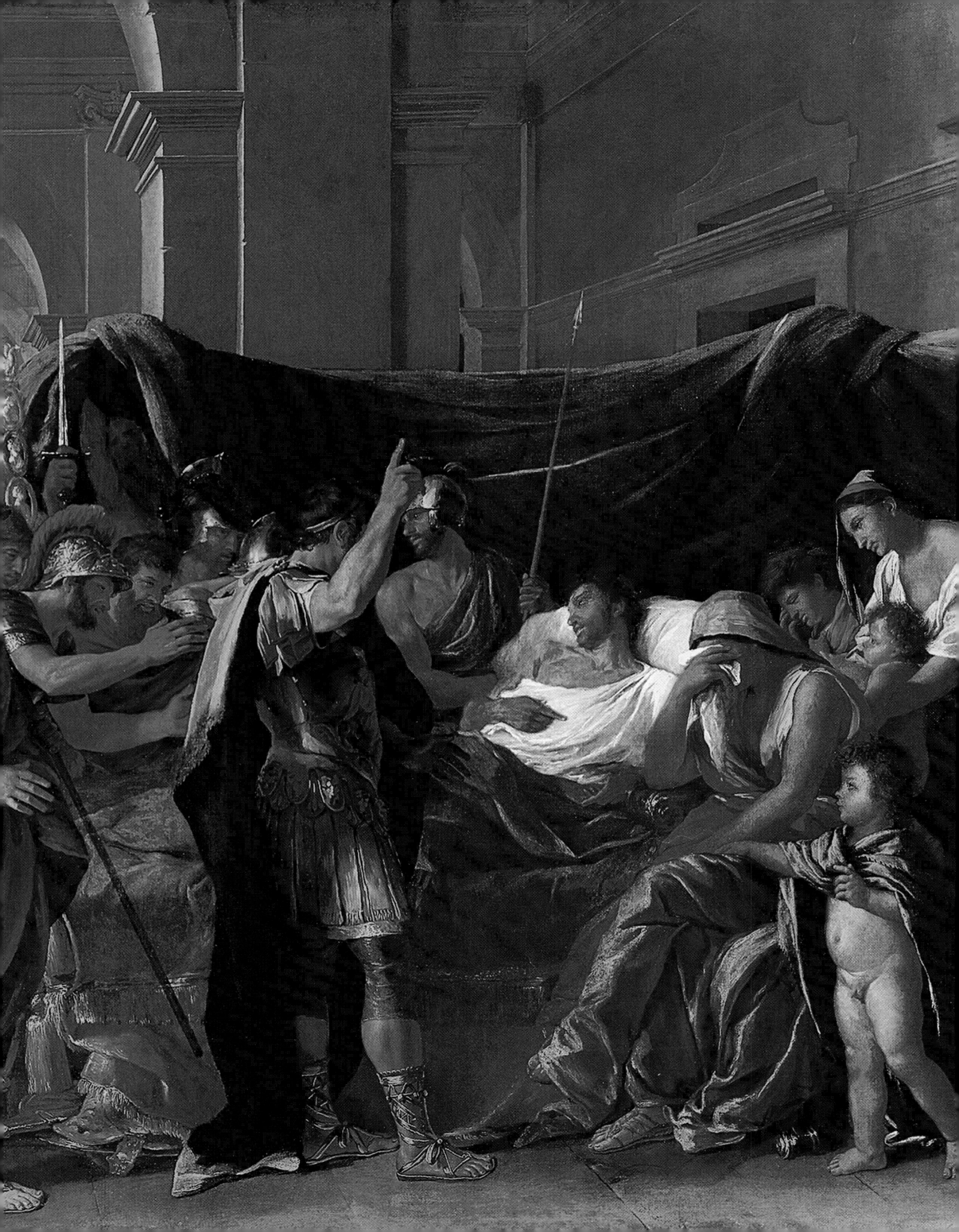

CHAPTER 21

The Baroque in France and England

DURING THE COURSE OF THE TUMULTUOUS SEVENTEENTH CENTURY, the great monarchies of France and England served as the greatest patrons of the arts. Expanding civic projects, notably in architecture, symbolized the wealth of each nation. England, led by an absolute ruler, and France, governed by a king who shared power with the Parliament, underwent

dramatic change. Devastated by the previous era's religious wars and dynastic struggles, both nations saw their treasuries sorely drained, their populations severely reduced, and their societies bitterly divided. The theological controversies that had characterized the earlier Reformation and Counter-Reformation continued in this period, with Catholicism becoming the dominant religion in France (ever since the public conversion of Henry IV in 1593 when he is reputed to have declared, "Paris is well worth a Mass") and Protestantism in England (since the establishment of the Church of England under Henry VIII). Each successive French and English monarch sought to strike a delicate balance between these competing religious forces while attempting to favor the religion of his choice. The same was true throughout Europe, where isolated skirmishes eventually coalesced into a conflict that encompassed nearly all nations—the Thirty Years' War (1618–48).

England faced still more upheavals (**map 21.1**) and its situation degenerated in 1642 into a civil war that led to the trial of King Charles I, who was convicted of treason and beheaded in 1649. With the abolishment of the monarchy, the puritan Oliver Cromwell was named head of state and Lord Protector. Although he restored political stability, upon his death in 1658 his government foundered. Two years later, in 1660, Parliament offered the throne to the son of the beheaded king, Charles II (r. 1660–1685),

thus ushering in the period known as the Restoration. Unfortunately, old religious rivalries and economic crises persisted, and the reign of Charles II's successor, James II (r. 1685–1688), was soon in jeopardy. In the so-called Glorious Revolution of 1688, a relatively peaceful and bloodless event, members of the governing classes of Whigs and Tories proclaimed the prince of Orange, ruler of the Dutch Republic, as king of England; he reigned as William III from 1689 to 1702. The Bill of Rights (1689) established Parliament's supremacy, thus creating a unique form of government that would gradually influence nations worldwide, notably the British colonies in North America.

Waging war was an expensive undertaking and sovereigns throughout Europe realized the pressing need to consolidate the state's power and exert economic control. In France, which by midcentury had emerged as Europe's most powerful nation both militarily and culturally, this centralization was most successfully implemented by Louis XIV (r. 1643–1715). Louis evoked the age-old Divine Right of Kings—the idea that the monarch received his authority directly from God. He used this to increase the state's power over the nobility and over local authorities, amassing revenue through taxation. He relied on a form of royal government known as absolutism, which gave full power to the monarch. The absolute monarchy in France differed from England's post-Restoration constitutional monarchy, which divided power between the ruler and other institutions. In his quest to assert the preeminence of France, Louis XIV embarked

Detail of figure 21.4, Nicolas Poussin, *The Death of Germanicus*

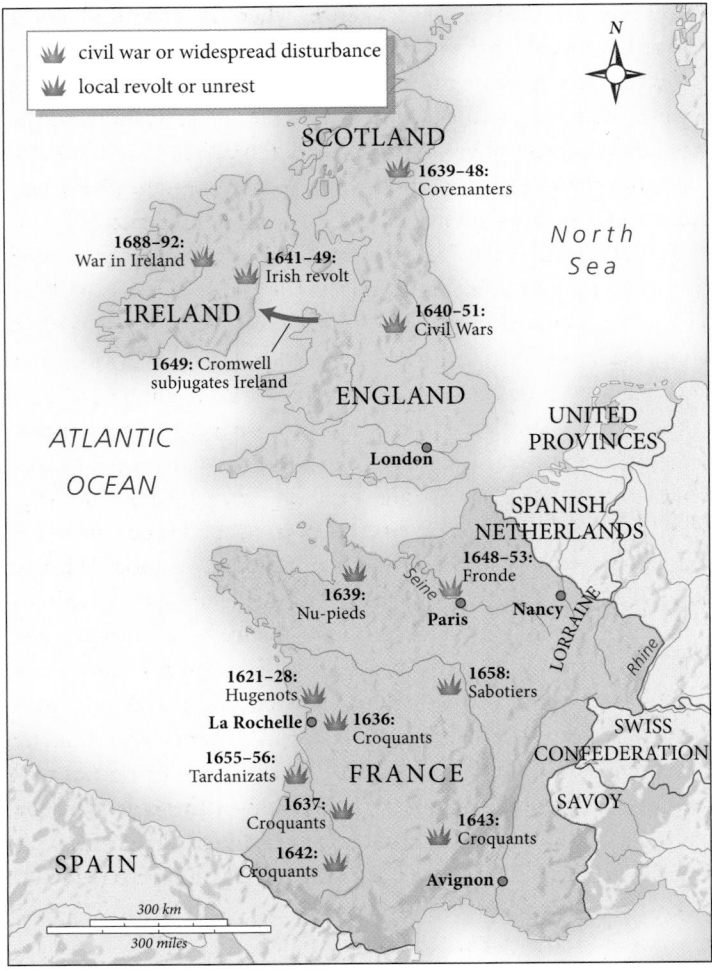

Map 21.1 Political resistance and unrest in France and England in the seventeenth century

Map labels:
- civil war or widespread disturbance
- local revolt or unrest
- N
- SCOTLAND
- 1639–48: Covenanters
- North Sea
- 1688–92: War in Ireland
- 1641–49: Irish revolt
- IRELAND
- 1640–51: Civil Wars
- 1649: Cromwell subjugates Ireland
- ENGLAND
- ATLANTIC OCEAN
- UNITED PROVINCES
- London
- SPANISH NETHERLANDS
- 1648–53: Fronde
- Seine
- 1639: Nu-pieds
- Paris
- Nancy
- LORRAINE
- Rhine
- 1621–28: Hugenots
- 1658: Sabotiers
- La Rochelle
- 1636: Croquants
- SWISS CONFEDERATION
- 1655–56: Tardanizats
- FRANCE
- SAVOY
- 1637: Croquants
- 1643: Croquants
- SPAIN
- 1642: Croquants
- Avignon
- 300 km
- 300 miles

imperial grandeur of Rome. Although the Mannerist style of the later School of Fontainebleau persisted in France until about 1625 (see page 629), classicism soon became the hallmark of seventeenth-century French art. It was the official court style of painting between 1660 and 1685, the climactic phase of Louis XIV's reign. Classical principles also dominated architecture, with the new Louvre and Versailles palaces representing the most visible accomplishments in France.

In England, too, classicism dominated art and architecture, notably the hospitals, churches, and country houses designed by Inigo Jones and Sir Christopher Wren. In the wake of the Great Fire of London in 1666, architecture thrived as massive reconstruction projects were undertaken to rebuild the city. Yet England's most lasting artistic successes in the seventeenth century were in literature, including the works of William Shakespeare, John Donne, and John Milton as well as the royal committee's translation of what would become known as the King James Bible.

FRANCE: THE STYLE OF LOUIS XIV

By the late seventeenth century Paris was vying with Rome to become Europe's art center. The French kings Henry IV (r. 1589–1610), Louis XIII (r. 1610–1643), and Louis XIV (r. 1643–1715)—aided by ambitious and able ministers and advisors such as the duc de Sully, cardinals Richelieu and Mazarin, and Jean-Baptiste Colbert—created the climate for this exciting turn of events. The rulers and their officials recognized the power of art to convey the majesty and strength of the monarchy, and they set out on a massive program of patronage of all the arts and sciences—painting, sculpture, architecture, landscape design, decorative arts, theoretical and applied science, philosophy, and literature. Louis XIV especially manipulated art to serve as propaganda for his absolutist policies. He adopted the symbolic imagery of the sun as well as the Greek god of the sun, Apollo, and came to be called the Sun King. This symbolism provided an ancient lineage for Louis and his status as absolute ruler. The ideal of *gloire* (glory), seen in the portraits and architecture he commissioned, reflected his desire to give concrete form to the majesty of his rule, and of France too.

Because the Palace of Versailles (see figs. 21.12–21.15) and other vast building projects glorified the French king, we are tempted to think of French art in the age of Louis XIV as merely an expression of absolute rule. This perception perhaps holds true for the period 1660–85, but by that time seventeenth-century French painting and sculpture had already attained their distinctive Classical character. French historians are reluctant to call this style Baroque but refer to it instead as the "Style of Louis XIV" (art created during his reign). They also use this term to describe art created prior to Louis XIV, particularly that produced at the court of his father, Louis XIII. In addition, scholars often describe the period's art and literature as "classic." In this context, the word has three meanings. It is a synonym for "highest

on a series of military campaigns from 1688 to 1713 against his rivals, Spain, the Dutch Republic, Germany, and England. Despite eventual defeat, France remained a world power upon Louis's death in 1715.

The wars and social turmoil took perhaps their harshest toll on peasants and commoners, who reeled from continually increasing taxes as well as from devastating natural disasters and the ensuing food shortages, famine, and rising prices. Yet despite the abject poverty endured by some members of society, others enjoyed new wealth and prosperity. Both England and France reaped enormous profits from investments in their colonial empires, and established trade routes that delivered a wider range of goods and enhanced the lifestyles of many Europeans. The development of mercantilism and a worldwide marketplace brought about the rise of a class of increasingly wealthy urban merchants seeking art to furnish and decorate their homes.

Classicism is the style now associated with the art of these two nations. Through its use of a Classical vocabulary—from columns, capitals, and pediments in architecture to styles of dress in painting—it draws on the example of the ancient world to suggest authority, order, and enduring tradition by evoking the achievement," which suggests that the Style of Louis XIV is the equivalent of the High Renaissance in Italy or the age of Perikles in ancient Greece. It also refers to the imitation of the forms and subject matter of Classical antiquity. Finally, it suggests qualities of balance and restraint shared by ancient art and the Renaissance. The last two meanings describe what could more accurately be called Classicism. Because the Style of Louis XIV reflects Italian Baroque art, although in modified form, we may call it Baroque Classicism.

Painting and Printmaking in France

The many foreign artists working in France drew inspiration from that country's styles and traditions, whereas French artists often traveled to Italy and the Netherlands to work. In the hopes of creating a nucleus of artists who would shape the Baroque style in France, Louis XIII began to recall these artists to Paris. That is, French artists who were abroad were then required to come home. Among the summoned artists were painters Nicolas Poussin and Simon Vouet, who had been working in Rome, and the printmaker Jacques Callot, who returned from Florence to his home in northern France. The influences of foreign artists were significant.

JACQUES CALLOT: A TRANSITIONAL FIGURE One of the most important early seventeenth-century artists was Jacques Callot (1592/93–1635), an etcher and engraver whose small-scale prints recording actual events inspired his compatriot Georges de La Tour (discussed below) and the young Rembrandt (see page 718). Callot's exploitation of the medium's ability to produce stark tonal contrasts and intricate details reflects the tradition, dating from the fifteenth century, of using mass-produced prints to disseminate information. Yet his poignant representations of contemporary figures and events places him firmly in the art of his own time. Callot spent much of his early career at the court of Cosimo II de' Medici in Florence, where he produced prints inspired primarily by the theater and especially the *commedia dell'arte*. After returning to his native town of Nancy in 1621, he began to concentrate almost exclusively on the technique of etching and the subject of his work changed. He visited Breda in 1626, soon after the surrender of Dutch troops there (see fig. 19.36), and executed six plates showing a large panorama of the site.

Callot's insight into the personal and political geography of battle can best be seen in the series *The Great Miseries of War*, which represents a distillation of his experience of the Thirty Years' War. (Scholars once thought Callot executed the series in 1633 but now consider it to be from 1629–32.) In the 18 etchings in the series, Callot reveals the misery, destruction, and poverty brought by the invading army. Several prints are devoted to soldiers' crimes, whereas others, including *Hangman's Tree* (fig. 21.1), focus on the punishments dealt out to the French army for their own excesses. The inscription at the bottom reads: "Finally these thieves, sordid and forlorn, hanging like unfortunate pieces of fruit from this tree, experience the justice of Heaven sooner or later." Despite the work's small size (it measures only a few inches), nearly 50 figures inhabit the scene. The awkward perspective emphasizes the tiny, elongated, Mannerist-style figures; in the figures on the right, however, Callot shows a naturalism in costume and attitude that is characteristic of the new Baroque style. The bleak scene is as disturbing as Hieronymus Bosch's vision of Hell in *The Garden of Earthly Delights* (see fig. 14.22); indeed, it may be even more so, for it is based on the artist's own experience of the horrors of war.

GEORGES DE LA TOUR AND THE INFLUENCE OF CARAVAGGIO Many French painters in the early seventeenth century were influenced by Caravaggio, although how they came to be exposed to the Italian artist's style remains unclear. Besides being named a painter to King Louis XIII, Georges de La Tour (1593–1652) received important commissions from the governor

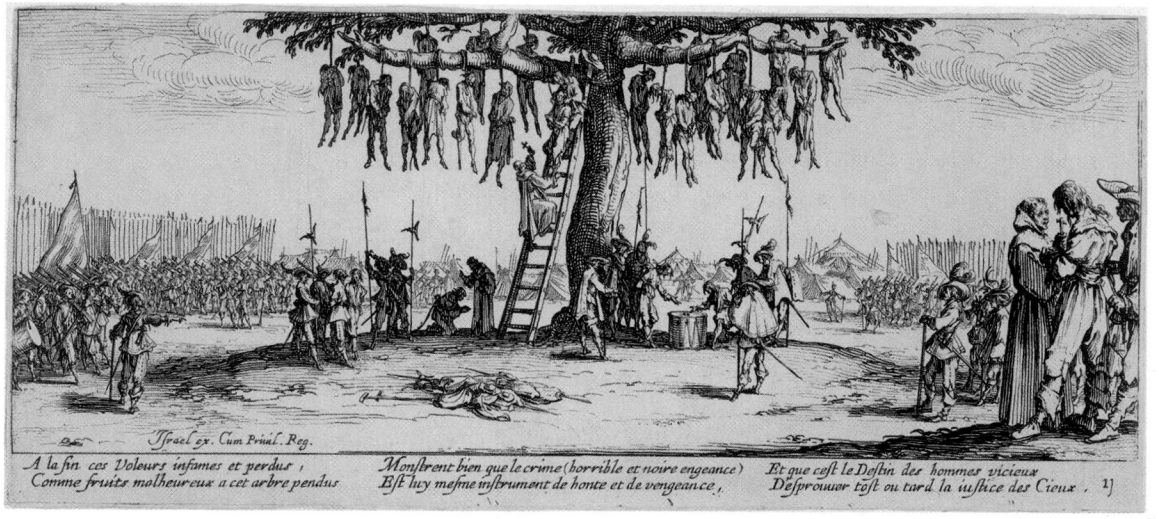

21.1 Jacques Callot, *Hangman's Tree*, from *The Great Miseries of War*. ca. 1629–32. Etching, 3½ × 9" (9 × 23 cm). The British Museum, London

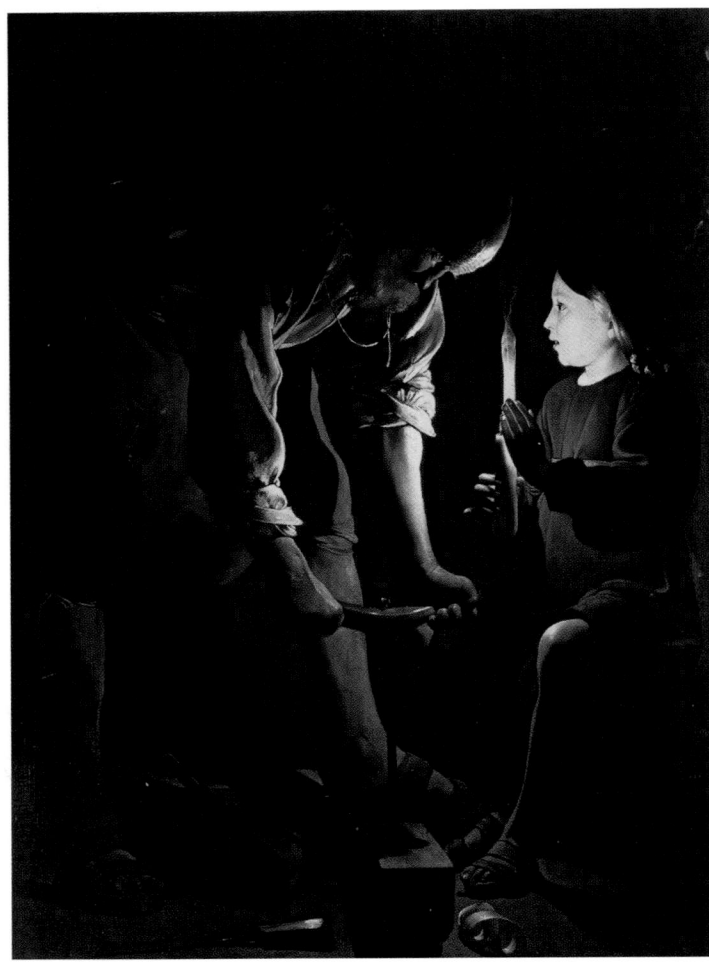

21.2 Georges de La Tour, *Joseph the Carpenter*. ca. 1642.
Oil on canvas, 51⅛ × 39¾" (130 × 100 cm). Musée du Louvre, Paris

in Rome, although he painted in many styles throughout his career. At an early age he accompanied his artist father to England and Constantinople, but his most significant foreign journey took him to Rome, where he lived from 1613 to 1627. There, he became an adherent of Caravaggio's style but was also later influenced by the Bolognese artist Annibale Carracci. Vouet was so well respected that he was elected president of the Academy of St. Luke in Rome. Officially recalled to France in 1627 by Louis XIII, he settled in Paris and became the leading painter of his day. Vouet quickly shed all traces of Caravaggio's manner and developed a colorful style, which won such acclaim that he was named first painter to the king. It is from Vouet's studio that the official style in France emanated in the 1630s and 1640s. His paintings, influenced by Venetian artists, were known for their rich colors and use of light and thus provided the interiors of royal residences and a growing number of French aristocratic houses with a new vibrant decorative style.

The Toilet of Venus (fig. **21.3**), possibly painted for one of the king's mistresses, is one of several on this theme that Vouet

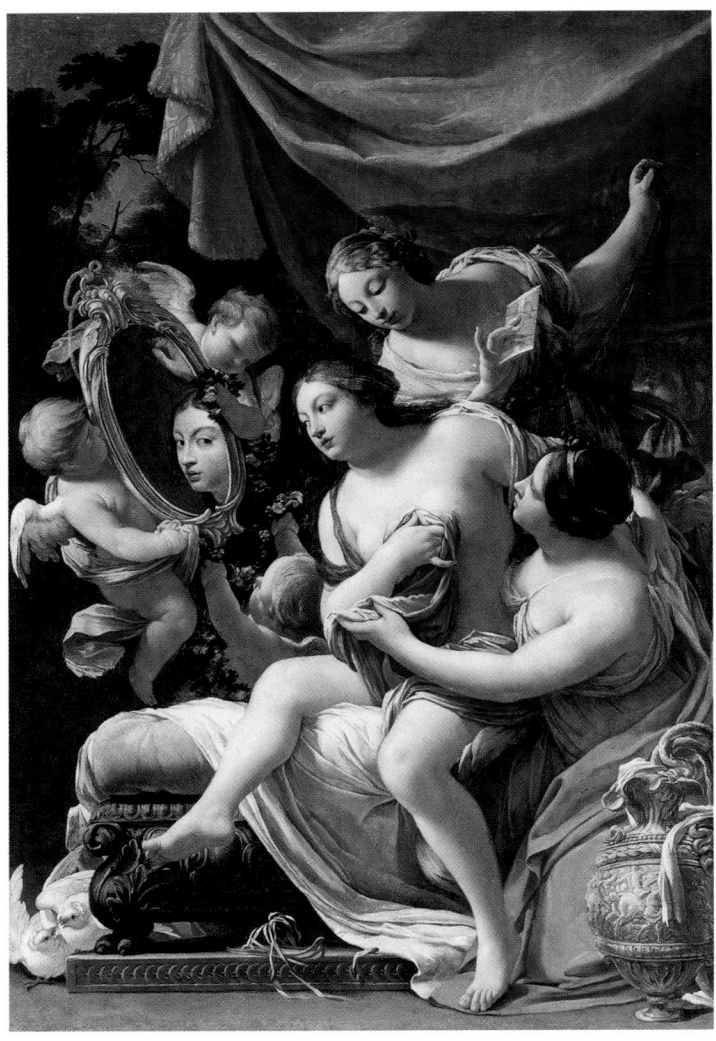

21.3 Simon Vouet, *The Toilet of Venus*. ca. 1640. Oil on canvas, 65¼ × 45" (165.7 × 114.3 cm). The Carnegie Museum of Art, Pittsburgh. Gift of Mrs. Horace Binney Hare (52.7)

of Lorraine, his hometown in northeast France. His use of light and his reliance on detailed naturalism derived largely from Caravaggio's northern European followers (see page 664), whom he may have visited in the Dutch Republic.

La Tour's mature religious pictures effectively convey the complex mysteries of the Christian faith. With its carefully observed details and seemingly humble subject, *Joseph the Carpenter* (fig. **21.2**) might initially be mistaken for a genre scene, but its devotional spirit soon overwhelms us. The two figures are set in profile, thus yielding little by their expressions. La Tour lends maximum significance to each gesture, each look. The boy Jesus holds a candle, a favorite device of the artist, whose flame reinforces the devotional mood and imbues the scene with intimacy and tenderness. The painting has the power of Caravaggio's *The Calling of St. Matthew* (see fig. 19.2), but the simplified forms, warm palette, and arrested movement are characteristic of La Tour's restrained and focused vision.

SIMON VOUET AND THE DECORATIVE STYLE Although Simon Vouet (1590–1649) may be little known today, he was the most important French painter in the first third of the seventeenth century. He was the leader of the French Caravaggesque painters executed. It depicts a subject popular in Venice, notably treated by Titian and Veronese, and also by Rubens (compare also the introspective toilet scene of Bathsheba by Rembrandt, see fig. 20.25). Vouet's central figure recalls Correggio's *Jupiter and Io* (see fig. 17.26) but lacks that work's frank eroticism. Instead, Vouet has imbued his Venus with an elegant sensuousness that is uniquely French. The continuous swirling circles, near-nudity, interest in fabric, and luminous colors only suggest the erotic, whose appeal would continue well into the eighteenth century and provide the basis for the Rococo style in painting. Vouet taught the next generation of artists, including those who worked on Louis XIV's palace at Versailles, the landscape designer and royal gardener André Le Nôtre, and Charles Le Brun, the royal painter who would later establish the French Royal Academy (from which he would exclude his teacher).

NICOLAS POUSSIN AND BAROQUE CLASSICISM Despite Vouet's earlier influence on painting, after the 1640s Classicism reigned supreme in France. The artist who contributed most to its rise was Nicolas Poussin (1594–1665), one of the most influential French painters of the century. Aside from an ill-fated two-year sojourn in Paris (he was "recalled" there by Louis XIII), Poussin spent his entire career in Rome. There, he hosted and taught visiting French artists, absorbing the lessons of Raphael's and Carracci's classically ordered paintings and developing his own style of rational classicism. Patrons brought Poussin's paintings back to Paris, where they influenced the royal court. Indeed, when establishing the curriculum of the French Royal Academy in the 1660s, Jean-Baptiste Colbert, the king's chief advisor, and Charles Le Brun chose Poussin's classical style to serve as a model for French artists.

POUSSIN AND HISTORY PAINTING: ANCIENT THEMES IN THE GRAND MANNER Arriving in Rome via Venice in early 1624, Poussin studied perspective and anatomy and examined ancient sculpture, such as the *Laocoön* (see page 183), the *Belvedere Torso*, and the *Apollo Belvedere*, the reliefs on ancient sarcophagi and vases, and the paintings of Raphael. His *The Death of Germanicus* (fig. **21.4** and page 736) reflects these studies. The work served as a model for artistic depictions of heroic deathbed scenes for the next two centuries and may in fact be the first example of this subject in the history of art. In some respects a typical history painting, the work relates the powerful themes of death, loyalty, and revenge. The story comes from Tacitus and is set in the year 19 CE. Germanicus was a Roman general who had led campaigns against the Germanic tribes. At the urging of Tiberius, Germanicus' adoptive father, the ruler in Syria, poisoned the powerful general. Poussin depicts Germanicus on his deathbed; on the left his loyal soldiers are swearing revenge and on the right his mournful family weeps. The promise to avenge is set at the center, commanding attention, as figures gesture their grief, loyalty, and suffering. Framed by the two groups, Germanicus becomes the focus of the composition, which is based on antique scenes of the death of Meleager (see fig. 7.69).

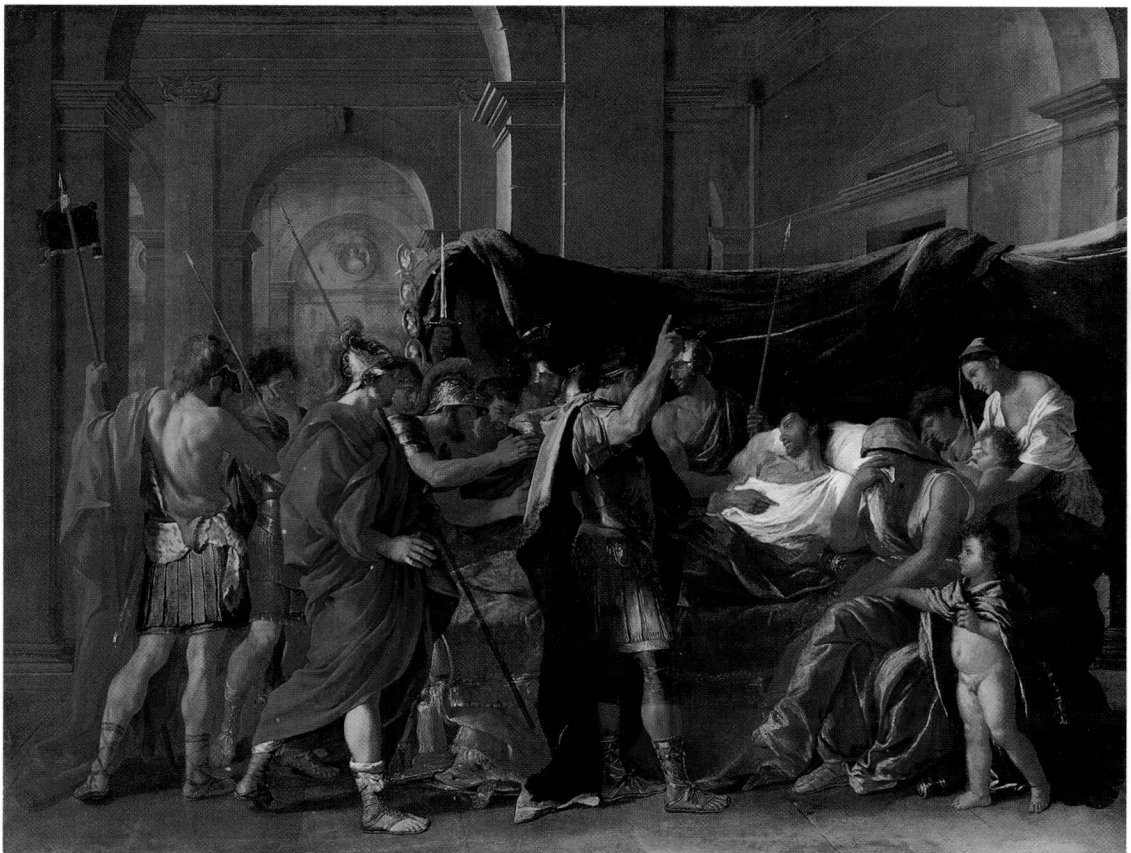

21.4 Nicolas Poussin, *The Death of Germanicus*. 1627–28. Oil on canvas, 4'10¼" × 6'6" (1.48 × 1.98 m). Minneapolis Institute of Art, Minneapolis, Minnesota. The William Hood Dunwoody Fund. 58.28

Nicolas Poussin (1594–1665)

From an undated manuscript

Poussin's ideas on art were central to the formation of the French Academy in 1648 and, because of the preeminence of that body, to the entire European academic movement of the seventeenth through the nineteenth centuries.

The magnificent manner consists of four things: subject, or topic, concept, structure and style. The first requirement, which is the basis for all the others, is that the subject or topic should be great, such as battles, heroic actions and divine matters. However, given the subject upon which the painter is engaged is great, he must first of all make every effort to avoid getting lost in minute detail, so as not to detract from the dignity of the story. He should describe the magnificent and great details with a bold brush and disregard anything that is vulgar and of little substance. Thus the painter should not only be skilled in formulating his subject matter, but wise enough to know it well and to choose something that lends itself naturally to embellishment and perfection. Those who choose vile topics take refuge in them on account of their own lack of ingenuity. Faintheartedness is therefore to be despised, as is baseness of subject matter for which any amount of artifice is useless. As for the concept, it is simply part of the spirit, which concentrates on things, like the concept realized by Homer and Phidias of Olympian Zeus who could make the Universe tremble with a nod of his head. The drawing of things should be such that it expresses the concept of the things themselves. The structure, or composition of the parts, should not be studiously researched, and not sought after or contrived with effort but should be as natural as possible. Style is a particular method of painting and drawing, carried out in an individual way, born of the singular talent at work in its application and in the use of ideas. This style, and the manner and taste emanate from nature and from the mind.

Source: Alain Merot, *Nicolas Poussin*, tr. Fabia Claris (London: Thames & Hudson, 1990)

The architecture sets the stage for the figures, which are arranged horizontally in a rectangular space, as in a Classical frieze. The curtain in the rear restricts the action to a shallow space, heightening the drama and creating a more intimate environment.

This early work by Poussin, painted just a few years after he arrived in Rome, was probably created for Cardinal Francesco Barberini's secretary, Cassiano dal Pozzo (1588–1657), a major patron of the arts. Its composition, setting, and heroic historical subject (see *Primary Source*, above), are typical of Poussin's classicism and his concept of the Grand Manner.

THE ABDUCTION OF THE SABINE WOMEN Demonstrating Poussin's allegiance to classicism, *The Abduction of the Sabine Women* (fig. **21.5**) displays the severe discipline of his intellectual

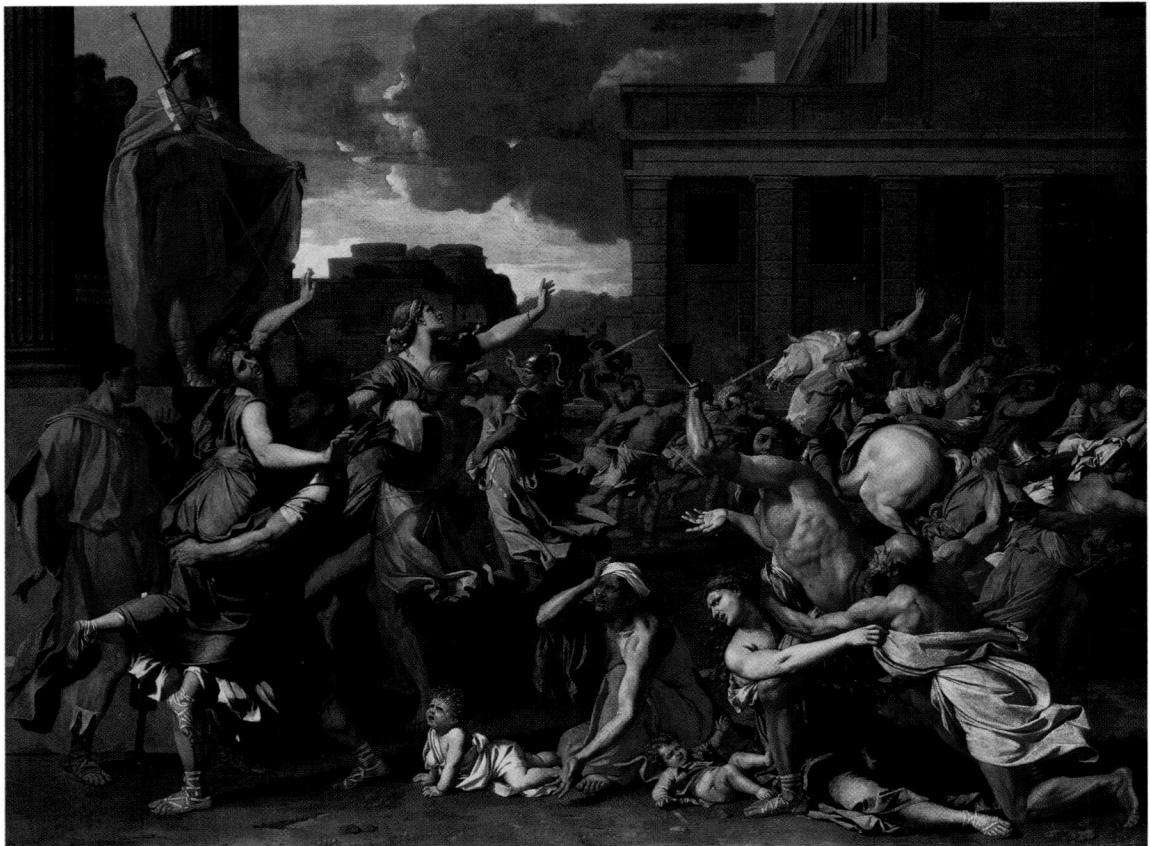

21.5 Nicolas Poussin, *The Abduction of the Sabine Women*. ca. 1633–34. Oil on canvas, 5'7⅞" × 6'10⅝" (1.54 × 2.09 m). Metropolitan Museum of Art, New York. Harris Brisbane Dick Fund, 1946 (46.160)

style, which developed in response to what he regarded as the excesses of the High Baroque. The strongly modeled figures are "frozen in action," like statues. Many are, in fact, derived from Hellenistic sculpture, but the main group is directly inspired by Giovanni Bologna's *The Rape of the Sabine Woman* (see fig. 17.13). Poussin has placed them before reconstructions of Roman architecture that he believed to be archaeologically correct.

Poussin thought the highest aim of painting was to represent noble and serious human actions. Emotion is abundantly displayed in the dramatic poses and expressions of the figures here, but there is a lack of spontaneity that perhaps causes it to fail to touch us. In part, this is due to their derivation from sculpture. The scene has a theatrical air, and for good reason. Before beginning the painting, Poussin, besides making preliminary drawings, arranged wax figurines on a miniature stage until he was satisfied with the composition.

Poussin believed that the viewer must be able to "read" the emotions of each figure as they related to the story. Such beliefs later proved influential to his student Charles Le Brun when establishing an approved court style for French painting. These ideas were not really new. We recall Horace's motto *Ut pictura poesis* ("As is painting, so is poetry"), and Leonardo's statement that the highest aim of painting is to depict "the intention of man's soul" (see page 564). Before Poussin, however, no artist had made the analogy between painting and literature so closely or put it into practice so singlemindedly.

The historical event portrayed in *The Abduction of the Sabine Women* was admired as an act of patriotism ensuring the future of Rome. According to the accounts of Livy and Plutarch, the Sabines were young women abducted by the Romans to become their wives; the women later acted as peacemakers between the two opposing sides. Clearly, in the painting the women do not go willingly as swords are drawn, babies are abandoned, and the elderly suffer. But Poussin's apparent detachment and lack of sympathy for those suffering has caused the work to be labeled "heroic." His work appeals to the mind, that is, to the larger view of history, rather than to the senses. Poussin suppresses color and instead stresses form and composition.

This method accounts for the visual rhetoric in *The Abduction of the Sabine Women* that makes the picture seem so remote. This preliminary drawing (fig. **21.6**) (made in fact for a different version of the painting) suggests how deliberate the artist's process was. Using pen and ink and wash, Poussin worked out many of his compositions beforehand, as did Rubens. We have already mentioned his employment of wax figurines. In this drawn example, he placed figures in the foreground and ancient architecture as a stage set in the background. Such studies con-trast sharply with the methods of Caravaggio and the Caravaggisti, who supported painting "from nature," that is, from living models and without the aid of preparatory drawings. Poussin, on the other hand, regarded history painting as more intellectual and as derived from the imagination; he reportedly told a contemporary that "Caravaggio had come into the world to destroy painting."

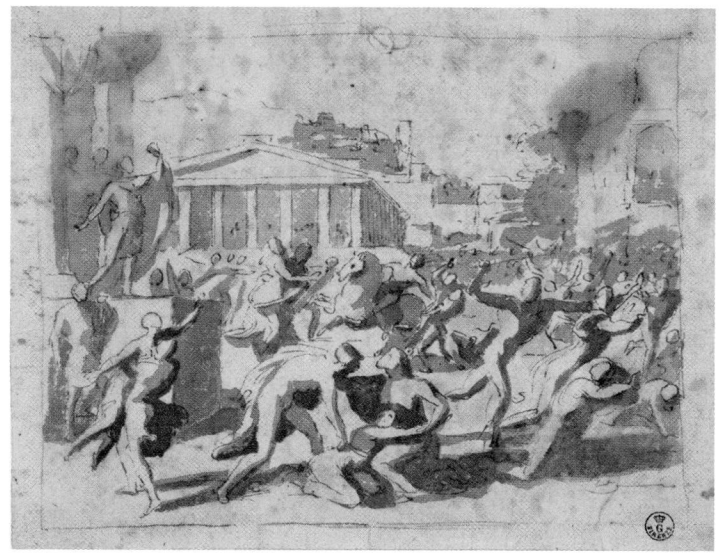

21.6 Nicolas Poussin,. *The Abduction of the Sabine Women*. ca. 1630. Brush drawing, 6¼ × 8⅛" (16.1 × 20.7 cm). Archivio del Gabinetto Disegni e Stampe, Galleria degli Uffizi, Florence

POUSSIN AND THE IDEAL LANDSCAPE The "ideal" landscape, serene and balanced, does not represent a particular locale but rather a generalized and often beautiful place. Poussin's ideal landscape is the opposite of those of his Dutch contemporaries (Van Goyen and Ruisdael, see figs. 20.27–20.29) and their topographical views. Indeed, because figures play only a minor role in landscapes, it is surprising that Poussin chose to explore this subject at all. The austere beauty and somber calm of Poussin's work can be seen in his *Landscape with St. John on Patmos* (fig. **21.7**), which continues the Classical landscape tradition of Annibale Carracci; with this work, Poussin is considered to have invented the ideal landscape. The brilliantly lit, ancient landscape strewn with architectural ruins suggests both the actual site and the concept of antiquity upon which early Christianity was founded. Trees on either side balance the composition, and many of the ruins are set parallel to the picture plane. A reclining St. John, who at the end of his life lived on the island of Patmos, reportedly in somewhat abject circumstances, is shown in profile facing left. Poussin's pendant (paired) painting, *Landscape with St. Matthew*, shows that saint facing right, yet the works were created independently. Poussin may have conceived the project as four paintings of the four Evangelists; if so, those featuring St. Luke and St. Mark were never executed. Both known paintings were made in Rome for the secretary to Pope Urban VIII. The composition suggests the physical, rational arrangement of a spiritual, eternal, ideal world—a concept well suited to and best explored by Baroque Classicism. Poussin's mythological landscapes show a similar blend of the physical, rational, and mythic.

CLAUDE LORRAIN AND THE IDYLLIC LANDSCAPE While Poussin developed the heroic qualities of the ideal landscape, the great French landscapist Claude Lorrain (Claude Gellée, also called Claude; 1604/05?–1682) brought its idyllic aspects of both

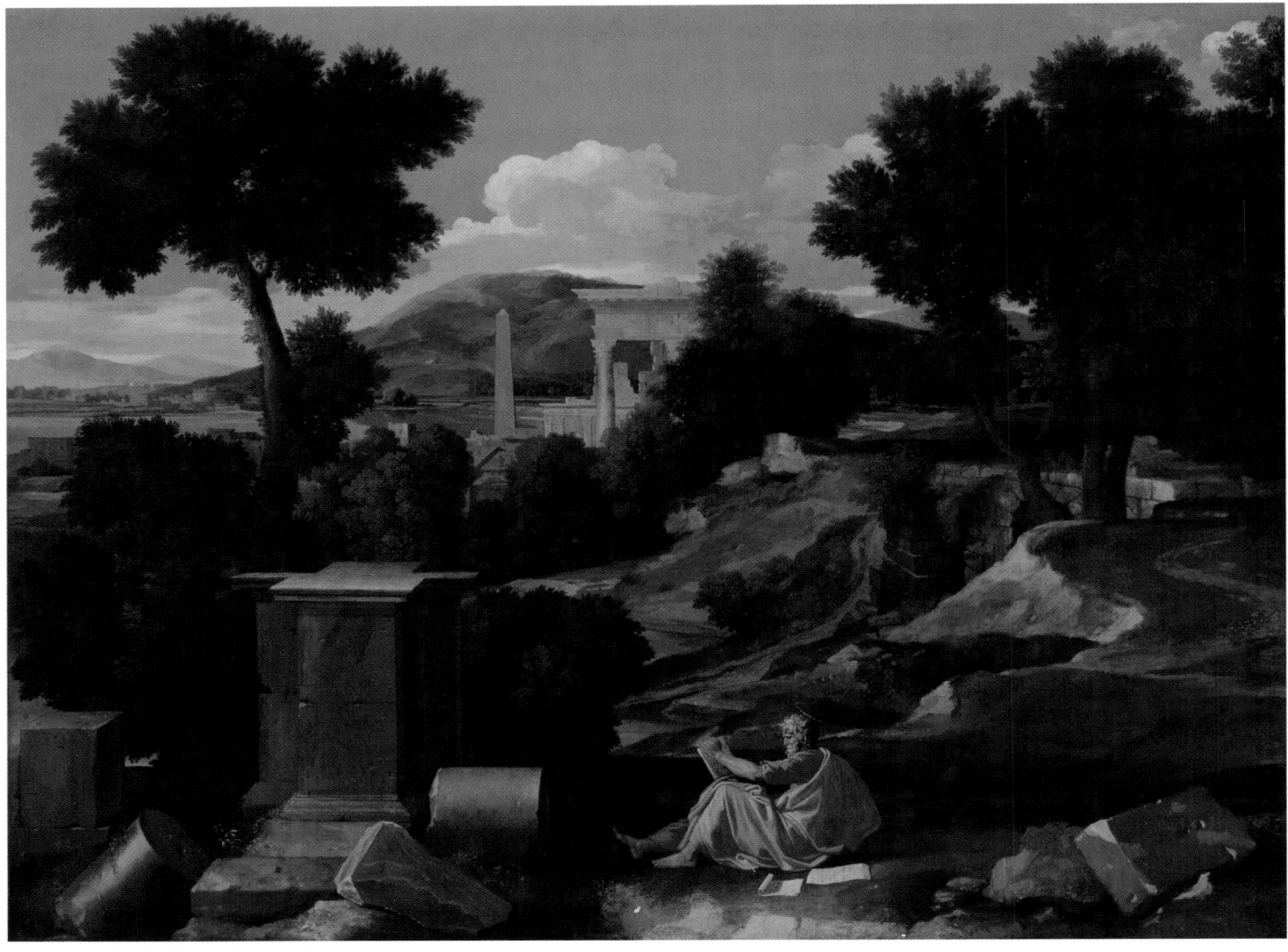

21.7 Nicolas Poussin. *Landscape with St. John on Patmos*. 1640. Oil on canvas, 39½ × 53¾" (100.3 × 136.4 cm).
Art Institute of Chicago. A. A. Munger Collection. (1930.500)

landscapes and seascapes. He, too, spent nearly his entire career in Rome, beginning as a pastry chef. From 1625 to 1627, however, he returned briefly to Nancy, where he was familiar with fellow resident Jacques Callot. He later copied Callot's etchings from *The Great Miseries of War* series (see fig. 21.1). Claude's family in Nancy had been victims of the Thirty Years' War and so the series may have had a particularly personal meaning for him. While in Rome, Claude worked with several artists and was a pupil and assistant to Agostino Tassi (see fig. 19.10). Like many northern Europeans, Claude thoroughly explored the surrounding countryside, the *campagna*, of Rome and his countless drawings made on site reveal his powers of observation. He is also the first artist known to have painted oil studies outdoors. Such sketches, however, were only the raw material for his landscapes. To guard against forgeries, about 1635 Claude began making drawings of his paintings, which he kept as a record in a book known as *Liber Veritatis* (*The Book of Truth*). (See *The Art Historian's Lens*, page 747.) It is from annotations made on the backs of these drawings that we have learned the subjects of his paintings known as

"pastorals," a literary genre that flourished in Venice in the sixteenth century in works by painters such as Giorgione and Titian (see figs. 16.29 and 16.30).

Claude's themes are often historical or pastoral, as in *A Pastoral Landscape* (fig. 21.8). He does not aim for topographic accuracy in his paintings but instead evokes the poetic essence of a countryside filled with echoes of antiquity. Many of Claude's paintings are visual narratives drawn from ancient texts, such as the epic tales and poetry of Vergil. Often, as in this painting, the compositions have the hazy, luminous atmosphere of early morning or late afternoon. One can refer to Claude as painting "into the light." That is, his sunlight (often sunsets) is at the center and at the horizon line of the painting so that the architecture and other elements in the foreground or middleground appear almost as silhouettes. This example is painted on copper, a material seventeenth-century artists frequently employed for small works. The surfaces of copper paintings are luminous. Here, the space expands serenely rather than receding step by step as in works by Poussin. An air of nostalgia, of past experience enhanced by memory, imbues the scene. It is this nostalgic mood founded in ancient literature that forms its subject.

Claude succeeded in elevating the landscape genre, which had traditionally been accorded only a very low status. Prevailing artistic theory had ranked the rendering of common nature at the bottom of the hierarchy of painting genres, with landscape only just above still life. Claude, encouraged by sophisticated patrons, progressively moved away from showing the daily activity of life at the ports, and embellished his seascapes and landscapes with historical, biblical, and mythological subjects, thereby raising the status of the genre.

CHARLES LE BRUN AND THE ESTABLISHMENT OF THE ROYAL ACADEMY In art as in life, the French monarchy sought to maintain strict control, and thus the Royal Academy of Painting and Sculpture was founded in Paris in 1648. One of the 12 founding members was artist Charles Le Brun (1619–1690), who helped reorganize the academy in the 1660s into a formal institution.

Although it came to be associated with the absolutism of Louis XIV's reign, at its inception the king was only ten years old, his mother Anne was regent, and Cardinal Mazarin effectively controlled affairs of state. Yet the ideology of academy and throne would increasingly coincide and strengthen each other in the ensuing years.

When Louis XIV assumed control of the government in 1661, Jean-Baptiste Colbert, his chief advisor, began to build an administrative apparatus capable of supporting the power of the absolute monarch. In this system, aimed at controlling the thoughts and actions of the nation, the task of the visual arts was to glorify the king. As in music and theater, which shared the same purpose, the official "royal style" was Classicism. Centralized control over the visual arts was exerted by Colbert and Le Brun, who became supervisor of all the king's artistic projects. As chief dispenser of royal artistic patronage, Le Brun's power was so great that for all practical purposes he acted as dictator of the arts in France.

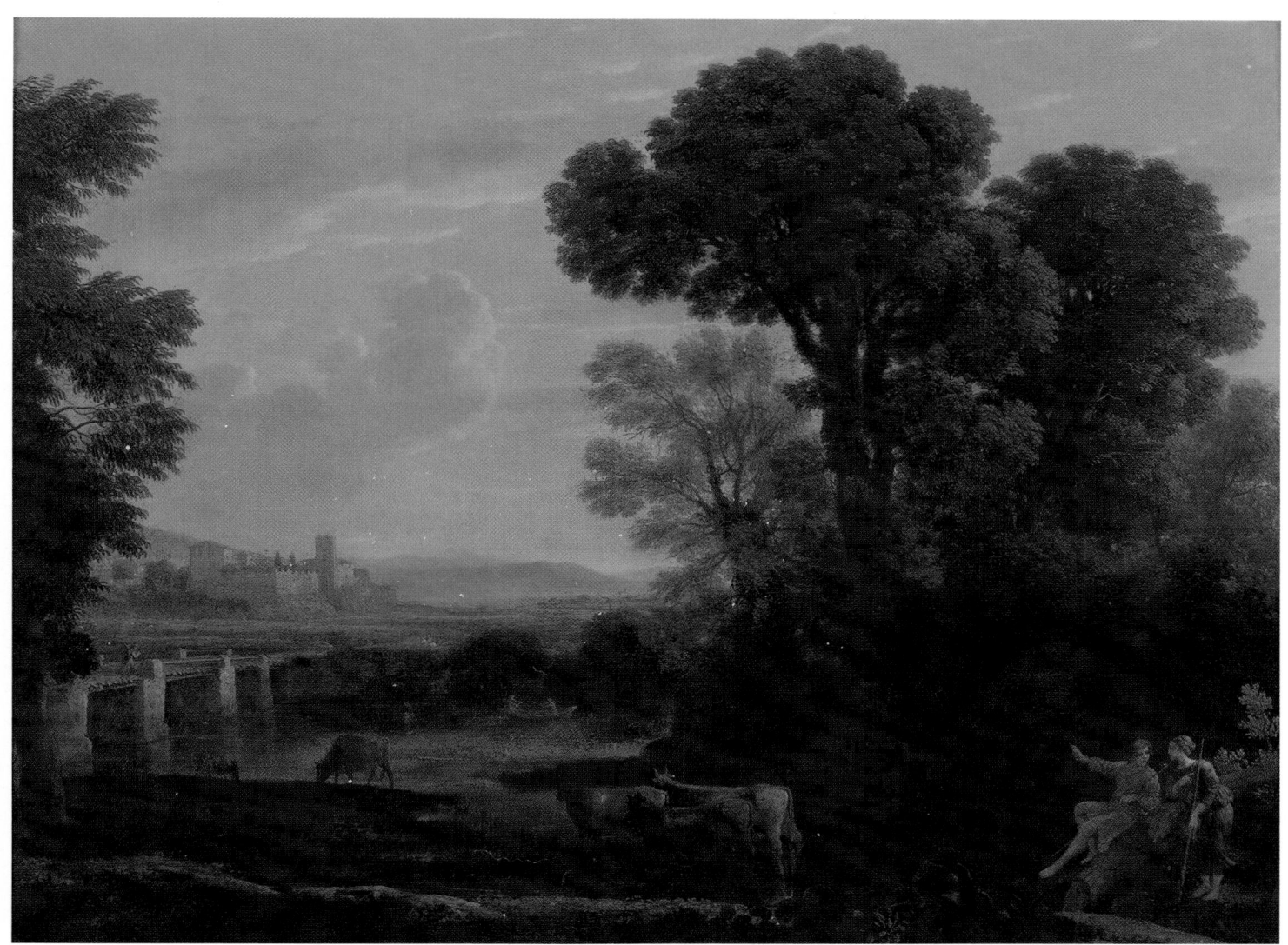

21.8 Claude Lorrain, *A Pastoral Landscape*. ca. 1648. Oil on copper, 15½ × 21" (39.3 × 53.3 cm). Yale University Art Gallery, New Haven, Connecticut. Leonard C. Hanna, Jr., B. A. 1913, Fund. 1959.47

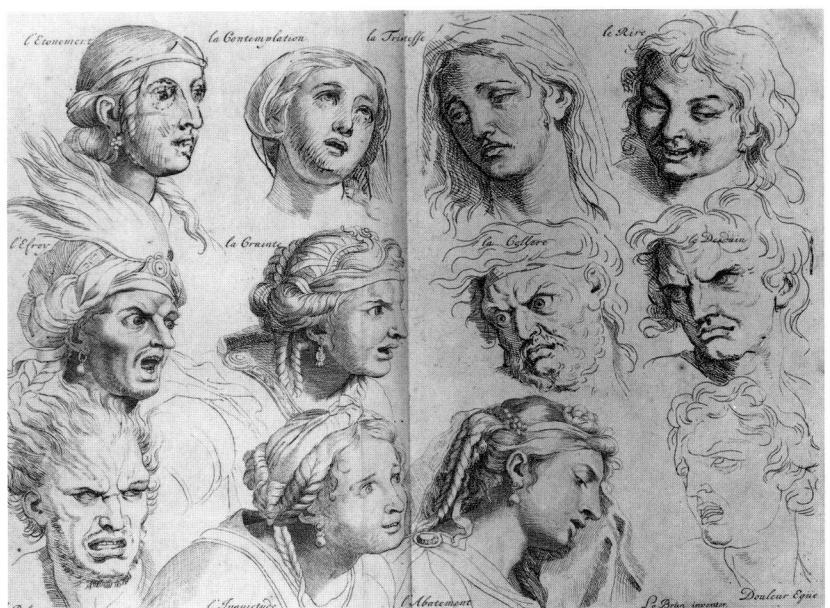

21.9 Henri Testelin after Charles Le Brun, *The Expressions*, 6th plate in Henri Testelin's *Sentiments des plus habiles peintres* (Paris, 1696). Etching (with later additions in ink), 13 1/16 × 17 3/4" (33.1 × 45.1 cm). Metropolitan Museum of Art, Rogers Fund, 1968. (68.513.6(6))

Upon becoming the academy's director in 1663, Le Brun established a rigid curriculum of practical and theoretical instruction. He lectured extensively at the academy; several lectures were devoted to examining the art of Poussin, venerating the works of Raphael, and studying physiognomy (facial expressions). Probably about 1668, he codified facial expressions in a series of annotated drawings published posthumously as engravings (fig. **21.9**). His lectures documented the movements of eyes, eyebrows, and mouths to show passions and emotions such as fear, anger, and surprise, corresponding to those described in the *Passions of the Soul*, published in 1649 by Descartes. Le Brun's schemata were intended to be used as formulas by artists to establish narratives in their paintings that could be easily "read" by viewers.

Much of Le Brun's doctrine was derived from Poussin, with whom he had studied for several years in Rome. The academy also devised a method for assigning numerical grades to artists past and present in such categories as drawing, expression, and proportion. The ancients received the highest marks, followed by Raphael and his school, and then Poussin. Venetian artists, who "overemphasized" color, ranked low, while the Flemish and Dutch were placed lower still. Subjects were also classified: At the top was history (that is, narrative subjects, whether Classical, biblical, or mythological) and at the bottom was still life, with portraiture falling in between.

HYACINTHE RIGAUD AND THE SPLENDOR OF LOUIS XIV

The monumental *Portrait of Louis XIV* (fig. **21.10**) by Hyacinthe Rigaud (1659–1743) conveys the power, drama, and splendor of the absolutist ruler. The king is shown life-size and full-length, much like Charles I in Van Dyck's portrait (see fig. 20.8). The resemblance is intentional, and the work follows the formulaic nature of royal portraiture of the time to espouse power and authority through the use of the insignias of rulership and the symbols of the opulence of the monarch's reign. Louis is shown

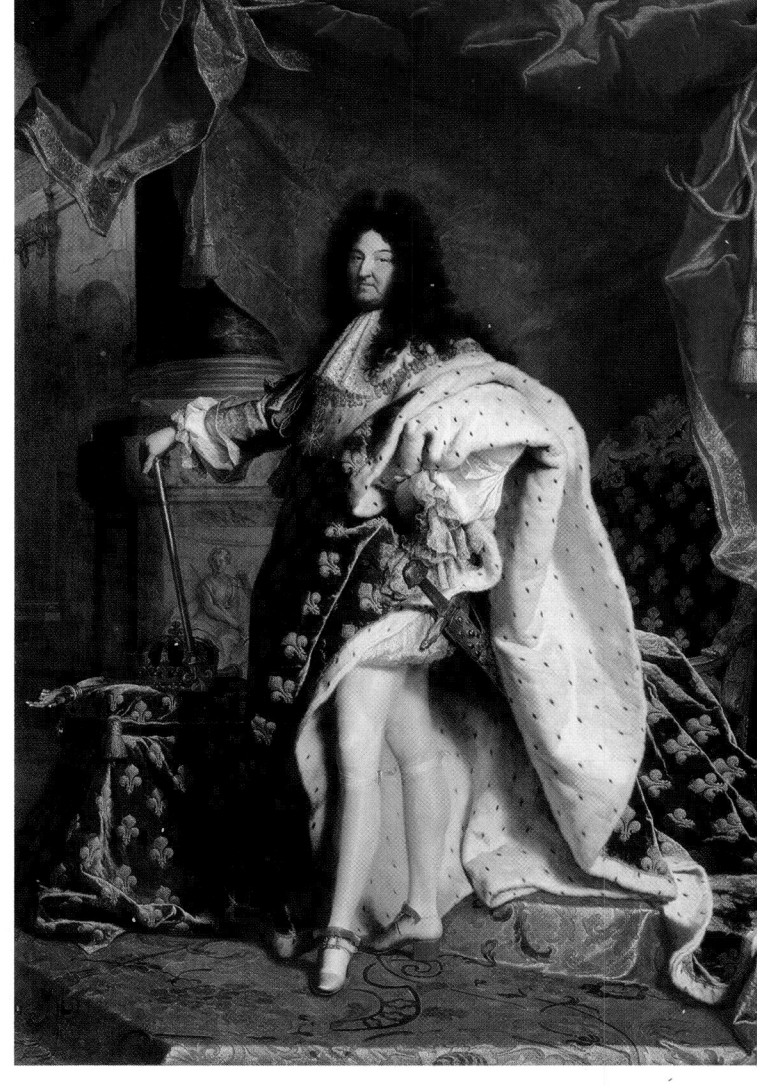

21.10 Hyacinthe Rigaud, *Portrait of Louis XIV*. 1701. Oil on canvas, 9'2" × 6'3" (2.8 × 1.9 m). Musée du Louvre, Paris. Inv. 7492

Forgeries and The Book of Truth

Art forgery—the deliberate copying or creation of a work of art without permission and with the intention to deceive—has long posed a serious threat to both artists and collectors. Art forgers have targeted jewelry, sculpture, painting, and prints, usually in the hopes of selling their fakes for personal gain.

Forgers may copy the works or styles of artists from either the past or present. In ancient times, reports surfaced of forgeries being made of the works of Myron and Praxiteles (see Chapter 5). We know, too, that Michelangelo made "antique" forgeries by burying sculpture to produce a patina imitating the effects of time and wear. To create the look of an older product, forgers may use materials such as old paper, homemade paints, previously used canvases, and wood that has been peppered with buckshot to resemble aged wood infested with wormholes.

Not only are artists deprived of monetary compensation by a forgery, but their reputation can also be jeopardized by art of lesser quality being passed off as theirs. Such was the case with Albrecht Dürer (see Chapter 18), who discovered upon his visit to Venice in 1506 that the well-known printmaker Marcantonio Raimondi (ca. 1480–ca. 1527) was selling engravings that he had created in the manner of Dürer's woodcuts and bearing Dürer's monogram. Dürer sued, and although Raimondi was allowed to continue producing the engravings, he could no longer include Dürer's signature on them.

Claude Lorrain experienced a similar problem, for which he developed a unique solution. We know from the writer Filippo Baldinucci (1625–1697) that Claude discovered that another artist, Sébastien Bourdon (1616–1671), was adept at imitating the light and tonal effects in Claude's paintings. In fact, Bourdon's skill in producing them was so great that, after visiting Claude's studio, he painted a landscape and sold it as a work purportedly by Claude. Other artists also found it easy to imitate Claude's techniques and compositions.

To safeguard against any such dishonest practices, around 1635 Claude decided to compile the *Liber Veritatis* (*The Book of Truth*), an album of drawings reproducing all of his paintings from that time on. On the verso, or back, he annotated each drawing with the name of the patron, buyer, or place to which the work was sent; he sometimes included the date and a reference to the work's subject as well. Collectors could consult the book and verify whether a painting was included—and thus foil any potential forger.

By the time of his death, Claude had made drawings of 195 of his paintings. He did not record paintings made before 1635, and therefore an estimated 50 works are missing from the album. Claude was a prolific draftsman—over 1,200 drawings by him are known, although the album records only drawings of his finished paintings (see Claude's drawing of *A Storm off the Coast*, above). The *Liber Veritatis*,

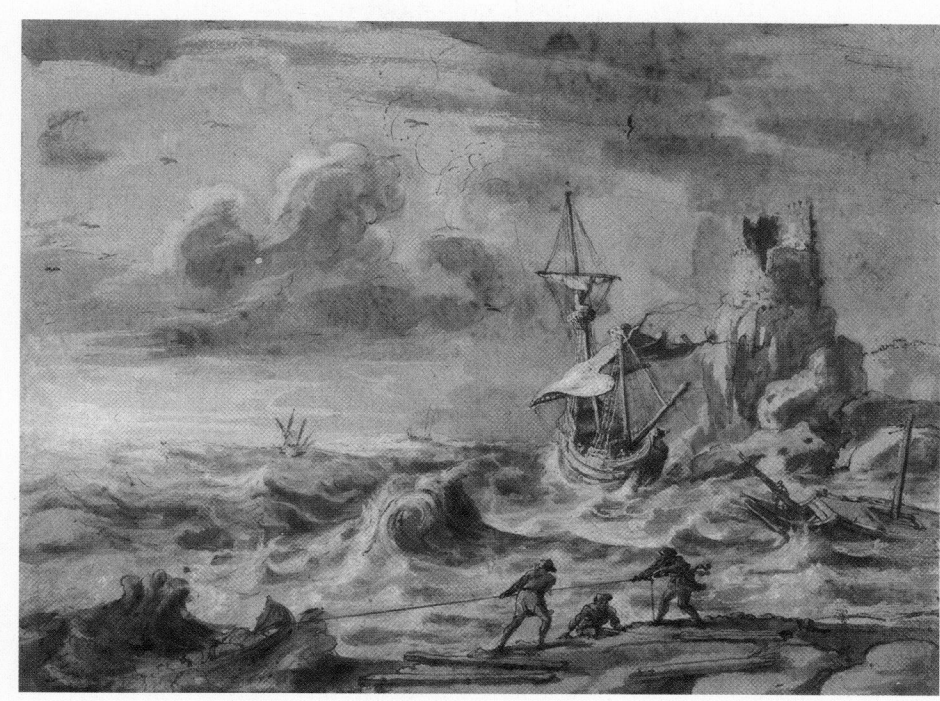

Claude Lorrain, *A Storm off the Coast*. ca. 1635. Pen and brown wash, heightened with white highlights on blue paper, 7¹¹⁄₁₆ × 10¼" (195 × 260 mm). The British Museum, London

now in the collection of the British Museum, consists of sheets measuring 7¹¹⁄₁₆ by 10¼ inches (195 × 260 mm) that are organized in groups of four white sheets alternating with four blue ones. Scholars have speculated that Claude chose these paper colors to reflect the light effects in his paintings. It also suggests that he probably did not execute the drawings in chronological order. To create them, he used pen and ink with brown and sometimes gray washes. He added highlights with white chalk and touches of gold. Such time-consuming details, especially evident in the book's later drawings, show that Claude began to use the album not just to reproduce paintings but also to create elaborate, finished drawings that stand on their own as accomplished works of art.

Dealers and collectors today often rely on a comparable type of book called a **catalogue raisonné**. Compiled by an expert after years of meticulous research, this publication describes and illustrates all the known, verified, and some attributed (but nonauthenticated) works by a particular artist as well as pertinent information about each object's dimensions, condition, and **provenance** (history of ownership). But perhaps most important in the fight against forgeries is the wide range of available technologies—from carbon dating to infrared spectroscopy—to analyze and date a work's materials and stages of creation. Still, even with these advanced detection methods, not all experts agree about the authenticity of a given work since these technologies can often only verify the time or place a work was produced and not the artist's hand. For that we still rely on connoisseurship and the experience and expertise of the art historian.

draped with his velvet coronation robes lined with ermine and trimmed with gold *fleurs-de-lis*. He appears self-assured, powerful, majestic—and also tall, an illusion created by the artist, for his subject actually measured only 5 feet 4 inches. The portrait proudly displays the king's shapely legs (emphasized by the high heels Louis himself designed to increase his height), which were his pride and joy as a dancer. Indeed, the king actively participated in the ballets of Jean-Baptiste Lully (1632–1687) from the 1650s until his coronation. All the arts, from the visual arts to the performing arts, fell under royal control—a fact exemplified in Rigaud's painting, which expresses Louis's dominance and unequaled stature as the center of the French state.

French Classical Architecture

Because they were large, ostentatious, and public, building projects, even more than paintings, transmitted the values of the royal court to a wide audience. In French architecture, the Classical style expressed the grandeur and authority of imperial Rome and confirmed the ideals of tradition, omnipotence, absolutism, strength, and permanence espoused by the monarchy. Mammoth scale and repetition of forms evoke these broad concepts, which were embodied in royal structures erected in the heart of Paris as well as outside the city, in the palace and gardens at Versailles.

In 1655, Louis XIV declared: "*L'état, c'est moi*" ("I am the state"). This statement was not just political but represented an artistic and aesthetic idea as well. Louis's projects for his palace and court took on colossal proportions and represented not a single individual, or even a single monarch, but the entirety of France. He began by renovating the Louvre, a project begun by his father, but that proved insufficient. Louis wanted to move his entire royal court to a more isolated location where he could control them more efficiently, and so he began construction on the palace and gardens at Versailles, located a few miles outside Paris. These complex building projects all share a single style—that of Baroque Classicism.

THE LOUVRE Work on the palace had proceeded intermittently for more than a century, following Pierre Lescot's original design under Francis I; what remained was to close the square court on the east side with an impressive façade. Colbert was dissatisfied with the proposals of French architects including François Mansart (1598–1666), who submitted designs not long before his death. Colbert then invited Bernini to Paris in the hope that the most famous artist of the Roman Baroque would do for the French king what he had done for the popes in Italy. Bernini spent several months in Paris in 1665 and submitted three innovative designs on a scale that would have dwarfed the existing palace. After much argument and intrigue, Louis XIV rejected them and turned the problem over to a committee: Charles Le Brun, his court painter; Louis Le Vau (1612–1670), his court architect who had already done much work on the Louvre (including the

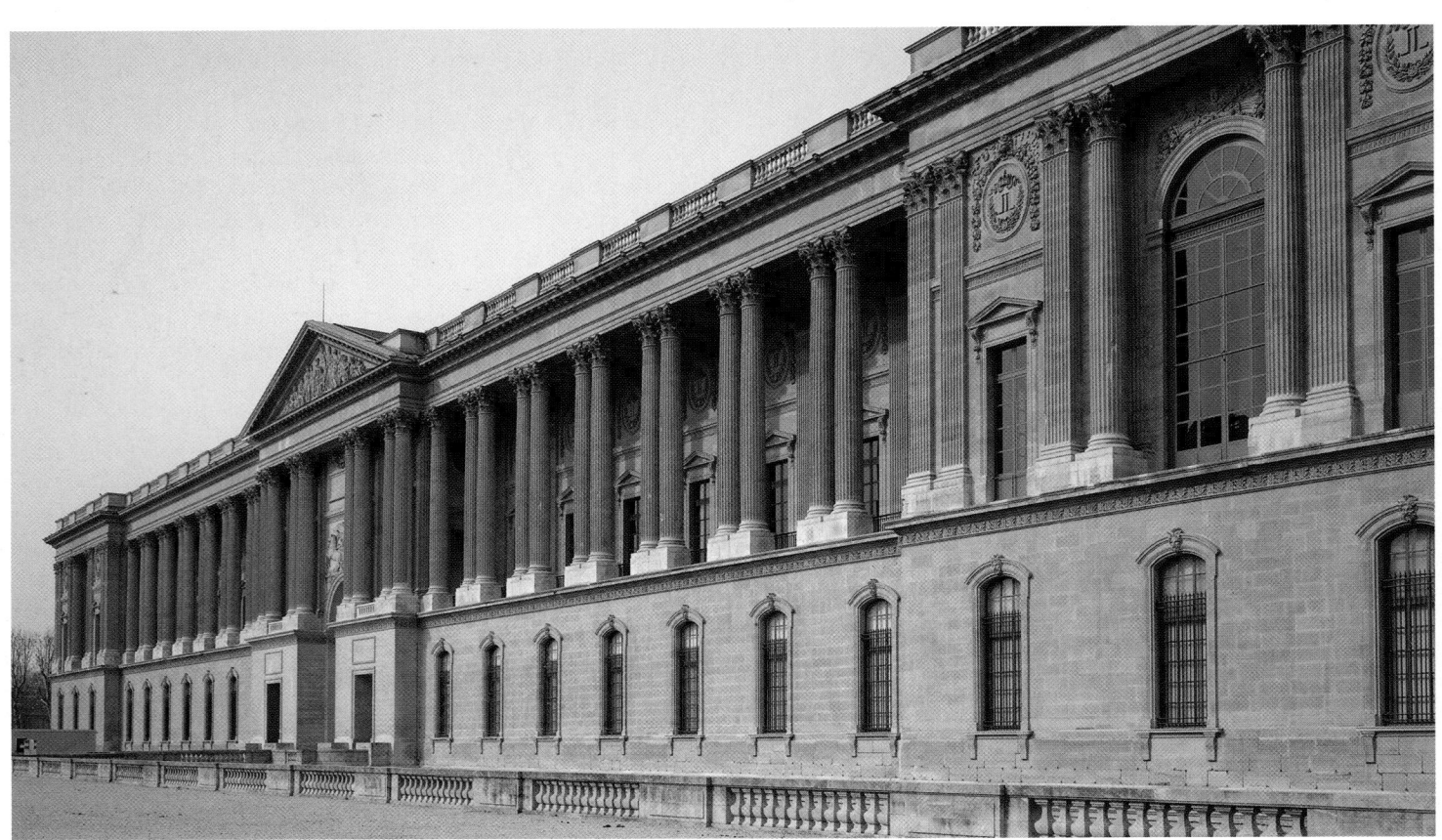

21.11   Louis Le Vau, Claude Perrault, and Charles Le Brun. East front of the Louvre, Paris. 1667–70

Gallery of Apollo, the Queen's Court, and the south façade); and Claude Perrault (1613–1688), an anatomist and student of ancient architecture. All three men were responsible for the structure of the new Louvre (fig. 21.11), but Perrault is rightly credited with the major share. Certainly his detractors at the time thought so, and he was often called upon to defend his design.

Perrault based the center pavilion on a Roman temple front, and the wings look like the sides of a temple folded outward. The colonnade was controversial because of its use of paired columns, but this treatment quickly became a characteristic of French Classicism in architecture.

The east front of the Louvre signaled the victory of French Classicism over the Italian Baroque as the royal style. It further proclaimed France as the new Rome, both politically and culturally, by linking Louis XIV with the glory of the Caesars. This revitalization of the antique, both in its conception and its details, was Perrault's main contribution.

Claude Perrault owed his position to his brother Charles (1628–1703), who, as Colbert's master of buildings under Louis XIV, had helped undermine Bernini during his stay at the French court. It is likely that Claude Perrault shared the views set forth some 20 years later in his brother's *Parallels Between the Ancients and Moderns* in which Charles claimed that "Homer and Vergil made countless mistakes which the moderns no longer make [because] the ancients did not have all our rules." The Louvre's east front presents not simply a Classical revival but a vigorous distillation of what Claude Perrault considered to be the eternal ideals of beauty, intended to surpass anything built by the Romans themselves. Indeed, Perrault annotated Vitruvius and wrote his own treatise on the Classical orders.

THE PALACE OF VERSAILLES Louis XIV's largest enterprise was the Palace of Versailles (fig. 21.12), located 11 miles (18 km) from the center of Paris. By forcing the aristocracy to live under royal scrutiny outside Paris, the king hoped to prevent a repeat of the civil rebellion known as the Fronde, which had occurred during his minority in 1648–53.

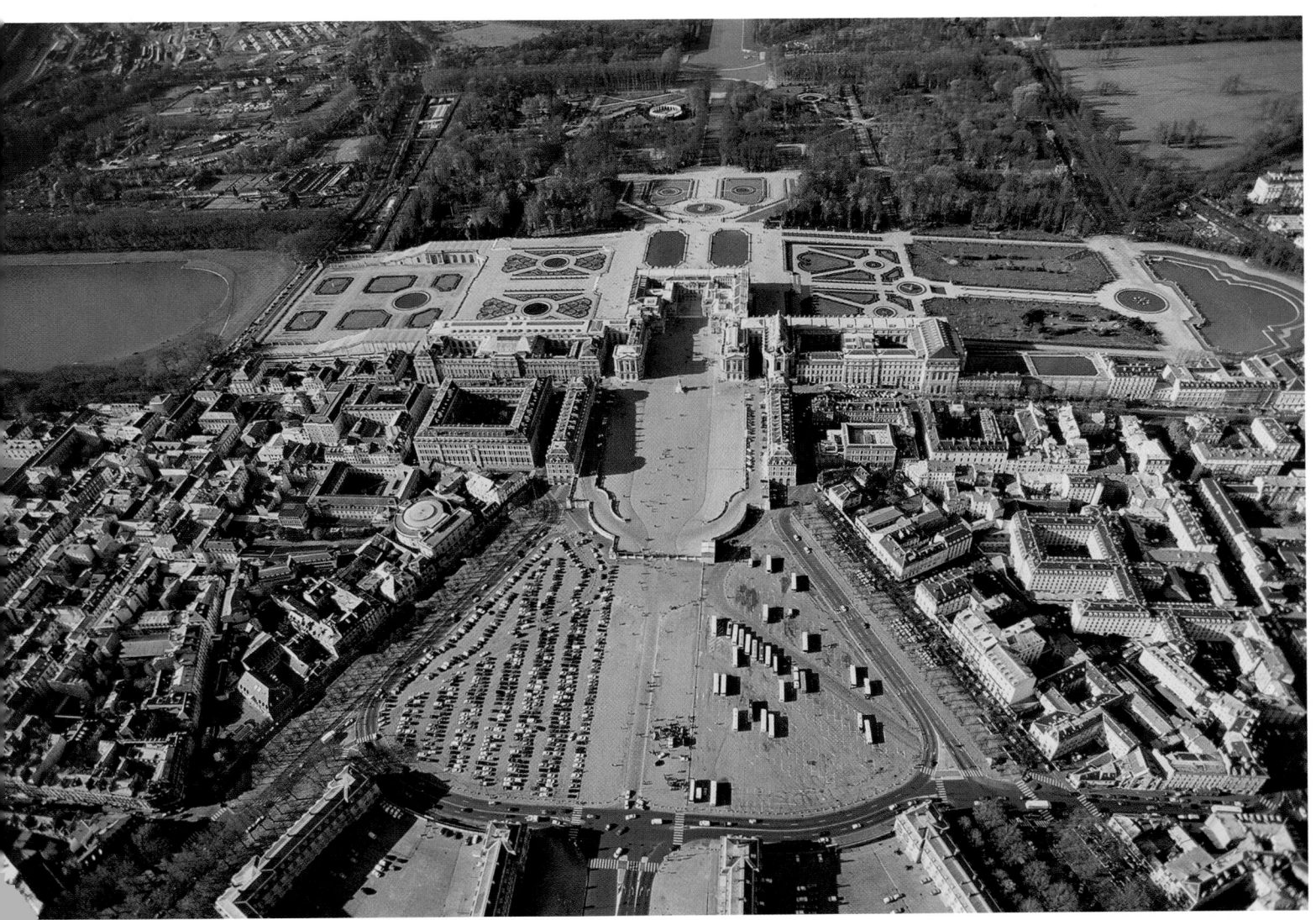

21.12 Aerial view of Versailles

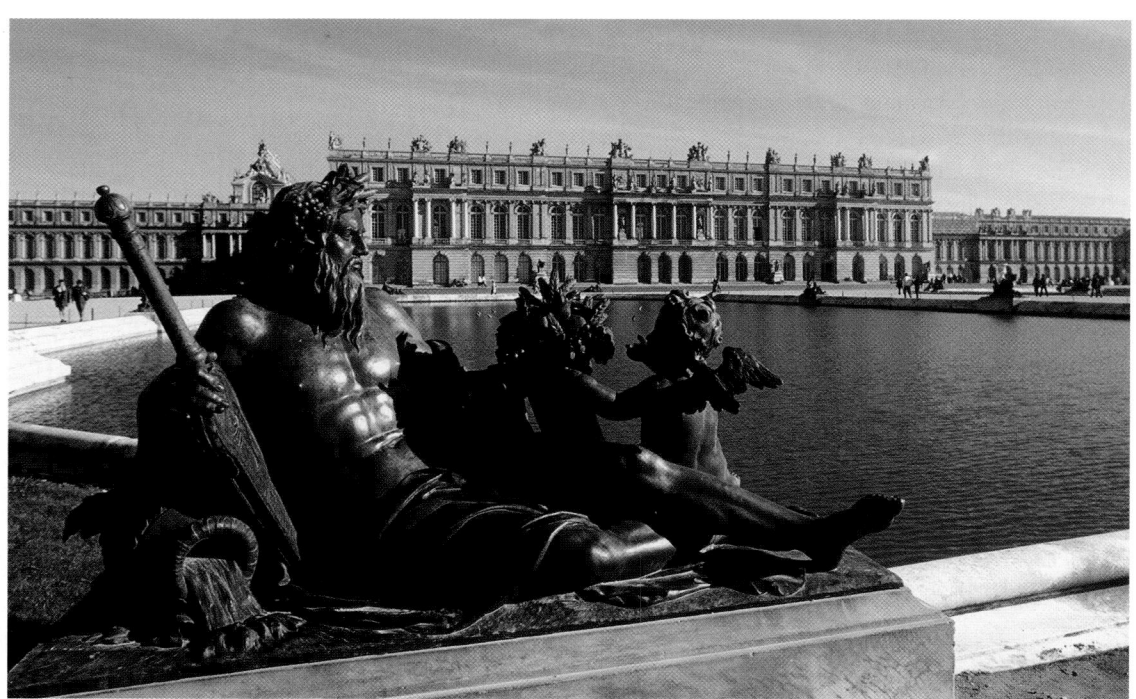

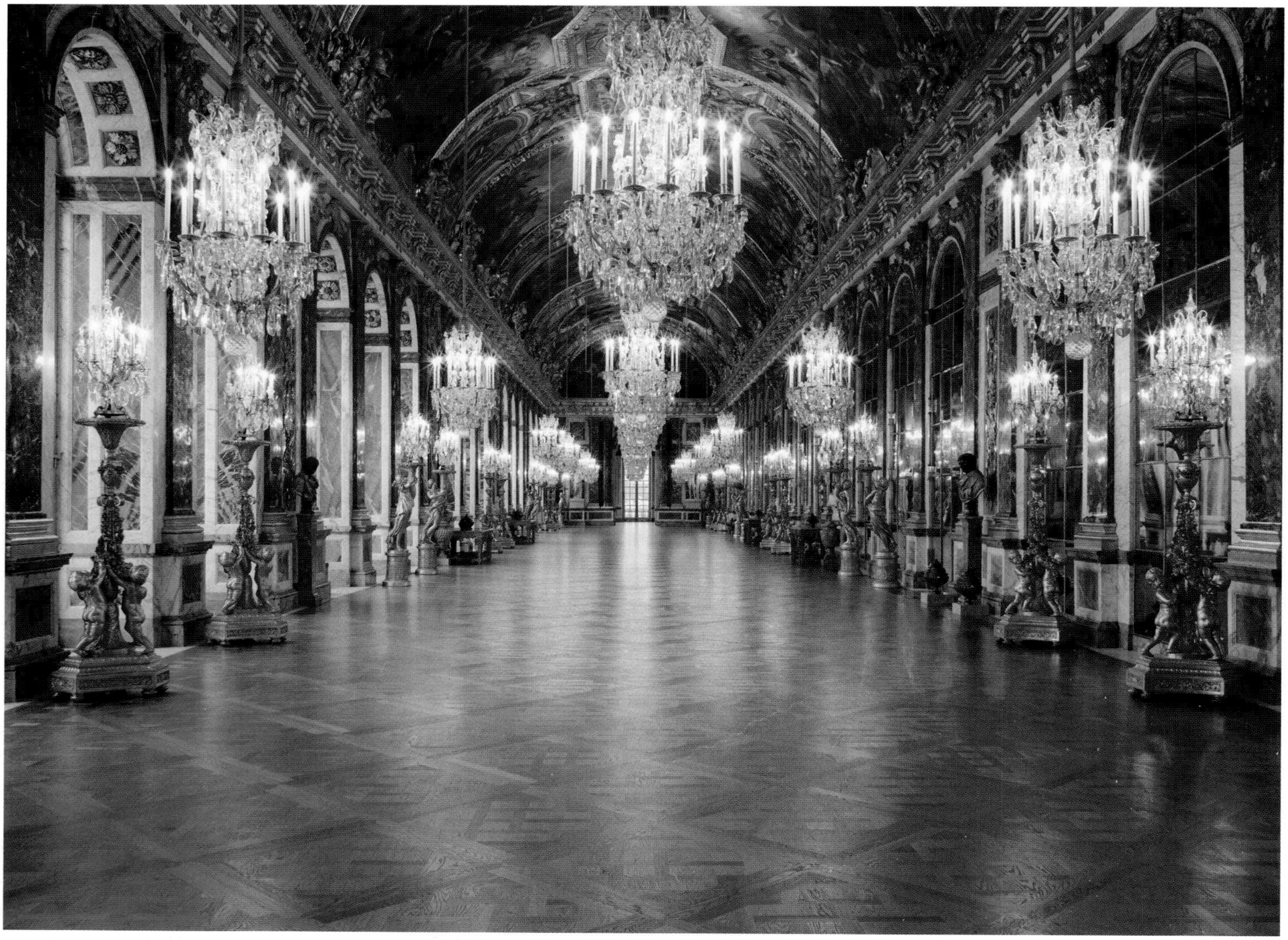

21.14 Jules Hardouin-Mansart, Louis Le Vau, and Charles Le Brun. Galerie des Glaces (Hall of Mirrors), Palace of Versailles. Begun 1678

The project was begun in 1669 by Le Vau, who designed the elevation of the garden front (fig. **21.13**); within a year of doing so he had died. Under the leadership of Jules Hardouin-Mansart (1646–1708), the structure was greatly expanded to accommodate the ever-growing royal household. The garden front, intended by Le Vau to be the main view of the palace, was stretched to an enormous length but with no change in the architectural elements. As a result, Le Vau's original façade design, a less severe variant of the Louvre's east front, now looks repetitious and out of scale. The center block contains a single room measuring 240 feet in length, the spectacular Galerie des Glaces, or Hall of Mirrors (fig. **21.14**). At either end are the Salon de la Guerre (Salon of War) and its counterpart, the Salon de la Paix (Salon of Peace). The sumptuous effect of the Galerie des Glaces recalls the gallery of Francis I at Fontainebleau, but the use of full-length mirrors was unique: They represented a great investment on the part of the monarchy. The art of large mirror-making was invented in Venice and brought to France by agents of Colbert. Such extravagant details were meant to reinforce the majesty of both Louis's reign and of France. The mirrors were placed in such a way as to reflect the gardens outside, making the room appear larger by day. At night, myriad reflections of candlelight illuminated the grand space. Whether by day or by night, the effect was impressive.

Baroque features, although not officially acknowledged by the architects, appeared inside the palace. This shift reflected the king's own taste. Louis XIV was interested less in architectural theory and monumental Classical exteriors than in the lavish interiors that would provide suitable settings for himself and his court. Thus, the man to whom he listened most often was not an architect but the painter Charles Le Brun, whose goal was to subordinate all the arts to the expression of the king's power. To achieve this aim, he drew freely on his memories of Rome; the great decorative schemes of the Italian Baroque must have impressed him. Although a disciple of Poussin, Le Brun had studied first with Vouet and became a superb decorator. At Versailles, he employed architects, sculptors, painters, and decorators to produce ensembles of unprecedented splendor. The Salon de la Guerre (fig. **21.15**), which includes a relief of *The Triumph of Louis XIV* by Antoine Coysevox (see page 753), is close in many ways to the theatricality and variety of mediums of Bernini's Cornaro Chapel (see fig. 19.31). Although Le Brun's ensemble is less adventurous than Bernini's, he has given greater emphasis to surface decoration. As in many Italian Baroque interiors, the separate components are less impressive than the effect of the whole.

THE GARDENS AT VERSAILLES Apart from its magnificent interior, the most impressive aspect of Versailles is its park designed by André Le Nôtre (1613–1700), who had become director of the gardens of Louis XIII in 1643 and whose family had served as royal gardeners for generations. Versailles and its gardens are vast: The completed palace and park covers almost 18,000 acres (the wall around it is 27 miles long). The type of formal gardens found at Versailles had their beginnings in Renaissance Florence but had never been attempted on the scale

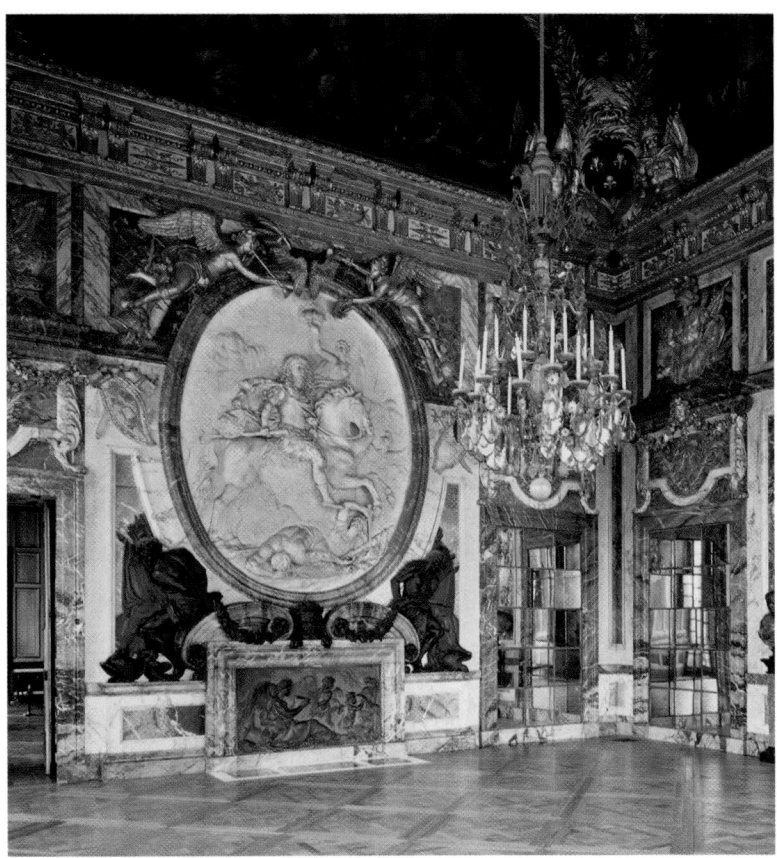

21.15 Jules Hardouin-Mansart, Charles Le Brun (the room and decoration), and Antoine Coysevox (for the relief, *The Triumph of Louis XIV*). Salon de la Guerre (Salon of War), Palace of Versailles. Begun 1678

achieved by Le Nôtre, who transformed an entire natural forest into a controlled park, a massive and expensive enterprise that reflected the grandeur of the king. The park follows its Grand Axis from east to west, intended to imply the course of the sun as it rises in the east over the king (the Sun King) in the palace and sets in the west at the farthest end of the gardens. Conceptually, the landscape is as significant as the palace—perhaps more so, for it suggests the king's dominion over nature. The landscape design is so strictly correlated with the plan of the palace that it in effect continues the architectural space. Like the interiors, the formal gardens were meant to provide a suitable setting for the king's public appearances. They form a series of "outdoor rooms" for the splendid fêtes and spectacles that were an integral part of Louis's court.

The spirit of absolutism is apparent in Le Nôtre's plan, which called for the taming of nature: Forests were thinned to create stately avenues, plants were shaped into manicured hedges, water was pumped into exuberant fountains and serene lakes. The formal gardens consist of a multitude of paths, terraces, basins, mazes, and parterres (designed flower beds) that create a unified geometric whole. Farther from the palace, the plan becomes less formal and incorporates the site's densely wooded areas and open meadows. Throughout, carefully planned vistas give rise to visual surprises. An especially important aspect of the landscape design was the program of sculpture, much of which incorporated images of Apollo, the sun-god, a favorite symbol of Louis XIV.

Versailles was called by a contemporary "pure harmony. Everything there is part of the unity of a perfect work of art." But the elaborate and expensive gardens had their detractors as well. From these critics we are able to ascertain what life was like at Versailles. The duc de Saint-Simon, a member of the court but no admirer of Louis, recorded in his diary:

> Versailles…the dullest of all places, without prospect, without wood, without water without soil; for the ground is all shifting sand or swamp, the air accordingly bad.…You are introduced [in the gardens] to the freshness of the shade only by a vast torrid zone.…The violence everywhere done to nature repels and wearies us despite ourselves. The abundance of water forced up and gathered together in all parts is rendered green thick and muddy; it disseminates humidity, unhealthy and evident; and an odor still more so. I might never finish upon the monstrous defects of a palace so immense.

> *Memoirs of Louis XIV and His Court and of the Regency by the Duke of Saint-Simon*, II (New York: P. F. Collier and Son, 1910)

THE STYLE OF JULES HARDOUIN-MANSART Constrained at Versailles by the design of Le Vau, Jules Hardouin-Mansart's own style can be better appreciated in the church of the Invalides (fig. **21.16**), best known today for housing the tomb of Napoleon. Originally the structure formed part of a hospital that served as a hostel for the many disabled soldiers returning from Louis's continuous wars, gathering them off the streets of Paris where they might incite disorder. The complex consists of a series of dormitories, dining halls, infirmaries, and two chapels—a simple, unadorned one for the soldiers and an elaborate, domed space for the king, where he could be seen high above them during his visits. Hardouin-Mansart's design visually connected the sacrifice of the soldiers to their allegiance to the king and the absolute authority of the monarchy.

In plan, the Invalides consists of a Greek cross with four corner chapels (fig. **21.17**); it is based on Michelangelo's and Bramante's centralized plans for St. Peter's. The dome, too, reflects the influence of Michelangelo, but consists of three shells instead of the usual two. The façade breaks forward repeatedly in the crescendo effect introduced by Maderno (see fig. 19.13), and the façade and dome are as closely linked as at Borromini's Sant'Agnese in the Piazza Navona (see fig. 19.23). The dome itself is the most original, as well as the most Baroque, feature of Hardouin-Mansart's design. Tall and slender, it rises in a single continuous curve from the base of the drum to the spire atop the lantern. On the first drum rests a second, short drum. Its windows provide light for the paintings on the dome's interior. The windows are hidden behind a "pseudo-shell" with a large opening at the top so that the painted visions of heavenly glory seem to be mysteriously illuminated and suspended in space. The bold theatrical lighting of the Invalides places it firmly within the Baroque style.

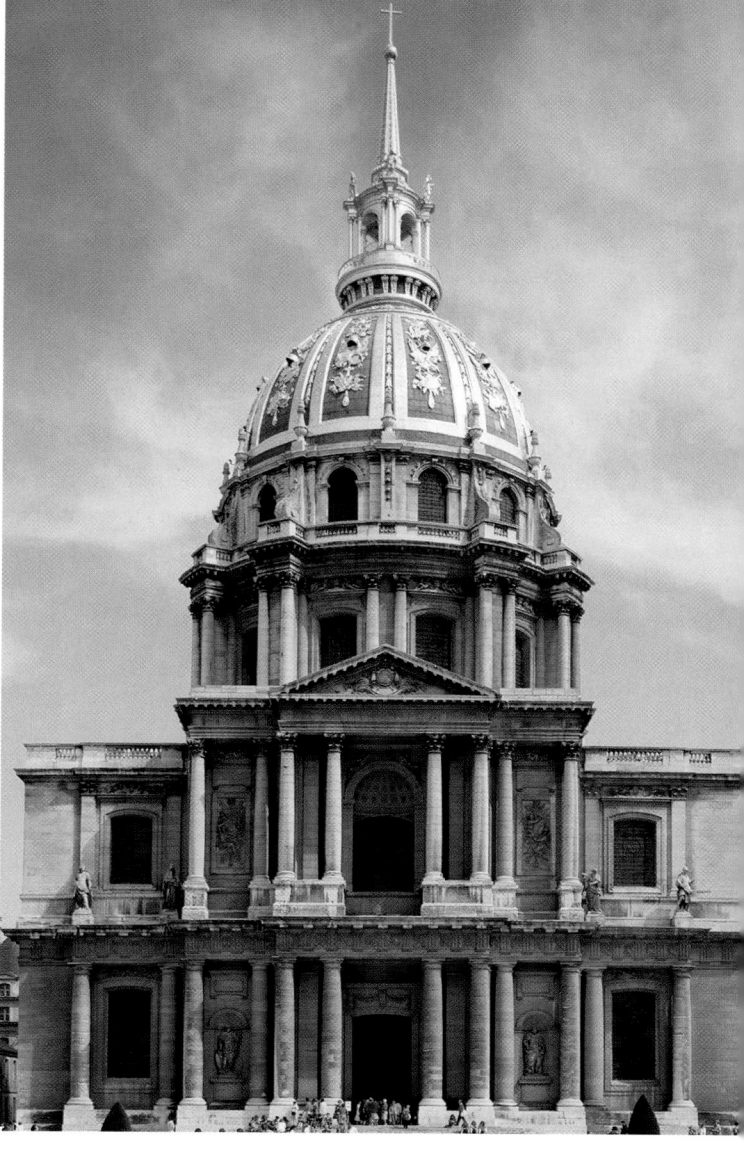

21.16   Jules Hardouin-Mansart. Church of the Invalides, Paris. 1677–91

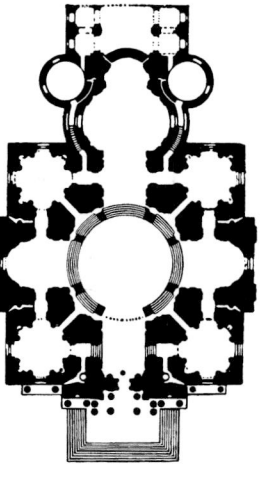

21.17   Plan of the church of the Invalides

Sculpture: The Impact of Bernini

Sculpture evolved into an official royal style in much the same way as architecture—through the influence of Rome and the impact of Bernini's visit to the royal court in 1665. While in Paris, Bernini carved a marble bust of Louis XIV. He was also commissioned to create an equestrian statue of the king, which he later executed in Rome and sent back to Paris, where it was reworked. It is now at Versailles.

ANTOINE COYSEVOX Bernini's influence can be seen in the work of Antoine Coysevox (1640–1720), the first in a long line of distinguished French portrait sculptors and one of the artists employed by Charles Le Brun at Versailles. The large stucco relief of the victorious Louis XIV that Coysevox made for the Salon de la Guerre (see fig. 21.16) retains the pose of Bernini's equestrian statue, although it has more restraint. In a vivacious terra-cotta portrait of the influential Le Brun (fig. **21.18**), Coysevox shows the artist with head turned to the side and slightly parted lips in a "speaking likeness" of the kind we have already seen in the paintings of Frans Hals (see fig. 20.17). The drapery folded over itself below the shoulder line recalls the general outline of Bernini's bust of Louis XIV. Le Brun's face, however, shows a naturalism and subtle characterization that are Coysevox's own.

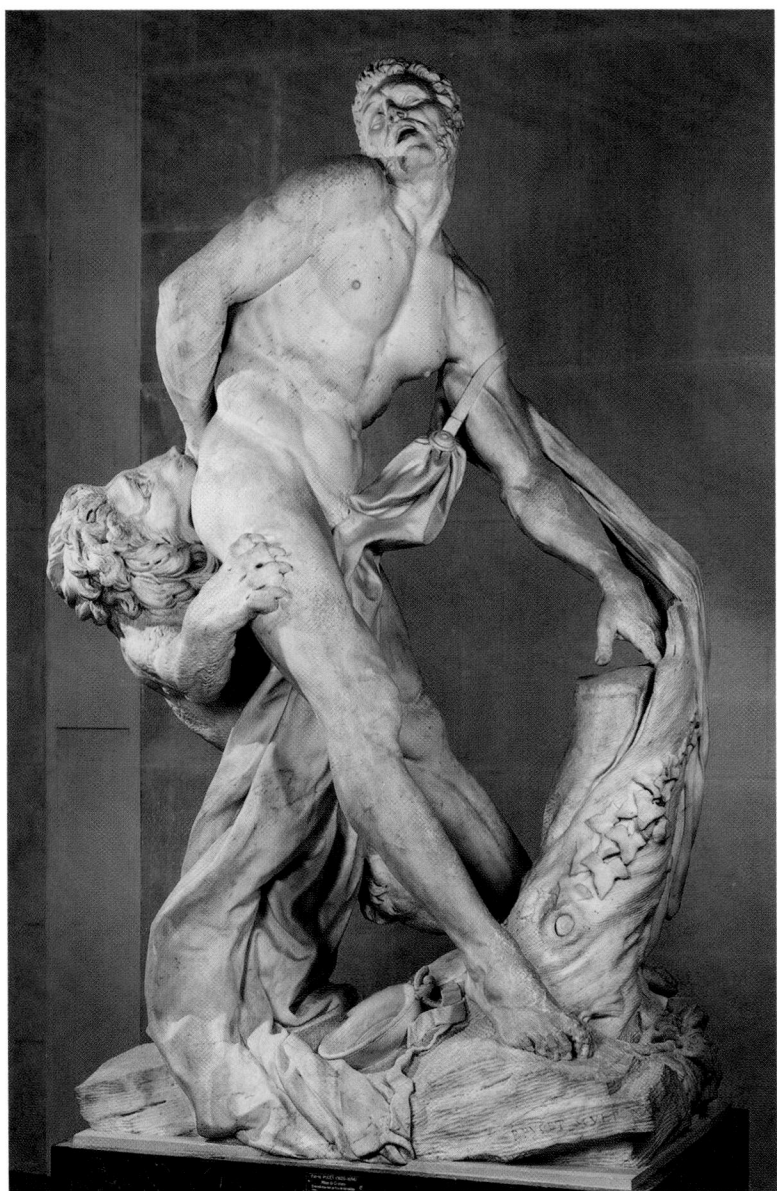

21.19   Pierre-Paul Puget, *Milo of Crotona*. 1671–82. Marble, height 8'10½" (2.7 m). Musée du Louvre, Paris

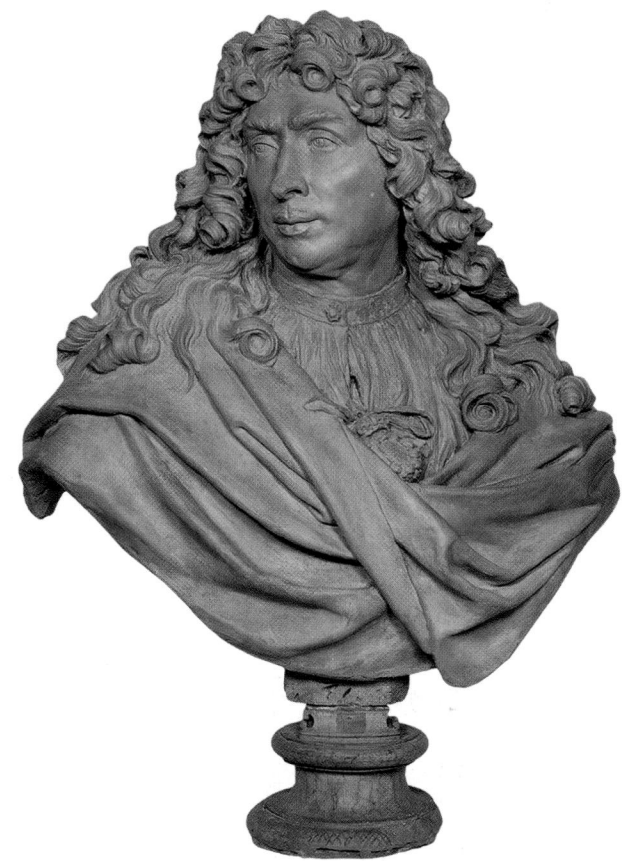

21.18   Antoine Coysevox, *Charles Le Brun*. 1676. Terra cotta, height 26" (66 cm). The Wallace Collection, London. Reproduced by Permission of the Trustees

PIERRE-PAUL PUGET Of all the seventeenth-century French sculptors, Pierre-Paul Puget (1620–1694) best represents the High Baroque style. Puget had no success at court until after Colbert's death, when Le Brun's power began to decline. His finest statue, *Milo of Crotona* (fig. **21.19**), owes its fierceness and drama to the impact of Bernini's trip to Paris and benefits from a comparison with Bernini's *David* (see fig. 19.30). Although Puget's composition is more contained, he nevertheless successfully conveys the dramatic force of the hero as he is attacked by a lion while his hand is trapped in a tree stump. The creature attacks from behind and digs its claws deeply into the thigh of Milo, who twists painfully and cries out in agony. The violent action imbues the statue with an intensity that also recalls the *Laocoön* (see page 183). This reference to antiquity, one suspects, is what made the work acceptable to Louis XIV.

BAROQUE ARCHITECTURE IN ENGLAND

The English contribution to the Baroque came mostly in the form of architecture since in painting it was artists from Italy, Flanders, and the Dutch Republic (Orazio and Artemisia Gentileschi, Anthony van Dyck and Peter Paul Rubens—the latter two were knighted during their stays—who dominated the English royal court through the century. Orazio Gentileschi and Rubens worked for James I, while Charles I's court painter Van Dyck executed both portraits and allegorical paintings (see figs. 20.7 and 20.8). After Van Dyck's death, many artists continued his style of portraiture for wealthy patrons, initiating little in the visual arts until the Restoration of Charles II in 1660. After the Great Fire of London in 1666, the rebuilding of the city gave priority to architecture, which thereafter represented the most important English artistic achievement.

Inigo Jones and the Impact of Palladio

The first significant English architect was Inigo Jones (1573–1652), architect to James I and Charles I as well as the era's leading English theatrical designer. Jones's style developed from the country-house tradition of large private mansions in parklike settings. Jones took two lengthy trips to Italy in 1597–1603 and 1613–14, with an interlude in Paris in 1609. Upon returning from his second trip to Italy, he was appointed surveyor of the king's works, a post he held until 1643. Jones was now an affirmed disciple of Antonio Palladio, whose work he saw in Venice and whose treatises (along with those of Alberti) he owned and annotated. Before Jones, English architecture was a pastiche of medieval and Renaissance forms; its high point was the English Gothic cathedral (see figs. 12.49–12.54). Jones is responsible for introducing Palladio's Renaissance Classicism to England, although the style took root only in the early decades of the eighteenth century, when a building boom resulted in the trend called the Palladian Revival.

The Banqueting House Jones built at Whitehall Palace in London (fig. 21.20) conforms to the principles set out in Palladio's treatises, although it does not copy any specific Palladian project. It was originally intended to be used for court ceremonies and performances called masques (a spectacle combining dance, theater, and music), although evening entertainments were halted after 1635 because smoke from torchlights was damaging Rubens's ceiling painting, the *Apotheosis of James I*. The Banqueting House is essentially a Vitruvian "basilica," a double cube with an apse for the king's throne, which Jones has treated as a Palladian villa. It is more like a Renaissance palazzo than any other building north of the Alps that had been designed at that time. Jones uses an ordered, Classical vocabulary and the rules of proportion to compose the building in three parts. The Ionic and composite orders of the pilasters add an understated elegance, and alternating segmental and triangular pediments over the first-floor windows create a rhythmic effect. The sculpted garland below the roofline and the balustrade above decoratively enhance the overall structure. The building is perhaps starker than originally conceived; it bore colored stones for each of the stories before the façade was resurfaced. Jones's spare style stood as a beacon of Classicist orthodoxy in England for 200 years.

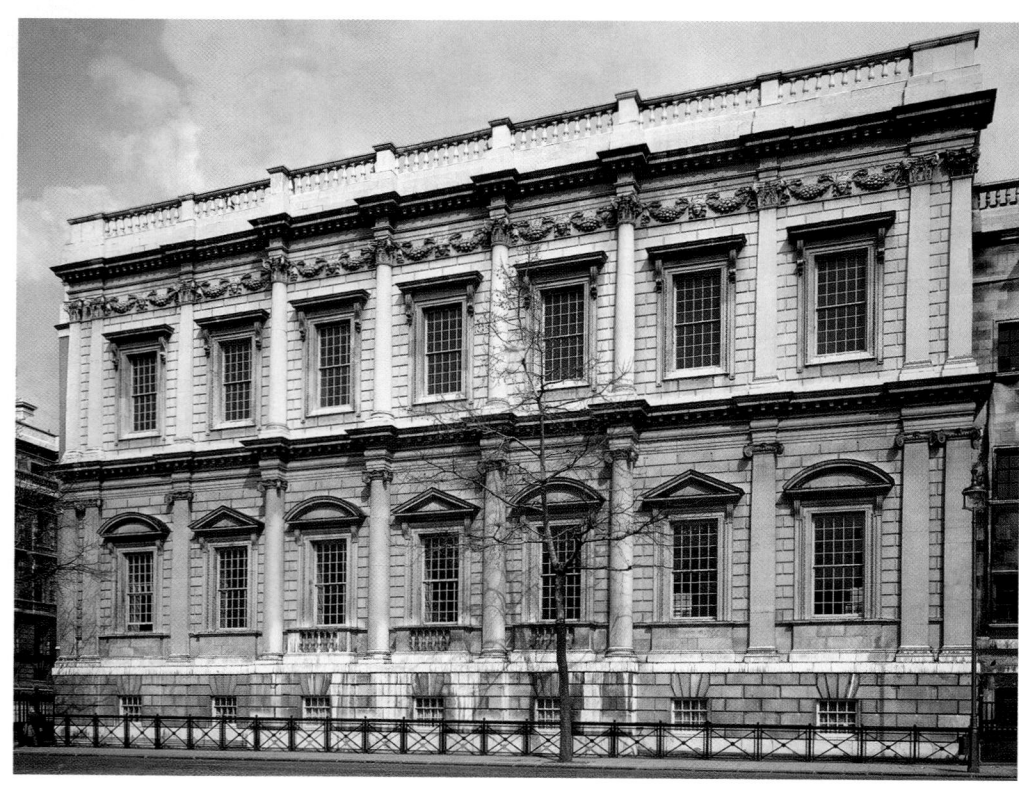

21.20 Inigo Jones. West front of the Banqueting House, Whitehall Palace, London. 1619–22

Sir Christopher Wren

But for the destruction caused by the Great Fire of London of 1666, Sir Christopher Wren (1632–1723), the most important English architect of the late seventeenth century, might have remained an amateur. Wren may be considered the Baroque counterpart of the Renaissance artist-scientist. An intellectual prodigy, he first studied anatomy and then physics, mathematics, and astronomy, and he was highly esteemed by Sir Isaac Newton for his understanding of geometry. Early in his career, Wren held the position of chair in the astronomy department at Gresham College, London, and then professor of mathematics at Oxford University. His interest in architecture did not surface until he was about 30 years old. His technical knowledge may have affected the shape of his buildings; certainly, no previous architect had gone to such lengths to conceal a building's structural supports. Only an architect thoroughly grounded in geometry and mathematics could have achieved such results, and the technical proficiency of Wren's structures has continually confounded his critics.

THE GREAT FIRE OF LONDON In early September 1666, the city of London was devastated by a catastrophic, uncontrollable fire covering 373 acres; four-fifths of the city was razed; 400 streets smoked and over 100,000 people made homeless. One observer famously wrote: "London was, but is no more." Within a few days, Wren had already planned a new London: The burned areas would be cleared and the builders would start anew. His drawing of September 11, 1666 has been translated three-dimensionally here (fig. **21.21**) and shows the influence of the planning of Renaissance Rome, known to him through engravings, and of Paris, a city he had only recently visited. The plan includes wide avenues and focal points punctuated by church steeples he would design (see fig. 21.24); the focal point (in the detail) is Wren's Monument to the Great Fire of London, which was erected between 1671 and 1677. Although his plan proved too radical for the crown to adopt, Wren was named to the short-lived royal commission to reconstruct the city (see www.myartslab.com) and many of his ideas were incorporated into the new urban planning: for example, concern about materials (limitations on the use of wood), and provisions for pavements and treatment of sewage.

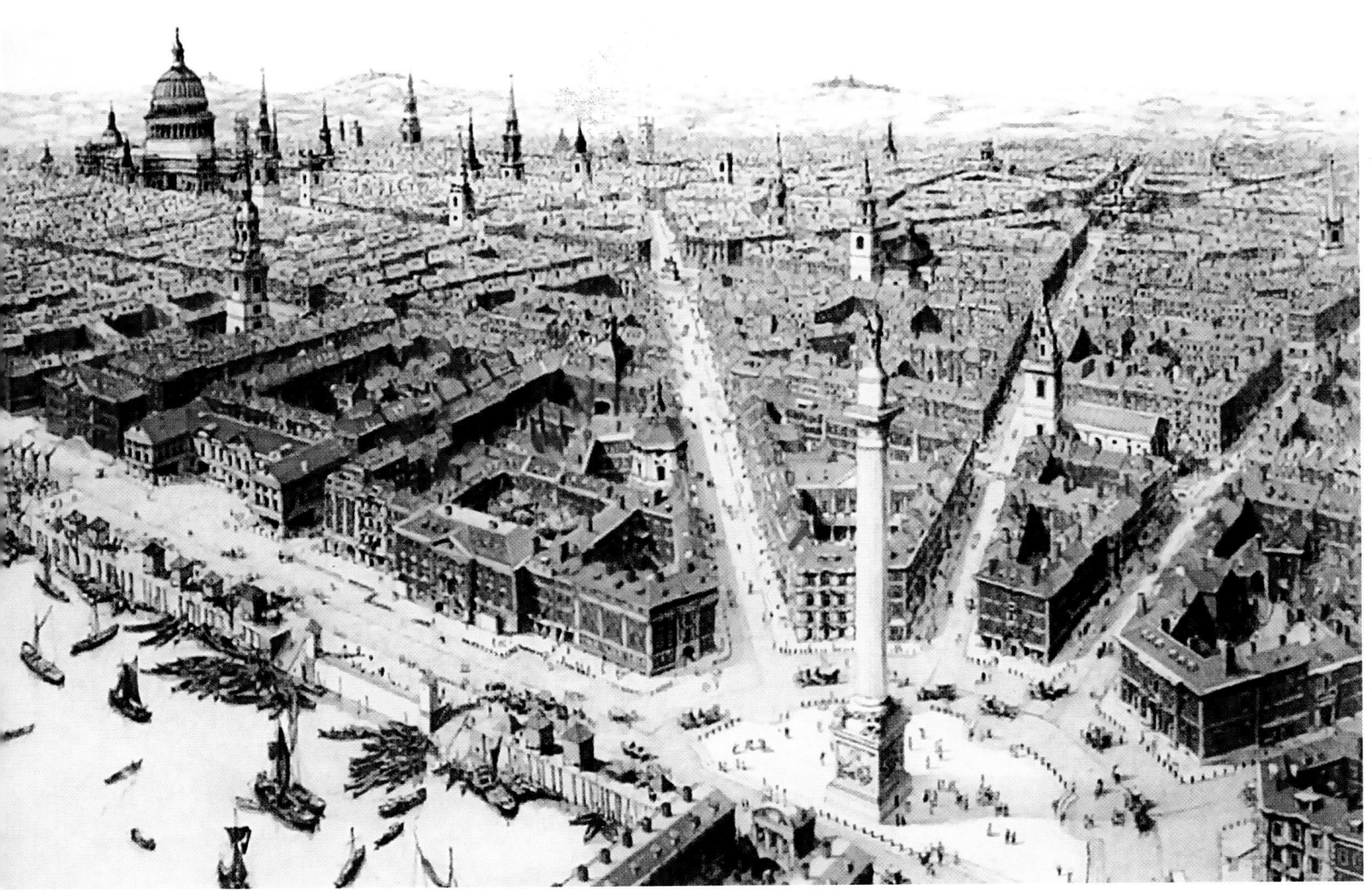

21.21   Paul Draper. Reconstruction (detail) of Sir Christopher Wren's plan for the City of London created from Wren's September 11, 1666 drawing after the Great Fire

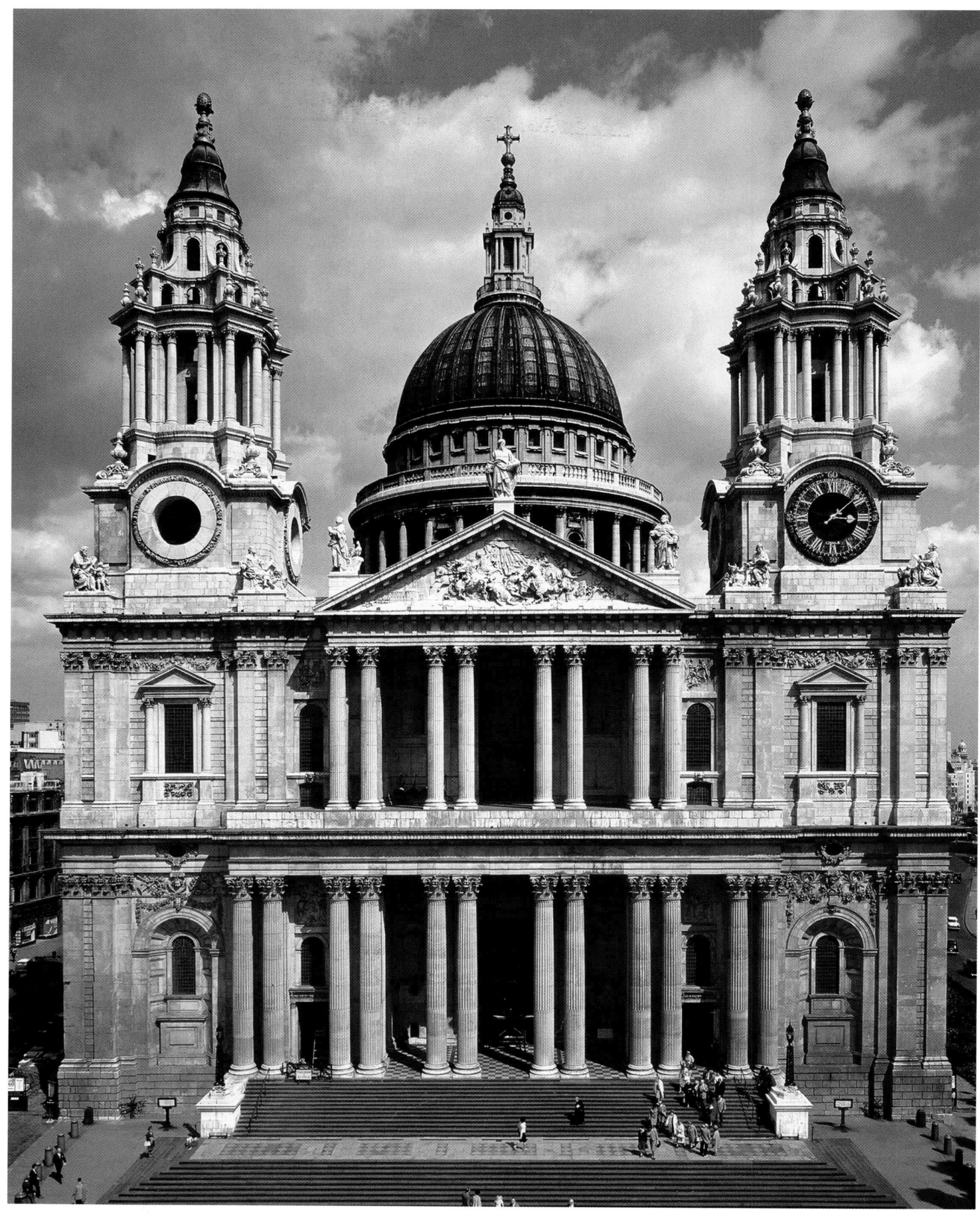

21.22   Sir Christopher Wren. Façade of St. Paul's cathedral, London. 1675–1710

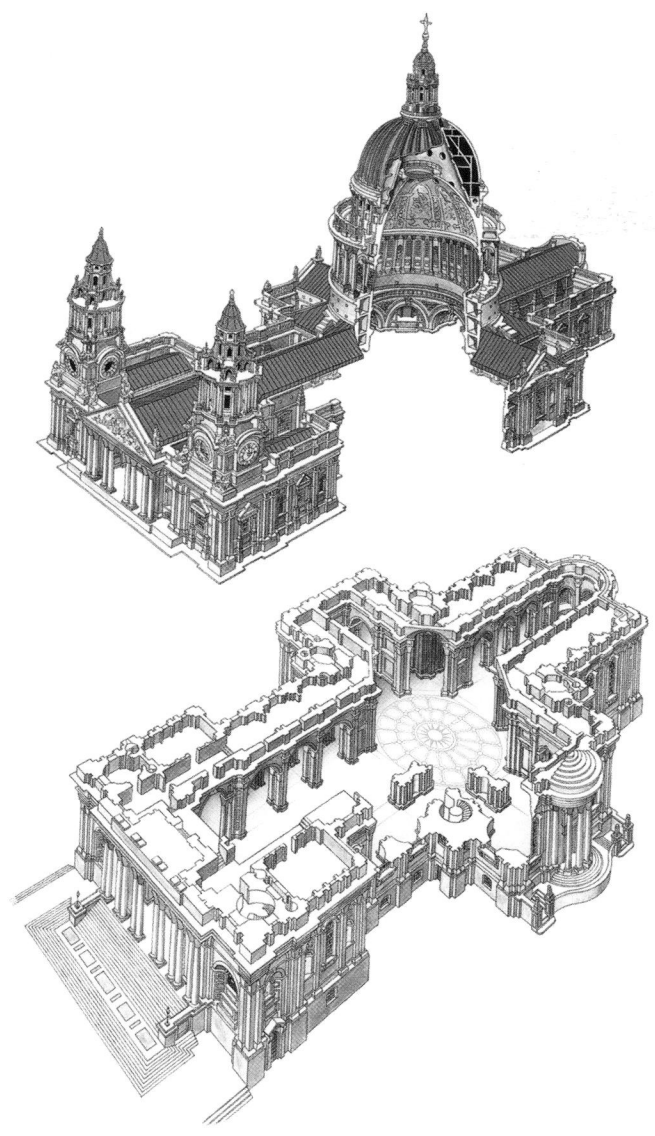

21.23 Cutaway 3D reconstruction of St. Paul's cathedral

XIV to design and complete the Louvre. The influence of this trip can be seen on the façade of St. Paul's (as well as in Wren's new street plans for London), where the impact of contemporary architecture in Paris can be discerned—the double columns of the Louvre and the three-part dome of Hardouin-Mansart's church of the Invalides. Unlike St. Peter's, St. Paul's dome (see fig. 21.22) rises high above the main body of the building and dominates the façade. It looks like a much-enlarged version of Bramante's Tempietto (see fig. 16.8). St. Paul's is an up-to-date Baroque design that reflects Wren's thorough knowledge of the Italian and French architecture of the day. Indeed, Wren believed that Paris provided "the best school of architecture in Europe," and he was equally affected by the Roman Baroque. The lantern and upper part of the bell towers suggest that he knew Borromini's Sant'Agnese in Piazza Navona (see fig. 19.23), probably from drawings or engravings. The present structure reflects not only the complex evolution of the design but also later changes made by the commission overseeing construction, which dismissed Wren in 1718.

For Wren as for Newton (who was appointed a commissioner of St. Paul's in 1697), mathematics and geometry were central to the new understanding of the universe and humanity's place in it. In Wren's *Five Tracts*, written toward the end of his life and presented by his son to the Royal Society in 1740, he stated that architecture must conform to "natural reason," which is the basis of eternal Beauty. In other words, architecture must use rational (that is, abstract) geometrical forms, such as the square and the

The Great Fire of London provided Wren with the opportunity to rebuild and reframe the city and its skyline.

A few years later he began his designs for the rebuilding of the almost totally destroyed St. Paul's cathedral (figs. **21.22**). Wren favored central-plan churches and originally conceived of St. Paul's in the shape of a Greek cross with a huge domed crossing, based on Michelangelo's plan of St. Peter's. This idea was also inspired by a previous design by Inigo Jones, who had been involved with the restoration of the original Gothic structure of St. Paul's earlier in the century. Wren's proposal was rejected by the church authorities, however, who favored a conventional basilica. In the end, the plan is that of a Latin cross (as can be seen in the cut-away reconstruction fig. **21.23**), the same followed for most Catholic churches, including St. Peter's. This was an ironic outcome given that the building program could have provided an opportunity to create a new vocabulary for the Protestant Church of England.

On his only journey abroad in 1665–66, Wren visited France and met with Bernini, who was in Paris at the invitation of Louis

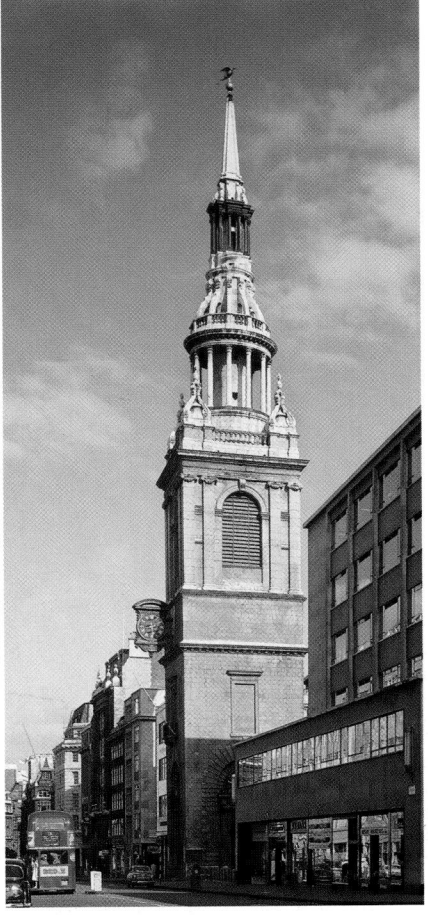

21.24 Sir Christopher Wren. Steeple of church of St. Mary-le-Bow, London. 1680

circle, as well as proportion, perspective, and harmony—but it must not sacrifice variety. Such rationality and diversity are clearly evident in Wren's design for St. Paul's.

Besides St. Paul's, Wren worked on 52 of the 87 damaged or destroyed churches, designing distinctive steeples for many of them. The steeple of the church of St. Mary-le-Bow (fig. 21.24) provides us with the most famous example. (It should be noted that many of these churches, including this one, were damaged during the bombing of London in World War II and have been reconstructed.) The steeple is exceptionally tall (225 feet high) and even today soars over surrounding buildings. The height is achieved through an unusual stacking of components: a two-story base (with arched entrance), plain attic, bell housing with paired pilasters, and a colonnaded temple surmounted by buttresses that support a lantern and obelisklike pinnacle as seen in the church of the Invalides. To indicate the church's dedication, Wren designed 12 "bows"—actually inverted brackets—at the base of the round temple. The result is an elaborate, multistoried steeple, Gothic in its verticality yet based on Classical motifs. Nothing like it had ever been seen before. Wren's innovations in this church and the others built after the Great Fire gave English Baroque church architecture its distinctive character.

John Vanbrugh and Nicholas Hawksmoor

The marriage of English, French, and Italian Baroque elements is still more evident in Blenheim Palace (fig. 21.25), a grandiose structure designed by Sir John Vanbrugh (1664–1726), a gifted amateur, with the aid of Nicholas Hawksmoor (1661–1736), Wren's most talented pupil. Although Blenheim is considered to be Vanbrugh's greatest work, the building was in fact completed by Hawksmoor; yet the architecture is seamless. Blenheim skillfully combines the massing of an English castle with the breadth of a country house, the rambling character of a French chateau such as Fontainebleau (see fig. 18.1), and a façade inspired by Sir Christopher Wren, Vanbrugh's rival. However, when Blenheim and its framing colonnade are compared with the piazza of St. Peter's (see fig. 19.14), Vanbrugh's design reveals itself to be even closer to Bernini. The main block uses a colossal Corinthian order to wed a temple portico with a Renaissance palace, while the wings rely on a low-slung Doric order. Such an eclectic approach, extreme even by the relaxed standards of the period, is maintained in the details. Vanbrugh, like Inigo Jones, had a strong interest in the theater and was a popular playwright. Blenheim's theatricality and massiveness make it a symbol of English power, a fitting, but more modest, counterpart to Versailles in both its structure and its grounds. Designed mainly for show and entertainment, it was presented by a grateful nation to the duke of Marlborough for his victories over French and German forces at the Battle of Blenheim in 1704, during the War of Spanish Succession.

The power and massiveness of Baroque architecture from Bernini to Blenheim changed the look of western Europe in the seventeenth century. It also provided the foundation for the art and architecture of the Rococo—both in continuation and in contrast.

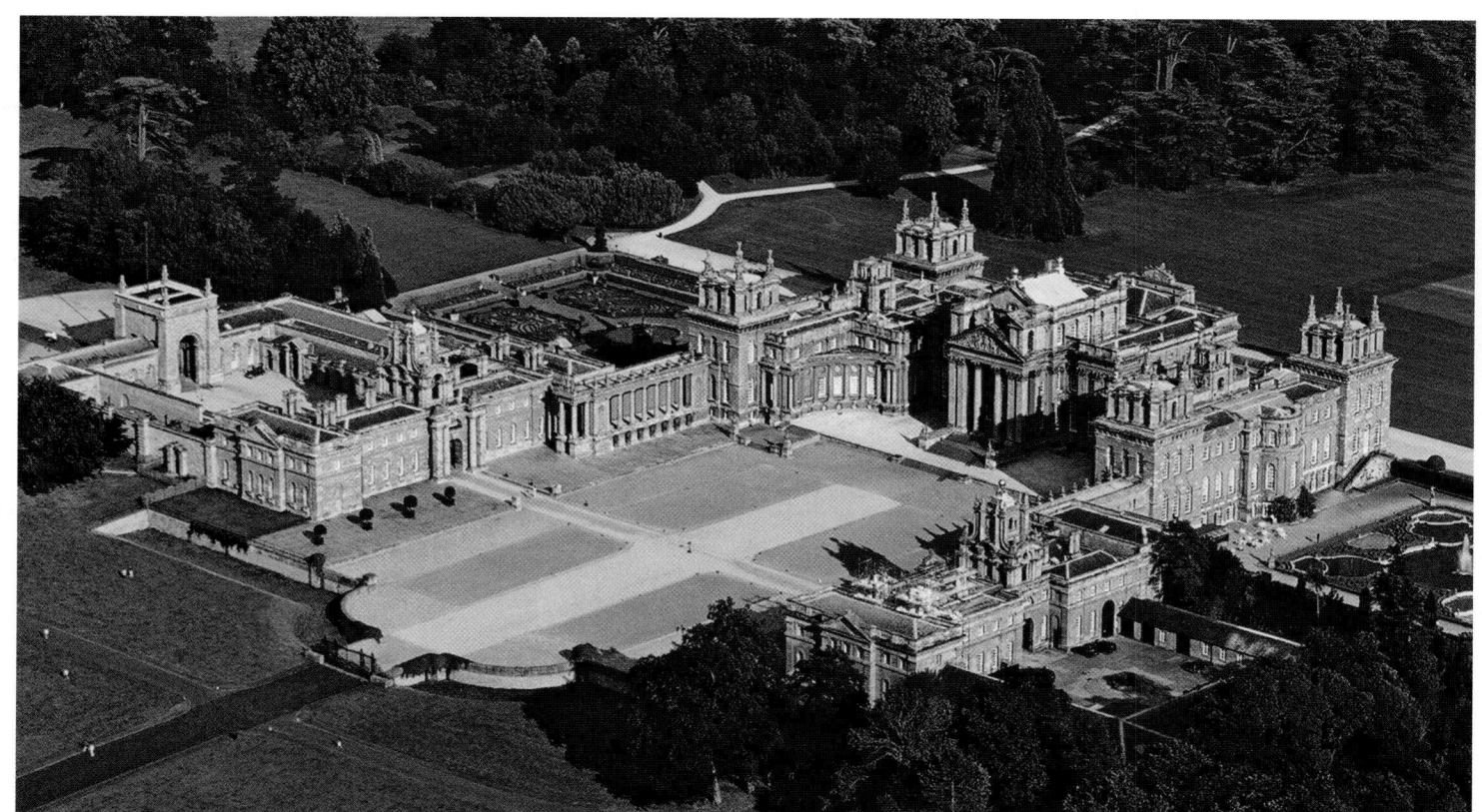

21.25 Sir John Vanbrugh and Nicholas Hawksmoor. Blenheim Palace, Woodstock, England. Begun 1705

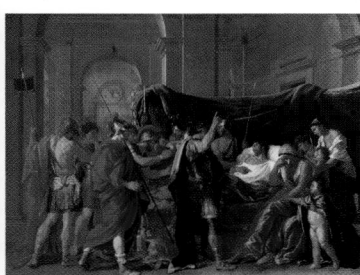

1627-28 Poussin's
Death of Germanicus

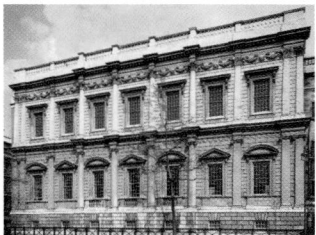

1619-22 Inigo Jones, Banqueting
House, Westminster

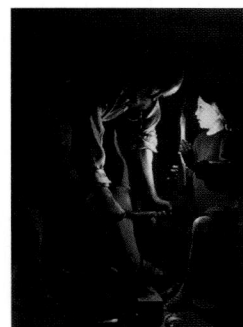

ca. 1642 La Tour,
Joseph the Carpenter

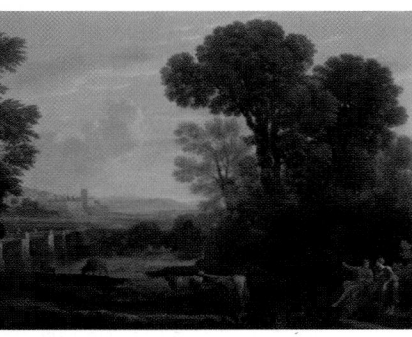

648 Claude's *A Pastoral Landscape*

1667-70 East front of
Louvre built

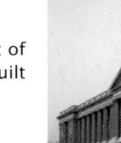

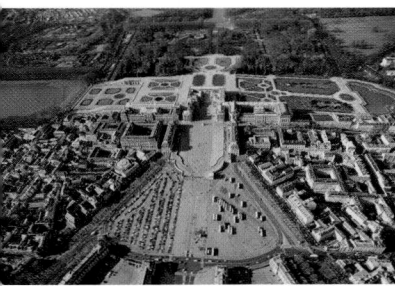

669-85 Palace of Versailles built

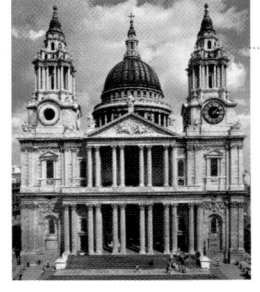

1675-1710
Sir Christopher Wren's
St. Paul's cathedral
built in London

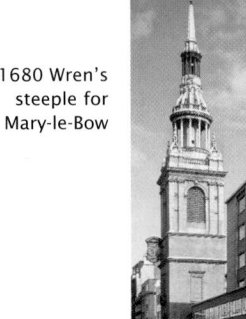

1680 Wren's
steeple for
Mary-le-Bow

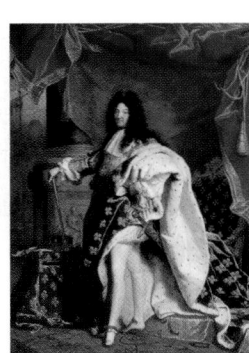

1701 Rigaud's
Portrait of Louis XIV

The Baroque
in France
and England

1610

1620

1623 Bernini's *David*

1630

1635 Van Dyck's *Portrait of Charles I on Horseback*
1638 Rubens's *The Garden of Love*
ca. 1638 Gentileschi's *Self-Portrait as the Allegory of Painting*

1640

◀ 1642-51 English civil war
◀ 1643 Louis XIV crowned king of France
1645 Bernini's *Ecstasy of St. Teresa*
◀ 1648 French Royal Academy of Painting and Sculpture founded
◀ 1649 Charles I of England beheaded
1650 Velázquez's *The Maids of Honor*

1650

1654 Rembrandt's *Bathsheba with King David's Letter*

1660

◀ 1664 New York City (formerly New Amsterdam) claimed for the English
◀ 1665-66 Bernini in Paris
◀ 1666 The Great Fire of London

1670

ca. 1670 Ruisdael's *Bleaching Grounds Near Haarlem*
1672-79 Gaulli's *Triumph of the Name of Jesus*

1680

◀ 1687 Newton formulates the law of gravity
◀ 1688 Glorious Revolution: William III of the Dutch Republic ruled England

1690

1700

1710

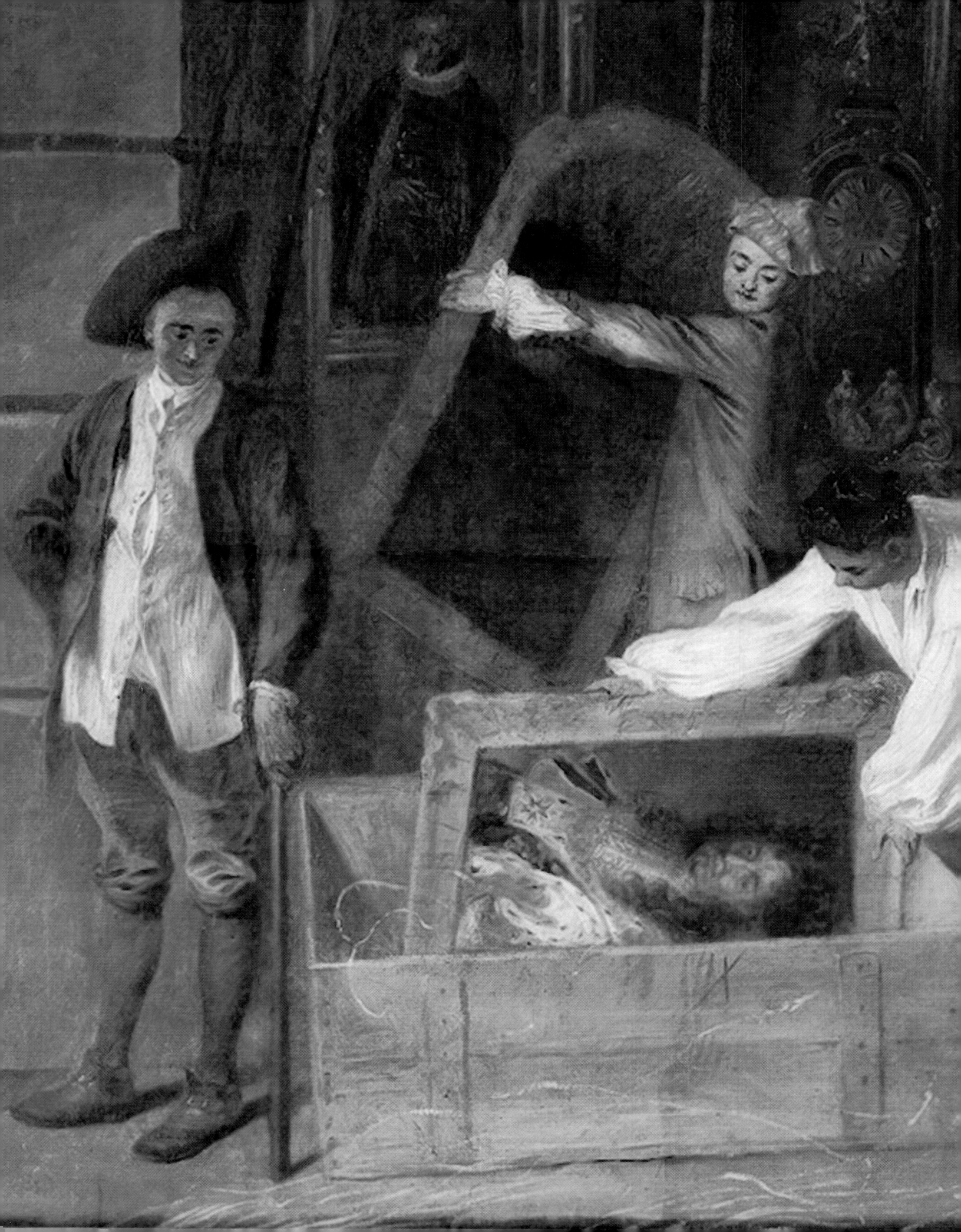

CHAPTER 22

The Rococo

N FRANCE THE ROCOCO STYLE IS LINKED WITH LOUIS XV (1710–1774) because it corresponds roughly to his lifetime—the heart of the eighteenth century. But the first signs of the Rococo style had appeared as much as 50 years before Louis's birth, at the height of the late seventeenth-century Baroque style, and it continued on through the excesses of the reign of Louis XVI (r. 1774–1792)

and his wife, Marie Antoinette, to the French Revolution of 1789. As noted by the philosopher François-Marie Arouet, better known by his pen name, Voltaire (1694–1778), the eighteenth century lived indebted to the past. In art, Poussin and Rubens cast long shadows over the period. The controversy between their followers, in turn, goes back much further to the debate between the supporters of Michelangelo and those of Titian over the merits of *disegno* (expressed through drawing or line) versus color (see page 584). In this sense, the Rococo, like the Baroque, still belongs to the Renaissance world.

Despite similarities between the Baroque and Rococo, a fundamental difference exists between the two styles. In a word, it is fantasy. If the Baroque presents theater on a grand scale, the Rococo stage is smaller and more intimate. Its artifice evokes an enchanted realm that presents a diversion from real life. In some ways, the Rococo in France manifests a shift in taste among aristocrats, who reasserted their power as patrons and began to favor stylized motifs drawn from nature and a more domestic art—private rather than public—with which to decorate their new homes in Paris.

The word Rococo fits well, for it implies both a natural quality and a sense of ornamentation well suited to court life. It was coined in the nineteenth century as a disparaging term, taken from the French word *rocaille* (meaning "pebble") and the Portuguese

barocco ("**baroque**"), to refer to what were then perceived as the excessively ornate tastes of the early eighteenth century. The word Rococo, then, in the first place refers to the playful, irregular pebbles, stones, and shells that decorated grottoes of Italian gardens and became the principal motifs of French interior designs.

Although sometimes viewed as the final phase of the Baroque, the Rococo asserted its own stylistic traits and represents a period of independent intense creative and intellectual activity. French artists continued to be trained in the tradition of the Royal Academy of Painting and Sculpture, which stressed working from live models, studying anatomy, and practicing perspective and proportion—lessons supplemented by lectures on the art of Raphael and Poussin. Yet artists also began exploring new subjects and treating old themes in new ways. The interest in the poetic genre of the pastoral, as practiced by Baroque artists including Claude (see pages 743–44), with subjects of love and loss, romantic trysts, and poetic musings took on growing importance in the eighteenth century. Patrons were increasingly taken with the notion of the "simple man" existing in an idealized nature. By way of response, the French Academy even established a new category to reflect this new interest, called the *fête galante*, a type of painting introduced by Jean-Antoine Watteau. The style celebrated the tradition of love and eroticism in art, and broadened the range of human emotion depicted there.

Although most directly associated with France, the Rococo exerted a wide geographical influence and affected the arts in most

Detail of figure 22.4, Jean-Antoine Watteau, *Gersaint's Signboard*

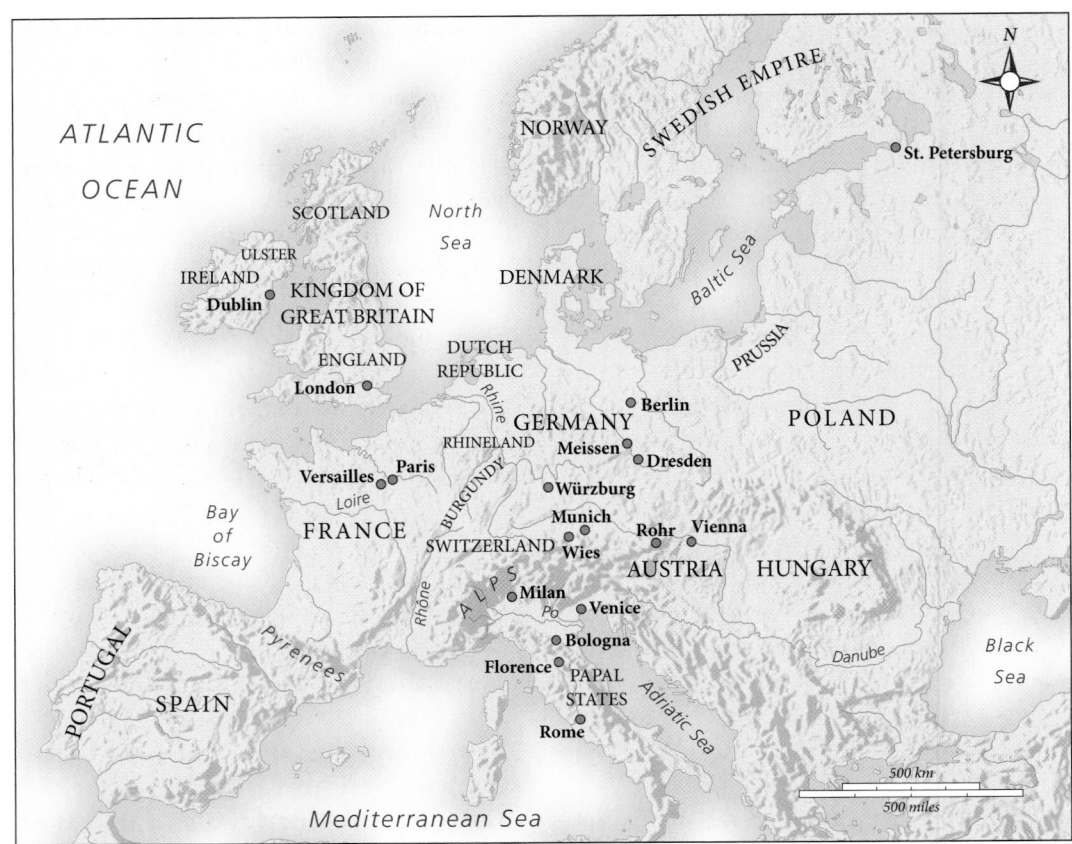

Map 22.1 Map of western Europe in the eighteenth century

of western and central Europe (map **22.1**). In Germany and Austria, the devastation of the Thirty Years' War (1618–1648) was followed in the eighteenth century by a period of rebuilding and a growth in the number of pilgrimage churches, whose architecture and decoration reflected both the transformation of the Baroque and the new Rococo style. Italian artists such as Tiepolo, with his assistants, painted ceiling frescoes in central European churches and palaces in this new elaborate and elegant style and produced similar works for their native city of Venice as well. There, Canaletto painted *vedute*, or scenes of the city, which provided foreign visitors with souvenirs of their Venetian stay.

European colonization of the New World continued in the eighteenth century. Armies battled to secure these distant lands, depleting their nations' treasuries but succeeding in sending back to their homelands exotic objects, including feathers, jewels, and metals that collectors coveted and artists used in the creation of new art. In the performing arts, the Venetian composer Antonio Vivaldi (1678–1741) and the German composer Johann Sebastian Bach (1685–1750) produced extraordinary music, and London became home to established theater, notably in Haymarket, Drury Lane, and Covent Garden.

FRANCE: THE RISE OF THE ROCOCO

After the death of Louis XIV in 1715, the nobility, formerly attached to the court at Versailles, found themselves freer from royal control. Louis XV, only five years old at his father's death, would not be crowned until 1723. This early period of the Rococo—between 1715 and 1723—is known as the Regency, so-called because France was governed by Louis's cousin Philip, duke of Orléans, who was acting as regent. With a nobleman in power, the aristocracy regained much of their former authority, and they abandoned the strict, demanding court life of Versailles. Rather than returning to their chateaux in the provinces, many chose to live in Paris, where they built elegant town houses with small intimate rooms. These *hotels particuliers* developed into social centers, known as **salons**, for intellectual gatherings. The rooms were decorated with paintings, porcelain, and small sculptures that created a lavish, light-hearted mood. Paintings, therefore, were just one element in the creation of an ambiance of refinement that permeated pre-revolutionary France. These paintings, as well as interior designs, would influence the decor of western and central Europe throughout the century.

Painting: Poussinistes versus Rubénistes

Toward the end of the seventeenth century, a dispute arose among the members of the French Academy, who formed themselves into two factions: the Poussinistes and the Rubénistes. Neither Poussin nor Rubens was still alive at the time of this debate, which focused on the issue of drawing versus color. French artists were familiar with Poussin's paintings, which had been sent from Rome back to Paris throughout his career, and they knew Rubens's work from the *Marie de' Medici Cycle* (see fig. 20.5) in the Luxembourg Palace. The conservative **Poussinistes** defended Poussin's view that line, which appealed to the mind, was superior to color, which appealed to the senses. The **Rubénistes** (many of whom were of Flemish descent) favored color, rather than drawing, as being truer to nature. They also pointed out that drawing, while admittedly based on reason, appealed only to the expert few, whereas color appealed to everyone. This argument had important implications. It suggested that the layperson should be the judge of artistic values, which challenged the Renaissance notion that painting, as a liberal art, could be appreciated only by the educated mind. The colorists eventually won the day, due in part to the popularity of painter Jean-Antoine Watteau.

JEAN-ANTOINE WATTEAU The greatest of the Rubénistes was Jean-Antoine Watteau (1684–1721). Born in Valenciennes, which until a few years before his birth had still been part of the Southern Netherlands, Watteau showed an affinity for the work of Rubens, the region's greatest artist. After moving to Paris in 1702, he made many drawings styled after Rubens's French

works, including the *Marie de' Medici Cycle* (see fig. 20.5). Watteau was a significant contributor to the new Rococo style as well as to the new subjects associated with it. His painted visions show idyllic images of aristocratic life, with elegant figures luxuriously dressed in shimmering pastel colors and set in dreamlike outdoor settings. He often seamlessly interweaves theater and real life in his works, incorporating well-known characters from the *commedia dell'arte* (a type of improvisational Italian theater) and creating stagelike settings that serve as backdrops for his actors. The carefully posed figures evoke forlorn love, regret, or nostalgia, and imbue the scenes with an air of melancholy. Such works became increasingly sought after by collectors in France, and the popularity of such themes soon spread throughout Europe.

Because Watteau's fantasies had little historical or mythological basis, his paintings broke many academic rules and did not conform to any established category. In order to be able to admit Watteau as a member, the French Academy had to create a new classification of painting, *fêtes galantes* (meaning "elegant fêtes" or "outdoor entertainments"). This category joined the hierarchy of genres that had been established in the seventeenth century by academy member André Félibien (1619–1695). The premier category was history painting, considered to be the highest form of art because it was thought to require the most imagination and was therefore the most difficult to execute. Next came portraits, landscapes, and finally still lifes. Watteau's reception piece for the French Academy, required when he became a member in 1712, was not delivered until five years later. The work, *A Pilgrimage to Cythera* (fig. **22.1**), is an evocation of love and includes elements of classical mythology. Cythera, which came to be viewed as an

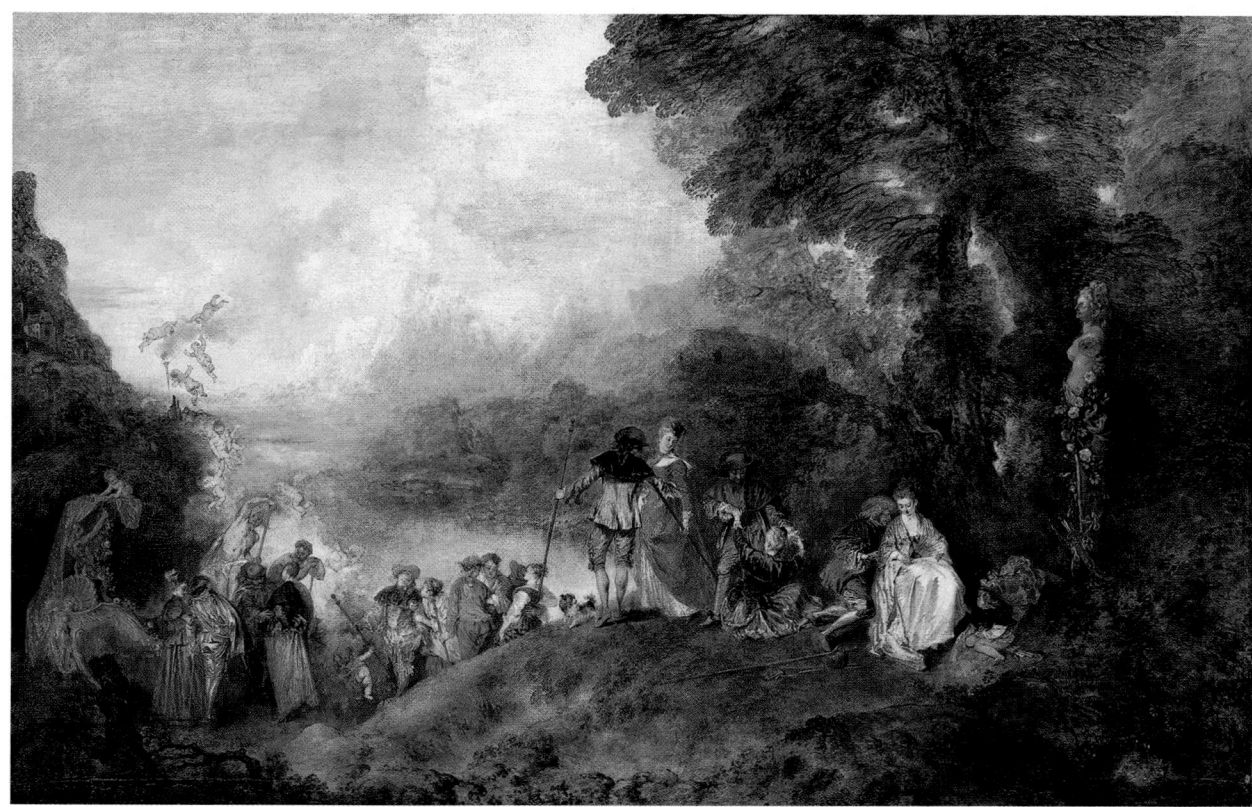

22.1 Jean-Antoine Watteau, *A Pilgrimage to Cythera*. 1717. Oil on canvas, 4'3" × 6'4½" (1.3 × 1.9 m). Musée du Louvre, Paris

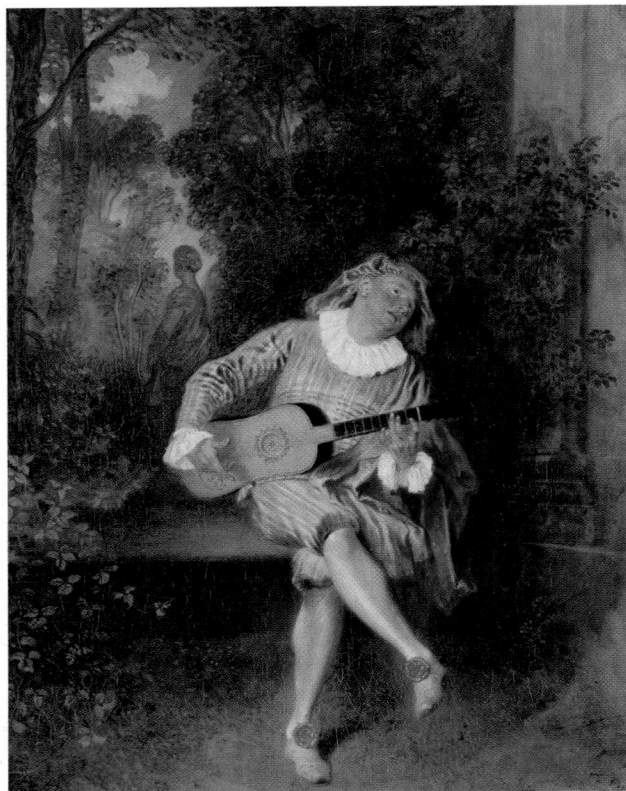

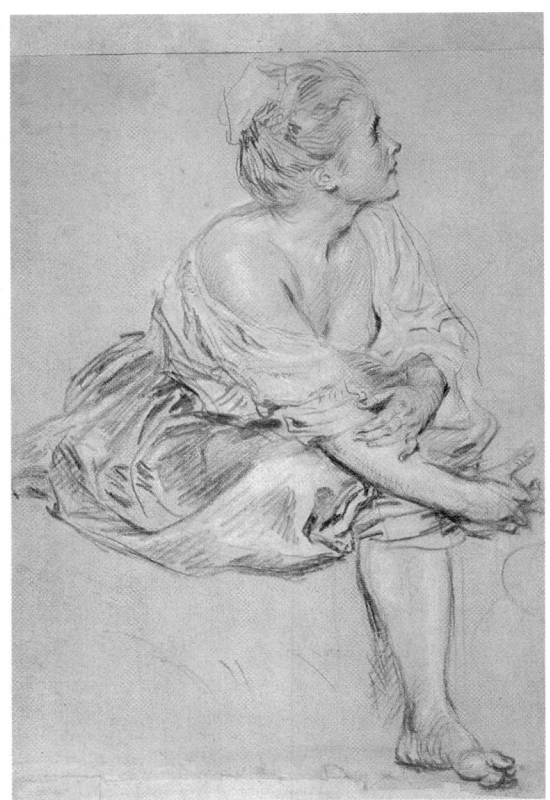

22.2   Jean-Antoine Watteau, *Mezzetin*. ca. 1718. Oil on canvas, 21¾ × 17" (55.3 × 43.2 cm). Metropolitan Museum of Art, New York. Munsey Fund, 1934 (34.138)

22.3   Jean-Antoine Watteau, *Seated Young Woman*. ca. 1716. Red, black, and white chalks on cream paper, 10 × 6¾" (25.5 × 17.1 cm). The Pierpont Morgan Library, New York

island of love, was one of the settings for the Greek myth of the birth of Aphrodite (Venus), who rose from the foam of the sea. The title suggests this traditional subject, but the painting was described in the French Academy records as a *fête galante*, perhaps the first use of this term.

Watteau has created a delightful yet slightly melancholic scene. It is unclear whether the couples are arriving at or leaving the island. The action unfolds in the foreground from right to left like a continuous narrative, which suggests that the figures may be about to board the boat. Two lovers remain engaged in their amorous tryst; behind them, another couple rises to follow a third pair down the hill as the reluctant young woman casts a longing look back at the goddess's sacred grove. Young couples, accompanied by swarms of cupids, pay homage to Venus, whose garlanded sculpture appears on the far right. The delicate colors—pale greens, blues, pinks, and roses—suggest the gentle nature of the lovers' relationships. The subtle gradations of tone showed Watteau's debt to Rubens and helped establish the supremacy of the Rubénistes.

As a fashionable conversation piece, the scene recalls the elegant figures in the courtly scenes of the Limbourg brothers' illuminations and those in Rubens's *The Garden of Love* (see figs. 14.3 and 20.6), but Watteau has altered the scale and added a touch of poignancy reminiscent of Giorgione and Titian. Watteau's figures are slim, graceful, and small in scale; they appear even

more so when compared with most Baroque imagery. The landscape does not overwhelm the scene but echoes its idyllic and somewhat elegiac mood. Watteau produces a sense of nostalgia, with its implications of longing and unrealized passion. This is achieved not only through the figures and their gentle touching and hesitancy, but also through the sympathetic parallel found in his landscape and the sculptures in it.

A similarly nostalgic atmosphere is evoked in Watteau's *Mezzetin* (fig. **22.2**), a painting of a stock figure from the *commedia dell'arte*, whose name means "half-measure" and who played the role of an amorous suitor. He sings a pleading love song while playing his guitar in a parklike setting decorated with a statue of a woman in the background. Scholars presume that he is playing his music to her. It has been suggested that the painting, which was owned by Watteau's friend Jean de Jullienne (the author of a biography of the artist; see *Primary Source*, page 766), may have related to Jean's courtship of his wife. The wistful musician strains to look up to the right, out of the picture. Yet the fantastical, delicately striped costume of rose, pale blue, and white, paired with yellow shoes and rose beret and cape, transforms the scene from melancholic to magical. The small, single figure in pastel colors, set amid this pale verdant setting, is typical of the Rococo in terms of spirit, figure type, and color of costume and setting.

As already stated, Watteau's use of color planted him firmly in the Rubéniste camp. However, his innovations and creativity as a

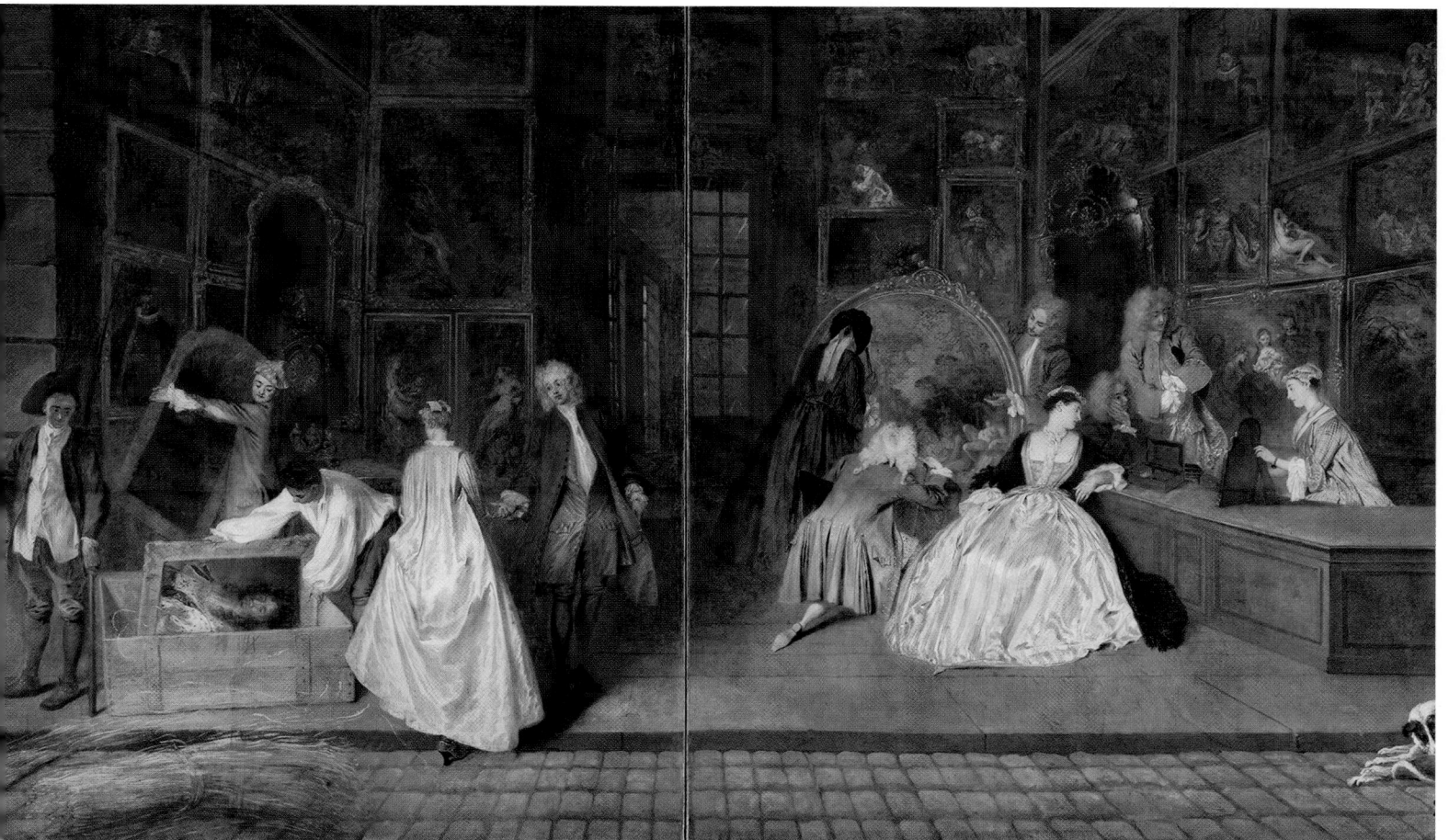

22.4 Jean-Antoine Watteau, *Gersaint's Signboard*. 1721. Oil on canvas, 5'5¼" × 10' (1.63 × 3.08 m). (Later cut in two pieces and then rejoined.) Schloss Charlottenburg, Staatliche Schlösser und Gärten, Berlin

draftsman (which would have implied a Poussiniste status) combined both color and line. (See *Materials and Techniques*, page 769.) Although previous artists, including Rubens, may have drawn with red or black chalk heightened with white, Watteau excelled in this technique, known as **trois crayons**. In *Seated Young Woman* (fig. **22.3**), he uses the three chalks to best effect, so that the red color that defines her body—legs, hands, parts of her face (lips, tip of nose), nape, breast—suggests a vivacious quality when contrasted against the black and white of her clothing, eyebrows, and upswept hair. The colors enliven and add a spontaneity to this life drawing. In numerous sketches, Watteau worked out poses, movements, gestures, and expressions, many of which (although apparently not this drawing) served as studies for figures in his paintings.

The same informality can be seen in one of Watteau's best-known works, *Gersaint's Signboard* or *The Shop Sign* (fig. **22.4** and page 760). Created to advertise the wares of his friend and art dealer Edmé Gersaint, the sign does not in fact show Gersaint's gallery. Gersaint wrote about this commission and indicated that it was made at Watteau's suggestion to allow him to "stretch his fingers" after he had returned from a trip to London. Watteau had been ill (he would die soon after of tuberculosis), and the implication was that the artist used this work as part of his hoped-for

convalescence. This account has since been disputed, but the work remains Watteau's last. The painting (originally arched at top) reportedly took only eight mornings to complete. It was meant to be exhibited outside but was shown for only 15 days (perhaps due to the weather or because it sold quickly). Gersaint reported that the painting attracted many artists as well as passersby who admired the natural, elegant poses of the figures— traits still admired today. The voluminous rose satin dress of the woman on the left, seen from the back, draws the eye; this figure is balanced by the languidly leaning woman on the right. Sophisticated and comfortable in the setting, the women are attended to by a solicitous staff as they admire paintings in the shop, arranged three to four high on the walls. Scholars do not believe these are copies of actual paintings but rather variants on Flemish and Venetian works, a theory that seems plausible when this work is compared with Jan Brueghel the Elder's *Allegory of Sight* and its real painting gallery (see fig. 20.10). The shop's stock also includes a variety of clocks and mirrors, which create an atmosphere of opulence and would remind the viewer of the world of the *ancien régime*. This association is supported by a portrait of Louis XIV based on Rigaud's (see fig. 21.10), seen on the left, which is being placed in a crate. Although on one level the presence of the king's image suggests the departure of the old (he had

Jean de Jullienne (1686–1767)

A Summary of the Life of Antoine Watteau, 1684–1721

Jullienne, a dyer and later the director of the Gobelin tapestry manufactory, was a lifelong friend of Watteau's and a collector of his works. At Watteau's death, he had all of the artist's drawings engraved and later did the same with his paintings, after buying many of them. His biography of the artist was first published in two volumes in 1726–28, along with 350 engravings after Watteau's paintings and drawings. Another two volumes followed.

Watteau, inclined more and more to study, and excited by the beauties of the gallery of this palace [the Luxembourg Palace] painted by Rubens, often went to study the color and the composition of this great master. This in a short time gave him a taste much more natural and very different from that which he had acquired with Gillot. …

Watteau was of medium height and weak constitution. He had a quick and penetrating mind and elevated sensibilities. He spoke little but well, and wrote likewise. He almost always meditated. A great admirer of nature and of all the masters who have copied her, assiduous work had made him a little melancholy. Cold and awkward in demeanor, which sometimes made him difficult to his friends and often to himself, he had no other fault than that of indifference and of a liking for change. It can be said that no painter ever had more fame than he during his life as well as after his death. His paintings which have risen to a very high price are today still eagerly sought after. They may be seen in Spain, in England, in Germany, in Prussia, in Italy, and in many places in France, especially in Paris. Also one must concede that there are no more agreeable pictures for small collections than his. They incorporate the correctness of drawing, truth of color and an inimitable delicacy of brushwork. He not only excelled in *gallant* and rustic compositions, but also in subjects of the army, of marches, and bivouacs of soldiers, whose simple and natural character makes this sort of pictures very precious. He even left a few historical pieces whose excellent taste shows well enough that he would have been equally successful in this genre if he had made it his principal objective.

Although Watteau's life was very short, the great number of his works could make one think that it was very long, whereas it only shows that he was very industrious. Indeed, even his hours of recreation and walking were never spent without his studying nature and drawing her in the situations in which she seemed to him most admirable.

The quantity of drawings produced by his study and which have been chose to be engraved and to form a separate work is a proof of this truth.

Source: *A Documentary History of Art*, II, ed. Elizabeth Gilmore Holt (Princeton, NJ: Princeton University Press, 1982)

died only a few years before in 1715), it is actually a pun on the name of the shop, Au Grand Monarque. Watteau's extraordinary abilities as a painter are apparent as he transforms this commercial venture into a sensitive work of sophistication and tender beauty.

FRANÇOIS BOUCHER Following the untimely death of Watteau in 1721, François Boucher (1703–1770) rose to prominence in French painting. Boucher built his reputation on his imaginative compositions, pastoral landscapes, and scenes of bourgeois daily life. He served as court painter to Madame de Pompadour (1721–1764), who has been called the "godmother of the Rococo." She was Louis XV's mistress, as well as his frequent political advisor and a major patron of the arts.

Boucher painted her portrait numerous times and with his 1756 life-size painting: *Portrait of Madame de Pompadour* (fig. 22.5) he established—even orchestrated—her self-fashioning as a *femme-savante*—an educated, cultured, accomplished woman who was also elegant, beautiful, and sophisticated. Born Jeanne-Antoinnette Poisson, she became the Royal Mistress (an actual title) in 1746. She had come from a nonaristocratic family, but because of her relationship with the king had been made a duchess, a marquis, and in the year this painting was done (when she was 35 years old and no longer his mistress, but lifelong confidante), she was named Lady-in-Waiting to the Queen, the highest nonroyal title at court. It has even been suggested that the background clock indicates the actual time she was given this title (although 8:20 is often the time set on old clocks for display purposes).

Madame de Pompadour is shown amid luxurious surroundings wearing a dress that signals opulence. The voluminous nature of the shimmering fabric, its turquoise blue color, and the intricacy of its bows and sewn roses also show off her small, narrow waist. She sits in her boudoir/library, which reflects the range of her accomplishments. The rosewood writing table set with pen, ink, and envelopes and the well-used book in her hand as well as the many in the cabinet and on the floor (truly an overflow) further confirm—even define—her level of literacy and qualify her as an educated woman. She also identified herself with Venus. The cupid by the clock, the roses on her dress and at her feet, and the pearl bracelets (pearls from the sea in which Venus was born) are each attributes that suggest her affinity with the love-goddess. She doesn't just sit on the day bed (*chaise longue*), but leans on its pillows, much like the languid female customer in Watteau's *Gersaint's Signboard* (see fig. 22.4). It suggests a relaxed, casual mood—the nonchalance of the leisurely aristocracy.

We can also compare the portrait to Rubens's life-size *Marchesa Brigida Spinola Doria* (see fig. 20.3), who strides from her palazzo. The Rococo portrait uses the play of diagonals (in her posture) and verticals (the pilasters, bookcase, and mirror's gilt frame) in much the same way Rubens uses these design elements. But the pastel colors, detail, and opulence anchor Boucher's painting in the Rococo world. The painting mirrors the luxurious and exuberant lifestyles of Madame de Pompadour, and the French aristocracy, for whom Boucher's works held great appeal.

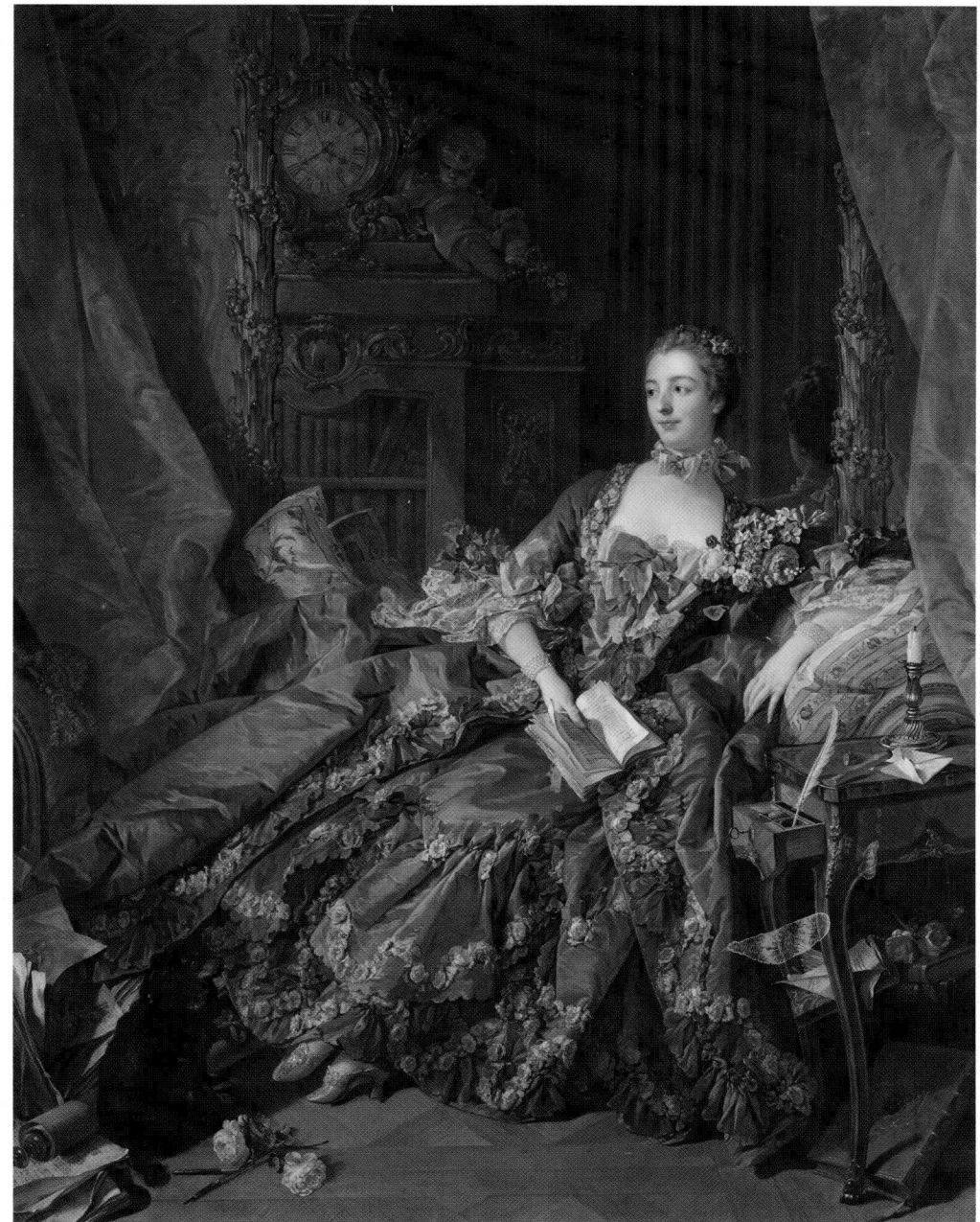

22.5 François Boucher, *Portrait of Madame de Pompadour*. 1756. Oil on canvas, 6'7⅛" × 5'1⅞" (2.01 × 1.57 m). Alte Pinakothek, Munich

JEAN-HONORÉ FRAGONARD Transforming fantasy into reality in paint was the forte of Jean-Honoré Fragonard (1732–1806)—or at least that was the reputation of this star pupil of Boucher. Also a brilliant colorist, Fragonard won the distinguished Rome Prize in 1752 and spent five years in Rome, beginning in 1756. Upon his return to Paris, he worked mostly for private collectors. Fantasy, flirtation, and licentiousness—in short, the spirit of the Rococo and the tradition that began with Watteau—coalesce in his painting *The Swing* (fig. **22.6**). An anecdote provides an interpretation of the painting. According to the story, another artist, Gabriel-François Doyen, was approached by the baron de Saint-Julien to paint his mistress "on a swing which a bishop is setting in motion. You will place me in a position in

which I can see the legs of the lovely child and even more if you wish to enliven the picture." Doyen declined the commission but directed it to Fragonard.

The painting, an example of an "intrigue," suggests a collusion in erotic fantasy between the artist and patron, with the clergy as their unwitting dupe. This "boudoir painting" (on the subject of sexual intimacy) offers the thrill of sexual opportunity and voyeurism but translated to a stagelike outdoor setting. The innocence of the public arena heightens the teasing quality of the motion of the swing toward the patron-viewer. The painted sculpture of a cupid to the left, holding a finger to his lips, suggests the conspiracy in the erotic escapade in which we as viewers are now participants. Fragonard used painted sculpture in many

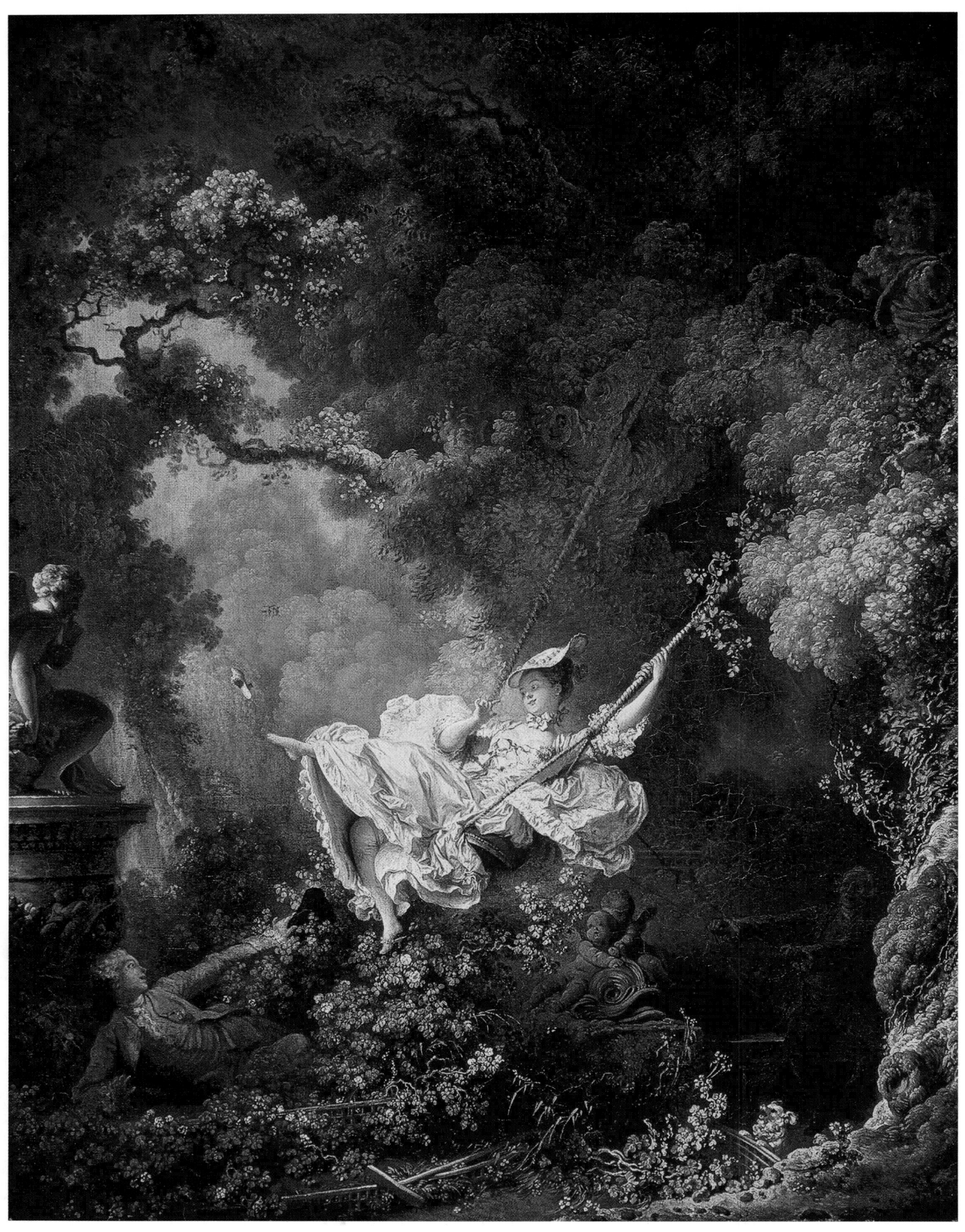

Pastel Painting

Pastels are a form of colored chalks or powders that are mixed (or filtered) with glue, juice, gum arabic, or whey and then rolled into a cylindrical tube. They are made and sold today in much the same way as they were in the Rococo era. The fillers and water enable the pastels to be applied smoothly. Pastels can be soft or hard, but they must be dried out to be packaged as pastel crayons.

Leonardo worked with pastels in the late fifteenth century (for his portrait of Isabella d'Este, 1499), but they really gained popularity among artists in the sixteenth century. Yet artists used them only to execute preparatory drawings, not to create finished works. In the eighteenth century, however, artists realized the possibilities of the medium and began making pastel paintings as finished works. Pastels, as well as the popular trois crayons technique (see fig. 22.3), had the advantage of suggesting both line and color at the same time. Since much debate arose in the late seventeenth and early eighteenth centuries about drawing (i.e., line) versus color, and since critics lauded artists such as Raphael who could combine both, the use of pastels may be considered a response to this issue. The lines could be smudged, built on each other, or hatched so that a single line could become an area of color and several together could create an even more vibrant patch.

Artists chose pastels primarily to make portraits, applying flicks of color to suggest animation, emotion, or expression and thus giving the sitter a more vivid and lifelike appearance. One of the greatest pastel portraitists is Rosalba Carriera (1675–1757), a Venetian artist known for revealing the psychological intensity of her sitters. Carriera was famous in her own time and had an international clientele of British, French, German, and Polish patrons. She became a member of the Academy of St. Luke of Rome in 1705, the Academy Clementina of Bologna in 1720, and the French Academy in 1721. Upon traveling to Paris in 1720–21, she was hailed by both the French court and French artists including Hyacinthe Rigaud (see Chapter 21) and Watteau (see pages 763–66), who made several drawings of her. The intimacy and

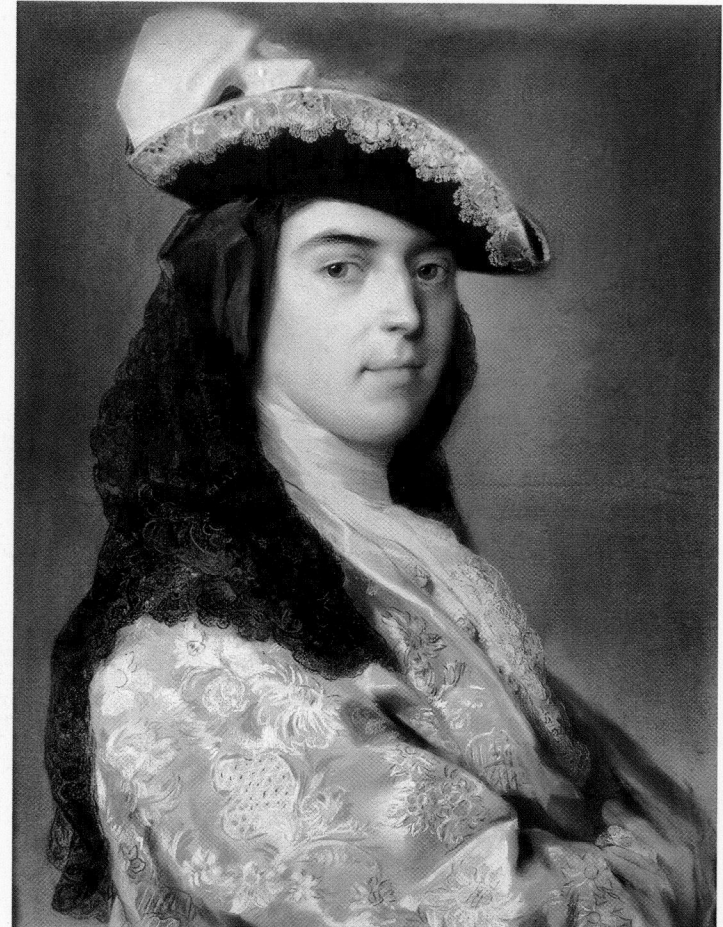

Rosalba Carriera, *Charles Sackville, Second Duke of Dorset*. ca. 1730. Pastel on paper, 25 × 19" (63.5 × 48.3 cm). Private collection

immediacy of her technique, combined with the indistinct, even hazy, quality of the resulting images, suggest a tantalizingly allusive sensuality, as seen in this portrait of the second duke of Dorset.

of his works to echo or reinforce their themes. Set in a lush arbor, this scene encapsulates the secluded "place of love" that provides secrecy for this erotic encounter. The dense and overgrown landscape, lit by radiant sunlight, suggests the warmth of spring or summer and their overtones of sexuality and fertility. The glowing pastel colors create an otherworldly haze that enhances the sensuality of this fantasy spun by Fragonard.

Fragonard epitomized the sensuality of the Rococo, and his works are marked by an extraordinary virtuosity in their use of color. His paintings range from erotic fantasies to intimate studies and pastoral landscapes, subjects that provided a distraction for his wealthy patrons.

22.6   Jean-Honoré Fragonard, *The Swing*. 1767. Oil on canvas, 32⅝ × 26" (82.9 × 66.0 cm). Wallace Collection, London

JEAN-SIMÉON CHARDIN   Raised in a bourgeois household, Jean-Siméon Chardin (1699–1779) rose to become treasurer of the French Academy as well as its *tapissier*, responsible for installing the paintings at its exhibitions. Chardin's expertise in still life as well as in genre painting was indebted to the many Dutch and Flemish seventeenth-century paintings then in France (many of these small, highly portable paintings were sold at auction). Indeed, some of Chardin's own patrons were important collectors of seventeenth-century Dutch and Flemish art.

To Chardin's patrons, members of the rising bourgeoisie in France, such genre scenes and domestic still lifes proclaimed the virtues of hard work, frugality, honesty, and devotion to family. Chardin's quiet household scenes struck a chord with his sophisticated patrons, and demand for them was so high that he often painted copies of his most popular subjects. His paintings were also reproduced as prints, making them affordable to those who lacked the means to buy an original work.

Soap Bubbles (fig. **22.7**) is very much an outgrowth of Dutch genre painting and the vanitas symbols frequently seen in the still-life tradition. The bubble, intact only for a moment, symbolizes the brevity of life, which serves as one of the painting's underlying themes. However, Chardin has chosen a charming, endearing way to send his message to a viewer. He presents two children: an older boy who is possibly instructing a younger one, who eagerly looks on—play was a common theme in Chardin's work. Unlike most Rococo painting, the figures in this work are half-length, life-size rather than diminutive, and their scale affects our understanding of the reality, reinforcing the possibility that we could encounter a similar scene in our own world.

Back from the Market (fig. **22.8**) shows life in a Parisian bourgeois household. We see the large room but cannot ignore the potentially amorous scene taking place outside on the left. The maid's posture, leaning to her left with her shoes pointed to the right, suggests informality (we have seen this leaning in figs. 22.4 and 22.5). The beauty hidden in everyday life and a clear sense of spatial order beg comparison with the Dutch artist Jan Vermeer (see fig. 20.35). However, Chardin's brushwork is soft at the edges and suggests objects rather than defines them. In the still-life

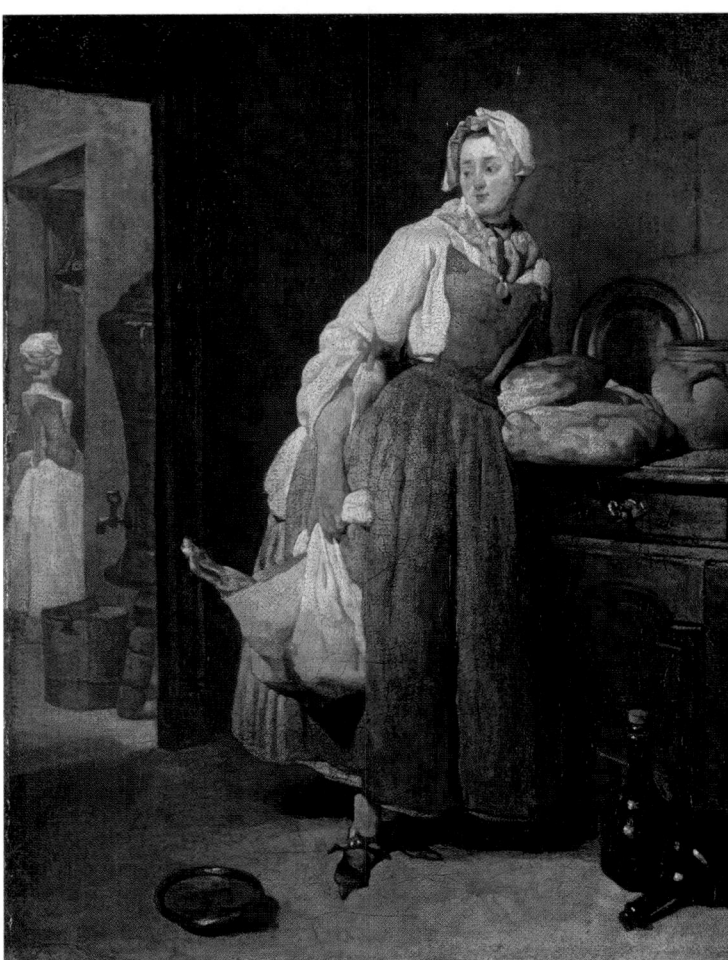

22.8 Jean-Siméon Chardin, *Back from the Market*. 1739. Oil on canvas, 18½ × 14¾" (47 × 37.5 cm). Musée du Louvre, Paris

elements in the painting (the floured loaves of bread are especially notable), he summarizes forms and subtly alters their appearance and texture. Thus, one can understand the appeal of pastel painting (see *Materials and Techniques*, page 769) as Chardin often turned to this medium late in life, when his eyes were failing him.

Still-life painting was important to Chardin (see page 769) as it was as a still-life artist (considered the lowest rank of painting) that he was admitted to the French Academy. But he raised this form of painting in its simplicity and elegance to a newly appreciated level. *The Brioche* (*The Dessert*), named for the center roll, displays a variety of textures set on a ledge that we view at eye level (fig. **22.9**). We can compare Chardin's painting to Heda's *Still Life with Oysters, Roemer, a Lemon, and a Silver Bowl* (see fig. 20.31). Texture in the Dutch work is created by the defined, sparkling edges of the broken glass, the shine of the silver, and the distinct reflections in the roemer. In Chardin's work, we are mostly impressed by the blurring of the edges: on the brioche topped with an orange branch, in the difficult-to-discern facets of the glass liqueur bottle on the right, and in the gilt-edged Meissen tureen on the left. Chardin used contemporary ceramics and porcelain in his paintings: German Meissen porcelain (celebrated French Sèvres would be its rival later in the century) was produced

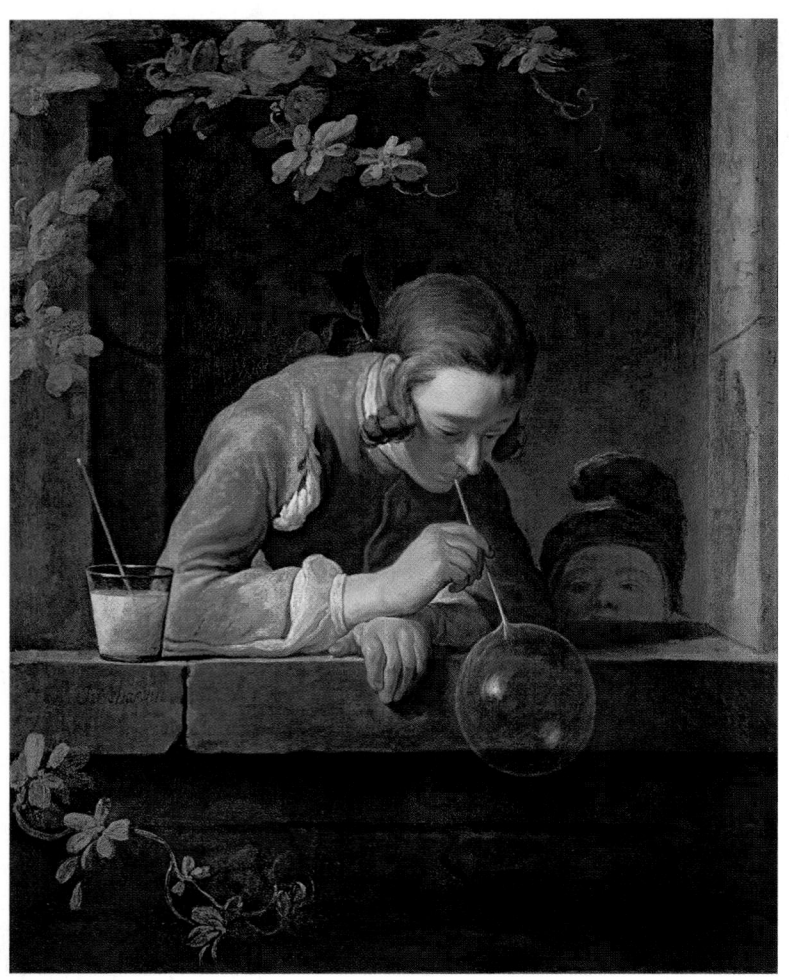

22.7 Jean-Siméon Chardin, *Soap Bubbles*. ca. 1733. Oil on canvas, 36⅝ × 29⅜" (93 × 74.6 cm). The National Gallery of Art, Washington, D.C. Gift of Mrs. John W. Simpson (1942.5.1)

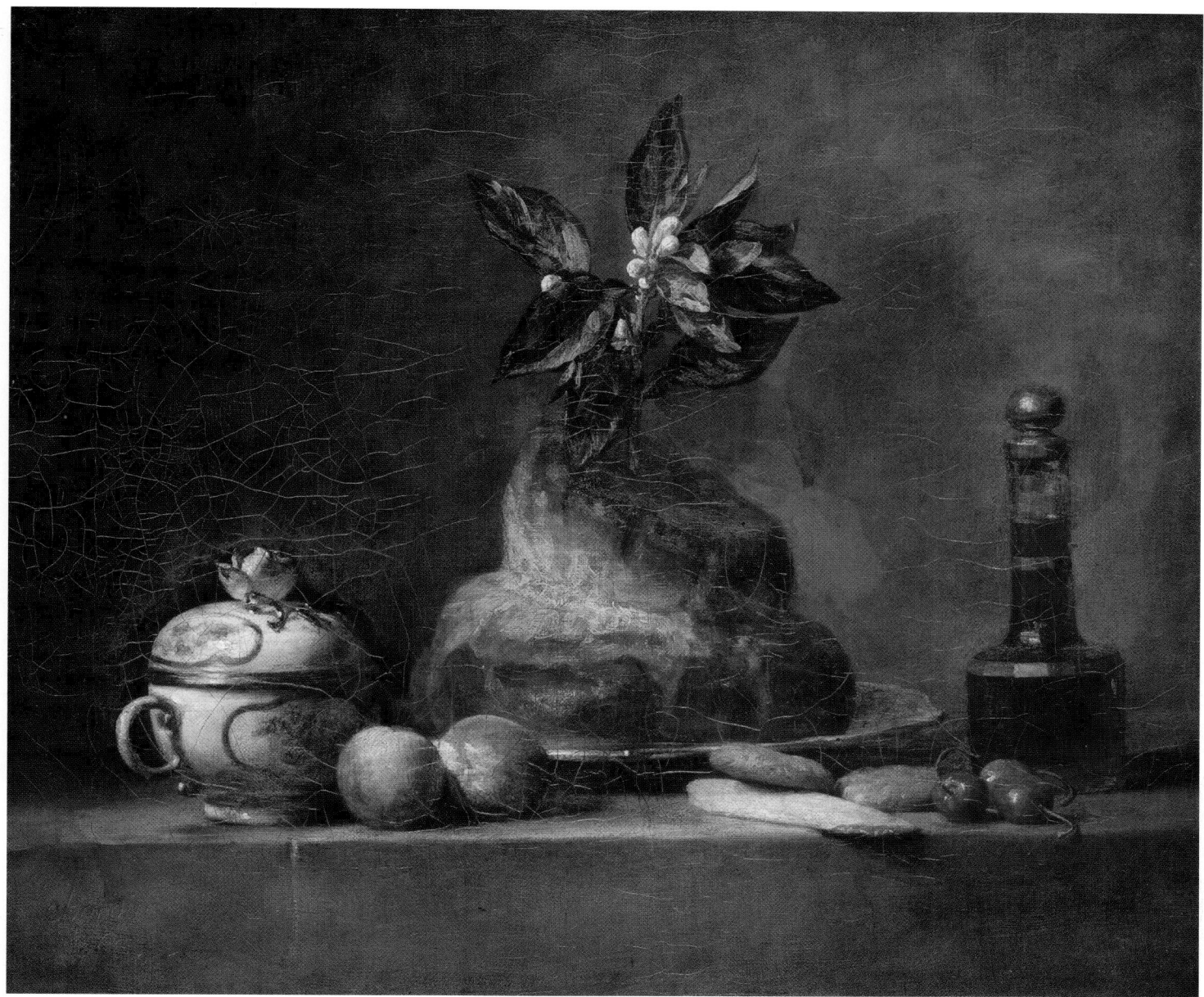

22.9   Jean-Siméon Chardin, *The Brioche (The Dessert)*. 1763. Oil on canvas, 18½ × 22" (47 × 56 cm). Musée du Louvre, Paris

in imitation of Chinese porcelain. In fact, in the eighteenth century, the tureen in the painting was described as Chinese (although, as is clear from the painted images on it, it is not).

Chinoiserie

Chinese wares—in the Netherlands spurred on by the Dutch East India Company (see page 700), in France, and throughout Europe—were wildly popular. As such, the Chinese also began making pieces for export to fulfill the desires of the European market, and European manufacturers developed products and designs in imitation of the Chinese. These items in Chinese style were known as **Chinoiserie** (*chinois* means "Chinese" in French) and belonged mostly to the decorative arts: silk, furniture (desks, cabinets), screens, garden décor, lacquerware, and of course,

porcelain. But perhaps the most significant Chinese export to Europe was tea, which first came to Europe through the Dutch East India Company in 1610.

Drinking tea changed both the daily routines of individuals and the economies of nations. It was only in the eighteenth century that tea sets (teapots, cups and saucers, sugar bowls, creamers and the utensils for them) in a variety of materials (porcelain, silver, pewter) were first created. Jean-Étienne Liotard's (1702–1789) *Still Life Tea Set* (fig. **22.10**) is an example of several levels of Chinoiserie—the tea, the porcelain Chinese-style tea set with images of Chinese figures and decoration (an example of Chinese export ware), all assembled on a lacquer tray.

Both Watteau and Boucher created designs in Chinoiserie for various patrons in prints, lacquerware and tapestry designs. Nicolas Pineau (see fig. 22.11), who designed salon interiors, also

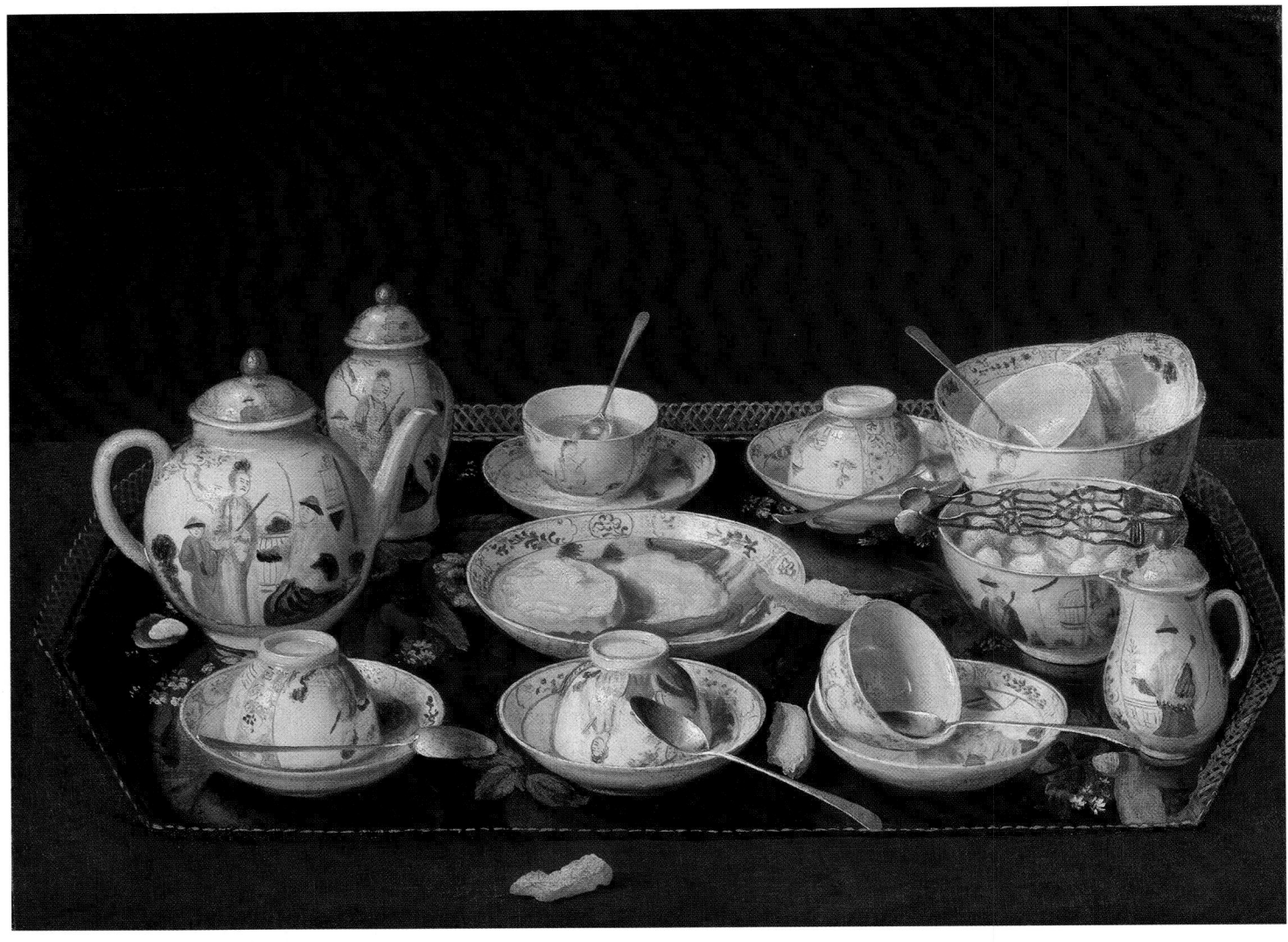

22.10 Jean-Étienne Liotard, *Still-Life: Tea Set*. ca. 1781–83. Oil on canvas mounted on board, 14⅞ × 20⅓" (37.8 × 51.6 cm). The J. Paul Getty Museum, Los Angeles

used Chinoiserie elements in his work. This was a style that artists could adapt to their own ends.

The French Rococo Interior

It is in the intimate spaces of early eighteenth-century interiors that the full elegance and charm of the Rococo are shown. The Parisian *hôtels* of the dispersed nobility soon developed into social centers. The field of "design for private living" took on new importance at this time. Because these city sites were usually cramped and irregular, they offered few opportunities for impressive exteriors. Hence, the layout and décor of the rooms became the architects' main concern. The *hôtels* demanded an intimate style of interior decoration that gave full scope to individual fancy, uninhibited by the classicism seen in the monumentality of Versailles.

Crucial to the development of French décor was the new importance assigned to interior designers. Their engravings established new standards of design that were expected to be followed by artisans, who thereby lost much of their independence. Designers also collaborated with architects, who became more involved in interior decoration. Along with sculptors, who often created the architectural ornamentation, and painters, architects helped to raise the decorative arts to the level of the fine arts, thus establishing a tradition that continues today. The decorative and fine arts were most clearly joined in furniture. Gilt, metals, and enamels were often applied to interior décor to create the feathery ornamentation associated with the Rococo. Many of these artisans came originally from the Netherlands, Germany, and Italy.

The decorative arts played a unique role during the Rococo. *Hôtel* interiors were more than collections of objects: They were total environments assembled with extraordinary care by discerning collectors and the talented architects, sculptors, decorators, and dealers who catered to their exacting taste. A room, like an item of furniture, could require the services of a wide variety of artisans: cabinetmakers, wood carvers, gold- and silversmiths, upholsterers, and porcelain makers. The products of these artisans were set in white rooms decorated with gilt molding and pastel-colored Rococo paintings, the overall effect being enhanced by mirrors and lighting. The artisans involved were dedicated to producing an ensemble, even though each craft was, by tradition, a separate specialty subject to strict regulations. Together they fueled the insatiable hunger for novelty that swept the aristocracy and haute bourgeoisie of Europe.

NICOLAS PINEAU Few of these Rococo rooms survive intact; the vast majority have been destroyed or greatly changed, or the objects and decorations have been dispersed. Even so, we can get a good idea of their appearance through the reconstruction of one such room (perhaps from the ground floor behind the garden elevation) from the Hôtel de Varengeville, Paris (fig. **22.11**), designed about 1735 by Nicolas Pineau (1684–1754) for the duchesse de Villars. Pineau had spent 14 years in Russia collaborating with other French craftsmen on Peter the Great's elaborate new city of

St. Petersburg. His room for the duchess incorporates many contemporary Rococo features. To create a sumptuous effect, the white walls are encrusted with gilded stucco ornamentation in arabesques, C-scallops, S-scrolls, fantastic birds, bat's wings, and acanthus foliage sprays. The elaborately carved furniture is embellished with gilt bronze. Everything swims in a sea of swirling patterns united by perhaps the most sophisticated sense of design and materials the world has ever known. No clear distinction exists between decoration and function in the richly designed fireplace and the opulent chandelier. The paintings, too, have been completely integrated into the decorative scheme, with works by Boucher set over two of the doors (such paintings even established a new type of work called "overdoors"). Similarly elaborate, gilt-decorated white walls became the hallmark of the Rococo, not only in its private spaces, but in church and palace decoration as well, especially in central Europe (see pages 776–77).

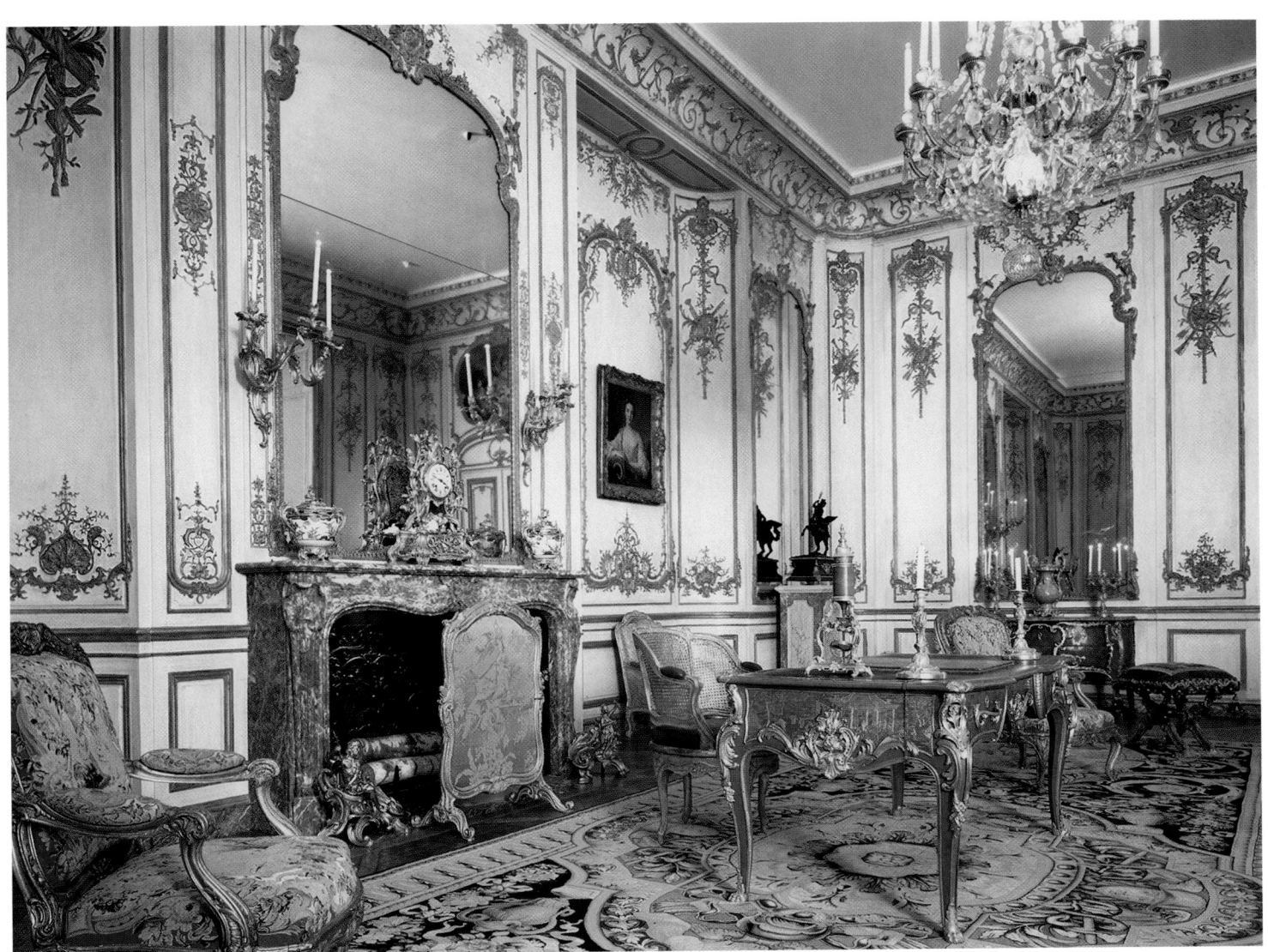

22.11 Nicolas Pineau. Room in the Hôtel de Varengeville, 217 Boulevard St.-Germain, Paris. ca. 1735. (The chimneypiece on the wall at left is not original to room.) Original paneling probably commissioned by Pineau. Carved, painted, and gilded oak, 18'3¾" × 40'6½" × 23'½" (5.58 × 12.35 × 7.07 m). Photographed about 1995. Metropolitan Museum of Art, New York. Purchase, Mr. and Mrs. Charles Wrightsman Gift, 1963. (63.228.1)

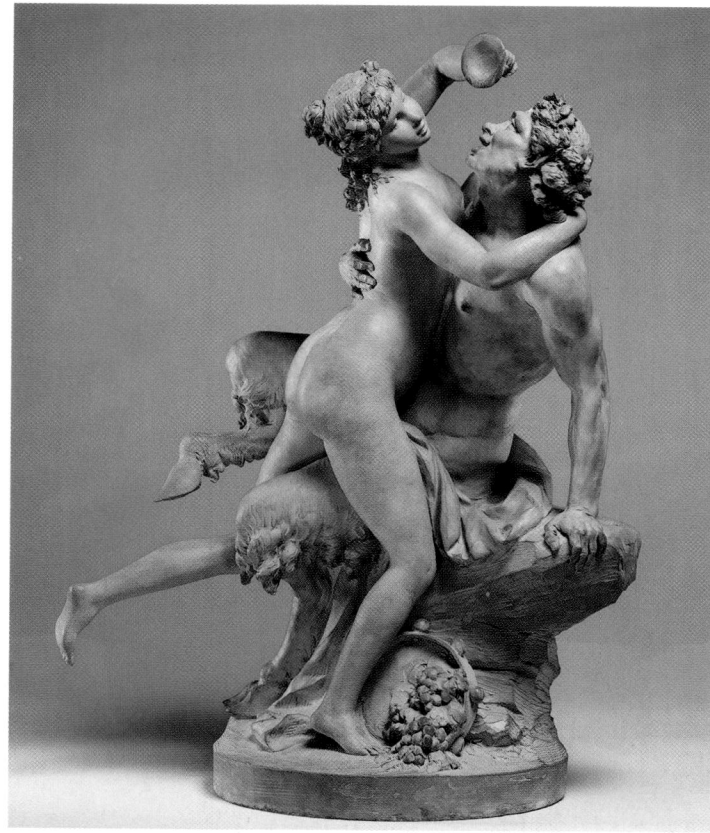

22.12 Clodion, *Nymph and Satyr Carousing*. ca. 1780. Terra cotta, height 23¼" (59 cm). Metropolitan Museum of Art, New York. Bequest of Benjamin Altman, 1913. (14.40.687)

CLODION AND FRENCH ROCOCO SCULPTURE Used to adorn interiors, French Rococo sculpture took many forms and was designed to be viewed at close range. A typical example is the small *Nymph and Satyr Carousing* (fig. **22.12**) by Claude Michel (1738–1814), known as Clodion, a successful sculptor of the Rococo period who later effectively adapted his style to the more austere Neoclassical manner. Clodion began his studies at Versailles and won the prestigious Rome Prize. His greatest contribution to the Rococo was transforming the fantasies of Boucher and Fragonard into three-dimensional works of coquettish eroticism. The open and airy composition of this sculpture is related to a work by Bernini, but its miniature scale produces a more intimate and sensual effect. Although Clodion undertook several large sculptural cycles in marble, he reigned supreme in the more intimate medium of terra cotta.

THE ROCOCO IN WESTERN EUROPE OUTSIDE OF FRANCE

The French Rococo exerted a major influence across the English Channel. There, foreign artists—Holbein, Gentileschi, Rubens, Van Dyck—had flourished for generations, and the works of Dutch and Italian artists were widely collected. Although foreign artists still reigned supreme, the Rococo helped to bring about the first school of English painting since the Middle Ages that had more than local importance. As we have seen with the works of Chardin and Rubens, among others, printmaking was used not just to create new compositions but to disseminate painted works, giving them a larger audience and broader appeal. This medium proved most beneficial for genre paintings and landscapes, areas of great interest to, and increasingly collected by, the British public.

William Hogarth and the Narrative

William Hogarth (1697–1764) was the first major native English artist since Nicholas Hilliard (see fig. 18.25). He began his career as an engraver and soon took up painting. Although he must have learned lessons about color and brushwork from Venetian and French examples, as well as from Van Dyck, his work is entirely original. He made his mark in the 1730s with a new kind of painting, which he described as "modern moral subjects … similar to representations on the stage." Hogarth's work is in the same vein as John Gay's *The Beggar's Opera* of 1728, a biting social and political stage satire that Hogarth illustrated in one of his paintings. Hogarth's morality paintings teach, by bad example, solid middle-class virtues and reflect the desire for a return to simpler times and values. They proved enormously popular among the newly prosperous middle class in England.

In the scene reproduced here both as a painting and an engraving (figs. **22.13** and **22.14**), taken from his *The Rake's Progress* series, the artist shows a young man, Tom Rakewell, who has just received an inheritance and is now spending his fortune by overindulging in wine and women. He is seen disheveled and drunk. (Later in the series, the rogue enters into a marriage of convenience, is arrested for debt, turns to gambling, goes to debtors' prison, and dies in Bedlam, the London insane asylum.) This scene is set in a famous London brothel, The Rose Tavern. The young woman adjusting her shoe in the foreground is a stripper preparing for a vulgar dance involving the mirrorlike silver plate and the candle behind her; to the left, a chamber pot spills its foul contents over a chicken dish; and in the background, a singer holds sheet music for a bawdy song of the day. A candle held to a map on the back wall indicates that Tom's world will burn—as did Nero's, the only Roman emperor whose image is not defaced in the paintings in the room. The scene is full of witty visual clues to its overall meaning, which the viewer would discover little by little, adding a comic element to this satire of social evils.

Hogarth combines Watteau's sparkling color with Jacob Jordaens's or Jan Steen's emphasis on narrative (see figs. 22.1, 20.9, and 20.33). Hogarth's moral narratives are so entertaining and popular that viewers can enjoy his sermon without being overwhelmed by the stern message. Of course, the "progress" of the rake was really his downfall. This series was the counterpart to Hogarth's earlier set, *The Harlot's Progress* (1731), where an innocent girl, Molly Hackabout, upon comes to the city and is tricked into becoming a prostitute, which leads to her demise.

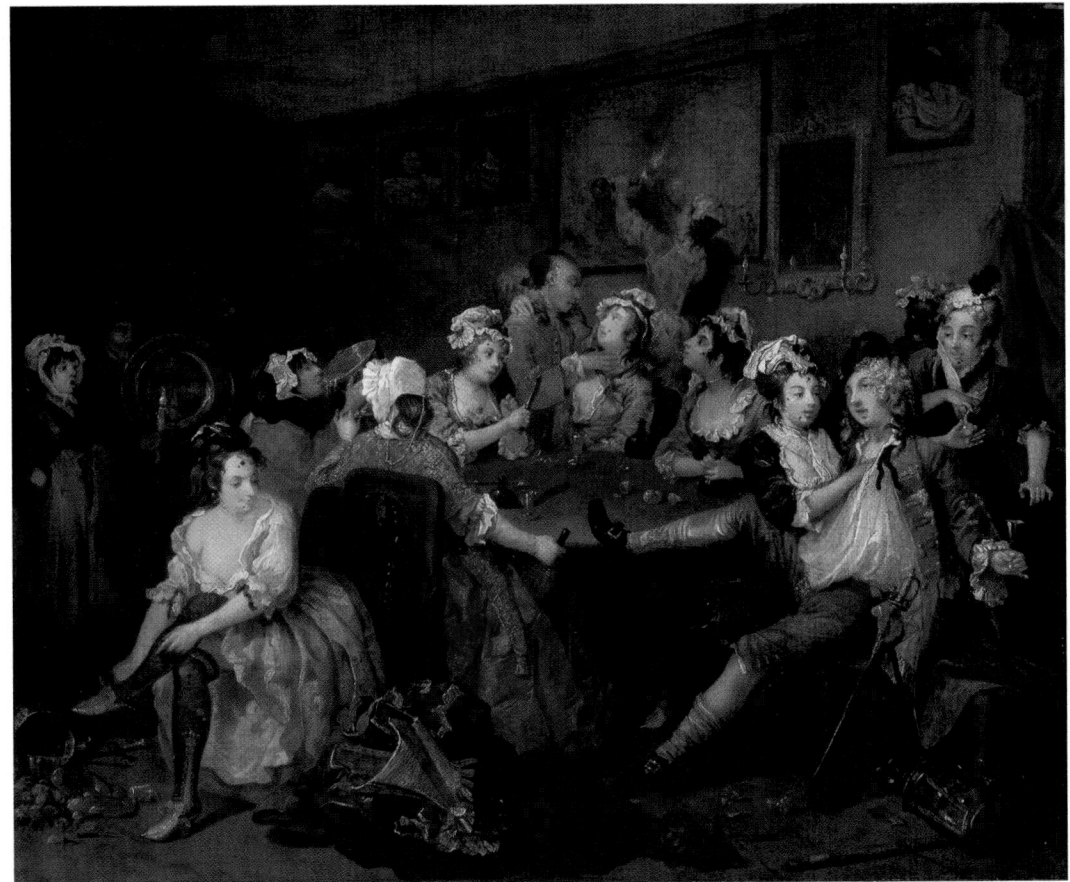

22.13   William Hogarth, *The Orgy*, scene III of *The Rake's Progress*. ca. 1734.
Oil on canvas, 24½ × 29½" (62.2 × 74.9 cm). Sir John Soane's Museum, London

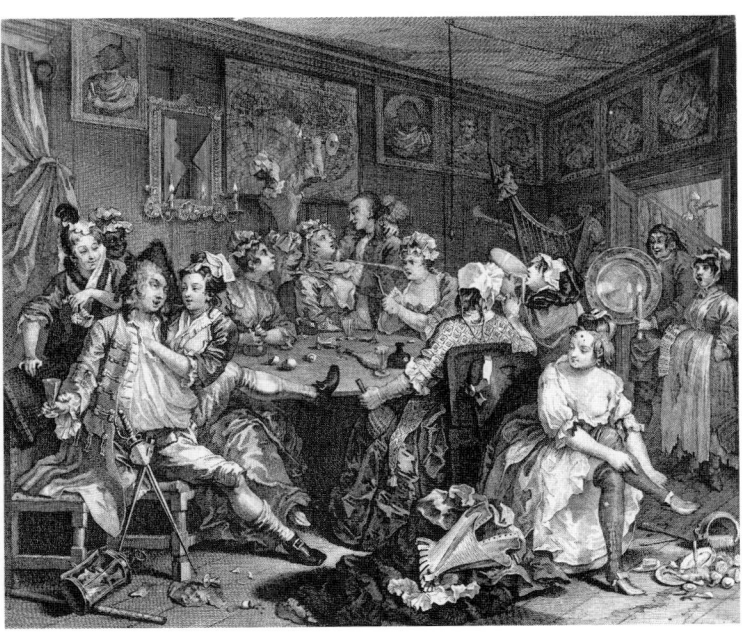

22.14   William Hogarth, *He Revels (The Orgy)*, scene III of
The Rake's Progress. 1735. Engraving. Metropolitan Museum of Art, New
York. Harris Brisbane Dick Fund, 1932. (32.35(30))

After executing the paintings, Hogarth made prints to sell
to the public. For *The Rake's Progress*, he made the prints only
after the passing of the Engraver's Copyright Act of 1735 which
provided protection from the many imitators who sought to
copy his works (see *The Art Historian's Lens*, page 747 for other
artists' concerns about counterfeiters). Prints made Hogarth a
wealthy man.

Canaletto

The paintings of the Venetian artist Canaletto (Giovanni Antonio
Canal, 1697–1768), known for his *vedute* (meaning "view" paintings) were especially popular with the British, particularly young
men on the Grand Tour (planned trips through western Europe to
complete their education) after their formal schooling. They
brought these scenes of Venice (and elsewhere) home as souvenirs.
This new form of subject can be traced back to the seventeenth
century, when many foreign artists, such as Claude Lorrain (see
fig. 21.8), specialized in depicting the Roman countryside, or to
the *Haarlempjes*, the local Dutch landscapes of Ruisdael (see fig.
20.28). After 1720, however, *vedute* took on a specifically urban
identity, focusing more narrowly on buildings or cityscapes.
During the eighteenth century, landscape painting in Italy evolved
into a new form in keeping with the character of the Rococo.

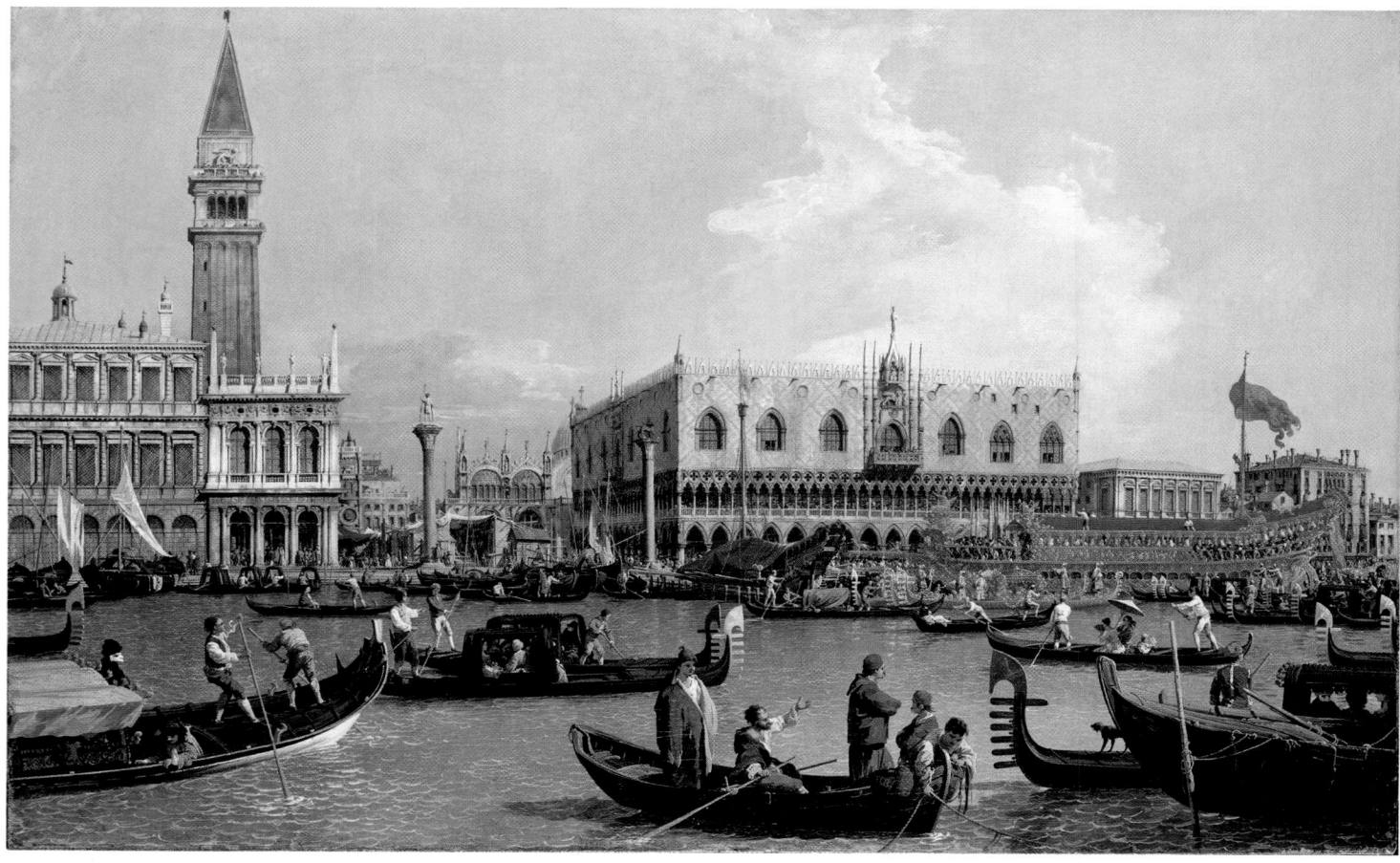

22.15   Canaletto, *The Bucintoro at the Molo*. ca. 1732. Oil on canvas, 30¼ × 49½" (77 × 126 cm).
The Royal Collection, copyright Her Majesty Queen Elizabeth II

The Bucintoro at the Molo (fig. **22.15**) is one of a series of paintings of Venice commissioned by Joseph Smith, an English entrepreneur (later named British consul to Venice) living there. Smith then issued the paintings as a suite of etchings to meet the demand for mementos of Venice from those who could not afford an original canvas by the artist. This work shows a favorite subject: the Doge returning on his magnificent barge to the Piazza San Marco from the Lido (the city's island beach) on Ascension Day after celebrating the Marriage of the Sea. Canaletto has captured the pageantry of this great public festival, which is presented as a brilliant theatrical display.

Canaletto's landscapes are, for the most part, topographically accurate. However, he usually made slight adjustments for the sake of the composition, and sometimes treated scenes with greater freedom or created composite views. He may have used a mechanical or optical device, perhaps a *camera obscura*, a forerunner of the photographic camera (see page 732), to render some of his views. The liveliness and sparkle of his pictures, as well as his sure sense of composition, sprang in large part from his training as a scenographer (a painter of stage sets for operas—including those by Antonio Vivaldi, 1678–1741). As in our example, Canaletto often included vignettes of daily life in Venice that lend greater human interest to his scenes and make them fascinating cultural documents as well.

Canaletto later became one of several Venetian artists to spend long sojourns in London, where he created views of the city's new skyline dotted with the church towers of Wren (see page 755). Other Venetian artists, such as Giovanni Battista Tiepolo (see page 781) and painters from his workshop had significant careers outside of Italy, in Germany and Austria, where the Rococo flourished.

THE ROCOCO IN CENTRAL EUROPE

Rococo architecture was a refinement in miniature of the curvilinear, "elastic" Baroque of Borromini and Guarini. It was readily united with the architecture of central Europe, where the Italian Baroque had firmly taken root. It is not surprising that the Italian style received such a warm response there. In Austria and southern Germany, ravaged by the Thirty Years' War, patronage for the arts was limited and the number of new buildings remained small until near the end of the seventeenth century. The Baroque here was an imported style, practiced mainly by visiting Italian artists. Not until the 1690s did native architects come to the fore. By the eighteenth century, however, these countries, especially the Catholic parts, were beginning to rebuild on a larger scale. A period of intense building activity in the first half of the

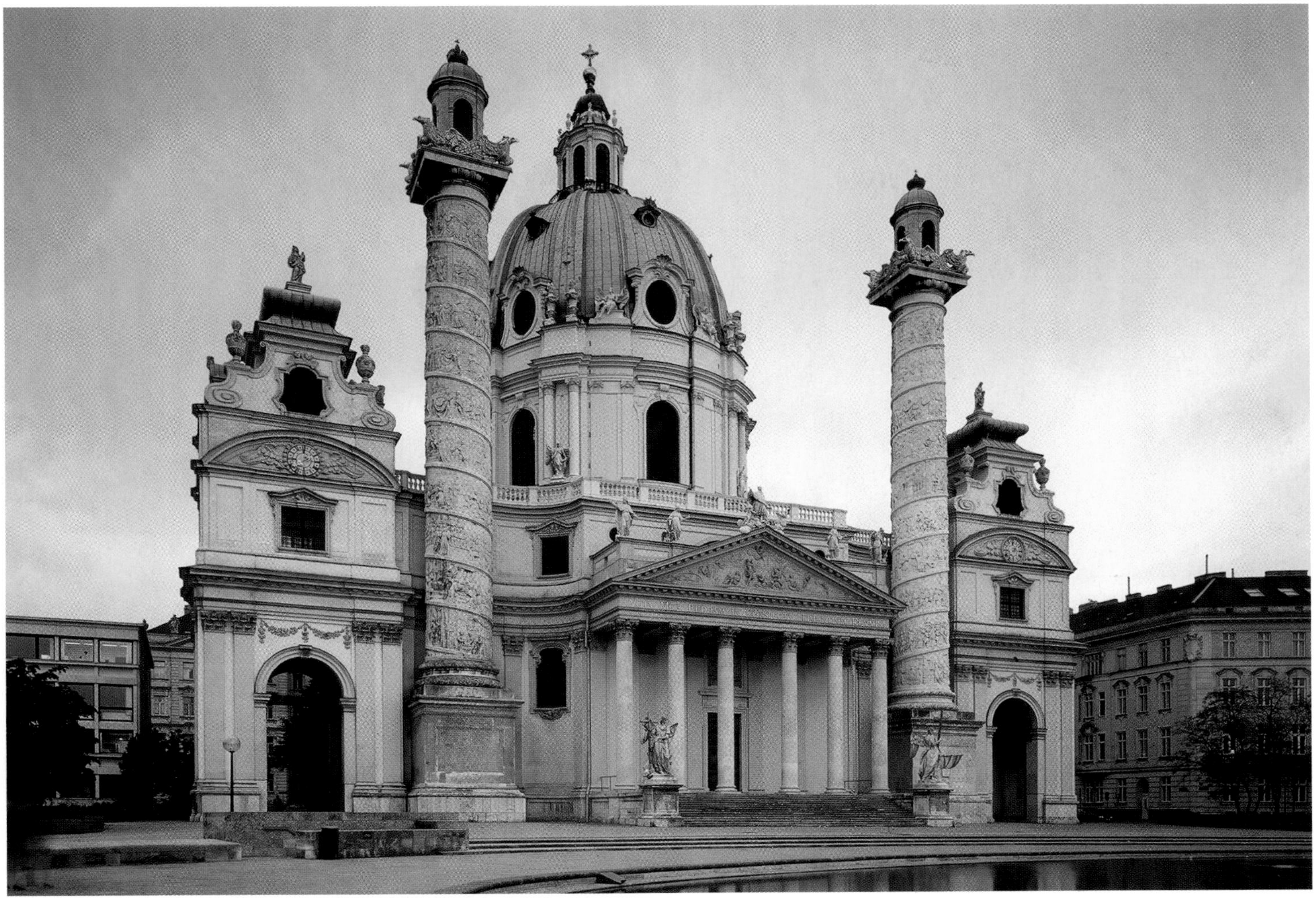

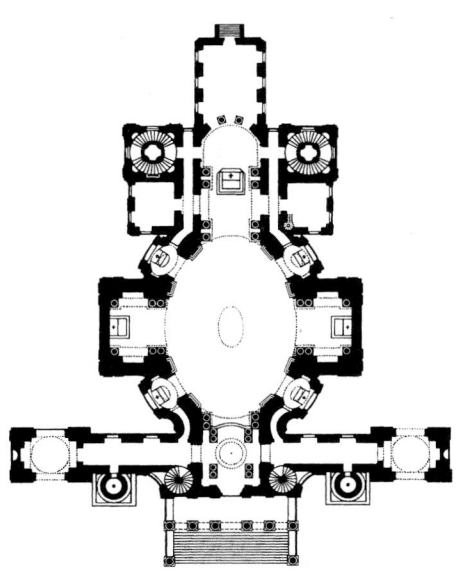

22.16 Johann Fischer von Erlach. Façade of the Karlskirche (church of St. Charles Borromeo), Vienna. 1716–37

eighteenth century gave rise to some of the most imaginative creations in the history of architecture. These monuments were built to glorify princes and prelates, who are generally remembered now only as lavish patrons of the arts. Rococo architecture in central Europe is larger in scale and more exuberant than that in France. Moreover, painting and sculpture are more closely linked with their settings. Palaces and churches are decorated with ceiling frescoes and sculpture unsuited to domestic interiors, however lavish, although they reflect the same taste that produced the Rococo French *hôtels*.

Johann Fischer von Erlach

The Austrian Johann Fischer von Erlach (1656–1723), the first important architect of the Rococo in central Europe, studied in Rome and was closely linked to the Italian tradition. His work represents the decisive shift of the center of architecture from Italy to north of the Alps. He is best known for the Karlskirche (the church of St. Charles Borromeo, literally "Charles's church") in Vienna (figs. **22.16** and **22.17**), built in thanks for the ending of the plague of 1713, much like the church of Santa Maria della

22.17 Plan of the Karlskirche

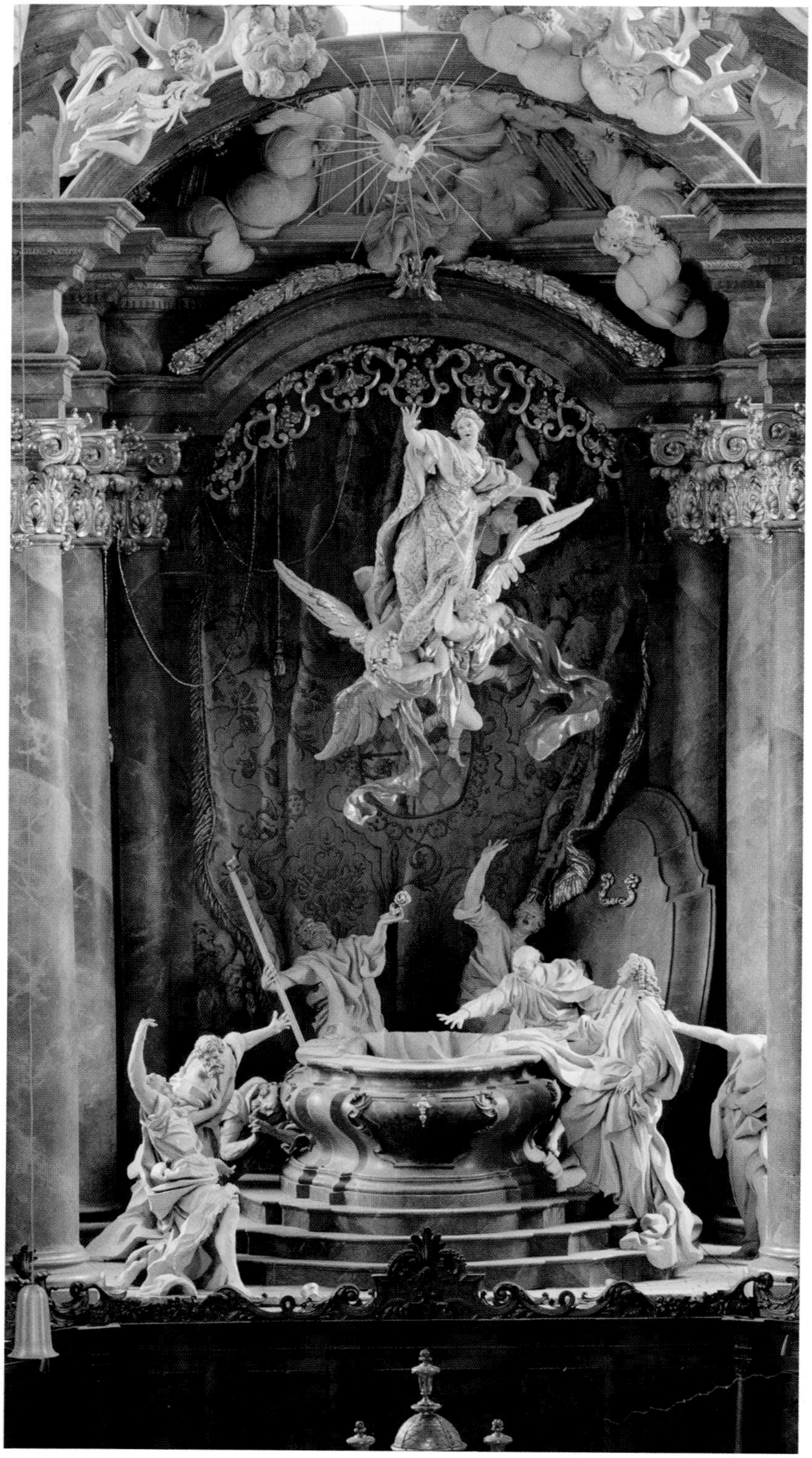

Salute in Venice in the previous century (see fig. 19.28). It was dedicated to the Counter-Reformation saint Charles Borromeo, for whom Emperor Charles VI was named and whose life is celebrated throughout the building. Fischer von Erlach uses several Italian and French architectural features to new effect, combining the façade of Borromini's Sant'Agnese and the Pantheon portico (see figs. 19.23 and 7.23). He added a pair of huge columns, derived from the Column of Trajan (see fig. 7.39) and decorated with scenes from the life of the saint. The two columns symbolize the Pillars of Hercules—the Straits of Gibraltar—a reference to Charles VI's claim to the throne of Spain. They also take the place of towers, which have become corner pavilions reminiscent of Lescot's Louvre court façade (see fig. 18.2). The church proclaims the emperor Charles VI as a Christian ruler and assures us of his domination over the Turks, who repeatedly menaced Austria and Hungary. They had been defeated only recently—at the Siege of

Vienna in 1683—but only with the aid of John III of Poland. The Turks remained a serious threat as late as 1718.

Fischer von Erlach uses aspects of major works of the canon of Western architecture here to create an entirely new work that brings with it all the grandeur and esteem of the old traditions. The extraordinary breadth of this architectural ensemble is due to the site itself (see fig. 22.16), which obscures the equally long main body of the church. With the inflexible elements of Roman imperial art embedded into the elastic curves of his church, Fischer von Erlach expresses, more boldly than any Italian architect of the time, the power of the Christian faith to transform the art of antiquity.

Egid Quirin Asam

The Rococo made stirring claims in the heart of southern Germany—Bavaria—where new buildings or renovations of old ones transformed churches into extravagant liturgical stage sets. Egid Quirin Asam (1692–1750) and his brother, Cosmas Damian Asam (1686–1739), were responsible for the complete design and decoration of several churches and palaces in Bavaria. The brothers traveled to Rome (1711–13) where they studied the works of Bernini and his influence in their work is palpable.

Egid Quirin Asam's magnificent contribution to the renovation of the Benedictine abbey at Rohr (his brother was to execute paintings here, but they were never completed) reveals a clear debt to the Roman Baroque master. The original Romanesque church had been remodeled several times before the eighteenth century, but Asam completely transformed the interior. The main altar is set as a stage with larger than life-size stucco figures depicting *The Assumption of the Virgin* (fig. **22.18**). The Virgin with the help of angels ascends into the golden heavens (the dome lit by windows), welcomed by the Trinity in the clouds as the white stuccoed apostles who surround her open sarcophagus (the huge lid is standing on the right) gesticulate wildly in amazement at this miracle. Their grand, broad gestures fill the space and are mirrored by the Virgin's own outstretched arms and fluttering fabrics. The scene is set before a flowing blue-gold curtain and framed by four columns. It is as if Bernini's *Ecstasy of St. Teresa* (see fig. 19.31) has met his *Baldacchino* and *Cathedra Petri* (see fig. 19.15). The lightness of the stucco (rather than marble) allowed for the use of wires and supports to raise the Virgin and to support the extended arms of the saints. The ensemble of exaggerated drama from the tomb to the golden heavens is an extravagant fulfillment of the Baroque in the eighteenth century.

Dominikus Zimmermann

Dominikus Zimmermann (1685–1766) created what may be the finest architectural design of the mid-eighteenth century: the rural Bavarian pilgrimage church nicknamed *"Die Wies"* ("The Meadow"). The exterior is so plain that by comparison the interior seems overwhelming (figs. **22.19** and **22.20**). This richness reflects the fact that the architect and his brother, Johann Baptist

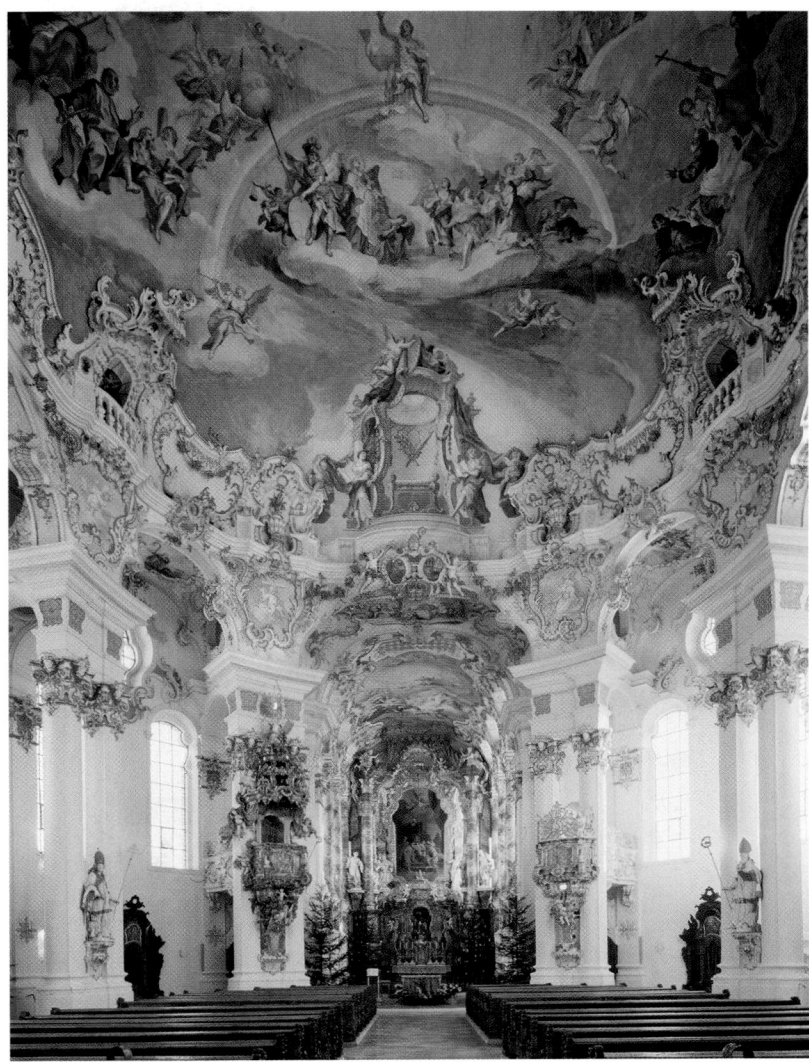

22.19 Dominikus Zimmermann. Interior of *"Die Wies,"* Upper Bavaria. 1757

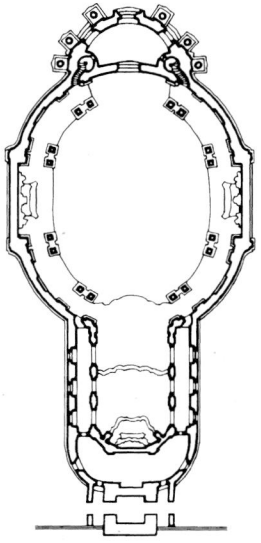

22.20 Plan of *"Die Wies"*

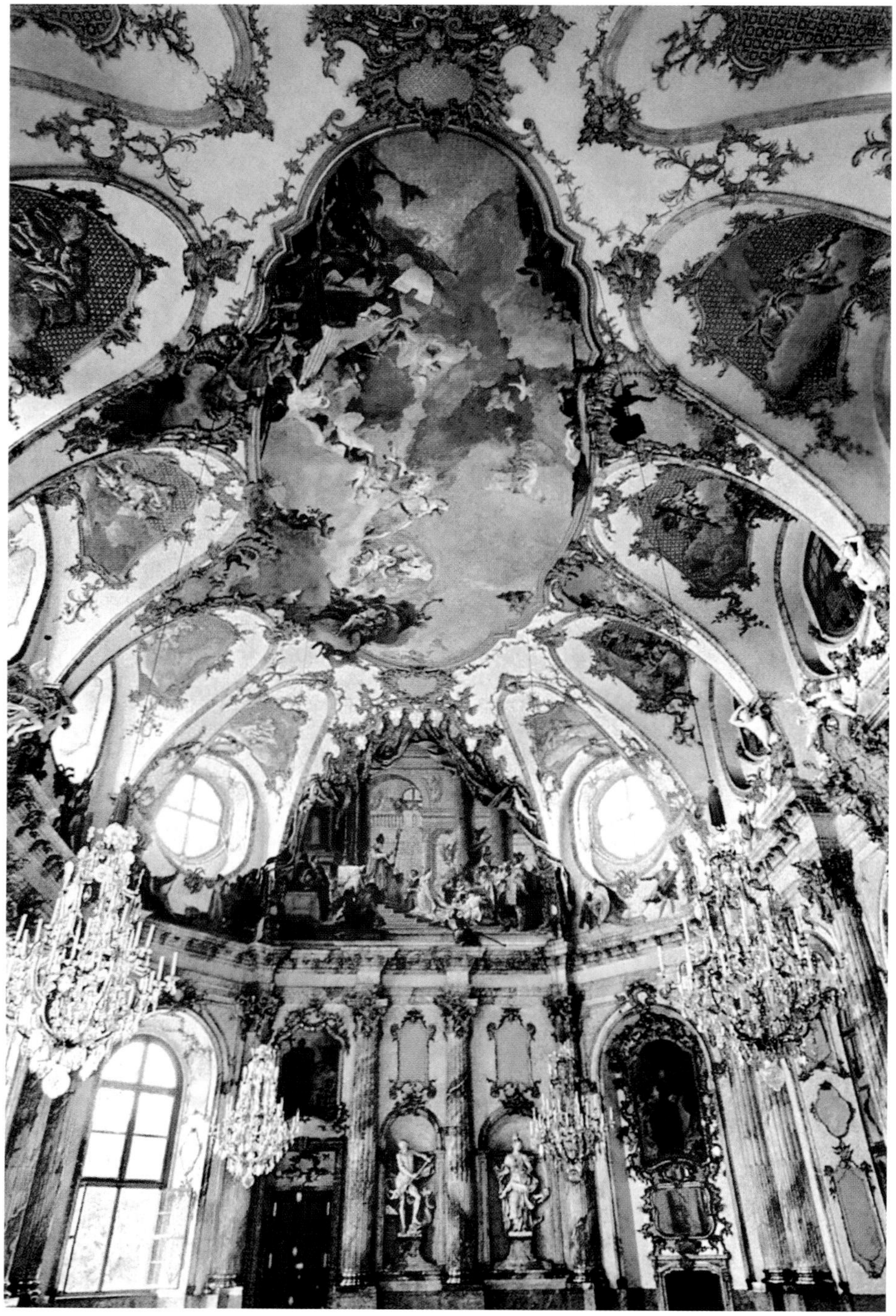

Zimmermann (1680–1758), who was responsible for the frescoes, trained initially as stucco workers. The interior design includes a combination of sculptural painted stucco decoration and painting. Like Fischer von Erlach's Karlskirche, the church's basic shape is oval. Yet because the ceiling rests on paired, free-standing supports, the space is more fluid and complex, recalling a German Gothic *Hallenkirche* (hall church). Even the way the Rococo décor tends to break up the ceiling recalls the webbed vaults of the Gothic Heiligenkreuz in Schwäbisch-Gmünd (see fig. 12.56). Here Guarini's prophetic reevaluation of Gothic architecture has become reality.

Balthasar Neumann

The work of Balthasar Neumann (1687–1753), a contemporary of Zimmerman's who designed buildings exuding lightness and elegance, represents one of the high points of the Rococo in central Europe. Trained as a military engineer, he was named a surveyor for the Residenz (Episcopal Palace) in Würzburg after his return from a visit to Milan in 1720. Although the basic plan was already established, Neumann was required to consult the leading architects of Paris and Vienna in 1723 before he made his extensive modifications. The final result is a skillful blend of the latest German, French, and Italian ideas. The breathtaking Kaisersaal (fig. **22.21**)

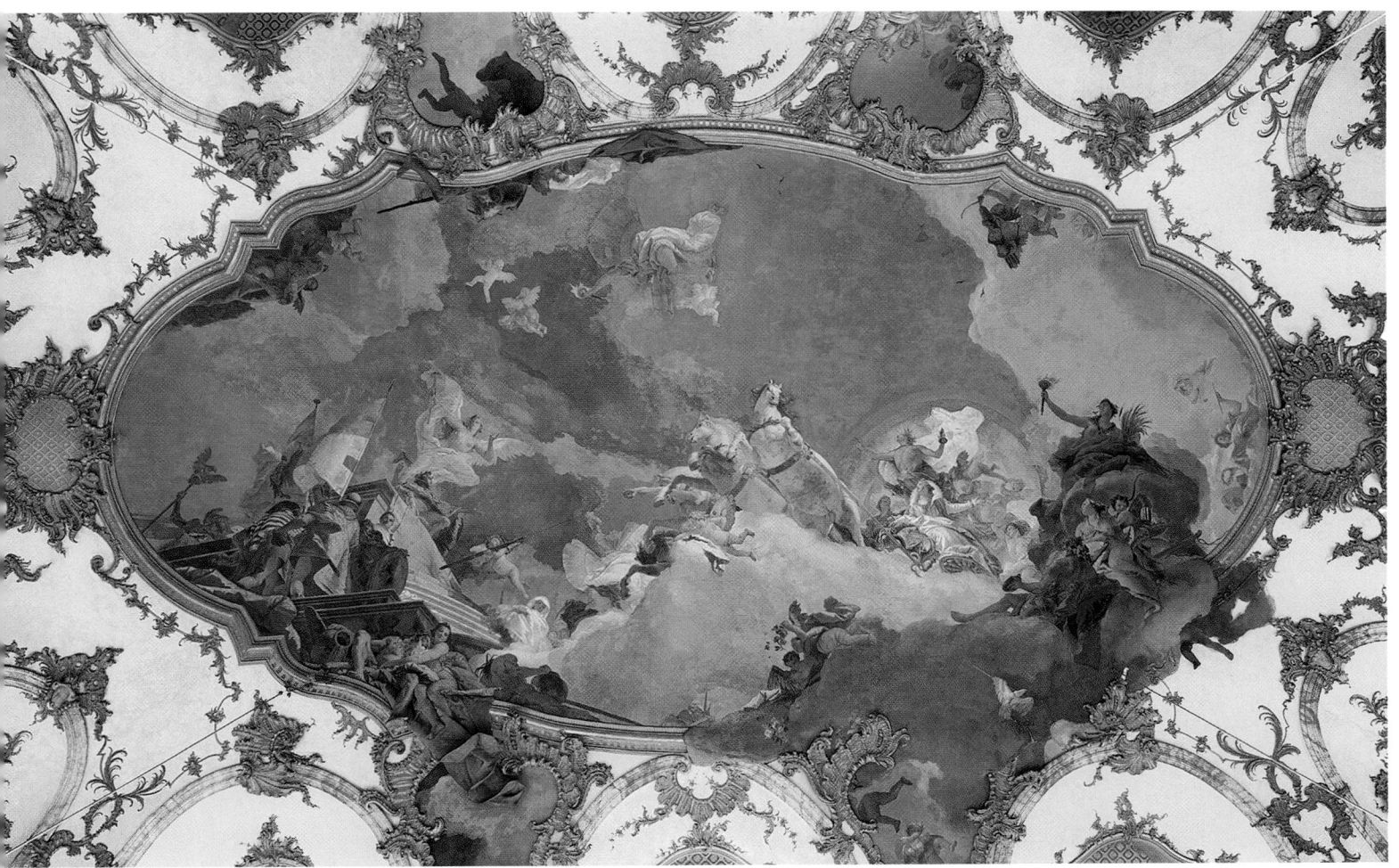

22.22 Giovanni Battista Tiepolo. Ceiling fresco (detail), Kaisersaal, Residenz, Würzburg. 1751

is a great oval hall decorated in the favorite color scheme of the mid-eighteenth century: white, gold, and pastel shades. The structural importance of the columns, pilasters, and architraves has been minimized in favor of their decorative role. Windows and vault segments are framed by continuous, ribbonlike moldings, and the white surfaces are covered with irregular ornamental designs. These lacy, curling motifs, the hallmark of the French style (see fig. 22.11), are happily combined with German Rococo architecture. (The basic design recalls an early interior by Fischer von Erlach.) But it is the painted decoration that completes the rich organic structure. The abundant daylight, the play of curves and countercurves, and the weightless grace of the stucco sculpture give the Kaisersaal an airy lightness far removed from the Roman Baroque. The vaults and walls seem thin and pliable, like membranes easily punctured by the expansive power of space.

Giovanni Battista Tiepolo and Illusionistic Ceiling Decoration

Central European Rococo churches and palaces required paintings to complement the architecture and achieve the full effect of extensive, overwhelming, yet light decoration (through the use of white, gold trim, and pastel colors). Venetian colorists with a revived appreciation of Veronese's colorism and pageantry, but with an airy sensibility that is new, were skilled in the Baroque illusionism of the previous century and were able to adapt it to Rococo architecture. They were active in every major center throughout Europe, especially in London, Dresden, and Madrid. And the most sought-after of these Venetian artists—both in Venice and throughout central Europe in the eighteenth century—was Giovanni Battista Tiepolo (1696–1770).

The last and most refined stage of Italian illusionistic ceiling decoration can be seen in the works of Tiepolo, who spent most of his life in Venice, where his works defined the Rococo style. Tiepolo spent two years in Germany, and in the last years of his life he worked for Charles III in Spain. His mastery of light and color, his grace and masterful touch, and his power of invention made him famous far beyond his home territory. When Tiepolo painted the Würzburg frescoes (figs. 22.22 and 22.23), his powers were at their height. The tissuelike ceiling gives way so often to illusionistic openings, both painted and sculpted, that it no longer feels like a spatial boundary. Unlike Baroque ceilings (see figs. 19.11 and 19.12), these openings do not reveal avalanches of figures propelled by dramatic bursts of light. Rather, pale blue skies

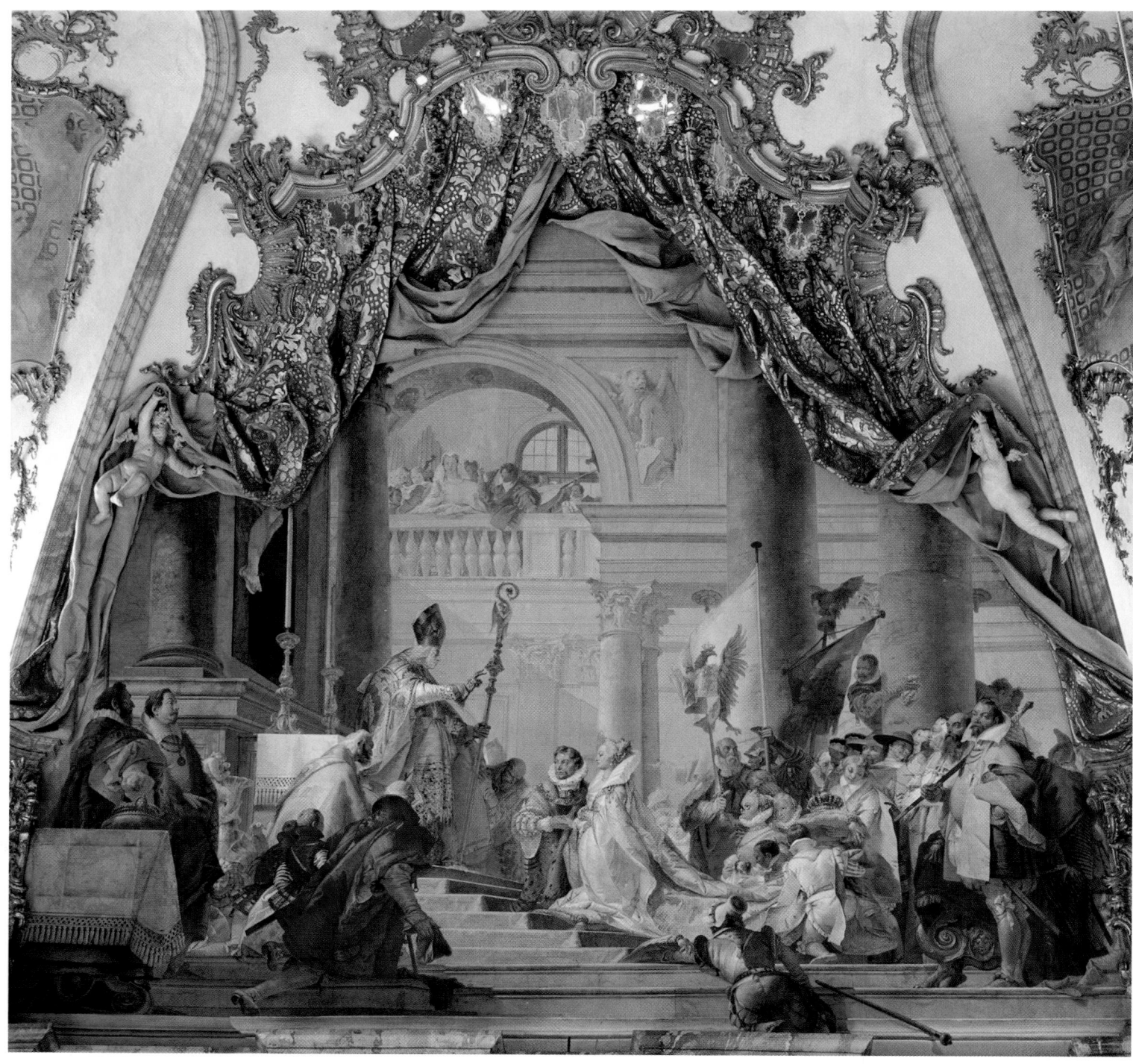

22.23 Giovanni Battista Tiepolo, *The Marriage of Frederick Barbarossa* (partial view), Kaisersaal, Residenz, Würzburg. 1752. Fresco

and sunlit clouds are dotted with an occasional winged creature soaring in the limitless expanse. Only along the edges of the ceiling do solid clusters of figures appear.

At one end, replacing a window, is *The Marriage of Frederick Barbarossa* (see fig. 22.23). As a public spectacle, it is as festive as *The Feast in the House of Levi* by Veronese (see fig. 17.38). The artist has followed Veronese's example by putting the event, which took place in the twelfth century, in a contemporary setting. Its allegorical fantasy is "revealed" by the carved putti opening a gilt-stucco curtain onto the wedding ceremony in a display

of theatrical illusionism worthy of Bernini. Indeed, it parallels the drama orchestrated by Egid Quirin Asam at Rohr (see fig. 22.18). Unexpected in this festive procession is the element of classicism, which gives an air of noble restraint to the main figures, in keeping with the solemnity of the occasion.

Tiepolo later became the last in the long line of Italian artists who were invited to work at the Royal Court in Madrid where he worked for Charles III. There, he encountered the German painter Anton Raphael Mengs, a champion of the classical revival, whose presence signaled the end of the Rococo.

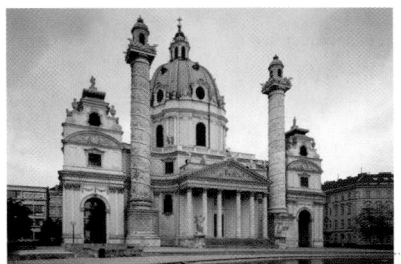

1716-37 Fischer von Erlach's Karlskirche
built in Vienna

The Rococo

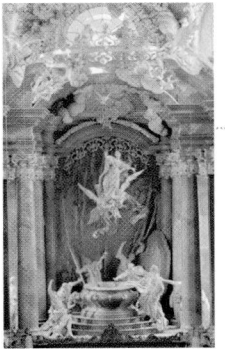

1717-23 Asam's
Assumption of the Virgin

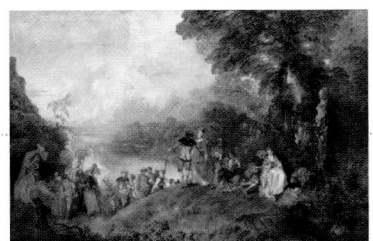

1717 Watteau's *A Pilgrimage to Cythera*

1685 Versailles Palace completed

1710

◄ 1710 Meissen porcelain factory established

◄ 1715 Louis XIV dies

1720

◄ 1723 Louis XV crowned king of France

◄ 1725 Antonio Vivaldi writes *Four Seasons* concerto

◄ 1728 John Gay, *The Beggar's Opera*

1730

◄ 1732 Theatre Royal in Covent Garden, London
opens

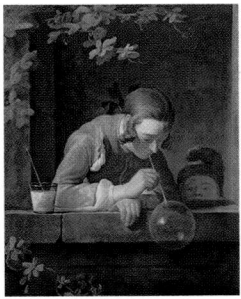
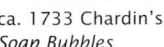

ca. 1733 Chardin's
Soap Bubbles

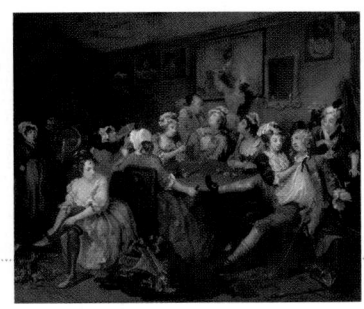

1733-35 Hogarth's
The Rake's Progress

1740

◄ 1741 Johann Sebastian Bach publishes *"Goldberg"
Variations*

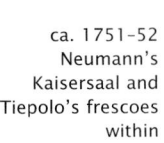

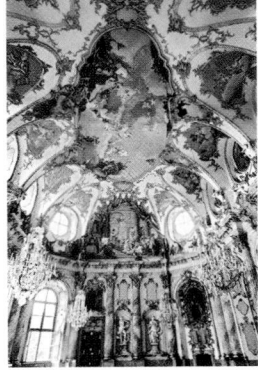

ca. 1751-52
Neumann's
Kaisersaal and
Tiepolo's frescoes
within

1750

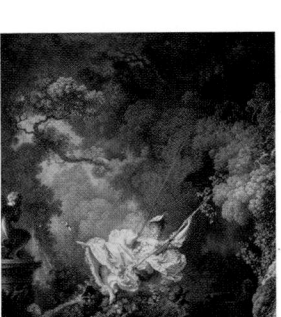

1756 Boucher's *Portrait of
Madame de Pompadour*

◄ 1759 Louis XV becomes sole owner of Sèvres
porcelain factory

1760

1770

1767 Fragonard's *The Swing*

783

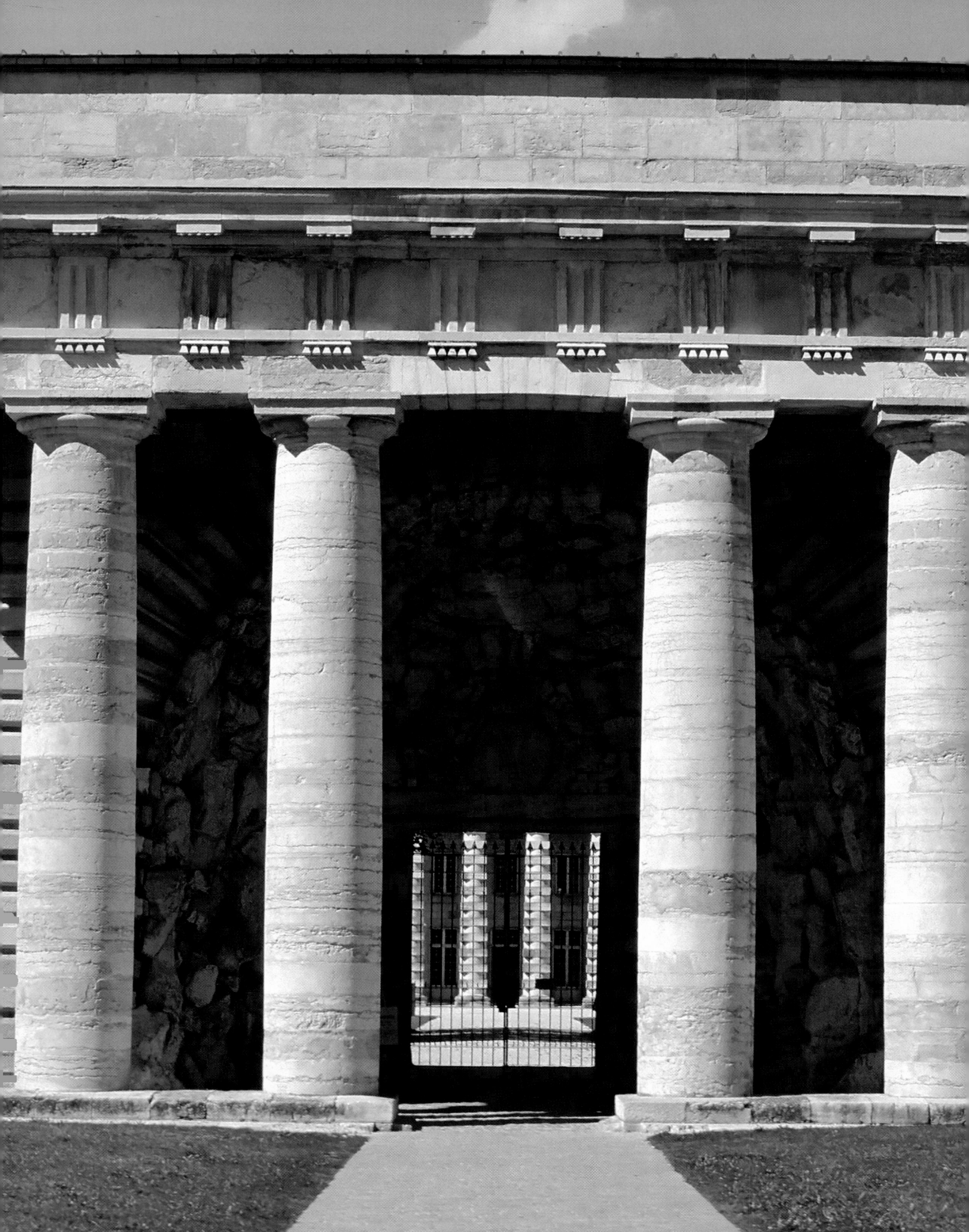

CHAPTER 23

Art in the Age of the Enlightenment, 1750–1789

A most remarkable change in our ideas is taking place, one of such rapidity that it seems to promise a greater change still to come. It will be for the future to decide the aim, the nature, and the limits of this revolution, the drawbacks and disadvantages of which posterity will be able to judge better than we can.

—Jean d'Alembert

W HEN THE FRENCH PHILOSOPHER AND SCIENTIST JEAN d'Alembert made this prophetic statement in 1759, the Western world was indeed embarking on a revolution, one that is still unfolding today. This revolution ushered in a radically new way of viewing the world, one that would lead to the social, scientific, economic, and

political values that govern our present lives. Little did d'Alembert realize that he was witnessing the birth of the modern world.

This new world was heralded by twin revolutions: the Industrial Revolution, which began first in Britain in the middle of the eighteenth century and gradually spread worldwide in the nineteenth century; and the political revolutions of the United States and France in 1776 and 1789, respectively. Democracy, personal liberty, capitalism, socialism, industrialization, technological innovation, urbanization, and the "doctrine of progress," that is, a continuous upward march toward an improved life through science and knowledge, are just some of the many modern concepts that emerged from this period.

The force behind this transformation was the Enlightenment, a term that refers to the modern philosophy that emerged largely in Britain, France, Germany, and the United States in the eighteenth century. The foundation for this new thought lay in late seventeenth-century Britain with the philosopher John Locke (1632–1704) and the physicist and mathematician Isaac Newton (1642–1727), perhaps the two most influential thinkers of their

age. Both stressed empiricism—the idea that knowledge comes from practical experience rather than abstract thought or religious revelation—as the basis for philosophy and science. For Newton, this meant proceeding from personally collected data and observation—not superstition, mysticism, religion, hearsay, or whimsy—and applying this information in a rational, logical fashion. For Locke, empiricism established experience as the only basis for formulating theory and principle. No longer could ideas be considered innate or ordained by God. Locke upset the applecart of Original Sin when he declared that all humans are born good and have a natural right to life, liberty, and property. He defined the function of government as the protection of these natural rights, and failure to do so granted citizens the license to remove their government, even if that required revolution.

What began as a trickle of influence evolved into a torrent as the basic premises behind the innovative ideas of Locke and Newton produced an explosion of treatises and theories throughout the eighteenth century. Leading this philosophical charge were the *philosophes*, as the leading French intellectuals of the time are commonly called. Among the best known are Voltaire (1694–1778), Jean-Jacques Rousseau (1712–1778), and Denis Diderot (1713–1784), who, along with d'Alembert, edited the 52-volume *Encyclopédie*, the world's first encyclopedia, which in its

Detail of figure 23.22, Claude-Nicolas Ledoux. Main entrance, saltworks, Arc-et-Senans

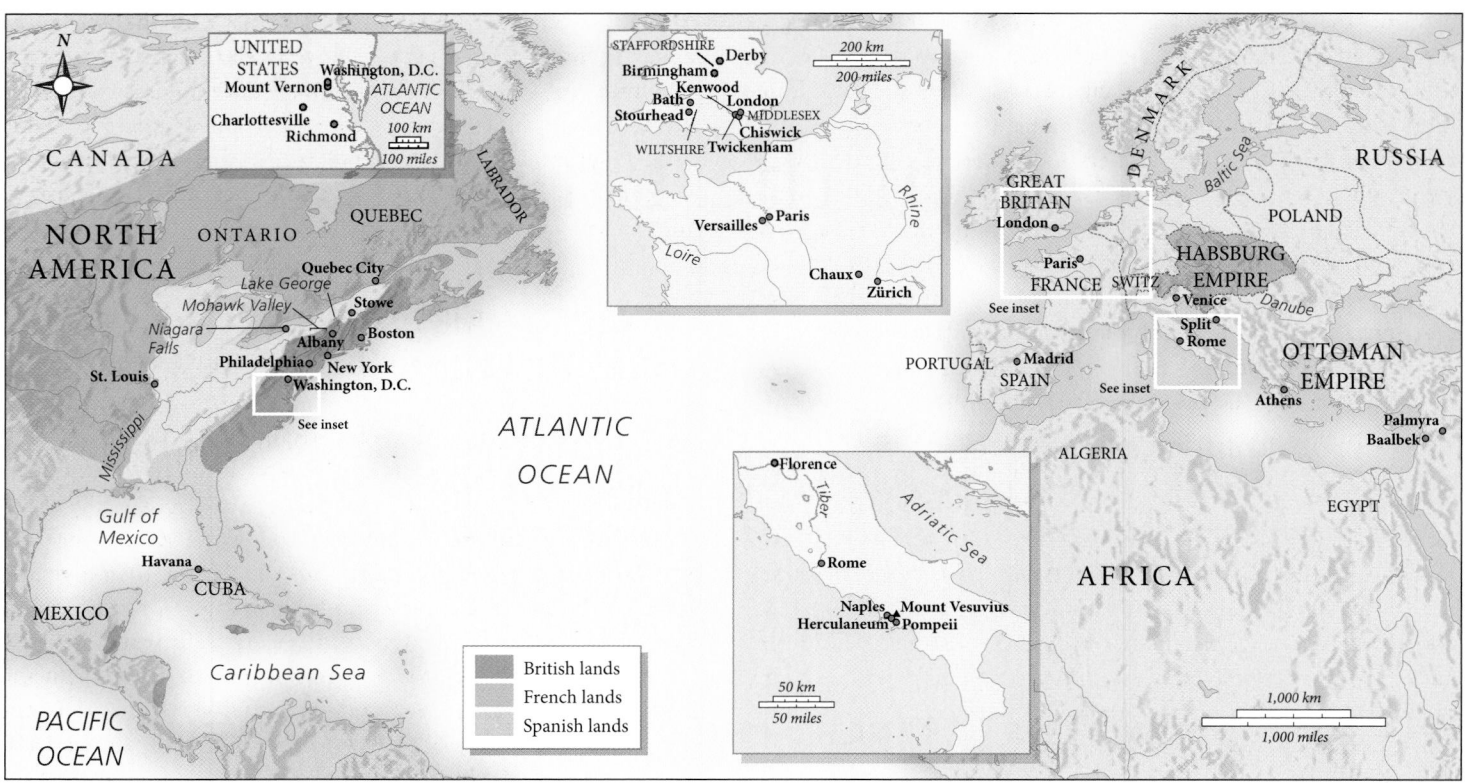

Map 23.1   Europe and North America in 1763

attempt to document the world and knowledge epitomizes Enlightenment empiricism.

In addition to establishing basic human rights and a new moral order, Enlightenment thought also ushered in modern science. Electricity and oxygen were discovered, for example, and chemistry and natural science as we know it today were established. Science helped launch the Industrial Revolution. By midcentury, the first mills were churning out yards of fabric at an unimaginable rate in the Midlands of England, and the notion of labor was redefined as the first factory workers, employed at subsistence wages, were tethered to clattering looms in enormous spaces filled with deafening noise. Miners excavated coal and ore to produce iron, permitting construction of the first metal bridge. Perfection of the steam engine by Scottish engineer James Watt from 1765 to 1782 aided the mining and textile industries and enabled Robert Fulton, in 1807, to send a steamboat chugging up the Hudson River in the face of a swift current and public incredulity, arriving in Albany from Manhattan in unimaginably quick time.

The second half of the eighteenth century was a period of transition as the world moved from the old to the modern, from rule by aristocracy and church to democracy, from agriculture to industry, and from rural to urban. The art of this time reflects this transformation, for it is often changing and complex, with several almost contradictory attitudes existing in a single work. The dominant style associated with this transitional period is **Neoclassicism,** meaning the "New Classicism," which often illustrated what were considered the virtuous actions and deeds of the

ancient Greeks and Romans. As we shall see, however, not all works labeled Neoclassical are set in historical antiquity; they may be contemporary genre scenes or major events that have the look or feel of classical antiquity and that embrace similar moral values.

Neoclassicism embraced the logic and morality of the Enlightenment, which were perhaps best encapsulated in the works of Voltaire. In his plays, poems, novels, and tracts, Voltaire used logic to attack what he called "persecuting and privileged orthodoxy," mainly meaning Church and State, but any illogical institution or concept was fair game for his satire. He believed science could advance civilization and that logic presumed a government that benefitted the people, not just the aristocracy. It is from Voltaire that we get the "doctrine of progress." The models for Voltaire's new civilization were the republics of ancient Greece and Rome, which in addition to being the first democracies provided the first rationalist philosophers. Taking its vocabulary directly from ancient art, Neoclassicism would reject the sensual pastel colors and bold painterly flourishes of the Rococo and instead return to the hard line and cool paint handling of the Italian Renaissance (see Chapters 15, 16, and 17) and French Classicism (see Chapter 21).

While Neoclassicism is the style generally associated with the second half of the eighteenth century, simultaneously, a second and seemingly antithetical thread appears in art: **Romanticism.** As we shall see in the next chapter, Romanticism really comes of age about 1800, when the term was actually coined in order to describe the sweeping changes in worldview then occurring. Instead of Neoclassicism's logic and its desire to control the forces of nature through science, Romanticism values emotion and intuition and believes in the supremacy of raw, unrestricted nature. Like Neoclassicism, however, early Romanticism often stems from Enlightenment thought, in particular its emphasis on morality. Jean-Jacques Rousseau is the principal proponent of this view, which he articulated in his *Discourse on the Arts and Sciences* (1750). Here, he advocated a return to nature, arguing, like Locke, that humans are born good, not in sin, and that they use their innate sense or instincts to distinguish between good and bad, that is, between what makes them happy and sad. Feeling determines their choices, not rational thought, which one uses to explain choices, not to make them. Society, he believed, through its mores, values, and conventions, eventually imposes its own rationalized standards on humans, distracting them from their first true and natural instincts. Rousseau praised what he called the sincere "noble savage," steeped in nature, and he denounced contemporary Western civilization for its pretensions, artificiality, and, in general, for those social restraints that prevent us from tapping into the power of our basic emotions.

Rousseau, in turn, inspired the German proto-romantic movement known as *Sturm und Drang* and conventionally translated as "Storm and Stress," although "Passion and Energy" or "Energy and Rebellion" is perhaps more accurate. This literary movement, which centered on the Weimar region, appeared from roughly the late 1760s through the early 1780s. Its best-known representative was Johann Wolfgang von Goethe (1749–1832), author of *The Sorrows of Young Werther* (1774), one of the most widely read novels of its day. Like Rousseau, the group supported personal freedom, which in part was a reaction to the repressive despotism of the German states and of contemporary moral and social conventions. Similarly, the movement advocated powerful emotions and extreme passion as an expression of the unique, creative individual, and it likewise called for a return to nature, a pre-civilization state.

While Neoclassicism is the style generally associated with the period, we must remember that the rational and the emotional survived side by side in art, flip sides of the same Enlightenment coin. Proponents of both attitudes aggressively rejected Rococo art (see Chapter 22), which they perceived as licentious, frivolous, even immoral, and which was generally associated with aristocracy and privilege, the twin evils condemned by the Enlightenment. While there was a call for a new art, one based on Classical values, no one was sure what it should look like. Not until the 1780s, with the paintings of Jacques-Louis David and the sculpture of Antonio Canova, did the Neoclassical style crystallize. In the meantime, Neoclassicism would appear in many guises, sometimes even containing elements of Rococo elegance, a reminder that the Rococo still survived—Boucher did not die until 1771, and Fragonard and Clodion lived on into the nineteenth century. Simultaneously, the Romantic fascination with strong emotions, with the irrational and unexplainable, and with the powerful forces of nature, was developing, which ironically would overshadow Neoclassicism by the 1790s, the decade following David's and Canova's rise as well as the French Revolution of 1789. While Britain and France dominate art in the second half of the century and are the focus of our discussion, Neoclassicism, like the Enlightenment, was an international movement, well represented in Scandinavia, Austria, Germany, and Russia.

ROME TOWARD 1760: THE FONT OF NEOCLASSICISM

Rome was the center of the art world in the eighteenth century, and virtually anyone aspiring to become a painter, sculptor, or architect wanted to study there, experiencing first hand the antiquities of Greece and Rome and the riches of the Renaissance and Baroque periods. Not just artists came to Rome, for no gentleman's education was complete without making a "Grand Tour" of Italy, including the North Country (Florence, Tuscany, Umbria, and Venice) and Naples, the jumping-off point for Herculaneum and Pompeii, perfectly preserved Roman cities that were in the process of being excavated from 1738 and 1748, respectively. These archaeological excavations, as well as those in Athens (of the Akropolis, 1751), Palmyra (1753), Baalbek (1757), Split (Spalato, 1757), and Ionia (1764), fueled an interest in antiquity and fired the imagination of artists, largely through illustrations published in lavish **folio** format. But the climax of the Grand Tour was Rome, which was itself one large excavation site, with antiquities dealers furiously digging for artifacts and sculpture to sell to tourists.

Equally responsible for creating a renewed preoccupation with antiquity were the writings of the German scholar Johann Winckelmann (1717–1768, see page 157), librarian to the great antiquities collector Cardinal Albani, whose Villa Albani in Rome was one of the antiquities museums—along with the Villa Borghese and the Capitoline Hill—that every gentleman on the Grand Tour had to visit. In 1755, Winckelmann published *Reflections on the Imitation of Greek Art in Painting and Sculpture*, and in 1765, he produced his *magnum opus, History of Greek Art*. The latter was one of the most widely read books of its day, which accounts for its influence. In both publications, Winckelmann elevated Greek culture to a position of supremacy it never quite held in the Classical tradition: an era of perfection that was followed only by imitation and decline. But Winckelmann did not just see beauty in Greek art; he also saw moral qualities that paralleled Enlightenment thought: "the general and predominant mark of Greek masterpieces is *noble simplicity and calm grandeur*, both in gesture and in expression. The expression of all Greek statues reveals even in the midst of all passions a great and grave soul [*italics added*]." He concludes that "the only way for us to become great, and if possible, even inimitable, is through imitation of the ancients." In response to Winckelmann's influence, the rallying cry of Neoclassicism would be the creation of moral works embodying "noble simplicity and calm grandeur."

Artistic Foundations of Neoclassicism: Mengs and Hamilton

Influenced by the revived interest in antiquity, two artists working in Rome began to lay the foundation for Neoclassicism: Anton Raphael Mengs (1728–1779) and the Scottish painter Gavin Hamilton (1723–1798). Mengs, a German who worked in Rome on and off from 1740 to 1765, gained notoriety when Cardinal Albani, at Winckelmann's urging, commissioned him to paint a ceiling fresco for the Villa Albani. Completed in 1761 and with Winckelmann assisting with the iconography, his *Parnassus* (fig. **23.1**) depicts the cardinal as Apollo surrounded by the seven female Muses, most of whom can be identified as the cardinal's friends. The composition is based on Raphael's Vatican fresco of the same title. Stylistically, Mengs drew on Raphael, as well as ancient sources. His painting combines Raphael's **planarity** (objects and figures are parallel to the picture plane) and **linearity** (objects and figures have crisply drawn contours). The figures themselves are copied from Raphael and from the recently unearthed murals at Herculaneum and Pompeii. Apollo's pose recalls the *Apollo Belvedere* (see page 157), a work in the Vatican collection and made famous by Winckelmann. For the sake of

planarity, Mengs dispensed with the Baroque device of an illusionistic ceiling (see fig. 19.10), one that opens up to the sky. Instead he made his ceiling look like a wall painting by Raphael, simply hung on a ceiling. He also daringly replaced the lush Rococo brushwork then in fashion (see page 766) with tight brushwork that dissolves into a smooth, hard surface. An even lighting models solid, three-dimensional forms. All of these elements—planarity, linearity, tight brushwork, even lighting, sculptural forms, and Classical figures and themes—played a prominent role in the development of the Neoclassical style.

The one element absent from Mengs's painting that would be crucial for the development of Neoclassicism is an austere, moralistic subject, such as a scene of self-sacrifice. This missing ingredient was provided by the painter and antiquities dealer Gavin Hamilton, who in the early 1760s began painting deathbed scenes, such as *Andromache Bewailing the Death of Hector* (ca. 1761), a subject taken from Homer showing Andromache bent over the body of her husband, Hector, the Trojan leader who had been killed by the Greek Achilles. The painting was reproduced in a widely circulated engraving of 1764 (fig. **23.2**), a reminder of the importance of prints in giving currency to images before the invention of photography, as well as an additional way for artists

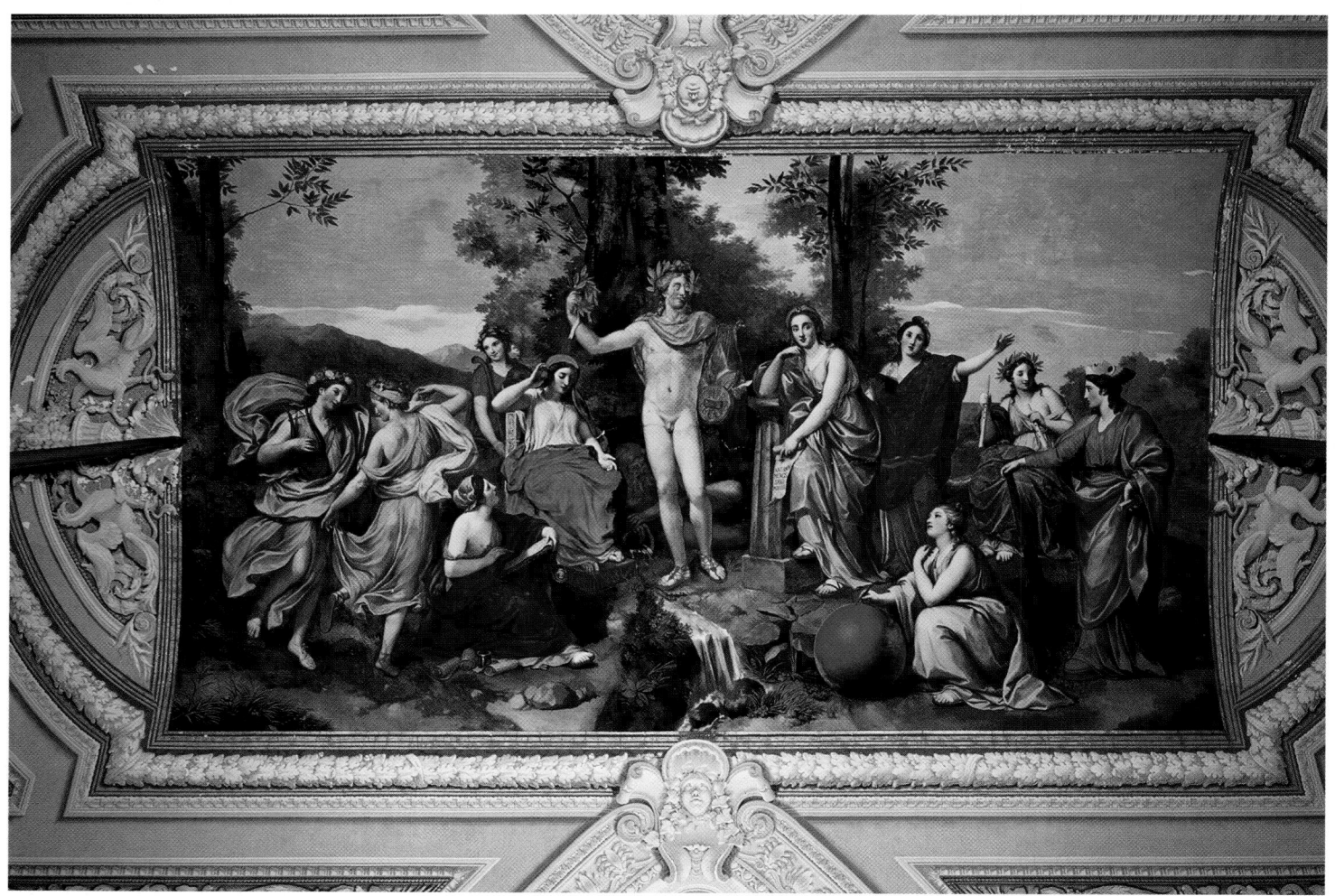

23.1 Anton Raphael Mengs, *Parnassus*, Villa Albani, Rome. 1761. Fresco

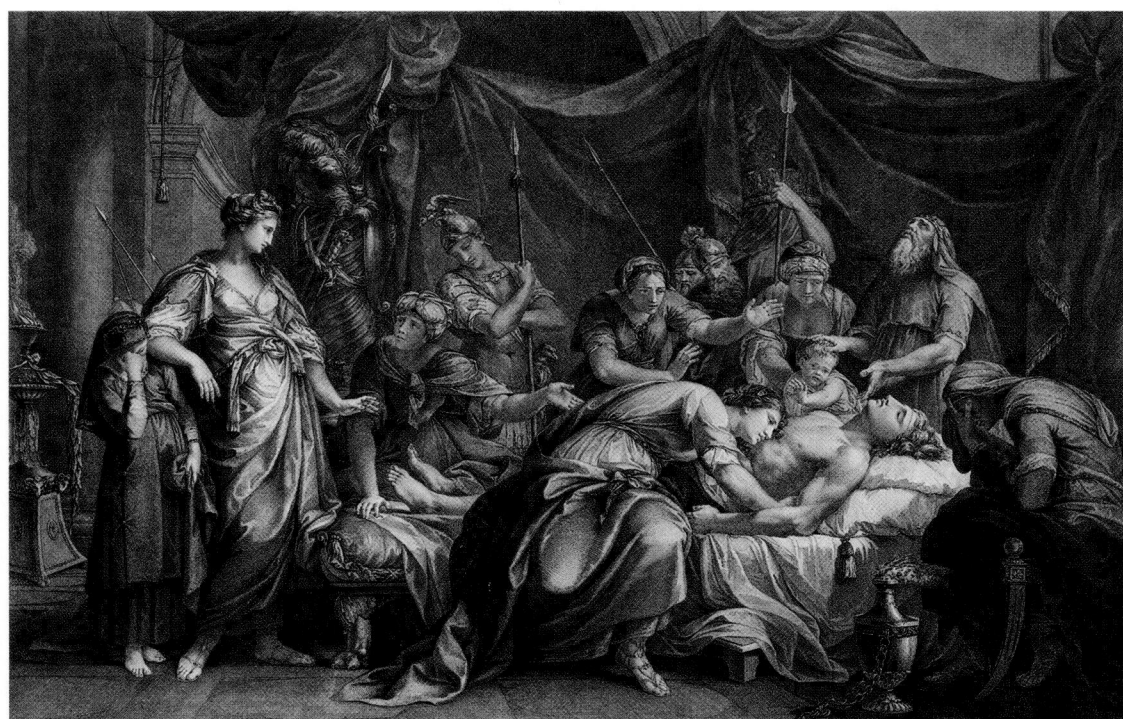

23.2 Gavin Hamilton, *Andromache Bewailing the Death of Hector*. 1764. Engraving by Domenico Cunego, after a painting of ca. 1761. Yale Center for British Art. Paul Mellon Collection

to earn a living. Everyone who went to Rome would have seen this picture in Hamilton's studio, since at the time he was one of the must-see painters. For those who did not get to see the work in Rome, it was available for viewing at a 1764 exhibition of the Society of Artists in London, an organization providing an annual exhibition for members and considered the premier venue in the British capital until the Royal Academy opened in 1768. This painting of mourning must have shocked eyes accustomed to Rococo gaiety, fantasy, and pleasure. Its moral is matrimonial devotion as opposed to marital indiscretion, unwavering dedication rather than titillating deception, virtue not vice. Elements of the composition were inspired by reliefs on Roman sarcophagi and sepulchral buildings, but Hamilton's prime source was Poussin's *Death of Germanicus* (see fig. 21.4), which was then in the Palazzo Barberini in Rome. The two pictures share the receding barrel vault on the left and the same planar composition established by the lateral spread of the bed with canopy and recumbent body. Hamilton would paint other works on the themes of virtue and moral fortitude, and while he was not the first to reintroduce themes that had been of extreme importance to artists until the advent of the Rococo, his pictures seem to have been a catalyst. Increasingly in the 1760s and 1770s, artists in all mediums turned to this kind of moralistic subject matter.

ROMANTICISM IN ROME: PIRANESI

As discussed in the introduction, Neoclassicism was not the only movement to evolve after 1750. Concurrently, the first signs of a Romantic spirit were emerging, a spirit that evoked strong emotional responses from the viewer. In Rome, the source of this current was Giovanni Battista Piranesi (1720–1778), a printmaker who would have a powerful impact on eighteenth-century artists, especially architects, as we shall see. By the 1750s, Piranesi was renowned for his *vedute*, or views, of Rome, which gentlemen on the Grand Tour took home as souvenirs of their visit. (In Venice, they would buy *vedute* by Canaletto and other artists—see page 775.) Winckelmann's glorification of the Greeks and belittling of the Romans had infuriated Piranesi, who set out to defend his Roman heritage by producing *Roman Antiquities*, a four-volume work completed in 1757 and illustrated with several hundred etchings of Roman ruins. These etchings are hardly mere documentation of sites in and around Rome. Often presenting worm's-eye views of the structures (fig. 23.3), Piranesi transformed them into colossal, looming monuments that not only attested to the Herculean engineering feats of the ancient Romans but also the uncontested might and supremacy of Roman civilization. The frightening scale of the monuments dwarfs the awestruck tourists who walk among the dramatically lit ruins. These structures seem erected not by mere humans, but by a civilization of towering giants who mysteriously vanished. Time, however, has taken a toll on their monuments, now crumbling and picturesquely covered by plants. Tourists such as Goethe, who before only knew Rome from Piranesi's *vedute*, were shocked to discover how small the ruins actually were upon seeing them for the first time.

These images embody Piranesi's own sense of awe in the face of Roman civilization and constitute a melancholic meditation on the destructive ability of time to erode that once-great empire. The prints are not intended just to inform; they are also meant to evoke a sense of astonishment, even fright. In them we see the beginnings of a sensitivity that is antithetical in spirit to the noble simplicity and calm grandeur of Neoclassicism.

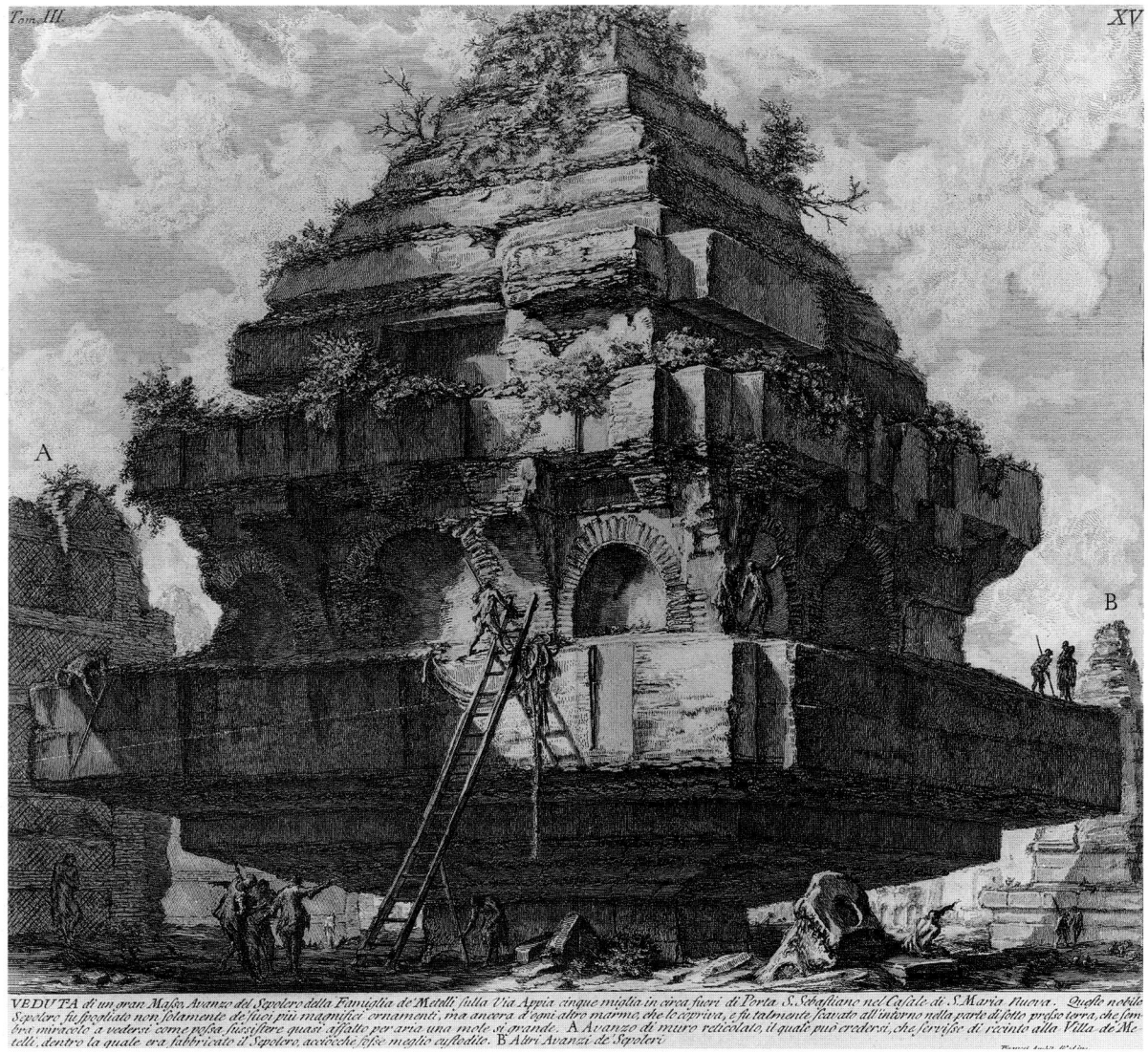

VEDUTA di un gran Masso Avanzo del Sepolcro della Famiglia de Metelli sulla Via Appia cinque miglia in circa fuori di Porta S.Sebastiano nel Casale di S.Maria Nuova. Questo nobile Sepolcro, fu spogliato non solamente de suoi più magnifici ornamenti, ma ancora d'ogni altro marmo, che lo copriva, e fu talmente scavato all'intorno nella parte di sotto presso terra, che sembra miracolo a vedersi come possa sussistere quasi affato per aria una mole sì grande. A Avanzo di muro reticolato, il quale può credersi, che servisse di recinto alla Villa de'Metelli, dentro la quale era fabbricato il Sepolcro, acciocché fosse meglio custodito. B Altri Avanzi de Sepoleri

23.3   Giovanni Battista Piranesi, *Tomb of the Metalli*, plate XV from *Antichità Romane III*. ca. 1756. Etching, 16¾ × 18⅜" (42.5 × 46.5 cm). Metropolitan Museum of Art, Rogers Fund, 1941, transferred from library. (41.71.3(15))

Before the eighteenth century was out, the sense of awe that Piranesi produced would be identified as being caused by what the period called the "sublime." The sublime is not a style, but a quality or attribute. Interestingly, the word became current in 1756, a year before Piranesi's publication, when the British statesman Edmund Burke (1729–1797) published a treatise titled *A Philosophical Inquiry into the Origin of Our Ideas of the Sublime and Beautiful*. Burke's study was directed more toward psychology than aesthetics, but its impact on the world of art was tremendous. He defined beauty as embodying such qualities as smoothness, delicacy, and grace, which produced feelings of joy, pleasure, and love. The **sublime** he defined as obscurity, darkness, power, vastness, and infinity, anything that generated feelings of fright, terror, being overwhelmed, and awe. The sublime, he wrote, produced "the strongest emotion which the mind is capable of feeling." As the century progressed, more and more artists embraced this quality, catering to viewers' demands to be awed or moved by paintings, sculpture, and architecture.

NEOCLASSICISM IN BRITAIN

It almost seems as though the British were predisposed to embracing Neoclassicism, not only because the birth of Enlightenment occurred in Britain but also because the nation already had an intense involvement with antiquity in literature, which dated to the opening decades of the eighteenth century. The Augustan or Classical Age of British poetry was in full bloom by then, with its leading authors, such as John Dryden, Alexander Pope, and Samuel Johnson, emulating the form and content of the writers active during the reign of the first Roman emperor, Augustus Caesar (63 BCE–14 CE), many of whose works these same British poets translated. Britain at this time was enjoying unprecedented peace and prosperity, which, in part, was responsible for the identification with Augustus Caesar's reign, similarly marked by stability, economic success, and the flourishing of culture. The liberal faction of the British aristocracy modeled itself on ancient Rome, relating the British parliamentary government that shared power with the king to the democracy of the Roman Republic. As we shall see, by the 1720s, these liberals, who compared themselves with Roman senators, had come to desire country homes based on Roman prototypes.

Sculpture and Painting: Historicism, Morality, and Antiquity

The British were particularly receptive to the Neoclassical foundation established by Mengs and Hamilton. Hamilton's moralistic antique scenes in particular had a major impact, and the list of artists inspired by them is extensive, starting with a handful in the 1760s and extending to dozens more in the following decades. However, the taste for the classical could also be just that, a taste for a style or look, with little consideration for the underlying moral message. This was especially true in the decorative arts (see *Materials and Techniques*, page 792).

THOMAS BANKS Hamilton's impact was so great it extended beyond painting to sculpture, as seen in the work of Thomas Banks (1735–1805). From 1772 to 1779 Banks studied in Rome, where he chiseled a marble relief of *The Death of Germanicus* (fig. **23.4**). Reflecting the Enlightenment emphasis on logic and credibility, Banks authenticated his scene by making his setting as real and as historical as possible, using archaeologically correct architectural details and furniture (note the klismos chair, for instance, which was especially popular in the fifth century BCE). To make his image more antique, he aligned his Classical figures in a flat, shallow frieze composition, idealizing faces and putting them in Greek profile. The unusual stance of the soldier on the far right is a mourning pose that Banks copied from Roman reliefs. As in Hamilton's *Andromache Bewailing the Death of Hector*, the devoted women and children express intense sorrow for the dying general, while the dedicated soldiers, with raised oath-swearing arms, probably inspired by Hamilton's 1763–64 *Oath of Brutus*, vow to avenge his murder. Similarly sweeping curves augment the intense emotion of both groups, although Hamilton's figures, especially Andromache, appear to imitate the explosive monumentality of Michelangelo's sibyls and prophets. As we shall see, Neoclassicism, in its climax in France in the 1780s, will abandon curvilinear design and embrace a severe geometric grid that underscores the intense moralistic resolve of the figures.

ANGELICA KAUFFMANN Angelica Kauffmann (1741–1807) was among the most important artists for the development of Neoclassicism in Britain. She was born in Switzerland, studied in Rome in the 1760s, and moved to London in 1766. She befriended Joshua Reynolds, who was to become the first president of the Royal Academy when it was founded in 1768, and she herself was a founding member. Prior to the twentieth century, she was one of only two women admitted into the academy. As a woman, she was denied access to studying the male nude, then considered critical to a history painter's success, which makes her accomplishments all the more remarkable. Of the few eighteenth-century

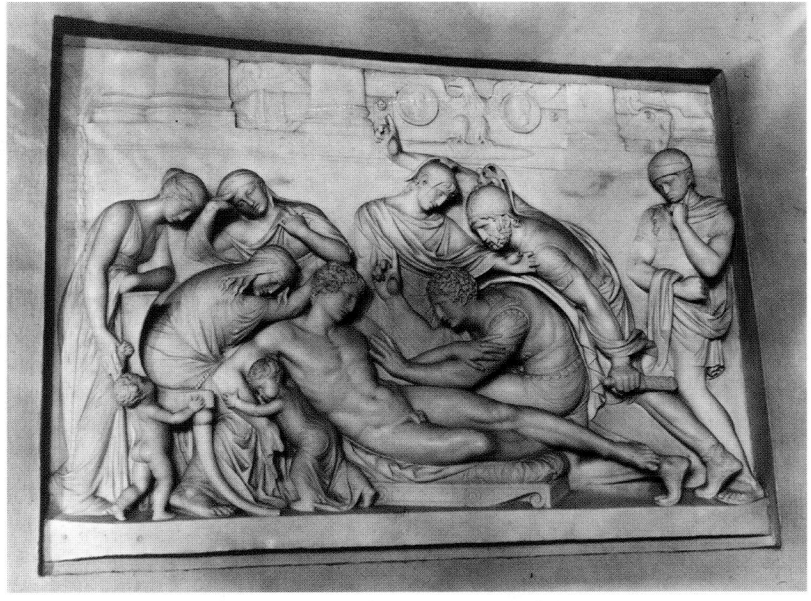

23.4 Thomas Banks, *The Death of Germanicus*. 1774. Marble, height 30" (76.2 cm). Holkham Hall, Norfolk, England. By Kind Permission of the Earl of Leicester and the Trustees of the Holkham Estate

women artists to carve out a successful career in a man's world, Kauffmann was the only one who became a history painter. The others were either still-life painters, like the Parisian Anne Vallayer-Coster (1744–1818), or portraitists, like Marie-Louise-Élisabeth Vigée-Lebrun (see page 816), who was the French queen Marie-Antoinette's favorite artist, and Adélaïde Labille-Guiard (1749–1803). Male prejudice was so strong against the latter two French women, both of whom rank among the finest painters of the period, that they were accused of employing men to make their works. Enlightenment philosophy, with its emphasis on equality, may have provided a theoretical premise for greater social, economic, and political freedom for women, but in reality female artists remained second-class citizens throughout the eighteenth century, only occasionally gaining access to the academies in London and Paris (the French Academy only allowed four women members at a time). Furthermore, male artists continued to depict women stereotypically, as wives and mothers who in addition to being fertile and pretty are helpless, passive, grieving, and immobile, as we saw in Hamilton's *Andromache Bewailing the Death of Hector* and Banks's *The Death of Germanicus*.

Like so many of her contemporaries, Kauffmann raided Greek and Roman literature for her subjects. In 1769, at the first Royal Academy exhibition, she presented *Hector Taking Leave of Andromache*, and three years later she showed *Andromache and Hecuba Weeping over the Ashes of Hector*, two pictures portraying unwavering marital fidelity. A classic example of Kauffmann's moralistic pictures is *Cornelia Presenting Her Children as Her Treasures (Mother of the Gracchi)* (fig. **23.5**) of about 1785. Here she champions child-rearing and family duty over materialism. While portraying a woman as a mother, she nonetheless counters traditional male stereotyping by presenting her subject as proactive and in control. In this second-century BCE story from

Josiah Wedgwood and Neoclassical Jasperware

Reflecting the rising demand in Britain for all things Classical was jasperware porcelain, invented by Josiah Wedgwood and produced by the mid-1770s in his factory named Etruria in Staffordshire. **Jasperware** is a durable, unglazed porcelain decorated with Classically inspired bas-relief (low-relief) or cameo figures. Most jasperware is ornamented in white relief on a colored ground, especially blue and sage green. In 1775, Wedgwood hired the sculptor John Flaxman (1755–1826) to produce many of his designs, which were largely based on ancient Greek vases in the collection of William Hamilton. The Greek vases, not discovered until the middle of the eighteenth century, were considered Etruscan, hence the name Etruria for Wedgwood's plant. Hamilton's collection, housed in Naples and sold to the newly founded British Museum in 1772, was published in enormous folio volumes in the 1760s and readily available for copying.

Reproduced here is a Flaxman vase depicting *Hercules in the Garden of the Hesperides*, designed in 1785, although not produced until later. Flaxman translated the two-dimensional drawing on a Hamilton vase into the shallow three-dimensionality appropriate for jasperware. While he retained the strong contours, profiles, and basic configuration of the figures on Hamilton's vase, he subtly increased the elegance of the original Greek design, largely by simplifying the drawing and making it more graceful.

Like most Wedgwood images, the scene is not one of action, resolve, or a decisive moment reflecting nobility of character. Instead, Flaxman shows Hercules in repose in the garden where his eleventh task required him to steal the golden apple belonging to Zeus, which was protected by the multi-headed Hydra and the Hesperides, the daughters of Atlas. The image looks more like a Classical *fête galante* than a heroic act of Herculean courage and might. The prettiness of the color and delicacy of the design echo Rococo sensitivity and are a reminder that the taste for the Classical could also be just that, a taste for a style or look, with little consideration for a moralistic message, as we saw in the Neoclassical images of Hamilton, Banks, and Kauffmann.

The rise of Wedgwood coincided with the Industrial Revolution: the company was based upon mass production. Wedgwood produced the same Flaxman design on different objects: vases, fireplace panels, plaques, medallions, and jardinières (large, ornamental flowerpot holders). With his partner Thomas Bentley, who was responsible for the firm's preoccupation with Classical art and for hiring Flaxman, Wedgwood opened a showroom in London to promote their wares and innovatively published a well-distributed catalogue of their products. The two men were not only mass-producing art, they were also mass-marketing it, making high-quality work available to a broad public at a reasonable price. They also fulfilled a growing public infatuation with celebrities, for their medallions included portraits of famous people, in effect anticipating the role of photography some 75 years later and the mass media in the twentieth century. Flaxman designed profiles of such renowned figures as the writer Samuel Johnson and the sensation of London, the actress Sarah Siddons.

The Industrial Revolution was increasing wealth and creating an upper middle class in Britain, and Wedgwood was meeting the needs of this new clientele—art was no longer just for royalty, the aristocracy, and the church. Demand was so great that Wedgwood installed his first steam engine at Etruria in the early 1780s to make his plant more efficient.

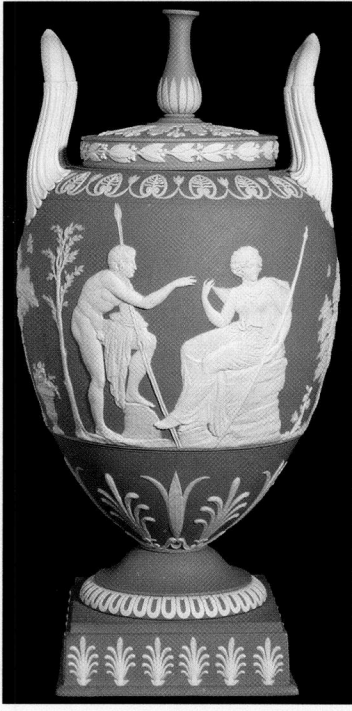

John Flaxman, *Hercules in the Garden of the Hesperides*. Designed 1785 and produced by Wedgwood ca. 1790. Jasperware, height 14" (35.7 cm). The Potteries Museum and Art Gallery, Stoke-on-Trent

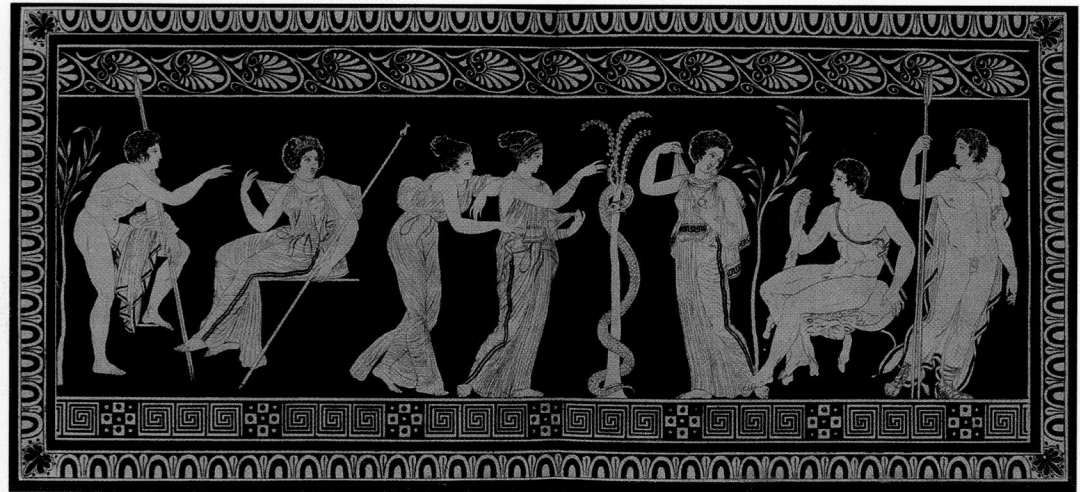

Hercules in the Garden of the Hesperides. Illustration in Pierre-François Hugues d'Hancarville, *Collection of Etruscan, Greek and Roman Antiquities from the Cabinet of the Honorable William Hamilton*. 1766–67. Vol. II, Plate 127

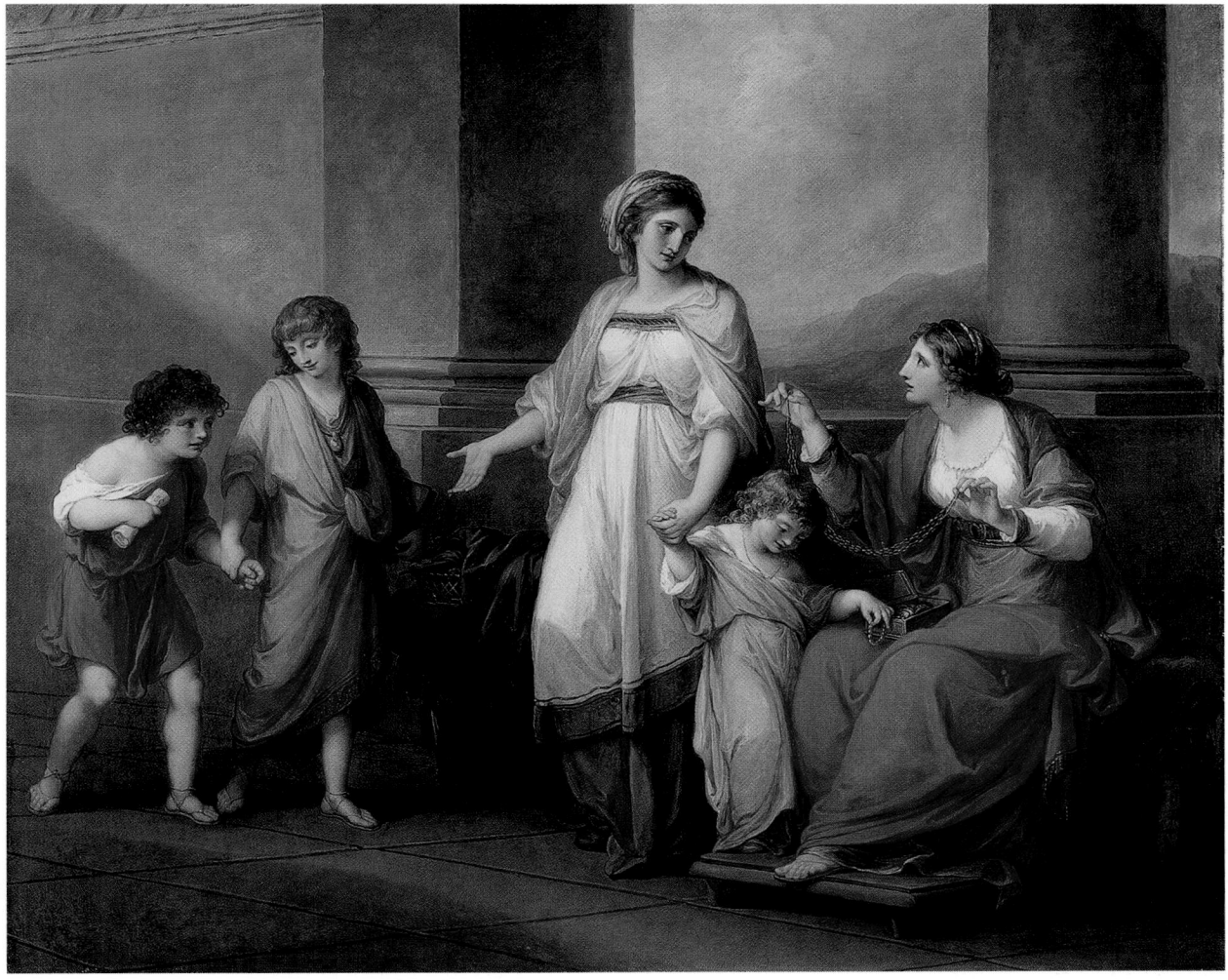

23.5   Angelica Kaufmann, *Cornelia Presenting Her Children as Her Treasures (Mother of the Gracchi).* ca. 1785. Oil on canvas, 40 × 50" (101.6 × 127 cm). Virginia Museum of Fine Arts, Richmond. The Adolph D. and Wilkins C. Williams Fund. 75.22

Roman history, a visiting friend has just shown off her jewelry to Cornelia Gracchus. Instead of displaying her own gems, Cornelia proudly presents her children, two of whom, Tiberius and Gaius, would become great politicians. To prepare her sons for leadership, Cornelia acquired the finest tutors in the world, and it was said that she "weaned" them on conversation, not her breasts. She remained an ally and advisor to both, and in addition to her reputation for virtue and intelligence, she was one of the most powerful women in the history of the Roman Republic. Kauffmann, a woman artist struggling in a man's world, must have identified with the successful Cornelia, whose features in the painting resemble the artist's own.

In *Cornelia Presenting Her Children*, Kauffmann has created an austere and monumental painting that reinforces the strength and nobility of the mother. The picture is dominated by the bareness of the floor and walls, the carefully modeled statuesque figures, and a stable composition anchored by a solid triangle culminating in Cornelia. The Cornelia theme was not unique to Kauffmann, but was quite popular with other artists. Not only did it illustrate virtue, it also reflected the new interest in the importance of the family unit that stemmed from the

Enlightenment teachings of Jean-Jacques Rousseau, who advocated that parents should nurture their children at home, rather than sending them off to wet nurses and nannies until they were adolescents.

The Birth of Contemporary History Painting

Enlightenment empiricism had a major impact on history painting in two ways. One was the strong emphasis on historicism—when portraying a scene set in the historical past, costume, setting, and props all had to be convincing and true to the period. The second impact affected the presentation of major contemporary events that the future would perceive as historically important. Until now, such moments had generally been shown using allegory and symbols, not by portraying the actual scene, or figures would be dressed in Classical garb in order to provide the sense of decorum and importance the event apparently required. But with the Enlightenment, paintings increasingly had to be logical and real and every bit as convincing to contemporaries as we expect period films to be today. This applied not only to the historical past but to contemporary events as well.

BENJAMIN WEST The artist perhaps most responsible for popularizing contemporary history painting is Benjamin West (1738–1820), one of the most successful British Neoclassical history painters. A Quaker born and raised just outside of Philadelphia, West went to Rome in 1760 where he studied with Mengs, befriended Gavin Hamilton, and immersed himself in antiquity and the Classically influenced Renaissance masters, especially Raphael. By 1763, he had settled permanently in London, and within three years had found success, in part because of his innovative handling of Neoclassicism's emerging vocabulary. He was a founding member of the Royal Academy in 1768, and he became its president in 1792 when Joshua Reynolds died. Throughout his life, he was a mentor for many American artists, and always remained proud of his New World heritage, even supporting the American Revolution. (For a discussion of art in colonial America, see the Introduction.)

Among the pictures that established West's reputation are his *Agrippina with the Ashes of Germanicus* of 1768, a picture that falls into the moral category of the dedicated widow, and *The Departure of Regulus from Rome* from 1769, which reflects the stoic self-sacrifice of a Roman general to save his country.

Employing Enlightenment historicism, the pictures are set in convincingly real ancient Roman cities, with figures aligned in relief, parallel to the picture plane, against a backdrop of Classical buildings.

West shocked the London art world in 1770 when he announced he was working on a *contemporary* history painting, *The Death of General Wolfe* (fig. **23.6**), and placing the event in the realistic setting of 1759 Quebec during the French and Indian War. Wolfe won the Battle of Quebec, which became a turning point in the war and made him a national hero. Upon hearing of West's plan, King George III declared he would never purchase a picture with his soldiers shown in modern uniforms, and Reynolds frowned on the picture's breach of decorum, which required an allegorical apotheosis scene. But when exhibited at the Royal Academy, the painting was immediately applauded by the public. The costumes, setting, and Indian warrior all lend the image an air of authenticity, despite inaccuracies (see *The Art Historian's Lens*, page 795), and in an era before photography and film, made the audience feel as though it were indeed witnessing its great national hero at the very moment he sacrificed his life for his country.

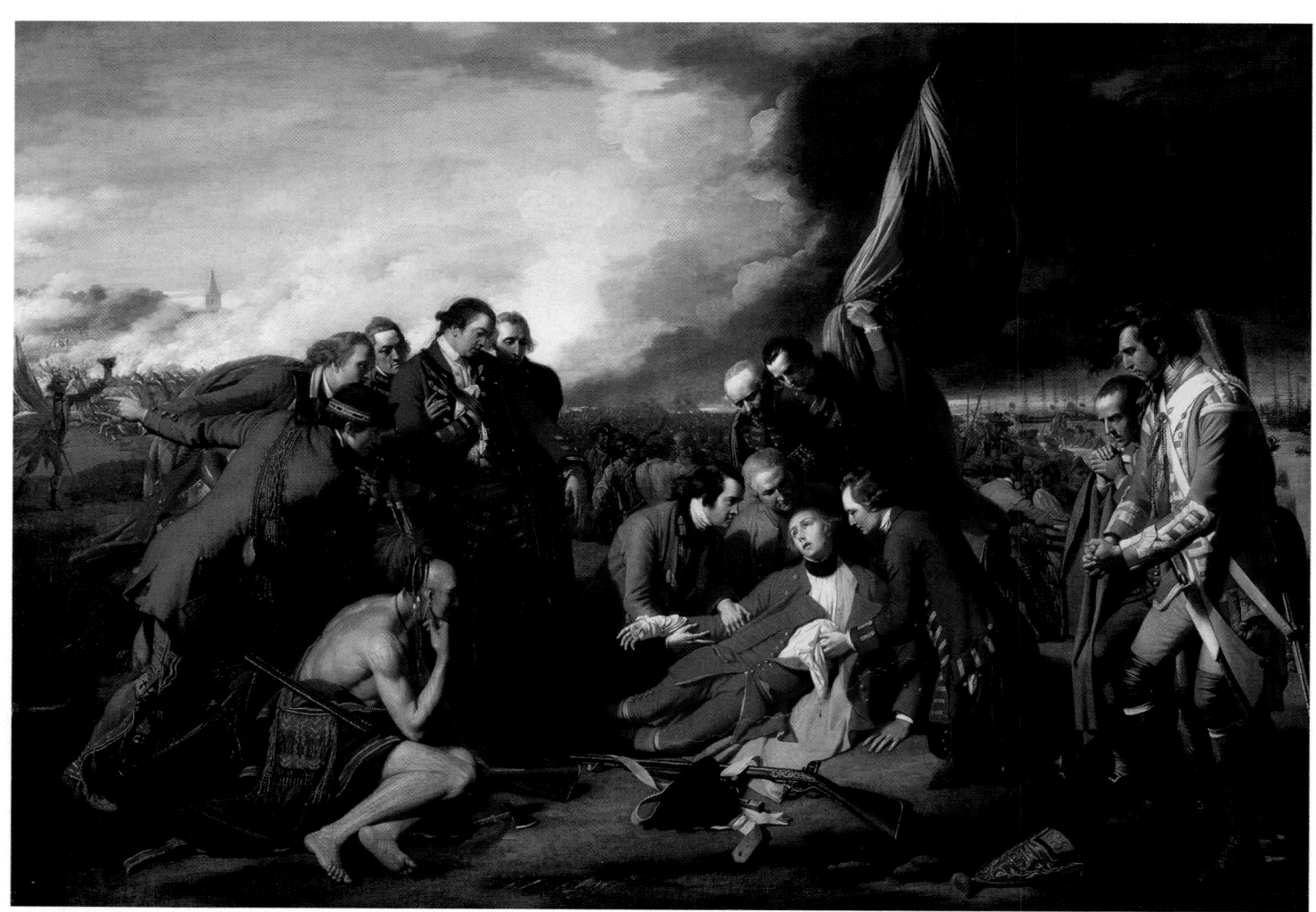

23.6 Benjamin West, *The Death of General Wolfe.* 1770. Oil on canvas, 59½ × 84" (1.51 × 2.13 m). National Gallery of Canada, Ottawa. Gift of the Duke of Westminster

The Elusive Meaning of West's The Death of General Wolfe

The history of art is filled with mysteries, and among the most common unknowns for art made before 1900 are the authorship and date of a piece, the reason it was made, and its message. Art historians are often forced to rely on speculation, a tactic filled with risk but one that has the advantage of beginning an intellectual dialogue that may lead to firm answers. Benjamin West's *The Death of General Wolfe* raises probing questions. The most obvious question is, why did West depict this particular subject? The key to the answer may be the figure of William Johnson, who is shown in a green coat to the left (see fig. 23.6). His name and a map with "Mohawk Valley" and "Ontario" on it are etched on his powder horn. These territories had been ceded to him as superintendent of Indian affairs by the Native Americans. More important, he had been the hero at the battles of Lake George and Fort

Niagara and therefore was a symbol of the important role that Americans played in winning the French and Indian War. Despite the picture's historicism, West's image is a fiction: Johnson had not been at Quebec, and the Indians aided the French, not the British. West made this picture on the threshold of the American Revolution (the Boston Massacre was in 1770), and his ahistorical inclusion of Johnson was perhaps designed to make the British aware of their indebtedness to the colonists, represented here by Johnson, who as faithful citizens had supported Britain, and of the need to be more conciliatory in granting the concessions they felt they had earned. This interpretation accounts for many of the unusual components in the painting, although the fact that the explanation is so logical is its only proof. Although conjecture, it certainly provides a new way to think about the picture.

The painting was also successful because West aggrandized and classicized his figures and the event, in effect creating a modern Classical scene. Contemporary viewers recognized they were in the presence of what amounted to a traditional Lamentation scene (for instance, see fig. 14.15), and that their hero was a modern-day Christ or martyr. The surrounding "apostles" express remorse and concern, but their powerful emotions, worthy of Poussin according to contemporary reviewers, are noble and controlled, in keeping with the Classical rule of decorum. Figures strike contrapposto poses, stand in Classical profile, and have the sculptural quality of a shallow ancient relief or Raphael saint, apostle, or Greek philosopher (see fig. 16.24); they are simultaneously modern and Classical. The one unemotional figure is the Iroquois, Rousseau's "noble savage," whom West presents with the grandeur and composure of an ancient river-god. West's painting technique was influenced by that of Hamilton and Mengs, both of whom he knew in Rome, for he first drew and then colored in the figures, allowing crisp contours to ennoble them.

Grand Manner Portraiture in the Neoclassical Style: Joshua Reynolds

Portraiture dominated British painting, for it was extremely difficult to earn a living as a history painter—there just was not much demand for it. Nonetheless, it was a fashionable "face painter," as portraitists were derogatorily called, who played a major role in encouraging British artists to turn to working in a grand manner that aspired to match the great accomplishments of the ancients and their Classical heirs in the Renaissance and Baroque. This proselytizer was Joshua Reynolds (1723–1792), who studied in Rome from 1750 to 1752 and returned to London determined to elevate British art in the mold of the great masters. Working behind the scenes, Reynolds played a role in establishing the Royal Academy of Art in 1768, and as a favorite of George III, he was appointed the body's first president, a position he held until his death in 1792. From 1769 to 1790, Reynolds delivered his

Fifteen Discourses on Art, in which he laid out theories similar to those of Charles Le Brun, the first director of the French Royal Academy (see page 745). He advocated history painting in the grand manner, emulation of the great masters, and an idealization in art.

While Reynolds was financially forced to spurn history painting for portraiture, he elevated the genre by encasing his figures in Classical poses and layering the images with recondite references of the kind that could be found in great history painting. Upon returning from Rome, for example, he painted a monumental full-length portrait of Commodore Keppel (1753), which shows the subject walking on a beach after a shipwreck. But Keppel is ennobled, for his pose is clearly based on the *Apollo Belvedere* (see page 157), then considered one of the great monuments of Greek art that Reynolds saw during his time in Rome. In his 1765 portrait *Lady Sarah Bunbury Sacrificing to the Graces* (fig. 23.7), Reynolds fills his picture with Classicisms. The presentation of the Three Graces on an antique pedestal at the upper left of the picture is based on a well-known Hellenistic sculpture. Lady Sarah's gown is not contemporary dress but rather ancient drapery, pinned at the shoulder and with a band at the waist. The brazier, urn, and architecture are also antique. The sitter's pose is based on a figure in a Guido Reni painting (see page 672).

Like a history painter, Reynolds has loaded his image with symbols. Using Cesare Ripa's *Iconologia* or Andrea Alciatii's *Emblemata*, books of symbols dating to the Renaissance that were vital resources for history painters, Reynolds selected the Three Graces because they were a representation of *amicitia*, or friendship. Ripa declared that the three figures symbolize the three stages of friendship, which are the giving, receiving, and constant exchange of friendship between friends. The intertwined arms represent this exchange, and the nudity the openness of friendship. The myrtle wreath held by the central figure signifies friendship's self-propagation, while the roses on the pedestal represent its beauty and pleasure. The figure pouring a sacrificial libation has been identified as Lady Sarah's lifelong friend, Lady

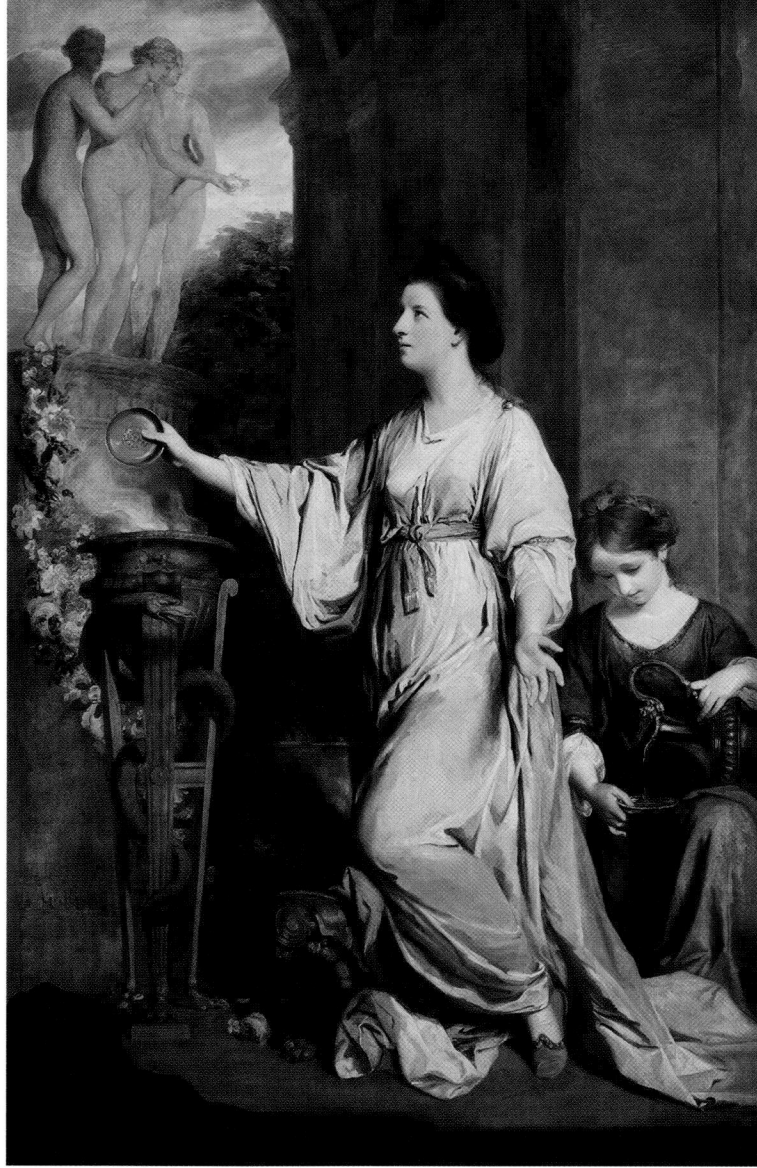

23.7 Joshua Reynolds, *Lady Sarah Bunbury Sacrificing to the Graces*. 1765. Oil on canvas, 7'10" × 5' (2.42 × 1.53 m). The Art Institute of Chicago, Mr. and Mrs. W.W. Kimball Collection, 1922.4468

Susan Fox-Strangways. While little is known about the commission for this picture, scholars believe the painting is as much about the platonic dedication of the women to one another as it is a portrait of Lady Sarah.

In the 1750s and 1760s, Reynolds made countless portraits that could be described as Neoclassical, pictures filled with Classical references and executed in a style that has a strong linear quality as well as smooth modeling and even lighting that sculpturally forms figures and objects. But in his quest to emulate the Old Masters, as he advocated in his Discourses, Reynolds was a stylistic chameleon, at one moment taking his cue from Raphael, the next Guido Reni, the next Rubens, and the next Rembrandt. One artist who is lurking behind most of his pictures in some form, however, is Anthony van Dyck, the Flemish painter who

ended his brief career painting royalty in London. His enormous full-lengths portraits with grandly yet elegantly posed figures (see fig. 20.8) challenged most portraitists in eighteenth-century Britain, and despite the Neoclassical look of Lady Sarah Bunbury, this almost 8-foot-high canvas, which would proudly preside in a public room of the sitter's imposing home, reflects the scale and grandeur of Van Dyck's work.

Architecture and Interiors: The Palladian Revival

In Britain, a Classical revival began much earlier in architecture than it did in painting and sculpture, and its origins date to the architectural treatises of Anthony Ashley Cooper, third earl of Shaftesbury, and of Colen Campbell, published in the 1710s. Both writers argued for a British architecture based on antiquity and Antonio Palladio's classically inspired villas, which not only evoked antiquity but projected a perfect harmony using geometry, mathematics, and logic (see pages 614–17). Sounding much like Winckelmann did when he was discussing sculpture some 50 years later, Shaftesbury, in his *Letter Concerning Art, or Science of Design* (1712), wrote that the proportions and geometry of ancient architecture reflected the nobility and beauty of the Greek and Roman soul, which have a powerful effect on the enlightened "man of taste." Architecture was beauty, not function.

The works of both Campbell and Shaftesbury reflect a British antagonism toward Roman Catholicism. In Britain, Baroque architecture was associated with two evils: papist Rome and French royalty. Shaftesbury, a patron and student of John Locke, was an advocate of individual freedom, and he equated ancient architecture with democracy. He was also a member of the Whigs, the liberal antimonarchy political party. (The Tories, the conservative promonarchy party, had backed the Roman Catholic Stuart king James II, who died in 1701.) In 1714, the Whig party came to power, ending 13 years of political turmoil. Its democratic members especially identified with Classical-revival architecture, for they saw themselves as the modern equivalent of Roman senators, who had country villas in addition to city houses. Campbell, who was virtually unknown prior to the publication of *Vitruvius Britannicus* (1715–25), could hardly fill singlehandedly the demand from Whigs who wanted Palladian-style country homes. His three-volume treatise consisted of dozens of his own Palladio-inspired designs, which formed a pattern book for architects for the remainder of the century. Most British architects had a copy of Campbell's *Vitruvius Britannicus* as well as Vitruvius' *Ten Books of Architecture* and Palladio's *Four Books*.

THE COUNTRY VILLA: CHISWICK HOUSE We can see the impact of *Vitruvius Britannicus* on Campbell's patron, Lord Burlington (1694–1753), who after a trip to Italy in 1719 became an amateur architect and eventually supplanted Campbell as the leading Palladian. In 1725, Burlington with the artist William Kent (1684–1748) designed Chiswick House (fig. **23.8**), located on Burlington's estate outside of London and one of the most

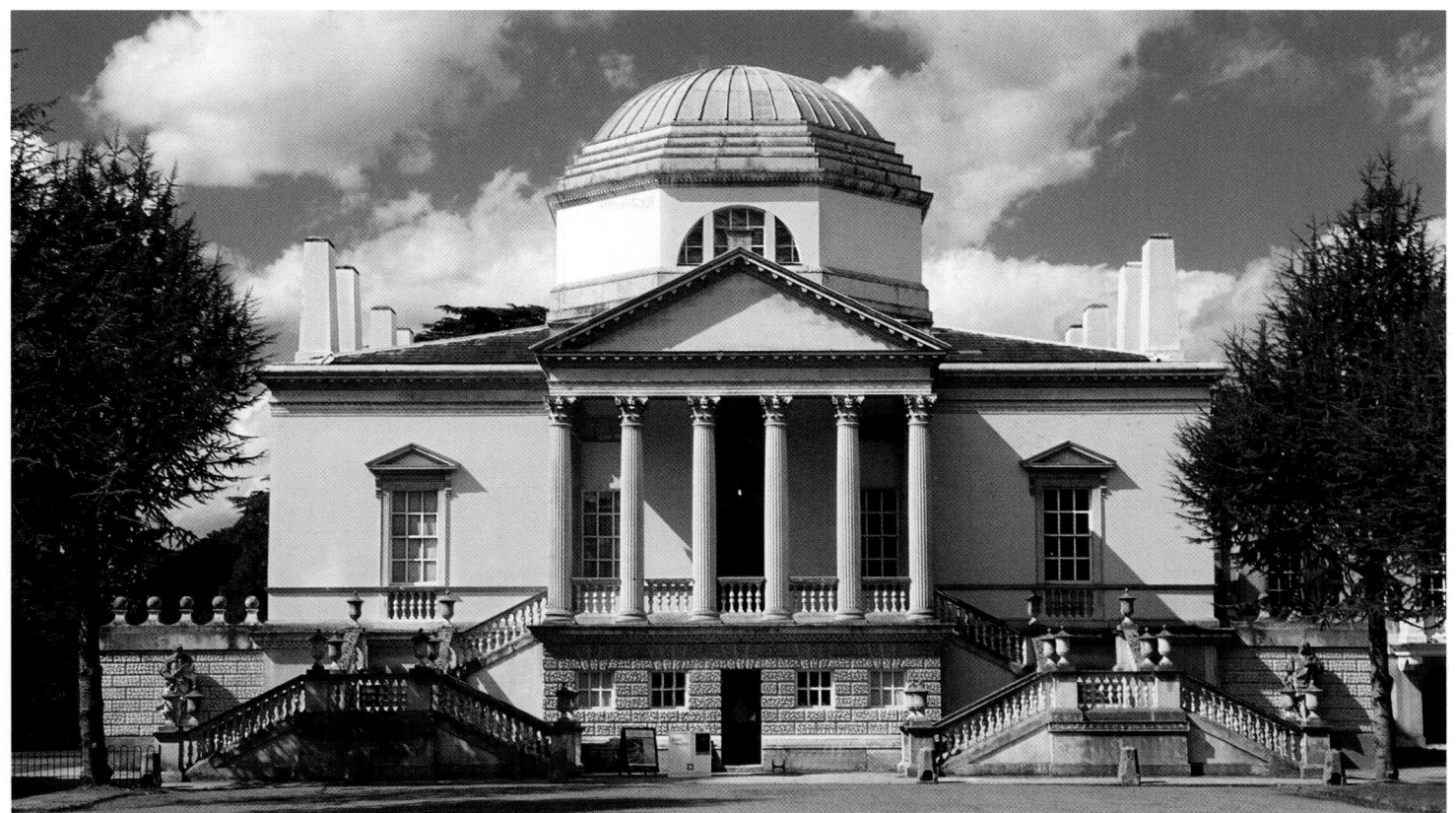

23.8 Lord Burlington and William Kent. Chiswick House, near London. Begun 1725

famous Palladian-revival houses. This stately home is based on Palladio's Villa Rotonda (see fig. 17.34), which Lord Burlington had studied on his Grand Tour. The exterior staircase, however, could just as well have come from Campbell's 1715 design for the façade of Wanstead House, which appears in volume one of *Vitruvius Britannicus*.

Chiswick House is remarkable for its simplicity and logic, making it easy to understand why Lord Burlington was such a success as an architect. The building is a cube. Its walls are plain and smooth, allowing for a distinct reading of their geometric shape and the form of the windows. The Greek temple portico protrudes from the wall, again creating a simple and clear form. Even the prominent domed octagonal rotunda is geometric, as are its tripartite semicircular clerestory windows, based on windows in Roman baths. Here we have reason and logic clearly stated, and put in the service of the ideals of morality, nobility, and republican government. Like Shaftsbury, Burlington believed architecture to be an autonomous art dealing in morality and aesthetics, not function.

URBAN PLANNING: BATH Perhaps the greatest example of the Classical revival in Britain is in Bath, a resort that had been a spa town since Roman times. Local architects John Wood the Elder (ca. 1704–1754) and the Younger (1728–1782) played a major role in developing the sleepy town as it expanded to accommodate the flood of wealthy Londoners who as a result of the burgeoning economy at midcentury came to "take the waters." In

the 1740s and 1750s, John Wood the Elder, influenced by the Classical revival, aspired to evoke ancient Rome and designed an imperial gymnasium, forum, and circus. Only the last was realized with success. Built in 1764, it consists of 33 attached houses surrounding a circle and divided by three streets. The façades are identical and continuous, and resemble the Colosseum turned outside in (see fig. 7.20). John Wood the Younger upstaged his father in 1767 when he designed the Royal Crescent (fig. **23.9**), a crescent-shaped space containing 30 houses. Wood the Younger used a colossal Palladian Ionic order mounted on a podium basement, giving the façade a magnificent unified grandeur. The Woods' urban planning of circuses was so innovative it would be replicated in Britain right through the nineteenth century.

THE NEOCLASSICAL INTERIOR The British taste for the Classical extended to interior design and was largely created by one man, Robert Adam (1728–1792). Adam was a wealthy Scottish architect who made the Grand Tour from 1754 to 1758. He scrambled over the Roman ruins, assisting Piranesi in measuring and documenting the deteriorating structures and reconstructing them on paper. Upon returning to Great Britain, he began practicing in London and was soon the city's most fashionable architect. Although he designed several houses, his specialty was renovating interiors and designing additions, especially for country homes. Along with Joshua Reynolds, Adam played a major role in developing a taste for the Neoclassical in London in the late 1750s.

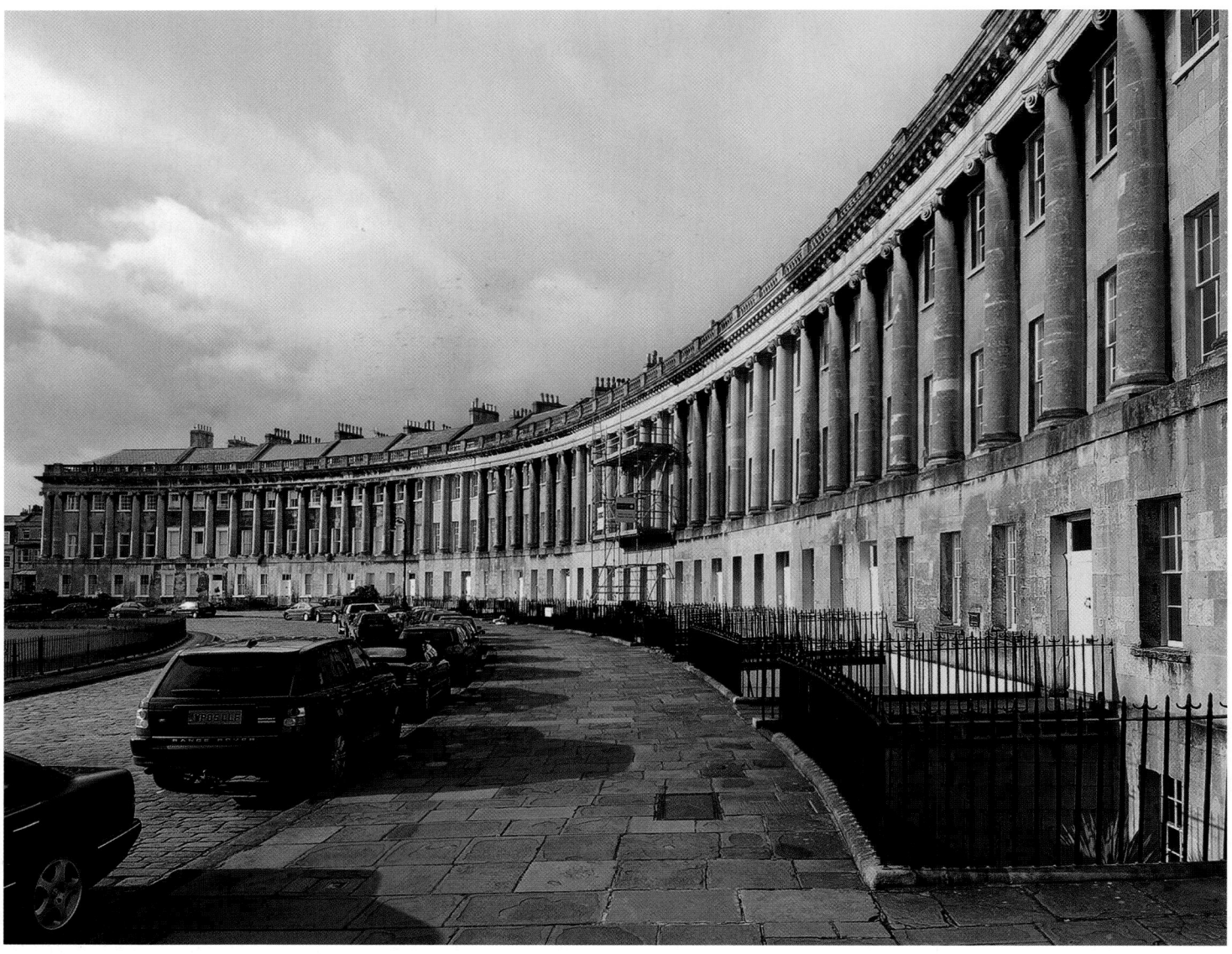

23.9 John Wood the Younger. Royal Crescent, Bath, England. 1767–ca. 1775

A fine example of his work is the library wing at Kenwood (fig. **23.10**), built in 1767–69. The ceiling of the room is a Roman barrel vault, and at either end is an apse separated from the main room by Corinthian columns. This concept comes largely from Palladio. The decoration is based on Classical motifs, which Adam could copy from the many archaeological books then being published. On the one hand, the library is quite Classical, not just because of the motifs, but also because it is symmetrical, geometric, and carefully balanced. On the other hand, it is filled with movement, largely because of the wealth of details and shapes that force the eye to jump from one design element to the next. Adam's palette is pastel in color and light in tone; light blues, white, and gold prevail. Curving circles, delicate plant forms, and graceful fluted columns with ornate capitals set a festive, elegant, and refined tone closer to Rococo playfulness than to Neoclassical morality. For the decorative wall paintings, Adam often turned to the Italian Antonio Zucchi and occasionally to Angelica Kauffmann, whom Zucchi married in 1781.

EARLY ROMANTICISM IN BRITAIN

The architect Sir John Vanbrugh was not only one of the leading figures of the British Baroque (see page 758), he was also responsible for introducing Gothic design to domestic architecture when he built his own London mansion, Claremont, in 1708, silhouetting the roofline with massive medieval crenelations. This decision to depart from the Baroque or Classical may at first seem incongruous, but within Vanbrugh are the seeds of Romantic longing for emotional experience. Vanbrugh argued not to destroy old buildings but rather to conserve them because they inspire "more lively and pleasing Reflections on the Persons who have inhabited them; on the remarkable things which have been transacted in them, or the extraordinary occasions of erecting them." This longing for exotic experience, of being transported mentally to a distant past, gradually became a prevailing sentiment in British art, surfacing in painting, architecture, and landscape design. By the closing decades of the eighteenth century,

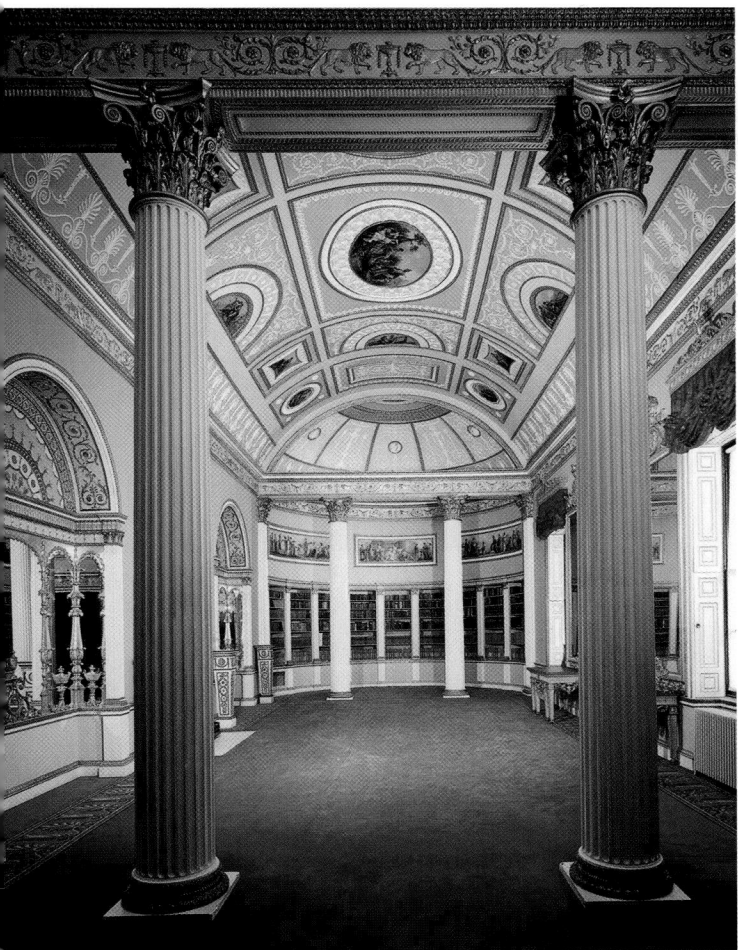

23.10   Robert Adam. Library, Kenwood, London. 1767–69

exotic experience alone would not be sufficient; audiences would want to be awed or terrified, just as they do today when they go to see a horror film.

Architecture and Landscape Design: The Sublime and the Picturesque

We do not know precisely what motivated Edmund Burke to write his 1756 treatise *A Philosophical Inquiry into the Origin of Our Ideas of the Sublime and Beautiful* (see page 790), but he must in part have been prompted by the period's increasing desire to undergo powerful subjective experiences, an emphasis that existed alongside a strong belief in the primacy of logic and empiricism. We have already seen how Piranesi created a sense of awe and melancholy in his etchings of Roman monuments, which were popular throughout Europe and were often labeled "sublime" once the word became current. The British, however, were principally responsible for developing a taste for the sublime in the visual arts—for the experience of undergoing the most primal of emotions, those verging on terror—and it first appears in architecture and garden design.

Simultaneously, the British also developed two other concepts or principles, neither of which is a style. One is the **picturesque**.

Initially the term was used in the guidebooks to the Lake District in the north of England to mean a scenic view that resembled a landscape painting. It gradually came to mean as well that something had variety and delightful irregularities that made it interesting to look at, and the concept was offered as an alternative to, on the one hand, the sublime, which caused awe and fear, or as Burke claimed, a feeling of a need for self-preservation, and, on the other hand, beauty, which was manifest in smooth, symmetrical, and harmonious qualities that generated feelings of joy, pleasure, and love. The British writer William Gilpin, who played a major role in defining the term picturesque in several late eighteenth-century treatises, wrote that a Gothic castle would be infinitely more interesting and picturesque if it were in a state of decay, a crumbling ruin covered with vegetation. In a painting, this ruin would offer greater variety for the eye if it were executed with a large range of colors instead of just a few, and were lit with a strong light that resulted in a play of dark and light as opposed to even, uniform illumination. Although not discussed by Gilpin, this same Gothic castle could be considered beautiful if exquisitely proportioned and in perfect condition, and it would be sublime if it were enormous, dark, and foreboding, seeming to harbor unseen dangers. The picturesque, in contrast to the sublime, generated visual interest, not fright or awe.

The other major concept developed at the time was **associationism**, a term invented by twentieth-century historians to describe the eighteenth century's love of layering architecture and garden design with numerous associations, many exotic, that were often designed to elicit emotional responses as well as to edify. Enlightenment research and publications vastly increased the knowledge of history and the world, and this knowledge was now poured into art. Winckelmann and Piranesi, for example, gave separate identities to Greek and Roman art, which had previously been combined under the banner of Classical art; now artists could make reference to the "noble simplicity and calm grandeur" of the Greeks or to the imperial might of the Romans. We have already seen, for example, how British architects evoked republican Rome in their buildings in order to elicit a sense of democracy. While architecture had always been representational, that is, containing associations, now these associations became more extensive, precise, formal, and literary.

THE ENGLISH LANDSCAPE GARDEN Burlington and Kent landscaped the grounds surrounding the Palladian-revival Chiswick House to look natural, that is, unplanned and without human intervention. This was a radical departure from the style of the house itself and from the geometric gardens that were then in vogue, such as those at Versailles (see fig. 21.12). Winding paths, rolling lawn-covered hills, serpentine ponds, and irregular stands of trees greeted visitors making their way to the mansion. Picturesque asymmetry rather than orderly geometric symmetry prevailed. However, these natural-looking grounds were not intended to be a re-creation of untamed nature; rather, they were an idealized vision of the Classical past as if rendered in a landscape painting by Claude Lorrain (see fig. 21.8), who was

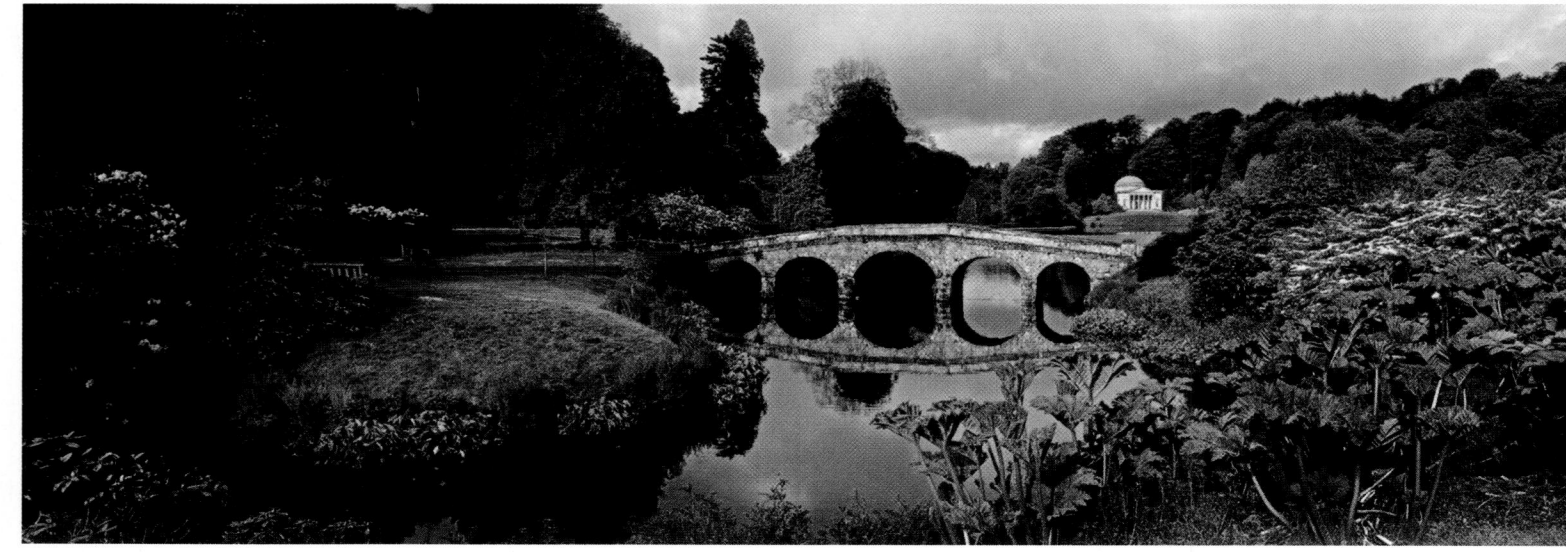

23.11 Henry Flitcroft and Henry Hoare II. Park at Stourhead, Wiltshire, England. Designed 1743, executed 1744–65, with later additions

extremely popular among British collectors. Aristocrats arriving in their carriages even had special yellow-tinted "Claude" glasses that gave the view the same warm twilight glow found in the French master's paintings. On the one hand, we can label the grounds as Neoclassical, since they are meant to evoke the Classical past as seen through the eyes of Claude. But on the other hand, they are Romantic, for they are designed to transport viewers psychologically into a lost Arcadian world, an immersion accompanied by powerful emotions.

Kent was probably responsible for most of the landscaping at Chiswick, and he became renowned as a landscape designer, rather than as an architect. He is credited with establishing the English style of landscape garden, his finest perhaps being the one he developed at Stowe in the 1740s. There, Kent sprinkled the grounds with carefully sited Classical temples and Gothic "ruins." Unfortunately, there is very little left of Kent's gardens. The best-preserved picturesque landscape garden is by two followers of Kent and Burlington, the architect Henry Flitcroft (1697–1769) and the banker Henry Hoare II (1705–1785), who started developing the grounds on the latter's estate at Stourhead in Wiltshire in 1743 (fig. **23.11**). In the carefully orchestrated view reproduced here, we look across a charming bridge and artificial lake to see nestled in the distant trees a Pantheon-like structure that is a replica of the Temple of Apollo in Claude's *Coast View of Delos with Aeneas*, a picture based on Vergil's epic poem *The Aeneid*. The path around the lake is meant to be an allegorical reference to the journey of Aeneas through the underworld, for the lake itself represents Lake Avernus, the entrance to the underworld. A grotto by the lake contains statues of a nymph and river-god. Thus, not only are there picturesque variety and views in the park at Stourhead, but there are also layers of historical and literary associations. Nor is the park limited to Greek and Roman motifs, for it includes rustic cottages, a Gothic spire, a Turkish tent, and Chinese bridges, an encyclopedic compendium reflecting Enlightenment discoveries. And there are also the sham ruins

that Kent popularized at Stowe "to raise the imagination to sublime enthusiasm, and to soften the heart to poetic melancholy," as contemporaries themselves described them.

In other words, the English garden did more than just evoke the nobility of the Classical past, in which case it would simply be described as Neoclassical. It also catered to a Romantic sensibility developing at the time—a sensibility characterized by delight in the exotic as well as a desire to experience powerful emotions. It was, in fact, a Piranesian contemplation of the destructive power of time and mortality as seen in the ruins. Burke had put the word sublime into play, and, as we saw in the previous quote about sham ruins, the period was using it.

THE GOTHIC REVIVAL: STRAWBERRY HILL While the Woods were developing Bath to look like a Roman city and Palladian country houses were springing up all over Britain, a Gothic revival was also taking place. An interest in Gothic architecture—which was then perceived as a national architecture because it was believed to have originated in Britain—was sparked in part by the appearance of some of the first literature on the style, which until then had been so little studied that no one knew when the buildings were made or that they even belonged to different periods of the Gothic, each with a different style. After midcentury, books began to identify the major buildings and their dates, and to define a development of Gothic architecture. But the Gothic style's appeal in large part lay in its sublime qualities. The cathedrals were cold, dark, and gloomy, and contained vast overwhelming spaces. Gothic ruins, which could be seen everywhere, evoked associations of death, melancholy, and even horror. In 1764, the Gothic novel emerged as a genre with the publication of Horace Walpole's *The Castle of Otranto: A Gothic Story*, which was set in a haunted castle. The book started a medieval craze that peaked with Victor Hugo's 1831 *Notre-Dame de Paris*, in which the dark, foreboding cathedral is the home of the terrifying hunchbacked recluse Quasimodo.

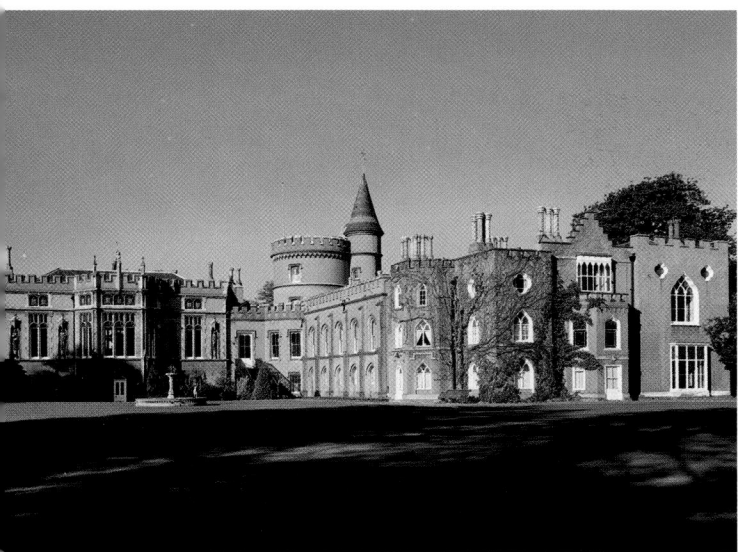

23.12 Horace Walpole, with William Robinson and others. Strawberry Hill, Twickenham, England. 1749–77

Horace Walpole (1717–1797) also deserves credit for making the Gothic revival fashionable when, with a group of friends, he redesigned Strawberry Hill (fig. **23.12**), his country house in Twickenham, just outside of London. Started in 1749, the renovation took over 25 years to complete. The house is distinctly medieval; the walls are capped with crenelated battlements and pierced by tracery windows. While Walpole may have thought of these features as eliciting a sublime quality, they are not really sublime. Instead they have a Rococo delicateness. The crenelations are petite, not massive, and the windows sit near the surface, making the walls look delicate, not fortresslike. Instead, Walpole's concept of the Gothic revival is more limited to just

being picturesque; the L-shaped building is irregular, asymmetrical, and looks like an accretion of additions from different periods, which it actually is because the building was erected piecemeal over a long period, with each section being designed by a different person. (The Neoclassical architect Robert Adam, for example, contributed the turret.) A Rococo lightness also characterizes the interior, as in the Picture Gallery (fig. **23.13**). Walpole insisted on historical accuracy for his rooms and had architectural details copied from engravings of medieval buildings that were being researched at that time. The gallery ceiling, for example, is taken from the Lady Chapel of Henry VII at Westminster Abbey (see fig. 12.54). The walls may be richly brocaded, but they look dainty, as though covered with lace-paper doilies, while the thin, gilded fan vault is elegant and lighthearted. Walpole verbally expressed the playfulness with which he approached the past when he wrote about "the charming venerable Gothic" and "whimsical air of novelty" the style lent contemporary buildings. Walpole's Gothic revival was in many respects as playful and decorative as Adam's Classical revival, a reminder that both represent a transition from the Rococo to the true Romantic revival, which would be much more somber, awe-inspiring, and even horrific, as seen in Fonthill Abbey of 1796 (see fig. 24.28).

Early Romantic Painting in Britain

Just as the Gothic revival thrived alongside the Classical revival in Britain, Romantic painting coexisted with Neoclassical. Romantic undercurrents even appeared in pictures that are essentially Classical, a paradox that underscores the limitations of labeling. Like a moth to a flame, the taste of the period was increasingly drawn to the awesome power of nature, the experience of unfettered elemental emotions and instincts, and even the wonder of the irrational. In effect, the Enlightenment at moments could deny its very foundation of logic and empiricism and permit itself to be swept away by the emotional pull of the exotic, wondrous, terrifying, and unexplainable. But we must remember that this thirst for sublime experiences stems from an identifiably Enlightenment mentality. Burke's treatise on the sublime, for example, reflects the Enlightenment inquiry into the operation of the human mind, while the cataloguing of the emotions and experiences parallels the compendious nature of Diderot and d'Alembert's *Encyclopedia*.

GEORGE STUBBS While we can only speculate as to whether Piranesi in his prints of Roman monuments was at all influenced by Burke's concept of the sublime, we know for sure that the treatise spurred George Stubbs (1724–1806) in the early 1760s to paint his series of approximately 21 paintings of a lion attacking either a horse or a stag, works that represent some of first examples of Romantic painting. Stubbs, who was from Liverpool, was a largely self-taught artist. He started as portrait painter in the north of England in the 1740s, and from 1745 to 1751 studied and taught human anatomy at York County Hospital. In 1754, he went to Italy, only to declare that he could learn nothing from the

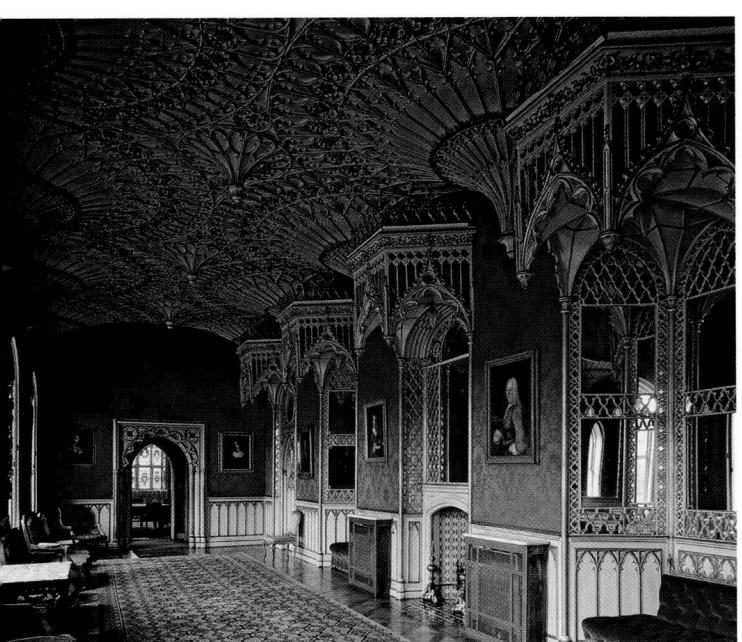

23.13 Picture Gallery at Strawberry Hill

Greeks and Romans; nature instead would be his only source of inspiration. Upon returning to England, he moved to Lincolnshire, where he practiced this professed Enlightenment empiricism by dissecting horses in order to study their anatomy. In 1766, he published his studies in *Anatomy of a Horse*. This was after he had moved to London, where he almost instantly became the country's foremost painter of horses, portraits that often also included an owner or groom holding the horse's lead. Never before had horses been painted with such scientific precision, a quality that in part accounted for Stubbs's acclaim.

While returning via ship from Rome in 1755, Stubbs saw a lion attack a horse in Morocco. When he repeatedly painted the scene, he was clearly under the influence of Burke's treatise, as seen in a fine 1770 example (fig. **23.14**). Here, Stubbs quite deliberately set out to create a horrifying natural event that would evoke a sublime emotion in a viewer. Stubbs's protagonists are animals, who, unlike humans, are immersed in nature and at one with it, virtual personifications of unleashed natural forces. We identify with the horse, which is white, a symbol of goodness and purity. Its mouth, eye, mane, and legs are taut with fear and pain. Evil is represented by the lion's dark powerful legs, which seem almost nonchalant as they rip into the horse's back, pulling the skin away to expose a skeletal ribcage. The lion's body disappears into the blackness of the landscape, identifying its evil force with a frightening darkness and elemental powers that surge from the earth. Ominous storm clouds announce the horse's fate as they threaten to cast the entire scene into dark shadow at the moment, we assume, the doomed horse expires. West, in *The Death of General Wolfe*, similarly harnessed the forces of nature to reinforce the emotional intensity and psychology of his figures.

JOSEPH WRIGHT Joseph Wright (1734–1797), born and raised in Derby in the Midlands, went to London in 1751 to study painting with a well-known portraitist, Thomas Hudson, with whom he later worked. However, Wright then returned to the Derby area, where he essentially spent his entire life. From here, he sent pictures to London, first to the Society of Artists and, after 1778, to the Royal Academy. While Wright earned his living largely from portraiture, he is best known today for his genre paintings and landscapes and has been hailed as "the first professional painter to express the spirit of the Industrial Revolution," of which he was in the middle since Derby is near Birmingham, the center of the Industrial Revolution. This acclaim is largely due to his paintings of iron forges and factories. He also made pictures of science experiments, and was himself a member of the Lunar Society, a Birmingham scientific organization that included many major figures, such as the physiologist and natural philosopher Erasmus Darwin, the grandfather of Charles Darwin. Many of

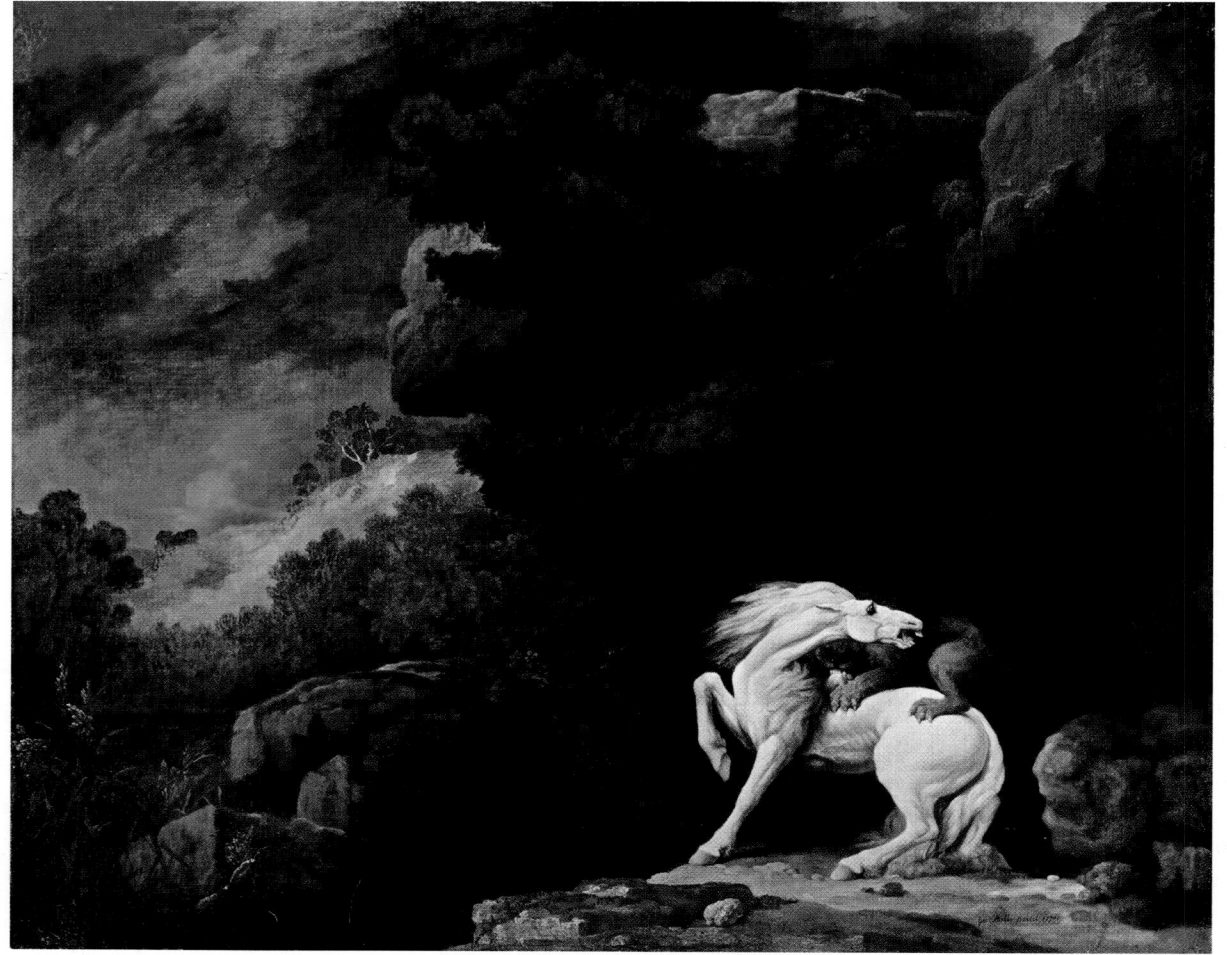

23.14 George Stubbs, *Lion Attacking a Horse*. 1770. Oil on canvas, 38 × 49½" (96.5 × 125.7 cm). Yale University Art Gallery, New Haven, Connecticut. Gift of the Yale University Art Gallery Associates 1961.18.34

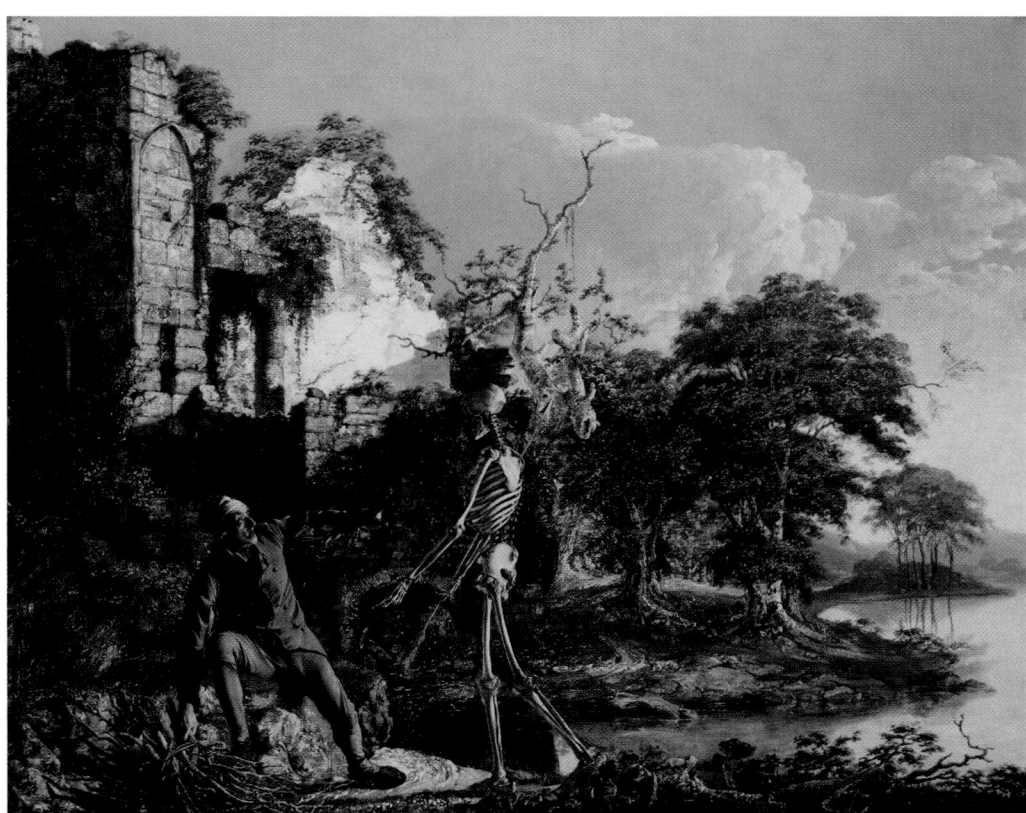

23.15 Joseph Wright, *The Old Man and Death*. ca. 1773. Oil on canvas, 40 × 50⅟₁₆" (102 × 127 cm). Wadsworth Atheneum, Hartford, Connecticut, The Ella Gallup Sumner and Mary Catlin Sumner Collection

Wright's images were set at night so that he could indulge in his scientific love of painting complicated light effects, which sometimes emanated from an artificial light source, including newly invented gas lamps.

In many of his images, Wright sought to create a sense of the miraculous or the unusual, thus reflecting the Romantic curiosity for new experiences and powerful emotions. A fine example of this is *The Old Man and Death* (fig. **23.15**), painted toward 1773. The theme comes from Aesop's fables (also recounted by Jean de La Fontaine), in which an old man, exhausted from carrying his load of faggots, falls to the ground and summons Death to come and take him away so that he need not return to his labor. Death instantly appears, terrifying the wearied worker, who now insists that he is fine, picks up his bundle, and continues about his business. In his painting Wright shows us Death, in the form of a skeleton with an arrow resting in his right palm, approaching the fatigued elder, who suddenly develops the energy of a horse. Although a daylight scene, Wright blasts the startled faggot-gatherer with an eerie powerful light, which seems to make him reel backwards. Adding to the sense of doom and gloom is the Gothic ruin, covered in plants, as were Piranesi's Roman ruins. Moss dangles from surrounding trees, contributing further to the lugubrious atmosphere. Employing his scientific approach to image making, Wright shuns Rococo paint handling and color, and instead carefully picks out each and every detail in the scene—every pebble on the ground, brick on the Gothic ruin, and leaf on the plants and trees. After finishing this frightening picture, Wright left for Italy, where instead of studying Greek and Roman art, he headed off to Naples. There, he watched the awesome eruption of Mount Vesuvius, which he painted, as well as sublime cavernous caves that he explored on the Bay of Naples.

JOHN HENRY FUSELI Early Romanticism in Britain culminated in the art of the Swiss-born painter John Henry Fuseli (1741–1825), whose special province was plumbing the innermost recesses of the mind and the incomprehensible forces within nature. Fuseli initially intended to be a theologian. In Zurich, he studied with the famous philosopher Johann Jakob Bodmer (1698–1783), who introduced him to the works of Shakespeare, Dante, Homer, and Milton, and to the *Nibelungenlied*, a medieval Norse epic that Germans believed was the northern equivalent of Homer's *The Odyssey* and *The Iliad*. He also befriended Johann Kaspar Lavater, a poet and physiognomist, who was an antagonist of rationalism despite his scientific interest in the way facial features reflected states of mind and personality. Lavater's interest in psychology heavily influenced Fuseli. As important, Lavater put Fuseli in direct contact with the German *Sturm und Drang*, which clearly influenced his development as an artist. He was especially captivated by the concept of the antihero, found, for example, in Goethe's *The Sorrows of Young Werther* (1774). The novel tells the tale of a young man, Werther, who rejects society, falls in love with a woman who spurns him, and in depression kills himself, suicide, in effect, being an extreme form of withdrawal from civilization and return to nature. The antihero was an important new kind of hero, one who established personal moral codes and followed personal passions to attain freedom and fulfill individual needs. These values would become part of the foundation of Fuseli's art.

In 1764, Fuseli moved to London. Encouraged by Reynolds, he took up painting and in 1770 went to Rome, where he became the leading figure in a circle of British and Swedish artists that included Thomas Banks. Dismissing Winckelmann's adulation of the calm grandeur and noble simplicity of Greek sculpture, as well as the perfect harmony of the High Renaissance as represented by Raphael, he gravitated to Michelangelo's colossal, twisting, muscular figures on the Sistine Chapel ceiling and especially the *Last Judgment* (see fig. 17.14). He was also inspired by the distorted anatomies of such Mannerists as Parmigianino (see fig. 17.29) and Rosso Fiorentino (see fig. 17.1).

Fuseli's selection of subjects was as unique as his style. Instead of noble, virtuous scenes drawn from the Roman historians Livy and Plutarch, he chose psychologically and physically agonizing events from Homer, Shakespeare, Milton, Spenser, and Ossian (a fake ancient Gaelic epic poet invented by James Macpherson and foisted on the public in the 1760s), many with erotic overtones. The more horrific and tortured the scene, the better, and the artists surrounding Fuseli in Rome favored similar themes. By the 1780s, Fuseli's subject matter dominated British painting, with

even the Neoclassicist Benjamin West painting lurid scenes from Shakespeare and the Bible.

Upon Fuseli's return to London in 1779, his themes and style were fixed, as we can see in *Thor Battering the Midgard Serpent* (fig. **23.16**) of 1790. The subject comes from the *Nibelungenlied*, an epic tale of the doom that results in the demise of the gods and the end of the cosmos and all morality. The wolf Skoll devours the sun and his brother Hatii eats the moon, plunging the world into darkness. Earthquakes shatter the world, releasing such monsters as Jormugand, the Midgard Serpent, who arises from the sea intent on poisoning the land and sky. Gods and giants fight fierce battles with the monsters, and here Thor, the god of thunder, is charged with slaying Jormugand, although ultimately he dies from the serpent's poison. The scene radiates sublime horror, from which the boatman shrinks and the ghost-white Wotan, king of the gods, cowers. Neoclassical planarity, tight drawing, consistent lighting, and the smooth handling of paint are replaced by an explosion of light, a flurry of Baroque brushwork, and a dramatic composition. The bold elements of this composition include the tensely coiled serpent, the deep recession of both the boat and boatman, and the violent upward thrust of Thor, whose Michelangeloesque proportions seen from the low vantage point of the serpent itself endow him with an appearance of Herculean strength. The image is all blood, water, rippling flesh, the heat of the serpent's breath, and the darkness of night, and because of the serpent's-eye perspective, a viewer is immersed in nature and put directly in the midst of the violent, frightening struggle.

While Thor epitomizes courage and sacrifice, Fuseli was often interested in portraying unconventional heroes who follow personal passion and exemplify individual freedom, especially in the face of societal pressure to conform and repress desires. How else to explain Fuseli's admiration for the Satan of Milton's epic poem *Paradise Lost*, whom he painted numerous times within the circle of Chaos, calling up his legions to launch a futile attack on the unfallen world of the Garden of Eden? Fuseli himself exemplified artistic freedom in his unique style and unconventional subjects, as well as in highly personal images, such as *The Nightmare* (fig. **23.17**) of 1781. The meaning of this work remains a puzzle. Clearly, sex permeates the picture, from the figure's erotic pose, to the mare's penetration of the "vaginal" parting of the curtain, and the sensual red of the fabric. But does the incubus (an evil spirit that has sexual intercourse with women while they sleep) on the woman's stomach represent her own psychotic monster or Fuseli's own repressed desires? A portrait of a woman on the back of the canvas suggests the exposed libido is Fuseli's, for although the figure is not identified, it may be of a Zurich woman who spurned the artist's offer of marriage in 1779 when he was passing through the city *en route* to London.

Regardless of the answer, this very personal painting is an extraordinary image, powerful, unique, and filled with sublime terror. It explores the erotic depths of the human mind and shrugs off expectations of what painting is supposed to be about. With Fuseli we have moved into the full-blown Romantic era, which begins to emerge throughout Europe toward 1800.

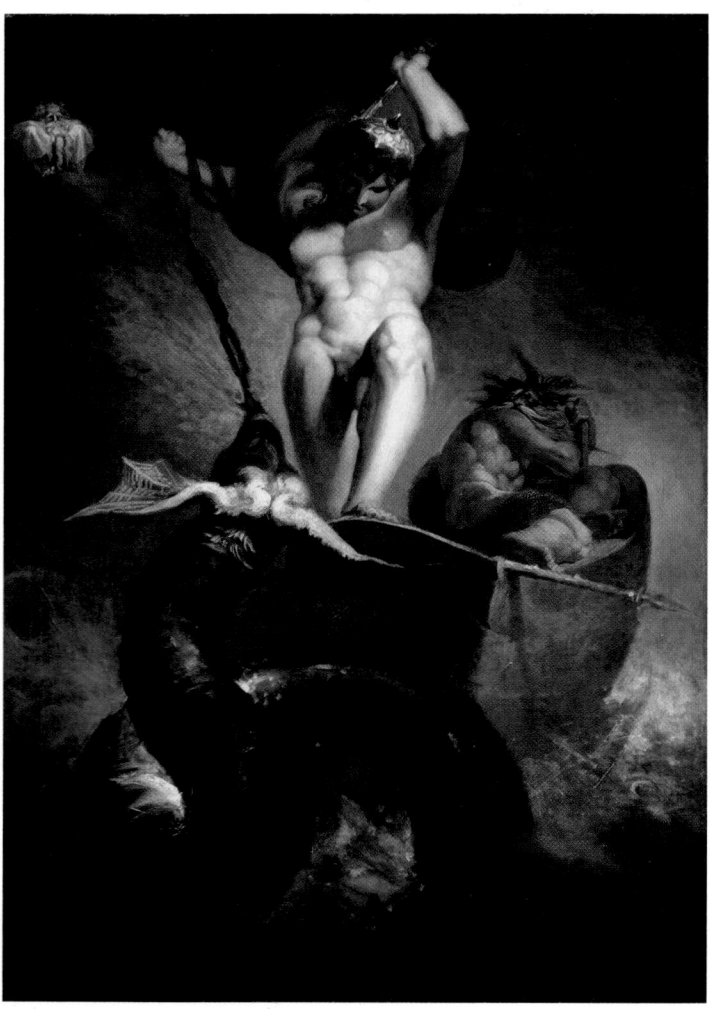

23.16   John Henry Fuseli, *Thor Battering the Midgard Serpent*. 1790. Oil on canvas, 51½ × 36¼" (133 × 94.6 cm). Royal Academy of Arts, London

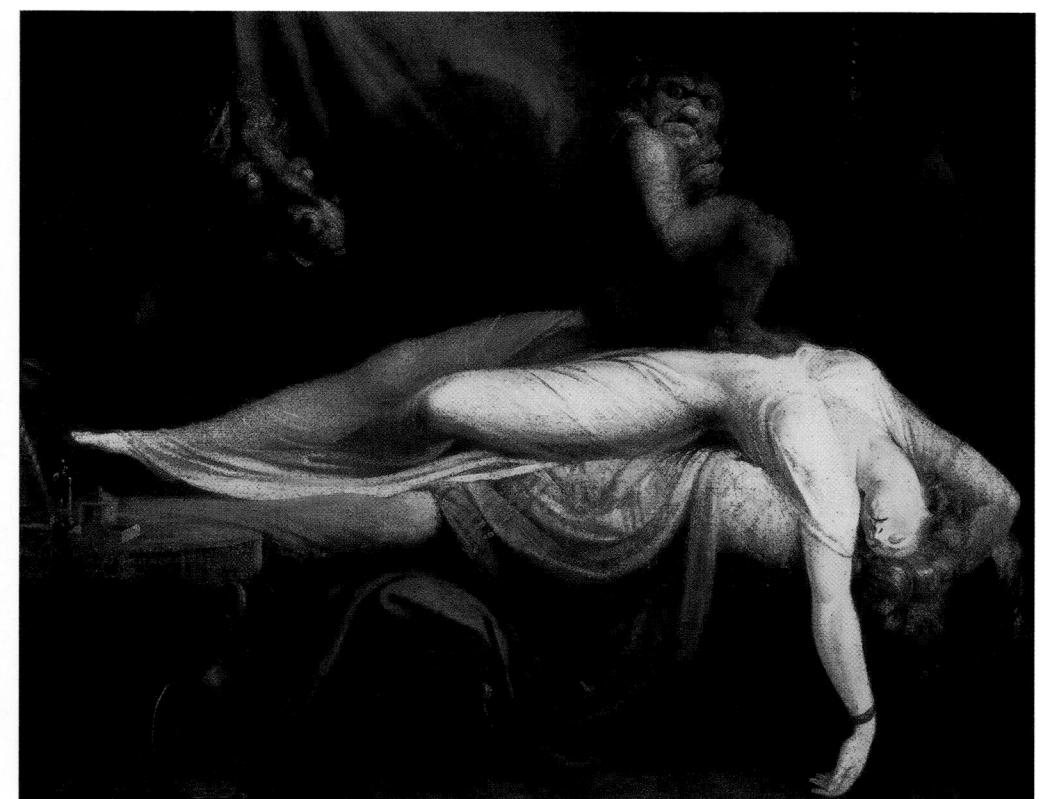

23.17 John Henry Fuseli, *The Nightmare*. 1781. Oil on canvas, 39¾ × 49½" (101 × 127 cm). The Detroit Institute of Arts. Gift of Mr. and Mrs. Bert Smokler and Mr. and Mrs. Lawrence A. Fleischmann

Romanticism in Grand Manner Portraiture: Thomas Gainsborough

Just as we saw that Neoclassicism affected portraiture in the work of Sir Joshua Reynolds, so too did burgeoning Romanticism. It is best exemplified in the portraits of Reynolds's nemesis, Thomas Gainsborough (1727–1788). Gainsborough was born into a prosperous Sudbury manufacturing family, and after studying painting in London with a French Rococo painter in the 1740s, he returned to his native Suffolk, initially painting landscapes. But to earn a living, he soon turned to portraiture, and in 1759 moved to Bath to take advantage of the wealthy clientele who came there to vacation. He did not move to London until 1774, but the appearance of his works at the Society of Artists from 1761 and the Royal Academy after 1769 established him as one of the leading artists of his day.

Like Reynolds, Gainsborough took his cue from Van Dyck, and his forte was enormous, life-size, full-length portraits, the figures often having elegant proportions and poses. While Reynolds created bold, modeled forms, Gainsborough dissolved figures and objects in lush, feathery brushwork, as can be seen in his 1785 *Portrait of Mrs. Richard Brinsley Sheridan* (fig. **23.18**), the sitter being a celebrated soprano married to the playwright responsible for the comedy of manners *The School for Scandal*. Not only does

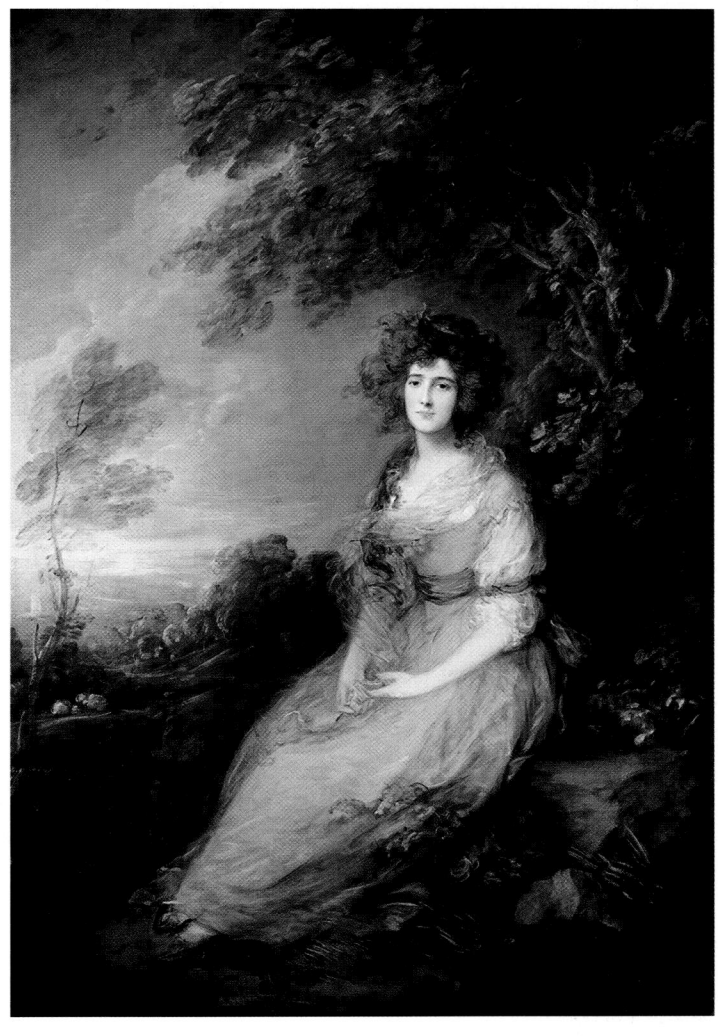

23.18 Thomas Gainsborough, *Portrait of Mrs. Richard Brinsley Sheridan*. 1785. Oil on canvas, 7'2⅝" × 5'⅜" (2.2 × 1.54 m). National Gallery of Art, Washington, D.C. Andrew W. Mellon Collection (1937.1.92)

Gainsborough's gossamer-thin touch give an elegance to the surface, it also animates it, making it seethe with motion and tying all of the objects together. More important, Gainsborough has integrated Mrs. Sheridan into the landscape. Her hair is windswept, following the pattern of the tree above and behind her, which forms a halo of sky around her head. Her body also echoes the thrust of the land, her drapery rippling in the same direction as the leaves, clouds, and rock. Mrs. Sheridan is steeped in nature, virtually swept away by it. Here we see demonstrated Rousseau's return to nature, the locus of innocence, beauty, and moral perfection.

NEOCLASSICISM IN FRANCE

As in Britain, the reaction against the Rococo in France first appeared in architecture, but it surfaced in the 1750s and 1760s, rather than the 1710s and 1720s. At first elegant and rational and largely based on seventeenth-century French Classical architecture, it moved into an austere, awe-inspiring, and even visionary stage by the late 1770s. This sublime phase of Neoclassicism had a profound impact on painting. Despite repeated appeals from numerous sources, including Enlightenment exponents and the government, painters were slow to meet the challenge to create a new moralistic art based on antiquity. It was not until the late 1770s that large numbers of painters took up the cause, and it was not until the 1780s, with the advent of Jacques-Louis David and his austere brand of Neoclassicism, that a new style emerged, one that thrived well into the nineteenth century.

Architecture: Rational Classicism

The first phase of French Neoclassical architecture was a reaction to the excesses of the Rococo, which had been about asymmetry, graceful movement, decorative flourishes, and curvilinear elegance. The new architecture was about rational design, and hence is often called "Rational Classicism." All components of a building had to be geometric, symmetrical, and logical in the sense that they should be essential to the structure. While this rational phase of Neoclassical architecture was theoretically based on nature, it nonetheless took its lead from seventeenth-century French Classical architecture.

THEORETICAL BEGINNINGS Launching the attack on the Rococo was the architect Jacques-François Blondel (1705–1774), who in a speech at the opening of the Royal School of Architecture in 1747 condemned the ornate flamboyance of that style. Here, and in his later publications, he called for a return to the Classicism of great seventeenth-century architects: Claude Perrault, Nicolas-François Mansart, and Louis Le Vau (see pages 748–51). Applying Enlightenment reason, Blondel demanded that buildings be logical, simple, functional, and symmetrical. They should be constructed with right angles, not curves, and there should be no superfluous ornament. Façades were to reflect interior layout and social use.

Blondel's rationalism was seconded by the influential writer Abbé Marc-Antoine Laugier (1713–1769), who in his *Essay on Architecture* (1753) and *Observations on Architecture* (1765) declared that function, not beauty, should determine the style of a building. Denouncing decorative ornament as well, his theory permitted only columns, architraves, pediments, and walls, all of which were essential and therefore natural. He condemned pilasters, niches, and any nonfunctional wall decoration or shape. Architectural components had to be based on nature, as illustrated by the famous engraving on the frontispiece of his *Essay*: a primitive hut, in essence the first building, consisting of four crude tree trunks dug into the ground in a rectangular configuration, with a gable roof made of twigs. This structure was the primordial forerunner of the Greek post-and-lintel system and the pedimented façade. Laugier's aesthetics also accommodated Gothic architecture, for he viewed its soaring stone columns as logical and natural, like a forest of trees, and he loved its spaciousness and light. Buttressing was structural, thus allowed.

But the theoretician who stripped rational architecture down to a barebones austerity that pointed to the future was Jean-François de Neufforge (1714–1791). Drawing on antiquity and Palladio but mostly on the British Palladians, his multivolume treatise *Basic Collection of Architecture* (1757–68) was filled with his own designs that reduced architecture to simple geometric forms: cubic houses, bare walls, severe unframed rectangular windows. Although he was otherwise virtually unknown, his treatise became a major source book for the period, one that many French architects owned and from which they lifted ideas.

A second major force for the Classical revival in architecture was the marquis de Marigny, who in 1751 became director general of buildings, a position that gave him artistic control over France, since he oversaw all royal commissions for art and buildings, as well as the French Academy. In preparation for the appointment, he went on the Grand Tour with the architect Jacques-Germain Soufflot from 1749 to 1751, receiving a Classical education that would prepare him to revolutionize French taste. Upon returning, he hired Soufflot to finish Perrault's Louvre (see fig. 21.11), which at the time was literally a ruin and slated for demolition. After the completion of the Louvre, he instructed Ange-Jacques Gabriel (1698–1782), the newly appointed first architect to Louis XV, to erect two enormous government buildings on the north side of what is today the Place de la Concorde, where they can still be seen: two huge identical façades framing the Rue Royale. Gabriel had never been to Rome, and for him Classicism largely meant seventeenth-century French Classicism. His two buildings are so similar to Perrault's Louvre they almost do not need illustrating: The major differences are that the double columns of Perrault's façade are now single, and the center pediment is removed, reappearing again at either end of the colonnade to become "bookends" framing the colonnade.

JACQUES-GERMAIN SOUFFLOT It was Soufflot (1713–1780), an ardent follower of Blondel, who designed the most famous rationalist building. Unfortunately, his masterpiece, the church of

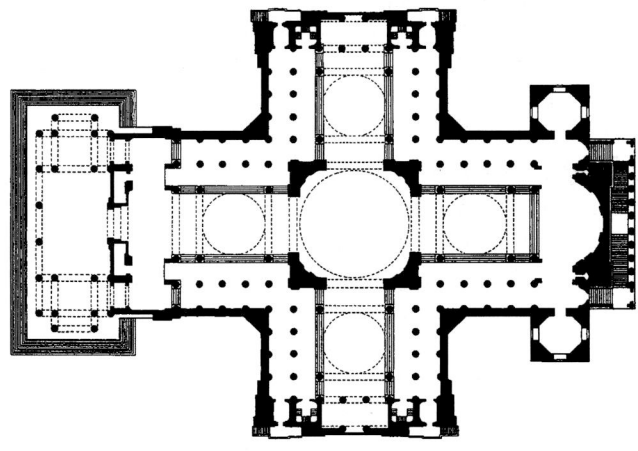

23.19 Jacques-Germain Soufflot. Initial plan for the Panthéon (formerly Sainte-Geneviève), Paris. 1757.

center crossing would have a hemispherical dome (modeled on the Pantheon in Rome) sitting on a drum supported by narrow piers consisting of four triangles, each triangle formed by three columns. Perrault's Louvre was his model. The pedimented section of the Louvre's east façade inspired the portico, and the Louvre colonnade provided the idea for the rows of interior Corinthian columns supporting an entablature. The drum for the dome largely derives from the circular peristyle Perrault used for the dome at the Louvre chapel. But Soufflot, following Laugier's vision of combining the clarity and grandeur of the Classical with the lightness and spaciousness of the Gothic, filled his church with light. Using a daring system of hidden buttresses, he was able to remove the wall mass and open the building up with enormous vertical windows.

Unfortunately, the clergy and public attacked Soufflot's 1757 plan, and the church was heavily compromised. An apse was added and the transept extended, destroying the symmetry of the first design. To adjust to these new proportions, Soufflot had to increase the size of the dome, with the result that it looks more like the Baroque dome on Christopher Wren's St. Paul's Cathedral (see fig. 21.22). But the greatest abuses came with the French Revolution. In its ardor to erase religion and honor French heroes, the Directoire government of the new republic in 1793 declared the building a pantheon to the nation's leaders (fig. 23.20). To convert the church into a lugubrious mausoleum, the windows were walled in and the interior ornamentation removed. Additional changes well into the nineteenth century further destroyed Soufflot's vision.

Sainte-Geneviève, has been so altered, including its name and function, that its current appearance can be quite misleading. In 1755, Marigny commissioned Soufflot to design the church. Within two years, the architect had completed his initial plan, which had a clearly stated geometry: an equilateral Greek cross with a six-column portico entrance (fig. 23.19). The wide square

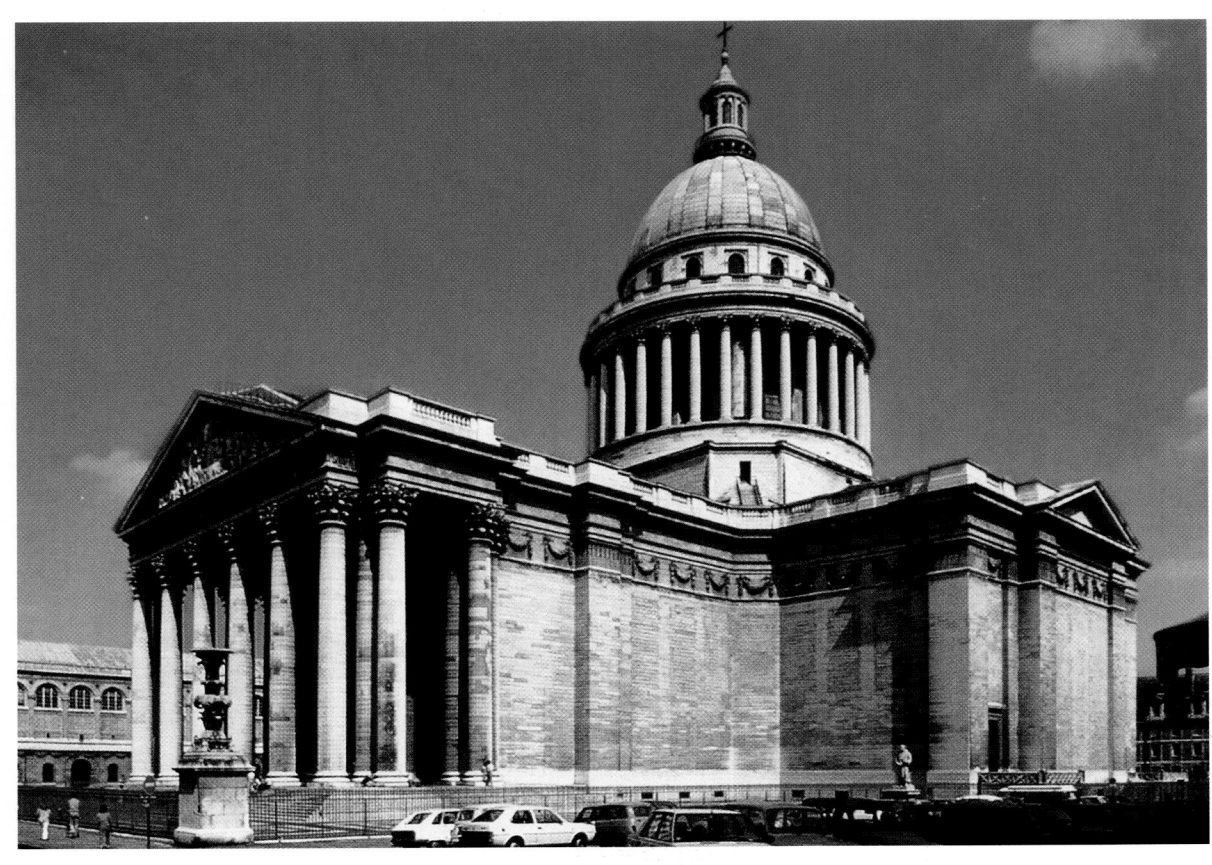

23.20 Jacques-Germain Soufflot. The Panthéon (formerly Sainte-Geneviève), Paris. 1757–90

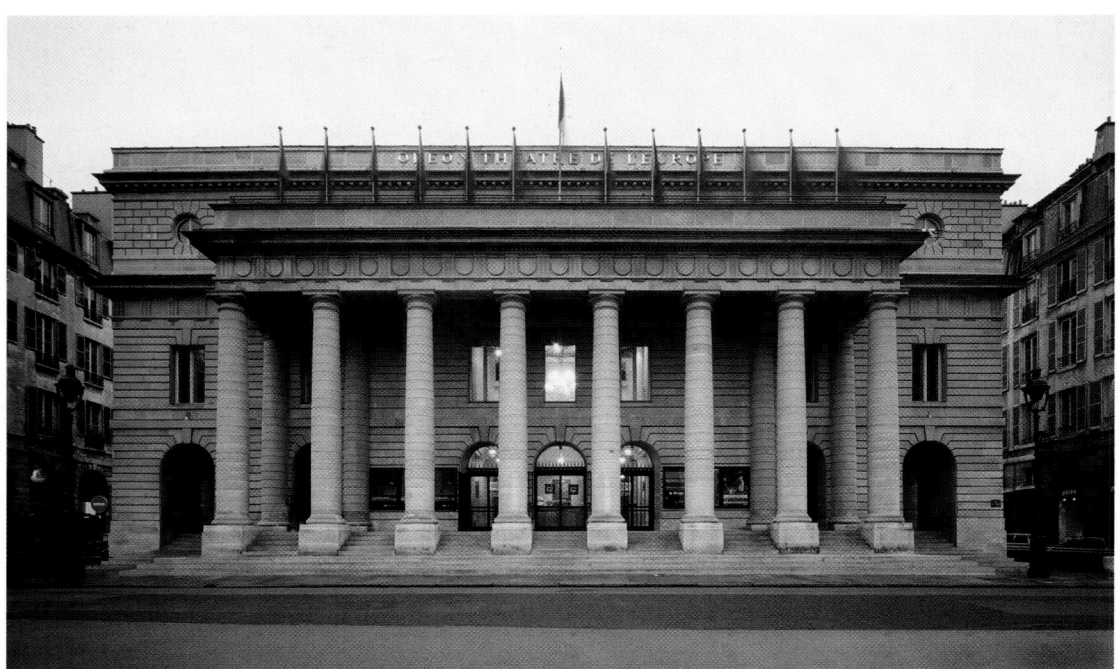

The Sublime in Neoclassical Architecture: The Austere and the Visionary

French architecture started to move into a new, more austere phase in the 1770s, one less interested in following the rules of the ancients and more preoccupied with reducing architecture to elemental geometric forms that operate on a monumental scale and create a Piranesian sense of awe and power. Among the architects largely responsible for this aesthetic were Claude-Nicolas Ledoux and Étienne-Louis Boullée.

MARIE-JOSEPH PEYRE Marie-Joseph Peyre (1730–1785) was a student of Blondel's, and in 1751 he won the Rome Prize. He met Piranesi and with his new mentor surveyed the baths of Caracalla and Diocletian (see figs. 7.58 and 7.63). This determined the course of his career, for he turned his back on the rules and propriety of Vitruvius and Palladio, and instead dreamed of making monumental, sublime architecture. In 1765, Peyre published *Architectural Works*, which included his plans for ideal buildings and the philosophy behind them. He emphasized the importance of scale and enormous cavernous spaces, especially advocating the use of vaults and domes that reflected the engineering prowess of the Romans. Modern architecture had to aspire to the sublime, to be awesome and grand—and he used the word "sublime" as defined by Burke. Decoration and detail were to be curtailed as the architect instead relied on the monumentality of the Romans to generate powerful emotional responses—shock, fear, awe, reverence, and passion.

Peyre's Théâtre Français (the present-day Théâtre de l'Odéon, fig. **23.21**), designed from 1767 to 1770 with another likeminded architect, Charles de Wailly, reflects the severity and monumentality that he advocated in his treatise, although it falls a bit short of a sense of the sublime, largely due to the practical restrictions of the commission. Nonetheless, the building seems austere compared to any eighteenth-century French building that preceded it. The façade consists of a towering two-story, unpedimented portico. Instead of elegant Corinthian or Ionic columns, Peyre used the harsh, unfluted Tuscan Doric. The only "decoration" is the striations and rustication of the stone. There are no frames around the arched doors and windows, and these openings penetrate deep within the wall, making it seem formidable and weighty. Geometry prevails in the form of circles and rectangles, and in the strong horizontals of the entablatures. Peyre's theater is a forceful block of a building, imposing in scale, awesome in its massiveness, and rational in its geometry.

CLAUDE-NICOLAS LEDOUX Even more severe than Peyre's Théâtre Français were the buildings of Claude-Nicolas Ledoux (1736–1806), also a student of Blondel. Ledoux was heavily influenced by Peyre's *Architectural Works*, Piranesi's publications, and Neufforge's *Basic Collection of Architecture*. He had no need of going to Italy. By the mid-1760s he was a fashionable Parisian architect designing many of the most prestigious *hotels particuliers*, as grand private homes were called, and by the 1770s, he was designing austere Palladian residences. In 1771, Ledoux became inspector of the royal salt mine at Chaux in the Franche-Comté region of southeastern France, designing many of its buildings from 1774 to 1779. The entrance portico to the gatehouse of the salt mine (fig. **23.22**) was in the Tuscan Doric style, which meant columns had neither flutes nor base and instead brutally sprang directly from a platform. The wall behind these primitive columns had an enormous primordial arch made of raw, uncut stone.

At Chaux, Ledoux developed a utopian vision of architecture, one that provided for the needs of employees of every rank. He was heavily influenced by Rousseau's vision of a world without

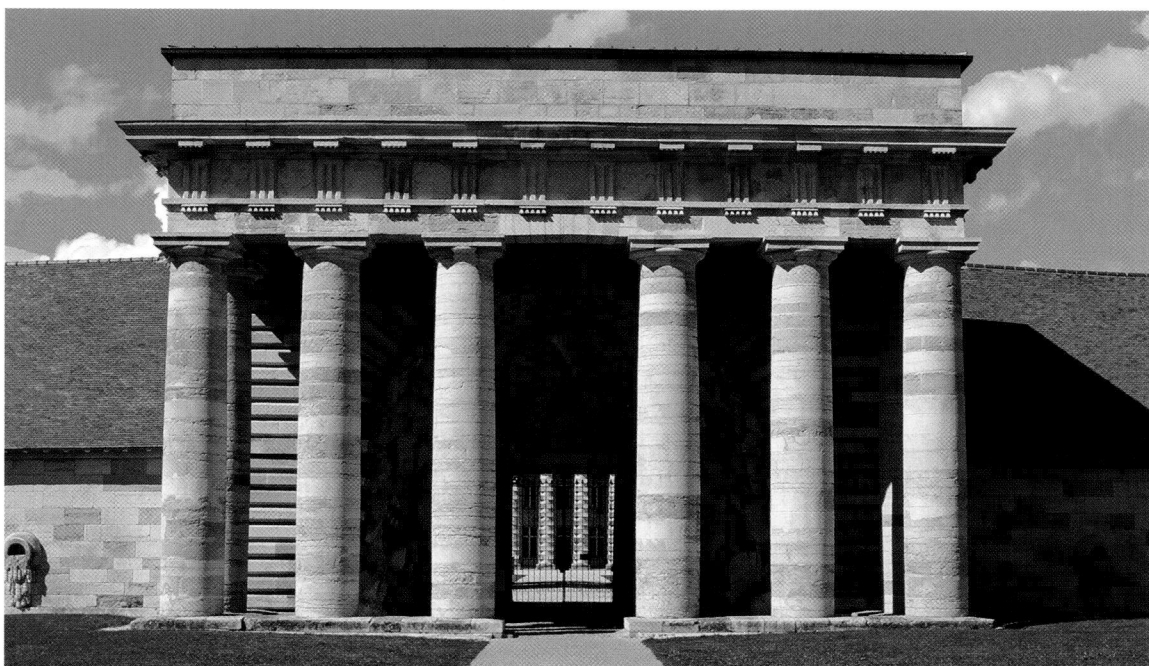

social barriers as well as by the social philosophy of an Enlightenment economic group called the Physiocrats, who advocated a basically agrarian economy that operated not only to benefit the proprietor class of landowners but also the productive class of laborers, thus giving workers a respected and essential position. Ideally, Ledoux wanted to lay out Chaux in concentric circles, with the most important functions symmetrically located in the center and the least farthest away. An essential component of the design had the concentric circles of buildings gradually dissolve into the surrounding countryside, thus becoming immersed in nature. Homes were often designed based on the dweller's job. The river authority's house, for example, was an enormous segment of pipe that the Chaux River would have literally run through if the house had actually been built (fig. 23.23). Hoopmakers would reside in houses shaped like wheels. Regardless of the owner's rank, each home had an austere

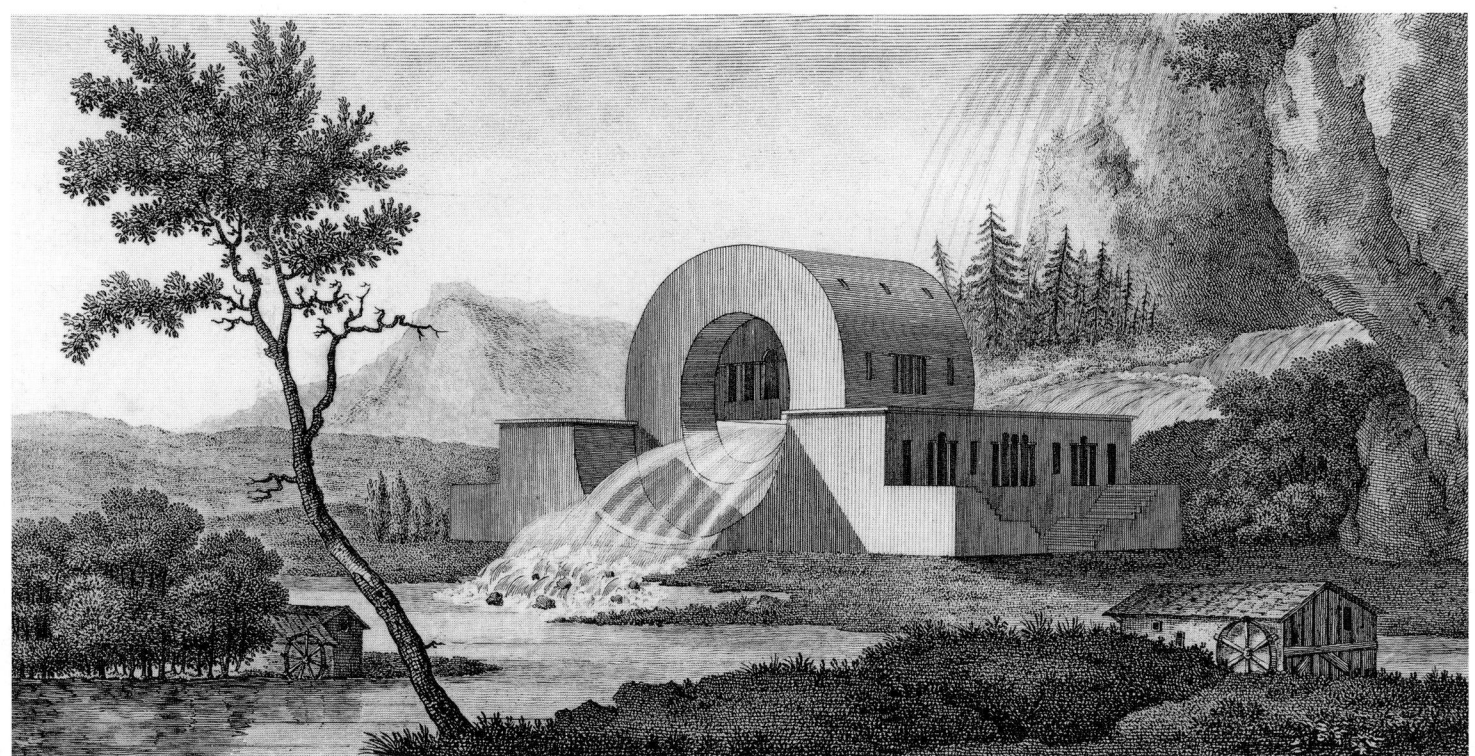

23.23 Claude-Nicolas Ledoux. House of the river authority, ideal city of Chaux. ca. 1785. Bibliothèque Nationale, Paris

stripped-down geometry that gave it a sense of importance and monumentality worthy of a noble civilization. While Ledoux's visionary architecture romantically conjured up the power and might of long-gone great civilizations, it simultaneously freed itself from the architectural vocabulary of the historical past as it radically reduced buildings to abstract forms, mutating Neoclassicism from a revival of the Classical past to a futuristic vision of purity and perfection.

ÉTIENNE-LOUIS BOULLÉE Ledoux's contemporary Étienne-Louis Boullée (1728–1799) shared his quest to create a monumental architecture using a basically abstract vocabulary. Like Ledoux, he did not go to Italy and took his cue from Piranesi, Neufforge, and Peyre. After a modest career designing relatively severe Palladian *hôtels*, he retired in 1782 to teach at the Royal Academy of Architecture, which gave him considerable influence over the next generation of architects throughout Europe. He also designed and published visionary structures that were so impractical they could never be built, which he knew. They are important nonetheless because they reflect the growing taste for the sublime that was welling up in France by the 1780s and that could be expressed, if not in real buildings, then at least on paper.

One of Boullée's most famous visions is his design for a tomb for Isaac Newton (fig. **23.24**). Conceived as a 500-foot-high hollow sphere resting in three concentric circles, it was meant to suggest a planet tracking three orbits. The top quarter or so of the orb was perforated with small holes to allow in light, making the ceiling from inside look like a night sky filled with stars. Below lay Newton's **cenotaph**, dwarfed by the immense scale of the structure and lost in the low lighting. The dramatic shadows and dark clouds of Boullée's drawing augment the frightening monumentality of his structure and help transform the edifice into an

awesome meditation on the power of universal forces and the insignificance of human existence. How ironic that Boullée should conceive of such a sublime building using a rational, geometric vocabulary—and have meant it to honor one of the most logical thinkers of all time.

Painting and Sculpture: Expressing Enlightenment Values

There was no parallel in French history painting to the swing toward Classicism occurring in French architecture in the 1750s and 1760s. Until the 1780s, the Enlightenment emphasis on reason and morality was best presented not by history painting but by the lower stratum of genre painting. In sculpture, it appeared in portraiture.

JEAN-BAPTISTE GREUZE One artist alone created the vogue for genre painting, Jean-Baptiste Greuze (1725–1805), and from 1759 until the 1770s his scenes of everyday life were the sensation of the Paris Salons. The Salon was an exhibition of members of the Royal Academy held in the Louvre. While conceived in the seventeenth century, the show was held only a handful of times before 1737, when it was first instituted as an annual that gradually evolved into a biennial presented in the *Salon carré* of the Louvre, hence its name. Pictures literally wallpapered the high walls, with smaller works and landscapes appearing at eye level, above which hung portraits, and above them, enormous history paintings. A narrow staircase leading to the Salon was packed with small still lifes and genre scenes. The Salons, which opened on August 25, the feast-day of St. Louis, and lasted between three and six weeks, were attended by some 20,000 to 100,000 people, who came from all strata of society, resulting in bakers and

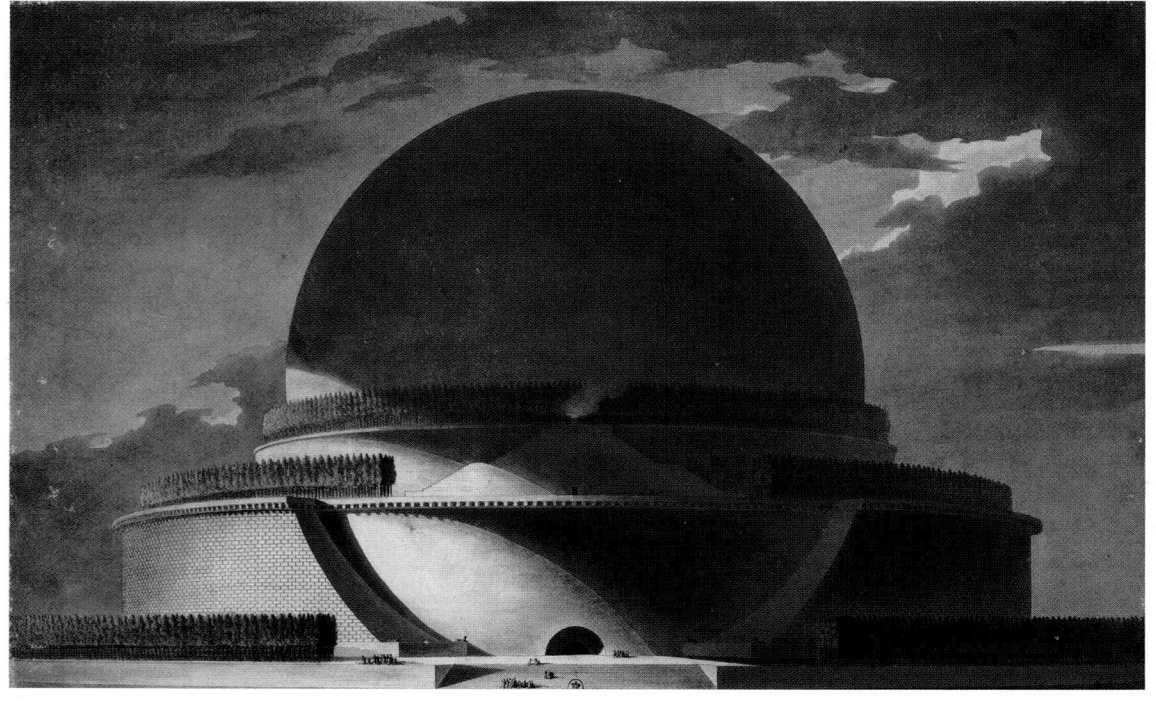

23.24 Étienne-Louis Boullée, *Project for a Tomb to Isaac Newton*. 1784. Ink and wash drawing, 15½ × 25½" (39.4 × 64.8 cm). Bibliothèque Nationale, Paris

blacksmiths literally rubbing shoulders with dukes and duchesses in the crowded room. With the Salons critics emerged, their commentaries, often scathing, appearing in brochures that were generally published anonymously.

Greuze emerged from a working-class background in the Lyon region and went to Paris in the mid-1750s to make his mark at the Royal Academy. A wealthy collector sponsored a trip to Italy for him from 1755 to 1759, but Greuze left Paris a genre and portrait painter and returned as one as well. Nonetheless, he became the rage of Paris with *The Village Bride* (fig. **23.25**), his submission to the Salon of 1761, which shows a Protestant wedding the moment after a father has handed his son-in-law a dowry, dutifully recorded by a notary, seated on the right. The scene seethes with virtue as the various members of this neat, modest, hardworking religious family express familial love, dedication, and respect. Here is the social gospel of Rousseau: The naïve poor, in contrast to the more cultivated, yet immoral aristocracy, are closer to nature and thus full of "natural" virtue and honest sentiment. Greuze draws a parallel between the human family and the hen and her chicks, each with one member separated, thus reinforcing the point about the natural instinct of common folk. Critics and public alike raved about the authenticity of the gestures and emotions, comparing them favorably with those of the noble figures of Poussin (see fig. 21.5). While Greuze was certainly attempting to match the intensity of emotion and gesture found in history painting, he was also inspired by contemporary theater, which accounts for the arrangement of the figures in a *tableau vivant* (a "living painting," when actors onstage freeze as in a painting to portray a pregnant moment) just as the father is declaiming his poignant speech about the sanctity of marriage.

Greuze was also heavily influenced by his friend Diderot, who championed him in his Salon reviews, which appeared anonymously in the *Correspondence littéraire*, a paper circulated privately throughout Europe and Russia. (See *Primary Source*, page

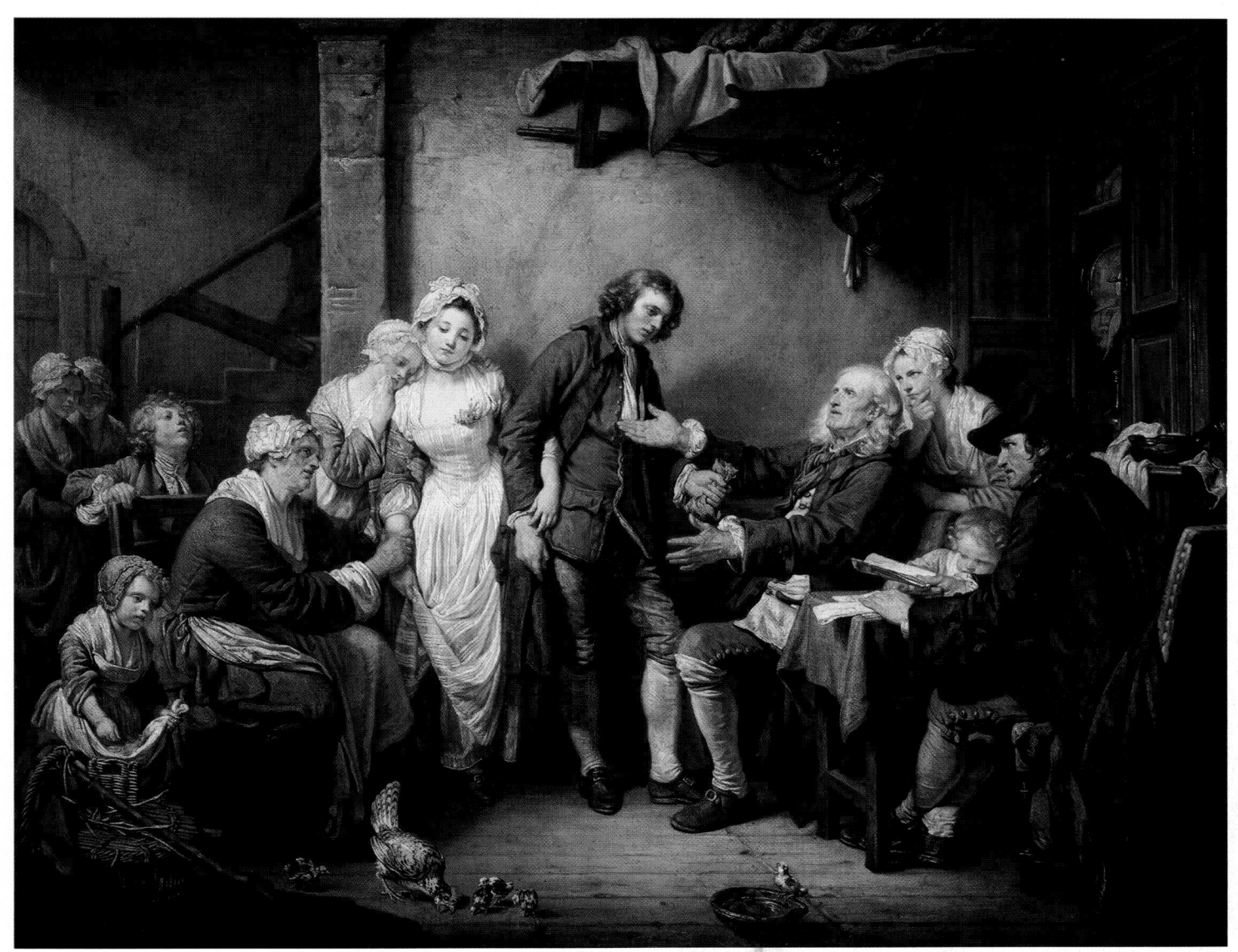

23.25 Jean-Baptiste Greuze, *The Village Bride*, or *The Marriage: The Moment When a Father Gives His Son-in-Law a Dowry*. 1761. Oil on canvas, 36 × 46½" (91.4 × 118.1 cm). Musée du Louvre, Paris

Denis Diderot (1713–1784)

From *Salon of 1763*, Greuze

Diderot's reviews of the biennial Salons, published in the outlawed newspaper Correspondence littéraire, *are generally considered the beginning of art criticism. The full title of the painting discussed below is* The Paralytic Succoured by His Children, *or* The Fruit of a Good Education, *which was subsequently acquired by Catherine II of Russia, with Diderot acting as intermediary. In a setting similar to* The Village Bride, *Greuze placed in the painting a paralyzed old man being affectionately attended by his large family.*

Now here is the man for my money, this Greuze fellow. Ignoring for the moment his smaller compositions … I come at once to his picture *Filial Piety,* which might better have been entitled the *Reward for Providing a Good Upbringing.*

To begin with, I like this genre: it is a painting with a moral. Come, now, you must agree! Don't you think the painter's brush has been employed long enough, and too long, in the portrayal of debauchery and vice? Ought we not to be glad to see it competing at last with dramatic poetry in moving us, instructing us, correcting us, and encouraging us to virtue? Courage, Greuze, my friend; you must go on painting pictures like this one!

812.) In his painting, Greuze perfectly captures Diderot's *drame bourgeois,* the new sentimental theater that this *philosophe* developed in the 1750s and that focused on ordinary middle-class people. As important as the bourgeois settings and sentimentality supporting virtue is Diderot's Enlightenment emphasis on logic and naturalism in theater. The dialogue was to be in prose, not verse, and the actors were to be instructed to stay in character and play to each other, not to the audience, which would destroy the illusion of reality. In other words, he wanted the audience to forget they were in a theater and be transported to the world of his drama. Likewise, Greuze wanted his viewers to forget the gallery they were standing in as they became immersed in the scene he magically painted.

Largely derived from Dutch and Flemish genre painting and certainly playing to an audience that loved Chardin's illusionism (see page 769), *The Village Bride* is filled with realistic detail, including attention to textures. The figures are individualized, rather than portrayed as ideal types: They are so real that when Greuze used them again in later paintings, the public decided it was witnessing the continuation of the story of the same family. As we shall see, Greuze's realism and morality as well as his pregnant *tableau vivant* moment will figure prominently in French Neoclassicism when it emerges some 20 years later.

JEAN-ANTOINE HOUDON The French sculptor who perhaps best exemplifies Enlightenment empiricism is Jean-Antoine Houdon (1741–1828). Both Greuze and Houdon used realism in their works, but Houdon, unlike Greuze, incorporated realism into a façade of Classicism. Son of the concierge at the Royal Academy school and thus literally growing up in the academy, he had little education but was extremely hardworking. His artistic vision was not given to flights of fantasy; rather, it was firmly rooted in Enlightenment empiricism. The elegant, mythological frolics of Clodion (see fig. 22.12) and the complex allegories favored by many French sculptors were foreign to his sensibility. Instead he approached the world scientifically. While a pensioner at the French Academy in Rome from 1765 to 1768, Houdon studied realistic Roman portrait busts, not idealized Greek sculpture, and in 1767 he executed in plaster a life-size flayed male

torso revealing in detail every muscle of the body while it leans against a support in perfect contrapposto, like Praxiteles' *Hermes* (see fig. 5.57).

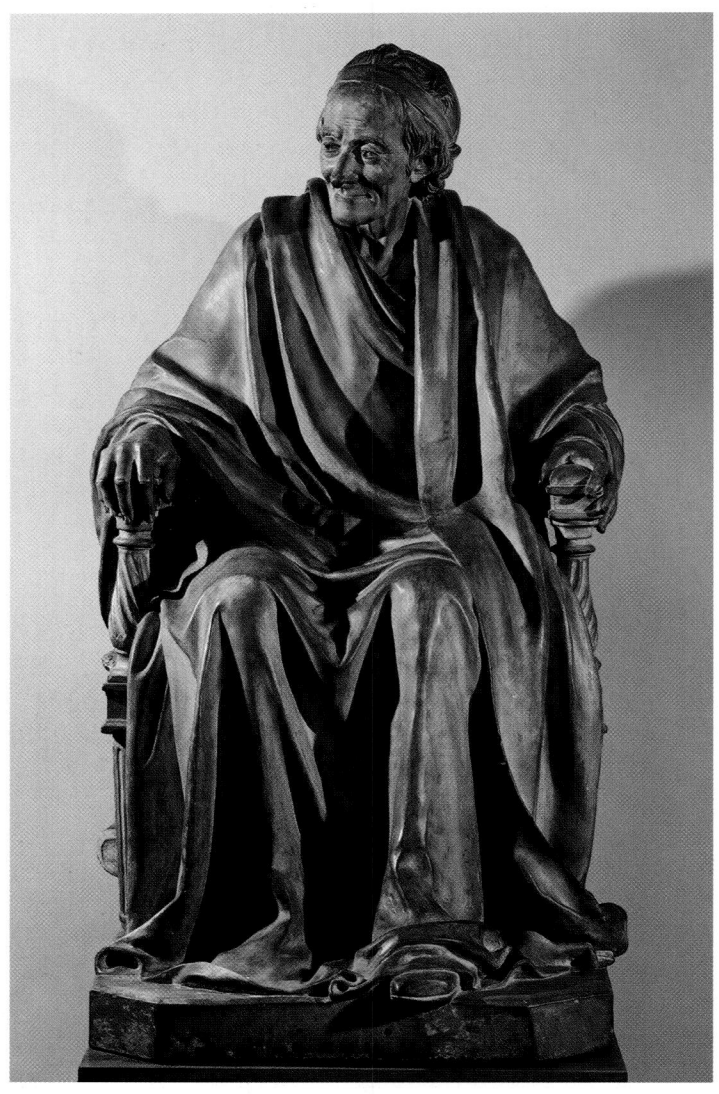

23.26 Jean-Antoine Houdon, *Voltaire Seated.* 1781. Terra-cotta model for marble original, height 47" (119.3 cm). Institut et Musée Voltaire, Geneva

Étienne-Jean Delécluze (1781–1863)

From *Louis David, son école et son temps*

In the early 1820s, David related the following to his student Étienne-Jean Delécluze, who published it in his 1855 book on David. Here, David describes the impact his 1779 discovery of Caravaggio and the Caravaggisti had on him. He ends his statement, however, by renouncing Caravaggio and embracing Raphael, an attitude that reflects a shift in style in his late work.

W hen I arrived in Italy, the most striking characteristic of the Italian pictures I saw was the vigor of the color and the shadows. It was the quality most radically opposed to the weakness of French painting; this new relationship between light and dark, this imposing vivacity of modeling, of which I had no idea, impressed me to such an extent that in the early days of my stay in Italy, I thought the whole secret of art consisted in reproducing, as had certain Italian colorists at the end of the sixteenth century, the bold uncompromising modeling that we see in nature. … I could understand and appreciate nothing but the brutally executed but otherwise commendable pictures of Caravaggio, Ribera, and Valentin who was their pupil. There was something barbarous about my taste, my formation, even my intelligence; I had to get rid of this quality in order to arrive at the state of erudition, or purity, without which one can certainly admire the Stanze of Raphael, but vaguely, without understanding, and without the ability to profit from them.

Source: Anita Brookner, *Jacques-Louis David* (New York: Harper & Row, 1980)

As would be expected of such an empirical mentality, Houdon specialized in portraits, and he became portraitist in chief to the Enlightenment, depicting virtually every one of the era's major personalities, including Diderot, Rousseau, Louis XVI, Catherine II of Russia, and Benjamin Franklin. Houdon's uncanny ability to capture both the look and essential character of his sitter is apparent in *Voltaire Seated* (fig. **23.26**), here shown as a terra-cotta cast from the original plaster, which is lost. The sculptor classicizes his sitter by dressing him in a Roman toga and headband, and seating him in an antique-style chair. But then Houdon's empiricism takes over. He gives us the sagging folds of skin on Voltaire's neck, the sunken toothless mouth, the deep facial wrinkles, and the slumping shoulders, all of which mark the sitter's age and frailty. Simultaneously, Houdon has brilliantly seized the *philosophe*'s sharp intellect and wit: The head is turning and the mouth smiling, and while one hand droops over the arm of the chair, suggesting age, the other grasps it firmly.

The Climax of Neoclassicism: The Paintings of Jacques-Louis David

The reign of genre painting in Enlightenment France was short, with Greuze's popularity peaking by 1765. The tide began to turn toward history painting in 1774 when Charles-Claude d'Angiviller was appointed director-general of buildings by Louis XVI. It became his personal mission to snuff out what he considered Rococo licentiousness and replace it with moralistic history painting. Beginning in 1777, he regularly commissioned "grand machines," as these enormous oils were called (they required special installation equipment), based on the noble and virtuous deeds of the ancients as well as exemplary moments from French history, which included a number of pictures set in the Middle Ages and Renaissance. The resulting paintings are largely forgotten today, but the project triggered a quest, and even a heated competition, among artists to produce *the* great history painting. The fruit of d'Angiviller's program appeared in the mid-1780s

with the emergence of Jacques-Louis David (1748–1825), whose images were so revolutionary they have virtually come to epitomize Neoclassicism, thus simplifying a very complex period and a very complicated term that encompasses much more than David's style.

It took David almost two decades to find his artistic voice, his distinctive mature style. He began his studies at the Royal Academy school in 1766. He did not win the Rome Prize until 1774, and then studied in Rome from 1775 to 1781. His progress was painfully slow, and he only seemed to find himself in 1780 after copying a painting the year before of a Last Supper by Valentin de Bologne, a French follower of Caravaggio, in the Palazzo Barberini. De Bologne's powerful naturalism and dramatic lighting, which carved out crisp sculptural figures and objects, triggered something in him (see *Primary Source* above), and in 1781 he submitted to the academy a painting of the Roman general Belisarius that incorporated this newly discovered aesthetic world. The work became his academic acceptance piece and garnered him a large following of students. It also won him his first major commission from d'Angiviller.

It took David three years to complete d'Angiviller's commission, *The Oath of the Horatii* (fig. **23.27**), which he finished in Rome in 1784. When David unveiled *The Oath* in his Rome studio, it instantly became an international sensation, with an endless procession of visitors filing through to see this revolutionary work. *The Oath* arrived in Paris from Rome a few days after the opening of the 1784 Salon, its delayed grand entrance enhancing the public clamor.

The theme for the picture comes from a Roman seventh-century BCE story found in both Livy and Plutarch recounting how a border dispute between Rome and neighboring Alba was settled by a sword fight involving three soldiers from each side. Representing Rome were the three Horatii brothers, and Alba the three Curiatii brothers. Complicating the story, a Horatii sister, Camilla, was engaged to a Curiatii brother, while one of the Horatii brothers was married to a Curiatii sister. Only Horatius of the Horatii brothers survived the violent fight, and David was instructed by d'Angiviller to paint the moment when Horatius returns home and slays his sister after she curses him for killing her fiancé. Instead, David painted a scene that does not appear in the literature: the Horatii, led by their father, taking an oath to fight to the death. The composition is quite simple and striking: David contrasts the virile stoic men, their bodies locked in rigorous determination, with the slack, curvilinear heap of the distressed women, Camilla and the Curiatii wife, who, either way, will lose a brother, husband, or fiancé.

David was undoubtedly inspired by the many oath-taking paintings that had appeared since Gavin Hamilton had made an *Oath of Brutus* in 1764. The dramatic, pregnant moment, which David made one of the hallmarks of Neoclassical history painting, allowed him to create a *tableau vivant* championing noble and virtuous action dedicated to the supreme but necessary sacrifice of putting state before family. The severity of the Horatii's dedication is reinforced by the severity of the composition. It can be seen in the austerity of the shallow space, and even in David's selection of stark, baseless Tuscan Doric columns, which Ledoux had made fashionable in France the decade before. It also appears in the relentless planarity that aligns figures and architecture parallel to the picture plane and in the harsh geometry of the floor, arches, and grouping of the warriors. It surfaces as well in the sharp linear contours of the figures, making them seem as solid and frozen as statues. In his planarity and linearity, David is more "Poussiniste" than his idol Poussin, from whom he borrows figures. Line and geometry, the vehicles of reason, now clearly prevail over the sensual color and brushwork of the Rococo.

But it is the Caravaggesque naturalism and intensity that make this image so powerful and distinguish it from Renaissance and Baroque Classicism. Sharpening edges and heightening the drama of the painting is a harsh light that casts precise shadows, an effect derived from Caravaggio (see fig. 19.2), as is the attention to textures and such details as chinks in the floor marble. The picture is startlingly lifelike, with the setting and costumes carefully researched to re-create seventh-century BCE Rome.

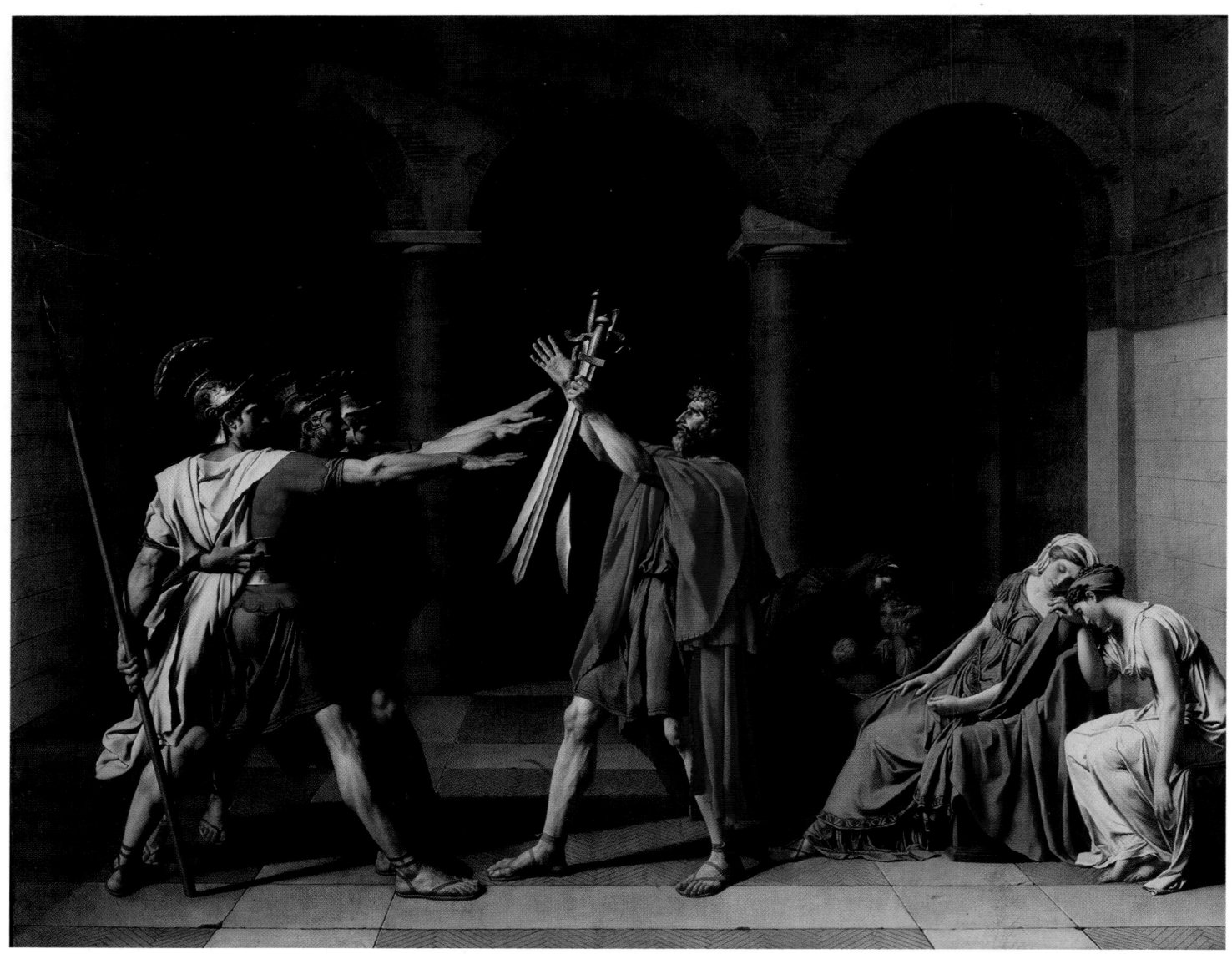

23.27 Jacques-Louis David, *The Oath of the Horatii*. 1784. Oil on canvas, 10'10" × 13'11" (3.3 × 4.25 m). Musée du Louvre, Paris

While *The Oath* is generally perceived as the quintessential Neoclassical picture, one of several David made that came to define the style, it is filled with undercurrents of Romanticism. It is a horrific scene, one that frightened onlookers, sending chills down their spines. This is not *just* an image of moral resolve and logic, reflecting the words of Cassius when he declares in Voltaire's play *Death of Caesar* that "a true republican's only father and sons are virtue, the gods, law, and country." Under the frozen Neoclassical stillness of this scene lies the tension of the bloodbath soon to come. We see this in the father's brightly lit fingers, which echo the stridency of the swords. This enormous 13-foot painting is about the impending violence, from which the woman in the ominous background shadow tries to shield the children.

David was a rabid revolutionary once the French Revolution began in 1789, and he became a powerful figure in the new republic when it was established in 1792. He was a member of the National Convention, the legislative assembly holding executive power in the early years of the French Republic, and was in charge of artistic affairs, in effect becoming the republic's minister of propaganda. He voted to execute the king, sent the revolutionary leader Georges-Jacques Danton to the guillotine, and successfully closed the Royal Academy. He was too busy signing arrest warrants and death sentences to make much art at the time.

Two major works from the early 1790s, however, are portraits of assassinated revolutionaries and were conceived as pendants. Only one survives: *The Death of Marat* (fig. **23.28**), which was exhibited with its mate at the Louvre in May 1793, after which the

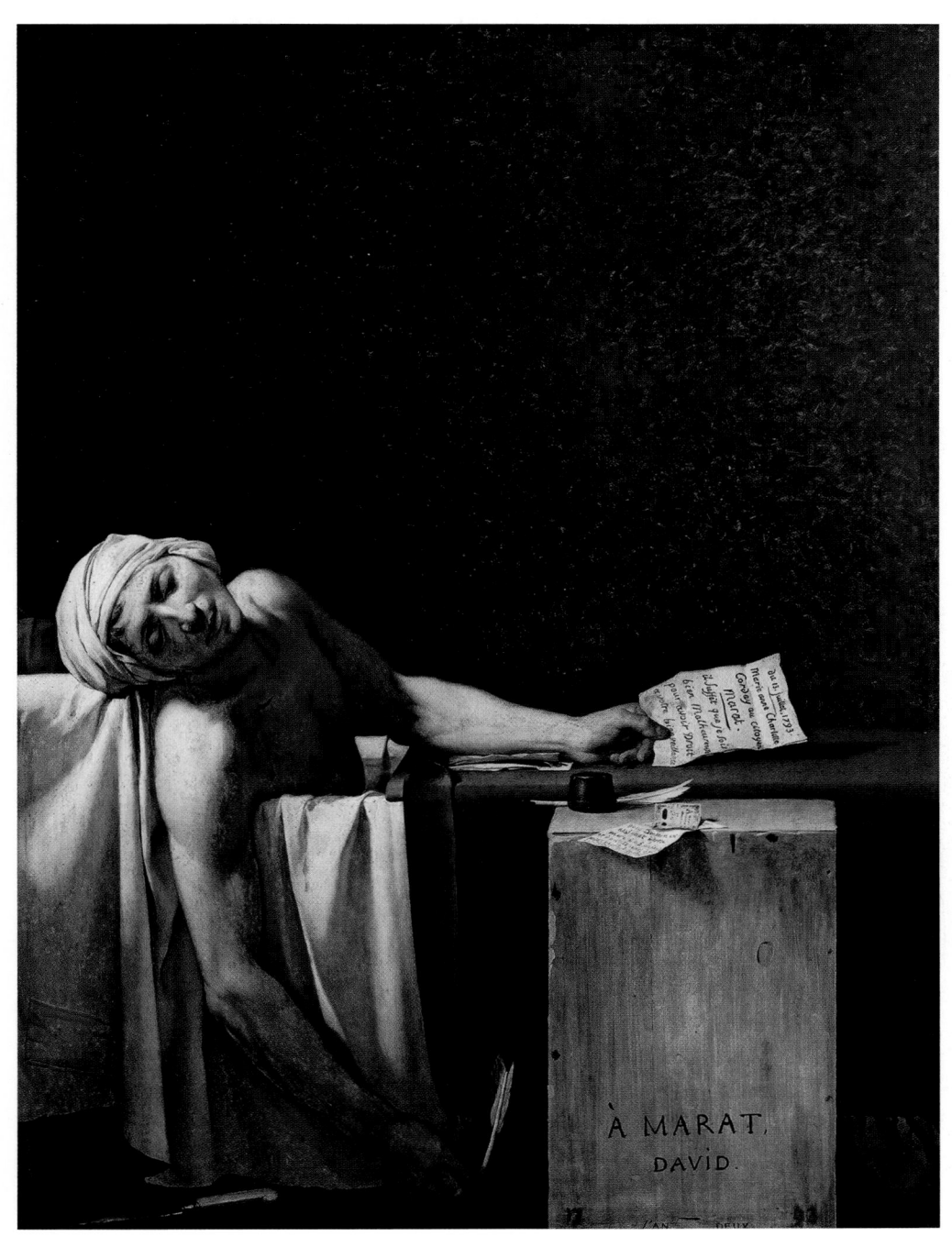

23.28 Jacques-Louis David, *The Death of Marat*. 1793. Oil on canvas, 65 × 50½" (165.1 × 128.3 cm). Musées Royaux des Beaux-Arts de Belgique, Brussels

government declared it would hang in perpetuity in the hall of the National Convention. The picture was propaganda. Marat was a deputy in the National Convention and the editor of a populist newspaper. He was a dedicated revolutionary and a defender of the people. But he was also a ruthless man, who was hated and feared. He was so despised that a counterrevolutionary from Caen, one Charlotte Corday, plunged a knife into his chest while he was writing on a portable desk laid across his bathtub, where he spent most of his time due to a lethal skin condition that grossly disfigured him.

David, who had visited Marat the day before, shows him expiring in the tub, still holding in one hand the quill with which he defended the French Republic, and in the other the fake petition Corday used to divert his attention before stabbing him. Like *The Oath*, David presented this scene with realism, attention to detail, sharp lighting, and planarity. But now he pushes the image much closer to the picture plane, almost to the surface of the canvas, with Marat's writing crate and Corday's blood-stained knife dramatically thrust into the viewer's space and the figure of Marat just inches behind.

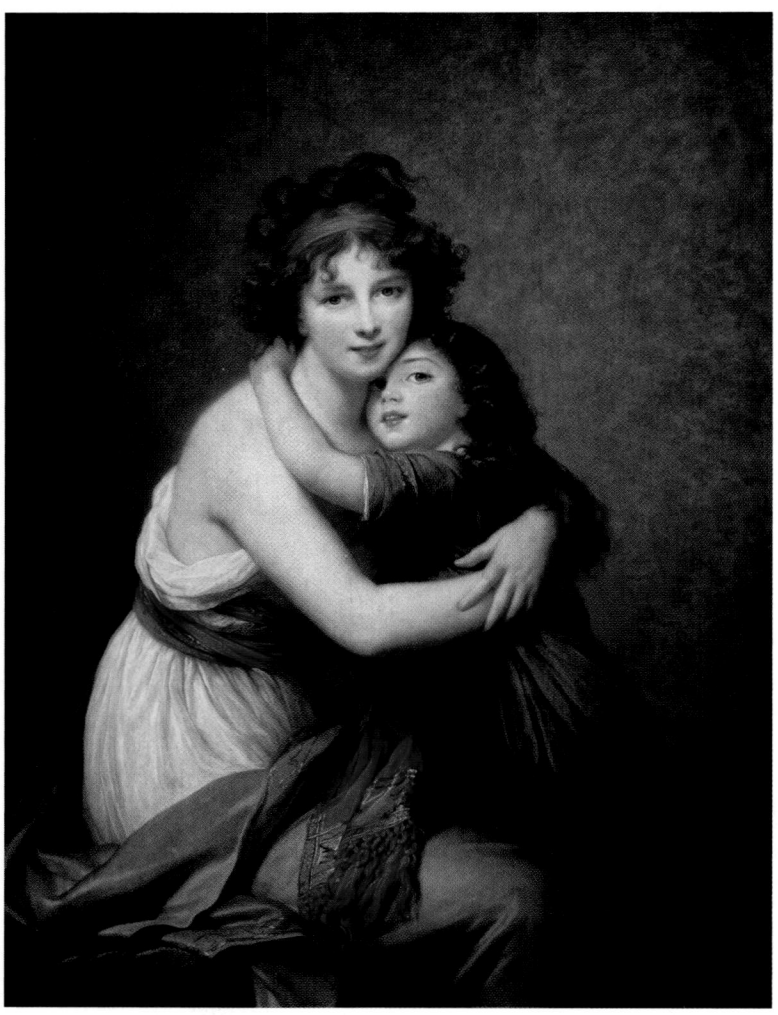

23.29 Marie-Louise-Élisabeth Vigée-Lebrun, *Self-Portrait with Daughter*. 1789. Oil on canvas, 47⅔ × 35½" (121 × 90 cm). Musée du Louvre, Paris

To contemporaries, this must have seemed like modern reportage. No matter that it was a propagandistic lie. Marat's bathroom was quite lavish, not the monastic republican interior seen here, which is so frugal the sheets are patched and a crate is used as a writing surface. Marat was notoriously unattractive, but here he has the physique of a Greek god and a seraphic face. The pose of the slumped arm is unmistakably that of Christ in a Deposition, Lamentation, or Pietà scene (see figs. 16.12 and 17.37), and derives from a Pietà by David's student Anne-Louis Girodet made the year before. The sheets recall Christ's shroud. The mundane writing crate is elevated to a time-worn tombstone. Like West in *The Death of General Wolfe* (see fig. 23.6), David appropriated religious iconography for secular glorification. He has also given the picture a personal twist, for on the crate he has written "À Marat" ("To Marat") with his signature below. Although a commission, the painting was one that David, as a member of the government, in a sense commissioned from himself, and one that he wanted to make. The dedication certainly makes the picture seem like a personal statement, almost a declaration that the powerful emotions expressed in it are particular to him as much as they are an expression of collective grief. The look of the painting has roots in a long Classical tradition going back to Poussin, Raphael, Caravaggio, and antiquity, but its personal intensity, as we shall see, is not far removed from that of the Romantic era, which is looming just around the corner and will be the subject of Chapter 24.

Neoclassical Portraiture: Marie-Louise-Élisabeth Vigée-Lebrun

The impact of David's Neoclassicism was powerful, not just on history painting but portraiture as well. We can see this impact on the 1789 *Self-Portrait with Daughter* (fig. **23.29**) by Marie-Louise-Élisabeth Vigée-Lebrun (1755–1842). Born in Paris to a father who was a minor painter and who died when she was 12, Vigée-Lebrun, as a woman, was denied access to the Royal Academy. Consequently, she was essentially self-taught. In her teens, she began painting portraits, which were illegal since she did not have a license from the academy, which forced her to seek admission to the less prestigious Academy of St. Luke, where she exhibited in 1774. The following year, in a marriage of convenience, she wed Jean-Baptiste-Pierre Lebrun, a painter and prominent art dealer, who gave her access to powerful contacts. Her exceptional talent, vibrant personality, and sophistication soon had her circulating among the aristocracy and the wealthy, and she became a favorite of Queen Marie-Antoinette, whose portrait she painted many times, beginning in 1778. Thanks to the queen's influence, the Royal Academy in 1783 accepted her as a painter of historical allegory.

Lebrun is generally labeled a Rococo painter, her portraits having an affableness, liveliness, intimacy, and colorful palette associated with the style (see page 761). But throughout her career, Vigée-Lebrun was attuned to the latest artistic fashions, and she was a forceful arbiter in the world of couture, introducing, for example, shawls, and making "an arrangement with broad scarfs lightly intertwined around the body and on the arms, which was an attempt to imitate the beautiful drapings of Raphael and Domenichino," as she said in her memoirs. Vigée-Lebrun's 1789 portrait of herself with her daughter reflects the taste for the Classical that was then becoming pervasive in Paris. (In 1788, Vigée-Lebrun famously gave a *souper grec*, or Greek supper, considered one of the great social events of the reign of Louis XVI.) In this portrait, we see the sitters attired *à la* antique, wearing togas, Vigée-Lebrun's cinched above the waist with a scarf. The artist wears an antique headband and sports a Roman-style coiffure. Instead of a lavish Rococo interior, she and her daughter pose against an austere, although warm, wall.

Vigée-Lebrun loved her daughter, but the powerful intimacy and affectionate nature of the scene should also be seen as a reflection of the new Rousseauian attitude toward children that called for greater parental involvement in child-rearing, a quality that was increasingly apparent in portraiture in the second half of the century as young children began to be featured more frequently in portraits with their parents. But despite these Neoclassicisms and Enlightenment influences, this spectacular painting still retains an undercurrent of the Rococo, seen in its warm colors, affable glances, soft Correggioesque contours, and curvilinear patterning of arms and drapery.

ITALIAN NEOCLASSICISM TOWARD 1785

This chapter began in Rome toward 1760, and our story comes full circle by ending there as well, toward 1785, no longer looking at foreigners, such as Mengs and Hamilton, but at an Italian sculptor. It took over 20 years for Neoclassical painting to crystallize into a distinctive style in the work of David, and the same happened almost simultaneously in sculpture in the work of Antonio Canova. Canova emerged in Rome in the 1780s, and by the 1790s he was the most famous sculptor in the world, receiving commissions from all over Europe and America. He was the artist the majority of sculptors in both the Old and New World emulated and tried to equal, deep into the nineteenth century.

Neoclassical Sculpture: Antonio Canova

Antonio Canova (1757–1822) came from a family of stonecutters in the region around Venice. When he was nine his artistic talent was brought to the attention of a Venetian senator, under whose patronage he was able to study sculpture in Venice, becoming a teenage prodigy. By 1780, he was in Rome, financed by the Venetian senate, and the following year he took the city by storm with his marble sculpture *Theseus Vanquishing the Minotaur*. The work was a sensation in part because it looked Classical, like an excavated sculpture, although it was not based on a specific antique source—it was entirely Canova's creation.

We can see Canova's originality in *Cupid and Psyche* (fig. **23.30**), commissioned in 1787 by a tourist for his home in Britain. Canova first modeled the work in plaster, and then had assistants rough it out in marble. Afterward he completed the carving, which included creating an impressive variety of surface textures,

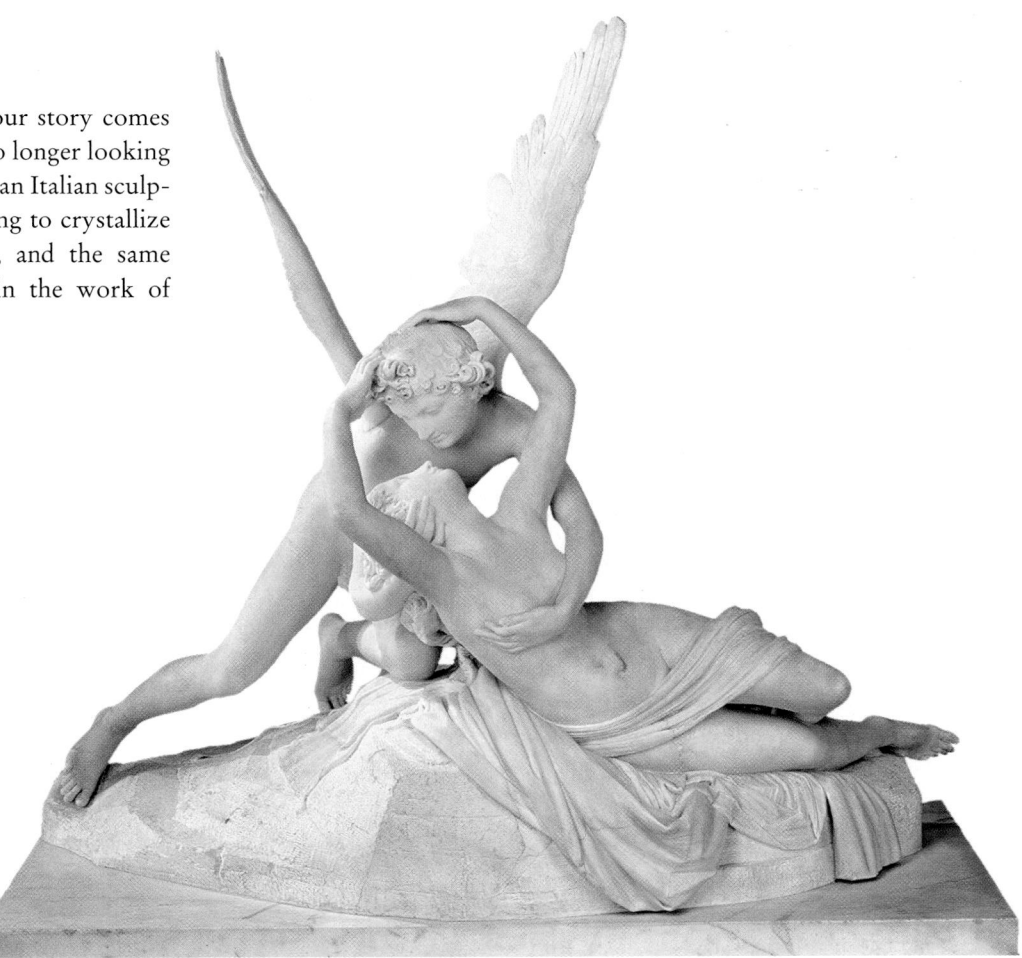

23.30 Antonio Canova, *Cupid and Psyche.* 1787–93. Marble, 6'1" × 6'8" (1.55 × 1.73 m). Musée du Louvre, Paris

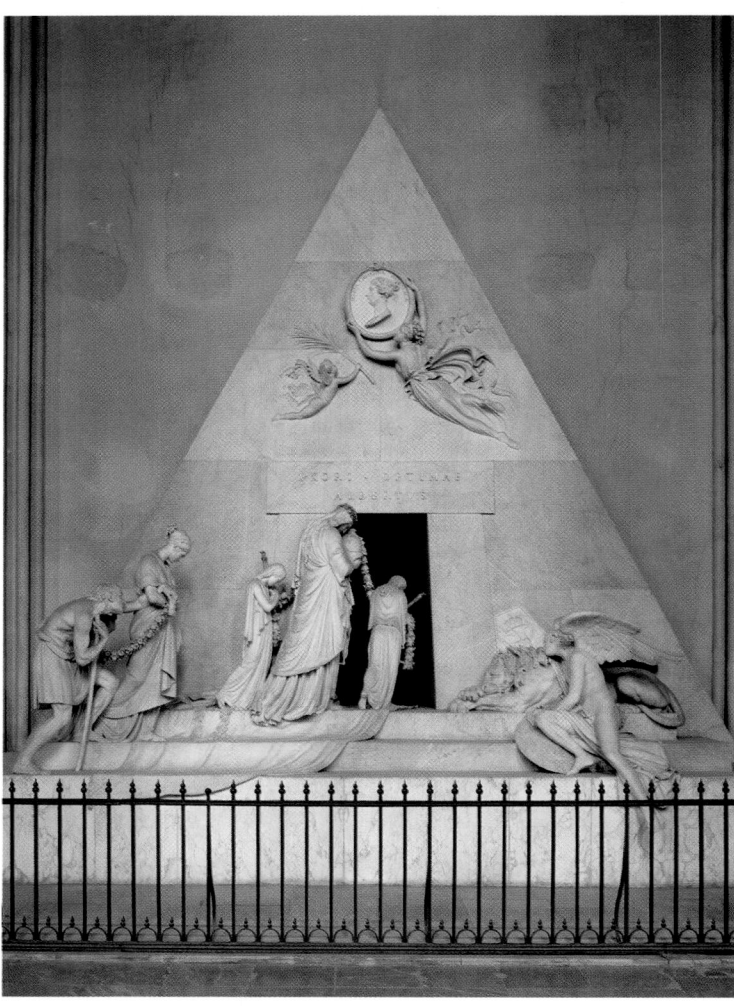

23.31 Antonio Canova, *Tomb of the Archduchess Maria Christina*, Augustinerkirche, Vienna. 1798–1805. Marble, life-size

especially the remarkable cold-perfect finish for flesh that was often copied but never equaled by his many imitators. Nor did anyone match his exquisite compositions of continuous elegant contours, which in *Cupid and Psyche* are visible in the curving pattern of the sensuous arms and legs, as well as in the flowing drapery and the oval mound gently elevating the figures.

Canova delivers more than beautiful idealized Classical models, more than noble simplicity and calm grandeur—he also presents intense emotion. Here, he portrays the moment when Cupid, having fallen in love with the human Psyche, gives her a kiss that awakens her from the eternal sleep into which she has been cast by the jealous Venus. With this kiss, she becomes immortal, like Cupid. Canova captures a tenderness and passion in both expression and gestures that was unthinkable before 1780, and this reflects the interest in states of mind that preoccupied the Fuseli circle in Rome in the 1770s and consumed British artists in the 1780s. Canova was a close friend of Gavin Hamilton, who in addition to introducing Canova to the antiquities of Rome undoubtedly brought to his attention the emotional intensity that his British colleagues were exploring in their art.

We can see this emotional intensity stated in a very different way in the *Tomb of the Archduchess Maria Christina* (fig. **23.31**) in the church of the Augustins in Vienna. One of the many

commissions that flooded Canova's studio by the 1790s, the monument projects a chill pallor and deathly silence appropriate to a scene of mourning. Classically robed figures with bowed heads, one holding an urn supposedly containing ashes, trudge in Classical profile ever so slowly into the pyramidal tomb. The cold melancholy is reinforced by the severe geometry of the pyramid, including its austere Egyptian **pylon**like post-and-lintel door. Above the door is a sculpture of two flying genii, one holding a portrait of the deceased, which is framed by a snake biting its tail, a symbol of eternity. On the right, a winged genius of war leans on a lion, representing Austria, both mourning the archduchess, while the three leftmost figures represent the Three Ages of Life. But for the most part, these symbols and allegories are subservient to the highly palpable realism of the event, so that we feel as though we are watching a real funeral procession taking place in real space and time. The scene is so convincing that we believe that the archduchess's ashes are indeed in the urn and the pyramid is the actual burial place—in fact, neither is the case, and the sculpture is only a monument. Despite Canovas's classicizing qualities of ideal beauty and drawing upon the antique, his work, like David's, contains a powerful emotional intensity that we have seen in early Romanticism and, as we will see in the next chapter, are the hallmarks of nineteenth-century Romanticism.

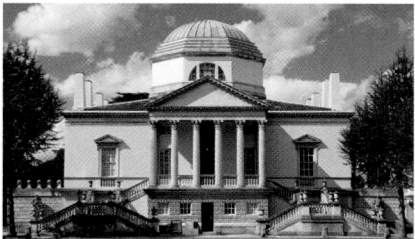

1725 Burlington and Kent begin construction of Chiswick House

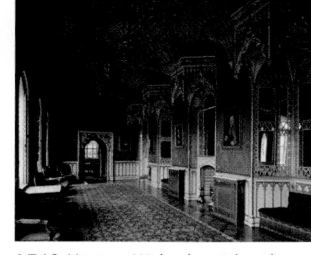

1749 Horace Walpole with others begins design of Gothic Strawberry Hill

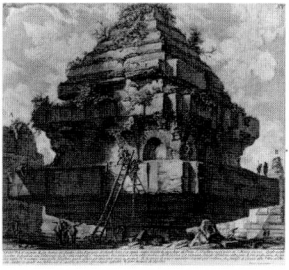

1757 Giovanni Battista Piranesi finishes *Roman Antiquities*

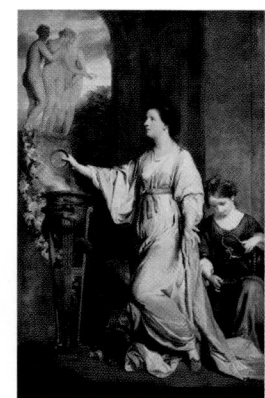

1765 Joshua Reynolds's *Lady Sarah Bunbury Sacrificing to the Graces*

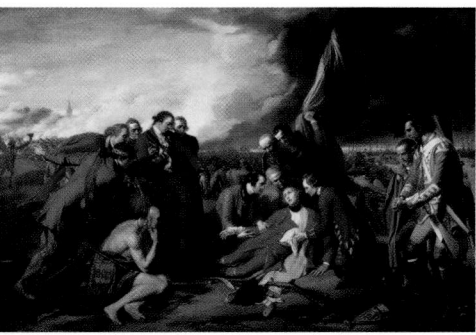

1770 Benjamin West's *The Death of General Wolfe*

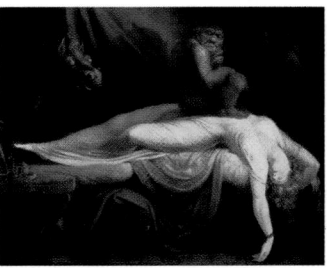

1781 John Henry Fuseli's *The Nightmare*

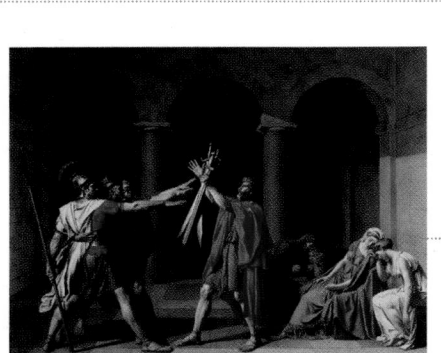

1775 Claude-Nicolas Ledoux designs main entrance to the saltworks, Arc-et-Senans

1787 Antonio Canova's *Cupid and Psyche*

1784 Jacques-Louis David's *Oath of the Horatii*

Art in the Age of the Enlightenment, 1750–1789

1720

1730

◄ 1734 Voltaire publishes *Philosophical Letters*

◄ 1738 Excavation of Herculaneum begins

1740

1750

◄ 1750 Jean-Jacques Rousseau publishes *Discourse on the Arts and Sciences*
◄ 1751 Denis Diderot and Jacques d'Alembert begin publishing the *Encyclopédie*

◄ 1755 Johann Winckelmann publishes *Reflections on the Imitation of Greek Art in Painting and Sculpture*
◄ 1756 Edmund Burke publishes *A Philosophical Inquiry ... the Sublime and the Beautiful*
◄ 1759 The British pottery firm of Josiah Wedgwood and Sons is founded
◄ 1756–63 French and Indian War

1760

◄ 1765–82 James Watts perfects the steam engine

◄ 1768 Royal Academy of Arts, London, founded

1770 · · · · · · · · · · 1770 George Stubbs's *Lion Attacking a Horse*

◄ 1774 Johann Wolfgang von Goethe writes *The Sorrows of Young Werther*
◄ 1775–84 American Revolution

◄ 1779 First iron bridge constructed, Coalbrookdale, England

1780

◄ 1789 French Revolution begins

1790

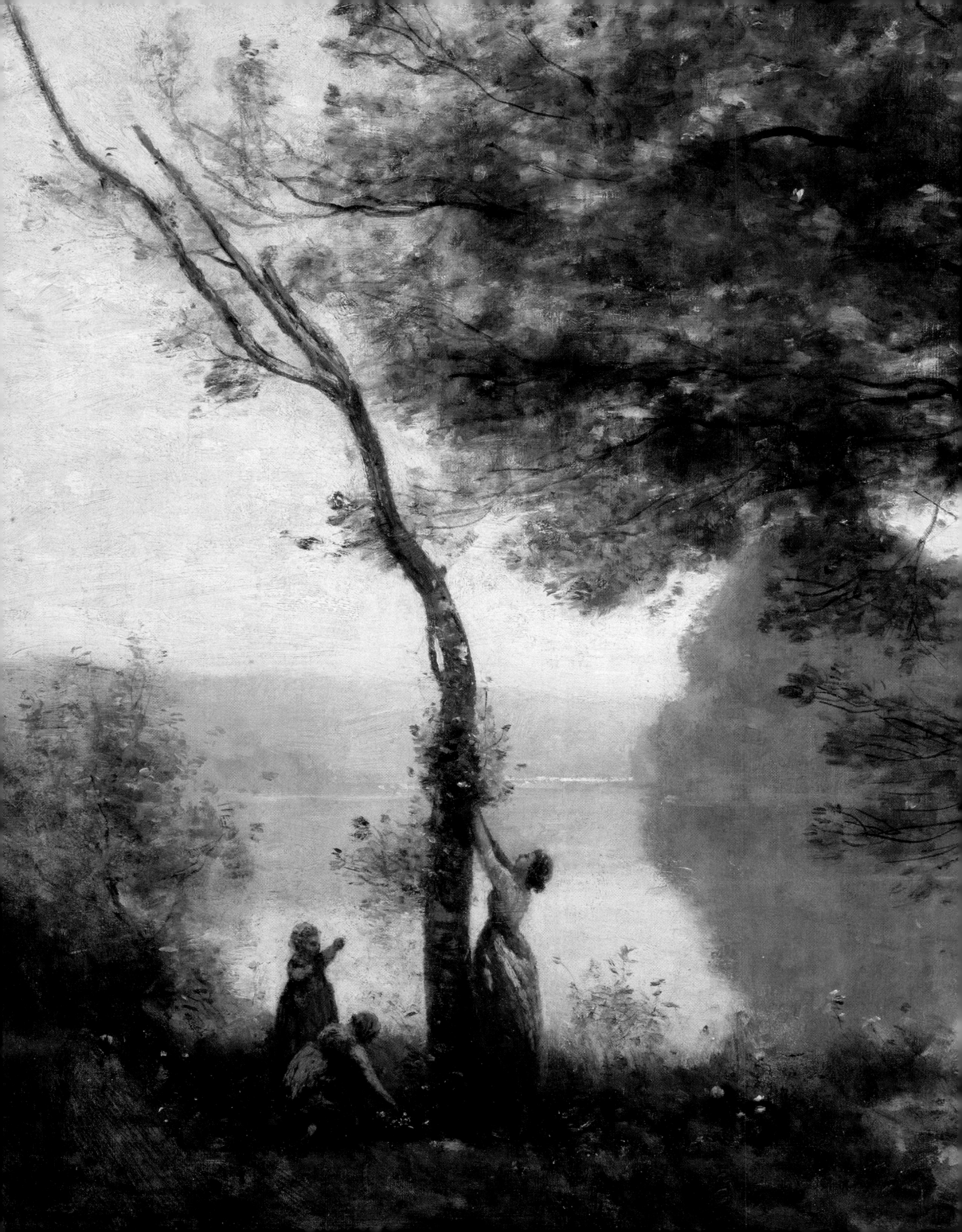

CHAPTER 24

Art in the Age of Romanticism, 1789–1848

THERE IS NO PRECISE MOMENT WHEN NEOCLASSICISM WAS ABSORBED into Romanticism, and Romanticism itself emerged as a full-blown movement that dominated Western art. But generally this change is ascribed to the turn of the century. The word "Romanticism" did not appear until 1798, when the German writer and poet Friedrich von Schlegel

(1772–1829) applied it to poetry. The term itself derived from the Gothic novels of such writers as Horace Walpole in England (see page 800), which were based on medieval heroic literature called *romanz* in Old French, and projected an aura of gloom that became popular in the second half of the eighteenth century. By 1800, the Western world had begun to sense a fundamental transformation in consciousness occurring, a transformation that reached its peak in the first half of the nineteenth century.

This change in consciousness was an indirect result of the upheavals that accompanied the French Revolution, the Napoleonic Wars, and the rise of industrialization and urbanization. The Enlightenment seemed to have failed. Instead of social reform and progress, there was turmoil and dislocation, often accompanied by pessimism and a concomitant search for truth within the inner self rather than in society. The French Revolution may have given rise to republican government, political enfranchisement, nationalism, and public institutions, including museums, but it had also thrown most of Europe into war by 1792 and resulted in the execution of some 17,000 people under Robespierre's Reign of Terror in 1793–94. Fearful that Enlightenment reform spawned only revolution, European governments cracked down on liberals, instituting a harsh reactionary

conservatism. The rise of Napoleon Bonaparte from commander of the Army of Italy under the Directory to self-proclaimed hereditary emperor in 1804 quashed the French Republic and initiated the Napoleonic Wars, which at their peak saw France occupy most of Europe and lasted until 1815. Napoleon's reign further increased the fervor of nationalism initiated by the French Revolution, and his military campaigns, covered in detail by the press, which proliferated in the opening decades of the century, provided the public with wondrous tales of valor and excitement that fed the Romantic imagination.

The military needs of war hastened the pace of the Industrial Revolution begun in Britain the previous century, and the return to peace with the defeat of Napoleon in 1815 hardly served as a brake. Waves of people fled the poverty of the countryside for the city to work in manufacturing. This new proletariat class, separated from the comforting predictability of the timeless rural world and needing to sell its labor, now experienced oppressive working conditions and subsistence wages, as well as poor housing in cities not designed to accommodate such a dramatic increase in population. The period saw the birth of modern labor and worker–management conflict, which culminated in 1848 with the publication of Karl Marx and Friedrich Engels's *Communist Manifesto* and a Europe-wide workers' revolution. The Industrial Revolution also gave rise to a powerful bourgeoisie, a wealthy middle class that controlled the means of production and demanded a greater voice in government.

Detail of figure 24.24, Jean-Baptiste-Camille Corot, *Souvenir de Mortefontaine (Oise)*

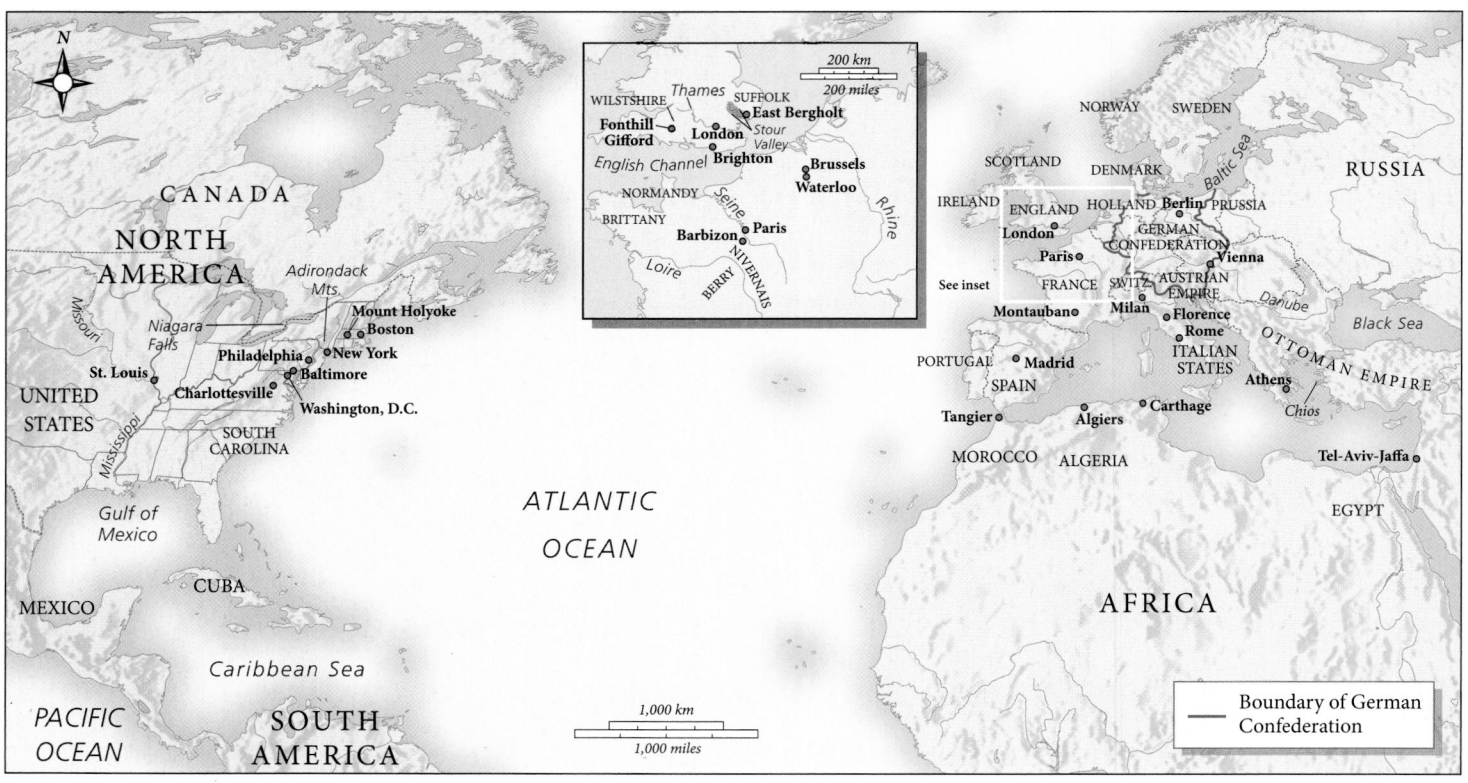

Map 24.1   Europe and North America in 1815

With this seemingly endless succession of crises, the West found a need to believe in something other than the Enlightenment values of logic and scientific empiricism. There arose a turning inward to the self, and a belief in the subjective emotion of the individual, promoted by Jean-Jacques Rousseau in France and the *Sturm und Drang* movement in Germany (see Chapter 23). What had been a strong undercurrent in the eighteenth century surfaced as the defining psychology of the West by the end of the century. Artists, writers, composers, and intellectuals now placed a premium on powerful emotion, intuition, and unrestrained creative genius. The era itself is often described as being dedicated to the "Cult of the Individual." For the intellectual and cultural elite, total liberation of the imagination and creative freedom replaced rules, standards, and logic. As expressed by the French Romantic writer Victor Hugo, "All systems are false; only genius is true." From this perspective, the mind was the conduit of nature, the only means of accessing elemental universal forces, God, and the goal of the artist was to tap into this reservoir of higher reality and express it. Sincerity and truthfulness were therefore now critical. Enlightenment morality was not applicable. Powerful emotions in response to violence, suffering, chaos, and ugliness replaced virtuous and noble actions and the perfection associated with ideal beauty. Romanticism produced a cult not only for exotic experiences but also for frightening, horrific, and extreme situations. Uniqueness became a strong value in art; copying someone else's genius, originality, or individualism was the manufacture of something false.

Consequently, Romanticism was not a style, but an attitude. It was a license to abandon logic and to follow one's genius wherever it led. It could lead to the distant past, the exotic present, the most grotesque and horrific aspects of human behavior, and the awesome forces of nature. It also resulted in a welling up of nationalistic spirit, as citizens were swept together not out of allegiance to a king but to a collective experience and language, eventually resulting in the rise of Italy and Germany as united countries in 1871. It also meant artists would no longer paint idealized Classical arcadias; instead they painted with pride and loving detail the countryside in which they themselves grew up, a countryside once considered too banal to render but that was now an emblem of God's presence, or filled with the powerful emotions of personal experience. And Romanticism meant artists were swept away by the emotions of liberty and freedom, the surge toward democracy, which, for example, was the driving force behind Ludwig van Beethoven's Symphony Number 3 in C Major, *The Eroica*, of 1804, originally dedicated to Napoleon and the civil liberties he instituted before he became emperor. While Romanticism may seem stylistically diverse, its attitude was cohesive, both passionate and powerful, as reflected in the work of some of the great names of the Romantic era: Beethoven, Hector Berlioz, Franz Liszt, Frédéric Chopin, Lord Byron, Mary and Percy Shelley, Samuel Taylor Coleridge, William Wordsworth, François-Renée de Châteaubriand, Victor Hugo, Henri-Marie Stendal, Herman Melville, and Edgar Allan Poe.

PAINTING

Of all the visual arts, painting is most closely associated in our minds with Romanticism because, unlike sculpture and architecture, it allowed for a spontaneous outpouring of emotion. In fact, many art historians think of the study or sketch, whether painted or drawn, as the quintessential Romantic medium. While some of the most famous Romantic paintings are Baroque in their dramatic handling of paint and energetic compositions, Romantic paintings can just as readily be tightly painted and composed in accordance with Neoclassical planes, resulting in frozen images that project chilling emotions.

Spain: Francisco Goya

In the opening decades of the nineteenth century, Spanish art was dominated by Francisco Goya y Lucientes (1746–1828), an artist whose work in many ways encapsulates the new psychology and issues pervading Europe. Born and raised in Aragon, he initially studied with Anton Raphael Mengs in Madrid. Goya did not much care for Mengs, and left to tour Italy in 1770 and 1771. Upon returning to Aragon, he studied with the painter Francisco Bayeu, developing a colorful, painterly Rococo style. Bayeu, a member of the Royal Academy of Fine Art in Madrid, arranged for Goya to design images for the Royal Tapestry Workshop, which brought him to Madrid again and gave him access to the royal court and Madrid aristocracy. Charles III (r. 1759–1788) appointed Goya royal painter in 1786, and his son Charles IV, in 1789, made him first painter to the king, putting him in the tradition of Velázquez, who had previously held the position (see page 691). For Goya, an Enlightened Spaniard who admired the French *philosophes*, there was not necessarily a conflict between supporting the monarchy and advocating liberal reform. The king recognized the need to bring a stagnant Spain into the eighteenth century and permitted a degree of economic and social development, which gave hope to the progressive forces. Goya was a member of this group that favored social reform, and his social circle, including many of his aristocratic clients, shared his outlook. But the French Revolution terrified heads of state throughout Europe and ushered in reactionary oppression, for now the Enlightenment became associated with revolution, not reform. Both Church and State suppressed the liberal reformers. Spain went to war with France, forging an alliance with its old enemy, Britain. On top of these reversals, Goya fell mysteriously ill in 1793, only just surviving and going deaf in the process. Now, Goya's art focused on exploring the human condition and the emerging modern psychology, on exposing wanton cruelty, misery, ignorance, and greed as universal constants, and on expressing the reality of death as a frightening, unknown void.

THE SLEEP OF REASON We can get some idea of Goya's reaction to the period's crises by looking at *The Sleep of Reason Produces Monsters* (fig. **24.1**), one of 80 etching-and-aquatint prints from the series *Los Caprichos* (*The Capriccios*), conceived

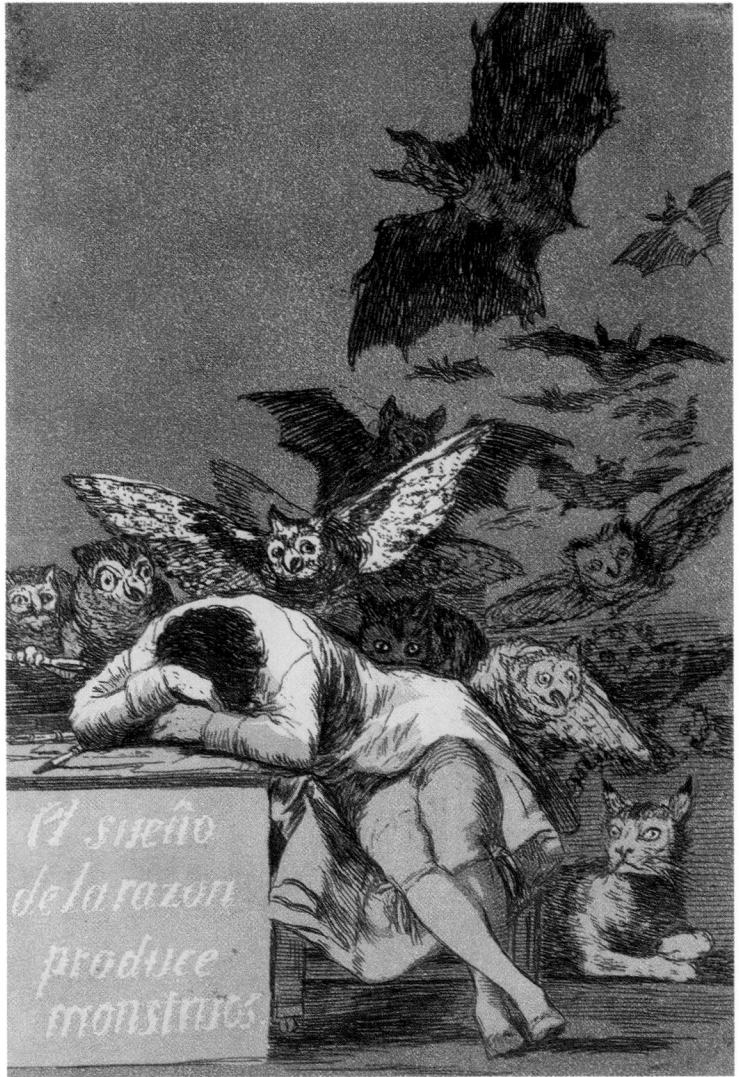

24.1 Francisco Goya, *The Sleep of Reason Produces Monsters*, from *Los Caprichos*. ca. 1799. Etching, aquatint, drypoint, and burrin, 8⅞ × 6" (21.5 × 15.2 cm). Metropolitan Museum of Art, New York. Gift of M. Knoedler & Co., 1918. (18.64(43))

by the artist in 1797 and published at his own expense at a financial loss. Here, we see the artist asleep on the geometric block of reason, while behind him rises an ominous disarray of owls and bats, symbols of folly and ignorance, respectively. In the margin of a study for this image, Goya wrote, "The author's…intention is to banish harmful beliefs commonly held, and with this work of *caprichos* to perpetuate the solid testimony of truth." This print introduces the second half of the series, which satirizes a range of sins, superstitions, and forms of ignorance, and is populated with witches, monsters, and demons, in effect showing what the world is like when Enlightenment logic is suspended.

But it is just as easy to interpret *The Sleep of Reason* as exposing a second, non-Enlightenment side to Goya's personality—the emotional and illogical rather than the rational. We sense that the owls and bats, rather than being real, are released from the inner recess of Goya's mind, so that this nightmarish scene becomes an expression of the artist's own emotional state of despair or horror at the terrible turn of events transforming the Western world. In effect, in *The Capriccios* Goya is announcing his right to abandon reason and use his imagination to express his deepest feelings, his innermost psychology—to free his demons and employ whatever stylistic tools and symbols he needs in order to do so. We are now far from Neoclassicism and the Rococo as we enter a dramatic graphic world energized by Baroque contrasts of light and dark, asymmetrical composition, the febrile patterning of the wings of bats and owls, and the rasping lines of the Goya's rich intaglio process. (See *Materials and Technique*s, page 501.)

ROYAL COMMISSIONS Goya continued to work for Church and State, which, in addition to painting portraits, is how he earned a living. In 1800, the king commissioned him to paint *The Family of Charles IV* (fig. **24.2**). This work is hardly a simple documentation of the royal family's likeness. And it is certainly not a grand machine designed to reaffirm the family's divine privilege and superiority, for the painting undermines this traditional premise by exposing their basic humanness, their ordinariness. The key to interpreting the picture is knowing that Goya meant it to be compared with Velázquez's *The Maids of Honor* (see fig. 19.38), a picture in the royal collection and known to everyone at court. In each painting, the artist is present and the royal family appears before a shadowy backdrop of two large oils. In addition, Goya's Queen Maria Luisa, standing in the center, strikes the same pose as Velázquez's *infanta*. Missing from Goya's portrait, however, is the all-important mirror, which in *The Maids of Honor* reveals the royal parents, the keystone that holds the picture together compositionally and thematically because it not only explains the scene but also establishes the hierarchical order of the figures. But where is the mirror in *Charles IV*? We must ask another question first, one that is always posed about Goya's picture: What is everyone gaping at so intently? The most likely answer is themselves. They are looking in a mirror—the unaccounted-for mirror—and Goya, standing *behind* his sitters, shows himself painting their reflection as they see themselves.

Théophile Gautier, a nineteenth-century French critic, cleverly noted their discomfort when he described the royal couple as looking like "the corner baker and his wife after they have won the lottery." Goya reduces his sitters to human animals, uncomfortable with themselves. Their clothes may be royal, but the family members are as awkward in them as in their false aristocratic poses, which lack the assuredness we saw in royal portraits by Van Dyck and Rigaud (see figs. 20.8 and 21.10). The figures appear lonely, isolated, even afraid. Goya presents each one as an individual, plagued by the same doubts about the meaning of existence and the same sense of alienation that haunt all humans. This Romantic sense of awe when confronting the infinite is Goya's creation, superimposed onto the royal family. Based on the principle of empiricism, many Enlightenment *philosophes* denied the existence of God, which the French Revolution did as well, suppressing the Catholic Church. Without God and religion, the meaning of existence is unknowable and beyond comprehension. This shockingly modern psychology casts a dark shadow over the

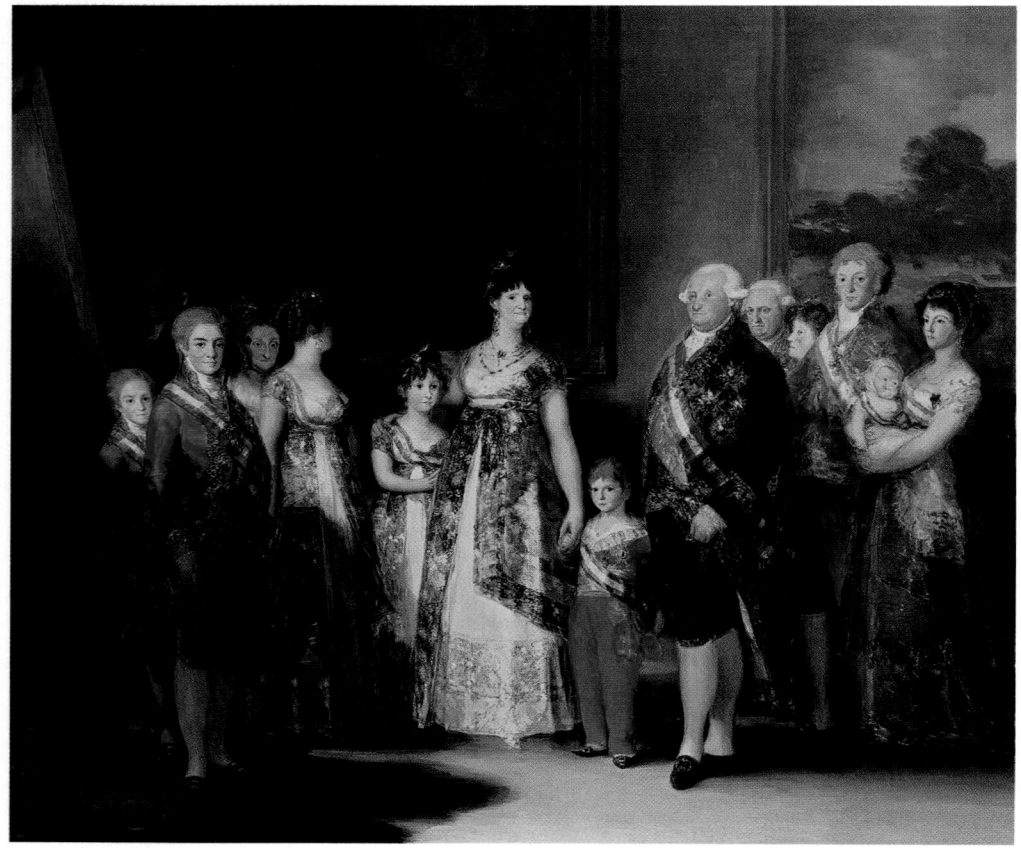

24.2 Francisco Goya, *The Family of Charles IV*. 1800. Oil on canvas, 9'2" × 11' (2.79 × 3.35 m). Museo del Prado, Madrid

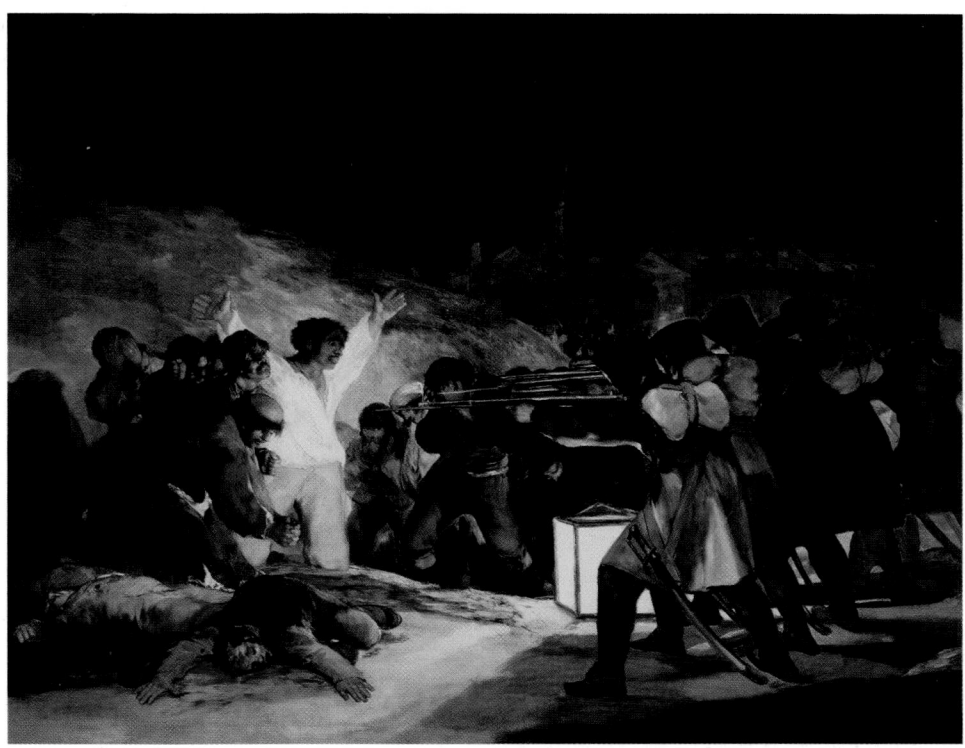

24.3 Francisco Goya, *The Third of May, 1808*. 1814. Oil on canvas, 8'9" × 13'4" (2.67 × 4.06 m). Museo del Prado, Madrid

room. Surprisingly, Charles IV did not reject the portrait, although he did not particularly like it either. Conceivably, the royal family overlooked the disturbing truths lying beneath the surface of the picture because they were blinded by Goya's brilliant flamboyant brushwork (difficult to see in reproduction), which surpassed even Velázquez's Baroque bravura. Goya's dynamic paint handling animates the surface—it is sparkling and dazzling, especially as seen in the clothes, jewelry, and medals.

An even more powerful mood of futility pervades *The Third of May, 1808* (fig. 24.3), painted in 1814 and one of many paintings, drawings, and prints that Goya made from 1810 to 1815 in response to the French occupation of Spain in 1808. The corruption of the Spanish administration forced Charles IV to abdicate in 1807. He was replaced by his son Ferdinand VII, who was deposed in 1808 when Napoleon's troops marched into Madrid and put the emperor's brother, Joseph Bonaparte, on the throne. Enlightened Spain was initially optimistic that the Enlightened French would bring political reform. But in Madrid a people's uprising spurred by nationalism resulted in vicious fighting and wholesale slaughter on both sides, within days fanning out across the entire country and then dragging on for six years. Goya's enormous, dramatic picture, painted after Napoleon had been deposed and Ferdinand reinstated, shows the mass execution of Spanish rebels that took place on May 3, 1808, on a hill outside Madrid.

How different it is from Neoclassical history painting that presented great and famous exemplars of nobleness, morality, and fortitude! Goya presents anonymous nobodies caught up in the powerful forces of history. Here we see the mechanical process of the slaughter. One rebel with raised arms, dressed in the yellow and white colors of the papacy, has the pose of Christ on the Cross. His right hand has a wound suggesting the stigmata. But

ironically Goya denies the rioters the status of martyrs. They are consumed by the fear of death, not the ecstasy of sacrifice. No divine light materializes to resurrect them, and the church in the background of this imaginary scene remains dark. When the stable lantern—which in its geometry and light could be construed as an emblem of Enlightenment logic and progress—is extinguished, there will be only eternal night, symbolized by the inert foreground body, whose face is reduced to a gory mass of paint. The faceless executioners, also small cogs in the wheel of history, are indifferent to their victims' fear of death and frantic pleas for mercy. Goya whips up the horror and emotional turmoil of his scene by rejecting tight Neoclassical paint handling, linearity, planarity, and even lighting, and by replacing this aesthetic with feverish loose brushwork, intense colors, compositional turmoil on the left, and a dramatically receding line of soldiers on the right.

Goya painted *The Third of May, 1808* at a time when he was desperate for work: He wanted to gain royal favor with this picture, hence his scripting of it so that it could be read as being about the sacrifice of the Spanish to the agents of political tyranny. But the real themes of the image are the anonymity of death and the senseless brutality of war. Its power lies in its ability to instill in a viewer an intense sense of terror that makes one confront the inescapable knowledge of one's own mortality.

Britain: Spiritual Intensity and the Bond with Nature

The road taken by Goya in *Los Caprichos* into a fantasy world that allowed his imagination and passions to go wild was most closely followed in Britain by William Blake, who viewed himself as a history painter. However, many British painters during the

Romantic era took the same path as Romantic poets such as William Wordsworth (1770–1850) and Percy Bysshe Shelley (1792–1822) and steeped themselves in nature, being emotionally swept away by its beauties and moods or awed by its sublime power and intimations of the infinite.

WILLIAM BLAKE Across the English Channel in London, the artist William Blake (1757–1827) was also retreating into a personal visual world as he responded to issues very similar to those affecting Goya. Blake was an ardent admirer of Jean-Jacques Rousseau and his theories about the inherent goodness of humans, who are born innocent primitives before becoming corrupted by the restrictive artificialities of society. He detested European civilization for its rules and conventions, which he felt hindered personal freedom, including equality for women. He loathed European materialism and its lack of spirituality, and condemned institutional religion for being as autocratic as government and society in general. His passion to find spiritual truths in a physical world led him to flirt with fringe religions in the 1780s.

Blake began his career as an artisan engraver. He then enrolled in the Royal Academy in 1779 but left within a year, declaring its president, Joshua Reynolds, and the institution itself a microcosm of society, repressing imagination, creativity, and progress. As a result, he was largely self-taught. While never a recluse, Blake was quite insular, functioning on the edge of society. He did not show at the academy after the mid-1780s and received virtually no critical notice throughout his career.

Despite his intense dislike of the Royal Academy, Blake was a proponent of history painting, which he saw as a vehicle for reforming society. However, he shunned oil painting, which he associated with the artificial hierarchies of the academy, and instead turned to medieval manuscript illumination for inspiration, producing illustrated books of his own poetry that were designed to evoke the same kind of spirituality found in his model. Before becoming a visual artist, Blake was a poet, garnering an impressive reputation. In the late 1780s, he started self-publishing his poetical works, which praised nature, freedom, youth, and imagination while denouncing the corruption of all

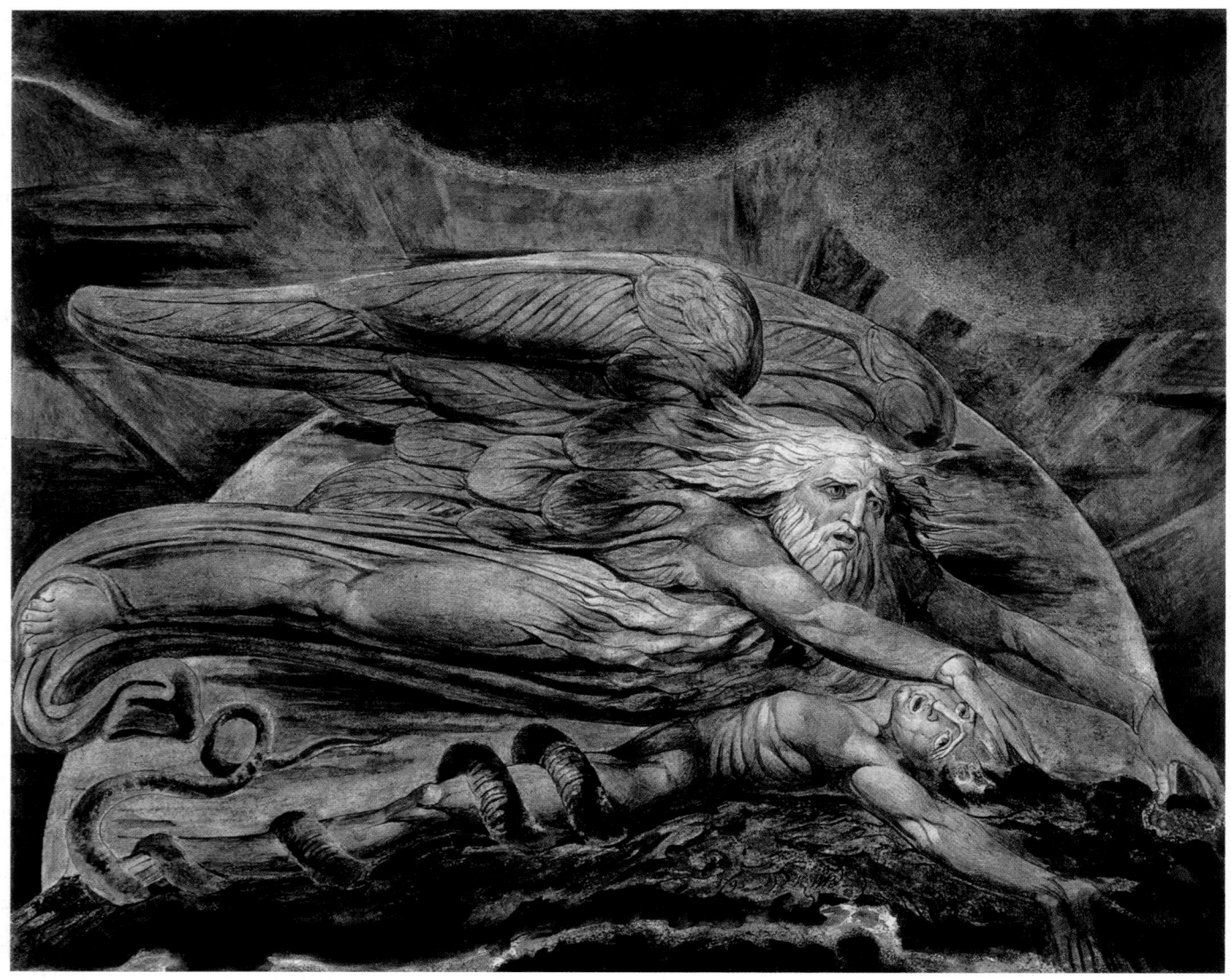

24.4 William Blake, *Elohim Creating Adam*. 1795. Monotype with pen and watercolor, 17 × 21⅛" (43.1 × 53.6 cm). Tate Gallery, London

Blake's Printing Process

For the series of 12 prints that included *Elohim Creating Adam* (see fig. 24.4), William Blake invented a process that is similar to **monotype**, a printing technique that would become popular by the end of the nineteenth century but was rarely used earlier. Monotype involves painting an image on one surface and then pressing paper against this wet surface to attain a counterimage, which unlike the original has a mottled, softer-looking surface. As the word monotype implies, generally only one impression is taken. However, a few impressions can be obtained before all of the original paint is consumed, with each successive image lighter than the previous.

Blake's process for the series was to first outline his image in black paint on a piece of millboard (a thick paperboard), often adding a small amount of modeling and detail as well. He would pull roughly three paper impressions from the millboard, using low pressure so as not to extract too much paint at one time. This would produce a simple black design without color. To finish his image, he would paint the millboard again but with colors, and press it on top of the pulled impressions with the black design. He then touched up the works with watercolor. Blake is said to have used oil paint for his printing, but considering his distaste for the medium he most likely used an egg-based tempera.

---

components of civilization, a corruption stemming from an over-reliance on reason. Toward 1793–94, Blake spiraled into a deep depression, triggered by the violence and chaos of the French Revolution, Britain's declaration of war on France, and the repressive policies that British Prime Minister William Pitt instituted in response to the most radical phase of the French Revolution. Like Goya, Blake was witnessing the failure of the Enlightenment.

At this point the visual imagery began to dominate the poetry in Blake's books. Simultaneously, his art reached maturity in twelve unusually large color prints made mostly in 1795, such as *Elohim Creating Adam* (fig. 24.4). These works were never bound and presented in book form, so we do not know for sure the order in which they were meant to be seen or how Blake intended to use them. (See *Materials and Techniques*, above.) However, all of the prints relate to the artist's vision of the early history of the world, in which humans, when born, are still attached to the infinite from which they have just come, and are morally good, free, and filled with imagination. As they age, they begin to be ruled by reason, lose their freedom and morality, and become consumed by materialism, thus trapped in the finite. The subjects for this series are not all invented: Some come from Shakespeare, Milton, and the Bible, which, as we have discussed (see page 804), were favorite sources for sublime imagery in the period. Blake appropriated these themes because they could be integrated into his own philosophical system and thus support it.

Elohim Creating Adam comes from the Bible, Genesis 2:7: "And the Lord God formed man of the dust of the ground." Blake presents Adam's birth as an aspect of the Fall, for this is a representation of his material birth, not his spiritual one. His body is tense, his face even tortured and apprehensive, and his pose is that of Christ on the Cross. Around his legs is a giant worm, a symbol of the material world. Elohim, the Hebrew word for "Jehovah," projects an expression of foreboding, knowing full well the fate of humans. We need but compare this image to Michelangelo's *The Creation of Adam* (see fig. 16.21) on the *Last Judgment* wall of the Sistine Chapel to see how disturbing and negative Blake's presentation is.

Since the mid-1770s, Blake had been influenced by Michelangelo and the Mannerists as well as by medieval art, and the presence of all can be detected in this picture, though transformed by Blake's own style. We see Michelangelo's overstated musculature (see fig. 16.21), as well as the curvilinear line of manuscript illumination (see fig. 10.8). The absence of an environmental setting and the emphasis on figures alone, as well as the selection of a sublime, horrifying situation derives from Fuseli (see figs. 23.16 and 23.17), whom Blake greatly admired and periodically tried to befriend, without success.

The degree to which Blake mentally immersed himself in his fictitious worlds is remarkable. He claimed his visions were revealed to him by spirits: "I am under the direction of Messengers from heaven, Daily and Nightly." While we have to take this statement with a grain of salt, nonetheless, his art was not naturalistic (a faithful representation of reality), but a conceptual fantasy world in which he could play out his passionate moral beliefs, historical views, and vision of a utopian future. Objects are relatively flat, with space kept to a minimum, an artistic strategy that reinforces the ideal concepts behind his images.

JOHN CONSTABLE Landscape gradually became a major vehicle in the period's search for truth. This is not surprising considering the importance of nature in Romantic ideology—the need to bond with it and to express its essence as personally experienced. John Constable (1776–1837) is one of two British artists who stand out in the period for their landscapes. Constable was born and raised in the village of East Bergholt, in the Stour Valley in Suffolk, and spent most of his life painting this rich farmland, which until then had been considered too ordinary to be used as artistic subject matter. Instead of working at the family's prosperous farm and mill, Constable, in 1799, was permitted to study at the Royal Academy School in London. He eventually realized that he was just learning to replicate painting conventions, and returned to Bergholt to make "laborious studies from nature," drawings and oil sketches that he worked up into finished pictures in the studio but that retained the freshness and details of the original source. Constable even considered painting landscape scientific: "Painting is a science, and should be pursued as an inquiry into the laws of nature. Why, then, may not landscape painting be considered as a branch of natural philosophy, of which pictures are but experiments?" Constable was especially adept at capturing the ephemeral properties of nature—clouds, light, and atmosphere. He made countless studies of just the sky, "the key note, standard scale, and chief organ of sentiment."

Constable's pictures are packed with the emotion that welled within him when experiencing the beauty of the Stour Valley—"painting is with me but another word for feeling," he claimed. (See *Primary Source*, page 829.) His pictures were both scientific and subjective, as in *The Haywain* (*Landscape: Noon*) (fig. **24.5**) of 1821, shown at the Royal Academy, where he had been exhibiting since 1811. We do not just see but feel a blue sky pushing out darker clouds, and an invisible layer of moisture that makes everything glisten. Vibrant flecks of paint and color dissolve the material world and make the atmosphere sparkle. The sky is a symphony of subjectivity, presenting a range of emotions, as does the land. It can be dark and undulating, as in the dramatic, energized twisting of tree branches, or bright and placid, as in the light-filled horizontal spread of the distant hayfield. Constable fills his picture with detailed anecdote; besides the haywain, there is the dog, the boat, the harvesters in the distant field, and the puffs of smoke coming from the mill. This is no perfect world, representing ideal beauty or a Classical Arcadia. Rather, it is a particular site presented in all of its heartfelt specificity. One of the new emotions experienced in the Romantic era was national pride and artists now passionately painted their own countries—not just the Italian landscape—and they painted it with loving detail, not idealized to look like the Classical past.

The 6-foot canvas—an unusually large size for a genre painting and a controversial strategy for elevating landscape to a higher status as well as an attempt to gain attention—was based on numerous outdoor studies, mostly made from 1814 to 1816, and

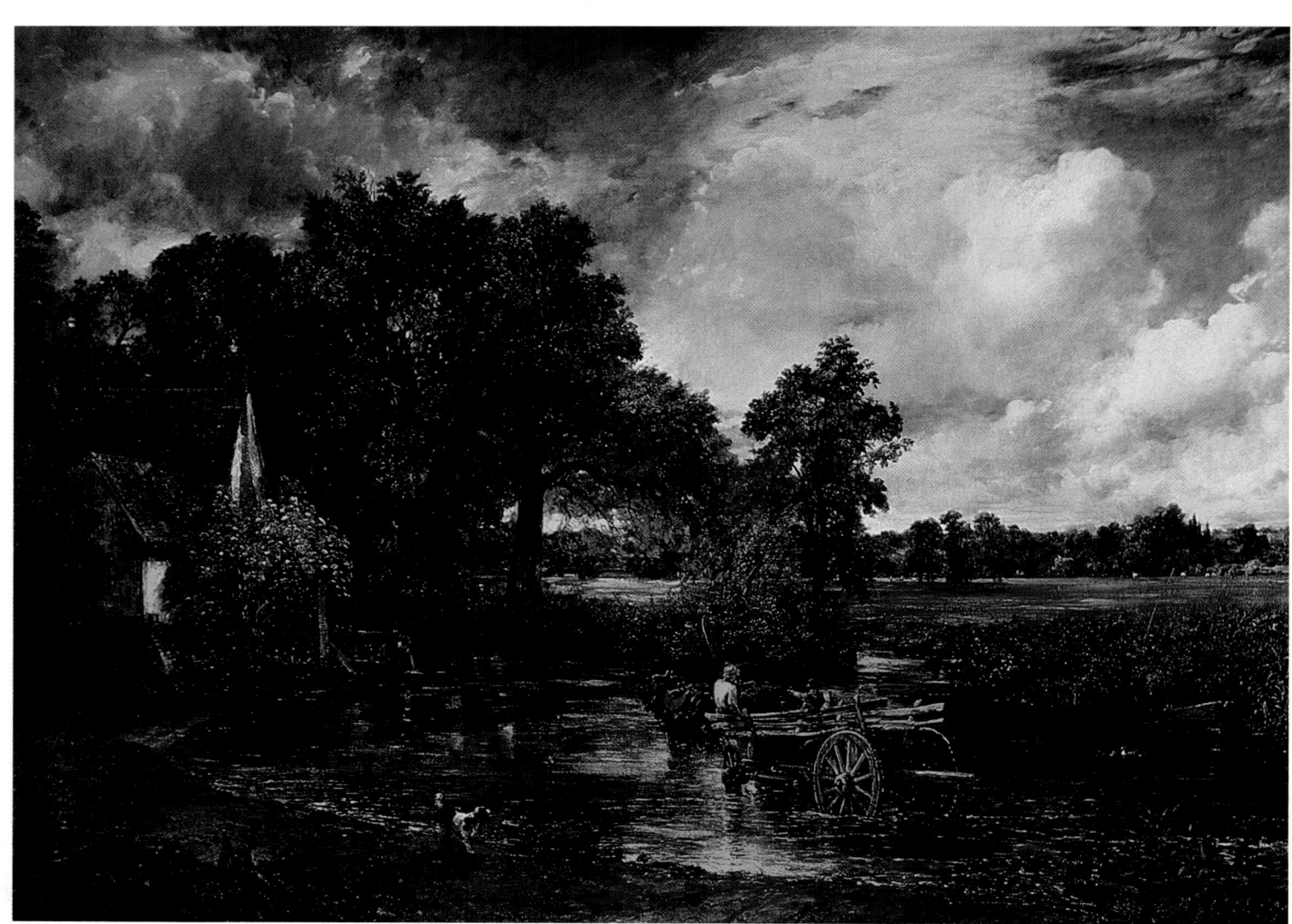

24.5 John Constable, *The Haywain* (*Landscape: Noon*). 1821. Oil on canvas, 51¼ × 73" (1.3 × 1.85 m). The National Gallery, London

John Constable (1776–1837)

From a letter to John Fisher

Fisher, the archdeacon of Salisbury Cathedral, was a lifelong friend of the artist. This letter of October 23, 1821, reflects Constable's sensitivity to the beauties of the English landscape.

How much I wish I had been with you on your fishing excursion in the New Forest! What river can it be? But the sound of water escaping from mill-dams, etc., willows, old rotten planks, slimy posts, and brickwork, I love such things. Shakespeare could make every-thing poetical; he tells us of poor Tom's haunts among "sheep cotes and mills." As long as I do paint, I shall never cease to paint such places. They have always been my delight, and I should indeed have been delighted in seeing what you describe, and in your company, "in the company of a man to whom nature does not spread her volume in vain." Still I should paint my own places best; painting is with me but another word for feeling, and I associate "my careless boyhood" with all that lies on the banks of the Stour; those scenes made me a painter, and I am grateful; that is, I had often thought of pictures of them before I ever touched a pencil.

Source: Charles Robert Lesslie, *Memoirs of the Life of John Constable*, ed. J. Mayne (London: Phaidon Press, 1951)

developed into this large presentation format in the artist's London studio, where he worked in the winter. Typically for his Stour pictures, life in *The Haywain* moves slowly, with rural laborers routinely doing what they have done for millennia in blissful harmony with nature. This was a period of social and economic unrest in the British agricultural community, putting tremendous financial pressure on the Constable property, then run by the artist's brother. This labor crisis is absent from Constable's poetic picture, which instead focuses on personal attachment to the land and the life the artist knew as a boy.

JOSEPH MALLORD WILLIAM TURNER The second major British landscape artist in this period is Joseph Mallord William Turner (1775–1851). In their basic operating premises, Constable and Turner could not be further apart. Whereas Constable painted with scientific accuracy the land he intimately knew, Turner aspired to rival great history painting and consequently invested his views with a rich overlay of historical motifs, references to the Old Masters, and metaphorical themes. His work was also often cataclysmic and horrific, portraying the powerful, uncontrollable forces of nature, and giving visual expression to the sublime as defined by Burke.

Turner began his career in the early 1790s as a for-hire topographical watercolorist. By 1799, at the unprecedentedly young age of 24, he became an associate of the Royal Academy. While he made numerous landscape studies of specific rural scenes as Constable did of Stour, his drive to artistic greatness led him to take on the great landscape and marine painters of the past—Claude Lorrain and Jacob Ruisdael—whose works his landscapes resemble in composition, subject, and atmosphere. The reason for this mimicry was to outdo the Old Masters at their own game: Turner's sun was brighter, his atmosphere moister, haze hazier, and perspectival space deeper. Like Constable, his handling of the intangible properties of nature—wind, light, reflections, atmosphere—was magical.

Turner's quest for the grandiose and his rich imagination led him to embed spectacular mythological and historical moments in his landscapes, creating historical landscape on an epic, sublime scale. *Snowstorm: Hannibal and His Army Crossing the Alps* (fig. **24.6**) of 1812 is one of his best-known historical landscapes, a genre he had developed by the late 1790s. In this work, the Carthaginian general Hannibal leads his troops across the French Alps in 218 BCE to launch a surprise attack on the Romans during the Punic Wars. A human sea of turmoil reigns in the valley below as Hannibal's troops plunder the alpine villages for desperately needed supplies. Above, the cataclysmic forces of nature—a wild snowstorm, turbulent wind, crashing storm clouds, and a blinding light from an ominous sun—threaten to engulf the insignificant figures below, too preoccupied with their immediate survival to notice. The great Hannibal is barely present, reduced to a speck on an elephant in the background. Dramatic light, diagonal recession, and bold brushwork reinforce the chaos and hysteria of the scene.

During the Napoleonic Wars, Turner made several pictures about Carthage, with which, as a great maritime empire, the British identified. In *Snowstorm*, however, the reference is probably to Napoleon's 1800 march across the Alps to invade Italy. Whether the precise allusion is to France or Britain probably does not matter, for the work's wider theme is the folly of empire, and imperial expansion was a hotly debated issue in both France and Britain at the time. The picture is also about the folly of existence. When Turner exhibited *Snowstorm* at the Royal Academy, he accompanied it with several lines from his unfinished poem "The Fallacies of Hope," which moralized about the plundering and ultimate defeat of Hannibal's army. This picture, like his later Carthage paintings, including the 1817 *Decline of the Carthaginian Empire*, is not meant to glorify or condemn human activity. Instead it is designed to put human activity and civilization into a grander cosmic scheme, in which they appear insignificant compared to the relentless, uncontrollable power of sublime universal forces. Turner's goal is the Romantic notion of making a viewer feel nature's unfathomable enormity, not to reproduce a landscape (although the painting is based on studies he made in the Alps). Consequently, an atmospheric haze shrouds the insignificant figures and a dramatically receding vortex ends in a blaze of eternal light. With Turner, Edmund Burke's idea of the sublime (see page 790) reaches a terrifying pitch. But more horrifying than the sheer power of nature are "the fallacies of hope," the Romantic notion of the infinity of the universe and the permanency of death, a modern psychology we have already seen in Goya.

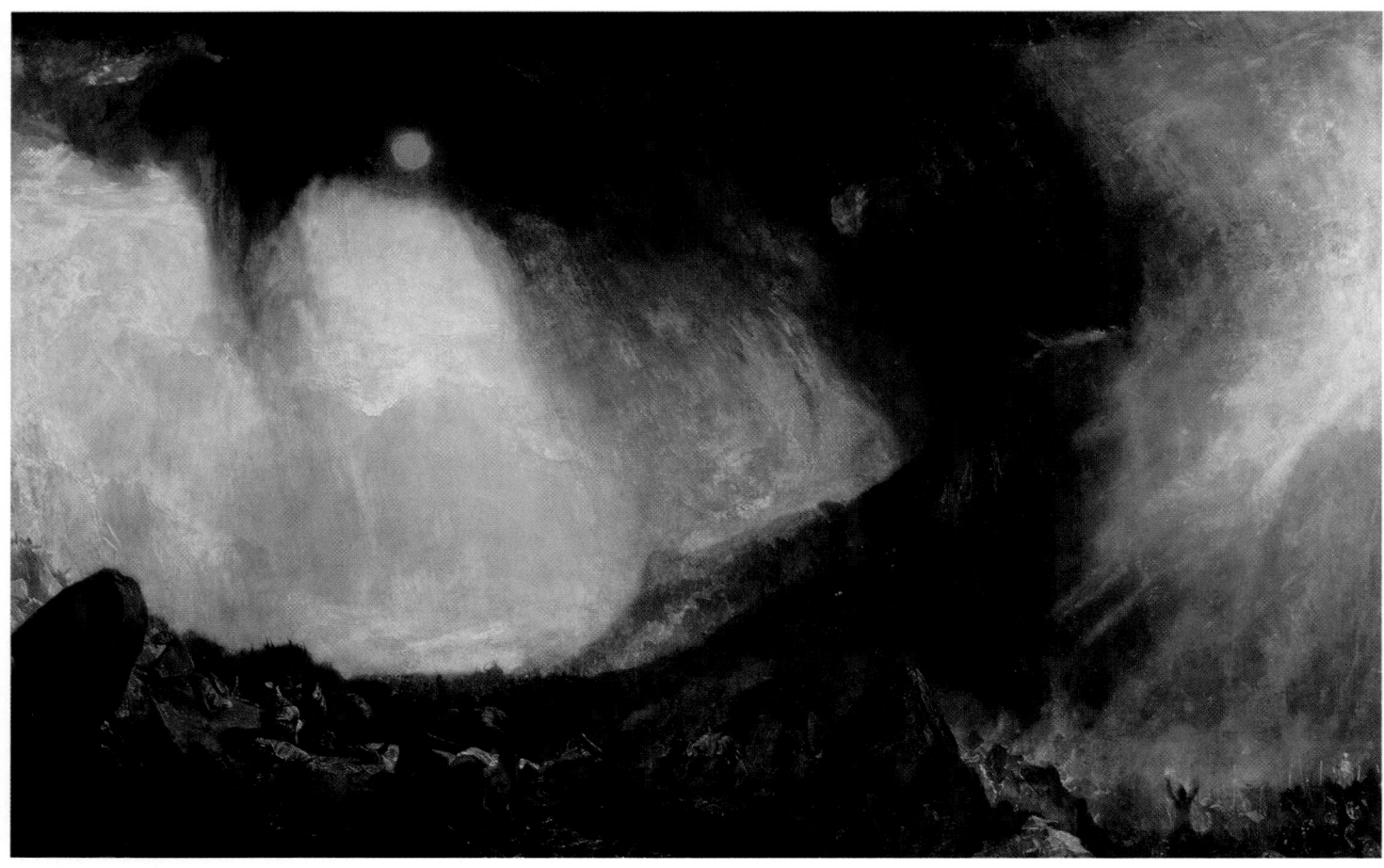

24.6 Joseph Mallord William Turner, *Snowstorm: Hannibal and His Army Crossing the Alps*. 1812. Oil on canvas, 4'9" × 7'9" (1.45 × 2.36 m). Tate Gallery, London

The direct experience of nature becomes stronger in Turner's late work. Now, the image begins to disappear, replaced by an atmospheric blur of paint and color that seems to sit on the surface of the canvas, making a viewer feel immersed in it. Today, Turner is best known for this late abstract style, which he developed toward 1838 and is seen in *The Slave Ship* or *Slavers Throwing Overboard the Dead and Dying—Typhoon Coming On* (fig. **24.7**) of 1840. These late works were condemned in Turner's own time. His contemporaries thought he had gone mad, for they found the works virtually unreadable, and certainly unintelligible. Furthermore, his epic stories were no longer drawn from mythology or history but from seemingly minor contemporary events. His earlier work may have been atmospheric, but there was always enough drawing to suggest precise objects, a distinct composition, and legible spatial recession and relationships, as we see in *Snowstorm*. Later, this readability evaporates in a haze of color and paint that represents the essence of mist, light, and atmosphere.

The Slave Ship shows the sick and dying human cargo being thrown into the sea during a typhoon. Turner was inspired by James Thomson's *The Seasons* (1730), where the poet describes how sharks follow a slave ship during a typhoon, "lured by the scent of steaming crowds, or rank disease, and death." Turner was also influenced by a recent newspaper account of a ship's captain who had jettisoned slaves in order to collect insurance, which paid for cargo lost at sea but not for death from illness. Here, Turner gives us a close-up of human suffering. Outstretched hands pleading for help, a leg about to disappear into the deep for a last time, the gruesome blackness of flailing chains and manacles, the frenzied predatory fish, and bloodstained water all dominate the immediate foreground. In the background is the slave ship, heading into the fury of the typhoon and its own struggle for survival, its distance and silence a metaphor for the callous indifference of the slavers. The searing brilliance of the sun bathes the sky in a blood-red aura, its seemingly infinite reach complementing the omnipotence of the raging sea.

This is a tragic, horrific scene, made a few years after Britain banned slavery entirely in the Abolition of Slavery Act (1833; the Atlantic slave trade had been outlawed in 1807). Turner certainly makes us feel the hardened inhumanity of the slavers, encouraging us to despise them. And yet, the picture has a haunting thematic and moral ambiguity: Birds eat fish and human carcasses, fish feed on other fish and discarded slaves, and slavers fight for their lives in the face of a storm. The picture is as much about the struggle of daily life and the role of fate as it is about the immorality of the slavers, the only constant being the frightening power of nature.

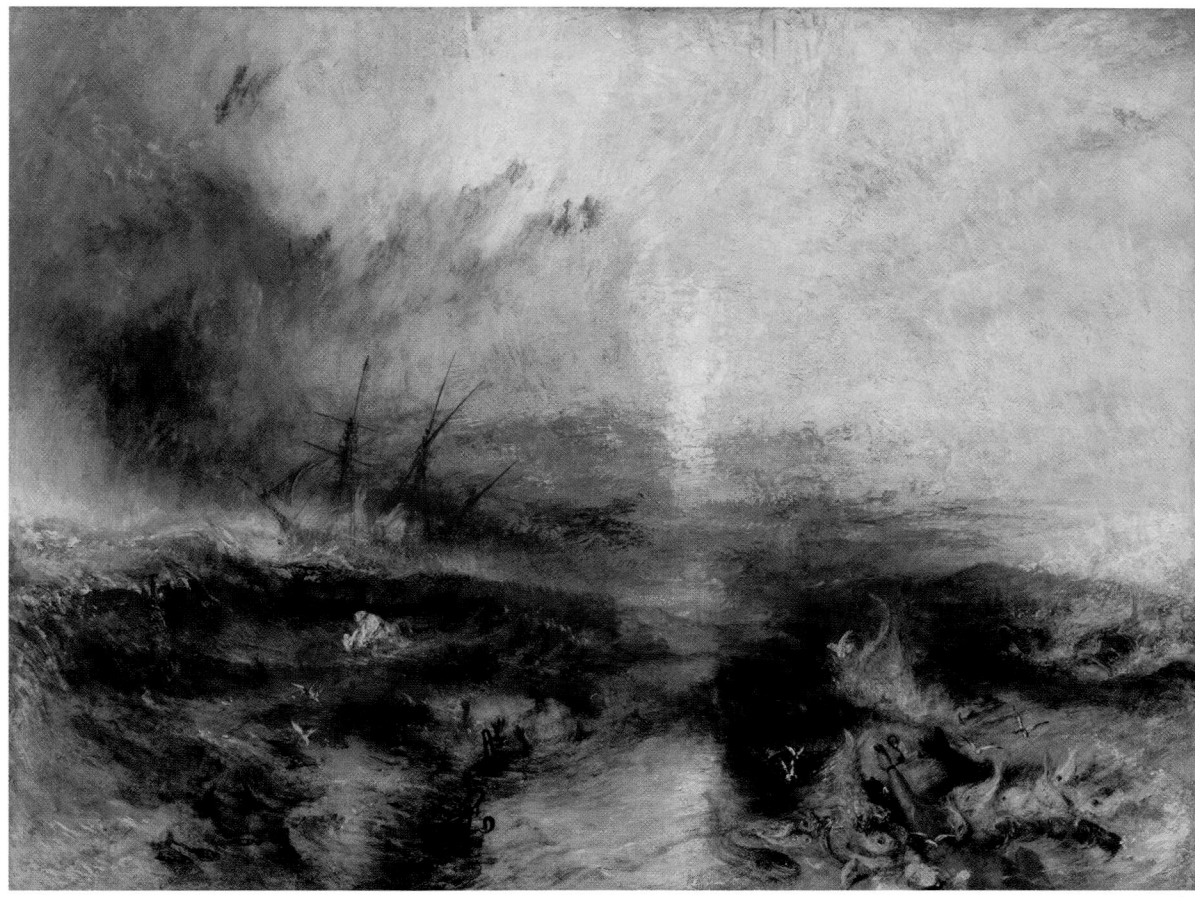

24.7 Joseph Mallord William Turner, *The Slave Ship* or *Slavers Throwing Overboard the Dead and Dying— Typhoon Coming On.* 1840. Oil on canvas, 35¼ × 48" (90.8 × 122.6 cm). Museum of Fine Arts, Boston. Henry Lillie Pierce Fund, Purchase. 99.22

Germany: Friedrich's Pantheistic Landscape

Human destiny is treated with a chilling bleakness and unsettling silence in the sublime landscapes of the German artist Caspar David Friedrich (1774–1840). While Turner focuses on the insignificance of human and animal life in the face of the all-powerful cosmos, Friedrich's concern is the passage from the physical way station of earth to the spiritual being of eternity. His landscapes are virtually pantheistic (seeing God's presence in nature), an especially German phenomenon, as he invests his detailed, realistic scenes with metaphysical properties that give them an aura of divine presence.

Friedrich was born into a prosperous bourgeois family of candle and soap manufacturers in the Baltic harbor town of Greifswald, then part of Sweden. Here, he found the austere landscape that served as the source material for his drawings and formed the foundation of many of his paintings. He studied drawing at the Academy of Copenhagen from 1794 to 1797 and then continued his training in Dresden, where he would maintain a studio throughout his life. Until 1807, he worked exclusively in drawing, shunning historical themes and instead making topographical landscapes, including many of the Baltic region. His paintings would retain the hard linear draftsmanship he developed in these years.

Gradually, his landscape drawings became metaphorical, often presented in groupings with cyclical themes, such as the times of

the day or the four seasons. He continued this practice in his early paintings, which include *Monk by the Sea*, which was paired with *Abbey in an Oak Forest* (fig. 24.8), made in 1809–10. The former, which would be hung on the left and read first, pits the small vertical figure of a standing monk, back to viewer, against the vastness of the sea and an overwhelming explosive sky in a landscape so barren and abstract that the beach, sea, and sky are virtually reduced to vague horizontal bands. Traditionally, art historians interpret the funeral depicted in *Abbey* as that of this monk, in part because the coffin-bearing Capuchins wear the same habit as that of the *Monk by the Sea*. If the first picture depicts life contemplating death, the void represented by the sky and sea, this second is an image of death, as suggested by a frozen snow-covered cemetery, a lugubrious funeral procession, distraught barren oak trees, the skeletal remains of a Gothic abbey, and a somber winter sky at twilight. The abbey and oaks, obviously equated and imbuing nature with a spirituality and vice versa, form a gate that the burial cortege will pass under. Religious hope is stated in the crucifix scene mounted on the portal. The oval at the peak of the tracery window is echoed by the sliver of new moon in the sky, a symbol of resurrection. We sense a rite of passage, a direct connection, between abbey and sky. Just as the moon goes through a cycle as it is reborn, twilight yields to night followed by sunrise and day, and winter gives way to spring, summer, and fall; so also, it is suggested, death will be followed by an afterlife or rebirth. And yet, this is a very gloomy picture that

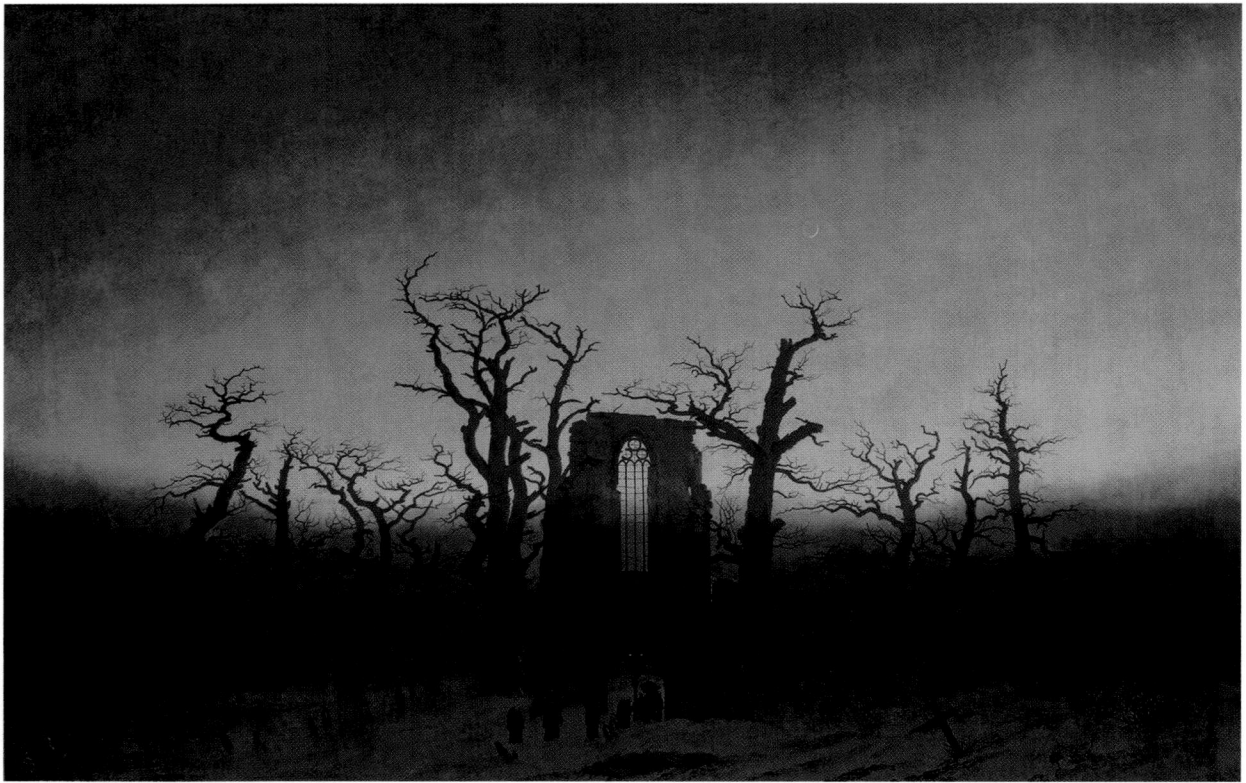

24.8 Caspar David Friedrich, *Abbey in an Oak Forest*. 1809–10. Oil on canvas, 44 × 68½" (111.8 × 174 cm). Nationalgalerie, Staatliche Museen zu Berlin

leaves our fate after death in doubt, making us dread the unknown on the other side of the horizon. Friedrich's cold, marmoreal paint handling reinforces the lifelessness of the scene.

Friedrich's equating nature with religion was influenced by the pantheism of his friend the theologian Gotthard Ludwig Kosegarten, who delivered his dramatic sermons on the shores of the Isle of Rügen in the Baltic, using the awesome and desolate coastal landscape as a metaphor for God. Kosegarten's pantheism was far from unique in Germany, and was in large part a product of the *Sturm und Drang* movement (see pages 787 and 803). Two leading members of the movement, Goethe and Johann Gottfried Herder (1744–1803), also played a major role in stimulating late eighteenth-century German nationalism, the political manifestation of Romanticism, which is also reflected in Friedrich's painting. In *Origin of Language* (1772), Herder argued that language was not divinely endowed but stemmed from the collective experience of a people, triggering a search to define this experience. Herder, for example, collected an anthology of German folk songs, while the Grimm brothers did the same for folktales. This delving into the distant primitive past in search of one's roots was distinctly Romantic, for it created an emotional bond among people that in intensity was quite different from their former shared practical allegiance to an aristocracy. For his part, Goethe declared that Gothic architecture was native to Germany, and, unlike Classical buildings, was premised not on calculation but Romantic intuition, Gothic cathedrals rising up like the towering oak trees that make up the great northern forests.

Friedrich's most salient motifs in *Abbey* are the Gothic ruin and barren oak trees, motifs he knew his audience would immediately recognize as national emblems. The picture was made at a moment of national crisis. There was no Germany in 1810, only a loose confederation of some 300 German-speaking states and free cities called the Holy Roman Empire, nominally ruled by Austrian emperors of the Habsburg dynasty. The emotional surge toward unification was crushed when Napoleon's troops overwhelmed the country. Friedrich's crumbling abbey and striped oaks are symbols of the demise of nationalism, while the winter chill, deadening silence, and gloomy light of a disappearing sun are a reflection of the national mood, and especially Friedrich's.

America: Landscape as Metaphor

Art had not been a priority in the struggling British colonies in America during the seventeenth and eighteenth centuries, and the only art market that existed there was largely for portraiture. Sculpture was mostly limited to weather vanes and tombstones. This did not change dramatically in the Federalist period (1789–1801) and the opening decades of the nineteenth century, although the first academies and galleries were founded in the first quarter of the century—the Pennsylvania Academy of Fine Arts (1802), the Boston Atheneum (1807), and New York's National Academy of Design (1825). By 1825, New York had surpassed Philadelphia as the largest and wealthiest city in the nation—in large part due to the opening of the 383-mile (613-km) Erie Canal that ran from Buffalo to the Hudson River at Albany, funneling the raw materials and produce of the hinterlands into New York City. New York simultaneously became the nation's art capital, and consequently our discussion of American art will center on New York well into the twentieth century.

In the 1820s, landscape painting began to acquire status and, by the 1840s, it had eclipsed portraiture as the most esteemed form of American art. A young nation with little history, the United States became preoccupied with a search for its own identity, one that would distinguish it from its Old World roots. Literary figures such as William Cullen Bryant (1794–1878) and Ralph Waldo Emerson (1803–1882) identified the land itself as America's wealth and contrasted its unspoiled virginity to the densely populated, resource-impoverished lands of Europe. America was overflowing with natural resources, a veritable Garden of Eden. They also interpreted this pristine land as a manifestation of God, whose presence was to be seen in every blade of grass, ray of sun, and drop of water. To meditate on nature was to commune with God. This belief stemmed not only from the metaphysics of German philosophers—the same thought we saw expressed in Friedrich's paintings—but also from the American Transcendentalist movement, which surfaced in the 1830s and is perhaps best known today from such works as Emerson's *Nature* (1836) and Henry David Thoreau's *Walden* (1852). In this famous quote from *Nature*, Emerson expresses the spiritual unification with nature and the consequent role of the artist or writer to channel this unification into art: "Standing on the bare ground—my head bathed by the blithe air, and uplifted into infinite space—all mean egotism vanishes. I become a transparent eyeball; I am

nothing; I see all; the currents of the Universal Being circulate through me; I am part or parcel of God." Elsewhere, Emerson wrote: "The poet must be a rhapsodist—his inspiration a sort of bright casualty; his will in it only the surrender of will to the Universal Power." The American landscape became the emblem of the young nation.

THOMAS COLE AND THE HUDSON RIVER SCHOOL

America's first art movement, based on landscape and born in the 1820s, is called the Hudson River School, because the artists, most with studios in New York, were initially centered on the Hudson River Valley before fanning out through all of New England in the 1830s through the 1850s. Spring through fall, the artists traveled through New York and New England making studies, generally drawings, of this unique land, which they then developed into large paintings in their New York studios during the winter. The lead figure in this group was Thomas Cole (1801–1848), a founding member of the National Academy of Design who produced his first major landscapes after an 1825 summer sketching trip up the Hudson. Initially, his views were sublime, presenting a wild, primordial nature, often with storms pummeling the forests, dark clouds blackening the earth, and lightning-blasted trees. Despite depicting specific sites, his style relied on European landscape conventions and formulas, with little attention given to detail.

By the 1830s, however, Cole's paint handling became tighter and his pictures less formulaic and more specific, embracing a Romantic truth to nature that we saw in Constable. This is apparent in *The Oxbow* (fig. **24.9**), made in 1836 for exhibition at the National Academy of Design. In this breathtaking view from atop

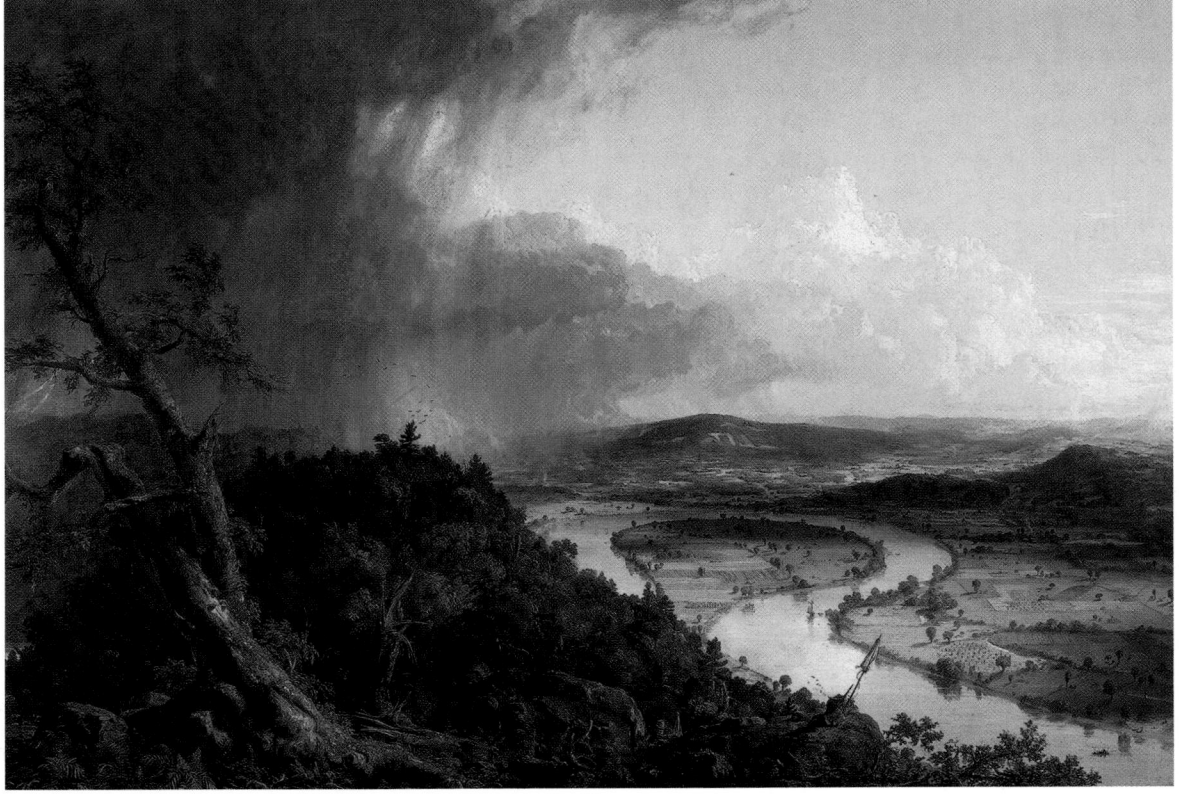

24.9 Thomas Cole, *The Oxbow (View from Mount Holyoke, Northampton, Massachusetts, after a Thunderstorm)*. 1836. Oil on canvas, 51½ × 76" (1.31 × 1.94 m). Metropolitan Museum of Art, New York. Gift of Mrs. Russell Sage, 1908 (08.228)

Mount Holyoke in western Massachusetts, Cole presents the natural wonder of the American landscape. The foreground is sublime wilderness, with blasted and windswept trees and dark storm clouds dumping sheets of rain. Except for the representation of Cole next to his parasol looking up at us (and in effect declaring his preference for primordial nature), there is no sign of humans in the foreground. Far below in the sunlit valley, separated by distance, height, and the sharp contour of the mountain ridge, are the Connecticut River and its plain. Closer inspection reveals not just a natural plain but also cultivated fields and settlements. But they are in such harmony with nature that they seem to blend in. Here is the "Garden of Eden," as Americans described their land, blessed by the divine light breaking through the clouds. Cole underscores God's presence in the land by roughly etching, under the guise of cleared forest, the name "Noah" into the distant hill; upside down, these same letters become Hebrew letters for *Shaddai*, meaning "the Almighty."

Cole's settlers respect nature as well as its cycles, fitting right in. In the wilderness foreground, the dead trees and seedlings represent this cycle of life, death, and resurrection. First and foremost, the picture is a paean to the glory of the American land. Cole captures the immense scale of the American landscape and its many moods, from the wild sublimity of the foreground, to the pastoral tranquility of the valley, to the majestic vastness of the distant hills. In *The Oxbow*, we see the artist rhapsodizing in Romantic fashion as Emerson prescribed, bonding with nature and God.

The Oxbow was also a political painting, as viewers at the 1836 exhibition would have recognized. While most Hudson River School painters depicted the glory of God as manifested in the American land, a handful, following Cole's lead, also used landscape painting to comment on the economic and social issues consuming the nation. An 1829–32 trip to Europe gave Cole first-hand knowledge of Turner's paintings and reinforced Cole's interest in using landscape as a vehicle for themes of historical significance. In 1836, for example, Cole painted a five-picture series titled *The Course of Empire*, which traced the transformation of the same site from a primitive state, to an agrarian society, to a thriving empire, to a decadent empire, and lastly to a state of ruin. Just as Turner's landscapes were metaphors for social and political issues, so were Cole's. His audience would recognize in *The Course of Empire* a statement reflecting the heated debate about progress then consuming the country. On one side were those Americans arguing for a Jeffersonian agrarian America; on the other were the advocates of Jacksonian *laissez-faire* economics, which embraced unrestricted industrial, commercial, and financial development. Cole, who like the novelist James Fenimore Cooper (1789–1851) was an early environmentalist, found the rapid destruction of the wilderness and disrespect for the land disheartening. His vision of healthy development stopped at the Jeffersonian agrarian society, where Americans lived in harmony with the land. He equated Jacksonian politics with empire, which would result not only in the destruction of the land but also the eventual downfall of America. In *The Oxbow*, Cole proclaims his

own personal preference for the wilderness, while championing the virtue of an agrarian civilization, one where Americans respect their covenant with God.

FREDERIC CHURCH AND NATIONAL LANDSCAPE Cole's only student, Frederic Edwin Church (1826–1900), fully understood how landscape could be used to make powerful political statements. Born into a wealthy family in Hartford, Connecticut, he joined Cole at his summer home in Catskill, New York, on the Hudson in 1844. In 1848, the year Cole died, he was made a member of the National Academy and was living in New York City. By 1850, Church had inherited Cole's mantle as America's foremost landscape painter, largely making pastoral or rural scenes showing man harmoniously living in nature. But throughout the 1850s, Church's work became increasingly sublime. He traveled to Niagara Falls to capture the awesome scale, power, and deafening roar of this famous landmark. His search for the sublime even took him to locales outside the United States, first going to the Andes in Ecuador and Columbia in 1853 to paint the exotic trappings of the tropics, and then sailing to the Arctic in 1859 to portray foreboding icebergs in Newfoundland and Labrador.

By January 1860, Church had begun working on *Twilight in the Wilderness* (fig. **24.10**), which he finished that year, exhibiting it to wild acclaim, first in the Tenth Street Studio Building, where he had a studio, and then at the Goupil Gallery in New York. While working on this painting, he was also finishing up *The Heart of the Andes*, the result of a second trip to South America in 1857, and starting *Icebergs*, his first major iceberg painting. *Twilight* represents the wonders of the American wilderness, most viewers associating it with Maine and New Hampshire. The picture represents a temperate environment and nicely complements the tropical and Arctic themes of the other two works in Church's studio at the time, the trilogy in effect presenting a compendium of New World climates as described by the German explorer and naturalist Alexander von Humboldt in his five-volume book *Cosmos* (1845).

As its title suggests, the picture represents the American wilderness, a pure, unspoiled Garden of Eden, with no sign of human presence. Americans considered brilliantly colored sunsets unique to their country, thus an emblem of the nation, just as they did the spectacular autumnal foliage, which was especially popular with painters. But Church's use here of twilight probably has a second function, that of referring to the twilight *of* the wilderness as New England especially was being settled and crisscrossed with railroad tracks, and pioneers, driven by Manifest Destiny (the compulsion to settle the entire continent), were swarming west toward the Pacific. And twilight has a third function in the image. We must remember the painting was made in 1860, a year before the Civil War, which most everyone knew was looming on the horizon as the slavery issue violently divided the nation. Church makes the country the focus of his picture by putting an American eagle on top of the dead tree in the left foreground, the tree serving as a pole for the American flag of fiery

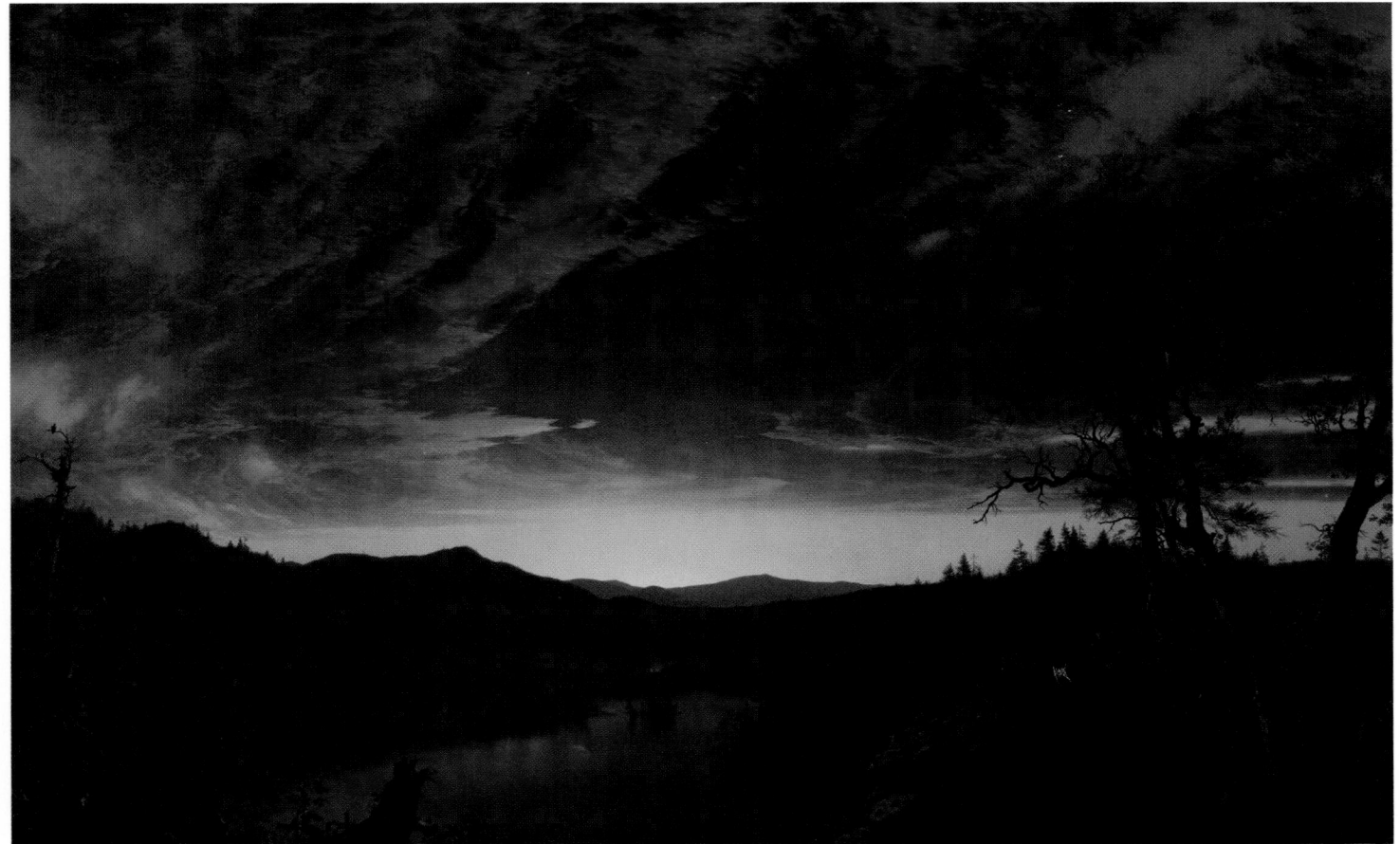

24.10　Frederic Edwin Church, *Twilight in the Wilderness*. 1860. Oil on canvas, 40 × 64" (101.6 × 162.6 cm).
The Cleveland Museum of Art, purchase, Mr. and Mrs. William H. Marlatt Fund (65.233)

red altocumulus clouds and blue sky. As the sun sets behind the horizon, Church casts doubts on the future of both the wilderness and the nation itself.

France: Neoclassical Romanticism

Neoclassicism dominated French art in the late eighteenth and early nineteenth centuries. This was because of Jacques-Louis David's powerful impact on painting (see pages 813–16). In his lifetime, David had some 400 students, and after 1800 his most gifted followers from the 1790s began to rival him for public attention. David convinced the new Republican government to abolish the French Royal Academy, although the biennial Louvre Salon exhibitions were still held during the Directory (1794–1799) and the Napoleonic era (1799–1814) and remained critical for an artist's success. David himself received major commissions from Napoleon, and was the emperor's official court painter. With Napoleon's defeat at Waterloo, David exiled himself to Brussels. But by then he had long been superseded by his students and followers. Despite the Neoclassical look of their paintings, these works were made in the Romantic era, and thematically we can describe them as belonging not to Neoclassicism but to Neoclassical Romanticism.

ANNE-LOUIS GIRODET AND THE PRIMITIVES Anne-Louis Girodet (1767–1824), one of David's most brilliant pupils, introduced a new type of Neoclassical painting in 1791 when he sent *The Sleep of Endymion* (fig. **24.11**) back to Paris from Rome, where he was a pensioner at the French Academy, having won the Rome Prize. The painting was shown at the Salon of 1793 to universal praise. Rome Prize students were required to execute an oil painting of a nude. Girodet's figure conforms to the Neoclassical paradigm: It is a Classical nude with sharp contours and is carefully painted with tight brushwork. Rather than virile and virtuous, however, Girodet's nude is androgynous and sensuous. The choice of subject was also startling. Derived from Classical mythology, its theme was an indulgent hedonism at a time when everyone else was portraying noble sacrifice, as in David's *The Oath of the Horatii* (see fig. 23.27). Girodet presents the story of the moon-goddess Selene (Diana), who fell desperately in love with the mortal shepherd Endymion and put him into an eternal sleep so she could visit him every night. Here, we see one of these nocturnal visits, with Zephyr pulling back the branches of a tree so that Selene can seduce the sleeping shepherd. David's harsh, raking light gives way to a softer, more sensual illumination that gently caresses Endymion, creating a chiaroscuro that emphasizes the slow undulation of his soft, beautiful flesh.

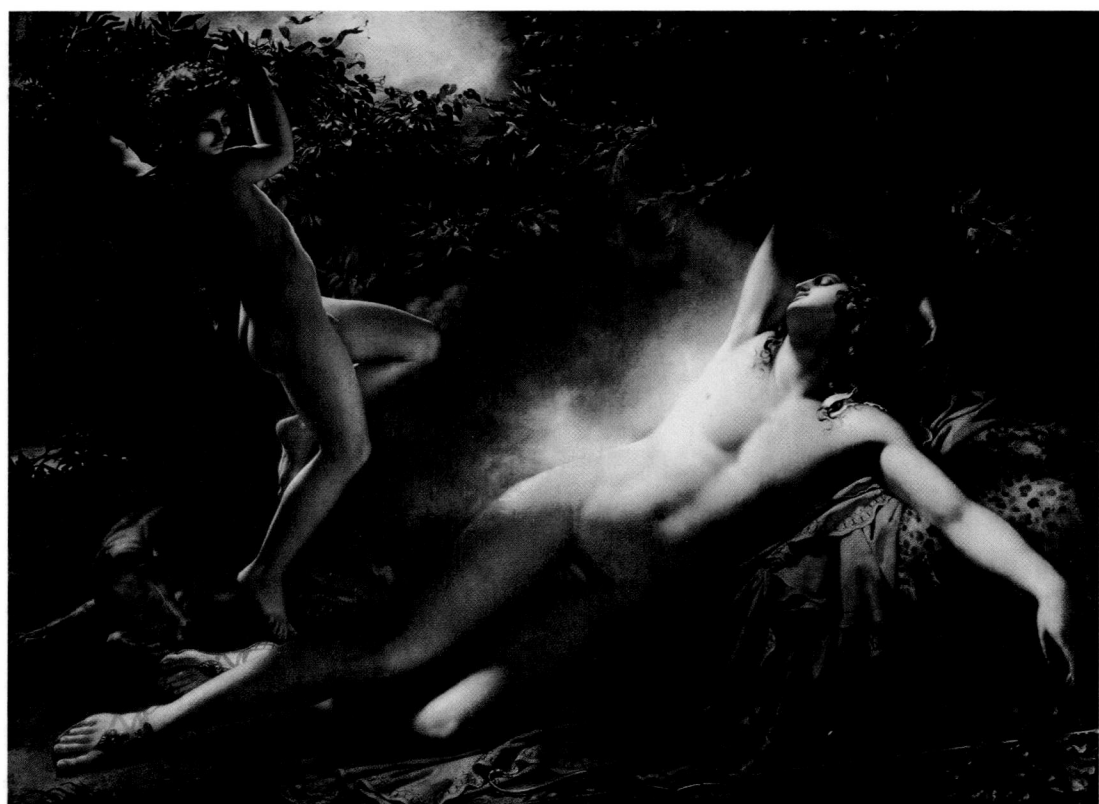

Moonbeams dramatically backlight the figures, etching strong, elegant curvilinear contours.

Despite the erotic content, this is hardly a titillatingly playful Rococo picture, for the work has a powerful mood of primal sensuality, brought about in part by the mysterious moonlight. Combining Correggio's chiaroscuro and vaporous sfumato (see fig. 17.26) with the grace of Bronzino's contours (see fig. 17.11), two artists Girodet studied first hand in Rome, the painter created a picture that does not illustrate a story so much as it projects a state of mind characterized by powerful elemental urges, a quality that is distinctly Romantic.

In the late 1790s, a number of David's followers, who called themselves the Primitives, took their cue from Girodet's *Endymion*. Themes of sensuous love based on Classical myth, such as Cupid and Psyche and the death of Hyacinth in the arms of Apollo, became popular. Figures were backlit to highlight strong contours and create a sensuous undulating line. Reinforcing this taste for prominent outlines was the publication of John Flaxman's engraved illustrations of Homer's *The Iliad* and *The Odyssey*, made in Rome in 1792–93 and based on Greek vase painting. (See *Materials and Techniques*, page 792.) Flaxman's startlingly severe engravings, in which he reduced figures and objects to a simple line with no **shading** or modeling, were popular throughout Europe and exerted a tremendous influence over the style and motifs of art during the Romantic era. While the Primitives in David's studio were heavily influenced by Flaxman and Girodet, they also admired the stripped-down clarity of Greek vase painting and the simple forms of fifteenth-century Italian painting, then considered "primitive" compared with the High Renaissance, hence the group's name.

JEAN-AUGUSTE-DOMINIQUE INGRES The painter Jean-Auguste-Dominique Ingres (1780–1867) was briefly in the Primitives group, and a strong emphasis on contour and line became one of the hallmarks of his Neoclassical style. He entered David's studio in 1797 and won the Rome Prize in 1801, although in part because of the Napoleonic Wars he could not take advantage of his award until 1806. Before leaving for Italy, he received a commission from the French Legislative Assembly for a *Portrait of Napoleon on His Imperial Throne* (fig. **24.12**), which he showed at the Salon of 1806, where it was heavily criticized, even by Napoleon. Ingres's Neoclassical roots are evident in the harsh Davidian planarity, compressed space, and emphasis on line or contour, although Ingres's edge is sharper, more lively, almost seeming to have a life of its own, as, for example, in the white border of Napoleon's robe.

But here the comparison with David and the Primitives stops and Ingres's Romanticism begins, although it does not overwhelm his Neoclassicism: He would be recognized as the great standard-bearer of the latter style in the first half of the nineteenth century. Ingres fills every square inch of his portrait of Napoleon with opulence—gold, gems, ermine, marble, tapestries, rare objects. In one hand Napoleon holds the golden scepter of Charlemagne, in the other the ivory hand of justice of the French medieval kings, both certifying his royal legacy. The elaborate gilt throne looks as if it is from imperial Rome. Its curved back

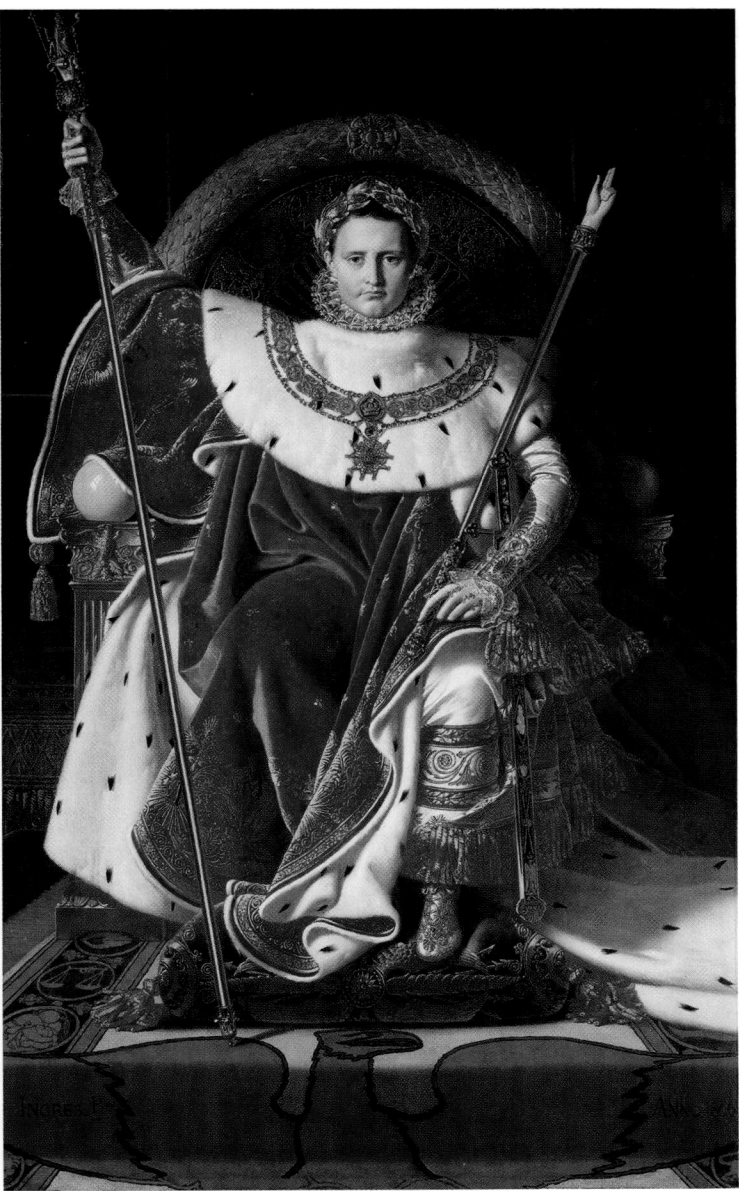

24.12 Jean-Auguste-Dominique Ingres, *Portrait of Napoleon on His Imperial Throne*. 1806. Oil on canvas, 8'9" × 5'3" (2.66 × 1.6 m). Musée de l'Armée, Palais des Invalides, Paris

audience at the Salon of 1806. While preferring tight brushwork and a hard icy surface to painterly gesture, Ingres was clearly a magnificent colorist. In *Napoleon*, his hues match the objects in opulence and have the same gemlike quality he found in the sparkling oils of the Van Eycks' paintings. They have a similar level of realism in capturing various lush textures. Ingres was as concerned with harmonizing complex relationships of deeply saturated color as he was in balancing the intricate designs of his compositions.

In Italy, Ingres studied ancient art and fell in love with the Classicism of Raphael. But as a Romantic—which is what he considered himself to be—his interests were broad, even exotic, and led him to medieval, Byzantine, and Early Renaissance art. After his four-year stipend expired, Ingres stayed on in Italy at his own expense for an additional 14 years, often impoverished and, like a true Romantic artist, painting what he wanted, not what the academy dictated. Periodically, he sent pictures back to Paris for exhibition, where they were generally met with derision. An example is *Grande Odalisque* (fig. **24.13**), commissioned in 1814 by Caroline Murat, Napoleon's sister and the queen of Naples, and submitted to the Salon of 1819.

This painting is even more exotic than his portrait of Napoleon, for it represents a Turkish concubine and is one of the earliest examples of **Orientalism**, as the Western fascination with the culture of the Muslim world of North Africa and the Near East was then called. (Byron's Romantic poem *The Corsair*, also featuring a harem slave, was published the same year the painting was commissioned.) This fascination was, in part, sparked by Napoleon's campaign in Egypt in 1798–99 and by the detailed description of the region and its culture and customs in the 24-volume government-sponsored publication *Description de l'Égypte*, which appeared from 1809 to 1822. Orientalism reflects European imperialism and its accompanying sense of superiority that viewed non-Christian Arab culture as not only different and exotic but also inferior—backward, immoral, violent, and barbaric. Here, the exotic subject gave Ingres license to paint a female nude who was not a Greek goddess, although she recalls numerous Renaissance and Baroque paintings of a reclining Venus and sculptures of Ariadne from antiquity. To make his figure more appealing to a Paris audience, Ingres gave his odalisque European features, even a Raphaelesque face and coiffure. Although the figure is alluringly sensual, and the hashish pipe, incense burner, fan, and turban "authenticate" the exotic scene, the painting as a whole projects a soothing sense of cultivated beauty, refinement, and idealization that seems Classical. In other words, Ingres treats a Romantic subject in an essentially Neoclassical manner, including idealization.

Ingres's trademark is a beautiful Classical line, which we can see as he focuses on the odalisque's flesh. Bathed in a caressing chiaroscuro, the body gently swells and recedes with delectable elegance. Its contours languidly undulate with sensuality, the sharply defined edges and tan color contrasting with the objects around it. The opulent color of the objects and the lush fabrics and peacock feathers enhance the sensual aura of the picture.

forms a halo around the emperor's head, which contemporaries recognized as a reference to God the Father in the central panel of Jan and Hubert van Eyck's *Ghent Altarpiece* (see fig. 14.10), then installed in the Napoleon Museum in the Louvre and part of the immense booty of Napoleon's conquests. Ingres even has Napoleon strike the same pose as the Van Eycks' God, which when combined with his iconic frontal position suggests that Napoleon is endowed with the same qualities, or at least that his actions are sanctioned by God. Ingres's deification of Napoleon is also strengthened by a resemblance to Zeus in a Flaxman line engraving.

Ingres's frozen larger-than-life image presents Napoleon as imperial, aloof, and divine, and its wondrously exotic and even fantastical Romantic content must have fascinated, even awed, the

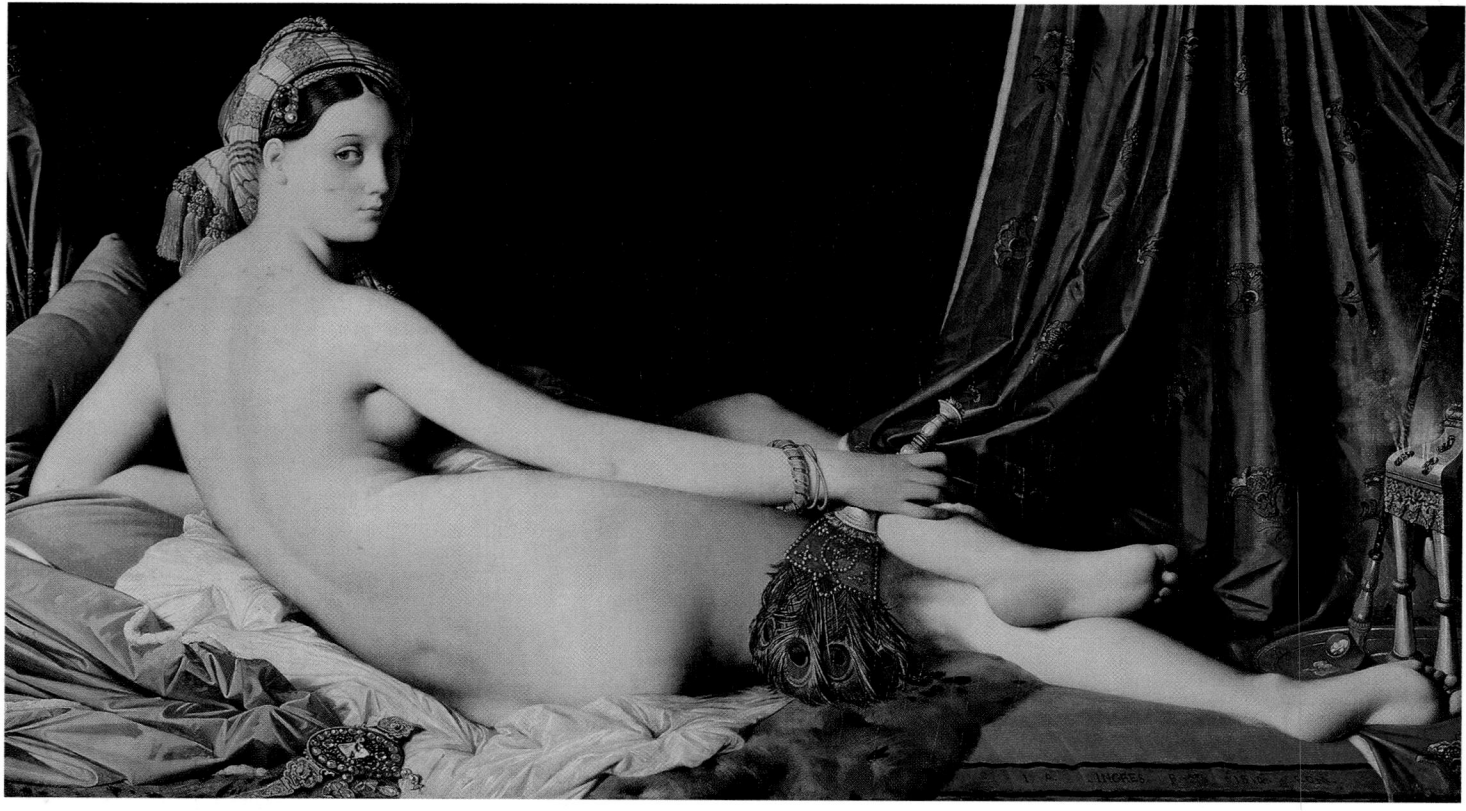

24.13   Jean-Auguste-Dominique Ingres, *Grande Odalisque*. 1814. Oil on canvas, 35⅞ × 63" (91 × 162 cm). Musée du Louvre, Paris. Inv. RF1158

Salon viewers noted the concubine's back had too many verte-
brae, and certainly her elbowless right arm is too long; but as far
as Ingres was concerned, the sweeping curves of both were essential components of the graceful composition, the line of the right
arm even being continued into the folds of the drapery.

In 1821, Ingres received a commission to make an enormous
painting of *The Vow of Louis XIII* for the cathedral in Montauban
in his hometown. Penniless, otherwise forgotten, and living in
Florence, with this painting Ingres turned his life around. He
showed the picture at the Salon of 1824 to rave reviews and was
hailed as the great savior of the Classical tradition. With the
final fall of Napoleon in 1815, David, who had been named
painter to the emperor in 1801, skulked off to Brussels, and the
careers of all of his students had stalled at the same time, displaced
by a new generation of painterly Romantic artists. Almost by
default, Ingres, because of *The Vow of Louis XIII*, was now
crowned the protector of Classicism, the champion of line over
color, and the savior of the "wholesome traditions of great art"
and ideal beauty from the unfettered emotionalism of the
painterly Romantics. In 1825, he was elected to the French
Academy, which as a Romantic he had disdained, and soon
became its director. He was also awarded the Legion of Honor,
the highest award in France for service to the state, established by
Napoleon in 1802. His studio became the destination of choice
for aspiring young history painters.

While Ingres defined himself as a history painter, since it
held the greatest prestige within the academy, his strength was
portraiture, especially of women. His 1856 *Portrait of Madame
Inès Moitessier* (fig. **24.14**) is a good example. The work was commissioned in 1844, and over the next 12 years the guardian of ideal
beauty transformed the wife of a wealthy banker into an image of
Classical perfection, an earthly goddess. He gave her creamy
smooth skin, beautiful curvilinear shoulders, arms, and hands,
and a Raphaelesque face. He enriched her with a lavish rose-pat-
terned gown lined with a fashionable fringe, opulent Renaissance-
revival jewelry on the raised right arm and cabochon garnets surrounded with diamonds on the left, and a peacock-feather fan.
Behind her is Chinese vase, a fanlike shield to protect her from
fireplace heat in the winter, and an imposing gilt-frame mirror.
Also contributing to her perfection are the immaculately smooth
paint surface (free of painterly brushwork), the precise drawing,
and the harmonious blending of a complicated composition with
a richly colored palette.

Madame Moitessier's pose suggests various Classical prototypes, while her contemplative hand-to-head gesture derives
from Roman murals at Herculaneum. The profile in the mirror,
an obvious distortion, could not be more Greek. It also super-
imposes an eerie psychological veil on the work, reinforcing the
introspection of her gesture and tinting the painting with a
mysterious mood that converts the realistic materiality of
Moitessier's physical surroundings into a spiritual embodiment
of beauty. While the style is distinctly Neoclassical, this
mysterious mood and the intensely lush setting give the picture
Romantic overtones.

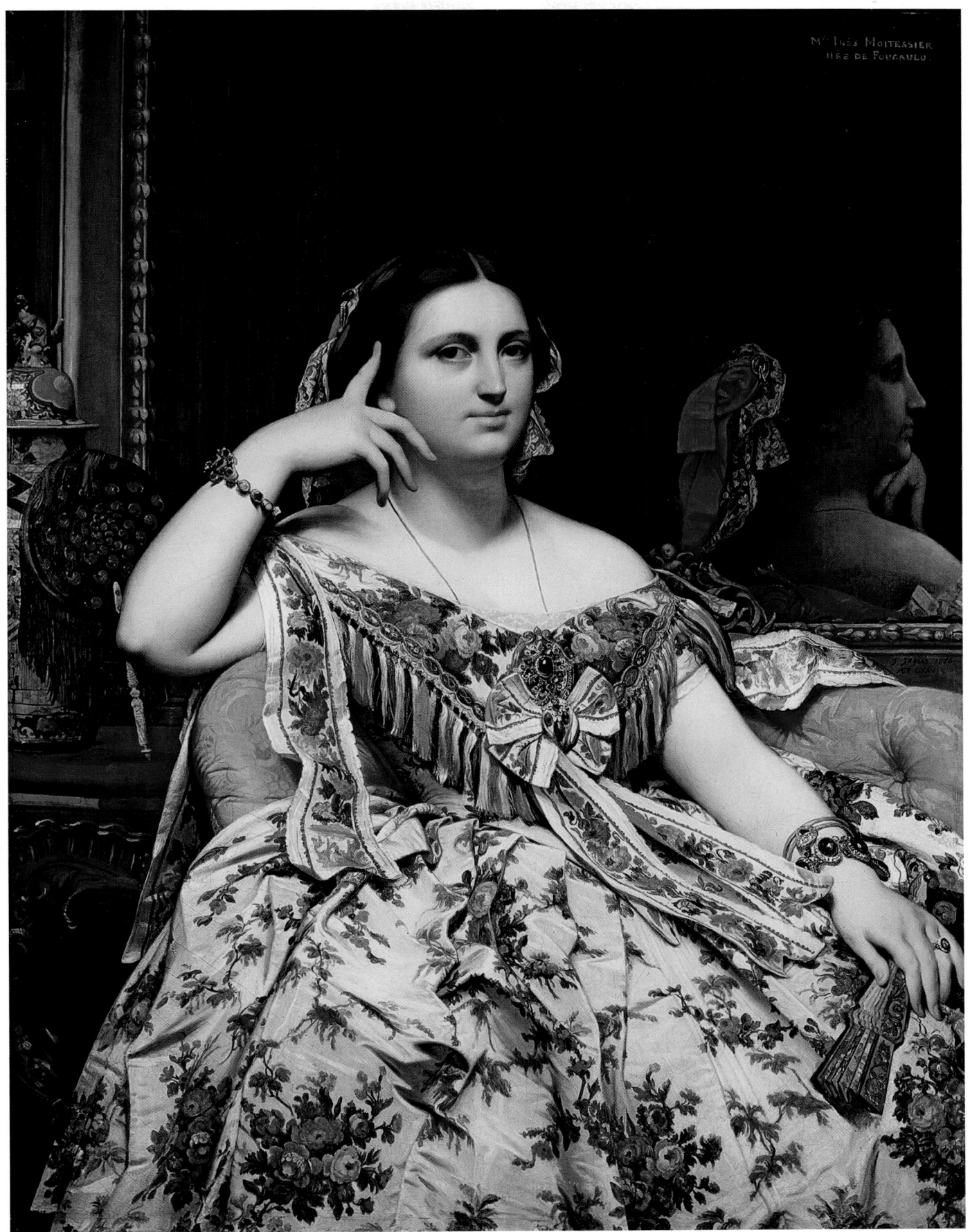

24.14 Jean-Auguste-Dominique Ingres, *Portrait of Madame Inès Moitessier*. 1856. Oil on canvas, 47¼ × 36¼" (120 × 92.1 cm).
The National Gallery, London

France: Painterly Romanticism and Romantic Landscape

While Ingres was taking Neoclassicism deep into the nineteenth century, but now within the context of Romanticism, Antoine-Jean Gros, a second student of David's, opened up an alternative course, one that would abandon line, order, clear rational space, evenly diffused light, ideal beauty, and Classical repose for bold brushstrokes, dazzling color, impetuous drama, confused space, irrational lighting, and extreme emotions. In his wake came Théodore Géricault and Eugène Delacroix, who brought painterly Romanticism to the fore in the 1820s, resulting in contemporaries finally applying the word Romanticism, previously reserved for literature and music, to art. In the 1820s as well, landscape painting began to emerge from under the shadow cast by Neoclassicism. French Romantic landscape was never as apocalyptic as its British counterpart nor as pantheistic as in Germany and America. Instead it was more serene and poetic.

ANTOINE-JEAN GROS Gros (1771–1835) entered David's studio in 1785. During the turmoil of the French Revolution, David

was able to secure a pass for Gros to go to Rome, although by the time he arrived there the city was closed to the antipapist French. Through Napoleon's wife, Josephine, he met Napoleon in Milan, traveled with his army, and impressed the general with his art. Napoleon charged Gros with painting his battles and glorifying his campaigns. Bonaparte, who was as brilliant at propaganda as he was at military strategy, carefully controlled his public image and relied heavily on art to reinforce his political position. He made sure his commissions were shown at the Salons, where they would be seen by everyone and reported in the press, which was becoming more important in the opening decades of the century due to increased literacy and decreased paper and printing costs.

The Napoleonic era was a catalyst for French Romanticism. The drama, glory, valor, and adventures of the Napoleonic Wars provided endless material for the artistic imagination. The North African campaigns took Europeans into the forbidden Arab world and introduced them to a wondrous exotic subject matter that they brought back to Europeans anxious for new experiences. Gros's first commission, *Napoleon in the Pesthouse at Jaffa, March 11, 1799* (fig. **24.15**), came in 1804 and was exhibited in that year's Salon to huge success. This 23-foot-wide picture was

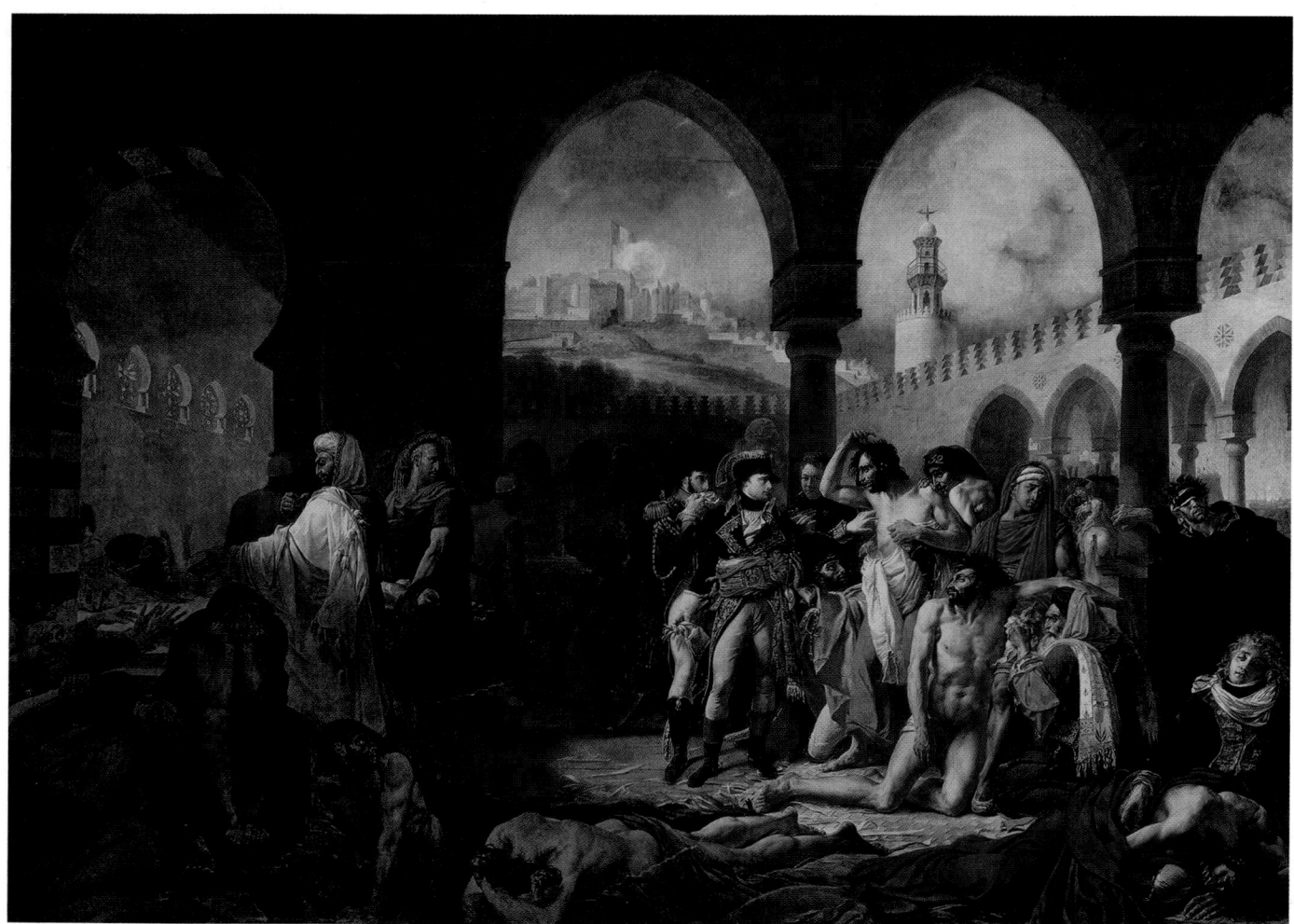

24.15   Antoine-Jean Gros, *Napoleon in the Pesthouse at Jaffa, March 11, 1799*. 1804. Oil on canvas, 17'5½" × 23'7½" (5.32 × 7.20 m). Musée du Louvre, Paris

commissioned not only to promote the emperor's bravery and leadership but to reinforce his humanitarian image, which was propagandistically essential considering the enormous human loss tallied in many of his battles, especially in Jaffa (then in Palestine but today a section of Tel Aviv, Israel). During the campaign, the bubonic plague broke out among the French ranks. Legend has it that, to calm his troops, Napoleon fearlessly entered the pesthouse and walked among the patients. Here we see the general, like Christ healing the sick, courageously touching the open sore of a victim, his presence virtually willing the dying to rise. The painting ignores the fact that Napoleon poisoned these same sick troops when he retreated from Jaffa.

While Gros's drawing and brushwork are relatively tight and Davidian, the picture is one of overt, turbulent drama, created by the dark shadows, bursts of light, splashes of bright red, rapidly receding perspective of the arcades, and cloud-filled sky. Chaos prevails. Although Napoleon is placed in the center as a compositional anchor, he momentarily gets lost in the turmoil of the scene. Our eye goes to the circle of the dead, dying, and sick surrounding him, which includes the Michelangelesque figures in the foreground shadows and the "resurrected" nudes next to Bonaparte. The male nude is now neither heroic, as in David, nor lovely, as in Girodet, but helpless and horrifying. Napoleon's courageous act has to vie for a viewer's attention with the dark mood of psychological and physical suffering and the exoticism, to Western eyes, of the Arab attendants and Islamic architecture. (This picture helped launch the vogue for Oriental subjects that we saw in Ingres's *Grande Odalisque*.) The monumental arches compositionally may pay homage to David's *The Oath of the Horatii* (fig. 23.27), but instead of supporting a narrative of Neoclassical stoicism and clarity they contribute a Romantic exoticism and sense of foreboding of horrifying uncertainty.

THÉODORE GÉRICAULT Without the Napoleonic campaigns to feed his imagination, Gros's career soon waned. David's other outstanding students and followers, such as Girodet, were simultaneously eclipsed. The future was now represented by Théodore Géricault (1791–1824) and those who followed him. Géricault was independently wealthy and largely self-taught, frequenting the Napoleon Museum, where he copied the great colorists: Rubens, Van Dyck, and Titian. Gros, however, was his role model, and Gros and Rubens were clearly the artistic sources for Géricault's submission to the Salon of 1812, *Charging Chasseur* (fig. **24.16**). The energetic brushwork, the sharp diagonal recession of the horse, the bold contrast of light and dark, the rippling contours on the horse's right legs, and the flashes of color could not be further from David or closer to Rubens. Completely gone is the Davidian planarity that structured the turmoil of Gros's pesthouse. Made during Napoleon's Russian campaign, the picture functions as an emblem of heroic valor. It is not meant to represent a specific event or person. Instead, the twisting *chasseur* (cavalryman) and rearing horse embody the psychological and physical forces that consume combatants in the heat of battle, and it is interesting how many compositional parallels there are

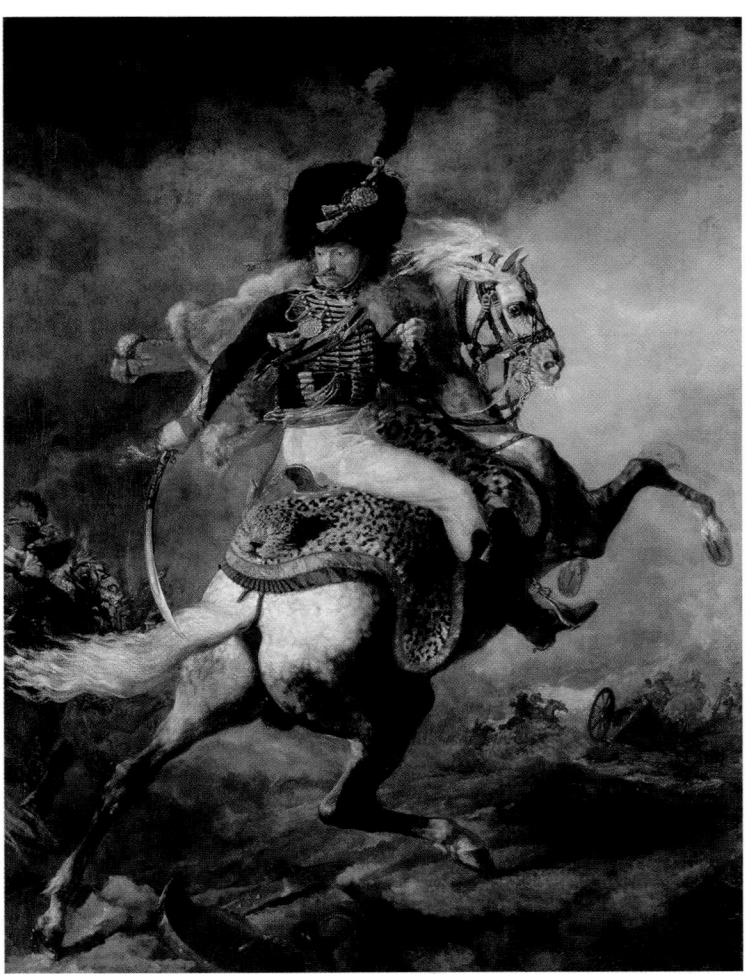

24.16   Théodore Géricault, *Charging Chasseur*. 1812. Oil on canvas, 11'5" × 8'9" (3.49 × 2.66 m). Musée du Louvre, Paris

between rider and horse, suggesting the sheer animalistic forces driving the cavalryman's heroism. This is a picture of raw emotion and physical tension, devoid of Neoclassical reason and the rules of beauty and morality. As the great Romantic writer Stendhal (pseudonym of Marie-Henri Beyle, 1783–1842) said in his review of the 1824 Salon, "The school of David can only paint bodies; it is decidedly inept at painting souls."

Charging Chasseur revealed Géricault's lack of formal training; namely, his inability to draw as seen in the oddly twisted head of the cavalryman, for example. Continuing his independent study, he now worked from Classical models, copying High Renaissance painters at the Royal Museum, as the Louvre was called after the second fall of Napoleon in 1815 and with the establishment of Louis XVIII's Restoration monarchy. In 1816, he went to Italy, stopping in Florence to draw Michelangelo's Medici tombs (see fig. 17.5), before going to Rome to study the antiquities. Not long after his return to Paris in late 1817, he began thinking about the third and last painting he would exhibit at the Salons, *The Raft of the Medusa* (fig. 24.17), painted between 1818 and 1819 after many studies. In 1816, the *Medusa*, a government vessel, foundered off the West African coast with approximately 400 people aboard. The captain commandeered the

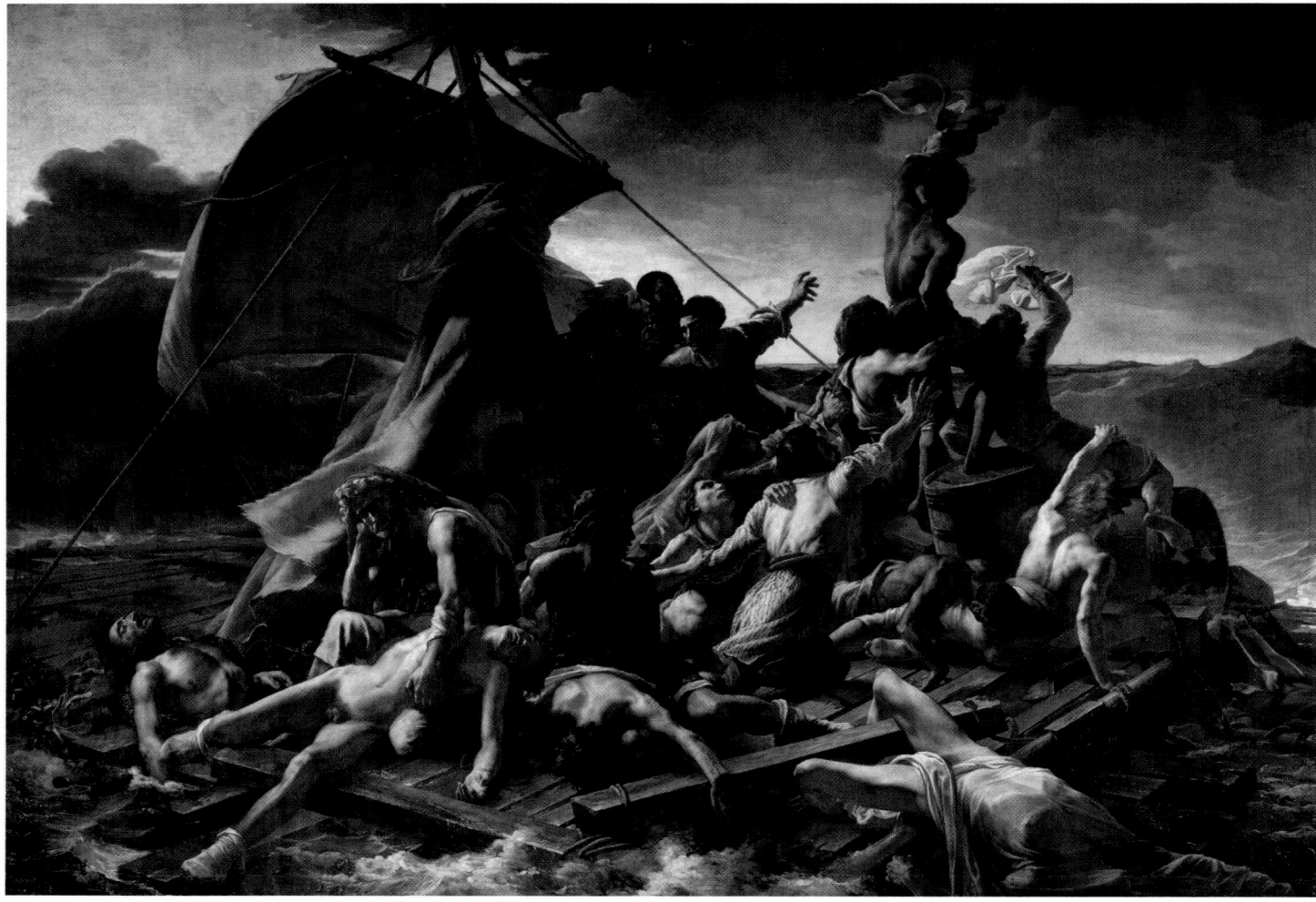

24.17 Théodore Géricault, *The Raft of the Medusa*. 1818–19. Oil on canvas, 16'1" × 23'6" (4.9 × 7.16 cm). Musée du Louvre, Paris

six lifeboats for government officials and officers, with the remaining 150 passengers being consigned to a makeshift raft that was set adrift by the crew at the mercy of the sea. When the passengers were finally rescued some two weeks later, only a handful were still alive. The callous captain was incompetent, an aristocrat who had been appointed for political reasons by the government of Louis XVIII. The headline-making event was condemned in the press as a reflection of the corruption of Louis's administration.

Géricault decided to paint the moment when the survivors first sighted a ship, not the more politically charged moment when the captain set the raft adrift. The painting is thus about the harrowing mental and physical experience of survival rather than an accusation of injustice. Géricault seems to have latched onto his subject after revisiting Gros's *Napoleon in the Pesthouse*, for the foreground is littered with Michelangelesque nudes. From the bodies of the dead and dying in the foreground, the composition recedes in a dramatic Baroque diagonal (see fig. 20.1), climaxing in the group supporting the frantically waving black man. As our eye follows this line of writhing, twisting bodies, we move from death to hope. But this is not a painting that is at root about hope, for there are no heroes, no exemplary moral fortitude.

Rather the theme is the human species against nature, and Géricault's goal was to make a viewer feel the trials and tribulations of the castaways. The academic, Classically proportioned monumental figures are a catalogue of human misery, reflecting the death, cannibalism, fighting, insanity, sickness, exhaustion, hunger, and thirst that tormented the victims. The stark realism, obtained in part through tighter brushwork, heightens our visceral connection to the dramatically lit event; we too are on the crude raft, pitched about on the high seas, and aimlessly buffeted by the wind.

Géricault would never exhibit again in a Salon and within six years would be dead at the age of 32. His later work, unlike *The Raft*, was not monumental; nor does it show off the artist's ability to draw and incorporate Classical models into an otherwise Baroque composition with a Romantic mood. Rather, it was largely painterly, a commitment reinforced by a trip to London in 1820 where he saw the work of Constable and Turner. His technique is apparent in a remarkable series of ten portraits of insane men and women made during the winter of 1822–23, his last active months. Only five exist today, and they belonged to a physician named Georget, who specialized in psychiatry, leading scholars to think he may have commissioned the paintings for documentary purposes. Géricault's contemporaries, following Caspar Lavater's theories (see page 803), believed there was a correlation between mental health and physiognomy, and that mental illness could be diagnosed by reading facial features. Having no need of money, Géricault obviously undertook the work for personal interest, and in addition to this series also painted guillotined heads and hospital inmates. The series allowed him to explore the mind and human suffering, as seen in *Portrait of an Insane Man (Man Suffering from Delusions of Military Rank)* (fig. **24.18**). Using energetic brushwork that seems virtually to signify mental energy, he exposes the psychotic derangement plaguing his subject, including nervousness, fear, and a sternness that implies a delusion of importance. The presentation is sympathetic, reflecting the period's recognition of mental illness as a disease, but it does not undermine the powerful mood of alienation and irrationality that consumes the sitter. In contrast to the goddesslike perfection and poise of Ingres's *Portrait of Madame Inès Moitessier*, Géricault's insane man is an emblem of imperfection, embodying a range of human psychoses and foibles—a reflection of the Romantic interest in the psychological and physical suffering of the socially marginalized.

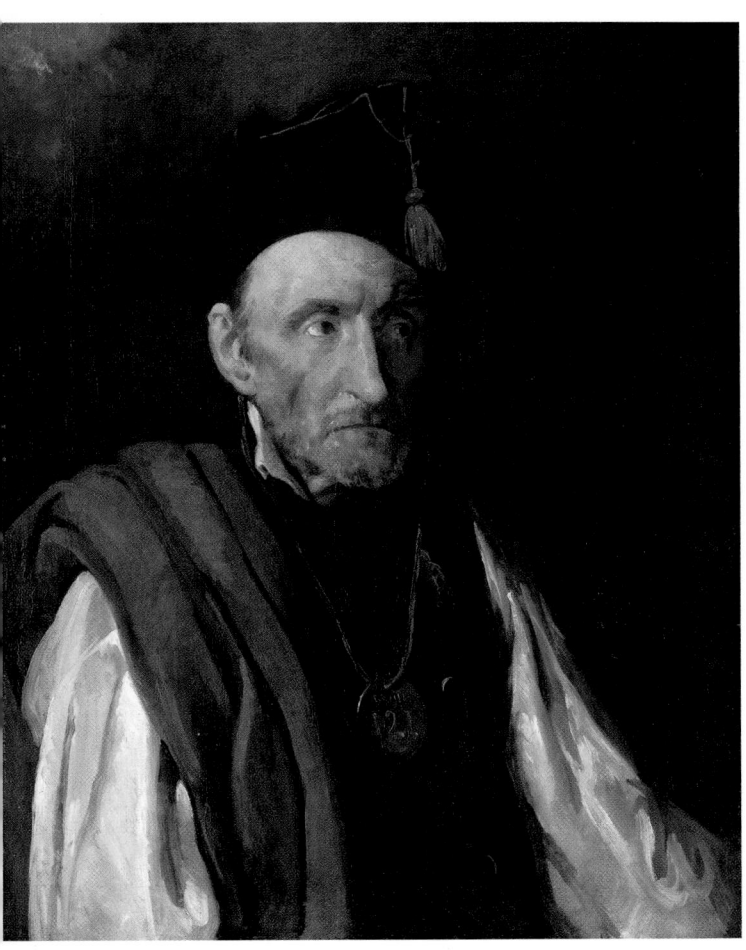

24.18 Théodore Géricault. *Portrait of an Insane Man (Man Suffering from Delusions of Military Rank)*. 1822–23. Oil on canvas, 32½ × 26" (81 × 65 cm). Collection Oskar Reinhart "Am Römerholz," Winterthur, Switzerland. Inv. no. 1924.7

EUGÈNE DELACROIX In 1822, Eugène Delacroix (1798–1863) emerged as the standard-bearer of painterly Romanticism, the position Géricault so dearly coveted. Delacroix was seven years younger than Géricault and came from a similar background—Parisian and wealthy. Like Géricault, he was essentially independent and self-taught, studying the great masterpieces at the Louvre, especially Rubens, Titian, and Veronese. His greatest excitement came when visiting the studios of Gros and Géricault. He befriended the latter in 1818 and posed for one of the figures in *The Raft of the Medusa*. His submission to the Salon of 1824, *Scenes from the Massacre at Chios* (fig. **24.19**), presents a compendium of misery and suffering in the foreground and was obviously inspired by the groupings of the dead and dying in Gros's *Pesthouse at Jaffa* and Gericault's *The Raft of the Medusa*. The picture was inspired by the Greek war of independence. In 1820, the Greeks revolted against the ruling Ottoman Empire, and the following year the Turks raided the Greek island of Chios, destroying villages and either massacring or enslaving virtually the entire population of 20,000. Delacroix's painting was based upon this event and was in part made to show support for Greek independence as well as to express the Romantic passion for democracy and individual freedom.

In the middle- and background, Delacroix presents burning and slaying transpiring in a blur of smoke and confusion, while in the foreground, he presents a group of Greeks rounded up for execution or enslavement, a scene that is, by contrast, remarkably devoid of violence. Resignation, desperation at the impending loss of loved ones, and hopelessness reign, this pessimism being symbolized by the foreboding silhouette of the armed Ottoman guard. Delacroix reinforces the turmoil of the brutality in the background by the twisting and turning of the foreground figures and their undulating contours as well as by the chaotic piling up of bodies. The intense colors of the painting have darkened considerably over time, especially the blues and reds, which originally created an optical snap that was reinforced by the bravura of the brushwork and sharp value contrasts. Clearly, Rubens is behind these qualities as well as the two asymmetrical compositional pyramids organizing the foreground group and the diagonal recession into deep space. (Delacroix, however, subverts the traditional device of putting a hero at the apex of the pyramids by instead placing villains, the Turkish guards, there.) Delacroix was also influenced by the color and brushwork of Constable, who had three landscapes, including *The Haywain* (see fig. 24.5), in the same Salon. Upon seeing these, Delacroix repainted the sky at the last minute, giving it a brilliant luminosity, and he worked vivid colors into the garments.

This "terrifying hymn in honor of doom and irremediable suffering," as the poet and critic Charles Baudelaire (1821–1867) described the painting, established Delacroix as the great Romantic painter. It was the first time the term "Romantic" had been applied to a visual artist, making him the artistic equivalent of composer Hector Berlioz (1803–1869) and writer Victor Hugo (1802–1885). And certainly Delacroix shared their Romantic spirit. (See *Primary Source*, page 845.) The year 1824 was therefore

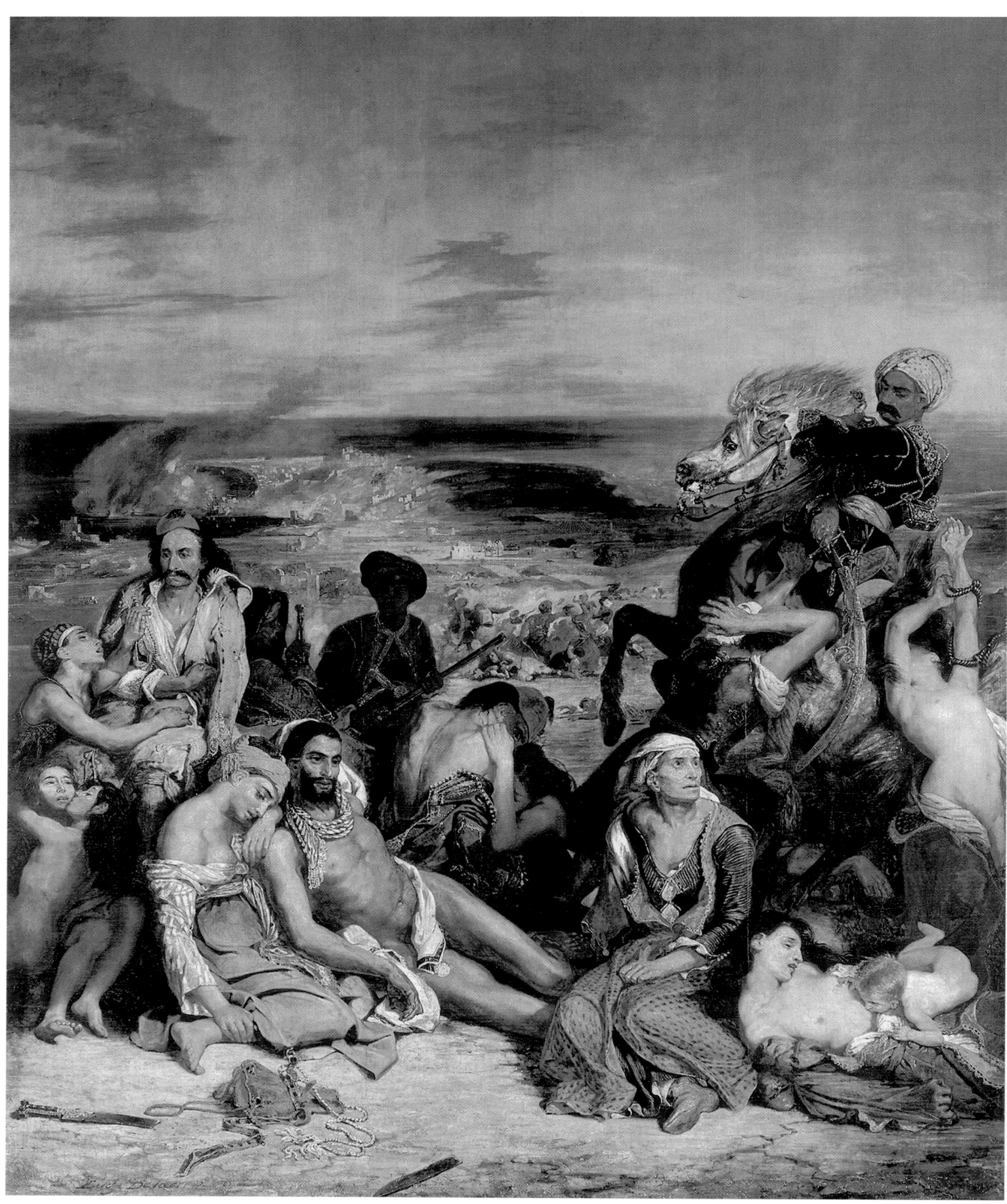

24.19   Eugène Delacroix, *Scenes from the Massacre at Chios*. 1824. Oil on canvas, 13'8" × 11'7" (4.17 × 3.54 m). Musée du Louvre, Paris

Eugène Delacroix (1798–1863)

From His *Journal*

Delacroix began his Journal in 1822 and maintained it irregularly until his death in 1863. He wrote it, he said, "for myself alone" in the hope that it would "do me a lot of good." This excerpt is from an entry for May 14, 1824.

What torments my soul is its loneliness. The more it expands among friends and the daily habits or pleasure, the more, it seems to me, it flees me and retires into its fortress. The poet who lives in solitude, but who produces much, is the one who enjoys those treasures we bear in our bosom, but which forsake us when we give ourselves to others. When one yields completely to one's soul, it opens itself completely. …

Novelty is in the mind that creates, and not in nature, the thing painted.

Source: *Journals of Eugène Delacroix*, tr. Walter Pach (New York: Crown Publishers, 1948)

---

a critical one. It was the year Géricault died, Constable was introduced in Paris, and Ingres returned from Italy, unaware that he would be anointed the guardian of the Classical tradition.

In 1825, Delacroix went to England, like Géricault before him, reinforcing his appreciation of British landscape and literature, especially the plays of Shakespeare, the poetry of Lord Byron (1788–1824), and the novels of Walter Scott (1771–1832).

Delacroix would turn to their imagery, and to that of Dante and Goethe, to fire his imagination and cultivate his moods. One product of his reading was the 1827 painting *Death of Sardanapalus* (fig. **24.20**), based on Byron's 1821 unrhymed poem *Sardanapalus*. Sardanapalus, the last Assyrian king, was overthrown by rebels because of his licentiousness and apathy. Too lethargic either to fight or to flee, he committed suicide.

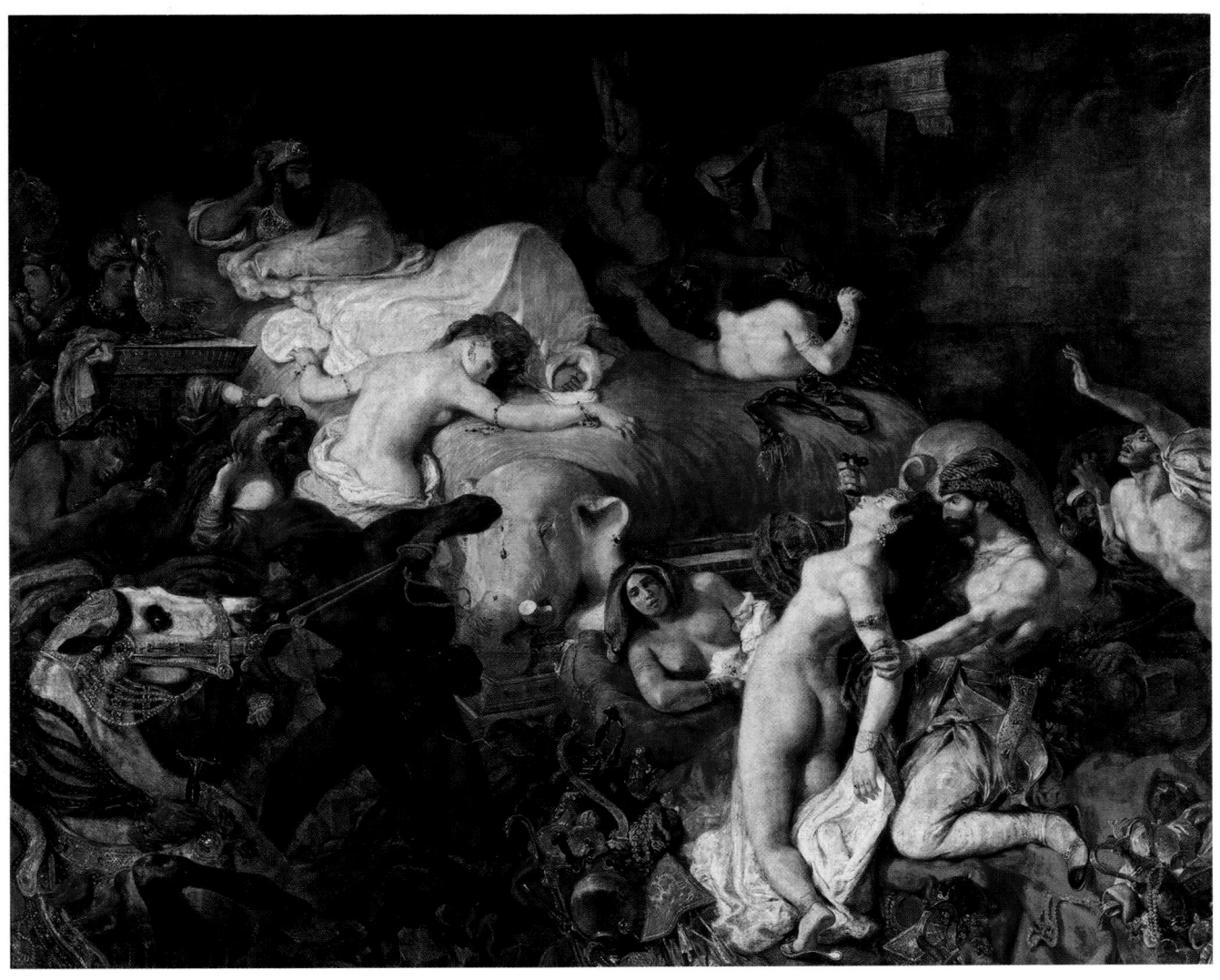

24.20   Eugène Delacroix, *Death of Sardanapalus*. 1827. Oil on canvas, 12'1½" × 16'2⅞" (3.69 × 4.94 m). Musée du Louvre, Paris

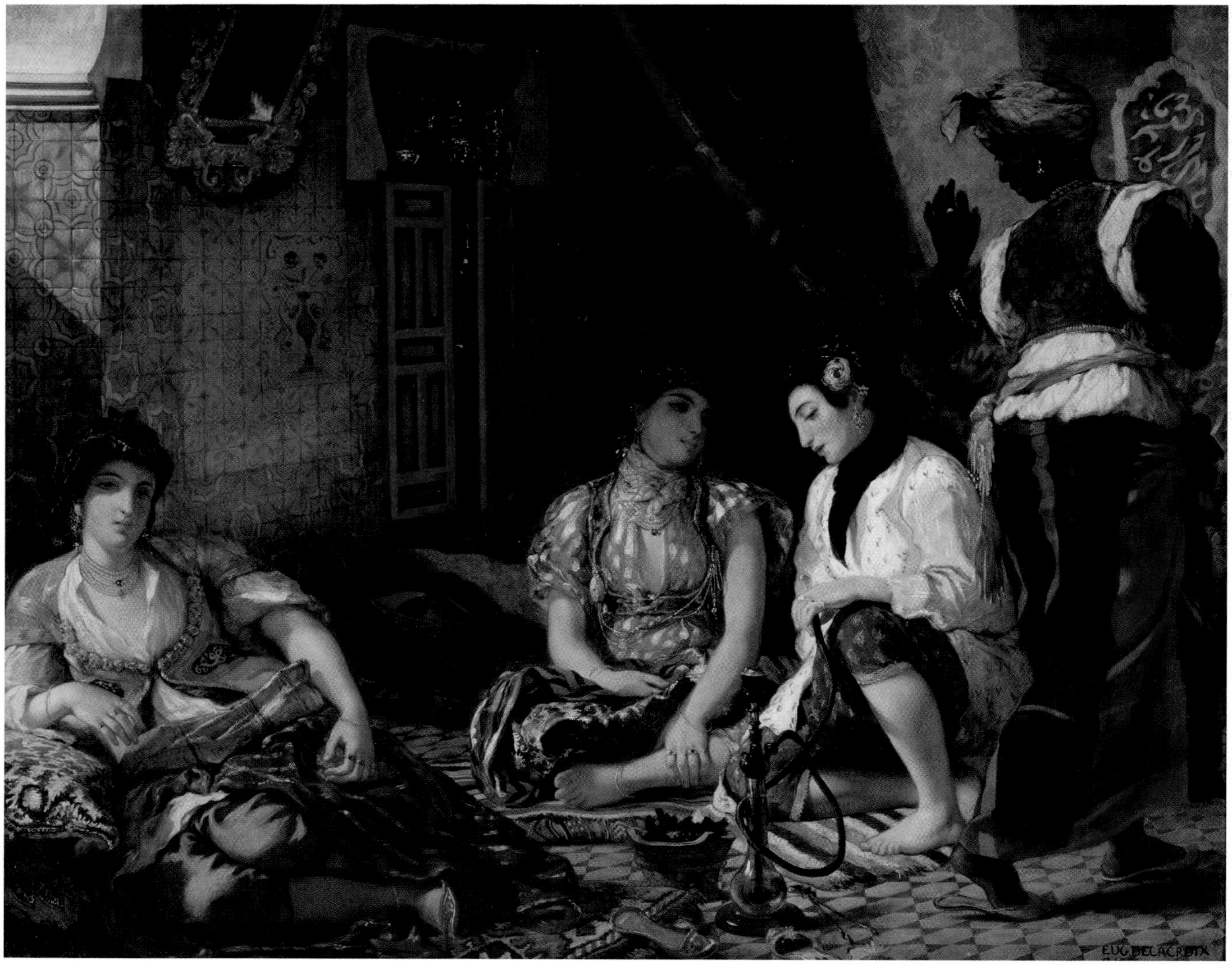

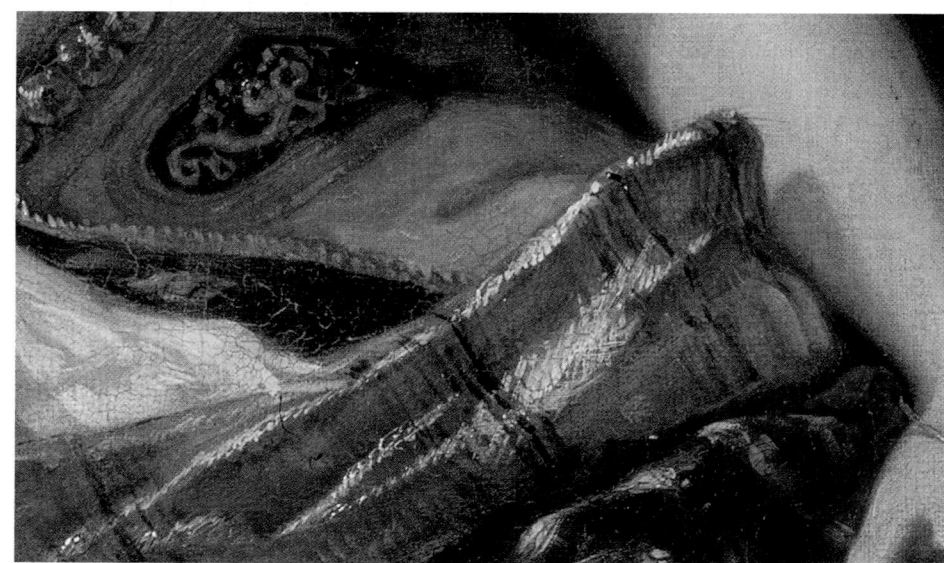

24.21 Eugène Delacroix,
Women of Algiers. 1834. Oil on canvas,
5'10⅞" × 7'6⅛" (180 × 229 cm).
Musée du Louvre, Paris

24.22 Eugène Delacroix. Detail of
Women of Algiers. 1834

Immersing himself in the king's mind as developed by Byron, Delacroix invented the scene of his death: He commands his eunuchs to bring to his bed, which is on a pyre, all of his prized possessions, including wives, pages, horse, and dog. The

Rubenesque traits we identified in the foreground of *Massacre at Chios* are intensified in this claustrophobic, chaotic composition. The only unifying element is the red bed, the perspective of which is so skewed it acts as a funnel, channeling all of the writhing energy and jumble of precious and exotic opulence to the anchor of the composition, the inert, indifferent king. He is the epitome of *ennui* and impotence. As in *Massacre at Chios*, Delacroix ignores Classical space and volume, allowing undulating contours, riotous color, and compositional pandemonium to project simultaneously the disparate moods of destruction, fear, violence, power, despair, sensuality, and indifference. With this enormous canvas of wanton annihilation, Delacroix offended just about everybody at the Salon of 1827, for in it there was nothing left of David's Classical formula, and there was no redeeming moral, just fascinating horror.

Delacroix's style underwent a change in the 1830s after a trip to North Africa; his palette became brighter and his paint handling looser. In 1832–33, Delacroix was asked to visually document the duc de Mornay's diplomatic mission to Morocco, and he excitedly made hundreds of watercolors that provided him with wondrous Oriental themes for the rest of his life. In Morocco, Delacroix entered a world of exotic architecture, clothing, and landscape, of intense light, and of unimaginably bright colors in fabrics, tiles, and interior design that displayed a *horror vacui* rivaling his own. That his palette became more colorful can be seen in *Women of Algiers* (fig. **24.21**), painted in Paris in 1834 from studies. To enter the secluded world of a harem, Delacroix had to obtain special permission, and the mood of the painting captures the sultry, cloistered feeling of this sensual den. We can almost smell the aroma of incense, the fragrance of flowers, and the smoke from the hookah. Delacroix's hues are as sensual as his subject. Color is dappled, and contours are often not continuous or drawn but just materialize through the buildup of adjacent marks (fig. **24.22**). A sea of paint and color covering the entire surface dissolves Neoclassical planarity and space. This technique began to free paint from what it was supposed to represent and established a platform for a new artistic style just over the horizon, Impressionism.

Romantic Landscape Painting

David's Neoclassicism was so dominant it even cast its shadow over French landscape painting in the opening decades of the nineteenth century, which was planar and stylized, largely modeled on Poussin and Claude Lorrain. The exhibition of Constable's landscapes at the pivotal Salon of 1824 opened up new possibilities in the genre, and a younger generation impressed by the Englishman's powerful naturalism and Romantic moods made it the foundation of their work. By the following decades, they had established landscape as a viable genre in France, one that could rival history painting in popularity and paved the way for the rise of Impressionism in the 1860s.

JEAN-BAPTISTE-CAMILLE COROT The first major nineteenth-century French landscape painter was Jean-Baptiste-Camille Corot (1796–1875), who was already committed to a vision of landscape that had Romanticism's fidelity to nature when Constable's *Haywain* was exhibited at the Salon of 1824. Uninfluenced by Constable, Corot's landscapes had Classical underpinnings. In 1822, he studied with a Parisian Classical landscape painter, Victor Bertin, who taught him the rudiments of drawing and, more important, emphasized making small **plein-air** ("open-air") studies called **pochades**, rapidly executed color studies in oil. In the studio, Bertin developed his sketches into large, formulaic Salon-oriented canvases. Corot rarely did, at least not initially; his small plein-air sketches often remained the final products until many years later, although he did not exhibit them either. When he later enlarged his pochades, he generally retained their accurate depictions of the land, refusing to idealize his scenes.

In 1825, Corot went to Italy and produced his first major body of work, about 150 small paintings, most of famous sites. *View of Rome* (fig. **24.23**), an oil on paper, is typical. Made on the spot in an hour or so, it is a literal, objective presentation of "the

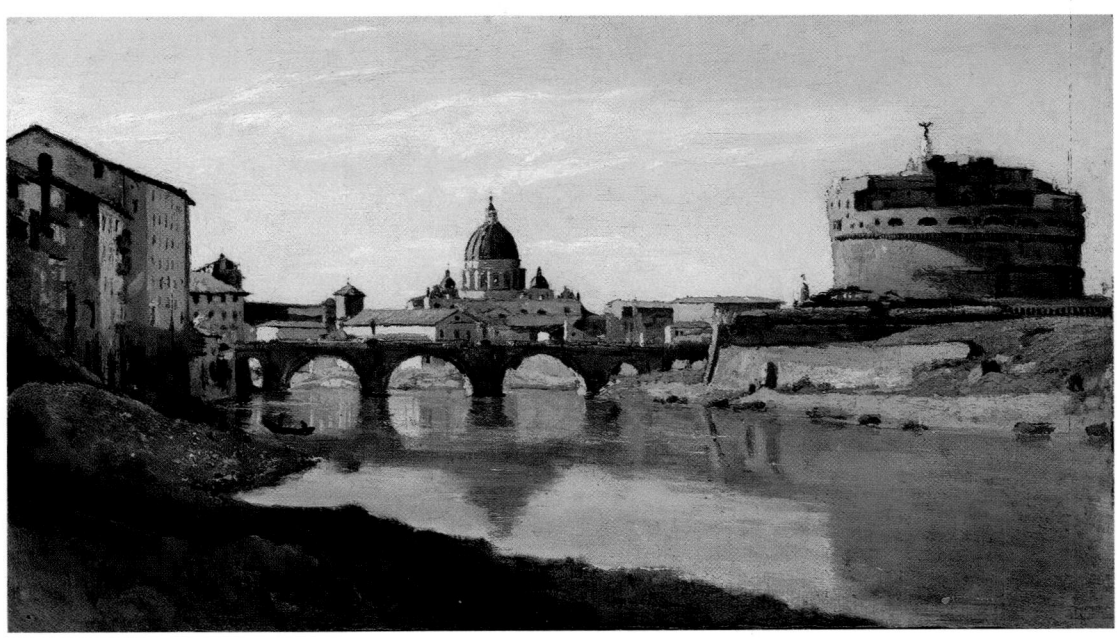

24.23 Jean-Baptiste-Camille Corot, *View of Rome: The Bridge and Castel Sant'Angelo with the Cupola of St. Peter's.* 1826–27. Oil on paper mounted on canvas, 10½ × 17" (26.7 × 43.2 cm). Fine Arts Museum of San Francisco. Museum Purchase, Archer M. Huntington Fund. 1935.2

truth of the moment," as Constable would say. We are convinced we are looking at the Castel Sant'Angelo and St. Peter's Basilica and real, not stylized clouds. We can feel the sun's intense heat bouncing off the stone and see the clear late-afternoon light crisply delineating the buildings and bridge. Without idealizing his landscape, Corot displays an instinct for Classical clarity and stability that recalls Poussin and Claude. Strong verticals and horizontals anchor his composition to its surface of creamy brushwork, and his buildings, no matter how loosely painted and insignificant, have a monumental presence. Nature inspired Corot to create little poems of beautifully harmonized tones and colors, generally browns and greens, and a seamless integration of painterly brushwork and Classical grid.

After a second trip to Italy in 1834, Corot made a concerted effort to attract attention at the Salons and added to his output large historical landscapes, such as *Hagar in the Wilderness*, which gained him occasional sales and some interest. But it was not until

the late 1840s, when he developed his third category of picture, the lyrical landscape, that he became popular, financially successful, and famous. Corot was no longer inspired directly by nature, but by his memories of landscape and the Romantic moods it provoked, as in his *Souvenir de Mortefontaine (Oise)* (fig. **24.24**), painted in 1864. We sense that Corot's vision has been filtered through the haze of memory. The canvas is covered with thin, almost transparent brushstrokes, layered one over another, making everything somewhat indistinct, as if gently floating. A magical light pervades the scene, shimmering off the water, flickering through the trees, and prancing dotlike along the ground. Everything is light, ethereal, and insubstantial, like the reflections of the trees in the water, which seem to levitate. Corot gives us very little to look at in this idyllic scene, simply a rural woman who appears to be removing leaves from a tree while accompanying children pick flowers. Instead we look at the artist's beautiful tonal palette that gracefully shifts from brown, to green, to gray,

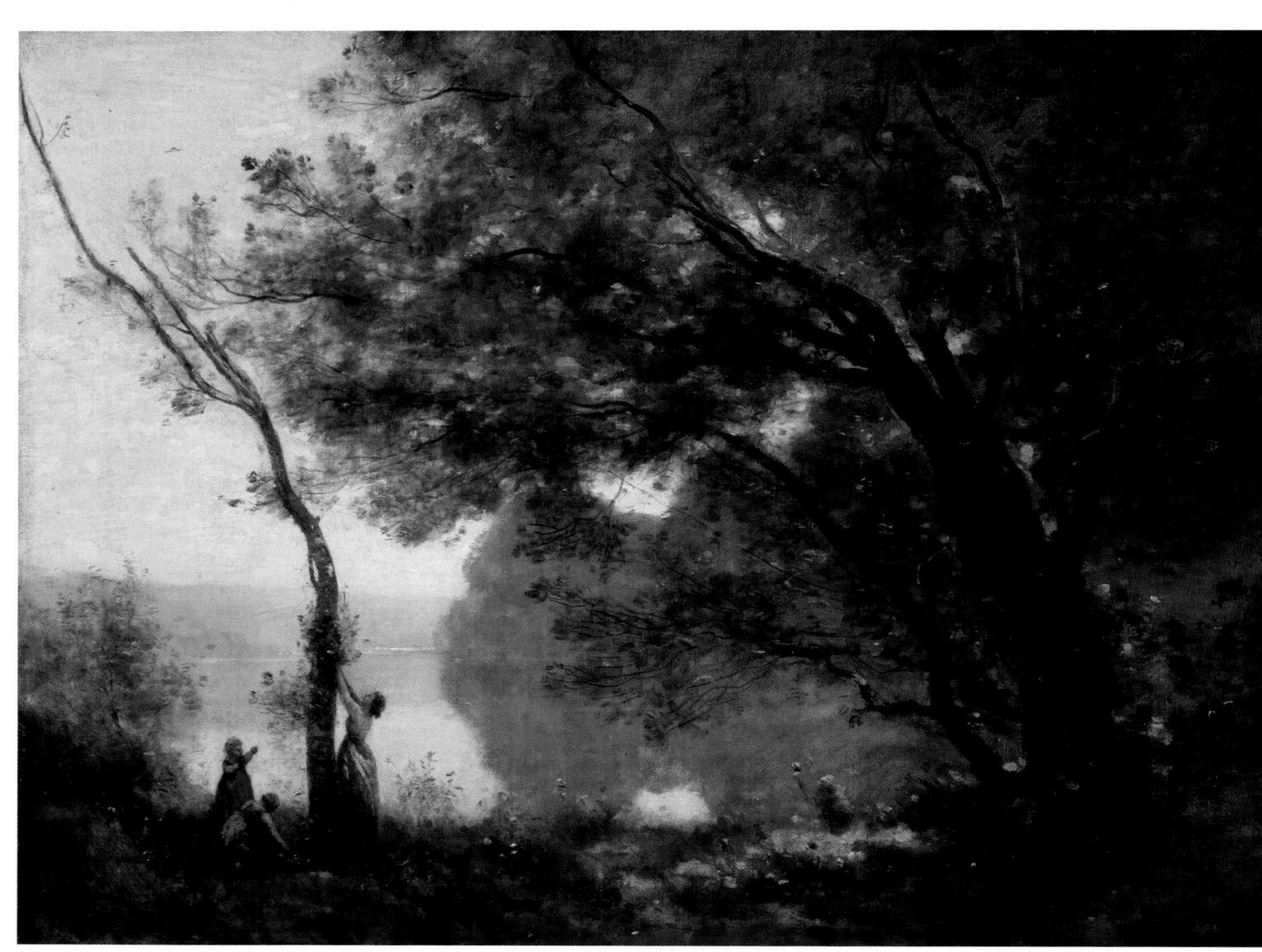

24.24   Jean-Baptiste-Camille Corot, *Souvenir de Mortefontaine (Oise)*. 1864. Oil on canvas, 25½ × 35" (65 × 89 cm). Musée du Louvre, Paris

to silver. We look at the powerful patterning of the trunks and branches of the foreground trees, and we delight in the magic of his gossamer brushwork. The picture is about creating a poetic mood, using abstract means to reinforce an idyllic vision that, while reminiscent of Claude Lorrain, reflects the Romantic yearnings of its author.

THÉODORE ROUSSEAU AND THE BARBIZON SCHOOL

Unlike Corot, a group of academically trained painters called the Barbizon School took their aesthetic lead directly from Constable, augmenting his direct impressions of nature with a study of the great seventeenth-century Dutch landscapists, such as Ruisdael (see fig. 20.28), who were exhibited in the Louvre. The group emerged in the 1830s and got its name from the village of Barbizon, which bordered the forest of Fontainebleau, where the artists painted and many settled. (Corot, who had a house in nearby Ville d'Avray, also often painted there.) The forest had been a royal hunting preserve, and as a result it offered nature in a relatively unspoiled state, undisturbed by the Industrial Revolution smoldering just 40 miles (64 km) away in Paris. The best-known Barbizon painter is Théodore Rousseau (1812–1867). He learned the rudiments of painting from two academically trained artists and by copying landscapes in the Louvre.

In the early to mid-1830s, his work was occasionally accepted at the Salons, from which he was then banished from 1837 to 1848, his view of nature being deemed too unseemly. He led a rather bohemian existence and permanently settled in Barbizon in 1848.

Under the Birches, Evening (fig. **24.25**) of 1842–43 is a fine example of Rousseau's work, which is perhaps the most diverse of all of the Barbizon painters. Produced in the studio from studies made on a seven-month trip to the Berry region in central France, the painting, like those of Constable and Corot, avoids artificial compositional and stylized motifs and instead captures the essence of nature. We readily sense this is a specific site; each tree seems individualized, for example, and each wisp of cloud unique. We can feel the onset of twilight and the cool damp atmosphere of autumn. While the blue-green sky and brownish-orange foliage offer a touch of color, Rousseau's palette is somber and earthy, evoking soil, decaying plant and animal matter, and the interior gloom of a thicket. Like Constable's, Rousseau's brushwork is stippled, applied in small flecks that make the landscape pulse with energy, reinforced by the nervous outline of trees and bushes. We sense growth and the constant movement of nature. It is little wonder Rousseau was rejected at the Salons. His dark, honest pictures with their turgid brushwork must have been considered ugly and depressing by conservative taste.

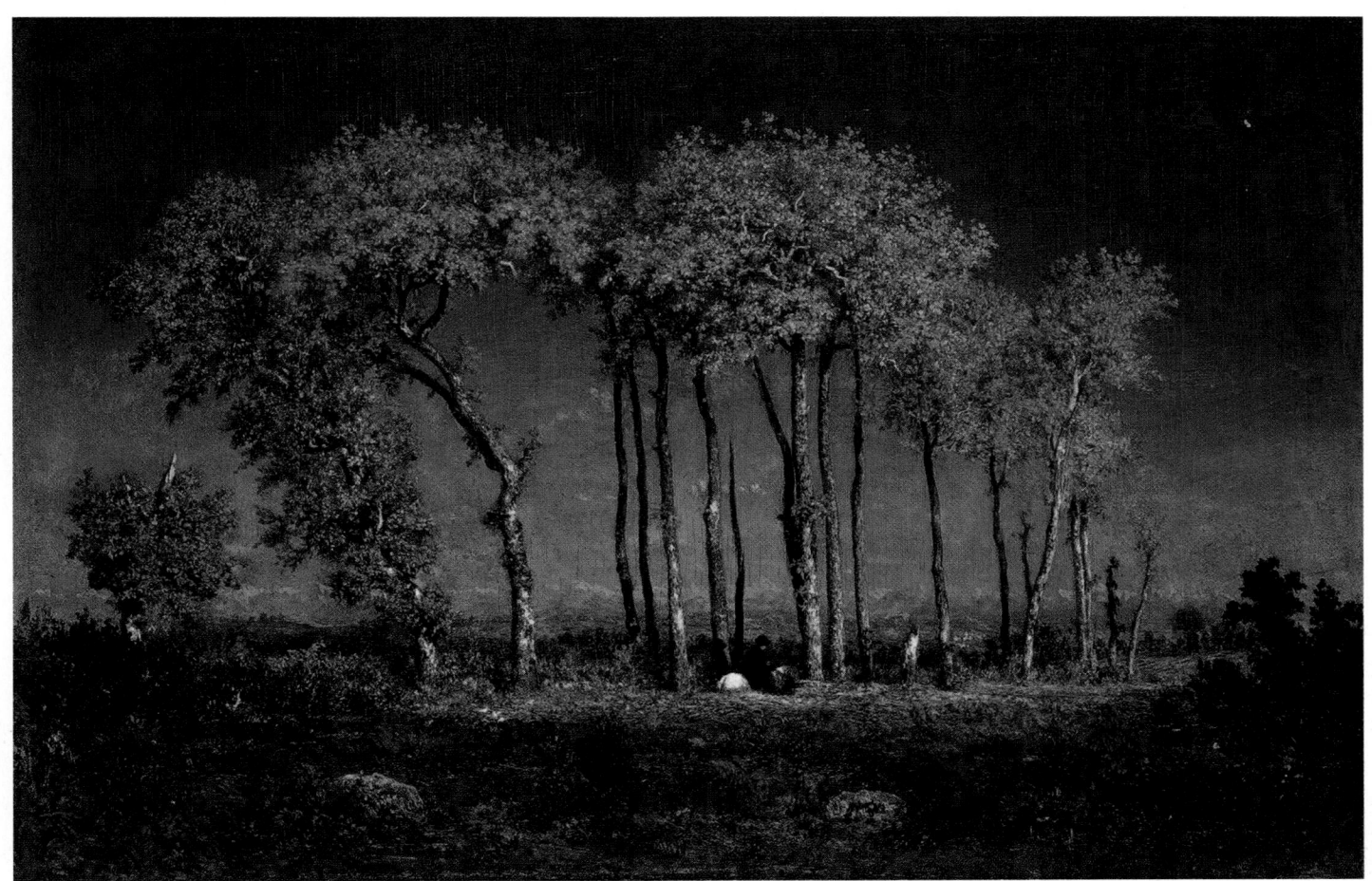

24.25   Pierre-Étienne-Théodore Rousseau, *Under the Birches, Evening*. 1842–43. Oil on wood panel, 16⅝ × 25⅜" (42.2 × 64.4 cm). Toledo Museum of Art, Ohio. Gift of Arthur J. Secor. 1933.37

ROMANTIC SCULPTURE

Compared with painting, sculpture was a severely limiting medium for an artist at the opening of the nineteenth century. In its most monumental form, free-standing historical sculpture, it was mostly restricted to the human figure, and since the Renaissance the sculpted figure had been largely based on antique models. Nineteenth-century sculptors throughout Europe would overwhelmingly follow the Classical paradigm of one or two figures based on Greek and Roman prototypes and embodying some notion of virtue or beauty. In France, however, a dramatic change in the artistic climate toward 1830 allowed a small gap for experimentation. The rise of Delacroix and Romantic painting in the 1820s was followed by the new, more liberal constitutional monarchy of Louis-Philippe (the July Monarchy) that emerged after the 1830 revolution, which resulted from Charles X censoring newspapers and Parisians rising up en masse, forcing the king to abdicate. The bourgeoisie had more of a presence in the new government and in society in general, ushering in an era of middle-class taste. These two forces gave a handful of artists the courage to create Romantic sculpture, which rejected the Classical model of beauty, morality, and perfection, and instead explored new subjects, emotions, and compositions.

ANTOINE-LOUIS BARYE Antoine-Louis Barye (1796–1875) surprised his colleagues when he submitted a painted plaster of a tiger devouring a gavial (a species of crocodile) to the Salon of 1831 (fig. **24.26**), winning a gold medal. There was no tradition of animal sculpture at the Salons, and previously, in 1828, Barye had shown portrait busts. Barye, however, loved animals, and drew them at the zoo. He was also a friend of Delacroix, whose Romantic themes included animal hunts and fights, thus providing Barye with a thematic vehicle for his interest in animal anatomy. Like Stubbs's *Lion Attacking a Horse* (see fig. 23.14), *Tiger Devouring a Gavial of the Ganges* is filled with Romantic terror, brute strength, and raw instinct unleashed without regard to morality, law, or decorum. It is a fierce fight to the death in the wilds of nature. Appealing to the Romantic imagination, Barye selected exotic animals, and often animals that traditionally do not prey on one another (tigers do not eat crocodiles). He also set his struggles in exotic locales, such as on the banks of the Ganges in India. His composition is filled with movement and a variety of shapes and textures, reinforcing the chaotic struggle and animal energy. In the 1840s, Barye began mass-producing his animals in bronze in a variety of sizes, successfully marketing them to a worldwide middle-class audience, including in America, and becoming quite famous.

FRANÇOIS RUDE Fame eluded François Rude (1784–1855), a sculptor who brought nationalistic fervor to his figurative work and is best remembered for the bas-relief often known as *La Marseillaise* (fig. **24.27**) on the Arc de Triomphe in Paris. Rude enrolled in the École des Beaux-Arts in 1809, studying sculpture; as a Napoleon sympathizer, he fled to Brussels when Bonaparte was defeated in 1815. He returned to Paris in 1827, and with a nationalistic zeal we associate with the Romantic era, he began studying French sculptural history—first the French Renaissance tradition of the School of Fontainebleau and Giovanni Bologna (see pages 601–03), and then delving deeper into the past to Claus Sluter (see pages 471–72).

It was a perfect match, then, when in 1833 Rude received one of the four sculptural commissions for the Arc de Triomphe, since the works were about patriotic fervor. The arch had been left unfinished when Napoleon was exiled in 1815, and Louis-Philippe and his minister of the interior saw the monument's completion as an opportunity to demonstrate that the new government supported national reconciliation. Hence the sculptural program consisted of four works by different artists, each surrounding the arch opening and offering something to every segment of the French political spectrum. Rude received the assignment thanks to the success of a rather Neoclassical-looking sculpture of a nude Neapolitan fisherboy playing with a turtle

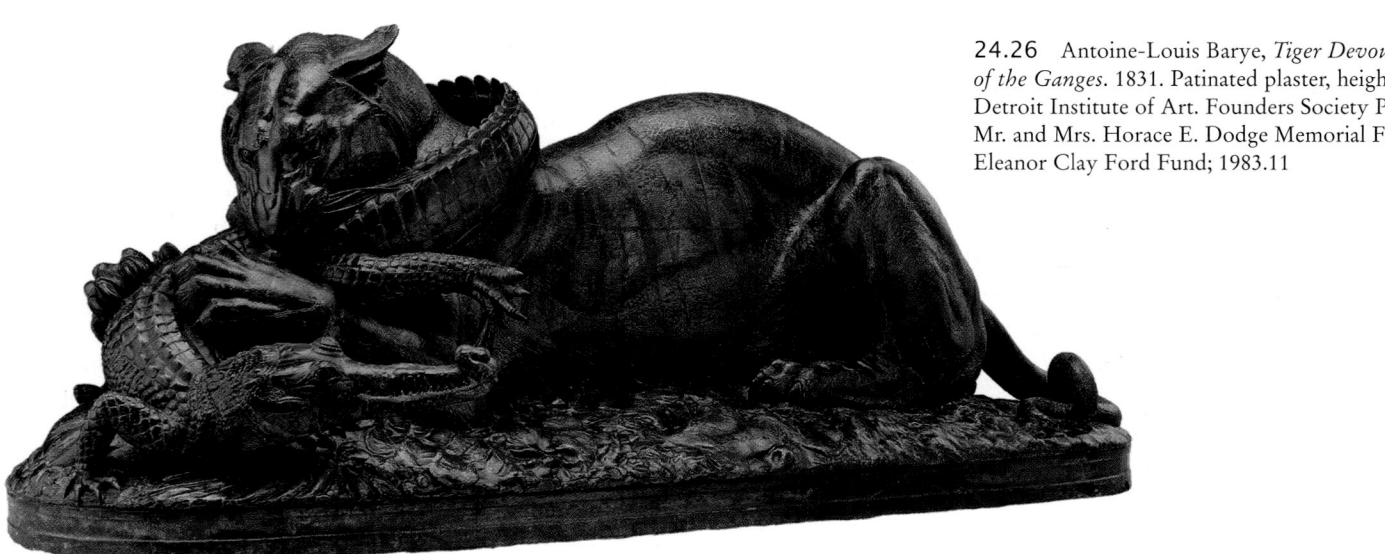

24.26 Antoine-Louis Barye, *Tiger Devouring a Gavial of the Ganges*. 1831. Patinated plaster, height 17" (43 cm). Detroit Institute of Art. Founders Society Purchase, Mr. and Mrs. Horace E. Dodge Memorial Fund, and Eleanor Clay Ford Fund; 1983.11

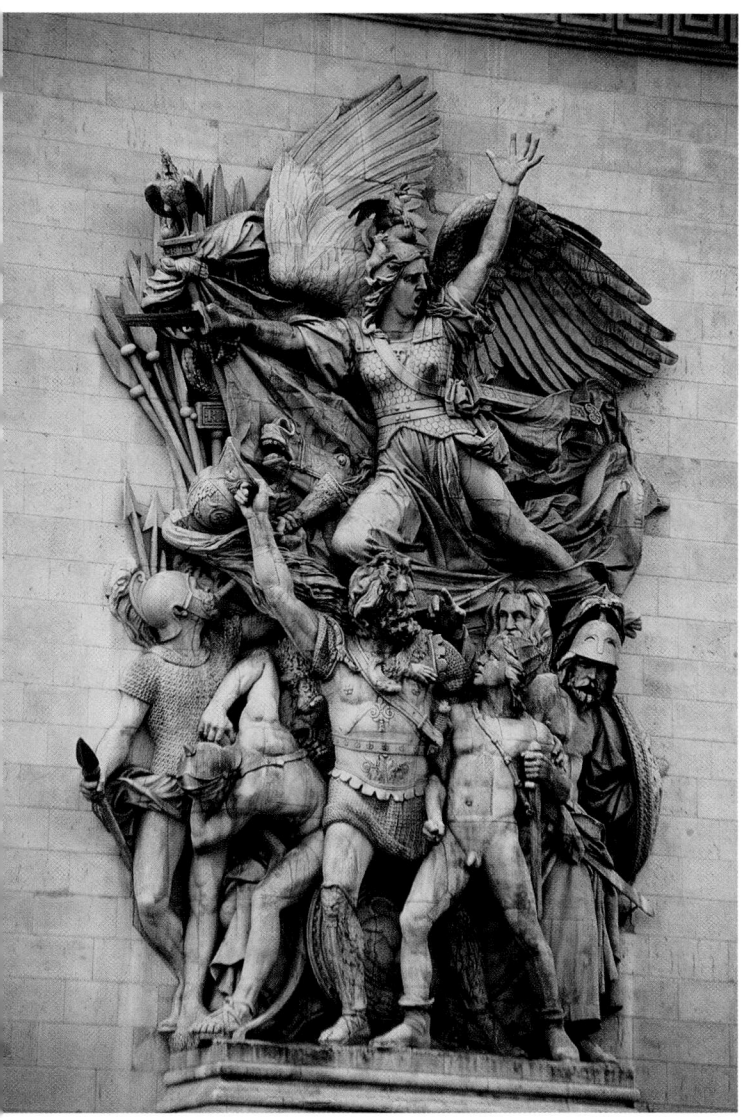

24.27 François Rude, *The Departure of the Volunteers of 1792* (*La Marseillaise*). 1833–36. Stone, approx. 42 × 26' (12.8 × 7.9 m). Arc de Triomphe, Paris

that he had submitted to the Salon of 1833. The Salon submission hardly anticipated the chaotic explosion we see in *The Departure of the Volunteers of 1792*, the formal title for *La Marseillaise*.

The scene honors the volunteers who rallied to defend the new French Republic from an Austro-Prussian threat in 1792. A winged allegorical figure representing both France and Liberty leads a collection of soldiers from different periods of the nation's past. Rather than a specific event, Rude evokes an eternal, all-powerful nationalistic spirit that emanates from the people and arises when called upon. While the figures have a Classical anatomy, strike Classical poses, and are aligned parallel to the wall in shallow relief, the composition is frenetic, a whirligig of arms, legs, and twisted bodies that energize the outpouring of patriotism that is swept along by Liberty above. This claustrophobic jumble of figures brings to mind Delacroix's turbulent pile of victims and objects in his *Death of Sardanapalus* (see fig. 24.20). When unveiled in 1836, *The Departure* was unanimously hailed

the best of the four works on the Arc de Triomphe and was nicknamed *La Marseillaise* after the French national anthem, because it so successfully embodied the national spirit. Rude himself attained no lasting fame from the project, and without commissions, which sculptors, unlike painters, rely on, he had no opportunity to develop further the innovative aesthetic implications of *The Departure*.

ROMANTIC REVIVALS IN ARCHITECTURE

The social and political turmoil that rocked Europe from 1789 to 1848 resulted in a search for stability and comfort, which in architecture came in the form of revival styles. Instead of developing new forms, architects resurrected the past, its familiarity providing solace and continuity in a world that otherwise seemed fractured, uncertain, and in constant flux. Intellectually justifying this appropriation of the past was the theory of evolution, developed by the German philosopher Georg Wilhelm Friedrich Hegel (1770–1831), who saw history, and thus reality, as a continuous, step-by-step unfolding of events reacting to one another in a dialectic. The present thus builds on the past, which it absorbs. Hegel's theory of evolution was the foundation for much nineteenth-century thinking and was the critical force behind Charles Darwin's theory of the evolution of the species (1859) and Karl Marx's dialectical materialism, which viewed history as a class struggle (1867). In architecture, Hegel's theory resulted in the appropriation of more or less every known architectural style, selected for their associations, picturesque qualities, or exoticism. Egyptian, Greek, Roman, Romanesque, Gothic, Renaissance, Baroque, Chinese, Turkish, Queen Anne, rustic thatched cottage—everything and anything could be found revived in nineteenth-century European architecture. It was not unusual for an architect to submit several proposals for a single project, each in a different style. Nor was it unusual to find several periods represented in a single building.

Britain: The Sublime and the Picturesque

Although British architects experimented with every conceivable revival style in the first half of the nineteenth century, Gothic and Classical were the clear favorites, Gothic-revival buildings probably only being outnumbered by Classical-revival ones. However, it is an overarching eclecticism that characterizes British architecture in the Romantic era.

GOTHIC REVIVAL In Britain, sublime architecture peaked in the 1790s. In terms of the Gothic revival, this can be seen in James Wyatt's (1746–1813) Fonthill Abbey (fig. **24.28**), in Fonthill Gifford, Wiltshire, whose owner, William Beckford, wanted to upstage the playfulness of Strawberry Hill (see fig. 23.12) and build a medieval home that embodied the awe and gloom of Gothic romance novels. Rising to a breathtaking 120 feet, it not

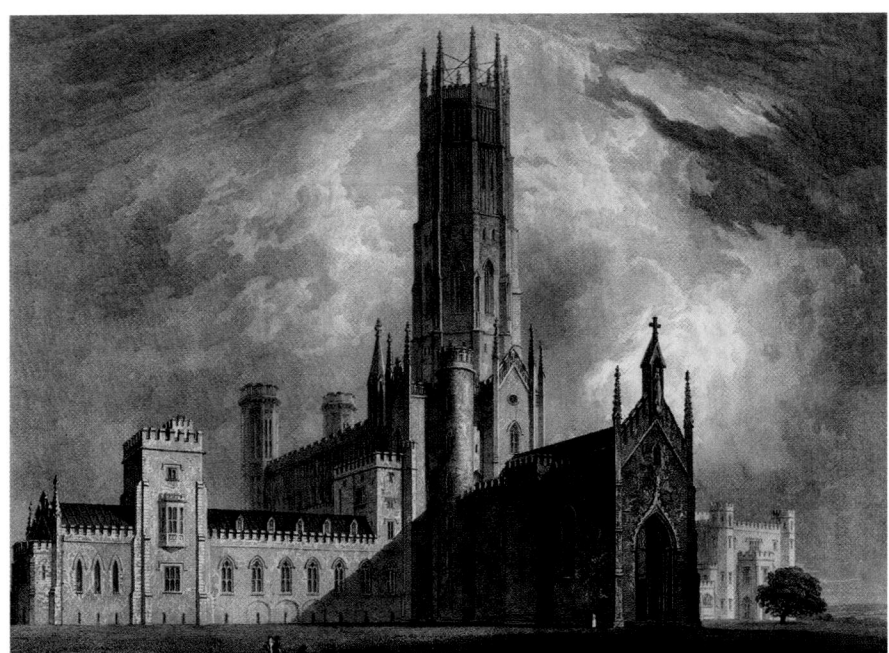

24.28 James Wyatt. Fonthill Abbey, Fonthill Gifford, Wiltshire, England. 1796–1813. (Engraving from John Rutter's *Delineations of Fonthill and its Abbey*)

only looked like a Gothic cathedral, it was scaled like one. (The tower was originally 300 feet high, but it collapsed twice.) The entrance door was 35 feet high. The interior was filled with endless dark, narrow corridors, which along with its immense soaring tower provided a sensation of Burke's "infinite sublime." The exterior was not only awesome in its bold massing, it was also picturesque in its syncopated accretion of parts. Beckford, at one time one of the richest men in the world, sold Fonthill Abbey in 1822. In 1825, the tower collapsed once again, and the building was essentially destroyed.

Most revival architects did not aspire to the sublime but satisfied their Romantic desires through historicism, exoticism, the picturesque, and associational qualities (see page 799). The most famous Gothic-revival building is the Houses of Parliament (fig. **24.29**) by Sir Charles Barry (1795–1860) and A. W. N. Pugin (1812–1852). It was commissioned in 1836 after the former building burned down, and the competition required the new Houses be designed in one of two "English" styles, Gothic or Elizabethan—91 of the 97 entries were Gothic. Barry, best known for his work in Classical- or Renaissance-revival styles, was the

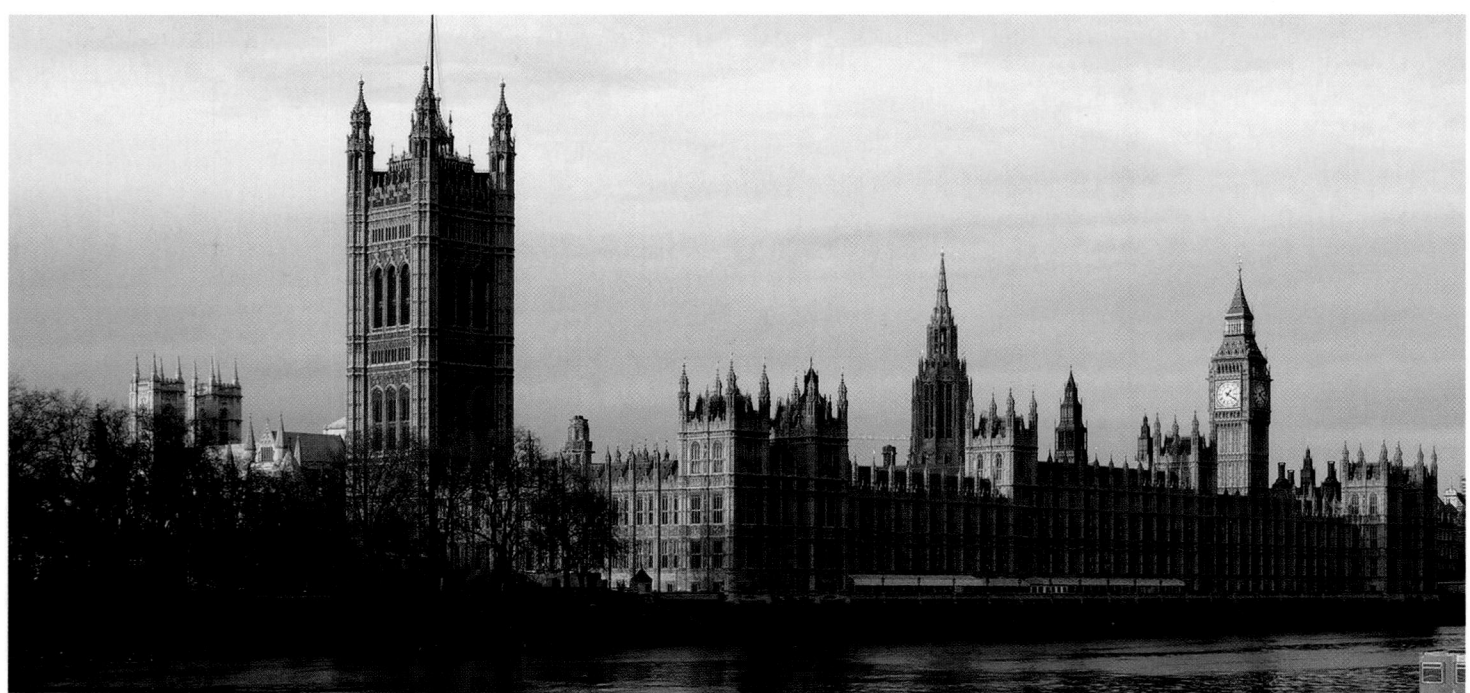

24.29 Sir Charles Barry and A. W. N. Welby Pugin. Houses of Parliament, London. Begun 1836

head architect. Predictably, he laid out the building in a symmetrical, orderly fashion. He wisely hired Pugin, Britain's leading expert on the Gothic, to design the Gothic details on both exterior and interior, which he did with meticulous historical accuracy in the florid Perpendicular style (see pages 428–29). The picturesque towers are believed to be Pugin's contribution as well. Instead of being sublime, Gothic revival now is largely picturesque and associational, the style having been specifically selected to conjure up a sense of national pride.

CLASSICAL REVIVAL The vast majority of nineteenth-century Classical-revival buildings are straightforward imitations of ancient sources. Virtually entire cities, like Glasgow and Edinburgh, were built in the Neoclassical style. In the Classical-revival style, the sublime is perhaps best represented by John Soane (1753–1837), especially in his Bank of England. In 1788, Soane was made the surveyor (chief architect) of the bank, a position he held almost until his death. During this time the bank expanded into a complex aggregate of dozens of enormous buildings, all of which Soane designed (most were destroyed in a fire in 1927). As seen in the Consols Office (fig. **24.30**), Soane's scale, inspired by Piranesi, was enormous, and his interior was austere, a reflection of the influence of Laugier (see page 806), whose treatises he owned in multiple copies. The interior of the Consols Office was meant to summon up the sublime grandeur of ancient Rome, for the enormous central space that expands into groin- and barrel-vaulted bays evokes the Baths of Diocletian, an association reinforced by the segmented bathhouse-type windows, which for the sake of austerity and emphasis on geometric shape were left unframed.

ECLECTICISM John Nash (1752–1835) is one of the most eclectic architects of this period and in a sense epitomizes it. A contemporary of Soane (who was also quite eclectic), he moved from one style

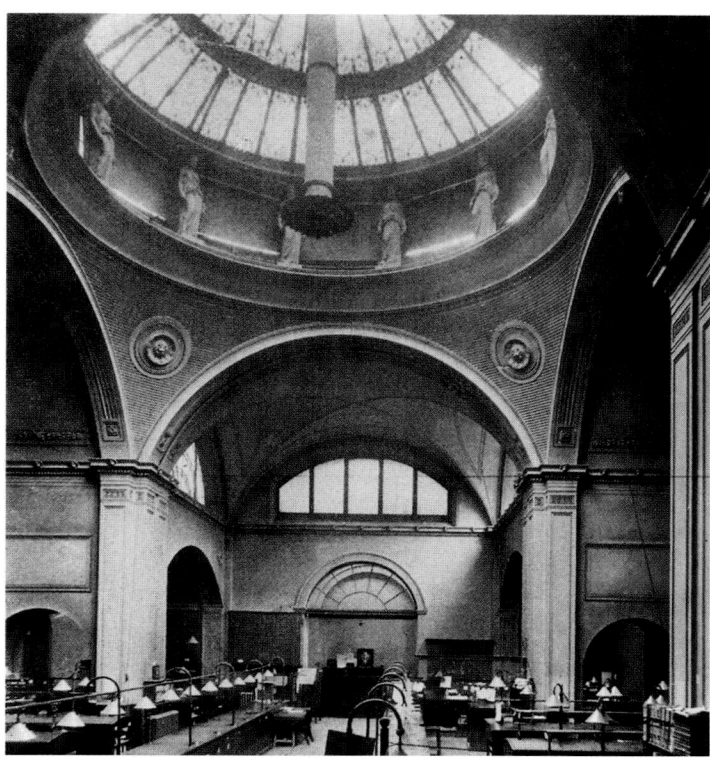

24.30 Sir John Soane. Consols Office, Bank of England, London. 1797–99. Destroyed in 1927

to the next with agility and lightning speed, often creating designs of extraordinary daring. Regardless of style, his hallmark was picturesque variety, with most of his buildings having an asymmetrical massing that made them look like a buildup of additions. One day he might design a hamlet with a thatched roof, the next an Italianate villa, followed by a mansion with medieval battlements.

In 1815, Nash turned to the fashionable "Oriental" mode for the prince regent's Royal Pavilion at Brighton (fig. **24.31**). The

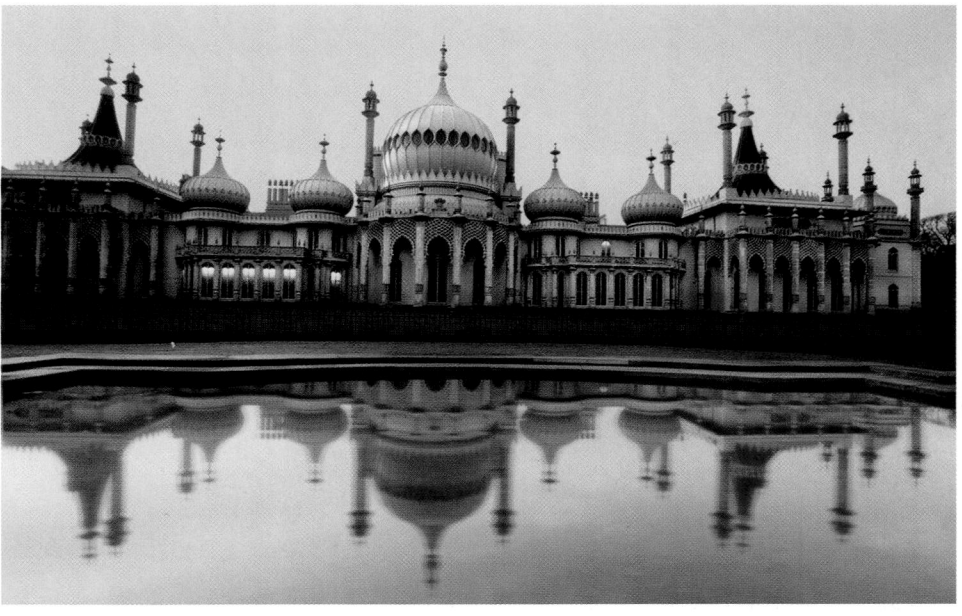

24.31 John Nash. Royal Pavilion, Brighton, England. 1815–23

building had already been partially erected in a Palladian style when he took over, so he was handicapped from the start. He quickly solved the problem, however, by throwing an iron armature over the Palladian façade to support cast-iron onion domes and minarets. Quoting Gothic, Chinese, Islamic, and Indian architecture, both inside and out, he created a rich fantasy world that played to the Romantic desire to be transported to exotic places and into the distant past.

Germany: Creating a New Athens

Although Prussian architects were as eclectic as their British counterparts, they designed some of the finest Classical-revival buildings. The most renowned architect is perhaps Karl Friedrich Schinkel, named state architect in 1815 by Friedrich Wilhelm III.

KARL FRIEDRICH SCHINKEL Like many architects of the day, Karl Friedrich Schinkel (1781–1841) worked in every imaginable revival style—Classical, Romanesque, Gothic, Renaissance, and *Rundbogen*, the German term for Italian vernacular construction. He began as a Neoclassicist, however, as can be seen in the Altes Museum in Berlin (fig. 24.32), his second major commission. Designed in 1824, it was modeled on a Greek temple, in part with the intention of endowing the building with the aura of being a temple of aesthetic treasures, a place where one came not to worship the gods but to contemplate art. The entrance is on what looks like the side of a temple (the real sides—their edges seen at either end of the colonnaded façade—are plain stone walls with rectangular windows), a brilliant device to suggest a temple without actually copying one and avoiding the use of the pedimented façade so common in the Classical revival. The museum is raised on a high podium and accessed by a centralized staircase, which along with the colossal Grecian order gives the building a serene monumentality and strong sense of axis. The width of the staircase is echoed above by a second-floor attic, which encases a

domed room for the display of sculpture. Schinkel is a master of perfect proportions and scale, and the symmetrical and logical interior echoes the exterior harmony.

Prussia emerged as a major political force at the Congress of Vienna, held after the fall of Napoleon in 1815, and the ambitious building program instituted by Friedrich Wilhelm III was designed to reinforce his imperial ambitions. Part of the idea behind the Altes Museum was to link Berlin with the glory and grandeur of ancient Athens.

America: An Ancient Style for a New Republic

The Classical-revival style was ubiquitous in America, since the new republic modeled itself on the democracies of ancient Greece and Rome. The White House and nation's Capitol are Neoclassical, and most churches, banks, and government buildings were designed with a Graeco-Roman temple façade, although the Gothic was also very popular for churches.

THOMAS JEFFERSON Thomas Jefferson, an amateur architect, designed his home Monticello (1770–1782) as a Palladian villa, like Burlington's Chiswick House (see fig. 23.8), and he based his Virginia State Capitol (1785) on the Maison Carrée in Nîmes (see fig. 7.44). His best-known project in the Romantic era is the University of Virginia campus in Charlottesville (fig. 24.33). Like Monticello and the Virginia State Capitol, the campus is based on antiquity in order to evoke the democratic heritage from Greece and Rome as well as the grandeur of these two great civilizations, which form the bedrock of Western art and culture. Designed from 1804 to 1817, the campus consists of two rows of five Palladian villas connected by a roofed colonnade, off which are rooms for students. Each of the ten villas, which housed the professors and classrooms, was different, conceptually symbolizing individualism and aesthetically introducing picturesque variety. Each has a different Classical association: One with a Doric

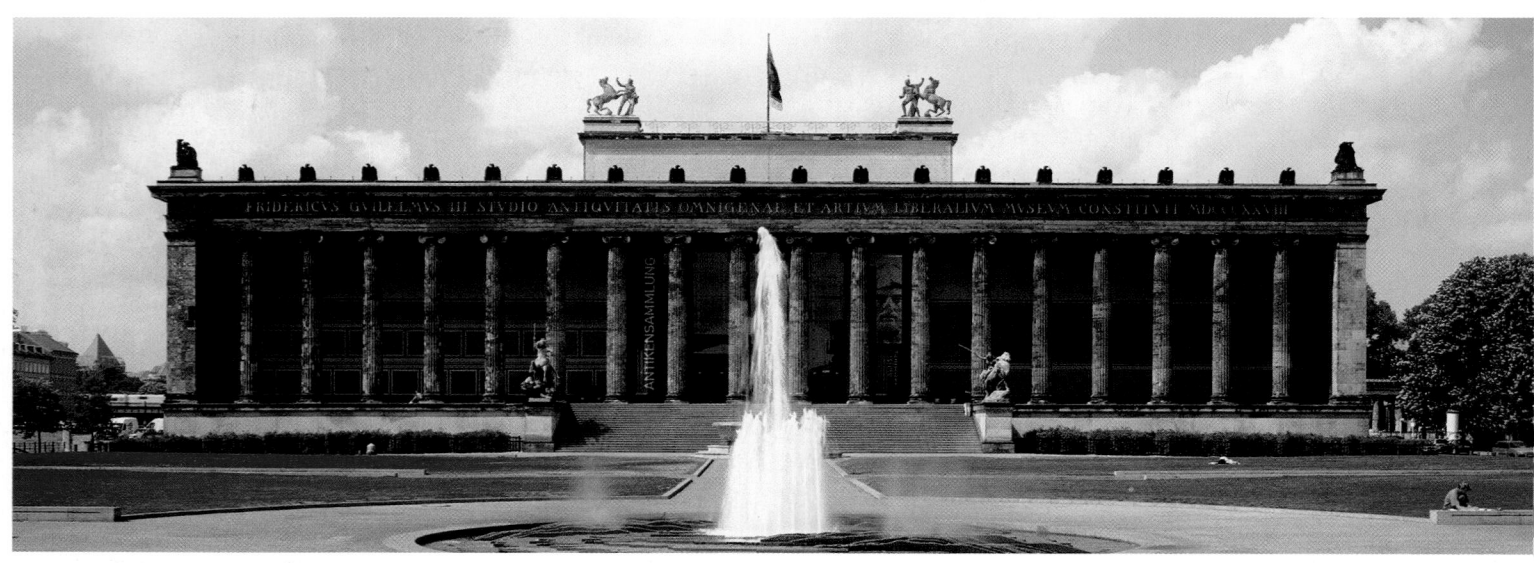

24.32 Karl Friedrich Schinkel. Altes Museum, Berlin. 1824–30

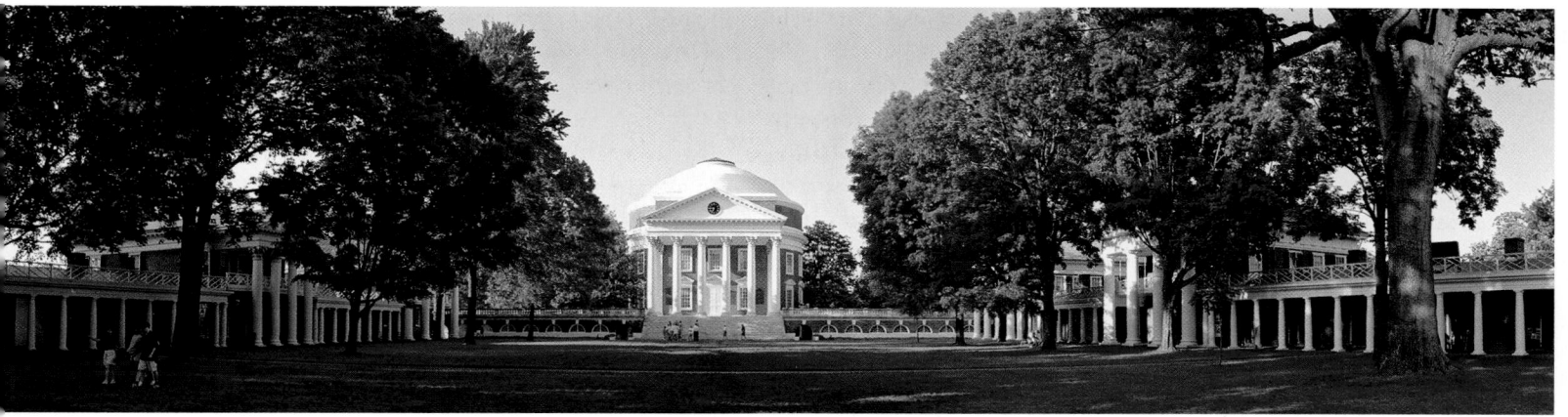

24.33 Thomas Jefferson. University of Virginia, Charlottesville. Designed 1804–17, constructed 1817–28

order refers to the Baths of Diocletian in Rome, a second with an Ionic order to the Temple of Fortuna Virilis, also in Rome. At one end of the two rows and tying them together is a Pantheon-like rotunda, the library, suggested by fellow architect Benjamin Latrobe and built in 1823–26. Lastly, the tree-lined lawn separating the two rows of villas imparts the complex with the naturalism of a picturesque English garden. Jefferson's genius in Charlottesville was to use the Classical revival to create a metaphor for the new republic that expresses both the individual-ism and the unity that defined the new nation. His use of picturesque variety in the buildings and landscape as well as his use of a style that evokes a lost, distant past are qualities that are distinctly Romantic.

BENJAMIN LATROBE The most famous American architect during the Federal period was Benjamin Latrobe (1764–1820), who in 1795 emigrated from England, where he had been heavily influenced by John Soane and the Parisian Claude-Nicolas Ledoux (see page 808). A friend of Jefferson—which in part accounts for his winning the commission for the U.S. Capitol—he built the first Greek-revival building in the United States (1798, the severe Bank of Pennsylvania in Philadelphia) and later the first Gothic-revival house (Sedgeley Gatehouse, also in Philadlephia, where Latrobe lived). His most esteemed building is Baltimore Cathedral, designed in 1804–8. The exterior is a rather undistinguished Graeco-Roman temple façade with Ionic columns. (Latrobe also submitted a Gothic proposal for the building.) The interior, however, is an impressive sequence of vaulted spaces, the centerpiece of which is a Pantheon-like dome springing from an arcade of segmental arches (fig. **24.34**). The arches and austere piers were inspired by Soane's 1792 Bank Stock Office at the Bank of England, while the elegant coffered vaulting recalls Robert Adam (see fig. 23.10). The vast interior was meant to evoke sublime Roman structures, an interest that can be traced back to Piranesi through Soane.

While Baltimore Cathedral may rank among Latrobe's most successful buildings, his most famous is the nation's Capitol, which along with the White House (another project Latrobe

advised on when Jefferson became president) firmly established Neoclassicism as the nation's official architectural style. Latrobe's many students were equally committed to Neoclassicism, result-ing in most major buildings in America being designed in a Neoclassical style.

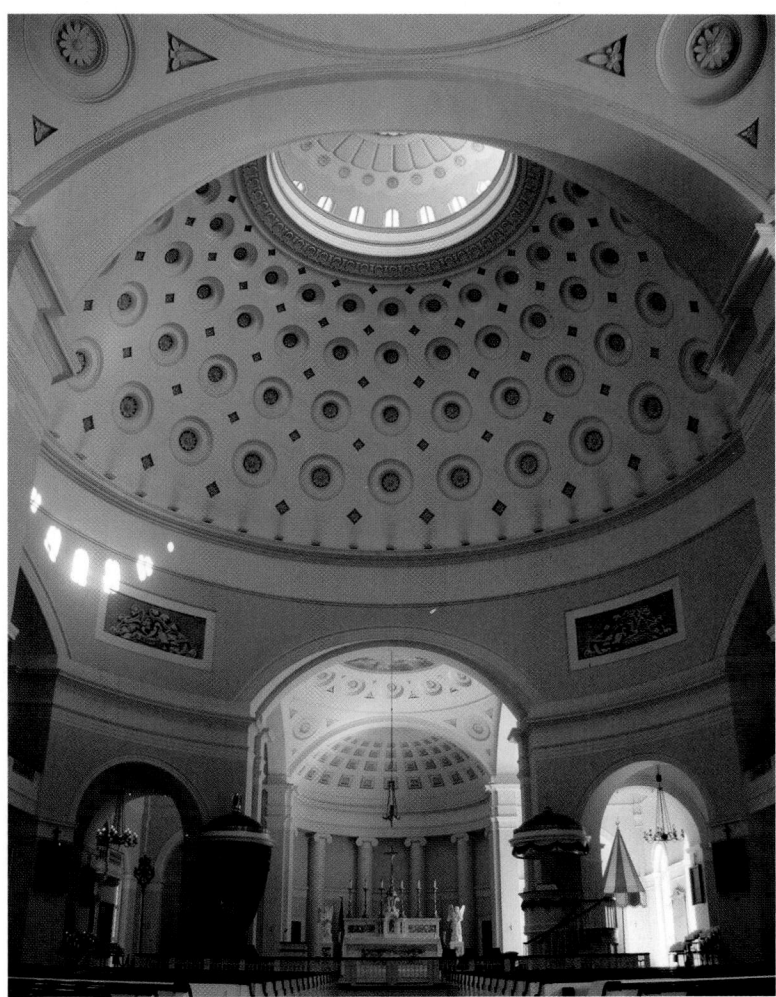

24.34 Benjamin Latrobe. Interior of Baltimore Cathedral (Basilica of the Assumption), Baltimore, Maryland. Begun 1805

France: Empire Style

The course of the Classical revival in France was set by Napoleon, who commissioned several Roman structures in Paris to reinforce his imperial image. What is today the church of Mary Magdalene, in the Place de la Madeleine, was commissioned as a "Temple of Glory" to French soldiers and directly modeled on a Roman Corinthian temple, the Maison Carrée (see fig. 7.44). The Arc de Triomphe, of course, was meant to evoke Roman triumphal arches, while the 130-foot-high bronze Vendôme Column, initially called the Column of the Great Army, was modeled on the Column of Trajan (see fig. 7.39) and commemorated Napoleon's victory at Austerlitz in 1805. Little was actually built during Bonaparte's reign, however, and his greatest influence perhaps resulted from the interior-design style developed for his residences: Empire Style.

One of the finest examples is the state bedroom that the architects Charles Percier (1764–1838) and Pierre-François Fontaine (1762–1853) designed for Josephine Bonaparte at the Chateau de Malmaison outside of Paris (fig. 24.35). The style is opulent, using exotic materials and a saturated palette similar to those we saw in Ingres's 1806 portrait of Napoleon (see fig. 24.12). The bed, decorated with swans and cornucopias, is Roman-inspired, while the canopy resembles a military tent and is crowned by an imperial eagle. The tripod washstand is based on the discoveries at Herculaneum and Pompeii, although the sphinxes supporting the bowl are Egyptian, and the decoration of the bowl itself is Greek, an eclecticism characteristic of the Romantic taste for picturesque variety and associational references. Despite the rich materials, the room does not seem busy; rather, it appears serious and ponderous, the result of the deep hues, the weight of the objects (even the drapery seems monumental), and an underlying geometry. For Napoleon, Percier and Fontaine created an august imperial style that corresponded perfectly to the image of the new French emperor.

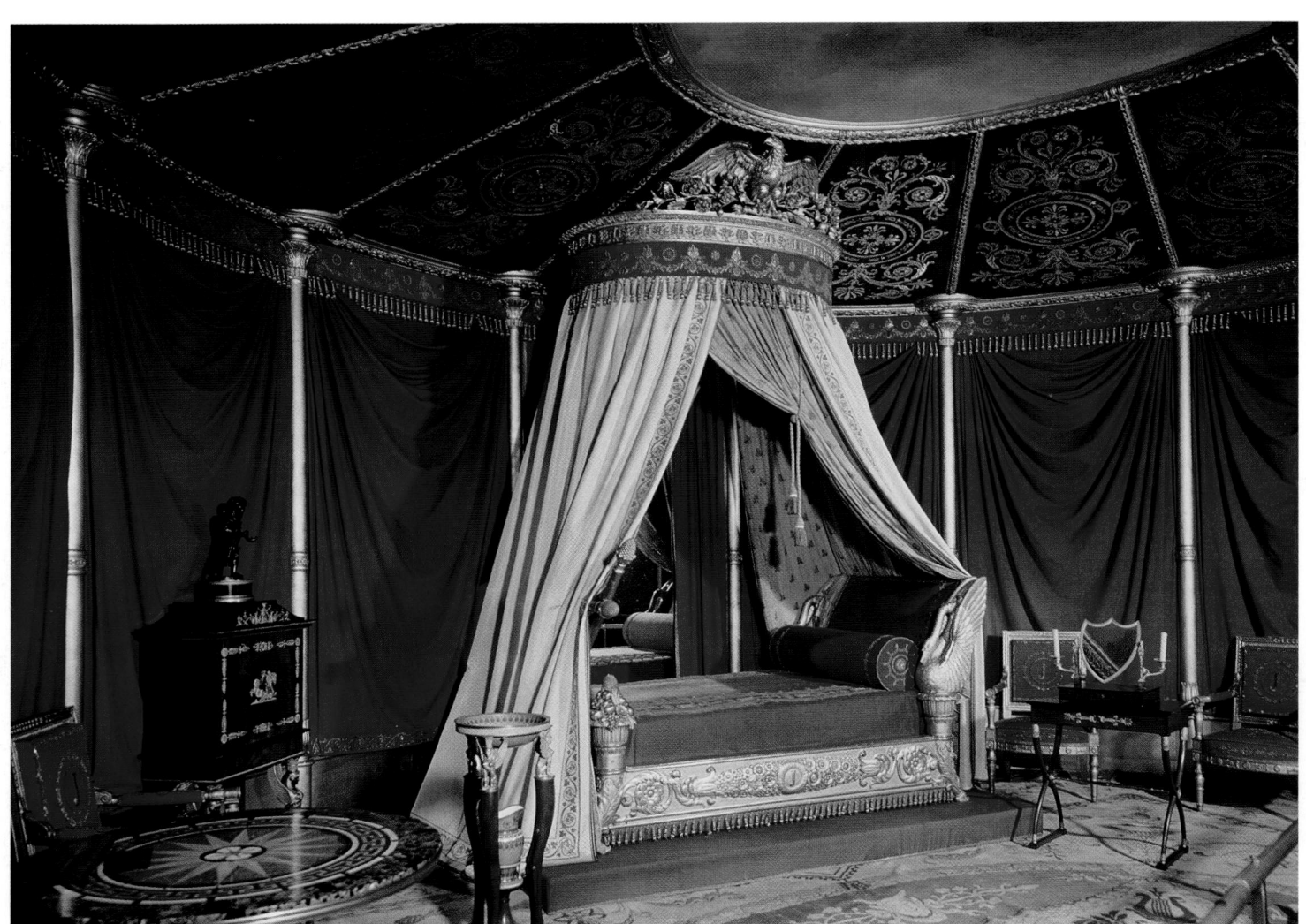

24.35 François-Honoré Jacob-Desmalter (after a design by Charles Percier and Pierre-François Fontaine). Bedroom of Empress Josephine Bonaparte. ca. 1810. Chateau de Malmaison, Rueil-Malmaison, France

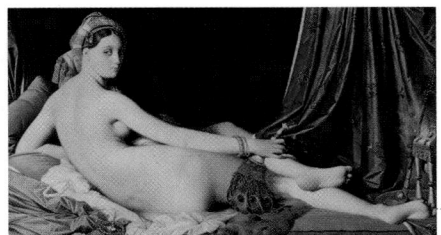

1814 Jean-Auguste-
Dominique Ingres's
Grande Odalisque

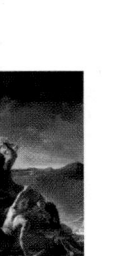

1814 Francisco Goya's *The Third of May,
1808*

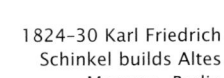

1818–19 Théodore Géricault's
The Raft of the Medusa

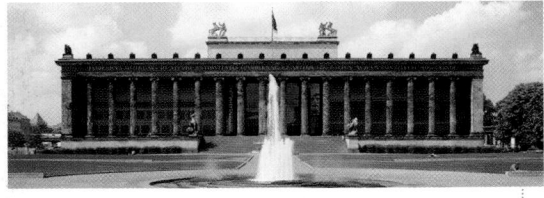

1824–30 Karl Friedrich
Schinkel builds Altes
Museum, Berlin

1827 Eugène
Delacroix's *Death of
Sardanapalus*

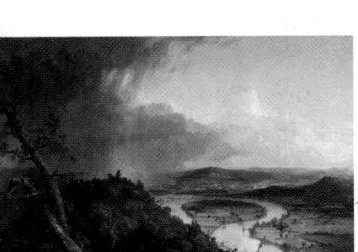

836 Thomas Cole's *The Oxbow*

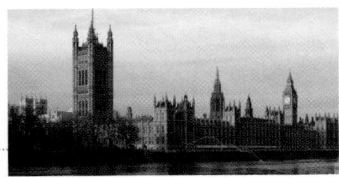

1836 Sir Charles Barry and
A. W. N. Pugin begin the Houses
of Parliament

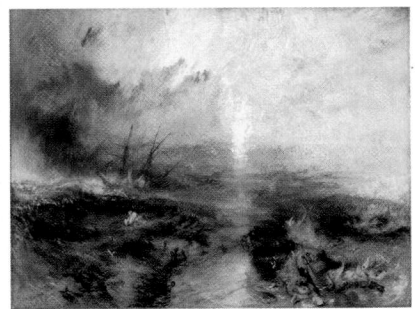

1840 Joseph Turner's
The Slave Ship

Art in the Age of
Romanticism,
1789–1848

1780

1790

◄ 1789 French Revolution begins

◄ 1798 First edition of *Lyrical Ballads* by
Wordsworth and Coleridge

1800

◄ 1804 Napoleon crowned emperor of France
1804 Ludwig van Beethoven finishes his Third
Symphony, the *Eroica*

◄ 1808 France occupies Spain, completing
occupation of much of Europe

1810

1814 Lord Byron publishes *The Corsair*
◄ 1814 Louis XVIII restores monarchy in France
◄ 1815 Battle of Waterloo, final defeat of Napoleon

1820

1830 The Liverpool and Manchester Railway
opens, first steam passenger railway service
◄ 1830 Revolution of 1830, Paris, and July
Monarchy, Louis-Philippe becomes king of France
◄ 1831 Victor Hugo publishes *The Hunchback of
Notre Dame*
◄ 1832 Ralph Waldo Emerson publishes *Nature*
◄ 1833 Slavery Abolition Act, banning slavery in
British Empire

1830

◄ 1839 The daguerreotype and calotype, the first
photography, are made commercially available

1840

◄ 1848 Revolution of 1848, European-wide worker's
revolt

1850

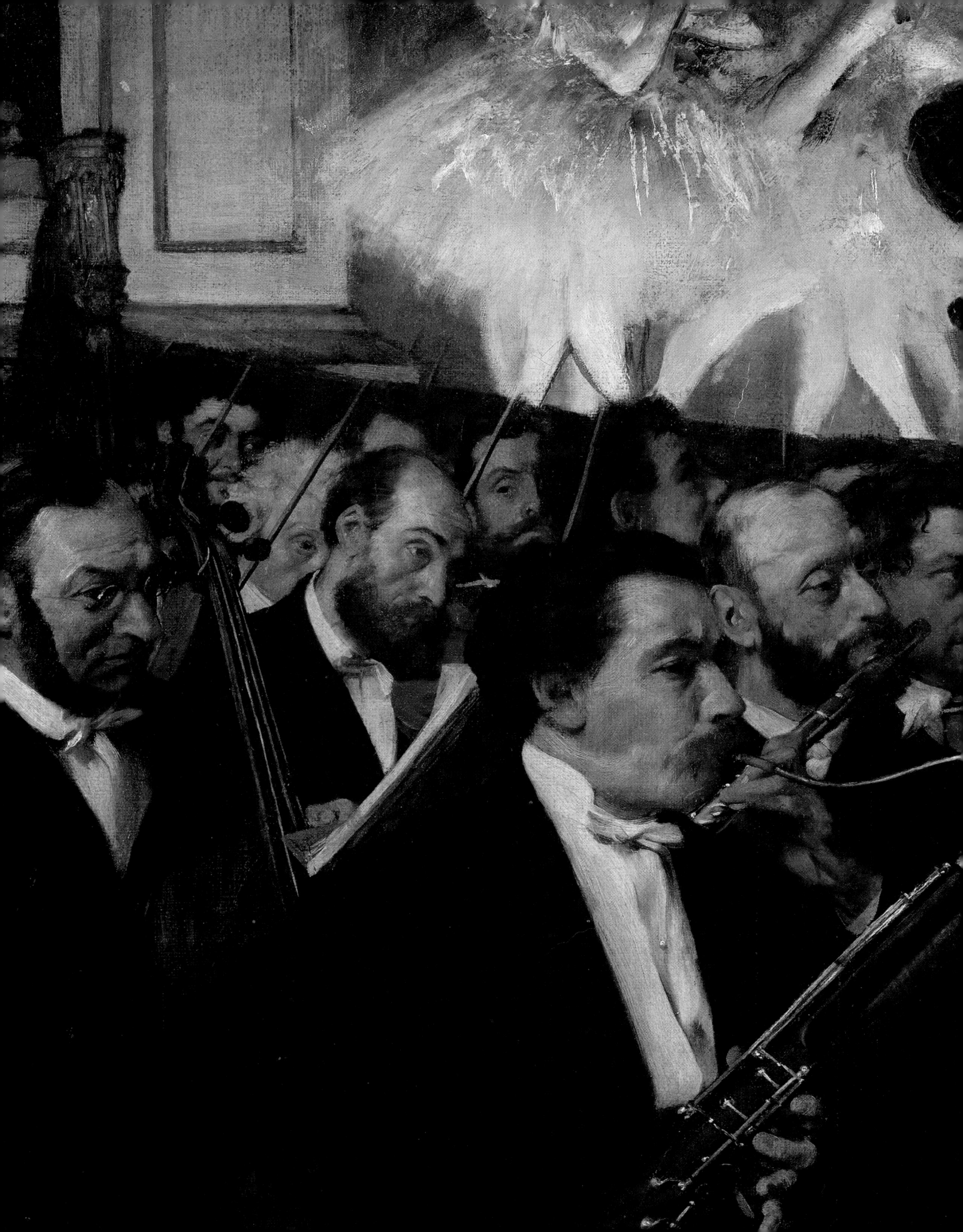

The Age of Positivism: Realism, Impressionism, and the Pre-Raphaelites, 1848–1885

R OMANTICISM BEGAN TO DISSIPATE IN EUROPE AS AN INTELLECTUAL attitude and stylistic trend after 1848 and was gradually superseded by Realism. Increasingly, people came to rely on the physical, physiological, empirical, and scientific as a way to understand nature, society, and human behavior. Hard facts, not feelings, became the bricks and mortar of

knowledge. Positivism is the term often used to describe the new mentality of pragmatism and materialism that emerged in the 1840s. The word was coined by the French philosopher Auguste Comte (1798–1857), who in 1830 began to write a multivolume series called *Positive Philosophy*. Comte called for social progress to be based on observable fact and tested ideas—in other words, on science. This new scientific approach to studying society came to be called sociology.

Paralleling Comte's sociology was the appearance in the 1830s and 1840s of popular and widely distributed pamphlets called *physiologies*. These were short essays that analyzed in tremendous detail different niches of French society, not just professions and types, such as the Lawyer, the Nun, the Society Woman, but also such specific categories as the Suburban Gardener and the Woman of 30. In a world undergoing tremendous flux due to rapid industrialization and urbanization, the *physiologies* were a means of understanding the dramatic transformations that were occurring.

In politics, this new tough pragmatism was called *Realpolitik*, a German word meaning the "politics of reality," a concept that Otto von Bismarck (1815–1898), first chancellor of the German Empire, deftly used to create a united Germany toward 1870. In religion, Positivism brought about a renewal of eighteenth-century skepticism. Epitomizing Positivism is the rise of photo-

graphy in the 1840s, which most people perceived not as an art form but as a tool for faithfully recording nature and documenting the rapidly changing world.

In the arts, Positivism resulted in Realism. Now, artists and writers did not bury their heads in the Classical, historical past nor view the modern world through rose-tinted glasses or Romantic notions of the exciting and exotic. Instead they concentrated on contemporary life, and they presented it unembellished and unidealized. And because it was changing so rapidly, they presented it as fleeting too. As early as 1846, the poet and critic Charles Baudelaire called for an art based on modern life, writing that "The pageant of fashionable life and the thousands of floating existences—criminals and kept women—which drift about in the underworld of a great city…all prove to us that we have only to open our eyes to recognize our heroism." By the 1850s, *réalisme* was the rallying cry of the new art and literature. The evangelist of Realism was critic Jules-Antoine Castagnary (1831–1888), who in his 1857 Salon review wrote: "There is no need to return to history, to take refuge in legends, to summon powers of imagination. Beauty is before the eyes, not in the brain; in the present, not in the past; in truth, not in dreams."

Instead of valuing wild flights of imagination, the exotic, and the sublime, Realists planted both feet firmly on the ground and, generally without emotion, bluntly depicted modern life. This ranged from the grim existence of country peasants and the downtrodden urban poor to the leisure activities of the rapidly

Detail of figure 25.12, Edgar Degas, *The Orchestra of the Paris Opéra*

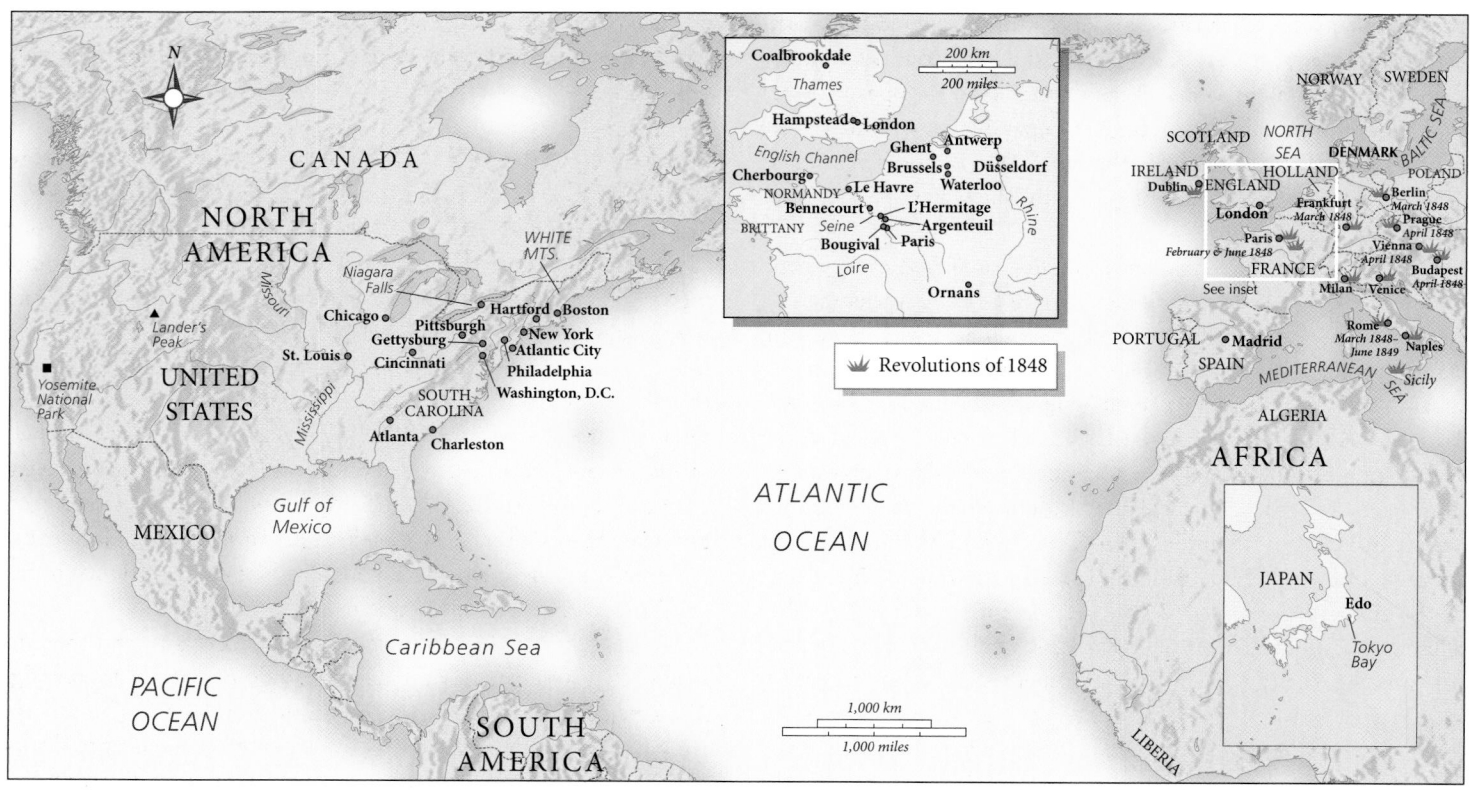

Map 25.1 Europe and North America in 1848

growing metropolitan middle class and *nouveau riche*. In landscape painting, this Realism evolved into Impressionism. Often working in the environs of Paris as well as in the city itself, the Impressionist painters documented the transformation of the landscape from rural to suburban, recording the incursion into the countryside of factories and railroads. They observed, too, the influx of moneyed Parisians, who built fancy weekend villas in farm villages, raced sailboats in regattas on such waterways as the Seine and Oise rivers, and dined, danced, and swam at fashionable riverside establishments. Painting rapidly outdoors with bold brushstrokes and strong colors, the Impressionists empirically captured the world before their very eyes, the shimmering sketchiness of their finished paintings reflecting the impermanence of a constantly changing contemporary world.

While the Impressionists were committed to creating an empirical representational art—a realistic art—a byproduct of their stylistic developments was the advent of Modernism. To the following generations, their bright colors and broad brushwork—that is, the abstract qualities of their works—seemed to challenge the representational components as the subject matter of the painting. In the early twentieth century, critics and historians would label this shift in art toward abstraction as "Modernism." Impressionism also marked the appearance of the **avant-garde**, the notion that certain artists and ideas are strikingly new or radical for their time. This meant, in effect, that artists began making art that was only understood by a handful of people, namely other avant-garde artists and a few art experts, including

collectors. The disconnect between the avant-garde and the general public, including the working class, who felt comfortable attending the highly publicized academy exhibitions, is reflected in the rise of commercial art galleries as the principal venue for the display of new art and the corresponding decline in power of academic Salons throughout the Western world. But while Realism served as a springboard for the abstraction of Modernism, we must remember that first and foremost it was a movement preoccupied with the dramatic changes occurring in society, and that its birth coincides with the great European-wide revolutions of 1848.

REALISM IN FRANCE

The year 1848 was one of uprising in France. Republicans, liberals, and socialists (those advocating a classless society in which either a popular collective or the government controls the means of production) united that year to demand an increased voice in government, and when King Louis-Philippe refused, armed conflict was imminent. The king abdicated. A provisional government was soon replaced by the Constituent Assembly. But the working class was still not represented; already organized into labor camps instituted by the new government, it revolted, storming Parliament. War raged in the streets of Paris, and 10,000 people were killed or wounded. This proletarian rebellion produced shock waves of class revolution that radiated throughout Europe, resulting in similar uprisings in major cities. Even Britain was threatened, as the Chartists, a socialist group, agitated for workers' rights, going so far as to gather arms and conduct military drills. As one contemporary French writer said, European society was "prey to a feeling of terror incomparable to anything since the invasion of Rome by the barbarians." It is no coincidence that Karl Marx and Friedrich Engels published their *Communist Manifesto* the same year.

The forces of conservatism ultimately prevailed everywhere. In France, Louis Napoleon Bonaparte (1808–1873), the emperor's nephew, was elected president of the Second Republic, largely on name recognition. In 1852, however, he dissolved Parliament and arranged to have himself "elected" emperor, becoming Napoleon III and establishing the Second Empire. France prospered under his reign, which ended in 1870 with the Franco-Prussian War.

The pace of the Industrial Revolution, which had not gained momentum in France until the 1840s, now increased dramatically, largely due to new financial systems instituted by Louis Napoleon, systems that also created unprecedented wealth. Dominated by financiers, industrialists, manufacturers, lawyers, and merchants, the bourgeoisie flourished, as did their hunger for material possessions. Reflecting the new consumerism was the 1855 Paris Universal Exposition, or World's Fair, in which countries from all over the world displayed their products. The Parisian exposition was a competitive response to the first international trade fair presented in London in 1851, the Great Exhibition of the Works of Industry of All Nations. In Paris, the new wealth and increased time for leisure activities gave rise to grand restaurants, cafés, department stores, theaters, clubs, parks, and racetracks, where people, often from different social classes, congregated and shopped.

Paris itself received a makeover, taking on its glorious modern-day form when, beginning in 1853, Georges-Eugène Haussmann (1809–1891), Louis Napoleon's minister of the interior, initiated huge municipal improvements. Among them was the creation of magnificent wide avenues that cut through the dark, dank, medieval rabbit warren of the Old City and that were flanked by chic modern apartment buildings. The result was spectacular perspectives (and arteries that permitted the rapid deployment of troops in the event of more insurrections), punctuated by beautifully landscaped parks, gardens, and squares, and anchored by grand civic buildings, including an opera house and stately railway stations. The boulevards opened up the city, permitting increased light and color, making the urban environment seem more salubrious, which it was. This new city is what the Impressionists would capture on their canvases.

Realism in the 1840s and 1850s: Painting Contemporary Social Conditions

French Realism arose simultaneously with the revolution of 1848. Especially in the hands of Gustave Courbet, the self-proclaimed banner-carrier of this art movement, and Jean-François Millet, the painter of peasants, Realism was a highly political style. It championed laborers and common country folk, groups that challenged the authority and privilege of the Parisian aristocracy and bourgeoisie and were in part responsible for the upheavals of 1848.

GUSTAVE COURBET Gustave Courbet (1819–1877) came from Ornans, a town at the foot of the Jura mountains near the Swiss border, where his father, a former peasant, was a prosperous landowner and vintner. He went to Paris in 1839 to study painting, and by the late 1840s had become a dominant figure at the new bohemian cafés on the Left Bank. There, Courbet met the literary avant-garde, befriending Baudelaire, the socialist journalist Pierre-Joseph Proudhon, and the critic and writer Champfleury. Largely under the influence of Proudhon, Courbet, already a republican, became a socialist. Meanwhile, Champfleury swayed him toward Realism. Champfleury, who collected folk art and was interested in such nonelitist art forms as popular prints, children's art, and caricatures, convinced Courbet to return to his rural roots and paint the simple world of Ornans.

In the fall of 1849, Courbet returned to Ornans, and there in his family's attic painted the 22-foot-wide *Burial at Ornans* (fig. **25.1**), which was accepted at the Salon of 1850–51. The picture was an affront to many viewers. It presented common provincial folk, portrayed in a coarse, heavy form, without a shred of elegance or idealization. The people of Ornans, many of whom can be identified, posed for Courbet, and the artist not only documented their clothes and bearing but their distinguishing facial features, which included bulbous noses, grotesquely wrinkled faces, and unkempt hair. The bleak overcast landscape is equally authentic, based on studies made at Ornans cemetery. Courbet's Realism extends to the democratic presentation of the figures. Despite bold brushwork and a chiaroscuro vaguely reminiscent of his favorite artists, Rembrandt and Velázquez, the picture has no Baroque drama and no compositional structure to emphasize one figure over another—the dog is as important as the priest or mayor. Nor does it use Classical formulas, as Benjamin West did in his pyramidal groupings in *The Death of General Wolfe* (see fig. 23.6). Instead, the image embraces the bold, simple compositions found in such popular art forms, as broadsides, almanacs, and song sheets—the art of the people, not the academy.

The picture seems so matter-of-fact it is difficult to know what it is about. We see pallbearers and the coffin on the left, then a priest and assistants, followed by small-town patricians and, to the right, womenfolk. An open grave is in the foreground center. We do not even know whose funeral it is. Nor is it clear that this is a statement about the finality of death, although that is the strongest candidate for an overriding theme. Clearly, the picture is a document of social ritual that accurately observes the distinctions of gender, profession, and class in Ornans. More important, it brazenly elevates provincial bourgeois events to a lofty status equal to that of historical events. In effect, it is an assault on the highly esteemed genre of history painting. As such, Courbet's work repulsed many Parisians. Equally unsavory was the political threat represented by the Ornans bourgeoisie, who under the Second Republic had considerable voting power, capable of

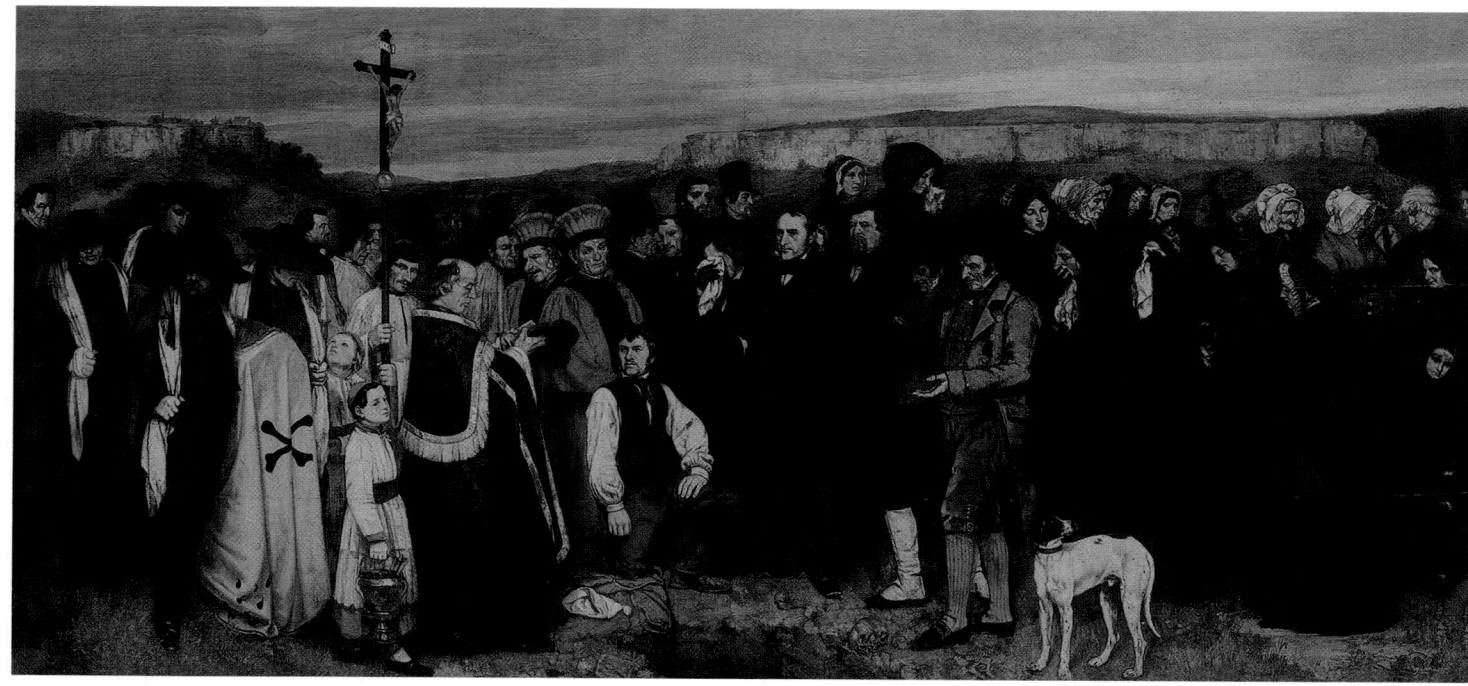

25.1   Gustave Courbet, *Burial at Ornans*. 1849–50. Oil on canvas, 10'3½" × 21'9½" (3.13 × 6.64 m). Musée d'Orsay, Paris

swaying national elections. Furthermore, they were a sobering reminder to many members of the Parisian bourgeoisie of their own provincial and even peasant origins, which many tried to hide.

Courbet exhibited a second Ornans painting in the Salon of 1850–51, *The Stone Breakers* (fig. **25.2**). Here, he presents on a confrontational, life-size scale two workers he met on the outskirts of town who were pounding stones to make gravel for a road. Again, Courbet portrays the figures with complete veracity, their poverty and social class announced by their ragged clothes, by the coarseness of their labor, and by the dirt under their fingernails. He gives the workers the same detailed intensity as the stones, and the fact that their faces cannot be seen virtually transforms them into inanimate objects, like the rocks and tools. Once more, the composition lacks conventional structure, resulting in our eye jumping from one fact to another.

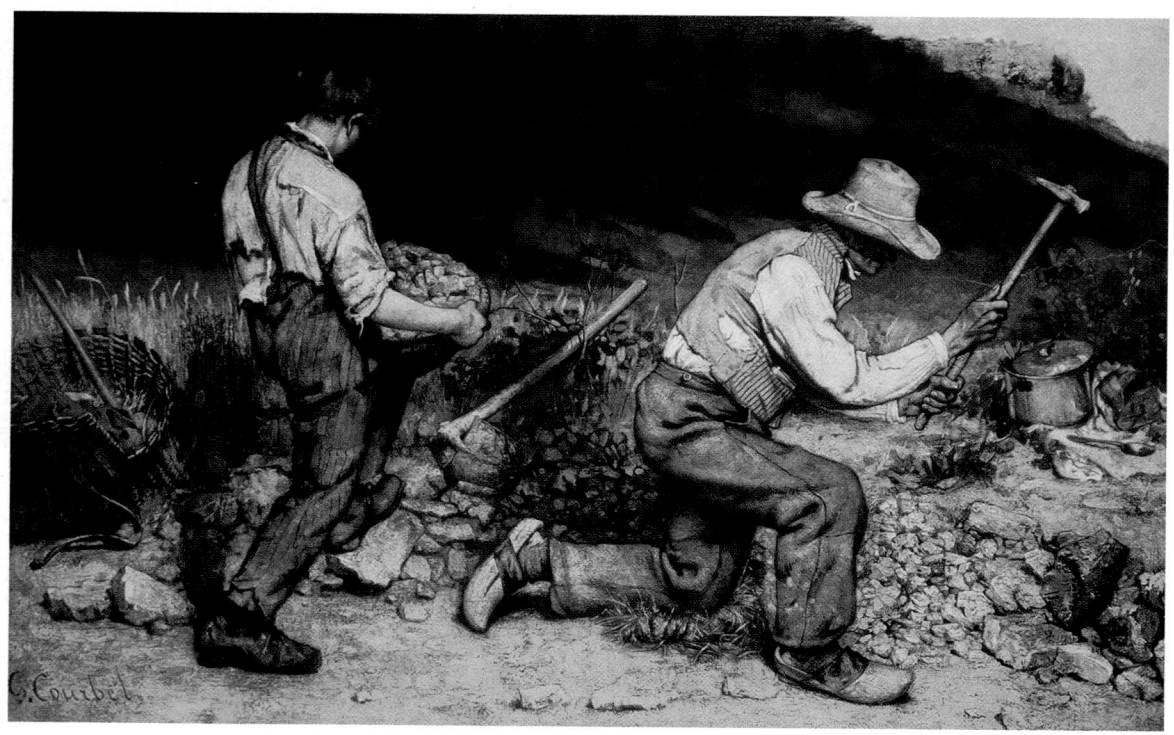

25.2   Gustave Courbet, *The Stone Breakers*. 1849. Oil on canvas, 5'3" × 8'6" (1.6 × 2.59 m). Formerly Gemäldegalerie, Dresden (believed to have been destroyed in World War II)

While the public variously condemned and praised the picture for having a socialist message, both political sides admired the image's materiality. As in the *Burial*, Courbet used a broad application of paint, sometimes troweling it on with a palette knife, in effect transforming the artist into an artisan-laborer. This bold paint application reinforces the powerful physicality of the figures and by its physical presence virtually stands in for the material objects. In both *Burial* and *Stone Breakers*, figures are sandwiched into a shallow space. They are pushed up to the surface of the canvas, and the landscape behind is so flat it seems like a backdrop that forces our eye to stay in the foreground. Courbet would never admit to having a socialist agenda in *Stone Breakers*, but this "complete expression of human misery," as the artist himself described it, is obviously about social injustice and a product of the revolution of 1848. Rather than presenting rural life as pastoral or comic, as had been traditional in art, Courbet depicts its harsh reality.

In 1855, Courbet had 11 paintings accepted for the Paris Universal Exposition, a world trade fair designed to promote French commerce and industry. The fair's fine-art section replaced the Salon exhibition that year and featured such famous French masters as Ingres and Delacroix. To promote his career, Courbet created a sensation by doing what no living artist had ever done before: He commissioned a Classically inspired building near the fair where he mounted his own one-person show, which included *Burial at Ornans*. He titled his exhibition *Du Réalisme* (On Realism) and sold a pamphlet, a "Manifesto of Realism." In it, he made the following proclamation: "To be in a position to translate the customs, the ideas, the appearance of my epoch according to my own estimation: to be not only a painter, but a man as well, in short to create living art—this is my goal." At every turn, Courbet challenged academic values. He replaced the hallowed Greek and Roman tradition with bold images of the contemporary world, images that contained no references, either iconographic or compositional, to the Classical tradition or history painting. He daringly troweled paint onto the canvas, undermining the refinement of academic paint handling, whether the Neoclassical hard smooth surface of Ingres or the painterly Venetian and Rubensian tradition found in Delacroix; and while not rejecting the Salons, he refused to rely on them to promote his career and instead turned to commercial exhibition.

JEAN-FRANÇOIS MILLET We can see how matter-of-fact in presentation and unemotional Courbet's pictures are if we compare them with another Realist entry at the Salon of 1850–51, *The Sower* (fig. **25.3**), by Jean-François Millet (1814–1875). Like Courbet, Millet had a rural upbringing. Born into a family of well-to-do farmers near Cherbourg in Normandy, he grew up steeped in the land and the timeless seasonal cycle of farm life. He was well educated and well read, and after choosing a career in painting and studying in both Cherbourg and Paris, he began by making portraits, using a dark palette that reflected his love of seventeenth-century Spanish painting and Rembrandt. In the late 1840s, when back in Paris, he befriended several of the landscape

painters of the Barbizon School (see page 849), and in 1848 he produced his first peasant picture, *Le Vanneur* (*The Grain Sifter*). Pictures of peasant life would be his specialty for the remainder of his life. In 1848, after an outbreak of cholera in Paris, Millet settled permanently in Barbizon.

Coming on the heels of the revolution of 1848, Millet's pictures dignifying the peasantry were read politically. As seen in *The Sower*, his workers, like Courbet's, are poor and downtrodden: They wear tattered clothing and are consigned to a life of grueling work on the land. Shadowy and enormous, they were frightening to a Parisian audience still reeling from the revolution of 1848. More threatening yet, Millet ennobled them. The anonymous sower is monumental in size, a massive dynamic form consuming most of the picture frame. He is not so much an individual, as are Courbet's figures in *Burial at Ornans*, but a type—the noble farmworker, who is poorly paid for his labor. Using a dark chiaroscuro reminiscent of Rembrandt, Millet casts the laborer in murky shadow, making him blend in with the soil from which he seems to emerge. He is the embodiment of the earth, a reading enhanced by the gritty coarseness of Millet's paint. The dramatic

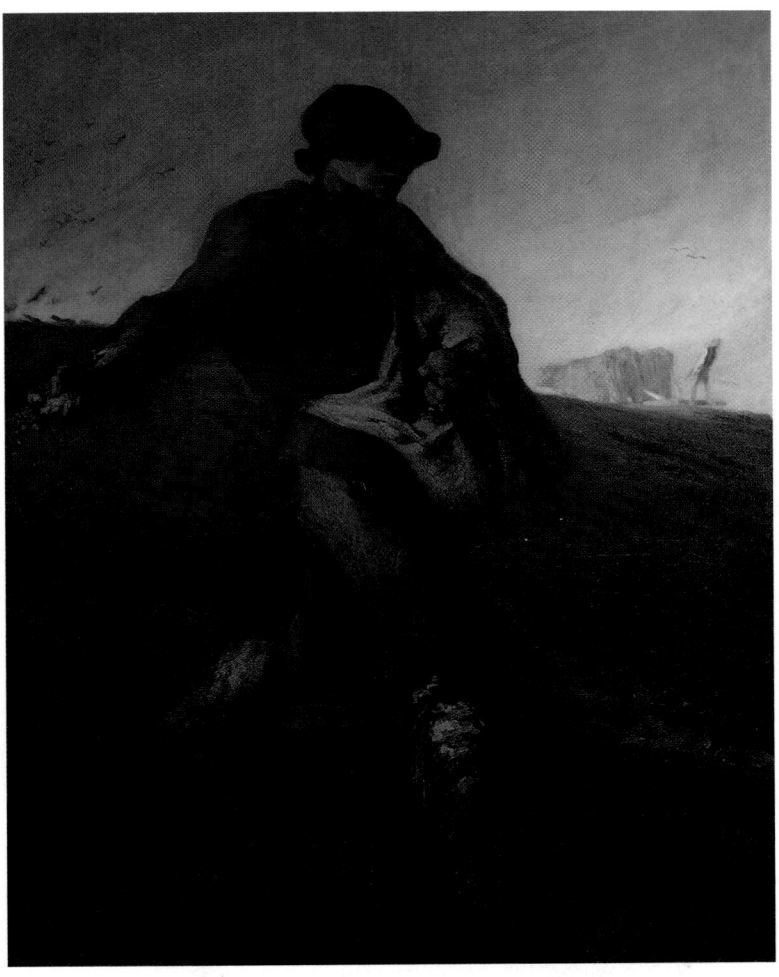

25.3 Jean-François Millet, *The Sower*. ca. 1850. Oil on canvas, 40 × 32½" (101.6 × 82.6 cm). Museum of Fine Arts, Boston. Gift of Quincy Adams Shaw through Quincy A. Shaw. Jr., and Mrs. Marion Shaw Haughton. 17.1485

sweep of the gesture and the undulating contours of the body align him with the eternal cyclical forces of nature itself. While a Realist in his peasant subject, Millet is clearly a Romantic in sensibility, his pictures aspiring to poetry and mood, not sheer fact.

HONORÉ DAUMIER Also appearing for the first time in the Salons at this time was Honoré Daumier (1808–1879). Daumier was famous as a caricaturist but virtually unknown as a painter. His lithographs began appearing regularly in Paris newspapers about 1830. (See *Materials and Techniques*, page 911.) The emergence of a sizeable and literate bourgeois public and the development of inexpensive paper and printing processes resulted in the modern-day newspaper, made all the more popular by being illustrated with lithographs and woodcuts. Daumier worked mostly for the socialist newspapers *La Caricature* and *Le Charivari*, both devoted to political and social satire. This was a perfect match, for Daumier was passionate about social causes, dedicating his life to exposing evil, from the corrupt and repressive activities of the government to the avarice and vanity of the *nouveau riche*. His brilliant lithographs quickly and subtly documented the different professions, classes, and types emerging in a rapidly growing and changing Paris, in some respects paralleling the lengthy factual descriptions of the physiology pamphlets. His characterizations anticipated the observations of types found in the urban Realists and Impressionists of the 1860s and 1870s. We can see Daumier's sharp eye, caustic humor, and succinct draftsmanship in *It's Safe to Release This One!* (fig. **25.4**), made in 1834 after a workers' uprising in Paris that resulted in the deaths of numerous poor and innocent citizens at the hands of government forces. It presents a caricature of the overweight pear-shaped King Louis-Philippe,

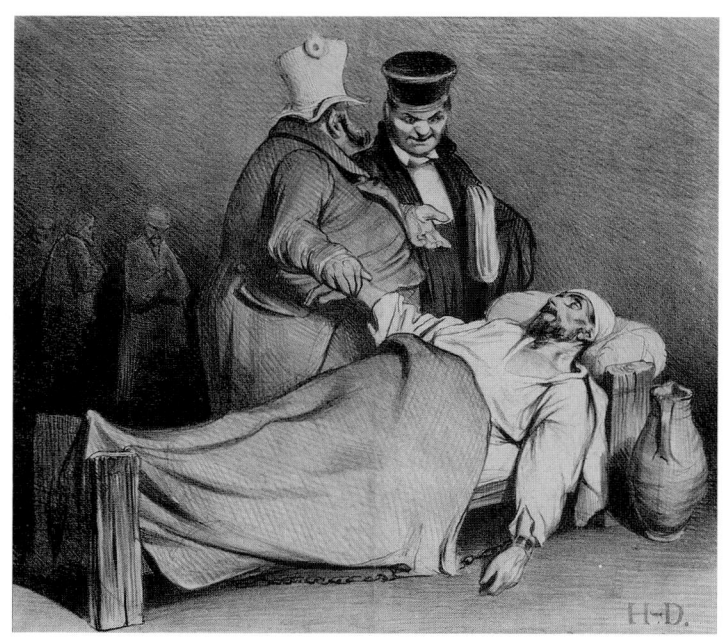

25.4 Honoré Daumier, *It's Safe to Release This One!* 1834. Lithograph

who, feeling no pulse in a chained emaciated worker, announces he is now free to go.

Daumier undoubtedly wanted to be considered a fine artist, and with this in mind exhibited a handful of paintings at the Salons of 1849 and 1850–51. He was ignored, however. For the rest of his life he painted privately, exhibiting only once more, 1877, the year before he died, at Durand-Ruel, a major commercial gallery in Paris. His paintings were therefore essentially unknown. It appears Daumier taught himself to paint during the

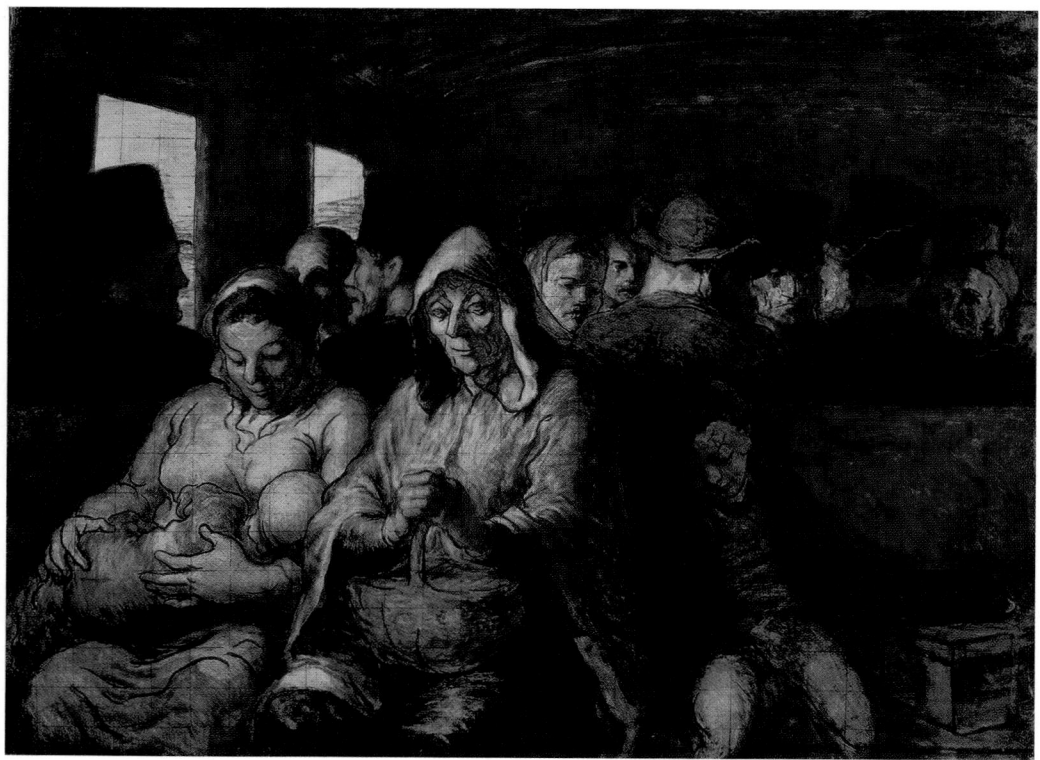

25.5 Honoré Daumier, *The Third-Class Carriage*. ca. 1863–65. Oil on canvas, 25¾ × 35½" (65.4 × 90.2 cm). Metropolitan Museum of Art, New York. Bequest of Mrs. H. O. Havemeyer, 1929. The H. O. Havemeyer Collection (29.100.129)

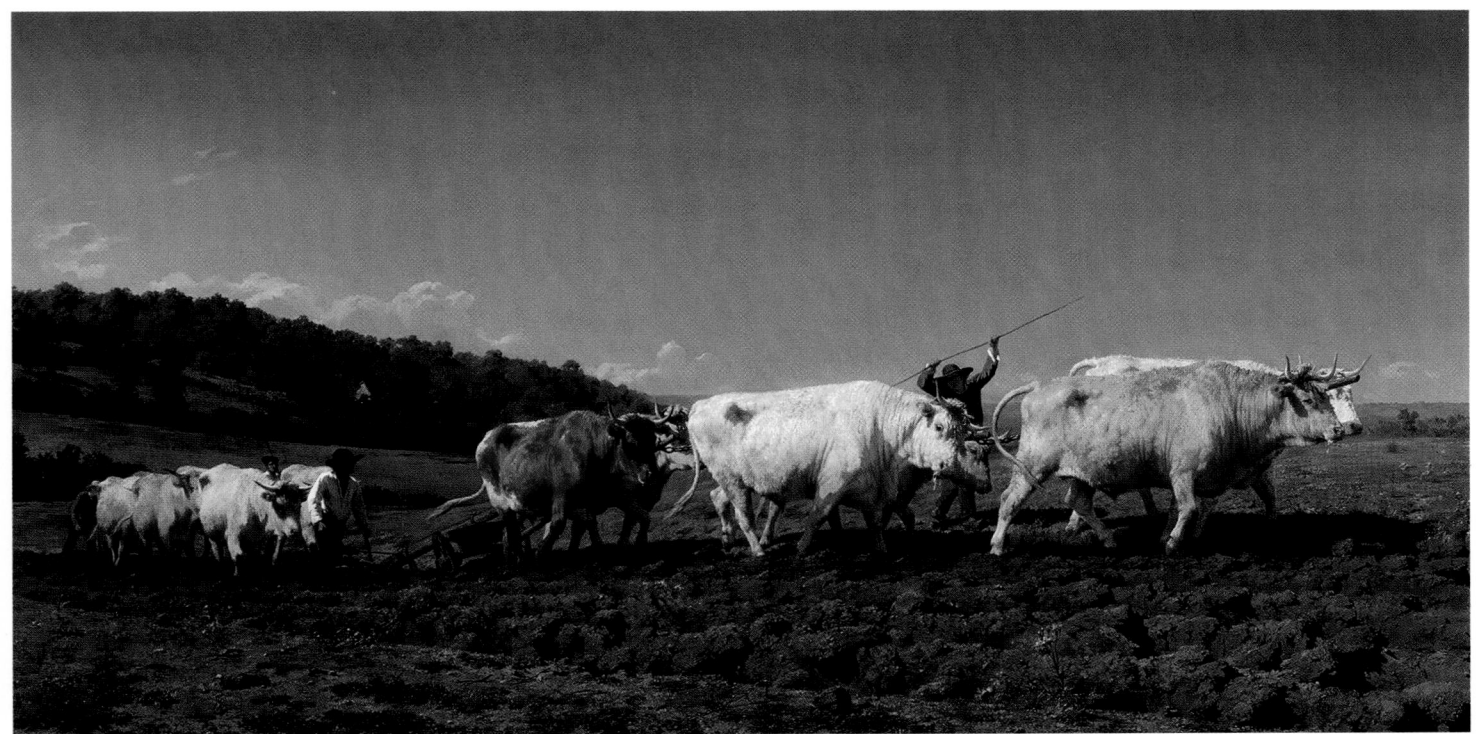

25.6 Rosa Bonheur, *Plowing in the Nivernais: The Dressing of Vines*. 1849. Oil on canvas, 5'9" × 8'8" (1.75 × 2.64 m). Musée d'Orsay, Paris

1840s. In contrast to his commercial work, his oils are pure compassion. He dispensed with humor and satire and, relying on his caricaturist's ability to concisely capture character and types, uncannily nailed the psychology of contemporary urban life, as seen in *The Third-Class Carriage* (fig. **25.5**), made about 1863–65. Here, he renders a peculiarly modern condition, "the lonely crowd," in which throngs of workers are jammed into a third-class railway car, consigned to hard benches in contrast to the wide plush seats of first-class cars. A range of types, all anonymous, and part of the growing urban masses, endure their daily commute. The weary family in the foreground is the focus of the picture. They are simpler and poorer than the top-hatted petits bourgeois behind them and seem to represent the uprooted rural poor who have come to Paris in search of opportunity, only to become victims of modern urbanism. Silent and tired, they are imprisoned in a turgid gloom, shut off from the wholesome bright light seen through the windows. But Daumier presents them with fortitude and dignity, for the two women have the monumental forms we saw in Millet's *Sower*. What appears to be a simple peasant family is transformed into the Mother and Child with St. Elizabeth. Like Millet, whom he admired, Daumier is alternately labeled a Realist and a Romantic, his paintings similarly combining Realist subject matter with the powerful compassion of a Romantic.

ROSA BONHEUR A fourth Realist exhibiting at the Salon of 1850–51 was Rosa Bonheur, who garnered considerable attention. She studied with her father, a drawing instructor and socialist, who advocated full equality for women. From early on, Bonheur was determined to become a successful woman in a man's world.

Instead of making the small still lifes and watercolors traditionally associated with women, Bonheur became an animal painter and worked on a large scale, displaying the technical finesse of the finest academicians. Rather than the exotic animals of the Romantic world of Delacroix and Barye, Bonheur painted farm animals, including cows, horses, and sheep. Influenced by the scientific empiricism of natural history, she presented specific species, carefully studying each and accurately rendering them, often in minute detail. Bonheur began showing at the Salon of 1841, and during the course of the decade, her reputation grew. (See www.myartslab.com.)

In 1848, the new Second Republic, reflecting a Positivist compunction to document French regional agriculture, commissioned a large painting from Bonheur. At the Salon of 1850–51, she unveiled the 8-foot-wide result, *Plowing in the Nivernais: The Dressing of Vines* (fig. **25.6**). The inspiration for this subject is believed to be *The Devil's Pool* (1846), a novel by George Sand (1804–1876), who, as a successful woman author, was a role model for Bonheur. In the book's preface, Sand announced that the novel "brings back civilized man to the charms of primitive life." As industrialization was beginning to transform France, creating complex urban centers filled with such ills as overcrowding, poor housing, class conflict, and dislocated migrants, Sand advocated a return to nature, to a simple "primitive" world, a theme also found in Millet's paintings and one that would become popular with the cultural community in the closing decades of the century. Bonheur's interest in animals in part reflected her own interest in nature, and after 1860, she left Paris and permanently settled in the rural forest of Fontainebleau, near Barbizon. There she lived with her companion, Nathalie Micas, and challenged societal conventions about women by wearing men's clothing, cropping her hair short, and smoking in public.

To create *Plowing in the Nivernais*, Bonheur spent weeks in the region, a rural area in central France, studying the unique qualities of the land, animals, farm tools, and regional dress, all of which Salon-goers recognized in her tightly painted detailed picture and responded to favorably. Unlike Millet's *Sower*, her image is factual and unemotional, and in contrast to Courbet's Ornans paintings, it plays down the unseemly qualities of rural life. We may see the ponderous weight of the enormous Nivernais oxen, but we experience no stench of animals, no sweat of labor, and no smell of earth, although it is all represented. Like the *physiologies*, Bonheur documents, catalogues, and presents. The large size of the oxen and the processional planar alignment lend a grandeur to the scene, which, combined with the tight paint handling, give the picture something of a Classical or academic aura that made it more palatable to a conservative public than Courbet's and Millet's more threatening images.

The Realist Assault on Academic Values and Bourgeois Taste

By presenting the provincial bourgeoisie and peasants on a scale usually reserved for history painting, Courbet launched an assault on the values of the French Academy and bourgeois taste. In effect, he declared contemporary life, and especially contemporary social conditions, just as valid (if not more so) a subject for painting as historical events, and his emergence signals the death knell for the traditional hierarchy of the genres that can be traced back to the establishment of the academies. (Ironically, vanguard artists would return to history and religious painting in the closing decades of the century.) Courbet's rejection of academic values in order to depict the social conditions of the modern world was taken up by Édouard Manet (1832–1883) in the 1860s. Focusing on urban rather than rural life, he painted musical gatherings in the Bois de Boulogne, the new park on the western outskirts of Paris where the upper classes came to be seen, and he painted the fashionable throngs who congregated at Longchamp, the new racetrack, also in the Bois. He painted chic masked balls held at the opera, courtesans with their clients, and the leisure activities at the new cafés, dance halls, and restaurants. His pictures are often complex, loaded with references, and densely layered with multiple readings. They are so rich as to be able to comment on academic values while capturing the energy, psychology, and changes occurring in modern society. This is especially true of *The Luncheon on the Grass* (see fig. 25.10), which he submitted to the Salon of 1863. To understand this picture, it is first necessary to look at the academic values that prevailed in the 1860s and that were used by the Salon jury.

OFFICIAL ART AND ITS EXEMPLARS While it is dangerous to characterize any one kind of art as being "academic" and promoted at the École des Beaux-Arts in Paris in the 1860s, many if not most of the academicians still believed in the supremacy of history painting, the Graeco-Roman paradigm, and the highly finished Neoclassical style of paint handling epitomized by Ingres. Among the more popular subjects was the female nude, and images of nudes plastered the walls of the Salons. However, these were not ordinary nudes, for they were all Venuses, Dianas, bacchantes, or nymphs: that is, they were noble beings with a Classical pedigree. Equally popular were nudes in genre scenes located in an exotic setting, such as a harem, as seen in Ingres's *Grande Odalesque* (see fig. 24.13), or in the distant past, such as ancient Rome. Nonetheless, the pictures were esteemed since they continued the Classical tradition of beauty and perfection.

The most prominent academic painter of the period was Adolphe-William Bouguereau (1824–1905), who became president of the Institute of France and the French Legion of Honor. In addition to gypsies, peasant girls, and religious themes, he painted mythological scenes, such as *Nymphs and a Satyr* (fig. **25.7**) of 1873. Here, nymphs playfully tug a satyr into the water in an image that is overtly erotic, as epitomized by the background nymph clutching the satyr's horn in unabashed ecstasy. Heightening the sensuality of flesh, gesture, and expression is

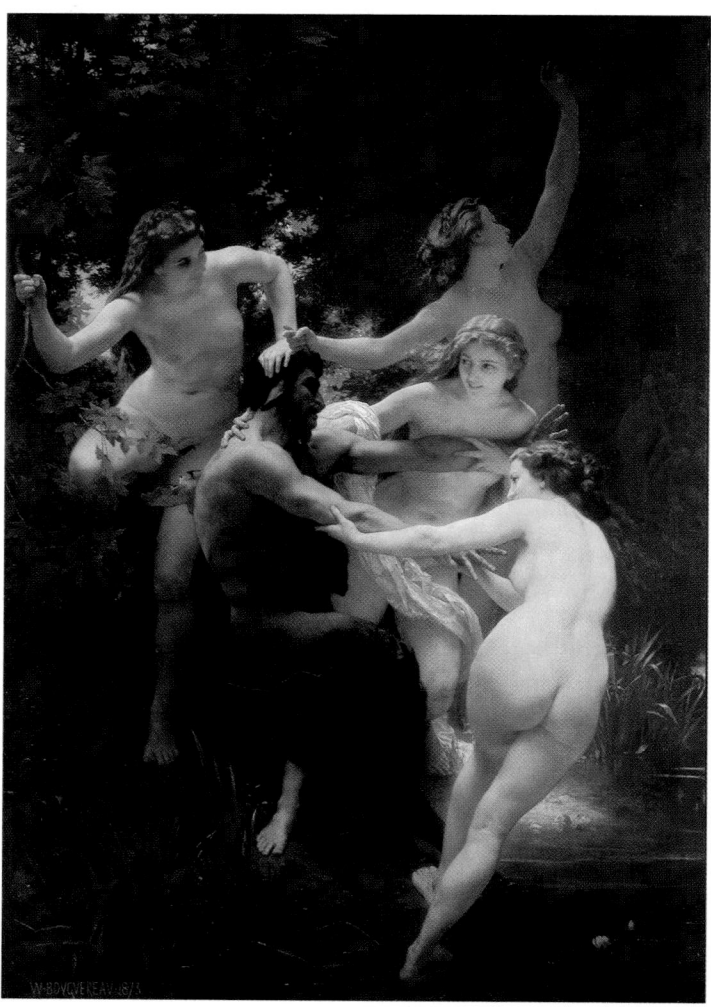

25.7 Adolphe-William Bouguereau, *Nymphs and a Satyr*. 1873. Oil on canvas, 9'3⅛" × 5'10⅞" (2.8 × 1.8 m). Sterling and Francine Clark Art Institute, Williamstown, MA

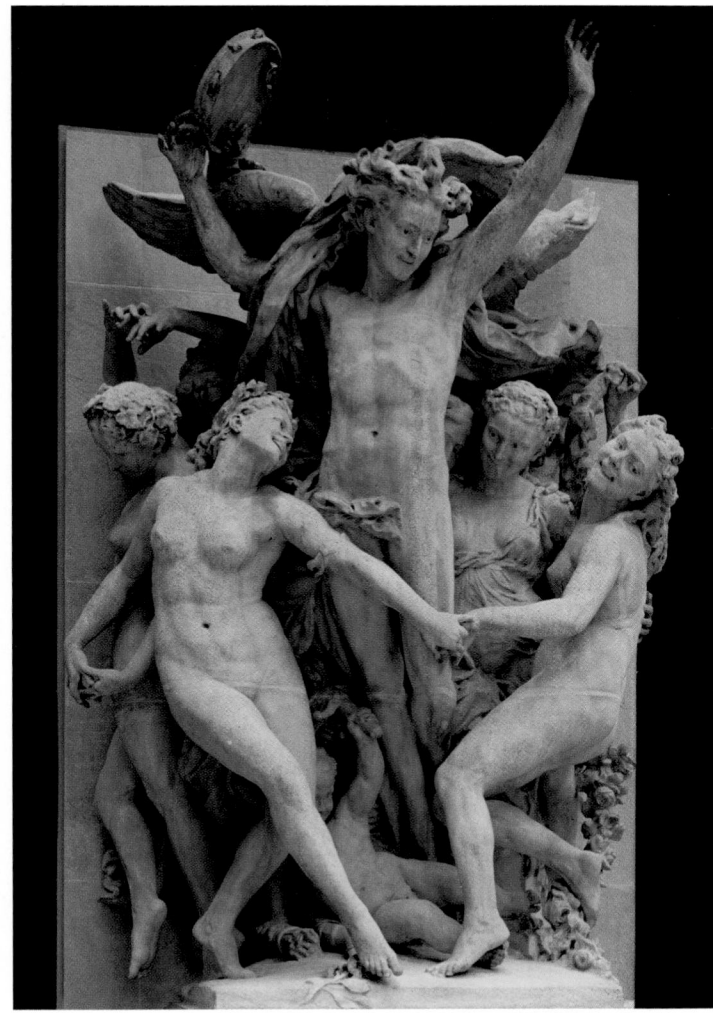

25.8 Jean-Baptiste Carpeaux, *The Dance*. 1867–69. Plaster, 13¾ × 9¾"
(420 × 298 cm). Musée de l'Opéra, Paris

Bouguereau's detailed naturalism, which reflects a Positivist penchant to record. Even Bouguereau's idealized women seem real and not goddesslike, not just because of their naturalistic flesh but also because they are voluptuous—they look more contemporary than Greek or Roman.

Despite upholding the Classical tradition into the twentieth century, Bouguereau is far from being just a standard-bearer of a dying tradition. Besides his remarkable technical finesse, his pictures are distinguished by a powerful psychology—here of erotic abandonment—which will preoccupy artists later in the nineteenth century. His images are often set against a backdrop of nature, reinforcing the expression of elemental desires and reflecting the period's desire to escape from the complex world of urbanization and industrialization to simpler times of Arcadian and rural retreats.

Sculpture remained tied to the Classical tradition and similarly often focused on the female nude. One of the outstanding sculptors from the period was Jean-Baptiste Carpeaux (1827–1875), and among his best-known works is *The Dance* (fig. **25.8**), one of four marbles commissioned in 1867 for the public façade of the new Paris Opéra, each sculpture representing a component of

opera as an art form. In the plaster model reproduced here—which is livelier and more precise than the finished marble—Dance is represented by an erect, winged allegorical male, who serves as an erotic maypole around which gleeful, well-proportioned bacchantes worshipfully prance. The satyr lurking under Dance's cape underscores the licentious intentions of their ritualistic play, which is presented within a more serious, artistic concept of dance.

When *The Dance* was unveiled in 1869, critics panned it, declaring that the figures looked drunk, vulgar, and indecent. The naturalism certainly makes the dancers look undressed rather than nude; we see elbows, kneecaps, and rolls of flesh on bodies that Canova (see fig. 23.30) would have presented perfectly smooth. While the figures may evoke antiquity, they do not look quite Greek or Roman but rather Second Empire. Within a year, however, eyes had adjusted to Carpeaux's naturalism and the egregiously erotic work was hailed as a great monument in the Classical tradition.

Because of its dynamic Baroque composition and excessiveness (too much flesh, too much mirth), *The Dance* was a perfect complement for its setting, the Opéra (fig. **25.9**) designed by Charles Garnier (1825–1898), which was built from 1861 to 1874 and shared the same qualities. The Opéra has become an emblem of the opulence and extravagance of the Second Empire, reflecting the pretentious taste of the bourgeois audience that patronized the academic or Classical tradition. The building was a lynchpin in Haussmann's design for Paris, the dramatic focal point for the Avenue de l'Opéra, as well as the hub for several other major arteries.

The Opéra marks the extension of nineteenth-century revival styles to the Baroque, rivaling the Classical and Gothic revivals before 1860. With the double-columned colonnade Garnier suggests Perrault's Louvre (see fig. 21.11), thereby putting Louis

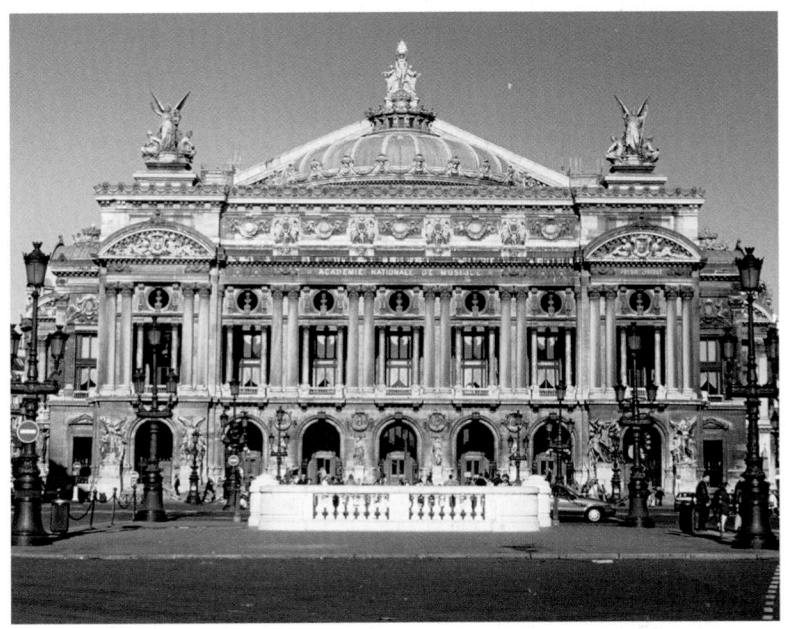

25.9 Charles Garnier. The Opéra, Paris. 1861–74

Napoleon in a line of descent from Louis XIV. The segmented arches springing from the columns at either end of the façade recall Lescot's Square Court of the Louvre (see fig. 18.2). The endless variety of colors and textures, the dazzling accretion of sculpture and decoration, and the extensive borrowing and recombining of architectural forms from the Renaissance and the Baroque—just the sheer density of *everything*—resulted in an opulent, ostentatious style that paralleled the materialistic conspicuous consumption of the period and appealed to *nouveau riche* tastes, although it was disdained by the old-moneyed aristocracy. The focal point of the interior was a dramatic grand staircase, which served as a stage on which high society paraded in order to be seen.

ÉDOUARD MANET Manet's *The Luncheon on the Grass* (fig. 25.10) was a condemnation of bourgeois values and academic taste as well as a statement of what art should be about—the modern world. Manet himself came from a Parisian bourgeois background, and studied with a famous academician, Thomas Couture (1815–1879). His true masters were the painterly artists he copied at the Louvre—Hals, Titian, Velázquez, and Goya. He was a regular at the cafés, befriending Courbet, who was his role model, as well as Baudelaire and the Realist novelist and art critic Émile Zola (1840–1902). Like many Realist writers and artists, Manet was a *flâneur*, a social type that surfaced as early as the 1830s, when the physiology pamphlets began appearing. The *flâneur* was an impeccably dressed man with perfect manners who kept abreast of current events through newspapers and gossip. His day

was spent inconspicuously strolling the streets of Paris and observing the fleeting moments of modern life, which he then translated into a painted or written image. The *flâneur* was witty and gregarious and delighted in shocking the bourgeois. Manet's close friend Baudelaire ranks among the most famous *flâneurs* of the period.

Out of this background Manet produced the *Luncheon*, which shows two couples picnicking in the Bois de Boulogne. The painting was rejected by the 1863 Salon jurors. But that year the jurors rejected a record number of artists, causing such a popular outcry that Louis Napoleon declared there would be a *Salon des Refusés* (*Salon of the Refused*), to be held in a separate building but in conjunction with the official Salon of 1863. Many of the rejected artists preferred not to participate in what was perceived as an inferior exhibition. Manet, however, did take part.

The public showed up in record numbers to laugh at the rejects, and especially to view Manet's *Luncheon*, which was front-page news in the papers. *Luncheon* created a scandal by presenting a contemporary scene of a naked woman in a park with two nattily dressed men. The public was outraged, for obviously the nude had to be a prostitute. It did not matter that critics acknowledged that the painting was inspired by the well-known Renaissance *Fête Champêtre* (see fig. 16.30) in the Louvre, which similarly presented a nude seated with two dressed men. One writer even correctly recognized that the seated group exactly replicates the poses of river-gods in a print of about 1520 by Marcantonio Raimondi after Raphael's *The Judgment of Paris* (see fig. 16.28). No mention was made, however, that the woman in a

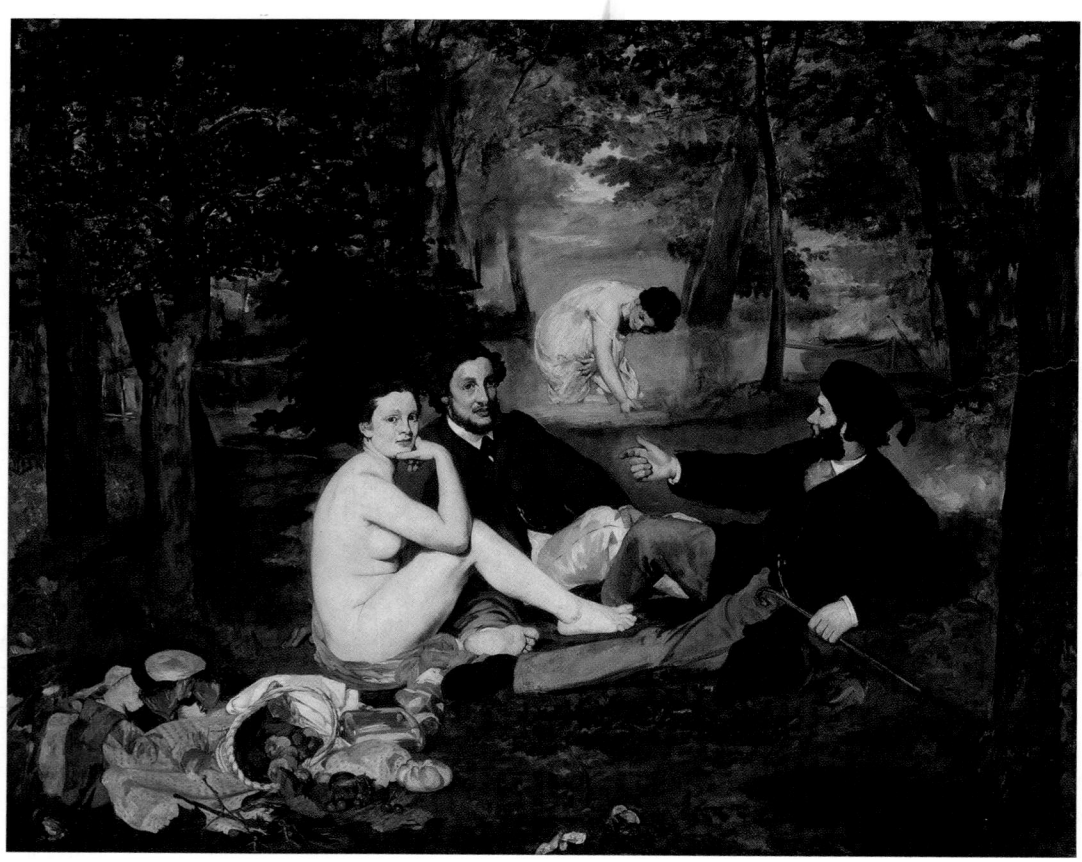

25.10 Édouard Manet, *The Luncheon on the Grass* (*Le Déjeuner sur l'Herbe*). 1863. Oil on canvas, 7' × 8'10" (2.13 × 2.69 m). Musée du Louvre, Paris

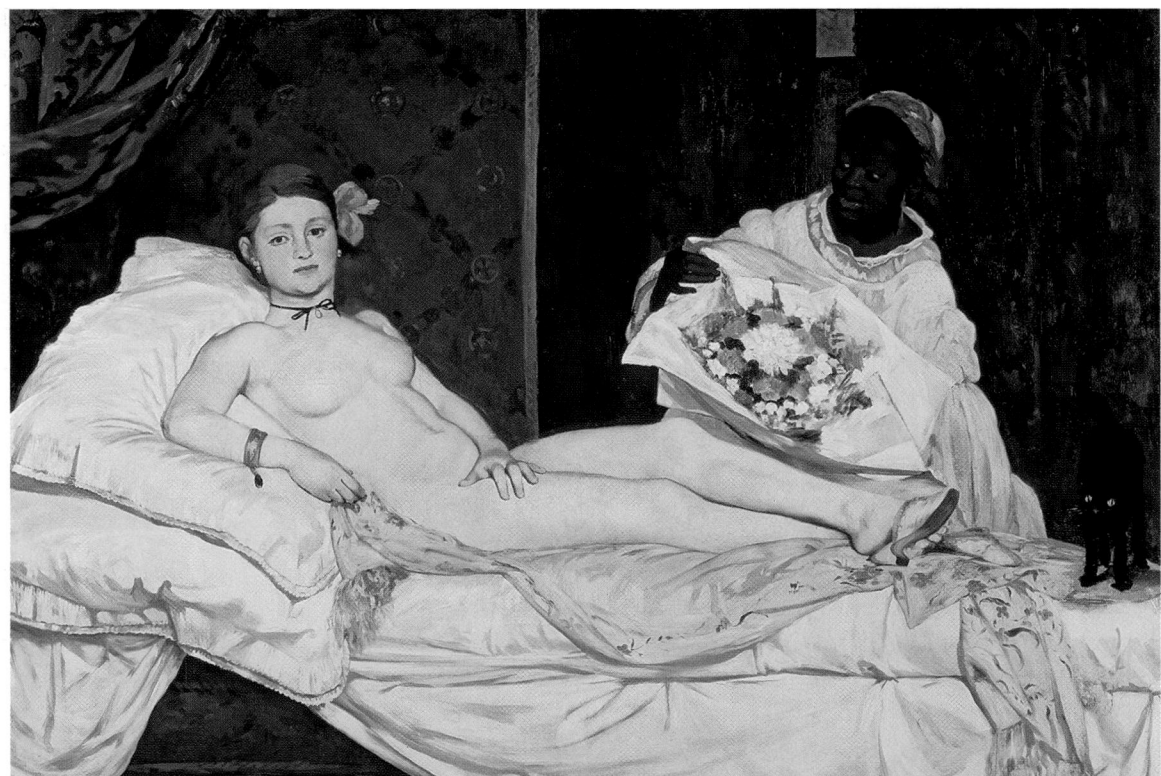

shift in the background is based on Watteau's *The Bather*, also in the Louvre. In fact, Manet originally used this title for his painting.

As far as the critics were concerned, referencing these august sources was not enough to justify Manet's flagrant lack of decorum, a crime he brazenly committed on a canvas roughly 7 by 9 feet, a scale generally reserved for history painting. So, why did Manet base his contemporary scene on historical sources? The answer may lie in the seemingly deliberate artificiality of his figures. As pointed out by one art historian, they look like École des Beaux-Arts students posing to re-create a famous painting. In effect, Manet is telling us the present cannot live in the past, which many academicians chose to do. As trumpeted by Baudelaire in 1846, Manet was declaring that artists must find their subject matter, their heroes, in the modern world. Furthermore, he was exposing the disguised eroticism that the tradition of the Classical nude had now stooped to. It is possible that Manet also used historical sources as a device to put himself into the long tradition of great art. In effect, he is announcing that his Realism is not only the most valid direction for art to take, but in addition that it is as important and vital as the great art of the past.

What convinced the jurors and public that Manet was an incompetent sensationalist who deserved to be relegated to the *Salon des Refusés* was his style. To their academically focused eyes, he could neither model nor create convincing space. The picture looked like a preliminary sketch, not a finished picture. The figures are two-dimensional cutouts, flattened by their crisp, silhouetting contours and a flourish of broad brushstrokes that dispense with the halftones between dark and light needed to mold volume—a shadow indicating a fold on a pant's leg, for example,

is rendered with one bold, black sweep of the brush. Cogent space is upended by making the woman wading in the background too large for her recessed location so that she seems to float over the seated group in front of her. All of the objects—figures, trees, the colorful still life of clothes and basket—hover in space, failing to connect and assemble into a coherent spatial structure.

Manet has undermined the order of the illusionistic Renaissance window and replaced it with a new unifying logic— a sensual sea of brushwork composed of lush, oily, and thickly applied paint that dramatically covers the entire surface of his canvas. Our eyes delight in the lusciousness of his brushwork, the wonderful variety of his Velázquez- and Goya-inspired blacks, the range of greens in the grass, and the deft play of darks next to lights that makes our eyes jump from one light area to another and from one dark patch to the next. These abstract qualities— paint handling and value contrasts, for example—are the new structure of painting, not illusionistic space and modeling. With *The Luncheon on the Grass*, Manet began what twentieth-century critics would consider the Modernist tradition, a tradition that emphasized the abstract qualities of art and that would continue for the next 100 years. Manet undoubtedly delighted in how the unfinished, sketchy look of his paintings irreverently countered the slick drawing and modeling of the academic tradition and shocked bourgeois taste. Additionally, he used it to create a sense of dynamic energy and of the momentary that reflected the quickly changing modern world, the world captured by the *flâneur*'s perspicacious eye.

Surprisingly, Manet was accepted into the Salon of 1865, for his *Olympia* (fig. **25.11**), painted in 1863, is unequivocally a courtesan, a prostitute with a wealthy, upper-class clientele. This nude, based on Titian's *Venus of Urbino* (see fig. 17.35), is the Second Empire gentleman's idea of a modern-day goddess, and everyone in Paris knew it, since Olympia was a common name adopted by powerful courtesans and kept women. With its Classical ring, the name was also a sly attack on the allegorical veiling of erotic nudes that appeared in the Salons.

Manet's *Olympia* portrays a reality of contemporary Paris: Many wealthy men—the same ones who bought academic nudes for their eroticism, not for their smokescreen Classicism—kept mistresses and visited prostitutes. Unlike Titian's Venus, Manet's Olympia is more real than idealized—she is angular, awkward, and harsh rather than voluptuously curvilinear. Furthermore, she is all business, returning our gaze with a daringly confident stare, a power stare that made men uncomfortable and fulfilled their worst fears of controlling, independent women. She engages the viewer in a way rarely seen in genre painting, reflecting Manet's interest in the new Parisian social mobility, the interaction of classes, and the importance of money and commodities in contemporary life.

EDGAR DEGAS AND JAPONISME Like Manet, Edgar Degas (1834–1917) came from a wealthy background, his father heading up the Paris branch of a family bank. And like Manet, he was something of a *flâneur*, although too much of a recluse to be considered a full-blown one. Initially he aspired to be a history painter. An admirer of Ingres, Degas emphasized drawing and modeling in his early work. By 1865, he had entered Manet and Baudelaire's orbit at the Café Guerbois, and now he turned to capturing modern Paris in his work. He developed a Manet-inspired painterly approach to his subject matter, as well as innovative compositional devices that give his images a spontaneous, transitory quality. Furthermore, he put a viewer in the voyeuristic position of the unobserved *flâneur*. Now he started painting the new Haussmann boulevards, the millinery shops, Longchamp racetrack, café concerts, opera, bars, cafés, and ballet dancers at the Opéra. His sharp eye captured types from all levels of society, from the bourgeoisie and performers, to the socially marginalized and the working class.

A classic work from the 1860s is *The Orchestra of the Paris Opéra* (fig. **25.12**). The painting began as a portrait of the bassoonist, in the center foreground, but was extended to include the other musicians and the dancers onstage. Essentially the picture is a genre scene of the orchestra pit, an unusual subject for a painting, although a precedent had been created by Daumier. Yet the subject here is not just the talented, toiling performers but the intensity, excitement, and fragmentation of contemporary life itself, which is presented in a matter-of-fact way. Degas has put us virtually in the pit, and we feel like unobserved voyeurs. Our view is not head-on but at an angle, which is unusual for a painting but certainly typical for a theatergoer. The bass violinist is arbitrarily cropped on the right, suggesting we are looking at the left side of the orchestra, seeing only a fragment of a complete view. The same is true of the ballet dancers, whose heads and legs are chopped off. X-rays have revealed that Degas cut the painting down at the top and sides after finishing it in order to further fragment the image.

Building on this energy are the planes of the wall, the stage, the front row of the orchestra, and the ballet dancers, all of which are slightly skewed, along with the angular thrust of the instruments and dancers' legs and arms. Space seems compressed, as far and near are dramatically juxtaposed, for example in the dark head of the bass and brightly colored tutus. The image seems to climb up the picture plane rather than recede in space. A precise line, retained from Degas's academic studies, still outlines figures and objects, but a sporadic spray of dashing brushwork, readily seen in the dancers' tutus, adds spontaneity and a fragmentary quality, giving us a feeling of the fleeting moment.

Scholars often attribute Degas's innovative compositions to the influence of Japanese prints, which flooded the Parisian market in the late 1850s. In 1853, American Commodore Matthew Perry steamed into Tokyo Bay with four warships and forced Japan to open its doors to the West after two centuries of isolation. By the early 1860s, the world was saturated with Japanese products. Fans, vases, kimonos, lacquer cabinets, folding screens,

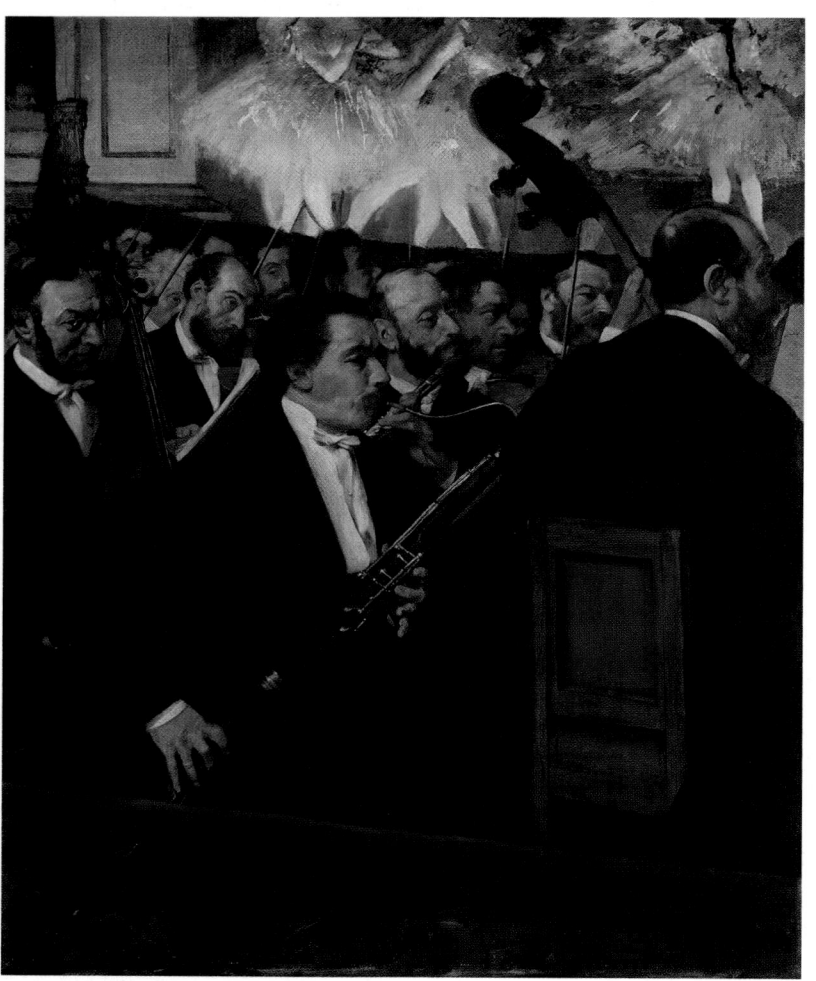

25.12 Edgar Degas, *The Orchestra of the Paris Opéra*. 1868–69. Oil on canvas, 22¼ × 18³⁄₁₆" (56.5 × 46.2 cm). Musée d'Orsay, Paris

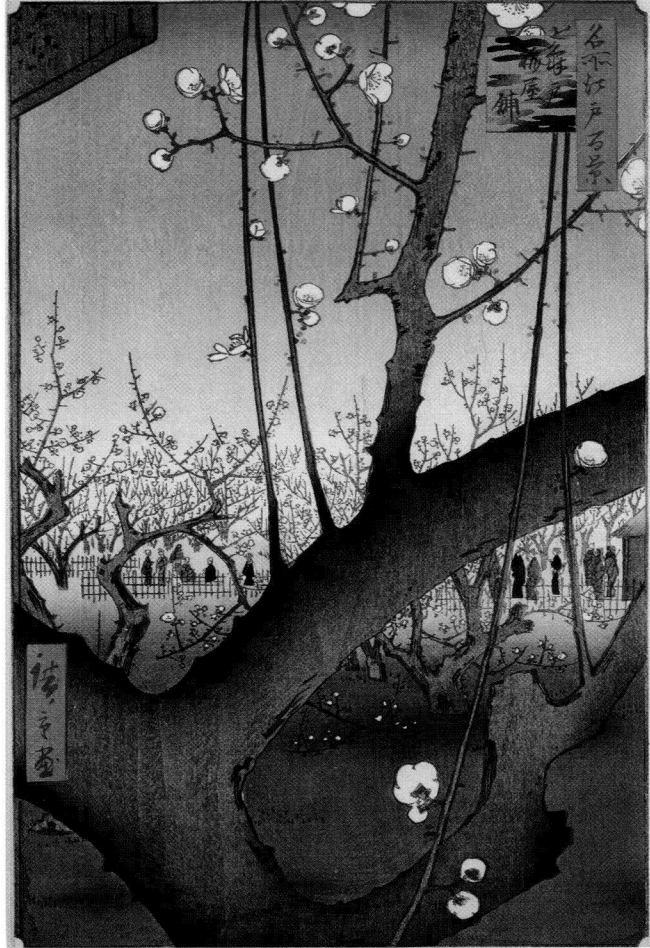

25.13 Andō Hiroshige, *Plum Estate, Kameido*, from the series *One Hundred Famous Views of Edo*. 1857. Woodblock print, 13⅜ × 8⅝" (34 × 22.6 cm). Brooklyn Museum of Art, New York. Gift of Anna Ferris. 30.1478.30

Impressionism: A Different Form of Realism

The label "Impressionism" was coined by a hostile conservative critic in 1874 when reviewing the first exhibition of an artists' collaborative called the *Société Anonyme des Artistes* (best translated as "Artists, Inc."). We now refer to that show as the first Impressionist exhibition (there would be eight altogether between 1874 and 1886). Like the general public, the writer found the paintings so sketchy that he felt they were just impressions, not finished paintings. Actually, the word impression had already been applied to the Realism of Manet and Degas. It appears in the title of an oil by Claude Monet of the harbor at Le Havre, which he exhibited in the first Impressionist exhibition and called *Impression, Sunrise* (see fig. 25.15) and Monet used the term on occasion when explaining his ideas on art to friends. (See *Primary Source*, page 872.)

Impressionism shares with the Realism of Manet and Degas a sketchy unfinished look, a feeling of the moment, and a desire to appear modern. It also presents its subjects matter-of-factly. Many scholars even apply the term Impressionism to the work of Manet and Degas, in part to distinguish their Realism from the earthy, rural Realism of Courbet and Millet and to indicate how Impressionism often shares with them a sense of the urbane and the modern. Like Manet and Degas, the Impressionists were interested in recording the transformations occurring in French society, especially the leisure activities of the *nouveau riche*. While they, too, painted city scenes and genre, they focused more on the evolution of the sleepy rural villages surrounding Paris into bustling suburbs containing factories, commercial wharves, and railroad trestles, on the one hand, and restaurants, regattas, and boating for Parisian weekenders on the other. Rather than the figure, the Impressionists focused more on landscape and cityscape, and instead of constructing their compositions in the studio using models, they worked empirically, outdoors, where they recorded the landscape and weather conditions that they witnessed as an evanescent moment. They painted not so much objects as the colored light that reflected off them. In effect, they painted what they saw, not what they knew.

CLAUDE MONET The leader in developing Impressionism was Claude Monet (1840–1926), who was raised in Le Havre in Normandy. He studied with an accomplished local landscape painter, Eugène Boudin (1824–1898), who worked outdoors. But in order to get financial support from his grocer father, Monet was forced to study in Paris, and chose the academically minded but liberal painter Charles Gleyre. In the latter's studio he met Auguste Renoir, who along with the much older Camille Pissarro would form the core of the Impressionists. In the early 1860s, Monet was forced to serve in the army in Algeria, and like Delacroix before him (see page 847), he experienced intense light and color that were foreign to the cloud-covered temperate Normandy coast. Throughout the 1860s, Monet and his friends painted the landscape surrounding Paris, meeting Corot and the Barbizon artists, who further encouraged their working outdoors

jewelry, and tea services were common items in most fashionable Western homes. The French were especially taken by Japanese culture, and their infatuation was called **Japonisme**, a term also used by the British and Americans. The most popular display at the 1867 Universal Exposition in Paris was the Japanese pavilion. Especially intriguing for artists were Japanese prints, works that first arrived in France as packing material for fragile objects but that were being collected by the late 1850s by the artists in Manet's circle, who found them visually fascinating.

As can be seen in *Plum Estate, Kameido* (fig. **25.13**) by Andō Hiroshige (1797–1858), Japanese image making was quite foreign to a Western way of seeing. Forms are flat with sharp contours, while space is compressed, the foreground pressed up against the viewer's nose, the background pulled right into the foreground space. There is no transition between near and far. Just the concept of situating a viewer in a tree from which to see the main activity miniaturized in the distance would have been radical to the eye of a Western artist. However, the flat contours, abrupt cropping, and spatial contraction of Japanese prints certainly influenced Degas and Manet, although in a far from obvious manner and never approaching direct copying.

Lila Cabot Perry (1848?–1933)

From "Reminiscences of Claude Monet from 1889 to 1909"

Perry was an American expatriate painter working in France in an Impressionist vein. Monet did not publicly theorize about art, and Perry's statement gives us one of the best insights into his ideas.

He never took any pupils, but he would have made a most inspiring master if he had been willing to teach. I remember his once saying to me:

"When you go out to paint, try to forget what objects you have before you—a tree, a house, a field, or whatever. Merely think, here is a little square of blue, here an oblong of pink, here a streak of yellow, and paint it just as it looks to you, the exact color and shape, until it gives your own naïve impression of the scene before you."...

He held that the first real look at the motif was likely to be the truest and most unprejudiced one, and said that the first painting should cover as much of the canvas a possible, no matter how roughly, so as to determine at the outset the tonality of the whole. ...

Monet's philosophy of painting was to paint what you really see, not what you think you ought to see; not the object isolated as in a test tube, but the object enveloped in sunlight and atmosphere, with the blue dome of Heaven reflected in the shadows.

Source: *The American Magazine of Art*, March 18, 1927

---

directly from nature. For Monet and his colleagues, however, these plein-air (outdoor) paintings were not small studies but large finished products. Painting rapidly with bold brushwork, they sought to capture light (and the color it carried) as it bounced off objects. Unlike Manet, who added oil to his store-bought paints to make them unctuous, Monet added none or very little, leaving them chalky and allowing color to supersede the plasticity of the paint. Nor did he varnish his finished oils, which would diminish their color. Monet's extensive use of primary and secondary colors, the principal hues on the traditional color wheel, was in part influenced by recent scientific research about color that demonstrated that the intensity of complementary colors (e.g., blue and orange, red and green, and yellow and violet) is increased when they are placed next to one another. (See *Materials and Techniques*, page 874.)

We can see the effectiveness of Monet's palette in *On the Bank of the Seine, Bennecourt* (fig. **25.14**), painted in 1868 in a village not unlike the many Seine and Oise river locations that Parisians took the train to on summer weekends and where the more affluent built impressive villas alongside rural cottages. The artist works with glaring sun-drenched whites and bright blues and greens accented with touches of red and yellow. Objects in shadow, such as leaves and grass, retain color and do not go black. Browns are not muddy but a light-filled tan. Monet maintains the strength of his colors by keeping the imagery close to the picture plane, not allowing it to suggest depth. As with Manet, there is no

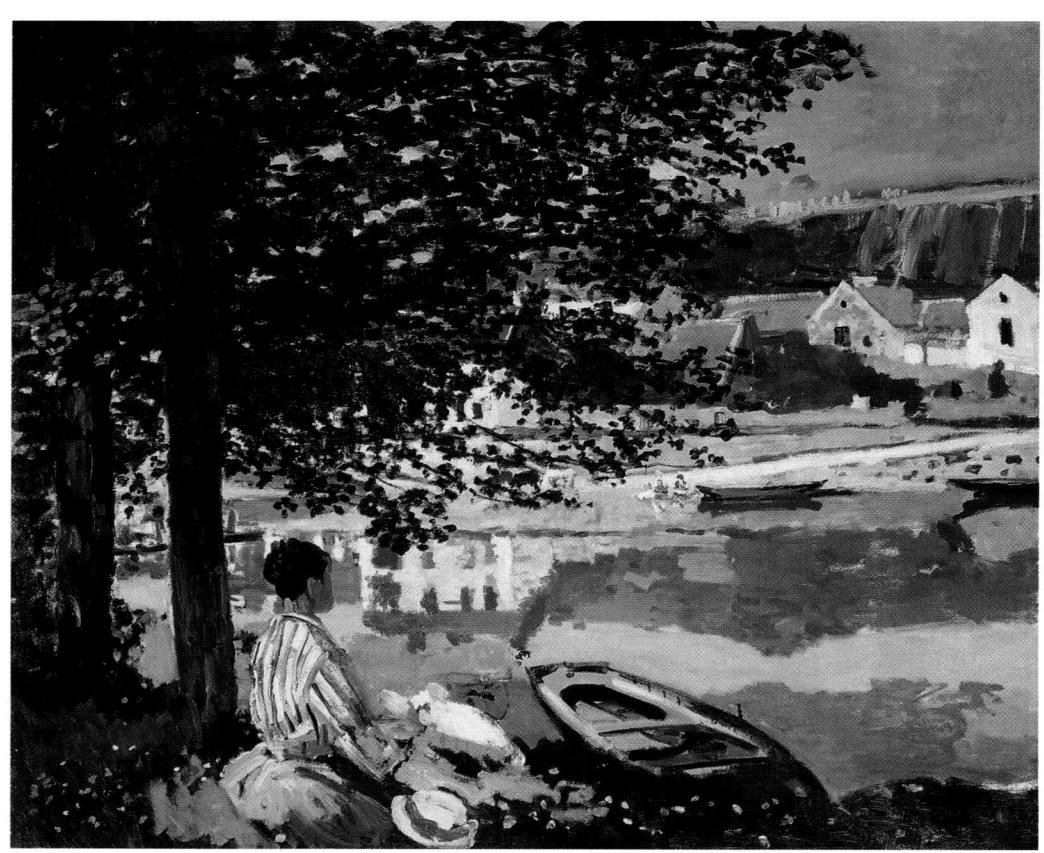

25.14 Claude Monet, *On the Bank of the Seine, Bennecourt*. 1868. Oil on canvas, 32⅛ × 39⅝" (81.6 × 100.7 cm). The Art Institute of Chicago. Mr. and Mrs. Potter Palmer Collection. 1922.427

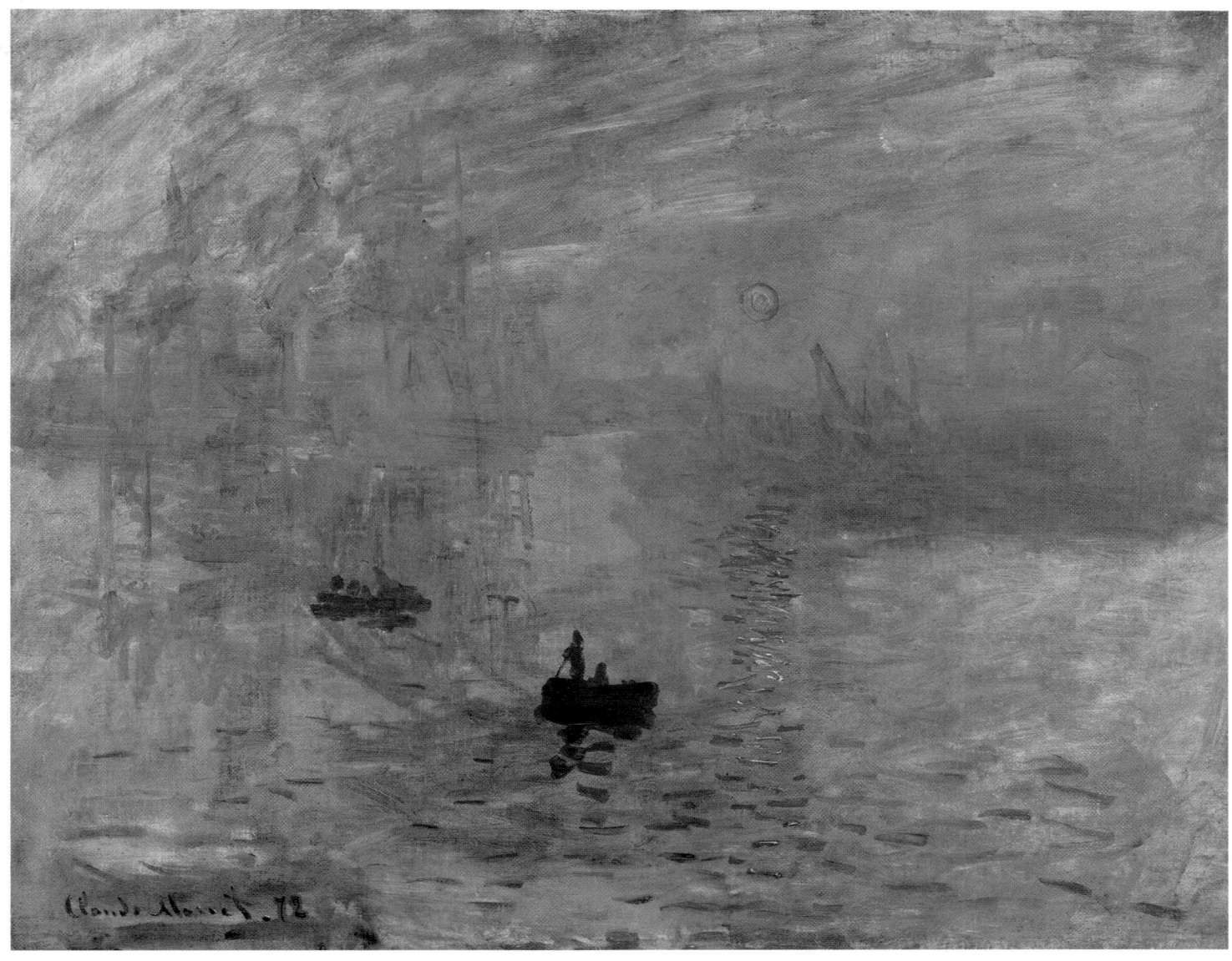

25.15 Claude Monet, *Impression, Sunrise*. 1872. Oil on canvas, 48 × 63" (122 × 160 cm). Formerly Musée Marmottan (stolen)

chiaroscuro to model forms. The tree foliage is a two-dimensional silhouette, while the blue sky behind is equally flat. The reflection of the house on the water runs up and down the picture plane, reinforcing the two-dimensionality of the broad smears of light and dark blue in the river just below. The solid blue sky is virtually the same shade as the darker blue in the water, a correlation that momentarily pulls the sky to the foreground. The only motif that suggests depth is the rowboat running diagonally back in perspective. Also asserting the surface of the canvas is Monet's bold, variegated brushwork, which changes character from one object to the next and gives the picture a shimmering quality that suggests we are witnessing a split second in time.

Equally important, contemporaries realized the brushwork represented the unstable, rapidly changing qualities of modern life. These pictures looked nothing like previous landscapes; they lacked the Classical look of Claude Lorrain, the Baroque conventions of the Dutch landscape painters and their earthy palette, and the emotional constructions of the Romantics. Their very appearance

was considered modern, as was their subject matter. We can safely assume that the fashionably dressed woman (Monet's wife) is meant to represent a vacationing Parisian who has been boating.

If in a work like *On the Bank* Monet painted with a range of colors, he was also capable of restricting his palette, as *in Impression, Sunrise* (fig. **25.15**) of 1872, the work that spawned the name of the Impressionist movement. In this fog-shrouded view of the harbor at Le Havre in the early morning, we see Monet basically using only two colors, the complements blue and orange. Blue prevails, defining water and ships with their tall masts, while orange is restricted to the rising sun, the fiery sky, and reflections on the water. Instead of a symphony of color, we now get a single powerful note of orange playing off the blue ground. Monet titled the picture *Impression* instead of naming it after the port because, as he himself said, "it really couldn't pass for a view of Le Havre." Sunrises and sunsets were popular themes with artists and were prevalent at the Salons, but they were usually dramatic Romantic events set in a landscape or over

Impressionist Color Theory

Impressionism was more than just the result of a Realist premise based on spontaneously and empirically capturing color and light on canvas. Scientific discoveries, technical developments, and mundane practicalities also went into the evolution of the style. One of these was the development of the theory of color by chemist Michel-Eugène Chevreul (1786–1889) that appeared in his 1839 book *The Principles of Harmony and Contrast of Colors*. Chevreul worked in the dyeing department of the tapestry workshop of Les Gobelins in Paris, and he noticed the intensity of a color was determined not just by the color itself but also by its relationship to a neighboring color. Primary colors (red, yellow, and blue) and secondary colors (green, orange, and violet), which were made by combining two primaries, became stronger when placed next to one another, a relationship he called **simultaneous contrast**. (Tertiary colors combine two secondaries.) Value contrast, placing a light hue next to a dark one, also affected the power of a color. The greatest intensity came from the juxtaposition of complements—red and green, blue and orange, purple and yellow—colors opposite one another on the traditional color wheel. Place a pure green next to a pure red and the red becomes redder and the green greener, the energy of each color escalating to the point where they seem to vibrate and "pop."

Eugène Delacroix was probably the first artist influenced by Chevreul's theories, although he had intuitively developed similar ideas earlier and placed small marks of strong contrasting colors next to one another (see page 847). However, the Impressionists were the first to work principally with primary and secondary color, though their palette was hardly restricted to just these hues. To maintain color intensity, the Impressionists began working on a primed surface that was light, instead of the traditional somber brown or brownish-red ground. Camille Corot pioneered a lighter primed canvas when he started using silver, which helped harmonize his tight palette of greens, silvers, and blues. It is unlikely that any of the Impressionists read Chevreul. But by the 1860s, his theories were common knowledge among many artists interested in color, and in 1867 they were repeated in Charles Blanc's *The Grammar of Painting and Engraving*, along with a discussion of Delacroix's use of simultaneous contrast.

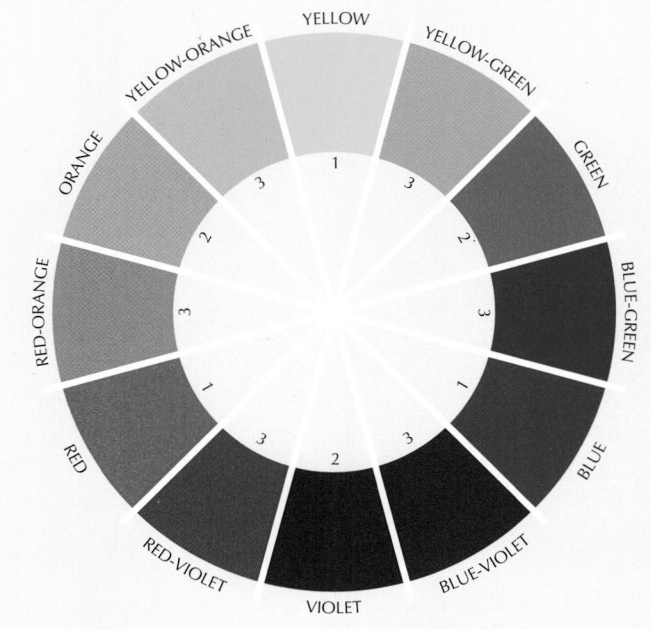

The traditional color wheel

the sea. It is tempting to see Monet satirizing this Romantic nostalgic imagery in his picture, which eulogizes not so much the glory of nature but rather the dynamic rhythms of a large, commercial port.

Monet's quest in the 1860s and 1870s to capture the dramatic changes brought on by industrialization naturally took him to the great urban center of Paris. Here he pictured such modern icons as the Boulevard des Capucines, one of the new Haussmann avenues located near the Opéra and lined with fashionable apartment buildings and shops, and the Gare Saint-Lazare train shed. In 1876–77, Monet made ten paintings of the shed recording the hustle and bustle of travelers, workmen, and trains (fig. **25.16**). It is as though one painting alone was not enough to take in the complexity of energy and activity beneath the glass-covered shed (for a discussion of these train sheds, see page 898), and each view represents a fragment of the constant flux of people, machines, and equipment. Again, we see Monet's variegated brushwork creating a blurry, pulsating world, in which we can make out a workman, passengers, and trains, and on the ground the shadow of the ironwork frame above. In the background, we see a railway trestle (the setting for one of Manet's most famous paintings),

and beyond, the new grand apartment buildings lining a Haussmann boulevard. Monet's haze of color and brushwork softens everything, giving the steel of the tracks, locomotive, columns, and grid of glass roof almost the same ethereal, transitory quality as the charming, blue-shaded puffs of smoke floating upward. The harsh, impersonal, geometric qualities of modernity dissolve in a flood of light and color that virtually transforms this smoke-filled scene of stifling pollution, heat, and noise into a visual paradise.

AUGUSTE RENOIR After meeting and befriending Monet in Gleyre's studio, Auguste Renoir (1841–1919) also developed an Impressionist style employing bright color, bold paint handling, and modern subjects. Often working beside Monet, Renoir painted landscapes. But he was attracted to the figurative tradition as well, and his career straddles the two genres.

Among his best-known genre paintings is *Luncheon of the Boating Party* (fig. **25.17**) of 1881. The picture is set in the Restaurant Fournaise on an island in the Seine at Chatou, a small village 9 miles (14 km) from Paris's Gare Saint-Lazare. Chatou was especially popular with boaters, and restaurants like this

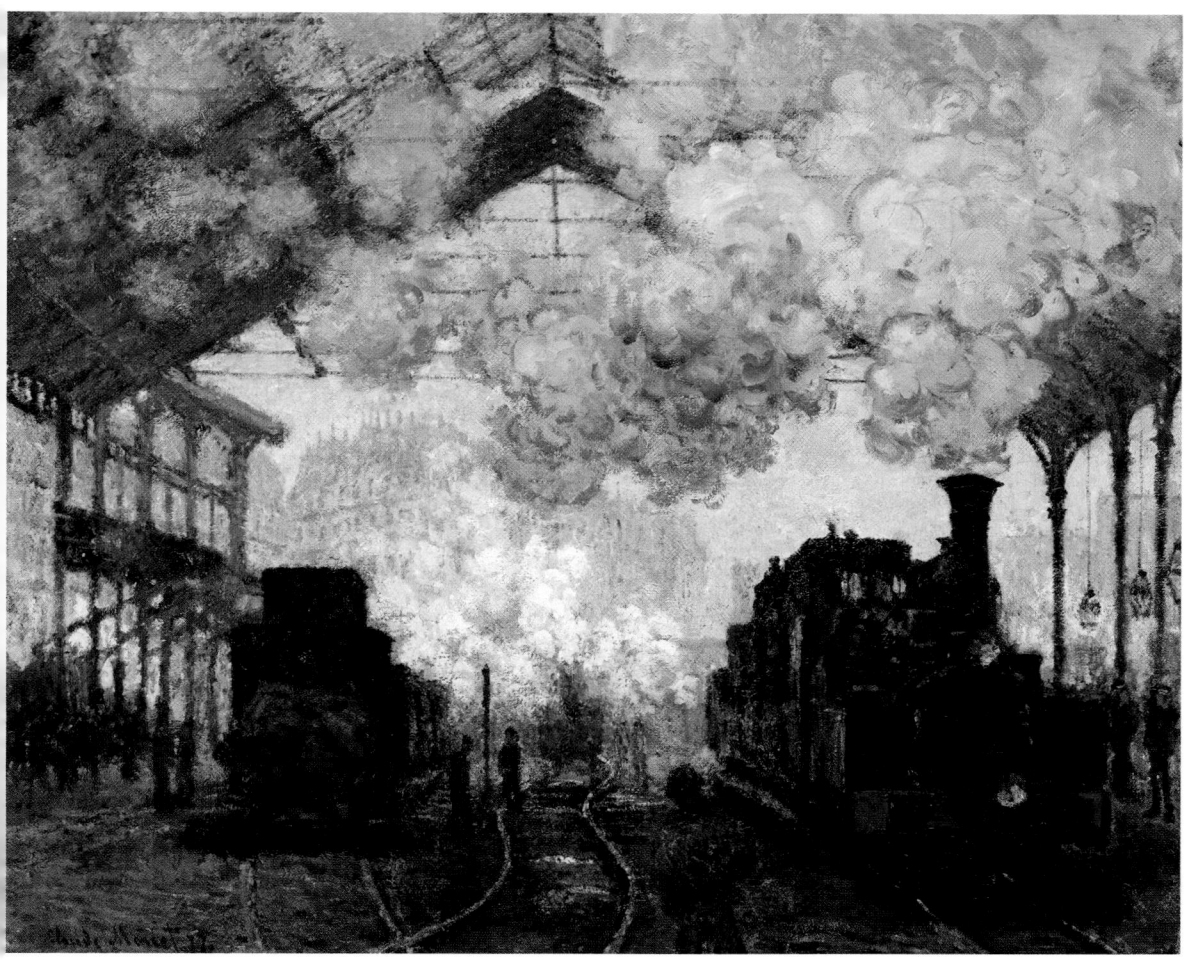

25.16 Claude Monet,
*The Gare Saint-Lazare:
Arrival of a Train*. 1877.
Oil on canvas, 31⅝ × 38⅝"
(83.3 × 102.8 cm).
Harvard Art Museum/Fogg
Art Museum, Bequest from
the Collection of Maurice
Wertheim, Class of 1906,
1951.53

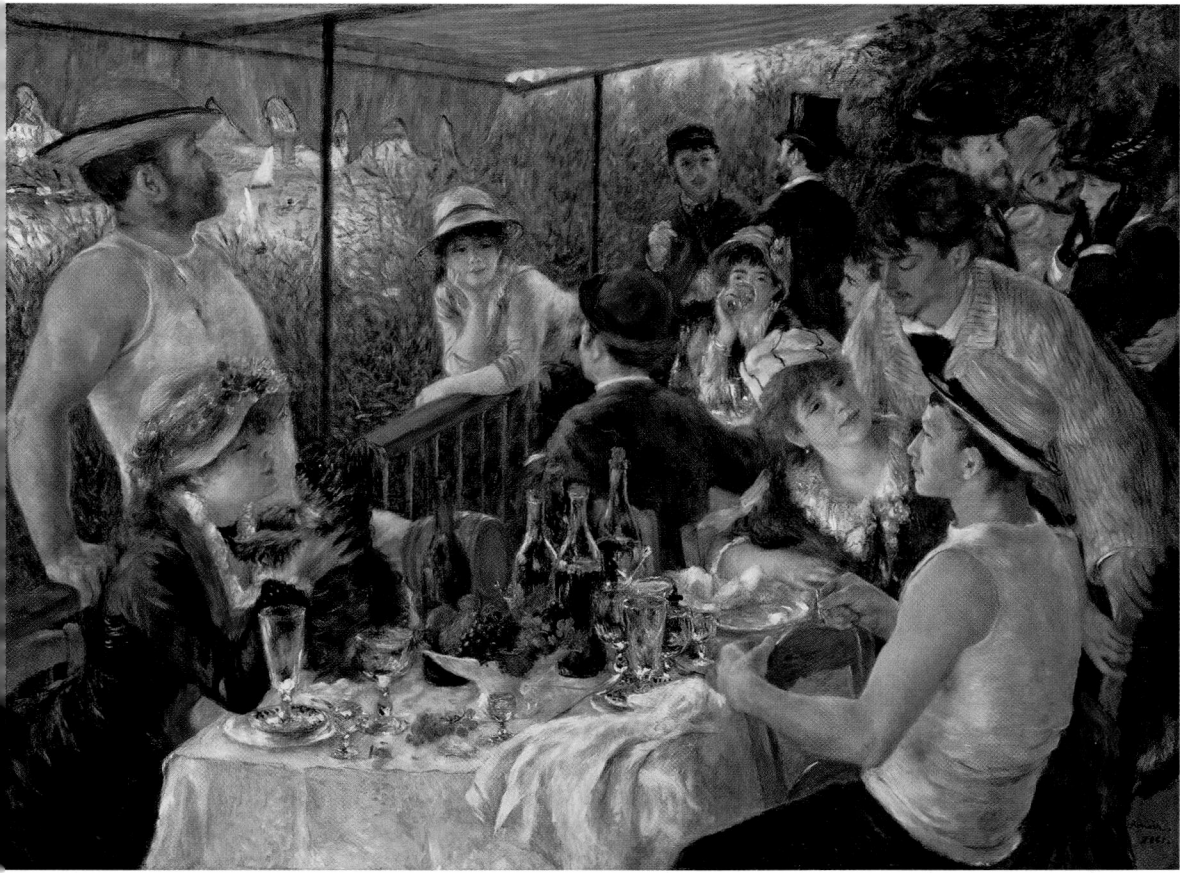

25.17 Auguste Renoir,
*Luncheon of the Boating
Party*. 1881. Oil on canvas,
51 × 68" (130.2 × 175.6 cm).
Acquired 1923.
The Philips Collection,
Washington, D.C.

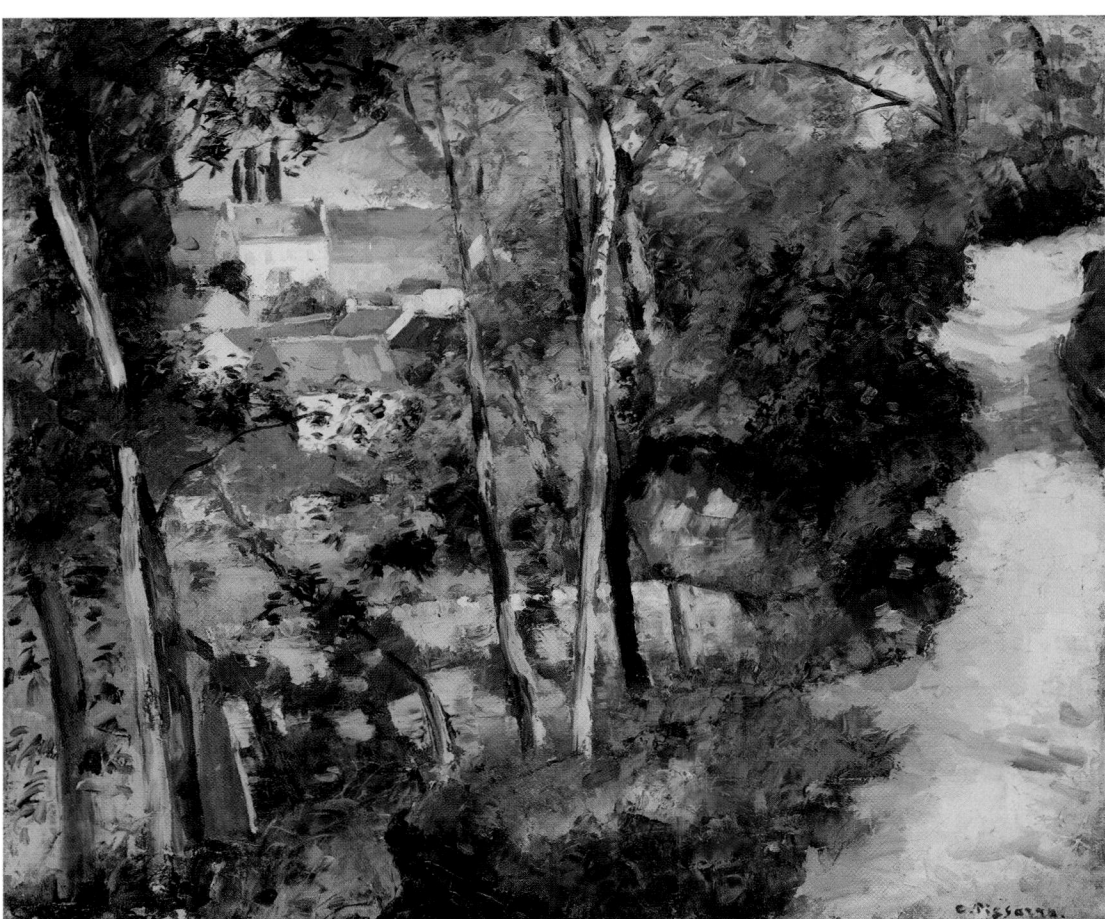

25.18 Camille Pissarro, *Climbing Path, L'Hermitage, Pontoise*. 1875. Oil on canvas, 21⅛ × 25¾" (54 × 65 cm). Brooklyn Museum of Art, New York. Purchased with Funds Given by Dikran K. Kelekian 22.60

catered to Parisians. In the background, on the river, we can just make out sailboats, a rowboat, and a commercial barge. We also get a glimpse of a train bridge.

The restaurant party consists of urban types, with the exception of Alphonese Fournaise, the restaurant owner's son, who leans against the railing, his muscular biceps the result of hauling rental boats into the water. Renoir carefully observes his figures' attire, allowing us to identify each type. The top-hatted man, for example, appears to be more conservative and moneyed (the model was a collector) than the younger men wearing straw boating caps—the models were Renoir's friends. Renoir even presents a range of boating caps, from a citified version worn by the seated figure on the lower right, to a country version on the man on the upper right, to an old-fashioned mariner's cap popular some 20 years earlier, worn by the man to the left of the top-hatted gentleman. The colorful sun-drenched scene of suburban leisure is pleasurable and relaxed, its sensuality enhanced by the lavish spread on the table and the gloriously lush brushwork of the tablecloth. The picture has the momentary quality we associate with Realism, achieved in part by the flickering, feathery brushwork and the asymmetrical composition that runs off the right side of the canvas, the picture being cropped and fragmented like Degas's *The Orchestra of the Paris Opéra*.

Luncheon of the Boating Party was made shortly before Renoir abandoned Impressionism. Renoir, like several of his colleagues, began to believe the critics' claim that the Realists could not draw and that their art lacked the timeless, monumental, and enduring qualities found in the great art of the past. In *Luncheon of the Boating Party*, Renoir began to model his figures and even give distinctive contours to his objects and figures. As we shall see, avant-garde artists in the 1880s would return to many values we associate with Classical art.

CAMILLE PISSARRO Pissarro (1830–1903) was the elder statesman of the Impressionists. A decade older than the others, he came to Paris in 1855 from his native St. Thomas in the Caribbean. During the 1860s, he sought out Corot (see page 847), who advised him, and he also studied the landscapes of Courbet and Charles Daubigny, a famous Barbizon-style artist, who worked outdoors and was especially known for painting landscape from a boat. As much as Pissarro was committed to landscape, he was also dedicated to developing a radical modern art, and by the late 1860s he had arrived at a style that like Monet's was empirical, spontaneous, and used bright color. Unlike Manet, Monet, Degas, and Renoir, he never considered himself a Parisian, and instead lived in the surrounding countryside, which was becoming suburban. While he occasionally painted factories and trains, he was a social anarchist who was dedicated to the people. Peasants and farms, not city dwellers and suburban pleasures, were his preferred subject matter. When in Paris, he socialized with his fellow artists at the Café Guerbois, and not only mentored the younger artists but also served as the arbitrator for Artists, Inc., of which he was a member, participating in all eight exhibitions.

Pissarro was a cautious, intellectual, and deliberate painter, who, like Monet in the 1860s, worked outdoors, where he developed a colorful palette and bold paint handling that captured weather conditions and a sense of fleeting imagery. His compositions were often extremely complex, as seen in *Climbing Path, L'Hermitage, Pointoise* (fig. **25.18**) of 1875, set in Pontoise, a suburb of Paris. Here, in a light-speckled landscape, he places a dense flat screen of trees in front of a deep view back to a village. This peek into the distance is contrasted by the path to the right, which seems to rise up the picture plane rather than recede. While the tree trunks, leaves, and rocks are painted with broad brushwork and bold sweeps of a palette knife that render them as flat, almost abstract objects, the distant houses are constructed in perspective, as dense three-dimensional cubic forms whose solidity contrasts with the flatness of the foreground. While reflecting a Barbizon-style love of nature and rural life, Pissarro simultaneously emphasized the abstract qualities of picture making, playing flat off solid, straight geometric line off unstructured organic forms, or a deep view through flat trees off a trail that rises up the picture plane. As we shall see, Pissarro's complex, highly structured compositions would have an enormous impact on fellow Impressionist Paul Cézanne, who in turn influenced Pablo Picasso and Cubism.

MANET AND IMPRESSIONISM The landscape styles of Monet, Renoir, and Pissarro resembled one another the most from the late 1860s to the mid-1870s. However, what is called the first Impressionist exhibition in 1874 was not designed to promote a particular style or artistic movement, although most of the 36 artists could be described as painterly and often used bright color, many of them working *en plein air*. Rather, the exhibition was meant to provide an alternative to the annual Salons. Degas, who participated in most of the exhibitions and was one of the most vociferous in promoting them, repeatedly disclaimed being an Impressionist. His lack of emphasis on color and light certainly separates him from the core group. Manet never exhibited with the Impressionists, holding out for Salon recognition and acceptance into the academy. By the early 1870s, however, he had adopted Impressionist color, and in 1873 was painting outdoors next to Monet in Argenteuil, just outside of Paris, although his paint application remained unctuous and his colors were never quite as intense.

We can see this more colorful palette in his last great Realist masterpiece, *A Bar at the Folies-Bergère* (fig. **25.19**), of 1881–82. Typical of Manet, the picture is rich in ideas and filled with references and hidden meanings, qualities generally not found in Realism or Impressionism. Manet has painted a second-floor bar, overlooking the main floor below, above which we can see the legs of a woman on a trapeze entering the picture in the upper left

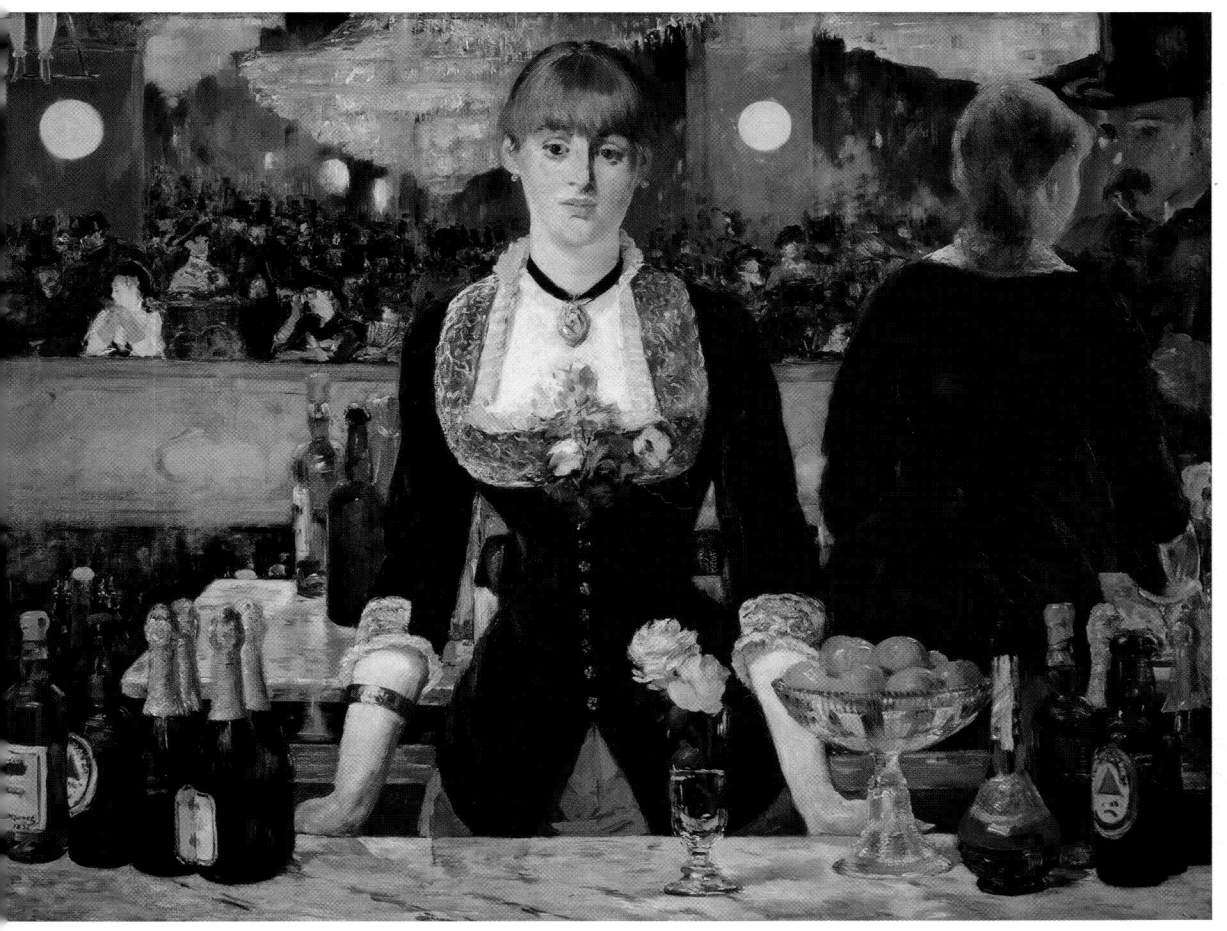

25.19 Édouard Manet, *A Bar at the Folies-Bergère*. 1881–82. Oil on canvas, 37½ × 52" (96 × 130 cm). The Samuel Courtauld Trust, Courtauld Institute of Art Gallery, London. P.1934.SC.234

corner. Most of the image, however, occurs in a mirror, a flat surface, like a painting, that presents an illusion. The illusion reflected behind the barmaid is that modern life is gay and festive. We see the densely packed sparkling interior of the dance hall that virtually symbolized Parisian nightlife at the time. But the barmaid, who is real, not a reflection, looks out at us with a sad blank expression, suggesting alienation, the reality of contemporary urban life. She, too, appears in the mirror, although her image is distorted, as she leans slightly forward and appears active and engaged. The mirror reveals that she has been approached by a dapper top-hatted gentleman, supposedly intent on buying the sensual drink and fruit at the bar. Some historians suggest he is propositioning the barmaid, citing evidence that some barmaids were also prostitutes and that they were as much an attraction of the Folies-Bergère as the entertainment and general conviviality. This theory would certainly account for the distortion of the barmaid in the mirror, suggesting she has two identities or roles. Regardless of the interpretation, this quiet interaction, removed from the festivity in the mirror, reflects the reality of modern life—anonymous, arbitrary encounters and urban alienation. The picture also seems to comment on the materialism pervading contemporary values. The Folies-Bergère was very expensive, catering to the well-to-do, and the remarkable still life on the bar captures the lavish richness of the music hall. But despite the illusion of gaiety in the mirror, an emptiness and sadness fills the picture, evoking the inability of money to buy meaningful happiness. But Manet's pictures are often elaborate puzzles, which generally defy a secure reading, remaining open to wide and controversial interpretation.

BERTHE MORISOT Berthe Morisot (1841–1895) was a key figure in the Impressionist circle. Born into a comfortable Paris family, she and her sister Edna took up painting seriously in the late 1850s. Women were not permitted to attend the École des Beaux-Arts, but the sisters studied independently with minor but supportive and knowledgeable artists. When they gravitated toward landscape in the early 1860s, they sought out Corot, who, struck by the quality of their work, met with them often, even giving them one of his paintings to study. Both Morisots had Corot-like landscapes accepted at the Salon of 1864, and Berthe had a figure painting accepted the following year. Edna married in 1869 and stopped painting, but Berthe continued her artistic career.

As a woman, Morisot could not go to the Café Guerbois. She nonetheless became an intimate of and even a favorite within the avant-garde circle, socializing with Manet, Degas, and other Realists at dinners and *salons*—weekly evening receptions at someone's home, such as the one that Manet's mother hosted. She developed a close friendship with Manet, posing for him in seven paintings and eventually marrying his brother. Morisot's brushwork became looser and her palette brighter. She made landscape and figure paintings, depicting the modern leisure activities of the city, suburbs, and the seashore. Her figures are generally women and children, the models most readily available to her. While her women are fashionably dressed, they are not pretty, frivolous, and mindless; rather, they are meditative and thoughtful, sophisticated, and in control of their image. They are never presented as appendages to men (unlike in Renoir's *Luncheon of the Boating Party*). We sense Morisot defining a woman's world, one that is as valid and meaningful as a man's.

Morisot's pictures are virtually a catalogue of a well-to-do woman's activities: gathering flowers, taking tea, child-rearing, reading, sewing, and vacationing in the suburbs and by the sea. But undoubtedly what impressed Morisot's avant-garde colleagues was her brilliant technique and finesse: Her bold brushwork magically defined figures and objects while creating an

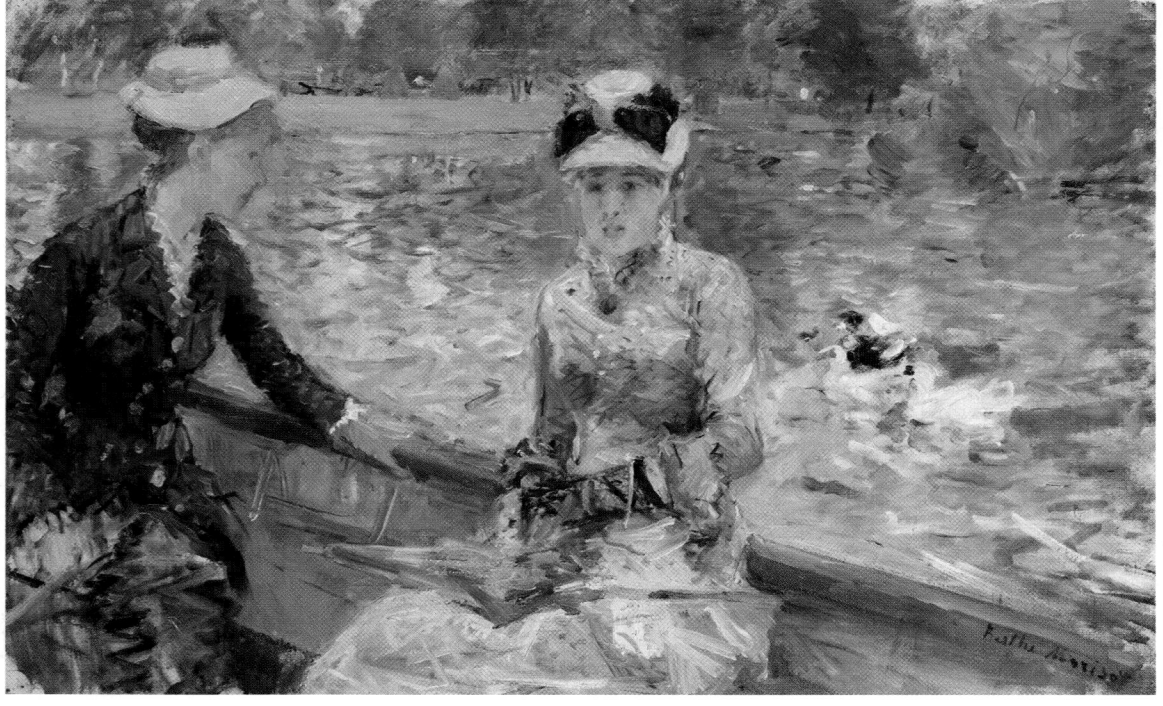

25.20 Berthe Morisot, *Summer's Day (The Lake in the Bois de Boulogne)*. ca. 1879. Oil on canvas, 17¹³⁄₁₆ × 29⁵⁄₁₆" (45.7 × 75.2 cm). The National Gallery, London. Lane Bequest, 1917

abstract tapestry of paint across the surface of the canvas, a deft balancing act that even Manet had to admire. (The hanging committee for her memorial exhibition at the Durand-Ruel gallery in 1894 consisted of Monet, Degas, and Renoir.) We can see her painterly brilliance in *Summer's Day (The Lake in the Bois de Boulogne)* (fig. **25.20**), which presents the classic Realist/Impressionist theme of a leisure activity taking place at a trendy venue. Typical of Morisot, the fashionably dressed figures do not interact, but instead are deep in thought, or perhaps are even regarding the scene like a *flâneur*, which was then generally considered the prerogative of a man, not a woman. While the palette is closer to Manet's and Corot's than to Monet's, the scene is a summer's day with light flickering off objects. Morisot enhances the spontaneity created with her brushmarks by using the sort of asymmetrical, cropped composition first developed by Degas.

MARY CASSATT Like Morisot, Mary Cassatt (1844–1926) approached Impressionism from a woman's perspective, her Realism reflecting the social concerns developing within the women's movement of her time. Cassatt was an American. She trained at the Pennsylvania Academy of Art in Philadelphia, where her wealthy family moved from Pittsburg, in part to support her career as an artist, a most unusual attitude for the time. In 1866, she went to Paris and studied with the renowned academician Jean-Léon Gérôme. She also studied in Parma and Rome before returning to Paris in 1874, where she spent the remainder of her life. In Paris, she befriended Degas and abandoned her academic style for Realism. Invited by Degas, she participated in the fourth Impressionist exhibition in 1879. Now, she displayed a bright palette, strong brushwork that hugged the surface, and the compositional devices of asymmetry and cropping.

Like Degas and Manet, Cassatt was a figure painter, and her most famous themes from the late 1870s include women in *loges* at the opera, a subject also treated by Renoir and Degas. She also painted women at home: reading, visiting, taking tea, sewing, or bathing an infant. Like Morisot, she presents the modern sophisticated woman in dress, manners, and leisure activities. In the 1880s, she abandoned her *loge* theme and focused increasingly on domestic scenes, especially of women and children.

Scholars often attribute Cassatt's subject matter to the restrictions she faced as a female: As a respectable woman, she could not go unattended to the same places as her male counterparts. But more at issue was her belief in the importance of women in society, even if this importance was largely restricted to the home. Her views coincided with developments then occurring in the women's movement. In 1878, the International Congress of Women's Rights was held in Paris, and at the top of its agenda was the need for better education for women, which would mean free and compulsory education through secondary school; France enacted this as law in the 1880s. Education would not only allow women to become professionals but also to better manage their homes and families. The congress also focused on the important role that women played in nurturing children, advocating that

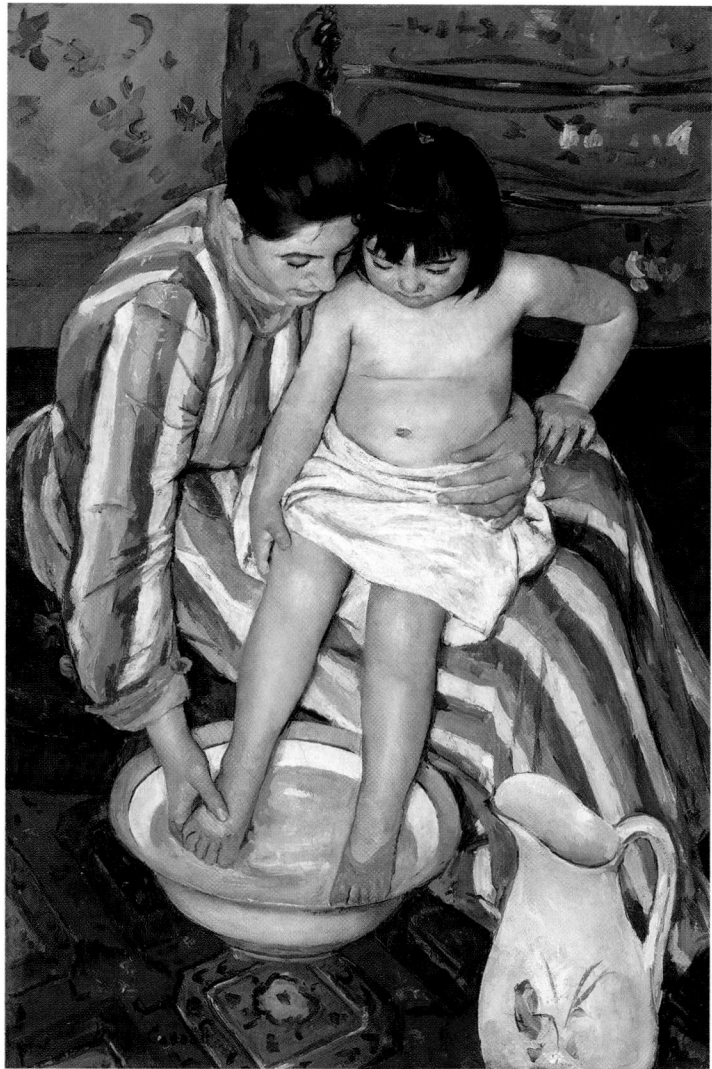

25.21 Mary Cassatt, *The Child's Bath*. 1891–92. Oil on canvas, 39½ × 26" (100.3 × 66 cm). The Art Institute of Chicago. Robert S. Waller Collection. 1910.2

mothers should nurse and care for their offspring rather than hiring wet nurses. This position reflects the increased importance sociologists placed on the care of children in general in the 1870s, which in part stemmed from a concern about the high infant mortality rate in Europe, especially in France. The path to a healthier society and nation, many argued, began in the home and was in the hands of the mother who nurtured her own children, both physically and emotionally, including attending to hygiene.

Cassatt's many domestic scenes of mothers tending their children, such as *The Child's Bath* (fig. **25.21**) of 1891–92, came out of this context. The pitcher and basin may seem quaint and old-fashioned to us today (only America had widespread indoor plumbing at this point), but regular bathing was a modern phenomenon for late nineteenth-century Paris, when people generally bathed only once a week. Not only is the picture about health, but also about intense emotional and physical involvement, as is reflected in the sensual yet tender manner with which the mother touches the child.

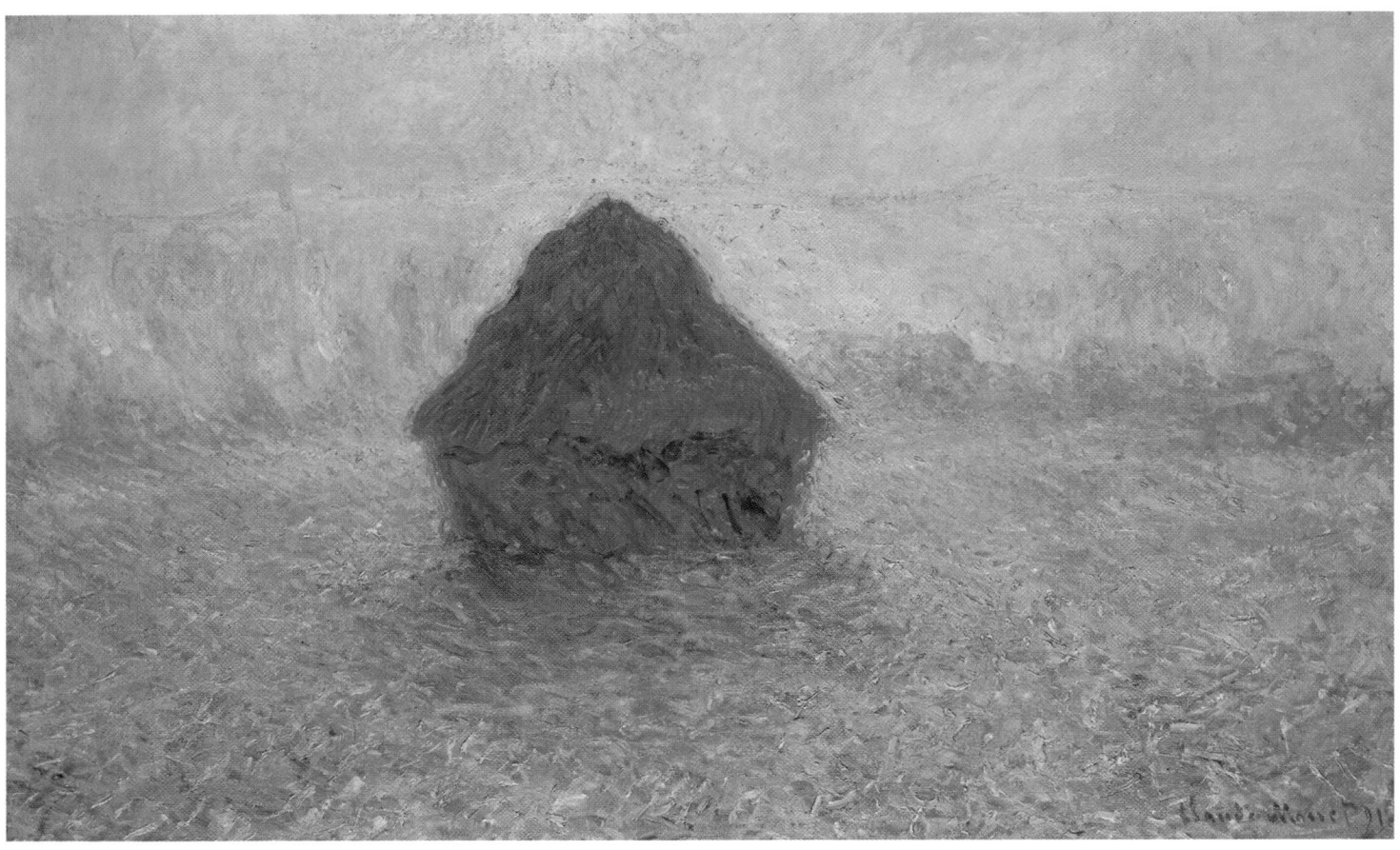

25.22 Claude Monet. *Wheatstack, Sun in the Mist*. 1891. Oil on canvas, 25⅝ × 39⅜" (65 cm × 100 cm). The Minneapolis Institute of Arts. Gift of Ruth and Bruce Dayton, The Putnam Dana McMillan Fund, The John R. Van Derlip Fund, The William Hood Dunwoody Fund, The Ethel Morrison Van Derlip Fund, Alfred and Ingrid Lenz Harrison and Mary Joann and James R Jundt

The picture contains all the ingredients we associate with Realism—the fashionable bourgeois décor and dress, the bright colors, and the sense of spontaneity in the brushwork and the skewed composition with its high viewpoint. The style of the picture reflects Cassatt's intense attraction to Japanese prints at this point in her career, an interest that is reflected in the overhead viewpoint as well as in the boldness of her forms and contours. Cassatt was also influenced by Renaissance art. Her palette has a chalky softness resembling tempera, and the strong line-defining contours have the same crispness as is found in fifteenth-century Italian painting. Many of Cassatt's presentations of a mother and child resemble Renaissance depictions of the Madonna and Child, an allusion that sanctifies the important role of women in creating a better society. But it also reflects the direction that Realism took after 1880, as many artists, as we saw in Renoir's *Luncheon of the Boating Party*, began to make a more monumental art that recalled the Classical art of the past.

MONET IN THE 1890S By the time the last Impressionist exhibition took place in 1886, any cohesiveness the core group had possessed was long gone, replaced by new concerns and styles. Manet's death in 1883 symbolically marks the death of the Realist movement that began with Courbet in the 1840s. Monet,

however, would live well into the twentieth century, and, while never abandoning the Realistic premise for his art and his commitment to Impressionism, he succeeded in making paintings that were among the most abstract of their day. At the same time, they became increasingly dreamlike, visionary, and poetic.

In the early 1890s, Monet began working more regularly in a series format, painting the same subject over and over, as he first did in the Gare Saint-Lazare series. His motifs included wheatstacks, Rouen Cathedral, and a line of poplar trees. The stack paintings came first, and he painted 30 of them, beginning in 1890. His goal was to show the same subject at different times of day and year, and under different weather conditions, believing life is not fixed but in continual flux. Working in a series format meant that the composition remained largely the same from one picture to the next. Again and again Monet painted a two-dimensional triangular wheatstack (occasionally he painted two) superimposed on top of a field in the foreground, with a line of trees, farmhouses, and distant hills at the horizon, and with the sky above. With compositional matters out of the way, Monet concentrated on color, his first love, which he changed from one painting to the next, theoretically to capture changing atmospheric and light conditions but also simply to give himself freer rein to improvise.

In *Wheatstack, Sun in the Mist* (fig. 25.22) of 1891, Monet used basically two complementary colors, orange and blue, in the haystack, pitting them against each other to make the stack vibrate. The remainder of the image is constructed with primary and secondary colors, similarly placed alongside one another, causing the entire scene to pulsate. Monet's flickering brushwork, now uniform streaks of varying length and direction, increases the shimmering effect and gives his wheatstacks a dreamy, haunting quality. Like the English landscapists Constable and Turner, Monet theoretically focused on capturing atmospheric effects, although it can be argued that because of his interest in color he was not as dedicated to transforming paint into atmosphere. He heavily reworked the *Wheatstack* canvases in his studio, suggesting that he was not solely dedicated to painting empirically. Critic Gustave Geffroy, in the introduction to the catalogue that accompanied the presentation of the *Wheatstack* at the Durand-Ruel gallery in Paris in 1891, strongly implied that the series is about experience and not seeing—that the paintings are about Monet's emotional reaction to the stacks and to nature. Geffroy gave the images a poetic reading, describing the stacks in one painting as "glow[ing] like heaps of gems," and in another as "hearth fires." By the 1880s, images of wheatstacks by French painters populated the Salons, the stacks an emblem of the nation's agricultural abundance, and Monet may have thought of the stacks similarly. Scholars have noted that his stacks sometimes echo the silhouetted shape of farmers' cottages lining the distant field, Monet thereby drawing a parallel between the two and paying homage to the farmers whose labor provides for the nation's food. Regardless of any such underlying messages, however, Monet's *Wheatstack* paintings seem more imaginary than realistic. Despite his claims to the contrary, Monet had moved well beyond the empiricism of 1870s Impressionism to create poetic, visionary images that paralleled the dreamlike fantasy worlds then being created by the Symbolist avant-garde, whom we will meet in the next chapter.

BRITISH REALISM

Realism took a very different form across the Channel, although the word itself was never applied to the art there. In Britain, Positivism produced a detailed naturalism, an intense truth to nature, and an interest in social types. There the Industrial Revolution had an almost 100-year head start over France. Industrialization and urbanization accounted for the poverty and other social ills so familiar to us today from the serialized novels of Charles Dickens (1812–1870), which were typically set in a cruel, corrupt metropolis suffocated by grime and soot. Materialism and greed were rampant. Cheap, ugly mass-produced objects replaced the highly refined handmade products that the aristocracy and upper class had once demanded. No longer were workers highly trained artisans with pride in their work but human machines suffering the drudgery of dawn-to-dusk mindless labor to turn out inferior consumer items with which they had no personal identity. It was precisely these conditions that

gave rise to the most radical of socialist organizations, the Chartists, and gave new energy to Christian socialism, the biblically based belief in community service and in the renunciation or sharing of personal wealth. It was also these conditions that the German political philosopher Karl Marx (1818–1883) and socialist Friedrich Engels (1820–1895) addressed in their *Communist Manifesto*, published in 1848 in England, where they were then living and working. It was artist, educator, writer, art critic, and environmentalist John Ruskin (1819–1900), however, who took the lead in attempting to arrest this decline into industrial hell. After Queen Victoria, he ranks as one of the greatest forces in the Victorian era, his influence extending well beyond Great Britain to mold American taste as well, beginning with the publication of the first of his four volumes of *Modern Painters* in 1843, and continuing with his *Seven Lamps of Architecture* after 1851.

Among Ruskin's most prominent beliefs was the need for contemporary society to aspire to a new spirituality and moral pride, which required adherence to truth and identification with what he considered the divinity of nature. He advocated art education for all social classes, for the working-class producer as well as the bourgeois consumer. He believed art was a necessity, not a luxury, for it molded people's lives and moral values—great art made great people. And by art Ruskin meant not only painting, sculpture, and architecture but also the decorative arts, all of which had to be as handcrafted, beautiful, and sincere as they had been in the Middle Ages.

Ruskin's emphasis on nature and religion marks the beginning of the nineteenth-century search for a simpler life, one that rejected the advances of urbanization and industrialization. As we've seen, Rosa Bonheur and George Sand were at virtually the same moment advocating a return to a "primitive" world—the countryside. For Ruskin, this purer primitive world could be found either in the spirituality of nature or medieval Christianity. By the end of the century, escape from the modern world and the search for the primitive would become dominant themes.

The Pre-Raphaelite Brotherhood

Ruskin championed the Pre-Raphaelite Brotherhood, a secret society started in September 1848 by three students at the Royal Academy School: William Holman Hunt, John Everett Millais, and Dante Gabriel Rossetti, who was the leader and spokesperson. The PRB, as they initially signed their paintings, denounced the art of the Royal Academy and most painting since early Raphael. They found the work decadent in that it clouded truth and fact with a muddy chiaroscuro and placed a premium on such artificial formal qualities as elegant contours or pleasing compositional patterning. Like Ruskin, the PRB abhorred bourgeois materialism and taste. Their heroes were the fifteenth-century Italian and Netherlandish primitives, such as Fra Angelico (see page 531) and Jan van Eyck (see pages 479–85), whose work they perceived as simpler, more direct, and hence sincere in its attempt to represent nature. They also considered this work more spiritual and moral because it was identified with the intensely religious Late Gothic period.

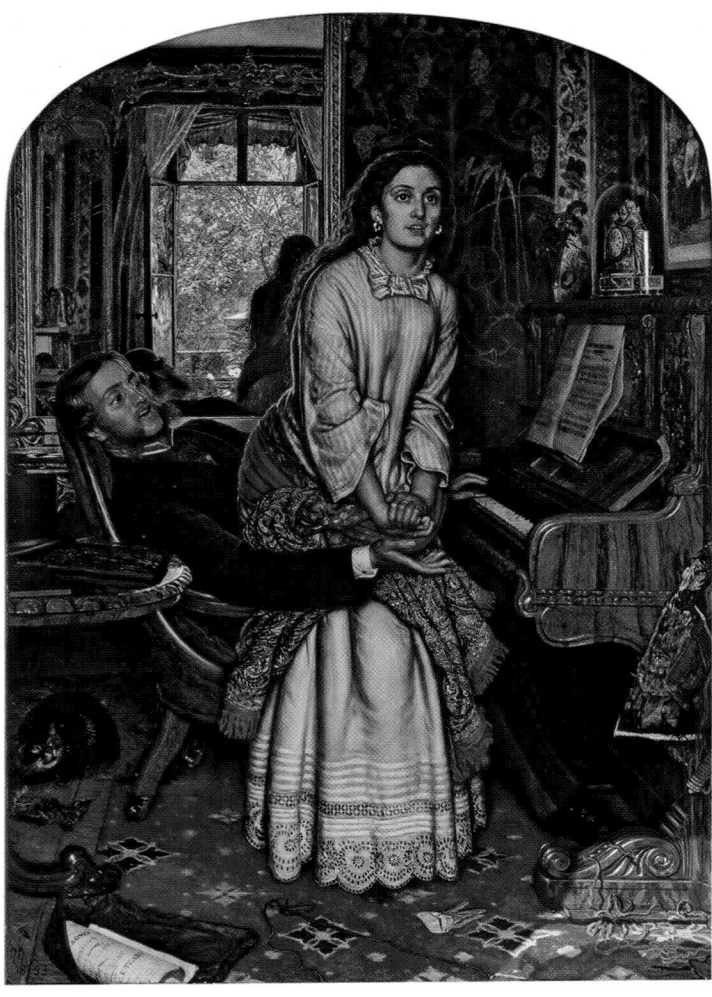

WILLIAM HOLMAN HUNT The most religious of the Pre-Raphaelite Brotherhood was William Holman Hunt (1827–1910), who came from a poor working-class family. His work is characterized by a combination of Victorian moral didacticism and intense naturalism. *The Awakening Conscience* (fig. **25.23**) of 1853–54 was inspired by a passage in Dickens's *David Copperfield* where David's friend, the simple fisherman Peggoty, goes searching for his beloved Emily, who has run off with an amoral dandy. Hunt tells the tale of one of the thousands of poor women appearing in the Realist literature of the period who perceived prostitution as their only hope of improvement even though it would inevitably lead to ruin. While sitting on her lover's lap and singing a song, a kept woman becomes aware of the lyrics, thinks of her family, and suddenly abhors her sinful situation, from which she must immediately escape. Hunt renders the room, cluttered with the shiny, vulgar products of crass consumerism, with a microscopic attention to detail worthy of Jan van Eyck, whose "*Arnolfini Portrait*" (see fig. 14.14) entered the collection of the National Gallery in London in 1842. In his review of the 1854 annual academy exhibition, Ruskin described the objects in Hunt's painting as having a "terrible lustre" and a "fatal newness" that reflected "the moral evil of the age." As in the "*Arnolfini Portrait*," every object seems to function symbolically. The cat chasing the bird under the table reflects the kept woman's position, and the clock approaching high noon denotes that the time left for decisive action is quickly expiring. The background mirror reflects an open window—redemption—since beyond we see the purity, beauty, and spirituality of nature, gloriously bathed in a bright divine light. Biblical warnings appear throughout the image, and on the bottom of the frame is a moralistic passage from Proverbs. The density of objects and figures in the painting

25.23   William Holman Hunt, *The Awakening Conscience*. 1853–54. Oil on canvas, 29½ × 22" (76.2 × 55.9 cm). Tate Gallery, London

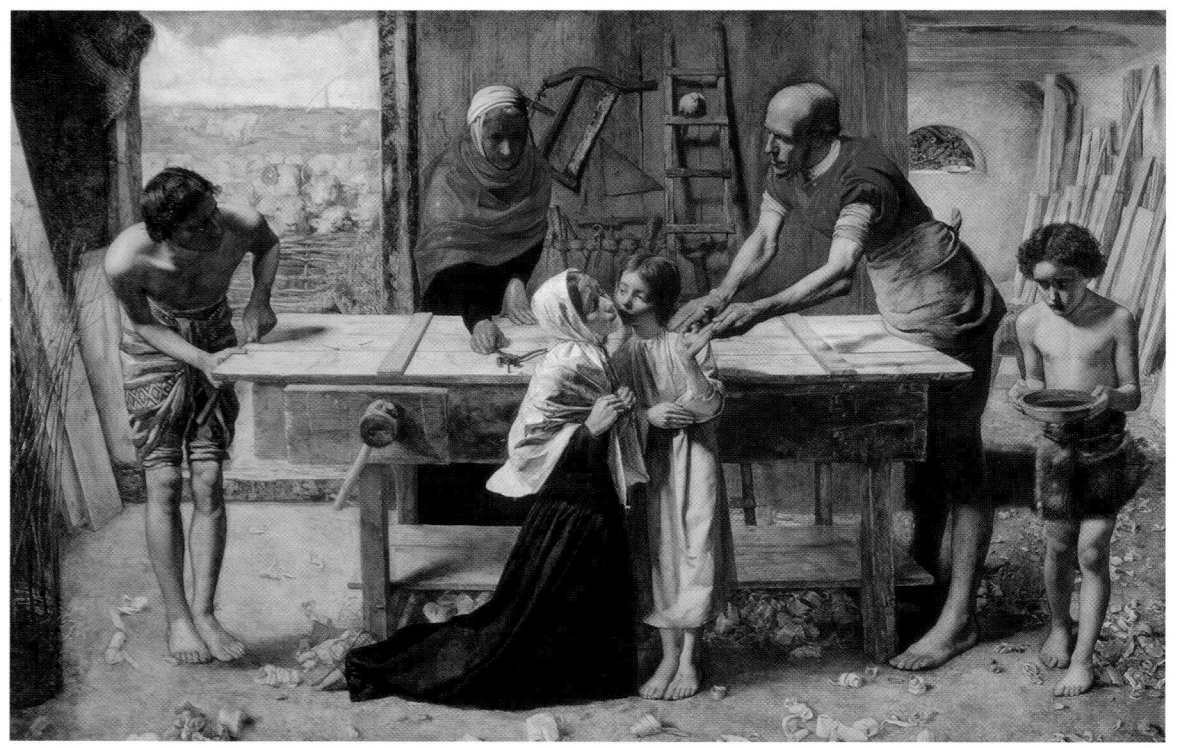

25.24   John Everett Millais, *Christ in the Carpenter's Shop* (*Christ in the House of His Parents*). 1849–50. Oil on canvas, 34 × 55" (86.4 × 140 cm). Tate Gallery, London

eliminates the compositional patterning and pleasing aesthetic contours that the Pre-Raphaelites disdained.

JOHN EVERETT MILLAIS The PRB was initially best known for biblical and literary pictures. While the subjects were drawn from a spiritual past, the themes were selected for their parallels with contemporary London and served as moral lessons. This is clear in *Christ in the Carpenter's Shop* (fig. 25.24), by John Everett Millais (1829–1896) and shown at the Royal Academy in 1850, where it was poorly received. The painting shows Jesus as a young boy in his stepfather's shop being comforted by his parents over a wound to his hand. Virtually every object in the room is a disguised symbol prefiguring the future role of Jesus as Savior. His cut palm anticipates the stigmata, his cousin John the Baptist carries a bowl that prefigures his calling, the flock beyond the door represents the congregation, and the tools on the wall, including the ladder, announce the Crucifixion. Millais's attention to realistic detail was perhaps the most intense of any member of the Pre-Raphaelites. To paint this picture, he went to a carpenter's shop to make studies of wood shavings and the musculature of a woodworker. He painted the sheep from severed heads.

The picture is more than an uncanny re-creation of a genre scene set during Jesus' boyhood. Rather, it is a Ruskinian political and social statement supporting quality workmanship and labor, spirituality being an attribute of hard-working artisans. Further identifying Christ with the working class, Millais depicts dirt beneath Jesus' fingernails, just as Courbet did with his stonebreakers, a detail that especially offended viewers.

WILLIAM MORRIS About 1856, two young painters befriended the Pre-Raphaelites: William Morris (1834–1896) and Edward Burne-Jones (1833–1898). Morris would dabble in architecture and become a renowned poet, but his true calling was implementing Ruskin's theories about replacing shoddy mass-produced products with beautifully designed handcrafted ones that, as in the Middle Ages, workers would take pride in producing. After collaborating in 1859 with architects, painters, and designers in the PRB and Ruskin's circle to design and furnish his own house, Morris in partnership with some of these same artists opened a company in 1865, which came to be called Morris & Co. It manufactured beautifully crafted fabrics, wallpaper, tapestries, carpets, tiles, furniture, and stained glass, with Morris himself designing most of the wallpaper and fabrics, a talent that translated easily into the many book designs he also undertook.

The palette and motifs of the Morris company products were organic and Gothic, creating an aura of nature and spirituality. This aesthetic is apparent in the dining room (fig. **25.25**) that Morris designed in 1867 for a new applied-arts museum called the South Kensington Museum, known today as the Victoria & Albert Museum. The gold-ground panels at the top of the wainscoting were painted principally by Morris's good friend Burne-Jones and represent the 12 months of the year, and thus the cycle of life. Because of the gold ground, they evoke the Early Renaissance (see fig. 13.22) and its intense spirituality. Morris's wallpaper, laboriously handprinted from wood blocks, is a flat abstract pattern based on an olive branch. The simple chest, decorated by Burne-Jones and also recalling the early Renaissance

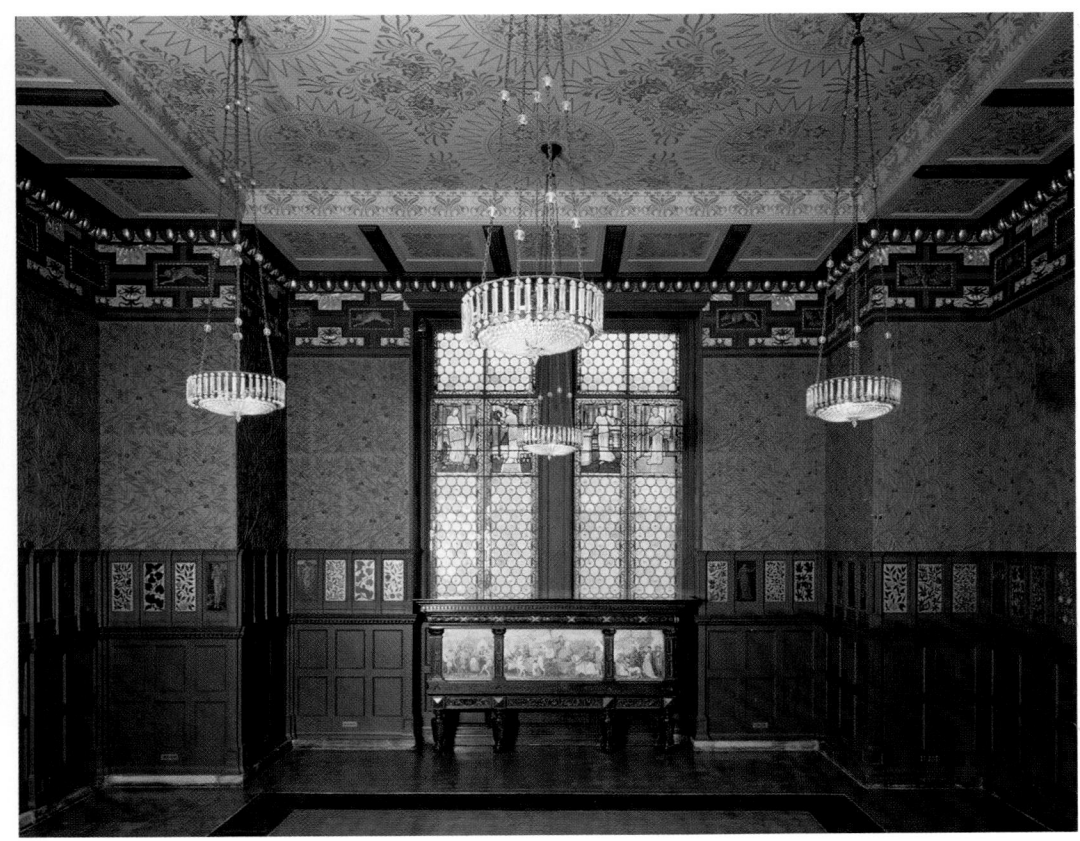

25.25 William Morris (Morris & Co.). Green Dining Room (William Morris Room). 1867. Victoria & Albert Museum, London

with its gold ground, is by the architect Philip Webb, who also designed the ceiling and the frieze above the wallpaper, abstract patterns largely based on botanical sources. As important as the handcrafting was the principle of truth to materials that Ruskin had advocated—that a material cannot be disguised as something it is not. Prefabricated plaster moldings, brackets, and decoration, then especially popular, were not allowed. In-vogue wallpaper mimicking the lush fabric that before the 1840s covered the walls of upper-class homes was condemned. Inferior wood could no longer be painted to resemble the grain of expensive wood. Morris and his collaborators' impact on the applied arts was far-reaching, launching what is known as the Arts and Crafts Movement, which soon spread to the United States.

The Aesthetic Movement:
Personal Psychology and Repressed Eroticism

While William Morris kept the moral and spiritual program of Ruskin alive with his Arts and Crafts Movement, the Pre-Raphaelite group had dissolved by 1860. Millais, for example, turned to anecdotal genre painting, and not only became a member of the Royal Academy but in 1896, the year of his death, its president. Rossetti, who had not been very productive in the 1850s, meanwhile gravitated toward a visionary, medieval-style art that expressed his own personal psychology, not social morality. Burne-Jones followed Rossetti down this path toward a visionary art that eventually developed into what is known as the Aesthetic Movement. Running through the paintings of both Rossetti and Burne-Jones is an undercurrent of repressed sexuality, a reflection of the strict moral code of Victorian Britain that outlawed even the discussion of sex.

DANTE GABRIEL ROSSETTI Today, Dante Gabriel Rossetti (1828–1882) is best known and most appreciated for his post-Pre-Raphaelite work. As the initial leader and spokesperson for the PRB, his shift away from its principles was significant for it anticipated the direction art was going to take in the closing decades of the century as Realism waned, to be replaced by a personal devotion to portraying strong emotions and imagination. The direct catalyst for this attitude was the poet Algernon Charles Swinburne (1837–1909), who in turn was influenced in the 1850s by the French critic Théophile Gautier. Gautier was a leading advocate of "art for art's sake," a theory maintaining that art's function was first and foremost to be beautiful, to appeal to the senses, and not to project moral values or tell stories. Rossetti came under Swinburne's spell, and the two men even shared a house in Chelsea after Rossetti's wife died in 1862.

This new aesthetic can be seen in Rossetti's *Proserpine* (fig. **25.26**) of 1874. The model was Jane Burden, William Morris's wife, with whom Rossetti was passionately in love, a sentiment she reciprocated. The artist presents her as Proserpine, the goddess abducted by Pluto, god of the underworld. Pluto forced her to eat six pomegranate seeds, which condemned her to spend six months of the year in Hades, the other half being spent above

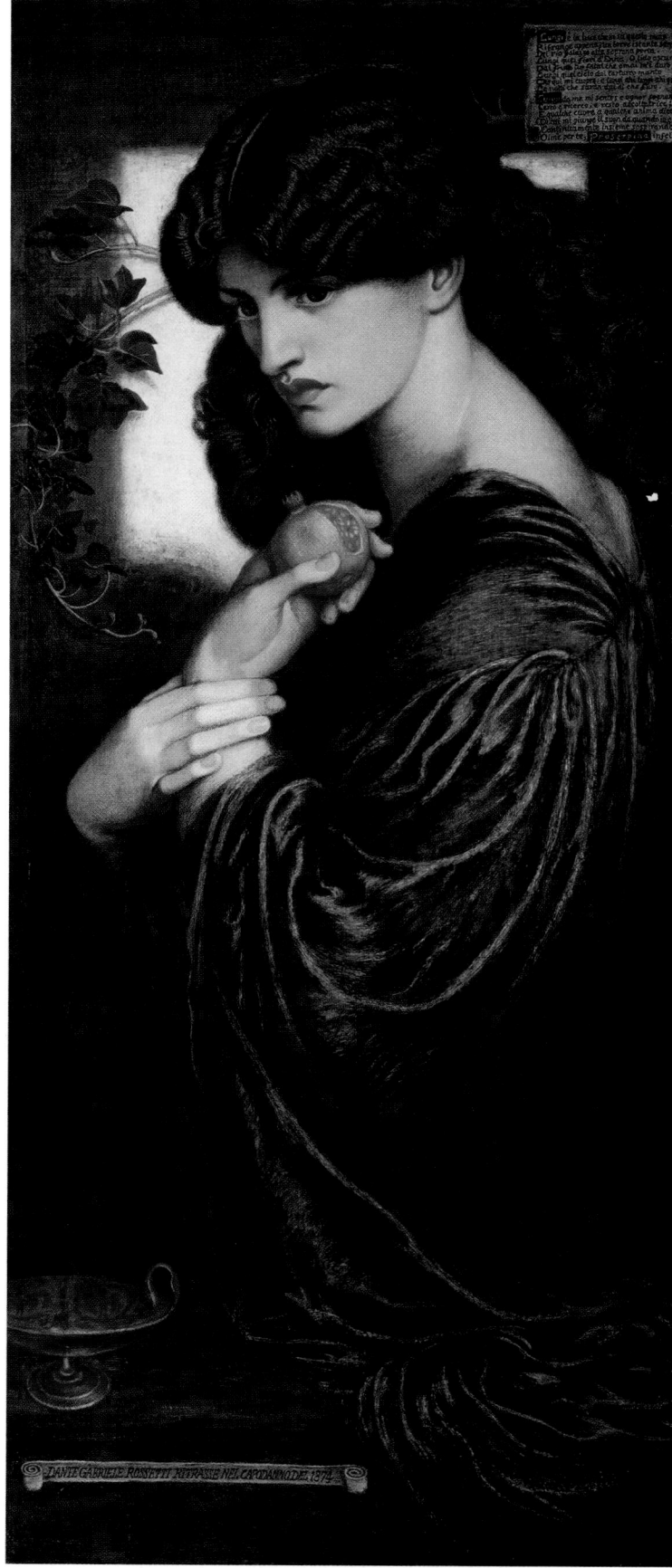

25.26 Dante Gabriel Rossetti, *Proserpine*. 1874. Oil on canvas, 49¼ × 24" (125.1 × 61.0 cm). Tate Gallery, London. Presented by W. Graham Robertson, 1940

James Abbott McNeill Whistler (1834–1903)

From *The Gentle Art of Making Enemies*

The Gentle Art of Making Enemies *(1893) is Whistler's autobiography.*

As music is the poetry of sound, so is painting the poetry of sight, and the subject matter has nothing to do with harmony of sound or of color.

The great musicians knew this. Beethoven and the rest wrote music—simply music; symphony in this key, concerto or sonata in that. …

This is pure music as distinguished from airs—commonplace and vulgar in themselves, but interesting from their associations, as for instance, "Yankee Doodle. …"

Art should be independent of all clap-trap—should stand alone, and appeal to the artistic sense of eye or ear, without confounding this with emotions entirely foreign to it, as devotion, pity, love, patriotism, and the like. All these have no kind of concern with it, and that is why I insist on calling my works "arrangement" and "harmonies."

Source: James Abbot McNeill Whistler, *The Gentle Art of Making Enemies* (NY: Putnam, 1925)

ground with her mother Ceres, goddess of the earth. Rossetti himself provides us with a succinct description of the painting:

> Proserpine is represented in a gloomy corridor of her palace, with the fatal fruit in her hand. As she passes, a gleam strikes on the wall behind her from some inlet suddenly opened, and admitting for a moment the sight of the upper world; and she glances furtively toward it, immersed in thought. The incense-burner stands beside her as the attribute of a goddess. The ivy branch in the background may be taken as a symbol of clinging memory.

Rossetti was in part attracted to Burden because of her classic Pre-Raphaelite looks, including her long, elegant neck and hands, and rich, flowing raven hair. Here, she wears a sumptuous Renaissance robe, the folds picking up the curvilinear rhythm of the ivy and her hair, face, neck, back, and hands. She stands behind a table that recalls the ubiquitous ledge found in Italian Renaissance portraiture.

By presenting Burden as Proserpine, Rossetti was expressing how he perceived her as trapped in a cold, loveless marriage with Morris. The picture is ultimately about the artist's own feelings of longing, as expressed in the line from his poem in the upper right, "And still some heart until some soul doth pine." Rossetti, also a serious poet and a translator of the works of his hero Dante, has in effect created a pictorial poem, dominated by the slow sensuous curvilinear surface patterning, the lush deeply saturated robe, and rich, lustrous, flowing hair. While Burden is presented as chaste (their relationship was apparently never consummated) and spiritual, dripping with Renaissance piety, she is also sensual and alluring. Instead of Realism, reality, and social issues, Rossetti has presented us with a torpid dream world filled with his own sexual yearning.

JAMES ABBOTT MCNEILL WHISTLER By the late 1870s, Rossetti was depressive, paranoid, and reclusive, and rarely exhibited. His friend Burne-Jones thus became the standard-bearer for the Aesthetic Movement and showed at the Grosvenor Gallery, a new space dedicated to this new art. But the most famous and notorious proponent of Aestheticism is the American painter

James Abbott McNeill Whistler (1834–1903). Raised in New England and Russia, Whistler studied with Charles Gleyre in Paris, where he lived from 1855 to 1859. He met Monet, befriended Courbet, and made his mark as a Realist, painting scenes of contemporary life that captured the underbelly of the city. After moving to London in 1859 (he never returned to America), he continued to spend long periods in Paris, maintaining his Parisian connections and friendships as well as submitting work to the Salons. He knew Gautier through Courbet and Manet, and in London befriended Swinburne.

By 1863, Whistler had abandoned French Realism to pursue Aestheticism, an example of which is his *Symphony in White No. I: The White Girl*, a title only applied later and probably inspired by Gautier's poem "Symphony in White Major." Whistler submitted the picture to the 1863 *Salon des Refusés*, where it hung not far from Manet's *The Luncheon on the Grass*. Like Gautier's poem, which is a complex interfacing of different white visions, the painting orchestrates a range of whites, soft yellows, and reds in a full-length portrait of the artist's mistress Jo, who is dressed in white against a largely white ground. While Gautier and Swinburne influenced Whistler conceptually, visually the artist came under the spell of Japonisme, an influence more clearly stated in *Symphony in White No. II: The Little White Girl* (fig. **25.27**) of 1864. Here, Jo leans on the mantel of Whistler's London home, surrounded by a Japanese blue-and-white vase, fan, and a spray of cherry blossom, often identified with Japan. At one level, the painting is a sensual display of abstract color and shapes. Using thin, delicate brushstrokes and almost transparent layers of paint, Whistler orchestrates a graceful symphony of whites, yellows, reds, pinks, and blues across the picture plane. He plays the softness of his paint and such forms as Jo's dress against the rectangular linearity of the mantel, mirror, and reflected picture frames. The flowers entering the composition on the right are another delicate touch, a Japanese compositional device used earlier by Degas to create fragmentation and spontaneity but here to make the petals seem to float magically.

The painting was conceived as a tribute to Ingres, compositionally echoing his *Portrait of Madame Inès Moitessier* (see fig. 24.14) and acknowledging the great Neoclassicist's ability to create perfect beauty. But in psychology it is closer to Rossetti's

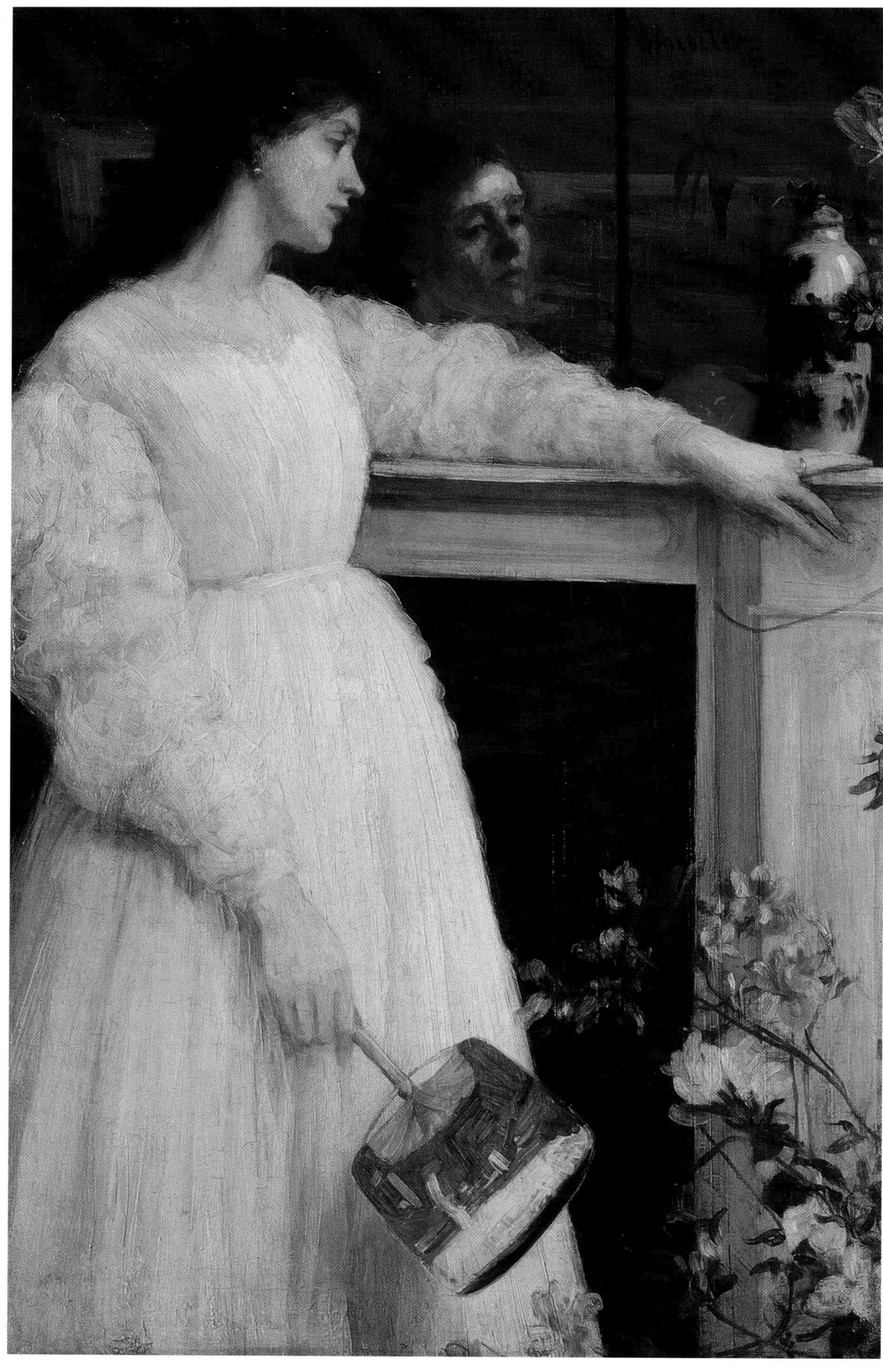

25.28 James Abbot McNeill Whistler, *Nocturne in Black and Gold: The Falling Rocket*. ca. 1875. Oil on panel, 23¾ × 18⅜" (60.2 × 46.8 cm). The Detroit Institute of Arts. Gift of Dexter M. Ferry, Jr.

Proserpine, for Whistler depicts a similarly dreamy, meditative, yet sensual mistress with long flowing hair. Jo's reflection levitates ghostlike in the mirror, an image that inspired Swinburne to write a poem, which Whistler affixed to the back of the canvas.

In the following decade, Whistler's work became increasingly abstract, as in *Nocturne in Black and Gold: The Falling Rocket* (fig. **25.28**) of about 1875. He exhibited the painting in 1877 at the Grosvenor Gallery with seven other ethereal, thinly painted blue-gray **nocturnes** (a musical term meaning "night scenes") of the Thames River, all meant to support his art-for-art's-sake position. *The Falling Rocket* is by far the most abstract, to the point that the aging Ruskin accused Whistler of "throwing a pot of paint in the public's face," for which Whistler sued him for slander. The painting is a picture of fireworks at Cremorne Gardens, a popular nightspot in the Chelsea section of London. Although based on real events, the work was nonetheless concocted in the studio according to more subjective dictates. As Whistler explained at the Ruskin trial, "It is an artistic arrangement. That is why I call it a nocturne." As suggested by his titles, which include words such as symphony and sonata as well as

nocturne, Whistler considered painting visual music, declaring it, in essence, abstract. (See *Primary Source*, page 885.) Without the words "The Falling Rocket" in the title, we would be hard-pressed to describe an actual subject; we would be left savoring Whistler's abstract display of orange and yellow sprinkles lazily drifting down over a gray-blue-brown ground of gossamer-thin brushstrokes. As in *Symphony in White No. II*, Whistler's surface has a delicate Japanese sensitivity, so refined that shapes and marks barely exist as one color bleeds through the haze of another. With his Grosvenor Gallery exhibition, Whistler moved art into a subjective, nonempirical realm. Unwittingly, he was presenting a preview of the art of the next two decades, as we shall see in the next chapter.

REALISM IN AMERICA

The ripple effect of the European revolutions of 1848 did not reach America, although it did produce waves of new immigrants. A more significant defining benchmark for the United States is the Civil War, which had a devastating physical, psychological, and economic impact on the nation. The Garden of Eden was ravaged. After the war, this metaphor for the country disappeared, displaced by the "Gilded Age," a term coined by Mark Twain and his coauthor for an 1871 book of the same name describing a new page in American history largely dominated by the robber barons, one that brought about tremendous wealth and ostentation. Twain's robber barons were the American speculators, manufacturers, industrialists, real-estate investors, and railway, coal, and iron magnates who made vast fortunes, often exploiting workers. Their new wealth transformed them into an American aristocracy with aspirations to all things European. The robber barons and their families traveled to Europe, brought back European furniture and art, and built European-style villas and chateaux. The result was a nostalgia by many for a more innocent, lost past, one perceived as pre-industrial.

The period is also defined by continued westward expansion, fulfilling what the nation saw as its God-given Manifest Destiny to overrun the North American continent. Survey teams mapped the new territories, and the Transcontinental Railroad, connecting East and West, was completed in 1869. By 1890, the government had subdued the Native American nations, either by containment in restricted territories or by violent annihilation. It honored Native Americans in 1913 by putting an Indian warrior, in headdress and Greek profile, on the American nickel. The reverse side portrayed the buffalo, also made "extinct" by westward expansion.

Scientific Realism: Thomas Eakins

Thomas Eakins (1844–1916), a Philadelphian, was among the earliest and most powerful Realist painters in America. His scenes of the modern world included not only middle-class leisure activities and the popular sports and pastimes of post-Civil War America but also surgery clinics portraying surgeons as modern heroes

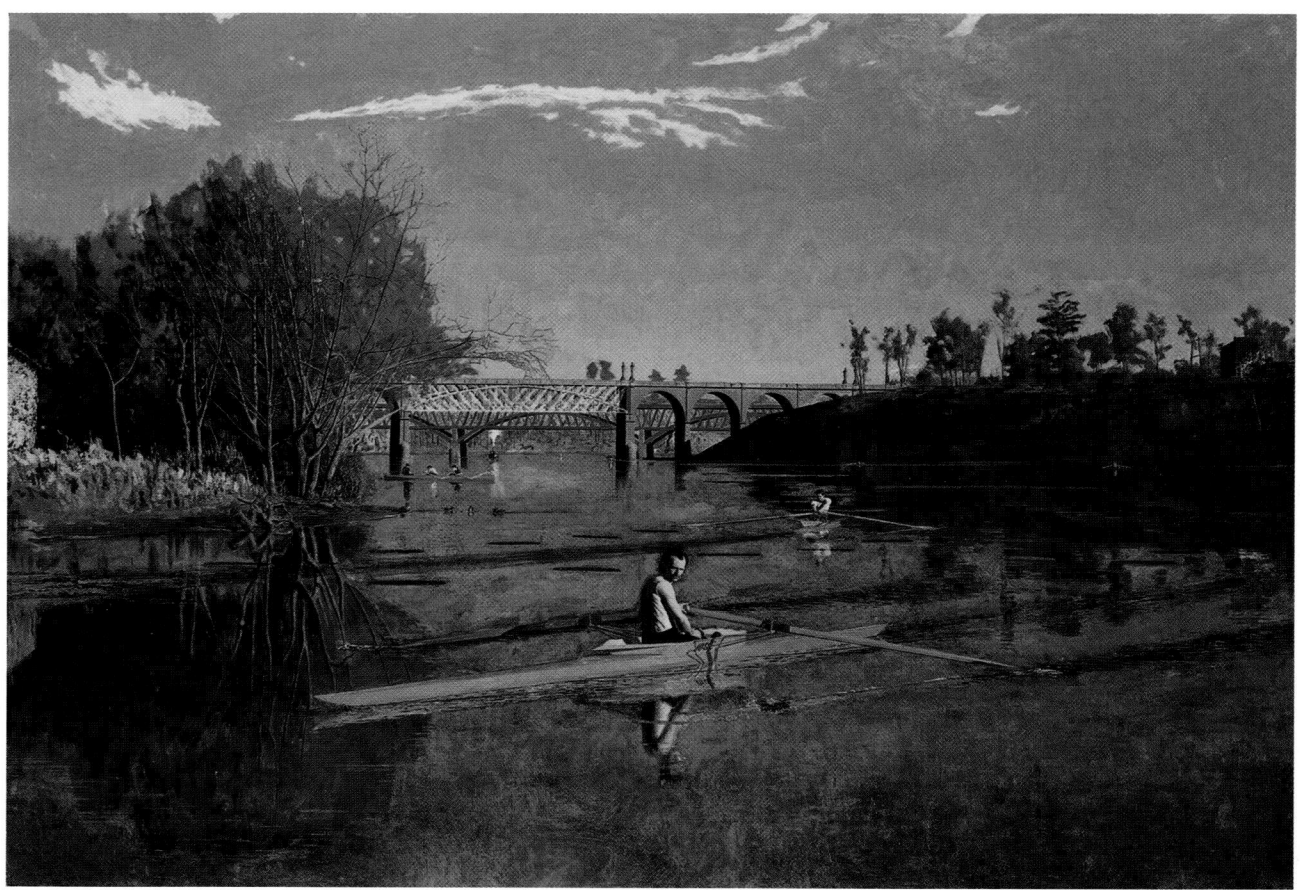

25.29 Thomas Eakins, *Max Schmitt in a Single Scull* (*The Champion Single Sculls*). 1871. Oil on canvas, 32¼ × 46¼" (82 × 117.5 cm). Metropolitan Museum of Art, New York. Alfred N. Punnett Endowment Fund and George D. Pratt Gift, 1934. (34.92)

and highlighting new scientific techniques such as anesthesia and antiseptic surgery. Eakins even brought a scientific approach to his Realism, which made it quite different from the Realism of Manet and Degas that he had witnessed while studying with a renowned academician in Paris in the late 1860s.

Among Eakins's first works upon returning to Philadelphia was a series of sculling pictures, such as *Max Schmitt in a Single Scull* (also called *The Champion Single Sculls*) (fig. **25.29**), an 1871 painting that reflects the rising popularity of the sport and presents Max Schmitt, the winner of a championship race on the Schuylkill River in Philadelphia, as a hero of modern life. While the picture looks like a plein-air painting, what we see is not a quickly recorded Impressionist moment but a painstakingly reconstructed event. Eakins's paintings are grounded in intense scientific inquiry designed to ensure the accuracy of his Realism. He made numerous perspective studies of the skulls and oars, which result in the river receding with breathtaking mathematical precision, firmly locking the boats in space. He studied light effects and anatomy, and, as a teacher at the Pennsylvania Academy of Art, outraged his colleagues and suffered public scorn by having his students, including women, work from the nude model, rather than imitate plaster casts of Classical figures. His quest for Realism drove him to record minute details, including a steamboat and landscape behind the distant bridges, details

beyond the reach of normal vision. (Shortly afterward he would begin using photographs in addition to drawings as preliminary studies.) The second bridge is an emblem of modernity, for it is a railroad bridge, on which we can just make out a train and its puffs of smoke. Eakins's Realism even extends to modern psychology, for Schmitt's isolation in the broad expanse of the river seems a form of alienation, as does his expression of unfamiliarity as he twists to squint at *us*, not Eakins, who is in the scull behind Schmitt.

Iconic Imagery: Winslow Homer

Winslow Homer (1836–1910) was in Paris about the same time as Eakins. He was already disposed toward painting the modern world, for he began his career in 1857 as a magazine illustrator, recording the latest fashions and social activities and later covering the Civil War. He was in Paris in 1866–67, where he saw the work of Courbet, Millet, and Manet, but he was too early to experience the full impact of Impressionism. Upon returning to New York, he painted outdoor scenes of the middle class engaged in contemporary leisure activities, such as playing croquet, swimming at the newest New Jersey shore resorts, and taking horseback tours in the White Mountains of New Hampshire, diversions now accessible by train.

An Artist's Reputation and Changes in Art-Historical Methodology

A change in the methodology of art history can sometimes affect scholars' attitudes toward artists, sometimes resurrecting figures who had once been renowned but had gradually disappeared from the history books. A case in point is the American painter John Singer Sargent (1856–1925). In his day, he was one of the most famous and financially successful artists. He can even be considered the quintessential American artist at that time, for he lived and worked in Europe and his art appeared to embrace the European values that so many *nouveau riche* Americans aspired to emulate.

Sargent was born and raised in Florence, studied at the École des Beaux-Arts in Paris, and by 1879 was winning medals at the Salons. In part due to the encouragement of novelist Henry James, he moved permanently to London in 1886. He made his first professional trip to America in 1887, and immediately became the portraitist to high society, painting William Henry Vanderbilt of New York and Isabella Stewart Gardner of Boston, among others. By 1892, he was the most fashionable portraitist in London and perhaps on the Continent as well. Sargent's success was in part based on the luxuriousness of his imagery—expensive fabrics and furnishings—reinforced by his dramatic sensual brushwork.

Sargent was a proponent of the avant-garde. He befriended Claude Monet and acquired his paintings as well as Manet's. His own work reflects the painterly bravura of Manet, and like Manet he admired Velázquez. He also made numerous Impressionist landscapes and urban views, often in watercolor. Ironically, Sargent fell into oblivion because of the Modernism that evolved in the twentieth century. His consummate handling of paint may have had the abstract qualities that the Modernists admired, but his work was perceived as conservative. It failed to offer anything new. Worse yet, his avant-garde brushwork was carefully packaged in the old-fashioned formulas of society portraiture.

Sargent's reevaluation began in the 1950s, with a renewed appreciation of the paint handling in his Impressionist watercolors. In succeeding decades his reputation gradually inched its way up as Modernism was replaced by Postmodernism and its broader values. (See Chapter 30.) Representational art became fashionable again, and art historians began to appreciate art for the way in which it reflected the spirit of its age. Sargent's portraiture was now perceived as the embodiment of Victorian and Edwardian society and of the Gilded Age.

For example, gender studies, which began appearing in the 1970s, looked at his daring presentation of women, as can be seen in his 1897 portrayal of New York socialite Edith Stokes in *Mr. and Mrs. I. N. Phelps Stokes*. Instead of giving us a demure and feminine woman, Sargent presents a boldly aggressive Mrs. Stokes, who represents the "New Woman" who emerged in the 1890s (see page 904). In a period when the women's movement was fiercely advocating equal rights, many women were asserting their independence and challenging conventional gender roles. This New Woman was independent and rebelled against the conventional respectability of the Victorian era that sheltered women in domesticity. She went out in public; she was

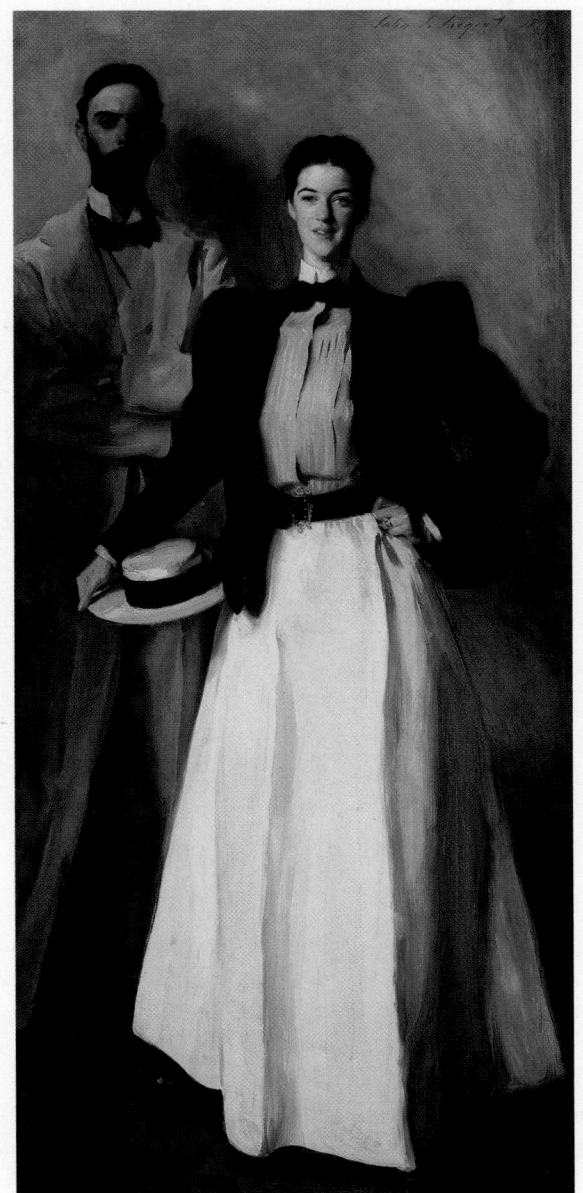

John Singer Sargent, *Mr. and Mrs. I.N. Phelps Stokes*. 1897. Oil on canvas, 84¼ × 39¾" (214 × 101 cm). Metropolitan Museum of Art, New York. Bequest of Edith Mintum Phelps Stokes (MRS. I. N.), 1938. (38.104)

educated; and she was athletic, spirited, and flaunted her sexual appeal. Not only did she wear comfortable clothes, she even wore men's attire, or a woman's shirtwaist based on a man's shirt. Instead of self-sacrifice, she sought self-fulfillment. Sargent presents Edith Stokes as just such a woman, even having her upstage her husband. The placement of her hat over her husband's crotch was especially controversial. For its time, this was a radical presentation of a woman and a reflection not only of the sitter's personality and identification with women's issues, but also of Sargent's willingness to buck portrait conventions and societal expectations.

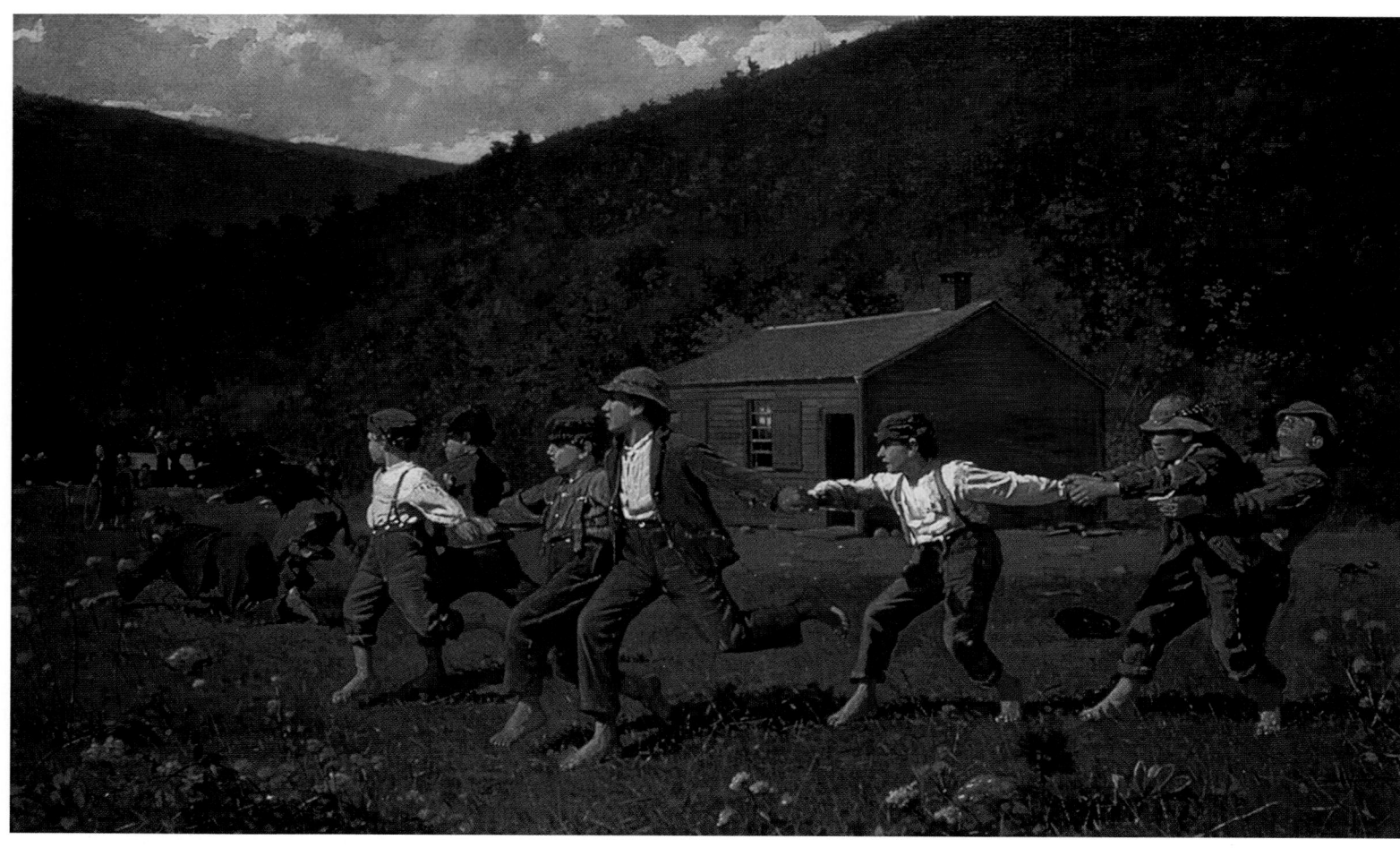

25.30 Winslow Homer, *Snap the Whip*. 1872. Oil on canvas, 22¼ × 36½" (56.5 × 92.7 cm). The Butler Institute of American Art, Youngstown, Ohio

Rather than portraying a world in flux, however, Homer created iconic symbolic images of American life and issues, as had Millet of the French peasant. We can see this emblematic approach in his *Snap the Whip* (fig. **25.30**) of 1872. At first glance, this visual record of a children's game appears to be an Americanization of Impressionism, for the image is a sun-filled scene rendered with fairly strong color and flashy passages of brushwork. But Homer's color is not as intense as the Impressionists', nor his brushwork as loose. The picture is not about color and light and empirically capturing a specific moment: This image is frozen. The figures are carefully outlined, modeled, and monumental, their solidity reinforced by the geometry of the one-room schoolhouse and the bold backdrop of the mountain, which parallels the direction of the boys' movement. The barefoot children in their plain country clothes, like the one-room schoolhouse behind them, are emblems of simplicity and wholesomeness, their youth projecting innocence and hope for a recently reunified country. The game itself is symbolic of union, since the chain of boys is only as strong as its weakest link. At a time when the nation was staggering under the weight of the disillusionment brought on by the Civil War and the turmoil of rampant industrialization, *Snap the Whip* embodied the country's lost innocence and was a nostalgic celebration of values that were quickly fading into memory.

PHOTOGRAPHY: A MECHANICAL MEDIUM FOR MASS-PRODUCED ART

In 1839, photography was commercially introduced almost simultaneously in both France and Britain. As a mechanical process that would eventually lend itself to mass production and popular culture, it was a perfect fit with the Industrial Revolution and seems a natural consequence of it. It was also a perfect tool for the Positivist era, for initially it was largely perceived as a recording device for cataloguing, documenting, and supporting scientific inquiry. It had the appearance of being objective, paralleling the matter-of-fact presentation of much Realism and Impressionism.

The potential for photography had existed since antiquity in the form of the *camera obscura*, a box with a small hole in one end that allowed the entrance of light, projecting an upside-down image of an object outside to be cast on the inside wall at the opposite end of the box. An artist could then trace the projected image. We know that Vermeer and Canaletto, for example, occasionally used a *camera obscura* for their paintings. However, the problem that remained was how to *fix* the image mechanically, that is, how to give it permanence without the intervention of drawing.

First Innovations

In the early eighteenth century, silver salts were discovered to be light-sensitive, but it was not until 1826 that the French inventor Joseph-Nicéphore Niépce (1765–1833) made the first photographic image, a blurry view out of his window that required an eight-hour exposure time. He teamed up with artist Louis-Jacques-Mandé Daguerre (1787–1851), who, after discovering the light-sensitive properties of silver iodide and the use of mercury fumes to fix a silver iodide-coated copper plate, unveiled the **daguerreotype** in 1838. The French government acquired the process and offered it free to the rest of the world, excepting Britain, with whom the French were in fierce economic competition. The invention represented both a nationalistic and imperialistic triumph, for it enabled the French to document not only the monuments of France but of its colonies as well, especially Egypt. And it was also viewed as a "Republican" medium since, unlike painting and sculpture, it was affordable, making portraits available to all social classes.

Meanwhile, in Britain, William Henry Fox Talbot (1800–1877) announced in 1839 that he could fix an image on paper, rather than on metal or glass, and in 1841 he took out a patent for the new negative-positive photograph he called a **calotype**, a salted paper print. Unlike the daguerreotype, which resulted in a single image, the calotype generated endless positive paper prints from one paper negative.

Both the daguerreotype and calotype were displaced in the early 1850s by the simultaneous invention in France and Britain of the **wet-collodion process**. This technique used a very sensitive emulsion, collodion (gun-cotton dissolved in alcohol ether), that cut exposure time to under a second and produced a sharp, easily reproducible negative. However, the process was cumbersome, for it required the photographic glass plate to be both prepared and processed as soon as it had been used. This meant keeping the plate chemically wet at all times and transporting a portable darkroom. At about the same time, Louis-Désiré Blanquart-Évrard (1802–1872) developed the **albumen print**, which used salted egg white on paper, creating a smooth, more refined surface that revealed greater detail with less graininess. For the next 30 to 40 years, photographers used wet-collodion plates for recording images and then printed them on albumen paper.

In 1846, Talbot published a photographically illustrated book, *The Pencil of Nature*, the title being a reference to light, "Nature's pencil," which "draws" on an emulsion-coated surface. (The word *photograph* is from the Greek words for "light" and "drawing.") Here, Talbot framed many of the basic issues that would surround photography well into the future. He not only saw the medium as a *recording* process capable of scientifically documenting the world, but also as an *interpretative vehicle* that would allow for new ways of perceiving and understanding reality, thus permitting artistic vision. Well into the twentieth century, this latter insight did not prevent the general public from viewing photography primarily as a tool for recording truths as well as a symbol of the mechanization of the Industrial Revolution and its accompanying social ills.

Recording the World

By the 1850s, the most prevalent use of photography was for recording the world: people, sights, and objects. These pictures were generally viewed as fact, which is ironic since, as we shall see, photographers could manipulate images in various ways, including the selection of motifs and objects to be included in, or excluded from, a photograph.

PORTRAITURE Americans especially took to photography, which the artist and inventor Samuel Morse (1791–1872) brought back to New York from France just weeks after the French government made it available in 1839. Soon every American city had photography studios offering daguerreotype portraits, and this form of photograph remained popular in the United States long after it had been superseded in Europe by the albumen print. Americans especially loved its wealth of details and simple factuality, which was reinforced by the blunt presentation of the sitter, posed against a plain background that did not detract from his or her physical presence. The daguerreotype could record the most minute details clearly, a clarity that holds up even under a magnifying glass. (Do the same with an albumen print and you get a blur.)

In the daguerreotype portrait of the abolitionist John Brown (fig. **25.31**) taken by Augustus Washington (1820–1875), we can

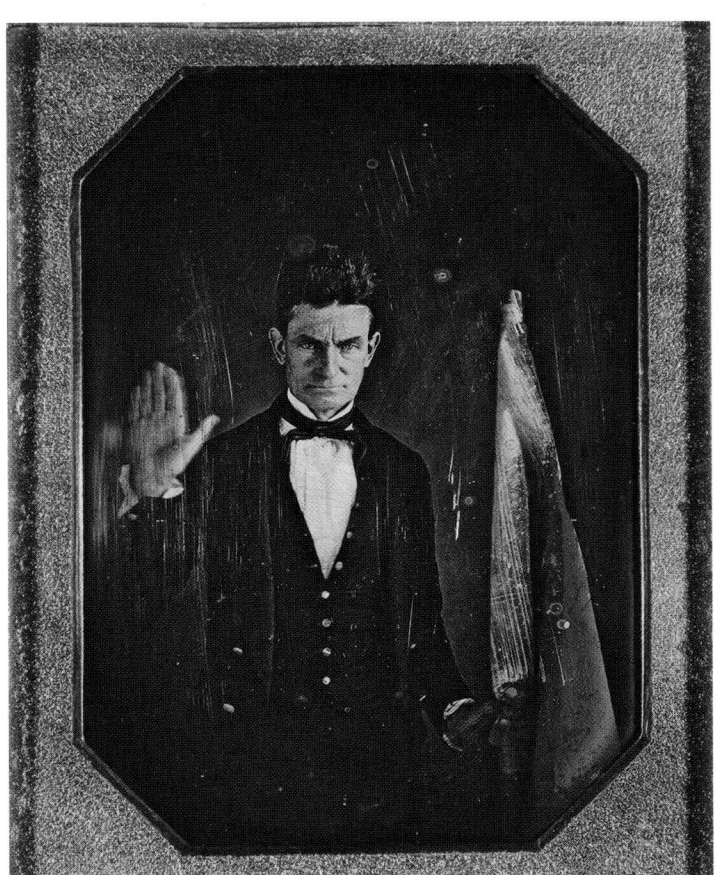

25.31 Augustus Washington, *John Brown*. ca. 1846–47. Quarter-plate daguerreotype, 3⅗ × 3¼" (10 × 8.2 cm). National Portrait Gallery, Smithsonian Institution, Washington, D.C.

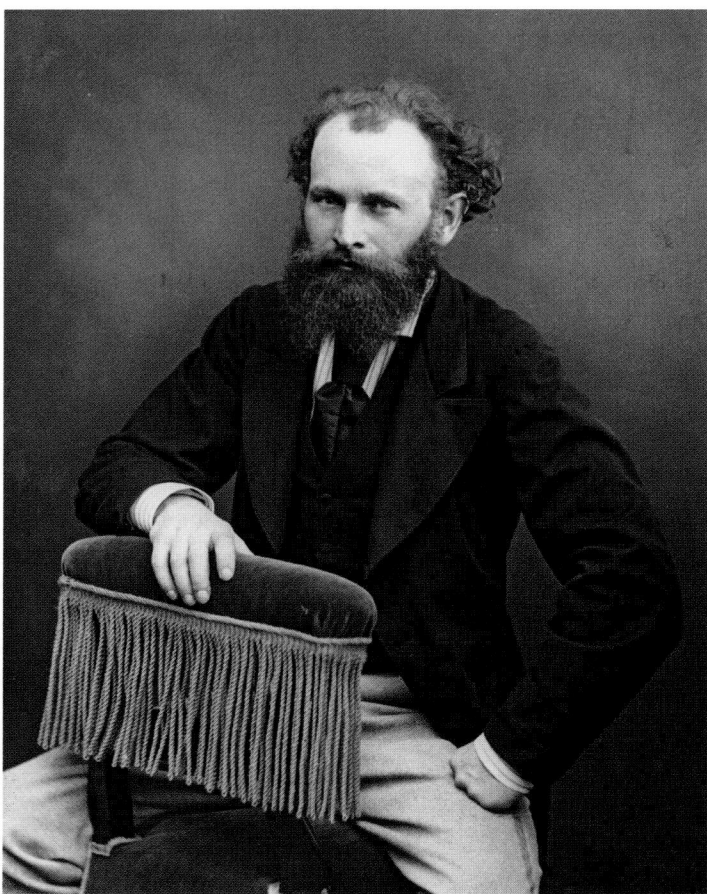

25.32 Nadar, *Édouard Manet*. 1870s. Albumen salted paper print, mounted on Bristol board. Musée d'Orsay, Paris

aspirations of Disdéri's bourgeois patrons. In 1854, he increased the popularity of photographs when he invented the **carte-de-visite**, a 2½ × 4" visiting card with the visitor's portrait, which by 1859 were widely collected, a phenomenon called "cardomania."

Among the most celebrated early portraitists of the era was the Parisian Gaspard-Félix Tournachon (1820–1910), known simply as Nadar. He began his career as a journalist and caricaturist and may have taken up photography as an aid in making the lithographic caricatures for his planned compendium of the 1,000 most prominent personalities of the day, which he called *Le Panthéon Nadar*. He began cashing in on the public infatuation with celebrities by mass-producing albumen prints of the famous, in particular writers, actors, performers, and artists of bohemian Paris. His skill as a caricaturist proved invaluable in setting up his shots, enabling him to create incisive portraits that captured the essence of his sitter's mystique.

We can see this skill in Nadar's 1870s portrait of the painter Édouard Manet (fig. **25.32**). Although of bourgeois origin, Manet is not presented as moneyed. The sitter may wear expensive clothes and be seated in a lavish chair, but there is no pretentious Classical column or billowing drapery. Instead the emphasis is on Manet's forceful personality. He has turned his chair around in a businesslike, if not argumentative manner, grasping the top with his right hand, and with a gesture of confidence placing the other hand on his hip. His meticulously trimmed beard and mustache and dapper clothes confirm his renown as a dandy. Nadar, especially noted for his lighting, has backlit Manet's head, making the entire figure seem to thrust forward and reinforcing the intensity of the painter's stare.

count the hairs on Brown's head, trace the wrinkles on his face and hands, and even inspect the thread holding his buttons on. Unlike most of their European counterparts, American portraitists encouraged their clients to project a personality for their photographs. The photographer here captured Brown, in a stern, determined, and almost confrontational pose, taking a vow and holding what historians believe to be a flag for the Subterranean Pass Way, the name he gave to an "underground railroad" he was planning for transporting runaway slaves north. Washington had the most successful studio in Hartford, Connecticut, but Brown undoubtedly went to him as a fellow abolitionist, which the portraitist, a free African American and political activist, most likely was. But convinced that blacks would never achieve equality during his lifetime, Washington sold his business shortly before the Civil War and emigrated to the Republic of Liberia, meaning "liberty," founded in West Africa as a sanctuary for former slaves, who started arriving there in 1822.

In Europe, the largest portrait studio in the 1850s and 1860s belonged to Adolphe-Eugène Disdéri, whose business was headquartered in Paris but had branches in Madrid and London. His enormous staff churned out formulaic portraits using the same props and settings, often a Classical column and a pompous swag of drapery. These same props are found in royal portraiture (see fig. 21.10), and were now used to fulfill the upwardly mobile social

VIEWS Along with portraits, views dominated photography, for they allowed people to travel the world without leaving their living room. Fulfilling the French government's vision of documenting its African conquests, Maxime Du Camp (1822–1894), a Parisian journalist, photographed the French territories in Africa and the Middle East, and in 1852 published 125 images in his book *Egypt, Nubia, Palestine and Syria*. More popular than such albums, which could be quite expensive, were **stereocards**, which by the 1860s were as prevalent as musical compact disks are today. Stereocards are side-by-side photographs of the same image taken by a camera with two lenses, replicating human binocular vision. When put into a special viewer, the twin flat pictures appear as a single three-dimensional image. To accommodate the tremendous demand for these images, distributing companies stocked as many as 300,000 different stereocards at one time. The quality of the rapidly reproduced prints was generally low, a problem compounded by their 2-by-5-inch size, although larger versions also existed. An awestruck world now slid the cards into their viewers and saw in three dimensions not only the dramatic changes occurring in Europe, such as new buildings, parks, and monuments, but such exotic climes as China, India, and Africa.

Of course, these same stereocards were available in the United States, which was an enormous market. American photographers were mostly preoccupied with documenting their own nation. A

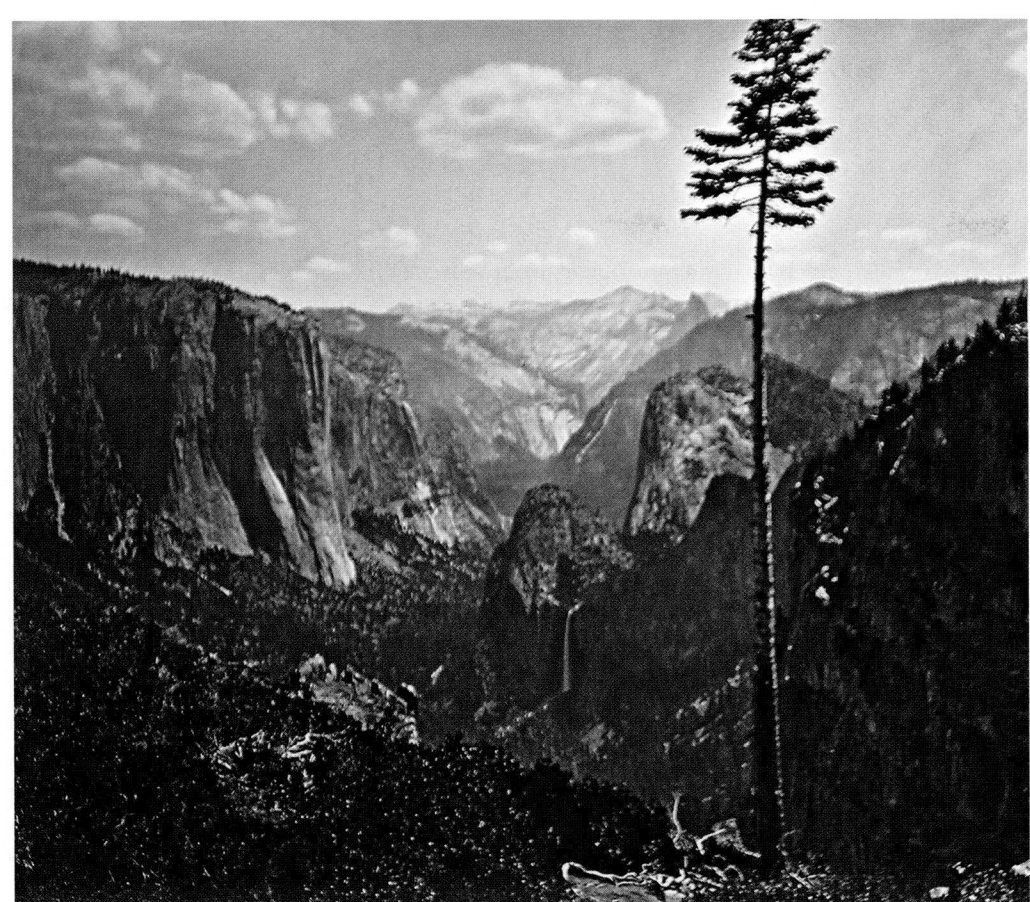

large contingent of them, like their fellow painters, specialized in landscape, traveling west, often with survey teams, to record the sublime wilderness that symbolized the nation. One of the first and most famous of this group is Carleton Watkins (1829–1916), who beginning in 1861 made hundreds of glass stereographic views of Yosemite along with some 1,000 18-by-22-inch albumen prints. Despite his strong commercial sense, Watkins thought of his work as art, not documentation. Originally from Oneonta, New York, he went west to San Francisco with the Gold Rush in 1851, eventually making daguerreotype portraits and photographically documenting land for surveys. Hearing about the visual wonders of Yosemite, he took off in 1861 to photograph this awesome, primeval landscape. In order to capture the vast scale of the land, he felt it was necessary to make large prints, and consequently he developed a mammoth camera that used large glass plates. He then set off in a covered wagon with a ton of equipment, which included wet-glass plates and a darkroom to process them immediately after they were exposed.

The results, as seen in *Yosemite Valley from the Best General View* (fig. **25.33**), made on a second trip to Yosemite in 1865–66, were so breathtaking that when shown to President Lincoln they helped convince him to preserve Yosemite as a park. Watkins captures the sublime scale of the American wilderness, the mountain peaks dramatically dwarfing Yosemite Falls, one of the highest waterfalls in America. Watkins produced a lush image by working up extremely rich textures in the developing process and a sense of drama by

creating powerful value contrasts and a composition of forceful diagonals descending from both right and left. To keep the sky from going a monotonous white, which would have happened had he used the proper exposure for the land, Watkins employed a second negative to add clouds. If we take into consideration the degree of manipulation of the camera, including depth of focus, aperture time, the decisions that went into selecting and framing the composition, and the numerous tools used in the darkroom, we can understand why Watkins declared his photographs art, even exhibiting them in 1862 at the prestigious Goupil Gallery in New York.

DOCUMENTATION Photography was also put in the service of categorizing the social types so central to the Positivist mentality. Perhaps the best example of this use of photography is Adolphe Smith's *Street Life in London* (1878), initially issued monthly as illustrated brochures, much like the *physiologies* in France. Smith was the nom-de-plume for Adolphe Smith Headingley (1846–1924), a social activist, who teamed up with photographer John Thomson (1837–1921), who also wrote some of the lengthy text for each social type. As stated in their introduction, they viewed the photograph as an objective tool for validating their descriptions: "[We wish to bring] to bear the precision of photography in illustration of our subject. The unquestionable accuracy of this testimony will enable us to present true types of the London Poor and shield us from the accusation of either underrating or exaggerating individual peculiarities of appearance."

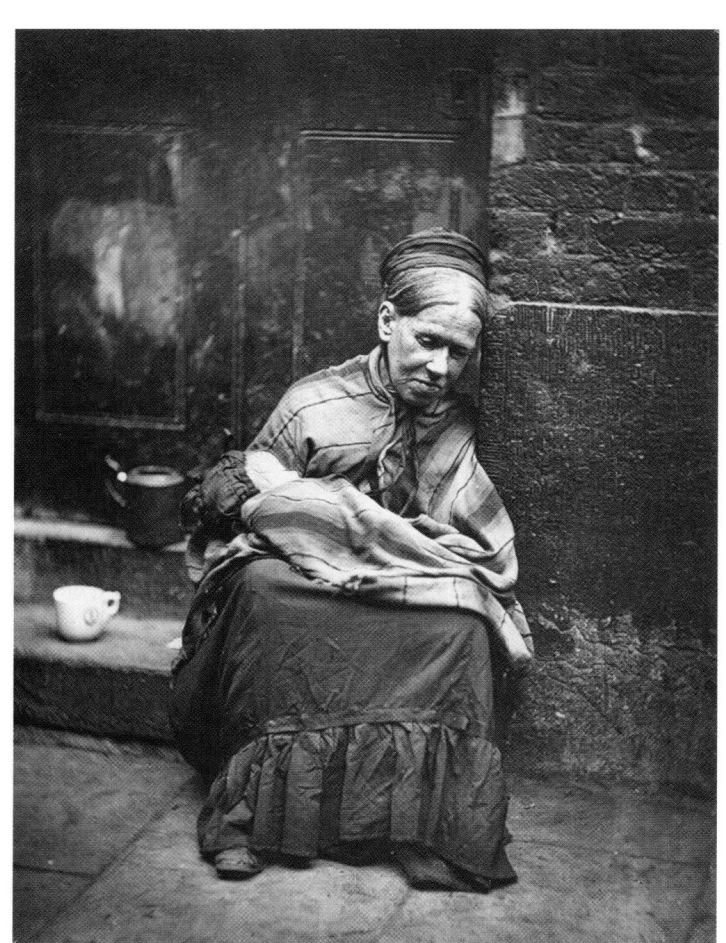

25.34 John Thomson. *The Crawlers*, 1877–78. Woodburytype. Victoria & Albert Museum, London

While most of Thomson's images seem quite objective and unbiased, some, like *The Crawlers* (fig. **25.34**), are powerful and compassionate, making the viewer sympathize with the plight of the poor. Here, a homeless widow minds the child of a working mother. The photo appeared in a brochure called *The Crawlers*, a reference to the indigent street dwellers who occasionally got enough money to buy tea and then, being too weak to walk, crawled to a pub for hot water.

Reporting the News: Photojournalism

Early photography also recorded famous events—a forerunner of photojournalism. Among the most outstanding examples are images of the Civil War, such as *A Harvest of Death, Gettysburg, Pennsylvania, July 1863* (fig. **25.35**) by Timothy O'Sullivan (ca. 1840–1882), who like Watkins became one of the great photographers of the American West. Before setting off to document the Civil War, O'Sullivan began his career as an apprentice to Mathew Brady (1823–1896), owner of the most famous photographic portrait gallery in America, located in New York. (Abraham Lincoln sat for Brady over 30 times and credited Brady's flattering

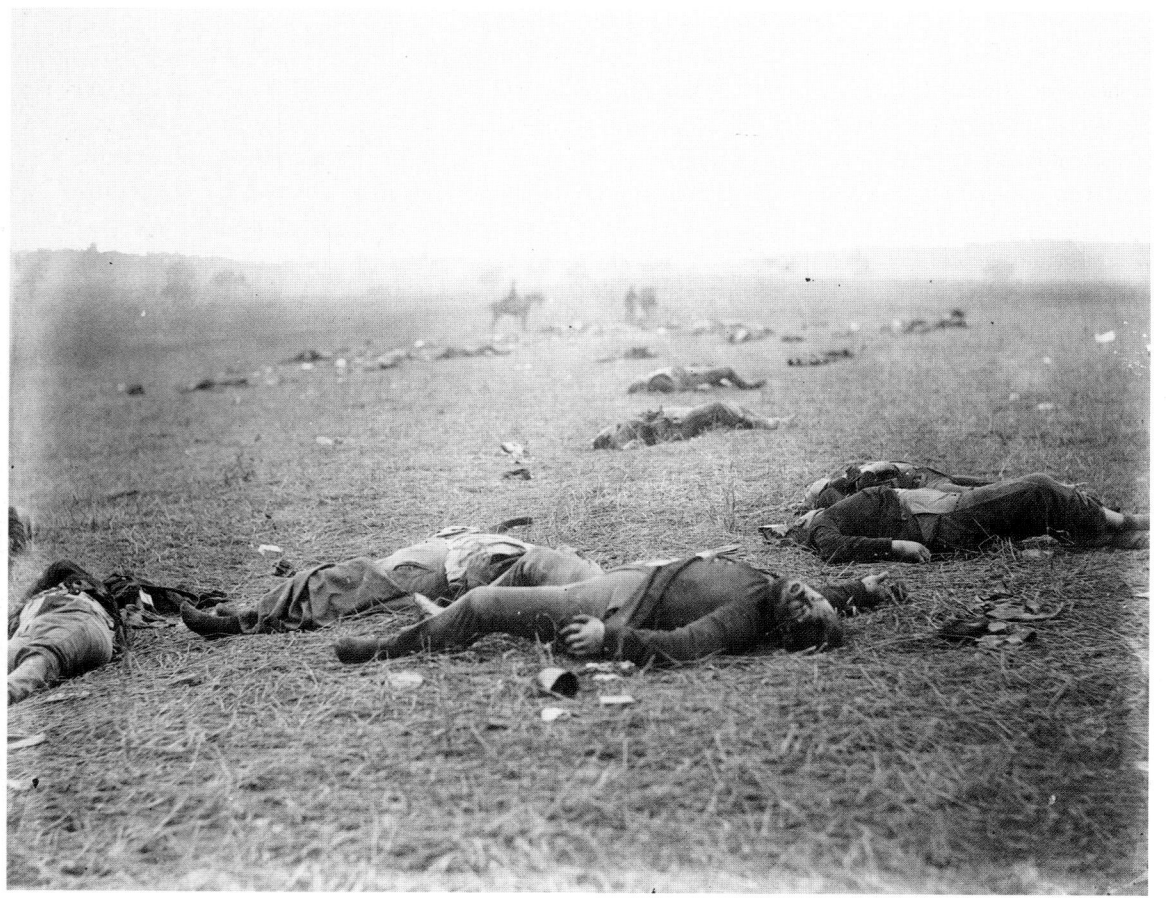

25.35 Timothy O'Sullivan, *A Harvest of Death, Gettysburg, Pennsylvania, July 1863*, from Alexander Gardner's *Gardner's Photographic Sketchbook of the War*. 1866. Albumen print (also available as stereocard), 7 × 8¹¹⁄₁₆" (17.8 × 22 cm). Brady Civil War Collection. Library of Congress, Washington, D.C.

1860 albumen print portrait with helping him win that November's presidential election.) In 1862–63, O'Sullivan signed up with the photographic team of Alexander Gardner and contributed 44 images to the album *Gardner's Photographic Sketchbook of the War* (1866). Unlike the banal European photographic images of the 1854–56 Crimean War, the Civil War photographs of O'Sullivan and his colleagues captured the horrific devastation wrought by the American conflict, despite the fact that the exposure time required by their cameras did not permit action pictures.

In *A Harvest of Death*, we feel the power of the documentary reality of photography, which a painted image can never have. We see *real* people and *real* death—images of an actual event on a definite date, the Battle of Gettysburg on July 3, 1863—not a fictitious image. Although we know that the war photographers often moved objects and bodies for the sake of their pictures, there is no evidence to suggest that O'Sullivan did so here. In any case he conveys the grim reality of war. The anonymous corpses are as lifeless as bales of hay waiting to be collected, hence the title. Their dark forms are hauntingly contrasted with the void of the overcast sky. The cropped bodies at right and left add to the brutality of the scene, so convincingly registered with the gaping mouth on the face of the dead soldier in the foreground. The living are pushed deep into the background, shrouded in the morning mist, as though life during this seemingly endless national conflict is itself dissolving into just the barest memory.

Photography as Art: Pictorialism and Combination Printing

Not all nineteenth-century photographers saw the new medium as primarily a tool to document reality. Some viewed it as high art and deliberately explored photography's aesthetic potential, confident it was as valid an art form as painting and sculpture. This attitude, which some critics found threatening (see *Primary Source*, page 896), was more prevalent in Europe than in America in the first 50 years of photography. Many artists experimented with the camera. Degas, for example, made photographs, although they had no obvious impact on or relationship to his painting, and Eakins used the photograph as he would a preliminary drawing, employing it to establish his compositions, which ultimately do not look photographic. Many painters and sculptors had collections of photographs, especially of models, which were used as source material. Courbet in particular is known to have used photographs from the 1860s for both his figurative paintings and landscapes. Arguments have been made that the look of photographs influenced artists, particularly Realists and Impressionists, but these claims remain controversial.

BRITISH PICTORIALISM In London, a group headed by Oscar Gustave Rejlander (1813–1875), a former painter who has been called "the father of art photography," and Henry Peach Robinson (1830–1901), another former painter who at one time was perhaps the most famous photographer in the world, began making **composite images** designed to look like Old Master and contemporary paintings. Both artists posed and costumed figures, whom they put in staged settings. To make their final photograph, they would take numerous photographs, producing multiple negatives (Rejlander as many as 30), which they then laboriously arranged in what was basically a cut-and-paste assemblage. The resulting images were often heavy-handed, far from seamless and not at all lifelike. Contemporaries derogatorily referred to them as "patchwork quilts." Their style is called Pictorialism, because the staged images were meant to look like paintings. Despite the fame of its principal practitioners, Pictorialist combination printing did not remain popular.

More successful were those Pictorialists who had a personal aesthetic vision and instead of using multiple negatives used just one, manipulating the camera and printing process to meet their needs. Although far less well known during her lifetime, Julia Margaret Cameron (1815–1879) is perhaps the most celebrated today of the British Pictorialists. Unlike Rejlander and Robinson, she did not use combination printing. Her trademark was an out-of-focus blurring to make her images seem painterly, as seen in *Sister Spirits* (fig. **25.36**) of about 1865. Born in Calcutta and settling on the Isle of Wight in 1860 after the death of her

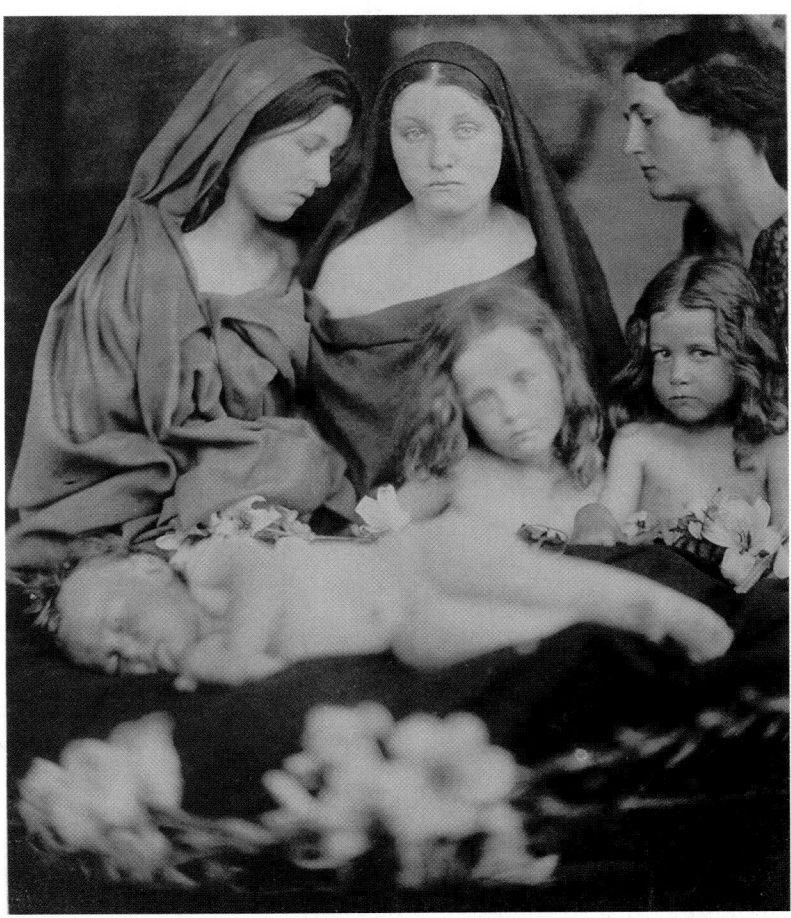

25.36 Julia Margaret Cameron, *Sister Spirits*. ca. 1865. Albumen print, 12^{7}/$_{16}$ × 10½" (31.6 × 26.6 cm). George Eastman House, Rochester, New York. Gift of Eastman Kodak Company

Charles Baudelaire
(1821–1867)

"The Modern Public and Photography," from Part 2 of *The Salon of 1859*

Baudelaire, now known primarily for his poetry, was an important art critic at midcentury and a powerful advocate for artists painting contemporary life.

I am convinced that the badly applied advances of photography, like all purely material progress for that matter, have greatly contributed to the impoverishment of French artistic genius. ... Poetry and progress are two ambitious men that hate each other, with an instinctive hatred, and when they meet along a pathway one or other must give way. If photography is allowed to deputize for art in some of art's activities, it will not be long before it has supplanted or corrupted art altogether, thanks to the stupidity of the masses, its natural ally. Photography must, therefore, return to its true duty, which is that of handmaid of the arts and sciences. ... Let photography quickly enrich the traveller's album, and restore to his eyes the precision his memory may lack; let it adorn the library of the naturalist, magnify microscopic insects, even strengthen, with a few facts, the hypotheses of the astronomer; let it, in short, be the secretary and record-keeper of whomsoever needs absolute material accuracy for professional reasons. ... But if once it be allowed to impinge on the sphere of the intangible and the imaginary, on anything that has value solely because man adds something to it from his soul, then woe betide us!

Source: *Art in Paris, 1845-1862*, tr. Jonathan Maynes (London: Phaidon Press, 1965)

husband, Cameron soon became an intimate of leading poets and scientists, and a thorn in the side of the photography world when she challenged the supremacy of crisp, focused imagery. Like Rejlander and Robinson, she staged scenes using actors, costumes, and sets, and illustrated such literary sources as the Bible, Shakespeare, and the poet laureate Alfred, Lord Tennyson (1809–1892). Stylistically, her images recall artists as diverse as Rembrandt and Pietro Perugino (see page 553).

Sister Spirits reflects the impact of the Pre-Raphaelites and Aesthetic Movement, in particular their preference for spiritual images set in the Late Gothic or Early Renaissance periods. Her women look as though they have stepped out of a Perugino painting and suggest such saints as Mary and Anne. The two children look like angels, and the sleeping baby like the Christ Child. One can also view the picture as the Three Ages of Woman, since the title suggests that the baby is most likely female. Cameron's blurred foreground is more than just a gimmick to give the image a painterly touch. It also carries psychological and symbolic meaning, for by visually dissolving the flowers and baby, Cameron makes the focused women consciously aware of the undetermined fate of the sleeping infant. Concern, pensiveness, and questioning are registered on the faces, and we sense a spiritual female bonding in this tight grouping of figures, who are closed off in the background as the image again goes fuzzy. While the photograph has soft sensual elements, it does not present women as objects meant for a male viewer, nor as appendages to a male world. Instead it reflects a powerful female vision as it embraces a female spirituality.

Cameron was generally criticized not only for her blurry images, which were attributed to incompetence, but also for the very act of making photographs. As a female photographer in a sexist society, she found it difficult getting men to participate in her Pictorialist photographs, although they would pose for their own portraits. She was criticized for exhibiting her art, which was a rare event for respectable Englishwomen in the Victorian era, and she was admonished for selling her photographs through a major London print dealer—it was deemed inappropriate for women to earn money. By redefining camera focus, Cameron challenged not only what was becoming the normative approach to photographic vision but also a vocation that was specifically male. Ironically, by the end of the century, male photographers would adopt her vision.

COMBINATION PRINTING IN FRANCE In France, one of the most passionate champions of art photography was Gustave Le Gray (1820–1884). Initially a painter, he turned to photography and became one of the medium's technical innovators, being the first to use double printing (using two negatives), which he used to compensate for the bleaching out of the sky in his marine photographs. While he pioneered paper negatives and the wet-collodion process, both of which, as discussed, allowed for finer images and greater detail, his approach to the medium was often quite painterly, focusing on a dramatic contrast of dark and light. To accomplish this, he invented processes that produced extremely fine gradations of tone and one technique that allowed him to develop a print for up to two weeks after it was exposed, during which he could manipulate the image. He also touched up negatives with a brush to alter their tonality and remove objects, and he toned his prints with a solution of gold chloride in hydrochloric acid, resulting in a lush violet-purple quality.

These techniques can be seen in *Brig on the Water* (fig. **25.37**) of 1856, an especially rich albumen print made from two wet-collodion glass negatives, one for the sky, the other for the sea, since at the time sky and sea required very different exposure times. What makes this image so exceptional is the rich range of tones that Le Gray was able to achieve, largely due to his dark-room technique. This technique allowed him to darken the sides of the image to dramatically frame the sea. It also allowed for the rich patterning of the dark clouds, which are contrasted with

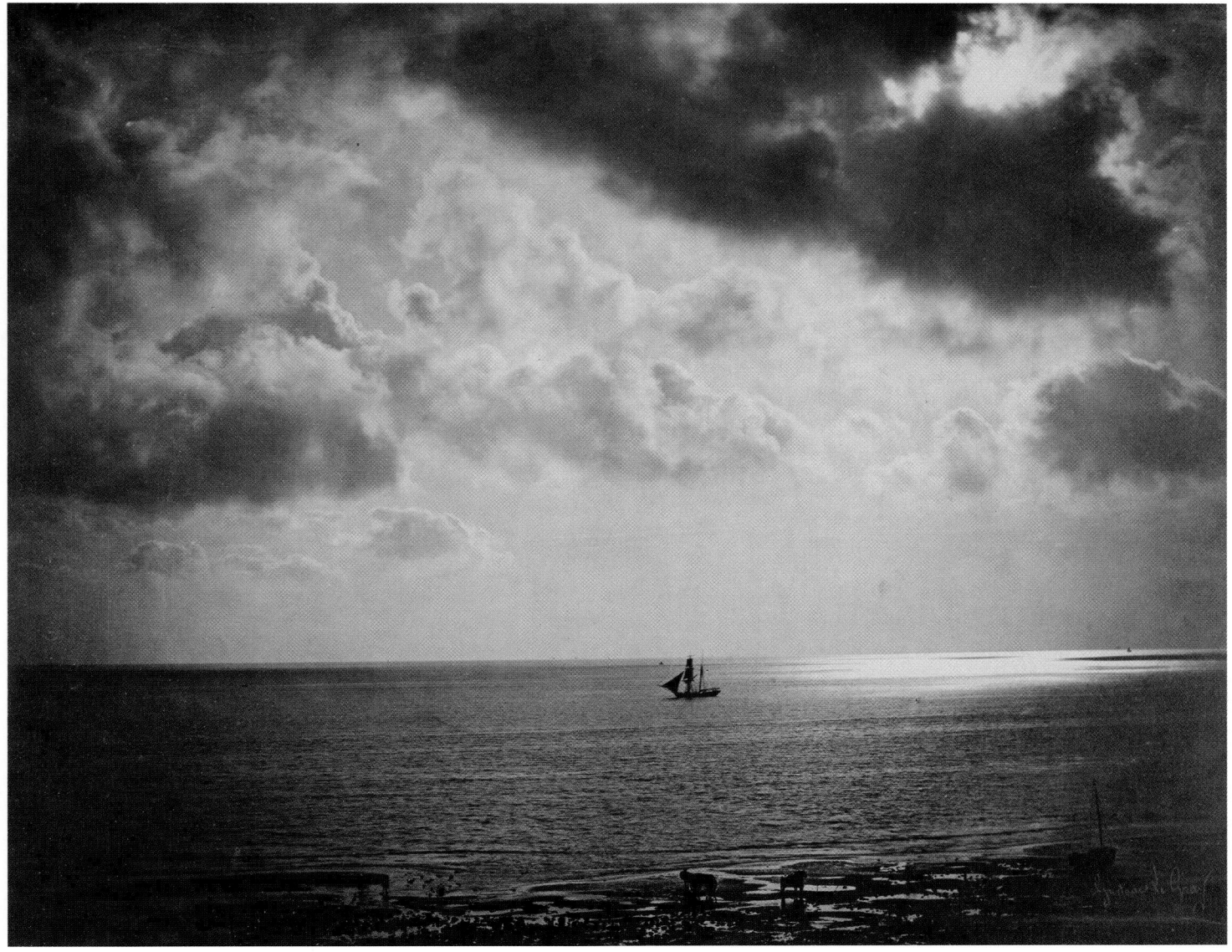

25.37 Gustave Le Gray, *Brig on the Water*. 1856. Albumen silver print from glass negative, 12⅝ × 16¹⁄₁₆" (32.1 × 40.8 cm). The J. Paul Getty Museum, Los Angeles. (84.XM.637.2)

lighter clouds in the center. And, finally, it allowed Le Gray to heighten the reflection of the setting sun on the water at the horizon, and to make light flicker among the waves in the foreground. The play of light and dark throughout the image is dramatic and the product of Le Gray's technical finesse. The result is a transcendental seascape where the drama of clouds, light, and sea dwarfing a lone silhouetted boat seems to embody the elemental forces of nature. Not surprisingly, *Brig on the Water* ranked among the most popular photographs of its day, one London dealer even claiming it had "800 copies subscribed for in two months."

Le Gray is believed to have been the first photographer to appear in the graphic-arts section of the Salons. He passionately felt photography was art, writing "the future of photography does not lie in the cheapness but in the quality of a picture....it is my wish that photography, rather than falling into the domain of an industry or of commerce, might remain in that of an art."

ARCHITECTURE AND THE INDUSTRIAL REVOLUTION

Iron was another product of the Industrial Revolution, and its relationship to architecture was as nebulous as that of photography to fine art. Initially, in the late eighteenth and early nineteenth centuries, iron was used for civil engineering, to build bridges and factories. Britain, home of the Industrial Revolution, began mass-producing cast iron in 1767 and remained its greatest producer through the first half of the nineteenth century. It led the way in the architectural adaptation of iron, erecting in 1779 the first iron bridge, an arched structure spanning the narrow Severn River at Coalbrookdale. Soon, the metal was used for the columns in textile factories and, by 1796–97, for an entire internal structure.

Revival styles continued to dominate architecture up to the closing decades of the nineteenth century, but the use of iron, while quite limited, freed buildings and civic structures from historicism because form (design) was now determined by the material and by engineering principles, thus setting the stage for the advent of modern architecture—not in Britain but in Chicago—in the 1880s. The pragmatism of iron construction and the blunt presentation of the medium's structural properties parallel the pragmatism and realism of the Age of Positivism.

Ferrovitreous Structures: Train Sheds and Exhibition Palaces

In the early nineteenth century, builders often used cast iron for the columns of Gothic-revival churches, and in the 1830s, with the rise of railroads, they employed it for train sheds as well. The sheds had to span parallel tracks and platforms and be high enough to allow steam and smoke to dissipate. The first of these sheds, London's Euston Station (1835–39), spanned 40 feet. The grandest was London's St. Pancras Station (1863–76), the girded metal arches of which spanned 263 feet (fig. **25.38**) and when extended in depth formed the largest undivided enclosed space up to that time. The cast-iron skeleton supported a roof of glass. This combination of iron and glass is often called ferrovitreous (for another example of a ferrovitreous train shed, see the Gare Saint-Lazare as represented in Monet's 1877 painting of the same title, fig. 25.16). Each arch of St. Pancras Station is actually a double arch, one on top of the other, tied together with a truss, a reinforcing structure composed of two or more triangles sharing sides. Known since Roman times when it was used for wood construction and hence by all roof and bridge builders, by 1860 the truss was ubiquitous in metal structures spanning large spaces.

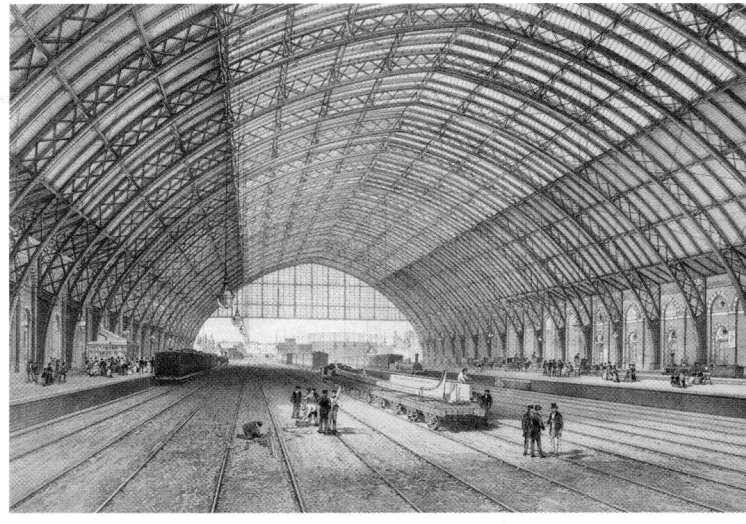

25.38 St. Pancras Station, London. 1863–76. Lithograph. Science Museum, London

As spectacular an engineering feat as a train shed like St. Pancras was, it paled in comparison to the new railway bridges, which had to cross deep canyons and broad rivers. Train sheds were nothing more than small-scale pieces of bridge architecture, the arches girded together to whatever depth was needed. The regularized repetition of arches is itself symbolic of mass production, reflecting the ability of industry to churn out an endless supply of the exact same product at a constant rhythm.

Perhaps the most famous ferrovitreous building of the nineteenth century is the Crystal Palace (fig. **25.39**), built in London in 1851 to house the first great international trade fair, the Great

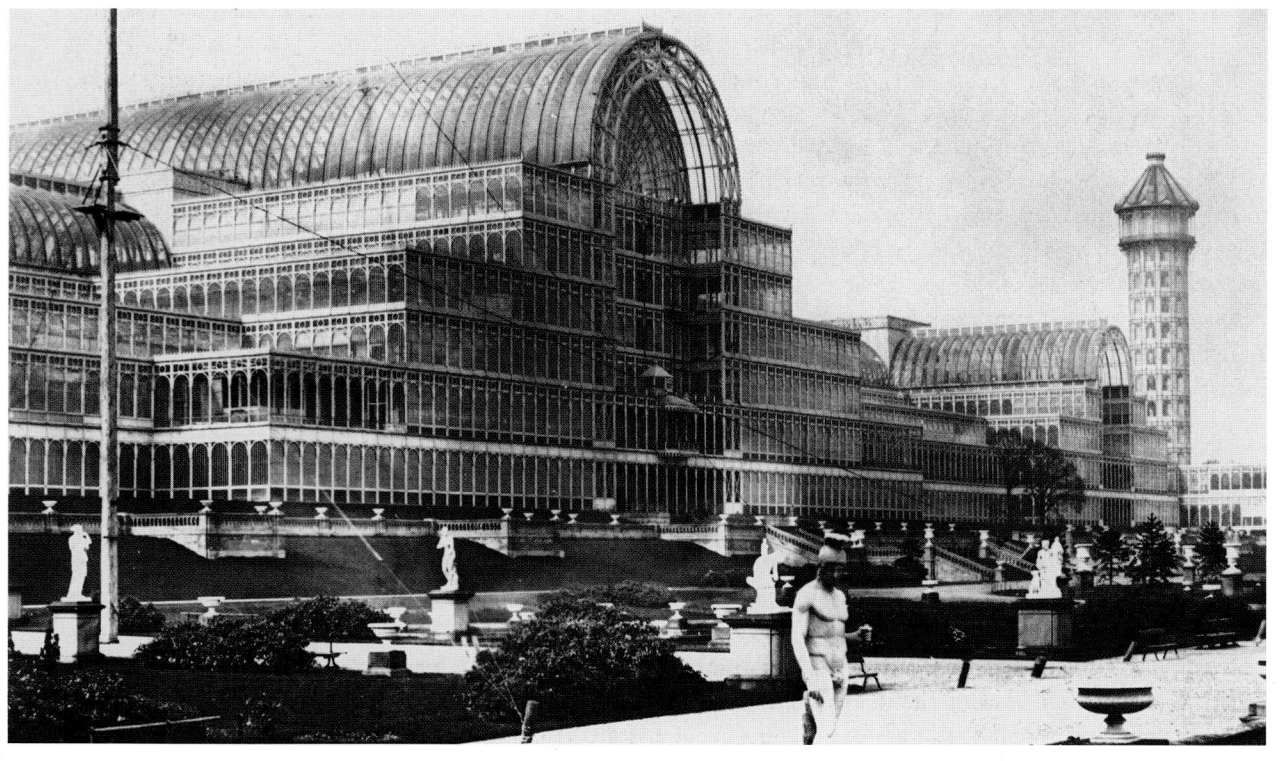

25.39 The Crystal Palace at Sydenham, showing the main dome and entrance from the ornamental gardens and paths; probably by Phillip Henry Delamotte (1820–89). The Victoria & Albert Museum, London. Museum no. 39284

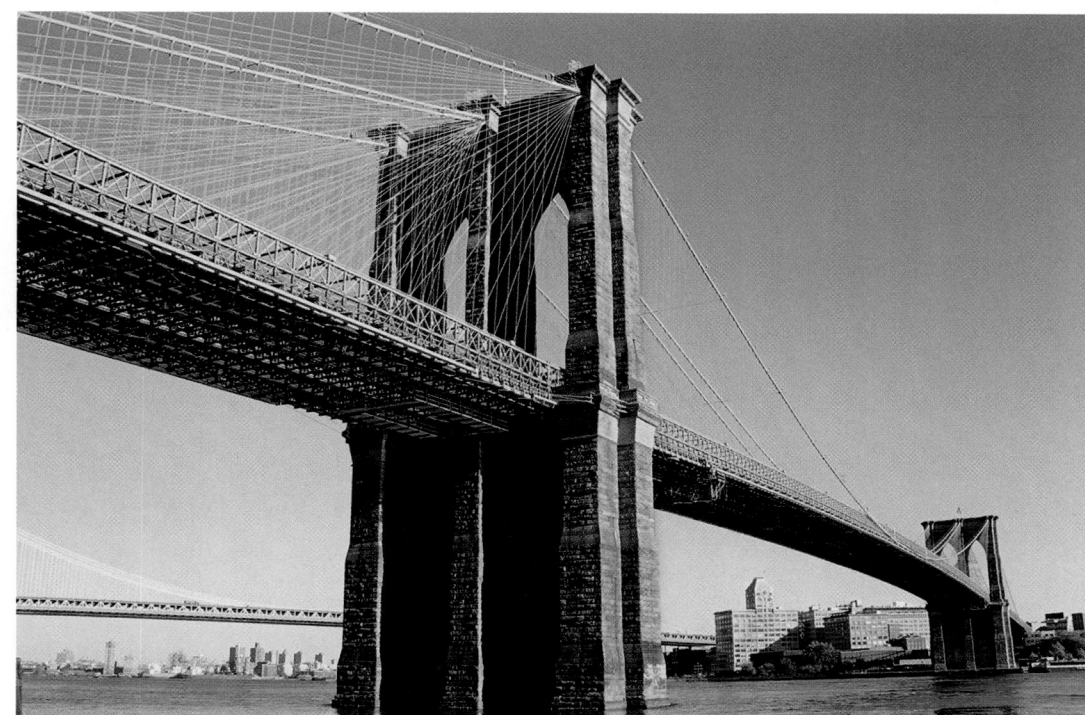

Exhibition of the Works of Industry of All Nations. The fair was designed to showcase the product development, technological advances, agricultural improvements, and fine and applied arts of the new industrial nations, with Britain expecting to shine as the most advanced. The exposition was not just a trade fair but a celebration of Western industrialization. Britain's preeminent greenhouse architect, Sir Joseph Paxton (1801–1865), designed the building and with engineers erected what is essentially a giant greenhouse. While the ferrovitreous materials are the same as in Paxton's earlier greenhouses, the form is not, for it resembles an English cathedral, with a long, barrel-vaulted center nave, a lower barrel-vaulted transept, and stepped-down side aisles. (After the exposition closed, the building was dismantled and moved to nearby Sydenham, where another transept was added. It was destroyed in a fire in 1936.) The building was a cathedral of industry, which had become the new religion. The familiar form and human scale of the building's small component parts, such as panes of sheet glass, must have helped put people at ease within this looming, visionary, 1,851-foot-long structure—its length determined by the year of the exhibition, 1851.

Historic Eclecticism and Technology

The Crystal Palace had a strong technological look, perhaps because it was conceived as a temporary, nontraditional building designed to host an exposition dedicated to technology and industry. Generally, monumental, stately buildings, such as courthouses, theaters, and parliaments, were not built of iron. Instead they were executed in stone and were associational or "representational," designed in a revival style that established a lineage to the Classical, Gothic, or Renaissance past. We saw, for example,

how Garnier incorporated elements of the Louvre into the Paris Opéra in order to link Louis Napoleon to Louis XIV. Iron was reserved for industrial buildings, such as train sheds and bridges and enormous food markets (Les Halles, Paris, 1850s) and urban shopping malls (Galleria Vittorio Emmanuele, Milan, 1865–77).

BROOKLYN BRIDGE The need to cloak technology in historic eclecticism is apparent in what is perhaps the greatest spanning structure of the nineteenth century, the Brooklyn Bridge (fig. **25.40**), designed by John Roebling (1806–1869) in 1867 and finished by his son Washington Roebling (1837–1926) in 1883. When announced, the bridge was considered a folly; when finished, a wonder of the world. Suspension bridges already existed, but on a much smaller scale, and no one imagined it possible to dig piers in such a deep waterway as New York's East River, to have them rise 300 feet above the water, and then to span the vast distance from Brooklyn to Manhattan *while* supporting fives lanes of traffic for railroads, carriages, and pedestrians. To accomplish this feat, John Roebling not only used vertical cables attached to the main drooping suspension cables, but also wire cables running from the top of the piers to regular intervals on the bridge, creating triangular units that he considered trusses.

Typical of the taste of the times, the two enormous piers are an eclectic combination of revival styles, with Gothic revival prevailing. In the original plan, however, the piers were Egyptian pylons, a motif retained in the final version only in the gorge moldings where the cables thread the top of the granite structure. As everyone at the time noted, the piers functioned like enormous Roman triumphal arches. The bridge was declared "America's Arch of Triumph," a reference not only to its awesome scale and achievements but also to America's technological superiority.

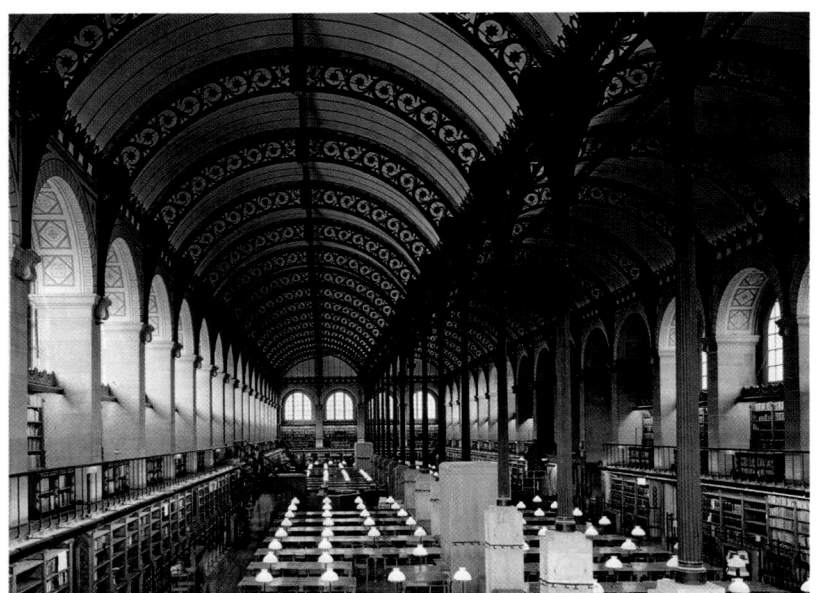

25.41 Henri Labrouste. Main reading room, Bibliothèque Sainte-Geneviève, Paris. Designed 1842, built 1842–51

BIBLIOTHÈQUE SAINTE-GENEVIÈVE By the 1850s, New York excelled at the production of cast-iron façades, where five- and six-story buildings, generally used for light manufacturing, were entirely sheathed in skins of iron arches and columns resembling stone. The more monumental and nonindustrial the building, the less likely the overt use of iron. The most innovative use of iron in an important civic structure is in Paris, where the Bibliothèque Sainte-Geneviève was designed in 1842 by Henri Labrouste (1801–1875). The exterior of the library is designed in a Renaissance revival style that evokes Jacopo Sansovino's famous Library of San Marco (1536) in Venice and the Medici Bank in Milan (ca. 1460). The exterior gives no hint of the radical technology displayed within. The main reading room (fig 25.41), located on the second floor, consists of two airy barrel vaults, their columns and arches made of cast iron (the ceiling is mesh-reinforced plaster). Instead of the Italian Renaissance of the exterior, the interior suggests the Gothic, specifically a Romanesque refectory. But to a Parisian, the metal arches would immediately bring to mind the new train sheds, suggesting not only modern life but also a sense of voyage, which indeed is the function of books.

Labrouste did not *need* to use iron in his library: He chose to do so for metaphorical and symbolic purposes. In effect, he was announcing the importance of technology in fashioning a new and better world. This symbolic use of iron even appears in the first-floor entrance, where a dense arrangement of fluted square Classical columns suggesting an Egyptian hypostyle hall supports metal arches resembling modern iron bridges, a reminder to the visitor that books and technology are a bridge to the future.

Announcing the Future: The Eiffel Tower

The most famous iron structure from the period is the Eiffel Tower (fig. 25.42), erected by the French engineer Gustave

Eiffel (1832–1923) in 1887–89 as an entrance to the 1889 Paris International Exposition. To create his tower, Eiffel basically appropriated a trussed **pylon** from the many bridges he had already constructed. At 984 feet high, twice the height of any other structure then in the world, it dominated the city, and because its design was largely determined by its structural integrity rather than adherence to a particular architectural style, it initially affronted Parisians, who declared it an eyesore. The lacework tower was so thin it looked fragile and unstable; Eiffel added arches at the base and organic decoration on the two platforms (removed in the 1930s) to make visitors more comfortable with his radical, visionary structure.

As with the Brooklyn Bridge, however, the public, grasping at the familiarity of the arches at the base, soon came to view the tower as a triumphal arch, one heralding the triumph of French technology and industry. It also saw the tower as a declaration of the triumph of the people: For a pittance, anyone could take the elevator to the upper platforms. Here, common citizens could look down on the churches and palaces, the bastions of tradition and privilege, which the century's continuous march toward democracy had undermined. The Eiffel Tower became a tower of the people and a symbol of Paris, if not France as well. More important, it pointed to the architecture of the next century, one of Modernism that would shed historical references and instead allow style to reflect the nature of the new building materials.

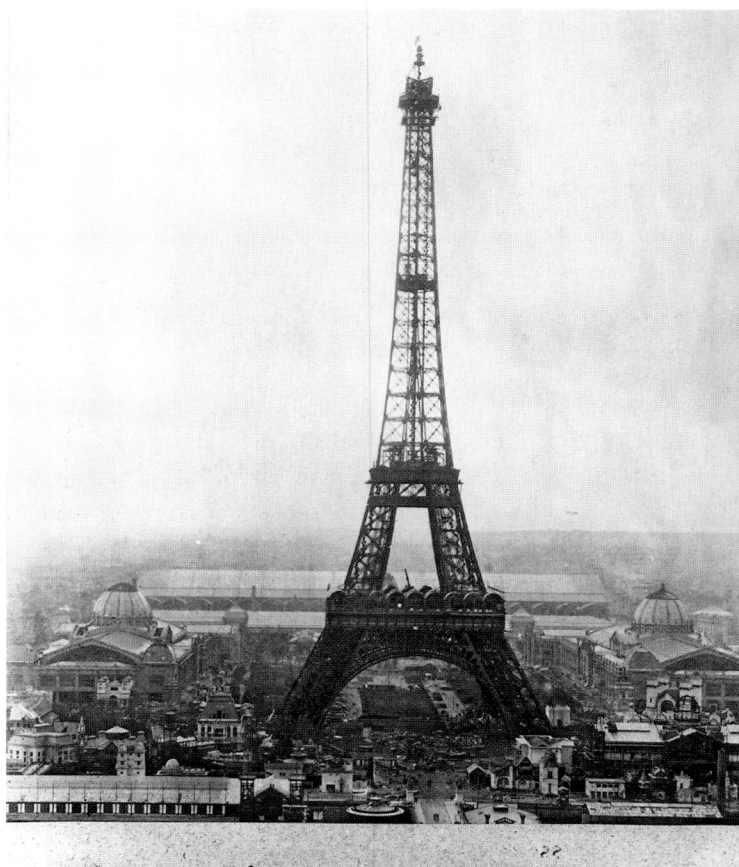

25.42 Gustave Eiffel. Eiffel Tower, Paris. 1887–89

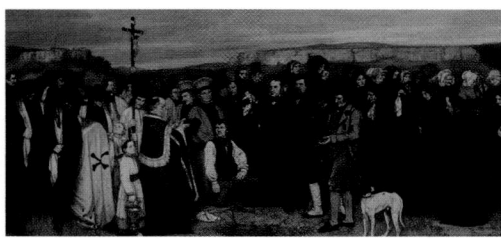

1849–50 Courbet's
Burial at Ornans

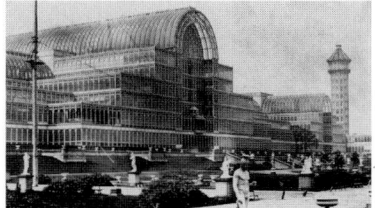

1851 Crystal Palace built to house
the Great Exhibition of the Works of
Industry of All Nations, London

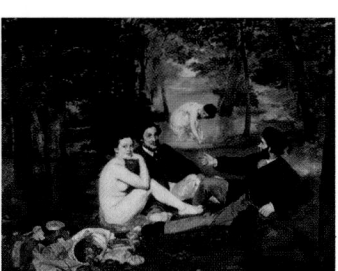

1863 Manet's *The Luncheon
on the Grass*

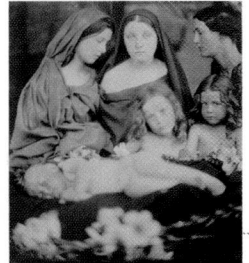

1865 Julia Margaret
Cameron's *Sister Spirits*

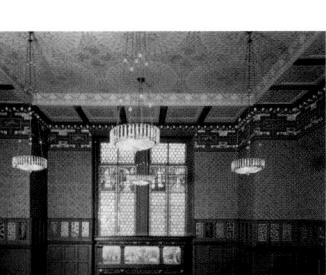

1867 William Morris designs Green Dining
Room at the South Kensington Museum,
today the Victoria & Albert Museum,
London

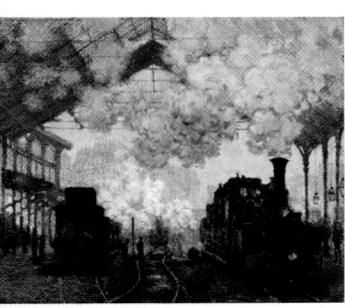

877 Claude Monet's *Gare Saint-Lazare*

1872 Winslow Homer's *Snap the Whip*

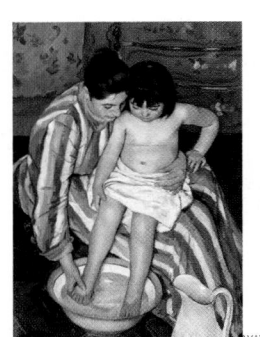

1892 Mary
Cassatt's *The
Child's Bath*

1887 Construction begins of
Eiffel Tower, Paris, opens
1889

1840

1850

1860

1870

1880

1890

The Age of
Positivism: Realism,
Impressionism, and
the Pre-Raphaelites,
1848–1885

◄ 1830 Auguste Comte begins publishing the
multivolume *Positive Philosophy*, establishing
sociology

◄ 1846 Ruskin publishes volume one of *Modern Painters*
1848 Karl Marx and Friedrich Engels publish *The
Communist Manifesto*
◄ 1848 European-wide workers' revolutions
1848 Seneca Falls Convention, Seneca, New York,
first women's rights convention in the United States
1850 Frederic Church's *Twilight in the Wilderness*

1852 Hausmann begins redesign of Paris, ends 1870
◄ 1852 Louis Napoleon, nephew of Napoleon I, proclaims
himself Napoleon III, emperor of Second Empire
◄ 1853 Commodore Perry of the United States opens up
Japan to trade with the West

1856 Jean-Auguste-Dominque Ingres's *Portrait of
Madame Inès Moitessier*

◄ 1861–65 American Civil War

◄ 1864 President Lincoln establishes Yosemite as a park

◄ 1869 First Transcontinental Railroad completed in
Promontory Summit, Utah
◄ 1871 Foundation of Germany and Italy

◄ 1873 Mark Twain and Charles Dudley Warner publish
The Gilded Age
◄ 1874 First Impressionist exhibition

◄ 1878 First International Congress of Women's Rights,
Paris

Progress and Its Discontents: Post-Impressionism, Symbolism, and Art Nouveau, 1880–1905

THE CLOSING DECADES OF THE NINETEENTH CENTURY presented a cultural dichotomy. On one side were those who optimistically reveled in the wealth, luxury, and technological progress of the industrialized world. On the other were those who perceived these same qualities as signs of decadence, excess, moral turpitude, and a spiritual

decline. Ther former experienced exuberance and pride, the latter despair and anxiety. Depending on one's viewpoint, the period was either the *Belle Époque*, "the beautiful era," or the *fin de siècle*, "the end of the century," immersed in anxiety about impending change. Often associated with the *fin de siècle* is the Decadent movement, a literary fashion that started in France in the 1880s and focused on exotic, bizarre, self-indulgent characters obsessed with leading anti-bourgeois lifestyles of visionary splendor that rejected the rational and the mechanization of modernity. The movement spread throughout Europe in the following decade. In Britain, it was best represented by the writer Oscar Wilde, whose homosexuality, dandified dress, and appreciation for the precious and unusual virtually epitomized the movement.

The end of the century, as well as the 14 years leading up to World War I, indeed constituted a period of unprecedented economic growth and prosperity, nurtured by some 40 years of peace following the 1870 Franco-Prussian War. National consolidation was largely complete, with many countries functioning as republics. Germany and France joined Britain and Belgium as truly industrialized countries, with Germany even leapfrogging over Britain, producing twice as much steel by 1914. The United States was included as well in this exclusive group. Spurred by

both capitalism and a heated nationalism was a dramatic increase in imperialism, which resulted in the carving up of Africa as well as parts of Asia and the Pacific islands into fiefdoms to be economically exploited.

The modern era, which began in the eighteenth century, now evolved into a new phase called modernity, often labeled the "New Industrial Revolution." The steam engine was refined and improved. Electricity, the telephone, the internal combustion engine, gasoline, automobiles, submarines, airplanes, moving pictures, and machines increasingly defined modern life, whose pace quickened even as it became, at least for many, more comfortable and efficient. In 1901, Guglielmo Marconi sent a wireless signal across the Atlantic, further shrinking the globe.

The late nineteenth century saw a dramatic increase in a sense of European superiority. Despite the sharp political divisions arising from nationalism, Europeans and such European-linked countries as the United States, Canada, Australia, and New Zealand shared a similar way of life and attitudes. They felt their world constituted the "civilized" world, and everything—and everyone—else was "backward." Enlightenment philosophy and science, Europeans believed, had reached a climax, creating the most sophisticated and elevated branch of humankind. As never before, Europeans became race-conscious, with whites considering themselves superior. Charles Darwin's theory of evolution, set forth in the *Origin of Species* (1859) and *Descent of Man* (1871), was twisted to reinforce this view of white supremacy. If

Detail of figure 26.29, Victor Horta. Interior stairwell of the Tassel House, Brussels

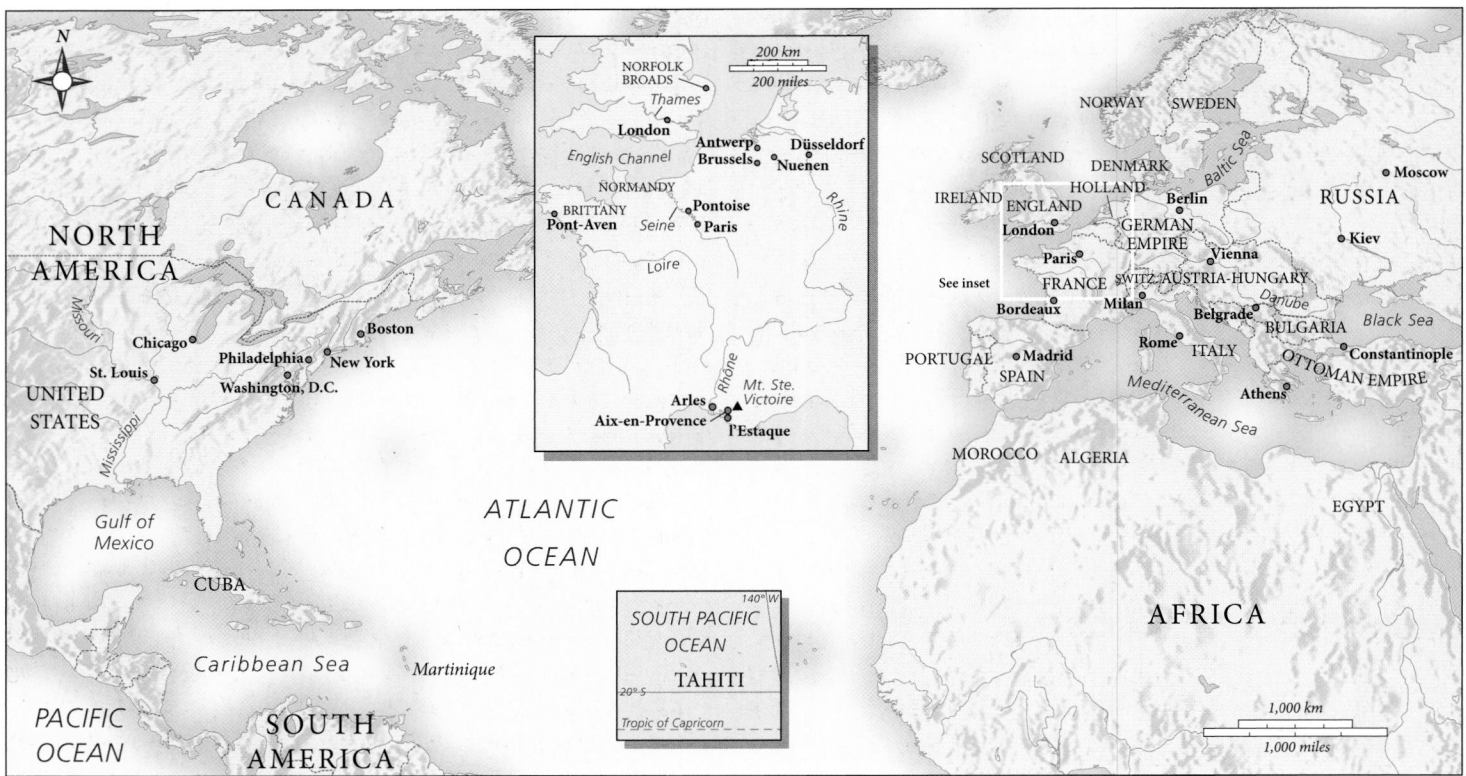

Map 26.1   Europe and North America at the end of the nineteenth century

life was a struggle that resulted in the "survival of the fittest" through "natural selection" of the "most favored races," then clearly, it seemed, advanced Western civilization was the "most favored race."

Many cultural anthropologists, however, refused to label any society as better than any other, and found tribal societies to be just as complex as Western civilization. The mores and values of any culture, they argued, were appropriate to its environment and circumstances. And then there were Europeans who found tribal cultures to be superior; lamenting industrialization and suspicious of unchecked progress in the West, they perceived the newly colonized, exploited territories in Africa and the Pacific as unspoiled utopias, havens from the materialistic evils of modern civilization. Continuing the tradition launched by Jean-Jacques Rousseau in the eighteenth century, they viewed these so-called primitive societies as still steeped in nature and thus virtuous and pure, as well as connected to universal spiritual forces.

Modernity also resulted in a renewed search for the spiritual in the closing decades of the century. Anthropologists demonstrated that the rituals, practices, and beliefs of Christianity were not unique at all, but had parallels in tribal cultures and Eastern religions. The strongest expression of this attitude appeared in Sir James Frazer's (1854–1941) multivolume *The Golden Bough*, which even declared that magic and religion were separated by a very fine line. As growing numbers of people fled progress by embracing an intense spirituality, they were drawn to orthodox Western religions as well as to Eastern-inspired practices such as

Theosophy and Rosicrucianism. Many were also drawn to animism and the occult, the period witnessing a dramatic increase in the appearance of psychic and spiritual mediums.

The late nineteenth century also marks the rise of psychology. The German physiologist Wilhelm Wundt (1832–1920) transformed psychology from a philosophy to a natural science by basing it on scientific method, which he detailed in his 1874 *Principles of Physiological Psychology*. Meanwhile, the research of the Russian Ivan Pavlov (1849–1936) sparked an intense interest in how human behavior is conditioned by experience and environment. And in Vienna, the neurologist Sigmund Freud began to formulate his theories of the unconscious, publishing his *Interpretation of Dreams* in 1900. This interest in the mind and the elemental forces driving human responses went well beyond the scientific community to permeate popular and high culture, and artists as diverse as Auguste Rodin and Edvard Munch increasingly focused on the unseen forces residing deep within the mind that produced such outward manifestations as sexual urges and anxiety.

Another major influence molding this period was the emergence of the "New Woman": women bent on changing the restrictive laws and conventions of Victorian society. The women's movement, launched in the second quarter of the nineteenth century in both Europe and America, became a powerful force in the last quarter, as women organized and forcefully demanded political, economic, educational, and social equality. By the 1890s, the term "New Woman" had been coined, and the mass media, especially in America, developed a visual image to describe her: She was tall, athletic, and independent, and she rejected the onerous probity of the Victorian era, wearing comfortable, masculine-inspired clothing while also flaunting her sexuality. This New Woman threatened most Victorian men, who viewed her independence as a challenge to their power, preferring women to stay at home, uneducated and without financial independence. Male artists were no exception, and the castrating, dominating *femme fatale* became a popular theme, a visual expression of male fears. At the same time, an increasing number of women artists presented women from a female viewpoint, one that gave them social importance and dignity, as Mary Cassatt and Julia Margaret Cameron had done before (see Chapter 25). These artists broke with the male tradition of depicting women as sex objects or as being defined only by their dependence on men.

In many respects, progress was the watchword of the late nineteenth century, and the force to which artists responded. The vast majority rejected it, seeking a spiritual, utopian, or primitive alternative. The result was a range of styles or movements, chief among them Post-Impressionism, Symbolism, and Art Nouveau. Most of the artists built on the brilliant formal innovations of Manet and the Impressionists and created work that was more abstract than representational. Their art was also highly personal, not reflecting a group vision. Consequently many artists, such as Vincent Van Gogh and Paul Cézanne, cultivated their own distinctive form of mark making. Often their work was visionary, depicting fantasies and dreamworlds, and often it was spiritual, as it sought relief from the crass, empty materialism of modernity and a more meaningful explanation for existence. Many artists found their subject matter in the sanctuary of the Classical, medieval, and biblical past, which the Realists had so fiercely rejected. Even modern architecture indulged in fantasy and spirituality. Art Nouveau, for example, succeeded in freeing architecture from the dominance of the eclecticism of revival styles by creating buildings that eerily resembled strange but marvelous organic forms. At the same time, the great Chicago architects of the 1880s and 1890s developed the first glass and steel skyscrapers and, in the case of Frank Lloyd Wright, complex houses made up of a relentless modern geometry of horizontals and verticals. Still, they often invested their modern buildings and houses with a powerful spirituality that tied them as much to cosmic forces as they did to the constant march of progress. While Realism and Impressionism had sought to capture the essence of the modern world, Post-Impressionism, Symbolism, and Art Nouveau largely struggled to escape it and to provide an antidote.

POST-IMPRESSIONISM

The early twentieth-century British art critic Roger Fry coined the term Post-Impressionism to describe the avant-garde art that followed Impressionism, work that became a springboard that took art in new directions. Each of the Post-Impressionist artists—Paul Cézanne, Georges Seurat, Vincent van Gogh, and Paul Gauguin—developed a unique style. Still, there are artistic conditions that unify the period from 1880 to 1904. The Post-Impressionists rejected the empiricist premises of Realism and Impressionism in order to create art that was more monumental, universal, and even visionary. Post-Impressionists, with the exception of Seurat, also rejected a collective way of seeing, which we found in Impressionism. Instead, each artist developed a personal aesthetic. Like the Impressionists, however, many Post-Impressionists continued to mine Japanese art for ideas. They also maintained the anti-bourgeois, anti-academic attitude of the Impressionists, similarly turning to artists' cooperatives and private galleries to promote their art.

Paul Cézanne: Toward Abstraction

Actually, Cézanne (1839–1906) is of the same generation as the Impressionists, developing his Post-Impressionism in tandem with the rise of that style. Born into a wealthy but socially isolated family in Aix-en-Provence in southern France, he rejected studying law and went to Paris to study art in 1861. He enrolled at a drawing academy, but was essentially self-taught, copying paintings in the Louvre by Delacroix and Courbet, among others. From l864 to 1869, Cézanne submitted intentionally crude, dark, intensely worked paintings depicting mysterious, morbid, and anonymous orgies, rapes, and murders to the Salon. These works were rejected, as the anti-bourgeois, anti-academic Cézanne knew they would be. In part, they were meant to shock and disgust the jurors. He painted with a palette knife and the dark pigments of Courbet, and he was also inspired by the Romantic imagery of Delacroix as well as the thematic brazenness of Manet. He even painted several *Modern Olympia*s, inspired by Manet's *Olympia* (see fig. 25.11), one of which he showed at the first Impressionist exhibition in 1874. (He would participate in the first three shows.)

In 1872, Cézanne left Paris for Pontoise and then nearby Auvers at the suggestion of Camille Pissarro (see page 876), who was already living there. The older artist became his mentor, and they bonded in their desire to make an art that stylistically looked modern. He began painting landscapes, occasionally at Pissarro's side. With this steadying influence, Cézanne's emotionalism dissipated, his palette lightened, even becoming colorful, and his compositions took on a powerful structural integrity, which had been suggested in his earlier work but now blossomed. As he would state later in life, he wanted "to make of Impressionism something solid, like the art in the museums."

We can see how he achieved this goal in a work from the next decade, *Mont Sainte-Victoire* (fig. **26.1**), painted around 1885 to 1887 in Provence, where the reclusive artist settled in the early 1880s. Typical of Impressionism, this canvas presents a light-filled landscape painted with broad brushstrokes and fairly bright color. The picture seems to shimmer at first, then it freezes. Cézanne has locked his image into a subtle network of shapes that echo one another. The curves and bends of the foreground tree branches can be found in the distant mountain and foothills. The diagonal lines on the edges of the green pastures reverberate in the houses, mountain slopes, and the directionality of the clusters of parallel

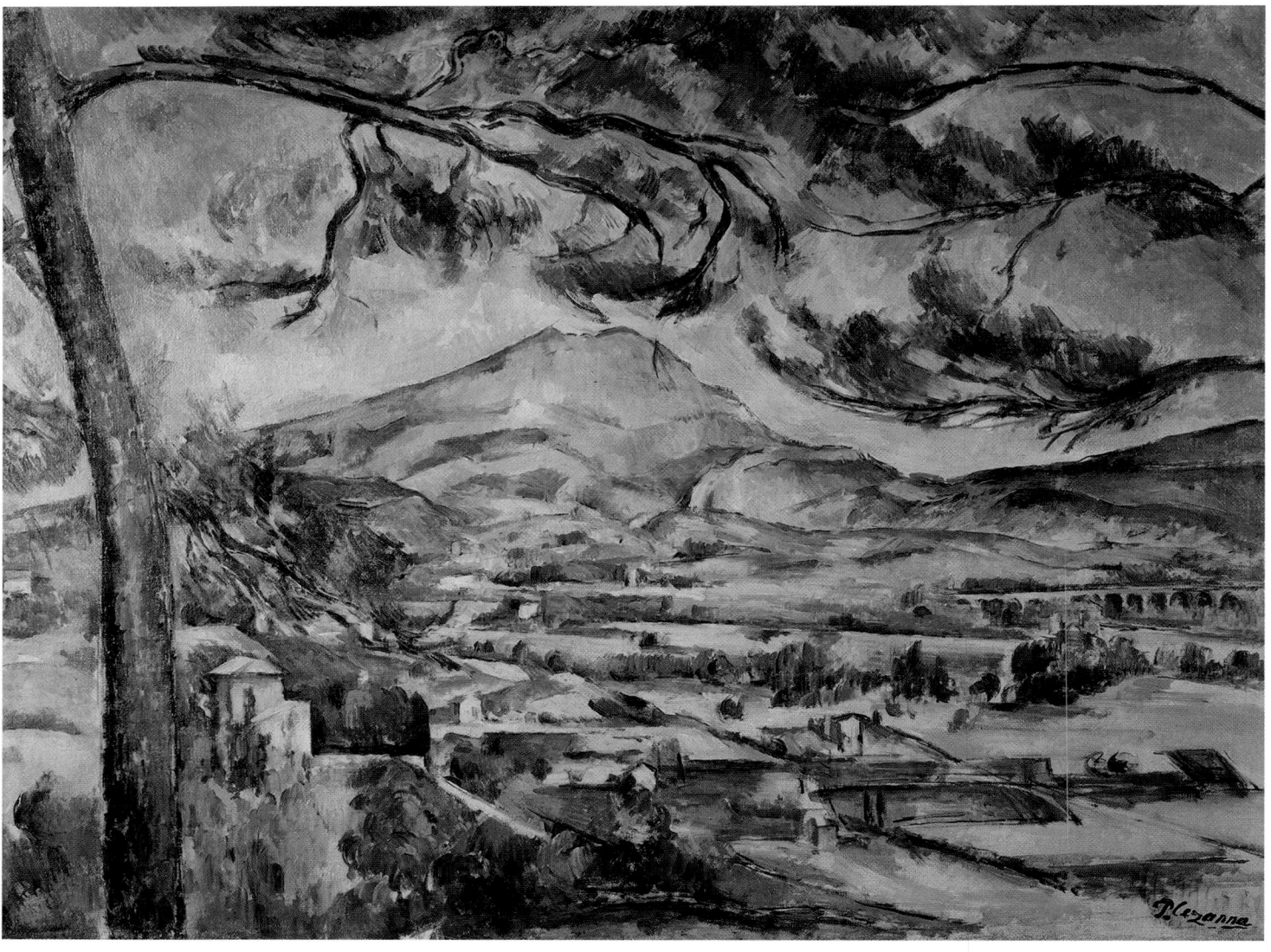

26.1 Paul Cézanne, *Mont Sainte-Victoire*. ca. 1885–87. Oil on canvas, 25½ × 32" (64.8 × 92.3 cm).
The Samuel Courtauld Trust, Courtauld Institute of Art Gallery, London. P. 1934. SC. 55

dashlike brushstrokes, perhaps best seen in the green pine needles. Just as the building to the right of the tree has a solid cubic presence, combinations of contiguous flat green pastures and ocher fields cause blocklike forms to emerge from the earth, before they dissolve once again in thin planes of color. A fair number of vertical stresses, often quite minute, are tucked into the landscape and play off strong horizontals to suggest an underlying grid.

Many aspects of the picture can be read in two diametrically opposed ways. There is an Impressionistic flicker, but it is a structurally frozen image. The picture is a deep panoramic view, and yet it is also flat and compressed, for the distant sky sits on the same plane as the foreground tree branches. This conflation is in part due to the tapestry of aligned, off-white brushstrokes that seem simultaneously to encase the pine needles and be woven into the sky. Every brushstroke sits on the surface of the canvas as a flat mark asserting the surface; and yet the strokes overlap one another, causing a sense of space or depth to exist between them. Even line has a dual function, for it can be read as shadow, as on

the top of the mountain, making depth happen, or it can be seen as a flat contour. There is a conflict here between figuration and abstraction, for while the picture obviously depicts a real world, we are never allowed to forget that we are looking at flat paint, lines, and patches of color applied to a flat canvas. We can sense the enormous amount of time that went into resolving all of these conflicts and achieving a balance between two- and three-dimensional space. Most pictures took Cézanne years to paint as he meticulously pondered every mark. (See *Primary Source*, page 907.)

In addition to landscape, Cézanne made portraits of acquaintances (never commissions, since his father provided him with a modest income), still lifes, and figure paintings, especially bathers in a landscape, and in every genre we can see the same conflicts and suppression of tension. In his 1879–83 *Still Life with Apples in a Bowl* (fig. **26.2**), we can immediately sense a Chardinesque monumentality (see fig. 22.9). There is a balancing of apples in the compote (stemmed bowl) with those on the dish, and a balancing of the folds of the white cloth with the wallpaper's leaf motif.

Paul Cézanne (1839–1906)

From a letter to Émile Bernard

Bernard had worked with Gauguin to formulate the style of the Pont-Aven School. He began a correspondence with Cézanne after meeting him at Aix-en-Provence in the spring of 1904, when this letter was written.

May I repeat what I told you here: treat nature by the cylinder, the sphere, the cone, everything in proper perspective so that each side of an object or a plane is directed towards a central point. Lines parallel to the horizon give breadth, that is a section of nature or, if you prefer, of the spectacle that the Pater Omnipotens Aeterne Deus spreads out before our eyes. Lines perpendicular to this horizon give depth. But nature for us men is more depth than surface, whence the need of introducing into our light vibrations, represented by reds and yellows, a sufficient amount of blue to give the impression of air.

Source: *Paul Cézanne: Letters*, Ed. John Rewald, Tr. Marguerite Kay (London: Bruno Cassirer, 1946)

Everything is framed by the forceful horizontal edges of the table. Each apple has a powerful physical presence as it is built up out of slablike brushstrokes, its form also carefully delineated with a distinct line. The folds of the cloth are equally plastic, their illusionistic tactility reinforced by the concrete presence of parallel bricks of paint. But the picture also has a nervous energy and ethereal flatness: The compote refuses to recede in space because its back lip tips forward. The same is true of the dish. Its edges disappear behind the apples and we have difficulty imagining their connection to each other in space. The tabletop is also spatially disorienting, for it tilts forward and up the canvas rather than moving back into space. The chunks of brushstrokes are obviously flat marks, and they cover the surface with a nervous energy. This energy is epitomized by the strange interior life that the folds of the cloth seem to have. Meanwhile, the wallpaper's leaf pattern momentarily does a reversal as it escapes its two-dimensional assignment to take on a three-dimensional life, one as concrete as that of the apples or folds of cloth. Cézanne has abandoned faithfully observed reality to create his own pictorial world, one that adheres to a private aesthetic order and

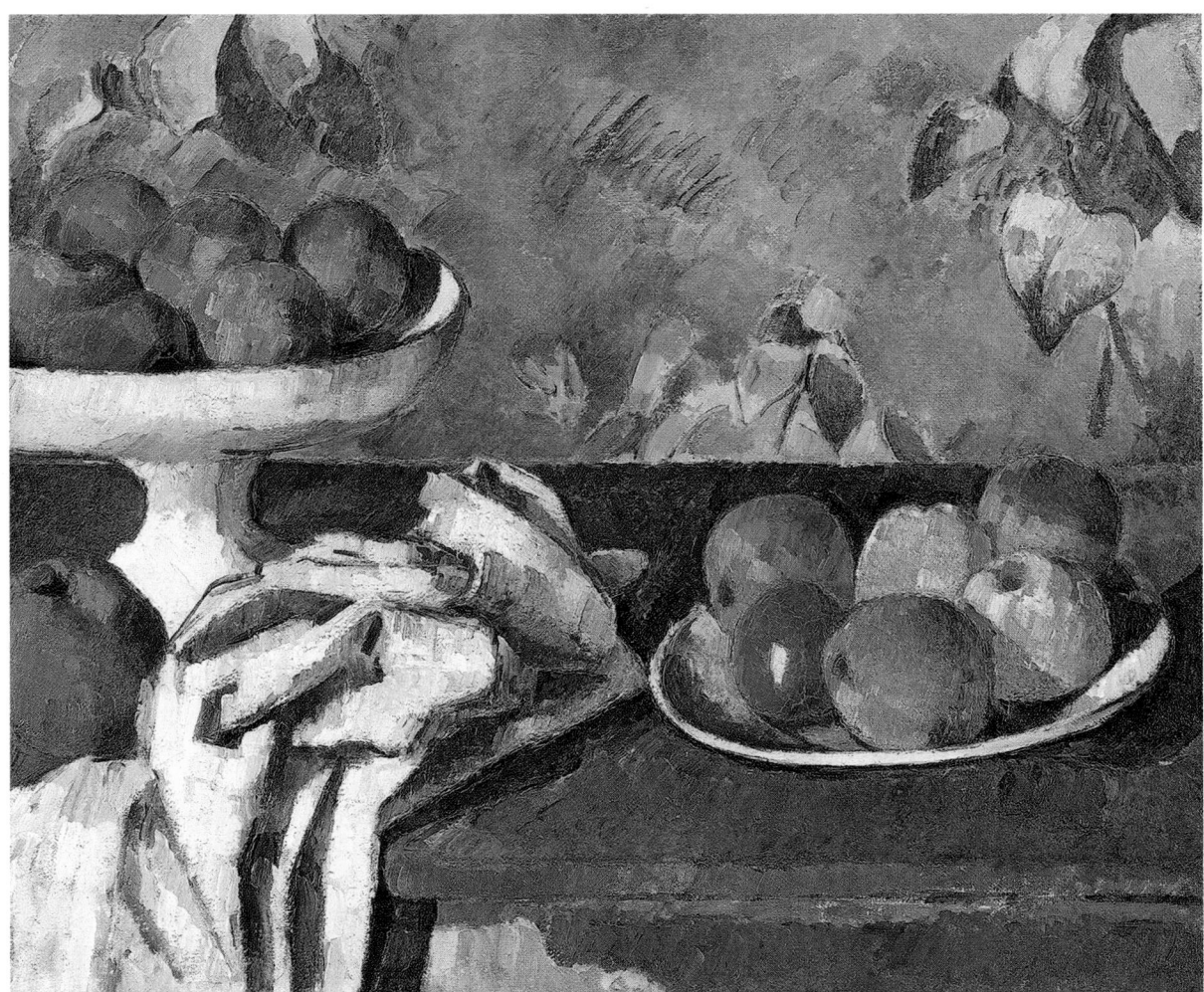

26.2 Paul Cézanne, *Still Life with Apples in a Bowl.* 1879–83. Oil on canvas, 17⅛ × 21¼" (43.5 × 54 cm). Ny Carlsberg Glyptotek, Copenhagen, Denmark

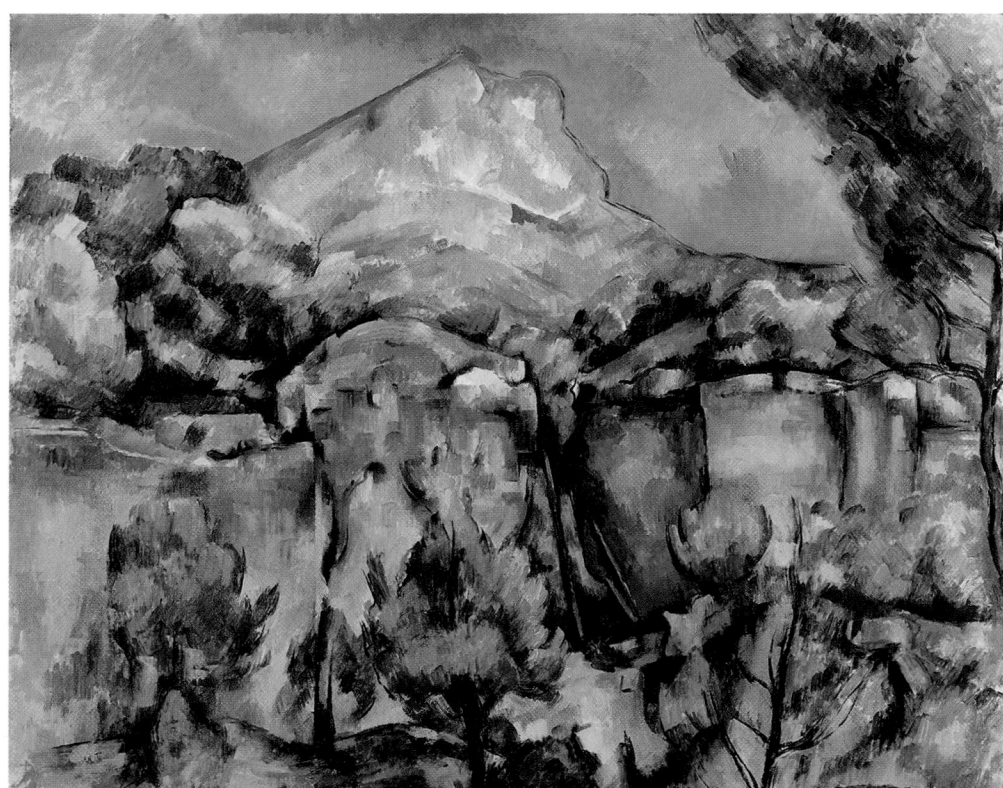

26.3 Paul Cézanne, *Mont Sainte-Victoire Seen from Bibemus Quarry*. ca. 1897–1900. Oil on canvas, 25½ × 31½" (65.1 × 80 cm). The Baltimore Museum of Art. The Cone Collection, Formed by Dr. Claribel Cone and Miss Ette Cone of Baltimore, Maryland. (BMA 1950.196)

acknowledges with every move that art is inherently abstract—painting is first and foremost about putting paint on canvas to create an arrangement of line and color.

Cézanne's art became increasingly abstract in the last ten years of his life, as can be seen in *Mont Sainte-Victoire Seen from Bibemus Quarry* (fig. **26.3**), painted from 1897 to 1900. Mont Sainte-Victoire was a favorite motif, almost an obsession, as it appeared in over 60 late paintings and watercolors. The deep vista we saw in the earlier view of the mountain has now been replaced with a more compressed version. The overlapping of representational objects is one of the few devices suggesting depth. Otherwise, the image is an intense network of carefully constructed brushstrokes, lines, and colors that begs to be read as an intricate spaceless tapestry. The foreground trees bleed into the quarry rock, or on the upper right into the sky. The sky in turn melds into the mountain, from which it is distinguished only by the defining line of the summit. No matter how flat and airless, the image, as with any Impressionist picture, paradoxically is also filled with light, space, and movement. Looking at this hermetic picture, we cannot help but feel how the tension and energy of his early romantic pictures were suppressed and channeled into a struggle to create images that balanced his direct observation of nature with his desire to abstract nature's forms. Here is the work of the painter most responsible for freeing the medium from a representational role and giving artists license to invent images that instead adhered to painting's own inherent laws. The Paris gallery Durand-Ruel began exhibiting the withdrawn, unknown Cézanne in the late 1890s, and in 1907, at his death, he had a retrospective at the avant-garde *Salon d'Automne* exhibition, which had a powerful influence on contemporary artists, especially Pablo Picasso and Henri Matisse, as we shall see in the next chapter.

Georges Seurat: Seeking Social and Pictorial Harmony

Like Cézanne, Georges Seurat (1859–1891) wanted to make Impressionism more like the great art of the past. He studied briefly in 1878 at the École des Beaux-Arts with a follower of Ingres, and after a year of compulsory military service in Brittany returned to Paris, where he spent the rest of his short life. He set up a studio, where he worked intensively in isolation, and in 1884 he unveiled his new style with a large picture called *A Bathing Place, Asnières*, which depicts a group of laborers swimming in the Seine in a working-class suburb of Paris, not far from where Seurat grew up. The picture, refused at the Salon, was shown in 1884 at the first exhibition of the Independent Artists, a new artists' cooperative whose shows were unjuried like those of the Impressionists' Artists', Inc. Seurat next participated in what would be the last Impressionist exhibition, in 1886, submitting *A Sunday Afternoon on the Island of La Grande Jatte* (fig. **26.4**). The dates of the two shows are significant, for they mark the end of the Impressionist era and the rise of Post-Impressionism.

La Grande Jatte's roots in the Realism of Manet and in Monet's Impressionist canvases are obvious, since this is a scene of the middle class taking its Sunday leisure on a sunny, color-filled afternoon. The painting presents a compendium of types that contemporaries would have easily recognized, such as the courtesan, shown walking a monkey, and the boatman, who is the

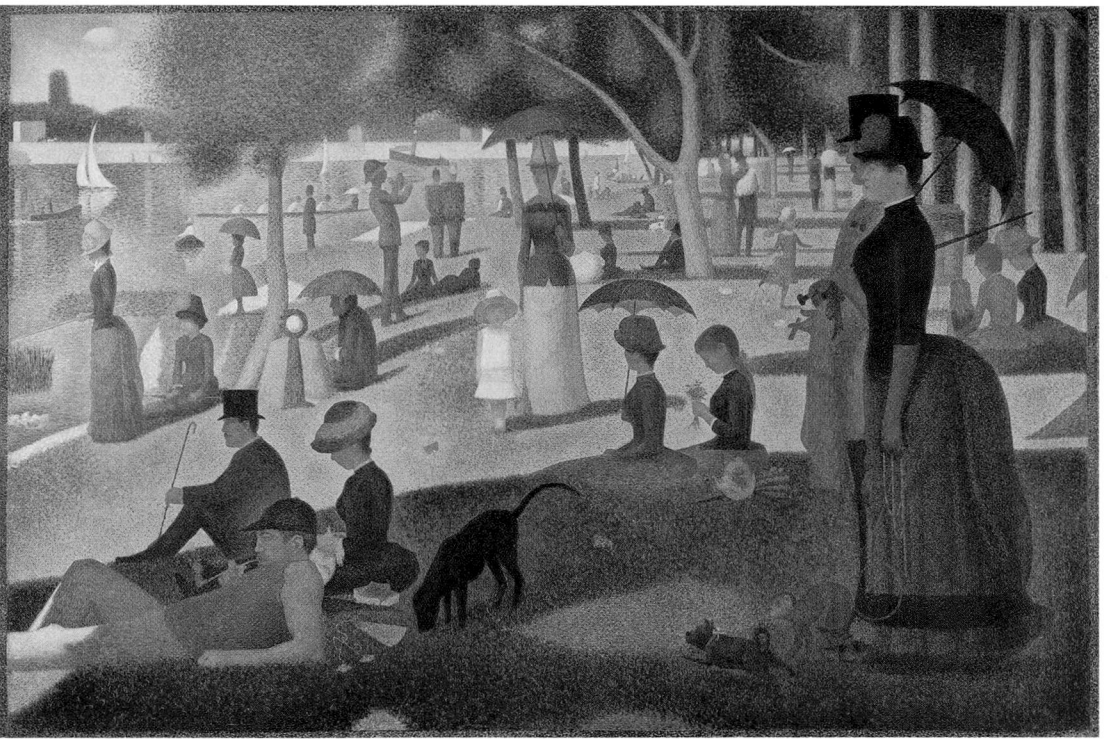

26.4 Georges Seurat, *A Sunday Afternoon on the Island of La Grande Jatte*. 1884–86. Oil on canvas, 6'10" × 101¼" (2.08 × 3.08 m). The Art Institute of Chicago. Helen Birch Bartlett Memorial Collection. 1926.224

sleeveless man smoking a pipe in the left corner. (Seurat's cataloging of types extends to the dogs in the foreground and boats on the Seine.) Seurat renders his figures as icons, for each is silhouetted in profile, frontally, or in a three-quarter view, following the prescription of the famous Roman architect Vitruvius for the arrangement of sculptural figures on temples. Seurat declared that he wanted "to make the moderns file past like figures on Pheidias' Panathenaic frieze on the Parthenon, in their essential form." And this was no idle claim. The 6-by-10-foot canvas was meant to function on the scale of great history painting and be seen in the tradition of Poussin and David. Like a history painter, Seurat

made detailed studies for every component of his work, even producing a painting of the landscape alone, before the insertion of the figures, and looking like a stage set.

INFLUENCE OF PUVIS DE CHAVANNES Critics noted that Seurat's *La Grand Jatte* recalls the Classical murals of Pierre Puvis de Chavannes (1824–1898), whose work was so ubiquitous that his fame was widespread by the 1880s. His paintings, such as *The Sacred Grove, Beloved of the Arts and Muses* (fig. **26.5**), are set in an idyllic mythical or biblical past where life is serene, bountiful, and carefree. In Puvis's world there is little movement, and

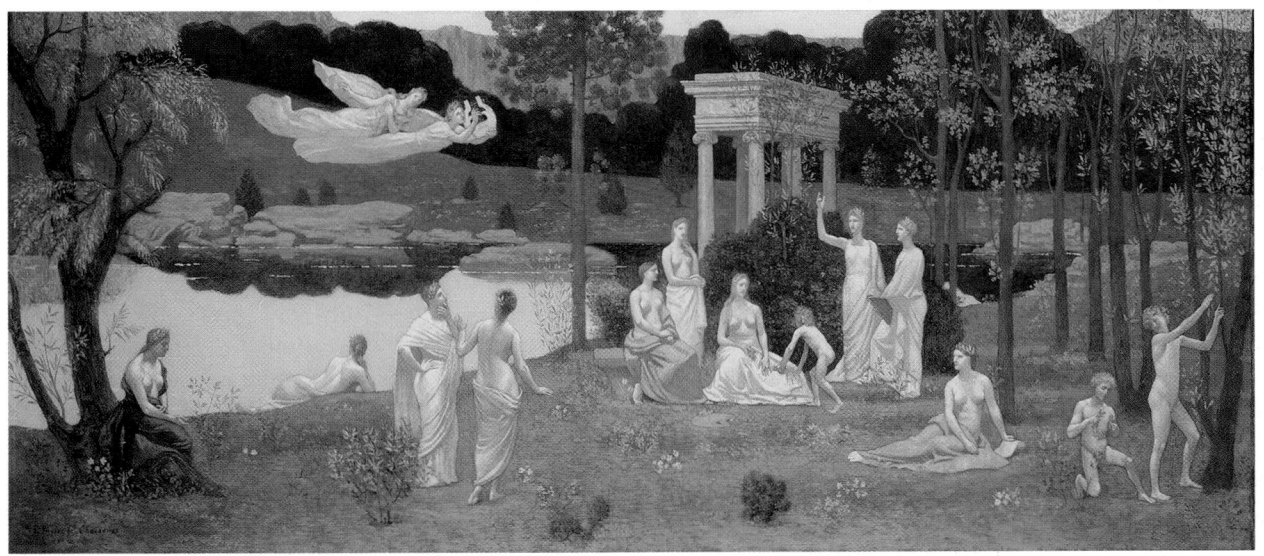

26.5 Pierre Puvis de Chavannes, *The Sacred Grove, Beloved of the Arts and Muses*. 1884. Oil on canvas, 3½ × 7½" (93 × 231 cm). The Art Institute of Chicago. Potter Palmer Collection. 1922.445

certainly no exertion. Without appearing geometric, everything is orderly, either vertical or horizontal, with a soothing planarity bringing everything into harmonious alignment. The decorative flatness evokes ancient murals as well as fourteenth- and fifteenth-century Italian frescoes. There is a minimum of detail, endowing the picture with a tranquil and unencumbered look. His figures tend to be silhouetted in profile or frontal, and often have an archaic angularity and simplicity that adds to the aura of primitive purity and innocence. Puvis, who emerged from the academic ranks in the early 1860s, provided a startling Classical alternative to Bouguereau (see page 866), although his classicizing, dreamy images often appealed to the same conservative audience. By the 1880s, they would attract the avant-garde as well, which saw in their visionary world and abstract simplicity the same sanctuary from modern life that they too were trying to attain.

SEURAT AND NEO-IMPRESSIONISM As much as Seurat was influenced by Puvis, his agenda could not have been more different, for instead of escaping into a distant past his goal was to create a utopian present, a poetic vision of middle- and working-class tranquility and leisure. His religion was not just Classicism, but also science. Familiar with the color theory of the American physicist Ogden Rood, he believed that colors were more intense when mixed optically by the viewer's eye rather than on the palette. Consequently, he would build up his paint surface, first laying down a thin layer of a partially mixed local color, over which came a layer of short strokes of related hues, and finally a top layer of equally sized dots of primary and binary color (fig. **26.6**). As explained in an 1886 article by Seurat's friend, the art critic Félix Fénéon, this top layer of "colors, isolated on the canvas, recombine on the retina: we have, therefore, not a mixture of material colors (pigments), but a mixture of differently colored rays of light." It does not matter that Seurat misinterpreted Rood and that the claim is not true. Seurat believed his colors were more luminous than the Impressionists', and certainly his technique, which he called "Chromoluminarism" and scholars later labeled

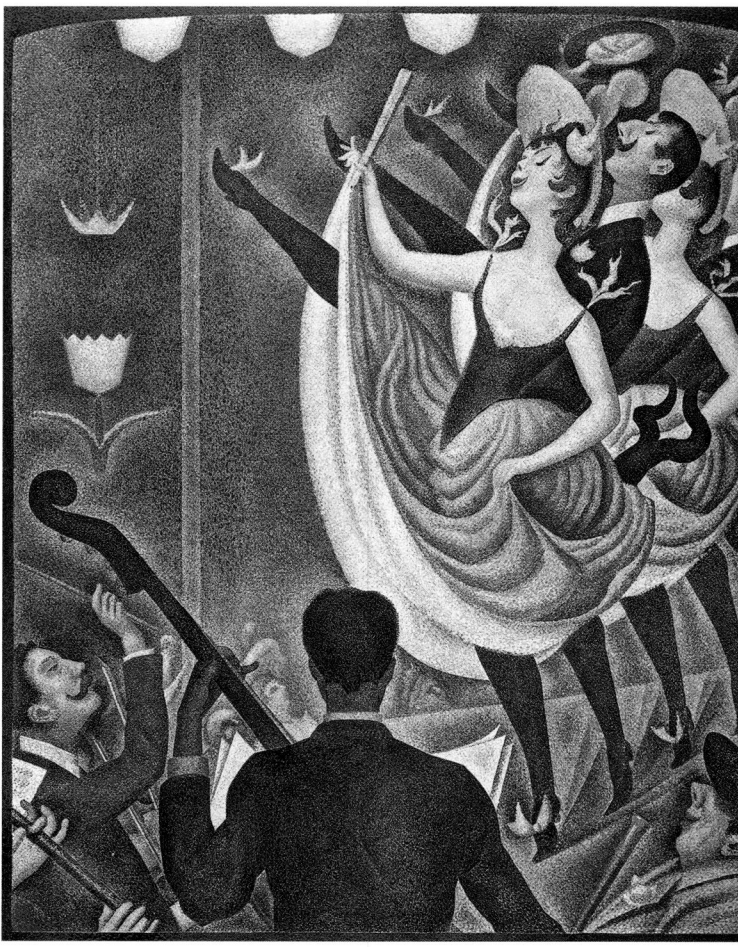

26.7   Georges Seurat, *Le Chahut*. 1889–90. Oil on canvas, 66½ × 54¾" (169 × 139 cm). Rijksmuseum Kröller-Müller, Otterlo, the Netherlands

"Pointillism" or "Divisionism," created a uniform, if vibrant, surface that was a kind of systematized Impressionism. Like the figures, the regularized surface of Seurat's pictures seem mechanical, as though the subjective hand–eye reaction of the Impressionist has been replaced by a machine capable of recording color and light with uniform dots of paint.

In his review of the 1886 Impressionist show, Fénéon labeled Seurat's style Neo-Impressionism—the "New Impressionism"—and before the decade was out, it had an army of practitioners who were attracted to its scientific approach, monumentality, and modern look. Many worked well into the twentieth century. As distinctive as the technique is, it would be a mistake to emphasize it at the expense of the meaning of the art. Seurat was a socialist sympathizer and was dedicated to creating a utopia of middle- and working-class tranquility and leisure. His socialist vision of a harmonious, perfect world and belief in science as the force to make this happen characterize his method.

Seurat's experimental approach led him to the theories of French psychophysiologist Charles Henry as outlined in his treatise *A Scientific Aesthetic* (1885). Henry claimed that colors, as well as lines, carried specific emotional meaning (e.g., yellow or a

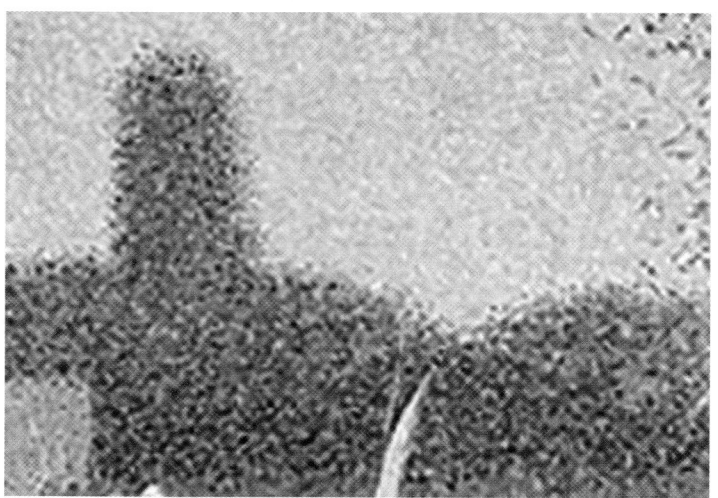

26.6   Detail of fig. 26.4

Lithography

Grease rejects water. Starting with that principle, Aloys Senefelder, an inspector of maps at the royal printing office in Munich, invented the process of lithography shortly before 1800. Essentially, an artist draws on stone with greasy crayon or ink, called **tusche**. The stone is then dampened with water, which is absorbed into the porous stone, except where there is *tusche* drawing. The printmaker next applies printer's ink, which adheres only where there are *tusche* marks. The stone is then put through a press, and the image is printed in reverse on paper. The process requires such technical proficiency that artists usually work with skilled lithographers who do the technical work and "pull" the prints, that is, they run the paper through the press. A later variation of the process allowed artists to draw with *tusche* on paper, which was then transferred onto the stone. Artists immediately embraced lithography, and it became one of the most popular print mediums of the nineteenth and twentieth centuries.

Unlike engraving plates (see *Materials and Techniques*, page 501), which wear down with repeated printing and require frequent strengthening of the lines, lithography needs no maintenance, and a seemingly unlimited number of prints could be produced from a single stone. Toward 1830, paper was becoming less expensive and literacy was growing, a combination that increased the medium's appeal to newspaper and magazine publishers, whose print runs were rising. Of the many newspaper illustrators who worked in lithography, Honoré Daumier became the most celebrated (see fig. 25.4).

With the development of larger printing presses and the ability to print in several colors, lithography became the preferred medium for posters, which in the closing decades of the nineteenth century began to feature images in addition to words. Advertisers now wanted pictures of their products and strong colors so that their poster would stand out from other advertisements. Artists responded. Large colored lithographic posters began to plaster the sides of buildings, commercial wagons, and omnibuses, reflecting the consumerism overtaking Europe. The art world quickly recognized the aesthetic merits of many such posters, and in 1889 a poster exhibition was mounted for the International Exposition at the Palace of Liberal Arts in Paris. Collectors began buying posters, galleries began selling them, and artists made them with collectors in mind. Today, Henri de Toulouse-Lautrec is among the most acclaimed of the artists who made colored lithographic posters (see fig. 26.8).

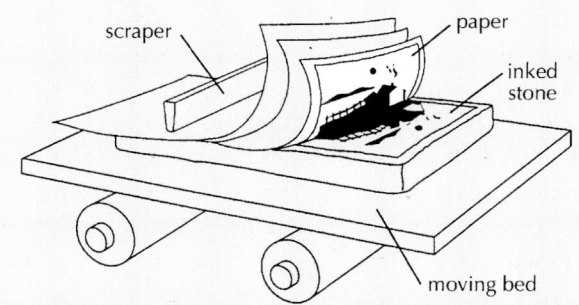

line rising from a horizontal connotes happiness, while blue or a descending line evokes sadness). Seurat put this theory into practice in the major paintings of his last five years, genre paintings of popular urban entertainment, such as circuses and cabarets. In the joyous and festive *Le Chahut* (fig. **26.7**) of 1889–90, we cannot miss the dominant yellow hue and upward thrusting lines. The scene represents the finale of a cancanlike dance at a nightclub near Seurat's studio, a scene so closely based on reality that the actual performers can be identified, although they, like the audience to either side of the runway, function as a catalogue of types as well. Seurat uses a Degas-like skewered, cropped, and conflated composition, which he then freezes, transforming figures and even furniture, such as the gas lamps, into powerful icons. We can never mistake Seurat's images for Realism; instead he presents an idealized world. His passionate belief in science, technology, and machines as the tools to attain progress and equality will be shared by later generations of artists, especially following World War I.

Henri de Toulouse-Lautrec: An Art for the Demimonde

Paradoxically, Seurat, along with the other Post-Impressionist artists, constituted a new avant-garde that would lead art down a path that made it esoteric and thus incomprehensible for mass audiences. The artist who succeeded in capturing urban exuberance

and decadence at the close of the nineteenth century for the wider public was Henri de Toulouse-Lautrec (1864–1901). His pictures of the Cirque Fernando were exhibited at the circus, while those of dancehalls, cabarets, and nightclubs (that is, the shadowy nightlife of the demimonde, or fringe society) were shown at those same venues, although he also exhibited with the new artists' cooperatives. His widest impact, however, was made through his large colorful lithographic posters advertising these popular spectacles, which were plastered in public places all over Paris. His images of urban nightlife became the public's perception as well, and his work continues to form our image of *fin-de-siècle* Paris. (See *Materials and Techniques*, above.)

Toulouse-Lautrec was a master of caricature, as can be seen in *La Goulue* (fig. **26.8**), which features the popular Moulin Rouge dancer Louise Weber, nicknamed La Goulue (The Glutton), who is credited with creating the French dance the cancan. The Moulin Rouge was a cabaret located in Montmartre, a bohemian neighborhood notorious for its raucous, low-class nightclubs. Lautrec himself settled there after coming to Paris in 1882 from his hometown in the Midi-Pyrénées region of France, where he was born into an aristocratic but not particularly wealthy family. He was crippled by a genetic disease and childhood leg injuries, which resulted in his having a man's torso on a child's legs, and being only 5'1" tall. This handicap did not prevent him from thriving in the thick of the bohemian nightlife of Montmartre, where he was

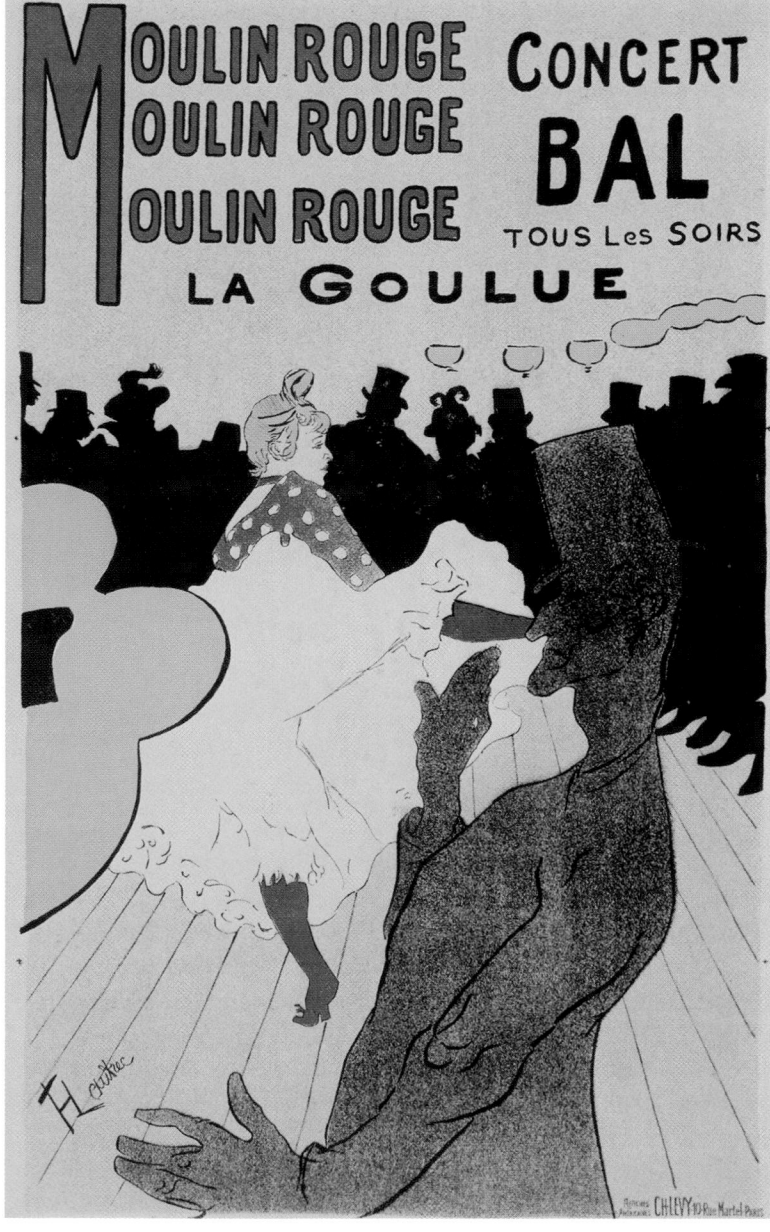

26.8 Henri de Toulouse-Lautrec, *La Goulue*. 1891.
Colored lithographic poster, 6'3" × 3'10" (1.90 × 1.16 m).
Private collection

a regular at the clubs and brothels, the subject of his art, before dying of alcoholism at the age of 36.

Toulouse-Lautrec initially studied privately with an academic painter, but embraced the avant-garde upon discovering the art of Degas. In addition, he was heavily influenced by Japanese art. Both sources can be seen in the flat silhouettes, cropping, and conflated space of *La Goulue*, and Degas in the subject matter. But Toulouse-Lautrec is more abstract than Degas, abandoning naturalism for **cartoonish** fantasy and working with a minimum of marks and flat planes of color and line. Unlike Seurat, who creates a three-dimensional monumental world, Toulouse-Lautrec's vision is paper-thin. And it is satirical. With this stripped-down vocabulary, he captures La Goulue's physical exertion as well as

her psychological isolation and detachment. He poignantly contrasts the animated La Goulue with the bizarre, zombielike profile of Valentin *le désossé* ("Valentin the Boneless"), famous for his idiosyncratic dancing. Toulouse-Lautrec is able to succinctly elicit the collective spirit and rhythm of the dancing through the repetition of silhouetted feet, a rhythm picked up by the repetition of the words "Moulin Rouge" above and the three yellow gas lamps. Even the lettering, with its staggered placement and shifts in scale, adds to the beat of the picture, as does the syncopation of the limited color. The floorboards streaking back add to the pace of the image. With minimal effort, Toulouse-Lautrec even tells us much about the shadowy audience, for he has catalogued a range of types by presenting the shapes of their hats. But despite the illusion of gaiety, there is something empty and soulless in this picture, suggested by La Goulue's weary expression, the distorted, if not ominous Valentin *le désossé*, and the dark anonymous onlookers. Toulouse-Lautrec presents a dissolute world, one he knew all too well, and one that represented the fruit of advanced civilization. This is the decadent *fin-de-siècle* Paris from which artists like Van Gogh and Gauguin will try to escape.

Vincent van Gogh: *Expression Through Color and Symbol*

Before becoming a painter, the Dutch artist Vincent van Gogh (1853–1890) had tried his hand at, among other things, preaching and teaching. Drawn to these vocations by his desire for a life both spiritually fulfilling and socially useful, Van Gogh eventually determined that art alone could provide access to the ideal world he sought. After receiving a rudimentary art training, he spent the years 1883 through 1885 painting at the family's vicarage (his father was a pastor) in the village of Nuenen in Holland, where he was deeply affected by the dignity, spirituality, and stolid sturdiness of the impoverished peasants. His major work from this period, *The Potato Eaters* (fig. 26.9), reflects his compassion and respect for the underclasses, as described in one of the 650 pages of letters he wrote to Theo, his brother: "I have tried to emphasize that these people eating their potatoes in the lamplight, have dug the earth with those very hands they put in the dish, and so it speaks of manual labor, and how they have honestly earned their food. I have wanted to give an impression of a way of life quite different from us civilized human beings." Here, we see Van Gogh's admiration and respect for a simple life based on direct contact with nature as well as his suspicion of bourgeois values and urban modernity. His artistic role models include Millet, whose powerful and sympathetic depictions of peasants are echoed in Van Gogh's, and his countryman Rembrandt, whose tenebrism shrouds this humble, almost ritualistic supper in a reverential cloak. What especially distinguishes this image is Van Gogh's excited expressionism, which gives the picture a raw, crude energy that simultaneously endows the peasants with a surging elemental vitality and reflects the artist's own uncontainable enthusiasm and passion for his subject matter. Gnarled fingers and hands, prominent twisted physiognomies, rippling

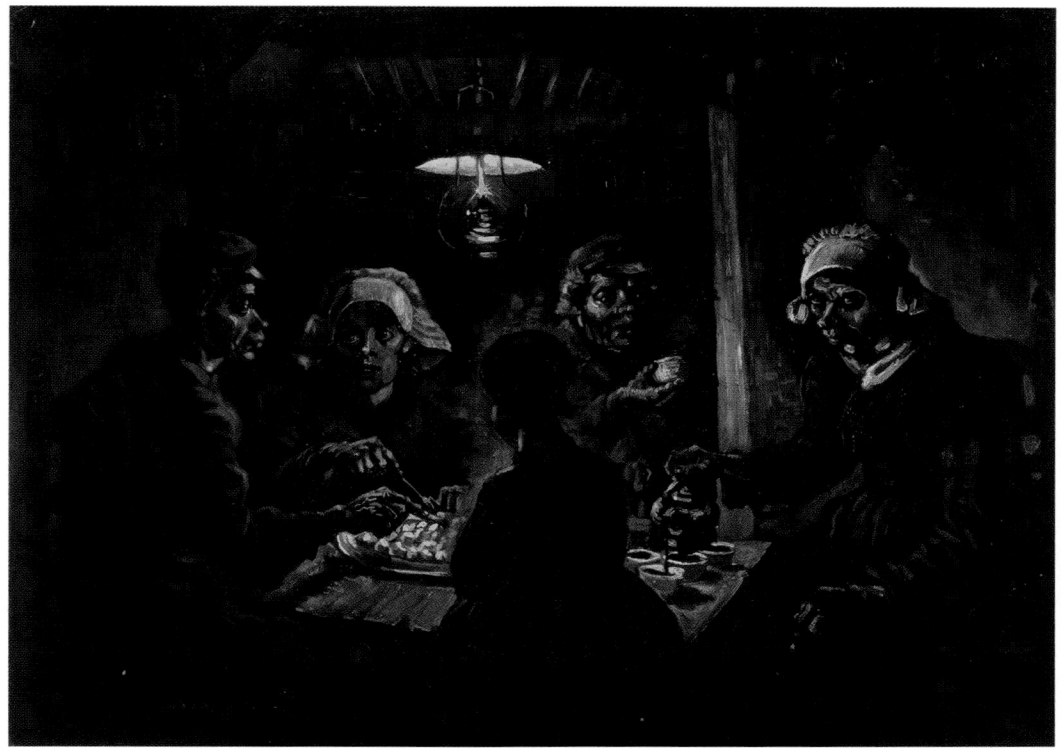

26.9 Vincent van Gogh, *The Potato Eaters*. 1885. Oil on canvas, 32¼ × 45" (82 × 114.3 cm). Vincent van Gogh Foundation/Van Gogh Museum, Amsterdam

folds of clothing, ceiling beams that recede with eruptive force, a clock and a picture of the Crucifixion that seem to jump off rather than hang on the wall—everything explodes within the picture, despite the tranquility of this event of work-weary laborers taking their frugal evening meal. Van Gogh's thick excited marks, which convey his overbearing enthusiasm and compassion, reinforce the powerful physical presence of his peasants.

In 1885, Van Gogh briefly enrolled at the Academy of Fine Arts in Antwerp, where he studied Rubens's paintings and collected Japanese prints, which he admired for their abstract qualities and because of their bright colors and nonindustrial imagery mistakenly believed presented a rural, utopian world. Unhappy in Belgium, Van Gogh then went to Paris to be with his brother, who handled the contemporary painting department at an art gallery. Here, from 1886 to 1888, he experienced Impressionism and Neo-Impressionism first hand, consuming their lessons with the same fervor he applied to everything else. His bold energetic brushwork now carried primary and binary hues and his pictures were filled with color and light. Restless as always, he started hounding fellow painters to join him in starting an artists' commune in the sun-drenched south of France, a "Studio of the South," which he envisioned as an Occidental Japan.

Only Paul Gauguin bought into this dream, and even he only lasted two months, finding Van Gogh's intense troubled personality insufferable. Alone in Arles, Van Gogh thrived in the Provençal landscape, fiercely generating from 1888 to 1889 his strongest body of work, including *Night Café* and *Starry Night*. His intense uncontrollable emotions took over and his painting became increasingly expressionistic, using color and brushwork abstractly to convey emotion rather than to document reality and employing a personal symbolic vocabulary. In *Night Café* (fig. 26.10), he registered his revulsion at an Arles den of iniquity, claiming he wanted "to express the terrible passions of humanity by means of red and green." This symbolic use of complementary color visually creates a harsh acidic atmosphere, made all the more sour by the jarring range of off-greens that appear on the billiard table, tabletops, bar, ceiling, and even in the waiter's hair. The morbid blood-red of the walls bleeds into the strident floorboards, whose fiery yellow seems to connote hell, not happiness, an aura reinforced by the rays emanating from the gas ceiling lamps.

The personality that prevailed in the majority of Van Gogh's pictures, however, is the one that painted *The Potato Eaters*, the one that belonged to the secular evangelist who celebrated all life and longed for universal harmony. This can be seen in *Starry Night* (fig. 26.11), painted after the artist committed himself to a mental institution near Saint-Rémy in Provence. Here, we see the inviting hearth-lit homes of plain rural folk, snugly ensconced in a valley, which is pervaded by a spiritual, celestial blue, the same color as the sky, uniting both. The yellow glow from the rectangular windows visually ties the homes with the yellow round stars in the universe above, their contrasting shapes a kind of yin and yang of elemental harmony. An upwardly spiraling cypress tree, filled with life, which it symbolizes, dominates the foreground. Its verticality echoes that of the church steeple, suggesting its spirituality, and both penetrate the fiery, star-filled sky, linking earth

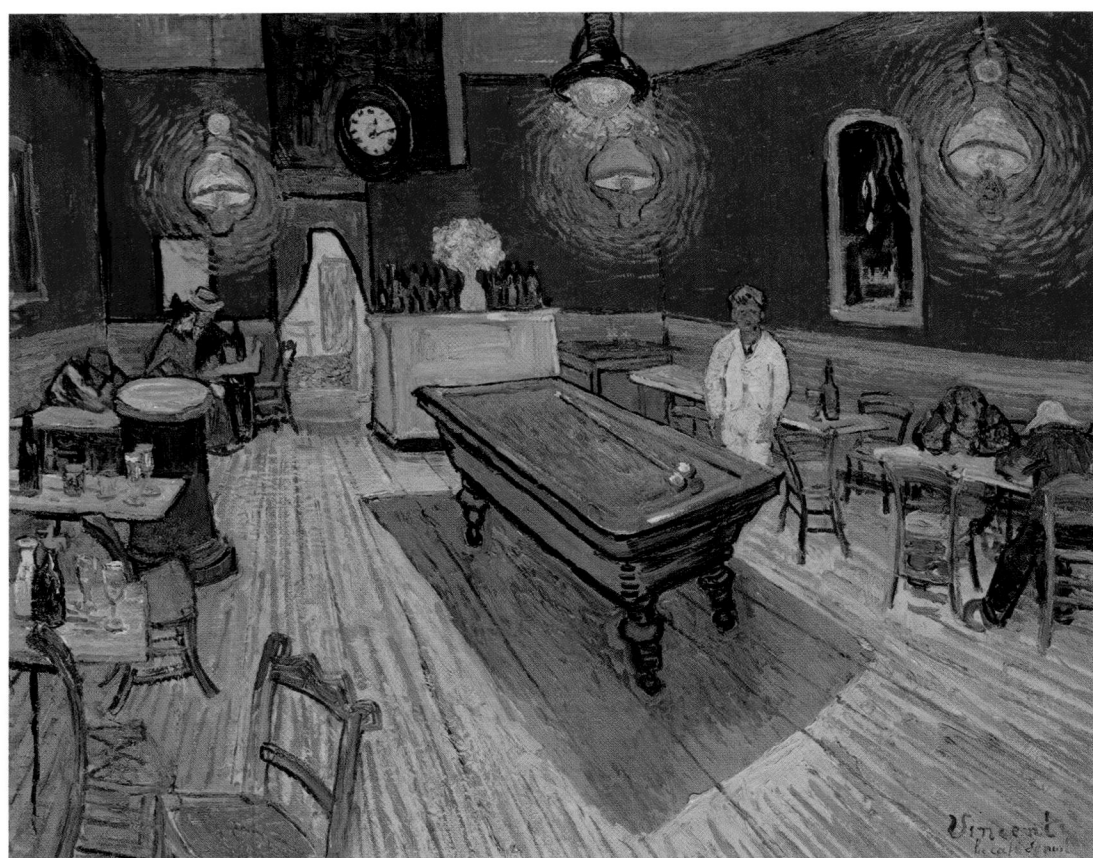

26.10 Vincent van Gogh, *Night Café*. 1888. Oil on canvas, 8½ × 36¼" (72.4 × 92.1 cm). Yale University Art Gallery, New Haven. Bequest of Stephen Carlton Clark, B.A. 1903.1961.18.34

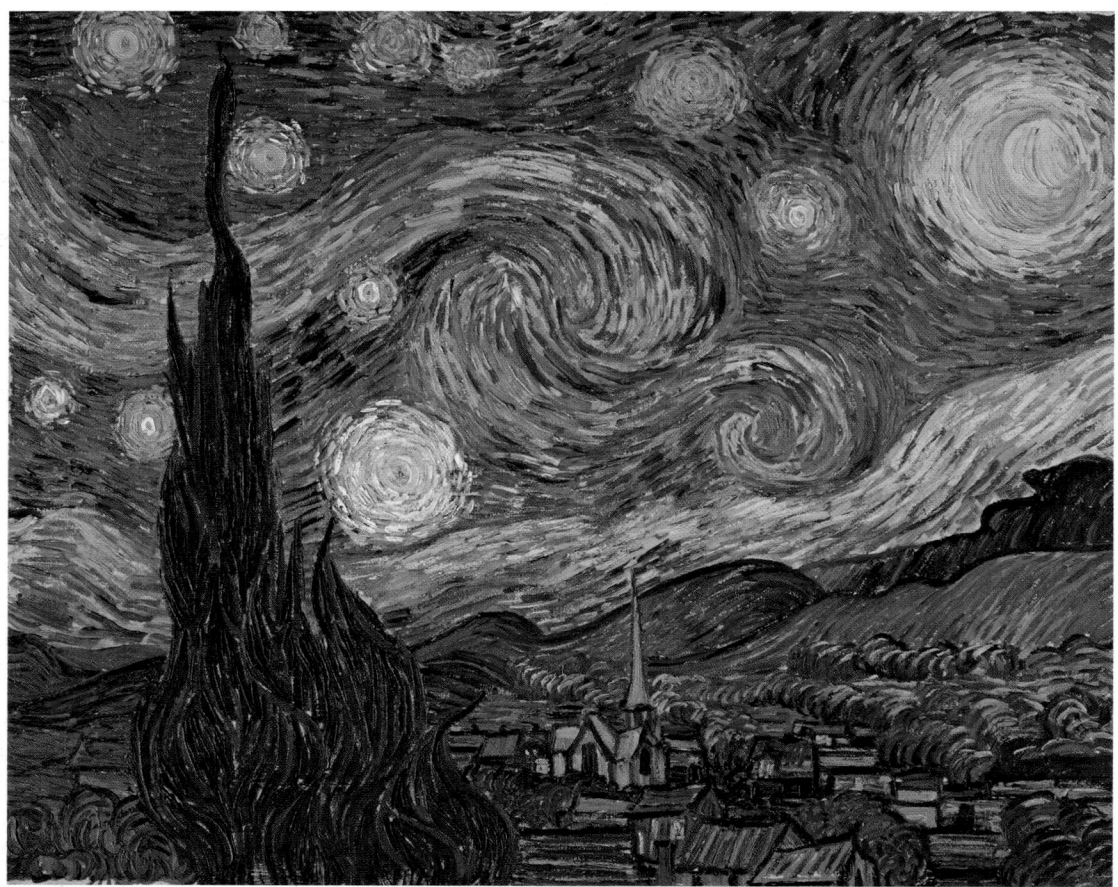

26.11 Vincent van Gogh, *Starry Night*, 1889. Oil on canvas, 28¾ × 36¼" (73 × 93 cm). Museum of Modern Art, New York. Acquired through the Lillie P. Bliss Bequest (472.1941)

with the transcendental. The sky is alight with spectacular cosmic fireworks—haloes of stars and joyous tumbling clouds reflect the undulation of the mountains and trees below. There is no mistaking this visionary painting, filled with expressionistic, abstract color and brushwork and personal symbolism, for a Realist or Impressionist picture. Here, Van Gogh created the primitive world and utopia he always dreamed of inhabiting: the peaceful tranquility of simple, unpretentious people, nurtured by nature and in harmony with universal forces. Despite his frenetic output and humanitarian commitment, Van Gogh, deeply troubled, depressed, and suffering from seizures, committed suicide within a year of painting *Starry Night*.

Paul Gauguin: The Flight from Modernity

Paul Gauguin (1848–1903), the fourth of the major Post-Impressionists, shared Van Gogh's distaste for advanced civilization and likewise yearned for a utopian alternative. His abandonment of society, however, was perhaps the most radical of any artist of his time. A Parisian stockbroker, he was attracted to art, collected the Impressionists, and, by the early 1870s, had taken up painting himself. He lost his job in 1882 and began to paint full time. He studied with his friend Pissarro, who introduced him to the work of Cézanne, and participated in the last four Impressionist exhibitions between 1881 and 1886. In 1886, he abandoned Paris to begin a nomadic search for a more meaningful existence,

which he believed existed in a simpler society in tune with nature. He first went to the village of Pont-Aven, a remote, rural community in Brittany. Here, locals wore a distinctive regional costume and displayed an intense, charismatic piety.

After briefly leaving Brittany for the Caribbean island of Martinique in 1887, Gauguin returned to Pont-Aven in 1888, where he painted with a colleague, Émile Bernard. They were joined by other artists, who came to be called the "Pont-Aven School." Together they developed a style they called Synthetism, a reference to their synthetic production of images based on imagination and emotion as opposed to a mimetic, empirical replication of reality. In their search to produce an authentic, direct art, as free of civilized influences as possible, they turned to a variety of vernacular and primitive sources, including crude popular illustrations (especially religious) and folk, children's, and medieval art. They were also attracted by what they viewed as archaic styles, such as the fourteenth-century Italian primitives and both Egyptian and Mesopotamian art, art that was not naturalistic. Especially appealing to them were medieval stained-glass windows, because of their spiritual function and saturated colors, and **cloisonné** enamels, which similarly use curvilinear lead dividers to separate areas of flat color.

The impact of medieval glass and cloisonné is apparent in Gauguin's *The Vision after the Sermon* (fig. **26.12**), where an undulating blue line encases flat planes of color. Gauguin presents a group of Breton women just after they have heard a sermon about

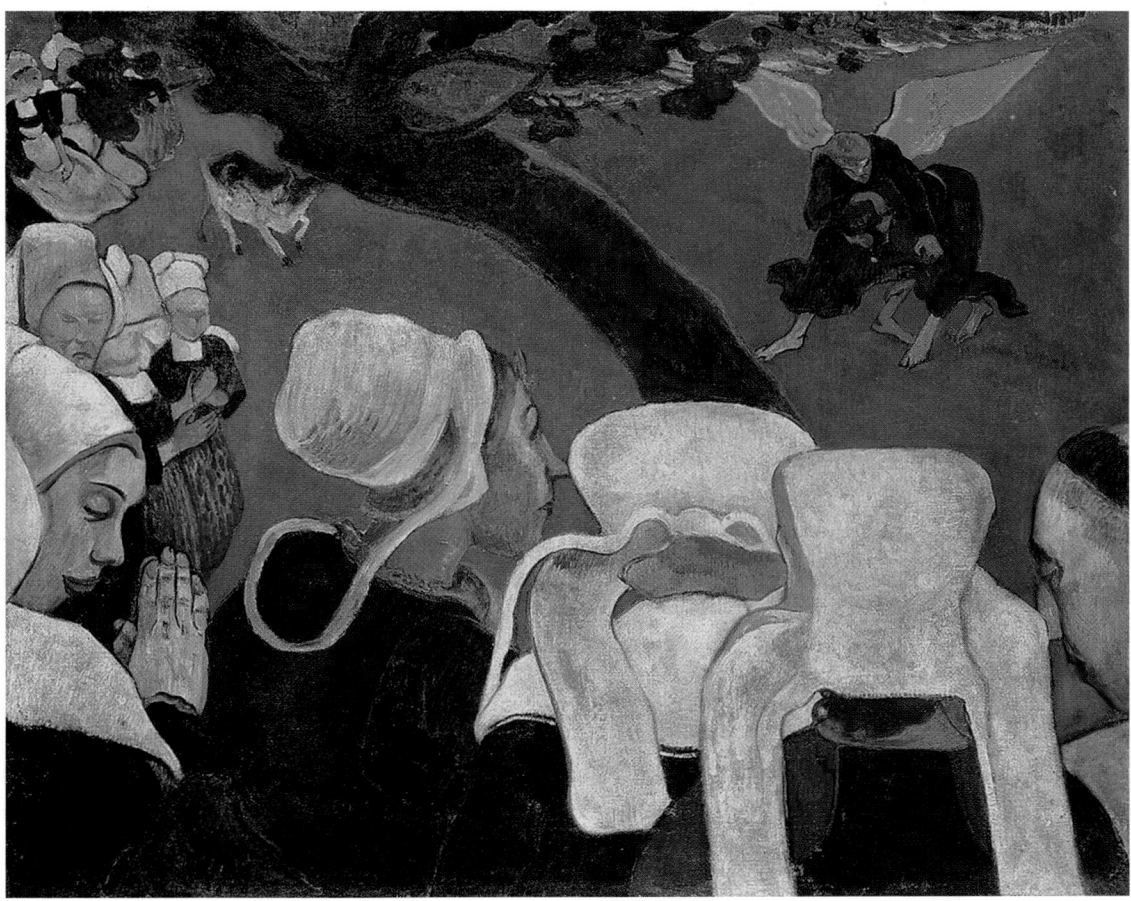

26.12 Paul Gauguin, *The Vision after the Sermon (Jacob Wrestling with the Angel)*. 1888. Oil on canvas, 28¾ × 36½" (73 × 92.7 cm). The National Galleries of Scotland, Edinburgh

Jacob wrestling with the angel. The artist attributes to the women a blind, naïve piety that allows them to see spirituality in such mundane objects as a cow, whose shape resembles the two struggling biblical figures the priest has just described. In a bold composition that conceptually comes from Japanese prints (see fig. 25.13), Gauguin places the cow and the wrestlers to either side of a tree, sharply contrasted on an intense mystical field of red. The objects of the women's vision clearly exist in an otherworldly sphere, where they appear to float magically. Everything seems possessed in Gauguin's picture, invested with an unseen religiosity. The string ties on two of the women's caps are animated and snakelike, while the silhouettes of the hats on the two women seen from the back on the right seem to take on a life all their own. Flat, curvilinear forms, and even forms within forms, can be found throughout the image, levitating, just as the cow and the wrestling figures do.

Despite its provincial charm and remove from Paris, Brittany for Gauguin was geographically far too close to modern civilization and its decadent materialism. (Seasonally, it was also overrun with tourists.) In 1891, therefore, he left for the French colony of Tahiti in the South Pacific, convinced that on this remote island he would find Jean-Jacques Rousseau's "noble savage," an elemental, innocent human, "a primitive" steeped in nature and in harmony with the universe. In Tahiti, he also felt he would be able "to go back…as far back as the *dada* from my childhood, the good old wooden horse." (*Dada* is French for "rocking horse.") He expected to live in a tropical Garden of Eden, uncovering the most basic truths about human existence. And a Garden of Eden is what he depicts in *Where Do We Come From? What Are We? Where Are We Going?* (fig. **26.13**) from 1897. Fruit hangs from the trees for the picking, while a statue of a god oversees the welfare of the islanders, bestowing blessings and an intense spirituality on

every aspect of daily life, while pointing to heaven and the afterlife. The tropical landscape is dense, lush, and sensuous, an abstract tapestry of deeply saturated, flat curvilinear forms in which everything seems to gently float. Life is languorous and untroubled, and time has stopped. When the picture was shown in Paris, critics, not surprisingly, compared it with Puvis's Classical worlds of milk and honey (see page 909).

As the title suggests, the painting represents the three stages of life—birth is pictured on the right, youth in the center, and old age at the far left. The entire painting is a remarkable synthesis of cultures, religions, and periods, testifying to Gauguin's desire to portray the elemental mythic forces underlying all humanity. The center figure is a Tahitian Eve. The statue of the deity on the left is a compilation of the Tahitian goddess Hina, a Javanese Buddha, and an Easter Island megalith. The old woman on the left is derived from a Peruvian mummy Gauguin saw at a Paris ethnological museum. Torsos are twisted so that they resemble Egyptian figures, and the bright gold upper corners with title and signature recall Byzantine and Early Renaissance icons. Pervading the image is the spirituality and look of medieval stained glass, as well as the bold forms and colors of Japanese prints.

Where Do We Come From? is a reflection of Gauguin's belief that the renewal of Western art and civilization as a whole must come from outside its own traditions, which he perceived as being corrupt. He advised other artists to shun Graeco-Roman forms and to turn instead to Persia, the Far East, and ancient Egypt for inspiration. This idea itself was not new. It stems from the Romantic myth of the noble savage and the ideas of the Enlightenment more than a century earlier, and its ultimate source is the age-old belief in an earthly paradise where people once lived, and might one day live again, in a state of nature and innocence. No artist before Gauguin had gone as far in putting this

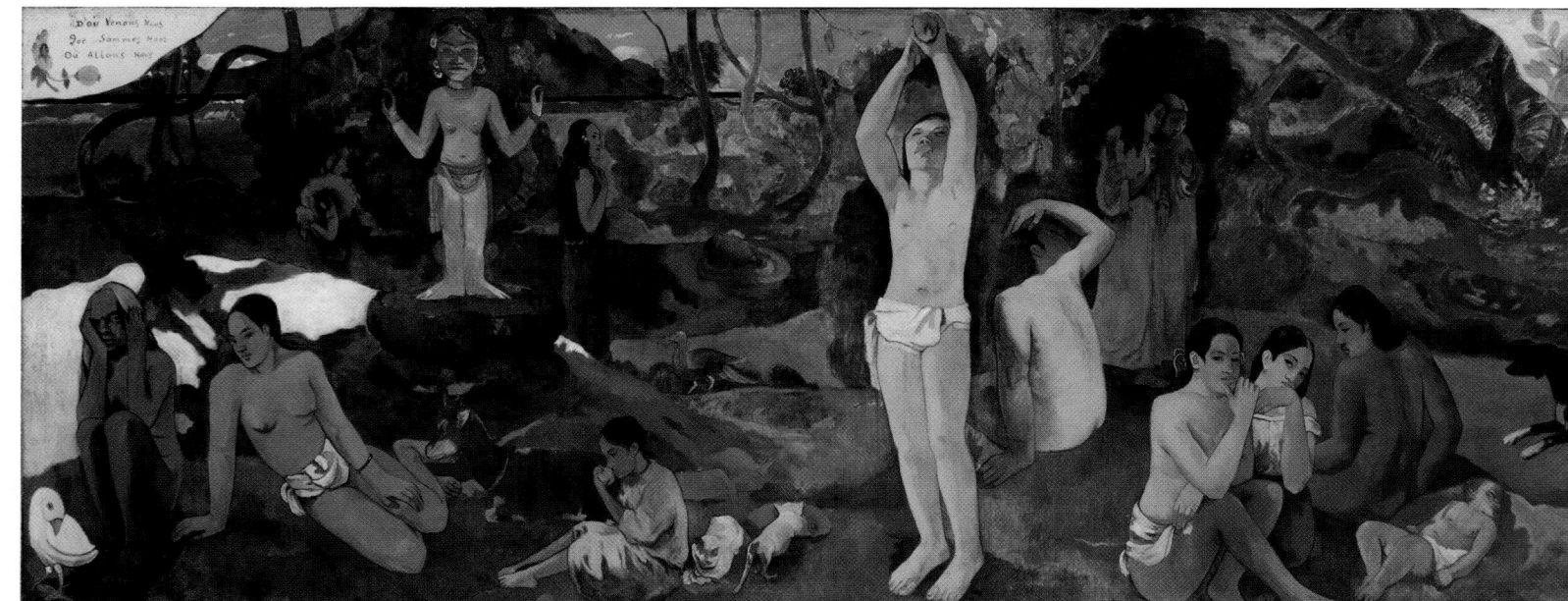

26.13   Paul Gauguin, *Where Do We Come From? What Are We? Where Are We Going?* 1897. Oil on canvas, 4'5¾" × 12'3½" (1.39 × 3.74 m). Photograph © Museum of Fine Arts, Boston. Arthur Gordon Tompkins Residuary Collection. 36.270

Paul Gauguin (1848–1903)

From a letter to J. F. Willumsen

The Danish painter J. F. Willumsen was a member of Gauguin's circle in Brittany. Gauguin wrote this letter to him in the autumn of 1890, before his departure for the South Seas.

As for me, my mind is made up. I am going soon to Tahiti, a small island in Oceania, where the material necessities of life can be had without money. I want to forget all the misfortunes of the past, I want to be free to paint without any glory whatsoever in the eyes of the others and I want to die there and to be forgotten there. ... A terrible epoch is brewing in Europe for the coming generation: the kingdom of gold. Everything is putrefied, even men, even the arts. There, at least, under an eternally summer sky, on a marvellously fertile soil, the Tahitian has only to lift his hands to gather his food; and in addition he never works. When in Europe men and women survive only after unceasing labor during which they struggle in convulsions of cold and hunger, a prey to misery, the Tahitians, on the contrary, happy inhabitants of the unknown paradise of Oceania, know only sweetness of life. To live, for them, is to sing and to love. ... Once my material life is well organized, I can there devote myself to great works of art, freed from all artistic jealousies and with no need whatsoever of lowly trade.

Source: *The Genesis of Modernism*, Ed. Sven Loevgren (New York: Hacker Art Books, 1983)

PRIMARY SOURCE

doctrine of **"primitivism"**—as it was called—into practice. His pilgrimage to the South Pacific had more than a purely private meaning: It symbolized the end of the 400 years of expansion that had brought most of the globe under Western domination. Colonialism, once so cheerfully—and ruthlessly—pursued by the empire builders, was, for many, becoming a symbol of Western civilization's corruption. Gauguin was disappointed to discover that large portions of Tahiti had already been spoiled by colonization, the French absorbing it as a protectorate in 1842 and making it a fully fledged colony in 1880.

SYMBOLISM

Although Gauguin devised the label Synthetism to describe his art, he was soon heralded as a Symbolist. Symbolism was a literary movement announced in a manifesto issued by poet Jean Moréas (1856–1910) in the newspaper *Figaro Littéraire* in 1886. The poet Charles Baudelaire, author of a book of poems titled *Flowers of Evil* (1857), was considered a forebear of the movement, and the poets Stephen Mallarmé and Paul Verlaine ranked among its salient representatives. Another poet, Gustave Kahn, succinctly encapsulated the movement's essence when he wrote shortly after the appearance of Moréas's manifesto that the writer's goal was to "objectify the subjective...instead of subjectifying the objective," meaning the everyday, contemporary world was to be rejected, and replaced by one of dreams that abstractly expressed sensations, moods, and deepseated fears and desires. The label was soon extended to the visual arts, and Gauguin's name always topped anyone's list of important Symbolists. Van Gogh, with his expressionist fantasies, was considered a Symbolist as well. In 1891, art critic Georges-Albert Aurier defined Symbolism with five adjectives: "ideal, symbolist, synthetist, subjective, and decorative." Gauguin himself felt compelled to use Symbolist terminology to describe his painting *Where Do We Come From?* when it was exhibited at Ambroise Vollard's gallery in Paris in 1898. Writing from Tahiti, he stressed the picture was "musical," declaring that it communicated via the abstract qualities of line, color, and form, and not through anecdote. At this time, the rich, chromatic operas of Richard Wagner (1813–1883), filled with intense passion and psychological urges, were the rage in Paris, as they were throughout Europe and America, and they inspired Symbolist writers and painters alike to use abstract means to project powerful emotional yearnings and tap into the most elemental states of mind.

The Nabis

Gauguin's impact was tremendous, and by the 1890s, flat curvilinear organic patterning was ubiquitous. For example, it is the basis for Toulouse-Lautrec's posters, and it is apparent in many of his oils as well. Gauguin was also the formative influence on the Nabis, a secret organization founded in 1888 by young Parisian artists, including Édouard Vuillard and Pierre Bonnard, who were stunned by the novelty and spirituality of Gauguin's Pont-Aven paintings. *Nabi* is Hebrew for "prophet," and as the name suggests, the members immersed themselves in religion of all kinds as well as in the occult and the supernatural.

Although the Nabis broke up by the mid-1890s, Édouard Vuillard (1868–1940), along with Bonnard, developed into a major artist. Abandoning the group's religious thrust, he retained its emphasis on emotion expressed through abstraction, which fellow Nabis member Maurice Denis summed up in a famous quote when he wrote, "A picture—before being a warhorse, a female nude, or some anecdote—is essentially a flat surface covered with colors in a particular order." Reality dissolving into an abstraction of emotion can be seen in Vuillard's small intimate oil of 1893, *The Suitor* (fig. **26.14**). Here, we see the artist's favorite theme, interiors, which are magical, not mundane. He presents his dressmaker mother, his sister, and her husband, a respected painter and member of the Nabis. The real world disappears in a poetry of paint. Lush, dappled brushwork and a subdued but colorful, rich palette create a tranquil, sensuous mood. Tables, chairs, figures, and bolts of fabric are two-dimensional ghosts floating in an enchanting sea of paint, color, and form that embodies the sweet intimacy and languid pace of bourgeois domesticity.

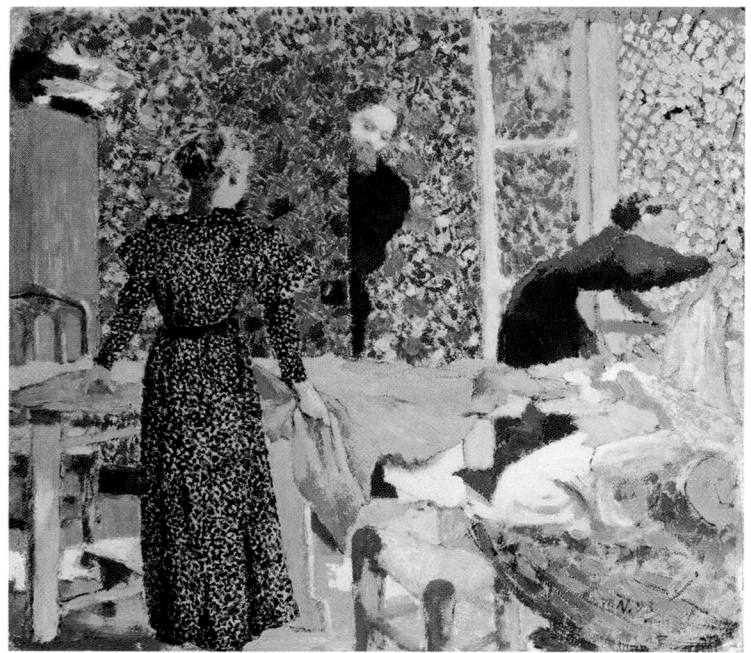

26.14 Édouard Vuillard, *The Suitor (Interior with Work Table)*. 1893. Oil on millboard panel, 12½ × 14" (31.8 × 35.6 cm). Smith College Museum of Art, Northampton, Massachusetts. Purchased, Drayton Hillyer Fund, 1938. SC. 1938:15.

Other Symbolist Visions in France

Two artists predating Symbolism were embraced by the movement: Gustave Moreau and Odilon Redon. Moreau emerged in the 1860s, and Redon the following decade. Both gained in notoriety when they were featured in Joris-Karl Huysmans's notorious 1884 Symbolist novel *À Rebours* (*Against Nature*). Huysmans's protagonist, Des Esseintes, an aristocrat, is a jaded decadent eccentric who leaves Paris and retreats to a remote village. Here, the self-obsessed recluse transforms his house into a strange dreamworld, filled with wondrous objects reflecting his personal dissolute aesthetic. In one famous chapter, Des Esseintes, in order to display his gems, has them affixed to a tortoise, which, heavily laden with the stones, collapses and dies after a few steps. His walls are decorated with prints of artworks by Moreau and Redon.

GUSTAVE MOREAU The imagery of Gustave Moreau (1826–1898) combined exotic Romantic motifs with an unsettling, mysterious psychology set in a supernatural world. In his large watercolor *The Apparition* (fig. **26.15**) of about 1876, we see the New Testament tale of Salome being presented with the head of St. John the Baptist. Herod, touched by his stepdaughter's dance at his birthday feast, granted Salome one wish, and at her mother's request, she asked for the Baptist's head. But instead of appearing on a charger, as is traditional, the head, encased in a radiant halo and gushing blood that pools on the floor, magically levitates. We see a bold stare-down between good and evil and between wanton sexuality and stern morality, as suggested by Salome's scant costume and erotic pose and John's stoic, condemning visage. The

decoration and costumes are Near Eastern, and the vast Classical hall dazzles with imperial opulence. Flowers, clothing, columns, and walls are created with minute, gemlike brushstrokes that are reminiscent of Delacroix (see page 843) and make everything sparkle. (Even the palette is Delacroix's.) In Moreau's hands, the story of Salome is not simply illustrated, but becomes a macabre hallucination of sex and death, presented through a dazzling haze of jewel-like marks and a smoldering, golden light.

ODILON REDON Even more visionary and dreamlike are the intense images of another artist claimed by the Symbolists, Odilon Redon (1840–1916). His drawings and prints deliver crepuscular fantasies enveloped in a velvety blurring of black charcoal or lithographic crayon. Among many sources, he especially drew inspiration from the grim, horrifying prints of Goya (see fig. 24.1). Redon's style can be seen in the lithograph reproduced here from an 1878 series dedicated to Edgar Allan Poe (fig. **26.16**). Translated into French by Baudelaire and Mallarmé, Poe's terrifying

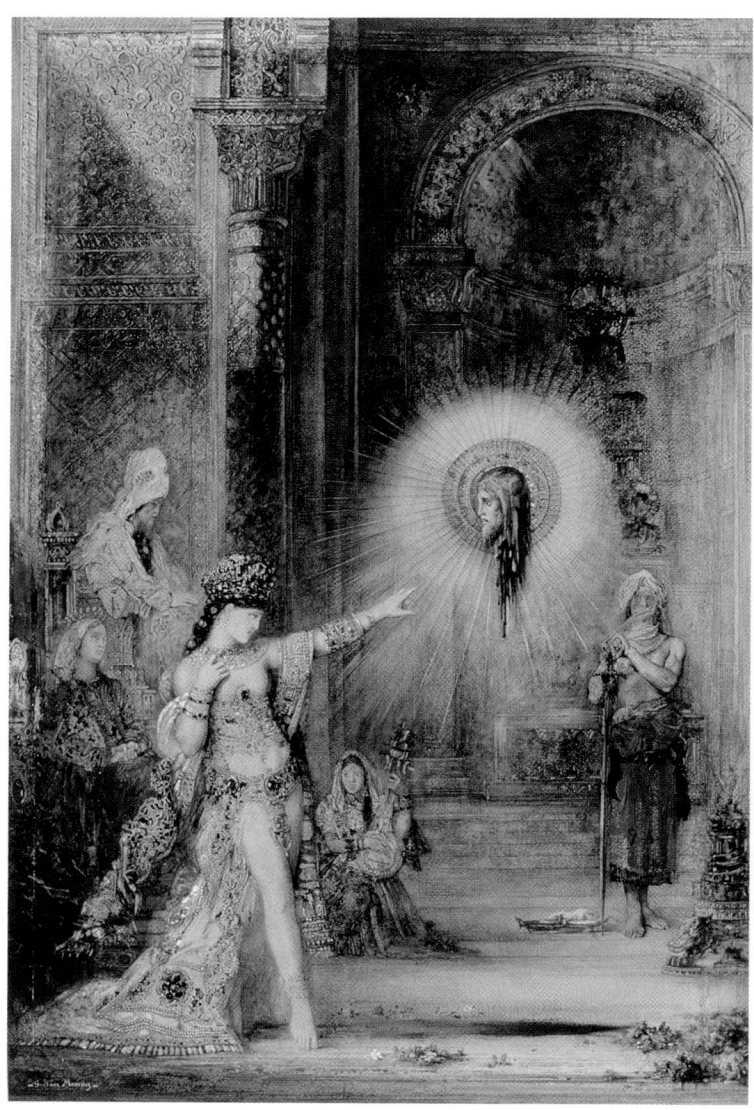

26.15 Gustave Moreau, *The Apparition (Dance of Salomé)*. ca. 1876. Watercolor, 41¾ × 28⅜" (106 × 72 cm). Musée du Louvre, Paris. RF 2130

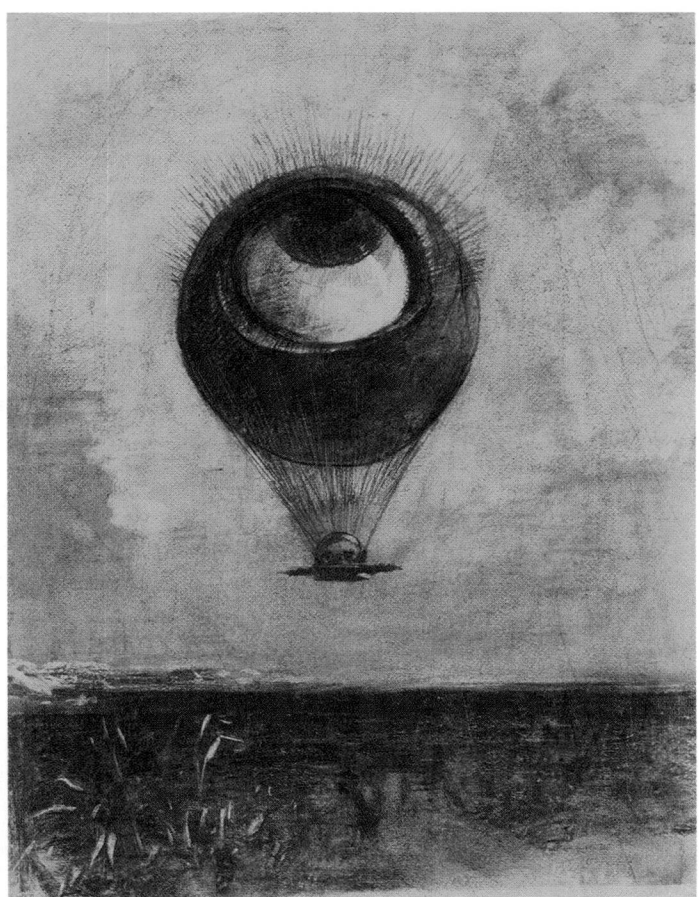

26.16 Odilon Redon, *The Eye Like a Strange Balloon Mounts Toward Infinity*, from the series *Edgar A. Poe*. 1878. Charcoal on paper, 16⅝ × 13⅛" (42.2 × 33.2 cm). Museum of Modern Art, New York. Gift of Larry Aldrich 4.1964

psychological tales were popular in France. Redon was inspired by Poe's Romantic mood, but his lithographs do not illustrate Poe directly: They are "visual poems" in their own right, evoking the macabre, hallucinatory world of Poe's imagination. If Goya created very pointed horrific nightmares, Redon envisions nebulous poetic dreams. Things float, glide, and hover, and edges are soft, grainy, and indistinct. Everything in Redon's world is in doubt and in some kind of strange evolutionary flux. Here, a balloon quietly morphs into a hairy eye and parts the sky as it rises up to heaven carrying a head severed at the nose. Below, a primordial plant with pyrotechnic fronds glows against a forbidding dark sea. Connotations of resurrection, transcendence, a rite of passage, life, death, eternity, and the unknown are embedded in *The Eye*, but the image's narrative meaning remains shrouded in mystery. Instead, what prevails is a troubling psychology and a feeling of frightening uncertainty.

HENRI ROUSSEAU A Symbolist preoccupation with portraying fundamental human urges and the psychology of sexual desire can also be seen in the work of Henri Rousseau (1844–1910), who was essentially self-taught and because of his naïve style is labeled a "primitive painter." A retired customs officer who started painting in the mid-1880s, Rousseau took as his ideal the hard-edged academic style of the followers of Ingres (see fig. 24.13), which in his autodidactic hands took on a charming, simplistic look. He sought inspiration in illustrated books and the botanical gardens in Paris. "When I go into the glass houses [of the botanical gardens] and I see the strange plants of exotic lands, it seems to me that I enter a dream." We see such a dream in this 1910 painting (fig. **26.17**), in which he presents a nude woman mysteriously

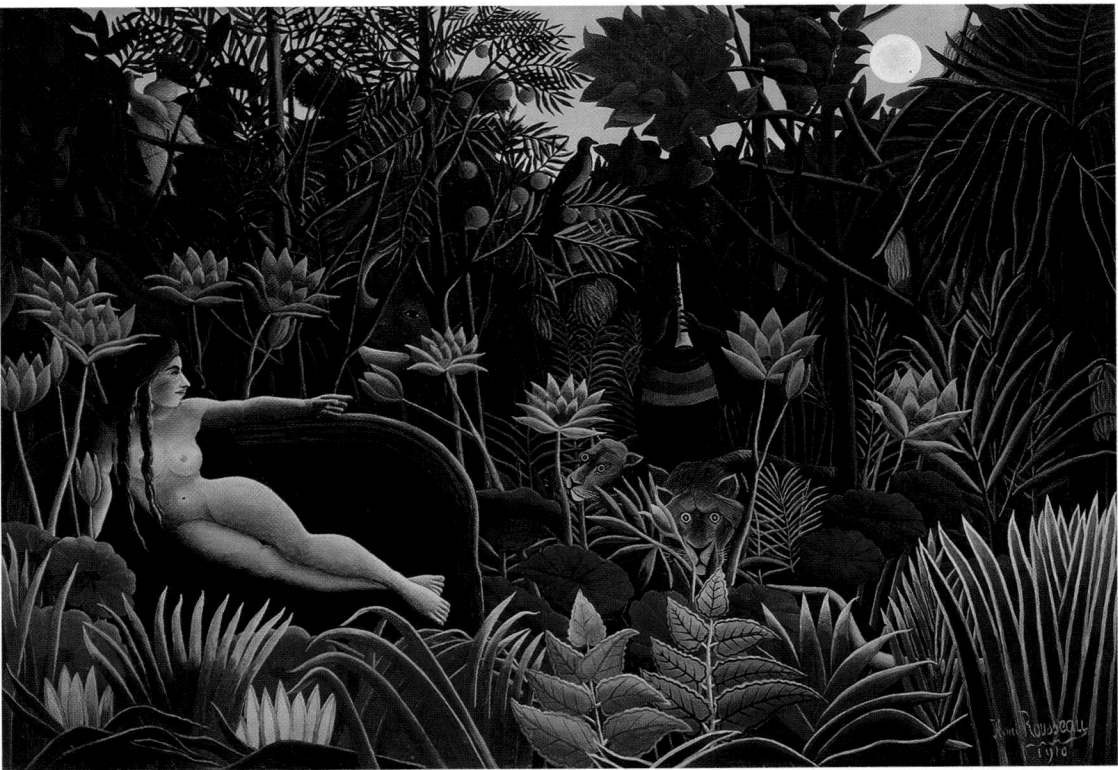

26.17 Henri Rousseau, *The Dream*. 1910. Oil on canvas, 6'8½" × 9'9½" (2.05 × 2.96 cm). Museum of Modern Art, New York. Gift of Nelson A. Rockefeller

lying on a sofa in a cardboard stage-set fantasy of a playfully colored, luxuriant jungle. Wide-eyed animals stare voyeuristically at her. We assume they are male, as suggested by the phallic orange snake and the musician playing a flute, an overt symbol of masculine sexual desire. Rousseau gives us an image of sexual longing, reinforced by the primordial pull of the jungle with its voluptuous iridescent flowers and fruit and the cosmic glow of a full moon presiding in the sky. Beginning in 1886, Rousseau showed at the Salon des Indépendants (an annual exhibition of independent artists), receiving little recognition during his lifetime. But in 1905, he was discovered by Pablo Picasso and his circle, who admired his naïve paintings for their flatness and abstraction as well as for their creative honesty and directness.

Symbolism Beyond France

Strange dreamlike imagery was not unique to Paris. By the late 1880s, a Symbolist otherworldly aesthetic of fantasy, escapism, and psychology could be found throughout the Western world, including America.

JAMES ENSOR AND LES VINGT In Belgium, Symbolism surfaced in the extraordinarily crude and visually aggressive paintings of James Ensor (1860–1949), who like Gauguin was repulsed by modernity and led a reclusive life above his parents' souvenir shop at the seaside resort of Ostend. In 1877, he enrolled in the Brussels Academy of Fine Arts, lasting three years, even though he described it as "that establishment for the near-blind" and declared, "All the rules, all the canons of art vomit death like their bronze brethren." He identified with socialists and anarchists and, in 1883, helped found in Brussels the counterpart of the Parisian Independent Artists. Called Les Vingt (The Twenty),

it offered unjuried exhibitions for a wide range of avant-garde Belgium artists, from Impressionists to Neo-Impressionists to Symbolists. But when the group started showing Whistler, Seurat, and Redon and became international, Ensor, a Belgian nationalist, permanently retreated to Ostend, where he immersed himself in his own world, one of disgust at the pretenses, artificiality, corruption, and lack of values of modern civilization. Turning his back on the cold refinement of academic art, he embraced popular culture, declaring, "Long live naïve and ignorant painting!" His nationalism and loathing of insincere refinement led him to admire the grotesque depictions often found in the work of Breugel and Bosch (see pages 655–58 and 492–93). The carnivals they painted still lived on in Ostend in annual festivals, for which the Ensor souvenir shop sold masks.

Ensor's mature style can be seen in his enormous 14-foot-wide *Christ's Entry into Brussels in 1889* (fig. **26.18**), painted in 1888 and representing a Second Coming of Christ. Beneath a banner declaring "Long Live Socialism" and swallowed up in the crowd and pushed into the background is a diminutive Christ on a donkey. The crowd wear masks, which reveal as opposed to hide the greed, corruption, and immorality that resides behind the false face of contemporary society. Not only does Ensor appropriate the masks from his parents' shop to give his image a primitive grotesqueness, but he paints everything with a crudeness and distortion we associate with popular art forms—caricature, graffiti, and naïve and children's art. A garish red intensified by its complement, green, hypes the stridency of this repulsive, claustrophobic image. Here, we see the philosophical antithesis of Seurat's genteel *La Grande Jatte*, which was shown at a Les Vingt exhibition the year before and seen by Ensor. The similar scale of *Christ's Entry* suggests Ensor's chaotic vision of ubiquitous evil is a sarcastic response to Seurat's Pollyanna rendition of modernity.

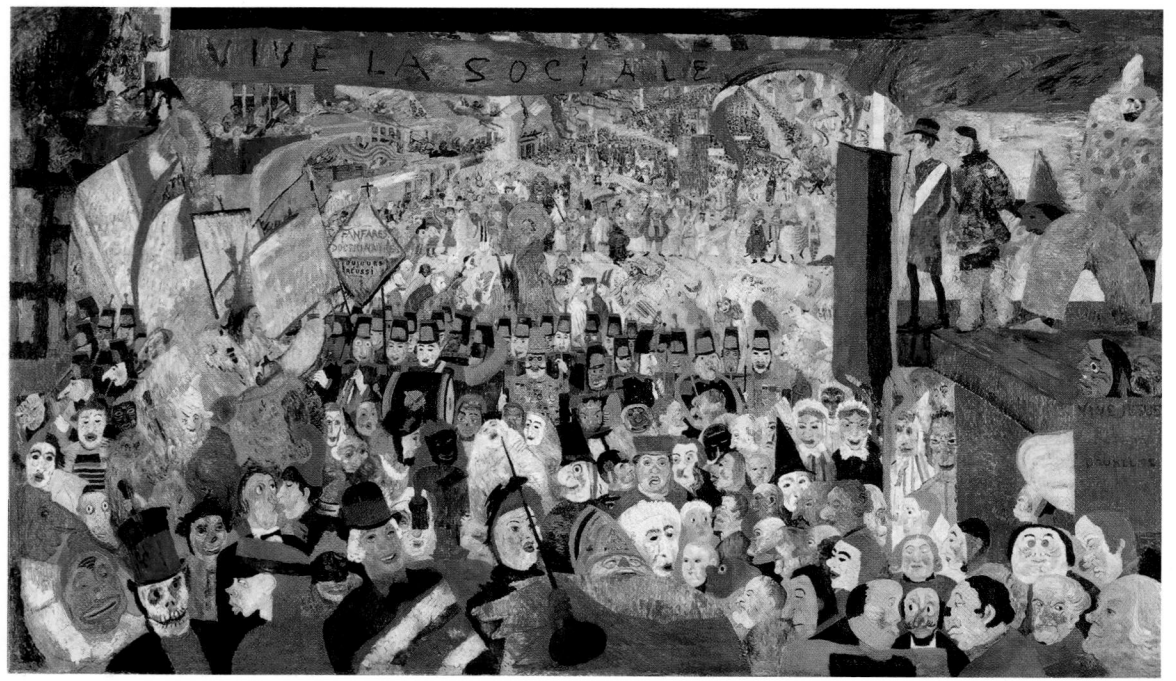

26.18   James Ensor, *Christ's Entry into Brussels in 1889*. 1888. Oil on canvas, 8'6½" × 14'1½" (2.6 × 4.3 m). Collection of the J. Paul Getty Museum, Los Angeles. 87. PA. 96.

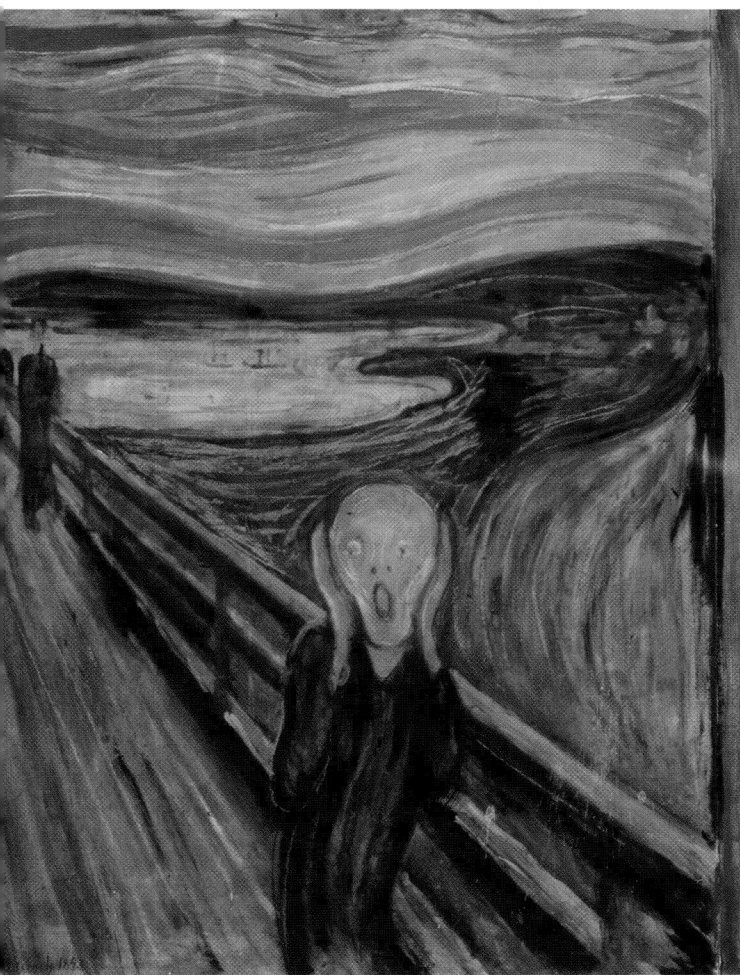

26.19 Edvard Munch, *The Scream*. 1893. Tempera and casein on cardboard, 36 × 29" (91.4 × 73.7 cm). Munch Museet, Oslo, Norway. (Stolen in May 2003.)

the thin streaking brushwork elevates the hysteria to a frightening feverish pitch.

The Scream was perhaps in part prompted by the 1883 eruption of the Indonesian volcano Krakatoa, which was so violent it generated the loudest sound heard by any human (the soundwaves traveled 1,500 miles [2,400 km]) and spewed forth ashes that circled the globe, immersing Europe in frightening blood-red or blue sunsets for some six months. After witnessing such an apocalyptic display of color in Christiania (now Oslo), Munch, already in a melancholic mood, wrote in his diary, "I sensed a great, infinite scream pass through Nature."

AUBREY BEARDSLEY While a morbid, fear-of-the-infinite psychology appears in much of Munch's work, perhaps his most prevalent subject is the uncontrollable yearnings of the libido, along with the sexual conflict it produces, especially as expressed by the *femme fatale* theme. This is a topic that preoccupied contemporary artists and writers. One of the most famous examples is Oscar Wilde's French play *Salomé*, which launched a vogue for Salome imagery. Wilde, an Irish *fin-de-siècle* writer and notorious aesthete, rewrote the biblical story. In the New Testament version, Salome asks for John's head at her mother behest. In Wilde's rewrite, she asks for it herself, because the saint spurns her sexual advances. The theme is distinctly sexual passion, with overtones of perversion, and its outrageous, bizarre behavior is characteristic of the sort of material relished by the British decadents. The play was published in French in 1893, with pictures by the British illustrator Aubrey Beardsley (1872–1898), who was in Wilde's circle of decadent writers and artists. In the image reproduced here (fig. **26.20**), Salome possessively holds John's severed head, which although dead still projects disdain. His snakelike hair and her octopus coif transform them into a pair of irrational Medusas driven by base hatred. John's blood drips into a dark pool, nourishing phallic plants that, like an insidious vine, slither around Salome. Their nightmarish confrontation takes place in a flat abstract world of curvilinear elegance, one so precious that the line virtually disappears at times as it twists in a sultry rhythm. As we shall shortly see, this plantlike, tendril quality is stylistically characteristic of Art Nouveau (see page 927), an architectural and decorative arts style that emerged in the 1890s. But thematically, the motif is used by Beardsley to reinforce the oppressive decadence of his image.

GUSTAV KLIMT A fascination with organic patterns and the psychological meanings they might convey also pervades the work of Gustav Klimt (1862–1918), whose career unfolded primarily in Vienna. Beginning in 1902, Klimt made a series of paintings centering on the theme of "The Kiss," the best-known version dating from 1907 to 1908 (fig. **26.21**). Although reflecting Klimt's own personal life (the model was his lover), the theme is Symbolist-inspired and relates directly to an 1897 painting by Munch of the same title. (In turn, both pictures were inspired by Rodin's sculpture *The Kiss*.) Munch's image presents a couple in a similarly unified form, but they are a simple dark mass, with the

EDVARD MUNCH Much Symbolist painting was influenced by Gauguin's mysterious sinuous patterning and abstraction, as well as by a desire to explore visually the most elemental psychological forces underlying modern civilization. Perhaps no one did this better than the Norwegian painter Edvard Munch (1863–1944), whose style matured in the early l890s after he spent time in Paris, where he experienced first hand the curvilinear planes of Gauguin's Pont-Aven paintings and the intense brushwork and color of Van Gogh's Arles pictures. His themes, however, could not be more different, for his painting investigated the psycho-logy of sex and the meaning of existence, thus delving into the deepest recesses of the mind, as did the plays of his two Scandinavian friends, the playwrights Henrik Ibsen and August Strindberg.

Munch crafts an image of horrifying anxiety in *The Scream* (fig. **26.19**), painted in 1893 after he had moved to Berlin. Clasping hands to a skull-like head, a grotesquely compressed, writhing figure gives voice to a base fear that appears funneled into it from the oozing, unstable landscape behind. The violent perspective of the uptilted walkway and rapidly receding railing combined with lovers' faces frighteningly merging as if consuming one another. Klimt's version of the theme with its rich surface patterning shows a faceless lustful male losing his identity as he is lured by passion and consumed by an enticing but indifferent *femme fatale*, who draws him perilously close to the abyss below. (For a discussion of the *femme fatale* theme, see *The Art Historian's Lens*, page 923.)

Formally inspired by the divine shimmer of Byzantine mosaics, which he studied first-hand in Ravenna (see page 256), Klimt cloaks his figures in richly patterned gold-leafed robes and encases them in a halo of bright light. Set on a mountain carpet of wild flowers and floating high above a celestial neverland, the painting simultaneously suggests the beauty and the spiritual pull of passion as well as its fleeting nature and painful consequences. In his intricate designs and shifting surfaces, Klimt hints at the instability inherent in individual subjectivity and social relations.

The Kiss has a strong decorative component, most evident in the lovers' exotic robes. In 1897, Klimt was one of 22 founders and the first president of the Vienna Secession, an avant-garde artists' organization. It was part of a loosely allied international

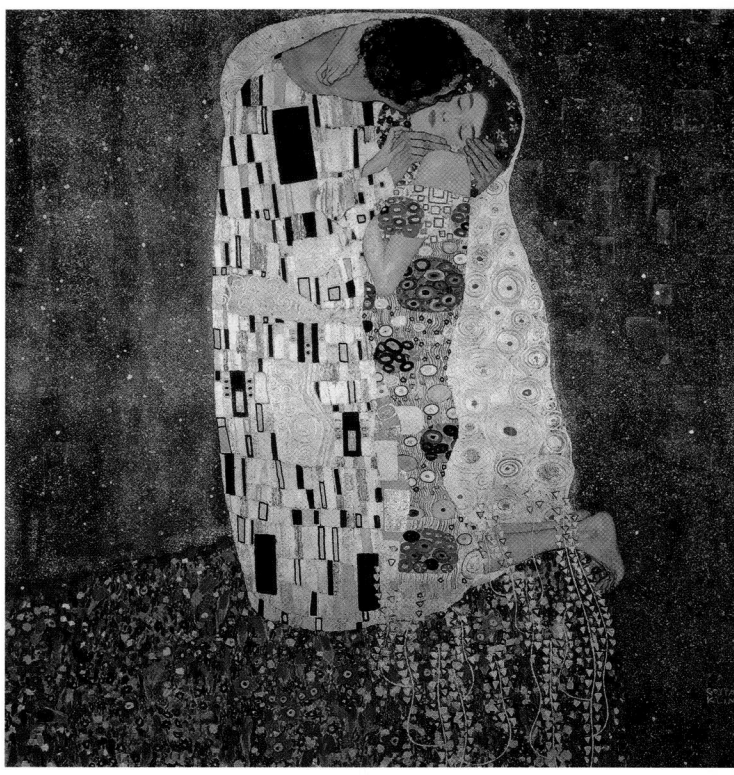

26.21 Gustav Klimt, *The Kiss*. 1907–08. Oil on canvas, 5'10⅞" × 5'10⅞" (1.80 × 1.80 m). Österreichische Nationalbibliothek, Vienna

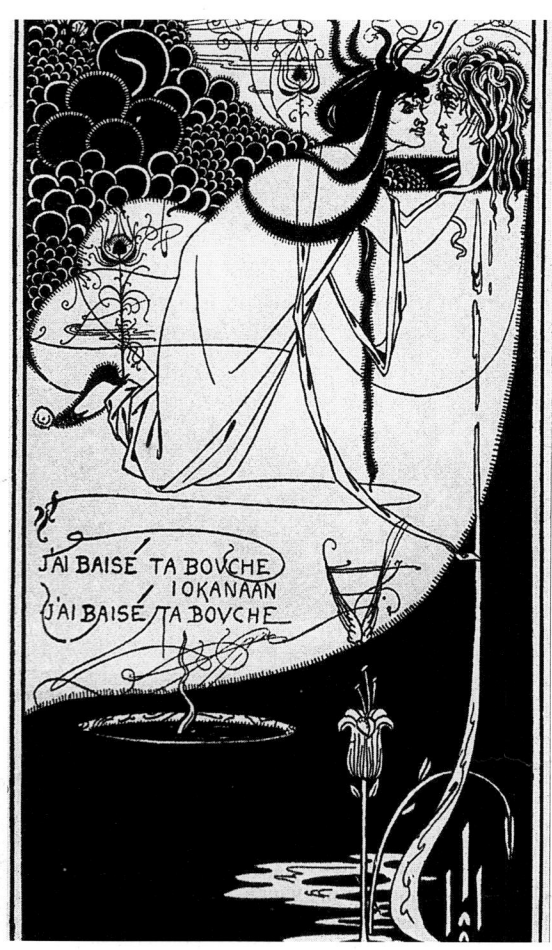

26.20 Aubrey Beardsley, *Salomé*. 1892. Pen drawing, 11 × 6" (27.8 × 15.2 cm). Aubrey Beardsley Collection. Manuscripts Division, Department of Rare Books and Special Collections, Princeton University Library, New Jersey. Special Collections, Princeton University Library, New Jersey

secession movement that started in Munich in 1892 and spread to Berlin that same year as progressive artists broke ranks with academic institutions. Not only did the Vienna Secession provide an alternative to the conservative academy, but its objectives included showcasing the applied arts and breaking down the hierarchy that placed painting and sculpture at the pinnacle and the decorative arts in the artisanal lower ranks. The secession movements equally embraced photography.

Symbolist Currents in American Art

In the 1880s, a small number of American artists also began to make more ethereal, otherworldly pictures. Today often labeled Tonalists, their imagery was more poetic and music-inspired, in many respects reflecting Whistler's Aestheticism (see page 885). Generally, no American is grouped with European Symbolism. Putting labels aside, however, two artists have strong parallels with the movement: Albert Pinkham Ryder and Henry Ossawa Tanner.

ALBERT PINKHAM RYDER Albert Pinkham Ryder (1847–1917), a somewhat reclusive New York artist, especially later in life, abandoned empirical observation to abstractly express his emotions. Born in New Bedford, Massachusetts, and moving to New York in 1867, he studied at the National Academy of Arts. Rather than the modern world, it was literature that inspired him, in particular works by the medieval English poet Geoffrey

Feminist Art History

It is tempting to view Gustav Klimt's *The Kiss* as just another example of *fin-de-siècle* decadence and indulgence, and a preoccupation with the psychology of sexual urges. But we can begin to read the image in other ways if we ask how this picture and others of its kind from this period present women, recognizing that it was made by a male and reflects male attitudes toward women. Now we can place the picture within the context of the late nineteenth-century feminist movement and the emergence of the New Woman, both of which threatened male dominance. Interestingly, this new approach to interpreting images like *The Kiss* is itself a product of another feminist movement that began late in the twentieth century.

Feminism emerged from the social radicalism of the 1960s, and its effects on the practice of art history were felt almost immediately. Feminist art historians began to reconstruct the careers and examine the work of women artists including Berthe Morisot, Mary Cassatt, Paula Modersohn-Becker, and Käthe Kollwitz. These studies demonstrated that women artists, far from being peripheral oddities, contributed importantly to the nineteenth-century avant-garde. In her groundbreaking essay of 1971, "Why Have There Been No Great Women Artists?", Linda Nochlin examined Western notions of genius and artistic success and concluded that social and economic factors prevented women from achieving the same status as their male counterparts. These factors, rather than inherent ability, were responsible for the relative paucity of "great women artists." Nochlin's essay spurred the historical study of artists' training, exhibition practices, and the effects of the art market on artists' careers. Other scholars, including Griselda Pollock and Rozsika Parker, went even further, examining art-historical language with its gender-based terms such as "Old Master" and "masterpiece."

Nochlin's essay also sparked an interest in studying artistic genres, such as the female nude and scenes of everyday life. Feminist scholars revealed the unspoken commercial and ideological interests vested in these scenes. In particular, feminist art historians brought to light previously ignored connections between depictions of women and late nineteenth-century attitudes toward gender roles and female sexuality. Quite often in the art of this period, images of women conform to simplistic (yet socially powerful) stereotypes of good or bad women. Mothers, virginal heroines, and martyrs represent the good women; prostitutes, adulteresses, and the myriad *femmes fatales*, such as vampires and incubuses, represent the bad.

The second wave of feminist art history, which would continue throughout the 1980s, was launched as early as 1973 when British film critic Laura Mulvey used psychoanalytic methods to introduce the concept of the controlling power of the male viewer's gaze. Studying Impressionist and Post-Impressionist imagery in terms of who gets to look and who is watched, feminist art historians exposed the operations of power, visual pleasure, and social control. "Men look at women, women watch themselves being looked at," the critic John Berger wrote in *Ways of Seeing* (1972). For Berger, Western art reflects the unequal status of men and women in society. Griselda Pollock analyzed the "Spaces of Femininity" in Impressionist paintings, and examined the ways in which some respectable bourgeois women artists like Cassatt and Morisot depicted a very different experience of modern life from their male peers. And the working-class Montmartre model-turned-artist Suzanne Valadon, who grew up in the studios of Impressionists such as Degas, painted revolutionary nudes from the position of someone who knew what it meant to pose for the artist's gaze.

Beginning in the 1990s, a third generation of feminist art historians broadened the scope of feminist art history to include gender studies, queer theory, the politics of globalization, and post-colonial studies. Nineteenth-century art remains fertile ground, however, for such interdisciplinary study, and new feminist investigations of this period continue to shape the discipline of art history.

Chaucer and Edgar Allan Poe. He was also influenced by the Bible, and, as with so many artists on both sides of the Atlantic, by Wagner's operas. In 1881, Ryder painted *Siegfried and the Rhine Maidens* (fig. **26.22**), beginning at midnight after attending a performance of Wagner's *Götterdämmerung* in New York, and obsessively painting nonstop for 48 hours. He continued to rework the painting until 1891, when it was exhibited at the Society of American Artists, an organization established, like the Impressionists' "Artists, Inc." (see page 871), to provide an alternative exhibition opportunity to that of the academy, in this case the restrictive staid National Academy of Fine Arts. Here, we see again a variant of the *femme fatale* theme, as a sexual struggle is embedded in the legend of the alluring Rhine maidens who

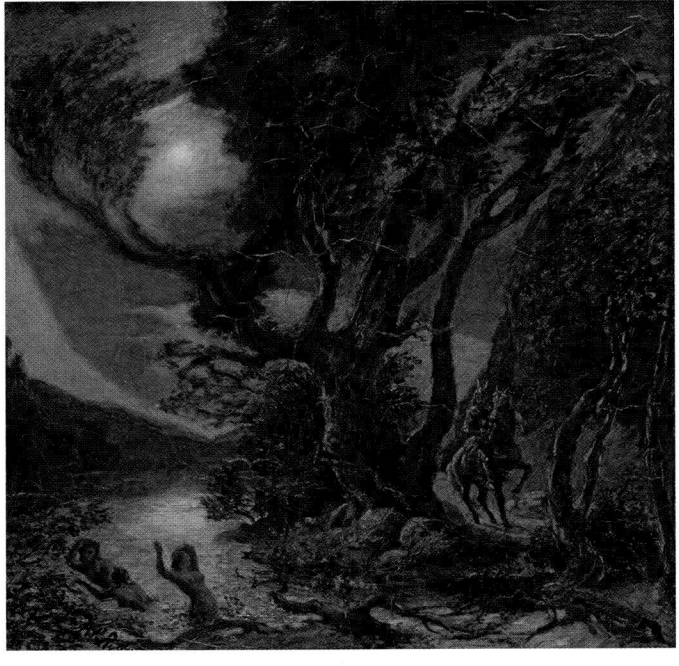

26.22 Albert Pinkham Ryder, *Siegfried and the Rhine Maidens.* 1888–91. Oil on canvas, 19⅞ × 20½" (50.5 × 52.1 cm). National Gallery of Art, Washington, D.C. Andrew W. Mellon Collection

foretell Siegfried's doom for refusing to return to them an all-powerful ring. Echoing the power of Wagner's music, often designed to project mythic Nordic forces, the broadly painted, fantastical landscape erupts with seething trees and a wild curvilinear sky, all seeming to emanate from the writhing forms of the maidens. who even seem to have at their command the supernatural pull of the moon. We sense uncontrollable power, reflecting uncontainable emotions, channeled through every brushstroke and distorted form.

HENRY OSSAWA TANNER The African-American artist Henry Ossawa Tanner (1859–1937) fell under the spell of Symbolism in Paris. Tanner studied in the 1880s under the liberal and supportive Thomas Eakins in Philadelphia, becoming a Realist. With little hope of achieving artistic parity in racist America, he went to Paris in 1892, where he settled permanently. There, his work began to show the influence of Symbolism as he experimented with abstraction and pursued new themes, even producing several Salome paintings. Tanner was the son of a preacher, and his work is dominated by religious imagery, such as *Angels Appearing before the Shepherds* (fig. **26.23**). The composition of this visionary painting is ingenious, for Tanner positions us in the sky with the angels. From this vantage point, we see the Holy Land: a breathtaking abstraction of lines and marks that nonetheless unmistakably contains hills, terraces, walls, and a city. We can even make out the shepherds' fire, the only note of strong color in what is otherwise a tonal symphony dominated by blue. Using rich, lush brushwork, Tanner dissolves the material world, making it ethereal and ephemeral, and as weightless as the transparent angels. Humanity is reduced to a speck in the vast scheme of the universe.

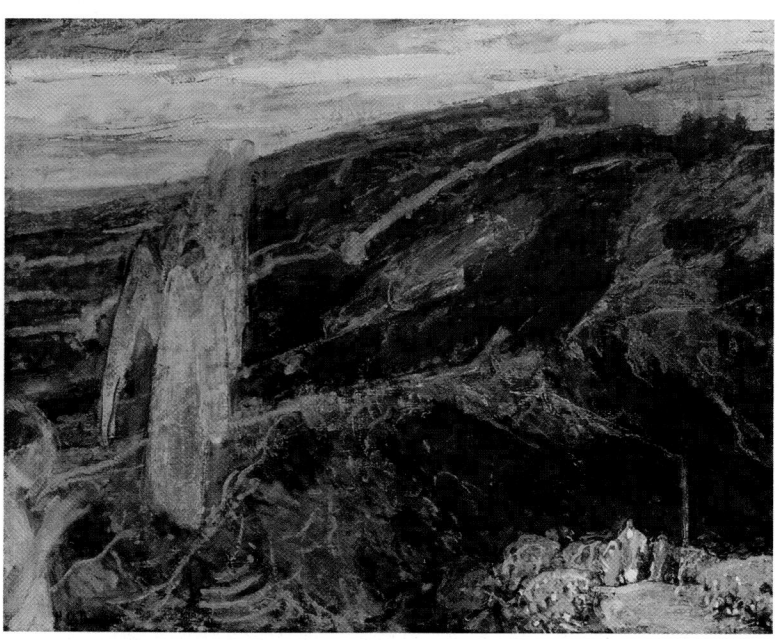

26.23 Henry Ossawa Tanner. *Angels Appearing before the Shepherds.* ca. 1910. Oil on canvas, 25¾ × 31⅞" (65.3 × 81.1 cm). Smithsonian American Art Museum. Gift of Mr. and Mrs. Norman Robins

The Sculpture of Rodin

The Symbolist desire to penetrate and portray the innermost essence of being had a parallel in sculpture in the work of Auguste Rodin (1840–1917). The most influential sculptor of the late nineteenth century, who singlehandedly laid the foundation for twentieth-century sculpture, Rodin's career started slowly. He was rejected by the École des Beaux-Arts, forcing him to attend the Petite École, which specialized in the decorative arts. His big break came in 1880, when he won a prestigious commission to design the bronze doors for a new decorative arts museum. Although the project eventually fell through, Rodin continued to work on it right up to his death. Called *The Gates of Hell* (fig. **26.24**), the 17-foot-high doors were inspired by Baudelaire's *Flowers of Evil* and Dante's *Inferno* from the *Divine Comedy*—indeed, at one point the thinker sitting in the tympanum contemplating the chaotic ghoulish scene below was to be Dante. Ultimately, the doors became a metaphor for the futility of life, the inability to satisfactorily fulfill our deepest uncontrollable passions, which is the fate of the sinners in Dante's second circle of hell, the circle that preoccupied Rodin the most. It is the world after the Fall, of eternal suffering, and Adam and Eve are included among the tortured souls below. Despite Rodin's devotion to the project, *The Gates of Hell* was never cast during his lifetime.

Rodin made independent sculptures from details of *The Gates*, including *The Thinker* (fig. **26.25**) and *The Three Shades*, the group mounted at the very peak of *The Gates*, which shows the same figure turned in three different positions. While his figures are based on familiar models—*The Thinker*, for example, recalls the work of Michelangelo, his favorite artist—they have an unfamiliar, organic quality. Rodin preferred to mold, not carve, working mostly in plaster or terra cotta, which artisans would then cast in bronze for him. We see where Rodin's hand has worked the malleable plaster with his fingers, for his surfaces ripple and undulate. His medium, instead of being smoothed out, remains intentionally rough and uneven, unlike Canova, for example, whose marble aspires to an uninterrupted graceful perfection (see figs. 23.30 and 23.31). With Rodin, we are made to feel privy to the creation of the figure, as if watching God making Adam out of clay. This primal quality is reinforced by his figures' nudity, which is less a Classical reference than a device to present an elemental form, stripped down to the very core of its humanity to expose primordial fears and passions.

For the sake of expression, Rodin does not hesitate to distort his figures, shattering Classical notions of the idealized figure and beauty. Look, for example, at *The Shades* atop the doors of *The Gates of Hell*. Their Michelangelesque musculature has been yanked and twisted, endowing these specters with a form that is at once familiar and unfamiliar. These uncanny messengers have arisen from tombs and now cast their message of eternal gloom on the teeming humanity below. We can even see this distortion to a lesser degree in *The Thinker*. Here, massive hands and feet project a ponderous weight that underscores the thinker's psychological

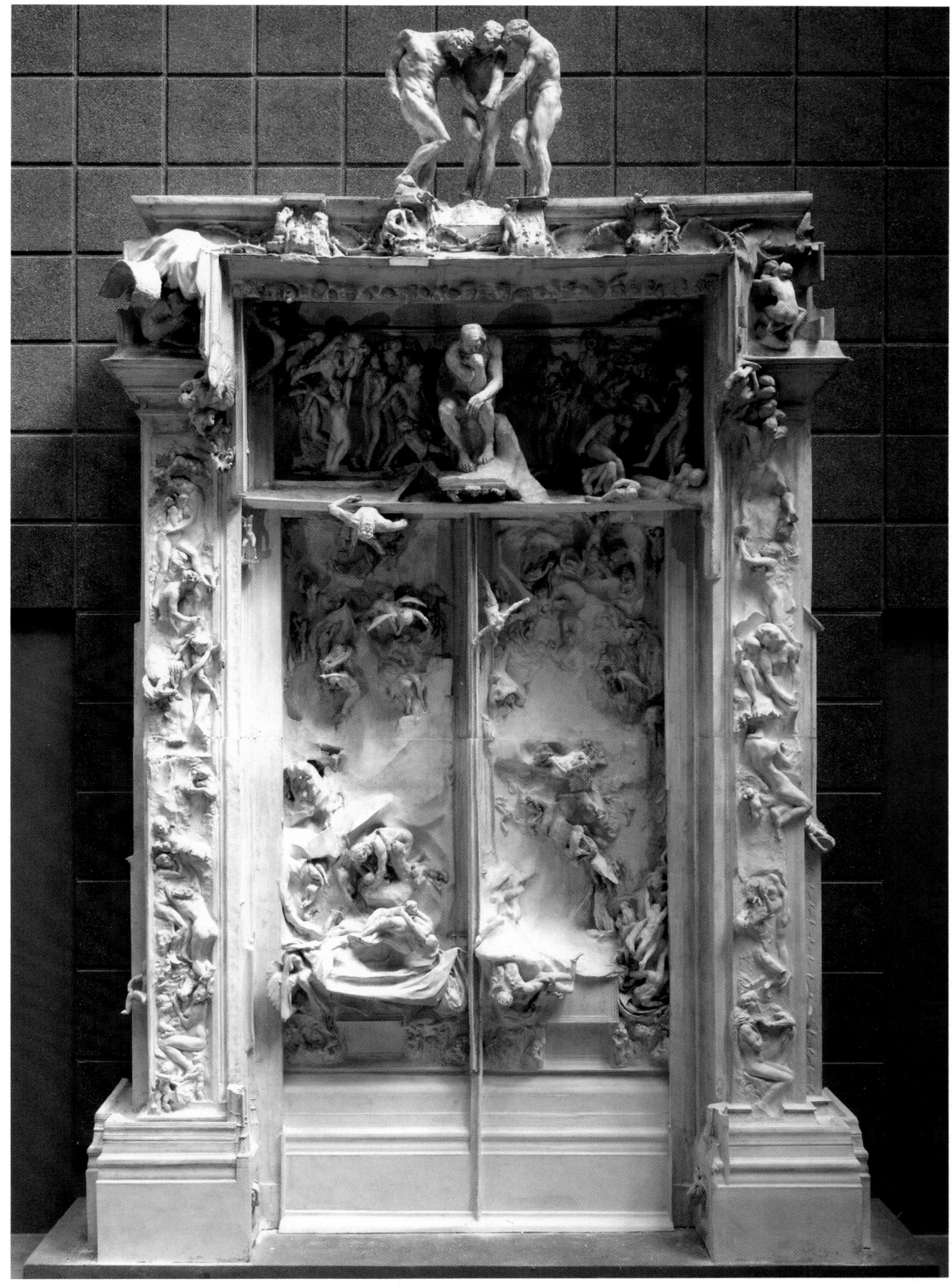

26.24 Auguste Rodin, *The Gates of Hell* (entire structure). 1880–1900. Plaster, height 18'1" × 13'1" × 3'1" (5.52 × 4.00 × 0.94 m). Musée d'Orsay, Paris

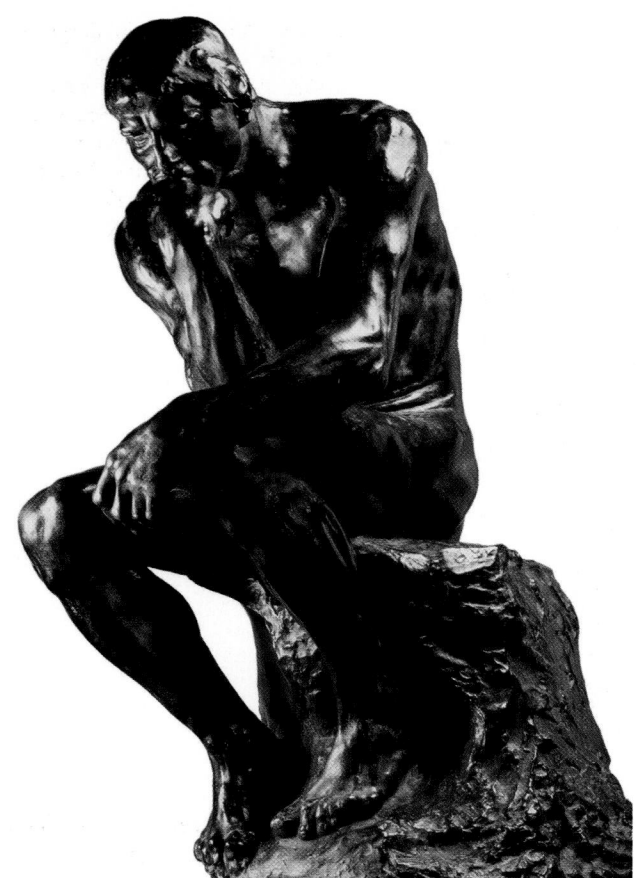

26.25   Auguste Rodin, *The Thinker*. 1879–87. Bronze, height 27½" (69.8 cm). Musée Rodin, Paris

town and the rest of its citizens. Rodin depicts the volunteers in crude burlap sacks and snakelike ropes trudging to their imprisonment and death. (Ultimately, they were freed.) Instead of courageous, noble heroes, he presents six men confronting death and displaying, among their emotions, fear, resignation, and anguish. They are not a united group but a chaotic mass, each alone with his thoughts. Massive distorted hands and feet, slumped bodies, and awkward gestures make the figures human. Rodin wanted the monument to sit on the ground in a plaza outside the town hall, so it would appear that the figures were walking from the building, thus allowing viewers to share the space of the burghers and experience their trauma. The ignoble, blunt monument embarrassed the town council, however, which hid it on a desolate site, mounted on a high pedestal.

Clearly, Rodin's preoccupation with expressing elemental fears and passions relates him to the Symbolist quest to plumb the depths of the mind. His thematic interests were stated as early as 1864, and in some ways it is possible to view him as a late Romantic. What ultimately marks him as a Symbolist, though, is

load, while his elongated arm is draped limply over his knee, suggesting inertia and indecision.

Equally expressive is Rodin's use of fragments; works that are just a hand or a torso, for example. The part not only represents the whole, embodying its essence, but it serves to strip away the inessential and focus on specifics. In *The Walking Man* (fig. **26.26**), which he began in 1877–78 as a preliminary study for a sculpture of St. John, we see another example of this distortion. The anatomy was again inspired by Michelangelo, while the partial body evokes damaged Classical statues. By not including a head, Rodin removed the distraction of the face and any associations it might carry such as identity and psychology, allowing him instead to stress movement, specifically forward motion. Initially just a study, Rodin eventually identified it as a self-sustaining work, recognizing that the headless, armless figure projected a powerful sense of humanity in its organic quality as well as providing an endless wealth of visual delight in the handling of the plaster. He had a first version cast in bronze before 1888, when it was exhibited at the Georges Petit gallery in Paris.

Rodin's emphasis on psychology can be seen in the *Burghers of Calais* (fig. **26.27**), a monument commissioned by the Calais city fathers to commemorate six citizens who agreed to sacrifice themselves during the 1347 English siege of Calais, a major event in the Hundred Years' War. In exchange for the execution of the six burghers, the English agreed to lift the siege and spare the

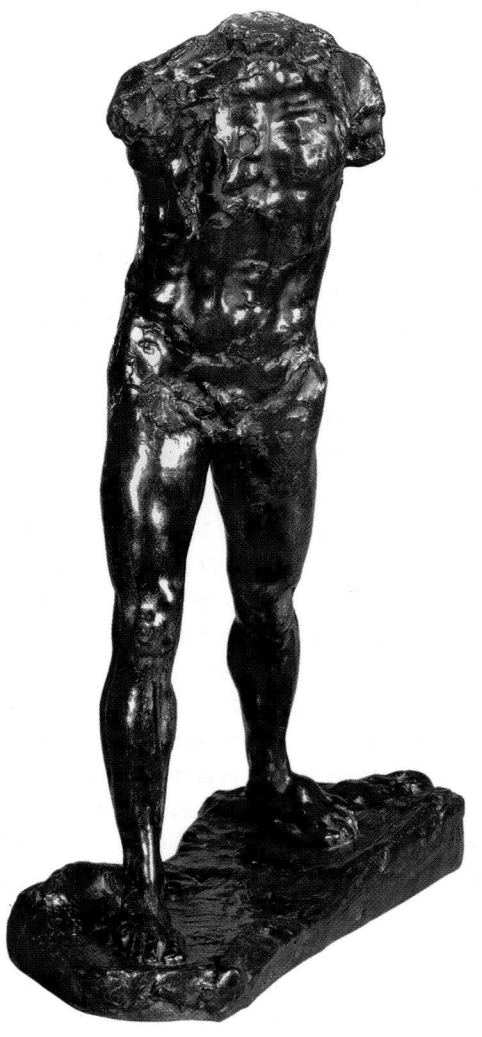

26.26   Auguste Rodin, *The Walking Man*. Model 1878–1900, cast ca. 1903. Bronze, height 33¼" (84.45 cm). National Gallery of Art, Washington, D.C. Gift of Mrs. John W. Simpson

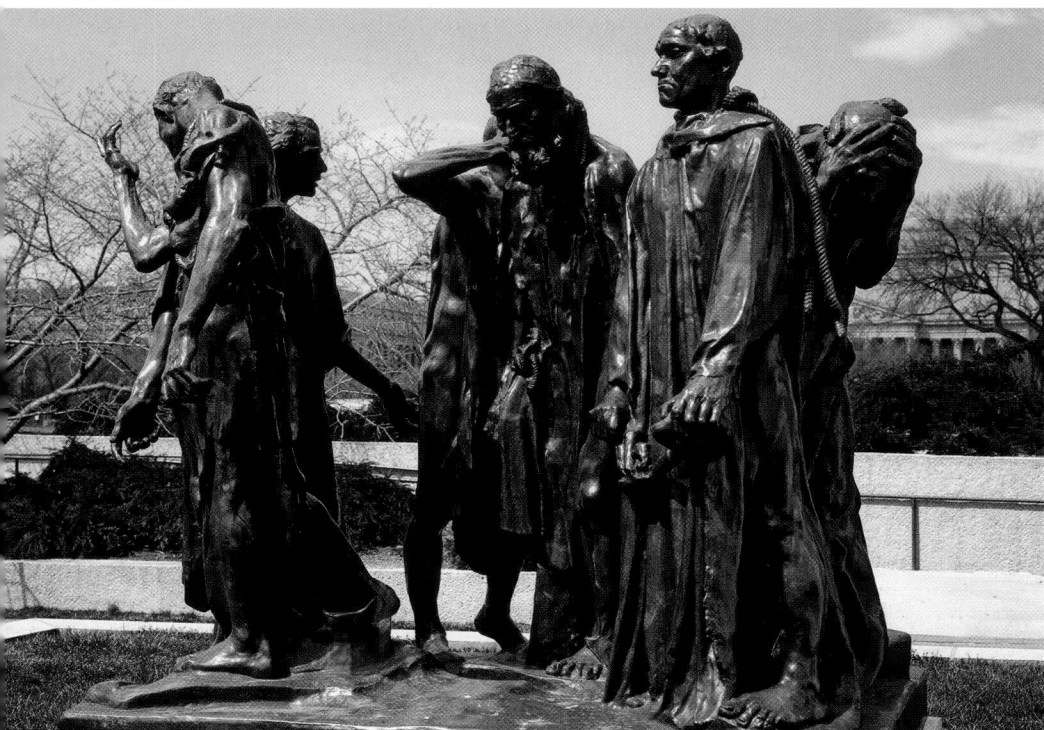

26.27 Auguste Rodin, *Burghers of Calais*. 1884–89. Bronze, 6'10½" × 7'11" × 6'6" (2.1 × 2.4 × 2 m). Hirshhorn Museum and Sculpture Garden, Smithsonian Institution, Washington, D.C. Gift of Joseph H. Hirshhorn, 1966. 66.4340

his interest in the psychic toll exacted on the individual by civilization. Whether he is exploring the crushing effects of war or the emotional costs of creative effort, Rodin emphasizes the psychological consequences of modern life. His ability to convey intense psychological states through forms at once familiar and abstract confirms his kinship with Symbolism. It was the hidden, inner struggle that Rodin, the Symbolists, and the nascent science of psychology sought to understand and render visible.

ART NOUVEAU AND THE SEARCH FOR MODERN DESIGN

In 1895, a German entrepreneur, Siegfried Bing, opened a decorative-arts shop called La Maison de l'Art Nouveau (The House of New Art) in Paris. Bing had made a fortune importing Japanese art and furnishings, and now sought to promote the Japanese principle of total design: Every detail of an interior space should be integrated into a single style. Aiming to eliminate any distinction between the fine and decorative arts, he hired famous architects, artists, and designers to develop every detail of entire rooms for his shop, as well as to design individual products, including furniture, vases, tiles, and stained-glass windows. This new style was called Art Nouveau, after Bing's shop. Elsewhere in Europe it took on different names, such as the Jugendstil (Youth Style) in Germany and the Secession Style in Vienna. Though varying somewhat from one country to the next, the style, which is particular to architecture and the decorative arts, is usually characterized by abstract organic forms and arabesques.

Art Nouveau can be seen in part as a response to William Morris's Arts and Crafts Movement, and certainly the emphasis

on handcrafted, finely designed products reflects this. The design products of Louis Comfort Tiffany (1848–1933) were another important influence on Art Nouveau, especially his stained-glass windows (fig. **26.28**) and glass lampshades with their organic motifs. Having a gemlike luster and the spiritual glow of medieval stained glass, Tiffany products are generally based on nature, depicting wooded landscapes, flowers, and trees. Coming on the heals of the Arts and Crafts Movement and anticipating Art Nouveau, Tiffany technically falls into neither category, and is a category unto itself. Tiffany's New York store, however, was the inspiration for Bing's La Maison de l'Art Nouveau.

Important differences exist between the Arts and Crafts Movement and Art Nouveau. Unlike the Arts and Crafts designers, many Art Nouveau artists embraced mass production and new industrial materials. And while Art Nouveau designs are clearly organic, they are often purely abstract rather than based on identifiable botanical specimens, as is the case in Morris's and Tiffany's designs.

The Public and Private Spaces of Art Nouveau

Compared with dark, ponderous Victorian interiors, the buoyant naturalism of Art Nouveau was a breath of fresh air, exuding youth, liberation, and modernity. It shared with Symbolism the element of fantasy, in this case biomorphic fantasy, which can especially be seen in architecture. Art Nouveau architects concerned themselves equally with exterior finish and interior space. Their typically complex, animated façades endow Art Nouveau buildings with a sculptural quality that engages viewers as they approach. This energy continues in the interior, for Art Nouveau spaces pulsate with a sense of movement—interior

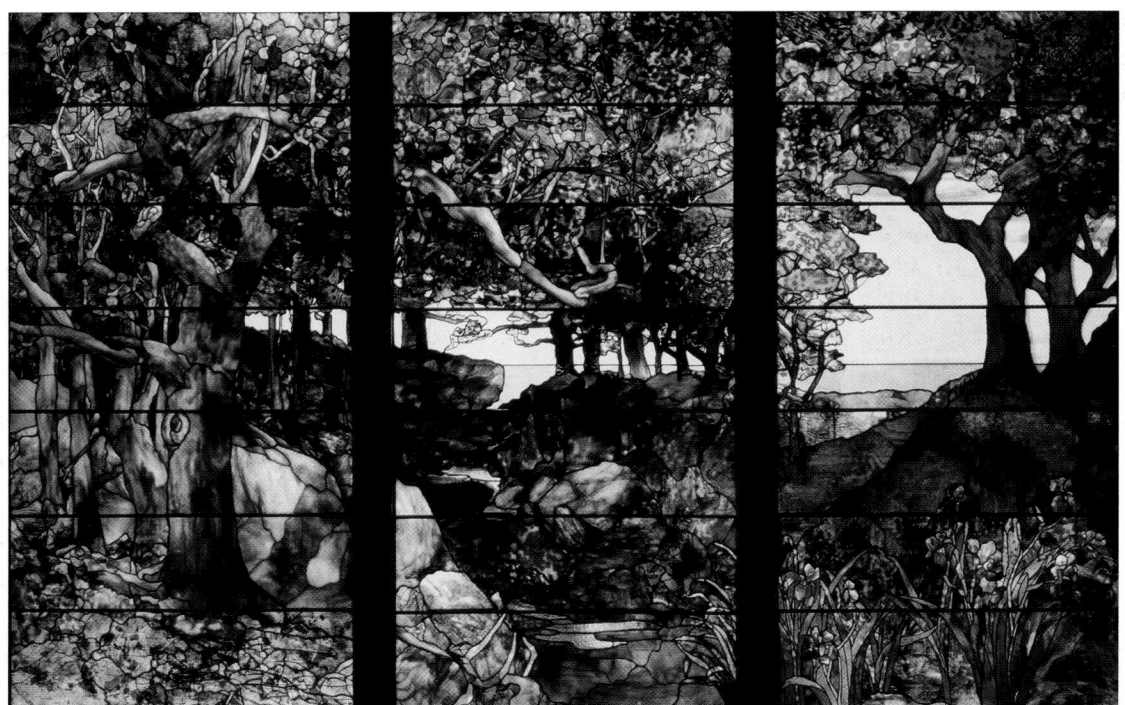

26.28 Louis Comfort Tiffany. Manufactured by Tiffany Studios. *A Wooded Landscape in Three Panels*. ca. 1905. Glass, copper-foil, and lead, $86^1/_2 \times 131^9/_{16} \times 1^3/_4$" (219.7 × 334.2 × 4.4 cm). Museum of Fine Arts, Houston, Museum Purchase with funds provided by the Brown Foundation Accessions Endowment Fund. 96.765. A, B, C

decoration and furnishings give the impression of having germinated and grown *in situ*. This effect is often enhanced by the admission of sunlight through glass ceilings or skylights, lending the space the fecundity of a greenhouse where everything seems to have grown spontaneously.

VICTOR HORTA The style began in Brussels with Belgian architect Victor Horta (1861–1947). Born in Ghent, Horta studied drawing, textiles, and architecture at the city's Académie des Beaux-Arts, and worked in Paris before returning to Belgium to start his own practice. In 1892, Horta designed the Tassel House in Brussels. The centerpiece of this is the ironwork of the stairwell (fig. **26.29**), the malleable wrought-iron columns and railings that were shaped into vines that evolve into whiplash tendrils on the walls, ceiling, and mosaic floor. The supporting role of the columns has been downplayed by making them as slender as possible. In a play on the Corinthian capital, they sprout ribbon-like tendrils that dissolve into arches. The linear patterns extend to the floor and wall, a device that further integrates the space visually. Sunlight filters through the glass ceiling, heightening the organic quality of the space. The curvilinear patterning derives from a variety of sources, including Japanese prints and Gauguin's cloisonnism (see fig. 26.12), although Horta's undulating linearity would in turn influence contemporary art, as seen in Beardsley's *Salomé* (see fig. 26.20). Everything has an organic fluidity, a springlike sense of growth and life, which has the effect of destroying the conventional boxlike quality of interior space.

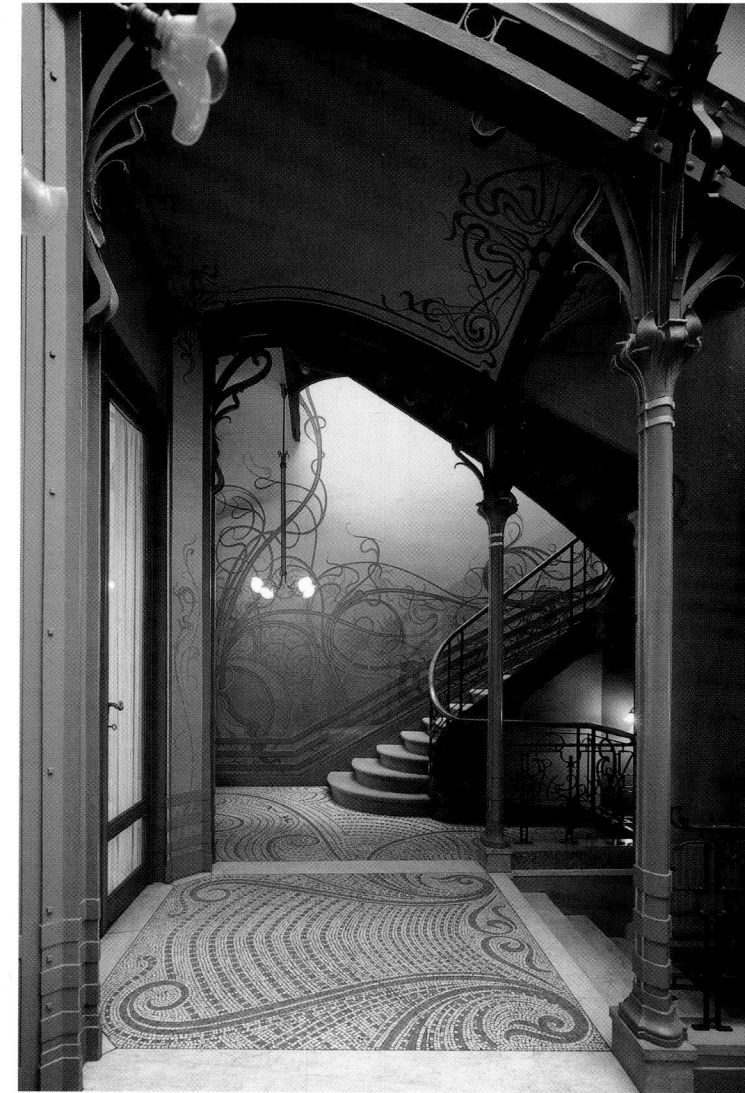

26.29 Victor Horta. Interior stairwell of the Tassel House, Brussels. 1892–93.

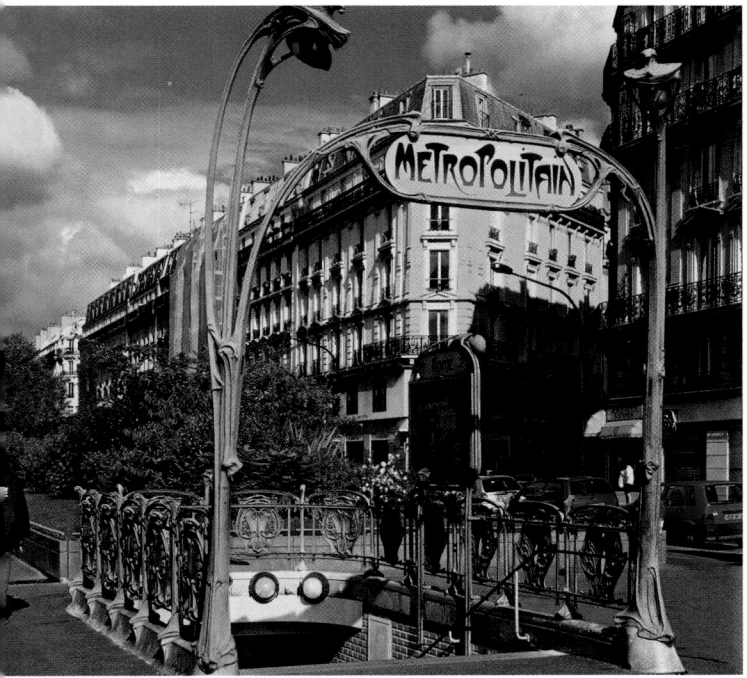

26.30 Hector Guimard. Métro station, Paris. 1900

HECTOR GUIMARD Art Nouveau next migrated to Paris, where its most famous practitioner was the architect Hector Guimard (1867–1942), who is especially renowned for designing the entrances to the Paris Métro, or subway, which opened in 1900 (fig. **26.30**). Like Horta, he worked with wrought and cast iron, patinated a soft, earthy green, but his sensitivity, while still organic, is quite different. If Horta suggests dynamic whiplash tendrils, Guimard evokes a lethargic prehistoric world, part plant-like, suggesting stalks and tendrils, and part zoomorphic, evoking praying mantises and dinosaurs. Even the lettering of the word "Métropolitain" morphs into strange organic characters, irregular, primitive, and foreboding. How appropriate for an architecture marking entrances to a new underworld. And how revealing that the style for a high-tech, machine world should be an escapist fantasy that is emphatically organic. Aside from his very public designs for the Métro, Guimard's practice was largely limited to private houses and apartment buildings for the haute bourgeoisie. He remained faithful to Art Nouveau even after it passed from fashion, around 1910.

ANTONI GAUDÍ Among the most bizarre Art Nouveau creations sprung from the wild imagination of Antoni Gaudí (1853–1926). Gaudí worked in Barcelona, the next and last major stop for the short-lived Art Nouveau, and his style reflects the fervent Catalan nationalism of the period, drawing heavily upon Mediterranean architectural traditions. His remarkable Casa Milà (fig. **26.31**), a large apartment house, expresses his fanatical devotion to the ideal of "natural" form, one quite different from Horta's plantlike designs. On the one hand, the building conjures up the Spanish Baroque, the Plateresque (indigenous Renaissance architecture suggesting elaborate silver plate), and the Moorish mosques of southern Spain. On the other, it is pure nature. Believing there are no straight lines in nature, Gaudí created an undulating façade and irregularly shaped interior spaces (fig. **26.32**), in effect destroying the architectural box. With its huge

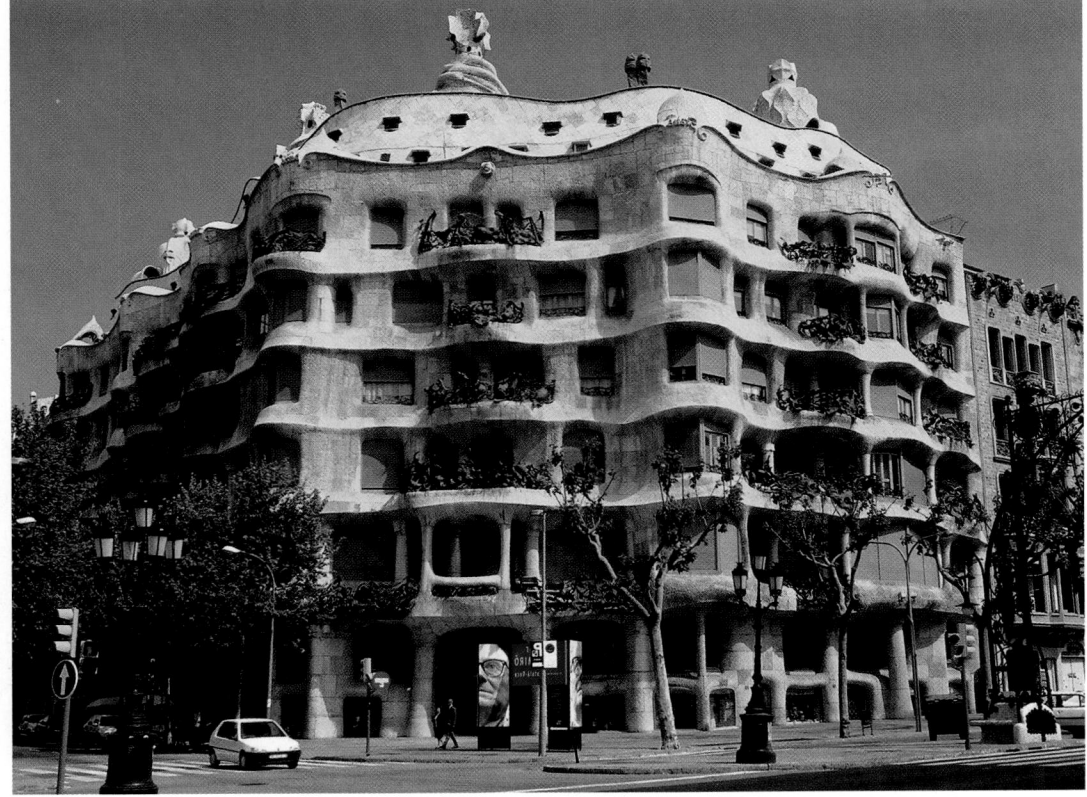

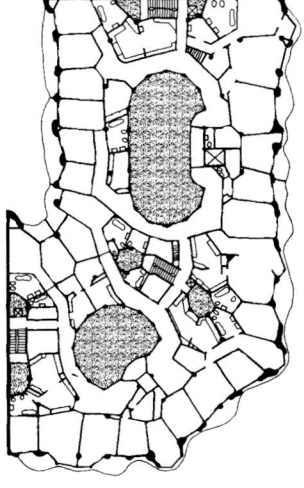

26.31 Antoni Gaudí. Casa Milà, Barcelona. 1905–10

26.32 Antoni Gaudí. Plan of typical floor, Casa Milà

stone blocks, the exterior evokes austere seaside cliffs while the wrought-iron balconies resemble seaweed and the scalloped cornice mimics ocean waves. To twenty-first-century eyes, the chimneys may recall soft ice-cream cones, but in 1905, they would have evoked, among other things, sand castles. These references to the seashore suggest Barcelona's distinctive geographic, cultural, and economic relationship to the Mediterranean. Gaudí was a fervent supporter of Catalan nationalism, so Barcelona, the capital of Catalonia, was especially symbolic for him. Perhaps more important, Gaudí was extremely religious, an ardent Catholic, and he viewed nature as a spiritual sanctuary and escape hatch from modernity. He spent the last decades of his life building an enormous Art Nouveau cathedral, La Sagrada Família, so vast in scale that it remains unfinished today.

CHARLES RENNIE MACKINTOSH Just as Gaudí's buildings evoke the landscape and culture of Catalonia, the work of the Glasgow architect Charles Rennie Mackintosh (1868–1928) speaks to a decidedly northern, Scottish sensibility. Mackintosh's designs are often labeled Art Nouveau, and he certainly began in this camp, especially adhering to Arts and Crafts values, and retaining organic qualities in his work throughout his career. As can be seen in his most famous building, the Glasgow School of Art (fig. **26.33**), built from 1897 to 1909, his work is infinitely more mainstream than Gaudí's, Guimard's, or Horta's. The façade is largely rectangular. Its austere windows, which hint at the Queen Anne revival style, dominate the building, making it look very geometric. The grid of the windows is reinforced by the horizontal overhang above the entrance. The entrance section evokes a Scottish baronial tower, within which is set an arched Baroque **aedicula**, or altar, with a Queen Anne **oriel**, or picture window, in a niche above. In other words, the building is an abstract presentation of

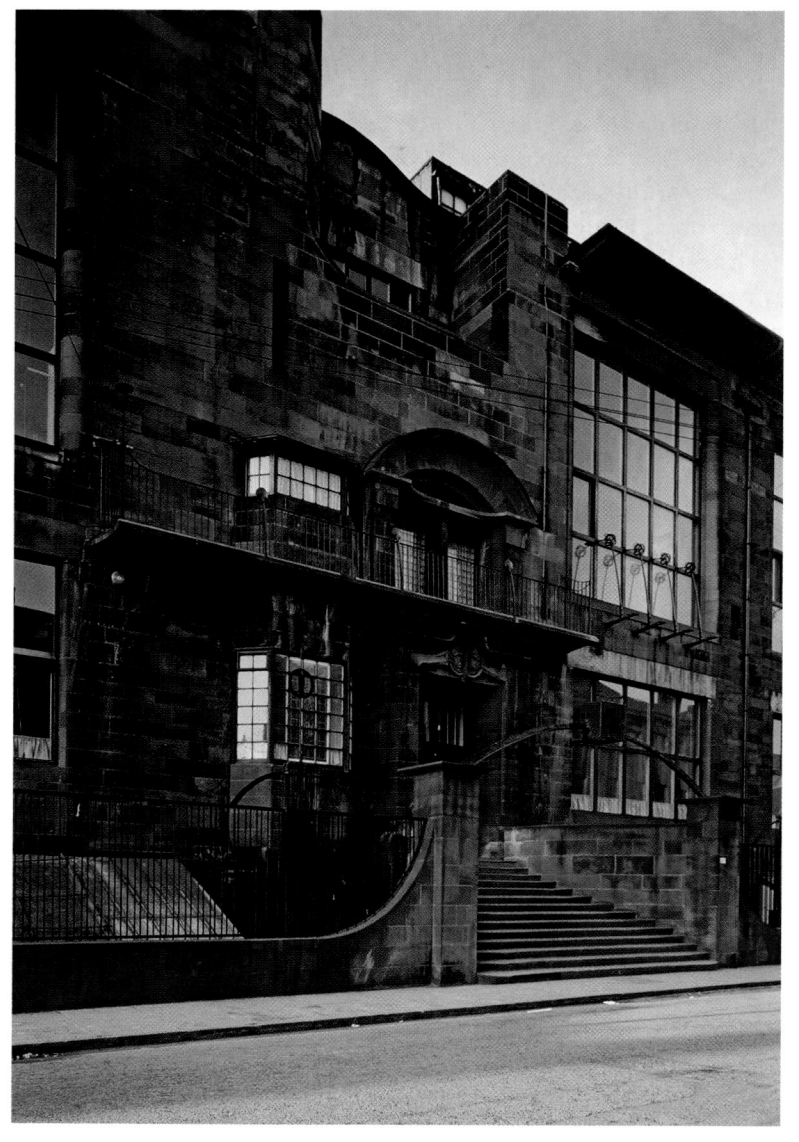

26.33   Charles Rennie Mackintosh.
North façade of the Glasgow School of Art,
Glasgow, Scotland. 1897–1909

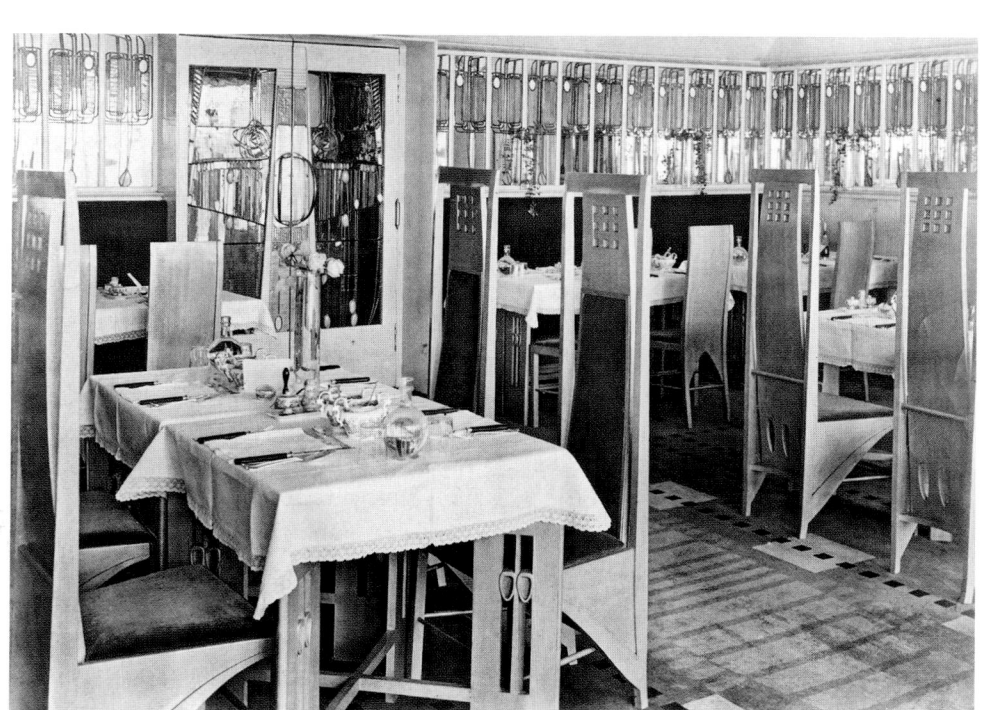

26.34   Charles Rennie Mackintosh.
Salon de Luxe, Willow Tea Rooms,
Sauchiehall Street, Glasgow. 1904

revival styles, but those styles are so reduced to a geometric essence that they almost disappear. Modern architects, especially in Vienna, would be especially inspired by this abstracting process. The only suggestion of the curvilinear Art Nouveau is in the eccentric, organic ironwork, including the railings and fences, the entrance arch with lantern, and the strange plantlike brackets used by windowcleaners.

Mackintosh's interiors, for which he is most noted, retain more of a balance between the geometric and organic, as seen in his 1904 Salon de Luxe at the Willow Tea Rooms in Glasgow (fig. **26.34**). The door and walls have a frail linear patterning suggesting willow branches, and the backs of the chairs gracefully buckle and taper, while their leg brackets curve. A severe grid of verticals and horizontals, however, epitomized by the nine squares on the backs of the chairs, sharply organizes the room, which nonetheless is quite elegant and refined. Regardless of labeling, Macintosh's design is certainly "new" and also total, encompassing every detail in the room, down to the door handle, all of which are beautifully handcrafted. While not the botanical and zoological fantasies of Horta and Guimard, Macintosh's vision equally dispatches the historical past and certainly charts strange territory, making tearoom guests feel as though they have passed through a magic door into a marvelous unidentifiable wonderland.

AMERICAN ARCHITECTURE: THE CHICAGO SCHOOL

Little did anyone know in 1871 that Chicago's devastating Great Fire would launch modern architecture and make American architects for the first time the most advanced in the world. Once the flames of the fire were extinguished, the issue at hand was not just one of rebuilding. Chicago had been growing rapidly, putting a premium on real estate, and now there was a need to maximize land use by building vertically. This was made possible by the invention of the safety elevator, perfected in New York in the 1850s and 1860s by Elisha Otis. Ambitious construction was delayed for ten years, however, due to the national financial collapse of 1873, which lasted through the decade. When rebuilding finally proceeded in the 1880s, it was dominated by young designers who had largely been trained as engineers with virtually no architectural background. This meant they were not hampered by strong preconceived notions of what buildings should look like and were open to allowing their structures to reflect the new technologies and materials they employed. They abandoned the historicism of revival architecture and designed abstract structures as they allowed form to follow function. The buildings they erected were technically so complicated and the workload was so great that the major architects paired off into complementary teams: Burnham and Root, Holabird and Roche, and Adler and Sullivan. Of this group, only Louis Sullivan had attended architectural school, one year at MIT and a half-year at the École des Beaux-Arts in Paris.

Henry Hobson Richardson: Laying the Foundation for Modernist Architecture

Designed by Boston architect Henry Hobson Richardson (1838–1886), the Marshall Field Wholesale Store (fig. **26.35**) provided an intellectual challenge to the new generation of Chicago architects. Born in New Orleans and educated at Harvard, Richardson rose to international fame for his Romanesque-revival work, which became so renowned that the style was eventually named after him. Made of stone, his buildings were massive, bold, and highly textured. They were also quite simplified, emphasizing volumetric forms. With the Marshall Field Wholesale Store, a seven-story building that took up an entire Chicago block, Richardson's style evolved to its most refined form, one that moved beyond the Victorian Romanesque revival. The building was composed of weighty stone walls made of red granite and red sandstone, and because it took up the entire city block, it felt massive, giving it a powerful physical presence. The scale and rough texture of the blocks as well as the dark hollows of the recessed windows added to the building's sculptural quality.

The building was highly associational, or referential. The arches, especially when used by Richardson, recalled the Romanesque, although they evoked a fifteenth-century Florentine palazzo as well (see fig. 15.32). The three-tier layering of the building also calls to mind Beaux-Arts architecture (see fig. 25.9), a reference to the rigorous architectural program of the Paris École des Beaux-Arts that established strict design

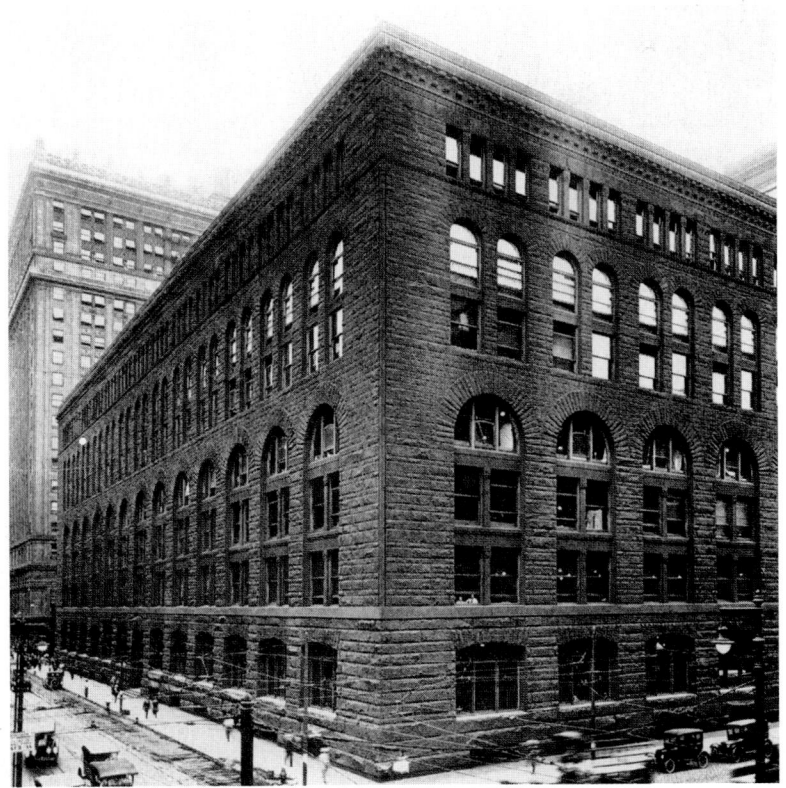

26.35 Henry Hobson Richardson. Marshall Field Wholesale Store, Chicago. 1885–87. Demolished 1931

principles. These rules included a stylobate-column-entablature configuration, that is, a base, rise, and crown format. In the Marshall Field building, the stylobate, or platform, was represented by the basement level, with the next two tiers representing the columnated level and the entablature. Despite parallels to past architecture, the building was remarkably abstract: There were no columns, piers, capitals, or entablatures per se. Instead the uniform stone, despite its rustication, was like a continuous skin covering the building. This innovative design that abstracted historical style would pose a major challenge for Chicago architects.

Louis Sullivan and Early Skyscrapers

Richardson did not consider himself a Modernist, and he was not one. But the abstraction of the Marshall Field building helped spawn Modernist architecture. As important as Richardson's influence were technical developments. As the Chicago fire clearly demonstrated, iron is not fire-resistant; intense heat makes it soften, bend, and, if hot enough, melt. To avoid towering infernos,

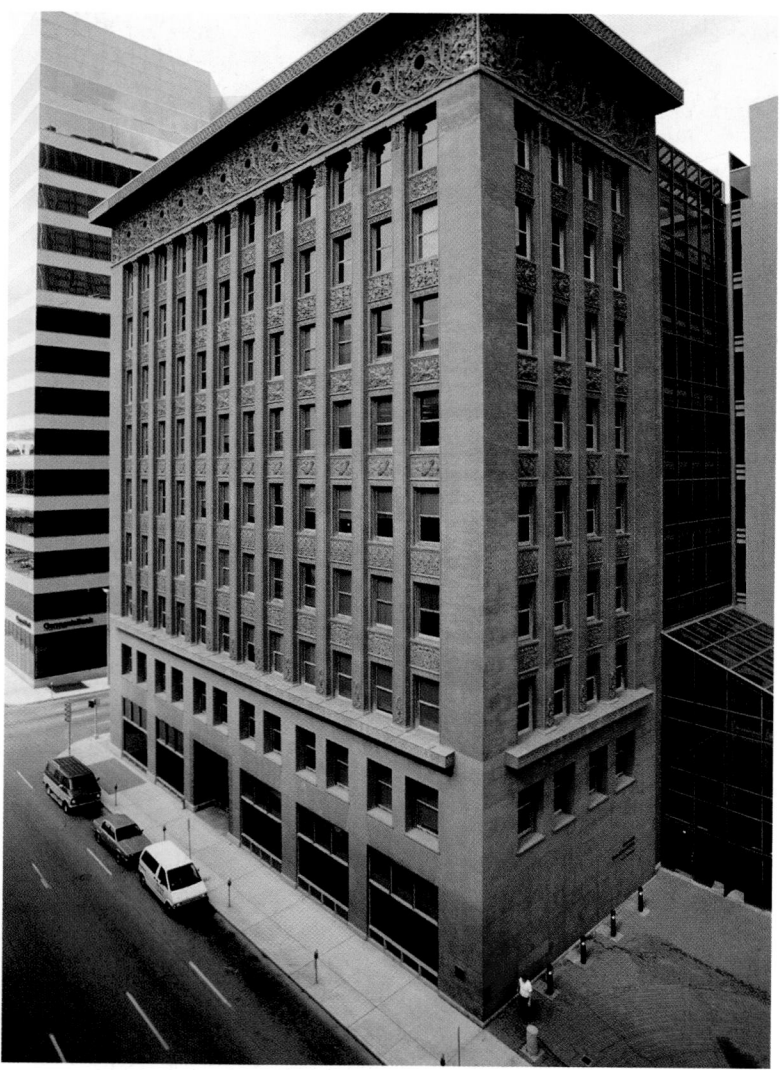

26.36 Louis Sullivan. Wainwright Building, St. Louis, Missouri. 1890–91. Destroyed

it was necessary to fireproof the metal, enveloping iron, and shortly thereafter steel (which was only developed as we know it today in the early twentieth century) with terra-cotta tiles and later in a coating of concrete (modern concrete, called Portland cement, was invented in England in 1825). The insulation also prevented corrosion.

An equally important technological development was the invention of the **curtain wall**. Unlike a self-supporting wall, the type Richardson used for the Marshall Field Wholesale Store, a curtain wall hangs from the lip of a horizontal beam at floor level on each story. Without this innovation, the base of the wall for a tall building would have to be extremely thick in order to support the weight of the wall above, severely limiting the number of floors. Furthermore, curtain walls allowed for entire walls to be made of glass, and with the development toward midcentury of plate glass, that is, large sheets of glass, it was now possible to design glass towers. The first extensive use of the curtain wall was in Chicago for the 1884–85 Home Insurance Building, which had a steel skeleton, and was designed by William Jenney, the elder statesman of the Chicago architects.

The architect generally credited with playing the main role in developing the aesthetic implications of the steel skeleton into powerful architecture is Louis Sullivan (1856–1924). In 1880, Sullivan joined the Chicago firm of Dankmar Adler, which in 1883 became Adler and Sullivan (Adler left the firm in 1891). Adler was the engineer, planner, and project manager who kept building construction moving forward, while Sullivan was the idealistic visionary who provided the design concepts.

Sullivan's early masterpiece is the Wainwright Building (fig. **26.36**), erected in St. Louis in 1890–91. (Most of his major buildings, however, are in Chicago.) Using the curtain wall, Sullivan designed a building that reflects the grid structure of the steel skeleton, although for aesthetic purposes he doubled the number of external piers, with only every other one having a structural beam behind it. The major problem for the early architects of skyscrapers was how to design a building that rose so many floors, while maintaining a visually interesting exterior that did not rely on outmoded revival styles. Sullivan's solution was ingenious. Like Richardson's Marshall Field Wholesale Store, his building is largely abstract. The end piers are widened, as in Marshall Field, dramatically framing the building, and the spandrels (the decorated horizontal panels between piers) are recessed, both elements giving the building a monumental sculptural quality and the sense of a building evolving from a solid block. The seven-story colossal piers and the enormous one-story cornice add to this grandeur. Again, we see the Beaux-Arts stylobate-column-entablature configuration of the Marshall Field building, which feels even more Classical in the Wainwright Building because of the grid and absence of Romanesque arches.

While the building's exterior presents a compilation of abstract, geometric forms, largely reflecting the substructure, Sullivan did not hesitate to design terra-cotta panels for the cornice and spandrels that feature a pattern based on an antique rinceau motif (an ornamental vine, leaf, or floral design). Sullivan intended these biomorphic decorations to symbolize his belief that architecture should utilize new technologies to promote social harmony and progress and to be part of a natural organic evolution of the world. Sullivan fervently believed in the spiritual theories of Emmanuel Swedenborg (1688–1772), a Swedish philosopher, theologian, and Christian mystic who preached that universal forces run through and unite all things, each of which is otherwise unique and an individual. His building reflects Swedenborgianism, which became popular at this time along with so many other nontraditional religions and cults. The decoration, for example, allowed Sullivan to distinguish the various parts of the building, giving each a separate identity (e.g., the upper story, the spandrels), and yet at the same time, all of these distinctive parts are tightly woven together into a unified whole, as suggested by the powerful grid of piers and spandrels. The flowering plant life energizes the building, reflects the vitality of the human element within, and relates both to the universal current flowing through all things. Although he was down-to-earth, practical, and

26.38 Louis Sullivan. Cast-iron ornament, Schlesinger and Meyer Store

functional—it was Sullivan who issued the famous dictum that "form ever follows function"—he was also a visionary Symbolist. (See www.myartslab.com.)

Sullivan's style became considerably lighter, airier, and abstract by 1900, anticipating the floating, geometric, glass boxes of twentieth-century Modernist architecture. This style can be seen in the Schlesinger and Meyer Store in Chicago (fig. 26.37), which was originally a commission for the three-bay, nine-story section on the left but evolved into the twelve-story structure we see today. Now, the thin vertical piers actually reflect the skeleton behind, and the mechanomorphic façade echoes the structural steel grid behind it. The wall has virtually disappeared, giving way to glass. Instead of the enormous monumental one-story cornice we saw on the Wainwright Building, Sullivan's top-floor "entablature" is actually a hollow recessed balcony, capped by a sliver of a cornice, which instead of being a weighty lid seems to be a floating piece of cardboard, in keeping with the airy lightness of the building. There is still a Beaux-Arts "base," but it seems recessed (although it is not) because of the horizontal molding above, making the nine floors of horizontal windows seem to float. The first floor dissolves in a wild flurry of Art Nouveau plant forms that cover cast-iron panels (fig. 26.38), in effect unifying the building with cosmic forces. With the Schlesinger and Meyer Store, the aesthetic for the Modernist skyscraper had perhaps reached its finest expression to date.

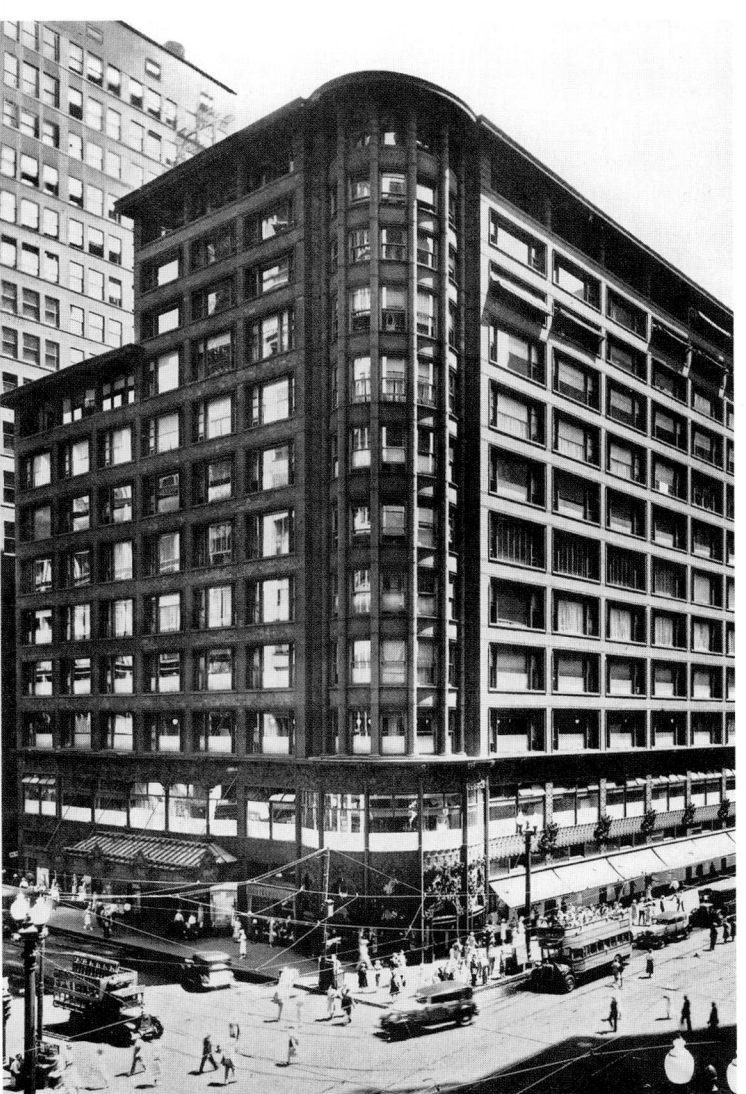

26.37 Louis H. Sullivan. Schlesinger and Meyer Store, then Carson-Pirie-Scott store (now the Sullivan Center). Chicago. 1899–1904

Frank Lloyd Wright and the Prairie House

After studying engineering at the University of Wisconsin, Frank Lloyd Wright (1867–1959) worked for Sullivan from 1888 until 1893. His sensitivity and strengths, however, could not have been more different. While Sullivan specialized in commercial buildings, Wright's forte was domestic architecture, although his public buildings are brilliant. Sullivan's innovations were largely in façades, whereas Wright's were in space, including interior space and its relationship to the exterior. Wright's architecture, like Sullivan's, is based on nature, and his reputation was established with what are known as his Prairie Houses, so-called because their strong horizontal sweep echoes the planarity of the Midwest landscape where the homes were built.

The crowning achievement of Wright's Prairie Houses, which he began designing in the early 1890s, is the Robie House (fig. 26.39), designed in Chicago in 1908. The building was so shockingly modern it would take architects a good ten to 20 years to understand it and develop its implications. As can readily be seen from the exterior, the house is an abstract play of not only horizontals and verticals, but also of open spaces and enclosed volumes. The dramatic cantilevered roofs (which are not flat as suggested by our reproduction, but slightly sloping) define one space, while the floor of the terrace, or the balcony below, charts another. The interior spaces not only flow into the exterior, but into one another, for rooms, especially public rooms, generally do not have doors and four walls (fig. 26.40).

Wright always claimed that his extraordinary ability to envision complex space and design came from playing with the Froebel blocks that his mother bought for him at the 1876 World's Fair in Philadelphia. Developed by Friedrich Froebel as part of his campaign to institute kindergarten throughout Germany, the blocks were designed to serve as a child's first building blocks, and were part of a program that progressed to working with sticks and clay, folding paper, and weaving various materials. The Froebel "gifts," as each stage was called, not only taught Wright to think in terms of abstract form, but also organic growth. Froebel was influenced by crystallography and consequently emphasized pattern making, not construction, with the pattern spreading out uniformly from a center row (the child was required to use all of the blocks). When it was complete, the child was encouraged to attach symbolic content to the shapes, relating

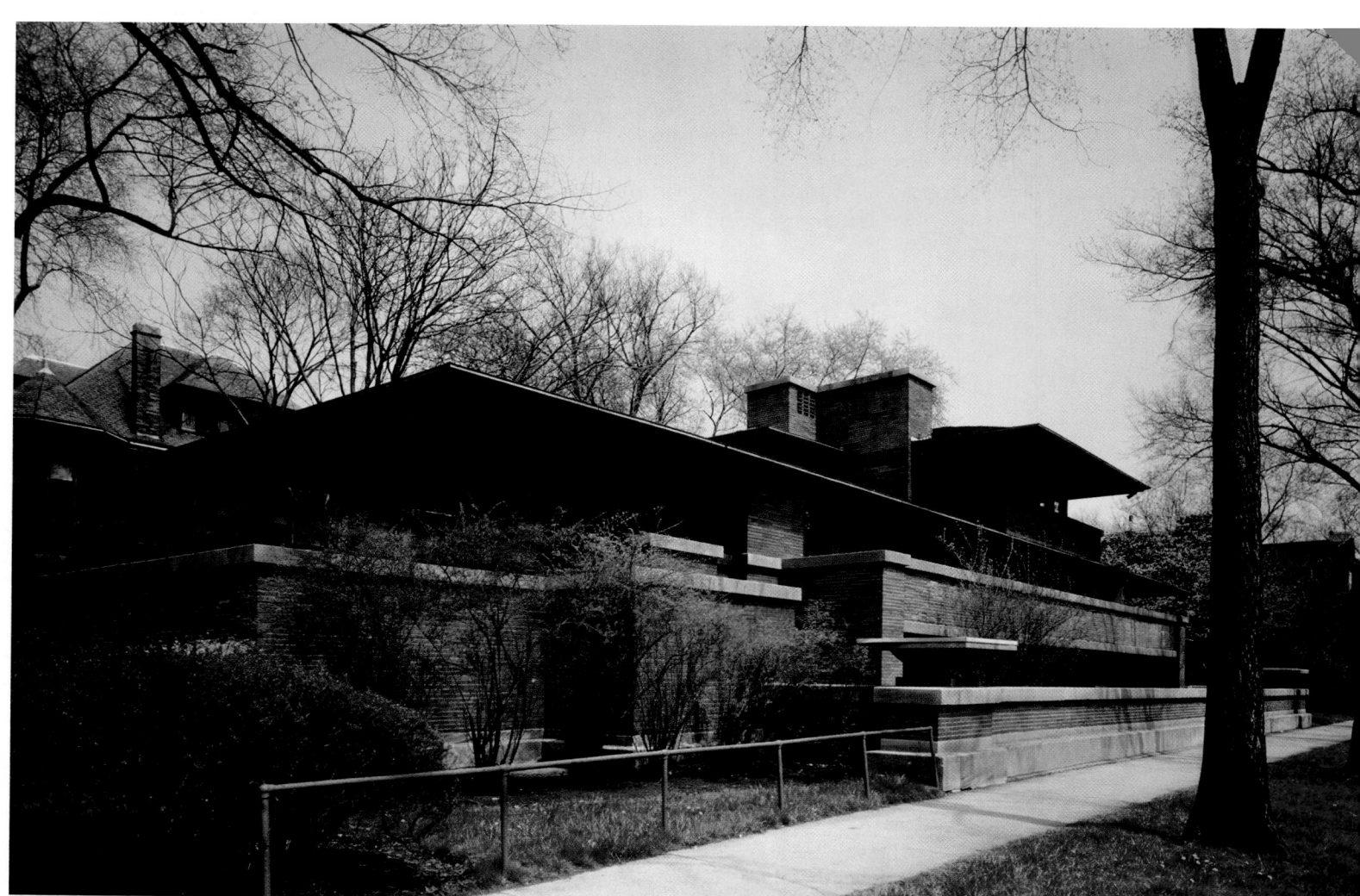

26.39 Frank Lloyd Wright. Robie House, Chicago. 1908–10.

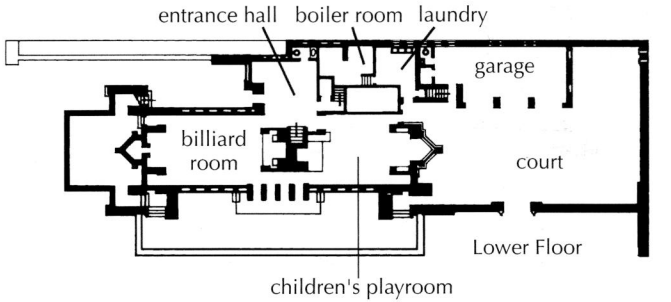

entrance hall   boiler room   laundry

garage

billiard room

court

Lower Floor

children's playroom

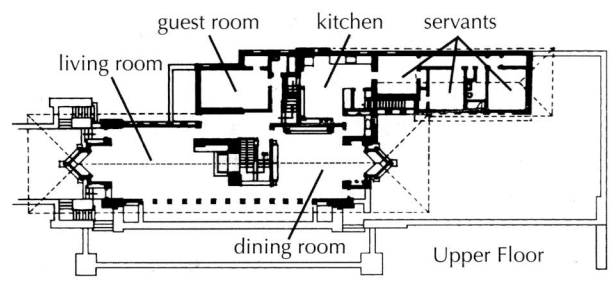

guest room   kitchen   servants

living room

dining room

Upper Floor

26.40   Plan of Robie House

the patterns to the living world of plants and the cosmos (suns and stars, for example). Equally important for Wright's development was a visit to the Japanese temple at the 1893 Chicago World's Fair. Here, he saw the dramatic projection of eaves, and severely geometrically shaped rooms that had sliding doors, which allowed one room to flow into another. Everything in a Japanese building was as tightly interlocked as in a Froebel project.

As abstract and geometric as the Robie House is, the home resonates with nature and the organic. Even in our reproduction, the house, made of a horizontal brick manufactured to Wright's specifications (the face is 1½ by 5 inches), appears perfectly integrated into the land, its lateral spread paralleling the surrounding plains. Wright thought of his architecture as organic, evolving much as a crystal develops or a tree grows. The Robie House, like many of his domestic designs, radiates from a large masonry fireplace, which Wright saw as a domestic altar to the "gods of shelter." The rest of the house develops organically from this fulcrum, with one room naturally flowing into another and into the

exterior, which in turn is integrated into the surrounding land. This sense of growth can readily be seen from the exterior, where the lateral spread of roofs, terraces, and balconies seems to be in constant movement. The picturesque variety of overhangs and recesses creates a play of light and shadow that we do not normally associate with architecture, but rather with nature.

Wright's interior design also embraces this organic note. Reproduced here is the living room from the Francis W. Little House (fig. 26.41), perhaps his finest extant early interior. Influenced by William Morris's Arts and Crafts Movement as well as the principles, if not the look, of Art Nouveau, Wright, when possible, designed every detail of his interiors, with everything hand-made and of the highest quality. Like his architecture, his furniture and designs are geometric, continuing the spatial interplay of his buildings. But the geometric designs that appear on the leaded stained-glass windows and ceiling grillwork are actually abstractions of plant and landscape motifs, and the palette of the room features somber, yet warm, earth colors. As much as

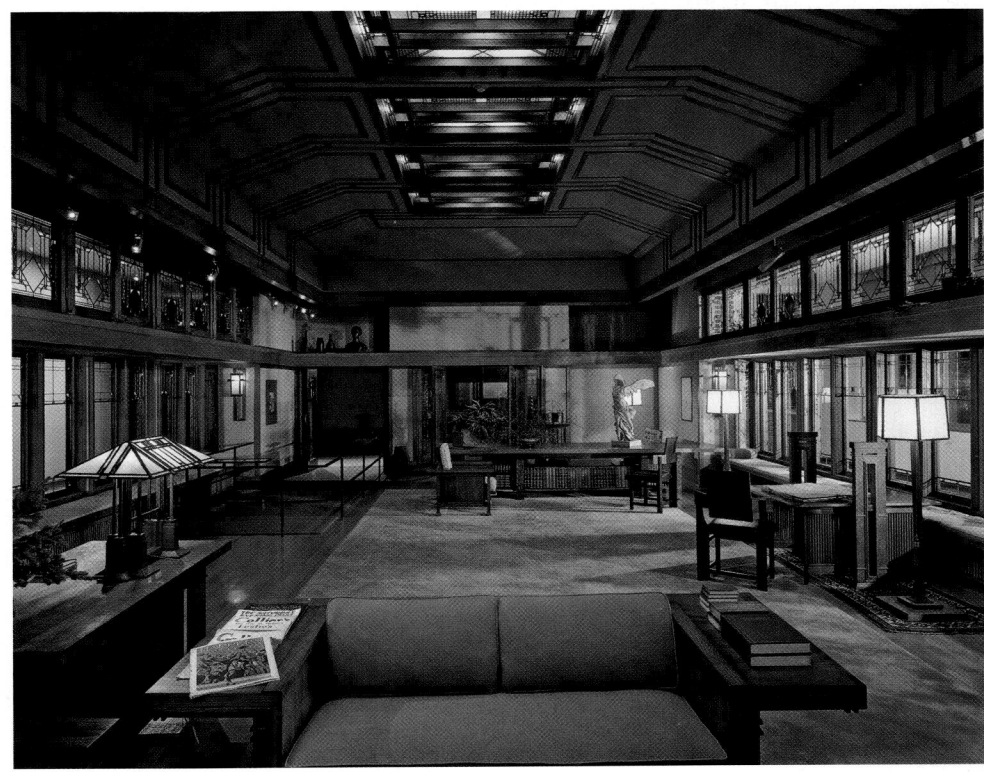

26.41   Frank Lloyd Wright. Living room of the Francis W. Little House, Wayzata, Minnesota, designed 1912–14, as installed at the Metropolitan Museum of Art, New York. Purchase Bequest of Emily Crane Chadbourne, 1972. 1972.60.1

we may want to see early Wright as an abstract, machine-age thinker conceptually playing with spaces and completely breaking with tradition, his theories and sensitivity are very much of the 1890s—he still has one foot planted in the Symbolist nineteenth century that advocated a retreat from modernity into the arms of nature and its rejuvenating spiritual forces.

PHOTOGRAPHY AND THE ADVENT OF FILM

The primary preoccupation of photographers at the end of the century was the ongoing debate about whether photography was art. Complicating the matter was the dramatic increase in nonart photography. The invention of the half-tone printing process was one reason for this upsurge, for it resulted in photographs being printed directly in newspapers, magazines, and books using either lithographic or relief printing. It also brought about the rise of the picture postcard, which during the height of its popularity in 1907–8 resulted in some 667 million postcards, most with pictures, being sent through the U.S. Mail. Another reason for the proliferation of photographs was the invention of dry plates, which replaced the awkward and impractical wet-plate process. Now, photographers could work faster and go anywhere. The process reduced exposure time to one-fiftieth of a second, and hand-held cameras with shutters were invented, making tripods unnecessary. Cameras could now record movement. And now cameras and prints were readily available at low cost to everybody. In 1888, the

Eastman Dry Plate Company of Rochester, New York, introduced the Kodak camera. It came loaded with a paper roll containing 100 frames, which, once exposed, were sent back to the company in the camera for developing and printing. The company's advertisement declared, "You press the button—We do the rest." Also appearing about this time was the single-lens reflex camera, which had a mirror that allowed the photographer to see the image in a viewer. Suddenly, everyone was taking pictures, and the word "snapshot" came into common parlance. Toward 1890, there were 161 photographic societies worldwide and 60 photographic journals. The medium became so popular that many newspapers carried an amateur photography column.

Pictorialist Photography and the Photo Secession

To counter the image of photography as a ubiquitous, mindless popular tool best suited for documenting the visual world, organizations sprang up dedicated to promoting the medium as high art. The first was the Wien Kamera Klub (Vienna Camera Club), founded in 1891, soon followed by the Linked Ring in London and the Photo-Club de Paris (1894). The Berlin, Munich, and Vienna Secessions, dedicated to breaking down any hierarchical ranking of the arts, showed art photography. In 1902, Alfred Stieglitz quit the conservative Camera Club of New York to form the Photo Secession, taking its name from the European secession groups. All of these photography organizations had international memberships, often with some of the same members, mounted

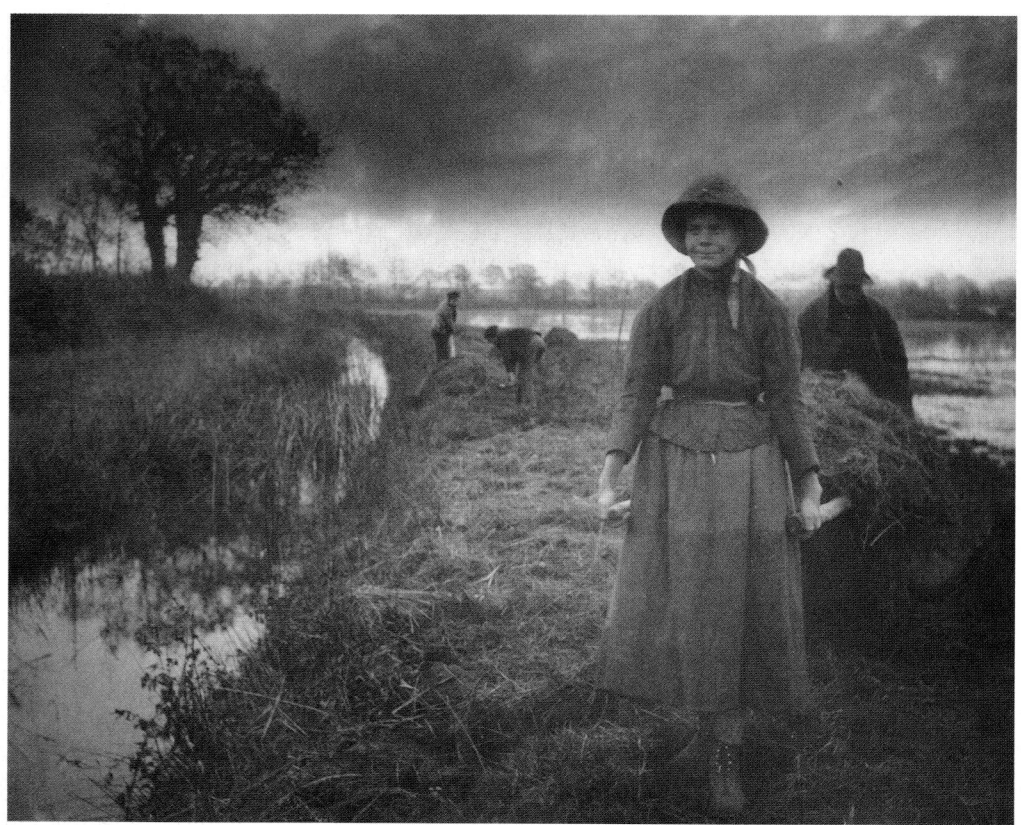

26.42 Peter Henry Emerson,
Poling the Marsh Hay. 1886.
Platinum print. Gernsheim Collection.
Harry Ransom Humanities Research
Center, University of Texas, Austin

exhibitions, and published magazines. And they all promoted a Pictorialist aesthetic, placing a premium on a painterly, artistic look, countering the sharp focus that characterized postcard, stereoscope, newspaper, and magazine images and the single fixed focus of the Kodak camera. Photographs by art photographers were taken out of focus, like those of Julia Margaret Cameron, whose work experienced a resurgence of interest. Pictorialist photographs were often highly textured, as a result of gum being brushed onto the printing paper before exposure or due to the use of a rough, pebbly paper.

PETER HENRY EMERSON The British photographer Peter Henry Emerson (1856–1936) became a role model for Pictorialist photography, although ironically his own aim was to combine art and science by applying a scientific approach to the creation of the image: His pictures were meant to look scientific, not artistic. Emerson was a medical doctor, who abandoned the profession for photography in 1885. He was influenced by the German scientist Hermann von Helmholtz's theory of vision, which maintains that the eye at any one time can only focus on one area, with everything else becoming hazy. Wanting to make a realistic photography based on scientific principle, Emerson set out to produce images that replicated Helmholtz's optical premise. In *Poling the Marsh Hay* (fig. **26.42**), the foreground woman is most in focus while the rest of the image is mildly blurred or indistinct. The picture appeared in Emerson's book *Life and Landscape on the Norfolk Broads* (1888), a folio of 40 mounted platinum prints, a photographic process that yielded an extraordinarily fine range of soft gray tones since the platinum lies directly on the surface of the paper, and is not embedded in albumen or a gelatin emulsion. Emerson was fascinated by the rural world of southeast England, where time seemed to stand still and hay was harvested by hand, not with the new steam-driven tractors. In this nostalgic image, we are presented with a Romantic view of an idyllic life of humans immersed in nature. Ironically, Emerson's scientific goal to realistically replicate the world as the eye sees it resulted in a poetic timeless vision, a soft-focused dreamworld of indistinct lush grays and of mysteriously floating darks and lights, such as a ghostly silhouetted tree and the light mystically shimmering on the canal and marshes.

GERTRUDE KÄSEBIER The international Pictorialists took their lead from Emerson and Cameron, among others, and similarly created painterly, dreamlike images. New Yorker Gertrude Käsebier (1852–1934) was one of the more prominent figures in the group, becoming a member of the Linked Ring in 1900, less than five years after taking up photography, and one of the founding members of Stieglitz's Photo Secession in 1902. Fleeing a wretched marriage, she enrolled in art classes at the Pratt Institute in 1889, and soon took up the camera with the intention of making art, although she supported herself through studio portraiture. In *Blessed Art Thou Among Women* (fig. **26.43**), an 1899 platinum print on Japanese tissue, a thin paper, we see Käsebier displaying the hallmarks of Pictorialism: a soft, grainy image,

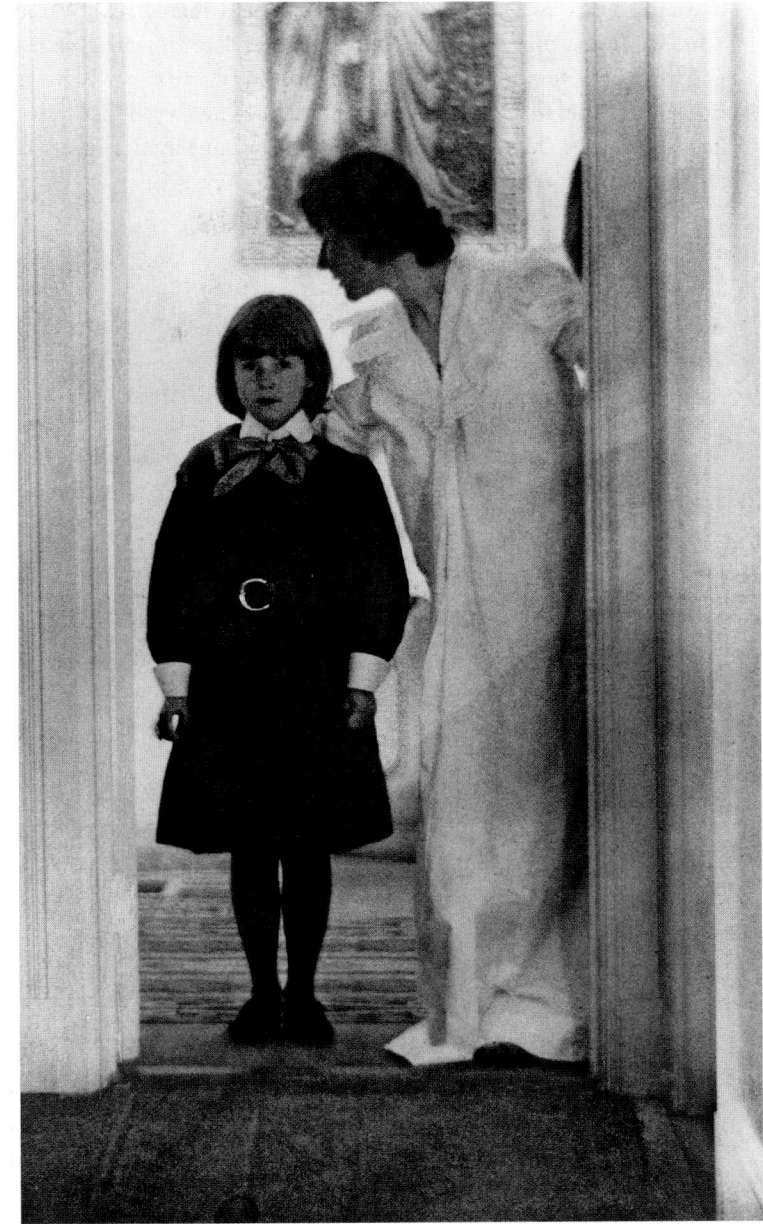

26.43 Gertrude Käsebier, *Blessed Art Thou Among Women*. 1899. Platinum print, 9¹⁄₁₆ × 5³⁄₁₆" (23 × 13.2 cm). Metropolitan Museum of Art, New York. Alfred Stieglitz Collection, 1933. (33.43.132)

slightly out of focus, and with a spectacular range of lush grays that only a platinum print can provide, made all the more delicate by being printed on a gossamerlike Japanese tissue. The mother wears a white Pre-Raphaelite-looking house robe and conspicuously stands before a religious image of the Annunciation on the back wall. The daughter, who is about to cross the threshold to go out into the world, is encased in a mandorlalike divine light created by the brilliant white that surrounds her, especially defined by the small gap between her and her mother. The scene has a spiritual quality, set within a sanctum dedicated to maternal protection and nurturing. In a modern urban society becoming increasingly fast, fragmented, and materialistic, Käsebier creates a tranquil domestic sanctuary based on, as the title suggests, the nurturing care of a mother. Käsebier's image shares with Mary Cassatt's *The Child's Bath* (see fig. 25.21) the same late nineteenth-century feminist belief in the important role that women play in the development of children, and with Cameron's *Sister Spirits* (see fig. 25.36) a female bonding or spiritual sisterhood designed to protect the rights and future of their gender.

EDWARD STEICHEN Along with Käsebier and Stieglitz, Edward Steichen (1879–1973) also helped to found the Photo Secession. Steichen's early contributions to this movement were painterly and moody, his landscapes having the same poetic and mystical quality found in the Tonalist painting that was inspired by Whistler's Aestheticism. His early style can be seen in his 1902 portrait *Rodin with His Sculptures "Victor Hugo" and "The Thinker"* (fig. **26.44**), a gum print. Using the painterly effect of the gum combined with the fuzziness of the focus, he created an image that looks more handcrafted than mechanically reproduced, demonstrating that the photographer made aesthetic decisions that profoundly affected the meaning of the image. Picturing together the brooding silhouettes of Rodin and *The Thinker*, Steichen uses them to frame a brightly lit, phantomlike *Victor Hugo*. Clearly, Steichen identifies Rodin with *The Thinker*. One of the readings of the famous sculpture is that it is meant to represent Rodin and the daunting creative process and mental struggle behind the development of a work of art. This interpretation certainly accounts for this image, as suggested by the light striking Rodin's "brain" and the emergence of Victor Hugo as an apparition, a figment of Rodin's imagination. While in some respects Rodin is portrayed here as a Romantic genius, we also sense a Symbolist psychology at work—ideas do not gush from

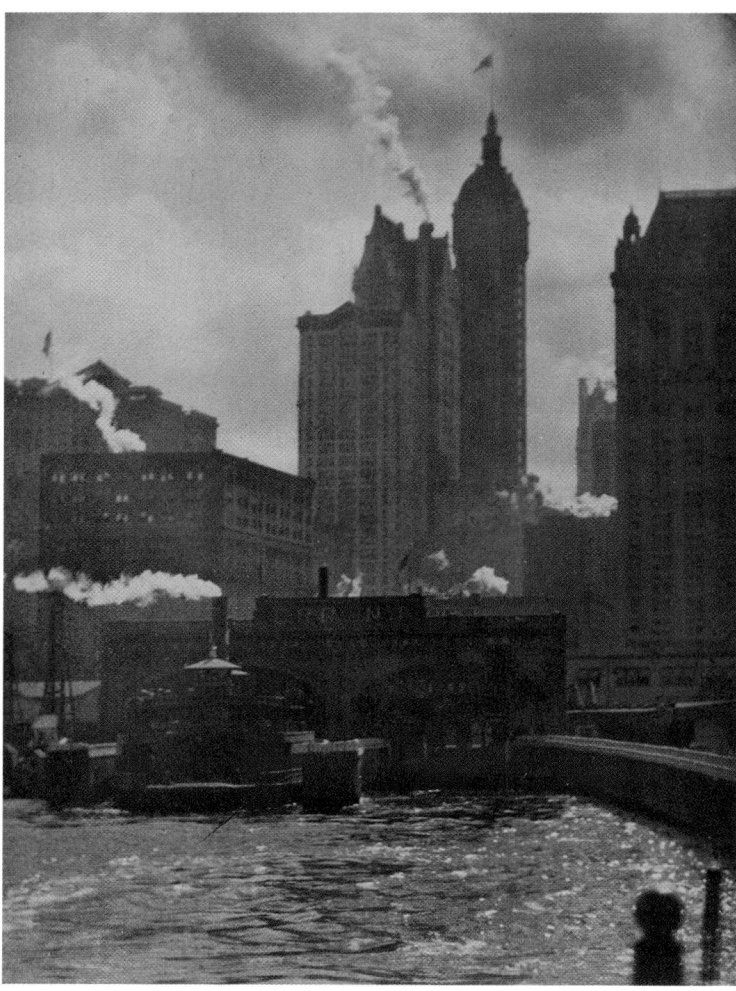

26.45   Alfred Stieglitz, *The City of Ambition*. 1910. Photogravure on Japanese tissue mounted on paperboard, 13⅜ × 10¼" (34 × 26 cm). Metropolitan Museum of Art, Alfred Stieglitz Collection. 1949. (49.55.15)

his imagination and emotions, but instead they are the result of a long creative struggle, a prolonged search into the dark recesses of the mind.

ALFRED STIEGLITZ Several of the Pictorialists in the Stieglitz circle photographed New York City, although paradoxically their images have a Romantic atmospheric quality more appropriate to landscape than the hard geometric look we associate with urban concrete and steel. By 1900, New York, not Chicago, was the city of skyscrapers, and as America attained global technological and financial superiority, New York and its "cathedrals of capitalism" became an emblem of this superiority. Even though Stieglitz (1864–1946) abhorred modernity and lamented the city's "mad, useless Materiality," he repeatedly photographed Gotham from the early 1890s up to 1910, as seen in *The City of Ambition* (fig. **26.45**) of 1910. Typical of Pictorialist images of New York, his pictures allow meteorological effects, such as snow, mist, steam, and fog, to upstage the buildings. In *The City of Ambition*, Stieglitz uses the Pictorialists' characteristic soft focus. The metropolis looms large, but buildings are indistinct and in

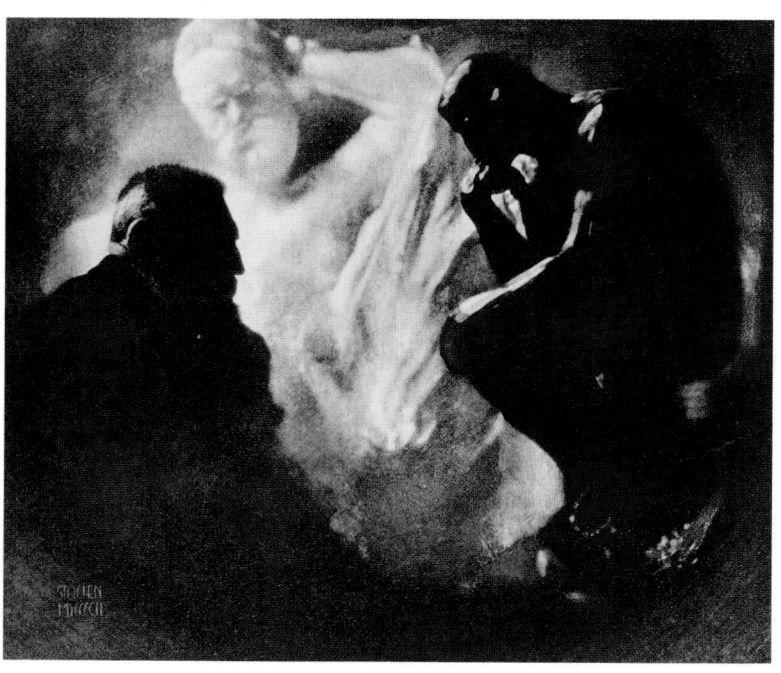

26.44   Edward Steichen, *Rodin with His Sculptures "Victor Hugo" and "The Thinker."* 1902. Gum print, 14¼ × 12¾" (36.3 × 32.4 cm). Courtesy George Eastman House

shadow, softened by puffs of smoke and the clouds behind. Light shimmering on the water gets as much attention as the skyline, and we are very much aware of the glow of the sun setting behind the buildings. Stieglitz capitalizes on this light to orchestrate a beautiful symphony of gray rectangular forms harmonizing with rich darks and bright whites. He captures the awesome scale of the city, this "monster" as he described it, and he suggests, by immersing it in an atmospheric veil, that it seems to comfortably coexist with the awesome forces of nature.

Documentary Photography

Among the most powerful documentary photographs made in the closing decades of the nineteenth century were those chronicling the horrific working and living conditions of the modern city. Some of the best-known work was made in New York, a crowded, fast-growing metropolis teeming with indigent immigrants and migrants readily victimized by unscrupulous landlords and employers. These masses were unsupported by social services and unprotected by the government. Conditions were especially appalling in the immigrant slums on the Lower East Side and the violent, lawless bars and brothels of Five Points, a district largely centering on the Bowery. Unlike the Pictorialists, whose techniques and subjects often softened the realism of their images, documentary photographers embraced the medium's capacity to produce direct, seemingly truthful records. Some documentary photographers felt that their work attained the status of art due to its apparent ability to convey "truth." Others pursued documentary photography for commercial or even political ends. Jacob Riis numbered among the latter.

JACOB RIIS Emigrating from Denmark in 1870, Jacob Riis (1849–1914) became a police reporter in the roughest neighborhoods of New York City, and was so appalled by the degradation and squalor he found there that he began photographing it in order to generate support for social reform. He made lantern slides of his images to illustrate his lectures, and published others in newspapers and magazines. Although Riis did not consider himself an artist, his works are undeniably striking. In order to create authentic, unposed, spontaneous images, he used a "flash," a magnesium flash powder (the predecessor of the flashbulb), which allowed him to enter tenements, flop houses, and bars at night and instantaneously take a picture, temporarily blinding his shocked subjects but capturing a candid image, as seen in *Five Cents a Spot* (fig. **26.46**). Here, he has burst into an overcrowded sleeping den on Bayard Street, creating an image that documents the greedy abuse of the homeless and leaves no doubt as to the unsanitary conditions that made such squalid, illegal quarters a breeding ground for disease. Riis published his photographs in a groundbreaking book, *How the Other Half Lives* (1890), which in part resulted in the bulldozing of the shanties in the Bayard Street neighborhood and the transformation of the site into a park. An army of social photographers emerged around and after the turn of the century, among the best known Lewis Hine and Jessie Tarbox Beals.

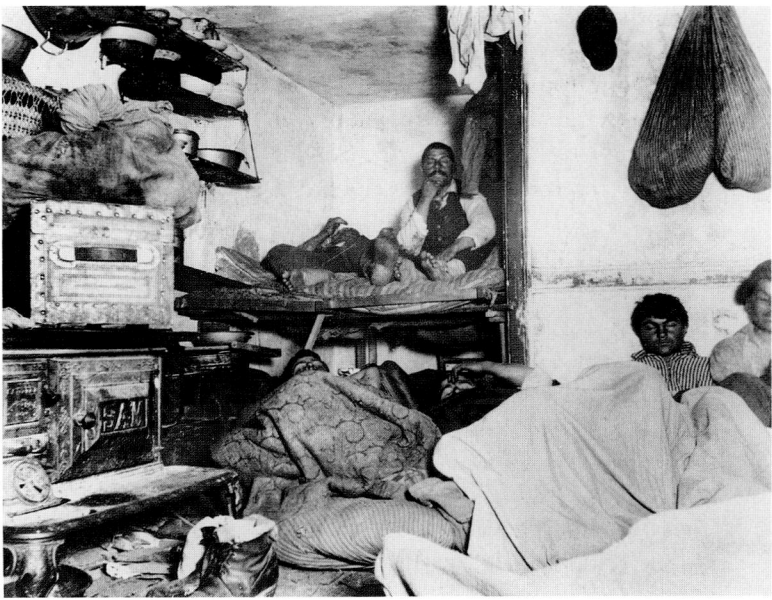

26.46 Jacob Riis, *Five Cents a Spot, Unauthorized Lodgings in a Bayard Street Tenement.* ca. 1889. Gelatin silver print, 8 × 10" (20.3 × 25.4 cm). Museum of the City of New York, Jacobs Riis Collection #155

Riis's work has something of the look of a snapshot, an uncomposed, quickly taken photograph, and with the advent of small hand-held cameras, this look was common to amateur photography. The snapshot, like the documentary photograph, returns us to the issue of photography as art. Since 1890, virtually everyone in developed countries has accumulated albums, drawers, and boxes filled with snapshots, visual memories of the past. Are they art? In a sense, they are all art, as will be discussed in the next chapter when we study Marcel Duchamp. What is really at issue is whether it is good art, and the answer here is obvious. The vast majority of the billions of images are generic, banal, and predictable, and their value is largely personal, which is no small matter. And yet, there is that rare person with an extraordinary aesthetic sensitivity who, with little technical instruction, produces remarkable images.

HENRI LARTIGUE Such a person was Henri Lartigue (1894–1986), born into a wealthy French family who gave him his first camera when he was six years old. With this expensive toy, Lartigue proceeded to document his privileged family, filling some 120 albums with images that also captured the advent of modernity—automobiles and airplanes, for example. His images, such as *My Hydroglider with Propeller*, are often humorous, if not outright uproarious. Made in 1904 at the age of ten, the picture shows Lartigue in his bathtub, his head surrealistically cut off at the neck by the water line and "floating" alongside his toy hydroplane, a toy based on a modern invention. Reproduced here is a later work, *Avenue du Bois du Bologne* (fig. **26.47**), made at the age of 17 and part of a series of photographs the teenage artist made in one day of fashionably dressed women parading their wealth on the main thoroughfare in the famous Paris park

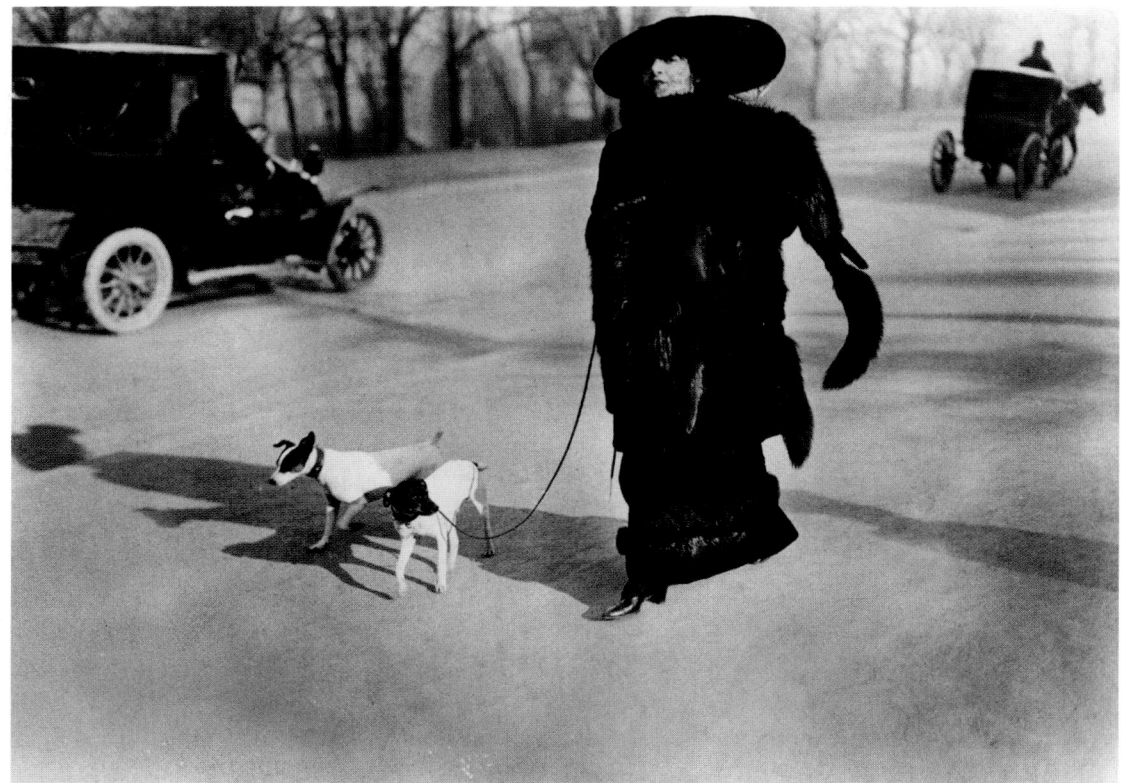

26.47 Henri Lartigue, *Avenue du Bois du Bologne* (*Woman with Furs*, or *Arlette Prevost, called "Anna la Pradvina," with her dogs "Chichi" et "Gogo"*) *15 Janvier 1911, Avenue du Bois de Boulogne, Paris*. 1911. Gelatin silver print, 2⅔ × 4⅓" (6.6 × 11.1 cm). Donation Jacques Henri Lartigue, Paris

of the same name. Here, Lartigue has captured an amply fur-draped "animal lover" walking her dogs, their scrawny build humorously contrasted with her materialistic bulk, and their nervousness with the inanimate drooping skins of her hand-warmer. This wonderful composition, which has the voyeuristic quality of a Degas painting, also includes an automobile and a horse-drawn carriage—the new and the old. Its representation of affluence and the inclusion of a car have made it one of the icons of the *Belle Époque*.

Lartigue eventually attended art school and became known as a painter as well as a professional photographer, producing numerous portraits and society photographs. However, his boy-hood photographs went unknown until he was 69, and when discovered they were shown at the Museum of Modern Art in New York and in a large spread in *Life* magazine, touted not only for their quality but also because they captured the essence of the time. Their legacy also includes the introduction of humor into the medium, which would become a regular feature of twentieth-century fine-art photography. Meanwhile, it was not until the 1990s that the aesthetic value of the anonymous snapshot was appreciated, driving collectors and curators to scour flea markets and estate sales for that rare remarkable work, that one-in-a-million shot with riveting subject matter or compelling aesthetic qualities. Called folk, vernacular, and sometimes "found" photography, it is today collected and exhibited by several of the world's best-known museums.

Motion Photography and Moving Pictures

In 1878, Eadweard Muybridge (1830–1904), who had made some of the most remarkable photographs of Yosemite the decade before, was hired by Leland Stanford, a business tycoon, politician, and founder of Stanford University, to use photography to resolve one of the great questions plaguing horse trainers and artists for centuries: Do all four legs of a horse leave the ground when it is running? Setting up 12 cameras on a raceway and creating a calibrated backdrop, he made a series of sequential photographs (fig. **26.48**) that once and for all answered the question: Yes. Artists ever since have used these images to draw a horse in motion, including Degas in 1879. Muybridge became a celebrity, and was invited to the University of Pennsylvania in Philadelphia to make studies in locomotion, producing in the 1880s some 100,000 images of nudes and animals. He published 781 plates in *Animal Locomotion* (1887). These motion studies convey a peculiarly modern sense of dynamics, reflecting, especially in their regularly repeated serial imagery, the new tempo of life in the machine age.

The French physiologist Étienne-Jules Marey (1830–1904) saw Muybridge's horse-in-motion photographs reproduced in the magazine *La Nature*, and became obsessed with studying motion as well. He used a single camera, the lens open, placed behind a rotating disk with regularly placed slots. When a slot appeared, an image was recorded, so that a moving object would appear in a different position each time. Since he was interested in the

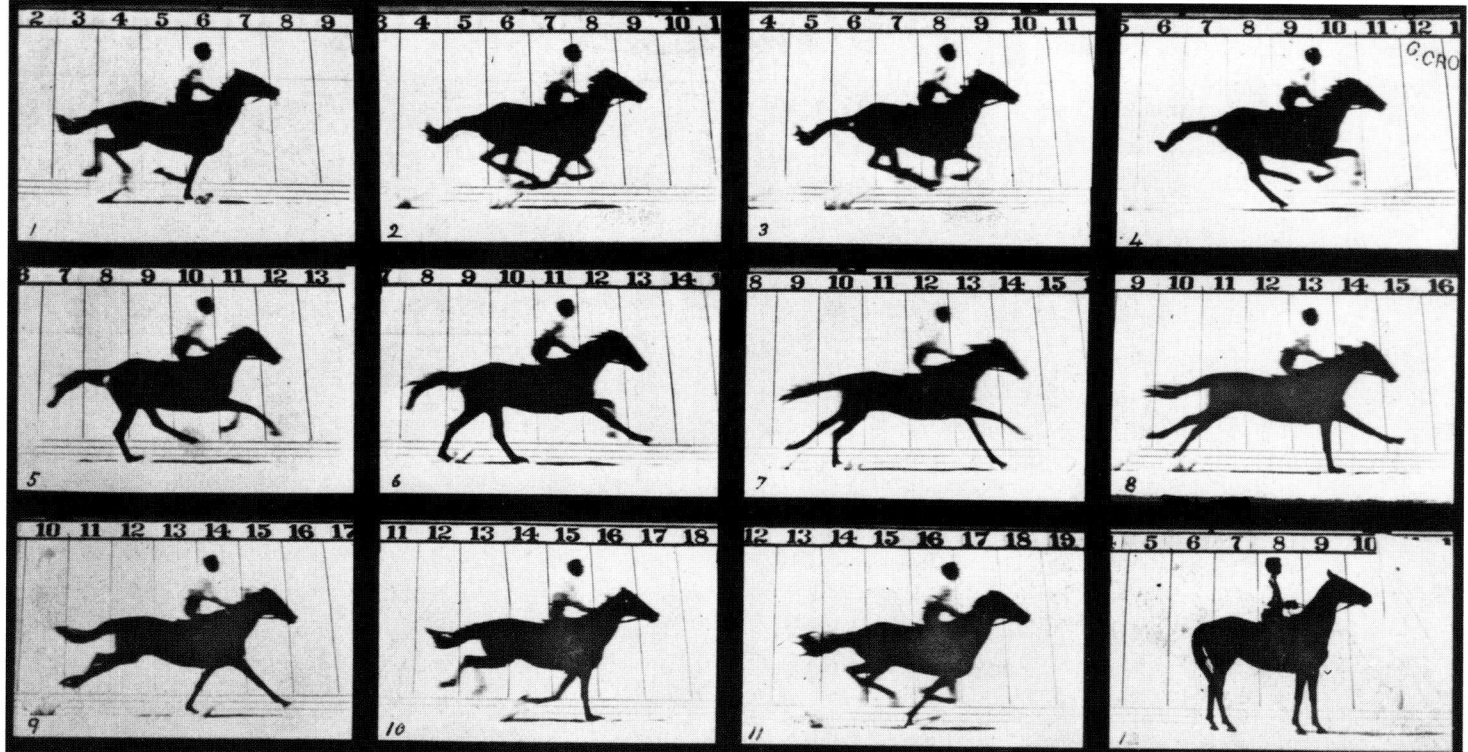

26.48 Eadweard Muybridge, *Untitled* (sequence photographs of the trot and gallop), from *La Nature*, December 1878. Gravures. George Eastman House, Rochester, New York

mechanics of locomotion and not the figure itself, he clothed his models in black body suits with a white stripe running along the length of the side. The models were then photographed in action against a black wall. Thus, only the white line of movement is visible in his photographs (fig. **26.49**). Though Marey saw no artistic merit in these studies, the results offer fascinating abstractions. And, as we shall see, they would influence artists who were interested in rendering the movement of an object through space.

As important, Marey's and Muybridge's studies reflected a rapidly increasing interest in creating moving pictures. They were building on the popular parlor-game amusements that created images in motion. One device, called a zoetrope, consisted of slotted cylinders with a sequence of images of, for example, a moving horse on the inside. When spun and viewed through the rapidly moving slots, the horse would appear to be trotting. Muybridge invented an apparatus he called the zoöpraxiscope,

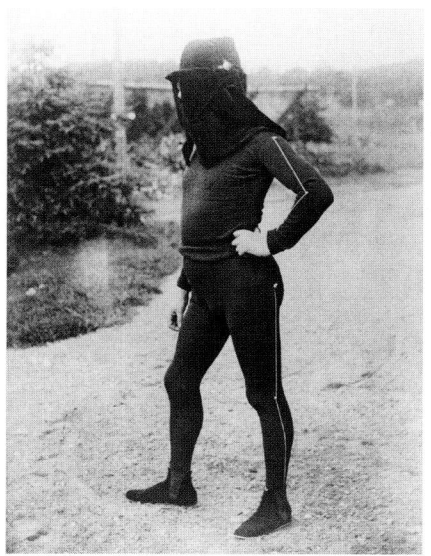
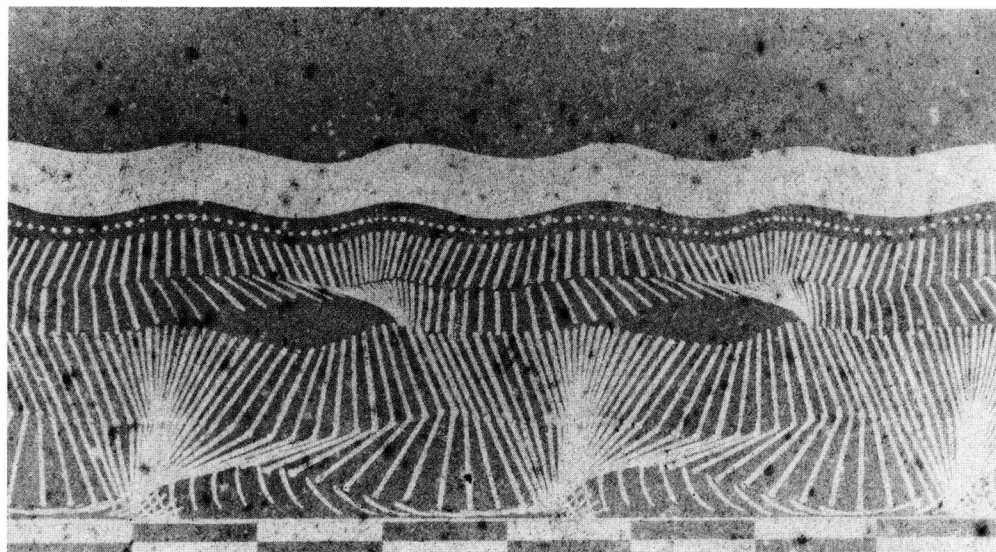

26.49 (a and b) Étienne-Jules Marey, *Man in Black Suit with White Stripes Down Arms* and *Legs, Walking in Front of a Black Wall*. ca. 1884. Chronophotograph. Institut Marey, Beaune, France

which similarly used a cylinder, but the image was projected, like a magic lantern slide, onto a wall. Enticed by the implications of Muybridge's zoöraxiscope, Thomas Edison in 1894 patented the kinetoscope, which consisted of moving images recorded on a 50-foot roll of flexible film that were viewed in a peepshowlike box. The show lasted 13 seconds. The following year, the French Lumière brothers, Louis and Auguste, introduced the hand-cranked camera and electric film projector and produced the first moving picture, which lasted 25 seconds. It showed workers leaving their father's factory at the end of the day.

In America, movie production was dominated by two companies, Thomas Edison and American Mutascope, which sent crews around the world to record various monuments, sites, and events. The pictures lasted only a few minutes at best and were presented in vaudeville houses in between acts. Filmmakers were now confronted by the same crisis that photographers had faced in 1839: What to film and how to film it. Generally, they focused on movement and action, as can be seen in Edison's 1899 moving picture of a train crossing the Brooklyn Bridge (fig. **26.50**; to view the film *New Brooklyn to New York via Brooklyn Bridge, No. 2*, see hdl.loc.gov/loc.mbrsmi/edmp.1734), filmed by a fixed camera positioned at the front of the first car. The Brooklyn Bridge film is revealing on many levels. First, it is a reminder that the early films, like those of today, had to appeal to a mass audience and present subjects of popular interest. Technological inventions and moving images of modernity, such as subways, skyscraper construction, the one million electric lights at the new Coney Island Amusement Park, and sleek ocean-liners and battleships coming into New York harbor, seem to make up a large portion of the existing Edison inventory from the late 1890s. Second, the film is remarkable for its modern attitude toward speed and space. As the train travels through the trussed structure, we become mesmerized by the rhythm of the wooden supports passing by and feel the speed of the electrified cars. Soon, the square structure becomes just an abstraction of squares within squares (fig. 26.50). As we shall see in the next chapter, objects, space, and time were understood much differently in a modern mechanized era dominated by electricity, vertiginous 55-story office towers, high-speed trains, cars, and, soon, airplanes and moving pictures.

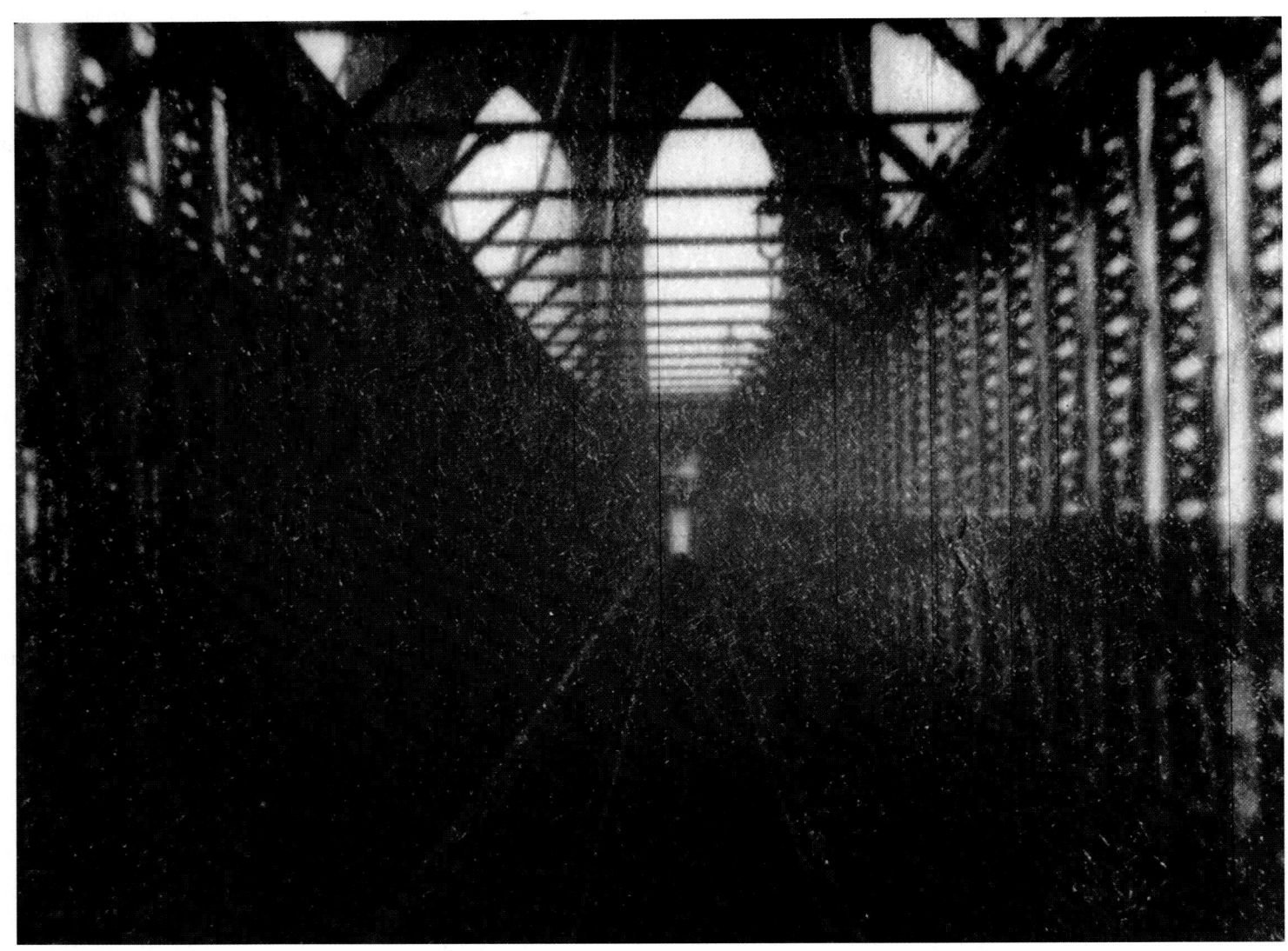

26.50   Thomas Edison. Still from the film *New Brooklyn to New York via Brooklyn Bridge, No. 2*. September 22, 1899. Black-and-white film, 2'13"

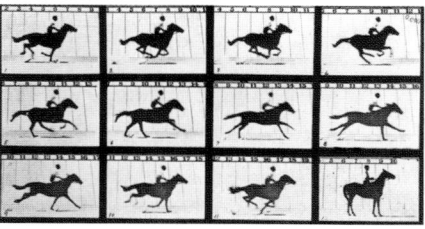

1878 Eadweard Muybridge makes sequence photographs of a horse galloping

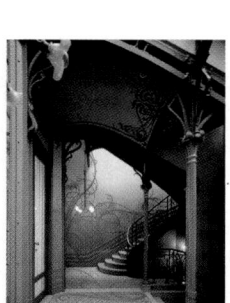

880 Rodin begins
ʾhe Gates of Hell

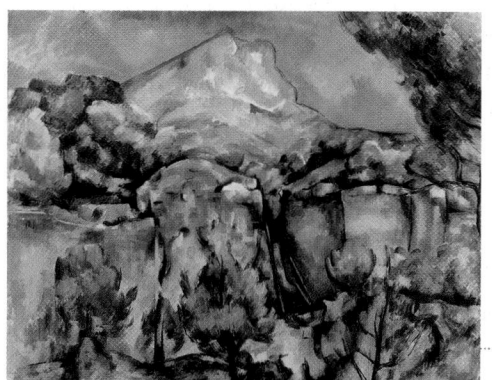

1885-87 Cézanne's *Mont Sainte-Victoire*

1886 Seurat shows *La Grande Jatte* at the last Impressionist exhibition, marking the end of Impressionism and the beginning of Postimpressionism

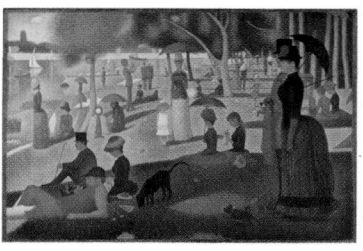

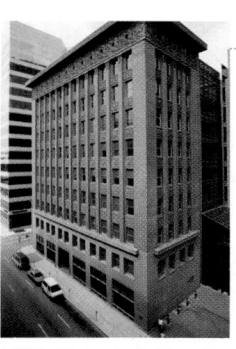

889 Van Gogh's *Starry Night*

1890-91 Louis Sullivan's Wainwright Building is erected, St. Louis, Missouri

1892 Victor Horta designs Tassel House, Brussels

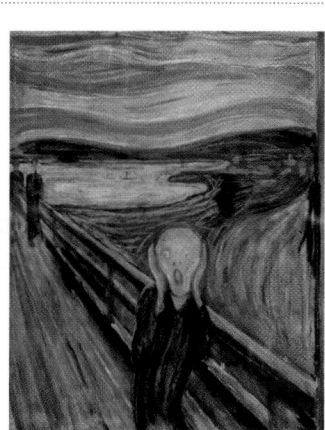

1893 Edvard Munch's
The Scream

Progress and its Discontents: Post-Impressionism, Symbolism, and Art Nouveau, 1880–1905

1870

1880

1890

1900

1910

◀ 1878 First International Congress of Women's Rights, Paris

◀ 1880s European nations colonize Africa

◀ 1882 The Edison Illuminating Electric Company provides electricity to lower Manhattan

◀ 1884 Seurat shows *A Bathing Place* at first exhibition of Independent Artists, Paris

◀ 1886 Jean Moréas publishes a Symbolist manifesto in *Figaro Littéraire*

◀ 1888 Van Gogh and Gauguin go to Arles
1888 The Nabis are founded in France
1888 Karl Benz begins manufacturing a combustion-engine automobile in Germany

◀ 1890 The National American Woman Suffrage Association formed
1891 Gauguin goes to Tahiti
1891 Claude Monet's *Wheatstack, Sun in the Mist*

◀ 1895 Siegfried Bing opens La Maison de l'Art Nouveau in Paris

◀ 1897 Vienna Secession founded, with Gustav Klimt as its first president

◀ 1900 The Paris Métro opens
1900 Sigmund Freud publishes *The Interpretation of Dreams*
1901 First transatlantic radio signal

◀ 1903 Wright brothers' first flight

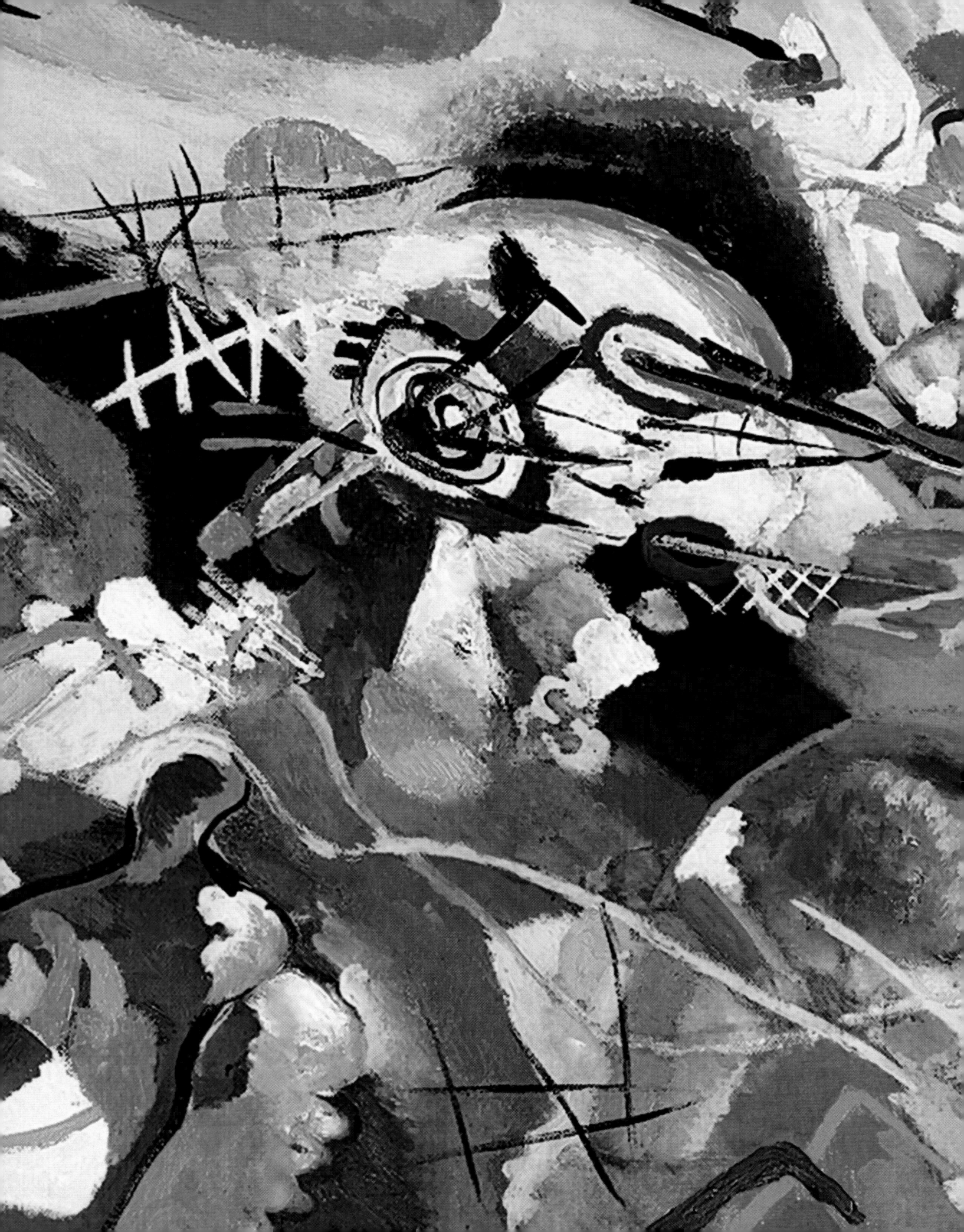

CHAPTER 27

Toward Abstraction: The Modernist Revolution, 1904–1914

THE OPENING DECADES OF THE TWENTIETH CENTURY SAW THE continued upward march of modernity. But, as in the preceding decades, artists both embraced and fled from progress. In some instances, they even clung to tradition while they purveyed the new, which we shall see, for example, in the work of Pablo Picasso and Henri Matisse, two artists who

successfully knitted together the new and revolutionary in style with the familiar and enduring in subject matter. The period is marked by landmark scientific developments that artists, like the public at large, could not ignore. In 1890, the German physicist Max Planck (1858–1947) proved that energy was not distinguishable from matter, in effect beginning a line of thought that led to quantum physics. He showed that energy was emitted and absorbed in bundles called quanta, disproving the idea that energy existed in a stable, uniform state. Energy and, therefore, matter were in constant flux. This concept was especially pertinent to the discovery of radioactivity in 1902 by British physicist Ernest Rutherford (1871–1937). In 1913, the atom itself was further redefined when the Dane Niels Bohr (1885–1962) declared that it consisted of electrons traveling in specific orbits around an atom's nucleus, and that matter was not solid but instead in constant movement. But the greatest amendment to classical physics was proposed by Albert Einstein (1879–1955). Einstein's revolutionary concepts appeared in a series of papers published in 1905 and 1916, and they included his theory of relativity, which claimed that time, space, and motion were not fixed but all relative, especially in relation to the observer's own position. The Newtonian world order, based on notions of energy and matter that remained stable, was now supplanted by a more complex and contingent notion of the universe.

Similar ideas emerged in accounts of human behavior by philosophers and psychologists. Henri Bergson (1859–1941), a French philosopher, was so influential in the first years of the twentieth century that he was well known even to the general public. Bergson postulated that we experience life not as a series of continuous rational moments, but as intuited random memories and perceptions that we then piece together to form ideas. The world, therefore, is complex and fractured, or as expressed by the Harvard philosopher and psychologist William James (1842–1910), whose theories independently paralleled Bergson's, a "booming buzzing confusion." Only intuition transcended this chaos. The mind, according to Bergson, was pure energy, an *élan vital* ("vital force") that penetrated the essence of all things. While Bergson was philosophically redefining consciousness, the Viennese neurologist and founder of psychoanalysis Sigmund Freud (1856–1939) continued to refine his ideas of the unconscious through observations made during clinical practice, an approach that he felt gave his conclusions a scientific basis. Despite taking a different approach from Bergson, Freud likewise developed a model of human consciousness as fragmented and conflicted.

Artists now pictured this new, constantly shifting, even fractured world discovered by scientists, philosophers, and psychologists. Some artists, such as Picasso and Georges Braque, in a sense emulated scientists, treating their studios like laboratories

Detail of figure 27.14, Vasily Kandinsky, *Sketch I for "Composition VII."*

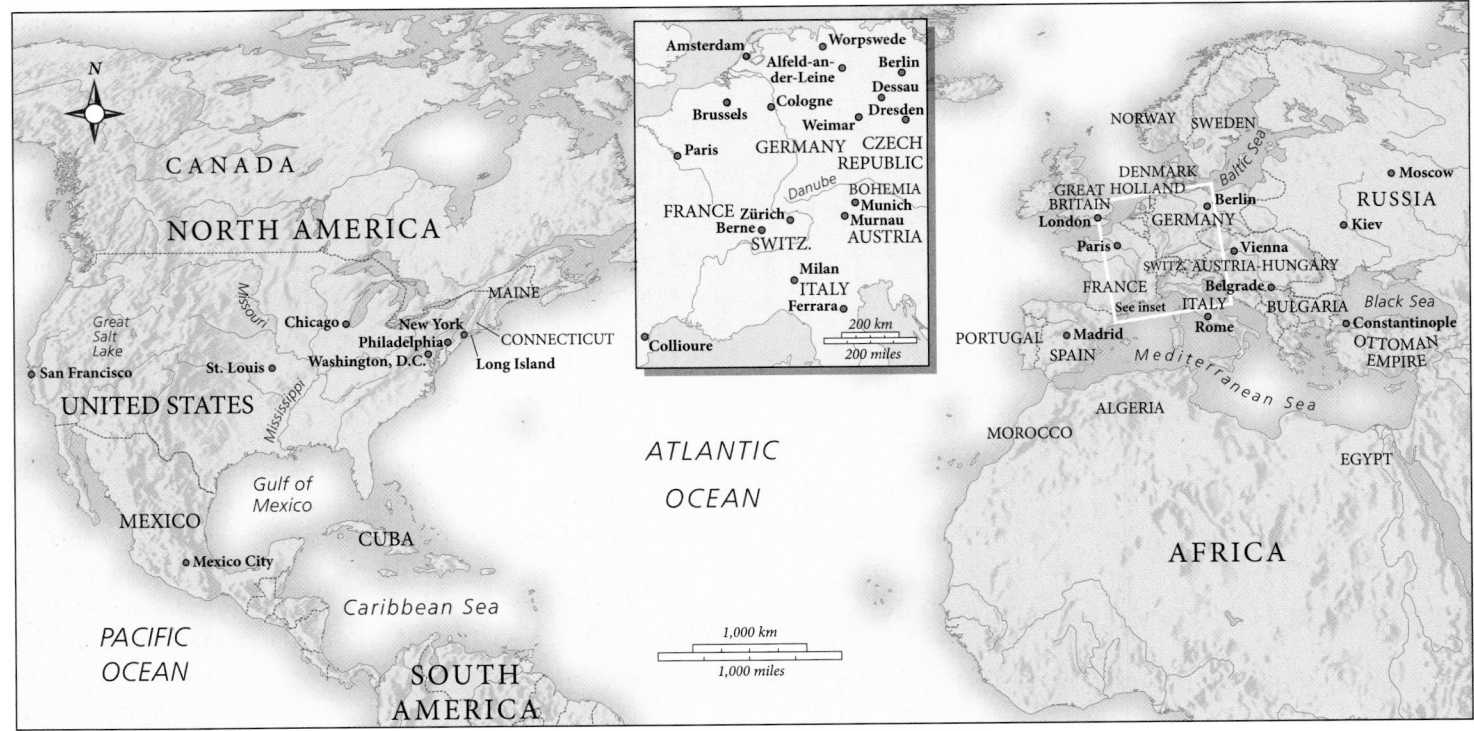

Map 27.1   Europe and North America in August 1914

FAUVISM

in which to analyze the very language of painting and where each creative breakthrough served as a steppingstone to the next as they sought to develop a new model of visual perception. Others, such as the Italian Futurists, embraced modernity and used new scientific discoveries, along with the radical stylistic developments of Picasso and Braque, to express the psychology of modern life and the impact of the technological wonders transforming the world.

Other artists, however, especially many of the German Expressionists, sought an antidote to the cold, impersonal tenor and crass materialism of modernity and tried to invest contemporary life with spirituality. Continuing Gauguin's quest to find a spiritual peace in a so-called primitive world that was in tune with nature, many artists turned to the direct, more abstract vocabulary of tribal art as well as to children's, folk, and medieval art. Many of these artists were heavily influenced by Theosophy, a brand of mysticism that dates back to Plato, but that in the nineteenth century took new form in the Theosophical Society, founded in New York in 1875 by the Russian émigrée, occultist, medium, and mystic Madame Helena Blavatsky. Basically, Theosophists claimed all religions are the same, with each containing an essential component of one larger grand religion. Therefore, all had to be studied. More important, Theosophists claimed that all creation is part of one eternal life, a "Radical Unity," and that everything is therefore mystically interconnected. For artists attempting to visualize the spiritual, the essence of which cannot be seen and is therefore abstract, the new stripped-down vocabulary of art was the perfect vehicle.

The rise of Fauvism, the first major style to emerge in the twentieth century, is part of a colorist tradition that can be traced back through Van Gogh, Gauguin, Monet, and Delacroix to Titian and the Venetians. The Fauves, however, took the free, expressive use of color to new heights. Van Gogh and Gauguin had the greatest impact on the group, as is readily apparent in the work of Henri Matisse (1869–1954) and André Derain (1880–1954). Matisse was well aware of the aesthetic traditions with which he was wrestling. Trained in the studio of Gustave Moreau (see page 918), Matisse had received an exacting academic education at the École des Beaux-Arts. He therefore understood the extent to which he was both continuing and breaking tradition when, in 1905, he presented his latest pictures at the *Salon d'Automne*, or Autumn Salon, an important annual venue for vanguard artists established in 1903 by Matisse and Derain, among other artists. As exhibitions of avant-garde art proliferated in Paris at the turn of the century, the *Salon d'Automne* enjoyed a special status as a juried show where critics anticipated seeing the best of the new work. Few critics or other viewers for that matter were prepared for what they saw there in 1905.

By that year, Matisse had not only moved beyond his academic training with Moreau, but had passed through an Impressionist phase in the 1890s, then a Cézannesque period, and finally a Neo-Impressionist stage. Strongly influenced by the Post-Impressionists' use of color for formal and expressive ends, Matisse pushed the independence of color even further. His experiments proved

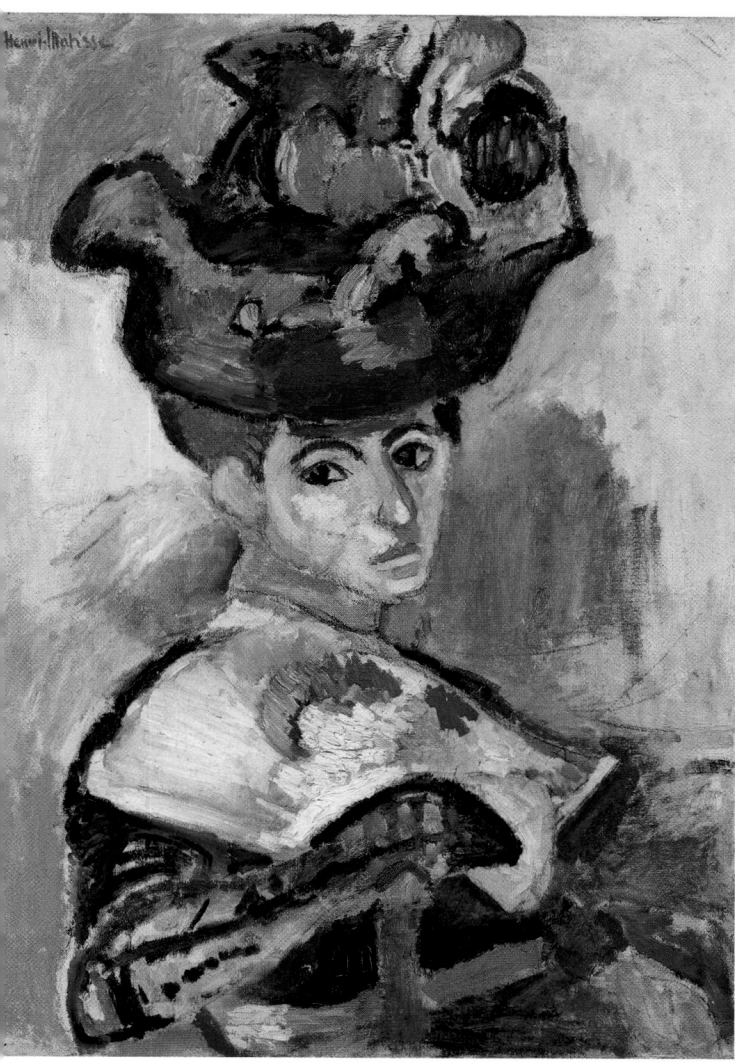

27.1 Henri Matisse, *Femme au chapeau* (*Woman with a Hat*). 1905. Oil on canvas, 31¾ × 23½" (80.6 × 59.7 cm). San Francisco Museum of Modern Art. Bequest of Elise S. Haas. 91.161.

too radical for some. Art critic Louis Vauxcelles was so shocked by the "orgy of pure colors" that he encountered in the work of Matisse, Derain, and their colleagues at the *Salon d'Automne*, that he declared the pictures *fauves*, or "wild beasts."

A classic example of the Fauve work exhibited in 1905 is *Femme au chapeau* (fig. 27.1). While the subject evokes a tradition of coloristic, virtuoso portraiture that stretches back to Vigée-Lebrun, Rubens, and Titian (see figs. 23.29, 20.3, and 16.33, respectively), Matisse's use of color is totally new. As with Impressionism, the color is intense, the image constructed of primary and secondary colors that look as if they have been squeezed directly from the tube. But now color does not have a representational function, adhering to a specific object. Instead it seems to have a life all its own, with patches of color sitting next to one another in what seems like random fashion. Along with the brushwork, color seems to reside uniformly on the surface of the image, reflecting Matisse's careful study of Cézanne's paintings. On the one hand, the background splashes of greens, yellows,

reds, and blues appear to exist on the same plane as the head and body in the foreground, locking all together as in one continuous flat mosaic. On the other, there is just enough overlapping of representational objects, such as arm and torso, to create space, and of course there is the abstract pictorial space suggested by contiguous planes of color and brushstroke, as we saw in Cézanne. Matisse, however, has dispensed with Cézanne's structure and monumentality, and instead achieves compositional coherence by balancing intense, complementary hues applied with brash, seemingly spontaneous brushwork.

Traditionally, art historians have placed the work of the Fauves in the category of Expressionism, but this is problematic, since the term generally applies to work displaying an outpouring of emotion—a tortured, anguished, or a pained state of mind. Despite the riot of color and chaos of brushstrokes, *The Woman with the Hat* is not about the sitter's or the artist's psychology. The figure is nothing more than an armature for an exercise in design and the release of color from a naturalistic or documentary function. The same is true of Matisse's landscapes and still lifes from this period as well.

André Derain, likewise, understood painting as an intellectual rather than an emotional medium. His *Mountains at Collioure* (fig. 27.2), a subject located in the south of France, where he was painting with Matisse in 1905, may seethe with Van Gogh's energetic brushwork and Gauguin's arabesques, but Derain did not intend it to embody those artists' spirituality or primitivism. Like the figure for Matisse, the landscape is just a vehicle for Derain's complex play of joyous color and surface design. Derain's overriding interest is in the *formal*—meaning abstract—qualities of image making, with special emphasis on bright color functioning in a nonrepresentational role.

The Fauves were never an organized group. The term was applied by critics to artists, many of whom had been friends since 1900, who used bright color and happened to show together at the *Salon d'Automne* of 1905, where the similarity of their work was recognized. By 1908, Fauvism had disintegrated. For Matisse, it was just one more stage toward making art that was, as he put it, "something like a good armchair in which to rest from physical fatigue." In other words, Matisse sought to use color in an abstract way that was beautiful, peaceful, serene, and sensuous.

We can see Matisse beginning to move out of Fauvism in his 1905–06 painting *Le Bonheur de Vivre* (*The Joy of Life*) (fig. 27.3). This work shows the influence not only of Derain's curvilinear patterning but also of first-hand experience with Gauguin's paintings; Gauguin's estate was being stored in Collioure, and Matisse visited the collection twice. The color in *Le Bonheur* remains intense and nonrealistic, but now it is contained in graceful arabesques. Matisse's most innovative move here is to dispense with logical space and scale while increasing the abstraction. No matter how abstract and flat Derain's and Matisse's Fauvist pictures of just a year earlier are, they still project a rational progression of space. Now, in Matisse's work, that space is gone, as two enormous reclining nudes in the middle ground are as large as, if

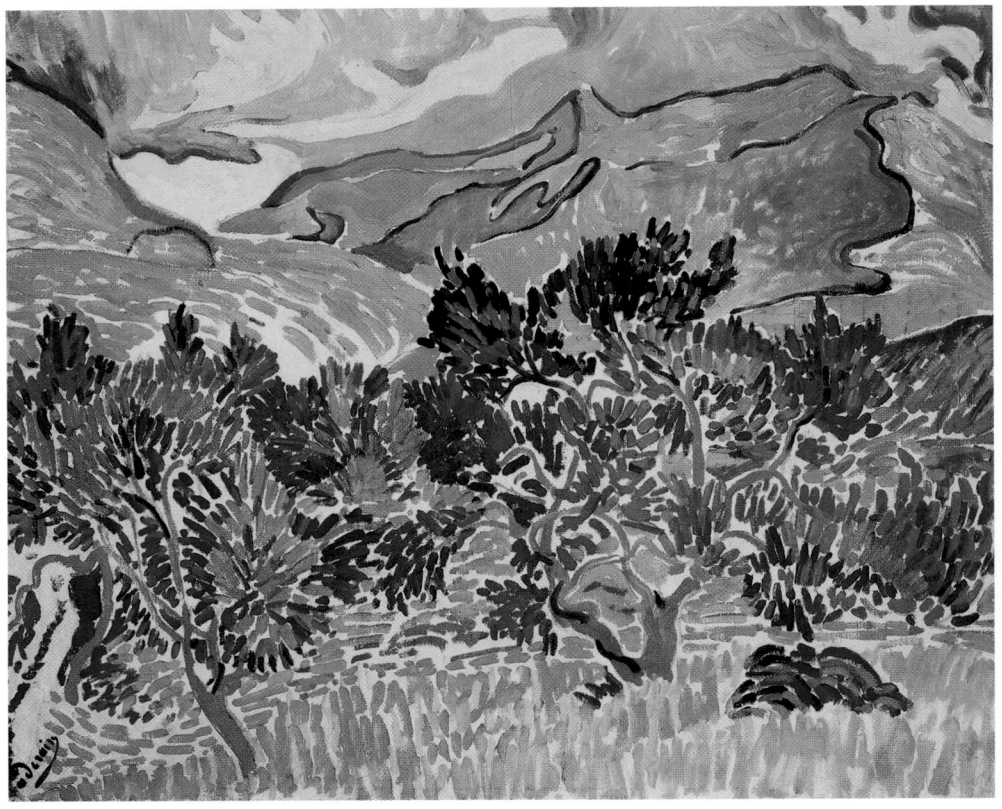

27.2 André Derain, *Mountains at Collioure*. 1905. Oil on canvas, 32 × 39½" (81.5 × 100 cm). National Gallery of Art, Washington, D.C. John Hay Whitney Collection

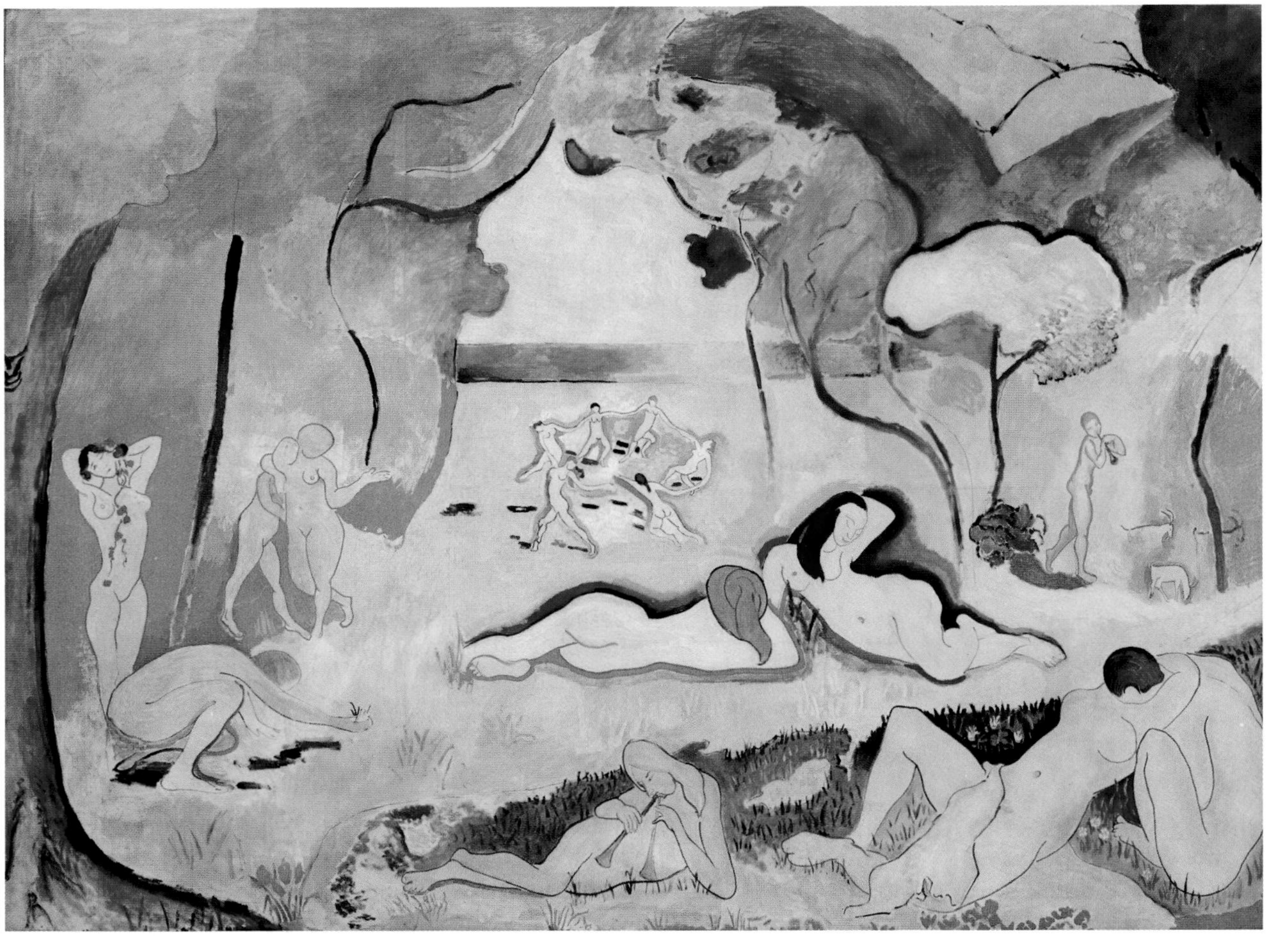

27.3 Henri Matisse, *Le Bonheur de Vivre (The Joy of Life)*. 1905–06. Oil on canvas, 5'8" × 7'9¾" (1.74 × 2.38 m). The Barnes Foundation, Merion, Pennsylvania

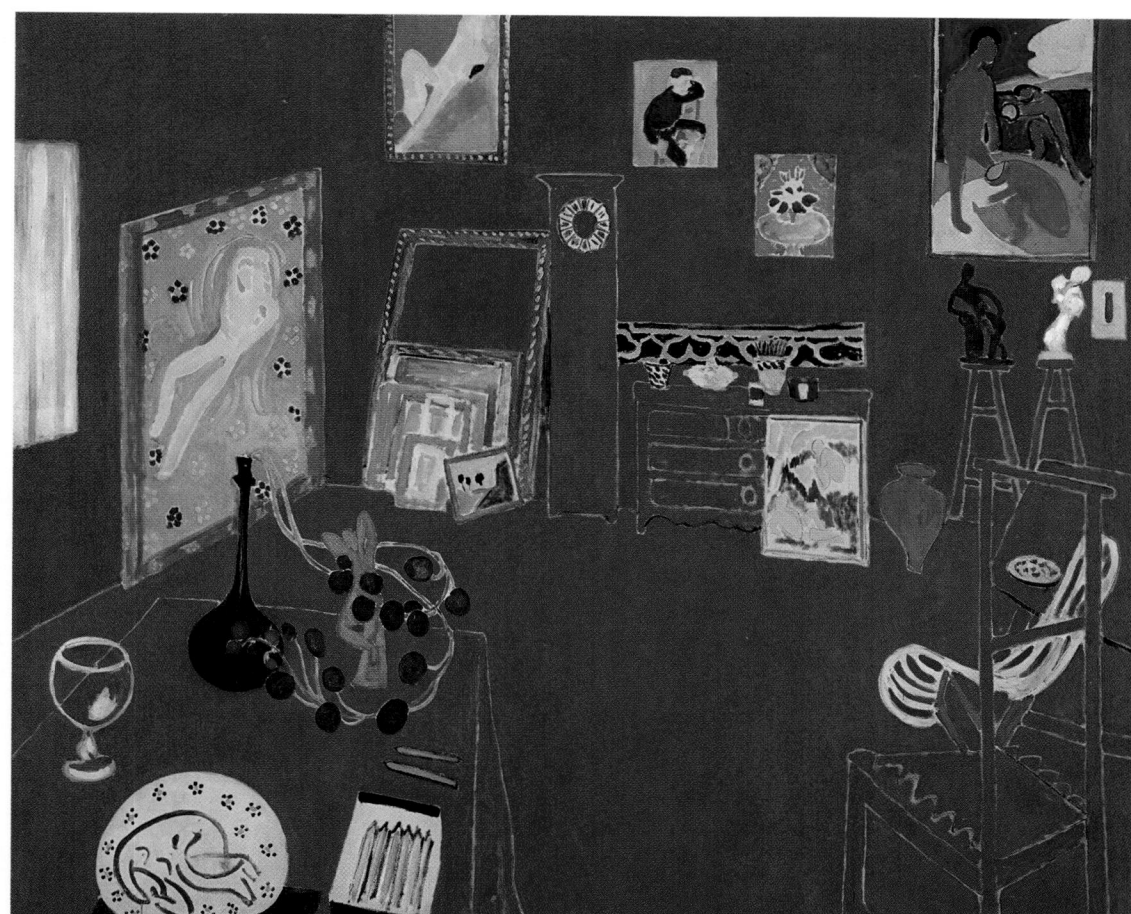

27.4 Henri Matisse, *The Red Studio*. 1911. Oil on canvas, 5'11¼" × 7'2¼" (1.81 × 2.19 m). Museum of Modern Art, New York. Mrs. Simon Guggenheim Fund

not larger than, the pipe player and kissing couple in the foreground. Figures dissolve into one another and trees into sky and hills, so that it is nearly impossible to tell which sits in front of which. Reality gives way to a joyous abstract orchestration of colored lines and planes, which takes its hedonistic cue from the Classical idylls of ritual, dance, and music making of Puvis de Chavannes (see fig. 26.5). The pipes, garlands, shepherd, and sense of Graeco-Roman nudity evoke an archaic Classical world, the same world conjured by such French painters as Poussin and Claude (see figs. 21.7 and 21.8).

Because of the intensity of its color, *Le Bonheur* is generally labeled a Fauvist picture. By 1907, however, Matisse's palette, while still colorful, was subdued, becoming sensuous and serene rather than joyfully riotous. We can see this new sensitivity in his 1911 *The Red Studio* (fig. **27.4**). While the subject is again a conventional one—in this case, the artist's studio—in Matisse's hands, the theme takes on new import. On the one hand, reassuringly familiar objects appear, such as pencils, a collection of studio props arranged as a still life, and several of Matisse's own canvases and along the right wall his sculpture. On the other hand, *The Red Studio* offers a viewer a completely novel visual experience through the manipulation of color and line to radically redefine pictorial space.

As the title indicates, the painting's keynote is the color red, which is like a flat window shade pulled through the entire canvas.

Basically unvarying in tone, it momentarily becomes floor, wall, and tablecloth because of the white-line drawing, before popping back to the surface as a perfectly flat red shade. Even the white lines that delineate the table, high-backed chair, and wall, for example, and suggest recession and thus space, ironically reinforce the two-dimensionality of the image, for they are not painted lines. Rather, they are slivers of canvas that Matisse has allowed to show through.

Matisse's slightly rust-colored red is highly evocative. It is enticing, lush, sensuous, soothing, and comforting, telling us with extraordinary efficiency and immediacy that this studio is warm, cheerful, and relaxing. The paintings on the wall seem to float on this red field, popping up to the surface of the image and asserting themselves as objects of pride and accomplishment. Matisse similarly highlights his box of pencils, plate, flowers, and chair, personal objects that must have been special to him. Only by dispensing with conventional space and volume, meaning realism, could Matisse push these objects to the fore and make them so prominent. The flat red field also serves as a foil that allows Matisse to create a wonderful syncopated rhythm with the paintings and other objects, producing a vitality that suggests artistic creativity, which complements the peacefulness of the room. Without entirely dispensing with the representational world, Matisse has used an abstract vocabulary to convey his soothing message.

CUBISM

The second major style to emerge in the new century was Cubism, largely under the leadership of Pablo Picasso and Georges Braque. Cubism was not just an innovative style that sparked new ways of thinking about the look of art. It was also important because it introduced new ways of thinking about the purpose of art, which happened when its subject matter became not so much the still lifes and portraits that were embedded within Cubist abstraction but rather an analysis of the very language of painting. Picasso was the first to push the limits of the abstraction observed in the work of Cézanne, Derain, and Matisse.

Reflecting and Shattering Tradition: Les Demoiselles d'Avignon

Pablo Picasso (1881–1973) was born in the Spanish town of Malaga, on the Mediterranean coast, where he began his artwork under the direction of his father, who was a painter. At age 15, he moved to Barcelona and continued his training at the Escuela de Bellas Artes. He was soon a major figure in Barcelona's art community, working primarily in a Symbolist style. After roughly four years of shuttling back and forth between Barcelona and Paris and leading a desperate, abject existence, he settled permanently in Paris, moving into a run-down building nicknamed the *bateau-lavoir* ("laundry boat") in bohemian Montmartre, the rural hill overlooking the city. The neighborhood was a center for the impoverished cultural avant-garde, and Picasso quickly became part of the group's inner circle, which also included writers Max Jacob (1876–1944) and Guillaume Apollinaire (1880–1918). In 1907, Picasso shocked even his closest companions when he unveiled in his studio *Les Demoiselles d'Avignon* (*The Young Ladies of Avignon*) (fig. **27.5**). The painting's style departed sharply from Picasso's previous work. To his contemporaries, this large, frightening picture seemed to come out of nowhere.

Of course, the painting did not emerge from an aesthetic vacuum. Among Picasso's sources were the great French history

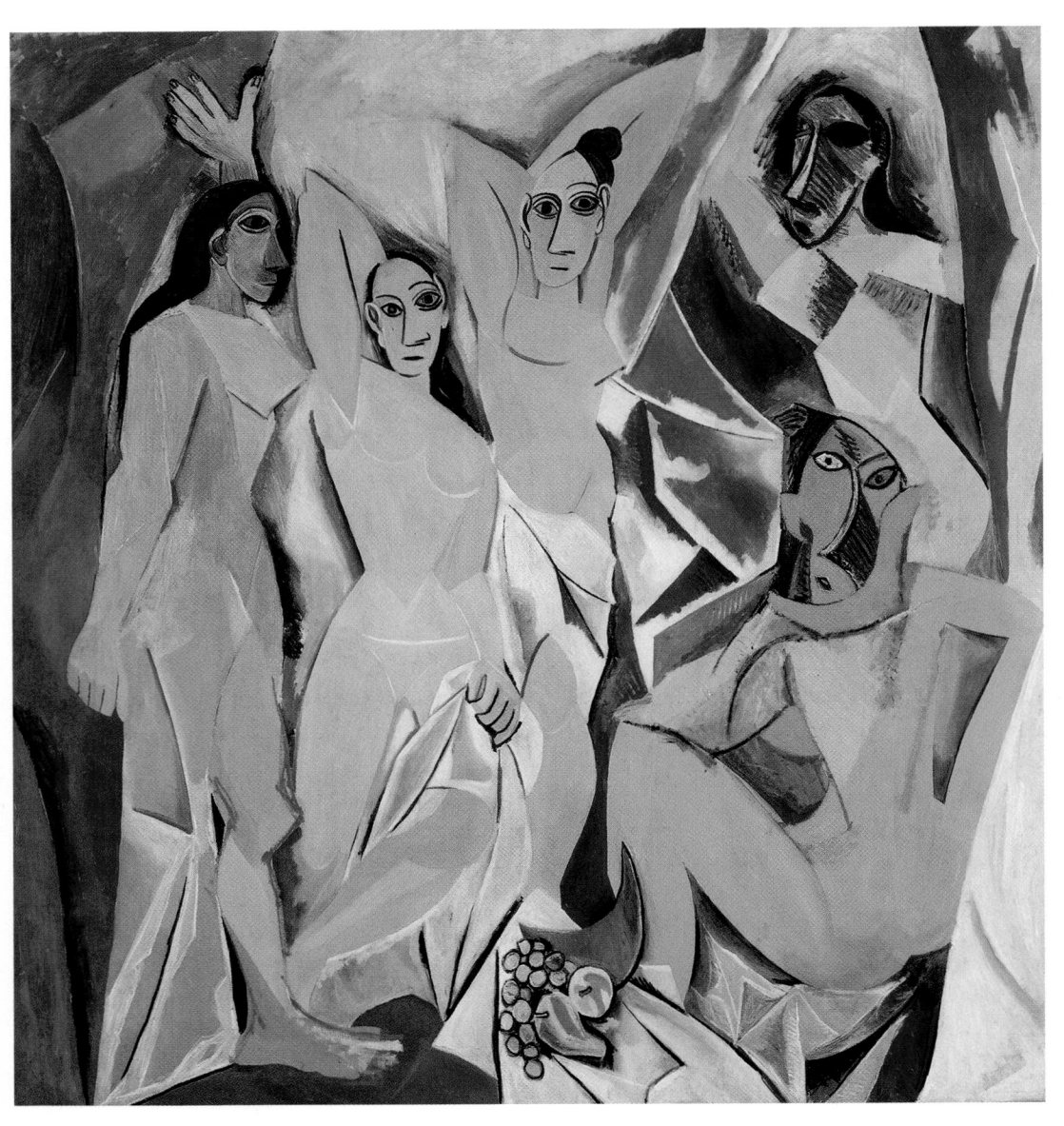

27.5 Pablo Picasso, *Les Demoiselles d'Avignon* (*The Young Ladies of Avignon*). 1907. Oil on canvas, 8' × 7'8" 2.44 × 2.34 m). Museum of Modern Art, New York. Acquired through the Lillie P. Bliss Bequest

The Myth of Primitivism

European countries began trading with Africa shortly before 1600 and the South Pacific (Oceania) in the late eighteenth century. But it was not until the nineteenth century that serious attempts were made to collect the art of these regions. Missionaries, traders, and government administrators sent home native objects, their activities increasing dramatically with the colonization of Africa and the Pacific in the closing decades of the century. The result of this collecting was the founding of ethnographic museums or ethnographic departments in fine art museums in major cities in Europe and the United States.

Despite the fact that tribal art was housed and presented in museums, including some that even specialized in antiquities, the works were perceived as artifacts, not art. It was ethnographic material. Paul Gauguin was the first artist to take a serious interest in tribal objects as art, incorporating Polynesian motifs and stylistic components into his paintings, prints, and sculpture, work that sought to escape the corrupting influence of decadent Western civilization by turning to so-called "primitive" cultures, which he perceived as more pure, natural, and unspoiled (see page 915). But it was not until about 1905 that tribal art began to have a broad impact on contemporary artists. The Fauves, including Henri Matisse and André Derain, were among the first artworld figures to begin collecting the sculpture of Africa and Oceania, soon followed by Pablo Picasso and Constantin Brancusi, as well as the German Expressionists, especially Ludwig Kirchner, who are discussed in this chapter.

The attraction of tribal art was twofold. First, much of it was abstract (although much was also naturalistic), reinforcing the abstraction of modern art. Its simplification of form, color, line, and composition and rejection of naturalism paralleled developments occurring in avant-garde art. For some artists, such as Picasso and Kirchner, the work was probably attractive for its expressionistic qualities, qualities that they perceived as frightening, even barbaric, and that could be incorporated into their work to express powerful emotions and a strained psychological state.

Second, tribal art was alluring to the avant-garde because, as for Gauguin, it represented humanity in an unspoiled, more natural state, a perception that can be traced to Jean-Jacques Rousseau's Enlightenment concept of the "noble savage" (see page 787). Before the discovery of tribal art, this return to nature and a simpler, more primordial time when humans were directly connected to universal forces was reflected by an interest in rural, even peasant, life, the Middle Ages, or Classical arcadias, as seen in the art or theory of George Sand, Rosa Bonheur, John Ruskin, the Pre-Raphaelites, William Morris, and Puvis de Chavannes (see Chapters 25 and 26).

The process of deriving inspiration from tribal cultures is called primitivism, and the term is often expanded to include appropriations of other art forms perceived as simple, naïve, and direct, such as Pre-Columbian, Native American, Archaic Greek, medieval, children's, and self-taught art. The first major publication on the subject, Robert Goldwater's *Primitivism in Modern Art*, came out in 1938. The book said little or nothing about the nature of tribal art, which Goldwater loved, and presented it as primitive, even inferior, in comparison to Western art, ignoring the aesthetic and social issues embedded in the work that would demonstrate that it was as sophisticated, complex, and rich as European fine art. With the advent in the 1960s of Postmodern philosophy (see page 1075), which argued that all viewpoints are biased and contain hidden agendas, scholars themselves began to realize their own prejudices and stopped perceiving tribal art as primordial, as had the modernist artists. Postcolonial scholarship, the scholarship coming out of the African independence movement that began in the 1950s, similarly attacked Western scholarship. Particularly influential was Edward Said's *Orientalism* (1978), which argued that the Western mind, because it had always considered Islamic culture as the inferior "other," could never responsibly report on North Africa and the Near East.

paintings of the seventeenth and eighteenth centuries; the canvas he chose for the work is uncharacteristically large, consistent with the dimensions of a painting destined for the traditional Salon. And the nude was a classic academic subject. An antithetical and more immediate influence was the avant-garde work of Matisse, with whom Picasso maintained a friendly rivalry until the older artist's death in 1954. In the case of *Les Demoiselles*, he was responding to the spatial ambiguity of Matisse's *Le Bonheur de Vivre*, which Picasso felt compelled to upstage. These sources were not immediately apparent to visitors to Picasso's studio, and *Les Demoiselles* initially outraged Matisse and everyone else. But once understood, it provided inspiration for untold artists for decades to come.

The title of the painting refers to the "red-light" district in Barcelona. Early studies show a sailor in a brothel, seated before a table with a plate of fruit and surrounded by prostitutes. In the final painting, the sailor is gone, but the theme remains, for we, the viewers, become the sailor seated at the table in front of the

fruit, an age-old symbol of lust. Coming through the brothel curtains and staring directly at us are perhaps five of the most savage, confrontational nudes ever painted. Thematically, then, the picture began as a typical Symbolist painting about male lust and castrating women, a continuation of the *femme fatale* theme prevalent in late nineteenth-century art and literature, as well as a reflection of Picasso's personal sexual conflict with women and his intense fear of venereal disease.

Instead of relying on conventional forms of pictorial narrative to tell his tale, Picasso allowed the abstract qualities of the medium to speak for him. For example, the formal qualities are threatening and violent, while the space is incoherent and jarring, virtually unreadable. The entire image is composed of what looks like enormous shards of glass that overlap in no comprehensible way. Instead of receding, they hover on the surface of the picture plane, jostling each other. Sometimes the facets are shaded, as in the diamond-shaped breast of the harlot parting the curtain on the right, but Picasso has reversed the shading, in effect detaching the

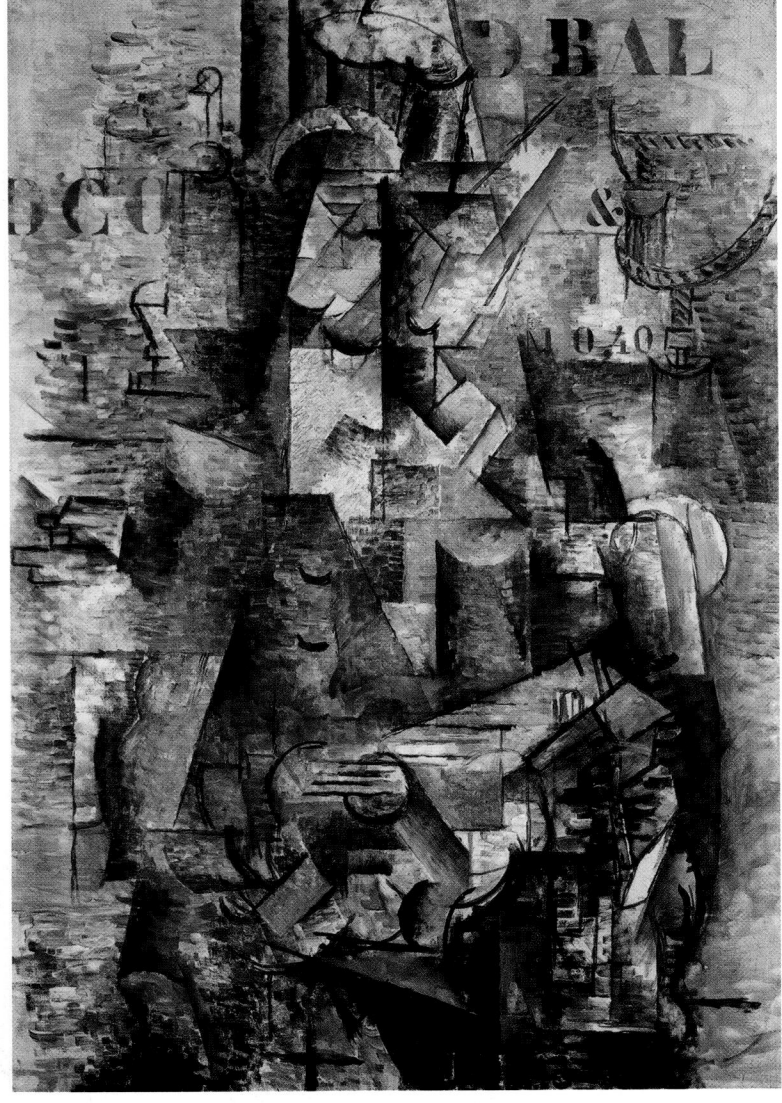

27.6 Georges Braque, *The Portuguese*. 1911. Oil on canvas, 45⅞ × 32⅛"
(116 × 81.6 cm). Kunstmuseum, Basel. Gift of Raoul LaRoche, 1952

breast from the body. Even more incomprehensible is the seated figure below her, who has her back to us yet simultaneously faces us. The table with fruit is tilted at such a raking angle that it would shock even Cézanne, who provided the most immediate model for this spatial distortion (see fig. 26.3) and was the subject of a major retrospective in Paris in 1907. The menacingly pointed melon sets the shrill tone for the picture and through its unsubtle phallic erection announces the sexual theme.

The use of conflicting styles within a single picture is another disturbing quality. The three nudes to the left with their almond-shaped eyes and severe facial features were inspired by ancient Roman Iberian sculptures, which Picasso collected. But the frightening faces on the right are entirely different. At this point in the creation of the painting, or so the story goes, Picasso's Fauve friends took him to the Trocadéro Museum of ethnographic art, where he saw African masks, providing the source for the ski-jump noses, facial scarifications, and lopsided eyes. The

story seems logical enough. We know Matisse and Derain were already collecting African art, attracted to its abstract qualities and admiring how Africans had relinquished naturalism for the sake of expression. And Picasso and Matisse had known one another since 1905. Direct sources for Picasso's borrowings can be found in African sculpture, and the abstraction and "barbarism" of the masks must have appealed to the artist's sensibility. (See *The Art Historian's Lens*, page 951.)

Picasso adamantly denied the influence at this time of *art nègre*, as African art was then called, although he would soon collect it himself. And, sure enough, in the early 1990s, art historians discovered that his source was possibly his own imagination, a claim based on doodlings in his sketchbooks that predate his exposure to African art. The striations, for example, were notational marks for shadow, while the head of the crouching *demoiselle* was actually the result of a witty transformation of a female torso into a face (visual double-entendres occur frequently in Picasso's art). But given Picasso's friendship with the Fauves, it is hard to imagine that he had not heard about and visited the Trocadéro Museum before he finished the painting.

Regardless of his sources, what cannot be denied is Picasso's willingness to look anywhere for inspiration, from the lowly source of his own caricaturing to African masks (then considered artifacts and not art), to Classical Greek sculpture, reflected here by the tradition of the monumental nude, which Matisse had presented so differently in *Le Bonheur de Vivre*. But most important about *Les Demoiselles* is the new freedom it announced for painting, for now line, plane, color, mass, and void were freed from their representational role to take on a life all their own. The picture laid the foundation for Analytic Cubism.

Analytic Cubism: Picasso and Braque

It may seem incredible that *Les Demoiselles* owes anything to the methodical, highly structured paintings of Cézanne, but Picasso had carefully studied Cézanne's late work and found in his abstract treatment of volume and space the basic units from which to derive the faceted shapes of what became Analytic Cubism. Picasso did not arrive at this style on his own, however, and even seemed creatively stalled after *Les Demoiselles*. To help him move beyond this point, the emotional Spaniard needed an interlocutor, a rational steadying force, someone with whom he could discuss his ideas and experiment. This intellectual partner was the French artist Georges Braque (1882–1963), who conveniently lived around the corner from him in Montmartre. From 1908 to 1910, the two fed off each other, their styles developing from representational pictures of fractured forms and space, as seen in *Les Demoiselles*, to shimmering evanescent mirages of abstract lines and brushwork, as found in Braque's 1911 painting *The Portuguese* (fig. **27.6**). Picasso and Braque were so intertwined during this period that their styles began to merge by 1910.

The Portuguese is a classic example of the Analytic Cubism that had emerged in 1910. Gone is the emotional terror and chaos of *Les Demoiselles*. Braque arranged a grid of lines following the shape of the canvas and an orderly geometric pattern of diagonal lines and curves, all recalling Cézanne's vision of a tightly structured world. Despite being abstract, however, these shapes also function as signs or hieroglyphs. The circle at the lower center is the sound-hole of a guitar, and the horizontal lines are the strings, although Braque used the same sign to indicate fingers, a confounding or visual punning of objects that is characteristic of Cubism and a declaration that art is a signing system, like language. The stenciled letters and numbers come from a poster that probably read "Grand Bal" and listed the price of admission (10 francs 40 centimes). The lines and shadows suggest arms, shoulders, and the frontal or three-quarter pose of a figure that tapers toward the head. In the upper right, we see lines that suggest rope and a pier. By providing these subtle visual clues, Braque prompts the viewer to recognize that the painting shows a guitar player, in a Marseille bar, with a view of the docks through a window. As with *Les Demoiselles*, we find a conventional subject—a genre scene—presented in a radical new artistic language. The light that floods the picture and falls on individual facets seems real or naturalistic but fails to create coherent space and volume. Ultimately everything is in a state of flux without absolutes, including a single interpretation of reality. The only reality is the pictorial world of line and paint, which Braque is telling us is as much a language as the hieroglyphic signs that he has embedded in his image.

In a 1909 review of Braque's earlier work, Louis Vauxcelles, who had named Fauvism, labeled the paintings "Cubism," influenced by Matisse's description of earlier Cubist works as appearing to be made of little cubes. The word was then applied to the analytic experiments of Braque and Picasso.

Synthetic Cubism: The Power of Collage

To focus on structure, line, and space, Picasso and Braque painted monochrome images, thus removing the problem of color from their Analytic Cubism. This situation changed in 1912, however, when they began working in collage, pasting flat objects, generally paper, onto canvas. Picasso made the earliest known example in May 1912, when he glued onto the surface of a Cubist painting a sheet of imitation chair caning, a product not unlike contact paper. (These oilcloth sheets with a chair-caning pattern printed on them were normally pasted on wood as an inexpensive way to repair a broken seat.) This device allowed him to complicate notions of the real and the illusionistic, for the chair caning was simultaneously real—a piece of real imitation chair caning—and illusionistic, a picture of chair caning. Clearly, collage allowed Picasso to continue parsing the language of painting,

Picasso and Braque realized immediately the broader implication of collage—the pasted image now literally sat on top of the canvas, a statement Matisse had made a year earlier about painted imagery in *The Red Studio* when he revealed the canvas to emphasize how paint sat atop its surface. Once and for all, the Renaissance conception of the picture plane as a window into an illusionistic world was shattered. Instead of a window, the picture surface became a tray on which art was served. Art occurred in front of, not behind, the canvas, a fact Édouard Manet had implied some 50 years earlier (see page 868).

Collage completely changed the way in which Braque and Picasso made their images. Instead of breaking down or abstracting an object into essential forms, the artists now synthetically constructed it by building it up or arranging it out of cut pieces of paper, hence the name Synthetic Cubism. Constructing the image out of large, flat shapes meant that they could introduce into Cubism a variety of textures and colors, as seen in Picasso's *Guitar, Sheet Music, and Wine Glass* (fig. **27.7**) of 1912. Because music is abstract, like their art, it became a favorite theme for the Cubists, who wished to establish parallels between the two art forms. Picasso built his composition on a background of real wallpaper that, like the imitation chair caning used earlier, serves as a visual pun on illusion and reality.

Picasso puns with solid forms and intangible space as well. The guitar sound-hole, an element that should be negative space

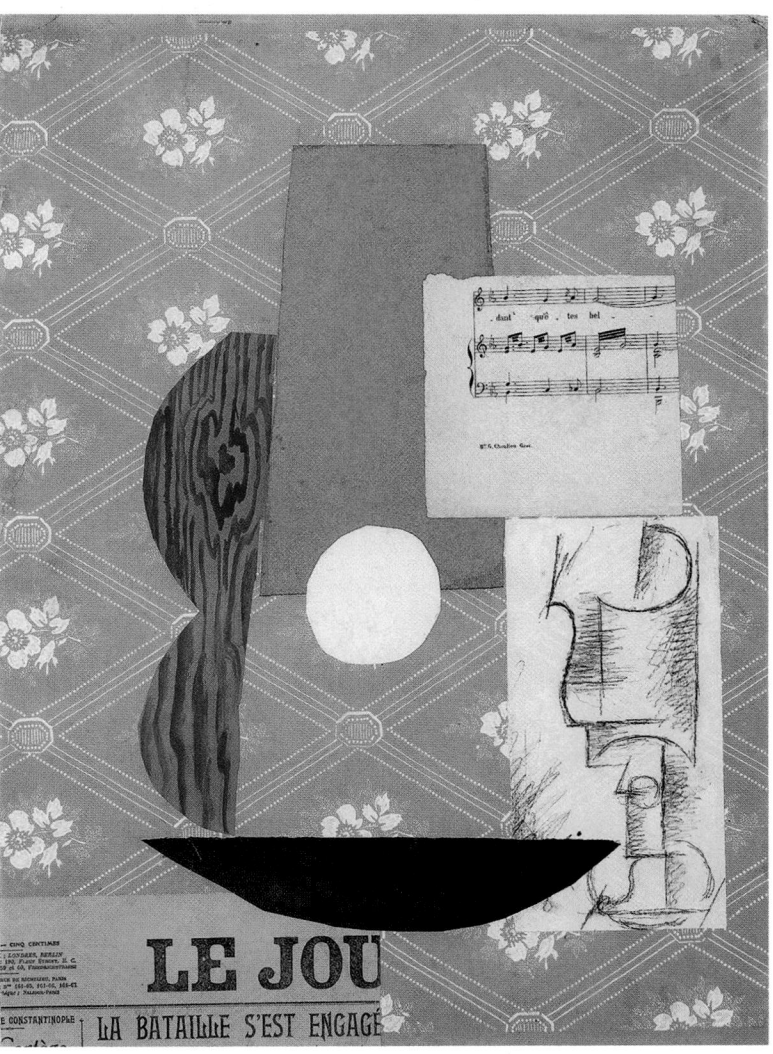

27.7 Pablo Picasso, *Guitar, Sheet Music, and Wine Glass*. 1912. Charcoal, gouache, and pasted paper, 24⅝ × 18½" (62.5 × 47 cm). The McNay Art Institute, San Antonio, Texas. Bequest of Marion Koogler McNay

but appears as a solid circle of paper, contrasts with the wine glass in the Analytic Cubist drawing, which should be three-dimensional and solid but instead consists of lines on a flat piece of off-white paper that has more physical presence than the drawn glass. Picasso even tells us he is punning, for he has cropped the newspaper collage at the bottom to read "LE JOU," a shortening of *Le Journal*, or "newspaper," which in French sounds like the verb *jouer*, meaning "to play." The headline for the article is "*La Bataille s'est engagé*," which translates as "The Battle Has Started," and refers to the violent war then raging in the Balkans, with Greece, Serbia, Bulgaria, and Montenegro fighting for independence against the Ottoman Empire (see map **27.1**). Picasso uses the announcement to signal the friendly rivalry between himself and Braque. Possibly, he is subtly contrasting the sensual pleasure of his still life and its implied comfortable bourgeois lifestyle with the horrendous suffering of the Balkan conflict, in effect commenting on French or middle-class indifference to the tragedy occurring to the east.

The logical peak of Cubism occurred when Picasso extended Synthetic Cubism to sculpture and created the first **construction**, a three-dimensional assemblage of materials. Although his earliest construction was made in 1912 (and evidence suggests Braque had made some even earlier), Picasso did not produce a large number of these sculptures until 1914–15. Most were musical instruments, such as *Violin* (fig. **27.8**) of 1915. Instead of pasting paper onto canvas, he assembled flat or slightly bent sheets of painted metal into a low relief. Just as he had for painting, he now redefined sculpture. Instead of being carved, chiseled, or molded, his sculpture was assembled, and, unlike most sculpture since the Renaissance, it was painted. He used paint perhaps with a bit of irony, since the cross hatching used to represent shading in his paintings is unnecessary for a sculpture, the three-dimensional form not requiring illusionistic shadow. Again Picasso puns with his medium as he comments on the language of art, describing the properties of sculpture and how it functions. While the subject of the work is a violin, we would never know this for certain were it not for the title. Recognizing a violin is not the issue, however, for Picasso is more concerned with creating a visual equivalent to music—here a staccato rhythm of shape, color, and texture—that transforms the individual metal components into playful musical notes that we can almost hear.

The outbreak of war in 1914 disrupted daily life, bringing an end to the brilliant visual game between Picasso and Braque. By then, the two artists had completely transformed painting and sculpture, undermining some 700 years of tradition by destroying notions about what art forms could be. Conventional systems for representing perspectival space were demolished, and now line and color conveyed formal or expressive content instead of serving to duplicate observed reality.

Braque and Picasso sparked a revolution in our perception of reality as radical as those of Freud and Einstein. Music and literature were undergoing similar transformations. For example, Russian composer Igor Stravinsky (1882–1971) changed the face of music with his primitive, rhythmic ballet score *The Rite of*

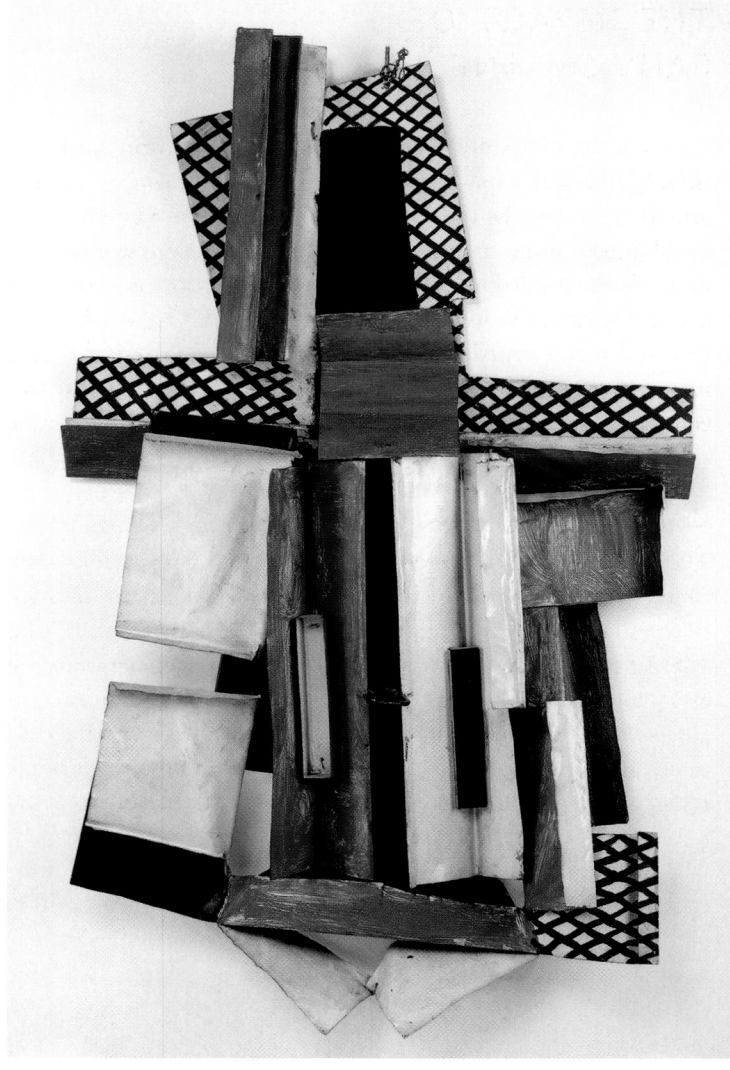

27.8 Pablo Picasso, *Violin*. 1915. Construction of painted metal, 37½ × 25⅝ × 7½" (94.5 × 65 × 19 cm). Musée Picasso, Paris

Spring, first performed in 1913 in Paris, where it caused a riot because people found it merely cacophonous noise that abandoned all musical rules. Irish author James Joyce (1882–1941) similarly dismantled and restructured the novel in *Ulysses*, begun in 1914, in which he disrupted the continuity of the narrative by giving a reader multiple views of the characters' personalities and psychologies.

Especially close to the Cubists, however, was the writer Gertrude Stein (1874–1946), who with her brother Leo amassed an astonishing collection of works by Picasso and Matisse, which they displayed in their Paris apartment. Stein is famous for such phrases as "Rose is a rose is a rose is a rose" or "Out of kindness comes redness and out of rudeness comes rapid same question, out of an eye comes research, out of selection comes painful cattle." Inspired by Cézanne, her novels and poems have a stream-of-consciousness and fractured abstract quality meant to evoke "the excitingness of pure being." Like Cubism, Stein's rhythmic "word-paintings" deny any absolutes.

THE IMPACT OF FAUVISM AND CUBISM

Matisse's and Picasso's liberation of color and line from illusionistic roles marked important steps in the development of modern art. As innovative as their achievements were, their interests and sensibilities during these years were limited. Their works were rational, intellectual, and pleasurable, and they focused on such traditional subjects as still life, portraiture, and the figure. Yet they provided a new artistic vocabulary for artists with very different interests and concerns, artists who used this new language to project powerful emotions, spirituality, and the intensity of modernity.

German Expressionism

The long tradition of Expressionism in German art extends back to the grotesque physical and psychological tensions of such Renaissance artists as Matthias Grünewald (see fig. 18.10) and Albrecht Dürer (see fig. 18.14). German Expressionism surfaced as a cohesive movement toward 1905, and although it encompassed a range of issues and styles, it can be characterized as tortured, anguished, brutally primitive, or passionately spiritual, reflecting elemental cosmic forces.

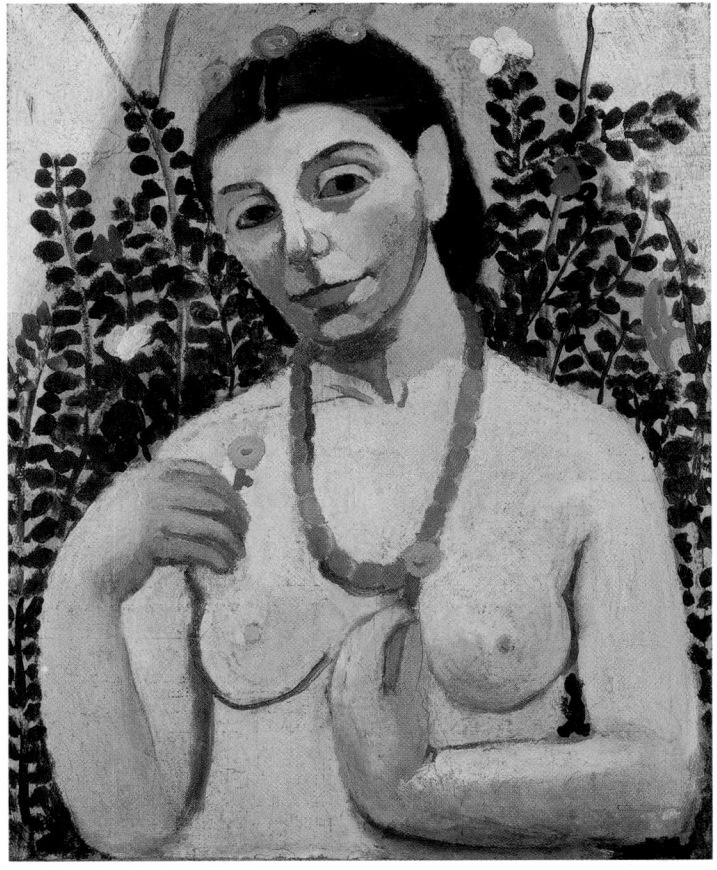

27.9 Paula Modersohn-Becker, *Selbstbildnis, Halbakt mit Bernsteinkette* (Self-Portrait with an Amber Necklace). 1913. Oil on canvas, 24 × 19¾" (61 × 50.2 cm). Kunstmuseum, Basel

A precursor of the first German Expressionist movement is Paula Modersohn-Becker (1876–1907), whose career was cut short by her early death at the age of 31. Her artistic activity was limited to two mature years, during which she produced remarkable pictures that promised a brilliant future. In 1898, she settled in the commune of Worpswede, a haven for artists and intellectuals seeking escape from modern urban life, just outside Bremen in north Germany. There, she befriended two major Symbolist writers, the poet Rainer Maria Rilke (1875–1926) and the novelist Carl Hauptmann (1862–1946), both of whom urged her to seek the spiritual in her art and to reject the naturalistic. Modersohn-Becker visited Paris regularly, and in 1905–06 she was especially influenced by exhibitions of works by Gauguin and Cézanne.

The emergence of her individual style is represented by her 1913 *Selbstbildnis, Halbakt mit Bernsteinkette* (Self-Portrait with an Amber Necklace) (fig. **27.9**). In this radical picture, the artist presents herself nude. With this gesture, Modersohn-Becker reclaims the nude female form for women, endowing it with a creative vitality and meaning that challenges the tradition of the passive nude Venuses and bathers popular since the Renaissance. The artist presents herself as an emblem of fertility, an earth-goddess, from which all life flows. Showing herself frontally, like an icon, she reduces her contours to a Gauguin-like curvilinear simplicity. Her awkward yet charming pose suggests the primitive, recalling especially Gauguin's Tahitian women (see fig. 26.13). Her amber necklace even resembles a lei, or garland of flowers. She poignantly displays two small flowers, symbols of fertility, which she has colored and shaped similarly to her nipples, drawing a parallel between the two. Also symbolic of fecundity is the garden that she stands in. A celestial blue halo deifies her and reinforces her elemental presence. What is revealing about the image is Modersohn-Becker's German primitivism, which differs so radically from that of Gauguin. There is a cultivated crudeness throughout the picture, reflected in the pasty application of paint, particularly in the masklike face and neck, and the awkward gestures, especially of her left hand. It appears as well in the ungainly flat ear and coarse fingers of the right hand. Despite the beautiful, colorful palette, we sense a raw, primal energy and an earthiness, characteristics of much German Expressionism.

DIE BRÜCKE (THE BRIDGE) Scholars generally assert that German Expressionism began with Die Brücke (The Bridge), a group conceived in 1903 when four Dresden architecture students, including Ernst Ludwig Kirchner (1880–1938) and Erich Heckel (1883–1970), decided to form an art alliance "to clear a path for the new German art." In 1905, the group officially formed and went public with no artistic program other than to oppose "older well-established powers" and to create a "bridge" to the future. Like so many progressive Germans, their vision was formed by the philosopher Friedrich Nietzsche (1844–1900). In his most famous book, *Thus Spoke Zarathustra* (1883–85), Nietzsche called for the rise of an *Übermensch*, or "superhuman," a youthful noble of superior intellect, courage, fortitude, creativity, and beauty who would dominate the inferior masses huddling safely in the conventional, restrictive past. This strong-willed *Übermensch* would be the "bridge" that would lead the world into a glorious future of new ideas.

The initial problem confronting these largely self-taught artists, who shared a communal studio in a former butcher's shop, was to find appropriate subject matter and a way to express it. Initially they focused on the unsettling psychology of modern Germany and turned to intense color to convey their message. Kirchner, the leader of Die Brücke, was perhaps the first to mature artistically, about 1907, as seen in his *Street, Dresden* (fig. 27.10) of 1908. The group's love of Van Gogh and their recent discovery of Matisse are reflected in the intense Fauvist color liberated from a representational role. As important is the impact of Edvard Munch (see fig. 26.19), who exhibited throughout Germany and often resided in Berlin after 1892. The disturbing psychological undertones and arabesque patterning are decidedly Munch-like, and Kirchner's crowded street evokes a claustrophobic anxiety worthy of the Norwegian symbolist. Like most Munch images, this one focuses on sexual confrontation. Wraithlike women stare out. One, dressed in yellow, lifts her dress to reveal her petticoat. Searing pinks, yellows, and oranges contrast with electrifying blues and greens, creating a disturbing dissonance and sexual excitement. This picture could never be mistaken for a Matisse. For the Bridge artists, prostitutes were emblems of the decadence of urban life, embodying the immorality and materiality of the city.

In 1906, the Berlin painter Emil Nolde (1867–1956) had a one-person show at the Galerie Arnold in Dresden. The Brücke artists were so captivated by Nolde's powerful use of color that they invited him to join the group. Older than the other members,

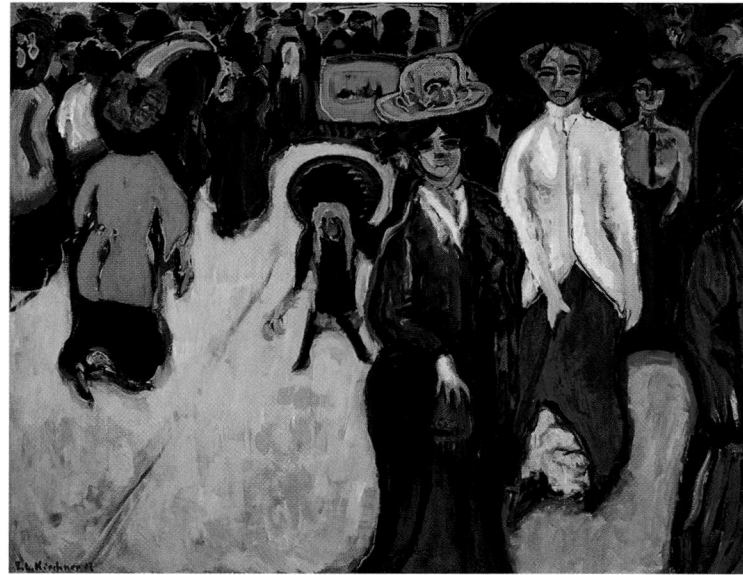

27.10 Ernst Ludwig Kirchner, *Street, Dresden*. 1908 (dated 1907 on painting). Oil on canvas, 4'11¼" × 6'6⅞" (1.51 × 2 m). Museum of Modern Art, New York

he lasted only a year, for his brooding nature and highly personal style were not really compatible with the group's communal mission. Still, his preoccupation with intense emotion and color conformed to the direction in which the group was heading, in part due to his influence. In 1909, after recovering from a serious illness, he made a series of religious pictures, including *The Last Supper* (fig. 27.11). Nolde claimed that in this picture he "followed an irresistible desire to represent profound spirituality, religion,

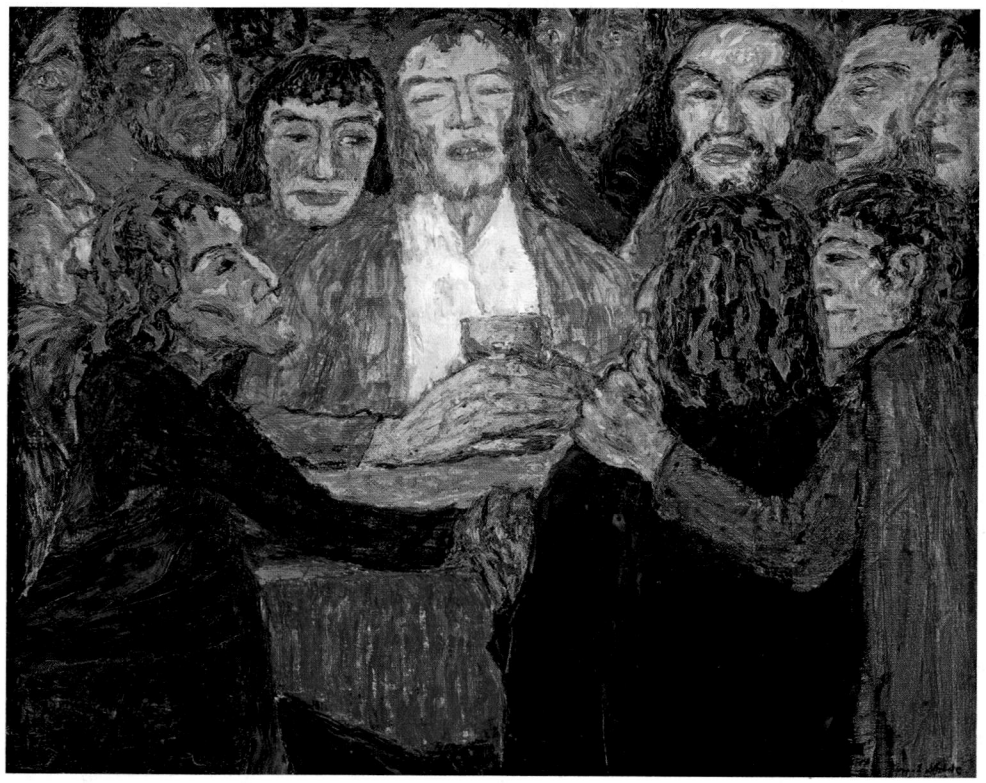

27.11 Emil Nolde, *The Last Supper*. 1909. Oil on canvas, 32½ × 41¾" (86 × 107 cm). Kopenhagen Statens Museum for Kunst Wvz Urban 316

and tenderness." This painting, created in a passionate fervour over several days, is about emotion, his own as well as that of Jesus and the apostles. Nolde crowds the figures and presses them to the surface of the picture plane, making their passions ours. A somber yet ardent red dominates, contrasted by its complement green and laced with yellows and blues, making the surface appear to burn with emotion. He used bold slabs of paint to crudely construct faces and bodies, an effect difficult to see in reproductions. A brutal angularity occasionally appears in chins and noses, and color patterns have jagged edges, as in the hair of the foreground figures.

At first the faces look like masks and are almost grotesque. These are not Ensor masks (see fig. 26.18), however, nor are they masks at all. The distortions and strident gestures, both figural and painterly, underscore the expressive power of the scene. The rawness of the figures, a quality we saw in Modersohn-Becker, enhances the direct emotional force. It also makes the protagonists appear more human and earthy, paradoxically more real despite their sketchiness. By this point in his career, Nolde regularly visited the Völkerkundemuseum in Berlin, drawn to the spirituality and expressionism of the tribal artifacts displayed there. Here, we can sense his adoption of the abstracting, simplification, and directness found in much African art and see him using it to create similar powerful psychological effects.

The ranks of Die Brücke gradually expanded to eight or nine artists, but by 1909, the members began moving one by one to Berlin. There, they found a more sophisticated art scene, dominated by Herwarth Walden's avant-garde art publication *Der Sturm*, begun in 1910, a concept he had expanded into a gallery of the same name by 1911. By that year, all the Brücke artists had relocated, although the group did not disband until 1913. Heavily influenced by Cubism, their style began to change as well. Most abandoned the undulating contours of Munch and the Jungendstil (German Art Nouveau) and embraced a fractured planarity and geometric linearity.

This new style that emerged toward 1910 can be seen in Erich Heckel's *A Crystal Day* (fig. **27.12**) of 1913. Although Die Brücke artists retained the linear look of Cubism, they generally used it to create psychological tension rather than a complicated pictorial space. In this work, Heckel uses Cubist line and fracturing of space to portray abstract, universal ideals. While Kirchner portrayed the psychologically debilitating and moralistically bankrupt side of modernity, Heckel presented the antidote, a Rousseauian elemental, almost primitive, unification with nature and its universal forces. In *A Crystal Day*, Heckel captures cosmic energy through the power of his long streaking lines that, especially in sky and lake, look like a painterly abstract Cubist composition. Similar asymmetrical jagged shapes are echoed throughout, locked in a tight mosaic. Even the angular figure, reduced to a simplified form and vaguely reminiscent of the African sculpture the group so admired for what it considered its primal directness, is closely woven into the linearity of the land. Heckel gives us the feeling of a common life force surging through all of nature, binding everything together. This reading is

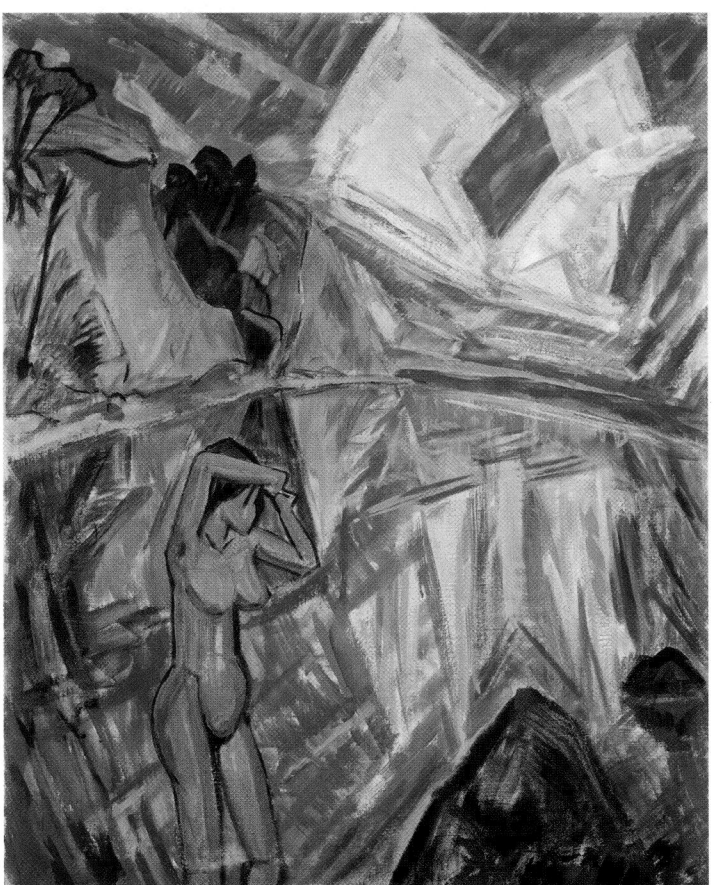

27.12   Erich Heckel. *A Crystal Day*. 1913. Oil on canvas, 47¼ × 37¾" (120 × 96 cm). Pinakothek der Moderne, Munich. Loan from Collection of Max Kruss, Berlin

confirmed by the clouds and their reflections in the water, which have been transformed into the crystals of the title and reflect the belief that crystals held spiritual properties, a perception popularized by the poet Paul Scheerbart in 1914 (see page 979).

In their quest to create a nationalistic art, Die Brücke artists revived the printmaking technique of woodcut, favored by German artists during the early Renaissance. (See *Materials and Techniques*, page 958.) Adding to the medium's attraction was its expressive rawness—one can sense the grain of the wood, which gives not only a stridency but also an earthly, organic feeling to the images. These qualities can readily be seen in Kirchner's *Peter Schlemihl: Tribulations of Love* (fig. **27.13**) of 1915, one of a series Kirchner created to illustrate the prose tale *Peter Schlemihl's Wondrous History* (1814) by Adelbert von Chamisso (1781–1838), which tells the tale of a man who sells his shadow, thus his soul, for a pot of gold. This colored woodcut shows the use of the ambiguous space of Cubism to project the invisible inner workings of the mind and to juxtapose that with the representational world. Here, we see a man next to a manifestation of his psychosexual conflict. Spatial dislocation, a splintering sharpness to the edges, a chaotic composition, and the touches of emotion-evoking color (a passionate violent red and a chilling melancholy blue)—all abstract qualities—create an unsettling and distressing image.

The Woodcut in German Expressionism

Some of the best-known European artists in the fifteenth and sixteenth centuries practiced the printmaking medium of the woodcut, but by the early nineteenth century this method had been eclipsed by new commercial printing technologies, such as wood engraving and lithography. These technologies produced images of great detail that could be executed rapidly and mass-produced. In the late nineteenth century, however, European painters and sculptors returned to the woodcut as an artistic medium precisely because it produced a crude, unsophisticated look in contrast to the slick techniques of modern image reproduction.

Japanese woodblock prints were the elaborate product of a series of designers, block cutters, and printers, and Europeans in the mid-nineteenth century avidly collected them. In the 1890s, Edvard Munch and Paul Gauguin reinvented a very different form of the woodblock print, or woodcut, as did such German Expressionists as Ernst Ludwig Kirchner (see fig. 27.13) and, somewhat later, Käthe Kollwitz in the early 1900s. Their simplified, hand-made process contributed to the planar effect of flat, simplified shapes, which can evoke strong emotional tensions. Unlike the division of labor characteristic in the production of Japanese prints and in those of northern Renaissance artists such as Albrecht Dürer, these modern artists designed, cut, and printed the woodcuts themselves. They could thus exploit unforeseeable expressive qualities in the wood grain that became evident only during the carving process. Munch developed an influential technique in which he cut the block into jigsaw pieces that were inked individually, reassembled, and printed, resulting in a multicolor print produced in one pull through the press. The Kirchner woodcut seen in figure 27.13 was printed from two blocks.

Although many prints by these artists appear spontaneous or perhaps haphazard, they are in fact the result of deliberate forethought: The block had to be cut in such a way that the wood remaining in relief, when rolled with ink, produced the sought-after image. There was no room for error, for the artist had not only to plan the positive and negative spaces but also to reverse his intended picture because, when printed, the impression created is a mirror image of the original woodblock design.

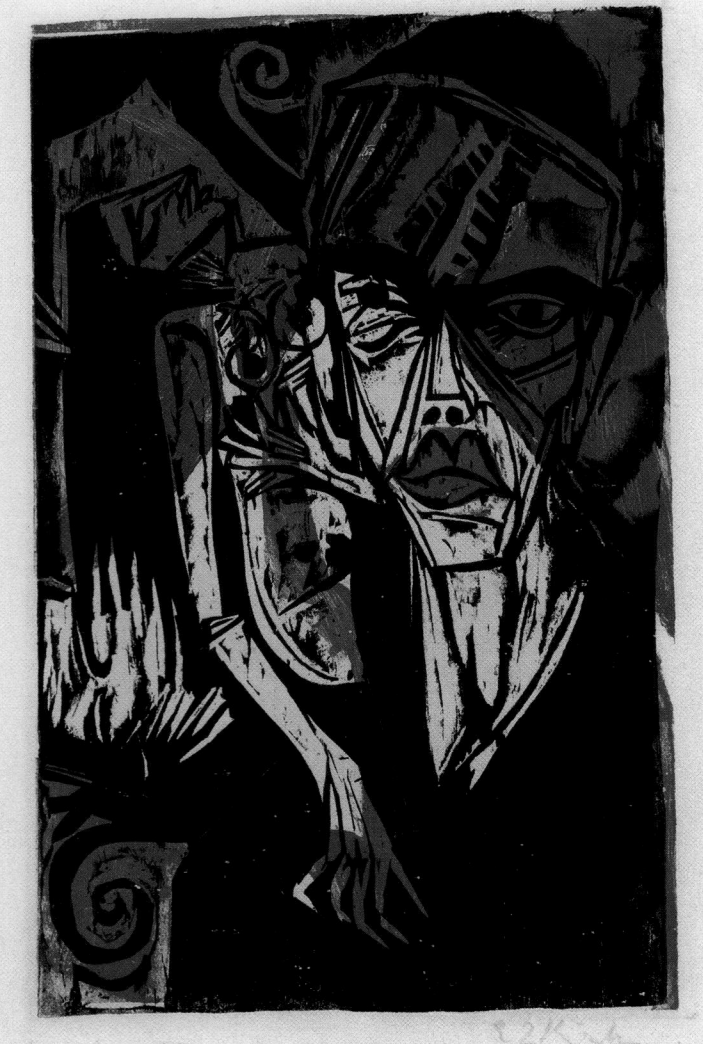

Kirchner, like Heckel, displays a Brücke reliance on the expressive distortions of African sculpture, seen especially in the sharp angularity and faceting of the man's face.

DER BLAUE REITER (THE BLUE RIDER) The second major German Expressionist group, Der Blaue Reiter (The Blue Rider), developed in Munich, in southern Germany. It officially lasted but four months, from December 1910 to March 1911. Like their Brücke counterparts, the artists associated with Der Blaue Reiter drew on art forms from Western art history as well as non-Western and folk-art traditions to create images that reveal their skepticism toward modern, industrial life. The group focused on expressing a spirituality they believed resided beneath the surface of the visual world.

The key figure in Der Blaue Reiter was the Russian artist Vasily Kandinsky (1866–1944). He left Moscow in 1896 to study art in Munich and brought with him Russian influences, namely the spirituality of native religious icons and the robust, emotional colors of folk art. His interest in folk culture was rekindled when, in 1908, he moved with painter and partner Gabriele Münter (1877–1962) to Murnau, just south of Munich in the Bavarian Alps. There he immersed himself in folk culture and was deeply affected by the powerful colors and the directness of the folk decorations and paintings on glass, a medium that he and Münter adopted.

27.13 Ernst Ludwig Kirchner, *Peter Schlemihl: Tribulations of Love.* 1915. Color woodcut from two blocks on wove paper, 13⅛ × 8¼" (33.6 × 21.7 cm). National Gallery of Art and Brücke Museum. Collection of Karl and Emy Schmidt-Rottluff

When in Munich, the couple lived in the Schwabing neighborhood of Munich, a bohemian enclave of cafés and liberalism. The area was a breeding ground for explorations of spirituality and the occult, especially Theosophy, which was a daily topic of conversation for many. Kandinsky owned the book *Theosophie* by German philosopher Rudolf Steiner (1861–1925) and attended his Theosophy lectures in Berlin in 1908. Inspired in part by Steiner's ideas, Kandinsky in 1910 wrote *Concerning the Spiritual in Art*, published the next year and read worldwide. In it, he proclaimed the need to paint one's connectedness with the universe and to use an abstract vocabulary, one that functioned much like music, to portray the abstract qualities of spirituality. He wrote that "color directly influences the soul. Color is the keyboard, the eyes are the hammers, the soul is the piano with many strings. The artist is the hand that plays, touching one key or another purposively, to cause vibrations in the soul." (See *Primary Source*, page 960.) Because of this parallel with music, Kandinsky titled his works "composition," "improvisation," and "concert." Kandinsky, a well-read intellectual, was also influenced by the recent scientific discoveries of Einstein and Rutherford, which demonstrated that

matter was not solid and stable but instead existed in a state of flux, convincing Kandinsky that a spiritual force coursed through all matter.

While Kandinsky advocated abstract art by 1910, it was not until 1911 that his own work became entirely nonobjective. In 1910, he began a series of ten paintings called "Compositions." The first works were abstract but still readable, with objects reduced to simple childlike forms vaguely recognizable as figures, trees, horses, mountains, or churches, for example. (A rider on a horse, often blue, occasionally appears, the horse and rider motif being common in Kandinsky's oeuvre and often interpreted as a reference to the artist himself and his idol St. George, the Christian dragonslayer, and their parallel quest to bring a new spirituality into the world. As is apparent, the motif became the group's name.) In these 1910 paintings, forms are often reduced to flat color and encased in a dark line, the deeply saturated color and line resembling the spiritual stained glass of churches. The total abstraction that appeared in 1911 can be seen in his 1913 painting *Sketch I for "Composition VII"* (fig. **27.14**). This was one of numerous preliminary studies for a large final version that

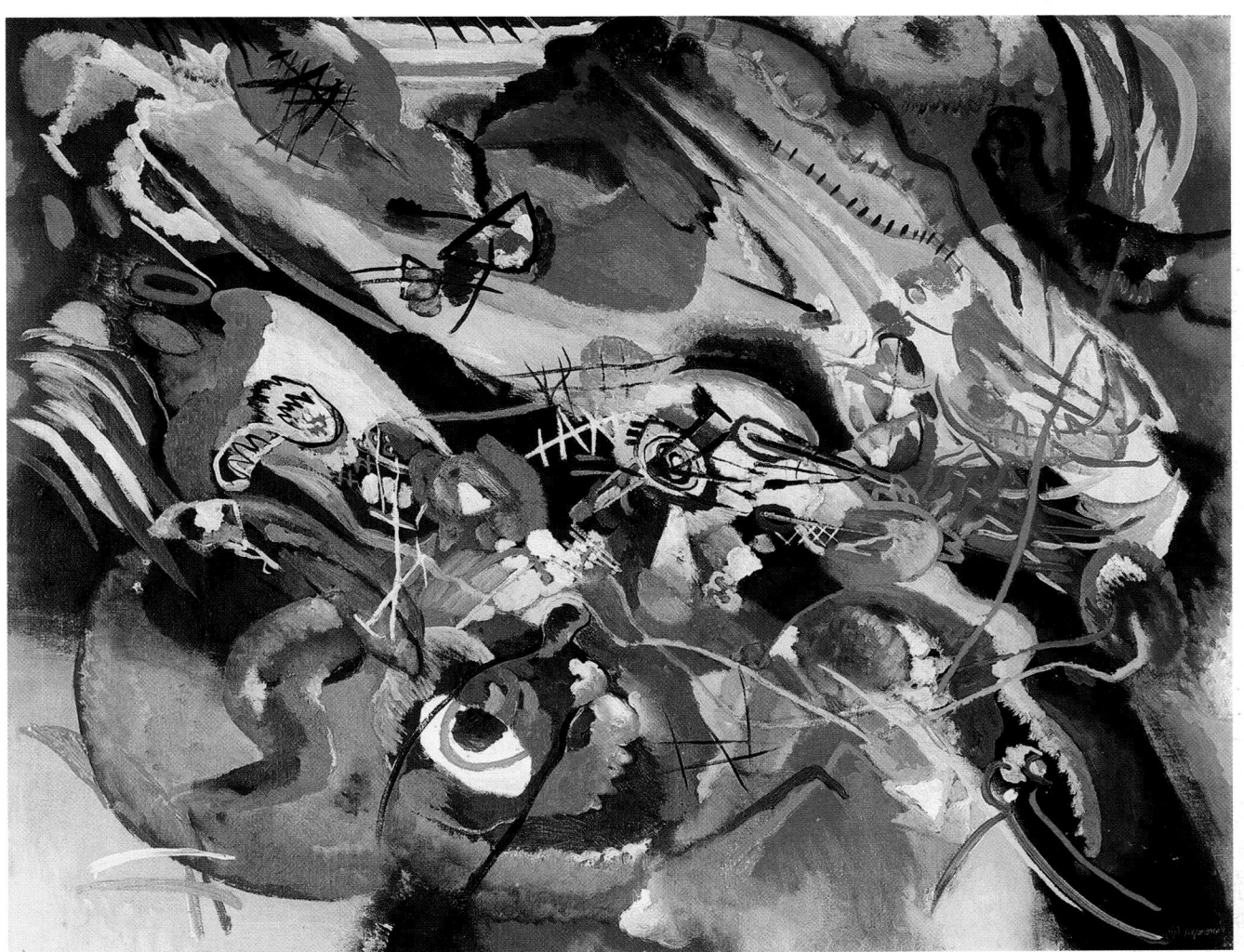

27.14 Vasily Kandinsky, *Sketch I for "Composition VII."* 1913. Oil on canvas, 30¾ × 39⅜" (78 × 100 cm). Felix Klee Collection

Vasily Kandinsky (1866–1944)

From *Concerning the Spiritual in Art*

Kandinsky hoped to inaugurate a new spiritual era for modern human beings through his art. These remarks first appeared in 1911.

If you let your eye stray over a palette of colors, you experience two things. In the first place you receive *a purely physical effect*, namely the eye itself is enchanted by the beauty and other qualities of color. You experience satisfaction and delight, like a gourmet savoring a delicacy. Or the eye is stimulated as the tongue is titillated by a spicy dish. But then it grows calm and cool like a finger after touching ice. These are physical sensations, limited in duration. They are superficial, too, and leave no lasting impression behind if the soul remains closed.

And so we come to the second result of looking at colors: their psychological effect. They produce a correspondent spiritual vibration, and it is only as a step towards this spiritual vibration that the physical impression is of importance. …

Generally speaking, color directly influences the soul. Color is the keyboard, the eyes are the hammers, the soul is the piano with many strings. The artist is the hand that plays, touching one key or another purposively, to cause vibrations in the soul.

It is evident therefore that color harmony must rest ultimately on purposive playing upon the human soul.

Source: Vasily Kandinsky, *Concerning the Spiritual in Art*, tr. Francis Golffing, Michael Harrison and Ferdinand Ostertag (NY: Wittenborn, Schultz, 1947)

retains some of the same compositional elements but has a different palette. While Kandinsky's hues still have the deep resonance of stained glass, the recognizable motifs of the earlier works are gone, yielding to an abstract play of color and painted line and form. The image may appear apocalyptic and chaotic, but these dynamic qualities are meant to capture the universal spiritual forces as the artist himself felt them. Despite the total abstraction, the image still feels like landscape—it has a horizontal spread we associate with the genre, and there is still a feeling of recession due to overlapping forms. But this "landscape" can be read as cosmic as much as earthly, and it is so abstract it can even be interpreted as microcosmic as well (portraying a microscopic view of nature).

Which is precisely Kandinsky's point since it is a picture of ubiquitous abstract mystical powers as the artist himself felt or experienced them.

Franz Marc (1880–1916), who met Kandinsky in 1910 or 1911, shared many of the same objectives, especially the quest to portray spirituality. Both artists discussed how animals instinctively bonded with nature and thus with the cosmos. (This belief as well accounts for Kandinsky's repeated use of the horse and rider motif, which dates to 1903.) Marc claimed that "animals with their virginal sense of life awakened all that was good in me." This statement conveys a feeling shared by all the artists of Der Blaue Reiter: the belief that Western, industrialized society was

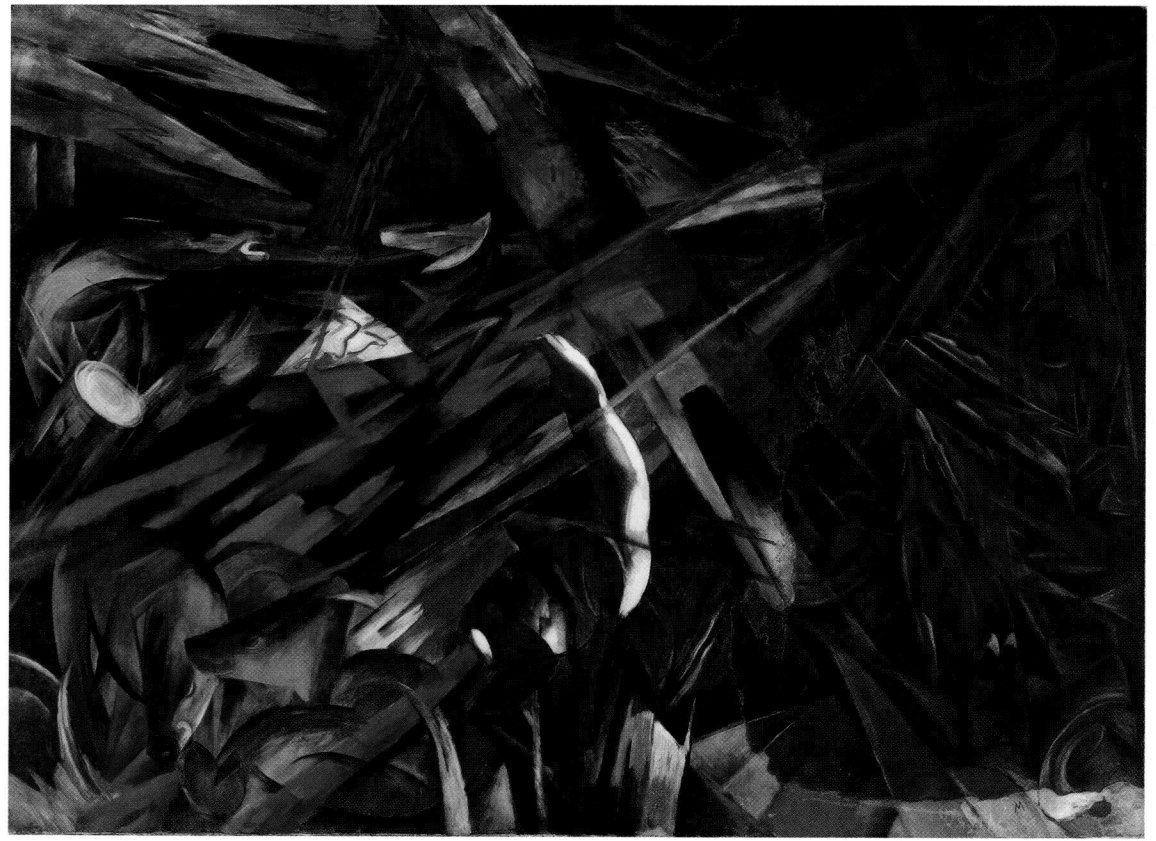

27.15 Franz Marc, *Animal Destinies (The Trees Showed Their Rings, The Animals Their Arteries).* 1913. Oil on canvas, 6'4½" × 8'7" (1.94 × 2.62 m). Öffentliche Kunstsammlung Basel, Kunstmuseum, Basel, Switzerland. 1739

spiritually bankrupt and therefore the need to return to nature. By 1911, Marc was interweaving animals, often horses, into tightly composed landscapes, and by early 1912, he was using Cubism to effect this instinctual interlocking of animal, nature, and primordial forces, as seen in *Animal Destinies* (fig. **27.15**) of 1913.

In this work Marc has transformed Cubist facets into dynamic rays of light that seem to have passed through an unseen mystical crystal. The horses, foxes, and deer dissolve into these spiritual bolts of light, becoming one with them and a universal life force. A sense of a cataclysmic finale pervades the image, suggesting death, or the end of the life cycle, at which point living matter fulfills its destiny by being absorbed back into the cosmos. On the reverse of the canvas, Marc wrote, "And all being is flaming suffering," suggesting the inevitability of a spiritual redemption and the innate ability of animals to accept this course. Marc's colors are the deep saturated hues of stained-glass windows, this reference to mystical illumination being reinforced by the illusionistic light streaming through the image.

By 1911, Der Blaue Reiter had dissolved. The group had two shows. The first was in the Galerie Thannhauser in Munich in December 1911. It then toured Germany, often to harsh reviews, closing at Der Sturm Galerie in Berlin. Clearly, the German viewing public was not ready to embrace the group's striking and abstracted images of nature, despite the works' evocation of traditional art forms such as stained-glass windows and religious icons. The second exhibition featured works on paper and was mounted at a Munich bookstore. Perhaps more important than their exhibitions was the *Der Blaue Reiter Almanac* (*The Blue Rider Yearbook*), which included members' work along with reproductions of examples of Egyptian, Gothic, Asian, tribal, and folk art. Even works by children found a place in the *Yearbook*. Further enhancing the publication's eclecticism was an article on the spirituality of music by the great tonalist composer and Theosophist Arnold Schönberg (1874–1951), who was also a painter and member of Der Blaue Rieter. The *Yearbook* was in effect a catalogue of art that was simple, direct, and spiritual—art that Kandinsky and Marc believed tapped into the cosmos and shared their own goals.

PAUL KLEE One artist whose long career touched on many of the elements expressed in the *The Blue Rider Yearbook* is the Swiss painter Paul Klee (1879–1940). Officially, Klee was only minimally involved with Der Blaue Reiter. He had come to Munich in 1898 to study painting and had settled there in 1906. On friendly terms with Kandinsky and other members of Der Blaue Reiter, Klee's understanding of Expressionism and other modern art movements came from his travels throughout Europe, although no voyage had a more decisive effect on him than a two-week trip to Tunisia. As had been the case with Delacroix and Monet the century before, the bright light and color of North Africa overwhelmed Klee. Soon after arriving, he wrote in his diary, "Color has taken hold of me....That is the meaning of this happy hour: Color and I are one. I'm a painter." But equally important for his development was his connection to

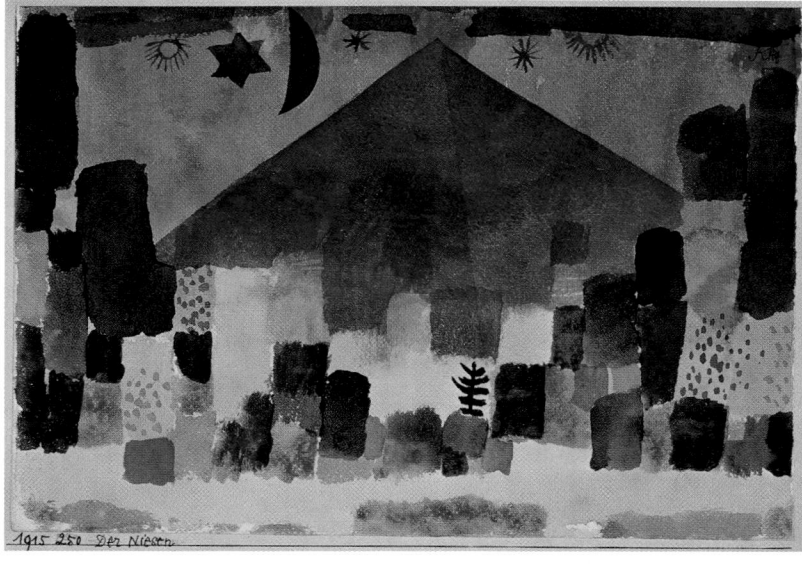

27.16   Paul Klee, *The Niesen*. 1915. Watercolor and pencil on paper, 7⅛ × 9½" (17.7 × 26 cm). Hermann and Marguerite Rupf-Stiftung

Der Blaue Reiter, for his art was the most comprehensive amalgam of all the sources listed in the *Yearbook*, especially children's art, tribal art, and music. (Klee himself was an accomplished flutist.)

Klee's new Tunisia-inspired palette appears in *The Niesen* (fig. **27.16**) of 1915. Combined within the grid of Cubism is an abstract use of color reminiscent of Matisse and Kandinsky. The image echoes the directness and naïveté of children's and folk art, as well as the luminescent, saturated colors of stained-glass windows, the white of the paper flickering through the transparent watercolor to create a glowing illumination. We instantly sense the spirituality that is the foundation of this picture and almost feel as though we can retrace Klee's steps in its creation. The triangular mountain, the Niesen, dominates the image, its rock-hard geometry providing a sense of permanence and eternity while reflecting the Theosophical belief in the spirituality of the triangle, which represents, among other things, the mystical correspondence of the universe. The night sky is filled with religious symbols, such as the Jewish Star of David and the Islamic crescent moon, which mingle with primitive hieroglyphic suns. The branches of the sole tree, suggesting life and all living things, rhythmically correspond to the rays emanating from the stars and suns above and are further linked to them by the Niesen, the shape of which powerfully connects earthly elements with cosmic ones. Through their color, the rectangular planes in front of the mountain evoke trees and plants, light, sun, fire, sky, and earth.

Using an abstract vocabulary of color and shape, into which are inserted a handful of representational signs, Klee has stripped away everything inessential. He reveals in a poetic, understated way his innermost feelings about the nature of life and the universe. Or as he himself said, "Art does not render the visible; rather it makes visible." Adding to the charm and intimacy of Klee's art is its small scale and childlike "draftsmanship."

Austrian Expressionism

Another major center for Expressionism was Vienna. Home of Sigmund Freud, it was an especially repressive city, socially and culturally dominated by a conservative bourgeoisie and an aloof aristocracy resistant to change. In reaction, many avant-garde artists led bohemian lifestyles, shunning middle-class morals and standards. Not surprisingly, Viennese artists generated some of the era's most neurotic and disturbing visual imagery, their art reflecting their psychic distance from conventional society.

OSKAR KOKOSCHKA Perhaps the most prominent Viennese Expressionist is Oskar Kokoschka (1886–1980), who entered the Vienna School of Arts and Crafts in 1905 and specialized in portraiture. In 1908, he exhibited with Gustav Klimt (see page 921) and other avant-garde artists at the *Vienna Kunstschau*, an exhibition for modern art, where his violent portraits, inspired by Van Gogh, generated so much controversy he was expelled from art school. Kokoschka called his expressionistic portraits "black portraits," and the sitters appeared to be so troubled that he became known as "the Freud of painting" who "paints the dirt of one's soul." Kokoschka described his process similarly: "From their face, from the combination of expressions and movement, I tried to guess the true nature of a person, recreating with my own pictorial language, what would survive in the memory." The following year, Kokoschka produced an exceptionally violent and sexual stage play, in the process capturing some of the deepest passions of the mind. The reaction to the play was so negative Kokoschka was forced to flee Vienna, going to Berlin for two years before returning.

We can get a sense of how expressionistic his portraits looked from the figures in *The Bride of the Wind* (fig. **27.17**), Kokoschka's 1914 self-portrait with his lover Alma Mahler, the notoriously beautiful and sophisticated widow of the famous Austrian composer Gustav Mahler (1860–1911). By 1914, their passionate relationship was threatened, and it ended the following year. *The Bride of the Wind* reflects the artist's distress. Originally,

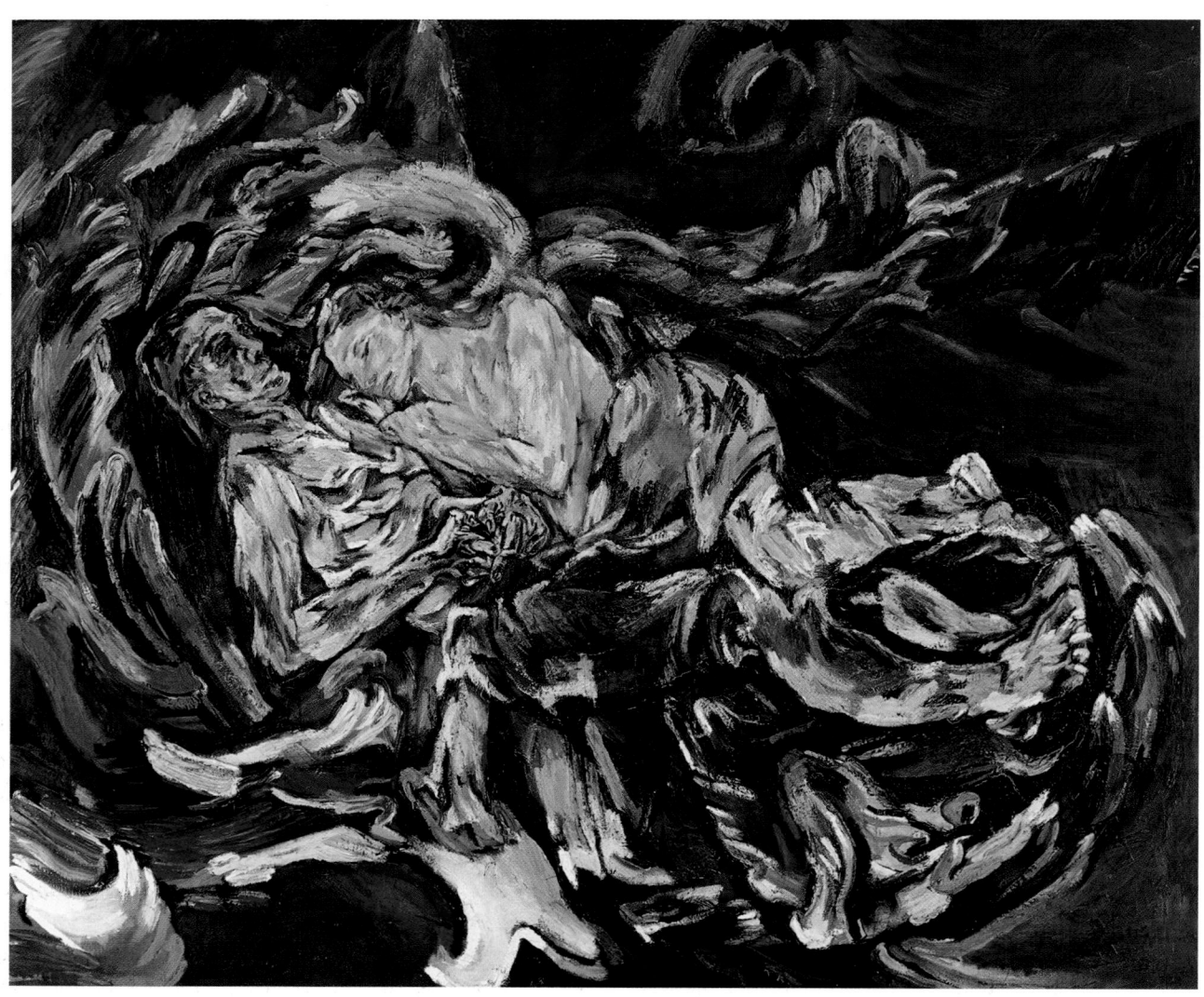

27.17 Oskar Kokoschka, *The Bride of the Wind*. 1914. Oil on canvas, 5'11¼" × 7'2⅝" (1.81 × 2.20 m). Öffentliche Kunstsammlung Basel, Kunstmuseum, Basel, Switzerland

Kokoschka intended to disguise this personal dilemma by calling the work *Tristan and Isolde*, after Wagner's opera about two tragic lovers. The final title comes from Georg Trakl (1887–1914), a bohemian Viennese poet who produced morbid and nightmarish work. Kokoschka expresses his anxiety through coarse, violent brushstrokes and a seething, swirling composition. Oblivious to this turmoil, Mahler is shown peacefully sleeping, while Kokoschka restlessly worries, his body transformed into a flayed corpse, his hands grotesquely gnarled. The couple are contained in a monstrous shell-like cradle adrift in a landscape that is bleak, uncontrollable, and subject to cosmic forces, as suggested by the gravitational pull of a distant moon. This lunar force seems to represent a Freudian sexual drive, for the moon is recessed in a vaginalike tube and framed by phallic peaks. The bizarre environment seems liquid and insubstantial, the entire image transformed into a threatening quagmire of paint and representing psychological urges and instability.

EGON SCHIELE Egon Schiele (1890–1918), another major Viennese painter, likewise defied bourgeois mores. He watched his father's painful death from syphilis, which probably accounts in part for his preoccupation with sickness and mortality. He then feuded bitterly with his conservative middle-class uncle in order to become an artist. He attended the Vienna Academy of Fine Art, and Gustav Klimt soon took him under his wing. At Klimt's invitation, Schiele exhibited at the same 1908 and 1909 *Vienna Kunstschau* exhibitions as Kokoschka. He soon dropped out of art school and with friends established yet another secessionist organization, the Neukunstgruppe (New Art Group). Inspired by Klimt's defiance toward bourgeois conservatism, he led a bohemian life, and in 1911 fled Vienna with his mistress to live in nearby small villages.

Schiele's art is dominated by images of nudes—of himself, prostitutes, and lovers—and although he worked in oil, many of his finest works are on paper, such as *Self-Portrait (Man Twisting Arm Around Head)* (fig. **27.18**) of 1910. The nude had dominated Western art since antiquity, but Schiele's presentation of the unclothed body departs from the tradition of the heroic male nude introduced in Classical antiquity and revived in the Renaissance. Here instead is an outright affront in its frank presentation of the body and its sickly and grotesque distortions. Schiele made the drawing most likely just after his uncle had cut him off financially, and it seems to represent the conflict between conformist bourgeois guardian and independent bohemian painter. Schiele is defiant, not only in his demonic glare and bold, contorted gestures but also in his willingness to present himself as disfigured and ghoulish. However, we also sense an element of self-scrutiny. The 20-year-old artist reveals ribs, underarm hair, and nipple. We sense the body's skeleton, its physicality, and, despite the confrontational stare, its vulnerability. Schiele's evocative handling of the medium, the velvety quality of the charcoal and splashes of watercolor, reinforce the sensuality of the flesh exposed to deterioration, one of the work's dominant themes. Just as his career was taking off in 1918, Schiele fell victim to the

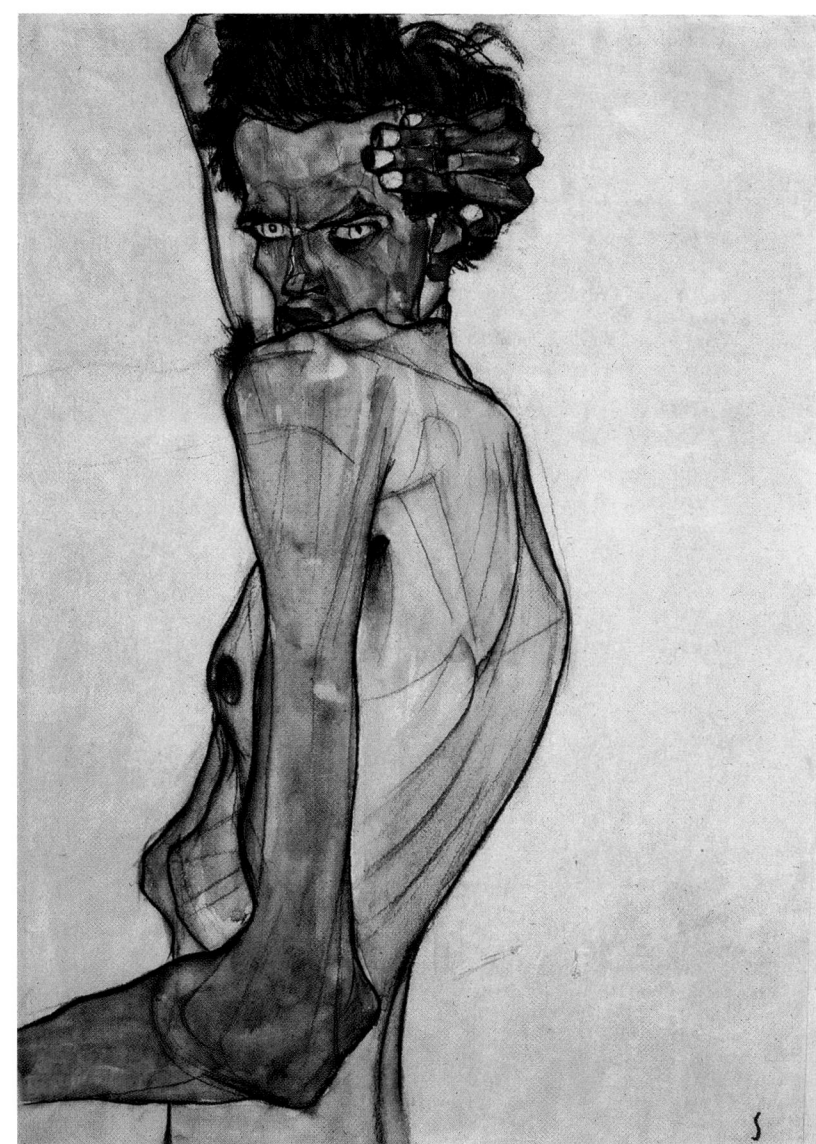

27.18 Egon Schiele, *Self-Portrait (Man Twisting Arm Around Head)*. 1910. Watercolor, gouache and charcoal on paper, 17¾ × 12½" (45 × 31.75 cm). Private collection, New York

pandemic influenza that killed 20 million people worldwide, including his pregnant wife who died three days before him.

Cubism after Picasso and Braque: Paris

In France, Cubism was thoroughly entrenched by 1911–12, expanding well beyond Picasso and Braque. A handful of individual painters had closely followed Picasso's and Braque's developments in 1909–10, and in late 1910 they began exhibiting together at the large Paris Salons and at a private gallery, calling themselves the Section d'Or (Golden Section). Original members Robert Delaunay, Albert Gleizes, Jean Metzinger, and Henri Le Fauconnier were soon joined by Fernand Léger, Roger de La Fresnaye, Marcel Duchamp, and his brother Raymond Duchamp-Villon. In 1912, Gleizes and Metzinger published *Du Cubisme* (*Cubism*), the first book on the subject.

ROBERT DELAUNAY Of this group, Robert Delaunay (1885–1941) was among the most influential. Unlike concurrent Analytic Cubist works by Braque and Picasso, Delaunay's 1910 Cubist paintings of the Eiffel Tower, an icon of modern technology, incorporated color, reflecting the artist's background as a Neo-Impressionist toward 1905. They also differed in their subject: the movement and energy of modernity and the constant flux of the contemporary world.

Delaunay's preoccupation with the dynamism of the modern world is evident in his 1914 *Homage to Blériot* (fig. **27.19**), honoring the French aviator Louis Blériot (1872–1936), inventor of the single-wing airplane and the first person to fly across the English Channel. Delaunay integrates emblems of the modern world—airplanes, propellers, and the Eiffel Tower—into a Cubist composition that is a kaleidoscope of floating balls and rotating disks suggesting whirling propellers and blazing suns. He creates movement not only through the shifting forms of Cubist space but also through the use of what Delaunay called "simultaneous contrasts," the placement of flat planes of primary and secondary colors next to one another, not only creating movement but also light and space, none of which is illusionistic.

Two years before, Delaunay had exhibited total abstractions called *Simultaneous Disks* or *Simultaneous Contrasts*, paintings consisting entirely of the multihued concentric circles seen in *Homage to Blériot*. While Delaunay's color theory was derived

from that of the nineteenth-century color theorist Michel-Eugène Chevreul (see page 874), his move into total abstraction was prompted by his contact with Marc and Kandinsky, who included him in the first Blaue Reiter exhibition. Some of these abstract paintings contain overlapping circles, suggesting a relationship among spheres in space, a reading reinforced by the subtitle *Sun and Moon*. The critic Guillaume Apollinaire, in his review of the 1913 Salon des Indépendants, even drew a parallel between Delaunay's paintings of simultaneous disks and music when he labeled his abstract work "Orphism," a reference to the mythological lyre player Orpheus. But despite numerous parallels with Kandinsky, Delaunay's interests lay in depicting modernity and using an abstract vocabulary of simultaneous contrasts of color to create space, light, and movement, especially the fast tempo of a modern world of trains, planes, automobiles, electricity, telephones, and movies.

Italian Futurism: The Visualization of Movement and Energy

In January 1909, Filippo Tommaso Marinetti (1876–1944), a free-verse poet based in Milan, launched the Futurist movement when he published his *Manifesto of Futurism*, a pamphlet sent to thousands of artists and poets. On February 20, it appeared on the front page of the Parisian newspaper *Le Figaro*. Marinetti called for a rebirth of Italy, a country he saw as mired in the dusty, anachronistic Classical past. He advocated an uncompromising acceptance of modernity in all its manifestations, including electricity, automobiles, and machines, writing that "all subjects previously used must be swept aside in order to express our whirling life of steel, of pride, of fever and of speed." (See www.myartslab.com.)

For Marinetti, Futurism was a continual process, a permanent revolution. As soon as one change is effected, a new one must begin. Artists were no longer the manufacturers of a high-end product for a wealthy clientele, but rather they were vital forces operating within the community and influencing such daily concerns as fashion, games, toys, graphics, interior design, sports, food, and behavior. Marinetti toured Italy, enrolling artists, musicians, playwrights, architects, and designers into his movement. He arranged Futurist *soirées*, where from a stage he expounded upon his theories, often provoking, if not insulting, the audience in his attempt to incite them to action or even violence, which Marinetti perceived as socially cleansing and productive. Marinetti was intent on generating constant activism, which he saw as the conduit for the cultural *risorgimento*, or rebirth, of Italy.

After a 1909 lecture in Milan presented to the avant-garde art group Famiglia Artistica (Artistic Family), Marinetti enlisted a handful of its members, including Umberto Boccioni (1882–1916), to become Futurists. In 1909, these artists were mostly Neo-Impressionists who transformed the color and energy of Divisionism to portray the dynamism of modernity. Their manifesto claimed that "Motion and light destroy the materiality of bodies" and that their concern would be the visualization of

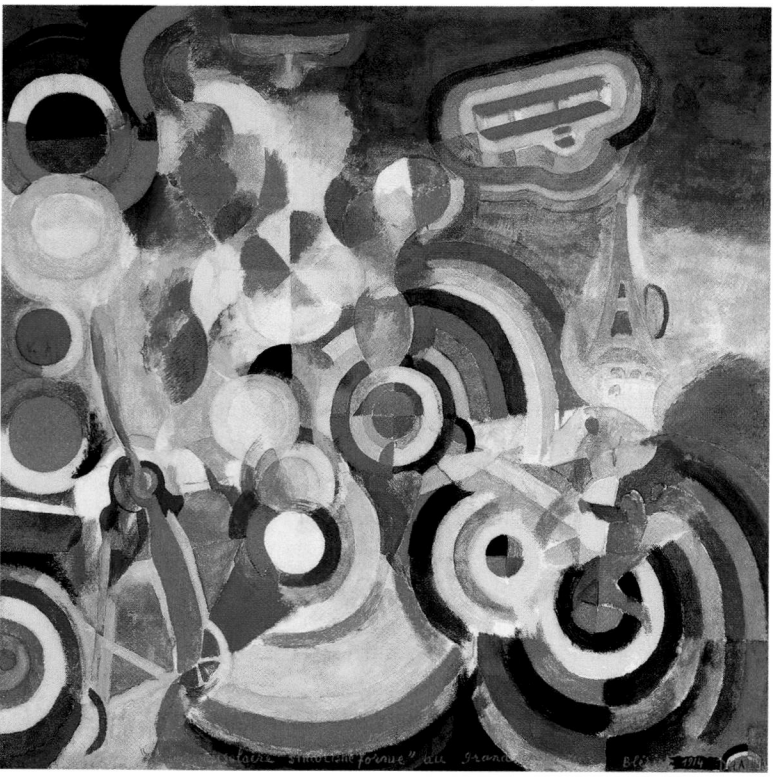

27.19 Robert Delaunay, *Homage to Blériot*. 1914. Tempera on canvas, 8'2½" × 8'3" (2.5 × 2.51 m). Öffentliche Kunstsammlung Basel, Kunstmuseum, Basel, Switzerland. Emanuel Hoffman Foundation. (1962.6)

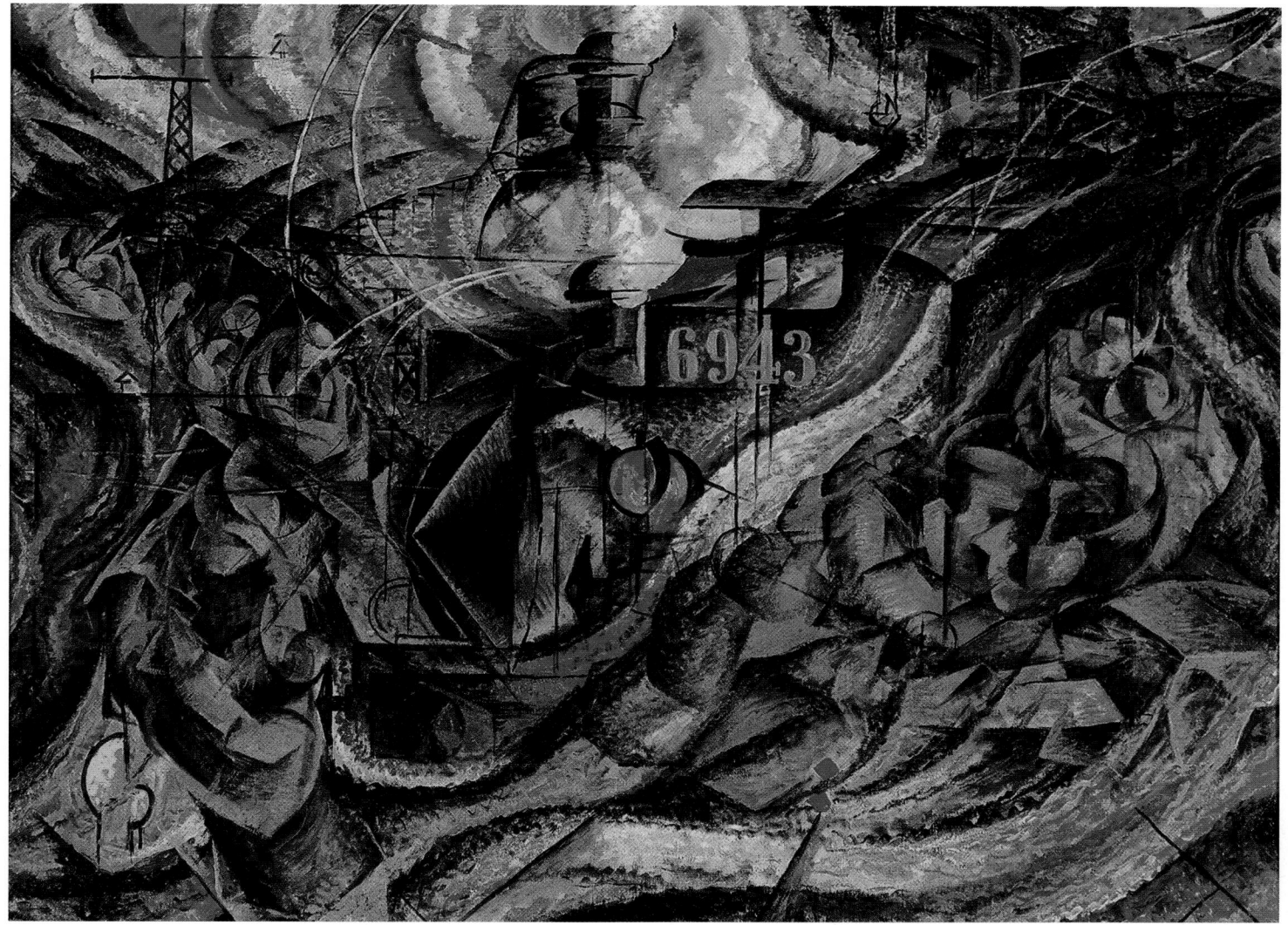

27.20 Umberto Boccioni, *States of Mind I: Farewells*. 1911 (second version). Oil on canvas, 28 × 37⅞" (70.7 × 96 cm). Museum of Modern Art, New York. Gift of Nelson A. Rockefeller

movement and energy. For their visual vocabulary, they rejected anything redolent of Classical Italian culture and instead turned to science: the motion studies of Marey and Muybridge (see page 940), Ernst Mach's graphic representations of shock waves, and Wilhelm Konrad Röentgen's x-rays, which, like Rutherford's discovery of the structure of the atom, proved the physical world was not stable but in constant flux. Much like Seurat, they wanted to create a new artistic language based on science, but without prescribing any one style. Their goal was to capture the intensity of movement—physical, psychological, and universal. In effect, they wanted to visualize Bergson's *élan vital*.

Initially following Marinetti's lead, the Futurists were activists. By the end of 1911, however, they had become disenchanted with Marinetti's politics and instead chose to concentrate on art. More important, they turned from Neo-Impressionism to Cubism in their search for aesthetic direction. Their interest in Cubism, however, departed from the concerns of Braque and Picasso because the Futurists wanted to convey motion, dynamic energy, and social progress. After visiting Paris and seeing Cubist

works in 1911, Boccioni painted *States of Mind I: Farewells* (fig. **27.20**). Embedded in a fractured world of Cubist facets is an eruption of steam, sound, moving objects, and psychic energy. The white curving lines over the locomotive reflect Mach's lines of thrust, whereas the repetition of the vaguely rendered green-tinted embracing couple is inspired by Muybridge's motion sequences. Boccioni is championing not just modern technology, as represented by the train, electric railroad signals, and trussed steel towers, but the perpetual movement of all objects and energy. In a May 1911 lecture in Rome, he proclaimed that painting had to capture the energy in all matter, energy in perpetual motion that dissolves the object while fusing it with surrounding space, an effect he called "plastic dynamism."

In *States of Mind I: Farewells*, we sense not only the dematerialization of the train and figures through time and movement, in part created by Boccioni's application of Divisionism, but also the simultaneous presence of space as something plastic and as vital as form. Swirling throughout the chaotic image is also an emotional energy—a sense of painful separation and disappearance—which

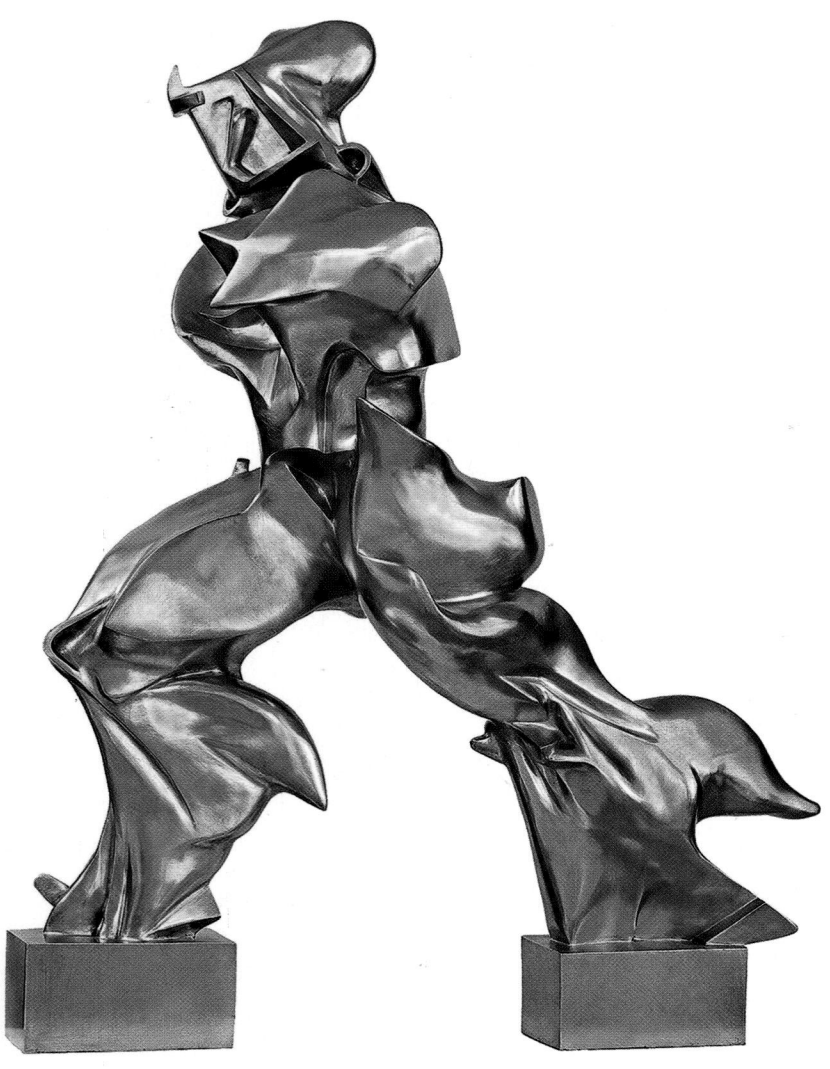

27.21 Umberto Boccioni, *Unique Forms of Continuity in Space*. 1913 (cast 1931). Bronze, 43⅞ × 34⅞ × 15¾" (111.4 × 88.6 × 40 cm). Museum of Modern Art, New York. Acquired through the Lillie P. Bliss Bequest. (231.1948)

the title reveals as a theme of the work. This "plastic dynamism," or the fusing of object and space, is evident in Boccioni's sculpture *Unique Forms of Continuity in Space* (fig. **27.21**) of 1913. The pointed forms trailing off legs and torso capture the direction of the energy, as if the displaced space were itself worn like a mantle.

Cubo-Futurism and Suprematism in Russia

Of all the major European countries in the 1910s, Russia was the least industrialized. Nevertheless, it became an important center for avant-garde art. Most of the population were serfs ruled by an indifferent czar and dominated by the Orthodox Church. Despite a recent rush to modernize and become a world power, Russia in some respects remained trapped in the Middle Ages. In a culture dominated by folk-art and icon-painting traditions, how did radical art emerge? Part of the explanation may lie in the country's desperate need for reform. When, in 1917, the October (or

Bolshevik) Revolution was led by Vladimir Ilyich Lenin (1870–1924), marking the first officially Communist-led revolution of the twentieth century, the change it brought about was far more radical than it had been in eighteenth-century America or France. The transformation in Russia was so revolutionary that it even embraced equality for women, who had proved integral to developing the radical art of the preceding years.

THE RUSSIAN AVANT-GARDE In Moscow, Sergey Shchukin and Ivan Morozov, two of the greatest collectors of contemporary art, made available to Russian artists their extraordinary holdings of works by Matisse and Picasso, among other vanguard artists. In response to these works and to growing ties with the western European avant-garde, Russian artists began to explore Cubism and other approaches to abstraction. In 1910, a group of Russian artists formed an avant-garde art association called the Jack of Diamonds to support exhibitions of experimental work. Two years later, a splinter group, The Donkey's Tail, emerged. The latter especially was modeled on the Futurists. These groups embraced the modern, emphasizing the machine and industry, both critical to bringing Russia into the twentieth century.

One of the outstanding painters in this avant-garde circle was Lyubov Popova (1889–1924), who studied in Paris in 1912 and in Italy in 1914, experiencing first hand the latest developments in Cubism and Futurism. These influences are reflected in *The Traveler* (fig. **27.22**) of 1915. In this depiction of a woman wearing a yellow necklace and holding a green umbrella, Popova combines the fracturing of Cubism with the energy and movement of Futurism.

KAZIMIR MALEVICH By 1913, many of the Russian artists were calling themselves Cubo-Futurists, a term coined by Kazimir Malevich (1878–1935) that reflects the dual origins of the style. Malevich had exhibited with both the Jack of Diamonds and The Donkey's Tail. In 1913, he designed Cubo-Futurist costumes and sets for what was hyped as the "First Futurist Opera" and titled *Victory over the Sun*. Presented in St. Petersburg, this radical "opera" embraced the principle of *zaum*, a term invented by progressive Russian poets. Essentially, *zaum* was a language based on invented words and syntax, the meaning of which was supposedly implicit in the basic sounds and patterns of speech. The poets' intention was to return to the nonrational and primitive base of language that, unencumbered by conventional meaning, expressed the essence of human experience. In *Victory over the Sun*, performers read from nonnarrative texts often consisting of invented words while being accompanied by the clatter of an out-of-tune piano. Malevich's geometric costumes and sets were equally abstract. A stack of triangles ran up and down the legs of one costume, while one backdrop was a square divided in half to form two triangles, one white, the other black.

27.22 Lyubov Popova, *The Traveler*. 1915. Oil on canvas, 56 × 41½" (142.2 × 105.4 cm). Norton Simon Art Foundation, Pasadena, California

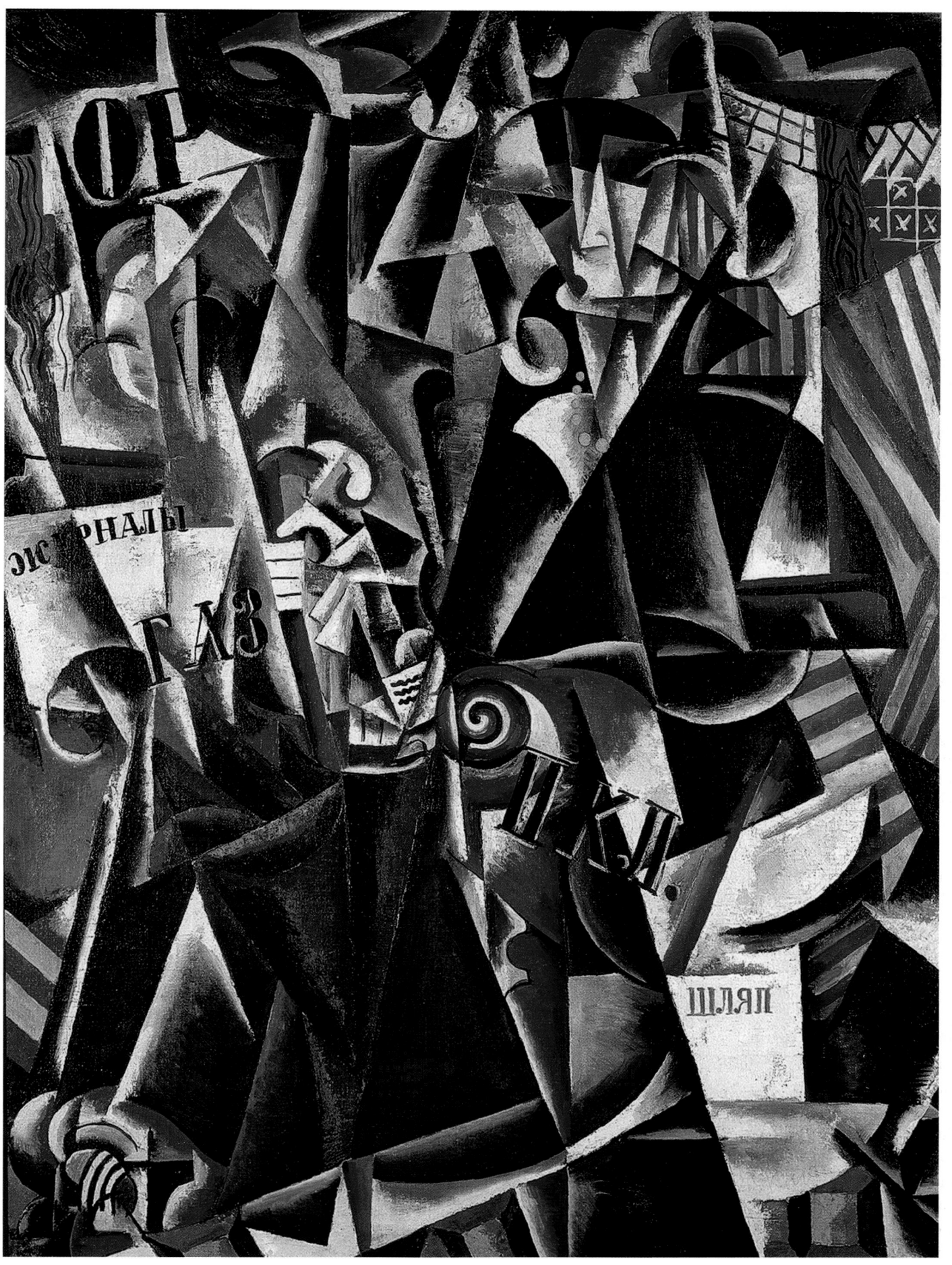

Kazimir Malevich (1878–1935)

From *The Non-Objective World*

Kazimir Malevich first published The Non-Objective World *in 1919 in the catalogue for the 10th State Exhibition in Moscow. Here, he emphasizes how nonobjective art represents feeling, not objects, as it strips away all of the accumulations of civilization to get at the essence of existence, much as so-called primitive artists do.*

Under Supremitism I understand the supremacy of pure feeling in creating art. ...

Hence, to the Suprematist, the appropriate means of representation is always the one which gives fullest possible expression to feeling as such and which ignores the familiar appearance of objects. ...

Even I was gripped by a kind of timidity bordering on fear when it came to leaving "the world of will and idea," in which I had lived and worked and in the reality of which I had believed.

But a blissful sense of liberating non-objectivity drew me forth into the "desert," where nothing is real except feeling ... and so feeling became the substance of my life.

This was no "empty square" [referring to the *Black Square*] which I had exhibited but rather the feeling of non-objectivity. ...

The black square on the white field was the first form in which non-objective feeling came to be expressed. The square = feeling, the white field = the void beyond this feeling. ...

The Suprematist square and the forms proceeding out of it can be likened to the primitive marks (symbols) of aboriginal man which represented, in their combinations, *not ornament but a feeling of rhythm.*

Suprematism did not bring into being a new world of feeling, but, rather, an altogether new and direct form of representation of the world of feeling.

Source: Kazimir Malevich, *The Non-Objective World*, tr. Howard Dearstyne (Chicago: Theobald, 1959)

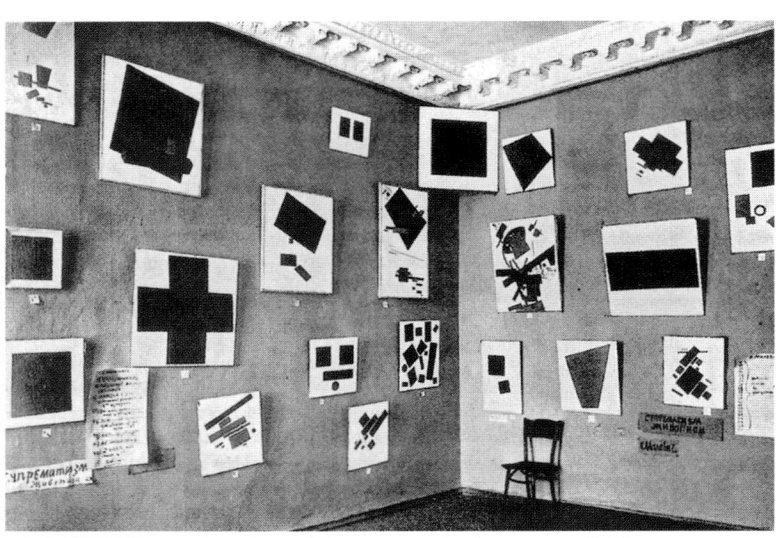

27.23   Kazimir Malevich. Installation photograph of the artist's paintings in *0, 10 (Zero–Ten): The Last Futurist Exhibition*. St. Petersburg, December 1915

It took Malevich two years to realize the implications of *zaum* for his art. In 1915, after working in a Cubo-Futurist style similar to Popova's, Malevich presented 39 nonobjective geometric paintings in a St. Petersburg exhibition entitled *0, 10 (Zero–Ten): The Last Futurist Exhibition* (fig. **27.23**). The best-known work in the show is *Black Square*, seen in the installation photograph hanging in the manner of a Russian icon across the corner of a room. Malevich labeled his new work "Suprematism." In his 1919 Suprematist treatise *The Non-Objective World*, Malevich explained that Suprematism refers to the supremacy of feeling. (See *Primary Source*, above.) This feeling is not just personal or emotional but revelatory, for the abstract essence of the world is

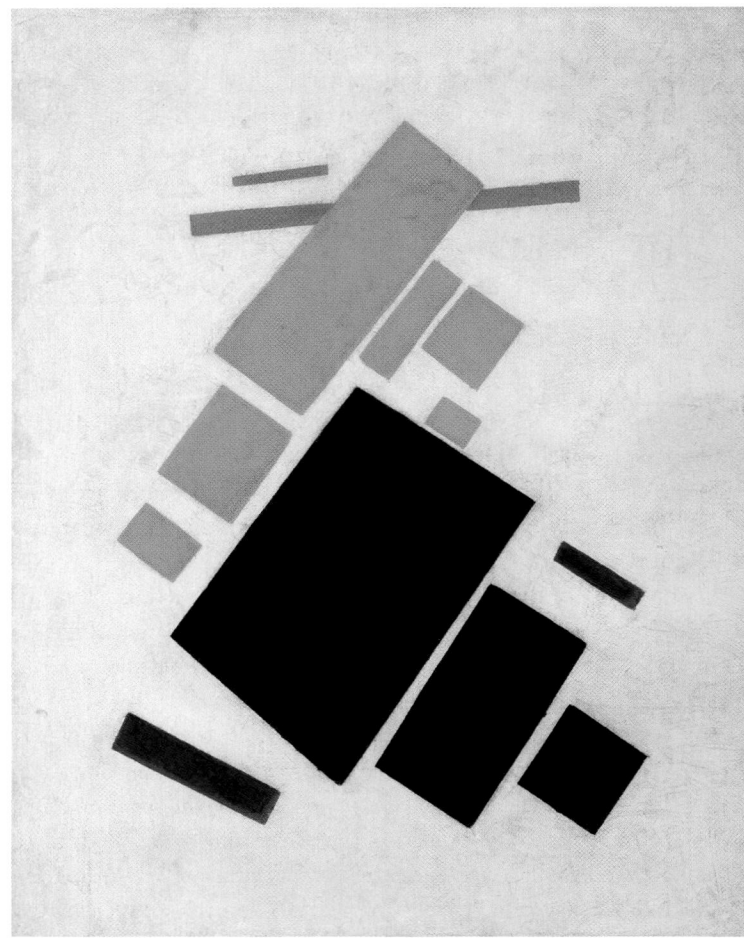

27.24   Kazimir Malevich, *Suprematist Composition: Airplane Flying.* 1915 (dated 1914). Oil on canvas, 22⅞ × 19" (58 × 48.3 cm). Museum of Modern Art, New York. Purchase. Acquisition confirmed in 1999 by agreement with the Estate of Kazimir Malevich and made possible with the funds from the Mrs. John Hay Whitney Bequest (by exchange). (248.1935)

translated into painting using an entirely new abstract language, stripped of any vestiges of realism. Like his fellow Russian Kandinsky, Malevich was a mystic, searching for cosmic unity, even a utopian world, as did supporters of the Bolshevik Revolution of 1917. *Black Square* embodies both the legacy of simple, otherworldly Russian icons and the mysticism of folk art. Its simple black form is as iconic as a frontal Madonna or saint, with the white ground extending off the four sides and projecting a sense of infinity.

Malevich's abstract language included different geometric shapes and colors. In *Suprematist Composition: Airplane Flying* (fig. **27.24**), also painted in 1915, he used red, yellow, and blue shapes in addition to black to create a sensation of movement and floating. Color, size, and shape produce a unique rhythm against the white ground. From one composition to the next, Malevich altered the rhythm by changing these formal characteristics. Although the title includes the word "airplane" and suggests an infatuation with technology, the image itself relates to the experience of air travel and the new relationship to the universe brought about by this mode of transportation.

Unfortunately, reproductions of Malevich's paintings almost never show their organic quality. The shapes in *Airplane Flying* may appear to be hard-edged, geometric, and machine-made, but in person one can see that their boundaries waver ever so slightly and there is a sense of a human hand applying paint to canvas. Malevich's paintings contain the same human presence, even if not as overtly stated, that is evident in the work of Kandinsky. And like Kandinsky, Malevich, through his white ground which evokes infinity, suggests a connection with the universe.

Cubism and Fantasy: Marc Chagall and Giorgio de Chirico

Malevich reduced Cubist geometry to the point that Cubist structure itself disappeared. Fellow Russian Marc Chagall (1887–1985), however, embraced Cubist composition in many of his works and remained a representational artist. With its ability to juxtapose and integrate the most disparate objects, Cubism was a perfect tool for creating dreamlike fantasy worlds. Chagall grew up in the Jewish quarter of Vitebsk, and his paintings evoke his memories of the simpler times, values, and rituals that he had experienced in the shtetl. In 1910, Chagall moved to Paris, where he immediately converted to Cubism, as seen in *I and the Village* (fig. **27.25**) of the following year. But this dream image is hardly a Cubist intellectual dissection of form. Using the saturated colors of a stained-glass window and the simple shapes of Russian folk art, Chagall conjures up the most elemental issues of life itself. Man and animal are equated in almost mirrorlike symmetry, and the translucent, ephemeral quality of their heads makes the scene appear ethereal and mystical. The circular composition suggests the cycle of life, with birth as the blooming bush and death as the farmer carrying a scythe. Or it could be interpreted as the four seasons. Chagall did not explain his works and adamantly denied they had any links to storytelling or fairy tale.

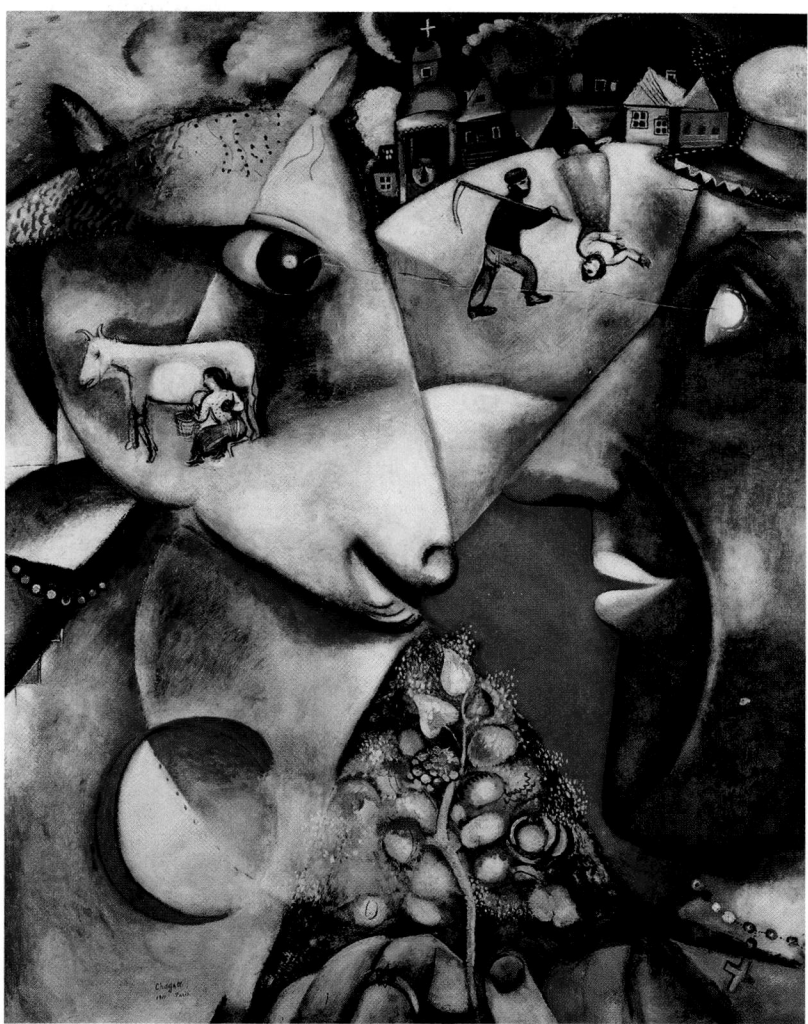

27.25 Marc Chagall, *I and the Village*. 1911. Oil on canvas, 6'3⅝" × 4'11½" (1.92 × 1.51 m). Museum of Modern Art, New York. Mrs. Simon Guggenheim Fund

Instead his dreamscapes are a Cubist kaleidoscope of objects and incidents evoking the most elemental issues of life and often embedded in a wondrous fairy-tale scene that has powerful psychological repercussions.

Arriving in Paris at virtually the same moment as Chagall was the Italian artist Giorgio de Chirico (1888–1978). While studying in Munich from 1905 to 1909, de Chirico was heavily influenced by German Symbolist artists, the Theosophy of Schopenhauer, and the philosophy of Friedrich Nietzsche, who described life as a "foreboding that underneath this reality in which we live and have our being, another and altogether different reality lies concealed." He moved to Italy in 1909, settling in Florence in 1910, where, influenced by the strong southern light of Italy and the arcades of the Piazza Santa Croce, he made the first of his "Metaphysical Town Squares," images of an empty piazza formed by austere buildings rendered as bold simple forms and carefully delineated by strong line. His compositions and use of space became increasingly complex after his arrival in Paris in 1911, as seen in his 1914 *Mystery and Melancholy of a Street* (fig. **27.26**), made after his permanent return to Italy in 1914. His reliance on strong diagonal lines, such as the receding buildings and shadows, and his use of unstable disjointed space make his works vaguely echo Cubism.

And yet de Chirico's pictures are stylistically conventional, even suggesting stage sets. Unlike his Futurist compatriots, de Chirico idolized rather than rejected the Classical past, although he subverted its austere authority by evoking a Romantic melancholy, using ominous shadows, intense light, and skewed perspective to create an unsettling eeriness. In *Mystery and Melancholy of a Street*, railroad tracks, darkened windows and arches, the empty van, and the girl with the hoop seem to be symbols, but de Chirico provides no clues about their meaning, insisting none existed. Instead, the painting offers a dreamscape, one with a poetic mood and wide open to interpretation. De Chirico called his work "Metaphysical Painting," revealing the reality underlying the appearance of things. As we shall see in the next chapter, his psychologically provocative poetic reveries would serve as a springboard for representational Surrealism in the coming decade.

MARCEL DUCHAMP AND THE ADVENT OF AN ART OF IDEAS

Along with Picasso and Matisse, Marcel Duchamp (1887–1968) played a major role in defining the art of the first half of the century, his influence then surging in the second half to the point that he almost singlehandedly molded post-1950 art. His great contribution was declaring that art was as much about ideas, thus residing in the mind, as it was about the beauty of what can be seen, thus of the retina. Realizing that Picasso and Braque, among others, were calling into question the meaning of art as they made the very nature of art visible, Duchamp took their development one step further by looking at the cerebral rather than formalist components of art and calling into question its very status as art by asking: What is art, and how does art function?

Working in Paris in the 1910s, Duchamp quickly digested Impressionism and Post-Impressionism. Toward 1911, he took on Cubism, as seen in *Nude Descending a Staircase, No. 2* (fig. **27.27**), which he attempted to exhibit at the 1912 Salon des Indépendants.

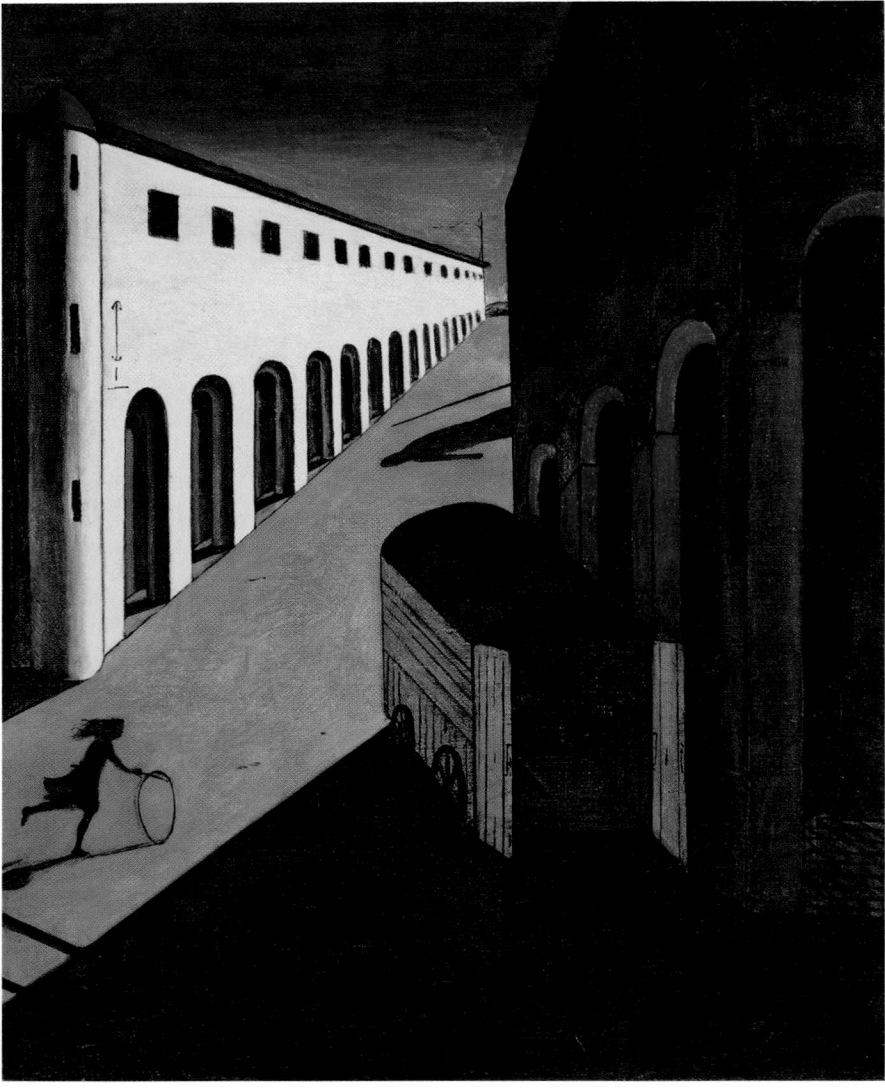

27.26   Giorgio de Chirico,
Mystery and Melancholy of a Street. 1914.
Oil on canvas, 34¼ × 28½" (87 × 72.4 cm).
Private collection

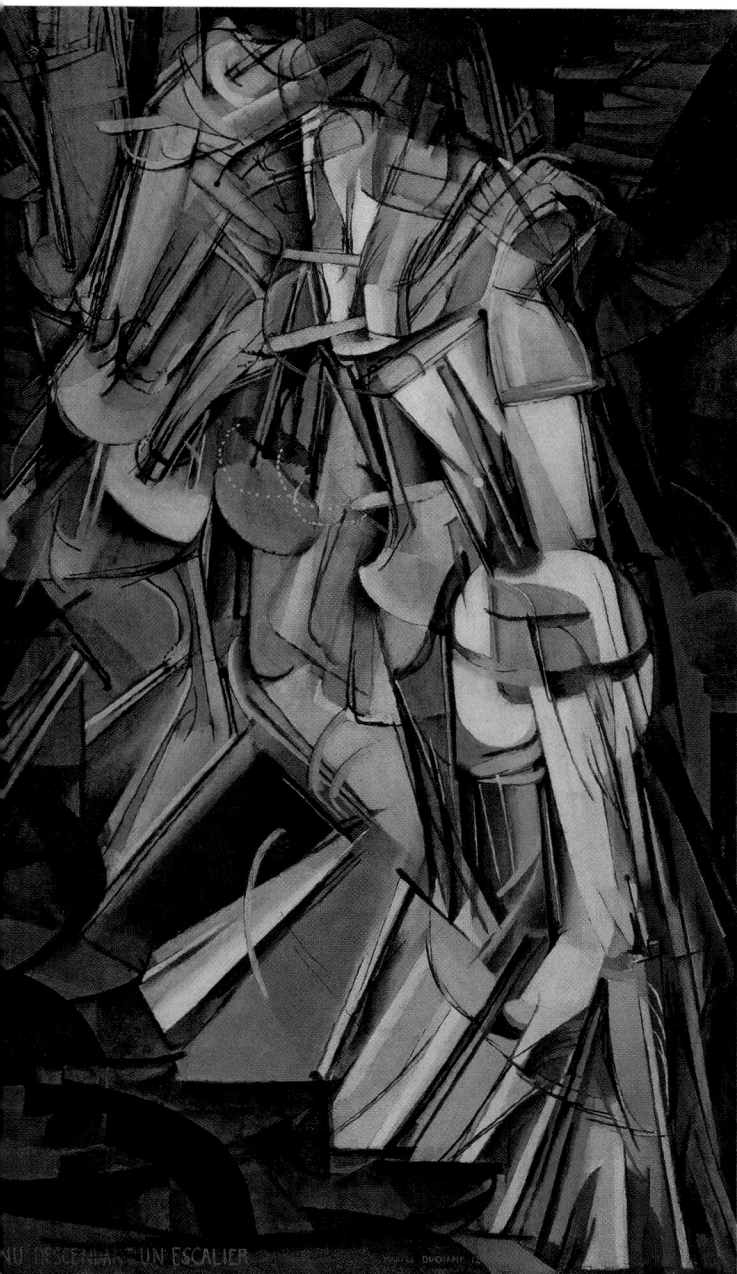

27.27 Marcel Duchamp, *Nude Descending a Staircase, No. 2.* 1912. Oil on canvas, 58 × 35" (147 × 90 cm). Philadelphia Museum of Art. Louise and Walter Arensberg Collection. 1950–134-59

The hanging jury, which included some of his friends and even his two brothers, Raymond Duchamp-Villon and Jacques Villon, found the painting neither serious nor Cubist enough, so Duchamp withdrew it. The work began as an illustration for a poem that described a figure ascending a stairway to the stars. Ever the iconoclast, Duchamp portrayed a nude figure, mechanical-looking and grandly descending a staircase, as he described it, "More majestic you know, the way it's done in music halls." Duchamp was fascinated by Marey's chronophotographs, which inspired the sequential movement of his "nude." Because one needs to know the title to understand that the figure is unclothed,

Duchamp underscores the way in which words become an integral part of an artwork, going so far as to paint the title on the front of the work. With this gesture, Duchamp makes an important move in his exploration of the essence of art. A title, which defines a work, circumscribes its meaning, and also serves as a tool for remembering the work, fulfilling a role as important as the artwork itself. Here, then, Duchamp makes plain the inseparability not only of artwork and title, but of visual and linguistic experience.

Duchamp's machinelike figure was not unique for 1912. By then, the theme was becoming commonplace in Cubist art, reflecting the era's worship of technology as a symbol of modernity and science's ability to improve the world. For example, Duchamp's older brother, Raymond Duchamp-Villon (1876–1918), was a Cubist sculptor who on occasion rendered living forms as machines, as in *Horse* (fig. **27.28**). Initial drawings show a realistic horse, but the final sculpture is an abstract monument to horsepower: The body has become a tapering cylinder with the tension of a coiled spring, and the legs look like thrusting pistons. Cubist facets and geometry have been ordered into an animal of twisting dynamism. Duchamp-Villon's horse, like most other mechanomorphic figures from the period, underscores the import role of industry in fashioning the modern age. In contrast, Marcel Duchamp's mechanical nude is humorous, sarcastic, and sacrilegious.

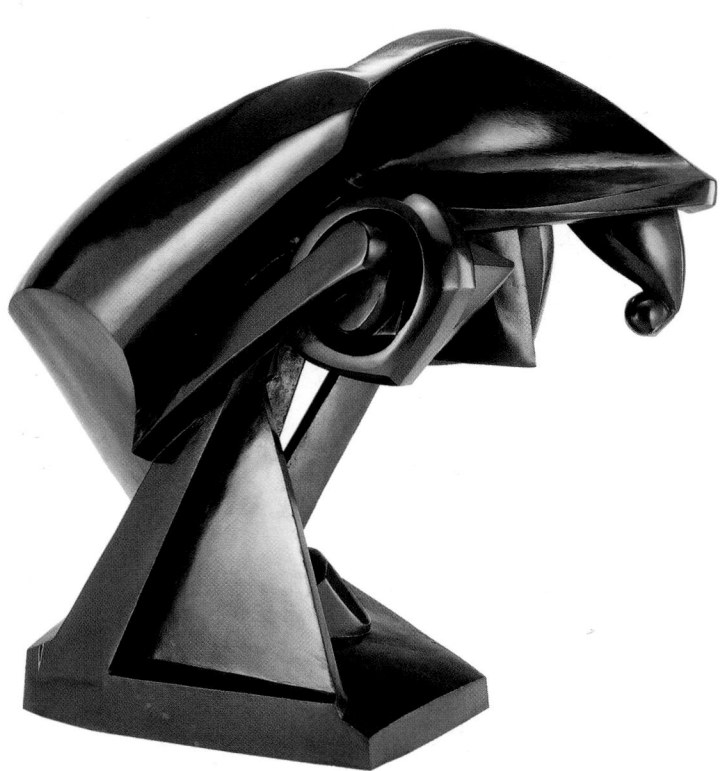

27.28 Raymond Duchamp-Villon, *Horse.* 1914 original, 1955–57 version from an edition of seven. Bronze, 39 × 24 × 36" (99 × 61 × 91.4 cm). The Art Institute of Chicago. Gift of Margaret Fisher in memory of her parents, Mr. and Mrs. Walter L. Fisher. (1957.165)

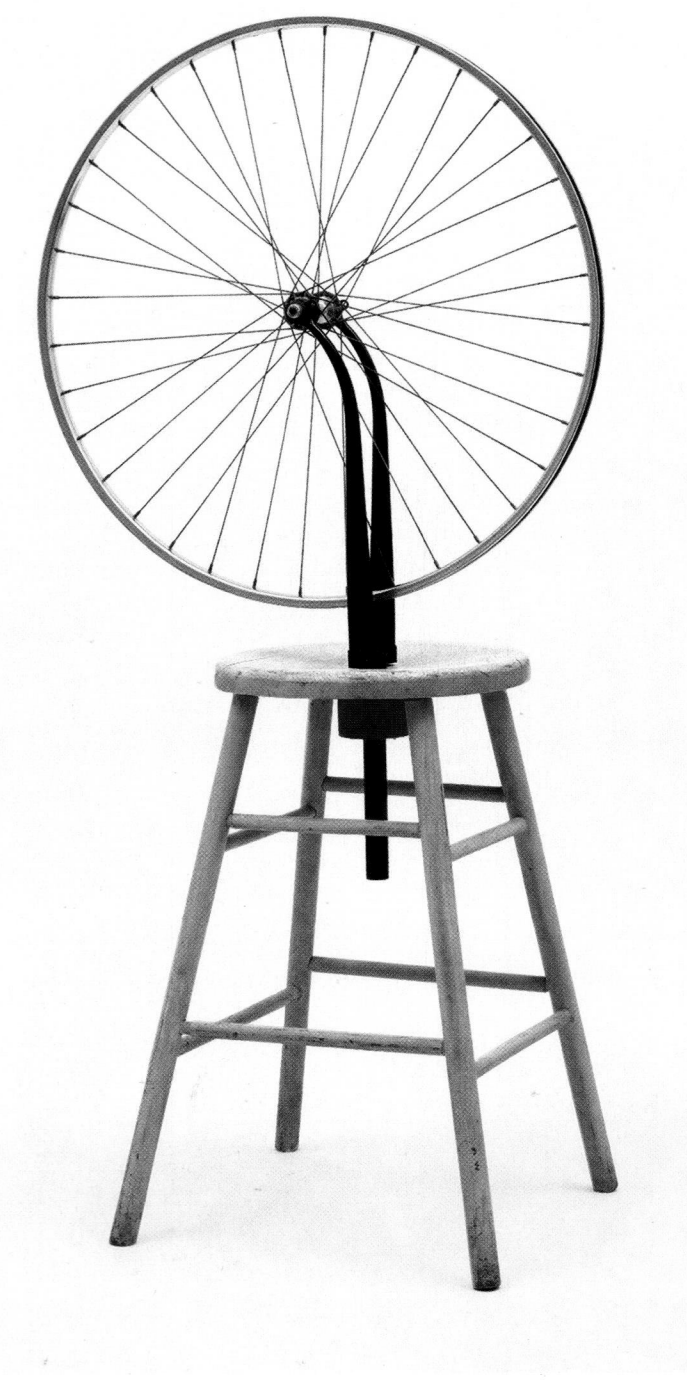

later labeled his sculpture an "Assisted **Readymade,**" because he had combined two found objects—a witty challenge to the notion that art involved only technical skill and craft. As important, he demonstrated that context determines the meaning of art, since by uniting these disparate objects, taking each out of its normal context and putting it in a new one, he gave each component of his sculpture a new meaning. Actually, *Bicycle Wheel* is so enigmatic it provokes wild interpretations, demonstrating that the meaning of a work of art also comes from viewers who bring their experiences to bear on the work. To an art historian, for example, the stool may suggest a pedestal and the wheel a head, an interpretation that can be seen as a clever engagement with artistic tradition, evoking the countless sculpted portrait busts that line museum galleries. A cyclist or a barfly most likely would come up with an entirely different scenario for the piece.

Duchamp was adamant that his Assisted Readymades had no aesthetic value. The act of combining stool and wheel, placing each in a new context, was more important to him than the resulting object. Duchamp made two other Assisted Readymades prior to World War I; none was exhibited. Only during the war years was his revolution fully unleashed on the art world, as we shall see in the next chapter (see page 986). But it is important to introduce Duchamp as prewar artist, for although he became a major figure in the Dada movement, which arose in large part as a reaction to World War I, it must be understood that his revolutionary art was not initially made as a political and social statement but rather as an artistic one that came on the heals of the investigations of Picasso and Braque.

CONSTANTIN BRANCUSI AND THE BIRTH OF MODERNIST SCULPTURE

Like Picasso's constructions and Duchamp's "Assisted Readymades," the sculptures of Constantin Brancusi (1876–1957) were among the most innovative artworks being produced before the war. Indeed, Brancusi's work is so minimal-looking and abstract it has come to symbolize modern sculpture itself. Ironically, Brancusi's background could not have been more removed from the modern world. The son of Romanian peasants, he grew up herding sheep in the remote village of Tîrju-Jiu in the Carpathian mountains. The region had a long tradition of ornate folk carving, in which Brancusi excelled. After studying art in Bucharest and passing through Munich in 1903, he settled in Paris and became an assistant to Auguste Rodin. Declaring that "Nothing can grow under big trees," he struck out on his own.

Escaping the far-reaching shadow of Rodin, an artist with strong ties to nineteenth-century art, Brancusi steered a radical course that, aesthetically if not thematically broke, with sculptural tradition and laid a foundation for much twentieth-century sculpture. Brancusi's mature style began to evolve as early as 1907, and by 1910 it had reached a minimal essence, as seen in *The Newborn* (fig. **27.30**) of 1915. Here, he reduces his subject to an ovoid resembling an egg, which suggests fertility and birth. The

27.29 Marcel Duchamp, *Bicycle Wheel.* 1913/1951 (third version, after lost original of 1913). Assemblage: metal wheel mounted on painted wood stool, 50½ × 25½ × 16⅝" (128.3 × 64.8 × 42.2 cm). Museum of Modern Art, New York. The Sidney and Harriet Janis Collection. 595.1967 a-b

The following year Marcel Duchamp's humorous inquiry into the nature of art culminated in a revolution as monumental as Picasso's *Les Demoiselles d'Avignon.* Duchamp placed a bicycle wheel upside down on a stool (fig. **27.29**) and declared it art. He

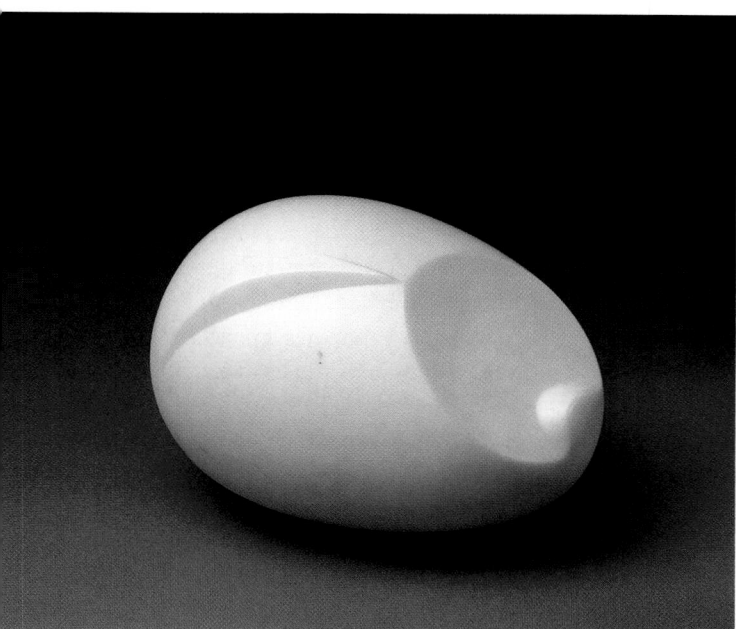

27.30 Constantin Brancusi, *The Newborn*. 1915. Marble, 5¾ × 8¼ × 5⅞" (14.6 × 20.9 × 14.9 cm). Philadelphia Museum of Art. Louise and Walter Arensberg Collection. 1950–134-10

form also resembles a head, with the concave depression as the mouth releasing its first cry and the slender triangular piercing as the nose. Yet the whole is so abstract that we are left with a sense of the simple form of the marble, which seems to harbor the hidden mysteries of life. The work has the elemental power of the Cycladic sculpture (see pages 82–84) and simplified, geometric African masks that Brancusi, like Picasso and Matisse, knew so well. Brancusi understood that by using a minimalist vocabulary, he was able to shed in works like *The Newborn* the clutter of visual reality to pursue invisible essential truths that revealed the very core of existence. As Brancusi explained, "Simplicity is not an end in art, but one arrives at simplicity in spite of oneself in approaching the real sense of things." His works evoke an essence of perfection, as though the scale, the smooth unblemished surfaced, and the composition are so precise that they cannot be altered one iota without destroying their purity and the sense that they capture a primordial reality underlying all life.

Brancusi's sculpture focuses on only a handful of themes, which he repeated numerous times, often in different mediums, including bronze, wood, stainless steel, and stone of different kinds. The shift in medium allowed Brancusi to explore both the visual and psychological associations of his material. His meticulous control over his work included designing the bases and pedestals, as can be seen in *Bird in Space* (fig. **27.31**), where the

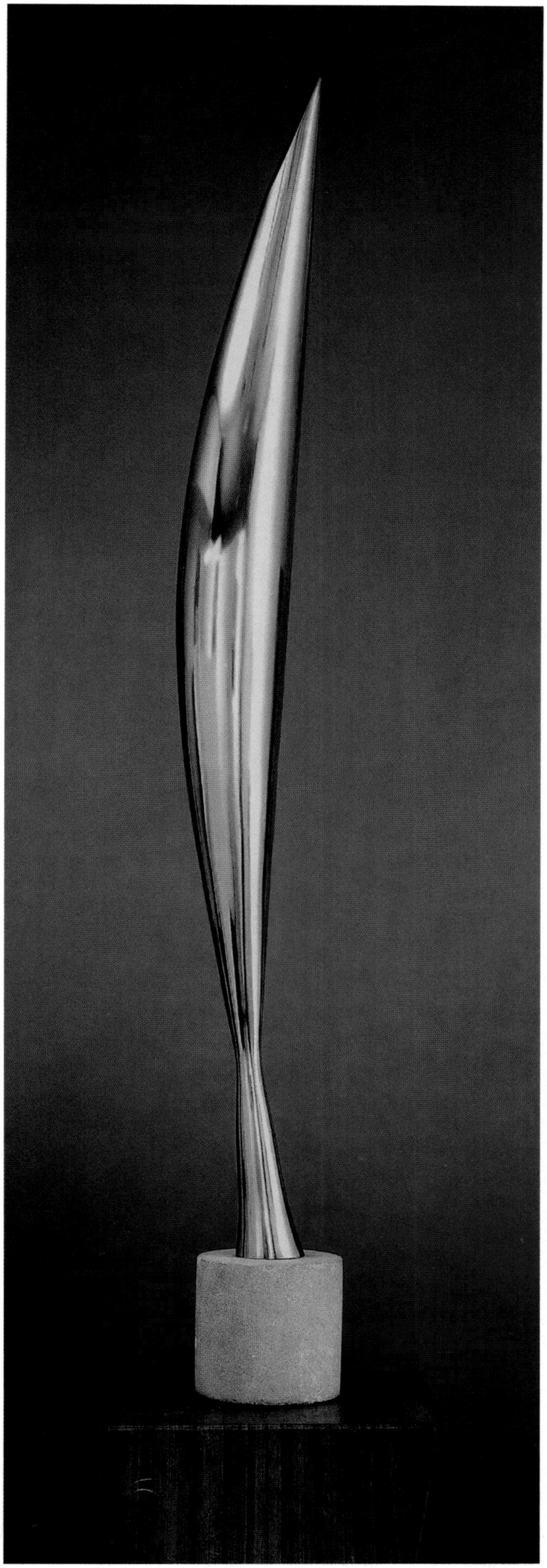

27.31 Constantin Brancusi, *Bird in Space*. 1928 (unique cast). Bronze, 54 × 8½ × 6½" (137.2 × 21.6 × 16.5 cm). Museum of Modern Art, New York. Given anonymously

sculpture includes the cylindrical stone base and the hourglass-shaped wood pedestal. This stacked system of presentation has the effect of distancing the sculpture from the space of the room and placing it within its own perfect world. Brancusi also realized the height of the presentation of his sculpture affected a viewer's physical and psychological relationship to it, and thus reading of it. Brancusi insisted, for example, that *The Newborn* be exhibited on a low pedestal, forcing a viewer to lean over the piece, placing his viewers in the position of an adult looking down at an infant in a cradle. In contrast, *Bird in Space* would be presented very high, like a soaring bird.

Brancusi introduced the bird motif as early as 1910. *Maiastra* was based on Romanian legends about a magical golden bird whose song held miraculous powers. By the 1920s, Brancusi showed the same bird soaring, as in *Bird in Space*, instead of perched. The elegantly streamlined form balances on a short, tapering column, the pinched section suggesting the juncture of legs and body. But of course we do not really see a bird. Instead Brancusi has presented us with the spirit of flight, as suggested by the smooth streamlined form that seems to gracefully and effortlessly cut through the air. Using an entirely different vocabulary, Brancusi, like Malevich, sought to reveal "the real sense of things."

AMERICAN ART

Modernism did not come to America until the second decade of the twentieth century. It first appeared in New York at "291," the nickname for the Little Galleries of the Photo Secession, the progressive art gallery owned by Alfred Stieglitz (see page 936). Beginning in 1909, Stieglitz started featuring such seminal Modernists as Picasso, Matisse, Henri Rousseau, Rodin, and Brancusi as well as African art and children's art. The key breakthrough Modernist event in New York was the 1913 *International Exhibition of Modern Art*, known as the Armory Show after the 26th Street armory where it was held. Exhibited were over 400 European works, mostly French, from Delacroix, through Courbet, Monet, Gauguin, Van Gogh, and Cézanne, to Picasso, Brancusi, and Matisse. Three times as many American artists were represented, but by comparison their work often looked provincial and was largely ignored.

Ruthless newspaper reviews lambasted the radical contemporary French art, and the public came out in droves—75,000 people attended the four-week show. They came especially to ridicule Duchamp's *Nude Descending a Staircase No. 2*, which one reviewer claimed looked like an "explosion in a shingle factory."

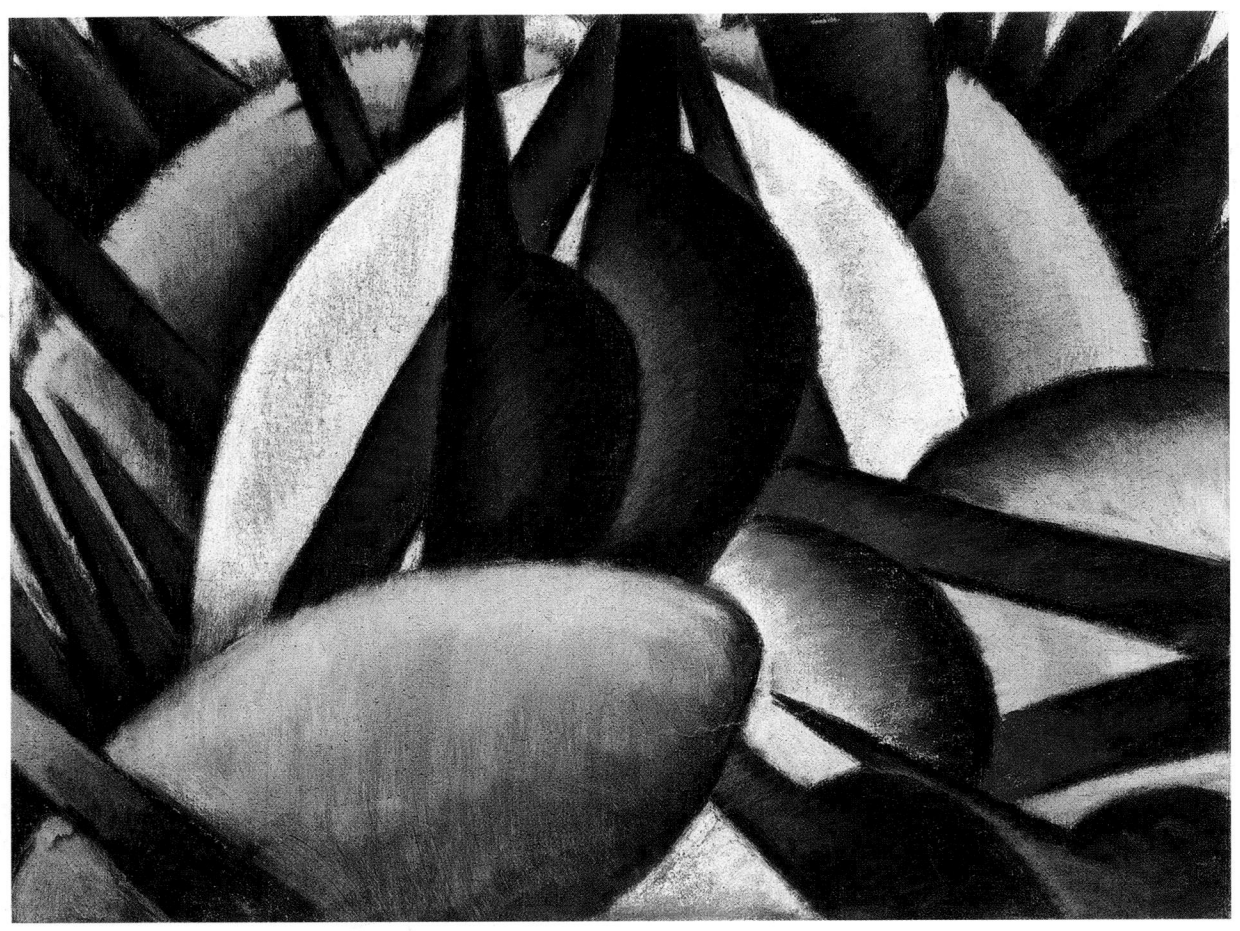

27.32 Arthur Dove, *Plant Forms*. ca. 1912. Pastel on canvas, 17¼ × 23⅞" (43.8 × 60.6 cm). Whitney Museum of American Art, New York. Collection of the Whitney Museum of American Art. Purchase with Funds from Mr. and Mrs. Roy R. Neuberger 51.20

The exhibition's slogan was "The New Spirit," and its symbol was the pine-tree flag of Revolutionary Massachusetts. The American organizers intentionally set out to create their own revolution, to jolt conventional bourgeois taste and bring about an awareness and appreciation of contemporary art. Despite the public's derision, the show spawned several modern art galleries and collectors adventurous enough to dedicate themselves to supporting radical art.

America's First Modernists: Arthur Dove and Marsden Hartley

American artists digested European Modernism almost as quickly as it was made, but those resident in Europe, especially in Paris, absorbed most rapidly the new movements of Fauvism and Cubism. In 1908, a young Arthur Dove (1880–1946) was in Paris, where he saw work by Matisse and the Fauves. When he returned to New York, he met Stieglitz and began showing at "291."

While remaining involved in the New York City art world throughout his life, Dove lived in rural areas in New York State and Connecticut, even spending several years on a houseboat anchored off Long Island. His art focused on nature, not modernity, and capturing universal forces. By 1910, he was painting complete abstractions, two years before Kandinsky and Delaunay, and this abstraction can be seen in a work from 1912, *Plant Forms* (fig. **27.32**), from a series of pastels titled *The Ten Commandments*, a title invoking spirituality.

In this work, Dove has supplied aspects of nature without painting them illusionistically. As with Cubism, the composition is made up of abstract components, although they overlap in a logical, consistent fashion to suggest continuous recession in space. The work has light and atmosphere as well as an organic quality, largely due to the elliptical, oval, and round forms and the biomorphic shapes suggesting plants and trees. We associate the colors green, ocher, and brown with earth and vegetation, and white and yellow with light. The curved white and yellow forms evoke suns, moons, and hills, and although the frondlike shapes recall plants and trees, they also seem like symbols of an unidentifiable burst of energy. We feel the powerful surge of nature and an elemental life force, and because each form suggests many different objects, Dove is able to convey the universal interconnectedness of all things. The picture is cosmic in its scope, yet provides an intimate view of nature. Dove's preoccupation with portraying potent natural forces will become a major theme in American art and, as we shall see, one of the major issues for artists in Stieglitz's circle.

Stieglitz's stable of artists also included Marsden Hartley (1877–1943), a Maine native who was making Pointillist paintings of the New England woods when the two met in 1909. In 1912, Hartley set off for Paris, where he became infatuated with the tribal art on view at the Trocadéro Museum, declaring, with an air of Western supremacy, that one "can no longer remain the same in the presence of these mighty children who get so close to the universal idea in their mud-baking." He stated that art had to be

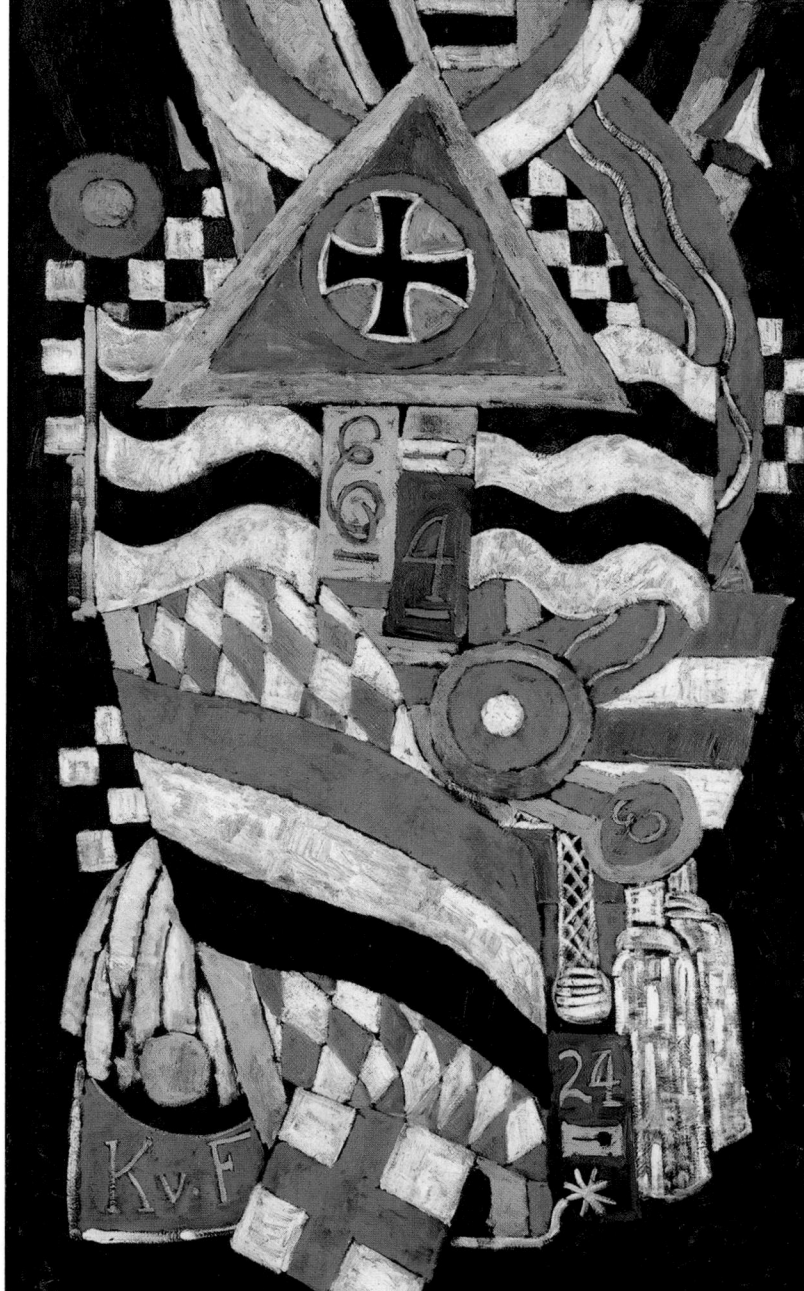

27.33 Marsden Hartley, *Portrait of a German Officer*. 1914. Oil on canvas, 68¼ × 41⅜" (173.4 × 105.1 cm). Metropolitan Museum of Art, New York. The Alfred Stieglitz Collection, 1949. (49.70.42)

"created out of spiritual necessity" and, finding French art superficial and lacking soul, he went to Berlin in 1913. There he read the writings of the great German mystics, such as Jakob Boehme (1575–1624). He then developed a unique form of Synthetic Cubism, which he combined with Fauvist and German Expressionist color to produce paintings filled with spiritual content, as can be seen in *Portrait of a German Officer* (fig. **27.33**), completed in 1914 and later bought by Stieglitz.

This large painting is one in a series dedicated to the memory of Karl von Freyburg, Hartley's lover, who was among the first soldiers killed in World War I. Shown in the painting are such German military paraphernalia as iron crosses, insignia, helmets, boots, service stripes, badges, flags, spurs, and tassels. In a sense, this abstraction is a still life that in spirit recalls Victorian keepsake boxes made for the deceased and containing photographs, clothing, hair, and memorabilia—all pressed under glass. The painting is dominated by a triangle and is filled with circles that reflect Kandinsky's Theosophical belief in the symbolism of geometry. In its jumble of color, form, and composition, *Portrait of a German Officer* expresses a cosmic force similar to Kandinsky's "Compositions" (see fig. 27.14) from the same period, and at times its abstraction seems to suggest landscape almost as readily as it does still life. With the outbreak of World War I, Hartley returned to the United States and to making landscapes, using an Expressionist style that revealed the elemental, spiritual power of nature.

EARLY MODERN ARCHITECTURE IN EUROPE

In Chapter 26, we saw the emergence of two distinct approaches to modern architecture, one in the United States and another in Europe. American artists such as Louis Sullivan and Frank Lloyd Wright challenged historicism and conventional revivalism when they eliminated the distinction between the form of a building and its proposed function. In Europe, we also saw a rejection of revival styles when Art Nouveau defined modern architecture as an organic style of growth and movement. Throughout the twentieth century, modern architecture followed these opposite poles set by the Chicago School and Art Nouveau—the rational, geometric and functional versus the personal, referential, and expressive.

Austrian and German Modernist Architecture

Austria and Germany shaped modern architecture in the opening decades of the century. Charles Rennie Mackintosh, discussed in the previous chapter (see page 930), became the rage in Europe in the 1890s and was particularly idolized in Vienna at the turn of the century by young architects searching for an alternative to Art Nouveau.

ADOLF LOOS An especially influential Viennese architect was Adolf Loos (1870–1933). After graduating from the Dresden College of Technology, Loos traveled to Chicago to attend the 1893 Columbian Exposition and stayed three years, digesting the functionalism of the Midwest architects and especially coming under the spell of Louis Sullivan. Upon returning to Vienna, he designed interiors and wrote for a liberal magazine, in which he railed against the extravagant ornamentation of Art Nouveau. In 1908, he published his functionalist theories in a book titled *Ornament and Crime*. He declared that except for tombs and monuments, buildings should be functional. "Modern man, the

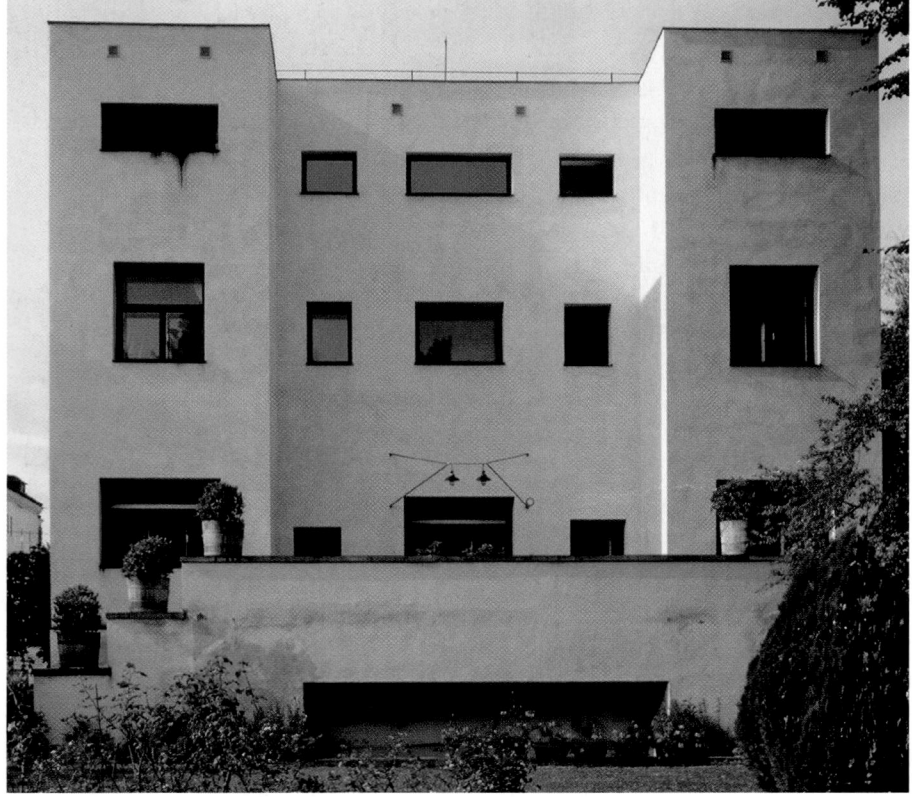

27.34 Adolf Loos. Garden façade of Steiner House, Vienna. 1910

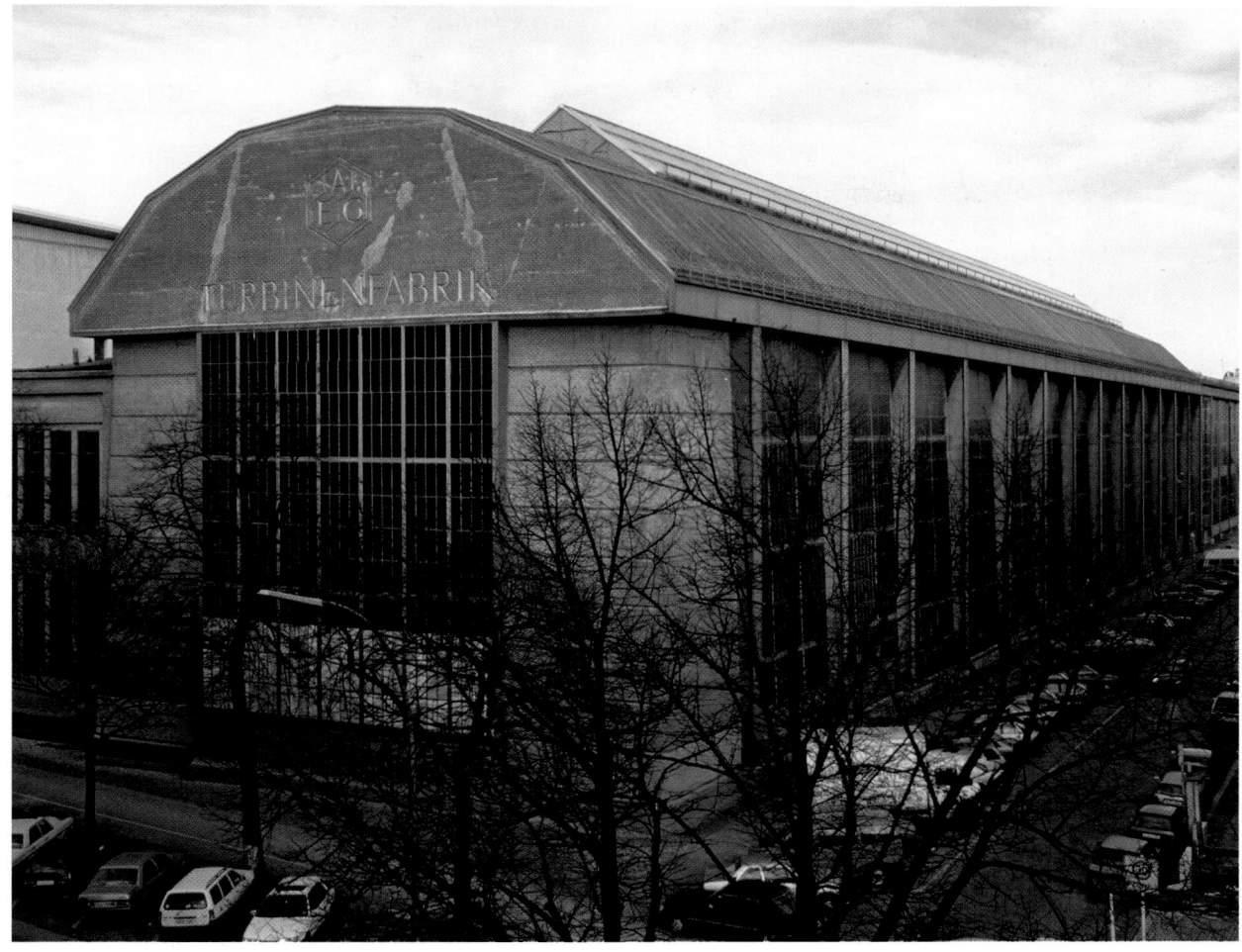

27.35 Peter Behrens. A.E.G. Turbinenfabrik (Turbine Factory), Berlin. 1909–10

man with modern nerves, does not need ornamentation; it disgusts him," he wrote. He even drew a parallel between ornament and scatological graffiti. Furthermore, as a socialist, he found decoration and historicism particularly offensive because of their associations with the wealthy as well as with the oppression of the artisan.

Loos put his theories into practice in the Steiner House (fig. **27.34**) of 1910. In the U-shaped garden façade seen here, Loos used a severe design that emphasizes geometric blocklike components of the structure. Loos's unadorned building even results in the cornice almost disappearing, being reduced to a thin, almost undetectable strip. The windows, especially the horizontal ones, seem more functional than aesthetic. In 1923, Loos migrated to Paris, where, as we shall see, High Modernist architects embraced his antiornamentalism, and viewed his Steiner House as an important model.

HERMANN MUTHESIUS AND PETER BEHRENS In Germany, government and industry nurtured Modernist architecture. In 1896, government officials sent architect Hermann Muthesius to London, then the world leader in quality mass production, to study British industry and design. Upon returning home in 1904, Muthesius was appointed to the Prussian Trade

Commission and given the task of restructuring education in the applied arts. To dominate world markets, he advocated mass production of functional objects executed in a well-designed machine style. In 1907, he was instrumental in establishing the Deutsche Werkbund, an association of architects, designers, writers, and industrialists whose goal was "selecting the best representatives of art, industry, crafts, and trades, and combining all efforts toward high quality in industrial work." In architecture he called for a new monumental style based on Schinkel's Classicism (see page 854), but reflecting modern industrial values, meaning mass production and modular components.

One of Muthesius's appointments to the Werkbund was architect Peter Behrens (1868–1940), who had been head of an applied-arts school in Düsseldorf. Also in 1907, Behrens was named design consultant to A.E.G., the German General Electric Company; he was responsible for the design of their buildings, products, and marketing materials. Between the Werkbund and A.E.G., Behrens had a mandate to implement the German belief in industrialization as its Manifest Destiny, and he was charged with finding a visual expression for the brute reality of industrial power. He accomplished this goal in his finest A.E.G. building, the 1909 Berlin Turbinenfabrik (Turbine Factory) (fig. **27.35**).

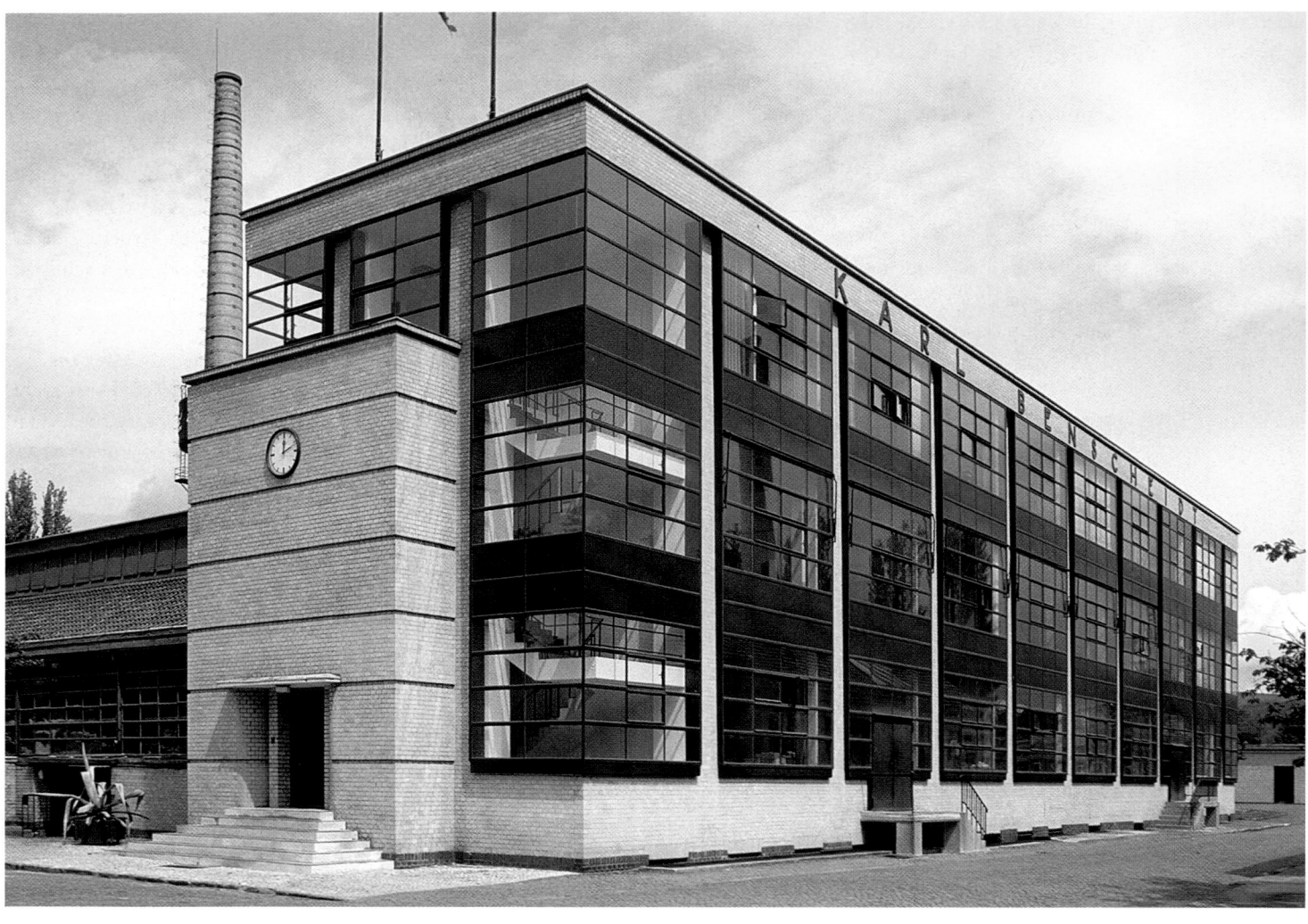

27.36 Walter Gropius and Adolf Meyer. Fagus Factory, Alfeld-an-der-Leine, Germany

This temple to industry is a veritable symbol of industrial might. The enormous main space is constructed of a row of hinged steel arches (their shape echoed in the roofline on the façade) like those used for nineteenth-century ferrovitreous train stations and exhibition halls (see figs. 25.38 and 25.39). Instead of a greenhouse encased in a historical façade, however, Behrens produces an abstract monumental structure that evokes a noble Classical temple and Egyptian entrance gateway. The corners are massive rusticated Egyptian pylons that support an enormous gable, whereas the windows on the side walls are recessed so that the lower portion of the steel arches is exposed, making the row of arches resemble a colonnade. Yet Behrens declares the building's modernity not only in its austere abstract vocabulary but also in the enormous window on the end—an unmistakably Modernist transparent curtain wall that seems to hang from the "pediment."

Although Behrens aggrandized industry in the monumental Turbinenfabrik, he did not produce the machine style that Muthesius was advocating—the *Typisierung*, a type or a basic unit, the equivalent of a mass-produced modular building that could be used by all architects. This machine style would be developed by the three architects in Behrens's office: Walter Gropius, Ludwig Mies van der Rohe, and Le Corbusier.

WALTER GROPIUS Of the architects in Behrens's office in 1910, Walter Gropius (1883–1969) was the most advanced. With associate Adolf Meyer, he was commissioned in 1911 to design the Fagus Factory (fig. **27.36**), a shoe plant in Alfeld-an-der-Leine. Well versed in the achievements of Loos and Behrens, Gropius nonetheless reached back to the Chicago School and utilized their steel-grid skeleton, sheathed in a ferrovitreous curtain wall. The factory's glass façade appears to be magically suspended from the brick-faced entablature above. It even turns corners unobstructed. The building feels light and transparent, the window mullions thin and elegant. Horizontal opaque panels, the exact size and shape of the glass, indicate each of the three floors and continue the modular composition of the windows. The only nod to the past is the prominent Beaux-Arts entrance and the thin pseudo-piers faced in brick that support the entabla-ture. Otherwise, with the Fagus Factory, Gropius created the machine style Muthesius was seeking: an unadorned building that adheres to a grid skeleton. This building type was so efficient and reproducible it would serve as the prototype for the glass-box structures that would dominate world architecture for the rest of the century.

German Expressionist Architecture

Not all German architects embraced technology, the Machine Age, and Muthesius's concept of the *Typisierung*. Some instead designed expressive spiritual structures meant to counter the cold impersonal impact of modernity.

HENRI VAN DE VELDE Another Werkbund architect was Henri van de Velde (1863–1957), a native of Belgium, where he was initially a successful Neo-Impressionist painter and then an Art Nouveau architect and designer. In 1901, he became consultant to the craft industries in the Grand Duchy of Saxe-Weimer. Van de Velde was a strong advocate of Nietzsche's theory of the *Übermensch* and believed in the importance of designing powerful, expressive architecture. He was also heavily influenced by the Munich psychologist Theodor Lipps and his theory of *Einfühlung*, meaning "empathy," the mystical projection of the ego onto the art object. This background led him to examine Wilhelm Worringer's 1908 book *Abstaktion und Einfühlung* (*Abstraction and Empathy*), which advocated attaining transcendence through abstraction as well as championing an aesthetic of emphatic expression of vital psychic states.

On a 1903 trip to Greece and the Middle East, Van de Velde became entranced by the powerful simplicity and purity of Assyrian and Mycenaean buildings (see pages 34–37 and 93–99), which he translated into modern terms in the theater he built for the 1914 Werkbund Exhibition in Cologne (fig. **27.37**). This structure was deliberately designed to counter Mathesius's *Typisierung*, as best represented by Gropius's model factory at the 1914 fair. Despite its massive abstraction, Van de Velde's structure seems like a living organic body rather than a cold, rigid box. Each space within the building is readable from the exterior and has its own identity. Because of the curves, the building seems to swell and breathe. However, this is no longer the springtime effervescence of Art Nouveau; rather, it is a reflection of a need to invest architecture with a spirituality and life force and to enhance these qualities by echoing the powerful monumentality and purity of the forms of ancient Near Eastern civilizations.

BRUNO TAUT A more overt spiritual contribution at the 1914 Werkbund Exhibition was Bruno Taut's (1880–1928) Glass Pavilion (fig. **27.38**), built for the glass industry and reflecting his belief in the mystical properties of crystal. The guru of glass was poet Paul Scheerbart, whose 1914 essay "Glasarchitektur," published in *Der Sturm*, had a tremendous impact on artists and architects. (See www.myartslab.com.) The entablature of Taut's Glass Pavilion is even etched with Scheerbart's aphorisms about the power of glass.

Scheerbart claimed that only a glass architecture that opened all rooms to light could raise German culture to a new spiritual

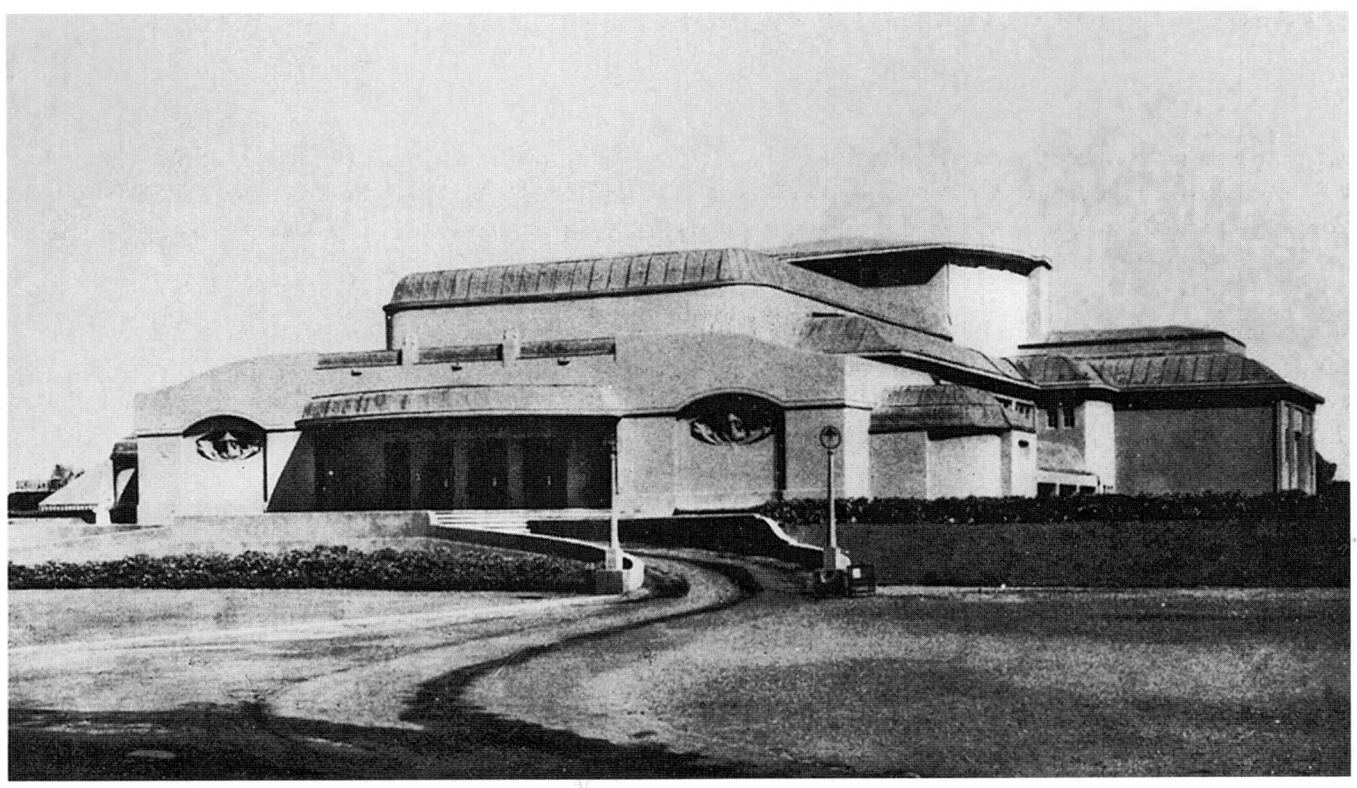

27.37   Henri van de Velde. Werkbund Theater, Cologne. 1913–14. Demolished 1920

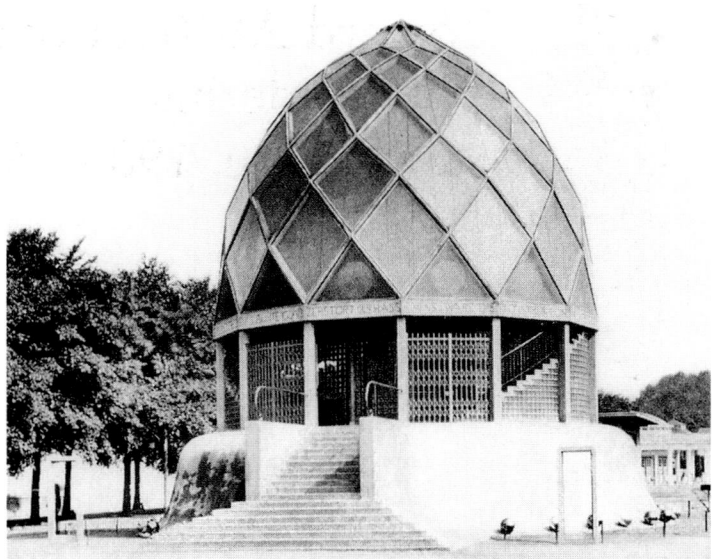

27.38 Bruno Taut. Glass Pavilion, Werkbund Exhibition, Cologne. 1914

main space had a central oculus that emitted a shower of colored spiritual light.

MAX BERG The year before, the mystically inspired architect Max Berg (1870–1947) used a similar ocular motif for his Jahrhunderthalle (Centennial Hall) (fig. **27.39**) in Breslau, erected to celebrate the 100th anniversary of Germany's liberation from Napoleon's rule. Berg's Expressionism is quite Romantic, for the enormous building, made possible by ferroconcrete (steel-reinforced concrete), conjures the sublime grandeur of Piranesi's fantasies of Rome (see fig. 23.3) and Boullée's visionary monuments (see fig. 23.24). (See *Materials and Techniques*, page 1013.) Massive elliptical arches resemble an ancient Roman aqueduct or bridge bent into a circle and springing from the floor. The ribbing of the ceiling recalls the Pantheon, but solid and void have been reversed since the coffered section is now windows, creating an aura of celestial light that makes the dome seem to float. The Pantheon's ocular opening is now closed. At the time, critics likened this dark disk to the iris of an eye, and the entire levitating dome to a giant eyeball connected to the universe. As expressed by one contemporary writer, "the cosmos opened to reveal the courses of the stars and the empyrean."

In 1925, Berg abandoned architecture to dedicate his life to Christian mysticism. But in 1912, when Die Brücke and Der Blaue Reiter were committed to leading Germany into a world of higher spirituality through painting, prints, and drawings, Berg sought to achieve the same in ferroconcrete and glass.

level. Consequently, Taut used glass brick for the walls and floors. The bulbous dome, which resembles a giant crystal, is made of two layers of glass; the outer one reflective, the inner one a myriad of colored-glass pieces resembling medieval stained glass. Taut also considered his cupola to be Gothic, its facets evoking the *élan vital* of the ribbing of the Flamboyant style. The ceiling of the

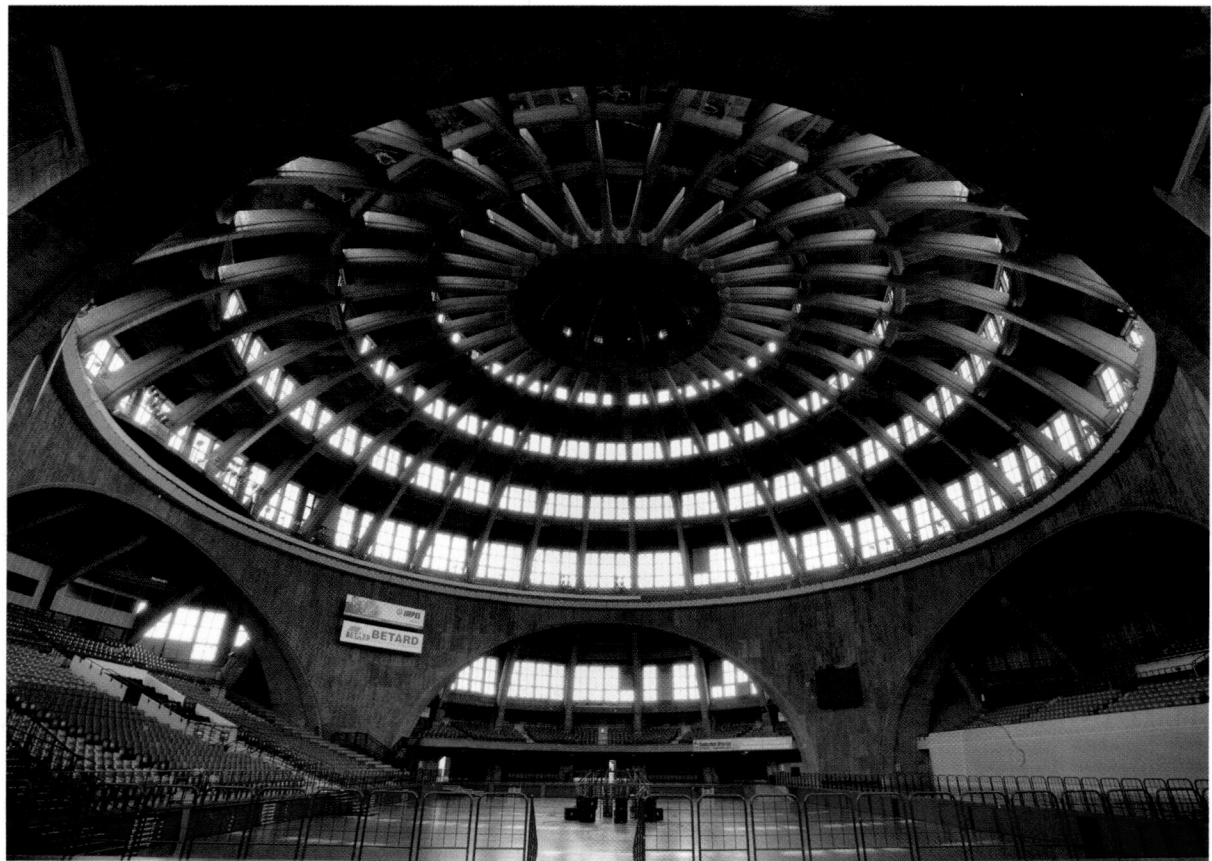

27.39 Max Berg. Interior of the Jahrhunderthalle (Centennial Hall), Breslau, Germany. 1912–13

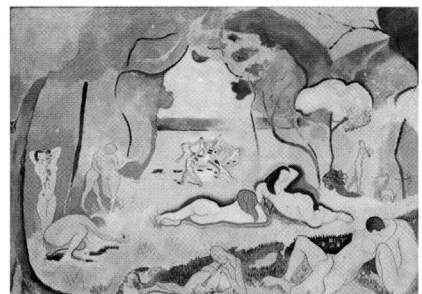
1905-06 Matisse's *Le Bonheur de Vivre*

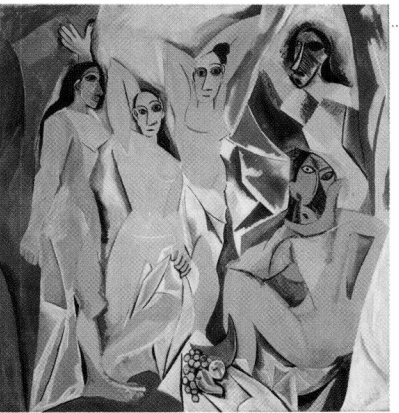
1907 Picasso's *Les Demoiselles d'Avignon*

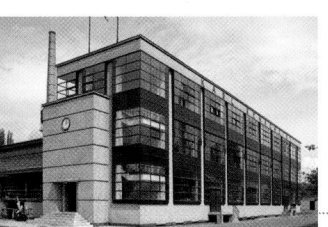
1911-13 The Fagus Factory, designed by Walter Gropius and Adolf Meyer, is erected

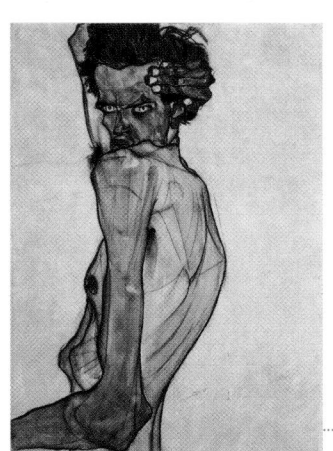
1910 Egon Schiele's *Self-Portrait with Twisted Arm*

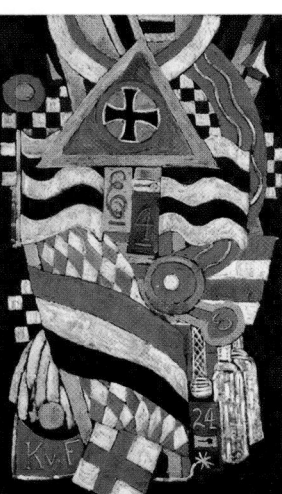
1914 Marsden Hartley's *Portrait of a German Officer*

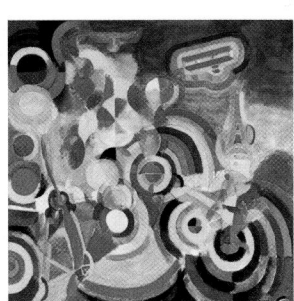
1914 Delaunay's *Homage to Blériot*

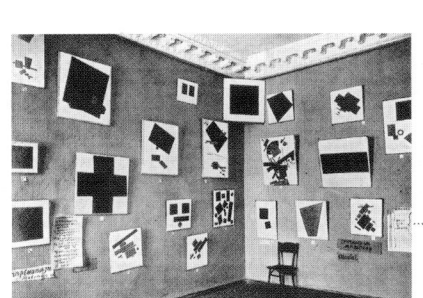
1915 Malevich's *Black Square*

Toward Abstraction: The Modernist Revolution, 1904–1914

1870

1880

1890

1900

1905

1910

1915

◀ 1875 Madame Blavatsky and Henry Steel Olcott found the Theosophical Society in New York

◀ 1900 Sigmund Freud publishes *The Interpretation of Dreams*

◀ 1905-15 Albert Einstein introduces the theory of relativity
1905 Critic Louis Vauxcelles names Fauvism
1905 Die Brücke (The Bridge) formed
1905 Alfred Stieglitz opens his gallery "291"

◀ 1907 Henri Bergson publishes *Creative Evolution*
1907-8 Gustav Klimt, *The Kiss*

◀ 1908 Henry Ford introduces the Model T Ford

1909 Critic Louis Vauxcelles names Cubism
◀ 1909 Filippo Tommaso Marinetti issues a *Manifesto of Futurism*
1909 Louis Blériot flies across the English Channel
◀ 1910 Der Blaue Reiter (The Blue Rider) formed

◀ 1911 Vasily Kandinsky publishes *Concerning the Spiritual in Art*
1912 Picasso creates first collage and the first-known construction
1913 First performance of Igor Stravinsky's *The Rite of Spring*
◀ 1913 Niels Bohr introduces atomic theory
1913 Armory Show in New York City

◀ 1914 James Joyce begins *Ulysses*
1914 World War I begins

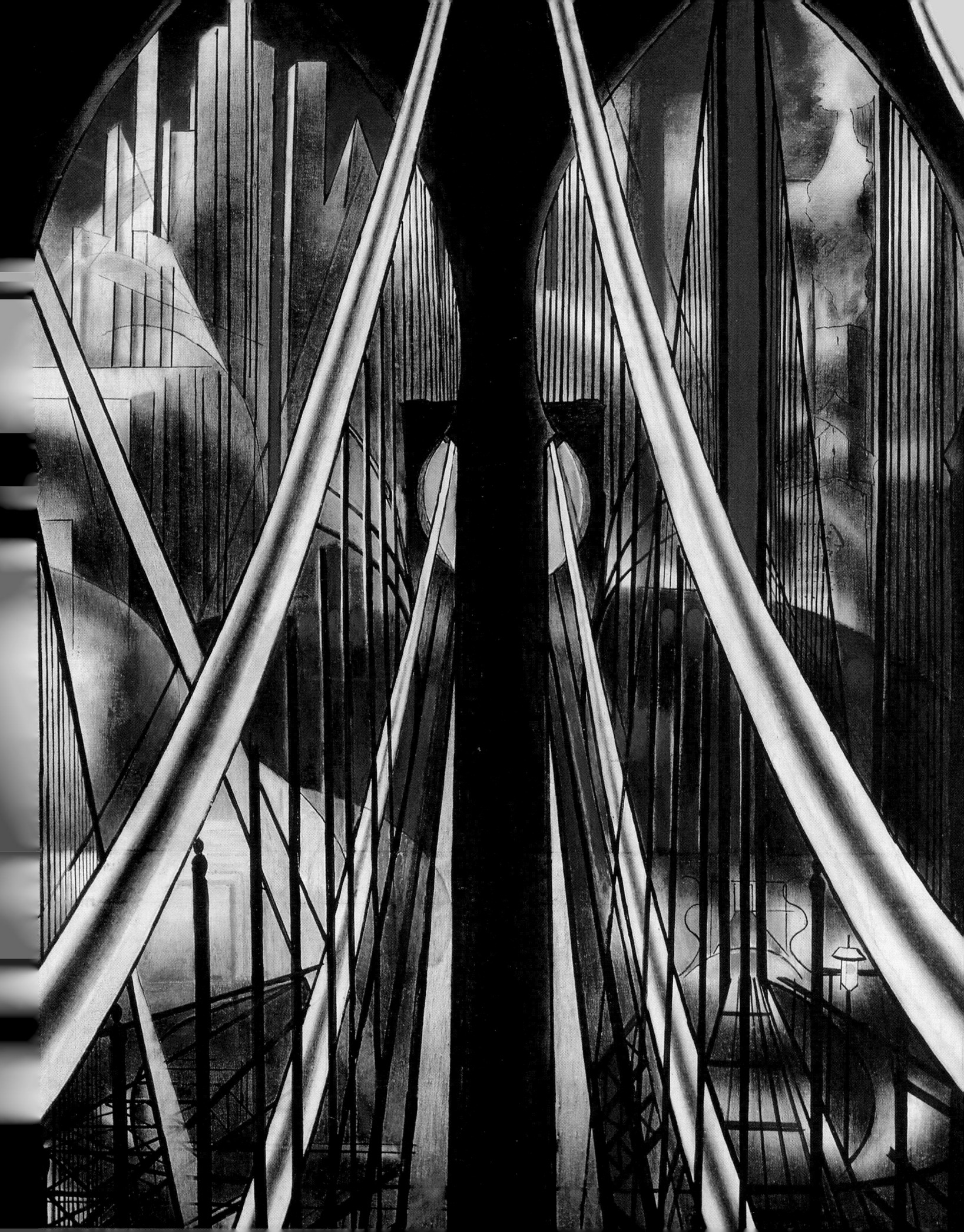

Art Between the Wars

PHYSICALLY AND PSYCHOLOGICALLY, WORLD WAR I DEVASTATED Western civilization. The destruction and loss of life were staggering, with hundreds of thousands of soldiers dying in single battles. The logic, science, and technology that many thought would bring a better world had gone horribly awry. Instead of a better world, the advancements of the nineteenth century

had produced such hi-tech weapons as machine guns, long-range artillery, tanks, submarines, fighter planes, and mustard gas.

To many, the very concept of nationalism now seemed destructive, and the rise of the first Communist government in Russia in 1917 offered some the hope of salvation. Around the world, branches of the Communist Party sprang up, with the goal of creating a nationless world united by the proletariat, the working class that provides the labor force for the capitalist system. Others maintained that a new world order could not be attained without first destroying the old; they advocated anarchy, which remained a constant threat in the postwar decades. Despite this drive to create a nationless and classless world, by the 1930s, it was fascism that had taken hold of European politics. Fascism, a totalitarian political system that exalts the nation over the individual and demands allegiance to a single leader, held a special appeal in nations defeated in World War I. Germany, in particular, had been humiliated by the terms of the Treaty of Versailles, and had suffered extreme inflation and then economic collapse. Germans gradually came under the spell of Adolf Hitler (1889–1945) and the Nazis, who skillfully used economic crises and anti-Semitism to consolidate their power. In Italy, Spain, and Japan, as well, fascists, under the command of charismatic leaders, took control. Armed with new technological tools of

destruction, these nations would plunge the world into another great war by 1939.

While fascism, communism, anarchy, and democracy jockeyed for dominance in Europe, America enjoyed unprecedented prosperity in the 1920s. Historians have called the economic and cultural exuberance of the postwar years the Roaring Twenties; it was a time of jazz, speakeasies, radio, and film. The 1920s also saw the rise of the city as the emblem of the nation. Technology and machines were king in America, where the world's largest skyscrapers could be erected in a year. This economic exhilaration came to a screeching halt with the stock market crash of October 1929, which sent the entire world into a downward economic spiral known as the Great Depression, which lasted throughout the 1930s. A reactionary backlash then occurred in both Europe and America: fascism in the former, and a conservative regionalism and isolationism in the latter. Nonetheless, the 1930s marked the advent in America of liberal social and economic programs, instituted by Franklin Delano Roosevelt's administration (1932–44). Believing that economic markets were inherently unstable, Roosevelt advocated the New Deal, which created millions of government-sponsored jobs, including many for artists.

Perhaps the strongest defining influence for artists between the wars was the Great War itself and the technology, science, and Enlightenment rationalism that allowed it to be so devastating. The war directly produced Dada, a movement that created a nonsensical nihilistic art that attacked bourgeois values and

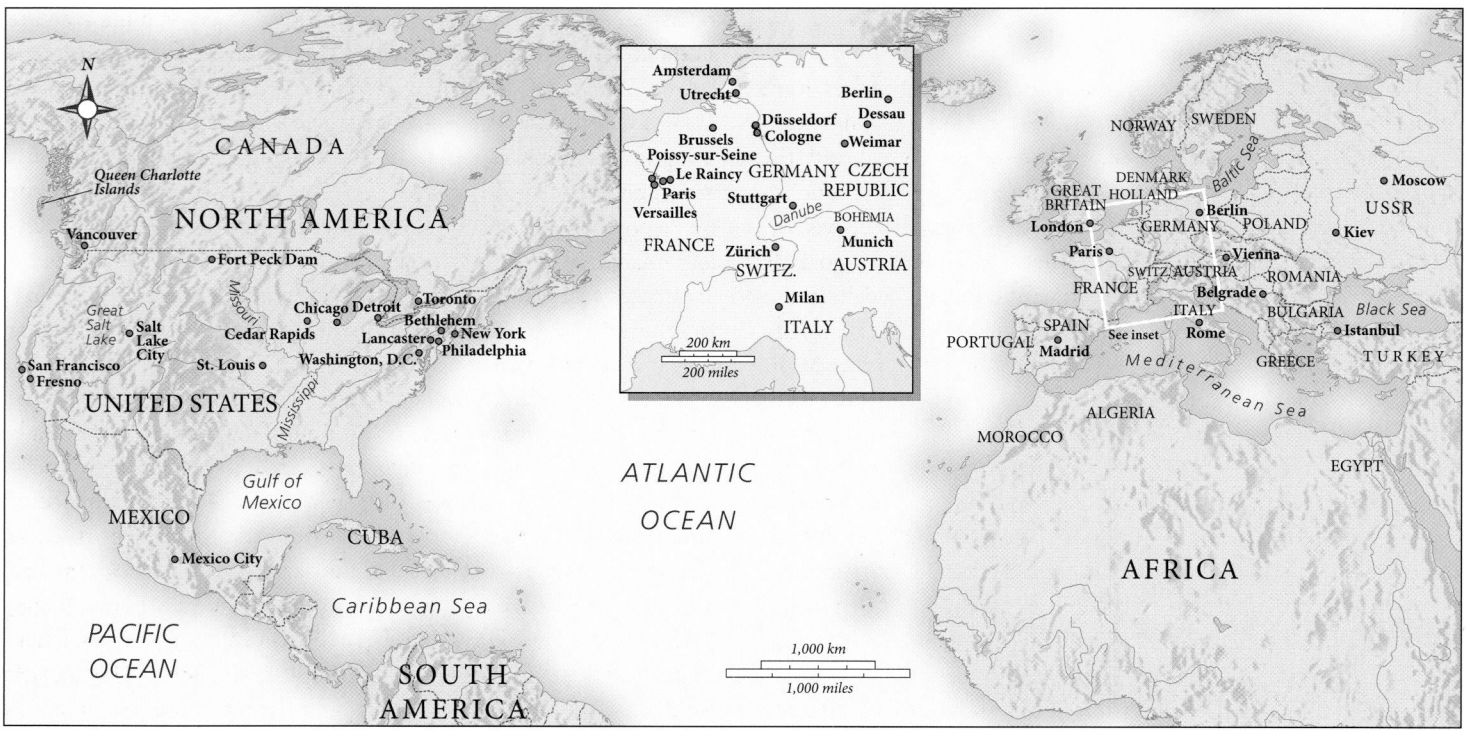

Map 28.1 Europe and North America in the 1920s and 1930s

conventions, including a faith in technology. The Dadaists aimed to wipe the philosophical slate clean, leading the way to a new world order. Other artists embraced the modernity of the Machine Age (as this interwar period is sometimes called), seeing it as a means to create classless utopias; still others rejected it, seeking higher truths or a meaningful spirituality in an increasingly materialistic, soulless world. Both groups often turned to abstraction to implement their vision. Those supporting technology embraced the geometry and mechanical look of the Machine Age, while those who rejected it sought higher truths often using an organic or biomorphic vocabulary.

A second major force for the period was Sigmund Freud, whose theories about the unconscious and dreams were a formative influence on Surrealism, a prevailing movement in the 1920s and 1930s. Like many abstract artists, the Surrealists sought to reveal invisible realities—not spiritual ones, but elemental universal forces that drove all humans. These unseen realities were deeply embedded in the mind and symbolically revealed in dreams. Freud maintained that the conventions of civilization had repressed the elemental needs and desires that all people shared, and that this suppressed, invisible world of desires and sexual energy was fundamental to human behavior, the driving force within all humans. Freud acknowledged that civilized societies required the repression and channeling of those desires, but asserted that individuals paid a price in the form of neuroses and discontent. For Surrealist artists, as well as writers and intellectuals,

Freud's theory of the unconscious confirmed the existence of realities unseen by the eye or unperceived by the conscious mind, and they served as the springboard for the development of Surrealist imagery and style.

Politics also strongly shaped the art of the period. Many, if not most, avant-garde artists were socialists and Communists, or at least sympathizers, and their utopian dreams and aesthetic visions stem in part from these political ideologies. The narrative, representational murals of the great Mexican artists directly champion Communism, especially when paired with science, as the vehicle for creating a classless utopian society. With the rise to power of Hitler and his National Socialist Party, many avant-garde artists turned their attention to making antifascist imagery and exposing the insane thinking and sadistic brutality of the new German government.

This period also saw a growing interest in racial and ethnic identity, which was expressed in Mexican art and African-American art. The Mexican muralists were preoccupied with national identity, which they associated with the indigenous population, not Euro-Mexicans, while African Americans sought to uncover their heritage and culture. Just as Mary Cassatt, Berthe Morisot, and Margaret Julia Cameron sought to present women from a female viewpoint, obtaining very different results from male artists, the Mexicans and African Americans did the same for native and African cultures. These artists presented a very different image of and attitude toward non-European civilizations.

DADA

The Great War halted much art making, as many artists were enlisted in their countries' military service. Some of the finest were killed, such as the German Expressionist Marc and the Italian Futurist Boccioni. But the conflict also produced one art movement: Dada. Its name was chosen at random, the story goes, when two German poets, Richard Huelsenbeck and Hugo Ball, plunged a knife into a French–German dictionary and its point landed on *dada*, the French word for "hobbyhorse." The word's association with childishness as well as the random violence of the poets' act of word choice fit the postwar spirit of the movement perfectly. As the birth story of Dada suggests, the foundations of the movement lay in chance occurrences and the absurd. Logic and reason, the Dada artists concluded, had led only to war. For them, the nonsensical and the ridiculous became tools to jolt their audience out of their bourgeois complacence and conventional thinking. The movement was profoundly committed to challenging the status quo in politics as well as in culture. Dada began in 1916 in neutral Zurich, where a large number of writers and artists had sought refuge from the war and dedicated themselves, as Ball declared, "to remind the world that there are independent men, beyond war and nationalism, who live for other ideals." The Dada spirit spread across the West and to parts of Eastern Europe and would become a reference point for artists throughout the twentieth century.

Zurich Dada: Jean Arp

In Zurich, the poet Hugh Ball founded the Cabaret Voltaire in 1916 as a performance center where writers and artists could protest the absurdity and wastefulness of the Great War. (The name Voltaire referred to the great Enlightenment *philosophe* whose ideas epitomized the logic that the Dadaists were attacking; see page 786.) Ball was soon joined by the Romanian poet Tristan Tzara, who became Dada's most vociferous proponent. The artists and writers at the Cabaret Voltaire attacked the rational thinking that, in their view, produced the depraved civilization responsible for the war. Their target was all established values—political, moral, and aesthetic—and their goal was to level the old bourgeois order through "nonsense" and anarchy. In the end, they hoped to produce a *tabula rasa*, a clean slate, that would provide a new foundation for a fresh understanding of the world.

The Cabaret Voltaire group, which included the Alsatian painter and poet Jean Arp, mounted boisterous performances. Wearing fanciful costumes, including primitive cardboard masks, they recited abstract phonetic poems of nonwords. ("Zimzum urallal zumzum urallal zumzum zanzibar zumazall zam" went one line in Hugo Ball's *O Gadji Beri Bimba*. To listen to Ball's sound poems, go to www.myartslab.com.) The readings were virtually drowned out by an accompanying "music," a cacophony of sounds, often the arrhythmic beating of a drum. The performers' chaos whipped the audiences into frenzies of catcalls,

whistles, and shouts. Some evenings, Tzara harangued the audience with rambling, virtually incomprehensible Dada manifestos. And, just as chance had named the Dada movement, it was used to create works themselves. Dada poems were "written" by pulling words out of a hat. Sometimes one poem was read simultaneously in different languages, or different verses of the same poem were read simultaneously in one language. The resulting chance weaving of words together in a new way created a fresh unpredictable poetic fabric, both in sound and meaning. Some performances included *danses nègres* and *chants nègres*, as African dance and music were called, reflecting the group's interest in so-called primitive cultures, cultures supposedly free of the evils of advanced civilization. Furthermore, the Dada artists believed that the directness and simplicity of African cultures put those cultures in touch with the primal essence of nature itself. Perhaps the most far-reaching influence of Dada performances was that they tore down the boundaries that had separated the various arts as visual artists, musicians, poets, actors, and writers worked together. Furthermore, the Dadaists destroyed any hierarchy of medium and genre. The Zurich Dadaists exhibited a broad range of avant-garde art, such as paintings by Klee and de Chirico (see pages 961 and 969, respectively)—as long as the art undermined bourgeois taste and standards. Most of the art presented at the Cabaret Voltaire and its successor, the Galerie Dada, was abstract. Among the strongest visual artists in the group was Jean (or Hans—his name changed with the shifting national status of his hometown Strasbourg) Arp (1886–1966), whose abstract collages hung on the walls of the Cabaret Voltaire on opening night. Arp made his collages by dropping pieces of torn rectangular paper on the floor; where they fell determined the composition. Although he claimed that chance alone arranged the papers, Arp probably manipulated them.

Arp believed that chance itself replicated nature. For him, life, despite the best-laid plans, was pure happenstance. Arp had been in Munich with Kandinsky (see pages 958–60), and there he adopted a mystical view of the world that envisioned a life force running through all things, binding them together in no particular order. Like Kandinsky, Arp sought to capture abstract universal forces. This spiritual outlook can be seen in the low-relief sculptures he began making at about this time, such as *The Entombment of the Birds and Butterflies (Head of Tzara)* (fig. **28.1**). The different shapes were determined by doodling on paper. He then had a carpenter cut the shapes out of wood, which Arp painted and assembled into abstract compositions evoking plant and animal forms as well as clouds, cosmic gases, and celestial bodies. The title came last, and, as it suggests, the image can be also seen as a head, suggesting an elemental connection between humans and nature.

The Cabaret Voltaire closed by the summer of 1916 and was replaced by a succession of other venues. Meanwhile, Tzara's magazine, *Dada*, spread the word about the movement worldwide. By the end of the war in late 1918, Zurich had been abandoned by many of the major artists, and by early 1919, Zurich

Perhaps the highlight of New York Dada is Duchamp's *Fountain* (fig. **28.2**). Duchamp submitted this sculpture to the 1917 exhibition of the Society of Independent Artists, an organization begun several decades earlier to provide exhibition opportunities for artists who did not conform to the conservative standards of New York's National Academy of Design, which had been the primary exhibition venue. Duchamp labeled his *Fountain* an "Assisted Readymade." He took the term Readymade from American readymade clothing, and applied it to his sculptures that simply re-presented a found object, such as a snow shovel, which Duchamp hung from the ceiling and entitled *In Advance of a Broken Arm*. Objects that he "assisted," by joining them with other objects, as in *Bicycle Wheel* (see fig. 27.29), or by signing, as in *Fountain*, he called an "Assisted Readymade." As we saw in Chapter 27, Duchamp began working with found objects when he made his *Bicycle Wheel* in 1913, although he did not exhibit his Readymades and coin the term until he was in New York. *Fountain* was, in fact, a urinal manufactured by J. L. Mott Iron Works in New York. Duchamp selected it, purchased it, turned it 90 degrees, set it on a pedestal, and crudely signed it with the fictitious name of "R. Mutt"—a reference not only to the manufacturer but also to the character Mutt in the popular *Mutt and Jeff* comic strip. The sculpture was

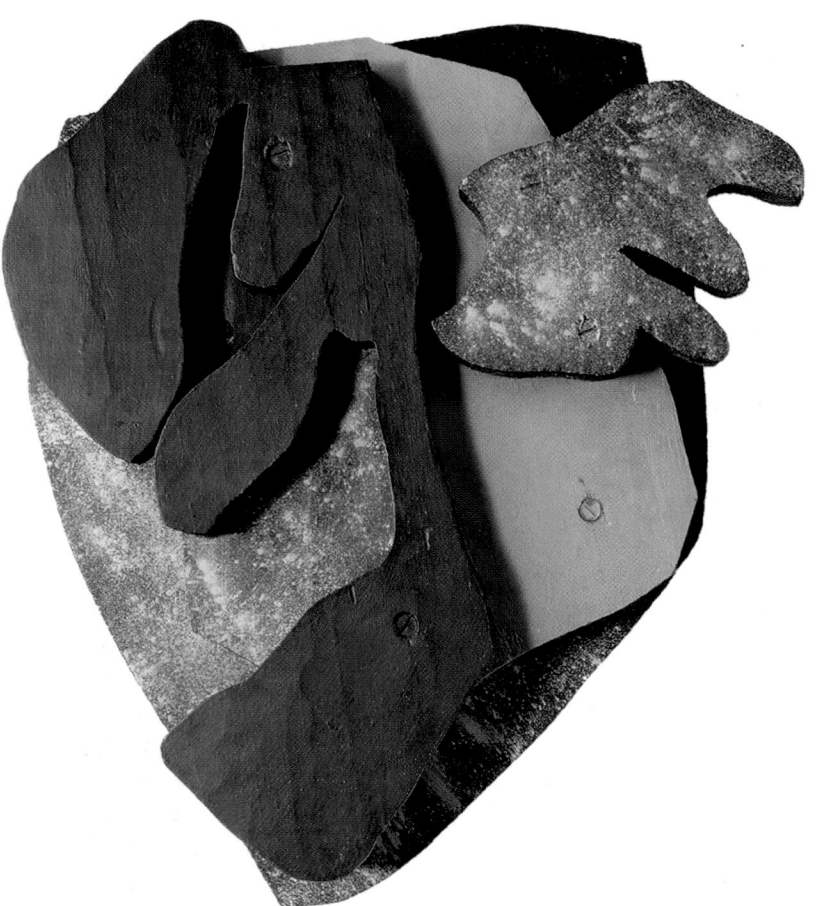

28.1 Jean (Hans) Arp, *The Entombment of the Birds and Butterflies (Head of Tzara)*. 1916–17. Painted wooden relief, 15¾ × 12¾" (40 × 32.5 cm). Kunsthaus, Zurich

Dada had drawn to a close. Only after the war was over did Tzara hear that there was a New York Dada movement happening simultaneously, if not in name, at least in spirit.

New York Dada: Marcel Duchamp

New York Dada was centered on Marcel Duchamp and Francis Picabia, both of whom fled Paris and the war in 1915. Picabia was notorious for his satirical portraits in which the subject is represented by a machine. In one, the photographer Alfred Stieglitz (see pages 936, 938, and 974) was portrayed as a camera, which takes on human qualities embodying Stieglitz's personality. The New York artists had no Cabaret Voltaire, no manifestos, and no performances, although they did hold a weekly salon at the home of the wealthy writer Walter Arensberg and his wife, Louise. From 1915 to 1916, they published their avant-garde art and ideas in a magazine entitled *291*, which was sponsored by Alfred Stieglitz, who as well as being a photographer was one of the first dealers of avant-garde art in America. The word Dada was never used at the time to describe their art; it was only applied in retrospect because their spirit was similar to that found in Zurich.

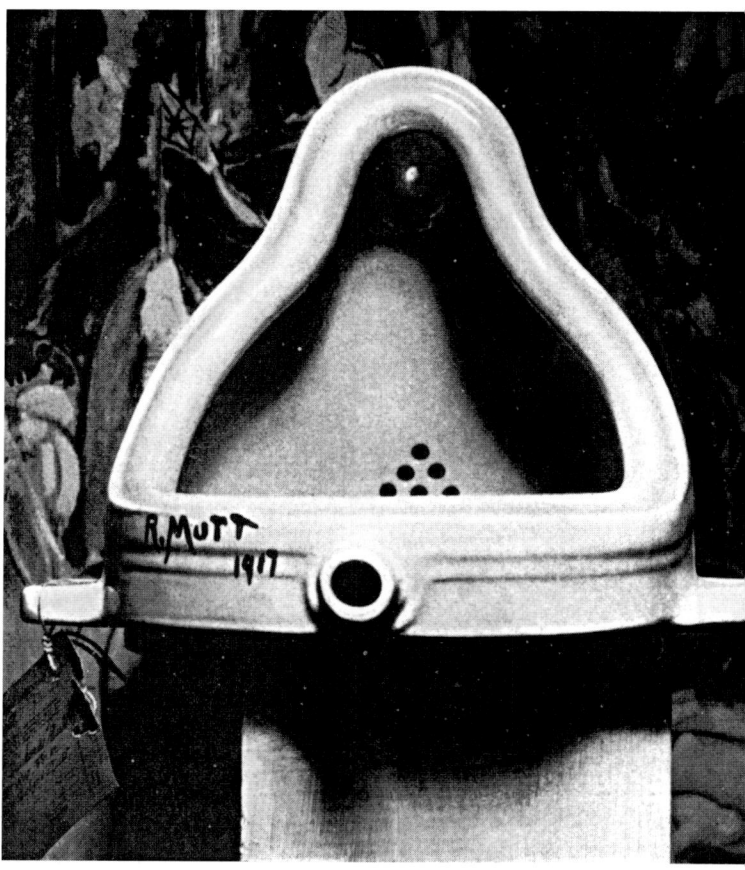

28.2 Marcel Duchamp, *Fountain*. 1917. Photograph by Alfred Stieglitz, from *The Blind Man*. May 1917. Philadelphia Museum of Art, Louise and Walter Arensberg Collection

submitted to the society's exhibition under Mutt's name, not Duchamp's. According to the society's rules, anyone paying the $6 admission fee would have his or her work accepted. But Duchamp knew the hanging committee would not consider *Fountain* art and so not allow it to go on view, and when it was removed at the opening, his friends formed a rowdy procession that drew attention to its rejection.

Duchamp continued the hoax of R. Mutt's authorship of the work when he wrote an article about the piece in a small newspaper he published with artist Beatrice Wood, *The Blind Man*, which only survived two issues but was well circulated in the avant-garde art world. The article was illustrated by a Stieglitz photograph of *Fountain* placed before a painting by Marsden Hartley (see fig. 27.33), an arrangement that underscored that the proper context for the appropriated urinal was the art world. The article defended Mutt's right to create a Readymade: "Whether Mr. Mutt with his own hands made the fountain or not has no importance. He chose. He took an ordinary article of life, placed it so that its useful significance disappeared under a new title and point of view…[creating] a new thought for that object."

Like all of Duchamp's works, *Fountain* is rich in ideas, and it stands as one of the seminal works of twentieth-century art, although the original has disappeared. The sculpture is all about ideas. A viewer of *Fountain* must ask: What is the work of art? Is it the urinal, the provocation of submitting it to the exhibition, the flamboyant parade when it was removed from the show, or the article about it in *The Blind Man*? Obviously, it is all of these things. Even the title is essential to the work, since it is an essential part of the sculpture, and it allows Duchamp to make it clear that he is attacking one of the more revered art forms, the fountain, which is the centerpiece for most European towns and city squares and is, in some respects, a symbol for the tradition of fine art. The satirical title also reinforces the humor of the piece, an ingredient found in much of Duchamp's work. Duchamp is telling us art can be humorous; it can defy conventional notions of beauty, and while intellectually engaging us in a most serious manner, it can also make us smile or laugh. Duchamp challenges the notion of what art is and the importance of technique or craft, as well as of the artist's signature. He also asks how a work of art takes on meaning. Here, Duchamp emphasizes the relationship between context and meaning: By taking a urinal out of its normal context he has changed its meaning. (For a more extensive discussion of Duchamp, focusing on his *Mona Lisa* with a moustache, see the Introduction, pages xxvi–xxvii.) He even allows a viewer to assign meaning to the work, underscoring how this is a reality for all art, not just his. Ironically, unlike all art that preceded his, his Readymades have no aesthetic value and theoretically no intended meaning. They are merely a device to launch ideas.

Because *Fountain* is industrially manufactured and can be easily replaced if broken or lost (the original is lost, and in 1964 the work was editioned, that is to say, several identical examples were produced), Duchamp also questions the significance attached to the uniqueness of a work of art. As we shall see, in the second half of the twentieth century, Duchamp will become the dominant figure in art as artists worldwide make what will be called Conceptual Art. For those artists, an idea or conceptual premise is the most important component of their work, in effect replacing the visual component.

In contrast to Zurich Dada, New York Dada was very quiet. In Manhattan, the group was far removed from the war, and it did not have a political agenda. Its focus was largely on defining art, following Duchamp's lead. More important, New York Dada was light-hearted and witty, as in Picabia's humanoid machines and Duchamp's *Fountain*. Dada art with a more acute sense of social mission was produced in wartorn Germany.

Berlin Dada

With the end of the war, the Dada poet Richard Huelsenbeck (1892–1974) left Zurich for Berlin. There, he found a moribund city, which like the rest of Germany was without food, money, medicine, or a future. Germans, especially the working class, loathed the military-industrial machine, which they felt had betrayed their interests by leading them into war. With the surrender, conditions worsened as Germany was punished by harsh and, some thought, unrealistic reparation demands. Inflation was rampant, and the value of the German currency plunged. Open class conflict in 1919 resulted in Communist-led worker uprisings in Berlin and Munich that were brutally repressed by right-wing armed units. The Weimar Republic government, which had replaced the Kaiser (emperor) and represented Germany's first experience with democracy, failed to revive the economy. Its refusal in 1923 to make war reparations only resulted in further humiliation when the French military occupied the Ruhr Valley and seized the German assets in that coalmining region.

For many, hope lay in the East, in Russia, where the Bolshevik Revolution established the prospect for a nationless world governed by the proletariat. The artists and writers of Berlin Dada looked to international worker solidarity as Germany's salvation. Here was a situation where Dada anarchy and nihilism could be put to practical use. Almost without exception, the Berlin Dada contingent made political art and were political activists, with some members, such as George Grosz and John Heartfield, joining the Communist Party.

In Berlin, the poet Huelsenbeck employed the usual Dada devices. He created an organization, Club Dada, and published manifestos calling for the overthrow of the bourgeois establishment and the creation of an egalitarian society. The principal members of the group included Raoul Hausmann, Hannah Höch, George Grosz, and John Heartfield. In 1920 they organized the first Dada International Fair, which featured worldwide Dada art. In the center of the fair, hanging from the ceiling, was an army-uniformed dummy with the head of a pig and wearing a sign saying "Hanged by the Revolution." The work, a collaboration by Hausmann and Grosz, epitomized Dada's abhorrence of the establishment.

RAOUL HAUSMANN Hausmann (1886–1971) quickly became the leader of Berlin Dada, and was perhaps the most visually inventive, as can be seen in his 1920 assemblage *Mechanical Head (Spirit of the Age)* (fig. **28.3**). He used found objects, which at the time were so foreign to the art world they were considered junk: a hairdresser's dummy, a collapsible cup, a crocodile wallet, labels, nails, a bronze segment of an old camera, a typewriter cylinder, a length of measuring tape, and a ruler. But now we see a new approach to making sculpture: The found objects are assembled together, an approach generally labeled "assemblage." Through this accumulation of objects, Hausmann presents a mindless, lifeless dummy, the contemporary German, whose actions and thoughts are molded by external forces, rendering it mechanical, even robotic, and with no personal identity. Hausmann claimed the typical German "has no more capabilities than those which chance has glued onto the outside of his skull; his brain remains empty."

Hausmann, however, is best known for his use of language and collage. Like Hugo Ball in Zurich, he wrote and performed phonetic poems made according to the laws of chance. (To listen to his Dada poems, go to www.myartslab.com.) His interest in words, letters, and sound led him in 1919 to innovative experiments with typography, in which he used different typefaces and

sizes for individual letters cut from magazines and newspapers, the shifts in scale indicating how the letter should be emphasized when sounded. These words were incorporated into ingenious collages made from material cut from different printed sources and rearranged in new contexts.

HANNAH HÖCH Some of the most elaborate and powerful Dada collages from the period were created by Hannah Höch (1889–1978), who was Hausmann's companion from roughly 1915 to 1922. Her Dada collages mimic manipulated portraits made for German soldiers. Individuals or entire battalions hired photographers to create fictitious portraits by photographing them, then cutting out their heads and pasting them onto pre-existing pictures of, for example, mounted militia. (See *Primary Source*, page 991.) *Cut with the Kitchen Knife Dada Through the Last Weimar Beer Belly Cultural Epoch of Germany* (fig. **28.4**) speaks volumes about the agenda of Berlin Dada. Using a chaotic, cramped composition of crowds, words, machinery, and lettering of different sizes and styles, Höch captures the hectic social, political, and economic intensity of the Weimar Republic. Her collage of photographs represents images of contemporary life made by photographers for the popular press. To Höch and her Dada colleagues, the camera was another machine that could be associated with the technological advances that had led to the war. With her "kitchen knife," she "killed" the machine, and rearranged the imagery to create a *hand-made* photograph, thus humanizing the mechanical. The resulting image is a spinning, gearlike composition with a portrait of the radical antiwar artist Käthe Kollwitz at the center. German masses and the new leaders of their government, the Weimar Republic, are pushed to the sides and villainously labeled as the "anti-Dada," meaning against Dada and leftist politics.

Collage, of course, was not new. But previously it had been used in a more refined manner, particularly by the Cubists, who had generally transformed the found materials taken from popular culture into beautiful art (see fig. 28.12). With Hausmann and Höch, however, collage retained the look and feeling of popular culture, especially the advertising look seen in the mass media. The Berlin Dadaists did not call their works collages, which suggests fine art. Instead, they labeled them **photomontages**, which evoked machine-made, mass-produced images. Their photomontages looked like antiart, and their powerfully abrupt compositions embodied the group's political stridency.

KÄTHE KOLLWITZ Though not a Dada artist, Käthe Kollwitz (1867–1945), spotlighted by Höch in *Cut with the Kitchen Knife*, provided an important precedent for the political and expressive nature of Berlin Dada and is often simply labeled an Expressionist. A generation older than Höch, she was denied admission to the Berlin Academy because she was a woman. She studied at a women's art school, and after marrying a doctor, settled in a working-class neighborhood in Berlin. There, her husband treated the poor, who became the subject of her art. She shunned painting as an elitist medium of the academy and

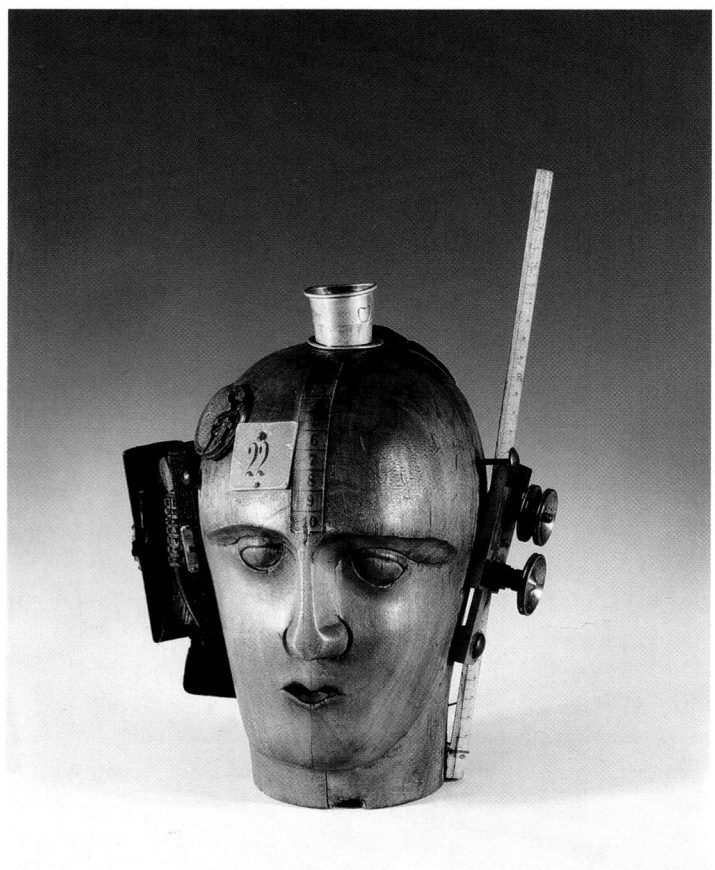

28.3 Raoul Hausmann, *Mechanical Head (Spirit of the Age)*. ca. 1920. Assemblage, height 12¾" (32.5 cm). Musée National d'Art Moderne, Centre Georges Pompidou, Paris

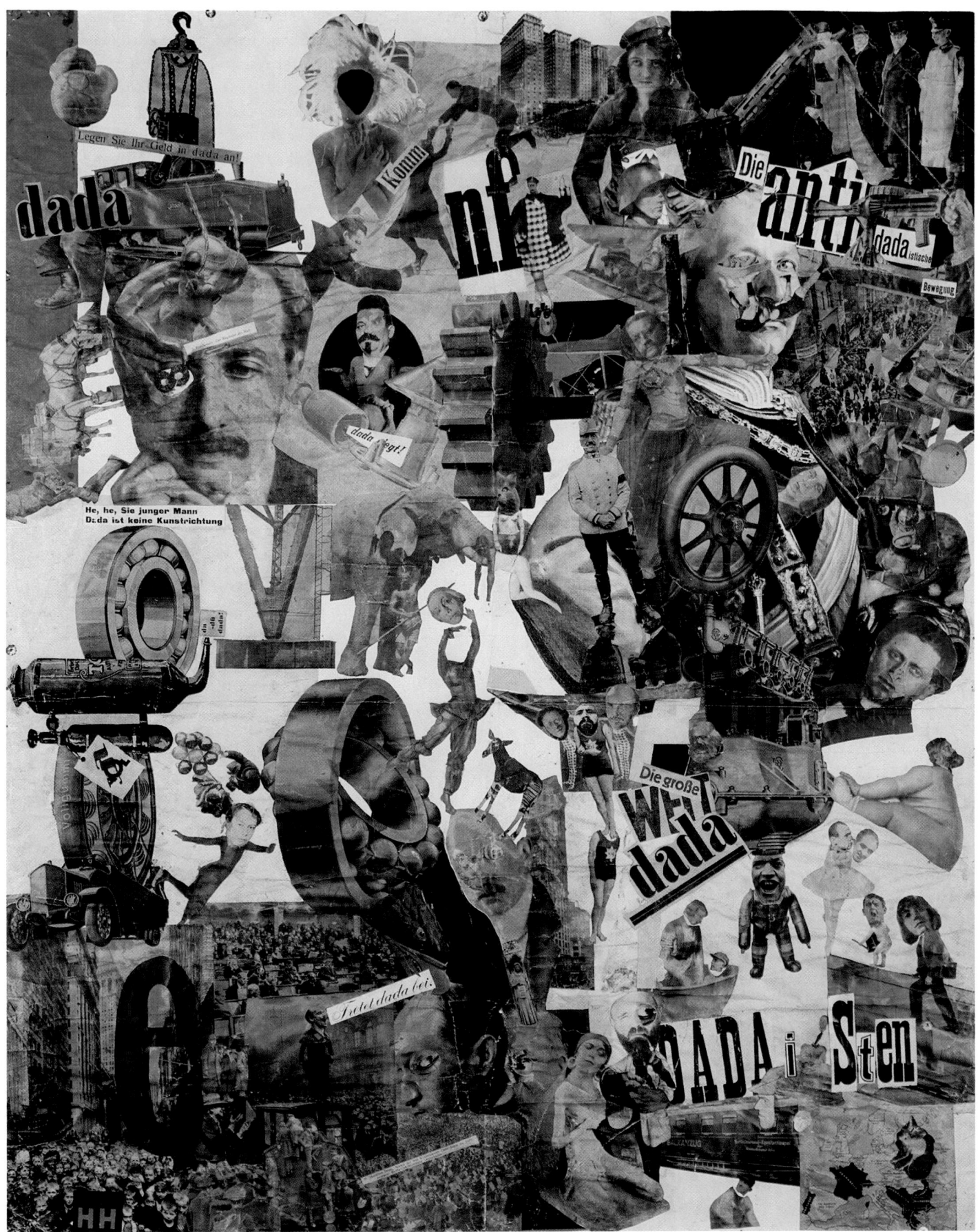

28.4 Hannah Höch, *Cut with the Kitchen Knife Dada Through the Last Weimar Beer Belly Cultural Epoch of Germany.* ca. 1919. Collage, 44⅞ × 35⅜" (114 × 90.2 cm). Staatliche Museen, Berlin

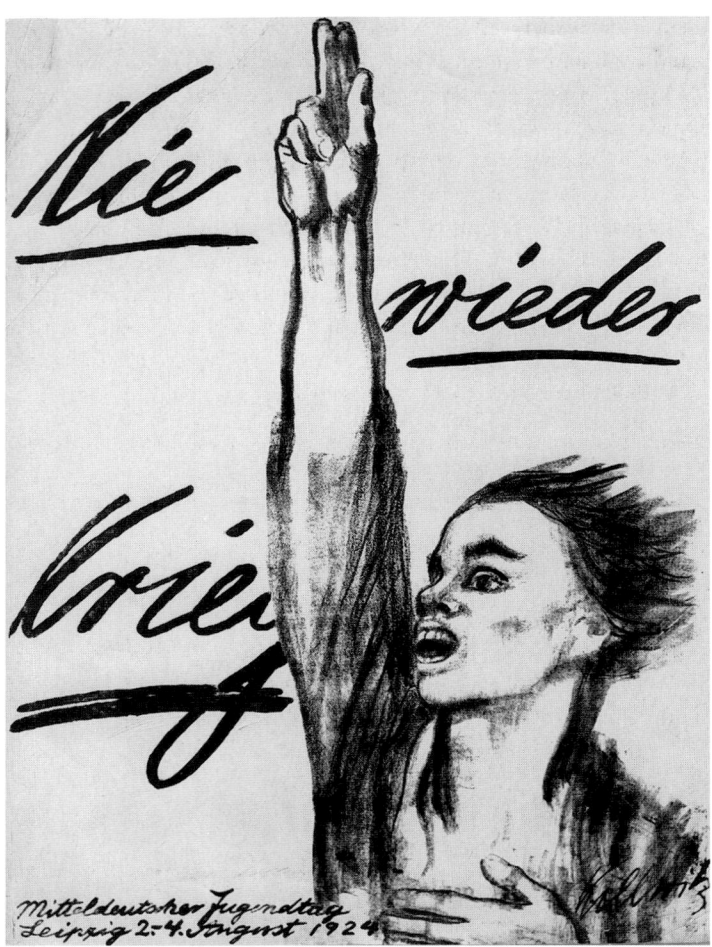

28.5 Käthe Kollwitz, *Never Again War!* 1924. Lithograph, 37 × 27½"
(94 × 70 cm). Courtesy Galerie St. Étienne, New York

the war and had suffered a mental breakdown, was especially bitter about the disastrous course charted by Germany's leaders. Upon convalescing and returning to Berlin, he was stylistically inspired by the expressive Cubism of the Futurists and worked in this style at the same time as he produced his more radical photomontages. A fine example of his Cubist style is *Germany, A Winter's Tale* (fig. **28.6**) of 1918. Here, the city of Berlin forms the kaleidoscopic, chaotic background for several large figures, which are superimposed on it as in a collage. They include the marionette-like "good citizen" at his table and the sinister forces that have molded him: a hypocritical clergyman, a brutal general, and an evil schoolmaster. For Grosz, this triumverate reflects the decadent world of the bourgeoisie that he, like many German intellectuals, hoped would be overthrown by Communism. In 1920, he, along with Kollwitz and other artists, joined the International Workers Aid, a Communist organization.

the bourgeoisie, and instead made drawings and prints, which could be mass-produced and circulated to wider audiences. For the Berlin Dada artists, who were committed to clear political messages, Kollwitz was an inspiration. Although for the 1920s, her representational style was somewhat conservative, her message was influential, for she had created a large body of powerful Expressionist work that conveyed her sympathies with the working class, and victims of war. In addition, her imagery contains far more women than does that of her male counterparts and reflects her socialist vision of women playing an equal role in the ideal Germany of the future. Typical of her Expressionist style of strident marks, strong value contrasts, and powerful emotions is her antiwar poster *Never Again War!* (fig. **28.5**), a lithograph published in 1924 and embodying personal content, since Höch lost a son in World War I. In 1920, Höch became the first woman ever admitted to the Prussian Academy of Fine Arts.

GEORGE GROSZ An early maker of Dada photomontages, George Grosz (1893–1959), provides a clear example of the Expressionist element in Berlin Dada and its direct connection with Kollwitz. (Like Höch, Grosz is often labeled a postwar Expressionist.) Grosz, who had been seriously wounded twice in

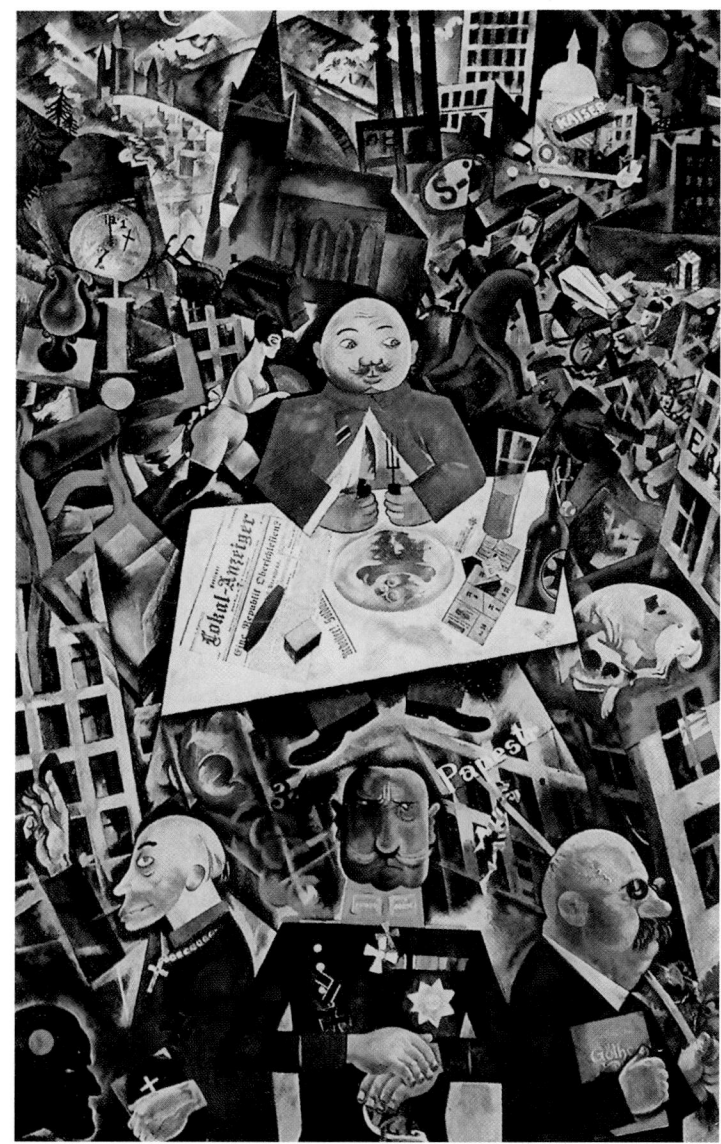

28.6 George Grosz, *Germany, A Winter's Tale.* 1918. Oil on canvas.
Formerly Collection Garvens, Hannover, Germany

Hannah Höch (1889–1978)

From an interview with Édouard Roditi

In an interview with art historian Édouard Roditi, the German Dada artist Hannah Höch talks about the inspiration for her Dada photomontages.

Actually, we borrowed the idea from a trick of the official photographers of the Prussian army regiments. They used to have elaborate oleolithographed mounts, representing a group of uniformed men with a barracks or a landscape in the background, but with the faces cut out; in these mounts, the photographers then inserted photographic portraits of the faces of their customers, generally coloring them later by hand. But the aesthetic purpose, if any, of this very primitive kind of photomontage was to idealize reality, whereas the Dada photomonteur set out to give to something entirely unreal all the appearances of something real that had actually been photographed. …

Our whole purpose was to integrate objects from the world of machines and industry in the world of art. Our typographical collages or montages also set out to achieve similar effects by imposing, on something which could only be produced by hand, the appearances of something that had been entirely composed by a machine; in an imaginative composition, we used to bring together elements borrowed from books, newspapers, posters, or leaflets, in an arrangement that no machine could yet compose.

Source: Édouard Roditi, *Dialogues: Conversations with European Artists* (Bedford Arts Publishers, 1990)

Cologne Dada

In the city of Cologne, Dada initially took its lead from Berlin, but it was never as political. Dada artists here were intrigued by Freud's theory of the unconscious and favored figures that combined mechanical and human forms (sometimes called mechanomorphic art), reminiscent of the work of Duchamp and Picabia. The key Cologne Dada artists were Max Ernst (1891–1976) and Johannes Baargeld (a pseudonym based on the German word *Bargeld*, meaning "cash"), both of whom appropriated the Berlin artists' collage techniques. Ernst and Baargeld were iconoclasts, not social evangelists, who delighted in submitting their witty low-end irreverent collages to the staid Cologne Kunstverein Exhibition in 1919, creating a scandal. When prohibited from showing there the following year, Ernst mounted a solo exhibition at a nearby brewery, forcing visitors to walk past the lavatory to get to the "gallery," where the central work was a sculpture that visitors were instructed to destroy with an axe he provided.

Typical of Ernst's work from this very productive period is *1 Copper Plate 1 Zinc Plate 1 Rubber Cloth 2 Calipers 1 Drainpipe Telescope 1 Piping Man* (fig. **28.7**), a gouache, ink, and pencil drawing on an illustration from a 1914 book about chemistry equipment. With a line here and a dab of paint there, Ernst transformed the picture of laboratory utensils into bizarre robotic figures set in a stark symbol-filled landscape. Perhaps we should say dreamscape, for the glazed-over stares and skewed de Chirico-like perspective, which culminates in a mystifying square, give this little collage an elemental power that suggests some otherworldly sphere—one of the imagination. Ernst was influenced by others who had made dream imagery, but he was also familiar with de Chirico's metaphysical paintings, to which he was introduced by his friend Jean Arp. The dreamlike quality of Ernst's image endows his figures with heavy psychological overtones. Not surprisingly, Ernst was fascinated by Sigmund Freud's theories about the unconscious and the importance of dreams.

Through Arp, Ernst was put in contact with two leaders of the Paris Dada movement, poets André Breton and Paul Éluard, both

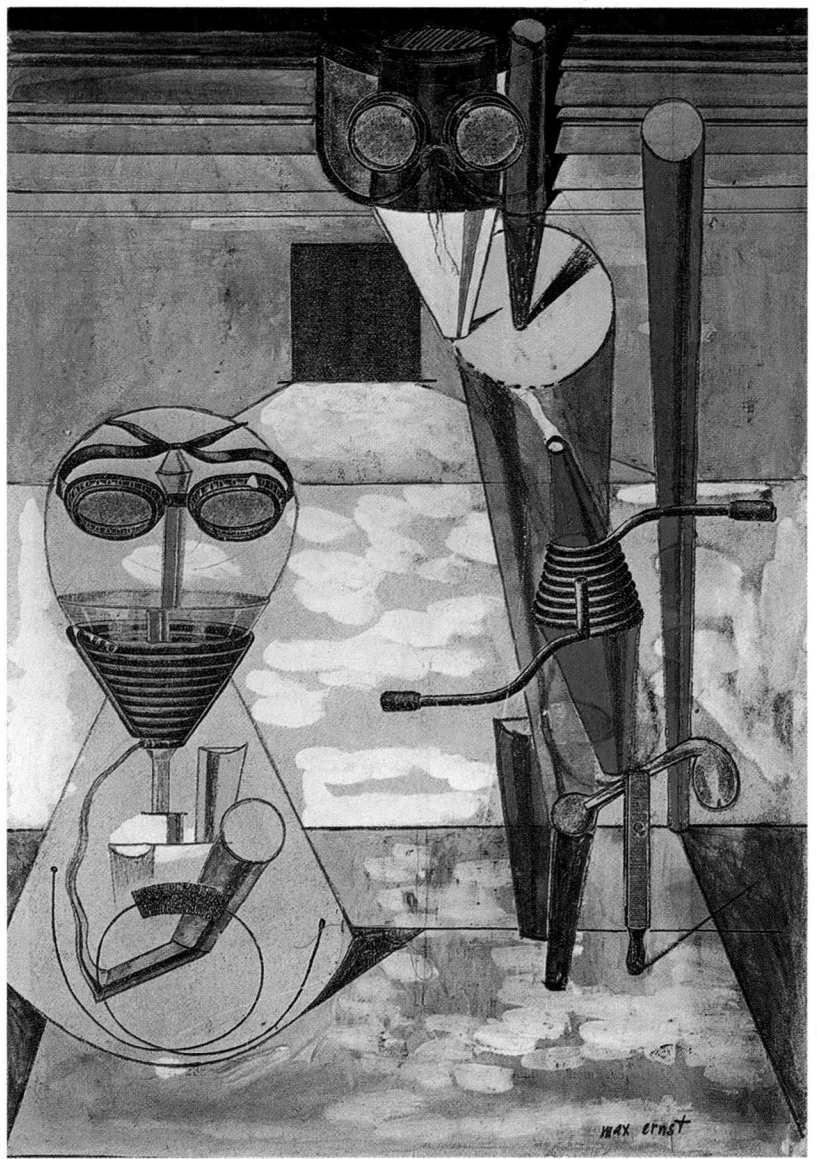

28.7 Max Ernst, *1 Copper Plate 1 Zinc Plate 1 Rubber Cloth 2 Calipers 1 Drainpipe Telescope 1 Piping Man*. 1920. Gouache, ink, and pencil on printer paper, 12 × 9" (30.5 × 22.9 cm). Estate of Hans Arp

of whom had also come under Freud's spell, entranced by the idea that the unconscious contained realities that had been suppressed by civilization. In 1921, they arranged for Ernst to show his Dada collages at a small avant-garde exhibition in Paris, where they made such a sensation he was hailed as the "Einstein of painting." The following year, Ernst emigrated to Paris. In 1924, Breton issued his *Surrealist Manifesto*, anointing Ernst's 1921 show, because of its dreamlike images, as the first Surrealist exhibition.

Paris Dada: Man Ray

The transition from Dada to Surrealism was well under way by 1922, and it occurred in Paris. Dada had established a foothold in the French capital with the return of Duchamp at the end of 1918 and with the arrival of Picabia from Barcelona in 1919. As in Zurich, the thrust behind Paris Dada came from the literary contingent. Inspired by Tzara's *Dada* magazine, three young poets— Louis Aragon, André Breton, and Philippe Soupault—founded a journal called *Littérature*. It was so avant-garde that there was hardly anything in it that the literary establishment would consider literature. In addition to phonetic poems by Tzara, it included Breton and Soupault's collaborative poem "Les Champs magnétique" ("Magnetic Fields") of 1920, which was written in a stream-of-consciousness style that was derived from working sessions lasting up to ten hours.

One artist who moved in and out of the Paris Dada circle was the independent American Man Ray (1890–1976). He had befriended Duchamp in New York, participated in New York Dada, and followed Duchamp to Paris in 1921. Best known as a photographer, Man Ray was extraordinarily inventive and worked in many mediums, some, such as airbrush painting, being quite innovative. Most important, Man Ray was the first artist to consistently use photography within a Dada context, often using the same conceptual premises, favoring idea over technique, as are found in Duchamp's work, thus freeing the medium from the merely representational restrictions placed on it by fine-art photographers. Man Ray helped establish photography, at least within Dada and Surrealist circles, as a medium that was viewed on a par with painting and sculpture.

In 1922, Man Ray had a major impact on the development of photography, as well as on Dada and abstract art, when he popularized the **photogram**—a one-of-a-kind cameraless photograph made by putting objects directly on photographic paper and then exposing both the object and paper to light (fig. **28.8**). Solid objects block light from striking the white paper, so they appear white in the image, while the spaces between and around the objects become black, since there is nothing to prevent the light from exposing the paper. Tzara dubbed Man Ray's print a "rayograph," and that year, using cover prints (photographic copies of the original print) made by Man Ray, Tzara published a limited-edition book, entitled *Champs délicieux* ("Delicious Fields," a pun on "Magnetic Fields"), containing 12 rayographs.

Our reproduction is one of these untitled works, which reveals the silhouettes of a brush and comb, a sewing pin, a coil of paper, and a strip of fabric, among the identifiable items. The image, like much of Man Ray's work, helps demonstrate the close relationship between the random and defiant art of Dada and the evocative, often sensual, art of Surrealism. The objects appear ghostlike and mysterious and float in a strange environment where darks and lights have been reversed and a haunting overall darkness prevails. Shapes and lines move in and out of dark shadows, sometimes vibrating, as with the brush-and-comb silhouette, other times crisply stated, as in the center oval. Because Man Ray exposed the paper with a light bulb that he moved several times during the process, he created multiple light sources, which caused the edges of some objects to shimmer and allowed other forms to recede back in space instead of just existing as flat silhouettes. His pictures, as with the Surrealist art that would follow, are a magical blend of the real and nonreal. We feel the presence of a real comb and sewing pin, and yet they seem to exist in a poetic otherworldly realm, even evoking the inner world of the mind and black-and-white world of dreams. Just as strange and inexplicable is the relationship of these objects and shapes to one another.

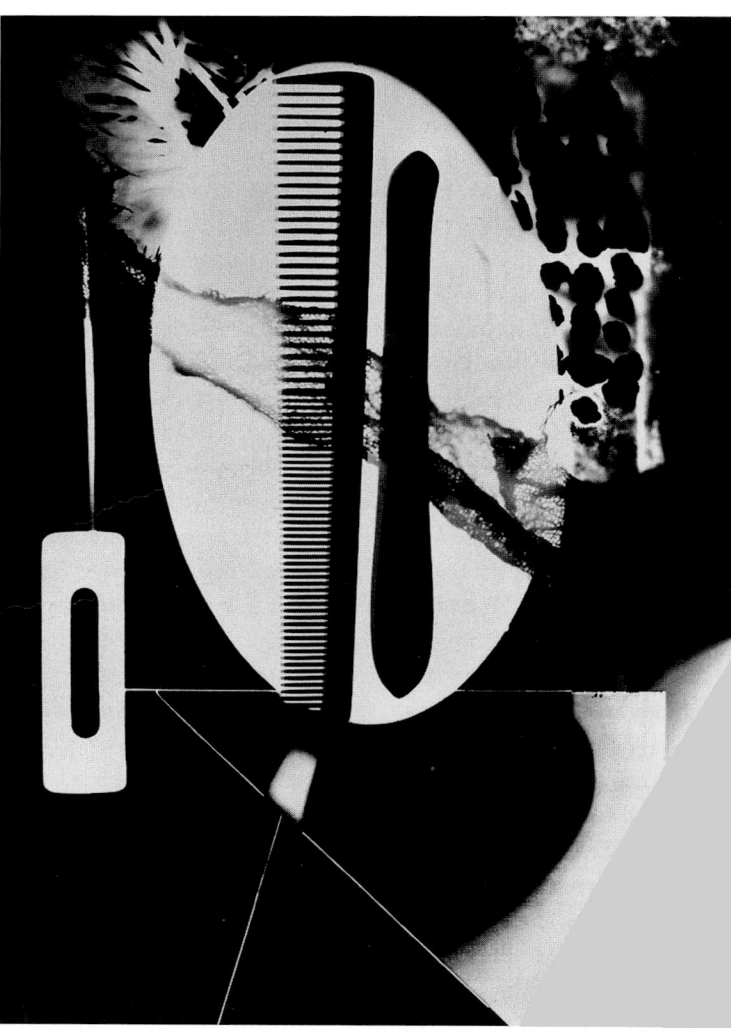

28.8 Man Ray. Untitled, from *Champs délicieux*. 1922. Gelatin silver print

Man Ray also used the same process to make films, which have the same dreamlike quality as his rayographs. At Tzara's invitation, he participated in what turned out to be the final major Dada event in Paris, *La Soirée de la Coeur de la Barbe* (The Bearded Heart *Soirée*) in 1923. To make his film, Man Ray sprinkled sand on a segment of unexposed film, and, nails, and tacks on another, creating a three-minute abstract movie titled *The Return to Reason* (to view the film, visit www.myartslab.com), an ironic title because the hallucinatory flickering of white objects floating in pitch-blackness creates a sense of chaos that is far from rational. To flesh out the film, Man Ray added segments of a carousel photographed at night, a tic-tac-toe-gridlike mobile dancing with its own shadow, and a nude model dissolved in harsh striped lighting, which are equally abstract and dreamlike. Like the rayographs, the film represented a new way to view the world, one that was essentially Surrealist, although the term had yet to be coined or the movement recognized. This short movie, Man Ray's first, not only introduced film to the Parisian fine-art world, but it also helped spawn a flurry of experimental films by other artists. Shortly after Man Ray's movie was screened that evening, a riot broke out when Breton, Éluard, and Soupault, all uninvited, stormed the stage screaming that Dada was dead. Though Dada continued to provide the intellectual foundation for challenging art throughout the century, the spirit of the moment was clearly shifting away from chance and nonsense to the psychological investigations of Surrealism.

SURREALISM

Surrealism existed in spirit, if not in name, well before 1924, but the movement was formally launched by Breton that year with his *Surrealist Manifesto*. Surrealism, Breton wrote, is "pure psychic automatism, by which it is intended to express, either verbally, or in writing, or in any other way, the true functioning of thought. Thought expressed in the absence of any control exerted by reason, and outside all moral and aesthetic considerations." Banished was the Neoclassical god of reason, the sureness of logic, and the need to portray an observable reality. Also gone was Dada nihilism, replaced by an intensive exploration of the unconscious. Surrealists argued that we see only a surface reality. More important was uncovering the reality that, as Freud maintained, resided in the deep-seated secrets and desires of the unconscious mind. For Freud, the basic human desires, particularly the sexual ones, that define our individual identities are repressed by the conventions of civilization but are revealed in dreams. Random dream images are, for Freud, charged with meaning and provide the "royal road to the unconscious." They contain symbols of our desires and anxieties. Using his own and his patients' dreams as "raw material," Freud decoded dream images into what he believed to be their true meaning, claiming sexual desires or concerns were often disguised as ordinary objects. A vase, for example, is a symbol of female sexuality, the vagina, while a tall building or a mountain suggests phallic maleness.

Breton's manifesto proposed several ways to tap into the unconscious. He encouraged the use of dreamlike images, the juxtaposition of unrelated objects that would jar the imagination, and stream-of-consciousness writing. He called for "the future resolution of these two states, dream and reality, which are seemingly so contradictory, into a kind of absolute reality, a surreality." He emphasized the concept of creating "the marvelous," images, either verbal or visual, that are mysterious, chance, and poetic, and that jolt the audience into a new, unknown plane of reality—surreality.

Surrealism was first a literary style. Breton traced its roots to several sources, including the comte de Lautréamont's 1869 novel *Chants de Maldoror*, which included wondrous passages of surreal images, the most famous perhaps being "as beautiful as a chance encounter of a sewing machine and an umbrella on an operating table." Breton's literary circle delighted in such "chance encounters" of words, even devising a game in which each participant provided words for a sentence, not knowing what had already been written. One such game produced "The exquisite corpse will drink the new wine," and "Exquisite Corpse" became the game's name. Surrealist visual artists played Exquisite Corpse as well. Folding a piece of paper, each artist drew on his or her segment without seeing what the others had done, only where they had left off. The result was a provocative image of unrelated objects or a strange form. But visual art had little place in Breton's manifesto, and visual artists were only mentioned as a footnote, appearing in a single sentence. Among those listed were Ernst, Man Ray, de Chirico, and Picasso.

Picasso and Surrealism

Perhaps the most surprising name on Breton's list is Picasso's. The Dada artists found little of interest in the analytic logical thinking of the Cubists. But Breton saw Picasso's Cubism as the first step toward loosening the grip of reality on the artistic imagination, and he declared Picasso's 1907 *Les Demoiselles d'Avignon* (see fig. 27.5) one of the first Surrealist images. Beginning in the mid-1920s, Picasso's work paralleled that of the Surrealists. They shared many symbols and myths, mostly sexual, including the female praying mantis, which eats it male partner upon mating, and the suffering, tortured male minotaur, which has the head of a bull on the body of man. But Picasso was very independent, and though he provided artwork for Surrealist publications and participated in some Surrealist shows, he did not consider himself a Surrealist.

With Breton's 1924 *Surrealist Manifesto*, the primal sexual forces seen in *Les Demoiselles* and smoldering beneath the surface of many of his Synthetic Cubist paintings of the mid- to late 1910s burst into the foreground of Picasso's works, as seen in *Three Dancers* (fig. **28.9**), made in 1925, less than a year after Breton published his manifesto. These are not the Three Graces, but rather disquieting nudes engaged in a strange performance. The figure in the center—the most conventionally rendered—appears at one moment to be completing a pirouette, at the next moment a midnight Dionysian bacchanal at the next. What remains consistent, however, is the pivotal role of the female body, whether as a symbol of erotic athleticism, threatening sexual frenzy, or spiritual suffering. Just as Freud attributed to the female body the power to incite desire as well as dread in men, Picasso, like the Surrealists, places the female form at the service of a male viewer's contradictory libidinal impulses.

WELDED SCULPTURE Picasso also turned to sculpture to express his urge to portray the unseen deep-seated psychological passions that drive physical urges, and it led him to revolutionize sculpture for a second time (see page 954). By late 1928, he was welding metal, which he experimented with for the next five years, starting a trend that by the 1940s established welded steel as a major sculptural process rivaling cast bronze and chiseled stone. Picasso began working in the medium when he decided to make sculpture based on the linear drawing of the figures in his

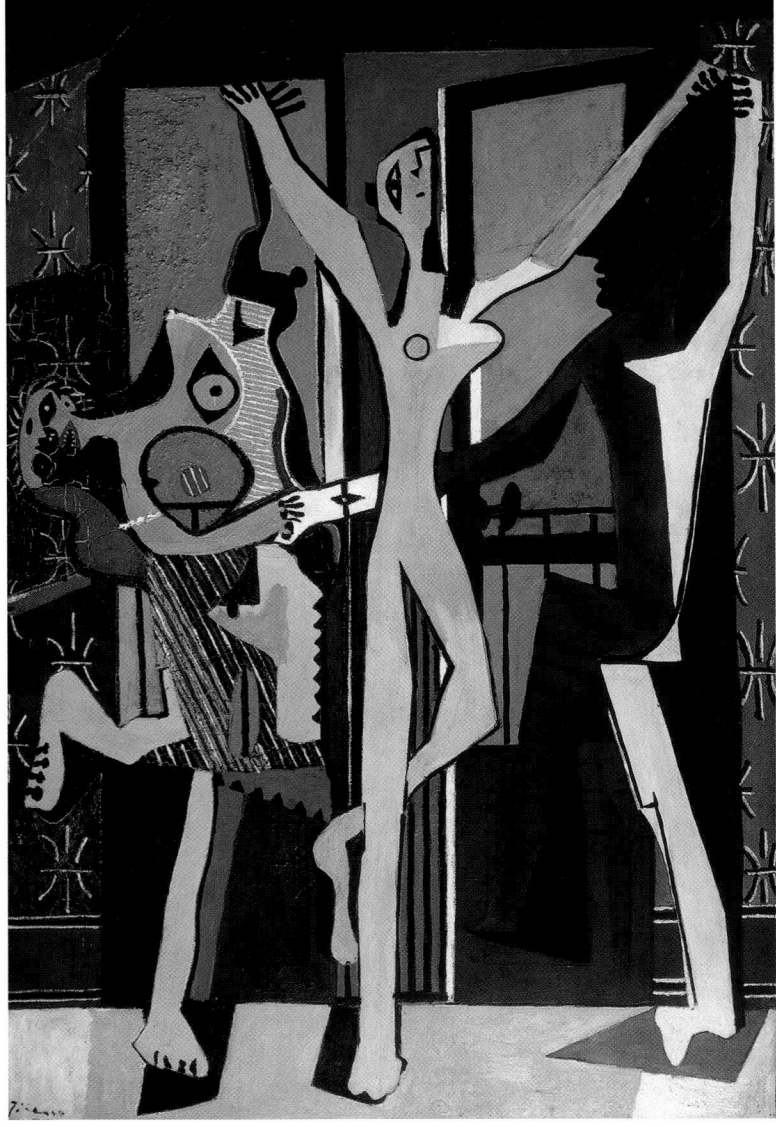

28.9 Pablo Picasso, *Three Dancers*. 1925. Oil on canvas, 7'1½" × 4'8¼" (2.15 × 1.4 m). Tate Gallery, London

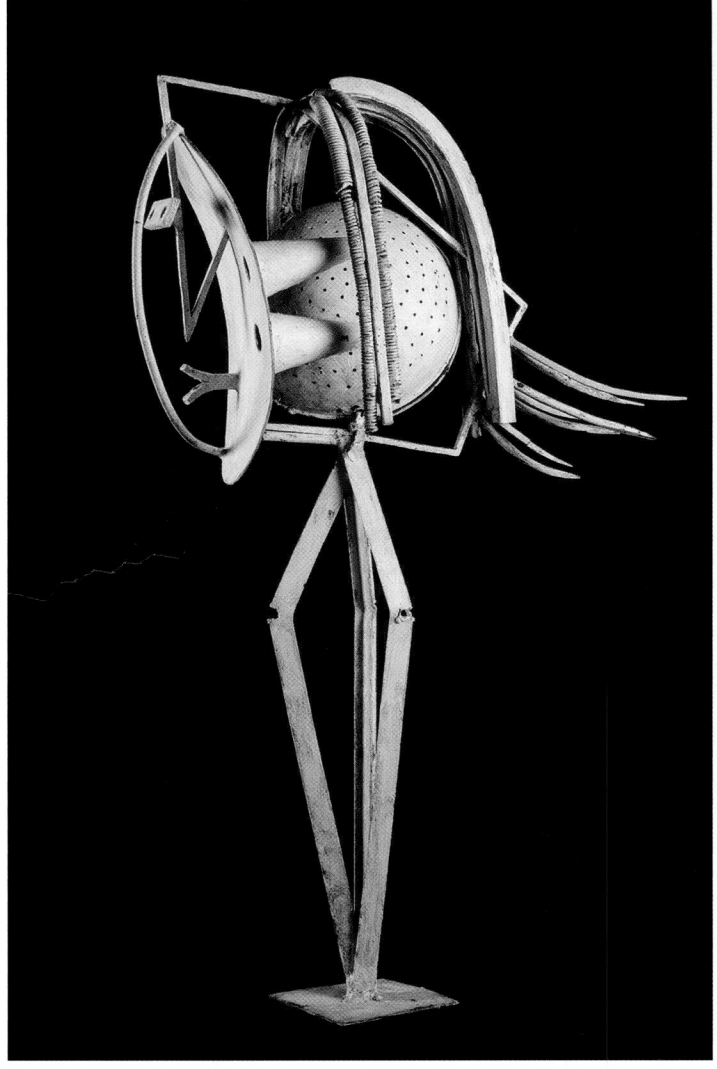

28.10 Pablo Picasso, *Head of a Woman*. 1929–30. Painted iron, sheet metal, springs, and colanders, 39⅜ × 14½ × 23¼" (100 × 37 × 59 cm). Musée Picasso, Paris

to be crucified. The contorted figure to the left has been reduced to an assemblage of abstruse hieroglyphic forms, which never quite coalesce into a single meaning. Her head is shaped like a quarter-moon, and it has been placed against a backdrop of a night sky filled with stars as represented by the abstracted *fleurs-de-lis* of the wallpaper. Some scholars claim the head resembles a Torres Strait, New Guinea mask that Picasso had in his personal collection of tribal art, and is thus a reflection of the artist's interest in the expressive primordial power of so-called primitive art, which Surrealists felt penetrated into the deepest recesses of the mind. The figure on the right is the most sedate or controlled of the three, causing some art historians to view the dancers as emblems of love, sex, and death. At every turn, Cubist fracturing dissolves the forms into disorienting shapes and colors, permitting multiple interpretations of the scene. What seems to be a dance rehearsal in a light-filled studio at one moment turns into

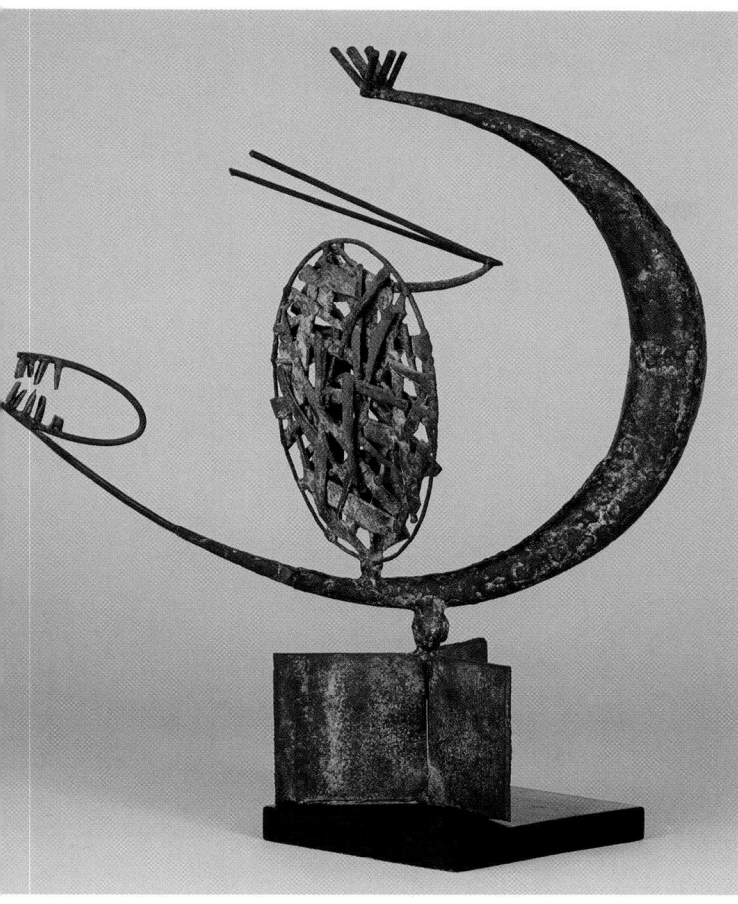

28.11 Julio González, *Head*. ca. 1935. Wrought iron, 17¾ × 15¼" (45.1 × 38.7 cm). Museum of Modern Art, New York. Purchase (266.1937)

current paintings, figures that were in effect skeletal stick figures. The resulting three-dimensional sculptures were made up of metal rods that represented the painted lines, and they looked like a line drawing in space.

Gradually, Picasso turned from metal rods to working with metal in a variety of shapes and sizes, including the use of found objects, as seen in *Head of a Woman* (fig. **28.10**) from 1929–30, which was made from colanders, springs, iron, and sheet metal. Picasso is still drawing in space, as seen in the hair, face, skull, and body—if this is indeed what these abstract shapes are. He has pared his figure down to a barebones essence, peeling away the superficial layers of physicality to reveal the psychological core of the woman that lies beneath, a rather strident, threatening psychology that reflects a male perception and fear of the opposite sex. The sculpture's overall resemblance to African masks, and the use of tribal hieroglyphic notations for different parts of the body, such as the stick legs, reinforce its elemental quality.

To do his welding, Picasso hired fellow Spaniard Julio González (1876–1942), who had learned the skill in a Renault automobile factory. By the 1930s, González was making his own work, such as *Head* (fig. **28.11**) of around 1935, which would garner him a reputation as the world's foremost practitioner of welded sculpture. González specialized in figures and heads,

which, like Picasso's *Head of a Woman*, project primitive, psychological, and hallucinatory qualities. Here, the sculptor reduces the figure to a pernicious clamplike mouth, stalklike eyes, spiky hair, and frazzled face (or is it the mind?), all attached to a moonlike crescent not only suggesting a skull but also the cosmos, a parallel we saw Jean Arp make as well in *The Entombment of the Birds and Butterflies* (see fig. 28.1)

Surrealism in Paris: Spurring the Imagination

In 1925, Breton, like everyone, was having doubts about the possibility of Surrealist painting or sculpture. Many argued that the visual arts, unlike writing, did not allow for a stream of consciousness since artists always had the work in front of them and, while creating, could see where they had been and think about where they were at that moment. The resulting imagery might seem surreal, but the method was not. Initially, many of the visual artists Breton championed relied on automatic drawing and chance to produce their images. In late 1925, Breton organized the first Surrealist exhibition, which featured Ernst, Picasso, André Masson, and Joan Miró, but also included de Chirico, Klee, Man Ray, and Arp.

MAX ERNST The use of automatic drawing had been initiated by the French painter André Masson (1896–1987) the year before, in 1924. In this process, Masson first made a series of lines while in a trancelike state, lines that he then used to spur the imagination to further develop the image. In 1926, he began prompting his unconscious by also randomly putting glue on his canvases and then sprinkling sand over the surface, the sand adhering where there was glue. The result of these chance techniques was the creation of mysterious environments inhabited by primitive organic forms, suggesting both the origin of life and the powerful universal urges that drive it.

Not to be outdone by Masson, Ernst in 1925 developed frottage, one of several devices he developed throughout his career to spur his imagination. **Frottage** consists of rubbing graphite, crayon, or charcoal over paper placed on an object, such as floorboards, chair caning, or pressed flowers, and then discerning an image in the irregular pattern of the wood grain or in the botanical geometry. When wiping paint over canvas, the technique is called **grattage**. In either case, the process often spurred Ernst's imagination to create a primeval forest filled with birds, animals, and bizarre, frightening creatures. While the pictures often have a mythic force similar to Masson's imagery, they are also filled with a frenetic sexual energy. Grattage is the basis for *Die Ganze Stadt* (*The Entire City*) (fig. **28.12**) of 1935–36, one of several paintings made on this theme at about this time for which Ernst placed canvas over boards and then rubbed dried paint over the surface. The result in each case is an austere and massive Mayan-like structure evoking an extinct monumental civilization, swallowed by the forces of nature and time, as suggested in this picture by the dominance of the enormous acidic-colored celestial body in the sky and the crawling animallike plantlife with lush buds in the

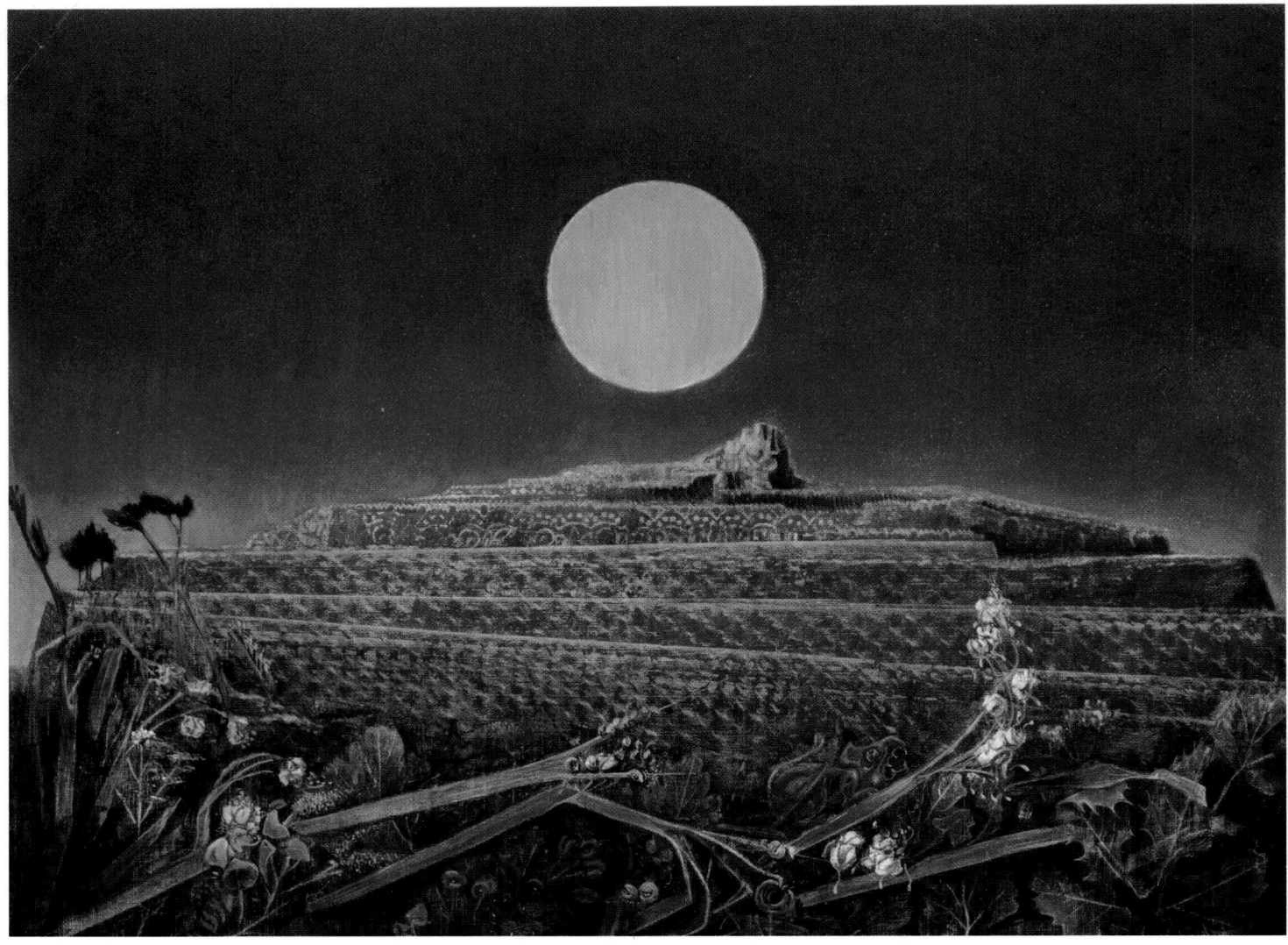

28.12 Max Ernst, *Die Ganze Stadt* (*The Entire City*). 1935–36. Oil on canvas, 23½ × 31¾" (60 × 81 cm). Kunsthaus, Zurich

foreground. A dark mood of twilight prevails, underscoring a sense of futility about humans trying to permanently achieve the goals of their primary, elemental desires.

JOAN MIRÓ A Catalan from Barcelona, Joan Miró (1893–1983) came to Paris in 1920 and took a studio next to Masson's. Soon after, through a hole in their adjoining wall, Masson whispered to Miró to go see Breton, not Picasso—because "he was the future." Within a short time Miró had abandoned Cubism and begun painting from his imagination. (Actually, he claimed he was working from hallucinations brought on by starvation—"I was living on a few dry figs a day.") He adopted Masson's wiry line and the childlike drawing and atmospheric quality of Klee (see fig. 27.16). Miró's pictures became abstractions of biomorphic and geometric forms set against a minimal color field that suggested a landscape or watery environment. Miró's paintings became increasingly abstract, as seen in *Composition* (fig. **28.13**), a 1933 oil. The work was one in a series based on collages on cardboard made from images cut out of catalogues with the idea that the shape

and even details of the objects would fire his imagination. The setting of *Composition* is a hazy atmospheric environment of washes, suggesting the same kind of primeval landscape as in Masson's abstractions. This eerie world is populated by strange curvilinear floating forms that suggest prehistoric and microscopic creatures, as well as spirits, ghosts, or souls. We can even find a story in places, such as two figures playing with or fighting over a ball in the upper left corner. Or are they? Other features in the painting express ideas about sex, struggle, and fear. Miró uses a minimal vocabulary, which includes color as well as form, to create a mythic image evoking humans' most primal urges and needs.

Representational Surrealism: Magritte and Dalí

Initially, Breton's strongest support was for an abstract Surrealism that was based on chance, spontaneity, and trance. Over the next decade, however, artists with all kinds of styles would move in and out of the movement, most abandoning it, in part because of

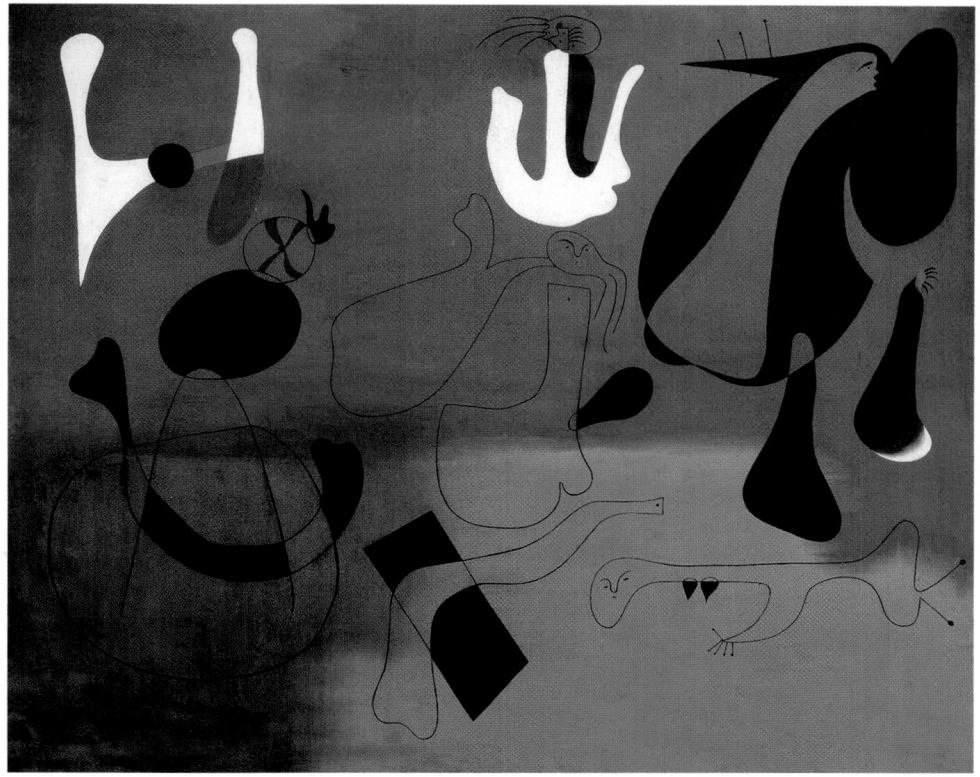

28.13 Joan Miró, *Composition*. 1933. Oil on canvas, 51¼ × 63½" (130.2 × 161.3 cm). Wadsworth Atheneum, Hartford, Connecticut. Ella Gallup Sumner and Mary Catlin Sumner Collection Fund

the group's strong socialist and Communist stance, but also because of Breton himself, who was rather controlling and functioned as though he were the Pope of Surrealism, capriciously anointing or not anointing and even excommunicating artists as Surrealists for the flimsiest of reasons.

RENÉ MAGRITTE By the late 1920s, more and more artists were working in a representational or quasi-representational style. One such was René Magritte (1898–1967), who was from Brussels. There, he was a member of the Surrealist circle, a group of artists and intellectuals who were also very involved with Communism. Magritte spent 1927 to 1930 in Paris, but Breton never officially recognized him as a Surrealist. He then returned to Belgium, where he spent the remainder of his life, not achieving fame until late in his career. His *The False Mirror* (fig. **28.14**), painted in 1928, reads like a manifesto of Surrealism, proclaiming the superior reality of the unconscious mind. We see an uncanny close-up of an eye, which reflects a distant sky. The iris, however, is transformed into an eerie eclipsed sun, behind which, Magritte suggests, lies the unconscious, which perceives the reality of things. The eye absorbs only the visual, not the real, world.

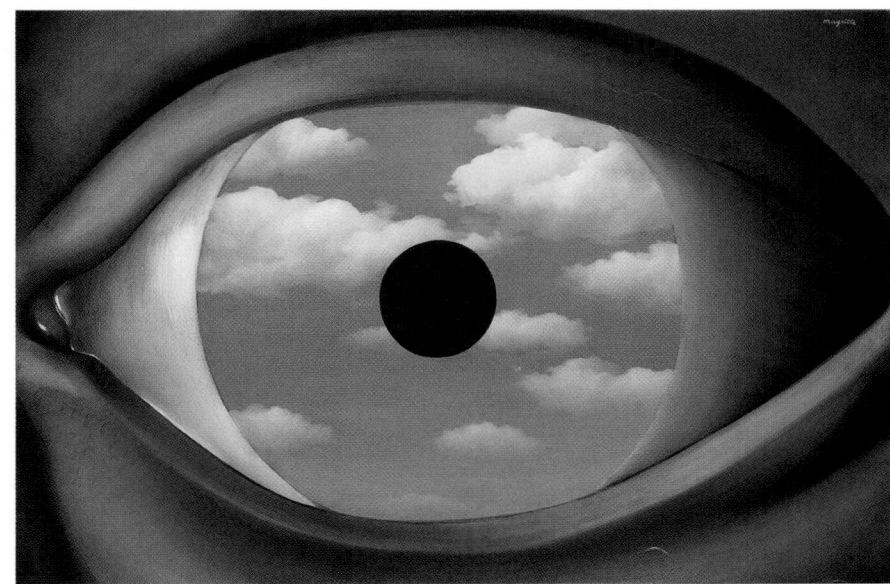

28.14 René Magritte, *The False Mirror*. 1928. Oil on canvas, 21¼ × 31⅛" (54 × 81 cm). Museum of Modern Art, New York

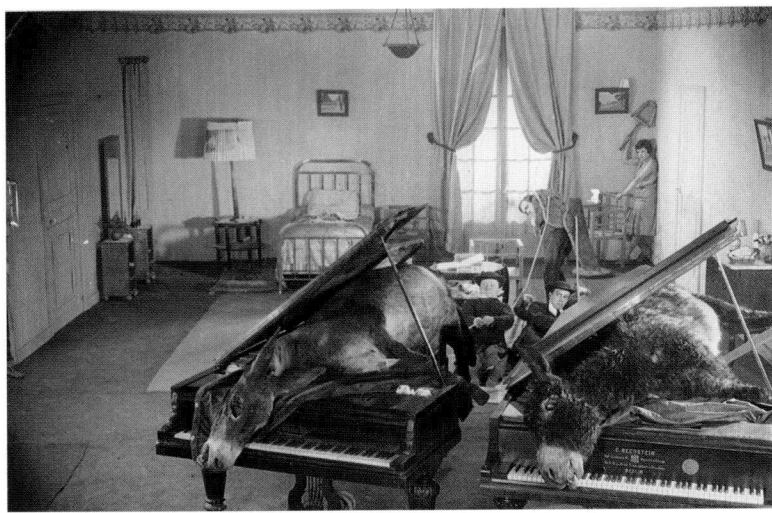

28.15 Salvador Dalí and Luis Buñuel. A still from the film *An Andalusian Dog (Un Chien Andalou)*. 1929. France

SALVADOR DALÍ Arriving in Paris a few years after Magritte was another major representational Surrealist. Salvador Dalí (1904–1989) came from Madrid, where he had already developed a meticulously detailed Realist style heavily based on the psycho-

logical complexes that Freud described in his writings. He made a grand entrance into the world of Parisian Surrealism with his 17-minute film *An Andalusian Dog* (see www.myartslab.com), which he made with fellow Spaniard, the filmmaker Luis Buñuel (1900–1983). The movie opens with Buñuel on a balcony with a woman and, as a cloud mysteriously passes behind them, the camera goes to a close-up of an eye, we assume the woman's, which is then dramatically sliced by a straight razor. This opening scene has been interpreted as a reference to the Oedipus complex and fear of castration, which is symbolized by a fear of blindness, two major themes in Freud's writings about male psychological development. The entire film, which consists of one unexplainable, bizarre sequence after another, lends itself to similar Freudian analysis. To produce their Surrealist effects, Dalí and Buñuel rely on montage, juxtaposing unrelated objects to create dream sequences that constantly put objects into new contexts designed to generate the "marvelous" and to jolt the unconscious. In one famous sequence, a needley sea urchin morphs into a woman's hairy armpit; in another, a man's mouth first disappears, then becomes a woman's crotch; and in yet other, ants swam over a hand appearing in a crack in a door. In yet another famous sequence, the film's protagonist drags across a room two priests and two grand pianos, each containing a putrefying dead donkey

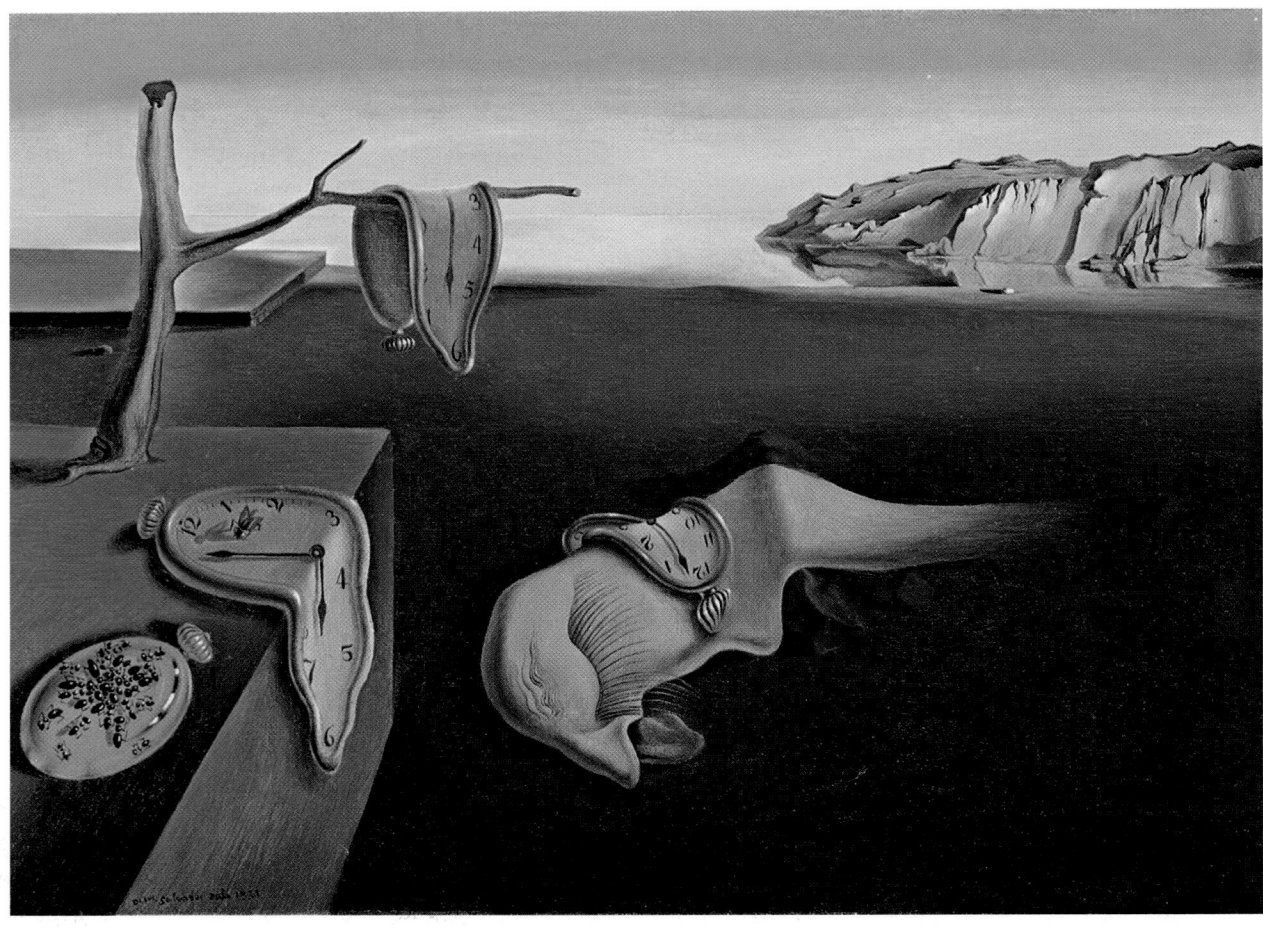

28.16 Salvador Dalí, *The Persistence of Memory*. 1931. Oil on canvas, 9½ × 13" (24.1 × 33 cm). Museum of Modern Art, New York. Given anonymously (162.1934)

(fig. **28.15**), a sequence suggesting among other things the admonishments of the church about sex and how they suppress basic human urges.

Similar themes and Freudian psychology appear in Dalí's visual art. Dalí made his paintings using a process he called "paranoiac-critical"—"[a] spontaneous method of irrational knowledge based upon the interpretative-critical association of delirious phenomena." He created paintings in a frenzy, a self-induced paranoid state where he would begin with a single object in mind. Then, he would respond to that object and so on, developing a mysterious image reflecting an irrational process that released the unconscious. *The Persistence of Memory* (fig. **28.16**) began with the strange amorphous head with an elongated trailing neck lying on the ground. A plate of soft Camembert cheese then inspired him to paint the soft pocket watches. While allowing no certain "final" reading, the picture evokes a host of associations, the most obvious being the crippling passage of time that leads to inevitable deterioration and death, although the title suggests we are looking backward to the past, not forward to the future. Many scholars interpret the flaccid watches as symbols of impotence. In any case, Dalí has created a provocative dreamscape of mysterious objects that can be read as metaphors for the deepest desires, fears, and anxieties, especially sexual, of the mind, and that can unleash multiple interpretations from a viewer's own unconscious.

Surrealism and Photography

Photographers, following Man Ray's lead, were discovering that their medium, which could both manipulate reality and create dreamlike sequences, were perfect vehicles for Surrealism. Many major photographers, not in Breton's circle, were deeply affected by Surrealism. One of the most famous outsiders was the Frenchman Henri Cartier-Bresson, who neither manipulated nor staged his images.

HENRI CARTIER-BRESSON Cartier-Bresson (1908–2004) made some of the most extraordinary images of the twentieth century. Trained as a painter, he turned to photography in the early 1930s when, influenced by the Surrealists, he sought to find the extraordinary in the ordinary and decided that the best means for accomplishing this was through photography. Armed with the new small, portable 35mm Leica camera, he took to the street to photograph what he called "the decisive moment," which he defined as "the creative fraction of a second when you are taking a picture," and "using intuition you ask your artistic question and decide almost simultaneously." We can see this decisive moment in his *Behind the Gare Saint-Lazare* (fig. **28.17**) of 1932. All over the world, Cartier-Bresson made photograph after photograph that miraculously captured the same supernatural magic we see in this fleeting, ghostlike image of a silhouetted man inexplicably suspended in midair. A master of strong value contrasts, Cartier-Bresson was able to transform stones, ladder, and arcs into strange hieroglyphic shapes that materialize out of the water. Like Dalí and Ernst, he establishes a powerful eerie dialogue among objects,

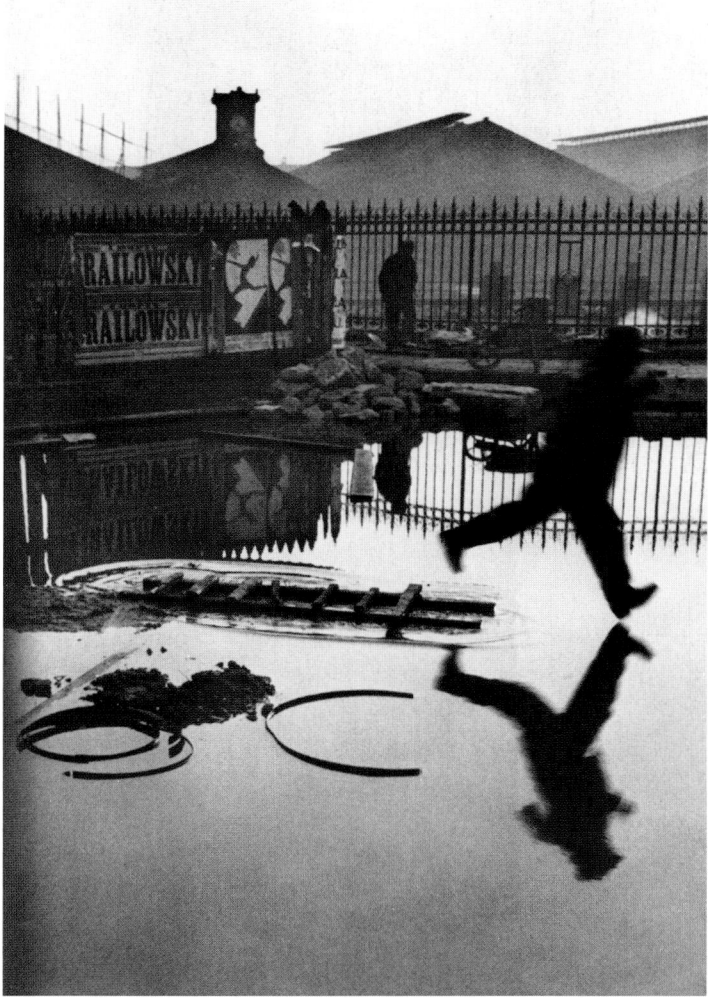

28.17 Henri Cartier-Bresson, *Behind the Gare Saint-Lazare*. 1932. Gelatin silver print

such as the man, clock, ladder, and reflections, sending the mind on an endless journey of associations and interpretations.

The Surrealist Object

When Joan Miró began work on his *Composition*, he started with an image that, like a dream, took him on a journey of psychological exploration and formal invention. Surrealists created objects that would initiate such journeys for viewers as well as for themselves. In fact, some of the most succinct Surrealist artworks were fetishistic objects, mysterious poetic things, that were found and created, and had no narrative, but jolted the unconscious and spawned infinite associations, mostly sexual and often violent. As early as 1921, Man Ray had already made one of the first Surrealist objects, *The Gift* (fig. **28.18**), a gift for the composer Erik Satie. The work is nothing more than tacks glued onto the flat side of a clothing iron. It is a shocking dislocation of both a household item and hardware that creates something unidentifiable, without logic or narrative, but filled with innuendoes of violence, pain, and sex.

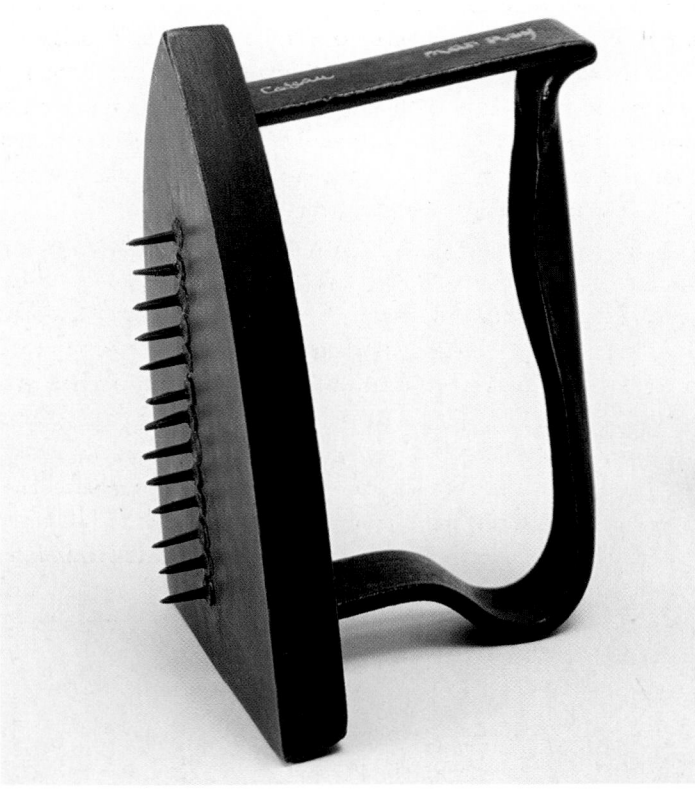

28.18 Man Ray, *The Gift*. 1921 (1958 replica). Painted flatiron with row of 13 tacks with heads glued to the bottom, 6⅛ × 3⅝ × 4½" (15.5 × 9.2 × 11.43 cm). Museum of Modern Art, New York. James Thrall Soby Fund (249.1966)

Probably the most famous Surrealist object was made by Meret Oppenheim (1913–1985). Oppenheim, the daughter of a Jungian psychologist, went to Paris as an 18-year-old in 1932. For a period she was Man Ray's model and assistant. Inspired by an off-hand comment she made when lunching with Picasso in 1936,

she covered a teacup, saucer, and spoon with gazelle fur and called it *Object* (fig. **28.19**), although Breton, when he included it in a Surrealist exhibition, retitled it *Luncheon in Fur*, punning on Manet's sexually fraught *Luncheon on the Grass* (see fig. 25.10). Oppenheim presents us with eroticism offered and eroticism denied, for, individually, fur and beverage are sensual, but juxtaposed as they are, they are disconcerting, if not outright repulsive. The fur anthropomorphizes the porcelain and spoon, and suggests, among other things, pubic hair. The work is designed to trigger the unconscious, to evoke infinite associations that deal with the repressed realities of eroticism, sensuality, desire, and anxiety. Using minimal means, Oppenheim created the "marvelous" that takes a viewer into the realm of the surreal.

ORGANIC SCULPTURE OF THE 1930S

The abstraction of such Surrealists as Masson and Miró inspired many artists to search for universal truths residing beneath the surface of things. As had the Romantic landscape painters of the previous century, they focused on nature, trying to pry loose the unseen pulse of the cosmos that coursed through the natural world. To reveal these higher truths and realities, a number of artists, including Alexander Calder in Paris and Henry Moore and Barbara Hepworth in England, turned to working with abstract organic forms. Often, they showed in Surrealist exhibitions and were occasionally labeled Surrealists, especially since their work dealt with hidden realities. But despite many parallels, their interests were quite different from Breton's as they evolved in the 1930s. Breton was more concerned with the psychology of anxiety, desire, and sex, while the artists working with abstract organic forms were more interested in the powerful forces of the universe. With the exception of Calder, they did not use chance or

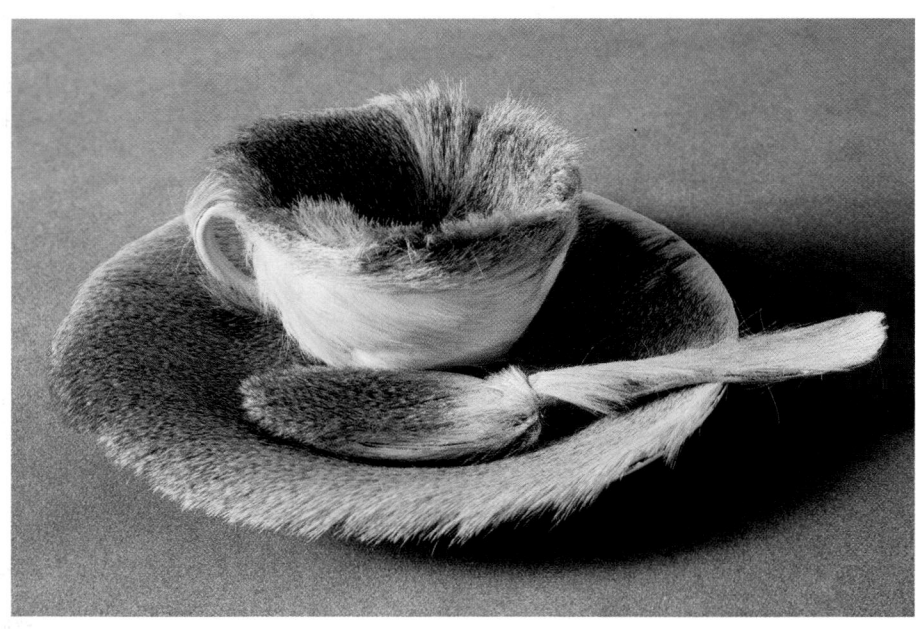

28.19 Meret Oppenheim, *Object (Luncheon in Fur)*. 1936. Fur-covered teacup, saucer, and spoon; diameter of cup 4¾" (12.1 cm); diameter of saucer 9⅜" (23.8 cm); length of spoon 8" (20.3 cm). Museum of Modern Art, New York

other devices to spur their imaginations. In some respects, their work relates more to Malevich, Kandinsky, and Mondrian than to the card-carrying Breton Surrealists. Some artists, like Jean Arp, whom we met in a Dada context but who became one of the first Surrealists, abandoned Breton's circle in the early 1930s and joined an international Paris-based group called Abstraction-Création, which was dedicated to abstract art. Similarly, Miró as well, without changing style, quit the Surrealist movement, claiming he was not a Surrealist.

Alexander Calder in Paris

Arp convinced his friend Alexander Calder (1898–1976) to become a member of Abstraction-Création as well. Calder, an American from Philadelphia, had settled in Paris in 1926, where he also befriended Miró and the abstract Dutch painter Piet Mondrian, whom we shall meet shortly. In the early 1930s, he started making mobiles, a name that Duchamp gave his kinetic sculptures. Calder's first mobiles were propelled by motors, but later mobiles were constructed of painted sheet metal attached to metal wires that were hinged together and perfectly balanced. With the slightest gust of air, the mobile seems to glide, tilting and turning in space. Some of his mobiles make a chiming sound as 'hammers' periodically swing around to strike gonglike elements. The mobiles vary in size from tabletop models to others with a 30-foot span that are suspended from a ceiling.

Like Miró and Arp, Calder generally used organic shapes, as seen in *Lobster Trap and Fish Tail* (fig. **28.20**) from 1939. The forms suggest marine life, but generally they are abstract and, like Miró's paintings, simultaneously suggest the microscopic and macroscopic. The black forms in *Lobster Trap* can be seen as a school of fish, but viewed together suggest something skeletal, even primeval. Calder was inspired to develop kinetic sculpture to suggest growth and cosmic energy. He kept his colors basic, generally using primary and secondary colors, as well as black and white. All colors stem from these, so Calder's palette symbolized the basic building blocks of life, a notion he shared with Mondrian (see page 1005), whose Paris studio he visited in 1930.

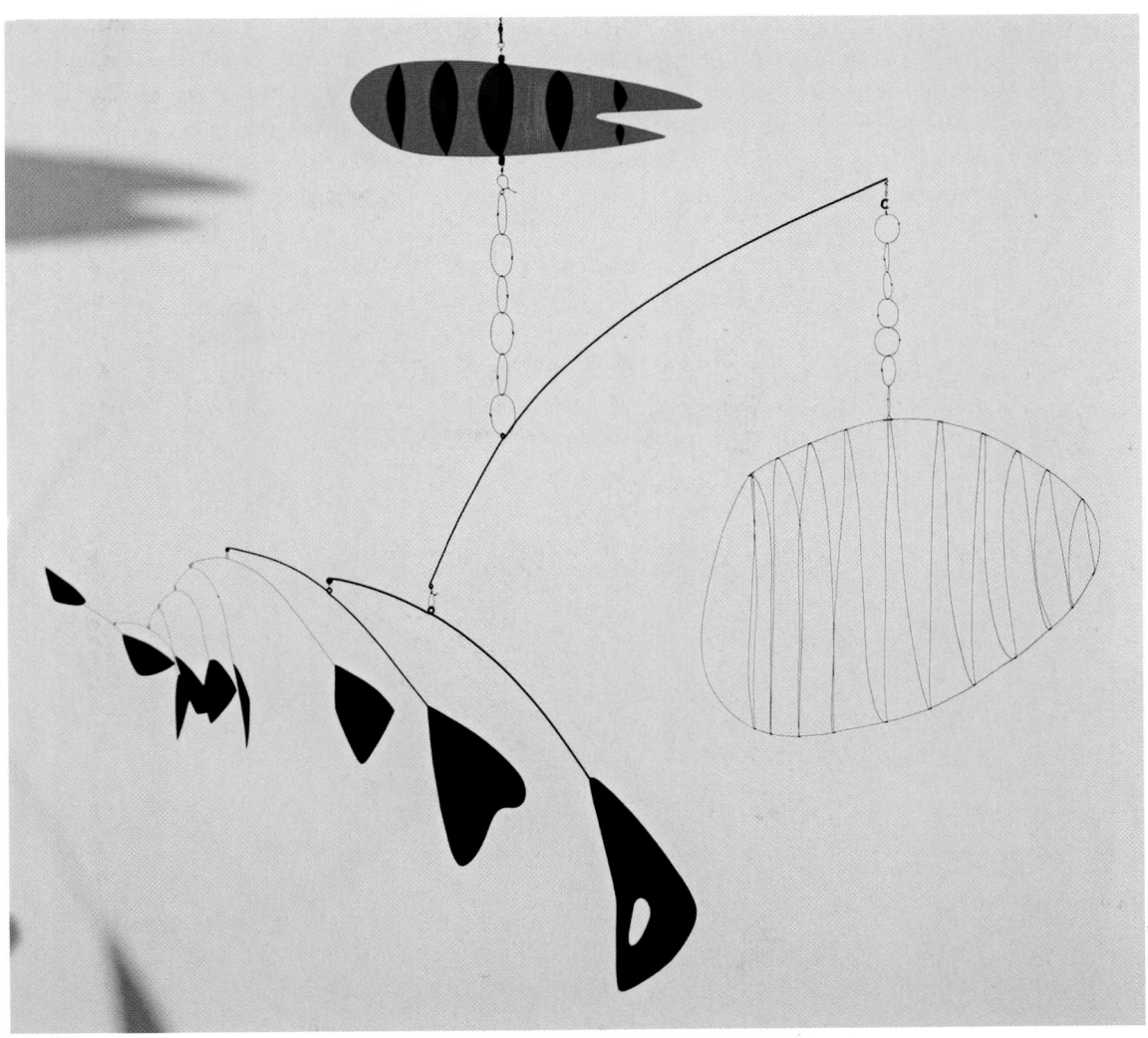

28.20   Alexander Calder, *Lobster Trap and Fish Tail*. 1939. Painted steel wire and sheet aluminum, approx. 8'6" × 9'6" (2.59 × 2.89 m). Museum of Modern Art, New York, Commissioned by the Advisory Committee for the Stairwell of the Museum

Henry Moore and Barbara Hepworth in England

The organic abstract style favored by Miró, Arp, and Calder jumped the English Channel in the 1930s, surfacing in the work of Henry Moore (1898–1986) and Barbara Hepworth. Moore studied at the Royal College of Art in London from 1921 to 1925, and in the following five years, from extensive museum visits in England and on the Continent, and through art publications, he digested the contemporary art of Brancusi, Arp, Miró, and Picasso. He was also influenced by the period's intense interest in non-Western art, including the Pre-Columbian art of Mexico.

By the early 1930s, Moore's mature style had emerged, represented here by *Recumbent Figure* (fig. **28.21**), made in 1938. The work is reminiscent of a Classical reclining river-goddess, although it is based more directly on Pre-Columbian figures. The sculptor is more interested in projecting the elemental and universal than in Classical antiquity as he explores the associations between the forms of nature and the shape of the figure. We see a woman, but the stone retains its identity as stone, looking like a rock that has been eroded by the elements for millions of years. Moore ingeniously suggests that figure and rock are one and the same, even making the female form harmonize with the striations of the stone. The universal forces present in the rock are transferred to the figure, which becomes an earth-goddess or fertility figure. The undulation of her abstract body virtually transforms

her into a landscape. Adding to the mystical aura is Moore's brilliant interplay between solid and void, each having the same weight in the composition and evoking the womblike mystery of caves or tidal pools embedded in seashore rocks.

Moore felt comfortable showing works similar to *Recumbent Figure* at the International Surrealist Exhibition held in London in 1936; he may have seen an affinity with the Surrealists in his attempts to express a higher reality lying beneath the surface of things. But Moore felt equally comfortable exhibiting in shows of abstract art, and his sculpture poses a classic case of the problematic nature of labeling art.

Barbara Hepworth (1903–1975) identified entirely with abstraction, and was a member of Abstraction-Création. She traveled to Paris in 1933 and visited the studios of Arp and Brancusi; she also met Picasso. She was in Paris again in 1935 and met Mondrian. Like Moore, who was with her for a time at the Leeds School of Art and was a lifelong friend, she was interested in investing her abstract forms with a sense of the unseen forces of nature. She began working in abstraction in the early 1930s, and within a few years her sculpture became geometric. Instead of seeming hard-edged and mechanical, however, they are organic and mysterious, a quality that became even stronger after she moved to a cottage overlooking St. Ives Bay in Cornwall on the southwest tip of England when war broke out in 1939. Her sculpture was a personal response to nature. (See *Primary Source*, page 1003.) In *Sculpture with Color (Deep Blue and Red) [6]* (fig. **28.22**), the egglike form, vaguely reminiscent of Brancusi's heads and

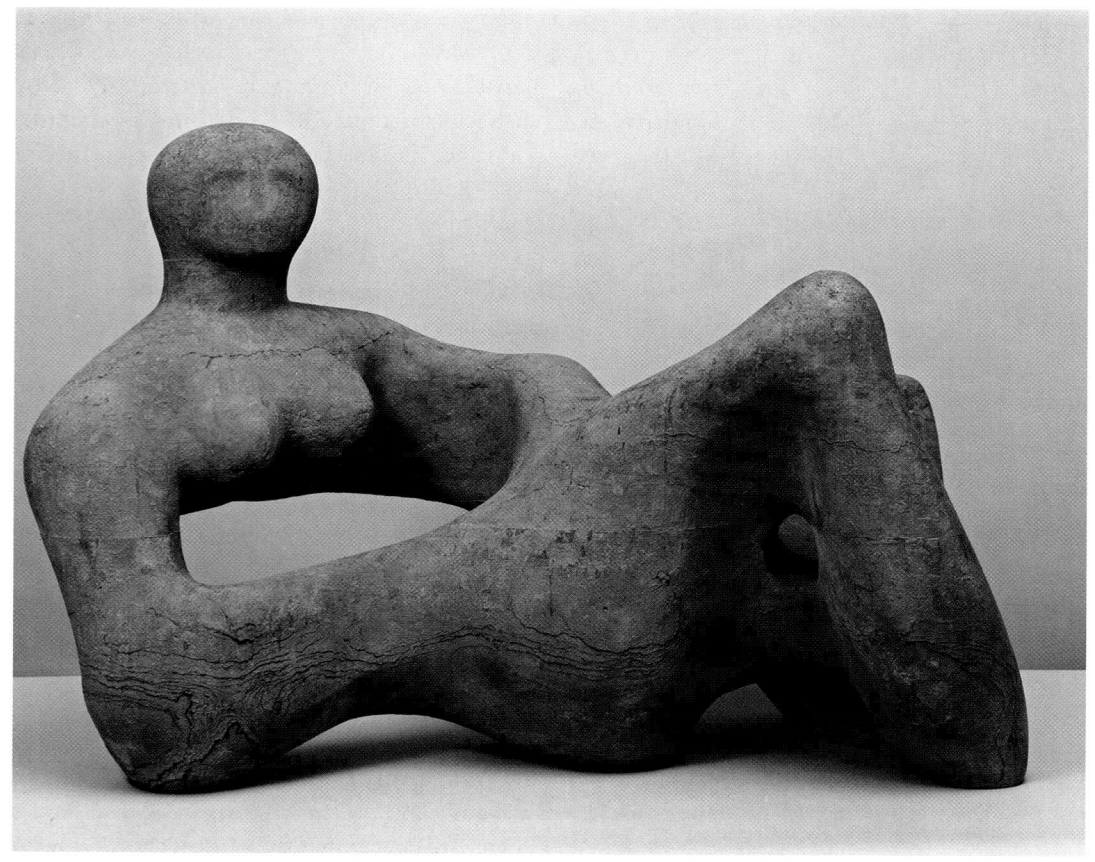

28.21 Henry Moore, *Recumbent Figure*. 1938. Green Horton stone, length approx. 54" (137.2 cm). Tate Gallery, London

Barbara Hepworth (1903–1975)

"On Sculpture" (1937)

In a 1937 book of artists' statements, British abstract sculptor Barbara Hepworth made the following statement about how her work reflects universal truths and an individual's relationship to nature.

The whole life force is in the vision which includes all phantasy, all intuitive imagination, and all conscious selection from experience. Ideas are born through a perfect balance of our conscious and unconscious life and they are realized through this same fusion and equilibrium. The choice of one idea from several, and the capacity to relate the whole of our past experience to the present idea is our conscious mind: our sensitivity to the unfolding of the idea in substance, in relation to the very act of breathing, is our unconscious intuition. ...

Contemporary constructive work does not lose by not having particular human interest, drama, fear or religious emotion. It moves us profoundly because it represents the whole of the artist's experience and vision, his whole sensibility to enduring ideas, his whole desire for a realization of these ideas in life and a complete rejection of the transitory and local forces of destruction. It is an absolute belief in man, in landscape and in the universal relationship of constructive ideas. The abstract forms of his work are now unconscious and intuitive—his individual manner of expression. His conscious life is bent on discovering a solution to human difficulties by solving his own thought permanently, and in relation to his medium. ... [Abstraction] is no escapism, no ivory tower, no isolated pleasure in proportion and space—it is an unconscious manner of expressing our belief in a possible life. The language of colour and form is universal and not one for a special class (though this may have been in the past)—it is a thought which gives the same life, the same expansion, the same universal freedom to everyone.

Source: *Circle—International Survey of Constructive Art*, ed. J. L. Martin, B. Nicholson, and N. Gabo (London: Faber and Faber, 1937)

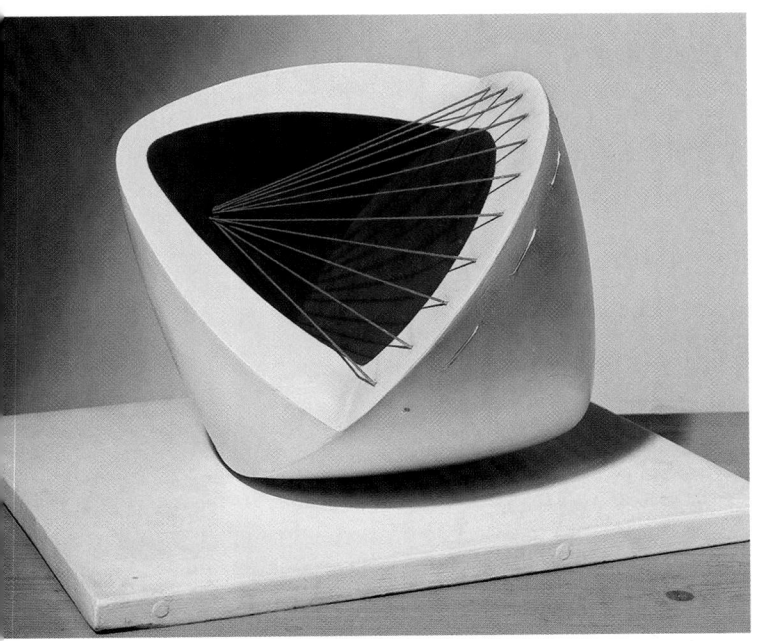

28.22 Barbara Hepworth, *Sculpture with Color (Deep Blue and Red) [6]*. 1943. Wood, painted white and blue, with red strings, on a white painted wooden base, 11 × 10" (27.9 × 26 cm). Private collection

newborns, is an elemental shape, suggesting fertility and birth. The carved wood is finely polished and covered with an immaculate sheen of white paint, producing a surface that, like the shape of the work, evokes purity. In addition, the white of the shell heightens the mystery of the dark cavity, which harbors a sky or water of deep blue. The stretched red strings have the intensity of the sun's rays and perpetual energy of life forces. Hepworth herself said, "the strings were the tension I felt between myself and the sea, the wind or the hills."

CREATING UTOPIAS

While Dada and Surrealism constituted a major force for the period between the wars, they were not the only movements. Many twentieth-century artists remained committed to exploring abstract art. Surrealists and abstract artists often shared similar social goals: Both groups championed individual freedom, and both wished to undermine bourgeois values, to eradicate nationalism, to destroy capitalism, and to create a classless society. (See www.myartslab.com.) Many Dadaists and Surrealists were socialists who also participated in Communist Party activities. Similarly, many abstract artists were socialists and Communists, but they viewed abstract art itself as a vehicle for creating a utopian society.

Two major centers of geometric abstraction emerged simultaneously: Constructivism appeared with the Russian Revolution in 1917, and De Stijl (The Style) appeared in Amsterdam. A third center was the Bauhaus in Germany, an art school founded in 1919 that succeeded as a significant force in the following decade and was often influenced by Constructivist refugees from Russia and De Stijl artists. Constructivism and the Bauhaus were especially influenced by the period's belief that industry and machines would create a better world, and the inter-war era, which indeed was dominated by tremendous technological advances, is often referred to as "The Machine Age."

Russian Constructivism: Productivism and Utilitarianism

The most direct connection between abstract art and radical politics came in the revolutionary society that developed in Russia. There, before and after the October Revolution of 1917, artists committed themselves to developing new art forms that they hoped would bring about a new utopian society. Building on the innovations of Malevich's Suprematism (see page 966), several movements followed, each attempting to put art at the service of the new revolutionary society.

VLADIMIR TATLIN As Malevich was developing his Suprematist painting in Moscow, a fellow Russian, Vladimir Tatlin (1885–1953), was working in Berlin and Paris. In 1914, Tatlin visited Picasso's Paris studio and saw his constructions (see page 954). Upon returning to Russia, he then made his own constructed reliefs (fig. **28.23**), which he called "counterreliefs," for which he used cardboard, wood, and metal covered with a variety of materials, including glazes, glass, and plaster. Similar to Russian icons and Malevich's *Black Square* (see fig. 27.23), some of the counterreliefs spanned corners, in effect using the space of the room to create a small environment. Unlike Picasso's constructions, which were generally musical instruments, Tatlin's were nonobjective, that is, they were totally abstract like Malevich's paintings, and not meant to evoke real objects. Following Tatlin's lead, other Russian sculptors began making abstract sculpture from geometric forms, a movement that in 1922 was formally called Constructivism.

With the Bolshevik Revolution in 1917, Tatlin's attitude toward his art changed. He embraced Communism and focused his efforts on supporting the party's goal of creating a utopian society. He worked for the Soviet Education Commissariat and turned his attention to architecture and engineering. A major component of his teachings was his passionate belief in the utility of modern machinery, the democratic quality of mass-produced objects, and the efficiency of industrial materials. Technological modernity was the future and the new religion, and industrial efficiency and materials had to be incorporated into art, design, and architecture, where they would produce a new, better, classless world. In other words, the social revolution had to be complemented with an aesthetic revolution. According to Tatlin's theory

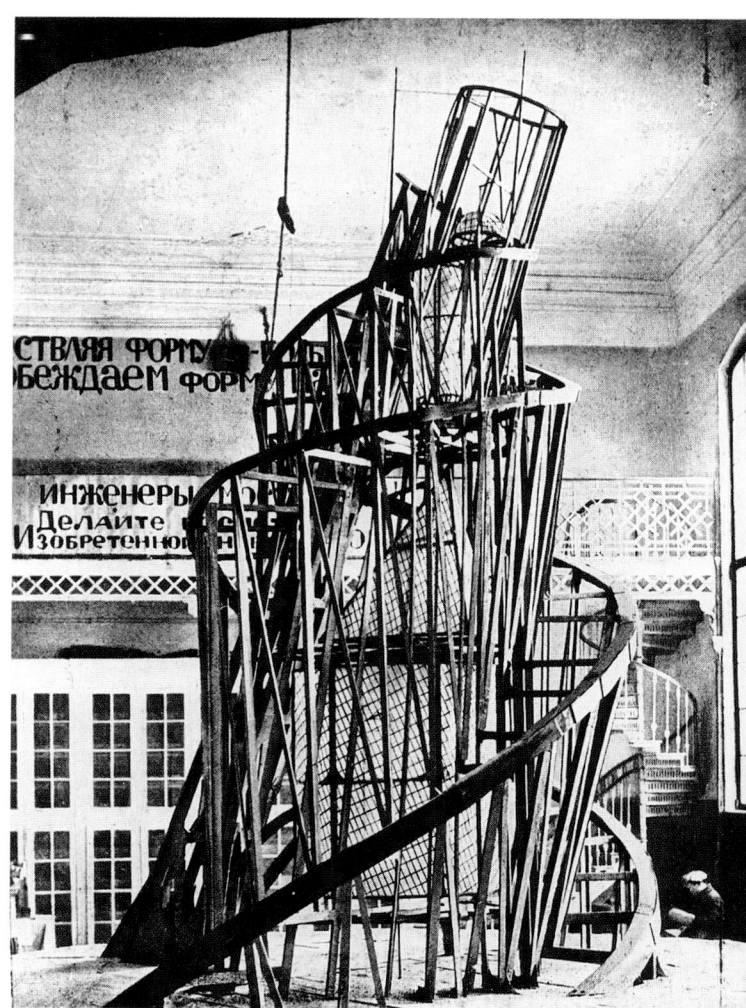

28.24 Vladimir Tatlin, *Project for "Monument to the Third International."* 1919–20. Wood, iron, and glass, height 20' (6.10 m). Destroyed; contemporary photograph

of Constructivist Productivism, everything—from appliances to clothing, from living spaces to theaters—now had to be machine-like and streamlined. Form must follow function and objects were to be stripped of all ornamentation, which was associated with bourgeois values and aristocratic ostentation.

Tatlin's most famous work is his *Project for "Monument to the Third International"* (fig. **28.24**), begun in 1919 and exhibited in Petrograd (St. Petersburg) and Moscow in December 1920. The project was actually a model for a building—which was never built—that was supposed to be 1,300 feet high, which would have made it the tallest structure in the world at that time. It was to have a metal spiral frame tilted at an angle and encompassing a glass cube, cylinder, and cone. These steel and glass units, housing conference and meeting rooms, were to revolve, making a complete revolution once a year, month, and day, respectively. The industrial materials of steel and glass and the dynamic, kinetic nature of the work symbolized the new Machine Age and the dynamism of the Bolshevik Revolution. The tower was to function as a propaganda center for the Communist Third

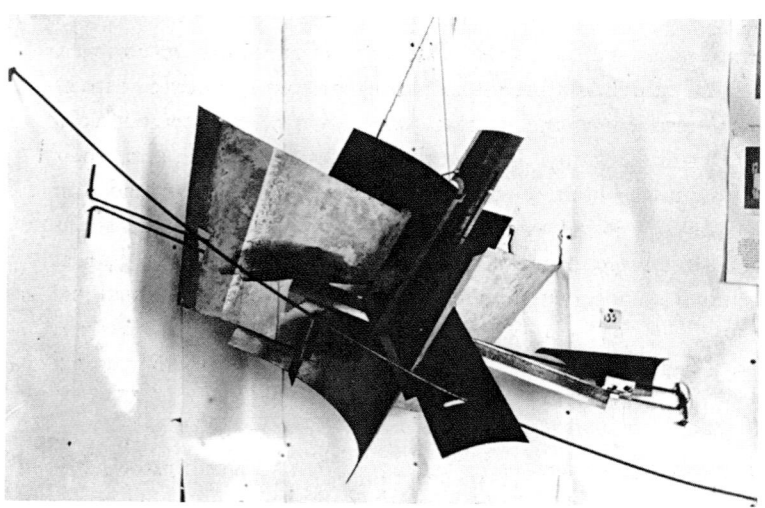

28.23 Vladimir Tatlin, *Corner Counterrelief.* 1915. Mixed media, 31½ × 59 × 29½" (80 × 150 × 75 cm). Presumed destroyed

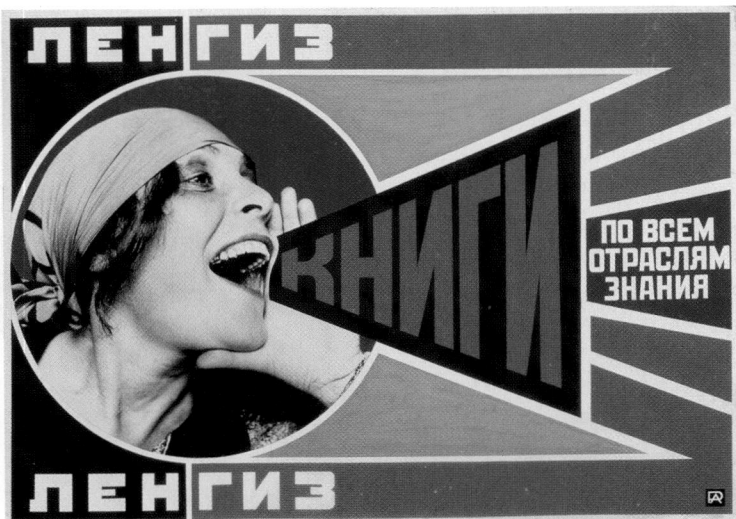

28.25 Alexander Rodchenko, *Advertisement: "Books!"* 1925. Rodchenko Archive, Moscow, Russia

International, an organization devoted to world revolution, and its rotating, ascending spiral symbolized the aspirations of Communism.

Following Tatlin's dictum of "Art into Life," many artists, at least temporarily if not completely, gave up making conventional art in order to design functional objects that would help create the great classless utopia. Both Aleksandr Rodchenko (1891–1956) and his wife Varvara Fedorovna Stepanova (1894–1958) fall into this category. In the early 1920s, Rodchenko stopped making Suprematist paintings and Constructivist assemblages to focus on graphic design, as seen here in a poster promoting literacy (fig. **28.25**). We are far removed from the organic and human Art Nouveau posters of Toulouse-Lautrec (see fig. 26.8), for example. Instead, a bold mechanical geometry prevails, with a nearly space-less image pressed to the surface. Even the letters are austere and geometric. Bold color creates an energy that is reinforced by the design, where the word "Books," for example, is shaped like a megaphone that emits the phrase "In All Spheres of Knowledge." At the time, Stepanova was the designer for a Moscow textile factory. In the sportswear reproduced here (fig. **28.26**), we again see bright colors and a simple yet energetic machinelike geometry. There is no ornamentation or reference to the past, nothing that could be associated with any class, time period, ethnic type, or region. Confronted with the problem of creating a new society, the Constructivist designers invented a new graphic language, one that was distinctly modern, utilitarian, and classless.

De Stijl and Universal Order

In 1917 in Amsterdam, Piet Mondrian (1872–1944), with painter Theo van Doesburg (1883–1931) and several other artists and architects, founded a movement called De Stijl (The Style). Architect Gerrit Rietveld (1888–1964) joined the group in 1919. Though not backed by a revolutionary government, as were the

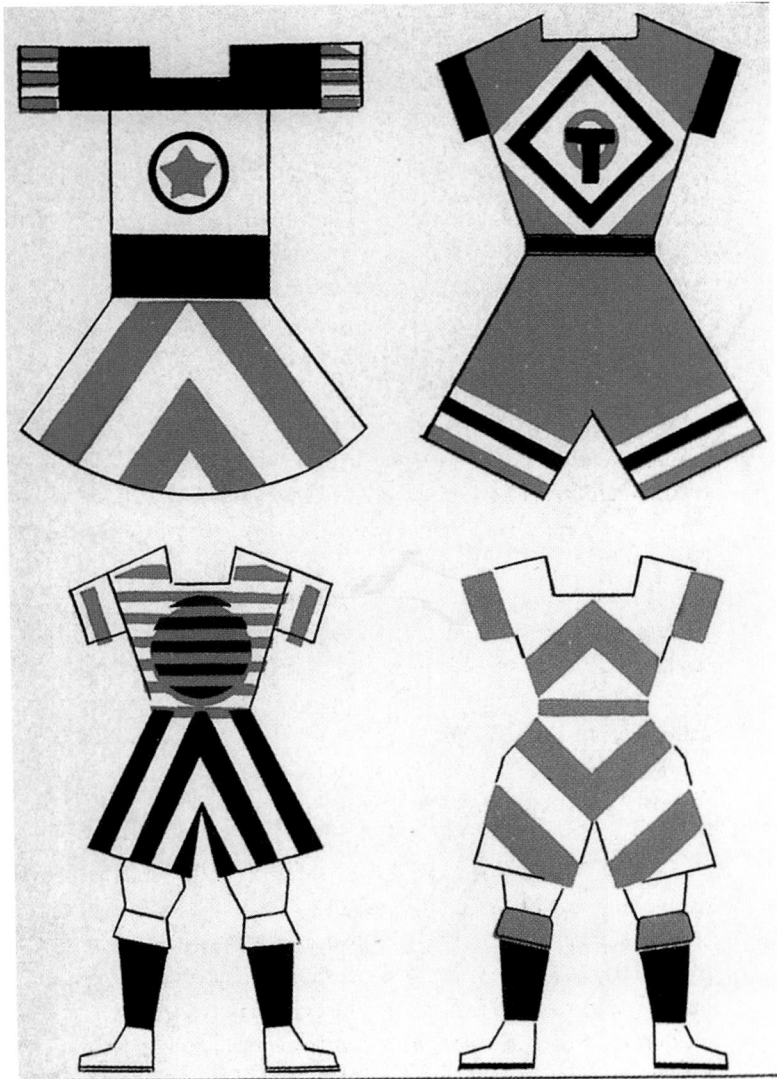

28.26 Varvara Fedorovna Stepanova, *Design for Sportswear*. 1923. Gouache and ink on paper, 11⅞ × 8½" (30.2 × 21.7 cm). Collection Alexander Lavrentiev

Russian artists, their goal was every bit as radical and utopian, for De Stijl artists sought to create, through geometric abstraction, total environments that were so perfect they embodied a universal harmony. Unlike their Russian counterparts, their mission was literally spiritual. Driven by Mondrian and Van Doesburg's intense commitment to Theosophy, De Stijl artists, as did the Communists, sought a universal order that would make nationalism obsolete. They called their style the International Style, applying it most often to a new architecture of glass and steel that was modern, pure, and universal, with no national identification.

PIET MONDRIAN In the magazine *De Stijl*, the group's publication, the artist Piet Mondrian (1872–1944) presented his theory of art in a series of articles. (See *Primary Source*, page 1007.) His philosophy was based on Theosophy (see page 946), which he was

28.27 Piet Mondrian, *Composition No.II/Composition I// Composition en Rouge, Bleu et Jaune (Composition with Red, Blue, and Yellow).* 1930. Oil on canvas, 20⅛ × 20⅛" (51 × 51 cm). The Fukuoka City Bank Ltd., Japan. © 2009 Mondrian/Holtzman Trust, c/o HCR International, Warrenton, Virginia, USA

square canvas is assigned its own identity. Every line exists in its own right, not as a means of defining the color rectangles. (The thickness of the lines often varies in his paintings, a function of individual identity.) Each component in the painting sits on the same plane on the surface—there is no foreground or background, no one object sitting on top of another. Despite this perfectly interlocking surface, the painting has a feeling of tremendous space, even of infinity, largely due to the rectangles expanding off the edges of the canvas. Space and mass have merged into a harmonious whole in what Mondrian called "dynamic equilibrium," where everything is energized yet balanced. Mondrian has attempted to capture the complexity of the universe—the individuality of its infinite components and the harmony and spiritual sameness that holds everything together.

Mondrian did endless variations of these motifs. Even the color did not change, since these elementary hues, from which all colors are derived, are symbolic of the building blocks of the cosmos. But in principle, painting was not the end product of Mondrian's aesthetic program. He considered it just a stop-gap measure until perfect abstract environments of architecture, furniture, and objects embodying all of these same principles could be achieved. Until then, the world needed his painting.

GERRIT RIETVELD Mondrian's De Stijl colleagues sought to implement his theories in architecture and interior design. In 1917, Gerrit Rietveld (1888–1964), a furniture maker who became a self-taught architect, designed the "Red-Blue" chair (fig. **28.28**), representing the first attempt to apply Neo-Plasticism to the

interested in before his move to Paris in 1911. After returning to neutral Amsterdam during the Great War, he was further influenced by the ideas of mystical lay philosopher and close acquaintance M. H. J. Schoenmaekers and especially Schoenmaekers's book *New Image of the World,* the only book other than his own publications in his library. Schoenmaekers argued that there was an underlying mathematical structure to the universe that constituted true reality. He believed that an artist could access and present this structure through rational manipulations of geometric forms. Mondrian developed an art based on such geometry and, using Schoenmaekers's term, he called it Neo-Plasticism, meaning "New Plasticism." By "plastic" in painting, he meant that the world of the painting had a plastic, or three-dimensional, reality of its own that corresponded to the harmonious plastic reality of the universe. In other words, he sought to replicate in his art the unseen underlying structure of the cosmos.

Beginning in 1917, Mondrian struggled to achieve this using total geometric abstraction, and only succeeded in his efforts upon returning to Paris in late 1919. After establishing his style, he pretty much retained it for the rest of his life, as seen in *Composition en Rouge, Bleu et Jaune* (fig. **28.27**) of 1930. His paintings, which are always asymmetrical, are remarkable for their perfect harmony. Mondrian very precisely gives every element in his painting equal weight. Each line and rectangle in this

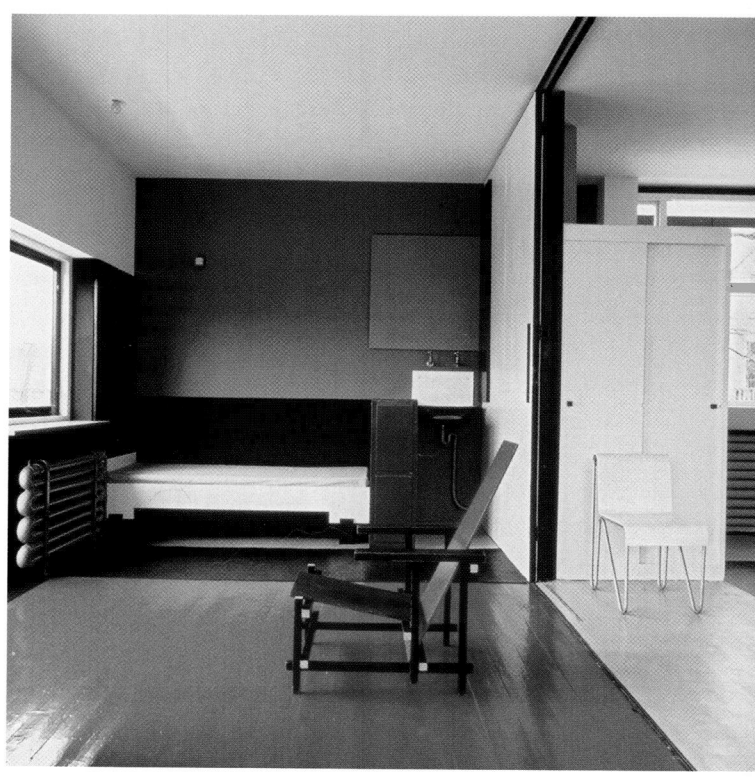

28.28 Gerrit Rietveld. Interior of Schröder House, with "Red-Blue" chair, Utrecht, Holland. 1924

Piet Mondrian (1872–1944)

From "Natural Reality and Abstract Reality" (1919)

This is an excerpt from an essay originally published in the magazine De Stijl in 1919. Here Mondrian explains how Neo-Plastic painting, using an abstract vocabulary, captures universal harmony.

The cultivated man of today is gradually turning away from natural things, and his life is becoming more and more abstract.

Natural (external) things become more and more automatic, and we observe that our vital attention fastens more and more on internal things. The life of the truly modern man is neither purely materialistic nor purely emotional. It manifests itself rather as a more autonomous life of the human mind becoming conscious of itself.

Natural man—although a unity of body, mind and soul—exhibits a changed consciousness: every expression of his life has today a different aspect, that is, an aspect more positively abstract.

It is the same with art. Art will become the product of another duality in man: the product of a cultivated externality and of an inwardness deepened and more conscious. As a pure representation of the human mind, art will express itself in an aesthetically purified, that is to say, abstract form.

The truly modern artist is aware of abstraction in an emotion of beauty; he is conscious of the fact that the emotion of beauty is cosmic, universal. This conscious recognition has for its corollary an abstract plasticism, for man adheres only to what is universal.

The new plastic idea cannot, therefore, take the form of a natural or concrete representation, although the latter does always indicate the universal to a degree, or at least conceals it within. This new plastic idea will ignore the particulars of appearance, that is to say, natural form and color. On the contrary, it should find its expression in the abstraction of form and color, that is to say, in the straight line and the clearly defined primary color. ...

We find that in nature all relations are dominated by a single primordial relation, which is defined by the opposition of two extremes. Abstract plasticism represents this primordial relation in a precise manner by means of the two positions which form the right angle. This positional relation is the most balanced of all, since it expresses in a perfect harmony the relation between two extremes, and contains all other relations.

If we conceive these two extremes as manifestations of interiority and exteriority, we will find that in the new plasticism the tie uniting mind and life is not broken; thus, far from considering it a negation of truly living life we shall see a reconciliation of the matter-mind dualism.

Source: *De Stijl*, Vol. I, 1919

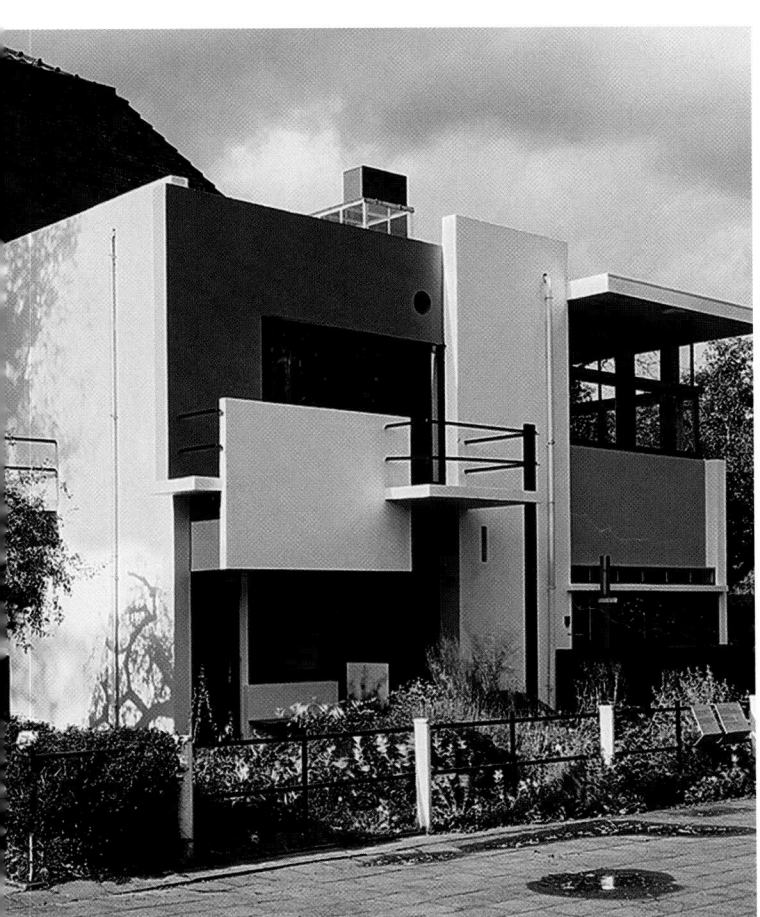

28.29   Gerrit Rietveld. Schröder House, Utrecht, Holland. 1924

decorative arts. One of the more uncomfortable chairs ever made, its emphasis was on spiritual aesthetics, employing flat planes and primary colors to implement Mondrian's dynamic equilibrium. Once the De Stijl members discovered and understood Frank Lloyd Wright (see page 934), whose works were published and available in Europe in 1911, they were able to apply architectural solutions to the theoretical ideas of Neo-Plasticism. They recognized that Wright had destroyed "the box," and declared "the new architecture will be anticubic." Combining the color and floating planes of Mondrian and the fluid spaces of Wright, Rietveld produced the definitive De Stijl building in 1924, the Schröder House in Utrecht (fig. **28.29**), which was built onto the end of existing row houses. On the façade, we can find Mondrian's "floating" rectangles and lines. Even the Wright-like cantilevered roof appears to float. The interior (see fig. 28.28) is designed according to the same principles, with wall-to-ceiling sliding panels allowing for a restructuring of the space. Both inside and out, the Schröder House is a three-dimensional Mondrian painting—ethereal, buoyant, and harmonious, embodying dynamic equilibrium.

The Bauhaus: Creating the "New Man"

As we have seen, most Dadaists, Surrealists, and abstract artists were socialists or Communists who believed the Bolshevik Revolution in Russia would save the world from bourgeois materialism and decadence and would establish a worldwide utopian society. Left-wing artists flocked to Berlin in 1922 to see the first

Russian Art Exhibition, which presented the Constructivists for the first time in the West. Twice more that year, the avant-garde held conferences in Germany, attempting to commit to a social program that would put art at the service of restructuring society. All of these attempts came to naught. Instead, it was the Bauhaus, an art and design school, that gradually emerged as the strongest center for advocating social progress through art.

The Bauhaus was founded in Weimar, Germany, in 1919 by the great Modernist architect Walter Gropius (see page 978). In many respects, the Bauhaus School was the embodiment of Muthesius's German Werkbund (see page 977), since the goal of the workshops was to design modern high-quality production-line products. Its guiding principle, however, was more utopian and less commercial, for the Bauhaus (meaning House of Building) was dedicated to the creation of utilitarian design for "the new man" through the marriage of art and technology. The school was formed by the merger of two Weimar arts and crafts schools, and designed to combine the fine and applied arts, giving each equal weight, as had the earlier Secessionist movements (see page 922). The artists were called artisan/craftspeople, and their mission was to create an abstract environment of the most progressive modernity. Their design ethic was based on "the living environment of machines and vehicles." Only "primary forms and colors" could be used, all in the service of creating "standard types for all practical commodities of everyday use as a social necessity." Like De Stijl, this was a philosophy oriented toward environments, not just painting and sculpture, and the Bauhaus is

often more associated with the work that came out of the textile, metal, and ceramic workshops, such as Marcel Breuer's 1927 aluminum tubular chairs and Anni Albers's abstract textiles, than with the paintings of Klee, Kandinsky, and Josef Albers, who also taught at the school.

MARCEL BREUER We can see the Bauhaus machine aesthetic at work in the living room of a Gropius house built in 1927 for a Werkbund housing development in Stuttgart (fig. **28.30**). The furniture and lighting were designed by Marcel Breuer (1902–1981), a former Bauhaus student who became a faculty member in 1925, heading the furniture workshop. All of Breuer's objects are geometric, made of modern materials, and easily mass-produced. On the far right is perhaps his most famous product, the "Wassily" armchair, made of polished, nickel-plated tubular steel and cotton fabric. In its planarity, Breuer was clearly influenced by the Rietveld "Red-Blue" chair (which Van Doesburg had introduced to the Bauhaus in 1921 when he taught there and Breuer was a student). But now heavy wood has been replaced by a strong but light metal tube that is geometrically structured in an airy, open pattern. The feeling that results echoes the transparency and weightlessness of Suprematist painting and Constructivist sculpture, qualities that can even be seen in Tatlin's *Project for "Monument to the Third International"* (see fig. 28.24). Breuer described a practical side to his design when in the product catalogue he wrote that the chair "provides a light, fully self-sprung sitting opportunity, which has the comfort of the upholstered

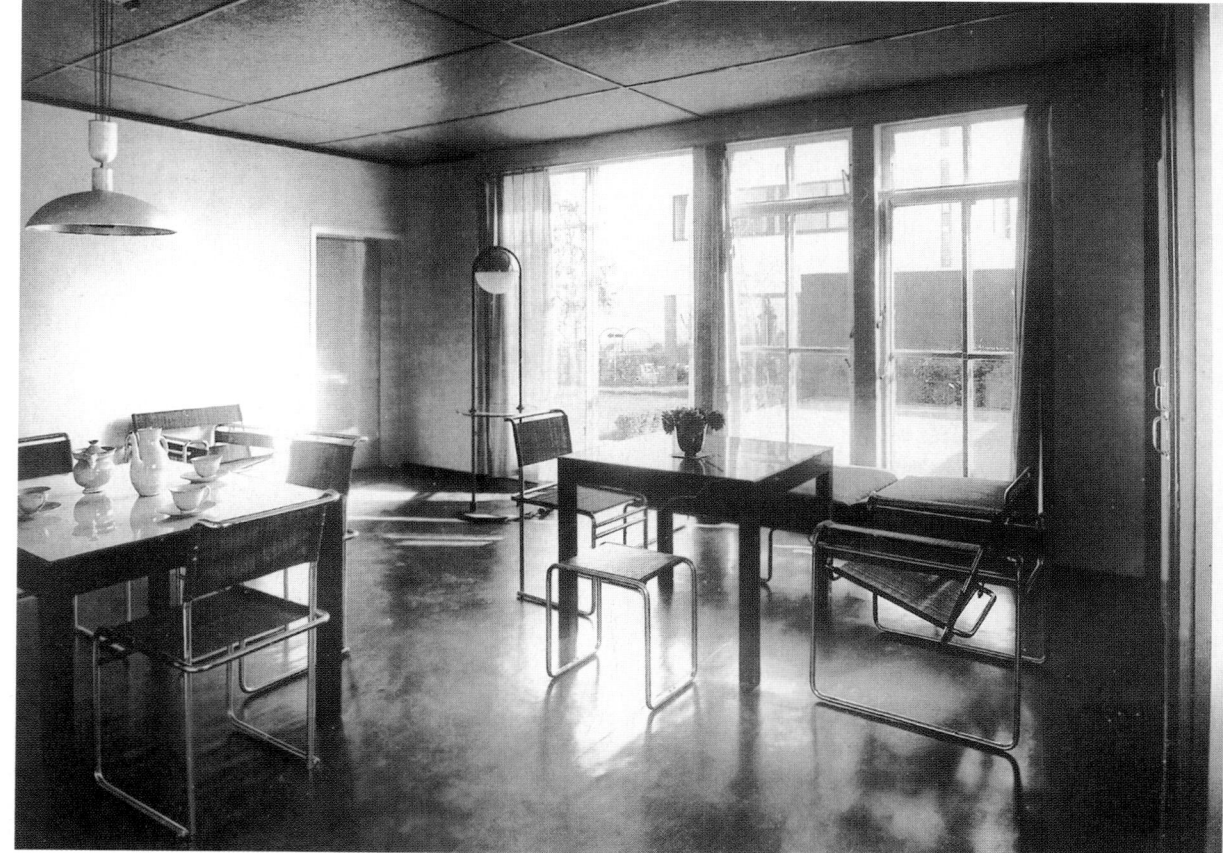

28.30 Walter Gropius. Two houses for the Werkbund housing development Weissenhof Settlement, Stuttgart, with furniture by Marcel Breuer. 1927

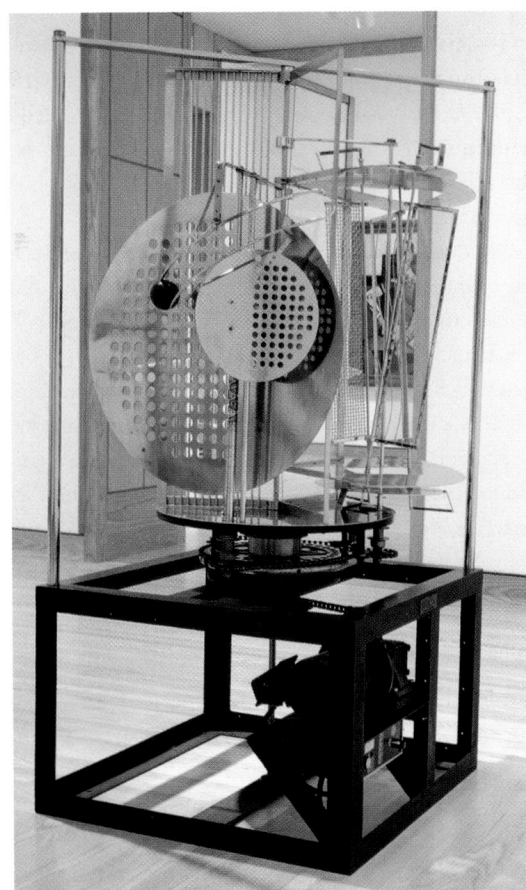

28.31 László Moholy-Nagy, *Light-Space Modulator*. 1922–30. Exhibition replica, 2006, constructed courtesy of Hattula Maholy-Nagy. Steel, plastic, wood, and other materials with electric motor, 59½ × 27½ × 27½" (151.1 × 69.9 × 69.9 cm). Harvard Art Museum, Busch-Reisinger Museum, Hildegard von Gontard Bequest Fund, 2007.105

armchair, but with the difference that it is much lighter, handier, more hygienic."

LÁSZLÓ MOHOLY-NAGY One of the strongest advocates of Constructivism at the Bauhaus, and perhaps the most influential figure there, was the Hungarian László Moholy-Nagy (1895–1946). Gropius hired Moholy-Nagy in 1923 as head of the metal workshop, but gradually he became the school's primary theoretician, concerned particularly with light and movement. As early as 1922, he began designing Constructivist sculptures that generated light, as seen in *Light-Space Modulator* (fig. **28.31**). This machinelike construction of planes of plastic, steel, and wood was propelled in a circle by a motor and projected an ever-changing light spectacle onto its surroundings. It was used as a prop in a 1930 ballet at the Bauhaus, but Moholy-Nagy also viewed it as a tool to study light and space, hoping to uncover new applications for environmental or stage lighting.

WALTER GROPIUS Many art historians consider the crowning aesthetic achievement of the Bauhaus to be the building itself, designed by Gropius in 1925–26 when the school moved from Weimar to Dessau. The building consists of three L-shaped wings coming off a central hub: The Shop Block, a workshop wing, is shown in figure **28.32**; a second wing had classrooms; and a third wing held an auditorium/theater, dining hall, and dormitory with studios. From the air, the complex looked like a Constructivist sculpture of rectangular blocks. The Bauhaus is dominated by a clearly articulated geometry. The workshop wing looks like an empty glass box, the glass curtain wall on two sides continuing around corners and flush with the stuccoed parapet above and

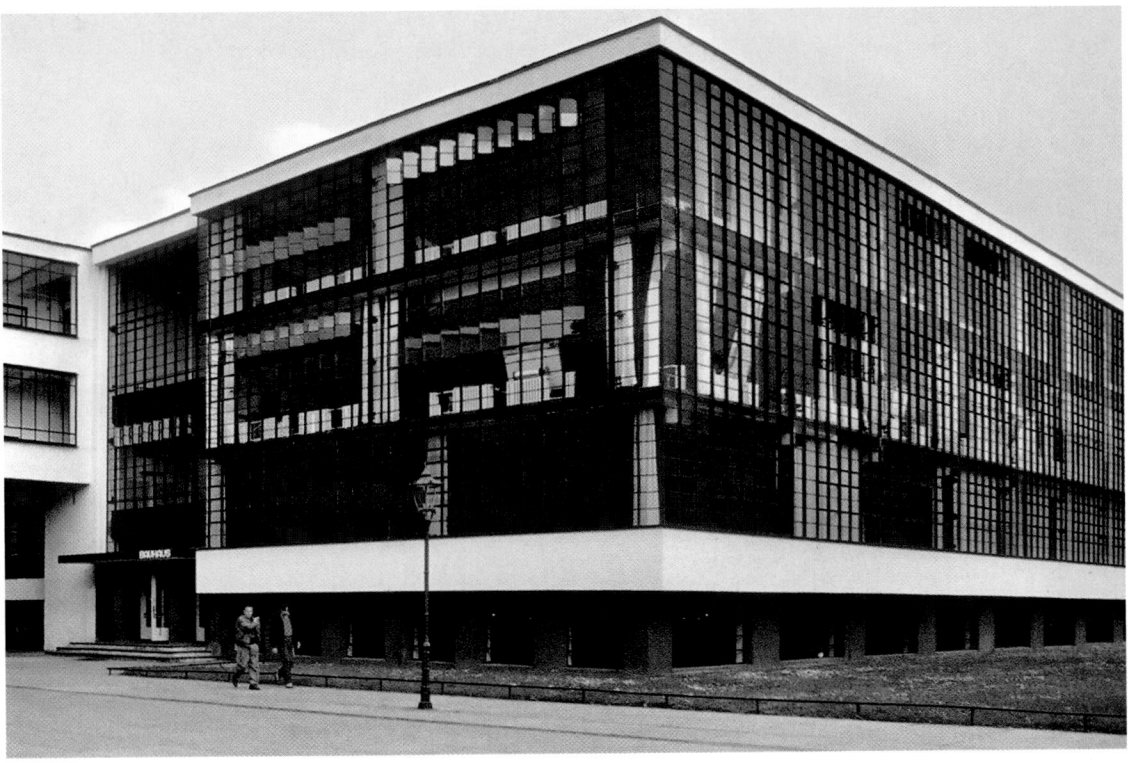

28.32 Walter Gropius. Shop Block, Bauhaus, Dessau, Germany. 1925–26

socle, or projecting molding underlying the wall, below. Instead of mass, we feel a weightless volume as defined by the metal and glass wall. And because the building projects over a setback half-basement, it seems to float.

Perhaps more than anything designed by De Stijl, Gropius's Bauhaus came to epitomize High Modernist architecture—the architecture that evolved out of Early Modernism (see pages 976–80) in the period between the two wars. With High Modernism, buildings became more severely geometric and so light they seemed to float. Their unadorned geometric shapes represented volume, not mass. Their walls, regardless of material, were thin membranes of a taut veneer that encased the building, and, as with the Bauhaus workshop, often this veneer was a curtain of glass, although horizontal strips of windows were generally favored by High Modernist architects. But High Modernism was more than just a style; it was a social movement predicated on a utopian socialist philosophy and a rationalist belief in progress. Life could be improved, the theory went, by creating a Machine Age environment. Ultimately, the movement was reduced to a style in 1932 when Philip Johnson and historian Henry-Russell Hitchcock organized an exhibition entitled *The International Style* at the newly opened Museum of Modern Art in New York. Their concern was with the look of the architecture, not its social premises. The exhibition brought the style to the attention of Americans, and resulted in the label "International Style," coined by De Stijl, being used to describe High Modernist architecture.

LUDWIG MIES VAN DER ROHE In 1930, architect Ludwig Mies van der Rohe (1886–1969) became the last director of the Bauhaus, which closed in 1933. In the 1920s, Mies had been at the center of the Berlin avant-garde. A student of Peter Behrens, he became a leading Modernist, and in 1927 organized the experimental Weissenhof Estate exhibition in Stuttgart, where leading architects were invited to build inexpensive but quality housing for workers. At this point he was converted to High Modernism, or the International Style, and was heavily influenced by the floating planes of De Stijl and the complex spaces of Wright. His motto, however, was "Less is more," and his architecture is characterized by a severe geometry and simplicity. Nonetheless, his buildings never seem austere; they invariably have elegant proportions and a sense of refinement that makes them seem rich and lush. When budget allowed, he augmented this refinement by using luxurious materials, such as expensive marble and travertine, bronze, chrome, and tinted glass.

We can see these qualities in his German Pavilion (fig. **28.33**), designed for the 1929 Barcelona Exposition and dismantled after the fair closed. (A reconstruction exists in the same site today.) The pavilion itself was the German exhibit, and the building simply consists of spaces with no specific uses attached to them. There is nothing overtly innovative here; the overlapping horizontal and vertical planes, the interlocking open-form space, and canterlevering had been used previously in the work of Wright and the De Stijl architects. Mies's innovation is subtle, and it resides in its simplicity of style. Geometry is everywhere. The pavilion sits on an enormous rectangular platform of beautiful travertine, and is partially enclosed by rectangular walls of travertine or Tinian marble. At either end, the platform is not covered and there is an asymmetrically placed but perfectly balanced rectangular pool lined with lush-looking black glass. The cantilevered flat roof is supported by a grid of eight slender piers, each a chrome x, between which are five partition walls, two in onyx, and the three others made of different kinds of glass—clear, frosted, and green—and encased in chrome mullions (fig. **28.34**). Using a minimal vocabulary, Mies created a sumptuous, elegant feast for the eye. Even the cantilevered chair he designed for the pavilion, known as the "Barcelona" chair and seen in figure 28.34, is simultaneously simple and posh, and, in contrast to the Rietveld "Red-Blue" chair, exceptionally comfortable.

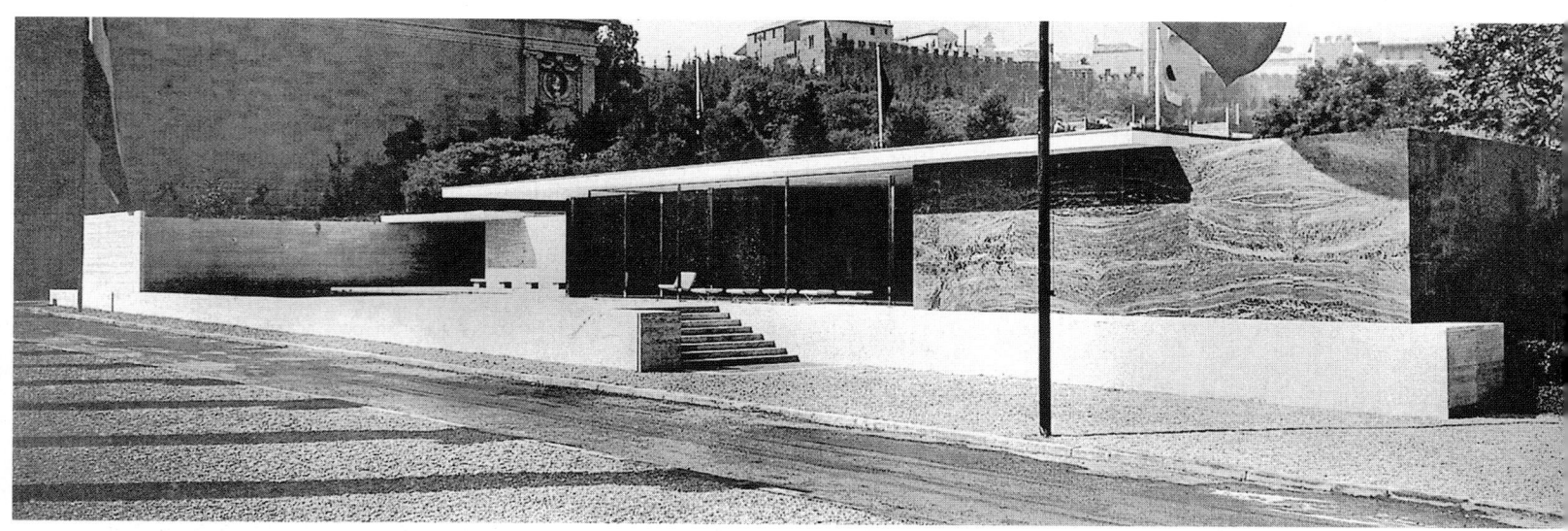

28.33 Ludwig Mies van der Rohe. German Pavilion, 1929. Guggenheim International Exposition, Barcelona

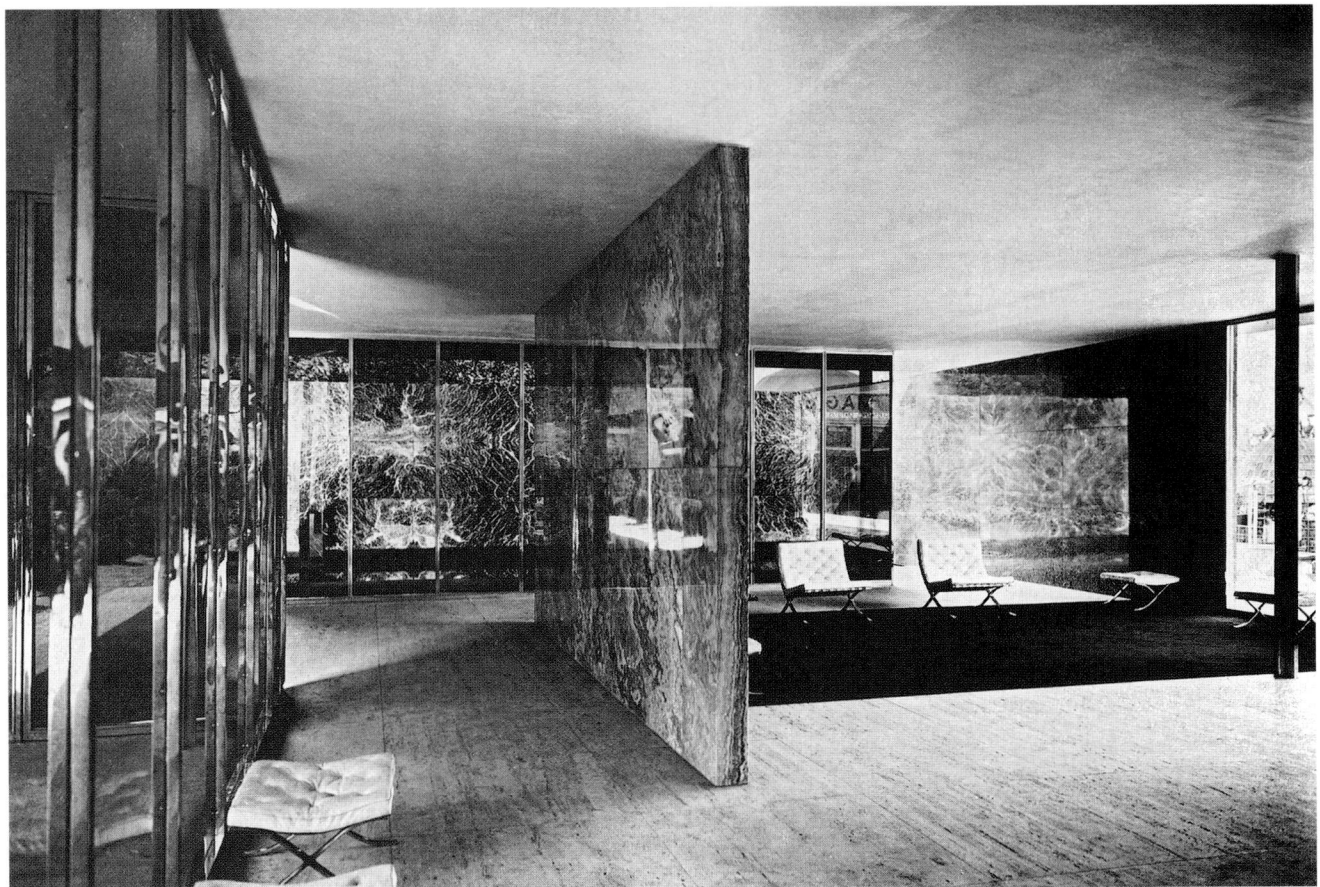

28.34 Ludwig Mies van der Rohe. Interior of the German Pavilion, with Barcelona Chairs, 1929. Guggenheim International Exposition, Barcelona

The Machine Aesthetic in Paris

The machine aesthetic and the utopian dream that accompanied it also made their way to Paris, where they found a rather different voice in the architecture of Charles-Édouard Jeanneret, called Le Corbusier (1886–1965). While developing his radical architectural theories, Le Corbusier also practiced as a painter, working under his given name Jeanneret. He created a style of painting that he called Purism, which reflected his belief in the supremacy of a machine aesthetic that embodied a Classical spirit. Purism influenced the French Cubist Fernand Léger, who was already well disposed toward glorifying the efficiency and purity of modern technology. Unlike Moscow, Amsterdam, and Dessau, Paris had no art schools or major artistic movements pushing for a utopian vision. Instead, the cause there was undertaken by individuals.

LE CORBUSIER'S IDEAL HOME Le Corbusier was Swiss, and led a rather peripatetic life prior to settling in Paris in the 1910s. In 1907, in Lyon, France, he met architect Tony Garnier, who had developed an ideal industrial city, the Cité Industrielle, which influenced Le Corbusier to think in terms of socialist utopian architecture and the creation of an easily reproducible architectural type that would provide superior housing for everyone. The following year in Paris, he worked part time for Auguste

Perret, the architect responsible for popularizing ferroconcrete—steel-reinforced concrete—as an architectural material. Most important, however, he demonstrated, as Max Berg had in his Breslau Jahrhunderthalle in 1912–13 (see fig. 27.39), the practicality of ferroconcrete: It is inexpensive, adaptable, easy to use, and very strong, combining the tensile strength of steel with the compressive resistance of concrete. (See *Materials and Techniques*, page 1013.) It is the medium Le Corbusier would adopt for most of his buildings. The last major influence on Le Corbusier was his experience in 1910 working in Peter Behrens's office in Berlin, where his colleagues included Walter Gropius and Mies van der Rohe. Here, he worked first hand with the German avant-garde architects who would be responsible for developing the International Style, and even then he was talking about creating a machine-based, easily reproduced architecture.

In 1922, Le Corbusier opened an architectural firm with his cousin Pierre Jeanneret, and over the course of the next two decades, he designed a series of houses that allowed him to develop and implement his theories of the ideal house, one that could serve as a prototype for all homes. (See *Primary Source*, page 1012.) He called his first type, developed in 1914, the Dom-Ino, because the house consisted of concrete floors with ceilings that sat on concrete columns arranged in a grid pattern that resembled the dots on a domino. By 1923, he had developed the

Le Corbusier (1886–1965)

From *Towards a New Architecture* (1923)

First published in 1923, Towards a New Architecture *codified ideas that were being widely discussed among architects, and it became the first manifesto of the International Style. The following excerpts are from the opening argument.*

The Architect, by his arrangement of forms, realizes an order which is a pure creation of his spirit; by forms and shapes he affects our senses to an acute degree and provokes plastic emotions; by the relationships which he creates he wakes profound echoes in us, he gives us the measure of an order which we feel to be in accordance with that of our world, he determines the various movements of our heart and of our understanding; it is then that we experience the sense of beauty.

Primary forms are beautiful forms because they can be clearly appreciated.

The great problems of modern construction must have a geometrical solution. …

The house is a machine for living in.

Standards are a matter of logic, analysis, and minute study. …

Man looks at the creation of architecture with his eyes, which are 5 feet 6 inches from the ground.

Industry, overwhelming us like a flood which rolls on towards its destined ends, has furnished us with new tools adapted to this new epoch, animated by the new spirit.

The problem of the house is a problem of the epoch.

If we eliminate from our hearts and minds all dead concepts in regard to the house, and look at the question from a critical and objective point of view, we shall arrive at the "House-Machine," the mass-production house, healthy (and morally so, too) and beautiful. …

Source: Le Corbusier, *Towards a New Architecture* (New York: Dover, 1986)

---

principles for his ideal home, which he published in an article entitled "Five Points of a New Architecture." His five points were the following: (1) no ground floor, with the house raised on columns called **pilotis**; (2) a flat roof, which would be used as a garden terrace; (3) an open floor plan, with partitions slotted between supports; (4) free composition of the exterior curtain walls; and (5) preferably ribbon (horizontal) windows. The raised house allowed for privacy and light and made the outdoors accessible by putting a garden on the roof. Much later, Le Corbusier remarked that "a house is a machine for living in," which suggested—wrongly—to many critics that he advocated a brutal functionalism that was not concerned with beauty and comfort. In fact, Le Corbusier wanted to create a Classical purity based on

geometry and a machine-age look. "Architecture is the masterly, correct, and magnificent play of masses brought together in light," he wrote. "Cubes, cones, cylinders, and pyramids are the primary forms which light reveals to advantage." Within this aesthetic, however, his emphasis was on the human being and "living." Machine Age values and technology were meant to serve humans, and consequently his houses, using the latest technology, would have a Machine Age look and efficiency. And they would be filled with light.

The 1928–29 Villa Savoye (fig. **28.35**) in Poissy-sur-Seine, outside Paris, is Le Corbusier's best-known house, and here we can see most of the elements called for in his "Five Points": the pilotis, the raised living space, the ribbon windows, and the flat-roof

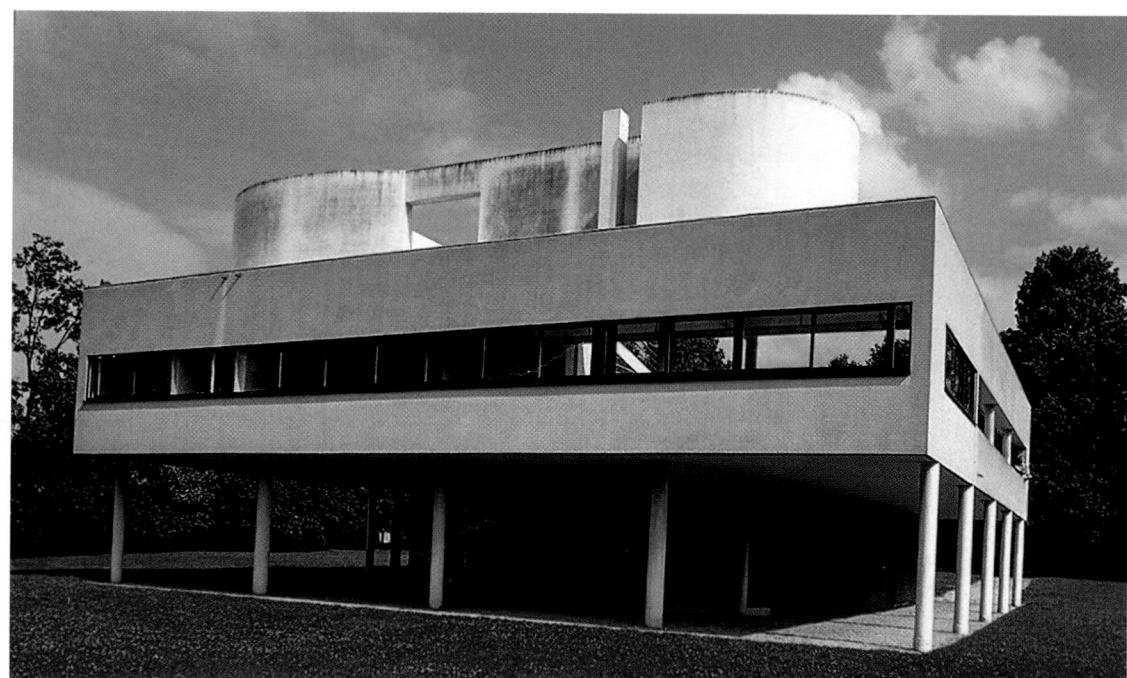

28.35 Le Corbusier. Villa Savoye, Poissy-sur-Seine, France. 1928–29

Reinforced Concrete

Reinforced concrete became one of the most popular building materials in the twentieth century. Concrete is a cement mixture of sand, limestone, and water that contains small stones or other (generally solid) small objects. While its history dates to 5600 BCE in the Balkans, the Romans were the first to use it extensively, starting in the second century BCE (see pages 186–87). Romans builders used concrete for bridges, docks, pavements, and aqueducts, but it was also used for homes and major civic buildings, such as the Pantheon (see fig. 7.23).

Concrete virtually disappeared from architecture after the Fall of Rome. Its revival began in 1824, when an English mason, Joseph Aspdin, patented an improved cement. Because it resembled a natural stone found on the Isle of Portland, the new material was called Portland cement. To make it, Aspdin heated clay and limestone to especially high temperatures, a process still used today. While concrete is fire-resistant and can stand extremely high compression, or

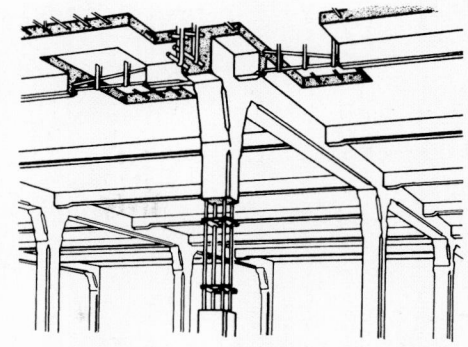

François Hennebique. System for reinforced concrete. 1892 (After Curtis)

engineer François Hennebique designed a ferroconcrete post-and-slab construction where each floor/ceiling was an integral part of the structure, not a separate element lying on top of a supporting frame (see fig.). Hennebrique's engineering was applied largely to industrial buildings and simply imitated traditional post-and-lintel styles.

Credit for introducing ferroconcrete to "high" architecture generally goes to the French architect Auguste Perret, who designed apartment buildings and parking garages using steel-reinforced concrete in the opening decades of the twentieth century. One of his most famous buildings is the Raincy Church, outside Paris, built in 1922 (see fig.), which conceptually uses the Rationalism we saw in Soufflot's Saint-Geneviève (see fig. 23.19) while aspiring to implement the lightness and airiness of a Gothic cathedral. Max Berg's Jahrhunderthalle (see fig. 27.39) in Breslau, built in 1912–13, also played a major role in popularizing ferroconcrete. Ultimately, it became the principal medium for Le Corbusier and a favorite for Frank Lloyd Wright (see page 934).

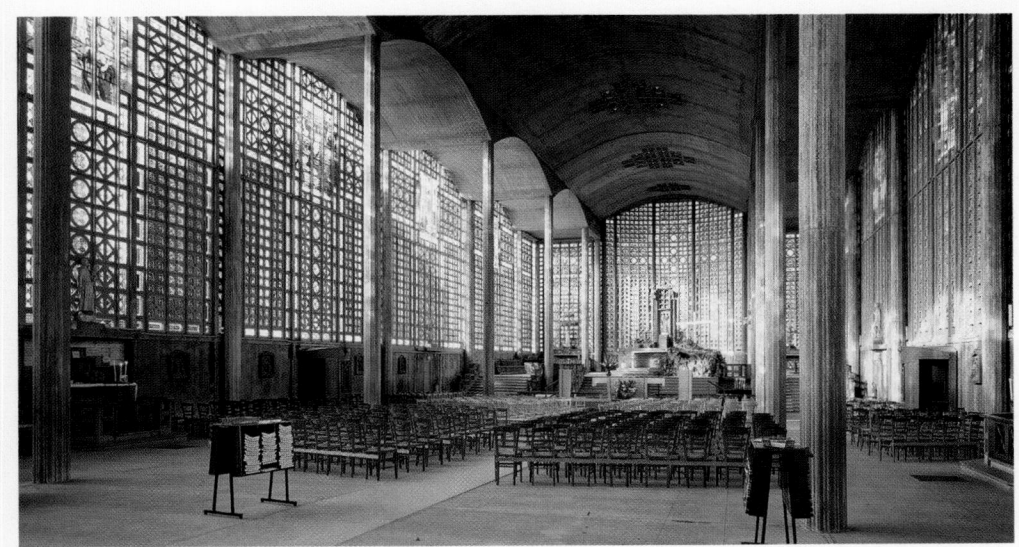

Auguste Perret. Notre Dame, Le Raincy, France. 1923–24

evenly applied weight, it does not have much tensile strength. That is, it does not hold up under unevenly applied stresses. To solve the problem, engineers reinforced the concrete by embedding iron rods within it. Steel rods replaced iron rods in the late nineteenth century. (A form of steel first appeared in the second half of the nineteenth century, although modern steel was not invented until toward the end of the century.) Iron and concrete were a perfect match, since the materials complemented each other. Concrete protected the iron, which otherwise melted and corroded easily, while iron provided the tensile strength that concrete lacked.

Almost simultaneously in England and France, inventors began to patent ferroconcrete, as steel-reinforced concrete is called. A British plasterer patented concrete floors and roofs made with iron bars and wire rope, while a French gardener took out a patent on steel-reinforced concrete planters, eventually designing guardrails, posts, and beams as well. But it was not until the 1890s that the French

became the principal medium for Le Corbusier and a favorite for Frank Lloyd Wright (see page 934).

In addition to its strength, ferroconcrete is attractive because it is inexpensive. The concrete component is readily available. The steel, the most expensive and rare component, makes up only 1 to 6 percent of the structure. By 1904, ferroconcrete was being used in skyscrapers; the first use was in the Ingalls Building in Cincinnati, which was 16 stories and rose to 210 feet. By 1962, it was being used in modern high-rises, including the 60-story twin towers of Marina City in Chicago. From 1998 to 2003, the largest building in the world was the ferroconcrete Petronas Towers in Kuala Lampur, Malaysia, designed by Cesar Pelli, who is based in Hartford, Connecticut. Rising 88 stories and 1,483 feet, the building would have been prohibitively expensive without ferroconcrete, since Malaysia does not manufacture steel. Like much of the world, however, Malaysia readily produces high-quality concrete.

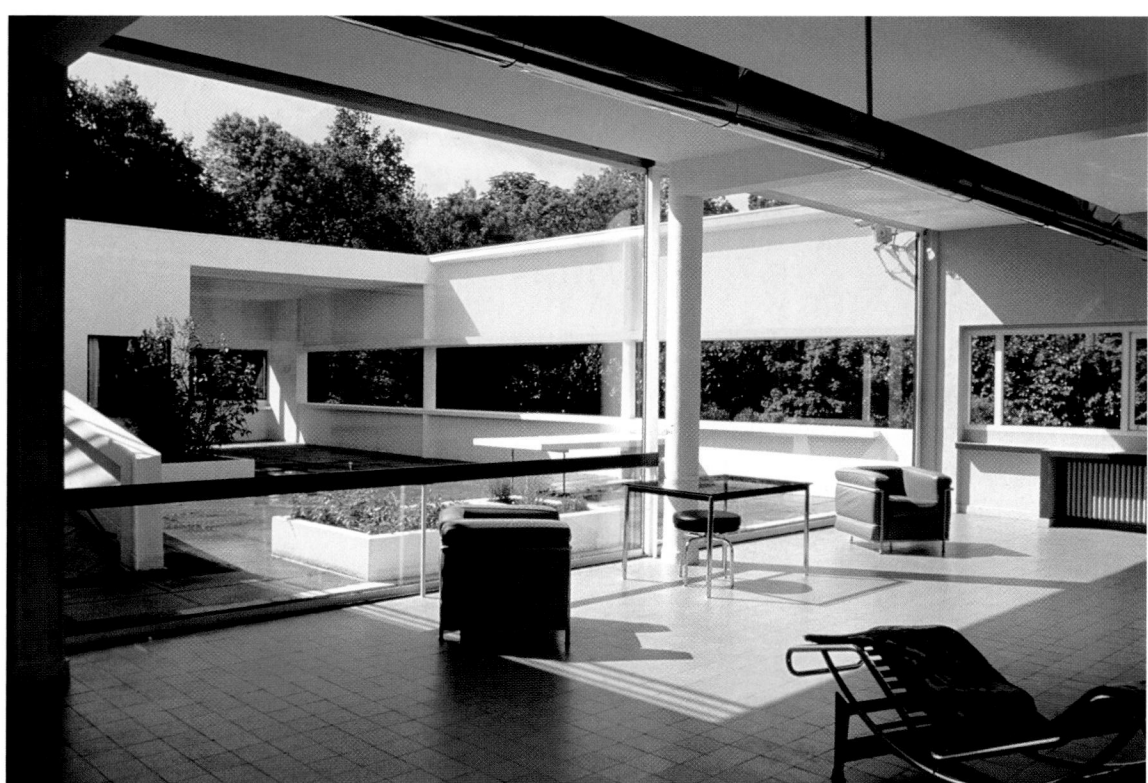

terrace, which is protected behind the enormous cylindrical wind-screens that look like oceanliner smokestacks. The main floor, the second, has an open-space plan using partition walls, and it faces into a court (fig. **28.36**), from which a ramp leads up to the roof. Everywhere we look we see a beautiful classicizing geometry, the building blocks of Le Corbusier's design aesthetic. The building is a perfect square box precisely defined by its taut skin of concrete. The pilotis are cylinders, and the windbreakers are enormous arcs. Obscured by the shadow in figure 28.35 is another geomet-ric curve on the ground floor, which encloses the garage and servants' quarters. Like the Bauhaus and the Schröder House, the villa appears light, virtually floating on its pilotis.

But as abstract and futuristic as the house may seem, it resonates with the past. We can project onto it the classic, white stuccoed Mediterranean house, oriented around a central court, that sits on a hill overlooking the sea. Le Corbusier also described his villa as a *jardin suspendu*, a hanging garden reflecting the mythical gardens of Babylon. The building also recalls Palladio in the perfection of the square, while the colonnade of pilotis echoes a Doric temple. The ramps (there is a circular staircase as well) linking the floors have reminded scholars of the great entrance ramps of Mycenae. In one of the great statements of High Modernism, Le Corbusier presents the Modernist, Machine Age update of the great Greek temple perched on a hill, overlooking nature, and permeated with light and air.

PURISM AND FERNAND LÉGER In 1917, Le Corbusier met the painter Amédée Ozenfant (1886–1966), and together they developed a theory called Purism, which in essence was a

Neo-Platonic concept that reduced all artistic expression to an abstract Classical purity reflecting a machine aesthetic. Clean line, pure forms, and mathematical clarity were highly valued. In 1918, they published an essay entitled "After Cubism" that railed against the distortions of the Cubist style, and in 1920 they published another essay, "Purism," which gave a label to their theory. As stated before, Le Corbusier was a painter as well. Working and writing under his given name Charles-Édouard Jeanneret, and like his colleague, Ozenfant, he made mostly still lifes, which used the multiple perspectives of Cubism but reduced objects to geometric mechanomorphic forms that run parallel to the picture plane.

The Cubist Fernand Léger (1881–1955) became an adherent of Purism, although he never defined himself as such. He was cer-tainly predisposed to its ideas, for in the early 1910s, he had made abstract, mechanical-looking Cubist figures, and was an outspo-ken socialist and champion of modernity and technological advancement. In the early 1920s, however, his style reflected the machinelike geometry and Classicism advocated by Jeanneret and Ozenfant, as can be seen in *Three Women* (*Le Grand Déjeuner*) (fig. **28.37**) of 1921. His almost identical-looking nudes are con-structed of circles and cylinders. Their body parts, such as hair and faces, are so similar they could be interchangeable. Virtually all of the objects look machine-made, and, as with the figures, they are reduced to cubes, cones, cylinders, and pyramids. Organic and man-made elements are virtually indistinguishable, and both types are ordered in a tight grid of horizontal and verti-cals and run parallel to the picture plane. Color is also kept to essentials—the primary and binaries—the building blocks of the

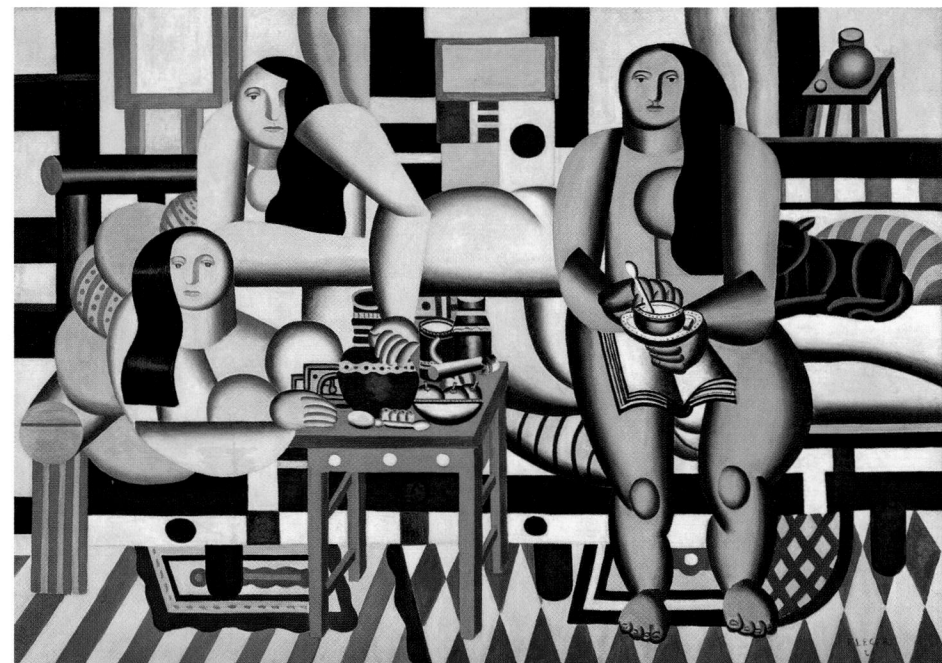

28.37 Fernand Léger, *Three Women* (*Le Grand Déjeuner*). 1921. Oil on canvas, 6'1¼" × 8'3" (1.8 × 2.5 m). Museum of Modern Art, New York. Mrs Simon Guggenheim Fund. 189.1942

color spectrum. Léger has taken the Classical theme of the monumental nude (although here we seem to be in a brothel) and updated it by placing it in a contemporary world of technological harmony and perfection, in effect telling us, as Seurat had 30 years earlier (see page 908), that the new Classicism and world order are based on the machine and science.

ART IN AMERICA: MODERNITY, SPIRITUALITY, AND REGIONALISM

Perhaps more than Europe, the United States could embrace the machine as the emblem of progress, for after World War I, America was the undisputed technological world leader. In contrast to the European avant-garde that sought a classless, nationless world, Americans were preoccupied with national identity. And generally they did not have a utopian vision. Instead they viewed skyscrapers, factories, and machines as symbols of the nation's technological superiority. But not everyone embraced modernity. As the economy boomed in the postwar years, culminating in the dizzying exuberance of the Roaring Twenties, many artists rejected materialism and looked to the spiritual. While some artists turned to nature in search of universal truths, others sought strength in old-fashioned American values that could be found in the American heartland, especially in the mythic conservative lifestyle of its hearty, hard-working, God-fearing farmers.

Still others responded to the poverty and social discontent that coexisted with the boom years. The period was marked by the oppression of labor, violent labor strikes, and anarchist threats. Racism escalated in the South, led by the dramatic growth of the Ku Klux Klan and increased lynchings of black men. The Twentieth Amendment granted women the right to vote in 1920, but it had no impact on granting social and economic parity, as women continued to be restricted to "women's jobs" and less pay. The Great Depression exacerbated these injustices, resulting in the rise in the 1930s of a representational art called Social Realism.

The City and Industry

Arriving in New York harbor for the first time in 1915, Marcel Duchamp marveled at the towering skyscrapers and pronounced them the epitome of modernity. He saw in America the future of art. The skyscraper and modern industry did indeed become the emblems of America, replacing landscape, which had dominated painting in the previous century. Skyscrapers were symbols of modernity, industry, and commerce, and thus of the country's technological and financial superiority, for the United States entered the century as the wealthiest and most modern country in the world. World War I fueled the economy, ushering in an era of unprecedented consumerism and materialism. Known as the Roaring Twenties and the Jazz Age, the 1920s were dominated by the culture of the city, for by 1920 more people lived in cities than in the countryside.

The symbol of the nation was New York, dominated by skyscrapers. Beginning in the late 1910s, these "cathedrals of capitalism" or of "commerce" became the favorite subject for painters and photographers—and for sculptors and designers—who presented the icon in all its technological splendor. Skyscrapers were shown soaring toward the heavens without a hint of the streets or humanity below. Bridges, factories, dams, refineries—anything that demonstrated America's advanced modernity—were also transformed into monuments as grand as the pyramids of Egypt and as sacred as the Gothic cathedrals of France.

JOSEPH STELLA Perhaps the greatest single visual icon of the city was made by the Italian immigrant Joseph Stella (1877–1946). Entitled *The Voice of the City (New York Interpreted)* (fig. **28.38**) and completed in 1922, it is an 8-foot-high, five-panel work that features on its center panel an abstraction of the city's towers, with the famous Flatiron building in the foreground, surrounded by both actual and fictitious buildings. The panels flanking the center panel represent the "Great White Way," Broadway, which has been reduced to an abstraction of color and light. The far-left panel presents the harbor on the Hudson River on the west side of lower Manhattan, while the right panel shows the Brooklyn Bridge on the east side. Every image features the technological wonders of Manhattan. We see communication towers, air-venting systems, and elevated trains in the harbor picture. The Great White Way panels present the dazzling illumination of Times Square at night, which at the time had no equivalent anywhere else in the world. In effect, these two panels are a homage to electricity and the energy of the city. And even 35 years after opening, the Brooklyn Bridge still remained one of the world's great feats of engineering.

Stella came to America in 1896, thus witnessing the rise of modern New York City at the turn of the century. He temporarily returned to Italy to study in 1910, where he met the Futurists (see pages 964–66). Through the Stieglitz gallery and his friendship with Duchamp and Man Ray, among others, he kept in touch with European trends, with Cubism becoming his primary artistic language in the 1910s. The Great White Way panels especially reflect the tenets of Futurism, for here we see the sound waves and Mach-like indications of motion that we saw in Boccioni's *States of Mind I* (see fig. 27.20). Their dizzying kaleidoscope of color powerfully captures the intense visual experience of Times Square at night. But in the skyscraper and Brooklyn Bridge panels, Stella is not only representational, he is iconic, centering his motifs and transforming them into emblems of modernity. His palette is deeply saturated, and color is often encased in heavy black-line drawing, in effect transforming his image into a medieval stained-glass window. He reinforces the religious motif by adding a predella at the bottom (see page 525), which itemizes the different tunnels and utility tubes running beneath the city. In effect, Stella is declaring technology and modernity the religion of the twentieth century.

PAUL STRAND Photography, it turns out, was especially well suited for capturing the triumphs of the Machine Age. However, the first photographs of modern New York, such as Alfred Stieglitz's *The City of Ambition* (see fig. 26.45), romanticized the metropolis by immersing it in a soft pictorial haze. A breakthrough occurred when a young New Yorker, Paul Strand (1890–1976), from 1915 to 1917 made a large body of work of

28.38 Joseph Stella, *The Voice of the City (New York Interpreted)*. 1920–22. Oil and tempera on canvas, five panels, 8'3¾" × 22'6" (2.53 × 6.86 m). The Newark Museum, Newark. 37.288 a–e

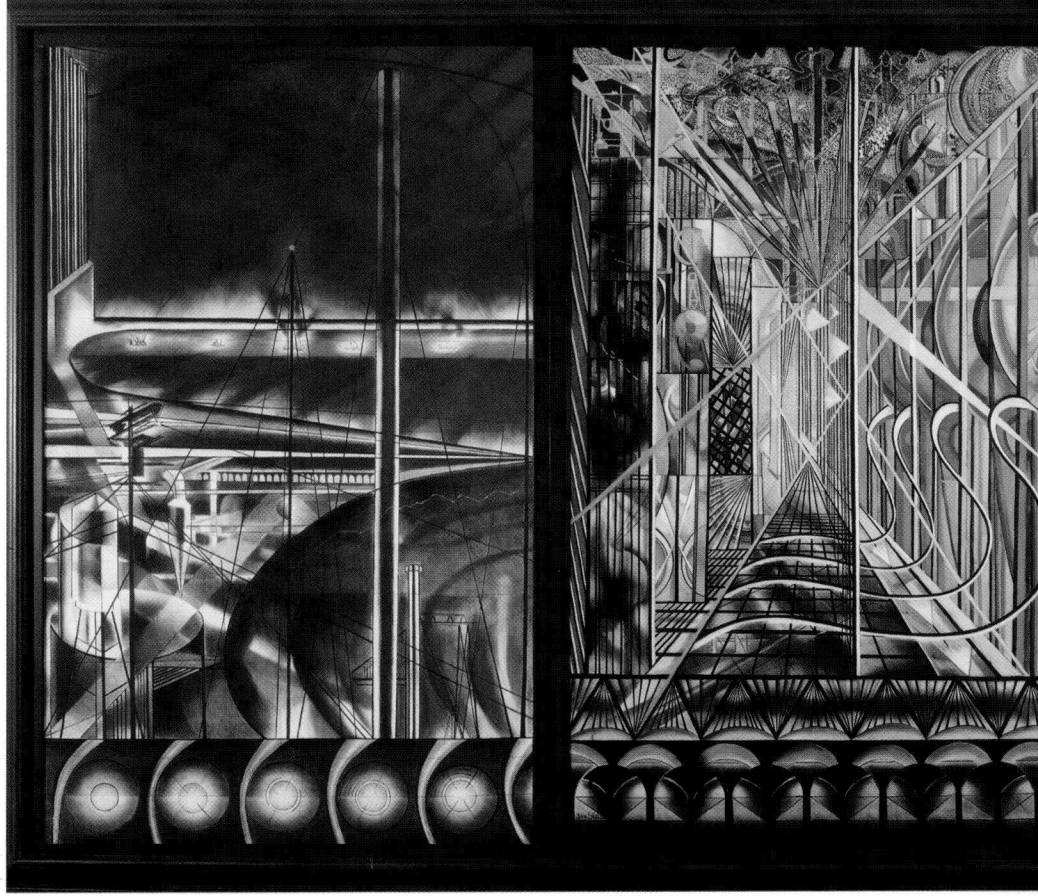

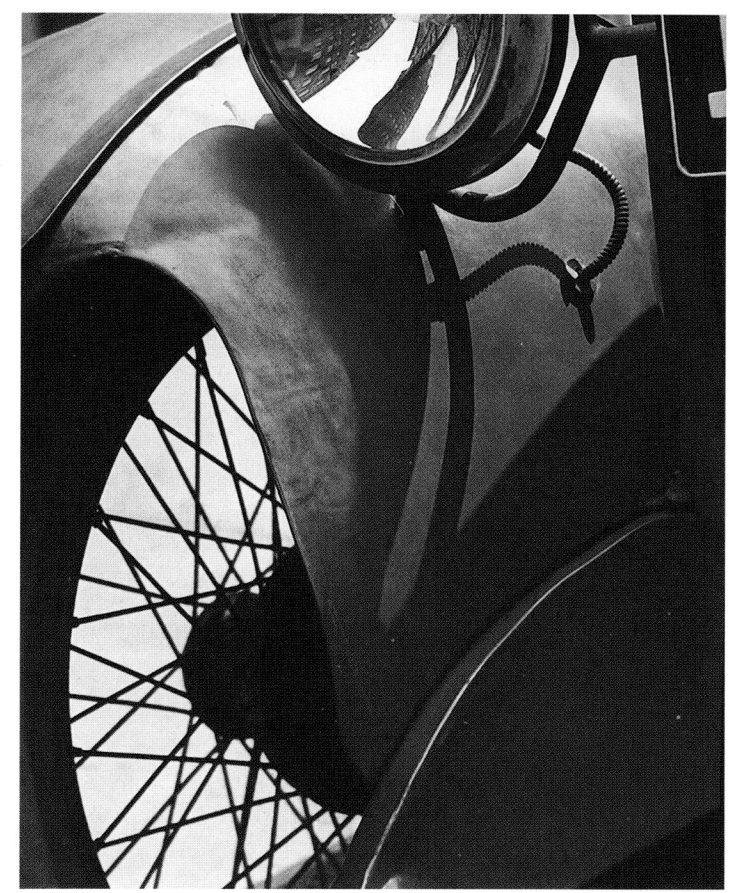

28.39 Paul Strand, *Wire Wheel*. 1917. Platinum print from enlarged negative, 13 × 10¼" (33.1 × 26.1 cm). George Eastman House

sharply focused, high-contrast photographs. Stieglitz immediately recognized their importance and showed a selection of them at "291." *Wire Wheel* (fig. **28.39**) is from this period. Its abstracted subject is a Model T Ford, an icon of the Machine Age since it marked the advent of the assembly line. The picture rejects the "painterliness" of turn-of-the-century pictorial photography. In its place is a new compositional style based on the Cubism that Strand saw displayed at Stieglitz's "291." By taking a close-up of the car, Strand created a skewed perspective and tight cropping, resulting in a difficult-to-read image with a flattened and complicated space.

In 1920, Strand collaborated with painter/photographer Charles Sheeler (1883–1965) to make a film intended to capture the energy and grandeur of New York. Entitled *Manhatta (New York the Magnificent)* (see www.myartslab.com), it opens with commuters arriving by ferry in lower Manhattan, spilling off the boat in teeming masses, and swarming through the financial district on their way to work. At the end of the film, the crowds get back on the boat at sunset. Rapid editing, vertiginous shots

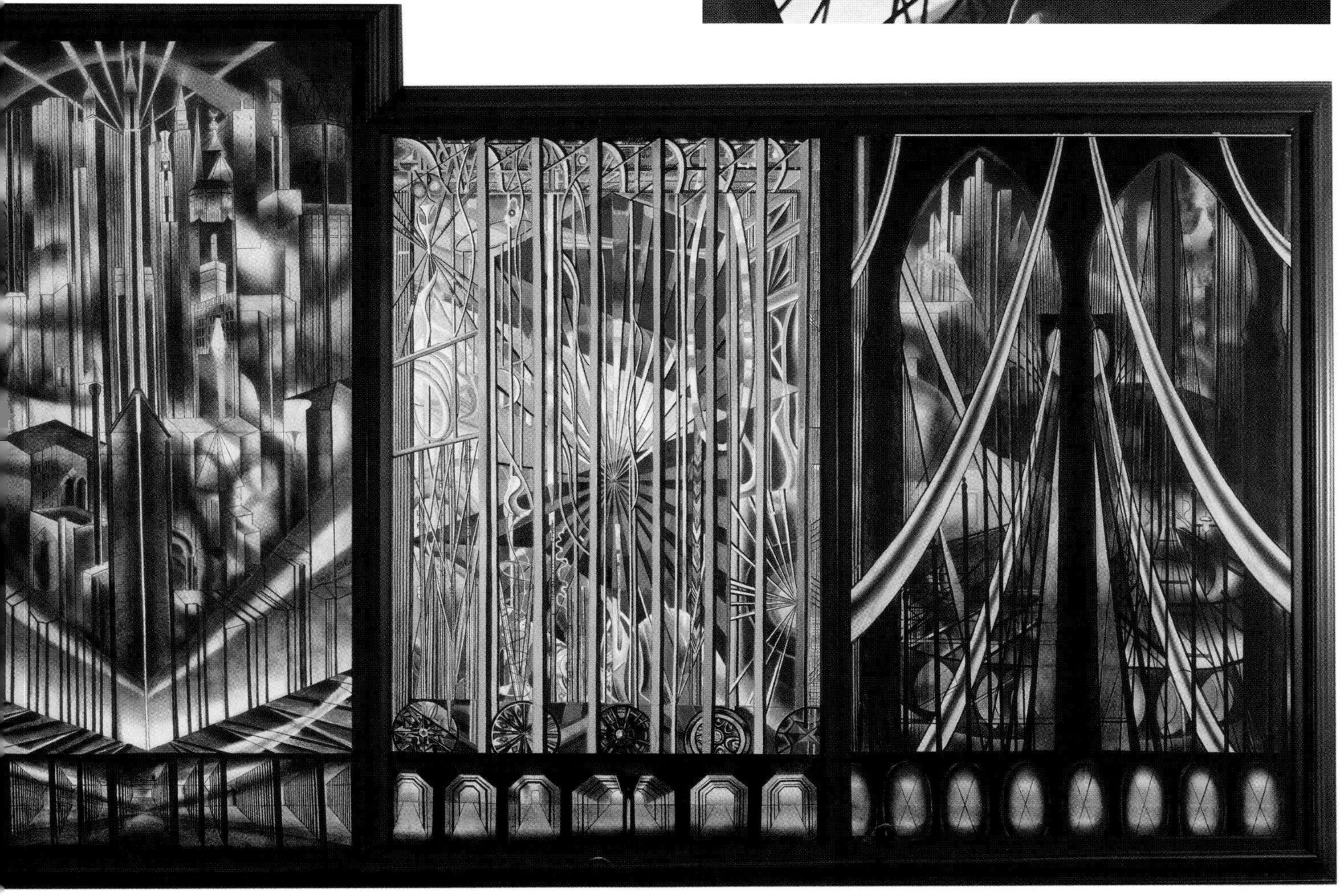

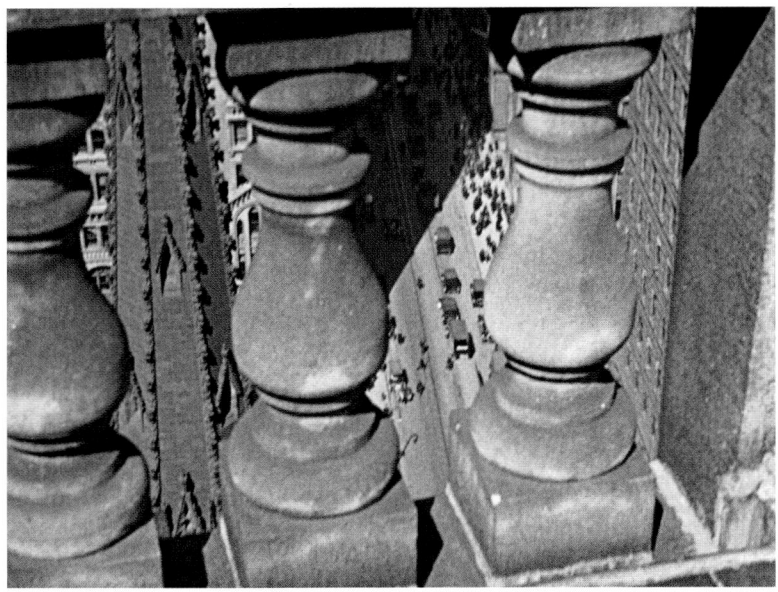

28.40 Paul Strand and Charles Sheeler. Still from the film *Manhatta* (*New York the Magnificent*). 1920. Black-and-white film, no sound, 10 minutes. Frame enlargement from 2008 2k digital restoration by Lowry Digital

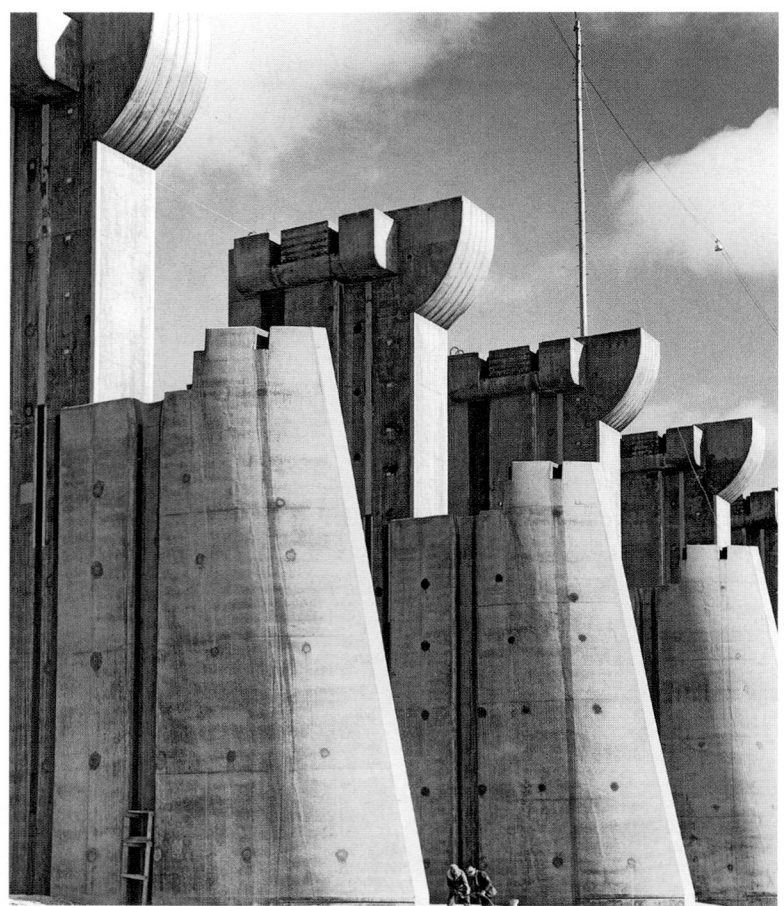

28.41 Margaret Bourke-White *Fort Peck Dam, Montana*. 1936. Time-Life, Inc.

taken from the top of skyscrapers (fig. **28.40**), raking angles, and sharp value contrasts—all simulating a Cubist fracturing—are among the formalist devices that give this movie a sense of surging energy and constant movement designed to capture the rapid pace of modernity and the powerful current of the urban experience. Interspersed throughout the film are fragments of Walt Whitman's 1860/1881 poem *Mannahatta* which proclaims the greatness, energy, and might of New York.

MARGARET BOURKE-WHITE Strand's hard-edged aesthetic transformed photography, not only in America, but eventually throughout the world. His style was especially appropriate for technological and industrial images, reinforcing the machine-made precision of the subject. Photojournalist Margaret Bourke-White especially embraced this new aesthetic and was drawn to technological imagery, especially machines, airplanes, and dirigibles. In *Fort Peck Dam, Montana* (fig. **28.41**), she presents a symbol of American technology. The picture was the cover image for the very first issue of *Life*, published on November 23, 1936. The photograph's power lies in its severe austerity, which reinforces the mammoth scale of the dam, dwarfing the antlike workers below. Each of the dam's pylons is identical, looking as though they were pressed out of an enormous machine mold, and because the photograph of the dam is cropped on either side, these gigantic assembly-line towers seem endless as well. Owing to their severe monumentality, they take on the grandeur of ancient Assyrian or Egyptian monuments. Again we find an artist declaring modern technology to be the new Classicism.

CHARLES DEMUTH In his 1927 painting *My Egypt* (fig. **28.42**), depicting contemporary grain elevators near his native Lancaster, Pennsylvania, Charles Demuth (1883–1935) similarly transformed American modernity into a Classical icon. Demuth had studied in Paris from 1912 to 1914, absorbing European Modernism, and by the 1920s he was traveling in the most sophisticated artistic circles and showing with Alfred Stieglitz. His work is quite varied in style, even in a given period, and here we see him working in the American counterpart of Purism, a style called Precisionism. In the 1920s, a group of American artists, including Demuth, developed a look that had the hard-edged geometric quality of Cubism but was far more representational. It came to be called Precisionism not only because of its precise geometry and drawing, but also because it seemed to capture the precision of mechanization and industry, which was often its subject matter. Brushwork was meticulous, and at one point these artists, who rarely showed together and did not think of themselves as a group, were called Immaculates.

At first glance, *My Egypt* seems quite Cubist. But the physical integrity of the grain elevators is barely compromised, and what seems like Cubist fracturing are mysterious, almost mystical, beams of light that only slightly distort the objects but quite successfully invest the building with a brute power, if not a mystical transcendence. The title suggests that such agricultural architecture as grain elevators were America's pyramids. The smokestack

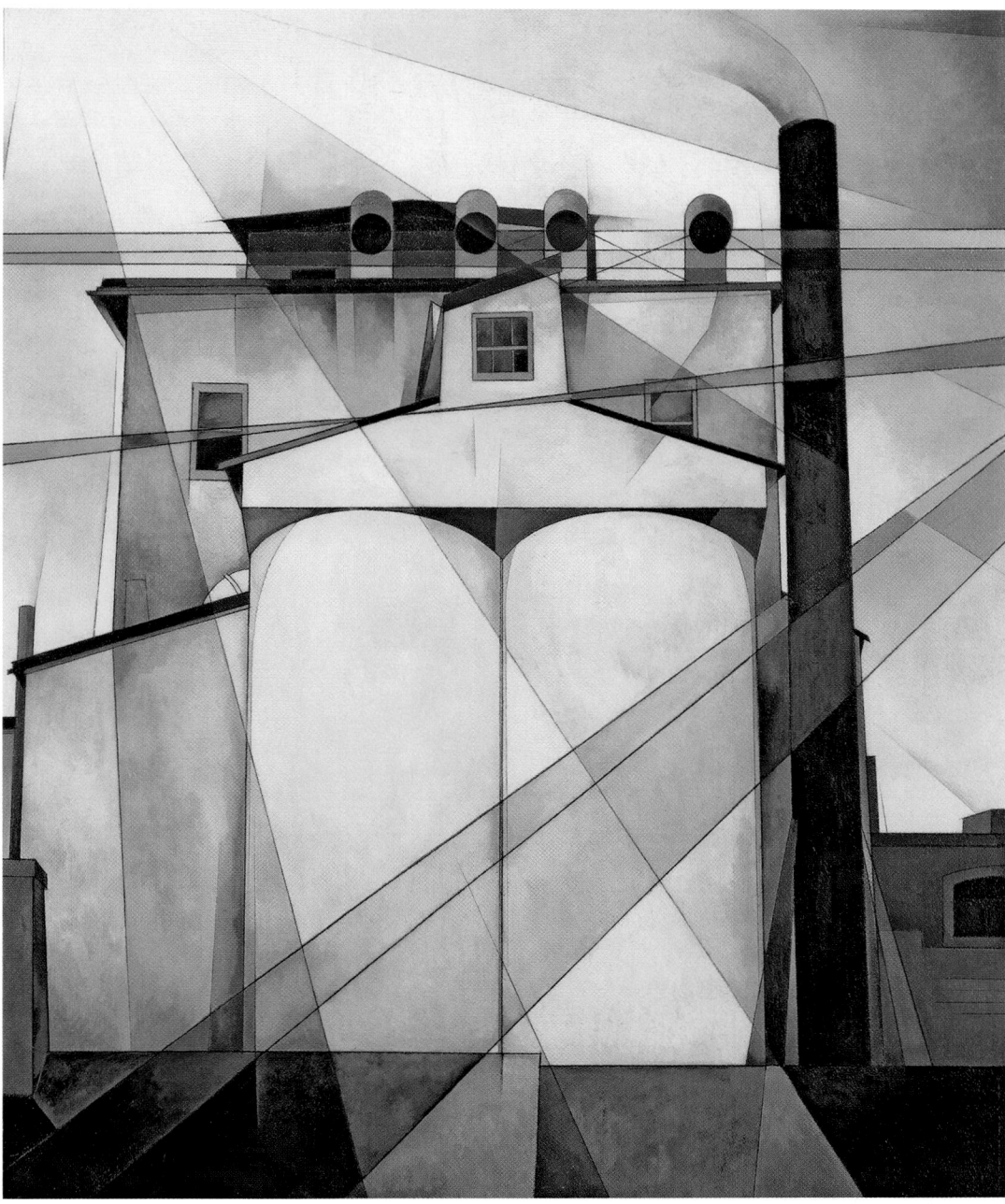

28.42 Charles Demuth, *My Egypt*. 1927. Oil and graphite on composition board, 2'11¾" × 2'6" (91 × 76 cm). Whitney Museum of American Art, New York. Purchase, with Funds from Gertrude Vanderbilt Whitney. 31.172

endows the grain elevators with an industrial might, and the geometry of the ventilation ducts and massive cylinders of the storage tanks virtually transform the building itself into an efficient machine.

STUART DAVIS Among the American artists who captured the essence of the modern experience using abstraction was Stuart Davis (1892–1964). The 1913 Armory Show in New York (see page 974) converted Davis into a dedicated Modernist, and by the 1920s his work was becoming increasingly abstract. Just as Mondrian tried to find an abstract equivalent for invisible life forces, Davis wanted to create the plastic equivalent for experiencing modern life—flying in an airplane, looking down from a towering skyscraper, listening to jazz music, or riding in a speeding car, motorcycle, or train. He wanted to capture the experience

of the "new lights, speeds, and spaces which are uniquely real in our time." To do this, he used a Synthetic Cubist vocabulary, and by the 1930s his palette had become bright, limited to primary, secondary, and tertiary colors, and his forms quite jaunty and their juxtaposition raucous, as seen in *Hot Still-Scape for Six Colors—Seventh Avenue Style* (fig. **28.43**) of 1940. After describing how his colors were used like musical instruments to create a composition (Davis loved jazz and swing), he went on to describe his picture, painted in his Seventh Avenue studio: "The subject matter…is well within the experience of any modern city dweller. Fruit and flowers; kitchen utensils; fall skies; horizons; taxi cabs; radio; art exhibitions and reproductions; fast travel; Americana; movies; electric signs; dynamics of city sights and sounds; these and a thousand more are common experience and they are the basic subject matter which my picture celebrates." Embedded

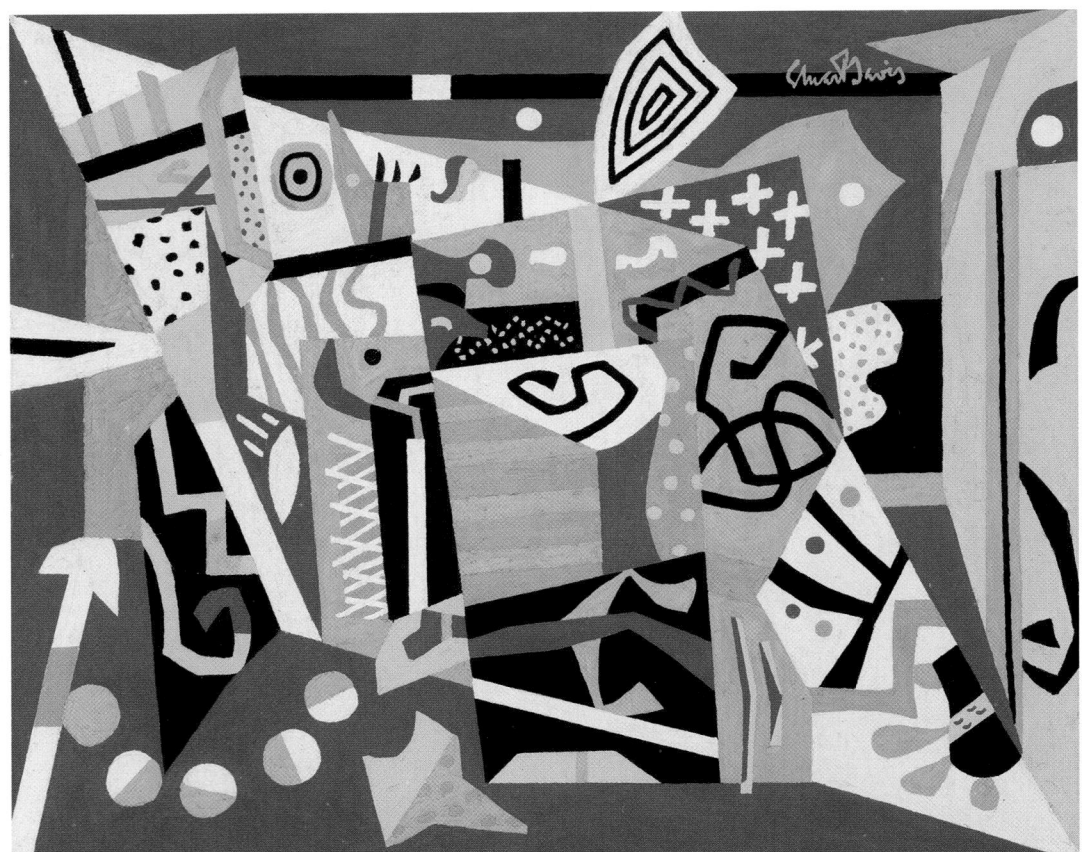

28.43 Stuart Davis, *Hot Still-Scape for Six Colors—Seventh Avenue Style*. 1940. Oil on canvas, 36 × 45" (91.4 × 113.9 cm). Photograph © Museum of Fine Arts, Boston. Gift of the William H. Lane Foundation and the M. and M. Karolik Collection, by Exchange, 1983.120

within this playful jumble of color and shapes and overlapping planes are smokestacks, seascapes, and brick walls, all reduced to funky hieroglyphic notations, which in their cartoony character seem to tap into American popular culture. In an almost indefinable way, Davis's sensitivity captures the pulse of America—its gaudy advertising, its love of the new, its jazz, its mobility, its intensity and speed, even its rootlessness.

Art Deco and the International Style

While the skyscraper became the national emblem of America's modernity, the buildings themselves were aesthetically conservative compared with European architectural developments, especially the International Style. Their distinguishing characteristic was their height. By 1900, New York had become the home of the skyscraper, taking the lead from Chicago. Buildings became progressively taller, with Cass Gilbert's 792-foot Woolworth Building dominating the cityscape in 1913. Aesthetically the new towers were very nineteenth-century, reflecting a variety of historical styles, often the Gothic. The wealth of the Roaring Twenties produced furious building campaigns, as architects competed to design the world's tallest building. Almost simultaneously, the 77-story Chrysler Building and 102-story Empire State Building went up in 1930.

The Chrysler Building (fig. **28.44**) designed by little-known architect William van Alen (1883–1954), is often considered the finest Art Deco skyscraper. Art Deco is a decorative-arts style that emerged in 1925 at the Exhibition of Decorative and Industrial Art held in Paris. Like the Bauhaus school, Art Deco concepts aimed to close the gap between quality design and mass production. It was an outgrowth of Art Nouveau, but it replaced the organic forms with a Machine Age geometric and streamlined look. Unlike the Bauhaus, Art Deco had no utopian goal; it was largely bourgeois, indulging in fantasy and lavishness. It was about decorative veneer, not idealistic substance. Within the geometry and streamlining of the machine aesthetic, it absorbed a wide range of historical references, from Cubist fracturing to the zigzag patterning of Native American and Pre-Columbian design. Deco designers loved lush colors, opulent materials, and shiny surfaces. Inspired by the geometry of machines, it generally drew together a variety of angular forms, often in jagged, staccato rhythms, and set them off against organic motifs that recall Art Nouveau or Jugendstil. We can see these qualities in the Chrysler Building. The geometry is streamlined in the tapering tower with its steadily receding arches. The flamelike triangular windows create a staccato rhythm, and the entire crown is sheathed in glistening stainless steel. Gargoyles duplicating the hood ornament for the 1929 Chrysler decorate the corners.

The International Style came to America about this same time, appearing in Raymond M. Hood's 1931 McGraw-Hill Building in New York and in the 1929–32 Philadelphia Savings Fund Society Building (fig. **28.45**) by George Howe (1886–1955) and William E. Lescaze (1896–1969). That Howe and Lescaze got to design a modern building is itself quite remarkable, since there was nothing else like it in America when it was planned. The building already presented an enormous financial risk, as potential renters were becoming scarce as the Great Depression deepened. Their building has many of the characteristics of High Modernism, but its floating, cantilevered blocks with glass curtain walls were compromised when the client insisted the piers get pushed to the outer perimeter of the building, creating strong vertical accents and interfering with the horizontal windows and the thin tautness of the wall. As a result, the building seems more massive than its light, floating European counterparts (see fig. 28.32). But the Philadelphia

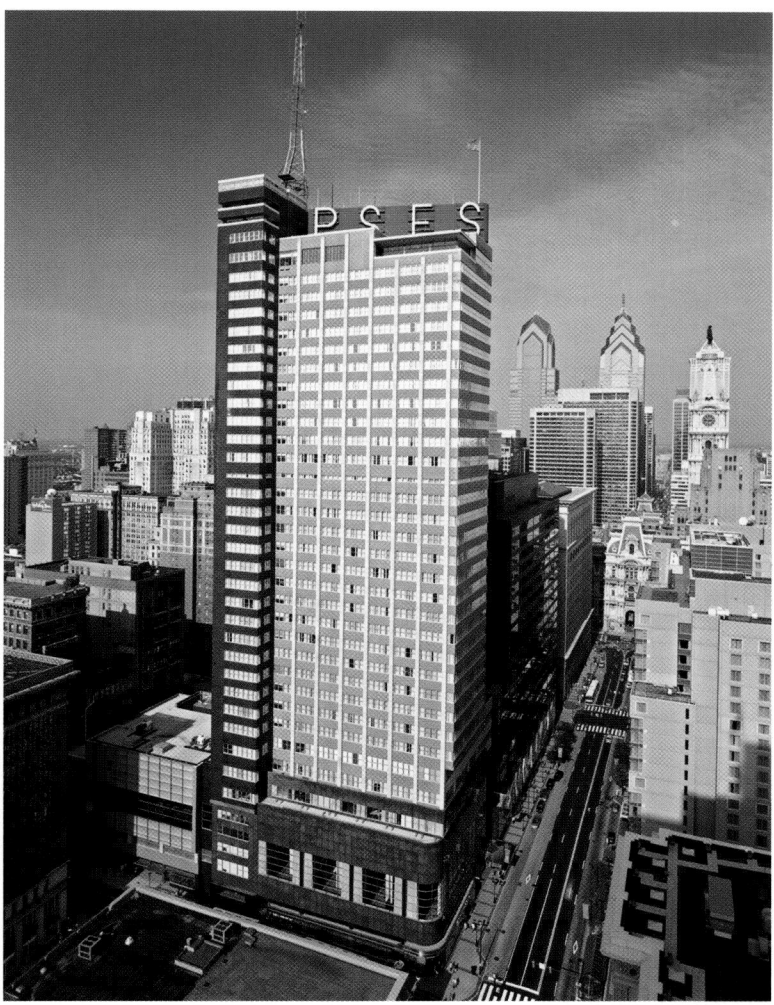

28.45   George Howe and William E. Lescaze. Philadelphia Savings Fund Society Building, Philadelphia. 1929–32

Savings Fund Society Building reflects its functionalism well, as each of the Constructivist-like blocks that we can see on the exterior was designed to accommodate a different purpose.

Seeking the Spiritual

In the 1910s, much of the American creative community turned its attention to producing a specifically American art. Writers, musicians, artists, and poets all felt that American culture was derived from Europe; now, they would seek to discover what was unique about the American experience and try to express it in an indigenous way. For some artists, like Stella in *The Voice of the City (New York Interpreted)* and Demuth in *My Egypt*, the answer lay in American modernity. Others looked to nature, going back to the pantheistic Romanticism of the Hudson River School and its successors. Stieglitz especially became preoccupied with this issue of an American art, deciding in the 1920s to represent only American artists and naming his last gallery, which he opened in 1928, An American Place. Stieglitz himself became increasingly intolerant of modernity, initially resisting buying a radio or a car,

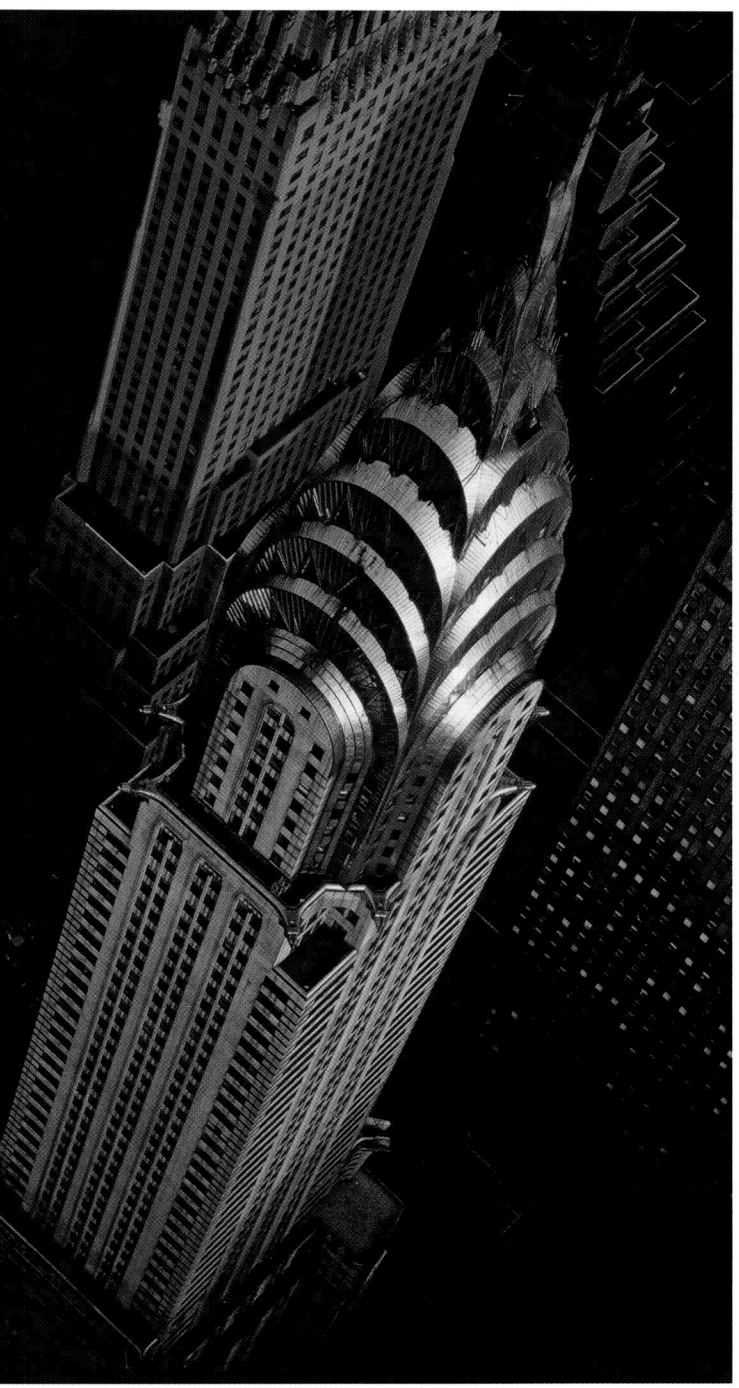

28.44   William van Alen. Chrysler Building, New York. 1928–30

and like so many others at the time shunning materialism to seek a spirituality in modern America. Stieglitz, who had published sections of Kandinsky's *Concerning the Spiritual in Art* (see page 959) in *Camera Work*, himself became preoccupied with visually capturing an equivalent of his emotions when confronting sublime nature.

The artists that Stieglitz showed from the early 1920s until his death in 1946 were generally, but not always, preoccupied with finding a higher meaning in life within a materialistic modern world, often focusing on nature. One was Georgia O'Keeffe, with whom Stieglitz became romantically involved in 1918 and later married.

GEORGIA O'KEEFFE When Stieglitz first showed her work in 1916, Georgia O'Keeffe (1887–1986) was making small abstract minimalist watercolors that evoked sublime landscapes. Toward 1920, her presentation of nature evolved into close-ups of flowers, as seen in *Black Iris III* (fig. **28.46**) of 1926, where the image is so magnified it virtually becomes abstract. We do not have to look far to find the pictorial source for O'Keeffe: Paul Strand. O'Keeffe briefly fell in love with the young, handsome Strand in

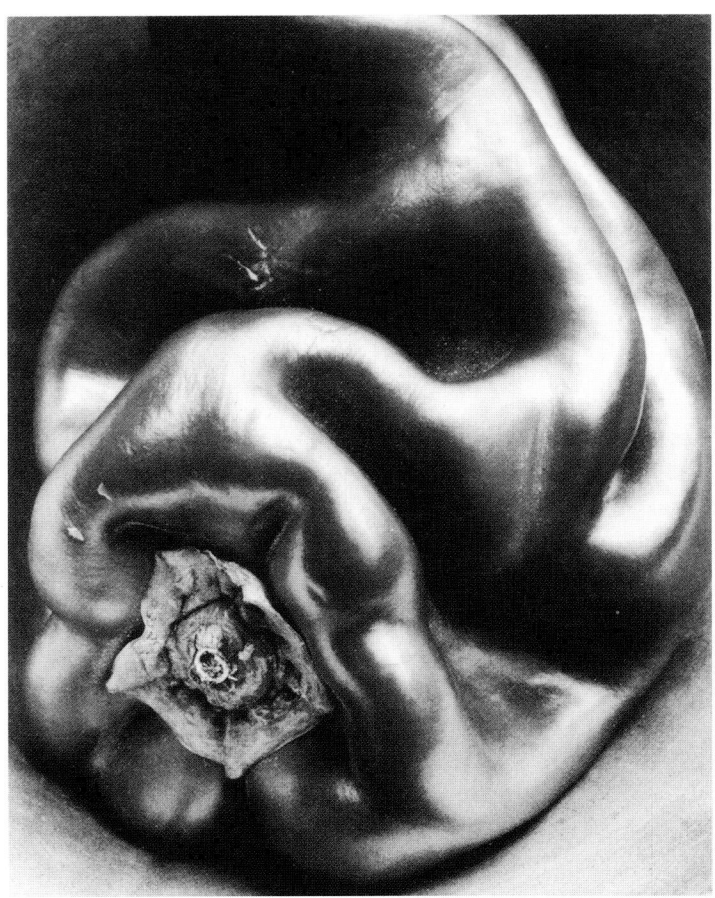

28.47   Edward Weston, *Pepper*. 1930. Gelatin silver print. Center for Creative Photography, Tucson, Arizona

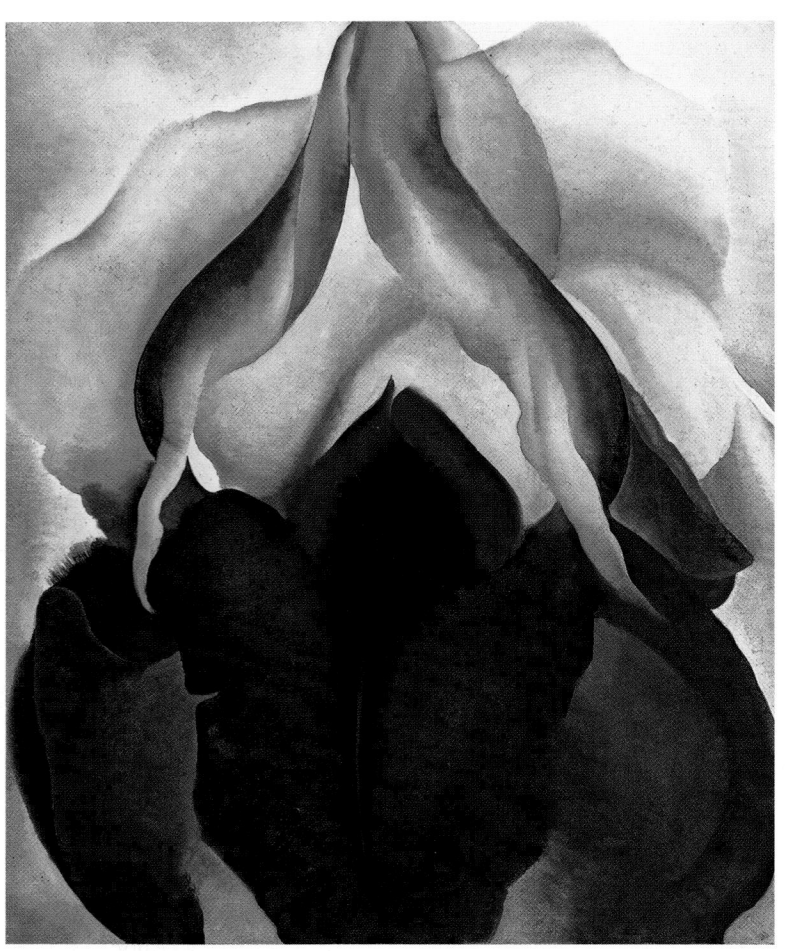

28.46   Georgia O'Keeffe, *Black Iris III*. 1926. Oil on canvas, 36 × 29⅞" (91.4 × 75.9 cm). Metropolitan Museum of Art, New York. The Alfred Stieglitz Collection, 1949

1917 and was smitten as well by the power of his photography, especially the use of the close-up image. This compositional device, she wrote, forced a viewer to see flowers with the same intensity that she did. But by abstracting the close-up, O'Keeffe accomplished much more: The forms of the flowers morph into the parts of a woman's body, and the iris is redolent of female sexuality. The petals ethereally dissolve into their surroundings, seeming to become one with the rest of nature.

Partly because of Stieglitz's marketing, critics described O'Keeffe's flowers as overtly erotic and sexual, which the new loose morality of the Roaring Twenties could accommodate. This interpretation outraged O'Keeffe, who denied that her pictures were about sexuality *per se*. And they are not. As with the banned sexually explicit novels of her friend the English author D. H. Lawrence, her paintings were not about lust but the uncontainable surging force of nature, which includes the urge to procreate. Sexuality was portrayed as being natural, beautiful, and as essential as a flower blossoming, disseminating pollen, and reproducing. And if her wonderful organic flower, which seems to be growing before our very eyes, begins to take on the look of other objects, such as clouds, smoke, buttocks, and flesh, it only increases the sense of universal equivalence that she believed ran through all things. In this microcosm of an iris, O'Keeffe presents a macrocosm so large it encompasses the entire universe.

EDWARD WESTON Due to both Strand and O'Keeffe, the close-up became a popular device with both painters and photographers in the 1920s, and in the hands of some artists it had the same spiritual dimensions found in O'Keeffe's paintings. *Pepper* (fig. **28.47**) by the Californian Edward Weston (1886–1958) falls into this category, as the rippling gnarled vegetable is transformed through lighting and cropping to resemble, in some places, a curled up figure (the back facing the upper right corner, buttocks to the lower right) and, in other places, breasts, arms, and so on. Weston was inspired to work with sharp-focus photography after a visit to New York in 1922, where he met Stieglitz and Strand. He then abandoned Pictorialist photography. Using a large-format camera that allowed him to print from 4-by-5 inch or 8-by-10-inch negatives, he was able to achieve rich detail and highly refined, beautiful textures. In 1932, he founded, with Ansel Adams, Imogen Cunningham, and others, a San Francisco photography group called f/64, a reference to the very small camera aperture that allowed for tremendous depth of field, and thus sharp, crisp images.

Regionalism and National Identity

While the New York avant-garde sought a national identity and spirituality using either images of modernity or compact abstract styles, a group of Midwest artists, headed by Grant Wood, Thomas Hart Benton, and John Stewart Curry, turned to "old-fashioned" representational art and regional imagery. Although trained in modern-art centers (Benton and Wood studied in Europe as well as in New York and Chicago), they generally preferred to work in the Midwest, where they came from and with which they identified.

The most famous image produced by this group is *American Gothic* (fig. **28.48**) by Grant Wood (1891–1942) of Cedar Rapids, Iowa. The picture was shown at the Art Institute of Chicago in 1930, where it caused a stir and brought Wood to national attention. It was intended as a window into the Midwest world in which the artist grew up and lived. A fictitious father and spinster daughter are presented as the God-fearing descendants of stalwart pioneers who first worked the soil. They are dressed in old-fashioned clothes

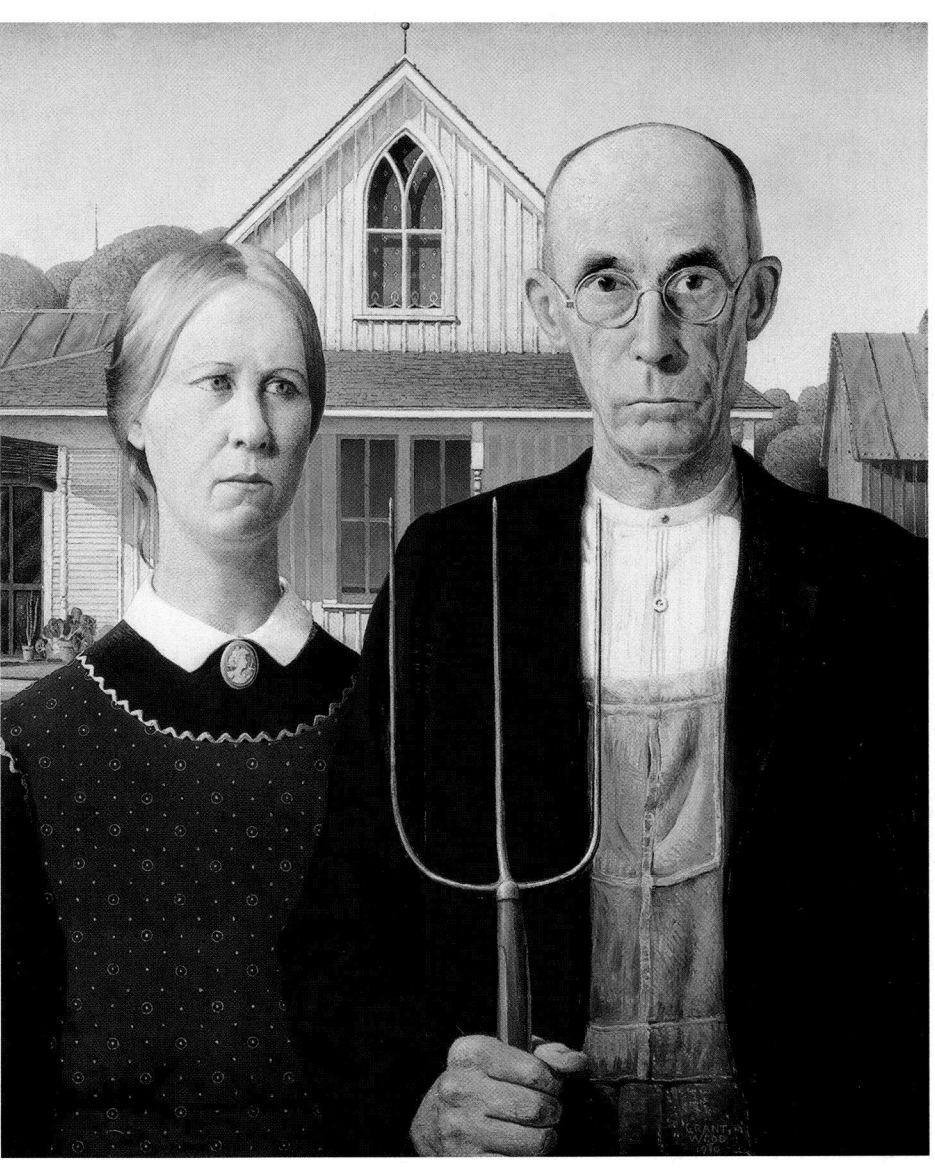

28.48 Grant Wood, *American Gothic*. 1930. Oil on beaverboard, 30¹¹⁄₁₆ × 25¹¹⁄₁₆" (78 × 65.3 cm). Unframed. The Art Institute of Chicago, Friends of American Art Collection. 1930.934

and stand firmly against the march of progress. The style of their house, from which the title of the painting is taken, is Carpenter Gothic, a nineteenth-century style evoking both the humble modesty and old-fashioned ways of the residents as well as their religious intensity, which parallels the fervor of the medieval period when Gothic cathedrals were built. Wood further emphasizes his characters' faith by developing numerous crosses within the façade, and by putting a church steeple in the distant background.

In addition to being hard-working and reverent, we also know these farmers are orderly and clean, as suggested by the crisp drawing and severe horizontal and vertical composition. This propriety also stems from the primness of the woman's conservative dress and hair and the suggestion that she carefully tends to the house, as she does to the plants on the front porch. The figures' harsh frontality, the man's firm grasp on his pitchfork, and his overalls suggest that they are industrious and strong. There is no hint of modernity, and the simplicity and austerity of the setting suggests they are frugal. Nonetheless, many critics viewed Wood as ridiculing his sitters and their lifestyle, and indeed the painting does contain humor, such as the woman warily looking off to the side as if to make sure nothing untoward is occurring. But regardless of interpretation, no one seemed to deny that the picture captured something fundamentally American, and especially Midwestern.

The Harlem Renaissance

From 1910 to 1940, approximately 1.6 million African Americans fled the racism and poverty of the rural South for the cities of the industrial north, where they hoped to find jobs as well as justice and equality. In the North, the new migrants often discovered they had exchanged rural poverty for urban slums, and the racism encoded in Southern Jim Crow laws for prejudice, segregated neighborhoods, and second-class citizenship. Nonetheless, the confluence of blacks in New York's Harlem and Chicago's South Side resulted in a cultural flourishing devoted to self-discovery and to establishing a black identity, something white America had methodically denied African Americans. The movement was then called the New Negro Movement, although today it is generally known as the Harlem Renaissance, after its primary center, often described as its "capital."

Leading this movement in literature, music, theater, and art was the Howard University philosopher Alain Locke (1886–1954), who called for a distinctive style that evoked a black sensibility and perspective. He advocated recapturing the African past and its art, which white avant-garde artists had already done, although presenting it from their own narrow perspective and using it to reflect their own needs and interests. Locke encouraged representations of African Americans and their lives as well as a

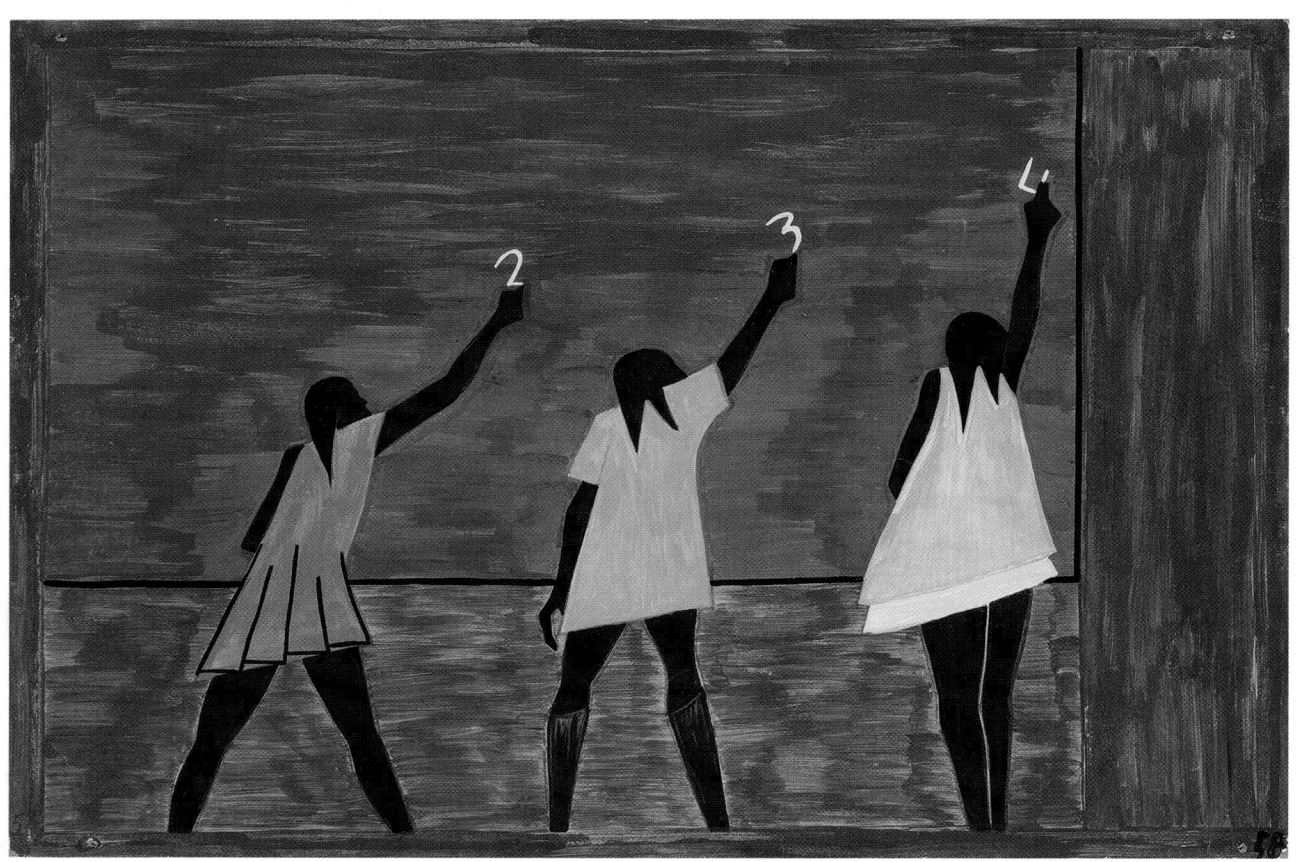

28.49 Jacob Lawrence, *In the North the Negro Had Better Educational Facilities*, from the series *The Migration of the Negro*, number 58. 1940–41. Casein tempera on hardboard, 12 × 18" (30.5 × 45.7 cm). Museum of Modern Art, New York. Gift of Mrs. David M. Levy

portrayal of the distinctive physical qualities of the race, just as African masks often stressed black physiognomy. In effect, he was advocating artists and writers to declare that Black is beautiful. In his promotion of a black aesthetic, he encouraged artists to depict a distinct African-American culture, one that departed from the Euro-American tradition and reflected the enormous contributions Americans of African descent had made to American life and identity.

Prior to the Harlem Renaissance, African-American fine artists made art that was inspired by the art that their Euro-American counterparts were producing, with the intention of "fitting in," conforming, and appealing to market values, which were determined by white artists. They made the same landscapes, still lifes, and genre scenes, all devoid of black content. (However, in the crafts and folk art, such as quilts, metalwork, and furniture, and in music as well, African Americans were often influenced by African traditions.) With the Harlem Renaissance, artists began making African Americans the subject of their art. Although most major African-American artists worked within the Modernist tradition, they also offered an alternative to this tradition by making racial identity a prominent theme in their work. In effect, they made the subject of race and the power of its presentation as important as formal innovation.

JACOB LAWRENCE The most famous painter to emerge from the Harlem Renaissance was Jacob Lawrence (1917–2000), who received his training as a teenager in the 1930s at the federally sponsored Harlem Art Workshop and Harlem Community Art Center. Lawrence regularly went to midtown to take in all the art the city had to offer, from a 1935 exhibition of African Art at the Museum of Modern Art, to Mexican textiles, to all of the latest European styles. In the late 1930s, he began making large narrative series dedicated to black leaders, including Harriet Tubman, Toussaint L'Ouverture, and Frederick Douglass. The images were small and modest, made of poster paint on cardboard or posterboard.

Lawrence is best known for his *Migration Series*, begun in 1940. In 60 images, Lawrence presented the reasons for blacks migrating north and their experiences in both the North and the South. While the series is anecdotal, the images did much of the talking through their abstraction, as seen in number 58, *In the North the Negro Had Better Educational Facilities* (fig. **28.49**). Three girls write numbers on a blackboard, but we do not see their faces, which would make them individuals. Instead, we see numbers and arms rising higher, suggesting elevation through education, and we see a clean slate for a clean start. The girls' brightly colored dresses affirm life and happiness, while the jagged and pointed edges in their hair and skirts impart an energy and a quality of striving. Lawrence generally shows a collective black spirit, not an individual or individual expression. He is interested in a human spirit that relentlessly and energetically moves forward, building a better future. His sparse and beautifully colored pictures embody a remarkable psychology, which is often reinforced by the Modernist space of his pictures. Here, a flat field pushes the figures to the surface, prominently displaying them, and the composition's geometry seems to reinforce the discipline of the students' dedication to education.

MEXICAN ART: SEEKING A NATIONAL IDENTITY

The Mexican Revolution, which began in 1910 with the overthrow of the dictatorship of General Porfirio Díaz and ended in 1921 with the formation of the reformist government of Alvaro Obregón, triggered a wave of nationalism within the cultural community, one that focused on indigenous traditions while rejecting European influences. A government building campaign resulted in a large number of impressive mural commissions, which in turn gave rise to a school of artists headed by Diego Rivera, David Siquieros, and José Clemente Orozco. Either socialists or Communists, the muralists proclaimed murals as the true art of the people. The Mexican muralists gained international renown and were especially popular in the United States, where they received important commissions, ironically from major capitalists such as the Rockefeller family.

Diego Rivera

Diego Rivera (1886–1957) is perhaps the best known of the three major muralists. He lived in Europe, primarily in Paris, from 1907 to 1921, and was an accomplished Cubist. By the late 1910s, Rivera was consumed by the idea of creating a nationalistic revolutionary art through mural painting, and he traveled to Italy to study Renaissance murals. Upon returning to Mexico, he jettisoned his elite esoteric Cubism for the straightforward representational art of fifteenth-century Italy, giving it a monumentality that also echoed the strong simple forms of Aztec and Mayan art. Furthermore, he shunned easel painting, declaring it a bourgeois capitalistic art form, a commodity for the rich. He viewed his fresco murals as a public art, an art for the masses. He also felt his art should be about the indigenous people, not the Euro-Mexicans and their European customs. Consequently, many of his mural commissions are about national identity and the uniqueness of Mexican customs and tradition.

Rivera was a Communist, and his politics, especially his championing of the common folk and labor, appear in his murals. From 1930 to 1934, he received numerous commissions in the United States, and his representational art had a tremendous impact on American mural painting, which was proliferating due to support from Franklin D. Roosevelts's New Deal administration which provided artists with work. One major project was the lobby of the RCA building in Rockefeller Center. Entitled *Man at the Crossroads Looking with Hope and High Vision to a New and Better Future*, it included a portrait of the Communist leader Lenin, which outraged the Rockefellers, who had commissioned the mural. The Rockefellers paid Rivera but then destroyed the mural. Rivera remade it as *Man, Controller of the*

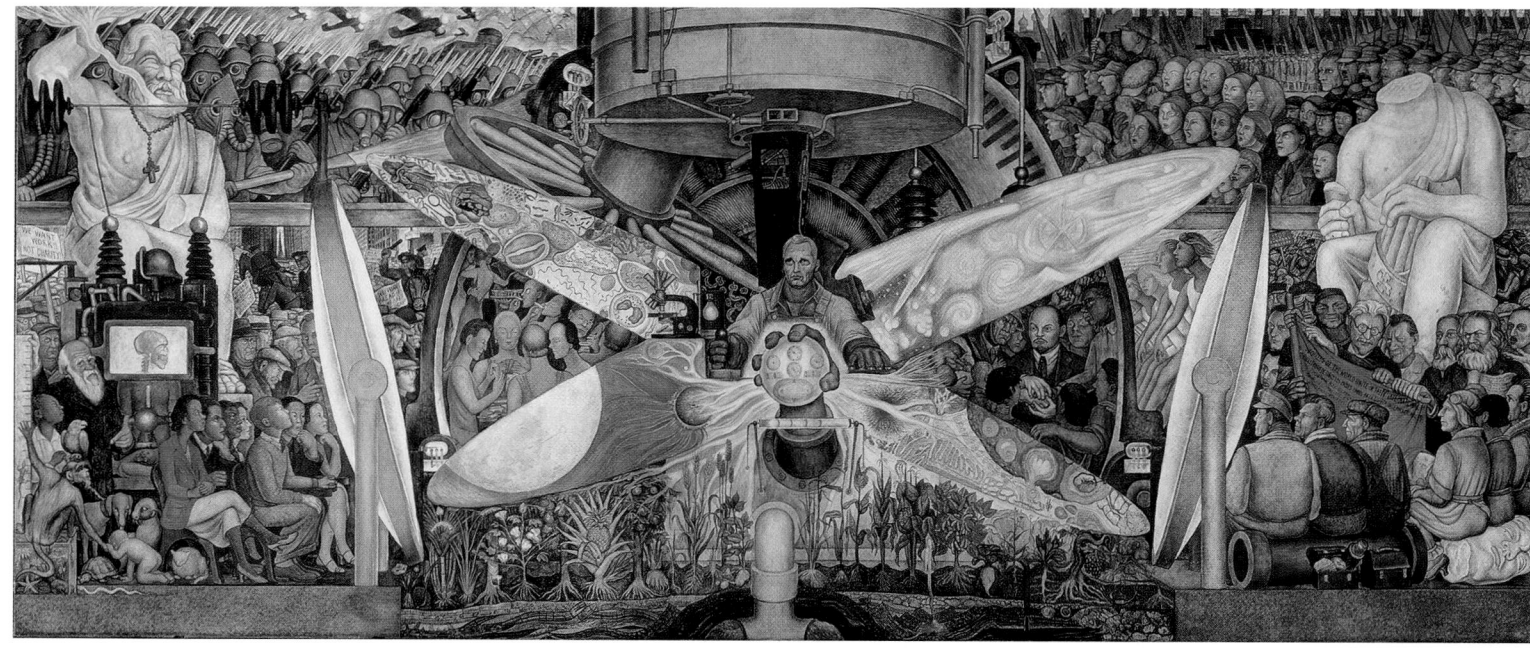

28.50 Diego Rivera, *Man, Controller of the Universe*. 1934. Fresco, 15'11" × 37'6" (4.85 × 11.45 m). Museo del Palacio de Bellas Artes, Mexico City

Universe (fig. **28.50**) at the Museo del Palacio de Bellas Artes in Mexico City in 1934. The painting champions science and Communism, which, for Rivera, were the twin tools of progress. In the center of the composition we see Man, positioned under a telescope and with a microscope to his right (our left), indicating that humankind will control the future through science. Two crisscrossing ellipses of light seem to emanate from Man, one depicting a microscopic world, the other the cosmos. Below him is the earth, and the superior agricultural products generated by scientific discovery. To Man's left (our right), we see, sandwiched between the healthy microorganisms and a harmonious cosmos, Lenin holding hands with workers of different races. Beyond is a scene of healthy unified labor. To Man's right (our left) are the evils of capitalism. Between the ellipses showing diseased organisms and a clashing cosmos is a decadent bar scene depicting the well-heeled bourgeoisie, including John D. Rockefeller, Jr. Beyond are frightening soldiers and discontented, protesting laborers.

FRIDA KAHLO A more remarkable, if less influential, artist from this period was Rivera's wife, Frida Kahlo (1907– 1954). She was almost killed in a traffic accident when she was 18, and, when recuperating, she started painting, cultivating a folk style that reflected her strong interest in the power of naïve Colonial pictures (art often made by self-taught or little-trained artists) and such folk imagery as ex-votos (a Catholic folk image of religious devotion often created in gratitude for a special event in someone's life). Kahlo's imagery was personal, focusing on her state of mind, generally her tumultuous relationship with her philandering husband or her lifelong excruciating suffering from her injuries. She made easel pictures, often quite small, which, while focusing on herself, nonetheless deliberately placed her in a Mexican context. She often presented herself in traditional Mexican clothing and jewelry, and with attributes associated with folk beliefs and superstition.

We can see this focus on her own identity and psychology in her 1939 painting *The Two Fridas* (fig. **28.51**), made when she and Rivera were divorcing. On the left is the European Frida, light-skinned, even sickly pale, and in Victorian dress, reflecting her father's Hungarian Jewish ancestry. To the right sits the Mexican Frida, dark-skinned and in peasant costume, reflecting her mother's Indian and Creole background. More important, this is the Frida that Rivera wanted her to be. She holds a miniature portrait of Rivera as a boy, the source of the blood coursing through her and into the European Frida, who has cut the connection back to her Mexican self, in effect draining the blood, and life, out of the indigenous self. The exposed heart, dripping blood, and the miniature have the surreal drama found in the Mexican ex-votos that Kahlo so admired, while the crisp contours and minimal modeling of the figures and the bench, for example, echo their plain direct folk-art style. Contrasted with these simple unarticulated passages are meticulously detailed motifs, such as the hearts and lace, which change the texture of the image, making it all the more bizarre. André Breton was in Mexico in 1938 and declared Kahlo a Surrealist, a label she objected to, declaring she was not painting dreams but rather the reality of her life. Her pictures were not meant to churn the unconscious, but rather to reflect her own pain and suffering, both physical and psychological.

MANUEL ÁLVAREZ BRAVO Breton also added photographer Manuel Álvarez Bravo (1902–2002) to his roster of Surrealists. Bravo, who was self-taught, was in the muralist circle in Mexico City and was equally preoccupied with creating a Mexican art.

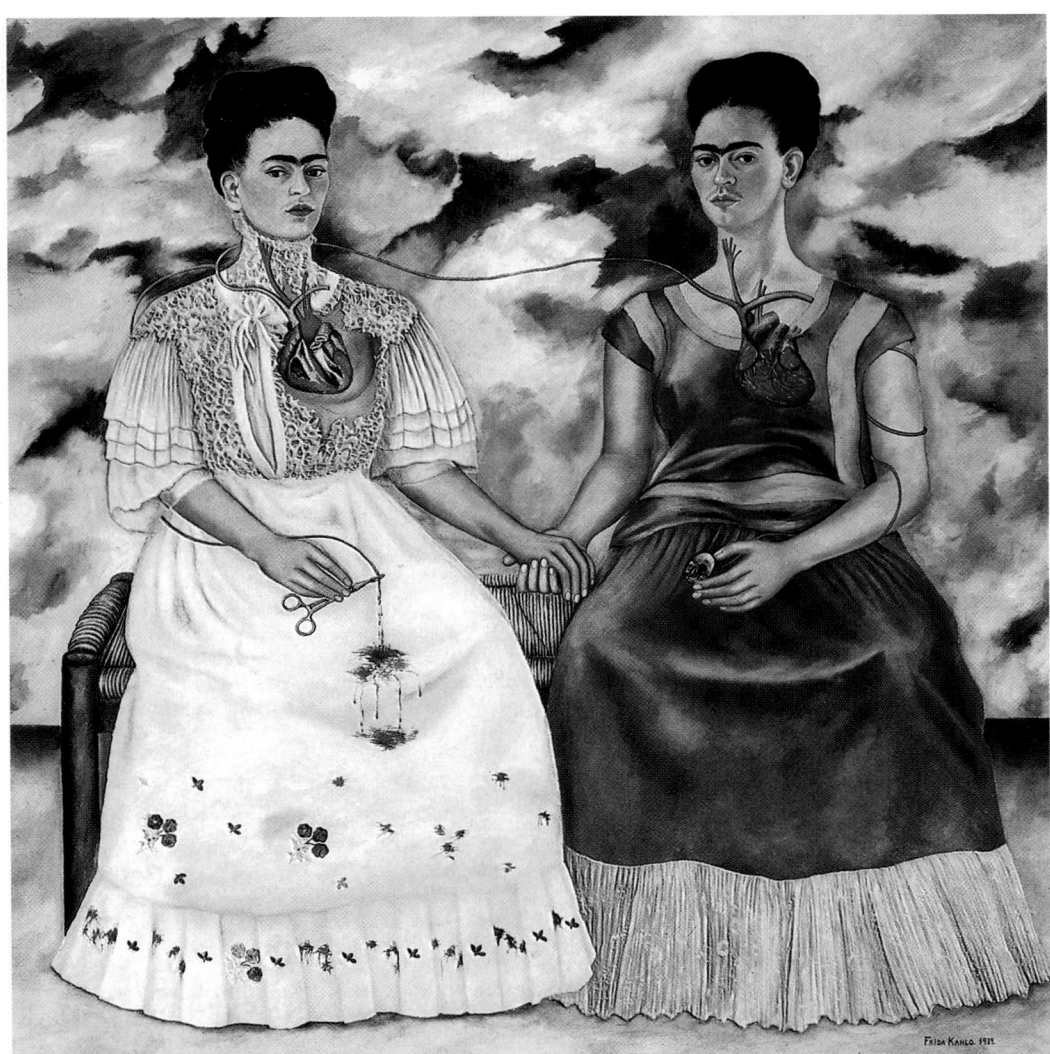

28.51 Frida Kahlo, *The Two Fridas*. 1939. Oil on canvas, 5'8½" × 5'8½" (1.74 × 1.74 m). Museo de Arte Moderno, Instituto Nacional de Bellas Artes, Mexico City

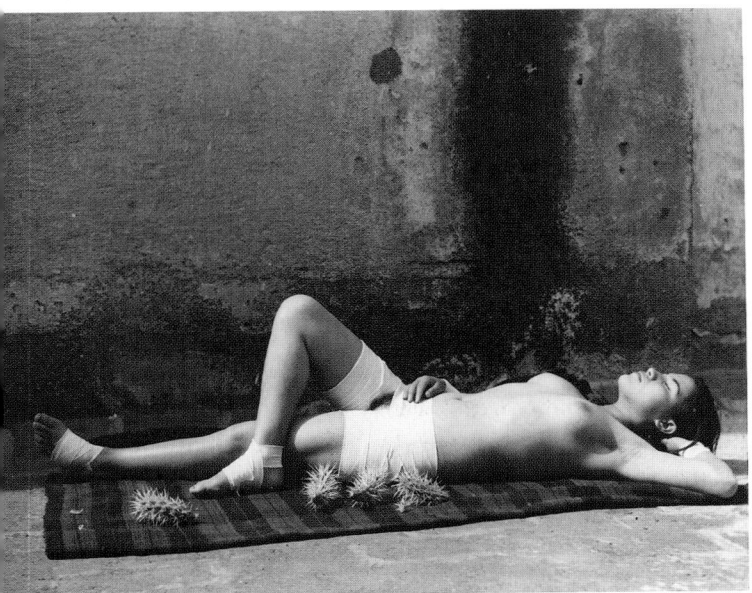

28.52 Manuel Álvarez Bravo, *La Buena Fama Durmiendo* (*Good Reputation Sleeping*). 1938–39. Gelatin silver print. Museum of Photographic Arts, San Diego, California

Like Cartier-Bresson's images, Bravo's have an uncanny quality, sometimes due to an unusual juxtaposition of objects, sometimes simply because of a strange silence and mysterious shadows. In some respects, his Surrealism was the result of his quest to capture the magical essence of folk myths and superstitions, as seen in *La Buena Fama Durmiendo* (*Good Reputation Sleeping*) (fig. **28.52**). Here, Bravo posed his model on the roof of the national arts school where he was teaching, having her lie on a Mexican blanket and binding her wrists, ankles, and feet as well as her pelvis and upper legs in bandages. He allows her pubic hair to show, and surrounds her with thorny cactus pears. Breton wanted to use this image for the cover of a 1940 international Surrealist exhibition he was organizing for Mexico City. Owing to the jarring relationship of prickly pears to the model, the exposed crotch, the strange tightly wound bandages, and the violent stains on the wall, it is not difficult to understand why. But Bravo's motivation was not just about evoking the pain, suffering, violence, and desire associated with sex; he also wanted to encompass the intensity of local legends that went back centuries. In Mexican folklore, for example, the thorny pears are supposed to ward off danger during sleep. The bandages were inspired by watching dancers bind their feet, which reminded Bravo of Pre-Columbian sculptural reliefs of dancers, which were related to the earth-goddess Coatlicue, who was conceived without sexual intercourse. The image is a wonderful exercise in doctrinaire Surrealism, but at the same time it is steeped in the myth and magic of Mexican tradition, especially drawing upon indigenous and folk culture.

THE EVE OF WORLD WAR II

In October 1929, the New York stock market crashed, unleashing the Great Depression that fanned out around the globe. The deprivation it inflicted lasted an excruciating 16 years. In Europe and Asia, fascists rose to power—Mussolini in Italy, Hitler in Germany, Franco in Spain, and Hirohito in Japan. Communist Russia became totalitarian with the emergence of Stalin in the late 1920s. In 1931, Japan invaded continental Asia.

For European artists, the rise of Hitler was the defining influence. To those bent on establishing a democratic classless world, his policies were insane. He was aggressively militaristic, believing great nations are based on a powerful, ruthless military. He declared Aryans, Germans of Scandinavian and Teutonic descent, to be a master race, superior to all others, and claimed Germany's economic and political decline resulted from its ethnic and linguistic diversity. He especially faulted Jews and Communists for undermining German superiority, and by the late 1930s, Jews,

Slavs, Gypsies, gays, the mentally and physically impaired, as well as Communists and political dissenters, were imprisoned, sent to work camps, or executed. The utopian dream of Dada, Surrealism, De Stijl, Constructivism, and the Bauhaus proved to be just that, a dream. Hitler forced the closing of the Bauhaus in 1933, and in 1937, the Nazis staged a "Degenerate Art" exhibition in Munich, denigrating German avant-garde artists in full public view. In America, social realism and representational regional art gained at the expense of avant-garde art. While regionalists painted stoic or dynamic scenes of American fortitude and drive, others focused on the plight of the urban poor.

America: The Failure of Modernity

The avant-garde continued to work in abstraction through the 1930s, but in an era dominated by the terrible social ills of the Great Depression, it became increasingly difficult for artists not to be socially concerned. Many in the avant-garde got involved by becoming socialists or Communists and by supporting the labor movement, even forming their own unionlike organizations. But for many artists, political activity was not enough. Now, more and more artists worked in a style called Social Realism, a representational format that focused on such pervasive problems as poverty, labor oppression, suffering migrant workers, alienation resulting from increased urbanization and industrialization, and racism, especially as seen in the Ku Klux Klan lynchings.

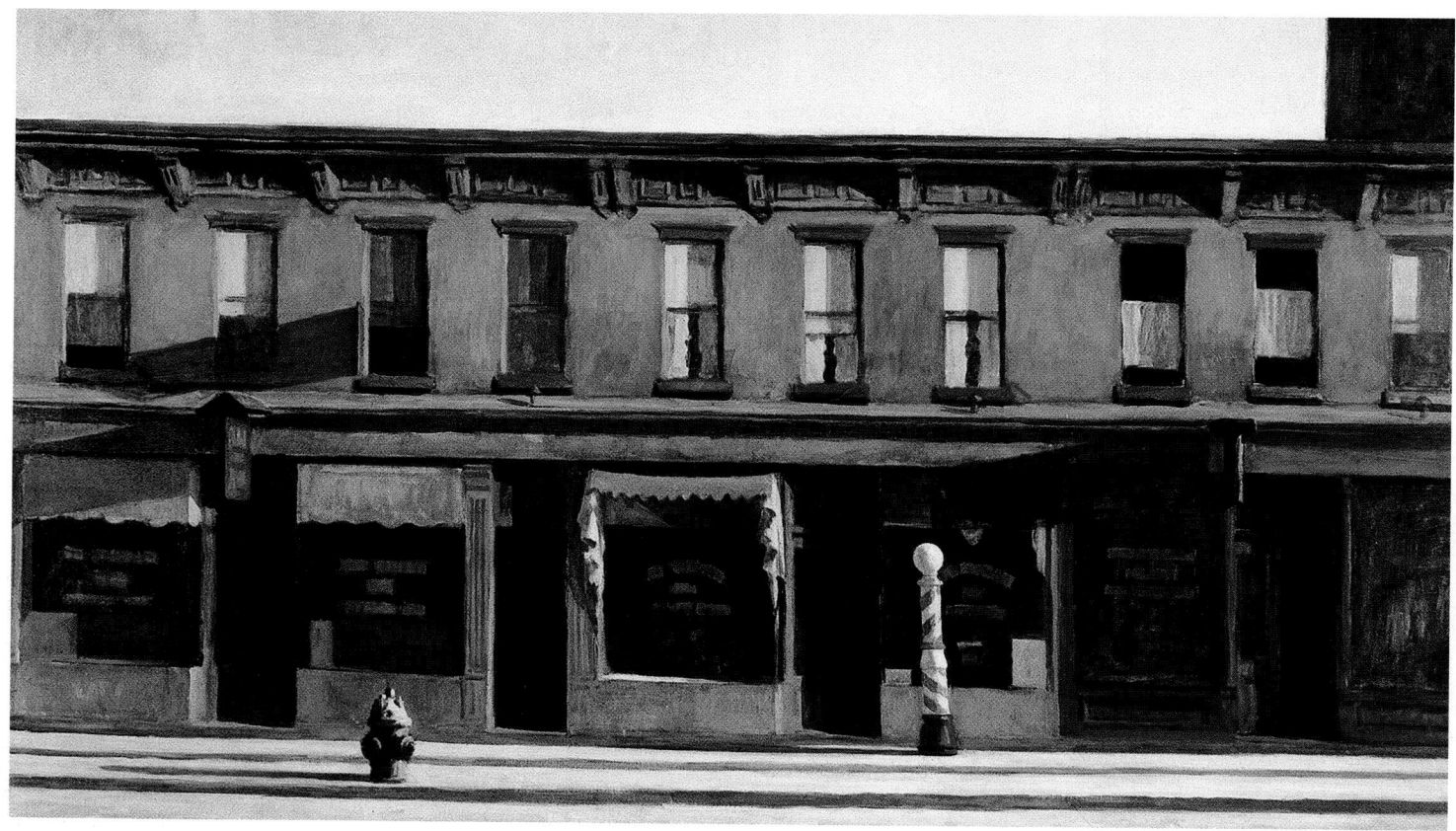

28.53 Edward Hopper, *Early Sunday Morning*. 1930. Oil on canvas, 35 × 60" (88.9 × 152.4 cm). Whitney Museum of American Art. Purchase with funds from Gertrude Vanderbilt Whitney (31.426)

EDWARD HOPPER One of the most powerful representational painters of the period was Edward Hopper (1882–1967), who was based in New York. His pictures are saturated with the alienation associated with life in the big city, and more generally with modern America. A classic Hopper is *Early Sunday Morning* (fig. **28.53**) of 1930. The image is frightening in its uncanny quiet and emptiness, qualities reinforced by the severe frozen geometry of the composition. The second-floor windows suggest a different story for each apartment, but none is forthcoming as their inhabitants remain secreted behind curtains and shades. A strange relationship exists between the fire hydrant, the barber-shop pole, and the void of the square awning-framed window between them, an uneasiness that we project onto the unseen inhabitants of the building. The harsh morning light has a theatrical intensity. Hopper's only loves outside of art were film and theater, and his paintings have a cinematic and staged quality that intimates that something is about to happen. His pictures are shrouded in mystery, and because their settings are distinctly American, the dreary psychology he portrays becomes distinctly American as well.

WALKER EVANS The largest art patron during the Great Depression was the United States government, which put tens of thousands of unemployed artists to work through the Works Project Administration and Federal Art Project, important components of Franklin D. Roosevelt's New Deal. What was so remarkable about these programs was their lack of racial, ethnic, or gender discrimination, which resulted in financial support for women and minorities. One especially influential project was the Farm Security Administration (FSA). Designed to document the suffering and poverty of both rural and urban Americans, the FSA hired about 20 photographers at a time to record the desperate

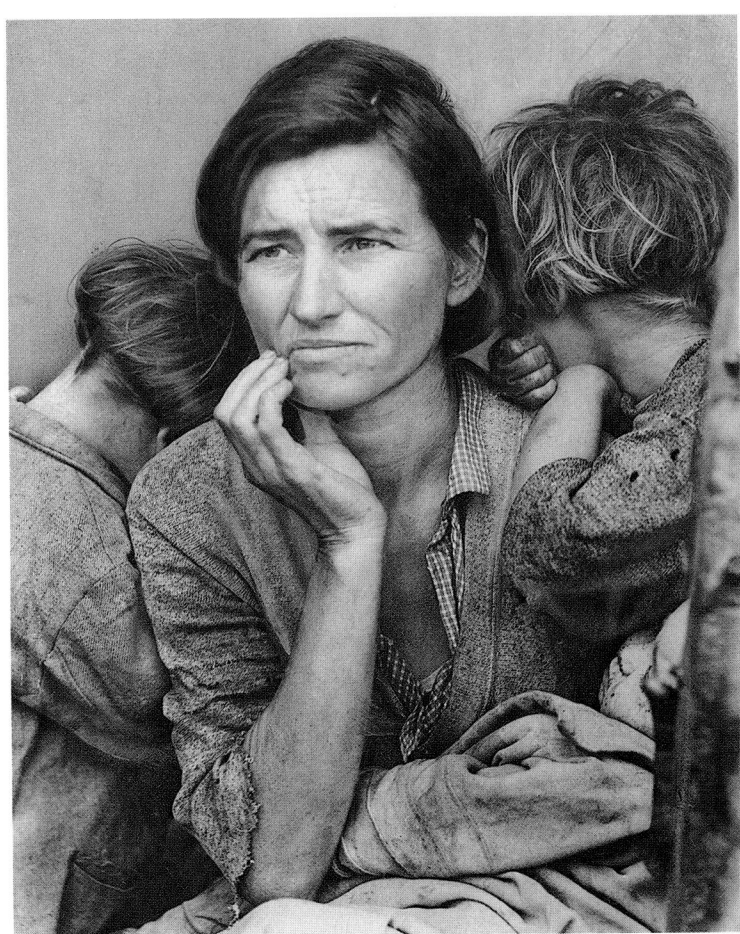

28.55 Dorothea Lange, *Migrant Mother, California*. 1936. Gelatin silver print, Library of Congress, Washington, D.C.

conditions of the poor. Their images were then distributed to the media, where they often had a powerful impact on public opinion.

One of the first photographers hired in 1935 was Walker Evans (1903–1975), who was fired two years later because he was stubbornly difficult and did not make the sort of images that the FSA was looking for: images that dramatically portrayed how wretched the conditions were in America. Instead, his subtle photographs focus on the nation's psychology, showing its gloom and alienation, much as Hopper's paintings did. This can be readily seen in the work reproduced here (fig. **28.54**). We see a town without people, where the cemetery, workers' row houses, and treeless industrial landscape of smokestacks and telephone poles summarize the denizens' lives, succinctly conveying the meaningless, rote, empty life cycle of the American worker. In addition to creating a tragic mood, Evans's genius lies in the brilliant formal play of his detailed compositions that subtly pit light against dark and vertical against horizontal.

DOROTHEA LANGE One of the most famous images from the FSA project is Dorothea Lange's (1895–1965) *Migrant Mother, California* (fig. **28.55**). Using the sharp-focus photography that had become commonplace by the 1930s, Lange created a powerful image that in its details captures the sitter's destitution, and in

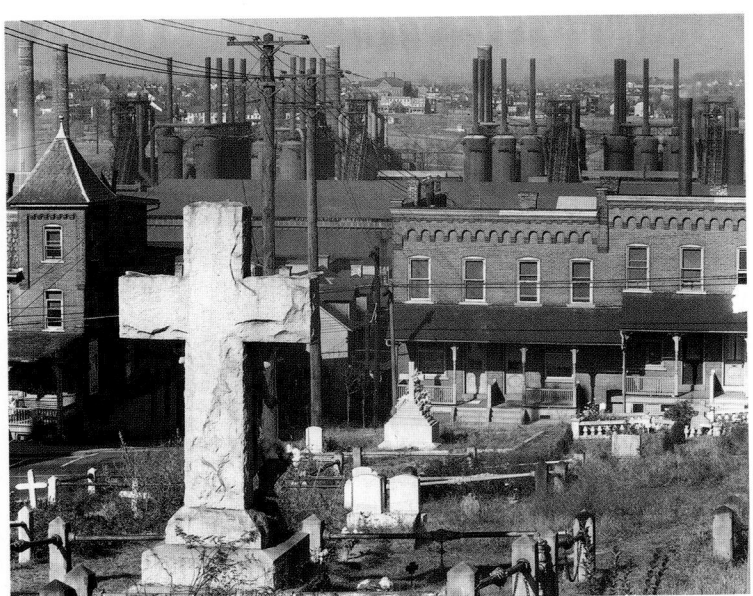

28.54 Walker Evans, *Graveyard, Houses, and Steel Mill, Bethlehem, Pennsylvania*. 1935. Film negative, 8 × 10" (20.3 × 25.4 cm). Museum of Modern Art, New York. Gift of the Farm Security Administration (569.1953)

its complex composition of hands, arms, and turned heads, the family's emotional distress. Because of this photograph and an accompanying news story, the government rushed food to California, and eventually opened relief camps for migrant workers. The immediate impact of this poignant photograph testifies to the overpowering credibility that the medium of photography can have, and we have to wonder if the article about the migrant workers had not included Lange's photograph if the government would have sent aid.

Europe: The Rise of Fascism

If America had to contend with economic deprivation in the 1930s, the situation was even worse in Europe, where the dark cloud of fascism added to the gloom of the worldwide financial collapse. In rapid succession, Italy, Germany, and Spain became fascist dictatorships, depriving citizens of their civil liberties and threatening the peace and security of the surrounding nations. The Enlightenment logic that had ushered in some 200 years of progress seemed to be crumbling, replaced by a world that had lost its sense as a large portion of the European population gave up their freedom and followed Mussolini, Hitler, and Franco down an authoritarian path that ended in World War II. Many artists responded to this threat to civilization. Among the first

was Max Ernst, who, by the late 1920s in Paris presciently saw the threat that was coming to Western civilization. *Die Ganze Stadt* (see fig. 28.12), which Ernst made in 1935–36 after the rise of Hitler and which was discussed earlier in the chapter in the context of Surrealism, is more than just a dreamscape prompted by grattage and aimed at provoking our own subconscious—it is an announcement that such basic human urges as greed and pride will condemn humans to failure and is a premonition of World War II.

MAX BECKMANN AND GERMAN EXPRESSIONISM No one movement or style had a monopoly on making art protesting the rise of fascism. Certainly, postwar German Expressionists, such as Köllwitz, and Berlin Dadaist were predisposed to political protest. German Expressionism continued throughout the 1920s and 1930s, taking on forms quite different from Die Brücke and Der Blaue Reiter but nonetheless retaining a sense of violence, suffering, and the grotesque that can be traced back to the Renaissance. Although we looked at George Grosz within the context of Berlin Dada, he is generally viewed as a postwar German Expressionist, which considering the clear political nature and narrative character of a work like *Germany, A Winter's Tale* (see fig. 28.6) is perhaps a more accurate label. Another postwar Expressionist active since the 1910s was Max Beckmann

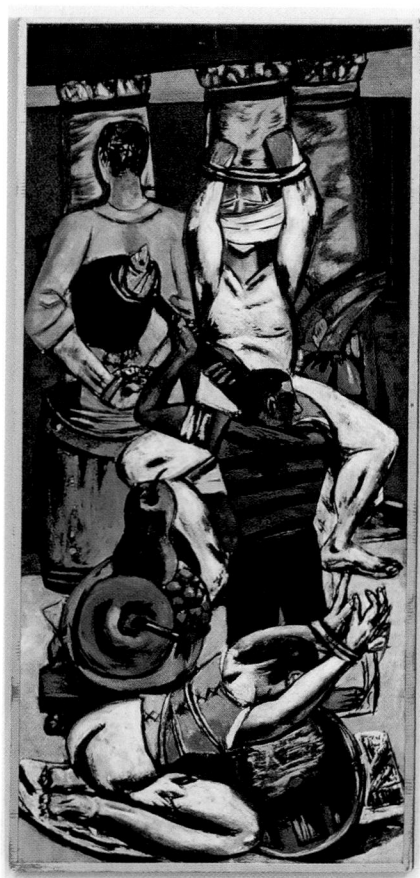 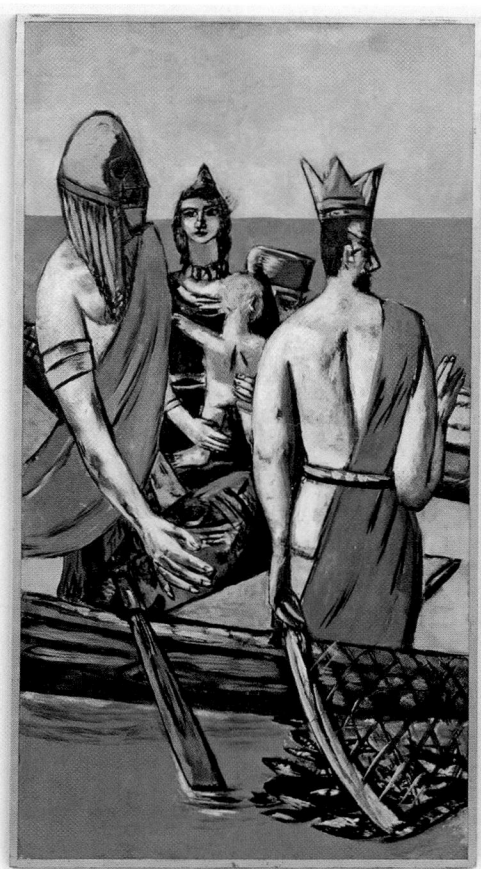 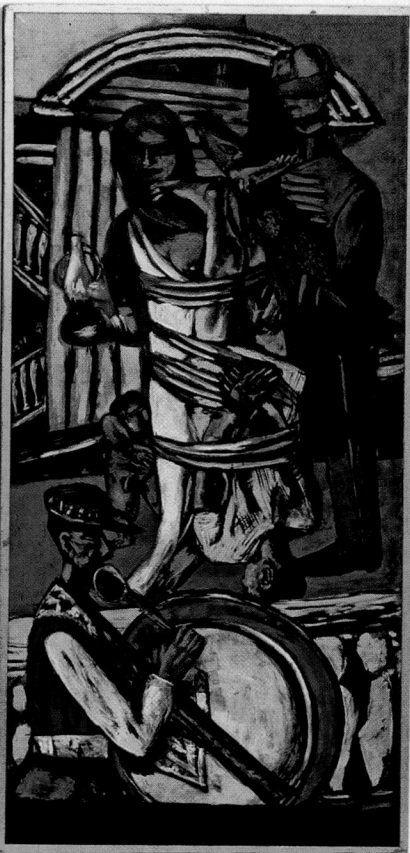

28.56 Max Beckmann, *Departure*. 1932–33. Oil on canvas, 21'2¼" × 3'9⅜" (6.45 × 3.45 m). Museum of Modern Art, New York. Given Anonymously by Exchange

(1884–1950), whose art tended to be more universal than Grosz's, focusing on the folly and despair of existence. Beckmann's pessimistic view of human nature stems from his experience in World War I, which caused him to become an Expressionist in order to "reproach God for his errors." In the early 1930s, he began working in his final style, seen in *Departure* (fig. **28.56**), which is one of nine enormous triptychs (inspired by the triptychs of Hieronymus Bosch) that the artist made in the last 20 years of his life. The complex symbolism in the flanking panels represents life itself, seen as endless misery filled with all kinds of physical and spiritual pain. The bright-colored center panel represents "the King and Queen hav[ing] freed themselves of the torture of life." Beckmann assigned specific meaning to each action and figure: The woman trying to make her way in the dark with the aid of a lamp is carrying the corpse of her memories, evil deeds, and failure, from which no one can ever be free so long as life beats its drum. But Beckmann believed that viewers did not need a key to his iconography; any interpretation would inevitably be similar to his, at least in spirit, if not in the details. The grotesquely distorted figures, strident angular lines, jagged forms, compressed claustrophobic space, and heavy, morbid black line encasing everything reinforce the insane, hell-on-earth mood of this nightmarish image.

The triptych's rich allegory and symbolism reflects Beckmann's early study of the Old Masters and his deep appreciation for the grim and disturbing imagery of Bosch and Grünewald (see pages 492–93 and 635–37). But such narratives of mythic proportions, which only start appearing in Beckmann's art in the 1930s, seem to reflect the artist's familiarity with Parisian Surrealism. The Frankfurt-based Beckmann was a regular visitor to Paris, and it appears he returned with more than just a semblance of Picasso's palette, for he seems to have also brought home the Surrealist emphasis on myth. His hell-on-earth nightmare of bizarre and sadistic events relies on disjointed puzzling motifs that parallel the devices he saw in the dream imagery of the Surrealists.

Shortly after Beckmann began *Departure*, life itself became surreal in Germany, for Hitler became chancellor in 1933. Now the Nazis turned from bullying and threats to overt violence toward their perceived enemies and inferiors, anyone they viewed as being at odds with the "Aryan" ideals of the Third Reich. German avant-garde art was deemed depraved and therefore ridiculed. The artists were forbidden from buying art supplies. Eventually, their work was confiscated from museums and either destroyed or sold in Switzerland to raise money. In 1937, the Nazis removed some 650 pieces of German modern art from museums and presented them in an exhibition entitled *Degenerate Art*, which opened in Munich and then toured Germany for three years. Beckmann was represented in this humiliating exhibition, an event that contributed to Ernst Ludwig Kirchner's suicide. But by 1937, Beckmann was in the United States, a path taken by numerous other artists, including Moholy-Nagy, who established a new Bauhaus in Chicago, today the Institute of Design at the Illinois Institute of Technology.

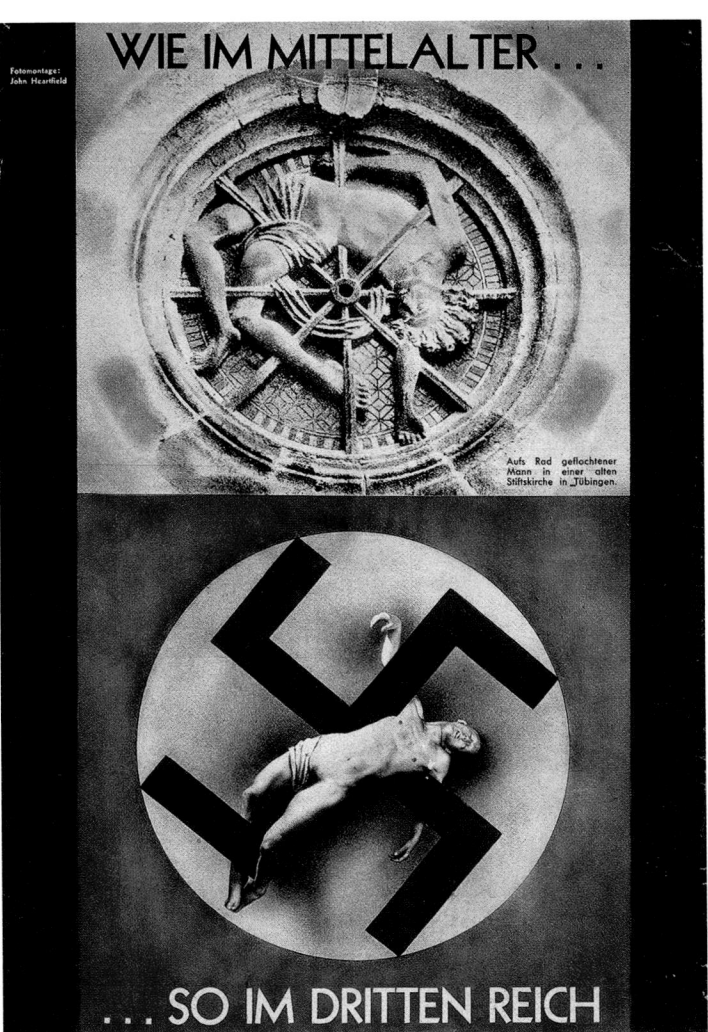

28.57 John Heartfield, *As in the Middle Ages, So in the Third Reich*. 1934. Poster, photomontage. Akademie der Künste, John Heartfield Archiv, Berlin

JOHN HEARTFIELD John Heartfield, the Berlin Dadist who, along with Grosz, Hausmann, and Höch, played a seminal role in the development of photomontage in the early 1920s, now took aim at the Nazis, creating some of his most powerful work. *As in the Middle Ages, So in the Third Reich* (fig. **28.57**) is a wonderful example of his montage technique, which consisted of collaging disparate images together and then photographing them. In this poster, he juxtaposes a Nazi victim crucified on a swastika with a Gothic image of the figure of humanity punished for its sins on the wheel of divine judgment. Heartfield was not interested in the original meaning of the Gothic motif; he used it to imply that the Nazis had ruthlessly transported the nation back to what he viewed as the dark barbaric past of the Middle Ages.

PABLO PICASSO In 1936, civil war broke out in Spain when conservatives loyal to the king and under the leadership of Franco (the Nationalists) tried to overthrow the popularly elected leftist, republican government (the Republicans or Loyalists). In some ways, it was a rehearsal for World War II. Hitler and Mussolini

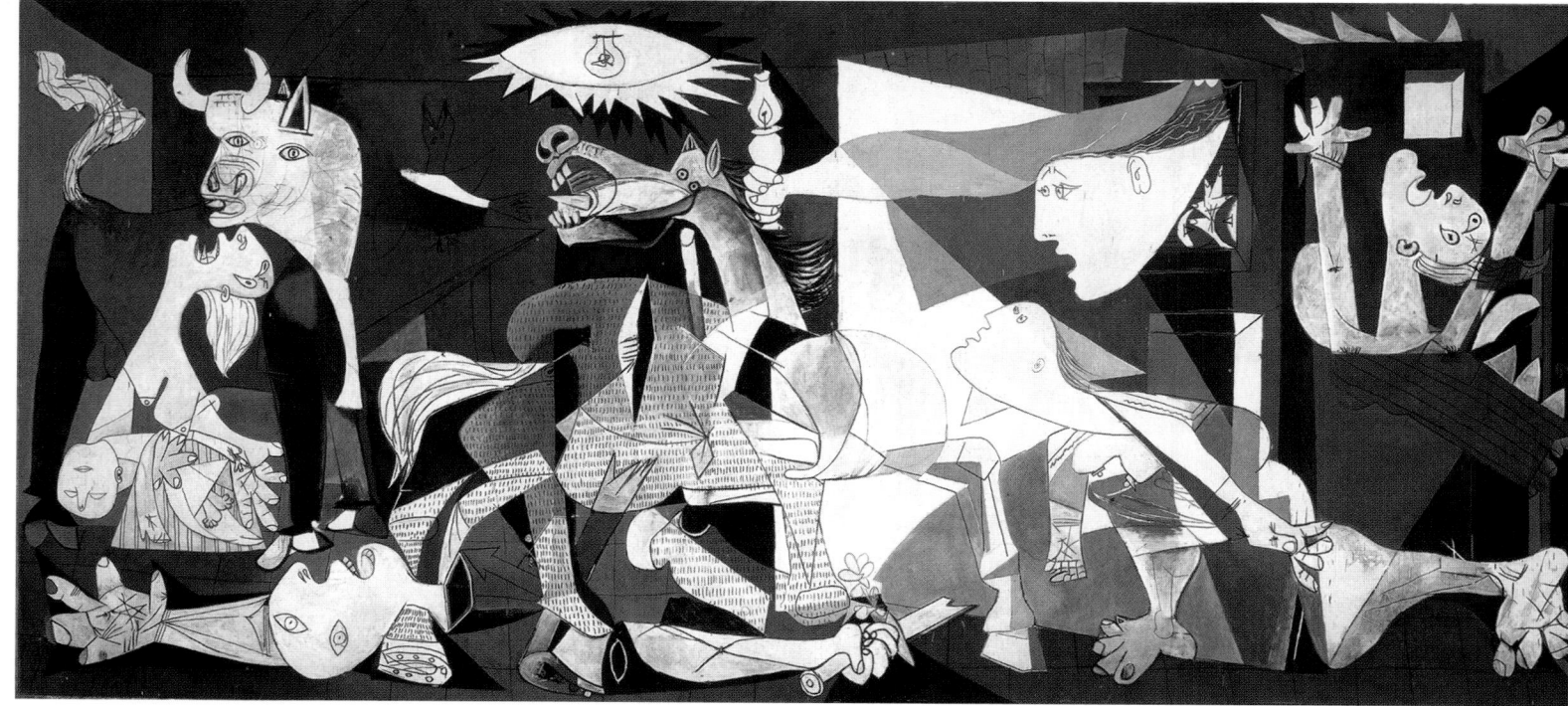

28.58 Pablo Picasso, *Guernica*. 1937. Oil on canvas, 11'6" × 25'8" (3.51 × 7.82 m).
Museo Nacional Centro de Arte Reina Sofia, Madrid. On Permanent Loan from the Museo del Prado, Madrid

provided military and political support for the Nationalists, who included monarchists, fascists, and Catholics. The Loyalists consisted of Communists, socialists, and Catalan and Basque separatists, as well as the International Brigade, made up of volunteers from all over the world. On April 26, 1937, Hitler's Nazi pilots used saturation bombing to attack the undefended Basque town of Guernica, killing thousands of civilians. Picasso, like most of the free world, was outraged, and responded by painting *Guernica* (fig. **28.58**), an enormous black, white, and gray mural that he exhibited as a protest at the Spanish Republican Pavilion of the 1937 Paris International Exposition. He pulled every artistic device out of his Cubist and Surrealist arsenal to create a nightmarish scene of pain, suffering, grief, and death. We see no airplanes and no bombs, and the electric lightbulb is the only sign of the modernity that made the bombing possible.

The symbolism of the scene resists exact interpretation, despite several traditional elements: The mother and her dead child are descendants of the Pietà, the woman with the lamp who vaguely recalls the Statue of Liberty suggests enlightenment, and the dead fighter clutching a broken sword is a familiar emblem of heroic resistance. We also sense the contrast between the menacing human-faced bull, which we know Picasso intended to represent the forces of brutality and darkness, and the dying horse, which stands for the people.

Picasso insisted, however, that the mural was not a political statement about fascism, and it is interesting that many of the figures were used quite differently in Picasso's earlier work. The horse and bull are motifs from the bullfight, which Picasso had

been using since the early 1930s as a metaphor for sexual conflict. The presence of the huge vulva-shaped tear on the side of the horse is certainly not a coincidence. Nor is that of the same sexual orifice on the inside of the sword-holding arm broken off of a Classical statue of a soldier. Nor is it coincidence that the flames on the back of the supplicating woman on the right remind us of the sawtooth groin of the sexually aggressive dancer in *Three Dancers* (see fig. 28.9), or that the quarter-moon silhouetted against a rooster's head just beyond her flailing breast reminds us of the same dancer's moon-shaped head. And is it coincidence that this figure, who resembles a Mary Magdalene at the Cross, also brings to mind Goya's supplicating rebel in *The Third of May, 1808* (see fig. 24.3)? If it were not for the title, there is not much to indicate this is not another of Picasso's images about the tormenting psychology of sexual conflict that we saw as far back as *Les Demoiselles d'Avignon* (see fig. 27.5) of 1907.

But the title cannot be ignored—nor the smashed statue of a soldier, the suffering women and children, the political use of the painting at the International Exposition, and the fact that it was made in response to the destruction of Guernica. When Picasso denied that this was an antifascist picture, he may very well have meant in part that this monumental mural was more than just mundane propaganda against Franco and his ilk. Like Beckmann's *Departure*, we cannot help but feel that this horrifying image is meant to portray the psychology of a world in perpetual conflict and misery—albeit using sexual imagery to convey this message, but this is what Picasso knew best. In *Guernica*, however, Picasso, unlike Beckmann, does not provide a boat to take us away to safety.

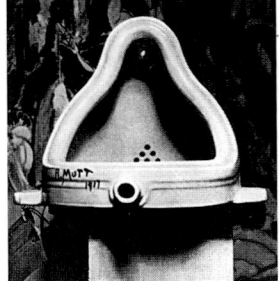
1917 Duchamp's *Fountain*

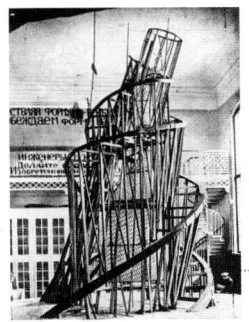
1919-20 Vladimir Tatlin's *Project for "Monument to the Third International"*

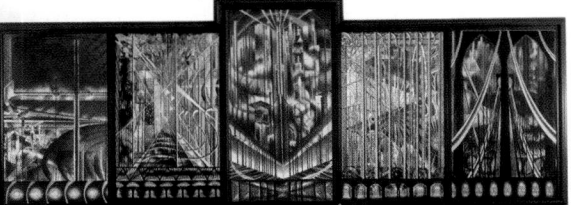
1920-22 Joseph Stella's *The Voice of the City*

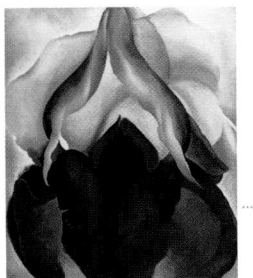
1926 Georgia O'Keefe's *Black Iris III*

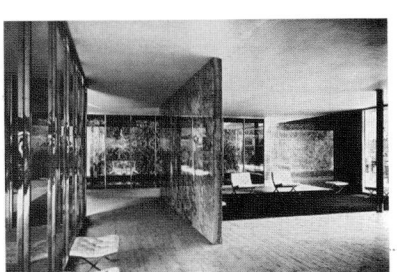
1929 Ludwig Mies van der Rohe designs German Pavilion for International Exposition, Barcelona

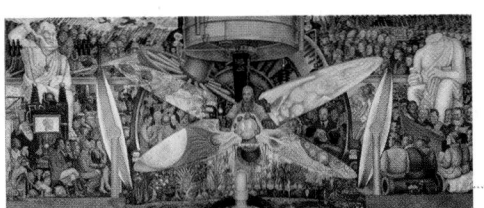
1934 Diego Rivera's *Man, Controller of the Universe*, Museo del Palacio de Bellas Artes, Mexico City

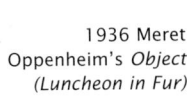
1936 Meret Oppenheim's *Object (Luncheon in Fur)*

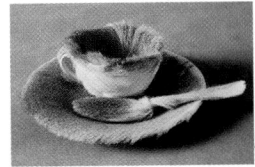
1936 Dorothea Lange's *Migrant Mother, California*

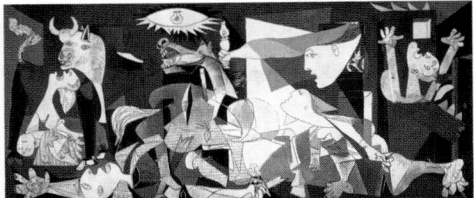
1937 Picasso's *Guernica*

Art Between the Wars

1900
◄ 1900 Sigmund Freud publishes *The Interpretation of Dreams*

1910
◄ 1910-20 Mexican Revolution
ca. 1910-40 The Great Migration, as 1.6 million African Americans move from the South to the North, Midwest, and West

1917 Piet Mondrian with others forms De Stijl

◄ 1919 Walter Gropius founds the Bauhaus which is relocated to Dessau in 1925

1920
◄ 1920 First Dada International Fair, Berlin
1920 19th Amendment to the U.S. Constitution passed giving women the right to vote

◄ 1924 André Breton publishes his first *Surrealist Manifesto*
◄ 1925 Exhibition of Decorative and Industrial Art, Paris, launching Art Deco style

◄ 1929 Great Depression begins

1930

◄ 1933 Hitler comes to power in Germany
1933 Franklin D. Roosevelt launches the New Deal

◄ 1936 Spanish Civil War begins, with rise of Francisco Franco as dictator

1939 John Steinbeck publishes *The Grapes of Wrath*
◄ 1939 World War II begins

1940

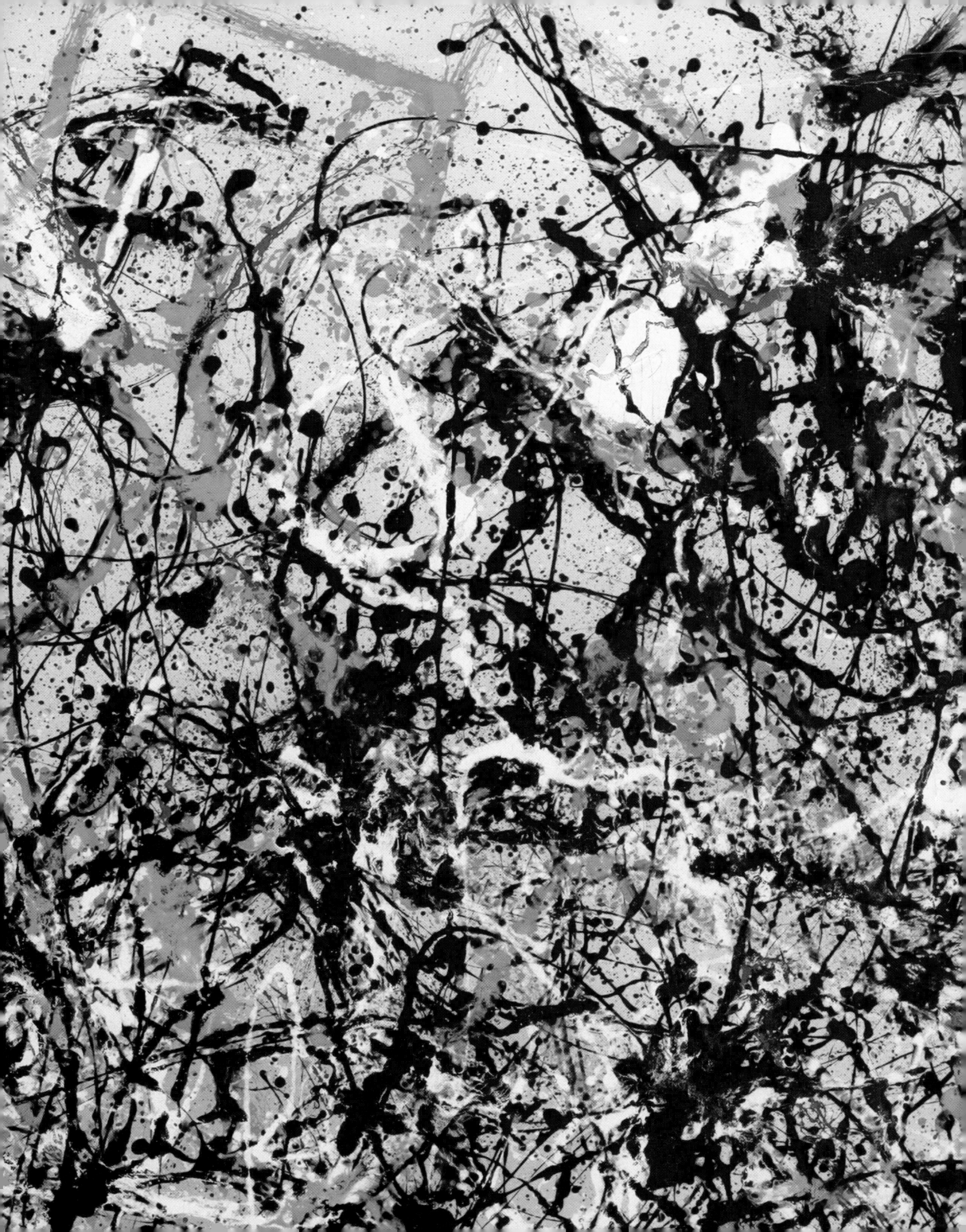

CHAPTER 29

Postwar to Postmodern, 1945–1980

S CHOLARS TRADITIONALLY VIEW WORLD WAR II (1939–45) AS A turning point for the art world, the time when its focus shifted from Paris to New York and when America's first major art movement, Abstract Expressionism, captured the world's attention, even dominating world art. In fact, the 1950s, not the 1940s, were the watershed for the second half of the

century. It was then that Duchamp's preoccupation with how art functions became a driving force as the decade progressed. Likewise, many artists became obsessed with the concept, also rooted in the early Cubism of Picasso and Braque, that art and image making were a form of language, and they dedicated their work to revealing the structure of this visual language and the complex ways it could be used to present ideas and opinions, even to deceive and manipulate.

It was also in the 1950s that artists, again following Duchamp's lead, realized that art need not be limited to the traditional mediums, such as oil on canvas or cast bronze or chiseled marble. It did not have to hang on a wall or sit on a pedestal. Artists could use anything to make art, and by the late 1950s and 1960s, they did. They made art with televisions, film, junk, earth, fluorescent lights, steel tiles, acrylics, entire environments, postcards, and words. **Performance Art**, **Earthworks**, Conceptual Art, Mail Art, **Happenings**, and Video Art are just a handful of the movements and mediums that sprang up from the mid-1950s through the 1970s.

In part, this burst of new mediums reflects the expansive spirit of the period, especially in America. World War II ended 16 years of financial depression and deprivation, and by the 1950s, the

United States had become a nation of consumers. Returning soldiers, eager to resume their lives, married and had children in record numbers, creating the baby-boom generation. Americans in large numbers moved from cities to new cookie-cutter tract houses in the suburbs. And as never before, they shopped—these new homes often had several cars, power boats, barbeque grills and lawn furniture, washing machines, self-cleaning ovens, televisions sets, transistor radios, stereo record players, and home-movie cameras and projectors. As suggested by these last items, Americans as never before chased the latest technology, which was developing quickly in part due to World War II and now the Cold War waged between the Communist U.S.S.R and the democratic West and which was characterized by fighter jets, helicopters, the hydrogen bomb, missiles, rocket ships, satellites, and space travel.

The new postwar American lifestyle, however, was not equally available to all. Magazines, newspapers, film, and the new medium of television reflected the reality of a distinct hierarchy within American democracy, with white males heading up a patriarchal society that viewed women, people of color, and gays as second-class citizens. It was a decade of conformity, symbolized at one extreme by the white businessman in a gray flannel suit climbing the corporate ladder while the prim housewife tended the family and house, played golf and tennis at the country club, and participated in the PTA and church activities. Beatniks, Zen Buddhists, avant-garde jazz musicians, bikers, and urban gangs of

Detail of figure 29.2, Jackson Pollock, *Autumn Rhythm: Number 30*

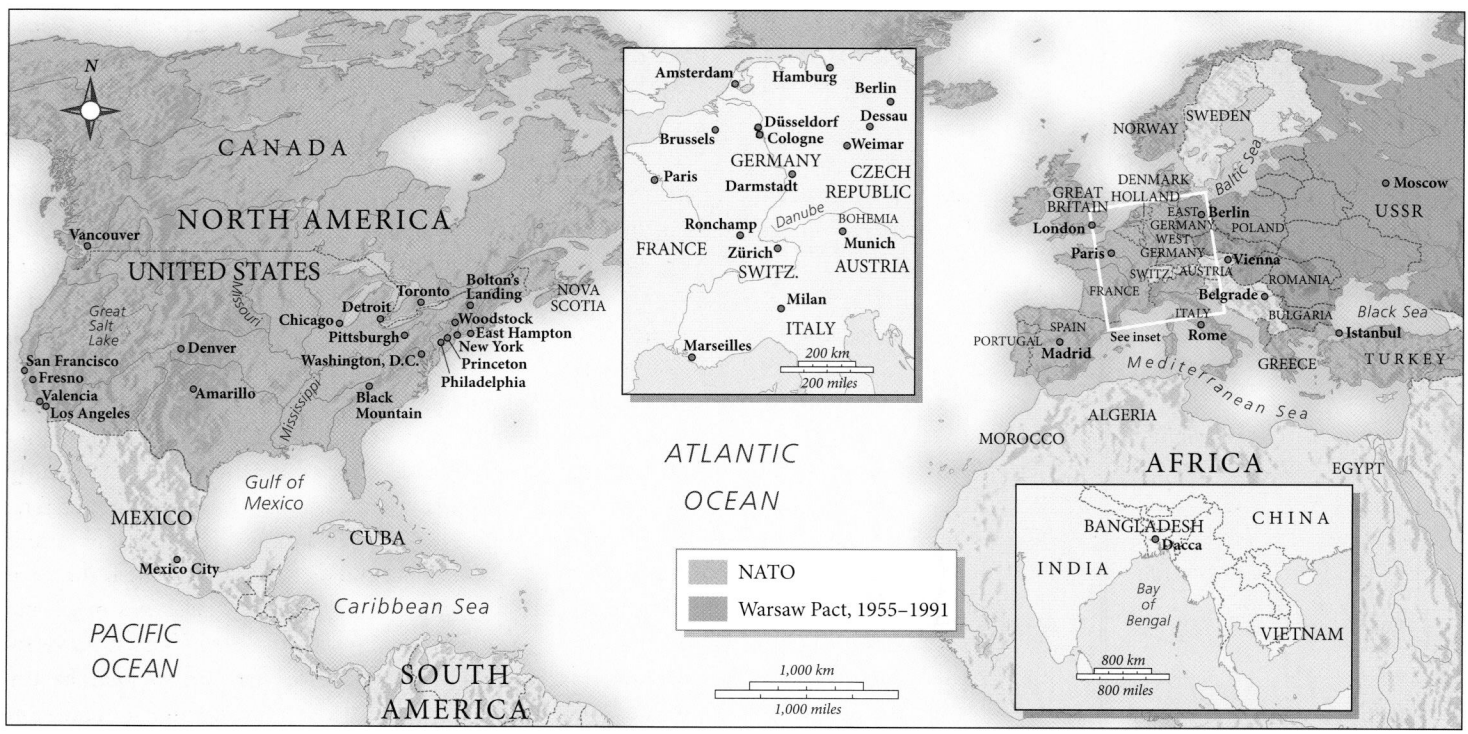

Map 29.1   Cold War alliances

juvenile delinquents established alternative lifestyles in the late 1940s and 1950s.

But it was the Civil Rights Movement that first seriously challenged the status quo in the second half of the 1950s, gaining tremendous momentum in the following decade. Spurred also by the Vietnam War (1959–75), which generated persistent antiwar protests, the mid-1960s began a period of social upheaval that reached a feverish pitch in the 1970s, producing the feminist movement, Gay Pride, Black Power, Gray Power, and environmental groups such as Greenpeace. It was an age of liberation aimed at shattering the status quo and questioning the validity of any claim to superiority or fixed truth. And in the forefront was art, which by the 1950s was challenging the existence of absolutes. But before this artistic revolution could occur, the center of the art world had to move from Paris to New York. This "coup," often referred to as the "Triumph of New York Painting," coincided with the rise of Abstract Expressionism in the late 1940s.

EXISTENTIALISM IN NEW YORK: ABSTRACT EXPRESSIONISM

Abstract Expressionism evolved out of Surrealism, which traced its roots to the Dada movement of the 1910s (see page 985). Like the Surrealists, the Abstract Expressionists were preoccupied with a quest to uncover universal truths. In this sense, their heritage goes back to Kandinsky and Malevich as well (see pages 958 and 966). In many respects, Abstract Expressionism is the culmination of the concerns of the artists of the first half of the twentieth century. But the Abstract Expressionists were also driven by a deep-seated belief in Existentialism, a philosophy that came to the fore with the devastation caused by World War II. The war shattered not only faith in science and logic, but even the very concept of progress, the idea that it was possible to create a better world. A belief in absolute truths had been abandoned.

Existentialism maintains that there are no absolute truths—no ultimate knowledge, explanations, or answers—and that life is a continuous series of subjective experiences from which each individual learns and then correspondingly responds in a personal way. Essential to this learning process is facing the direst aspects of human existence—fear of death, the absurdity of life, and alienation from individuals, society, and nature—and taking responsibility for acts of free will without any certain knowledge of what is right or wrong, good, or bad. The Abstract Expressionists, like so many intellectuals after the war, embraced this subjective view of the world. Their art was a personal confrontation with the moment, reflecting upon their physical, psychological, and social being.

The Bridge from Surrealism to Abstract Expressionism: Arshile Gorky

Surrealism dominated New York art in the early 1940s. In late 1936, the seven-year-old Museum of Modern Art mounted the blockbuster exhibition *Fantastic Art, Dada, and Surrealism*, an eye-opener for many New York artists. Some artists not converted by the exhibition were nevertheless swayed by the dramatic influx of European artists who fled the Continent shortly before and during World War II. André Breton, Marcel

Duchamp, André Masson, and Max Ernst were just a few of the many artists and intellectuals who sought the safety of Manhattan and were a powerful presence in the art world. Peggy Guggenheim, a flamboyant American mining heiress who had been living in Europe, returned to New York and opened a gallery, Art of This Century, which featured Surrealism. Surrealism was *everywhere*, and many New York artists took to it enthusiastically.

Just as Dada developed into Surrealism, New York Surrealism seamlessly evolved into Abstract Expressionism. The transformation occurred when all of the symbols and suggestions of myths and primordial conditions disappeared, and images dissolved into a complete abstraction containing no obvious references to the visible world. We can see the beginning of this process in the paintings of Arshile Gorky (1904–1948), an Armenian immigrant, whose family fled Armenia to escape the genocide of the ruling Turks of the Ottoman Empire. Gorky's mother died of starvation in his arms in a Russian refugee camp. By the 1930s, Gorky was in New York, where, over the next decade, his Cubist style began to evolve toward complete abstraction. At his wife's farm in Connecticut, he would dash off minimal abstract line drawings inspired by nature. In the studio, he would then develop, often using preparatory drawings, these linear patterns into paintings, similar to his 1944 surrealistically titled *The Liver Is the Cock's Comb* (fig. **29.1**).

Here, we see wiry black-line drawing and washes of predominantly red, blue, yellow, and black playing off of one another, giving a sense of how the composition developed as a series of psychological reactions with one mark or color triggering the next, and so on until completion. While the painting has echoes of Miró's biomorphic shapes (see fig. 28.13), Masson's automatic drawing (see page 995), and Kandinsky's color and cosmic chaos (see fig. 27.14), it is more abstract and flatter than the work of his predecessors, with the image kept close to the surface. We cannot safely read much into the picture other than a feeling of a landscape filled with some kind of organic animation, perhaps genitalia and figures, which seem eruptive, violent, and in conflict. In fact, many scholars have suggested that Gorky's abstractions refer to the Turkish slaughter of Armenians, but again, the picture is too abstract to interpret. What stands out as a prominent theme is the art process itself, our sense of how the image was made and how it seems to have been determined by Gorky's own powerful emotions. Gorky was one of the last two artists that Breton anointed a Surrealist, a label Gorky rejected, since he undoubtedly saw himself as expressing his innermost feelings and memories, not exploring his repressed self.

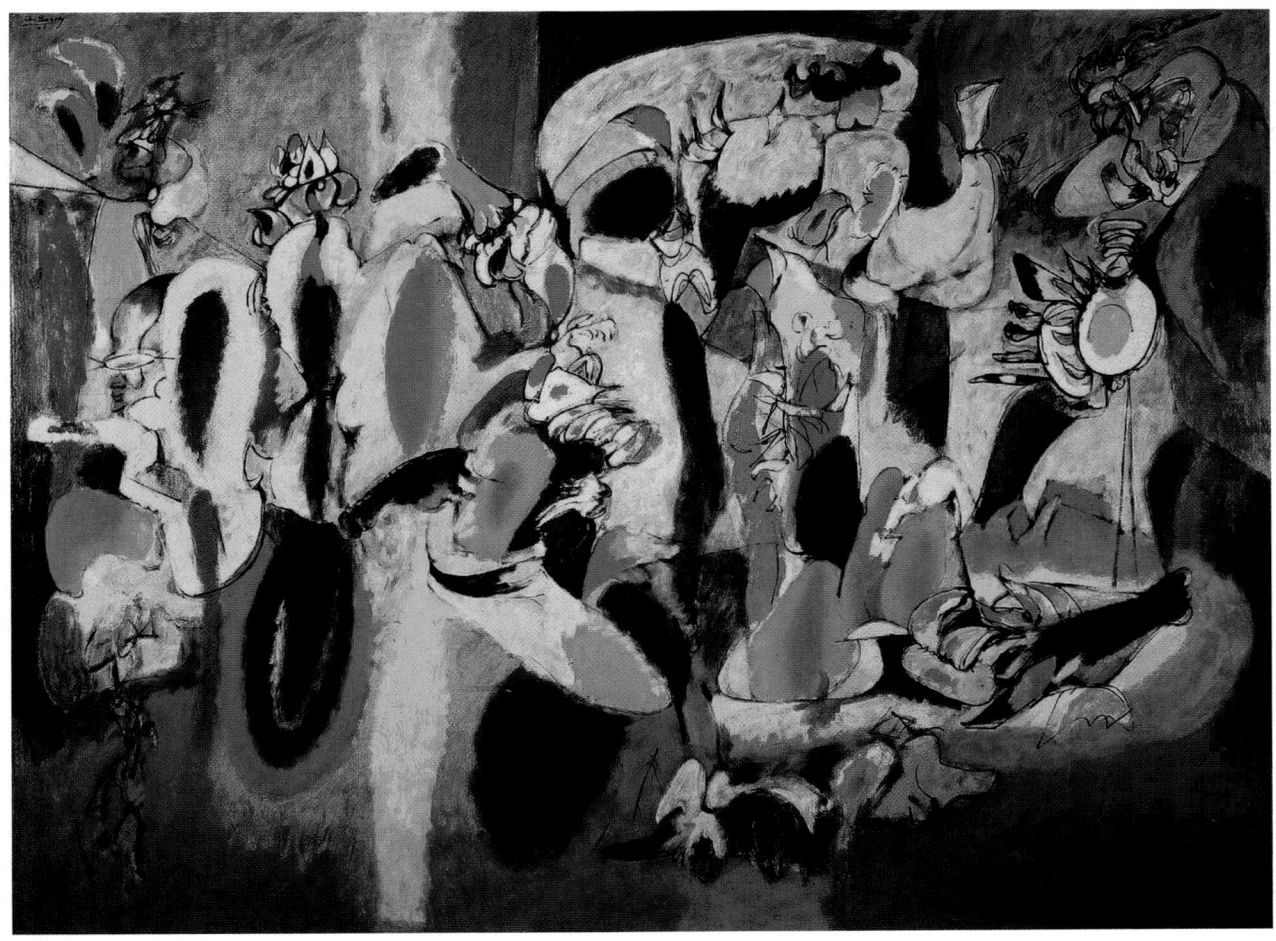

29.1 Arshile Gorky, *The Liver Is the Cock's Comb*. 1944. Oil on canvas, 6'¼" × 8'2" (1.86 × 2.49 m). Albright-Knox Art Gallery, Buffalo, New York. Gift of Seymour H. Knox, 1956

Jackson Pollock (1912–1956)

From "My Painting"

In 1947, when these remarks were recorded, Pollock rejected the usual easel format by placing his unstretched canvases directly on the floor. Using ordinary paint, he claimed he was not just throwing paint but delineating some real thing in the air above the canvas.

My painting does not come from the easel. I hardly ever stretch my canvas before painting. I prefer to tack the unstretched canvas to the hard wall or the floor. I need the resistance of a hard surface. On the floor I am more at ease. I feel nearer, more a part of the painting, since this way I can walk around it, work from the four sides and literally be in the painting. This is akin to the method of the Indian sand painters of the West.

I continue to get further away from the usual painter's tools such as easel, palette, brushes, etc. I prefer sticks, trowels, knives and dripping fluid paint or a heavy impasto with sand, broken glass and other foreign matter added.

When I am *in* my painting, I'm not aware of what I'm doing. It is only after a sort of "get acquainted" period that I see what I have been about. I have no fears about making changes, destroying the image, etc., because the painting has a life of its own. I try to let it come through. It is only when I lose contact with the painting that the result is a mess. Otherwise there is pure harmony, an easy give and take, and the painting comes out well.

The source of my painting is the unconscious. I approach painting the same way I approach drawing. That is direct—with no preliminary studies. The drawings I do are relative to my painting but not for it.

Source: *Possibilities*, I (winter 1947-48), p. 79. Reprinted in by Francis V. O'Conor, *Jackson Pollock* (NY: Museum of Modern Art, 1967)

Abstract Expressionism: Action Painting

Three years later, in 1947, Jackson Pollock made the physical act of energetically applied paint—the gesture—the undisputed focus of painting. This is not to say that his abstract **gesture paintings** are just about the art process, because that process is now a metaphor for the human condition, which previously had been represented through hieroglyphs and biomorphic forms. Almost simultaneously, a second artist emerged, Willem de Kooning, who similarly employed bold gestural abstraction to express his innermost feelings.

JACKSON POLLOCK Through the 1930s, Jackson Pollock (1912–1956) was a marginal figure in the art world who worked odd jobs, including being a custodian at what is today called the Solomon R. Guggenheim Museum. In the early 1940s, just when he started Jungian psychoanalysis, he became a hardcore Surrealist, making crude but powerful paintings filled with

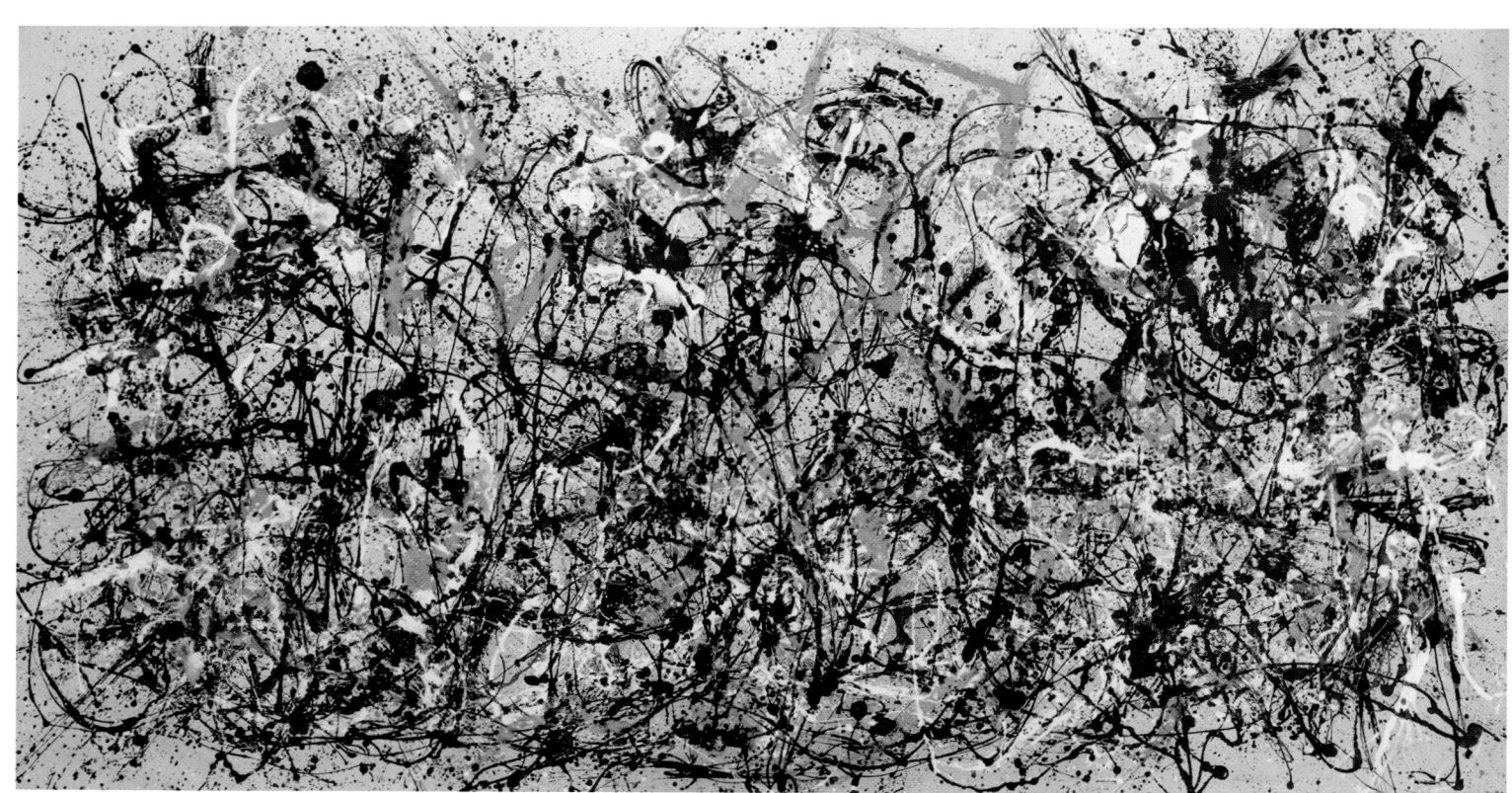

29.2 Jackson Pollock, *Autumn Rhythm: Number 30*. 1950. Enamel on canvas, 105 × 207" (266.7 × 525.8 cm). Metropolitan Museum of Art, New York, George A. Hearn Fund, 1957 (57.92)

slapdash hieroglyphs, totems, and references to primitive myth, whipped about in a swirling sea of paint. His big break came in 1943 when Peggy Guggenheim exhibited his work at her gallery, Art of This Century, and gave him a stipend to paint.

At the Betty Parsons Gallery in 1948, Pollock unveiled his first gesture or **action paintings**, the latter term being coined in the 1950s by art critic Harold Rosenberg (1906–1978). A famous example of this style is *Autumn Rhythm: Number 30* (fig. **29.2**) of 1950, an 8-by-17-foot wall of house paint that was applied by dripping, hurling, pouring, and splattering when the unstretched canvas was on the floor. Pollock had worked on it from all four sides, and he claimed that its source was his unconscious. (See *Primary Source*, page 1038.) Despite the apparent looseness of his style, Pollock exerted great control over his medium by changing the viscosity of the paint, the size of the brush or stick he used to apply the paint, and the speed, reach, and direction of his own movements, and he rejected many paintings when the paint did not fall as anticipated. The energy of the painting is overwhelming, and from its position on a wall the work looms above us like a frozen wave. Our eye jumps from one stress to another—from a white blob, to a black splash, to a Masson-like automatic line, and so on. There is no focus upon which the eye can rest. Because of these even stresses throughout the image, Pollock's compositions are also often described as **allover paintings**.

Pollock constructed his picture as he went along, with each new move playing off the previous one, and emotional intuition dictating the next gesture. The resulting image is not just a record of the physical self, but also of the psychological being. Because the artist must face the challenge of the bare canvas and the risk-taking responsibility of making each mark, painting becomes a metaphor for the challenges of the human condition and the risks inherent in taking responsibility for one's actions, particularly in an Existentialist world. World War II dashed the blind belief in the superiority of science, progress, and utopian societies. The one thing that could be trusted and believed in was the self, and *that* became the sole subject of Abstract Expressionist painting.

WILLEM DE KOONING Pollock's style was too personal to spawn significant followers. The gesture painter who launched an entire generation of painters was Willem de Kooning (1904–1997), a Dutch immigrant, who quietly struggled at his art for decades in New York's Greenwich Village. Encouraged by his friend and mentor Arshile Gorky, de Kooning made Picasso-inspired Cubist-Surrealist paintings in the 1940s, mostly of women. He finally got his first one-person show in 1948, at the Egan Gallery, when he was 44. The radical works he presented appeared to be total abstractions of dramatically painted curving lines and shapes that entirely covered the canvas with the same evenness as in Pollock's allover paintings.

Despite the spontaneity implied by the bravura paint handling, the pictures were laboriously crafted, often using methods similar to those of the Surrealists. For example, de Kooning fired his imagination by pinning line drawings on his canvas, not only at the beginning but throughout the process. Charcoal lines

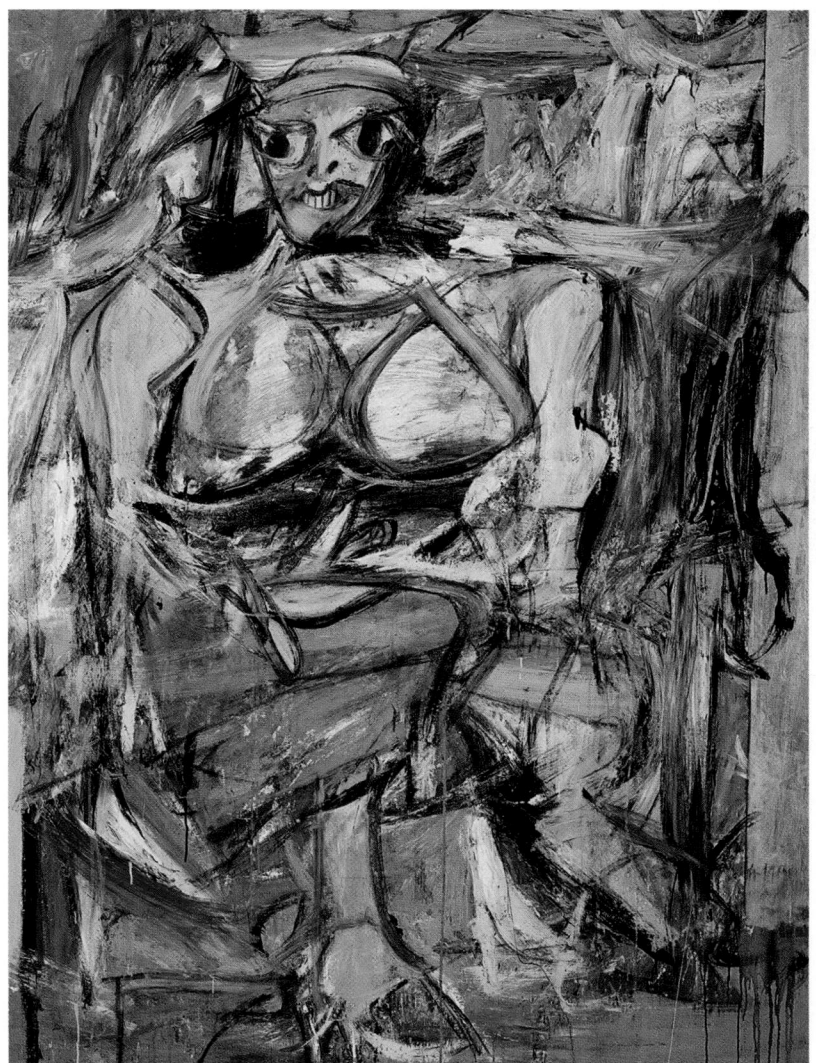

29.3 Willem de Kooning, *Woman I*. 1950–52. Oil on canvas, 75⅞ × 58" (1.93 × 1.47 m). Museum of Modern Art, New York. Purchase

drawn on dried paint to both provoke and experiment with composition sometimes remained in the final picture. He jump-started other paintings by inscribing large letters across the canvas. Like Pollock, he constructed the paintings through a continuous process of gestural reactions based on intuition and emotion, with the resulting marks reflecting his presence, feeling, and uncontrollable urges. Unlike Pollock, however, de Kooning's Expressionist paint handling retained the push-pull of Cubist space and composition, with one painterly form residing above or below another.

De Kooning shocked the art world with his second exhibition, held at the Sidney Janis Gallery in 1953. He did the unthinkable for an Abstract Expressionist: He made representational paintings, depicting women, as seen in *Woman I* (fig. **29.3**), a work he struggled with from 1950 to 1952. It now became clear that the curvilinear patterning of the earlier abstractions was as sexual as everyone had suspected, or as the critic Tom Hess put it, the works were "covert celebrations of orgiastic sexuality." De Kooning reportedly painted and completely repainted *Woman I* hundreds of times on the same canvas, and he also made numerous other paintings of women in the summer of 1952 when he was in East Hampton on Long Island, New York. The process of making the picture was almost as important as the final product, as though it were a ritualistic catharsis of sorts.

Woman I is by far the most violent and threatening of numerous paintings in the *Women* series, the other women having a neutral appearance and embodying a broad range of attributes. Nonetheless, de Kooning intended *Woman I* to be equally unfixed in meaning, or as open to interpretation. He was surprised that viewers did not see the humor in his threatening, wide-eyed, snarling figure, which was based as much on contemporary advertisements of models smoking Camel cigarettes as on primitive fertility goddesses, such as the Paleolithic *Woman of Willendorf* (see fig. 1.14), both of which the artist cited as sources. In the *Women* series, as in all of his paintings, de Kooning played out his own ambivalent emotions, which, because they constantly changed, allowed him to keep repainting his figure.

Abstract Expressionism: Color-Field Painting

Abstract Expressionism had a flip side. If one side was gestural painting, then the other was **color-field painting**. Instead of bombastic brushstrokes and the overt drama of paint, these painters used large meditative planes of color to express the innermost primal qualities that linked them to universal forces. The objective of the color-field painters, like that of their gestural counterparts, was to project the sublime human condition as they themselves felt it. The principal color-field painters—Mark Rothko, Barnett Newman, and Clifford Still—all started out by making myth-inspired abstract Surrealist paintings in the 1940s and were close friends until 1952.

MARK ROTHKO Mark Rothko (1903–1970) ranks among the best-known color-field painters. His paintings from the 1940s draw heavily from Greek tragedy, such as Aeschylus' *Oresteia*, and from Christ's Passion cycle and death—scenes with a harrowing psychology where the lone individual faces ultimate truths about existence, death, and spirituality. But all suggestion of figuration disappeared in 1947. In 1949, Rothko arrived at his mature style, from which he did not deviate for the remainder of his life.

Now, Rothko's paintings consisted of flat planes of color stacked directly on top of one another, as in the 10-foot-high 1953 work *No. 61 (Rust and Blue)* (fig. **29.4**). There is no longer any storytelling, nor any hieroglyphics or symbols, even in the title. But the painting is still mythic, for the artist has painted what he himself has confronted, the inevitable void of our common future and our sense of mystical oneness with unseen cosmic forces, a theme reminiscent of Caspar David Friedrich's *Abbey in an Oak Forest* (see fig. 24.8). Rothko's subject, he explained, was "tragedy, ecstasy, doom, and so on." His ethereal planes are so thin, color glimmers through from behind and below, creating a shimmering spiritual light. Their edges are ragged, and like clouds dissipating in the sky, they seem precariously fragile. Although the painting

29.4   Mark Rothko. *No. 61 (Rust and Blue)* (also known as *Brown, Blue, Brown on Blue*). 1953. Oil on canvas, 115¾ × 91¼" (2.94 × 2.32 m). Museum of Contemporary Art, Los Angeles. The Panza Collection

is not about process, we feel Rothko's hand building up the planes with individual marks, giving the work a poignant organic quality. Space is paradoxically claustrophobic and infinite. On the one hand, the planes literally crowd the picture to the edges and hover at the very front of the picture plane, while on the other hand, the pervasive blue ground seems to continue forever, uncontained by the edge of the canvas and suggesting infinity. Enormous shifts in scale give a sense of the sublime. Note, for instance, the tiny, thin wisp of soft white on the bottom of the middle plane, which seems so insignificant in comparison to the enormous planes and the vast size of the canvas.

Regardless of the palette, whether bright yellows and oranges or the more moody blues and browns in *No. 61*, the colors in a Rothko painting have a smoldering resonance that makes the image seem to glow from within and evoke a spiritual aura. Rothko wanted viewers to stand close to his enormous iconic images, which would tower over them, and where they would be immersed in this mystical void of the unknown future, as if standing on the precipice of infinity and death. After making a series of predominantly dark paintings, Rothko committed suicide in 1970.

New York Sculpture: David Smith and Louise Nevelson

Like the Abstract Expressionist painters, the avant-garde sculptors of the postwar period were originally Surrealists, and most were similarly steeped in Existentialist philosophy. Some, like David Smith, developed their compositions as they worked on their sculptures, which were largely abstract. Others, like Louise Nevelson, retained the hieroglyphic signs of Surrealism but now began working on an enormous scale, in part spurred by the scale of Abstract Expressionist painting.

Along with Alexander Calder (see page 1001), who returned to America with World War II, David Smith (1906–1965) was perhaps the most visible American sculptor at midcentury. He began as a painter, but upon seeing illustrations of welded steel sculpture by Picasso and González (see pages 994–95), he adopted the blowtorch as his tool and metal as his medium, which he used throughout his career. He was friendly with the Abstract Expressionist painters, and even after moving to a farm in Bolton's Landing in upstate New York in 1940, he periodically came to the city for long periods and socialized with them in Greenwich Village.

Smith was steeped in the Existentialist philosophy of his circle, and, like his colleagues, he dedicated his work to expressing his physical and psychological being. His career follows a path similar to Rothko's, moving from Surrealist sculptures that were basically drawings of organic forms in space, suggestive of Miró, to totally abstract iconic forms. Beginning in the mid-1940s, Smith constructed his sculptures from large reserves of metal that he always had on hand, working not so much from preliminary sketches and preconceived notions of a finished product but, like de Kooning and Pollock, by a continuous chain of reactions to each gesture, which in his case would be made in a welded material. Despite his working method, which allowed him to work and think in the round, he generally conceived his sculptures like paintings, to be seen almost two-dimensionally from a single viewpoint.

An example of Smith's late, iconic style is the *Cubi* series (fig. **29.5**), begun in 1961 and consisting of 18 works. Because of its severe geometry, the *Cubi* series is unusual for Smith. He did not have equipment to cut stainless steel, and consequently was forced to order it from the manufacturer in precut rectangular shapes, which he assembled into boxes of different sizes that he welded together based on intuition and personal emotion. Despite their relentless geometry, these enormous sculptures are hardly mechanical and unemotional. They are both anthropomorphic and totemic, evoking giant figures and ritualistic structures. They have the sublime presence of a prehistoric monument and embrace a powerful spirituality. It is as though the elemental forms, placed on a tabletop altar, are the very building blocks of the universe itself, their sense of movement and solidity reflecting the essence of life, their precarious arrangement the inevitable impermanence of all things. Smith ended by burnishing the steel, giving it a textured finish. And because we can feel his touch here, the work takes on a surprising organic quality.

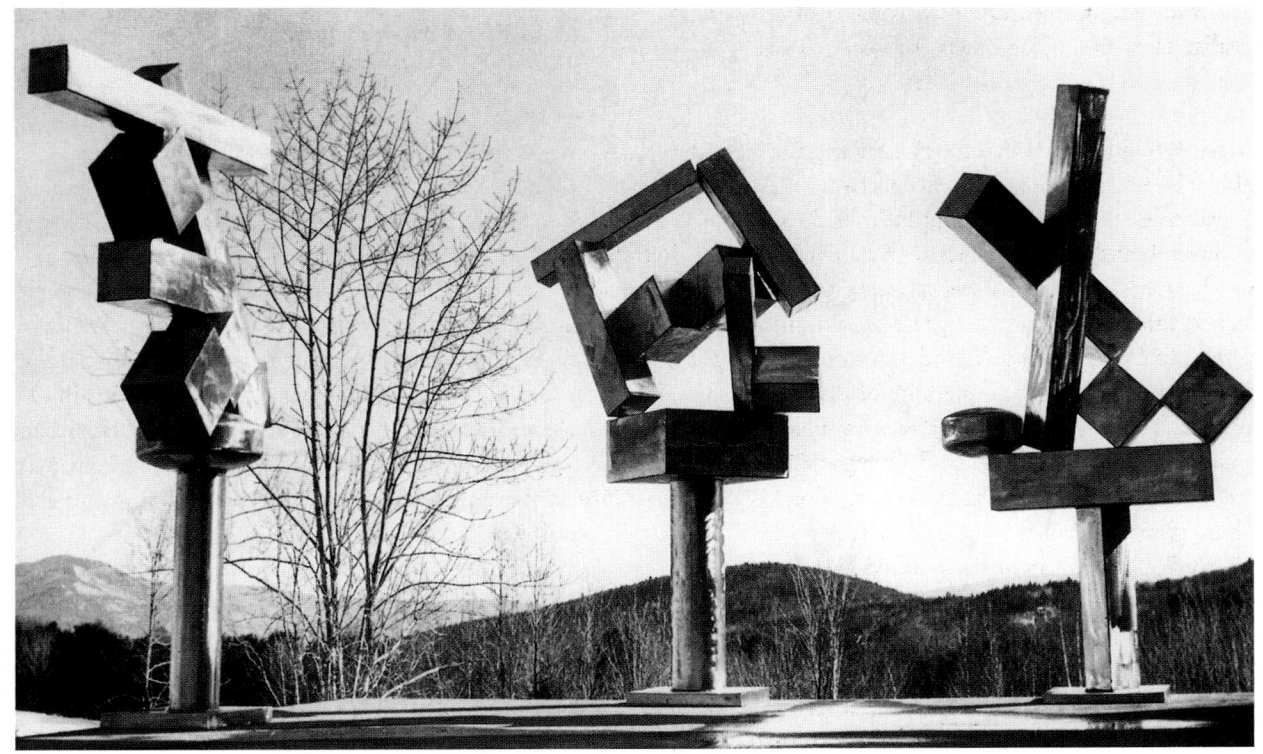

29.5 David Smith, *Cubi* series as installed at Bolton's Landing, New York. Stainless steel. Left: *Cubi XVIII*. 1964. Height 9'8" (2.95 m). Museum of Fine Arts, Boston. Center: *Cubi XVII*. 1963. Height 9' (2.74 m). Dallas Museum of Art. Right: *Cubi XIX*. 1964. Height 9'5" (2.87 m). Tate Gallery, London

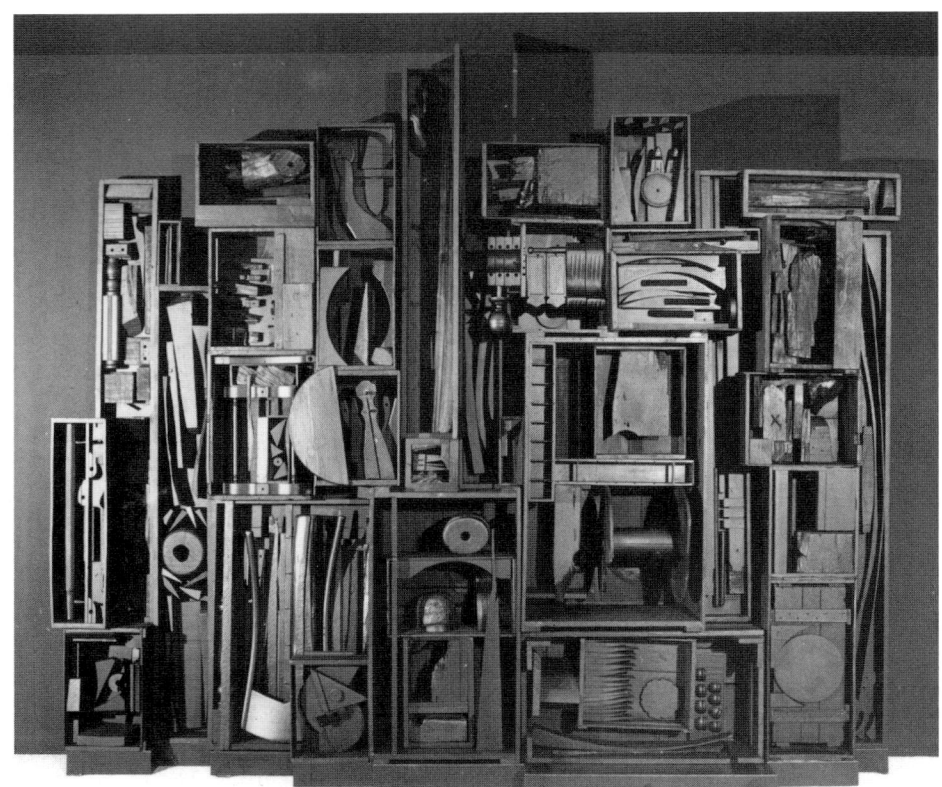

29.6 Louise Nevelson, *Sky Cathedral—Moon Garden Plus One*. 1957–60. Painted wood, black, 9'1" × 10'2" × 1'7" (2.78 × 3.1 × 0.5 m). Collection of Milly and Arne Glimcher, New York. Courtesy PaceWilderstein, New York

Smith's work became dramatically larger in the 1950s, influenced, in part, by the scale of Abstract Expressionist painting. Another Surrealist sculptor followed suit: Louise Nevelson (1900–1988), who emerged in the 1940s. By the 1950s, she was working with fragments of black-painted wood assembled in mysterious black boxes, and by the end of the decade, she began making enormous walls of these boxes.

One of these is *Sky Cathedral—Moon Garden Plus One* (fig. **29.6**), produced from 1957 to 1960. In it, fragments of furniture and architecture become provocative Surrealist objects in a poetic dreamlike setting. We sense we are looking at the flotsam and jetsam of civilization, the fragments of people's lives, of people long gone. But as the title suggests, Nevelson's forms also evoke landscape and the cosmos, the round shapes suggesting the planets and moons, the splintered wood the mountains, and the accumulation of boards the rock formations. Nevelson wanted her black works (others are all gold or white) illuminated by a blue light, which would suggest twilight, the moment of transformation, when things begin to look different and to change into something else, swallowed up by unseen mystical forces.

EXISTENTIALISM IN EUROPE: FIGURAL EXPRESSIONISM

Abstract Expressionism was identified with the United States, which in the late 1950s began exporting the work to Europe in exhibitions sponsored by the federal government. These shows, ostensibly for the sake of good international public relations, strutted the country's artistic superiority and virility, and complemented its military, financial, and technological dominance. They were cultural pawns in the Cold War. While Europeans developed a counterpart to Abstract Expressionism, perhaps the best-known Existentialist painting was figurative. Two especially powerful artists were Jean Dubuffet and Francis Bacon. Both were loners, with no group or movement affiliations, and artistically kept to themselves, independently developing their own responses to the existential loneliness of human existence.

Jean Dubuffet

As a young man, the Frenchman Jean Dubuffet (1901–1985) was an unlikely candidate for artistic fame. Until the early 1940s, his commitment to, and even his belief in, art was intermittent, and he often worked for a family wine business. Many of his attitudes paralleled Dada: He was antiart and antibourgeois. What interested him most was finding a way to see beyond the blinders of civilization, with its limited concepts of beauty and reality. As had Kandinsky, Malevich, and Mondrian before him, Dubuffet sought to reveal higher truths, namely the interconnectedness of all things in the universe.

Critical to Dubuffet's development was his discovery in the early 1940s of the art of the untrained and insane, which he called **Art Brut** (literally, "Raw Art") and collected. He felt artists untouched by conventional training were uninhibited by the superego and expressed primal urges and desires that were directly connected to mystical forces. Graffiti, children's art—anything equally unrestrained and spontaneously produced—fell

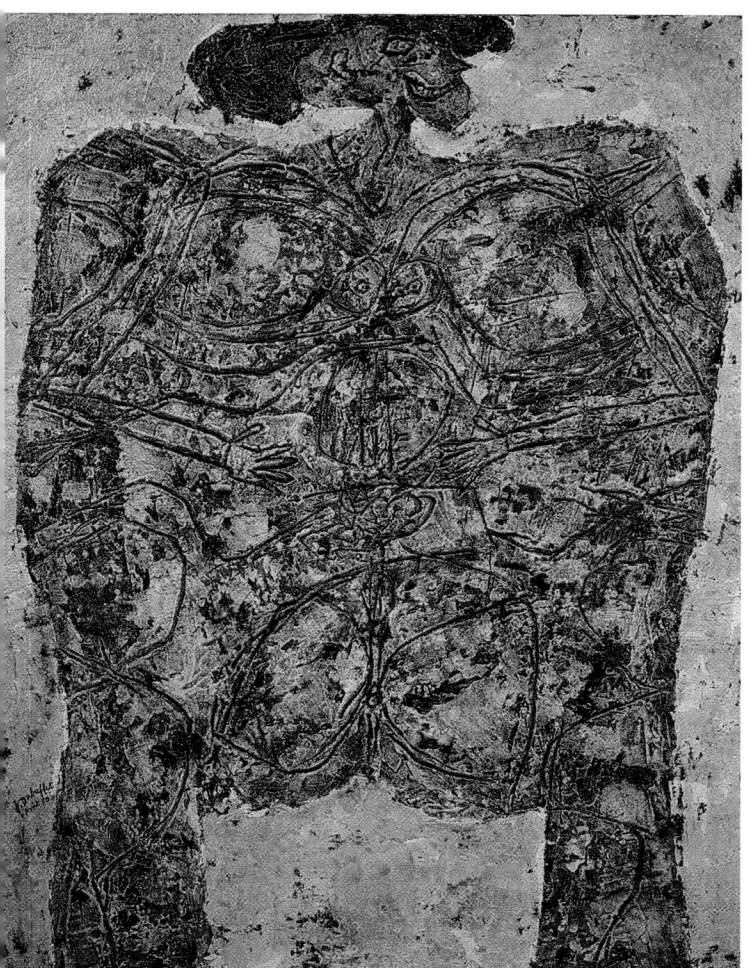

29.7 Jean Dubuffet, *Le Métafisyx*, from the *Corps de Dames* series. 1950. Oil on canvas, 45¾ × 35¼" (116.2 × 89.5 cm). Musée d'Art Moderne, Centre Georges Pompidou, Paris

into this same category. Dubuffet adopted these direct untutored styles in his own art because he believed they represented a universal language that anyone could understand and appreciate.

The second major ingredient in Dubuffet's worldview is the concept that all things are equally consecrated because everything is composed of the same matter and energy. We can see this virtually illustrated in *Le Métafisyx* (fig. **29.7**), painted in 1950 in his Art Brut style. Here, he literally etches his woman into a deep bed of paint, which is crude and rough, suggesting earth, ancient plaster walls, and stone. Not only is this comic-repulsive, soil-encrusted woman identified with mineral matter, she is also timeless, for she resembles an archaeological find excavated from a remote prehistoric site. The frenetic graffitilike style is so abstract, we can read the figure in endless ways and even see the scratchy wiry lines as representing an unseen energy that courses through all things. There is even the suggestion of the body dissolving back into elemental matter. *Le Métafisyx* is part of a series called *Corps de Dames* (*Women's Bodies*), which in its crude drawing and grating texture was meant to shock, challenging the art world's conventional notions of beauty and art.

Francis Bacon

Across the English Channel in London, Francis Bacon (1909–1992), a second loner, was stirring up the art world by expressing his own existential angst. One look at his *Head Surrounded by Sides of Beef* (fig. **29.8**) of 1954 and we realize we are in the presence of one of the more frightening images of the twentieth century. Bacon emerged as a force on the London art scene right after World War II, and it is tempting to view his horrific pictures as a statement about the senseless savagery he had just witnessed. But Bacon's themes were already in place well before the war, and presumably they stem largely from his own horrible circumstances, which included abuse as a child and an adult life dominated by the classic vices of alcohol, gambling, and promiscuous sex.

We cannot be sure that these experiences account for Bacon's work, for unlike Dubuffet and the Abstract Expressionists, for example, Bacon did not pontificate about art, issue manifestos, or declare that painting had to fill social voids. Like his Existentialist contemporaries, he painted from the gut, claiming that when he started a picture he had no idea where he would end up. His first painting based on Velázquez's *Pope Innocent X* (there are 45 versions), which is the source for the central figure in *Head*

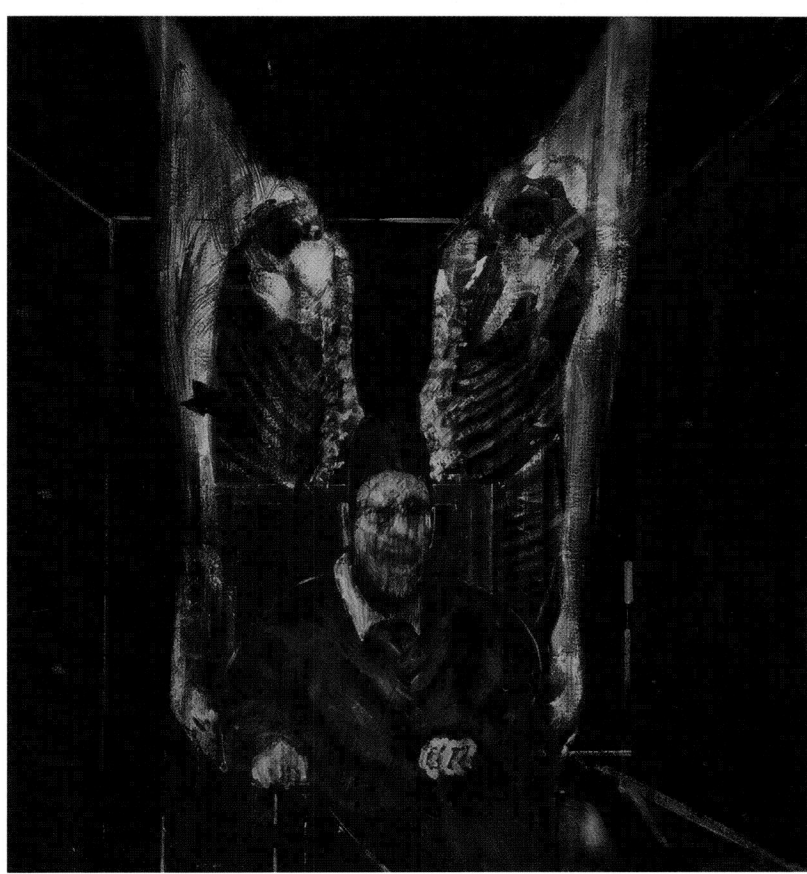

29.8 Francis Bacon, *Head Surrounded by Sides of Beef*. 1954. Oil on canvas, 51⅛ × 48" (129.9 × 121.9 cm). Unframed. The Art Institute of Chicago. Harriott A. Fox Fund. 1956.1201

Surrounded by Sides of Beef, supposedly began as a garden scene. Our painting not only refers to the Velázquez portrait, but also to a contemporary photograph of Pope Pius XII (whose bespectacled head we see), a Rembrandt painting of a flayed ox, and a still of a nurse screaming in the 1925 classic silent film *Battleship Potemkin* by Sergei Eisenstein (1898–1948). In most of Bacon's paintings based on Velázquez's *Pope Innocent X*, the focal point is the primal scream of the sitter, the wide dark pit of the opened mouth. In our figure, however, this motif is not nearly as prominent, as it is balanced by the crucified slab of beef that frames the sitter. Add the black void, the claustrophobic compression of the glass cage, and the gritty quality of sections of the paint surface, and we have a house of horror, obviously the chamber of the artist's grim psyche. A viewer cannot get back from the scene, which seems thrown in one's face by the bold brushwork that prominently sits on the surface of the canvas, pulling the image along with it and toward us. Bacon said of his paintings, "You can't be more horrific than life itself."

REJECTING ABSTRACT EXPRESSIONISM: AMERICAN ART OF THE 1950s AND 1960s

By the mid-1950s other styles were already beginning to overshadow Abstract Expressionism. The 1950s planted the seeds of a cultural revolution, producing a thirst for freedom of expression that required the invention of radically new art forms. Combines, **environments**, Happenings, Minimal Art, and Conceptual Art took art into uncharted territory, breaking down the barriers that had previously narrowly restricted art to certain standard mediums.

Re-Presenting Life and Dissecting Painting

No one person or event triggered the dramatic change that occurred in art in the 1950s, but artist Robert Rauschenberg and musical composer John Cage certainly played major roles. Rauschenberg probably spoke for many when he explained why he rejected Abstract Expressionism: "It was all about suffering and self-expression and the State of Things. I just wasn't interested in that, and I certainly did not have any interest in trying to improve the world through painting." Jasper Johns, Rauschenberg's close friend at the time, similarly rejected Abstract Expressionism. While both artists made paintings that had the gestural mark making of the Abstract Expressionists, these works were an intellectual, impersonal analysis of art rather than an explosion of feelings and primal urges.

ROBERT RAUSCHENBERG AND JOHN CAGE Robert Rauschenberg (1925–2008) was a Texan from a working-class family who ended up in New York studying painting by 1947. A critical component of his development was attending the avant-garde

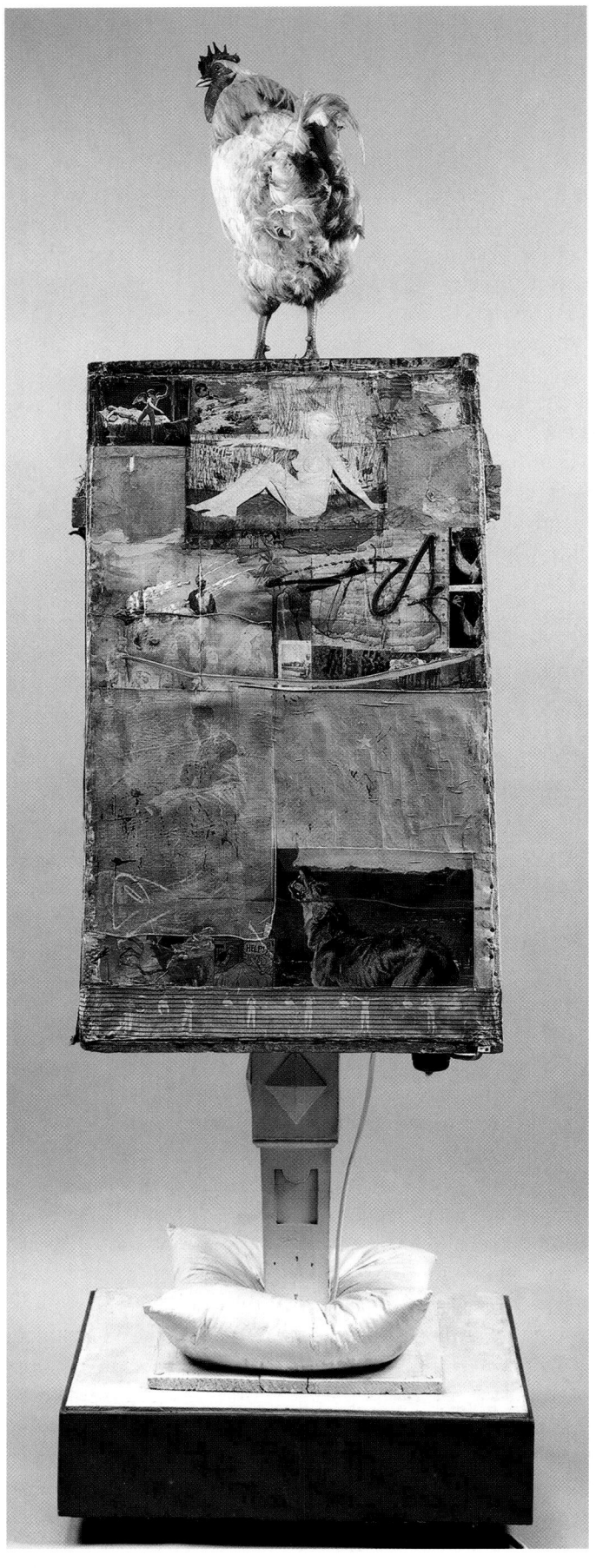

29.9 Robert Rauschenberg, *Odalisk*. 1955–58. Mixed media, 6'9" × 2'1" × 2'1" (205.7 × 63.5 × 63.5 cm). Museum Ludwig, Cologne

Black Mountain College in North Carolina in the fall of 1948, and again in 1951 and 1952. The painting department at the small liberal arts school was headed by Josef Albers (1888–1976), who, with his wife, Anni (1899–1994), had taught at the Bauhaus, in Germany (see pages 1007–10). Rauschenberg did not care for Albers as a teacher, but the institution encouraged experimentation, which turned Rauschenberg away from pure painting, toward an analysis of the very concept of art. At Black Mountain in 1951, he made a series of *White Paintings*, which he exhibited at the Stable Gallery in New York in 1953. These were large canvases painted a solid white, with no evidence of brushwork. Viewers wondered what they were supposed to see. Themselves, for one thing. Their shadows were cast on the canvases, which also caught reflected colored light and accumulated dust and dirt. These canvases captured real life, which was presented without comment or meaning. Viewers could read anything into them that they wanted. Like Duchamp, Rauschenberg was making Conceptual Art, determined by chance, and aimed at capturing the world without attaching any firm meaning in that process. In their objective neutrality, these extraordinary paintings were the antithesis of the intensely personal Abstract Expressionism, which ruled the day.

One of the people who thoroughly understood the *White Paintings* was John Cage (1912–1992), an avant-garde composer who was garnering a reputation for his works for altered piano, a piano with objects placed under the strings to change their sound. In response to the *White Paintings*, Cage wrote *4'33"*, a piano piece first performed in Woodstock, New York, in 1952. The work was "played" by a pianist who sat down and opened the keyboard and did nothing else for 4 minutes and 33 seconds. During this time the audience listened to the sounds of the real world: the shuffling, coughing, and whispering in the recital hall and the sounds of falling rain and chirping birds coming in through an open window. The last sound was the keyboard case being shut, signaling the end of the piece.

These and many other conceptual works from this period were designed to remove the artist from the work of art as well as to ask such questions as: What is art? How does it function? Rauschenberg picked up where Duchamp had left off. His art, however, is never meant to shock or destroy, and his attitude and approach are always positive. He is a presenter, not a nihilist. He is a collector of life, which he gathers up and energetically presents for us to think about and interpret for ourselves. Furthermore, he was not interested in painting life, but in *representing* it. "I don't want a picture to look like something it isn't. I want it to look like something it is. And I think a picture is more like the real world when it's made out of the real world."

In 1955, Rauschenberg incorporated the real world into his art when he began making **combines**, innovative works that combined painting, sculpture, collage, and found objects, as in his *Odalisk* (fig. **29.9**) of 1955–58. This four-sided "lamp"—there is an electric light inside—is crowded with collaged material culled from contemporary magazines and newspapers as well as detritus from the street and from thrift shops. Even the title is part of this busy collage, for it has to be considered when we try to construct a narrative for the work. But is there a narrative in this poetic collage of disparate materials? Obviously, *Odalisk* has a subject, for it is filled with sexual innuendo: the phallic pole jammed into the pillow on the bottom, the stuffed cock mounted above the nude pinup with a dog howling at her from below, the comic strip of a woman in bed being surprised by a man (on a side of the sculpture not pictured here). Even the title, which is a pun on the female *odalisque* (see fig. 24.13) and phallic *obelisk* (a tall, tapering stone monument), can be interpreted sexually. But the artist places no value on materials, suggests no interpretation, makes no grand statement. The work just is. It is our materials, our time, our life. Rauschenberg re-presents it with extraordinary formal powers and with a poetry of paint and collage. In its energy and fragmentation, the work powerfully captures the spirit of the constantly changing world and the fractured way we experience it.

JASPER JOHNS In 1954, Rauschenberg met Jasper Johns (b. 1930) and moved into a loft in the same run-down building in lower Manhattan. Although Johns incorporated objects into his paintings before Rauschenberg made his combines, he is primarily a painter, and his works are literally about painting. This can be seen in *Three Flags*, a work of 1958 (fig. **29.10**). Because of the Americana theme, many writers talk about this painting as Pop Art, a style that in New York emerges in the early 1960s and derives its imagery from popular culture. American pride surged in the postwar period as the United States emerged as the most powerful and wealthiest nation in the world. More than ever before, images of the flag were everywhere and an integral part of vernacular culture. *Three Flags*, however, is not about popular culture, for it is part of series in which the artist repeatedly painted flat objects, such as numbers, targets, and maps, with the intention of eliminating the need to paint illusionistic depth. Here, he has painted a flat object (a flag) on a flat surface (the canvas), so we are not tempted to read, for example, a white star as sitting on top of a blue field because we know it does not. Furthermore, Johns does not place the flag in any context that allows us to read specific meaning or emotion into it. The flag is a sign to which Johns has attached no specific meaning or emotion. In other words, Johns has created a nonillusionistic, impersonal image. What we are left to look at is *how* the picture was made. Johns's very beautiful and methodical application of wax-based encaustic paint reminds us that a painting consists of paint on canvas. And, of course, painting can be about color, here red, white, and blue. Lest we forget that a painting is a three-dimensional object, Johns has stacked three flag paintings one atop another. We see their sides and hence their depth. Lastly, Johns reminds us that painting can produce an image. However, he does not give us an illusionistic image; we would never mistake Johns's flag for a real flag. As such, Johns tells us an image is a sign, that painting is an abstract language, just like verbal language. Just as a word is a sign, standing for something else, so too is painting; it signifies something else, just as numbers and maps are signs for something else.

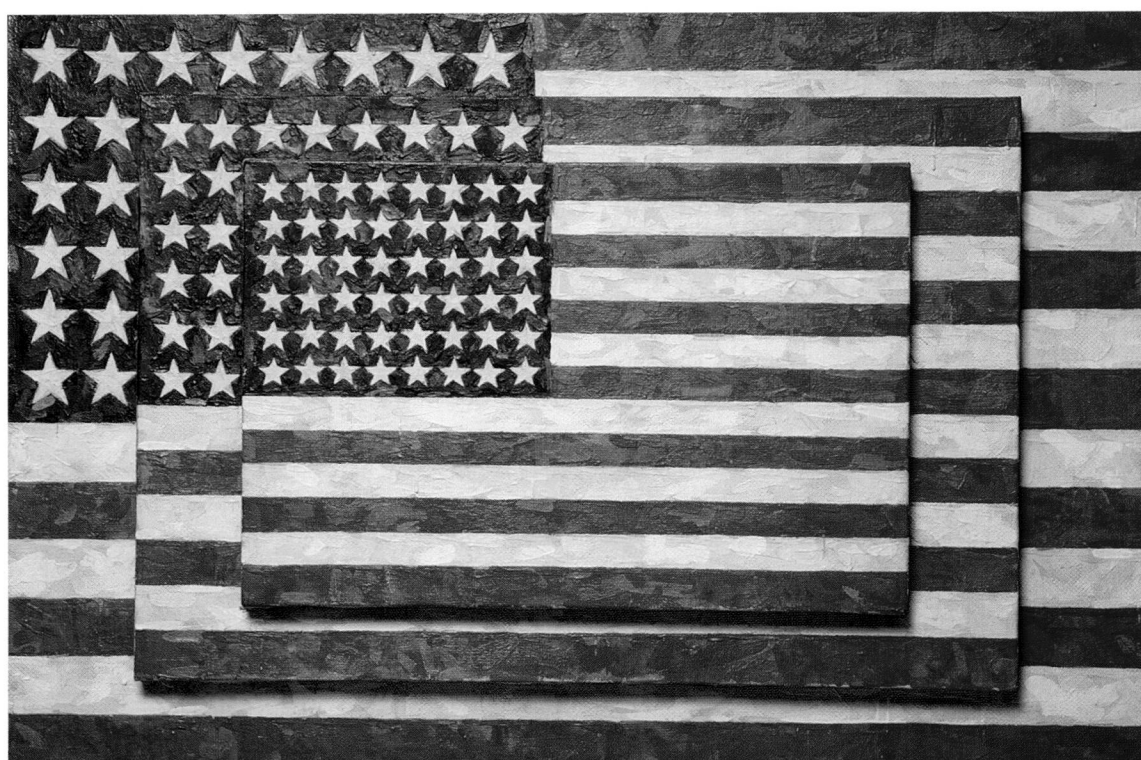

While the intellectual gymnastics in Johns's paintings are complex and rigorous, the works themselves are objective, devoid of any emotion. Like Rauschenberg, Johns paved a way for artists to break away from the subjectivity and vocabulary of Abstract Expressionism. His powerful assertion of the properties of painting and its inherent flatness would inspire numerous artists in the following decades.

Environments and Performance Art

Rauschenberg's combines played a major role in setting off a chain reaction that caused an explosion of art making that entirely redefined art. Art was no longer just painting, sculpture, and work on paper; now, it took on the form of limitless mediums and moved out of galleries and museums into the real world, sometimes interacting with daily life, other times taking place in such faraway locations that few people ever got to see it. Art was often no longer an object; rather it could be temporary and ephemeral, something that could not be bought and sold.

ALLAN KAPROW In 1956, months after Pollock's death in a car crash, Allan Kaprow (1927–2006), a painter teaching at Rutgers University in New Brunswick, New Jersey, published an article in *Art News* entitled "The Legacy of Jackson Pollock." He described how Pollock's action paintings, often because of their scale and the fact that some contained real objects, had started to become environmental. The next step, he claimed, was to make environmental art: "Pollock, as I see him, left us at the point where we must become preoccupied with and even dazzled by the space and objects of our everyday life, either our bodies, clothes, rooms, or,

if need be, the vastness of Forty-second Street." Kaprow knew Rauschenberg's work (he was awed by the *White Paintings*), and this pronouncement about incorporating everyday life into art sounds like a description of the Texan's combines.

In 1958, Kaprow began to make what he called environments, constructed installations that a viewer can enter. His most famous environment, *Yard* (fig. **29.11**), came in 1961. Filled mostly with used tires, the work had the allover look and energy of a Pollock painting, but visitors to the town-house garden where it was installed were expected to walk through it, experiencing it physically, including its smell. Like Rauschenberg in his combines, Kaprow attached no firm meaning to his works, although the discarded synthetic materials suggest a modern industrial urban environment, as well as a sense of waste, even death.

To learn how to add sound to his environments, Kaprow sat in on John Cage's music composition course at the New School for Social Research, a class filled with artists—not musicians— almost all of whom went on to become famous. Music was made by chance and generally without traditional instruments. A typical exercise would be to compose a piece with radios and use a method governed by chance, such as the I-Ching, an ancient Chinese system of divination based on random number-generation procedures, to determine when and by whom each radio would be turned on and off and the length of the piece.

The class inspired Kaprow to add the live human figure to his environments, which, unlike *Yard*, initially were made of a variety of collaged nonart materials that ran from floor to ceiling, vaguely resembling a Rauschenberg combine. He unveiled the result to the New York art world in 1959 at the Reuben Gallery as *18 Happenings in 6 Parts.* Using polyfilm walls, Kaprow divided his

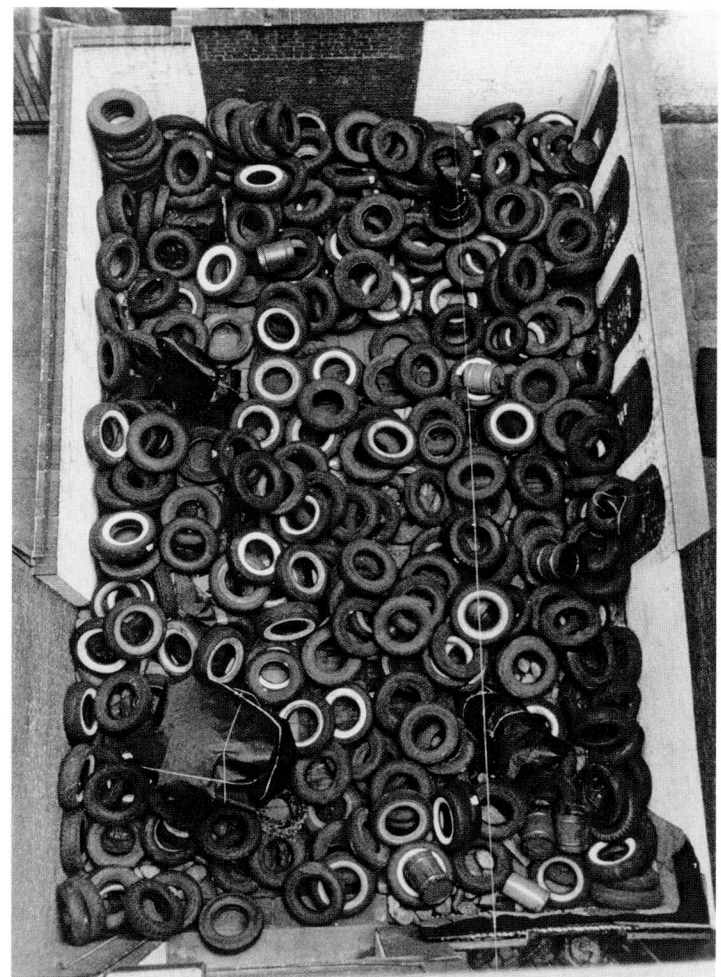

29.11 Allan Kaprow, *Yard*. 1961. Environment of used tires, tar paper, and barrels, as installed at the Martha Jackson Gallery, New York, life-size. Destroyed. Research Library, The Getty Research Institute, Los Angeles, California (980063)

collaged environment into three rooms, in which seated spectators watched, listened, and smelled as performers carried out such tasks as painting (Rauschenberg and Johns participated), playing records, squeezing orange juice, and speaking fragments of sentences, all determined by chance. In a sense, the work was like a Rauschenberg combine that took place in time and space and with human activity. Because of the title of Kaprow's innovative work, a Happening became the term for this new visual art form, in which many of the major artists of the day, including Rauschenberg, started working. While many artists accepted this term, others used different labels, all of which can be grouped under the umbrella term Performance Art, which is distinguished from theater in that it takes place in an art context.

ROBERT WHITMAN *18 Happenings* unleashed a flurry of Happenings, or Performance Art, which lasted through the mid-1960s. Soon-to-be-famous artists like Claes Oldenburg, Jim Dine, Robert Morris, and Red Grooms along with Rauschenberg created works. The artist who has dedicated his life to the

genre, which he prefers to call Theater Pieces, is Robert Whitman (b. 1935), a student of Kaprow's at Rutgers and also another vagabond in Cage's famous New School composition class. In 1960, he presented *American Moon* at the Reuben Gallery. The set was made up largely of paper, cardboard and polyfilm, yet these banal materials were leant a poetic beauty by the strange, non-narrative actions of the performers, which occurred at a lyrical pace. All of these elements—common materials, poetic imagery, and lyrical pacing—would characterize his work, defying interpretation while evoking a broad range of responses. (To view the performance and a documentary film on this and other Theater Pieces, see www.myartslab.com.) If Kaprow's performance pieces were prosaic, mundane, and very down-to-earth, Whitman's were abstract and dreamlike, garnering him a reputation with art historians as the master of the medium and one of its most innovative practitioners. Whitman thought of his Theater Pieces as one continuous image that unfolds in space and time. Abandoning words, he took the most mundane objects, such as a candle, piece of fruit, or lightbulb, and over time, using light, color, movement, and pacing, transformed it into something magical and mysterious. An especially radical feature of *American Moon* was film projection, which he used in many of his performances, as seen in *Prune Flat* (fig. **29.12**) of 1965, where film, shadow, and the real-life performers are hauntingly juxtaposed, creating multiple layers of imagery and an oneiric sense of mystery. Whitman's use of film, which he also used in 1964 installations he called Cinema Pieces, were made before the advent of video, and anticipated the Video Art and installations of later decades.

GEORGE BRECHT Also in John Cage's class with Kaprow in 1958 was another unregistered student, George Brecht (1926–2009), who for a class assignment wrote a composition for automobiles entitled *Motor Vehicle Sunset Event*. For this work, participants drew cards with instructions and at sundown in a city parking lot they revved engines, honked horns, rolled down windows, slammed doors shut, and opened and closed hoods and trunks. Brecht began typing up this and other **Events**, as he called

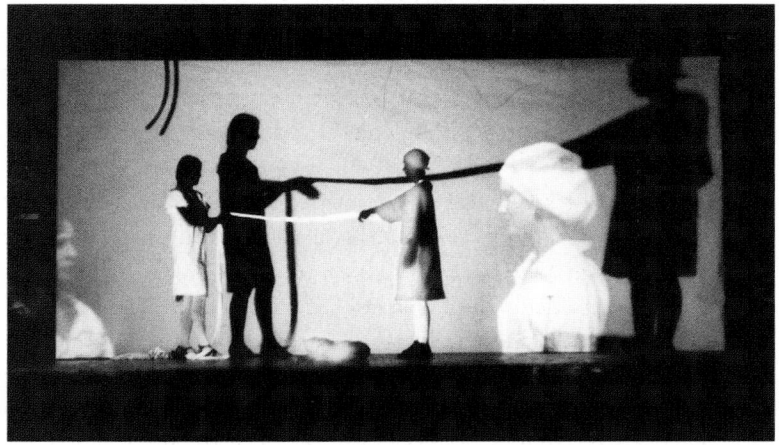

29.12 Robert Whitman, *Prune Flat*. 1965. As performed in 1976. Courtesy of Dia Art Foundation

these compositions, on white cards and mailing them to acquaintances, an act that initiated an art form that came to be called Mail Art. (Brecht's good friend, Rutgers University art teacher Robert Watts, began designing art stamps to mail their Event cards, thus inventing Stamp Art.)

By 1960, Brecht's Events had become quite minimal. *Three Aqueous Events*, printed on a roughly 2-by-3-inch card, consisted of the title and under it three bulleted words: "water," "ice," and "steam" People receiving the card in the mail could respond in any way they wanted—they could even frame the card. Allan Kaprow, for example, thought of making iced tea. What is the work of art in *Three Aqueous Events*? The idea? The card itself? The execution of the piece? And who is actually the artist in this work that allows the recipient to be the creator? Brecht was posing the classic Duchampian questions while simultaneously integrating art into daily life and taking it off the aesthetic and intellectual pedestal reserved for high art. By 1962, Brecht's example had helped spawn a New York-based international art movement called Fluxus, similarly dedicated to making a conceptual art that violated the conventional distinctions between art and life, artist and nonartist, museum and street, and which included Performance Art as a major component. One of the group's most famous works is Brecht's *Drip Music* (1959), which was executed by having the performer mount a stepladder and pour water at varying rates and intervals into a bowl on the floor.

GEORGE SEGAL Living down the road from Kaprow in rural New Jersey was George Segal (1924–2000), who responded to his friend's environments and Happenings by creating representational,

not abstract, environments out of real objects and populated by plaster figures, as in *The Gas Station* (fig. **29.13**) of 1963. Now, the performers are frozen, reduced to ghost-white mannequins. To create them, Segal used real people, making castings of them by using plaster medical bandages. Like Rauschenberg and Kaprow, he was breaking down the barrier between art and life. But his art is far from neutral; it is emotional and makes a statement. Segal's work highlights the alienation he perceived in contemporary life. This alienation can be seen in his figures, which are left white, as though drained of life. Generally they are lethargic, exhausted, and alone, and seem trapped by a harsh geometry of the horizontals and verticals of their setting.

The works even contain symbols used in more traditional art. *Gas Station*, for example, is dominated by a Bulova clock, a *memento mori* ("reminder of death") motif, which floats in a 10-foot expanse of darkness. Its shape mysteriously resonates with the tire on the floor. The vending machine, tires, cans of high-performance oil, and the gas station itself suggest modernity, technology, and fast, efficient living. Missing from this materiality, however, is something meaningful—human interaction and spirituality. Segal retains the existential angst of his Abstract Expressionist background by questioning the meaning of modern existence. Although he often used contemporary branded objects, such as Coke bottles, to give his environments the look of reality and modernity, Segal never celebrated the products of consumer culture, nor questioned how mass-media imagery, including advertising, manipulates its audience. His sculpture is closer in spirit and style to the paintings of Edward Hopper (see fig. 28.53) than to Pop Art, with which he has been mistakenly associated.

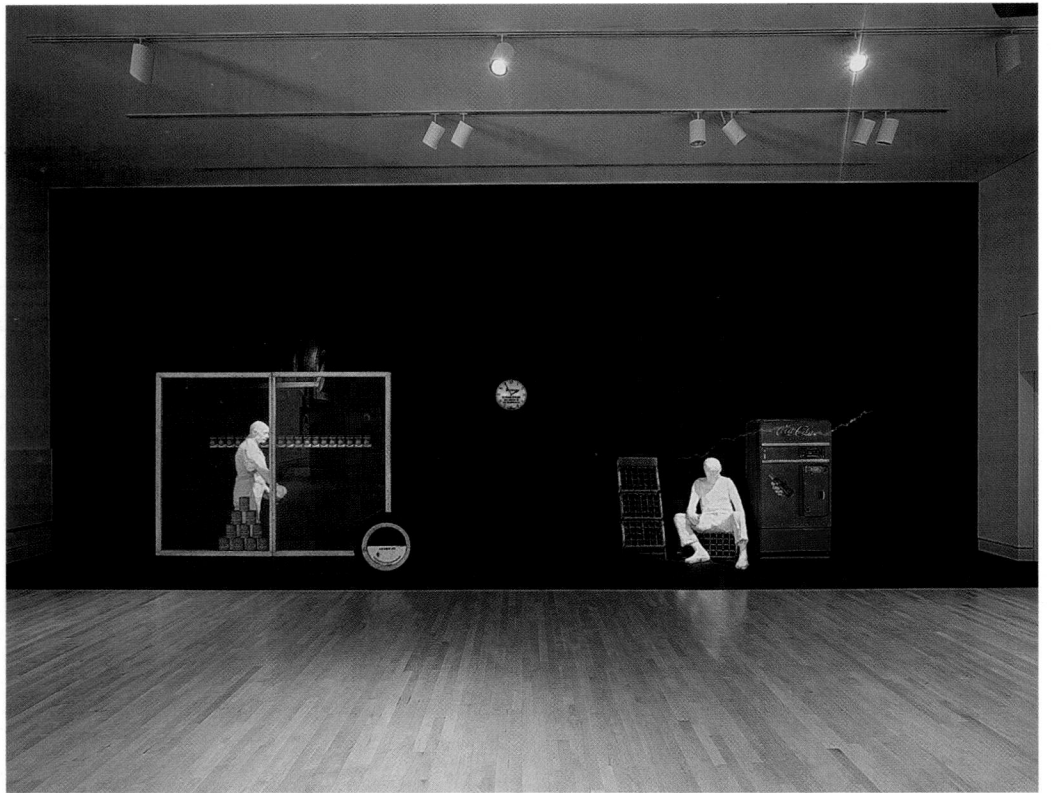

29.13 George Segal, *The Gas Station*. 1963. Plaster figures, Coca-Cola machine, Coca-Cola bottles, wooden Coca-Cola crates, metal stand, rubber tires, tire rack, oil cans, electric clock, concrete blocks, windows of wood and plate glass, 8'6" × 24' × 4' (2.59 × 7.32 × 1.22 m). National Gallery of Canada, Ottawa

Pop Art: Consumer Culture as Subject

Pop Art is a style that emerged in New York in the early 1960s, although it had appeared in a very different guise and with less fanfare in Britain a decade earlier—this incarnation had no impact on the development of American Pop. The style got its name because it derives its imagery from popular or vernacular culture. Like Rauschenberg and Kaprow, Pop artists re-presented the artifacts of the world they lived in, namely the imagery of the mass media, although they did it using conventional painting rather than new mediums. Unlike Johns and Segal, both of whom occasionally used popular imagery, Pop artists focused on the products of popular culture by taking what art historians often describe as a *low* art form, that is commercial art, and incorporating it into one that is considered *high*, meaning fine art. By doing so, however, they subversively revealed the manipulative impact of the mass media. Among the best-known Pop artists are the Americans Roy Lichtenstein, and Andy Warhol, as well as the British collagist and painter Richard Hamilton. Although not labeled a Pop artist, the German Sigmar Polke similarly appropriated imagery from mass culture as he not only critiqued that culture but also explored the meaning and language of art.

ROY LICHTENSTEIN Another close friend of Kaprow's was Roy Lichtenstein (1923–1997), who was hired in 1960 to teach painting at Rutgers University. When he arrived he was an Abstract Expressionist painter. Within a year, however, he was making what would be considered Pop paintings, in part influenced by Kaprow's dictum to make art that did not look like art. (See *Primary Source*, page 1050.)

The contemporary life that Lichtenstein scavenged and re-presented was not the urban streets, as was the case with Kaprow, Rauschenberg, and Segal, but the crude black-and-white advertisements in telephone books and newspapers and the prosaic drawings in comic books. These he cropped and adjusted into visually riveting images, such as *Drowning Girl* (fig. **29.14**). Traditionally, Lichtenstein is appreciated for seeing the beauty of "low art" and elevating it to "high art," in effect celebrating popular culture, and in particular American culture. When first shown, however, his paintings were so radical they were thought hideous and were not even considered art by many. After all, they looked like images from comic books. Furthermore, art, and particularly Modernist art, was supposed to move art forward, investigating new aspects of abstraction. High art was not supposed to look like low art, and it was not supposed to be representational.

Lichtenstein's work does more than just blur the distinctions between fine art and mass culture. Like Johns, whose *Flag* paintings had a profound impact on him, Lichtenstein was interested in the language of art, particularly in regard to issues of perception. He does not just imitate the comic strip, he also plays with that genre's technique of making an image out of benday dots, the small dots that when massed together create color and shading in

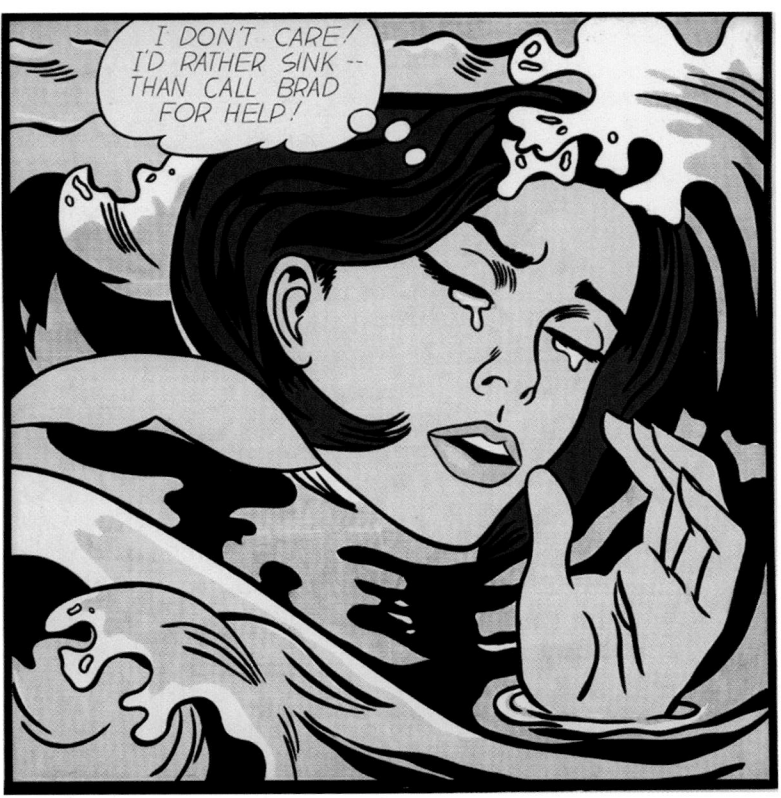

29.14 Roy Lichtenstein, *Drowning Girl*. 1963. Oil on canvas, 5'7⅝" × 5'6¾" (1.72 × 1.69 m). Museum of Modern Art, New York. Philip Johnson Fund and Gift of Mr. and Mrs. Bagley Wright

printed material. He was intrigued by how an illusion of three-dimensional volume could be made using flat dots and flat black lines. When viewed from close up, Lichtenstein's large images dissolve into flat abstract patterns, virtually becoming Abstract Expressionist compositions.

Lichtenstein did not randomly select his sources or select them just for aesthetic purposes, for the images that he used for his paintings from 1961 to 1964 tend to fall into a distinct pattern: Men are portrayed as strong, virile soldiers and fighter pilots, whereas women are shown as emotionally distraught, dependent on men, and happily slaving around the house doing domestic chores. With deadpan brilliance, Lichtenstein made his paintings a mirror of contemporary society, revealing the stereotyping deeply embedded in the media. But the paintings themselves appear objective and unemotional, giving little suggestion of a polemical agenda or a sense of the artist's presence, whether his hand (brushwork) or emotions.

ANDY WARHOL Andy Warhol (1928–1987) was making art based on comic books at exactly the same time as Lichtenstein. When the dealer Leo Castelli decided to represent Lichtenstein and not him, Warhol turned to other kinds of popular imagery, namely product design and newspaper photographs. Warhol was from Pittsburgh, and in the 1950s in New York he established himself as a successful illustrator of women's shoes, learning first

Roy Lichtenstein (1923–1997)

From an interview with Joan Marter

In this 1996 interview with the art historian Joan Marter, Roy Lichtenstein talks about the enormous impact Allan Kaprow's environments and New York happenings had on the development of his Pop Art.

JOAN MARTER: In one of your interviews, you say that "although I feel that what I am doing almost has nothing to do with Environments, there is a kernel of thought in Happenings that is interesting to me." Can you comment?

ROY LICHTENSTEIN: Well, there's more than a kernel of thought in Happenings that is interesting to me. ... Many of them tended to have American objects rather than School of Paris objects. I'm thinking of the tires, and the kind of advertising sort of things in [Claes] Oldenburg's and [Jim] Dine's Happenings. They were like an American street, maybe from Pollock in a certain way. The Environments are like expanded Pollocks; they are allover in the same kind of sense. If I look at Pollock now, I think they're really beautiful; I don't get all of the gutsy stuff—the cigarette butts and house paint, and everything they're made out of. They had a big

influence on Happenings. Because the Environment would envelop you the way that we thought that Pollock's paintings enveloped you—they were big and seemed to have no end. They were allover, all of that. Some of that, I think, went into Environments, which were kind of a background for Happenings. ... But the thing that probably had the most influence on me was the American rather than the French objects.

JM: Do you remember anything specifically [about Allan Kaprow's work] that interested you?

RL: The tires he did [*Yard* at the Martha Jackson Gallery, 1961; see fig. 29.11]. Also other things with strips of paper and things written on them [*Words*, at the Smolin Gallery, 1962]. I think the thing I most got from him was this kind of statement about it doesn't have to look like art, or how much of what you do is there only because it looks like art. You always thought artists should be original, whatever it was. I was doing Abstract Expressionism very late, 1961, and much of that was because it looked like art to me. ... I was amazed at how much he [Kaprow] actually liked [my *Look Mickey* and the other first Pop paintings]. Most people hated it at first.

Source: *Off Limits: Rutgers University and the Avant-Garde, 1957–1963*, ed. Joan Marter (NJ: Rutgers University Press, 1999)

---

hand the deceiving and manipulative role of advertising and product packaging. He was also fascinated by the impact of the mass media on public opinion. Among his most famous works and among the first he made after abandoning cartoon imagery is the first that he mass-produced, *Campbell's Soup Cans* (fig. **29.15**). He painted 32 Campbell's soup can images for his first exhibition, in 1962, at the Ferus Gallery in Los Angeles, which at the time had a burgeoning contemporary art scene. The Campbell company then offered 32 varieties of canned soup, hence 32 paintings, which Warhol hand-painted. Warhol installed the works as

29.15 Andy Warhol, *Campbell's Soup Cans*. 1961–64. Acrylic on canvas, 32 works, each 20 × 16" (50.8 × 40.6 cm). Museum of Modern Art, New York. Gift of Irving Blum; Nelson A. Rockefeller Bequest, gift of Mr. and Mrs. William A. M. Buirden, Abby Aldrich Rockefeller Foundation

monotonously as possible, evenly spacing them and placing them on a shelf, as soup cans would be presented in a supermarket. (In our illustration, the works, some later and **silkscreened**, are arranged in a grid.) Just as the soup came off a mass-production assembly line, Warhol, soon after his Ferus Gallery exhibition, began mass-producing his paintings in his studio, which he called "the Factory." Assistants made the works to his specifications, using a silkscreen process to print a photographic image of a soup can onto canvas, or onto paper, as he did to make prints. (For a more extensive discussion of this process as well as of his portrait of Marilyn Monroe, see the Introduction, pages xxi and xxvi.) Although a workaholic and highly involved with the production of his art, Warhol gave the public the illusion that he barely touched his own paintings and prints, just signing them on the back. With this Duchampian gesture, Warhol tells us that paintings are commodities, that people are buying a name product—that is, a Warhol—and that art is about ideas, not necessarily about technique or craftsmanship.

But Warhol is also commenting on the camouflaging function of product design, how it tells us nothing about the mass-produced product it promotes and how the packaging lures us into buying it. Warhol's art underscores how Campbell's soup is everywhere, having penetrated the farthest reaches of the country, and that mass production, uniformity, and consumerism dominate American society. In effect, his *Soup Cans* are a portrait of America. Like Lichtenstein, Warhol neither praises nor condemns.

BRITISH POP While Pop Art emerged in America in the early 1960s, it had already appeared in London in the mid-1950s. Protesting the conservatism of the Institute of Contemporary Arts, which largely promoted prewar painters and sculptors, a handful of artists formed the Independent Group, dedicated to bringing contemporary life into contemporary art. The war had left Britain commercially weak and with few creature comforts. Thus, the British were more than ready to appreciate the celebrity promotion and advertisements for appliances, cars, and homes that they found in the American magazines that flooded London. Well before their American counterparts, the British were fascinated by the technology and consumerism they saw taking over American society. The Independent Group, led by artists Richard Hamilton (b. 1922) and Eduardo Paolozzi (1924–2005) and critic Lawrence Alloway (1926–1990), embraced American mass culture and celebrated it in their art.

Using the photomontage technique developed by the Berlin Dadaists (see page 988), Richard Hamilton cut images from comic books and body-building and pinup magazines, as seen in his *Just What Is It That Makes Today's Homes So Different, So Appealing?* (fig. **29.16**) of 1956. Sprinkled around the room depicted in this small collage are the latest hi-tech commodities: a tape recorder, television, and Space Age vacuum cleaner. A Ford logo decorates a lampshade, while a can of ham sits on a coffee table as though it were a sculpture. The weightlifter carries a lollipop inscribed with the word "pop," a term coined by Alloway, announcing that this is Pop Art. Sex permeates the image as Hamilton exposes, and perhaps even celebrates, the powerful role sexual innuendo plays in advertising.

THE IMPACT OF POP ART IN GERMANY During the 1960s and 1970s, the art world was focused so heavily on New York that other art centers, especially those in Europe, were all but ignored. Artists in Düsseldorf were producing some of the most important work of the period, yet only Joseph Beuys, whom we shall meet later in this chapter, was well known internationally. It was not until the mid-1980s that the New York art world discovered Sigmar Polke (b. 1941) and Gerhard Richter (b. 1932), two East German transplants, who toward 1963 cultivated a kind of German Pop Art.

Polke and Richter were heavily influenced by the combines of Robert Rauschenberg and by Pop Art, especially the works of Roy Lichtenstein and Andy Warhol, which they knew from magazines. They were also well versed in the Dada antiart movement, since the first postwar Dada exhibition took place in Düsseldorf in 1958, and they were mesmerized by Fluxus, the group that like Dada rejected high art and was dedicated to transforming life into art. Fluxus literally came to Düsseldorf in 1963 when the group presented a festival of performances, Festum Fluxorum. Combined with these artistic forces was the impact of the "economic miracle" of the Marshall Plan (European Recovery Program) in Germany,

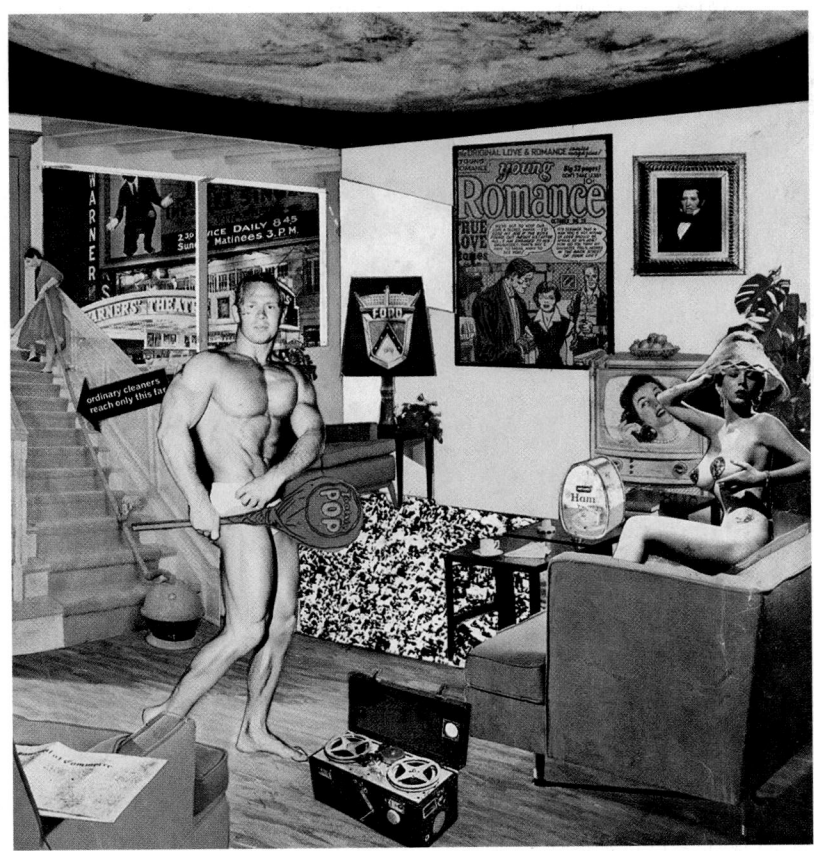

29.16 Richard Hamilton, *Just What Is It That Makes Today's Homes So Different, So Appealing?* 1956. Collage on paper, 10¼ × 9¾" (26 × 24.8 cm). Kunsthalle Tübingen. Sammlung Zundel, Germany

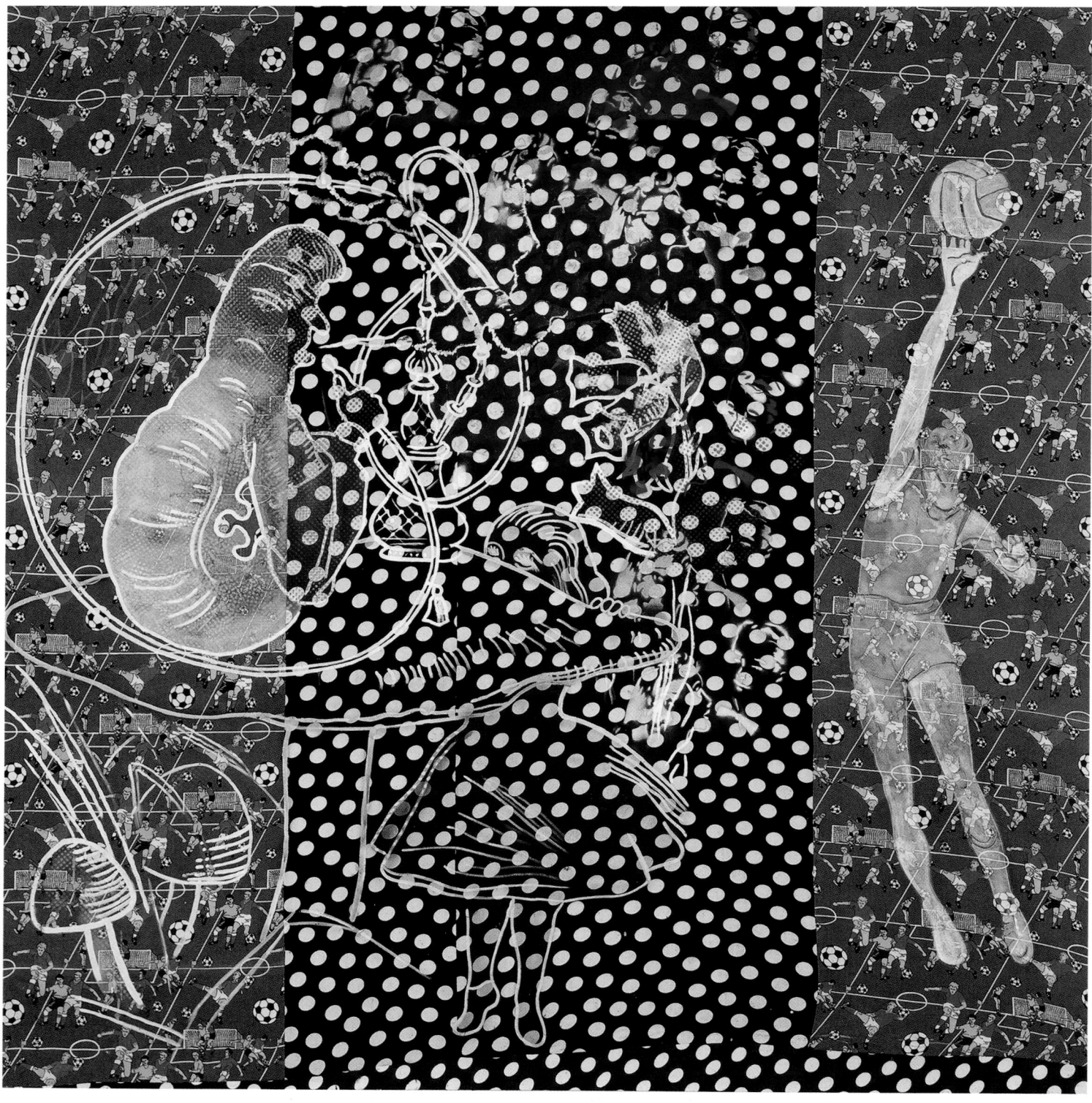

29.17 Sigmar Polke, *Alice in Wonderland.* 1971. Mixed media on fabric strips, 10'6" × 8'6¾" (3.2 × 1.6 m). Private collection, Cologne

which by 1963 brought about a stable economy and a degree of consumerism. As a result, Polke and Richter, to varying degrees, were preoccupied with mass-media imagery, commodity culture, and analyzing art, revealing how it functions and takes on meaning. For a brief period they called their art "Capitalist Realism," a pun on Socialist Realism, the official representational propaganda art of East Germany and the rest of the Soviet Union. Richter, in his paintings, largely focused on appropriating photographs, both mass-media and family, using a blurry presentation to undermine the reality of the image and turn it into a fictitious haze, thus revealing the artifice of painting and suggesting the ambiguity of the meaning of the original photograph.

Polke's work was more varied at this time; throughout his career, the look of his work and the issues he has dealt with have changed constantly. In the 1960s, he made countless drawings, often based on images in magazines and advertising, showing common products. He used a range of styles, such as a slick dead-ened illustrational look and a crude cartoony style. He also often used nonart materials, such as blue ballpoint pen on notebook paper. These works were a rejection of the refinement of the high-art tradition, and at the same time they were quite cynical, not only toward artistic values but also the mass media and how it transformed commercial products into appealing objects: The objects in Polke's drawings weren't appealing. Polke also made drawings and paintings using Raster dots, the small dots used in commercial printing. He blew up the original magazine photo-graph so large the image became a fascinating grid of dots. In a 1966 painting entitled *Bunnies* a re-presentation of a magazine photograph of bunnygirls at a Playboy club (here the commodity is sex), the original image became a pixilated blur, the bunnies reduced to vibrating dots of different shades of black and gray and just barely visible. In *Bunnies*, Polke exposes the artificiality of image making, revealing how the original magazine photo was not reality but just an image consisting of dots.

Before the decade was out, Polke was creating art on a wide range of surfaces and with a wide range of materials, as suggested by *Alice in Wonderland* (fig. **29.17**) of 1971, which is paint printed on store-bought printed fabric, not canvas. One fabric is covered with soccer players and the other with polka dots, the latter a visual pun on the artist's name but also a reference to his use of Raster dots, and thus the media. Like Warhol, Polke printed appropriated images on his fabric—a ghost-white image of a basketball player, pirated from a magazine, and the caterpillar with a hookah and Alice biting into a mushroom, taken from the illustrations by Sir John Tenniel for Lewis Carol's 1865 *Alice in Wonderland*. Difficult to see in reproductions are the appropri-ated 1950s-style outlines of the heads of a man and woman, hand-stamped several times in red and yellow. Polke bombards us with a variety of pilfered images, images executed in a range of styles and from many different periods. In effect, he is telling us that we both see and know the world through images, and that this picto-rial world becomes the real world, our reality. Supposedly, the painting was inspired by watching sports on television while under the influence of drugs, the theme of hallucination being suggested by the caterpillar's hookah and Alice's mushroom. If this is the case, we can add portraying the experience of sensory perception to the long list of issues we find in this painting. Another issue is how context structures meaning. Polke demon-strates this by layering his motifs, for the narrative of his scav-enged images would change if they were juxtaposed differently. Ultimately, it is virtually impossible to attach a fixed meaning to *Alice in Wonderland*, allowing us to assume that Polke sees art, and images in general, as not having fixed meanings—only interpreta-tions depending on context and who is doing the interpreting.

Ultimately, Polke and Richter did not consider their art Pop Art, and despite Polke re-presenting media images, as did Warhol

and Lichtenstein, there is no mistaking his art for theirs. In his work, there is no sense of fun or light humor and no sense of celebrating low art, even if the Americans were actually being subversively ironic in their celebration. To the contrary, his paint-ings and drawings often have a sense of parody, or as seen in *Alice in Wonderland*, and a sense of loss or sadness, as evoked by the ghostlike figures, the chaos of the imagery, and the emptiness of the "television snow" of polka dots. Instead of seeming objective and unemotional, his art appears subjective and emotional. As we shall see in the next chapter, Polka's art, heavily influenced by Pop, anticipated many of the fundamental issues of Postmodernism, and his layering of imagery and interest in how images and art function and take on meaning would prove quite influential.

FORMALIST ABSTRACTION OF THE 1950s AND 1960s

The most influential art critic in the United States in the 1940s and well into the 1960s was Clement Greenberg, who wrote art reviews for *The Nation* and *The Partisan Review*. He began by championing Pollock's formalism, but as the 1940s progressed he increasingly promoted an art that was totally abstract and nonref-erential and dealt with just those qualities inherent to the medium, that is color, texture, shape of field, and composition. Such work, which emphasized the formalist or abstract qualities of the medium, could make no reference beyond itself. Greenberg's theories had an enormous impact on the way painters, sculptors, and other critics thought about art. His criticism helped lay a foundation for the Post-Painterly painting and Minimalist Art of the 1950s and 1960s.

Formalist Painting

Formalist painting emerged in the heyday of Abstract Expressionism, the early 1950s, and in large part as a reaction to it. Just as Rauschenberg, Johns, Kaprow, and the Pop artists rejected the subjective components of Pollock and de Kooning, the formalist painters sought to make unemotional art. They replaced bold, gestural brushwork with smooth surfaces that gave no hint of the artist's hand or feelings. Instead of the push-pull of Cubist space of de Kooning's style of Abstract Expressionism, they powerfully asserted the flatness of the canvas, virtually elim-inating any sense of space. Led by Greenberg, they were attracted to the formalist implications of Abstract Expressionism, not its emotional content. They also embraced the style's enormous scale. Among the formalist styles of the period are Post-Painterly Abstraction, Hard-Edge Abstraction, and Minimalism.

HELEN FRANKENTHALER Greenberg championed Helen Frankenthaler (b. 1928) as one of the new formalists. Franken-thaler was inspired by Jackson Pollock, who, toward 1950, in an attempt to expand his art beyond drip paintings, began working on unprimed canvases, using just black enamel paint and allowing

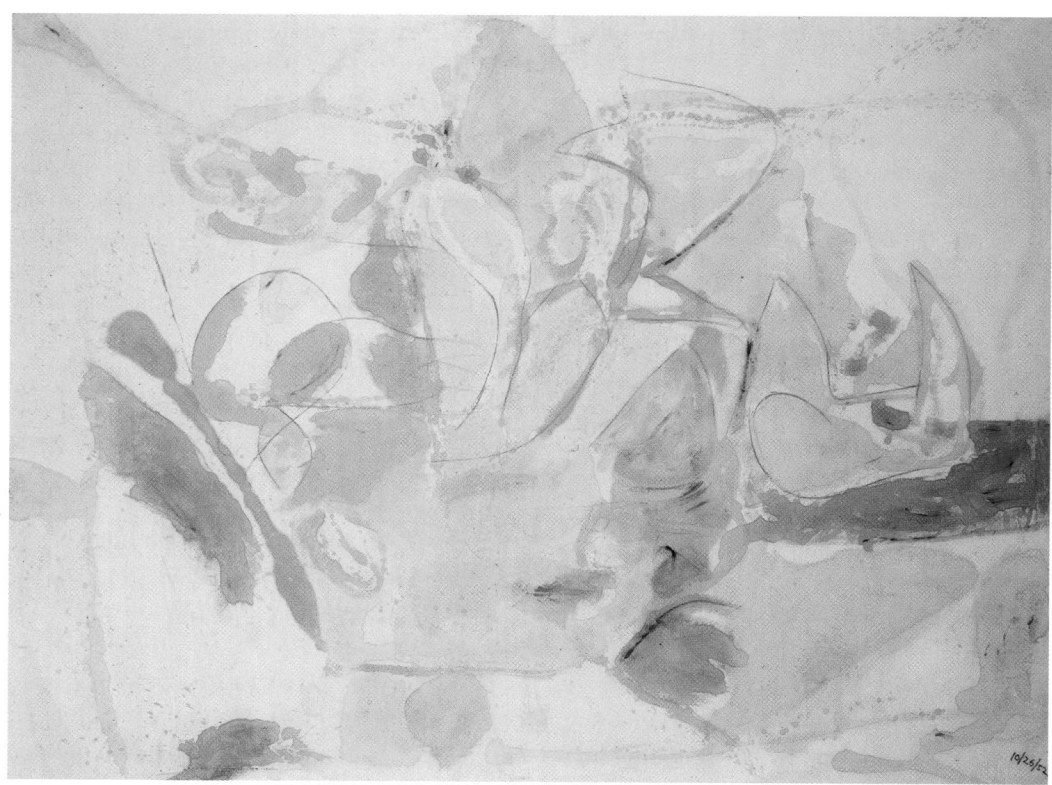

29.18 Helen Frankenthaler, *Mountains and Sea.* 1952. Oil and charcoal on canvas, 7'2¾" × 9'8¼" (2.2 × 2.95 m). Helen Frankenthaler Foundation, Inc. (on extended loan to the National Gallery of Art, Washington, D.C.)

it to seep into the fabric, creating a smooth surface. Frankenthaler built on the implications of this technique. In a breakthrough work of 1952, *Mountains and Sea* (fig. **29.18**), she developed **stain painting**. Frankenthaler had just returned from Nova Scotia, and using charcoal on unprimed canvas, she quickly laid in a composition suggesting landscape. Working like Pollock, she put her canvas on the floor. She then poured thin oil paint on it, tilting it to allow the paint to run, drawing and painting by changing the angled tilt of the canvas rather than using a brush. The thin oil bled into the canvas, becoming one with it and having the translucency of watercolor. Greenberg admired the picture's flatness and the fact that the paint was not tactile, a three-dimensional quality

29.19 Ellsworth Kelly, *Red Blue Green.* 1963. Oil on canvas, 7'8" × 11'4" (2.34 × 3.45 m). Museum of Contemporary Art, San Diego, La Jolla, CA. Gift of Jack and Carolyn Farris

that he felt would result in the illusion of space. He declared you could not sense the artist's hand, and thus her presence, and praised the picture's nonreferential "decorativeness" as opposed to its "expressionistic" qualities. While Pollock first used unprimed canvas, it was Frankenthaler's example of thin translucent oils that spawned in the 1950s and 1960s legions of stain painters, of whom the best known are the Washington Color School painters. Unlike Frankenthaler, however, her followers' work was entirely abstract.

Greenberg's personal infatuation with Frankenthaler apparently blinded him to the Abstract Expressionist side of her work. Like her many followers, she is now often labeled a Post-Painterly Abstractionist, a term that refers to the smooth nongestural nature of this kind of abstraction, but in the 1950s and 1960s she was generally considered a second-generation Abstract Expressionist. As the title implies, *Mountains and Sea* reflects her experience of the Nova Scotia landscape. The energy of the curving, explosive composition seems to embody the sublime force of nature, while the soft translucent colors and white unprimed canvas evoke the brilliant glare of sunlight. Although essentially abstract, the picture is filled with references, which is generally true of her work up to the present day.

ELLSWORTH KELLY In contrast, there are no references whatsoever to be found in the abstraction of Ellsworth Kelly (b. 1923). Kelly developed a distinctly American brand of formalist painting in Paris from 1948 to 1954. During these years, he began to reduce painting to a barebones simplicity, which some critics called Hard-Edge Abstraction. To free his mind from earlier art, he based his abstractions on shapes he saw in the world around him, especially negative spaces, such as the opening under a bridge, a shadow, or a window. His paintings use just a handful of geometric shapes in solid primary and secondary colors to explore how forms move through space, how colors interact, and how "figure" relates to "ground," that is, how image relates to background. Kelly generally locks his figure and ground so tightly into a single unit they seem to coexist on the same spatial plane.

In *Red Blue Green* (fig. **29.19**), a 1963 work, Kelly plays a red rectangle and a blue curved shape off a green ground. The left side of the painting appears fixed, whereas the right has movement. When standing in front of this enormous work, which is more than 11 feet wide, a viewer can feel at one moment the green ground consuming the blue and at the next moment the blue plunging down into the green. In other words, the figure–ground relationship is reversed. But never to be forgotten is the sheer intensity of the color, especially as presented on such a large scale. Kelly's genius is the simplicity of his gesture: He stripped everything else away, including any sense of himself, to make a painting that is about color—in this case red, blue, and green—and movement.

FRANK STELLA Just as Kelly was returning from Europe, a young Frank Stella (b. 1936) began his studies at Princeton University, opting for an art education at a university rather than an art school, which became commonplace after the war. Within a year of graduating, he was in New York and the talk of the town because of his "Black Paintings," included in a 1959 Museum of Modern Art exhibition called *Sixteen Americans*. These were total abstractions consisting of black parallel bands created by allowing white pinstripe lines of canvas to show through. He soon began working in color, as in *Empress of India* (fig. **29.20**) of 1965, and on an enormous scale, here over 18 feet across. Inspired by the inherent flatness of Johns's *Flag* paintings (fig. 29.10), Stella made entirely flat works as well.

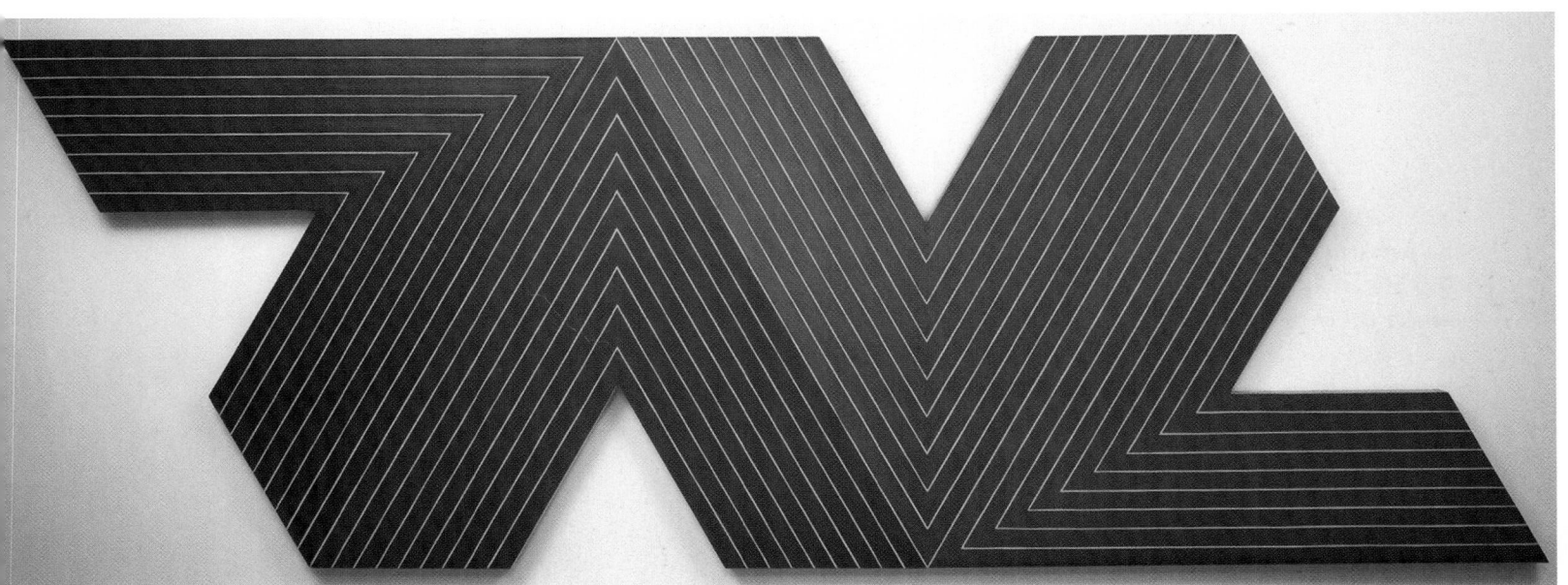

29.20 Frank Stella, *Empress of India*. 1965. Metallic powder in polymer emulsion on canvas, 6'5" × 18'8" (1.96 × 5.69 cm). Museum of Modern Art, New York. Gift of S. I. Newhouse, Jr.

Frank Stella (b. 1936)

Pratt Institute Lecture

In 1959, Stella gave a lecture to students at New York's Pratt Institute in which he discussed his paintings then being shown in the Museum of Modern Art's Sixteen Americans *exhibition. He specifically addressed what he saw as one of the most pressing formalist issues facing painters at the time: how to make a composition that was not about the relationship of its parts.*

There were two problems which had to be faced. One was spatial and the other methodological. In the first case, I had to do something about relational painting, i.e., the balancing of the various parts with and against each other. The obvious answer was symmetry—make it the same all over. The question still remained, though, of how to do this in depth. A symmetrical image or configuration placed on an open ground is not balanced out in the illusionistic space. The solution I arrived at—and there are probably quite a few, although I know of only one other, color density—forces illusionistic space out of the painting at a constant rate by using a regulated pattern. The remaining problem was simply to find a method of paint application which followed and complemented the design solution. This was done by using the house painter's technique and tools.

Source: Pratt Institute Lecture, 1959

There is no figure–ground relationship in *Empress of India*, and no push-pull of Cubist and Abstract Expressionist space. In fact, there is no hierarchy to the composition, which is determined by the V-shape of each of the four canvases that have been butted together. Stella said of his work, "What you see is what you see." In other words, the painting has nothing that you do not see—no hidden meanings, symbols, or references. Despite giving his work suggestive titles such as *Empress of India*, Stella wanted his canvases viewed simply as objects with an independent life of their own, free from associations. (See *Primary Source*, above.)

Fellow artists and critics evaluated this kind of abstract art on its ability to invent new formalist devices (for example, Stella's ability to create perfectly flat, spaceless painting or the innovative shapes of his canvases). However, the power of such work lies in the sheer force of its scale and dramatic sense of movement as the Vs change direction to create new lines of movement. Because Stella used a stripped-down artistic vocabulary and often determined his compositions using a geometric premise, critics often describe his paintings from this period as Minimal Art.

Formalist Sculpture: Minimal Art

A group of sculptors emerged in the early 1960s who generally composed their work using a mathematical or conceptual premise, paralleling in sculpture what Stella was doing in painting. Their reliance upon geometry in this new work emphasized conceptual rather than emotional content, and it favored the means and materials of mass production. Their sculpture came to be known as Minimal art. Artists often avoided making the objects themselves, preferring to send specifications to an artisan, or more likely a factory, for production. Like Pop paintings, Minimal

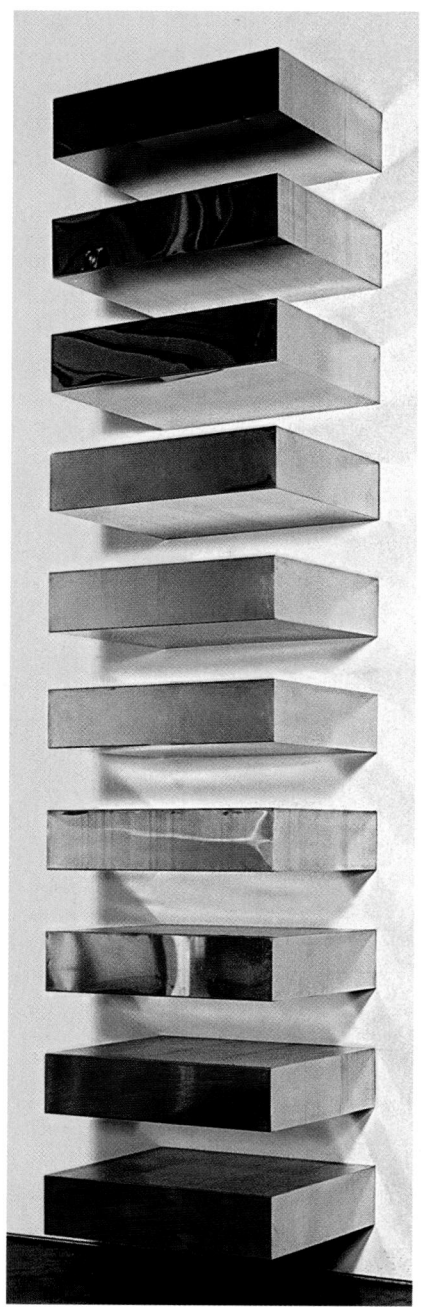

29.21 Donald Judd, *Untitled*. 1969. Copper, ten units, 9 × 40 × 31″ (22.8 × 101.6 × 78.7 cm) each, with 9″ (22.8 cm) intervals; 170 × 40 × 31″ (432 × 101.6 × 106.7 cm) overall. Solomon R. Guggenheim Museum, New York. Panza Collection. 91.37.13

sculpture lacks the evidence of the artist's touch that traditionally served as the sign of personal emotion and expression as well as proof of the artist's technical accomplishment. There is no sign of the artist at all. Furthermore, the artists used unconventional nonart materials to make art—Plexiglas, fluorescent tubes, galvanized steel, magnesium tiles—continuing the exploration of new materials that characterized so much of the art making of the late 1950s and 1960s. Similarly, one of their concerns was to make art that did not look like art. Like Stella, they wanted their artworks to be perceived as independent objects, having no reference to things beyond themselves.

DONALD JUDD The characteristics of Minimalism are apparent in *Untitled*, a 1969 sculpture of copper boxes (fig. **29.21**) by Donald Judd (1928–1994). The sculptor determined the shape and spacing of the boxes by mathematical premise (each box is 9-by-40-by-31 inches, with 9 inches between boxes), not by intuition or artistic sensitivity, as David Smith, for example, operated (see fig. 29.5). Like Stella's paintings, Judd's work was constructed by serial repetition of elements so there is no hierarchy of composition and no evocation of emotion. A viewer can take in and readily understand his composition at a glance.

Judd described his sculpture as a "specific object," meaning it was a real object that had no references beyond itself. Viewers were to admire it for its scale, color, texture, and proportions, for example. In addition to possessing the properties of a well-made "real thing," Judd's boxes occupy space like ordinary things as well. They are not presented on a base, and there is no glass case

to protect them. By relinquishing the props that announce an object to be a work of art, Minimalism heightens our awareness of the spaces in which we view art. In other words, the space around the object becomes an integral part of the work and of the art experience.

DAN FLAVIN The Minimalist whose work was perhaps most severely limited to mathematical formulas is the light sculptor Dan Flavin (1933–1996), renowned for working with common fluorescent tubes, which he used to sculpt with colored and white light. Flavin's tubes were store-bought and came in 2-, 4-, 6-, and 8-foot lengths.

Although difficult to tell from reproductions, Flavin's deceivingly simple works are spectacularly beautiful, even when they use just white light, as in *the nominal three (to William of Ockham)* (fig. **29.22**). The magical quality of the light as it radiates through the surrounding space is mesmerizing, even calming, often projecting a Classical serenity. For some viewers, it even embodies spirituality. The work, however, is strictly formalist and is determined by geometric premises, here a progression from one to two to three lights. No references are intended, despite the suggestion of the title, which Flavin attached upon finishing the work.

Flavin's sculpture is often extremely simple, consisting of a single tube of white or colored light, sometimes placed vertically on the wall and sitting on the floor, other times coming off a corner along a wall at a 45-degree angle. With Minimalism, art reached "Ground Zero." Reduced to bare essentials, it *seemed* to have no place left to go.

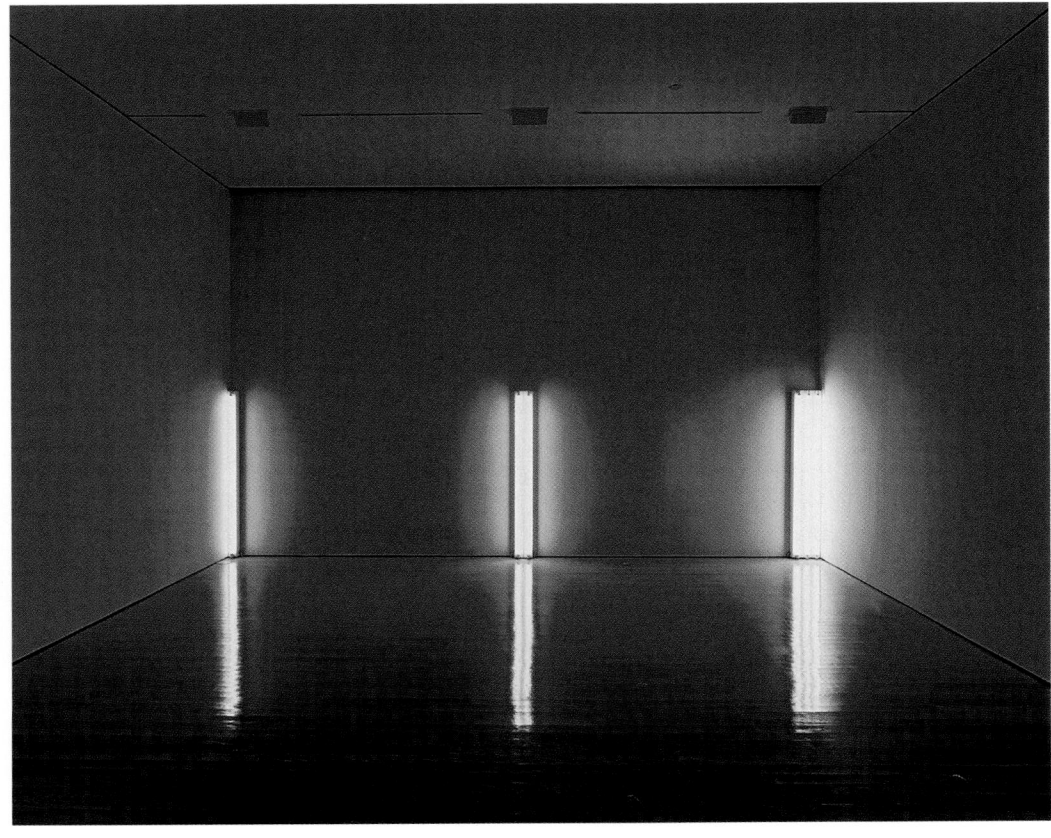

29.22 Dan Flavin. *the nominal three (to William of Ockham)*. 1963. Fluorescent light fixtures with daylight lamps, each 6' (1.83 m). Solomon R. Guggenheim Museum, New York. Panza Collection. 91.3698

THE PLURALIST 1970S: POST-MINIMALISM

The cold objectivity of Minimalism and formalist abstraction dominated contemporary art in the mid-1960s and into the 1970s, overshadowing styles that focused on subjectivity and the human figure. Even Pop Art seemed unemotional and machine-made. But as the 1960s developed, so did an interest in an art based on emotion, the human being, and referential and representational subject matter. In the midst of the Vietnam War and the civil rights-led social revolution that challenged the status quo, artists began to view formalist abstraction as an escapist indulgence. With Minimalism, many artists felt that the Modernist avant-garde had completely lost touch with society, retreating into a hermetic world of its own. By the mid-1960s, artists could no longer remain removed from their emotions and the hotly contested social and political issues of the day. By the late 1960s, American artists began to put the human component back into art, and many addressed the issues tearing the nation apart. The responses were diverse, with artists using what seems like an endless array of mediums to deal with an endless array of issues. Now, many artists made art that was temporary or conceptual and could not be collected, in effect dematerializing the art object and reflecting the antimaterialist stance of the 1960s social revolution. (See *The Art Historian's Lens*, page 1059).

Artists themselves became quite political as they attacked the bastions of white male art, museums and commercial galleries. Women, African Americans, Latinos, American Indians, and Asian Americans vociferously protested their exclusion from the art world by picketing museums and denouncing the prejudices of those organizations. More important, they began making art that dealt with issues that museum curators and directors did not consider mainstream or valid aesthetic concerns—issues such as gender, ethnic and racial identity, as well as sexual orientation. Disenfranchised artists, like the Impressionists 100 years earlier, began opening their own galleries to provide an alternative to museums. Because the pluralism of the 1970s came on the heels of Minimalism, and in many respects is a response to its hermetic aesthetics, the art from this decade is often called Post-Minimalism.

Post-Minimal Sculpture: Geometry and Emotion

Some of the first Post-Minimal sculptors retained the geometry of Minimalism, but they were hardly creating insular, discreet objects. To the contrary, their geometric forms were loaded with powerful emotional issues.

EVA HESSE One of the outstanding Post-Minimalists in the 1960s was Eva Hesse (1936–1970). Her accomplishment is astonishing when one considers that her career was cut short when she died of a brain tumor at age 34. Born in Hamburg, Germany,

she was raised in New York after her Jewish parents fled Nazi persecution. Hesse worked with a variety of unusual materials, such as acrylic paint on papier-mâché slathered over balloons. Her sculptures were abstract and had a basis in geometry. But because they reveal the dripping, pooling, flowing, stretching, and drying by which they took shape, they also suggest organic forms and processes, and growth and sexuality. In 1968, she began using fiberglass, which became her trademark material and was perhaps responsible for her brain cancer.

A classic work is *Untitled* (fig. **29.23**), which has as its starting point the geometric form of Minimalism. The four rectangular units of which it is composed imply boxes or framed paintings because of their curled edges. Contradicting their geometry are the uneven rippling surfaces and sides, which transform the fiberglass into an organic substance, especially recalling skin. The strange ropelike latex appendages eccentrically flopping from either side of center suggest arms or legs, momentarily transforming the boxes or frames into a family of individuals. Ultimately, these appendages are nothing more than abstract elements, like the rectangular units. The work is full of contradictions: It is simultaneously funny and morbid, geometric and organic, erotic and repulsive, abstract and referential. (See www.myartslab.com.) Perhaps the most powerful quality in Hesse's sculptures is the sense of frailty, wear, decay, and aging—best expressed in *Untitled* by the wobbly "legs."

RICHARD SERRA Emerging at the same time was sculptor Richard Serra (b. 1939), who befriended Hesse. He explored the properties of sculpture in a series of works that included making **process art**, in which the creative act itself was the art, such as

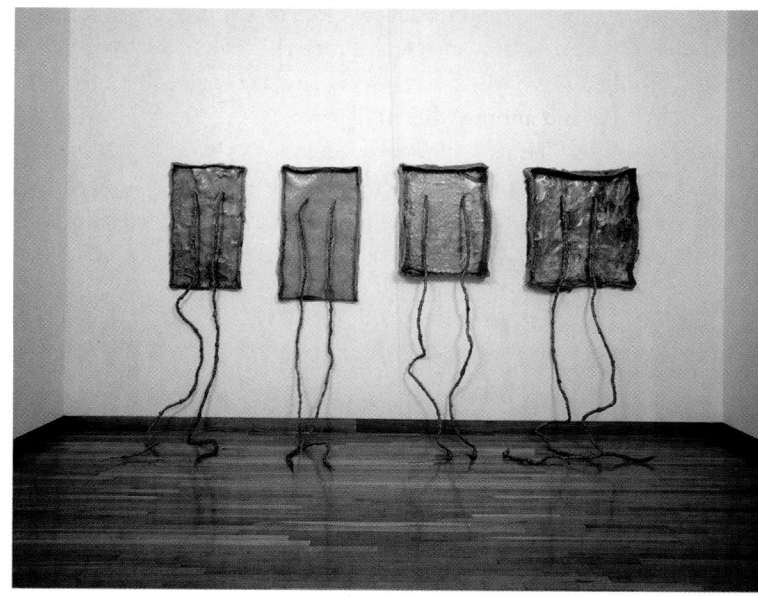

29.23 Eva Hesse, *Untitled*. 1970. Fiberglass over wire mesh, latex over cloth and wire (four units), 7'6⅞" × 12'3⅝" × 3'6½" (2.31 × 3.75 × 1.08 m), overall. Des Moines Art Center, Des Moines, IA. Purchased with Funds from the Coffin Fine Arts Trust, Nathan Emory Coffin, Collection of the Des Moines Art Center, 1988 (1988.b.a-d)

Studying the Absent Object

By the 1970s, art historians and critics were talking about the "dematerialization of the art object" in contemporary art. By this, they meant that art was no longer exclusively an object. Art was also something that could *not* be bought and sold, something so temporary that it could be seen only for a brief time, making it difficult for scholars and critics to study, analyze, and write about it. Artists were now making temporary sculpture out of crumpled paper, bread placed on the mouth of a volcano, or patterns made in the snow. Many of the artists making temporary art photographed their work. The photographs became works of art in themselves and allowed scholars to study the artists' output.

A handful of artists worked almost entirely in temporary mediums and left no record in photographs, films, or drawings. Not surprisingly, their careers along with their contributions and accomplishments are today underrecognized, if not virtually lost to art historians. Perhaps the most vulnerable artists were the performance artists who emerged

toward 1960 (see page 1046). Yvonne Rainer and Robert Whitman, for example, had a wide following and strongly influenced art in the 1960s, but today they are largely forgotten. Their work was performed, sometimes once, sometimes for several weeks, and then it disappeared. During the 1960s, Whitman, especially, had tremendous visibility. His integration of film projection into his Performance Pieces (see fig. 29.12) was startlingly innovative, anticipating the video installations that would become popular in the 1980s (see page 1047). Like his performances, Whitman's installations disappeared when they were dismantled and put into storage, where they cannot be seen, unlike conventional paintings or sculptures. Today, his Theater Pieces are occasionally performed, and one work, *Prune Flat*, has been acquired by a museum, the Dia Center for the Arts in New York, which owns the "score," the detailed drawings for costumes, and instructions for performance.

---

throwing molten lead at the spot where floor and wall meet, a kind of Jackson Pollock action sculpture that resulted in a violent, energetic splattering on wall and floor. It also resulted in **site-specific art**, since it could not be removed from the site of its creation without substantially altering the work.

By the late 1960s, Serra was making objects—now extremely heavy geometric lead forms—and invoking such themes as gravity, fear, and life and death. In *Corner Prop* (fig. **29.24**), an enormous lead cube weighing thousands of pounds is precariously propped up against the wall with a lead rod, with *nothing* securing either element. The piece, like much of Serra's sculpture from this period, communicates an unmistakable threat of violent collapse and an aura of danger that can be terrifying. In an even more frightening piece, Serra placed an enormous rectangular lead plate on the floor and another directly above, at a right angle, attached to the ceiling. The viewer was expected to walk on the one plate, thereby passing under the other. Serra's sculptures may look like Minimal Art, but they are loaded with narrative and emotion.

Earthworks and Site-Specific Art

By the late 1960s, the Post-Minimal aesthetic operated on an enormous scale, not only far beyond the confines of the gallery but far away from the art world, and in many instances in uninhabited remote areas. Several artists began sculpting with earth, snow, volcanoes, lightning, and deep-sea sites, their work often temporary and existing today only in photographs and drawings. Often the work had a strong geometric component, reflecting the influence of Minimal Art and Hard-Edge Abstraction. But in contrast, this sculpture generally was filled with references, including environmental, ontological (concerned with the nature of being), and political issues, as we will see in the work of Robert Smithson and the team of Christo and Jeanne-Claude.

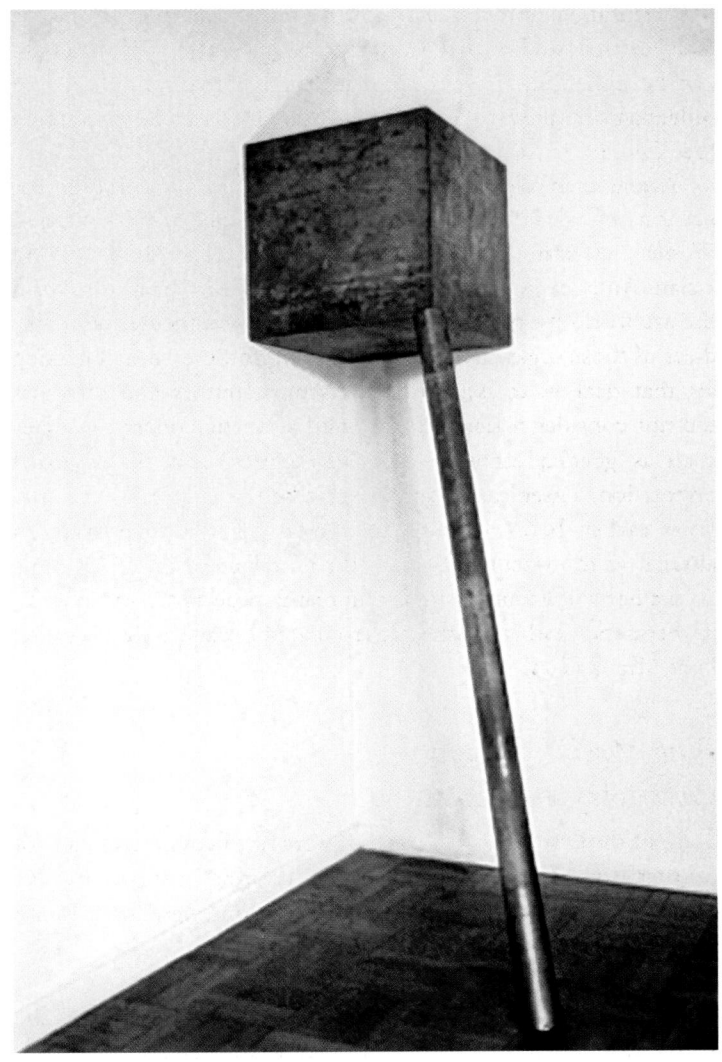

29.24   Richard Serra, *Corner Prop*. 1969. Lead antimony, box 25 × 25 × 25" (63.5 × 63.5 × 63.5 cm), pole 6'8" (2.03 m)

ROBERT SMITHSON One of the most famous earthworks, works of art created by manipulating the natural environment, is *Spiral Jetty* (fig. **29.25**), a site-specific sculpture made by Robert Smithson (1938–1973) in 1970. Smithson, who was a friend of Serra's, became a prominent figure in the New York art world in the mid- to late 1960s because of his articles on art, which often took an environmental approach to discussing land and nature. He also became known for his nonsite sculptures, which were "landscapes" consisting of rocks and stones from specific sites (often in neighboring New Jersey) that Smithson put into geometrically shaped metal bins or mirrored boxes on a gallery floor. A map or aerial photograph showed the actual site of the "landscape." Instead of painting a landscape, Smithson was re-presenting the real thing in the form of what looks like a Minimal sculpture. What a viewer was witnessing was the entropy, or steady degradation, of the land as it was removed from one site and taken to another.

Like Hesse's sculpture, Smithson's Minimalist-looking sculpture is full of references and issues, which is apparent in *Spiral Jetty*. The work is 1,500 feet long, 15 feet wide, and involved moving 6,650 tons of earth and black basalt. It is located at Rozel Point, a remote area of Utah's Great Salt Lake, whose surrounding landscape looks like an industrial wasteland because of the rusting, discarded mining equipment littering the vicinity. Just as time consumes civilization, and all things for that matter, so too will the jetty eventually disappear as it erodes into the lake. The spiral form, as it wraps around itself, going nowhere, and trapping microorganisms that turn the water red, seems like the relic of a prehistoric civilization. Rather than just a minimal geometric shape to be admired for its own sake, *Spiral Jetty* is a powerful sculpture that utilizes time as a major component to speak about the entropy of all things.

CHRISTO AND JEANNE-CLAUDE Christo (Christo Javacheff, b. 1935) is a Bulgarian-born American artist. He met his French-born American wife and collaborator Jeanne-Claude (Jeanne-Claude de Guillebon, b. 1935) in Paris in 1958. There, the couple were interested in creating a social dialogue and provoking their audience to think about their immediate world. In one work, Christo and Jeanne-Claude dammed up a narrow Paris street with a neat Minimalist-looking stack of barrels, preventing passage. However, they are best known for wrapping unidentified objects in fabric, stimulating viewer curiosity about the object as well as the reason for the gesture. In 1964, they moved to New York.

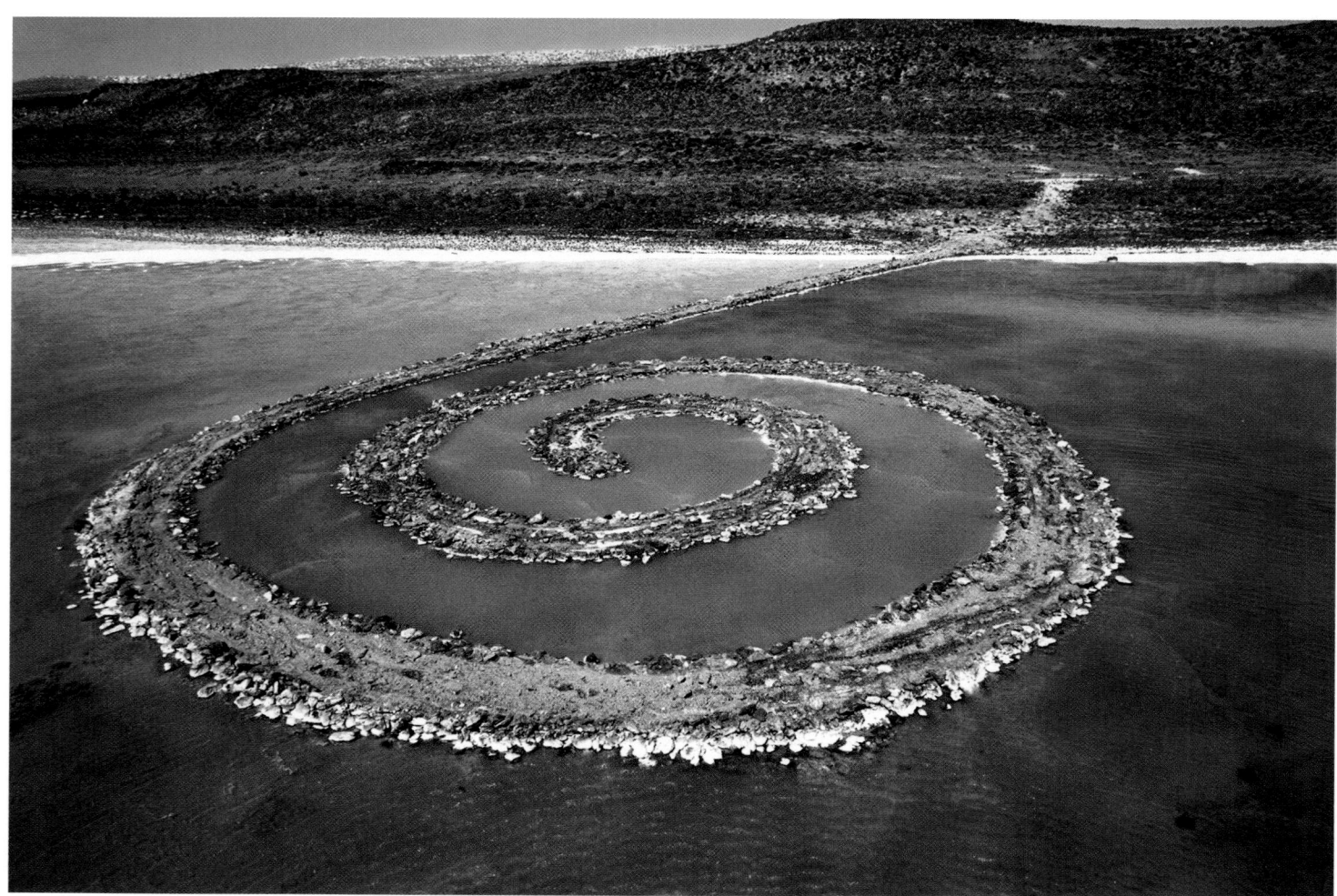

29.25 Robert Smithson, *Spiral Jetty*. 1970. Total length 1,500' (457.2 m); width of jetty 15' (4.57 m). Great Salt Lake, Utah

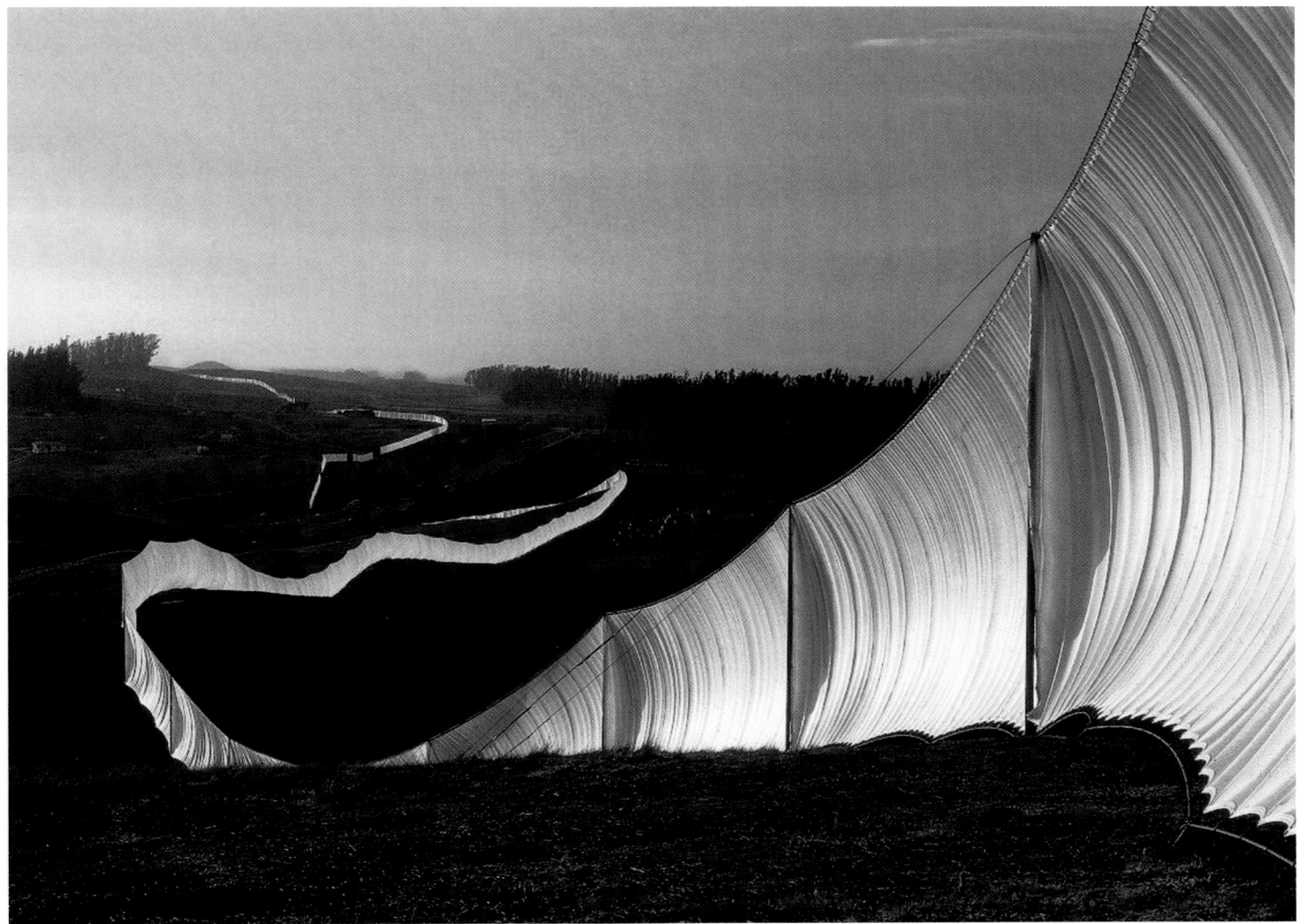

29.26 Christo and Jeanne-Claude, *Running Fence*, Sonoma and Marin counties, California. 1972–76. Fabric, 18' × 24½ miles (5.5 m × 39.4 km)

Their goal was to operate on an environmental or architectural scale, which they first did on a small scale in 1961 in Cologne (*Dockside Packages*) and on a large scale in 1969 when they wrapped a 1-million-square-foot section of a rocky coast in Australia. Since then they have wrapped enormous buildings, and a bridge, and surrounded 11 islands with floating fabric, creating site-specific sculptures.

Reproduced here is *Running Fence* (fig. **29.26**), proposed in 1972 and executed in 1976. On the one hand, the work looks like Minimal Art, since it consists of predetermined mathematical units that extend to fill an allocated space, here the 24½-mile (39.5-km) hilly terrain in California's Sonoma and Marin counties, with one terminus literally ending in the ocean. Each segment is 18 feet high and consists of cloth attached to steel poles. But this work is not only about the object itself, which was removed by the artists after being displayed for two weeks. Rather, it includes the entire process of implementing the concept: from the endless negotiations with government officials and landowners (mostly ranchers), the acquiring and supervising of an enormous workforce, the manufacturing of the work, and removal of it. It took four years to produce, the largest stumbling block being the tremendous community resistance. But the dialogue resulted in a raised consciousness about the land. It forced people to look at the land, and to think about it, recognizing how it was financially, emotionally, and aesthetically valued. The use of the word "fence" in the title specifically raised issues about how the land was to be used, and for whom.

Once installed, *Running Fence* transformed the landscape. The fence itself was like a fleet of ships sailing across hill and dale. Probably hundreds of thousands of people came to experience it. In a documentary of the project, one rancher, who had fought the installation, described how he and his son slept next to the fence one night—listening to it ripple in the wind, watching the stars—in effect undergoing a transformative experience. And then it was gone. Nothing was left, except memories of experiences, pieces of the cloth, which were given to the landowners, and hundreds of drawings that Christo had made to finance the $3.2 million project, which Christo and Jeanne-Claude paid for themselves.

Conceptual Art: Art as Idea

Although the Frenchman Marcel Duchamp had made ideas the focus of art beginning in the 1910s (see page 970) and American George Brecht had begun to create a kind of conceptual art in the 1950s (see page 1047), the term itself did not become commonplace until the late 1960s, when a large number of artists started producing art that emphasized ideas rather than the aesthetics of style. Of course, ideas appear in all art, but the ideas are closely tied to the formal qualities of the art and cannot exist without them. In Conceptual Art, the art generally exists solely as an idea, with no visual manifestation other than words. Or the idea or information can appear as a graph, chart, map, or documentary photograph. In addition to works that are entirely Conceptual, we can also talk about art that is basically visual and aesthetic but has a Conceptual component as well. For example, Smithson's *Spiral Jetty* has such an element for we *know* that the work is going to very slowly disappear, which is something that was not visible when it was made in 1970. But with the Conceptual artists, idea, concept, or information will be the consuming quality of the work.

JOSEPH KOSUTH By the late 1960s, more and more artists were making art based on ideas, and in 1970, the Museum of Modern Art in New York mounted an exhibition entitled *Information*, dedicated to Conceptual Art and taking as its thesis that art provides information and ideas, not visual aesthetics. The show's cocurator was artist Joseph Kosuth (b. 1945). Characteristic of Kosuth's own work is *One and Three Chairs* (fig. **29.27**) of 1965, in which he combined a large gelatin-silver print of a folding chair with the real chair and a photograph of a dictionary definition of a chair. By using words instead of just an image, Kosuth tells us how cerebral and nonaesthetic his intentions are.

The work appears to be a textbook study in semiotics—the science of signs—a popular topic in universities and in a small segment of the art community at the time. In the language of semiotics, the real chair is the "signified," the photograph is the "signifier," signifying that particular chair, and the dictionary definition is the idealized nonspecific chair. By arranging three versions of a chair in this particular way, Kosuth has determined their context, which leads a viewer to consider issues of language and meaning, rather than such typical art issues as beauty and expression. Reading the definition, we tend to think of the real chair next to it. If it were not present, we would probably think of some other chair from our own experience. If we look only at the photograph of a chair, we may even think the subject of the photograph is not necessarily the chair but the absence of a person sitting in the chair. The title is an important part of the work, for it too provides context, suggesting we can view the chairs as the same chair (one chair) or as three different chairs with very different stories. In other words, this work is about ideas as much as it is about the aesthetics of the visual presentation, which is as unemotional and straightforward as Minimalism. Ultimately, the task of establishing meaning is the viewer's.

One and Three Chairs also reflects a new approach to photography that appeared in the mid-1960s: The medium was no longer the sacred preserve of professional photographers, who worked on a modest scale, carefully took their own photographs, and often slaved over their prints. Now, photographs were used by Installation, Earthwork, Performance, and Conceptual artists, who in their primary medium often worked on a large scale.

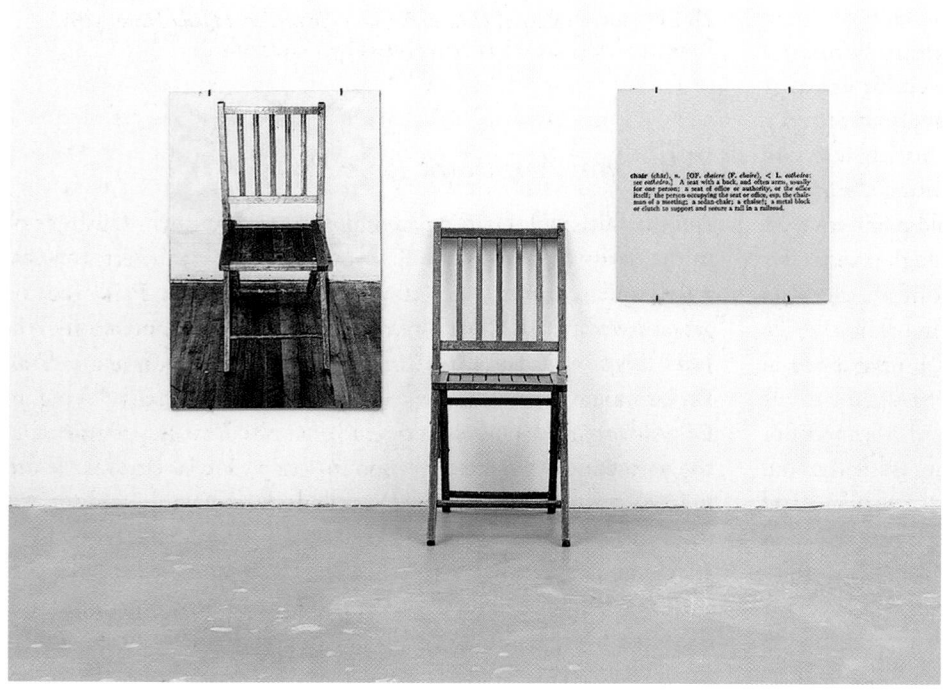

29.27 Joseph Kosuth, *One and Three Chairs.* 1965. Wooden folding chair, photographic copy of chair, and photographic enlargement of dictionary definition of chair; chair, 32⅜ × 14⅞ × 20⅞" (82.2 × 37.8 × 53 cm); photo panel, 36 × 24⅛" (91.5 × 61 cm); text panel, 24 × 24⅛" (61. × 62.2 cm). Museum of Modern Art, New York. Larry Aldrich Foundation Fund

They now made photographs based on their work, and produced large photographs to suggest the scale of their primary work, the photographs even rivaling painting in size. Generally, they did not take their own pictures, and few if any did their own printing. Most shocking to traditional photographers, they often integrated photography into other mediums, as Kosuth did in *One and Three Chairs*, thus violating the time-honored integrity of the medium.

JOSEPH BEUYS Beuys (1921–1986) was a German Conceptual artist who produced work so complex and rich in ideas it is nearly impossible to pin down exactly what his art is. His objects, diagrams, photographs, and performances interrelate so tightly that no one piece can comfortably stand on its own. He was based in Düsseldorf, a city that by the 1970s was home to many of the world's leading artists, its art scene perhaps second only to New York's. Beuys played a major role in developing this artistic climate. His impact included spurring German artists to confront their nation's Nazi past, to rediscover the German Romantic tradition, and to invest their art with spirituality, much as the German Expressionists had done in the early twentieth century.

Two key factors in Beuys's development were his experiences in World War II as a fighter pilot in Hitler's Luftwaffe (airforce) and the 1963 arrival in Düsseldorf of the Fluxus artists. Beuys propagated a myth that his plane was shot down in 1943 in a snowstorm over Crimea, and that nomadic Tartars saved him from freezing to death by covering him in animal fat and layers of felt, materials that became a foundation for much of his sculptural work. Whatever Beuys's war experience actually was, it was clearly traumatic, for after attending the Düsseldorf Art Academy in the late 1940s, he disappeared into the German countryside to work as a farmhand and purge himself of his guilt and anxiety.

In 1961, Beuys was teaching at the Düsseldorf Art Academy, and two years later he was introduced to Fluxus, adopting Performance Art and joining them for a segment of their European tour. In 1965, he performed *How to Explain Pictures to a Dead Hare* (fig. **29.28**). For three hours he moved his lips as if silently lecturing the dead hare cradled in his arm about the pictures surrounding him on the walls. Attached to his left sole was felt, and to his right, steel, the one representing "spiritual warmth," the other "hard reason." Honey and gold paint covered Beuys's head, transforming him into a shaman, a high priest who uses magic to cure ills. The honey represented a life force. This mysterious ritualistic performance was about the meaninglessness of conventional picture making—art that had to be explained—and about the need to replace it with a more spiritual and natural form of communication, an art the meaning of which could be felt or intuited by a viewer rather than understood intellectually. The performance was designed to create a magical art that would cause people to invest their own lives with spirituality. Everyone who watched the performance apparently found it riveting and unforgettable, even if they did not understand it. His objects, too, such as a worn wooden chair with a pile of fat on its seat, affected people similarly.

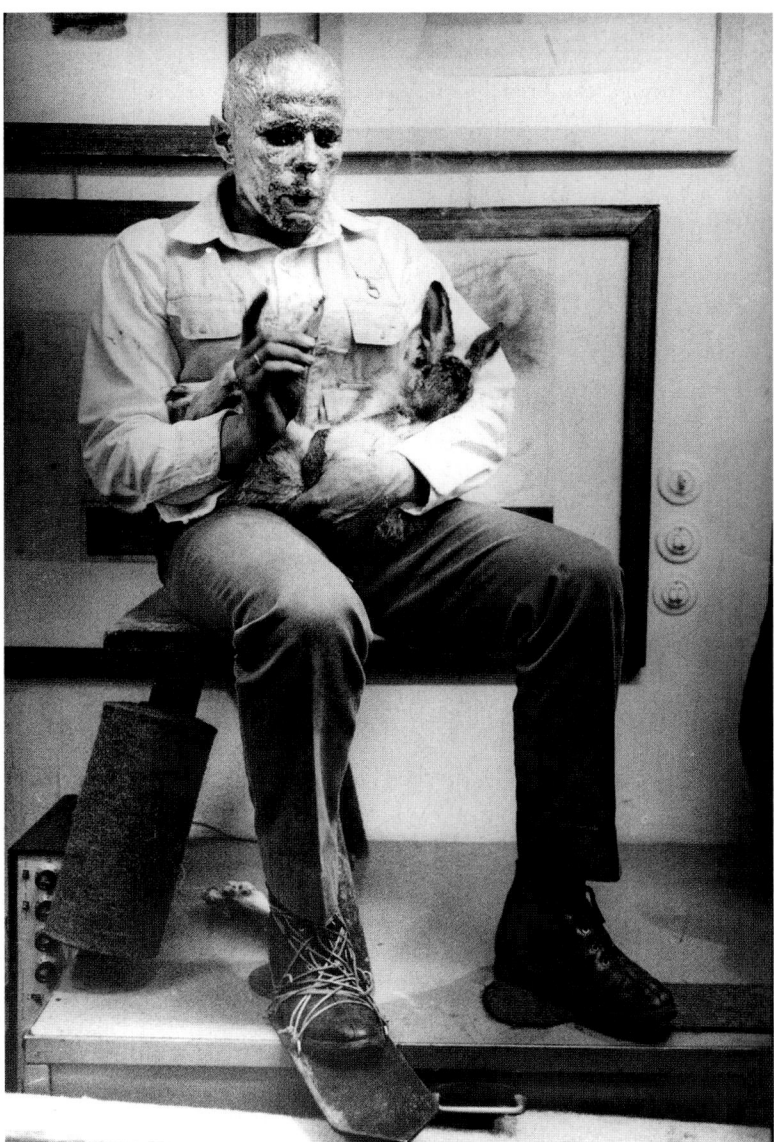

29.28 Joseph Beuys, *How to Explain Pictures to a Dead Hare*. 1965. Performed at Galerie Schmela, Düsseldorf, Germany

Television Art: Nam June Paik

Another artist who participated in Fluxus activities in Düsseldorf in the early 1960s was the Korean-born musician, Performance artist, and sculptor Nam June Paik (1932–2006). Paik's background was in music, but shortly after studying composition with John Cage in Darmstadt, Germany, in 1958, he became a radical Performance artist, exploring unconventional mediums. Living in Düsseldorf in 1963 and performing in the Fluxus program, he began making art using television monitors. He labeled television the "electronic superhighway" and declared it the medium of the future, dedicating his life to working with it. His earliest television art used single monitors with simple abstract patterns, such as a single horizontal or vertical line. Or using a magnet, he distorted a television signal to create arclike or wavy compositions. In 1964, he moved to New York, and with the launch of the

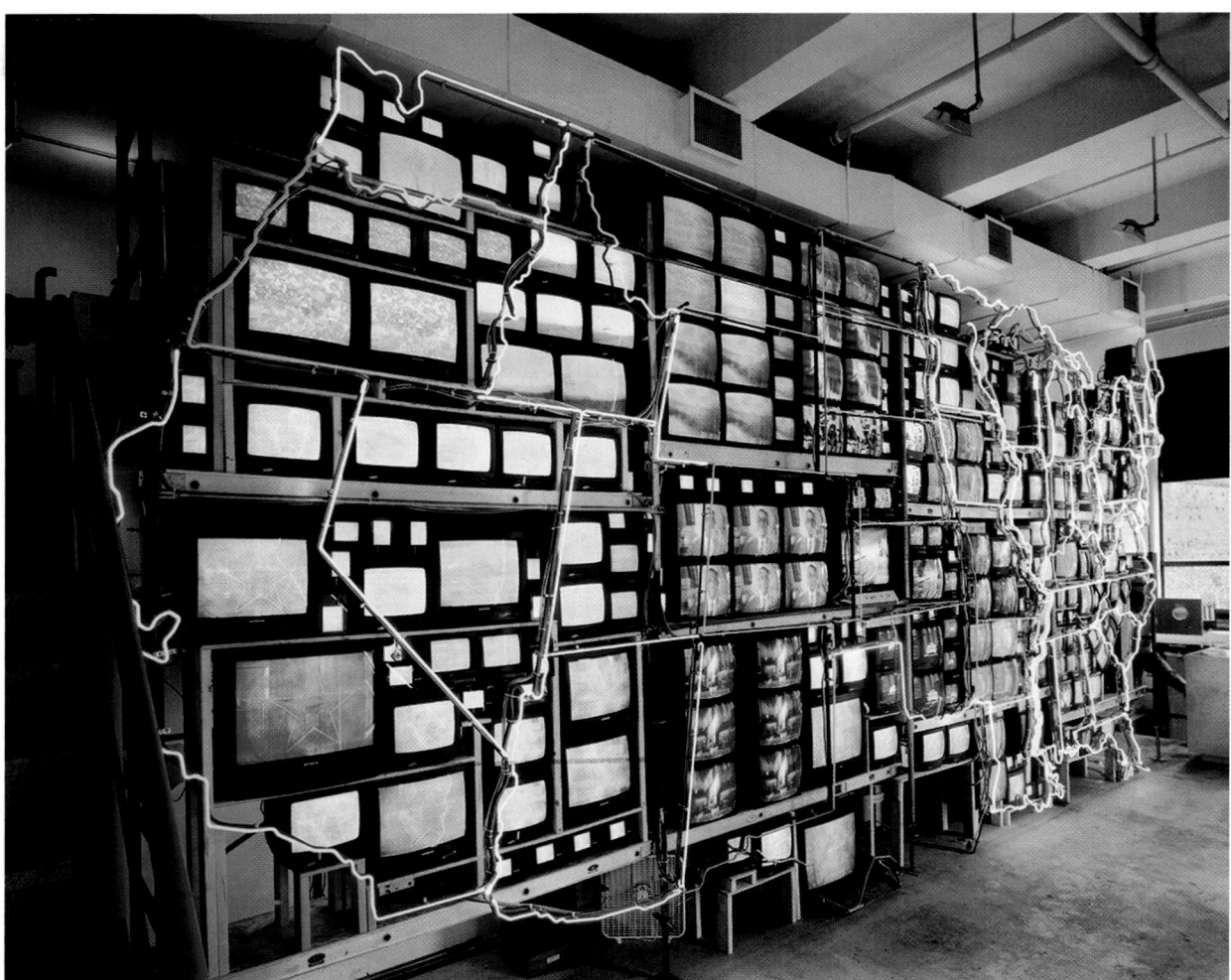

29.29 Nam June Paik, *Electronic Superhighway: Continental U.S.* 1995. Installation: Forty-seven-channel closed-circuit video installation with 313 monitors, laser disk images with sound, steel structure and neon, 15 × 32 × 4' (4.57 × 9.75 × 1.2 m). Courtesy Nam June Paik Studio, New York

first affordable video camera by Sony, he began to use video as well as live-broadcast television.

Paik's work in the 1970s became increasingly grand and complex. Typical of the more elaborate structure of the later work is a piece from 1995, *Electronic Superhighway: Continental U.S.* (fig. **29.29**). Fed by numerous computer-controlled video channels, this installation consists of dozens of monitors inserted in a neon map of the 48 continental states. The rapidly changing images generally relate to the respective states, except for New York, which was fed from a live camera in the New York Holly Solomon Gallery, where the work was shown and from where our reproduction originates.

In *Electronic Superhighway*, Paik reaffirms the prevalence of television in American society, presenting his work with the fast-paced continuous stream of information characteristic of broadcast television. The work celebrates American vernacular culture, both in its use of neon and television as mediums and in the Americana presented on the videos. Television is America, Paik tells us. It is, in effect, real life, because most Americans experience the world through their television screens. Paik is not condemning the medium, which would be antithetical to the objective position of a Fluxus artist, but simply revealing its power to define contemporary life.

ART WITH A SOCIAL AGENDA

Most of the postwar artists discussed thus far did not have a social agenda. Even some who did, such as Lichtenstein and Warhol, subversively buried their message so that it was not readily visible, especially to the groups they criticized. While an atmosphere of counterculture dominated the vanguard art world paralleling the social revolution occurring not only in America but also worldwide by the late 1960s, few artists made political art. By the 1970s, however, the trickle of artists making work that dealt with social issues began to swell into a torrent. So great was its influence that we now think of social issues as playing a major role in avant-garde art for the last 35 years. An art with a social agenda became a key component of 1970s Post-Minimalism.

Street Photography

Not everyone was caught up in the economic boom and technological euphoria of the 1950s. Some observers, including many outstanding photographers, perceived serious problems within American society. In part inspired by the powerful photographs of Walker Evans (see fig. 28.54), they trained their cameras on the injustices smoldering beneath the placid surface of society and made what is often called **street photography**, a reference to their taking to the streets to find their imagery. They were free to do so because photography was not handcuffed by the Modernist aesthetics of painting and sculpture that demanded an increasingly abstract nonreferential art.

Perhaps the best known of the postwar street photographers is Robert Frank (b. 1924), who emigrated from Switzerland in the 1940s. In 1955, Frank crisscrossed the nation, taking candid, unposed photographs in banal public settings, which he then published as a photoessay in a book called *The Americans* (1958). American publishers found his view of America so grim that Frank had to go to France to find someone to produce the book. An American edition finally came out in 1959 with an introduction by Jack Kerouac (1922–1969), author of the classic Beatnik novel *On the Road* (1957).

Like his friend George Segal, Frank used his work to reflect his concerns about the alienation and lack of spirituality in twentieth-century America. *Drug Store, Detroit* (fig. **29.30**) is characteristic of his national portrait of emptiness, alienation, and despair. Under a barrage of bold advertising (reminding us of Andy Warhol's *Campbell's Soup Cans*), some 15 men order, among other items, artificial orange whips, each patron seemingly unaware of the others. On the other side of the counter dutifully serving the white males are African-American women, undoubtedly working for a minimum wage. Just as the cake is trapped in the airless foreground case, the waitresses seem trapped behind the counter in the drudgery of their menial jobs. The glare of bare fluorescent bulbs bouncing off linoleum, Formica, and plastic is a reminder of the period's deadening aesthetic of efficiency and modernity, while the monotonous lineup of jukeboxes on the counter opposite the patrons underlines the "sell, sell, sell" mentality of American business.

Unlike Bourke-White, Evans and Lange (see pages 1018 and 1029), Frank avoids refinement in his documentary photographs. His prints are blurry and gritty, and grimy blacks violently contrast with whites. Their harsh crudeness projects an undercurrent of unease and disquiet. We sense the speed with which Frank operated in the informal settings he encountered, wielding his 35mm single-lens reflex camera as spontaneously as his instinct dictated. It should come as no surprise that the downtown Detroit where this photograph was taken was largely destroyed during the race riots of the late 1960s. (For a discussion of a second documentary photographer, Lee Friedlander, from this period, see the Introduction.)

African-American Art: Ethnic Identity

Other American artists soon joined the street photographers and began doing what had been unthinkable in the art world of the 1960s: turning their backs on both Minimalism and abstraction in general and instead making art about the nation's problems and issues, particularly those concerning race, ethnic background, gender, and sexual orientation. Because of the Civil Rights Movement, African-American artists were challenged to make art about their

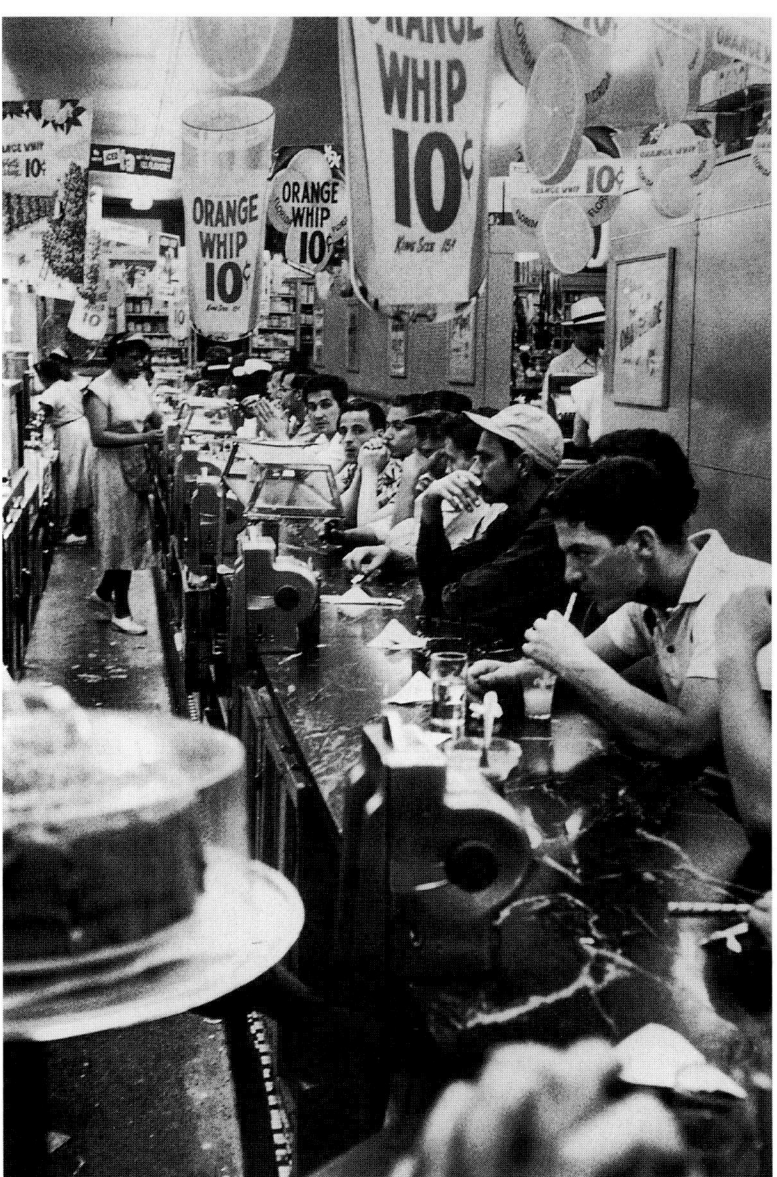

29.30 Robert Frank, *Drug Store, Detroit*. 1955. Gelatin silver print, 11 × 14" (27.9 × 35.5 cm). Courtesy of the Pace MacGill Gallery, New York

heritage. At college and in art school, they were trained like everyone else to make abstract art. But their communities pressured them to do the exact opposite: Make narrative art and take up the black cause. To balance both claims was a challenge.

ROMARE BEARDEN In New York in 1963, a number of African-American artists formed a loose group called Spiral, dedicated to supporting the Civil Rights Movement. They met in the studio of Romare Bearden (1911–1988), a New York University-educated mathematician and philosopher who in the 1940s increasingly became a committed artist. Influenced by Martin Luther King, Jr.'s 1963 March on Washington, D.C., Bearden suggested a collaborative project for Spiral that involved the members all contributing to a large photocollage about black

PRIMARY SOURCE

Romare Bearden (1911–1988)

From a 1984 interview with Joseph Jacobs

Romare Bearden talks about why collage was so important for him and its relationship to jazz.

One of the attractions of collage for me is it allows me to work quickly, which is a very twentieth-century attitude. The development of the machine, and now of the computer, killed man's capacity for patience. It is too nervous a century for people to paint the way Jan van Eyck painted, for example. Many modern super-realist paintings, which may look as detailed as a Van Eyck, are made from photographs or slides which get projected onto the canvas and are then painted. Collage is the cutting out rather than the painting of things, and it allows a more direct way to get something down. Just cut it out and put it down.

No, the physicality of the medium did not attract me to collage. Also, I don't think of my use of collage as an extension of Abstract Expressionism. Rather I would like to think of it within the context of Cubism. My quarrel with Abstract Expressionism, if any, is that sometimes the space is naturalistic. If you place in one area of the canvas a large field of blue, and then in another area you put an orange, you have painted sunlight, which is naturalistic space and light. I prefer to bring things forward, not just for the sake of making Cubism, but to make flat painting and not fool the eye with depth and perspective. And that is achieved by having the collage sit on the surface. …

Yes, you can draw parallels between my work and jazz. As you just said, there is a spirit that is there before a work is begun and develops with the work that is similar to the kind of improvisation that one gets in jazz. … [Jazz] has a rhythmic component, and it also has interval. When you listen to the piano of Earl Hines, what really counts is the silences between the notes struck. … The same importance of interval can be seen in confetti thrown at a wedding; the confetti dazzles the eye, but it is the spaces between the pieces that really causes things to happen.

Source: Joseph Jacobs, *Since the Harlem Renaissance: 50 Years of Afro-American Art* (The Center Gallery of Bucknell University, 1985). Lewisburg, Pennsylvania. 1985

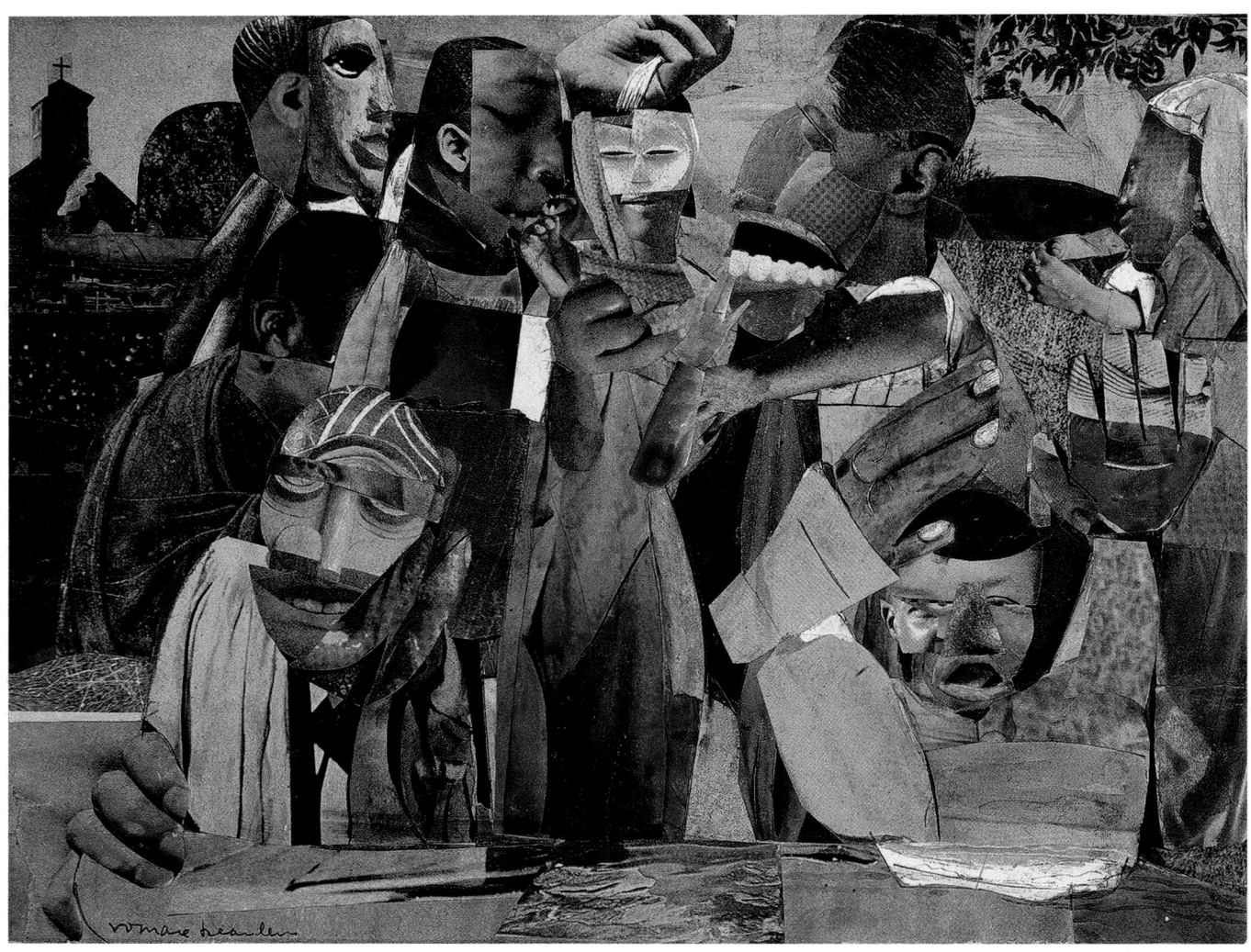

29.31   Romare Bearden, *The Prevalence of Ritual: Baptism.* 1964. Collage of photochemical reproduction, synthetic polymer, and pencil on paperboard, 9⅛ × 12" (23.2 × 30.5 cm). Hirshhorn Museum and Sculpture Garden, Smithsonian Institution, Washington, D.C. Gift of Joseph H. Hirshhorn, 1966

identity. When no one turned up, Bearden undertook the project by himself, cutting up newspapers and magazines to make collages, for which he became famous.

The composition of Bearden's collages is based on Cubism, as seen in *The Prevalence of Ritual: Baptism* (fig. **29.31**), created in 1964, but the subject matter is distinctly African-American. Bearden grew up in Charlotte, North Carolina, before moving to New York City's Harlem, and the fractured image shows a baptism, reflecting the importance of religion in black culture. The faces not only express the African physiognomy but in some instances also suggest African masks. This work has the effect of tracing American culture back to its African roots and reinforcing the continuous importance of ritual and community. The collage composition has a wild syncopation and even a sense of improvisation that seems to relate to the black jazz musicians of the period, such as Charlie Parker or John Coltrane. (See *Primary Source*, page 1066.) The power of Bearden's work lies in the artist's ability to pack so much information and energy into a single image that it overflows with the vitality and essence of the African-American experience, an energy we saw as well in the small temperas of Jacob Lawrence (see fig. 28.49).

MELVIN EDWARDS At virtually the same moment, Melvin Edwards (b. 1937) took an entirely different approach to reflecting his racial background. Raised in Houston, Texas, and studying welded-steel sculpture and formalist aesthetics at the University of Southern California in Los Angeles, Edwards was outraged at the lynchings of blacks in the South, which were increasing as the Ku Klux Klan responded to the Civil Rights Movement. In 1963, he began to make a series of relief sculptures entitled *Lynch Fragments* (fig. **29.32**), incorporating chains and spikes and brutal metal fragments, all of which took on a brown tonality when oiled to prevent rusting.

While there is no set reading of these works—which Edwards, a New York resident, continues to make today along with monumental sculpture—they evoke oppression, bondage, violence, and anger, as well as skin color. They also appear to refer to African masks (which the artist denies is intended) and ritual, and in their bold frontality they display a sense of confrontation and dignity. These basically abstract works, which fulfilled the demands of his university teaching to make nonrepresentational art, are so open to interpretation that we can view them as autobiographical as well. A horseshoe that appears in many of the *Lynch Fragments* is the artist's reminiscence of visits to his uncle's ranch outside of Houston. Edwards's political and expressive abstraction stands in stark contrast to the Minimalist Art being produced at the same time and anticipated Post-Minimal sculpture.

BETYE SAAR With Betye Saar (b. 1926), there is no attempt to accommodate the art establishment by catering to formalist abstraction. Her work is brazenly representational and, like Bearden, her themes are obviously dedicated to her African-American heritage. Saar, who is from Los Angeles, where she still lives, got her B.A. in design from the University of California,

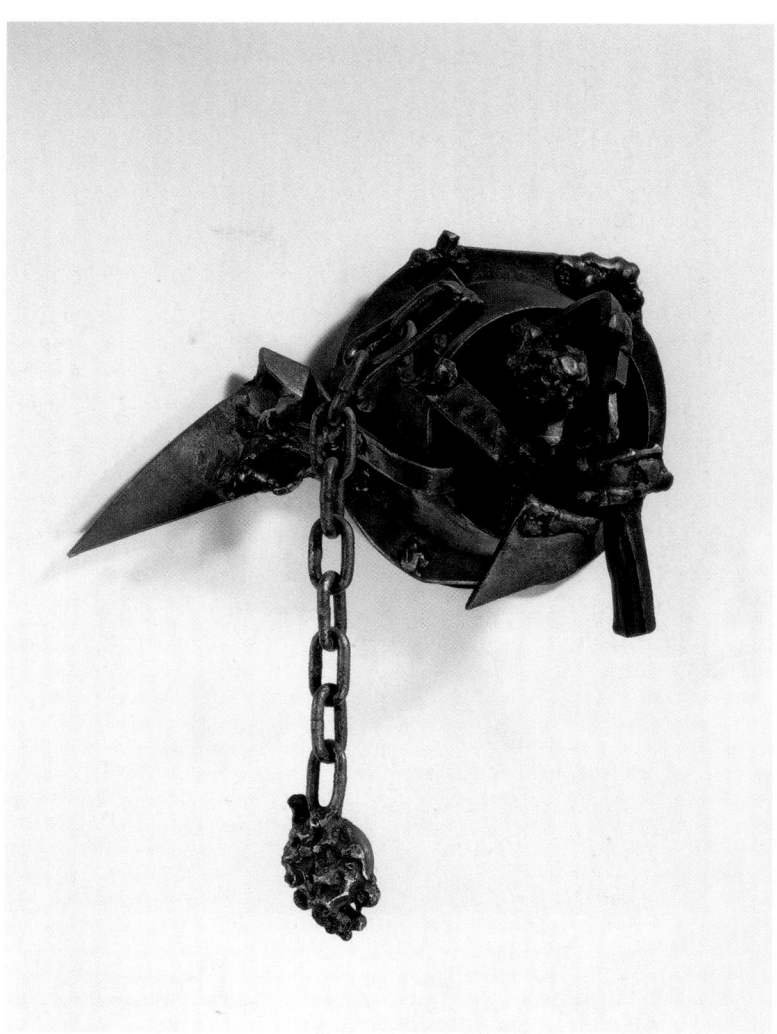

29.32 Melvin Edwards, *Lynch Fragment: Some Bright Morning*. 1963. Welded steel, 14¼ × 9¼ × 5" (36.2 × 23.5 × 12.7 cm). Collection of the artist

Los Angeles, and graduate degrees in education and printmaking from nearby universities. But it was not until she experienced first hand the Surrealist assemblage boxes of the New Yorker Joseph Cornell in 1968 that she found her mature artistic voice. She began working in the same technique, as can be seen in *Shield of Quality* (fig. **29.33**) of 1974. The work is part of a series of boxes inspired by the death of the artist's great-aunt. Each is like a Victorian keepsake box, containing relics of the ancestor—a glove, a feather from a hat, lace, buttons, and a baby spoon, for example. Vintage photographs are arranged in a triptych, transforming the box into a portable altar. The shrine pays homage to the values the great-aunt handed down, values reflected in the quality and propriety of the objects themselves. And the box counters America's racial stereotyping by presenting African Americans as middle-class, a reminder that Saar was born in 1926 and grew up in precivil-rights America.

Like so much of Saar's work, *Shield of Quality* focuses on women and is also about female pride and the important role of

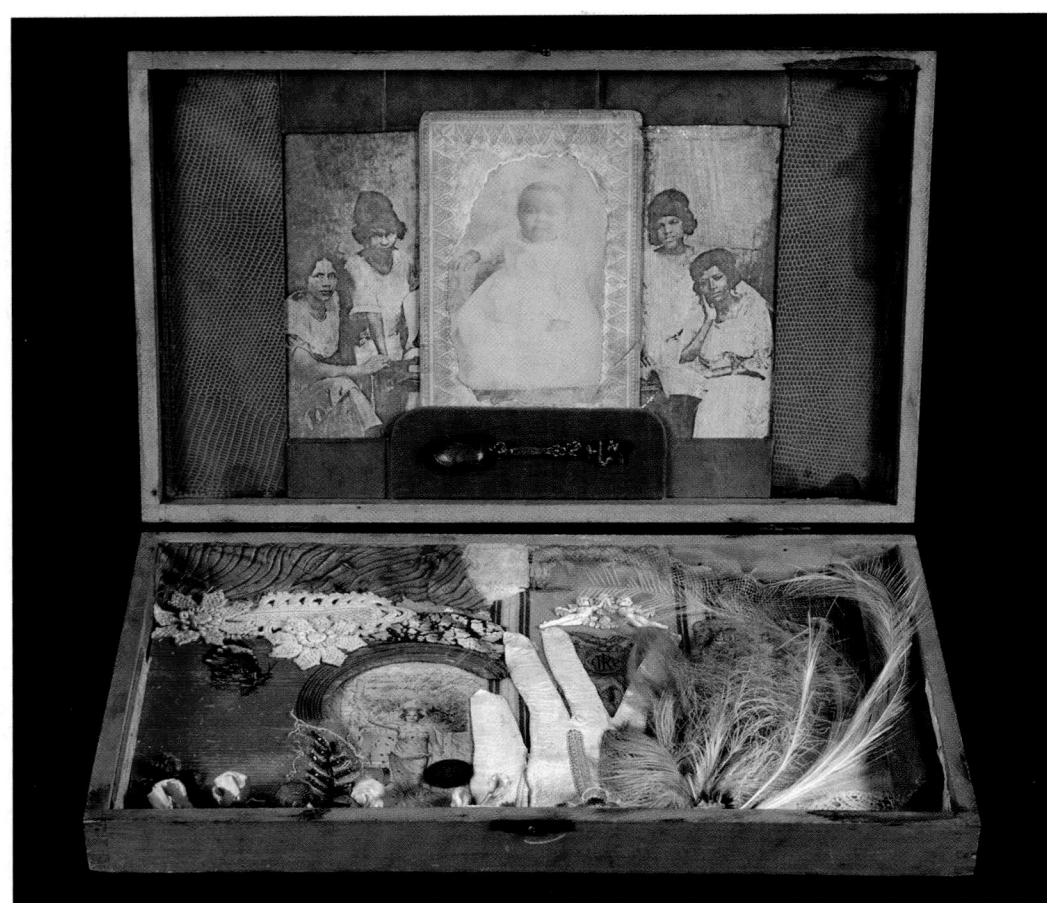

29.33 Betye Saar, *Shield of Quality*. 1974. Mixed media, 18 × 14¾ × 1" (45.7 × 36.4 × 2.5 cm). Collection of the Newark Museum. Purchase 1998, The Members' Fund (98.37). Photograph courtesy of Michael Rosenfeld Gallery, LLC, New York

women in society. Clearly, by working on a small-scale and making delicate effeminate work, Saar was defying the art establishment, turning her back on the enormous canvases and sculptures being churned out by white males. With Saar, we have stepped into the feminist era.

Feminist Art: Judy Chicago and Gender Identity

Betty Friedan's 1963 book *The Feminine Mystique* signaled the start of the feminist movement. Almost simultaneously a number of women artists began making work that dealt with women's issues. Nancy Spero (b. 1926) made simple but powerful expressionistic drawings depicting violence toward women, while Mimi Smith (b. 1942) made what is now recognized as the first American clothing art, objects such as a Minimalist *Girdle* (1966), constructed of rubber bathmats that capture the discomfort of women's clothing. And, as just discussed, Betye Saar made boxes that paid homage to women.

The best-known work coming out of the women's movement is *The Dinner Party* (fig. **29.34**), orchestrated by Judy Chicago (b. 1939) and made by over 400 women between 1974 and 1979. By the late 1960s, Chicago was a dedicated feminist, who in the early 1970s established a Feminist Art Program, the first of its kind, at California State University at Fresno. Shortly thereafter, with artist Miriam Schapiro (b. 1923), she started a second similar program at the California Institute of the Arts in Valencia. The thrust of these courses was to encourage women to make art and deal with gender issues, which the art world, including university and art-school faculties, said she could not do because the work did not conform to the aesthetic norms of Modernist formalism that signified serious art. The Feminist Art Program was designed to provide support for women artists and to redefine aesthetic values in contemporary art.

The Dinner Party reflects Chicago's shift from a maker of abstract Minimalist objects and paintings to works on feminist themes in alternative mediums and installations. It pays homage to the many important women who Chicago felt were ignored, underrated, or omitted from the history books. Chicago laboriously researched these lost figures. She then designed a triangular table with 39 place settings, 13 to a side, each honoring a significant woman, ranging from ancient goddesses to such twentieth-century icons as Georgia O'Keeffe. In addition, 919 other women's names are inscribed on the white floor tiles lying in the triangular intersection of the tables. Each place setting included a hand-painted ceramic plate that pictured a vagina executed in a period style. American poet Emily Dickinson's sex, for example, is surrounded by lace, and French queen Eleanor of Aquitaine's is encased in a *fleur-de-lis*. Under each place setting is an embroidered runner, often elaborate and again in period style.

Instead of using bulldozers, chainsaws, hoists, and welding equipment as men did for their environments, Chicago intention-

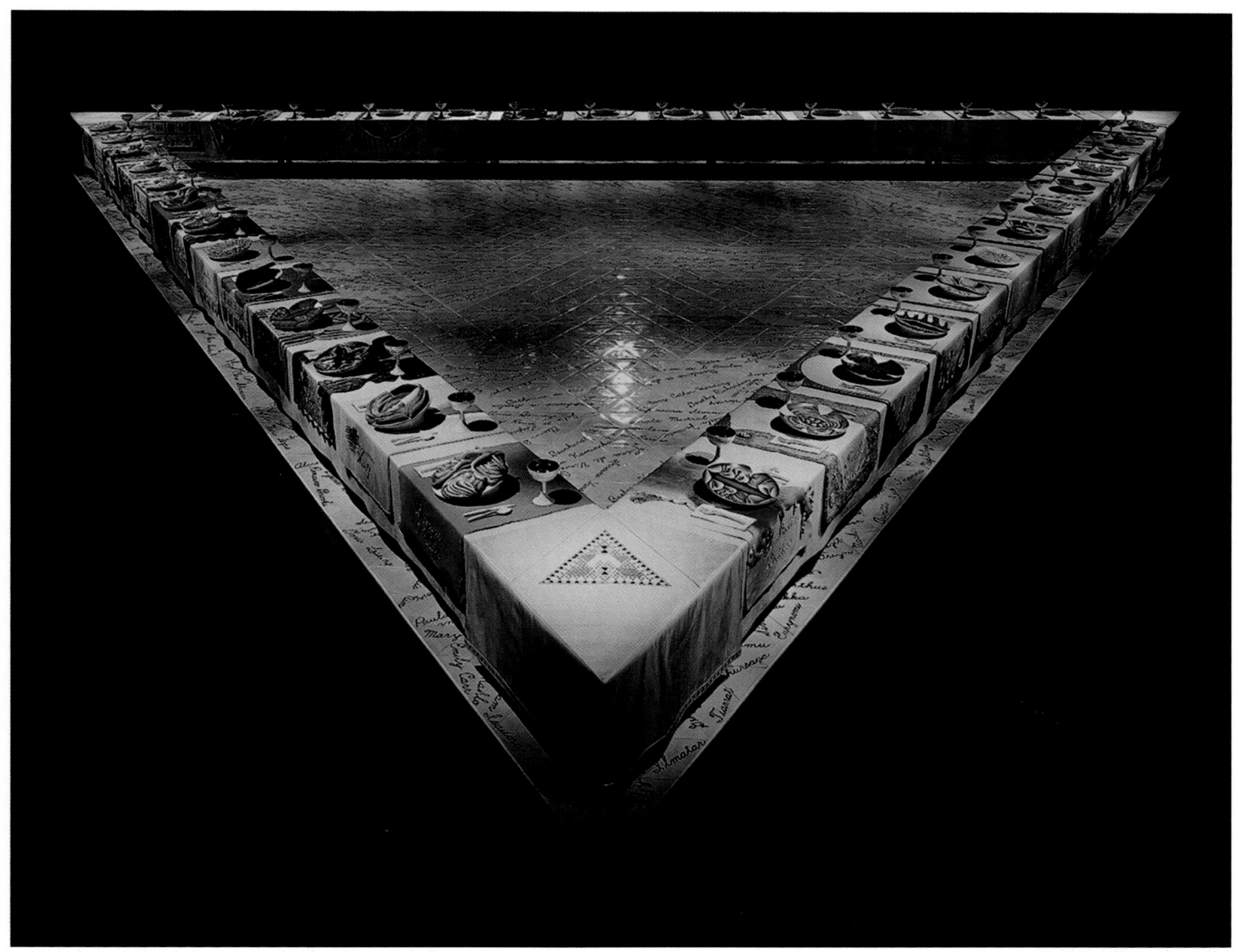

29.34 Judy Chicago, *The Dinner Party*. 1979. Mixed media, 3 × 48 × 42' (0.9 × 17.6 × 12.8 m).
Brooklyn Museum of Art, New York

ally turned to mediums associated with women—painted china, ceramics, and embroidery—and created an elegant, beautiful work that subtly operates on an epic scale, spanning millennia. Also present is a sense of community and ritual, for we feel as though Chicago has appropriated and transformed the Christian male theme of the Last Supper into a spiritual communion of women.

LATE MODERNIST ARCHITECTURE

Modernist architecture thrived after World War II, especially in America, which had previously preferred traditionalist architecture (skyscrapers, for example, in a Gothic style) as discussed in the previous chapter (see pages 1020–21). But now Modernist architecture was only a look or style. It no longer had the utopian vision and revolutionary zeal to improve the world that we saw in the High Modernism of De Stijl and the Bauhaus (see pages

1007–10), and in the art and design of Constructivist Productivism (see pages 1003–05). However, some of the most influential buildings of the period continued to be built by the major High Modernist architects: Wright, Mies van der Rohe, and Le Corbusier. While Mies continued the International Style aesthetic of light, floating geometric buildings with taut, thin glass walls, Frank Lloyd Wright and Le Corbusier, joined by the emerging Philadelphia architect Louis Kahn, developed a sculptural architecture that emphasized mass and the physical presence of a building, and they were not afraid to be referential.

Continuing the International Style: *Ludwig Mies van der Rohe*

Postwar Late Modernism resulted in glass boxes sprouting up in urban centers and dotting the beltways that circled American cities, especially beginning in the 1960s and 1970s. The glass box begin to approach the perfection that Mies achieved with his aesthetic of "Less is more" (see page 1010).

We can see these minimal gestures in the Seagram Building. Mies began by removing the 38-story building from its urban environment and placing it on a pedestal, that is a plaza elevated above street level. The plaza is simple but sumptuous; it is made of pink granite, has two shallow pools placed symmetrically on either side of the building, and is surrounded by a low serpentine marble wall. The weightless tinted glass-and-bronze tower sits on a colonnade of pilotis that leaves the first floor open, and every detail, including the paving stones, is carefully proportioned to create a sense of perfection and elegance. With the rise of Hitler in Germany, Mies had joined Moholy-Nagy at the new Bauhaus in Chicago, and in the Seagram Building we can see the influence of the nineteenth-century Chicago School in the emphasis on the skeletal grid of the building. To acknowledge the functionalism of the grid, Mies used thin I-beams for the mullions between windows. They provide the vertical accent that the proportions of the horizontal spandrels so perfectly counterbalance with their thin ridges on top and bottom. Inside and out, lavish, beautifully harmonized materials embellish the building's exquisite proportions.

Sculptural Architecture: Referential Mass

Mies's architecture was essentially nonreferential, just like Minimalist sculpture. However, his contemporaries Le Corbusier and Frank Lloyd Wright took Late Modernist architecture in a different direction. Their buildings contain references and are organic, if not outright expressionistic. Made of poured concrete, they are massive monumental buildings that have a powerful sculptural presence.

LE CORBUSIER In his late style, Le Corbusier abandoned the taunt, light walls and floating architecture of his early villas for a massive, sculptural, and even referential style. This late work can be quite expressive, even to the point of being oppressively massive and harsh, and it is often referred to as Brutalist. Especially abrasive is his use of concrete, which instead of being smooth and highly finished is now left raw, having a rough texture and revealing the pattern of the wood forms.

A sculptural masterpiece from this period is Notre-Dame-du-Haut (fig. **29.36**), a chapel in Ronchamp, France, built from 1950 to 1955. While the main interior space is basically simple, an oblong nave, the exterior erupts with diagonals and curves. The concrete-covered masonry walls are thick and massive, and the poured concrete roof, which is hollow and the concrete left raw, is ponderous, even if it paradoxically seems to float. Visitors enter the front through an enormous fissure in the wall, giving them a sense of slipping through a cleft in a rock formation. The pointed façade reminds us of a ship's prow, while the roof recalls the bottom of a boat, allusions to such vessels of salvation as Noah's Ark and St. Peter's fishing boat. But these shapes also suggest a nun's cowl, praying hands, and a church spire. The vertical towerlike

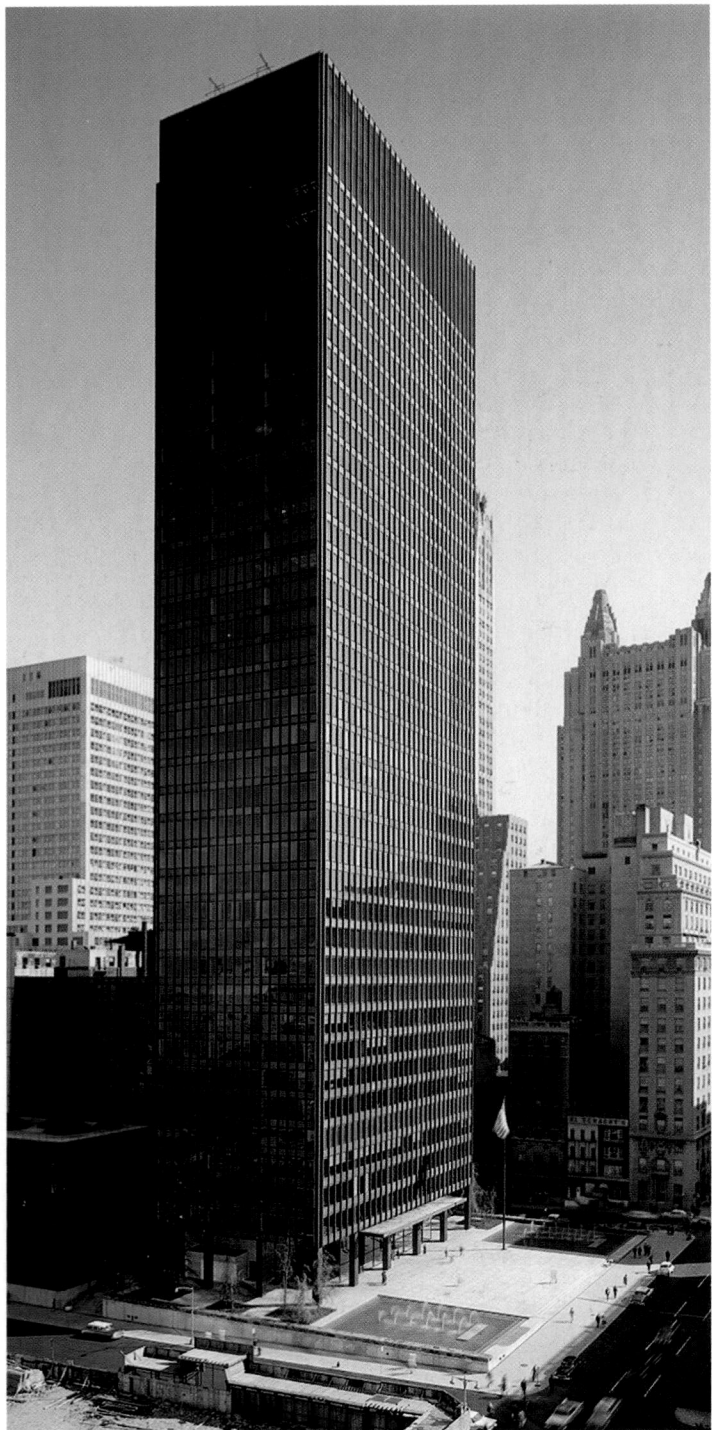

29.35 Ludwig Mies van der Rohe and Philip Johnson. Seagram Building, New York. 1954–58

became the required image for corporate headquarters, such as I. M. Pei and Henry N. Cobb's John Hancock Center in Boston (1977) and Skidmore, Owens, and Merrill's Sears Tower in Chicago (1974). If one were to choose a single building to epitomize the Late Modernist skyscraper it would have to be Mies van der Rohe's Seagram Building (fig. **29.35**) in New York, built from 1954 to 1958, with interiors by Philip Johnson (1906–2005). This building was imitated worldwide, but rarely did the imitations

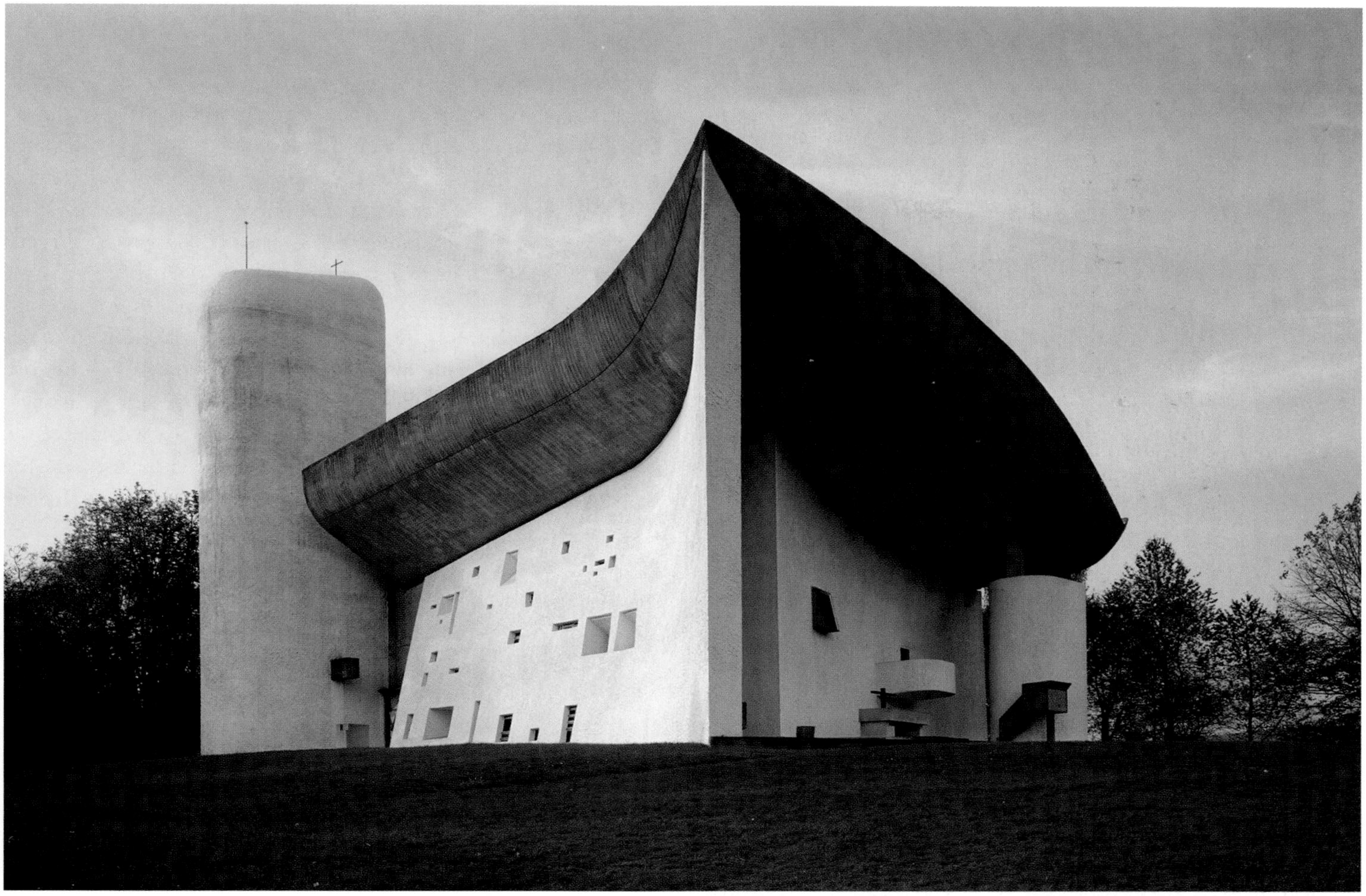

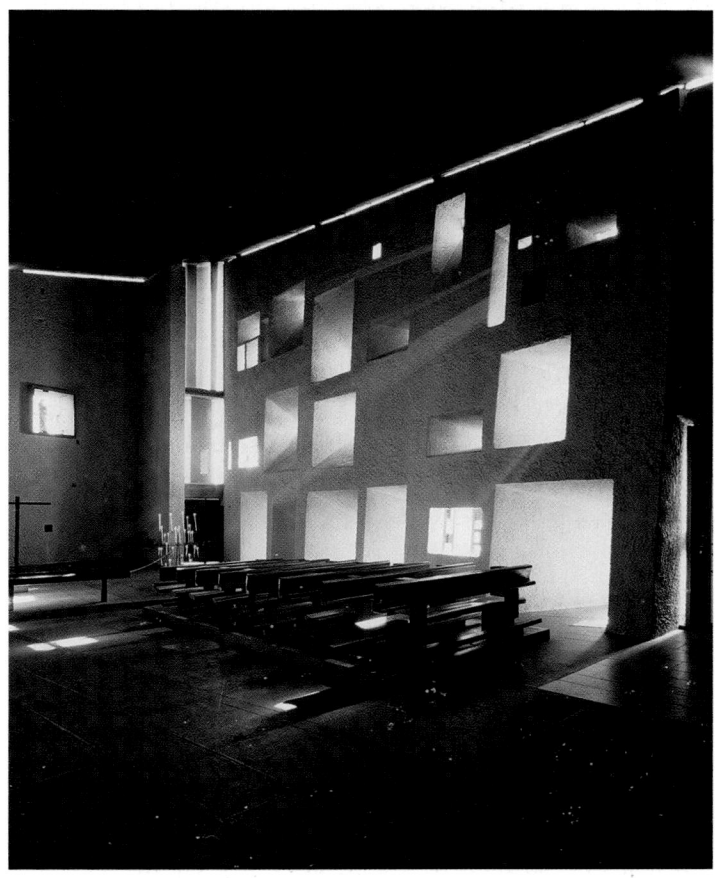

29.36 Le Corbusier. Notre-Dame-du-Haut (from the southeast), Ronchamp, France. 1950–55

forms to the left, a bell tower, and right resemble the nearby prehistoric dolmens of Carnac (see fig. 1.24). A sense of the primordial continues in the cavelike interior, where the ceiling precipitously drops from 32 feet over the altar to 16 feet in the center of the room. Faint streams of colored light pierce the stained-glass windows set in the thick walls (fig. **29.37**), gently illuminating the space and giving it a mystical aura. Regardless of religion, anyone visiting Notre-Dame-du-Haut is likely to be transported to the realm of the mysterious and magical.

FRANK LLOYD WRIGHT Rising almost simultaneously in New York as Mies van der Rohe's Seagram Building was Frank Lloyd Wright's Solomon R. Guggenheim Museum, located some 50 blocks north in Manhattan. For a discussion of this building, see the Introduction and fig. I.16.

29.37 Le Corbusier. Interior of Notre-Dame-du-Haut.

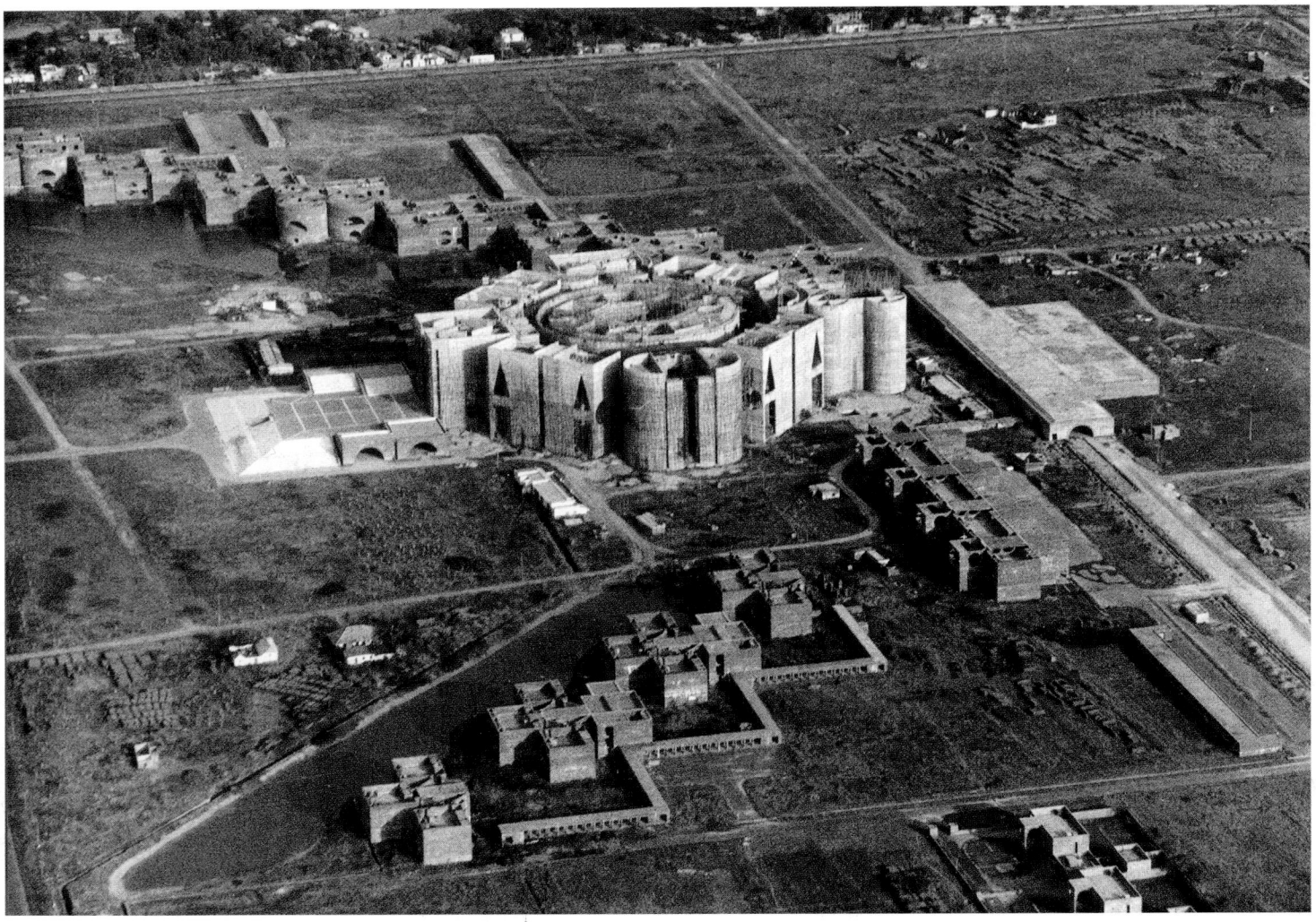

29.38 Louis Kahn. National Assembly Building, Dacca, Bangladesh. 1962

LOUIS KAHN Louis Kahn (1901–1974) is a difficult artist to place and is alternatively labeled an Expressionist, a Brutalist, and a Proto-Postmodernist. He was in his fifties when he finally found his architectural voice, largely due to a year spent at the American Academy in Rome in 1950–51. Here, he awakened to the importance and power of the ancient monuments of the Mediterranean, from the pyramids of Egypt to the baths and aqueducts of Rome to the Athenian Akropolis. Their bold, sculptural forms and pure geometry evoked a timeless serenity and Classical grandeur and became the building blocks of his Modernist aesthetic. In the late 1950s, Kahn discovered the Expressionist, Brutalist style of late Le Corbusier, of whom Kahn said, "He was my teacher, although he didn't know it." He rejected High Modernism's emphasis on light volume defined by a taut membrane as he instead designed massive, weighty structures that evoked ancient civilizations that seemed capable of defying the ravages of time.

We can see these qualities in his 1962 ferroconcrete National Assembly Building in Dacca, Bangladesh (fig. 29.38). The assembly chamber is in the center, surrounded by concentric circles of meeting rooms, press offices, and a mosque, each building separated by unroofed walkways, creating a veritable light-filled city. Monumental triangles, rectangles, and circles puncture the massive walls of each ring of rooms, allowing light to filter in and virtually structure the space. The entire complex looks like a fortress, the outer wall projecting the sublime presence of antiquity, although functionally it is designed to keep out the harsh sun of the Indian subcontinent. As we shall see in the next chapter, Kahn's referential architecture would inspire the next generation of architects.

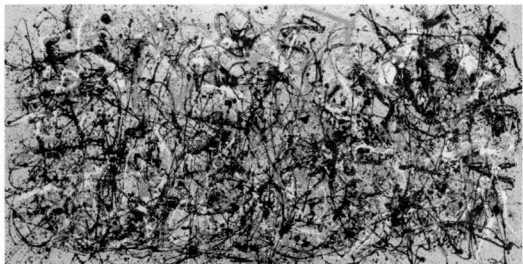

1950 Jackson Pollock's *Autumn Rhythm: Number 30*

1954-58 Ludwig Mies van der Rohe's Seagram Building

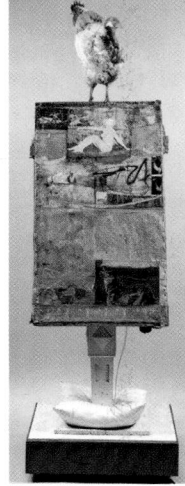

1955-58 Robert Rauschenberg's *Odalisk*

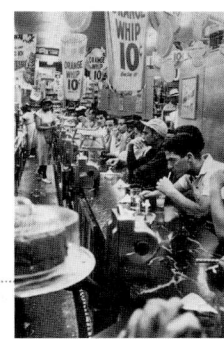

1955 Robert Frank's *Drugstore, Detroit*

1962 Andy Warhol's *Campbell's Soup Cans*

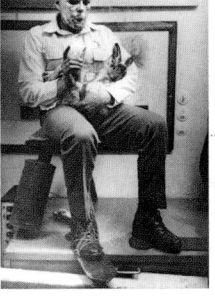

1965 Joseph Beuys's *How to Explain Pictures to a Dead Hare*

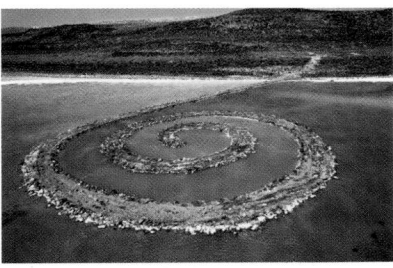

1970 Robert Smithson, *Spiral Jetty*

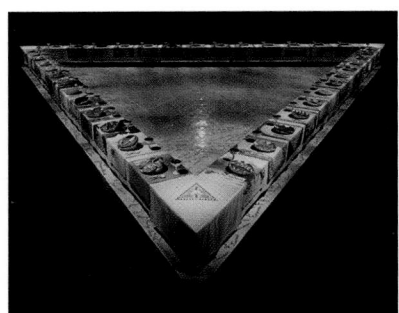

1979 Judy Chicago's *The Dinner Party*

Postwar to Postmodern, 1945–1980

1940

1950

1960

1970

1980

◄ 1945-49 Jean-Paul Sartre publishes his existential trilogy *Les Chemins de la Liberté* (*The Roads to Freedom*)

◄ 1950-53 Korean War

◄ 1955-68 First phase of the civil rights movement
◄ 1956 Tunisia gains independence from France, launching the independence movement in Africa
1956 William H. Whyte publishes *The Organization Man*, a description of impact of mass organization, especially corporations, on the United States
◄ 1957 Jack Kerouac publishes *On the Road*
1957 Russia launches Sputnik I

◄ 1963 Betty Friedan publishes *The Feminine Mystique*
◄ ca. 1965 Commercial portable video cameras become available
1965 United States enters the Vietnam War
◄ 1966 Jewish Museum, New York, mounts *Primary Structures*, first exhibition of Minimal Art
◄ 1968 The leftist student protest and strikes in Paris in May that eventually brought about the fall of the De Gaulle government
◄ 1969 Stonewall riots in New York City as gays respond to police persecution
◄ 1969 Woodstock Festival, Bethel, New York
◄ 1969 Moon landing
◄ 1970 Museum of Modern Art, New York presents *Information*, first exhibition of Conceptual Art
◄ 1971 Greenpeace Foundation founded

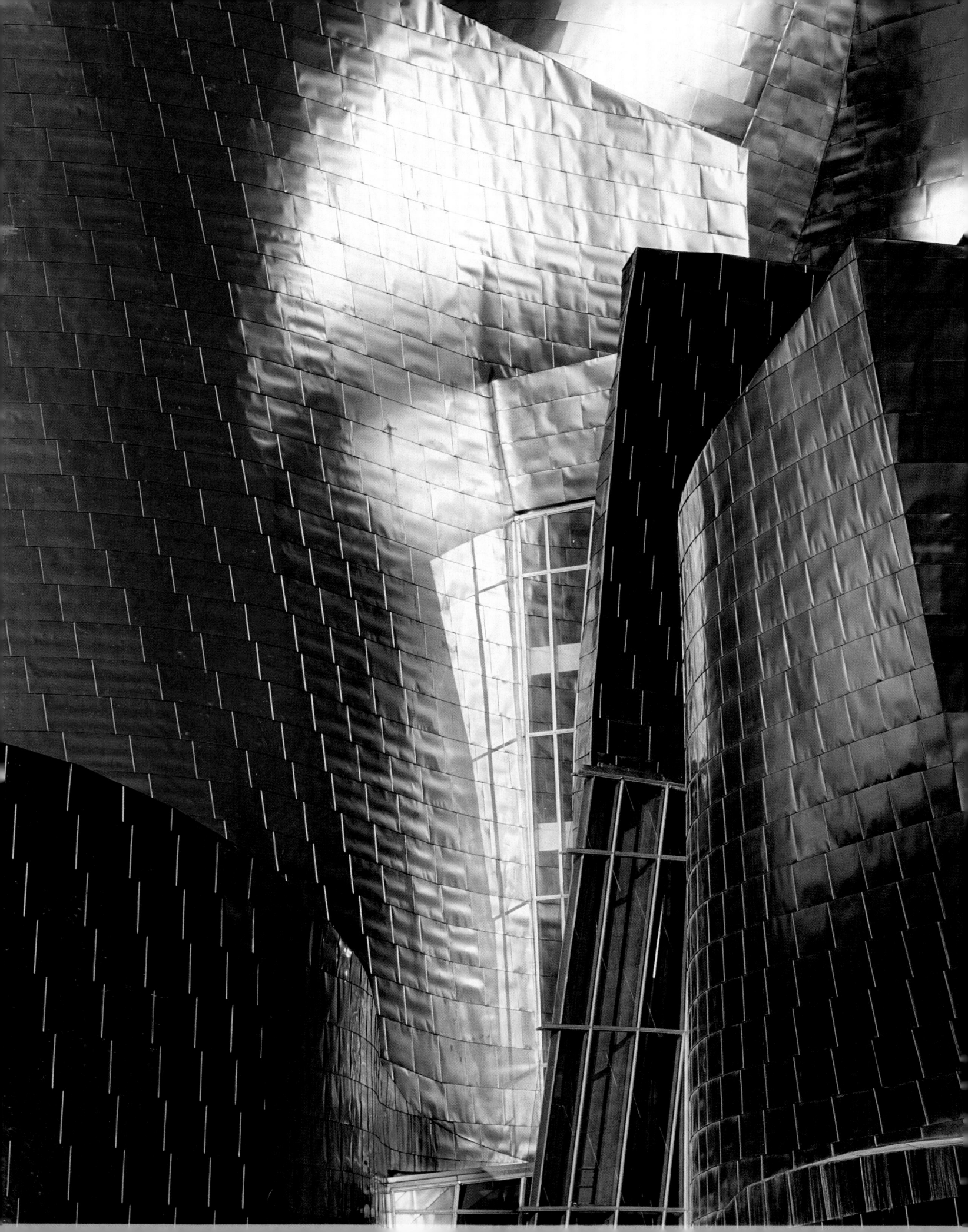

CHAPTER 30

The Postmodern Era: Art Since 1980

THE ART THAT CAME TO THE ART WORLD'S ATTENTION TOWARD 1980 is generally known as Postmodern art. The term was coined in the mid-1960s by European literary critics, and was applied to the theories of such French philosophers as Jacques Derrida (1930–2004), Roland Barthes (1915–1980), and Michel Foucault (1926–1984), as well as to the sociologist

and cultural critic Jean Baudrillard (1979–2007) and psychoanalyst Jacques Lacan (1901–1981). At the heart of much European Postmodernism, which is also called Deconstructionism or Post-Structuralism, is the premise that all text, and by extension visual art, contains hidden hierarchies of meaning "by which," as Derrida expressed it, "an order is imposed on reality and by which a subtle repression is exercised, as their hierarchies exclude, subordinate, and hide the various potential meanings." In other words, any text or artwork has an agenda, or point of view, as does any interpretation or use of a text or art. Revealing this agenda means "deconstructing" it. The result is there are no fixed truths or realities, no absolutes—just "hierarchies," which are forever changing. We shall see an especially fine example of this theory later in the chapter when we look at the art of Fred Wilson, who in 1992 placed slave manacles in a case of fine silver at the Maryland Historical Society in Baltimore (see fig. 30.19). The society was presenting the silver as refined aesthetic objects, reflecting the evolution of style. By inserting the manacles, Wilson changed the context of the silver, and thus he changed its meaning as well—now the goblets, pitchers, and teapots became icons of wealth brought about by the enslavement of blacks. As reflected in Wilson's deconstruction of the historical society's display, artists and critics starting in the late 1970s began to digest

European Postmodernism and were applying it to art. They were especially interested in how art functioned as a visual language, particularly as one of propaganda, manipulation, and power that determined taste and values and structured, for example, ethnic, sexual, racial, and gender identities.

In a sense, these ideas were not entirely new to the 1970s art world. We have already seen Marcel Duchamp dealing with similar issues in the 1910s, and Robert Rauschenberg, George Brecht, Joseph Kosuth, Roy Lichtenstein, Andy Warhol, and especially Sigmar Polke touching on them as well in the 1950s and 1960s. While the immediate seeds of Postmodernism in the visual arts date from this time, a self-consciousness about entering a new era only occurred in the art world in the late 1970s. In large part, this new awareness stemmed from the critical writing in a new art magazine, *October*, founded in 1976, which reflected European Postmodern philosophy. (See www.myartslab.com.) As a result, a large number of artists and critics asked more overtly and persistently: How do words and images acquire meaning? What is the message? Who originates it? What—and whose—purpose does it serve? Who is the audience and what does this tell us about the message? Who controls the media—and for whom? More and more artists, such as Fred Wilson, began using familiar images in new contexts, revealing—or *deconstructing*—their deeper social, political, economic, and aesthetic meanings. The preferred mediums for many of these artists were those of the mass media, namely photography, electronic signs, billboards, and video.

Frank Gehry. Guggenheim Museum, Bilbao, Spain. See also figure 30.9

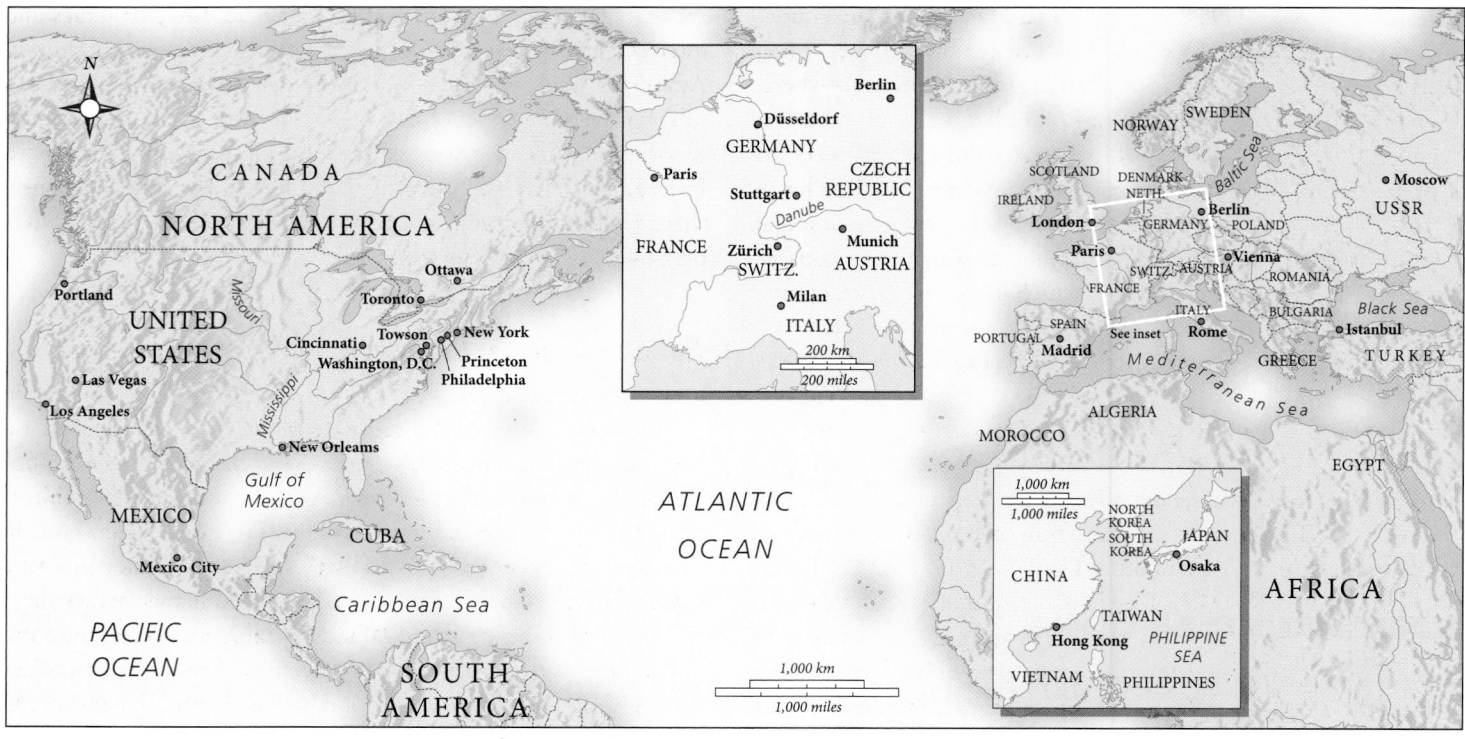

Map 30.1 Europe and North America in the 21st century

While this Postmodernist attitude emerged toward 1980, it has been only one of numerous issues that have preoccupied the art world in the last 30 years. The period is characterized by pluralism, in effect continuing the pluralism associated with 1970s Post-Minimalism (see pages 1058–69). Now, however, pluralism had a philosophical foundation in Postmodern theory. By denying any one system, reading, interpretation, or truth, Postmodern theory destroyed the credibility of the authoritarian hierarchies of styles, mediums, issues, and themes, and it opened the door for everything and everyone. It also had an enormous impact on art history, as art historians began to question the validity of the traditional story of art, generally told from a narrow viewpoint, generally male-centric and European-American, and emphasizing the evolution of style. Now, scholars approached art from countless angles, using issues of gender, sexual orientation, ethnicity, race, economics, and politics to demonstrate the many layers of meaning and ideas embedded in a work of art. In part, this trend had begun in the late 1960s, a result of the social revolution that accompanied the civil rights movement and the Vietnam War and challenged the validity of the status quo.

Postmodernism marked the end of the Modernist era, which peaked in the 1950s and 1960s with such styles as Abstract Expressionism and Minimal Art. Modernism viewed modern art as a linear progression of one style building upon the last, continuously advancing art toward the "new." Because of this emphasis on style, tremendous importance was placed on the individual and stylistic originality. But the pluralism of the 1970s accompanied by Postmodern theory ended the need for artists to invent the new. By the 1980s, artists had license *not* to be new. Not only did

they appropriate art in every imaginable style and medium from the history of civilization and combine them as they saw fit, many of the leading artists, such as Felix Gonzalez-Torres, Jeff Koons, Kiki Smith, and Damien Hirst, did not even concern themselves with cultivating a distinguishable style as they jumped from one medium to the next, relying on a theme rather than a look to tie their work together. Message was more important than a readily identifiable, single style, a hallmark of Modernism. Artists also challenged the premium that Modernism placed on individuality and authorship, with many artists collaborating or working in groups, such as the Guerrilla Girls and Group Material.

The Postmodern era also redefined the nature of the art world itself. The art establishment widened to embrace artists of all ethnicities and races, accepting all kinds of mediums, styles, and issues without placing a value on one over another. In this new environment, often referred to as multiculturalism, artists who had been marginalized in the 1970s became mainstream. Furthermore, in the 1990s, artists from all over the world, not just America and Europe, played a major role in molding contemporary art. A benchmark exhibition for presenting this new world view was *Magiciens de la Terre*, organized in 1988 by the National Museum of Modern Art (Pompidou Center) in Paris and featuring artists from all the continents.

The acceptance of artists worldwide mirrors the global restructuring of the last 20 years. The Cold War ended as the Berlin Wall fell in 1988 and the U.S.S.R. was dissolved soon after. Political and economic realignments resulted as first Russia and then China abandoned a strict adherence to Communism, experimented with capitalism, and opened up to foreign trade and investment. In the 1990s, Europe formed the European Union, and the United States, Mexico, and Canada signed the North American Free Trade Agreement. Barriers were falling everywhere, with people crossing borders more readily than ever before. Another important force behind the creation of a world art is the long-term impact of the independence movements, especially in Africa and Asia, of the 1950s and 1960s. These new post-colonial nations asserted their cultural traditions as viable and valuable alternatives to mainstream culture, which in the last 25 years have increasingly been woven into the fabric of a world culture.

But perhaps the communications field more than anything else was responsible for the creation of the "Global Village." Television, cellular phones, satellites, computers, global positioning systems, and the Internet have linked the world, reminding us that the Post-Industrial era is also the Information Age. Today, the world's leading artists come from countries as varied as Lebanon, Iran, Israel, Cambodia, Thailand, Korea, India, Japan, China, South Africa, Mali, Russia, Colombia, Brazil, Cuba, and Iceland. They readily travel the globe, often have studios in numerous countries, and exhibit regularly worldwide, especially participating in the international explosion of contemporary art fairs and annual or biennial art shows that take place in such disparate venues as Istanbul, Dubai, Moscow, Johannesburg, Saigon, Havana, and Shanghai.

In this world of complex media and changing interpretations, scholars do not always agree on the meaning of Postmodernism. While the term initially was applied specifically to the European philosophy that emerged in the 1960s, today scholars and art historians use it quite loosely to encompass all of the art made since 1980. In effect, they use it to mean art made after Modernism, and we will use it in the same way here. But the sign that we have nonetheless entered a new era is the fact that we can no longer treat art as a succession of isms or styles. While some historians and critics have tried to identify movements or styles, such as Neo-Expressionism, Neo-Geo, and Neo-Conceptualism, these are forced labels that do not hold up to scrutiny. Unlike the other chapters in this book, the fine art will be presented not within the context of style but instead under headings of theme or issue.

ARCHITECTURE

Postmodernism appeared in architecture in the 1960s and was accompanied by a manifesto of sorts. In his book *Complexity and Contradiction* (1966), the architect Robert Venturi called for a new architecture, one that rejected the cold, abstract Modernist International Style. The new architecture would be referential, that is, buildings would recall earlier architectural styles, or contain motifs that referred to the past and present. By the 1980s, an architecture that the architectural community labeled "Postmodern" had emerged. The term, however, was used specifically to describe work that made references to earlier periods and styles.

Since fundamental to European Postmodern theory is the concept that no one authoritative style or set of principles can prevail,

architecture since the 1980s reflects a broad range of issues and interests, going well beyond just designing referential buildings. Among them is a revised Modernism, one strain of which we can call Hi-Tech because of its highly technological appearance. Another strain is Deconstructivism, a concept relating to Derrida's theories of Deconstruction and embracing the notion that architecture should not have a fixed structure or logic, thus being wide open to interpretation.

Postmodern Architecture: A Referential Style

Modernist architecture, best characterized by High Modernism or the International Style (see page 1010), was rule-bound and abstract. Some architectural critics—as well as the general public—found it cold and impersonal. With Postmodernist architecture, buildings, as in the nineteenth century, once again contain references to earlier architectural styles. Sometimes they project a sense of place, imparting an aura of uniqueness that makes them special to those using them. While Postmodern architecture did not come to the fore until about 1980, a handful of architects had been advocating and practicing a new architecture by the 1960s, among them Robert Venturi.

ROBERT VENTURI Robert Venturi (b. 1925) upset the architectural establishment by attacking Modernist architecture in *Complexity and Contradiction*. He challenged Mies van der Rohe's dictum "Less is more" with "Less is a bore" and argued that architecture could be whatever the architect wanted it to be. He asserted that art and the architectural past, as well as life itself, are filled with complexity and contradiction, and buildings should be too. Instead of being pure, simple, and conventional, buildings should be complicated, rich, and filled with references to the past and to the present as well. Buildings should contain meanings, even if these are contradictory, as had been the case in Mannerist architecture (see page 592). And structures could be fun and humorous as well as serious. Venturi's idol was Louis Kahn, who was also based in Philadelphia and whose Modernist buildings, such as the National Assembly Building (see fig. 29.38) in Dacca, Bangladesh, are filled with overt historical references. Venturi admired Kahn's daring use of symbolism and historical layering. Venturi outraged the architectural world again in 1972, when he published *Learning from Las Vegas* with his wife, the architect Denise Scott Brown. The couple declared Los Angeles and Las Vegas to be the modern-day equivalents of ancient Rome and Renaissance Florence, and they proposed that the strip malls, neon signs, and highways of these American cities reflected contemporary needs and a new architectural language, one that should be embraced by architects.

Venturi practiced what he preached. In 1962, he designed a house for his mother in Chestnut Hill, Philadelphia (fig. **30.1**). The structure resembles a Modernist abstraction of flat planes, strict geometry, clean lines, and a play of forms and spaces, notably in the enormous cleft in the center of the façade. But the house is also referential, for it is a parody of a conventional

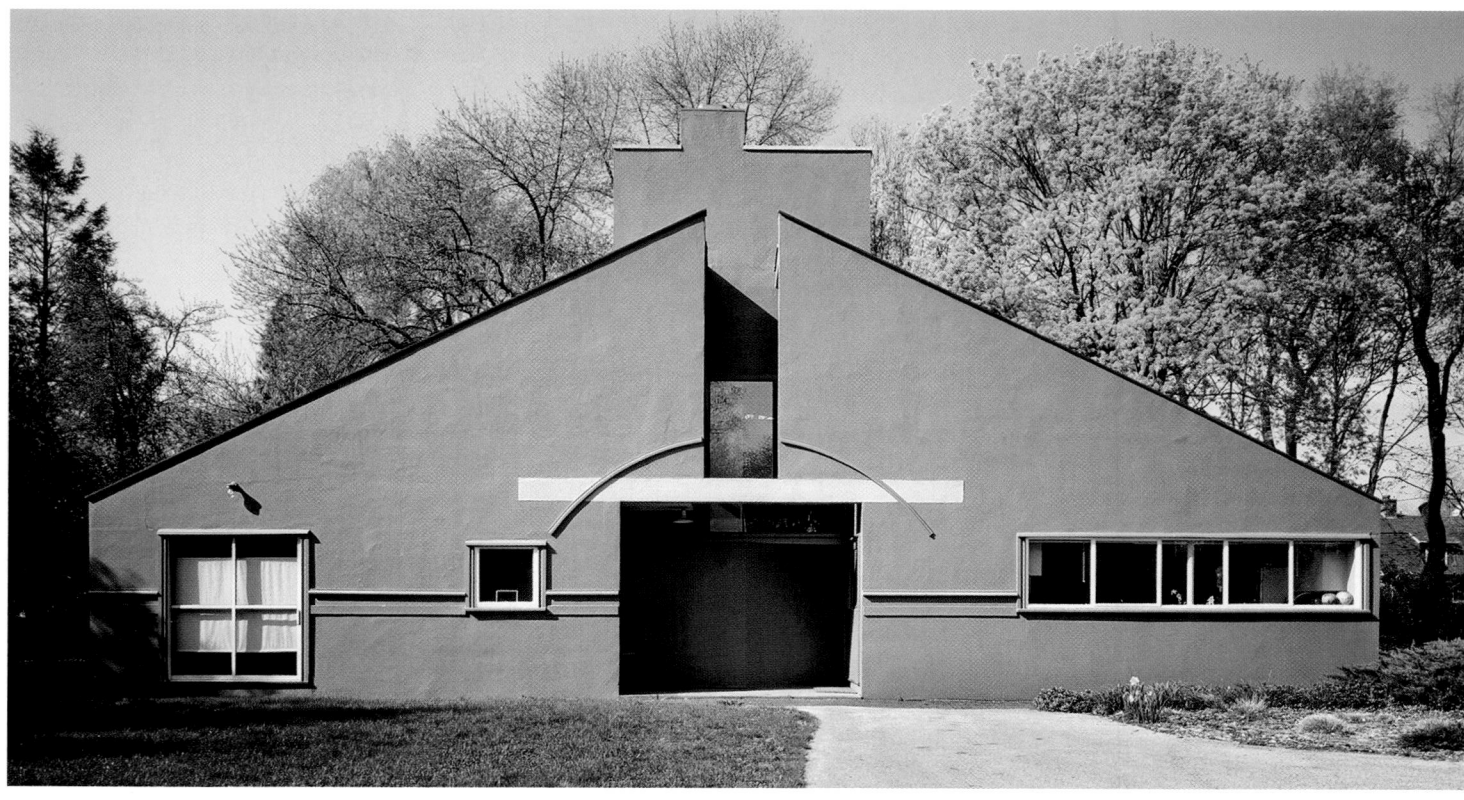

30.1   Robert Venturi. Vanna Venturi House, Chestnut Hill, Philadelphia. 1962. Venturi, Scott Brown and Associates, Inc.

American home, complete with a slanted gable (the actual roof is much lower), a nineteenth-century pane-glass window, twentieth-century tract-house sliding-glass windows, a front porch, and behind that a large rectangular block that looks like a chimney but is not, since the real chimney, much smaller, pokes up out of it. Venturi then complicates the house with endless architectural references—the cleft, for example, derives from Kahn's medieval-city buildings with slotted parapets and lintels embedded in the wall. The use of the "lintel," which seems to support the two halves of the façade, combined with the opening of the porch, recalls an Egyptian pylon, while the broken segmental arch, functioning like a molding, brings to mind Pierre Lescot's Square Court at the Louvre (see fig. 18.2). Venturi has imbued the overscale house with humor, irony, and allusions, transforming the traditional American home into a rich architectural statement.

MICHAEL GRAVES   The American architect whose name is perhaps most synonymous with Postmodern architecture is Michael Graves (b. 1934), who is based in Princeton, New Jersey. He rose to national attention in 1980 when he received a commission for the Public Services Building (fig. **30.2**) in Portland, Oregon. The design is filled with paradox, as every element on the building's surface begs to be seen in several ways: flat and sculptural, representational and abstract, historical and modern.

The form of the building is a Palladian cube sitting atop a platform, with the square or near-square motif echoed in the outline of the façade and in additional squares within (for example, the

enormous mirror-glass window, which encases a square defined by the maroon vertical piers). The individual windows are each 4 feet square. The wall can be read as a flat mural, a thin Modernist membrane stretched over the metal skeleton; but suddenly it becomes three-dimensional and sculptural, an effect heightened by the maroon-colored vertical shafts in front of the large mirror window. These mullionlike shafts become the fluting of pilasters, topped with bracket capitals, which support an enormous keystone above. Yet, if you read the keystone with the beige-colored wall, it becomes part of a flat arch framing the mirror window. The façade can even be described as anthropomorphic, for the pilasters and keystone can be read as a huge face, the capitals as eyes, and the pilasters as legs. The building has a whimsical sense of play, but it is also serious, recalling such great historical models as Palladio, Mannerism, and one of Graves's favorite predecessors, John Soane, who is reflected here in the sublime pilasters (see fig. 24.30). The enormous curtain-wall window, massive corner piers, and prominent "pediment" bring to mind Behrens's Turbinenfabrik (see fig. 27.35), not coincidentally one of the great Early Modernist buildings made just before Modernism abandoned all overt reference to the historical past.

JAMES STIRLING   As subtle, complex, and difficult as Graves is the London architect James Stirling (1926–1992), as can be seen in his Neue Staatsgalerie in Stuttgart (fig. **30.3**). This museum and theater complex is located on the side of a steep hill, with a highway at its base and a city street above. Like Kahn's National

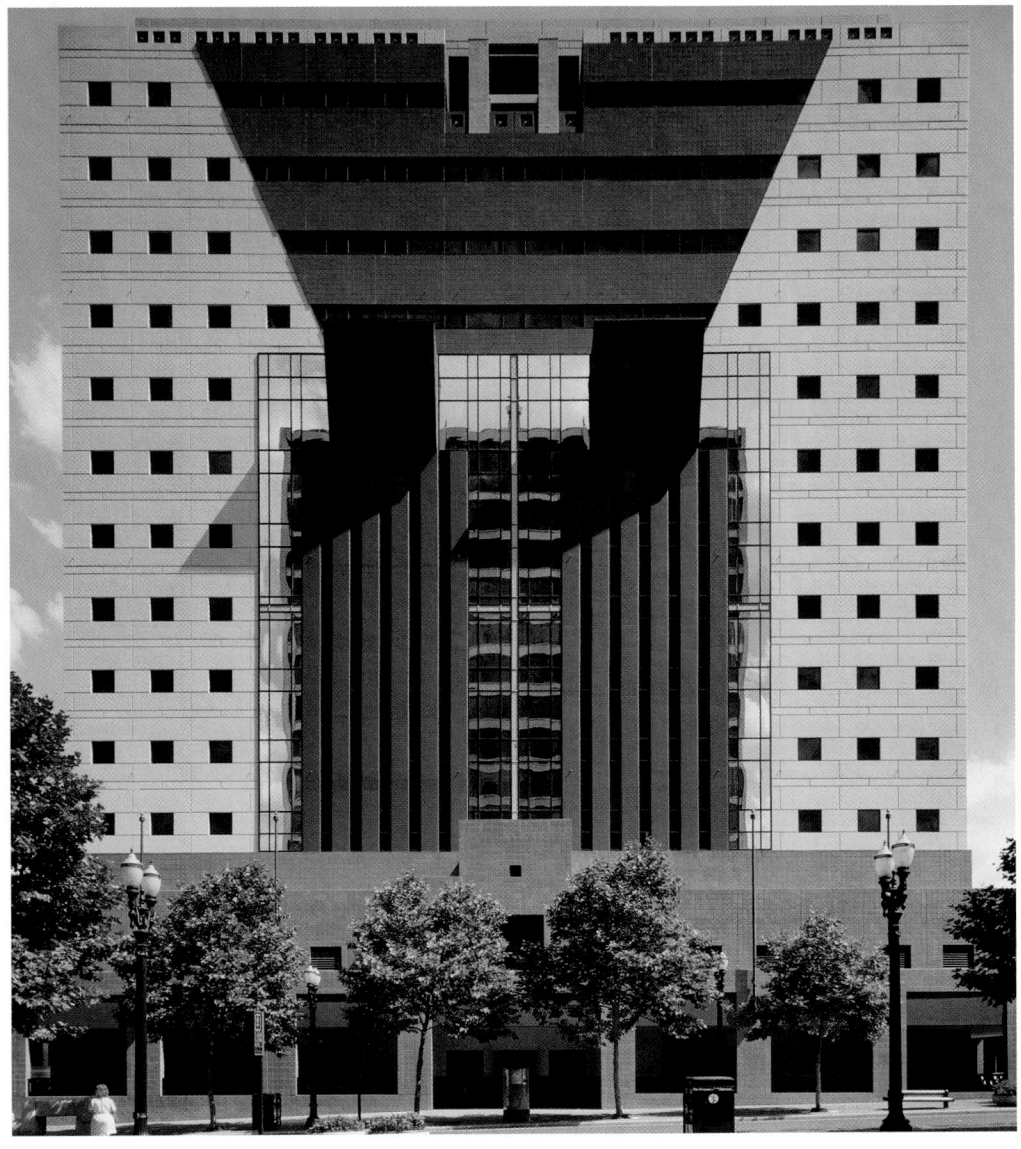

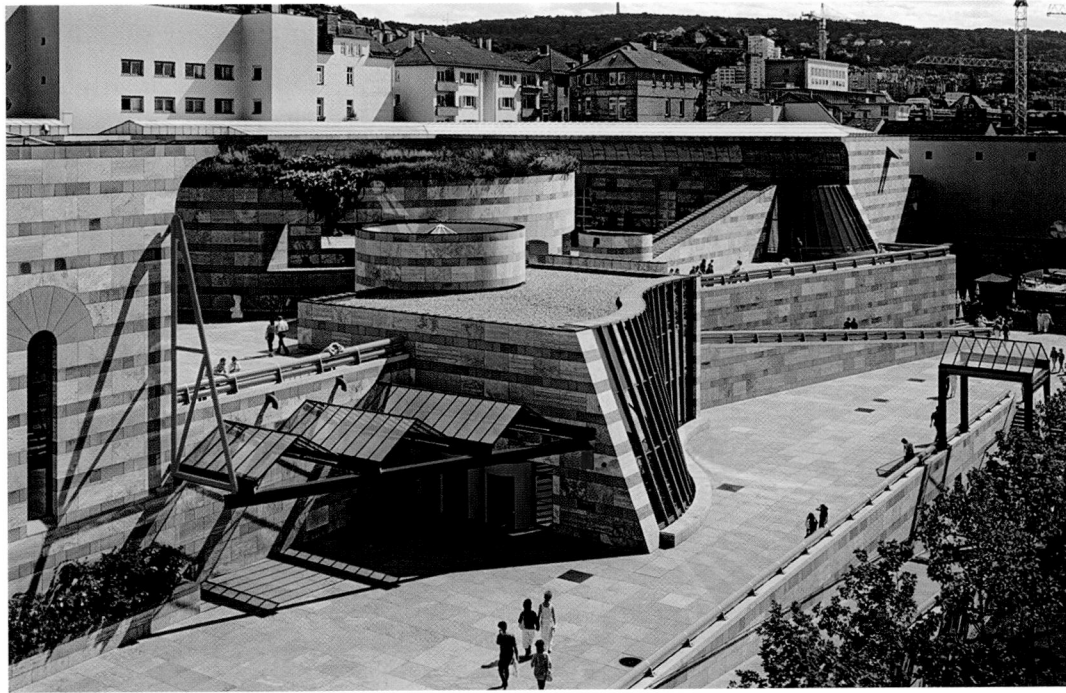

30.3 James Stirling. Neue Staatsgalerie, Stuttgart. 1977–83

Assembly Building, Stirling's bold massing of simple forms and switchback ramps evoke ancient civilizations. Egypt especially comes to mind because of the large pylonlike forms and clefts that allow for narrow passageways. The pattern of alternating sandstone and travertine suggests medieval Italian structures, while the enormous wavelike window of the museum reverberates with memories of Paxton's Crystal Palace (see fig. 25.39) and the great curtain-wall window in Behrens's Turbinenfabrik. The curving window also suggests a grand piano, reminding us of the building's function as a performance hall. The pink and blue tubular railing and the blue I-beam support for the "pedimented" museum entrance are Hi-Tech and industrial. The same can be said for the skeletal taxi stand, whose ferrovitreous construction is also reminiscent of Paxton, while its form recalls a Greek temple. As in the work of Venturi and Graves, all these familiar sources are seamlessly melded into a unified vision that brings the past into the present. The result is a building that is distinctly modern yet imparts a Kahn-like monumentality and aura of importance.

New Modernisms: High-Tech Architecture

Late 1970s and 1980s Postmodernist architecture, with its historicism and symbolism, was important for launching new architectural freedoms. Released from the narrow constraints of pure Modernism, architects were free to explore a new range of possibilities that went well beyond the eclectic historical references of Postmodernism. Facilitating and even encouraging artistic license was the worldwide economic boom of the 1980s and 1990s, when unprecedented amounts of private and corporate money poured into building projects, dramatically energizing architecture and architectural vision. Just as New York real-estate developers in the 1920s had competed to create the tallest building, so clients worldwide now strove to erect the most spectacular, exciting structure, one with international cachet. At every level, the public was no longer settling for undistinguished generic Modernist buildings. Even the American strip malls of the 1980s were designed as Mediterranean minicities (Victorian, Queen Anne, Tudor, and Romanesque were popular styles as well), with many

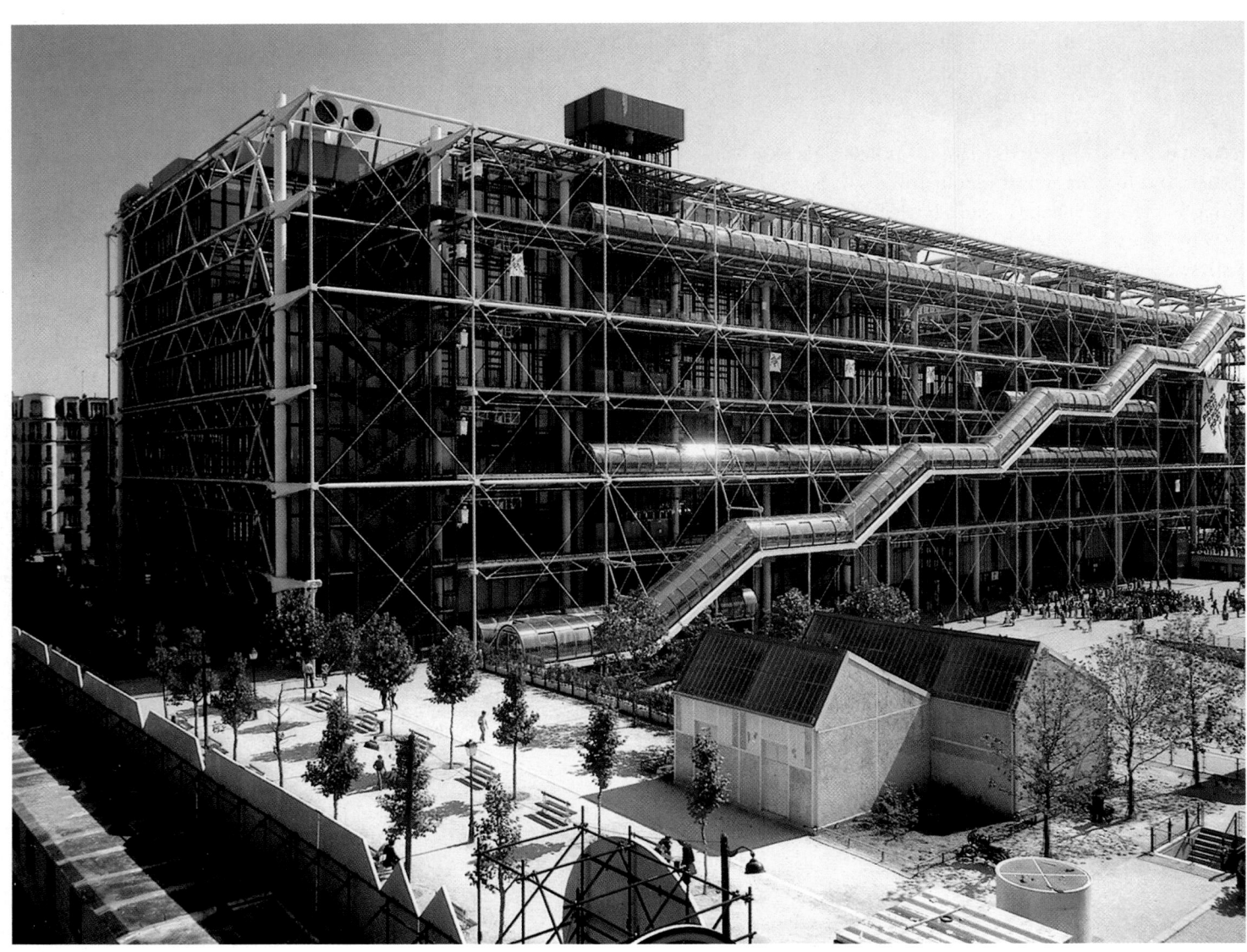

30.4 Richard Rogers and Renzo Piano. Centre National d'Art et Culture Georges Pompidou, Paris. 1971–77

of those built in earlier decades in a Modernist style getting Postmodern facelifts.

Major Postmodern architecture in the vein of Venturi and Graves faded in the 1990s, superseded by an exhilarating diversity that expanded architecture to a true Postmodernism, if we use the term in its broadest sense to mean pluralism. Many architects now revisited Modernism, reinvigorating it with the new artistic license that had emerged during the late 1970s. An extreme version of this New Modernism is Hi-Tech, whose buildings resemble powerful industrial machines. Like Postmodern architecture, the most immediate roots of Hi-Tech design can be found in a few examples in the 1950s and 1960s, one of the earliest being James Stirling's 1959–63 Engineering School in Leicester, England. Perhaps the most famous prototype for Hi-Tech Modernism is the 1971–77 Pompidou Center (fig. **30.4**) in Paris. There, architects Richard Rogers (b. 1933) and Renzo Piano (b. 1937) exposed the building's utilities—instead of being buried within the interior, they are displayed on scaffolding around the perimeter of what is otherwise a classical Modernist glass box. Elevators, escalators, and plumbing, electrical, and ventilation ducts are all prominently displayed as exterior "ornament." Besides challenging architectural aesthetics, this device has the advantage of completely opening up the interior space, allowing for any necessary configuration.

NORMAN FOSTER By the late 1970s, Hi-Tech Modernism had come to the fore, its arrival announced in part by the eye-popping Hong Kong and Shanghai Bank (HKSB) (fig. **30.5**), designed in 1979 by Norman Foster (b. 1935) at a cost of $1 billion. Here was a skyscraper that did not look like a skyscraper. Gone is the grid of the typical office tower, replaced by a complex structural apparatus that looks like a machine. The building is composed of four units, each consisting of four colossal piers that are pushed to either end of the rectangular building. Mammoth trusswork supports are cantilevered from these piers, and the floors then hang from these cantilevers in five stacked groups of six to nine floors each, groups that Foster called "villages." Elevators stop only on the communal floor of each village, and escalators then connect the remaining floors. All the services, including elevators, are placed in sleek shafts at either end of the building, allowing the interior to be virtually free of obstructions (fig. **30.6**). Foster transformed the ground floor into a piazza, opening it up to the surrounding streets and leaving it unlevel since the streets themselves are at different elevations. The piazza has an enormous curved ceiling, penetrated by escalators that ascend to a spectacular atrium, extending ten stories and 170 feet high, as seen in our reproduction, off which are balconies of workspace. On the south side of the building, computer-driven mirrors, called "sun scoops," track the sun and reflect light onto a second set of

30.5 Norman Foster. Hong Kong and Shanghai Bank, Hong Kong, China. 1979–86

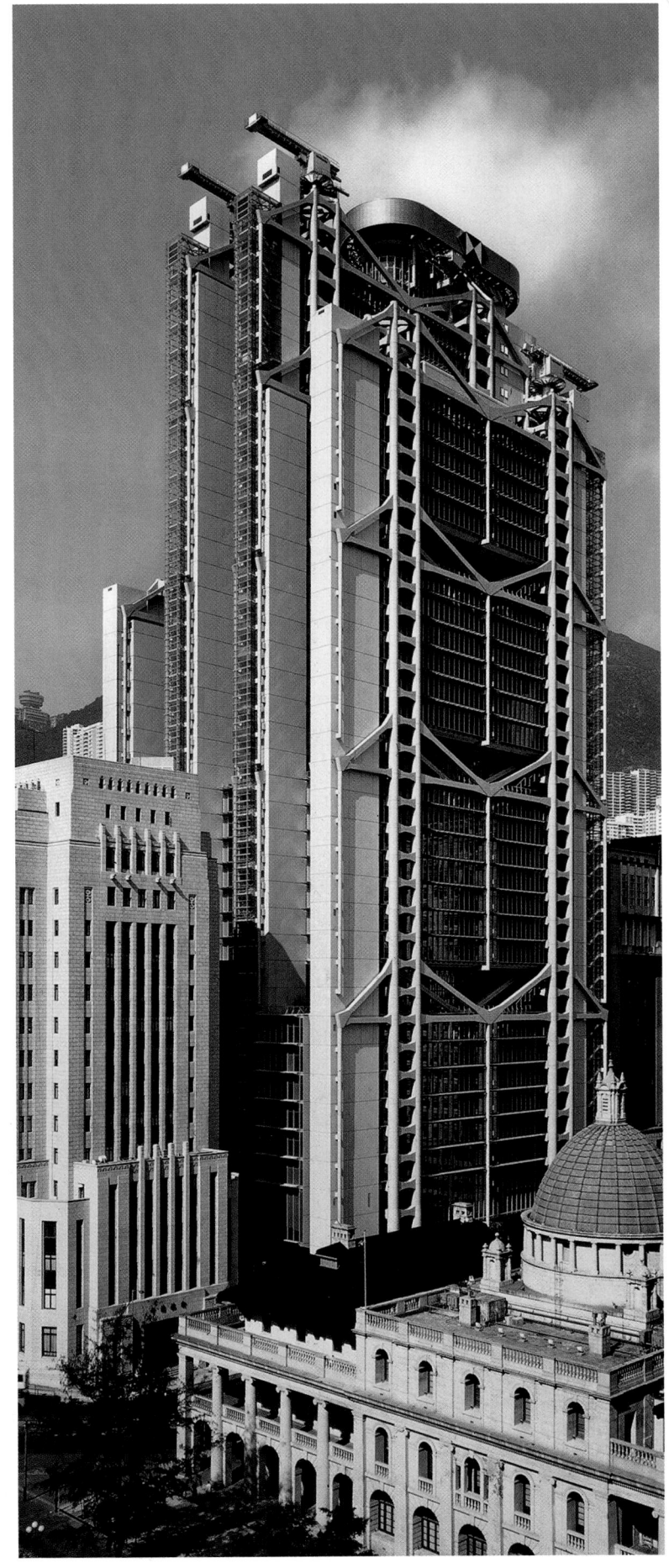

Deconstructivism: Countering Modernist Authority

In 1988, the Museum of Modern Art in New York mounted an exhibition titled *Deconstructivism*. The show included seven architects whose work displayed a Constructivist geometry (see page 1003) and planarity that created an architecture of "disruption, dislocation, deviation, and distortion," as Mark Wigley, who cocurated the exhibition with architect Philip Johnson, wrote in the accompanying catalogue. Originally the show was to have been called "Violated Perfection," which would have spared everyone from struggling to determine what Deconstructivism actually is. The label caught on, however, with none of its advocates agreeing on a definition or even who the core Deconstructivists were. The show's curators derived the term from Derrida's theory of Deconstruction. Essentially, Derrida posits that there are no firm meanings to any written text; outside of the text there are infinite forces that continually restructure its meaning and provide endless readings and interpretations. Similarly, Deconstructivist architecture had no fixed meaning. Wigley linked architectural Deconstructivism with Russian Constructivism. This connection is based on style and not theory, since Constructivism was about establishing a new order and a utopian perfection, whereas Deconstructivism focused on denying any fixed structure or logic.

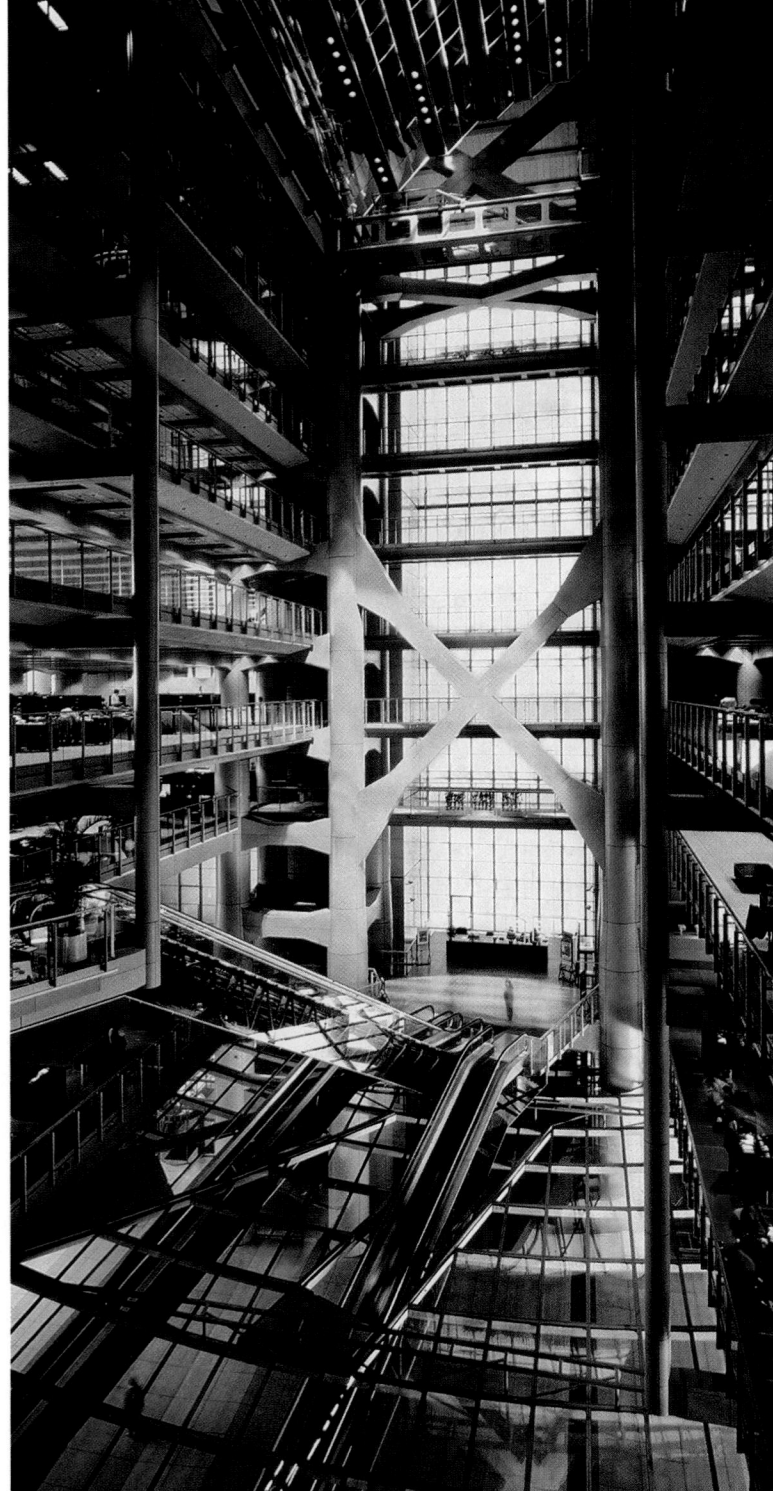

30.6   Norman Foster. Interior of the Hong Kong and Shanghai Bank

mirrors that in turn direct it down into the piazza, which becomes filled with spectacular natural light strong enough to cast shadows. Inside and out, machines, mechanics, a megastructure of trusswork, rooftop maintenance hoists, and sleek service shafts define the building, giving it an appearance of industrial strength, efficiency, and functionalism.

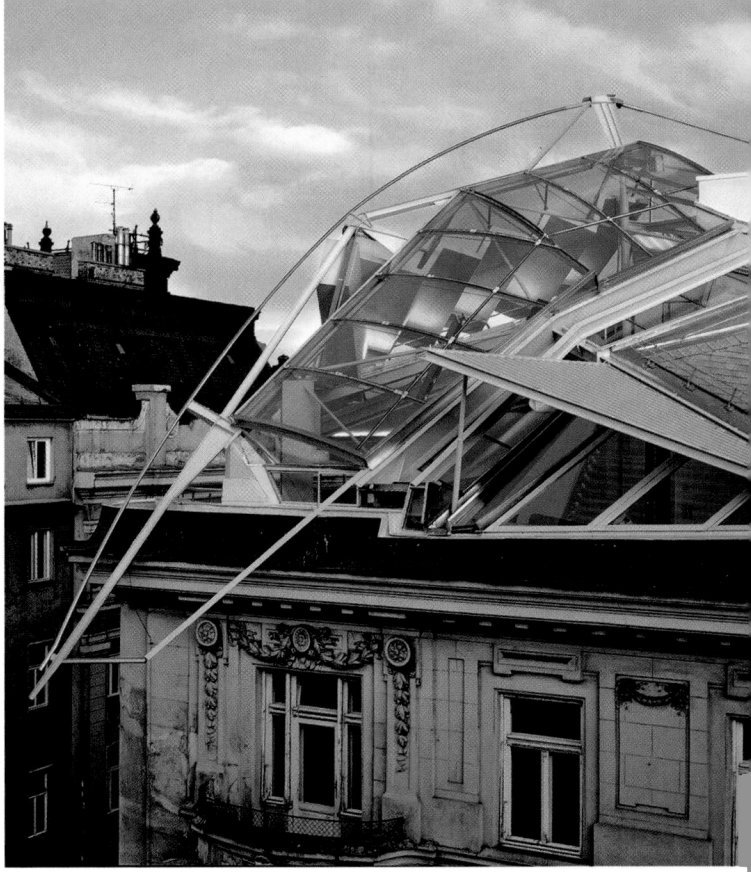

30.7   Coop Himmelblau. Rooftop Office, Vienna. 1983–88

Ironically, most of the architects in the show had no or little interest in Derrida, and if they did, it was through indirect associations rather than a reading of his abstruse writings. That said, a major trend emerged in the 1980s that challenged the idea that architecture had to adhere to any single concept or ideal. These architects rebelled against the notion that architecture had to aspire to some kind of perfection, order, or logic.

COOP HIMMELBLAU Early advocates of this movement are Wolf Prix (b. 1942) and Helmut Swiczinsky (b. 1944), whose Viennese firm Coop Himmelblau was included in the 1988 *Deconstructivism* exhibition. Their aesthetic is prominently displayed in the rooftop conference room (fig. **30.7**) they designed in 1983 for a law firm in Vienna. No explanation or logic can be applied to this architectural phenomenon, in which the roof seems to explode, creating a sense of catastrophe wholly at odds with the staid conservatism usually associated with the legal profession. Even the materials are jarring, conflicting violently with the nineteenth-century apartment building below. The planarity of the

forms may suggest Constructivist sculpture, but the design lacks the clarity, structure, and logic of the Russian movement. The project is devoid of historicist and architectural references. Replacing order and logic is a sense of slashing, thrusting, tilting, fragmentation, and skewing. Yet these attributes are not about destruction, demolition, dismantling, or disaster. Rather, the architects aspired to disrupt preconceived notions of architecture.

ZAHA HADID Zaha Hadid (b. 1950) is the one artist who is on everyone's list of Deconstructivist architects, although she has little interest in Derrida and claims her work is not based in theory, but instead is intuitive. Born in Iraq and trained and based in London, she was heavily influenced by the energized geometric forms of Suprematism (see pages 966–69). Hadid's projects generally show her concern for creating easily perceived fluid spaces that encourage people to come into and move about her structures.

In the Lois and Richard Rosenthal Center for Contemporary Art in Cincinnati (fig. **30.8**), which opened in 2003, broad shifting Suprematist-like planes and Constructivist-like boxes move up

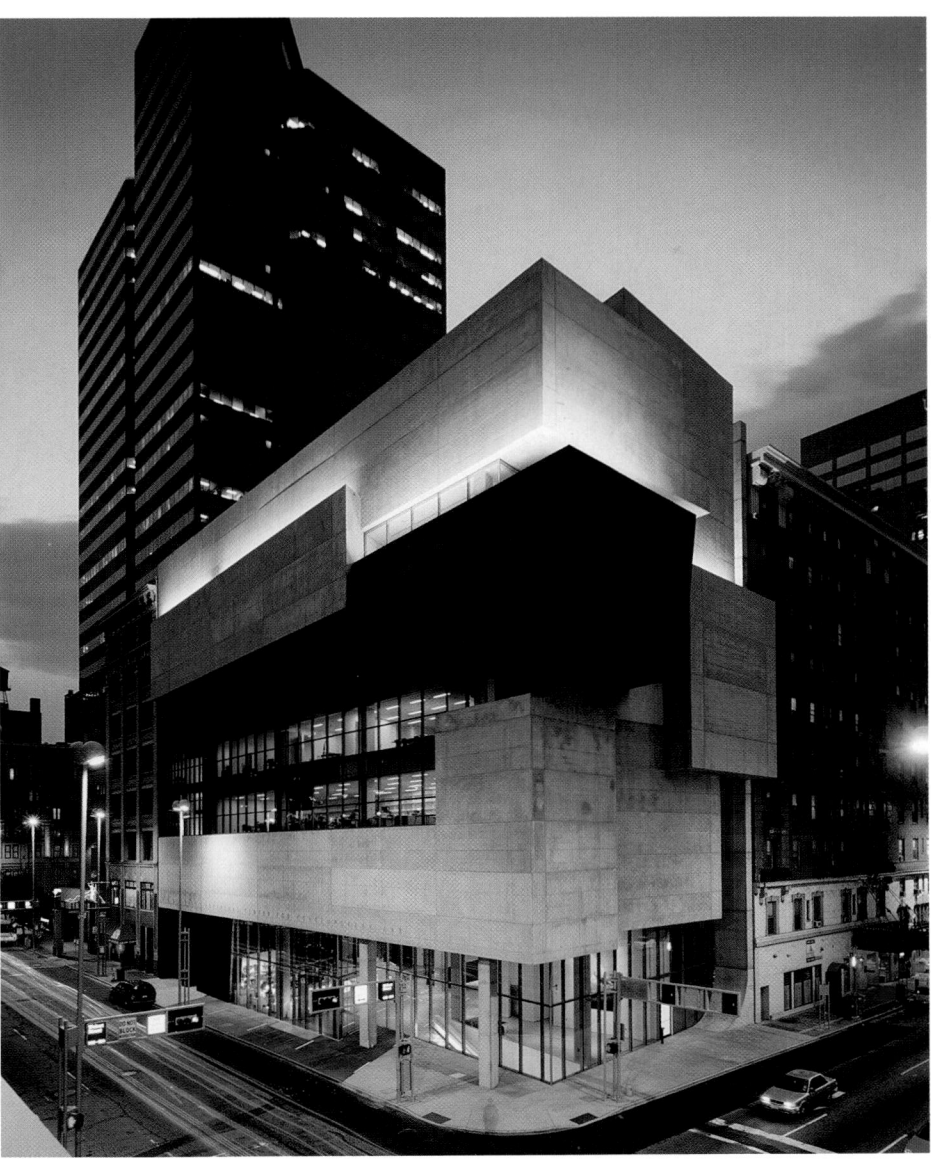

30.8 Zaha Hadid. Lois and Richard Rosenthal Center for Contemporary Art, Cincinnati. Opened 2003

and down and in and out on the museum's façade. Hadid describes the façade as an "Urban Carpet," and in fact, the sidewalk curves slowly upward into the building, encouraging people to enter. The ground floor is a landscaped lobby, serving as an enclosed park, further attracting visitors. It is dominated by a dramatic series of lobby ramps that run the length of the entire space. The ramps lead to a mezzanine that opens onto galleries. The galleries and their shapes are visible from the street, further enticing the public to enter the museum. Because the museum does not have a permanent collection and only mounts temporary exhibits, Hadid designed a wide range of spaces to accommodate all kinds of art objects. The galleries appear to be suspended in space, floating on a variety of levels. This sense of energized fluidity, not only within the museum but also in the relationship of the street and sidewalk with the building, is one of the hallmarks of Hadid's work.

FRANK GEHRY Frank Gehry (b. 1929) was also one of the seven architects included in the 1988 *Deconstructivism* show, but he views himself as an independent, refusing to be associated with any style or group. Nevertheless, his projects share with Coop Himmelblau's rooftop office a sense of disorder, fragmentation, and energy, as seen in his most famous project, the Guggenheim Museum, Bilbao (fig. **30.9**). Its unique forms and vocabulary make it impossible to establish any specific meaning or architectural references. People have described the building's forms as a boat, a fish, and a blossoming flower—Gehry's own description—but ultimately the structure is an exploration of the abstract

sculptural play of enormous volumes, and it shows clearly the architect's pure delight in architectural freedom.

The building's curvilinear masses are contrary to orthodox Deconstructivism, which emphasizes flat planes and angularity. Gehry designed their complex forms using computer technology, an integral tool in the fabrication of the building as well. (See *Materials and Techniques*, page 1085.) The museum even feels Hi-Tech, for covering the steel skeleton is a thin skin made up of thousands of tiny titanium shingles. These shimmer in the light, changing color—silver, blue, gold—as the time of day or the weather changes. The interior is equally spectacular. A handful of conventional, rectilinear rooms containing modern art (that is, art made before 1960) contrast with large, irregularly shaped galleries that accommodate contemporary works. One such space is the so-called boat gallery, a long corridor created by two massive concave walls. Perhaps the most sensational area is the vast entrance atrium. Crisscrossed by catwalks and lined with elevator cages, it contains spiraling ribbons of piers and opens up to a sea of windows and skylights.

The Guggenheim, Bilbao is an example of the architectural diversity that had emerged by the end of the twentieth century, when all rules about design were suspended. As important, it reflects how architecture has moved beyond just being about designing buildings. Architects have, once again, begun to create prominent symbols for a city. From its conception, the museum was intended to be more than just a museum; it was meant to change the image of this Spanish industrial port, giving it cultural cachet and transforming it into a tourist destination. That is

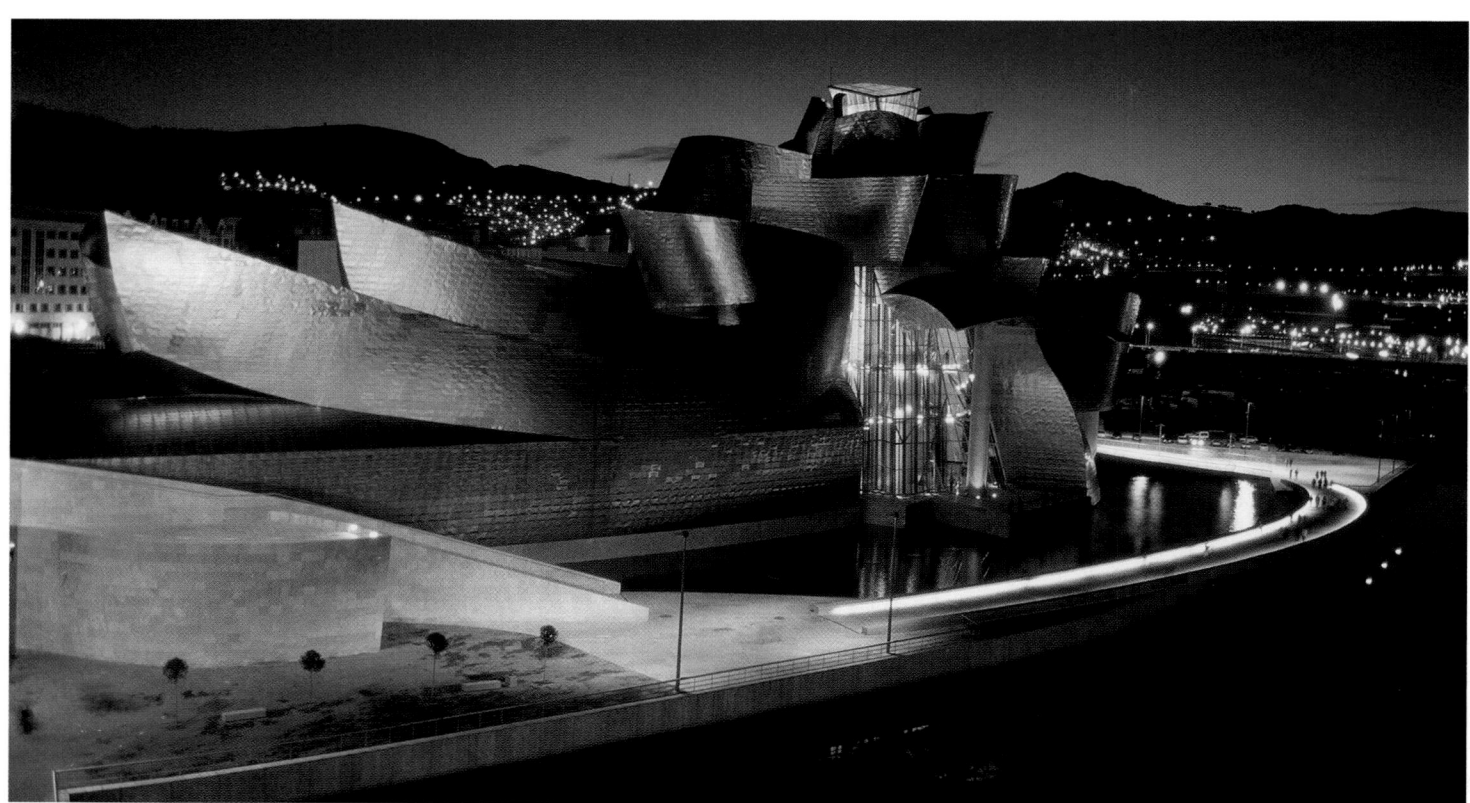

30.9 Frank Gehry. Guggenheim Museum, Bilbao, Spain. 1992–97

Computer-Aided Design in Architecture

In the early 1990s, architects began using CAD (computer-aided design) to create their buildings. In the "paperless studio," plans were developed using computer programs. This approach to design was initially quite controversial, since it forsook the age-old intuitive process of creating by putting hand to paper or modeling with wood or cardboard.

Frank Gehry used a CAD program to produce the extremely complicated forms of the Guggenheim, Bilbao, and without this advanced technology, the structure and its titanium veneer probably would have been difficult to achieve, or at least the building would have been prohibitively expensive. The CAD program that Gehry, with his associate Him Glymph, selected is called CATIA, originally developed by Dessault Systems of France to digitally design and precisely produce extremely complicated products, such as airplane wings and fuselages for the French aerospace industry.

Perhaps more important for Gehry and Glymph than facilitating the design, CATIA made the fabrication possible. Without CATIA, Gehry would have had to hand his plans over to artisans and workers, who then would have been challenged to translate them precisely into three-dimensional forms, a daunting if not impossible task. (Frank Lloyd Wright had tremendous difficulty finding a contractor willing to build his highly irregular, organic Solomon R. Guggenheim Museum in New York.) Instead, Gehry and Glymph sent computer files to fabricators, who fed the digitized information into computer-robotic equipment that then manufactured the forms. Every detailed component of the building could be produced this way, from each unique, oddly

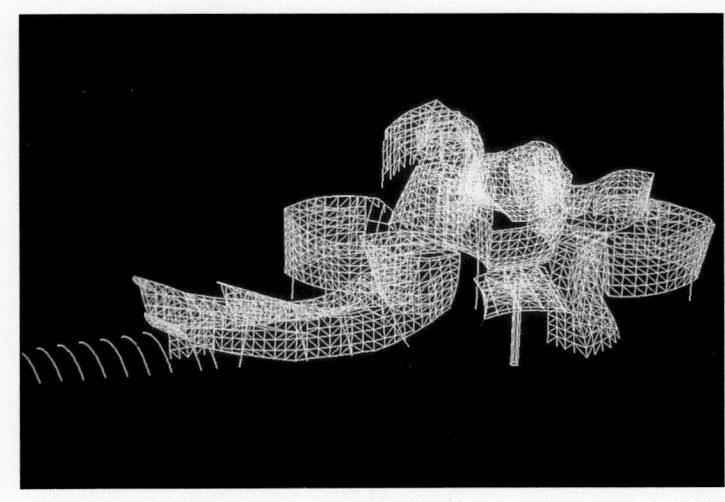

Computer-generated diagram of the Guggenheim Museum, Bilbao, Spain

shaped window to each irregular titanium slate. CATIA also kept costs down. It no longer mattered that large segments of the building were uniquely sized and shaped and therefore could not be cost-effectively mass-produced. The computer program could manufacture each unique product with virtually the same expediency and cost as those of a Modernist building that has thousands of uniform windows and I-beams.

precisely what happened: Gehry designed one of the seminal buildings of the twentieth century, a satellite of Frank Lloyd Wright's sensational 1950s Solomon R. Guggenheim Museum in New York (see figs. I.16 and I.17), which it rivals in audacity and individuality.

POST-MINIMALISM AND PLURALISM: LIMITLESS POSSIBILITIES IN FINE ART

Beginning in the late 1960s, the Post-Minimalists had rejected the austerity of Minimalism (see pages 1058–69) and once again returned the human figure, the artist's hand, subjectivity, and references back to art. The reaction to Minimalism was accompanied by the rise of a broad range of issues, styles, and mediums in the 1970s. During the 1980s, this pluralism began to gain widespread acceptance as it moved from marginalized art to the mainstream. At the same time, Postmodern theory provided a philosophical basis for pluralism, as it argued against all authoritative aesthetics and philosophical positions. The Modernist notion that one and only one style was correct and could move art forward at any given moment was dead. Indeed, if a single word could encapsulate the art made since the 1980s, it would be "diverse." The art market, too, became truly global, with artists from every continent

developing individual styles expressing a wide range of subjects in almost limitless mediums. Art's complexity now made it difficult to comfortably place an artist in a single category or hang a label on her or him.

Among the many developments of the last 30 years are a revival of interest in painting and the ascendance of installation art, photography, and video as leading mediums. Among the more popular themes are racial, ethnic, and gender identity, a preoccupation with the body and death, and a Postmodern analysis, or Deconstruction, of how images and art take on meaning. But if there is anything that unites this period, it is the belief that Modernism with its authoritarian posturing is dead, and that the possibilities of what art can be and be about are limitless.

The Return of Painting

Painting was back by 1980. Not that it had ever disappeared, but in the late 1960s and 1970s it had been overshadowed by Conceptual, Video, Performance, and Earth Art, for example. The Postmodern art critics of the late 1970s associated painting with Modernism and were talking about "the death of painting," even though a stream of shows featuring the medium opened in London, New York, Germany, and Italy in the period. In the introduction to his book about painting's revival, *The*

International Trans-avantgarde (1982), critic Achille Bonito Oliva wrote, "The dematerialization of the work and the impersonality of execution which characterized the art of the seventies, along strictly Duchampian lines, are being overcome by the reestablishment of manual skill through a pleasure of execution which brings the tradition of painting back into art." Another staunch advocate of painting, Christos Joachimides, in the introduction to the catalogue for his 1981 London show, *A New Spirit in Painting*, lauded the medium because now "Subjectivity, the visionary, myth, suffering and grace have all been rehabilitated." The demand for painting was fueled by an explosion of personal and corporate wealth in the 1980s in America, western Europe, and Japan, especially driven in America by the takeovers and mergers encouraged by Reaganomics. As the recession of the 1970s and early 1980s ended, demand grew for art that could be bought and hung on a collector's wall or in a corporate lobby.

The new type of painting that emerged came to be known as Neo-Expressionism, an appropriate label for works that are often both painterly and expressionistic, although not always, which makes the term problematic, along with the fact that the range of issues these artists deal with are quite broad in range and unrelated. The painting labeled Neo-Expressionist appeared first in Germany and Italy in the 1970s and then migrated to New York. In Germany, painters self-consciously recalled the Northern Romanticism and Expressionism so deeply ingrained in that

nation's culture. Joseph Beuys (see page 1063), through his mystical performances, was the catalyst for this resurrection of the German past. Among the themes he and other artists began to explore was the legacy of Hitler's Third Reich.

ANSELM KIEFER Among Beuys's students at the Düsseldorf Art Academy was Anselm Kiefer (b. 1945). Kiefer created images of mythical themes and epic scope that evoke centuries of German history, as seen in his enormous painting *To the Unknown Painter* (fig. **30.10**). The picture explodes with the energy of flailed paint and the dramatic perspective of crop furrows rushing toward an eerie monumental tomb. Cold, bleak, and lifeless, this largely colorless image, except for shots of blood-red, seems to exude an atmosphere of death. Or does it? Crops lying fallow in the winter will be reborn in the spring, and the cycle of life continues. Kiefer's expressive use of paint and dramatic composition can be interpreted as a metaphor for the constant movement and forces of nature. Inspired by Beuys's use of symbolic objects, Kiefer often incorporated real materials into his paintings, imbuing them with a similar ritualistic magic. In this work, he embedded straw into the paint, and viewers could smell its scent for years. Nature is not just illustrated, it is physically present.

The focus of the image is the tomb, a mausoleum for painters, as suggested by the title. We can assume the painters are German because the tomb is not painted but rendered in a large woodcut,

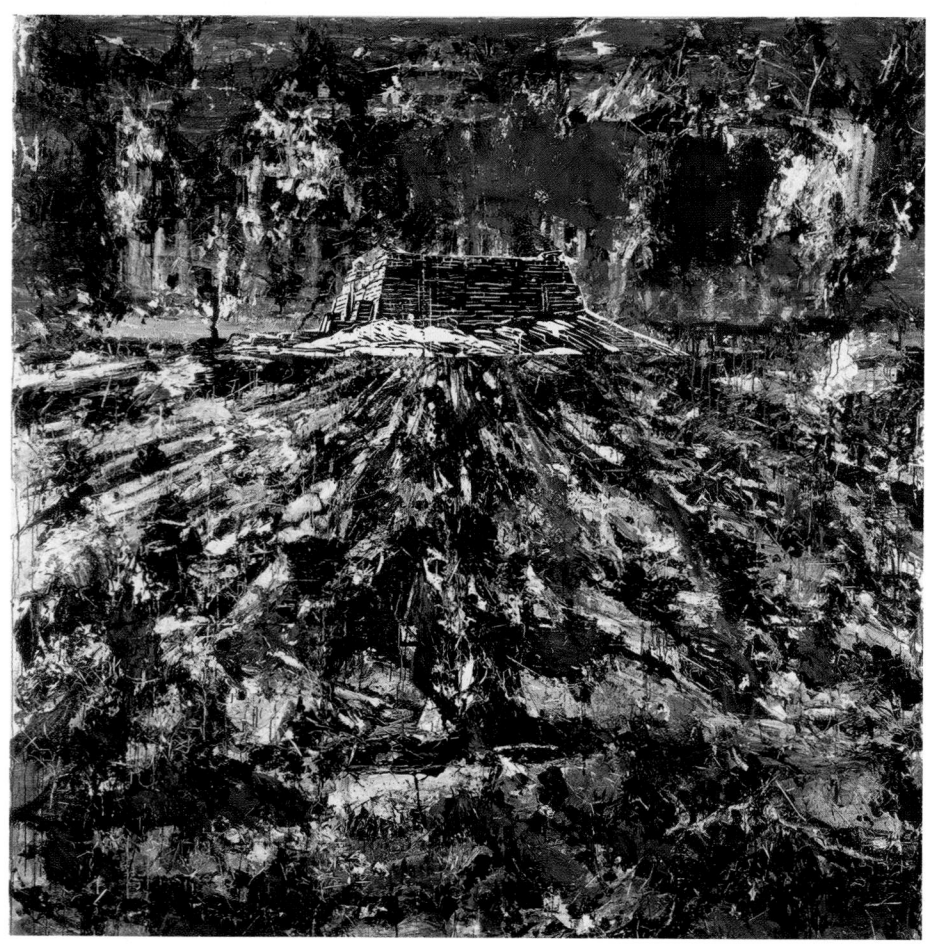

30.10 Anselm Kiefer, *To the Unknown Painter.* 1983. Oil, emulsions, woodcut, shellac, latex, and straw on canvas, 9'2" × 9' × 2" (2.79 × 2.79 × 0.05 m). The Carnegie Museum of Art, Pittsburgh. Richard M. Scaife Fund; a. w. Mellon Acquisition Endowment Fund. 83.53

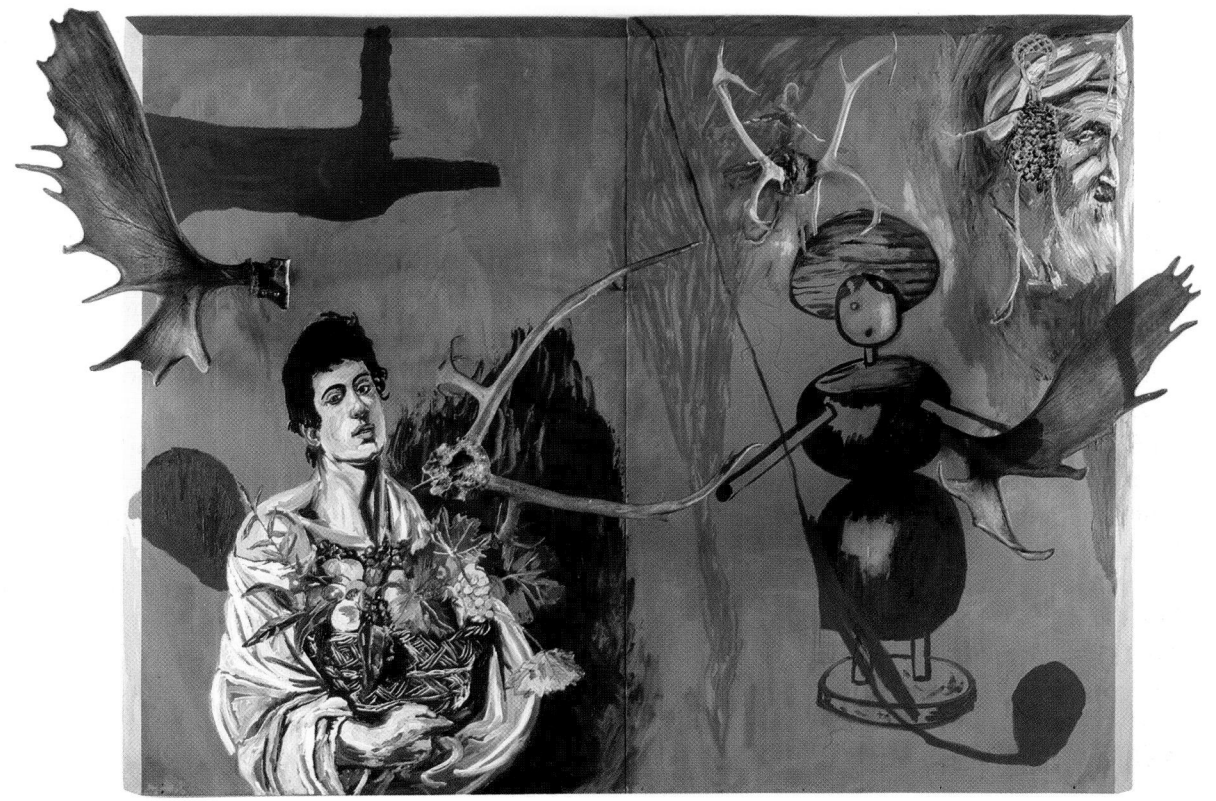

30.11 Julian Schnabel, *The Exile*. 1980. Oil, antlers, gold pigment, and mixed media on wood, 90 × 120 x 24⅝" (229 × 305 × 63 cm). Bischofberger Collection, Switzerland

a medium associated with German art since being widely used by northern European artists during the Renaissance as well as by the Expressionists in the early twentieth century (see page 958). The bunkerlike shape suggests a shelter, and the isolated but well-anchored monument seems to be surrounded by the swirling forces of nature, representing not only the German mythical past but also the Romantic spirit that has driven German artists for centuries. We know from other works by Kiefer that these destructive forces are meant to symbolize Hitler's perversion of the German Romantic tradition, which he manipulated to serve his racist agenda and justify the suppression of avant-garde German artists, whom the Nazis labeled "Degenerates" (see page 1031).

In a painting about national identity, Kiefer's Expressionist style and use of Romantic themes proclaim his place within the northern European Romantic tradition. He assures us that this tradition is once again in safe hands. With its wealth of symbols, metaphors, and overlapping and interlocking interpretations, the resulting image is varied and complex, reflecting the epic scale Kiefer covers and the mythical themes he evokes.

JULIAN SCHNABEL The artist who became emblematic of Neo-Expressionism in America is Julian Schnabel (b. 1953), a New Yorker raised in Texas, where he went to the University of Houston. While today perhaps better known by the general public for his films, such as *The Diving Bell and the Butterfly* (2007), Schnabel dominated the New York art world in the 1980s, or, as one critic put it, he "created a bonfire over Manhattan," which he ignited with a 1981 exhibition that was so large it was held at both the Leo Castelli Gallery, the premier blue-chip gallery, and the Mary Boone Gallery, the hottest new gallery in town. Everything about Schnabel was oversize, including his ego, reflected in such statements as "I'm the closest thing to Picasso." His paint surfaces are enormous, 16 feet in one direction not being unusual, and range from traditional canvas, to Kabuki backdrops, to tarpaulins, to animal skins, to the disreputable black velvet found in gas-station art. Often, his pictures are encased in extremely ornate and wide baroque frames. He covers his surfaces with violent, crude-looking, and dramatic slathers of paint, as well as with objects of all kinds, including broken crockery, for which he became especially renowned, the skeleton of a fir tree, and antlers, as seen here in his 1980 painting *The Exile* (fig. **30.11**). Demonstrating a Postmodern penchant to raid the art of the past and present, as well as popular culture, his motifs are often appropriated, as is the figure holding a fruit basket in *Exile*, which was taken from a painting by Caravaggio. Despite the bombast, there is no point in trying to interpret Schnabel's picture, since there is no narrative to be found in the Caravaggio figure, the spool-like diagrammatic doll, the bearded man, the antlers, and the often odd trailings of paint. The inspiration for Schnabel's appropriation of objects and images that are juxtaposed in no particular narrative is Sigmar Polke (see fig. 29.17), whose work Schnabel saw in Europe in the 1970s. Like Polke, Schnabel's painting exudes a mood, rather than a story. In *The Exile*, we can sense the eruptive gestures and vitality of the artist locking horns with death, as evoked by the lifelessness of the appropriated figures and the sad, one-eyed doll, and, of course, the antlers themselves, the remains of once-living animals. As expressed by the artist, his paintings "are icons that present life in terms of our death." Although he is Jewish, his imagery is often Catholic, the crucified Christ being one favorite motif. While reflecting his personal experience as a student at a Catholic school in Brownsville, Texas, this kind of imagery is hardly spiritual, instead reinforcing a sense of physical suffering, loss, and isolation that haunts his baroque pictures.

JEAN-MICHEL BASQUIAT AND GRAFFITI ART Of the many American Neo-Expressionists to emerge in the 1980s, among the most exciting was Jean-Michel Basquiat (1960–1988). Born in New York to a middle-class family, Basquiat's father was Haitian and his mother was of Puerto Rican descent. He dropped out of school at age 17, first writing poetry and then becoming a street artist using the tag name SAMO, suggesting the phrase "same old." By studying art books, he became knowledgeable about art history and began painting. By the time he was 22, he had achieved international stardom. He died of a drug overdose at age 27.

In *Horn Players* (fig. **30.12**) of 1983, Basquiat combines both poetry and graffiti. More important, he draws upon the lessons of the pluralistic 1970s by brilliantly incorporating the era's strategies of using texts, making process art, working with narratives, and dealing with social politics, here racial identity. Basquiat also owes a debt to Abstract Expressionism, seen in his dynamic handling of paint, and to Pop Art, visible in his cartoonlike imagery and popular-culture references.

Basquiat was prolific, working quickly and with the stream-of-consciousness intensity sensed here. We can feel him painting, writing, crossing out. He draws us into the canvas by forcing us to read and piece it together. He makes us experience the sounds coming out of the saxophone, think about the repetition of words and the rhythms they make, and analyze his masterful use of color—a brilliant pink and blue here, yellow and green there. Because they are so powerfully presented, we cannot dismiss Basquiat's use of words such as "alchemy," a reference to the alchemy of jazz, "ornithology," a nod to jazz musician Charlie Parker, nicknamed "Bird,", and "ear," an allusion to musical instinct. His works evoke the raw energy of the 1950s—Beat poetry, improvisational jazz, and Abstract Expressionism.

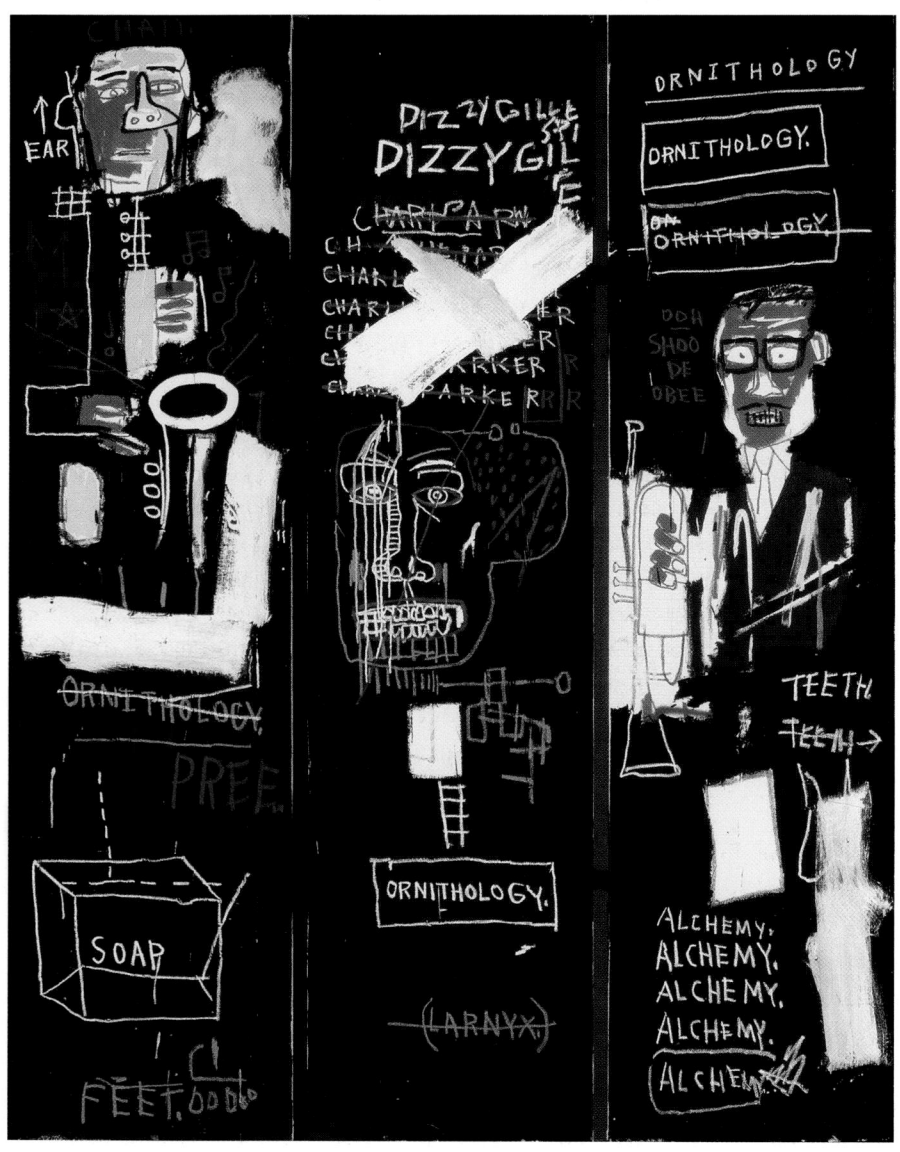

30.12 Jean-Michel Basquiat, *Horn Players*. 1983. Acrylic and oil paintstick on canvas, three panels, overall 8' × 6'5" (2.44 × 1.91 m). Broad Art Foundation, Santa Monica, CA

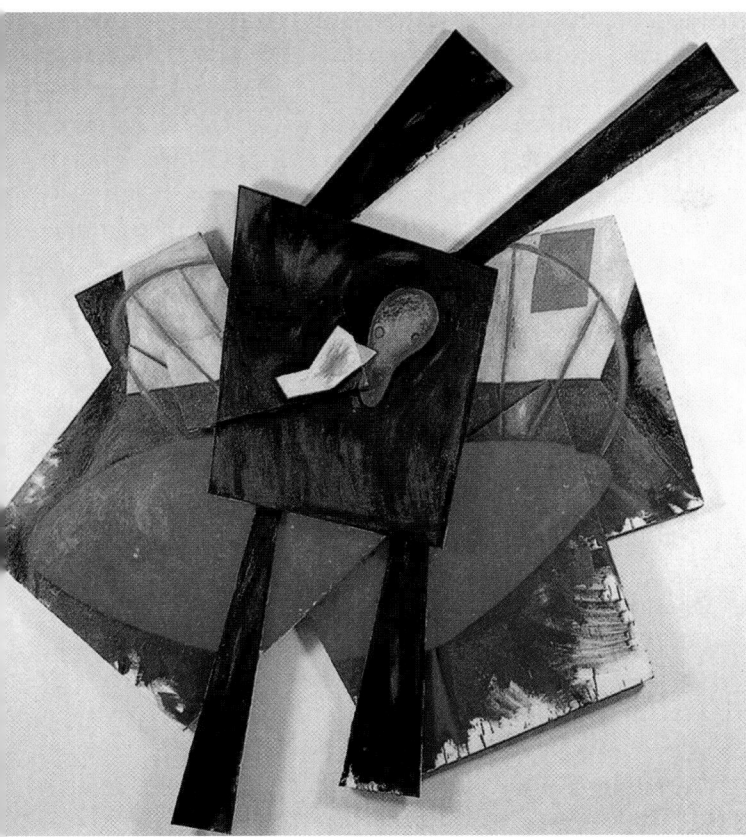

30.13 Elizabeth Murray, *More Than You Know*. 1983. Oil on ten canvases, 9'3" × 9' × 8" (2.82 × 2.74 × 0.20 m). Estate of Elizabeth Murray. Courtesy PaceWildenstein Gallery, New York

sweeping organic curve playing off a blue-gray Constructivist rectangle is the back of a spindleback chair. We then recognize the mostly gray rectangle as a painting hanging on a yellow wall. Finally, the green anthropomorphic shape evolves into a table with collapsed legs. On the table lie a white form resembling a piece of paper and a disturbing biomorphic shape that recalls the skull in Munch's *The Scream* (see fig. 26.19). Tension dominates the image, symbolized by the collapsed table as well as the strident colors, the unfinished-looking paint handling, and the violent tilt of the floor. Even the shape of the painting is frenzied. Murray combines ten canvases, overlapping them and producing a ragged profile that transforms the painting into a wildly spinning pinwheel. Nothing seems to be anchored in this composition as objects shift like detritus adrift in a stormy sea. In her three-dimensional, heaving paintings, Murray continually focuses on the psychological tension of daily life, the edgy reality that lies beneath the façade of domestic harmony. Because her work often deals with the psychology of the home as experienced from a woman's viewpoint, many critics place her within the context of feminist art. In any case, her work reflects the increasing interest in women's issues that characterize the 1980s.

Sculpture

The Post-Minimal aesthetic in sculpture, which combined the geometry of Minimalism with references and emotion that we saw in the work of Eva Hesse and Richard Serra (see pages 1058–59), continued unabated into the 1980s and 1990s. It could appear in such diverse forms as beautifully crafted, mysterious objects, as in the work of Martin Puryear, or readily understood public monuments, as in the *Vietnam Veterans Memorial* by Maya Lin.

MARTIN PURYEAR One of the many outstanding sculptors who made objects rather than installations is Martin Puryear (b. 1941). Puryear fulfills in sculpture "the reestablishment of manual skill through a pleasure of execution," as the critic Oliva had said about painting. After serving in the Peace Corps in the West African nation of Sierra Leone, studying printmaking and woodworking in Sweden, and visiting Japan, Puryear settled in Brooklyn in 1973, where he soon emerged, by the 1980s becoming a leading sculptor of his generation.

One of the first things we notice in his 1985 wood and steel sculpture *The Spell* (fig. 30.14) is his craftsmanship. We marvel at the beauty of the curved shapes, the elegant tapering of the cone, the playful variety of its rectangular openings, and the sensuous texture of the flat, striated wood strips that make up the "webbing" of what looks like a basket. The allusion to basket making suggests crafts and craftsmanship, which in turn implies a human presence—we sense the hand that carefully constructed this object, unlike Minimal Art, which seemed mass-produced and machine-made. We also sense Puryear's background not only in Africa, where he would have seen magnificently crafted utilitarian and ceremonial wooden objects, but also in Sweden, where he

But 1980s hip-hop also comes to mind. Like Schnabel, Basquiat appropriates motifs, styles, and ideas from different periods— a hallmark of Postermodernism. This approach allows him to create a powerful, sensuous experience as he shares his passionate feelings about the black musicians Dizzy Gillespie and Charlie Parker, with whom he clearly identifies. Much of his work features African-American musicians, singers, and athletes, and is a reflection of the importance artists were increasingly giving to racial, ethnic, and gender identities, as will be discussed below.

ELIZABETH MURRAY AND NEW IMAGE PAINTING In 1978, the Whitney Museum of American Art in New York mounted an exhibition of American artists entitled *New Image Painting*. The show not only claimed that painting was alive and well, it heralded the arrival of a new kind of painting, one that had representational objects embedded within seemingly abstract paintings. At the time, Elizabeth Murray (1940–2007) was producing totally abstract work and was not included in the exhibition. But within a few years, she had begun adding representational components to her abstractions. Because of their associations, these recognizable elements served as metaphors for a psychological state. Murray's evolution to referential abstraction can be seen in *More Than You Know* (fig. 30.13) of 1983. At a glance, the painting appears to consist of entirely abstract shapes. But we soon realize that the

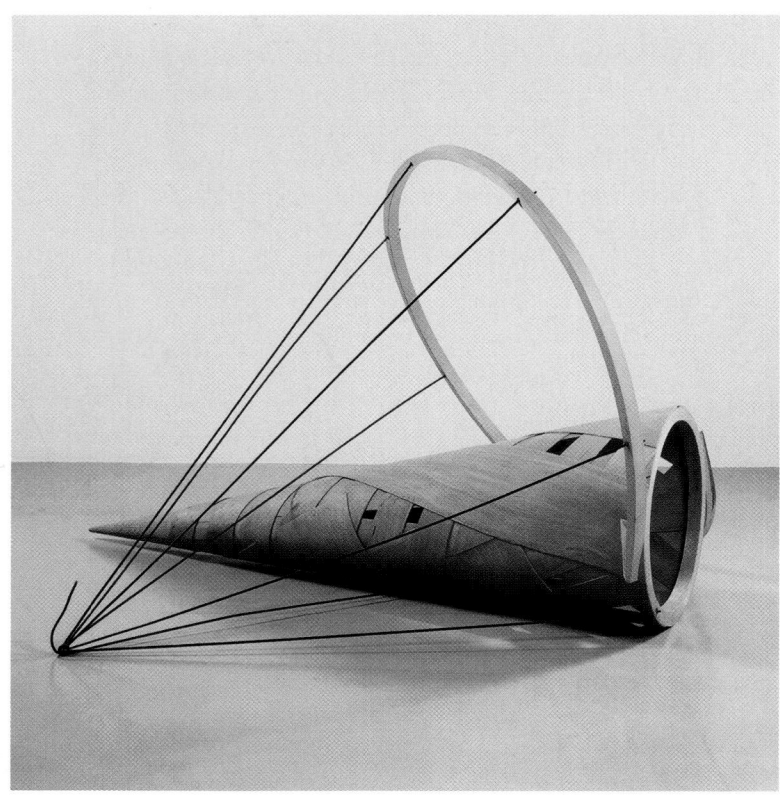

30.14 Martin Puryear, *The Spell*. 1985. Pine, cedar, and steel, 4'8" × 7' × 5'5" (1.42 × 2.13 × 1.65 m). Collection of the artist. Courtesy of the McKee Gallery, New York

trained in woodworking, and in Japan, a culture with a long tradition of crafting wood into functional and decorative objects. It would be a mistake, however, to interpret Puryear's references to African art as just an acknowledgment of his African-American background. His sculpture is generally not about ethnic identity and politics, although there are exceptions, but instead it reflects his broader experiences in diverse cultures well versed in using wood as an artistic medium.

The Spell defies interpretation. Resembling a trap lying on the floor, the sculpture appears to be utilitarian but is not. Despite its title, suggestive of mystery and sorcery, there is nothing clearly ritualistic or shamanistic about the work. Rather, we sense the essence of the wood itself, and therefore the sculpture evokes nature. Yet it is the human component—the craftsmanship—that prevails. Like Eva Hesse, but working in a radically different style, Puryear transforms the austerity of Minimalist geometry into an enigmatic yet warm organic object loaded with powerful human allusions.

MAYA LIN One of the best-known Post-Minimal sculptures of the 1980s is the *Vietnam Veterans Memorial* (fig. **30.15**) by Maya Lin (b. 1959). Lin received the commission while still a student in the architecture program at Yale University. A daunting project because of the strong emotions and opinions surrounding the Vietnam War, Lin's solution proved beautiful in its simplicity, ingenious in its neutrality, and sublime in its emotional impact. Lin presents

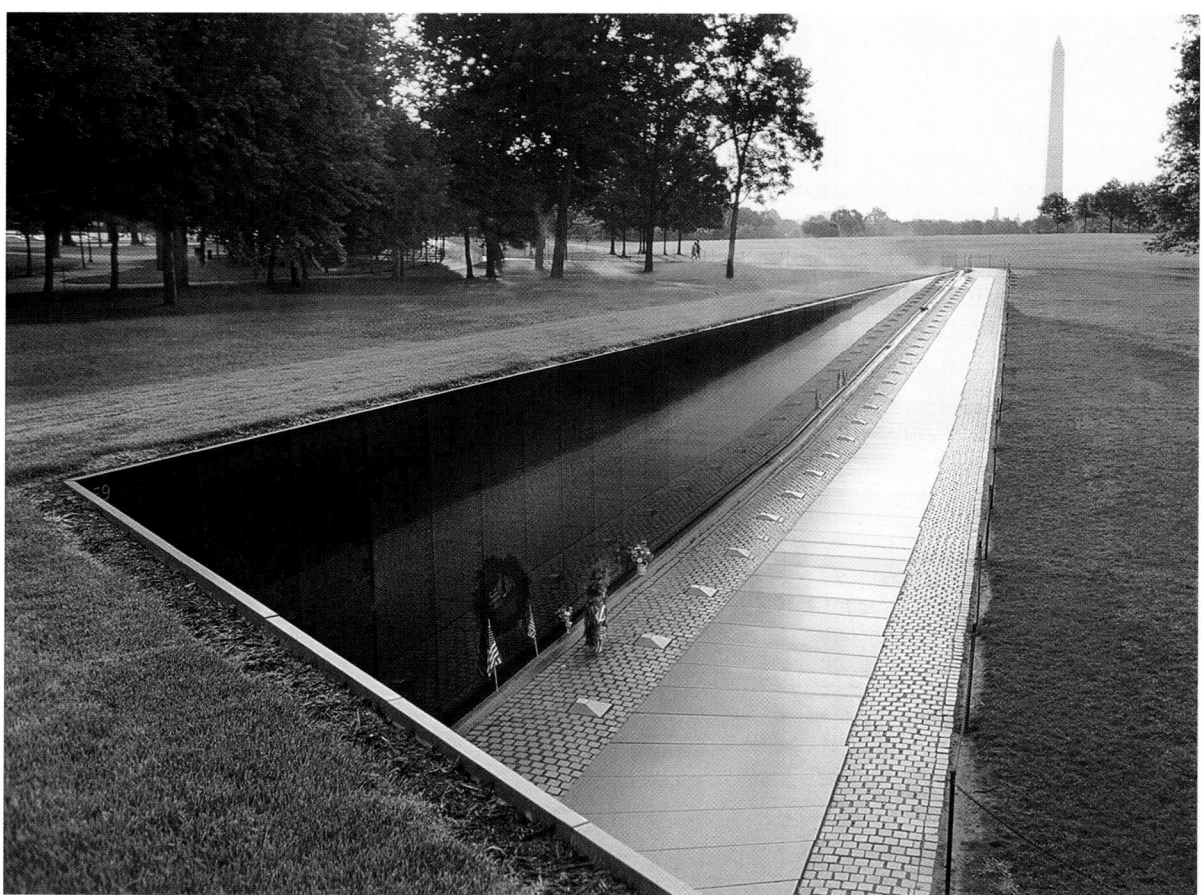

30.15 Maya Lin, *Vietnam Veterans Memorial*. 1982. Two black granite walls, length of each 246'9" (75m). The Mall, Washington, D.C.

Cindy Sherman (b. 1954)

PRIMARY SOURCE

From an interview

In these excerpts from a 1988 interview with Jeanne Siegel, Sherman discusses the role-playing in her photographs.

CINDY SHERMAN: I still wanted to make a filmic sort of image, but I wanted to work alone. I realized that I could make a picture of a character reacting to something outside the frame so that the viewer would assume another person.

Actually, the moment that I realized how to solve this problem was when Robert [Longo] and I visited David Salle, who had been working for some sleazy detective magazine. Bored as I was, waiting for Robert and David to get their "art talk" over with, I noticed all these 8 by 10 glossies from the magazine which triggered something in me. (I was never one to discuss issues—after all, at that time I was "the girlfriend.")

JEANNE SIEGEL: In the "Untitled Film Stills," what was the influence of real film stars? It seems that you had a fascination with European stars. You mentioned Jeanne Moreau, Brigitte Bardot, and Sophia Loren in some of your statements. Why were you attracted to them?

CS: I guess because they weren't glamorized like American starlets. When I think of American actresses from the same period, I think of bleached blonde, bejeweled, and furred sex bombs. But, when I think of Jeanne Moreau and Sophia Loren, I think of more vulnerable, lower-class types of characters, more identifiable as working-class women.

At that time I was trying to emulate a lot of different types of characters. I didn't want to stick to just one. I'd seen a lot of the movies that these women had been in but it wasn't so much that I was inspired by the women as by the films themselves and the feelings in the films.

JS: And what is the relationship between your "Untitled Film Stills" and the real film stills?

CS: In real publicity film stills from the 40s and 50s something usually sexy/cute is portrayed to get people to go see the movie. Or the woman could be shown screaming in terror to publicize a horror film.

My favorite film images (where obviously my work took its inspiration) didn't have that. They're closer to my own work for that reason, because both are about a sort of brooding character caught between the potential violence and sex. However, I've realized it is a mistake to make that kind of literal connection because my work loses in the comparison. I think my characters are not quite taken in by their roles so that they couldn't really exist in any of their so-called "films," which, next to a real still, looks unconvincing. They are too aware of the irony of their role and perhaps that's why many have puzzled expressions. My "stills" were about the fakeness of role-playing as well as contempt for the domineering "male" audience who would mistakenly read the images as sexy. …

JS: Another critical issue attached to the work was the notion that the stereotypical view was exclusively determined by the "male" gaze. Did you see it only in this light or did it include the woman seeing herself as well?

CS: Because I'm a woman I automatically assume other women would have an immediate identification with the roles. And I hoped men would feel empathy for the characters as well as shedding light on their role-playing. What I didn't anticipate was that some people would assume that I was playing up to the male gaze. I can understand the criticism of feminists who therefore assumed I was reinforcing the stereotype of woman as victim or as sex object.

Source: *Artwords*, II, ed. Jeanne Siegel (NY: Da Capo Press, 1990). Copyright © 1988 by Jeanne Siegel. Reprinted by permission of Jeanne Siegel

---

the names of the dead and missing in action in a chronological list from 1959 to 1975. The names are etched into slabs of black granite that carve out a V-shaped gash in the earth. Viewers start reading from the left, representing the year 1959, where the first killed are listed and the granite rises out of the ground. The name-laden stone gradually rises along its 247-foot (75.2-m) length as more and more Americans die. The names keep coming, and the viewer soon becomes emotionally overwhelmed by their number.

At its 10-foot peak, the granite turns at a 130-degree angle and then descends along another 247-foot length, with fewer soldiers listed as the 1973 withdrawal from Vietnam approaches. At the end, as the granite again disappears into the ground, many viewers are left with a feeling of existential nothingness. Adding to this sense of loss is the impact of the granite's polished surface, which acts like a mirror casting reflections of the living onto the names of the dead. This memorial is a sharp departure from traditional representational monuments to heroism, like Rude's *La Marseillaise* (see fig. 24.27), which glorified nationalistic spirit and dedication. In a sense, the granite wall acts as an enormous tombstone. While the monument takes the form of Minimal sculpture, and like Minimal sculpture was manufactured, it has been transformed through references into a brilliant Postmodern monument of powerful emotions.

APPROPRIATION ART: DECONSTRUCTING IMAGES

While painting and sculpture were exciting the art world in the first half of the 1980s and garnering the bulk of the attention, more and more artists came under the spell of Postmodern ideas. These artists turned to photography, video, film, billboards, and LED (light-emitting diode) boards, that is, mediums associated with the mass media. Rarely did they make paintings, which were identified with Modernism, although Julian Schnabel's appropriated images that he put into a new context, thus changing their meaning, could just as easily be discussed in this section as under Neo-Expressionism. This new generation of artists began to deconstruct the visual world, exploring how images, which include three-dimensional objects, function largely to establish power, prestige, and value, but also demonstrating how objects take on meaning in general. This Postmodern questioning parsed image making, exposing hidden agendas or hierarchies, and demystifying the authority of the image. Feminist theory especially propelled this Postmodernist art, as large numbers of women artist explored how women were presented in the media, and for whom.

Photography and LED Signs

While *October* magazine played a major role in introducing Postmodern theory to American artists, an exhibition titled *Pictures*, presented in 1977 at Artists Space, an alternative gallery in lower Manhattan, was also instrumental in bringing Postmodernism to the art world's attention. The art in the show consisted largely of pictures, both paintings and photographs, that were appropriations of preexisting images, thus demonstrating how all pictures, to varying degrees, are based on earlier art and calling into question such issues as originality, uniqueness, and authorship in art. Sherrie Levine, one of the artists in the exhibition, soon after became notorious for making photographs of photographs by such major male artists as Edward Weston and Walker Evans (see pages 1023 and 1029) and drawings of drawings by Joan Miró and Piet Mondrian (see pages 996 and 1005). Her copies, or re-presentations, called into question how art takes on value and the importance granted to the original artist, who, himself, was always borrowing from predecessors. In effect, Levine was declaring that no art was new. Furthermore, Levine re-presented the work of men, her appropriations underlining the status accorded male artists. Not only did many of the early appropriation artists work in photography, but many, such as Cindy Sherman, Louise Lawler, Barbara Kruger, and Laurie Simmons, were women, who often dealt with women's issues. By the end of the 1980s, Neo-Expressionism was on the wane, overtaken by Deconstruction, much of which was photography.

BARBARA KRUGER If anyone knows how the mass media operates, it is Barbara Kruger (b. 1945), who has a background in graphic design at the magazines *Mademoiselle* and *House and Garden*. Kruger appropriates photographs from magazines, which she re-presents in gelatin silver prints, often quite large, with wording across the image, similar to the wording in advertising. Over the frontally presented head of an attractive woman, for example, she put "Your body is a battleground," a reference to the abortion debate engulfing the nation in the 1980s as Jerry Falwell's Moral Majority ramped up the attack on Roe vs. Wade, the 1973 supreme court decision upholding the right to abortion. Over the image of a stone sculpture bust of a woman seen in profile she placed "Your gaze hits the side of my head," a reference to art being made specifically for the male gaze, as described in Jacques Lacan's psychoanalytic theories, with women being presented for male pleasure. This same theme is presented in *Untitled (We Won't Play Nature to Your Culture)* (fig. **30.16**). The woman does not have the power of the gaze for she is blinded, not because she is stone, but here because her eyes are covered with leaves. By using words such as "we" and "our" versus "you" and "your,"

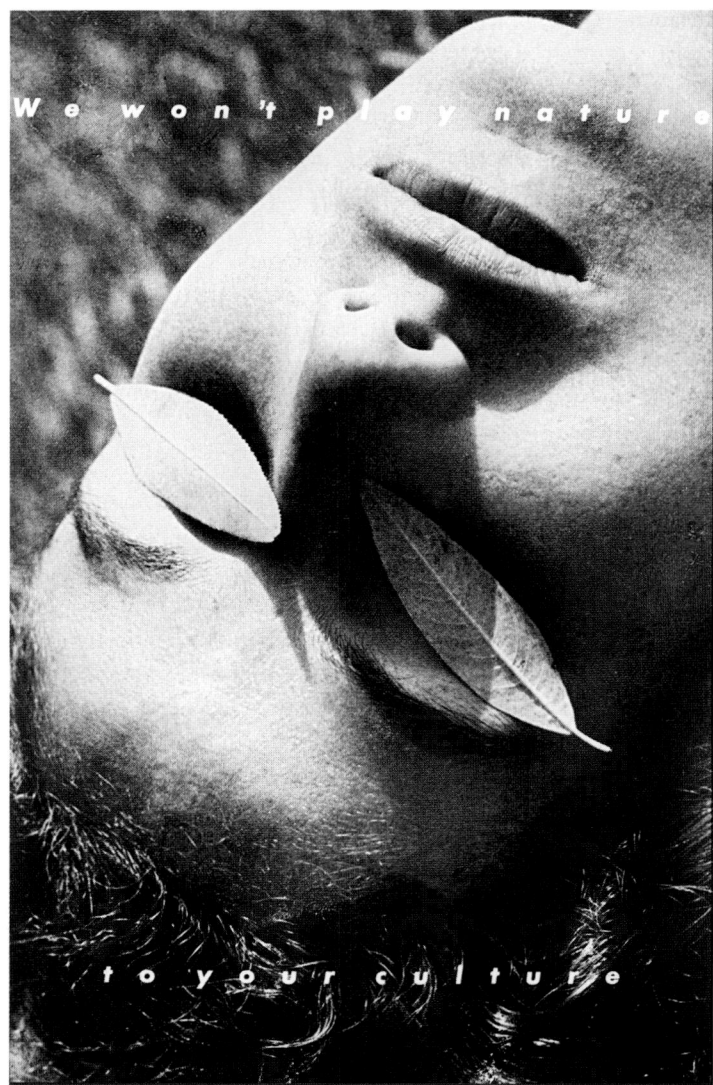

30.16 Barbara Kruger, *Untitled (We Won't Play Nature to Your Culture)*. 1983. Photograph, 73 × 49" (185 × 124 cm.) Courtesy Mary Boone Gallery, NY

Kruger sets up a dichotomy between the maker/manipulator of the image on the one hand, and the target/manipulated on the other. Besides the male/female dichotomy, Kruger sets up a nature/culture opposition, "nature" referring to the neutral state of nature, and "culture" to the two-dimensional visual image in which one person's agenda is imposed on another.

Kruger's deconstruction not only reflects European Postmodernism, it is also driven by a dramatic increase in feminist theory in general, which appeared in such journals as *Camera Obscura* and *Differences*. The feminist movement also produced a journal specifically for feminist art, *Heresies*, started in 1976. The late 1970s and 1980s saw an enormous increase in women artists dealing with feminist issues. Among the most vociferous and effective was a collaborative called the Guerrilla Girls, founded in New York in 1985 and with cells throughout the United States. They produced printed matter, especially posters, and gave presentations, wearing gorilla masks, a feminist ploy meant to undermine the Modernist emphasis on the individual artist and shift focus to the issues. They especially spotlighted how women were marginalized by the art establishment. Among their more famous posters is one made in 1989 presenting Ingres's *Grande Odalisque* (see fig. 24.13) wearing a gorilla mask, above which is printed "Do women have to be naked to get into the Met. Museum? Less than 5% of the artists in the Modern Art sections are women, but 85% of the nudes are female." The Guerilla Girls are confrontational interventionists, taking their art out of the gallery and to the public by plastering their posters and billboards in public places, often around museums and galleries that they were viciously critiquing. Kruger as well on occasion has worked in the public domain, using billboards.

CINDY SHERMAN AND THE *UNTITLED FILM STILL*

While Kruger and the Gorilla Girls appropriate the propagandistic look and power of advertising, Cindy Sherman (b. 1954) focuses more on how film structures identity and sexuality. She is also interested in revealing how viewers impose meaning on images. Beginning in 1977, Sherman began a series called *Untitled Film Stills*, in which she photographed herself in situations that resemble stills from B movies. For each, she created a set and a female character that she played herself, wearing different clothes, wigs, and accouterments so that she is unrecognizable as the same

person from one 10-by-8-inch still to the next. It is conceptually important that she is always the actress, for her metamorphosis represents the transformation women undergo subliminally as they conform to societal stereotypes reinforced, if not actually determined, by the mass media. In *Untitled Film Still # 15*, Sherman plays the "sexy babe" who seems to be anxiously awaiting the arrival of a date or lover (fig. **30.17**). But is this really what is happening? Sherman leaves the viewer guessing. She may suggest a narrative, but in her *untitled* works, she never provides enough information to securely determine one. In effect, the story a viewer imagines says more about their own backgrounds, experiences, and attitudes than it does about the picture itself, which remains ambiguous. Her "babe" could very well be dressed for a costume party instead of a date, and her look of concern could be for something occurring on the street below. Innumerable stories can be spun from this image, taking into account such details as her cross pendant or the spindleback chair and exposed-brick wall, which seem to conflict with her youth and the lifestyle her clothing suggests. Remove any one of these motifs, and the story would change. Through what seems a simple strategy, Sherman brilliantly reveals the complex ways in which images become invested with meaning and how we are programmed by the media to interpret them. (See *Primary Source*, page 1091.)

JENNY HOLZER AND LED BOARDS

Like Kruger and Sherman, Jenny Holzer (b. 1950) works in the very medium she wants to expose. For Holzer, the target is the advertising slogan that passes as truth. In 1977, she began writing what she calls "truisms," which she printed on posters, flyers, T-shirts, and hats. Eventually, she moved on to electronic signs, even using the big electronic board in New York's Times Square in 1982. In the mid-1980s, she began working with LED boards, the medium with which she is now most associated. Holzer's truisms were homespun aphorisms, one-liners that express a broad range of attitudes and biases, such as "Murder has its sexual side," "Raise boys and girls the same way," "Any surplus is immoral," and "Morality is for little people." In effect, she presents either side of the "us versus you" conflict exposed by Kruger, but the impact is the same. Her works provoke an awareness that one person is trying to impose a position on another. Holzer created the installation of truisms reproduced here (fig. **30.18**) for the Solomon R. Guggenheim Museum in 1989. LED boards run up the side of museum's spiral ramp, while below, arranged in a ritualistic circle, are benches with truisms etched on their seats. Wherever visitors turn, they are being talked to, and in a sense, manipulated, harangued, preached to, and controlled. Left unanswered, however, are such questions as: What is the truth? And who is talking, and for whom?

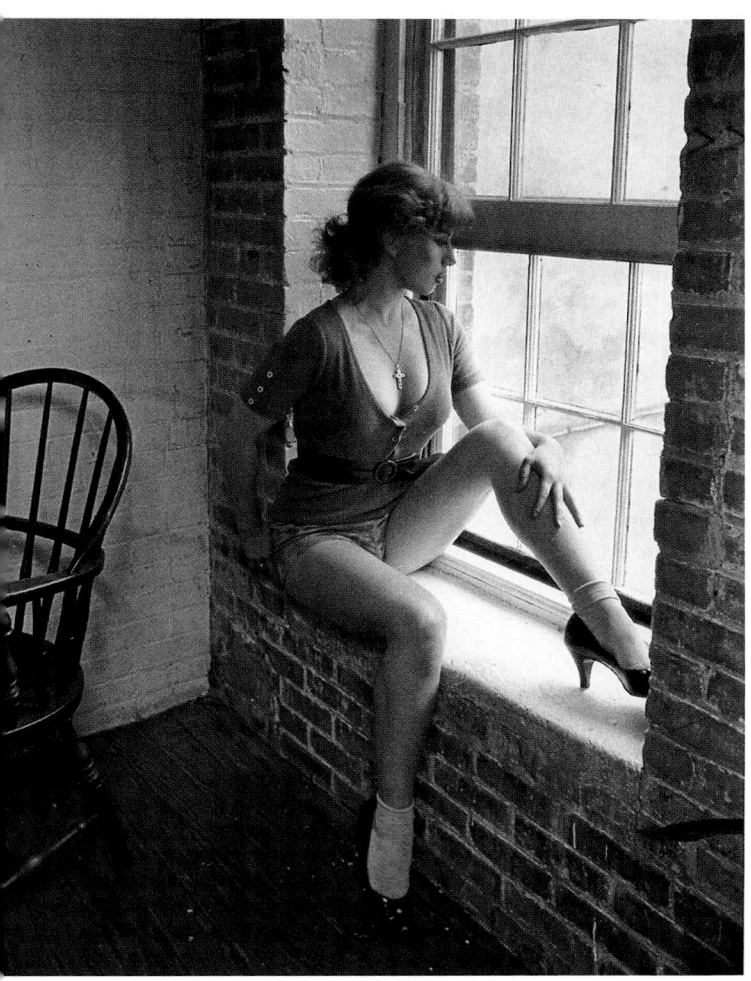

30.17 Cindy Sherman, *Untitled Film Still #15*. 1978.
Gelatin silver print, 10 × 8" (25.4 × 20.3 cm).
Courtesy of the artist and Metro Pictures, New York

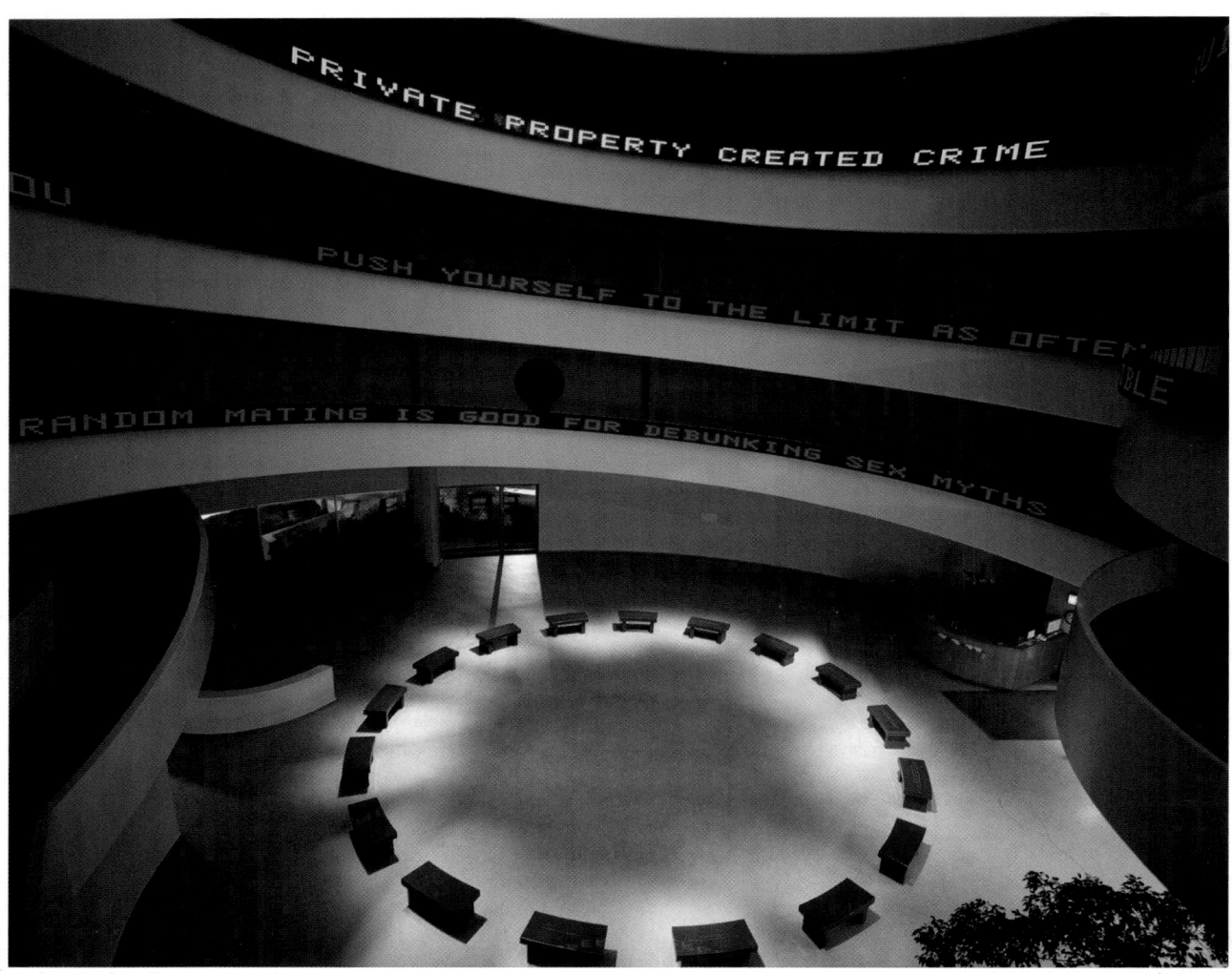

30.18 Jenny Holzer, *Untitled* (selections from *Truisms, Inflammatory Essays, The Living Series, The Survival Series, Under a Rock, Laments,* and *Child Text*). 1989. Extended helical tricolor LED electronic display signboard, 16" × 162' × 6" (40.6 × 4,937.8 × 15.2 cm). Site-specific dimensions. Solomon R. Guggenheim Museum, New York. Partial gift of the artist, 1989. 89.3626

Context and Meaning in Art: The Institutional Critique and Art as Commodity

Not all Postmodern artists deconstructed the mass media. Some, such as Fred Wilson, used appropriation to explore how museums control meaning and manipulate visitors, which we have already seen the Guerrilla Girls doing as well. Others, such as Jeff Koons, scavenged images from mass culture, especially nonart kitsch objects, and transformed them into high art. By putting the work in a high-art context, Koons demonstrates how art functions, how it differs from popular culture, and how taste is fashioned.

THE INSTITUTIONAL CRITIQUE: FRED WILSON Fred Wilson (b. 1954) is a New York Conceptual artist who generally works with found objects that he puts into new contexts in order to reveal the hidden meanings or agendas of their previous uses. Or, as he himself said, "I get everything that satisfies my soul from bringing together objects that are in the world, manipulating them, working with spatial arrangements, and having things

presented in the way I want to see them." He is especially renowned for deconstructing museums, that is, reinstalling collections to reveal how museums have an agenda when they present art and how the interpretation of this art can change when it is put into a new context. His most famous work is titled *Mining the Museum* (fig. **30.19**), a commission from the Museum of Contemporary Art in Baltimore. For this project, Wilson "mined" the collection of the nearby Maryland Historical Society, pulling works out of storage that probably had not seen the light of day in decades, and then inserting them into existing installations, the new item creating a new context for the display and powerfully deconstructing the original objects. Wilson, for example, uncovered slave manacles in storage, which he then inserted in a case of fine silver. Silver pitchers, teapots, and goblets, which had been presented as examples of superb craftsmanship and design, were now seen as valuable commodities, their production and acquisition made possible by the proceeds of slave labor. The manacles also raised a second issue, which is that without the manacles, African Americans, who constitute as large portion of

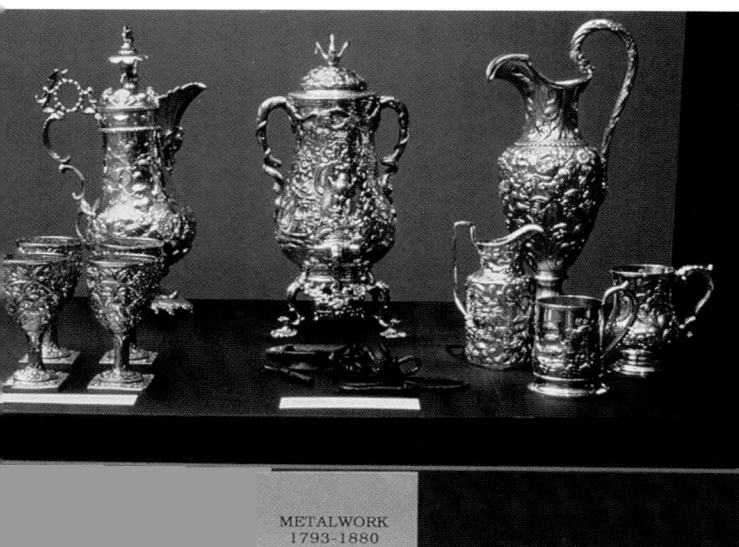

30.19 Fred Wilson, 'Metal Work, 1793–1880,' from *Mining the Museum: An Installation by Fred Wilson*. The Contemporary Museum and Maryland Historical Society, Baltimore, 4 April 1992–8 February 1993. Photograph courtesy PaceWildenstein, New York

Baltimore's populace, would not be represented at all in the museum. The unadorned, painfully functional manacles sit in powerful contrast to the glistening polished silver, creating a new context that radically undermines the story formerly told by the historical society.

ART AS COMMODITY: JEFF KOONS Unlike Wilson, Jeff Koons (b. 1955) makes objects, although he does not do the work himself, preferring to contract out the actual labor. But he likewise scavenges objects and images in order to explore the relationship of fine art, often sculpture, to mass culture. He is particularly interested in issues of taste and how art functions as a commodity. Despite making objects, Koons is basically a Conceptual artist, and the wealth of his ideas drives the diverse styles and mediums in which he works. He continuously pushes the limits of sculpture, creating objects that range from Hoover vacuum cleaners presented in Plexiglas boxes to stainless-steel train cars filled with bourbon based on actual Jim Beam train cars, and from a rabbit-shaped chrome balloon to a 43-foot-tall puppy made of flowers.

Entirely different is the ceramic sculpture *Michael Jackson and Bubbles* (fig. **30.20**) of 1988. Like a Warhol print, the sculpture was factory-produced, made to Koons's specifications in a limited edition by craftsmen in Italy. The image was not drawn or designed by the artist but rather chosen by him, in Duchampian fashion, from a publicity photograph of the singer with his pet chimpanzee, a process that on another occasion resulted in a copyright lawsuit against him. Its ornateness recalls seventeenth-century Italian Baroque sculpture (see Chapter 19) and eighteenth-century French porcelain, while the tawdry gold paint and rouged lips, along with the pop-culture imagery, give the work a crass look associated with mass-produced gift-shop figurines. Koons realized that by presenting his subject life-size, like a Classical sculpture of a Greek god, he was placing a mass-media image in the context of fine art, and giving it a new meaning. He transformed it from a kitsch souvenir into a compelling statement about what constitutes art, exploring the differences between fine art and "low" art. And because souvenirs are commodities, Koons reminds us that art, too, is merchandise. Again, with a hint of Warhol, Koons captures and parodies the glitz of celebrity promotion. But the tawdriness of the image and the porcelain medium give the sculpture a poignant sense of fragility and impermanence, suggesting

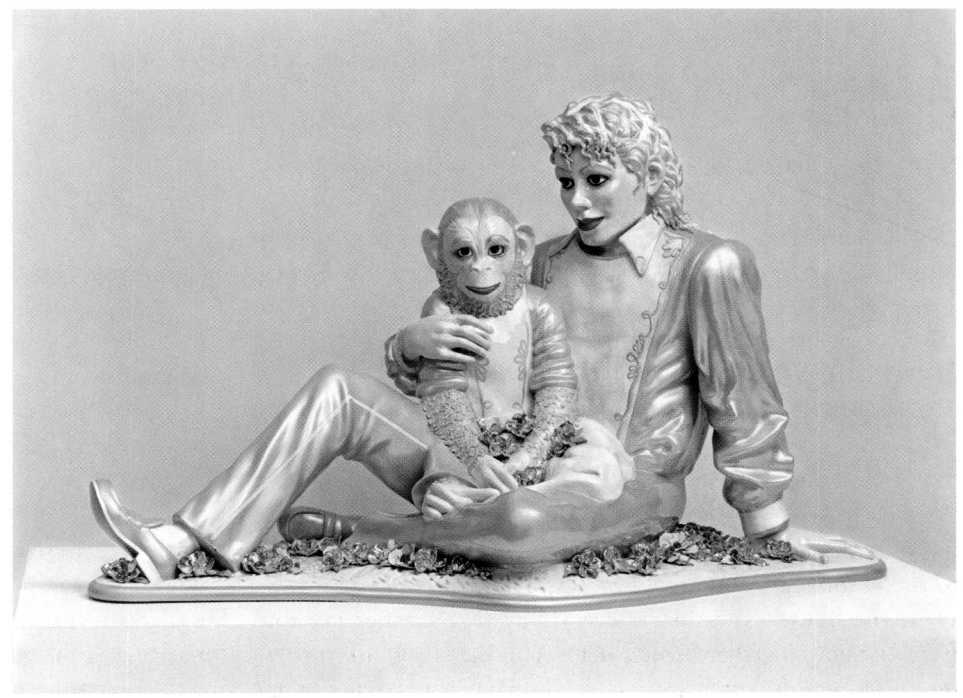

30.20 Jeff Koons, *Michael Jackson and Bubbles*. 1988. Porcelain, 42 × 70½ × 32½" (107 × 179 × 83 cm). Courtesy Sonnabend Gallery, New York

the temporary nature of life and fame. Koons rolls the influences of Duchamp, Warhol, and Postmodern deconstruction into one package and updates it for the consumption-oriented 1980s.

MULTICULTURALISM AND POLITICAL ART

We have looked at Fred Wilson within the context of appropriation, deconstruction, and the institutional critique, but we could have just as easily incorporated him in a section devoted to racial identity. Part and parcel of the Postmodern 1980s is the tremendous surge in art dealing with issues of race, ethnicity, gender, and sexual orientation, as well as a full range of social and economic issues. Goading many artists was the adversarial position of the neoconservativism of Ronald Reagan's administration (1981–89) and Jerry Falwell's Moral Majority, founded in 1979. Their extreme-right philosophy defeated the women's Equal Rights Amendment in 1982, sought to outlaw abortion, reduced funding for social welfare, and ignored the AIDS epidemic, which struck mostly gays, blacks, and Latinos.

African-American Identity

There are almost as many approaches to dealing with racial issues as there are artists. While Fred Wilson uses site-specific installation, others, like Lorna Simpson and Carrie-Mae Weems, use photography with text, like Kruger. In one of her best-known works, *Cornered* (1988), the Conceptual artist Adrien Piper used video installation. She barricaded a television monitor, draped in black cloth, in a corner of a room behind an upturned table. Above the monitor on the wall were two death certificates for her father, one describing him as white, the other as octoroon, that is, one-eight African-American. On the screen, Piper, well dressed and softly spoken, gives a 20-minute monologue describing how people become cornered due to stereotyping and labeling. Radically different is Conceptual artist David Hammons, whose work is often imbued with humor and takes place in the community. In contrast again, Kara Walker's cut-paper silhouette wall drawings are charged with horror, exposing the conflicting feelings of hatred, lust, sadism, and fascination that lie beneath racial tensions.

DAVID HAMMONS Emerging in the late 1960s, David Hammons (b. 1943) is a wonderfully quirky Conceptual artist who, for most of his career, shunned showing in prestigious galleries (he does now), often presenting his art surreptitiously in New York shops owned by friends, where customers would chance upon it while looking at the store's regular nonart merchandise. Or he creates work specifically for African-American communities, as is the case with *Higher Goals* (fig. **30.21**) of 1982, originally installed in his Harlem neighborhood and here photographed at a Brooklyn site. The sculpture was provoked by a group of neighborhood teenagers, who were playing basketball

when they should have been attending school and who told the artist that the road to success lay in sports, not education.

Hammons' response was to design 40-foot-high basketball hoops decorated with wind chimes (which suggest native American spirit catchers meant to filter out bad dreams) and bottle caps, often associated with winos and thus wasted lives and arranged in colorful geometric patterns suggesting African motifs, designs, textiles, and beadwork. As stated in the title, the work is about setting realistic higher goals, such as getting an education, as opposed to unrealistic objectives, such as becoming a professional basketball player, as suggested by the unreachable 40-foot-high baskets. Its brightly decorated objects have a ritualistic, even totemic quality, and they raise the issue of what is to be revered and where ancestral spirit is to be placed. While clearly humorous, Hammons's works are extremely intellectual, although they communicate at a "cool" accessible level with the neighborhood and in the neighborhood.

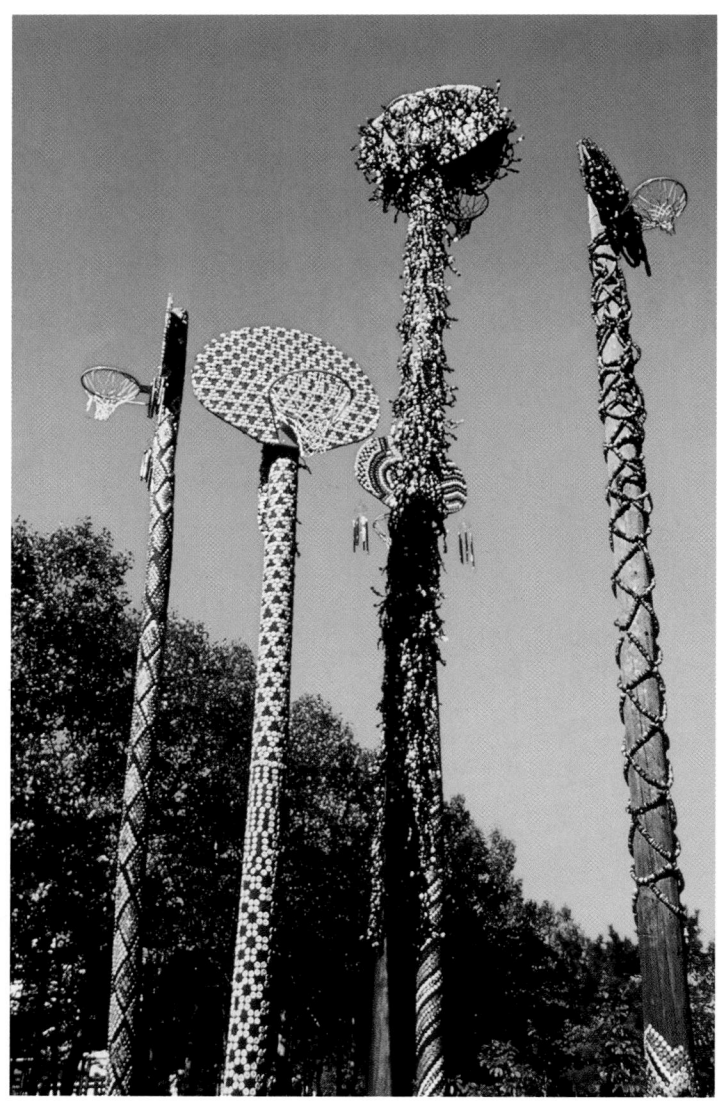

30.21 David Hammons, *Higher Goals*. 1982. Wood poles, basketball hoops, bottle caps, and other objects, height 40' (12.19 m). Shown installed in Brooklyn, New York, 1986

KARA WALKER Among the most sensational, and perhaps the most controversial, African-American artists to appear in recent years is Kara Walker (b. 1969), who emerged in 1994 fresh out of the M.F.A. program at the Rhode Island School of Design. Heavily influenced by her readings of such black feminist writers as Michele Wallace, Octavia Butler, and Toni Morrison, and especially the latter's *Tar Baby*, Walker found her subject matter in African-American history and, often, in her feelings as a black woman living in racist America. Simultaneously, her research led her to nineteenth-century silhouette portraits, simple black cut-paper silhouettes of the sitter, made by privileged white girls as part of their education and by itinerant portraitists for clients who could not afford full-blown portraits, whether on paper or canvas.

Walker exploded onto the New York art world in 1994 with a 13-by-50-foot installation of life-size black cutouts titled *Gone, An Historical Romance of a Civil War As It Occurred Between the Dusky Thighs of One Young Negress and Her Heart*, presented at the Drawing Center, a not-for-profit space. The scene is set in the antebellum South, filled with moss-laden oaks that frame such vignettes as white lovers leaning together to kiss, a small male slave mysteriously strangling a bird that appears to emerge from the opened legs of a female slave while the sword of a white gentleman appears to pierce the backside of the boy, and a slave girl performing fellatio on a white man. By 2000, Walker was adding projected silhouettes and colored lighting to her cut-paper installations, as can be seen in *Insurrection (Our Tools Were Rudimentary, Yet We Pressed On)* (fig. **30.22**), containing such lurid or unseemly events as a plantation owner surreptitiously propositioning a naked female slave behind a tree, a group of whites torturing a black, and a female slave, with a tiny baby on her head, trying to escape a lynching. Everything is exaggerated and caricatured, playing to stereotypes; many of the figures in her works are outright grotesques, having, for example, four legs or giant phalluses, thus hammering home the perversion and abnormality driving the emotions in her anecdotal, chimerical world. The cut paper is executed in unmitigated black, and the scene has the quality of a dream, actually a nightmare, its sense of violence, hysteria, and horror pushed to a feverish pitch by Walker's contours, which are jagged, spiky, and erupting with piercing sword- or daggerlike projections. This simple, detailless, flat, dark world seems to penetrate beneath the visual overload and superficiality of the fact-filled real world to expose the essence of human relations—a frightening psychological realm where the basic human urges and emotions of sex, desire, hatred, cruelty, love, sodomy, masochism, bestiality, castration, murder, and lust are played out. Walker's world is not just that of the antebellum South, it is also the world of today, where fraught race relations still plague American society and racial, ethnic, and religious conflict steeps the world in perpetual conflict. For besides giving *Insurrection* an oneiric quality, the projections pull Walker's antebellum scene into the present, for the light casts shadows of the viewers on the wall, thereby integrating the present, us, into Walker's nightmare and making us complicit in this horrific timeless occurrence.

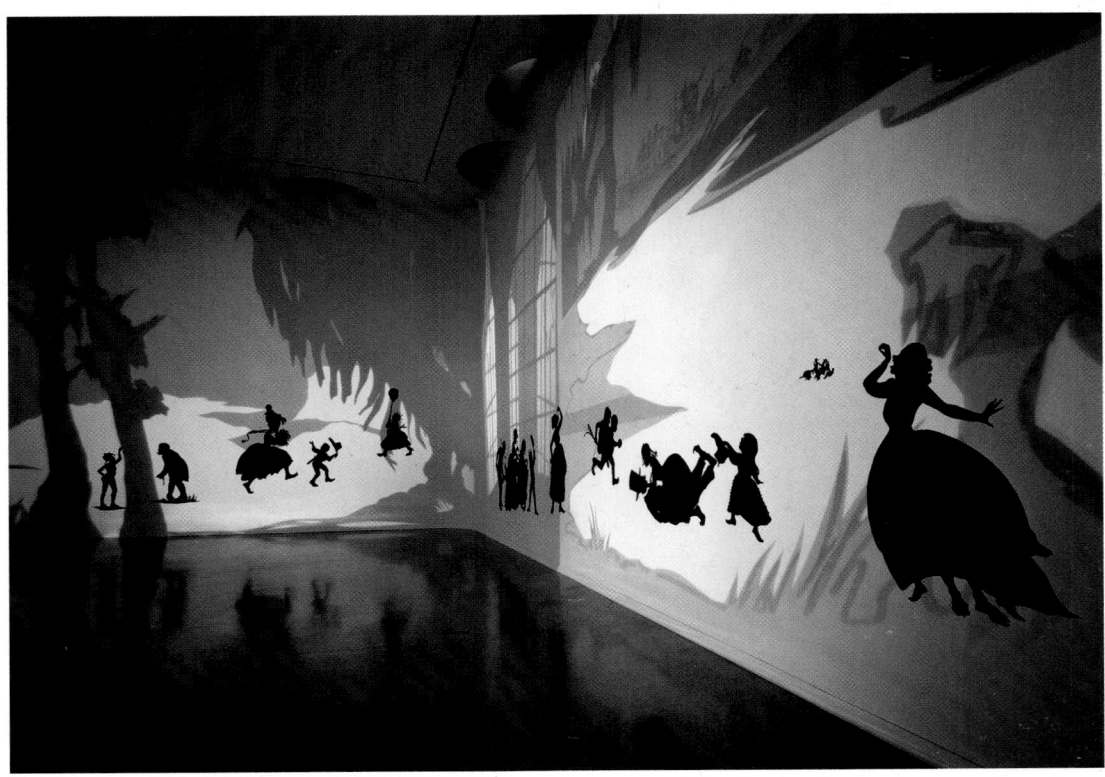

30.22 Kara Walker, *Insurrection (Our Tools Were Rudimentary, Yet We Pressed On)*. 2000. Cut paper silhouettes and light projections, dimensions variable. Solomon R. Guggenheim Museum, New York. Purchased with funds contributed by the International Director's Council and Executive Committee Members, 2000. 200.68

The AIDS Pandemic and a Preoccupation with the Body

One of the most embattled fronts in the 1980s artistic war with right-wing politics was the struggle to bring about government support to deal with the AIDS epidemic, a disease of the immune system first identified in 1981 that to date has affected over 33 million people worldwide. Triggered by ACT-UP, the acronym for the AIDS Coalition to Unleash Power, artists, many gay, began making art dealing with the crisis of thousands of people dying while the government did nothing. Much of the art was made by groups, such as Gran Fury and Group Material, these collaborative artists being a reflection of the Postmodern rejection

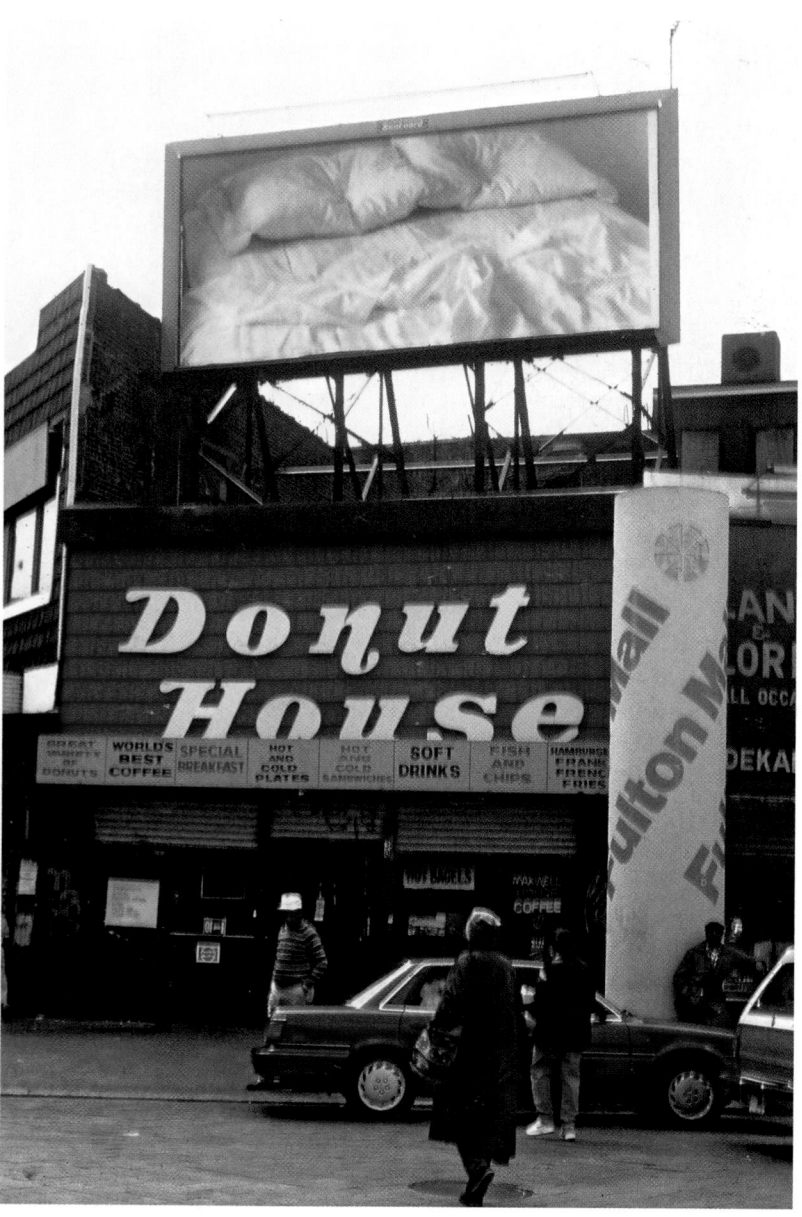

30.23 Felix Gonzalez-Torres, *Untitled* (billboard of an empty unmade bed). 1991. Billboard, overall dimensions vary with installation. The Felix Gonzalez-Torres Foundation. Courtesy of Andrea Rosen Gallery, New York and Museum of Modern Art, New York

of the importance placed on the individual in the production of art. Gran Fury, a spin-off of ACT-UP, its name taken from the Plymouth automobile used by the then-repressive New York Police Department, made posters, such as the 1988 *The Government Has Blood on Its Hands*, the bold type of the title appearing above and below a large blood-red handprint.

THE AIDS CRISIS: FELIX GONZALEZ-TORRES Felix Gonzalez-Torres (1957–1996), a founding member of the collaborative Group Material in 1980, produced some of the most powerful AIDS-related art, although his work encompasses a wide range of social issues. Gonzalez-Torres, who was born in Cuba and came to Florida in the 1981 in the mass-exodus called the Mariel boatlift, can best be described as a Conceptual artist working in a Minimalist mode. He is the quintessential Postmodern artist, since his art is issue-drive and seemingly oblivious to the concept of style. His mediums include, for example, two identical wall clocks hung side by side, which can be viewed as lovers who fade and die as the batteries wear out; a string of lightbulbs hanging from the ceiling, the lights evoking tears, or even souls, and like the clocks, eventually burning out; and a pile of brightly wrapped candy, the weight of the artist's lover, which visitors may take and eat, the gradual disappearance of the candy reflecting, among other things, the lover's body being consumed by AIDS.

Like so many artists of the 1980s, Gonzalez-Torres took his work out of a specifically art context and into the public domain. As part of a 1991 exhibition at the Museum of Modern Art in New York, he arranged for a black-and-white photograph of an empty, unmade bed, in which two people had slept, to be installed on 24 billboards around the city (fig. **30.23**). A classic Postmodern picture, it was highly suggestive and subject to broad interpretation. Despite being devoid of text, the simple image of an unmade bed spoke volumes. It conjured thoughts of intimacy, relationships, and love, as well as of loss, absence, and death. For some viewers, the image of the empty bed evoked the thousands of men, women, and children who had become victims of the AIDS epidemic, creating public awareness and discussion of the disease. In contrast to the overt propaganda of Gran Fury, Gonzalez-Torres's work is poetic and understated. Gonzalez-Torres died of AIDS at the age of 38.

A PREOCCUPATION WITH THE BODY: KIKI SMITH The death and suffering of AIDS victims brought about a new awareness of the body, especially its vulnerability and frailty. One artist to explore the vincibility of the body and the brevity of life is New Yorker Kiki Smith (b. 1954). In the 1980s, she created a work consisting of eight identical jars of blood, and another presenting silver-coated watercooler bottles etched with the names of bodily fluids such as tears, milk, saliva, vomit, semen, urine, and sweat that a viewer is led to believe is in the jars. Because these works contain repeated elements, they resemble Minimal Art. Yet the Conceptual component—the thoughts we have when confronting any of these bodily fluids—packs a powerful, visceral

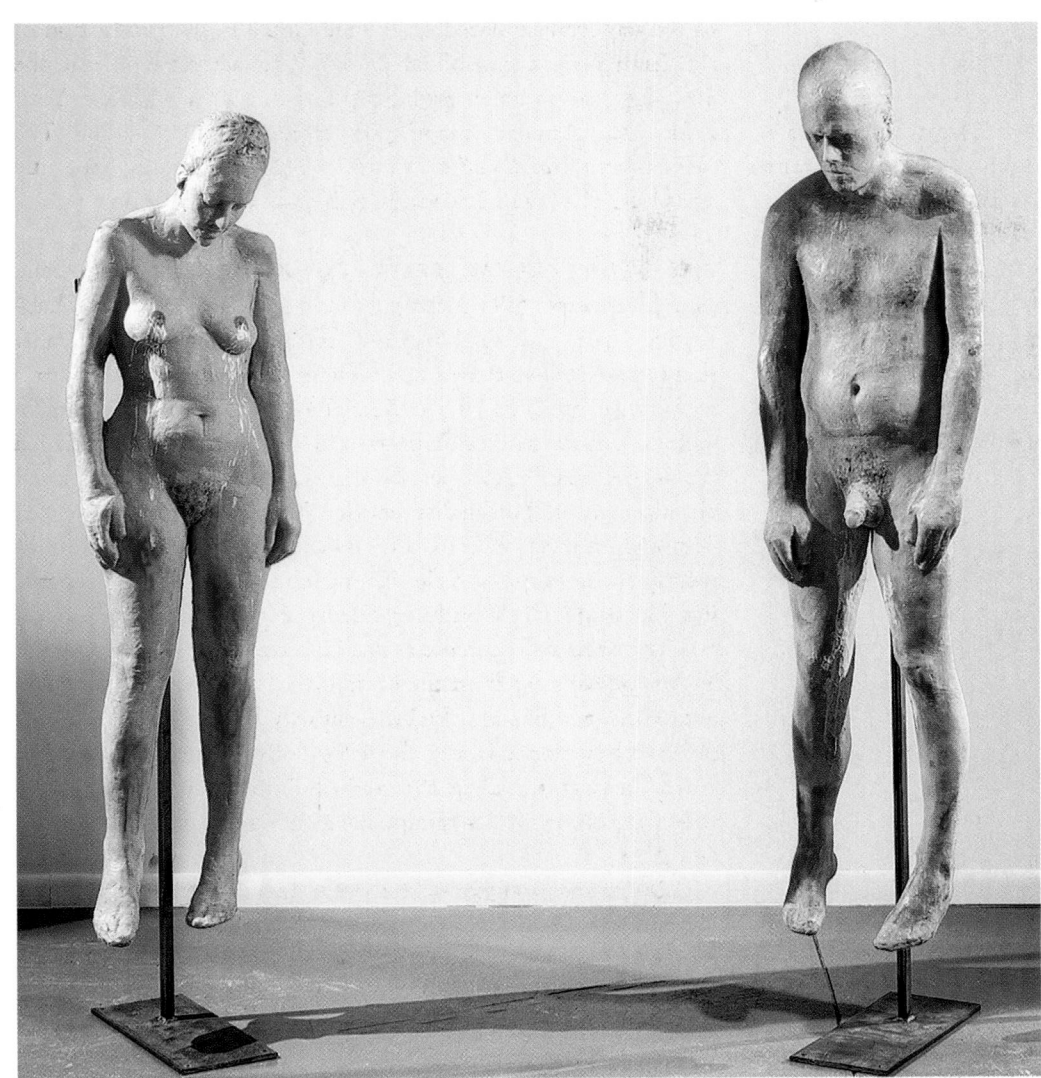

30.24 Kiki Smith, *Untitled*. 1990. Beeswax and micro-crystalline wax figures on metal stands, female figure installed height 6'4¹⁵⁄₁₆" (1.95 m). Collection Whitney Museum of American Art, New York. Purchase, with funds from the Painting and Sculpture committee. 91.13 (a–d)

response and emotional punch. Smith has reduced existence to an elemental essence, stripping away individuality and uniqueness to reveal the basic elements of life.

Toward 1990, Smith began constructing entire figures, usually using such impermanent materials as paper, papier-mâché, and wax, which served as a metaphor for the fragility of the body and the transience of life. In the untitled 1990 work reproduced here (fig. **30.24**), Smith cleverly revives the Classical tradition of the nude figure. However, we are viewing neither Greek gods and goddesses nor heroic athletes and soldiers. Rather, Smith portrays flesh-and-blood mortals. The woman oozes milk from her breast and the man semen from his penis, attributes of nourishment, procreation, and life. But death prevails, seen in the form of the limp figures slumped on their poles and the repulsive discoloration of the skin. Smith presents the entire life cycle, but it is the sadness of deterioration and our ultimate fate of death that prevail.

THE FUTILITY OF PRESERVING LIFE: DAMIEN HIRST

One of the most powerful statements about death, decay, and impermanence comes from the British artist Damien Hirst (b. 1965). Hirst, who has a flamboyant personality and is often accused of being a publicity hound, headed a group of London artists who came to the fore in 1988, when Hirst organized a student exhibition entitled *Freeze* in a London warehouse. The group created a public sensation and a critical storm due to their outrageous subject matter. Their imagery got even more outrageous in the 1990s, highlighted by Hirst's *The Physical Impossibility of Death in the Mind of Someone Living*, consisting of a dead shark floating in a tank of formaldehyde and shown in a 1992 Saatchi Gallery exhibition titled *Young British Artists*. The show also included Hirst's 1990 *One Thousand Years*, a glass case filled with flies and maggots feeding off a rotting cow's head. In addition, Hirst has made beautiful, ethereal paintings incorporating dead butterflies and abstractions using dead flies stuck to an enormous canvas. In *Mother and Child Divided* (fig. **30.25**), shown at the Venice Biennale in 1993, a cow and a calf, each divided in two, float in four tanks of formaldehyde. Using a Minimalist seriality, Hirst placed the bisected cows into identical tanks, thus creating a feeling of scientific objectivity. Even the nearly identical halves of each cow are multiples, that is, a repetition of the same form. The Minimalist tanks function as frames, the cow and calf as "realist pictures." The beauty and repulsiveness of this daring

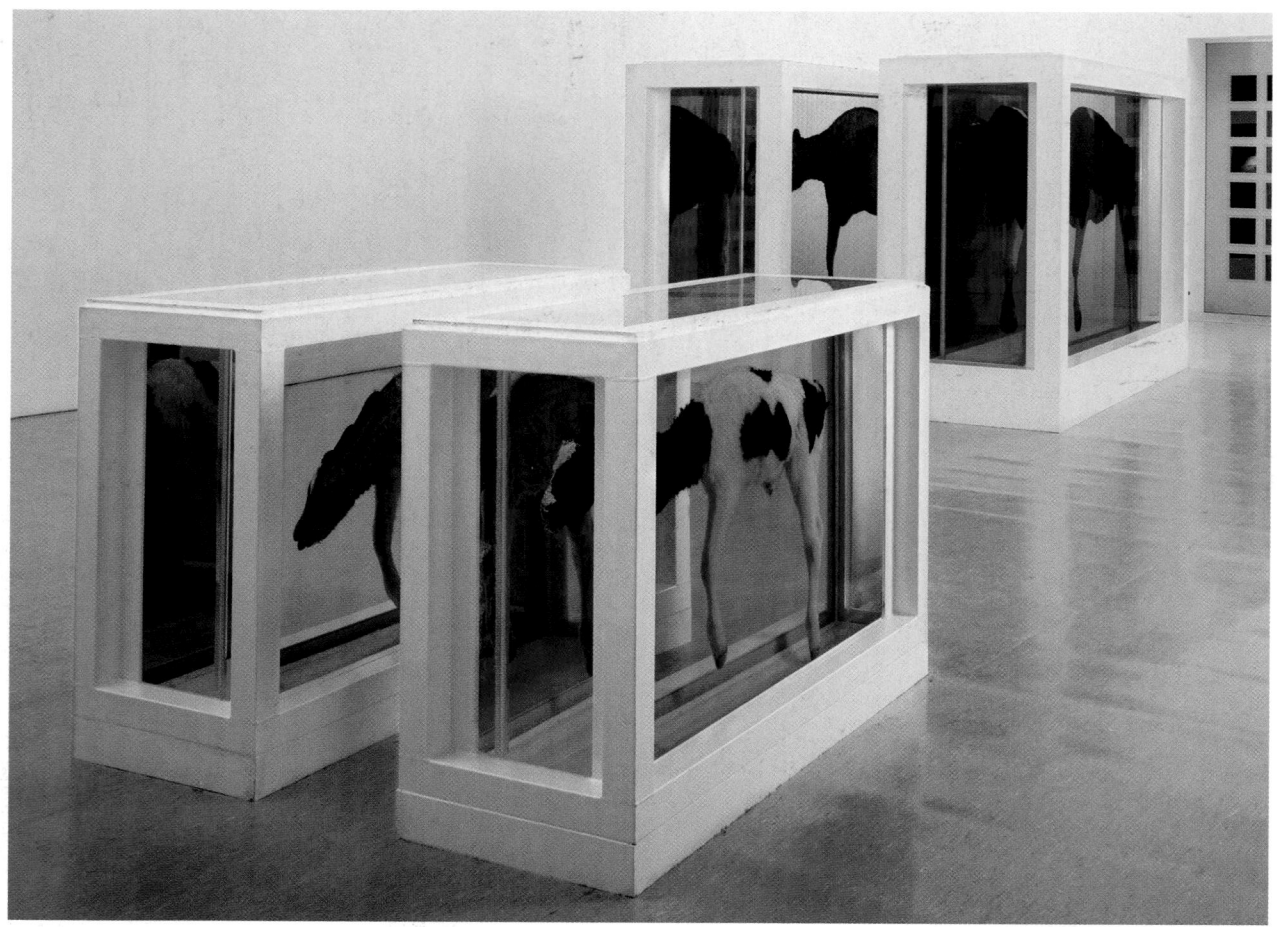

30.25 Damien Hirst, *Mother and Child Divided*. 1993. Steel, GRP composites, glass, silicone, cow, calf, and formaldehyde solution, two tanks at 74⅞ × 126⅞ × 43" (190 × 322 × 109 cm) and two tanks at 40⅛ × 66½ × 24⅝" (102.5 × 169 × 62.5 cm). Astrup Fearnley Museet for Moderne Kunst

presentation is fascinating. And because we are looking at real objects, we are literally confronting death, which is a powerful experience. We are also witnessing a vain attempt to prolong the physical existence of the animals. An especially poignant aspect of this work is the separation of mother from calf, a reminder of the life that once was and the emotional attachment of mother and child. While Hirst's subject matter may seem sensational, the animals he displays in formaldehyde tanks are powerful and unforgettable metaphors of life and death.

The Power of Installation, Video, and Large-Scale Photography

As we saw in the last chapter, installation art had existed since the late 1950s, when introduced by Alan Kaprow and called Environments. And by the early 1960s, we saw Robert Whitman integrating film into installation, thus anticipating video installation, and Nam June Paik taking a lead role in popularizing Video Art. At the same time, avant-garde artists, such as Joseph Kosuth, redefined photography, using the medium on a large scale and integrating it with other mediums. But in the 1980s, installation, video, and large-scale photography entered a new stage, their popularity

exploding to new heights again in the 1990s. Not only did all three art forms become more popular, they got bigger, more sophisticated, and more refined, moving away from the more experimental, tentative, or temporary look of these mediums in the 1960s and 1970s. And now artists often worked primarily in these mediums, not being part-time practitioners as before. And like art in the Postmodern era, the work often drew heavily on earlier styles and historical periods, and showed no fear of being anecdotal, often having elaborate narratives as opposed to being abstract.

ILYA KABAKOV Of the legions of installation artists who emerged in the 1980s, one of the most engaging is the Russian Ilya Kabakov (b. 1933), who emigrated from Moscow to New York in 1988. In Russia from 1981 to 1988, he made a series of rooms he called *Ten Characters* that replicated the types of seedy communal apartments assigned to people by the Russian state under the Communist regime. Each was inhabited by an imaginary person with an "unusual idea, one all-absorbing passion belonging to him alone." One spectacular cubicle was *The Man Who Flew into Space from His Apartment* (fig. 30.26). We see the room after its occupant has achieved his dream of being ejected into outer space, hurled through the ceiling from a catapult suspended by springs

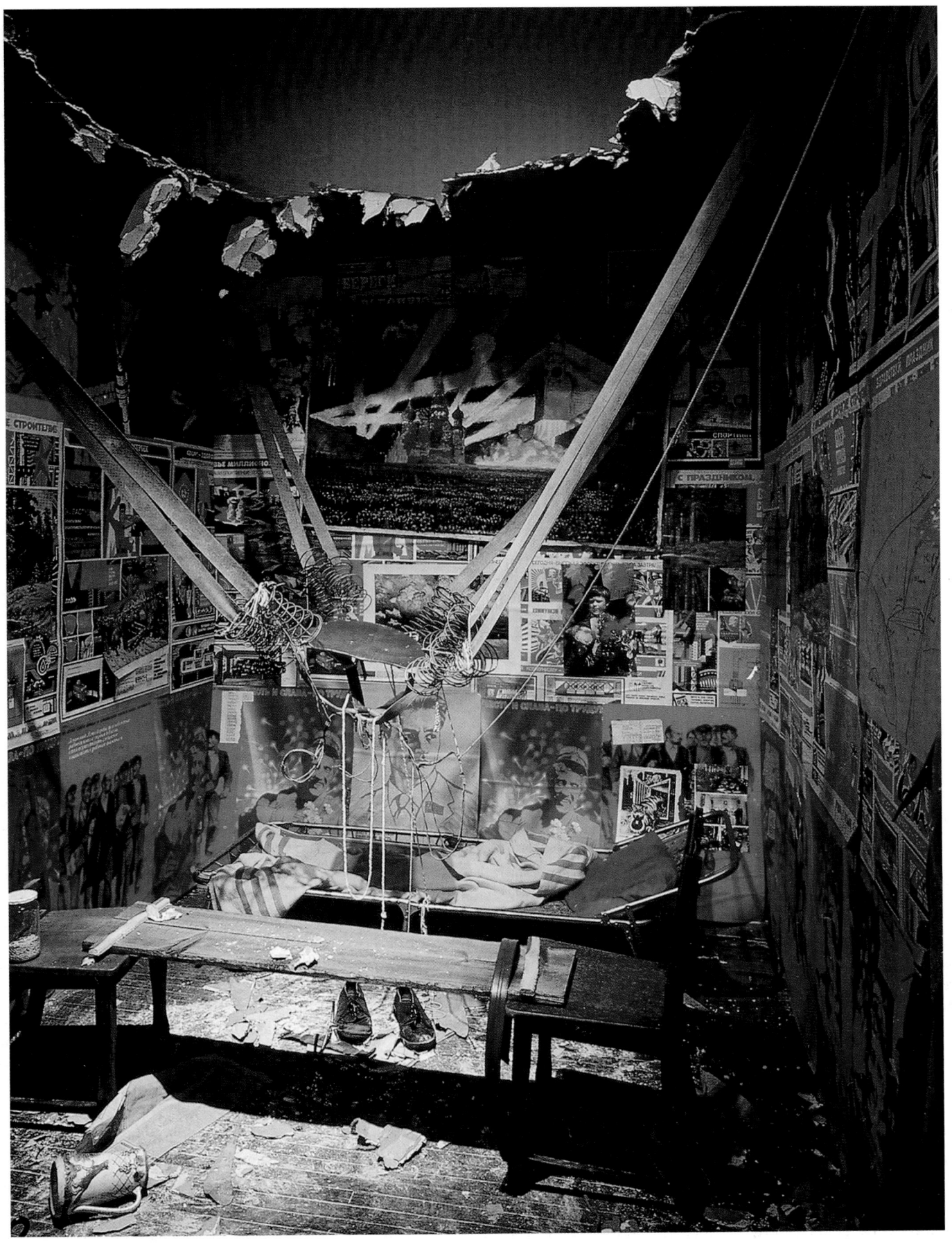

30.26 Ilya Kabakov, *The Man Who Flew into Space from His Apartment*, from *Ten Characters*. 1981–88.
Mixed-media installation, life-size

Ilya Kabakov (b. 1933)

On installations

Kabakov discusses his installations entitled Ten Rooms, *which deal with life in Soviet Russia. He especially emphasizes the importance of the space in his installations, claiming the rooms have a spirit that establishes the mood and meaning of the work.*

How does this "spirit of the place" seize you? In the first place, the rooms are always deconstructive, asymmetrical to the point of absurdity or, on the contrary, insanely symmetrical. In the second place, they look dull, oppressing, semidark, but this is not so because the windows are small or weak lamps are on. The main thing is the light both during the day and at night is arranged so excruciatingly, so awkwardly that it creates a peculiar discomfort distinctive to that place alone. The third important feature of our rooms' effect is their wretched, ridiculous preparation from the planning stage to the realization: everything is crooked, unfinished, full of stains, cracks; even in the most durable materials, there is something temporary, strange, made haphazardly, just to "pass."

What is especially depressing is the fact that everything is old, but at the same time it isn't clear when it was made, it doesn't have all the noble "patina of time," the marks of "wonderful days of old"; it is old in the sense of being decrepit and useless. All of this is despite the fact that it might have been made and painted only yesterday—it already appears outdated, marked for disposal. There is an impression of dust and dirt in every place and in everything—on the walls, at the ceiling, on the floor, in the corners. But the sensation is even stronger that these rooms, including private apartments, do not belong to anyone, that they are no-one's and that, in essence, no-one cares in the least about them. No-one loves them, people live in them temporarily and will leave not remembering them at all, like a train station, an underground crosswalk or a toilet at the bus station. ...

Sociality, being completely interlinked, was the natural means of survival, the very same traditional Russian "commune" which later also entered Soviet reality, in which you as a voluntary or subordinated participant were forever drowned, dissolved. But on the other hand, the commune saved you, supported you, didn't let you disappear or perish in loneliness, in despair, in a state of material or moral neglect. Every second of your life, you belonged to some kind of community....The atmosphere of the surrounding space was, in essence, its "spirit." ... And you caught this spirit immediately, all you had to do was to enter this or that space.

Source: Ilya Kabakov, *The Text as the Basis of Visual Expression*, ed. Zdenek Felix (Cologne: Oktagon, 2000)

and alluding to the space race between the U.S. and Russia. Like the other rooms, this one is accompanied by a grim story, worthy of the Russian novelist Fyodor Dostoevsky. The text, the collapsed ceiling, limp sling, and clutter become a tableau of life in Communist Russia, where claustrophobic squalor has brought about a hopeless delusional state, and flights of fantasy are the only escape from the drudgery of daily life. The ruin we are witnessing in *The Man Who Flew into Space* is not just the devastation of one man's life, but rather the shattered dream of the utopia in which Tatlin, the Constructivists, the Dadaists, and the Communist world in general had so firmly believed. Kabakov's installation is presented as a relic of an actual event, and like any relic, it possesses a powerful aura, almost impossible to achieve in conventional painting and sculpture. (See *Primary Source*, above.)

BILL VIOLA An especially popular form of installation is video or film installation. Among the best-known video artists is Bill Viola (b. 1951), who was also one of the first to specialize in video, coming at the tail end of the first generation of video artists. He started working with the medium in the 1970s after graduating from Syracuse University, his earliest work being primarily single-channel video presented on a television monitor. By the early 1980s, he was projecting video onto large walls and incorporating

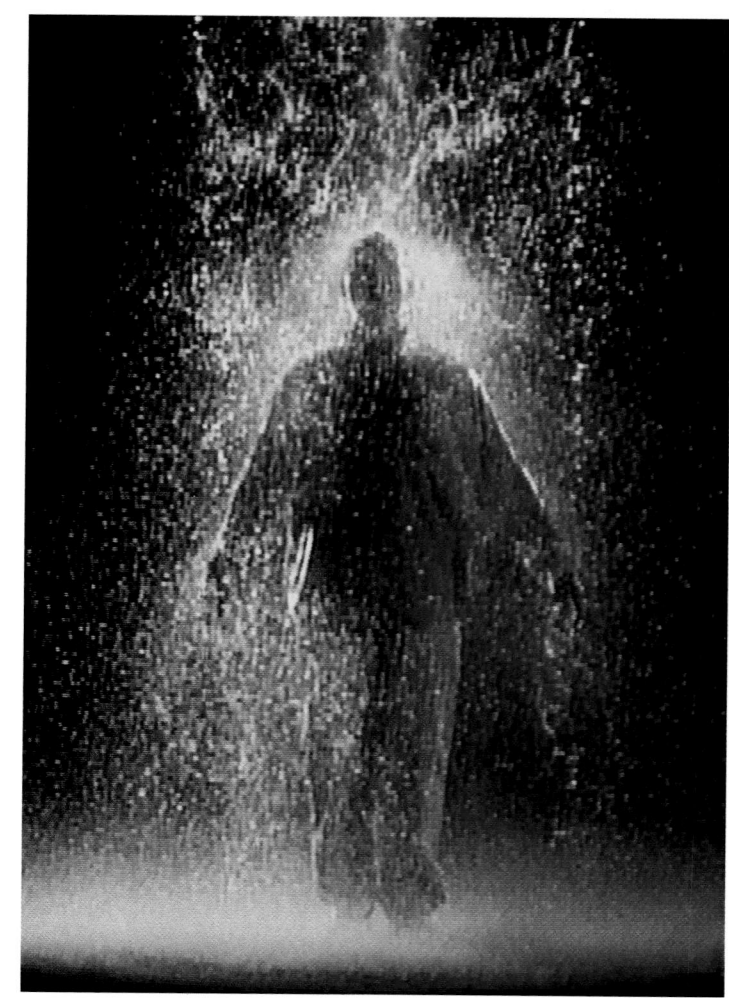

30.27 Bill Viola, *The Crossing*. 1996. Video/sound installation with two channels of color video projected onto 6-foot-high (1.83 m) screens, 10½ minutes. View of one screen at 1997 installation at Grand Central Market, Los Angeles. Courtesy of the Artist

it into installations or environments containing real objects. Although Viola's work does not always have a clear sequential narrative, it always has a theme, usually an unsettling, intense questioning of the meaning of existence that in part is brought about through intense sensory experience for a viewer.

One of Viola's best-known—and simplest—video projections is *The Crossing* (fig. **30.27**). In two simultaneous, approximately ten-minute projections, shown side by side, or on either side of a single screen, a plainly dressed man approaches from the distance, passing through an empty, darkened space and stopping when his body, now nearly 12 feet tall, fills the screen. In one projection, water begins to drip on him, eventually becoming a deluge that washes him away. In the other, a small fire erupts at his feet, increasingly swelling into a bonfire that ultimately consumes him. The projections end with water hauntingly dripping in one, and a fire mysteriously smoldering in the other. Both videos are accompanied by a deafening soundtrack of pouring water and crackling fire, which intensifies the force of the imagery and heightens its visceral impact. Viola's elemental symbols of fire and water seem to have destroyed the figure. Or perhaps the two forces have brought about a transformative process, as the body dissolves into a spiritual state, crossing into a higher reality and becoming one with the unseen universal forces. We do not know. The video relentlessly instills a sense of the physical and sensory, and then suddenly leaves us in an existential void. Viola's work is a quest for the spiritual, reflecting the influence of Zen Buddhism, Islamic Sufism, and Christian mysticism. Viola summed up the thrust of much of his work when he said, "And those two realizations: that you are connected deeply to the entire cosmos and at the same time you are mortal and you are fragile and inconsequential; the search for meaning that human beings have been engaged with since the beginning of time is part of the reconciliation of those two things."

LARGE-SCALE PHOTOGRAPHY: ANDREAS GURSKY As we have already seen when discussing Joseph Kosuth in the last chapter (see page 1062), photography underwent a dramatic change beginning in the late 1960s as the medium was appropriated by visual artists who, because they were not trained as photographers, broke all of photography's traditions. These new photographers worked on a large scale, often did not take their own photographs, generally did not print their own work, and occasionally integrated photography into other mediums. Beginning in the 1980s, large-scale photography entered a new stage. For one thing, by the end of the 1980s, it became more prevalent, to the point that it may very well have superseded painting for the art world's attention. Second, it got bigger, with more and more artists working on a larger and larger scale. Cindy Sherman and Barbara Kruger, for example, made 6- and 8-foot pictures, while the Canadian Jeff Wall worked on a billboard scale, backlighting his images, which were transparencies in lightboxes. And third, it was increasingly being made by artists for whom it was their primary medium. Düsseldorf especially produced a large number of major photographers, mainly due to the

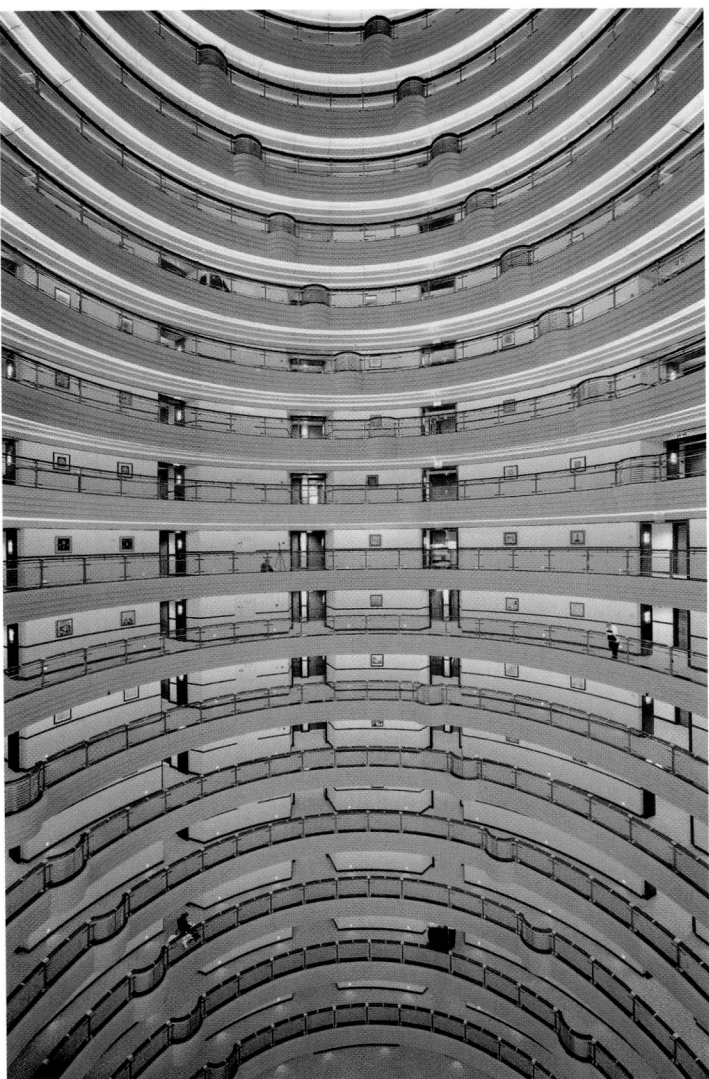

30.28 Andreas Gursky, *Shanghai*. 2000. Chromogenic color print, 9'11¹¹⁄₁₆" × 6'9½" (2.80 × 2.00 m). Courtesy: Monika Sprueth/Philomene Magers, Cologne

innovative black-and-white photography of Bernd (1931–2007) and Hilla (b. 1934) Becher, and because Bernd, like Joseph Beuys, taught at the Art Academy. Becher's students included such renowned photographers as Thomas Struth, Thomas Ruff, Candida Höffer, and Elger Esser.

They also included Andreas Gursky (b. 1955). We can get a sense of his scale from his 2000 Chromogenic color print *Shanghai* (fig **30.28**), which is over 9½ feet high. Looking at this work, we get the impression that Gursky has an exceptional eye that has allowed him to discover remarkable compositions in the real world. Here, as in so many of his works, he seems to have discovered a wonderful geometry, which gives his image the look of Minimalist Art (see page 1056), yet another example of a Postmodern appropriation of an earlier style. But in fact he has digitally manipulated his images—sharpening lines, emphasizing certain colors while suppressing others, heightening value contrasts or minimizing them, and, on occasion, removing

The Changing Art Market

The world of contemporary art is as complex and varied as the art itself. Museums, commercial galleries, private dealers, auction houses, art fairs, international exhibitions, collectors from all strata of society, critics, curators, art historians, books, and a vast mass media that includes the Internet are some of the pieces that form the kaleidoscopic art market of the twenty-first century.

How different this conglomerate of influences is from the late medieval and Early Renaissance world that was largely defined by artists' guilds, the apprentice system, and a patronage system dominated by aristocrats and the Church. The rise of academies in the sixteenth and seventeenth centuries, especially the French Royal Academy in 1648, marked a shift of power to the academy system and its accompanying exhibitions (called Salons in Paris) which showcased the work of members and students. Historians published the first books on artists during this period. The eighteenth century witnessed the rise of prominent art auctions in Paris and London, the opening of the first public art museums in those cities, and the beginning of what many consider to be the first art criticism (see pages 811–12). In the nineteenth century, the French Salon changed from a members' exhibition into an open show that was juried and that presented hundreds of artists and thousands of works. Artists from all over Europe and the Americas aspired to exhibit at the Paris Salon, which, although dominated by the French, in effect became the first international showcase and an important venue for attracting patrons and commercial success. By the end of the nineteenth century, art dealers, who had virtually always been around, became a major force in the art world, especially in Paris.

Today, one of the strongest influences on an artist's career is representation by a prestigious dealer with a reputation for selecting "important" artists. Also significant is exhibiting and being collected by major museums, such as the Museum of Modern Art in New York, the Museum of Contemporary Art in Los Angeles, the Tate Gallery in London, the Ludwig Museum in Cologne, and the National Museum of Modern Art in Paris. These are just a few of the many museums known for presenting prestigious exhibitions and collecting contemporary art.

Artists also aspire to be included in the big international exhibitions, the twentieth- and twenty-first-century equivalent of the nineteenth-century French Salons, although the artists are generally invited by curators and do not submit work to a jury. One of the oldest international exhibitions is the Venice Biennale, established in 1903 and located in a park in Venice. Today, the show occurs once every two years and takes place in permanent pavilions owned by the various countries which present their own artists. Such international shows were often conceived to promote the host cities and to encourage their economic development. For example, Andrew Carnegie founded the Carnegie Museum of Art in Pittsburgh in 1895, and the following year he established what is now known as the Carnegie International in order to draw international attention to Pittsburgh. Both the Venice Biennale and the Carnegie International, however, only gained their current prestige after World War II, when they were joined by other major international shows, such as the Documenta in Kassel, Germany, which is held every four years, and the São Paulo Biennale in Brazil. In the last few decades, many other international biennials have joined the art scene, including those in Istanbul, Havana, Cairo, and Johannesburg. A major venue for American artists has been New York's Whitney Museum of American Art, which was founded in 1930 and has always held an annual or biennial exhibition.

Despite the excitement generated by fairs and galleries, however, contemporary art has largely lived in the shadow of Old Masters and Impressionism, and, as the twentieth century progressed, early European Modernism. It was not until the 1970s that contemporary art became fashionable. Triggering the stampede to buy work by living artists was the sensationally successful auction of the Pop Art collection of Robert and Ethel Scull at Sotheby's in New York in 1973. Such major auction houses as Sotheby's and Christie's, both dating to eighteenth-century London, had long sold contemporary art, but in small quantities and with little fanfare. But after the Scull auction, countless collectors rushed into the contemporary arena, and in the last 25 years, auctions of contemporary art have shared the limelight with sales of Impressionism and European Modernism. This collecting fever spurred the appearance of numerous international art fairs, including Art Basel in Basel, Switzerland; Art Basel Miami in Miami Beach; the Frieze Art Fair in London; the Armory Show in New York; and the Foire Internationale d'Art Contemporain or FIAC (International Fair of Contemporary Art) in Paris. Every year, these high-end art fairs are flooded with tens of thousands of collectors and visitors scouting for new work and new artists.

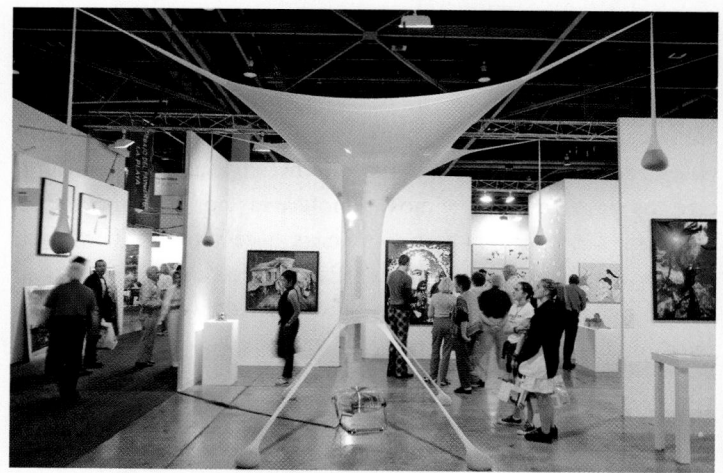

International Art Fair. Art/Basel/Miami Beach/1–4/Dec/05

objects. In some respects, he colors and draws like a painter. And his extremely realistic-looking images, which *have* to be fact since after all they are photographs, are a deconstruction of photography since they serve as evidence of how all images are artificial and reflect what Derrida would describe as one person's hierarchy.

If it were not for the title, *Shanghai*, we would have no idea where Gursky's photograph was shot, for there is nothing to give

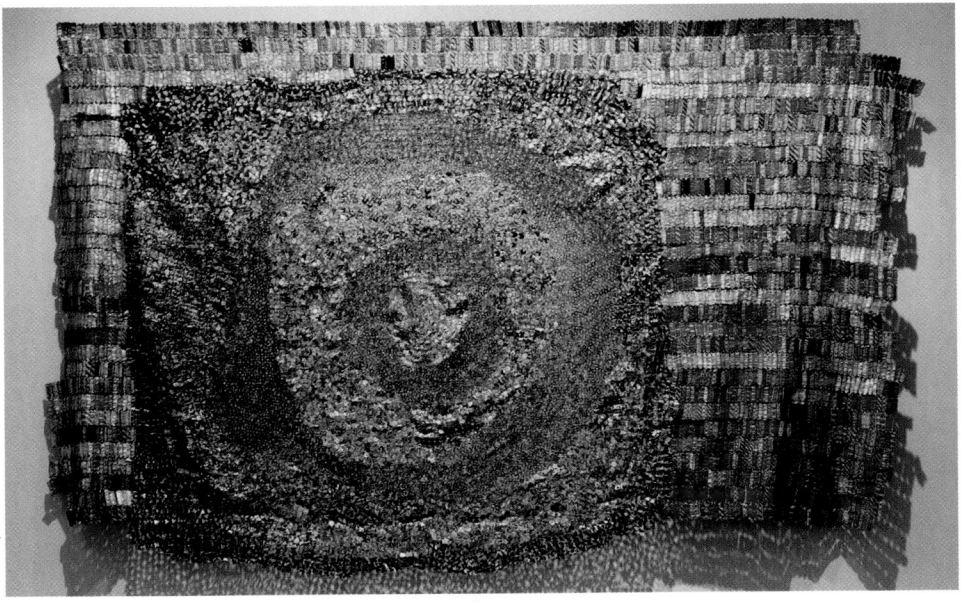

30.29 El Anatsui, *Dzesi II*. 2006.
Aluminum liquor bottle caps and copper wire,
9'9" × 16'3" × 8" (2.97 × 4.95 × 0.20 m).
Collection of the Akron Art Museum, Akron
Ohio. Courtesy Artist and Jack Shainman
Gallery, New York

this building a sense of place. And that is the point. From a deconstruction standpoint, the title is in a sense an integral part of the visual work, underscoring how the title affects meaning. As social commentary, the work points up how global all cultures have become. Gursky travels the world to acquire his images, photographing such motifs as hotel lobbies, stock exchanges, office towers, department stores, and crowds at rock concerts: The latter, instead of appearing Minimalist, have the allover look of a Jackson Pollock painting, another stylistic appropriation. In every instance, if it were not for the title, we would be clueless not only about the locale but even the nation or hemisphere featured in Gursky's highly objective and unemotional images, which suggest how homogeneous the world has become.

GLOBAL ART

The closing decade of the twentieth century marked the rise of a world art. With the arrival of the Internet and satellite communications, artists in even the most remote areas no longer operate in isolation. More artists than ever have access to what is being produced in New York, London, Paris, Düsseldorf, Beijing, and Tokyo. Jet travel circulates artists from Korea to Cairo, from Johannesburg to São Paulo, and from Basel to Dubai, for exhibitions and art fairs. (See *The Art Historian's Lens*, page 1104.) The entire world is artistically bound together, transforming it into one large art gallery and making it nearly impossible to talk about art in one hemisphere without talking about developments occurring everywhere else. Now, artists worldwide use the same art language, deal with similar issues, and avidly follow each other's work.

Many critics predicted that the rise of a global art world would result in a global art, art that is basically homogeneous. But this is hardly the case. Since Postmodernism emphasizes issues and not style, artists often make work that is very personal and that reflects their personal experience. As we have seen, gender, race,

ethnicity, sexual orientation, politics, and economics have been dominant themes in Western culture since the 1980s, and the same holds true worldwide, with contemporary art from Lebanon, Vietnam, India, Iran, and Colombia, for example, embracing issues specific to these countries. Or, as expressed by the Ghanaian artist El Anatsui, "Art is something that is environment-based. It takes its roots from a certain soil."

El Anatsui, Adinkra Signs, and Postmodern Ambiguity

El Anatsui (b. 1944) was born in Ghana, and studied art at the University of Science and Technology in Kumasi, his education focusing on contemporary art, largely made in a formalist, Modernist tradition. In 1975, he began teaching at the University of Nigeria in Nsukka, where he lives today. Initially working in clay and wood and reflecting traditional Ghanaian and Nigerian art and themes, he now works with the flattened metal caps and bottleneck foil of liquor bottles, weaving this metal together with copper wire to create what look like enormous, luxurious tapestries or fabrics. These brightly colored aluminum mosaics, such as *Dzesi II* (fig. **30.29**), evoke Nigerian and Ghanaian textiles and designs, the hard metal being visually transformed into something soft. For Anatsui, these caps are a reminder of the liquor that European traders brought to Africa as barter and therefore could be seen as a reference to trade, commodity, and even the beginning of globalization. The artist has also said that "metals and liquor in many cultures, especially African, have this association with the spiritual, with healing. Just think about the many ways a hand must open metal caps to pour out schnapps for prayers and libations."

In *Dzesi II*, the protrusion of concentric circles placed within a square suggests something ritualistic. According to the artist, this form came about "with thoughts about the zero sign, Ø— which can mean a lot or nothing. And I think is a kind of harking to Adinkra symbols I had worked with earlier." Adinkra, which translates as saying farewell, are West African symbols, printed on fabric originally worn at funerals, although they have wider uses now. The symbols encapsulate aphorisms that help mourners meditate on life, and the concentric circles, according to Antasui, are the "king of these signs, the most conspicuous and attention-grabbing, which I think has focus-inducing properties." The central zero is thus a form upon which to mediate. And it is also a Postmodern void to which viewers can assign meaning. Not only does the meaning of the work have a Postmodern ambiguity, but so does the form of the sculpture itself. For travel, the artist folds these enormous reliefs until they are small enough to fit into a box; when unfurled, they do not automatically resume their original shape, allowing curators and collectors in the artist's absence, and with his blessing, to restructure the work, implementing what Anastui calls a "nomadic aesthetic."

Cai Guo-Qiang: Projects for Extraterrestrials

It seems only fitting to end this book with Cai Guo-Qiang (b. 1957), a Chinese artist living in New York since 1995, with a second house in Beijing, which he needed as the director of Visual and Special Effects for the 2008 Olympics. With the adoption of capitalism, China has become a powerhouse in art, not only saturating the art world with artists but becoming a major art center and market for art itself. Cai is among the most visible artists working today, and he brings to the new global art a Chinese background and perspective. Like Gonzalez-Torres, Cai is primarily a Conceptual artist working in a broad range of mediums. His oeuvre, however, is dominated by installation art and the use of explosions, namely fireworks, which he used so effectively in the opening ceremonies at the 2008 Olympics and which have become his signature style. By using gunpowder, a Chinese invention, Cai is able to underscore his cultural identity, which he does as well by working with Chinese calligraphy, dragons, Chinese medicine, and feng shui, an ancient art and science that reveals how to balance the energy of any given space to assure health and good fortune. He started working with explosives while living in Japan between 1986 and 1995, reveling in the spontaneity and chance of the medium and finding it an emotional release from the stifling artistic and social environment of precapitalist 1980s China. As the artist explains: "Explosions make you feel something intense at the very core of your being because, while you can arrange explosives as you please, you cannot control the explosion itself. And this fills you with a great deal of freedom." Cai "draws" with explosives, on a small scale by drawing with gunpowder on large sheets of paper that he then ignites, and on a large scale with fireworks, which sometimes resemble Chinese calligraphy.

In 2003, Cai was commissioned by New York City and the Central Park Conservancy to create an explosion piece in Central Park. Titled *Light Cycle: Explosion Project for Central Park* (fig. **30.30**), the work lasted four minutes and was divided into three parts: "Signal towers" (pillars of light), "The Light Cycle" (a series of haloes), and "White Night" (small-shell explosions of brilliant white light). The degree to which Cai controls the explosions is remarkable. He draws and paints with the medium. Through his work, Cai seeks to capture a spiritual essence. He has said that his work is for extraterrestrials, and he has subtitled many of his explosions "Project for Extraterrestrials." Just as the art world has become global, so Cai, perhaps with a little wink, is looking beyond earth, seeking to create art for the universe.

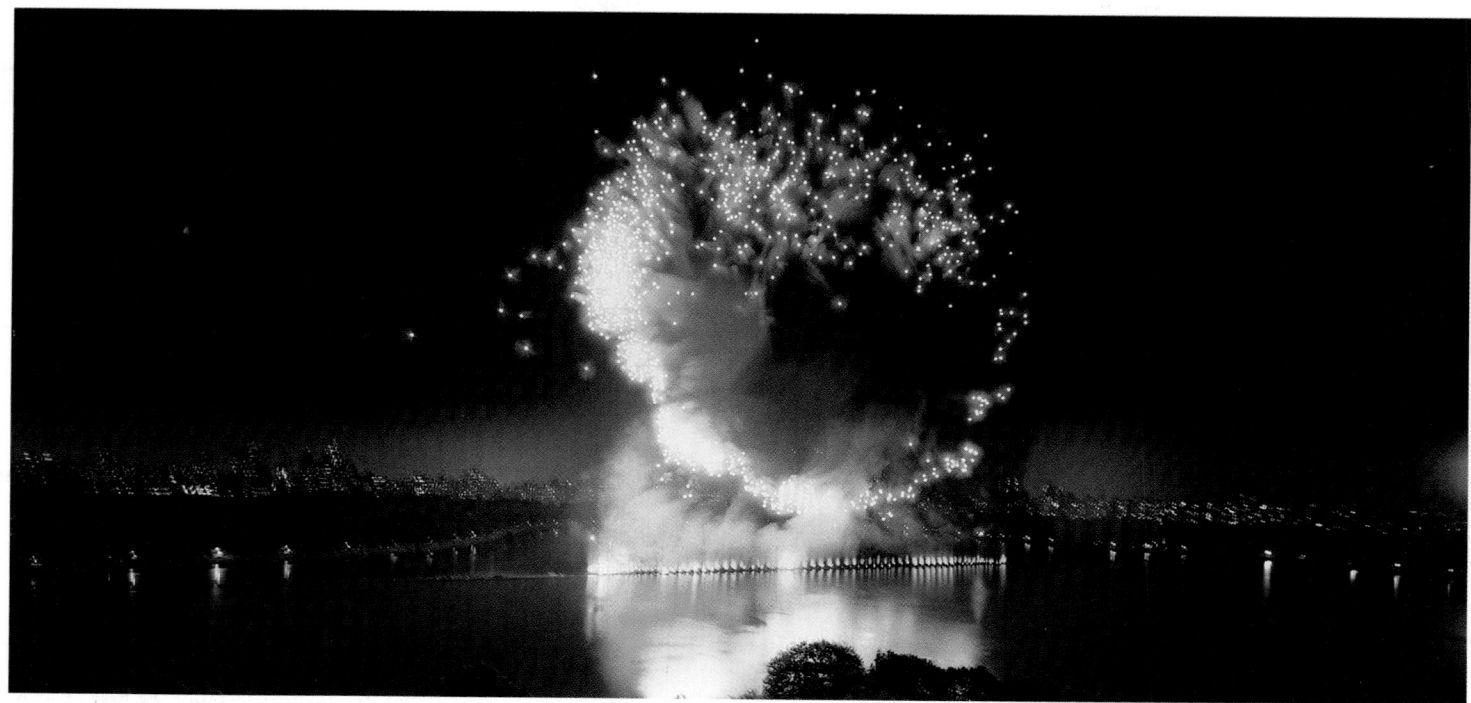

30.30 Cai Guo-Qiang, *Light Cycle: Explosion Project for Central Park*. Tiger tails, titanium solutes fitted with computer chips, shells with descending stars, 4 minutes. Realized at Central Park, New York, 7:45 p.m. September 15, 2003.

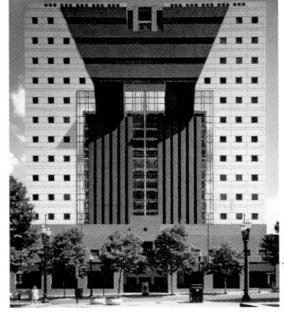

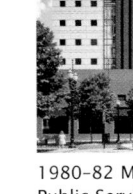

1980–82 Michael Graves's Public Services Building, Portland, Oregon

1982 Maya Lin's *Vietnam Veterans Memorial*

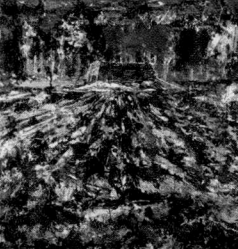

1983 Anselm Kiefer's *To the Unknown Painter*

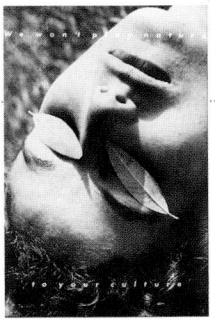

1983 Barbara Kruger's *We Won't Play Nature to Your Culture*

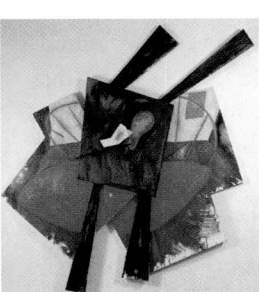

1983 Elizabeth Murray's *More Than You Know*

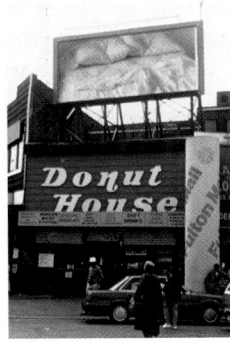

1991 Felix Gonzalez-Torres's *Untitled* (billboard of an empty bed)

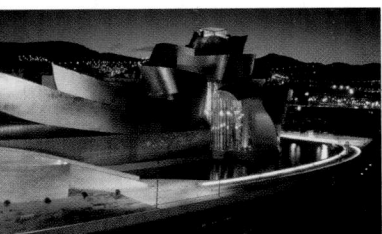

92–97 Frank Gehry's
ggenheim Museum, Bilbao,
ain

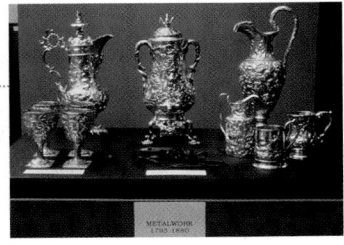

1992 Fred Wilson's *Mining the Museum*

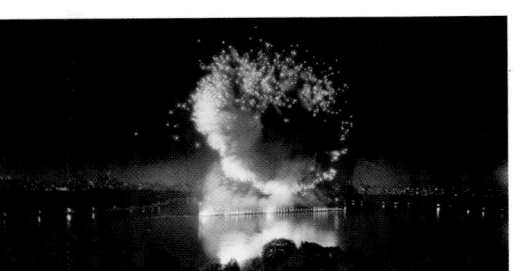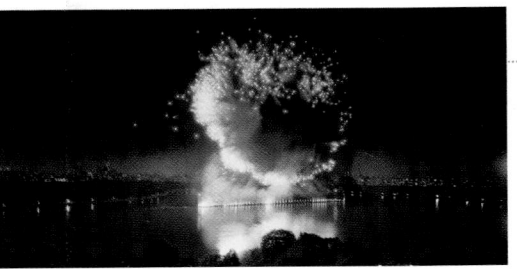

2003 Cai Guo-Qiang's *Light Cycle: Explosion Project for Central Park*

The Postmodern Era: Art Since 1980

1979–89 Soviet-Afghan War
1979–90 Margaret Thatcher, leader of the Conservative Party, is Prime Minister of the United Kingdom
◀ 1979 Jerry Falwell forms Moral Majority

1981–89 Ronald Reagan is President of the USA
1981 Sandra Day O'Connor is the first woman appointed to the Supreme Court
◀ 1981 First AIDS cases reported
········· 1981 *A New Spirit in Painting*, a painting exhibition at the Royal Academy of Arts, London
◀ 1982 Equal Rights Amendment defeated

1986 Chernobyl Nuclear Power Plant disaster
1986 Ivan Boesky, an arbitrageur specializing in
◀ corporate takeovers and mergers, is on the cover of *Time* December 1
◀ 1987 The Intermediate-Range Nuclear Forces Treaty between the U.S. and the Soviet Union

········· 1988 *Magiciens de la Terre*, an exhibition dedicated to global art, presented at the Pompidou Center,
◀ 1989 Berlin Wall torn down
1989 Student protests in Tiananmen Square, Beijing
◀ 1990 Germany Reunited
1990–91 Persian Gulf War
◀ 1991 U.S.S.R. is dissolved
1991–92 Republic of South Africa repeals apartheid
········· 1992 Saatchi Gallery, London mounts exhibition *Young British Artists*

1994 Nelson Mandela elected president of South Africa
◀ 1994 World Wide Web launched
1994 North American Free Trade Agreement

◀ 2001 Al Qaeda terrorists attack the United States

◀ 2003 United States invades Iraq

2008 Beijing hosts Olympics; Cai Guo-Qiang artistic director of opening and closing ceremonies
◀ 2008 Barack Obama is elected the first African-American President of the United States

1980
1985
1990
1995
2000
2010

Glossary

ABACUS. A slab of stone at the top of a Classical capital just beneath the architrave.

ABBEY. (1) A religious community headed by an abbot or abbess. (2) The buildings that house the community. An abbey church often has an especially large choir to provide space for the monks or nuns.

ACROTERION (pl. **ACROTERIA**). Decorative ornaments placed at the apex and the corners of a pediment.

ACTION PAINTING. In Abstract art, the spontaneous and uninhibited application of paint, as practiced by the avant-garde from the 1930s through the 1950s.

AEDICULA. A small shrine or altar that dates to ancient Rome.

AEOLIC. An early style of Greek architecture, found in northwestern Asia Minor. The Aeolic style is often considered a precursor to the Ionic style.

AISLE. The passageway or corridor of a church that runs parallel to the length of the building. It often flanks the nave of the church but is sometimes set off from it by rows of piers or columns.

ALABASTRON. A perfume container, similar to an aryballos, crafted by Greek vase-painters and often imported into Etruria.

ALBUMEN PRINT. A process in photography that uses the proteins found in eggs to produce a photographic plate.

ALLEGORY. A representation in which figures or events stand for ideas beyond themselves as symbols or metaphors, to create a moral or message for the viewer.

ALLOVER PAINTING. A painting in which the texture tends to be consistent throughout and which has no traditional compositional structure with a dominant focus of interest but, rather, even stresses throughout the image, as in Jackson Pollock's Abstract Expressionist action paintings.

ALTAR. A mound or structure on which sacrifices or offerings are made in the worship of a deity. In a Catholic church, a tablelike structure used in celebrating the Mass.

ALTARPIECE. A painted or carved work of art placed behind and above the altar of a Christian church. It may be a single panel or a *triptych* or a *polytych*, both having hinged wings painted on both sides. Also called a reredos or retablo.

AMBULATORY. A covered walkway. (1) In a basilican church, the semicircular passage around the apse. (2) In a central-plan church, the ring-shaped aisle around the central space. (3) In a cloister, the covered colonnaded or arcaded walk around the open courtyard.

ANAMORPHIC. Refers to a special form of perspective, which represents an object from an unusual or extreme viewpoint, so that it can only be understood from that viewpoint, or with the aid of a special device or mirror.

ANDACHTSBILD. German for "devotional image." A picture or sculpture with imagery intended for private devotion. It was first developed in Northern Europe.

ANIMAL STYLE. A style that appears to have originated in ancient Iran and is characterized by stylized or abstracted images of animals.

ANNULAR. From the Latin word for "ring." Signifies a ring-shaped form, especially an annular barrel vault.

APOTROPAIC DEVICE. An object deployed as a means of warding off evil. Often a figural image (such as a Medusa head) or a composite image (like a Near Eastern lamassu), inserted into an architectural setting.

APSE. A semicircular or polygonal niche terminating one or both ends of the nave in a Roman basilica. In a Christian church, it is usually placed at the east end of the nave beyond the transept or choir. It is also sometimes used at the end of transept arms.

APSIDIOLE. A small apse or chapel connected to the main apse of a church.

ARCADE. A series of arches supported by piers or columns. When attached to a wall, these form a blind arcade.

ARCH. A curved structure used to span an opening. Masonry arches are generally built of wedge-shaped blocks, called *voussoirs*, set with their narrow sides toward the opening so that they lock together. The topmost *voussoir* is called the *keystone*. Arches may take different shapes, such as the pointed Gothic arch or the rounded Classical arch.

ARCHAIC SMILE. A fixed, unnaturalistic smile characteristic of many archaic Greek sculpted images. Artists ceased to depict figures smiling in this way once they began to explore greater naturalism.

ARCHITRAVE. The lowermost member of a classical entablature, such as a series of stone blocks that rest directly on the columns.

ARCHIVOLT. A molded band framing an arch, or a series of such bands framing a tympanum, often decorated with sculpture.

ARCUATION. The use of arches or a series of arches in building.

ART BRUT. Meaning "raw art" in French, *art brut* is the direct and highly emotional art of children and the mentally ill that served as an inspiration for some artistic movements in Modern art.

ARYBALLOS. A perfume jar, generally small in size, and often minutely decorated. This was a favorite type of vessel for Corinthian vase-painters.

ASHLAR MASONRY. Carefully finished stone that is set in fine joints to create an even surface.

ASSOCIATIONISM. A 20th-century art historical term that refers to the concept that architecture and landscape design can have motifs or aspects that associate them with earlier architecture, art, history, or literature.

ATMOSPHERIC PERSPECTIVE. Creates the illusion of depth by reducing the local color and clarity of objects in the distance, to imply a layer of atmosphere between the viewer and the horizon.

ATRIUM. (1) The central court or open entrance court of a Roman house. (2) An open court, sometimes colonnaded or arcaded, in front of a church.

AVANT-GARDE. Meaning "advance force" in French, the artists of the avant-garde in 19th- and 20th-century Europe led the way in innovation in both subject matter and technique, rebelling against the established conventions of the art world.

BALDACCHINO. A canopy usually built over an altar. The most important one is Bernini's construction for St. Peter's in Rome.

BAROQUE. A style of Hellenistic Greek sculpture, characterized by extreme emotions and extravagant gestures, as seen on the Great Altar of Zeus at Pergamon. The term is usually used to describe a style of 17th-century CE art, and scholars of ancient art coin it in recognition of similarities of style.

BARREL VAULT. A vault formed by a continuous semicircular arch so that it is shaped like a half-cylinder.

BAR TRACERY. A style of tracery in which glass is held in place by relatively thin membranes.

BAS-DE-PAGE. Literally "bottom of the page." An illustration or decoration that is placed below a block of text in an illuminated manuscript.

BASILICA. (1) In ancient Roman architecture, a large, oblong building used as a public meeting place and hall of justice. It generally includes a nave, side aisles, and one or more apses. (2) In Christian architecture, a longitudinal church derived from the Roman basilica and having a nave, an apse, two or four side aisles or side chapels, and sometimes a narthex. (3) Any one of the seven original churches of Rome or other churches accorded the same religious privileges.

BATTLEMENT. A parapet consisting of alternating solid parts and open spaces designed originally for defense and later used for decoration. See *crenelated*.

BAY. A subdivision of the interior space of a building. Usually a series of bays is formed by consecutive architectural supports.

BELVEDERE. A structure made for the purpose of viewing the surroundings, either above the roof of a building or free-standing in a garden or other natural setting.

BLACK-FIGURED. A style of ancient Greek pottery decoration characterized by black figures against a red background. The black-figured style preceded the red-figured style.

BLIND ARCADE. An arcade with no openings. The arches and supports are attached decoratively to the surface of a wall.

BLOCK BOOKS. Books, often religious, of the 15th century containing woodcut prints in which picture and text were usually cut into the same block.

BOOK OF HOURS. A private prayer book containing the devotions for the seven canonical hours of the Roman Catholic church (matins, vespers, etc.), liturgies for local saints, and sometimes a calendar. They were often elaborately illuminated for persons of high rank, whose names are attached to certain extant examples.

BUON FRESCO. See *fresco*.

BURIN. A pointed metal tool with a wedged-shaped tip used for engraving.

BUTTRESS. A projecting support built against an external wall, usually to counteract the lateral thrust of a vault or arch within. In Gothic church architecture, a *flying buttress* is an arched bridge above the aisle roof that extends from the upper nave wall, where the lateral thrust of the main vault is greatest, down to a solid pier.

CALOTYPE. Invented in the 1830s, calotype was the first photographic process to use negatives and positive prints on paper.

CAMEO. A low relief carving made on agate, seashell, or other multilayered material in which the subject, often in profile view, is rendered in one color while the background appears in another, darker color.

CAMES. Strips of lead in stained-glass windows that hold the pieces of glass together.

CAMPANILE. From the Italian word *campana*, meaning "bell." A bell tower that is either round or square and is sometimes free-standing.

CANON. A law, rule, or standard.

CAPITAL. The uppermost member of a column or pillar supporting the architrave.

CARAVANSARAY. A wayside inn along the main caravan routes linking the cities of Asia Minor, usually containing a warehouse, stables, and a courtyard.

CARTE-DE-VISITE. A photographic portrait mounted on thicker card stock measuring 2½ x 4 inches (6 x 10 cm) that people commissioned and distributed to friends and acquaintances. They were developed in 1854 by the French photographer Adolphe-Eugène Disdéri, and by the end of the decade were so popular that they were widely collected in Europe and America, a phenomenon called "cardomania."

CARTOON. From the Italian word *cartone*, meaning "large paper." (1) A full-scale drawing for a picture or design intended to be transferred to a wall, panel, tapestry, etc. (2) A drawing or print, usually humorous or satirical, calling attention to some action or person of popular interest.

CARYATID. A sculptured female figure used in place of a column as an architectural support. A similar male figure is an *atlas* (pl. *atlantes*).

CASEMATE. A chamber or compartment within a fortified wall, usually used for the storage of artillery and munitions.

CASSONE (pl. **CASSONI**). An Italian dowry chest often highly decorated with carvings, paintings, inlaid designs, and gilt embellishments.

CATACOMBS. The underground burial places of the early Christians, consisting of passages with niches for tombs and small chapels for commemorative services.

CATALOGUE RAISONNÉ. A complete list of an artist's works of art, with a comprehensive chronology and a discussion of the artist's style.

CATHEDRAL. The church of a bishop; his administrative headquarters. The location of his *cathedra* or throne.

CAVEA. The seating area in an ancient theater. In a Greek theater, it was just over semicircular; in a Roman theater, it was semicircular. Access corridors divided the seating into wedges (*cunei*).

CELLA. (1) The principal enclosed room of a temple used to house an image. Also called the *naos*. (2) The entire body of a temple as distinct from its external parts.

CENOTAPH. A memorial monument to honor a person or persons whose remains lie elsewhere.

CENTERING. A wooden framework built to support an arch, vault, or dome during its construction.

CHAMPLEVÉ. An enameling method in which hollows are etched into a metal surface and filled with enamel.

CHANCEL. The area of a church around the altar, sometimes set off by a screen. It is used by the clergy and the choir.

CHIAROSCURO. Italian word for "light and dark." In painting, a method of modeling form primarily by the use of light and shade.

CHIASTIC POSE. From the Greek letter chi: an asymmetrical stance, where the body carries the weight on one leg (and often bears a weight with the opposite arm). Also described as *contrapposto*.

CHINOISERIE. Objects, usually in the decorative arts (screens, furniture, lacquerware) made in a Chinese or pseudo-Chinese style, most popular in the 18th century.

CHITON. A woman's garment made out of a rectangle of fabric draped and fastened at the shoulders by pins. The garment is worn by some Archaic Greek *korai*, where it provides a decorative effect.

CHRYSELEPHANTINE. Usually refering to a sculpture in Classical Greece, signifying that it is made of gold and ivory. Pheidias' cult statues of Athena in the Parthenon, and Zeus at Olympia, were chryselephantine.

CLASSICISM. Art or architecture that harkens back to and relies upon the style and canons of the art and architecture of ancient Greece or Rome, which emphasize certain standards of balance, order, and beauty.

CLASSICIZING. To refer to the forms and ideals of the Classical world, principally Greece and Rome.

CLERESTORY. A row of windows in the upper part of a wall that rises above an adjoining roof. Its purpose is to provide direct lighting, as in a basilica or church.

CLOISONNÉ. An enameling method in which the hollows created by wires joined to a metal plate are filled with enamel to create a design.

CLOISTER. (1) A place of religious seclusion such as a monastery or nunnery. (2) An open court attached to a church or monastery and surrounded by an ambulatory. Used for study, meditation, and exercise.

COFFER. (1) A small chest or casket. (2) A recessed, geometrically shaped panel in a ceiling. A ceiling decorated with these panels is said to be coffered.

COLONNETTE. A small, often decorative, column that is connected to a wall or pier.

COLOPHON. (1) The production information given at the end of a book. (2) The printed emblem of a book's publisher.

COLOR-FIELD PAINTING. A technique of Abstract painting in which thinned paints are spread onto an unprimed canvas and allowed to soak in with minimal control by the artist.

COLOSSAL ORDER. Columns, piers, or pilasters in the shape of the Greek or Roman orders but that extend through two or more stories rather than following the Classical proportions.

COMBINES. The label the American artist Robert Rauschenberg gave to his paintings of the mid-1950s that combined painting, sculpture, collage, and found objects.

COMPOSITE CAPITAL. A capital that combines the volutes of an Ionic capital with the acanthus leaves of the Corinthian capital. Roman architects developed the style as a substitute for the Ionic style, for use on secular buildings.

COMPOSITE IMAGE. An image formed by combining different images or different views of the subject.

COMPOUND PIER. A pier with attached pilasters or shafts.

CONSTRUCTION. A type of sculpture, developed by Picasso and Braque toward 1912, and popularized by the Russian Constructivists later in the decade. It is made by assembling such materials as metal or wood.

CONTINUOUS NARRATION. Portrayal of the same figure or character at different stages in a story that is depicted in a single artistic space.

CONTRAPPOSTO. Italian word for "set against." A composition developed by the Greeks to represent movement in a figure. The parts of the body are placed asymmetrically in opposition to each other around a central axis, and careful attention is paid to the distribution of weight.

CORBEL. (1) A bracket that projects from a wall to aid in supporting weight. (2) The projection of one course, or horizontal row, of a building material beyond the course below it.

CORBEL VAULT. A vault formed by progressively projecting courses of stone or brick, which eventually meet to form the highest point of the vault.

CORINTHIAN CAPITAL. A column capital ornamented with acanthus leaves, introduced in Greece in the late fifth century BCE, and used by Roman architects throughout the Empire.

CORNICE. (1) The projecting, framing members of a classical pediment, including the horizontal one beneath and the two sloping or "raking" ones above. (2) Any projecting, horizontal element surmounting a wall or other structure or dividing it horizontally for decorative purposes.

CORPUS. In carved medieval altarpieces, the corpus is the central section which usually holds a sculpted figure or design.

COURT STYLE. See *Rayonnant*.

CRENELATIONS. A sequence of solid parts, and the intervals between them, along the top of a parapet, allowing for defense and to facilitate firing weapons. The effect is of a notched termination of a wall. Generally used in military architecture.

CROSSING. The area in a church where the transept crosses the nave, frequently emphasized by a dome or crossing tower.

CRYPT. A space, usually vaulted, in a church that sometimes causes the floor of the choir to be raised above that of the nave; often used as a place for tombs and small chapels.

CUBICULUM (pl. **CUBICULA**) A bedroom in a Roman house. A cubiculum usually opened onto the atrium. Most were small; some contained wall-paintings.

CUNEUS (pl. **CUNEI**). A wedgelike group of seats in a Greek or Roman theater.

CUNEIFORM. The wedge-shaped characters made in clay by the ancient Mesopotamians as a writing system.

CURTAIN WALL. A wall of a modern building that does not support the building; the building is supported by an underlying steel structure rather than by the wall itself, which serves the purpose of a façade.

DADO. The lower part of an interior wall. In a Roman house, the dado was often decorated with paintings imitating costly marbles.

DAGUERREOTYPE. Originally, a photograph on a silver-plated sheet of copper, which had been treated with fumes of iodine to form silver iodide on its surface and then after exposure developed by fumes of mercury. The process, invented by L. J. M. Daguerre and made public in 1839, was modified and accelerated as daguerreotypes gained popularity.

DEËSIS. From the Greek word for "entreaty." The representation of Christ enthroned between the Virgin Mary and St. John the Baptist, frequent in Byzantine mosaics and depictions of the Last Judgment. It refers to the roles of the Virgin Mary and St. John the Baptist as intercessors for humankind.

DIKKA. An elevated, flat-topped platform in a mosque used by the muezzin or cantor.

DIPTERAL. Term used to describe a Greek or Roman building—often a temple or a stoa—with a double colonnade.

DIPTYCH. (1) Originally a hinged, two-leaved tablet used for writing. (2) A pair of ivory carvings or panel paintings, usually hinged together.

DOLMEN. A structure formed by two or more large, upright stones capped by a horizontal slab. Thought to be a prehistoric tomb.

DOME. A true dome is a vaulted roof of circular, polygonal, or elliptical plan, formed with hemispherical or ovoidal curvature. May be supported by a circular wall or drum and by pendentives or related constructions. Domical coverings of many other sorts have been devised.

DOMUS. Latin word for "house." A detached, one-family Roman house with rooms frequently grouped around two open courts. The first court, called the *atrium*, was used for entertaining and conducting business. The second court, usually with a garden and surrounded by a *peristyle* or colonnade, was for the private use of the family.

DORIC COLUMN. A column characterized by a simple cushionlike abacus and the absence of a base. One of three styles of column consistently used by Greek and Roman architects.

DRÔLERIES. French word for "jests." Used to describe the lively animals and small figures in the margins of late medieval manuscripts and in wood carvings on furniture.

DROMOS. A pathway, found, for instance, in Bronze Age, Aegean and Etruscan tomb structures.

DRUM. (1) A section of the shaft of a column. (2) A circular-shaped wall supporting a dome.

DRYPOINT. A type of *intaglio* printmaking in which a sharp metal needle is use to carve lines and a design into a (usually) copper plate. The act of drawing pushes up a burr of metal filings, and so, when the plate is inked, ink will be retained by the burr to create a soft and deep tone that will be unique to each print. The burr can only last for a few printings. Both the print and the process are called drypoint.

EARLY ENGLISH STYLE. A term used to describe Gothic architecture in England during the early- and mid-13th century. The style demonstrates the influence of architectural features developed during the Early Gothic period in France, which are combined with Anglo-Norman Romanesque features.

EARTHWORKS. Usually very large scale, outdoor artwork that is produced by altering the natural environment.

ECHINUS. In the Doric or Tuscan Order, the round, cushionlike element between the top of the shaft and the abacus.

ENCAUSTIC. A technique of painting with pigments dissolved in hot wax.

ENGAGED COLUMN. A column that is joined to a wall, usually appearing as a half-rounded vertical shape.

ENGRAVING. (1) A means of embellishing metal surfaces or gemstones by incising a design on the surface. (2) A print made by cutting a design into a metal plate (usually copper) with a pointed steel tool known as a burin. The burr raised on either side of the incised line is removed. Ink is then rubbed into the V-shaped grooves and wiped off the surface. The plate, covered with a damp sheet of paper, is run through a heavy press. The image on the paper is the reverse of that on the plate. When a fine steel needle is used instead of a burin and the burr is retained, a drypoint engraving results, characterized by a softer line. These techniques are called, respectively, engraving and drypoint.

ENNEASTYLE. A term used to describe the façade of a Greek or Roman temple, meaning that it has nine columns.

ENTABLATURE. (1) In a classical order, the entire structure above the columns; this usually includes architrave, frieze, and cornice. (2) The same structure in any building of a classical style.

ENTASIS. A swelling of the shaft of a column.

ENVIRONMENT. In art, environment refers to the Earth itself as a stage for Environmental art, works that can be enormously large yet very minimal and abstract. These works can be permanent or transitory. The term Earth art is also used to describe these artworks.

EVENTS. A term first used by John Cage in the early 1950s to refer to his multimedia events at Black Mount College in North Carolina that included dance, painting, music, and sculpture. The term was appropriated by the conceptual artist George Brecht in 1959 for his performance projects, and shortly thereafter by the conceptual and performance group Fluxus, which included Brecht.

EXEDRA (pl. **EXEDRAE**). In Classical architecture, an alcove, often semicircular, and often defined with columns. Sometimes, exedrae framed sculptures.

FAIENCE. (1) A glass paste fired to a shiny opaque finish, used in Egypt and the Aegean. (2) A type of earthenware that is covered with a colorful opaque glaze and is often decorated with elaborate designs.

FIBULA. A clasp, buckle, or brooch, often ornamented.

FILIGREE. Delicate decorative work made of intertwining wires.

FLAMBOYANT. Literally meaning "flamelike" in French, describes a late phase of Gothic architecture where undulating curves and reverse curves were a main feature.

FLUTES. The vertical channels or grooves in Classical column shafts, sometimes thought to imitate the faceting of a hewn log.

FLYING BUTTRESS. An arch or series of arches on the exterior of a building, connecting the building to detached pier buttresses so that the thrust from the roof vaults is offset. See also *Buttress*

FOLIO. A leaf of a manuscript or a book, identified so that the front and the back have the same number, the front being labeled *recto* and the back *verso*.

FORESHORTENING. A method of reducing or distorting the parts of a represented object that are not parallel to the picture plane in order to convey the impression of three dimensions as perceived by the human eye.

FRESCO. Italian word for "fresh." Fresco is the technique of painting on plaster with pigments ground in water so that the paint is absorbed by the plaster and becomes part of the wall itself. *Buon fresco* is the technique of painting on wet plaster; *fresco secco* is the technique of painting on dry plaster.

FRIEZE. (1) A continuous band of painted or sculptured decoration. (2) In a Classical building, the part of the entablature between the architrave and the cornice. A Doric frieze consists of alternating triglyphs and metopes, the latter often sculptured. An Ionic frieze is usually decorated with continuous relief sculpture.

FRONTALITY. Representation of a subject in a full frontal view.

FROTTAGE. The technique of rubbing a drawing medium, such as a crayon, over paper that is placed over a textured surface in order to transfer the underlying pattern to the paper.

GABLE. (1) The triangular area framed by the cornice or eaves of a building and the sloping sides of a pitched roof. In Classical architecture, it is called a *pediment*. (2) A decorative element of similar shape, such as the triangular structures above the portals of a Gothic church and sometimes at the top of a Gothic picture frame.

GALLERY. A second story placed over the side aisles of a church and below the clerestory. In a church with a four-part elevation, it is placed below the triforium and above the nave arcade.

GEISON. A projecting horizontal cornice. On a Greek or Roman temple, the geison will often be decorated.

GENRE PAINTING. Based on the French word for type or kind, the term sometimes refers to a category of style or subject matter. But it usually refers to depictions of common activities performed by contemporary people, often of the lower or middle classes. This contrasts with grand historical themes or mythologies, narratives or portraits.

GEOMETRIC ARABESQUE. Complex patterns and designs usually composed of polygonal geometric forms, rather than organic flowing shapes; often used as ornamentation in Islamic art.

GESTURE PAINTING. A technique in painting and drawing where the actual physical movement of the artist is reflected in the brushstroke or line as it is seen in the artwork. The artist Jackson Pollock is particularly associated with this technique.

GISANT. In a tomb sculpture, a recumbent effigy or representation of the deceased. At times, the gisant may be represented in a state of decay.

GLAZE. (1) A thin layer of translucent oil color applied to a painted surface or to parts of it in order to modify the tone. (2) A glassy coating applied to a piece of ceramic work before firing in the kiln as a protective seal and often as decoration.

GLAZED BRICK. Brick that is baked in a kiln after being painted.

GOTHIC. A style of art developed in France during the 12th century that spread throughout Europe. The style is characterized by daring architectural achievements, for example, the opening up of wall surfaces and the reaching of great heights, particularly in cathedral construction. Pointed arches and ribbed groin vaults allow for a lightness of construction that permits maximum light to enter buildings through stained-glass windows. Increasing naturalism and elegance characterize Gothic sculpture and painting.

GRANULATION. A technique of decoration in which metal granules, or tiny metal balls, are fused to a metal surface.

GRATTAGE. A technique in painting whereby an image is produced by scraping off paint from a canvas that has been placed over a textured surface.

GREEK CROSS. A cross with four arms of equal length arranged at right angles.

GRISAILLE. A monochrome drawing or painting in which only values of black, gray, and white are used.

GRISAILLE GLASS. White glass painted with gray designs.

GROIN VAULT. A vault formed by the intersection of two barrel vaults at right angles to each other. A groin is the ridge resulting from the intersection of two vaults.

GUILLOCHE PATTERN. A repeating pattern made up of two ribbons spiraling around a series of central points. A guilloche pattern is often used as a decorative device in Classical vase-painting.

GUILDS. Economic and social organizations that control the making and marketing of given products in a medieval city. To work as a painter or sculptor in a city, an individual had to belong to a guild, which established standards for the craft. First mentioned on p.211. Emboldened entry on p.258

GUTTAE. In a Doric entablature, small peglike projections above the frieze; possibly derived from pegs originally used in wooden construction.

HALL CHURCH. See *hallenkirche*.

HALLENKIRCHE. German word for "hall church." A church in which the nave and the side aisles are of the same height. The type was developed in Romanesque architecture and occurs especially frequently in German Gothic churches.

HAN. In Turkish, an establishment where travelers can procure lodging, food, and drink. Also called a *caravansaray*.

HAPPENING. A type of art that involves visual images, audience participation, and improvised performance, usually in a public setting and under the loose direction of an artist.

HARMONY. In medieval architecture, the perfect relationship among parts in terms of mathematical proportions or ratios. Thought to be the source of all beauty, since it exemplifies the laws by which divine reason made the universe.

HATAYI. A style of ornament originated by the Ottomans and characterized by curved leaves and complex floral palmettes linked by vines, sometimes embellished with birds or animals.

HATCHING. A series of parallel lines used as shading in prints and drawings. When two sets of crossing parallel lines are used, it is called *crosshatching*.

HERALDIC POSE. A pose where two figures are mirror images of one another, sometimes flanking a central object, as in the relieving triangle above the Lioness Gate at Mycenae.

HEROÖN. The center of a hero cult, where Classical Greeks venerated mythological or historical heroes.

HEXASTYLE. A term used to describe the façade of a Greek or Roman temple, meaning that it has six columns.

HIERATIC SCALE. An artistic technique in which the importance of figures is indicated by size, so that the most important figure is depicted as the largest.

HIEROGLYPH. A symbol, often based on a figure, animal, or object, standing for a word, syllable, or sound. These symbols form the early Egyptian writing system, and are found on ancient Egyptian monuments as well as in Egyptian written records.

HOUSE CHURCH. A place for private worship within a house; the first Christian churches were located in private homes that were modified for religious ceremonies.

HUMANISM. A philosophy emphasizing the worth of the individual, the rational abilities of humankind, and the human potential for good. During the Italian Renaissance, humanism was part of a movement that encouraged study of the classical cultures of Greece and Rome; often it came into conflict with the doctrines of the Catholic church.

HYDRIA. A type of jar used by ancient Greeks to carry water. Some examples were highly decorated.

HYPOSTYLE. A hall whose roof is supported by columns.

ICON. From the Greek word for "image." A panel painting of one or more sacred personages, such as Christ, the Virgin, or a saint, particularly venerated in the Orthodox Christian church.

ICONOCLASM. The doctrine of the Christian church in the 8th and 9th centuries that forbade the worship or production of religious images. This doctrine led to the destruction of many works of art. The iconoclastic controversy over the validity of this doctrine led to a division of the church. Protestant churches of the 16th and 17th centuries also practiced iconoclasm.

ICONOGRAPHY. (1) The depicting of images in art in order to convey certain meanings. (2) The study of the meaning of images depicted in art, whether they be inanimate objects, events, or personages. (3) The content or subject matter of a work of art.

IMPASTO. From the Italian word meaning "to make into a paste"; it describes paint, usually oil paint, applied very thickly.

IMPLUVIUM. A shallow pool in a Roman house, for collecting rain water. The impluvium was usually in the atrium, and stood beneath a large opening in the roof, known as a compluvium.

INFRARED LIGHT. Light on the spectrum beyond the comprehension of the naked eye is referred to as infrared. Special filters are needed to perceive it.

INFRARED REFLECTOGRAPHY. A technique for scientifically examining works of art. Special cameras equipped with infrared filters can look below the top layer of paintings to record the darker materials, such as carbon, which artists used to create drawings on panels or other supports.

INLAID NIELLO. See *niello*.

INSULA (pl. **INSULAE**). Latin word for "island." (1) An ancient Roman city block. (2) A Roman "apartment house": a concrete and brick building or chain of buildings around a central court, up to five stories high. The ground floor had shops, and above were living quarters.

INTAGLIO. A printing technique in which the design is formed from ink-filled lines cut into a surface. Engraving, etching, and drypoint are examples of intaglio.

INTERCOLUMNIATION. The space between two columns, measured from the edge of the column shafts. The term is often used in describing Greek and Roman temples.

INVERTED PERSPECTIVE. The technique, in some 16th- and 17th-century paintings, of placing the main theme or narrative of a work in the background and placing a still life or other representation in the foreground.

IONIC COLUMN. A column characterized by a base and a capital with two volutes. One of three styles of column consistently used by Greek and Roman architects.

IWAN. A vaulted chamber in a mosque or other Islamic structure, open on one side and usually opening onto an interior courtyard.

JAMBS. The vertical sides of an opening. In Romanesque and Gothic churches, the jambs of doors and windows are often cut on a slant outward, or "splayed," thus providing a broader surface for sculptural decoration.

JAPONISME. In 19th-century French and American art, a style of painting and drawing that reflected the influence of the Japanese artworks, particularly prints, that were then reaching the West.

JASPERWARE. A durable, unglazed porcelain developed by the firm of Josiah Wedgwood in the 18th century. It is decorated with Classically inspired bas relief or cameo figures, and ornamented in white relief on a colored ground, especially blue and sage green.

KORE (pl. **KORAI**). Greek word for "maiden." An Archaic Greek statue of a standing, draped female.

KOUROS (pl. **KOUROI**). Greek word for "male youth." An Archaic Greek statue of a standing, nude youth.

KRATER. A Greek vessel, of assorted shapes, in which wine and water are mixed. A *calyx krater* is a bell-shaped vessel with handles near the base; a *volute krater* is a vessel with handles shaped like scrolls.

KUFIC. One of the first general forms of Arabic script to be developed, distinguished by its angularity; distinctive variants occur in various parts of the Islamic worlds.

KYLIX. In Greek and Roman antiquity, a shallow drinking cup with two horizontal handles, often set on a stem terminating in a foot.

LAMASSU. An ancient Near Eastern guardian of a palace; often shown in sculpture as a human-headed bull or lion with wings.

LANCET. A tall, pointed window common in Gothic architecture.

LANTERN. A relatively small structure crowning a dome, roof, or tower, frequently open to admit light to an enclosed area below.

LATIN CROSS. A cross in which three arms are of equal length and one arm is longer.

LEKYTHOS (pl. **LEKYTHOI**). A Greek oil jug with an ellipsoidal body, a narrow neck, a flanged mouth, a curved handle extending from below the lip to the shoulder, and a narrow base terminating in a foot. It was used chiefly for ointments and funerary offerings.

LIGHT WELLS. Open shafts that allow light to penetrate into a building from the roof. These were a major source of light and ventilation in Minoan "palaces."

LIMINAL SPACE. A transitional area, such as a doorway or archway. In Roman architecture, liminal spaces were often decorated with apotropaic devices.

LINEARITY. A term used to refer to images that have a strong sense of line that provides sharp contours to figures and objects.

LITURGY. A body of rites or rituals prescribed for public worship.

LOGGIA. A covered gallery or arcade open to the air on at least one side. It may stand alone or be part of a building.

LUNETTE. (1) A semicircular or pointed wall area, as under a vault, or above a door or window. When it is above the portal of a medieval church, it is called a *tympanum*. (2) A painting, relief sculpture, or window of the same shape.

LUSTER. A metallic pigment fired over glazed ceramic, which creates an iridescent effect.

MACHICOLATIONS. A gallery projecting from the walls of a castle or tower with holes in the floor in order to allow liquid, stones, or other projectiles to be dropped on an enemy.

MAIDAN. In parts of the Near East and Asia a large open space or square.

MANDORLA. A representation of light surrounding the body of a holy figure.

MANUSCRIPT ILLUMINATION. Decoration of handwritten documents, scrolls, or books with drawings or paintings. Illuminated manuscripts were often produced during the Middle Ages.

MAQSURA. A screened enclosure, reserved for the ruler, often located before the *mihrab* in certain important royal Islamic mosques.

MARTYRIUM (pl. **MARTYRIA**). A church, chapel, or shrine built over the grave of a Christian martyr or at the site of an important miracle.

MASTABA. An ancient Egyptian tomb, rectangular in shape, with sloping sides and a flat roof. It covered a chapel for offerings and a shaft to the burial chamber.

MATRIX. (1) A mold or die used for shaping a ceramic object before casting. (2) In printmaking, any surface on which an image is incised, carved, or applied and from which a print may be pulled.

MEANDER PATTERN. A decorative motif of intricate, rectilinear character applied to architecture and sculpture.

MEGALITH. From the Greek *mega*, meaning "big," and *lithos*, meaning "stone." A huge stone such as those used in cromlechs and dolmens.

MEGARON (pl. **MEGARONS** or **MEGARA**). From the Greek word for "large." The central audience hall in a Minoan or Mycenaean palace or home.

MENHIR. A megalithic upright slab of stone, sometimes placed in rows by prehistoric peoples.

METOPE. The element of a Doric frieze between two consecutive triglyphs, sometimes left plain but often decorated with paint or relief sculpture.

MEZZOTINT. Printmaking technique developed in the late 17th century where the plate is roughened or "rocked" to better retain the ink and create dark images.

MIHRAB. A niche, often highly decorated, usually found in the center of the *qibla* wall of a mosque, indicating the direction of prayer toward Mecca.

MINA'I. From the Persian meaning "enameled," polychrome overglaze-decorated ceramic ware produced in Iran.

MINARET. A tower on or near a mosque, varying extensively in form throughout the Islamic world, from which the faithful are called to prayer five times a day.

MINBAR. A type of staircase pulpit, found in more important mosques to the right of the mihrab, from which the Sabbath sermon is given on Fridays after the noonday prayer.

MINIATURIST. An artist trained in the painting of miniature figures or scenes to decorate manuscripts.

MODULE. (1) A segment of a pattern. (2) A basic unit, such as the measure of an architectural member. Multiples of the basic unit are used to determine proportionate construction of other parts of a building.

MONOTYPE. A unique print made from a copper plate or other type of plate from which no other copies of the artwork are made.

MOSQUE. A building used as a center for community prayers in Islamic worship; it often serves other functions including religious education and public assembly.

MOZARAB. Term used for the Spanish Christian culture of the Middle Ages that developed while Muslims were the dominant culture and political power on the Iberian peninsula.

MUQARNAS. A distinctive type of Islamic decoration consisting of multiple nichelike forms usually arranged in superimposed rows, often used in zones of architectural transition.

NAOS. See *cella*.

NARTHEX. The transverse entrance hall of a church, sometimes enclosed but often open on one side to a preceding atrium.

NATURALISM. A style of art that aims to depict the natural world as it appears.

NAVE. (1) The central aisle of a Roman basilica, as distinguished from the side aisles. (2) The same section of a Christian basilican church extending from the entrance to the apse or transept.

NECROPOLIS. Greek for "city of the dead." A burial ground or cemetery.

NEMES HEADDRESS. The striped cloth headdress worn by Egyptian kings, and frequently represented in their sculpted and painted images.

NEOCLASSICISM. An 18th-century style that emphasizes Classical themes, sometimes with strong moral overtones, executed in a way that places a strong emphasis on line, with figures and objects running parallel to the picture plane. Paintings and drawings are typically executed with sharp clarity, by way of tight handling of paint and clearly defined line and light.

NIELLO. Dark metal alloys applied to the engraved lines in a precious metal plate (usually made of gold or silver) to create a design.

NIKE. The ancient Greek goddess of victory, often identified with Athena and by the Romans with Victoria. She is usually represented as a winged woman with windblown draperies.

NOCTURNE. A painting that depicts a nighttime scene, often emphasizing the effects of artificial light.

NOMAD'S GEAR. Portable objects, including weaponry, tackle for horses, jewelry and vessels, crafted by nomadic groups such as the tribes of early Iran, and sometimes buried with their dead.

OBELISK. A tall, tapering, four-sided stone shaft with a pyramidal top. First constructed as *megaliths* in ancient Egypt, certain examples have since been exported to other countries.

OCTASTYLE. A term used to describe the façade of a Greek or Roman temple, meaning that it has eight columns.

OCULUS. The Latin word for "eye." (1) A circular opening at the top of a dome used to admit light. (2) A round window.

OPISTHONAOS. A rear chamber in a Greek temple, often mirroring the porch at the front. The opisthonaos was sometimes used to house valuable objects. Access to the chamber was usually from the peristyle rather than the cella.

OPTICAL IMAGES. An image created from what the eye sees, rather than from memory.

ORANT. A standing figure with arms upraised in a gesture of prayer.

ORCHESTRA. (1) In an ancient Greek theater, the round space in front of the stage and below the tiers of seats, reserved for the chorus. (2) In a Roman theater, a similar space reserved for important guests.

ORIEL. A bay window that projects from a wall.

ORIENTALISM. The fascination of Western culture, especially as expressed in art and literature, with Eastern cultures. In the 19th-century, this fascination was especially focused on North Africa and the Near East, that is, the Arab world.

ORTHOGONAL. In a perspective construction, an imagined line in a painting that runs perpendicular to the picture plane and recedes to a vanishing point.

ORTHOSTATS. Upright slabs of stone constituting or lining the lowest courses of a wall, often in order to protect a vulnerable material such as mud-brick.

POUSSINISTES. Those artists of the French Academy at the end of the 17th century and the beginning of the 18th century who favored "drawing," which they believed appealed to the mind rather than the senses. The term derived from admiration for the French artist Nicolas Poussin. See *Rubénistes*.

PALETTE. (1) A thin, usually oval or oblong board with a thumbhole at one end, used by painters to hold and mix their colors. (2) The range of colors used by a particular painter. (3) In Egyptian art, a slate slab, usually decorated with sculpture in low relief. The

small ones with a recessed circular area on one side are thought to have been used for eye makeup. The larger ones were commemorative objects.

PARCHMENT. From Pergamon, the name of a Greek city in Asia Minor where parchment was invented in the 2nd century BCE. (1) A paperlike material made from bleached animal hides used extensively in the Middle Ages for manuscripts. Vellum is a superior type of parchment made from calfskin. (2) A document or miniature on this material.

PEDIMENT. (1) In Classical architecture, a low gable, typically triangular, framed by a horizontal cornice below and two raking cornices above; frequently filled with sculpture. (2) A similar architectural member used over a door, window, or niche. When pieces of the cornice are either turned at an angle or interrupted, it is called a *broken pediment*.

PENDENTIVE. One of the concave triangles that achieves the transition from a square or polygonal opening to the round base of a dome or the supporting drum.

PERFORMANCE ART. A type of art in which performance by actors or artists, often interacting with the audience in an improvisational manner, is the primary aim over a certain time period. These artworks are transitory, perhaps with only a photographic record of some of the events.

PERIPTERAL TEMPLE. In Classical architecture, a temple with a single colonnade on all sides, providing shelter.

PERISTYLE. (1) In a Roman house or *domus*, an open garden court surrounded by a colonnade. (2) A colonnade around a building or court.

PERPENDICULAR GOTHIC STYLE. Describes Late Gothic architecture in England, characterized by dominant vertical accents.

PERSPECTIVE. A system for representing spatial relationships and three-dimensional objects on a flat two-dimensional surface so as to produce an effect similar to that perceived by the human eye. In *atmospheric* or *aerial* perspective, this is accomplished by a gradual decrease in the intensity of color and value and in the contrast of light and dark as objects are depicted as farther and farther away in the picture. In color artwork, as objects recede into the distance, all colors tend toward a light bluish-gray tone. In *scientific* or *linear* perspective, developed in Italy in the 15th century, a mathematical system is used based on orthogonals receding to vanishing points on the horizon. Transversals intersect the orthogonals at right angles at distances derived mathematically. Since this presupposes an absolutely stationary viewer and imposes rigid restrictions on the artist, it is seldom applied with complete consistency. Although traditionally ascribed to Brunelleschi, the first theoretical text on perspective was Leon Battista Alberti's *On Painting* (1435).

PHOTOGRAM. A shadowlike photograph made without a camera by placing objects on light-sensitive paper and exposing them to a light source.

PHOTOMONTAGE. A photograph in which prints in whole or in part are combined to form a new image. A technique much practiced by the Dada group in the 1920s.

PICTOGRAPH. A pictorial representation of a concept or object, frequently used by Egyptian artists, sometimes in conjunction with hieroglyphs.

PICTURESQUE. Visually interesting or pleasing, as if resembling a picture.

PIER. An upright architectural support, usually rectangular and sometimes with capital and base. When columns, pilasters, or shafts are attached to it, as in many Romanesque and Gothic churches, it is called a compound pier.

PIETÀ. Italian word for both "pity" and "piety." A representation of the Virgin grieving over the dead Christ. When used in a scene recording a specific moment after the Crucifixion, it is usually called a Lamentation.

PILE CARPET. A weaving made on a loom in which rows of individual knots of colored wool are tied so that the ends of each knot protrude to form a thick pile surface.

PILGRIMAGE PLAN. The general design used in Christian churches that were stops on the pilgrimage routes throughout medieval Europe, characterized by having side aisles that allowed pilgrims to ambulate around the church. See *pilgrimage choir.*

PILOTIS. Pillars that are constructed from *reinforced concrete (ferroconcrete).*

PINAKOTHEKE. A museum for paintings. The first known example may have been in the Propylaia on the Athenian Akropolis.

PINNACLE. A small, decorative structure capping a tower, pier, buttress, or other architectural member. It is used especially in Gothic buildings.

PISÉ. A construction material consisting of packed earth, similar to wattle and daub. Etruscan architects used pisé for houses, with the result that little survives of them.

PLANARITY. A term used to described a composition where figures and objects are arranged parallel to the picture plane.

PLATE TRACERY. A style of tracery in which pierced openings in an otherwise solid wall of stonework are filled with glass.

PLEIN-AIR. Sketching outdoors, often using paints, in order to capture the immediate effects of light on landscape and other subjects. Much encouraged by the Impressionists, their *plein-air* sketches were often taken back to the studio to produce finished paintings, but many *plein-air* sketches are considered masterworks.

POCHADES. Small outdoor oil paintings made by landscape painters, serving as models for large-scale pictures that would be developed in the artist's studio.

POLIS. A city-state, in the Classical Greek world. City-states began to develop in the course of the 7th and 6th centuries BCE, and were governed in a variety of different ways, including monarchy and oligarchy.

POLYPTYCH. An altarpiece or devotional work of art made of several panels joined together, often hinged.

PORTRAIT BUST. A sculpted representation of an individual which includes not only the head but some portion of the upper torso. Popular during the Roman period, it was revived during the Renaissance.

POST AND LINTEL. A basic system of construction in which two or more uprights, the posts, support a horizontal member, the lintel. The lintel may be the topmost element or support a wall or roof.

POUNCING. A technique for transferring a drawing from a cartoon to a wall or other surface by pricking holes along the principal lines of the drawing and forcing fine charcoal powder through them onto the surface of the wall, thus reproducing the design on the wall.

PREDELLA. The base of an altarpiece, often decorated with small scenes that are related in subject to that of the main panel or panels.

PREFIGURATION. The representation of Old Testament figures and stories as forerunners and foreshadowers of those in the New Testament.

PRIMITIVISM. The appropriation of non-Western (e.g., African, tribal, Polynesian) art styles, forms, and techniques by Modern era artists as part of innovative

and avant-garde artistic movements; other sources were also used, including the work of children and the mentally ill.

PROCESS ART. Art in which the process is the art, as when Richard Serra hurled molten lead where a wall meets the floor, or Hans Haacke put water in a hermetic acrylic cube, which resulted in condensation forming on it.

PRONAOS. In a Greek or Roman temple, an open vestibule in front of the *cella.*

PRONK. A word meaning ostentatious or sumptuous; it is used to refer to a still life of luxurious objects.

PROPYLON. A monumental gateway, often leading into a citadel or a precinct, such as the Akropolis of Mycenae or Athens.

PROTOME. A decorative, protruding attachment, often on a vessel. Greek bronze-workers attached griffin-shaped protomes to tripod cauldrons in the 7th century BCE.

PROVENANCE. The place of origin of a work of art and related information.

PSALTER. (1) The book of Psalms in the Old Testament, thought to have been written in part by David, king of ancient Israel. (2) A copy of the Psalms, sometimes arranged for liturgical or devotional use and often richly illuminated.

PYLON. Greek word for "gateway." (1) The monumental entrance building to an Egyptian temple or forecourt consisting either of a massive wall with sloping sides pierced by a doorway or of two such walls flanking a central gateway. (2) A tall structure at either side of a gate, bridge, or avenue marking an approach or entrance.

PYXIS. A lidded box, often made of ivory, to hold jewelry or cosmetics in daily life, and, in the context of the Christian church, used on altars to contain the Host (Communion wafer).

QIBLA. The direction toward Mecca, which Muslims face during prayer. The qibla wall in a mosque identifies this direction.

QUADRANT VAULT. A half-barrel vault designed so that instead of being semicircular in cross-section, the arch is one-quarter of a circle.

QUATREFOIL. An ornamental element composed of four lobes radiating from a common center.

RAYONNANT. The style of Gothic architecture, described as "radiant," developed at the Parisian court of Louis IX in the mid-13th century. Also referred to as *court style.*

READYMADE. An ordinary object that, when an artist gives it a new context and title, is transformed into an art object. Readymades were important features of the Dada and Surrealism movements of the early 20th century.

RED-FIGURED. A style of ancient Greek ceramic decoration characterized by red figures against a black background. This style of decoration developed toward the end of the 6th century BCE and replaced the earlier *black-figured* style.

REGISTER. A horizontal band containing decoration, such as a relief sculpture or a fresco painting. When multiple horizontal layers are used, registers are useful in distinguishing between different visual planes and different time periods in visual narration.

RELIEF. (1) The projection of a figure or part of a design from the background or plane on which it is carved or modeled. Sculpture done in this manner is described as "high relief" or "low relief" depending on the height of the projection. When it is very shallow, it is called *schiacciato,* the Italian word for "flattened out." (2) The apparent projection of forms represented in a painting or drawing. (3) A category of printmaking in which lines raised from the surface are inked and printed.

RELIEVING TRIANGLE. A space left open above a lintel to relieve it of the weight of masonry. This device was used by Bronze Age architects in gate and tomb construction.

RELIQUARY. A container used for storing or displaying relics.

RENAISSANCE. Literally, rebirth. During the 14th and 15th centuries, Italian writers, artists, and intellectuals aimed to revive the arts of the ancient world. From their accomplishments, the term has been applied to the period, and is used generally to refer to a cultural flowering.

REPOUSSÉ. A metalworking technique where a design is hammered onto an object from the wrong side. Sasanian craftsmen used this techniques for silver vessels.

RESPOND. (1) A half-pier, pilaster, or similar element projecting from a wall to support a lintel or an arch whose other side is supported by a free-standing column or pier, as at the end of an arcade. (2) One of several pilasters on a wall behind a colonnade that echoes or "responds to" the columns but is largely decorative. (3) One of the slender shafts of a compound pier in a medieval church that seems to carry the weight of the vault.

RHYTON. An ancient drinking or pouring vessel made from pottery, metal, or stone, and sometimes designed in a human or animal form.

RIBBED GROIN VAULTS. A vault is a stone or brick roof. Groin vaults result from the intersection of two barrel vaults; the places where the arched surfaces meet is called the groin. Adding ribs or thickenings of the groins increases the strength of the roof.

RIBBED VAULT. A style of vault in which projecting surface arches, known as ribs, are raised along the intersections of segments of the vault. Ribs may provide architectural support as well as decoration to the vault's surface.

ROCOCO. The ornate, elegant style most associated with the early-18th-century in France, and which later spread throughout Europe, generally using pastel colors and the decorative arts to emphasize the notion of fantasy.

ROMANESQUE. (1) The style of medieval architecture from the 11th to the 13th centuries that was based upon the Roman model and that used the Roman rounded arch, thick walls for structural support, and relatively small windows. (2) Any culture or its artifacts that are "Roman-like."

ROMANTICISM. A cultural movement that surfaced in the second half of the 18th century and peaked in the first half of the 19th century. The movement was based on a belief in individual genius and originality and the expression of powerful emotions, as well as preference for exotic themes and the omnipotent force of nature, often viewed as manifestation of God.

ROSE WINDOW. A large, circular window with stained glass and stone tracery, frequently used on façades and at the ends of transepts in Gothic churches.

ROSTRUM (pl. **ROSTRA**). (1) A beaklike projection from the prow of an ancient warship used for ramming the enemy. (2) In the Roman forum, the raised platform decorated with the beaks of captured ships from which speeches were delivered. (3) A platform, stage, or the like used for public speaking.

ROTULUS (pl. **ROTULI**). The Latin word for scroll, a rolled written text.

RUBÉNISTES. Those artists of the French Academy at the end of the 17th century and the beginning of the 18th century who favored "color" in painting because it appealed to the senses and was thought to be true to nature. The term derived from admiration for the work of the Flemish artist Peter Paul Rubens. See *Poussinistes.*

RUSTICATION. A masonry technique of laying rough-faced stones with sharply indented joints.

SALON. (1) A large, elegant drawing or reception room in a palace or a private house. (2) Official government-sponsored exhibition of paintings and sculpture by living artists held at the Louvre in Paris, first biennially, then annually. (3) Any large public exhibition patterned after the Paris Salon.

SARCOPHAGUS (pl. **SARCOPHAGI**). A large coffin, generally of stone, and often decorated with sculpture or inscriptions. The term is derived from two Greek words meaning "flesh" and "eating."

SAZ. Meaning literally "enchanted forest," this term describes the sinuous leaves and twining stems that are a major component of the *hatayi* style under the Ottoman Turks.

SCHIACCIATO. Italian for "flattened out." Describes low relief sculpture used by Donatello and some of his contemporaries.

SCHOLASTICISM. A school of medieval thought that tries to reconcile faith and reason by combining ancient philosophy with Christian theology.

SCIENTIFIC PERSPECTIVE. See *perspective*.

SCRIPTORIUM (pl. **SCRIPTORIA**). A workroom in a monastery reserved for copying and illustrating manuscripts.

SECTION. An architectural drawing presenting a building as if cut across the vertical plane at right angles to the horizontal plane. A *cross section* is a cut along the transverse axis. A *longitudinal section* is a cut along the longitudinal axis.

SELECTIVE WIPING. The planned removal of certain areas of ink during the etching process to produce changes in value on the finished print.

SEPTPARTITE VAULT. A type of vault divided into seven sections.

SERDAB. In Egyptian architecture, an enclosed room without an entrance, often found in a funerary context. A sculpture of the dead king might be enclosed within it, as at Saqqara.

SEXPARTITE VAULT. See *vault*.

SFUMATO. Italian word meaning "smoky." Used to describe very delicate gradations of light and shade in the modeling of figures. It is applied especially to the work of Leonardo da Vinci.

SGRAFFITO ORNAMENT. A decorative technique in which a design is made by scratching away the surface layer of a material to produce a form in contrasting colors.

SHADING. The modulation of volume by means of contrasting light and shade. Prehistoric cave-painters used this device, as did Greek tomb-painters in the Hellenistic period.

SILKSCREEN PRINTING. A technique of printing in which paint or ink is pressed through a stencil and specially prepared cloth to produce a previously designed image. Also called serigraphy.

SILVERPOINT. A drawing instrument (stylus) of the 14th and 15th centuries made from silver; it produced a fine line and maintained a sharp point.

SIMULTANEOUS CONTRAST. The theory, first expressed by Michel-Eugène Chevreul (1786–1889), that complementary colors, when placed next to one another, increase the intensity of each other (e.g., red becoming more red and green more green.)

SITE-SPECIFIC ART. Art that is produced in only one location, a location that is an integral part of the work and essential to its production and meaning.

SKENE. A building erected on a Greek or Roman stage, as a backdrop against which some of the action took place. It usually consisted of a screen of columns, arranged in several storeys.

SOCLE. A portion of the foundation of a building that projects outward as a base for a column or some other device.

SPANDREL. The area between the exterior curves of two adjoining arches or, in the case of a single arch, the area around its outside curve from its springing to its keystone.

SPATIAL PERSPECTIVE. The exploration of the spatial relationships between objects. Painters were especially interested in spatial perspective in the Hellenistic period in Greece.

SPIRE. A tall tower that rises high above a roof. Spires are commonly associated with church architecture and are frequently found on Gothic structures.

SPOLIA. Latin for "hide stripped from an animal." Term used for (1) spoils of war and (2) fragments of architecture or sculpture reused in a secondary context.

SPRINGING. The part of an arch in contact with its base.

SQUINCHES. Arches set diagonally at the corners of a square or rectangle to establish a transition to the round shape of the dome above.

STAIN PAINTING. A type of painting where the artist works on unprimed canvas, allowing the paint to seep into the canvas, thus staining it.

STELE. From the Greek word for "standing block." An upright stone slab or pillar, sometimes with a carved design or inscription.

STEREOBATE. The substructure of a Classical building, especially a Greek temple.

STEREOCARDS. Side-by-side photographs of the same image taken by a camera with two lenses, replicating human binocular vision. When put into a special viewer, the twin flat pictures appear as a single three-dimensional image.

STILL LIFE. A term used to describe paintings (and sometimes sculpture) that depict familiar objects such as household items and food.

STIPPLES. In drawing or printmaking, stippling is a technique to create tone or shading in an image with small dots rather than lines.

STREET PHOTOGRAPHY. A term applied to American documentary photographers such as Walker Evans, who emerged in the 1930s, and Robert Frank, who surfaced in the 1950s, who took to the streets to find their subject matter, often traveling extensively.

STYLOBATE. A platform or masonry floor above the stereobate forming the foundation for the columns of a Greek temple.

SUBLIME. In 19th-century art, the ideal and goal that art should inspire awe in a viewer and engender feelings of high religious, moral, ethical, and intellectual purpose.

SUNKEN RELIEF. Relief sculpture in which the figures or designs are modeled beneath the surface of the stone, within a sharp outline.

SYMPOSIUM. In ancient Greece, a gathering, sometimes of intellectuals and philosophers to discuss ideas, often in an informal social setting, such as at a dinner party.

SYNCRETISM. The act of bringing together disparate customs or beliefs. Historians usually describe Roman culture as syncretistic, because Romans embraced many of the the practices of those they conquered.

SYNOPTIC NARRATIVE. A narrative with different moments presented simultaneously, in order to encapsulate the entire story in a single scene. The device appears in early Greek pediment sculpture.

TEMPERA. Medium for painting in which pigments are suspended in egg yolk tempered with water or chemicals; this mixture dries quickly, reducing the possibility of changes in the finished painting.

TENEBRISM. The intense contrast of light and dark in painting.

TESSERA (pl. **TESSERAE**). A small piece of colored stone, marble, glass, or gold-backed glass used in a mosaic.

THOLOS. A building with a circular plan, often with a sacred nature.

TONDO. A circular painting or relief sculpture.

TRANSEPT. A cross arm in a basilican church placed at right angles to the nave and usually separating it from the choir or apse.

TRANSVERSALS. In a perspective construction, transversals are the lines parallel to the picture plane (horizontally) that denote distances. They intersect orthogonals to make a grid that guides the arrangement of elements to suggest space.

TRIBUNE. A platform or walkway in a church constructed overlooking the *aisle* and above the *nave*.

TRIFORIUM. The section of a nave wall above the arcade and below the clerestory. It frequently consists of a blind arcade with three openings in each bay. When the gallery is also present, a four-story elevation results, the triforium being between the gallery and clerestory. It may also occur in the transept and the choir walls.

TRIGLYPH. The element of a Doric frieze separating two consecutive metopes and divided by grooves into three sections.

TRILITHIC. A form of construction using three stones—two uprights and a lintel—found frequently in Neolithic tomb and ritual architecture.

TRIPTYCH. An altarpiece or devotional picture, either carved or painted, with one central panel and two hinged wings.

TRIUMPHAL ARCH. (1) A monumental arch, sometimes a combination of three arches, erected by a Roman emperor in commemoration of his military exploits and usually decorated with scenes of these deeds in relief sculpture. (2) The great transverse arch at the eastern end of a church that frames altar and apse and separates them from the main body of the church. It is frequently decorated with mosaics or mural paintings.

TROIS CRAYONS. The use of three colors, usually red, black, and white, in a drawing; a technique popular in the 17th and 18th centuries.

TROMPE L'OEIL. Meaning "trick of the eye" in French, it is a work of art designed to deceive a viewer into believing that the work of art is reality, an actual three-dimensional object or scene in space.

TRUMEAU. A central post supporting the lintel of a large doorway, as in a Romanesque or Gothic portal, where it is frequently decorated with sculpture.

TRUSS. A triangular wooden or metal support for a roof that may be left exposed in the interior or be covered by a ceiling.

TUMULUS (pl. **TUMULI**) A monumental earth mound, often raised over a tomb. Etruscan builders constructed tumuli with internal chambers for burials.

TURRET. (1) A small tower that is part of a larger structure. (2) A small tower at a corner of a building, often beginning some distance from the ground.

TUSCAN STYLE. An architectural style typical of ancient Italy. The style is similar to the Doric style, but the column shafts have bases.

TUSCHE. An inklike liquid containing crayon that is used to produce solid black (or solid color) areas in prints.

TYMPANUM. (1) In Classical architecture, a recessed, usually triangular area often decorated with sculpture. Also called a pediment. (2) In medieval architecture, an arched area between an arch and the lintel of a door or window, frequently carved with relief sculpture.

TYPOLOGY. The matching or pairing of pre-Christian figures, persons, and symbols with their Christian counterparts.

VANISHING POINT. The point at which the orthogonals meet and disappear in a composition done with scientific perspective.

VANITAS. The term derives from the book of Ecclesiastes I:2 ("Vanities of vanities, …") that refers to the passing of time and the notion of life's brevity and the inevitability of death. The vanitas theme found expression especially in the Northern European art of the 17th century.

VAULT. An arched roof or ceiling usually made of stone, brick, or concrete. Several distinct varieties have been developed; all need buttressing at the point where the lateral thrust is concentrated. (1) A barrel vault is a semicircular structure made up of successive arches. It may be straight or annular in plan. (2) A groin vault is the result of the intersection of two barrel vaults of equal size that produces a bay of four compartments with sharp edges, or groins, where the two meet. (3) A ribbed groin vault is one in which ribs are added to the groins for structural strength and for decoration. When the diagonal ribs are constructed as half-circles, the resulting form is a domical ribbed vault. (4) A sexpartite vault is a ribbed groin vault in which each bay is divided into six compartments by the addition of a transverse rib across the center. (5) The normal Gothic vault is quadripartite with all the arches pointed to some degree. (6) A fan vault is an elaboration of a ribbed.groin vault, with elements of tracery using conelike forms. It was developed by the English in the 15th century and was employed for decorative purposes.

VELLUM. See *parchment*.

VERISTIC. From the Latin *verus*, meaning "true." Describes a hyperrealistic style of portraiture that emphasizes individual characteristics.

VIGNETTE. A decorative design often used in manuscripts or books to separate sections or to decorate borders.

VOLUTE. A spiraling architectural element found notably on Ionic and Composite capitals but also used decoratively on building façades and interiors.

VOUSSOIR. A wedge-shaped piece of stone used in arch construction.

WARP. The vertical threads used in a weaver's loom through which the weft is woven.

WEBS. Masonry construction of brick, concrete, stone, etc. that is used to fill in the spaces between groin vault ribs.

WEFT. The horizontal threads that are interlaced through the vertical threads (the warp) in a woven fabric. Weft yarns run perpendicular to the warp.

WESTWORK. From the German word *Westwerk*. In Carolingian, Ottonian, and German Romanesque architecture, a monumental western front of a church, treated as a tower or combination of towers and containing an entrance and vestibule below and a chapel and galleries above. Later examples often added a transept and a crossing tower.

WET-COLLODION PROCESS. A 19th-century photographic technique that uses a very sensitive emulsion called collodion (gun-cotton dissolved in alcohol ether), that reduces exposure time to under a second and produces a sharp, easily reproducible negative.

WHITE-GROUND. Vase-painting technique in which artists painted a wide range of colors onto a white background. This was a favorite technique for decorating lekythoi (vases used in a funerary context in ancient Greece.)

WOODCUT. A print made by carving out a design on a wooden block cut along the grain, applying ink to the raised surfaces that remain, and printing from those.

X-RADIOGRAPHIC. Using a form of electromagnetic radiation called X-rays, researchers can examine the layers of paint or other materials used by artists to construct works of art.

ZIGGURAT. From the Assyrian word *ziqquratu*, meaning "mountaintop" or "height." In ancient Assyria and Babylonia, a pyramidal mound or tower built of mud-brick forming the base for a temple. It was often either stepped or had a broad ascent winding around it, which gave it the appearance of being stepped.

Books for Further Reading

This list is intended to be as practical as possible. It is therefore limited to books of general interest that were printed over the past 20 years or have been generally available recently. However, certain indispensable volumes that have yet to be superseded are retained. This restriction means omitting numerous classics long out of print, as well as much specialized material of interest to the serious student. The reader is thus referred to the many specialized bibliographies noted below.

REFERENCE RESOURCES IN ART HISTORY

1. BIBLIOGRAPHIES AND RESEARCH GUIDES

Arntzen, E., and R. Rainwater. *Guide to the Literature of Art History*. Chicago: American Library, 1980.

Barnet, S. *A Short Guide to Writing About Art*. 8th ed. New York: Longman, 2005.

Ehresmann, D. *Architecture: A Bibliographical Guide to Basic Reference Works, Histories, and Handbooks*. Littleton, CO: Libraries Unlimited, 1984.

———. *Fine Arts: A Bibliographical Guide to Basic Reference Works, Histories, and Handbooks*. 3d ed. Littleton, CO: Libraries Unlimited, 1990.

Freitag, W. *Art Books: A Basic Bibliography of Monographs on Artists*. 2d ed. New York: Garland, 1997.

Goldman, B. *Reading and Writing in the Arts: A Handbook*. Detroit, MI: Wayne State Press, 1972.

Kleinbauer, W., and T. Slavens. *Research Guide to the History of Western Art*. Chicago: American Library, 1982.

Marmor, M., and A. Ross, eds. *Guide to the Literature of Art History 2*. Chicago: American Library, 2005.

Sayre, H. M. *Writing About Art*. New ed. Upper Saddle River, NJ: Pearson Prentice Hall, 2000.

2. DICTIONARIES AND ENCYCLOPEDIAS

Aghion, I. *Gods and Heroes of Classical Antiquity*. Flammarion Iconographic Guides. New York: Flammarion, 1996.

Boström, A., ed. *Encyclopedia of Sculpture*. 3 vols. New York: Fitzroy Dearborn, 2004.

Brigstocke, H., ed. *The Oxford Companion to Western Art*. New York: Oxford University Press, 2001.

Burden, E. *Illustrated Dictionary of Architecture*. New York: McGraw-Hill, 2002.

Carr-Gomm, S. *The Hutchinson Dictionary of Symbols in Art*. Oxford: Helicon, 1995.

Chilvers, I., et al., eds. *The Oxford Dictionary of Art*. 3d ed. New York: Oxford University Press, 2004.

Congdon, K. G. *Artists from Latin American Cultures: A Biographical Dictionary*. Westport, CT: Greenwood Press, 2002.

Cumming, R. *Art: A Field Guide*. New York: Alfred A. Knopf, 2001.

Curl, J. *A Dictionary of Architecture*. New York: Oxford University Press, 1999.

The Dictionary of Art. 34 vols. New York: Grove's Dictionaries, 1996.

Duchet-Suchaux, G., and M. Pastoureau. *The Bible and the Saints*. Flammarion Iconographic Guides. New York: Flammarion, 1994.

Encyclopedia of World Art. 14 vols., with index and supplements. New York: McGraw-Hill, 1959–1968.

Fleming, J., and H. Honour. *The Penguin Dictionary of Architecture and Landscape Architecture*. 5th ed. New York: Penguin, 1998.

———. *The Penguin Dictionary of Decorative Arts*. New ed. London: Viking, 1989.

Gascoigne, B. *How to Identify Prints: A Complete Guide to Manual and Mechanical Processes from Woodcut to Inkjet*. New York: Thames & Hudson, 2004.

Hall, J. *Dictionary of Subjects and Symbols in Art*. Rev. ed. London: J. Murray, 1996.

———. *Illustrated Dictionary of Symbols in Eastern and Western Art*. New York: HarperCollins, 1995.

International Dictionary of Architects and Architecture. 2 vols. Detroit, MI: St. James Press, 1993.

Langmuir, E. *Yale Dictionary of Art and Artists*. New Haven: Yale University Press, 2000.

Lever, J., and J. Harris. *Illustrated Dictionary of Architecture, 800–1914*. 2d ed. Boston: Faber & Faber, 1993.

Lucie-Smith, E. *The Thames & Hudson Dictionary of Art Terms*. New York: Thames & Hudson, 2004.

Mayer, R. *The Artist's Handbook of Materials and Techniques*. 5th ed. New York: Viking, 1991.

———. *The HarperCollins Dictionary of Art Terms & Techniques*. 2d ed. New York: HarperCollins, 1991.

Murray, P., and L. Murray. *A Dictionary of Art and Artists*. 7th ed. New York: Penguin, 1998.

———. *A Dictionary of Christian Art*. New York: Oxford University Press, 2004, © 1996.

Nelson, R. S., and R. Shiff, eds. *Critical Terms for Art History*. Chicago: University of Chicago Press, 2003.

Pierce, J. S. *From Abacus to Zeus: A Handbook of Art History*. 7th ed. Englewood Cliffs, NJ: Pearson Prentice Hall, 2004.

Reid, J. D., ed. *The Oxford Guide to Classical Mythology in the Arts 1300–1990*. 2 vols. New York: Oxford University Press, 1993.

Shoemaker, C., ed. *Encyclopedia of Gardens: History and Design*. Chicago: Fitzroy Dearborn, 2001.

Steer, J. *Atlas of Western Art History: Artists, Sites, and Movements from Ancient Greece to the Modern Age*. New York: Facts on File, 1994.

West, S., ed. *The Bulfinch Guide to Art History*. Boston: Little, Brown, 1996.

———. *Portraiture*. Oxford History of Art. New York: Oxford University Press, 2004.

3. INDEXES, PRINTED AND ELECTRONIC

ARTbibliographies Modern. 1969 to present. A semiannual publication indexing and annotating more than 300 art periodicals, as well as books, exhibition catalogues, and dissertations. Data since 1974 also available electronically.

Art Index. 1929 to present. A standard quarterly index to more than 200 art periodicals. Also available electronically.

Avery Index to Architectural Periodicals. 1934 to present. 15 vols., with supplementary vols. Boston: G. K. Hall, 1973. Also available electronically.

BHA: Bibliography of the History of Art. 1991 to present. The merger of two standard indexes: *RILA* (*Répertoire International de la Littérature de l'Art/International Repertory of the Literature of Art*, vol. 1. 1975) and *Répertoire d'Art et d'Archéologie* (vol. 1. 1910). Data since 1973 also available electronically.

Index Islamicus. 1665 to present. Multiple publishers. Data since 1994 also available electronically.

The Perseus Project: An Evolving Digital Library on Ancient Greece and Rome. Medford, MA: Tufts University, Classics Department, 1994.

4. WORLDWIDE WEBSITES

Visit the following websites for reproductions and information regarding artists, periods, movements, and many more subjects. The art history departments and libraries of many universities and colleges also maintain websites where you can get reading lists and links to other websites, such as those of museums, libraries, and periodicals.

http://www.aah.org.uk/welcome.html Association of Art Historians

http://www.amico.org Art Museum Image Consortium

http://www.archaeological.org Archaeological Institute of America

http://archnet.asu.edu/archnet Virtual Library for Archaeology

http://www.artchive.com

http://www.art-design.umich.edu/mother/ Mother of all Art History links pages, maintained by the Department of the History of Art at the University of Michigan

http://www.arthistory.net Art History Network

http://artlibrary.vassar.edu/ifla-idal International Directory of Art Libraries

http://www.bbk.ac.uk/lib/hasubject.html Collection of resources maintained by the History of Art Department of Birkbeck College, University of London

http://classics.mit.edu The Internet Classics Archive

http://www.collegeart.org College Art Association

http://www.constable.net

http://www.cr.nps.gov/habshaer Historic American Buildings Survey

http://www.getty.edu Including museum, five institutes, and library

http://www.harmsen.net/ahrc/ Art History Research Centre

http://icom.museum/ International Council of Museums

http://www.icomos.org International Council on Monuments and Sites

http://www.ilpi.com/artsource

http://www.siris.si.edu Smithsonian Institution Research Information System

http://whc.unesco.org/ World Heritage Center

5. GENERAL SOURCES ON ART HISTORY, METHOD, AND THEORY

Andrews, M. *Landscape and Western Art*. Oxford History of Art. New York: Oxford University Press, 1999.

Barasch, M. *Modern Theories of Art: Vol. 1, From Winckelmann to Baudelaire. Vol. 2, From Impressionism to Kandinsky*. New York: 1990–1998.

———. *Theories of Art: From Plato to Winckelmann*. New York: Routledge, 2000.

Battistini, M. *Symbols and Allegories in Art*. Los Angeles: J. Paul Getty Museum, 2005.

Baxandall, M. *Patterns of Intention: On the Historical Explanation of Pictures*. New Haven: Yale University Press, 1985.

Bois, Y.-A. *Painting as Model*. Cambridge, MA: MIT Press, 1993.

Broude, N., and M. Garrard. *The Expanding Discourse: Feminism and Art History*. New York: Harper & Row, 1992.

———., eds. *Feminism and Art History: Questioning the Litany*. New York: Harper & Row, 1982.

Bryson, N., ed. *Vision and Painting: The Logic of the Gaze*. New Haven: Yale University Press, 1983.

———., et al., eds. *Visual Theory: Painting and Interpretation*. New York: Cambridge University Press, 1991.

Chadwick, W. *Women, Art, and Society*. 3d ed. New York: Thames & Hudson, 2002.

D'Alleva, A. *Methods & Theories of Art History*. London: Laurence King, 2005.

Freedberg, D. *The Power of Images: Studies in the History and Theory of Response*. Chicago: University of Chicago Press, 1989.

Gage, J. *Color and Culture: Practice and Meaning from Antiquity to Abstraction*. Berkeley: University of California Press, 1999.

Garland Library of the History of Art. New York: Garland, 1976. Collections of essays on specific periods.

Goldwater, R., and M. Treves, eds. *Artists on Art, from the Fourteenth to the Twentieth Century*. 3d ed. New York: Pantheon, 1974.

Gombrich, E. H. *Art and Illusion*. 6th ed. New York: Phaidon, 2002.

Harris, A. S., and L. Nochlin. *Women Artists, 1550–1950*. New York: Random House, 1999.

Holly, M. A. *Panofsky and the Foundations of Art History*. Ithaca, NY: Cornell University Press, 1984.

Holt, E. G., ed. *A Documentary History of Art: Vol. 1, The Middle Ages and the Renaissance. Vol. 2, Michelangelo and the Mannerists. The Baroque and the Eighteenth Century. Vol. 3, From the Classicists to the Impressionists*. 2d ed. Princeton, NJ: Princeton University Press, 1981. Anthologies of primary sources on specific periods.

Johnson, P. *Art: A New History*. New York: HarperCollins, 2003.

Kemal, S., and I. Gaskell. *The Language of Art History*. Cambridge Studies in Philosophy and the Arts. New York: Cambridge University Press, 1991.

Kemp, M., ed. *The Oxford History of Western Art*. New York: Oxford University Press, 2000.

Kleinbauer, W. E. *Modern Perspectives in Western Art History: An Anthology of Twentieth-Century Writings on the Visual Arts*. Reprint of 1971 ed. Toronto: University of Toronto Press, 1989.

Kostof, S. A. *History of Architecture: Settings and Rituals*. 2d ed. New York: Oxford University Press, 1995.

Kruft, H. W. *A History of Architectural Theory from Vitruvius to the Present*. Princeton, NJ: Princeton Architectural Press, 1994.

Kultermann, U. *The History of Art History*. New York: Abaris Books, 1993.

Langer, C. *Feminist Art Criticism: An Annotated Bibliography*. Boston: G. K. Hall, 1993.

Laver, J. *Costume and Fashion: A Concise History*. 4th ed. The World of Art. London: Thames & Hudson, 2002.

Lavin, I., ed. *Meaning in the Visual Arts: Views from the Outside: A Centennial Commemoration of Erwin Panofsky (1892–1968)*. Princeton, NJ: Institute for Advanced Study, 1995.

Minor, V. H. *Art History's History*. Upper Saddle River, NJ: Pearson Prentice Hall, 2001.

Nochlin, L. *Women, Art, and Power, and Other Essays*. New York: HarperCollins, 1989.

Pächt, O. *The Practice of Art History: Reflections on Method*. London: Harvey Miller, 1999.

Panofsky, E. *Meaning in the Visual Arts*. Reprint of 1955 ed. Chicago: University of Chicago Press, 1982.

Penny, N. *The Materials of Sculpture*. New Haven: Yale University Press, 1993.

Pevsner, N. *A History of Building Types*. Princeton, NJ: Princeton University Press, 1976.

Podro, M. *The Critical Historians of Art*. New Haven: Yale University Press, 1982.

Pollock, G. *Differencing the Canon: Feminist Desire and the Writing of Art's Histories*. New York: Routledge, 1999.

———. *Vision and Difference: Femininity, Feminism, and the Histories of Art*. New York: Routledge, 1988.

Prettejohn, E. *Beauty and Art 1750–2000*. New York: Oxford University Press, 2005.

Preziosi, D., ed. *The Art of Art History: A Critical Anthology*. New York: Oxford University Press, 1998.

Rees, A. L., and F. Borzello. *The New Art History*. Atlantic Highlands, NJ: Humanities Press International, 1986.

Roth, L. *Understanding Architecture: Its Elements, History, and Meaning*. New York: Harper & Row, 1993.

Sedlmayr, H. *Framing Formalism: Riegl's Work*. Amsterdam: G+B Arts International, © 2001.

Smith, P., and C. Wilde, eds. *A Companion to Art Theory*. Oxford: Blackwell, 2002.

Sources and Documents in the History of Art Series. General ed. H. W. Janson. Englewood Cliffs, NJ: Prentice Hall. Anthologies of primary sources on specific periods.

Sutton, I. *Western Architecture*. New York: Thames & Hudson, 1999.

Tagg, J. *Grounds of Dispute: Art History, Cultural Politics, and the Discursive Field*. Minneapolis: University of Minnesota Press, 1992.

Trachtenberg, M., and I. Hyman. *Architecture: From Prehistory to Post-Modernism*. 2d ed. New York: Harry N. Abrams, 2002.

Watkin, D. *The Rise of Architectural History*. Chicago: University of Chicago Press, 1980.

Wolff, J. *The Social Production of Art*. 2d ed. New York: New York University Press, 1993.

Wölfflin, H. *Principles of Art History: The Problem of the Development of Style in Later Art*. Various eds. New York: Dover.

Wollheim, R. *Art and Its Objects*. 2d ed. New York: Cambridge University Press, 1992.

PART ONE: THE ANCIENT WORLD

GENERAL REFERENCES

Baines, J., ed. *Civilizations of the Ancient Near East*. 4 vols. New York: Scribner, 1995.

Boardman, J., ed. *The Oxford History of Classical Art*. New York: Oxford University Press, 2001.

De Grummond, N., ed. *An Encyclopedia of the History of Classical Archaeology*. Westport, CT: Greenwood, 1996.

Fine, S. *Art and Judaism in the Greco-Roman World: Toward a New Jewish Archaeology*. New York: Cambridge University Press, 2005.

Holliday, P. J. *Narrative and Event in Ancient Art*. New York: Cambridge University Press, 1993.

Redford, D. B., ed. *The Oxford Encyclopedia of Ancient Egypt*. 3 vols. New York: Oxford University Press, 2001.

Stillwell, R. *The Princeton Encyclopedia of Classical Sites*. Princeton, NJ: Princeton University Press, 1976.

Tadgell, C. *Origins: Egypt, West Asia and the Aegean*. New York: Whitney Library of Design, 1998.

Van Keuren, F. *Guide to Research in Classical Art and Mythology*. Chicago: American Library Association, 1991.

Wharton, A. J. *Refiguring the Post-Classical City: Dura Europos, Jerash, Jerusalem, and Ravenna*. New York: Cambridge University Press, 1995.

Winckelmann, J. J. *Essays on the Philosophy and History of Art*. 3 vols. Bristol, England: Thoemmes, 2001.

Wolf, W. *The Origins of Western Art: Egypt, Mesopotamia, the Aegean*. New York: Universe Books, 1989.

Yegül, F. K. *Baths and Bathing in Classical Antiquity*. Architectural History Foundation. Cambridge, MA: MIT Press, 1992.

CHAPTER 1. PREHISTORIC ART

Bahn, P. G. *The Cambridge Illustrated History of Prehistoric Art*. New York: Cambridge University Press, 1988.

Chauvet, J.-M., É. B. Deschamps, and C. Hilaire. *Dawn of Art: The Chauvet Cave*. New York: Harry N. Abrams, 1995.

Clottes, J. *Chauvet Cave*. Salt Lake City: University of Utah Press, 2003.

———. *The Shamans of Prehistory: Trance and Magic in the Painted Caves*. New York: Harry N. Abrams, 1998.

Cunliffe, B., ed. *The Oxford Illustrated Prehistory of Europe*. New York: Oxford University Press, 1994.

Fitton, J. L. *Cycladic Art*. London: British Museum Press, 1999.

Fowler, P. *Images of Prehistory*. New York: Cambridge University Press, 1990.

Leroi-Gourhan, A. *The Dawn of European Art: An Introduction to Paleolithic Cave Painting*. New York: Cambridge University Press, 1982.

McCold, C. H., and L. D. McDermott. *Toward Decolonizing Gender: Female Vision in the Upper Palaeolithic*. American Anthropologist 98, 1996.

Ruspoli, M. *The Cave of Lascaux: The Final Photographs*. New York: Harry N. Abrams, 1987.

Sandars, N. *Prehistoric Art in Europe*. 2d ed. New Haven: Yale University Press, 1992.

Saura Ramos, P. A. *The Cave of Altamira*. New York: Harry N. Abrams, 1999.

Twohig, E. S. *The Megalithic Art of Western Europe*. New York: Oxford University Press, 1981.

White, R. *Prehistoric Art: The Symbolic Journey of Mankind*. New York: Harry N. Abrams, 2003.

CHAPTER 2. ANCIENT NEAR EASTERN ART

Amiet, P. *Art of the Ancient Near East*. New York: Harry N. Abrams, 1980.

Aruz, J., ed. *Art of the First Cities: The Third Millennium B.C. from the Mediterranean to the Indus*. Exh. cat. New York: Metropolitan Museum of Art; Yale University Press, 2003.

Collon, D. *Ancient Near Eastern Art*. Berkeley: University of California Press, 1995.

———. *First Impressions: Cylinder Seals in the Ancient Near East*. Chicago: University of Chicago Press, 1987.

Crawford, H. *The Architecture of Iraq in the Third Millennium B.C.* Copenhagen: Akademisk Forlag, 1977.

Curtis, J., and N. Tallis. *Forgotten Empire: The World of Ancient Persia*. Exh. cat. London: British Museum, 2005.

Frankfort, H. *The Art and Architecture of the Ancient Orient*. 5th ed. Pelican History of Art. New Haven: Yale University Press, 1997.

Goldman, B. *The Ancient Arts of Western and Central Asia: A Guide to the Literature*. Ames: Iowa State University Press, 1991.

Harper, P. O., ed. *The Royal City of Susa: Ancient Near Eastern Treasures in the Louvre*. New York: Metropolitan Museum of Art; Dist. by Harry N. Abrams, 1992.

Leick, G. *A Dictionary of Ancient Near Eastern Architecture*. New York: Routledge, 1988.

Lloyd, S. *The Archaeology of Mesopotamia: From the Old Stone Age to the Persian Conquest*. Rev. ed. New York: Thames & Hudson, 1984.

Moscati, S. *The Phoenicians*. New York: Abbeville Press, 1988.

Oates, J. *Babylon*. Rev. ed. London: Thames & Hudson, 1986.

Reade, J. *Mesopotamia*. 2d ed. London: Published for the Trustees of the British Museum by the British Museum Press, 2000.

Zettler, R., and L. Horne, eds. *Treasures from the Royal Tombs of Ur*. Exh. cat. Philadelphia: University of Pennsylvania, Museum of Archaeology and Anthropology, 1998.

CHAPTER 3. EGYPTIAN ART

Aldred, C. *The Development of Ancient Egyptian Art, from 3200 to 1315 B.C.* 3 vols. in 1. London: Academy Editions, 1972.

———. *Egyptian Art*. London: Thames & Hudson, 1985.

Arnold, D., and C. Ziegler. *Building in Egypt: Pharaonic Stone Masonry*. New York: Oxford University Press, 1991.

———. *Egyptian Art in the Age of the Pyramids*. New York: Harry N. Abrams, 1999.

Bothmer, B. V. *Egyptian Art: Selected Writings of Bernard V. Bothmer*. New York: Oxford University Press, 2004.

Davis, W. *The Canonical Tradition in Ancient Egyptian Art*. New York: Cambridge University Press, 1989.

Edwards, I. E. S. *The Pyramids of Egypt*. Rev. ed. Harmondsworth, England: Penguin, 1991.

Egyptian Art in the Age of the Pyramids. New York: Metropolitan Museum of Art; Dist. by Harry N. Abrams, 1999.

Grimal, N. *A History of Ancient Egypt*. London: Blackwell, 1992.

Mahdy, C., ed. *The World of the Pharaohs: A Complete Guide to Ancient Egypt*. London: Thames & Hudson, 1990.

Malek, J. *Egypt: 4000 Years of Art*. London: Phaidon, 2003.

———. *Egyptian Art. Art & Ideas*. London: Phaidon, 1999.

Mendelssohn, K. *The Riddle of the Pyramids*. New York: Thames & Hudson, 1986.

Parry, D. *Engineering the Pyramids*. Stroud, England: Sutton, 2004.

Robins, G. *The Art of Ancient Egypt*. Cambridge, MA: Harvard University Press, 1997.

Schaefer, H. *Principles of Egyptian Art*. Oxford: Clarendon Press, 1986.

Schulz, R., and M. Seidel. *Egypt: The World of the Pharaohs*. Cologne: Könemann, 1998.

Smith, W., and W. Simpson. *The Art and Architecture of Ancient Egypt*. Rev. ed. Pelican History of Art. New Haven: Yale University Press, 1999.

Tiradritti, F. *Ancient Egypt: Art, Architecture and History*. London: British Museum Press, 2002.

Walker, S. and P. Higgs, eds. *Cleopatra of Egypt: From History to Myth*. Exh. cat. Princeton, NJ: Princeton University Press, 2001.

Wilkinson, R. *Reading Egyptian Art: A Hieroglyphic Guide to Ancient Egyptian Painting and Sculpture*. New York: Thames & Hudson, 1992.

CHAPTER 4. AEGEAN ART

Akurgal, E. *The Aegean, Birthplace of Western Civilization: History of East Greek Art and Culture, 1050–333 B.C.* Izmir, Turkey: Metropolitan Municipality of Izmir, 2000.

Barber, R. *The Cyclades in the Bronze Age*. Iowa City: University of Iowa Press, 1987.

Dickinson, O. T. P. K. *The Aegean Bronze Age*. New York: Cambridge University Press, 1994.

Elytis, O. *The Aegean: The Epicenter of Greek Civilization*. Athens: Melissa, 1997.

German, S. C. *Performance, Power and the Art of the Aegean Bronze Age*. Oxford: Archaeopress, 2005.

Getz-Preziosi, P. *Sculptors of the Cyclades*. Ann Arbor: University of Michigan Press, 1987.

Graham, J. *The Palaces of Crete*. Rev. ed. Princeton, NJ: Princeton University Press, 1987.

Hampe, R., and E. Simon. *The Birth of Greek Art from the Mycenean to the Archaic Period*. New York: Oxford University Press, 1981.

Higgins, R. *Minoan and Mycenaean Art*. Rev. ed. The World of Art. New York: Oxford University Press, 1981.

Hood, S. *The Arts in Prehistoric Greece*. Pelican History of Art. New Haven: Yale University Press, 1992.

———. *The Minoans: The Story of Bronze Age Crete*. New York: Praeger, 1981.

Hurwit, J. *The Art and Culture of Early Greece, 1100–480 B.C.* Ithaca, NY: Cornell University Press, 1985.

McDonald, W. *Progress into the Past: The Rediscovery of Mycenaean Civilization*. 2d ed. Bloomington: Indiana University Press, 1990.

Preziosi, D., and L. Hitchcock. *Aegean Art and Architecture*. New York: Oxford University Press, 1999.

Renfrew, C. *The Cycladic Spirit: Masterpieces from the Nicholas P. Goulandris Collection*. London: Thames & Hudson, 1991.

Vermeule, E. *Greece in the Bronze Age*. Chicago: University of Chicago Press, 1972.

CHAPTER 5. GREEK ART

Beard, M. *The Parthenon*. Cambridge, MA: Harvard University Press, 2003.

Beazley, J. D. *Athenian Red Figure Vases: The Archaic Period: A Handbook*. The World of Art. New York: Thames & Hudson, 1991.

———. *Athenian Red Figure Vases: The Classical Period: A Handbook*. The World of Art. New York: Thames & Hudson, 1989.

———. *The Development of Attic Black-Figure*. Rev. ed. Berkeley: University of California Press, 1986.

———. *Greek Vases: Lectures*. Oxford and New York: Clarendon Press and Oxford University Press, 1989.

Boardman, J. *The Archaeology of Nostalgia: How the Greeks Re-created Their Mythical Past*. London: Thames & Hudson, 2002.

———. *Athenian Black Figure Vases: A Handbook*. Corrected ed. The World of Art. New York: Thames & Hudson, 1991.

———. *Early Greek Vase Painting: 11th–6th Centuries B.C.: A Handbook*. The World of Art. New York: Thames & Hudson, 1998.

———. *Greek Art*. 4th ed., rev. and expanded. The World of Art. New York: Thames & Hudson, 1996.

———. *Greek Sculpture: The Archaic Period: A Handbook*. Corrected ed. The World of Art. New York: Thames & Hudson, 1991.

———. *Greek Sculpture: The Classical Period: A Handbook*. Corrected ed. New York: Thames & Hudson, 1991.

———. *The History of Greek Vases: Potters, Painters, and Pictures*. New York: Thames & Hudson, 2001.

Burn, L. *Hellenistic Art: From Alexander the Great to Augustus*. London: The British Museum, 2004.

Carpenter, T. H. *Art and Myth in Ancient Greece: A Handbook*. The World of Art. New York: Thames & Hudson, 1991.

Carratelli, G. P., ed. *The Greek World: Art and Civilization in Magna Graecia and Sicily*. Exh. cat. New York: Rizzoli, 1996.

Fullerton, M. D. *Greek Art*. New York: Cambridge University Press, 2000.

Hampe, R., and E. Simon. *The Birth of Greek Art*. Oxford: Oxford University Press, 1981.

Haynes, D. E. L. *The Technique of Greek Bronze Statuary*. Mainz am Rhein: P. von Zabern, 1992.

Himmelmann, N. *Reading Greek Art: Essays*. Princeton, NJ: Princeton University Press, 1998.

Hurwit, J. M. *The Acropolis in the Age of Pericles*. New York: Cambridge University Press, 2004.

———. *The Art & Culture of Early Greece, 1100–480 B.C.* Ithaca, NY: Cornell University Press, 1985.

Lawrence, A. *Greek Architecture*. Rev. 5th ed. Pelican History of Art. New Haven: Yale University Press, 1996.

L'Empereur, J. *Alexandria Rediscovered*. London: British Museum Press, 1998.

Osborne, R. *Archaic and Classical Greek Art*. New York: Oxford University Press, 1998.

Papaioannou, K. *The Art of Greece*. New York: Harry N. Abrams, 1989.

Pedley, J. *Greek Art and Archaeology*. 2d ed. New York: Harry N. Abrams, 1997.

Pollitt, J. *The Ancient View of Greek Art: Criticism, History, and Terminology*. New Haven: Yale University Press, 1974.

———. *Art in the Hellenistic Age*. New York: Cambridge University Press, 1986.

———., ed. *Art of Ancient Greece: Sources and Documents*. New York: Cambridge University Press, 1990.

Potts, A. *Flesh and the Ideal: Winckelmann and the Origins of Art History*. New Haven: Yale University Press, 1994.

Rhodes, R. F. *Architecture and Meaning on the Athenian Acropolis*. New York: Cambridge University Press, 1995.

———., ed. *The Acquisition and Exhibition of Classical Antiquities: Professional, Legal, and Ethical Perspectives*. Notre Dame, IN: University of Notre Dame Press, 2007.

Richter, G. M. A. *A Handbook of Greek Art*. 9th ed. New York: Da Capo, 1987.

———. *Portraits of the Greeks*. Ed. R. Smith. New York: Oxford University Press, 1984.

Ridgway, B. S. *Hellenistic Sculpture: Vol. 1, The Styles of ca. 331–200 B.C.* Bristol, England: Bristol Classical Press, 1990.

Robertson, M. *The Art of Vase Painting in Classical Athens*. New York: Cambridge University Press, 1992.

Rolley, C. *Greek Bronzes*. New York: Philip Wilson for Sotheby's Publications; Dist. by Harper & Row, 1986.

Schefold, K. *Gods and Heroes in Late Archaic Greek Art*. New York: Cambridge University Press, 1992.

Smith, R. *Hellenistic Sculpture*. The World of Art. New York: Thames & Hudson, 1991.

Spivey, N. *Greek Art*. London: Phaidon, 1997.

Stafford, E. *Life, Myth, and Art in Ancient Greece*. Los Angeles: J. Paul Getty Museum, 2004.

Stansbury-O'Donnell, M. *Pictorial Narrative in Ancient Greek Art*. New York: Cambridge University Press, 1999.

Stewart, A. F. *Greek Sculpture: An Exploration*. New Haven: Yale University Press, 1990.

Whitley, J. *The Archaeology of Ancient Greece*. New York: Cambridge University Press, 2001.

CHAPTER 6. ETRUSCAN ART

Boethius, A. *Etruscan and Early Roman Architecture*. 2d ed. Pelican History of Art. New Haven: Yale University Press, 1992.

Bonfante, L., ed. *Etruscan Life and Afterlife: A Handbook of Etruscan Studies*. Detroit, MI: Wayne State University, 1986.

Borrelli, F. *The Etruscans: Art, Architecture, and History*. Los Angeles: J. Paul Getty Museum, 2004.

Brendel, O. *Etruscan Art*. Pelican History of Art. New Haven: Yale University Press, 1995.

Hall, J. F., ed. *Etruscan Italy: Etruscan Influences on the Civilizations of Italy from Antiquity to the Modern Era*. Provo, UT: Museum of Art, Brigham Young University, 1996.

Haynes, Sybille. *Etruscan Civilization: A Cultural History*. Los Angeles: J. Paul Getty Museum, 2000.

Richardson, E. *The Etruscans: Their Art and Civilization*. Reprint of 1964 ed., with corrections. Chicago: University of Chicago Press, 1976.

Spivey, N. *Etruscan Art*. The World of Art. New York: Thames & Hudson, 1997.

Sprenger, M., G. Bartoloni, and M. Hirmer. *The Etruscans: Their History, Art, and Architecture*. New York: Harry N. Abrams, 1983.

Steingräber, S., ed. *Etruscan Painting: Catalogue Raisonné of Etruscan Wall Paintings*. New York: Johnson Reprint, 1986.

Torelli, M., ed. *The Etruscans*. Exh. cat. Milan: Bompiani, 2000.

CHAPTER 7. ROMAN ART

Allan, T. *Life, Myth and Art in Ancient Rome*. Los Angeles: J. Paul Getty Museum, 2005.

Andreae, B. *The Art of Rome*. New York: Harry N. Abrams, 1977.

Beard, M., and J. Henderson. *Classical Art: From Greece to Rome*. New York: Oxford University Press, 2001.

Bowe, P. *Gardens of the Roman World*. Los Angeles: J. Paul Getty Museum, 2004.

Brilliant, R. *Commentaries on Roman Art: Selected Studies*. London: Pindar Press, 1994.

———. *My Laocoon: Alternative Claims in the Interpretation of Artworks*. University of California Press, 2000.

Claridge, A. *Rome: An Oxford Archaeological Guide*. New York: Oxford University Press, 1998.

D'Ambra, E. *Roman Art*. New York: Cambridge University Press, 1998.

———., comp. *Roman Art in Context: An Anthology*. Englewood Cliffs, NJ: Prentice Hall, 1993.

Davies, P. *Death and the Emperor: Roman Imperial Funerary Monuments from Augustus to Marcus Aurelius*. Austin: University of Texas Press, 2004.

Dunbabin, K. M. D. *Mosaics of the Greek and Roman World*. New York: Cambridge University Press, 1999.

Elsner, J. *Imperial Rome and Christian Triumph: The Art of the Roman Empire, A.D. 100–450*. New York: Oxford University Press, 1998.

Gazda, E. K. *Roman Art in the Private Sphere: New Perspectives on the Architecture and Decor of the Domus, Villa, and Insula*. Ann Arbor: University of Michigan Press, 1991.

Jenkyns, R., ed. *The Legacy of Rome: A New Appraisal*. New York: Oxford University Press, 1992.

Kleiner, D. *Roman Sculpture*. New Haven: Yale University Press, 1992.

———., and S. B. Matheson, eds. *I, Claudia: Women in Ancient Rome*. New Haven: Yale University Art Gallery, 1996.

Ling, R. *Ancient Mosaics*. London: British Museum Press, 1998.

———. *Roman Painting*. New York: Cambridge University Press, 1991.

Nash, E. *Pictorial Dictionary of Ancient Rome.* 2 vols. Reprint of 1968 2d ed. New York: Hacker, 1981.

Pollitt, J. J. *The Art of Rome, c. 753 B.C.– A.D. 337: Sources and Documents.* New York: Cambridge University Press, 1983.

Ramage, N., and A. Ramage. *The Cambridge Illustrated History of Roman Art.* Cambridge: Cambridge University Press, 1991.

———. *Roman Art: Romulus to Constantine.* 4th ed. Upper Saddle River, NJ: Pearson Prentice Hall, 2005.

Richardson, L. *A New Topographical Dictionary of Ancient Rome.* Baltimore, MD: Johns Hopkins University Press, 1992.

Rockwell, P. *The Art of Stoneworking: A Reference Guide.* Cambridge: Cambridge University Press, 1993.

Strong, D. E. *Roman Art.* 2d ed. Pelican History of Art. New Haven: Yale University Press, 1992.

Vitruvius. *The Ten Books on Architecture.* Trans. I. Rowland. Cambridge: Cambridge University Press, 1999.

Ward-Perkins, J. B. *Roman Imperial Architecture.* Reprint of 1981 ed. Pelican History of Art. New York: Penguin, 1992.

Zanker, P. *The Power of Images in the Age of Augustus.* Ann Arbor: University of Michigan Press, 1988.

PART TWO: THE MIDDLE AGES

GENERAL REFERENCES

Alexander, J. J. G. *Medieval Illuminators and Their Methods of Work.* New Haven: Yale University Press, 1992.

———., ed. *A Survey of Manuscripts Illuminated in the British Isles.* 6 vols. London: Harvey Miller, 1975–1996.

Avril, F., and J. J. G. Alexander, eds. *A Survey of Manuscripts Illuminated in France.* London: Harvey Miller, 1996.

Bartlett, R., ed. *Medieval Panorama.* Los Angeles: J. Paul Getty Museum, 2001.

Cahn, W. *Studies in Medieval Art and Interpretation.* London: Pindar Press, 2000.

Calkins, R. G. *Medieval Architecture in Western Europe: From A.D. 300 to 1500.* New York: Oxford University Press, 1998.

Cassidy, B., ed. *Iconography at the Crossroads.* Princeton, NJ: Princeton University Press, 1993.

Coldstream, N. *Medieval Architecture.* Oxford History of Art. New York: Oxford University Press, 2002.

De Hamel, C. *The British Library Guide to Manuscript Illumination: History and Techniques.* Toronto: University of Toronto Press, 2001.

———. *A History of Illuminated Manuscripts.* Rev. and enl. 2d ed. London: Phaidon Press, 1994.

Duby, G. *Art and Society in the Middle Ages.* Polity Press; Malden, MA: Blackwell Publishers, 2000.

Hamburger, J. *Nuns as Artists: The Visual Culture of a Medieval Convent.* Berkeley: University of California Press, 1997.

Katzenellenbogen, A. *Allegories of the Virtues and Vices in Medieval Art.* Reprint of 1939 ed. Toronto: University of Toronto Press, 1989.

Kazhdan, A. P. *The Oxford Dictionary of Byzantium.* 3 vols. New York: Oxford University Press, 1991.

Kessler, H. L. *Seeing Medieval Art.* Peterborough, Ont. and Orchard Park, NY: Broadview Press, 2004.

Luttikhuizen, H., and D. Verkerk. *Snyder's Medieval Art.* 2d ed. Upper Saddle River, NJ: Prentice Hall, 2006.

Pächt, O. *Book Illumination in the Middle Ages: An Introduction.* London: Harvey Miller, 1986.

Pelikan, J. *Mary Through the Centuries: Her Place in the History of Culture.* New Haven: Yale University Press, 1996.

Ross, L. *Artists of the Middle Ages.* Westport, CT: Greenwood Press, 2003.

———. *Medieval Art: A Topical Dictionary.* Westport, CT: Greenwood Press, 1996.

Schütz, B. *Great Cathedrals.* New York: Harry N. Abrams, 2002.

Sears, E., and T. K. Thomas, eds. *Reading Medieval Images: The Art Historian and the Object.* Ann Arbor: University of Michigan Press, 2002.

Sekules, V. *Medieval Art.* New York: Oxford University Press, 2001.

Stokstad, M. *Medieval Art.* Boulder, CO: Westview Press, 2004.

Tasker, E. *Encyclopedia of Medieval Church Art.* London: Batsford, 1993.

Watson, R. *Illuminated Manuscripts and Their Makers: An Account Based on the Collection of the Victoria and Albert Museum.* London and New York: V & A Publications; Dist. by Harry N. Abrams, 2003.

Wieck, R. S. *Painted Prayers: The Book of Hours in Medieval and Renaissance Art.* New York: George Braziller in association with the Pierpont Morgan Library, 1997.

Wixom, W. D. *Mirror of the Medieval World.* Exh. cat. New York: Metropolitan Museum of Art; Dist. by Harry N. Abrams, 1999.

CHAPTER 8. EARLY JEWISH, EARLY CHRISTIAN, AND BYZANTINE ART

Beckwith, J. *Studies in Byzantine and Medieval Western Art.* London: Pindar Press, 1989.

Bowersock, G. W., ed. *Late Antiquity: A Guide to the Postclassical World.* Cambridge, MA: Belknap Press of Harvard University Press, 1999.

Cormack, R. *Icons.* London: British Museum Press, 2007.

Demus, O. *Studies in Byzantium, Venice and the West.* 2 vols. London: Pindar Press, 1998.

Drury, J. *Painting the Word: Christian Pictures and Their Meanings.* New Haven and London: Yale University Press in association with National Gallery Publications, 1999.

Durand, J. *Byzantine Art.* Paris: Terrail, 1999.

Evans, H. C., ed. *Byzantium: Faith and Power, 1261–1557.* Exh. cat. New York: Metropolitan Museum of Art; New Haven: Yale University Press, 2004.

Evans, H. C., and W. D. Wixom, eds. *The Glory of Byzantium: Art and Culture of the Middle Byzantine Era, A. D. 843–1261.* Exh. cat. New York: Metropolitan Museum of Art; New Haven: Yale University Press, 1997.

Galavaris, G. *Colours, Symbols, Worship: The Mission of the Byzantine Artist.* London: Pindar, 2005.

Grabar, A. *Christian Iconography: A Study of Its Origins.* Princeton, NJ: Princeton University Press, 1968.

Henderson, G. *Vision and Image in Early Christian England.* New York: Cambridge University Press, 1999.

Kalavrezou, I. *Byzantine Women and Their World.* Exh. cat. Cambridge, MA and New Haven: Harvard University Art Museums; Yale University Press, © 2003.

Kleinbauer, W. *Early Christian and Byzantine Architecture: An Annotated Bibliography and Historiography.* Boston: G. K. Hall, 1993.

Krautheimer, R., and S. Curcic. *Early Christian and Byzantine Architecture.* 4th ed. Pelican History of Art. New Haven: Yale University Press, 1992.

Lowden, J. *Early Christian and Byzantine Art.* London: Phaidon Press, 1997.

Maguire, H. *Art and Eloquence in Byzantium.* Princeton, NJ: Princeton University Press, 1981.

Mango, C. *The Art of the Byzantine Empire, 312–1453: Sources and Documents.* Reprint of 1972 ed. Toronto: University of Toronto Press, 1986.

Mark, R., and A. S. Çakmak, eds. *Hagia Sophia from the Age of Justinian to the Present.* New York: Cambridge University Press, 1992.

Matthews, T. *Byzantium from Antiquity to the Renaissance.* New York: Harry N. Abrams, 1998.

———. *The Clash of Gods: A Reinterpretation of Early Christian Art.* Princeton, NJ: Princeton University Press, 1993.

Milburn, R. *Early Christian Art and Architecture.* Berkeley: University of California Press, 1988.

Rodley, L. *Byzantine Art and Architecture: An Introduction.* New York: Cambridge University Press, 1994.

Simson, O. G. von. *Sacred Fortress: Byzantine Art and Statecraft in Ravenna.* Reprint of 1948 ed. Princeton, NJ: Princeton University Press, 1987.

Webster, L., and M. Brown, eds. *The Transformation of the Roman World A.D. 400–900.* Berkeley: University of California Press, 1997.

Weitzmann, K. *Late Antique and Early Christian Book Illumination.* New York: Braziller, 1977.

CHAPTER 9. ISLAMIC ART

Asher, C. E. B. *Architecture of Mughal India.* New Cambridge History of India, Cambridge, England. New York: Cambridge University Press, 1992.

Atil, E. *The Age of Sultan Süleyman the Magnificent.* Exh. cat. Washington, DC: National Gallery of Art; New York: Harry N. Abrams, 1987.

———. *Renaissance of Islam: Art of the Mamluks.* Exh. cat. Washington, DC: Smithsonian Institution Press, 1981.

Behrens-Abouseif, D. *Beauty in Arabic Culture.* Princeton, NJ: Markus Wiener, 1998.

Bierman, I., ed. *The Experience of Islamic Art on the Margins of Islam.* Reading, England: Ithaca Press, 2005.

Blair, S., and J. Bloom. *The Art and Architecture of Islam 1250–1800.* Pelican History of Art. New Haven: Yale University Press, 1996.

Brookes, J. *Gardens of Paradise: The History and Design of the Great Islamic Gardens.* New York: New Amsterdam, 1987.

Burckhardt, T. *Art of Islam: Language and Meaning.* London: World of Islam Festival, 1976.

Creswell, K. A. C. *A Bibliography of the Architecture, Arts, and Crafts of Islam.* Cairo: American University in Cairo Press, 1984.

Denny, W. B. *The Classical Tradition in Anatolian Carpets.* Washington, DC: Textile Museum, 2002.

Dodds, J. D., ed. *al-Andalus: The Art of Islamic Spain.* Exh. cat. New York: Metropolitan Museum of Art; Dist. by Harry N. Abrams, 1992.

Erdmann, K. *Oriental Carpets: An Essay on Their History.* Fishguard, Wales: Crosby Press, 1976, © 1960.

Ettinghausen, R., O. Grabar, and M. Jenkins-Madina. *Islamic Art and Architecture, 650–1250.* 2d ed. Pelican History of Art. New Haven: Yale University Press, 2002.

Frishman, M., and H. Khan. *The Mosque: History, Architectural Development and Regional Diversity.* London: Thames & Hudson, 2002, © 1994.

Goodwin, G. *A History of Ottoman Architecture.* New York: Thames & Hudson, 2003, © 1971.

Grabar, O. *The Formation of Islamic Art.* Rev. and enl. ed. New Haven: Yale University Press, 1987.

Hillenbrand, R. *Islamic Architecture: Form, Function, and Meaning.* New ed. New York: Columbia University Press, 2004.

Komaroff, L., and S. Carboni, eds. *The Legacy of Genghis Khan: Courtly Art and Culture in Western Asia, 1256–1353.* Exh. cat. New York: Metropolitan Museum of Art; New Haven: Yale University Press, 2002.

Lentz, T., and G. Lowry. *Timur and the Princely Vision: Persian Art and Culture in the Fifteenth Century.* Exh. cat. Los Angeles: Los Angeles County Museum of Art; Washington, DC: Arthur M. Sackler Gallery; Smithsonian Institution Press, 1989.

Lings, M. *The Quranic Art of Calligraphy and Illumination.* 1st American ed. New York: Interlink Books, 1987, © 1976.

Necipolu, G. *The Age of Sinan: Architectural Culture in the Ottoman Empire.* Princeton, NJ: Princeton University Press, 2005.

———. *The Topkapı Scroll: Geometry and Ornament in Islamic Architecture.* Topkapı Palace Museum Library MS H. 1956. Santa Monica, CA: Getty Center for the History of Art and the Humanities, 1995.

Pope, A. U. *Persian Architecture: The Triumph of Form and Color.* New York: Braziller, 1965.

Robinson, F. *Atlas of the Islamic World Since 1500.* New York: Facts on File, 1982.

Ruggles, D. F. *Gardens, Landscape, and Vision in the Palaces of Islamic Spain.* University Park: Pennsylvania State University Press, 2000.

———., ed. *Women, Patronage, and Self-Representation in Islamic Societies.* Albany: State University of New York Press, 2000.

Tabbaa, Y. *The Transformation of Islamic Art During the Sunni Revival.* Seattle: University of Washington Press, 2001.

Thompson, J., ed. *Hunt for Paradise: Court Arts of Safavid Iran, 1501–1576*. Milan: Skira; New York: Dist. in North America and Latin America by Rizzoli, 2003.

———. *Oriental Carpets from the Tents, Cottages, and Workshops of Asia*. New York: Dutton, 1988.

Vernoit, S., ed. *Discovering Islamic Art: Scholars, Collectors and Collections, 1850–1950*. London and New York: I. B. Tauris; Dist. by St. Martin's Press, 2000.

Welch, S. C. *Imperial Mughal Painting*. New York: Braziller, 1978.

———. *A King's Book of Kings: The Shah-nameh of Shah Tahmasp*. New York: Metropolitan Museum of Art; Dist. by New York Graphic Society, 1972.

CHAPTER 10. EARLY MEDIEVAL ART

Backhouse, J. *The Golden Age of Anglo-Saxon Art, 966–1066*. Bloomington: Indiana University Press, 1984.

———. *The Lindisfarne Gospels: A Masterpiece of Book Painting*. London: British Library, 1995.

Barral i Altet, X. *The Early Middle Ages: From Late Antiquity to A.D. 1000*. Taschen's World Architecture. Köln and New York: Taschen, © 1997.

Conant, K. *Carolingian and Romanesque Architecture, 800–1200*. 4th ed. Pelican History of Art. New Haven: Yale University Press, 1992.

Davis-Weyer, C. *Early Medieval Art, 300–1150: Sources and Documents*. Reprint of 1971 ed. Toronto: University of Toronto Press, 1986.

Diebold, W. J. *Word and Image: An Introduction to Early Medieval Art*. Boulder, CO: Westview Press, 2000.

Dodwell, C. R. *Anglo-Saxon Art: A New Perspective*. Ithaca, NY: Cornell University Press, 1982.

———. *The Pictorial Arts of the West, 800–1200*. New ed. Pelican History of Art. New Haven: Yale University Press, 1993.

Graham-Campbell, J. *The Viking-age Gold and Silver of Scotland, A.D. 850–1100*. Exh. cat. Edinburgh: National Museums of Scotland, 1995.

Harbison, P. *The Golden Age of Irish Art: The Medieval Achievement, 600–1200*. New York: Thames & Hudson, 1999.

Henderson, G. *The Art of the Picts: Sculpture and Metalwork in Early Medieval Scotland*. New York: Thames & Hudson, 2004.

Kitzinger, E. *Early Medieval Art, with Illustrations from the British Museum*. Rev. ed. Bloomington: Indiana University Press, 1983.

Lasko, P. *Ars Sacra, 800–1200*. 2d ed. Pelican History of Art. New Haven: Yale University Press, 1995.

Mayr-Harting, M. *Ottonian Book Illumination: An Historical Study*. 2 vols. London: Harvey Miller, 1991–1993.

Megaw, M. R. *Celtic Art: From Its Beginnings to the Book of Kells*. New York: Thames & Hudson, 2001.

Mosacati, S., ed. *The Celts*. Exh. cat. New York: Rizzoli, 1999.

Nees, L. *Early Medieval Art*. Oxford History of Art. New York: Oxford University Press, 2002.

Ohlgren, T. H., comp. *Insular and Anglo-Saxon Illuminated Manuscripts: An Iconographic Catalogue, c. A.D. 625 to 1100*. New York: Garland, 1986.

Rickert, M. *Painting in Britain: The Middle Ages*. 2d ed. Pelican History of Art. Harmondsworth, England: Penguin, 1965.

Stalley, R. A. *Early Medieval Architecture*. Oxford History of Art. New York: Oxford University Press, 1999.

Stone, L. *Sculpture in Britain: The Middle Ages*. 2d ed. Pelican History of Art. Harmondsworth, England: Penguin, 1972.

Webster, L., and J. Backhouse, eds. *The Making of England: Anglo-Saxon Art and Culture, A.D. 600–900*. Exh. cat. London: Published for the Trustees of the British Museum and the British Library Board by British Museum Press, 1991.

CHAPTER 11. ROMANESQUE ART

Barral i. Altet, X. *The Romanesque: Towns, Cathedrals, and Monasteries*. Cologne: Taschen, 1998.

Bizzarro, T. *Romanesque Architectural Criticism: A Prehistory*. New York: Cambridge University Press, 1992.

Boase, T. S. R. *English Art, 1100–1216*. Oxford History of English Art. Oxford: Clarendon Press, 1953.

Cahn, W. *Romanesque Bible Illumination*. Ithaca, NY: Cornell University Press, 1982.

Davies, M. *Romanesque Architecture: A Bibliography*. Boston: G. K. Hall, 1993.

Focillon, H. *The Art of the West in the Middle Ages*. Ed. J. Bony. 2 vols. Reprint of 1963 ed. Ithaca, NY: Cornell University Press, 1980.

Hearn, M. F. *Romanesque Sculpture: The Revival of Monumental Stone Sculpture*. Ithaca, NY: Cornell University Press, 1981.

Mâle, E. *Religious Art in France, the Twelfth Century: A Study of the Origins of Medieval Iconography*. Bollingen series, 90:1. Princeton, NJ: Princeton University Press, 1978.

Minne-Sève, V. *Romanesque and Gothic France: Architecture and Sculpture*. New York: Harry N. Abrams, 2000.

Nichols, S. *Romanesque Signs: Early Medieval Narrative and Iconography*. New Haven: Yale University Press, 1983.

O'Keeffe, T. *Romanesque Ireland: Architecture and Ideology in the Twelfth Century*. Dublin and Portland, OR: Four Courts, 2003.

Petzold, A. *Romanesque Art*. Perspectives. Upper Saddle River, NJ: Prentice Hall, 1996.

Platt, C. *The Architecture of Medieval Britain: A Social History*. New Haven: Yale University Press, 1990.

Sauerländer, W. *Romanesque Art: Problems and Monuments*. 2 vols. London: Pindar, 2004.

Schapiro, M. *Romanesque Art*. New York: Braziller, 1977.

Stoddard, W. *Art and Architecture in Medieval France*. New York: Harper & Row, 1972, © 1966.

Stones, A., J. Krochalis, P. Gerson, and A. Shaver-Crandell. *The Pilgrim's Guide to Santiago de Compostela: A Critical Edition*. 2 vols. London: Harvey Miller, 1998.

Toman, R., and A. Bednorz. *Romanesque Architecture, Sculpture, Painting*. Cologne: Könemann, 2008.

Zarnecki, G. *Further Studies in Romanesque Sculpture*. London: Pindar, 1992.

CHAPTER 12. GOTHIC ART

Barnes, C. F. *Villard de Honnecourt, the Artist and His Drawings: A Critical Bibliography*. Boston: G. K. Hall, 1982.

Belting, H. *The Image and Its Public: Form and Function of Early Paintings of the Passion*. New Rochelle, NY: Caratzas, 1990.

Blum, P. *Early Gothic Saint-Denis: Restorations and Survivals*. Berkeley: University of California Press, 1992.

Bony, J. *French Gothic Architecture of the Twelfth and Thirteenth Centuries*. Berkeley: University of California Press, 1983.

Camille, M. *Gothic Art: Glorious Visions*. Perspectives. New York: Harry N. Abrams, 1997.

———. *The Gothic Idol: Ideology and Image Making in Medieval Art*. New York: Cambridge University Press, 1989.

———. *Sumptuous Arts at the Royal Abbeys of Reims and Braine*. Princeton, NJ: Princeton University Press, 1990.

Cennini, C. *The Craftsman's Handbook (Il Libro dell'Arte)*. New York: Dover, 1954.

Coldstream, N. *Medieval Architecture*. Oxford History of Art. New York: Oxford University Press, 2002.

Erlande-Brandenburg, A. *Gothic Art*. New York: Harry N. Abrams, 1989.

Frankl, P. *Gothic Architecture*. Rev. by P. Crossley. Pelican History of Art. New Haven, CT: Yale University Press, 2001.

Frisch, T. G. *Gothic Art, 1140–c. 1450: Sources and Documents*. Reprint of 1971 ed. Toronto: University of Toronto Press, 1987.

Grodecki, L. *Gothic Architecture*. New York: Electa/Rizzoli, 1985.

———. *Gothic Stained Glass, 1200–1300*. Ithaca, NY: Cornell University Press, 1985.

Hamburger, J. F. *The Visual and the Visionary: Art and Female Spirituality in Late Medieval Germany*. Zone Books. Cambridge, MA: MIT Press, 1998.

Jantzen, H. *High Gothic: The Classic Cathedrals of Chartres, Reims, Amiens*. Reprint of 1962 ed. Princeton, NJ: Princeton University Press, 1984.

Kemp, W. *The Narratives of Gothic Stained Glass*. New York: Cambridge University Press, 1997.

Limentani Virdis, C. *Great Altarpieces: Gothic and Renaissance*. New York: Vendome Press; Dist. by Rizzoli, 2002.

Mâle, E. *Religious Art in France, the Thirteenth Century: A Study of Medieval Iconography and Its Sources*. Ed. H. Bober. Princeton, NJ: Princeton University Press, 1984.

Marks, R., and P. Williamson, eds. *Gothic: Art for England 1400–1547*. Exh. cat. London and New York: Victoria & Albert Museum; Dist. by Harry N. Abrams, 2003.

Murray, S. *Beauvais Cathedral: Architecture of Transcendence*. Princeton, NJ: Princeton University Press, 1989.

Panofsky, E. ed. and trans. *Abbot Suger on the Abbey Church of Saint-Denis and Its Art Treasures*. 2d ed. Princeton, NJ: Princeton University Press, 1979.

———. *Gothic Architecture and Scholasticism*. Reprint of 1951 ed. New York: New American Library, 1985.

Parnet, P., ed. *Images in Ivory: Precious Objects of the Gothic Age*. Exh. cat. Detroit, MI: Detroit Institute of Arts, © 1997.

Sandler, L. *Gothic Manuscripts, 1285–1385*. Survey of Manuscripts Illuminated in the British Isles. London: Harvey Miller, 1986.

Scott, R. A. *The Gothic Enterprise: A Guide to Understanding the Medieval Cathedral*. Berkeley: University of California Press, 2003.

Simson, O. von. *The Gothic Cathedral: Origins of Gothic Architecture and the Medieval Concept of Order*. 3d ed. Princeton, NJ: Princeton University Press, 1988.

Toman, R., and A. Bednorz. *The Art of Gothic: Architecture, Sculpture, Painting*. Cologne: Könemann, 1999.

Williamson, P. *Gothic Sculpture, 1140–1300*. New Haven: Yale University Press, 1995.

Wilson, C. *The Gothic Cathedral: The Architecture of the Great Church, 1130–1530*. 2d rev. ed. London: Thames & Hudson, 2005.

PART THREE: THE RENAISSANCE THROUGH THE ROCOCO

GENERAL REFERENCES AND SOURCES

Campbell, L. *Renaissance Portraits: European Portrait-Painting in the 14th, 15th, and 16th Centuries*. New Haven: Yale University Press, 1990.

Chastel, A., et al. *The Renaissance: Essays in Interpretation*. London: Methuen, 1982.

Cloulas, I. *Treasures of the French Renaissance*. New York: Harry N. Abrams, 1998.

Cole, A. *Art of the Italian Renaissance Courts: Virtue and Magnificence*. London: Weidenfeld & Nicolson, 1995.

Gascoigne, B. *How to Identify Prints: A Complete Guide to Manual and Mechanical Processes from Woodcut to Inkjet*. New York: Thames & Hudson, 2004.

Grendler, P. F., ed. *Encyclopedia of the Renaissance*. 6 vols. New York: Scribner's, published in association with the Renaissance Society of America, 1999.

Gruber, A., ed. *The History of Decorative Arts: Vol. 1, The Renaissance and Mannerism in Europe. Vol. 2, Classicism and the Baroque in Europe*. New York: Abbeville Press, 1994.

Harbison, C. *The Mirror of the Artist: Northern Renaissance Art in its Historical Context*. New York: Harry N. Abrams, 1995.

Harris, A. S. *Seventeenth-Century Art and Architecture*. 2d ed. Upper Saddle River, NJ: Pearson Education, 2008.

Hartt, F., and D. Wilkins. *History of Italian Renaissance Art*. 6th ed. Upper Saddle River, NJ: Pearson Prentice Hall, 2007.

Hopkins, A. *Italian Architecture: from Michelangelo to Borromini*. World of Art. New York: Thames & Hudson, 2002.

Hults, L. *The Print in the Western World*. Madison: University of Wisconsin Press, 1996.

Impey, O., and A. MacGregor, eds. *The Origins of Museums: The Cabinet of Curiosities in Sixteenth- and Seventeenth-Century Europe*. New York: Clarendon Press, 1985.

Ivins, W. M., Jr. *How Prints Look: Photographs with a Commentary*. Boston: Beacon Press, 1987.

Landau, D., and P. Parshall. *The Renaissance Print*. New Haven: Yale University Press, 1994.

Lincoln, E. *The Invention of the Italian Renaissance Printmaker*. New Haven: Yale University Press, 2000.

Martin, J. R. *Baroque*. Harmondsworth, England: Penguin, 1989.

Millon, H. A., ed. *The Triumph of the Baroque: Architecture in Europe, 1600–1750*. New York: Rizzoli, 1999.

Minor, V. H. *Baroque & Rococo: Art & Culture*. New York: Harry N. Abrams, 1999.

Norberg-Schultz, C. *Late Baroque and Rococo Architecture*. New York: Harry N. Abrams, 1983.

Olson, R. J. M. *Italian Renaissance Sculpture*. The World of Art. New York: Thames & Hudson, 1992.

Paoletti, J., and G. Radke. *Art in Renaissance Italy*. 3d ed. Upper Saddle River, NJ: Pearson Prentice Hall, 2006.

Payne, A. *Antiquity and Its Interpreters*. New York: Cambridge University Press, 2000.

Pope-Hennessy, J. *An Introduction to Italian Sculpture: Vol. 1, Italian Gothic Sculpture. Vol. 2, Italian Renaissance Sculpture. Vol. 3, Italian High Renaissance and Baroque Sculpture*. 4th ed. London: Phaidon Press, 1996.

Richardson, C. M., K. W. Woods, and M. W. Franklin, eds. *Renaissance Art Reconsidered: An Anthology of Primary Sources*. Wiley-Blackwell, 2007.

Smith, J. C. *The Northern Renaissance*. Art & Ideas. London: Phaidon Press, 2004.

Snyder, J. *Northern Renaissance Art: Painting, Sculpture, the Graphic Arts, from 1350–1575*. 2d ed. New York: Harry N. Abrams, 2005.

Strinati, E., and J. Pomeroy. *Italian Women Artists of the Renaissance and Baroque*. Exh. cat. Washington, DC: National Museum of Women in the Arts; New York: Rizzoli, 2007.

Tomlinson, J. *From El Greco to Goya: Painting in Spain 1561–1828*. Perspectives. New York: Harry N. Abrams, 1997.

Turner, J. *Encyclopedia of Italian Renaissance & Mannerist Art*. 2 vols. New York: Grove's Dictionaries, 2000.

Vasari, G. *The Lives of the Artists*. Trans. with an introduction and notes by J. C. Bondanella and P. Bondanella. New York: Oxford University Press, 1998.

Welch, E. *Art in Renaissance Italy, 1350–1500*. New ed. Oxford: Oxford University Press, 2000.

Wiebenson, D., ed. *Architectural Theory and Practice from Alberti to Ledoux*. 2d ed. Chicago: University of Chicago Press, 1983.

Wittkower, R. *Architectural Principles in the Age of Humanism*. 5th ed. New York: St. Martin's Press, 1998.

CHAPTER 13. ART IN THIRTEENTH- AND FOURTEENTH-CENTURY ITALY

Bellosi, L. *Duccio, the Maestà*. New York: Thames & Hudson, 1999.

Bomford, D. *Art in the Making: Italian Painting Before 1400*. Exh. cat. London: National Gallery of Art, 1989.

Christiansen, K. *Duccio and the Origins of Western Painting*. New York: Metropolitan Museum of Art and Yale University Press, 2009.

Derbes, A. *The Cambridge Companion to Giotto*. New York: Cambridge University Press, 2004.

———., and M. Sandona. *The Usurer's Heart: Giotto, Enrico Scrovegni, and the Arena Chapel in Padua*. University Park: Pennsylvania State University Press, 2008.

Kemp, M. *Behind the Picture: Art and Evidence in the Italian Renaissance*. New Haven: Yale University Press, 1997.

Maginnis, H. B. J. *The World of the Early Sienese Painter*. With a translation of the Sienese Breve dell'Arte dei pittori by Gabriele Erasmi. University Park: Pennsylvania State University Press, 2001.

Meiss, M. *Painting in Florence and Siena after the Black Death: The Arts, Religion, and Society in the Mid-Fourteenth Century*. Princeton, NJ: Princeton University Press, 1978, © 1951.

Nevola, F. *Siena: Constructing the Renaissance City*. New Haven and London: Yale University Press, 2008.

Norman, D., ed. *Siena, Florence, and Padua: Art, Society, and Religion 1280–1400*. New Haven: Yale University Press in association with the Open University, 1995.

Schmidt, V., ed. *Italian Panel Painting of the Duecento and Trecento*. Washington, DC: National Gallery of Art; New Haven: Dist. by Yale University Press, 2002.

Stubblebine, J. H. *Assisi and the Rise of Vernacular Art*. New York: Harper & Row, 1985.

———. *Dugento Painting: An Annotated Bibliography*. Boston: G. K. Hall, 1983.

Trachtenberg, M. *Dominion of the Eye: Urbanism, Art, and Power in Early Modern Florence*. New York: Cambridge University Press, 2008.

White, J. *Art and Architecture in Italy, 1250–1400*. 3d ed. Pelican History of Art. New Haven: Yale University Press, 1993.

CHAPTER 14. ARTISTIC INNOVATIONS IN FIFTEENTH-CENTURY NORTHERN EUROPE

Ainsworth, M. W., and K. Christiansen. *From Van Eyck to Bruegel: Early Netherlandish Painting in the Metropolitan Museum of Art*. New York: Metropolitan Museum of Art, 1998.

Borchert, T., ed. *The Age of Van Eyck: the Mediterranean World and Early Netherlandish Painting, 1430–1530*. New York: Thames & Hudson, 2002.

Chapuis, J., ed. *Tilman Riemenschneider, Master Sculptor of the Late Middle Ages*. Washington, DC: National Gallery of Art; New York: Metropolitan Museum of Art; New Haven: Dist. by Yale University Press, 1999.

Cuttler, C. *Northern Painting from Pucelle to Bruegel*. Fort Worth: Holt, Rinehart & Winston, 1991, © 1972.

De Vos, D. *Rogier van der Weyden: The Complete Works*. New York: Harry N. Abrams, 1999.

Dhanens, E. *Hubert and Jan van Eyck*. New York: Alpine Fine Arts Collection, 1980.

Dixon, L. *Bosch*. Art & Ideas. London: Phaidon Press, 2003.

Friedländer, M. *Early Netherlandish Painting*. 14 vols. New York: Praeger, 1967–1973.

Hand, J. O., C. Metzger, and R. Spronk. *Prayers and Portraits: Unfolding the Netherlandish Diptych*. Exh. cat. Washington DC, National Gallery of Art; New Haven: Yale University Press, 2006.

Koldeweij, J., ed. *Hieronymus Bosch: New Insights into His Life and Work*. Rotterdam: Museum Boijmans Van Beuningen: NAi; Ghent: Ludion, 2001.

Muller, T. *Sculpture in the Netherlands, Germany, France, and Spain, 1400–1500*. Pelican History of Art. Harmondsworth, England: Penguin, 1966.

Nuttall, P. *From Flanders to Florence: The Impact of Netherlandish Painting, 1400–1500*. New Haven: Yale University Press, 2004.

Pächt, O. *Van Eyck and the Founders of Early Netherlandish Painting*. London: Harvey Miller, 1994.

Panofsky, E. *Early Netherlandish Painting*. 2 vols. New York: Harper & Row, 1971. Orig. published Cambridge, MA: Harvard University Press, 1958.

Rothstein, B. L. *Sight and Spirituality in Early Netherlandish Painting*. Cambridge: Cambridge University Press, 2005.

Van der Velden, H. *The Donor's Image: Gérard Loyet and the Votive Portraits of Charles the Bold*. Turnhout: Brepols, 2000.

Williamson, P. *Netherlandish Sculpture 1450–1550*. London: V & A; New York: Dist. by Harry N. Abrams, 2002.

CHAPTER 15. THE EARLY RENAISSANCE IN ITALY

Ahl, D. C. *The Cambridge Companion to Masaccio*. New York: Cambridge University Press, 2002.

Aikema, B. *Renaissance Venice and the North: Crosscurrents in the Time of Bellini, Dürer and Titian*. Exh. cat. Milan: Bompiani, 2000.

Ajmar-Wollheim, M., and F. Dennis, eds. *At Home in Renaissance Italy*. Exh. cat. London: Victoria & Albert Museum; V&A Publications, 2006.

Alberti, L. B. *On Painting*. Trans. C. Grayson, introduction and notes M. Kemp. New York: Penguin, 1991.

———. *On the Art of Building, in Ten Books*. Trans. J. Rykwert, et al. Cambridge, MA: MIT Press, 1991.

Ames-Lewis, F. *Drawing in Early Renaissance Italy*. 2d ed. New Haven: Yale University Press, 2000.

Baxandall, M. *Painting and Experience in Fifteenth-Century Italy: A Primer in the Social History of Pictorial Style*. 2d ed. New York: Oxford University Press, 1988.

Blunt, A. *Artistic Theory in Italy, 1450–1600*. Reprint of 1940 ed. New York: Oxford University Press, 1983.

Bober, P., and R. Rubinstein. *Renaissance Artists and Antique Sculpture: A Handbook of Sources*. New York: Oxford University Press, 1986.

Borsook, E. *The Mural Painters of Tuscany: From Cimabue to Andrea del Sarto*. 2d ed. New York: Oxford University Press, 1980.

Cole, B. *The Renaissance Artist at Work: From Pisano to Titian*. New York: Harper & Row, © 1983.

Fejfer, J. *The Rediscovery of Antiquity: The Role of the Artist*. Copenhagen: Museum Tusculanum Press, University of Copenhagen, 2003.

Gilbert, C. E. *Italian Art, 1400–1500: Sources and Documents*. Englewood Cliffs, NJ: Prentice Hall, 1980.

Goldthwaite, R. *Wealth and the Demand for Art in Italy, 1300–1600*. Baltimore, MD: Johns Hopkins University Press, 1993.

Gombrich, E. H. *New Light on Old Masters*. New ed. London: Phaidon Press, 1994.

Heydenreich, L., and W. Lotz. *Architecture in Italy, 1400–1500:* Rev. ed. Pelican History of Art. New Haven: Yale University Press, 1996.

Humfreys, P., and M. Kemp, eds. *The Altarpiece in the Renaissance*. New York: Cambridge University Press, 1990.

———., ed. *The Cambridge Companion to Giovanni Bellini*. New York: Cambridge University Press, 2004.

Huse, N., and W. Wolters. *The Art of Renaissance Venice: Architecture, Sculpture, and Painting, 1460–1590*. Chicago: University of Chicago Press, 1990.

Janson, H. W. *The Sculpture of Donatello*. 2 vols. Princeton, NJ: Princeton University Press, 1979.

Kempers, B. *Painting, Power, and Patronage: The Rise of the Professional Artist in the Italian Renaissance*. New York: Penguin, 1992.

Kent, D. V. *Cosimo de' Medici and the Florentine Renaissance: The Patron's Oeuvre*. New Haven: Yale University Press, © 2000.

Krautheimer, R., and T. Krautheimer-Hess. *Lorenzo Ghiberti*. Princeton, NJ: Princeton University Press, 1982.

Lavin, M. A. *Piero della Francesca*. Art & Ideas. New York: Phaidon Press, 2002.

Murray, P. *The Architecture of the Italian Renaissance*. New rev. ed. The World of Art. New York: Random House, 1997.

Musacchio, J. M. *Art, Marriage, and Family in the Florentine Renaissance Palace*. New Haven: Yale University Press, 2009.

Pächt, O. *Venetian Painting in the 15th Century: Jacopo, Gentile and Giovanni Bellini and Andrea Mantegna*. London: Harvey Miller, 2003.

Panofsky, E. *Perspective as Symbolic Form*. New York: Zone Books, 1997.

———. *Renaissance and Renascences in Western Art*. Trans. C. S. Wood. New York: Humanities Press, 1970.

Pope-Hennessy, J. *Italian Renaissance Sculpture*. 4th ed. London: Phaidon Press, 2000.

Randolph, A. *Engaging Symbols: Gender, Politics, and Public Art in Fifteenth-Century Florence*. New Haven: Yale University Press, 2002.

Saalman, H. *Filippo Brunelleschi: The Buildings*. University Park: Pennsylvania State University Press, 1993.

Seymour, C. *Sculpture in Italy, 1400–1500*. Pelican History of Art. Harmondsworth, England: Penguin, 1966.

Turner, A. R. *Renaissance Florence*. Perspectives. New York: Harry N. Abrams, 1997.

Wackernagel, M. *The World of the Florentine Renaissance Artist: Projects and Patrons, Workshop and Art Market*. Princeton, NJ: Princeton University Press, 1981.

Wood, J. M., ed. *The Cambridge Companion to Piero della Francesca*. New York: Cambridge University Press, 2002.

CHAPTER 16. THE HIGH RENAISSANCE IN ITALY, 1495–1520

Ackerman, J., *The Architecture of Michelangelo*. 2d ed. Chicago: University of Chicago Press, 1986.

Beck, J. H. *Three Worlds of Michelangelo*. New York: W. W. Norton, 1999.

Boase, T. S. R. *Giorgio Vasari: The Man and the Book*. Princeton, NJ: Princeton University Press, 1979.

Brown, P. F. *Art and Life in Renaissance Venice*. Perspectives. New York: Harry N. Abrams, 1997.

———. *Venice and Antiquity: The Venetian Sense of the Past*. New Haven: Yale University Press, 1997.

Chapman, H. *Raphael: From Urbino to Rome*. London: National Gallery; New Haven: Dist. by Yale University Press, 2004.

Clark, K. *Leonardo da Vinci*. Rev. and introduced by M. Kemp. New York: Penguin, 1993, © 1988.

Cole, A. *Virtue and Magnificence: Art of the Italian Renaissance Courts*. Perspectives. New York: Harry N. Abrams, 1995.

De Tolnay, C. *Michelangelo*. 5 vols. Some vols. rev. Princeton, NJ: Princeton University Press, 1969–1971.

Freedberg, S. *Painting in Italy, 1500–1600*. 3d ed. Pelican History of Art. New Haven: Yale University Press, 1993.

———. *Painting of the High Renaissance in Rome and Florence*. 2 vols. New rev. ed. New York: Hacker Art Books, 1985.

Goffen, R. *Renaissance Rivals: Michelangelo, Leonardo, Raphael, Titian*. New Haven: Yale University Press, 2002.

Hall, M. B. *The Cambridge Companion to Raphael*. New York: Cambridge University Press, 2005.

Hersey, G. L. *High Renaissance Art in St. Peter's and the Vatican: An Interpretive Guide*. Chicago: University of Chicago Press, 1993.

Hibbard, H. *Michelangelo*. 2d ed. Boulder, CO: Westview Press, 1998, © 1974.

Kemp, M. *Leonardo*. New York: Oxford University Press, 2004.

———., ed. *Leonardo on Painting: An Anthology of Writings*. New Haven: Yale University Press, 1989.

Nicholl, C. *Leonardo da Vinci: Flights of the Mind*. New York: Viking Penguin, 2004.

Panofsky, E. *Studies in Iconology: Humanist Themes in the Art of the Renaissance*. New York: Harper & Row, 1972.

Partridge, L. *The Art of Renaissance Rome*. Perspectives. New York: Harry N. Abrams, 1996.

Rowland, I. *The Culture of the High Renaissance: Ancients and Moderns in Sixteenth Century Rome*. Cambridge: 1998.

Rubin, P. L. *Giorgio Vasari: Art and History*. New Haven: Yale University Press, 1995.

Steinberg, L. *Leonardo's Incessant Last Supper*. New York: Zone Books, 2001.

Wallace, W. *Michelangelo: The Complete Sculpture, Painting, Architecture*. Southport, CT: Hugh Lauter Levin, 1998.

Wölfflin, H. *Classic Art: An Introduction to the High Renaissance*. 5th ed. London: Phaidon Press, 1994.

CHAPTER 17. THE LATE RENAISSANCE AND MANNERISM

Ackerman, J. *Palladio*. Reprint of the 2d ed. Harmondsworth, England: Penguin, 1991, © 1966.

Barkan, L. *Unearthing the Past: Archaeology and Aesthetics in the Making of Renaissance Culture*. New Haven: Yale University Press, 1999.

Beltramini, G., and A. Padoan. *Andrea Palladio: Complete Illustrated Works*. New York: Universe; Dist. by St. Martin's Press, 2001.

Cole, M., ed. *Sixteenth-Century Italian Art*. Oxford: Blackwell, 2006.

Ekserdjian, D. *Correggio*. New Haven: Yale University Press, 1997.

Fortini Bown, P. *Private Lives in Renaissance Venice: Art, Architecture, and the Family*. New Haven: Yale University Press, 2004.

Friedlaender, W. *Mannerism and Anti-Mannerism in Italian Painting*. Reprint of 1957 ed. Interpretations in Art. New York: Columbia University Press, 1990.

Furlotti, B., and G. Rebecchini. *The Art and Architecture of Mantua: Eight Centuries of Patronage and Collecting*. London: Thames & Hudson, 2008.

Goffen, R. *Titian's Women*. New Haven: Yale University Press, 1997.

Jacobs, F. H. *Defining the Renaissance "Virtuosa": Women Artists and the Language of Art History and Criticism*. New York: Cambridge University Press, 1997.

Klein, R., and H. Zerner. *Italian Art, 1500–1600: Sources and Documents*. Reprint of 1966 ed. Evanston, IL: Northwestern University Press, 1989.

Kliemann, J., and M. Rohlmann. *Italian Frescoes: High Renaissance and Mannerism, 1510–1600*. New York: Abbeville Press, 2004.

Partridge, L. *Michelangelo—The Last Judgment: A Glorious Restoration*. New York: Harry N. Abrams, 1997.

Rearick, W. R. *The Art of Paolo Veronese, 1528–1588*. Cambridge: Cambridge University Press, 1988.

Rosand, D. *Painting in Sixteenth-Century Venice: Titian, Veronese, Tintoretto*. New York: Cambridge University Press, 1997.

Shearman, J. K. G. *Mannerism*. New York: Penguin Books, 1990, © 1967.

Smyth, C. H. *Mannerism and Maniera*. 2d ed. Bibliotheca artibus et historiae. Vienna: IRSA, 1992.

Tavernor, R. *Palladio and Palladianism*. The World of Art. New York: Thames & Hudson, 1991.

Valcanover, F., and T. Pignatti. *Tintoretto*. New York: Harry N. Abrams, 1984.

Wundram, M. *Palladio: The Complete Buildings*. Köln and London: Taschen, 2004.

CHAPTER 18. EUROPEAN ART OF THE SIXTEENTH CENTURY: RENAISSANCE AND REFORMATION

Bartrum, G. *Albrecht Dürer and His Legacy: The Graphic Work of a Renaissance Artist*. Princeton, NJ: Princeton University Press, 2002.

Baxandall, M. *The Limewood Sculptors of Renaissance Germany*. New Haven: Yale University Press, 1980.

Campbell, T. P. *Tapestry in the Renaissance: Art and Magnificence*. Exh. cat. New York: Metropolitan Museum of Art; New Haven: Yale University Press, 2006.

Eichberger, D., ed. *Durer and His Culture*. New York: Cambridge University Press, 1998.

Hayum, A. *The Isenheim Altarpiece: God's Medicine and the Painter's Vision*. Princeton, NJ: Princeton University Press, 1989.

Hitchcock, H.-R. *German Renaissance Architecture*. Princeton, NJ: Princeton University Press, 1981.

Honig, E. A. *Painting and the Market in Early Modern Antwerp*. New Haven: Yale University Press, 1998.

Hulse, C. *Elizabeth I: Ruler and Legend*. Urbana: Published for the Newberry Library by the University of Illinois Press, 2003.

Hutchison, J. C. *Albrecht Dürer: A Biography*. Princeton, NJ: Princeton University Press, 1990.

Jopek, N. *German Sculpture, 1430–1540: A Catalogue of the Collection in the Victoria and Albert Museum*. London: V & A, 2002.

Kavaler, E. M. *Pieter Bruegel: Parables of Order and Enterprise*. New York: Cambridge University Press, 1999.

Koerner, J. *The Moment of Self-Portraiture in German Renaissance Art*. Chicago: University of Chicago Press, 1993.

———. *The Reformation of the Image*. Chicago: University of Chicago Press, 2004.

Mann, R. *El Greco and His Patrons: Three Major Projects*. New York: Cambridge University Press, 1986.

Melion, W. *Shaping the Netherlandish Canon: Karel van Mander's Schilder-Boeck*. Chicago: University of Chicago Press, 1991.

Moxey, K. *Peasants, Warriors, and Wives: Popular Imagery in the Reformation*. Chicago: University of Chicago Press, 1989.

Osten, G. von der, and H. Vey. *Painting and Sculpture in Germany and the Netherlands, 1500–1600*. Pelican History of Art. Harmondsworth, England: Penguin, 1969.

Panofsky, E. *The Life and Art of Albrecht Dürer*. 4th ed. Princeton, NJ: Princeton University Press, 1971.

Smith, J. C. *Nuremberg: A Renaissance City, 1500–1618*. Austin: Published for the Archer M. Huntington Art Gallery by the University of Texas Press, 1983.

Stechow, W. *Northern Renaissance Art, 1400–1600: Sources and Documents*. Evanston, IL: Northwestern University Press, 1966, © 1966.

Van Mander, K. *Lives of the Illustrious Netherlandish and German Painters*. Ed. H. Miedema. 6 vols. Doornspijk, Netherlands: Davaco, 1993–1999.

Wood, C. *Albrecht Altdorfer and the Origins of Landscape*. Chicago: University of Chicago Press, 1993.

Zerner, H. *Renaissance Art in France: The Invention of Classicism*. Paris: Flammarion; London: Thames & Hudson, 2003.

CHAPTER 19. THE BAROQUE IN ITALY AND SPAIN

Avery, C. *Bernini: Genius of the Baroque*. London: Thames & Hudson, 1997.

Bissell, R. W. *Masters of Italian Baroque Painting: The Detroit Institute of Arts*. Detroit, MI: Detroit Institute of Arts in association with D. Giles Ltd., London, 2005.

Brown, B. L., ed. *The Genius of Rome, 1592–1623*. Exh. cat. London: Royal Academy of Arts; New York: Dist. in the United States and Canada by Harry N. Abrams, 2001.

Brown, J. *Francisco de Zurbaran*. New York: Harry N. Abrams, 1991.

———. *Painting in Spain, 1500–1700*. Pelican History of Art. New Haven: Yale University Press, 1998.

———. *Velázquez: The Technique of Genius*. New Haven: Yale University Press, 1998.

Dempsey, C. *Annibale Carracci and the Beginnings of Baroque Style*. 2d ed. Fiesole, Italy: Cadmo, 2000.

Enggass, R., and J. Brown. *Italy and Spain, 1600–1750: Sources and Documents*. Reprint of 1970 ed. Evanston, IL: Northwestern University Press, 1992.

Freedberg, S. *Circa 1600: A Revolution of Style in Italian Painting*. Cambridge, MA: Harvard University Press, 1983.

Garrard, M. D. *Artemisia Gentileschi: The Image of the Female Hero in Italian Baroque Art*. Princeton, NJ: Princeton University Press, 1989.

Marder, T. A. *Bernini and the Art of Architecture*. New York: Abbeville Press, 1998.

Montagu, J. *Roman Baroque Sculpture: The Industry of Art*. New Haven: Yale University Press, 1989.

Nicolson, B. *Caravaggism in Europe*. Ed. L. Vertova. 3 vols. 2d ed., rev. and enl. Turin, Italy: Allemandi, 1989.

Schroth, S., R. Baer, et al. *El Greco to Velázquez: Art During the Reign of Philip III*. Exh. cat. Boston: Museum of Fine Arts; MFA Publications, 2008.

Smith, G. *Architectural Diplomacy: Rome and Paris in the Late Baroque*. Cambridge, MA: MIT Press, 1993.

Spear, R. E. *From Caravaggio to Artemisia: Essays on Painting in Seventeenth-Century Italy and France*. London: Pindar Press, 2002.

Spike, J. T. *Caravaggio*. Includes CD-ROM of all the known paintings of Caravaggio, including attributed and lost works. New York: Abbeville Press, © 2001.

Varriano, J. *Italian Baroque and Rococo Architecture*. New York: Oxford University Press, 1986.

Wittkower, R. *Art and Architecture in Italy, 1600–1750*. 4th ed. Pelican History of Art. New Haven: Yale University Press, 2000.

———. *Bernini: The Sculptor of the Roman Baroque*. 4th ed. London: Phaidon Press, 1997.

CHAPTER 20. THE BAROQUE IN FLANDERS AND HOLLAND

Alpers, S. *The Art of Describing: Dutch Art in the Seventeenth Century*. Chicago: University of Chicago Press, 1983.

———. *The Making of Rubens*. New Haven: Yale University Press, 1995.

Chapman, H. P. *Rembrandt's Self-Portraits: A Study in Seventeenth-Century Identity*. Princeton, NJ: Princeton University Press, 1990.

Fleischer, R., ed. *Rembrandt, Rubens, and the Art of Their Time: Recent Perspectives*. University Park: Pennsylvania State University, 1997.

Franits, W. E. *Dutch Seventeenth-Century Genre Painting: Its Stylistic and Thematic Evolution*. New Haven: Yale University Press, 2004.

Grijzenhout, F., ed. *The Golden Age of Dutch Painting in Historical Perspective*. New York: Cambridge University Press, 1999.

Kiers, J. and E. Runia, eds. *The Glory of the Golden Age: Dutch Art of the 17th Century*. 2 vols. Exh. cat. Rijksmuseum, Amsterdam: Waanders: 2000.

Logan, A. S. *Peter Paul Rubens: The Drawings*. Exh. cat. New York: Metropolitan Museum of Art; New Haven: Yale University Press, 2004.

Salvesen, S., ed. *Rembrandt: The Master and His Workshop*. 2 vols. Exh. cat. New Haven: Yale University Press, 1991.

Schama, S. *The Embarrassment of Riches: An Interpretation of Dutch Culture in the Golden Age*. New York: Alfred A. Knopf, 1987.

Schwartz, G. *Rembrandt: His Life, His Paintings*. New York: Viking, 1985.

Slive, S. *Dutch Painting, 1600–1800*. Pelican History of Art. New Haven: Yale University Press, 1995.

———. *Frans Hals*. Exh. cat. Munich: Prestel-Verlag, 1989.

———. *Jacob van Ruisdael: Master of Landscape*. London: Royal Academy of Arts, 2005.

Sluijter, E. J. *Rembrandt and the Female Nude*. Amsterdam University Press, 2006.

Sutton, P. *The Age of Rubens*. Exh. cat. Boston: Museum of Fine Arts, 1993.

Vlieghe, H. *Flemish Art and Architecture, 1585–1700*. Pelican History of Art. New Haven: Yale University Press, © 1998.

Westermann, M. *Art and Home: Dutch Interiors in the Age of Rembrandt*. Exh. cat. Zwolle: Waanders, 2001.

———. *Rembrandt*. Art & Ideas. London: Phaidon Press, 2000.

———. *A Worldly Art: The Dutch Republic 1585–1718*. Perspectives. New York: Harry N. Abrams, 1996.

Wheelock, A. K., ed. *Johannes Vermeer*. Exh. cat. New Haven: Yale University Press, 1995.

———., et al. *Anthony van Dyck*. Exh. cat. New York: Harry N. Abrams, 1990.

White, C. *Peter Paul Rubens*. New Haven: Yale University Press, 1987.

CHAPTER 21. THE BAROQUE IN FRANCE AND ENGLAND

Blunt, A. *Art and Architecture in France, 1500–1700*. 5th ed. Pelican History of Art. New Haven: Yale University Press, 1999.

Brusatin, M., et al. *The Baroque in Central Europe: Places, Architecture, and Art*. Venice: Marsilio, 1992.

Donovan, F. *Rubens and England*. New Haven: Published for The Paul Mellon Centre for Studies in British Art by Yale University Press, 2004.

Downes, K. *The Architecture of Wren*. Rev. ed. Reading, England: Redhedge, 1988.

Garreau, M. *Charles Le Brun: First Painter to King Louis XIV*. New York: Harry N. Abrams, 1992.

Kitson, M. *Studies on Claude and Poussin*. London: Pindar, 2000.

Lagerlöf, M. R. *Ideal Landscape: Annibale Carracci, Nicolas Poussin, and Claude Lorrain*. New Haven: Yale University Press, 1990.

Mérot, A. *French Painting in the Seventeenth Century*. New Haven: Yale University Press, 1995.

———. *Nicolas Poussin*. New York: Abbeville Press, 1990.

Porter, R. *London: A Social History*. Cambridge, MA: Harvard University Press, 1995.

Rosenberg, P., and K. Christiansen, eds. *Poussin and Nature: Arcadian Visions*. Exh. cat. New York: Metropolitan Museum of Art; New Haven: Yale University Press, 2008.

Summerson, J. *Architecture in Britain, 1530–1830*. Rev. 9th ed. Pelican History of Art. New Haven: Yale University Press, 1993.

Tinniswood, A. *His Invention So Fertile: A Life of Christopher Wren*. New York: Oxford University Press, 2001.

Verdi, R. *Nicolas Poussin 1594–1665*. London: Zwemmer in association with the Royal Academy of Arts, 1995.

Vlnas, V., ed. *The Glory of the Baroque in Bohemia: Essays on Art, Culture and Society in the 17th and 18th Centuries*. Prague: National Gallery, 2001.

Waterhouse, E. K. *The Dictionary of Sixteenth and Seventeenth Century British Painters*. Woodbridge, Suffolk, England: Antique Collectors' Club, 1988.

———. *Painting in Britain, 1530–1790*. 5th ed. Pelican History of Art. New Haven: Yale University Press, 1993.

Whinney, M. D. *Wren*. World of Art. New York: Thames & Hudson, 1998.

CHAPTER 22. THE ROCOCO

Bailey, C. B. *The Age of Watteau, Chardin, and Fragonard: Masterpieces of French Genre Painting*. New Haven: Yale University Press in association with the National Gallery of Canada, 2003.

Brunel, G. *Boucher*. New York: Vendome, 1986.

———. *Painting in Eighteenth-Century France*. Ithaca, NY: Cornell University Press, 1981.

Cuzin, J. P. *Jean-Honoré Fragonard: Life and Work: Complete Catalogue of the Oil Paintings*. New York: Harry N. Abrams, 1988.

François Boucher, 1703–1770. Exh. cat. New York: Metropolitan Museum of Art, © 1986.

Gaunt, W. *The Great Century of British Painting: Hogarth to Turner*. 2d ed. London: Phaidon Press, 1978.

Kalnein, W. von. *Architecture in France in the Eighteenth Century*. Pelican History of Art. New Haven: Yale University Press, 1995.

Levey, M. *Giambattista Tiepolo: His Life and Art*. New Haven: Yale University Press, 1986.

———. *Painting and Sculpture in France, 1700–1789*. New ed. Pelican History of Art. New Haven: Yale University Press, 1993.

———. *Painting in Eighteenth-Century Venice*. 3d ed. Pelican History of Art. New Haven: Yale University Press, 1993.

———. *Rococo to Revolution: Major Trends in Eighteenth-Century Painting*. Reprint of 1966 ed. The World of Art. New York: Thames & Hudson, 1985.

Links, J. G. *Canaletto*. Completely rev., updated, and enl. ed. London: Phaidon Press, 1994.

Paulson, R. *Hogarth*. 3 vols. New Brunswick: Rutgers University Press, 1991–1993.

Pointon, M. *Hanging the Head: Portraiture and Social Formation in Eighteenth-Century England*. New Haven: Yale University Press, 1993.

Posner, D. *Antoine Watteau*. Ithaca, NY: Cornell University Press, 1984.

Rococo to Romanticism: Art and Architecture, 1700–1850. Garland Library of the History of Art. New York: Garland, 1976.

Rosenberg, P. *Chardin*. Exh. cat. London: Royal Academy of Art; New York: Metropolitan Museum of Art, 2000.

———. *From Drawing to Painting: Poussin, Watteau, Fragonard, David & Ingres*. Princeton, NJ: Princeton University Press, 2000.

Scott, K. *The Rococo Interior: Decoration and Social Spaces in Early Eighteenth-Century Paris*. New Haven: Yale University Press, 1995.

Sheriff, M. D. *The Exceptional Woman: Elisabeth Vigée-Lebrun and the Cultural Politics of Art*. Chicago: University of Chicago Press, 1996.

Wintermute, A. *Watteau and His World: French Drawing from 1700 to 1750*. Exh. cat. London: Merrell Holberton; New York: American Federation of Arts, 1999.

PART FOUR: THE MODERN WORLD

GENERAL REFERENCES

Arnason, H. H. *History of Modern Art: Painting, Sculpture, Architecture, Photography*. 5th ed. Upper Saddle River, NJ: Pearson Prentice Hall, 2004.

Atkins, R. *Artspoke: A Guide to Modern Ideas, Movements, and Buzzwords, 1848–1944*. New York: Abbeville Press, 1993.

Baigell, M. *A Concise History of American Painting and Sculpture*. Rev. ed. New York: Icon Editions, 1996.

Banham, R. *Theory and Design in the First Machine Age*. 2d ed. Cambridge, MA: MIT Press, 1980, © 1960.

Bearden, R., and H. Henderson. *A History of African-American Artists from 1792 to the Present*. New York: Pantheon, 1993.

Bergdoll, B. *European Architecture 1750–1890*. Oxford History of Art. New York: Oxford University Press, 2000.

Bjelajac, D. *American Art: A Cultural History*. Upper Saddle River, NJ: Pearson Prentice Hall, 2005.

Boime, A. *A Social History of Modern Art. Vol. 1, Art in the Age of Revolution, 1750–1800. Vol. 2, Art in the Age of Bonapartism, 1800–1815. Vol. 3, Art in the Age of Counterrevolution, 1815–1848*. Chicago: University of Chicago Press, 1987–2004.

Bown, M. C. *A Dictionary of Twentieth Century Russian and Soviet Painters 1900–1980s*. London: Izomar, 1998.

Campany, D., ed. *Art and Photography*. Themes and Movements. London: Phaidon Press, 2003.

Castelman, R. *Prints of the Twentieth Century: A History*. Rev. ed. London: Thames & Hudson, 1988.

Chiarmonte, P. *Women Artists in the United States: A Selective Bibliography and Resource Guide to the Fine and Decorative Arts, 1750–1986*. Boston: G. K. Hall, 1990.

Chilvers, I. *A Dictionary of Twentieth-Century Art*. New York: Oxford University Press, 1998.

Chipp, H., ed. *Theories of Modern Art: A Source Book by Artists and Critics*. Berkeley: University of California Press, 1968.

Colquhoun, A. *Modern Architecture*. New York: Oxford University Press, 2002.

Crary, J. *Techniques of the Observer: On Vision and Modernity in the Nineteenth Century*. Cambridge, MA: MIT Press, 1990.

Craven, W. *American Art: History and Culture*. New York: Harry N. Abrams, 1994.

Crook, J. *The Dilemma of Style: Architectural Ideas from the Picturesque to the Post Modern*. Chicago: University of Chicago Press, 1987.

Crow, T. *Modern Art in the Common Culture*. New Haven: Yale University Press, 1996.

Cummings, P. *Dictionary of Contemporary American Artists*. New York: St. Martin's Press, 1988.

Documents of Modern Art. 14 vols. New York: Wittenborn, 1944–1961. Anthologies of primary source material. Selected titles listed individually, below.

The Documents of Twentieth-Century Art. Boston: G. K. Hall, Anthologies of primary source material. Selected titles listed individually, below.

Doss, E. *Twentieth-Century American Art*. Oxford History of Art. New York: Oxford University Press, 2002.

Drucker, J. *The Century of Artists' Books*. New York: Granary Books, 2004.

Eisenman, S. *Nineteenth Century Art: A Critical History*. New York: Thames & Hudson, 2002.

Eitner, L. *An Outline of Nineteenth-Century European Painting: From David Through Cézanne*. 2 vols. New York: Harper & Row, 1986.

Elderfield, J., ed. *Modern Painting and Sculpture: 1880 to the Present at the Museum of Modern Art*. New York: Museum of Modern Art; Dist. by D.A.P./Distributed Art Publishers, 2004.

Evans, M. M., ed. *Contemporary Photographers*. 3d ed. New York: St. James Press, 1995.

Farrington, L. E. *Creating Their Own Image: The History of African-American Women Artists*. New York: Oxford University Press, 2005.

Frampton, K. *Modern Architecture: A Critical History*. 3d ed. New York: Thames & Hudson, 1992.

Frascina, F. and J. Harris, eds. *Art in Modern Culture: An Anthology of Critical Texts*. New York: Harper & Row, 1992.

Gaiger, J., ed. *Art of the Twentieth Century: A Reader*. New Haven: Yale University Press in association with the Open University, 2003.

———. *Frameworks for Modern Art*. New Haven: Yale University Press in association with the Open University, 2003.

Goldberg, R. *Performance Art: From Futurism to the Present*. Rev. and exp. ed. The World of Art. New York: Thames & Hudson, 2001.

Goldwater, R. *Primitivism in Modern Art*. Enl. ed. Cambridge: Harvard University Press, 1986.

Gray, J. *Action Art: A Bibliography of Artists' Performance from Futurism to Fluxus and Beyond*. Westport, CT: Greenwood Press, 1993.

Harrison, C., and P. Wood, eds. *Art in Theory, 1815–1900: An Anthology of Changing Ideas*. Malden, MA: Blackwell, 1998.

————. *Art in Theory, 1900–2000: An Anthology of Changing Ideas.* New ed. Malden, MA: Blackwell, 2003.

Heller, N. *Women Artists: An Illustrated History.* New York: Abbeville Press, 2003.

Hertz, R., ed. *Theories of Contemporary Art.* 2d ed. Englewood Cliffs, NJ: Prentice Hall, 1993.

————., and N. Klein, eds. *Twentieth-Century Art Theory: Urbanism, Politics, and Mass Culture.* Englewood Cliffs, NJ: Prentice Hall, 1990.

Hitchcock, H. R. *Architecture: Nineteenth and Twentieth Centuries.* 4th rev. ed. Pelican History of Art. New Haven: Yale University Press, 1987, © 1977.

Hughes, R. *American Visions: The Epic History of Art in America.* New York: Alfred A. Knopf, 1997.

Hunter, S., and J. Jacobus. *Modern Art: Painting, Sculpture, Architecture.* 3d rev. ed. New York: Harry N. Abrams, 2000.

Igoe, L. *250 Years of Afro-American Art: An Annotated Bibliography.* New York: Bowker, 1981.

Joachimides, C., et al. *American Art in the Twentieth Century: Painting and Sculpture, 1913–1933.* Exh. cat. Munich: Prestel, 1993.

Johnson, W. *Nineteenth-Century Photography: An Annotated Bibliography, 1839–1879.* Boston: G. K. Hall, 1990.

Kostelanetz, R. *A Dictionary of the Avant-Gardes.* New York: Routledge, 2001.

Lewis, S. *African American Art and Artists.* Berkeley: University of California Press, 1990.

Marien, M. *Photography: A Cultural History.* Upper Saddle River, NJ: Pearson Prentice Hall, 2002.

McCoubrey, J. *American Art, 1700–1960: Sources and Documents.* Englewood Cliffs, NJ: Prentice Hall, 1965.

Meikle, J. L. *Design in the USA.* Oxford History of Art. New York: Oxford University Press, 2005.

Modern Arts Criticism. 4 vols. Detroit, MI: Gale Research, 1991–1994.

Newhall, B. *The History of Photography from 1830 to the Present.* Rev. and enl. 5th ed. New York: Museum of Modern Art; Dist. by Bulfinch Press/Little, Brown, 1999.

Nochlin, L. *The Politics of Vision: Essays on Nineteenth-Century Art and Society.* New York: Harper & Row, 1989.

Osborne, H., ed. *Oxford Companion to Twentieth-Century Art.* Reprint. New York: Oxford University Press, 1990.

Patton, S. F. *African-American Art.* Oxford History of Art. New York: Oxford University Press, 1998.

Pevsner, N. *Pioneers of Modern Design: From William Morris to Walter Gropius.* 4th ed. New Haven: Yale University Press, 2005.

Piland, S. *Women Artists: An Historical, Contemporary, and Feminist Bibliography.* Metuchen, NJ: Scarecrow Press, 1994.

Powell, R. J. *Black Art and Culture in the 20th Century.* New York: Thames & Hudson, 1997.

Robinson, Hilary. *Feminism-Art-Theory: An Anthology, 1968–2000.* Oxford and Malden, MA: Blackwell, 2001.

Rose, B. *American Art Since 1900.* Rev. ed. New York: Praeger, 1975.

————. *American Painting: The Twentieth Century.* New updated ed. New York: Rizzoli, 1986.

Rosenblum, N. *A World History of Photography.* 3rd ed. New York: Abbeville Press, 1997.

Rosenblum, R., and H. W. Janson. *19th Century Art.* Rev. and updated ed. Upper Saddle River, NJ: Pearson Prentice Hall, 2005.

Schapiro, M. *Modern Art: Nineteenth and Twentieth Centuries.* New York: Braziller, 1982.

Scharf, A. *Art and Photography.* Reprint. Harmondsworth, England: Penguin, 1995.

Sennott, S., ed. *Encyclopedia of 20th Century Architecture.* 3 vols. New York: Fitzroy Dearborn, 2004.

Stiles, K., and P. Selz. *Theories and Documents of Contemporary Art.* Berkeley: University of California Press, 1996.

Tafuri, M. *Modern Architecture.* 2 vols. New York: Rizzoli, 1986.

Taylor, J. *The Fine Arts in America.* Chicago: University of Chicago Press, 1979.

————., ed. *Nineteenth-Century Theories of Art.* California Studies in the History of Art. Berkeley: University of California Press, 1987.

Tomlinson, J. *Readings in Nineteenth-Century Art.* Upper Saddle River, NJ: Prentice Hall, 1995.

Upton, D. *Architecture in the United States.* New York: Oxford University Press, 1998.

Varnedoe, K., and A. Gopnik, eds. *Modern Art and Popular Culture: Readings in High and Low.* New York: Harry N. Abrams, 1990.

Waldman, D. *Collage, Assemblage, and the Found Object.* New York: Harry N. Abrams, 1992.

Weaver, M. *The Art of Photography, 1839–1989.* Exh. cat. New Haven: Yale University Press, 1989.

Wilmerding, J. *American Views: Essays on American Art.* Princeton, NJ: Princeton University Press, 1991.

Witzling, M., ed. *Voicing Our Visions: Writings by Women Artists.* New York: Universe, 1991.

CHAPTER 23. ART IN THE AGE OF THE ENLIGHTENMENT, 1750–1789

Bryson, N. *Tradition and Desire: From David to Delacroix.* Cambridge: Cambridge University Press, 1984.

————. *Word and Image: French Painting in the Ancient Régime.* Cambridge: Cambridge University Press, 1981.

Crow, T. *Painters and Public Life in Eighteenth-Century Paris.* New Haven: Yale University Press, 1985.

Eitner, L. E. A. *Neoclassicism and Romanticism, 1750–1850: Sources and Documents.* Reprint of 1970 ed. New York: Harper & Row, 1989.

Fried, M. *Absorption and Theatricality: Painting and Beholder in the Age of Diderot.* Chicago: University of Chicago Press, 1980.

Friedlaender, W. *David to Delacroix.* Reprint of 1952 ed. New York: Schocken Books, 1968.

Goncourt, E. de, and J. de Goncourt. *French Eighteenth-Century Painters.* Reprint of 1948 ed. Ithaca, NY: Cornell University Press, 1981.

Honour, H. *Neoclassicism.* Reprint of 1968 ed. London: Penguin, 1991.

Irwin, D. G. *Neoclassicism.* Art & Ideas. London: Phaidon Press, 1997.

Licht, F. *Canova.* New York: Abbeville Press, 1983.

Miles, E. G., ed. *The Portrait in Eighteenth-Century America.* Newark: University of Delaware Press, 1993.

Ottani Cavina, A. *Geometries of Silence: Three Approaches to Neoclassical Art.* New York: Columbia University Press, 2004.

Picon, A. *French Architects and Engineers in the Age of Enlightenment.* New York: Cambridge University Press, 1992.

Rebora, C., et al. *John Singleton Copley in America.* Exh. cat. New York: The Metropolitan Museum of Art, 1995.

Rosenblum, R. *Transformations in Late Eighteenth Century Art.* Princeton, NJ: Princeton University Press, 1967.

Rosenthal, M., ed. *Prospects for the Nation: Recent Essays in British Landscape, 1750–1880.* Studies in British Art. New Haven: Yale University Press, © 1997.

Saisselin, R. G. *The Enlightenment Against the Baroque: Economics and Aesthetics in the Eighteenth Century.* Berkeley: University of California Press, 1992.

Solkin, D. *Painting for Money: The Visual Arts and the Public Sphere in Eighteenth-Century England.* New Haven: Yale University Press, 1993.

Vidler, A. *The Writing of the Walls: Architectural Theory in the Late Enlightenment.* Princeton, NJ: Princeton Architectural Press, 1987.

Watkin, D., and T. Mellinghoff. *German Architecture and the Classical Ideal.* Cambridge: MIT Press, 1987.

CHAPTER 24. ART IN THE AGE OF ROMANTICISM, 1789–1848

Boime, A. *The Academy and French Painting in the Nineteenth Century.* New ed. New Haven: Yale University Press, 1986.

Brown, D. B. *Romanticism.* Art & Ideas. New York: Phaidon Press, 2001.

Chu, P. *Nineteenth-Century European Art.* Upper Saddle River, NJ: Pearson Prentice Hall, 2002.

Eitner, L. E. A. *Géricault: His Life and Work.* Ithaca, NY: Cornell University Press, 1982.

Hartley, K. *The Romantic Spirit in German Art, 1790–1990.* Exh. cat. London: South Bank Centre, © 1994.

Herrmann, L. *Nineteenth Century British Painting.* London: Giles de la Mare, 2000.

Honour, H. *Romanticism.* New York: Harper & Row, 1979.

Johnson, E. *The Paintings of Eugène Delacroix: A Critical Catalogue, 1816–1863.* 6 vols. Oxford: Clarendon Press, 1981–1989.

————. *The Paintings of Eugène Delacroix: A Critical Catalogue.* 4th supp. and reprint of 3d supp. New York: Oxford University Press, 2002.

Joll, E. The *Oxford Companion to J. M. W. Turner.* Oxford: Oxford University Press, 2001.

Koerner, J. *Caspar David Friedrich and the Subject of Landscape.* New Haven: Yale University Press, 1990.

Licht, F. *Goya: The Origins of the Modern Temper in Art.* New York: Harper & Row, 1983.

Middleton, R. *Architecture of the Nineteenth Century.* Milan: Electa, © 2003.

Noon, P. J. *Crossing the Channel: British and French Painting in the Age of Romanticism.* Exh. cat. London: Tate, 2003.

Novak, B. *Nature and Culture: American Landscape and Painting, 1825–1875.* Rev. ed. New York: Oxford University Press, 1995.

Novotny, F. *Painting and Sculpture in Europe, 1780–1880.* 3d ed. Pelican History of Art. New Haven: Yale University Press, 1992.

Pérez Sánchez, A., and E. A. Sayre. *Goya and the Spirit of Enlightenment.* Exh. cat. Boston: Bulfinch Press, 1989.

Rosenblum, R. *Jean-Auguste-Dominique Ingres.* New York: Harry N. Abrams, 1990.

Tomlinson, J. *Goya in the Twilight of Enlightenment.* New Haven: Yale University Press, 1992.

Vaughn, W. *Romanticism and Art.* World of Art. London: Thames & Hudson, © 1994.

CHAPTER 25. THE AGE OF POSITIVISM: REALISM, IMPRESSIONISM, AND THE PRE-RAPHAELITES, 1848–1885

Adriani, G. *Renoir.* Cologne: Dumont; Dist. by Yale University Press, 1999.

Broude, N. *Impressionism: A Feminist Reading.* New York: Rizzoli, 1991.

Cachin, F., et al. *Cézanne.* Exh. cat. New York: Harry N. Abrams, 1995.

Cikovsky, N., and F. Kelly. *Winslow Homer.* Exh. cat. New Haven: Yale University Press, 1995.

Clark, T. J. *The Absolute Bourgeois: Artists and Politics in France, 1848–1851.* Berkeley: University of California Press, 1999, © 1973.

————. *The Painting of Modern Life: Paris in the Art of Manet and His Followers.* Rev. ed. Princeton, NJ: Princeton University Press, 1999.

Denvir, B. *The Chronicle of Impressionism: A Timeline History of Impressionist Art.* London: Thames & Hudson, 2000, © 1993.

————. *The Thames & Hudson Encyclopaedia of Impressionism.* New York: Thames & Hudson, 1990.

Elsen, A. *Origins of Modern Sculpture.* New York: Braziller, 1974.

Fried, M. *Courbet's Realism.* Chicago: University of Chicago Press, 1990.

————. *Manet's Modernism, or, The Face of Painting in the 1860s.* Chicago: University of Chicago Press, 1996.

Goodrich, L. *Thomas Eakins.* 2 vols. Exh. cat. Cambridge, MA: Harvard University Press, 1982.

Gray, C. *The Russian Experiment in Art, 1863–1922.* Rev. ed. The World of Art. New York: Thames & Hudson, 1986.

Hamilton, G. H. *Manet and His Critics.* Reprint of 1954 ed. New Haven, CT: Yale University Press, 1986.

Hares-Stryker, C., ed. *An Anthology of Pre-Raphaelite Writings.* New York: New York University Press, 1997.

Herbert, R. *Impressionism: Art, Leisure, and Parisian Society.* New Haven: Yale University Press, 1988.

Higonnet, A. *Berthe Morisot.* New York: Harper & Row, 1990.

House, J. *Impressionism: Paint and Politics.* New Haven: Yale University Press, 2004.

———. *Monet: Nature into Art*. New Haven: Yale University Press, 1986.

Jenkyns, R. *Dignity and Decadence: Victorian Art and the Classical Inheritance*. Cambridge, MA: Harvard University Press, 1991.

Kendall, R., and G. Pollock, eds. *Dealing with Degas: Representations of Women and the Politics of Vision*. New York: Universe, 1992.

———. *Degas: Beyond Impressionism*. Exh. cat. London: National Gallery; Chicago: Art Institute of Chicago; New Haven: Dist. by Yale University Press, 1996.

Krell, A. *Manet and the Painters of Contemporary Life*. The World of Art. New York: Thames & Hudson, 1996.

Lipton, E. *Looking into Degas*. Berkeley: University of California Press, 1986.

Mainardi, P. *Art and Politics of the Second Empire: The Universal Expositions of 1855 and 1867*. New Haven: Yale University Press, 1987.

———. *The End of the Salon: Art and the State in the Early Third Republic*. Cambridge: Cambridge University Press, 1993.

Miller, D., ed. *American Iconology: New Approaches to Nineteenth-Century Art and Literature*. New Haven: Yale University Press, 1993.

Needham, G. *Nineteenth-Century Realist Art*. New York: Harper & Row, 1988.

Nochlin, L., ed. *Impressionism and Post-Impressionism, 1874–1904: Sources and Documents*. Englewood Cliffs, NJ: Prentice Hall, 1976.

———. *Realism and Tradition in Art, 1848–1900: Sources and Documents*. Englewood Cliffs, NJ: Prentice Hall, 1966.

Novak, B. *American Painting of the Nineteenth Century: Realism and the American Experience*. 2d ed. New York: Harper & Row, 1979.

———. *Nature and Culture: American Landscape and Painting, 1825–1875*. New York: Oxford University Press, 1995.

Pollock, G. *Mary Cassatt: Painter of Modern Women*. New York: Thames & Hudson, 1998.

Prettejohn, E. *The Art of the Pre-Raphaelites*. Princeton, NJ: Princeton University Press, 2000.

Reff, T. *Manet and Modern Paris*. Exh. cat. Washington, DC: National Gallery of Art, 1982.

Rewald, J. *Studies in Impressionism*. New York: Harry N. Abrams, 1986, © 1985.

Rubin, J. H. *Impressionism*. Art & Ideas. London: Phaidon Press, 1999.

Spate, V. *Claude Monet: Life and Work*. New York: Rizzoli, 1992.

Tucker, P. H. *Claude Monet: Life and Art*. New Haven: Yale University Press, 1995.

———. *The Impressionists at Argenteuil*. Washington, DC: National Gallery of Art; Hartford, CT: Wadsworth Atheneum Museum of Art, 2000.

———. *Monet in the '90s: The Series Paintings*. Exh. cat. New Haven: Yale University Press, 1989.

Walther, I., ed. *Impressionist Art, 1860–1920*. 2 vols. Cologne: Taschen, 1996.

Weisberg, G. *Beyond Impressionism: The Naturalist Impulse*. New York: Harry N. Abrams, 1992.

Werner, M. *Pre-Raphaelite Painting and Nineteenth-Century Realism*. New York: Cambridge University Press, 2005.

CHAPTER 26. PROGRESS AND ITS DISCONTENTS: POST-IMPRESSIONISM, SYMBOLISM, AND ART NOUVEAU, 1880–1905

Brettell, R., et al. *The Art of Paul Gauguin*. Exh. cat. Boston: Little, Brown, 1988.

Broude, N. *Georges Seurat*. New York: Rizzoli, 1992.

Denvir, B. *Post-Impressionism*. The World of Art. New York: Thames & Hudson, 1992.

Dorra, H., ed. *Symbolist Art Theories: A Critical Anthology*. Berkeley: University of California Press, 1994.

Gibson, M. *The Symbolists*. New York: Harry N. Abrams, 1988.

Hamilton, G. H. *Painting and Sculpture in Europe, 1880–1940*. 6th ed. Pelican History of Art. New Haven: Yale University Press, 1993.

Herbert, R. L. *Georges Seurat, 1859–1891*. New York: Metropolitan Museum of Art; Dist. by Harry N. Abrams, 1991.

Hulsker, J. *The New Complete Van Gogh: Paintings, Drawings, Sketches: Revised and Enlarged Edition of the Catalogue Raisonné of the Works of Vincent van Gogh*. Amsterdam: J. M. Meulenhoff, 1996.

Mosby, D. *Henry Ossawa Tanner*. Exh. cat. New York: Rizzoli, 1991.

Schapiro, M. *Paul Cézanne*. New York: Harry N. Abrams, 1988.

———. *Vincent Van Gogh*. New York: Harry N. Abrams, 2000, © 1983.

Shiff, R. *Cézanne and the End of Impressionism: A Study of the Theory, Technique, and Critical Evaluation of Modern Art*. Chicago: University of Chicago Press, 1984.

Silverman, D. *Art Nouveau in Fin-de-Siècle France*. Berkeley: University of California Press, 1989.

Théberge, P. *Lost Paradise, Symbolist Europe*. Exh. cat. Montreal: Montreal Museum of Fine Arts, 1995.

Troy, N. J. *Modernism and the Decorative Arts in France: Art Nouveau to Le Corbusier*. New Haven: Yale University Press, 1991.

Varnedoe, K. *Vienna 1900: Art, Architecture, and Design*. Exh. cat. New York: Museum of Modern Art, 1986.

CHAPTER 27. TOWARD ABSTRACTION: THE MODERNIST REVOLUTION, 1904–1914

Bach, F., T. Bach, and A. Temkin. *Constantin Brancusi*. Exh. cat. Cambridge: MIT Press, 1995.

Behr, S. *Expressionism*. Movements in Modern Art. Cambridge: Cambridge University Press, 1999.

Bowlt, J. E., ed. *Russian Art of the Avant-Garde: Theory and Criticism, 1902–1934*. New York: Thames & Hudson, 1988.

Brown, M. *The Story of the Armory Show*. 2d ed. New York: Abbeville Press, 1988.

Duchamp, M. *Marcel Duchamp, Notes*. The Documents of Twentieth-Century Art. Boston: G. K. Hall, 1983.

Edwards, S. *Art of the Avant-Gardes*. New Haven: Yale University Press in association with the Open University, 2004.

Elderfield, J. *Henri Matisse: A Retrospective*. Exh. cat. New York: Museum of Modern Art; Dist. by Harry N. Abrams, 1992.

Golding, J. *Cubism: A History and an Analysis, 1907–1914*. 3d ed. Cambridge, MA: Harvard University Press, 1988.

Goldwater, R. *Primitivism in Modern Art*. Enl. ed. Cambridge, MA: Belknap Press, 1986.

Gordon, D. *Expressionism: Art and Idea*. New Haven: Yale University Press, 1987.

Green, C. *Cubism and Its Enemies*. New Haven: Yale University Press, 1987.

Herbert, J. *Fauve Painting: The Making of Cultural Politics*. New Haven: Yale University Press, 1992.

Hoffman, K., ed. *Collage: Critical Views*. Ann Arbor, MI: UMI Research Press, 1989.

Kallir, J. *Egon Schiele: The Complete Works*. Exp. ed. New York: Harry N. Abrams, 1998.

Krauss, R. *The Originality of the Avant-Garde and Other Modernist Myths*. Cambridge: MIT Press, 1986.

Kuspit, D. *The Cult of the Avant-Garde Artist*. New York: Cambridge University Press, 1994.

Rosenblum, R. *Cubism and Twentieth-Century Art*. New York: Harry N. Abrams, 2001.

Rubin, W. S. *Picasso and Braque: Pioneering Cubism*. Exh. cat. New York: Museum of Modern Art, 1989.

Taylor, B. *Collage: The Making of Modern Art*. London: Thames & Hudson, 2004.

Washton, R.-C., ed. *German Expressionism: Documents from the End of the Wilhelmine Empire to the Rise of National Socialism*. The Documents of Twentieth-Century Art. Boston: G. K. Hall, 1993.

Weiss, J. *The Popular Culture of Modern Art: Picasso, Duchamp and Avant Gardism*. New Haven: Yale University Press, 1994.

CHAPTER 28. ART BETWEEN THE WARS, 1914–1940

Ades, D. *Photomontage*. Rev. and enl. ed. London: Thames & Hudson, 1986.

Arbaïzar, P. *Henri Cartier-Bresson: The Man, the Image and the World: A Retrospective*. New York: Thames & Hudson, 2003.

Bayer, H., et al., eds. *Bauhaus, 1919–1928*. Reprint of 1938 ed. Boston: New York Graphic Society, 1986.

Blaser, W. *Mies van der Rohe*. 6th exp. and rev. ed. Boston: Birkhauser Verlag, 1997.

Campbell, M., et al. *Harlem Renaissance: Art of Black America*. New York: Harry N. Abrams, 1987.

Chadwick, W., ed. *Mirror Images: Women, Surrealism, and Self-Representation*. Cambridge, MA: MIT Press, 1998.

Corn, W. *The Great American Thing: Modern Art and National Identity, 1915–1935*. Berkeley: University of California Press, 2001.

Curtis, W. *Modern Architecture Since 1900*. 3rd ed. New York: Phaidon Press, 1996.

Durozoi, G. *History of the Surrealist Movement*. Chicago: University of Chicago Press, 2002.

Fer, B., et al. *Realism, Rationalism, Surrealism: Art Between the Wars*. Modern Art—Practices and Debates. New Haven: Yale University Press, 1993.

Fiedler, J., ed. *Photography at the Bauhaus*. Cambridge, MA: MIT Press, 1990.

Foster, S. C., ed. *Crisis and the Arts: The History of Dada*. 10 vols. New York: G. K. Hall, 1996–2005.

Gale, M. *Dada & Surrealism*. Art & Ideas. London: Phaidon Press, 1997.

Gössel, P., and G. Leuthäuser. *Architecture in the Twentieth Century*. Cologne: Taschen, 1991.

Greenough, S., and J. Hamilton. *Alfred Stieglitz: Photographs and Writings*. New York: Little, Brown, 1999.

Haskell, B. *The American Century: Art & Culture, 1900–1950*. New York: W. W. Norton, 1999.

Hight, E. M. *Picturing Modernism: Moholy-Nagy and Photography in Weimar Germany*. Cambridge, MA: MIT Press, 1995.

Hitchcock, H. R., and P. Johnson. *The International Style*. With a new forward. New York: W. W. Norton, 1996.

Hochman, E. S. *Bauhaus: Crucible of Modernism*. New York: Fromm International, © 1997.

Hopkins, D. *Dada and Surrealism: A Very Short Introduction*. New York: Oxford University Press, 2004.

Kandinsky, W. *Kandinsky: Complete Writings on Art*. Orig. pub. in The Documents of Twentieth-Century Art. New York: Da Capo Press, 1994.

Krauss, R. *L'Amour Fou: Photography and Surrealism*. New York: Abbeville Press, 1985.

Kultermann, U. *Architecture in the Twentieth Century*. New York: Van Nostrand Reinhold, 1993.

Lane, B. *Architecture and Politics in Germany, 1918–1945*. New ed. Cambridge, MA: Harvard University Press, 1985.

Le Corbusier. *Towards a New Architecture*. Oxford: Architectural Press, 1997, © 1989.

Lodder, C. *Russian Constructivism*. New Haven: Yale University Press, 1983.

McEuen, M. A. *Seeing America: Women Photographers Between the Wars*. Lexington, KY: University Press of Kentucky, 2000.

Miró, J. *Joan Miró: Selected Writings and Interviews*. The Documents of Twentieth-Century Art. Boston: G. K. Hall, 1986.

Mondrian, P. *The New Art, the New Life: The Complete Writings*. Eds. and trans. H. Holtzmann and M. James. Orig. pub. in the Documents of Twentieth-Century Art. New York: Da Capo, 1993.

Motherwell, R., ed. *The Dada Painters and Poets: An Anthology*. 2d ed. Cambridge, MA: Harvard University Press, 1989.

Nadeau, M. *History of Surrealism*. Cambridge, MA: Harvard University Press, 1989.

Phillips, C., ed. *Photography in the Modern Era: European Documents and Critical Writings, 1913–1940*. New York: Metropolitan Museum of Art; Aperture, 1989.

Roskill, M. *Klee, Kandinsky, and the Thought of Their Time: A Critical Perspective*. Urbana: University of Illinois Press, 1992.

Silver, K. E. *Esprit de Corps: The Art of the Parisian Avant-Garde and the First World War, 1914–1925*. Princeton, NJ: Princeton University Press, 1989.

Spiteri, R., ed. *Surrealism, Politics and Culture*. Aldershot, Hants., England and Burlington, VT: Ashgate, 2003.

Wood, P., ed. *Varieties of Modernism*. New Haven: Yale University Press in association with the Open University, 2004.

Wright, F. L. *Frank Lloyd Wright, Collected Writings.* 5 vols. New York: Rizzoli, 1992–1995.

CHAPTER 29. POST-WORLD WAR II TO POSTMODERN, 1945–1980

Archer, M. *Art Since 1960.* World of Art. New York: Thames & Hudson, 2002.

Ashton, D. *American Art Since 1945.* New York: Oxford University Press, 1982.

Atkins, R. *Artspeak: A Guide to Contemporary Ideas, Movements, and Buzzwords, 1945 to the Present.* New York: Abbeville Press, 1997.

Baker, K. *Minimalism: Art of Circumstance.* New York: Abbeville Press, 1989.

Battcock, G., comp. *Idea Art: A Critical Anthology.* New ed. New York: Dutton, 1973.

———., ed. *Minimal Art: A Critical Anthology.* Berkeley: University of California Press, 1995.

———., and R. Nickas, eds. *The Art of Performance: A Critical Anthology.* New York: Dutton, 1984.

Beardsley, J. *Earthworks and Beyond: Contemporary Art in the Landscape.* 3d ed. New York: Abbeville Press, 1998.

———., and J. Livingston. *Hispanic Art in the United States: Thirty Contemporary Painters and Sculptors.* Exh. cat. New York: Abbeville Press, 1987.

Burgin, V., ed. *Thinking Photography.* Communications and Culture. Houndsmills, England: Macmillan Education, 1990.

Carlson, M. A. *Performance: A Critical Introduction.* 2d ed. New York: Routledge, 2004.

Causey, A. *Sculpture Since 1945.* Oxford History of Art. New York: Oxford University Press, 1998.

Crane, D. *The Transformation of the Avant-Garde: The New York Art World, 1940–1985.* Chicago: University of Chicago Press, 1987.

Crow, T. *The Rise of the Sixties: American and European Art in the Era of Dissent.* London: Laurence King, 2005, © 1996.

Frascina, F. *Pollock and After: The Critical Debate.* 2d ed. New York: Routledge, 2001.

Gilbaut, S. *How New York Stole the Idea of Modern Art.* Chicago: University of Chicago Press, 1983.

———., ed. *Reconstructing Modernism: Art in New York, Paris, and Montreal, 1945–1964.* Cambridge: MIT Press, 1990.

Greenberg, C. *Clement Greenberg: The Collected Essays and Criticism.* 4 vols. Chicago: University of Chicago Press, 1986–1993.

Griswold del Castillo, R., ed. *Chicano Art: Resistance and Affirmation, 1965–1985.* Exh. cat. Los Angeles: Wight Art Gallery, University of California, 1991.

Hopkins, D. *After Modern Art: 1945–2000.* New York: Oxford University Press, 2000.

Joselit, D. *American Art Since 1945.* The World of Art. London: Thames & Hudson, 2003.

Landau, E. G., ed. *Reading Abstract Expressionism: Context and Critique.* New Haven: Yale University Press, 2005.

Leggio, J., and S. Weiley, eds. *American Art of the 1960s.* Studies in Modern Art, 1. New York: Museum of Modern Art, 1991.

Leja, M. *Reframing Abstract Expressionism: Subjectivity and Painting in the 1940s.* New Haven: Yale University Press, 1993.

Linder, M. *Nothing Less Than Literal: Architecture After Minimalism.* Cambridge, MA: MIT Press, 2004.

Lippard, L. R., ed. *From the Center: Feminist Essays on Women's Art.* New York: Dutton, 1976.

———. *Overlay: Contemporary Art and the Art of Prehistory.* New York: Pantheon, 1983.

Livingstone, M. *Pop Art: A Continuing History.* New York: Thames & Hudson, 2000.

Lucie-Smith, E. *Movements in Art Since 1945.* The World of Art. New York: Thames & Hudson, 2001.

McCarthy, D. *Pop Art.* Movements in Modern Art. New York: Cambridge University Press, 2000.

McEvilley, T. *Sculpture in the Age of Doubt.* New York: School of Visual Arts; Allworth Press, 1999.

Meisel, L. K. *Photorealism at the Millennium.* New York: Harry N. Abrams, 2002.

Ockman, J., ed. *Architecture Culture, 1943–1968: A Documentary Anthology.* New York: Rizzoli, 1993.

Orvell, M. *American Photography.* The World of Art. New York: Oxford University Press, 2003.

Pincus-Witten, R. *Postminimalism into Maximalism: American Art, 1966–1986.* Ann Arbor, MI: UMI Research Press, 1987.

Polcari, S. *Abstract Expressionism and the Modern Experience.* New York: Cambridge University Press, 1991.

Rosen, R., and C. Brawer, eds. *Making Their Mark: Women Artists Move into the Mainstream, 1970–85.* Exh. cat. New York: Abbeville Press, 1989.

Ross, C. *Abstract Expressionism: Creators and Critics: An Anthology.* New York: Harry N. Abrams, 1990.

Sandler, I. *Art of the Postmodern Era: From the Late 1960s to the Early 1990s.* New York: Icon Editions, 1996.

———. *The New York School: The Painters and Sculptors of the Fifties.* New York: Harper & Row, 1978.

———. *The Triumph of American Painting: A History of Abstract Expressionism.* New York: Praeger, 1970.

Sayre, H. *The Object of Performance: The American Avant-Garde Since 1970.* Chicago: University of Chicago Press, 1990.

Seitz, W. *Abstract Expressionist Painting in America.* Cambridge, MA: Harvard University Press, 1983.

Self-Taught Artists of the 20th Century: An American Anthology. Exh. cat. San Francisco: Chronicle Books, 1998.

Sontag, S. *On Photography.* New York: Picador; Farrar, Straus & Giroux, 2001, © 1977.

Weintraub, L. *Art on the Edge and Over.* Litchfield, CT: Art Insights; Dist. by D.A.P., 1997.

Wood, P., et al. *Modernism in Dispute: Art Since the Forties.* New Haven: Yale University Press, 1993.

CHAPTER 30. THE POSTMODERN ERA: ART SINCE 1980

Barthes, R. *The Pleasure of the Text.* Oxford: Blackwell, 1990.

Belting, H. *Art History After Modernism.* Chicago: University of Chicago Press, 2003.

Broude, N., and M. Garrad., eds. *Reclaiming Female Agency: Feminist Art History After Postmodernism.* Berkeley: University of California Press, 2005.

Brunette, P., and D. Wills, eds. *Deconstruction and the Visual Arts: Art, Media, Architecture.* New York: Cambridge University Press, 1994.

Capozzi, R., ed. *Reading Eco: An Anthology.* Bloomington: Indiana University Press, © 1997.

Derrida, J. *Writing and Difference.* London: Routledge Classics, 2001.

Eco, U. *A Theory of Semiotics.* Bloomington: Indiana University Press, 1976.

Foster, H., ed. *The Anti-Aesthetic: Essays on Postmodern Culture.* New York: New Press; Dist. by W. W. Norton, 1998.

Ghirardo, D. *Architecture After Modernism.* New York: Thames & Hudson, 1996.

Harris, J. P. *The New Art History: A Critical Introduction.* New York: Routledge, 2001.

Jencks, C. *New Paradigm in Architecture: The Language of Post-Modernism.* New Haven: Yale University Press, 2002.

———., ed. *The Post-Modern Reader.* London: Academy Editions; New York: St. Martin's Press, 1992.

———. *What Is Post-Modernism?* 4th rev. ed. London: Academy Editions, 1996.

Lucie-Smith, E. *Art Today.* London: Phaidon Press, 1995.

Mitchell, W. J. T. *The Reconfigured Eye: Visual Truth in the Post-Photographic Era.* Cambridge, MA: MIT Press, 1992.

Norris, C., and A. Benjamin. *What Is Deconstruction?* New York: St. Martin's Press, 1988.

Papadakes, A., et al., eds. *Deconstruction: The Omnibus Volume.* New York: Rizzoli, 1989.

Paul, C. *Digital Art.* New York: Thames & Hudson, © 2003.

Pearman, H. *Contemporary World Architecture.* London: Phaidon Press, © 1998.

Risatti, H., ed. *Postmodern Perspectives.* Englewood Cliffs, NJ: Prentice Hall, 1990.

Senie, H. *Contemporary Public Sculpture: Tradition, Transformation, and Controversy.* New York: Oxford University Press, 1992.

Steele, J. *Architecture Today.* New York: Phaidon Press, 2001.

Thody, P. *Introducing Barthes.* New York: Totem Books; Lanham, MD: National Book Network, 1997.

Tomkins, C. *Post to Neo: The Art World of the 1980s.* New York: Holt, 1988.

Wallis, B., ed. *Art After Modernism: Rethinking Representation.* Documentary Sources in Contemporary Art, 1. Boston: Godine, 1984.

Index

Credits

INTRODUCTION

I.1 © 2009. Digital Image, The Museum of Modern Art, New York/Scala, Florence, © The Andy Warhol Foundation for the Visual Arts / Artists Rights Society (ARS), New York / DACS, London 2009; I.2 © 2005. Photo The Newark Museum/Art Resource/Scala, Florence; I.3 Image © The Board of Trustees, National Gallery of Art, Washington I.4 akg-images / Erich Lessing; I.5 Werner Forman Archive; I.6 © Grant Wood/ Licensed by VAGA, New York. Photography © The Art Institute of Chicago; I.8 Photograph by Lorene Emerson/Images © The Board of Trustees, National Gallery of Art, Washington; I.9 © 1990. Photo Scala, Florence; I.10 Photograph by Lynn Rosenthal, Philadelphia Museum of Art, © Succession Marcel Duchamp/ADAGP, Paris and DACS, London 2009; I.11 Photo by O. Zimmermann, © Musée d'Unterlinden, Colmar; I.12 © Estate of Duane Hanson/VAGA, New York/DACS, London 2009; I.13 © Lee Friedlander, courtesy Fraenkel Gallery, San Francisco; I.14 © Aerocentro; I.15 akg-images / Erich Lessing; I.16 Ezra Stoller © Esto, © ARS, NY and DACS, London 2009; I.17 Ben Mangor / SuperStock, © ARS, NY and DACS, London 2009.

CHAPTER 1

1.0 © Centre des Monuments Nationaux, Paris; 1.1 National Geographic / Getty Images; 1.2 Jean Clottes, Ministère de la Culture et des Communications; 1.3 Jean Vertut; 1.4 Jean Vertut; Box p5 Ministère de la Culture et des Communications; 1.6 Jean Vertut; 1.8 © Centre des Monuments Nationaux, Paris; 1.9 Thomas Stephan, © Ulmer Museum; 1.10 Kunsthalle Tubingen; 1.11 Photo by Max Begouen; 1.12 Jean Vertut; 1.13 © Jean-Gilles Berizzi/Reunion des Musees Nationaux; 1.14 akg-images/Erich Lessing; 1.15 Harry N. Abrams; 1.16 akg-images / © Erich Lessing; 1.17 Zev Radovan; 1.18 R. Sheridan, The Ancient Art & Architecture Collection; 1.19 Dr. Gary/Prof. Nasser D Khalili; 1.20 Courtesy McDonald Institute for Archaeological Research; 1.22 akg-images / Erich Lessing; 1.23 Alamy; 1.24 © Yan Arthus-Bertrand / Corbis; 1.25 © English Heritage, NMR.

CHAPTER 2

2.0 © 2007. Image The Metropolitan Museum of Art/Art Resource/Scala, Florence; 2.1 © The Trustees of the British Museum; **Box images** Penelope Davies; 2.3 World Tourism Organization: Iraq; 2.4 © 2008. Photo Scala, Florence/BPK, Bildagentur fuer Kunst, Kultur und Geschichte, Berlin; 2.5 Courtesy of The Oriental Institute of the University of Chicago; 2.6 University of Pennsylvania Museum of Archaeology and Anthropology; 2.7 © The Trustees of the British Museum; 2.8 University of Pennsylvania Museum of Archaeology and Anthropology; 2.9 University of Pennsylvania Museum of Archaeology and Anthropology; 2.10 © 2005. Photo Scala, Florence/BPK, Bildagentur fuer Kunst, Kultur und Geschichte, Berlin; 2.11 © 1990. Photo Scala, Florence; 2.12 © Chuzeville/Réunion des Musées Nationaux; 2.13 The Ancient Art & Architecture Collection Ltd; 2.14 Photograph © 2010, Museum of Fine Arts, Boston; 2.15 © Réunion des Musées Nationaux; 2.16 © Herve Lewandowski / Réunion des Musées Nationaux; 2.17 Courtesy of The Oriental Institute of the University of Chicago; 2.18 World Tourism Organization: Iraq; 2.19 © The Trustees of the British Museum; 2.20 © The Trustees of the British Museum; 2.21 © 2005. Photo Scala, Florence/BPK, Bildagentur fuer Kunst, Kultur und Geschichte, Berlin; 2.22 The Art Archive / Alfredo Dagli Ort; 2.23 © The Trustees of the British Museum; 2.24 PhotoEdit Inc; 2.25 © Réunion des Musées Nationaux; 2.26 © Kurt Scholz / SuperStock; 2.27 © 1990. Photo Scala, Florence; 2.28 © Gerard Degeorge, Corbis; 2.29 akg-images / Erich Lessing; 2.30 Courtesy of The Oriental Institute of the University of Chicago; 2.31 Corbis; 2.32 © Robert Harding/Getty Images; 2.33 © 2007. Image The Metropolitan Museum of Art/Art Resource/Scala, Florence.

CHAPTER 3

3.0 © The Trustees of the British Museum; 3.1 The Art Archive / Egyptian Museum Cairo / Dagli Orti; 3.2 Werner Forman Archive; 3.4 The Art Archive / Gianni Dagli Ort; 3.5 © The Trustees of the British Museum; 3.6 Peter A. Clayton; 3.7 Nature Picture Library; 3.8 Photo by Carl Andres, © President and fellows of Harvard College for the Semitic Museum; 3.9 Roger Wood/Corbis; 3.10 Araldo de Luca/Index, Florence; 3.11 Photograph © 2010, Museum of Fine Arts, Boston; 3.12 The Art Archive / Egyptian Museum Cairo / Alfredo Dagli Orti; 3.13 akg-images / Andrea Jemolo; 3.15 © Herve Lewandowski Réunion des Musées Nationaux; 3.16 © Araldo de Luca; 3.17 © 2007. Image copyright The Metropolitan Museum of Art/Art Resource/Scala, Florence; 3.18 Photograph © 2010, Museum of Fine Arts, Boston; 3.19 Jean Vertut; 3.20 © Graham Harrison; 3.21 Peter A. Clayton; 3.22 © The Trustees of the British Museum; 3.23 © Jurgen Liepe; 3.24 Robert Frerck, Woodfin Camp & Associates, Inc; 3.26 Photograph Schecter Lee/© 1986 The Metropolitan Museum of Art; 3.27 Dorling Kindersley Media Library; 3.28 Jean Vertut; 3.29 The Art Archive / Gianni Dagli Orti, 3.30 Gianni Dagli Orti, The Art Archive/Picture Desk; 3.31 Hervé Champollion / akg-images; 3.32 © 2008. Photo Scala, Florence/BPK, Bildagentur fuer Kunst, Kultur und Geschichte, Berlin; 3.33 © The Trustees of the British Museum; 3.34 © 1997. Photo Scala, Florence; 3.35 Araldo De Luca, Index, Florence; 3.36 © 2005. Photo Scala, Florence/BPK, Bildagentur fuer Kunst, Kultur und Geschichte, Berlin; 3.37 © 2005. Photo Scala, Florence/BPK, Bildagentur fuer Kunst, Kultur und Geschichte, Berlin; 3.38 © 2005. Photo Scala, Florence/BPK, Bildagentur fuer Kunst, Kultur und Geschichte, Berlin; 3.39 The Stapleton Collection / Art Resource, NY; 3.40 Jurgen Liepe Photo Archive; 3.41 © The Trustees of the British Museum.

CHAPTER 4

4.0 © 1990. Photo Scala, Florence; 4.1 © Studio Kontos/Photostock; 4.2 John Bigelow Taylor; 4.3 © 1990. Photo Scala, Florence; 4.4 From John Griffiths Padley, *Greek Art and Archaeology, 2/e*, Prentice Hall 1988, fig 3.1, p.65; 4.5 Courtesy McRae Books Srl, Florence; 4.6 © Roger Wood, Corbis; 4.7 From: Donald Preziosi and Louise, A. Hitchcock, *Aegean Art and Architecture*, Oxford University Press, Oxford, 1999, fig 54, pg. 96; 4.8 © Studio Kontos/ Photostock; 4.9 © Studio Kontos/ Photostock; 4.10 akg-images / Nimatallah; 4.11 © Studio Kontos/ Photostock; 4.12 © 1990. Photo Scala, Florence; 4.13 akg-images / Nimatallah; 4.14 akg-images / Nimatallah; 4.15 akg-images / Erich Lessing; 4.16 akg-images / Nimatallah; 4.17 © Studio Kontos/ Photostock; 4.19 From John Griffiths Pedley, *Greek Art and Archaeology, 2/e*, Prentice Hall 1988, fig 3.40, p.95; 4.20 © 1990. Photo Scala, Florence; 4.22 © Studio Kontos/ Photostock; 4.23 © Studio Kontos/ Photostock; 4.24 © Vanni Archive, Corbis; 4.26 The Art Archive / Gianni Dagli Ort; 4.27 Hirmer Verlag, Munich; 4.28 akg-images / Nimatallah; 4.29 akg-images / Nimatallah; 4.30 akg-images / Nimatallah.

CHAPTER 5

5.0 © The Trustees of the British Museum; 5.2 akg-images / Nimatallah; 5.4 © 2007. Image copyright The Metropolitan Museum of Art/Art Resource/Scala, Florence; 5.5 Photograph © 2010, Museum of Fine Arts, Boston; 5.6 © The Trustees of the British Museum; 5.9 © Marco Cristofori, Corbis; 5.10 © John Heseltine, Corbis; 5.12 © The Trustees of the British Museum; 5.13 © Hervé Lewandowski/Réunion des Musées Nationaux; 5.14 © 2007. Image copyright The Metropolitan Museum of Art/Art Resource/Scala, Florence; 5.15 © 1990. Photo Scala, Florence; 5.16 The Art Archive / Acropolis Museum Athens / Gianni Dagli Orti; 5.17 The Art Archive / Archaeological Museum Corfu / Gianni Dagli Orti; 5.21 Penelope Davies; 5.22 Vanni, Art Resource, NY; 5.23 Staatliche Antikensammlungen und Glyptothek Munich; 5.24 Staatliche Antikensammlungen und Glyptothek Munich; 5.25 A. Bracchetti, © Photo Vatican Museums; 5.26 Photograph © 2010, Museum of Fine Arts, Boston; 5.27 Staatliche Antikensammlungen und Glyptothek Munich; 5.28 Giraudon, Art Resource, NY; 5.29 akg-images / Nimatallah; 5.30 Pubbliphoto; 5.31 National Archaeological Museum, Athens, Greece; 5.32 Foto Vasari/Index, Firenze; 5.33 © 2003, Photo Scala, Florence, courtesy of the Ministero Beni e Att. Culturali; 5.34 Soprintendenza per i Beni Archeologici della Calabria; 5.35 © Studio Kontos/Photostock; 5.36 © Studio Kontos/Photostock; 5.38 © Studio Kontos/Photostock; 5.40 © Studio Kontos/Photostock; 5.41 Box p134 © The Trustees of the British Museum; 5.43 © The Trustees of the British Museum; 5.44 © The Trustees of the British Museum; 5.45 © Studio Kontos/Photostock; 5.46 © The Trustees of the British Museum; 5.47 akg-images / Nimatallah; 5.48 akg-images / Nimatallah; 5.49 © Studio Kontos/Photostock, 5.50 © Studio Kontos/Photostock; 5.51 Bettmann, Corbis; 5.52 From Howard Colvin, *Architecture and the After Life*, Yale University Press, 1991, fig. 31, p.35; 5.54 John Decopoulos; 5.55 Hirmer Verlag, Munich; 5.56 © Photo Vatican Museums; 5.57 © Studio Kontos/Photostock; 5.58 © 1990. Photo Scala, Florence; 5.59 © Réunion des Musées Nationaux; 5.60 akg-images / Nimatallah; 5.61 Reprinted with permission from Cambridge University Press. From Jerome Politt, *Art in the Hellenistic Age*, 1986, fig.31, p.35; 5.62 ZUMA Press – Gamma; 5.63 Reprinted with permission from Cambridge University Press. From Jerome Politt, *Art in the Hellenistic Age*, 1986, fig.31, p.35; 5.64 © 2005 Photo Scala, Florence/BPK, Bildagentur fuer Kunst, Kultur und Geschichte, Berlin; 5.65 Advance Illustration Ltd, Congleton, Cheshire, UK; 5.66 © Bednorz-Images; 5.68 akg-images; 5.69 © Réunion des Musées Nationaux/Musee du Louvre; 5.71 © Araldo de Luca/CORBIS; 5.72 © 2009. Photo Scala, Florence/BPK, Bildagentur fuer Kunst, Kultur und Geschichte, Berlin; 5.73 Staatliche Museen, Berlin, Germany / Photo © AISA / The Bridgeman Art Library; Box p157 © 1990. Photo Scala, Florence; 5.74 © Réunion des Musées Nationaux; 5.75 akg-images / Nimatallah; 5.76 Staatliche Antikensammlungen und Glyptothek Munich; 5.77 © Studio Kontos/Photostock; 5.78 © Fotografica Foglia, Naples.

CHAPTER 6

6.0 Soprintendenza Beni Archeologici Etruria Meridionale, Roma; 6.1 INDEX/Ricciarini; 6.2 O Louis Mazzatenta, National Georgraphic/Getty Images; 6.3 *Etruscan Life and Afterlife: A Handbook of Etruscan Studies*, © 1986 Wayne State University Press, with the permission of Wayne State University Press; 6.4 © 1990. Photo Scala, Florence – courtesy of the Ministero Beni e Att. Culturali; Box p6 © G. Blot/C. Jean/Réunion des Musées Nationaux; 6.5 © Soprintendenza Beni Archeologici Etruria Meridionale; 6.7 Canali Photobank, Milan Italy; 6.9 © 1990, Photo Scala, Florence – courtesy of the Ministero Beni e Att. Culturali; 6.10 © Nicolo Orsi Battaglini; 6.11 Photograph © 2010, Museum of Fine Arts, Boston; 6.12 © 1990. Photo Scala, Florence; 6.13 *Etruscan Life and Afterlife: A Handbook of Etruscan Studies*, Copyright © 1986 Wayne State University Press, with the permission of Wayne State University Press; 6.14 © 2005, Photo Scala, Florence – courtesy of the Ministero Beni e Att. Culturali; 6.15 Penelope Davies; 6.16 Canali Photobank, Milan Italy; 6.17 © 1990. Photo Scala, Florence; 6.18 © Vincenzo Pirozzi, Rome fotopirozzi@inwind.it; 6.19 Canali Photobank, Milan Italy; 6.20 Canali Photobank, Milan Italy.

CHAPTER 7

7.0 akg-images / Nimatallah; Box p7 © 1996. Photo Scala, Florence – courtesy of the Ministero Beni e Att. Culturali; 7.1 from *"La Grande Roma dei Tarquini. Alterne civvende di un felice intuizione"*, Bullcom (2000), fig. 7-26, p.25; 7.2 Canali Photobank, Milan Italy; 7.4 From Amanda Claridge, *An Archaeological Guide*, Oxford University Press, 1988, fig. 188, p.389; 7.5 Gianni Vanni / Art Resource, NY; 7.8 © Archivio Fotografico Musei Capitolini; 7.9 Penelope Davies; 7.10 Foto Marburg, Art Resource, NY (top), Photo: Chuzeville. Louvre, Paris, France, © Réunion des Musées Nationaux (bottom); 7.11

TEXT CREDITS

Page 25 From *The Epic of Gilgamesh*, translated by Maureen Gallery Kovacs with an Introduction and Notes (California: Stanford University Press, 1989), copyright © 1985, 1989 by the Board of Trustees of the Leland Stanford Junior University. All rights reserved. Used with the permission of Stanford University Press, www.sup.org. **Page 33** Henri Frankfort. From *The Art and Architecture of the Ancient Orient*, 4th edition (New Haven: Yale University Press, 1970). Reprinted by permission of the publisher. **Page 58** "The Resurrection of King Unis" from *Ancient Egyptian Literature: An Anthology*, translated by John L. Foster (Austin, TX: University of Texas Press, 2001). By permission of the University of Texas Press. **Page 266** St. Theodore the Studite. From "Second and Third Refutations of the Iconoclasts" from *On the Holy Icons*, translated by Catherine P. Roth (Crestwood, NY: St. Vladimir's Seminary Press, 1981). Reprinted by permission of the publisher. **Page 309** Abd al-Hamid Lahori. From "Padshah Nama" from *Taj Mahal: The Illumined Tomb*, compiled and translated by W.E. Begley and Z.A. Desai (Cambridge, Mass: Aga Kahn Program for Islamic, Architecture 1989). Reprinted by permission of the Aga Khan Program Publications. **Pages 352, 353** From *The Pilgrim's Guide to Santiago de Campostela*, edited and translated by Willliam Melczer (New York: Italica Press, 1993). Copyright 1993 by William Melczer. Used by permission of Italica Press. **Page 359** St. Bernard of Clairvaux. From "Apologia to Abbot William of Saint-Thierry" from *The "Things of Greater Importance": Bernard of Clairvaux's Apologia and the Medieval Attitude Towards Art*, edited by Conrad Rudolph (Philadelphia: University of Pennsylvania Press, 1990). Reprinted by permission of the publisher. **Page 369** C. Edson Armi. "Report on the Destruction of Romanesque Architecture in Burgundy" from *Journal of the Society of Architectural Historians*, volume 55 (1996). Reprinted by permission of the publisher. **Page 393** Suger of Saint-Denis. From "On the Consecration of the Church of Saint-Denis" from *Abbot Suger on the Abbey Church of Saint-Denis and Its Art Treasures*, edited and translated by Erwin Panofsky (Princeton, NJ: Princeton University Press, 1946), © 1947, 1958, 1982 Princeton University Press. Reprinted by permission of Princeton University Press. **Page 461** Inscriptions on the Frescoes in the Palazzo Pubblico; Siena from *Arts of Power: Three Halls of State in Italy, 1300-1600*, edited by Randolph Starn and Loren Partridge (Berkeley: University California Press, 1992), copyright © 1992 The Regents of the University of California. Reprinted by permission of the University of California Press. **Page 494** Fray Jose de Siguenza. From *Bosch in Perspective*, edited by James Snyder (NY: Simon & Schuster, 1973), © 1973 Prentice Hall Inc. Reprinted with permission of Simon & Schuster, Inc. All rights reserved. **Page 562** Leonardo da Vinci. From his undated manuscripts from *The Literary Works of Leonardo da Vinci*, edited by Jean Paul Richter (London: Phaidon Press, 1975), © 1975 Phaidon Press Limited, reprinted by permission of the publisher. **Page 568** Michelangelo. From Commentary on his 'Pieta' by Ascanio Condivi from *Life, Letters and Poetry*, edited and translated by George Bull (Oxford: Oxford University Press, 1987). Reprinted by permision of Oxford University Press. **Page 572** From *The Poetry of Michelangelo*, translated by James Saslow (New Haven, CT: Yale University Press, 1991), copyright © 1991 by Yale University Press. Reprinted by permission of the publisher. **Page 603** Michelangelo. Sonnet, "The Smith" from *Life, Letters and Poetry*, edited and translated by George Bull (Oxford: Oxford University Press, 1987). Reprinted by permission of Oxford University Press. **Page 620** From a Session of the Inquisition Tribunal in Venice of Paolo Veronese from *A Documentary History of Art, volume 2*, edited by Elizabeth Gilmore Holt (Princeton, NJ: Princeton University Press, 1982), copyright © 1947, 1958, 1982 Princeton University Press. Reprinted by permission of Princeton University Press. **Page 656** Karel van Mander. From *Dutch and Flemish Painters*, translated by Constant van de Wall (Manchester, NH: Ayer Co, 1978). Reprinted by permission of the publisher. **Page 766** Jean de Jullienne. "A Summary of the Life of Antoine Watteau" from *A Documentary History of Art, Volume 2*, edited by Elizabeth Gilmore Holt (Princeton, NJ: Princeton University Press, 1982), copyright © 1947, 1958, 1982 by Princeton University Press. Reprinted by permission of Princeton University Press. **Page 1050** Roy Lichtenstein. Interview with Joan Marter. From *Off Limits: Rutgers University and the Avant-Garde, 1957-1963*, edited by Joan Marter (NJ: Rutgers University Press, 1999), copyright © 1999 by Rutgers, the State University and The Newark Museum. Reprinted by permission of Rutgers University Press.